THE NEW NELSON JAPANESE-ENGLISH CHARACTER DICTIONARY

NOTE CONCERNING CHART INSIDE FRONT COVER The use of the Radical Chart is explained in the first five appendices. The tables in Appendix 5, in particular, indicate whether a given element of a character is likely to be a radical in the position in which it occurs. If the reader is unable to locate the radical or cannot find the character under the radical selected, Appendix 15 crosslists characters under every radical or radical-like element appearing in the character.

The chart shows all 214 historic radicals arranged by stroke count, together with their numbers and variants. The *large numeral* indicates the stroke count of the radicals that follow it. An unadorned *small numeral* shows the number of the radical. *Small numbers in parentheses* show a variant form of the radical with the same stroke count as its parent. A *small number in brackets* designates a variant form having a different stroke count than its parent or a second entry of a radical that may appear to have more strokes than traditionally counted.

WINGATE
FIDES
SCIENTIA
PIETAS
1896
UNIVERSITY

新版ネルソン漢英辞典

The New Nelson

JAPANESE-ENGLISH CHARACTER DICTIONARY

Based on the Classic Edition
by Andrew N. Nelson

COMPLETELY REVISED
by JOHN H. HAIG
and the Department of
East Asian Languages and Literatures
University of Hawai'i at Manoa

TUTTLE PUBLISHING
Tokyo • Rutland, Vermont • Singapore

Published by Tuttle Publishing, an imprint of Periplus Editions (HK) Ltd.

www.tuttlepublishing.com

LCC Card No. 96060004

ISBN 978-0-8048-2036-3
ISBN 978-4-8053-0738-0 (for sale in Japan only)

New Nelson edition, 1997

Distributed by

North America, Latin America & Europe
Tuttle Publishing
364 Innovation Drive, North Clarendon,
VT 05759-9436 U.S.A.
Tel: 1 (802) 773-8930; Fax: 1 (802) 773-6993
info@tuttlepublishing.com
www.tuttlepublishing.com

Japan
Tuttle Publishing
Yaekari Building, 3rd Floor
5-4-12 Osaki, Shinagawa-ku,
Tokyo 141-0032
Tel: (81) 3 5437-0171; Fax: (81) 3 5437-0755
tuttle-sales@gol.com

Asia Pacific
Berkeley Books Pte. Ltd.
61 Tai Seng Avenue, #02-12, Singapore 534167
Tel: (65) 6280-1330; Fax: (65) 6280-6290
inquiries@periplus.com.sg
www.periplus.com

14 13 12 11 10 13 12 11 10 9 8
Printed in Hong Kong

TABLE OF CONTENTS

FOREWORD

Without the original *The Modern Reader's Japanese-English Character Dictionary*, there, of course, could have been no *New Nelson*. Besides being a trailblazer, Nelson's dictionary also incorporated the Radical Priority System, which gave a hierarchically ordered algorithm for finding characters, but essentially retained the traditional radical system. Given its proven usefulness, we were reluctant to abandon the Radical Priority System, but we have replaced it with the **Universal Radical Index**, which cross-indexes each entry by every radical or radical like element in it. The advantages of the unprecedented level of cross-referencing and the ease of use offered by the URI, as well as the transfer of skills and knowledge to the use of traditional dictionaries offered by the reversion to the traditional radical system, more than compensate for the loss of the Radical Priority System. In addition, the incorporation of the URI has allowed us to eliminate crosslisting of the same character within the body of the dictionary.

Under the philosophy that one should be able to check on any character generated by one's wordprocessor, we have incorporated all of the JIS level 1 and 2 characters (JIS X 0208). This has meant an extension of the numbered entries from 5446 characters to 7107. One of the unique features of the original Nelson's dictionary was that it incorporated such a large number of numbered and unnumbered variant characters; we have tried to maintain this advantage. However, we have reduced the number somewhat by ignoring some predictable variations. These are primarily of two types. In the first case, the element 亠 appears with the top stroke vertical as pictured or as horizontal (亠). In the original Nelson's, both were listed as separate entries, often under different radicals, but we have listed only the common variant, usually with the vertical upper stroke. Also, the element 八 occurs both with the two strokes pointing out at the bottom and with the two strokes pointing in at the bottom. This variation occurs in many positions, but generally only the inward-pointing variation has been listed herein for Jōyō characters and the outward-pointing variation for traditional forms. Where a variation changes the appearance of the character significantly or changes the stroke-count, both forms of the character have been retained and given reference numbers.

The *on-kun* index has been expanded to include compounds that have readings not predictable from their component characters (e.g., 明日 *asu*, *ashita*, 海豚 *iruka*). The addition of the original *on-kun* index made the "reader's" dictionary a "writer's" dictionary as well, and we hope this expansion will prove to be useful to writers. No attempt has been made to indicate which of these compounds are in common use and which are comparatively rare, however.

All of the entries were examined and changes, additions, and deletions were suggested by the compound judges Haruko Minegishi Cook, Kakuko Shōji, Hisami Konishi Springer, and Nobuko Miyama Ochner. The Universal Radical Index was developed by several people with Stewart A. Curry, who also entered the index into the database, doing the majority of the index development. Jim K. Yoshioka, John D. Creamer, Mariko Yamashita Shawback, Dianne S. J. Lim, Blaine Erickson, and Zachry A. Matheson worked on text inputting, editing, and proofreading. Other people who contributed in significant ways on the project include Michael S. Wenzel, Dina Rudolph Yoshimi, Jeffrey J. Hayden, Arthur Thornhill, J. Marshall Unger, and Timothy Vance. The support and advice of editors Patrick J. Mahany and Tatsuya Tamura, and operations manager Richard S.

Keirstead at Charles E. Tuttle Co., have been invaluable. Support and encouragement were also provided by the Department of East Asian Languages and Literatures and the College of Languages, Linguistics, and Literature of the University of Hawai'i at Mānoa.

In addition to the references cited in the original Nelson, we consulted the following works in deriving definitions for new entries and tightening the definitions of existing entries.

Daikangorin. T. Kamata et al. Taishūkan Shoten: Tōkyō. 1992.
Daikanwa Jiten. T. Morohashi. Taishūkan Shoten: Tōkyō. 1955–1960.
Gakken Kanwa Daijiten. A. Tōdō. Gakushū Kenkyūsha: Tōkyō. 1978.
Guide to Reading and Writing Japanese, A. F. Sakade. Tuttle: Rutland, Vermont and Tōkyō. 1959.
Imidas 1994. Shūeisha: Tōkyō. 1993.
Kadokawa Daijigen. Y. Ozaki et al. Kadokawa Shoten: Tōkyō. 1992.
KANJIDIC Database of JIS X 0208 Kanji and Associated Details, The. J. Breen et al. Monash University: Australia. 1995. (ftp:ftp.cc.monash.edu.au:pub/nihongo/kanjidic).
Kanji Dictionary, The. M. Spahn and W. Hadmitzky. Tuttle: Rutland, Vermont and Tōkyō. 1996.
Kōjien. I. Shinmura. Iwanami Shoten: Tōkyō. 1969.
New Japanese-English Character Dictionary. J. Halpern. Kenkyūsha: Tōkyō. 1990.
Nihon Kokugo Daijiten. Nihon Kokugo Daijiten Kankōkai. Shōgakkan: Tōkyō. 1972.
Taishūkan Shin-Kanwa Jiten. T. Morohashi. Taishūkan Shoten: Tōkyō. 1992.

TYPOGRAPHICAL EXPLANATIONS

THE PAGE IN GENERAL

N.B. The first five items below pertain to the first main-character entry on a left-hand page and to the last on a right-hand page.

1. The topmost boldface numeral in the upper, outer corner shows the traditional number of the radical under which the main character entries on the page are classified.

2. The vertical string of radicals in the outer margin shows all the radicals containing the relevant number of strokes, plus their more important variants.

3. The heavy brackets enclose the radical (and important variants) under which the main character entries on the page are classified. As the reader spins the pages, the brackets will seem to run up and down the string of radicals, providing a rapid visual aid to locating the relevant radical.

4. The boldface number at the head of a radical string shows the number of strokes in the radicals in the string.

5. The tiny numeral outside the radical (and variants) enclosed by the brackets show the number of strokes in the non-radical part of the main character entries on the page.

6. Boldface numbers in the lower, outer corner show the inclusive numbers of the character entries on the page.

7. Numerals centered at the bottom of each page are page numbers.

8. A column-wide divider consisting of a boldface numeral flanked by horizontal lines shows the beginning of a group of characters each having the indicated number of strokes in its non-radical part.

9. A page-wide divider consisting of a radical and its traditional number flanked by heavy horizontal lines shows the beginning of a new radical section. Shown immediately below the divider are the variants of the radical, its names in Japanese and English, and other pertinent information. Each radical is also given an English "nickname" in an effort to standardize the English nomenclature of the radicals.

THE ENTRIES

10. The large boldface character at the left of a column indicates a main entry character.

11. Three numbers separated by horizontal lines immediately follow each main entry. The top number is the character's Nelson number and is assigned sequentially through the dictionary to every main entry. This number is used in all cross-references. The middle number, preceded by a J, is the character's Japan

Industrial Standard code number. "J-X" indicates that the character is not found in the JIS character set. The bottom number, preceded by an M, is the number assigned to the character in Morohashi's *Dai Kanwa Jiten*. "M-X" means that the character is not found in Morohashi.

12. A capital A immediately to the left of a main character entry indicates that the character is one of the 1006 characters designated by the Ministry of Education to be learned in the six years of elementary school (See Appendix 13). A capital B indicates that the character is one of the other 939 characters in the Jōyō Kanji List. If no small capital letter precedes a main entry character, it is to be understood that the character, while outside the 1,945 list, is still sufficiently common in modern literature to be important in a wide mastery of Japanese.

13. Other large boldface characters to the right of a main entry show alternative forms of the character. The Nelson, JIS, and Morohashi numbers of these variants are also given.

14. Readings of a character in small capital letters show the *on* or Sino-Japanese readings. These are defined only if they have distinctive meanings; otherwise they partake of the English meanings which follow other readings of the character. (Note that many on readings have gone out of use. As a rule, only those on that have independent use or appear in compounds in this dictionary are listed. For a complete listing of all the on readings of a character, see the Morohashi dictionary. See our character 6997 for an example of the great number of on readings that a character may have.)

15. Readings of a character in italics show the *kun* or native Japanese readings. The Hepburn system of romanization is employed in this dictionary. In general, the order of listing of the *kun* readings is, first, verbs, then other parts of speech, and finally prefixes and suffixes. The punctuation of the *on* and *kun* readings provides information about their uses and meanings as shown in the following examples: (a) "ON meaning. *kun* meaning." or "ON meaning. ON meaning. *kun* meaning. *kun* meaning." shows *on* and *kun* readings with separate meanings. (b) "ON. *kun* meaning." shows that the *on* reading is not used alone, but partakes of the *kun* meaning in compounds. (c) "ON. ON meaning. *kun* meaning." shows that the first *on* is not used alone, but partakes of the meanings of the other readings in compounds. (d) "ON *kun* meaning." or "ON, ON *kun* meaning." shows that the *on* may be used alone and share the meaning of the *kun* readings.

16. Syllables of a reading enclosed in parentheses show syllables comprising the *okurigana*, i.e., the inflected part of the word written in the kana syllabary. We follow recent Ministry of Education recommendations, but there is considerable variation in actual use. The auxiliary verbs *suru*, *nasu*, and *naru* and particles (*na*, *no*, *ni*, *de*, etc.) are not parts of the preceding words and are therefore not enclosed in parentheses; they should, of course, be written in the kana syllabary in a text.

17. The characters 国字 (*kokuji*) following a main entry indicate that the character is made in Japan and not inherited from China.

18. A radical enclosed in heavy brackets at the end of a main entry shows the character's traditional radical, which may differ from the radical under which we

have classified it in several cases. These cases are described in the material described in Paragraph 9 above.

THE COMPOUNDS

19. Small characters at the left of a column following a main entry are the compound entries and are followed by their readings in italics. No distinction is made between *on* and *kun* readings in compound entries. Parentheses are used to indicate *okurigana* as described in Paragraph 16 above. Note that in listing compounds the main-entry character is not repeated since it is the first member of every compound.

20. Superscript numerals immediately to the left of a list of compounds show the full stroke count of the second character of the compound (the main-character entry being counted as the first character). A new numeral appears whenever the stroke count changes.

THE CROSS-REFERENCES

The two types of cross-references used in the text are illustrated below.

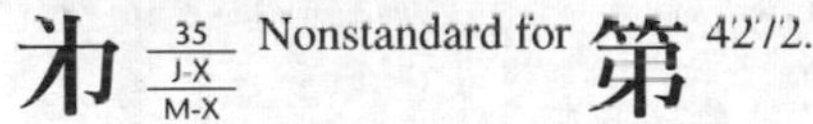

才 is not on the Jōyō list and is not one of the traditional variants listed in standard character dictionaries, but is quite widely used for 第 4272.

區 593 / J523f / M2691 See 区 585.

The information concerning the character 區 is to be found under its Jōyō equivalent 区 585.

The New Nelson Japanese-English Character Dictionary

1-STROKE RADICALS

一 RAD. 1

Ichi one. Variant: a shorter horizontal. Nickname: One.

一 A 1 J306c M1 ICHI one; a. ITSU one. *hi* one. *hito(tsu)* one, a unit; the same; just; once. *itsu wa, hito(tsu) wa* for one thing, partly. *itsu ni* solely, entirely, only; or. *hitotsu ni* as one. *hitotsu ni wa* for one thing, partly. *ichi-* one, a certain; the whole; the same (time); petty, worthless. *-ichi* the best, the first. *hito-* one; a.

1 一 *ichi-ichi, hito(tsu)-hito(tsu)* one by one, separately; everything; in detail

2 入 *hitoshio* still more, especially

八 *ichi(ka)bachi(ka)* sink or swim

了簡 *ichiryōken* at one's discretion

二及 *ichini(ni)oyo(buzu)* without going into details

二無 *ichi(mo)ni(mo)na(ku)* unhesitatingly

丁 *itchō* one block; counter for guns, ink sticks, oars, candles, palanquins, or jinrickshas

丁字 *itteiji* a single letter

刀 *ittō* a sword, a blade, a (single) stroke

刀両断 *ittō-ryōdan* cutting in two with one stroke; a swift and decisive action or measure

刀彫 *ittōbo(ri)* a one-knife carving

人 *hitori, ichinin* one person. *hitori de* alone; by oneself, voluntarily, spontaneously, automatically

人一人 *hitoribitori* one by one

人子 *hitorigo, hitorikko* an only child

人芝居 *hitori shibai* a one-man show

人当 *hitoria(tari), hitoria(te)* per person

人歩 *hitoriaru(ki)* walking alone

人者 *hitorimono* a single person; someone alone

人物 *ichijimbutsu* a man of some importance, a character

人乗 *hitorino(ri)* a single-seater

人前 *hitorimae, ichinimmae* full manhood, adult; a plate, one helping

人娘 *hitori musume* an only daughter

人旅 *hitoritabi* traveling alone

人残 *hitori noko(razu)* everyone

人称 *ichininshō* first person (in grammar)

人息子 *hitori musuko* an only son

人寝 *hitorine* sleeping alone

人舞台 *hitori butai* one's unrivaled field

3 山 *hitoyama* a mountain; the whole mountain; a pile (of something)

己 *ikko* oneself. *ikko no* personal, private

丸 *ichigan* a lump, (into) one

才 *issai* one year old

ヶ月 *ikkagetsu* one month

夕 *isseki* one evening, some evening

大 *ichidai* very important

大事 *ichidaiji* a serious matter

子 *hitorigo* an only child. *isshi* a child, especially the son and heir; an only child

子相伝 *isshi-sōden* transmission of a trade secret from a father to one child only

寸 *issun* one. *chotto* just a minute; a short time; just a little, somewhat; easily, readily, rather

寸先 *issun saki* an inch ahead, the immediate future. *chotto saki* a little ahead

寸逃 *issunnoga(re)* quibbling, prevarication

寸法師 *issumbōshi* dwarf, midget

口 *hitokuchi* a mouthful, a bite, a sip, a draft

口同音 *ikku-dōon* reading in unison; saying the same thing

口咄 *hitokuchibanashi* joke, anecdote

口商 *hitokuchi akina(i)* an immediate definite deal

口話 *hitokuchibanashi* joke, anecdote

口噺 *hitokuchibanashi* joke, anecdote

4 戸 *ikko* a house, a household

月 *Ichigatsu* January. *hitotsuki, ichigetsu* one month

0 木 *ichiboku* one tree
水 *issui* a current (of water); a drop
片 *ippen* a piece, a bit
円 *ichien* the whole area; one yen
区 *ikku* a district, a ward, a lot
匹 *ippiki* one animal; two-*tan* bolt of cloth
反 *ittan* one-tenth hectare; a roll of cloth (of about ten meters)
双 *issō* a pair (of screens)
介 *ikkai no* mere, only a...
辺倒 *ippentō* complete devotion to one side
手 *itte* a move (in a game); one method; a monopoly. *itte ni* single-handed. *hitote* one hand; one's own effort
手販売 *itte hambai* sole agency
毛 *ichimō* one-tenth of a *rin* (厘)
毛作 *ichimōsaku* a single crop
六勝負 *ichiroku-shōbu* gambling, speculation
六銀行 *ichiroku ginkō* pawnshop
夫一婦 *ippuippu* monogamy
夫多妻 *ipputasai* polygamy
心 *isshin, hito(tsu)kokoro* one mind, the whole heart, wholeheartedness
心不乱 *isshin-furan ni* wholeheartedly, intently
心同体 *isshin-dōtai* one flesh, union
方 *ippō* a quarter, a side; one direction; one hand; the other hand; one party; the other party; on the other hand; meanwhile; only, simply; in turn. *hitokata(naranu)* extraordinary; special. *hitokata(narazu)* unusually, greatly
方交通 *ippō kōtsū* one-way traffic
方的 *ippōteki* one-sided, unilateral, arbitrary
方通行 *ippō tsūkō* one-way traffic
切 *issai* all, everything, the whole; entirely, absolutely. *hitoki(re)* a slice, a small piece. *hitoki(ri)* a pause, a period, a step; once, some years ago
切合財 *issai-gassai* any and every thing; altogether, without reserve
切経 *Issaikyō* complete Buddhist scriptures
切衆生 *issai-shujō* all creatures
天 *itten* the whole sky, firmament
天万乗 *itten-banjō* a sovereign of the whole realm
天四海 *itten-shikai* the world, the universe
元 *ichigen no* unitary
元化 *ichigenka* unification, centralization
元的 *ichigenteki* monistic, unitary, unified, centralized
元論 *ichigenron* monism
分 *ippun* a minute. *ichibu* one tenth; one hundredth, one percent; one tenth of a *sun*; one quarter *ryō* (an old coin). *ichibun* duty, honor
分別 *hitofumbetsu* careful consideration
分金 *ichibukin* a gold quarter *ryō*
分銀 *ichibugin* a silver quarter *ryō*
文 *ichimon* one *mon*. one-tenth of a *sen*; something of insignificant value. *ichibun* a sentence
文字 *ichimonji* a straight line, a beeline
文惜 *ichimon-oshi(mi)* stinginess; miser
文商 *ichimon akina(i)* a penny store; business on a small scale
文無 *ichimonna(shi)* penniless
日 *ichinichi, ichijitsu, hitohi* one day, a day. *tsuitachi* the first day (of the month)
日一日 *ichinichi-ichinichi* gradually, day by day
日一夜 *ichijitsu-ichiya* all day and all night
日千秋 *ichijitsu-senshū* many a weary day
日片時 *ichijitsu-henshi* a short time
日中 *ichinichijū* all day long
日長 *ichijitsu(no)chō* superiority
日路 *ichinichiji* a day's journey
日増 *ichinichima(shi) ni* day by day
5 矢 *isshi* an arrow; a retort
穴 *hito(tsu)ana* the same hole; one gang. *ikketsu* a hole
皿 *hitosara* a plate, a dish (of food)
句 *ikku* a phrase, a verse, a line; a *haiku*-poem counter
巡 *hitomegu(ri)* a turn, a round; one full year. *ichijun* a beat, a round
打 *hito-u(chi), ichida* a stroke, a blow. *ichi dāsu* one dozen
札 *issatsu* a document, a bond
礼 *ichirei* a bow, a salute, a greeting
旦 *ittan* once; one morning; temporarily
半 *ippan* a half; a part
失 *isshitsu* a disadvantage; a defect; an error

冊 *issatsu* one copy (of a book)
号 *ichigō* number one
仕事 *hito shigoto* a task
汁一菜 *ichijū-issai* a one-plate meal, a simple meal
石 *isseki* one game (of *go*); a stone
石二鳥 *isseki-nichō* killing two birds with one stone
代 *ichidai* one generation; a lifetime; an age
代記 *ichidaiki* a biography
生 *isshō* a lifetime, one's (whole) life; all through life
生涯 *isshōgai* a lifetime, one's (whole) life; all through life
生懸命 *isshōkemmei ni* with all one's might
目 *hitome* glimpse, a glance. *ichimoku* a glance, a look. *hito(tsu)me* a one-eyed monster
目惚 *hitomebo(re)* love at first sight
目散 *ichimokusan ni* at full speed
目瞭然 *ichimoku-ryōzen* very clear
世 *issei* a first generation immigrant. *isse, issei* one existence, a lifetime, a generation, an age; the era
世一代 *isse-ichidai* once a lifetime
世紀 *isseiki* a century
本 *ippon* one (long object); one version; a certain book; a blow; a full-fledged geisha
本立 *ipponda(chi)* independence
本気 *ippongi* a one-track mind, single-minded
本建 *ipponda(te)* a single standard
本道 *ippommichi* a direct unforked road
本釣 *ipponzu(ri)* fishing with a pole
本槍 *ippon'yari* one's sole talent; a guiding principle
本調子 *ipponchōshi, ipponjōshi* monotone
本橋 *ippombashi* a log bridge
6 色 *isshoku, hitoiro* one color; one kind. *isshiki* one color; pure; one article
行 *ichigyō, ikkō* a line, a row. *ikkō* a party; a troupe; an act
同 *ichidō* all present, all concerned, all of us
旬 *ichijun* ten days
団 *ichidan* a body, a group, a party, a gang, a troupe
因 *ichiin* a cause
式 *isshiki* a complete set, all, the whole, everything
曲 *ikkyoku* a tune, a melody, a piece of music
向 *ikkō* (not) at all. *hitasura* earnestly
任 *ichinin suru* entrust (to someone)
件 *ikken* a matter, an item
休 *hitoyasu(mi)* a rest
会 *ichie* one meeting
如 *ichinyo* oneness
列 *ichiretsu* a row, a line
汗 *hitoase* doing a job; riding and sweating up a horse
再 *issai* once or twice. *issai narazu* repeatedly
先 *hitomazu* for the present; in outline; tentatively
朶 *ichida* a branch (of flowers); a cluster, a mass (of clouds)
考 *ikkō* consideration, a thought
名 *ichimei* one person; another name
存 *ichizon* one's own discretion; one's own idea; one's own responsibility
安心 *hitoanshin* a feeling of relief
合目 *ichigōme* the start of a climb up a mountain
肌脱 *hitohadanu(gu)* pitch in and help
衣帯水 *ichiitai-sui* a narrow strait
糸 *isshi* a thread
糸一毫 *isshi-ichigō* tiny amount
気 *ikki ni* at a breath, at a stroke, at a sitting
気呵成 *ikki-kasei ni* at a breath, at a stroke, at a sitting
字 *ichiji* a character, a letter
字千金 *ichiji-senkin* a word of great value
死 *isshi* one out (in baseball); dying
死報国 *isshi-hōkoku* dying for one's country
次 *ichiji* the first; a linear (equation)
次電流 *ichiji denryū* primary current
両 *ichiryō* one *ryō* (an old coin); one vehicle
両日 *ichiryojitsu* a day or two
両年 *ichiryōnen* a year or two
年 *ichinen* one year. *hitotose* one year; some time ago
年中 *ichinenjū* through the year
年生 *ichinensei* first-year student; annual (plant)

1 年草 *ichinensō* an annual (plant)
回 *ikkai* once, a time, one time, a round, a game, a bout, a heat, an inning. *hitomawa(ri)* a turn, a round
回分 *ikkaibun* a dose; an installment
回忌 *ikkaiki* first death anniversary
回転 *ikkaiten, ichi kaiten* one revolution; one rotation
回戦 *ikkaisen* first game, first round (of tennis, etc.)
7 走 *hitohashi(ri), hito(p)pashi(ri)* a spin, a run
応 *ichiō* once; tentatively; in outline
位 *ichii* first place, first rank; unit's place (in figures)
吹 *hitofu(ki)* a blast, puff, whiff, gust
役 *hitoyaku* a part to play. *ichiyaku* an office; an important office
折 *hitoo(ri)* one box. *hitoo(re)* a segment (of music, dance)
対 *ittsui* a pair (of screens, vases, etc.)
決 *ikketsu suru* be agreed, be settled
別 *ichibetsu* parting
助 *ichijo* a help
更 *ikkō* first watch, 7–9 p.m.
呑 *hitono(mi)* swallowing in one gulp; an easy prey
系 *ikkei* a single-family lineage
声 *hitokoe, issei* a voice, a cry, a shout
条 *ichijō* a line, a streak; a matter, a quotation
男 *ichinan* a boy; eldest son
芸 *ichigei* an art; one talent
花 *hitohana* a flower; success
束 *issoku, hitotaba* a bundle, a hundred
私人 *isshijin, ichishijin* a private individual
卵性双生児 *ichiransei sōseiji* identical twins
見 *ikken* a look, a glimpse; first meeting; apparently. *ichigen* first meeting; first-time (customer)
見識 *ichikenshiki* an opinion
角 *ikkaku* corner, section; point; a narwhal. *hitokado, ikkado* superiority, something uncommon. *hitokado no* respectable; full-fledged
角獣 *ikkakujū* unicorn; a narwhal
足 *issoku* a pair (footwear). *hitoashi* a step
足飛 *issokuto(bi) ni* at one bound
身 *isshin* throughout the body; oneself, one's own interests. *hito(tsu)mi* baby clothes
身上 *isshinjō no* personal (affairs)
里 *ichiri* 2.44 miles
里塚 *ichirizuka* milestone, mileposts (standing one *ri* apart)
局 *ikkyoku* one game (of checkers, etc.)
局部 *ikkyokubu* one part
利 *ichiri* one advantage
利一害 *ichiri-ichigai* advantages and disadvantages
体 *ittai* one body, one flesh; what on earth, really, in fact, properly speaking; originally. *ittai ni* generally
体化 *ittaika* unification, integration
体全体 *ittai-zentai* Whatever (is the matter)?; What on earth (is going on)?
言 *hitokoto, ichigen, ichigon* a word, a single word
言一行 *ichigen-ikkō* every word and act
言二言 *hitokoto-futakoto* a word or two
言半句 *ichigen-hanku, ichigon-hanku* a word, a few words
言居士 *ichigen-koji* a person who always has to have his say
8 門 *ichimon* the family, dependents, the household
雨 *hitoame* a shower, a rain
例 *ichiretsu* one example, an instance
味 *ichimi* one flavor; an ingredient (of medicine); a touch, a tinge; conspirators, a gang
帖 *ichijō* a quire (of paper); one mat; ten sheets (of seaweed)
往 *ichiō* once, tentatively, in outline; go once
抱 *hitokaka(e)* an armful, one bundle
抹 *ichimatsu* a touch of, a tinge of, a wreath (of smoke)
泡 *hitoawa* a shock; a surprise
版 *ippan* an edition
物 *ichimotsu* an article, a thing; plot, ulterior motive, secret intention. *ichibutsu* a thing
服 *ippuku* a dose; a puff, a smoke; lull, dull market; short rest
命 *ichimei* a life; a command
念 *ichinen* a determined purpose
宗 *isshū* a sect, a denomination
宛 *hito(tsu)zutsu, hito(tsu)ate* one each
具 *ichigu* one set

昔 *hitomukashi* antiquity
事 *ichiji* one thing. *hito(tsu)koto* the same thing
切那 *issetsuna* a moment, an instant
炊夢 *issui (no) yume* an empty dream
直線 *itchokusen* a straight line
長一短 *itchō-ittan* good points and shortcomings
知半解 *itchi-hankai* superficial knowledge
妻多夫 *issai-tafu* polyandry
泊 *ippaku* stopping one night
泊行軍 *ippaku kōgun* an overnight march
所 *ik(ka)sho, hitotokoro, issho* one place; the same place
所懸命 *isshokemmei ni* with all one's might
杯 *ippai* a cup of; a drink; full; to the utmost; up to (one's income)
杯機嫌 *ippai-kigen* slight intoxication
定 *ittei suru* fix, settle, regularize, define; unify; standardize. *ichijō* something definitely settled. *ittei no* certain, uniform, prescribed, standard, regular, fixed, definite
定不変 *ittei-fuhen* invariable, permanent
刻 *ikkoku* a moment, an instant. *ikkoku na* stubborn, hotheaded
刻千金 *ikkokusenkin* an extremely important time
刻早 *ikkoku(mo) haya(ku)* immediately
周 *hitomegu(ri)* a turn, a round; one full year. *isshū* once around, a revolution, a tour, a lap
周年 *isshūnen* one full year
周忌 *isshūki* first death anniversary
周期 *isshūki* a period (in astronomy)
国 *ikkoku* stubborn, hotheaded; the whole country
国一党主義 *ikkoku-ittō shugi* one-party system
国一票 *ikkoku-ippyō* one vote per nation
国者 *ikkokumono* an ultranationalist; a hot-tempered person, a stubborn person
枚 *ichimai* one sheet
枚下 *ichimai shita* one step lower
枚上 *ichimai ue* one step higher
枚貝 *ichimaigai* univalve
枚看板 *ichimaikamban* one's only suit, only coat; leading actor, prima donna; slogan, motto; sole aim
斉 *issei ni* simultaneously, all at once
斉安 *isseiyasu* all-round (market) decline
斉高 *isseidaka* all-round (market) advance
斉射撃 *isseishageki* volley firing, fusillade, a broadside
斉検挙 *isseikenkyo* wholesale arrest, round-up
歩 *ippo* a step
歩一歩 *ippo-ippo* step by step, by degrees
歩前進 *ippo zenshin* a step forward
歩金 *ichibukin* a gold quarter *ryō*
歩銀 *ichibugin* a silver quarter *ryō*
夜 *ichiya, hitoyo* one night, all night, one evening, overnight
夜大臣 *ichiya daijin* overnight millionaire
夜乞食 *ichiya kojiki* a person made homeless by fire; overnight beggar
夜中 *ichiyajū, hitoyojū* all night through
夜妻 *ichiyazuma, hitoyozuma* temporary consort, prostitute
夜造 *ichiyazuku(ri)* built in a night; stopgap; hastily written
夜漬 *ichiyazuke* salted just overnight; cramming
9 食 *isshoku* a meal. *ichijiki* one meal (a day)
首 *isshu* a poem (esp. waka or tanka)
度 *ichido, hitotabi* once, one time, on one occasion
通 *ittsū* one copy (of a document). *hitotō(ri)* in general, briefly. *hitotō(ri) no* ordinary, usual
連 *ichiren* a series, a chain; 1,000 sheets (of paper)
途 *itto* a way, a course; the only way. *ichizu ni* wholeheartedly
律 *ichiritsu* evenness, uniformity, equality, monotony. *ichiritsu ni* in the same way
指 *isshi* a finger
括 *ikkatsu* one lump, one bundle; summing up. *hitokuku(ri)* a bundle. *hitokuru(me)* a bunch, a bundle, a lot
派 *ippa* a school, a sect, a party
級 *ikkyū* one grade; first class
計 *ikkei* a plan

1 【一】 0 丨 丶 丿 乙 亅

陣 *ichijin* vanguard; a gust of wind
封 *ippū* a sealed letter; a sealed document; an enclosure
変 *ippen* complete change
軍 *ichigun* an army, the whole army
星 *hito(tsu)boshi* evening star; morning star
思 *hitoomo(i) ni* instantly, resolutely
発 *ippatsu* a shot, a round, a charge
荒 *hitoa(re)* a squall, a burst of anger
巻 *ikkan* one volume. *hitomaki* one roll
洗 *issen suru* thoroughly wash away
昼夜 *itchūya* a whole day and night, 24 hours
院制 *ichiinsei* unicameral system
神教 *isshinkyō* monotheism
音節 *ichionsetsu* monosyllable
姫二太郎 *ichihime-nitarō* It's good to have a girl first and then a boy.
風呂 *hitofuro* a quick bath
風変 *ippūkawa(tta)* eccentric, queer; unconventional, original
段 *ichidan* more, still more, much more, all the more; a part (of a talk). *ittan* $\frac{1}{10}$ hectare
段落 *ichidanraku* a pause
品 *ippin* an item; a dish, a course; the best item
品料理 *ippin-ryōri* service à la carte
点 *itten* a speck, dot, point, particle; a very little; one item
点張 *ittemba(ri)* persistence
面 *ichimen* one side, one phase; the whole surface; first page (of a newspaper); (on) the other hand; all over
面観 *ichimenkan* one-sided view
面識 *ichimenshiki* a passing acquaintance
重 *hitoe* one layer; single. *hitokasa(ne)* a suit; a set of boxes
重桜 *hitoezakura* a cherry tree bearing single blossoms; single cherry blossoms
重継 *hitoetsu(gi)* sheet bend (knot)
昨日 *issakujitsu, ototoi, ototsui* day before yesterday
昨年 *issakunen, ototoshi* year before last
昨夜 *issakuya* night before last
昨昨日 *issakusakujitsu, sakiototoi, sakiototsui* two days before yesterday
昨昨年 *issakusakunen, sakiototoshi* two years before last
昨晩 *issakuban* night before last
10 座 *ichiza* the party; those present; a troupe; the first seat
席 *isseki* a sitting; a speech; a feast
閃 *issen* a flash
俵 *ippyō* one straw-bagful
倍 *ichibai* the same amount; double; still more
挺 *itchō* counter for guns, ink sticks, oars, candles, palanquins, or jinrickshas
桁 *hitoketa* a unit (in figures)
流 *ichiryū* a school (of art); foremost, first-class, top-notch; unique
将 *isshō* a general
眠 *hitonemu(ri)* a nap. *ichimin* the first sleep (of silkworms)
脈 *ichimyaku* a vein, a thread (of connection)
郭 *ikkaku* a city block; an enclosure
員 *ichiin* a member
案 *ichian* an idea, a plan
差 *hitosa(shi)* a dance; a match (of sumo)
書 *hito(tsu)ga(ki)* an item, itemization. *issho* one letter; one book
息 *hitoiki* a breath, a pause; without a pause; a little effort
荷 *ikka* a load
帯 *ittai* a region, a zone; the whole place
能 *ichinō* one talent; one ability
個人 *ikkojin, ichikojin* a private person, an individual
進一退 *isshin-ittai* advance and retreat, ebb and flow, seesawing, fluctuating
紙半銭 *isshi-hansen* a small sum; things of little value
殺多生 *issetsu-tashō, issatsu-tashō* destroying one to save many
党 *ittō* a party or clique
笑 *isshō* a laugh, a smile
笑付 *isshō ni fu(su)* laugh (someone) down
致 *itchi* agreement, conformity, consistency; union, cooperation
致点 *itchiten* point of agreement
隻 *isseki* one boat, one ship; one of a pair
隻眼 *issekigan* one eye; a discerning eye; an opinion
週 *isshū* a week
週間 *isshūkan* a week
部 *ichibu* a part; a copy (of a publication)

部分 *ichibubun* a part
部始終 *ichibu-shijū* full particulars
家 *ikka, ikke* a house, a home, a family, a household, one's family, one's folks; a style
家団欒 *ikka-danran* a family get-together
家言 *ikkagen* a private opinion, a personal view
軒 *ikken* a house
軒一軒 *ikken-ikken* house to house
軒屋 *ikken'ya* an isolated house
軒家 *ikken'ya* an isolated house
挙 *ikkyo* one effort, one action
挙一動 *ikkyo-ichidō* one's every action
挙手一投足 *ikkyoshu-ittōsoku* a slight effort, one's every action
挙両得 *ikkyo-ryōtoku* killing two birds with one stone
時 *ichiji* one o'clock; a time; temporarily; at one time. *hitotoki* a little while, at one time. *ittoki* 12th part of a day; a short period. *ichidoki ni* at a time, at one time
時払 *ichijibarai* lump sum payment
時金 *ichijikin* lump sum
時逃 *ichijinoga(re), ittokinoga(re)* quibbling, temporizing
時的 *ichijiteki* temporary
時凌 *ichiji-shino(gi)* makeshift, temporary expedient
時預 *ichijiazu(kari)* (baggage) checking, temporary custody. *ichijiazu(ke)* (baggage) checking, temporary depositing
時賜金 *ichiji shikin* lump sum grant
般 *ippan no* general, universal, ordinary, average
般人 *ippanjin* an ordinary person
般化 *ippanka* generalization, popularization
般投票 *ippan tōhyō* referendum, popular vote, plebiscite
般性 *ippansei* generality
般法 *ippanhō* general law
般的 *ippanteki* general
般概念 *ippan gainen* general idea
般論 *ippanron* general consideration
11 遍 *ippen* once; at one time; perfunctory; in a general way
道 *ichidō* one road; a ray (of hope)
頃 *hitokoro* once, some time ago
掃 *issō* a clean sweep
掬 *ikkiku* one scoop (of water)
族 *ichizoku* a family, dependents, relatives, a household
渉 *hitowata(ri)* briefly, in general, glancing through
理 *ichiri* a principle, a reason
眸 *ichibō* one sweep, an unbroken view
眼 *ichigan* one eye; single-lens
組 *hitokumi, ichikumi* one class. *hitokumi* one set
敗 *ippai* one defeat
隊 *ittai* a party, a gang, a squad, a company (of soldiers)
隅 *ichigū, hitosumi* a corner, a nook
階 *ikkai* ground floor, first floor
毫 *ichigō* a trifle
堂 *ichidō* a building, a hall; a room; same place
票 *ippyō* a vote, a ballot
雫 *hitoshizuku* a drop (of water)
盛 *hitosaka(ri)* temporary prosperity. *hitomo(ri)* a pile
絃琴 *ichigenkin* one-stringed instrument
帳羅 *itchōra* one's only (good) suit (or kimono)
陽来復 *ichiyō-raifuku* return of spring
過 *ikka suru* pass away
過性 *ikkasei* transient (pain or fever)
問 *ichimon* family, kin, clan
問一答 *ichimon-itō* answering each question one by one
張一弛 *itchō-isshi* tension and relaxation
張羅 *itchōra* one's only (good) suit (or kimono)
得 *ittoku* one advantage, a merit
得一失 *ittoku-isshitsu* an advantage and a disadvantage, a merit and a demerit
視同仁 *isshidōjin* impartiality, universal brotherhood, universal benevolence
転 *itten* a turn, complete change
転機 *ittenki, ichitenki* a turning point
宿 *isshuku* staying one night
宿一飯 *isshuku-ippan* just staying for a night and a meal
貫 *ikkan* consistency, coherence, integration; $8\frac{1}{3}$ pounds
貫番号 *ikkan bangō* serial number
望 *ichibō* one sweep, an unbroken view
望千里 *ichibō-senri* the boundless (ocean)

粒 *hitotsubu* a grain
粒選 *hitotsubuyo(ri), hitotsubue(ri)* careful selection
粒種 *hitotsubudane* an only child
12 間 *ikken* one *ken*, six feet. *hitoma* one room, one *ken*
喝 *ikkatsu* a roar, a thundering cry
場 *ichijō* one time, one place. *ichiba* one scene (of a play)
項 *ikkō* an item
幅 *ippuku* a scroll
握 *ichiaku, hitonigi(ri)* a handful
揃 *hitosoroi, hitosoroe* a set, a suit
揆 *ikki* a riot, an insurrection; union
晩 *hitoban* one evening; a night; all night; overnight
晩中 *hitobanjū* all night long
棟 *hitomune* one house; the same house
斑 *ippan* a spot; a glimpse, an outline; a part
統 *ittō* a lineage, a line; unification; all (of you)
飲 *hitono(mi)* a mouthful; a swallow, a sip
飯 *ippan* a bowl (of rice); a meal
割 *ichiwari* ten percent
散 *issan ni* at top speed
期 *ichigo* one's life, a lifetime. *ikki* a term, the first term
策 *issaku* an idea, a plan
畳 *ichijō* one mat
着 *itchaku* first arrival; first (in the race); a suit (of clothes); wear clothes
葦 *ichii* one reed; a small boat
葉 *ichiyō* a leaf; a page; a copy (of a photo); a small boat
報 *ippō* information; a report
閑張 *ikkamba(ri)* lacquered papier-mâché
喜一憂 *ikki-ichiyū* alternation of hope and fear, alternation of joys and sorrows
朝 *itchō* a short period; once; one morning
朝一夕 *itchō-isseki ni* in a day, in a brief interval
筆 *hitofude, ippitsu* a few lines, a stroke of the pen
筆書 *hitofudega(ki)* a one-stroke sketch
塁 *ichirui* first base; a fort
塁手 *ichiruishu* first baseman
塁線 *ichiruisen* first base line
筋 *hitosuji* a line; earnestly, blindly, straightforwardly
筋道 *hitosuji michi* a straight road
筋縄 *hitosuji nawa* an ordinary method
番 *ichiban* number one, the first; most, best; a game, a round, a bout, an event (in a meet). *hitotsugai* a pair, a couple, a brace
番手 *ichibante* initial-assault force; first player, first worker
番茶 *ichibancha* the first pick of tea; the first brew of tea
番乗 *ichibannori* leader of a charge; first to arrive
番鶏 *ichibandori* first cockcrow
等 *ittō* first class, first rank, A-1; the most, the best
等車 *ittōsha* first-class coach
等兵 *ittōhei* private first class (Marine Corps); private (army)
等卒 *ittōsotsu* private first class
等国 *ittōkoku* first-class power
等星 *ittōsei* first-magnitude star
等賞 *ittōshō* first prize, blue ribbon
等親 *ittōshin* first-degree relative
13 廉 *hitokado, ikkado* superiority, something uncommon. *hitokado no* respectable; full-fledged
塩 *hitoshio* slightly salted
塊 *hitokatama(ri)* a group, a lump. *ikkai* a lump
睡 *issui, hitonemuri* a nap, a short sleep
話 *hito(tsu)banashi* anecdote; favorite topic
路 *ichiro* one road, one way; straight; earnestly
際 *hitokiwa* noticeably, remarkably; still more, especially
戦 *issen* a battle, a game, a bout
献 *ikkon* one cup (of saké)
群 *ichigun, hitomu(re)* a group; a flock, a crowd, a herd, a cluster (of flowers)
歳 *issai* one year old
置 *hito(tsu)o(ki)* alternate, every other one
夢 *ichimu* a dream; a fleeting thing
寝入 *hitone-i(ri)* a nap
溜無 *hitotama(ri) (mo) na(ku)* easily, irresistibly, helplessly
蓮托生 *ichiren-takushō* sharing one's lot with another; being reborn on the same lotus in Buddhist Heaven

触即発 *isshoku-sokuhatsu* delicate situation, explosive situation
新 *isshin* complete change, reform, remodeling, renewal
新紀元 *ichi shinkigen* a new era
節 *issetsu* a verse (in the Bible), a stanza, a paragraph, a passage. *hito fushi* a joint, section; a tune, note, strain, measure
節切 *hitoyogi(ri)* one-jointed bamboo musical instrument
義 *ichigi* a reason, a principle, a meaning; the first meaning, the first principle
義的 *ichigiteki* having a single meaning; being the first principle
幕 *hitomaku* one act
幕物 *hitomakumono* a one-act play
意 *ichii* earnestness; one idea; same thought
意専心 *ichii senshin* wholeheartedly
14 層 *issō* more, still more, much more, all the more
旗 *hito hata* a flag; an undertaking
概 *ichigai ni* unconditionally, sweepingly
様 *ichiyō* uniformity, evenness, similarity, equality, impartiality
滴 *itteki* a drop
種 *hitokusa* one kind. *isshu* a kind, a species, a variety
端 *ittan* one end; a part
緒 *issho* the same; company. *issho ni* together (with); at the same time, in a lump. *issho ni suru* unite, confuse with. *issho(kuta)* mix up; heterogeneous mixture
読 *ichidoku* a perusal; one reading
説 *issetsu* an opinion; a report; another opinion
駄 *ichida* a horse load
管 *ikkan* a pipe; one flute; one brush; flute solo in noh plays
髪 *ippatsu* a hair, a hair's breadth
網打尽 *ichimō-dajin* a big haul; wholesale arrest
酸化炭素 *issanka tanso* carbon monoxide
語 *ichigo* one word
語一語 *ichigo-ichigo* word for word
箇 *ikko* one; a piece
箇月 *ikkagetsu* one month
箇年 *ikkanen* one year
15 億 *ichioku* one hundred million
儀 *ichigi* a matter; that matter
撮 *hitotsumami* a pinch (of something)
稼 *hitokasegi* a job; a gain
線 *issen* a line; line of demarcation
諾 *ichidaku* a consent
輛 *ichiryō* one vehicle
審 *isshin* first instance; first trial
撃 *ichigeki* a blow, a hit, a poke
徹 *ittetsu na* obstinate, stubborn, inflexible
徹者 *ittetsu mono* stubborn person
輪 *ichirin* a flower; a wheel
輪車 *ichirinsha* unicycle, wheelbarrow
輪挿 *ichirinzashi* a vase for one flower
16 樹 *ichiju* one tree
獲 *ikkaku* one grab
艘 *issō* a ship, a vessel
頻 *hitoshiki(ri)* for a while, at one time
興 *ikkyo* amusement, fun
覧 *ichiran* a look, a glance; a summary
覧表 *ichiranhyō* list, table, schedule, catalog
頭 *ittō* a head (of cattle)
頭立 *ittōda(te)* one-horse (carriage)
膳 *ichi (no) zen* first course at a banquet. *ichizen* a bowl (of rice); a pair (of chopsticks)
膳飯屋 *ichizemmeshiya* a diner
17 闋 *hitokusari* passage in a discourse, one scene
擲 *itteki suru* abandon
環 *ikkan* a link
縷 *ichiru* a thin wreath (of smoke); a ray (of hope); a thread; very little
瞥 *ichibetsu* a glance, a look
臂 *ippi* an elbow, an arm; (helping) hand
瞬 *isshun* a blink; a moment, an instant
瞬間 *isshunkan* a moment, an instant
18 癖 *hitokuse* a trait, a peculiarity, an idiosyncrasy
儲 *hitomōke* making a profit
難 *ichinan* one difficulty, one danger
類 *ichirui* same kind; accomplices, companions; same clan
叢 *hitomura* a copse; a crowd; a herd
瀉千里 *issha-senri* moving rapidly; fast writing; eloquence
騎 *ikki* one horseman
騎打 *ikkiu(chi)* a man-to-man fight

騎当千 *ikki-tōsen no* matchless (warrior)
騎討 *ikkiu(chi)* personal combat
19 蹴 *isshū, hitoke(ri)* a kick; a rejection; easy victory
20 議 *ichigi* a word, an opinion, an objection; a discussion
齣 *hitokusari* a passage in a discourse, one scene. *hitokoma* a scene
籌 *itchū* a point, a degree
籌輸 *itchū (o) yu(suru)* admit defeat
21 躍 *ichiyaku* one bound; at one bound
顧 *ikko* a notice
纏 *hitomato(me)* a bunch, a bundle
22 驚 *ikkyō* suprise, amazement
23 攫 *ikkaku* one grab
攫千金 *ikkaku-senkin* getting rich quick
24 顰一笑 *ippin-isshō* a mood; a smile or a frown

1

A 丁 2 / J437a / M2 TEI D, fourth; adult male; servant. CHŌ counter for guns, tools, orders of food, leaves, blocks, or cakes of something; even number. TŌ. *hinoto* fourth calendar sign. *-chō.* leaf (of paper), block, cake (of something).
2 丁 *tōtō* ringing of an ax. *chōchō* clashing of swords; felling of trees
5 目 *chōme* city block (of irregular size)
付 *chōzu(ke)* pagination, numbering
半 *chōhan* odd and even numbers; dice game; gambling
6 年 *teinen* majority, adulthood, age twenty
年者 *teinensha* adult
字 *teiji* the letter T
字形 *teijikei* T-shaped
字形定規 *teijikei jōgi* T square
8 定規 *teijōgi* T square
9 度 *chōdo* exactly, just right
重 *teichō* courtesy; politeness
13 数 *chōsū* number of pages; even numbers
稚 *detchi* apprentice
稚奉公 *detchibōkō* apprenticeship
14 寧 *teinei* politeness, courtesy, care, conscientiousness

A 七 3 / J3c37 / M6 SHICHI *nana(tsu), na, nana* seven.
2 七日 *shichishichinichi, nanananuka* 49th day after death
十 *shichijū, nanajū* 70
十人訳 *Shichijūnin'yaku* Septuagint
十路 *nanasoji* age 70
3 夕 *Tanabata, shichiseki* July 7 Festival of the Weaver; prayer ceremony for children's artistic development
4 日 *nanoka, nanuka* seven days; the seventh day (of the month)
月 *Shichigatsu* July
辺形 *shichihenkei* heptagon
不思議 *nanafushigi* the seven wonders
五三 *shichi-go-san* the lucky numbers seven, five, and three; shrine visit by children aged seven, five, and three
五三縄 *shimenawa* sacred shrine rope
五調 *shichigochō* seven-and-five-syllable meter
分三分 *shichibu-sambu* seven to three (chances)
分袖 *shichibusode* three-quarter sleeves
分搗 *shichibuzu(ki)* seventy percent polished (rice)
5 生 *shichishō* seven lives
6 色 *nanairo, shichishoku* the seven prismatic colors
曲 *nanamaga(ri)* tortuous or spiral (path)
回忌 *shichikaiki* seventh anniversary of a death
年忌 *shichinenki* seventh anniversary of a death
7 角形 *shichikakkei* heptagon
8 夜 *shichiya* celebration of a child's seventh day
宝 *shippō* the seven treasures (gold, silver, pearls, agate, crystal, coral, and lapis lazuli); cloisonné
宝焼 *shippōyaki* cloisonné
9 海 *nanatsu no umi* the seven seas
重 *nanae* sevenfold, seven-ply
星 *shichisei* the Big Dipper, Ursa Major
草 *nanakusa* the seven spring flowers; the seven fall flowers
面鳥 *shichimenchō* turkey
面倒 *shichimendō* great trouble, difficulty
10 週祭 *Nanashū (no) Matsu(ri), Nanamawari (no) Iwai* the Feast of Weeks, Pentecost
11 道 *shichidō* the seven districts of ancient Japan

絃琴 *shichigenkin* seven-stringed koto
党伽藍 *shichidōgaran* complete seven-structure temple compound
転八起 *nanakoro(bi)-yao(ki)* the vicissitudes of life; always rising after a fall
顛八倒 *shittembattō* writhing in agony
13 福神 *Shichifukujin* Seven Gods of Luck
14 種 *nanakusa* the seven spring flowers; the seven fall flowers
15 輪 *shichirin* earthen brazier (for cooking)
賢 *shichiken* the seven wise men
18 曜 *shichiyō* the seven luminaries (sun, moon, and five planets); the seven days of the week
19 顛八起 *shichiten-hakki* always rising in spite of repeated failures; the vicissitudes of life
顛八倒 *shittembattō* writhing in agony

2

丂 4 / J-X / M-X Nonstandard for **工** 1532.

B **丈** 5 / J3e66 / M11 Jō 10 feet; length, measure; Mr. or Mrs. (re: artists). *dake* only; alone; no more; merely.
4 比 *takekura(be)* comparison of statures
夫 *masurao, jōfu* a hero; a gentleman; warrior. *jōbu na* healthy, strong, robust; solid, durable
7 余 *jōyo* over ten feet
8 長 *takenaga* tall

B **与** 6 / J4d3f / M20 **與** 4911 / J6750 / M30212 Yo. *ata(eru)* give, award, impart, provide, allot, cause (pain or damage). *azuka(ru)* participate in. *kumi(suru)* take part in; be implicated in; side with; support.
2 力 *yoriki* feudal-era police sergeant; help
4 太 *yota* nonsense, idle talk, good-for-nothing fellow. *yota(ru)* live a wicked life; say silly things
太郎 *yotarō* slow-witted fellow, liar
太者 *yotamono, yotamon* good-for-nothing fellow, hoodlum
太話 *yotabanashi* idle gossip; wild talk
6 件 *yoken* postulate, given conditions, data
8 国 *yokoku* ally; nations in alliance
10 党 *yotō* party in power
11 野党 *yoyatō* majority and minority parties
14 奪 *yodatsu* giving and taking

A **万** 7 / J4b7c / M10 **萬** 5103 / J685f / M31339 MAN ten thousand; myriad. BAN ten thousand, myriad; fully; if by any chance. *yorozu* ten thousand, myriads, all, everything.
1 一 *man'ichi, man(ga)ichi* if by any chance, 10,000 to 1
2 力 *manriki* vise, jack
人 *bannin, banjin* all people, everybody
人向 *bannimmu(ki)* all-purpose, suiting everyone
3 口 *bankō* the mouths of many people; words of many people
千 *bansen* a tremendous number; manifold
丈 *banjō* 10,000 *jō*; unfathomable height (depth); full vent
万 *bamban* very much, fully; (with neg.) never
万一 *bamban'itsu, mamman'ichi* by any chance, 10,000 to one
4 戸 *banko* all houses, many houses
方 *bampō* many directions; many lands; many means
化 *banka* many changes
引 *mambiki* shoplifting; shoplifter
天 *banten, manten* the whole world; the whole sky
夫 *bampu* many men; many warriors
分一 *mambun(no)ichi* one ten thousandth
止得 *ban'ya(muo)e(zu)* unavoidable. *ban'ya(muo)e(nakereba)* if necessary, when unavoidable
5 目 *bammoku* many eyes
仞 *banjin* 10,000 fathoms; great depth; great height
古 *banko* perpetuity, eternity
民 *bammin* all people; the whole nation
代 *bandai* eternity, all ages. *yorozuyo* thousands of years, all generations, eternity
代不易 *bandai fueki* eternally unchanging; perpetuity
世 *bansei* all ages, eternity. *yorozuyo* thousands of years, all generations, eternity

1 2【一】丨 丶 丿 乙 亅

世一系 *banseiikkei* unbroken line through all ages
世不易 *bansei-fueki* eternally unchanging; perpetuity
6 死 *banshi* certain death; dying many times
邦 *bampō, mampō* all nations
朶 *banda* many branches
全 *banzen* perfection
全策 *banzen (no) saku* a carefully thought-out plan
灯 *mandō* many votive lanterns; festival lanterns
灯会 *mandōe* Buddhist lantern festival
有 *ban'yū* all things, all creation
有引力 *ban'yū inryoku* universal gravitation
有神教 *ban'yū shinkyō* pantheism
年 *mannen* 10,000 years; eternity
年床 *mannendoko* always leaving bedquilts unfolded
年候補 *mannen-kōho* ever unsuccessful candidate, persistent candidate
年雪 *mannen'yuki* perpctual snow
年筆 *mannenhitsu* fountain pen
年新造 *mannenshinzō* woman of perennial youth
7 言 *mangon* many words
状 *banjō* diversity, multifariousness
別 *bambetsu* various differentiations
劫 *mangō, magō* eternity; extremely long time
芸 *bangei* all-around accomplishments
来 *banrai* many guests coming
寿 *banju* longitivity. *Manju* era name
里 *banri* 10,000 miles; great distance
里長城 *Banri (no) Chōjō* Great Wall of China
8 金 *mankin, bankin* immense sum of money; great value
物 *bambutsu* all things, all creation
物霊長 *bambutsu (no) reichō* mankind
卒 *bansotsu* host of soldiers
宝 *bampō, mambō* many treasures
事 *banji* all, everything
事休 *banjikyū(suru)* There is nothing more that can be done.
事窮 *banjikyū(suru)* There is nothing more that can be done.
国 *bankoku* all nations
国史 *bankokushi* world history
国旗 *bankokki, bankokuki* flags of all nations
9 屋 *yorozuya* general store; a Jack-of-all-trades
乗 *banjō* sovereignty
点 *manten* perfect, perfect score
巻 *bankan, mangan* many scrolls; many books
10 骨 *bankotsu* thousands of lives; many skeletons
病 *mambyō* all kinds of sickness
般 *bampan* all things
華鏡 *bankakyō, mangekyō* kaleidoscope
能 *bannō, mannō* all-purpose; all-around. *bannō* omnipotence
能薬 *bannōyaku* cure-all, panacea
11 頃 *bankei* vast expanse
斛 *bankoku* great quantity; copious (tears)
遍無 *mambenna(ku)* equally, uniformly, without exception, all around
12 尋 *banjin* 10,000 fathoms; great depth; great height
策 *bansaku* all means
善 *manzen* all good deeds
象 *banshō* manifold forms; all creation, all the universe
鈞 *mankin, bankin* very heavy
場 *manjō* all (present)
場一致 *manjō-itchi de* unanimously
葉仮名 *man'yōgana* an early Japanese syllabary composed of Chinese characters used phonetically
葉集 *Man'yōshū* Japan's oldest anthology of poems
13 福 *bampuku* all happiness and blessings
障 *banshō* all obstacles
歳 *banzai* hurrah; long life; congratulations. *manzai* strolling dancer for New Year's celebration; a pair of comic dialogists
雷 *banrai* heavy thunder; thundrous sound
感 *bankan* flood of emotions; many thoughts
愚節 *Bangusetsu* April Fool's Day
14 境 *bankyō* all places; all circumstances
端 *bantan* all, everything
緑 *banryoku* myriad green leaves
態 *bantai* endless variety of forms
16 機 *banki* all affairs of the State; all important political matters
燈 *mandō* many votive lanterns; festival lanterns

17 謝 *bansha* many thanks; sincere apologies
18 難 *bannan* innumerable difficulties, all obstacles
19 願 *bangan* completion of a round of Buddhist prayers
22 籟 *banrai* sounds of wind blowing against all things in nature

三 8 / J3b30 / M12 SAN three. *mi(tsu), mi(ttsu), mi* three.
A

2 七日 *minanuka, minanoka* 21st day after death (also Buddhist rite on that day). *sanshichinichi* 21 days; 21st day after death; 21st day after birth
人 *sannin* three people
人称 *sanninshō* third person (in grammar)
人組 *sanningumi* trio, gang of three, threesome
十二分音符 *sanjūnibu ompu* a 32nd note
十八度線 *Sanjūhachido Sen* the Thirty-eighth Parallel
十三所 *Sanjūsansho* the thirty-three temples sacred to the bodhisattva Kannon
十日 *sanjūnichi* 30th. *misoka* last day of the month
十六計 *sanjū-rokkei* 36 strategems; many plans
十年戦争 *Sanjūnen Sensō* the Thirty Years' War
十路 *misoji* age thirty
3 口 *mi(tsu)kuchi* harelip
子 *mi(tsu)go* three-year old; triplets
才 *sansai* the three powers (heaven, earth, and man); all things in the universe
寸舌 *sanzun (no) shita* eloquent tongue
三九度 *sansan-kudo* exchange of nuptial cups
三五五 *sansan-gogo* by twos and threes
千 *sanzen* 3,000; many
千世界 *sanzen-sekai* the whole world, the universe
叉 *sansa, mitsumata* three-pronged fork. *sansa no* three-pronged
叉路 *sansaro* three-forked road
大国 *sandaikoku* three major countries
大都市 *sandaitoshi* the three largest cities
大節 *sandaisetsu* the three big national holidays
4 方 *sambō* three sides; small offering stand. *sampō* three sides
分 *sambun suru* trisect; divide by three. *sambu* $\frac{3}{10}$ (of various units). *sampun* three minutes
巴 *mi(tsu)domoe* three fat comma shapes arranged to form a circle; three parties in mutual conflict
月 *Sangatsu* March. *mitsuki* three months
月節句 *Sangatsu (no) Sekku* Girls' Doll Festival (in March)
毛作 *sammōsaku* three crops a year
毛猫 *mikeneko* tricolored cat
文 *sammon* three coppers; farthing; cheapness
文小説 *sammon shōsetsu* dime novel
文文士 *sammon-bunshi* hack writer
文判 *sammomban* ready-made seal
尺 *sanjaku* three Japanese feet; waistband, belt
尺秋水 *sanjaku (no) shūsui* a sharpened sword
尺帯 *sanjaku obi* waistband, belt
尺童子 *sanjaku (no) dōji* a mere child
日 *mikka* three days; the third day (of the month)
日三夜 *mikka-miyo* three days and three nights
日三晩 *mikka-miban* three days and three nights
日月 *mikkazuki* crescent moon, new moon
日天下 *mikkatenka* a very brief reign
日坊主 *mikkabōzu* unsteady worker
5 冬 *santō* three winter months
本足 *sambon ashi* three legs (two legs and a cane)
号雑誌 *sangōzasshi* short-lived magazine
半 *mi(tsu)ban* three-stroke alarm
半規管 *sanhan-kikan* semicircular canals
世 *sanze* past, present, and future existences; three generations. *sansei* three generations; the third generation (of immigrants); the third monarch of the same name
世相 *Sanzesō* the Book of Divination

1 〔一〕2 丨 丶 丿 乙 亅

6 死 *sanshi* three outs
曲 *sankyoku* instrumental trio; three most important pieces or numbers
次元 *sanjigen* three dimensions
羽烏 *sambagarasu* triumvirate, trio
行半 *mikudarihan* letter of divorce. *sangyōhan* three lines and a half
行広告 *sangyō kōkoku* three-line classified advertisement
行広告欄 *sangyō kōkokuran* classified ads
百 *sambyaku* 300; petty sum; cheap
百代言 *sambyaku-daigen* pettifogging lawyers
百諸候 *sambyaku-shokō* all the daimyos
色 *sanshoku* three colors. *sanshiki* three colors; three kinds
色印刷法 *sanshoku insatsuhō* three-color process
色版 *sanshokuban* three-color printing (red, yellow, and blue)
色菫 *sanshiki sumire, sanshoku sumire* pansy
色旗 *sanshokki, sanskokuki* tricolor flag
7 身 *mi(tsu)mi* kimono for little children
体 *santai* three forms; the three character styles: square, semicursive, and grass
役 *san'yaku* the three highest sumo ranks below the grand champion; the three highest officials (in companies, etc.)
折 *mitsuo(ri)* threefold, folded in three
助 *sansuke* male bathhouse attendant
更 *sankō* midnight, dead of night; the wee hours; 11 p.m.–1 a.m., the third of five night watches
災 *sansai* the three calamities (fire, flood, and storm)
男 *sannan* third son
位 *sammi, san'i* the third rank; the Christian Trinity
位一体 *Sammiittai* doctrine of the Trinity
角 *mi(tsu)kado* three corders; three-forked intersection. *sankaku* triangle
角巾 *sankakukin* triangle bandage
角帆 *sankakuho* jib sail
角形 *sankakukei* triangle
角波 *sankakunami* choppy waves
角定規 *sankaku jōgi* triangles (used in mechanical drawing)
角函数 *sankaku kansū* trigonometrical function
角洲 *sankakusu* delta
角帽 *sankakubō* three-cornered hat
角測量 *sankaku sokuryō* triangulation
角旗 *sankakuki* pennant
角関係 *sankaku kankei* love triangle
角錐 *sankakusui* triangular pyramid
角闘争 *sankaku tōsō* three-cornered fight
8 府 *Sampu* the Three Urban Prefectures (Tokyo, Kyoto, Osaka)
門 *sammon* large triple gate to a temple; three "gates" to Buddhist enlightenment
弦 *sangen* three-stringed instrument, 「samisen
板 *sampan* a sampan
股 *sammata, mi(tsu)mata* forked stick
宝 *sambō* three treasures; the three treasures of Buddhism (Buddha, the doctrine, and the priesthood); another name for Buddha
拍子 *sambyōshi* triple time (in music); three important requisites
枚目 *sammaime* comedian
味 *sami, shami* three-stringed lute
味線 *samisen, shamisen* three-stringed lute
拝 *sampai* worshiping three times
拝九拝 *sampai-kyūhai* kowtowing, bowing repeatedly
国 *sangoku* three countries
国一 *sangoku-ichi* unparalleled in Japan, China, and India
国同盟 *sangoku dōmei* triple alliance
者 *sansha* the three parties
者凡退 *sansha-bontai* three batters-three outs
者会談 *sansha kaidan* a three-way talk
9 食 *sanshoku* three meals (a day)
昧 *sammai* concentration, absorption
軍 *sangun* a great army, three sections of an army, the whole army; three armed services
思 *sanshi* deep reflection
界 *sangai* the threefold world in Buddhism; the whole world; past, present, and future existences; as far away as
竿 *sankan* the height of three bamboo poles; (the sun or moon) high in heaven
春 *sanshun* three spring months; three years

省 *sansei* reflecting on oneself three times a day; frequent self-reflection
途川 *Sanzu (no) Kawa* the River Styx
相 *sansō* three phases
相交流 *sansōkōryū* three-phase alternating current
秋 *sanshū* three fall months; three years
秋思 *sanshū (no) omo(i)* longing for one's loved ones
乗 *sanjō* cube (in math); three vehicles to truth (in Buddhism)
乗根 *sanjōkon* cube root
面 *sammen* three sides, three faces; page three (of a newspaper)
面六臂 *sammen-roppi* having three faces and six arms; one person doing the work of many; versatility
面記事 *sammenkiji* page-three news, police news, human-interest stories
段跳 *sandantobi* triple jump
段構 *sandangama(e)* triple, three-way
段論法 *sandanrompō* syllogism
重 *mie* three-fold, triple, three-ply. *sanjū* triple, treble, three-fold, three-ply, triplicate
重奏 *sanjūsō* instrumental trio
重殺 *sanjūstsu* triple play
重唱 *sanjūshō* vocal trio
重盗 *sanjūtō* triple steal (in baseball)
重結 *sanjū musu(bi)* magnus hitch
10 倍 *sambai* threefold, three times
振 *sanshin* three strikes, a strikeout
時 *sanji* three o'clock; afternoon snack; three seasons important in agriculture (spring, summer, fall); three ages of Buddhist law after Buddha's entering nirvana. *(o)sanji* three-o'clock snack
校 *sankō* third proof
桁 *miketa* hundreds (in figures)
流 *sanryū* third rate
紋 *mi(tsu)mon* having a family crest in three places (on kimono)
夏 *sanka* three summer months
原色 *sangenshoku* three primary colors
部合奏 *sambu-gassō* an ensemble of three parts
部合唱 *sambu-gasshō* a chorus of three parts
11 唱 *sanshō* three cheers; singing three times
絃 *sangen* three-stringed instrument; samisen
組 *mi(tsu)gumi* set of three. *sankumi, mikumi* three sets, three classes, three teams, three groups
教 *Sankyō* Three Teachings: Confucianism, Buddhism, Taoism (or Shinto); Three Religions (Buddhism, Shinto, Christianity); Three Teachings of Buddha
脚 *sankyaku* tripod; three legs
脚架 *sankyakuka* tripod
12 揃 *mi(tsu)zoro* three-piece suit; a set of three items
景 *sankei* three famous scenic places
筆 *sampitsu* three famous calligraphers, esp. Emperor Saga, Kūkai, and Tachibana no Hayanari
幅対 *sampukutsui* set of three; triptych; triad
寒四温 *sankan-shion* alternation of three cold days and four warm days
等 *santō* third class; third rate; third place
等分 *santōbun suru* trisect
番鳥 *sambandori* a cock crow at dawn
番鶏 *sambandori* a cock crow at dawn
塁 *sanrui* third base
塁手 *sanruishu* third baseman
塁打 *sanruida* three-base hit, triple
塁線 *sanruisen* third-base line
13 嘆 *santan* repeated praise or admiration; repeated lamentation
猿 *san'en* three monkeys who see, hear, and speak no evil
稜鏡 *sanryōkyō* prism
業 *sangyō* three types of business in the pleasure quarters (restaurant, *machiai*, and geisha service)
業地 *sangyōchi* licensed red-light quarters
14 選 *sansen* third-term election
徳 *santoku* three primary virtues (i.e., wisdom, benevolence, and valor)
箇日 *sanganichi* January first through third
種神器 *Sanshu (no) Jingi* the three Sacred Treasures (Mirror, Sword, and Jewel); three status symbols
15 論 *Sanron* the three basic scriptures of the Sanron sect of Buddhism
論宗 *Sanronshū* one of the six major Buddhist sects in Nara

1 【二】 丨 丶 丿 乙 亅

権 *sanken* the three powers of government (legislative, executive, and judicial)
権分立 *sanken bunritsu* separation of powers (executive, legislative, and judicial)
線 *sanshin* Okinawan three-stringed lute
輪 *sanrin* three wheels; three underground wheels that support the earth (in Buddhism)
輪車 *sanrinsha* tricycle, three-wheeled truck
16 頭政治 *santō-seiji* triumvirate
18 鞭酒 *shampen* champagne
韓 *Sankan* the Three Han States (of Korea); the Three Countries of Korea (Silla, Paekche, Koguryo)
21 顧礼 *sanko(no)rei* most politely requesting a person to take on a job

A **下** 9 / J323c / M14 KA, GE low class; inferiority; second, or last volume. *kuda(ru)* come down, go down; get down, descend; be given; be less than; have diarrhea; retire; leave the capital. *kuda(saru)* give, confer; oblige, favor with. *kuda(sai)* please give me. *kuda(su)* let down, lower; give, confer; issue (orders); hand down (decisions); have diarrhea; lay (hands) on. *o(riru)* come down, go down, step down, descend; get off; swoop down; land. *o(rosu)* take down, lower, pull down, lift down, let down, drop; launch; let off (passengers); wear (for the first time); cause (abortion); grate; invoke; exercise; borrow (in subtraction); lock. *sa(garu) vi* hang down, dangle; fall, go down, come down; abate; wane; retire; stand back; go behind; be granted. *sa(geru) vt* hang; wear (a decoration); reduce (rank); move back; let go, dismiss; remove; grant; draw (money), withdraw. *shita* lower part, bottom, base, foot; downstairs; subordinate place; below average; part payment; under, lower; sub-, subordinate; preliminary. *kuda(ranai)* trivial, worthless; absurd, silly; nasty. *kuda(ri)* descent; leaving the capital; diarrhea. *kuda(shi)* purgation, evacuation. *o(roshi)* grating; grater; grated radish. *(o)sa(gari)* former offering to deities; used clothes; leavings (of food). *sa(gari)* decline. *shimo* bottom, lower part, the foot; lower stream; latter; lower part of the body; the masses, the servants; the governed. *shimo ni* below, down, downward. *moto* vicinity. *moto de, moto ni* under (a tree); under (the jurisdiction of).

2 人 *genin* low-rank person, menial
3 山 *gezan, gesan* descent from the mountain; leaving a temple
下 *shimojimo, shitajita* the lower classes, the common people
上 *o(ri)-nobo(ri)* going up and down; going to and from the capital
大根 *oro(shi) daikon* grated radish
士 *kashi* noncommissioned officer
士官 *kashikan* noncommissioned officer
女 *gejo* maidservant
女下男 *gejo-genan* servants
女中 *shimojochū* kitchen maid
4 心 *shitagokoro* secret intention, motive
戸 *geko* nondrinker, temperance man
方 *kahō* lower part. *kahō ni* below
火 *shitabi* burning low; decline, waning
刈 *shitaga(ri)* weeding
水 *gesui* sewer, drain, ditch, gutter; sewerage
水道 *gesuidō* drainage system; drain; sewer
水管 *gesuikan* sewer pipe
手 *heta* unskillful, awkward. *shimote* lower part; stage right. *shitade, shitate* lower part; humble position; underhand grip (in sumo)
手人 *geshunin* murderer; the perpetrator
手物 *getemono* ordinary ware, folk ware; an odd thing
手屎 *hetakuso* extreme clumsiness
5 生 *shitaba(e)* underbrush, undergrowth
田 *geden* worn-out rice land
目 *shitame* downward glance; contemptuous look. *saga(ri)me* eyes slanting downward; beginning of decline
立 *o(ri)-ta(tsu)* go down and stand
句 *shimo (no) ku* the second half (of a *tanka*)
札 *sa(ge)fuda* tag, label
司 *gesu* vulgar, lowly; petty official. *geshi, shitazukasa* petty official; resident manager of medieval estates
民 *kamin, gemin* the masses, the lower classes, the common people

仕事 *shitashigoto* spade work; subcontract
台所 *shimo daidokoro* servants' kitchen
世話 *gesewa* common saying; common people's talk
付 *kafu suru* grant, issue
付金 *kafukin* grant; bounty
半 *kahan* lower half
半身 *shimo hanshin, kahanshin* lower half of the body
半期 *shimo hanki* the second half of the year, the second half of a term
6 臣 *kashin* low-rank retainer
血 *geketsu* bloody bowel discharge
旬 *gejun* last ten days (of a month)
同 *shitamawa(ri)* subordinate part; menial service; subordinate; utility man (in theater). *shitamawa(ru)* be less than, be lower than
向 *shitamu(ki)* downward look; beginning of decline; downturn. *shitamu(ku)* look down; decline. *gekō suru* leave the capital; move from high to low
地 *shitaji* groundwork, foundation; inclination, makings; elementary knowledge of, grounding in; prearrangement, spadework; first coat of plastering; soy
阪 *gehan* proceeding from Tokyo to Osaka
劣 *geretsu na* base, mean, vulgar
名 *kamei* the undermentioned, the undersigned
吏 *kari* lower official
列車 *kuda(ri) ressha* trains going away from the capital
7 車 *gesha* alighting
図 *shitazu* rough sketch. *kazu* the lower illustration
作 *gesaku* poor manufacture
位 *kai* low rank, subordinate position
体 *katai* lower part of the body; lower limbs
坂 *kuda(ri)zaka* downhill; decline; waning
役 *shitayaku* subordinate official; underling
男 *genan* manservant
克上 *gekokujō* a retainer supplanting his lord; juniors dominating seniors

見 *shitami* preliminary inspection, preview; siding (on a house)
見板 *shitami ita* siding (on a house)
町 *shitamachi* downtown section
町風 *shitamachifū* downtown style
足 *gesoku* footgear checked at public places
足料 *gesokuryō* footwear-checking charge
足番 *gesokuban* footwear checker
附 *kafu suru* grant, issue
8 金 *shitagane* basic metal (in an art object); old metal. *oro(shi)gane* grater
国 *gekoku suru* leaving for the province
刷 *shitazu(ri)* proof printing
姓 *geshō* person of humble birth
押 *shitao(su)* decline (stock market). *shitaoshi* press downward; bearish market
放 *shitabana(re)* slump (on the stock market)
松 *saga(ri) matsu* drooping pine
物 *kabutsu* accompaniment of saké. *o(ri)mono* afterbirth; discharge from the womb
知 *gechi, geji* command, order
肥 *shimogo(e)* night soil, manure
肢 *kashi* lower extremities, legs
郎 *gerō* servant, valet, menial
垂 *kasui* drooping, hanging down
命 *kamei* order, command
弦 *kagen* last quarter (of the moon)
弦月 *kagen (no) tsuki* waning moon
9 風 *kafū* subordinate position, lower position
城 *gejō* withdrawing from the castle
拵 *shitagoshira(e)* preparation, spadework
降 *kakō* descent, fall; drop, subsidence
降線 *kakōsen* downward curve
院 *kain* the lower (legislative) body
剃 *shitazori* barber's apprentice; preliminary shave
段 *gedan* lower (horizontal) column (of print); lowest step, lowest tier, lower berth; low positioning (of sword, spear)
乗 *gejō* dismounting; prohibition against entering the sacred precincts in a vehicle or on horseback
卑 *gebi(ru)* become vulgar, coarsen. *gebi* vulgar, coarse

1 【一】 2 丨 丶 丿 乙 亅

品 *gehin* vulgarity, coarseness, indecency; inferior article. *kahin* inferior article; person of low birth
界 *gekai* this world; the lower world; the earth
草 *shitakusa* weeds beneath a tree
巻 *gekan* last volume (in a set of 2 or 3)
剋上 *gekokujō* a retainer supplanting his lord; juniors dominating seniors
屋敷 *shimo yashiki* villa, daimyo's suburban residence in Edo
相場 *sa(ge) sōba* bearish market
相談 *shita sōdan* preliminary consultation, arrangements ⌈(officer)
級 *kakyū* lower grade, low class; junior
級生 *kakyūsei* underclassmen
級審 *kakyūshin* lower court
級職 *kakyūshoku* subordinate post
10 座 *geza* to get off one's seat and kowtow; lower seat; musician's box. *shimoza* lower seat; stage right
疳 *gekan* chancre
唇 *shita kuchibiru, kashin* lower lip
値 *shitane* lower price
振 *sa(ge)fu(ri)* plummet, plumb bob
紐 *shita himo* undersash, belt
記 *kaki no* the following
剤 *gezai* laxative
家 *shitaya* small attached annex
穿 *shitabaki* undershorts
書 *shitaga(ki), gesho* rough copy, draft
帯 *shita obi* loincloth, waistcloth; undersash
流 *karyū* downstream, lower reaches of a river; lower classes
流社会 *karyū shakai* lower classes
部 *kabu* lower part, lower order; subordinate (offices)
部機関 *kabu kikan* subordinate offices or institutions
馬 *geba* dismounting
馬先 *gebasaki* dismounting place
馬評 *gebahyō* outsider's irresponsible talk, hearsay, rumor
11 達 *katatsu suru* command a subordinate
問 *kamon suru* inquire, consult. *kamon* one's subordinate
婢 *kahi* servant girl
張 *shitaba(ri)* lining, lining paper
情 *kajō* condition of the common people
掛 *shimogaka(ru)* talk about indecent things
略 *geryaku, karyaku* the rest omitted (in quoting)
組 *shitagu(mu)* preliminary assembling
脚 *kakyaku* lower limbs
船 *gesen* going ashore
野 *geya* retirement from public office
萌 *shitamoe* sprouts, shoots; sprouting unseen
宿 *geshuku* room and board, lodging; boarding house
宿人 *geshukunin* lodger, roomer
宿屋 *geshukuya* lodginghouse
宿料 *geshukuryō* room-and-board
12 歯 *shitaba* lower teeth ⌊charge
痢 *geri* diarrhea
御 *gegyo suru* dismount (used for emperors and empresses)
渡 *sa(ge)wata(su)* (government) grant; (superiors) hand down (to inferiors)
湯 *shimoyu* sitz bath
絵 *shitae* rough sketch, design
脹 *shimobukure* swelling in the lower part; full-cheeked (face)
貼 *shitabari* lining, lining paper
期 *shimoki* second half (of the year)
策 *gesaku* poor plan
着 *shitagi* underwear
落 *geraku* depreciation, decline, fall, slump
葉 *shitaba* lower leaves
衆 *gesu* person of humble rank, humble person
番 *kaban* going off duty
検分 *shita kembun* preliminary examination
検査 *shita kensa* preliminary inspection
等 *katō* low grade, lower class. *katō na* inferior, base, vulgar
等動物 *katō dōbutsu* lower animals
等植物 *katō shokubutsu* lower plants
13 殿 *geden* leaving the palace
働 *shitabatara(ki)* subordinate work; assistant, servant
僧 *gesō* low-rank priest
腿 *katai* lower leg
馴 *shitanara(shi)* training; warming-up
幕 *sa(ge)maku* drop curtain
意 *kai* feelings of the people
塗 *shitanu(ri)* first coat; undercoating
準備 *shita jumbi* preliminary arrangements, spade work

腹 *shitahara, shita(p)para, shitabara, kafuku* abdomen. *kudaribara* diarrhea
腹部 *kafukubu* abdominal region
14 聞 *shitagi(ki)* inquiring beforehand
僚 *karyō* subordinates, petty officials
僕 *geboku, kaboku* servant; your humble servant
摺 *shitazu(ri)* proof printing
様 *shitazama* lower classes, common people; lower part
獄 *gegoku suru* be sent to prison
端 *katan* lower end. *shita(p)pa* underling
緒 *sageo* sword knot
読 *shitayo(mi)* preparatory reading; lesson study
髪 *sa(ge)gami* hair tied at the back; plaited hair
種 *gesu* person of humble rank; vulgar person. *gesubaru* be vulgar
種女 *gesu onna* woman of low rank; a term of degradation for a woman
種根性 *gesu konjō* base, vulgar nature
層 *kasō* lower strata; lower classes
層土 *kasōdo* subsoil
層社会 *kasō shakai* lower strata of society
層階級 *kasō kaikyū* lower classes
駄 *geta* wooden clogs, geta
駄直 *getanao(shi)* repairing clogs; clog repairer
駄屋 *getaya* clog shop
駄掛 *getaka(ke)* wearing wooden clogs
駄番 *getaban* footwear checker
駄履 *getaba(ki)* wearing clogs
駄箱 *getabako* cupboard (for shoes and clogs)
15 履 *shitabaki* footgear for outdoors
潮 *sa(ge)shio* ebb tide
縫 *shitanu(i)* basting, temporary sewing
調 *shitashira(be)* preliminary investigation; preparation
賜 *kashi* imperial grant
賤 *gesen* humble birth
敷 *shitaji(ki)* desk pad; something lying underneath; model, pattern; a thin plastic board (laid under writing paper); pinned under, crushed beneath
輩 *kahai, gehai* an inferior, a low-class person
熱 *genetsu* alleviation of fever
請 *shitauke* subcontractor
請業者 *shitau(ke) gyōsha* subcontractor
16 積 *shitazu(mi)* goods piled beneath; being in a subservient position
膨 *shimobuku(re)* full-cheeked (face); swelling in the lower part
薬 *geyaku, kuda(shi)gusuri* laxative. *o(roshi)gusuri* abortifacient, abortion drug
稽古 *shitageiko* rehearsal, preparation
17 瞰 *kakan suru* look down (from a height), get a bird's-eye view
翼 *sa(ge)yoku* wing flap
18 瞼 *shita mabuta* lower eyelid
顎 *shita ago, kagaku* lower jaw
21 露 *shita tsuyu* dew under the trees; dew dripping from the trees
22 鬚 *shita hige* beard below the mouth
24 齶 *shita ago* lower jaw

A 上 10 / J3e65 / M13 Jō top; best; first volume. Shō upper part; government. *ue* up, upper part, top, summit; surface; far better; higher; (in) authority; as far as... is concerned; besides; after; emperor, sovereign; upon (examination); influence of (liquor); lord, shogun; superior. *a(garu)* rise, go up; climb up; advance, appreciate; be promoted; improve; enter, call on; be offered; accrue; be finished; (expenses) come to; go bankrupt; begin spinning (cocoons); be caught; get ruffled; eat, drink; die; weaken (as a battery); let up (rain). *a(geru)* raise, elevate; fly (kites); praise; increase, advance; promote, elevate; vomit; usher in, admit; send (to school); offer; present, leave with; finish; arrange (expenses); observe, perform; quote, mention, give (examples); bear (a child); improve (talents); do up (the hair); arrest; engage; fry; (rains) stop. *a(gattari)* poor business. *a(gari)* ascent, rise, advance; yield; death; spinning; completion; stop; finish. *nobo(ru)* rise, ascend, go up, climb; go to (the capital); add up to; be promoted; advance (in price); sail up; come up (on the agenda). *nobo(su), nobo(seru)* raise; record; bring up (a matter); serve (food); send some one out (from Kyoto). *nobo(ri)* ascent; up train (toward the capital). *kami* top;

head; upper part; upper stream; emperor; a superior; upper part of the body; the above. *-ue* my dear (father). *-jō* aboard a ship or vehicle; from the standpoint of; as a matter of (fact). *jō-* governmental; imperial; best; high class; going up; presenting; showing. *uwa-* upper, upward, outer, surface, top. *-a(gezu)* every (two days, etc.). *-a(gari)* after (rain); ex- (official, etc.).

2 人 *shōnin* Buddhist saint, priest
3 口 *nobo(ri)guchi* starting point for a mountain ascent. *a(gari)guchi, a(gari)kuchi* entrance
上 *jōjō* the best
女中 *kamijochū* head servant
下 *shōka, jōge* high and low; the government and the people; going up and down. *a(ge)oro(shi)* raising and lowering; loading and unloading. *a(ge)sa(ge)* raising and lowering; praising and blaming; modulation. *nobo(ri)kuda(ri)* going up and down. *a(gari)sa(gari)* rise and fall, fluctuation. *kamishimo* samurai garb; old ceremonial garb; the government and the people; the upper and lower parts of the body
下水道 *jōgesuidō* water and sewer services
下動 *jōgedō* vertical motion (in earthquakes)
下線 *jōgesen* both (railway) tracks
4 戸 *jōgo* drinker; drinker's habits
文 *jōbun* the foregoing
辺 *uwabe* exterior, surface, outside; outward appearance. *jōhen* the upper side
込 *a(gari)-ko(mu)* enter, step in
中下 *jō-chū-ge* excellent-good-poor; first-second-third (class)
分別 *jōfumbetsu* good idea, wise policy
手 *uwate, kamite* upper part; upper stream; overhand grip (in sumo); left side (of a stage). *jōzu na* skillful, dexterous
手者 *jōzumono* flatterer
方 *jōhō* upper part. *kamigata* Kyoto and vicinity. *ue(tsu)gata* nobles, the upper class.
方贅六 *kamigata-zeiroku* people of the Kyoto area
水 *jōsui* water supply
水道 *jōsuidō* waterworks
天 *jōten* heaven; God, Providence, the Supreme Being, the Absolute
天気 *jōtenki* fair weather
5 玉 *jōdama* fine jewel; best article; pretty woman
田 *jōden* high rice field; very fertile rice
白 *jōhaku* first-class rice
皮 *jōhi, uwakawa* outer skin, cuticle, epidermis
目 *uwame* upward glance, upturned eyes. *a(gari)me* eyes slanting upward; rising tendency
石 *uwaishi* upper millstone
句 *kami (no) ku, jōku* the first part of a poem or verse
代 *jōdai* ancient times
付 *uwatsu(ku)* be fickle, be flippant, be restless
包 *uwazutsu(mi)* cover, wrapper, envelope
司 *jōshi* superior authorities
世 *jōsei, kamitsuyo* antiquity; ancient times
出来 *jōdeki* good performance
甲板 *jōkampan* upper deck
申 *jōshin* report to a superior
申書 *jōshinsho* written report
古 *jōko* ancient times
古史 *jōkoshi* ancient history
半 *jōhan* first half, upper half
半身 *jōhanshin* bust, upper half of the body
半期 *kamihanki* first half of a year
6 米 *jōmai* first-class rice
臼 *uwausu* upper millstone
衣 *uwagi, jōi* coat, tunic, jacket, outer garment
旬 *jōjun* first ten days of a month
回 *uwamawa(ru)* exceed
気 *jōki* dizziness; rush of blood to the head
汲 *uwagu(mu)* draw off the top liquid
旨 *jōshi* the emperor's thoughts
列車 *nobo(ri) ressha* trains going toward the capital
向 *uwamu(ku), uemu(ku)* look upward, turn upward, rise. *uwamu(ki), uemu(ki)* upturn; tendency; looking upward
向線 *jōkōsen* upswing

7 足 *jōsoku* high retainer
図 *jōzu* the upper illustration
述 *jōjutsu* the above-mentioned
位 *jōi* high rank, precedence
体 *jōtai* upper part of the body
作 *jōsaku* good crop; masterpiece
坂 *nobo(ri)zaka* ascent, upgrade
役 *uwayaku* senior official, one's superior
告 *jōkoku* appeal (of a case)
8 長 *jōchō* one's superior, a senior, an elder
底 *a(ge)zoko* false bottom
使 *jōshi* shogun's envoy
弦 *jōgen* first quarter (of a moon); a crescent moon
板 *a(ge)ita* movable floor boards; trap door
物 *a(gari)mono* food offering; yield; waste. *jōmono* quality goods
服 *uwafuku* outer garment
肢 *jōshi* upper limbs, arms
限 *jōgen* maximum (in math)
官 *jōkan* superior officer
空 *uwa(no)sora* inattention, absentmindedness. *jōkū* high-altitude sky, upper air
京 *jōkyō* proceeding to the capital
京中 *jōkyōchū* in the capital
表 *jōhyō* memorial to the emperor
表紙 *uwahyōshi* cover, front cover, wrapper, jacket
昇 *jōshō suru* rise, ascend, climb
昇気流 *jōshō kiryū* ascending air current
昇限度 *jōshōgendo* ceiling (in aviation)
昇線 *jōshōsen* rising curve
9 面 *jōmen* surface, top, exterior. *uwatsura, uwa(t)tsura* surface, appearances
廻 *uwamawa(ru)* be more than
映 *jōei* screen projection
枯 *uwaga(reru)* die at the top
洛 *jōraku* proceeding to the capital
計 *jōkei* best policy
降 *a(gari)o(ri)* ascent and descent
段 *jōdan* dais, raised part of the floor; seats of honor, upper row of seats; upper berth; upper (horizontal) column (of print). *a(gari)dan* staircase, doorsteps
乗 *jōjō* the best. *uwano(ri)* supercargo
帝 *jōtei* Shangti, God, Lord, Creator, the Supreme Being
前 *uwamae* outer skirt; percentage, commission
品 *jōhin* refinement, decency; first-class article. *jōbon* Buddhism's highest paradise
客 *jōkyaku* guest of honor; good customer
界 *jōkai* upper world, heaven
皇 *jōkō* retired emperor
巻 *jōkan* volume one
背 *uwazei* stature, height
首尾 *jōshubi* success, happy result
相場 *a(ge)sōba* bullish market
草履 *uwazōri* indoor sandals, slippers
屋 *uwaya* a shed
屋敷 *kamiyashiki* a daimyo's main Tokyo mansion
級 *jōkyū* higher grade, advanced class, high class
級生 *jōkyūsei* upperclassman
院 *jōin* Upper House, Senate, Lords
院議員 *jōin giin* senator, member of the upper house
奏 *jōsō* report to the throne
奏文 *jōsōbun* report to the throne
10 馬 *jōba* excellent horse
高 *a(gari)daka* revenue, income, receipts, yield
席 *jōseki* seniority, precedence; upper seat
座 *jōza, kamiza* chief seat, seat of honor
唇 *uwakuchibiru, jōshin* upper lip
値 *uwane* higher price; price rise
酒 *jōshu* high-class saké
紙 *uwagami* paper cover, wrapper, wrapping paper
紐 *uwahimo* outside string (on a package)
航 *jōkō* going upstream
記 *jōki no* the above-mentioned
陸 *jōriku* landing, disembarkation
荷 *uwani* top cargo; top of the load
書 *uwaga(ki)* address; superscription. *jōsho* memorial to the throne
帯 *uwaobi* outer sash, outer obi
流 *jōryū* upper stream; upper classes
流社会 *jōryū shakai* upper classes
部 *jōbu* upper part, top, upper side, surface

1 2 [一] 丨 丶 丿 乙 亅

部構造 *jōbu kōzō* superstructure
納 *jōnō* payment to the government
納米 *jōnōmai* rice-tax delivery
納金 *jōnōkin* money paid to the government
11 道 *nobo(ri) michi* uphill road
達 *jōtatsu* progress, proficiency
側 *uwakawa, uwagawa, uwa(k)kawa* upper side, surface
張 *uwaba(ri)* face, coat, veneer. *uwa(p)pa(ri)* overalls, wrapper, duster, smock
掲 *jōkei no* the above mentioned
宿 *jōyado* first-class inn
盛 *uwamo(ri)* adding to the top; what's placed on top
菓子 *jōgashi* quality cakes
掛水車 *uwaga(ke) suisha* overshot water wheel
12 歯 *uwaba* upper teeth
場 *a(gari)ba* landing, landing place
提 *jōtei* introducing (a bill)
湯 *a(gari)yu* clean hot bath water for rinsing
疏 *jōso suru* report to the emperor
程 *jōtei* departure on a journey; introducing (a bill)
絵 *uwae* printed figures (on cloth or pottery)
腕 *jōwan* upper arm
訴 *jōso* appeal (in court)
貼 *uwabari* finishing coat of paper
畳 *a(ge)datami* a *tatami* finished on both sides
策 *jōsaku* excellent plan; best policy
着 *uwagi* coat, tunic, jacket, outer garment
番 *jōban* being on duty
智 *jōchi* Sophia University; supreme wisdom
裁 *jōsai* imperial decision
景気 *jōkeiki* boom, prosperity
御一人 *kamigoichinin* the emperor
棟 *jōtō* raising the ridgepole
棟式 *jōtōshiki* ridgepole-raising ceremony
等 *jōtō* superiority, first class, very good
等兵 *jōtōhei* superior private
等兵曹 *jōtōheisō* chief petty officer
等品 *jōtōhin* first-class article
13 働 *uwabatara(ki)* housemaid
滑 *uwasube(ri)* superficial, careless, inattentive
腿 *jōtai* thigh
詰 *nobo(ri)-tsu(meru)* go to the top; be engrossed in
靴 *uwagutsu* overshoes, rubbers, galoshes
筵 *uwamushiro* thin padded mat laid on the *tatami*
蓆 *uwamushiro* thin padded mat laid on the *tatami*
蓋 *a(ge)buta* trap door; removable floor boards
意 *jōi* the emperor's wishes
塗 *uwanu(ri)* last plaster coat, last painting, finish
14 聞 *jōbun* an imperial hearing
様 *uesama* emperor, shogun, honored person. *uwazama* up. *(o)nobo(ri)san* visitor from the country
演 *jōen* stage performance
端 *jōtan* top, tip, upper end
膊 *jōhaku* upper arm
蔟 *jōzoku* spinning of cocoons; the silkworm's last sleep
製 *jōsei* superior make; superior binding
製本 *jōseibon* best binding
層 *jōsō* upper layer; upper air; upper story; higher class
層土 *jōsōdo* topsoil
層気流 *jōsō kiryū* upper air currents
層風 *jōsōfū* winds aloft
層建築 *jōsō kenchiku* superstructure; upper stories
層階級 *jōsō kaikyū* upper classes, high society
層雲 *jōsōun* upper clouds
15 履 *uwabaki* hallway slippers, inside shoes
潮 *a(ge)shio* incoming tide
澄 *uwazu(mi)* the clear top of a liquid
謁 *jōetsu* interview with an important person
敷 *uwashi(ki), uwaji(ki)* bordered matting
箱 *uwabako* outer box, outer casing
質 *jōshitsu* fine quality
調子 *uwachōshi* high pitch, higher tone. *uwa(t)chōshi na* flippant, frivolous, shallow
16 燗 *jōkan* top quality hot saké
積 *uwazu(mi)* deck cargo; upper layer of goods

臈 *jōrō* court lady, noblewoman
諭 *jōyu* imperial edict
覧 *jōran* imperial inspection
機嫌 *jōkigen* good humor
17 擦 *uwazu(ru)* sound shallow, sound hollow (in speaking)
翼 *jōyoku* upper wing of a plane
18 瞼 *uwamabuta* upper eyelid
顎 *jōgaku, uwaago* upper jaw; palate
覆 *uwaō(i)* cover, covering
噛合 *uwakamia(wase)* overbite
19 離 *a(ge)-hana(su)* cut off (the head)
20 騰 *jōtō* advance, rise, jump
議 *jōgi suru* place on the agenda
欄 *jōran* top or preceding horizontal column

3

丐 11 / J5022 / M22 KAI. *ko(u)* ask, request; invite, pray for; beg, solicit.

丑 12 / J3121 / M23 CHŪ. *ushi* 1–3 a.m.; second zodiac sign; cow.

A **不** 13 / J4954 / M19 FU negation; bad; clumsy; ugly. BU bad; clumsy; ugly. *-zu* negation.

1 乙 *fuitsu, fuichi* Sincerely yours; Yours truly
一 *fuitsu, fuichi* Sincerely yours; Yours truly
一致 *fuitchi* discord, disagreement, dissonance
2 二 *fuji* peerless, unparalleled; Sincerely yours
入 *fui(ri)* small attendance, poor house
十分 *fujūbun* insufficiency, imperfection
人気 *funinki* unpopularity
人情 *funinjō* unkindness, inhumanity, heartlessness
3 才 *fusai* lack of talent, incompetency
干渉 *fukanshō* nonintervention, noninterference
4 日 *fujitsu* in a few days, at an early date; not writing dates
仁 *fujin* heartlessness, inhumanity
予 *fuyo* indisposition; emperor's illness; unhappiness
分明 *fubummei* indistinct, obscure
介入 *fukainyū* noninvolvement, nonintervention, neutrality
心得 *fukokoroe* indiscretion, imprudence
手回 *futemawa(shi)* poor preparation, poor arrangements
手際 *futegiwa* clumsiness, ineptitude
毛 *fumō* barren, sour, unproductive (land)
毛地 *fumōchi* unproductive land
公平 *fukōhei* unfairness, injustice, partiality
公正 *fukōsei* injustice, unfairness
文 *fubun* unwritten; illiterate, uneducated; poor writing
文法 *fubunhō* unwritten law, common law
文律 *fubunritsu* unwritten law, unwritten rule, common law
5 払 *fubara(i)* nonpayment, default
世出 *fuseishutsu* rare, extraordinary, unparalleled
出来 *fudeki* poor workmanship, bad job, bungle
必要 *fuhitsuyō* unnecessary
本意 *fuhon'i* reluctance, unwillingness
生産的 *fuseisanteki* nonproductive; unprofitable, unfruitful
甲斐無 *fugaina(i)* spiritless, cowardly, worthless
仕合 *fushia(wase)* unhappiness, misfortune, ill luck
平 *fuhei* discontent, dissatisfaction, complaint
平不満 *fuhei-fuman* discontent and grumbling
平等 *fubyōdō* inequality; unequal (treaties)
用 *fuyō* of no use; waste (products)
用心 *buyōjin, fuyōjin* insecurity; carelessness
用品 *fuyōhin* disused article
用意 *fuyōi* unpreparedness, carelessness
正 *fusei* injustice, iniquity, impropriety, irregularity, dishonesty, illegality
正行為 *fusei kōi* unfair practices, wrongdoing, malpractice, cheating, foul play
正直 *fushōjiki* dishonesty
正事件 *fusei jiken* scandal, bribery case, graft case
正乗車 *fusei jōsha* stealing a ride
正視 *fuseishi suru* consider wrong or unjust

正規 *fuseiki* irregularity
正規軍 *fuseikigun* irregular troops
正確 *fuseikaku* inaccuracy, uncertainty
可 *fuka* wrong, bad, improper, unjustifiable, inadvisable
可入性 *fukanyūsei* impenetrability
可欠 *fukaketsu na* indispensable
可分 *fukabun* indivisibility
可抗力 *fukakōryoku* act of God; irresistible force; inevitability
可知 *fukachi na* unknowable, mysterious
可知的 *fukachiteki* agnostic
可知論 *fukachiron* agnosticism
可侵 *fukashin* inviolability, nonaggression
可侵条約 *fukashin jōyaku* nonaggression pact
可思議 *fukashigi* mystery, wonder, miracle
可能 *fukanō* impossibility
可解 *fukakai* mystery, incomprehensibility
可避 *fukahi* inescapable, inevitable, unavoidable
6 臣 *fushin* disloyalty, unfaithfulness
尽 *fujin* Sincerely yours; incompleteness
印 *fujirushi* poor results
向 *fumu(ki) na* unfit, unsuitable, unmarketable
仲 *funaka* discord
次 *fuji* irregularity; disorganized writing (humble reference to one's own)
好 *busu(ki) na* no liking for, no interest in
朽 *fukyū* immortality
全 *fuzen* partial, incomplete, imperfect
吉 *fukitsu* bad luck, ill omen, inauspiciousness
充分 *fujūbun* insufficiency, shortage, imperfection, inadequacy
似合 *funia(i)* unbecoming, improper, unsuitable, ill-matched, unworthy of
気味 *bukimi* ill feeling. *bukimi na* uncanny, weird, ghastly, ominous
如意 *funyoi* contrary to one's wishes; short of money
自由 *fujiyū* inconvenience, discomfort; destitution; disability
自然 *fushizen* unnatural, artificial, affected, strained
合格 *fugōkaku* failure (in an examination), rejection, disqualification
合理 *fugōri na* unreasonable, irrational, absurd, inconsistent
名数 *fumeisū* abstract number
名誉 *fumeiyo* dishonor, disgrace, shame
老 *furō* perennial youth
老不死 *furō-fushi* perennial youth and immortality
老泉 *furōsen* fountain of youth
同 *fudō* difference, diversity, irregularity; disorder
同化 *fudōka* nonassimilation
同意 *fudōi* disagreement, objection
成立 *fuseiritsu* failure, rupture, rejection
成功 *fuseikō* failure
成績 *fuseiseki* poor result, bad record, failure
死 *fushi* immortality, eternal life
死鳥 *fushichō* phoenix bird
死身 *fujimi* invulnerability, immortality, insensibility to pain
行状 *fugyōjō* misconduct, profligacy, immorality
行届 *fuyu(ki)todo(ki)* negligence, carelessness, incompetence, mismanagement
行跡 *fugyōseki* misconduct, profligacy, immorality
行儀 *fugyōgi* bad manners, rudeness
安 *fuan* anxiety, uneasiness; insecurity; suspense
安心 *fuanshin* uneasiness, uncertainty, anxiety, apprehension, restlessness, insecurity, suspense, fear
安気 *fuange na* uneasy
安定 *fuantei* instability; insecurity; crankiness
当 *fua(tari)* failure, unpopularity. *futō na* unjust, unreasonable, undeserved. *futō* injustice, impropriety, unreasonableness
当利得 *futō ritoku* excessive profit, unjust enrichment
当労働行為 *futō rōdō kōi* unfair labor practices
当廉売 *futō rembai* dumping
在 *fuzai* absence
在地主 *fuzai jinushi* absentee landlord
在投票 *fuzai tōhyō* absentee voting
在証明 *fuzai shōmei* alibi
7 図 *futo* suddenly, casually, accidentally,

incidentally, unexpectedly, unintentionally
快 *fukai* displeasure, discomfort; indisposition, malaise
抜 *fubatsu* firm, steadfast, indomitable, invincible, unswerving
肖 *fushō* being unlike one's father; unworthy, incompetent; I, myself, your humble servant
孝 *fukō* disobedience to parents, lack of filial piety
束 *futsutsuka* a rude, inexperienced, stupid, or incompetent person; ignoramus
完全 *fukanzen na* imperfect, incomplete, faulty, defective
沙汰 *busata* silence, neglect to write, neglect to call
身持 *fumimo(chi)* misconduct, profligacy, licentiousness, inconstancy
条理 *fujōri* irrationality, absurdity, inconsistency
体裁 *futeisai, buteisai* bad form, bad manners, improper appearance, indecency
即不離 *fusoku-furi* neutral, noncommittal
労所得 *furō shotoku* unearned income
作 *fusaku* poor crop, crop failure
作法 *busahō* bad manners, discourtesy
妊 *funin* sterility, barrenness
妊症 *funinshō* sterility, barrenness
決定 *fukettei* pending, unsettled, undecided
決断 *fuketsudan* irresolution, indecision, vacillation
利 *furi* disadvantage, drawback, handicap
利益 *furieki* disadvantage, handicap, drawback, inadvisability, inexpediency
見目 *mijime na* sad, pitiful, wretched
見転芸者 *mizuten geisha* a loose geisha
見識 *fukenshiki na* undignified, unprincipled, disgraceful
言 *fugen* silence
言不語 *fugen-fugo* silence
言実行 *fugen-jikkō* no talk and all deeds
足 *fusoku* shortage, lack, deficiency, dearth
足前 *tarazumae* deficit, shortage
足勝 *fusokugachi* needy
均斉 *fukinsei* asymmetry
均等 *fukintō* imbalance, inequality, unevenness
均質 *fukinshitsu no* of uneven quality; heterogeneous
均衡 *fukinkō* out of balance, imbalance, disparity, inequality
承 *fushō* dissent, objection, disapproval, refusal; a reluctant consent
承不承 *fushō-bushō* reluctant, unwilling
承知 *fushōchi* dissent, disagreement, objection, refusal
承認 *fushōnin* disapproval, dissent, veto
良 *furyō* bad, poor, inferior; wicked, delinquent
良化 *furyōka* degradation, downfall
良少年 *furyōshōnen* juvenile delinquent
良児 *furyōji* juvenile delinquent
良貸付 *furyō ka(shi)tsu(ke)* bad debts
良導体 *furyōdōtai* insulator, nonconductor, poor conductor
8 斉 *fusei* irregularity, unevenness, asymmetry, lack of uniformity
屈 *fukutsu* fortitude, indomitability
届 *futodo(ki)* careless, bad, outrageous, insolent
例 *furei* indisposition; sickness
味 *mazu(i)* unpalatable, insipid; homely; awkward, bungling; unwise. *fumi* unsavoriness
拘 *kakawarazu* in spite of, regardless of
況 *fukyō* depression, slump, recession
治 *fuchi, fuji* incurability
服 *fufuku* dissatisfaction, discontent; disagreement, disapproval; objection, protest, complaint
幸 *fukō* unhappiness, misfortune; death (of family or relative)
実 *fujitsu* faithlessness, inconstancy, insincerity; falsehood
易 *fueki* immutability, constancy
拡大 *fukakudai* nonexpansion, nonaggravation, localization
始末 *fushimatsu* mismanagement, wastefulness, carelessness, misconduct
夜城 *fuyajō* nightless pleasure quarters; nightless city
退転 *futaiten* firm determination, indomitableness
注意 *fuchūi* carelessness, negligence
所存 *fushozon* imprudence, indiscretion

所存者 *fushozonsha* thoughtless person
知 *fuchi* ignorance; foolishness
知火 *shiranuhi, shiranui* strange lights floating over the sea
和 *fuwa* discord, trouble, dissension, disagreement
服 *fufuku* dissatisfaction; disapproval; protest
服従 *fufukujū* insubordination, disobedience
参 *fusan* nonattendance, default, nonappearance
参加 *fusanka* nonparticipation
具 *fugu* deformity; distortion; disability; cripple; Sincerely yours (letter ending)
具者 *fugusha* cripple, disabled person
忠 *fuchū* disloyalty, infidelity
忠実 *fuchūjitsu* disloyalty, faithlessness
明 *fumei* obscurity, indistinctness, uncertainty, ambiguity; ignorance, lack of wisdom
明朗 *fumeirō* gloomy; dubious; underhand
明瞭 *fumeiryō* indistinctness, dimness, obscurity
法 *fuhō* lawlessness, injustice, illegality, unlawfulness
法入国 *fuhō nyūkoku* illegal entry
法占有 *fuhō sen'yū* unlawful detention (of shipping), unlawful occupation (of a house or land)
法侵入 *fuhō shinnyū* trespassing, intrusion
法集会 *fuhō shūkai* unlawful assembly
定 *futei* uncertainty, indefiniteness, indeterminateness, mutability. *fujō* uncertainty, mutability
定法 *futeihō* infinitive mood
定冠詞 *futei kanshi* indefinite article
定詞 *futeishi* infinitive
定期 *futeiki* indeterminate (sentence); irregular (service); tramp (steamer)
9 通 *futsū* suspension, stoppage, tie-up, cessation, impassability
便 *fuben* inconvenience, inexpediency. *fubin* inconvenience; caring; pity, compassion
軌 *fuki* lawlessness; rebellion
変 *fuhen* unchangeability, immutability, constancy, permanence; indestructibility
宣 *fusen* Sincerely yours
要 *fuyō* unnecessary; waste (products)
急 *fukyū* nonessential (industry); in no hurry
為 *futame na* disadvantageous, unprofitable, harmful
面目 *fumemmoku, fumemboku* shame, disgrace
品行 *fuhinkō* unchastity, misconduct, dissipation, loose conduct
格好 *bukakkō* unshapeliness; clumsiness
相応 *fusōō, busōō* unsuited, inappropriate, improper, undeserved
首尾 *fushubi* failure, fizzle; disgrace, disfavor. *bushubi* inconsistency
透明 *futōmei* opacity
風流 *bufūryū* lack of refinement
侵略 *fushinryaku* nonaggression
連続 *furenzoku* discontinuity
祝儀 *bushūgi* an occasion for mourning; a funeral
則不離 *fusoku-furi* close relationship
浄 *fujō* uncleanliness, impurity, filthiness, defilement; menses; toilet, latrine
浄場 *fujōba* unclean place; toilet, latrine
活発 *fukappatsu na* dull, slow, sluggish, inactive, quiet
活動 *fukatsudō* inaction, lethargy
思議 *fushigi* wonder, mystery, marvel, miracle; curiosity
可思議 *fukashigi* wonder, mystery, marvel, miracle; curiosity
発 *fuhatsu* misfire
発弾 *fuhatsudan* dud, unexploded shell; unexploded bomb
貞 *futei* unchastity, unfaithfulness, (conjugal) infidelity
貞寝 *futene* staying in bed out of spite
貞腐 *futekusa(reru)* become sulky, become irresponsible
信 *fushin* unfaithfulness, insincerity; perfidy; mistrust, distrust, discredit
信心 *fushinjin, bushinjin* impiety, unbelief, infidelity
信用 *fushin'yō* distrust, discredit
信任 *fushinnin* nonconfidence
信任投票 *fushinnin tōhyō* a nonconfidence (no-confidence) vote
信任案 *fushinnin an* nonconfidence (no-confidence) motion
信仰 *fushinkō* lack of faith, unbelief, impiety, infidelity

信実 *fushinjitsu* insincerity, unfaithfulness
信義 *fushingi* faithlessness, insincerity
10 逞 *futei* insubordination; outlawry
倫 *furin* impropriety, immorality; infidelity, unfaithfulness
埒 *furachi* unresolved, unsettled; lawless, outrageous, wicked; insolence, misconduct
振 *fushin* dullness, depression, slump, stagnation
祥 *fusho* misfortune; inauspicious, ill-omened
粋 *busui na* inelegant, lacking in polish
納 *funō* nonpayment, default
敏 *fubin* inability, dullness, slowness
党 *futō* nonpartisanship
能 *funō* incompetency, lack of ability; impossibility; weak point; impotence
帰 *fuki* returning no more; dying
案内 *fuannai, buannai* ignorance, inexperience, unfamiliarity
都合 *futsugō* inconvenience, inexpedience; trouble, harm; impropriety, wrongdoing
流通 *furyūtsū* nonnegotiable
倒翁 *okiagarikoboshi, futōō* tumbler, self-righting toy
勉強 *fubenkyō* idleness, lack of application, lazy study habits
従順 *fujūjun* disobedience
料簡 *furyōken* indiscretion
耕作地 *fukōsakuchi* nonfarming land; untilled land
真面目 *fumajime* unsteadiness; lack of sincerity
倶戴天 *fugutaiten* irreconcilable (enemy)
起 *fuki* rising no more (as in illness and death)
起訴 *fukiso* nonprosecution, nonindictment
消化 *fushōka* indigestion
消化物 *fushōkabutsu* indigestible materials
純 *fujun* impurity, adulteration; dishonesty; irregularity
純物 *fujumbutsu* foreign matter, impurities
時 *fuji* emergency, unexpectedness
時着 *fujichaku* emergency landing
時着陸 *fuji chakuriku* emergency landing

眠 *fumin* wakefulness, sleeplessness
眠不休 *fumin-fukyū* without sleep or rest, day and night
眠症 *fuminshō* insomnia, sleeplessness
随 *fuzui* paralysis, palsy
随意 *fuzuii* involuntary
随意筋 *fuzuiikin* involuntary muscles
凍海 *futōkai* ice-free sea
凍剤 *futōzai* antifreeze
凍液 *futōeki* antifreeze
凍港 *futōkō* ice-free port
11 達 *futatsu* nondelivery
運 *fuun* misfortune, bad luck, fate
遇 *fugū* misfortune, bad luck, obscurity
猟 *furyō* poor catch
敗 *fuhai* invincibility
悉 *fushitsu* Very sincerely yours
細工 *busaiku* clumsy work; poor shape; awkward, clumsy; homely, plain
問付 *fumon (ni) fu(su)* ignore, disregard, overlook, connive at
釣合 *futsuria(i)* unbalance, asymmetry, disparity
経済 *fukeizai* poor economy, waste
道理 *fudōri* unreasonableness, absurdity, irrationality
道徳 *fudōtoku* immorality, iniquity
健全 *fukenzen* unhealthful
健康 *fukenkō* poor health; unhealthiness
偏 *fuhen* impartiality, fairness
偏不党 *fuhen-futō* neutrality
断 *fudan* usually, habitually, continually; constantly; indecision, irresolution
断着 *fudangi* ordinary clothes
動 *fudō* immobility, firmness, steadfastness; fixed, motionless, idle
動心 *fudōshin* imperturbability
動産 *fudōsan* real estate
規律 *fukiritsu na* irregular, undisciplined, disorganized, slipshod
規則 *fukisoku* irregularity, unsteadiness
規則動詞 *fukisoku dōshi* irregular verb
得手 *fuete* weak point; unskillfulness
得要領 *futokuyōryō* vague, ambiguous, irrelevant, noncommittal

1 【一】丨 丶 ノ 乙 亅 (3)

得策 *futokusaku* unwise plan, bad policy, inexpediency
得意 *futokui* one's weak point
12 間 *buma* clumsiness, stupidity, blunder
備 *fubi* deficiency, imperfection , defect, inadequacy; Yours in haste
順 *fujun* irregularity, unseasonableness
揃 *fuzoroi, fusoroi* unevenness, irregularity, lack of uniformity
渡 *fuwata(ri)* nonpayment, dishonoring (a bill); bouncing (check)
測 *fusoku* unexpectedness
期 *fuki* unexpected, accidental
着 *fuchaku* nonarrival, nondelivery
惑 *fuwaku* past forty; following the right course
統一 *futōitsu* disunity, disharmony
勝手 *fukatte* inconvenience; a hard living
裁可 *fusaika* veto, rejection
景気 *fukeiki* hard times, depression; gloom, sullenness, cheerlessness
量見 *furyōken* indiscretion
愉快 *fuyukai* unpleasantness, disagreeableness, unhappiness
検束 *fukensoku* nonrestraint
結果 *fukekka* failure, poor results
然者 *shikarazumba* if not so
換紙幣 *fukan shihei* inconvertible paper money, fiat money
満 *fuman* dissatisfaction, displeasure, discontent
満足 *fumanzoku* dissatisfaction, displeasure, discontent
評 *fuhyō* bad reputation, disgrace, unpopularity
評判 *fuhyōban* bad reputation, disgrace, unpopularity
善 *fuzen* evil, sin, vice; mischief
善感 *fuzenkan* negative reaction, unsuccessful vaccination
等 *futō* disparity, inequality
等辺 *futōhen* unequal sides
買 *fubai* not buying
買同盟 *fubai dōmei* boycott, buyer's strike
敬 *fukei* disrespect, irreverence, impiety, blasphemy, profanity
敬虔 *fukeiken* impiety, irreverence
敬罪 *fukeizai* lese majesty
覚 *fukaku* fault, failure, negligence, indiscretion
覚一投 *fukaku-ittō* pitcher's misjudgment
覚者 *fukakumono* shallow thinker; indecisive person; coward
13 虞 *fugu* emergency
遜 *fuson* arrogance, insolence, disrespect
嗜 *butashinami* poor preparation
滅 *fumetsu* immortality, indestructibility
詳 *fushō* unknown, unidentified
馴 *funare* inexperience, unfamiliarity
戦 *fusen* antiwar, war renunciation
勢 *buzei* few, numerical inferiority
愍 *fubin* pitiful
摂生 *fusessei* neglect of health, intemperance
節制 *fusessei* intemperance, excesses
寛容 *fukan'yō* intolerance
感症 *fukanshō* sexual frigidity
寝番 *fushimban* night watch; sleepless vigil, vigilance. *nezuban, nezu(no)ban* sleepless vigil
誠実 *fuseijitsu* insincerity, dishonesty, untruthfulness, bad faith
誠意 *fuseii* insincerity, dishonesty, untruthfulness, bad faith
隠 *fuon* disturbed conditions
隠当 *fuontō na* disturbed (conditions); unfortunate (expression)
義 *fugi* immorality; injustice; impropriety; misconduct; adultery; perfidy
義理 *fugiri* dishonesty, injustice; dishonor; ingratitude
適 *futeki* unfitness, inappropriateness, inadequacy, impropriety
適切 *futekisetsu na* unsuitable, inappropriate
適格 *futekikaku, futekkaku* disqualification, unfitness
意 *fui* suddenness, unexpectedness
意打 *fuiu(chi)* surprise attack
意気 *buiki* vulgarity, lack of refinement
意討 *fuiu(chi)* surprise attack
意試験 *fui shiken* surprise examination
14 慣 *funa(re)* inexperience, unfamiliarity
様 *buzama na* unshapely, unsightly, unpresentable, uncouth, clumsy
漁 *furyō* poor catch
語 *fugo* silence
徳 *futoku* depravity, immorality, unworthiness

徳漢 *futokukan* a crook, swindler
認可 *funinka* disapproval, rejection
認証 *funinshō* nonrecognition
導体 *fudōtai* nonconductor
導性 *fudōsei* nonconductibility
精 *bushō* laziness, indolence
精不精 *fushō-bushō* grudgingly
精巧 *fuseikō na* clumsy, bungling
精者 *bushōmono* lazybones, a sluggard
精髭 *bushō hige* unshaven face
[15]慮 *furyo no* unforeseen, accidental
憫 *fubin* pity, compassion
撓 *futō* unbending; inflexibility, tenacity, indomitableness
撓不屈 *futō-fukutsu* inflexibility, tenacity, indomitableness
潔 *fuketsu* uncleanliness, dirtiness, impurity
縁 *fuen* divorce; unrealized marriage; dim marriage prospects
遇 *fugū* misfortune; obscurity
敵 *futeki na* bold, fearless, daring, tough
熱心 *funesshin* lack of enthusiasm, indifference, inattentiveness
衛生 *fueisei* unsanitary condition
養生 *fuyōjō* intemperance, neglect of health
履行 *furikō* nonperformance, default
賛成 *fusansei* disapproval, disagreement
徹底 *futettei* not thoroughgoing, unconvincing, inconclusive, inconsistent, illogical, indefinite, half-way
熟練 *fujukuren* unskillfulness
銹鋼 *fushūkō* stainless steel
確 *futashi(ka) na* unreliable, uncertain, indefinite
確実 *fukakujitsu na* uncertain, unreliable, inauthentic
審 *fushin* incomplete understanding; doubt, question; distrust, suspicion; strangeness; infidelity
審訊問 *fushinjimmon* questioning (by the police)
調 *fuchō* disagreement, break-off, disorder; slump; out of form
調法 *buchōhō* impoliteness; carelessness; misconduct; clumsiness
調和 *fuchōwa* discord, incongruity
器 *fuki* clumsiness, unskillfulness
器用 *bukiyō* clumsiness, unskillfulness
器用者 *bukiyōsha, bukiyōmono* bungler
器量 *bukiryō, fukiryō* ugliness, homeliness; lack of ability, incompetence
[16]磨 *fuma* permanence, immortality
興 *fukyō* displeasure, ill-humor
親切 *fushinsetsu* unkindliness, unfriendliness
整脈 *fuseimyaku* irregular pulse
機嫌 *fukigen* displeasure, ill humor, sullenness
錆鋼 *fuseikō* stainless steel
燃 *funen* incombustibility
燃性 *funensei* incombustibility
躾 *bushitsuke* ill-breeding, impoliteness, bad manners
躾者 *bushitsukemono* rude person
穏 *fuon* unrest, turbulence; impropriety
穏分子 *fuon bunshi* disturbing elements
穏文書 *fuon bunsho* inflammatory pamphlets
穏当 *fuontō* impropriety, inappropriateness, unfairness, unreasonableness
[17]鮮明 *fusemmei* blurring
謹慎 *fukinshin* indiscretion, imprudence
[18]謬性 *fubyūsei* papal infallibility
[19]離 *furi* inseparability
[22]羇 *fuki* freedom, liberty, independence
[24]羈 *fuki* freedom, liberty, independence

4

业 14 / J-X / M-X See **北** 581.

丗 15 / J5242 / M32 See **世** 20 and **卅** 602.

B **丙** 16 / J4a3a / M35 Hei C, third. *hinoe* third calendar sign.

B **且** 17 / J336e / M29 Sho. *katsu* also, furthermore.
[2]又 *katsumata* moreover

丕 18 / J5023 / M30 Hi large; plentiful; receive; source. *ō(kii)* large, immense.
[7]図 *hito* large-scale plans
[13]業 *higyō* immense undertaking; splendid job

1 【一】 丨 丶 丿 乙 亅

[18] 顕 *hiken* extremely clear

B 丘 19/J3556/M33 KYŪ. KU. *oka* hill, knoll, rising ground.

[3] 上 *kyūjō* hilltop
[4] 辺 *okabe* vicinity of a hill
[10] 疹 *kyūshin* pimple, papule
陵 *kyūryō* hill, hillock

A 世 20/J4024/M31 丗 16/J5242/M32 丗 605/J-X/M2713 卋 609/J-X/M2714 SE generation; world. SEI generation; age, world, counter for kings of the same name. *yo* world, society, public; life, existence, career, life-time; age, era, generation, times; reign.

[2] 人 *sejin* people, the public, the world
[3] 上 *sejō* the world
才 *sesai* worldly wisdom, practical wisdom, prudence, shrewdness
[4] 中 *yo (no) naka* society, the world, the times
[5] 立 *yo (ni) ta(tsu)* become famous
代 *sedai, seidai* generation; the world; the age
出 *yo (ni) de(ru)* become famous
世限無 *yoyokagi(ri)na(ku)* forever and ever
[6] 伝 *seiden no* hereditary (estates)
[7] 局 *seikyoku* worldly developments
直 *yonao(shi)* world reformation
事 *seji* worldly affairs
迷言 *yomaigoto* grumbling, muttering, nonsense
知 *sechi* worldly wisdom; stingy person
知辛 *sechigara(i)* a hard (life); a tough (world)
[9] 相 *sesō* phase of life; sign of the times; world conditions
柄 *yogara* world conditions, the times
故 *seko, seiko* worldly affairs
変 *seihen* change of times
紀 *seiki* century; era
紀末 *seikimatsu* end of a century
俗 *sezoku* common customs; worldliness; the world, the common people. *sezoku no* common, worldly, vulgar, popular
俗心 *sezokushin* worldliness
俗化 *sezokuka* secularization
俗主義 *sezokushugi* secularism
俗的 *sezokuteki* worldly
界 *sekai* the world; society; the universe
界一 *sekaiichi* best in the world
界一周 *sekaiisshū* round-the-world trip, circumnavigation, globe-trotting
界人 *sekaijin* a cosmopolitan, a world citizen
界大戦 *Sekai Taisen* World War
界中 *sekaijū* all over the world
界史 *sekaishi* world history
界市民 *sekai shimin* world citizen
界平和 *sekai heiwa* world peace
界主義 *sekai shugi* internationalism, cosmopolitanism
界的 *sekaiteki* world, world-wide, international, universal
界周航 *sekai-shūkō* circumnavigation of the earth
界国家 *sekai kokka* world state
界連邦 *Sekai Rempō* World Federation
界政策 *sekai seisaku* global policy
界記録 *sekai kiroku* world record
界経済 *sekai keizai* international economy
界遊歴 *sekai yūreki* globe-trotting, round-the-world tour
界遊歴者 *sekai yūrekisha* globe-trotter
界新記録 *sekai shinkiroku* new world record
界暦 *sekaireki* world calendar
界選手権 *sekai senshuken* world championship
界銀行 *Sekai Ginkō* the World Bank
界観 *sekaikan* world view
[10] 帯 *setai* household, home
帯主 *setainushi* householder
[11] 過 *yosu(gi)* living, livelihood
運 *seiun* course of events
情 *sejō* world conditions; worldly affairs; human nature
務 *seimu* public affairs, worldly affairs
常 *yo (no) tsune* common occurrence; custom
道 *sedō* morality
道人心 *sedō jinshin* public morals
捨 *yo (o) su(teru)* depart for a hermit's life
捨人 *yosu(te)bito* hermit, recluse; monk

12 渡 *yowata(ri)* living, subsistence, getting along in the world
統 *seitō* a long family line
評 *sehyō* popular opinion; popularity; rumor
覚 *yo (no) obo(e)* reputation, public esteem
智辛 *sechigara(i)* hard (life), tough (world)
間 *seken* world, society, life, people, the public; rumor, gossip
間口 *sekenguchi* reputation
間見 *sekemmi(zu)* ignorance of the world; a person ignorant of the world
間体 *sekentei* decency, reputation, appearance
間的 *sekenteki* worldly, earthly
間知 *sekenshi(razu)* ignorance of the world; a person ignorant of the world
間並 *sekenna(mi)* average, ordinary, common. *sekenna(mi) ni* according to custom
間通 *sekentsū* man of the world
間不見 *sekemmi(zu)* ignorance of the world; a person ignorant of the world
間話 *sekembanashi* gossip, chitchat
間擦 *sekenzure no* sophisticated
間離 *sekembana(re) shita* queer; uncommon; unworldly
13 嗣 *yotsugi, seishi* heir, successor
継 *yotsu(gi)* heir, successor
辞 *seji* flattery, compliment
路 *sero, seiro* the path of life
馴 *yona(reru)* get used to the world; grow worldly
話 *sewa* help, aid; good offices, service, recommendation; care, trouble; everyday life
話人 *sewanin* go-between, intermediary; sponsor; caretaker; manager
話女房 *sewa nyōbō* good housekeeper
話好 *sewazu(ki)* obliging person; officious person
話役 *sewayaku* go-between, intermediary; sponsor; caretaker; manager
話掛 *sewa (o) ka(keru)* bother someone about something
話場 *sewaba* low-life scene
話焼 *sewaya(ki)* busy body; arranger. *sewa (ga) ya(keru)* require a lot of care
14 塵 *sejin* the world, earthly affairs
嫡 *seiteki, seichaku* heir
慣 *yona(reru)* get used to the world; grow worldly
説 *sesetsu* public opinion; popularity; rumor
態 *setai, seitai* social conditions, world conditions; life; the world
15 論 *seron, seiron, yoron* public opinion
論投票 *seron tōhyō*
論調査 *seron chōsa* public-opinion research
18 職 *seishoku* hereditary occupation
22 襲 *seshū* heredity; heritage
襲的 *seshūteki* hereditary
襲権 *seshūken* hereditary right

5

㐂 21 / J-X / M-X Nonstandard for **喜** 858.

丞 22 / J3e67 / M40 JŌ, SHŌ help.

A **両** 23 / J4e3e / M46 **兩** 368 / J5140 / M1436 RYŌ old Japanese coin; both; two; vehicle counter. *tēru* tael.

2 人 *ryōnin* both people
刀 *ryōtō* two swords
刀使 *ryōtōtsuka(i)* two-sword fencer; expert in two lines; man of broad tastes, bisexual man
刀遣 *ryōtōtsuka(i)* two-sword fencer; expert in two lines; man of broad tastes; bisexual man
3 口 *ryōguchi* both openings; two people; a couple
刃 *ryōba no* double-edged
三日 *ryōsannichi* two or three days
4 方 *ryōhō* both
日 *ryōjitsu* both days; two days
氏 *ryōshi* both men
分 *ryōbun suru* bisect, cut in two
天秤 *ryōtembin* two alternatives
手 *ryōte* both hands
手利 *ryōtekiki* ambidextrous; ambidextrous person
手花 *ryōte (ni) hana* two blessings at once; a man with two women
5 立 *ryōritsu* coexistence, standing together, compatibility

生動物 *ryōsei dōbutsu* amphibious animal
用 *ryōyō* dual use
用機 *ryōyōki* amphibian plane
6 肌 *ryōhada* stripped to the waist
舌 *ryōzetsu* double-tongued
両 *ryōryō* both, two each
全 *ryōzen* mutual advantage
名 *ryōmei* both persons
成敗 *ryōseibai* two guilty parties tried and punished together
7 足 *ryōashi, ryōsoku* both feet; both legs
肘 *ryōhiji* both elbows
8 虎 *ryōko* two tigers; two rivals
岸 *ryōgan, ryōgishi* both banks (of a river)
者 *ryōsha* both persons; both things
国 *ryōkoku* both countries
国語 *ryōkokugo* both languages
性 *ryōsei* both sexes
性花 *ryōseika* bisexual flower
性的 *ryōseiteki* bisexual
9 度 *ryōdo* both times
便 *ryōben* urination and bowel movement
洋 *ryōyō* Orient and Occident; Atlantic and Pacific
院 *ryōin* both houses (of a legislative assembly)
軍 *ryōgun* both armies; both teams
陛下 *Ryōheika* Their Majesties
面 *ryōmen* both faces, both sides
面刷 *ryōmenzu(ri)* printing on both sides
10 脇 *ryōwaki* both sides
袖 *ryōsode* both sleeves
家 *ryōke* both families
党 *ryōtō* both political parties
部神道 *Ryōbu Shintō* Shinto-Buddhist amalgamation, dual-aspect Shinto
11 側 *ryōgawa, ryōsoku* both sides
得 *ryōtoku* double gain
眼 *ryōgan* both eyes
舷 *ryōgen* both sides of a ship
断 *ryōdan* bisection
脚 *ryōkyaku* both legs
脚器 *ryōkyakuki* a pair of compasses
12 開 *ryōbira(ki)* double (two-leaf) door
腕 *ryōude* both arms
雄 *ryōyū* two great men
棲動物 *ryōsei dōbutsu* amphibious animal
極 *ryōkyoku* both extremities; north and south poles, positive and negative poles
極地方 *ryōkyoku chihō* polar areas
極端 *ryōkyokutan* both extremes
替 *ryōgae* money exchange
替人 *ryōgaenin* money changer
替屋 *ryōgaeya* money-exchange shop
替商 *ryōgaeshō* money-exchange business
13 損 *ryōzon, ryōson* loss on both sides
義 *ryōgi* double meaning, two meanings
14 像 *ryōzō* both images
様 *ryōyō* two ways, both ways, two kinds
種 *ryōshu* both kinds
端 *ryōtan, ryōhashi* both ends, either end; both edges; sitting on the fence
15 論 *ryōron* both arguments; both theories
輪 *ryōrin* two wheels
16 頭 *ryōtō no* double-headed
親 *ryōshin, futaoya* parents, both parents
17 翼 *ryōyoku* both wings; both flanks
20 議院 *ryōgiin* both houses (of a legislative assembly)

7

A 並 24 J4a42 M54 竝 4230 J636d M25752 HEI. *nara(bu)* line up, be in a row; rank with, rival, equal. *nara(beru)* arrange, place in order, marshal, put side by side, display, serve (food); enumerate; compare with. *na(mi)* common, ordinary, average. *nara(bi) ni* and, besides, as well as. *nara(bi)* row, line, side. *na(bete)* all.
3 大抵 *na(mi)-taitei no* ordinary
4 方 *nara(be)kata* arrangement
木 *namiki* roadside tree; row of trees
木路 *namiki michi* avenue of trees
5 立 *nara(be)-ta(teru)* enumerate. *heiritsu* standing abreast
外 *na(mi)hazu(re)* above the average, extraordinary; abnormal; unreasonable
6 列 *heiretsu* arrangement; row, parallel
存 *heizon* coexistence
行 *heikō* parallel
行処理 *heikō shori* parallel processing
7 足 *na(mi)ashi* walking pace, slow march
8 居 *na(mi)-i(ru)* sit in a row
並 *na(mi)na(mi)* ordinary. *na(mi)na(minaranu)* extraordinary
歩 *na(mi)ashi* walking pace, slow march

[9] 型 *na(mi)gata* ordinary or regulation size
[10] 進 *heishin suru* keep pace with, keep abreast of
[12] 幅 *na(mi)haba* ordinary-width cloth (about 28 cm.)
無 *nara(bi)na(i), nara(bi)na(ki)* unparalleled, unequaled, unique
[13] 置 *heichi* juxtaposition, placing side by side
[14] 製 *namisei* ordinary make

丨 RAD. 2

Bō rod, stick, line. Variant: a shorter vertical. Nickname: Rod.

2

个 25 / J5024 / M70 See **個** 258.

丫 26 / J-X / M71 A a fork.

3

丯 27 / J-X / M75 Bō luxurious growth of grass; fat face.

A **中** 28 / J4366 / M73 Chū center, middle; middle (course); (golden) mean; medium, mediocrity, average; second volume (of three). *naka* inside, interior, midst, middle, mean, midway. *uchi* inside, interior; house, home; within; between, among, out of; mind; myself. *chū(suru)* reach the middle; reach the height (of prosperity). *-chū, -jū* through, throughout, during; all over (town); within, among, in.
[2] 入 *nakai(ri)* intermission (of a play)
二階 *chūnikai* mezzanine floor
[3] 口 *nakaguchi* central entrance; slander
小 *chūshō* medium and small
小企業 *chūshō kigyō* medium and small enterprises
小諸国家 *chūshō shokokka* medium and small nations
[4] 手 *nakate* mid-season rice; mid-season vegetables
日 *chūnichi* the middle day, the equinoctial day. *Chū-Nichi* China and Japan. *nakabi* the middle day
止 *chūshi* suspension, stoppage, interruption
中 *nakanaka* very, considerably; easily, readily; by no means (with negative)
天 *chūten* mid-air; mid-heaven, zenith
夭 *chūyō* dying young
元 *chūgen* 15th day of the seventh lunar month; last day of Bon Lantern Festival; Bon gifts
分 *chūbun suru* halve
支 *Chūshi* Central China
支那 *Naka Shina* Central China
心 *chūshin* center, heart; pivot, emphasis; balance
心人物 *chūshin jimbutsu* central personage
心地 *chūshinchi* center, metropolis
心点 *chūshinten* center
心思想 *chūshin shisō* central idea
[5] 皿 *chūzara* medium-sized dish
句 *chūku* middle part of the verse
外 *chūgai* home and abroad
正 *chūsei* impartiality, fairness
半 *chūhan* middle; half finished
丗 *chūsei* medieval times; Middle Ages
甲板 *chūkampan* main deck
仕 *nakashi* longshoreman, baggageman
仕切 *nakajikiri* partition
立 *chūritsu* neutrality
立地帯 *chūritsu chitai* neutral zone
立国 *chūritsukoku* neutral power
古 *chūko, chūburu* secondhand
古史 *chūkoshi* medieval history
古車 *chūkosha, chūburusha* secondhand car
古品 *chūkohin* secondhand goods
央 *chūō* center, middle
央突破 *chūō toppa* central breakthrough
央政府 *chūō seifu* central government
央集権 *chūō shūken* centralized authoritarian rule
央集権化 *chūō shūkenka* centralization of power

6 米 *Chūbei* Central America
糸 *chūito* medium-sized thread
老 *chūrō* middle age
旬 *chūjun* middle ten days of a month
気 *chūki* palsy, paralysis
休 *nakayasu(mi)* rest, recess
次 *nakatsugi* (electric) relay; intermediary; brokerage
弛 *nakadaru(mi)* a slump
近東 *Chūkintō* Near and Middle East
西部 *Chūseibu* Midwest
衣嚢 *nakagakushi* inside pocket
耳 *chūji* middle ear, tympanum
耳炎 *chūjien* tympanitis
肉 *chūniku* medium build; meat of medium quality
肉中背 *chūniku-chūzei* medium build
共 *Chūkyō* Chinese Communists; Communist China
共軍 *Chūkyōgun* Chinese Communist Army
年 *chūnen* middle age
年者 *chūnemmono* middle-aged person; a person who changes his line in middle life. *chūnensha* middle-aged person
年増 *chūdoshima* woman approaching middle age
7 身 *nakami* interior, contents, substance, filling; (sword) blade
低 *nakabiku, nakahiku* hollow, concave
佐 *chūsa* lieutenant colonel; commander (navy)
判 *chūban* medium size; cabinet size (in photography)
形 *chūgata* medium size
位 *chūi* medium, mediocrity, average. *chūgurai, chūkurai* about medium
位数 *chūisū* median
折 *nakao(ri)* folded in the middle. *nakao(re)* felt hat
折帽 *nakaorebō* felt hat
折帽子 *nakaorebōshi* felt hat
8 退 *chūtai* leaving school during a term
味 *nakami* interior, contents, substance, filling; (sword) blade
物 *a(te)mono* guessing; covering
和 *chūwa suru* neutralize, counteract
取 *naka (o) to(ru)* work out a compromise
欧 *Chūō* Central Europe
京 *Chūkyō* Nagoya
直 *nakanao(ri)* reconciliation
空 *chūkū* mid-air, the air; emptiness. *nakazora* mid-air
毒 *chūdoku* poisoning; addiction
東 *Chūtō* Middle East
波 *chūha* medium wave (in broadcasting)
波長 *chūhachō* medium wave
刳 *nakagu(ri)* boring
刳盤 *nakagu(ri)ban* boring machine
国 *Chūgoku* China; middle of a country; the Hiroshima area
国人 *Chūgokujin* a Chinese
性 *chūsei* neutral gender; (chemical) neutrality; sterility; indifference
性子 *chūseishi* neutron
性洗剤 *chūseisenzai* a detergent
枢 *chūsū* center, pivot, nucleus, backbone, central figure, mainstay, pillar, key man
枢性 *chūsūsei* central (nervous system)
枢神経系 *chūsū shinkei kei* central nervous system
学 *chūgaku* middle school; junior high school
学生 *chūgakusei* middle school pupil; junior high school pupil
学校 *chūgakkō* middle school; junior high school
9 風 *chūbu, chūbū, chūfū* palsy, paralysis
速 *chūsoku* intermediate gear
通 *nakadōri* intermediate street. *chūdōri* medium quality
垣 *nakagaki* middle fence
指 *nakayubi, chūshi* middle finger
柄 *chūgara* medium size, medium pattern, medium stature
柱 *nakabashira* middle pillar
秋 *chūshū* 15th day of the eighth lunar month; mid-autumn
段 *chūdan* half way up a slope or stairway, the landing; center of three (horizontal) columns (of print)
前 *chūzen* front of center field
点 *chūten* middle point, median point
巻 *chūkan* middle volume (of three)
背 *chūzei* average height
南米 *Chūnambei* Central and South America

級品 *chūkyūhin* fair average quality
途 *chūto* midway, half way
途半端 *chūto-hampa* half finished, incomplete
途退学 *chūto taigaku* leaving school during a term
10 座 *chūza suru* leave before an affair is over
庭 *nakaniwa* courtyard, quadrangle, middle court
核 *chūkaku* kernel, core, nucleus
将 *chūjō* lieutenant general, vice admiral
破 *chūha* half damage
耕 *chūkō* cultivation
島 *nakajima* island in a pond or river
宮 *chūgū* palace of the empress; empress; emperor's second consort
高 *nakadaka* convex
原 *chūgen* middle of a field; middle of a country; field of contest
原鹿 *chūgen (no) shika* the aim (in a campaign)
流 *chūryū* mid-stream; middle course; middle class
流社会 *chūryū shakai* middle class
部 *chūbu* central part, center, middle, heart
部太平洋 *Chūbu Taiheiyō* Central Pacific
華 *Chūka* Middle Kingdom, China
華人民共和国 *Chūka Jimmin Kyōwakoku* the People's (Communist) Republic of China
華民国 *Chuka Minkoku* Republic of China (Taiwan)
華料理 *Chūka ryōri* Chinese cooking, Chinese dishes
11 庸 *chūyō* mean, golden mean, moderation, middle path; Doctrine of the Mean
尉 *chūi* first lieutenant; lieutenant junior grade
頃 *nakagoro* about the middle
略 *chūryaku* omission of a part (of an article)
脳 *chūnō* midbrain
隊 *chūtai* company (in the army)
断 *chūdan* break, interruption, suspension
堂 *chūdō* main temple building
距離 *chūkyori* middle distance (race)
産階級 *chūsan kaikyū* middle class, bourgeoisie
道 *chūdō* the middle road, middle of the road, mean, moderation
道派 *chūdōha* middle-of-the roaders, neutrals
堅 *chūken* main body (of troops); center field, center fielder; nucleus, backbone, mainstay
堅手 *chūkenshu* center fielder
12 越 *chūgoshi* over center field
項 *chūkō* the mean
幅 *chuhaba* medium width
程 *nakahodo* middle, midway
絶 *chūzetsu* interruption, discontinuance, suspension, abeyance, abortion
軸 *chūjiku* axis, pivot, central figure, key man
隔 *chūkaku* septum
飯 *chūhan* the noonday meal
期 *chūki* middle period
尊 *chūzon* middle image (of three)
景 *chūkei* middle distance
葉 *chūyō* about the middle of (an era)
等 *chūtō* second grade, medium quality, average; middle class; secondary grade
等学校 *chūtō gakkō* secondary school
等教育 *chūtō kyōiku* secondary education
等教員 *chūtō kyōin* secondary teachers
間 *chūkan* middle, midway; interim
間子 *chūkanshi* meson, mesotron
間内閣 *chūkan naikaku* interim cabinet
間国 *chūkankoku* buffer state
間派 *chūkanha* middle-of-the roaders, neutrals, independents
間商人 *chūkan shōnin* middleman, broker
間景気 *chūkan keiki* temporary boom
間搾取 *chūkan sakushu* kickback
間層 *chūkansō* the middle class
間駅 *chūkan eki* way station
間選挙 *chūkan senkyo* by-election, interim election
13 傷 *chūshō* slander, libel, defamation
腰 *chūgoshi* half-sitting or half-standing posture
腹 *chūfuku* mountain side, halfway up
数 *chūsū* arithmetical mean

幕 *nakamaku* middle act
塗 *nakanuri* second (plaster) coat
農 *chūnō* middle-class farmer
継 *chūkei* (radio) relay, hookup
継所 *chūkeisho* relay station
継放送 *chūkei hōsō* relay broadcasting
継貿易 *chūkei bōeki* transit trade
14 稲 *nakate* mid-season rice
15 編 *chūhen* second part, second volume
篇 *chūhen* second part, second volume
盤戦 *chūbansen* the midst of a campaign
16 積 *nakazu(mi)* loading in the middle
興 *chūkō* restoration, revival, resurgence
興祖 *chūkō (no) so* an ancestor who rejuvenated a dynasty of a family

4

丱 29 J5025 M77 KAN young. *agemaki* young woman's hair style with hair worn up in a knot.
3 女 *kanjo* young woman with hair in *agemaki* style
12 童 *kandō* child; child with hair in *agemaki* style

6

串 30 J367a M80 KAN. KEN. SEN. *kushi* spit, skewer.
8 刺 *kushiza(shi)* skewering
9 柿 *kushigaki* persimmons dried on skewers
12 焼 *kushiya(ki)* food cooked on skewers

8

B **衷** 31 J436f M-X **衷** 5424 J-X M-X CHŪ heart, mind; inside. *uchi* the inside.
4 心 *chūshin* innermost feelings, true heart
11 情 *chūjō* innermost feelings, true heart

RAD. 丶 3

Ten dot, point (the Japanese comma, like the grave accent). Nickname: Dot.

丶 32 J5026 M91 CHU mark, dot.

1

〆 33 J213a M116 **〆** 40 J2561 M115 （国字） *shime* adding up; bundle; ream; seal. *kan* 8 $\frac{1}{3}$ pounds. *shime(te)* totalling. *shi(meru)* sum up.
4 切 *shimeki(ri)* closing; closing up
切日 *shimekiribi* deadline
10 高 *shimedaka* total
11 粕 *shimekasu* oil cake

2

A **丸** 34 J345d M94 GAN. *maru* full (month); perfection; purity; the ship-name suffix anciently used after the name of a sword or a child. *maru(meru)* make round, round off, roll up, curl up; seduce; cajole; explain away. *tama* pills. *maru de* quite, completely, absolutely; just like; as it were. *maru(i), maru(kkoi)* round, circular, spherical.
1 一 *maruichi* bisected-circle seal
2 十 *marujū* cross in a circle
3 丸 *marumaru* completely. *marumaru to* plump
4 込 *maru(me)-ko(mu)* coax, seduce
刈 *maruga(ri)* close clipping
切 *maruki(ri), maru(k)ki(ri)* quite, completely, absolutely; just like; as it were.
公 *marukō* official price
天井 *maru tenjō* arched ceiling
太 *maruta* log
太小屋 *marutagoya* log cabin, blockhouse
太材 *marutazai* round timber
太足場 *maruta ashiba* scaffolding
木 *maruki* log
木舟 *marukibune* dugout canoe
木造 *marukizuku(ri)* rustic work
木船 *marukibune* dugout canoe
木橋 *marukibashi* log bridge
5 瓦 *marugawara* concave roof tile

石 *maruishi* boulder, cobble
出 *maruda(shi)* bare, exposed, undisguised; broad (provincial accent)
本 *maruhon* reciter's book
6 行灯 *maru andon* round paper lantern
7 見 *marumi(e)* completely visible
形 *marugata* round shape, circle
呑 *maruno(mi)* swallowing whole
禿 *maruhage* complete baldness
坊主 *marubōzu* close-cropped head, bald hill
8 味 *marumi* roundness, rotundity
取 *marudo(ri) suru* monopolize
事 *marugoto* in its entirety, whole
9 首 *marukubi* round-necked (T shirt)
持 *marumo(chi)* moneyed man
洗 *maruara(i)* washing kimonos without taking them apart
負 *maruma(ke)* complete defeat
括弧 *marugakko* parentheses
10 帯 *maruobi* one-piece obi
砥石 *marutoishi* grindstone
11 彫 *marubo(ri)* three-dimensional sculpture
窓 *marumado* circular window
12 焼 *maruya(ke)* total fire loss; completely burned. *maruya(ki)* barbecue
勝 *maruga(chi)* complete victory; clean record
提灯 *marujōchin* round lantern
13 損 *maruzon* total loss
暗記 *maru anki* indiscriminate memorizing
腰 *marugoshi* unarmed
裸 *maruhadaka* nude
14 鼻蜂 *marubanabachi* bumblebee
15 潰 *marutsubu(re)* complete ruin, collapse
16 鋼 *marukō* round steel bar
鋸 *marunoko* circular saw
薬 *gan'yaku* pill
髷 *marumage* married woman's hair style
18 儲 *marumōke* clear gain
28 鑿 *marunomi* a gouge

3

丬 35 / J-X / M-X Nonstandard for 第 4272.

B **丹** 36 / J4330 / M99 TAN red; red lead; pills. *ni* red; red earth.
4 心 *tanshin* sincerity, faithfulness
6 色 *ni iro* red
朱 *tanshu* cinnabar, vermilion
8 青 *tansei* red and blue; painting
念 *tannen* application, diligence
毒 *tandoku* erysipelas
9 砂 *tansha* cinnabar
前 *tanzen* large padded kimono
13 誠 *tansei* sincerity; efforts, diligence
塗 *ninu(ri) no* red painted, vermilion lacquered
14 精 *tansei suru* work earnestly
碧 *tampeki* red and green

4

丼 37 / J5027 / M101 TON. TAN. *domburi* bowl; bowl of food
8 物 *domburimono* food served in a large bowl
13 鉢 *domburibachi* bowl

A **主** 38 / J3c67 / M100 SU. SHŪ. SHU Lord; lord, master, employer; aim; main thing. *aruji* head of the house, master, mistress, husband. *nushi* owner; master, husband; lover; a god; you. *omo(na), omo(naru)* main, principal, important. *omo(ni)* chiefly, principally, mostly. *shu(taru)* main, principal, major. *shu toshite* mainly, chiefly. *omo-* main.
2 人 *shujin, aruji* master, head (of a household), landlord; one's husband; employer; host
人公 *shujinkō* master, head (of a household); hero or heroine (of a story)
人役 *shujin'yaku* host, toastmaster
人持 *shujimmo(chi)* a samurai attached to daimyo
人顔 *shujingao* proprietary air
力 *shuryoku* main force, main strength
力株 *shuryoku kabu* leading shares
力艦 *shuryokukan* capital ship
力艦隊 *shuryoku kantai* main fleet
3 上 *shujō* emperor
4 文 *shubun* the text; the main clause (in grammar); the main part of a document

日 *Shujitsu, Shu (no) Hi* the Sabbath, the Lord's Day

5 用 *shuyō* the master's business; necessary business

犯 *shuhan* principal offense; principal offender

犯者 *shuhansha* principal offender

6 色 *shushoku* predominant color

因 *shuin* primary cause, prime factor

帆 *shuhan* main sail

刑 *shukei* principal penalty

旨 *shushi* opinion, idea; meaning, gist, tenor; aim, motive, purpose

成分 *shuseibun* main ingredient

任 *shunin* person in charge

任者 *shuninsha* person in charge, manager, chief, head

7 位 *shui* first place, leading position

役 *shuyaku* a major role; a big part; a star

君 *shukun* lord, master

我 *shuga* ego, self

我主義 *shuga shugi* egoism, love of self

体 *shutai* the subject; constituency, constituents

体的 *shutaiteki* subjective

体性 *shutaisei* independence, autonomy

8 法 *shuhō* main laws

物 *shubutsu* the main thing

祈 *Shu (no) Ino(ri)* the Lord's Prayer

取 *shūdo(ri)* enter the service of a daimyo

命 *shūmei, shumei* ruler's orders, master's orders

事 *shuji* manager, director, secretary

治医 *shujii* attending physician

治効能 *shuji kōnō* chief virtue (of a medicine)

知主義 *shuchi shugi* intellectualism

知的 *shuchiteki* intellectual

9 音 *shuon* tonic, keynote

持 *shumo(chi), shūmo(chi)* serving a master; employee

虹 *shuniji* primary rainbow

査 *shusa* chief investigator

思 *shūmo(i)* worrying about one's master's affairs; one who so worries

食 *shushoku* staple food; main article of diet

食物 *shushokubutsu* staple food; main article of diet

計 *shukei* paymaster, accountant

計局 *shukeikyoku* budget bureau

客 *shukaku, shukyaku* host and guest; principal and auxiliary

客転倒 *shukaku tentō* opposites; reverse order

客顛倒 *shukaku tentō* opposites; reverse order

要 *shuyō na* main, principal, chief, essential, staple

要人物 *shuyō jimbutsu* key people

要工業 *shuyō kōgyō* key industries

要国 *shuyōkoku* principal countries

要物価 *shuyō bukka* prices of staple commodities

要点 *shuyōten* main point, keynote

要駅 *shuyōeki* principal stations

10 馬 *shume* equerry

従 *shujū, shūjū* master and servant, lord and retainer, employer and employee

根 *omone, shukon* main root, taproot

将 *shushō* commander-in-chief; captain (of a team)

班 *shuhan* head position

砲 *shuhō* main battery, main armament

脈 *shumyaku* main mountain range

殺 *shūkoro(shi)* murder of one's master

部 *shubu* main part; complete subject

家 *shuka* employer's house

恩 *shuon* the favor of one's master

格 *shukaku* nominative case

格補語 *shukaku hogo* subject complement

流 *shuryū* main current

流派 *shuryūha* main faction

宰 *shusai* supervision; chairmanship

宰者 *shusaisha* chairman, president

席 *shuseki* head seat, head, chief, president, governor, chairman

席外交官 *shuseki gaikōkan* doyen of the diplomatic corps

席全権 *shuseki zenken* chief delegate

席判事 *shuseki hanji* chief judge

11 唱 *shushō* advocacy, promotion

婦 *shufu* housewife, mistress

張 *shuchō* assertion, claim, advocacy; emphasis, contention, insistence; opinion, tenet

情的 *shujōteki* emotional

情論 *shujōron* emotionalism

眼 *shugan* chief aim; main point

眼点 *shuganten* main point

務 *shumu* competent (authorities)
務大臣 *shumu daijin* the cabinet minister in charge
動 *shudō* leadership
動的 *shudōteki* autonomous
産地 *shusanchi* chief producing center
産物 *shusambutsu* main product
教 *shukyō* bishop, prelate, primate
教室 *shukyōshitsu* home room (in a school)
教冠 *shukyōkan* miter
12 訴 *shuso* main complaint
軸 *shujiku* main shaft
筆 *shuhitsu* editor in chief
筋 *shusuji* people close to the head person
晩餐 *Shu (no) Bansan* the Lord's Supper
13 意 *shui* main meaning; opinion, idea; aim, motive
幹 *shukan* chief editor, managing editor; manager
義 *shugi* principle, policy, basis; -ism
義者 *shugisha* advocate (of a theory or principle); man of principle, ideologist
催 *shusai* sponsorship, promotion
催者 *shusaisha* sponsor, promoter, organizer
催国 *shusaikoku* sponsoring nation
戦 *shusen* advocacy of war
戦投手 *shusen tōshu* top pitcher
戦論 *shusenron* war advocacy, jingoism, bellicose argument
14 語 *shugo* subject (of a sentence)
領 *shuryō* chief, leader
管 *shukan* supervision, management; supervisor, manager
監 *shukan* chief editor, managing editor; manager
製品 *shuseihin* main products
演 *shuen* starring, playing the leading part
演者 *shuensha* star, leading actor
導 *shudō* main leadership
導権 *shudōken* leadership, initiative
15 潮 *shuchō* main current
調 *shuchō* keynote; main melody
審 *shushin* chief umpire
賓 *shuhin* main guest, guest of honor
箱 *Shu (no) Hako* Ark of the Lord
権 *shuken* sovereignty, dominion
権在民 *shuken zaimin* the sovereignty of the people
権国 *shukenkoku* sovereign nation
権者 *shukensha* sovereign, ruler
権侵犯 *shuken shimpan* infringement of sovereignty
16 薬 *shuyaku* principal agent (in a medicine)
謀 *shubō* chief, leader
謀者 *shubōsha* leader
17 翼 *shuyoku* main wings (of an airplane)
18 題 *shudai* subject, theme, motif
題歌 *shudaika* theme song
観 *shukan* subjectivity; subject, ego
観主義 *shukan shugi* subjectivism
観性 *shukansei* subjectivity
観的 *shukanteki* subjective
観論 *shukanron* subjectivism

RAD. 丿 4

No (the katakana). At top: ノ *no kammuri*. Variants of varying lengths. Nickname: *Kana No*.

丿 39 / J5028 / M106 HETSU, HECHI left-to-right bend.

1

メ 40 / J2561 / M115 Nonstandard for 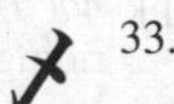 33.

乂 41 / J5029 / M111 GAI, GE govern, restrain. *osa(maru)* be at peace, calm down; be settled, be ruled. *osa(meru)* govern, manage, regulate; quell, subdue. *ka(ru)* trim, mow (grass).
6 安 *gaian* peaceful, calm

4

1 一 丨 丶 【丿】 乙 亅

乃 42 / J4735 / M113 DAI. NAI. *sunawa(chi)* whereupon, accordingly. *no* possessive particle. *soko de* then, thereupon, accordingly.
6 至 *naishi* from… to…; or

2

ケ 43 / J2531 / M-X **个** 27 / J5024 / M70 See **個** 258.

凢 44 / J-X / M123 See **凡** 433.

々 45 / J2139 / M97 Character repetition.

B **乏** 46 / J4b33 / M133 BŌ. *tobo(shii), tomo(shii)* meager, scarce, limited; destitute, hard up.

A **久** 47 / J3557 / M118 KYŪ. KŪ. *hisa(shii)* long, long-continued, an old (story). *hisa(shiku)* for a long time.
3 久 *hisabisa* a long time, many days
4 方 *hisakata* sky, moon
方振 *hisakataburi* a long time, many days
10 振 *hisa(shi)buri* a long time, many days
12 遠 *kuon, kyūen* eternity
16 懐 *kyūkai* a long-cherished hope

3

之 48 / J4737 / M125 SHI. *kore* this. *ko(no)* this.

4

乎 49 / J3843 / M131 KO. *ya, ka* question mark.
5 古止点 *okototen* marks to aid in reading classical Chinese

乍 50 / J4663 / M130 SA. *-naga(ra)* though, notwithstanding; while, during; both, all. *tachima(chi)* in a moment, instantly, immediately, all of a sudden.
12 然 *sarinagara* however, but

5

乑 51 / J-X / M139 SHŪ assemble.

6

乕 52 / J6949 / M148 See **虎** 5265.

7

乖 53 / J502a / M149 KAI oppose, disobey.
19 離 *kairi* estrangement, separation

8

A **乗** 54 / J3e68 / M153 **乘** 55 / J502b / M154 JŌ power (in math); multiplication; record; vehicle; vehicle counter. *no(ru), no(kkaru)* ride, board, mount; get up on; spread (paints); be taken in; share in, join; be found in (a dictionary); feel like doing; be mentioned in; be in harmony with. *no(seru)* place, put, lay, set; let (one) take part; impose on; record, mention. *no(ri-konasu)* manage (a horse). *jō(jiru), jō(zuru)* take advantage of; multiply (in math); follow blindly. *no(ri)* riding, ride; (two)-seater; spread (of paints).
2 入 *no(ri)-i(reru)* *vi* and *vt* ride or drive into (a place); extend (a line into a city). *no(ri)-i(ru)* ride or drive into (a place). *no(ri)-i(re)* driving into
3 上 *no(ri)-a(geru)* run aground, be stranded
4 手 *no(ri)te* passenger; rider; good rider
反 *no(ruka)-so(ruka)* win or lose, sink or swim
込 *no(ri)-ko(mu)* *vt* and *vi* board, embark on, get into (a car); ship (passengers); man (a ship); help (someone) into; march into, enter
切 *no(ri)-ki(ri)* overcome, get through; ride or sail across; weather, tide over
心地 *no(ri)gokochi* one's feeling while riding
5 付 *no(ri)-tsu(keru)* ride up to; get used to riding. *no(ri)tsu(ke)* one's regular (taxi)

出 *no(ri)-da(su)* set out, set sail; embark on; lean forward; begin to ride
号 *jōgō* sign of multiplication
用自動車 *jōyō-jidōsha* passenger auto
用車 *jōyōsha* passenger auto
6 回 *no(ri)-ma(waru)* ride around. *no(ri)-ma(wasu)* *vt* drive (a car) around, ride (a bicycle) around.
気 *no(ri)ki* interest, eagerness
合 *no(ri)-a(wasu), no(ri)-a(waseru)* happen to ride together, share a vehicle. *noriai* bus, stagecoach; riding together; fellow passenger; joint partnership
合馬車 *noriai basha* stagecoach
合船 *noriaibune* ferryboat
7 戻 *no(ri)-modo(su)* ride (a horse) back, drive (a car) back
良 *no(ri)yo(i)* easy to ride, riding well
車 *jōsha* entraining
車口 *jōshaguchi* entrance to a station
車券 *jōshaken* passenger ticket
車賃 *jōshachin* railway fare
車駅 *josha eki* entraining point
8 逃 *no(ri)ni(ge)* stealing a ride; stolen ride
法 *jōhō* multiplication
物 *no(ri)mono* vehicle
取 *no(t)to(ru), no(ri)-to(ru)* capture, occupy, usurp
取策 *no(t)to(ri)saku* a plot against (someone), hijack
9 飛 *no(ri)-to(basu)* tear along (the road)
通 *no(ri)-to(ru)* ride through, ride along
除 *jōjo* multiplication and division
客 *jōkyaku, jōkaku* passenger
降 *jōkō, no(ri)o(ri)* getting on and off
降者優先 *jōkōsha yūsen* priority to pedestrians
降場 *jōkōjō* (station) platform
10 進 *no(ri)-susu(meru)* ride forth
逸 *no(ri)-hagu(reru)* miss a train
員 *jōin* crew ⌈horse
馬 *jōba, no(ri)uma* riding horse; saddle
馬服 *jōbafuku* riding habit
馬隊 *jōbatai* mounted corps, cavalcade
馬靴 *jōbagutsu* riding boots
11 遅 *no(ri)-oku(reru)* miss (a train)
過 *no(ri)-su(gosu)* ride past
捨 *no(ri)-su(teru)* get off, abandon (a ship)
掛 *no(ri)-ka(keru), no(ri)-ka(karu)* be about to board; be riding on; get on top of; lean over; set about; collide with
移 *no(ri)-utsu(su)* transfer (a stowaway). *no(ri)-utsu(ru)* change (cars or horses), transfer; possess; inspire
船 *jōsen* embark; be on board
務員 *jōmuin* trainman, train crew
組 *no(ri)-ku(mu)* get on aboard; join a ship. *noriku(mi)* crew
組員 *norikumiin* crew
12 越 *no(ri)-ko(eru)* climb over; ride across; surmount. *no(ri)-ko(su)* ride past; pass; outdistance. *noriko(shi)* riding past (one's station)
場 *no(ri)ba* car stop, platform
替 *no(ri)-ka(eru)* transfer
換 *no(ri)-ka(eru)* transfer. *norika(e)* transfer
換券 *norikaeken* ticket for transfer
換場 *norika(e)ba* platform for transfer
換駅 *norikae eki* transfer point
13 損 *no(ri)-soko(nau)* miss (a train)
溢 *no(ri)-kobo(reru)* be crowded with passengers
馴 *no(ri)-na(rasu)* break in (a horse)
14 算 *jōzan* multiplication
15 潰 *no(ri)-tsubu(su)* ride (a horse) to death
16 積 *jōseki* product (in math)
18 冪 *jōbeki* power (in math)
20 艦 *jōkan* joining one's warship

—— **9** ——

乘 55 / J502b / M154 See **乗** 54.

RAD. 乙 5

Otsu second (in order). Variants: ⺃, ⺄ *tsuribari* fishhook. Nickname: Fishhook.

B **乙** 56 / J3235 / M161 ITSU. OTSU B, second; the latter; duplicate. *otsu na* strange, queer, quaint; witty; stylish, spicy, chic; tasty; romantic. *kinoto* second calendar sign.
3 女 *otome* virgin, maiden

女心 *otomegokoro* a girl's feeling, a maiden's mind

5 巡 *otsujun* second-class cruiser

8 夜 *otsuya, itsuya* about ten p.m.

9 姫 *otohime* youngest princess

1

A 九 57 / J3665 / M167 Kyū, Ku *kokono(tsu), ko* nine.

2 九表 *kuku (no) hyō* multiplication table

十九折 *tsuzurao(ri)* winding road

3 寸五分 *kusungobu* a dagger

4 日 *kokonoka* nine days; the ninth day (of the month)

月 *Kugatsu* September

牛一毛 *kyūgyū (no) ichimō* a mere fraction, a drop in the bucket

天 *kyūten* sky; heavens; palace

分 *kubu* nine parts; nine percent; nine cases out of ten

分九厘 *kubu-kurin* ten to one, nine cases out of ten

6 地 *kyūchi* very low land

回戦 *kyūkaisen* regulation game, ninth inning

死一生 *kyūshi-isshō* narrow escape from death

7 折 *kyūsetsu* many turns (in a road)

8 拝 *kyūhai* bowing many times (in apology)

9 泉 *kyūsen* Hades, nether regions

重 *kokonoe* ninefold; imperial palace, the court

重天 *kyūchō no ten* the palace

星 *kyūsei* astrology, horoscope

星家 *kyūseika* astrologer, star reader

星術 *kyūseijutsu* astrology, horoscopy

10 夏 *kyūka* summer

11 族 *kyūzoku* the nine nearest generations of relatives

13 腸 *kyūchō* intestines, bowels, entrails, viscera; the heart

14 穀 *kyūkoku* the nine grains

15 輪 *kurin* pagoda finial

2

也 58 / J4c69 / M171 Ya. *nari = desu* to be (classical).

乞 59 / J3870 / M170 Kitsu. Kotsu. *ko(u)* ask, request; invite; pray for; beg, solicit.

8 取 *ko(i)-to(ru)* ask for and receive

9 食 *kojiki* beggar; begging

10 高評 *kou kōhyō* with the author's compliments

12 婿 *koi muko* bridegroom who is loved by his bride

6

A 乱 60 / J4d70 / M187 亂 64 / J502c / M214 亂 65 / J-X / M-X

Ran, Ron riot, rebellion, war, disorder. *mida(re)* disorder, disturbance, agitation. *mida(su), mida(ru)* put in disorder; disturb, agitate; corrupt; derange (the mind). *mida(reru)* be out of order, be confused; be disturbed, be disorganized; be demoralized, be lax; be disheveled. *mida(ri) ni* without authority, without reason, arbitrarily, unnecessarily, indiscriminately, recklessly. *mida(rigamashii)* morally corrupt.

2 丁 *ranchō* mixed up pages (in a book)

入 *rannyū* intrusion, raid. *rannyū suru* intrude, break into

入者 *rannyūsha* intruder, trespasser

3 山 *ranzan* a jumble of high and low mountains

4 心 *ranshin* insanity, derangement

文 *rambun* careless writing (in composition)

反射 *ranhansha* diffused reflection

5 用 *ran'yō* misuse, abuse, misappropriation

立 *ranritsu* flood (of candidates)

打 *randa* pummeling, random blows

世 *ransei* troubled times

民 *rammin* insurgents, rioters, mob

6 臣 *ranshin* traitorous vassal, traitor

行 *rangyō* profligacy, debauchery, misconduct

伐 *rambatsu* indiscriminate deforestation

7 足 *mida(re) ashi* out of step

売 *rambai* underselling, panicky selling

8 国 *rangoku* a disturbed country, strife-torn country
拍子 *rambyōshi* out of tune
杭 *rangui* (defense) palisade; fence
杭歯 *ranguiba* irregular teeth
9 飛 *mida(re)-to(bu)* (rumors) spread wildly, run wild
造 *ranzō* overproduction; careless manufacture
後 *rango* after the rebellion
軍 *rangun* mixed fight, rough-and-tumble
発 *rampatsu* random or reckless firing
10 倫 *ranrin* immorality, immoral conduct
流 *ranryū* turbulent flow
酒 *ranshu* drunken frenzy; vicious drinker
脈 *rammyaku* confusion, disorder, chaos
射 *ransha* random firing, wild shot
書 *mida(re)ga(ki)* careless composition (of an article)
11 麻 *ramma* confusion, chaos, anarchy
視 *ranshi* astigmatism, distorted vision
酔 *ransui* dead drunk
12 筆 *rampitsu* bad writing, scribbling
雲 *ran'un* nimbus clouds, rain clouds, torn clouds
費 *rampi* waste, extravagance
13 賊 *ranzoku* gangsters, rebels
戦 *ransen* free-for-all fight, melee
痴気 *ranchiki* quarreling, carousing, disorderliness
痴気騒 *ranchikisawa(gi)* uproarious festivity
14 雑 *ranzatsu* disorder, confusion
髪 *mida(re)gami, mida(shi)gami, rampatsu* unkempt hair
舞 *rambu* boisterous dance
読 *randoku* indiscriminate reading
読家 *randokuka* indiscriminate reader
15 箱 *mida(re)bako* box for kimono and accessories
撃 *rangeki* confused fighting, melee
調 *ranchō* discord; ragtime; confusion, irregularity; market fluctuation
調子 *ranchōshi* discord; ragtime; confusion, irregularity; market fluctuation
暴 *rambō* violence, rudeness, rowdiness, carelessness, lawlessness, recklessness
暴者 *rambōmono* rowdy, vandal, rascal
16 獲 *rankaku* indiscriminate fishing or hunting
18 闘 *rantō* free-for-all fight, melee
19 離 *ranri* dispersion
22 籠 *mida(re)kago* clothes basket (in a bathhouse)

7

乳 61 / J467d / M190 NYŪ. *chi, chichi* milk; the breasts; loop.

4 牛 *chichiushi, nyūgyū* milk cow, dairy cattle
化 *nyūka* emulsification
5 汁 *nyūjū* milky juice; latex; milk
用牛 *nyūyōgyū* milk cow
兄弟 *chikyōdai* foster brother or sister
幼児 *nyūyōji* infant
石英 *nyūsekiei* milky quartz
母 *uba, nyūbo, omba* wet nurse, nursing mother
母車 *ubaguruma* baby buggy
白 *nyūhaku* milky white, lactescent
白色 *nyūhakushoku* milk white
6 色 *nyūshoku* milk white
7 呑子 *chinomigo* baby, suckling child
状 *nyūjō* milky
状液 *nyūjō eki* milky juice, latex
児 *nyūji* suckling, infant, baby
児死亡率 *nyūji shibōritsu* infant mortality
児脚気 *nyūji kakke* infantile beriberi
8 房 *chibusa, nyūbō* breast, nipple, udder
9 首 *chikubi, chichi kubi* teat, nipple
香 *nyūkō* frankincense, olibanum
臭 *nyūshū* boyishness, inexperience. *chichikusa(i)* smelling of milk; immature
10 剤 *nyūzai* emulsion
11 液 *nyūeki* latex
菓 *nyūka* emulsion
12 歯 *nyūshi* first set of teeth
棒 *nyūbō* pestle
飲児 *chino(mi)go* baby, suckling child
13 搾 *chichishibo(ri)* milking; milker
腺 *nyūsen* mammary gland
酪 *nyūraku* butter
鉢 *nyūbachi* mortar
業 *nyūgyō* the dairy business
14 製品 *nyūseihin* dairy products
様突起 *nyūyōtokki* mastoid
酸 *nyūsan* lactic acid

酸菌 *nyūsankin* lactic acid bacilli
16 濁 *nyūdaku* emulsion
糖 *nyūtō* milk sugar, lactose
頭 *nyūtō* nipple, teat
17 癌 *nyūgan* breast cancer
19 繰 *chichiku(ru)* have illicit sexual relations
離 *chibana(re), chichibana(re)* weaning

10

亀 62/J3535/M210 龜 7106/J737d/M48847 KI, KIN. *kame* turtle, tortoise.
2 卜 *kiboku, kameura* tortoise-shell divination
3 子 *kame (no) ko* young tortoise
4 手 *kame(no)te* barnacle
5 甲 *kikō, kikkō, kame(no)kō* tortoise shell
12 裂 *kiretsu* crack, crevice, fissure, chap
22 鑑 *kikan* pattern, model, example

B 乾 63/J3425/M204 KAN. KEN heaven; emperor. *ho(su) vt* dry; desiccate; drain (off); drink up; dry up. *ka(seru)* dry up, scab, slough; be poisoned (with lacquer). *kawa(ku)* dry, dry up; be dry. *kawa(kasu) vt* dry, desiccate. *kara(biru)* dry up, shrivel. *kawa(ki)* drying; dryness. *hoshi-* dried, cured.
3 干 *karabo(shi)* sun-dried fish or vegetables
上 *hiaga(ru)* dry up, parch; ebb away
5 田 *kanden* dry rice field
皮 *kampi* dried hides
生姜 *kanshōga* powdered ginger
生植物 *kansei shokubutsu* desert plants
生薑 *kanshōga* powdered ginger
6 肉 *hoshiniku* dried meat, pemmican
地農法 *kanchi nōhō* dry farming
7 材 *kanzai* dry lumber
8 固 *hikata(maru), kanko suru* dry and harden
杯 *kampai* a toast
板 *kampan, kamban* dry plate
季 *kanki* dry season
果 *kanka* dried fruit
坤 *kenkon* heaven and earth; universe
坤一擲 *kenkon'itteki* throwing all into a task; staking all on
性 *kansei* dryness, dry (pleurisy)
性油 *kanseiyu* drying oil, linseed oil
物 *kambutsu* groceries. *hoshimono* laundry on the line. *karamono* dried fish
物屋 *kambutsuya* grocery store
9 風 *kara(k)kaze, karakaze* dry wind
咳 *karazeki, karaseki* dry cough, hacking cough
拭 *karabuki* polishing with a dry cloth
枯 *kanko suru, hika(rabiru)* completely dry up
草 *kansō, magusa, hoshi kusa* hay, dry grass
海苔 *hoshinori* dried edible seaweed
10 留 *kanryū* dry distillation
芻 *kansū* hay
11 魚 *hoshiuo, hizakana, hiuo, kangyo* dried fish
舷 *kangen* freeboard
菜 *kansai* dried vegetables
菓子 *higashi* candy; cookies
船渠 *kansenkyo, kandokku* dry dock
12 飯 *hoshiii, karei, kareii* dried boiled rice
期 *kanki* dry season
裂 *kanretsu* cracks in drying lumber
葡萄 *hoshibudō* raisins
湿 *kanshitsu* degree of humidity
湿計 *kanshitsukei* humidity meter
13 溜 *kanryū* dry distillation
煎 *karai(ri)* roasting, broiling
電池 *kandenchi* dry cell
酪 *kanraku* cheese
酪素 *kanrakuso* casein
15 蝕 *kanshoku* the rotting of lumber stored with poor air circulation
16 瓢 *kampyō* dried gourd strings
17 燥 *kansō* drying; dryness, aridity; insipid; dehydrated
燥牛乳 *kansō gyūnyū* powdered milk
燥地 *kansōchi* dry land
燥材 *kansōzai* seasoned lumber
燥卵 *kansō tamago* dehydrated eggs
燥炉 *kansōro* drying furnace
燥季 *kansōki* dry season
燥果 *kansōka* dried fruit
燥室 *kansōshitsu* drying room
燥剤 *kansōzai* a drying agent
燥野菜 *kansō yasai* dehydrated vegetables
燥期 *kansōki* dry spell, dry period
燥腐朽 *kansō fukyū* dry rot
燥器 *kansōki* dryer
燥機 *kansōki* dryer

13

亂 64 J502c M214 亂 65 J-X M-X See 乱 60.

RAD. 亅 6

Hane bō feathered stick or *kagi* hook, barb. Nickname: Barb.

亅 66 J502d M224 KETSU hook.

1

B 了 67 J4e3b M226 RYŌ. *ryō(suru)* finish, complete; understand. *ryō to suru* acknowledge. *shima(u)* get through with.

7 見 *ryōken* idea, thought, intention, inclination, motive, decision; discretion; forgiveness; toleration
承 *ryōshō* acknowledgment
8 知 *ryōchi suru* know, understand, appreciate
12 覚 *ryōkaku suru* come to understand
13 解 *ryōkai* understanding, comprehension
18 簡 *ryōken* idea, thought, intention, inclination, motive, decision; discretion; forgiveness; toleration
簡違 *ryōkenchiga(i)* wrong idea; delusion; indiscretion, false step

3

A 予 68 J4d3d M231 豫 5751 J502e M36425 YO I, myself, the writer. *arakaji(me)* previously. *kane(te)* previously, already, lately.

4 予 *kanegane* often, lately, already
5 示 *yoji suru* show signs of, foreshadow
令 *yorei* preparatory command
6 行 *yokō* rehearsal
行演習 *yokō enshū* rehearsal
防 *yobō* prevention, protection against
防医学 *yobō igaku* preventive medicine; a prophylactic
防法 *yobōhō* precautionary measures
防注射 *yobō chūsha* immunization, shots
防接種 *yobō sesshu* immunization, vaccination
防策 *yobōsaku* precautionary measures
防戦争 *yobō sensō* preventive war
防線 *yobōsen* guard (against attack)
防薬 *yoboyaku* prophylactic medicine
7 見 *yoken suru* foresee, foreknow. *yoken* divination
告 *yokoku* previous notice, preliminary announcement
言 *yogen* prediction, prognostication. *kanegoto* prediction; promise
言者 *yogensha* predictor, prognosticator
8 波 *yoha* secondary effect, aftermath; trail (of a storm), sequel, consequence
知 *yochi* intimation, premonition, foreknowledge, prediction
定 *yotei* prearrangement; program, plan; expectation; estimate
定日 *yoteibi* scheduled date, expected date
定案 *yoteian* program, prospectus
定期日 *yotei kijitsu* prearranged date
定期限 *yotei kigen* target date
定説 *yoteisetsu* predestination
9 後 *yogo* prognosis, aftereffects, recuperation, convalescence
科 *yoka* preparatory course; preparatory department
科生 *yokasei* preparatory-department student
約 *yoyaku* contract, subscription, booking, reservation, pledge, advance order
約出版 *yoyaku shuppan* publication after securing subscriptions
約名簿 *yoyaku meibo* subscription list
約者 *yoyakusha* subscriber
約済 *yoyakuzu(mi)* reserved, engaged
10 納 *yonō* advance payment
11 習 *yoshū* lesson preparation; rehearsal
断 *yodan suru* guess, predict, conclude
12 測 *yosoku* forecast, estimate
期 *yoki* expectation, anticipation, hope, foresight, forecast

覚 *yokaku* hunch, foreboding, premonition
報 *yohō* forecasting, prediction, previous notification
報音 *yohōon* telephone time-warning sound
備 *yobi* preparation; preliminaries; reserve; spare
備工作 *yobi kōsaku* spade work, preliminaries
備士官学校 *yobi shikan gakkō* reserve officers' cadet school
備交渉 *yobi kōshō* preliminary negotiations
備会議 *yobi kaigi* preliminary conference
備兵 *yobihei* reservists
備役 *yobieki* service in the first reserve
備判事 *yobi hanji* supernumerary judge
備金 *yobikin* reserve fund, emergency fund
備知識 *yobi chishiki* background knowledge
備協約 *yobi kyōyaku* preliminary agreement
備科 *yobika* preparatory course
備品 *yobihin* spares, reserve supply
備室 *yobishitsu* spare room
備馬 *yobiba* spare horse
備校 *yobikō* preparatory school
備員 *yobiin* reserve men
備部品 *yobi buhin* spare parts
備座席 *yobi zaseki* rumble seat
備将校 *yobi shōkō* reserve officers
備隊 *yobitai* reserve corps
備運動 *yobi undō* limbering up
備費 *yobihi* reserve fund, emergency fund, preliminary expenses
備試験 *yobi shiken* preliminary exam
備選手 *yobi senshu* reserve player
備錨 *yobi ikari* spare anchor
備艦隊 *yobi kantai* reserve fleet
13 鈴 *yorei* first bell
感 *yokan* premonition, hunch
想 *yosō* anticipation, forecast, conjecture, imagination; estimate
想外 *yosōgai* unexpected, unforeseen, strange
想収穫高 *yosō shūkakudaka* crop estimate
想利益 *yosō rieki* estimate profits
想通 *yosōdō(ri)* as expected
想屋 *yosōya* crystal gazer, dopester
想高 *yosōdaka* estimate
14 選 *yosen* nomination, primary election, elimination match
選会 *yosenkai* primary caucus
算 *yosan* estimate, appropriation, budget
算上 *yosanjō no* budgetary
算外 *yosangai* outside the budget
算案 *yosan'an* budget proposal
算措置 *yosan sochi* budgetary provision
15 震 *yoshin* preliminary tremor
審 *yoshin* preliminary examination, pretrial hearing
審廷 *yoshintei* court of first instance
16 謀 *yobō* premeditation, aforethought
17 餞会 *yosenkai* farewell meeting, send-off

5

A 争 69/J4168/M236 爭 3510/J6027/M19663 Sō. *araso(u)* dispute, argue; be at variance; compete. *araso(i)* dispute, strife, quarrel, dissension, conflict; rivalry, contest. *araso(warenai)* indisputable, undeniable, unmistakable. *ika(de)* how.
6 好 *araso(i)zu(ki) na* quarrelsome, contentious
7 乱 *sōran* rioting, disturbances
8 事 *araso(i)goto* dispute
9 点 *sōten* point at issue
怒 *araso(i)-ika(ru)* be angry and quarrelsome
11 訟 *sōshō* dispute. *sōshō no* contentious
12 訴 *araso(i)-utta(eru)* accuse, rise up in judgment against
13 戦 *araso(i)-tataka(u)* fight with, contend with
14 端 *sōtan* beginning of a dispute
奪 *sōdatsu* contest, competition, struggle, challenge
奪戦 *sōdatsusen* contest, competition, struggle, challenge
15 論 *sōron* argument, dispute, controversy
18 闘 *sōtō* strife, struggle
19 覇 *sōha* contending for victory, struggling for supremacy
覇戦 *sōhasen* struggle for supremacy, championship game
20 議 *sōgi* dispute, conflict

6

事 70 / J502f / M-X Nonstandard for 事 71.

7

A 事 71 / J3b76 / M241 Jɪ thing, matter. *koto* thing, matter, fact, circumstances, business, reason, experience. *tsuka(eru)* serve, work for. *koto (ni yoru to)* possibly, probably. *koto to suru* deal in; take pleasure in; make it your business. *-ji* fact, matter. *-koto* alias.

3 大 *jidai* subserviency to the stronger
大主義 *jidai shugi* worship of the powerful
大思想 *jidai shisō* admiration of the powerful
4 欠 *kotoka(ku)* lack, be in need of
切 *kotoki(reru)* die, expire
5 立 *kotoda(teru)* do something different; make a big thing of
由 *jiyū* reason, cause
犯 *jihan* crime
6 好 *koto (o) kono(mu)* revel in trouble and discord
共 *kotodomo* things, matters
毎 *kotogoto ni* in everything; always
件 *jiken* event, incident, affair, case, plot, trouble, scandal
件表 *jikenhyō* docket
7 足 *kotota(ru), kotota(riru)* suffice, serve the purpose, be satisfied
局 *jikyoku* circumstances
8 例 *jirei* example; precedent
物 *jibutsu* things, affairs
宜 *jigi* a fitting thing
典 *jiten* encyclopedia
事 *kotogoto* everything. *kotogoto(shii)* bombastic, pretentious, exaggerated
実 *jijitsu* fact; reality; as a matter of fact
実上 *jijitsujō* actually, in fact
実無根 *jijitsu-mukon* contrary to fact
実調査 *jijitsu chōsa* fact-finding
9 迹 *jiseki* evidence, trace
相 *jisō* aspect, phase, phenomenon
柄 *kotogaru* matter, affair, circumstance
珍 *kotomezura(shiku)* like something strange
故 *jiko* accident, incident, trouble; circumstances, reasons
変 *jihen* accident, disaster; incident, uprising, emergency
後 *jigo-* after, post-, ex post facto
後承諾 *jigo shōdaku* ex-post-facto approval
前 *jizen no* prior, before the fact
前日付 *jizen hizuke* antedating
前同意 *jizen (no) dōi* prior consent
前割当 *jizen waria(te)* prearranged quota
前検閲 *jizen ken'etsu* pre-publication censorship
11 情 *jijō* circumstances, reasons
理 *jiri* reason, facts, propriety, sense
細 *kotokoma(kani), kotokoma(yakani)* minutely, in detail
寄 *kotoyo(su)* find an excuse. *kotoyo(seru)* pretend. *kotoyo(sete)* on the plea of, under the pretext of
務 *jimu* business, clerical work
務引継 *jimuhikitsu(gi)* taking over an office
務会 *jimukai* business meeting
務当局 *jimu tōkyoku* officials in charge
務次官 *jimu jikan* permanent vice-minister, undersecretary
務局 *jimukyoku* secretariat, executive office
務所 *jimusho* office
務的 *jimuteki* businesslike, practical
務服 *jimufuku* work clothes
務官 *jimukan* administrative official, secretary, commissioner
務長 *jimuchō* manager; purser
務長官 *jimu chōkan* chief secretary
務取扱 *jimutoriatsukai* acting director
務室 *jimushitsu* office
務員 *jimuin* clerk
務家 *jimuka* man of affairs
務量 *jimuryō* amount of business
務総局 *jimu sōkyoku* secretariat-general
務総長 *jimu sōchō* secretary-general, director
務器 *jimuki* business machines
12 項 *jikō* matters, facts, items
無 *koto(mo)na(ge) na* careless. *kotona(shi)* nothing; nothing to be done; safe; easy. *kotona(ku)* without accident, uneventfully
象 *jishō* phenomenon, a matter
13 跡 *jiseki* evidence, trace, vestige

新 *kotoatara(shiku)* anew; again, specially, formally
業 *jigyō* enterprise, business, industry; operation
業化 *jigyōka* industrialization
業年度 *jigyō nendo* fiscal year
業界 *jigyōkai* industrial or business world
業部 *jigyōbu* operations department
業家 *jigyōka* enterprising man; businessman; industrialist
業税 *jigyōzei* business tax
14 誤 *kotoayama(ri)* mistake in speaking
態 *jitai* situation, state of affairs
16 積 *jiseki* achievement, exploit; merits
18 蹟 *jiseki* evidence, trace, vestige

2-STROKE RADICALS

二 RAD. 二 7

Ni two. Variant: shorter horizontals. Nickname: Two.

二 72 J4673 M247 NI two; second. JI.
A二 *futa(tsu), fu, fū, futa* two.
2 八 *nihachi* 16
七日 *futananuka* second week's memorial service
人 *futari, ninin* two persons, pair, couple
人三脚 *nininsankyaku* three-legged race
人連 *futarizu(re)* a party of two
人前 *futarimae, ninimmae* the (work) of two; (meals) for two
人称 *nininshō* second person (in grammar)
人組 *niningumi* twosome
十日 *hatsuka* 20 days; 20th day (of the month)
十日大根 *hatsukadaikon* a small garden radish
十日鼠 *hatsukanezumi* mouse
十代 *nijūdai* one's twenties
十世紀 *nijisseiki* 20th century
十四時間制 *nijūyojikansei* around-the-clock-system
十重 *hatae* many-fold
十歳 *hatachi* age 20
3 子 *futago* twins; a twin
三 *nisan* two or three
丸 *ni (no) maru* outer citadel
口目 *futakuchime* a pet expression
大政党主義 *nidaiseitō shugi* two-party system
4 心 *futagokoro, nishin* duplicity, treachery
手 *futate* two groups, two bands
方 *futakata* both people
月 *Nigatsu* February. *futatsuki* two months
毛作 *nimōsaku* two crops a year
日 *futsuka* two days; the second day (of the month)
日酔 *futsukayoi* a hangover
王 *Niō* Guardian Deva Kings
王門 *Niōmon* temple gate guarded by fierce Deva Kings
分 *nibun suru* halve, bisect
分音符 *nibu ompu* half note
元的 *nigenteki* dual
元放送 *nigen-hōsō* a broadcast in which participants speak from different stations
元論 *nigenron* dualism
5 目 *futame to* for a second time
号 *nigō* number two; concubine
矢 *ni (no) ya* second arrow
乍 *futa(tsu)naga(ra)* both
句 *ni (no) ku* another word, answer
句出 *ni(no)ku ga de(nu)* be at a loss for words
本立 *nihonda(te)* double feature (movie)
本建 *nihonda(te)* dual system; double standard
本差 *nihonza(shi)* two-sworded (samurai)
世 *nise* two existences, the present and the future. *nisei* junior; the second (king of the same name); two generations; the second generation (of immigrants)
世固 *nise (no) kata(me)* marriage vows
世契 *nise (no) chigi(ri)* marriage vows
世約束 *nise (no) yakusoku* marriage vows
6 列 *niretsu* two rows; double file

字 *niji* two characters; name
共 *futa(tsu) tomo* both
死 *nishi* two out (baseball)
返事 *futa(tsu) henji* an immediate (happy) reply
交替制労働 *nikōtaisei rōdō* two-shift work program
色 *nishoku* two-color, dichromatic
色刷 *nishokuzu(ri)* two-color printing
百二十日 *nihyaku hatsuka* 220th day, end of the storm period
百十日 *nihyaku tōka* 210th day from the beginning, the storm day
次 *niji* second, secondary. *ni (no) tsugi* secondary, subordinate
次元 *nijigen* two dimensions
次方程式 *niji hōteishiki* quadratic equation
次会 *nijikai* a second party the same night
次的 *nijiteki* secondary
7 伸 *nishin* postscript
位 *nii* second place
役 *futayaku* double role
形 *futanari* hermaphrodite
更 *nikō* second watch, 9–11 p.m.
君 *nikun* two masters
束三文 *nisokusammon* cheap
言 *futakoto* two words; repetition. *nigon* double dealing, double tongue
言目 *futakotome* the constant burden of some people's talk
足 *ni (no) ashi* hesitation
足三文 *nisoku sammon* dirt cheap
足草鞋 *nisoku (no) waraji* many irons in the fire
足動物 *nisokudōbutsu* bipeds
8 念 *ninen* two ideas
拍子 *nibyōshi* double time
国間 *nikokukan no* bilateral
股 *futamata* bifurcation, fork, parting of the way
股膏薬 *futamatagōyaku* double dealing; timeserver; an opportunist
直 *nichoku* lining out to second base
直角 *nichokkaku* a straight angle
者 *nisha* two things; two persons
者選一 *nisha sen'itsu* an alternative
者選一法 *nisha sen'itsuhō* completion test (one out of two choices)
枚目 *nimaime* actor in a love scene
枚舌 *nimaijita* double tongue, double dealing
枚貝 *nimaigai* bivalve
枚折 *nimaio(ri)* a folio
9 食 *nishoku, nijiki* two meals (a day)
通 *nitsū* two copies. *futatō(ri)* duplicate pair; two kinds, two ways, twofold
俣 *futamata* bifurcation, fork, parting of the way
相 *nisō* two-phase
封 *nifū* forced out on second
段見出 *nidan mida(shi)* a two-line heading
院 *niin* the two houses of a legislature
院制 *niinsei* bicameral system
院制度 *niinseido* bicameral system
乗 *nijō suru* square, multiply (a number) by itself
乗根 *nijōkon* square root
連式 *nirenshiki* duplex
連発 *nirempatsu* double-barreled gun
連銃 *nirenjū* double-barreled gun
度 *nido* two times
度三度 *nido sando* again and again
度刈 *nidoga(ri)* getting two crops a year
度手間 *nido tema nidodema* double effort
度咲 *nidoza(ki)* second blooming
度添 *nidozo(i)* second wife
重 *futae, nijū* double, twofold
重人格 *nijū jinkaku* double personality
重写 *nijū utsu(shi)* double exposure
重外交 *nijū gaikō* dual diplomacy
重母音 *nijū boin* diphthong
重生活 *nijū seikatsu* double life
重否定 *nijū hitei* double negative
重底 *nijūzoko* double bottom; double sole
重抵当 *nijū teitō* second mortgage
重国籍 *nijū kokusei* dual nationality
重星 *nijūsei* double star
重奏 *nijūsō* instrumental duet
重釜 *nijūgama* jacketed kettle, double boiler
重唱 *nijūshō* vocal duet
重窓 *nijū mado* storm window
重道徳 *nijū dōtoku* double standard of morality
重税 *nijūzei* double duty
重焼付 *nijū yakitsu(ke)* double printing
重焦点 *nijū shōten* bifocal
重結婚 *nijū kekkon* bigamy
重橋 *Nijūbashi* Double Bridge at the Palace

重撮影 *nijū satsuei* double exposure
重織 *nijūo(ri)* double-weight cloth
重顎 *nijū ago* double chin
重露出 *nijū roshutsu* double exposure
10 倍 *nibai* double, twice, twofold
桁 *futaketa* tens (in figures)
核 *nikaku* binuclear
流 *niryū* second-rate, inferior
宮 *Nigū* the Two Ise Shrines
軒建 *nikenda(te)* duplex (house)
週間 *nishūkan* fortnight, two weeks
進三進 *nitchi(mo)satchi(mo)* in a dilemma
部 *nibu* two parts, two copies; the second part
部合奏 *nibu gassō* instrumental duet
部合唱 *nibu gasshō* vocal duet
部教授 *nibu kyōju* two-sessions system
11 道 *futamichi* branch roads, forked road, crossroads, two ways (of proceeding)
階 *nikai* second floor, upstairs
階建 *nikaidate* two-storied building
12 結 *futamusu(bi)* two half hitches
割 *futa(tsu)wa(ri)* half; cutting in two. *niwari* 20%
着 *nichaku* runner-up, second (in a race)
葉 *niyō* two flat things. *futaba* bud, sprout
筋道 *futasuji michi* branch roads, crossroads
塁 *nirui* second base
塁手 *niruishu* second baseman
塁打 *niruida* two-base hit, double
等 *nitō* second class; second
等辺三角形 *nitōhen sankakukei* isosceles triangle
等分 *nitōbun* bisection
等分線 *nitōbunsen* bisector
等賞 *niōshō* second prize
等親 *nitōshin* second-degree relative
番 *niban* second, number two, runner-up
番刈 *nibanka(ri)* second crop; aftermath
番作 *nibansaku* second crop
番抵当 *niban teitō* second mortgage
番星 *nabamboshi* second star of the evening
番煎 *nibansen(ji)* a rehash
13 置 *futa(tsu)o(ki)* every third
業地 *nigyōchi* entertainment quarters (food and geisha)
義的 *nigiteki ni* secondarily
14 様 *niyō* two methods
種 *nishu* second-class (mail)
舞 *ni(no)mai* repeating the same failure
15 輪 *nirin* two wheels, two flowers
輪車 *nirinsha* child's bicycle; two-wheeled vehicle
16 膳 *ni (no) zen* side dish
親 *futaoya* parents, both parents
頭立 *nitōda(te)* two-horse cart
頭建 *nitōda(te)* two-horse cart
頭筋 *nitōkin* biceps
頭膊筋 *nitōhakkin* (arm) biceps
18 繭 *futa(tsu) mayu* double cocoon

1

于 73 / J5032 / M252 U going; from.

20 蘭盆 *Urabon* Feast of Lanterns. *Obon* Feast of the Dead
蘭盆会 *Urabon'e* Feast of Lanterns. *Obon* Feast of the Dead

2

云 74 / J313e / M254 UN. *yu(u), i(u)* say, tell, talk, speak, declare; call, term, name.

4 云 *shikajika, unnun* and so forth, and so on, and the like
9 為 *un'i* words and deeds

B **互** 75 / J385f / M255 GO. *tagai ni, katami ni* mutually, reciprocally, reciprocally, together.

5 用 *goyō* using together; using in turn
市 *goshi* trade, commerce
同士 *tagaidōshi de* with each other
7 角 *gokaku* equality, evenness, par; good match
助 *gojo* mutual aid, co-operation
助会 *gojokai* a benefit society
助的 *gojoteki* friendly; cooperative
10 恵 *gokei* reciprocity, mutual benefits
12 違 *taga(i)chiga(i) ni* alternately
換性 *gokansei* compatibility
14 選 *gosen* co-optation; mutual election
20 譲 *gojō* mutual concession, compromise
譲的 *gojōteki* mutually conciliatory

B **井** 76 / J3066 / M258 SHŌ. SEI *i* well.

4 戸 *ido* well
戸水 *ido mizu* well water
戸車 *idoguruma* well pulley
戸屋形 *ido yakata* well roof
戸浚 *idosara(e)* well cleaning
戸側 *idogawa* well curb
戸掘 *idoho(ri)* well digging; well digger
戸替 *idoga(e)* well cleaning
戸綱 *idozuna* well rope
戸端 *idobata* well side
戸端会議 *idobata kaigi* well-side gossip
8 底 *seitei* well bottom; narrow place
底蛙 *seitei (no) kawazu* a frog in a well; narrow-minded person
9 泉 *seisen* well
10 桁 *igeta* well crib; parallel crosses
12 堰 *iseki* sluice, dam
蛙 *seia* a frog in a well; narrow-minded person
筒 *izutsu* well crib
然 *seizen(taru)* orderly, regular, systematic, trim, accurate, well-organized
14 綱 *izuna* well rope

A **五** 77 / J385e / M257 Go five. *itsu(tsu), itsu* five; five years old.
2 人組 *goningumi* five-family unit; five-man group
人噺子 *gonimbayashi* five court-musician dolls at the Girls' Festival (in March)
十三次 *gojūsan tsugi* the 53 Tōkaidō stages
十年祭 *gojūnensai* jubilee, semicentennial
十歩百歩 *gojippo-hyappo, gojuppo-hyappo* six of one and a half dozen of the other
十音 *gojūon* the Japanese syllabary
十音順 *gojūonjun* the syllabary order
十路 *isoji* 50 years; age 50
3 寸釘 *gosun kugi* long nail
大洲 *godaishū* the five continents (Asia, Europe, Africa, America, Australia)
大洋 *gotaiyō* the five oceans
4 日 *itsuka* five days; the fifth day (of the month)
斗米 *gotobei* small salary
辺形 *gohenkei* pentagon
分 *gobu* five-tenths of a *wari* (ten percent); five-tenths of a *sun* 寸 (3 cm); 50%, half; a tie; evenness. *gofun* five minutes
分刈 *gobuga(ri)* close haircut
分五分 *gobugobu* evenly matched; tie
分試 *gobudame(shi)* killing by inches
月 *Gogatsu* May. *satsuki* lunar fifth month
月人形 *Gogatsu ningyō* Boys' Festival dolls
月雨 *samidare, satsuki ame* early summer rain
月祭 *Gogatsusai* May Day; the May Festival
月晴 *satsikuba(re)* fine weather during the rainy season; fine weather in May
月節句 *Gogatsu no Sekku* Boys' Festival
月幟 *Gogatsu nobori, satsuki nobori* Boys' Festival carp streamers
月闇 *satsuki yami* dark night in the rainy season
月蠅 *urusa(i)* annoying, troublesome, irksome, inquisitive, importunate
月蠅方 *urusagata* disagreeable disposition; disagreeable person; faultfinder
月蠅型 *urusagata* disagreeable disposition; disagreeable person; faultfinder
5 目 *gomoku* a mixture; simplified game of *go*; *gomokumeshi* (飯) and *gomokuzushi* (鮨)
目飯 *gomokumeshi* boiled rice mixed with vegetables and fish
目鮨 *gomokuzushi* rice mixed with various delicacies and seasoned with vinegar
6 色 *goshiki, goshoku* five colors; variegated colors; the five cardinal colors; various kinds
行 *gogyō* the five elements (wood, fire, earth, metal, and water)
旬節 *Gojunsetsu* Pentecost
7 戒 *gokai* the five commandments (against murder, lust, theft, lying, and intemperance)
体 *gotai* five component parts of the body; the whole body; five styles of calligraphy
更 *gokō* fifth watch; 3–5 a.m.; the five night watches

児 *itsu(tsu)go* quintuplets. *goji* five children
角形 *gokakukei, gokakkei* pentagon
里霧中 *gori-muchū* in a fog, at sea, mystified, bewildered, in a maze
8 官 *gokan* the five sensory organs
弦 *gogen* five strings; a five-stringed musical instrument
9 指 *goshi* the five fingers
音音階 *goon onkai* pentatonic scale
重 *gojū, itsue* fivefold, five-storied, quintuplicate
重塔 *gojū no tō* five-storied pagoda
10 桁 *go keta* ten thousands (in figures)
倍子 *fushi, gobaishi* gallnut
倫 *gorin* the five Confucian human relationships
倫道 *gorin (no) michi* the five Confucian human relationships
11 情 *gojō* the five emotions (joy, anger, sorrow, pleasure, and hatred [or desire]) ⌈Classics
経 *Gokyō, Gokei* the Five Chinese
絃 *gogen* five strings; a five-stringed musical instrument
彩 *gosai* the five colors (blue, yellow, red, white, and black); five-colored porcelain
悪 *goaku* the five sins in Buddhism (murder, theft, adultery, falsehood, and drinking); violation of the five Confucian virtues
常 *gojō* the five cardinal Confucian virtues (justice, politeness, wisdom, fidelity, and benevolence)
13 感 *gokan* the five senses
節句 *gosekku* the five festivals (Jan. 7, Mar. 3, May 5, July 7, and Sept. 9)
14 徳 *gotoku* the five virtues; tripod; kettle stand
穀 *gokoku* the five grains (rice, *mugi* [wheat and barley], beans, and millet [*awa* and *kibi*])
種競技 *goshu kyōgi* pentathlon
15 畿内 *Gokinai* the Five Home Provinces
線 *gosen* staff (in music)
線紙 *gosenshi* music paper
線譜 *gosenfu* score (in music)
輪 *gorin* the five rings in Buddhism, representing the five component elements of all matter (earth, water, fire, wind, and air)
輪大会 *Gorin Taikai* Olympic Games
輪会議 *Gorin Kaigi* Olympic Congress
輪塔 *gorin (no) tō* a gravestone or monument composed of five pieces piled one upon another, representing the five component elements of all matter
輪聖火 *Gorin Seika* Olympic Torch
輪旗 *Gorinki* Olympic Flag
18 臟 *gozō* the five viscera (liver, lungs, heart, kidney, and spleen)
臟六腑 *gozō-roppu* the internal organs; inside one's mind

3

亙 78 J-X M-X See **亙** 80.

4

亘 79 J4f4b M262 SEN, KAN request. KŌ. *wata(ru)*

亙 80 J4f4a M265 **亙** 78 J-X M-X KŌ. *wata(ru)* range, reach, extend, last, cover, be spread over.

5

B **亜** 81 J3021 M272 **亞** 82 J5033 M274 A. *tsu(gu)* rank next, come after. -A- Asia. *a-* sub-, -ous (in acids).
6 成層圏 *aseisōken* substratosphere
米利加 *Amerika* America
米利加合衆国 *Amerika Gasshūkoku* The United States of America
米利加杉 *Amerika sugi* redwood
9 科 *aka* suborder
炭 *atan* lignite, brown coal
砒酸 *ahisan* arsenious acid
10 流 *aryū* adherent, follower, imitator
11 麻 *ama* flax, hemp, linen
麻仁 *amani* flaxseed, linseed
麻仁油 *amaniyu* linseed oil
麻布 *amanuno* linen
麻製 *amasei no* flaxen, linen
麻織物 *ama orimono* flax fabrics, linen
12 属 *azoku* subgroup
温帯 *aontai* subtemperate zone
寒帯 *akantai* subarctic zone

13 聖 *asei* a sage of the second order
鉛 *aen* zinc
鉛引 *aembi(ki)* galvanized
鉛末 *aemmatsu* zinc dust
鉛凸板 *aen toppan* photoengraving
鉛版 *aemban* zinc etching
鉛板 *aemban* zinc plate
鉛華 *aenka* zinc white, zinc oxide, flowers of zinc
鉛鉄 *aentetsu* galvanized iron
14 種 *ashu* subspecies
15 熱帯 *anettai* subtropics

— 6 —

亞 82/J5033/M274 See 亜 81.

亟 83/J5034/M279 KYOKU fast, busy. *sumi(yaka)* quick, speedy, prompt. *shibashiba* often, frequently.

些 84/J3a33/M268 SA. *chi(to), chit(to), isasaka* a little, a bit, sometimes.
4 少 *sashō no* trifling, little, few, slight
8 些 *sasa(taru)* trifling, trivial
事 *saji* something small or petty
11 細 *sasai na* trivial, small, petty

亠 RAD. 8

Nabebuta kettle lid, *ten'ichi* (Rad. 3 *ten* plus Rad. 1 *ichi*), or *keisan kammuri* (crown shaped like a Japanese paperweight). Variant: 亠. Nickname: Lid.

亠 85/J5035/M286 TŌ. ZU.

— 1 —

A 亡 86/J4b34/M287 BU. MU. MŌ. BŌ. my late, the late; dying; being destroyed. *na(ku)naru* be lost; run short, be used up; disappear; die. *na(ku)suru* lose. *horo(biru)* perish, be ruined. *horo(bosu)* ruin, destroy, overthrow. *na(ki)* the late, the deceased. *na(shi) ni, na(shi) de* without.
2 人 *na(ki)hito* the deceased
3 子 *bōshi* dead child
4 父 *bōfu* one's late father
友 *bōyū* deceased friend
夫 *bōfu* one's late husband
5 母 *bōbo* one's late mother
兄 *bōkei* one's late elder brother
失 *bōshitsu* loss
7 状 *bōjō* discourtesy; lawlessness
児 *bōji* one's dead child
君 *bōkun* one's late lord
8 国 *bōkoku* ruined country
姉 *bōshi* one's late elder sister
物 *na(ki)mono ni suru* do away with
妻 *bōsai* one's late wife
者 *mōja* the dead. *na(ki)mono ni suru* ⌈kill
命 *bōmei* exile
命者 *bomeisha* displaced persons, (political) refugees
9 後 *na(ki)ato* after one's death
11 婦 *bōfu* one's late wife; deceased lady
14 魂 *bōkon, na(ki)tama* departed soul, spirit
15 霊 *bōrei* the dead, departed spirits, apparition, ghost
16 骸 *nakigara* remains, corpse
親 *bōshin, na(ki)oya* one's late parent
18 軀 *nakigara* remains, corpse

— 2 —

亢 87/J5036/M288 KŌ high spirits.
10 進 *kōshin* rise, acceleration, exasperation
16 奮 *kōfun* excitement, agitation, stimulation

— 4 —

亦 88/J4b72/M293 EKI. YAKU. *mata* also, again.

亥 89/J3067/M292 GAI. *inoshishi, i* 9–11 p.m.; 12th zodiac sign; wild boar.

2 二 【亠】4 人 イ 𠆢 儿 入 八 ソ 冂 冖 冫 几 凵 刀 刂 力 勹 匕 匚 匸 十 卜 卩 厂 厶 又

A 交 90/J3872/M291 Kō coming and going; association; change of seasons. *maji(waru), maji(ru)* associate with, mingle with; interest; join. *maji(eru)* mix; converse with, cross (swords). *ma(zeru)* mix, blend, mingle; include, let in on. *ma(jiru) vi* be mixed, be blended; mingle with. *kawa(su)* exchange (messages); dodge, parry, avoid, turn aside.

3 叉 *kōsa* crossing, intersection
叉点 *kōsaten* crossing, intersection
4 互 *kōgo no* mutual, reciprocal, alternate
友 *kōyū* friend, companion
友関係 *kōyū kankei* one's associate
5 付 *kōfu suru* deliver, furnish with (copies)
付金 *kōfukin* grant, subsidy, bounty
付者 *kōfusha* deliverer, donor
代 *kōtai* alternation, change, relief, relay, shift
代投手 *kōtai tōshu* relief pitcher
代作業 *kōtai sagyō* working in shifts
代制 *kōtaisei* shift system
代員 *kōtaiin* a shift (of workmen)
代操業 *kōtai sōgyō* working in shifts
6 交 *komogomo* alternately, in succession
合 *kōgō* sexual union
7 尾 *kōbi* copulation (in animals)
8 易 *kōeki* trade, commerce
9 信 *kōshin* correspondence, communication
点 *kōten* point of intersection
通 *kōtsū* traffic; communication; transport; navigation
通公社 *kōtsū kōsha* travel bureau
通巡査 *kōtsū junsa* traffic officer
通安全 *kōtsū anzen* traffic safety
通妨害 *kōtsū bōgai* traffic obstruction
通事故 *kōtsū jiko* traffic accident
通信号 *kōtsū shingō* traffic signal
通違反 *kōtsū ihan* traffic violation
通規則 *kōtsū kisoku* traffic rules
通道徳 *kōtsū dōtoku* traffic ethics
通運輸業 *kōtsū un'yugyō* transportation business
通量 *kōtsūryō* traffic, traffic volume
通費 *kōtsūhi* traveling expenses, carfare
通路 *kōtsūro* traffic route
通網 *kōtsūmō* traffic network
通遮断 *kōtsū shadan* blockade, quarantine
通整理 *kōtsū seiri* traffic control
通機関 *kōtsū kikan* transportation facilities
10 配 *kōhai* mating, crossbreeding, cross-fertilization
流 *kōryū* alternating current; (cultural) exchange; intermingling
流人事 *kōryū jinji* personnel shuffle
差 *kōsa suru* to cross
差点 *kōsaten* crossing, intersection
11 遊 *kōyū* friend; friendship
情 *kōjō* intimacy, friendship
接 *kōsetsu* sexual intercourse
渉 *kōshō* negotiation, discussion; connection
渉委員 *kōshō iin* negotiation committee
渉員 *kōshōin* negotiators
12 番 *kawa(ri)ban(ko) ni, kawa(ri)ban ni* alternately. *kōban* police box
替 *kōtai* deliver, furnish, with (copies)
換 *kōkan* exchange, reciprocity, barter; substitution; clearing (of checks)
換手 *kōkanshu* switchboard operator
換円 *kōkan'en* convertible yen
換台 *kōkandai* (telephone) switchboard
換局 *kōkankyoku* (telephone) exchange
換所 *kōkanjo* clearing house
換学生 *kōkan gakusei* exchange student
換品 *kōkanhin* thing bartered, trade-in
換船 *kōkansen* repatriation ship
換教授 *kōkan kyōju* exchange professor
換貿易制 *kōkan bōekisei* barter system
換器 *kōkanki* (telephone) switchboard
13 詢 *kōjun* promotion of social intercourse
感 *kōkan* rapport, mutual sympathy
感神経 *kōkan shinkei* sympathetic nerves
戦 *kōsen* war, battle, hostilities
戦国 *kōsenkoku* belligerents
戦権 *kōsenken* right of belligerency
際 *kōsai* association, intercourse, comradeship, acquaintance
際上 *kōsaijō* as a matter of social courtesy
際好 *kōsaizu(ki) na* sociable
際社会 *kōsai shakai* society, social circles
際国 *kōsaikoku* friendly powers, treaty powers
際法 *kōsaihō* etiquette, social code
際家 *kōsaika* sociable person
際費 *kōsaihi* entertainment expenses

際場裡 *kōsaijōri* society
際嫌 *kōsaigira(i)* unsociable
際範囲 *kōsai han'i* circle of acquaintance
14 雑 *kōzatsu* mating, crossbreeding, cross-fertilization
読 *kōdoku suru* read responsively
読文 *kōdokubun* responsive readings
15 誼 *kōgi* friendship
霊術 *kōreijutsu* spiritism, spiritualism
歓 *kōkan* exchange of courtesies, fraternization
歓会 *kokankai* reception
16 錯 *kōsaku* mixture, blending, complication
18 織 *kōshoku, ma(ze)o(ri)* mixed weave
19 響曲 *kōkyōkyoku* symphony
響楽 *kōkyōgaku* symphony (orchestra)
響楽団 *kōkyōgakudan* symphony (orchestra)
20 譲 *kōjō* mutual concession, compromise
27 驩 *kōkan* exchange of courtesies, fraternization

5

亨 91 J357c M295 Kō. Kyō. *tō(ru)* pass through.
9 通 *kōtsū* pass through, get through
11 運 *kōun* good luck.

6

B 享 92 J357d M298 Kyō. *u(keru)* receive, take, get, obtain; accept, take, get, obtain; catch (a ball); stop (a blow), parry; answer (the phone); undergo (an operation); take (an exam); sustain (a loss); be exposed to (ridicule); face, front on; inherit; catch the public fancy.
6 年 *kyōnen* age at death
有 *kyōyū* possession, enjoyment
8 受 *kyōju suru* receive, accept, enjoy, be given
受者 *kyōjusha* recipient
9 持 *kyōji* securing rights and profits
13 楽 *kyōraku* enjoyment, pleasure
楽生活 *kyōraku seikatsu* pleasurable life
楽主義 *kyōraku shugi* epicureanism
楽的 *kyōrakuteki* pleasure-seeking

A 京 93 J357e M299 京 94 J5037 M307 Kei ten quadrillion. Kyō capital, metropolis; ten quadrillion; Kyoto. *miyako* capital, metropolis.
2 人 *keijin* citizen of the capital
人形 *kyōningyō* Kyoto doll
3 女 *kyōonna* Kyoto woman
4 方 *kyōgata* the direction of Kyoto; Kansai area; citizens of Kyoto; nobles
6 地 *kyōchi* the capital; Kyoto and its environs
阪 *Keihan* Kyoto and Osaka
阪神 *Keihanshin* Kyoto-Osaka-Kobe
7 形 *kyōgata* style current in the capital
8 物 *kyōmono* Kyoto products
表 *Kyōomote* vicinity of Kyoto
9 風 *kyōfū* Kyoto style; urbanity, refinement
洛 *keiraku, kyōraku* capital; Kyoto
10 師 *keishi* capital, metropolis; old Kyoto
浜 *Keihin* Tokyo and Yokohama
華 *keika* capital; flower capital
12 葉 *Keiyo* Tokyo and Chiba

7

京 94 J5037 M307 See 京 93.

亮 95 J4e3c M304 Ryō clear; help.
10 陰 *ryōan* national mourning (for an emperor)

B 亭 96 J4462 M303 Tei restaurant; mansion; arbor; cottage; vaudeville, music hall, stage name. Chin arbor, pavilion, summer house.
5 主 *teishu* master, host; landlord, innkeeper; husband
主関白 *teishu kampaku* autocratic husband
9 亭 *teitei(taru)* lofty, towering

8

亳 97 J5038 M-X Haku ancient Chinese place name.

——— 11 ———

亶 98 J5039 M328 TAN true; cordial. SEN. fly.

RAD. 人 9

Hito man. At left: 亻 *nimben.* At top: 𠆢 *yane* roof, *hito-yane* or *hitogashira.* Nickname: Man.

A **人** 99 J3f4d M344 JIN man, person, people. NIN man, person. *hito* man, human being, mankind, person, people; character, personality; true man; man of talent; adult; other people; messenger; visitor. *hito(rashii)* like a decent person, human. *hito(tonari)* hereditary disposition. *-jin* man; expert. *-nin* man, person. *-to* person.

1 一倍 *hito-ichibai* unusual; more than all others
2 人 *hitobito* men, people everybody. *ninnin* each person
力 *jinriki* human power. *jinryoku* human strength, human effort, human agency
力車 *jinrikisha* jinricksha
3 士 *jinshi* well-bred man; people
子 *Hito (no) Ko* the Son of Man, Christ. (with negative) *hito(k)ko* not a soul
山 *hitoyama* crowd of people
才 *jinzai* man of talent
才登用 *jinzaitōyō* selection for high ⌈office
口 *jinkō* population; common talk
口密度 *jinkō mitsudo* population density
口調査 *jinkō chōsa* census
口膾炙 *jinkō (ni) kaisha suru* become famous
工 *jinkō* human work, human skill; artificial; artificiality
工池 *jinkō ike* artificial pool
工気胸療法 *jinkō-kikyōryōhō* artificial respiration
工地震 *jinkō jishin* artificial earthquake
工林 *jinkōrin* planted forest
工的 *jinkōteki* artificial, unnatural
工雨 *jinkōu* artificial rain
工知能 *jinkō chinō* articial intelligence
工呼吸 *jinkō kokyū* artificial respiration
工呼吸法 *jinkō kokyūhō* artificial respiration
工受胎 *jinkō jutai* artificial insemination
工受粉 *jinkō jufun* artificial fertilization (of plants)
工受精 *jinkō jusei* artificial insemination
工降雨 *jinkō kōu* artificial rain
工栄養 *jinkō eiyō* bottle feeding
工栄養児 *jinkō eiyōji* bottle-fed child
工真珠 *jinkō shinju* artificial pearls
工流産 *jinkō ryūzan* abortion
工雪 *jinkō yuki* artificial snow
工港 *jinkōkō* artificial harbor
工雷 *jinkōrai* artificial lightning
工孵化法 *jinkō fukahō* artificial incubaton
工避妊法 *jinkō hininhō* contraception
工衛生 *jinkō eisei* manmade satellite
4 手 *hitode* a worker, a hand
込 *hitogo(mi)* a crowd of people
中 *hitonaka* society, company, the public, the world
夫 *nimpu, nimbu* coolie, laborer, carrier
心 *jinshin, hitogokoro* human nature; sentiment
心地 *hitogokochi* consciousness
文 *jimmon, jimbun* humanity; civilization
文史 *jimbunshi* history of civilization
文主義 *jimbun shugi* humanism
文地理 *jimbun chiri* descriptive geography
文学派 *jimbungakuha* humanists
文科学 *jimbun kagaku* human and cultural sciences; social sciences
5 立 *hitoda(chi)* a crowd of people
外 *jingai* breech of morals; inhuman treatment; absence of human habitation. *ningai* outcast, outlaw
払 *hitobara(i)* clearing out the people
出 *hitode* crowd, turnout

世 *jinsei* this world; life
本主義 *jimpon shugi, jimbon shugi* humanism, humanitarianism
代名詞 *jindaimeishi* personal pronoun
目 *hitome, jimmoku* a glimpse; public gaze
目余 *hitome ni ama(ru)* be too prominent
付 *hitozuki* reputation
付合 *hitozu(ki)a(i)* social disposition
民 *jimmin* people, subjects, the public
民投票 *jimmin tōhyō* plebiscite, referendum
民戦線 *jimmin sensen* popular front
生 *jinsei* human life
生派 *jinseiha* humanists
生案内欄 *jinsei-annai ran* personal-question column
生哲学 *jinsei tetsugaku* philosophy of life
生記録 *jinsei kiroku* human document
生観 *jinseikan* view of life
6 肉 *jinniku* human flesh
臣 *jinshin* subjects; retaincrs
死 *hitoji(ni)* death, casualty
任 *hitomaka(se)* leaving (it) to others
伝 *hitozute* hearsay; message
好 *hitozu(ki)* attractiveness, amiability, charm
肌 *hitohada* the skin; body warmth
交 *hitomajiwa(ri)* association with people
当 *hitoa(tari)* influence of one's manners
件費 *jinkenhi* personnel expenses
名 *jimmei* a person's given name
名辞典 *jimmei jiten* biographical dictionary
名辞書 *jimmei jisho* biographical dictionary
名録 *jimmeiroku* directory, name list
名簿 *jimmeibo* directory, name list
気 *ninki* popularity; business conditions; popular feeling. *hitoke* signs of life (in a place)
気役者 *ninki yakusha* stage favorite, star
気投票 *ninki tōhyō* popularity contest
気者 *ninkimono* popular person, favorite
気取 *ninkito(ri)* bid for popularity, publicity stunt
気商売 *ninki shōbai* occupations dependent on public favor
7 足 *ninsoku* coolie, laborer, carrier. *hitoashi* pedestrian traffic
車 *jinsha* jinricksha
位 *jin'i* a person's rank
材 *jinzai* man of talent
別 *nimbetsu* census taking
助 *hitodasu(ke)* act of mercy
形 *ningyō* doll, puppet, figure
形芝居 *ningyō shibai* puppet show
形回 *ningyōmawa(shi)* puppet operator
形使 *ningyōtsuka(i)* puppet operator
形師 *ningyōshi* doll maker
声 *hitogoe* a human voice, a cry
良 *hito (no) i(i)* of good character
君 *jinkun* sovereign, ruler
寿 *jinju* man's life span
見知 *hitomishi(ri)* shyness
応待 *hitoashirai* treatment of people
里 *hitozato* human habitation
里離 *hitozato-hana(reta)* lonely (place)
体 *jintai* human body. *nintei* personal appearance
体学 *jintaigaku* somatology
体実験 *jintai jikken* testing on a living person
体模型 *jintai mokei* anatomical model of the human body
身 *jinshin, hitomi* the human body, one's person
身売買 *jinshin baibai* slave trade; white slave trade
身攻撃 *jinshin kōgeki* personal attack
身保護 *jinshin hogo* habeas corpus
身保護令状 *jinshin-hogo reijō* writ of habeas corpus
身御供 *hitomi gokū* human sacrifice; victim
8 使 *hitozuka(i)* handling one's workmen
怖 *hitooji* a child's fear of a stranger
性 *jinsei* human nature, instinct, humanity, humanism
波 *hitonami* wave of humanity; stampede
泣 *hitona(kase)* annoyance, nuisance
知 *jinchi* human intellect, knowledge. *hitoshi(renu), hitoshi(rezu)* secret, hidden, unseen, inward
取 *hitoto(ri)* prisoner's base (a game)
並 *hitona(mi) no* ordinary
参 *ninjin* carrot; ginseng
受 *hitou(ke)* popularity
苛 *hitoiji(me)* bullying, teasing

妻 *hitozuma* a married woman
非人 *nimpinin* a brute of a man
的 *jinteki* human; personal
的資源 *jinteki shigen* man-power resources
命 *jimmei* (human) life
命救助 *jimmei kyūjo* lifesaving
物 *jimbutsu* person, man; character, personage; talented man
物寸描 *jimbutsu-sumbyō* thumb-nail sketch
物画 *jimbutsuga* portrait painting
物経済 *jimbutsu keizai* human engineering
物評 *jimbutsuhyō* personal criticism; character sketch
物像 *jimbutsuzō* statue; picture; a picture revealing character
事 *hitogoto* others' affairs. *jinji* personal affairs; personnel affairs
事不省 *jinji-fusei* unconsciousness
事行政 *jinji gyōsei* personnel administration
事院 *Jinjiin* National Personnel Authority
事異動 *jinji idō* personnel changes
事欄 *jinji ran* personal column
9 屋 *hitoya* prison, jail
通 *hitodō(ri), hitotō(ri)* pedestrian traffic
垣 *hitogaki* a crowd of people
後 *jingo* behind others, losing out to others
柱 *hitobashira* human pillar, human sacrifice
柄 *hitogara* character; personality; personal appearance; gentility
相 *ninsō* physiognomy
前 *hitomae* the public, company. *hitomae de* in public, in company
品 *jimpin* personal appearance; character, personality
待顔 *hitoma(chi)gao* a look of expectation
海戦術 *jinkai senjutsu* infiltration tactics, human-wave tactics
食 *hitoku(i)* cannibalism; biting (someone)
食人種 *hitoku(i) jinshu* cannibals
面 *jimmen* human face
面獣心 *nimmen-jūshin, jimmen-jūshin* a beast in human form
為 *jin'i* human work; human agency; art; artificiality
為的 *jin'iteki* artificial, unnatural
為淘汰 *jin'i tōta* artificial selection (in biology)
相 *ninsō* physiognomy, looks, countenance
相占 *ninsō urana(i)* divination by facial features
相見 *ninsōmi* physiognomist
相書 *ninsōga(ki)* personal description
造 *jinzō* artificial, synthetic; imitation
造人間 *jinzō ningen* robot
造氷 *jinzōgōri* artificial ice
造石油 *jinzō sekiyu* synthetic oil
造米 *jinzōmai* imitation rice
造宝石 *jinzō hōseki* artificial jewels
造真珠 *jinzō shinju* artificial pearls
10 馬 *jimba* men and horses
骨 *jinkotsu* human bones
倫 *jinrin* human relations; morality
時 *ninji* man-hour
称 *ninshō* person; personal (in grammar)
殺 *hitogoro(shi)* murder; murderer
家 *jinka* house, human habitation
畜 *jinchiku* men and animal
笑 *hitowara(ware)* laughingstock. *hitowara(wase) na* ridiculous, laughable. *hitowara(i), hitowara(e)* something people would laugh at
真似 *hitomane* mimicry, imitation
差 *hitosa(shi)* index finger
差指 *hitosa(shi) yubi* index finger
格 *jinkaku* character, personality, individuality
格化 *jinkakuka* impersonation; personification
格者 *jinkakusha* man of character; person
格権 *jinkakuken* personal rights
員 *jin'in* staff, personnel, crew; the number of persons
員淘汰 *jin'in tōta* personnel reduction
員整理 *jin'in seiri* personnel cut
員縮少 *jin'in shukushō* personnel reduction
11 魚 *ningyo* mermaid, merman
達 *hitotachi* people
探 *hitosaga(shi)* searching for someone
欲 *jin'yoku* human desires, human passions
寄 *hitoyo(se)* a gathering of people

雪崩 *hitonadare* a surging crowd
望 *jimbō* popularity
望家 *jimbōka* popular character
道 *jindō* humanity; sidewalk
道主義 *jindō shugi* humanism; humanitarianism
道的 *jindōteki* humane
情 *ninjō* humanity, sympathy, kindness; human nature; common sense; customs and manners
情本 *ninjōbon* a novel
情味 *ninjōmi* human interest, kindness
情負 *ninjoma(ke)* overcome by sympathy
情劇 *ninjōgeki* human-interest play
情噺 *ninjōbanashi* love story, real-life story
12 傑 *jinketsu* great man, hero
証 *jinshō, ninshō* testimony of a witness
買 *hitoka(i)* slave traffic; slave dealer
蒸 *hitoiki(re)* stuffiness
集 *hitodaka(ri)* a crowd
智 *jinchi* human intellect; knowledge
違 *hitochiga(i), hitochiga(e)* mistaken identity; a person so changed that it's hard to recognize him
無 *hitona(shi) hito(de)na(shi)* brute, miscreant, ungrateful fellow
喰 *hitoku(i)* cannibalism; biting (someone)
喰人種 *hitokui jinshu* cannibals
間 *ningen* man, person, human being
間工学 *ningen kōgaku* ergonomics
間以上 *ningen ijō no* superhuman
間以前 *ningen izen no* prehuman
間手作 *ningen tezuku(ri) no* manmade
間社会 *ningen shakai* human society
間味 *ningemmi* human kindness; human weakness
間性 *ningensei* human nature, humanity
間的 *ningenteki* human
間並 *ningenna(mi)* the common run of people
間苦 *ningenku* human suffering
間学 *ningengaku* anthropology
間界 *ningenkai* the world of humans
間嫌 *ningengira(i)* misanthropy; misanthropist
間愛 *ningen ai* human love
間業 *ningen waza* the work of man
間堕落 *ningen (no) daraku* the fall of man
間爆弾 *ningen bakudan* human bomb
間離 *ningembana(re)* unworldly; superhuman
13 嫌 *hitogira(i)* one who dislikes people; dislike of people
煙 *jin'en* smoke from human habitations
絹 *jinken* rayon, artificial silk
馴 *hitona(re)* used to people; tame
数 *ninzu, ninzū, hitokazu* the number of people
意 *jin'i* public sentiment
猿同祖説 *jin'en dōsosetsu* monkey-ancestry theory
跡 *jinseki, hitoato* signs of human habitation
跡未到 *jinseki-mitō* unexplored
跡未踏 *jinseki-mitō* unexplored
14 選 *jinsen* personnel selection
聞 *hitogi(ki)* reputation, respectability
境 *jinkyō* human habitation
徳 *jintoku, nintoku* personal virtue; natural virtue
様 *hitosama* (polite) other people, another
熅 *hitoiki(re)* stuffiness, lack of ventilation
語 *jingo* human speech
魂 *hitodama* will-o'-the-wisp; spirit of a dead person
蔘 *ninjin* carrot; ginseng
種 *jinshu* race of people
種改良 *jinshu kairyo* racial eugenics
種的 *jinshuteki* racial
種学 *jinshugaku* ethnology
15 膚 *hitohada* the skin; body warmth
影 *hitokage, jin'ei* a person's shadow, a form
質 *hitojichi* hostage, prisoner
権 *jinken* human rights
権蹂躙 *jinken-jūrin* trampling on human rights
16 懐 *hitonatsu(koi)* friendly, amiable. *hitonatsu(kashii)* lonesome for
頼 *hitodayo(ri), hitodano(mi)* reliance on others
頭 *jintō* the number of people, population
頭税 *nintōzei, jintōzei* poll tax
17 擦 *hitozure* sophistication
爵 *jinshaku* worldly honors
糞 *jimpun* night soil
18 騒 *hitosawa(gase)* false alarm

2 二亠【人イ𠆢】儿入八ソ冂冖冫几凵刀リカ勹匕匚匸十卜卩厂ム又

類 *jinrui* man, mankind, humanity
類史 *jinruishi* human history
類学 *jinruigaku* anthropology, ethnology
類学者 *jinruigakusha* anthropologist; ethnologist
類猿 *jinruien* anthropoid ape
類愛 *jinruiai* love for humanity
22 籟 *jinrai* instrumental music
23 攫 *hitosarai* kidnapping; kidnapper

2

仐 100 J-X M366 Nonstandard for 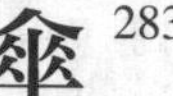 283.

仂 101 J503e M350 Nonstandard for 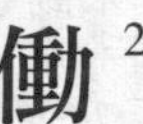 297.

从 102 J503a M362 Jū, Shō *shitaga(u)* obey, submit to, comply with, observe (a law); follow; accompany.

仆 103 J503d M354 Fu fall; lie down; bend.

仍 104 J503b M361 Jō. *yo(tte)* therefore, consequently.

什 105 J3d3a M348 Jū ten; utensil, thing.
1 一 *jūichi* tithe
8 物 *jūmotsu* furniture, fixtures; utensil; treasure
宝 *jūhō* treasured article
15 器 *jūki* utensil, appliance, furniture

仇 106 J3558 M355 Kyū. *ada, ata, kataki* foe, enemy; revenge; enmity, grudge, feud; harm, evil; ruin; invasion.
6 同士 *katakidōshi* enemy
10 討 *adauchi* vengeance, retaliation
15 敵 *kyūteki* bitter enemy
23 讎 *kyūshū* revenge; bitter enemy

仄 107 J503c M352 Soku. *hono(meku)* be seen dimly; glimmer. *hono(mekasu)* hint at, intimate, suggest, allude to. *hono(kana)* faint, indistinct. *hono(mekashi)* hint, intimation.
4 仄 *honobono to* dimly, faintly
5 白 *honojiro(i)* dimly white
13 暗 *honogura(i)* gloomy; obscure
14 聞 *sokubun suru* casually hear

B **介** 108 J3270 M359 Kai shell, shellfish. *kai(suru)* be in between; mediate; concern oneself with. *kai(shite)* through the medium of.
2 入 *kainyū* intervention
5 甲 *kaikō* crust-like shell
6 在 *kaizai* intervention
8 抱 *kaihō suru* nurse; look after
10 病 *kaibyō suru* nurse a patient
11 添 *kaizo(e)* helper, assistant, second
殻 *kaikaku* seashell
13 意 *kaii suru* worry about, care about
16 錯 *kaishaku suru* assist at harakiri
錯人 *kaishakunin* a second at harakiri; attendant; attendance, assistance
23 鱗 *kairin* fish and shellfish

A **以** 109 J304a M388 I. *mot(te)* with, by, by means of; because; in view of.
3 下 *ika* less than, under, below; and downward; not exceeding; the following; the rest
上 *ijō* more than, over, above; and up; beyond; the above-mentioned; since, as long as; the end
4 内 *inai* within, less than
心伝心 *ishin-denshin* telepathy; sympathy, quiet understanding
5 外 *igai ni* with the exception of; excepting. *mot(te) (no) hoka* absurd, unreasonable
北 *ihoku* north of; and northward
6 西 *isei* west of; and westward
7 来 *irai* since
8 往 *iō* hereafter; thereafter; the future; formerly; in ancient times
東 *itō* east of; and eastward
9 後 *igo* hereafter; thereafter
降 *ikō* on and after; hereafter; thereafter
前 *izen ni* ago, since, before, previously
南 *inan* south of; and south
12 遠 *ien* and beyond

A **仁** 110 J3f4e M349 Jin virtue, benevolence, humanity, charity; man. Nin kernel.
2 人 *jinnin* man of virtue, humanitarian
4 心 *jinshin* benevolence, humanity
王 *Niō* Guardian Deva Kings

王力 *niōriki* Herculean strength
王門 *niōmon* temple gate guarded by fierce Deva Kings
5 兄 *jinkei* term of address for a friend
7 君 *jinkun* benevolent ruler
8 者 *jinsha* man of virtue; humanitarian
9 侠 *ninkyō, jinkyō* chivalrous spirit
政 *jinsei* benevolent rule
10 恕 *jinjo* benevolence, magnanimity
恵 *jinkei* graciousness, mercy, charity
11 術 *jinjutsu* benevolent act; healing art
12 智 *jinchi* benevolence and wisdom
13 慈 *jinji* benevolence, mercy
愛 *jin'ai* benevolence, charity, love
義 *jingi* humanity and justice; duty; moral code (of a gang)
義礼智信 *jin-gi-rei-chi-shin* the five Confucian virtues (benevolence, justice, courtesy, wisdom, and sincerity)
14 徳 *jintoku* benevolence, goodness
15 輪加狂言 *niwaka kyōgen* farce, extravaganza

A **仏** 111/J4a29/M364 **佛** 146/J5047/M517 BUTSU Buddha, Buddhism. FUTSU French. *hotoke* Buddha; merciful person; Buddhist image; the dead.
2 力 *butsuriki* the power of Buddha
3 工 *bukkō* maker of Buddhist images and altar fittings
4 心 *busshin, hotokegokoro* the Buddha heart, the Buddha mind
文 *Futsubun* French, French writing, French literature
5 生会 *busshōe* Buddha's birthday celebration
6 式 *busshiki* Buddhist ritual
気 *hotokegi* a compassionate heart
印 *Futsu-In* French Indo-China
会 *butsue* Buddhist memorial service
寺 *butsuji* Buddhist temple
名 *butsumyō* a Buddha's name
7 陀 *Budda, Butsuda* Buddha
8 門 *Butsumon* Buddhism; priesthood
国 *Fukkoku* France
性 *hotokeshō, busshō* the Buddha nature
刹 *bussetsu, bussatsu* Buddhist temple
画 *butsuga* Buddhist picture
参 *bussan suru* visit a Buddhist temple
具 *butsugu* Buddhist altar equipment
典 *butten* Buddhist scriptures, sutras
学 *butsugaku* Buddhist learning
価 *bukka* Buddhahood, Nirvana
者 *bussha* a Buddhist; a Buddhist priest
事 *butsuji* Buddhist memorial service
舎利 *busshari* Buddha's ashes
法 *Buppō* Buddhism
法僧 *buppōsō* the Buddha, the doctrine, and the priesthood
9 祖 *Busso* Founder of Buddhism
前 *butsuzen* before the Buddha or a mortuary tablet
臭 *hotokekusa(i)* otherworldly, sanctimonious
10 座 *butsuza* Buddhist image seat; temple pulpit
師 *busshi* Buddhist image maker
徒 *butto* a Buddhist
家 *bukke* Buddhist priest
書 *bussho* Buddhist scriptures
恩 *butsuon* grace of Buddha; indebtedness to Buddha
11 道 *butsudō* Buddhism, Buddhist teachings
経 *bukkyō* Buddhist sutras
教 *Bukkyō* Buddhism
堂 *butsudō* Buddhist temple
貨 *fukka* francs
頂面 *butchōzura* sour look
12 間 *butsuma* Buddhist family chapel
葬 *bussō* Buddhist funeral
13 殿 *butsuden* Buddhist temple
僧 *bussō* Buddhist priest
滅 *butsumetsu* Buddha's death; unlucky day
跡 *busseki* a place sacred to Buddhism
14 閣 *bukkaku* Buddhist temple
像 *butsuzō* Buddhist image
様 *hotokesama* a Buddha; a deceased person
説 *bussetsu* Buddha's teaching
語 *Futsugo* French language. *butsugo* Buddhist term
領 *Futsuryō* French possession, French territory
15 縁 *butsuen* Buddha's providence
器 *bukki* Buddhist altar fittings
16 噸 *futsuton* metric ton
壇 *butsudan* Buddhist household altar
18 顔 *hotokegao* a gentle face
20 艦 *Futsukan* French warship
蘭西 *Furansu* France

A **今** 112/J3a23/M358 KIN. KON now, the present; the coming; this. *ima* now, present time; just now, soon, immediately; (one) more. *ima demo* even now, still, as yet. *ima dewa* now, nowadays. *ima ni* before long; even now, still. *ima nimo* at any time, soon. *ima ya* now. *ima(mekashii)* fashionable. *ima(mekasu)* modernize. *ima(motte)* until now. *ima-* modern.

1 一 *ima hito(tsu)* one more
一度 *ima ichido* once more
3 夕 *konseki, kon'yū* this evening, tonight
上 *Kinjō* the reigning emperor
上陛下 *kinjō heika* the reigning emperor
4 方 *ima(shi)gata, imagata* a moment ago
以 *ima mot(te)* still, yet, (not) yet
少 *ima suko(shi)* a little more
月 *kongetsu* this month
月分 *kongetsubun* (charge) for this month
今 *ima-ima* right now. *ima(ka)ima(ka)* eagerly waiting. *ima(ga)ima* just now
今迄 *ima (ga) ima made* till just now
日 *kyō, konnichi* today, this day. *Konnichi wa* Good afternoon
日迄 *kyō made, konnichi made* until today
日的 *konnichiteki* modern, up-to-date
日明日 *kyō-asu* today and tomorrow; today or tomorrow; in a day or two
5 生 *konjō* this life, this world
古 *kinko* now and anciently
迄 *ima made* till now
冬 *kontō* this winter; next winter; last winter
出来 *imadeki* something new
世界 *konsekai* this world
世紀 *konseiki* this century
6 回 *konkai* lately; this time
次 *konji* the present time. *konji no* new, recent
年 *konnen, kotoshi* this year
7 更 *imasara* now, at this late hour
8 夜 *kon'ya* tonight, this evening
尚 *ima nao* still, even now
昔 *konjaku, konseki* past and present
明日 *kommyōnichi* today and (or) tomorrow
9 風 *imafū* modern style
度 *kondo* this time, now; next time; another time
後 *kongo* after this, hereafter
秋 *konshū* this fall; next fall; last fall
春 *konshun* this spring; next spring; last spring
10 週 *konshū* this week
般 *kompan* now, recently; this time
夏 *konka* this summer; next summer; last summer
宵 *koyoi* this evening, tonight
時 *imadoki* recently, these days; at this hour
時分 *ima jibun* about this time
11 遅 *ima(ya)oso(shi) to* impatiently, eagerly
頃 *imagoro* about this time
道心 *ima dōshin* neophyte, novice
12 晩 *komban* tonight, this evening. *Komban wa* Good evening.
暁 *kongyō* this morning; this morning at dawn
程 *imahodo* recently; a moment before
期 *konki* the present term
朝 *kesa, konchō* this morning
朝方 *kesagata* this morning
13 際 *imawa* one's dying hour
14 様 *imayō* modern style
様歌 *imayō uta* a Heian poetry style

3

仟 113/J5042/M380 See 千 599.

仝 114/J2138/M378 See 同 717 and 全 145.

仞 115/J5040/M379 **仭** 116/J-X/M-X **仭** 117/J5041/M397
JIN fathom.

仗 118/J503f/M371 JŌ. *tsue* cane; whipping rod.

仔 119/J3b46/M367 SHI *ko-* (animal) offspring.

4 牛 *koushi* calf
犬 *koinu* puppy
6 羊 *kohitsuji* lamb
虫 *shichū* larva
11 細 *shisai* reasons, circumstances; significance; particulars; hindrance, obstruction, interference

B **仙** 120 / J4067 / M374 SEN hermit; wizard. *sento* cent.

2 人 *sennin* hermit; wizard; fairy; otherworldly person
人掌 *saboten, shaboten* cactus
3 女 *sennyo, senjo* fairy, nymph
4 丹 *sentan* the elixir (of life)
9 界 *senkai* dwelling place of hermits; a pure land away from the world
10 骨 *senkotsu* unusual physique, outstanding appearance; philosophic turn of mind; the sacrum, sacral bone
郷 *senkyo* fairyland, enchanted land
11 術 *senjutsu* wizardry; the secret of immortality
13 窟 *senkutsu* enchanted cave
14 境 *senkyō* fairyland, enchanted land
16 薬 *sen'yaku* panacea; elixir (of life)

A **令** 121 / J4e61 / M387 RYŌ ancient laws. REI order, command; ordinance, law, decree. *rei(suru)* command, order, dictate. *-shi(mu)* old causative verbal ending.

4 夫人 *reifujin* Mrs., Lady, Madam; your wife
5 兄 *reikei* your elder brother
6 色 *reishoku* servile looks
旨 *reishi, ryōji* a prince's message; command of a prince
名 *reimei* good reputation, fame
7 状 *reijō* warrant, summons; written order
弟 *reitei* your younger brother
8 姉 *reishi* your elder sister
妹 *reimai* your younger sister
9 姪 *reitetsu* your niece
10 娘 *reijō* your daughter, young lady
孫 *reison* your grandchild
息 *reisoku* your son
11 堂 *reidō* your home; your mother
望 *reibō* good reputation
12 婿 *reisei* your son-in-law
13 嗣 *reishi* heir
14 聞 *reibun* good reputation, fame
閨 *reikei* your wife, his wife, Mrs.
16 孃 *reijo* your daughter, your lady

A **他** 122 / J423e / M370 TA. another, the other, others, another thing; the rest; another place. *ta-* another, other. *hoka* some other place; outside; the rest.

2 力 *tariki* outside help; salvation by faith
力本願 *tariki-hongan* salvation by faith in Amida Buddha; reliance upon others
人 *tanin, adabito* another person, unrelated person, outsider, stranger
人扱 *tanin'atsuka(i)* treating like a stranger
人行儀 *tanin gyōgi* reserved manners
人空似 *tanin (no) sorani* accidental resemblance
3 山 *tazan* another mountain; another temple
山石 *tazan (no) ishi* object lesson, food for thought
4 心 *tashin* other intention, secret purpose, ulterior motive, ill will, fickleness, doublemindedness
方 *tahō* another side; different direction; (on) the other hand
日 *tajitsu* some day; hereafter, at some future time
5 出 *tashutsu* going out
世界 *tasekai* other worlds
生 *tashō* previous existence; future existence; transmigration
生縁 *tashō (no) en* karma from a previous existence
6 行 *tagyō* absence from home. *takō* going out
年 *tanen* some other year; some day
7 見 *taken* viewing by others; showing others
言 *tagen, tagon* telling others; revealing to others
村 *tason* another village
8 店 *taten* another shop, store, or firm
姓 *tasei* another surname
所 *yoso, tasho* another place
物 *tabutsu, ta(no)mono* the other thing, the other man's property
宗 *tashū* another sect
事 *taji* other matters, other people's affairs
念 *tanen* thinking about something else
念無 *tanenna(ku)* eagerly, intently
国 *takoku* foreign country; another province
国人 *takokujin* foreigner, alien, stranger
国民 *takokumin* other nations, other peoples
国者 *takokumono* stranger, a person from another place

9 面 *tamen* the other side; another direction; (on) the other hand
律 *taritsu* heteronomy, subjection, subordination
派 *taha* the other group
界 *takai suru* die. *takai* the next world; death
県 *taken* another prefecture
10 称 *tashō* third person (in grammar)
殺 *tasatsu* murder
郷 *takyō* another place; a foreign country
家 *take* another family
流 *taryū* another style; another school (of thought); different blood
流試合 *taryūjiai* contest between different schools (of fencing, etc.)
11 動詞 *tadōshi* transitive verb
12 覚的 *takakuteki* objective (symptoms)
覚症 *takakushō* objective symptoms, symptoms observed by the doctor
覚症状 *takaku shōjō* objective symptoms, symptoms observed by the doctor
13 愛 *taai* altruism
意 *tai* other intention, secret purpose, ulterior motive, ill will, fickleness, doublemindedness
14 聞 *tabun* publicity, reaching other ears
領 *taryō* another fief
16 薦 *tasen* recommendation

A **仕** 123 / J3b45 / M368 SHI official; civil service. *tsuka(eru)* serve, work for. *tsukamatsu(ru)* serve; do (polite).
2 入 *shi-i(reru)* laying in stock
入物 *shii(re)mono* stock of goods received
3 口 *shikuchi* method, way
上 *shi-a(garu) vi* be finished. *shi-a(geru) vt* finish
上工 *shiagekō* finishing workman
上払 *shia(ge)bara(i)* piecework pay
4 手 *shite* protagonist; hero; leading part
切 *shi-ki(ru)* partition, divide; mark off; settle accounts; toe the mark. *shiki(ri)* partition, division, boundary; compartment; settlement of accounts; toeing the mark. *shi-ki(renai)* impossible to do
分 *shi-wa(keru)* assort, classify; journalize (in accounting)
込 *shi-ko(mu)* train, bring up, educate; fit into, stock up on. *shiko(mi)* training; stocking up; preparation
込杖 *shiko(mi)zue* a sword cane
方 *shikata* way, method, resource, course, means
方無 *shikata (no) na(i), shikata (ga) na(i), shikatana(i)* it can't be helped, it's inevitable; it's no use; can't stand it; be impatient; be annoyed. *shikatana(ku), shikatana(shi) ni* helplessly, reluctantly
方話 *shikatabanashi* talking with gestures
5 打 *shiu(chi)* treatment; behavior, conduct
払 *shi-hara(u)* pay
末 *shimatsu* circumstances; management; disposal, settlement; control
付 *shi-tsu(keru)* be used to a job; begin to do; make; baste, tack; plant. *shitsu(ke)* rice planting; tacking, basting
付糸 *shitsu(ke) ito* tacking; basting (thread)
出 *shida(shi)* catering; shipment. *shi-da(su)* begin to do; cater
出来 *shi-deka(su)* finish up
出屋 *shida(shi)ya* caterer
立 *shi-ta(teru)* tailor; make; prepare; train; send (a messenger). *shita(te)* tailoring, dressmaking, sewing; making; preparation
立下 *shita(te)oro(shi)* brand-new (clothes)
立方 *shita(te)kata* style of clothes; method of tailoring; method of training
立券 *shitateken* free dressmaking ticket (with a purchase of cloth)
立物 *shitatemono* sewing, tailoring; newly-tailored clothes
立直 *shita(te)nao(shi)* making over (clothing)
立屋 *shita(te)ya* tailor; dressmaker
6 返 *shikae(shi)* doing over; tit for tat; retaliation, revenge
向 *shi-mu(keru)* treat, act toward, handle (men); send, forward to
合 *shiai* contest, match, game, bout, tournament, joust. *shia(wase)* fortune, luck; happiness, blessing

合者 *shia(wase)mono* fortunate person
7 形 *shikata* way, method, resource, course, means
来 *shikita(ri)* custom, conventional practice
8 送 *shioku(ri)* allowance, remittance
始 *shi-haji(meru)* begin, start
直 *shi-nao(su)* do over, remake, resume, begin again
官 *shikan* government service; samurai's service
奉 *tsuka(o) matsu(ru)* serve (polite); build as commanded
放題 *shihōdai* having one's own way
事 *shigoto* work, employment, occupation
事日 *shigotobi* work day
事台 *shigotodai* workbench, work table
事師 *shigotoshi* workman; enterpriser; schemer
事部屋 *shigotobeya* workroom
事場 *shigotoba* place where one works; construction site 「suit
事着 *shigotogi* work clothes; business
事箱 *shigotobako* workbox
9 度 *shitaku* preparation, arrangements; costume, dress; trousseau
拵 *shikoshira(e)* preparation
草 *shigusa* treatment; behavior, action; gestures
10 納 *shiosa(me)* finishing up
致 *shi (o) ita(su)* resign
兼 *shi-ka(neru)* be unable to do; hesitate, be reluctant. *shi ka(nenai)* be capable of anything
留 *shi-to(meru)* bring down (a bird), kill
11 遂 *shi-to(geru)* accomplish, finish, fulfill
済 *shi-su(masu)* succeed as planned
組 *shi-ku(mu)* devise, arrange, plan, plot. *shiku(mi)* construction; contrivance, arrangement; plan, plot
訳 *shi-wa(keru)* assort, classify; journalize (in accounting)
訳書 *shiwakesho* specifications
訳帳 *shiwakechō* bookkeeping journal
掛 *shi-ka(keru)* commence; lay (mines); set (traps); wage (war); challenge. *shikaka(ri)* commencement. *shika(ke)* mechanism, gadget; (small) scale; half-finished
掛花火 *shikake hanabi* a fireworks piece
12 着 *shiki(se)* livery, servant's clothes provided by employers
替 *shi-ka(eru)* do over, start anew
13 損 *shi-sokona(u), shi-son(jiru)* blunder, fail, make a mistake
馴 *shi-na(reru)* be used to doing, be experienced in
業 *shiwaza* act, action, deed
置 *shio(ki)* execution; punishment
置者 *shio(ki)mono* a criminal
置場 *shio(ki)ba* execution ground
14 種 *shigusa* method; attitude; actor's expressions, actions. 「help
様 *shiyō* way, method, resource; remedy,
様書 *shiyōga(ki), shiyōsho* specifications
様無 *shiyō (ga) na(i)* It can't be helped. *shiyō (no) na(i)* hopeless, good-for-nothing, incorrigible
舞 *shima(u)* finish, conclude; put away; save; close, wind up. *shimai* end, termination; informal noh play
舞込 *shima(i)-ko(mu)* lay away, stow away, hoard up
舞物 *shima(i)mono* goods left unsold
舞屋 *shimotaya* a store that has gone out of business; a household that lives without carrying on a business
15 儀 *shigi* situation, developments, outcome

A **付** 124/J1966/M373 FU. *fu(suru)* give to, submit to, refer to; affix, attach, append. *tsu(keru) vt* attach, join, stick, glue, fasten; sew on, furnish (a house with); wear, put on; make an entry; appraise, set (a price); apply (ointment); bring alongside; place (under guard or a doctor); follow, shadow; add, append, affix; load; give (courage to); keep (an eye on); establish (relations or understanding). *tsu(ku) vi* be connected with; be dyed; be stained; be scarred; be recorded; be attached to; (fires) start; follow; become allied to; accompany; study with; increase, be added to. *(o)tsu(ki)* attendant, escort. *tsu(ke)* bill, bill of sale. *(ni) tsu(ki)* per, apiece; because of; regarding. *tsu(ki)* (printing) impression; sociability; appearance. *tsu(ketari)* addition, accessory, appendage, supplement, appendix; complement; an excuse. *(ni)* *tsu(ite)* concerning; along; under; per. *-zu(ke)* dated. *-zu(ki)* attached to, furnished with. *tsu(ke)-* fixed, external. *-tsu(ke)* date. *-tsu(ki)* attached to, under, to.

2 人 *tsu(ke)bito* assistant, attendant; chaperon; suite

入 *tsu(ke)-i(ru)* take advantage of, impose on

3 上 *tsu(ke)-a(garu)* be elated; be spoiled; take advantage of

与 *fuyo* grant, allowance, endowment

4 文 *tsu(ke)bumi* love letter

火 *tsu(ke)bi* incendiarism

込 *tsu(ke)-ko(mu)* take advantage of, impose on; make an entry. *tsu(ke)ko(mi)* entry, booking

切 *tsu(ki)ki(ri), tsu(k)ki(ri)* constant attendance (by a doctor)

元気 *tsu(ke) genki* show of courage

不足 *tsu(ke)busoku* undercharge

5 目 *tsu(ke)me* aim; (to aim at) a weak point

札 *tsu(ke) fuda* tag, label

出 *tsu(ke)-da(su)* charge. *tsu(ke)da(shi)* bill, account

加 *tsu(ke)-kuwa(eru)* add to. *fuka* addition, annexation, supplement, appendage

加税 *fukazei* additional tax

6 回 *tsu(ke)-mawa(su), tsu(ke)-mawa(ru)* follow, shadow, hanker after, hover around

近 *fukin* neighborhood, environs, vicinity

会 *fukai* add to; twist the meaning

合 *tsu(ke)-a(waseru)* add to. *tsu(ki)-a(u)* keep company with, associate with, get along with. *tsu(ki)a(i)* association, fellowship, acquaintance, friendship. *tsu(ki)a(wase)* perfect occlusion; vegetable relish with meat

7 言 *fugen* postscript, additional remarks

足 *tsu(ke)-ta(su)* add to. *tsu(ke)ta(shi)* addition, appendix, supplement, postscript

図 *fuzu* attached map or plan

8 届 *tsu(ke)todo(ke)* tip, present

所 *tsu(ke)dokoro* viewpoint

注 *fuchū* annotation, comment

物 *tsu(ki)mono* accessory, appendage

狙 *tsu(ke)-nera(u)* prowl after, shadow, keep watch on

直 *tsu(ke)-nao(su)* repair again, join again

者 *tsu(ki)mono* attendant; curse; devil possession

表 *fuhyō* attached list

事 *tsu(kanu) koto* something sudden

具合 *tsu(ki) guai* (printing) impression; sociability; appearance

和 *fuwa* blindly following others

和雷同 *fuwa-raidō* following blindly

知恵 *tsu(ke)jie* hint, suggestion

9 則 *fusoku* additional rules, by-laws, supplementary provisions

10 馬 *tsu(ki)uma, tsu(ke)uma* bill collector for the night's entertainment; followers

値 *tsu(ke)ne* the bid, the offer

従 *tsu(ki)-shitaga(u)* follow, accompany, join up with; obey implicitly; flatter

根 *tsu(ke)ne* root, joint, base, crotch

紙 *tsu(ke)gami* tag, slip, label

紐 *tsu(ke) himo* child's sash

記 *fuki* appendix, addition, note

託 *futaku suru* commit to, refer to, submit to

随 *tsu(ki)-shitaga(u)* follow, accompany, cleave to. *fuzui* incidental, attendant, annexed, accompanying

帯 *futai* incidental, accessory, secondary, collateral

帯犯 *futaihan* accessory offense

帯事項 *futai jikō* supplementary item

帯費用 *futai hiyō* incidental expenses

11 掛 *tsu(ke)ka(ke)* overcharge

著 *fuchaku* adhesion, cohesion, agglutination

黒子 *tsu(ke)bokuro* artificial facial beauty spot

添 *tsu(ki)-so(u)* escort and wait on, accompany, chaperon. *tsukiso(i)* attendance on; attendant, escort, chaperon, retinue

添人 *tsukisoinin* attendant

添婦 *tsukisoifu* practical nurse

12 換 *tsu(ke)-ka(eru)* renew, replace, change for, attach anew

着 *fuchaku* adhesion, cohesion, agglutination

落 *tsu(ke)o(chi), tsu(ke)o(toshi)* omission in a bill

替 *tsu(ke)ka(e)* replacement

景気 *tsu(ke)geiki* borrowed prosperity
焼 *tsu(ke)ya(ki)* broiling with soy
焼刃 *tsu(ke)yakiba* pretension, affectation
属 *fuzoku* attached, annexed; affiliated, associated; subordinate, incidental, dependent, auxiliary
属物 *fuzokubutsu* belongings, appendage, accessory
属品 *fuzokuhin* accessory, fittings, appurtenances
属書 *fuzokusho* appendix, supplementary notes
属節 *fuzoku setsu* subordinate clause
14 鼻 *tsu(ke)bana* false nose, artificial nose
箋 *fusen* tag, slip, label
髪 *tsu(ke)gami* false hair
16 録 *furoku* supplement, appendix
薬 *tsu(ke)gusuri* ointment, lotion
19 離 *tsu(kazu)-hana(rezu)* indecision
20 議 *fugi suru* bring up a matter, discuss, debate
21 纏 *tsu(ki)-mato(u), tsu(ki)-matsu(waru), tsu(ke)-mato(u)* follow around, shadow, hang around (a woman)

A **代** 125 / J4265 / M386 DAI period, age, generation; charge, rate, fee, cost, price. *yo* world, society, public; life, existence, career, lifetime; age, era, generation, times; reign. *ka(eru)* change, turn, convert, exchange, renew, substitute, replace. *ka(waru)* replace, relieve. *kawa(ri)* substitute, deputy, proxy, alternate, relief; compensation; second helping. *shiro* price; substitution; materials. *kawa(ri) ni* instead of. *(sono) kawa(ri) ni* on the other hand.

2 人 *dainin* substitute, deputy, proxy, representative, agent
4 父 *daifu* godfather
5 母 *daibo* godmother
代 *daidai, yoyo* for generations; hereditary. *kawa(ru)gawa(ru), kawa(ri)gawa(ri)* alternately
打 *daida* pinch-hitting
打者 *daidasha* pinch hitter
弁 *daiben suru* pay by proxy; act for another; speak for another
弁者 *daibensha* spokesman, mouthpiece
用 *daiyō* substitution
用肉 *daiyō niku* meat substitute
用食 *daiyōshoku* substitute food
用品 *daiyōhin* a substitute
6 返 *daihen suru* answer a roll call for another
印 *daiin* signing by proxy
任 *dainin* agency, acting official
休 *daikyū* compensatory holiday
地 *daichi* substitute land
合 *kawa(ri)-a(u)* relieve each other, take turns
名詞 *daimeishi* pronoun
行 *daikō* acting as an agent
行者 *daikōsha* agent, proxy
行機関 *daikō kikan* agency
7 走 *daisō* substitute runner
位 *daii* substitution
作 *daisaku* ghostwriting
役 *daiyaku, kawa(ri)yaku* substitute actor, a stand-in, a double
言 *daigen* speaking for another; attorney
言人 *daigennin* attorney
8 価 *daika* price, cost, charge
拝 *daihai* vicarious, worship
物 *daibutsu* substitute. *shiromono* thing, article, goods; fellow; affair
参 *daisan* visiting a temple for another
官 *daikan* chief magistrate, governor, bailiff (Tokugawa era)
金 *daikin* price, cost, charge, the money, the bill
金引換 *daikin hikikae* C.O.D.
表 *daihyō* representation, type, example, model; delegate
表団 *daihyōdan* delegation
表作 *daihyōsaku* masterpiece, a representative work
表者 *daihyōsha* representative, delegate
表的 *daihyōteki* representative, exemplary, model
表部 *daihyōbu* diplomatic mission
9 待 *daima(chi)* waiting in place of someone else
品 *daihin* substitute article
栄 *kawa(ri)ba(e)* successful substitution
10 将 *daishō* brigadier general; commodore
納 *dainō* payment for another
員 *daiin* proxy
案 *daian* alternate plan
書 *daisho* scribe, amanuensis
書人 *daishonin* scribe, amanuensis
11 務 *daimu* vicarious management
執行 *daishikkō* carrying out by proxy

理 *dairi* representation, agency, proxy, deputy, agent, attorney; substitute, alternate; acting (principal, etc.)
理人 *dairinin* proxy, agent, substitute, deputy, alternate, representative, attorney
理大使 *dairi taishi* chargé d'affaires of an embassy
理公使 *dairi kōshi* chargé d'affaires of a legation
理投票 *dairi tōhyō* voting by proxy
理店 *dairiten* agency
理者 *dairisha* proxy, agent, substitute, deputy, alternate, representative, attorney
理委任状 *dairi ininjō* power of attorney
理牧師 *dairi bokushi* vicar
理部 *dairibu* mail-order department; branch store
理業 *dairigyō* agency
理領事 *dairi ryōji* acting consul
理権 *dairiken* agency; (attorney's) right of representation
12 診 *daishin* doctor's assistance; doctor's assistant; locum tenens
筆 *daihitsu* amanuensis
番 *kawa(ri)ban(ko) ni, kawa(ri)ban ni* alternately
替 *daiga(wari)* subrogation, change of ownership
替物 *daitaibutsu* substitute
替品 *daiga(e)hin* substitute article
13 僧 *daisō* substitute priest
署 *daisho suru* sign for another
置 *daichi suru* replace
数 *daisū* algebra
数式 *daisū shiki* algebraic expression
数学 *daisūgaku* algebra
14 演 *daien suru* substitute for an actor
読 *daidoku* reading for another
16 稽古 *daigeiko* substitute teaching
燃車 *dainensha* car running on substitute fuel
赭 *taisha* red ocher
赭色 *taisha iro* yellowish brown
17 償 *daishō* compensation, indemnification, reparation; consideration
講 *daikō* substitute lecturing
謝 *taisha* renewal, replacement, regeneration; metabolism
19 願 *daigan* paying by proxy; applying by proxy
願人 *daigannin* one who offers prayer in place of another
20 艦 *daikan* replacement warship
議 *daigi* representing others in a conference
議士 *daigishi* member of a congress
議制度 *daigi seido* parliamentary system
議政体 *daigi seitai* representative government
議政治 *daigi seiji* representative government
議員 *daigiin* representative, delegate
議員団 *daigiindan* delegation

4

价 126 / J5043 / M412 KAI good; big.

仿 127 / J-X / M420 BŌ, HŌ stand still; wander.

伜 128 / J5067 / M462 **倅** 223 / J5066 / M750 SAI. SOTSU. SOCHI. *segare* son, my son.

伉 129 / J5044 / M431 KŌ same kind; compare with.
10 配 *kōhai* spouse, married couple

A **件** 130 / J376f / M410 KEN matter, case, item. *kudan* example, precedent. *kudan no* the usual; the said; the above-mentioned. *kudari* the above-mentioned.
13 数 *kensū* number of cases or items

伍 131 / J3860 / M435 GO five; five-man squad; file, line. *go(suru)* rank with, associate with. *itsu(tsu)* five.
8 長 *gochō* corporal

B **伐** 132 / J4832 / M439 BATSU. *u(tsu)* strike, attack; punish. *ki(ru)* cut, chop, hash; carve; saw; clip, shear; slice, strip; fell, cut down; punch; sever (connections); pause, break off; disconnect, turn off; hang up; cross (a street); discount, sell below cost; shake (water) off.
4 木 *batsuboku* felling, logging
5 出 *ki(ri)-da(su)* quarry; cut (timber); cut and carry off; begin to talk, break the ice

10 倒 *battō* felling
11 採 *bassai* felling, deforestation, lumbering

伎 133 / J346c / M436 GI, KI deed; skill.

3 女 *gijo* woman entertainer
工 *gikō* artisan
7 芸 *gigei* arts, handicrafts, accomplishments
10 倆 *giryō* ability, talent, skill, capacity
能 *gino* skill, ability, capacity
13 楽 *gigaku* ancient music

伊 134 / J304b / M432 I that one. *I-, -I* Italy.

4 太利 *Itaria, Itarī* Italy
7 呂波 *i-ro-ha* the first three *kana* of the syllabary
11 達 *date na* vainglorious, showy
達女 *date onna* a flapper
達男 *date otoko* dandy, dude
達者 *datesha, datemono* dandy, dude
達姿 *date sugata* flashy appearance
達巻 *datemaki* undersash; omelet wrapper
達着 *dategi* showy clothes
達衆 *dateshū* a dandy, a gallant; chivalrous person
13 勢大神宮 *Ise Daijingū* the Grand Shrines of Ise
勢大廟 *Ise Taibyō* the Grand Shrines of Ise
勢参 *Isemai(ri)* Ise pilgrimage
勢蝦 *ise ebi* spiny lobster
14 語 *Igo* Italian language
20 艦 *Ikan* Italian warship

B **企** 135 / J346b / M422 KI. *kuwada(teru)* plan, plot, propose, design, intend, contemplate; attempt, undertake. *taku(ramu)* scheme, plan, play a trick, invent, conspire, frame up. *takura(mi)* plan, design, artifice; trick, intrigue. *kuwada(te)* plan, attempt, undertaking.

3 及 *kikyū* attempt
7 図 *kito* plan, project, scheme
8 画 *kikaku* plan; planning
13 業 *kigyō* an enterprise
業心 *kigyōshin* enterprising spirit
業化 *kigyōka* commercialization
業合同 *kigyō gōdō* a trust
業者 *kigyōsha* industrialist
業連合 *kigyō rengō* a cartel
業家 *kigyōka* industrialist
業整備 *kigyō seibi* curtailment of business operations
14 劃 *kikaku* plan; planning

A **任** 136 / J4724 / M416 JIN. NIN duty, responsibility; office; mission; term. *maka(su), maka(seru)* entrust to, leave to. *nin(jiru), nin(zuru)* appoint, nominate; assume (responsibility); pose as. *mama* as it is; as one likes; because.

5 用 *nin'yō* appointment, employment
6 地 *ninchi* one's post, appointment
8 官 *ninkan* appointment, investiture
免 *nimmen* appointments and dismissals
命 *nimmei* appointment, nomination, ordination, commission, designation
命式 *nimmeishiki* investiture
命状 *nimmeijō* written appointment
9 侠 *ninkyō* chivalry, generosity, heroism, chivalrous spirit
11 務 *nimmu* duty, function, office, mission
12 期 *ninki* term of office
期中 *ninkichū* during one's tenure
13 意 *nin'i* option, pleasure, discretion, free will
意出頭 *nin'i shuttō* voluntarily appearing for police questioning
18 職 *ninshoku* ordination

B **仰** 137 / J3644 / M400 GYŌ. KŌ. *ao(gu)* look up; look up to; ask for, depend on; seek; respect, revere; drink, take. *ao(muku), ao(noku)* look up. *ao(nokeru)* turn up (one's face or a card). *os(sharu)* say, speak, tell, talk (polite). *ō(serareru)* say, state (polite). *ō(se)* statement, command, wishes (of a superior).

3 山 *gyōsan* large quantity, plenty, abundance, a great many
4 反 *nokezo(ru)* bend back; throw (the head back)
天 *gyōten suru* be amazed, be horrified
5 付 *ō(se)-tsu(keru)* command; request; appoint. *ō(se)-tsu(karu)* receive a command
出 *ō(se)-da(su)* announce, proclaim
6 仰 *gyōgyō(shii)* exaggerated, bombastic, highly colored

向 *aomu(keru)* turn up (one's face or a card). *aomu(ku)* look up, lie face up
向様 *aomu(ke)zama* on one's back
7 見 *ao(gi)-mi(ru)* look up to, look up at; revere
角 *gyōkaku* angle of elevation
附 *ō(se)-tsu(keru)* command; request; appoint. *ō(se)-tsu(karu)* receive a command
8 奉 *ao(gi)-tatematsu(ru)* look up; look up to; ask for, depend on; seek; respect, revere; drink, take (polite)
臥 *gyōga* sleeping face up
臥位 *gyōgai* lying face up
11 視 *gyōshi suru* look up to, revere
望 *gyōbō suru, ao(gi)-nozo(mu)* look to (for help); look up to, revere
14 様 *nokezama ni* on one's back

A **似** 138 / J3b77 / M485 JI. *ni(ru)* resemble. *nise(ru)* copy, imitate; counterfeit, forge. *ni(tsukawashii)* suitable, appropriate, becoming. *-ni* takes after (a parent).
5 付 *ni-tsu(ku)* become, suit, be like, match well. *ni-tsu(kawashii)* suitable, becoming
6 合 *ni-a(u)* become, suit, be like, match well. *nia(i)* well matched; suitable, becoming. *nia(washii)* well matched, suitable, becoming
而非 *ese-* false, would-be, sham, pretended, mock, spurious, pseudo-, quasi-
気無 *nigena(i)* unlike, unbecoming, unworthy of, out of keeping with
8 者 *ni(ta)mono* similar people
非 *ni(te)hi(naru)* falsely similar, counterfeit. *ese-* false, would-be, sham, pretended, mock, spurious, pseudo-, quasi-
非者 *esemono* sham, fraud, counterfeit; impostor, pretender
非事 *esegoto* laughable affair, unlaudable affair, something unreliable
非笑 *esewara(i)* smirk, affected smile
非理窟 *eserikutsu* sophistry
非親 *eseoya* distant disinterested parent
9 通 *ni-kayo(u)* resemble closely
11 寄 *ni-yo(ru)* resemble. *niyo(ri)* similarity. *ni(tari)-yo(ttari)* much the same
18 顔 *nigao* likeness, portrait
顔書 *nigaoka(ki)* portrait painter; drawing portraits
顔絵 *nigaoe* likeness, portrait

B **伏** 139 / J497a / M438 FUKU. *fu(su) vi* bend down, bow down, lie prostrate. *fu(seru) vt* turn over, lay face down; cover; lay (pipes), lay (an ambush); hide. *fuku(suru)* stoop, bend down, crouch; lie down, prostrate oneself, fall prostrate; hide; yield to, submit to. *fu(shite)* bowing down; humbly, respectfully.
5 目 *fu(shi)me* downcast look
6 字 *fu(se)ji* asterisk, blank type (dots, circles, etc.)
在 *fukuzai suru* lie concealed, be hidden
7 兵 *fukuhei* ambush, troops in ambush
8 拝 *fu(shi)-oga(mu)* kneel and worship
9 屋 *fu(se)ya* humble cottage, hut
奏 *fukusō* report to the throne
10 倒 *fu(shi)-tao(reru)* fall down
射 *fukusha suru* to shoot lying prone
射濠 *fukushagō* sheltered trench
11 転 *fu(shi)-maro(bu)* fall and roll over; wriggle about
13 罪 *fukuzai* pleading guilty
勢 *fu(se)zei, fukuzei* ambush
14 樋 *fu(se)doi* covered drain
15 縫 *fu(se)nu(i)* hemming
線 *fukusen* underplot (in a novel); precautionary measures
22 籠 *fu(se)kago* coop, hen coop

A **仲** 140 / J4367 / M403 CHŪ. *naka* relation; relationship.
2 人 *nakōdo, chūnin* go-between; matchmaking
人口 *nakōdoguchi* matchmaker's story; saying nice things about a person
4 介 *chūkai* agency, intermediation
介物 *chūkaibutsu* intermediary, medium, channel
介者 *chūkaisha* mediator, go-between, middleman
5 仕 *nakashi* longshoreman; baggageman
兄 *chūkei* the younger of two elder brothers
冬 *chūtō* midwinter
立 *nakada(chi)* mediation, agency;

agent, mediator, middleman, go-between
立人 *nakadachinin* middleman, mediator, go-between
6 好 *nakayoshi* intimacy; chum
7 良 *nakayo(ku)* on cordial terms. *nakayo(shi)* intimacy; chum
8 居 *nakai* waitress
直 *nakanao(ri)* reconciliation. *nakane* average price
9 春 *chūshun* midspring
保 *chūho* mediation, intercession
保者 *chūhosha* mediator, intercessor
秋 *chūshū* eighth lunar month; midautumn
秋名月 *chūshū (no) meigetsu* harvest moon
10 値 *nakane* average price
核 *chūkaku* nucleus, core, kernel
夏 *chūka* midsummer
12 違 *nakataga(i)* discord, estrangement
買 *nakagai* brokerage
買人 *nakagainin* broker, jobber
裁 *chūsai* arbitration, mediation, peacemaking, intercession
裁人 *chūsainin* arbitrator, mediator
裁者 *chūsaisha* arbitrator, mediator
裁裁判 *chūsai saiban* arbitration
裁裁判所 *chūsai saibansho* court of arbitration
間 *nakama* company, circle, party; associate, confederate, accomplice. *chūgen* samurai's attendant, footman
間人 *nakamai(ri)* joining a group
間外 *nakamahazu(re)* being left out
間同士 *nakamadōshi* comrades
間値段 *nakama nedan* trade price
間割 *nakamawa(re)* split among friends, internal discord
間喧嘩 *nakamagenka* quarrel among friends
間褒 *nakamabo(me)* logrolling, mutual admiration
13 働 *nakabatara(ki)* maid, servant

A **伝** 141/J4541/M462′ **傳** 287/J5123/M1019 TEN. DEN legend, tradition; life, biography; commentary; communicating. *tsuta(u)* go along, walk along, follow. *tsuta(waru)* be transmitted, be circulated, be introduced into; go along, walk along. *tsuta(eru)* report, tell, impart, transmit, propagate, teach, bequeath. *tsuta(e)* legend, tradition. *tsute* intermediary, good offices, connections; someone to trust. *-zuta(i) ni* along (the wall).
5 世 *densei suru* transmit from generation to generation
令 *denrei* messenger, orderly, runner
令者 *denreisha* herald, orderly, messenger
7 来 *denrai suru* be transmitted, be handed down; be imported. *denrai no* ancestral, hereditary; imported
声器 *denseiki* speaking tube
言 *dengon* verbal message, word. *tsutegoto* verbal message; rumor
言板 *dengomban* message board
承 *denshō* transmission, legend, tradition, folklore
承文学 *denshō bungaku* oral literature
8 送 *densō* dissemination, circulation, diffusion, propagation; transmission, communication, delivery
法 *dembō* teaching Buddhism; rough person; bullying; ostentatious bravado
法肌 *dembō-hada* rough-and-tumble; a bullying disposition
奇 *denki* romance (fiction)
奇小説 *denki shōsetsu* romance (fiction)
奇的 *denkiteki* legendary
9 奏 *densō suru* deliver a message to the emperor
単 *dentan* leaflet
音器 *den'onki* megaphone, speaking tube; sound box
染 *densen* contagion
染毒 *densendoku* virus, germ
染病 *densembyō* contagious disease, infectious disease, epidemic
10 家 *denka* heirloom; trump card; last resort; family tradition
書鳩 *denshobato* carrier pigeon, homing pigeon
馬 *temma* post horse
馬船 *temmasen* large sculling boat
記 *denki* biography
記文学 *denki bungaku* biographical literature
記作者 *denki sakusha* biographer

記物 *denkimono* biographical writings
11 達 *dentatsu* transmission, communication, delivery
唱 *denshō* tradition
授 *denju* initiation, instruction
習 *denshū* learning
票 *dempyō* chit, sales slip, voucher
道 *dendō suru* evangelize. *dendō* evangelism, missionary work
道者 *dendōsha* evangelist, evangelistic worker
道師 *dendōshi* evangelist
道船 *dendōsen* missionary boat
道集会 *dendō shūkai* evangelistic meeting
12 統 *dentō* tradition, convention
統的 *dentōteki* traditional, conventional
13 話 *tsuta(e)banashi* legend
14 聞 *dembun suru, tsuta(e)-ki(ku)* learn by hearsay. *dembun* hearsay, rumor, report
説 *densetsu* legend, tradition
誦 *denshō* tradition
導 *dendō* conduction, transmission
導性 *dendōsei* conductivity
導度 *dendōdo* conductivity
15 播 *dempa* propagation, circulation, diffusion, dissemination
18 騎 *denki* mounted orderly

A **休** 142 / J3559 / M440 KYŪ. *yasu(mu), kyū(suru)* *vi* rest; take a day off; be absent; retire, sleep. *yasu(meru)* *vt* rest (oneself); let idle; suspend; have (someone) rest; set at ease, give relief to; fallow (land). *yasu(maru)* be rested, feel at ease, repose, be relieved. *yasu(maseru)* excuse (someone); give a holiday to; make (someone) rest. *yasura(u)* rest, relax. *yasu(mi)* rest, recess, respite, suspension; vacation, holiday; absence; molting.
4 心 *kyūshin* peace of mind, freedom from care; (sense of) relief or security; reassurance
火山 *kyūkazan* dormant volcano
日 *kyūjitsu* holiday, rest day
日明 *kyūjitsua(ke)* the day after a holiday
止 *kyūshi* pause, cessation, rest
止符 *kyūshifu* rest (in music); period, full stop
5 刊 *kyūkan* suspension of publication
6 休 *yasu(mi)-yasu(mi)* resting at times; thinking carefully
会 *kyūkai* adjournment, recess
会明 *kyūkaia(ke)* reassembling of a legislature
7 足 *kyūsoku* resting
廷 *kyūtei* court recess
廷日 *kyūteibi* no-court day ⌈of rest
8 所 *yasu(mi)dokoro* resting place, haven
学 *kyūgaku* temporary absence from school; suspension
泊所 *kyūhakujo* temporary quarters
9 神 *kyūshin* peace of mind, freedom from care; (sense of) relief
怠 *kyūtai* laziness, neglect
茶屋 *yasu(mi)jaya* wayside teahouse
10 校 *kyūkō* closing school (temporarily); dropping one's studies
祥 *kyūshō* good omen
航 *kyūkō* suspension of sailings
眠 *kyūmin* idle (facility); dormant
眠期 *kyūminki* dormant season
息 *kyūsoku* rest, relief, relaxation
息所 *kyūsokujo* restroom, lobby, lounge
息時間 *kyūsoku jikan* recess
11 戚 *kyūseki* weal and woe, welfare
転 *kyūten* (elevator) not running
12 場 *yasu(mi)ba* resting place. *kyūjō* theater closure; stage absence
閑 *kyūkan* fallowing
閑地 *kyūkanchi* fallow land
診 *kyūshin* no medical examinations (today)
診日 *kyūshimbi* doctor's no-consultation day
13 意 *kyūi* peace, tranquility
載 *kyūsai* nonappearance in print
暇 *kyūka* holiday, vacation, furlough
暇願 *kyūka nega(i)* application for leave
電 *kyūden* electricity cutoff
電日 *kyūdembi* no-electricity day
業 *kyūgyō* shop closed, business suspended, shutdown, holiday
業日 *kyūgyōbi* business holiday
戦 *kyūsen* truce, armistice
戦会談 *kyūsen kaidan* armistice conference
戦条約 *kyūsen jōyaku* armistice treaty
戦協定 *kyūsen kyōtei* cease-fire agreement
戦記念日 *Kyūsen Kinembi* Armistice Day

[14]演 *kyūen suru* suspend performance
[15]養 *kyūyō* rest, recreation
養室 *kyūyōshitsu* rest or recreation room
[16]錘 *kyūsui* idle spindles
憩 *kyūkei* rest, recess, intermission
憩所 *kyūkeijo* restroom, lounge
憩室 *kyūkeishitsu* restroom, lounge
[17]講 *kyūkō* lecture cancelled
[18]職 *kyūshoku* temporary retirement; suspension from office

A **会** 143 / J3271 / M460 **會** 2493 / J5072 / M14306 E Buddhist ceremony; understanding. Kai meeting, assembly; party; association, club. *a(u)* meet, interview. *a(waseru)* expose to, subject to. *kai(suru)* meet, assemble; join. *e(suru)* understand. *tamatama* casually, unexpectedly; few.

[4]心 *kaishin* congeniality, satisfaction
[5]主 *kaishu* sponsor of a meeting
[6]同 *kaido* an assembly, a meeting
式 *eshiki* a temple service
合 *kaigō* meeting, assembly
[7]社 *kaisha* company, corporation
社員 *kaishain* company employee
見 *kaiken* interview, audience
見者 *kaikensha* interviewer
見記 *kaikenki* record of an interview
[8]長 *kaichō* chairman, president (of a society)
所 *kaisho* meeting place; club
[9]食 *kaishoku* dining together; mess
則 *kaisoku* society regulations, constitution
計 *kaikei* account; finance; accountant; treasurer; paymaster; a reckoning; bill
計士 *kaikeishi* certified public accountant
計年度 *kaikei nendo* fiscal year
計官 *kaikeikan* accountant, treasurer
計学 *kaikeigaku* accountancy
計検査 *kaikei kensa* audit, auditing
[10]陰 *ein* the perineum
員 *kaiin* member; the membership
員証 *kaiinshō* membership certificate
席 *kaiseki* meeting place; restaurant dinner; seats for the public
席料理 *kaiseki ryōri* banquet
席膳 *kaisekizen* elaborate dinner tray
[11]得 *etoku* understanding, comprehension, grasp, perception, appreciation
釈 *eshaku* salutation, greeting, recognition, bow
規 *kaiki* society bylaws
商 *kaishō* negotiation, talks
堂 *kaidō* church, chapel, tabernacle, synagogue
堂司 *kaidōzukasa* ruler of a synagogue
[12]場 *kaijō* meeting place, the grounds
飲 *kaiin suru* drinking and carousing together
衆 *kaishū* audience, congregation
集 *kaishū* audience, assembly, meeting
費 *kaihi* membership fee
報 *kaihō* bulletin, report
期 *kaiki* session (of a legislature)
期中 *kaikichū* during a session
葬 *kaisō* attendance at a funeral
葬者 *kaisōsha* attendants at a funeral, mourners
[13]話 *kaiwa* conversation
戦 *kaisen* engagement, battle
意 *kaii* a type of characters made up of meaningful parts (e.g., 東 and 休)
意文字 *kaii moji* ideograph
[14]読 *kaidoku* a reading-and-discussion meeting
厭 *een* epiglottis
厭軟骨 *een nankotsu* epiglottis
[15]談 *kaidan* conversation, discussion, interview
[16]頭 *kaitō* society president
館 *kaikan* assembly hall
[20]議 *kaigi* conference, assembly, council, convention, congress, meeting
議日程 *kaigi nittei* conference program
議所 *kaigisho* place of assembly
議事項 *kaigi jikō* agenda
議室 *kaigishitsu* council room
議場 *kaigijō* place of assembly
議録 *kaigiroku* minutes, proceedings

A **仮** 144 / J323e / M398 **假** 261 / J5071 / M835 Ka. Ke (Buddhist) vanity. *kari no* temporary, provisional; informal, unauthorized; fleeting; assumed (name); interim; acting. *kari ni* temporarily, provisionally; for example; for argument's sake. *kari nimo* even for an instant, even as a joke.

[2]入学 *kari nyūgaku* provisional enrollment

3 小屋 *karigoya* booth, shack, hut, temporary shed
5 令 *tatoe, tatoi* if, even if, though, although
世 *kari (no) yo* this transient world
処分 *kari shobun* temporary measures
払 *karibara(i)* temporary advance (of money)
払金 *karibara(i)kin* temporary advance (of money)
出所 *kari shussho* parole; release on bail
出獄 *kari shutsugoku* parole; release on bail
6 死 *kashi* apparent death; asphyxiation
宅 *karitaku* temporary dwelling
字 *kana* Japanese syllabaries
名 *kana* Japanese syllabaries. *kamei, kemyō, karina* pseudonym, alias, pen name
名文 *kanabumi* publication in *kana* alone
名文字 *kana moji* the Japanese syllabary symbols
名手本 *kanadehon* Japanese *kana* copybook
名本 *kanabon* publication in *kana* alone
名交 *kanama(jiri)* mixed writing (characters and *kana*)
名交文 *kanama(jiri)bun* mixed writing (characters and *kana*)
名草紙 *kanazōshi* story in *kana*
名書 *kanaga(ki)* writing in *kana*
名遣 *kanazuka(i)* syllabary spelling
名勝 *kanaga(chi)* using more *kana* than characters
7 役 *kariyaku* temporary post
決 *kaketsu* conditional approval
初 *karisome* temporariness, transience; trifle; negligence. *karisome nimo* for a moment; even as a joke; even in the slightest degree
声 *kasei* falsetto
条約 *kari jōyaku* provisional treaty
住 *karizuma(i)* temporary residence
住居 *karizumai* temporary residence
8 刷 *karizu(ri)* proof printing
性 *kasei* false (symptoms)
枕 *kari makura* a nap
泊 *kahaku* emergency anchoring
臥 *karibushi* nap
命 *kari (no) inochi* this transient life
舎 *kariya* temporary dwellings
免状 *kari menjō* temporary certificate
定 *katei* assumption, supposition, hypothesis
定法 *kateihō* subjunctive mood
定款 *kari teikan* provisional articles
受金 *kariu(ke)kin* money temporarily receipted
受取 *kari uketori* temporary receipt
受取証 *kari uketorishō* temporary receipt
9 屋 *kariya* temporary residence; temporary shelter
拵 *karigoshira(e)* makeshift; temporary building
相 *kasō* appearance, phenomenon
政府 *kari seifu* provisional government
面 *kamen* mask, disguise
面舞踏会 *kamen butōkai* masquerade ball
10 病 *kebyō* feigned illness
借 *kashaku* borrowing; pardon, extenuation; a type of characters substituted for others of the same sound (e.g., 燕 for 宴)
埋 *kariu(me)* temporary burial
眠 *kamin* nap
称 *kashō* temporary name
託 *kataku* pretense, pretext
家 *kari ie* temporary house
宮 *kari miya* temporary shrine
記入 *kari kinyū* suspense account
差押 *kari sashiosa(e)* provisional seizure
進級 *kari shinkyū* conditional promotion
埋葬 *kari maisō* temporary burial
納 *kanō* deposit
納金 *kanōkin* deposit
納税 *kari nōzei* tax payment under protest
11 設 *kasetsu* temporary, provisional; hypothesis, supposition; fiction
宿 *kari (no) yado(ri)* temporary dwelling; this transient world
釈放 *kari shakuhō* release on parole
勘定 *kari kanjō* suspense account, outstanding account
庵 *kariio, kario, kariho* booth, tabernacle, temporary dwelling
12 歯 *kashi* false tooth
植 *kariu(e), kashoku* temporary planting
渡 *kariwata(shi)* temporary approximate payment

粧 *keshō* make-up
貼 *kariba(ri)* temporary pasting
寓 *kagū* temporary residence
葺 *karibuki* temporary roofing
普請 *karibushin* temporary building
装 *kasō* masquerade, disguise, fancy dress; converted (cruiser)
装巡洋艦 *kasō jun'yōkan* merchant cruiser
装舞踏会 *kasō butōkai* masquerade ball
13 殿 *karidono* temporary shrine
睡 *kasui, utatane* nap, siesta
寝 *karine* nap, siesta; stopping at an inn
想 *kasō* imagination, supposition; potential (enemy)
14 漆 *kashitsu* varnish
説 *kasetsu* hypothesis, supposition
綴 *karitoji* temporary binding; paper binding
綴本 *karitojihon* paper-bound book
15 縫 *karinu(i)* temporary sewing, basting
調印 *kari chōin* initialing (a pact)
16 橋 *karibashi* temporary bridge
親 *kari oya* adopted parents; temporarily assumed parents
17 繃帯 *kari hōtai* first-aid dressing
20 議長 *kari gichō* acting chairman, acting president

A 全 145 J4134 M1424 仝 114 J2138 M378 ZEN all. *mattō(suru)* accomplish, fulfill, complete, preserve (life). *matta(ki)* perfect, complete, whole, sound, intact. *matta(ku)* entirely, completely, wholly, perfectly; truly, indeed. *zen-* all, whole, entire, complete, overall; pan-. [人]
2 力 *zenryoku* all one's energy, full capacity
人 *zenjin* a saint; a person well-balanced morally and intellectually
人生 *zenjinsei* the whole life
人格 *zenjinkaku* one's whole personality
3 土 *zendo* the whole land, the whole country
山 *zenzan* the whole mountain
4 心 *zenshin* one's whole heart
戸 *zenko* all the houses (in town)
文 *zembun* whole sentence; full paragraph; full text
以 *matta(ku) mo(tte)* as a matter of fact
天 *zenten* all heaven
日制 *zennichisei* the full-day (school system)
反射 *zenhansha* total reflection
5 甲 *zenkō* an all-A (student)
史 *zenshi* complete history
世界 *zensekai* the whole world
生涯 *zenshōgai* one's whole life
民衆 *zemminshū* all the peoples
市 *zenshi* the whole city
市民 *zenshimin* all the citizens of the city
6 米 *zen Bei* all America, pan-American
休止符 *zenkyūshifu* a whole rest (in music)
地 *zenchi* the whole world, all lands
地方 *zenchihō* the whole area
会一致 *zenkai-itchi* unanimous
会衆 *zenkaishū* the whole assembly, the whole congregation
7 角 *zenkaku* em, em quad (in printing)
図 *zenzu* complete map, whole view
局 *zenkyoku* general situation, whole aspect
快 *zenkai* complete recovery of health
形 *zenkei* the whole form; a perfect form
住民 *zenjūmin* all the inhabitants
体 *zentai* the whole; whatever (is the matter). *zentai de* in all
体主義 *zentai shugi* totalitarianism
体主義国 *zentaishugikoku* totalitarian state
身 *zenshin* the whole body; full-length (portrait)
身不髄 *zenshin fuzui* total paralysis
身浴 *zenshin'yoku* full bath
身病 *zenshimbyō* general constitutional illness
身衰弱 *zenshin suijaku* general prostration
身麻酔 *zenshin masui* general anesthesia
身像 *zenshinzō* full-length portrait or statue
身黴毒 *zenshimbaidoku* syphilis of the whole system
8 長 *zenchō* over-all length, span
所 *matta(ku) (no) tokoro* entirely
治 *zenchi, zenji* complete recovery
乳 *zennyū* whole milk
欧 *zen-Ō* all Europe
岸 *zengan* all the banks (of a river)
免 *zemmen* complete exemption

2 波受信機 *zempa jushinki* all-wave receiver
店 *zenten* the whole store
店中 *zentenchū* throughout the store
知 *zenchi* omniscience
知全能 *zenchi-zennō* omniscience and omnipotence
4 国 *zenkoku, zengoku* the whole country; nationwide, national
国大会 *zenkoku taikai* national convention; national athletic meet
国区 *zenkokuku* national constituency
国中継 *zenkoku chūkei* nationwide hookup
国民 *zenkokumin* the whole nation
国的 *zenkokuteki* nationwide
国放送 *zenkoku hōsō* national network broadcast
9 通 *zentsū* opening of the whole (railway line)
科 *zenka* complete course
級 *zenkyū* the whole class
段 *zendan* the whole page
軍 *zengun* the whole army; the whole team
巻 *zenkan* the whole reel; the whole volume
封地 *zenhōchi* the whole fief
音 *zen'on* whole tone (in music)
音符 *zen'ompu* whole note
速 *zensoku* full speed
速力 *zensokuryoku* full speed
面 *zemmen* the whole surface
面的 *zemmenteki* all-out, general, overall, complete, extensive, full-scale
面戦争 *zemmen sensō* total war, all-out war
10 校 *zenkō* the whole school
納 *zennō* full payment
紙 *zenshi* the whole sheet; the whole newspaper
豹 *zempyō* the whole, all the rest
都 *zento* the whole metropolis
島 *zentō* the whole island; all the islands
員 *zen'in* all members; all hands, the whole crew
家 *zenka* the whole family, the whole house
容 *zen'yō* full portrait; whole aspect; full story
書 *zensho* complete book; complete set
荷重 *zenkajū* full load
般 *zempan* the whole. *zempan no* universal, general, whole
般的 *zempanteki ni* generally, universally, wholly
部 *zembu* all, the whole; entirely, altogether
部保険 *zembu hoken* full insurance
能 *zennō* omnipotence
能力 *zennōryoku* full capacity, all one's ability
能者 *zennōsha* the Almighty, The Omnipotent One
11 道 *zendō* all Hokkaido
域 *zen'iki* the whole area
船 *zensen* the whole ship
訳 *zen'yaku* complete translation
敗 *zempai* complete defeat
隊 *zentai* the entire force (of soldiers)
責任 *zensekinin* full responsibility
強風 *zenkyōfū* whole gale
盛 *zensei* height of prosperity
盛時代 *zensei jidai* golden age
盛期 *zenseiki* golden age
12 開 *zenkai suru* open fully. *zenkai* full throttle
備 *zembi* completeness, perfection, consummation
焼 *zenshō* total destruction by fire
量 *zenryō* the whole quantity
集 *zenshū* complete works
智 *zenchi* omniscience
然 *zenzen* wholly, entirely, completely, absolutely
幅 *zempuku* overall width; wing span. *zempuku no* all, every, utmost
幅的 *zempukuteki ni* fully
勝 *zenshō* complete victory
勝軍 *zenshōgun* ever-victorious army
景 *zenkei* panoramic view, bird's-eye view
景写真 *zenkei shashin* panoramic photo
廃 *zempai* total abolition
廃論 *zempairon* abolitionism
廃論者 *zempaironsha* abolitionist
13 損 *zenson* total loss
滅 *zemmetsu* annihilation, complete destruction
数 *zensū* the whole number, all
勢力 *zenseiryoku* full force
裸 *zenra* nude
裸体 *zenratai* stark naked body
14 貌 *zembō* full portrait; whole aspect; full story

製品 *zenseihin* manufactured article
15 潰 *zenkai* complete destruction
線 *zensen* the whole line; all lines
編 *zempen* whole book, whole volume
篇 *zempen* whole book, whole volume
霊 *zenrei* one's whole soul
質化 *zenshitsuka* transubstantiation
論点 *zenronten* the whole point
権 *zenken* plenipotentiary powers; full authority
権大使 *zenken taishi* ambassador plenipotentiary
権公使 *zenken kōshi* minister plenipotentiary
権委員 *zenken iin* plenipotentiaries
16 壊 *zenkai* complete destruction
17 優 *zen'yū* straight A's
翼飛行機 *zen'yoku hikōki* a flying wing
18 癒 *zen'yu* complete healing
軀 *zenku* the whole body
額 *zengaku* total, full amount

5

佛 146 J5047 M517 See 仏 111.

佝 147 J5048 M520 KU, KŌ bent, ugly; foolish; weak.

估 148 J5046 M467 KO price; business; selling.

伶 149 J4e62 M478 REI actor.
2 人 *reijin* court musician, minstrel

佑 150 J4d24 M507 U, YŪ help.
7 助 *yūjo* assistance

佃 151 J4451 M492 TEN. *tsukuda* cultivated rice field.
12 煮 *tsukudani* food preserved by boiling down in soy

佇 152 J504a M496 CHO. *tatazu(mu)* stop, linger, loiter. *tatazumai* appearance, shape, figure, bearing.
5 立 *choritsu suru* stand still

佚 153 J5045 M516 ITSU, TETSU be lost; peace; hide; mistake; beautiful; in turn.
10 書 *issho* a lost book
13 楽 *itsuraku* pleasure

B **但** 154 J4322 M495 TAN. DAN. *tadashi* but, however, excepting that.
5 付 *tadashizu(ki) no* conditional
10 書 *tadashiga(ki)* proviso

B **佐** 155 J3a34 M506 SA help.
8 官 *sakan* field officer
9 保姫 *saohime* goddess of spring
13 幕 *sabaku* adherence to the shogunate
14 様 *sayō* yes, indeed; well… *sayō na* such, of that kind, like that

B **伺** 156 J3b47 M483 SHI. *ukaga(u)* vt and *vi* visit; ask, inquire, question; hear, be told; implore (a god for an oracle).
8 事 *ukaga(i)goto* inquiry
10 候 *shikō suru* wait upon (someone)
11 探 *ukaga(i)-sagu(ru)* spy out
済 *ukaga(i)zu(mi)* instructions received

B **伴** 157 J483c M475 HAN. BAN. *tomona(u)* accompany, bring with; be accompanied by; be involved in. *tomo* companion, follower.
4 天連 *Bateren* Portuguese missionaries; Christianity
9 食 *banshoku* eating with a guest; nominal official (a slighting term)
侶 *hanryo* companion
奏 *bansō* accompaniment
奏部 *bansōbu* accompaniment
13 僧 *bansō* priests assisting at a Buddhist service

B **伯** 158 J476c M466 HAKU count; earl; eldest brother; uncle; chief official.
4 父 *oji, hakufu* uncle
5 母 *oba, hakubo* aunt
兄 *hakkei* the eldest son
6 仲 *hakuchū suru* be evenly matched
8 叔 *hakushuku* brothers; one's father's brothers
13 楽 *bakurō* horse trader
17 爵 *hakushaku* count; earl

伽 159 J3240 M486 GA. KA. KYA. *togi* nursing; nurse; attending; attendant; entertainer.

5 芝居 *(o)togi shibai* fairy play, pantomime
9 草子 *(o)togizōshi* fairy-tale book
13 話 *(o)togibanashi* fairy tale, nursery tale
17 藍 *garan* temple, monastery
藍洞 *garandō* hollowness, emptiness, void
藍鳥 *garanchō* pelican
19 羅 *kyara* aloes wood; aloes-wood perfume

侘 160 J5049 M513 TA. *wabi(ru)* be worried, be grieved, pine for. *wabi* subdued taste. *wabi(shii)* wretched, comfortless, lonesome.

2 人 *wabibito* lonesome person; unwanted person; poverty-stricken person
7 言 *wabigoto* sad words, anxious words
声 *wabigoe* sad voice
住 *wabizuma(i)* wretched abode; solitary life
住居 *wabizumai* wretched abode; solitary life
13 寝 *wabine* lonesome sleep
14 歌 *wabiuta* a sad song; singing in a lonesome tone

佞 161 J5524 M521 NEI flattery; insincerity.

2 人 *neijin* flatterer, smooth talker, crafty person
5 弁 *neiben* flattery, cajolery, adulation
6 臣 *neishin* crafty courtier; traitor
奸 *neikan na* treacherous, wicked, perverse
8 者 *neisha* smooth talker, crafty person
9 姦 *neikan na* treacherous, wicked, perverse
11 悪 *neiaku* perverseness; perverse person
12 智 *neichi* craftiness

A **位** 162 J304c M503 I rank, place, grade. *kurai* grade, rank; court order, dignity, nobility; situation; throne, crown. *kurai suru* occupy a position. *-kurai, -gurai* about, almost, as; rather; at least; enough to. *-i* rank, place.

6 次 *iji* order of rank; order of seating
地 *ichi* situation, position, rank
8 取 *kuraido(ri)* grade, class, quality; unit; digit
官 *ikan* rank and official position
9 相 *isō* phase (in science)
冠 *ikan* ancient headgear showing rank
負 *kuraima(ke)* being unworthy of one's rank; being outranked
10 倒 *kuraidao(re)* inability to live up to one's rank
記 *iki* court-rank diploma
記追贈 *iki-tsuisō* conferment of posthumous rank
11 階 *ikai* court rank
階勲等 *ikai-kuntō* court rank and honors
12 牌 *ihai* Buddhist mortuary tablet
牌堂 *ihaidō* mortuary chapel
13 置 *ichi* situation, position, location, place
15 勲 *ikun* rank and order of merit

B **伸** 163 J3f2d M481 SHIN stretching. *no(biru)* extend, lengthen, stretch, spread; be postponed; increase; grow; progress, develop; be straightened, be flattened, be smoothed; be exhausted. *no(basu)* lengthen, stretch, extend; let (nails) grow; straighten; uncoil; spread out; reach out; postpone; dilute; smooth out; develop (talents); amass (riches). *no(beru)* make (a bed); stretch, widen, lengthen. *no(su)* stretch, spread, smooth out; roll out; iron; stretch, extend; gain influence; knock out. *no(bi)* stretching (the body); excess, surplus; postponement; growth; spread. *no(biyakana)* comfortable, carefree. *noshi* an iron.

3 上 *no(shi)-a(geru)* promote; make richer. *no(shi)-a(garu)* stand on tiptoe; rise in the world; become arrogant. *no(bi)-a(garu)* stretch, reach to, stand on tiptoe
4 反 *no(ruka)-so(ruka)* win or lose, sink or swim
5 広 *no(be)-hiro(geru) vt* stretch out
7 伸 *no(bi)no(bi) suru* feel at ease, feel carefree
8 長 *shinchō* expansion, extension, elongation
9 度 *shindo* elasticity
10 展 *shinten* expansion, extension
悩 *no(bi)-naya(mu)* be sluggish (business)
11 張 *shinchō* expansion, extension, elongation

掛 *no(shi)-ka(karu)* lean on; bend over; come upon
[12] 筋 *shinkin* protractor muscle
[14] 暢 *shinchō* expansion, extension, elongation
[15] 餅 *noshimochi* flattened rice cakes
[17] 縮 *shinshuku, no(bi)chiji(mi)* expansion and contraction; elasticity, flexibility
縮自在 *shinshuku jizai na* elastic, flexible. telescoping. expandable
縮性 *shinshukusei* elasticity
縮法 *shinshukuhō* sliding scale
縮税率 *shinshuku zeiritsu* flexible tariff

A **住** 164 / J3d3b / M505 Jū dwelling, living. *su(mu), su(mau), jū(suru)* live, reside, inhabit. *su(mai)* residence.
[2] 人 *jūnin* resident, inhabitant
[4] 込 *su(mi)-ko(mu)* live in, live with
心地良 *su(mi)gokochi (no) yo(i)* comfortable to live in
[5] 処 *su(mi)ka* dwelling; den (of robbers); nest
生活 *jūseikatsu* manner of housing
民 *jūmin* inhabitants, residents, population
民税 *jūminzei* municipal tax
民登録 *jūmin tōroku* resident registration
[6] 宅 *jutaku* residence, house
宅地 *jūtakuchi* residential district
宅難 *jūtakunan* housing shortage
[8] 居 *jūkyo, sumai* dwelling, residence, address
居手当 *jūkyo teate* rent allowance
所 *jūsho, su(mi)dokoro* residence, address, domicile
所録 *jūshoroku* address book
[9] 持 *jūji* chief priest of a temple
荒 *su(mi)-a(rasu)* leave a house in bad shape
[10] 家 *sumika, jūka* dwelling, residence
[11] 著 *su(mi)-tsu(ku)* settle down
[12] 着 *su(mi)-tsu(ku)* settle down
替 *su(mi)-ka(eru)* change one's residence
[13] 僧 *jūsō* chief priest (of a Buddhist temple)
[14] 慣 *su(mi)-na(reru)* get used to living in
[18] 職 *jūshoku* chief priest (of a Buddhist temple)

難 *su(mi)niku(i)* inconvenient (residence), unpleasant (surroundings)

A **体** 165 / J424e / M509 **體** 6794 / J7173 / M45291 **躰** 5931 / J6d3c / M38065

TAI the body; substance, object; reality; style, form; image counter. TEI appearance, air; condition, state, form. *tai(suru)* obey, comply with; keep in mind. *karada* body; health.
[2] 力 *tairyoku* physical strength
[4] 内 *tainai* interior of the body
中 *karadajū* throughout the body
[5] 付 *karadatsu(ki)* body build, figure
[6] 刑 *taikei* corporal punishment; jail sentence
当 *taiata(ri)* body blow, ramming attack, sacrifice attack
[7] 言 *taigen* uninflected word
位 *taii* physical standard; physique
技 *taigi* boxing and jujitsu
形 *taikei* form, figure
良 *teiyo(ku)* decently, gracefully; plausibly; politely; tactfully
系 *taikei* system, organization
系化 *taikeika* organization, systematization
系的 *taikeiteki* systematic
[8] 長 *taicho* length of an animal
制 *taisei* structure, system, setup, organization
育 *taiku* physical education, gymnastics, athletics
育家 *taiikuka* physical culturist, athlete
育館 *taiikukan* gymnasium
[9] 面 *taimen* honor, reputation; dignity; prestige; appearances
重 *taijū* body weight
臭 *taishū* body odor; a characteristic (of someone)
[10] 粉 *karada (o) ko ni suru* work assiduously
格 *taikaku* physique, constitution
格検査 *taikaku kensa* physical examination
[11] 得 *taitoku* realization, experience; comprehension; mastery
惜 *karada (o) o(shimu)* be lazy
液 *taieki* body fluids
現 *taigen suru* personify, impersonate, embody
細胞分裂 *taisaibō bunretsu* mitosis

12 腔 *taikō, taikū* body cavity
腔壁 *taikōheki, taikūheki* body wall
量 *tairyō* body weight
量器 *tairyōki* scales for weighing
温 *taion* body temperature
温計 *taionkei* clinical thermometer
温器 *taionki* clinical thermometer
裁 *teisai* form, style; appearance, show; get-up, format; decency
裁上 *teisaijō* for appearance' sake
裁良 *teisaiyo(ku)* tastefully, respectfully, decently
裁振 *teisaibu(ru)* put on airs
13 感 *taikan* bodily sensation
14 様 *taiyō* situation; terms
認 *tainin* an understanding based on experience
貌 *taibō* appearance
罰 *taibatsu* corporal punishment
15 熱 *tainetsu* body heat
質 *taishitsu* physical constitution
16 積 *taiseki* volume, capacity
操 *taisō* gymnastics, calisthenics
操場 *taisōjō* gymnasium; drill ground
18 軀 *taiku* the body, stature, physique, constitution
験 *taiken* experience
験談 *taikendan* story of one's experience

A **低** 166/J4463/M504 **祇** 1727/J-X/M10069 TEI low. *hiku(i)* low, short; humble; low (voice).

3 下 *teika* fall, decline, lowering, deterioration
4 木 *teiboku* shrub, shrubbery
5 目 *hikume* low ball (in baseball)
圧 *teiatsu* low pressure; low voltage
丘陵 *teikyūryō* low hills
6 回 *teikai* loitering, lingering, reluctance to leave
地 *teichi* low ground, bottom land, plain
当 *teitō* mortgage, hypothec, security
劣 *teiretsu* low grade, inferiority; coarseness, vulgarity
気圧 *teikiatsu* low atmospheric pressure, cyclone; bad temper, tense situation
7 吟 *teigin suru* hum, sing in a low voice
声 *teisei* low voice, whisper
利 *teiri* low interest
利金 *teirikin* low-interest money
利金融 *teiri kin'yū* low-interest credit
利資金 *teiri shikin* low-interest funds
8 迷 *teimei* low-hanging (clouds)
佪 *teikai* loitering, lingering, reluctance to leave
学年 *teigakunen* lower grades in school
金利 *teikinri* low interest
物価 *teibukka* low prices
周波 *teishūha* low frequency
性能 *teiseinō* low efficiency
空 *teikū* low ceiling; low altitude
空飛行 *teikū hikō* low-altitude flying
9 度 *teido* low degree, low grade, low class
速 *teisoku* low (gear), slow speed
俗 *teizoku* vulgar
徊 *teikai* loitering, lingering, reluctance to leave
級 *teikyū* low grade; vulgar
音 *teion* bass (in music); low voice
音部記号 *teiombu kigō* bass clef
10 能 *teinō* low intelligence, feeblemindedness, imbecility
能児 *teinōji* feebleminded child; poor scholar
能者 *teinōsha* imbecile, moron
11 唱 *teishō suru* hum, sing softly
率 *teiritsu* low rate
教会 *Teikyōkai* the Low Church
12 温 *teion* low temperature
減 *teigen* decrease, reduction, fall, depreciation, mitigation
湿 *teishitsu* low and damp
落 *teiraku* fall, decline, slump
雲 *teiun* low-hanging clouds
開発国 *teikaihatsukoku* backward nations
13 廉 *teiren* cheap, inexpensive
置 *teichi* low (toilet tank)
資 *teishi* low-interest funds
賃金 *teichingin* low wages
障碍 *teishōgai* low hurdles
15 潮 *teichō* low tide
調 *teichō* low tone, undertone, dullness, (market) weakness
16 頭 *teitō suru* bow low
頭平身 *teitō-heishin suru* prostrate oneself
17 翼 *teiyoku no* low-wing
18 額 *teigaku* small amount

A **作** 167 / J3a6e / M518 SA. SAKU a work, a production; tillage; harvest; ridge (in a field). *tsuku(ru)* make, create, manufacture, prepare, draw up, write, compose; build; coin; cultivate; organize, establish; make up (a face), trim (a tree); fabricate; prepare food; commit (sin). *(o)tsuku(ri)* makeup; sliced raw fish. *tsuku(ri)* make, structure, construction; physique, build; workmanship; (a woman's) makeup; cultivation; a mounting.

3 土 *sakudo* surface soil
上 *tsuku(ri)-a(geru)* build up; complete
4 手 *tsuku(ri)te* maker, builder, creator; tenant farmer
文 *sakubun* composition, writing
方 *tsuku(ri)kata* way of making; recipe, how to grow (something); style of building; construction; workmanship
木 *tsuku(ri)gi* a well-trimmed tree
5 用 *sayō* action, operation, function, effect
立 *tsuku(ri)-ta(teru)* adorn, decorate, dress up; build up
付 *tsuku(ri)tsu(ke)* fixed. *sakuzuke* planting.
出 *tsuku(ri)-da(su)* manufacture, raise (crops), turn out, create, make; invent; dream up
6 成 *sakusei* framing, drawing up, making; writing
返 *tsuku(ri)-kae(su)* remake
合 *tsuku(ri)-a(waseru)* make two (things) and join (them) together; make a duplicate
当 *sakua(tari)* good crop
曲 *sakkyoku* musical composition
曲者 *sakkyokusha* composer (general)
曲家 *sakkyokuka* composer (professional)
7 言 *tsuku(ri)goto* fabrication, lie
図 *sakuzu suru* draw figures; construct (in geometry). *sakuzu* drawing
声 *tsuku(ri)goe* feigned voice; unnatural voice
男 *saku otoko* farm hand; tenant
8 例 *sakurei* model of writing
法 *sahō* manners, etiquette, propriety
泣 *tsuku(ri)na(ki)* make-believe crying
物 *sakumotsu* crops. *tsuku(ri)mono* artificial product; decoration; fake; crop. *sakubutsu* literary work
盲 *tsuku(ri) mekura* feigned blindness
直 *tsuku(ri)-nao(su)* remake, rebuild
事 *tsuku(ri)goto* fabrication, lie, fiction
者 *sakusha* author
者不知 *sakusha shirazu* anonymous
者未詳 *sakusha mishō* anonymous, author unknown
9 風 *sakufū* literary style
眉 *tsuku(ri) mayu* painted eyebrows
柄 *sakugara* crop conditions; quality (of art)
品 *sakuhin* work, performance, production, opus
為 *sakui* artificiality; act; commission (of a crime)
10 病 *tsuku(ri) yamai, sakubyō* feigned illness
家 *sakka* writer, novelist; artist
笑 *tsuku(ri)wara(i)* forced laugh
酒屋 *tsuku(ri)zakaya* saké brewer; saké brewery
12 場 *sakuba* farm; workshop
替 *tsuku(ri)-ka(eru)* remake, remold, convert, reconstruct, adapt; parody
13 損 *tsuku(ri)-sokona(u), tsuku(ri)-zokona(u), tsuku(ri)-son(jiru)* fail in making
話 *tsuku(ri)banashi* fable, fabrication, fiction, myth
意 *sakui* design, motif, idea, conception, intention
詩 *sakushi* writing poetry; poem
詩法 *sakushihō* versification
戦 *sakusen* military or naval operations
戦上 *sakusenjō no* operational, strategic
戦計画 *sakusen keikaku* campaign plan
業 *sagyō* work, operations, manufacturing; fatigue duty
業用 *sagyōyō* for work, for manufacturing
業衣 *sagyōi* work clothes
業服 *sagyōfuku* work clothes
業場 *sagyōba, sagyōjō* works; workshop
業費 *sagyōhi* operational expense
業療法 *sagyō ryōhō* occupational therapy
14 歌 *sakka* writing songs or poems; poem
製 *sakusei* manufacture
16 興 *sakkō suru* promote, arouse
機嫌 *tsuku(ri) kigen* feigning good feeling

18 顔 *tsuku(ri)gao* affected look, made-up face

A **余** 168 / J4d3e / M515 **餘** 6693 / J7131 / M44185 YO I, myself, the writer; surplus, other; remainder. *ama(ri)* rest, remainder, remnant; surplus, balance; excess; remains, scraps, residue; fullness. *ama(ru)* remain, be in excess, be too many. *ama(su)* leave, spare, save. *-yo* over, more than. *ama(ri) ni* too much, excessively, too. *yo no* other, the rest. *-ama(ri)* upward of, over, more than.

2 人 *yonin, yojin* others, other people
力 *yoryoku* remaining strength; reserve power; money to spare
4 日 *yojitsu* remaining time, days left
切 *yosetsu* cotangent (in trigonometry)
分 *yobun* extra, excess, surplus
水路 *yosuiro* spillway
5 生 *yosei* one's remaining years
世 *yosei* one's remaining years
白 *yohaku* blank space, margin
白注 *yohakuchū* marginal notes, glosses
6 色 *yoshoku* complementary color
地 *yochi* place, room, margin; scope
光 *yokō* afterglow, lingering light
7 角 *yokaku* complementary angle
技 *yogi* avocation, hobby
沢 *yotaku* blessings, benefits (of modern civilization)
芳 *yohō* lingering fragrance; continuing fame (after death)
8 弦 *yogen* cosine (in trigonometry)
波 *yoha* secondary effect, aftermath; trail (of a storm), sequel, consequence. *nagori* farewell; keepsake, remembrance; remains, relics
物 *ama(ri)mono* remains, leavings, remnant; surplus. *ama(shi)mono* something not needed; a person who is in the way
命 *yomei* one's remaining days
炎 *yoen* burning embers
事 *yoji* other things, the rest; leisure tasks
念 *yonen* another idea
念無 *yonenna(ku)* earnestly, intently
所 *yoso* another place
所目 *yosome* another's eyes, casual observer
所乍 *yosonaga(ra)* while at a distance, indirectly, casually
所行 *yosoyu(ki), yosoi(ki)* going out; company manners, one's best (clothes)
所見 *yosomi suru* look away
所余所 *yosoyoso(shii)* distant, cold, formal
所者 *yosomono* stranger
所事 *yosogoto* another's affair
所無 *ama(su) tokoro na(ku)* fully, thoroughly
9 音 *yoin* reverberation; swelling (of a hymn); trailing note; lingering memory
風 *yofū* surviving custom, holdover influence
香 *yokō* lingering odor
後 *yogo* prognosis, aftereffects, recuperation, convalescence
殃 *yoō* trouble brought on by sins of forebears
計 *yokei* abundance, surplus, excess, superfluity
臭 *yoshū* lingering odor
栄 *yoei* posthumous honors
10 病 *yobyō* secondary disease, complications
財 *yozai* spare cash, available funds, remaining fortune
烈 *yoretsu* ancestors' meritorious deeds; the evil effects of the lives of our predecessors
11 得 *yotoku* emoluments, additional profits
情 *yojō* suggestiveness (of a poem), lingering charm, lasting impression
剰 *yojō* surplus, balance, residue
習 *yoshū* old remaining customs
12 禄 *yoroku* additional gain
程 *yohodo, yo(p)podo* very, greatly, much, to a large extent
割 *yokatsu* cosecant (in trigonometry)
寒 *yokan* lingering winter
裕 *yoyū* surplus, margin, room, time, allowance, scope, rope
裕綽綽 *yoyū-shakushaku(taru)* composed, calm and broadminded
13 暇 *yoka* spare time, leisure
煙 *yoen* lingering smoke
賊 *yozoku* the remaining bandits
罪 *yozai* other crimes, further offenses
意 *yoi* implied meaning
勢 *yosei* surplus power, force, momentum, impetus, inertia

業 *yogyō* side line, avocation
義無 *yogina(ku)* unavoidably, necessarily, inevitably
14 塵 *yojin* trailing dust; aftereffects
聞 *yobun* gossip, rumor
徳 *yotoku* influence of great virtue; influence of ancestors
滴 *yoteki* drippings
15 慶 *yokei* fortunate heredity; blessings, the reward of virtue; something bequeathed to posterity
憤 *yofun* pent-up anger, rage
談 *yodan* sequel (of a story); digression
震 *yoshin* aftershock
弊 *yohei* resulting evil, a holdover
熱 *yonetsu* waste heat; remaining heat
儀 *yogi, yo(no)gi* another method; another problem
儀無 *yogina(ku)* unavoidably, necessarily, inevitably
16 薫 *yokun* lingering odor
興 *yokyō* side show, entertainment
17 齢 *yorei* life expectancy
18 燼 *yojin* smouldering fire, embers
類 *yorui* remnants of a party or a gang
19 韻 *yoin* reverberation; swelling (of a hymn); trailing note; lingering memory
蘊 *youn* inexhaustible supply

A 何 169 J323f M511 Ka. *nan, nani* what. *dore* which; who. *nan da* What! Why! Well! What do you mean! *nan da ka* some way or other. *nan dattara* if you like. *nan de* why, what for. *nan demo* anything; by all means, probably. *nani* Oh! What! why, well. *nani ka* something, anything. *nanikashira* something or other; I don't know what it is but… *nani kato* one way or another. *nanni(mo), nani(mo)* nothing, no (with neg.). *nan ni seyo, nani(shiro), nani(se)* at any rate, anyhow. *nani yori no* most, best. *nani yori mo* first of all. *nan nara* if you wish, if you can, if desirable. *nan no* what, what kind of. *nani, nan to, nan te* what, whatever; What! How! Look here! *nan toka* some way or other; so and so. *nan tomo* nothing; quite. *nan to nareba* for, because. *izu(re)* where, which, who. *izu(re) mo* both; (neg.) neither. *izu(re) ni seyo, izu(re) ni shitemo* either way, in any case. *nan da ga, nan da kedo* to speak frankly. *nani(ka), nani(yara)* some, any, something anything. *nan(narito)* anything, whatever. *nan(taru)* How! What! (beautiful, etc.). *dō(shite)* how; why; absurd, on the contrary. *dō(shitemo)* by all means, surely; no matter what you do; by no means; willy-nilly; after all; all things considered. *dō(se)* anyway, in any case, after all, at all (neg. implication). *nani(kanitsuke)* concerning many things. *nani(kuso)* an interjection of determination. *nani(watomoare)* nevertheless, anyway. *nan-* some (thousands).
2 人 *nannin* how many (people). *nampito mo, nambito mo* everyone, all
3 千 *nanzen* many thousands. *nanzen… ka* how many thousands
4 方 *donata* who. *dotchi, dochira* where, what place; which; who. *dochira demo, dochira ka* either
日 *nannichi* how many days, what day
月 *nangatsu* what month
分 *nanibun* anyway, please. *nanibun no* some, something or other, as much as possible
心無 *nanigokorona(ku)* without any special thought
5 用 *naniyō de* on what business
付 *nani(ka) (ni) tsu(kete)* one way or another
奴 *doitsu, doyatsu* who
代目 *nandaime* what ordinal number (of a president, daimyo, etc.)
処 *doko, dokoira, izuko, izuku* where. *doko ka* somewhere, anywhere, in some respects
処迄 *doko made* how far; to what extent. *doko made mo* anywhere; through thick and thin, to the utmost; persistently, stubbornly; in all respects; thoroughly
処其処 *dokosoko* such and such a place
処無 *doko(tomo)na(ku)* aimlessly; somehow. *doko(to)na(ku)* somehow, for some reason; vaguely
6 回 *nankai* how many times. *nankai mo* time and time again
共 *nan tomo* (neg.) nothing; quite
年 *nannen* how many years; what year

2 二 亠 人 5 イ 𠆢 儿 入 八 ソ 冂 冖 冫 几 凵 刀 リ 力 勹 匕 匚 匸 十 卜 卩 厂 厶 又

気無 *nanigena(i)* casual, unconcerned. *nanigena(ku)* unintentionally, calmly, innocently, inadvertently 「printing
色摺 *nanshokuzu(ri)* multicolored
7 言 *nan(to)i(u)* how (beautiful, etc.)
何 *dore-dore* Which (emphatic)! *nani(ga)nan(daka)* What's what! *naninani* What are the items?
条 *nanjō* how
呉 *nanikure to* in various ways
呉無 *nanikure (to) na(ku)* in various ways
8 彼 *nani(yara)-ka(niyara), nani(ka)-ka(nika), nani(ya)-ka(ya)* this and that. *nan(toka)-kan(toka), nan(da)-kan(da)* something or other. *nani(mo)ka(mo)* anything and everything
物 *nanimono* something; nothing (neg.)
卒 *nanitozo, dōzo* please
者 *nanimono* who, what kind of a person. *nanimono ka* someone
事 *nanigoto* what; something, everything, nothing (neg.)
9 屋 *nan(demo)ya* jack-of-all-trades
度 *nando* how many times, how often. *nando mo* many times, often. *nando demo* any number of times. *nando ka* many times
故 *naze, naniyue* why, how
某 *nanigashi, nanibō, nan (no) nanigashi* a certain person; a certain amount
食顔 *naniku(wanu) kao* innocent looks
10 個 *nanko* how many pieces
時 *itsu* when, how soon. *nanji, nandoki* what time. *itsu demo* any time; always; never (with neg.). *itsu ka* some time, some day; at one time, one day, the other day, before we know it. *itsu kara* since when, how long. *itsu mo* always, usually; never (with neg.); every time. *itsumo no* usual, habitual. *itsu demo, nandoki demo* whenever, at any time. *itsu shika* unawares, before you know it. *itsu zoya* once, some time ago
時迄 *itsu made* till when, how soon, how long. *itsu made mo* indefinitely
時何時 *itsu-itsu* when (emphatic). *itsu nandoki* at any time; every moment
時何時迄 *itsuitsumade mo* indefinitely; for a long time
時時分 *itsu jibun* about what time
時頃 *nanjigoro, itsugoro* about when, how soon
時間 *nan jikan* how many hours. *itsu(no)ma(nika), itsu(no)ma(niyara)* unawares, unnoticed; before you know it
時無 *itsu(ni)na(i)* unusual
11 遍 *namben* how many times, how often. *namben mo* repeatedly
12 程 *dorehodo* how much, how long, how far. *nanihodo* how much, how many
期 *nanki mo* many periods
等 *nanra, nanira* what, whatever, what sort of, any kind of, nothing whatever (with neg.). *nanra(ka) no* some… or other
番 *namban* what number
無 *nan(demo) na(i)* easy, trifling, harmless. *nani(ka)na(shi) ni* casually. *nan(towa)na(shi) ni, nan(to)na(ku), nani(to)na(ku)* somehow or other
13 歳 *nansai* how old (are you, is she)
14 様 *nanisama* what kind; how; indeed, truly; extremely; to be sure
箇 *nanko* how many pieces
箇月 *nankagetsu* how many months
18 曜日 *naniyōbi, nan'yōbi* what day of the week

6

侭 170 J4b79 M-X Nonstandard for 儘 327.

侠 171 J3622 M625 Nonstandard for 俠 213.

侫 172 J5525 M-X Nonstandard for 佞 161.

來 173 J5054 M581 See 来 2565.

佰 174 J5051 M553 See 百 3864.

佼 175 J3873 M570 Kō, Kyō attractive; clever; deceive; line up. *utsuku(shii)* beautiful, attractive.

侖 176 / J5055 / M599 RIN, RON think; be methodical. *omo(u)* think, consider.

侑 177 / J5052 / M594 YŪ gift.

佻 178 / J504f / M569 CHŌ frivolity.

佪 179 / J-X / M545 KAI go around.

侈 180 / J504c / M583 SHI luxury; pride; extravagance; arbitrariness; selfishness.

侘 181 / J504e / M602 TA be proud; be lonely. *wabi(shii)* lonely.

侃 182 / J3426 / M577 KAN strong; just; right; love of peace.

8 侃諤諤 *kankan-gakugaku no* outspoken

侏 183 / J504d / M592 SHU actor; supporting post (in a roof truss).

16 儒 *shuju* dwarf

佶 184 / J504b / M562 KITSU, KICHI healthy; correct.

8 屈 *kikkutsu* crouching; difficulty in explaining characters or writing

佯 185 / J5053 / M552 YŌ. *itsuwa(ru)* lie, falsify; deceive; pretend; cheat.

7 狂 *yōkyō* feigned madness

佩 186 / J5050 / M543 HAI. *ha(ku), o(biru)* wear, put on (a sword).

2 刀 *haitō suru* carry a sword

5 用 *haiyō* wearing

10 剣 *haiken suru* wear a sword

B **侮** 187 / J496e / M629' **侮** 197 / J-X / M630 BU. *anado(ru), anazu(ru)* despise, make light of. *anado(ri)* contempt, scorn.

7 言 *bugen* insult

10 辱 *bujoku* insult, contempt; slight; humiliation

14 慢 *buman* contempt, insult, offense

蔑 *bubetsu* contempt, scorn, slight

A **価** 188 / J3241 / M628' **價** 316 / J512b / M1163 KA. *atai* price, cost, value, worth. *atai suru* be worth, merit; cost, be valued at.

10 値 *kachi* value, merit

値有 *kachia(ru)* valuable

値高 *kachitaka(i)* valuable

格 *kakaku* price, cost, value

格表 *kakakuhyō* price list

格差 *kakakusa* price margin

18 額 *kagaku* valuation, amount

A **舎** 189 / J3c4b / M30278' **舍** 4918 / J6752 / M30278 SEKI. SHA inn; hut, house, mansion.

5 兄 *shakei* my elder brother

6 宅 *shataku* residence

7 弟 *shatei* my younger brother

利 *shari* bones of the Buddha or a saint

利別 *sharibetsu* syrup

利塩 *sharien* Epsom salts, magnesium sulfate

12 営 *shaei* billeting, quarters

14 監 *shakan* dormitory director; dormitory inspector

B **併** 190 / J4a3b / M561 **倂** 224 / J-X / M746 HEI. *awa(saru) vi* get together, unite. *awa(seru) vt* put together, unite. *awa(sete)* collectively, altogether; in addition, besides; at the same time. *shika(shi)* however, but. *shika(mo)* moreover, furthermore, nevertheless, and yet.

5 用 *heiyō suru, awa(se)-mochi(iru)* use jointly, use at the same time

乍 *shika(shi)naga(ra)* however

6 合 *heigō* annexation, merger, absorption

考 *awa(se)-kanga(eru)* consider together

有 *heiyū suru* own together; combine

行 *heikō* parallel

行線 *heikōsen* parallel railways

7 呑 *heidon* annexation, merger, swallowing up

9 発 *heihatsu* complications (in illness)

発症 *heihatsushō* complications (in illness)

10 起 *heiki suru* occur simultaneously

進 *heishin suru* advance together

称 *heishō suru* classify together
記 *heiki suru* line up together (in writing)
殺 *heisatsu* double play (in baseball)
13 置 *heichi* juxtaposition, placing side by side

B **依** 191 / J304d / M607 I. E. *yo(ru)* depend on. *yo(tte)* therefore, consequently. *(ni) yo(ri)* due to, depending on.
6 存 *izon, ison* dependence, reliance
7 估地 *ikoji* obstinacy, stubbornness
估贔屓 *ekohiiki* favoritism, partiality, prejudice, bias
8 拠 *ikyo* dependence
10 託 *itaku* dependence (on someone)
12 然 *izen toshite* still, as yet, as of old
15 嘱 *ishoku suru* entrust with
16 頼 *irai* request; trust; dependence
頼心 *iraishin* spirit of dependence
頼状 *iraijō* written request
19 願 *igan* in accordance with one's request
願免官 *igan menkan* retirement at one's own request

B **侍** 192 / J3b78 / M589 Jɪ. *habe(ru), ji(suru)* wait upon, serve. *samurai* warrior, samurai.
3 女 *jijo* lady attendant, a lady in waiting
5 立 *jiritsu suru* assist (a dignitary)
史 *jishi* private secretary; respectfully
6 臣 *jishin* courtier, attendant
気質 *samurai katagi* samurai spirit
7 医 *jii* court physician
8 者 *jisha* attendant, valet; altar boy
10 従 *jijū* chamberlain
従長 *jijūchō* grand chamberlain
従官 *jijūkan* chamberlain
従武官 *jijū bukan* emperor's aide-de-camp
従職 *jijūshoku* board of chamberlains
11 婢 *jihi* lady in waiting
13 僧 *jisō* acolyte
14 読 *jidoku* imperial tutor
15 衛 *jiei* bodyguard
衛長 *jieichō* captain of the guard
17 講 *jikō* imperial tutor

A **例** 193 / J4e63 / M587 Rᴇɪ custom, usage, precedent; case, example, parallel, illustration. *tato(eru)* compare to, speak figuratively, illustrate. *tatoe* parable, illustration, figure of speech. *tato(eba)* for example. *tameshi* instance, example, case, precedent, an experience.
4 文 *reibun* model sentence
日 *reijitsu* week day, ordinary day; appointed day
月 *reigetsu* every month
5 示 *reiji* illustration
外 *reigai* exception. *reigai na* exceptional
外無 *reigai na(ku)* without exception
6 式 *reishiki* regular ceremony, established form
会 *reikai* regular meeting
年 *reinen* normal year, average year; every year, annually
年祭 *reinensai* annual festival
7 言 *reigen* preface, foreword
8 刻 *reikoku* the regular time
10 時 *reiji* the usual time
11 規 *reiki* established rule
祭 *reisai* regular festival, annual festival
12 証 *reishō* illustration, example
13 解 *reikai* illustration, example
話 *reiwa* illustration
数 *reisū* number of cases
18 題 *reidai* example, exercises (in a textbook)

B **佳** 194 / J3242 / M557 Kᴀ beautiful; good; excellent. *i(i), yo(i), yo(shi)* good, good-natured; pleasing; precious; noble; lovely, beautiful, fine; lucky; efficacious; right; suitable; justifiable; appropriate, satisfactory; better; all right; unnecessary; no objection; intimate, friendly; easy; well; desirous.
2 人 *kajin* a beautiful woman
4 月 *kagetsu* a good month; bright moon
木 *kaboku* beautiful trees
什 *kajū* excellent poem
5 句 *kaku* beautiful passage of literature
7 言 *kagen* good words
辰 *kashin* lucky day, happy day, auspicious occasion
作 *kasaku* a good piece of work
良 *karyō na* good, favorable, successful
8 例 *karei* a good example
味 *kami* delicious taste
肴 *kakō* delicacy, rare treat; good-eating fish

9 品 *kahin* choice article
客 *kakyaku* a good visitor
10 酒 *kashu* good wine; a good drink
宴 *kaen* congratulatory banquet
容 *kayō* comely face
12 景 *kakei* beautiful view
13 話 *kawa* good story
節 *kasetsu* auspicious occasion
14 境 *kakyō* climax (of a story)
15 趣 *kashu* good taste; a good impression
編 *kahen* an outstanding poem
調 *kachō* good tune
賓 *kahin* good guest, interesting guest
篇 *kahen* an outstanding poem
19 麗 *karei* beauty
20 醸 *kajō* sweet saké; good wine

A **供** 195 / J3621 / M605 KYŌ. KU. GU. *kyō(suru)* offer, present, submit; serve (a meal); supply. *sona(eru)* offer, sacrifice, dedicate. *(o)tomo suru* accompany. *(o)sona(e)* offering. *tomo* attendant, companion, retinue.

2 人 *tomobito* companion
3 与 *kyōyo suru* give, furnish, provide
5 出 *kyōshutsu* delivery
出米 *kyōshutsumai* (farmers') rice deliveries
6 米 *kumai* rice offered to a god
回 *tomomawa(ri)* retinue, suite
7 応 *kyōō* treat, feast, banquet
述 *kyōjutsu* affidavit, deposition, testimony
述者 *kyōjutsusha* deponent, testifier
述書 *kyōjutsusho* affidavit, deposition, testimony
8 物 *kumotsu, sona(e)mono* an offering
物台 *kumotsudai* alter
9 待 *tomoma(chi)* attendant's waiting room
10 進 *gushin* giving offerings
料 *kyōryō* an offering
宴 *kyōen* banquet, dinner
託 *kyōtaku* deposit
託金 *kyōtakukin* deposit of money
託物 *kyōtakubutsu* something deposited
託者 *kyōtakusha* depositor
11 祭 *gusai* offerings; offerings and worship
12 御 *kugo, gugo* emperor's meal
揃 *tomozoroi* attendants, retinue
給 *kyōkyū* supply
給地 *kyōkyūchi* supply center
給者 *kyōkyūsha* supplier
給源 *kyōkyūgen* source of supply
給路 *kyōkyūro* supply route
15 養 *kuyō* memorial service
養塔 *kuyōtō* memorial tower
養塚 *kuyōzuka* unknown person's grave
16 覧 *kyōran* display, show

A **使** 196 / J3b48 / M573 SHI use; messenger. *tsuka(u)* use; handle, manipulate; employ; need, want; spend, consume; speak (English), practice (fencing); take (one's lunch); circulate (bad money). *tsuka(i) suru* go as an envoy. *tsuka(eru)* useful, serviceable. *tsuka(wasu)* send, dispatch; give, donate, bestow on; do for (someone). *tsuka(i-konasu)* handle (men); master (a tool); acquire a command of (a language). *-shi(mu)* old causative verbal ending. *tsuka(i)* mission, errand, message; messenger, bearer; trainer, tamer; familiar spirit.

2 丁 *shitei* servant, janitor, messenger
4 手 *tsuka(i)te* user, consumer; employer; prodigal, spendthrift; fencing master
方 *tsuka(i)kata* how to use, treatment, management (of help)
込 *tsuka(i)-ko(mu)* embezzle; accustom oneself to using
切 *tsuka(i)-ki(ru)* use up, exhaust, wear out
分 *tsuka(i)wa(ke)* proper use. *tsuka(i)-wa(keru)* use properly
5 立 *tsuka(i)da(te)* causing you trouble
処 *tsuka(i)dokoro* use
旧 *tsuka(i)-furu(su)* wear out (something)
古 *tsuka(i)-furu(su)* wear out (something)
出 *tsuka(i)de* lasting quality, good wearing
用 *shiyō suru* employ, use, utilize
用人 *shiyōnin* employee, servant
用例 *shiyōrei* examples showing the use (of a word)
用法 *shiyōhō* use, directions
用者 *shiyōsha* user, consumer
用価値 *shiyō kachi* utility value
用料 *shiyōryō* rent, hire
用量 *shiyōryō* amount used

用権 *shiyōken* use, right to use
6 臣 *shishin* envoy
尽 *tsuka(i)-tsuku(su)* use up, squander
先 *tsuka(i)saki* the place where one is sent on an errand
7 役 *shieki suru* employ, use, set to word; enslave
役動詞 *shieki dōshi* causative verb
8 所 *tsuka(i)dokoro* use
物 *tsuka(i)mono* gift; bribe; usable article
歩 *tsuka(i)aru(ki)* running errands
果 *tsuka(i)-hata(su)* use up, squander
者 *shisha* messenger; envoy
命 *shimei* mission, errand; message
命者 *shimeisha* messenger
9 途 *shito* purpose for which money is spent; the way money is spent
10 残 *tsuka(i)noko(ri), tsuka(i)noko(shi)* remnant, remainder, odds and ends, leavings
料 *tsuka(i)ryō* use
徒 *shito* apostle, disciple
徒行伝 *Shitogyōden* Acts of the Apostles
徒承伝 *shito shōden* apostolic succession
徒信条 *Shito Shinjō* Apostles' Creed
徒信教 *Shito Shinkyō* Apostles' Creed
徒書 *Shitosho* the Epistles (of the New Testament)
徒書簡 *Shito Shokan* the Epistles (of the New Testament)
徒達 *Shitotachi* the Apostles
徒継承 *shito keishō* apostolic succession
11 過 *tsuka(i)-su(giru)* use excessively, use too much; spend too much; overwork someone
道 *tsuka(i)michi* use
頃 *tsuka(i)goro* handy
13 聘 *shihei* exchange of diplomatic representatives
賃 *tsuka(i)chin* messenger tip or charge
節 *shisetsu* envoy; embassy, mission; delegate
節団 *shisetsudan* mission, delegation
14 嗾 *shisō* instigation, incitement
慣 *tsuka(i)-na(rasu)* accustom oneself to using; train; break in (horses). *tsuka(i)-na(reru)* get accustomed to using
様 *tsuka(i)yō* how to use

7

侮 197 / J-X / M630 See **侮** 187.

俞 198 / J5141 / M1437 Yu affirmative response. *shika(ri)* yes, that is correct. [入]

俔 199 / J5057 / M686 Ken *tato(eru)* compare, speak figuratively. *tatoe* metaphor, simile. *ukaga(u)* inquire.

俤 200 / J505f / M719 (国字) *omokage* visage, face; trace, shadow; memory.

俥 201 / J5060 / M720 (国字) *kuruma* jinricksha.

俣 202 / J4b73 / M718 (国字) *mata* crotch, thigh, groin.

俟 203 / J5058 / M705 Shi. *ma(tsu)* *vi* and *vt* wait, wait for; expect, watch for; depend on; treat, deal with.

俏 204 / J-X / M680 Shō. *yatsu(su)* disguise oneself as; adorn oneself; pine away; act shamefully; abbreviate (a character).

侶 205 / J3e37 / M647 Ryo. Ro. *tomo* companion, follower.
7 伴 *ryohan* companion

俑 206 / J505c / M683 Yō figure buried with the dead.
7 作 *yō (wo) tsuku(ru)* create a bad precedent

俛 207 / J505b / M700 Fu. Ben *fuse(ru)* turn over, lay face down.
6 仰 *fugyō suru* look up and down

俐 208 / J505e / M682 **悧** 1856 / J5826 / M10689 Ri clever.
5 巧 *rikō* cleverness, wisdom, intelligence
9 発 *rihatsu* cleverness, wisdom, intelligence

俎 209 / J5059 / M679 **爼** 3519 / J602c / M19743 So altar of sacrifice. *manaita* chopping board.
3 上 *sojō* on the chopping board
8 板 *manaita* chopping board

俘 210 / J505a / M697 Fu. *toriko* captive.
13 虜 *furyo* captive, prisoner of war
虜収容所 *furyo shūyōjo* concentration camp

B **侯** 211 / J3874 / M633 Kō marquis; lord, daimyo.
7 伯 *kōhaku* nobles; feudal lords
8 国 *kōkoku* principality
17 爵 *kōshaku* marquis, marquess
爵夫人 *kōshaku fujin* marchioness

B **促** 212 / J4225 / M664 Soku. Saku. *unaga(su)* urge, press, demand; stimulate; quicken; incite; invite (attention to).
6 成 *sokusei* growth promotion
成栽培 *sokusei saibai* raising out-of-season crops with artificial heat
9 音 *sokuon* assimilated obstruent sound (represented by つ [*tsu*] in Japanese)
10 進 *sokushin suru* promote, encourage, facilitate, accelerate, spur on
進剤 *sokushinzai* accelerant, stimulant

侠 213 / J-X / M706 Kyō chivalry. *kyan* tomboy, bobby soxer, flapper.
3 女 *kyōjo* gallant woman
6 気 *kyōki, otokogi,* chivalrous spirit
9 客 *kyōkaku, otokodate* one who champions the underdog
勇 *kyōyū* gallantry, chivalry
10 骨 *kyōkotsu* chivalrous spirit

俚 214 / J505d / M699 Ri rustic, ill-mannered.
6 耳 *riji* the ears of the public
7 言 *rigen* slang, dialect
14 語 *rigo* slang, dialect
16 謡 *riyō* ballad, folk song, popular song
諺 *rigen* proverb, saying

俄 215 / J3264 / M665 Ga. *niwaka* sudden, abrupt, unexpected; improvised, offhand.
4 分限 *niwaka bugen* overnight millionaire
5 仕込 *niwakajiko(mi)* hasty preparation
仕立 *niwakajita(te)* extemporary, improvised
6 成金 *niwaka narikin* overnight millionaire
8 雨 *niwaka ame* shower
盲 *niwaka mekura* sudden blindness; one suddenly blinded
9 造 *niwakazuku(ri)* makeshift, improvised
10 勉強 *niwuka benkyō* cramming
12 然 *gazen* suddenly, abruptly
景気 *niwakageiki* temporary boom

B **俊** 216 / J3d53 / M674 Shun excellence, genius.
3 士 *shunshi* a genius
才 *shunsai* genius; talented person, prodigy
7 足 *shunsoku* swift horse, talented person
抜 *shumbatsu* uncommon, above average
秀 *shunshū* genius; talented man, prodigy
8 英 *shun'ei* excellence; genius
10 馬 *shumme, shumba* swift horse
逸 *shun'itsu* excellence, genius
敏 *shumbin na* keen, quick-witted
11 偉 *shun'i* large and excellent
12 傑 *shunketsu* a genius, hero
童 *shundō* precocious child
14 徳 *shuntoku* great virtue
豪 *shungō* talent; a man of outstanding learning and virtue
15 賢 *shunken* excellent wisdom

A **係** 217 / J3738 / M663 Kei. *kakari, -gakari* duty; person in charge. *kaka(waru)* concern oneself in, have to do with; affect, influence; stick to (opinions). *kaka(ru)* is the work of. *kaka(wari)* relation, connection. *ka(karu) vi* hang on, be suspended from, be caught, be trapped; be built; begin; arrive at; require, cost; play against, oppose; be splashed; weigh (a pound); be levied; (the instrument or tool) works; attack, fall on; is now showing at; consult; depend (on a son); concern, affect, involve.
6 合 *kaka(ri)a(i)* unfortunate relationship
争 *keisō* dispute, contention
争物 *keisōbutsu* the legal point of contention

2 二 亠 【人 7 イ 𠆢】 儿 入 八 ソ 冂 冖 冫 几 凵 刀 刂 力 勹 匕 匚 匸 十 卜 卩 厂 厶 又

8 長 *kakarichō* chief clerk
官 *kaka(ri)kan* official in charge
10 員 *kaka(ri)in* clerk in charge
留 *keiryū* mooring, anchorage
11 船 *keisen* mooring a ship
累 *keirui* encumbrances, dependents; implication, complicity
12 属 *keizoku* relationship
13 数 *keisū* coefficient (in math)

B **侵** 218 / J3f2f / M646 SHIN. *oka(su)* invade, raid; violate, trespass, intrude on.
2 入 *shinnyū* invasion, raid, aggression, trespass
入者 *shinnyūsha* invader, trespasser, raider
入軍 *shinnyūgun* invading army
4 水 *shinsui* inundation, flood, submersion; leaking
5 犯 *shimpan* invasion, violation, infringement
9 食 *shinshoku* erosion; corrosion
10 害 *shingai* infringement, violation, trespass, impairment
11 掠 *shinryaku* aggression, invasion, raid
寇 *shinkō* invasion
略 *shinryaku* aggression, invasion, raid
略国 *shinryakukoku* aggressor nation
略的 *shinryakuteki* aggressive
略者 *shinryakusha* aggressor, invader
略軍 *shinryakugun* invading army
略戦争 *shinryaku sensō* aggressive war
15 蝕 *shinshoku* erosion; corrosion
撃 *shingeki suru* invade and attack

A **便** 219 / J4a58 / M659 BEN convenience, facility; excreta, stools; evacuation. BIN chance; mail, letter. *ben(jiru), ben(zuru)* will do, answer the purpose, make convenient. *tayo(ru)* rely on, have recourse to. *tayo(ri)* news, tidings; connection. *yosuga* way, means.
6 衣 *ben'i* convenient clothes, ordinary clothes
衣隊 *ben'itai* plainclothes soldiers, mufti corps
7 利 *benri na* convenient, handy, useful
利屋 *benriya* expressman, handyman, utility person
8 所 *benjo* lavatory, latrine, comfort station, toilet
法 *bempō* handy method, shortcut, expedient
服 *bempuku* civilian clothes
宜 *bengi* convenience, accommodation, advantage, expedience
宜上 *bengijō* for convenience sake
宜主義 *bengi shugi* opportunism, expediency
9 便 *bemben(taru)* protuberant, paunchy. *bemben to* idly
通 *bentsū* bowel movement
乗 *binjō* taking advantage of a ride or an opportunity, taking a ship
乗主義者 *binjō shugisha* opportunist
乗者 *binjōsha* hitchhiker; one who catches a ride (with a friend)
10 座 *benza* toilet seat
益 *ben'eki* convenience; benefit, profit
秘 *bempi* constipation
11 船 *binsen* available steamer
12 壺 *ben tsubo* night soil container
13 意 *ben'i* call of nature, bowel-movement inclination
14 箋 *binsen* stationery, writing paper
管 *benkan* sewer pipe
15 器 *benki* toilet; bedpan, chamber pot, urinal
16 覧 *benran* manual, handbook, compendium

B **俗** 220 / J422f / M695 ZOKU customs, manners; the world; worldliness; vulgarity; mundane things; the laity. *zoku(ppoi)* cheap (reading); vulgar, worldly-minded.
2 人 *zokujin* layman; worldling
3 才 *zokusai* worldly wisdom; practical wisdom
4 化 *zokka suru* vulgarize, secularize, popularize
文 *zokubun* colloquial style
文学 *zokubungaku* popular literature
5 用 *zokuyō* worldly matters
世 *zokusei* this world, earthly life
世界 *zokusekai* everyday world
世間 *zokuseken* the workaday world
6 耳 *zokuji* vulgar ears, attention of the masses
気 *zokki, zokke* vulgarity, worldliness, worldly ambition
向 *zokumu(ki)* popular (literature)
曲 *zokkyoku* folk song, ballad
字 *zokuji* popular characters; nonstandard characters

名 *zokumei* popular name; common name; secular name; bad reputation. *zokumyō* secular name
吏 *zokuri* petty official
7 見 *zokken* popular view, laymen's opinion
言 *zokugen* colloquial language
体 *zokutai* condition of the (Buddhist) laity
形 *zokugyō* the figure of the common man
8 姓 *zokusei* (a priest's) secular surname
物 *zokubutsu* worldly-minded person, vulgar person
念 *zokunen* worldliness, worldly ambition, unholy desires
受 *zokuu(ke)* popular appeal
事 *zokuji* worldly affairs; daily routine
9 界 *zokkai* secular life, workaday world
臭 *zokushū* vulgarity, worldly-mindedness
10 流 *zokuryū* populace, common run of men; worldly customs
称 *zokushō* popular name, common name
書 *zokusho* cheap fiction
11 情 *zokujō* worldly-mindedness; worldly affairs
眼 *zokugan* popular opinion
務 *zokumu* secular affairs, worldly cares, daily routine
悪 *zokuaku* worldliness, vulgarity, coarseness
累 *zokurui* worldly troubles; worldliness
習 *zokushū* custom, usage
12 間 *zokkan* the world; the public
衆 *zokushū* people, crowd, masses, the public
13 僧 *zokusō* a worldly priest
解 *zokkai* explanation in common language
話 *zokuwa* worldly story; gossip
楽 *zokugaku* secular music; popular music
14 塵 *zokujin* the world, earthly affairs
語 *zokugo* colloquial language; colloquialism
説 *zokusetsu* common saying, popular version; folklore, tradition
歌 *zokka* popular song, folk song, ditty, ballad
15 縁 *zokuen* worldly connection
調 *zokuchō* popular music, vulgar music
論 *zokuron* popular opinion
談 *zokudan* common talk, worldly conversation
輩 *zokuhai* worldlings, the crowd
趣味 *zokushumi* vulgar taste
16 儒 *zokuju* mediocre scholar
諦 *zokutai* simplified (Buddhist) teaching
謡 *zokuyō* popular song, folk song, ballad, ditty
諺 *zokugen* proverb, popular saying
20 議 *zokugi* popular opinion

A **信** 221 / J3f2e / M707 SHIN truth; faith, fidelity, sincerity; trust, confidence, reliance. *shin(jiru), shin(zuru)* believe; believe in; place trust in, confide in, have faith in. *makoto* sincerity, fidelity, devotion.
4 込 *shin(ji)-ko(mu)* believe implicitly. *shin(ji)-ko(masu)* lead to believe
天翁 *shinten'ō, ahōdori* albatross
心 *shinjin* faith, belief, devotion, godliness
心家 *shinjinka* pious man, religionist
心深 *shinjimbuka(i)* deeply religious, devout, godly, faithful
5 玄袋 *shingembukuro* cloth bag with reinforced bottom and drawstring
号 *shingō* signal, semaphore; signaling
号手 *shingōshu* flag man
号灯 *shingoto* signal light
号所 *shingōjo* signal station
号塔 *shingōtō* signal tower
号電波 *shingō dempa* beam (signal)
号旗 *shingoki* signal flag
号機 *shingōki* signal, semaphore
用 *shin'yō* confidence, trust, faith; dependence, reliance; belief, credence; credit
用状 *shin'yōjō* letter of credit
用状態 *shin'yō jōtai* credit standing
用取引 *shin'yō torihiki* credit transaction
用取引先 *shin'yō torihikisaki* charge customer
用協同組合 *shin'yō kyōdō kumiai* cooperative credit association
用借 *shin'yōga(ri)* debt of honor
用組合 *shin'yō kumiai* credit association

用貸 *shin'yōga(shi)* loans without collateral
用詐欺 *shin'yō sagi* confidence game
6 伏 *shimpuku suru* be convinced
任 *shinnin* trust, confidence, credence
任状 *shinninjō* credentials
任投票 *shinnin tōhyō* vote of confidence
7 任統治制度 *shinnin tōchi seido* trusteeship system
仰 *shinkō* belief, creed; religious faith
仰生活 *shinkō seikatsu* a life of faith; religious life
仰告白 *shinkō kokuhaku* profession of faith
仰的 *shinkōteki* religious, spiritual
仰者 *shinkōsha* believer, devotee
仰深 *shinkōbuka(i)* devout
仰箇条 *shinkō kajō* articles of faith
7 条 *shinjō* article of faith, creed, belief
8 服 *shimpuku suru* be convinced
念 *shinnen* belief, faith, conviction
実 *shinjitsu* sincerity, honesty, truth, faithfulness
受 *shinju suru* believe, accept (truths)
者 *shinja* believer, devotee, adherent; Christian
奉 *shimpō* belief, faith
奉者 *shimpōsha* adherent, devotee, believer
9 約 *shin'yaku* vow, promise
10 倚 *shinki* reliance, trust, confidence
書 *shinsho* letter, personal correspondence
徒 *shinto* layman, believer, adherent, follower, laity
徒伝道 *shinto dendō* lay evangelism
徒伝道者 *shinto dendōsha* lay missionary
託 *shintaku* trust; entrusting
託会社 *shintakugaisha* trust company
託投資 *shintaku tōshi* trust investment
託契約 *shintaku keiyaku* trust agreement
託統治 *shintaku tōchi* trusteeship
託業 *shintakugyō* trust business
託資金 *shintaku shikin* trust fund
11 経 *shinkyō* creed
望 *shimbō* confidence, popularity
教 *shinkyō* religion, faith, belief
教自由 *shinkyō (no) jiyū* religious liberty, liberty of conscience
12 愛 *shin'ai suru* love and believe in
義 *shingi* faith, fidelity, loyalty
14 認 *shinnin* acknowledge, acceptance, admission
管 *shinkan* fuse
疑 *shingi* belief or doubt
15 賞必罰 *shinshō-hitsubatsu* sure penalty and certain rewards
16 憑 *shimpyō* trust, credit, credence
憑性 *shimpyōsei* authenticity, credibility
頼 *shinrai* reliance, trust, confidence
頼性 *shinraisei* credibility, authenticity
頼為合 *shinraishi-a(u)* enjoy each other's confidence
頼感 *shinraikan* feeling of trust

A **保** 222 / J4a5d / M702 Ho. Hō. *ho(suru)* guarantee. *tamo(tsu)* keep, preserve, hold, retain, maintain; support, sustain; last, endure, keep well (food), wear well, be durable.

5 母 *hobo* kindergarten teacher
母養成所 *hobo yōseijo* kindergarten teacher institute
6 合 *mo(chi)a-(u)* maintain equilibrium; share expenses. *tamo(chi)a(i)* interdependence, steadiness. *mo(chi)a(i)* interdependence
存 *hozon* preservation, conservation, storage, maintenance
全 *hozen* integrity; preservation, conservation
全会 *hozenkai* (family) corporation
全会社 *hozen kaisha* (family) corporation
安 *hoan* peace preservation, security
安林 *hoanrin* forest reserve
安要員 *hoan yōin* mine guards (during a strike)
有 *hoyū* possession, retention, maintenance
有米 *hoyūmai* rice holdings
有者 *hoyūsha* owner
守 *hoshu* conservatism
守主義 *hoshu shugi* conservatism
守的 *hoshuteki* conservative
守党 *hoshutō* conservative party, the Right, Tories
7 身 *hoshin* self-protection
身術 *hoshinjutsu* art of self-protection
8 姆 *hobo* kindergarten teacher
育 *hoiku suru* nurse, nurture, rear
育所 *hoikujo* nursery school, nursery

育園 *hoikuen* nursery school, day nursery
9 持 *hoji* maintenance, preservation
持者 *hojisha* holder (of a record)
10 留 *horyū suru* reserve, defer
険 *hoken* insurance, guarantee
険付 *hokenzu(ki)* guaranteed; insured
険会社 *hokengaisha* insurance company
険医 *hoken'i* insurance doctor
険金 *hokenkin* insurance money
険金受取人 *hokenkin uketorinin* beneficiary
険料 *hokenryō* insurance premium
11 菌者 *hokinsha* germ carrier
釈 *hoshaku* bail
釈金 *hoshakukin* bail
健 *hoken* health preservation, hygiene, sanitation
健医 *hoken'i* public-health doctor
健所 *hokenjo* health center
健婦 *hokenfu* public-health nurse
12 温 *hoon* keeping warm; heat insulation
税 *hozei* customs bond
税倉庫 *hozei sōko* bonded warehouse
証 *hoshō* guarantee, security, pledge
証人 *hoshōnin* guarantor, bondsman
証牛乳 *hoshō gyūnyū* certified milk
証付 *hoshōtsu(ki)* guaranteed, certified
証金 *hoshōkin* security money, bond, deposit
13 障 *hoshō* guarantee, security
14 管 *hokan* custody, deposit, storage
管人 *hokannin* custodian, trustee
管会社 *hokangaisha* safety-deposit company
管物 *hokambutsu* goods in custody, property in trust
管金 *hokankin* money on deposit
管林 *hokanrin* managed forest
管料 *hokanryō* custody fee, storage charge
管証 *hokanshō* certificate of custody
15 線 *hosen* track maintenance
養 *hoyō* health preservation; recuperation; recreation
養地 *hoyōchi* health resort
養所 *hoyōsho* sanatorium
養院 *hoyōin* sanatorium
20 護 *hogo* care, shelter, protection; favor, patronage
護色 *hogoshoku* protective coloration
護金 *hogokin* subsidy
護国 *hogokoku* protectorate
護者 *hogosha* protector, guardian, patron
護委員 *hogo iin* rehabilitation worker
護鳥 *hogochō* protected bird
護税 *hogozei* protective duty
護検束 *hogo kensoku* protective arrest
護貿易 *hogo bōeki* protective trade
護領 *hogoryō* protectorate
護関税 *hogo kanzei* protective tariff
護関税率 *hogo kanzeiritsu* protective tariff
護観察 *hogo kansatsu* probation

8

倅 223/J5066/M750 See 伜 128.

併 224/J-X/M746 See 併 190.

倣 225/J-X/M725 See 傚 280.

倪 226/J5064/M792 GEI stare.

倢 227/J-X/M784 SHŌ fast, speedy.

倖 228/J3876/M771 KŌ happiness, luck.

倆 229/J506f/M751 RYŌ skill.

倩 230/J506a/M791 SEN. *tsuratsura* carefully, attentively, profoundly.

倏 231/J6047/M762 SHUKU sudden; shine. *tachimachi* immediately, suddenly.

們 232/J506e/M766 MON, *-ra* plural ending, and others. *tomogara* fellows, set, group.

倬 233/J506b/M794 TAKU large; superior; clear.

俾 234 J506c M740 Hɪ manage. *-shi(mu)* causative ending. Hᴇɪ stare. glare at.

B **倣** 235 J4a6f M785 Hō. *nara(u)* imitate, follow, emulate.

俶 236 J5068 M732 Sʜᴜᴋᴜ. Tᴇᴋɪ begin, excel. *yo(i)* good, pleasing; precious, noble; lovely, beautiful.
12 装 *shukusō* dress

倘 237 J-X M774 Sʜō if; dullness.
8 佯 *shōyō* wandering

倥 238 J5065 M787 Kō boorish; urgent.
11 傯 *kōsō* hurrying

倔 239 J5063 M769 Kᴜᴛsᴜ stubborn.
11 強 *kukkyō* strong health. *kukkyō na* strong, sturdy, stalwart, robust, burly, able-bodied

俺 240 J3236 M736 Eɴ. *ore* I.
12 等 *oira* I; we. *orera* we

倨 241 J5062 M790 Kʏᴏ pride; squatting with legs outstretched. *ogo(ru)* be proud.
13 傲 *kyogō* pride, arrogance

倭 242 J4f41 M796 Wᴀ *Yamato* ancient Japan.
2 人 *wajin* (an old word for) a Japanese
11 寇 *wakō* Japanese pirates

A **俵** 243 J4936 M730 Hʏō bag, bale, sack; bag counter. *tawara* straw bag.
8 物 *tawaramono* goods in straw bags
13 数 *hyōsū* number of straw bags

倚 244 J5061 M776 I. Kɪ. *yo(ru)* lean on, rest against.
3 子 *isu* chair, couch, seat; office, position
20 懸 *yo(ri)-ka(karu)* lean on, recline on; rely on

倶 245 J3666 M724 Gᴜ. Kᴜ. *tomo ni* both; alike; together, along with, including.
8 舎 *Kusha* Buddhist sect originating in the seventh century
9 発 *guhatsu* concurrence
13 楽部 *kurabu* club, fraternity, sorority; clubhouse

B **倫** 246 J4e51 M793 Rɪɴ companion.
11 理 *rinri* ethics, morals
理的 *rinriteki* ethical
理学 *rinrigaku* ethics, moral philosophy

倡 247 J5069 M783 Sʜō actor.
8 佯 *shōyō* wandering
和 *shōwa* cheering in chorus
11 婦 *shōfu* prostitute, harlot

B **倹** 248 J3770 M823 **儉** 315 J512d M1190 Kᴇɴ economy. *tsuma(shii)* thrifty, economical.
9 約 *ken'yaku* economy, frugality
約家 *ken'yakuka* thrifty person; economist
10 素 *kenso* economical and simple

B **俸** 249 J4a70 M734 Hō salary.
12 給 *hōkyū* salary, pay
給日 *hōkyūbi* pay day
給生活者 *hōkyū-seikatsusha* salaried man
給袋 *hōkyūbukuro* pay envelope
13 禄 *hōroku* retainer's stipend, pay, salary
禄米 *hōrokumai* rice allowance

A **候** 250 J3875 M775 Kō season, weather. *sōrō* classical verbal ending equivalent to colloquial *-masu.*
4 文 *sōrōbun* epistolary style
11 鳥 *kōchō* bird of passage, migratory bird
12 補 *kōho* candidacy
補生 *kōhosei* cadet
補地 *kōhochi* proposed site; site chosen
補者 *kōhosha* candidate, applicant

倦 251 J3771 M788 Kᴇɴ. *u(mu), aki(ru), agu(mu)* get tired of, lose interest in.

[9] 怠 *kentai* fatigue, weariness, boredom
怠期 *kentaiki* the stage of fatigue
怠感 *kentaikan* a washed-out feeling
[10] 疲 *u(mi)-tsuka(reru)* grow weary, get tired of
[14] 厭 *ken'en* weariness
[15] 撓 *u(mazu)-tayu(mazu)* untiringly, assiduously
[16] 憊 *kempai* extreme fatigue

A **倍** 252 J475c M760 BAI double, twice; times, -fold. *bai(suru) vi* and *vt* double, be doubled; increase.
[3] 大 *baidai* double size
[5] 旧 *baikyū no* redoubled, increased
加 *baika* doubling
[9] 音 *baion* overtone, harmonic
[11] 率 *bairitsu* magnification, magnifying power
[13] 数 *baisū* multiple
[14] 増 *baima(shi), baizō* doubling
[18] 額 *baigaku* double amount

俯 253 J506d M722 FU. *fu(su)* bend down, bow down, lie prostrate. *utsumu(keru)* turn upside down; turn (face) downward. *utsumu(ku)* look downward, stoop.
[6] 向 *utsumu(keru)* turn upside down; turn (face) downward. *utsumu(ku)* look downward, stoop. *utsumu(ke), utsumu(ki)* lying face down; upside down
伏 *utsubu(su)* lie on one's face. *fufuku* prostration
仰 *fugyō* looking up and down; actions; being obliging
仰角 *fugyōkaku* angle of elevation
[7] 角 *fukaku* angle of dip
[17] 瞰 *fukan suru* command a view of
瞰図 *fukanzu* bird's-eye view

A **俳** 254 J4750 M726 HAI actor.
[2] 人 *haijin* a haiku poet
[4] 文 *haibun* prose with a poetic haiku flavor
友 *haiyū* (haiku) poetry pals
[5] 句 *haiku* 17-syllable poem in three lines of five, seven, and five syllables; *hokku*
号 *haigō* pseudonym of a haiku poet
[6] 名 *haimei, haimyō* a haiku poet's pen name
[8] 味 *haimi* subdued taste, refined taste; a haiku (poetic) flavor
画 *haiga* briefly drawn picture, haiku picture
[9] 徊 *haikai* loitering, sauntering. *motō(ru)* wander around
[13] 聖 *haisei* famous haiku poet; the poet Bashō
[16] 壇 *haidan* the world of the haiku
諧 *haikai* 17- syllable poem, haiku; humorous haiku
諧師 *haikaishi* writer of *haikai* poems
[17] 優 *haiyū* actor, actress, player

A **倉** 255 J4152 M756 SŌ storehouse. *kura* warehouse, godown; cellar; depository, treasury; granary, elevator.
[2] 入 *kurai(re)* warehousing
[5] 主 *kuranushi* warehouse owner
出 *kurada(shi)* releasing stored goods
[7] 作 *kurazuku(ri)* warehouse style
[10] 荷 *kurani* warehouse goods
庫 *sōko* storehouse, godown; magazine
庫会社 *sōkogaisha* warehousing company
庫業 *sōkogyō* warehousing business
[12] 渡 *kurawata(shi)* ex-warehouse
[15] 敷 *kurashiki* storage charges
敷料 *kurashikiryō* storage charges
[16] 廩 *sōrin* rice granary

B **倒** 256 J455d M767 TŌ. *tao(reru), ko(keru)* fall, collapse, drop; break down, die, succumb to; fall senseless; be ruined; have a bad debt. *tao(su)* bring down, throw down, blow down, fell, knock down, trip up; defeat; ruin, overthrow; kill; leave unpaid; cheat. *tao(re)* bad debt. *saka(sa), saka(sama), saka(shima)* reverse, inversion, upside down.
[6] 死 *tōshi* dying by the wayside
伏 *tao(re)-fu(su)* fall down
[8] 事 *sakasamagoto* wrong order
[11] 産 *tōsan* insolvency, bankruptcy
[13] 睫 *sakasa matsuge* turned-in eyelashes
幕 *tōbaku suru* overthrow the shogunate
置 *tōchi* turning things upside down; placing nonessentials before essentials
置法 *tōchihō* inversion of the word order in a sentence

14 閣 *tōkaku suru* overthrow the cabinet
像 *tōzō* inverted image
15 潰 *tōkai suru* collapse, be destroyed
影 *tōei* reflection
16 壊 *tōkai suru* collapse, be destroyed
錯 *tōsaku* perversion
20 懸 *tōken* hanging (someone) upside down

A **値** 257/J434d/M786 CHI *atai, ne* price, cost, value. *atai suru* value.
3 巾 *nehaba* price range, price fluctuation
下 *nesa(gari)* price decline. *nesa(ge)* price reduction
上 *nea(gari)* price advance, increase in value. *nea(ge)* price hike, markup
4 引 *nebiki* price reduction, discount
切 *negi(ru)* haggle, bargain
5 打 *neuchi* value, worth, price; dignity
6 安 *neyasu* cheapness
9 段 *nedan* price, cost
段付 *nedanzu(ke) suru* price at
段表 *nedanhyō* price list
段書 *nedanga(ki)* price list
11 遇 *chigū* meeting (someone)
頃 *negoro* reasonable price
動 *neugo(ki)* price fluctuation
12 幅 *nehaba* price range or fluctuation
14 増 *nemashi* price hike, markup
15 踏 *nebu(mi)* appraisal, estimation, evaluation
16 積 *nezumo(ri)* estimation, valuation
鞘 *nezaya* margin, spread (in prices)

A **個** 258/J3844/M758 **介** 25/J5024/M70 **ケ** 43/J2531/M-X
KA article counter. KO individual; article counter.
2 人 *kojin* private person, individual. *kojin no* personal, private, individual
人用 *kojin'yō* for personal use
人主義 *kojin shugi* individualism
人名 *kojimmei* personal name
人性 *kojinsei* individuality, personality, idiosyncrasy
人的 *kojinteki* individual, personal, self-centered
人指導 *kojin shidō* personal guidance, tutoring
人差 *kojinsa* individual differences; personal equation
人個人 *kojin-kojin* individual, one by one
人展 *kojinten* one-man exhibition, one-man show
人教授 *kojin kyōju* private instruction
人経営 *kojin keiei* private management
人誤差 *kojin gosa* personal equation
7 体 *kotai* an individual
別 *kobetsu* a particular case
別的 *kobetsuteki ni* individually
条 *kajō* article, clause, item
条書 *kajōgaki* itemization
8 性 *kosei* personality; individuality, idiosyncrasy
性的 *koseiteki* personal, individual
10 展 *koten* personal exhibition
個 *koko* one by one; individuals. *koko ni* individually, separately
個別別 *koko-betsubetsu* each one separately
13 数 *kosū* number of articles

A **借** 259/J3c5a/M781 SHA, SHAKU borrowing. *ka(riru), ka(ru)* borrow; have a loan; hire, rent. *ka(ri)* borrowing; debt; loan.
2 人 *karinin* borrower
入 *ka(ri)-i(reru)* borrow, rent, lease, charter. *karii(re)* debt
入金 *kariirekin* loan, debt
3 上 *ka(ri)-a(geru)* hire, lease, requisition, charter
4 手 *ka(ri)te* borrower, debtor; tenant
方 *ka(ri)kata* debtor; debit; way of borrowing
火 *ka(ri)bi* borrowing fire; borrowed fire
込 *ka(ri)-ko(mu)* borrow
切 *ka(ri)-ki(ru)* reserve. *ka(ri)ki(ri)* reserved (car)
5 主 *karinushi* borrower, debtor; tenant
出 *ka(ri)-da(su)* borrow, check out
用 *shakuyō* borrowing, loan
用者 *shakuyōsha* borrower
用証書 *shakuyō shōsho* promissory note
6 字 *ka(ri)ji* characters borrowed (to represent the meaning)
名 *ka(ri)na* borrowed name
衣装 *ka(ri)ishō* borrowed clothes
地 *shakuchi, ka(ri)chi* leased land
地権 *shakuchiken* lease, leasehold
7 住 *ka(ri)zuma(i)* living in rented quarters
8 店 *ka(ri)dana* rented shop
逃 *ka(ri)ni(ge)* running away from a debt

放 *ka(rip)pana(shi)* borrowing without returning
物 *ka(ri)mono* something borrowed
取 *ka(ri)do(ri)* borrowing without returning
金 *shakkin* loan, debt, liabilities
金取 *shakkinto(ri)* bill collection; bill collector
受 *ka(ri)-u(keru)* borrow; have a loan; hire, rent; buy on credit
受人 *ka(ri)u(ke)nin* borrower, debtor; tenant
受金 *ka(ri)u(ke)kin* borrowed money
9 屋 *shakuya* rented house
10 倒 *ka(ri)-tao(su)* evade payment
料 *shakuryō* rent money
財 *shakuzai* loan, debt, liability
家 *shakuya, shakka, ka(ri)ie, ka(ri)ya* house for rent, rented house, renting a house
家人 *shakkanin, shakuyanin* tenant, renter
家争議 *shakka sōgi* tenancy troubles
家住居 *shakuyazumai* living in rented quarters
12 間 *ka(ri)ma* rented room
換 *ka(ri)-ka(eru)* convert (a loan). *ka(ri)ka(e)* conversion, refunding, renewal
款 *shakkan* loan
着 *ka(ri)gi* borrowed clothes
集 *ka(ri)-atsu(meru)* borrow money, call for loans
貸 *ka(ri)ka(shi), shakutai* loan; lending and borrowing
越 *ka(ri)-ko(su)* overdraw. *ka(ri)ko(shi)* outstanding debt; overdraft
越金 *karikoshikin* overdraft; outstanding debt
13 賃 *ka(ri)chin* rent, hire
14 銭 *shakusen* debt
16 覧 *shakuran suru* borrow and read

A **修** 260 / J3d24 / M721 SHŪ. SHU. *osa(maru)* govern oneself, conduct oneself well. *osa(meru)* study, complete (a course); cultivate; master; order (one's life); repair.
2 了 *shūryō* completion (of a course)
3 士 *Shūshi* Master of Arts
5 史 *shūshi* compilation of a history
正 *shūsei* amendment, revision, modification, alteration, correction, retouching
正者 *shūseisha* amender
正案 *shūseian* proposed amendment
6 好 *shūkō* amity, friendship
交 *shūkō* amity, friendship
行 *shugyō* training, practice, ascetic practices, discipline; pursuit of knowledge
行者 *shugyōsha* practitioner of (Buddhist) austerities
7 身 *shūshin* morals, ethics, moral training
改 *shūkai* personal reformation
8 法 *shūhō* (Buddhist) prayer and austerities
学 *shūgaku* learning
学旅行 *shūgaku ryokō* field trip
9 造 *shūzō, shuzō* repairing
訂 *shūtei* correction, revision
院 *shūin* friary
院長 *shūinchō* prelate, prior, abbot
11 得 *shūtoku* learning, acquirement
理 *shūri, shuri* repair, mending
理工 *shūrikō* repair man
理中 *shūrichū* under repair
道 *shūdō* learning, studying the fine arts
道士 *shūdōshi* (Catholic) monk, friar
道女 *shūdōjo* (Catholic) nun
道生活 *shūdō seikatsu* monasticism, monastic life
道会 *shūdōkai* (Catholic) order
道院 *shūdōin* monastery, convent, cloister
道院制度 *shūdōin seido* monasticism
道誓願 *shūdō seigan* vows of religious orders
12 復 *shūfuku* repair, mending
補 *shūho* repairing
営 *shūei* building work
13 煉 *shūren* culture, training
飾 *shūshoku suru* decorate, adorn; polish up (writing); modify (in grammar)
飾語 *shūshokugo* modifier
業 *shūgyō, shugyō* pursuit of knowledge
業年限 *shūgyō nengen* length of the course of study
辞 *shūji* figure of speech; rhetorical flourish
辞法 *shūjihō* rhetoric
辞学 *shūjigaku* rhetoric
14 練 *shūren* drill, practice, training, culture
練者 *shūrensha* (Catholic) neophyte

二 亠 【人 9 イ 𠆢】 儿 入 八 丷 冂 冖 冫 几 凵 刀 刂 力 勹 匕 匚 匸 十 卜 卩 厂 厶 又

15 撰 *shūsen* editing, compiling
養 *shūyō* culture, (mental) training, self-discipline
熟 *shūjuku* developing skill
16 錬 *shūren* culture, training
築 *shūchiku* repair, renovation, restoration
整 *shūsei* adjustment; retouching (in photography)
18 験者 *shugenja* mountaineering ascetic
繕 *shūzen* repairs, mending
繕工 *shūzenkō* repair man
繕工場 *shūzen kōjō* repair shop
繕費 *shūzenhi* repair expense
19 羅 *shura* fighting; scene of carnage
羅巷 *shura (no) chimata* scene of carnage
羅道 *shuradō* scene of carnage
羅場 *shuraba* fighting scene *shurajō* scene of carnage

9

假 261/J5071/M835 See 仮 144.

偐 262/J5074/M850 GAN. GEN false, fake, counterfeit.

傯 263/J5078/M889 SŌ feel pain, suffer.

做 264/J5076/M861 SA. *-na(su)* make.

偖 265/J5077/M856 **捨** 2268/J-X/M12728 SHA. *sate* well, now.

偲 266/J3c45/M895 SHI. SAI. *shino(bu)* recollect, remember.

偈 267/J5075/M836 KETSU, KEI healthy; fast. GE Buddhist text in verse.
13 頌 *geju* Buddhist text in verse

偓 268/J-X/M853 AKU fuss.
9 促 *akuseku to* fussily, sedulously, busily

偕 269/J5073/M855 KAI together.
6 老 *kairō* growing old together
老同穴 *kairō-dōketsu* a happy life partnership
13 楽 *kairaku* enjoying oneself with others

B **偵** 270/J4465/M898 TEI spy.
8 知 *teichi* spying, investigation
14 察 *teisatsu* scouting, reconnaissance
察隊 *teisatsutai* scouting party, patrol

偃 271/J5070/M830 EN dam, weir.
4 月 *engetsu* crescent moon
月刀 *engetsutō* scimitar
8 臥 *enga suru* lie face down

偸 272/J5079/M901 TSU, TŌ steal.
6 安 *tōan suru* snatch a moment of rest; dicker for time
11 視 *tōshi* stealthy glance
盗 *chūtō* robber; theft

A **停** 273/J4464/M864 TEI stopping. *todo(maru)* stop, halt, stay, remain, stay behind; be limited to. *todo(meru)* stop, cease, detain, put an end to; leave; fix; remain in (a certain condition); content oneself with. *to(maru)* stop, halt, stand still, pull up; cease, be interrupted, be discontinued; be choked; alight on, perch, roost; be held in position.
4 止 *teishi* suspension, ban; stop, standstill; deadlock, stalemate; interruption; abeyance
止価格 *teishi kakaku* pegged price
止線 *teishisen* stop line
6 会 *teikai* adjournment, suspension of a meeting; recess of a legislature
年 *teinen* mandatory retirement age
7 車 *teisha* stopping a vehicle
車場 *teishajō, teishaba* railway station; taxi stand
8 泊 *teihaku* anchorage moorings
学 *teigaku* suspension from school
9 音 *teion* rest (in music)
音符 *teiompu* rest (in music)
10 留 *teiryū suru* stop, halt
留所 *teiryūjo* bus or streetcar stop
11 船 *teisen* stopping a ship, detention, quarantine
船場 *teisenjō* ferry landing

13 滞 *teitai* stagnation, tie-up; retention, accumulation, congestion; failing into arrears
戦 *teisen* armistice, cease fire
頓 *teiton* standstill, stalemate, setback, abeyance
電 *teiden* electricity failure; interruption of electrical service
18 職 *teishoku* suspension from office

B **偶** 274/J3676/M899 Gū even number; couple, man and wife; friend; same kind; doll. *tama no* occasional, rare. *tamasaka* occasionally. *tamatama* casually, unexpectedly; accidentally.
2 人 *gūjin* puppet; doll
6 因 *gūin* contingent cause
成 *gūsei no* impromptu
7 作 *gūsaku* something accidentally accomplished; two working together
吟 *gūgin* impromptu poem (humble)
9 発 *gūhatsu* sudden outbreak; accidental, incidental
発的 *gūhatsuteki* accidental, incidental, occasional, casual
11 偶 *tamatama* casually, unexpectedly, accidentally
12 詠 *gūei* impromptu poem (humble)
然 *gūzen* chance, accident, fortuity
13 数 *gūsū* even number
感 *gūkan* random thoughts
14 像 *gūzō* image, idol, statue
像化 *gūzōka* idolization
像礼拝 *gūzō reihai* idolatry
像破壊 *gūzō hakai* iconoclasm, image breaking
像視 *gūzōshi* idolization
像教 *gūzōkyō* idolatry
像教徒的 *gūzōkyōtoteki* idolatrous
像崇拝 *gūzō sūhai* idol worship, idolatry

A **側** 275/J4226/M897 Soku. *soba(mu) vi* lean to one side, oppose, look aside, regret. *soba(meru)* shove to one side, look at out of the corner of one's eyes. *gawa* a side; surroundings; (watch) case. *hata* side, edge; a third person. *kawa* side; row. *soba* side, vicinity. *katawara* side; besides; while. *hono(kana)* faint, indistinct; stupid; few.
3 女 *sobame* concubine
4 辺 *sokuhen* corner
火山 *sokkazan* parasitic volcano
5 圧 *sokuatsu* lateral pressure
仕 *sobazuka(e)* personal attendant, valet, maid
6 近 *sobachika(ku),* nearby. *sokkin* close associate, braintruster
近者 *sokkinsha* close associate
7 役 *sobayaku* personal attendant
杖 *sobazue* blow received by a bystander
8 泳 *sokuei* side stroke
9 室 *sokushitsu* a noble's concubine
背 *sokuhai* flank
面 *sokumen* side, flank; sidelight; lateral
面図 *sokumenzu* side view
面観 *sokumenkan* side view
10 根 *sokkon* lateral root
射 *sokusha* flanking fire
部 *sokubu* the side
14 聞 *sokubun suru* hear casually
15 線 *sokusen* sidetrack, siding; side line (at a game)
16 壁 *sokuheki* side wall

B **偽** 276/J3536/M927' **僞** 303/J5126/M1105 Gi. *itsuwa(ru)* lie, falsify; deceive; pretend; deceive, cheat. *nise* sham, counterfeit, forgery, imitation, false (prophet).
5 札 *nise satsu, gisatsu* forged document, counterfeit money
史 *gishi* falsified history
本 *gihon* spurious book, a forgery
6 印 *giin* forged seal
名 *gimei* false name, assumed name
似症 *gijishō* suspected case
7 言 *gigen* falsehood
作 *gisaku* apocryphal work, forgery, spurious article
兵 *gihei* dummy soldiers
君子 *nise kunshi, gikunshi* hypocrite, snob
8 物 *nisemono, gibutsu* spurious article, a forgery, counterfeit
版 *gihan* pirated edition
学 *gigaku* false science; science out of line with the world of thought
者 *itsuwa(ri)mono* impostor, liar
9 計 *gikei* deceptive plan
造 *gizō* forgery, falsification, fabrication, counterfeiting
造罪 *gizōzai* forgery

2 二亠【人イ𠆢】儿入八ソ冂冖冫几凵刀刂力勹匕匚匸十卜卩厂厶又

10 称 *gishō suru* assume a false name
書 *gisho* spurious letter, apocryphal book, a forgery
11 悪 *giaku* pretense of evil
12 筆 *gihitsu* forged handwriting; plagiarism
装 *gisō* camouflage
報 *gihō* false report
善 *gizen* hypocrisy
善者 *gizensha* hypocrite
証 *gishō* perjury, false testimony
証者 *gishōsha* perjurer, false witness
証罪 *gishōzai* crime of perjury
13 電 *giden* false telegram
14 語 *itsuwa(ri)-kata(ru)* speak falsely
誓 *itsuwa(ri)-chika(u)* swear falsely. *gisei* perjury, false oath

B **偏** 277/J4a50/M848 HEN side; left radical of a character; inclining. *hen(suru)* incline toward, be biased. *katayo(ru)* lean, incline; be biased. *katayo(ri)* inclination; offset; polarization. *hitoe ni* earnestly; humbly; solely.
2 人 *henjin* eccentric person
3 土 *hendo* rural areas
4 心 *henshin* eccentricity (in mechanics)
片 *katahera* one of a pair; one side
辺 *katahoto(ri)* corner, remote country place
5 平 *hempei na* flat
6 向 *henkō* propensity, inclination; deflection
好 *henkō* partiality
光 *henkō* polarized light; polarization
在 *henzai* maldistribution
7 見 *katayo(ri)-mi(ru)* show partiality. *henken* prejudice, narrow view
狂 *henkyō* monomania; monomaniac
8 屈 *henkutsu* eccentricity, bigotry, obstinacy
性 *hensei* eccentric personality
9 食 *henshoku* unbalanced diet
狭 *henkyō* narrow-mindedness; narrowness
降 *katabu(ri)* rainy spell
重 *henchō suru* make too much of. *henchō, henjū* preponderance
10 流 *henryū* drift
針 *henshin* deflection
差 *hensa* declination, deflection, variation, deviation, drift
11 斜 *hensha* declination, deviation
執 *henshū* bias, eccentricity, obstinacy
13 愛 *hen'ai* partiality, favoritism
窟 *henkutsu* eccentricity, bigotry, obstinacy
照 *katade(ri)* a stretch of sunshine (after rain)
14 歴 *henreki* travels, pilgrimage
頗 *hempa* favoritism, discrimination
16 頭痛 *henzutsū, hentōtsū* headache on one side; migraine
18 癖 *hempeki* eccentricity, crankiness

A **健** 278/J3772/M875 KEN health, strength; stick-to-itiveness. *suko(yakana)* vigorous, healthy, sound. *shitataka ni* heartily; severely.
6 気 *kenage* courage. *kenage na* manly, heroic, brave; praiseworthy; industrious
全 *kenzen* health, soundness. *kenzen na* healthy, sound, wholesome
在 *kenzai* good health
7 投 *kentō* good pitching
児 *kenji* stalwart youth
忘 *kembō* forgetfulness
忘症 *kembōshō* amnesia, loss of memory
8 歩 *kempo* good walker
者 *shitatakamono* desperate character, scoundrel; strong-willed person
9 胃剤 *ken'izai* stomach medicine
胃錠 *ken'ijō* stomach tablets
10 祥 *kenshō* spirit, pep, energy
11 脳剤 *kennōzai* brain tonic
啖 *kentan* gluttony, voracity
啖家 *kentanka* glutton, gormandizer
脚 *kenkyaku* good walker
脚家 *kenkyakuka* good walker
康 *kenkō* health. *kenkō na* sound; wholesome
康地 *kenkōchi* healthy place, health resort
康体 *kenkōtai* healthy body
康児 *kenkōji* healthy child
康者 *kenkōsha* healthy person
康法 *kenkōhō* hygiene
康的 *kenkōteki* hygienic, healthful, sanitary
康美 *kenkōbi* physical beauty

康保険 *kenkō hoken* health insurance
康保険医 *kenkō hoken'i* health insurance doctor
康証明書 *kenkō shōmeisho* health certificate
康診断 *kenkō shindan* physical examination
12 棒 *kembō* good batting
勝 *kenshō* good health
筆 *kempitsu* powerful pen
筆家 *kempitsuka* ready writer
10 闘 *kento* good fight, strenuous efforts

10

僅 279 / J364f / M-X Nonstandard for **僅** 292.

傚 280 / J507h / M969 **効** 225 / J-X / M725 Kō. *nara(u)* imitate, follow, emulate.

傅 281 / J507c / M939 Fu instructor, tutor (to a prince). *kashizu(ku)* wait upon, serve.
8 育 *fuiku* bringing up; tuition, education

傀 282 / J507a / M928 Kai large.
17 儡 *kairai, kugutsu* puppet; dummy
儡政府 *kairai seifu* puppet government
儡師 *kairaishi, kugutsushi* puppet player; wirepuller

B **傘** 283 / J3b31 / M966 **仐** 100 / J-X / M366 San. *kasa* umbrella, parasol. *karakasa* paper umbrella.
3 下 *sanka* affiliated with; under the jurisdiction of
5 立 *kasata(te)* umbrella stand
6 地 *kasaji* umbrella cloth
7 形碍子 *kasagata gaishi* umbrella insulator
9 屋 *kasaya* umbrella shop
持 *kasamo(chi)* umbrella carrier
10 紙 *kasagami* oiled umbrella paper
12 歯車 *kasahaguruma* bevel gear

A **備** 284 / J4877 / M967 Bi. *sona(waru)* be furnished with, be endowed with, possess; be among, be one of. *sona(eru)* furnish, provide, equip, install; have ready; prepare; possess, have; be endowed with; be armed with. *sona(e)* preparation, provision, guarding. *tsubu(sa) ni* in detail, with great care; completely; again and again.
5 付 *sona(e)tsu(ke)* equipment, provision *sona(e)-tsu(keru)* provide, furnish, equip, install
6 考 *bikō* note, remarks, N. B.
7 忘 *bibō* reminder
忘録 *bibōroku* memorandum, notebook
9 品 *bihin* fixtures, furnishings, equipment
後表 *bingo omote* a quality *tatami* covering
荒 *bikō* provision for famine
荒食 *bikōshoku* emergency food
荒貯蓄 *bikō chochiku* famine-relief fund
10 砲 *bihō* armament
13 蓄 *bichiku* stored, reserved
蓄米 *bichikumai* reserved rice

B **偉** 285 / J304e / M837 I greatness. *era(garu)* be conceited. *era(i)* great, famous, remarkable, excellent.
2 人 *ijin* great man
力 *iryoku* power, might, authority, influence
3 大 *idai* greatness, grandeur
才 *isai* remarkable man
丈夫 *ijōfu* a hero, a great man, a big man
5 功 *ikō* great deed
8 物 *eramono, erabutsu* great man
効 *ikō* great effect
10 容 *iyō* majestic appearance, dignity
挙 *ikyo* excellent deeds
烈 *iretsu* great achievement
13 跡 *iseki* remaining works, results of one's labor
業 *igyō* great enterprise, exploits
14 徳 *itoku* outstanding virtue
15 勲 *ikun* great achievement
17 績 *iseki* glorious achievements
18 蹟 *iseki* remaining works, results of a man's labor
観 *ikan* grand sight

B **傍** 286 / J4b35 / M948 Hō. Bō *katawa(ra), waki, soba* side; besides; while. *katawa(ra) no* nearby. *katawa(ra) ni* beside, nearby. *hata* side; edge; a third person.

2 人 *bōjin* bystander
5 目 *okame, hatame* looking on by an outsider
目八目 *okame-hachimoku* superior observation by an outsider
6 耳 *katamimi* things overheard
7 見 *okami* looking on by an outsider
杖 *sobazue* blow received by a bystander
系 *bōkei* collateral family; subsidiary; affiliated
8 受 *bōju* interception, tapping
迷惑 *hata meiwaku* inconvenience to those nearby
若無人 *bōjaku-bujin* arrogance, audacity, insolence, defiance
9 点 *bōten* marks to facilitate reading of Chinese
10 訓 *bōkun* marginal notes. *fu(ri)gana* side *kana* (to show the pronunciation of characters)
11 惚 *okabore* unrequited love, secret affections
視 *bōshi suru* look on from the side
12 註 *bōchū* marginal notes
15 線 *bōsen* side line, underline
輩 *hōbai* term of address among retainers of the same lord; people working in the same office; students of the same teacher; companions
17 聴 *bōchō* hearing, attendance, auditing
聴人 *bōchōnin* hearer, auditor, audience
聴券 *bōchōken* admission ticket
聴席 *bōchōseki* visitor's gallery, seats for the public
聴料 *bōchōryō* admission fee
聴随意 *bōchō zuii* admission free
聴無料 *bōchō muryō* admission free
18 観 *bōkan suru* look on, remain a spectator
観者 *bōkansha* bystander, onlooker
観的 *bōkanteki ni* as a spectator

11

傳 287 / J5123 / M1019 See 伝 141.

僂 288 / J5124 / M1045 Rō, Ru bend over.

僊 289 / J-X / M1055 Sen hermit.

2 人 *sennin* hermit; wizard; fairy; otherworldly person

傴 290 / J507d / M1020 U, Ku bend over.

13 僂 *kuru, semushi* hunchback; rickets

僉 291 / J5121 / M1054 Sen. *mina* all, everyone.

20 議 *sengi* conference
議者 *sengisha* speaker, orator

僅 292 / J-X / M1048 **僅** 279 / J364f / M-X Kin. *wazu(ka)* a little, a small quantity.

4 少 *kinshō* few, little, insignificant
少差 *kinshōsa* narrow majority; a shade of difference
13 僅 *kinkin* merely, no more than

傑 293 / J3766 / M955 B Ketsu excellence. *sugu(reru)* excel.

2 人 *ketsujin* an outstanding person
3 士 *kesshi* hero, great man
5 出 *kesshutsu suru* excel, be foremost
7 作 *kessaku* masterpiece; gross mistake, blunder
8 物 *ketsubutsu* remarkable character, great man

傲 294 / J507e / M1015 Gō. *ogo(ru)* be proud.

8 岸 *gōgan* haughtiness, pride
10 倨 *gōkyo* arrogance
12 然 *gōzen(taru)* proud, haughty
14 慢 *gōman* pride, haughtiness, insolence, arrogance
慢不遜 *gōman-fuson na* haughty, arrogant, overbearing

傭 295 / J4d43 / M1007 Yō. *yato(u)* employ, hire.

2 人 *yōnin* employee
7 兵 *yōhei, yato(i)hei* mercenary soldier
11 船 *yōsen* chartered ship
船契約 *yōsen keiyaku* chartering ships
13 聘 *yōhei suru* employ

債 296 / J3a44 / M1022 B Sai debt; loan.

5 主 *saishu* creditor
8 券 *saiken* bond, debenture

¹⁰鬼 *saiki* cruel creditor; bill collector
¹¹務 *saimu* debt; liabilities
務者 *saimusha* debtor
¹⁵権 *saiken* credit; claim
権者 *saikensha* creditor

A **働** 297 / J462f / M1079 (国字) Dō. *hatara(ku)* work, labor; do, act, commit, practice; work on; come into play; be conjugated; reduce the price. *hatara(ki)* work, labor; action, function, operation, movement, motion; conjugation, inflection; talent; achievement.
²人 *hatara(ki)bito* a worker; a good worker
³口 *hatara(ki)guchi* position, opening
⁴手 *hatara(ki)te, hatara(ki)de* a worker; a good worker, a breadwinner, an able worker
⁸者 *hatara(ki)mono* hard worker
⁹通 *hatara(ki)tō(shi) de* working right on through
¹⁰振 *hatara(ki)bu(ri)* way of working, discharge of duty
¹¹掛 *hatara(ki)-ka(keru)* work on someone, influence, appeal to; begin to work
盛 *hatara(ki)zaka(ri)* prime of life
¹³蜂 *hatara(ki)bachi* worker bee

B **催** 298 / JJa45 / M1005 SAI. *moyō(su)* hold (a meeting); give (a dinner); feel; show signs of, develop symptoms of, feel (sick). *moyō(shi)* meeting, gathering; (bodily) urge.
⁶合 *moya(u)* cooperate (in enterprises)
⁷告 *saikoku* notification
⁸物 *moyō(shi)mono* points of interest; tourist attraction; an exhibit; events
⁹促 *saisoku suru* demand, request, urge (action), press for
促状 *saisokujō* dun, letter requesting money, etc.
¹⁰涙瓦斯 *sairui gasu* tear gas
涙弾 *sairuidan* tear-gas bomb
涙銃 *sairuijū* tear-gas gun
眠 *saimin* hypnotism
眠剤 *saiminzai* sleeping medicine
眠術 *saiminjutsu* hypnotism
眠薬 *saimin'yaku* sleeping medicine
¹¹淫剤 *saiinzai* an aphrodisiac

B **傾** 299 / J3739 / M1038 KEI. *kashi(gu) vi* lean, incline, tilt, list, tip, careen, lurch. *kashi(geru) vt* lean, incline, tilt. *katamu(ku), katabu(ku), kata(gu)* incline toward, tilt, slant, slope, lurch, heel over; be disposed to; trend toward, be prone to; go down (sun); wane, sink, decline. *katamu(keru) vt* incline, list, bend, lean, tip, tilt, slant; concentrate on; devote to; ruin; squander; empty. *kata(geru) vt* incline, tilt, slant. *nada(reru)* slope, descend, slide (snow, etc.). *katamu(ki)* slope, inclination, list; tendency, trend; bent; disposition, bias. *nada(re)* avalanche; snowslide; slope, sloping; surging (crowd).
⁴込 *nada(re)-ko(mu)* rush or crowd into
⁶向 *keikō* tendency, trend; disposition
⁷角 *keikaku* inclination
⁸国 *keikoku* a matchless beauty, a siren
注 *keichū* devotion, concentration
⁹度 *keido* inclination
城 *keisei* a matchless beauty, a siren
¹⁰倒 *katamu(ke)-tao(su)* cast down, lay low. *keitō suru* devote oneself to, concentrate on; admire, idolize
差 *keisa* dip (of the compass)
¹¹斜 *keisha* inclination, level, slope, list, dip
斜角 *keishakaku* angle of inclination
斜面 *keishamen* inclined plane, slope
斜度 *keishado* gradient
¹²落 *nada(re)-o(chiru)* slide down (snow, etc.)
¹⁷聴 *keicho* listening closely
¹⁸瀉 *keisha* decanting
覆 *keifuku suru* overthrow; rebel

B **僧** 300 / J414e / M1076 **僧** 304 / J-X / M1117 Sō monk, priest.
⁵尼 *sōni* monks and nuns
正 *sōjō* high priest of a Buddhist sect
号 *sōgō* priest's religious name
⁶寺 *sōji* Buddhist priest; a temple with priests resident (as opposed to nuns)
⁷位 *sōi* priestly rank
体 *sōtai* the form of a Buddhist priest; priestly attire
坊 *sōbō* priests' quarters
形 *sōgyō* the form of a Buddhist priest; priestly attire
兵 *sōhei* priest soldier

8 門 *sōmon* priesthood; Buddhism
房 *sōbō* priests' temple quarters
服 *sōfuku* priest's garb
9 俗 *sōzoku* priests and laymen
侶 *sōryo* (Buddhist) priest, monk
院 *sōin* monastery, temple
10 徒 *sōto* (Buddhist) priests, monks
家 *sōka* Buddhist temple
11 堂 *sōdō* temple meditation hall or certain other temple structures
庵 *sōan* priest's hermitage
庵生活 *sōan seikatsu* hermit life
18 職 *sōshoku* (Buddhist) priesthood
20 籍 *sōseki* (Buddhist) priesthood

A **傷** 301 / J3d7d / M1029 SHŌ wound, injury. *ita(mu)* feel a pain, hurt; be hurt, be damaged, be spoiled, be bruised, wear out, be worn out. *ita(meru)* hurt, injure, impair, spoil, worry, bother, afflict, cause pain. *kizu* wound, injury, hurt; cut, gash, bruise, scratch; scar; weak point. *ita(mi)* pain, ache.

3 口 *kizuguchi* wound
4 心 *shōshin* heartbreak, grief
5 付 *kizutsu(keru)* wound, injure; damage, mar; disgrace. *kizutsu(ku)* get injured, be wounded
7 悴 *shōsui* great grief
兵 *shōhei* wounded soldier
8 物 *kizumono* defective article, damaged goods
咎 *kizutogame* inflamed wound
者 *shōsha* wounded or injured person
10 害 *shōgai* wound, injury, accident, casualty
害保険 *shōgai hoken* accident insurance
病 *shōbyō* injuries and sickness
病兵 *shōbyōhei* sick and wounded soldiers
病捕虜 *shōbyō horyo* sick and wounded prisoners
11 痕 *kizuato, shōkon* scar
悴 *shōsui* great grief
痍 *shōi* wound, injury
痍軍人 *shōi gunjin* wounded soldier, disabled veteran
12 創 *shōsō* wound, injury
13 傷 *itaita(shii)* pitiful, pathetic
嘆 *shōtan* crying in pain
跡 *kizuato* scar
15 歎 *shōtan* crying in pain
16 薬 *kizugusuri* salve, ointment

12

僊 302 / J5122 / M-X Nonstandard for **僊** 289.

僞 303 / J5126 / M1105 See **偽** 274.

僧 304 / J-X / M1117 See **僧** 300.

僣 305 / J5129 / M1111 See **僭** 329.

僖 306 / J5125 / M1095 KI. *yoroko(bu)* rejoice, be glad, be pleased. *tanoshi(mu)* enjoy, amuse oneself; anticipate.

僑 307 / J3623 / M1088 KYŌ temporary home.

A **像** 308 / J417c / M1084 **像** 309 / J-X / M48923 ZŌ image, statue, figure, picture, portrait.

僮 310 / J512a / M1132 TŌ, DŌ child; servant; foolishness.

僥 311 / J5127 / M1113 GYŌ luck; seek; desire.

10 倖 *gyōkō* windfall, godsend, good fortune

儁 312 / J512e / M1175 SHUN excellence; talented person.

7 秀 *shunshū* genius, prodigy, talented man

B **僕** 313 / J4b4d / M1094 BOKU manservant, I (used by male speakers). *shimobe* manservant; servant (of God).

6 仲間 *shimobe nakama* fellow servant
11 婢 *bokuhi* male and female servants

B **僚** 314 / J4e3d / M1100 RYŌ official; companion.

4 友 *ryōyū* comrade, coworker
11 船 *ryōsen* consort ship
16 機 *ryōki* consort plane

20 艦 *ryōkan* consort ship

13

儉 315 / J512d / M1190 See **倹** 248.

價 316 / J512b / M1163 See **価** 188.

僵 317 / J512c / M1150 KYŌ. fall down, topple, collapse. *tao(reru)* fall, collapse, drop; break down, die, succumb to; fall senseless; be ruined. *tao(su)* bring down, throw down, blow down, fell, knock down, trip up; defeat, ruin, overthrow; kill.

儂 318 / J512f / M1176 NŌ, DŌ *washi, ware* I, me. *kare* he, she, that person.

儈 319 / J-X / M1189 KAI middleman.

儚 320 / J5133 / M1236 BŌ. *hakana(i)* fleeting, momentary, ephemeral; vain, empty, hopeless; fickle, inconstant, unstable; fragile, frail; pitiful, poor, sad, miserable.

A **億** 321 / J322f / M1178 OKU 100,000,000.
3 万長者 *okumanchōja* billionaire
6 兆 *okuchō* people, multitude, masses
7 劫 *okkū na* troublesome, annoying

B **舗** 322 / J4a5e / M30323' **舖** 4922 / J6754 / M30323 **鋪** 6269 / J4a5f / M40491
HO shop, store.
11 道 *hodō* pavement; paved street
12 装 *hosō* paving
装煉瓦 *hosō renga* paving brick

僻 323 / J4a48 / M1166 HEKI prejudice, bias; rural area. *heki(suru)* be biased, be warped. *higa(mu)* be prejudiced, be soured. *higami* prejudice, bias; inferiority complex. *higa-* evil, untrue, erroneous.
4 心 *higamigokoro* warped mind
5 目 *higame* squint; sight error; bias; misunderstanding, misjudgment
6 地 *hekichi* remote place
在 *hekizai* being off to one side; being away off in the country
7 見 *hekiken* prejudice
言 *hekigen* unreasonable talk
邑 *hekiyū* remote village
村 *hekison* remote village
8 事 *higagoto* immoral act; mistake
10 根性 *higami konjō* prejudiced mind
11 隅 *hekigū* corner, nook
12 遠 *hekien no* remote, outlying
14 境 *hekikyō* deep rural areas
説 *hekisetsu* prejudiced opinion
15 論 *hekiron* prejudiced opinion

B **儀** 324 / J3537 / M1172 GI rule; ceremony; affair, case, a matter.
2 刀 *gitō* ceremonial sword
5 仗 *gijō* cortege, guard
仗兵 *gijōhei* guard of honor
礼 *girei* courtesy, etiquette
礼兵 *gireihei* guard of honor
礼的 *gireiteki* formal
6 刑 *gikei* model, pattern, copy
式 *gishiki* ceremony, rite, ritual, service
式用 *gishikiyō no* ceremonial
式主義 *gishiki shugi* ritualism, ceremonialism
式張 *gishikiba(ru)* formalize, stick to formality, be ceremonious, be punctilious
8 典 *giten* ceremony, rite, ritual, service
表 *gihyō* a model
9 型 *gikei* model, pattern, copy
10 容 *giyō* bearing, manners
12 装 *gisō* ceremonial equipment
装馬車 *gisō basha* state carriage
15 範 *gihan* precedent, model

14

儖 325 / J5130 / M1229 RAN ugly.

儔 326 / J5132 / M1224 CHŪ companion; similar kinds.

儘 327 / J5056 / M1234 JIN. *mama* as it is; as one likes; because.

儕 328 / J5131 / M1227 SEI, SAI companion.
15 輩 *saihai* colleagues, fellows

僭 329 J5128 M1128 **僣** 305 J5129 M1111 SEN. *sen(suru)* boastfully usurp.
3 上 *senshō, senjō* audacity, forwardness
5 用 *sen'yō* using something belonging exclusively to someone else
主 *senshu* usurper, tyrant
7 位 *sen'i* usurpation of a throne
8 取 *senshu* usurpation
10 称 *senshō* pretension, assumption (of a title)
12 越 *sen'etsu* audacity, forwardness
14 奪 *sendatsu* usurpation

B **儒** 330 J3c74 M1220 JU Confucianism; Confucianist; Chinese scholar.
4 仏 *Ju-Butsu* Confucianism and Buddhism
5 生 *Jusei* Confucian scholar
6 艮 *jugon* dugong, sea pig
8 官 *jukan* official Confucian teacher
者 *Jusha* a Confucianist
学 *Jugaku* Confucianism
学者 *Jugakusha* Confucian scholar
学界 *Jugakkai* Confucian circles
10 家 *Juka* Confucianist
11 道 *Judō* Confucianism
教 *Jukyō* Confucianism
教主義 *Jukyō shugi* Confucianism
教的 *Jukyōteki* Confucian

15

儲 331 J4c59 M-X See **儲** 335.

儡 332 J5134 M1249 RAI defeat.

B **償** 333 J3d7e M1245 SHŌ. *tsuguna(u)* make up for, recompense, redeem (one's faults), compensate for, indemnify, atone for.
7 却 *shōkyaku* repayment, redemption, amortization
8 金 *shōkin* reparation, redemption
15 還 *shōkan* repayment, redemption, amortization

A **優** 334 J4d25 M1261 YŪ actor; superiority; gentleness. *sugu(reru)* excel, surpass; have advantages over; be excellent. *masa(ru)* excel, surpass, outrival. *yasa(shii)* gentle, tender, graceful, affectionate, kind, amiable, suave. *yasa-* gentle, affectionate. *yasa(shige) na* gentle, kind, sweet-looking. *yū ni* easily, amply, sufficiently, well, skillfully.
3 女 *yasaonna* gentle woman, affectionate woman
5 生学 *yūseigaku* eugenics
生結婚 *yūsei kekkon* eugenic marriage
6 劣 *yūretsu* superiority or inferiority, quality
先 *yūsen* preference, priority
先外貨 *yūsen gaika* preferred foreign currency
先的 *yūsenteki* preferential
先株 *yūsen kabu* preferred stock
先権 *yūsenken* priority, preference, preferential right
7 位 *yūi* predominance, ascendancy, superiority
利 *yūri na* advantageous, better, profitable
形 *yasagata* slender figure
男 *yasaotoko* man of gentle manners; man of delicate features
秀 *yūshū* excellence, superiority
秀品 *yūshūhin* high-grade merchandise
良 *yūryō* excellence, superiority
良児 *yūryōji* superior child
良品 *yūryōhin* superior articles
良馬 *yūryōba* thoroughbred horse
良株 *yūryō kabu* gilt-edged stock
8 長 *yūchō na* excellence, superiority
性 *yūsei* dominance
者 *yūsha* superior individual
9 美 *yūbi* grace, refinement, elegance
姿 *yasasugata* graceful figure
待 *yūtai suru* treat kindly, receive hospitably, welcome
待券 *yūtaiken* complimentary ticket
柔 *yūjū* indecisiveness
柔不断 *yūjū-fudan* indecisiveness
11 遇 *yūgū* hearty welcome, hospitality, good treatment
婉 *yūen na* elegant, grand
12 渥 *yūaku na* gracious
越 *yūetsu* supremacy, predominance

越性 *yūetsusei* supremacy, predominance
越感 *yūetsukan* superiority complex
越複合 *yūetsu fukugō* superiority complex
越権 *yūetsuken* special rights, predominant rights
等 *yūtō* excellency, superiority
等生 *yūtōsei* honor student
等卒業生 *yūtō sotsugyōsei* honors graduate
等賞 *yūtōshō* honor prize
等賞状 *yūtō shōjō* grand-prize diploma
勝 *yūshō* victory, championship
勝劣敗 *yūshō reppai* survival of the fittest
勝杯 *yūshōhai* championship cup
勝者 *yūshōsha* prize winner, pennant winner, victor
勝馬 *yūshōba* winning horse
勝旗 *yūshōki* championship pennant
13 雅 *yūga* elegance, refinement
勢 *yūsei* superiority, superior power, preponderance, predominance
19 艶 *yūen na* charming, fascinating

16

儲 335 J-X M1284 儲 331 J4c59 M-X CHO. *mō(karu)* be profitable, yield a profit. *mō(keru)* get, earn, gain. *mōke* profits, earnings.
3 口 *mōkeguchi* profitable job
6 尽 *mōkezu(ku) de* for investment, to make money
7 役 *mōkeyaku* lucrative position
8 物 *mōkemono* good bargain; a find
13 蓄 *chochiku* savings

19

儷 336 J5136 M1311 REI companion.

儺 337 J5135 M1317 NA, DA exorcism.

20

儻 338 J5130 M1323 TŌ superior. *sugu(reru)* excel, surpass; be excellent. *mo(shi)* if, perhaps.

儼 339 J5137 M1324 GEN serious; not to be touched. *gen (to shite)* solemnly, gravely, majestically, authoritatively.
12 然 *genzen to* solemnly, gravely, majestically, authoritatively

RAD. 儿 10

Hito-ashi human legs. Nickname: Legs.

儿 340 J5139 M1336 JIN, NIN.

1

兀 341 J513a M1337 KOTSU. GOTSU. GOCHI high and level; lofty; bald; ignorant; immobile; restless.
24 鷹 *hagetaka* vulture; condor

2

允 342 J3074 M1338 IN sincerity; permit.
11 許 *inkyo* permission, license

A 元 343 J3835 M1340 GAN, GEN yuan; origin; New Year's Day; first year of an era. GEN Mongol (dynasty). *moto* beginning, origin; foundation, basis, source; cause; root (of a tree); (raw) material, base; capital; principal; cost; forebears; formerly. *moto(yori)* originally; of course.
3 三 *Ganzan* New Year's Day; January 1 to 3
4 手 *motode* funds, capital, stock
方 *motokata* capitalist, wholesaler

日 *Ganjitsu* New Year's Day
凶 *genkyō* ringleader
元 *motomoto* from the first, originally; by nature, naturally
込 *motogo(me)* breech-loading
込銃 *motogo(me)jū* breechloader
5 払 *motobara(i)* prepayment
旦 *Gantan* New Year's morning; New Year's Day
本 *gampon* principal, capital
号 *gengō* era name
6 任 *gennin* return of an official to his former post
兇 *genkyō* ringleader
年 *gannen* first year (of a reign)
老 *genrō* elder statesman, veteran, authority
老院 *genrōin* (Roman) senate
気 *genki* vigor, energy, vitality, vim, stamina, spirit, courage, pep
気付 *genkizu(keru) vt* pep up, cheer up
気者 *genkimono* a live wire (a person)
7 利 *ganri* principal and interest
来 *ganrai* originally, primarily, logically, naturally, essentially
8 金 *motokin, gankin* capital, principal
価 *genka* cost price
服 *gempuku, gembuku* ceremony of attaining manhood
始 *genshi* origin
始祭 *Genshisai* Shinto Festival of Origins Jan. 3
9 首 *genshu* ruler, sovereign
通 *motodō(ri)* as ever, as before
祖 *ganso* originator, founder, pioneer, inventor
軍 *Gengun* the Mongol forces
帥 *gensui* (field) marshal, fleet admiral, general of the army
10 値 *motone* cost
素 *genso* element
11 帳 *motochō* ledger
悪 *gen'aku* head gangster
寇 *Genkō* the Mongol Invasion
12 結 *motoyu(i), motoi* paper cord for tying the hair
朝 *ganchō* New Year's morning
15 標 *gempyō* zero milestone
締 *motoji(me)* manager, boss, promoter
勲 *genkun* elder statesman
請人 *moto u(ke)nin* master contractor
請負人 *moto ukeoinin* master contractor

3

A 兄 344 / J373b / M1343 KEI brother; you. KYŌ. *ani, nii(san)* elder brother. *se* a women's familiar call for her husband or elder brother.
3 上 *aniue* elder brother
4 分 *anibun* one regarded as an elder brother
7 君 *anigimi* endearing term for elder brother. *senokimi* husband
弟 *kyōdai, keitei, anioto, aniotōto* brother, brethren
弟子 *anideshi* senior schoolmate, senior apprentice
弟分 *kyōdaibun* buddy, pal, sworn brother
弟会社 *kyōdaigaisha* affiliated companies
弟姉妹 *keitei-shimai* brothers and sisters, brethren
弟愛 *kyōdaiai* brotherly love
8 妹 *keimai* older brother and younger sister
事 *keiji suru* regard as one's senior
9 姫 *ehime* eldest daughter
10 息子 *animusuko* my eldest son
12 御 *anigo* elder brother (polite)
貴 *aniki* elder brother, one's senior
13 嫁 *aniyome* elder brother's wife
14 様 *niisama, niisan* elder brother

4

癸 345 / J-X / M1351 Nonstandard for 兌 353.

A 兆 346 / J437b / M1347 CHŌ sign, omen, indication, portent; trillion. *kiza(su)* show signs or symptoms of. *kizashi* signs, omen, symptoms.
5 民 *chōmin* the whole nation, all the people
10 候 *chōkō* sign, indication, omen, symptom

兇 347 / J3624 / M1348 KYŌ wickedness.
3 刃 *kyōjin* assassin's dagger
4 手 *kyōshu* assassin

6 行 *kyōkō* violence, murder, crime
7 状 *kyōjō* crime, offense
状持 *kyōjōmo(chi)* a criminal
8 具 *kyōgu* dangerous weapon
9 変 *kyōhen* catastrophe; assassination
10 徒 *kyōto* outlaw, rebel, rioter
悍 *kyōkan* heinousness, ferocity
11 猛 *kyōmō* fierce
悪 *kyōaku na* atrocious, fiendish, brutal
13 漢 *kyōkan* villain, outlaw, assassin
賊 *kyōzoku* villain
15 暴 *kyōbō* brutality, ferocity, atrocity
器 *kyōki* dangerous weapon
18 類 *kyōrui* wicked gang

B **充** 348 J3d3c M1345 Jū fill. *ate(ru)* apply, place, put; hit (the mark); guess; succeed; expose to; sit (on a cushion); assign, allocate; call on (a pupil). *mi(chiru)* be full; mature, expire. *mi(tasu)* fill; supply, make good; satisfy, appease, answer (the need), meet (the demand).

4 分 *jūbun* enough; satisfactory, adequate; perfect; thorough
5 用 *jūyō suru* appropriate to, earmark for
6 血 *jūketsu* congestion (medical); engorgement
行 *atega(u)* allot, fasten to, supply with, choose (a wife for); match with; patch; cover; apply to
当 *jūtō suru* allot, appropriate
当金 *jūtōkin* appropriation
7 足 *jūsoku* sufficiency
8 実 *jūjitsu* substantiality; fullness, completion, perfection. *jūjitsu shita* full, complete; replete with; substantial (meal), solid (reading)
10 員 *jūin* reserves, recruits, draftees
12 備 *jūbi* completion, perfection
満 *jūman suru, michimichi(te) iru* be filled with, be pregnant with, teem with
13 塡 *jūten suru* fill (up), plug; replenish. *jūten* filling (in a tooth)
溢 *jūitsu* overflow, abundance, exuberance
塞 *jūsoku suru vt* plug, fill up, block. *vi* be filled with, be stopped up
電 *jūden* charging (batteries)
電器 *jūdenki* charger

A **光** 349 J3877 M1350 Kō light. *hika(ru)* shine, glitter, sparkle, twinkle, flash. *hika(rakasu), hika(rasu)* show one's authority, strut around; shine (a light) on. *hikari* light, beam, flash, glare, gleam, twinkle, sparkle, glimmer, glow, brightness, radiance, glitter, luster; influence (of parents).

2 力 *kōryoku* intensity of light
4 化学 *kōkagaku* photochemistry
6 芒 *kōbō* shaft of light, flash of lightning
年 *kōnen* light year
合成 *kōgōsei* photosynthesis
行差 *kōkōsa* aberration (in astronomy)
7 体 *kōtai* luminous body
来 *kōrai* your visit, your company
束 *kōsoku* a beam of light
沢 *kōtaku* brilliance, polish, luster
沢紙 *kōtakushi* glossy paper
沢綿糸 *kōtaku menshi* mercerized cotton thread
8 波 *kōha* light wave
物 *hika(ri)mono* shooting star; luminous body; metal scraps; gold and silver coins
炎 *kōen* light and flames; energy
明 *kōmyō* light, hope, bright future; glory; halo
明度 *kōmeido* power (of binoculars)
学 *kōgaku* optics
学硝子 *kōgaku garasu* optical glass
9 速 *kōsoku* speed of light
神 *hikari (no) kami* Mazda (the sun god)
冠 *kōkan* corona
点 *kōten* luminous point
栄 *kōei* honor, glory; privilege
背 *kōhai* halo
風 *kōfū* a pleasant wind after a rain
風霽月 *kōfū-seigetsu* a bright moon after a storm; serenity of mind
度 *kōdo* brightness, luminosity
度計 *kōdokei* photometer
10 流 *kōryū* stream of light
被 *kōhi* permeating all
陰 *kōin* time
11 球 *kōkyū* photosphere
鹵石 *kōroseki* carnalite
彩 *kōsai* brilliance, splendor
彩陸離 *kōsai rikuri* splendor, brilliancy
12 焔 *kōen* flame
景 *kōkei* scene, spectacle; aspect
量 *kōryō* radiation intensity

覚 *kōkaku* optic sense, sensation of light
13 源 *kōgen* light source
暈 *kōun* halation, ghost (in photography)
照 *kōshō* shining
電 *kōden* photoelectricity
電池 *kōdenchi* photoelectric cell
電管 *kōdenkan* photoelectric cell
15 線 *kōsen* light; light ray, beam
輪 *kōrin* halo
輝 *hika(ri)-kagaya(ku)* shine, glitter. *kōki* brightness, splendor
熱 *kōnetsu* light and heat
熱費 *kōnetsuhi* fuel-and-light expense, utilities
16 頭 *kōtō* bald head
17 環 *kōkan* corona
臨 *kōrin* our visit, your company

A **先** 350 J4068 M1349 SEN the future; priority, precedence. *saki(njiru), saki(nzuru)* precede; forestall, anticipate. *saki* point, tip, end; nozzle; head (of a line); the first priority; the future; objective, destination; sequel, remainder; the other party; future. *saki no* previous, prior. *saki ni* before, earlier than; ahead, beyond, away; previously; recently. *ma(zu)* first (of all); about, almost, hardly (with neg.); anyway; well, now. *sen ni* formerly. *sen no* former, previous, old, late.

2 人 *senjin* predecessor, pioneer, ancestor
入 *sennyū* preconception, prejudice
入主 *sennyūshu* preconception, prejudice
入感 *sennyūkan* preconception, prejudice, preoccupation
入観 *sennyūkan* preconception, prejudice, preoccupation
3 口 *senkuchi* previous application; previous engagement
4 手 *sente* the first move; initiative, forestalling. *sakite* front lines, vanguard
方 *sempō* the other party, he, they; destination. *sakikata* the person in front; companion
日 *senjitsu, saki(no)hi* the other day, a few days ago
月 *sengetsu* last month
王 *sen'ō, sennō* the late king, the preceding king; good ancient kings
以 *ma(zu)mo(tte)* first of all, in the first place
太 *sakibuto* thicker toward the end, club-shaped
夫 *sempu* former husband; late husband
日付 *sakihizuke* dating forward
天性 *sentensei* hereditary
天的 *sententeki* inborn, innate, inherent, congenital, hereditary
天病 *sentembyō* hereditary disease
天梅毒 *senten-baidoku* congenital syphilis
5 生 *sensei* teacher, master, doctor
立 *sakida(tsu)* go before, precede; die before; take precedence *sakida(teru)* have (someone) go ahead
付 *sakizu(ke)* dating forward
代 *sendai* family predecessor; previous age; previous generation
払 *sakibara(i)* advance payment; payment on delivery; forerunner
主 *senshu* former master; late master
古 *senko* ancient times
世 *saki (no) yo* previous existence
史学 *senshigaku* prehistory
6 行 *sakiyu(ki), sakii(ki)* the future. *senkō* preceding, going first
回 *sakimawa(ri)* going on ahead; forestalling; anticipating; arrival before another
安 *sakiyasu* lower future quotations
年 *sennen* former years, formerly, a few years ago
先 *ma(zu)ma(zu)* tolerable. *sakizaki* the distant future; places one visits. *mama* well, well
先月 *sensengetsu* month before last
在 *senzai* pre-existence
在性 *senzaisei* priority
任 *sennin* seniority, predecessor
任者 *senninsha* senior official, senior members
任将校 *sennin shōkō* senior officer
任順 *senninjun* order of seniority
7 走 *sakibashi(ru)* be forward, be impertinent
攻 *senkō* batting first
役 *sen'yaku* former post; former occupant of the post
投 *sentō* starting pitcher
売 *sakiu(ri)* advance sale
君 *senkun* previous ruler; ancestors

見 *senken* foresight, anticipation
見明 *senken (no) mei* foresight, anticipation
見者 *senkensha* seer
住民族 *senjū minzoku* aborigines
住者 *senjūsha* former occupant
決 *senketsu* previous decision
決問題 *senketsu mondai* question to be settled first
8 金 *sakigane* advance payment
非 *sempi* past sin, past folly
例 *senrei* precedent
知 *senchi* foresight; speedy comprehension
制 *sensei* headstart (of several runs)
刻 *senkoku* already, a while ago
夜 *sen'ya* a few nights ago
妻 *sensai* former wife; late wife
物 *sakimono* futures
物売買 *sakimono baibai* dealing in futures
物買 *sakimonoga(i)* buying futures; speculation
取 *senshu suru* earn the first (runs); preoccupy. *sakido(ri)* taking before others
取特権 *senshu tokken* prior right
取得点 *senshu tokuten* first runs scored
9 度 *sendo* recently
途 *sendo* crisis in a battle; death
便 *sembin* previous letter
約 *sen'yaku* previous engagement; prior contract
陣 *senjin* vanguard, advance guard
客 *senkyaku* the preceding visitor
皇 *sennō, senkō* the previous emperor
祖 *saki(no)oya, saki(tsu)oya, senzo* ancestor
祖伝来 *senzo-denrai no* inherited
発 *sempatsu* forerunner, advance party. *sempatsu suru* go on ahead
発投手 *sempatsu tōshu* starting pitcher
発隊 *sempatsutai* advance party
10 高 *sakidaka* higher future quotations
週 *senshū* last week
師 *senshi* former teacher
借 *sakiga(ri)* borrowing in advance
哲 *sentetsu* ancient wise men
進 *senshin* seniority; advance; leadership
進国 *senshinkoku* advanced nations
般 *sempan* the other day, some time ago
般来 *sempanrai* for some time
11 達 *sendatsu* guide, leader, pioneer. *senda(tte)* recently, the other day
頃 *sakigoro, senkoro* recently, the other day
婦 *sempu* former wife; late wife
務 *semmu* the most important task
細 *sakiboso* tapering toward the end
12 棒 *sakibō* front palanquin carrier; cat's-paw
渡 *sakiwata(shi)* future delivery
程 *sakihodo* some time ago
勝 *senshō* scoring the first point; winning the first game
登 *sentō* the head, the lead, the van, the first; advance guard
着 *senchaku* first arrival
番 *semban* precedence; first move (in games)
貸 *sakiga(shi)* payment in advance
遣 *senken suru* send ahead
遣部隊 *senkembutai* advance troops, vanguard
覚 *senkaku* learned man, pioneer
覚者 *senkakusha* seer, pioneer, leading spirit, enlightened person
13 触 *sakibu(re)* previous or preliminary announcement
聖 *sensei* ancient sage; Confucius
14 様 *sakisama* the other party
端 *sentan* pointed end, tip; fine point; cusp; spearhead, vanguard
隣 *sakidonari* two doors away
導 *sendō* guidance, leadership
駆 *sakiga(keru)* be the first. *sakiga(ke)* charging ahead of others; the first to charge; the initiative, the lead; pioneer, forerunner, harbinger. *senku* outrider, forerunner; pilot car; pioneer, herald, precursor
駆者 *senkusha* pioneer, forerunner
15 潜 *sakikugu(ri)* forestalling, anticipating
鋒 *sempō* advance guard
鋭 *sen'ei* radical; acute
輩 *sempai* senior, superior, elder, older graduate; progenitor; old-timer
賢 *senken* ancient sage
16 頭 *sentō* the head, the lead, the van, the first; advance guard
頭打者 *sentō dasha* lead-off man (in baseball)

18 蹤 *senshō* precedent
鞭 *semben* initiative; pioneering
験的 *senkenteki* transcendental
験論 *senkenron* transcendentalism
19 繰 *sengu(ri) ni* in order, in turn
蹴 *senshū* the kick-off
20 議 *sengi* initiative, prior consideration
議権 *sengiken* right to prior consideration

5

免 351 J-X M-X See 免 361.

兔 352 J-X M1358 See 免 361.

兌 353 J513c M1356 兊 345 J-X M1351 Da exchange.
12 換 *dakan* conversion (of paper money)
換券 *dakanken* convertible banknotes
換銀行 *dakan ginkō* bank of issue

B 克 354 J396e M1355 Koku. *ka(tsu)* win; prevail, predominate, surpass. *yo(ku)* kindly; skillfully.
3 己 *kokki* self-denial, self-control
己心 *kokkishin* spirit of self-denial
8 明 *kokumei* faithfulness, diligence, conscientiousness
服 *kokufuku* subjugation, conquest
12 復 *kokufuku* restoration

A 児 355 J3b79 M1364 兒 357 J513b M1365 Ji, Ni child. *ko* child; the young of animals. *chigo* baby, child; page; festive children.
3 女 *jijo* boys and girls; children
10 孫 *jison* children and grandchildren, descendants
11 曹 *jisō* children
12 童 *jidō* child, juvenile
童文学 *jidō bungaku* juvenile literature
童心理学 *jidō shinrigaku* child psychology
童画 *jidōga* pictures drawn by a child
童福祉 *jidō fukushi* child welfare
童劇 *jidōgeki* juvenile play
15 戯 *jigi* mere child's play

兎 356 J-X M1359 兎 358 J4546 M-X 兔 359 J513d M1368 兔 360 J-X M1368' 兔 362 J-X M-X To. *usagi* rabbit, hare, cony.
3 口 *mitsukuchi* harelip
4 欠 *uguchi, toketsu* harelip
毛 *u(no)ke* just a hair
6 耳 *usagi mimi* long ears; a gossiper
肉 *toniku* rabbit meat
有 *to(mo)a(re)* anyhow, in any case
7 角 *to(nimo)kaku(nimo), to(ni)kaku, to(ya)kaku, to(mo)kaku(mo), to(mo)kaku, tokaku* anyhow, anyway, somehow or other, generally speaking, in any case. *tokaku* this and that; many; be apt to
9 狩 *usagiga(ri)* rabbit hunting
10 馬 *usagiuma* donkey
11 脣 *iguchi, mitsukuchi, toshin* harelip
12 結 *usagi musu(bi)* loop knot
斯 *to(ya)kō* this or that
14 網 *usagi ami* rabbit-catching net

6

兒 357 J513b M1365 See 児 355.

兎 358 J4546 M-X See 兎 356.

兔 359 J513d M1368 See 兎 356.

兔 360 J-X M1368' See 兎 356.

B 免 361 J4c48 M-X 兔 352 J-X M1358 免 351 J-X M-X Men dismissal. *manuga(reru), manuka(reru)* escape from, be rescued from, avoid, evade, avert, elude, be exempted, be relieved from pain, get rid of. *men(jiru), men(zuru)* dismiss; exempt. *(ni) men(jite)* in deference to.
5 囚 *menshū* discharged prisoner
7 役 *men'eki* release from office, military service, or prison
状 *menjō* diploma; license
8 官 *menkan* dismissal, discharge
9 除 *menjo* exemption, discharge, exoneration
疫 *men'eki* immunity; immunization

疫血清 *men'eki kessei* serum
疫性 *men'ekisei* immunity
10 租 *menso* tax exemption
租地 *mensochi* tax-exempt land
11 責 *menseki* exemption from responsibility
許 *menkyo* license, certificate, permit
許状 *menkyojō* license, certificate, permit
許証 *menkyoshō* license, permit
12 訴 *menso* acquittal, dismissal (of a case)
税 *menzei* tax exemption; duty exemption
税店 *menzeiten* duty-free shop
税表 *menzeihyō* duty-free list
税品 *menzeihin* duty-free articles
13 罪 *menzai* acquittal, pardon; papal indulgence
罪符 *menzaifu* an indulgence
17 黜 *menchutsu* dismissal
18 職 *menshoku* dismissal, discharge

7

免 362 J-X M-X See 兎 356.

8

A 党 363 J455e M1381 黨 7062 J735e M48132 Tō party, faction, clique; companions. *tō(suru)* side with, make common cause with.
2 人 *tojin* party member, partisan
3 与 *tōyo* companions; conspirators
4 内 *tōnai* intra-party
6 色 *tōshoku* partisan coloring
争 *tōsō* party rivalry
同伐異 *tōdō-batsui* partisanship, cliquism
7 利 *tōri* party interests
利党略 *tōri-tōryaku* (thinking of) party interests and policies
9 首 *tōshu* party leader
紀 *tōki* party discipline
則 *tōsoku* party rules
是 *tōze* party platform
派 *tōha* party, faction, clique
派心 *tōhashin* factiousness
派秘密会 *tōha himitsukai* party caucus
10 員 *tōin* party member, partisan
11 情 *tōjō* condition of the political party
略 *tōryaku* party policy, party platform
務 *tōmu* party affairs
規 *tōki* party regulations
12 費 *tōhi* party expenses; party dues
13 勢 *tōsei* party strength
14 閥 *tōbatsu* faction; cliquism
15 論 *tōron* party platform, party opinion
輩 *tōhai* associates, companions
弊 *tōhei* party evils
18 類 *tōrui* faction, partisans, gang
20 議 *tōgi* party policy, platform, party conference
籍 *tōseki* party registration, membership (in a party)

9

兜 364 J3375 M1386 Tō. To. *kabuto* helmet, headpiece.
0 虫 *kabuto mushi* beetle

12

兢 365 J513e M1395 KYŌ *tsutsu(shimu)* be discreet, be careful, be prudent, be cautious; restrain oneself, be moderate.
14 兢 *kyōkyō* fearfully; respectfully

RAD. 入 11

Iru enter. At top: 𠆢 *iri-yane* "entering" roof or *iri-gashira* "entering" top. Nickname: Entering.
Note that it is often very difficult to distinguish between Rads. 9 and 11 when these occur at the top as *hito-yane* and *iri-yane*; therefore, we have treated all such cases as Rad. 9.

A 入 366 J467e M1415 NYŪ. JU. *i(ru)* go in, come in; flow into; set; set in. *hai(ru)* enter; break into; join; enroll; contain, hold; accommodate; have (an income of). *i(reru)* put in, take in, bring in, let in, admit, introduce, commit (to prison), usher in; insert; set (jewels); employ; listen to; tolerate, comprehend; include; pay (interest); cast (votes). *i(ri)* entering, setting (of the sun); audience; capacity; income; beginning. *-i(re)* container, receptacle.

3 口 *irikuchi, iriguchi, hai(ri)guchi* entrance, gate, approach, mouth
子 *i(re)ko* nest (of boxes)
4 込 *i(re)-ko(mu)* put forth (effort). *i(ri)-ko(mu)* go into, come into, penetrate; become complicated. *i(ri)go(mi)* coming in together; unreserved seats for the public
日 *i(ri)hi* setting sun
木 *i(re)ki* wood inlay. *nyūboku* calligraphy
毛 *i(re)ge* false hair, switch
水 *jusui, nyūsui* suicide by drowning, drowning oneself
内 *judai* imperial bridal party's entry into the court
仏 *nyūbutsu* enshrining a Buddhist image
切 *i(ri)-ki(reru)* (all) are able to get in
夫 *nyūfu suru* marry into the wife's family
手 *nyūshu* receipt, procurement
手難 *nyūshunan* difficulty of obtaining
5 用 *i(ri)yō, nyūyō* need, demand, necessity
目 *i(ri)me* expenses. *i(re)me* artificial eye
立 *i(ri)-ta(tsu)* enter, penetrate; interfere in, be inquisitive
代 *i(ri)-ka(waru), i(re)-ka(waru) vi* change places, relieve (one another). *i(re)-ka(eru) vt* replace, substitute
母屋 *irimoya* hip-gable roof
札 *nyūsatsu* bid, bidding
札者 *nyūsatsusha* bidder
6 舟 *i(ri)bune, i(ri)fune* incoming ship; ship's arrival
江 *i(ri)e* inlet, cove, creek, bay
交 *i(ri)-ma(jiru)* mix with, be mixed. *i(re)-ma(zeru) vt* mix
合 *i(re)-a(waseru)* make up for
会 *nyūkai* admission, joining, enrollment
会式 *nyūkaishiki* initiation ceremony
会金 *nyūkaikin* admission fee, initiation fee
会者 *nyūkaisha* entrant, new member
7 廷 *nyūtei* admission to the courtroom
乱 *i(ri)-mida(reru)* be jumbled together
牢 *nyūrō, jurō* imprisonment
来 *nyūrai* an august visit, arrival
社 *nyūsha* joining a company
社試験 *nyūsha shiken* test for a position in a company
8 金 *nyūkin* payment, money received; money due
門 *nyūmon* entering an institute; primer; manual; introduction to
門者 *nyūmonsha* beginner
所 *nyūsho* entrance, admission; imprisonment, internment
波 *i(ri)nami* incoming wave
物 *i(re)mono* receptacle, container
京 *nyūkyō* entering the capital
念 *nyūnen ni* with scrupulous care
舎 *nyūsha* entering a dormitory
定 *nyūjō* Zen contemplation; death of a priest; nirvana; spiritual liberty
知恵 *i(re)jie* suggestion, hint
国 *nyūkoku, nyūgoku* entering a country
国税 *nyūkokuzei* alien tax, landing tax
苑 *nyūen* entering the garden
苑券 *nyūenken* ticket to the garden
学 *nyūgaku* matriculation
学生 *nyūgakusei* new student
学式 *nyūgakushiki* entrance ceremony
学考査 *nyūgaku kōsa* entrance examination
学志願者 *nyūgaku shigansha* applicants for admission
学金 *nyūgakukin* matriculation fee
学者 *nyūgakusha* new student
学試験 *nyūgaku shiken* entrance examinations
学難 *nyūgakunan* difficulty of getting into a college
学願書 *nyūgaku gansho* application for admittance to a school
9 信 *nyūshin* entering the faith
城 *nyūjō* triumphant entry into a castle
相 *i(ri)ai* sunset
海 *iriumi* bay, gulf, inlet, creek
洛 *juraku* proceeding to Kyoto
津 *nyūshin* entering a port
神 *nyūshin* inspiration; superhuman skill, genius
室 *nyūshitsu* entering a room; studying under a Buddhist teacher
院 *nyūin* hospitalization

院患者 *nyūin kanja* in-patients
10 庫 *nyūko* warehousing, storing; entering the car barn
梅 *nyūbai* entering the rainy season
校 *nyūkō* matriculation
浸 *i(ri)-bita(ru)* seep in; stay long
浜 *i(ri)hama* salt farm
浴 *nyūyoku* bath, bathing
党 *nyūtō* joining a political party
貢 *nyūkō suru* pay tribute
荷 *nyūka, i(ri)ni* arrival of goods; goods received
射 *nyūsha* incidence
射角 *nyūshakaku* angle of incidence
11 掛 *i(ri)-ka(keru)* be about to enter (a bath etc.). *irekake* called off
混 *i(ri)-maji(ru) vi* mix with, be mixed. *i(re)-ma(zeru) vt* mix
眼 *i(re)me* artificial eye
組 *i(ri)-ku(mu)* be or become complicated
船 *nyusen, i(ri)fune* ship's arrival
隊 *nyūtai* enlistment
寇 *nyūkō* invasion, encroachment
寂 *nyūjaku* death of a priest; nirvana; spiritual liberty
道 *nyūdō* entering the priesthood; priest
道雲 *nyūdōgumo* great columns of clouds; cumulo-nimbus
12 歯 *i(re)ba* artificial tooth, denture
超 *nyūchō* excess of imports
婿 *i(ri)muko* man who takes his wife's name
違 *i(re)-chiga(eru)* misplace. *i(re)chiga(i)* passing each other
御 *nyūgo* emperor's return to the inner palace
換 *i(re)-ka(eru)* replace, substitute, shift
揚 *i(ri)-a(geru), i(re)-a(geru)* lavish money on
棺 *nyūkan* placing in the coffin
植 *nyūshoku* settlement, immigration
殖 *nyūshoku* settlement, immigration
朝 *nyūchō* visiting Japan; arrival in Japan
営 *nyūei* entering the barracks; enlistment
渠 *nyūkyo* entering a dock
費 *nyūhi* expenses
智慧 *i(re)jie, i(re)chie* suggestion, hint
港 *nyūkō* entering a port
港料 *nyūkōryō* ship's harbor charges
湯 *nyūtō* taking a hot bath; bathing at hot springs
湯客 *nyūtōkyaku* a bathing guest at a hot spring
替 *i(re)-ka(waru), i(ri)-ka(waru) vi* change places, relieve (one another). *i(re)-ka(eru) vt* replace, substitute
替部品 *ireka(e) buhin* replacement parts
場 *nyūjō* admission; entrance, entering
場門 *nyūjōmon* admission gate
場券 *nyūjōken* admission ticket; platform ticket
場者 *nyūjōsha* visitors, attendance
場料 *nyūjōryō* admission fee, gate receipts
場断 *nyūjō (o) kotowa(ri)* No Admittance.
場税 *nyūjōzei* admission tax
場権 *nyūjōken* liberty of entrance
13 滅 *nyūmetsu* dying, entering nirvana; death (of a Buddhist saint)
試 *nyūshi* entrance examinations
電 *nyūden* telegram received
14 閣 *nyūkaku* joining the cabinet
獄 *nyūgoku* imprisonment
綿 *irewata* cotton padding
雑 *i(ri)-maji(ru) vi* mix with, be mixed. *i(re)-ma(zeru) vt* mix
魂 *jukon, jikkon, jukkon* intimacy
墨 *i(re)zumi* tattooing
監 *nyūkan* imprisonment
選 *nyūsen* chosen (in a competition)
選者 *nyusensha* winner, winning candidate
漁者 *nyūgyosha* fishing lot fisherman
漁料 *nyūgyoryō* fishing-lot charge
漁権 *nyūgyoken* fishing-lot rights
15 質 *i(re)jichi, nyūshichi* pawning
賞 *nyūshō* winning a prize
賞者 *nyūshōsha* prizewinner
20 籍 *nyūseki* entrance in the family register

2

内 367 / J-X / M1418 See **内** 386.

6

兩 368 / J5140 / M1436 See **両** 23.

RAD. 八 12

Hachi eight. At top: 八 or *hachigashira*. Variants: 八 and 丷. Nickname: Eight.

A 八 369 J482c M1450 HATSU, HACHI *ya(tsu), ya(ttsu), ya* eight. *(o)ya(tsu)* between-meal snack.

2 丁 *hatchō* skillfulness
九分 *hakkubu* nearly, almost
十路 *yasoji* 80 years of age
3 口 *ya(tsu)kuchi* kimono underarm sleeve opening
千代 *yachiyo* eternity, thousands of years
千年 *yachitose, hassennen* 8000 years; thousands of years; eternity
千草 *yachigusa* variety of plants, various herbs
千歳 *yachitose* thousands of years; eternity
4 日 *yōka* eight days; the eighth (day of the month)
月 *Hachigatsu* August
切 *ya(tsu)gi(ri)* cutting into eight parts; octavo
辺形 *hachihenkei* octagon
手 *ya(tsu)de* eight-fingered-leaf shrub
手網 *ya(tsu)de ami* eight-armed scoop net
分目 *hachibumme, hachibume* eight-tenths; moderation
分音符 *hachibu ompu* an eighth note
方 *happō* all sides, directions, quarters, or corners
方美人 *happō-bijin* a person beautiful from all angles; everybody's friend
方塞 *happō fusaga(ri)* all doors closed, blocked in every direction
5 目鰻 *ya(tsu)me unagi* lamprey eel
6 州 *Yashima* (an old name for) Japan
当 *ya(tsu)ata(ri)* outburst of anger. *ya(tsu)ata(ri) ni* indiscriminately, recklessly
字 *hachi (no) ji* figure eight
字髭 *hachiji hige* finely-trimmed moustache
百万 *yaoyorozu* myriads
百長 *yaochō* put-up job, prearranged affair, logrolling
百屋 *yaoya* vegetable store; Jack-of-all-trades; dabbling in all lines of knowledge
7 角形 *hakkakkei* octagon
折判 *ya(tsu)o(ri)ban* octavo
8 卦 *hakke* eight divination signs; divination
苦 *hakku* the eight pains (of Buddhism)
9 荒 *hakkō* the national boundaries
咫鏡 *Yata (no) Kagami* the Sacred Mirror (one of the Three Imperial Treasures)
面 *hachimen* eight faces; all sides
面六臂 *hachimen-roppi* eight faces and six arms; versatile, all-round, many-sided
面玲瓏 *hachimen-reirō* beautiful from all sides; perfect serenity, affability
重 *yae* double (blossom); eightfold
重咲 *yaeza(ki)* double blossom
重垣 *yaegaki* fences within fences
重桜 *yaezakura* double cherry blossoms
重歯 *yaeba* double tooth; oblique tooth
重雲 *yaegumo* layers of clouds
重潮路 *yae (no) shioji* distant seas
10 挺 *hatchō* skillfulness
釜 *yakama(shii)* noisy, boisterous; critical; troublesome; much-discussed; fastidious
紘 *hakkō* the eight directions; the whole land; the whole world
紘一宇 *hakkō-ichiu* universal brotherhood, all eight corners of the world under one roof
11 達 *hattatsu* (roads) running in all directions; convenient transportation; ability in any line
道 *hachidō* the eight districts of feudal Japan
掛 *hachiga(ke)* twenty percent discount. *hakke* divination
12 裂 *ya(tsu)za(ki)* tearing limb from limb, tearing apart, cutting (a person) to pieces
13 福 *Hachifuku* the Beatitudes
14 端 *hattan* twilled fabric
15 潮路 *yashioji* long sea voyage
幡 *Hachiman* God of War; shrine of the God of War

幡知 *yawatashi(razu)* labyrinth, maze
幡宮 *Hachimangū* Shrine of the God of War
幡藪知 *yawata (no) yabu shi(razu)* labyrinth, maze
16 橋 *ya(tsu)hashi* zigzag bridge
24 衢 *yachimata* multiple road crossing; road network

2

兮 370 / J5142 / M1455 KEI emphatic particle in Chinese poetry used to fill out rhythm of line; adjectival suffix.

A 六 371 / J4f3b / M1453 RIKU. ROKU *mu(tsu), mu(ttsu), mu* six. *mu(zukashii)* hard, difficult; delicate; troublesome; doubtful; hopeless; stern; sullen; hard to please; serious; technical.
2 十四分音符 *rokujūshibu ompu* 64th note
十余州 *rokujūyoshū* the 66-odd provinces of old Japan
十路 *musoji* age sixty
3 大州 *roku daishū* the six continents (Asia, Africa, North America, South America, Europe, Oceania)
三制 *roku-sansei* 6-3 system of education
4 方 *roppō* the six directions (north, south, east, west, up, and down)
日 *muika* six days; the sixth (day of the month)
月 *Rokugatsu* June
辺形 *rokuhenkei* hexagon
分儀 *rokubungi* sextant
6 合 *rikugō* the universe, the cosmos
百六号 *roppyakurokugō* salvarsan
7 花 *rikka, rokka* snow
角 *rokkaku* hexagon
角形 *rokkakukei* hexagon
角堂 *rokkakudō* hexagonal building
8 法 *roppō* six law codes
法全書 *Roppō Zensho* the Statute Books
9 連発 *roku rempatsu* six-chambered (revolver)
重奏 *rokujūsō* instrumental sextet
重唱 *rokujūshō* vocal sextet
10 部 *rokubu* Buddhist pilgrim; six copies
書 *Rokusho* Hexateuch. *rikusho* six classes of characters
根清浄 *rokkon shōjō* purification of the six roots of perception
11 情 *rokujō* the six emotions (joy, anger, sorrow, pleasure, love, and hatred)
12 腑 *roppu* the six internal organs
13 感 *rokkan* the six senses
16 親 *rokushin* the six blood relationships

A 公 372 / J3878 / M1452 KŌ prince, duke, lord; public. KU *ōyake* public, open; official, governmental; formal. *kimi* prince, lord. *-kō* lord, daimyo; companion; a subordinate.
2 人 *kōjin* public character
3 子 *kōshi* young nobleman
4 方 *kubō* public affairs; the court; the shogun; the shogunate
辺 *kōhen* public ceremonies; public affairs
分母 *kōbumbo* common denominator
公然 *kōkōzen to* publicly
文 *kōbun* official document; archives
文書 *kōbunsho* official document; archives
5 示 *kōji* public announcement
布 *kōfu* proclamation, announcement
司 *kōshi, konsu* company, firm (in China)
生活 *kōseikatsu* public life
生涯 *kōshōgai* public career, public life
立 *kōritsu* public (institution)
立学校 *kōritsu gakkō* public school
正 *kōsei* justice, fairness, impartiality
正証書 *kōsei shōsho* notarized document
用 *kōyō* government business; public use; public expense
用文 *kōyōbun* official terminology
用車 *kōyōsha* official vehicle
平 *kōhei* justice, fairness
平政策 *Kōhei Seisaku* Fair Deal
平無私 *kōhei-mushi* impartiality, fair play
民 *kōmin* citizens, freemen
民生活 *kōmin seikatsu* national life
民科 *kōminka* civics
民権 *kōminken* civil rights, citizenship, franchise
民館 *kōminkan* public hall, community center
6 団 *kōdan* public corporation
吏 *kōri* public official

休 *kōkyū* legal holiday
休日 *kōkyūbi* national holiday
安 *kōan* public welfare, public safety
安官 *kōankan* railway police
式 *kōshiki* formula; formality
式主義 *kōshiki shugi* formalism
式試合 *kōshiki shiai* championship match
式訪問 *kōshiki hōmon* official visit
会 *kōkai* public meeting
会堂 *kōkaidō* public hall; town hall
会問答 *kōkai mondō* catechism
有 *kōyū* public ownership
有地 *kōyūchi* public land
有林 *kōyūrin* public forest
有物 *kōyūbutsu* public property
共 *kōkyō* society, the community. *kōkyō no* public, communal
共心 *kōkyōshin* public spirit
共団体 *kōkyō dantai* public organization
共図書館 *kōkyō toshokan* public library
共物 *kōkyōbutsu* public property
共事業 *kōkyō jigyō* public utilities
7 言 *kōgen* declaration, profession
役 *kōeki* public service
私 *kōshi* government and people; public and personal affairs. *kōshi no* public and private
邸 *kōtei* official residence
売 *kōbai* public sale, public auction
告 *kōkoku* public notice
沙汰 *ōyakezata* public question
社 *kōsha* public corporation
社債 *kōshasai* public bonds
判 *kōhan* public hearing, trial
判廷 *kōhantei* court, courtroom
判調査 *kōhan chōsa* trial record
8 金 *kōkin* public funds
国 *kōkoku* dukedom, duchy, principality
的 *kōteki* public, official
表 *kōhyō* official proclamation
事 *kōji* government business
使 *kōshi* minister (of a legation)
使館 *kōshikan* legation
明 *kōmei* fairness, justice
明正大 *kōmei-seidai* fairness, justice
法 *kōhō* public law
法人 *kōhōjin* juridical person, public corporation
武 *kōbu* nobles and soldiers; imperial court and the shogunate
武合体 *kōbu-gattai* shogunate marital union with the Imperial Family
定 *kōtei* official (rate)
定価 *kōteika* ceiling or fixed price
定価格 *kōtei kakaku* ceiling or fixed price
定相場 *kōtei sōba* ceiling price, official quotation
9 侯 *kōkō* princes and marquises; great feudal lords
約 *kōyaku* public commitment or promise
海 *kōkai* high seas
海上 *kōkaijō* on the high seas
10 庫 *kōko* finance corporation
庭 *kōtei* place of ceremony; public place
租 *kōso* public tax
家 *kuge* Imperial Court; court noble
害 *kōgai* pollution
差 *kōsa* common difference (in math); allowance, margin, tolerance
孫樹 *ichō* gingko or maidenhair tree
称 *kōshō* public name, announcing publicly
称資本 *kōshō shihon* authorized capital
益 *kōeki* public good
益法人 *kōeki hōjin* legal person working for the public weal
益事業 *kōeki jigyō* public utilities
益質屋 *kōeki shichiya* public pawn shop
益優先 *kōeki-yūsen* public interest first
11 道 *kōdō* public highway; justice
達 *kindachi* kings, children of nobles, young nobleman. *kōtatsu* official announcement
理 *kōri* axiom, maxim, self-evident truth
許 *kōkyo* official government permission
転 *kōten* revolution (around the sun)
娼 *kōshō* licensed prostitution; registered prostitute
娼全廃 *kōshō zempai* abolition of licensed prostitution
設 *kōsetsu* public (institution)
設市場 *kōsetsu ichiba* public market
教 *Kōkyō* Roman Catholicism
教会 *Kōkyōkai* Roman Catholic Church
教要理 *Kōkyō yōri* Catholic catechism
務 *kōmu* public service, official business
務災害 *kōmu saigai* accidents in line of duty
務員 *kōmuin* government worker
務疾病 *kōmu shippei* sickness incurred in line of duty

12 評 *kōhyō* popular opinion
訴 *kōso* accusation, prosecution
卿 *kugyō, kuge* Imperial Court; court noble
葬 *kōsō* public funeral
募 *kōbo* public appeal, public contribution
営 *kōei* public management
費 *kōhi* public expenditure
報 *kōhō* official bulletin, communiqué
裁 *kōsai* judicial decision
然 *kōzen no* open, avowed, public, official
然秘密 *kōzen (no) himitsu* an open secret
証 *kōshō* authentication, notarization
証人 *kōshōnin* notary public
証役場 *kōshō yakuba* notary public's office
開 *kōkai suru* present to the public
開外交 *kōkai gaikō* open diplomacy
開状 *kōkaijō* open letter
開図書館 *kōkai toshokan* public library
開講座 *kōkai kōza* extension lectures
衆 *kōshū* the public
衆伝道 *kōshū dendō* public evangelism
衆便所 *kōshū benjo* public lavatory
衆浴場 *kōshū yokujō* public bathhouse
衆道徳 *kōshū dōtoku* public morals
衆電話 *kōshū denwa* public telephone
衆衛生 *koshu eisei* public health and sanitation
13 園 *kōen* park
傷 *kōshō* occupational accident
債 *kōsai* public debt, public bond or securities
暇 *kōka* leave of absence, furlough
試 *kōshi* national examinations
路 *kōro* public road; highway
署 *kōsho* government office
義 *kōgi* justice, equity
電 *kōden* official telegram
準 *kōjun* postulate (in math)
14 選 *kōsen* public election
僕 *kōboku* public servant
演 *kōen* public performance
領 *kōryō* duchy, dukedom, principality
算 *kōsan* probability
徳 *kōtoku* civic virtues
徳心 *kōtokushin* public spirit
認 *kōnin* official authorization, recognition, license, accreditation
認会計士 *kōnin kaikeishi* certified public accountant
認候補 *kōnin kōho* official candidate
認候補者 *kōnin kōhosha* official candidate
15 儀 *kōgi* imperial court; shogunate government; authorities; public affairs. *kōgi no* official, government
憤 *kōfun* public indignation
論 *kōron* public opinion, unbiased criticism
課 *kōka* public imposts, taxes
器 *kōki* public institution
敵 *kōteki* public enemy
敵一号 *kōteki ichigō* public enemy number one
16 館 *kōkan* official residence
17 聴会 *kōchōkai* public hearing
爵 *kōshaku* prince, duke
爵夫人 *kōshaku fujin* princess, duchess
18 職 *kōshoku* public office
職追放 *kōshoku tsuihō* purge of public officials
20 議 *kōgi* just view; public opinion

4

A 共 373 / J3626 / M1458 KYŌ. *tomo* both; neither (with neg.); all; and, as well as; including; with, together with; plural ending. *tomo ni suru* share with, participate in. *tomo ni* both; alike; together, along with, with; including. *(to) tomo ni* together with.

2 力 *kyōryoku* cooperation
4 切 *tomogi(re)* same cloth (for patching)
5 用 *kyōyō* common use
立 *kyōritsu* joint, common
布 *tomogire* same cloth (for patching)
白髪 *tomoshiraga* growing old together (a couple)
犯 *kyōhan* complicity
犯者 *kyōhansha* accomplice
6 共 *tomodomo ni* together, in company
存 *kyōson, kyōzon* coexistence
存共栄 *kyōson-kyōei* coexistence and coprosperity
有 *kyōyū* joint ownership
有地 *kyōyūchi* public land; a common
有物 *kyōyūbutsu* common property
有者 *kyōyūsha* joint owners, part owners

有財産 *kyōyū zaisan* community property
同 *kyōdō* cooperation, collaboration, association; joint (defense)
同一致 *kyōdō itchi* unanimous cooperation
同井戸 *kyōdō ido* common well
同水栓 *kyōdō suisen* common faucet
同生活 *kyōdō seikatsu* community life; cohabitation
同会見 *kyōdō kaiken* news conference
同防衛 *kyōdō bōei* joint defense
同体 *kyōdōtai* cooperative body; cooperative system
同社会 *kyōdō shakai* a communal society, community
同住宅 *kyōdō jūtaku* a settlement; an apartment house
同声明 *kyōdō seimei* joint declaration
同性 *kyōdōsei* cooperation
同者 *kyōdōsha* coworker
同炊事場 *kyōdō suijiba* community kitchen
同便所 *kyōdō benjo* public toilet
同相続人 *kyōdō sōzokunin* joint heir
同計算 *kyōdō keisan* pooling; joint account
同租界 *kyōdō sokai* international settlement
同責任 *kyōdō sekinin* joint responsibility; solidarity
同組合 *kyōdō kumiai* a cooperative; a partnership
同救済基金 *kyōdō kyūsai kikin* community chest
同経営 *kyōdō keiei* joint management
同募金 *kyōdō bokin* community chest
同疎開 *kyōdō sokai* community evacuation
同墓地 *kyōdō bochi* public cemetery
同農場 *kyōdō nōjō* collective farm
同戦線 *kyōdō sensen* united front
同管理 *kyōdō kanri* joint control
同線 *kyōdōsen* party line
7 助 *kyōjo* cooperation
労者 *kyōrōsha* coworker
8 学 *kyōgaku* coeducation
学制 *kyōgakusei* coeducational plan
和主義 *kyōwa shugi* republicanism
和国 *kyōwakoku* republic
和制 *kyōwasei* republicanism
和制度 *kyōwa seido* republicanism
和政体 *kyōwa seitai* republican form of government
和政治 *kyōwa seiji* republican government
和党 *Kyōwatō* Republican Party
9 食 *tomogu(i)* cannibalism (in animals), mutual destruction, internecine struggle, eating each other; damaging each other
栄 *kyōei* mutual prosperity
栄圏 *kyōeiken* coprosperity sphere
通 *kyōtsū no* common
通点 *kyōtsūten* common feature
通語 *kyōtsūgo* common term, common language
10 倒 *tomodao(re)* falling together, mutual destruction, joint bankruptcy
振 *kyōshin* resonance
益 *kyōeki* common profit
進会 *kyōshinkai* competitive exhibition, prize show
11 訳 *kyōyaku* joint translation
著 *kyōcho* coauthorship
済 *kyōsai* mutual aid
済組合 *kyōsai kumiai* a cooperative society, a mutual-benefit association
販 *kyōhan* cooperative selling
販会社 *kyōhangaisha* cooperative sales company
産化 *kyōsanka* communization
産分子 *kyōsan bunshi* communist elements
産中国 *Kyōsan Chūgoku* Communist China
産主義 *kyōsan shugi* communism, collectivism
産主義国 *kyōsan shugikoku* communist country
産主義者 *kyōsan shugisha* a communist
産地区 *kyōsan chiku* communist area
産系 *kyōsankei* communist controlled
産国家群 *kyōsan kokkagun* Communist bloc
産軍 *kyōsangun* communist army
産陣営 *kyōsan jin'ei* Communist camp
産党 *Kyōsantō* Communist Party
産党政治局 *Kyōsantō Seijikyoku* Politburo
産党細胞 *kyōsantō saibō* communist cell
産圏 *kyōsanken* communist sphere
12 営 *kyōei* joint management

13 催 *kyōsai* two or more organizations sponsoring a meeting together
裏 *tomoura* lining a kimono with the same material as the kimono itself
寝 *tomone* sleeping together
感 *kyōkan* sympathy, response
14 鳴 *kyōmei, tomona(ri)* resonance, sympathy
鳴者 *kyōmeisha* sympathizer, fellow traveler
演 *kyōen* coacting, costarring
演者 *kyōenshu* costar, coactor
15 稼 *tomokase(gi)* (husband and wife) earning a living together
編 *kyōhen* joint editorship
編者 *kyōhensha* coeditor
16 謀 *kyōbō* conspiracy, complicity
謀者 *kyōbōsha* conspirator, accomplice
18 襟 *tomoeri* same-colored neckband
観福音書 *kyōkan fukuinsho* diatessaron

5

A **兵** 374 / J4a3c / M1462 HEI, HYŌ soldier, private; troops, army; warfare; arms; strategy, tactics. *tsuwamono* soldier, warrior.
2 力 *heiryoku* military force; force of arms; strength of an army
3 士 *heishi* soldier
刃 *heijin* sword blade
4 戈 *heika* swords; arms; warfare
火 *heika* fire caused by war
5 仗 *heijō* arms; armed soldier
6 団 *heidan* army corps
式体操 *heishikitaisō* military drill
7 車 *heisha* war chariot
乱 *heiran* war, disturbance
児帯 *heko obi* waist band
役 *heieki* military service
役忌避 *heieki kihi* evading the draft
役免除 *heieki menjo* draft exemption
8 長 *heichō* lance corporal
制 *heisei* military system
卒 *heisotsu* soldier, private
舎 *heisha* barracks
事 *heiji* military affairs
法 *heihō* art of war, strategy, tactics
法家 *heihōka* tactician, strategist
学 *heigaku* military science, strategy, tactics
学者 *heigakusha* tactician, strategist
学校 *heigakkō* naval academy
9 革 *heikaku* arms; war
食 *heishoku* food for soldiers and noncommissioned officers
威 *heii* military power
科 *heika* branch of the army
変 *heihen* military disturbance
10 馬 *heiba* arms and cavalry; troops; war; military affairs
匪 *heihi* bandits
員 *heiin* military strength, military personnel
家 *heika* soldier; tactician, strategist
書 *heisho* book on military science
站 *heitan* supply train, communications
站学 *heitangaku* logistics
站部 *heitambu* commissariat
站基地 *heitan kichi* supply base
站線 *heitansen* supply line, line of communications
11 略 *heiryaku* strategy
船 *heisen* warship
隊 *heitai* soldier; sailor
曹 *heisō* warrant officer
曹長 *heisōchō* chief warrant officer
12 備 *heibi* war preparations
営 *heiei* barracks
13 禍 *heika* ravages of war
粮 *hyōrō* (army) provisions, food
数 *heisū* number of soldiers
14 種 *heishu* branch of an army
端 *heitan* hostilities, beginning of hostilities
語 *heigo* military term
15 権 *heiken* military authority
鋒 *heihō* the point of a sword; the advance of an army
器 *heiki* arms, ordnance
器工 *heikikō* armorer
器工場 *heiki kōjō* arsenal, ordnance factory, armory
器庫 *heikiko* armory
器廠 *heikishō* armory, arsenal, ordnance department
18 難 *heinan* distress of war
燹 *heisen* fire caused by war
糧 *hyōrō* (army) provisions; food
糧米 *hyōrōmai* army rice
糧攻 *hyōrōze(me)* starvation tactics
20 籍 *heiseki* military register

A **典** 375/J4535/M1474 TEN ceremony, celebration; law code. *nori* rule, law.
5 礼 *tenrei* ceremony; etiquette, courtesy; (Catholic) liturgy
8 侍 *tenji* maid of honor, lady in waiting
拠 *tenkyo* authority
物 *tembutsu* pawned article
9 則 *tensoku* regulations
故 *tenko* authentic precedent
型 *tenkei* type, pattern
型的 *tenkeiteki* typical, model, ideal
13 雅 *tenga na* refined, graceful, elegant, classic
14 獄 *tengoku* warden of a prison
15 範 *tempan* model, standard, law
16 薬 *ten'yaku* court physician
19 麗 *tenrei na* graceful
20 籍 *tenseki* books

A **具** 376/J3671/M1473 **具** 377/J-X/M-X GU tool; vessel; means; ingredients (in a dish); counter for armor, suits, sets of furniture. *gu(suru)* possess, have; be accompanied by. *sona(waru)* be furnished with, be endowed with, possess; be among, be one of. *sona(eru)* furnish, provide, equip, install; have ready; prepare; possess, have; be endowed with; be armed with. *tsubusa ni* minutely, fully.
5 申 *gushin* reporting (to a superior)
6 合 *guai* fitness, order, condition; way, style; convenience; decency; propriety; state of health; situation; arrangements
有 *guyū* preparedness. *guyū suru* have, possess, be endowed with
7 述 *gujutsu* speaking in detail
状 *gujō* full report. *gujō suru* tell the circumstances in detail
足 *gusoku* completeness; armor
足師 *gusokushi* armorer
体 *gutai* concreteness
体化 *gutaika* embodiment, materialization
体的 *gutaiteki* concrete, tangible, definite
体策 *gutaisaku* concrete plan
8 者 *gu(no)mono* companion, follower
10 陳 *guchin* formal statement
案 *guan* framing a plan; concrete plan
11 現 *gugen* incarnation, embodiment
現化 *gugenka* materialization, realization
眼 *gugan* discrimination
眼士 *gugan(no)shi* man of discernment
眼者 *gugansha* man of discernment
12 備 *gubi suru* have, possess, be endowed with
象 *gushō suru* embody, express concretely
象化 *gushōka suru* incorporate, materialize
象的 *gushōteki* concrete, material
14 徳 *gutoku* (Buddhist) merit

其 378/J4236/M1472 KI. *so(no)* that (adj.). *sore* that, it. *sore da kara* therefore. *sore datte* but. *sore de* thereupon, therefore. *sore de koso* all the more. *sore da noni, sore na noni* nevertheless. *sore wa sō toshite* be that as it may. *sore tomo* or. *sore ja, sore dewa* then, in that case; well. *sore demo* nevertheless. *sore kara* after that; since; and then, and; from then on. *sore koso* the very thing. *sore nara* if so. *sore ni* besides, moreover, what is more. *sore ni shite mo* even so, nevertheless. *sore ni shite wa* considering that. *sore wa sō to* but now, to change the subject.
3 上 *so(no)ue* on top of that, over and above, in addition, besides
丈 *sore dake* that much; only that; only that much. *soredake ni* all the more because
4 辺 *so(no) hen* thereabouts, in the neighborhood
手 *so(no) te* that trick, that move, that way
内 *so(no) uchi* soon, before long; some day; meanwhile; among the number
日暮 *so(no)higura(shi)* hand-to-mouth existence
日稼 *so(no)hi kasegi* day labor
方 *sochira, sonata, sochi, so(no)hō* over there, your place; you, your family; the other one. *sotchi, so(no)hō, sonata* that direction, that way, that one, that
方此方 *sochikochi* here and there; this and that
方達 *sochitachi, so(no)hōtachi* you (plural)

方等 *sotchira, sochira, so(no)hōra* you (plural)
5 付 *sore(ni)tsu(kete)mo, sore(ni)tsu(ki), sore(ni)tsu(ite)* concerning that
他 *so(no)ta* the others, the rest
奴 *soitsu* that guy; that one, that, it
外 *so(no) hoka* the rest, the others
迄 *sore made* till then; so long, so far, so much, to that extent; the end
処 *soko* that place, there; to that extent; when, at this juncture. *soredokoro ka* on the contrary, out of the question (too busy). *soko(ra), soko(ira)* about there, around there. *soko de* then, thereupon, accordingly
処当 *soko(ra) ata(ri)* about there, around there
処迄 *soko made* that far
処此処 *soko-koko ni* here and there, in places; sporadically
6 式 *soreshiki* only that much
成 *sorenari ni* in its own way; as it is
向 *so(no) mu(ki)* that direction; the person concerned
7 位 *sore kurai, soregurai, so(no) kurai, so(no)gurai* about that many, about so much
身其儘 *so(no)mi-so(no)mama* just as it is
8 居 *sore (de) i(te)* and yet
物 *so(no) mono* the thing itself
限 *sorekiri, sore(k)kiri, sore kagi(ri)* no more than that
実 *so(no)jitsu* really, in reality
其 *sore(wa) sore(wa)* exceedingly, terrific. *sorezore* each, respectively. *sore(wa) sore toshite* be that as it may
者 *so(no) mono* the person himself
9 通 *so(no) tō(ri)* That's right; exactly, just like that
後 *so(no)go* thereafter, later, since then
除 *so(tchi)no(ke) ni suru* neglect, lay aside, slight, ignore
故 *soreyue* therefore
相応 *sore sōō ni* in a corresponding degree
11 道 *so(no) michi* line of business, profession, trade, art
頃 *so(no) koro* about that time
許 *sore bakari* only that, about that much
12 程 *sore hodo* so, so far, to that extent; (not) very
筋 *so(no) suji* the authorities concerned
筈 *so(no) hazu* proper, just, reasonable
無 *sore (to) na(ku)* indirectly, by implication
場 *so(no)ba* the place, the spot, the occasion, the situation
場逃 *so(no)banoga(re)* temporizing, stopgap
場限 *so(no)bakagi(ri)* on the spur of the moment. *so(no)bakagi(ri) no* temporary, makeshift
13 節 *so(no) setsu* at that time
14 様 *sonna, so(no)yō na* that kind of. *so(no)yō ni* in that way
15 儀 *so(no)gi* such is the case
16 儘 *so(no)mama* as it is, in that condition
積 *so(no) tsumo(ri) de* with that in mind
18 癖 *so(no) kuse* nevertheless, still

7

荊 379 / J-X / M-X See **荊** 5026.

茲 380 / J-X / M-X See **茲** 3617.

8

B **兼** 381 / J3773 / M1483 KEN and, in addition, concurrently. *ka(neru)* combine with, serve as both; hold an additional post; use with. *ka(nete)* simultaneously. *-ka(neru)* cannot; hesitate to; be impatient.
5 用 *ken'yō* combined use, combination, serving two purposes
仕 *ka(ne)-tsuka(eru)* serve at the same time
6 行 *kenkō* doing simultaneously
任 *kennin* concurrent post
合 *ka(ne)a(i)* equilibrium, poise. *ka(ne)-a(u)* to balance, to poise
7 役 *ka(ne)yaku* carrying on a second line of work
8 併 *kempei suru* unite
官 *kenkan* additional post
10 修 *kenshū* studying two lines together (as a major and a minor)
兼 *ka(ne)ga(ne)* often, lately, already
帯 *kentai* combined use, combination, filling two positions; serving two purposes

11 務 *kemmu* additional post
12 備 *kembi suru* be proficient in both, combining both. *ka(ne)-sona(eru)* have both, combine with
補 *kempo* carrying on a second line of work
勤 *kenkin* additional post
営 *ken'ei suru* operate or carry on simultaneously
13 摂 *kensetsu* concurrent post
業 *kengyō* side line
業農家 *kengyō nōka* part-time farmer
18 職 *kenshoku* concurrent post
題 *kendai* subject for a poem

11

RAD. 冂 13

Dōgamae (enclosure like that of *dō* "same"), *makigamae*, or *keigamae*. Variants: 冂, 冂, 𠘨. Nickname: Upside-down Box.

冂 384 J5144 M1506 KEI border, far.

2

A **円** 385 J315f M1513 **圓** 961 J5424 M4819 EN circle; yen. *mado(ka) na* round; tranquil. *maru(i), maro(yaka) na* round, circular, spherical. *tsubura na* round, rotund. *maru* circle; money.
4 心 *enshin* center of a circle
内 *ennai* within the circle
5 丘 *enkyū* knoll, hummock
6 安 *en'yasu* cheap yen
光 *enkō* halo
虫類 *enchūrui* round worms
7 形 *enkei, marugata* circle, round shape
8 居 *madoi* small gathering, happy circle
価 *enka* value of the yen
味 *marumi* roundness, rotundity
弧 *enko* arc
周 *enshū* circumference
周率 *enshūritsu* circular constant, pi
卓 *entaku* round table
卓会議 *entaku kaigi* round-table conference
9 建 *enda(te)* yen base
柱 *enchū* column, shaft, cylinder. *marubashira* cylindrical column
陣 *enjin* circle, ring
盆 *marubon* round tray
型 *marugata* circle, circular form
屋根 *maru yane* dome, cupola
為替 *engawase* yen exchange
10 高 *endaka* exchange in favor of the yen, strong yen
座 *enza* sitting in a circle; round straw mat
11 域 *en'iki* yen bloc, yen area
規 *enki* a pair of compasses
頂 *enchō* dome, cupola
寂 *enjaku* nirvana; death of the Buddha or a priest
窓 *marumado* round window
貨 *enka* yen currency
運動 *en'undō* circular motion
転 *enten(taru)* orotund, spherical; smoothly rolling
転滑脱 *enten-katsudatsu* versatility, adaptability, tact
12 弾 *endan* round shot
満 *emman* perfection, harmony, peace, satisfaction, smoothness, integrity, completeness
筒 *entō* cylinder
13 滑 *enkatsu, enkotsu* smoothness, harmony
鉋 *maruganna* round carpenter's plane

兾 382 J-X M1494 See **冀** 383.

14

冀 383 J5143 M1500 **兾** 382 J-X M1494 KI. *koinega(u)* beg, request, pray, beseech; hope, desire.
7 図 *kito* hopefully planning
8 念 *kinen* hope, desire, aspiration, anticipation; request
11 望 *kibō* hope, desire, aspiration, anticipation; request

蓋 *engai* cupola, dome, vault
14 舞 *embu* waltz
15 墳 *empun* burial mound
熟 *enjuku* ripeness, mellowness, maturity, perfection
盤 *emban* disk; discus
盤投 *embanna(ge)* discus throw
16 錐 *ensui* cone. *marugiri* round gimlet
錐形 *ensuikei* cone
17 壔 *entō* cylinder
18 顔 *marugao* round face
19 鏡 *enkyō, maru kagami* round mirror
25 顱 *enro* tonsure, shaven head

A **内** 386 / J4662 / M1512 **内** 367 / J-X / M1418 DAI, NAI inside, interior, within, between, among. *uchi* inside, interior; house, home; within; between, among, out of; mind; myself. *uchi-* inner. *-nai* within, within the scope of.

2 力 *nairyoku* internal stress
3 大臣 *Naidaijin* Lord Keeper of the Privy Seal
4 心 *naishin* inmost heart, one's mind, in the heart
方 *naihō* inside; your wife (honorific)
内 *uchiuchi* family circle, the inside. *uchiuchi no, nainai* private, informal; secret, confidential
反脚 *naihankyaku* bowlegs
火艇 *naikatei* launch
分 *naibun* secret, confidential
分泌 *naibumpi, naibumpitsu* internal secretion
5 示 *naiji, naishi* unofficial announcement
圧 *naiatsu* internal pressure
払 *uchibara(i)* part payment
包 *naihō* connotation, comprehension
出血 *naishukketsu* internal hemorrhage
玄関 *uchi genkan, naigenkan* side entrance
弁慶 *uchibenkei* braggart
用 *naiyō* internal use; private business
用薬 *naiyōyaku* medicine taken internally
申 *naishin* unofficial report
申書 *naishinsho* pupil's record
外 *naigai* inside and outside; domestic and foreign; approximately. *uchi-soto* inside and out
外人 *naigaijin* nationals and foreigners
外野 *naigaiya* infield and outfield

6 因 *naiin* the actual reason
気 *uchiki* timidity, shyness, bashfulness
池 *uchi ike* garden pond
旨 *naishi* emperor's secret orders
争 *naisō* internal strife
向性 *naikōsei* introversion
交渉 *uchi kōshō* preliminary negotiations
耳 *naiji* inner ear
耳炎 *naijien* inner ear inflammation
地 *naichi* homeland; mainland; inland
地人 *naichijin* Japanese in Japan proper
地米 *naichimai* homegrown rice
在 *naizai* immanence, inherence, indwelling
在性 *naizaisei* immanence, inherence, indwelling
在的 *naizaiteki* immanent, internal, intrinsic
7 見 *naiken* preliminary inspection, preview
角 *naikaku* interior angle; inside corner (in baseball)
局 *naikyoku* a bureau in a ministry
応 *naiō* secret understanding, collusion; betrayal
廷 *naitei* harem; inside the palace; the palace
住 *naijū* indwelling (life)
攻 *naikō* (disease) settling in internal organs; quarreling among companions
状 *naijō* internal conditions; true state of affairs
乱 *nairan* civil war, rebellion
助 *naijo* a wife's help
含 *naigan* implication
弟子 *uchi deshi* live-in apprentice
沙汰 *uchizata* secret government business
8 金 *uchikin* bargain money, money paid on account
侍 *naishi* maid of honor
径 *naikei* bore, inside diameter
法 *uchinori* inside measure
治 *naiji, naichi* internal or domestic affairs
命 *naimei* private or secret orders
実 *naijitsu* the facts
定 *naitei* tentative decision
炎 *naien* inner flame
苑 *naien* inner garden, inner park
典 *naiten* sutras, Buddhist literature

妻 *naisai* common-law wife
事 *naiji* personal affairs; internal affairs
国 *naikoku* home country
国産 *naikokusan* domestic product
所 *naisho* kitchen; state of finances
所話 *naishobanashi* secret talk
的 *naiteki* inner, intrinsic, mental, inherited
的生活 *naiteki seikatsu* the inner life
服 *naifuku* internal use
服薬 *naifukuyaku* medicine taken internally
股 *uchimomo, uchimata* inner thigh. *uchimata ni* (walking) pigeon-toed
股膏薬 *uchimata-gōyaku* duplicity, double-dealing; double-dealer, turncoat, fence-sitter
9 造 *uchizuku(ri)* inside finishing (of a home)
相 *Naishō* prewar Home Minister
海 *uchi umi, naikai* inlet, bay, inland sea
約 *naiyaku* (marriage) engagement; secret treaty; tacit understanding; private contract
陣 *naijin* chancel, inner sanctuary
政 *naisei* internal administration; domestic affairs
界 *naikai* inner world, inner sphere
奏 *naisō* secret report to the emperor
冑 *uchi kabuto* inside of a helmet; hidden circumstances
省 *naisei* introspection, reflection
祝 *uchi iwai* family celebration; small present on such an occasion
祝言 *naishūgen* private wedding
面 *naimen* inside, interior
面的 *naimenteki* inner, internal, inside
通 *naitsū* secret understanding, collusion
通者 *naitsūsha* betrayer
科 *naika* internal medicine
科医 *naikai* physician, internist
10 庭 *uchiniwa, naitei* inner court, quadrangle
借 *uchiga(ri)* drawing ahead on salary
紛 *naifun* domestic or internal discord
航 *naikō* coastwise service
訌 *naikō* internal or domestic discord
訓 *naikun* private or secret orders
倉 *uchikura* a godown within a building or compound
宴 *naien* private dinner
宮 *Naikū, Naigū* Inner Ise Shrine

陸 *nairiku* inland
陸国 *nairikukoku* landlocked country
陸霧 *nairikumu* inland fog
部 *naibu* interior, inside. *naibu no* internal
部生活 *naibuseikatsu* the inner life
部的 *naibuteki* internal
容 *naiyō* contents, detail, import
容見本 *naiyō mihon* sample pages
容物 *naiyōbutsu* contents (of the stomach)
容証明 *naiyō shōmei* certification of contents
11 達 *naitatsu* unofficial notice
偵 *naitei* scouting
側 *uchigawa* inside, interior, inner part
堀 *uchibori* inner moat, moat within the castle walls
情 *naijō* internal conditions; true state of affairs
張 *uchiba(ri)* lining, ceiling, wainscoting
掛 *uchiga(ke)* throwing down by leg work
接 *naisetsu* inscribed (circle)
探 *naitan* private inquiry, secret investigation
済 *naisai* settlement out of court
訳 *uchiwake* items, breakdown; classification
規 *naiki* private regulations, bylaws, tradition
密 *naimitsu* privacy, secrecy. *naimitsu ni* confidentially, privately, off the record
兜 *uchi kabuto* inside of a helmet; hidden circumstances
患 *naikan* internal or domestic trouble
寄合 *uchi yoria(i)* family council
勘定 *uchi kanjō* secret account
遊星 *naiyūsei* inner planet
斜視 *naishashi* cross-eyed, strabismus
務 *naimu* internal or domestic affairs
務大臣 *Naimu Daijin* prewar Home Minister
務省 *Naimushō* prewar Ministry of Home Affairs
野 *naiya* infield, diamond
野手 *naiyashu* infielder, baseman
野席 *naiyaseki* infield bleachers
12 検 *naiken* preliminary inspection
港 *naikō* inner harbor
湯 *uchiyu* hotsprings water in the home, indoor bathplace

渡 *uchiwata(shi)* partial delivery; partial payment
腔 *naikō* lumen
診 *naishin* pelvic examination
勤 *naikin* office or indoor work
貸 *uchiga(shi)* advancing part of a salary
報 *naihō* secret information
割引 *uchi waribiki* bank discount
惑星 *naiwakusei* inner planet
証 *naishō* secret, privacy; internal evidence; one's circumstances
証事 *naishōgoto* a secret
証話 *naishōbanashi* confidential talk, whispering
13 殿 *naiden* inner shrine
債 *naisai* domestic loan
福 *naifuku* richer than it appears
隠 *uchi kaku(shi)* inside pocket
戦 *naisen* civil war
意 *naii* intention, personal opinion
裏 *dairi* imperial palace
裏雛 *dairibina* festival dolls representing the emperor and empress
蒙 *Naimō* Inner Mongolia
蒙古 *uchi Mōko* Inner Mongolia
幕 *uchimaku* inside curtain; inside information. *uchimaku, naimaku* the inside; hidden circumstances
幕話 *uchimakubanashi* inside information
14 層 *naisō* inner layers
聞 *naibun no* secret, private (information)
膜 *naimaku* lining membrane
需 *naiju* domestic demand
閣 *naikaku* cabinet, ministry
閣総理大臣 *Naikaku Sōri Daijin* Premier
緒 *naisho ni* secretly
緒話 *naishobanashi* secret talk
15 閲 *naietsu* private perusal
線 *naisen* indoor wiring; inner line
縁 *naien* common-law marriage
談 *naidan* private conversation
諾 *naidaku* informal consent
謁 *naietsu* private audience
踝 *uchi kurubushi* inner side of the ankle
憂 *naiyū* internal or domestic troubles
輪 *uchiwa* family circle, the inside. *uchiwa no* moderate, conservative; pigeon-toed
輪同志 *uchiwa dōshi* members of the family; insiders
輪揉 *uchiwamome* internal dissension; family trouble
輪喧嘩 *uchiwagenka* family quarrel; quarreling among themselves
16 懐 *uchibutokoro* inside pocket; one's heart, bosom
壁 *naiheki* inner wall
覧 *nairan* private audience
親王 *naishinnō* imperial or royal princess
燃機関 *nainen kikan* internal-combustion engine
17 濠 *uchibori* inner moat
18 職 *naishoku* home industry; side line
臓 *naizō* internal organs, intestines, viscera
観 *naikan* introspection
20 議 *naigi* secret conference; private consultation

3

冋 387/J5145/M1521 See 回 941.

冉 388/J5147/M1514 ZEN, NEN weak, slim; advance.

A 冊 389/J3a7d/M1515 册 390/J5146/M1516 SAKU. SATSU book counter; volume, book, letter.
3 子 *sasshi* book, booklet, pamphlet; notebook *sōshi* copy-book; storybook
13 数 *sassū* number of books

4

A 再 391/J3a46/M1524 SAI. *futata(bi)* again, twice. *sai-* re-; second time, again.
2 入学 *sainyūgaku* readmission to a school
入国 *sainyūkoku* re-entry into a country
入国許可書 *sainyūkoku kyokasho* re-entry permit
3 下付 *saikafu* reissue, renewal
上映 *saijōei* rerun (of a film)
三 *saisan* again and again, repeatedly
三再四 *saisan-saishi* repeatedly

[4]分配 *saibumpai* redistribution
[5]刊 *saikan* reprint, republication
犯 *saihan* second offense
犯者 *saihansha* second offender
出 *saishutu* reappearance, re-emergence
出発 *saishuppatu* restart, fresh start
生 *saisei* regeneration, resuscitation, return to life; rebirth, reincarnation; narrow escape; reclamation; recycling; reproduction
生品 *saiseihin* recycled goods
[6]任 *sainin* reappointment
再 *saisai* often, frequently
会 *saikai* another meeting; meeting again, reunion
交付 *saikōfu* reissue, regrant
考 *saikō* reconsideration
考慮 *saikōryo* reconsideration
[7]来 *sairai* return; second coming; Second Advent; reincarnation
来月 *saraigetsu* month after next
来年 *sarainen* year after next
来週 *saraishū* week after next
[8]征 *saisei* second punitive expedition
拝 *saihai* worshipping again; bowing twice; epistolary closing
版 *saihan* reprinting; reprint; second edition
服役 *saifukueki* re-enlistment; second imprisonment
放送 *saihōsō* rebroadcasting
武装 *saibusō* rearmament
注 *saichū* repeat order
注文 *saichūmon* repeat order
[9]度 *saido* twice, again, second time
変 *saihen* second change; second calamity
思 *saishi* reconsideration
洗礼 *saisenrei* rebaptism by sprinkling
保険 *saihoken* reinsurance
軍備 *saigumbi* rearmament
降臨 *Saikōrin* Second Advent
封鎖 *saifūsa suru* reblock, refreeze
訂 *saitei* second revision
訂版 *saiteihan* second revised edition
建 *saikon* (temple or shrine) rebuilding. *saiken* reconstruction, rebuilding
建築 *saikenchiku* reconstruction, rebuilding
発 *saihatsu* relapse; recurrence
発足 *saihossoku* restart, fresh start
[10]起 *saiki* a comeback, recovery, restoration, rally; reflexive (in grammar)
校 *saikō* second proof; reinvestigation
案 *saian* second plan, second draft
挙 *saikyo* another attempt
帰熱 *saikinetsu* recurrent fever
配分 *saihaibun* redistribution
配置 *saihaichi* reallocation, realignment
従兄 *saijūkei, mataitoko* elder second cousin
従兄弟 *mataitoko, saijū keitei, futaitoko* second cousin
従弟 *saijūtei, mataitoko* younger second cousin
[11]遊 *saiyū* revisit
婚 *saikon* second marriage
現 *saigen* reappearance, return; revival
設 *saisetsu* re-establishment, reorganization
敗 *saihai* second defeat
転 *saiten* changing directions, turning around
許可 *saikyoka* renewal of a permission
教育 *saikyōiku* retraining, re-education
組織 *saisoshiki* reorganization
[12]開 *saikai* reopening, resumption
勝 *saishō* another victory
勤 *saikin* reappointment
割引 *saiwaribiki* rediscount
評価 *saihyōka* reassessment, reappraisal
創造 *saisōzō* recreation
尋問 *saijimmon* re-examination
測量 *saisokuryō* resurvey
検査 *saikensa* re-examination
検討 *saikentō* re-examination, review, reappraisal
[13]嫁 *saika* remarriage
禁止 *saikinshi* reimposition of an embargo, reprohibition
感染 *saikansen* getting the same sickness again
試合 *saishiai* resumption of a game
試験 *saishiken* re-examination
[14]演 *saien* another showing (of a play); recapitulation (in biology)
説 *saisetsu* repeated explanation
読 *saidoku suru* reread
構成 *saikōsei* reconstruction, reorganization, reconstitution
選 *saisen* re-election
選挙 *saisenkyo* re-election
製 *saisei* remanufacture, reconditioning

製品 *saiseihin* reprocessed goods
15 縁 *saien* second marriage
誕 *saitan* resurrection (of a company or school, etc.)
鋳 *saichū* recasting
調査 *saichōsa* re-examination, reinvestigation
確認 *saikakunin* reaffirmation, reconfirmation
編 *saihen* reorganization, reshuffle
編成 *saihensei* reorganization, reshuffle
審 *saishin* re-examination, retrial, review
審査 *saishinsa* re-examination
16 燃 *sainen* recurrence, revival, resuscitation, rekindling
興 *saikō* revival, restoration, resuscitation, rehabilitation
輸入 *saiyunyū* reimportation
輸出 *saiyushutsu* re-exportation
17 臨 *Sairin* Second Advent
臨派 *Sairinha* Adventists
20 議 *saigi* reconsideration, redeliberation

5

冏 392 / J5148 / M1528 KEI, KYŌ clear, shining.

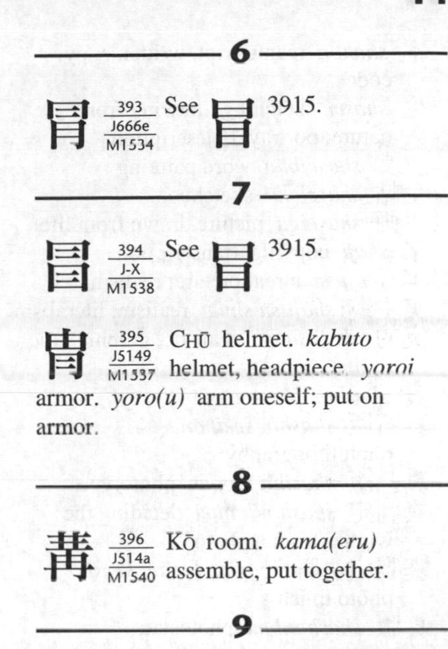

6

冒 393 / J666e / M1534 See 冒 3915.

7

冐 394 / J-X / M1538 See 冒 3915.

冑 395 / J5149 / M1537 CHŪ helmet. *kabuto* helmet, headpiece. *yoroi* armor. *yoro(u)* arm oneself; put on armor.

8

冓 396 / J514a / M1540 KŌ room. *kama(eru)* assemble, put together.

9

冕 397 / J514b / M1545 BEN crown.

冖 RAD. 14

Wa kammuri (crown shaped like the katakana *wa*) or *beki kammuri* "covering" crown. Nickname: *Kana Wa.*

冖 398 / J514c / M1565 BEKI. *ō(u)* cover.

2

B **冗** 399 / J3e69 / M1566 **宂** 1305 / J-X / M7056 JŌ uselessness.
4 文 *jōbun* redundancy
5 用 *jōyō* unnecessary work, unnecessary expense
句 *jōku* redundant phrase
6 多 *jōta* superabundance
8 長 *jōchō* verbosity, tediousness
物 *jōbutsu* redundancy, superfluity
官 *jōkan* supernumerary official
10 員 *jōin* supernumerary
12 筆 *jōhitsu* worthless painting and writing
費 *jōhi* unnecessary expenses
14 漫 *jōman* verbosity
語 *jōgo* redundancy
15 談 *jōdan* joke
談口 *jōdanguchi* joke
談事 *jōdangoto* joking matter

3

A **写** 400 / J3c4c / M1570 **寫** 1364 / J556d / M7320 **㝍** 1307 / J-X / M7076

冩 407 / J5150 / M-X SHA. *utsu(ru)* be photographed; be projected (on a screen); (light or shadows) fall on. *utsu(su)* copy, transcribe, duplicate, reproduce, trace; describe, picture, photograph. *utsu(shi)* copy, duplicate, facsimile, transcript.
5 出 *utsu(shi)-da(su)* reveal, show

二亠人亻𠆢儿入八丷冂【冖】3 冫几凵刀刂力勹匕匚匸十卜卩厂厶又

本 *shahon* manuscript, written copy, codex
生 *shasei* sketching; drawing from nature; portrayal, description
生文 *shaseibun* word painting
生帖 *shaseichō* sketchbook
生画 *shaseiga* picture drawn from life
6 字 *shaji* copying, transcription
8 実 *shajitsu* a real picture; realism
実主義 *shajitsu shugi* realism, literalism
実的 *shajitsuteki* realistic, graphic, true to life
10 真 *shashin* photograph
真石版 *shashin sekiban* photolithography
真凸版 *shashin toppan* phototype
真判定 *shashin hantei* deciding the winner from a photo
真判定決勝 *shashin hantei kesshō* photo finish
真版 *shashimban* photostat; photographic plate; photogravure
真屋 *shashin'ya* photographer, photo studio
真師 *shashinshi* photographer
真班 *shashinhan* (newspaper) cameramen
真嫌 *shashingira(i)* camera shy
真帳 *shashinchō* photograph album
真術 *shashinjutsu* photography
真望遠鏡 *shashin bōenkyō* photographic telescope
真植字 *shashinshokuji* photosetting (in printing)
真測量 *shashin sokuryō* photographic surveying
真結婚 *shashin kekkon* picture marriage
真電送 *shashin densō* phototelegraphy
真館 *shashinkan* photo studio
真機 *shashinki* camera
真顔 *shashingao* one's looks in a photo
11 経 *shakyō* copying Buddhist scriptures or sutras; a copied Buddhist scripture
12 植 *shashoku* photosetting (in printing)
絵 *utsu(shi)e* magic-lantern picture; child's copying pictures, shadowgraph
象 *shashō* image

7

B **冠** 401 / J3427 / M1580 KAN crown, diadem; first, best, peerless. *kamu(ru)* *vt* and *vi* wear, put on; take (the blame); pour on; be covered with; ship (a wave); have (labor pains); be accidentally exposed (a film). *kan(suru)* crown, cap; name, designate; entitle; initiate on coming of age. *kammuri* crown, diadem; a top character radical.
4 毛 *kammō* thistledown
水 *kansui* flooding, submergence
木 *kabuki* lintel, crossbar; gate with a crossbar; roofed gate
木門 *kabukimon* gate with a crossbar
7 位 *kan'i* system indicating court ranks by headgear colors
状 *kanjō no* coronary
8 枉 *kammuri (o) ma(geru)* become displeased; get stubborn
者 *kanja, kaja* young person; young servant, a young man come of age (at 16)
9 省 *kanshō* a letter salutation
11 動脈 *kandōmyaku* coronary artery
婚葬祭 *kankonsōsai* ceremonial occasion
12 絶 *kanzetsu suru* be unique, be unsurpassed
詞 *kanshi* article (in grammar)
13 辞 *kanji* stereotyped epithet

8

冦 402 / J514e / M1590 Nonstandard for **寇** 1339.

冢 403 / J514f / M1585 See **塚** 1060.

冤 404 / J514d / M1587 **寃** 1338 / J5563 / M7202 EN false charge; hatred.
8 枉 *en'ō* false charge
13 罪 *enzai* false charge

冥 405 / J4c3d / M1588 MEI, MYŌ dark.
3 土 *meido* hades, realm of the dead
4 王星 *Meiōsei* (planet) Pluto
5 加 *myōga* divine protection
加金 *myōgakin* votive offering; forced contributions (Edo era)
7 利 *myōri* providence, luck, favor, advantage
8 府 *meifu* hades, realm of the dead, sheol

[9] 途 *yomi, meido* hades, realm of the dead, sheol
界 *meikai* hades, realm of the dead
[13] 暗 *meian* gloom, shade
福 *meifuku* happiness in the next world
想 *meisō* meditation, contemplation
[14] 境 *meikyō* shades of the dead
罰 *meibatsu* retribution, divine punishment
[17] 闇 *meian* gloom, shade

9

冨 406/J495a/M1592 See 富 1349.

12

寫 407/J5150/M-X Nonstandard for 写 400.

13

冪 408/J5151/M1601 See 冪 4652.

RAD. 冫 15

Ni-sui (two-stroke "water," as distinguished from Rad. 85). Also known as the "ice" radical because of its use in the early form of the character for *kōri* "ice." Nickname: Ice.

冫 409/J5152/M1607 HYŌ. *kōri* ice.

3

冬 410/J455f/M1610 (A) TŌ *fuyu* winter. *fuyu(meku)* become wintry.
[4] 月 *tōgetsu* winter season; winter moon
天 *tōten* wintry sky, wintry weather
日和 *fuyubiyori* a fine winter day
支度 *fuyujitaku* winter preparations
木 *fuyuki, fuyugi, tōboku* deciduous trees in winter
木立 *fuyukodachi* deciduous trees in winter
[6] 向 *fuyumu(ki) no* for winter
休 *fuyu yasu(mi)* winter vacation, winter holidays
至 *tōji* winter solstice
至点 *tōjiten* winter solstice
至線 *Tōjisen* Tropic of Capricorn
[8] 物 *fuyumono* winter clothing
服 *fuyufuku* winter clothing
季 *tōki* winter season
空 *fuyuzora* winter sky
芽 *tōga* winter buds
[9] 枯 *fuyuga(re)* winter decay, winter withering, winter business slump
[10] 眠 *tōmin* hibernation
宮 *tōkyū* winter palace
将軍 *Fuyu Shōgun* Jack Frost
[12] 越 *fuyugo(shi)* wintering
場 *fuyuba* winter season
着 *fuyugi* winter clothing
営 *tōei* winter quarters; wintering
期 *tōki* winter season
期間 *tōkikan* winter season
[14] 構 *fuyugama(e)* preparations for winter
[22] 籠 *fuyugomori* hibernation, wintering

4

決 411/J5153/M1617 See 決 3070.

冰 412/J5156/M1612 See 氷 3032.

冲 413/J5155/M1616 See 沖 3065.

冱 414/J5154/M1613 GO, KO cold. *kō(ru)* freeze. *samu(i)* be cold. *sa(eru)* be clear; be skillful.

冴 415/J-X/M1615 冴 417/J3a63/M-X GO. *sa(eru)* be clear; be serene; be cold, be skillful.

6 行 *sa(e)-yu(ku)* gradually clear, gradually get cold
返 *sa(e)-kae(ru)* be very clear; be keenly cold
7 冴 *sa(e)za(e) shita* cheerful (look), healthy (complexion)
12 渡 *sa(e)-wata(ru)* get cold; freeze over
15 輝 *sa(e)-kagaya(ku)* shine clearly

5

況 416 / J5157 / M1620 See **況** 3086.

冴 417 / J3a63 / M-X See **冴** 415.

冶 418 / J4c6a / M1621 Ya melting.
3 工 *yakō* metallurgical worker
8 金 *yakin* metallurgy
金学 *yakingaku* metallurgy (the science)
金学者 *yakingakusha* metallurgist

A **冷** 419 / J4e64 / M1622 Rei cold, cool. *hi(eru)* cool down, grow cold; feel chilly. *hiya(su)* cool, refrigerate. *hi(yakasu)* cool (in water or ice); banter, make fun, speak playfully, tease; window-shop, look in at a shop. *same(ru) vi* cool, get cold; abate, subside; dampen, cool down (interest); come down (interest, enthusiasm, etc.). *sama(su) vt* cool, let cool; dampen, throw a damper on, spoil. *hi(e)* chilling, exposure. *hiya* cold drinking water. *hi(yayakana)* cold; chilly; indifferent, coldhearted; surly, curt, cool, composed. *(o)hi(ya)* cold water; cold boiled rice. *tsume(tai)* cold, chilly, icy, freezing; coldhearted. *hi(yari)* cool, chilly, *toshita* cold.
2 入 *hi(e)-i(ru)* become completely chilled
3 上 *hi(e)-a(garu)* get completely chilled
4 込 *hi(e)-ko(mu)* get colder; get chilled
切 *hi(e)-ki(ru)* get completely chilled
水 *hi(ya)mizu, reisui* cold water
水浴 *reisuiyoku* cold bath, cold shower
水摩擦 *reisui masatsu* cold rub
5 奴 *hi(ya)yakko* iced tofu
6 肉 *reiniku* cold meat
気 *reiki* cold, chill; cold weather; cold wave; cold air
汗 *hi(ya)ase, reikan* cold sweat
光 *reikō* cold light, luminescence
血 *reiketsu* coldbloodedness; coldheartedness
血動物 *reiketsu dōbutsu* coldblooded animal
血漢 *reiketsukan* coldblooded person
7 冷 *hi(ya)hi(ya) suru, hi(e)bi(e) suru* feel chilly; be fearful
麦 *hi(ya)mugi* iced noodles
却 *reikyaku* cooling, refrigeration
却期間 *reikyaku kikan* cooling-off period
却器 *reikyakuki* refrigerator, cooler, freezer; radiator (of a car)
8 雨 *reiu* chilly rain
性 *hi(e)shō* sensitivity to cold
房 *reibō* air conditioning, air-cooling
房完備 *reibō kambi* air-conditioned
房車 *reibōsha* air-conditioned car
房装置 *reibō sōchi* air-conditioning; air-cooling apparatus
9 泉 *reisen* cold mineral springs
10 剛 *reigō* chilling (steel)
酒 *hi(ya)zake, reishu* cold saké
害 *reigai* cold-weather damage
笑 *reishō* derisive smile, scornful laugh, sneer, cynicism
笑的 *reishōteki* sarcastic, derisive
凍 *reitō* refrigeration, freezing, cold storage
凍車 *reitōsha* refrigerator car
凍食品 *reitō shokuhin* frozen food
凍庫 *reitōko* freezer, freezer compartment
凍剤 *reitōzai* refrigerant
凍魚 *reitōgyo* refrigerated fish
凍船 *reitōsen* refrigerator ship
凍業 *reitōgyō* cold-storage business
凍器 *reitōki* deep freeze; freezer; refrigerating machine
11 遇 *reigū* frigid reception, cold treatment
淡 *reitan* indifference, coolness, lukewarmness; coldheartedness
眼 *reigan* cold look
12 評 *reihyō* sarcasm, sneer, jeer
飯 *hi(ya)meshi* cold rice
募 *hi(e)-tsuno(ru)* get colder, get chilled
然 *reizen* indifference, coolness, lukewarmness; coldheartedness
覚 *reikaku* sensation of cold
湿布 *reishippu* cold compress

[13] 腹 *hi(e)bara* abdominal chills, diarrhea
戦 *reisen* cold war
罨法 *reiampō* cold compress, cold pack
[14] 酷 *reikoku* cruelty; heartlessness; bitterness
静 *reisei* calmness, coolness, composure, serenity
蔵 *reizō* cold storage, refrigeration
蔵車 *reizōsha* refrigerator car
蔵法 *reizōhō* refrigeration
蔵庫 *reizōko* refrigerator
蔵船 *reizōsen* refrigerator ship
[15] 嘲 *reichō* mocking (someone)
罵 *reiba* sneer, scoffing, abuse
熱 *reinetsu* heat and cold, temperature
[17] 厳 *reigen na* grim, stern, stark, heartless

6

冽 420 J5158 M1637 RETSU cold.
[8] 冽 *retsuretsu* extremely cold

8

凉 421 J515a M1665 See **涼** 3198.

涸 422 J5139 M1659 KO, KU freeze, cold; close off, obstruct. *kō(ru)* freeze.

凋 423 J437c M1668 CHŌ. *shibo(mu)* droop, wither, wilt, fade; be downcast.
[6] 尽 *chōjin* withering, decay, decline
[10] 残 *chōzan* ruined blossoms
[11] 悴 *chōsui* becoming emaciated
[12] 落 *chōraku* decline, decay, fall, withering

凌 424 J4e3f M1669 RYŌ. *shino(gu)* endure; keep out (rain); stave off; tide over, pull through; defy; slight; surpass, excel, eclipse. *shinogi* tiding over.
[8] 波性 *ryōhasei* seaworthiness
[10] 辱 *ryōjoku* insult; outrage, rape
[12] 場 *shino(gi)ba* shelter
雲 *ryōun no* skyscraping, very high
[15] 駕 *ryōga suru* excel, surpass, outdo

凄 425 J4028 M1657 SEI. *sugo(mu)* threaten. *sugo(i)* uncanny, weird; ghastly, horrible; intimidating; enormous; amazing. *susama(jii)* terrible; amazing; absurd.
[4] 文句 *sugomonku* intimidating language
[8] 味 *sugomi* weirdness, ghastliness, dreadfulness
[11] 惨 *seisan* ghastliness, gruesomeness
[12] 絶 *seizetsu na* weird, gruesome, lurid
[13] 愴 *seisō na* desolate, dreary
[19] 艶 *seien na* weirdly beautiful

B **准** 426 J3d5a M1661 **準** 3278 J3d60 M17934 JUN quasi-, semi-, associate. *jun(jiru), jun(zuru)* apply correspondingly, correspond to, be proportionate to, conform to. *nazora(eru)* pattern after, liken to, imitate. *(ni) jun(jite)* in proportion (to).
[3] 士官 *junshikan* warrant officer
[6] 州 *junshū* a territory
[7] 決勝 *junkesshō* semifinals
[10] 将 *junshō* brigadier general; commodore
[11] 尉 *jun'i* warrant officer
許 *junkyo* approval, sanction

B **凍** 427 J4560 M1670 TŌ. *kō(ru), shi(miru), i(teru)* freeze; be frozen over; congeal. *kō(rasu) vt* freeze, refrigerate. *kogo(ru) vi* congeal, freeze. *kogo(eru)* freeze, be chilled, be frozen. *kogo(raseru) vt* freeze, congeal, condense.
[3] 土 *tōdo* frozen soil
土帯 *tōdotai* tundra
[5] 石 *tōseki* soapstone
付 *shi(mi)-tsu(ku), ko(ri)-tsu(ku), kogo(e)-tsu(ku)* freeze to, be frozen to
氷 *shi(mi)-kō(ru)* freeze hard, feel gloomy
[6] 肉 *tōniku* frozen meat
死 *kogo(e)ji(nu), kogo(e)-shi(nu), tōshi suru* freeze to death, die of cold
死者 *tōshisha* person frozen to death
[7] 豆腐 *shimidōfu* frozen tofu
[8] 雨 *tōu* winter rain; freezing rain
[10] 原 *tōgen* tundra
害 *tōgai* frost damage
[12] 寒 *tōkan* frost, bitter cold
結 *tōketsu* freezing
結資産 *tōketsu shisan* frozen assets

結器 *tōketsuki* freezer
13 傷 *shimoyake, tōshō* frostbite, chilblains
傷者 *tōshōsha* a case of frostbite
15 瘡 *tōsō* chilblains, frostbite
16 餒 *tōtai, tōdai* privation

9

準 428 / J5245 / M1695 See **準** 3278.

13

凜 429 / J7425 / M1717 **凛** 430 / J515b / M1718 RIN cold.
8 冽 *rinretsu na* biting, severe, intense, rigorous
10 烈 *rinretsu* biting, severe, intense, rigorous
12 然 *rinzen(taru)* commanding, awe-inspiring
15 凜 *rinrin(taru)* severe, intense, biting. *riri(shii)* gallant, chivalrous, manly, imposing, dignified, awe-inspiring

14

B **凝** 431 / J3645 / M1720 GYŌ. *kogo(rasu), kogo(raseru) vt* freeze, congeal. *ko(ru)* feel stiff, get stiff; be absorbed in, be devoted to, be a fanatic; elaborate. *kogo(ru)* congeal, freeze. *ko(rasu)* concentrate, devote, apply, strain, rack. *shiko(ru)* stiffen, harden. *kori* stiffness, swelling, hardening. *ko(tta)* elaborate, exquisite, tasty, refined, artistic. *shiko(ri)* muscle stiffness.
5 立 *gyōritsu* standing absolutely still
6 血 *gyōketsu suru* curdle. *gyōketsu* blood clot
8 性 *ko(ri)shō* enthusiasm for one thing; fastidiousness
乳 *gyōnyū* curd, curdled milk, rennet
念 *gyōnen* concentration of thought
固 *ko(ri)-kata(maru)* coagulate, curdle, clot; be fanatical. *korikata(mari)* coagulation, clot; enthusiast, fanatic. *gyōko* solidification, congealing, coagulation, condensation
固点 *gyōkoten* freezing point
10 脂 *gyōshi* solidified oil
11 視 *gyōshi* stare, steady gaze, fixation. *mitsu(meru)* stare at, gaze at, fix the eyes on
望 *gyōbō suru* look intently
12 結 *gyōketsu* coagulation, curdling, setting, congealing, freezing, refrigeration, condensation, solidification
然 *gyōzen toshite* quietly
集 *gyōshū* cohesion; condensation
集力 *gyōshūryoku* cohesive power
着 *gyōchaku* adhesion
着力 *gyōchakuryoku* adhesion
13 塊 *gyōkai* clot
滞 *gyōtai* delay
17 縮 *gyōshuku* condensation
20 議 *gyōgi* deliberation, consultation

RAD. 几 16

Tsukue table or *ki-nyō* "table" enclosure. Variant: 𠘨 *kazegamae* (enclosure like that of *kaze* "wind"). Nickname: Windy (cf. Rad. 182).

几 432 / J515c / M1737 KI table.
11 帳 *kichō* a screen
帳面 *kichōmen na* methodical, punctual, steady

1

B **凡** 433 / J4b5e / M1739 **凢** 44 / J-X / M123 HAN. Bon mediocrity. *oyo(so), ōyo(so)* as a rule; approximately. *sube(te)* all, the whole; entirely; in general. *a(rayuru)* all, every.
2 人 *bonjin, bonnin* ordinary person, mediocre
3 小 *bonshō* small and of mediocre talent
凡 *bombon(taru)* ordinary, usual
才 *bonsai* mediocrity, ordinary ability
4 手 *bonshu* mediocre ability, a person of ordinary skills

二 亠 人 亻 𠆢 儿 入 八 丷 冂 冖 9 【冫】 几 凵 刀 刂 力 勹 匕 匚 匸 十 卜 卩 厂 厶 又

夫 *bompu, bombu* ordinary man
5 打 *bonda* poor batting
失 *bonshitsu* a common mistake
6 百 *bompyaku* many, many kinds
7 作 *bonsaku* poor piece of writing
8 退 *bontai* put in 1-2-3 order
例 *hanrei* introductory remarks, explanatory notes
9 俗 *bonzoku* mediocrity; the masses, ordinary person
10 骨 *bonkotsu* ordinary person
流 *bonryū* ordinary style
書 *bonsho* ordinary book; ordinary handwriting
11 庸 *bon'yō* mediocrity; commonplace
庶 *bonsho* common people
眼 *bongan* (through) a layman's eyes
常 *bonjō na* ordinary, common
12 策 *bonsaku* commonplace policy
13 僧 *bonsō* unranked priest, ordinary priest
戦 *bonsen* dull game
愚 *bongu* common person; foolish commoner
15 慮 *bonryo* ordinary minds, ordinary people
器 *bonki* ordinary talent

3

凧 434 / J427c / M1749 (国字) *ikanobori, tako* kite.
12 揚 *takoa(ge)* kite flying

A **処** 435 / J3d68 / M1745 **處** 5268 / J515d / M32697 SHO. *sho(suru)* manage, deal with; sentence, condemn; act, behave, conduct oneself (well). *tokoro* place, spot, scene, site, seat; locality, district; room; distance; address; point, feature; passage (in a book), part; thing; time, moment; extent; matter of course. *-ka* place.
3 女 *shojo, otome* virgin, maiden
女地 *shojochi* virgin soil
女作 *shojosaku* one's first published work
女性 *shojosei* virginity, maidenhood
女峰 *shojohō* an unclimbed mountain
女航海 *shojo kōkai* maiden voyage
女期 *shojoki* virginity, maidenhood
女膜 *shojo maku* hymen
4 分 *shobun* disposition of, disposal, management; measure, action; punishment
方 *shohō* prescription, formula
方書 *shohōsho* (doctor's) prescription
方箋 *shohōsen* (doctor's) prescription
5 弁 *shoben* disposal, management; action, measure; treatment
生法 *shoseihō* secret of success
生術 *shoseijutsu* secret of success
処 *shosho* various places. *tokorodokoro* here and there
処方方 *shosho-hōbō* here and there
世 *shosei* conduct of life, getting on
世訓 *shoseikun* rules for living a good life
6 刑 *shokei* (infliction of) punishment, execution
刑台 *shokeidai* gallows
刑法 *shokeihō* means of execution
7 決 *shoketsu* decision, resolution, settlement, determination; resignation
8 法 *shohō* prescription, formula
11 遇 *shogū* treatment
理 *shori* procedure, management, treatment. *shori suru* manage, dispose of, settle, adjust
務 *shomu* management of affairs
断 *shodan* judgment, decision
12 違 *tokorochiga(i)* mistaking the place
13 置 *shochi* disposal, management; action, measure; treatment
14 罰 *shobatsu* penalty, punishment
罰令 *shobatsurei* penal regulations

4

凩 436 / J515e / M1757 (国字) *kogarashi* wintry wind.

凪 437 / J4664 / M1758 (国字) *nagi* lull, calm. *na(gu)* become calm, die down.

6

凭 438 / J515f / M1766 HYŌ. HEI. *mota(reru)* lean on, recline on; lie heavy (on the stomach). *yo(ru)* lean on, rest against.
11 掛 *mota(se)-ka(keru) vt* lean against, set against. *mota(re)-ka(karu), yo(ri)-ka(karu) vi* lean on, recline on; rely on
12 椅子 *mota(re) isu* reclining chair

9

凰 439 / J5160 / M1784 Ō. Kō female phoenix bird.

10

凱 440 / J332e / M1790 Gai victory song.

11 旋 *gaisen* triumphal return

旋門 *gaisemmon* arch of triumph

旋軍 *gaisengun* returning victorious army

14 歌 *gaika* victory song; victory

RAD. 凵 17

Ukebako open box or *kangamae* "open box" enclosure. Nickname: Open Box.

凵 441 / J5161 / M1800 Kan, Kon open the mouth.

2

B 凶 442 / J3627 / M1803 Kyō evil; bad luck; disaster; bad harvest.

3 刃 *kyōjin* assassin's dagger

4 手 *kyōshu* assassin

日 *kyōjitsu, kyōnichi* unlucky day

6 行 *kyōkō* violence, murder, crime

兆 *kyōchō* evil omen

年 *kyōnen* bad year, bad harvest

7 作 *kyōsaku* bad harvest, poor crop

状 *kyōjō* crime, offense

状持 *kyōjōmo(chi)* a criminal

8 具 *kyōgu* dangerous weapon

事 *kyōji* calamity, misfortune

9 音 *kyōin* bad news; news of a death

変 *kyōhen* catastrophe; assassination

荒 *kyōkō* poor crops; famine

10 徒 *kyōto* rioter, outlaw, rebel

党 *kyōtō* gang, gangsters

11 猛 *kyōmō* fierce

悪 *kyōaku na* atrocious, fiendish, brutal

12 報 *kyōhō* bad news

13 漢 *kyōkan* villain, outlaw, assassin

賊 *kyōzoku* villain

歳 *kyōsai* poor-crop year

夢 *kyōmu* bad dream, inauspicious dream

14 聞 *kyōbun* bad news

15 暴 *kyōbō* brutality, ferocity, atrocity

器 *kyōki* dangerous weapon

18 類 *kyōrui* wicked gang

3

B 凸 443 / J464c / M1809 Totsu *deko* projecting, beetle brow.

5 凹 *dekoboko, totsuō* unevenness, ruggedness, roughness

7 角 *tokkaku* convex angle

坊 *dekobō* beetle-browed boy; a mischievous boy

状 *totsujō* protrusion

8 版 *toppan* relief printing

9 面 *totsumen* convex surface

面鏡 *totsumenkyō* convex lens

19 鏡 *tokkyō* convex lens

B 凹 444 / J317a / M1810 Ō hollow, sunken. *heko(mu)* be dented, be indented, yield to, give, sink, collapse, cave in; be snubbed; be defeated. *heko(maseru), heko(masu) vt* dent, indent, depress; humiliate. *kubo(maru)* be low (as a hollow). *kubo(meru)* hollow out. *kubo, boko* hollow, depression. *heko(mi)* dent, hollow, depression.

5 田 *kubota* rice field in a low place

凸 *ōtotsu* unevenness, roughness, ruggedness

6 地 *ōchi* depression, hollow, pit, basin

7 形 *ōkei* intaglio; concavity

8 所 *ōsho* concavity, cavity, hollow, depression

版 *ōhan, ōban* intaglio (printing)

9 面 *ōmen* concavity

面鏡 *ōmenkyō* concave lens or mirror

[11] 眼 *ōgan* cavernous eyes
眼鏡 *ōgankyō* concave glasses
[13] 溜 *kubotama(ri)* a hollow; a pond in a hollow

A 出 445 J3d50 M1811 SUI. SHUTSU born of; appearing from; going out; sending out. *da(su), ida(su)* put out, take out, pull out, stick out; draw (a gun); stretch out, extend; save (from a fire); expose, bare; exhibit; send, forward, post; publish; hoist (a flag); hang out; present, send in, tender, submit; serve; run (extra trains); produce; pay, contribute; invest; advance (money). *de(ru)* appear, come out, emerge; haunt, infest; be found, get back; be served (meals); lead to, enter; find (oneself) at; come out (as a result); leave, go out, get out; attend, appear; work (at); participate; launch (into); run (for an office); be published; sell; depart; graduate; break out, originate; be raised, be produced; issue from, be traced to, derive from, stem from; protrude, stick out; exceed; interfere; intrude. *-de, de-* turnout, attendance, appearance, flow, outflow; pouring; outlay, expenditure, crop, yield, supply; sale, demand; start, outset, origin, birth, stock; one's turn; drawing (of tea). *de(shaburu)* intrude, butt in. *(o)i(de)* being; coming; going; come, come on. *(o)i(deninaru)* be; come; go. *da(shi)* broth, soup stock; pretext, excuse; cat's paw, a dupe, a tool. *da(su)* begin to.
[2] 力 *shutsuryoku* output (of a dynamo)
入 *de-i(ru)* go in and out; quarrel; have the freedom of the home. *de(zu)-i(razu)* moderation; neither gain nor loss. *da(shi)i(re)* taking in and out, depositing and withdrawing; receipts and expenditures. *shutsunyū* going in and out; entrance and exit; receipts and expenditures. *dei(ri), dehai(ri)* free association, going in and out, entrance and exit; receipts and payments, surplus and deficit; indentation (of a coast)
入口 *deiriguchi* entrance and exit, a doorway, a gateway
入国 *shutsunyūkoku* emigration and immigration
[3] 口 *deguchi* exit, way out; outlet, leak, vent
土 *shutsudo* appearance of an archeological find
土品 *shutsudohin* artifacts
刃 *deba* knife, pointed carver
刃庖丁 *debabōchō* knife, pointed carver
[4] 手 *da(shi)te* one who furnishes the money
方 *dekata* attitude; a move; theater usher
欠 *shukketsu* presence or absence
水 *shussui, demizu* flood, freshlet, inundation
火 *shukka* fire, outbreak of fire
切 *de-ki(ru)* be out of, have no more on hand
分 *da(shi)bun* one's share (in the expenses)
不精 *debushō* a stay-at-home; homekeeping
[5] 立 *i(de)-ta(tsu)* start, leave. *idetachi* start, departure; dress, attire, outfit. *shuttatsu* departure
払 *dehara(i)* be out of
外 *dehazu(re)* end, extremity (of a village)
汁 *da(shi)jiru* broth, stock, soup
目 *deme* protruding eyes
目金 *demekin* pop-eyed goldfish
処 *shussho, dedokoro* birthplace; origin; source, authority; exit
処進退 *shussho-shintai* advancing and retreating; appearance and disappearance; one's daily activities; one's course of action; one's attitude
仕 *shusshi* attendance, serving
仕事 *deshigoto* outside work
札 *shussatsu* issuing tickets
札口 *shussatsuguchi* ticket window
札所 *shussatsujo* ticket office
札係 *shussatsugakari* ticket agent
生 *shusshō* birth
生地 *shusshōchi* birthplace
生年月日 *shusshō nengappi* date of birth
生率 *shusshōritsu* birth rate
生証明書 *shusshō shōmeisho* birth certificate
生数 *shusseisū* number of live births
世 *shusse* successful career, eminence
世作 *shussesaku* a work of art or literature that brings fame

世間 *shusseken* monastic life
世間的 *shussekenteki* unworldly, religious
世頭 *shussegashira* most successful man
6 色 *shusshoku* prominence; excellence
回 *de-mawa(ru)* arrive on the market, be moving
迎 *de-muka(eru)* (go to) meet, (come to) meet, greet, receive. *demuka(e)* meeting, reception
向 *de-mu(ku), shukkō suru* go to, proceed to, leave for
任 *demaka(se)* random speech
帆 *shuppan* sailing, departure
会 *de-a(u)* meet, encounter, run across. *shukkai* an encounter
合 *de-a(u)* meet, encounter, run across, hold a rendezvous, have a date. *da(shi)-a(u)* contribute jointly
合頭 *dea(i)gashira ni* as one passes, as one happens to meet
先 *desaki* destination
先機関 *desaki kikan* branch office
血 *shukketsu* hemorrhage, bleeding
血死 *shukketsushi* bleeding to death
血性人 *shukketsusei (no) hito* bleeder, hemophiliac
血症 *shukketsushō* bleeders' affliction
血過多 *shukketsu kata* excessive bleeding
7 足 *deashi* start; turnout
戻 *demodo(ri)* divorced woman
抜 *da(shi)-nu(ku)* forestall, anticipate, jump the gun on, outwit, circumvent, steal a march on. *da(shi)nu(ke) ni* suddenly, without notice, unexpectedly
没 *shutsubotsu* appearance and disappearance
社 *shussha* going to the office
兵 *shuppei* dispatch of troops; expedition
花 *debana* first brew of tea
廷 *shuttei* appearance in court
廷日 *shutteibi* court day
初 *dezome* first appearance, debut; firemen's New Year's demonstrations
初式 *dezome shiki* firemen's New Year's demonstrations
身 *shusshin* graduate from; hailing from
身地 *shusshinchi* birthplace, native place
身者 *shusshinsha* alumnus
身校 *shusshinkō* alma mater
来 *deki(ru)* can, be able to; be possible; be done, be finished, be ready; be made of; be established, be set up; be formed; come into being; grow, be produced; break out; be good at; be versed in; become intimate with. *deka(su)* complete, accomplish praiseworthily. *deka(shita)* well done, bravo. *deki(ta)* fully developed, mature, cultured, well-balanced. *deki* make, workmanship; result; crop, harvest. *shuttai, shutsurai* occurrence; completion; fulfillment
来上 *dekia(garu)* be finished, be ready, be made for, be cut out
来丈 *deki(ru)dake* as…as possible
来心 *dekigokoro* sudden impulse, passing fancy
来立 *dekita(te)* new, newly made, fresh, brand-new
来合 *deki-a(u)* be ready-made; become intimate with. *dekia(i)* ready-made; common-law (wife)
来年 *dekidoshi* fruitful year
来次第 *dekishidai* as soon as completed
来物 *dekimono, dekibutsu* able man. *dekimono* tumor, growth, boil, ulcer, abcess, rash, pimple
来事 *dekigoto* incident, affair
来具合 *dekiguai* result, effect, performance, success
来映 *dekibae* result, effect, performance, success; excellently made; shape and quality of (an article)
来値 *dekine* selling price
来高 *dekidaka* yield, crop, production
来高払 *dekidakabara(i)* piecework payment
来高仕事 *dekidaka shigoto* piecework
来得限 *deki-u(ru) kagiri* as (much) as possible, as (far) as possible
来損 *deki-sokona(u)* be badly made; fail
8 門 *shutsumon* going out
国 *shukkoku* departure from a country
店 *demise* branch store
府 *shuppu* going to the capital; working in a government office ⌈to come in
始 *de-haji(meru)* begin to appear; begin
物 *demono* rash, boil; secondhand article. *da(shi)mono* performance, program

京 *shukkyō* proceeding to the capital
直 *de-nao(ru)* setting out again. *de-nao(su)* come again, call again, make a fresh start
歩 *de-aru(ku)* go out, take a stroll, go about
芽 *shutsuga* germination, sprouting
典 *shutten* source, authority
放 *da(ship)panasu, da(shi)-hana(su)* leave on, leave running, leave lying around, leave (a faucet) open
放題 *dehōdai* free flow (of water); random talk, nonsense. *da(shi)hōdai* free flow of water
奔 *shuppon* abscondence; flight
奔者 *shupponsha* absconder
金 *shukkin* payment, contribution, investment, financing
金者 *shukkinsha* contributer, investor, financier
金額 *shukkingaku* amount invested or contributed
所 *shussho, dedoko, dedokoro* origin, source; authority; exit; point of departure; release from prison
所進退 *shussho shintai* one's daily activities
所勝負 *de(ta)tokoshōbu* leaving a matter to chance
征 *shussei* departure for the front
征軍 *shusseigun* army in the field
征軍人 *shussei gunjin* soldier at the front
征家族 *shussei kazoku* family of a soldier at the front
版 *shuppan* publication
版元 *shuppammoto* publisher
版目録 *shuppan mokuroku* catalog of publications
版自由 *shuppan (no) jiyū* freedom of the press
版社 *shuppansha* publishing house
版法 *shuppanhō* press law, publication law
版物 *shuppambutsu* publications
版者 *shuppansha* publisher
版屋 *shuppan'ya* publishing house
版界 *shuppankai* the publishing world
版部 *shuppambu* publishing department
版部数 *shuppambusū* circulation, number printed
版許可 *shuppan kyoka* permission to publish
版費 *shuppanhi* publishing costs
版業 *shuppangyō* publishing business
版業者 *shuppan gyōsha* publisher
9 城 *dejiro* branch castle
這入 *dehai(ri)* going in and out
陣 *shutsujin* departure for the front
軍 *shutsugun* expedition
炭 *shuttan* coal production
前 *demae* restaurant delivery service. *da(shi)mae* one's share (in the expenses)
前持 *demaemo(chi)* boy who delivers take-out food
発 *shuppatsu* departure
発点 *shuppatsuten* starting point; point of departure
品 *shuppin* exhibit, display
品人 *shuppinnin* exhibitor
品国 *shuppinkoku* exhibiting country
品物 *shuppimbutsu* exhibit
品者 *shuppinsha* exhibitor
10 馬 *shutsuba suru* go on horseback; go in person; run for election
庫 *shukko* delivery from a storehouse
師 *suishi* dispatch of troops, expedition
捐 *shutsuen* contribution, subscription
時 *dedoki* time of departure
梅 *tsuyuake, shutsubai* end of the rainy season
航 *shukkō* departure, sailing
郷 *shukkyō* leaving one's hometown; a priest going out to teach
倚 *shukka* forwarding, shipping; outgoing freight
格子 *degōshi* projecting lattice; latticed bay window
家 *shukke* entering the priesthood; priest, monk
家遁世 *shukke-tonsei* monastic seclusion
納 *suitō* receipts and disbursements
納係 *suitōgakari* cashier, treasurer; teller
納簿 *suitōbo* cashbook
席 *shusseki* attendance
席者 *shussekisha* those present, attendance
席率 *shussekiritsu* percent of attendance
席簿 *shussekibo* attendance record

11 遅 *da(shi)oku(re)* belated
過 *de-su(giru)* project or protrude too much; be too forward, obtrude
惜 *da(shi)-oshi(mu)* grudge, be stingy, be unwilling to pay
掛 *de-ka(keru)* depart, go out, set out, start, be going out. *degake* about to start out
涸 *degarashi* washed out, insipid
渋 *da(shi)-shibu(ru)* grudge, be stingy, be unwilling to pay. *de-shibu(ru)* be unwilling to go out
猟 *shutsuryō* going hunting
現 *shutsugen* appearance, arrival
船 *debune, defune, idebune* weighing anchor, setting sail; outgoing ship
殻 *da(shi)gara, degara* grounds (of tea and coffee)
商 *deakina(i)* peddling
窓 *demado* bay window
渠 *shukkyo* leaving the (repair) dock
盛 *de-saka(ru)* appear in profusion. *desaka(ri), dezaka(ri)* best time for (corn, etc.), season for
動 *shutsudō* sailing, marching, going out
動命令 *shutsudō meirei* marching orders, sailing orders
産 *shussan* childbirth; production (of goods)
産数 *shussansū* number of births (including stillbirths)
張 *de-ba(ru), de(p)pa(ru)* project, stand out, jut out, protrude. *deba(ri)* projection, ledge. *shutchō* business trip, official trip
張店 *shutchōten* branch store
張所 *shutchōjo* branch office
張員 *shutchōin* agent, represenative, dispatched official
12 歯 *deba, de(p)pa* protruding tooth, overbite
超 *shutchō* excess of exports, favorable balance of trade
御 *shutsugyo* emperor's arrival (at his office, etc.)
揃 *de-soro(u)* appear all together, be all present
棺 *shukkan* carrying out a coffin
湯 *ideyu* hot springs
塁 *shutsurui* on base (in baseball)
番 *deban* one's turn
替 *de-kawa(ru) vi* take someone else's place. *degawa(ri), dekawa(ri)* periodical relief or replacement of workers
違 *de-chiga(u)* miss a visitor. *da(shi)-chiga(u)* miss sending, miss delivering
費 *shuppi* expenses, disbursements
場 *shutsujō* stage appearance, performance; participation. *deba* one's turn; place of projection; production center
場者 *shutsujōsha* participants, participating athletes
訴 *shusso* access to courts, bringing an action
訴期限法 *shusso kigenhō* statute of limitations
港 *shukkō* departure; clearance (of a ship)
港船 *shukkōsen* outgoing vessel
港停止 *shukkō teishi* embargo
勤 *shukkin* at work; going to work
勤日 *shukkimbi* employee's work day
勤者 *shukkinsha* workers on the job
勤時間 *shukkin jikan* hour for reporting to work
勤簿 *shukkimbo* employees' attendance record
13 嫌 *degira(i)* a stay-at-home
損 *de-sokona(u)* fail to go; fail to come
際 *degiwa* the time of setting out
群 *shutsugun* excellence, pre-eminence
資 *shusshi* investment, financing, contribution
資金 *shusshikin* capital
資者 *shusshisha* investor, financier
資額 *shusshigaku* amount invested
14 鼻 *debana, dehana* projecting part (of a headland, etc.); outset, starting out
様 *deyō* attitude; a move, measures (to take)
獄 *shutsugoku* release from prison
端 *deha* chance of going out, opportunity (to succeed). *debana* moment of departure, beginning of work
精 *shussei* diligence, industry
監 *shukkan* leaving prison
演 *shutsuen* stage appearance, performance
演者 *shutsuensha* performer, entertainer, actor
漁 *shutsugyo, shutsuryō* going fishing

漁区域 *shutsuryō kuiki* fishing area
漁期 *shutsuryōki* fishing season
漁権 *shutsuryōken* fishing rights
15 潮 *deshio* high tide
稼 *dekasegi* working away from home
撃 *shutsugeki* sortie, sally
駕 *shutsuga* departure (of a noble)
16 盧 *shutsuro suru* come out of retirement
頭 *shuttō* appearance, presence
稽古 *degeiko* giving lessons at pupils' homes
17 講 *shukkō suru* give lectures
藍 *shutsuran* a pupil excelling his master
18 臍 *debeso* protruding navel
額 *debitai* beetle brows, projecting forehead
題 *shutsudai* proposing a question
19 願 *shutsugan* application
願人 *shutsugannin* applicant
22 鱈目 *detarame* irresponsible utterance, nonsense

6

函 446 / J4821 / M1826 **凾** 447 / J5162 / M1830 KAN. *hako* box. *i(reru)* put into.
13 数 *kansū* function (in math)
蓋 *kangai* box and cover

7

凾 447 / J5162 / M1830 See **函** 446.

RAD. 刀 18

Katana sword. At right: 刂 *rittō* standing "sword." Nickname: Sword.

A **刀** 448 / J4561 / M1845 TŌ sword, saber, knife, engraving tool. *katana* sword, blade.
3 工 *tōkō* swordsmith
下 *tōka ni* under the sword
刃 *tōjin* sword blade
4 手前 *katana (no) temae* a samurai's face
5 礼 *tōrei* sword salute
6 自 *tōji* lady, matron, mistress, housekeeper
匠 *tōshō* swordsmith
圭 *tōkei* doctor
圭家 *tōkeika* doctor
7 身 *tōshin* sword blade
9 持 *katanamo(chi)* swordbearer
架 *tōka* sword rack
背 *tōhai, mine* back of a sword
背打 *mineu(chi)* striking with the back of the sword
10 剣 *tōken* sword
剣商 *tōkenshō* sword dealer
11 痕 *tōkon* sword scar
疵 *katana kizu* sword wound
掛 *katanaka(ke)* sword rack
12 筆吏 *tōhitsu (no) ri* minor official
13 傷 *tōshō* sword cut
14 鋩 *tōbō* point of a sword
17 鍛冶 *katana kaji* swordsmith
20 懸 *katanakake* sword rack

1

B **刃** 449 / J3f4f / M1850 **刄** 450 / J-X / M1848 **刄** 451 / J5163 / M1849 JIN blade, sword, cutting tool. NIN. *ha* blade, edge. *yaiba* blade, sword.
6 向 *hamu(kau)* strike at; bite back; turn on, rise against, oppose, defy
先 *hasaki* edge of a blade
8 物 *hamono* edged tool, cutlery
10 針 *habari* lancet
12 渡 *hawata(ri)* sword length, walking on a sword
13 傷 *ninjō* bloodshed
傷沙汰 *ninjōzata* bloodshed

2

B **刈** 452 / J3422 / M1859 KAI. *ka(ru)* cut, clip; shear; reap; trim, prune.
2 入 *ka(ri)-i(reru)* harvest, reap
入人 *kari-i(re)bito* reapers
3 干 *ka(ri)-ho(su)* cut and dry (in the sun)
上 *ka(ri)-a(geru)* reap completely; trim up (the hair); dress up
4 手 *ka(ri)te* mower, reaper
込 *ka(ri)-ko(mu)* cut, trim, clip; dress, prune. *kariko(mi)* haircut, pruning
5 田 *ka(ri)ta* harvested rice field

立 *karita(te)* new-mown (grass); newly cut (hair)
[8]取 *ka(ri)-to(ru)* mow, reap, harvest
取器 *karito(ri)ki* reaping machine
[9]除 *ka(ri)so(ku), ka(ri)nozo(ku)* remove, cut off
[10]株 *ka(ri)kabu* stubble
根 *ka(ri)ne* stubble
[12]葺 *ka(ri)-fu(ku)* thatch (a roof)
[13]跡 *ka(ri)ato* cut-over land
[15]穂 *ka(ri)ho* harvested grain

A **切** 453 / J405a / M1858 SETSU. SAI. *ki(ru)* cut, chop, hash; carve; saw; clip, shear; slice, strip; fell, cut down; punch; sever (connections); pause, break off; disconnect, turn off; hang up; cross (a street); discount, sell below cost; shake (water) off. *ki(reru)* cut well, be sharp; break, snap; wear out; be injured; burst, collapse; break off, be disconnected; be out of; expire; sever (connections) with; sharp, shrewd; less than. *ki(rasu) vt* be out of, be short of. *ki(re)* cloth; piece, cut, chop, strip, slice, scrap; counter for such. *ki(ri)* limits, end, bounds; period, place to leave off, closing sentence. *setsu na* earnest, eager; kind; keen, acute. *setsu(nai)* oppressive, suffocating; painful, trying. *-kitte no* the most… of all. *-ki(ru)* finish, be through, complete; be able to. *-ki(ri)* all there is; only; since.
[2]入 *ki(ri)-i(ru)* cut into, raid. *ki(ri)-*
[3]子 *ki(ri)ko* facet ⌊*i(reru)* cut and insert
干 *kiribo(shi)* dried daikon strips
下 *ki(ri)-o(rosu)* slash downward. *ki(ri)-sa(geru)* cut down, prune; cut and hang down; reduce, cut shorter
上 *ki(ri)-a(geru)* close, finish. *kiria(ge)* end, conclusion
口 *ki(ri)kuchi* cut end, section; opening, slit
口上 *ki(ri)kōjō* stiff formality, set terms
[4]戸 *ki(ri)do* low gate, side gate
方 *ki(ri)kata* how to cut, how to slice
火 *ki(ri)bi* Shinto fire-purification ceremony; flint sparks
片 *seppen* cut-off scraps
切 *ki(re)gi(re)* pieces, scraps. *setsusetsu* politeness; feeling of loneliness
支丹 *Kirishitan* (early) Japanese Christianity
手 *kitte* postage stamp; merchandise certificate. *ki(re)te* man of ability. *ki(ri)te* cutter, certificate
手蒐集 *kitte shūshū* philately
込 *ki(ri)-ko(mu)* cut into; raid, attack; cut up. *ki(re)-ko(mu)* cut into. *ki(re)ko(mi)* cut, notch, incision
込炭 *ki(ri)ko(mi)tan* unscreened coal
分 *ki(ri)-waka(tsu), ki(ri)-wa(keru)* cut up
分法 *setsubunhō* syncopation
[5]目 *ki(re)me* rift, gap, break; pause, interruption. *ki(ri)me* cut, section, notch, incision; end (of a task)
石 *ki(ri)ishi* hewn stone, quarried stone
立 *ki(ri)-ta(teru)* cut, slash, slay all. *ki(ri)-ta(tsu)* rise perpendicularly. *ki(ri)ta(te)* freshly cut. *ki(ri)ta(tta)* steep, precipitous
付 *ki(ri)-tsu(keru)* slash at a person
外 *ki(ri)-hazu(su)* miss in attempting to kill
払 *ki(ri)-hara(u)* clear away; clear land; prune, lop off
札 *ki(ri)fuda* trump card
去 *ki(ri)-sa(ru)* cut off
出 *ki(ri)-da(su), ki(ri)-ida(su)* quarry; cut (timber); cut and carry off; begin to talk, break the ice. *ki(ri)da(shi)* pointed knife; logging; (beef) scraps; starting to speak
[6]回 *ki(ri)-mawa(su)* run around killing; manage everything, control; cut carelessly (a cook or a surgeon)
死 *ki(ri)ji(ni)* fighting to the death (with swords)
返 *ki(ri)kae(shi)* railway switchback
伏 *ki(ri)-fu(seru)* slay, cut down (a foe)
地 *ki(re)ji* cloth; piece of cloth, swatch
合 *ki(ri)a(i)* crossing swords, fighting with swords, cutting each other (in fighting)
先 *ki(s)saki* point of a sword; spearhead
羽 *kiriha* coal face, working face
羽詰 *seppatsu(maru)* be at one's wit's end, be cornered
[7]言 *setsugen* urging, persuasion; declaration
身 *ki(ri)mi* slice, chop
迫 *seppaku* pressure, urgency; imminence; acuteness, tenseness
形 *ki(ri)kata* a way to cut, a way to slice
花 *ki(ri)bana* cut flowers

狂言 *ki(ri)kyōgen* last act
抜 *ki(ri)-nu(keru)* cut one's way through, tide over, struggle through. *ki(ri)-nu(ku)* cut out, clip from, extract. *kirinu(ki)* scraps
抜帖 *kirinu(ki)chō* scrapbook
売 *kiriu(ri)* selling by the piece
売主義 *kiriu(ri) shugi* prostitution
8 味 *ki(re)aji* sharpness (of the sword), the feel of a cutting edge
拡 *ki(ri)-hiro(geru)* cut and enlarge
放 *ki(ri)-hana(su), ki(ri)-hana(tsu)* cut loose, let loose, cut off, detach, dismember, cut in two
枝 *ki(ri)eda* slips (to plant)
杭 *ki(ri)kui* stump
物 *ki(re)mono* edged tool; cutlery; shrewd businessman
刻 *ki(ri)-kiza(mu)* hew, chop up, mangle, mince
実 *setsujitsu ni* strongly, keenly, vividly, sincerely, urgently
岸 *ki(ri)gishi* steep bank, cliff
妻 *ki(ri)zuma* gable
取 *ki(ri)-to(ru)* cut off, cut out; whittle down; tear out; cut down, amputate. *kirito(ri)* cutting; tearing off, cutting off; robbery with assault, burglary; robber, burglar
取強盗 *kirito(ri) gōtō* violent robbery, burglary; robber, burglar
取線 *kirito(ri) sen* perforated line
9 通 *ki(ri)-tō(su)* cut through (with a road, tunnel, or canal). *kiridō(shi)* (railway) cut
枯 *ki(ri)-ka(rasu)* destroy, kill off (trees)
畑 *ki(ri)hata, ki(ri)batake* hillside farm; fallow ground
除 *ki(ri)-no(keru), setsujo suru* cut off, cut out
炭 *ki(ri)zumi* cut-up charcoal
10 屑 *ki(ri)kuzu* scraps, chips. *ki(re)kuzu* cloth scraps
起 *ki(ri)-oko(su)* open up waste land for cultivation
倒 *ki(ri)-tao(su)* cut down, chop down, fell
株 *ki(ri)kabu* stump, stubble
破 *ki(ri)-yabu(ru)* cut to pieces
紙 *ki(ri)kami* cut paper, paper cut in half, paper scrap
釘 *ki(ri)kugi* brad; double-pointed nail
殺 *ki(ri)-koro(su)* slay
11 痔 *ki(re)ji* anal fistula
疵 *ki(ri)kizu* a cut, a gash
張 *kiriba(ri)* patching
得 *ki(ri)doku* no retribution for a samurai killing a commoner
情 *setsujō* ardent love
接 *ki(ri)tsu(gi)* grafting
捨 *ki(ri)-su(teru)* cut down, slay; omit, discard
掛 *ki(k)ka(ke)* chance; start; clue; excuse
捲 *ki(ri) maku(ru)* slash about, attack and scatter
据 *ki(ri)-su(eru)* cut down an enemy
組 *ki(ri)-ku(mu)* piece together; mortise; miter; dovetail
崩 *ki(ri)-kuzu(su)* level (a hill); cut through (a mountain); break (a strike); split (the opposition)
窓 *ki(ri)mado* windows cut out of a wall
苛 *ki(ri)-saina(mu)* hack to pieces
望 *setsubō* earnest desire, longing
盛 *kirimo(ri)* management, administration; preparing food
乾 *ki(ri)boshi* dried strips of daikon
細裂 *ki(ri)-komaza(ku)* cut up small
符 *kippu* ticket
符切 *kippuki(ri)* ticket punch; ticket puncher
符売 *kippuuri* ticket seller
符売場 *kippu uriba* ticket window; box office, ticket
断 *setsudan* section; cutting, severance, amputation
断図 *setsudanzu* sectional drawing
断面 *setsudammen* section (in drawing)
断患者 *setsudan kanja* amputee
断機 *setsudanki* cutter, cutting machine
12 開 *sekkai suru, ki(ri)-hira(ku)* clear (land), open up; cut through. *sekkai* incision, operation, section. *ki(ri)hira(ki)* clearing (land); excavating
間 *ki(re)ma* interval, break, rift (in clouds)
場 *ki(ri)ba* coal face, working face
揃 *ki(ri)-soro(eru)* cut and even up, cut several pieces to the same size
結 *ki(ri)-musu(bu)* cross swords with
貼 *kiriba(ri)* patching
創 *ki(ri)kizu* cut, gash; incision
割 *ki(ri)-wa(ru)* cut in two

散 *ki(ri)-chi(rasu)* cut down all, slash promiscuously
落 *ki(ri)-oto(su)* cut down, lop off, prune
無 *ki(ri) (no) na(i)* endless, boundless. *ki(ri)na(shi)* always, continuously. *-ki(re)nai* cannot, be unable to. *-ki(ra)na(i)* not through, not finished
裂 *ki(ri)-sa(ku)* cut off, cut up; cut to pieces
歯 *sesshi* gnashing of teeth
歯扼腕 *sesshi-yakuwan suru* be enraged, be indignant, be impatient, gnashing the teeth and clenching the arms on the breast (in anger or regret)
換 *ki(ri)-ka(eru)* change, exchange, convert, renew; throw a switch; replace; switch over
換時 *kirika(e)doki* time to switch over; time to renew (a license)
替 *ki(ri)-kawa(ru)* change completely. *ki(ri)-ka(eru)* change, exchange, convert, renew, throw a switch, replace; switch over
替時 *kirika(e)doki* time to switch over, time to renew (a license)
13 傷 *ki(ri)kizu* cut, gash
継 *ki(ri)tsu(gi) suru* cut and patch
腹 *seppuku* disembowelment, harakiri
解 *ki(ri)-hodo(ku)* cut open a tied bundle; releasing prisoners
詰 *ki(ri)-tsu(meru)* shorten, reduce, economize. *ki(ri)tsu(me)* retrenchment, curtailment
毀 *ki(ri)-kowa(su)* cut to pieces
愛 *setsuai* deep love
賃 *ki(ri)chin* brokerage, exchange, commission
暖簾 *ki(ri)noren* a short split entrance ⌈curtain
14 嘖 *ki(ri)-saina(mu)* hack to pieces
端 *ki(re)hashi, ki(rep)pashi, ki(ri)hashi* scraps, cut end, cut-off piece
髪 *ki(ri)gami* bobbed hair
15 線 *sessen* tangent (in trigonometry)
縄 *ki(ri)nawa* piece of rope cut for a certain purpose
論 *setsuron* persistent argument
調 *ki(ri)-totono(eru)* trim (hedges)
幣 *ki(ri)nusa* paper and sacred *sakaki* branches cut and mixed with rice to scatter before the gods
磋 *sessa* polishing (stone); polishing (character)
磋琢磨 *sessa-takuma* diligent application
16 諫 *sekkan* admonition, expostulation
整 *ki(ri)-totono(eru)* cut and prepare (stones)
17 縮 *ki(ri)-chiji(meru)* cut smaller; economize
19 願 *setsugan* entreaty, supplication
離 *ki(ri)-hana(reru)* cut off and separate
22 籠 *ki(ri)ko* facet

A **分** 454 / J4a2c / M1853 BUN dividing; part, segment; share; ration; rate; degree; one's lot, one's status; relation; duty; kind, lot. FUN a minute of time; one-sixtieth of a degree; one-tenth of a *momme* (see Weights and Measures). BU rate, part, percentage; one percent; thickness; odds; chance of winning; one-tenth of a *shaku* (see Weights and Measures); one quarter of a *ryō*. *wa(karu)* understand, comprehend; know, be known, be identified; be open to reason, be sensible; can tell (what will happen); appreciate; be announced; be discovered; recognize. *wa(keru)* divide, split, separate; isolate; distribute, share; distinguish; spare. *wa(katsu)* divide, separate; share with; distinguish between. *wa(kazu)* without differentiation. *wa(kare)* branch, fork; division, section; farewell. *wa(kareru)* branch off, diverge from, fork; split; be divided; part with; be divorced; bid farewell; break up, disperse, scatter. *wa(kari)* understanding, comprehension. *wa(ke)* sharing, division; draw, tie. *wa(kachi)* distinction, differentiation, discrimination. *bun-* branch, detached.
2 入 *wa(ke)-i(ru)* force one's way, push through
力 *bunryoku* component force
3 工場 *bunkōjō* branch factory
子 *bunshi* numerator; molecule; (bad) elements
子量 *bunshiryō* molecular weight
子説 *bunshi setsu* molecular theory
与 *wa(ke)-ata(eru), waka(chi)-ata(eru)* apportion to, share. *bun'yo suru* distribute. *bun'yo* distribution, allocation; dispensation; impartation
与税 *bun'yozei* tax allotment (to local government)

4 区 *bunku* subdistrict
化 *bunka* specialization, differentiation
切 *wa(kari)-ki(ru)* understand completely. *wa(kari)-ki(tta)* obvious, undeniable
分 *wa(kare)-waka(re) ni* separately, apart, severally, individually
水山脈 *bunsui sammyaku* watershed, divide
水界 *bunsuikai* watershed, divide
水線 *bunsuisen* watershed, divide
水嶺 *bunsuirei* watershed, divide
5 母 *bumbo* denominator
目 *wa(ke)me* dividing line; parting (of the hair); partition; crisis
立 *bunritsu* segregation, separation, independence
外 *bungai* not within proper limits, excessive; unmerited; special
出 *wa(kare)-de(ru)* branch out, diverge, radiate
布 *bumpu* distribution
冊 *bunsatsu* separate volume, installment
6 団 *bundan* branch, chapter
地 *bunchi* parceling out an estate
合 *wa(kachi)-a(u), wa(ke)-a(u)* share
会 *bunkai* branch, chapter
争 *wa(kare)-araso(u)* quarrel and separate
列 *bunretsu* filing off (in a parade)
列式 *bunretsushiki* military review
光 *bunkō* spectrum
光学 *bunkōgaku* spectroscopy
光器 *bunkōki* spectroscope
7 身 *bunshin* parturition, delivery; one's child; branch, offshoot; one's other self
局 *bunkyoku* branch office
体 *buntai* fission
社 *bunsha* branch shrine
利 *bunri* crisis (in an illness)
売 *bumbai, wa(ke)u(ri)* selling separately
良 *wa(kari)yo(i)* easy to understand. *wa(ke)yo(i)* easy to divide
別 *fumbetsu* discernment, judgment, wisdom. *bumbetsu* discrimination; separation, division; classification; distinction
別心 *fumbetsushin* prudence, distinction, discrimination
別盛 *fumbetsuzaka(ri)* the age of wisdom, around forty
岐 *bunki* divergence, ramification, forking
岐点 *bunkiten* diverging point; turning point; fork, crossroads; junction; parting of the ways
岐駅 *bunki eki* junction
岐線 *bunkisen* branch line, spur
8 店 *bunten* branch store, branch of a firm
明 *bummei, bummyō* clearness; clear understanding
取 *wa(kachi)-to(ru)* divide the spoils, receive a share. *wa(ke)-to(ru)* apportion, share. *wa(ke)do(ri)* sharing, division
易 *wa(kari)yasu(i)* easy to understand. *wa(ke)yasu(i)* easy to divide
泌 *bumpitsu, bumpi* secretion
泌液 *bumpitsu eki* a secretion
限 *bungen* social standing. *bugen* social standing; wealth
限者 *bungenja* a rich man
担 *buntan* apportionment
担金 *buntankin* share of expenses; contribution
担額 *buntangaku* amount allotted; contribution
析 *bunseki* analysis, assaying
析化学 *bunseki kagaku* analytical chemistry
析学 *bunsekigaku* analytics
析表 *bunsekihyō* analysis table
析試験 *bunseki shiken* assaying
9 厚 *buatsu na, buatsu(i)* thick, bulky, massive
厘 *funrin* (not) in the least, (not) a bit
屋 *wa(karazu)ya* obstinate person; blockhead
秒 *fumbyō* a moment
袂 *bumbei* parting (from someone)
院 *bun'in* branch (of an institution); branch temple; detached building
封 *bumpō* hiving off, swarming; dividing a fief
乗 *bunjō* riding separately
前 *wa(ke)mae* share, quota
点 *bunten* equinox; fork, junction
室 *bunshitsu* isolated room, detached office, annex
巻 *bumma(ki)* alternating-current winding
度器 *bundoki* protractor
県地図 *bunken chizu* prefecture maps
派 *bumpa* denomination, sect, branch, faction. *bumpa suru* separate from

派主義 *bumpa shugi* sectarianism; sectionalism
科 *bunka* department, section, branch; course; school
科会 *bunkakai* subcommittee meeting
界 *bunkai* delimitation, demarcation; border, boundary
界線 *bunkaisen* line of demarcation
10 骨 *bunkotsu* part of a person's ashes
校 *bunkō* branch school
流 *bunryū* tributary
納 *bunnō* installment payment or delivery
針 *funshin* minute hand
家 *bunke* branch family
党 *buntō* secession from a party
書 *wa(kachi)ga(ki)* leaving spaces between words in *kana* script
配 *bumpai* division, sharing; distribution, allotment
配金 *bumpaikin* dividend (on shares)
捕 *bundo(ru)* capture, seize, plunder
捕物 *bundo(ri)mono* loot, booty, plunder
捕品 *bundo(ri)hin* loot, booty, plunder
11 野 *bun'ya* field, sphere, division, branch
隊 *buntai* squad; division (in the navy); small unit
悪 *wa(kari)niku(i)* hard to understand
宿 *bunshuku* billeting
教場 *bunkyōjō* detached classroom
娩 *bumben* delivery, confinement, childbirth
娩作用 *bumben sayō* delivery, parturition
娩時 *bumbenji* time of delivery (of a child)
娩期 *bumbenki* time of delivery (of a child)
12 遣 *bunken* detachment, detail
疏 *bunso* explanation, justification, defense, excuse, apology
詞 *bunshi* participle
散 *bunsan* breakup, dispersion, decentralization, divergence; bankruptcy
掌 *bunshō* division of duties
量 *bunryō* quantity, amount, dose
営 *bun'ei* outpost, detached garrison
極 *bunkyoku* polarization; lining up with
極化 *bunkyokuka* polarization; lining up with
割 *bunkatsu* partition, division, dismemberment
割払 *bunkatsubara(i)* installment paying
裂 *bunretsu* dissolution, dismemberment, breakup, disintegration, segmentation, fission, split, schism, separation
裂性 *bunretsusei* fissionable
裂物質 *bunretsu busshitsu* fissionable materials
13 溜 *bunryū* cracking, fractional distillation (of gasoline)
際 *bunzai* social standing
数 *bunsū* fraction
署 *bunsho* substation, branch office
業 *bungyō* division of labor, specialization, assembly-line production
解 *bunkai* analysis; parsing; decomposition; dismantling; disintegration; dissolution; reduction (in chemistry)
解的 *bunkaiteki* analytical
解能 *bunkainō* power (of an optical instrument)
解蒸溜法 *bunkai jōryūhō* cracking (in chemistry)
14 銅 *fundō* weight, counterweight
15 権 *bunken* decentralization of authority
課 *bunka* subdivision, section, branch
賦 *bumpu* assignment, allocation
蝕 *bunshoku* partial eclipse
16 館 *bunkan* annex
餐 *bunsan suru* distribute (the emblems in Communion)
17 轄 *bunkatsu* separate jurisdiction
18 類 *bunrui* classification, group
類法 *bunruihō* classification system
類学 *bunruigaku* science of classification
類表 *bunruihyō* classified table
19 離 *bunri* division, separation. *wa(ke)-hana(su)* separate from, detach
離主義者 *bunri shugisha* separatists, schismatics
離機 *bunriki* separator
20 譲 *bunjō* selling (real-estate) lots
譲地 *bunjōchi* lots for sale

3

刋 455 / J5164 / M1866 SEN. *ki(ru)* cut.

A **刊** 456 J3429 M1865 KAN publishing; carve, engrave.
5本 *kampon* printed book
6行 *kankō* publication
行物 *kankōbutsu* a publication

4

刕 457 J-X M1899 Nonstandard for **州** 1529.

刔 458 J5165 M1897 See **抉** 2078.

刎 459 J5166 M1879 FUN. *ha(neru)* decapitate.
3上 *ha(ne)-a(garu)* jump up, spring up
6死 *funshi* decapitating oneself
16頸 *funkei* decapitation

A **列** 460 J4e/3 M1901 RETSU row, rank, tier, file, column, line; procession; queue. *res(suru) vi* attend, rank with. *vt* line up. *tsura(naru)* range, be connected with, join; stand in a row; attend; join one's people (in death). *tsura(neru)* put in a row, join.
4氏 *resshi* Reaumur (thermometer)
王 *retsuō* chronicles of the kings
王紀 *Retsuōki* the Book of Kings
6次 *retsuji* order, sequence, precedence
伝 *retsuden* series of biographies
伝体 *retsudentai* biographical style
7車 *ressha* train
8国 *rekkoku* the powers, all nations
9侯 *rekkō* many feudal lords
10座 *retsuza* presence, attendance, sitting in a row
記 *rekki* enumeration, listing
島 *rettō* archipelago, chain of islands
挙 *rekkyo* enumeration
席 *resseki* attendance, presence
席者 *ressekisha* those present, the guests, the attendance
11強 *rekkyō* the great powers
13福 *reppuku* beatification
福式 *reppukushiki* beatification ceremony
聖 *ressei* successive emperors; canonization
聖式 *resseishiki* canonization
18藩 *reppan* the various clans

B **刑** 461 J373a M1886 KEI penalty, sentence, punishment. *kei(suru)* sentence.
6死 *keishi* execution
名 *keimei* penalty designations
吏 *keiri* executioner
7余 *keiyo* previous conviction
余者 *keiyosha* ex-convict
8法 *keihō* criminal law
具 *keigu* instruments of punishment
典 *keiten* criminal law books
事 *keiji* criminal case; criminal
事上 *keijijō no* penal, criminal
事犯 *kaijihan* criminal offense
事処分 *keiji shobun* punishment of a criminal
事事件 *keiji jiken* criminal case
事被告 *keiji hikoku* the accused
事被告人 *keiji hikokunin* the accused
事裁判 *keiji saiban* criminal trial
事訴訟 *keiji soshō* criminal action
9律 *keiritsu* criminal law
10徒 *keito* condemned person, prisoner
11務作業 *keimu sagyō* prison industry
務官 *keimukan* prison guard
務所 *keimusho* prison, penitentiary
務所長 *keimushochō* warden
12場 *keijō* place of execution
期 *keiki* prison term
14獄 *keigoku* jail; punishment
罰 *keibatsu* judgment, penalty, punishment
15戮 *keiriku* punishment, penalty; execution

5

刧 462 J5167 M1927 **刦** 463 J-X M1926 See **劫** 529.

删 464 J5168 M1917 SAN cut down.
8定 *santei* revision of a passage
10修 *sanshū* revision, reform

A **判** 465 J483d M1923 HAN stamp, seal; a monogram signature; judgment. *han(jiru)* judge, decide; guess; solve, decipher, interpret; divine. *waka(ru)* understand, comprehend; know, be known, be identified; be open to reason, be sensible; can tell (what will happen);

2 二 亠 人 亻 𠆢 儿 入 八 丷 冂 冖 冫 几 凵 【刀 5 刂】 力 勹 匕 匚 匸 十 卜 卩 厂 厶 又

appreciate; be announced; be discovered; recognize. *-ban* size (of paper or books).
3 士 *hanshi* judge advocate
子 *hanko* personal seal
6 任官 *hanninkan* junior official
7 決 *hanketsu* judgment, decision, decree, sentence
別 *hambetsu* distinction, discrimination
8 例 *hanrei* judicial precedent
明 *hammei suru* become clear, be confirmed
物 *han(ji)mono* puzzle, riddle
官 *hangan* judge, magistrate
者 *hanja* judge (of literary contests)
事 *hanji* judge
取 *hanto(ri)* traveling around getting seal stamps
取帳 *hanto(ri)chō* chit book, delivery book
定 *hantei* judgment, decision, award, verdict
定勝 *hanteiga(chi)* winning on a decision
11 断 *handan* judgment, decision, adjudication, conclusion; decipherment; divination
断力 *handanryoku* judgment, discernment
12 絵 *han(ji)e* picture puzzle
然 *hanzen(taru)* clear, distinct, evident, definite
検事 *hankenji* judges and prosecutors
14 読 *handoku* decipherment, interpretation, making out
読難 *handoku(shi)gata(i)* illegible

A **利** 466 / J4d78 / M1932 RI advantage, benefit, gain; interest; victory. *ri(suru)* benefit, do good, profit, gain. *ki(ku)* take effect, do (a person) good; work, operate; tell (on one's strength); be available (bus or phone). *ki(kasu)* use (one's head); exert (influence). *ki(keru)* be influential. *kiki* efficacy.
2 刀 *ritō* sharp sword
3 子 *rishi* interest
下 *risa(ge)* lowering the interest rate
上 *ria(ge)* raising the interest rate
刃 *rijin* sharp sword
口 *rikō* cleverness, wisdom, intelligence
口者 *rikōmono* clever person
己 *riko* selfishness
己心 *rikoshin* selfishness
己主義 *riko shugi* egoism, selfishness
己性 *rikosei* selfishness
己説 *rikosetsu* egoism
4 方 *rikata* profitableness
水 *risui* irrigation, water utilization
5 目 *kikime* effect, efficacy, impression
払 *ribara(i)* interest payment
出 *ki(ki)-da(su)* begin to take effect
付 *ritsu(ki)* interest-bearing
付債券 *ritsuki saiken* coupon bond
巧 *rikō* skill and speed, cleverness
巧者 *rikōmono* clever person
札 *risatsu, rifuda* coupon, interest coupon
札付債券 *rifudazu(ki) saiken* coupon bond
他 *rita* altruism
他主義 *rita shugi* altruism
他的 *ritateki* altruistic
用 *riyō* use, utilization; improvement (of opportunities); making a tool of
用者 *riyōsha* user
用価値 *riyō kachi* usefulness, utility value
用厚生 *riyō kōsei* promotion of public welfare
6 回 *rimawa(ri)* interest, yield, profit
7 役 *kikiyaku* influential person
売 *riu(ri)* selling at a profit
男 *kikiotoko* man of ability
尿 *rinyō* urination
尿剤 *rinyōzai* diuretic
8 金 *rikin* interest, gain
所 *kikidokoro* effective points
者 *ki(ki)mono* influential person. *ki(ke)mono* able man, man of influence
9 食 *rigui* profit taking
便 *riben* convenience
点 *riten* advantage, point in favor
発 *rihatsu* cleverness, wisdom, intelligence
10 根 *rikon na* bright (child)
酒 *kikizake* wine tasting
害 *rigai* advantages and disadvantages, interests
害関係 *rigai kankei* interests
息 *risoku* interest
息算 *risokuzan* interest calculation
益 *rieki* profit, gain; benefit, advantage. *riyaku* the favor of a Buddha; answer to prayer; help

益代表国 *rieki daihyōkoku* a country representing the diplomatic interests of another
益交換 *rieki kōkan* reciprocity, reciprocal benefits
益金 *riekikin* amount of profit
益配当 *rieki haitō* distribution of profits; profit-sharing; dividend
11 達 *ritatsu* success in life
運 *riun* good fortune
欲 *riyoku* greed, covetousness
率 *riritsu* rate of interest
得 *ritoku* profit, benefit
得税 *ritokuzei* profits tax
12 殖 *rishoku* moneymaking
腕 *ki(ki)ude* the right arm, the whip hand
鈍 *ridon* sharp or blunt, bright or dull
13 福 *rifuku* public welfare, prosperity
15 潤 *rijun* profit
慾 *riyoku* greed, covetousness
器 *riki* sharp swords; good cutting knives; convenient machine; useful talents; a superior person
権 *riken* rights, concessions
権屋 *riken'ya* concession hunter, grafter
16 鞘 *rizaya, risaya* margin of profit
18 鎌 *togama* sharp sickle

A **別** 467 J4a4c M1924 **別** 468 J-X M1925 BETSU. *wa(keru)* divide, split, separate; isolate; distribute, share; distinguish; spare. *waka(tsu)* divide, separate; share with; distinguish between. *waka(reru)* branch off, diverge from, fork; split; be divided; part with; be divorced; bid farewell; break up, disperse, scatter. *betsu no* another, different, particular, separate; extra; exception; difference, distinction. *betsu ni* (with neg.) not especially, not particularly. *bes(shite)* especially, particularly. *waka(chi)* distinction, discrimination; differentiation. *waka(re)* branch, fork; division, section; farewell. *wake(te)* above all, especially, all the more. *-betsu* classified by.
2 人 *betsujin, betsunin* different person, changed man
3 口 *betsukuchi* different item, different lot, different kind
与 *waka(chi)-ata(eru)* divide and pass around
4 戸 *bekko* separate house
切 *waka(ri)-ki(ru)* understand completely
天地 *bettenchi* another world
5 目 *waka(re)me* turning point, junction, parting of the ways
冊 *bessatsu* separate volume, extra issue, supplement
号 *betsugō* another name
仕立 *betsushita(te)* tailor-made
世界 *bessekai* another world
6 行 *betsugyō* another line
宅 *bettaku* secondary residence
当 *bettō* groom, footman, stableman, equerry; intendant, steward
争 *waka(re)-araso(u)* separate and quarrel
名 *betsumei, betsumyō* another name, alias, pseudonym
7 言 *betsugen* other words. *betsugen (sureba)* in other words
状 *betsujō* a different situation
別 *betsubetsu ni, waka(re)-waka(re) ni* separately, apart, severally, individually
形 *bekkei* another form (of a character)
邸 *bettei* villa, detached residence
条 *betsujō* something unusual
8 居 *bekkyo* separation, limited divorce
送 *bessō* separate mail, separate shipment
使 *besshi* special messenger; another messenger
杯 *beppai* farewell cup, farewell dinner
法 *beppō* different method
物 *betsumono* another thing, exception, special case
表 *beppyō* an annexed (statistical) table
事 *betsuji* another affair, mishap
9 途 *betto* special, special reserve (account)
便 *betsubin de* by separate post
派 *beppa* different sect, party or school
珍 *betchin* velveteen
科 *bekka* special course; another course
院 *betsuin* branch temple
封 *beppū de* under separate cover
段 *betsudan* (with neg.) not in particular, not especially
盃 *beppai* farewell cup; farewell dinner
前 *wa(ke)mae* share, quota

品 *beppin* a beautiful woman (vulgar)
室 *besshitsu* separate room, special room
荘 *bessō* villa, second house
染 *betsuzo(me)* special dyeing
除権 *betsujoken* right of exclusion
10 席 *besseki* different seat, special seat, separate room
個 *bekko no* several, separate, different, another
時 *betsuji* another time; time of separation
格 *bekkaku* special, extraordinary
称 *besshō* another name, alias, pseudonym
紙 *besshi* enclosure
納 *betsunō* another method of payment
記 *bekki* separate paragraph; separate volume
宴 *betsuen* farewell dinner
書 *waka(chi)gaki* leaving spaces between words in *kana* script
配達 *betsu haitatsu* special delivery
11 道 *waka(re)michi* forked road, crossroads, branch road, parting of the ways
堂 *betsudō* separate building
勘定 *betsu kanjō* separate account
問題 *betsu mondai* a different thing, another question, a different case
12 間 *betsuma* separate room, special room
項 *bekkō* separate paragraph; special heading
棟 *betsumune* outbuilding, detached building
隔 *wa(ke)heda(te)* distinction, favoritism
無 *betsuna(ku)* without distinction
報 *beppō* another report
13 殿 *betsuden* palace annex, shrine annex
辞 *betsuji* farewell address, parting words
誂 *betsu atsura(e)* special order
路 *betsuro* different road. *waka(re)michi* forked road. *waka(re)ji* parting of the ways; the way to hades; one's way after the parting
意 *betsui* different opinion, ill will; intention to part
業 *betsugyō* villa, second house, country house; another line of work
働隊 *betsu dōtai* flying column, detached force
14 種 *besshu* another kind, distinct species, variety
箇 *bekko* several, separate, different, another
製 *bessei* special make
15 趣 *besshu* deep interest
儀 *betsugi* other affair, special matter
16 館 *bekkan* annex
17 嬪 *beppin* beauty, beautiful woman, pretty girl
懇 *bekkon* intimacy
19 離 *betsuri* parting, separation

A 初 469 / J3d69 / M1911 SHO beginning; first. *haji(meru) vt* begin, open, start, originate, inaugurate, initiate. *haji(maru) vi* begin, start, open; date from; (season) sets in; arise, break out; originate in. *haji(mete)* (for) the first time; not until. *hatsu* beginning, first, new. *haji(me)* beginning, origin. *-haji(me)* including, and, as well as. *-so(meru)* begin to. *ui-* first(time), beginning. *hatsu-* new, the first (snow), maiden (voyage). *-some* begin to.

1 一見 *shoikken* first sight, first glance
一念 *shoichinen* original intention, first desire
2 七日 *shonanuka* seventh day since death
3 口 *shokuchi* beginning, start
子 *hatsugo* first child
4 手 *shote* beginning, start
天辺 *shoteppen* topmost, first and foremost
公演 *hatsukōen* premiere
心 *shoshin* original aim, original intention; inexperience
心者 *shoshinsha* beginner
日 *hatsuhi* New Year's Day sunrise. *shonichi* first day, opening day, first performance. *shojitsu* first day; dawn
日出 *hatsuhi(no)de* New Year's Day sunrise
中後 *shochūgo* all the time, constantly, always
5 句 *shoku* first line (of a poem)
犯 *shohan* first offense; first offender
冬 *shotō* beginning of winter; tenth lunar month
号 *shogō* first number (of a magazine, etc.)
氷 *hatsugōri* the first ice
出 *shoshutsu* first appearance
生 *hatsunari* first fruit of the season

生児 *shoseiji* newborn infant
代 *shodai* the first generation; the founder
代教会 *Shodai Kyōkai* the Early Church
6 老 *shorō* age forty
耳 *hatsumimi* something heard for the first time
旬 *shojun* first ten days of the month
回 *shokai* first time; first inning
任 *shonin* first appointment
任給 *shoninkyū* initial salary
年 *shonen* first year, early years
年兵 *shonenhei* new conscript, raw recruit
年級 *shonenkyū* beginner's class
7 初 *uiui(shii)* innocent, artless, unsophisticated
更 *shokō* the first of five night watches, 8–10 p.m.
志 *shoshi* original aim, original intention
売 *hatsuu(ri)* first sale of the new year
花 *hatsuhana* the first flowers; the first cherry blossoms
対面 *shotaimen* first meeting, first interview
見 *shoken* seeing for the first time
見参 *uigenzan* first interview
8 刷 *hatsuzu(ri), shozu(ri)* first printing; first printing of the year
版 *shohan* first edition
物 *hatsumono* season's first product
夜 *shoya* first watch of the night; bridal night
歩 *shoho* first steps, elements, primer
空 *hatsusora* first springlike sky; first sky suggesting the new season
学 *shogaku* beginning to study; a person beginning a course of study
9 音 *hatsune* first song (of a bird)
速 *shosoku* initial velocity, muzzle velocity
便 *hatsudayo(ri)* first letter of the new year
秋 *hatsuaki, shoshū* early fall
級 *shokyū* beginners' class
陣 *uijin* one's first battle, baptism of fire
段 *shodan* lowest grade; first-degree black belt (martial arts)
茸 *hatsutake* a kind of mushroom
春 *hatsuharu, shoshun* early spring
信者 *shoshinja* new believer
紅葉 *hatsumomijiba, hatsumomiji* first colored maple leaves
発 *shohatsu* first, initial, incipient
10 値 *hatsune* first price
孫 *uimago, hatsumago* first grandchild
校 *shokō* first proof
夏 *shoka, hatsunatsu* early summer
恋 *hatsukoi* first love; puppy love
荷 *hatsuni* first load of the new year
時雨 *hatsushigure* first winter rain
航海 *hatsukōkai* maiden voyage
11 頃 *hajimegoro* near the beginning
婚 *shokon* first marriage
経 *shokei* first menstruation
終 *haji(me)-owa(ri)* beginning and end, particulars, circumstances
雪 *hatsuyuki* the first snow
教会 *Shokyōkai* the Early Church
産 *hatsusan, uizan, shozan* first childbirth
産婦 *shosampu* primipara, a woman having her first child
12 雁 *hatsukari* first wild goose
給 *shokyū* initial salary
期 *shoki* early days, early years, early stage, beginning
筆 *shohitsu, shofude* first writing
場所 *hatsubasho* New Year's sumo tournament
診 *shoshin* first medical examination
診料 *shoshinryō* first medical examination fee
等 *shotō* elementary
等科 *shotōka* elementary course, beginners' class
等教育 *shotō kyōiku* elementary education
13 詣 *hatsumōde* first shrine or temple visit in the new year
戦 *shosen* beginning of hostilities
幕 *shomaku* curtain raiser
夢 *hatsuyume* first dream of the new year
14 演 *shoen* first performance
舞台 *hatsubutai* stage debut
15 幟 *hatsunobori* first Boy's Festival streamer
潮 *shochō* first menstruation
穂 *hatsuho* first harvest, first fruits, first grains
縁 *shoen* first marriage
審 *shoshin* first trial
審裁判所 *shoshin saibansho* court of first instance
16 頭 *shotō* early, elementary; at first

興行 *hatsukōgyō* first performance
17 臨 *Shorin* First Advent (of Christ)
霜 *hatsushimo* the first frost
18 雛 *hatsubina* a girl's first Doll Festival
顔合 *hatsukaoa(wase)* first meeting

— 6 —

刲 470 / J-X / M1955 KEI pierce.

刮 471 / J-X / M1975 KATSU tear off.

刮 472 / J5169 / M1943 KATSU. *koso(geru)* scrape off.

A **券** 473 / J3774 / M1966 KEN ticket, coupon, bond, certificate.
9 面 *kemmen* the face of a bond, draft, or certificate

刹 474 / J516b / M1967 SECHI. SETSU. SATSU temple.
6 那 *setsuna* moment, instant, juncture
那的 *setsunateki* ephemeral, transitory

刳 475 / J516a / M1956 **刳** 476 / J-X / M-X KO. *egu(ru)* gouge, hollow out, bore, excavate. *ku(ru)* bore; gouge; scoop out, hollow out; excavate.
6 舟 *kuribune* dugout canoe
7 抜 *ku(ri)-nu(ku)* gouge out; excavate; bore, drill
形 *kurikata* molding
11 貫 *ku(ri)-nu(ku)* gouge out; excavate; bore, drill

B **到** 477 / J457e / M1950 TŌ. *ita(ru)* go, proceed, come; arrive, reach, attain; result in, lead to.
7 来 *tōrai* arrival, advent, visitation
来物 *tōraimono* something sent as a gift
8 底 *tōtei* after all, in the long run; (with neg.) (cannot) possibly, (none) at all, impossible; absolutely
11 著 *tōchaku* arrival
達 *tōtatsu* arrival
達地 *tōtatsuchi* destination
達局 *tōtatsukyoku* office of destination
達点 *tōtatsuten* destination
達港 *tōtatsukō* port of destination
12 着 *tōchaku* arrival
着早早 *tōchaku sōsō* immediately upon arrival
着地点 *tōchaku chiten* destination; objective (of an army)
着港 *tōchakukō* port of arrival
着駅 *tōchaku eki* arrival station
16 頭 *tōtō* at last, finally, after all

A **刻** 478 / J396f / M1970 KOKU time; carving, engraving, cutting. *kiza(mu)* cut fine, chop up; mince, hash; carve (images); engrave (seals); chisel, cut, notch. *ho(ru)* carve, engrave, chisel, sculpture, inscribe. *kiza(mi)* shredded tobacco; notch, nick. *kiza* scratch.
1 一刻 *koku-ikkoku* moment by moment; hour by hour
3 下 *kokka* the present
5 目 *kiza(mi)me* notch, nick, marks on a ruler
付 *kiza(mi)-tsu(keru)* engrave, carve out
出 *kiza(mi)-da(su)* carve out
本 *kokuhon* wood-block printed book
6 印 *kokuin* carved seal
字 *kokuji* carving characters; carved characters
7 足 *kiza(mi)ta(shi)* mincing steps
8 限 *kokugen* time, appointed time
刻 *kokukoku, kokkoku to* moment by moment; hour by hour
苦 *kokku* hard work
13 煙草 *kiza(mi) tabako* shredded tobacco
16 薄 *kokuhaku* cruelty

A **刷** 479 / J3a7e / M1964 SATSU. *su(ru)* print.
3 子 *sasshi, hake* brush; commutator brush
上 *su(ri)-a(garu)* be off the press. *su(ri)-a(geru)* finish printing, print off
4 込 *su(ri)-ko(mu)* insert (an illustration); stencil (a pattern)
毛 *hake* paint brush
毛目 *hakeme* brush marks
毛先 *hakesaki* brush tip
5 立 *su(ri)ta(te)* just off the press
出 *su(ri)-da(su)* print, publish; begin to print
本 *su(ri)hon* printed book
8 物 *su(ri)mono* printed matter
直 *su(ri)-nao(su)* reprint
12 違 *su(ri)chigai* misprint

[13] 損 *su(ri)-soko(nau)* misprint, spoil in printing
新 *sasshin* reform, renovation, innovation

B **刺** 480/J3b49/M1969 SHI calling card. *sa(su)* pierce, thrust, stab, prick; bite, sting; pin down; sew, stitch; put (a runner) out; pole (a boat); stick. *sa(saru)* stick, be stuck. *ira, toge* thorn, splinter; spine; biting words. *sashi* sharpened tube for testing rice in bags.

[3] 子 *sashiko* a lined garment with overall stitching
[7] 抜 *togenu(ki)* tweezers, forceps
身 *sashimi* sliced raw fish
身庖丁 *sashimibōchō* fish-slicing knife
[8] 青 *irezumi, shisei* tattooing
股 *sasumata* two-pronged weapon for catching a criminal
刺 *togetoge(shii)* sharp, harsh, stinging
[9] 通 *sa(shi) tō(su)* stab, pierce, run (a sword) through
客 *shikaku, sekkaku, shikyaku* assassin
草 *irakusa* nettle
[10] 殺 *sa(shi)-koro(su)* stab to death. *shisatsu suru* put out (in baseball); stab to death
[11] 貫 *sa(shi)-tsuranu(ku)* pierce
[12] 絡 *shiraku* bloodletting
違 *sa(shi)-chiga(eru)* stab at each other
戟 *shigeki* stimulus, impetus, incentive, excitement, irritation, encouragement
戟性 *shigekisei* stimulative, incentive, irritative
戟物 *shigekibutsu* stimulus, incentive
戟的 *shigekiteki* stimulating
戟剤 *shigekizai* stimulant
[13] 傷 *shishō, sa(shi)kizu* stab; puncture wound
[14] 網 *sa(shi)ami* gill net
[15] 衝 *shishō* stabbing; stimulation
[16] 激 *shigeki* stimulus, impetus, incentive, excitement, irritation, encouragement
激的 *shigekiteki* stimulating
[19] 繍 *shishū* embroidery. *nui* embroidery, sewing

A **制** 481/J4029/M1961 SEI system, organization; imperial command; laws, regulation. *sei(suru)* control, govern, suppress, restrain, hold back; establish.

[4] 止 *seishi* control, check, restraint, inhibition
[5] 圧 *seiatsu* oppression, control, mastery, ascendancy, supremacy
札 *seisatsu* roadside prohibition edict boards
令 *seirei* regulations
[7] 肘 *seichū* restraint, check, restriction, control, interference
作 *seisaku* production (of a painting, book, etc.)
作室 *seisakushitsu* studio, workshop
[8] 定 *seitei* enactment, establishment, creation
服 *seifuku* uniform
服制帽 *seifuku-seibō* cap and uniform
空 *seikū* mastery of the air
空権 *seikūken* mastery of the air
限 *seigen* limit, limitation, restriction
限速度 *seigen sokudo* speed limit
限漢字 *seigen kanji* restricted Chinese characters
[9] 度 *seido* system, organization, institution
約 *seiyaku* condition, limitation, restriction
海権 *seikaiken* control of the seas
[11] 欲 *seiyoku* control of passions, control of appetite
規 *seiki no* regular, legal, formal, established, legitimate
球 *seikyū* (pitcher's) control
球力 *seikyūryoku* (pitcher's) control
動 *seidō* braking (mechanism)
動手 *seidōshu* brakeman
動機 *seidōki* brake
[12] 帽 *seibō* regulation cap; school cap
勝 *seishō* victory, championship
馭 *seigyo* control, governing; checking, suppression; repression; restraint; mastery; management
裁 *seisai* restraint, punishment, sanctions
御 *seigyo* control, governing; checking, suppression; repression; restraint; mastery; management
御盤 *seigyoban* switchbox
御器 *seigyoki* controller, regulator
御機 *seigyoki* controller, regulator
[14] 酸剤 *seisanzai* anti-acid preparation
[17] 禦 *seigyo* control, governing; checking, suppression; repression; restraint; mastery; management
[19] 覇 *seiha* conquest, domination, supremacy, mastery; championship

剋 482 J-X M-X See 尅 486.

剄 483 J516d M1990 KEI beheading.

剌 484 J516f M2010 RATSU oppose; be biased.

剏 485 J516c M2024 SŌ, SHŌ begin; be damaged.

剋 486 J516e M2009 尅 1378 J5571 M7435 剋 482 J-X M-X
KOKU victory.

A 則 487 J4227 M1994 SOKU. *norito(ru), notto(ru)* follow (precedent), be based on, go by; live up to; model after; be in accordance with. *nori* law, rule; model, doctrine. *sunawa(chi)* whereupon, accordingly.

B 削 488 J3a6f M2000 SAKU. *kezu(ru)* plane, sharpen, whittle, pare, shave (leather); scrape off; cross out; reduce, curtail. *so(gu) vt* chip, slice off, cut aslant, split off; diminish, reduce; dampen, spoil, mar. *so(geru) vi* split, splinter; be sunken; be sharpened; miss the mark. *hatsu(ru)* cutting down little by little; taking a percentage.

4 片 *sakuhen* splinter, chip
5 氷機 *sakuhyōki* ice-shaving machine
8 取 *kezu(ri)-to(ru)* shave off, scrape off
9 除 *sakujo* elimination, cancellation, deletion, erasure
10 屑 *kezu(ri)kuzu* shavings
12 減 *sakugen* reduction, curtailment
落 *kezu(ri)-oto(su)* scrape off, plane off
13 節 *kezu(ri)bushi* flaked bonito
16 磨 *sakuma* denudation

剃 489 J4466 M1989 TEI. *so(ru), su(ru)* shave.

2 刀 *kamisori* razor
刀気触 *kamisori kabure* razor rash
刀研 *kamisoritogi* one who sharpens razors
刀負 *kamisorima(ke)* razor rash
刀砥 *kamisorido* razor strop; hone
5 立 *surita(te), sorita(te) no* clean shaven, freshly shaven
11 捨 *so(ri)-su(teru)* cut off the hair; take the tonsure 「off the hair
12 落 *so(ri)-oto(su), su(ri)-oto(su)* shave
14 髪 *teihatsu* tonsure, cutting off the hair

A 前 490 J4130 M2011 SEN. ZEN before. *mae* front, fore part; head (of a line); presence; ago, before; previously; (five minutes) to. *mae ni* ahead, before. *(o)mae(san)* you; my dear; hey. *-mae* a helping, portion; lady (So-and-so). *-zen* ago, before. *zen-* former, previous, one-time; the above. *saki ni* before, earlier that; ahead, beyond, away; previously; recently.

2 人 *zenjin* predecessor, former people
人未到 *zenjin-mitō* unexplored
人未踏 *zenjin-mitō* unexplored
3 山 *zenzan* foothills, first range of mountains
下 *maesa(gari)* front part low
口上 *mae kōjō* introductory remarks
4 文 *zembun* the above statement; preamble
方 *maekata* previously, some time ago. *zempō* front
日 *zenjitsu, maebi* the day before
厄 *maeyaku* the year before a critical age
以 *mae mot(te)* in advance, previously
夫 *zempu* former husband
5 生 *zenshō* previous existence
号 *zengō* preceding issue
払 *maebara(i)* advance payment
古 *zenko* old times, ancient days
立 *maeda(te)* plume, crest
立腺 *zenritsusen* prostate gland
史 *zenshi* prehistory 「ages
代 *zendai* previous generation; former
代未聞 *zendaimimon* unparalleled, unheard of, record-breaking
半 *zempan, zenhan* first half
半期 *zempanki, zenhanki* first half period
半戦 *zempansen, zenhansen* first half of the game
世 *zense, mae (no) yo, saki (no) yo* previous existence. *zensei* antiquity; the previous era

世生存 *zense seizon* pre-existence
世紀 *zenseiki* last century; ancient times
世界 *zensekai* prehistoric age
6 行 *zenkō* former conduct
回 *zenkai* last time; last session
向 *maemu(ki)* facing forward
兆 *zenchō* omen, portent, sign, premonition, harbinger
列 *zenretsu* front row
名 *zemmei* one's previous name
年 *zennen* the preceding year, last year
年度 *zennendo* preceding fiscal year
任 *zennin no* former (official)
任地 *zenninchi* former post
任者 *zenninsha* predecessor
7 言 *zengen* previous remarks
足 *mae ashi* forefeet
身 *zenshin* antecedents, ancestor; previous position; previous existence; predecessor organization
述 *zenjutsu no* the above-mentioned
条 *zenjō* preceding article, preceding entry
車 *zensha* the car ahead; front wheel
車軸 *zenshajiku* front axle
売 *maeu(ri)* advance sale, booking
売券 *maeu(ri) ken,* ticket sold in advance
8 門 *zemmon* front gate
非 *zempi* past folly, past sin
屈 *zenkutsu suru* bend forward. *maekaga(mi)* slouch
例 *zenrei* precedent
板 *maeita* dashboard; frontlet
知 *maeji(rase)* previous notice; omen, signs; premonition
肢 *mae ashi, zenshi* forefeet
垂 *maedare* apron
官 *zenkan* one's former post
者 *zensha* the former
表 *zempyō* omen, portent, sign, premonition, harbinger
金 *maekin, zenkin* advance payment
金払 *maekinbara(i)* payment in advance
夜 *zen'ya* last night, the previous night
夜祭 *zen'yasai* Christmas Eve
9 面 *zemmen* front part, frontage, façade
便 *zembin* one's last letter
祝 *mae iwa(i)* celebration in anticipation
約 *zen'yaku* previous engagement, previous promise
段 *zendan* preceding paragraph; first part
軍 *zengun* front-line troops
途 *zento* one's future prospects; outlook; the journey ahead
途有望 *zento yūbō* promising future
途多難 *zento tanan* a future fraught with difficulty
科 *zenka* criminal record, previous offense
科者 *zenkamono* person with a criminal record
前 *maemae* beforehand; for a long time
前回 *zenzenkai* the time before last
奏 *zensō* prelude (in music)
奏曲 *zensōkyoku* prelude, overture
後 *zengo, mae-ushi(ro)* front and back, before and behind, before and after. *zengo* about that (time); longitudinal; context, order, sequence. *-zengo* nearly, approximately
後不覚 *zengo-fukaku* unconsciousness
後左右 *zengo-sayū* in all directions
後策 *zengosaku* means of settling a problem
後撞着 *zengo-dōchaku* self-contradiction
10 庭 *zentei* front yard
座 *zenza* opening performance; minor performer
週 *zenshū* last week; the week before
納 *zenno* prepayment, advance payment
記 *zenki no* the above-mentioned
陳 *zenchin no* the above-mentioned
部 *zembu* front part, fore, front
書 *maega(ki)* preface, preamble. *zensho* first of two books; previous writing; previous letter
借 *maega(ri), zenshaku* getting an advance; a loan
借金 *zenshakukin* loan, advance
栽 *senzai* garden; trees and flowers in a garden
栽物 *senzaimono* greens, vegetables
進 *zenshin* advance, drive, progress
進力 *zenshinryoku* driving power
進部隊 *zenshin butai* advance troops
進基地 *zenshin kichi* advance base
進運動 *zenshin undō* forward motion
哨 *zenshō* outpost
哨地 *zenshōchi* outpost

哨勤務 *zenshō kimmu* outpost duty
哨戦 *zenshōsen* skirmish; prefinals (in games)
哨線 *zenshōsen* scouting line
哨騎兵 *zenshō kihei* outpost cavalry
11 婦 *zempu* previous wife
掛 *maeka(ke)* apron
略 *zenryaku* first part omitted; salutation of a brief letter
脚 *mae ashi, zenkyaku* forelegs
脳 *zennō* forebrain
著 *zencho* ibid.; the above-mentioned publication
菜 *zensai* appetizers, hors d'œuvres
章 *zenshō* preceding chapter
勘定 *mae kanjō* paying in advance
掲 *zenkei no* the above-named
掲書 *zenkeisho* op. cit.
12 歯 *maeba, zenshi* front tooth
開 *maebira(ki)* open in front
場 *zemba* morning market session
項 *zenkō* the preceding paragraph
提 *zentei* preamble, premise, reason, prerequisite
渡 *maewata(shi)* advance payment; advance delivery
腕 *maeude, zenwan* forearm
期 *zenki* first term, first half year, preceding period, early period
葉 *zen'yō* preceding page
貸 *maega(shi)* advance payment
景 *zenkei* foreground, front view
景気 *maegeiki* prospect, promise, outlook
装 *zensō* muzzle loading
13 触 *maebu(re)* previous notice; herald; harbinger, portent
節 *zensetsu* preceding paragraph, section, or verse
照灯 *zenshōtō* headlights
置 *zenchi, maeo(ki)* preface, introduction
置詞 *zenchishi* preposition
14 歴 *zenreki* personal history
徴 *zenchō* omen, portent, sign, premonition, harbinger
膊 *zempaku* forearm
説 *zensetsu* former opinion
髪 *maegami* forelock
舞台 *maebutai* apron stage
鼻緒 *maehanao* sandal or geta strap
駆 *zenku* vanguard, precursor, forerunner, leader
駆戦 *zenkusen* skirmish; prefinals (in games)
15 線 *zensen* front line; (weather) front
輪 *zenrin, maewa* front wheel
審 *zenshin* preliminary trials
篇 *zempen* first part, first volume
衛 *zen'ei* advance guard, vanguard
衛戦 *zen'eisen* skirmish; prefinals (in games)
16 頭部 *zentōbu* the front, the forehead
17 輿 *sakigoshi* front palanquin carrier
18 蹤 *zenshō* precedent
額 *zengaku* forehead
額部 *zengakubu* forehead. *zengakubu no* frontal
19 禱 *zentō* invocation

8

剞 491 / J5170 / M2054 KI curved chisel for carving. *kisa(mu)* carve.

B **剖** 492 / J4b36 / M2034 HŌ. BŌ divide.

B **剤** 493 / J3a5e / M2076′ **劑** 520 / J517d / M2241 ZAI medicine, drug, dose.

剔 494 / J5171 / M2031 TEKI cutting.

5 出 *tekishutsu* extraction, removal, excision
7 抉 *tekketsu suru* gouge, gouge out; expose
9 余 *tekijo* removal (in surgery)

剝 495 / J-X / M2049 **剥** 496 / J476d / M48939 HAKU. *ha(geru)* come off, peel off, be worn off; fade, discolor. *ha(gu), ha(gasu), he(gu)* tear off, peel off, rip off, strip off; skin, flay; disrobe; deprive of. *mu(keru)* peel off, come off, be taken off. *mu(ku)* peel, pare, hull. *hezu(ru)* pilfer, steal a portion. *muku(reru)* be tangled up with, be connected with.

5 出 *mu(ki)-da(su)* show, bare (the teeth). *mu(ki)da(shi)* nakedness; frankness
7 身 *sukimi* a meat or fish slicer. *mukimi* shellfish removed from the shell
8 取 *ha(gi)-to(ru)* tear off; strip; rob. *ha(gi)to(ri)* pad of paper

11 脱 *hakudatsu suru* come off, peel off
12 落 *hakuraku suru, ha(ge)-o(chiru)* peel off
14 暦 *haga(shi)goyomi* calendar pad
奪 *hakudatsu suru* deprive of, divest of
製 *hakusei* stuffing
製術 *hakuseijutsu* taxidermy
19 離 *hakuri suru vt* and *vi* peel off

B **剛** 497 / J3964 / M2042 GŌ strength.
2 力 *gōriki* herculean strength, mountain carrier-guide
4 毛 *gōmō* bristle
6 気 *gōki* bravery, stoutheartedness
7 体 *gōtai* a rigid body
8 性 *gōsei* hardness, rigidity
直 *gōchoku* integrity, moral courage
果 *gōka* valor and decisiveness
者 *gō(no)mono* very strong person, brave warrior, veteran
9 胆 *gōtan* boldness, hardihood, courage
勇 *gōyū* bravery, prowess
11 健 *gōken* vigor, virility, sturdiness, health
強 *gōkyō* strength, firmness
情 *gōjō* obstinacy, stubbornness
球 *gōkyū* fast ball
13 腹 *gōfuku* obstinacy, stubbornness
15 毅 *gōki* fortitude, firmness of character, hardihood, manliness
17 臆 *gōoku* bravery and cowardice

B **剣** 498 / J3775 / M2076 **劍** 514 / J5178 / M2228 **劒** 518 / J5179 / M2245

劔 519 / J517a / M2243 **剱** 499 / J517b / M-X KEN sword, saber, blade, bayonet; sting; clock hand. *tsurugi* sword.
3 士 *kenshi* fencer
5 玉 *kendama* ball-and-cup toy
付食 *kentsu(ku) (o) ku(wasu)* burst out in anger. *kentsu(ku) (o) ku(u)* be the victim of a burst of anger
付鉄砲 *kentsu(ki)deppō* fixed bayonet
6 先 *kensaki* point of a sword
7 状 *kenjō* sword-shaped
形 *kengata* sword shape
呑 *kennon na* risky, dangerous, insecure
8 法 *kempō* fencing
突 *kentsuku* rough scolding
9 客 *kenkaku* fencer, swordsman
10 帯 *kentai* sword belt
11 道 *kendō* fencing, swordmanship
術 *kenjutsu* fencing
12 戟 *kengeki* weapons, arms
13 幕 *kemmaku* threatening attitude
14 豪 *kengō* master fencer
舞 *kembu* sword dance
15 劇 *kengeki* sword play
18 難 *kennan* the calamity of being killed by the sword
19 璽 *kenji* sacred sword and jewels

9

剱 499 / J517b / M-X See **剣** 498.

剳 500 / J5175 / M2113 TŌ sickle. SATSU stay, remain.
8 青 *irezumi* tattooing

B **剰** 501 / J386a / M2107 **剩** 504 / J5174 / M2109 JŌ. *amatsusa(e)* besides.
7 余 *jōyo* surplus, balance
余金 *jōyokin* surplus, balance
10 員 *jōin* surplus people
12 費 *jōhi* unnecessary expenses
14 語 *jōgo* redundancy

剪 502 / J5172 / M2088 **翦** 4686 / J6648 / M28752 SEN. *hasa(mu)* clip, snip. *ki(ru)* cut.
2 刀 *sentō, hasami* scissors; punch
4 毛 *semmō* wool shearing
切 *hasa(mi)-ki(ru)* nip off, snip, clip, trim off
8 枝 *senshi* pruning
定 *sentei* pruning
定鋏 *senteibasami* pruning shears
9 除 *senjo suru* cut off, cut out
12 裁 *sensai suru* cut, trim, shear, prune
裁機 *sensaiki* shearing machine

A **副** 503 / J497b / M2097 FUKU duplicate, copy; assistant, associate. *so(u) vi* suit, meet, satisfy; marry; accompany; be added to; be adjusted to. *so(eru) vt* add to, attach, append; accompany; garnish; imitate. *fuku-* vice-, sub-, deputy, assistant, substitute; auxiliary, supplementary, additional; collateral.

[3]大統領 *fukudaitōryō* vice-president
[4]手 *fukushu* assistant, associate
木 *fukuboku* splint
尺 *fukushaku* vernier scale
[5]本 *fukuhon* duplicate, copy
収入 *fukushūnyū* additional income
司令 *fukushirei* deputy commander
[6]因 *fukuin* secondary cause
次的 *fukujiteki* secondary
会長 *fukukaichō* vice-president (of a society)
[7]見出 *fukumida(shi)* subtitle
作用 *fukusayō* reaction, secondary effect
社長 *fukushachō* vice-president of a firm
[8]使 *fukushi* vice-envoy, deputy delegate
官 *fukukan, fukkan* adjutant, aide, aide-de-camp
抵当 *fukuteitō* collateral security
牧師 *fukubokushi* associate pastor, curate
[9]虹 *fukuniji* secondary rainbow
食 *fukushoku* side dish; supplementary food
食物 *fukushokubutsu* side dish; supplementary food
[10]将 *fukushō* second in command
書 *fukusho* copy, duplicate
[11]産物 *fukusambutsu* by-product, side line
[12]詞 *fukushi* adverb
葬品 *fukusōhin* articles buried with the dead
[13]署 *fukusho* countersignature
業 *fukugyō* subsidiary business, side line
[14]読本 *fukutokuhon* supplementary reader
領事 *fukuryōji* vice-consul
[15]審 *fukushin* sub-umpire, sub-referee
賞 *fukushō* extra prize
[18]題 *fukudai* subtitle, subheading
[20]議長 *fukugichō* vice-chairman

10

剰 504 / J5174 / M2109 See **剩** 501.

剴 505 / J5173 / M2122 GAI scythe; suitability.

[4]切 *gaisetsu* appropriateness, adequacy, aptness

A **創** 506 / J414f / M2127 SŌ. *kizu* wound, injury, hurt; cut, gash, bruise, scratch; scar; weak point. *haji(meru)* start, originate.

[5]立 *sōritsu* establishment, founding, organization
立者 *sōritsusha* founder, organizer
刊 *sōkan* launching a magazine; first issue
刊号 *sōkangō* first issue
世 *sōsei* creation of the world
世記 *Sōseiki* Genesis
[7]見 *sōken* originality, creation, invention
作 *sōsaku* production, literary creation; work
作力 *sōsakuryoku* creative power, genius, creative originality
作的 *sōsakuteki* creative
作家 *sōsakuka* writer, novelist
作権 *sōsakuken* rights of authorship
[8]始 *sōshi* creation, founding, initiating
始者 *sōshisha* originator
[9]面 *sōmen* surface of a wound
建 *sōken* establishment, foundation
建者 *sōkensha* founder
造 *sōzō* creation
造力 *sōzōryoku* creative power
造主 *Sōzōshu, Sōzōnushi* Creator
造物 *sōzōbutsu* creature, creation
造的 *sōzōteki* creative
造者 *sōzōsha* creator; Creator
造説 *sōzōsetsu* creationism
[10]案 *sōan* original idea
案者 *sōansha* originator, inventor
[11]痍 *sōi* wound, scar
痕 *sōkon* scar
設 *sōsetsu* establishment, founding, organization
設者 *sōsetsusha* founder
[13]傷 *sōshō* wound
意 *sōi* original idea; originality
業 *sōgyō* establishment
業者 *sōgyōsha* founder, promoter
業費 *sōgyōhi* initial expenses
[14]製 *sōsei* invention, origination, discovery

A **割** 507 / J3364 / M2112′ KATSU. *wa(ru)* divide, cut, halve; separate; split, rip; break, crack, smash; dilute. *wa(reru)* break, split, cleave, fissure, be smashed. *sa(ku)* cut up, cleave; sever, separate, divide; spare (time); cede, alienate. *wa(re)* broken piece. *wa(ri)* rate, ratio, proportion, percentage, profit, assignment.

wa(ri) ni comparatively. *-wari* ten percent.
4 方 *wa(ri)kata* comparatively
木 *wa(ri)ki* split firewood
込 *wa(ri)-ko(mu)* wedge oneself in, cut in, muscle in on. *wa(ri)ko(mi)* sharing a theater box; muscling in on; wedging oneself in
切 *wa(ri)-ki(reru)* be divisible by. *wa(ri)-ki(ru)* divide; give a clear explanation. *wa(ri)-ki(renai)* indivisible; unconvincing; incomprehensible; unaccounted for
引 *wa(ri)-bi(ku)* discount. *waribiki* discount, reduction, rebate
引券 *waribikiken* a discount coupon
5 目 *wa(re)me* crevice, crack, split, rift, chasm, fissure
付 *wa(ri)-tsu(keru)* allot, assign, distribute, divide among. *waritsu(ke)* allotment, assignment, distribution; layout, editing
出 *wa(ri)-da(su)* calculate, compute; infer
礼 *katsurei* circumcision
6 竹 *wa(ri)dake* split bamboo
返 *warikae(shi)* rebate
印 *wa(ri)in* a seal over the edges of adjacent sheets
合 *wariai* rate, ratio, proportion, percentage. *wariai ni* comparatively; contrary to expectations
安 *wariyasu na* comparatively cheap
当 *wa(ri)-a(teru)* assign, allot, divide among, distribute, prorate, assess. *waria(te)* assignment, allotment, quota, rationing
当額 *wariategaku* allotment
7 材 *wa(ri)zai* split log, split timber
判 *wa(ri)ban* a seal over the edges of adjacent sheets
麦 *wa(ri)mugi* ground barley
戻 *wa(ri)-modo(su)* rebate
戻金 *wa(ri)modo(shi)kin* rebate money
8 拠 *kakkyo suru* hold one's ground; defend local authority
注 *wa(ri)chū* inserted note
物 *wa(re)mono* broken article; fragile article
易 *wa(re)yasu(i)* brittle, fragile, easily cracked, perishable
9 前 *wa(ri)mae* share, quota
前勘定 *wa(ri)mae kanjō* divide the bill equally, each person pays his or her own share
10 高 *waridaka na* comparatively high
振 *wa(ri)-fu(ru)* assign, allot, divide among, distribute, prorate, assess. *wa(ri)fu(ri)* assignment, allotment, quota, rationing
書 *wa(ri)ga(ki)* interlinear notes
栗石 *wa(ri)guri ishi* crushed rock, macadam
烹 *kappō* cooking, cuisine
烹店 *kappōten* restaurant
烹着 *kappōgi* coverall apron, cook's apron
11 勘 *wa(ri)kan* divide the bill equally, each person pays his or her own share
符 *wa(ri)fu* tally, check
12 普請 *wa(ri)bushin* dividing work among several contractors
13 楔 *wa(ri) kusabi* split wedge
腹 *kappuku* disembowelment, harakiri
愛 *katsuai suru* share, spare, part with reluctantly
14 算 *wa(ri)zan* division (in math)
増 *warima(shi)* extra wages, premium, bonus
増金 *warima(shi)kin* premium, bonus
15 線 *kassen* secant (in trigonometry)
賦 *kappu, wappu* allotment, quota
箸 *wa(ri)bashi* split chopsticks, disposable chopsticks
19 鏨 *wa(ri) tagane* ripping chisel
20 譲 *katsujō* cession of territory

11

剿 508 J5176 M2165 **勦** 509 J-X M2164 Shō. Sō destroy.
13 滅 *sōmetsu* clean sweep, annihilation

剽 510 J5177 M2160 Hyō threat.
9 窃 *hyōsetsu* piracy; plagiarism
10 悍 *hyōkan* fierceness; daring
11 盗 *hyōtō* highwayman
12 軽 *hyōkin* facetious, droll, funny
軽者 *hyōkimmono* a comical person

12

劄 511 J-X M-X See 箚 4305.

劂 512 / J-X / M2190 KETSU carve.
[2] 人 *ketsujin* sculptor; carver; seal engraver

劃 513 / J3344 / M2193 KAKU divide.
[1] 一 *kakuitsu* uniformity, standardization
[10] 時代的 *kakujidaiteki* epoch-making
[12] 然 *kakuzen(taru)* distinct, clear-cut
期 *kakki* epoch
期的 *kakkiteki* epoch-making

13

劍 514 / J5178 / M2228 See 剣 498.

劉 515 / J4e2d / M2224 RYŪ axe; kill.

劈 516 / J517c / M2223 HEKI. *tsunza(ku)* break, tear, pierce, split, burst.
[13] 開 *hekikai* cleavage (in gems)
[16] 頭 *hekitō* outset

A **劇** 517 / J3760 / M2218 GEKI drama, play. *hage(shii)* violent, vehement, furious, severe, acute, intense, extreme, passionate, heated, stormy (applause); tempestuous (temperament); mighty.
[4] 化 *gekika* dramatization
文学 *geki bungaku* dramatic literature
[6] 団 *gekidan* troupe, theatrical company
[7] 作 *gekisaku* play writing
作家 *gekisakuka* playwright, dramatist
[8] 的 *gekiteki* dramatic
毒 *gekidoku* deadly poison
[9] 通 *gekitsū* dramatic expert
変 *gekihen* sudden change, upheaval, convulsion, cataclysm
界 *gekikai* the stage, theatrical world
臭 *gekishū* strong odor
甚 *gekijin* intenseness, violence, severity, vehemence, keenness
映画 *geki eiga* film drama
[10] 剤 *gekizai* powerful medicine; violent poison
烈 *gekiretsu* violence, severity, intenseness, fierceness
[11] 道 *gekidō* drama, dramatic art
務 *gekimu* exhausting work
[12] 痛 *gekitsū* intense pain, sharp pain
評 *gekihyō* drama criticism
暑 *gekisho* severe heat
場 *gekijō* theater
場通 *gekijōkayo(i)* attending shows
[13] 詩 *gekishi* dramatic poetry
戦 *gekisen* severe fight
[15] 談 *gekidan* talk on drama
論 *gekiron* heated discussion
震 *gekishin* severe earthquake
[16] 壇 *gekidan* the stage, the theatrical world
薬 *gekiyaku* powerful medicine; violent poison
[18] 職 *gekishoku* exhausting work

14

劒 518 / J5179 / M2245 **劔** 519 / J517a / M2243 See 剣 498.

劑 520 / J517d / M2241 See 剤 493.

RAD. 力 19

Chikara strength. Nickname: Strong.

A **力** 521 / J4e4f / M2288 RIKI. RYOKU. *riki(mu)* strain, bear up, exert one's strength; swagger, bluff, boast. *tsuto(meru)* serve, fill a post, serve under; exert oneself, endeavor, work. be diligent; play (the part of). *chikara* strength, energy, force, might, power; agency; authority, influence; vigor; stress, emphasis; exertions, endeavors; efficacy; help, support, good offices; ability, faculty, capability, attainment; means, resources. *-riki* strength. *-ryoku* strength, power.
[1] 一杯 *chikaraippai ni* with all one's strength
[2] 入 *chikara (o) i(reru)* put forth effort

[3] 士 *rikishi* Japanese sumo wrestler; a strong man
及 *chikara oyo(bazu)* be unable to accomplish
[5] 石 *chikara ishi* a lifting stone
付 *chikarazu(ku) vi* be strengthened, revive, be invigorated, be encouraged. *chikarazu(keru) vt* strengthen (someone)
仕事 *chikara shigoto* physical work
[6] 行 *rikkō* strenuous efforts, exertion
尽 *chikarazu(ku) de* by sheer strength
任 *chikaramaka(se) ni* with all one's might
合 *chikaraa(wase)* test of strength
自慢 *chikara jiman* boasting of one's strength
[7] 走 *rikisō* hard running
足 *chikara ashi* strong legs
作 *rikisaku* literary masterpiece
役 *rikieki* physical labor
抜 *chikaranu(ke)* discouragement, disappointment
投 *rikitō* powerful pitching
[8] 泳 *rikiei* powerful swimming
学 *rikigaku* dynamics, mechanics
[9] 革 *chikaragawa* leather stirrup
持 *chikaramo(chi)* strong man
点 *rikiten* leverage; emphasis, importance
負 *chikarama(ke)* misdirection of one's strength
[10] 倆 *rikiryō* talent, skill
帯 *chikara obi* abdominal-support belt
弱 *chikarayowa(i)* weak
[11] 強 *chikarazuyo(i)* reassuring, emboldened
添 *chikarazo(e)* assistance
動的 *rikidōteki* dynamic
[12] 量 *rikiryō* physical strength; capacity, ability; tact
落 *chikara-o(toshi)* loss of energy, fatigue, discouragement, disappointment
無 *chikarana(ge) ni* feebly, dejectedly
[13] 試 *chikaradame(shi)* trial of strength, quiz
戦 *rikisen* hard fighting
業 *chikara waza* heavy work
[14] 漕 *rikisō suru* row hard
説 *rikisetsu* emphasis, stress
[15] 瘤 *chikarakobu* large biceps
瘤入 *chikarakobu (o) i(reru)* work earnestly; render aid
[18] 闘 *rikitō* hard fight
織機 *rikishokki* power loom
[20] 競 *chikara kurabe* trial of strength

3

A **功** 522 / J3879 / M2295 KŌ merits, meritorious deeds; success; credit, honor; effect; class (in court orders). KU merits. *isao, isaoshi* merit; meritorious deed.
[5] 田 *kōden* (ancient) rice-field reward
[6] 臣 *kōshin* meritorious retainer
伐 *kōbatsu* many exploits
名 *kōmyō* great achievement
名心 *kōmyōshin* ambition, love of fame
[7] 利 *kōri* utility; utilitarian
利主義 *kōri shugi* utilitarianism
利的 *kōriteki* utilitarian, businesslike
利説 *kōrisetsu* utilitarianism
労 *kōrō* meritorious deed; services
労金 *kōrōkin* reward for meritorious services
労者 *kōrōsha* man of distinguished service
労章 *kōrōshō* distinguished-service medal (police and railways)
[10] 能 *kōnō* work; efficiency
[11] 過 *kōka* merits and demerits
[13] 罪 *kōzai* merits and demerits
業 *kōgyō* exploit, achievement
[14] 徳 *kōtoku, kudoku* charity, virtue, merit
[15] 勲 *kōkun* meritorious service to ruler and country
[17] 績 *kōseki* meritorious service, merit

A **加** 523 / J3243 / M2297 KA addition, increase. *kuwa(waru)* join in; accede to; gain in (influence); increase. *kuwa(eru)* add, sum up; append; include; increase; inflict. *kuwa(uru) ni* besides, furthermore. *kuwa(ete)* and, in addition, furthermore.
[2] 入 *kanyū* joining, entry, admission, affiliation, adherence, signing, subscription
入金 *kanyūkin* admission fee
入者 *kanyūsha* member, entrant, participant; (telephone) subscriber
[3] 工 *kakō* processing, manufacturing, treatment

2 二亠人亻𠆢儿入八丷冂冖冫几凵刀刂【力】3 勹匕匚匸十卜卩厂厶又

工品 *kakōhin* processed goods, finished goods
工紙 *kakōshi* processed paper, coated paper
工歯 *kakōshi* dental bridge
工税 *kakōzei* processing tax
工費 *kakōhi* processing cost
工貿易 *kakō bōeki* processing trade
工賃 *kakōchin* processing fees
工業 *kakōgyō* processing industries
4 水分解 *kasui bunkai* hydrolysis
5 圧 *kaatsu* increasing pressure
号 *kagō* plus sign; sign of addition
6 年 *kanen* adding years
7 里 *kari* potassium, potash
役 *kayaku* temporary extra work
判 *kahan suru* affix a seal
判人 *kahannin* signatory
8 味 *kami* seasoning, flavoring
法 *kahō* addition
担 *katan* support; conspiracy, complicity
担者 *katansha* accomplice
9 持 *kaji* incantation, faith healing
重 *kajū, kachō* weighting (in averaging); aggravation
冠 *kakan* a man's coming-of-age ceremony
虐愛 *kagyakuai* sadism
速度 *kasokudo* acceleration
速運動 *kasoku undō* accelerated motion
除 *kajo* insertion and deletion
除式 *kajoshiki* looseleaf
10 俸 *kahō* extra allowance
留多 *karuta* playing cards
配 *kahai* additional ration
配米 *kahaimai* extra rice ration
害 *kagai* assault, violence, damaging (someone)
害者 *kagaisha* assailant
11 階 *kakai* promotion
12 湿 *kashitsu* humidification
禄 *karoku* increase in a samurai's stipend
給 *kakyū* raising salaries
筆 *kahitsu* correction, revision
硫 *karyū* vulcanizing
硫法 *karyūhō* vulcanization
減 *kagen* addition and subtraction; allowance for; degree; condition; seasoning, flavor; moderation; adjustment; influence (of the weather); state of health; chance
減抵抗器 *kagen teikōki* rheostat
減乗除 *kagenjōjo* the four arithmetical operations (addition, subtraction, mulitplication, and division)
13 勢 *kasei* assistance, backing, reinforcements; assistant
盟 *kamei* participation, affiliation
盟者 *kameisha* participants
盟国 *kameikoku* member nation, signatory
14 増 *kazō* increase, addition
算 *kasan, kuwa(e)zan* addition
15 養 *kayō* caring for the sick. *kayō suru* take care of oneself
熱 *kanetsu* heating
16 薬 *kayaku* spices, seasoning; adding ingredients (in medicine)
餐 *kasan* caring for one's health
糖粉乳 *katō funnyū* sweetened powdered milk
17 療 *karyō* medical treatment
齢 *karei* adding to one's years
20 護 *kago* divine protection

4

劣 524 / J4e74 / M2302 B RETSU. *oto(ru)* be inferior to, be worse than.
3 才 *ressai* inferior talents
8 者 *ressha* an inferior
10 弱 *retsujaku* inferiority
弱意識 *retsujaku ishiki* inferiority complex
11 情 *retsujō* animal passions, carnal desire, lust
敗 *reppai* defeat of the weaker
悪 *retsuaku na* inferior, coarse
12 等 *rettō* inferiority, low grade
等感 *rettōkan* inferiority complex
等複合 *rettō fukugō* inferiority complex
等観念 *rettō kannen* inferiority complex
13 勢 *ressei* numerical inferiority; weakness
勢感 *resseikan* inferiority complex

5

劬 525 / J5222 / M2317 KU, GU *tsuka(reru)* tire, become tired.

劭 526 / J5223 / M2318 SHŌ. JŌ beautiful. *tsuto(meru)* endeavor, persevere, persist; encourage.

A **努** 527 / J4558 / M2314 Do *tsuto(meru)* serve, fill a post, serve under; exert oneself, endeavor, work, be diligent; play (the part of). *tsuto(mete)* as much as possible; diligently.

2 力 *doryoku* endeavor, exertion, effort, labor, strain, industry

力家 *doryokuka* hard worker

B **励** 528 / J4e65 / M2326 **勵** 562 / J522f / M2472 Rei *hage(mu)* be diligent. *hage(masu)* encourage, inspire; raise (the voice). *hage(mi)* encouragement, stimulation; incentive.

6 行 *reikō suru* enforce strictly, carry out (regulations)

合 *hage(mi)-a(u)* vie with one another. *hage(mi)a(i)* encouragement, emulation

7 声 *reisei* shouts of encouragement

14 精 *reisei* diligence

劫 529 / J3965 / M2316 **刧** 462 / J5167 / M1927 **刦** 463 / J-X / M1926

Kō, Gō, Kyō threat; long ages. *obiya(kasu)* threaten.

4 火 *gōka* world-destroying conflagration

11 掠 *kyōryaku, gōryaku* pillage, plunder

略 *kyōryaku, gōryaku* pillage, plunder

盗 *gōtō* highway robber

14 罰 *gōbatsu* eternal punishment

A **助** 530 / J3d75 / M2313 Jo help, rescue. *tasu(karu)* be saved, be rescued, survive; be helpful. *tasu(keru)* help; save, rescue; give relief to; spare (life); reinforce; promote; abet. *su(keru)* help. *tasu(ke), suke* assistance. *jo-* assistant.

2 力 *joryoku* assistance, support

3 上 *tasu(ke)-a(geru)* help up; pick up, bring safely to land

4 手 *tasu(ke)te, su(ke)te* helper, helpmeet. *joshu* helper, assistant, tutor; intern

太刀 *sukedachi* assistance (in a fight), seconds (in a fight)

5 平 *sukebei* lewdness; lewd person

出 *tasu(ke)-da(su)* help out of (trouble), extricate

6 舟 *tasu(ke)bune* timely help

合 *tasu(ke)-a(u)* help each other, cooperate

守 *tasu(ke)-mamo(ru)* protect, preserve, keep

成 *josei* fostering, aiding

成金 *joseikin* subsidy, grant-in-aid

7 役 *joyaku* assistant official

言 *jogon, jogen* advice, suggestion

言者 *jogonsha, jogensha* adviser, counsellor

8 長 *jochō* promotion, fostering

命 *jomei* sparing a life, clemency, reconsidering a dismissal

10 起 *tasu(ke)-oko(su)* help up

11 船 *tasu(ke)bune* lifeboat; a friend in need, help

祭 *josai* (Catholic) deacon

動詞 *jodōshi* auxiliary verb

教 *jokyō* assistant teacher

教授 *jokyōju* assistant or associate professor

教諭 *jokyōyu* assistant or associate professor

産 *josan* midwifery

産所 *josanjo* maternity home

産院 *josan'in* maternity hospital

産婦 *josampu* midwife

12 詞 *joshi* a particle (in grammar)

13 辞 *joji* particle (in grammar); auxiliary word

勢 *josei* encouragement, backing. *sukezei* reinforcements

数詞 *josūshi* counters for various categories of objects

14 監督 *jokantoku* assistant director (in taking professional movies)

演 *joen* co-star

演者 *joensha* co-star

A **労** 531 / J4f2b / M2329 **勞** 550 / J5229 / M2410 Rō labor, toil, trouble. *rō(suru)* labor, toil, strive; put (someone) to work; thank (someone) for their efforts; comfort. *itawa(ru)* pity, sympathize with, console, care for, be kind to. *negira(u)* thank for, reward for. *itawa(ri)* trouble, service, labor; sympathy; illness; carefulness, attention. *itazuki* pain, trouble.

2 力 *rōryoku* labor; toil, trouble

5 功 *rōkō* meritorious deed

7 労 *rōrō(taru)* tired out

災保険 *rōsai hoken* worker's accident insurance

2 二 亠 人 イ 𠆢 儿 入 八 ソ 冂 冖 冫 几 凵 刀 リ 【力】 勹 匕 匚 匸 十 卜 卩 厂 厶 又

作 *rōsaku* toil, labor; laborious task
作教育 *rōsaku kyōiku* manual training
役 *rōeki* work, labor, toil
役場 *rōekijō* prison labor camp
8 使 *rōshi* laborers and employers
苦 *rōku* labor, toil, hardship
11 務 *rōmu* labor, work, service
務者 *rōmusha* laborer, workman
13 賃 *rōchin* wages
資 *rōshi* capital and labor; capitalists and laborers
農 *rōnō* workers and farmers
農政府 *Rōnō Seifu* Soviet Government
農党 *rōnōtō* labor-farmer party
働 *rōdō* manual labor, work, toil
働力 *rōdōryoku* labor, manpower, working force
働大臣 *Rōdō Daijin* Labor Minister
働収容所 *rōdō shūyōsho* labor camp
働市場 *rōdō shijō* labor market
働同盟 *rōdō dōmei* labor federation
働争議 *rōdō sōgi* labor trouble, strike
働条件 *rōdō jōken* working conditions
働攻勢 *rōdō kōsei* labor offensive
働者 *rōdōsha* laborer, worker
働委員会 *rōdō iinkai* labor-relations board
働省 *Rōdōshō* Labor Ministry
働党 *rōdōtō* labor party
働時間 *rōdō jikan* working hours; man hours
働祭 *Rōdōsai* Labor Day, May Day
働組合 *rōdō kumiai* labor union
働階級 *rōdō kaikyū* working classes
働運動 *rōdō undō* labor movement
働運動者 *rōdō undōsha* labor agitator
働歌 *rōdōka* songs of labor
14 銀 *rōgin* wages, labor wages

6

券 532 / J5225 / M2330 Ken tire; come to a halt.

劼 533 / J5224 / M2338 Katsu. *tsutsu(shimu)* be careful, be moderate; strive.

B **劾** 534 / J332f / M2342 Gai criminal investigation.
9 奏 *gaisō suru* report an official's offense to the emperor

A **効** 535 / J387a / M2334 **效** 2336 / J5a43 / M13186 Kō efficacy, benefit; efficiency; effect, result; success. *ki(ku)* be effective.
2 力 *kōryoku* effect, efficacy; validity
5 用 *kōyō* use, utility, effect, benefit
目 *kikime* effect, efficacy, impression
8 果 *kōka* effect, efficacy, result
果的 *kōkateki* effective, successful
10 能 *kōnō* effect, efficacy, virtue, benefit
能書 *kōnōga(ki)* statement of the efficacy of a medicine
11 率 *kōritsu* efficiency
18 験 *kōken* efficacy, effect

7

勉 536 / J-X / M2362 **勉** 537 / J-X / M-X See **勉** 543.

勁 538 / J5226 / M2349 Kei strong.
8 卒 *keisotsu* excellent soldier
10 悍 *keikan* strong and fierce
11 捷 *keishō* strong and nimble
15 敵 *keiteki* formidable foe

勃 539 / J4b56 / M2351 Botsu suddenness; rise.
9 勃 *botsubotsu(taru)* spirited, rising energetic
発 *boppatsu* outbreak, outburst, sudden occurrence
10 起 *bokki suru* stand erect, stiffen
12 然 *botsuzen to* suddenly; in fit of anger
16 興 *bokkō* sudden rise to power

B **勅** 540 / J443c / M2354 **敕** 2338 / J5a45 / M13225 Choku *mikotonori* imperial decree.
5 令 *chokurei* imperial edict
6 旨 *chokushi* imperial order, imperial will
任 *chokunin* imperial appointment
8 使 *chokushi* imperial messenger
命 *chokumei* imperial command
9 宣 *chokusen* imperial decree
10 書 *chokusho* imperial rescript
11 問 *chokumon* imperial question
許 *chokkyo* imperial sanction
勘 *chokkan* the emperor's censure
12 筆 *chokuhitsu* imperial autograph
答 *chokutō* emperor's reply; reply to the emperor

裁 *chokusai* imperial decision or sanction
13 意 *chokui* meaning or gist of a decree
14 語 *chokugo* imperial rescript
選 *chokusen* imperial nomination
選集 *chokusenshū* emperor-sponsored anthology
15 撰 *chokusen* compilation for the emperor; emperor's literary production
諚 *chokujō* imperial message
16 諭 *chokuyu* imperial instructions
18 額 *chokugaku* imperial scroll
題 *chokudai* theme of the Imperial Poetry Contest
19 願 *chokugan* imperial prayer

A 勇 541 / J4d26 / M2360 Yū bravery, courage, heroism. *isa(mu)* cheer up, be in high spirits. *isa(mashii)* courageous, valiant.
2 力 *yūryoku* courage
3 士 *yūshi* brave man, hero
4 夫 *yūfu* valiant man
5 立 *isa(mi)-ta(tsu)* cheer up, be encouraged (by)
6 壮 *yūsō* bravery, heroism
肌 *isa(mi)hada* gallantry
名 *yūmei* fame, great renown
気 *yūki* courage, bravery, valor, nerve, boldness.
気付 *yūkizu(ke)* have a burst of courage
7 図 *yūto* ambitious undertaking
決 *yūketsu* decisiveness
8 退 *yūtai suru* retire voluntarily, bow out
武 *yūbu* bravery, valor, military prowess
者 *yūsha* hero, man of valor
往 *yūō* spirited advance, energetically going forward
往邁進 *yūō-maishin suru* dash ahead, push forward
9 飛 *yūhi* flying jump, great achievement
姿 *yūshi* gallant figure
10 進 *yūshin suru* dash forward bravely
将 *yūshō* brave general, great soldier
烈 *yūretsu* bravery, valor, courage
11 健 *yūken* sound health
断 *yūdan* resolute decision
猛 *yūmō* daring, bravery, valor
猛心 *yūmōshin* intrepid spirit
12 敢 *yūkan* heroism, gallantry, bravery
13 戦 *yūsen* brave fight, desperate fight
15 邁 *yūmai na* heroic, courageous
21 躍 *yūyaku suru* take heart, be in high spirits

8

勍 542 / J5227 / M2370 Kei, Kyō strong.

A 勉 543 / J4a59 / M2384 勉 536 / J-X / M2362 勉 537 / J-X / M-X
Ben. *tsuto(meru)* serve, fill a post, serve under; exert oneself, endeavor, work, be diligent; play (the part of). *tsuto(mete)* as much as possible; diligently.
7 励 *benrei* diligence
8 学 *bengaku* study
11 強 *benkyō* study; diligence; discount, reduction
強中 *benkyōchū* while studying
強家 *benkyōka* scholar, diligent student

9

勖 544 / J5228 / M2392 Kyoku encourage, endeavor; persist, be diligent.

勒 545 / J7055 / M2386 Roku halter and bit. *roku(suru)* carve, engrave; lead; control.

A 務 546 / J4L33 / M2394 务 547 / J-X / M-X Mu. *tsuto(meru)* serve, fill a post, serve under; exert oneself, endeavor, work, be diligent; play (the part of). *tsuto(me)* service, duty, business; Buddhist religious services.
11 盛 *tsuto(me)zaka(ri)* a worker's prime

B 勘 548 / J342a / M2393 Kan perception, intuition; the sixth sense.
5 付 *kanzu(ku)* suspect, sense, scent
弁 *kamben* pardon, forgiveness, forbearance
6 気 *kanki* disfavor, disinheritance
当 *kandō* disinheritance
考 *kankō* consideration, deliberation
合 *kangō* checking and verifying
合貿易 *kangō bōeki* licensed trade
7 決 *kanketsu suru* investigate and decide

忍 *kannin* patient endurance
8 例 *kanrei* considering old precedents
所 *kandokoro* finger board (of an instrument); vital point
定 *kanjō* calculation; account; settlement of an account; consideration, allowance
定日 *kanjōbi* settlement day
定尻 *kanjōjiri* balance of an account
定尽 *kanjōzu(ku) de* in a mercenary spirit
定取 *kanjōto(ri)* bill collector
定係 *kanjōgakari* cashier, accountant, treasurer
定書 *kanjōga(ki)* bill, one's account
定高 *kanjōdaka(i)* calculating, mercenary, closefisted
定違 *kanjōchiga(i)* miscalculation
定場 *kanjōba* cashier's counter
9 査 *kansa* investigation
10 進 *kanshin* reporting after careful investigation
校 *kankō suru* examine and correct
案 *kan'an suru* think
11 責 *kanseki* reproving for a fault
12 検 *kanken suru* investigate
違 *kanchiga(i)* misunderstanding, wrong guess
15 審 *kanshin* careful investigation
19 繰 *kangu(ru)* be suspicious of

A **動** 549 / J4630 / M2390 Dō motion; change; confusion. *dō(jiru), dō(zuru)* be perturbed, be agitated. *ugo(ku) vi* move, stir, shift, shake, swing; operate, run, go, work; be touched, be influenced, waver, fluctuate, vary, change, be transferred. *ugo(kasu) vt* move, shift; set in motion, operate; inspire, rouse, influence; mobilize; deny; change. *ugo(ki)* movement, activity, trend, development, change. *yaya(mosureba), yaya(tomosureba)* be apt to, be liable to, be inclined to.

2 力 *dōryoku* power, motive power, dynamic force
力学 *dōryokugaku* kinetics, dynamics
力降下 *dōryoku kōka* power dive
力源 *dōryokugen* source of power
力資源 *dōryoku shigen* sources of power
4 天 *dōten* heaven-shaking event
6 回 *ugo(ki)-mawa(ru)* move around
因 *dōin* inducement, incentive, motive, cause, contributing factor
向 *dōkō* trend, tendency, movement, attitude
名詞 *dōmeishi* gerund
7 体 *dōtai* moving body
作 *dōsa* action, movements, motions; bearing, behavior, manners
乱 *dōran* agitation, commotion, riot
8 的 *dōteki* dynamic, kinetic
物 *dōbutsu* animal
物化 *dōbutsuka* animalization
物学 *dōbutsugaku* zoology
物相 *dōbutsusō* fauna
物界 *dōbutsukai* animal kingdom
物崇拝 *dōbutsu sōhai* zoolatry
物園 *dōbutsuen* zoo
物愛 *dōbutsu ai* love for animals
物誌 *dōbutsushi* fauna
物質 *dōbutsushitsu* animal matter
10 員 *dōin* mobilization
員令 *dōinrei* mobilization order
脈 *dōmyaku* artery
脈血 *dōmyakuketsu* arterial blood
脈硬化 *dōmyaku kōka* arteriosclerosis
脈硬化症 *dōmyaku kōkashō* arteriosclerosis, hardening of the arteries
11 悸 *dōki* palpitation, pulsation, throbbing
転 *dōten* being surprised and stunned; transition, change
産 *dōsan* personal property, personal effects
12 揺 *dōyō* shaking, trembling, pitching, rolling, oscillation; agitation, excitement; unrest, commotion
軸 *dōjiku* driving axle
量 *dōryō* momentum
植物 *dōshokubutsu* plants and animals, flora and fauna
詞 *dōshi* verb
詞状名詞 *dōshijō meishi* gerund
13 勢 *dōsei* state, condition, movements
滑車 *dōkassha* movable pulley
14 静 *dōsei* state, condition, movements
態 *dōtai* movement; vital (statistics)
15 輪 *dōrin* driving wheel
16 機 *dōki* motive, incentive
20 議 *dōgi* a motion

10

勞 550 J5229 M2410 See **労** 531.

B **募** 551 J4a67 M2416 Bo. *tsuno(ru)* gather (contributions); campaign (for students); float (a loan); enlist (troops); grow violent.

[7] 兵 *bohei* recruiting, enlistment, drafting
[8] 金 *bokin* fund raising
金運動 *bokin undō* fund-raising campaign
金趣意書 *bokin shuisho* subscription prospectus
[12] 集 *boshū* recruiting; invitation, collection; enrollment; solicitation; flotation
[13] 債 *bosai* loan flotation

A **勤** 552 J3650 M2415' Kin. Gon. *tsuto(maru)* be fit for, be equal to, function properly. *tsuto(meru)* serve, fill a post, serve under; exert oneself, endeavor, work, be diligent; play (the part of). *tsuto(me)* service, duty, business; Buddhist religious services.

[2] 人 *tsuto(me)nin* office worker, salaried man, white-collar worker
[3] 口 *tsuto(me)guchi* position, place of employment
上 *tsuto(me) a(geru)* serve out one's apprenticeship, serve out one's time
[4] 王 *kinnō* imperialism, loyalism
王家 *kinnōka* a loyalist
王攘夷 *kinnō-jōi* loyalty to the emperor and expulsion of the foreigners
[6] 行 *tsuto(me)-okona(u)* carry on (work). *gongyō* Buddhist religious service
気 *tsuto(me)gi* mercenary spirit
向 *tsuto(me)mu(ki)* one's business, one's duties
先 *tsuto(me)saki* place of work
[7] 求 *gongu* inquiring about the Buddha way
労 *kinrō* labor, exertion
労大衆 *kinrō taishū* working people
労者 *kinrōsha* working man
労奉仕 *kinrō hōshi* labor service
労所得 *kinrō shotoku* earned income
労階級 *kinrō kaikyū* salaried class, working class
労感謝日 *Kinrō Kansha no Hi* (Labor) Thanksgiving Day, November 23
[8] 苦 *kinku* toil and hardship
奉公 *tsuto(me)bōkō* apprenticeship
[9] 恪 *kinkaku* faithful service
怠 *kintai* diligence and indolence; diligence; attendance
皇 *kinnō* imperialism
皇家 *kinnōka* a loyalist
皇攘夷 *kinnō jōi* loyalty to the emperor and expulsion of the foreigners
[10] 倹 *kinken* industry, diligence, frugality
振 *tsuto(me)bu(ri)* assiduity; conduct
勉 *kimben* industry, diligence
[11] 盛 *tsuto(me)zaka(ri)* the prime of one's career
務 *kimmu* service, duty, work
務先 *kimmusaki* place of employment
務地手当 *kimmuchi teate* area allowance
務交代 *kimmu kōtai* change of shifts
務年限 *kimmu nengen* term of service
務者 *kimmusha* workers, men on duty
務実績 *kimmu jisseki* service record
務員 *kimmuin* worker, employee
務評定 *kimmu hyōtei* evaluation of workers
[12] 惰 *kinda* diligence and indolence; diligence; attendance
番 *kimban* on duty in Edo
[13] 働 *tsuto(me)-hatara(ku)* work diligently
続 *kinzoku* continuous service
続者 *kinzokusha* a man of long service

A **勝** 553 J3e21 M2409 Shō victory; beauty spot. *ka(tsu)* win; prevail, predominate, surpass. *masa(ru)* excel, surpass, outrival. *sugu(reru)* excel, surpass; have advantages over; be excellent. *ka(chi)* victory, success. *-ga(chi)* be apt to, be prone to, be liable to, tend to; predominating.

[4] 手 *katte* kitchen; condition, circumstances; one's own convenience; wilfulness, selfishness. *katte(gamashii)* selfish
手口 *katteguchi* back door, service door
手向 *kattemu(ki)* kitchen affairs; one's financial circumstances
手次第 *katteshidai* having one's own way

2 二亠人亻𠆢儿入八丷冂冖冫几凵刀刂【力】[10] 勹匕匚匸十卜卩厂厶又

手気盡 *kattekimama* selfishness
手道具 *katte dōgu* kitchen utensils
5 目 *ka(chi)me* chances of winning
6 色 *ka(chi)iro* signs of victory
因 *shōin* cause of victory
気 *ka(chi)ki* determination to win
向 *ka(chi)muka(i)* the defeated treating the victor
地 *shōchi* scenic spot
守 *ka(chi)mamo(ri)* victory charm
7 車 *shōsha* winning car
投手 *ka(chi) tōshu* winning pitcher
抜 *ka(chi)-nu(ku)* win one game after another
抜戦 *ka(chi)nu(ki)sen* tournament
利 *shōri* victory
利者 *shōrisha* winner, victor, conqueror
利投手 *shōri tōshu* winning pitcher
8 逃 *ka(chi)ni(ge)* running away with a game
味 *ka(chi)mi* chances of winning
放 *ka(chi)-hana(su)* win by a big score. *ka(chip)pana(shi)* string of victories
取 *ka(chi)-to(ru)* gain a victory
者 *shōsha* winner, victor, conqueror
9 通 *ka(chi)-tō(su), ka(chi)-dō(su)* win straight victories
乗 *ka(chi) (ni) no(ru)* win straight victories
軍 *shōgun* military victory; victorious army. *ka(chi) ikusa* victory
星 *ka(chi)boshi* winning mark
負 *shōbu* victory or defeat; game, bout. *ka(chi)ma(ke)* victory or defeat
負事 *shōbugoto* game of skill; gambling
負師 *shōbushi* gambler; chess or go player
負無 *shōbuna(shi)* a tie (in games)
10 馬 *ka(chi) uma* winning horse
残 *ka(chi)-noko(ru)* make the finals
栗 *ka(chi)guri* dried chestnut
11 得 *ka(chi)-u(ru), ka(chi)-e(ru)* achieve, win, earn, gain
敗 *shōhai* victory or defeat; the issue (of a battle)
率 *shōritsu* chances of victory
12 越 *ka(chi)ko(shi)* more wins than losses
訴 *shōso* winning a lawsuit
景 *shōkei* beautiful view, scenic spot
報 *shōhō* news of victory
13 鼓 *ka(chi)tsuzumi* drums of victory
続 *ka(chi)tsuzu(ke)* series of victories
誇 *ka(chi)-hoko(ru)* triumph, be elated with success
14 算 *shōsan* chances of victory
16 鬨 *ka(chi)doki* shout of victory; victory song
21 籤 *ka(chi) kuji* winning ticket

11

勤 554 / J-X / M2424 See **勤** 552.

勣 555 / J522a / M2423 SEKI, SHAKU exploit, feat, meritorious deed.

勠 556 / J522d / M2418 RIKU. *a(waseru)* join forces.
2 力 *rikuryoku* join forces, cooperate

勦 557 / J522b / M2426 SHŌ. SŌ destroy.
10 討 *sōtō* complete annihilation
13 滅 *sōmetsu* eradication, annihilation

A **勢** 558 / J402a / M2422 SE. SEI. energy; military strength. *ikio(izuku)* gather strength. *ikio(i)* force, vigor, energy, spirit, life; authority, influence, power, might; impetus; course (of events), tendency; necessarily. *hazumi* spring, bound, rebound; inertia, momentum; impetus, stimulus, impulse; instant; chance.
2 力 *seiryoku* influence, power, might, strength; force, energy
力下 *seiryokuka ni* under the influence or power of
力家 *seiryokuka, seiryokka* man of influence
力圏 *seiryokuken* sphere of influence
力範囲 *seiryoku han'i* sphere of influence
3 子 *seko* beater (on a hunt)
4 込 *ikio(i)-ko(mu)* brace oneself
7 車 *hazumiguruma* flywheel
良 *ikio(i)yo(ku)* vigorously
8 門 *seimon* influential family, the man in power
9 威 *seii* power, might, authority, influence; high spirits
10 家 *seika* influential family; the man in power

11 運 *seiun* trend, tendency
望 *seibō* power and popularity
12 揃 *seizoro(i)* array, muster, lineup; full force

B 勧 559 J342b M2433 勸 563 J5230 M2486 KAN. *susu(meru)* recommend, advise, encourage; offer (wine). *susu(me)* recommendation, advice, encouragement.

3 工 *kankō* encouragement of industry
工場 *kankōba* fair, bazaar
4 化 *kange* religious-fund soliciting; Buddhist preaching
5 世縒 *kanzeyori* twisted paper, twisted-paper string
7 告 *kankoku* advice, counsel, recommendation
告状 *kankokujō* letter of advice
告者 *kankokusha* adviser, counselor
告案 *kankokuan* recommendation
8 学 *kangaku* encouragement of learning
9 降 *kankō* call to surrender
10 進 *kanjin* temple solicitation
進元 *kanjimmoto* backer, promoter
進帳 *kanjinchō* temple solicitation book
12 善懲悪 *kanzen-chōaku* rewarding good and punishing evil; political justice; moral purpose
善懲悪劇 *kanzen-chōaku geki* morality play
13 奨 *kanshō* encouragement, stimulation
農 *kannō* encouragement of agriculture
業 *kangyō* encouragement of industry; industry
14 説 *kanzei suru* urge, persuade
誘 *kan'yū* invitation, inducement, solicitation, canvassing; persuasion, encouragement
誘員 *kan'yūin* canvasser, traveling salesman
15 賞 *kanshō* praise and encouragement

13

B 勲 560 J372e M2463 勳 561 J522e M2465 KUN merit, order of merit. *isao, isaoshi* meritorious deed; merit.

5 功 *kunkō* merits, distinguished services
6 臣 *kunshin* meritorious retainer
7 位 *kun'i* order of merit
状 *kunjō* letter of commendation with an award
労 *kunrō* merit, meritorious deed
10 記 *kunki* decoration diploma
11 章 *kunshō* decoration, order, medal
12 等 *kuntō* order of merit
17 爵 *kunshaku* peerage and order of merit

14

勳 561 J522e M2465 See 勲 560.

勵 562 J522f M2472 See 励 528.

17

勸 563 J5230 M2486 See 勧 559.

RAD. 勹 20

Tsutsumigamae "wrapping" enclosure. Nickname: Wrapping.

勹 564 J5231 M2493 Hō enclose.

1

B 勺 565 J3c5b M2495 SHAKU one-tenth of a *gō* (see Weights and Measures); dip, ladle.

2

B 匁 566 J4c68 M2502 (国字) *momme, me* $\frac{1}{100}$ *hyakume* (See Weights and Measures)

匂 567 J4677 M2503 (国字) *nio(u)* be fragant, smell; stink; glow, be bright. *nio(wasu), nio(waseru) vt* give out an odor, scent, or perfume; suggest,

insinuate. *nioi* smell, odor, scent; stench; fragrance, aroma, perfume.
8 油 *nioi abura* perfumed hair oil
11 袋 *nioibukuro* sachet
菫 *nioi sumire* a sweet violet
菖蒲 *nioi shōbu* aromatic cane, orris

勾 568 / J387b / M2500 Kō be bent.
4 引 *kadowaka(su)* kidnap. *kōin suru* arrest, seduce, abduct. *kadowaka(shi)* kidnapper. *kōin* arrest, custody.
引状 *kōinjō* summons, warrant of arrest
5 玉 *magatama* comma-shaped jewels
10 配 *kōbai* slope, incline, gradient, grade, pitch
留 *kōryū* detention, confinement

勿 569 / J4c5e / M2501 MOCHI. BUTSU. *naka(re)* must not, do not, be not.
7 忘草 *wasurenagusa* forget-me-not
体 *mottai* overemphasis. *mottai(buru)* assume airs. *mottai(rashiku)* exaggeratedly, importantly
体無 *mottaina(i)* sacrilegious; unworthy of; wasteful
8 怪 *mokke* something unexpected
怪幸 *mokke (no) saiwa(i)* stroke of luck, godsend, windfall
15 論 *mochiron* naturally, of course

3

匀 570 / J-X / M-X **匁** 571 / J5232 / M2511 See **忽** 1815.

A **包** 572 / J4a71 / M2506′ **包** 573 / J-X / M2506 Hō. *tsutsu(mu)* wrap, pack up; cover with; dress in; conceal. *kuru(mu)* wrap up, tuck in. *kuru(meru)* lump together, include, sum up; quibble. *tsutsu(mi)* bundle, package, parcel, bale. *tsutsu(minaku)* without concealment, without reserve, frankly.
2 丁 *hōchō* kitchen knife; cooking
4 込 *tsutsu(mi)-ko(mu)* wrap up
5 皮 *hōhi* foreskin
皮切断 *hōhi setsudan* circumcision
7 囲 *hōi* siege, encirclement
含 *hōgan suru* include, comprise, comprehend, cover, imply
8 金 *tsutsu(mi)gane* a money tip wrapped in paper
物 *tsutsu(mi)mono* bundle, package
直 *tsutsu(mi)-nao(su)* rewrap
9 括 *hōkatsu* include, comprise, comprehend, cover, imply
括的 *hōkatsuteki* inclusive, comprehensive
10 紙 *tsutsu(mi)gami* wrapping paper
容 *hōyō suru* comprehend, embrace, imply, tolerate
莖 *hōkei* phimosis
帯 *hōtai* bandage, dressing
11 釦 *tsutsu(mi) botan* covered button
12 装 *hōsō* packing, wrapping
13 摂 *hōsetsu* connotation
隠 *tsutsu(mi)-kaku(su)* conceal, keep secret, cover up. *tsutsu(mi)kaku(shi)* concealment
飾 *tsutsu(mi)-kaza(ru)* cover up and make a show
14 蔵 *hōzō suru* contain, keep, comprehend, imply, entertain (an idea)

4

匈 574 / J5233 / M2512 KYŌ turmoil, Hungary.
5 奴 *Kyōdo* Huns
牙利 *Hangari* Hungary

7

匍 575 / J5235 / M2527 HO crawl, creep.
11 匐 *hofuku* creeping, crawling, sneaking
球 *hokyū, goro* grounder (baseball)

9

匏 576 / J5237 / M2544 Hō. *hisago* gourd.

匐 577 / J5236 / M2545 FUKU, HOKU crawl.

RAD. 匕 21

Saji spoon or *hi* (the katakana). Variant: 匕. Nickname: *Kana Hi.*

匕 579 / J5238 / M2570 **匕** 578 / J-X / M2571 HI. *saji* spoon.

[9] 首 *aikuchi, hishu* dagger, dirk

2

A **化** 580 / J323d / M2572 KA influence. KE. *ba(kasu)* bewitch, enchant, confuse, delude. *ba(keru)* appear in disguise. *ka(suru), ka(su), ke(suru)* change into, convert into, transform, be reduced; influence, improve (someone). *fu(keru)* steam (rice); change with age, spoil from weathering. *(o)ba(ke)* goblin, apparition. *-ka* -ize (a verbal ending meaning "to change").

[5] 生 *kasei* growth, metamorphosis. *keshō* goblin
皮 *bake (no) kawa* masking one's true character, disguise
石 *kaseki* petrifaction, fossilization; fossil
石学 *kasekigaku* paleontology
石層 *kasekisō* fossil bed
[6] 合 *kagō* compounding (in chemistry)
合物 *kagōbutsu* chemical compound
成 *kasei* change, transformation
成工業 *kasei kōgyō* chemical industry
成肥料 *kasei hiryō* chemical fertilizer
[7] 身 *keshin* (Buddhist) incarnation; personification; impersonation
[8] 物 *ba(ke)mono* goblin, apparition
育 *kaiku* evolution, growth
学 *kagaku* chemistry
学工学 *kagaku kōgaku* chemical engineering
学工業 *kagaku kōgyō* chemical industry
学反応 *kagaku hannō* chemical reaction
学式 *kagaku shiki* chemical formula
学兵器 *kagaku heiki* chemical weapons
学者 *kagakusha* chemist
学肥料 *kagaku hiryō* chemical fertilizer
学変化 *kagaku henka* chemical change
学記号 *kagaku kigō* chemical symbols (for the elements)
学線 *kagakusen* actinic rays
学療法 *kagaku ryōhō* chemotherapy
学繊維 *kagaku sen'i* synthetic fibers
[10] 骨 *kakotsu* ossification
[12] 粧 *keshō* makeup
粧下 *keshō shita* makeup base
粧水 *keshōsui, keshō mizu* face lotion
粧代 *keshōdai* lady's pin money; cosmetics expense
粧台 *keshōdai* dressing table, dresser
粧石鹼 *keshō sekken* toilet soap
粧品 *keshōhin* toilet articles
粧室 *keshōshitsu* powder room, lavatory
粧料 *keshōryō* lady's pin money
粧部屋 *keshōbeya* lavatory; dressing room
粧道具 *keshō dōgu* toilet set
粧着 *keshōgi* dressing gown
粧煉瓦 *keshō renga* ornamental tile; facing bricks
粧箱 *keshōbako* vanity case; fancy box
[14] 導 *kadō* influencing (a person) for good
[17] 繊 *kasen* synthetic fibers
膿 *kanō suru* suppurate, fester, come to a head
膿菌 *kanōkin* suppurative germ

3

A **北** 581 / J4b4c / M2574 **业** 14 / J-X / M-X HOKU. *kita* north.

[3] 山 *kitayama* a northern hill
下 *kitaoro(shi)* cold wind from the northern uplands
上 *hokujo* going north
大西洋 *Kita Taiseiyō* North Atlantic
大西洋条約機構 *Kita Taiseiyō Jōyaku Kikō* North Atlantic Treaty Organization
[4] 辺 *hokuhen* northern extremity
方 *hoppō* north, northward; northern
方 *kita (no) kata* nobleman's true wife; facing the north
天 *hokuten* northern sky
支 *Hokushi* North China
支事変 *Hokushi Jihen* the Marco Polo Bridge Incident
斗七星 *Hokuto Shichisei* Big Dipper
斗星 *Hokutosei* Big Dipper
[5] 半球 *Kita Hankyū* Northern Hemisphere
氷洋 *Hokuhyōyō, Hoppyōyō* Arctic Ocean

北西 *hokuhokusei* north-northwest
北東 *hokuhokutō* north-northeast
6 行 *hokkō* northbound; sailing north
向 *kitamu(ki)* facing north, northern exposure
光 *hokkō* northern lights
米 *Hokubei* North America
回帰線 *Kita Kaikisen* Tropic of Cancer
西 *hokusei, kitanishi* northwest
西航路 *Hokusei Kōro* Northwest Passage
7 辰 *Hokushin* North Star
8 門 *kitamon* north gate
枕 *kitamakura* turning the head to the north in sleeping
郊 *hokkō* northern suburbs
受 *kitau(ke)* facing the north
東 *hokutō, kitahigashi* northeast
国 *hokkoku, kitaguni* northern provinces, northern countries
欧 *Hokuō* Northern Europe; land of the Norsemen, Scandinavia
岸 *hokugan* north coast; north bank
岸沿 *hokuganzo(i) ni* along the north coast; along the northern seashore
9 面 *hokumen* north face, north side; the north; facing north
風 *hokufū, kitakaze* north wind
海 *hokkai* northern sea, the North Sea
洋 *hokuyō* northern waters
10 進 *hokushin suru* proceed north
航 *hokkō* sailing north
部 *hokubu* north, northern part
叟笑 *hokusoe(mu)* chuckle, gloat over. *hokusowara(i)* smile of success
11 側 *kitagawa* north side, north bank. *hokusoku* north side
寄 *kitayo(ri)* northerly (wind)
清事変 *Hokushin Jihen* North China Incident; Boxer Uprising
12 満 *Hokuman* North Manchuria
朝 *Hokuchō* Northern Dynasty
極 *Hokkyoku* North Pole
極光 *hokkyokukō* northern lights, aurora borealis
極洋 *Hokkyokuyō* Arctic Ocean
極海 *Hokkyokukai* Arctic Ocean
極星 *Hokkyokusei* North Star
極圏 *Hokkyokuken* Arctic Circle
極熊 *hokkyokuguma* polar bear
14 境 *hokkyō* northern boundary
端 *hokutan* northern extremity
16 緯 *hokui* north latitude
17 鮮 *Hokusen* North Korea
嶺 *hokurei* northern mountain; Mt. Hiei

9

匙 582 / J3a7c / M2590 Shi. Ji. *saji* spoon.
5 加減 *saji kagen* about a spoonful; dosage, prescription; discretion, consideration, allowance
7 投 *saji (o) na(geru)* withdraw, give up as hopeless

RAD. 匚 22

Hakogamae (box-on-side enclosure). Variant: 匸. This variant is actually Rad. 23 but is treated herein as Rad. 22. Nickname: Box on Side.

匚 583 / J5239 / M2595 Hō enclosure.

2

B **匹** 584 / J4924 / M2673 Hitsu. Hiki head, counter (small animals); roll of cloth.
4 夫 *hippu* a man; a coarse man; a rustic
夫匹婦 *hippuhippu* coarse men and women
夫勇 *hippu (no) yū* rash courage
11 婦 *hippu* coarse woman; country woman
15 敵 *hitteki suru* compare with, match, rival, be equal to
16 儔 *hitchū* an equal, a match

A **区** 585 / J3668 / M2674 **區** 593 / J523f / M2691 Ku ward, district, section.
4 区 *kuku(taru), machimachi no* several, various, divergent, conflicting
内 *kunai* in the ward or borough
切 *kugi(ru)* punctuate; cut off; mark off. *kugi(ri)* punctuation

分 *kuwa(ke), kubun* division, section, demarcation; (traffic) lane; compartment; classification, sorting
5 処 *kusho* dividing for administrative purposes; partition; division
民 *kumin* ward residents
6 会 *kukai* ward assembly
会議員 *kukai giin* ward assemblyman
7 別 *kubetsu* distinction, difference; classification
役所 *kuyakusho* ward office
8 長 *kucho* ward headman
画 *kukaku* division, section; compartment; boundary; area; block
画整理 *kukaku seiri* land readjustment, town planning
11 域 *kuiki* limits, boundary; domain, zone, sphere, territory
12 検 *kuken* local prosecutor
費 *kuhi* ward expenses
裁判所 *ku saibansho* local court
間 *kukan* section (of track, etc.)
間列車 *kukan ressha* local train
14 劃 *kukaku* division, section; compartment; boundary; area; block
劃整理 *kukaku seiri* land readjustment, town planning
20 議 *kugi* ward assemblyman

3

匝 586 / J4139 / M2599 Sō go around.

4

匡 587 / J3629 / M2606 Kyō correct; save; assist.
5 正 *kyōsei* reform, correction, training

B **匠** 588 / J3e22 / M2605 Shō workman, artisan; means; idea. *takumi* artisan, mechanic; carpenter.
6 気 *shōki* affectation, desire to be impressive

5

匣 589 / J523a / M2610 Kō. *hako* box.

A **医** 590 / J3065 / M2680 **醫** 6190 / J6e50 / M40006 I medicine, the healing art; doctor. *i(suru), iya(su)* cure, heal; quench (thirst).
3 大 *idai* medical university
4 化学 *ikagaku* medical chemistry
6 会 *ikai* medical society
7 局 *ikyoku* medical office, dispensary
伯 *ihaku* doctor (polite)
8 長 *ichō* head doctor
官 *ikan* medical officer
者 *isha* doctor
事伝道 *iji dendō* medical missionary work
学 *igaku* medical science, medicine
学士 *Igakushi* Bachelor of Medicine, M.B.
学史 *igakushi* history of medicine
学生 *igakusei* medical student
学技術士 *igaku gijutsushi* medical technician
学界 *igakukai* medical world
学博士 *Igaku Hakushi, Igaku Hakase* M.D., Doctor of Medicine
9 界 *ikai* medical world
科 *ika* medical science; medical department
科大学 *ika daigaku* medical school
院 *iin* doctor's office, dispensary
院長 *iinchō* head doctor
10 員 *iin* medical staff; doctor
家 *ika* doctor
書 *isho* medical book
師 *ishi* doctor
師会 *ishikai* medical association
師法 *ishihō* medical practitioner's law
11 術 *ijutsu* medicine, healing art
務 *imu* medical affairs
務室 *imushitsu* medical office
13 業 *igyō* medical practice
16 薬 *iyaku* medicine
薬分業 *iyaku-bungyō* separation of medical and dispensary practice
薬品 *iyakuhin* medical supplies
17 療 *iryō* medical care; medical
療伝道 *iryō dendō* medical missionary work
療車 *iryōsha* clinic car, traveling clinic
療材料 *iryō zairyō* medical supplies
療法人 *iryō hōjin* medical corporation
療品 *iryōhin* medical supplies
療保険 *iryō hoken* medical-care insurance

2 二亠人イヘ儿入八ソ冂冖冫几凵刀刂力勹匕【匚匸】十卜卩厂ム又

療施設 *iryō shisetsu* medical facilities
療報酬 *iryō hōshū* medical fee
療器械 *iryō kikai* medical appliances, surgical instruments
療機関 *iryō kikan* medical institution
20 籍 *iseki* register of physicians

8

B 匿 591 / J463f / M2690 TOKU. *kakuma(u)* shelter, shield, hide.
6 名 *tokumei* anonymity; pseudonym

匪 592 / J485b / M2629 HI negation; wicked person.
6 団 *hidan* bandit gang
10 徒 *hito* bandit
躬 *hikyū* self-sacrificing service
13 賊 *hizoku* bandit, rebel

9

區 593 / J523f / M2691 See 区 585.

11

滙 594 / J523b / M2644 KAI swirl; gather.

12

匱 595 / J523c / M2651 KI. *hitsu* chest, coffer; rice tub.

13

匳 596 / J523d / M2655 REN box. *kushige* comb box.

RAD. 匸 23

Kakushi-gamae "hiding" enclosure. This radical is treated herein as a variant of Rad. 22. Nickname: Hiding.

匸 597 / J523e / M2672 KEI hide, cover.

8

RAD. 十 24

Jū ten. Variants: 十, ナ. The enclosure ナ is sometimes included as a variant of this, but not herein. Nickname: Cross.

A 十 598 / J3d3d / M2695 JŪ *tō, to* ten.
1 一月 *Jūichigatsu* November
一面観世音 *Jūichimen Kanzeon* 11-faced Goddess of Mercy
一面観音 *Jūichimen Kannon* 11-faced Goddess of Mercy
2 八番 *jūhachiban* No. 18; one's favorite stunt; one's hobby. *ohako* one's favorite stunt, one's hobby
人力 *jūninriki* the strength of ten
人十色 *jūnin-toiro* Everyone has his own interests and ideas.
人並 *jūninna(mi)* average, mediocrity
二支 *jūnishi* the 12 signs of the zodiac
二月 *Jūnigatsu* December
二分 *jūnibun* more than enough
二折 *jūnio(ri)* duodecimo (folding)
二使徒 *Jūni Shito* Twelve Apostles
二単衣 *jūnihitoe* lady's ceremonial court dress
二指腸 *jūnishichō* duodenum
二指腸虫 *jūnishichōchū* hookworm
二時 *jūniji* 12 o'clock; noon; midnight
二宮 *jūnikyū* the constellations of the zodiac
3 干 *jikkan* the ten calendar signs
三夜 *jūsan'ya* the 13th day (of the moon); the night of the 13th day of the ninth lunar moon

万 *jūman* 100,000
万億土 *jūman'okudo* eternity, paradise
4 手 *jitte* short metal truncheon
五夜 *jūgoya* night of the full moon; the night of the 15th day of the eighth lunar month
文字 *jūmonji* cross. *jūmonji no* cruciform. *jūmonji ni* crosswise
中八九 *jitchū-hakku* eight or nine cases out of ten
日 *tōka* ten days; the tenth (day of the month)
日菊 *tōka (no) kiku* coming too late
月 *Jūgatsu* October
月革命 *Jūgatsu Kakumei* the October Revolution
六分音符 *jūrokubun ompu* a 16th note
六夜 *izayoi* 16-day-old moon
分 *jūbun* enough, satisfactory; perfect; thorough. *juppun* ten minutes.
分一 *jūbun (no) ichi* the tithe; a tenth
5 目 *jūmoku* all eyes
代 *jūdai* the teens; the tenth generation
6 全 *jūzen* perfection, consummation; absolute safety
字 *jūji* cross. *jūji ni* crosswise. *jūji no* crossed, cruciform
字形 *jūjikei* cross. *jūjikei no* cruciform
字架 *jūjika* cross; the Cross (of Christ)
字架状 *jūjika no* cruciform
字架像 *jūjikazō* crucifix
字軍 *Jūjigun* Crusades; Crusaders
字軍騎士 *Jūjigun Kishi* the Crusaders
字砲火 *jūji hōka* crossfire
字街 *jūjigai* crossroads, street crossing
字路 *jūjiro* crossroads
字線 *jūjisen* cross hairs
字鍬 *jūjishū* a pick, a pickax
7 戒 *jikkai* the ten Buddhist precepts
把一絡 *jippa-hitokara(ge)* sweeping (criticism)
8 雨 *jūu* a refreshing rain once in ten days
9 指 *jisshi, jusshi* the ten fingers
重 *toe* tenfold
10 倍 *jūbai* ten times, tenfold
哲 *jittetsu, juttetsu* Basho's Ten Disciples; Confucius' Ten Disciples
能 *jūnō* fire shovel, fire pan
部門分類法 *Jūbumon Bunruihō* Dewey Decimal System
進 *jisshin no* decimal. *jisshin* decimal system
進分類法 *jisshin bunruihō* decimal classification system
進法 *jisshinhō* decimal system
進制 *jisshinsei* decimal system
13 数 *jūsū-* ten-odd
14 誡 *Jikkai* the Ten Commandments, the Decalog
種競技 *jisshu kyōgi* decathlon
15 億 *jūoku* a billion
21 露盤 *soroban* abacus

1

A 千 599/J4069/M2697 仟 113/J5042/M380 SEN *chi* thousand; many.

1 一夜 *Sen'ichiya* Thousand and One Nights
2 人力 *senninriki* strength of a thousand men
人針 *sennimbari* a 1,000-stitch belt (a soldier's charm)
3 千 *chiji* thousands. *chiji* a great number of; variety
万 *chiyorozu* a great many. *semman* 10,000,000; myriad. *semban* exceedingly, very many, very much, indeed
万長者 *semmanchōja* multimillionaire, billionaire
万無量 *samman-muryo* innumerable; unfathomable; unutterable
4 日 *sennichi* 1,000 days
木 *chigi* ornamental crossed rafter ends on shrine gables
切 *chigi(ru)* cut up fine; pick (fruit). *sengiri* short small pieces of vegetables
分 *sembun* division by 1,000; $\frac{1}{1000}$
分率 *sembunritsu* permillage, rate per thousand
5 生 *sennari* a great collection (of things)
古 *senko* all ages; great antiquity; eternity
石船 *sengokubune* large junk
仭 *senjin* great depth; great height
仭谷 *senjin (no) tani* bottomless ravine
代 *chiyo, sendai* 1,000 years; a very long period
代紙 *chiyogami* gaily colored paper
6 両 *senryō* 1,000 *ryō* (an old Japanese coin)
両役者 *senryō yakusha* star (actor), prima donna; leading figure

両箱 *senryōbako* box of 1,000 *ryo*
年 *sennen* millennium, 1,000 years
年期 *sennenki* millennium
年間 *sennenkan* a 1,000-year period
7 辛万苦 *senshin-banku* many hardships
言万語 *sengen-bango* many words
状万態 *senjō-bantai* various forms; various circumstances
里 *senri* 1,000 *ri*; a long distance
里眼 *senrigan* clairvoyance; clairvoyant
8 金 *senkin* 1,000 yen; 1,000 pieces of gold; pricelessness
夜 *chiya, sen'ya* many nights
卒長 *sensotsuchō* captain of a thousand
枚通 *semmaidō(shi)* an awl
波万波 *sempa-bampa* many waves, onrushing waves
9 度 *chitabi, sendo* 1,000 times
草 *chigusa* great variety of flowering plants
変万化 *sempembanka* innumerable changes, infinite variety
思万考 *senshi-bankō* deep meditation, mature consideration
客万来 *senkaku-banrai, senkyaku-banrai* flood of customers
軍万馬 *sengumbamba* series of battles
姿万態 *senshi-bantai* endless variety
秋 *senshū* 1,000 years; many years
秋楽 *senshūraku* the last day of a sumo tournament; the concluding program
10 倍 *sembai* 1,000-fold
般 *sempan* variety
島 *Chishima* the Kurile Islands
差万別 *sensa-bambetsu* infinite variety
11 遍一律 *sempen-ichiritsu* no change
鳥 *chidori* plover
鳥足 *chidori ashi* tottering steps
12 鈞 *senkin* 1,000 pounds; 1,000 *kan*; great weight
尋 *chihiro* 1,000 fathoms; great depth
紫万紅 *senshi-bankō* variegated colors (of flowers)
13 歳 *chitose* 1,000 years
載 *senzai* 1,000 years; a long time; a millennium; perpetuity
載一遇 *senzai-ichigū* experienced once in 1,000 times; once in a lifetime opportunity
14 態万様 *sentai-ban'yō* great diversity of form
15 慮 *senryo* much thought
慮一失 *senryo (no) isshitsu* the mistake of a wise man
篇 *sempen* many volumes
篇一律 *sempen-ichiritsu* monotony, lack of variety

2

卆 600 J5240 M2701 See 卒 615.

卍 601 J-X M48950 BAN. MAN. *manji* the Nazi swastika; the reversed swastika, a variant of 卍 611.

卅 602 J5241 M2700 **丗** 15 J5242 M32 SŌ. ZŌ. *sanjū* thirty.

B **升** 603 J3e23 M2702 SHŌ 1.8 liter. *masu* a measuring box.

A **午** 604 J3861 M2703 GO *uma* 11 a.m. – 1 p.m., seventh zodiac sign. *uma* horse; south.
6 后 *gogo* afternoon, p.m.
8 刻 *gokoku* noon
9 後 *gogo* afternoon, p.m.
後中 *gogojū* throughout the afternoon
前 *gozen* forenoon, a.m.
前中 *gozenchū* throughout the morning
10 砲 *gohō* noon gun
11 過 *hirusu(gi)* after noon
13 睡 *gosui* nap, siesta
16 餐 *gosan* lunch, dinner
餐会 *gosankai* luncheon party

3

卋 605 J-X M2713 See 世 20.

卉 606 J5243 M2706 KI grass.

卌 607 J-X M2712 SHŪ. *shijū* 40.

A **半** 608 J483e M2707 HAN half; odd number; semi-, hemi-, demi-. *naka(ba)* half, semi-, middle, halfway; partly.

[2] 人前 *hannimmae* half share; half a person
[3] 口 *hankuchi* half share
弓 *hankyū* small bow
ケ月 *hankagetsu* half a month
ケ年 *hankanen* half a year
[4] 日 *hannichi, hanjitsu* a half day
天 *hanten* half the sky, midair
分 *hambun* half. *hampun* half minute
円 *han'en* semicircle
円形 *han'enkei* semicircle
切 *hansetsu* half size. *hanki(re)* half a piece
切符 *hankippu* half-price ticket
月 *hantsuki, hangetsu* half moon; half month; semicircle
月刊 *hangekkan* a semimonthly
月形 *hangetsugata* semicircle, half moon
[5] 玉 *hangyoku* child geisha, apprentice entertainer
生 *hansei* half a lifetime. *hanshō* half death
田 *handa* solder; pewter
白 *hampaku* grayish color
句 *hanku* a brief word
半 *hanhan* half and half, fifty-fifty
母音 *hamboin* semivowel
世紀 *hanseiki* a half century
永久的 *han'eikyūteki* semipermanent
加工品 *hankakōhin* semiprocessed goods
可 *hanka* insufficiency, half ripe
可通 *hankatsū* superficial knowledge; smatterer
[6] 休 *hankyū* half holiday
死 *hanshi* half dead
死半生 *hanshi-hanshō* half dead
年 *hantoshi, hannen* a half year
年毎 *hannengoto ni* semiannually
[7] 里 *hanri* half a *ri* (see Weights and Measures)
作 *hansaku* half crop
折 *hansetsu* half size, half a piece, half length
狂乱 *hankyōran* half-crazed
身 *hanshin* half the body, half length
身不随 *hanshin fuzui* paralyzed on one side
身浴 *hanshin'yoku* sitz bath
身像 *hanshinzō* half-length statue or portrait, bust
[8] 金 *hankin* half the amount
周 *hanshū* semicircle
価 *hanka* half price
径 *hankei* radius
夜 *han'ya* midnight
季 *hanki* half a quarter, a half period
股引 *hammomohiki* knee-length underwear
盲 *hammō* half blind
盲症 *hammōshō* star blindness, half-blindness
官半民 *hankan-hammin* semi-governmental
官的 *hankanteki* semi-official
官報 *hankampō* semi-official paper
[9] 音 *han'on* half tone (in music)
途 *hanto* halfway; unfinished
神 *hanshin* demigod
独立 *handokuritsu* semi-independent
透明 *hantōmei* semi-transparency
信半疑 *hanshin-hangi* dubious, incredulous
封建制 *hanhōkensei* semi-feudalism
革装釘 *hankawa sōtei* half-leather binding
面 *hammen* half the face; one side, half; the other side the reverse; the contrary
面識 *hammenshiki* slight acquaintance
[10] 値 *hanne* half price
時 *hantoki* about an hour; a short time
紙 *hanshi* rice paper, thin Japanese writing paper
袖 *hansode* short sleeves
被 *happi* workman's livery coat
殺 *hangoro(shi)* half-killed
島 *hanto* peninsula
宵 *hanshō* midnight
病人 *hambyōnin* semi-invalid
流動体 *hanryūdōtai* semi-liquid
陰陽 *han'inyō* bisexualism
陰影 *han'in'ei* penumbra
夏 *hange* 11th day after the summer solstice, last seed-sowing day
[11] 道 *hammichi* half a *ri* (see Weights and Measures); halfway
張 *hamba(ri)* half sole
球 *hankyū* hemisphere
眼 *hangan de* with a half-opened eye
乾 *hankawa(ki)* half dry
過 *naka(ba)su(gi)* beyond the middle
過去 *hankako* imperfect tense
舷砲 *hangenhō* firing a broadside
[12] 間 *hamma* fragment; incomplete set; fraction, odd sum; remnant; incompleteness

2 二亠人亻𠆢儿入八丷冂冖冫几凵刀刂力勹匕匚匸【十】卜卩厂厶又

焼 *han'ya(ke)* half-burnt; half-done; half-baked; rare
期 *hanki* half term, half year, half period
畳 *hanjō* half mat; hissing, heckling
煮 *hanni(e)* half-boiled, half-done
貴石 *hankiseki* semiprecious stones
開 *hankai* semicivilized. *hambira(ki)* partly open, in half bloom
開国 *hankaikoku* underdeveloped country, half-civilized country
減 *hangen* reduction by half
減期 *hangenki* half life (in physical chemistry)
13 解 *hankai* only half understood
靴 *hangutsu, hanka* low shoes; shoes
数 *hansū* half the number
農 *hannō* part-time farming
搗米 *hantsukimai* half-polished rice
艇身 *hanteishin* half a boat length
裸体 *hanratai* seminude, half-naked
意識 *han'ishiki* subconsciousness
14 旗 *hanki* flag at half-mast
端 *hampa* fragment; incomplete set; fraction, odd sum; remnant; incompleteness
導体 *handōtai* semiconductor
製品 *hanseihin* semiprocessed goods
15 潰 *hantsubu(re)* half demolished
輪 *hanrin* semicircle; half-moon
影 *han'ei* penumbra
熟 *hanjuku* half-boiled
熟練工 *hanjuku renkō* semiskilled worker
16 壊 *hankai* partial destruction
濁点 *handakuten* circle used in *kana* to indicate p-sound
濁音 *handakuon* p-sound
諧音 *hankaion* assonance
18 襟 *han'eri* a quality collar for an under kimono
額 *hangaku* half price, half amount, half fare
20 鐘 *hanshō* fire alarm
鹹水 *hankansui* brackish water
21 纏 *hanten* short coat; workman's livery coat

4

卋 609 J-X M2714 See **世** 20.

卉 610 J-X M2720 See **卉** 606.

卍 611 J5244 M2724 **卐** 601 J-X M48950 BAN. MAN. *manji* gammadion, fylfot, swastika.
4 巴 *manji-tomoe* falling in swirls

6

卑 612 J-X M2738 See **卑** 618.

協 613 J-X M-X Nonstandard for **協** 617.

尭 614 J3646 M-X GYŌ high; valuable; rich; abundant.

A **卒** 615 J4234 M2740 **卆** 601 J5240 M2701 SOTSU soldier, private; graduate. *sos(suru)* die, pass away.
4 中 *sotchū* apoplexy, cerebral stroke
5 去 *sokkyo, shukkyo* death
6 伍 *sotsugo* rank and file, the ranks
先 *sossen* taking the initiative
8 直 *sotchoku* frankness, openheartedness
10 倒 *sottō* fainting, swooning
12 然 *sotsuzen* suddenly, unexpectedly
塔婆 *sotoba* wooden grave tablet; stupa
13 業 *sotsugyō* graduation
業生 *sotsugyōsei* graduate, alumnus
業式 *sotsugyōshiki* graduation exercises
業後 *sotsugyōgo* after graduation
業証書 *sotsugyō shōsho* graduation certificate
14 爾 *sotsuji na* abrupt, sudden

B **卓** 616 J426e M2741 TAKU table, desk; high.
3 子 *takushi, tēburu* table
上 *takujō* after-dinner (speech); on the table, on the desk
上電話 *takujō denwa* desk phone
5 用 *takuyō* desk (equipment); table use
出 *takushutsu* excellence, superiority, preeminence; prevalence
7 見 *takken* clearsightedness, penetration, farsightedness; excellent idea
抜 *takubatsu* excellence, superiority, preeminence; prevalence

8 効 *takkō* great efficiency
11 球 *takkyū* pingpong, table tennis
袱台 *chabudai* tea table
12 絶 *takuzetsu* excellence, superiority, preeminence; prevalence
筆 *takuhitsu* excellent literary work
越 *takuetsu* excellence, superiority, preeminence; prevalence
越風 *takuetsufū* prevailing wind
14 説 *takusetsu* excellent opinion
15 論 *takuron* sound argument, clever presentation
19 識 *takushiki* clearsightedness, penetration, farsightedness; excellent idea

A **協** 617/J3628/M2742 **恊** 613/J-X/M-X KYŌ cooperation.
2 力 *kyōryoku* cooperation
力者 *kyōryokusha* co-worker; cooperator
4 心 *kyōshin* unison, accord
6 会 *kyōkai* association, society
同 *kyōdō* cooperation, collaboration, association
同組合 *kyōdō kumiai* a cooperative; a partnership
同動作 *kyōdō dōsa* concerted action
8 和 *kyōwa* concord, harmony, concert
和音 *kyōwaon* consonance; concord
定 *kyōtei* pact, agreement
定案 *kyōteian* agreement, proposal
定書 *kyōteisho* agreement, protocol
9 奏曲 *kyōsōkyoku* concerto
約 *kyōyaku* pact, convention, agreement
約国 *kyōyakukoku* high contracting powers, signatories
約書 *kyōyakusho* written agreement
11 商 *kyōshō* negotiation; agreement
商国 *kyōshōkoku* allies
13 業 *kyōgyō* cooperative industry
15 賛 *kyōsan* mutual aid, cooperation; approval, authorization
調 *kyōchō* cooperation, conciliation, harmony; firm (market) tone
調主義 *kyōchō shugi* collaboration
20 議 *kyōgi* conference, deliberation
議会 *kyōgikai* council, conference, convention
議会員 *kyōgikaiin* conferees
議所 *kyōgisho* conference site
議官 *kyōgikan* conferees
議事項 *kyōgi jikō* agenda
議員 *kyōgiin* delegate

7

B **卑** 618/J485c/M2751 **卑** 612/J-X/M2738 HI. *iya(shii)* humble; base, mean, vile, vulgar; greedy. *iya(shimu), iyashi(meru)* despise.
3 小 *hishō* petty, trifling
下 *hige* humility, self-deprecation
6 近 *hikin* common, simple
劣 *hiretsu* meanness, foul play
劣漢 *hiretsukan* a despicable person
7 見 *hiken* my humble opinion
言 *higen* slang expression
8 屈 *hikutsu* meanness servility
怯 *hikyō* cowardice; meanness; unfairness
陋 *hirō* low rank; wickedness; vulgarity
金属 *hikinzoku* base metals
9 俗 *hizoku na* vulgar, coarse
10 称 *hishō* this wretch (oneself); you wretch
12 属 *hizoku* lineal descendants (beyond grandchildren)
猥 *hiwai* indecency, obscenity
14 語 *higo* slang
15 賤 *hisen* low class

A **南** 619/J466e/M2750 NAN. *minami, minnami* south.
2 十字星 *Minami Jūjisei* Southern Cross
3 下 *nanka suru* go south
山 *nanzan* southern mountain; Mt. Kōya
山寿 *nanzan (no) ju* longevity
4 中 *nanchū suru* crossing the meridian
天 *nanten* the southern sky
太平洋 *Minami Taiheiyō* South Pacific
支 *Nanshi* South China
支那海 *Minami Shinakai* South China Sea
方 *nampō* south; southern, southward
方産 *nampōsan* products of the south seas
5 瓜 *kabocha, nanka, tōnasu* squash, pumpkin
氷洋 *Nanhyōyō, Nampyōyō* Antarctic Ocean
半 *nanhan* southern half

半球 *Minami Hankyū* Southern Hemisphere
北 *namboku* north and south
北朝 *Nambokuchō* Northern and Southern Dynasties (1336 – 1392)
北戦争 *Namboku Sensō* (U. S.) Civil War
6 米 *Nambei* South America
行 *nankō* southbound
向 *minamimu(ki)* southern exposure, facing south
光 *nankō* southern lights
回帰線 *Minami Kaikisen* Tropic of Capricorn
西 *nansei, minaminishi* southwest
西諸島 *Nansei Shotō* Nansei Islands (the Ryūkyū and Satsunan Islands)
7 宋 *Nansō* the Southern Song
阿 *Nan'a* South Africa
阿連邦 *Nan'a Rempō* Union of South Africa
阿戦争 *Nan'a Sensō* Boer War
8 門 *nammon* south gate
国 *nangoku* southern countries
欧 *Nan'ō* Southern Europe
郊 *nankō* southern suburbs
東 *nantō, minamihigashi* southeast
征北伐 *nansei-hokubatsu* attacking in all directions
岸 *nangan* south coast; south bank
岸沿 *nanganzo(i) ni* along the southern coast; along the southern seashore
京 *Nankin* Nanking
京虫 *nankimmushi* bedbug
京豆 *nankimmame* peanut
京焼 *Nankin'ya(ki)* Nanking porcelain, chinaware
9 面 *nammen* south face, south side; the south. *nammen suru* face the south; ascend the throne; rule
風 *nampū, minami kaze* south wind
海 *nankai* southern sea
洋 *Nan'yō* South Seas
洋諸島 *Nan'yō Shotō* South Sea Islands
南西 *nannansei* south-southwest
南東 *nannantō* south-southeast
10 進 *nanshin suru* proceed south
航 *nankō* sailing south, southbound
部 *nambu* southern part
都 *nanto* southern capital, Nara
11 側 *minamigawa, nansoku* south side
偶 *nangū* southern corner
寄 *minamiyo(ri)* southerly (wind)
船北馬 *nansen-hokuba* constant traveling, restless wandering
12 満 *Namman* South Manchuria
朝 *Nanchō* Southern Dynasty
蛮 *namban* southern barbarians; red pepper
蛮人 *nambanjin* the southern barbarians, the early Europeans
蛮船 *nambansen* the early European ships
無 *namu* hail (in Buddhist prayers)
無阿弥陀仏 *Namu Amida Butsu* Hail Amida
無妙法蓮華経 *Namu Myōhō Rengekyō* Hail Lotus Sutra
極 *Nankyoku* South Pole
極大陸 *Nankyoku Tairiku* Antarctica
極光 *nankyokukō* aurora australis, southern lights
極星 *nankyokusei* the southern polar stars
極洋 *Nankyokuyō* Antarctic Ocean
極海 *Nankyokukai* Antarctic Ocean
極帯 *Nankyokutai* Antarctic Zone
極圏 *Nankyokuken* Antarctic Circle
14 端 *nantan* southern tip
16 緯 *nan'i* south latitude

A **単** 620 / J4331 / M2752 **單** 833 / J5345 / M3993 TAN one, single, simple, singular, individual. *tan(naru)* mere, simple, sheer. *tan ni* simply, merely, only, solely. *hitoe* one layer, single.

1 一 *tan'itsu na* single, simple, sole, individual
一化 *tan'itsuka* simplification
一性 *tan'itsusei* unitary
一神教 *tan'itsu shinkyō* monotheism
2 刀直入 *tantō-chokunyū* getting right into the subject, frankness
3 子葉 *tanshiyō* monocotyledon
4 文 *tambun* simple sentence
元 *tangen* a teaching unit
比 *tampi* simple ratio
比例 *tampirei* simple proportion
5 句 *tanku* simple phrase
打 *tanda* one-base hit
本位 *tanhon'i* single standard, monometallism
本位制 *tanhon'isei* single standard, monometallism

弁 *tamben* univalve
弁花 *tambenka* single-petaled flower
6 行本 *tankōbon* separate volume
衣 *tan'i, hitoe* unlined kimono
衣物 *hitoemono* unlined kimono
色 *tanshoku* single color
色光 *tanshokukō* monochromatic light
色画 *tanshokuga* a monochrome
式 *tanshiki* simple system; single-entry (bookkeeping)
式火山 *tanshiki kazan* simple volcano
式学級 *tanshiki gakkyū* single-grade (class-room)
式簿記 *tanshiki boki* single-entry bookkeeping
7 角 *tankaku no* one-horned
作 *tansaku* single crop
坐式 *tanzashiki no* single-seated
坐機 *tanzaki* single-seater
身 *tanshin* alone; unaided; away from home
身赴任 *tanshin funin* working separated from home and family
身銃 *tanshinjū* single-barreled gun
利 *tanri* simple interest
利表 *tanrihyō* simple-interest table
利法 *tanrihō* simple-interest method
位 *tan'i* unit, denomination; credit (in school)
位労働組合 *tan'i rōdō kumiai* local (labor) union
位制度 *tan'i seido* point system, credit system
位組合 *tan'i kumiai* local labor union
8 価 *tanka* unit cost, unit price
性 *tansei* unisexual, unisex
物 *hitoemono* unlined kimono
9 相 *tansō* single phase
級 *tankyū* single-grade (classroom)
軌 *tanki* monorail; single track
音 *tan'on* monosyllable; monotony
音節 *tan'onsetsu no* monosyllabic
音節語 *tan'onsetsugo* monosyllable
発 *tampatsu* single engine
発銃 *tampatsujū* single-barreled gun
発機 *tampatsuki* single-engined plane
独 *tandoku* solo (flight); independence; singleness. *tandoku no* single, sole, lone. *tandoku de* independently, individually, separately, alone, single-handed, unassisted
独内閣 *tandoku naikaku* one-party cabinet
独会見 *tandoku kaiken* exclusive interview
独行為 *tandoku kōi* individual action, unilateral act
独行動 *tandoku kōdō* independent action
独飛行 *tandoku hikō* solo flight
独講和 *tandoku kōwa* separate peace
10 帯 *hitoeobi* unlined obi
峰駱駝 *tampō rakuda* Arabian camel, dromedary, a one-hump camel
記 *tanki* single-entry (bookkeeping); voting for one person only
記投票 *tanki tōhyō* voting for one person only
純 *tanjun* simplicity
純化 *tanjunka* simplification
純性 *tanjunsei* simplicity
11 細胞 *tansaibō* single cell
眼 *tangan* one eye
眼鏡 *tangankyō* monocle
12 葉 *tan'yō* simple leaf; monoplane
葉飛行機 *tan'yō hikōki* monoplane
葉機 *tan'yōki* monoplane
13 試合 *tanshiai* singles (in tennis)
数 *tansū* singular number
数型 *tansūkei* singular form
14 複 *tanfuku* simplicity and complexity; singular and plural; single and double; single and doubles (in tennis)
語 *tango* word; vocabulary; single-character word
語集 *tangoshū* word book
語篇 *tangohen* glossary, vocabulary
15 線 *tansen* single line; solid wire; single track
調 *tanchō* monotone, monotony, dullness
16 機 *tanki* a lone plane
縦列 *tanjūretsu* Indian file, single file, single column
18 騎 *tanki* a single horseman

10

A **博** 621 / J476e / M2761′ HAKU. BAKU. *haku(suru)* command esteem, win acclaim; gain, receive. *-haku* doctor, PhD; exposition, fair, exhibition.

3 大 *hakudai* large and wide
士 *Hakase, Hakushi* PhD
士号 *hakushigō* doctor's degree, PhD
4 引旁証 *hakuin-bōshō* citing copious references

[5]打 *bakuchi* gambling
打打 *bakuchiu(chi)* gambling
[7]労 *bakurō* horse trader
[8]学 *hakugaku* erudition
学力行 *hakugaku-rikkō* wide learning and energetic activity
物 *hakubutsu* wide learning; natural history
物学 *hakubutsugaku* natural history
物館 *hakubutsukan* museum
[9]奕 *bakuchi, bakueki* gambling
奕打 *bakuchiu(chi)* gambling
[10]徒 *bakuto* gambler
[13]雅 *bakuga no* well-informed, accomplished
愛 *hakuai* charity, benevolence, philanthropy, humanity
愛家 *hakuaika* philanthropist
[14]聞 *hakubun no* well-informed, erudite
[16]覧 *hakuran* extensive reading, wide knowledge
覧会 *hakurankai* fair, exhibition, exposition
覧強記 *hakuran-kyōki* reading and recording
[19]識 *hakushiki* extensive knowledge

RAD. 卜 25

Uranai divination or *to* (the katakana). Variants: ⺊, ⺊. Nickname: *Kana To.*

卜 622 / J4b4e / M2774 Boku divining. *boku suru, urana(u)* tell a fortune, predict; choose, settle, fix. *uranai, ura* divination.
[8]居 *bokkyo suru* choosing a homesite by divination
者 *bokusha* fortuneteller, soothsayer, diviner
[10]書 *urabumi* fortuneteller's book
[13]筮 *bokuzei* fortunetelling, divination

2

卞 623 / J5246 / M2778 Ben, Hen law, rule, regulation; hasty
[9]急 *benkyū* short tempered, hasty

3

B **占** 624 / J406a / M2780 Sen. *shi(meru)* occupy, hold, have, get, take (a seat). *urana(u)* divine, forecast, augur. *uranai* divination, fortunetelling, soothsaying. *shi(meta)* I've got it; all right, fine.
[2]卜 *semboku* divination, fortunetelling, soothsaying
[5]用 *sen'yō* exclusive use
[6]当 *urana(i)-a(teru)* divine
有 *sen'yū* exclusive possession, occupancy
有権 *sen'yūken* right of exclusive possession
[7]住 *senjū suru* occupy
[8]居 *senkyo suru* occupy a certain place
法 *sempō* divination
者 *uranaisha* diviner, fortuneteller, soothsayer, palmist
拠 *senkyo* occupation
拠地 *senkyochi* occupied territory
取 *senshu* preoccupation
取権 *senshuken* right of preoccupancy
[9]星術 *senseijutsu* astrology
[10]師 *uranaishi* diviner, fortuneteller, soothsayer, palmist
[14]領 *senryō* capture, possession, occupation. *senryō suru* have a room to oneself
領下 *senryōka no* occupied (by an army)
領地 *senryōchi* occupied territory
領地帯 *senryō chitai* occupied zone
領軍 *senryōgun* army of occupation

6

卦 625 / J3735 / M2798 Ka. Ke a divination sign.
[14]算 *keisan* a paperweight

RAD. 卩 26

Warifu seal or *fushizukuri* right-side "joint." Variant: 㔾 *mage warifu* crooked seal. Nickname: Seal.

卩 626 J5247 M2836 SETSU sign, symbol, tally.

— 3 —

卮 627 J5248 M2846 SHI. *sakazuki* large wine vessel.

卯 628 J312c M2847 BŌ. *u* 5–7 am; fourth zodiac sign; rabbit; east.
4 木 *utsugi* Japanese snow flower
月 *uzuki* fourth lunar month
7 花 *u(no)hana* refuse from tofu; Japanese snow flower

— 4 —

A 危 629 J346d M2849 KI. *abu(nagaru)* be afraid of, feel uneasy about, shrink from. *aya(bumu)* fear, have misgivings, be doubtful, mistrust. *aya(meru)* wound; murder. *abu(nai), abu(nakkashii), ayau(i)* dangerous; critical, grave; uncertain, unreliable; limping; narrow, close; watch out.
6 気 *abu(na)ge* possibility of danger
地 *kichi* dangerous position, peril
7 局 *kikyoku* crisis
坐 *kiza suru* sit up straight
9 殆 *kitai* danger, jeopardy, distress
急 *kikyū* emergency, crisis
急存亡 *kikyū-sombō* a life-and-death matter
10 峰 *kihō* a high, steep peak
害 *kigai* injury, harm; danger
険 *kiken* danger, risk
険人物 *kiken jimbutsu* dangerous character
険地帯 *kiken chitai* danger zone
険角度 *kiken kakudo* critical angle
険性 *kikensei* riskiness, danger
険物 *kikembutsu* dangerous goods, explosives, combustibles
険信号 *kiken shingō* danger signal, red light
険思想 *kiken shisō* dangerous thoughts
険視 *kikinshi suru* regard as dangerous
11 惧 *kigu* fear, misgivings
12 極 *kikyoku* crisis; grave danger; serious depression
絵 *abu(na)e* suggestive or indecent picture
13 虞 *kigu* fear, misgivings
14 疑 *kigi* fear, misgivings
16 篤 *kitoku* on the verge of death
機 *kiki* crisis, emergency
機一髪 *kiki-ippatsu* critical moment
機打者 *kiki dasha* pinch hitter
機突破 *kiki toppa* crisis relief
18 難 *kinan* danger, hazard, distress
21 懼 *kiku* fear, misgivings

A 印 630 J3075 M2848 IN seal, stamp, mark. *in(suru)* print, imprint, impress. *shirushi* sign, mark; symbol, emblem; badge; evidence; souvenir; token; brand, trademark; signs, indications; omen; seal. *-In-* Indian.
2 刀 *intō* seal-engraving knife
5 本 *impon* printed book
半纏 *shirushibanten* livery coat
6 肉 *inniku* a seal stamp pad
行 *inkō suru* publish
池 *inchi* seal stamp pad
字 *inji* copying
字機 *injiki* typewriter; teletype
7 材 *inzai* seal stock
形 *ingyō* seal, signet
判 *imban, impan* seal, stamp
判師 *imbanshi* seal engraver
8 刻 *inkoku* seal engraving
刻師 *inkokushi* seal engraver
画 *inga* (photographic) print
画紙 *ingashi* (photographic) printing paper
刷 *insatsu* printing
刷人 *insatsunin* printer
刷工 *insatsukō* pressman, printer
刷用 *insatsuyō* for printing
刷所 *insatsujo* press, print shop
刷物 *insatsubutsu* printed matter
刷者 *insatsusha* printer
刷紙 *insatsushi* printing paper
刷術 *insatsujutsu* printing art

刷業 *insatsugyō* printing business
刷機 *insatsuki* printing press
8 度 *Indo* India, Hindustan. *Indo no* Indian, Hindu
度人 *Indojin* Indian, Hindu
度支那 *Indo-Shina* Indo-China
度洋 *Indoyō* Indian Ocean
10 紙 *inshi* revenue stamp
11 許 *shirushibaka(ri)* only a trifle
章 *inshō* seal, signet
12 棉 *Immen* Indian cotton
税 *inzei* royalty (on a book)
象 *inshō* impression
象付 *inshōzu(keru)* impress (someone)
象主義 *inshō shugi* impressionism
象的 *inshōteki* graphic, impressive
象派 *inshōha* impressionist school
14 綬 *inju* seal ribbon
綿 *Immen* Indian cotton
15 褥 *injoku* small thick desk pad
箱 *imbako* seal box
19 譜 *impu* book of seals
22 鑑 *inkan* seal impression
籠 *inrō* seal case; pill box, medicine case

5

B **却** 631/J3551/M2856 **卻** 638/J524a/M2867 KYAKU. *kae(tte)* instead, on the contrary; rather, all the more.
3 下 *kyakka suru* reject, dismiss, ignore
14 説 *sate* well, now

A **卵** 632/J4d71/M2857 RAN ovum. *tamago* egg; spawn, roe; (an expert) in the making.
3 子 *ranshi* ovum, ovule, egg cell
5 生 *ransei* oviparity; produced from eggs
白 *rampaku* white of an egg, albumin
6 色 *tamago iro* yellowish color
7 状 *ranjō* egg-shaped
形 *tamagogata, rankei* egg-shaped, oval
8 泡立器 *tamago awada(te)ki* egg beater
9 胞 *ranbō* egg sac
11 黄 *ran'ō* yolk of an egg
殻 *rankaku* eggshell
細胞 *ransaibō* ovum, egg cell
巣 *ransō* ovary
巣炎 *ransōen* ovaritis
12 焼 *tamagoyaki* fried eggs; omelet
塔 *rantō* oval tombstone
塔場 *rantōba* cemetery
14 管 *rankan* fallopian tube, oviduct
22 嚢 *rannō* egg case

B **即** 633/J4228/M2855 **卽** 639/J-X/M2872 **𠨚** 640/J-X/M2873
SOKU namely; as is. *soku(suru)* conform to, agree with; be adapted to; be based on. *sunawa(chi)* namely, viz. *tsu(ku)* ascend (a throne); take root; begin work; be settled (questions).
4 今 *sokkon* this moment
日 *sokujitsu* the same day
日速達 *sokujitsu sokutatsu* special delivery the same day
5 功 *sokkō* immediate effect
6 行 *sokkō* prompt execution
死 *sokushi* instant death
死者 *sokushisha* persons instantly killed
7 応 *sokuō* adaptation, compliance, conformity
応性 *sokuōsei* relevance
吟 *sokugin suru* improvise (poems or songs)
妙 *sokumyō* tact
売 *sokubai* sale on the spot
位 *sokui* enthronement, coronation, accession. *sokui suru* ascend the throne
位式 *sokuishiki* enthronement ceremony
決 *sokketsu* prompt decision, snap judgment
決処分 *sokketsu shobun* summary conviction
決裁判 *sokketsu saiban* summary trial
8 金 *sokkin, sokukin* spot cash, down payment
刻 *sokkoku* instantly, immediately
効 *sokkō* immediate effect
夜 *sokuya* the same night
事 *sokuji* the matters at hand
10 座 *sokuza* prompt; impromptu
納 *sokunō* prompt payment
席 *sokuseki* extemporaneous, offhand, ad lib
席料理 *sokuseki ryōri* quick lunch
時 *sokuji* promptly, immediately
時払 *sokujibarai* immediate payment
時渡 *sokujiwata(shi)* spot delivery
11 達 *sokutatsu* special delivery
断 *sokudan* prompt decision, snap judgment

[12] 答 *sokutō* prompt answer
買 *sokubai* buying on the spot
[14] 製 *sokusei* making on the spot
[15] 諾 *sokudaku* ready consent
[16] 興 *sokkyō* improvisation, impromptu
興詩 *sokkyōshi* impromptu poem
[18] 題 *sokudai* an impromptu composition; a school task to be done on the spot

6

巷 634 J-X M-X Nonstandard for 巷 1544.

巻 635 J524b M2860 See 巻 1545.

卹 636 J-X M2862 Shutsu, Jutsu have mercy on.

卺 637 J-X M2864 Kin cup.

7

卻 638 J524a M2867 See 却 631.

卽 639 J-X M2872 卽 640 J-X M2873 See 即 633.

B 卸 641 J3237 M2861 Sha. *oro(su)* sell at wholesale; grated (vegetables). *oroshi* wholesale.
[3] 大根 *oro(shi) daikon* grated daikon
[7] 売 *oroshiuri* wholesale
[8] 金 *oro(shi)gane* grater
[10] 値 *oroshine* wholesale price
[11] 商 *oro(shi)shō* wholesaler
問屋 *oro(shi) don'ya* wholesaler

8

卿 642 J362a M2878 See 卿 643.

10

卿 643 J-X M2880 卿 644 J-X M2879 卿 642 J362a M2878
Kei, Kyō you; lord; secretary; state minister.

RAD. 厂 27

Gandare trailing "cliff" or *ichidare* (a trailing *ichi* "one"). Also known as the "trailing goose" radical because it is the enclosure in the character for *gan* "wild goose." Nickname: Cliff.

厂 645 J524c M2890 *karigane* wild goose; also nonstandard for 歴 2964.

2

B 厄 646 J4c71 M2893 Yaku misfortune, bad luck, evil, disaster.
[4] 日 *yakubi* critical day, unlucky day
介 *yakkai* trouble, bother, worry; dependence, support; kindness; obligation
介払 *yakkaibara(i)* good riddance
介物 *yakkaimono* nuisance, encumbrance
介者 *yakkaimono* dependent, hanger-on
介事 *yakkaigoto* trouble, difficulty, burden
[5] 払 *yakubara(i)* good riddance; exorcism. *yakuhara(i)* exorcism
[6] 年 *yakudoshi* critical age, unlucky year
[7] 災 *yakusai* calamity, disaster, accident
[9] 除 *yakuyo(ke)* warding off evil
前 *yakumae* the year before the unlucky year
負 *yakuma(ke)* victimized by the unlucky year
[12] 落 *yakuoto(shi)* escape from evil, exorcism
[18] 難 *yakunan* calamity, misfortune

二亠人亻𠆢儿入八丷冂冖冫几凵刀刂力勹匕匚匸十卜卩【厂】厶又

4

𠩄 647/J-X/M-X Nonstandard for 歷 2964.

6

厓 648/J-X/M2930 See 崖 1488.

7

厖 649/J524d/M2942 Bō large; mix.
3 大 *bōdai* swelling; expansion

B 厘 650/J4e52/M2946 Rin one-tenth of a *sen;* one-tenth of a *bu* (See Weights and Measures).
4 毛 *rimmō* a farthing, a trifle

A 厚 651/J387c/M2949 Kō. *atsu(bottai)* very thick; heavy. *atsu(i)* thick; kind, cordial. *atsu(kamashii)* impudent, shameless, brazen. *atsu(sa)* thickness.
4 手 *atsude no* thick (paper, etc.)
切 *atsugi(ri)* thick slice
化粧 *atsugeshō* heavy makeup
5 皮 *atsugawa* thick hide; shamelessness
氷 *atsugōri* thick ice
生 *kōsei* public welfare, health promotion
生大臣 *Kōsei Daijin* Minister of Welfare
生年金 *kōsei nenkin* welfare pension
生省 *Kōseishō* Welfare Ministry
6 臼 *atsuusu* stone hand mill
地 *atsuji* thick cloth
7 利 *kōri* large profits
志 *kōshi* kindness, kind intention
8 味 *atsumi* thickness
板 *atsuita* plank, thick board; plate glass; heavy metal sheet; heavy brocaded obi
9 相 *Kōshō* Welfare Minister
10 紙 *atsugami* thick paper, cardboard
恩 *kōon* great favor; obligation
11 遇 *kōgū* cordial welcome, kind treatment
情 *kōjō* kindness, favor, hospitality
12 着 *atsugi* wearing thick clothes
13 意 *kōi* kindness, favor
15 誼 *kōgi* your kindness
16 薄 *kōhaku* thickness, partiality
18 顔 *kōgan* impudence, audacity

8

A 原 652/J3836/M2973 Gen original, primitive. *hara* field, plain, prairie, tundra, moor, wilderness. *hara(ppa)* plain. *gen-* original, primitive, primary, fundamental; raw.
2 人 *genjin* primitive man
3 寸 *gensun* actual size, full size
寸大 *gensundai* actual size, full size
子 *genshi* atom
子力 *genshiryoku* atomic energy
子力学 *genshi rikigaku* atomic mechanics
子兵器 *genshi heiki* atomic weapons
子価 *genshika* atomic value
子物理学 *genshi butsurigaku* atomic physics
子症 *genshishō* symptoms of radiation sickness
子病 *genshibyō* radiation sickness
子核 *genshikaku* atomic nucleus
子砲 *genshihō* atomic cannon
子時代 *genshi jidai* atomic age
子破壊機 *genshi hakaiki* cyclotron
子量 *genshiryō* atomic weight
子雲 *genshiun* atomic cloud
子弾頭 *genshi dantō* atomic warhead
子戦争 *genshi sensō* atomic war
子説 *genshi setsu* atomic theory
子爆発 *genshi bakuhatsu* atomic explosion
子爆弾 *genshi bakudan* atomic bomb
4 文 *gembun* the text, the original
木 *gemboku* pulpwood
毛 *gemmō* raw wool
水爆 *gensuibaku* atom and hydrogen bombs
5 句 *genku* the original passage (in a document)
由 *gen'yū* reason, cause
本 *gempon* the original, original copy, script primitive
民 *gemmin* aborigines
生 *gensei* spontaneous generation; primeval, primitive
生林 *genseirin* primeval forest, virgin forest
生動物 *gensei dōbutsu* protozoa

6 糸 *genshi* thread for weaving
虫 *genchū* a protozoan
成岩 *genseigan* primary rocks
成岩石 *gensei ganseki* primary rocks
色 *genshoku* primary color
色写真版 *genshoku shashimban* tricolor printing
因 *gen'in* root cause, factor, occasion, origin, source
因不明 *gen'in fumei* cause unknown
因結果 *gen'in-kekka* cause and effect, causality
7 図 *genzu* original drawing
状 *genjō* original state
告 *genkoku* plaintiff, accuser, prosecutor
住民 *genjūmin* natives, aborigines
判決 *genhanketsu* original decision
材料 *genzairyō* raw material
作 *gensaku* original work
作者 *gensakusha* the original author (of a translated work)
形 *genkei* original form
形質 *genkeishitsu* protoplasm, plasma
8 油 *gen'yu* crude oil
注 *genchū* the original notes
版 *gemban* original edition
物 *gembutsu* the original
画 *genga* original picture
典 *genten* original document
価 *genka* original price
価計算 *genka seisan* cost accounting
始 *genshi* origin; primitive, primeval
始人 *genshijin* primitive man
始林 *genshirin* primeval forest, primeval virgin forest
始的 *genshiteki* primitive, original, primeval
始時代 *genshi jidai* primitive times
始教会 *genshi kyōkai* the early church, the primitive church
9 音 *gen'on* fundamental tone
点 *genten* starting point
品 *gempin* the original article
泉 *gensen* fountainhead, wellspring, source, origin
茸 *haratake* common mushroom
型 *genkei* prototype; model, pattern
則 *gensoku* principle, general rule
則的 *gensokuteki* general
10 料 *genryō* raw materials
紙 *genshi* stencil; silkworm eggsheet
案 *gen'an* original bill, motion, draft, or plan
書 *gensho* the original document
素 *genso* chemical element
振動 *genshindō* fundamental vibration
11 理 *genri* principle, theory, basic truth
野 *gen'ya* waste land, wilderness, moor, field, plain. *harano* plain, field, wilderness, moor, prairie
隊 *gentai* one's home unit
票 *gempyō* stub (of a checkbook)
動 *gendō* motive
動力 *gendōryoku* motive power
著 *gencho* the original work
著者 *genchosha* author
産地 *gensanchi* place of origin; home, habitat
産物 *gensambutsu* primary product
12 註 *genchū* the original notes
裁判 *gensaiban* original judgment
裁判所 *gensaibansho* the original court, court of the first instance
13 詩 *genshi* original poem
鉱 *genkō* ore, raw ore
罪 *genzai* original sin
義 *gengi* original meaning
意 *gen'i* original meaning
14 像 *genzō* original statue
種 *genshu* pure breed
綿 *gemmen* raw cotton
語 *gengo* original word or language
15 論 *genron* theory, principle
審 *genshin* original sentence
器 *genki* standard (for weights and measures)
稿 *genkō* manuscript
稿用紙 *genkō yōshi* manuscript paper
稿料 *genkōryō* payment for a manuscript
稿稼 *genkō kasegi* living on one's writing
稿紙 *genkōshi* manuscript paper
16 糖 *gentō* unrefined sugar
頭 *gentō* the field, the parade ground
17 繊維 *gensen'i* raw fibers, minute fibers
19 簿 *gembo* ledger, original record
爆 *gembaku* atom bomb
爆症 *gembakushō* symptoms of atomic illness
20 籍 *genseki* original domicile, permanent address

2 二亠人亻𠆢儿入八ソ冂冖冫几凵刀刂力勹匕匚匸十卜卩【厂】8 厶又

9

厠 653 J524e M2981 **廁** 1627 J567a M9410 SHI. *kawaya* privy, toilet.

10

厩 654 J3139 M-X See **廐** 660.

厦 655 J524f M2993 KA. SA. SHA. *ie* house.

厥 656 J5250 M2992 KETSU that.
7 冷 *ketsurei* clamminess, coldness of the body

厨 657 J3f5f M3005 **廚** 1631 J-X M-X **廚** 1638 J5724 M9479
CHŪ. ZU. *kuriya* kitchen.
3 子 *zushi* miniature shrine in a temple
7 芥 *chūkai* garbage
芥箱 *chūkaibako* garbage box
8 房 *chūbō* kitchen, galley

12

厰 658 J5252 M3034 See **廠** 1643.

厲 659 J-X M-X REI whetstone; encourage.
6 行 *reikō* encouragement

廐 660 J-X M3006 **厩** 654 J3139 M-X **廏** 1635 J567e M9453 **廄** 1636 J567d M9454 KYŪ. *umaya* barn, stable.
8 肥 *kyūhi* manure, compost
舎 *kyūsha* barn

厮 661 J5251 M3026 **廝** 1641 J5723 M9487 SHI servant; someone of low status.
10 徒 *shito* servant, messenger
15 養 *shiyō* low-ranking servant

厭 662 J315e M3025 EN. YŌ. YŪ. *a(kiru)* get tired of, lose interest in, have enough. *a(kasu)* satiate, surfeit; bore, tire, weary. *ito(u)* dislike, hate; grudge (doing), spare (oneself); be weary of; take (good) care of, *agu(mu)* be weary of doing. *i(yarashii), ito(washii), i(yana)* detestable, diagreeable.
2 人 *enjin* misanthropy
人者 *enjinsha* misanthrope
5 世 *ensei* pessimism, weariness with life
世主義 *ensei shugi* pessimism
世的 *enseiteki* pessimistic
世家 *enseika* pessimist
世悲観者 *ensei-hikansha* pessimist
世観 *enseikan* pessimistic view of life, pessimism
8 味 *iyami* disagreeableness; gaudiness; mannerism; sarcasm
性 *a(ki)shō* fickle nature, flighty temperament
11 悪 *en'o suru* dislike, detest
13 戦 *ensen* war weariness

15

A **厳** 663 J3837 M3048′ **嚴** 924 J536e M4589 GON. GEN strictness, severity. *gen ni* strictly, severely, rigidly. *gen (ni) suru* fortify, strengthen, secure. *gen(taru)* strict, severe, stern. *ikame(shii)* solemn, majestic; dreadful, stern, ostentatious. *kibi(shii)* severe, strict, stern; intense (cold). *ogoso(kana)* austere, majestic, dignified, stately, awful, impressive. *ikatsu(i)* grim, stern.
4 父 *gempu* your honored father
5 冬 *gentō* severe winter
正 *gensei* strictness, impartiality, exactness, rigidness
正中立 *gensei chūritsu* strict neutrality
正科学 *gensei kagaku* exact science
6 刑 *genkei* severe punishment
旨 *genshi* strict order; your order
守 *genshu* strict observance
存 *genson* real existence
7 戒 *genkai* strict guard
君 *genkun* your honored father
8 命 *gemmei* strict order, peremptory command
9 律 *genritsu* strict law
科 *genka* severe punishment, rigorous measures
封 *gempū suru* seal hermetically

重 *genjū* strictness, rigor, severity. *genjū na* firm, strong, secure
10 格 *genkaku* strictness, rigor, austerity, severity
秘 *gempi* strict secrecy, top-secret
訓 *genkun* strict instruction
容 *gen'yō* stern expression
11 達 *gentatsu* strict order
探 *gentan* strict search, sharp lookout
密 *gemmitsu* strictness
粛 *genshuku* gravity, solemnity, seriousness, dignity, rigor, austerity
12 寒 *genkan* intense cold
暑 *gensho* extreme heat
然 *genzen to* solemnly, gravely, majestically, authoritatively
13 誅 *genchū suru* punish severely
禁 *genkin* ban, interdict, strict prohibition
14 選 *gensen* careful selection
酷 *genkoku* severity, rigor
罰 *gembatsu* severe punishment, rigorous measures
15 談 *gendan* strong protest, demand for an explanation, serious talk

RAD. 厶 28

Mu (the katakana). Nickname: *Kana Mu*.

厶 664 / J5253 / M3057 SHI. *watakushi* I.

3

A **去** 665 / J356e / M3070 KYO. KO. *sa(ru) vi* leave, move away, quit; pass, elapse, be gone, be over; be distant from., *vt* remove, eliminate, get rid of; divorce. *sa(ru)-* used in specifying a certain day in the past, last (June).
4 文 *sa(ri)bumi* bill of sale (for land); bill of divorcement
6 行 *sa(ri)-yu(ku)* go away
年 *kyonen, kozo* last year
7 状 *sa(ri)jō* bill of sale (for land); bill of divorcement
来 *kyorai* coming and going; past and future
11 頃 *sa(ru)koro* formerly, some years ago, a few days ago
12 就 *kyoshū* course of action; attitude
13 勢 *kyosei* castration; enervation; emasculation
勢牛 *kyoseigyū* bullock, ox, steer
18 難 *sa(ri)gata(i)* hard to part with

6

A  666 / J3b32 / M3090  667 / J5254 / M3098 SHIN. SAN three; going; coming; visiting. *mai(ru)* go; come; call, visit; visit a shrine; be defeated; be nonplussed; be madly in love; die. *mai(raseru)* beat, floor (someone), bring (someone) to his knees. *san(jiru), san(zuru)* go; visit; come. *(o)mai(ri)* visits to shrines or temples.
3 上 *sanjō suru* call on, visit
与 *san'yo* participation (in public affairs); counselor, consultant
与者 *san'yosha* participant
与官 *san'yokan* parliamentary councilor
4 内 *sandai* palace visit
5 加 *sanka* participation, joining, intervention
加者 *sankasha* participant, entrant
6 向 *sankō suru* proceed to
列 *sanretsu* attendance, presence, participation
列者 *sanretsusha* attendant
会 *sankai* attendance (at a meeting)
会者 *sankaisha* attendance, attendee
考 *sankō* reference, consultation
考人 *sankōnin* a person given as a reference
考図書館 *sankō toshokan* reference library
考品 *sankōhin* reference materials
考書 *sankōsho* reference book
考書目 *sankō shomoku* bibliography
考資料 *sankō shiryō* reference data
8 拝 *sampai* worship, visits to shrines or tombs
画 *sankaku suru* take part in planning
事 *sanji* secretary, councilor

2 二亠人亻𠆢儿入八丷冂冖冫几凵刀刂力勹匕匚匸十卜卩厂【厶】6 又

事会 *sanjikai* a council
事官 *sanjikan* counselor
9 洛 *sanraku* going to the capital
院 *San'in* House of Councilors
政 *sansei* participation in government
政官 *sanseikan* parliamentary under-secretary
政権 *sanseiken* suffrage, franchise
10 酌 *sanshaku suru* compare and choose the good; consult, refer to
宮 *sangū* visit to the Ise Shrine
差 *shinshi(taru)* uneven, of different lengths
11 道 *sandō* approaching a shrine
堂 *sandō* visiting a home or temple
12 着 *sanchaku* arrival; payment on sight
集 *sanshū* assembling (of people)
勤交代 *sankin kōtai* daimyos' alternating Edo residence
賀 *sanga* congratulatory palace visit
賀者 *sangasha* congratulatory visitors
賀帳 *sangachō* congratulatory visitors' book
13 殿 *sanden* palace visit
禅 *sanzen* Zen meditation
詣 *sankei* temple or shrine visit, pilgrimage, homage
戦 *sansen* participation in a war
照 *sanshō* reference, comparison
16 謀 *sambō* staff officer; participation in planning
謀本部 *Sambō Hombu* General Staff Headquarters
謀長 *sambōchō* chief of staff
18 観 *sankan* visit, inspection
観人 *sankannin* visitor
20 議 *sangi* councilor; participation in government
議院 *Sangiin* House of Councilors, Upper House
議院議員 *Sangiin giin* member of the House of Councilors
22 籠 *sanrō suru* retiring (to a temple or shrine) for prayer

— 9 —

參 667 J5254 M3098 See **参** 666.

RAD.  **29**

Mata again. Variant: 又. Nickname: Again.

B **又** 668 J4b74 M3115 Yū. *mata* again, and, furthermore; on the other hand. *mata (moya)* again. *mata (shitemo)* again. *mata (wa)* or.
2 又 *matamata* again and again
3 小作 *mata kosaku* subtenancy, sublease
4 日 *mata(no)hi* another day; the next day
木 *matagi* forked tree, forked branch
5 写 *matautsu(shi)* copying again
6 名 *mata (no) na* alias, another name
7 弟子 *mata deshi* indirect pupil
10 借 *mataga(ri)* subtenancy
候 *matazoro* again
家来 *matagerai* secondary retainer
12 買 *mataga(i)* buying through an agent
無 *mata na(i), mata (to) na(i)* unique, matchless, unparalleled, never again
貸 *mataga(shi)* sublease
14 聞 *matagi(ki)* hearsay
隣 *matadonari* second door from here
15 請 *matau(ke)* subcontract
請負 *mataukeoi* subcontract
16 頼 *matadano(mi)* indirect request

— 1 —

叉 669 J3a35 M3116 Sa. Sha. *mata* fork (of a road); crotch (of a tree).
4 手網 *sadeami* dip net, scoop net
10 庫 *azekura* ancient log cabin
14 銃 *sajū* stacked arms

— 2 —

B **及** 670 J355a M3118′ **夃** 671 J-X M3118 Kyū. *oyo(bosu)* exert, exercise, cause. *oyo(bu)* reach, come up to, amount to; befall, happen to; extend; match, equal. *oyo(banai)* unnecessary; unattainable. *oyo(bi)* and, as well as.

5 乍 *oyo(bazu)naga(ra)* to the best of my ability, poor though it may be
11 第 *kyūdai* passing an examination
第者 *kyūdaisha* successful examinee
第点 *kyūdaiten* passing grade
12 落 *kyūraku* success or failure (in exams)
13 腰 *oyo(bi)goshi* a bent back
18 難 *oyo(bi)gata(i)* hard to attain to

A **友** 672 J4d27 M3119 YŪ. *tomo* friend, companion, pal.
2 人 *yūjin* friend
6 邦 *yūhō* friendly nation, ally
交 *yūkō* friendship, amity, companionship
好 *yūkō* friendship, amity, companionship
好条約 *yūkō jōyaku* treaty of friendship
好国 *yūkōkoku* friendly nation
好的 *yūkōteki* friendly, amicable
好通商航海 *yūkō tsūshō kōkai* (treaty of) friendship, commerce, and navigation
8 朋 *yūhō* friend
宜 *yūgi* friendship, friendly relations
9 垣 *tomogaki* friend
軍 *yūgun* allied army, friendly troops
10 討 *tomou(chi)* friends shooting one another
党 *yūtō* allied political party
11 情 *yūjo* friendship, fellowship
釣 *tomozuri* fishing with decoys
達 *tomodachi* friend, companion
達付合 *tomodachizu(ki)a(i)* friendly relations
達中斐 *tomodachigai* true friendship
13 義 *yugi* friendship's responsibilities
愛 *yūai* friendship
愛結婚 *yūai kekkon* companionate marriage
15 誼 *yūgi* friendship, friendly relations
誼国家 *yūgi kokka* friendly nation

B **双** 673 J4150 M3125 **雙** 6511 J5256 M42116 SŌ a pair; a set; comparison; counter for pairs.
2 十節 *Sōjūsetsu* the Double Tenth, October 10, National Foundation Day of the Republic of China (Taiwan)
3 子 *futago* twins, twin
子葉 *sōshiyō* dicotyledon
子葉植物 *sōshiyō shokubutsu* dicotyledon
4 手 *sōshu* both hands
方 *sōhō* both sides, both parties. *sōhō no* mutual, both
互 *sōgo* mutual, reciprocal
六 *sugoroku* a child's dice game
5 生 *sōsei* bearing twins; twins
生児 *sōseiji* twins
6 成 *futana(ri)* hermaphrodite
曲線 *sōkyokusen* hyperbola
8 肩 *sōken* shoulders
9 発 *sōhatsu* two-motored
発機 *sōhatsuki* two-motored plane
10 紙 *sōshi* copybook; notebook; storybook; fiction; books
胴船 *sōdōsen* catamaran
胴機 *sōdōki* twin-fuselage plane
峰駱駝 *sōhō rakuda* two-humped camel, Bactrian camel
11 眸 *sōbō* the pupils of both eyes; both eyes
脚 *sōkyaku* both feet
務契約 *sōmu keiyaku* bilateral agreement
眼 *sōgan* both eyes; binocular
眼鏡 *sōgankyō* field glasses, binoculars
12 幅 *sōfuku* pair of hanging scrolls
葉 *futaba* bud, sprout
殻類 *sōkokurui* bivalves
13 暗車 *sōansha* twin propellers
15 輪 *sorin* two wheels
16 頭 *sōtō no* double-headed
蹄 *sōtei* cloven foot
蹄獣 *sōteijū* cloven-hoofed animal
17 翼 *sōyoku* both wings
18 璧 *sōheki* pair of bright jewels; matchless things; matchless people

A **反** 674 J483f M3127 HON. TAN roll of cloth (c. 10 yds.); .245 acres, 300 *tsubo*. HAN antithesis, opposite, antagonism; anti-. *so(ru) vi* warp; curve; lean backward. *so(rasu), so(raseru) vt* bend, warp. *han(suru)* be inconsistent with, oppose; contradict; transgress; rebel. *kae(ru) vi* change, turn over, turn upside down. *kae(su) vt* change, turn over, turn upside down. *sori* warp, curvature, curve, arch. *kae(tte)* instead, on the contrary; rather, all the more.
4 日 *hannichi* anti-Japanese
毛 *hammō* reclaimed wool
比 *hampi* inverse ratio

比例 *hampirei* inverse proportion
5 目 *hommoku* antagonism, hostility
古 *hogu, hogo* wastepaper
古籠 *hogukago* wastebasket
6 米 *hambei* anti-American
返 *so(ri)-ka(eru)* warp; bend backward; throw the head (or shoulders) back, throw out the chest
吐 *hedo* vomiting
合 *sori (ga) a(wanai)* be unable to cooperate
共 *hankyō* anticommunist
7 身 *hanshin* bending backward, strutting. *so(ri)mi* strutting, sticking out the chest
応 *hannō* reaction, response
攻 *hankō* counteroffensive
抗 *hankō* resistance, insubordination, defiance, opposition, hostility, rebellion
別 *tambetsu* acreage, land area
形 *so(ri)kata* warped shape
作用 *hansayō* reaction
社会的 *hanshakaiteki* antisocial
乱 *hanran* rebellion
乱者 *hanransha* rebel, insurgent
乱軍 *hanran gun* rebel army
対 *hantai* opposition, resistance, antagonism, hostility, contrast, objection, dissension; reverse, opposite, vice versa
対色 *hantaishoku* clashing colors
対者 *hantaisha* opposer, adversary, dissenter
対咬合 *hantai kōgō* cross bite (with lower jaw protruding)
対党 *hantaitō* opposition party
対訊問 *hantai jimmon* cross-examination
対側 *hantaigawa* the opposite side
対貿易風 *hantai bōekifū* antitrade winds
対語 *hantaigo* antonym
対論 *hantairon* opposing argument
8 逆 *hangyaku* treason, treachery, rebellion, insurrection, mutiny
歩 *tambu* one-tenth hectare (see Weights and Measures)
英 *han-Ei* anti-British
宗教改革 *Hanshūkyō Kaikaku* Counter Reformation
物 *tammono* cloth; textiles, drapery; dry goods, piece goods
物屋 *tammonoya* dry-goods store
9 面 *hammen ni* on the other hand
映 *han'ei* reflection, influence
独 *han-Doku* anti-German
則 *hansoku* transgression; default; foul; balk; irregularity
故 *hogu, hogo* wastepaper
省 *hansei* reflection, introspection; reconsideration; meditation, contemplation
革命 *hankakumei* counterrevolution
政府 *hanseifu* antigovernment
政府党 *hanseifutō* opposition party
軍 *hangun* antimilitary
軍的 *hangunteki* antimilitary
発 *hampatsu suru* repel, repulse; rebound; recover; resist
発力 *hampatsuryoku* repellent force; resiliency, elasticity
10 哺 *hampo* caring for one's parents in return
徒 *hanto* rebels, insurgents
芻 *hansū* chewing the cud, rumination
射 *hansha* reflection, reverberation
射作用 *hansha sayō* reflex action
射的 *hanshateki* reflective; reflecting; reflexive. *hanshateki ni* reminiscingly
射運動 *hansha undō* reflex action
射望遠鏡 *hansha bōenkyō* reflecting telescope
射鏡 *hanshakyō* reflector
11 問 *hammon suru* cross-examine; retort; ask in return
側 *hansoku suru* turn over in bed
転 *hanten suru* turn around, roll over, turn from side to side
動 *handō* reaction; recoil, kick
動主義 *handō shugi* reactionism
動的 *handōteki* reactionary
動派 *handōha* the reactionaries
動革命 *handō kakumei* counterrevolution
動思想 *handō shisō* reactionary ideas
動家 *handōka* a reactionary
12 歯 *soppa* projecting teeth
間 *hankan* counterintelligence
復 *hampuku* repetition
証 *hanshō* counterevidence
訴 *hanso* counteraction, counterclaim
落 *hanraku* reaction
植民主義 *hanshokumin shugi* anticolonialism

13 賊 *hanzoku* rebel
戦 *hansen* antiwar
数 *hansū* reciprocal number
感 *hankan* antipathy, animosity
照 *hanshō* reflection, influence
意語 *han'igo* antonym
14 旗 *hanki* standard of revolt
語 *hango* irony; rhetorical question; antonym; word in reverse
駁 *hambaku, hampaku* refutation, rebuttal
歌 *hanka* tanka appendage to a long poem
15 撥 *hampatsu* repel, repulse; rebound; recover; resist
論 *hanron* refutation; rebuttal
影 *han'ei* reflection, influence
撃 *hangeki* counterattack
16 噬 *hanzei* turning against one's master; returning evil for good
橋 *so(ri) hashi, so(ri)bashi* arched bridge
18 覆 *hampuku suru* reverse; repeat
19 響 *hankyō* echo, reverberation; repercussion, reaction, influence
繰返 *so(k)ku(ri)-ka(eru)* throw one's head back (boastfully)
20 騰 *hantō* reactionary price rise

3

A **収** 675 / J3L7U / M3128 **収** 676 / J-X / M3137 **收** 2329 / J5a40 / M13110

SHŪ income. *osa(meru)* obtain, reap; dedicate, consecrate; pay; supply; store; finish; collect; restore, replacc; accept (a present); bury, gather; rally (troops); sheathe (the sword). *osa(maru)* be paid; be restored; stay (in the stomach); look composed; be contented; be satisfied; be settled.

2 入 *shūnyū* receipts, income, revenue, proceeds, earnings
入印紙 *shūnyū inshi* revenue stamp
入役 *shūnyūyaku* government treasurer
入源 *shūnyūgen* source of income
4 支 *shūshi* income and expenditure
5 用 *shūyō* expropriation
7 没 *shūbotsu* confiscation of possessions
束 *shūsoku suru* tie up
8 金 *shūkin* collecting; collections
受 *shūju suru* receive
9 拾 *shūshū suru* get under control, save (the situation)
10 益 *shūeki* earnings, proceeds, returns
差 *shūsa* aberration
納 *shūnō* crop, harvest, receipts
納係 *shūnōgakari* receiving teller
納額 *shūnōgaku* amount received
容 *shūyō* accommodation, seating, housing custody, admission; entering (in a dictionary)
容力 *shūyōryoku* capacity, accommodation
容所 *shūyōjo* home, asylum, camp
容者 *shūyōsha* inmates
容能力 *shūyō nōryoku* capacity, accommodation
容患者 *shūyō kanja* inpatients
容設備 *shūyō setsubi* accommodations
11 得 *shūtoku suru* receive
12 着 *shūchaku* sorption (in physical chemistry)
集 *shūshū* gathering up; collection; accumulation
税 *shūzei* tax collection, taxation
税人 *shūzeinin* tax collector
税吏 *shūzeiri* tax collector
税所 *shūzeisho* tax-collection office
税官 *shūzeikan* revenue officer
13 賄 *shūwai* accepting bribes, corruption, graft
14 奪 *shūdatsu suru* rob
蔵 *shūzō* garnering, collection
監 *shūkan* imprisonment
監力 *shūkanryoku* cell capacity
監状 *shūkanjō* commitment warrant
16 縛 *shubaku suru* arrest and tie up
輯 *shūshū* gathering up
録 *shūroku suru* collect, record
覧 *shūran suru* grasp; win over
獲 *shūkaku* harvest, harvesting, ingathering, crop
獲感謝祭 *Shūkaku Kanshasai* Thanksgiving Day; harvest festival
17 斂 *shūren* exaction (of taxes); convergence, contraction, astriction
縮 *shūshuku* contraction, shrinking, constriction
縮期血圧 *shūshukuki ketsuatsu* systolic blood pressure
18 繭 *shūken* cocoon crop
穫 *shūkaku* harvest, harvesting, ingathering, crop

穫予想 *shūkaku yosō* crop estimate
穫物 *shūkakubutsu* the harvest, the yield
穫高 *shūkakudaka* the income, the crop, the yield
穫時 *shūkakuji* time of harvest
穫期 *shūkakuki* harvest time
24 攬 *shūran* grasping, winning over

6

B **叔** 677 / J3d47 / M3154 SHUKU uncle; youth.
4 父 *oji* uncle (parent's younger brother)
5 母 *oba* aunt (parent's younger sister)

A **受** 678 / J3c75 / M3159 JU receive. *u(keru)* receive, accept, take, get, obtain; catch (a ball); stop (a blow), parry; answer (the phone); undergo (an operation); take (an exam); sustain (a loss); be exposed to (ridicule); face, front on; inherit; catch the public fancy. *uka(ru)* pass (an examination). *u(ke)* receiving; receptacle; support, prop; (pot) holder; popularity; agreement.
2 入 *u(ke)-i(reru)* accept, receive; assent to, grant
入体制 *u(ke)i(re) taisei* preparedness (for new personnel), reception set-up (for immigrants)
入態勢 *u(ke)i(re) taisei* preparedness (for new personnel), reception set-up (for immigrants)
3 口 *u(ke)guchi, u(ke)kuchi* mouth with protruding lower lip
4 木 *u(ke)gi* support
止 *u(ke)-to(meru)* stop, catch; parry, ward off
太刀 *u(ke)dachi* defensive position
5 皿 *u(ke)zara* saucer
払 *u(ke)hara(i)* receipts and payment
出 *u(ke)-da(su)* redeem, ransom, buy out, pay off, take out of pawn
付 *u(ke)-tsu(keru)* receive, accept (an application). *uketsuke* receipt, acceptance; receptionist; information desk
付係 *uketsukegakari* receptionist, usher
6 肉 *juniku* incarnation
任 *junin suru* be nominated, accept an appointment
合 *u(ke)a(i)* guarantee, assurance
血者 *juketsusha* blood recipient
刑 *jukei suru* serve time
刑者 *jukeisha* convict, convicted person
7 身 *ukemi* being acted upon, passivity, defensive position; passive voice; safe ways to fall
戒 *jukai* Buddhist confirmation, becoming a Buddhist
戻 *u(ke)-modo(su)* redeem, ransom, buy out, pay off, take out of pawn
売 *ukeu(ri)* retailing; second hand (knowledge)
8 命 *jumei* commission (of an official)
直 *u(ke)-nao(su)* receive (baptism) again
苦 *Juku* the Passion (of Christ)
取 *u(ke)-to(ru)* receive, take delivery, accept; believe; understand, interpret. *uketori* receipt, acknowledgment
取人 *uketorinin* recipient, payee
取帳 *uketorichō* receipt book
取済 *uketorizu(mi)* payment received
取証 *uketorishō* receipt, voucher
9 胎 *jutai* conception, fertilization
持 *u(ke)-mo(tsu)* take charge of, be in charge of. *ukemo(chi)* charge (of something); matter in one's charge
持時間 *ukemo(chi) jikan* teaching hours
信 *jushin* receipt of a message; radio reception
信人 *jushinnin* addressee
信機 *jushinki* receiver
洗 *jusen* baptism (by sprinkling). *jusen suru* be baptized
洗者 *jusensha* a person baptized by sprinkling
洗数 *jusensū* number baptized (by sprinkling)
負 *u(ke)-o(u)* contract for, undertake. *ukeoi* a contract
負人 *ukeoinin* contractor
負仕事 *ukeoi shigoto* job work, contract work
負師 *ukeoishi* contractor
負賃金 *ukeoi chingin* piecework pay
10 流 *u(ke)-naga(su)* ward off, parry, turn aside
粉 *jufun* pollinization, fertilization
納 *junō* receipt, acceptance
託 *jutaku* trust, custody, charge
容 *u(ke)-i(reru), juyō suru* accept
配者 *juhaisha* recipient of rations
益 *jueki suru* benefit by

益者 *juekisha* beneficiary
浸 *jushin suru* be baptized (by immersion)
浸者 *jushinsha* a person baptized by immersion
浸数 *jushinsū* number baptized (by immersion)
11 授 *juju* receiving and giving
理 *juri suru* entertain (an action against), accept, take up (a report)
動 *judō* passiveness, passivity
動的 *judōteki* passive
動免疫 *judō men'eki* passive immunity
動態 *judōtai* passive voice
12 検 *juken suru* be subjected to an investigation
訴 *juso* acceptance of a legal suit
診 *jushin* getting a physical examination
答 *u(ke)kota(e)* reply, response
給者 *jukyūsha* pensioner
註 *juchū suru* accept an order
註額 *juchūgaku* volume of orders
渡 *ukewata(shi)* delivery, transfer, payment; give-and-take
渡日 *ukewata(shi)bi* settlement day, delivery day
渡期日 *ukewata(shi) kijitsu* delivery date
13 傷 *jushō suru* get hurt; get wounded
損 *u(ke)-sokona(u)* fail to parry; fail to catch, miss ⌈over
継 *u(ke)-tsu(gu)* inherit, succeed to, take
話器 *juwaki* receiver, headphones
話機 *juwaki* receiver, headphones
14 精 *jusei* fertilization, pollination
膏者 *jukōsha* anointed one
像 *juzō suru* receive TV broadcasts
像機 *juzōki* TV set
領 *juryō* receipt, acceptance
領者 *juryōsha* receiver, recipient
領高 *juryōdaka* amount received, receipts
領書 *juryōsho* receipt
領証 *juryōshō* receipt
15 諾 *judaku* acceptance
賞 *jushō* receiving a prize
賞者 *jushōsha* prize winner
17 講 *jukō* taking lectures
講生 *jukōsei* trainee; a person present at a lecture class; a participant
18 贈 *jusō suru, juzō suru* receive a present
難 *junan* ordeal, trouble, sufferings; the crucifixion
難日 *Junambi* Good Friday
難曲 *junankyoku* passion (a musical composition)
難者 *junansha* sufferer
難週 *Junanshū* Passion Week
難節 *Junansetsu* Lent
難劇 *junangeki* passion play
験 *juken suru* take an examination
験生活 *juken seikatsu* life while preparing for examination
験者 *jukensha* examinee
験学校 *juken gakkō* preparatory school, a school preparing students for examinations
験地獄 *juken jigoku* examination hell
験科 *jukenka* examination-coaching course
験料 *jukenryō* examination fee
験票 *jukenhyō* examination admission ticket
験資格 *juken shikaku* qualifications for taking an examination
験準備 *juken jumbi* preparing for examinations

A **取** 679 / J3c68 / M3158 SHU. *to(ru)* take, hold, seize, catch, capture; fetch; receive, procure, obtain; adopt (a measure); engage (graduates); choose; order (foodstuffs); pick, pluck; make, produce; eat; set up (camp); charge; administer; transact; take (pains); make out (the meaning); remove; take off (one's hat); take out (spots); strike out (words); weed, catch (fish); deprive of; steal; capture (territory), annex; need, require; reserve (rooms); subscribe to; press (a point home); take (a picture); possess. *to(reru)* can be held, can take; come off, come apart, be off, be removed; be relieved (of pain); be obtained, be produced; be caught; be earned; come out (well) (a photo); require (time); be interpreted as; can get; let (light) in; take (one's measure); can feel (the pulse); take (a pen and write). *to(tchimeru)* drive into a corner, take to task, take it out on. *to(ttoku), to(tte)o(ku)* keep, hold, save, reserve, set aside. *to(tte)* to, for, in the case of; including.

2 入 *to(ri)-i(reru)* take in, gather in, harvest; accept, adopt, introduce

(customs). *to(ri)-i(ru)* get into (someone's favor), win (another's heart), ingratiate oneself with. *to(ri)i(re)* ingathering, taking in, harvest

入口 *toriireguchi* intake

入祭 *To(ri)i(re) (no) Matsu(ri)* Harvest Festival

3 下 *to(ri)-sa(geru)* withdraw, dismiss. *to(ri)-o(rosu)* take down, lower, pull down, lift down, let down, drop

上 *to(ri)-a(geru)* take up, pick up; deal with; adopt, accept, listen to; dispossess, expropriate, confiscate, revoke; deliver (a baby)

4 手 *to(ri)te* receiver, recipient, taker. *to(t)te* handle, knob, grip

方 *to(ri)kata* way of taking (a photo)

止 *to(ri)-ya(meru)* stop, withdraw. *to(ri)-to(meru)* ascertain, make sure, save (a life). *to(ri)ya(me)* cancellation

切 *to(ri)ki(ri)* taking and not returning

分 *to(ri)-wa(keru)* divide, separate; distribute; assort. *to(ri)wa(ke), to(ri)wa(kete)* especially, particularly. *toribun* share, portion

片付 *to(ri)-katazu(keru)* put in order, put away dispose of, solve, finish; marry off; get married

込 *to(ri)-ko(mu)* take in; introduce into; embezzle; be in confusion; get into favor with

込事 *toriko(mi)goto* confusion, complications

込詐欺 *toriko(mi) sagi* confidence game

引 *torihiki* transactions, deal, business

引先 *torihikisaki* customer, client, business connection

引所 *torihikijo, torihikisho* stock exchange

引高 *torihikidaka* turnover, volume of business

引員 *torihikiin* broker

引量 *torihikiryō* volume of business

引銀行 *torihiki ginkō* one's bankers

5 広 *to(ri)-hiro(geru), to(ri)-hiro(meru)* enlarge, extend; widen; spread (to air something)

代 *to(tte) ka(waru)* supplant, supersede, replace

外 *to(ri)-hazu(su)* remove, take away; dismantle; demount

払 *to(ri)-hara(u)* remove, take away, demolish, dismantle

去 *to(ri)-sa(ru)* take away, remove, leave out

出 *to(ri)-da(su)* take out; produce; pick out

仕切 *to(ri)-shiki(ru)* manage alone

立 *to(ri)-ta(teru)* collect; employ, appoint; promote; patronize; exact (taxes). *torita(te)* collection, levy; appointment, employment; promotion; patronage. *torita(te) no* fresh, freshly picked. *torita(tete)* particularly

立金 *toritatekin* collected money

付 *to(ri)-tsu(keru)* draw, cash; patronize; furnish, install; establish (regulations). *to(ri)-tsu(ku)* hold fast to, catch hold of; possess, obsess, haunt. *toritsu(ke)* run on a bank; drawing, cashing; installation, furnishing. *toritsu(ke) no* regular (tradesman). *toritsu(ki)* beginning; rudiments; foot (of a hill road); edge (of town). *to(t)tsu(ki)* the beginning; the first you come to; first impression

付工事 *toritsuke kōji* installation (of built-in furnishings)

付品 *toritsu(ke)hin* fixtures, furnishings

付様 *to(tte) tsu(keta) yō na* artificial, affected, forced, unnatural

6 回 *to(ri)-mawa(su)* manage, treat

尽 *to(ri)-tsuku(su)* take all

成 *torina(shi)* arrangement; influence; mediation, intercession; good offices. *to(ri)-na(su)* mediate, intervene, intercede for, recommend

交 *to(ri)-ma(zeru)* mix, put together. *to(ri)-kawa(su)* exchange, interchange. *to(ri)maze(te)* all together, in all

合 *to(ri)-a(u)* take each other's (hand); scramble for; take notice of; have to deal with. *to(ri)-a(waseru)* assort, arrange, group, combine, mix; match, garnish. *toria(i)* a scramble. *toriawa(se)* combination

返 *tori-kae(su)* get back, regain, retrieve, recover; recuperate; recall; undo; make good, make up for, redeem; withdraw. *to(tte) kae(su)* turn back, hurry back. *to(ri)kae(shi)* recovery, making up for, catching up

返付 *to(ri)kae(shi) (no) tsu(kanai)* irrevocable, irretrievable, irreparable
次 *to(ri)-tsu(gu)* act as agent; intermediate; transmit, convey. *toritsu(gi)* agency; agent; intermediation; relaying (a telegram)
次店 *toritsugiten* agency
次所 *toritsugijo* agency
次商 *toritsugishō* agency
扱 *to(ri)-atsuka(u)* treat; manage; handle, manipulate; conduct, transact; take charge of; accept (telegrams). *toriatsuka(i)* treatment, dealing, service; handling, manipulation; transaction, management
扱人 *toriatsukainin* agent, person in charge
扱所 *toriatsukaijo* office, agency
扱法 *toriatsukaihō* method of handling
7 足 *to(runi)ta(ranai)* beneath notice, insignificant, trifling
囲 *to(ri)-kako(mu)* surround, crowd against
戻 *to(ri)-modo(su)* take back, regain, resume, recover, redeem, recapture
抑 *to(ri)-osa(eru)* catch, seize, capture; quiet (a horse)
材 *shuzai* choice of subject. *shuzai suru* gather material for a report
決 *to(ri)-ki(meru)* arrange, agree upon, settle, make an appointment. *toriki(me)* arrangement, agreement, settlement
糺 *to(ri)-tada(su)* ask, demand; investigate
乱 *to(ri)-mida(su)* mess up, disturb; be agitated
来 *to(tte) ku(ru)* fetch, go and get
沙汰 *to(ri)zata, to(ri)sata* rumor, gossip, criticism, comment
8 固 *to(ri)-kata(meru)* defend, fortify
逃 *to(ri)-ni(gasu)* let escape, fail to catch, miss
所 *to(ri)dokoro* worth, merit, redeeming feature
押 *to(ri)-osa(eru)* catch, seize, capture; quiet (a horse)
拡 *to(ri)-hiro(geru), to(ri)-hiro(meru)* enlarge, extend; widen; spread (to air something)
拉 *to(ri)-hishi(gu)* defeat, crush
取 *to(ri)do(ri) no* various

舎 *shusha* adoption or rejection, choice, option
並 *to(ri)-nara(beru)* arrange, place in order, marshal, put side by side, display, serve (food); enumerate; compare with
直 *to(rimo)nao(sazu)* namely, in other words. *to(ri)-nao(su)* recover, mend, change one's mind; get a firmer hold of, wrestle over again
逆上 *to(ri)-nobo(seru)* be dizzy, be feverish, get excited, be enthusiastic over
放題 *to(ri)hōdai* taking as much as you wish
9 持 *to(ri)-mo(tsu)* treat, entertain; mediate; recommend. *torimo(chi)* treatment, reception; mediation; recommendation
柄 *to(ri)e* worth, merit, redeeming feature
糾 *to(ri)-tada(su)* ask, demand; investigate
計 *to(ri)-haka(rau)* manage, arrange, dispose of, settle, deal with
除 *to(ri)-no(keru)* remove, clear away, get rid of; make an exception of; lay aside, reserve. *to(ri)-nozo(ku)* remove, take away; set apart
前 *to(ri)mae* portion, share
急 *to(ri)-iso(gu)* hurry. *to(ri)iso(gi)* in haste
巻 *to(ri)-ma(ku)* surround, encircle, enclose. *torima(ki)* followers, adherents
巻連 *torima(ki) ren* followers, adherents
10 高 *to(re)daka* catch, yield
進 *to(ri)-susu(mu)* go on to the finals
捉 *to(t)tsuka(maeru)* catch, seize, arrest, capture. *to(t)tsuka(maru)* be caught, can catch
捌 *to(ri)-saba(ku)* manage; settle, judge, try
残 *to(ri)-noko(su)* leave behind
紛 *to(ri)-magi(reru)* be in confusion; be perplexed; be busily engaged
粉 *to(ri)ko* rice meal
殺 *to(ri)-koro(su)* curse (a person) to death, haunt to death
留 *to(ri)-to(meru)* ascertain, make sure; save (a life)
留無 *to(ri)to(me)na(i),*

to(ri)to(meno)na(i) rambling, vague, incoherent, absurd
消 *to(ri)-ke(su)* cancel, nullify, revoke, rescind, withdraw, retract, take back, repeal, quash, abrogate, annul, countermand, recall
消不能 *torike(shi)-funō* irrevocable
消記事 *torike(shi) kiji* announcement for correction
消権 *torike(shi)ken* right to rescind
11 掛 *to(ri)-kaka(ru), to(k)kaka(ru)* begin, set to work, proceed to business. *to(ri)-ka(keru)* begin to take
捨 *shusha* adoption or rejection, choice, option
混 *to(ri)-ma(zeru)* mix
舵 *to(ri)kaji* port; turning (a ship) to port
寄 *to(ri)-yo(seru)* send for, write for, procure, order, obtain
崩 *to(ri)kuzu(su)* break down, dismantle; tear down, demolish
得 *to(ri)doku* gain, profit. *shutoku* acquisition, possession. *to(ri)e* worth, merit, redeeming feature
得権 *shutokuken* ownership
組 *to(ri)-ku(mu)* wrestle; be matched against, tackle. *torikumi* match, bout
組合 *to(k)ku(mi)-a(u)* grapple, tussle
12 遣 *to(ri)ya(ri)* exchange, give-and-take
違 *to(ri)-chiga(eru)* mistake, take the wrong one; misunderstand
揃 *to(ri)-soro(eru)* arrange; make even; complete, get ready
極 *to(ri)-ki(meru)* arrange, agree upon, settle, make an appointment. *toriki(me)* arrangement, agreement, settlement
結 *to(ri)-musu(bu)* conclude; act as go-between; curry favor
散 *to(ri)-chi(rasu)* scatter around, clutter up
敢 *to(ri)a(ezu)* immediately; for the present; first of all
落 *to(ri)-o(tosu)* drop, let fall, throw down; throw (a shadow); miss (a ball), fumble; lose; capture; omit; degrade; depreciate, detract from; decrease; make worse; drive away, exorcise; leave behind; knock down (an article); cause abortion; entrap; end (a story) with a punch; remove (stains)
集 *to(ri)-atsu(meru)* gather, collect, assort
税人 *shuzeinin* tax collector, publican
越 *to(ri)-ko(su)* anticipate, do ahead of time
越苦労 *torikoshigurō, torikoshi kurō* unnecessary worry
替 *to(ri)-ka(eru)* exchange; barter; change, renew. *torika(e), torika(ekko)* a swap, an exchange
替品 *torikaehin* substitute
13 損 *to(ri)-sokona(u)* fail to take, fail to get, miss
詰 *to(ri)-tsu(meru)* corner, take to task; brood over, pine for
毀 *to(ri)-kowa(su), tori-kobo(tsu)* break down, dismantle; tear down, demolish
置 *to(tte) o(ku)* keep, hold, save, reserve, set aside
14 様 *to(ri)yō* way of taking; interpretation
静 *to(ri)-shizu(meru)* quiet (someone)
15 澄 *to(ri)-su(masu)* put on airs, put on company manners
縋 *to(ri)-suga(ru)* cling to, hang on to, lean on; depend on, appeal to
調 *to(ri)-shira(beru)* investigate, examine
締 *to(ri)-shi(maru)* manage, control, oversee. *torishima(ri)* control, management, regulation, discipline, supervision; good order; supervisor, superintendent, director, foreman
締役 *torishimariyaku* director
締規則 *torishima(ri) kisoku* control regulations
16 壊 *to(ri)-kowa(su)* break down, dismantle; tear down, demolish
17 鍋 *to(ri)nabe* ladle
18 繕 *to(ri)-tsukuro(u)* mend, repair, patch; smooth over, temporize
19 離 *to(ri)-hana(su)* detach, remove, drop, let go of
20 競 *to(rik)kura* scramble
22 纏 *to(ri)-mato(meru)* settle, complete, agree upon, arrange; collect; put in order; unify; coordinate
籠 *to(ri)-ko(meru)* confine, surround

7

叛 680 / J4840 / M3166 HON. HAN rebellion. *somu(ku)* act contrary to, go back on, disobey, defy, rebel against, turn one's back on.

4 心 *hanshin* rebellious spirit
6 臣 *hanshin* rebellious retainer
7 乱 *hanran* rebellion
8 逆 *hangyaku* treason, treachery, rebellion, insurrection, mutiny
9 軍 *hangun* rebel army, mutinous troops
10 徒 *hanto* rebels, insurgents
将 *hanshō* rebel leader
13 賊 *hanzoku* rebel
跡 *hanseki* results of rebellion
意 *han'i* spirit of rebellion
14 旗 *hanki* standard of revolt

B 叙 681/J3d76/M3163 敍 2340/J5a46/M13205 敘 2341/J5a47/M13206
Jo. *jo(suru)* relate, narrate, describe, write; confer (a rank); write a preface.
4 文 *jobun* preface, introduction
6 任 *jonin* investiture
7 述 *jojutsu* description, narration
位 *joi* investiture
8 事 *joji* narration, description
事文 *jojibun* narration, description
事詩 *jojishi* descriptive poetry, epic poem
11 情 *jojō* description of feelings; lyricism
情詩 *jojōshi* lyric poetry; lyric poem
12 景 *jokei* scenery description
14 説 *josetsu* explanation, interpretation
15 賜 *joshi* distributing ranks, rewards, and pensions
勲 *jokun* conferring of decorations
17 爵 *joshaku* conferring a peerage

8

叟 682/J5257/M3176 Sō. Shū old person.

14

叡 683/J3143/M3214 睿 3949/J624f/M23536 Ei intelligence; imperial.
6 旨 *eishi* the emperor's instructions
8 知 *eichi* wisdom, intelligence; intellect
12 智 *eichi* wisdom, intelligence; intellect
13 感 *eikan* the emperor's approval
14 聞 *eibun ni* in the emperor's hearing
15 慮 *eiryo* the emperor's pleasure
16 覧 *eiran* the emperor's personal inspection

16

叢 684/J4151/M3220 Sō plexus. *kusamura* clump of bushes, grassy place, thicket, the bush. *mura-, mura(garu)* crowd, flock, swarm.
5 生 *sōsei* dense growth; healthy growth
立 *murada(chi)* standing in a group
氷 *sōhyō* pack ice
8 雨 *murasame* passing shower
林 *sōrin* Zen monastery
10 祠 *hokora, sōshi* small shrine
書 *sōsho* series (of publications); a library (of literature)
時雨 *murashigure* autumn shower
12 雲 *murakumo* cloud masses
15 談 *sōdan* collection of stories

3-STROKE RADICALS

RAD. 口 30

Kuchi mouth. At left: *kuchi hen*. Nickname: Mouth.

A 口 685/J387d/M3227 Ku. Kō mouth. *kuchi* mouth, lips; speech, words; one's taste, stopper, plug; nozzle, orifice, slit, aperture; door, gate, entrance; route, ascent; employment, job; call (for a doctor); share; kind, lot, brand; beginning; rumor, opening (of a boil).

2 八丁 *kuchihatchō* voluble, eloquent
入 *kuchii(re)* acting as go-between; good offices. *kuchi (o) i(reru)* throw in a suggestion
入屋 *kuchii(re)ya* employment agency
3 口 *kuchiguchi* each entrance, every

3 【口】0 口 土 士 夂 夊 夕 大 女 子 宀 寸 小 ⺌ 尢 尸 屮 山 川 巛 工 己 巾 干 幺 广 廴 廾 弋 弓 ヨ 彑 彡 彳

mouth. *kuchiguchi ni* severally, unanimously

0 巾 *kuchihaba(ttai)* acting smart, bragging

才 *kōsai* clever speech

下手 *kuchibeta* defective speech, slowness of speech; poor talker

小言 *kuchi kogoto* scolding, faultfinding

三味線 *kuchijamisen, kuchizamisen* humming a samisen tune

上 *kōjō* verbal message, statement; introduction

上手 *kuchijōzu na* smooth-speaking

上書 *kōjōga(ki)* verbal statement

4 中 *kōchū* interior of the mouth

切 *kuchiki(ri)* start broaching (a subject)

元 *kuchimoto* the mouth; the shape of the mouth; near an entrance

分 *kuchiwa(ke)* assortment

不調法 *kuchi buchōhō* poor talker

止 *kuchido(me) suru* forbid to speak, muzzle (a person)

火 *kuchibi* fuse; spark plug; cause (of war); origin (of a quarrel)

火切 *kuchibi (o) ki(ru)* start a conversation

辺 *kōhen ni* around the mouth

辺単純疱疹 *kōhen tanjun hōshin* cold sore

内 *kōnai* in the mouth

内炎 *kōnaien* stomatitis

5 外 *kōgai suru* tell, divulge

占 *kuchiura* gathering from another's words

号 *kōgō* hum, sing to oneself; compose impromptu (poems)

弁 *kōben* eloquence

出 *kuchida(shi)* interference. *kuchi (o) da(su)* interrupt a conversation

巧者 *kuchigōsha na* smooth-spoken

可笑 *kuchiokashi* witty talking, joking

付 *kuchizu(keru)* kiss. *kuchizu(ki)* the mouth; manner of speaking; mouthpiece (of a cigarette)

6 舌 *kōzetsu* words, tongue. *kōzetsu, kuzetsu* talking recklessly; quarreling; curtain lecture

回 *kuchimawa(shi)* an expression; phraseology

気 *kōki* bad breath; intimation

伝 *kuden, kuchizuta(e), kuchizute* oral tradition; tradition

任 *kuchimaka(se)* random talk

汚 *kuchigitana(i)* foul-mouthed, abusive. *kuchiyogo(shi)* tantalizing sample (of food)

当 *kuchia(tari)* taste; reception, hospitality

早 *kuchibaya* rapid talking

先 *kuchisaki* lips, mouth; snout; proboscis; professions, lip service, mere words

争 *kuchiaraso(i)* quarreling

返答 *kuchihentō* talking back, retort

耳 *kōji* mouth and ear

耳学 *kōji (no) gaku* shallow learning

7 走 *kuchibashi(ru)* speak carelessly, tell, blurt out

車 *kuchiguruma* cajolery

吟 *kōgin* humming to oneself. *kuchizusa(mu)* hum

吻 *kōfun* way of speaking; intimation

抜 *kuchinu(ki)* corkscrew

利 *kuchikiki* eloquent person; mouthpiece; man of influence; mediator, middleman

承 *kōshō* passing on by word of mouth, oral tradition

言葉 *kuchi kotoba* words in common use

角 *kōkaku* corners of the mouth

角力 *kuchizumō* war of words

述 *kōjutsu* oral statement, dictation, lecture

述試験 *kōjutsu shiken* oral examination

8 金 *kuchigane* bottle cap; clasp, base (of a light bulb)

固 *kuchigata(me)* verbal promise

味 *kōmi* taste, flavor, deliciousness

径 *kōkei* aperture, bore, caliber

明 *kuchia(ke)* start, beginning

取 *kuchito(ri)* groom, horse boy; side dish

直 *kuchinao(shi)* removing a bad taste by eating something else

実 *kōjitsu* excuse, pretext

受 *kōju* listening to someone talking

拍子 *kuchibyōshi* counting time aloud

忠実 *kuchimame na* talkative, voluble

性無 *kuchisagana(i)* gossipy abusive

奇麗 *kuchigirei* speaking elegantly; speaking clearly; not coveting food. *kuchigirei ni* speaking like an innocent person

供 *kōkyō* affidavit, deposition

供書 *kōkyōsho* affidavit, deposition

9 廻 *kuchimawa(shi)* an expression; phraseology
拭 *kuchifu(ki)* napkin
紅 *kuchibeni* lipstick; red-rimmed
重 *kuchiomo na, kuchiomo(i)* slow of speech ⌈profession
前 *kuchimae* way of speaking;
宣 *kōsen* oral statement
臭 *kōshū* bad breath, halitosis
茶 *kuchija* adding more tea
荒 *kuchiara* rough speaking
約 *kōyaku* verbal promise
約束 *kuchi yakusoku* verbal promise
10 座 *kōza* account
唇 *kōshin* lips, labia
凌 *kuchishino(gi)* hand-to-mouth living
振 *kuchiburi* way of speaking; intimation
脇 *kuchiwaki* edges of the mouth
書 *kuchiga(ki) suru* writing with the brush in the mouth. *kōsho, kuchiga(ki)* affidavit, written confession
恐 *kuchiosoro(shii)* terrible talker
真似 *kuchimane* mimicry
祥無 *kuchisagana(i)* gossipy, abusive
11 過 *kuchisu(gi) suru* make a living
遅 *kuchioso* slow of speech
遊 *kuchizusa(mu), kuchizusa(bu)* hum, sing to oneself; compose impromptu (poems)
惜 *kuya(shii)* vexing, regrettable, mortifying. *kuya(shigaru)* be chagrined (at one's failure); regret (a circumstance); resent (an insult). *kuchio(shii)* regrettable, mortifying
掛 *kuchi (ga) ka(karu)* be called (to entertain)
授 *kōju, kuju* oral instruction, dictation
添 *kuchizo(e)* advice, support, good offices
移 *kuchiutsu(shi)* mouth-to-mouth feeding; oral transmission, tradition
許 *kuchimoto* the mouth; shape of the mouth; near an entrance
悪 *kuchi (no) waru(i)* evil-mouthed. *kuchiwaru* reviling; abuser
寄 *kuchiyo(se)* spiritism, necromancy, telepathy; medium, sorceress
笛 *kuchibue* whistling
堅 *kuchigata(i)* closed mouthed, discreet
達 *kōtatsu, kōdatsu* verbal message, oral instructions
達者 *kuchidassha na* talkative
12 開 *kuchia(ke)* beginning
幅 *kuchihaba(ttai)* acting smart, bragging
減 *kuchibe(rashi)* cutting down personnel
絵 *kuchie* frontispiece
証 *kōshō* oral testimony
軽 *kuchi (ga) karu(i)* careless (talker). *kuchigaru* glibness, volubility
飲 *kuchino(mi)* drinking from the bottle
割 *kuchi (o) wa(ru)* confess to a crime
喧 *kuchiyakama(shii)* nagging, faultfinding, scolding; talkative, gossipy
喧嘩 *kuchigenka* quarreling
腔 *kōkō, kōkū* oral cavity
腔外科 *kōkū geka, kōkō geka* oral surgery
答 *kuchigota(e)* talking back, retort, oral answer. *kōtō* oral answer
答試問 *kōtō shimon* oral examination
13 煩 *kuchiurusa(i)* nagging
腹 *kōfuku* mouth and stomach
触 *kuchizawari* taste
試 *kōshi* oral examination
跡 *kōseki* manner of speaking
際 *kuchigiwa* around the mouth
馴 *kuchina(rashi)* vocal or oral drill. *kuchina(reru)* develop vocal or oral skill
数 *kuchikazu* number of dependents; words, speech; number of shares. *kōsū* number of accounts; number of times
塞 *kuchifusa(gi)* stopping someone from talking
話術 *kōwajutsu* lip reading
蓋 *kōgai* palate
蓋垂 *kōgaisui* uvula
14 慣 *kuchina(reru)* develop vocal or oral skill
演 *kōen* oral narration
滌 *kuchisusu(gu), kuchisoso(gu)* gargle; rinse
碑 *kōhi* legend, folklore, tradition
端 *kuchi(no)ha* rumor, gossip. *kōtan* mouth
網 *kuchiami* (dog) muzzle
誦 *kōshō* humming; reading aloud
酸 *kuchi (ga) suppa(ku) naru, kuchi (o) suppa(ku) suru* repeat tediously

銭 *kōsen* commission, brokerage; net profit
綺麗 *kuchigirei* speaking elegantly; speaking clearly; not coveting food. *kuchigirei ni* speaking like an innocent person
説 *kudo(ku)* persuade, entreat, woo, seduce. *kuzetsu* quarrel; curtain lecture; jabbering
説立 *kudo(ki)-ta(teru)* entreat, urge strongly
説掛 *kudo(ki)-ka(keru)* persuade
説落 *kudo(ki)-o(tosu)* persuade, talk (someone) into (something), seduce
語 *kōgo* colloquial language
語文 *kōgobun* colloquial language
語体 *kōgotai* colloquial style; colloquialism
語訳 *kōgoyaku* colloquial translation
語詩 *kōgoshi* a poem in colloquial style, a poem in the spoken language
15 論 *kōron* dispute, argument
輪 *kuchiwa* muzzle
慰 *kuchinagusa(mi)* relieving boredom by reading poetry or by munching food
賢 *kuchisaka(shii), kuchigashiko(i)* clever in talking
調 *kuchō* tone, expression
調法 *kuchi chōhō* clever speaking
16 頼 *kuchidano(mi)* oral requirement
髭 *kuchi hige* moustache
頭 *kōtō* oral
頭弁論 *kōtō benron* oral argument
頭投票 *kōtō tōhyō* voice vote
頭試問 *kōtō shimon* oral examination
頭試験 *kōtō shiken* oral examination
頭審問 *kōtō shimmon* court hearing
18 癖 *kuchiguse* way of saying, favorite phrase
穢 *kuchigitana(i)* foul-mouthed
糧 *kōryō* rations
覆 *kuchiō(i)* mask
19 鏡 *kōkyō* mouth speculum
22 籠 *kuchigomo(ru)* stammer, mumble, falter. *kugomo(ru)* mumbling

2

叨 686 J525b M3237 Tō covet, be greedy, indulge. *midari ni* without permission; arbitrarily, unnecessarily; at random, indiscriminately.

叭 687 J525c M3242 HATSU open.

叺 688 J525d M3267 (国字) *kamasu* straw bag; tobacco pouch.

叶 689 J3370 M3255 KYŌ. *kana(eru)* grant, answer, hear (a prayer). *kana(u)* suit, be capable of; measure up to expectations; match, rival, keep up with; stand (the work); bear (the heat).

叮 690 J525a M3244 TEI courtesy.
17 嚀 *teinei* politeness, courtesy; care, conscientiousness

叱 691 J3c38 M3247 SHITSU. *shika(ru)* scold, reprove.
5 付 *shika(ri)-tsu(keru)* scold severely
正 *shissei* correction, improvement
7 声 *shissei* hiss
8 呼 *shikko suru* shout
9 飛 *shika(ri)-to(basu)* scold severely, blow up at
咤 *shitta* scolding
11 責 *shisseki* rebuke, reprimand

A **号** 692 J3966 M3256 **號** 5271 J694b M32726 Gō number; item, title, pseudonym; Buddhist name. *gō(suru)* assume the name of; name, call, style; declare, announce. *-gō* suffix after a foreign ship name.
4 火 *gōka* signal fire
5 外 *gōgai* newspaper extra
令 *gōrei* order, command
6 叫 *gōkyō* calling in a loud voice
8 泣 *gōkyū* lamentation, wailing
9 音 *gōon* reverberating sound; audible signal, a call
10 砲 *gōhō* signal gun
哭 *gōkoku* lamentation, wailing
11 笛 *gōteki* whistle
14 旗 *gōki* signal flag; flag emblem
20 鐘 *gōshō* signal bell

A **句** 693 J3667 M3234 Kō. KU phrase, clause, sentence, passage, paragraph; expression; line, verse, stanza; 17-syllable poem.

4 切 *kugi(ru)* punctuate; cut off; mark off, stop *kugi(ri)* stopping place, punctuation, pause
5 句 *kuku* every clause
6 会 *kukai* a gathering of haiku poets
7 作 *kusaku* composing haiku poems
8 法 *kuhō* phraseology, diction
9 点 *kuten* period (in punctuation)
12 集 *kushū* collection of haiku poems
13 節 *kusetsu* phrases and clauses
義 *kugi* meaning of a phrase
意 *kui* meaning of a phrase
14 読 *kuto* punctuation, pause
読点 *kutōten* punctuation marks

只 694 J427e M3239 SHI. *tada* free; only, just. *tada sae* in addition to, to add to.
4 中 *tadanaka ni* in the midst of
今 *tadaima* now, at present; right now; soon; Here I am. I just got back. I'm home
切符 *tadagippu* free ticket, pass
5 只 *tadatada* only by
8 物 *tadamono* ordinary person
取 *tadato(ri)* getting something for nothing
者 *tadamono* ordinary person
奉公 *tadabōkō* serving without pay
9 独 *tada hito(ri)* only one
乗 *tadano(ri)* stolen ride, free ride
13 働 *tadabatara(ki)* working for nothing
11 管 *hitasura* earnestly

B **召** 695 J3e24 M3241 SHŌ. *me(su)* call, send for; wear, put on; take (a bath); ride in; buy; eat, drink; catch (a cold). *me(shi)* summons, a call. *(o)me (shi)* summons, a call; dressing; clothing; striped crepe.
2 入 *me(shi)-ire(ru)* call in
3 上 *me(shi)-a(garu)* eat (honorific). *me(shi)-a(geru)* forfeit, confiscate; call out
上物 *me(shi)a(gari)mono* food
5 出 *me(shi)-da(su)* call out, summon
7 状 *meshijō, shōjō* letter of invitation
8 使 *me(shi)tsuka(i)* servant. *me(shi)-tsuka(u)* employ
抱 *me(shi)-kaka(eru)* employ, engage, take into one's service. *me(shi)kaka(e)* mercenary troops
物 *(o)me(shi)mono* clothing (polite)
命 *shōmei* call; divine call
9 連 *me(shi)-tsu(reru)* bring along, accompany
10 捕 *me(shi)-to(ru)* arrest, apprehend
致 *shōchi suru* call together
11 寄 *me(shi)-yo(seru)* call (someone) to you, call together, call to come
12 募 *shōbo* levy, enlistment
替 *(o)me(shi)ka(e)* change of clothes (honorific)
喚 *shōkan* summons
喚状 *shōkanjō* call, summons, subpoena
集 *shōshū suru, me(shi)-atsu(meru)* call together
集令 *shōshūrei* draft order (military)
15 還 *shōkan* recall
請 *shōsei suru* call together

叩 696 J4321 M3238 KŌ *tata(ku)* strike, beat, hit, knock, knock, thrash, slap, rap, pat, pound, maul, clap (the hands); sound out (views); criticize. *tata(ki-nomesu)* knock down, beat up. *tata(ki)* dusting; duster.
3 上 *tata(ki)-a(geru)* work up; improve by training
大工 *tata(ki) daiku* clumsy carpenter
4 込 *tata(ki)-ko(mu)* drive into; throw (into prison); hammer in, inculcate
切 *tata(ki)-ki(ru)* hack down, chop down, mangle
5 立 *tata(ki)-ta(teru)* beat severely
付 *tata(ki)-tsu(keru)* beat, thrash, throw at
出 *tata(ki)-da(su)* begin to beat (a drum); beat and drive out; dismiss, send away
6 肉 *tata(ki)niku* meat loaf, meatball
伏 *tata(ki)-fu(seru)* knock down; utterly defeat
合 *tata(ki)-a(u)* fight, exchange blows. *tata(ki)-a(waseru)* strike (things) together
8 直 *tata(ki)-nao(su)* beat back into shape; correct by discipline
10 起 *tata(ki)-oko(su)* rouse, shake, awake
倒 *tata(ki)-tao(su)* knock down, beat down
消 *tata(ki)-ke(su)* beat out (a fire)
破 *tata(ki)-yabu(ru)* smash in, smash down

殺 *tata(ki)-koro(su)* beat to death
12 割 *tata(ki)-wa(ru)* break to pieces, smash
落 *tata(ki)-oto(su)* knock down, knock off
13 鉦 *tata(ki)gane* temple ceremonial gong
毀 *tata(ki)-kowa(su)* knock to pieces, smash up, wreck
15 潰 *tata(ki)-tsubu(su)* smash up, crushing defeat
16 頭 *nukazu(ku)* bow, kowtow, prostrate oneself. *kōtō* kowtow, bow
頭戦術 *kōtō senjutsu* kowtowing strategy

A **史** 697 / J3b4b / M3249 SHI history, chronicles; historian; book.
3 上 *shijō no* historical. *shijō ni* in history
6 伝 *shiden* history and biography; historical materials
8 官 *shikan* chronicler
実 *shijitsu* historical fact
的 *shiteki* historic, historical
的現在 *shiteki genzai* historical present
学 *shigaku* (study of) history
学者 *shigakusha* historian
10 料 *shiryō* historical records
家 *shika* historian
書 *shisho* history book
11 略 *shiryaku* outline history
眼 *shigan* historical view; historical insight
12 筆 *shihitsu* historical writing
13 詩 *shishi* historical poem
跡 *shiseki* historical landmark
15 劇 *shigeki* historical drama
談 *shidan* historical story
論 *shiron* historical treatise, historical discussion
18 蹟 *shiseki* historical landmark
観 *shikan* historical view
20 籍 *shiseki* historical works, annals

A **司** 698 / J3b4a / M3257 SHI official; government office. *tsukasado(ru)* rule, administer, conduct. *tsukasa* office, government office; director, head official.
5 令 *shirei* command, control; commander
令官 *shireikan* commanding officer
令長官 *shirei chōkan* commander-in-chief
令部 *shireibu* headquarters, the command
令塔 *shireitō* conning tower
6 会 *shikai* chairmanship; chairman
会者 *shikaisha* chairman, toastmaster, moderator
式 *shishiki* directing a ceremony; celebrant
式者 *shishikisha* leader, presiding minister, master of ceremonies
式聖職 *shishiki seishoku* celebrant
8 直 *shichoku* judicial authorities, the court, the bench, a judge
法 *shihō* administration of justice
法大臣 *Shihō Daijin* Minister of Justice
法官 *shihōkan* judicial official
法省 *Shihōshō* Justice Ministry
法保護 *shihō hogo* judicial protection
法部 *shihōbu* the judicature
法権 *shihōken* judicial powers, powers of jurisdiction
法警察 *shihō keisatsu* judicial police
9 政官 *shiseikan* civil administrator
政長官 *shisei chōkan* civil administrator
10 書 *shisho* librarian
11 教 *shikyō* (Catholic) bishop
教区 *shikyōku* diocese
祭 *shisai* (Catholic) priest
祭職 *shisaishoku* (Catholic) priesthood
12 税官 *shizeikan* assessor, tax officer

A **台** 699 / J4266 / M3246 **臺** 4905 / J674a / M30161 TAI. DAI stand, pedestal, rack, table, dais, bench, block; holder, support; mounting, setting. *utena* calyx; tower; platform. *tsukasa* office, government office; director, head official. *-dai* level, mark; the decade of one's age; plateau, height, eminence; counter for vehicles, machines, tables, benches, etc.
3 下 *daika* your honor; his honor
4 木 *daigi* (gun) stock, unworked block of wood; parent-tree stock (in grafting)
石 *daiishi* stone pedestal
尻 *daijiri* butt of a gun
6 地 *daichi* plateau, tableland, eminence
7 車 *daisha* push car; flatcar
形 *daikei* echelon formation; trapezoid
8 所 *daidokoro* kitchen
所用品 *daidokoro yōhin* kitchenware
9 颪 *taifū* typhoon
颪眼 *taifūgan, taifu (no) me* eye of a typhoon
10 座 *daiza* pedestal

秤 *daibakari* platform scales
紙 *daishi* cardboard; mat, mount
11 帳 *daichō* ledger, register
12 場 *daiba* fort, battery
無 *daina(shi) ni suru* spoil, mar, ruin, destroy, make a mess of
湾 *Taiwan* Taiwan
湾人 *Taiwanjin* a Taiwanese
詞 *serifu* speech, words, lines, remarks
詞回 *serifumawa(shi)* theatrical elocution
14 閣 *taikaku, daikaku* tall building, castle, the cabinet
16 頭 *taitō* raise one's head, come to the fore, become influential, gain power, become famous

A **右** 700 / J3126 / M3250 YŪ. U. *migi, migiri* right, right hand. *migi suru* turn to the right.
3 大臣 *Udaijin* Minister of the Right
4 手 *migite, mete* right hand
方 *uhō* the right
辺 *uhen* right side
中間 *uchūkan* between right field and center
心房 *ushimbō* right auricle
心室 *ushinshitsu* right ventricle
5 左 *migi-hidari* right and left
打者 *migi dasha* right-handed batter
6 回 *migimawa(ri)* right-handed rotation, clockwise
7 足 *usoku, migiashi* right foot
折 *usetsu suru* turn to the right
社 *usha* right wing socialist party
利 *migiki(ki)* right-handedness; right-hander
8 枕 *migimakura ni* (lying) on the right side
岸 *ugan, migi kishi* right bank, right shore (as you go down a river)
表 *uhyō* the chart at the right
往左往 *uōsaō suru* go right and left, go this way and that
9 派 *uha* rightists, the Right
前 *uzen, migimae* folding the left side of a kimono over the right. *uzen* in front of the right fielder
巻 *migima(ki)* clockwise
10 党 *utō* rightists, the Right
書 *migiga(ki)* written from right to left
11 眼 *ugan* right eye
舷 *ugen* starboard
寄 *migiyo(ri)* leaning toward the right; rightist
側 *usoku, migigawa* right hand, right side
側通行 *migigawa tsūkō* keep to the right
12 越 *ugo(shi)* over right field
腕 *migi ude, uwan* right arm
筆 *uhitsu* amanuensis, secretary
13 傾 *ukei* leaning to the right, rightist
14 端 *utan* right edge; right end; right lane
17 翼 *uyoku* right wing, rightists; right field; right flank
翼手 *uyokushu* right fielder
翼団体 *uyoku dantai* right-wing groups
21 顧左眄 *uko-saben suru* look right and left; vacillate, waver

A **可** 701 / J3244 / M3245 KOKU. KA good, passable; approval; safe to say, ability to do. *-be(karazu)* must not, should not; do not. *i(i), yo(i), yo(shi)* good, good natured; pleasing; precious; lovely, beautiful, fine; lucky; efficacious; right; suitable; justifiable; appropriate; satisfactory; better; all right; unneccessary; unobjectionable; intimate, friendly; easy, well; desirous. *-be(shi), -be(ki)* shall, should, must, ought to, be expected to; seem to, look like; can; will.
3 也 *kanari* considerably, fairly, quite
及的 *kakyūteki* as ... as possible
4 分 *kabun* divisible, separable
分性 *kubunsei* divisibility
5 圧性 *kaatsusei* compressibility
6 成 *kanari* considerably, fairly, quite
7 決 *kaketsu* approval, adoption
否 *kahi* right or wrong, propriety, advisability, pro and con
9 哀想 *kawaisō na* poor, pitiable, pathetic; pitiless; unjust
変 *kahen* variable, changeable, convertible,controllable
変抵抗器 *kahen teikōki* rheostat
10 笑 *oka(shii)* funny amusing, ridiculous
能 *kanō* possible
能性 *kanōsei* possibility
能法 *kanōhō* potential mood
能動詞 *kanō dōshi* potential verb
11 惜 *atara, attara* alas; regrettably
動 *kadō* movable, mobile

3 【口】2 口 土 士 夂 夊 夕 大 女 子 宀 寸 小 ⺌ 尢 尸 屮 山 川 巛 工 己 巾 干 幺 广 廴 廾 弋 弓 ヨ 彑 彡 彳

動性 *kadōsei* mobility
動堰 *kadōzeki* canal gates, river gates
動橋 *kadōkyō* movable bridge
13 塑物質 *kaso busshitsu* plastics
溶片 *kayōhen* fuse
溶性 *kayōsei* solubility
愛 *kawai(garu)* love, hold dear; *kawai(rashii)* lovely, sweet. *kawai(i)* dear, darling, charming, lovely, sweet
愛気 *kawaige* loveliness
15 憐 *karen na* poor, pitiful; cute, sweet, lovely
撓 *katō* flexible
16 燃性 *kanensei* combustibility, inflammability
燃物 *kanembutsu* a combustible, inflammables
17 聴度 *kachōdo* audibility
聴距離 *kachō kyori* audible distance
鍛性 *katansei* malleability
鍛鉄 *katantetsu* malleable iron
18 鎔性 *kayōsei* fusibility

A **古** 702 / J3845 / M3233 Ko old. *furu(i)* old, aged, ancient, antiquated; stale, threadbare; outmoded, obsolete article. *furu(biru)* look old, get old. *furu(bokeru)* look old; become musty; wear out. *furu, furu-* used, secondhand. *furu(ku)* anciently, formerly. *inishie* antiquity, ancient times. *(o)furu* used article. *furu(mekashii)* old and familiar.

2 人 *kojin* ancient people
刀 *kotō* an old sword
4 手 *furute* disused article, secondhand article; ex-soldier; retired official
木 *koboku* an old tree
切 *furugi(re)* old cloth, old rags
井戸 *furuido* an old unused well
文 *kobun, komon* ancient writing
文学 *kobungaku* paleography, the study of ancient writings
文書 *kobunsho, komonjo* ancient documents
今 *kokon* ancient and modern times, all ages, past and present
今東西 *kokon-tōzai* all times and places
今無類 *kokon-murui* best ever
5 句 *koku* an ancient expression; an old poem
史 *koshi* ancient history
写本 *koshahon* an old manuscript; a codex
生物 *koseibutsu* extinct plants and animals
生物学 *koseibutsugaku* paleontology
本 *furuhon, furubon* old book, secondhand book
本屋 *furuhon'ya* secondhand book store
代 *kodai* ancient times
代人 *kodaijin* the ancients
代史 *kodaishi* ancient history
代語 *kodaigo* ancient language
6 米 *komai* old rice
老 *korō* old people, seniors, elders
血 *furuchi* impure blood
式 *koshiki* old style; ancient rites
曲 *kokyoku* old music
池 *furuike* an old pool, an old pond
寺 *furudera, koji* an old temple
字 *koji* ancient writing
印紙 *koinshi, furuinshi* used stamps
自動車 *furujidōsha* used car
色 *koshoku* faded color, antique look
色蒼然 *koshoku-sōzen(taru)* antique-looking
伝 *koden* legend, tradition
伝説 *kodensetsu* old tradition
7 言 *kogen* obsolete word; old proverb
里 *furusato* hometown, birthplace; an old village; a historic village
体 *kotai* old custom, old style
址 *koshi* historic ruins
兵 *kohei* old soldier, veteran. *furutsuwamono* an old veteran, an old hand
希 *koki* seventy years of age
来 *korai* from time immemorial. *korai no* ancient, time-honored
社寺 *koshaji* old shrines and temples
8 金 *furugane* scrap iron, scrap metal
例 *korei* old precedent, tradition, custom
法 *kohō* old method; old law
注 *kochū* commentaries of the ancients
狐 *furugitsune* an old fox, old-timer, schemer
服 *furufuku* old clothes, old suit
制 *kosei* ancient establishment; ancient laws
刹 *kosatsu* ancient temple
画 *koga* ancient painting
学 *kogaku* classical studies
昔 *koseki* ancient times
武士 *kobushi* feudal warrior, samurai.

furutsuwamono an old veteran, an old hand

往今来 *koō-konrai* in all ages, since antiquity

版 *kohan* an old edition

版本 *kohambon* old edition

物 *furumono, kobutsu* antique, old article, secondhand goods

物商 *kobutsushō* curio or secondhand dealer

参 *kosan* seniority, long service

参者 *kosansha* senior, old timer

事 *koji* ancient events

事記 *Kojiki* Japan's Ancient Chronicle

典 *koten* old book; classics; classic

典文学 *koten bungaku* classical literature

典主義 *koten shugi* classicism

典的 *kotenteki* classical

典学 *kotengaku* the classics

典派 *kotenha* classical school

典語 *kotengo* classical or dead languages

9 音 *koon* old character pronunciation

風 *kofū* old customs, old style

俗 *kozoku* old custom

城 *kojō* old castle

柯 *koka* coca (source of cocaine)

臭 *furukusa(i)* stale, old fashioned; hackneyed, trite

茶 *kocha* last year's tea

草 *furukusa* last year's grass, dead grass

美術品 *kobijutsuhin* old art object

10 格 *kokaku* convention, usage; old customs, old etiquette

株 *furukabu* old-timer, veteran, senior

酒 *furuzake* last year's saké, old saké. *koshu* well-cured saké

流 *koryū* old manners, old style; old school (of art)

狸 *furudanuki* old badger, veteran, old-timer, schemer, old fox

祠 *koshi* an old small shrine

称 *koshō* old name

訓 *kokun* ancient instruction; an old reading of a character

記 *koki* ancient records

都 *koto* ancient city; former capital

衰 *furu(bi)-otoro(eru)* waste away

家 *furuie* old house, deserted house

書 *kosho* old book, rare book

11 疵 *furukizu* an old wound

趾 *koshi* historic ruins

巣 *furusu* old home, former haunt

道 *kodō* old road; ancient methods; ancient moral teachings; the way of learning

道具 *furudōgu, kodōgu* old furniture; curious; secondhand goods

道具屋 *furudōguya* secondhand store

12 渡 *kowata(ri)* an old imported item

稀 *koki* seventy years of age

註 *kochū* commentaries of the ancients

創 *furukizu* an old wound

着 *furugi* old clothes, secondhand clothing

筆 *kohitsu* old writing

筆家 *kohitsuka* an expert in old writing

13 傷 *furukizu* scar, old wound; old unpleasant incident

雅 *koga* classical elegance, antiquity

詩 *koshi* ancient poems

跡 *koseki, furuato* historic spot, ruins

鉄 *furugane, furutetsu* scrap iron, scrap metal

靴 *furugutsu* old shoes

義 *kogi* old meaning, old interpretation

意 *koi* ancient ways; the feelings of the ancients

楽 *kogaku* ancient music

聖 *kosei* ancient sage

戦場 *kosenjō* ancient battlefield

14 語 *kogo* obsolete word; old proverb

説 *kosetsu* ancient belief

歌 *furuuta, koka* old song, old poem

豪 *kogō* veteran, old-timer, a person of experience

墨 *koboku* old ink stick

銭 *kosen* old coin

銭学 *kosengaku* numismatics

15 廟 *kobyō* old shrine

儀 *kogi* ancient rite

墳 *kofun* old mound, old grave, ancient tomb

賢 *koken* ancient sage

器 *koki* an antique

16 諺 *kogen* an old proverb

18 蹟 *koseki* historic spot, ruins

顔 *furugao* familiar face, old-timer

吋 703 J3125 M3292 TŌ. *inchi* inch.

A **后** 704 J3921 M3298 KŌ. Go after; behind; back; later. *kisaki* empress, queen.
6 妃 *kōhi* queen
10 宮 *kōgū* harem; imperial consort; palace

吁 705 J525e M3275 KU, U. *ā* exclamation of surprise, sorrow, or doubt.
6 吁 *kuku, uu* exclamation of surprise, sorrow, or doubt
13 嗟 *usa* exclamation

B **吏** 706 J4d79 M3299 RI an official.
2 人 *rijin* officials
10 員 *riin* officials
党 *ritō* party of officials
11 道 *ridō* official ethics
務 *rimu* the work of the officials

吃 707 J3549 M3280 KITSU. *domo(ru)* stammer, stutter.
4 水 *kissui* draft (of a ship)
水線 *kissuisen* (loaded) water line
8 逆 *shakkuri, kitsugyaku* hiccups
9 音 *kitsuon* stammering, stuttering
14 緊 *kikkin* urgent
22 驚 *bikkuri suru* be surprised
驚仰天 *bikkuri-gyōten suru* be startled, be shocked, be stunned
驚箱 *bikkuribako* jack-in-the-box

B **叫** 708 J362b M3240 KYŌ. *sake(bu)* shout, exclaim, cry, yell, roar, howl; cry for, clamor for, advocate. *wame(ku)* shout, cry, yell, clamor.
5 出 *sake(bi)-da(su)* cry out
号 *kyōgō suru* cry aloud
7 声 *sake(bi)goe* shout, cry, yell, scream, wail, roar, howl
求 *sake(bi)-moto(meru)* cry for
8 呼 *sake(bi)-yo(bawaru)* wail
泣 *sake(bi)-na(ku)* wail
12 喚 *kyōkan* shout, scream
訴 *sake(bi)-utta(eru)* cry out against

B **吐** 709 J4547 M3300 TO. *ha(ku)* disgorge, vomit; belch, emit; give vent to; confess; tell (lies), speak. *tsu(ku)* breathe; disgorge; tell (lies).
3 口 *ha(ke)guchi* outlet, vent; *ha(ki)guchi* spillway; marketing.
下 *ha(ki)kuda(shi)* vomiting and purging
5 出 *ha(ki)-da(su)* vomit, disgorge, spit out; breathe out; send out (smoke); belch (fire and smoke); say (angrily)
6 血 *toketsu* vomiting blood
気 *ha(ki)ke* nausea
8 物 *tobutsu suru* vomit
乳 *tonyū suru* throw up milk
10 剤 *tozai* emetic
息 *toiki* sigh, a long breath
11 捨 *ha(ki)su(te)* exhaust, discharge
掛 *ha(ki)-ka(keru)* spit at, spit on
12 散 *ha(ki)-chi(rasu)* pour out (evil words)
16 薬 *ha(ki)gusuri* emetic
18 瀉 *tosha* vomiting and diarrhea
瀉物 *toshabutsu* vomit and bowel discharge
21 露 *toro suru* express one's mind, give vent to, open (one's heart)

吊 710 J445f M3291 CHŌ. *tsuru(su), tsu(ru)* hang, suspend; wear (a sword).
3 下 *tsu(ri)-sa(garu)* dangle, be suspended, be hung down from. *tsu(ri)-sa(geru)* dangle, suspend, hang down
上 *tsu(ri)-a(geru)* hang up, haul up, suspend, raise, hoist, weigh (an anchor). *tsuru(shi)a(ge)* kangaroo court; impeachment
4 天井 *tsuritenjō* suspended ceiling
太鼓 *tsuridaiko* suspended drum
5 出 *tsu(ri)-da(su)* pull out (a fish); decoy, lure
9 革 *tsurikawa* (hanging) strap. *tsu(ri)-oro(su)* hang, suspend, let down
柿 *tsuru(shi)gaki* dried persimmons
10 紐 *tsurihimo* supporting cord
索 *tsuri nawa* rope for hanging things up
11 眼 *tsurime* slant eyes
窓 *tsuru(shi) mado* vertically sliding windows
梯子 *tsuribashigo* rope ladder
12 棚 *tsuridana* hanging shelf
15 縄 *tsurinawa* rope for hanging things up
16 橋 *tsuribashi* suspension bridge

[17]環 *tsuriwa* flying ring (in a gym); watch fob
繃帯 *tsurihōtai* (arm) sling
[18]鎖 *tsurigusari* supporting chain
[22]籠 *tsurikago* hanging basket; nacelle, gondola

B **吉** 711 / J3548 / M3289 KICHI, KITSU *yoshi* good luck; joy, congratulations.
[4]方 *kippō, ehō* lucky direction
日 *kichinichi* , *kitsujitsu* lucky day
凶 *kikkyō* fortune, sunshine and shadow
[5]礼 *kichirei, kitsurei* auspicious ceremony; festival
旦 *kittan* lucky day
左右 *kissō* good news; good or bad news
[6]兆 *kitchō* lucky omen
[7]辰 *kisshin* lucky day
[8]例 *kichirei, kitsurei* time-honored custom
事 *kichiji, kitsuji* auspicious event
[9]相 *kissō* good omen
[10]祥 *kisshō* lucky omen
[11]野紙 *yoshinogami* tissue paper
野桜 *yoshinozakura* a common kind of cherry tree
[12]報 *kippō* good news
[13]瑞 *kichizui, kitsuzui* lucky omen
夢 *kichimu, kitsumu* good dream
[14]徴 *kitchō* lucky omen
[15]慶 *kikkei* congratulatory event, rejoicing

A **向** 712 / J387e / M3301 KŌ. KYŌ. *mu(kau)* face, confront; oppose, defy; proceed to; get, tend toward; approach. *mu(keru)* turn, face; point (a gun); send (a messenger or letter). *mu(ku)* turn towards, (a needle) points to; lean towards; face, front on; suit. *mu(kai)* opposite. *mu(ke), mu(kete)* bound for. *mu(ki)* direction; exposure; aspect; suitability; position (on a proposition). *mu(kō)* the other side; opposite direction; the other party; destination; the next (few years); opposition to.
[3]三軒 *mukō sangen* one's three neighbors across the way
上 *kōjō* advancement, progress, improvement, elevation, rise
上心 *kōjōshin* ambition, aspiration
[4]日性 *kōjitsusei, kōnichisei* disposition (in flowers) to turn toward the sun
日葵 *himawari* sunflower
[5]付 *mu(ki)tsu(ke)* ni to one's face, in one's presence
[6]向 *mu(ki)mu(ki)* suitability
合 *mu(kai)-a(waseru), mu(ki)-a(u), mu(kai)-a(u)* face, confront: be opposite to
地性 *kōchisei* the nature of plants to grow down and root
[7]見 *mu(kō)-mi(zu)* recklessness
[8]波 *mu(kai)nami* headsea
直 *mu(ke)-nao(ru) vi, mu(ke)-nao(su) vt* change direction
岸 *mu(kō)gishi* the opposite bank
学心 *kōgakushin* love of learning
[9]風 *mu(kai)kaze* headwind
後 *kōgo* hereafter
背 *kōhai* one's attitude; state of affairs
[11]疵 *mu(kō)kizu* frontal wound
側 *mu(kō)gawa* the opposite side; the other party
脛 *mu(kō)zune* shin, front of lower leg
[12]寒 *kōkan* facing the winter
暑 *kōsho* facing the heat
替 *mu(ke)-kae(ru)* change direction
[13]腹 *mu(kap)para* anger, passion
鉢巻 *mu(kō)hachimaki* folded or rolled head towel

A **吸** 713 / J355b / M3372' KYŪ. *su(u)* inhale; imbibe, sip; suck, suck out.
[2]入 *kyūnyū* inhalation. *su(i)-i(reru)* suck in
入剤 *kyūnyūzai* inhalant
入液 *kyūnyūeki* spray, vapor
入器 *kyūnyūki* inhaler
[3]口 *su(i)kuchi* cigarette holder, mouthpiece (on a pipe)
上 *su(i)-a(geru)* suck in, pump up. *suia(ge)* suction; sucking
[4]込 *su(i)-ko(mu)* inhale, imbibe; suck in; absorb, engulf, swallow up; suck down
引 *kyūin* absorption, suction, attraction
引力 *kyūinryoku* attraction, absorption
水 *kyūsui* suction
水管 *kyūsuikan* water pipe
[5]付 *su(i)-tsu(keru)* attract; light (a cigarette). *su(i)-tsu(ku)* adhere to, stick to
出 *su(i)-da(su)* suck out, draw out, pump out

出膏薬 *su(i)da(shi) kōyaku* poultice, an antiphlogistic
収 *kyūshū* absorption; suction; attraction; extinction (of light)
収力 *kyūshūryoku* absorptive power
収性 *kyūshūsei* absorptiveness
収剤 *kyūshūzai* an absorbent
収薬 *kyūshūyaku* an absorbent
6 気 *kyūki* breathing in
血 *kyūketsu* sucking blood
血鬼 *kyūketsuki* a vampire, an extortioner
血動物 *kyūketsu dōbutsu* bloodsucker
7 角 *kyūkaku* cupping glass
角子 *kyūkakushi* cupping glass
8 物 *su(i)mono* soup
物椀 *su(i)mono wan* soup bowl
取 *su(i)-to(ru)* suck up, soak up, suck out; extort, squeeze out (money)
取紙 *suitorigami* blotting paper, blotter
10 差 *su(i)sa(shi)* cigarette butt
12 殻 *su(i)gara* tobacco ashes
殻入 *suigarai(re)* ash tray
飲 *kyūin* (opium) smoking. *suino(mi)* feeding cup (for a patient)
飲器 *kyūinki* feeding cup (for a patient)
着 *kyūchaku suru* adhere, stick fast
着剤 *kyūchakuzai* an absorbent
14 管 *kyūkan* suction pipe, siphon
塵器 *kyūjinki* vacuum cleaner
15 盤 *kyūban* sucker (on an octopus)
16 瓢 *su(i)fukube* cupping glass

A **各** 714 / J3346 / M3281 KAKU each. *ono-ono* each, every, either, respectively. *kaku-* each.
2 人 *kakujin* each individual
4 戸 *kakko* every door
月 *kakugetsu* every month
方面 *kakuhōmen* every direction; all quarters
5 処 *kakusho* each place, various places
6 自 *kakuji* each individual
回 *kakukai* each time
地 *kakuchi* each place; various areas
州 *kakushū* all the provinces, all the states
各 *onoono* each, every, either, respectively
各方 *onoonogata* all of you
7 位 *kakui* gentlemen, sirs
別 *kakubetsu ni* individually, separately
条 *kakujō* each item
町村 *kakuchōson* each town and village
8 国 *kakkoku* all countries, various nations, each nation.
例 *kakurei* each illustration
所 *kakusho* each place, various places
宗 *kakushū* all sects
9 面 *kakumen* all phases
通 *kakutsū* each document; each letter
派 *kakuha* each party, all sects, each faction
科 *kakka* each subject, each department
点 *kakuten* each point
界 *kakkai* each field, various circles
巻 *kakkan* each volume
省 *kakushō* each ministry
10 般 *kakuhan no* all, every, various
部 *kakubu* every part; various parts; every department
員 *kakuin* each one
書 *kakusho* each book
個 *kakko* every one, each. *kakko ni* individually, respectively, each
個撃破 *kakko-gekiha* divide and conquer
11 階 *kakkai* each floor
階止 *kakkaidoma(ri)* stopping at every floor
12 項 *kakkō, kakukō* each item, each clause
14 層 *kakusō* each stratum; each class
様 *kakuyō* various
種 *kakushu* each kind, all kinds
種学校 *kakushu gakkō* miscellaneous schools
駅 *kakueki* every station
駅停車 *kakueki teisha* local train
15 論 *kakuron* detailed exposition
18 藩 *kakuhan* each clan

A **合** 715 / J3967 / M3287 GŌ one-tenth *shō* (see Weights and Measures); one of ten stations up a mountain. *a(u)* fit, suit; agree with, match, be correct; pay, be profitable. *a(wasu), a(waseru)* join together; be opposite, face; unite, combine, connect; add up; mix; match; overlap; compare; check with. *a(wasaru)* get together, unite. *gas(suru) vi* and *vt* join together; sum up; combine, unite, mix; agree with. *a(i)-* joint; associate, accomplice. *a(wase)-* joined together; opposite, facing.

1 一 *gōitsu* unification, union, oneness
2 力 *gōryoku* resultant force; cooperation. *gōriki* alms, assistance, contribution, Buddhist almsgiving
3 口 *a(i)kuchi* chum, pal
子 *a(ino)ko* mulatto, Eurasian; crossbreed; hybrid
4 手 *a(ino)te* interlude; accompaniment; sideshow; strain of music
方 *a(i)kata* accompaniment
切 *gassai* all; altogether
5 目 *a(wase)me* joint, seam
札 *a(i)fuda* check
弁 *gōben* joint management; pool
本 *gappon* a collection in one volume
冊 *gassatsu, gōsatsu* a collection in one volume
6 羽 *kappa* raincoat, foul-weather gear; an oil-skin
行 *a(wase)-okona(u)* carry on together; do at the same time
式 *gōshiki* formal, regular; valid; categorical
印 *a(i)jirushi* comradeship badge. *aiin* verification seal
名会社 *gōmeigaisha* unlimited partnership
同 *gōdō* union, combination, amalgamation, fusion; congruence
同会議 *gōdō kaigi* joint session
同軍 *gōdōgun* combined armies
同慰霊祭 *gōdō ireisai* joint service for the war dead
成 *gōsei* synthesis, composition; synthetic; composite, mixed, combined, compound
成力 *gōseiryoku* resultant force
成物 *gōseibutsu* a compound
成宝石 *gōsei hōseki* synthetic gems
成酒 *gōseishu* synthetic saké
成語 *gōseigo* compound word
成樹脂 *gōsei jushi* plastics, synthetic resins
成繊維 *gōsei sen'i* synthetic fiber
7 図 *aizu* sign, signal
体 *gattai* union, combination, alliance, annexation
作 *gassaku* joint work, collaboration
判 *a(i)ban* medium-sized paper; medium-sized book
言葉 *a(i)kotoba* password, watchword
8 金 *gōkin* alloy
性 *a(i)shō* affinity, compatibility
抱 *gōhō* an armful
板 *gōhan, gōban, a(wase)ita* veneer board, plywood
版 *gōhan* joint publication
物 *a(wase)mono* something joined together
祀 *gōshi suru* enshrine together
服 *aifuku* spring or fall wear
併 *gappei, gōhei* combination, union, amalgamation, consolidation, merger, coalition, fusion, annexation, affiliation, incorporation
併症 *gappeishō* complications (in an illness)
法 *gōhō* legality, legitimacy, lawfulness
法化 *gōhōka* legalization
法的 *gōhōteki* legal, lawful, legitimate, law-abiding, in order
法性 *gōhōsei* lawfulness, validity
9 計 *gōkei* total
乗 *a(i)no(ri)* riding together
点 *gaten, gatten* understanding, comprehension, grasp; consent
奏 *gassō* concert, ensemble
奏調 *gassōchō* concert pitch
10 流 *gōryū* confluence; union, linking up
砥 *a(wase)do* double whetstone
致 *gatchi* agreement, concurrence, conforming to
釘 *a(i)kugi* double-pointed nail
剤 *gōzai* medical compound
衾 *gōkin suru* sleep together
格 *gōkaku* passing an examination; eligibility
格者 *gōkakusha* successful applicant
格者名 *gōkakushamei* names of successful candidates
11 符 *a(i)jirushi* comradeship badge
著 *gōcho, gatcho* joint authorship
祭 *gōsai suru* enshrine together
宿 *gasshuku* lodging together
宿所 *gasshukujo* boardinghouse
唱 *gasshō* chorus
唱団 *gasshōdan* chorus, choir
唱隊 *gasshōtai* chorus, choir
唱隊長 *gasshōtaichō* choir leader
唱隊員 *gasshōtaiin* choir member
理 *gōri* rationality
理化 *gōrika* rationalization
理主義 *gōri shugi* rationalism

理性 *gōrisei* rationality, reasonableness
理的 *gōriteki* reasonable, rational, logical
12 間 *aima* interval
棒 *a(i)bō* companion
評 *gappyō* joint review, joint criticism
詞 *a(i)kotoba* password
掌 *gasshō* pressing palms together (in prayer)
着 *aigi* between-season wear
衆国 *Gasshūkoku* The United States of America; a federal state
13 戦 *kassen* battle, engagement
資 *gōshi suru* joint stocks, enter into partnership
資会社 *gōshigaisha* limited partnership
意 *gōi* agreement, consent, mutual understanding
意心中 *gōi shinjū* double suicide
意情死 *gōi jōshi* double suicide
14 憎 *ainiku* unfortunately
算 *gassan* totaling
15 調 *gōchō* tuning (in music)
歓 *gōkan* enjoying pleasure together
16 薬 *a(i)gusuri* specific remedy
壁 *gappeki* a neighbor with just a wall between
憲性 *gōkensei* constitutionality
17 鍵 *aikagi* pass key, duplicate key, master key
19 鏡 *a(wase) kagami* opposite mirrors
20 議 *gōgi* consultation, conference
議制 *gōgisei* parliamentary system
議制度 *gōgi seido* parliamentary system

A **名** 716 / J4c3e / M3297 MYŌ. MEI distinguished, noted; wise; name. *na* name; fame, reputation; pretext. *na(zukeru)* name, call. *na(ute) no* notorious, famous. *-mei* counter for persons.

2 刀 *meitō* noted sword, fine blade
人 *meijin* master, expert
人肌 *meijinhada* the eccentric spirit of artists
人芸 *meijingei* expert skill
人戦 *meijinsen* chess championship
3 士 *meishi* a celebrity
山 *meizan* famous mountain
工 *meikō* expert artisan
4 手 *meishu* expert
月 *meigetsu* moon of the 15th day of the eighth lunar month and the 13th day of the ninth month
木 *meiboku* historic tree; fine incense wood; choice wood
分 *meibun* moral duty; justice
文 *meibun* fine prose; beautiful passage
文句 *meimonku* a fine expression; famous words
文家 *meibunka* fine writer
5 立 *nada(taru)* famous, notorious
句 *meiku* happy expression; famous phrase; wise saying; excellent haiku poem
号 *myōgō* name of a Buddha or Bodhisattva. *meigō* fame
代 *myōdai* proxy, deputy, representative. *nadai* star (actor), famous, notorious
札 *nafuda* name plate; name card; place card; identification tag
主 *nanushi* (ancient) village head
付 *nazu(keru)* name, call, entitle, christen
付親 *nazu(ke) oya* godparent
目 *meimoku, myōmoku* title, name; pretext; nominal
目的 *meimokuteki ni* nominally
目論 *meimokuron* nominalism
6 臣 *meishin* illustrious retainer
匠 *meishō* master artisan
成 *na (o) na(su)* become famous
曲 *meikyoku* famous music
字 *myōji* surname
有 *naa(ru), na(no)a(ru)* famous, notorious
7 医 *meii* famous doctor
吟 *meigin* excellent haiku poem
妓 *meigi* famous geisha
折 *nao(re)* disgrace
状 *meijō suru* describe
売 *na (o) u(ru)* become famous
灸 *meikyū* famous moxa cautery
花 *meika* famous flower
君 *meikun* wise ruler
言 *meigen* beautiful words, famous words
言集 *meigenshū* analects
作 *meisaku* literary masterpiece
作選 *meisakusen* selection of masterpieces
利 *meiri, myōri* wealth and honor
利心 *meirishin* worldly spirit
声 *meisei* fame, reputation

声啧啧 *meisei-sakusaku* renowned
告 *nano(ri)* announcing one's candidacy; self-introduction
告出 *nano(ri)-de(ru)* give one's name
告合 *nano(ri)-a(u)* introduce each other
8 門 *meimon* noble or illustrious family
取 *natori* a professional name (in the arts) received from one's teacher
刹 *meisatsu* famous temple
宝 *meihō* rare treasure
所 *meisho* place of interest, beauty spot. *nadokoro* name and address; beauty spot
所旧跡 *meisho-kyūseki* scenic and historical places
物 *meibutsu* specialty, noted product
物男 *meibutsu otoko* popular figure
画 *meiga* famous picture, masterpiece
画伯 *meigahaku* famous artist
宛 *naate* address (on a letter)
宛人 *naatenin* addressee
実 *meijitsu* name and reality
実共 *meijitsu tomo ni* both in name and in fact
刺 *meishi* (calling) card
刺入 *meishii(re)* card case
刺受 *meishiu(ke)* card tray
9 香 *meikō* fine incense
城 *meijo* famous castle; sturdy castle
相 *meishō* famous premier; famous minister
前 *namae* name; given name
品 *meihin* perfect article, a gem
茶 *meicha* fine tea
負 *na(ni)o(u), na(nishi)o(u)* (reputation) agrees with facts; be famous
指 *naza(shi)* naming, designation. *naza(su)* name, mention by name
指選 *naza(shi)-era(bu)* designate by name
乗 *nano(ru)* profess to be, introduce oneself as. *nano(ri)* announcing one's candidacy; self-introduction
乗出 *nano(ri)-de(ru)* give one's name
乗合 *nano(ri)-a(u)* introduce each other
10 馬 *meiba* fine horse
高 *nadaka(i)* famous, notorious
酒 *meishu* superior saké
流 *meiryū* famous people. *na (o) naga(su)* become famous
将 *meishō* famous commander
称 *meishō* name, title, term
剣 *meiken* famous sword; excellent sword
家 *meika* good family; a celebrity, an authority
案 *meian* splendid idea, good plan
辱 *na (o) hazukashi(meru)* lose one's reputation
残 *nagori* farewell; keepsake, remembrance; remains, relics
残惜 *nagorio(shii)* reluctant to part
11 遂 *nato(geru)* become successful, become famous
惜 *na (o) osh(mu)* be careful to preserve one's reputation
訳 *meiyaku* excellent translation
産 *meisan* noted product, specialty
著 *meicho* famous work, masterpiece
望 *meibō* reputation, popularity
望家 *meibōka* popular person, a man highly esteemed
12 揚 *na (o) a(geru)* become famous
勝 *meishō* scenic spot
詞 *meishi* noun
答 *meitō* right answer, excellent answer
筆 *meihitsu* excellent calligraphy, excellent calligrapher
無 *nana(shi)* nameless, anonymous, unknown
13 園 *meien* famous garden
僧 *meisō* famous priest
辞 *meiji* term, name
跡 *myōseki* family name
数 *meisū* number of items, articles, etc.; a compound that contains a number
節 *meisetsu* fame and fidelity
義 *meigi* name; justice, moral duty
義人 *meiginin* nominal person
義上 *meigijō no* nominal
誉 *meiyo* honor, credit, glory; dignity; prestige; honorary
誉心 *meiyoshin* desire for fame
誉欲 *meiyoyoku* desire for fame
誉章 *meiyoshō* medal of honor
誉教授 *meiyo kyōju* professor emeritus
誉毀損 *meiyo kison* libel, defamation, slander
誉棄損 *meiyo kison* libel, defamation, slander
誉慾 *meiyoyoku* desire for fame
誉職 *meiyoshoku* honorary position
14 聞 *meibun, myōbun* fame, honor
説 *meisetsu* excellent idea

歌 *meika* famous poem
歌集 *meikashū* anthology of poetry
15 儀 *meigi* name; justice, moral duty
編 *meihen* literary masterpiece
論 *meiron* sound argument, excellent opinion
篇 *meihen* literary masterpiece
器 *meiki* rare utensil, curio
調子 *meichōshi* eloquence
16 親 *naoya, na(zuke)oya* godparent
薬 *meiyaku* famous medicine
17 優 *meiyū* great actor, star
18 題 *nadai* star (actor), famous, notorious; title of a play
19 簿 *meibo* register of names
22 鑑 *meikan* directory

A **同** 717/J4631/M3294 **仝** 114/J2138/M378 Dō the same, the same, the said, ibid. *dō(jiru), dō(zuru)* agree. *ona(ji), onna(ji)* same, identical, equal; uniform; equivalent; similar; common (origin); changeless. *ona(jiku) suru* make similar; have the same (idea). *ona(jiku)* the same (name).

1 一 *dōitsu* sameness, similarity, identity, equality; fairness
一人 *dōitsunin* the same person
一視 *dōitsushi suru* class with, put on a par with, regard in the same light
2 人 *dōjin, dōnin* same person, said person; clique; fraternity; kindred spirits; comrade, colleague
人種 *dōjinshu* racial identity, same race
人雑誌 *dōjin zasshi* a magazine of a society
3 上 *dōjō* same as above, ditto, ibid.
士 *dōshi* fellow, companion
士打 *dōshiu(chi)* killing each other by mistake
士討 *dōshiu(chi)* killing each other by mistake
4 日 *dōjitsu* the same day
月 *dōgetsu* the same month
氏 *dōshi* the same person, the said person
父母 *dōfubo* the same parents
分母 *dōbumbo* common denominator
文 *dōbun* same script; same language
心 *dōshin* same mind, unanimity; concentricity; policeman. *dōshin no* concentric
心円 *dōshin'en* concentric circles
仁 *dōjin* universal benevolence
仁教会 *Dōjin Kyōkai* Universalist Church
化 *dōka* assimilation, adaptation, absorption
化作用 *dōka sayō* assimilation, metabolism, anabolism
5 処 *dōsho* the same place
穴 *dōketsu* being buried in the same grave
巧異曲 *dōkō-ikyoku* practically the same
6 舟 *dōshū* shipmates, fellow passengers
色 *dōshoku* the same color
気 *dōki* same temperament, same turn of mind
地 *dōchi* the same place; that place
列 *dōretsu* same rank, same file; company; attendance
邦 *dōhō* the same country
字 *dōji* the same character
行 *dōkō* travelling together. *dōgyō* fellow pilgrim, fellow practicer of austerities
行者 *dōkōsha* fellow travellers
年 *ona(ji)doshi, ona(i)doshi* same age. *dōnen* that year, same year; same age
年輩 *dōnempai* persons of the same age
名 *dōmei, dōmyō* the same name
名異人 *dōmei-ijin* namesake; person with the same name
好 *dōkō* similar tastes
好会 *dōkōkai* association of like-minded people
好者 *dōkōsha* people of similar tastes
7 車 *dōsha suru* taking the same car or train
局 *dōkyoku* the said bureau, the same bureau
体 *dōtai ni* as one, together
役 *dōyaku* colleague
村 *dōson* the same village; that village
町 *dōchō* the same town; that town
社 *dōsha* the same firm
形 *dōkei* the same shape
系 *dōkei* affiliated, akin
坐 *dōza* sitting together; the same theater; involvement, entanglement, implication
伴 *dōhan suru* accompany, go with
伴者 *dōhansha* companion

位 *dōi* the same rank; the same digit
位元素 *dōi genso* isotope
労 *dōrō* working together
労者 *dōrōsha* fellow worker
志 *dōshi* same mind; kindred soul, comrade
志打 *dōshiu(chi)* internal strife, fighting among themselves
志会 *dōshikai* an association of kindred spirits
志的 *dōshiteki* companionable
8 門 *dōmon* fellow student
店 *dōten* the same store, the same shop
房 *dōbō* the same room; sharing a room; sharers of a room
価 *dōka* equivalent
姓 *dōsei* the same surname
所 *dōsho* the same place, the same address, the said place
朋 *dōbō* companions
夜 *dōya* the same night; that night
宗 *dōshū* the same sect
学 *dōgaku* the same school
事 *dōji* the same event; no change (on the stock market)
国 *dōkoku* the same country, the same province, the said country
国民 *dōkokumin* fellow countrymen
居 *dōkyo* living with (someone)
居人 *dōkyonin* a person living with the family
性 *dōsei* the same sex; homosexuality; homogeneity; congeniality
性愛 *dōseiai* homosexual love
9 信 *dōshin* the same faith
侶 *dōryō, dōryo* companion
相 *dōshō* the said (cabinet) minister
派 *dōha* the same sect
祖 *dōso* common ancestor
封 *dōfū* enclosure. *dōfū suru* enclose
乗 *dōjō* riding together
前 *dōzen* same as above, ditto, ibid.
点 *dōten* tie, draw
室 *dōshitsu* the same room
型 *dōkei* the same type, the same pattern
県 *dōken* the same prefecture
省 *dōshō* the said ministry, the same ministry
音 *dōon* the same sound; one voice
音語 *dōongo* homonym
級 *dōkyū* the same grade, same class
級生 *dōkyūsei* classmates
胞 *dōhō, harakara, dōbō* brothers, brethren, fellow countrymen, fellowmen
胞愛 *dōhōai* brotherly love
10 座 *dōza* sitting together; the same theater; involvement, entanglement, implication
席 *dōseki* sitting together, being present together
病 *dōbyō* the same sickness
格 *dōkaku* the same rank, equality; apposition
流 *dōryū* the same style; same school; common origin
紙 *dōshi* the same newspaper
郷 *dōkyō* same village, town, or province
衾 *dōkin* sharing the bed
家 *dōke* the said family; the same family
党 *dōtō* the same political party
書 *dōsho* the same book, the said book
時 *dōji* the same time. *dōji no* synchronous, simultaneous. *dōji ni* coincident with; on the other hand; while
時代 *dōjidai* the same age, same period
11 道 *dōdō suru* go with, accompany
視 *dōshi suru* treat alike
断 *dōdan* the same, ditto
宿 *dōshuku* lodging in the same hotel
異 *dōi* similarities and differences
船 *dōsen* the ship; taking the same ship
船人 *dōsen (no) hito* fellow voyager
情 *dōjō* sympathy
情心 *dōjōshin* sympathy, compassion
情者 *dōjōsha* sympathizer
族 *dōzoku* the same family, same tribe, same race
族会 *dōzokukai* family council, family company
族会社 *dōzokugaisha* family corporation, affiliated concern
窓 *dōsō* the same school
窓生 *dōsōsei* schoolmate, fellow student, alumnus
窓会 *dōsōkai* alumni meeting
12 棲 *dōsei suru* cohabit with, live together
筆 *dōhitsu* the same handwriting
等 *dōtō* equality, same rights; same rank
然 *dōzen* the same
期 *dōki* the same period; same class; synchronism
期生 *dōkisei* classmate

3 【口】口土士夂夊夕大女子宀寸小⺌尢尸屮山川巛工己巾干幺广廴廾弋弓ヨ彑彡彳

13 腹 *dōfuku* born of the same mother; kindred spirits
数 *dōsū* same number
罪 *dōzai* the same offense
勢 *dōzei* party, company
感 *dōkan* the same feeling, sympathy; concurrence
義 *dōgi* the same meaning
義語 *dōgigo* synonym
業 *dōgyō* the same trade, same business
業者 *dōgyōsha* person in the same business; the profession, the trade
業組合 *dōgyō kumiai* trade association, craft, guild
意 *dōi* the same meaning; same opinion; agreement, consent, approval
意見 *dōiken* the same opinion
意義 *dōigi* the same meaning
意語 *dōigo* synonym
盟 *dōmei* alliance, league, union
盟休校 *dōmei kyūkō* student strike
盟条約 *dōmei jōyaku* treaty of alliance
盟国 *dōmeikoku* ally (of another nation)
盟軍 *dōmeigun* allied armies
盟怠業 *dōmei taigyō* go-slow strike
盟罷業 *dōmei higyō* strike
14 僚 *dōryō* associate, colleague
様 *dōyō* same, same kind, identical, like, equal. *ona(ji) yō ni* similarly
説 *dōsetsu* the same opinion
誌 *dōshi* the same magazine
語反復 *dōgo-hampuku* tautology
種 *dōshu* the same kind; homogeneousness; the same race
種同文 *dōshu-dōbun* same race and same script
種類 *dōshurui* the same kind
15 慶 *dōkei* a matter for mutual congratulation
権 *dōken* the same rights, equal rights
輩 *dōhai* comrade, colleague, one's equal
趣味 *dōshumi* the same interests
調 *dōchō* alignment; tuning
調者 *dōchōsha* fellow traveler, sympathizer
質 *dōshitsu* the same quality, same nature, homogeneity
質的 *dōshitsuteki* homogeneous
18 職 *dōshoku* the same occupation; the said occupation
類 *dōrui* the same kind; accomplice
額 *dōgaku* the same amount
藩 *dōhan* the same clan

4

局 718 / J-X / M-X See 局 1412.

吴 719 / J-X / M3365 See 呉 741.

吸 720 / J-X / M3372 See 吸 713.

𠮷 721 / J-X / M3420 Nonstandard for 品 792.

呎 722 / J5268 / M3423 SHAKU. *fīto* foot, feet (distance measure).

听 723 / J5261 / M3352 KIN *wara(u)* laugh with open mouth. TEI, CHO hear, listen to. *pondo* pound.

吭 724 / J5262 / M3353 KŌ throat; neck; pivot; voice. *nodo* throat. *kubi* neck.

吩 725 / J5266 / M3347 FUN give orders; spout, emit. *fu(ku)* spout, emit, flush out.
8 咐 *fumpu* order

吮 726 / J5264 / M3356 SEN, SHUN suck, lick. *su(u)* inhale; imbibe, sip; suck, suck out.
6 血 *senketsu* sucking blood

吽 727 / J525f / M3378 KŌ, GŌ bark; bite. UN transcription of Sanscrit *hum.*
7 呀 *kōga* bark

呂 728 / J4f24 / M3386 RYO, RO backbone.
9 律 *roretsu* articulation, pronunciation

吻 729 / J4a2d / M3375 FUN proboscis. *kuchiwaki* sides of the mouth
6 合 *fungō* coincidence, conformity, concurrence; union; junction

吼 730 / J5263 / M3377 Kō. Ku. *ho(eru)* bark, bay, howl, bellow, roar, cry.
7 声 *ho(e)goe* bark, bellow, howl, roar

呀 731 / J5260 / M3383 Ga open mouth, bare teeth; be vacant, be empty.
7 呀 *gaga* open mouth wide, bare teeth; laugh with mouth open
12 然 *gazen* wide open, vacant, empty

吶 732 / J5265 / M3370 Totsu stutter.
12 喊 *tokkan* war cry
13 嗟 *tossa* moment, instant. *tossa ni* at once

吾 733 / J3863 / M3379 Go. *waga* my, our, one's own. *ware* I, oneself, self, ego.
8 妹 *wagimo* (ancient) my wife, my love
妹子 *wagimoko* (ancient) my wife, my love
12 等 *warera* we
15 輩 *wagahai* I

B **呈** 734 / J4468 / M3401 **呈** 735 / J-X / M3363 Tei *tei(suru)* offer, present; send (a letter); exhibit; develop (symptoms); assume (airs).
3 上 *teijō* presentation
5 出 *teishutsu* presentation
示 *teishi, teiji* presentation
示払 *teijibara(i)* payment on demand
6 色 *teishoku* color, coloring

吝 736 / J5267 / M3327 Rin. *shiwa(i), yabusa(kana)* miserly, stingy, unwilling, sparing (of praise). *kechi* stinginess.
7 坊 *shiwambō* miser, stingy fellow
13 嗇 *rinshoku, kechi* stinginess, miserliness
嗇坊 *kechimbō* miser, stingy fellow
嗇臭 *kechikusa(i)* stingy; shabby
嗇家 *rinshokuka* miser, stingy person
嗇漢 *rinshokukan* miser, stingy person

呑 737 / J465d / M3329 Don. *no(mu)* drink, taste, take; swallow, devour; smoke; conceal (a weapon); accept (an idea); despise.
3 口 *nomiguchi* bung hole; end of a pipe stem
4 込 *no(mi)-ko(mu)* swallow, gulp down; understand
6 気 *nonki* optimistic, carefree, careless, heedless
気者 *nonkimono* happy-go-lucky person
7 兵衛 *nombē* heavy drinker

呆 738 / J4a72 / M3395 Hō. Bō. *aki(reru)* be amazed, be aghast, be disgusted, be shocked. *boke* dullheadedness.
6 返 *aki(re)-kae(ru)* be amazed at, be disgusted with
気 *akke* blank amazement. *utsuke* stupid fellow
気者 *utsukemono* stupid fellow
気無 *akkena(i)* disappointing
8 果 *aki(re)-ha(teru)* be amazed at, be disgusted with
12 然 *bōzen to* in blank amazement
18 顔 *aki(re)gao* amazed look

吠 739 / J4b4a / M3331 Hai. Bei. *ho(eru)* bark, bay, howl, bellow, roar, cry.
5 付 *ho(e)-tsu(ku)* bark at
8 回 *ho(e)-mawa(ru)* run around barking; run around yelling
叫 *ho(e)-sake(bu)* howl, roar, cry out
7 声 *ho(e)goe* bark, howl, roar, bellow, baying
陀 *Bēda* the Vedas
陀文学 *Bēda bungaku* Vedic literature
9 面 *hoezura (o) ka(ku)* make a tearful face
11 掛 *ho(e)-ka(keru)* bark at
猛 *ho(e)-ta(keru)* roar

B **吟** 740 / J3663 / M3330 Gin singing; recital; song; poem. *gin(jiru), gin(zuru)* sing, chant, recite.
6 行 *ginkō* traveling minstrel
7 社 *ginsha* poetry club
声 *ginsei* reciting voice
8 味 *gimmi* testing, scrutinizing, careful inquiry
9 客 *ginkaku* poet
11 唱 *ginshō* recite, chant
遊詩人 *gin'yū shijin* troubadour, minnesinger, minstrel
12 詠 *gin'ei* singing, recital; song, poem
14 誦 *ginshō suru* recite, chant
16 嘯 *ginshō suru* recite, chant

B 呉 741/J3862/M3365' 呉 719/J-X/M3365 Go. *ku(reru)* give; do (something) for.
[4]手 *ku(re)te* donor; one who does something for you
[7]呉 *kuregure mo* repeatedly, sincerely, earnestly
[8]服 *gofuku* piece goods, dry-goods, draperies
服店 *gofukuten* dry-goods store
服物 *gofukumono* piece goods, dry-goods, draperies
服屋 *gofukuya* dry-goods store
服商 *gofukushō* dry-goods dealer
[9]音 *goon* Wu-dynasty pronunciation
[12]越同舟 *goetsu-dōshū* enemies in the same boat
遣 *kure(te) ya(ru)* give, do (something) for

A 否 742/J485d/M3340 Hi no, noes. *ina(mu)* refuse, decline; deny. *iya(mu)* detest, dislike. *ina* no, nay. *ina(ya)* as soon as, no sooner than, the moment; yes or no; objection; if, whether. *ie, iie* no. *iya, iiya* no, nay; yes, well.
[7]決 *hiketsu* rejection, voting down
応 *iya(demo)-ō(demo)* willy-nilly, whether willing or not. *iya-ō* an answer regarding an agreement or disagreement
応無 *iyaōna(shi) no* compulsory
否 *iyaiya* reluctantly; by no means
否乍 *iyaiyanaga(ra)* reluctantly
[8]定 *hitei* denial
定文 *hiteibun* negative sentence
定的 *hiteiteki* negative, contradictory
[11]運 *hiun* bad fortune, misfortune
[12]程 *iya (to iu) hodo* persistently, bitterly, extremely
[14]認 *hinin* denial, disapproval, repudiation, veto, nonrecognition

B 含 743/J345e/M3350 Gan. *fuku(mu)* hold in the mouth; bear in mind, understand; cherish, harbor; contain, comprise, have, hold, include, embrace; be charged or loaded with, be dripping with, be full of, be suffused with. *fuku(maseru), fuku(masu)* soak, saturate; suckle, make one hold something in the mouth; include; instruct, make one understand. *fuku(meru)* include, instruct, make one understand. *fuku(mi)* implication, hidden meaning; latitude; atmosphere, tone, sentiment; inclusion.
[4]水化合物 *gansuikagōbutsu* hydrate
水炭素 *gansuitanso* carbohydrate
[6]有 *gan'yū suru* contain, have, hold, include
有量 *gan'yūryō* content (of a mineral, etc.)
[7]声 *fuku(mi)goe* muffled voice
[8]味 *gammi suru* taste; think over carefully
油層 *gan'yusō* oil strata
金 *gankin* containing gold
[10]笑 *fuku(mi)wara(i)* suppressed laugh, smile, giggle, chuckle
[11]羞草 *ojigisō* sensitive plant, mimosa
[13]蓄 *ganchiku* implication, significance
[14]嗽 *gansō, ugai* gargling, rinsing
塵率 *ganjinritsu* dust content
[16]糖 *gantō* sugar content
糖量 *gantōryō* sugar content

A 告 744/J3970/M3381' 告 745/J-X/M3381 Koku. *tsu(geru)* tell, inform, announce, proclaim; bid, order. *tsu(ge)* oracle, revelation, inspiration.
[3]口 *tsu(ge)guchi* talebearing
[4]文 *kokubun* written appeal of a case
天子 *hibari* skylark
[5]白 *kokuhaku* confession, acknowledgment
示 *tsu(ge)-shime(su)* tell, proclaim. *kokuji* notification, bulletin
示板 *kokujiban* bulletin board
[6]回 *tsu(ge)-mawa(su)* noise abroad
[7]別 *kokubetsu* leave-taking, farewell
別式 *kokubetsushiki* funeral service
[8]知 *tsu(ge)-shi(raseru), tsu(ge)-shi(rasu), kokuchi suru* tell, notify, reveal. *kokuchi* notice, announcement
知板 *kokuchiban* bulletin board
知書 *kokuchisho* notice
[9]発 *kokuhatsu* prosecution; indictment; accusation, complaint, denunciation
発状 *kokuhatsujō* bill of indictment
発者 *kokuhatsusha* prosecutor, accuser, informant
[11]達 *kokutatsu* notification
[12]訴 *kokuso* accusation, complaint
訴人 *kokusonin* one who brings suit
[13]辞 *kokuji* address, farewell address

解 *kokkai* penance
16 諭 *kokuyu* official notice, proclamation

A 君 746 J372f M3323 KUN mister (familiar). *kimi* you (familiar); ruler.
3 子 *kunshi* true gentleman, wise man; an official
子人 *kunshijin* true gentleman, wise man
4 父 *kumpu* one's lord and father
王 *kunnō* king
辺 *kumpen* (at) the ruler's side
公 *kunkō* lord, master, ruler
5 代 *Kimi(ga)yo* Japan's national anthem
民 *kummin* the king and his people
主 *kunshu* ruler
主国 *kunshukoku* monarchy
主専制 *kunshu sensei* autocratic monarchy
主政 *kunshusei* monarchy
主政体 *kunshu seitai* monarchy
6 臣 *kunshin* ruler and ruled; master and servant
7 位 *kun'i* throne, crown
8 国 *kunkoku* king and country
命 *kummei* imperial command, one's lord's orders
10 家 *kunka* ruler's residence
恩 *kun'on* imperial benevolence
11 側 *kunsoku* the (palace) court
12 等 *kimira* you folks
17 臨 *kunrin suru* reign; control, dictate
19 寵 *kunchō* a lord's favor

B 吹 747 J3f61 M3373 SUI. *fu(ku) vi* and *vt* breathe, blow; play (a wind instrument); emit; smelt; mint; brag. *fu(kasu) vt* smoke, puff.
2 入 *fu(ki)-i(reru)* breathe into; blow into; (winds) blow in
3 口 *fu(ki)guchi* nozzle
下 *fu(ki)-o(rosu)* blow down (from a mountain)
上 *fu(ki)-a(garu)* be blown up high (as dust, or water in geysers). *fu(ki)-a(geru)* spout (water), blow up; wash ashore. *fu(ki)a(ge)* fountain, spouting, spray
4 手 *fu(ki)te* blower
止 *fu(ki)-ya(mu)* blow over, die down, subside
分 *fu(ki)-wa(keru)* winnow; smelt; assay; blow apart
井戸 *fu(ki)ido* artesian well, drilled well
込 *fu(ki)-ko(mu)* blow into, breathe into; record; inspire, instill. *fukiko(mi)* recording
5 矢 *fu(ki)ya* blowgun
立 *fu(ki)-ta(teru)* blow up (a fire); blow (a trumpet); brag
代 *fu(ki)ka(e)* substitute actor; dummy; stand-in; recasting, reminting
付 *fu(ki)-tsu(keru)* blow against (a house), blow (sparks) upon; blow ashore. *fu(ki)-tsu(ku)* (winds) blow against (something), blow (something) along; blow up (a fire in a brazier). *fu(ki)tsu(ke)* spraying; air blast
払 *fu(ki)-hara(u)* drive away (clouds)
去 *fu(ki)-sa(ru)* blow away
出 *fu(ki)-da(su)* begin to blow; breathe out; burst out laughing. *fu(ki)-de(ru)* begin to blow; break out (in sores)
出物 *fu(ki)demono* skin eruption, rash, pimple, eczema, boil, ulcer
6 竹 *fu(ki)dake* bamboo blowpipe (for a charcoal fire)
回 *fu(ki)-mawa(su)* blow around. *fu(ki)-mawa(shi)* blowing; stroke of fortune
返 *fu(ki)-kae(su)* blow and overturn; resuscitate
当 *fu(ki)-a(taru) vi* blow against, strike. *fu(ki)-a(teru) vt* (winds) blow against, hit (something) with a blow gun
7 伸 *fu(ki)-no(basu)* blow (glass)
抜 *fu(ki)-nu(ku)* blow through, blow over, blow itself out. *fu(ki)nu(ki)* ventilation, draft; streamer, pennant
折 *fu(ki)-o(ru)* break by blowing
8 送 *fu(ki)-oku(ru) vt* waft, blow over to
直 *fu(ki)nao(shi)* recasting, recoinage
9 飛 *fu(t)to(bu) vi* be blown off, blow off. *fu(ki)-to(basu) vt* blow away, blow off
通 *fu(ki)-tō(su)* blow through, penetrate; keep blowing. *fukitō(shi)* windy place
降 *fu(ki)bu(ri)* driving rain
荒 *fu(ki)-susa(mu), fu(ki)-susa(bu), fu(ki)-a(reru), fu(ki)-a(rasu)* blow violently, sweep over, devastate
奏 *suisō* playing wind instruments
奏者 *suisōsha* wind-instrument player
奏楽 *suisōgaku* wind-instrument music

奏楽団 *suisō gakudan* wind-instrument orchestra
奏楽隊 *suisō gakutai* brass band
奏楽器 *suisō gakki* wind instruments
10 起 *fu(ki)-oko(su)* blow up (a wind); fan up (a fire)
倒 *fu(ki)-tao(su)* blow down
値 *fukine* jump in prices, boom
晒 *fu(ki)-sara(su)* blow with unhindered sweep
消 *fu(ki)-ke(su)* blow out (a fire)
流 *fu(ki)-naga(su)* blow away, drive out of course. *fukinaga(shi)* streamer, pennant
破 *fu(ki)-yabu(ru)* blow to pieces
挙 *suikyo suru* propose (for office)
11 過 *fu(ki)-su(giru)* blow past, sweep past
捲 *fu(ki)-maku(ru) vi* (the wind) sweeps along; brag, boast. *fu(ki)-meku(ru) vt* blow off (a roof)
掛 *fu(ki)-ka(keru)* blow on, breathe on, spray. *fu(k)ka(keru)* blow on, breathe on, spray; challenge, pick (a quarrel); make an unreasonable demand
寄 *fu(ki)-yo(seru)* drift, blow together. *fu(ki)yo(se)* collection; drift (of sand or snow)
雪 *fubuki* snowstorm, blizzard. *fubu(ku)* (winds) blow hard; (snow) is driven
12 渡 *fu(ki)-wata(ru)* blow over (an area)
散 *fu(ki)-chi(rasu)* scatter, blow about
募 *fu(ki)-tsuno(ru)* blow with growing intensity
落 *fu(ki)-oto(su)* blow down (fruit)
替 *fu(ki)ka(e)* substitute actor; dummy; stand-in; recasting, reminting
13 溜 *fu(ki)damari* snowdrift
零 *fu(ki)-kobo(reru)* boil over
14 鳴 *suimei suru* blow (a whistle) *fu(ki)-na(rasu)* blow a blast
舞 *fu(ki)-mawa(su)* (winds) blow ⌈erratically
16 頻 *fu(ki)-shiki(ru)* blow hard
17 聴 *fuichō* announcement, publicity, advertisement, notification, recommendation
19 曝 *fu(ki)-sara(su)* blow with unhindered sweep. *fu(ki)sara(shi) no*, *fu(ki)zara(shi) no* exposed to the wind, weather-beaten, wind-blown, wind-swept, bleak, bare
離 *fu(ki)-hana(su)* blow off, blow apart; blow darts

5

咏 748 / J5269 / M3494 See **詠** 5584.

咜 749 / J-X / M-X See **咤** 781.

呰 750 / J526f / M3452 SHI blame, censure, scold; weak; damage, fault; this.

咋 751 / J5a70 / M3488 SAKU bite; loud voice, noisy. SA soon; clearly. *ku(u)* eat; subsist on; bite at; gnaw at.

咐 752 / J5275 / M3497 FU. BU. HO. order, exhale.

呟 753 / J526c / M3427 GEN. *tsubuya(ku)* mutter, grumble, murmur.

咆 754 / J5276 / M3484 HŌ bark, roar; get angry.
10 哮 *hōkō* yell, roar, howl

呶 755 / J5273 / M3460 DO noisy.
8 呶 *dodo* harping on the same point

呷 756 / J526e / M3461 KŌ bite, chew; suck; eat; quack. *su(u)* inhale; imbibe, sip; suck, suck out.
8 呷 *kōkō* quack of a duck

呱 757 / J526d / M3454 KO cry.
8 呱 *koko* baby's birth cry
呱声 *koko (no) koe* baby's birth cry

咀 758 / J5272 / M3476 SO bite; eat.
21 嚼 *soshaku* chewing, mastication
嚼面 *soshakumen* chewing surface

咎 759 / J526b / M3493 **咎** 760 / J-X / M-X KYŪ. *toga(meru)* blame, censure, reprimand, find fault with, rebuke; challenge; get inflamed. *toga* fault, blame; charge, offense, sin.
2 人 *toganin* criminal, offender

5 立 *togameda(te)* blame, censure, faultfinding, rebuke

咄 761 J5274 M3480 TOTSU pshaw, God forbid, Shame on you, exclamation of surprise. *hanashi* talk, chat, conversation; story; rumor; news; consultation, negotiations; facts, reasons.
8 咄 *totsutotsu* (tongue) clicking; groaning; exclamation of surprise
10 家 *hanashika* storyteller
13 嗟 *tossa* moment, instant. *tossa ni* at once

呻 762 J5271 M3470 SHIN. *ume(ku)* groan, moan. *umeki* groan, moan, moaning.
6 叫 *ume(ki)-sake(bu)* groan
7 吟 *shingin suru, ume(ku)* groan. *shingin* moaning, groaning; pining
声 *umekigoe* groan, moan, moaning

呵 763 J526a M3459 KA. *ka(su)* scold; blow on. *shika(ru)* scold, reprove.
5 付 *shika(ri)-tsu(keru)* scold severely
8 呵 *kaka* ha ha (laughing)
11 責 *kashaku* torture, maltreatment

呪 764 J3c76 M3443 **咒** 765 J5270 M3444 JU spell, curse, incantation. *majina(u)* charm, cast a spell over. *noro(u)* curse. *noroi* curse, anathema, malediction. *majinai* spell, charm, enchantment
4 文 *jumon* magic formula, incantation, curse, spell, charm
8 咀 *juso* curse, anathema
法 *juhō* enchanter's formula
物 *jubutsu* fetish
物神 *jubutsushin* fetish
物崇拝 *jubutsu sūhai* fetishism
11 符 *jufu* charm, amulet, talisman
術 *jujutsu* magic, incantation, sorcery
術的 *jujutsuteki* magical
12 詛 *juso* curse, anathema
16 縛 *jubaku* a spell

A **味** 766 J4c23 M3456 MI taste, flavor, dash; touch, tinge; counter for foods and drinks. *aji(wau)* taste; appreciate, experience. *aji, aji(wai)* taste, flavor, aroma; zest; experience; tinge. *aji na* clever, witty, smart.
4 方 *mikata* friend, ally, supporter. *ajiwa(i)kata* way to taste
5 付 *ajitsu(ke)* seasoning
加減 *aji kagen* seasoning
6 気無 *ajikena(i)* irksome, insipid, wretched, vain
7 見 *ajimi* sampling, foretaste
利 *ajikiki* taster
8 知 *ajiwa(i)-shi(ru)* taste and know
到 *mitō suru* taste thoroughly
11 得 *mitoku suru* taste thoroughly
淋 *mirin* sweet saké
12 覚 *mikaku* sense of taste
13 感 *mikan* sense of taste
楽 *aji(wai)-tano(shimu)* enjoy (art, etc.)
14 読 *midoku suru* appreciate a book
15 醂 *mirin* sweet saké
噌 *miso* fermented bean paste; flattery
噌付 *miso (o) tsu(keru)* make a mess of, fizzle
噌汁 *misoshiru, misojiru* bean-paste soup
噌豆 *miso mame* soy beans
噌歯 *miso(p)pa* decayed baby tooth; dirty black teeth
噌煮 *misoni* boiling with bean paste
噌漬 *misozuke* pickled in bean paste
噌漉 *misokoshi* bean-paste strainer

A **命** 767 J4c3f M3473 MYŌ. MEI command, decree; life; destiny. *mei(jiru), mei(zuru)* command; appoint. *inochi* life. *mikoto* words of a ruler; lord, prince.
3 乞 *inochigoi* pleading for one's life
4 日 *meinichi* death anniversary
中 *meichu* a hit
中弾 *meichūdan* (direct) hit; straight shot
中数 *meichūsū* number of hits
5 令 *meirei* command, decree, directive, order
令一下 *meirei-ikka* immediately, as soon as the order is given
令文 *meireibun* imperative sentence
令形 *meireikei* imperative form
令法 *meireihō* imperative mood
令書 *meireisho* decree, directive
6 名 *meimei* naming, christening
7 辛辛 *inochikaragara* for dear life; barely escaping alive

8 取 *inochito(ri) no* fatal
知 *inochishi(razu)* recklessness; daredevil. *inochishi(razu) no* long-lasting
9 拾 *inochibiro(i)* narrow escape from death
10 冥加 *inochi-myōga* providential protection
11 運 *meiun* fate, doom
掛 *inochiga(ke) de* at the risk of life
13 数 *meisū* span of life; destiny
14 綱 *inochi (no) tsuna* the thread of life
18 題 *meidai* thesis, proposition
20 懸 *inochigake no* risky, desperate. *inochigake de* at the risk of life

A **周** 768 / J3c7e / M3441' SHŪ circuit, lap, circumference, vicinity; Chou (dynasty). *mawa(ri)* rotation; circumference, girth; surroundings, border; detour; tour; efficacy or effect (of something taken); spread (of flames). *gururi* surroundings.
4 辺 *shūhen* circumference, perimeter; environs, outskirts
6 回 *shūkai* circumference, girth, surroundings
年 *shūnen* whole year; anniversary (used after number)
7 囲 *shūi* circumference, girth; surroundings
忌 *shūki* anniversary of a person's death (used after number)
8 到 *shūtō na* scrupulous, careful, meticulous, complete
易 *shūeki* divination
知 *shūchi* common knowledge
知徹底 *shūchi-tettei* (something) known to all
波 *shūha* cycle, wave, frequency
波変調 *shūha henchō* frequency modulation, FM
波帯 *shūhatai* frequency band
波数 *shūhasū* frequency (in electricity)
10 流 *shūryū* flowing around
航 *shūkō* circumnavigation; a circle tour by ship
11 密 *shūmitsu na* scrupulous, careful, meticulous, complete
遊 *shūyū* tour, round trip
遊券 *shūyūken* excursion ticket
章 *awa(teru)* be confused, lose one's head, be hurried, be hasty. *shūshō* agitation, frustration
旋 *shūsen* good offices, recommendation, mediation; (Tokugawa-era) employment office
旋人 *shūsennin* agent, middleman
旋屋 *shūsen'ya* broker, employment agency office
旋料 *shūsenryō* brokerage, commission
旋業 *shūsengyō* brokerage, commission agency
旋業者 *shūsengyōsha* broker, middleman; employment agency
12 智 *shūchi* common knowledge
極星 *shūkyokusei* circumpolar star
期 *shūki* period, cycle
期性 *shūkisei* cyclic, periodic
16 覧 *shūran* looking all around

A **呼** 769 / J3846 / M3471 KO. *yo(bu)* call, call out to; invoke; summon; invite; attract; send for; name, designate; bring about. *yo(bawaru)* shout, exclaim, cry, yell, roar, howl; cry for, clamor for, advocate. *-yo(bawari) suru* treat as, denounce as, call (someone something).
2 入 *yo(bi)-i(reru)* call in, restore (a disowned son)
3 下 *yo(bi)-o(rosu)* call down (from above)
上 *yo(bi)-a(geru)* call out, call up, call the roll
子 *yo(bu)ko, yo(bi)ko* police whistle
子鳥 *yobukodori* cuckoo
4 止 *yo(bi)-to(meru)* call (to someone) to stop, challenge; call back
水 *yo(bi)mizu* priming water
込 *yo(bi)-ko(mu)* call in; restore a disowned son
5 立 *yo(bi)-ta(teru)* call out, call (someone to) come, summon
付 *yo(bi)-tsu(keru)* call (to someone), send for, summon
号 *kogō suru* cry out, proclaim; appeal to; exaggerate
出 *yo(bi)-da(su)* call out, call before, call up; summon, subpoena; decoy; conjure up, involve
出状 *yobida(shi)jō* subpoena, summons
出符号 *yobida(shi) fugō* call letters
出電話 *yobida(shi) denwa* a telephone call to a nonsubscriber received at a neighbor's house

6 回 *yo(bi)-mawa(ru)* go around calling out (for someone)
気 *koki* exhalation
返 *yo(bi)-kae(su)* recall, call back
迎 *yo(bi)-muka(eru)* send for
叫 *yo(bawari)-sake(bu)* cry out to
合 *yo(bi)-a(u)* call each other (brethren); call to each other
名 *yo(bi)na* given name, popular name, alias
吸 *kokyū* breath, respiration; knack, secret; tone, time. *kokyū suru* breathe
吸運動 *kokyū undō* breathing exercises
吸器 *kokyūki* respiratory organs
吸器病 *kokyūkibyō* respiratory disease
7 応 *koō suru* hail each other; act in concert; respond to
戻 *yo(bi)-modo(su)* call back, call home; resuscitate, recall
声 *yo(bi)goe* call, yell, hail; street huckster's call; rumor
売 *yo(bi)u(ri)* hawking, peddling
求 *yo(bi)-moto(meru)* call upon, call for (help)
8 物 *yo(bi)mono* attraction, feature, main event
奉 *yo(bi)-matsu(ru)* call upon (a god or rulers)
10 起 *yo(bi)-oko(su)* *vt* wake, rouse, call; call up; recall
値 *yo(bi)ne* nominal price, price asked, bidding
格 *kokaku* vocative case
称 *koshō suru* call out, call (someone by name or title)
留 *yo(bi)-to(meru)* call (to someone) to stop, challenge; call back
11 掛 *yo(bi)-ka(keru)* call out to, accost; address (a crowd). *yo(bi)ka(ke)* a call (to prayer)
捨 *yobisu(te)* calling to someone disrespectfully
寄 *yo(bi)-yo(seru)* send for, summon, call together
12 集 *yo(bi)-atsu(meru)* assemble. *yo(bawari)-atsu(meru)* call together. *yo(bawari)-atsu(maru)* be called together
違 *yo(bi)chiga(e)* calling by the wrong name
覚 *yo(bi)-sa(masu)* *vt* wake up
13 鈴 *yo(bi)rin* buzzer, door bell, call bell
馴 *yo(bi)-na(reru)* be used to calling (someone by a certain name)
14 慣 *yo(bi)-na(reru)* be used to calling (someone by a certain name)
誤 *yo(bi)-ayama(ru)* call by the wrong name
16 醒 *yo(bi)-sa(masu)* *vt* wake up

A **和** 770 J4f42 M3490 **咊** 771 J-X M3489 KA. WA sum; peace, harmony, reconciliation, unity. *wa(suru)* harmonize, be in harmony with; make peace, be reconciled; respond, echo. *yawa(ragu)* *vi* soften, be reconciled; lessen; calm down. *yawa(rageru)* *vt* soften, moderate, ease, alleviate, mitigate, relax; appease; dilute (wine); tone down (colors); comfort; pacify, quiet. *nago(mu)* *vi* be softened; get quiet. *nago(meru)* *vt* soften, quiet down. *na(gu)* get calm, die down. *nago(yakana)* mellow, matured, refined, genial. *nagi* lull, calm.

2 人 *Wajin* (an old word for) a Japanese
4 毛 *nikoge* (bird's) down
牛 *wagyū* Japanese cow
文 *wabun* Japanese, Japanese writing
文英訳 *wabun'eiyaku* Japanese-English translation
5 平 *wahei* peace
本 *wahon* Japanese book, book bound in Japanese style
6 合 *wagō* harmony, unity, union
字 *waji* Japanese syllabaries; characters originating in Japan; Japanese literature
名 *wamyō, wamei* Japanese name
気 *waki* harmony, peacefulness
気藹藹 *wakiaiai* maturity; refinement; harmony
7 声 *kasei, wasei* harmony (in music), concord
8 協 *wakyō* harmony, concord
物 *aemono* vegetable side dish
服 *wafuku* Japanese clothes, kimono
尚 *oshō* chief priest of a temple
英 *Wa-Ei* Japanese-English
学 *wagaku* Japanese literature
9 音 *waon* the rare *on* pronunciations originating in Japan
風 *wafū* light breeze; Japanese style
食 *washoku* Japanese food
独 *Wa-Doku* Japanese-German

約 *wayaku* treaty of peace
姦 *wakan* fornication, adultery
室 *washitsu* Japanese-style room
臭 *washū* Japanese flavor, Japanism
衷 *wachū* harmony, concord
衷協同 *wachū kyōdō* harmonious cooperation
洋 *wayō* Japanese and Western
洋折衷 *wayō setchū* semi-European style
10 紙 *washi* Japanese paper
訓 *wakun* Japanese reading (of a character)
書 *washo* Japanese book, book bound in Japanese style
11 船 *wasen* Japanese-style ship
訳 *wayaku* Japanese translation
寇 *wakō* Japanese pirates
菓子 *wagashi* Japanese confectionery
12 順 *wajun* normal weather; docile; quiet (person)
硫 *waryū* vulcanization
装 *wasō* Japanese dress; Japanese binding
裁 *wasai* Japanese sewing
琴 *wagon* Japanese harp, ancient koto
13 睦 *waboku* reconciliation, conclusion of a peace treaty
解 *wakai* reconciliation; atonement; compromise. *wakai, wage* translation; rewriting Chinese *(kambun)* in mixed script
戦 *wasen* peace and war
楽 *wagaku* Japanese music. *waraku* peace and harmony
漢 *Wa-Kan* Japan and China; Japanese and Chinese
漢混淆文 *wa-kan konkōbun* (ancient) mixture of Japanese and Chinese writing
14 語 *wago* pure Japanese words
歌 *waka* thirty-one-syllable poem, tanka
算 *wasan* Japanese mathematics; abacus calculation
製 *wasei* Japanese manufacture
魂漢才 *wakon-kansai* Japanese spirit and Chinese learning
15 談 *wadan* a talk to settle differences
16 親 *washin* harmony, amity, friendship
親条約 *washin jōyaku* treaty of friendship
親国 *washinkoku* friendly country
親協商 *washin kyōshō* treaty of friendship
19 蘭 *Oranda* Holland, Netherlands
蘭語 *Orandago* Dutch language
20 議 *wagi* peace negotiations, reconciliation
22 讃 *wasan* (Buddhist) hymns of praise

6

呁 772 / J5326 / M-X Kō *saso(u)* invite, entice.

咥 773 / J527a / M3534 Ki laugh in a high voice. *wara(u)* laugh, smile. Tetsu *ka(mu)* bite, chew.

咸 774 / J5279 / M3563 Kan *mina* all, everything, everyone; same.

咼 775 / J5325 / M3573 Kai, Ka crooked mouth; wicked, dishonest, unjust. *yokoshima* dishonest, wicked.

咾 776 / J5324 / M3578 Rō *koe* voice.

哂 777 / J5322 / M3583 Shin. *wara(u)* laugh, smile, ridicule. *azawara(u)* ridicule, sneer at, laugh at.

哈 778 / J527d / M3594 Gō school of fish; fish's mouth moving; laugh; eat. *painto* pint.

哉 779 / J3a48 / M3596 Sai. *Kana* How! What! Alas! *ya* question mark.

咨 780 / J527e / M3538 Shi investigate, inquire; weep.

咤 781 / J5323 / M3533 **吒** 749 / J-X / M-X Ta clicking (with the tongue).

咢 782 / J5278 / M3529 Gaku be surprised; be outspoken; debate loudly; protrude; beat drum.
9 咢 *gakugaku* protrude; state directly

咫 783 / J5321 / M3542 Shi short; span.

⁴尺 *shiseki* a very short distance

喀 784 J533e M3550 KAKU quarrel.
⁶血 *kakketsu* lung hemorrhage

哇 785 J5277 M3593 AI. A voice of flattery; amorous voice.
⁹哇 *aa* laugh; child's voice
咬 *aiō* seductive voice; lecherous voice

哄 786 J527c M3588 KŌ resound, reverberate.
¹⁰笑 *kōshō* loud laughter
¹²然 *kōzen to* (laugh) broadly, loudly

咬 787 J527b M3543 KŌ. *ka(mu)* bite, gnaw, chew; gear with; (waves) dash against.
⁶合 *kōgō, kamiawa(se)* occlusion (in dentistry)
¹²痙 *kōkei* lockjaw
¹³傷 *kōshō* bite (injury)

咽 788 J3076 M3577 IN. EN. ETSU. *muse(ru), muse(bu)* be choked, be smothered. *muse(ppoi)* stuffy, suffocating. *nodo* throat, gullet, windpipe; voice.
⁶返 *mu(se)-kae(ru)* be severely choked
⁸泣 *muse(bi)-na(ku)* sob
¹²喉 *inkō* throat
喉炎 *inkōen* pharyngitis
頭 *into* pharynx
頭炎 *intōen* pharyngitis

咳 789 J3331 M3555 **欬** 2932 J-X M16061 GAI cough. *se(ku)* cough. *shiwabu(ku)* cough, clear one's throat. *seki* cough. *shiwabuki* cough, clearing one's throat.
²入 *se(ki)-i(ru)* cough persistently
³上 *se(ki)-a(garu)* have a coughing spell; sob convulsively
⁴止 *sekido(me)* cough medicine, throat tablet
込 *se(ki)-ko(mu)* have a fit of coughing
⁵払 *sekibara(i)* clearing the throat; coughing
⁶気 *gaike* severe coughing
返 *se(ki)-kae(su)* cough to relieve discomfort
¹⁰病 *gaibyō, shiwabuki yamai* illness accompanied by coughing
¹¹唾 *gaida* cough and spittle
¹⁴嗽 *gaisō* cough, coughing

B **咲** 790 J3a69 M3554 SHŌ. *sa(ku)* bloom, blossom. *-sa(ki)* blooming.
⁴匂 *sa(ki)-nio(u)* bloom beautifully and fragrantly
分 *sa(ki)-wa(keru)* bloom in many colors. *sa(ki)wa(ke)* variegated flowering
⁵出 *sa(ki)-de(ru), sa(ki)-da(su)* begin to bloom, come out
⁷乱 *sa(ki)-mida(reru)* bloom in profusion
初 *sa(ki)-so(meru)* begin to bloom
¹⁰残 *sa(ki)-noko(ru)* be still in bud; be still blooming
¹²揃 *sa(ki)-soro(u)* be in full bloom
渡 *sa(ki)-wata(ru)* bloom over a wide area, continue to bloom
勝 *sa(ki)-masa(ru)* bloom first; bloom beautifully
散 *sa(ki)-chi(ru)* (the blossoms) fall
¹³溢 *sa(ki)-kobo(reru)* bloom in profusion
誇 *sa(ki)-hoko(ru)* bloom in glory

B **哀** 791 J3025 M3580 AI. *awa(remu)* pity, have mercy on, sympathize with. *awa(re)* grief, sorrow; misery; compassion, pathos. *awa(reppoi)* plaintive, piteous, doleful.
⁴切 *aisetsu na* pathetic
弔 *aichō* sympathetic condolences
⁵史 *aishi* sad, sorrowful, pensive
号 *aigō* moan, wailing
⁶気 *awa(re)ge na* sad, sorrowful, pensive
⁷別 *aibetsu* sad parting
⁹音 *aion* sad voices; sad sounds
¹⁰哭 *aikoku* grief, mourning, lamentation
¹¹悼 *aitō* condolence, regret, sympathy, sorrow, lament
惜 *aiseki* grief, sorrow
情 *aijō* sadness
¹²痛 *aitsū* sorrowing with the bereaved
訴 *aiso* appeal, complaint
詞 *aishi* message of condolence
¹³傷 *aishō* sorrow, grief
詩 *aishi* elegy
話 *aiwa* sad tale
愁 *aishū* sorrow, grief
感 *aikan* pathos

愍 *aibin* pity
楽 *airaku* grief and pleasure
14 歌 *aika* elegy, dirge, sad song, lamentation
慕 *aibo* cherish the memory of, yearn for
15 憫 *aibin* pity
憐 *airen* pity, compassion
調 *aichō* mournful melody; minor key
歓 *aikan* sadness and joy
19 願 *aigan* appeal, entreaty, petition

A **品** 792 / J494a / M3581 HIN refinement, dignity; article. HON item, course (in a meal). *shina* article, goods, thing; quality; brand; kind, type; ways, conditions; character.
4 切 *shinagi(re)* out of stock, sold out
分 *shinawa(ke)* assortment
5 目 *himmoku* list of articles
6 行 *hinkō* conduct, behavior; moral character, respectability
行方正 *hinkō-hōsei* respectability
7 位 *hin'i* dignity, nobility; grade, quality, fineness; character
作 *shina (o) tsuku(ru)* pretend to be someone; attract attention to oneself
形 *shinakatachi* countenance, personal appearance
8 物 *shinamono* goods, stock, articles
定 *shinasada(me)* estimation, judgment, criticism (of goods)
性 *hinsei* character
性発達 *hinsei hattatsu* character development
性鍛錬 *hinsei tanren* character building
9 柄 *shinagara* quality, brand
枯 *shinaga(re)* shortage of goods
品 *shinajina* various articles
10 格 *hinkaku* grace, dignity
致 *hinchi* quality
書 *shinaga(ki)* catalog, inventory, itemization; bill of fare
12 詞 *hinshi* part of speech
等 *hintō* grade quality
評 *himpyō* criticism, comment
評会 *himpyōkai* competitive exhibition, a fair
13 数 *shinakazu, hinsū* number of articles, amount of stock
彙 *hin'i* quality, kind
14 種 *hinshu* kind, description, grade, variety, breed
15 調 *shinashira(be)* stock taking
質 *shishitsu* quality
16 薄 *shinausu* shortage of goods
18 類 *hinrui* kinds of articles

7

啄 793 / J426f / M-X Nonstandard for 啄 821.

唔 794 / J532a / M3741 See 吾 733.

唖 795 / J3022 / M3743 Nonstandard for 啞 827.

哭 796 / J532d / M3658 KOKU. *nage(ku), na(ku)* cry, weep, wail, moan. *koku(suru)* weep, wail, mourn for.

唳 797 / J533a / M-X REI bird cry; honking of crane or goose; drone of cicada.

哦 798 / J5328 / M3642 GA exclamation. *uta(u)* sing.

哽 799 / J532b / M3680 KŌ, KYŌ *muse(bu)* sob, be choked up.

唏 800 / J5329 / M3707 KI *nage(ku)* regret, deplore; grieve, lament, cry over.

哥 801 / J5327 / M3641 KA. KO. *ani* elder brother.

唄 802 / J3134 / M3694 BAI. *uta* songs accompanied by the samisen.

B **唆** 803 / J3a36 / M3696 SA. *sosonoka(su)* tempt, seduce; instigate; promote.

哮 805 / J532c / M3659 KŌ. *ta(keru)* roar, howl, growl, bellow.

哩 805 / J4b69 / M3649 RI. *mairu* mile.

哢 806 / J532f / M3635 RŌ *saezu(ru)* chirp, titter, warble.
7 吭 *rōkō* chirping of birds

B **唇** 807 J3f30 M3697 SHIN. *kuchibiru* lip.
[9]音 *shin'on* labial sound
[12]歯輔車 *shinshi-hosha* interdependence

A **員** 808 J3077 M3633 EN. IN *-in* member; number; the one in charge.
[4]内 *innai* within the membership
[5]外 *ingai* nonmembership
[13]数 *inzū, inzu, insū* number of members, things, or people

哨 809 J3e25 M3646 SHŌ scout, sentinel
[7]戒 *shōkai* patrol, patrolling
兵 *shōhei* sentry, sentinel
[8]舎 *shōsha* sentry box
[9]海艇 *shōkaitei* patrol vessel
[20]艦 *shōkan* patrol ship

哺 810 J532e M3676 HO taking in the mouth. *haguku(mu) vt* feed from mouth to mouth; tell simply. *fuku(mu) vi* hold in the mouth; keep in mind.
[8]育 *hoiku suru* suckle, nurse, nurture; rear
育所 *hoikusho* nursery school; nursery
乳 *honyū* lactation, suckling
乳児 *honyūji* suckling child
乳瓶 *honyubin* nursing bottle
乳動物 *honyū dōbutsu* mammal

B **哲** 811 J4521 M3667 TETSU clear.
[2]人 *tetsujin* wise man, sage, philosopher
[8]学 *tetsugaku* philosophy
学史 *tetsugakushi* history of philosophy
学的 *tetsugakuteki* philosophical
学者 *tetsugakusha* philosopher
学博士 *Tetsugaku Hakushi, Tetsugaku Hakase* Doctor of Philosophy
[11]理 *tetsuri* the philosophy (of something)

B **唐** 812 J4562 M3709' TŌ Tang (dynasty); China; foreign countries. *Kara* China; Cathay; Korea; foreign countries. *Kara-, Tō-* Chinese; Korean; foreign. *kara(meku)* look like something Chinese.
[2]人 *Tōjin, karabito* a Chinese; a foreigner
[3]土 *Tōdo, Morokoshi* China, Cathay
丸籠 *tōmaru kago* basket for transporting criminals
[4]戸 *karato* Chinese-style gate
手 *karate* a weaponless defense system
木 *karaki* rare foreign wood
犬 *karainu* foreign dog, lion-dog (statues in shrine gardens). *tōken* foreign dog
天 *tōten* velveteen
天竺 *Kara-Tenjiku* China and India
[5]本 *tōhon* books from China
[6]糸 *tōito* foreign thread, foreign yarn
臼 *kara usu* mortar for hulling grain
衣 *kara koromo, karagoromo* ancient Chinese clothes; strange clothes
[7]作 *karazuku(ri)* Chinese building style
辛子 *tōgarashi* red pepper
[8]金 *karakane* bronze
門 *karamon* arched Chinese-style gate
国 *Karakuni* China
松 *karamatsu* larch
物 *karamono* goods from China or Korea
画 *tōga* Chinese painting; Chinese-style painting
突 *tōtotsu* suddenly, unexpectedly
物 *tōbutsu* imported goods
物屋 *tōbutsuya* foreign-goods store
物商 *tōbutsushō* foreign-goods store
[9]音 *tōon* Tang-dynasty pronunciation
風 *karafū* Chinese style
紅 *karakurenai* deep crimson
竿 *karasao* flail
変木 *tōhemboku* a blockhead
津物 *karatsumono* earthenware, chinaware
胡麻 *tōgoma* castor-bean plant; castor beans
草 *karakusa* arabesque
草模様 *karakusa moyo* arabesque design
[10]馬 *kara uma* (ancient) foreign horse
桃 *karamomo* apricot
紙 *karakami* thick door paper; opaque sliding paper door
紙障子 *karakami shōji* opaque sliding paper door; Tang-dynasty yellow drawing paper
[11]船 *karafune, tōsen* Chinese ship; foreign ship
[12]硯 *tōken* Chinese ink slab
朝 *Tōchō* the Tang dynasty
傘 *karakasa* paper umbrella
黍 *karakibi* maize, Indian corn
筆 *tōhitsu* writing brush made in China
[13]詩 *tōshi* Tang-dynasty poem
獅子 *kara shishi* lion
[14]様 *karayō* Chinese style

語 *kara kotoba* ancient Chinese words; foreign language
歌 *kara uta* Chinese poem
箕 *tōmi* winnowing fan, fanning machine
墨 *kara sumi, tōboku* Chinese quality ink stick
15 鋤 *karasuki* Chinese plow
16 錦 *karanishiki* Chinese brocade
17 鍬 *tōguwa* a heavy-duty hoe
薯 *karaimo* sweet potato
縮緬 *tōchirimen* muslin
18 櫃 *tōbitsu* Chinese chest
20 繻子 *tōjusu* Korean silk satin

8

售 813 J5334 M3760 SHŪ *u(ru)* sell, vend.

唹 814 J5330 M3774 O. YO *wara(u)* laugh, smile.

啅 815 J5336 M3802 TAKU. TO noisy, chirping of birds; nibble.

啌 816 J5333 M3810 KŌ scold; angry voice; rinse the mouth.

唎 817 J533b M3833 KA. WA *shitaga(u)* follow, submit.

啗 818 J5338 M3825 TAN. *ku(rawasu)* allure, entice.

啖 819 J5337 M3824 TAN eat.
8 呵 *tanka* caustic words

啀 820 J5331 M3789 GAI. *iga(mu)* wrangle; growl at.
6 合 *iga(mi)-a(u)* wrangle; growl at each other

啄 821 J-X M3801 TAKU. *tsuiba(mu)* peck, pick up.
4 木鳥 *kitsutsuki* woodpecker

啜 822 J5335 M3832 SETSU. *susu(ru)* sip, suck up.
3 上 *susu(ri)-a(geru)* suck up
8 泣 *susu(ri)-na(ku)* sob

唸 823 J5339 M3773 TEN. *una(ru)* groan, moan; roar, howl, snarl, growl, bellow, trumpet, snort; hum, buzz; sough.
7 声 *una(ri)goe* grown, moan
9 独楽 *una(ri)goma* a humming top

B **喝** 824 J3365 M-X **喝** 834 J-X M3960 KATSU scold; get hoarse
8 采 *kassai* applause, cheers
10 破 *kappa suru* declare, proclaim

啣 825 J5332 M3876 KAN. GAN. *kuwa(eru)* take or hold in the mouth or between the teeth; bite.
4 込 *kuwa(e)-ko(mu)* (a prostitute) brings in a victim
11 煙草 *kuwa(e) tabako de* with a cigarette in the mouth
煙管 *kuwa(e)giseru de* with a pipe in the mouth

唾 826 J4243 M3785 DA. *tsuba, tsubaki* sputum; saliva.
11 液 *daeki* saliva
液腺 *daekisen* salivary glands
13 腺 *dasen* salivary glands
棄 *daki subeki* detestable, disgusting, revolting. *daki suru* spit; detest, hate, abhor, reject

啞 827 J-X M3835 A. *oshi* deaf-mute.
8 者 *asha* deaf-mute
12 然 *azen to* in mute amazement
13 鈴 *arei* dumbbell
18 蟬 *oshizemi* silent female cicada

B **啓** 828 J373c M3820 KEI open; say.
3 上 *keijō* speak respectfully
5 白 *keihaku* informing
示 *keiji* revelation
9 発 *keihatsu* enlightenment, development, improvement, education, edification
13 蒙 *keimō* enlightenment, instruction
14 慕 *keibo suru* revere and long for

A **唱** 829 J3e27 M3765 SHŌ. *tona(eru)* recite, chant; call upon; cry, yell (*banzai*); advocate, preach; quote (prices).
6 名 *shōmyō* reciting Buddha's name

8 和 *shōwa* cheering in chorus
11 道 *shōdō* advocacy
道者 *shōdōsha* proponent
14 導 *shōdō* advocacy
歌 *shōka* song; singing
歌隊 *shōkatai* choir
歌集 *shōkashū* collection of songs

A **問** 830 J4c64 M3814 MON question, problem, subject, discussion. *to(u)* ask, question, inquire; accuse. *to(i)* question, inquiry. *to(wazu)* without distinction, regardless of, irrespective.
6 返 *to(i)-kae(su)* ask again
合 *to(i)-a(waseru), to(i)-a(wasu)* inquire of
9 屋 *ton'ya, toiya* wholesaler, forwarding agent
屋業 *ton'yagyō* wholesale business
11 掛 *to(i)-ka(keru)* inquire of; begin to ask
責 *monseki* reproof, censure
12 尋 *to(i)-tazu(neru)* look for, inquire for, ask (someone) a question, question, accuse
答 *mondō* questions and answers; catechism; discussion; dispute
13 詰 *to(i)-tsu(meru)* press for an answer, cross-examine
罪 *monzai* accusation, indictment
14 語 *to(wazu)gata(ri)* voluntary remark, unasked-for remark
15 質 *to(i)-tada(su)* inquire of, question
18 題 *mondai* problem, question, issue, case, matter; discussion; trouble
題化 *mondaika suru* become an issue
題外 *mondaigai* beside the question
題点 *mondaiten* the point at issue

B **唯** 831 J4d23 M3761 YUI. I. *tatta* only, merely, solely, simply. *tada* only, merely, solely, simply; earnestly; perfectly, generally.
1 一 *yuiitsu, yuitsu* sole, unique, the one and only. *tada hitotsu* sole, only one
一神道 *Yuiitsu Shintō* Pure Shinto
4 今 *tadaima* now, at present; right now; soon; Here I am. I just got back. I'm home.
心論 *yuishinron* idealism
6 名論 *yuimeiron* nominalism
7 我的 *yuigateki* egoistic
我独尊 *yuigadokuson* feeling of supremacy
我論 *yuigaron* egoism
8 物主義 *yuibutsu shugi* materialism
物史観 *yuibutsu shikan* materialistic conception of history
物的 *yuibutsuteki* materialistic
物論 *yuibutsuron* materialism
物論的 *yuibutsuronteki* materialistic
9 美主義 *yuibi shugi* estheticism
美的 *yuibiteki* esthetic
美派 *yuibiha* esthetes
11 理論 *yuiriron* rationalism
唯 *ii toshite* willingly, meekly
唯諾諾 *iidakudaku toshite* quite willing; readily; submissively; meekly; at one's beck

A **商** 832 J3e26 M3803 SHŌ trade; merchant; quotient. *akina(u)* sell, handle, trade in. *akina(i)* trade, business.
2 人 *shōnin, akindo, akyūdo, akiudo* trader, shopkeeper, merchant
3 大 *shōdai* commercial college
才 *shōsai* business ability
工 *shōkō* commerce and industry
工会議所 *Shōkō Kaigisho* Chamber of Commerce and Industry
工業 *shōkōgyō* commerce and industry
工業者 *shōkōgyōsha* commercial and industrial men
5 号 *shōgō* firm name, trade name
用 *shōyō* business
用文 *shōyōbun* business correspondence
用語 *shōyōgo* commercial term
6 会 *shōkai* company, firm
行為 *shōkōi* commercial transaction
7 状 *shōjō* market conditions
社 *shōsha* company, firm
利 *shōri* commercial profit
売 *shōbai* trade, business, commerce; transaction, occupation, trade
売人 *shōbainin* merchant; professional, expert
売気 *shōbaigi* commercial spirit, profit motive
売気質 *shōbai katagi* mercenary spirit
売柄 *shūbaigara* nature of one's business; business instinct
売道具 *shōbai dōgu* stock-in-trade
売筋 *shōbai suji* business connections
売替 *shōbaiga(e)* change of occupation
売敵 *shōbaigataki* professional jealousy; business rivalry

8 況 *shōkyō* business conditions
法 *shōhō* trade, business, commerce; commercial law
取引 *shōtorihiki* business transaction
店 *shōten* shop, store
店街 *shōtengai* shopping district; shopping street
学士 *Shōgakushi* Bachelor of Commercial Science
学博士 *Shōgaku Hakushi* Doctor of Commercial Science
事 *shōji* commercial affairs
事会社 *shōjigaisha* commercial company
9 科 *shōka* commercial course
科大学 *shōka daigaku* commercial college
品 *shōhin* goods, stock, merchandise
品目録 *shōhin mokuroku* inventory, catalog
品現在高 *shōhin genzaidaka* amount of inventory
品券 *shōhinken* merchandise certificate
品学 *shōhingaku* (study of) merchandising
10 家 *shōka* mercantile house, store; merchant
11 運 *shōun* fortunes of business
略 *shōryaku* business policy
経 *shōkei* commerce and economics
務 *shōmu* commercial affairs
務官 *shōmukan* commercial attaché
船 *shōsen* merchant ship
船大学 *shōsen daigaku* merchantile-marine college
船学校 *shōsen gakkō* merchant-marine school
船隊 *shōsentai* merchant fleet
船旗 *shōsenki* merchant flag
12 港 *shōkō* commercial port
量 *shōryō* consideration, deliberation, discussion
策 *shōsaku* business policy
13 業 *shōgyō* commerce, trade, business
業文 *shōgyōbun* commercial correspondence
業化 *shōgyōka* commercialization
業史 *shōgyōshi* history of commerce
業主義 *shōgyō shugi* commercialism
業地 *shōgyōchi* business district
業学 *shōgyōgaku* commercial science
業学校 *shōgyō gakkō* commercial school
業放送 *shōgyō hōsō* commercial broadcast
業界 *shōgyōkai* commercial world
業美術 *shōgyō bijutsu* commercial art
業都市 *shōgyō toshi* commercial city
業組合 *shōgyō kumiai* guild, trade association
業道徳 *shōgyō dōtoku* business morality
業街 *shōgyōgai* shopping street
業港 *shōgyōkō* commercial port
業数学 *shōgyō sūgaku* commercial mathematics
業算術 *shōgyō sanjutsu* commercial arithmetic
14 魂 *shōkon* commercial spirit
慣習 *shōkanshū* commercial practice
慣習法 *shōkanshūhō* commercial law
15 権 *shōken* commercial supremacy, commercial rights
談 *shōdan* business transaction
舗 *shōho* shop, store
標 *shōhyō* trademark
標権 *shōhyōken* trademark rights
16 機 *shōki* business opportunity
館 *shōkan* firm, trading company
20 議 *shōgi* conference, consultation
議員 *shōgiin* counselor, trustee

9

單 833 / J5345 / M3993 See **単** 620.

喝 834 / J-X / M3960 See **喝** 824.

啻 835 / J5341 / M3886 SHI. *tada(naranu)* incomparable. *tada ni* merely, only, simply.

喨 836 / J534a / M3978 RYŌ, RŌ clear voice.

啼 837 / J5346 / M3887 TEI. *na(ku)* (animals and birds) cry, bark, chirp, etc.

喙 838 / J533c / M3951 KAI. *kuchibashi* (bird) bill.

喩 839 / J5348 / M3979 YU. *tato(eru)* compare, illustrate, speak figuratively.

tatoe, tatoi parable, illustration, figure of speech.

啾 840 J5342 M3892 SHŪ cry; childs voice. *na(ku)* (animal or bird) cry.
12 啾 *shūshū* (bird or insect) cry; whimper

喬 841 J362c M3990 KYŌ high; boasting.
4 木 *kyōboku* tall tree, forest tree, arbor

喟 842 J5340 M3963 KI moan.
12 然 *kizen* dejection

喊 843 J533f M3916 KAN cry, call.
7 声 *kansei* war cry, battle cry

喞 844 J-X M3961 喞 845 J5344 M-X SHOKU. SOKU. *kako(tsu)* speak resentfully.
18 顔 *kako(chi)gao* sorrowful countenance

喃 846 J5347 M3903 NAN chatter, rattle on.
12 喃 *nannan to* volubly, glibly, chatteringly. *nōnō* a word used in calling someone
14 語 *nango* love talk

喀 847 J533d M3896 KAKU vomit.
6 血 *kakketsu* lung hemorrhage
13 痰 *kakutan* expectoration, sputum

喘 848 J5343 M3946 ZEN. *ae(gu)* pant, gasp, breathe hard.
7 求 *ae(gi)-moto(meru)* long after
10 息 *zensoku* asthma; broken wind (in a horse)

喰 849 J3674 M4015 （国字） *kura(u), ku(u)* eat, drink; receive (a blow). *ku(u)* eat; subsist on; support oneself; consume; get (a scolding); encroach; bite at, gnaw at; (shoes) pinch; be cheated.
4 込 *kura(i)-ko(mu)* go to jail; shoulder a debt or other load; be deceived; abandon oneself to vice; fall heir (to trouble)
5 付 *kura(i)-tsu(ku)* bite

喋 850 J437d M3917 CHŌ. *shabe(ru), shabe(kuru)* talk, chat, chatter.
5 立 *shabe(ri)-ta(teru)* talk volubly
11 捲 *shabe(ri)-maku(ru)* talk volubly
12 散 *shabe(ri)-chi(rasu)* spread gossip, talk carelessly

喇 851 J5349 M3909 RATSU, RA chatter, rattle on.
5 叭 *rappa* trumpet, horn, bugle
叭手 *rappashu* bugler, trumpeter
叭飲 *rappano(mi)* drinking from the bottle
14 嘛 *rama* lama
嘛教 *Ramakyō* Lamaism

B 喚 852 J342d M3953 KAN. *ome(ku), wame(ku)* cry, scream, yell, shout, clamor. *yo(bu)* call, call out to; invoke; summon; invite; attract; send for; name, designate; bring about.
5 立 *wame(ki)-ta(teru)* bawl, squall, yell, cry out
7 声 *kansei, wame(ki)goe* shout, yell, scream, clamor
8 呼 *kanko suru* cry out
10 起 *kanki suru* arouse, evoke
11 問 *kammon* summons

B 喪 853 J4153 M3905 SŌ. *mo* mourning.
4 心 *sōshin* absentmindedness; stupor, dejection
中 *mochū* mourning
5 主 *moshu* chief mourner
失 *sōshitsu* loss, forfeit, forfeiture
8 服 *mofuku* mourning dress
具 *sōgu* funeral accessories
9 神 *sōshin* absentmindedness; stupor, dejection
10 家 *sōka* homeless; family in mourning
11 章 *moshō* sign of mourning
祭 *sōsai* funerals and festivals

喉 854 J3922 M3913 KŌ. *nodo* throat, voice.
4 仏 *nodobotoke* Adam's apple
元 *nodomoto* throat
6 自慢 *nodojiman* pride of voice
9 音 *kōon* guttural sound
首 *nodokubi* throat

彦 *nodobiko* uvula
16 頭 *kōtō* larynx
頭炎 *kōtōen* laryngitis
頭痛 *kōtōtsū* sore throat
頭蓋 *kōtōgai* epiglottis
頭癌 *kōtōgan* cancer of the larynx

B **喫** 855 / J354a / M3987 KITSU. KEKI. *kis(suru)* eat, drink, smoke; receive (a blow, etc.).
4 水 *kissui* draft (of a ship)
水線 *kissuisen* water line (of loaded ship)
9 茶 *kissa, kitcha* tea drinking, tea house
茶店 *kissaten* tea house, coffee shop
12 飯 *kippan* eating
13 煙 *kitsuen* smoking (tobacco)
煙車 *kitsuensha* smoking car
煙者 *kitsuensha* smoker
煙室 *kitsuenshitsu* smoking room
煙家 *kitsuenka* smoker
14 緊 *kikkin* very urgent
緊事 *kikkinji* a very urgent matter
22 驚 *bikkuri suru* be surprised. *kikkyō* surprise, astonishment

喧 856 / J3776 / M3976 KEN. *kamabisu(shii)* noisy, boisterous. *yakama(shii)* noisy, boisterous; critical; troublesome; much-discussed; fastidious.
6 伝 *kenden suru* noise abroad, circulate
7 狂 *kenkyō na* noisy and apparently crazy
9 屋 *yakama(shi)ya* exacting person, fault finder
12 喧囂囂 *kenken-gōgō* pandemonium
13 嘩 *kenka* quarrel, dispute
嘩好 *kenkazu(ki)* quarrelsome
嘩早 *kenkabaya(i), kenka(p)paya(i)* combative, pugnacious
嘩買 *kenka (o) ka(u)* stir up a quarrel
嘩腰 *kenkagoshi* defiant attitude
16 噪 *kensō* noisy, uproarious; nuisance
18 擾 *kenjō* noisy, uproar
騒 *kensō* noisy, uproar, a nuisance
21 轟 *kengō* noisy, uproar
囂 *kengō* noisy, uproar

A **営** 857 / J3144 / M4025 **營** 3491 / J535b / M19457 EI camp; performing. *itona(mu)* perform (ceremonies); build; conduct (business); follow (a profession), operate (a store); build. *itona(mi)* business, occupation, operation.
4 内 *einai* inside the barracks
中 *eichū* within the barracks
5 外 *eigai* outside the barracks
6 団 *eidan* corporation, foundation
7 利 *eiri* gain, money-making
利会社 *eirigaisha* commercial concern
利法人 *eiri hōjin* profit-making corporation
利事業 *eiri jigyō* business enterprise
8 門 *eimon* barracks gate
所 *eisho* barracks, camp
林 *eirin* forestry
舎 *eisha* barracks
9 造 *eizō* building, construction
造物 *eizōbutsu* building, structure, public works
10 庭 *eitei* barracks' parade ground
倉 *eisō* guardhouse, detention barracks
11 巣 *eisō* building a nest
12 営 *eiei to* strenuously, eagerly, diligently
13 業 *eigyō* business, trade
業区域 *eigyō kuiki* business district
業用 *eigyōyō* business purposes
業主 *eigyōshu, eigyōnushi* proprietor
業所 *eigyōsho* place of business
業者 *eigyōsha* trader
業費 *eigyōhi* operating expenses
18 繕 *eizen* upkeep (of equipment)

A **喜** 858 / J346e / M3957 KI. *yoroko(bu)* rejoice, be glad, be pleased. *yoroko(basu)* gladden, please, make happy. *yoroko(bi)* joy, delight, pleasure. *yoroko(bashii)* joyful, glad, pleasant.
6 色 *kishoku* joyful countenance
迎 *yoroko(bi)-muka(eru)* welcome, receive with joy
叫 *yoroko(bi)-sa(kebu)* shout with joy
字祝 *ki(no)ji (no) iwai* 77th birthday celebration
7 走 *yoroko(bi)-hashi(ru)* run for joy
寿 *kiju* 77th birthday
寿祝 *kiju (no) iwai* 77th birthday celebration
8 雨 *kiu* good rain
呼 *yoroko(bi)-yo(bawaru)* shout for joy
受 *yoroko(bi)-u(keru)* gladly accept
事 *yoroko(bi)goto* happy event, pleasant affair
9 祝 *yoroko(bi)-iwa(u)* joyously celebrate
勇 *yoroko(bi)-isa(mu)* be in high spirits, be cheerful

怒 *kido* joy and anger
怒哀楽 *kido-airaku* joy and anger, feelings
10 悦 *kietsu* gladness, delight
11 捨 *kisha* charity, donation
12 喜 *kiki(taru)* gleeful, joyful
集 *yoroko(bi)-tsudo(u), yoroko(bi)-atsu(maru)* meet with joy
13 楽 *yoroko(bi)-tano(shimu)* rejoice and be happy. *kiraku* joy, pleasure
誇 *yoroko(bi)-hoko(ru)* exult
14 踊 *yoroko(bi)-odo(ru)* dance for joy
歌 *yoroko(bi)-uta(u)* rejoice and sing
歌劇 *kikageki* comic opera
15 劇 *kigeki* comedy
憂 *kiyū* joy and sorrow, weal and woe

A **善** 859 / J4131 / M3904 ZEN good, goodness, right, virtue. *i(i), yo(i)* good, good-natured; pleasing; precious; noble; lovely, beautiful, fine; lucky; efficacious; right; suitable; justifiable; appropriate, satisfactory; better; all right; unnecessary; no objection; intimate, friendly; easy; well; desirous. *yo(ku) suru* be skilled in. *yo(shi)* good, all right, well, so. *yō(koso)* Well, good for you. Well, that's a rude thing to do.
2 人 *zennin* good people
4 心 *zenshin* virtue, moral sense, conscience
5 玉 *zendama* good person
用 *zen'yō* good use
処 *zensho suru* tide over, make the best of, use discretion
6 行 *zenkō* good deed, good conduct; benevolence
因善果 *zen'in-zenka* Good actions lead to good rewards.
7 良 *zenryō* goodness, virtue, excellence
男善女 *zennan-zennyo* pious men and women
8 性 *zensei* innate goodness of man
果 *zenka* good results
事 *zenji* good thing, good deed
9 政 *zensei* good government
美 *zembi* the good and the beautiful
哉 *zenzai* soft bean-jam; Well done!
後 *zengo* giving careful thought to the future; finishing up carefully
後策 *zengosaku* relief measure, remedy, countermeasure, means of settling a problem
10 根 *zenkon* good deeds, charity
書 *zensho* beautiful calligraphy; a calligrapher; a good book
11 道 *zendō* path of virtue, righteousness
悪 *zen'aku, zennaku* good and evil. *yo(shi)-waru(shi), yo(shi)-a(shi), yo(i)-waru(i)* good or bad; merits or demerits; quality; suitability. *yo(kare)-a(shikare)* good or bad, right or wrong
13 戦 *zensen suru* fight a good fight
意 *zen'i* good faith; good will, good intentions; favorable sense
感 *zenkan* successful vaccination, positive reaction
業 *zengō* good deeds
14 徳 *zentoku* virtues
隣 *zenrin* good neighbor
導 *zendo* proper guidance
15 霊 *zenrei* spirit of goodness

10

嗇 860 / J5427 / M4053 SHOKU. *yabusa(ka)* miserly, stingy, unwilling, sparing (of praise).

嘩 861 / J325e / M-X **譁** 5674 / J6b7b / M35928 KA noisy.

嗛 862 / J-X / M4088 KEN insufficient; put in the mouth.

嗉 863 / J-X / M4057 SO bird's craw.
22 嚢 *sonō* bird's craw, crop

嗤 864 / J5350 / M4110 SHI. *wara(u)* laugh, smile; ridicule; be in full bloom. *azawara(u)* ridicule.
10 笑 *shishō* ridicule

嗚 865 / J534b / M4084 U, O weep. *ā* ah, alas, an interjection of surprise or sadness.
9 咽 *oetsu* sobbing, weeping

嗔 866 / J5351 / M4074 SHIN anger. *ika(ru)* become angry.
10 恚 *shin'i* anger

13 詬 *shinkō* berate, scold angrily

嗄 867 / J534e / M4047 SA. *ka(rasu)* make one's throat hoarse. *ka(reru), shaga(reru), shiwaga(reru)* get hoarse. *kare(bamu)* get slightly hoarse.

7 声 *ka(re)goe, shaga(re)goe, shiwaga(re)goe* hoarse voice

13 嗄 *ka(re)ga(re)* hoarse

B **嗣** 868 / J3b4c / M4109 SHI heir. *tsu(gu)* succeed to, inherit; follow; patch.

3 子 *shishi* heir, successor

7 君 *shikun* heir of a ruler

13 業 *shigyō* inheritance

嗟 869 / J534d / M4102 SA be satisfied; grieve. *a* ah.

9 哉 *awaya* an instant

13 嘆 *satan suru* lament, deplore; admire, praise

15 歎 *satan suru* lament, deplore; admire, praise

嗜 870 / J534f / M4089 SHI. *tashina(mu)* like, have a taste for; be prudent, be modest, be temperate. *tashina(mi)* taste; prudence; modesty; etiquette; accomplishment; attention to appearance.

6 好 *shikō* taste, liking, preference

好品 *shikōhin* luxury articles

10 眠 *shimin* lethargy

11 欲 *shiyoku* fondness for, appetite, weakness for

嗅 871 / J534c / M4048 KYŪ. *ka(gu)* smell, sniff, scent.

2 入薬 *kyūnyūyaku* medicine inhaled through the nose

4 手 *kagite* a smeller

込 *ka(gi)-ko(mu)* smell deeply; investigate by smelling

分 *ka(gi)-wa(keru)* tell by scent

5 付 *ka(gi)-tsu(keru) vt* scent, sniff, smell; detect, sense

出 *ka(gi)-da(su)* sniff out, get wind of

6 当 *ka(gi)-a(teru)* smell out, investigate by smelling

8 官 *kyūkan* the olfactory organ

9 神経 *kyūshinkei* olfactory nerve

10 剤 *kyūzai* smelling medicine

12 覚 *kyūkaku* sense of smell

13 感 *kyūkan* sense of smell

煙草 *kagitabako* snuff

16 薬 *kagigusuri* smelling medicine; snuff

B **嘆** 872 / J4332 / M4138′ **嘆** 874 / J-X / M4171 TAN sigh. *nage(ku)* sigh, lament, moan, grieve; regret, deplore, sorrow. *tan(jiru), tan(zuru)* deplore, mourn, regret, be indignant. *nage(kawashii)* sad, wretched, deplorable.

2 入 *nage(ki)-i(ru)* be weeping inconsolately

6 叫 *nage(ki)-sake(bu)* wail

7 声 *tansei* sigh, lamentation; sigh of admiration

8 明 *nage(ki)-a(kasu)* cry all night; weep for a long period of time

9 美 *tambi* admiration, adoration

美者 *tambisha* admirer, adorer

10 称 *tanshō* praise, admiration, applause

衰 *nage(ki)-otoro(eru)* mourn and languish

息 *tansoku* sigh, grief, deploring

12 訴 *nage(ki)-utta(eru)* complain

悲 *nage(ki)-kana(shimu)* lament, mourn

13 辞 *tanji* interjection; admiration

15 賞 *tanshō* praise, admiration, applause

賞者 *tanshōsha* admirer

19 願 *tangan* entreaty, appeal, petition, suit

11

噌 873 / J4139 / M-X See **噌** 889.

嘆 874 / J-X / M4171 See **嘆** 872.

嗹 875 / J5358 / M4148 REN verbose, voluble; 1000 sheets of paper.

嘛 876 / J5357 / M4230 MA what.

嗾 877 / J5355 / M4155 ZOKU. SOKU. SŌ. *keshika(keru)* sick on, egg on, instigate.

嘗 878 / J3e28 / M4205 **甞** 3714 / J6133 / M21659 SHŌ. *na(meru)* lick; lap up; burn up; taste; undergo; underrate, despise. *katsu(te)* once, before, formerly; ever, never (neg.); former, ex-.

嘈 879/J-X/M4175 Sō noisy.
21 嘈雜 *munayake, sōzatsu* heartburn, sour stomach

嗷 880/J5353/M4142 **謷** 881/J-X/M4143 Gō noisy.
12 嗷訴 *gōso* direct petition

嘖 882/J5354/M4204 Saku. *saina(mu)* scold, torment, chastise.
14 嘖嘖 *sakusaku toshite* noisily, loudly

嗽 883/J5356/M4154 Sō. *susu(gu), yusu(gu)* rinse, wash, pour on. *kuchisusu(gu), kuchisoso(gu)* rinse the mouth, gargle. *ugai* gargling.
9 咳嗽 *sōgai* coughing

嘔 884/J5352/M4200 Ō. *mukatsu(ku)* feel nauseated; be angry. *ha(ku)* vomit.
6 嘔気 *ōki, hakike* nausea

噓 885/J-X/M4206 **嘘** 886/J3133/M-X Kyo. *uso* lie, falsehood, fib, fabrication.
2 嘘八百 *usohappyaku* full of lies
5 嘘皮 *uso(no)kawa* a pure fabrication
6 嘘吐 *usotsuki* liar, fibber
嘘字 *usoji* miswritten character
7 嘘言 *usogoto* lie, falsehood
9 嘘発見器 *uso hakkenki* lie detector
嘘発見機 *uso hakkenki* lie detector
13 嘘話 *usobanashi* fable, untruth

嘉 887/J3245/M4176 Ka. *yomi(suru)* applaud, praise, esteem, appreciate, approve of.
4 嘉手 *kashu* skilled calligrapher
嘉日 *kajitsu* auspicious day, good day
嘉月 *kagetsu* auspicious month; beautiful moonlight; lunar third month
嘉木 *kaboku* beautiful trees
5 嘉礼 *karei* congratulatory ceremony
嘉卉 *kaki* beautiful trees and plants
6 嘉兆 *kachō* auspicious omen
7 嘉言 *kagen* wise saying
嘉辰 *kashin* lucky day, auspicious occasion
8 嘉例 *karei* happy precedent
嘉味 *kami* fine taste
嘉尚 *kashō* friendship; respect
嘉典 *katen* congratulatory ceremony
嘉事 *kaji* happy event
10 嘉祥 *kashō* good omen
嘉納 *kanō suru* approve, appreciate, accept (a gift)
13 嘉瑞 *kazui* good omen
嘉節 *kasetsu* auspicious occasion
15 嘉儀 *kagi* auspicious occasion
嘉調 *kachō* good tune
嘉賞 *kashō* approval
17 嘉齢 *karei* a long happy life

12

噛 888/J337a/M-X See **嚙** 921.

噌 889/J-X/M4303 **噌** 873/J4139/M-X Sō, Zō, Shō throat.

噚 890/J-X/M4349 *Hiro, Ei-hiro, fazomu* fathom.

噀 891/J-X/M4284 Son blow out water (elephants and whales).

嘶 892/J535d/M4260 Sei. *inana(ku)* neigh, whinny, bray.

嘸 893/[illegible]/M4269 Bu. *sazo, sazo ya, sazo(kashi)* how, indeed, no doubt, I dare say.
15 嘸嘸 *sazosazo* emphatic for *sazo* how, indeed, no doubt, I dare say

B **嘱** 894/J3e7c/M4249 **囑** 935/J5376/M4654 Shoku requesting. *shoku suru* request; send a message.
5 嘱目 *shokumoku suru* pay attention to, notice, observe, watch
10 嘱託 *shokutaku suru* commission, charge (a person) with, give (a person) charge of. *shokutaku* part-time employment
11 嘱望 *shokubō* expectation

噎 895/J5359/M4307 Itsu. *mu(seru), muse(bu)* be choked, be smothered.
2 噎入 *muse(bi)-i(ru)* sob convulsively
6 噎返 *muse(bi)-kae(ru)* cough up (something)

[8] 鳴 *musebina(ki)* sobbing

噂 896 / J313d / M4286 SON. *uwasa* rumor, gossip, hearsay.
[5] 主 *uwasa (no) nushi* the person talked about
[13] 話 *uwasabanashi* rumor, gossip, hearsay
[14] 種 *uwasa (no) tane* source of rumor, subject of gossip

嘲 897 / J535e / M4254 CHŌ. *azake(ru)* ridicule, insult.
[7] 弄 *chōrō* ridicule
[10] 笑 *azawara(u)* jeer at. *chōshō* derisive smile, ridicule, sneer. *seserawara(u), azake(ri)-wara(u)* laugh to scorn
[15] 罵 *chōba* taunt, insult

A **器** 898 / J346f / M4349′ **噐** 899 / J535a / M4311 **器** 901 / J-X / M4376
KI container; utensil, instrument, tool, apparatus; set; ability. *utsuwa* vessel, receptacle, utensil, implement, instrument; capacity, ability.
[5] 用 *kiyō* cleverness, ingenuity; shrewdness; versatility
用人 *kiyōjin* a clever person
用貧乏 *kiyō-bimbō* Jack-of-all-trades and master of none
[7] 材 *kizai* machine parts
[8] 物 *utsuwamono, kibutsu* container, receptacle, utensil, tool, furnishings
官 *kikan* organ (of the body)
具 *kigu* utensil, appliance; apparatus; tool; fixtures
[10] 財 *kizai* tools
[11] 械 *kikai* appliance; apparatus; instrument
械体操 *kikai taisō* calisthenics using equipment
[12] 量 *kiryō* looks, features, personal beauty; ability; dignity
量人 *kiryōjin* talented person
量負 *kiryōma(ke)* good looks but poor luck; too smart for success
[13] 楽 *kigaku* instrumental music

B **噴** 900 / J4a2e / M4345 FUN. *fu(ku)* spout, emit, flush out.
[4] 井 *fukii* artesian well, drilled well
井戸 *fukiido* artesian well, drilled well
水 *funsui* jet of water, squirt, fountain
水孔 *funsuikō* jet, spout
水井戸 *funsui ido* artesian well
火 *funka* eruption, volcanic activity
火口 *funkakō* crater
火山 *funkazan* volcano
[5] 出 *fu(ki)-da(su)* spout out, gush out, spurt out, shoot out, send out, discharge, exude. *funshutsu* gushing, spouting, eruption
[6] 気 *funki suru* flutter, puff (as a locomotive)
[8] 沫 *fummatsu* splash, spray
[9] 泉 *funsen* fountain, spring, geyser
[10] 射 *funsha* jet, jet propulsion
射推進 *funsha suishin* jet propulsion
[11] 貫井戸 *fukinuki ido* artesian well, drilled well
[12] 飯 *fumpan suru* burst out laughing
[13] 煙 *fun'en* smoke (out of a chimney)
[19] 霧 *fummu* spray
霧器 *fummuki* atomizer, sprayer

13

器 901 / J-X / M4376 See **器** 898.

噬 902 / J5363 / M4382 ZEI bite.

噺 903 / J4838 / M4433 （国字） *hanashi* talk, chat, conversation; story; rumor; news; consultation, negotiations; facts, reasons.

嘯 904 / J5362 / M4246 SHŌ. *usobu(ku)* roar, howl; feign indifference; recite emotionally.

嘴 905 / J535c / M4256 **觜** 5546 / J6b39 / M35050 SHI beak, bill. *kuchibashi, hashi* (bird) bill.

噪 906 / J5364 / M4380 SŌ be noisy.
[9] 音 *sōon* noise, cacophony

噯 907 / J-X / M4394 AI breathe.
[6] 気 *aiki, okubi* belching

嚆 908 / J5365 / M4458 KŌ call.

[5]矢 *kōshi* the first, the pioneer

噤 909 J5361 M4364 KIN. *tsugu(mu)* shut (one's mouth).

[3]口 *kinkō* saying nothing, silence

噸 910 J4655 M4429 （国字） TON ton.

[12]税 *tonzei* tonnage dues

[13]数 *tonsū* tonnage

噫 911 J3360 M4381 I, AI. *a* exclamation, sigh; yawn.

[6]気 *aiki* exhalation

[13]嗚 *io* grieve

14

嚔 912 J536a M4493 Nonstandard for **嚏** 917.

嚊 913 J5367 M4467 HI moan; snort, breathe through the nose. *kaka, kakā* (one's own) wife.

嚀 914 J5366 M4445 NEI kindness.

嚇 915 J3345 M4459 B KAKU. *odo(su), odo(kasu)* threaten; frighten; intimidate.

[17]嚇 *kakukaku(taru)* brilliant, glorious

噦 916 J-X M-X KAI *mukatsu(ku)* feel nauseated; be angry. *shaku(ru)* to scoop; to hiccup. *shakkuri* hiccups.

[3]上 *shaku(ri)-a(geru)* sob convulsively

[8]泣 *shaku(ri)-na(ku)* sob

[13]溝 *shakuri mizo* groove

鉋 *shakuriganna* rabbet plane

15

嚏 917 J5369 M4501 TEI. *kushami, kusame, kusami* sneeze.

嚠 918 J5368 M4544 RYŪ, RU a clear sound.

[9]亮 *ryūryō(taru)* clear, sonorous

[12]喨 *ryūryō(taru)* clear, sonorous

嚮 919 J-X M4565 **嚮** 920 J536c M-X KYŌ. *saki ni* before, earlier than; ahead; beyond, away; previously; recently.

[4]日 *kyōjitsu* the other day; the day before

[14]導 *kyōdō* leadership, guidance; leader, guide

嚙 921 J-X M4516 **噛** 888 J337a M-X GŌ. *ka(mu)* bite, gnaw, chew; gear with; (waves) dash against.

[4]反 *ka(mi)-kae(su)* chew the cud

切 *ka(mi)-ki(ru)* bite off, gnaw off

分 *ka(mi)-wa(keru)* chew, tell by tasting; understand, appreciate

[5]付 *ka(mi)-tsu(ku)* bite at

[6]合 *ka(mi)-a(u) vi* fight or bite each other; engage (gears); occlude (teeth). *ka(mi)-a(waseru) vt* clench (teeth); engage (gears); set (animals fighting)

含 *ka(nde) fuku(meru)* teach very carefully

[9]砕 *ka(mi)-kuda(ku)* crunch, crush with the teeth

[10]破 *ka(mi)-yabu(ru)* bite to pieces

殺 *ka(mi)-koro(su)* bite to death; keep back, suppress

[12]裂 *ka(mi)-sa(ku)* tear by biting

[13]傷 *kamikizu* bite mark

煙草 *kamitabako* chewing tobacco

[14]鳴 *ka(mi)-na(rasu)* gnash the teeth

緊 *ka(mi)-shi(meru)* chew well; meditate on; digest (ideas); appreciate (kindness)

[15]潰 *ka(mi)-tsubu(su* crunch with the teeth

16

嚬 922 J-X M4562 HIN scowl.

嚥 923 J536b M4545 EN swallow.

[3]下 *enka, enge* swallowing

下痛 *engetsū* difficulty in swallowing

17

嚴 924 J536e M4589 See **厳** 663.

3
17【口】口土士夂夊夕大女子宀寸小⺌尢尸屮山川巛工已巾干幺广廴廾弋弓ヨ彑彡彳

嚶 925 / J536d / M4592 Ō birds crying together.

14 鳴 *ōmei* birds singing together

18

嚼 926 / J5370 / M4602 Shaku. *ka(mu)* bite, gnaw, chew; gear with; (waves) dash against.

囀 927 / J5373 / M4614 Ten. *saezu(ru)* sing, chirp, twitter, warble; prattle, chatter.

14 歌 *saezu(ri)-uta(u)* (birds) sing

囁 928 / J5371 / M4615 Shō. *sasaya(ku)* whisper, murmur.

6 合 *sasaya(ki)-a(u)* whisper together

囃 929 / J5372 / M4619 Satsu. Sō. *haya(su)* play (on an instrument); accompany; beat time; banter, jeer; applaud.

3 子 *hayashi* Japanese orchestra; band, accompaniment

子詞 *hayashi kotoba* meaningless words in a song (for rhythm)

囂 930 / J536f / M4616 Gō. *kashima(shii), kamabisu(shii), kashigama(shii)* noisy, boisterous.

12 然 *gōzen(taru)* noisy, uproarious, vociferous

21 囂 *gōgō(taru)* noisy, uproarious, vociferous

囈 931 / J5374 / M4629 Gei foolish talk.

7 言 *uwagoto* delirious utterances

14 語 *tawagoto, tawakoto* nonsense, jargon, talking in one's sleep

19

囎 932 / J5375 / M-X So（国字）used in proper names.

囊 933 / J-X / M4633 Nō pouch, purse. *fukuro* bag, sack, pouch.

4 中 *nōchū* pocket, purse. *nōchū ni* in the bag

7 状 *nōjō* sac shape

8 底 *nōtei* bottom of the bag

10 疱 *nōhō* cyst

剤 *nōzai* capsule

13 腫 *nōshu* cyst

20

嚙 934 / J5377 / M4659 See **齧** 7097.

21

囑 935 / J5376 / M4654 See **嘱** 894.

RAD. 囗 31

Kunigamae (enclosure as in *kuni* "country"). Nickname: Box.

囗 936 / J5378 / M4675 I. enclosure. Koku. country.

2

B **囚** 937 / J3c7c / M4680 Shū criminal, arrest. *tora(eru)* catch, arrest, capture. *torawa(reru)* be caught, be captured, be arrested; be a slave to; be seized with.

2 人 *meshiudo, shūjin, torawa(re)bito* prisoner, convict

6 衣 *shūi* a convict's clothes

7 役 *shūeki* prison work

8 者 *torawa(re)mono* prisoner, convict, criminal

10 徒 *shūto* prisoner, convict

13 虜 *shūryo* arrest; arrested person; captive

14 獄 *hitoya, shūgoku* prison house

16 縛 *shūbaku suru* arrest and tie up

A **四** 938 / J3b4d / M4682 Shi four. *yo(tsu), yo(ttsu), yo, yon* four.

2 十 *yonjū, shijū* 40

十雀 *shijūkara* a great titmouse, a chickadee

十雀雁 *shijūkaragan* Canada goose

十路 *yosoji* age 40
人 *yonin, yottari* four people
人乗 *yoninno(ri)* four-seater
人組 *yoningumi* foursome, quartet, group of four
3 女 *yonjo* fourth daughter
子 *yo(tsu)go* quadruplets
大節 *Shidaisetsu, Yondaisetsu* four main prewar Shinto festivals (New Year's, Empire Day, Emperor Showa's Birthday, and Emperor Meiji's Birthday)
4 日 *yokka* four days; the fourth day (of the month)
切 *yo(tsu)gi(ri)* quartering; quarter
天王 *shitennō* four heavenly kings; the Tokugawa Big Four
手網 *yo(tsu)de ami* four-armed scoop net
斗樽 *shitodaru* a four-*to* (about 20 gal.) barrel
爪錨 *yotsume ikari* grapnel
月 *Shigatsu* April. *yotsuki* four months
月馬鹿 *shigatsu baka* April fool
辺 *shihen* neighborhood; frontiers; four sides (of a quadrilateral)
辺形 *shihenkei* quadrilateral, quadrangle
六判 *shirokuhan* duodecimo
六時中 *shirokujichū* 24 hours, day and night; constantly, always
方 *shihō, yomo* four directions; all directions; four sides
方八方 *shihō happō* far and wide, in all directions
方山 *yomoyama no* various, sundry
方拝 *Shihōhai* Shinto New Year's Ceremony
分円 *shibun'en* quadrant
分六 *shiburoku* six-to-four ratio
分五裂 *shibun-goretsu* disruption
分板 *shibu ita* thin board, half-inch board
分音符 *shibu ompu* quarter note
分儀 *shibungi* quadrant (the instrument)
5 辻 *yo(tsu)tsuji* street crossing, four corners
民 *shimin* the four classes; the whole nation
半分 *shihambun* quarter, fourth
半世紀 *shihanseiki* a quarter of a century
半期 *shihanki* quarter (of a year)
目 *yo(tsu)me* crest of four squares; four eyes
目垣 *yo(tsu)megaki* trellis, rough bamboo fence
目格子 *yo(tsu)megōshi* lattice work; lattice window
目錐 *yo(tsu)megiri* square drill
6 夷 *shii* barbarians, foreigner
次元 *yojigen, yonjigen* fourth dimension
旬節 *Shijunsetsu* Lent
百四病 *shihyakushibyō* all human sickness
百余州 *shihyakuyoshū* all China
7 身 *yo(tsu)mi* a child's kimono
囲 *shii* circumference, girth; surroundings
折 *yo(tsu)o(ri)* quarto (a page or book size about $9\frac{1}{2}$ x $12\frac{1}{2}$ inches)
阿 *azumaya* arbor, summer house
更 *shikō, yonkō* fourth watch of the night, one to three a.m.
声 *shisei* the four (mandarin) tones
君子 *shikunshi* the four princely plants (plum, orchid, bamboo, and chrysanthemum)
足 *yo(tsu) ashi* four legs. *yo(tsu)ashi* beast, animal
足獣 *shisokujū* quadruped
角 *yosumi* all the corners, four corners. *yotsukado* four corners; intersection, street crossing. *shikaku* square; quadrilateral
角四面 *shikaku-shimen na* methodical, prim
角形 *shikakkei* quadrilateral, square
角張 *shikakuba(ru)* be formal
角錐 *shikakusui* quadrilateral pyramid
8 周 *shishū* surroundings
肢 *shishi* the limbs, the extremities, the arms and legs
苦八苦 *shiku-hakku* much agony
季 *shiki* the four seasons
季払 *shikibara(i)* quarterly payments
季咲 *shikiza(ki)* blooming all seasons; such a flower
9 則 *shisoku* the four arithmetical operations
発 *yompatsu* four-engined
重奏 *shijūsō* instrumental quartet
通八達 *shitsū-hattatsu* accessible from all directions
面 *shimen* four sides, all sides

面楚歌 *shimensoka* completely surrounded (by the enemy)
海 *shikai* the four seas, the seven seas; the whole world
海同胞 *shikai-dōhō* universal brotherhood
10 這 *yo(tsu)bai* crawling. *yo(tsum)bai* on all fours, falling flat, sprawling
時 *shiji* the four seasons; all year long. *yoji* four o'clock
桁 *yoketa* thousands (in figures)
部合奏 *shibu gassō* instrumental quartet
部合唱 *shibu gasshō* vocal quartet
書 *Shisho* the Four Chinese Classics
書五経 *Shisho-Gokyō* the Nine Chinese Classics
11 球 *shikyū* four balls, base on balls
組 *yo(tsu)gumi* foursome. *yo(tsu)gumi no* quadruple
絃 *shigen* four-stringed lute
隅 *yosumi* four corners
望 *shibō* wide view all around
捨五入 *shisha-gonyū* counting .5 and over as 1 and discarding .4 and less; rounding
12 幅 *yono* four-unit width (cloth)
割 *yo(tsu)wa(ri)* quartering. *yonwari, shiwari* 40%
散 *shisan suru* disperse, scatter
13 聖 *shisei* the world's four great sages (Gautama, Confucius, Socrates, and Christ)
福音書 *Shifukuinsho* the Four Gospels
14 選 *shisen* fourth-term election
境 *shikyō* boundaries
隣 *shirin* whole neighborhood, surrounding countries
15 輪車 *yonrinsha, shirinsha, yorinsha* four-wheeled vehicle
21 顧 *shiko suru* look around

3

A 因 939 / J3078 / M4693 IN cause, factor. *china(mu)* be associated with. *yo(ru)* depend on, be limited to. *yo(tte)* therefore, consequently. *chinami ni* by the way, in this connection.
3 子 *inshi* factor, element (in math)
5 由 *in'yu* cause
8 果 *inga* cause and effect; retribution, karma; fate, destiny; misfortune
果応報 *inga-ōhō* reward according to deeds, retribution
9 盾 *injun* indecision, vacillation
11 習 *inshū* custom, convention, tradition
12 循 *injun* indecision, vacillation
循姑息 *injunkosoku na* temporizing, tardy, time-serving
13 業 *ingō* causes and actions, results of one's actions in a former existence
数 *insū* factor (in math)
数分解 *insū-bunkai* factoring (in math)
15 縁 *innen* cause and effect; karma; fate; affinity, connection; origin, history; pretext
22 襲 *inshū* custom, convention, tradition

A 団 940 / J4344 / M4703' 團 964 / J5425 / M4834 TON. DON. DAN body, group, corps, gang, party, company, troupe; circle.
3 子 *dango* dumpling
子鼻 *dangobana* flat nose
4 円 *dan'en* roundness; peacefulness in the home; conclusion
6 交 *dankō* collective bargaining
7 体 *dantai* corporation, party, body, organization, group, association, entity
体行動 *dantai kōdō* collective action
体交渉 *dantai kōshō* collective bargaining
8 長 *danchō* leader of a group
服 *dampuku* association uniform
10 員 *dan'in* member of a group
匪 *dampi* bandits; Boxers
匪乱 *Dampi (no) Ran* Boxer Rebellion
扇 *uchiwa* round fan; referee's fan
扇太鼓 *uchiwa taiko* fan-shaped drum
栗 *donguri* acorn
栗眼 *donguri manako* goggle-eyed
12 結 *danketsu* unity, union, combination
結力 *danketsuryoku* cohesion; capacity for united action
結心 *danketsushin* feeling of unity, esprit de corps
14 旗 *danki* association flag
歌 *danka* association song
23 欒 *danran* family circle; harmony

A 回 941 / J3273 / M4690 囬 942 / J-X / M4713 囘 387 / J5145 / M1521 E. KAI time; round, game, bout, heat, inning, innings; go around. *megu(ru), mawa(ru)* *vi* and *vt* turn, go around; revolve, rotate, spin, gyrate; patrol, tour; take effect (medicine); be distributed; be past (time); be transferred. *mawa(rasu), mawa(su)* turn, revolve, rotate; circularize; pass around; forward, transmit; refer to; transfer; lend money. *motō(ru)* wander around. *mawa(ri)* rotation; circumference, girth, surroundings, border; detour; tour; efficacy or effect (of something taken); spread (of flames). *mawa(shi)* loin cloth; cape, mantle. *megu(rasu)* enclose, surround; turn, turn around; ponder; devise. *mawa(rikudoi)* circuitous. *-mawa(ri)* via; a round, a turn; a size; a cycle (12 years). (See also 廻 1659 for related compounds)

4 文 *kaibun, kaimon, mawa(shi)bumi* circular letter
天 *kaiten no* epoch-making, stupendous
心 *kaishin* conversion
心者 *kaishinsha* a convert
5 生 *kaisei* resurrection, resuscitation
旧 *kaikyū* longing for the old days
付 *kaifu suru* transmit, refer to, send to, pass on to
収 *kaishū* collection (of materials); recovery (of something)
右 *mawa(re) migi* right about face
礼 *kairei* round of complementary calls
礼客 *kaireikyaku* New Year's callers
6 米 *kaimai* rice transportation; rice deliveries
虫 *kaichū* round intestinal worm.
気 *mawa(ri)gi* distrust
向 *ekō* Buddhist memorial service
合 *mawa(ri)a(wase), megu(ri)awase)* turn of fortune, chance, fate. *kaigō* chance meeting
回 *mawa(ri)-mawa(tte)* after many vicissitudes
回教 *Fuifuikyō, Uiuikyō* Muhammedanism; Islam
7 折 *kaisetsu* diffraction
状 *kaijō* circular letter
忌 *kaiki* death anniversary
8 金 *mawa(ri)gane* money to invest
国 *kaikoku* pilgrimage, tour
歩 *mawa(ri)-aru(ku)* walk around
者 *mawa(shi)mono* spy, secret agent
送 *kaisō* forwarding, transportation
送車 *kaisōsha* out-of-service bus, train, or streetcar
9 持 *mawa(ri)mo(chi)* doing by turns
勅 *kaichoku* (papal) encyclical
春 *kaishun* return of spring; recovery (from an illness); rejuvenation
10 流 *kairyū* flowing around; a stream flowing
航 *kaikō* navigation, cruise
訓 *kaikun* the requested instructions
書 *kaisho* answer to a letter
根性 *mawa(ri) konjō* distrust
帰 *kaiki* revolution, recurrence. *kaiki suru* revolve, return, recur
帰年 *kaikinen* equinoctial year
帰線 *kaikisen* the tropics (of Cancer and Capricorn)
帰熱 *kaikinetsu* recurrent fever
11 廊 *kairō* corridor
道 *mawa(ri)michi* detour, roundabout way
旋 *kaisen* rotation, revolution, convolution
章 *kaishō* circular letter
梯子 *mawa(ri)bashigo* winding staircase
階段 *mawa(ri)kaidan* winding staircase
運業 *kaiungyo* marine transportation business
遊 *kaiyū* excursion, circular tour
遊船 *kaiyūsen* excursion steamer
遊券 *kaiyūken* excursion ticket
船 *kaisen* barge; cargo vessel
船問屋 *kaisendon'ya* shipping agency
船業 *kaisengyō* marine transportation business
教 *Kaikyō* Muhammedanism; Islam
教国 *Kaikyōkoku* Mohammedan country
教徒 *Kaikyōto* a Mohammedan, a Moslem
転 *kaiten* revolution, rotation; revolving, swivel; turnover
転戸 *kaitendo* revolving door
転木馬 *kaiten mokuba* merry-go-round
転灯 *kaitentō* revolving light
転炉 *kaitenro* rotary oven, revolving furnace
転計 *kaitenkei* revolution counter
転盆 *kaitenbon* Lazy Susan, revolving tray

3 口 4【囗】土 士 夂 夊 夕 大 女 子 宀 寸 小 ⺌ 尢 尸 屮 山 川 巛 工 己 巾 干 幺 广 廴 廾 弋 弓 ヨ 彑 彡 彳

3 転砲 *kaitenhō* swivel gun
転砲塔 *kaiten hōtō* revolving turret
転率 *kaitenritsu* rate of turnover
転窓 *kaiten mado* transom window
転椅子 *kaiten isu* swivel chair
転資金 *kaiten shikin* revolving fund
転儀 *kaitengi* gyroscope
転翼 *kaiten'yoku* rotor
転羅針儀 *kaiten rashingi* gyrocompass
12 遠 *mawa(ri)dōi* roundabout, long-winded
游 *kaiyū* a run of fish; traveling around for pleasure
診 *kaishin* doctor's hospital rounds
飲 *mawa(shi)no(mi)* drink in turn from one cup
答 *kaitō* reply
番 *mawa(ri)ban ni* alternately
報 *kaihō* circular; reply
復 *kaifuku* recovery, restoration, rehabilitation
復中 *kaifukuchū* convalescing period
復期 *kaifukuki* convalescence
13 禄 *kairoku* god of fire
路 *kairo* (electric) circuit
想 *kaisō* reflection, reminiscence
想録 *kaisōroku* memoirs
数 *kaisū* frequency, number of times
数券 *kaisūken* railway ticket book
数乗車券 *kaisū jōshaken* book of railway tickets
14 暦 *kaireki* arrival of the New Year
歴 *kaireki* round, patrol, tour
読 *kaidoku suru* read (a book in turn)
舞台 *mawa(ri)butai* revolving stage
漕 *kaisō* marine transportation
漕店 *kaisōten* shipping agency
漕問屋 *kaisōdon'ya* shipping agency
15 線 *kaisen* (electric) circuit
縁 *mawa(ri)en* veranda around two sides
避 *kaihi* evasion, shirking, dodging, circumvention, avoiding
避所 *kaihisho* place to pass (on a narrow road)
16 錐 *mawa(shi)giri* auger (tool)
燈籠 *mawa(ri)tōrō* revolving lantern
覧 *kairan* circulation
覧文庫 *kairanbunko* circulating library
覧板 *kairanban* circular letter
21 顧 *kaiko* recollection, retrospect
顧的 *kaikoteki* retrospective
顧録 *kaikoroku* memoirs, reminiscences

4

囬 942 / J-X / M4713 See **回** 941.

囯 943 / J-X / M4716 See **国** 950.

囮 944 / J5379 / M4715 KA. GA *otori* decoy, lure, stool pigeon.

A **囲** 945 / J304f / M4722 **圍** 959 / J5423 / M4806 I enclosure. *kako(mu), kako(u)* enclose, surround, encircle; besiege; preserve, store; keep. *kako(mi), kako(i)* enclosure, paling; tea arbor; storage.
2 入 *kako(mi)-i(reru)* gather in
8 者 *kako(i)mono* concubine
炉裏 *irori* sunken hearth
12 堰 *kako(i)zeki* cofferdam
13 障 *ishō* fence
碁 *igo* (the game of) *go*
18 繞 *inyō suru, ijō suru* surround

A **困** 946 / J3a24 / M4717 KON. *koma(ru)* be distressed be in trouble, be destitute, be embarrassed, be perplexed, be annoyed. *koma(raseru), koma(rasu)* embarrass, annoy.
4 厄 *kon'yaku* trouble, misfortune, hardship
切 *koma(ri)-ki(ru)* be greatly perplexed; be greatly embarrassed
7 抜 *koma(ri)-nu(ku)* be greatly perplexed; be greatly embarrassed
却 *konkyaku* embarrassment, perplexity, trouble
8 果 *koma(ri)-ha(teru)* be greatly perplexed; be greatly embarrassed
者 *koma(ri)mono* good-for-nothing person; source of trouble
苦 *konku* hardships, privation
苦欠乏 *konku-ketsubō* hardships, privation
10 悩 *koma(ri)-naya(mu)* be in deep trouble
12 惑 *konwaku* perplexity, embarrassment; doubt; confusion
15 窮 *konkyū* poverty, distress
窮者 *konkyūsha* the poor, the needy
16 憊 *kompai* exhaustion, fatigue
18 難 *konnan* trouble, distress, perplexity

A 図 947 J3f5e M4734′ 圖 963 J5426 M4832 To plan. Zu drawing, plan, figure, cut, chart, diagram, illustration, graph. *haka(ru)* measure, gauge, weigh; fathom, sound; compute, estimate; plan, devise, scheme; counsel with; have in mind; aim at; deceive, impose on. *haka(razaru)* unexpected. *haka(razu) mo* unexpectedly, unintentionally, accidentally.

2 入 *zui(ri)* illustrated (book)
3 工 *zukō* draftsman
上 *zujō* on the map
4 引 *zuhi(ki)* drafting, drawing; draftsman
太 *zubuto(i)* bold, audacious, impudent
5 示 *zushi* explanatory diagram, illustration
6 式 *zushiki* diagram, graph
当 *zu (ni) a(taru)* hit the mark; work well
7 図 *zūzū(shii)* impudent, audacious, bold, brazenfaced
体 *zūtai* body
抜 *zunu(keru)* tower above, be outstanding
形 *zukei* figure, diagram
形幾何学 *zukei kikagaku* descriptive geometry
8 法 *zuhō* drawing, draftsmanship
版 *zuhan* plate, figure, illustration
取 *zudo(ri)* sketching; sketch, plan
画 *zuga* drawing (the study); a drawing, a picture
表 *zuhyō* chart, diagram, graph
9 面 *zumen* drawing, plan, map, sketch
柄 *zugara* a design
星 *zuboshi* the bull's-eye, the mark
10 案 *zuan* design, plan, sketch, drawing
案家 *zuanka* designer
書 *tosho* books
書出版会社 *tosho shuppangaisha* publishing company
書出版者 *tosho shuppansha* publisher
書出納台 *tosho suitōdai* library charging desk
書目録 *tosho mokuroku* catalog of publications
書受入 *tosho u(ke)i(re)* library accessioning
書受入原簿 *tosho u(ke)i(re) gembo* accession book
書室 *toshoshitsu* library room
書票 *toshohyō* book label
書解題 *tosho kaidai* bibliography
書請求票 *tosho seikyūhyō* library call slip
書閲覧人 *tosho etsurannin* library reader
書閲覧用紙 *tosho etsuran yōshi* library call slip
書閲覧室 *tosho etsuranshitsu* reading room
書閲覧料 *tosho etsuranryō* library admission charge
書館 *toshokan* library
書館長 *toshokanchō* head librarian
書館学 *toshokangaku* library science
書館員 *toshokan'in* library clerk, librarian
12 葉 *zuyō* a map
13 解 *zukai* illustration, explanatory diagram
14 様 *zuyō* illustration; map; style
説 *zusetsu* explanatory diagram; illustrated book
像学 *zuzōgaku* iconology, iconography
18 題 *zudai* caption for an illustration
19 譜 *zufu* chart, picture, figure
22 鑑 *zukan* picture book

5

囹 948 J537a M4744 Rei prison.

10 圄 *reigo* prison

A 固 949 J3847 M4745 Ko. *kata(maru) vi* harden, stiffen, solidify, set, settle, congeal, clot, curdle, conglomerate, get together; be devoted to; settle down (weather). *kata(meru) vt* harden; tighten; freeze; curdle; strengthen; stabilize; defend, fortify; collect, amass; settle down, locate. *kata(me)* defense, fortification; guard; pledge, engagement. *katama(ri)* lump, chunk, cold, mass; clump, cluster, group; flock; bigotry; personification (of). *kata(i)* hard, solid; tough, rigid; tight; steady, firm; strict; safe, reliable, upright; chaste, constant; stiff; bookish; classical; stubborn. *moto(yori)* from the beginning; of course.

4 太 *katabuto(ri)* of firm build
6 守 *koshu* persistence, tenacity, adhering
有 *koyū no* personal, characteristic, peculiar to, inherent

有名詞 *koyū meishi* proper noun
有財産 *koyū zaisan* personal property
有語 *koyūgo* idiomatic expression
7 体 *kotai* a solid (body)
体化 *kotaika* solidification
体燃料 *kotai nenryō* solid fuel
形 *kokei* a solid (body)
形分 *kokeibun* solids
形体 *kokeitai* a solid (body)
形物 *kokeibutsu* a solid ; solid food
形便 *kokeiben* firm (ordinary) feces
形食物 *kokei shokumotsu* solid food
形燃料 *kokei nenryō* solid fuel
8 陋 *korō* perversity, bigotry, conservatism
苦 *katakuru(shii)* formal, ceremonious; awkward; punctilious; strict
定 *kotei* fixing, fixation, fixed; identification (of biological specimens)
定化 *koteika* fixation, freezing (credits)
定給 *koteikyū* fixed salary
定費 *koteihi* fixed charge
定資本 *kotei shihon* fixed capital
定資産 *kotei shisan* fixed assets
9 持 *koji suru* persist in (a belief), adhere to (a cause)
10 疾 *koshitsu* chronic illness
11 執 *koshū, koshitsu* adherence; persistence
唾飲 *katazu (o) no(mu)* be intensely anxious
12 着 *kochaku suru* adhere to
13 塩 *katashio* rock salt
辞 *koji suru* positively decline
14 飴 *kataame* hard candy

A  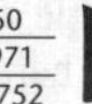 950 J3971 M4752  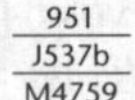 951 J537b M4759   956 J5422 M4798

国 943 J-X M4716 KOKU country. *kuni* country, land, realm; province; native land. *(o)kuni* your country; hometown, province.
2 人 *kunibito, kokujin* a people, natives
力 *kokuryoku* national strength, national resources
3 土 *kokudo* country, territory, domain
土防衛 *kokudo bōei* national defense
土計画 *kokudo keikaku* land planning
4 手 *kokushu* skilled doctor
父 *kokufu* father of his country
王 *kokuō* king, monarch
中 *kunijū* throughout the country
分寺 *kokubunji* ancient provincial temples
内 *kokunai* domestic; the interior of a country
内消費 *kokunai shōhi* domestic consumption
内産業 *kokunai sangyō* domestic industries
内戦 *kokunaisen* civil war
文 *kokubun* national literature; national language
文法 *kokubumpō* Japanese grammar
文学 *kokubungaku* Japanese literature
文学史 *kokubungakushi* history of Japanese literature
文科 *kokubunka* Japanese literature course
5 母 *kokubo* empress, empress dowager
号 *kokugō* name of a country
用 *kokuyō* national expenses, national resources, national use
巡 *kunimegu(ri)* touring countries
史 *kokushi* national history
払 *kunibara(i)* exile, deportation
主 *kokushu* feudal lord, governor of a medieval province *(kuni)*
司 *kunizukasa, kokushi* governor of a medieval province *(kuni)*
本 *kokuhon* foundation of the nation
外 *kokugai* overseas, outside the country
外追放 *kokugai tsuihō* deportation
立 *kokuritsu* national (institution)
立公園 *kokuritsi kōen* national park
立図書館 *kokuritsu toshokan* national library
立墓地 *kokuritsu bochi* national cemetery
民 *kokumin, kunitami* the people, a national; national
民化 *kokuminka* nationalization
民文学 *kokumin bungaku* national literature
民生活 *kokumin seikatsu* national life
民主義 *kokumin shugi* nationalism
民投票 *kokumin tōhyō* plebiscite
民性 *kokuminsei* national character
民的 *kokuminteki* national
民所得 *kokumin shotoku* national income
民軍 *kokumin gun* national army
民皆兵 *kokumin kaihei* universal conscription

民思想 *kokumin shisō* national sentiment
民党 *Kokumintō* Chinese Nationalist Party
民経済 *kokumin keizai* national economy
民道徳 *kokumin dōtoku* national morality, civic virtues
民登録 *kokumin tōroku* national registration
民感情 *kokumin kanjō* national sentiment
民精神 *kokumin seishin* national spirit
民精神総動員 *kokumin seishin sōdōin* national spiritual mobilization
6 交 *kokkō* diplomatic relations
安 *kokuan* national peace
守 *kokushu* medieval governor's executive officer
光 *kokkō* national glory, national prestige
名 *kokumei* name of a country
自慢 *kuni jiman* provincial pride
字 *kokuji* native script; the *kana* syllabary; characters made in Japan
字改良 *kokuji kairyō* reform of Japanese writing
防 *kokubō* national defense
防色 *kokubōshoku* khaki color
防服 *kokubōfuku* civilian wartime uniform
防軍 *kokubōgun* national defense force
防費 *kokubōhi* defense expenditures
会 *kokkai* national assembly, diet, congress, parliament
会図書館 *Kokkai Toshokan* Library of Congress, National Diet Library
会衛視 *kokkai eishi* sergeant-at-arms
会議事堂 *Kokkai Gijidō* Diet Building; House of Parliament; U.S. Capitol, National Assembly Building
会議員 *kokkai giin* national assemblyman
有 *kokuyū* national ownership
有化 *kokuyūka* nationalization
有地 *kokuyūchi* national land
有林 *kokuyūrin* national forest
有財産 *kokuyū zaisan* national resources
有鉄道 *kokuyū tetsudō* national railways
7 体 *kokutai* national structure, national polity; national athletic meet
技 *kokugi* national skills; national sport
状 *kokujō* condition of the country
乱 *kokuran* civil strife
別 *kunibetsu* classification by nations
花 *kokka* national flower
君 *kokkun* sovereign
言葉 *kuni kotoba* local dialect
利 *kokuri* national interests; profit to the country
利民福 *kokuri-mimpuku* the prosperity of the country and the happiness of the people
8 国 *kuniguni* nations
府 *kokufu* provincial capital; Nationalist government of China. *kokubu* (ancient) local government office
使 *kokushi* envoy
法 *kokuhō* national law, public law
育 *kunisodachi* brought up in the country
宝 *kokuhō* national treasure; national hero
歩 *kokuho* fortunes of state
典 *kokuten* state ceremony; national literature; Japanese book
定 *kokutei* stipulated by law, compiled by the state
定公園 *kokutei kōen* national park
学 *kokugaku* study of Japanese literature
学者 *kokugakusha* Japanese classical scholar
事 *kokuji* national affairs
事行為 *kokuji kōi* matters of state
事犯 *kokujihan* political offense, treason
9 風 *kokufū, kuniburi* national customs; popular songs, folk songs
廻 *kunimegu(ri)* touring the countries *(kuni)*
威 *kokui* national prestige
造 *kunizuku(ri)* founding a nation
俗 *kokuzoku* national customs
持 *kunimo(chi)* feudal lord
柄 *kunigara* national character. *kokuhei* reins of government
政 *kokusei* government, national administration
軍 *kokugun* Japanese armed forces
是 *kokuze* national policy
連 *Kokuren* United Nations
連安全保障理事会 *Kokuren Anzen Hoshō Rijikai* UN Security Council

連事務総長 *Kokuren Jimu Sōchō* UN Secretary General
連軍 *Kokuren Gun* UN Forces
連教育科学文化機構 *Kokuren Kyōiku Kagaku Bunka Kikō* UNESCO
連旗 *Kokurenki* UN flag
連総会 *Kokuren Sōkai* UN General Assembly
10 庫 *kokko* national treasury
辱 *kokujoku* national dishonor
師 *kokushi* Buddhist priest
恥 *kokuchi* national humiliation
訓 *kokkun* Japanese reading of a Chinese character that is used without regard to the real meaning of the character in China
都 *kokuto* national capital
益 *kokueki* national prosperity
書 *kokusho* credentials (to a ruler); a ruler's message; national record; national literature
華 *kokka* national pride or glory
恩 *kokuon* blessing received from one's country
粋 *kokusui* national characteristics
粋主義 *kokusui shugi* ultranationalism
家 *kokka* nation, country
家公務員 *kokka kōmuin* government officials
家主義 *kokka shugi* nationalism
家地方警察 *kokka chihō keisatsu* national rural police
家扶助 *kokka fujo* assistance from the government
家的 *kokkateki* national, state
家宗教 *kokka shūkyō* national religion
家神道 *Kokka Shintō* State Shinto
家経済 *kokka keizai* national economy
家群 *kokkagun* family of nations, group of nations
家試験 *kokka shiken* government examinations
家管理 *kokka kanri* state control
家総動員 *kokka sōdōin* national general mobilization
家憲章 *kokka kenshō* national charter
家警察 *kokka keisatsu* national police
11 道 *kokudō* national highway
運 *kokuun* national destiny, national fortunes
情 *kokujō* condition of the country
設 *kokusetsu* provided by the government
訛 *kuni nama(ri)* provincial accent
許 *kunimoto* birthplace, one's country, one's home province
教 *kokkyō* state religion, state church
章 *kokushō* national emblem
基 *kokki* foundation of a nation
患 *kokkan* national disaster
務 *kokumu* state affairs
務大臣 *kokumu daijin* minister of state; minister without portfolio
務長官 *Kokumu Chōkan* Secretary of State
産 *kokusan* domestic products
産品 *kokusanhin* domestic products
祭 *kokusai* national festival
祭日 *kokusaibi* national holiday
12 税 *kokuzei* national tax
朝 *kokuchō* imperial court
富 *kokufu* national wealth
策 *kokusaku* national policy
葬 *kokusō* state funeral
替 *kuniga(e)* transfer of a daimyo
費 *kokuhi* national expenditures
喪 *kokusō* national mourning
営 *kokuei* government-operated
営化 *kokueika* nationalization
営墓地 *kokuei bochi* national cemetery
13 債 *kokusai* national debt; national bonds, national securities
漢 *kokkan* Japanese and Chinese literature
賊 *kokuzoku* traitor, rebel
鉄 *kokutetsu* national railways
電 *kokuden* government electric line
禁 *kokkin* a national prohibition
勢 *kunizei* local armed forces. *kokusei* national strength; condition of the country
勢調査 *kokusei chōsa* national census
際 *kokusai* international (intercourse)
際人 *kokusaijin* citizen of the world
際化 *kokusaika* internationalization
際的 *kokusaiteki* international
際公法 *kokusai kōhō* international public law
際友誼 *kokusai yūgi* international friendship, comity of nations
際司法裁判所 *Kokusai Shihō Saibansho* International Court of Justice
際主義 *kokusai shugi* internationalism

際共産主義 *Kokusai Kyōsan Shugi* International Communism
際共産党 *Kokusai Kyōsantō* Comintern, International Communism
際仲裁裁判所 *Kokusai Chūsai Saibansho* International Court of Arbitration, the Hague Court
際赤十字 *Kokusai Sekijūji* International Red Cross
際社会 *kokusai shakai* community of nations
際私法 *kokusai shihō* international private law
際法 *kokusaihō* international law
際連合 *Kokusai Rengō* United Nations
際連合軍 *Kokusai Rengō Gun* United Nations Army
際連盟 *Kokusai Remmei* League of Nations
際通 *kokusaitsū* authority on international affairs
際通信社 *Kokusai Tsūshinsha* International News Services
際通貨基金 *Kokusai Tsūka Kikin* International Monetary Fund
際都市 *kokusai toshi* cosmopolitan city
際麻薬輸入団 *kokusai mayaku yunyūdan* international narcotics ring
際間 *kokusaikan no* international
際結婚 *kokusai kekkon* international marriage
際場裡 *kokusai jōri* international arena
際語 *kokusaigo* an international language
際管理 *kokusai kanri* international control
際警察軍 *kokusai keisatsu gun* international police force
14 旗 *kokki* national flag
構 *kunigama(e)* national structure; the closed-box radical (of a character)
歌 *kokka* national anthem
製品 *kokuseihin* Japanese product
選弁護人 *kokusen bengonin* counsel assigned by the court
語 *kokugo* national language; Japanese
語改良 *kokugo kairyō* reform of the Japanese language
語学 *kokugogaku* study of languages, study of Japanese
境 *kokkyō, kunizakai* frontier, national boundary
境刺戟 *kokkyō shigeki* border raid
境線 *kokkyōsen* boundary line
境警備 *kokkyō keibi* border guards
15 儀 *kokugi* state function
権 *kokken* sovereign rights; national prestige
論 *kokuron* public opinion, public discussion
賓 *kokuhin* national guest
勲 *kokkun* meritorious service for the state
器 *kokki* statesman
幣社 *kokuheisha* national shrine
16 憲 *kokken* national constitution
18 儲 *kokucho* imperial heir
難 *kokunan* national crisis, national disaster
19 璽 *kokuji* the seal of state
警 *kokkei* national police
20 籍 *kokuseki* nationality, citizenship

6

圀 951 / J537b / M4759 See 国 950.

囿 952 / J537c / M4756 YŪ, IKU. *sono* garden, park, preserve.
2 人 *yūjin* animal caretaker; gardener.
8 苑 *yūen* zoological or botanical gardens

7

圄 953 / J537d / M4775 GO prison; arrest.

圃 954 / J4a60 / M4774 HO field (for crops); garden.

8

圈 955 / J5421 / M4789 See 圏 960.

國 956 / J5422 / M4798 See 国 950.

圉 957 / J537e / M4793 GYO. GO. *ori* cage, corral; prison. *makiba* pasture.

圊 958 / J-X / M4797 SEI. *kawaya* privy, lavatory.

3 口 9【囗】 土 士 夂 夊 夕 大 女 子 宀 寸 小 ⺌ 尢 尸 屮 山 川 巛 工 己 巾 干 幺 广 廴 廾 弋 弓 ヨ 彑 彡 彳

9

圍 959 / J5423 / M4806 See **囲** 945.

B **圈** 960 / J3777 / M4815' **圏** 955 / J5421 / M4789 KEN sphere, circle, range, radius.
4 内 *kennai* within the range or orbit
5 外 *kengai* outside the range or orbit
9 点 *kenten* a circle (for emphasis)

10

圓 961 / J5424 / M4819 See **円** 385.

A **園** 962 / J3160 / M4818 EN garden, yard, plantation, farm. *sono* garden, park.
2 丁 *entei* gardener
5 生 *sonoo* garden
主 *enshu* garden of orchard owner
6 地 *enchi* park
7 児 *enji* kindergarten pupil
芸 *engei* horticulture, floriculture, gardening
芸家 *engeika* gardener, horticulturist
8 長 *enchō* kindergarten principal
9 亭 *entei* arbor, bower, summer house
10 圃 *empo* fields and gardens; truck farm, vegetable garden
11 遊会 *en'yūkai* garden party

11

圖 963 / J5426 / M4832 See **図** 947.

團 964 / J5425 / M4834 See **団** 940.

圜 965 / J5428 / M4851 EN round. KAN surround, enclose.
5 丘 *enkyū* rounded hill
11 視 *enshi* stare with round eyes. *kanshi* look all around.
18 繞 *kanjō* surround, enclose

RAD. 土 32

Tsuchi earth. At left: 𡈽 *tsuchi-hen*. Variant: 士. This variant is actually Rad. 33 but, except for the radical character itself, is herein treated as a variant of Rad. 32. Nickname: Earth.

A **土** 966 / J455a / M4867 **圡** 967 / J-X / M4871 To. Do earth, ground; Saturday; Turkey. *tsuchi* earth, soil, ground.
2 人 *dojin* natives, aborigines
人形 *tsuchi ningyō* clay doll
3 工 *dokō* earthwork; coolie, laborer
下座 *dogeza suru* prostrate oneself
4 戸 *tsuchido* earthen door
手 *dote* bank, dike, embankment
方 *dokata* laborer, coolie
不踏 *tsuchifu(mazu)* arch of the foot
木 *doboku* engineering, public works
木工学 *doboku kōgaku* civil engineering
木学 *dobokugaku* civil engineering
5 付 *tsuchitsu(kazu)* unbeaten, having a clean record
平 *tsuchinara(shi)* ground-leveling roller
台 *dodai* foundation, groundwork, base; fundamentally, entirely
民 *domin* natives, aborigines
左衛門 *dozaemon* drowned person
用 *doyō* dog days, midsummer
用干 *doyōbo(shi)* summer airing (of clothes)
用休 *doyōyasu(mi)* summer vacation
用波 *doyō nami* high waves in the dog days
6 色 *tsuchi iro* earth color
団子 *tsuchi dango* mud pie
気色 *tsuchike iro* earth color
百姓 *dobyakushō* dirt farmer, peasant
耳古 *Toruko* Turkey
耳古石 *toruko ishi* turquoise
耳古風呂 *torukoburo* Turkish bath
耳古帽 *Torukobō* fez
耳其 *Toruko* Turkey

地 *tochi* land, tract, lot; estate; soil; locality; territory; the neighborhood
地付 *tochitsu(ki)* land attached, with land
地収用 *tochi shūyō* expropriation of land
地台帳 *tochi daichō* land register
地会社 *tochigaisha* real-estate company
地私有 *tochi shiyū* private ownership of land
地改良 *tochi kairyō* land improvement
地言葉 *tochi kotoba* dialect
地国有 *tochi kokuyū* state ownership of land
地柄 *tochigara* nature of the locality
地家屋 *tochi-kaoku* real estate; land and buildings
地訛 *tochi namari* colloquial expression
7 足 *dosoku de* with footgear on
均 *tsuchinara(shi)* ground-leveling roller
兵 *dohei* local soldiers; native soldiers
牢 *tsuchirō* underground cell, dungeon
芥 *dokai* rubbish, dirt
8 国 *Dokoku* Turkey
肥 *tsuchiko(eta)* fertile
金属 *dokinzoku* earth metals
性骨 *doshōbone* (derisive for) disposition, nature
性根 *doshōne* disposition, nature
9 室 *tsuchimuro* mud house
星 *Dosei* Saturn
臭 *tsuchikusa(i)* earth-smelling; rustic, boorish
俗 *dozoku* local customs
俗学 *dozokugaku* folklore, ethnography
建 *doken* civil engineering and construction
建屋 *doken'ya* contractor
建業 *dokengyō* civil engineering and construction
砂 *dosha* earth and sand
砂降 *doshabu(ri)* downpour
砂崩壊 *dosha hōkai* landslide
10 匪 *dohi* rebellious natives
埃 *tsuchibokori, tsuchihokori* dust
倉 *tsuchigura, dosō* underground storehouse
釜 *tsuchigama* earthen pot
留 *tsuchido(me)* sand guard
俵 *dohyō* sandbag; ring, wrestling arena
俵場 *dohyōba* ring, arena
俵際 *dohyōgiwa* scaffold, place of execution
竜 *mogura, mugura* mole
竜色 *mogura iro* taupe
竜塚 *mogurazuka* molehill
竜戦術 *mogura senjutsu* underground campaign
11 黒 *tsuchiguro(i)* dark dirt color
偶 *dogū* earthen figure, wooden image, dummy, puppet
瓶 *dobin* earthen teapot
寄 *tsuchiyo(se)* covering the roots
袋 *dotai* sandbag
断場 *dotamba* place of execution, scaffold
崩 *dohō* collapse
崩瓦解 *dohō-gakai* collapse, downfall
蛍 *tsuchibotaru* glowworm
産 *miyage* souvenir, present
産物 *miyagemono* souvenir, present
産法案 *miyagehōan* pork barrel
産話 *miyagebanashi* story of one's travels
12 間 *doma* unfloored room; dirt floor
塀 *dobei* mud wall
焼 *tsuchiya(ki)* unglazed earthenware
塁 *dorui* earthwork, breastwork
筆 *tsukushi, tsukushimbo* horsetail
葬 *dosō* burial, interment
着 *dochaku no* aboriginal, indigenous, native
着民 *dochakumin* natives, aborigines
13 塊 *dokai, tsuchikure* clod, lump of earth
煙 *tsuchikemuri* cloud of dust
賊 *dozoku* bandit, rebel, insurgent
窟 *dokutsu* cave
14 語 *dogo* native tongue, dialect
管 *dokan* earthen pipe, drainpipe
蔵 *dozō* warehouse, storehouse, godown
製 *dosei, tsuchisei* earthen, terra cotta
豪 *dogō* (ancient) powerful provincial family
豪劣神 *dogō-resshin* oppressive landowner
15 墳 *dofun* grave mound
踏 *tsuchifu(mazu)* arch of the foot
蕃 *doban* natives, aborigines
質 *doshitsu* nature of the soil
器 *doki, kawarake* unglazed earthenware, earthenware, crockery, pottery
16 壌 *dojō* soil, earth
橋 *dobashi* earthen bridge

篩 *tsuchifurui* earth strainer
壁 *tsuchi kabe* mud wall
壇場 *dotamba* place of execution, scaffold
17 鍋 *donabe, tsuchi nabe* earthen pot
18 類金属 *dorui kinzoku* earth metals
曜 *Doyō* Saturday
曜日 *Doyōbi* Saturday
19 瀝青 *dorekisei, asufuaruto* asphalt
20 饅頭 *domanjū, tsuchi manjū* grave mound
21 竈 *dogama* soft-charcoal furnace; soft charcoal
22 嚢 *donō* sandbag

1

圡 967 J-X M4871 See 土 966.

壬 968 J3f51 M5639 NIN. JIN I, ninth. *mizunoe* ninth calendar sign. [士]

2

圦 969 J5429 M-X (国字) *iri* flood gate, sluice gate; spout.

A **圧** 970 J3035 M4879 **壓** 1104 J545a M5557 EN. ATSU. *as(suru)* press, oppress, dominate, overwhelm. *he(su)* push, press. *o(su)* push, shove; press, squash, compress; stamp, seal; do in spite of. *o(shi)-* emphatic verbal prefix.
2 力 *atsuryoku* pressure, stress
力団体 *atsuryoku dantai* pressure groups
力計 *atsuryokukei* pressure gauge
4 込 *he(shi)-ko(mu)* push into
5 石 *o(shi)ishi* stone weight
出 *asshutsu* pressing out
6 死 *asshi* crushing to death
伏 *appuku suru* overpower, subdue
合 *he(shi)-a(u)* jostle, push
舌器 *atsuzetsuki* tongue depressor
7 折 *he(shi)-o(ru)* smash, break
迫 *appaku* pressure, coercion, oppression
迫感 *appakukan* feeling of oppression
8 拉 *o(shi)-hishi(gu)* smash, suppress
服 *appuku suru* overpower, overwhelm, subdue, keep down
制 *assei* oppression, tyranny, despotism
制的 *asseiteki* oppressive, despotic
制者 *asseisha* oppressor, tyrant
延 *atsuen* rolling
延工場 *atsuen kōjō* rolling mill
延機 *atsuenki* rolling machine
延鋼 *atsuenkō* rolled steel
9 砕 *assai* crushing
巻 *akkan* best part (of a book); masterpiece; highlight; best in the lot
10 殺 *o(shi)-koro(su)* crush, stifle, or squeeze to death. *assatsu* crushing to death
倒 *attō suru* overwhelm, overpower, crush; outdo, surpass
倒的 *attōteki* overwhelming
12 勝 *asshō* complete victory
覚 *akkaku* sense of pressure
13 搾 *assaku* pressure, compressing
搾空気 *assaku kūki* compressed air
搾機 *assakuki* press, compressor
17 縮 *asshuku* compression, pressing, constriction, condensation
縮性 *asshukusei* compressibility
縮空気 *asshuku kūki* compressed air
縮率 *asshukuritsu* compressibility
縮器 *asshukuki* compressor
19 濾器 *atsuroki* filter press

3

圸 971 J542b M-X (国字) *mama* steep slope, cliff.

圷 972 J542a M4900 (国字) *akutsu* low-lying land.

圭 973 J373d M4887 KEI corner, angle, edge; jewel.
7 角 *keikaku* angle, corner
14 算 *keisan* paperweight

B **壮** 974 J4154 M5642 **壯** 977 J5463 M5643 SŌ manhood; prosperity. *saka(n)* prosperous. [士]
2 丁 *sōtei* a young man, an able-bodied youth
3 士 *sōshi* henchman, political bully
大 *sōdai* grandeur, splendor
4 夫 *sōfu* able-bodied man
6 年 *sōnen* the prime of life
行 *sōkō* a grand farewell
行会 *sōkōkai* farewell party

7 言 *sōgen* spirited words
図 *sōto* great undertaking; heroic attempt
快 *sōkai na* stirring, thrilling, exciting
志 *sōshi* ambition, aspiration
8 者 *sōsha* man in his prime
9 途 *sōto* ambitious course
重 *sōchō* solemnity, gravity, impressiveness
美 *sōbi* magnificence, grandeur
10 挙 *sōkyo* great undertaking; heroic attempt
烈 *sōretsu na* heroic, brave
11 健 *sōken na* healthy, robust
12 絶 *sōzetsu na* sublime, heroic, magnificent
14 語 *sōgo* bragging, exaggeration
17 厳 *sōgon* solemnity, sublimity, impressiveness, magnificence, majesty
齢 *sōrei* prime of life, around thirty
18 観 *sōkan* grandeur, grand spectacle
19 麗 *sōrei* splendor, grandeur

A **在** 975 J3a5f M4881 Zᴀɪ outskirts, suburbs, country. *a(ru)* there is, have, exist; occur; be located, be contained in; (it) measures; happen; be found; be held; consist of. *owa(su)* to be (polite). *a(ri) to arayuru* all, every. *zai-* located in.
4 方 *a(ri)kata* way something should be; the way something is
天 *zaiten no* heaven, heavenly
中 *zaichū* within
中物 *zaichūbutsu* contents
日 *zai Nichi* resident in Japan. *ari(shi)hi* bygone days; during one's lifetime
日中 *zai-Nichichū* while resident in Japan
日本 *zai-Nihon* resident in Japan
5 処 *arika* one's whereabouts, retreat, refuge, hiding place; location (of something)
世 *zaisei* on the earth. *ari(shi)yo* on the earth; past days
世中 *zaiseichū* during one's lifetime
外 *zaigai* abroad ⌈abroad
外邦人 *zaigai hōjin* Japanese residents
外事務所 *zaigai jimusho* overseas agency
外研究員 *zaigai kenkyūin* overseas research personnel
6 合 *a(ri)-a(u)* happen to have
宅 *zaitaku suru* be in, be at home
米 *zai-Bei* resident in America
米中 *zai-Beichū* while resident in America
任 *zainin suru* hold office
任中 *zaininchū* while in office
7 廷 *zaitei* serving in the imperial court; appearing in court
役 *zaieki* being employed; serving in the army; (ships) being commissioned
社 *zaisha suru* be in office
来 *zairai, a(ri)ki(tari)* usage, tradition
村地主 *zaison jinushi* resident landlord
位 *zaii* reigning
位中 *zaiichū* during the reign of
住 *zaijū suru* live, reside, dwell
住者 *zaijūsha* resident
8 国 *zaikoku* living in one's province
所 *zaisho* the country; one's residence; one's home town. *a(ri)dokoro* one's whereabouts, retreat, refuge, hiding place; location (of something)
英 *zai-Ei* resident in England
英中 *zai-Eichū* while resident in England
京 *zaikyō* resident in the capital
京中 *zaikyōchū* while in the capital
官 *zaikan* tenure of office
官中 *zaikanchū* while in office
官者 *zaikansha* officeholder
学 *zaigaku* enrolled in school
学生 *zaigakusei* student; undergraduate
学年限 *zaigaku nengen* time limit for completing a curriculum
9 室 *zaishitsu suru* be in the room
10 家 *zaika* farmhouse; in the country. *zaike* a formal Buddhist
華 *zai-Ka* resident in China
荷 *arini, zaika* goods on hand, inventory
庫 *zaiko* stock, stockpile
庫品 *zaikohin* goods on hand, inventory
校 *zaikō suru* be in school
校生 *zaikōsei* present students
郷 *zaigō, zaigo* rural districts. *zaikyō* in the country
郷者 *zaigōsha* person from the country
郷軍人 *zaigō gunjin* veteran, reservist
留 *zairyū suru* reside temporarily
留民 *zairyūmin* residents
留外人 *zairyū gaijin* foreign residents
留邦人 *zairyū hōjin* Japanese in foreign lands

11 宿 *zaishuku suru* be in, be at home
貨 *zaika* goods on hand, inventory
野 *zaiya* out of office; the party out of power
野党 *zaiyatō* the party out of power
12 勤 *zaikin suru* serve, hold office
無 *a(riya)-na(shiya)* to be living or not to be living; be true or not true. *a(ruka)-na(ika)* too small; existing or not existing; to be held or not to be held
番中 *zaibanchū* on duty
場所 *aribasho* one's whereabouts, retreat, refuge, hiding place; location (of something)
14 銘 *zaimei* maker's signature
獄 *zaigoku* in prison
獄中 *zaigokuchū* while in prison
監 *zaikan* in prison
監者 *zaikansha* prisoner; prison population
18 韓 *zai-Kan* resident in Korea
職 *zaishoku suru* hold office, remain in office
職年限 *zaishoku nengen* tenure of office
職期間 *zaishoku kikan* tenure of office
20 籍 *zaiseki* be enrolled
籍学生数 *zaiseki gakuseisū* school enrollment

A **地** 976 / J434f / M4890 CHI earth, land, ground, the surface of the earth; soil; place, region; territory; room, space; position; site; foundation. *ji* ground, land, earth; the surface of the earth; foundation, soil; texture, weave, fabric; field (of a flag); region; disposition; respectability; accompaniment; narrative part; fact. *ji(beta)* the ground, the earth. *tsuchi* earth, soil, ground.
2 力 *chiryoku* fertility
3 口 *jiguchi* play on words
久節 *Chikyūsetsu* Empress' Birthday (ancient term)
上 *chijō no* terrestrial, earthly, mundane, temporal. *chijō ni* on the ground, on earth, in this world
上力 *chijō (no) chikara* temporal power
上水 *chijōsui* surface water
上軍 *chijō gun* ground forces
上権 *chijōken* lease
下 *jige* ordinary officials; common people. *chika* underground, subterranean; basement
下水 *chikasui* subterranean water
下牢 *chikarō* underground dungeon
下足袋 *jika tabi* heavy-soled work tabi
下茎 *chikakei* rhizome
下室 *chikashitsu* basement, cellar
下政府 *chika seifu* underground government
下道 *chikadō* underground passage
下細胞 *chika saibō* underground elements
下運動 *chika undō* underground movement
下街 *chikagai* underground market
下鉄 *chikatetsu* subway
下鉄道 *chika tetsudō* subway
下資源 *chika shigen* underground resources
下権 *chikaken* subsurface rights
下線 *chikasen* underground cable or wire
4 心 *chishin* earth's center, earth's core
区 *chiku* area, region, lot
辷 *jisube(ri)* landslide
中 *chichū* underground, subterranean
中海 *Chichūkai* Mediterranean Sea
元 *jimoto no* local. *jimoto* that country
太 *jibuto no* coarse (texture)
文 *chimon, chibun* physiographical features
文学 *chimongaku, chibungaku* physiography
水 *chisui* subterranean water
水火風 *chi-sui-ka-fū* the four elements; earth, water, fire, and wind
引 *jibiki* seine fishing
引網 *jibikiami* dragnet, seine (for inshore fishing)
方 *chihō* locality, region, area, section; the country; vicinity, neighborhood. *jigata* rural locality; coastal waters
方区 *chihōku* prefectural or local constituencies
方化 *chihōka* localization
方主義 *chihō shugi* provincialism
方色 *chihōshoku* local color
方回 *chihō mawa(ri)* provincial tour
方性 *chihōsei* local color
方版 *chihōban* provincial edition
方的 *chihōteki* local
方官 *chihōkan* local authorities

方制度 *chihō seido* local government system
方風 *chihōfū* local wind
方病 *chihōbyō* endemic disease; animal disease
方時 *chihōji* local time
方訛 *chihō namari* provincialism, local dialect, local accent
方税 *chihōzei* local taxes
方債 *chihōsai* local bonds
方新聞 *chihō shimbun* local newspaper
方闘争 *chihō tōsō* local strike
5 目 *chimoku* land category
代 *jidai, chidai* land rent
玉 *jitama* home-grown eggs; local eggs
玉子 *jitamago* home-grown eggs; local eggs
主 *jinushi* landlord
主層 *jinushisō* the landowner class
平 *chihei* ground level
平面 *chiheimen* horizontal plane
平線 *chiheisen* horizon, skyline
6 米 *jimai* locally produced rice
糸 *jiito* homespun thread
色 *jiiro* ground color
虫 *jimushi* grub, ground beetle
衣 *chii* lichen
気 *chiki* earth vapors
肌 *jihada* texture, grain
合 *jia(i)* texture, weave, fabric
先 *jisaki* frontage
名 *chimei* place name
団駄 *jidanda* stamping with vexation
回 *jimawa(ri)* neighborhood, neighboring districts, provincial, local; a street tough
回船 *jimawa(ri)sen* coastwise steamer
曳 *jibiki* seine fishing
曳網 *jibiki ami* dragnet, seine (for inshore fishing)
7 車 *jiguruma* a wagon
図 *chizu* map, chart, plan
位 *chii* position, status, place, office, post
利 *chiri* excellent topography. *chi(no)ri* geographical advantage
声 *jigoe* natural voice
牢 *jirō* dungeon
卵 *jitamago* home-grown eggs; local eggs
吹雪 *jifubuki* drifting snow
役権 *chiekiken* easement, servitude
均 *jinarashi* ground leveling
均機 *jinarashiki* bulldozer
形 *chikei* topography. *jigyō* ground leveling; groundwork
形図 *chikeizu* topographical map
形学 *chikeigaku* physiography, geomorphology
8 金 *jigane* metal, ore, ground metal; true character
固 *jigata(me)* ground leveling; ground tamping
底 *chitei* the bowels of the earth; underground
価 *chika* land value
味 *chimi* nature of the soil. *jimi na* plain, simple, quiet, sober, modest, conservative
坪 *jitsubo* ground area
板 *jiita* flooring, planking
炉 *jiro* fireplace in the ground
物 *chibutsu* natural objects, landmarks, places to hide. *jimono* local product
取 *jido(ri)* ground plan, layout
歩 *chiho* one's ground, one's stand, standing, position, footing
券 *chiken* title deed
学 *chigaku* physiography
表 *chihyō* surface of the earth
所 *jisho* land, ground, tract, plot
所持 *jishomo(chi)* landowner
所熱 *jisho netsu* land fever, land hunger
9 廻 *jimawa(ri)* neighborhood, neighboring districts; provincial, local; a street tough
峡 *chikyō* isthmus
相 *chisō* divination by the lay of the land; topography
狭 *chikyō* isthmus
神 *chijin* earthly deities
変 *chihen* natural calamity
点 *chiten* spot, point, place, position
界 *chikai* boundary
政学 *chiseigaku* geopolitics
面 *jimen* surface (of land), ground, land, lot
面持 *jimemmo(chi)* landowner
10 唄 *jiuta* ballad, folk song
核 *chikaku* earth's nucleus
酒 *jizake* locally brewed saké
祇 *chigi* earthly deities
租 *chiso* land tax
紋 *jimon* pattern
帯 *chitai* zone, belt, region, area

紙 *jigami* fan paper
紙形 *jigamigata* fan shape
11 道 *chidō* tunnel; slow but sure method. *jimichi* leisurely walk. *jimichi na* fair, honest
階 *chikai* basement
殻 *chikaku* the earth's crust
異 *chii* physiographical changes
袋 *jibukuro* cupboard near the floor
動 *chidō* earth tremors; earth's rotation
動説 *chidōsetsu* heliocentric or Copernican theory
域 *chiiki* region area zone
域的 *chiikiteki* local, regional
域差 *chiikisa* regional differences
理 *chiri* geography, topography
理学 *chirigaku* geography
理学者 *chirigakusha* geographer
理書 *chirisho* geography book
球 *chikyū* earth, globe
球人 *chikyūjin* earthdwellers
球物理学 *chikyū butsurigaku* geophysics
球照 *chikyūshō* earthshine
球儀 *chikyūgi* terrestial globe
12 温 *chion* underground temperature
税 *chizei* land tax
軸 *chijiku* earth's axis
割 *jiwa(re)* earth fissure or crack. *jiwa(ri)* land allotment
13 続 *jitsuzu(ki)* land contiguity
腫 *jibare* swelling around a wound
蜂 *jibachi* digger wasp
隙 *chigeki* chasm, cleft, fissure
勢 *chisei* topography
塗 *jinu(ri)* first coat. *chi ni mami(reru)* be defeated; fail (in business)
雷 *jirai* land mine
雷火 *jiraika* land mine
雷弾 *jiraidan* high-explosive shell
14 歴 *chireki* geography and history
鳴 *jina(ri), chimei* earth tremor
境 *jizakai* landmark, boundary
誌 *chishi* topography
磁気 *chijiki* terrestial magnetism
模様 *jimoyō* background pattern (woven into cloth)
層 *chisō* stratum, layer
層学 *chisōgaku* stratigraphy
獄 *jigoku* hell
獄耳 *jigoku mimi* sharp ears
獄行 *jigokuyu(ki)* going to hell
蔵 *Jizō* a Buddhist guardian deity of children
蔵眉 *jizō mayu* arched eyebrows
蔵菩薩 *Jizō Bosatsu* a Buddhist guardian deity of children
蔵顔 *jizōgao* round cheerful face
15 線 *chisen* ground wire
熱 *chinetsu, jinetsu* subterranean heat
盤 *jiban* base, foundation, the ground; footing, foothold; sphere of influence; constituency
質 *chishitsu* geology, geological features; nature of the soil. *jishitsu* texture
質物理学 *chishitsu butsurigaku* geophysics
質分析 *chishitsu bunseki* soil analysis
質図 *chishitsuzu* geological map
質学 *chishitsugaku* geology
震 *jishin* earthquake
震図 *jishinzu* seismogram
震国 *jishinkoku* an earthquake-ridden country
震学 *jishingaku* seismology
震計 *jishinkei* seismograph
震帯 *jishintai* earthquake belt
震観測 *jishinkansoku* seismometry
16 積 *chiseki* acreage
錦 *tsuta* ivy
18 類 *chirui* land category
鎮祭 *jichinsai* ground-breaking ceremony
19 霧 *chimu* ground fog
響 *jihibi(ki)* earth tremor
瀝青 *jirekisei, chirekisei* asphalt
20 籍 *chiseki* land register

4

壯 977 / J5463 / M5643 See 壮 974. [士]

坐 978 / J3a41 / M4931 See 座 1619.

坙 979 / J-X / M4963 Nonstandard for 堅 1038.

圻 980 / J542d / M4903 Kɪ. Gɪɴ *sakai* border; limit; boundary.

坎 981 / J542c / M4928 KAN. KON. hide; bury; dangerous. *ana* hole; pitfall.

址 982 / J542e / M4908 SHI ruins.

B **壱** 983 / J306d / M5647 ICHI, ITSU one. [士]

坏 984 / J542f / M1930 HAI. *tsuki* bowl.

A **坂** 985 / J3a64 / M4910 HAN. *saka* incline, slope, hill.

3 下 *sakamoto, sakashita* bottom of the hill

11 道 *sakamichi* hill road

13 路 *hanro* hill road

B **坊** 986 / J4b37 / M4924 BŌ priest's residence; (Buddhist) priest; boy. *bō(ya)* boy. *bo(tchan)* your, his, or her boy. *tsukasa* office, government office; director, head official.

4 中 *bōchū* inside a temple; in the streets

5 本 *bōhon* books published unofficially

主 *bōzu* Buddhist priest, monk; shaven head; boy; rascal

主山 *bōzuyama* bare mountain

主刈 *bōzuga(ri)* closely cropped hair

主臭 *bōzukusa(i)* smacking of Buddhism

主読 *bōzuyo(mi)* singsong reading

主頭 *bōzu atama* tonsure, shaven head

6 守 *bōmori* sexton; low-rank priest; priest's wife

8 門 *bōmon* town gate, street

舎 *bōsha* priests' quarters

12 間 *bōkan* all over town

14 様 *bōsan, bōsama* priest

B **坑** 987 / J3923 / M4932 KŌ pit, hole.

3 口 *kōkō* mine entrance

4 区 *kōku* mine area

木 *kōboku* mine pillars

水 *kōsui* mine-pit water

夫 *kōfu* miner

内 *kōnai* mine pit, shaft

内夫 *kōnaifu* underground miner

5 外 *kōgai* surface, out of the pit

外夫 *kōgaifu* surface (mine) worker

8 底 *kōtei* mine-pit bottom

11 道 *kōdō* (mine) level; tunnel

A **均** 988 / J3651 / M4916 KIN. *nara(su)* to level, to average. *hito(shii)* equal, similar, alike, equivalent.

1 一 *kin'itsu* uniformity, equality

一説 *kin'ichisetsu, kin'itsusetsu* uniformitarianism

4 分 *kimbun* equal division

5 圧 *kin'atsu* equal pressure

8 斉 *kinsei* symmetry, balance

並 *hitona(mi)* same, ordinary

12 等 *kintō* equality, uniformity, evenness, identity

等待遇 *kintō taigū* equal treatment

等割 *kintōwa(ri)* per-capita rate

13 勢 *kinsei* balance of power, uniformity

15 質 *kinshitsu* homogeneity

16 衡 *kinkō* equilibrium, balance

整 *kinsei* symmetry, balance

A **声** 989 / J403c / M5645 **聲** 4736 / J6661 / M29166 SHŌ. SEI *koe* voice; tone; alarm, cry; (bird) song, chirp. [士;耳]

5 立 *koe (o) ta(teru)* speak

6 合 *koea(wase)* singing or talking in unison

名 *seimei* fame, popularity

自慢 *koe jiman* pride of voice

色 *seishoku* voice and countenance; songs and women. *kowairo* tone of voice

色遣 *kowairo (o) tsuku(u)* imitate someone's speech

7 呑 *koe (o) no(mu)* keep quiet, say nothing

8 価 *seika* good reputation, fame, popularity

並 *koena(mi)* voice quality

明 *seimei* declaration, statement, proclamation

明書 *seimeisho* public statement

9 音 *kowane* tone of voice, timber of the voice. *seion* voice quality, vocal sound

柄 *koegara* voice quality

変 *koegawa(ri)* change of voice. *seihen* a break in one's voice

10 高 *kowadaka ni, koetaka(rakani), koedaka(ku), koetaka(ku)* with a loud voice

涙 *seirui* tears in the voice
息 *seisoku* news, message
帯 *seitai* vocal chords
帯模写 *seitai mosha* vocal mimicry
11 問 *seimon* news, message
掛 *koe (o) ka(keru)* call to (someone). *koegaka(ri)* influence, recommendation
望 *seibō* popularity, fame
12 援 *seien* encouragement, support, rooting, cheering
量 *seiryō* voice volume
13 誉 *seiyo* fame, honor, glory
楽 *seigaku* vocal music
楽家 *seigakuka* vocalist
14 聞 *seibun* fame, honor, glory
様 *koezama* voice quality
15 調 *seichō* tone of voice
17 優 *seiyū* radio actor

A **売** 990/J4764/M5647' **賣** 5808/J6c4e/M36825 MAI. BAI selling. *u(ru)* sell, deal in, betray, deceive, impose on, tell on, pick (a quarrel). *u(reru)* sell, be in demand, enjoy a large sale; be well known. *u(ri)* sale, selling. *u(re)* sale, demand. [士;貝]

2 人気 *u(ri) ninki* bearish sentiment, selling support
卜 *baiboku* divination, divining for money, fortunetelling
卜者 *baibokusha* diviner, fortuneteller
3 口 *u(re)kuchi, u(ri)guchi* outlet, market, demand
女 *baita, baijo* harlot, prostitute
子 *u(rek)ko* popular person. *u(ri)ko* sales clerk
下 *u(ri)-sa(geru)* sell, dispose of. *u(ri)sa(ge)* official sale by the government
上 *u(ri)-a(geru)* sell out. *uria(ge)* sales, proceeds; sale, closing sale
上元帳 *uria(ge)motochō* sales ledger
上金 *uriagekin* amount sold, sales
上高 *uria(ge)daka* amount sold, sales
上帳 *uria(ge)chō* sales book
上証 *uria(ge)shō* bill of sale
4 方 *u(ri)kata* salesmanship; seller
止 *u(ri)dome* suspension of sale
切 *u(ri)-ki(reru)* be sold out. *u(ri)-ki(ru)* sell out, clear out. *uriki(re)* sold out, a sellout
手 *urite* seller
手形 *u(ri) tegata* bill of sale
文 *baibun* hack writing
文業 *baibungyō* hack writing
込 *u(ri)-ko(mu)* sell, find a market for
込戦 *uriko(mi)sen* competitive selling to limited customers
5 立 *urita(te)* selling off, an auction
広 *u(ri)-hiro(geru), u(ri)-hiro(meru)* extend the sale of, find a market for
代 *u(ri)shiro* sales, proceeds; sale, closing sale
付 *u(ri)-tsu(keru)* palm off, force a sale
叩 *u(ri)-tata(ku)* make a bear drive, undersell
払 *u(ri)-hara(u)* sell off, close out
主 *urinushi* seller, vendor
出 *u(ri)-da(su), u(ri)-ida(su)* offer for sale; gain a reputation. *urida(shi)* sale
6 舟 *u(ri)bune* boats for sale
色 *baishoku* prostitution
行 *ureyu(ki), urei(ki)* sale, demand, a run
回 *u(ri)-mawa(ru)* go around selling
尽 *u(ri)-tsuku(su)* sell off, clear out
気 *u(ri)ki* bearish sentiment, selling support
先 *u(ri)saki, u(re)saki* market, outlet, demand, buyer
名 *baimei* self-advertisement
7 足 *u(re)ashi* selling; a sale
戻 *u(ri)modo(shi)* resale (on the stock market)
位 *baii* buying a rank
初 *u(ri)zome* placing on sale for the first time; first New Year's sale
却 *baikyaku* sale
余 *u(ri)-ama(su)* reserve some (not selling all)
声 *u(ri)goe* peddler's cry
見本 *u(ri)mihon* sample
言葉 *u(ri)kotoba* tit-for-tat; exchange of complements
8 店 *baiten* booth, stand, store
退 *u(ri)-no(ku)* realize, liquidate
価 *baika* selling price
放 *u(ri)-hana(su)* sell off, close out
物 *urimono* article for sale, offerings, for sale
官 *baikan* selling appointments
歩 *u(ri)-aru(ku)* peddle
国 *baikoku* treason

国奴 *baikokudo* traitor
9 飛 *u(ri)-toba(su)* sell off
食 *urigu(i)* live by selling one's property
約 *baiyaku* sales contract
品 *baihin* article for sale
急 *u(ri)-iso(gu)* push the sale, be anxious to sell
相場 *u(ri) sōba* bear market; selling rate (of exchange)
為替 *u(ri)gawase* selling exchange
春 *baishun* prostitution
春婦 *baishunfu* prostitute
10 高 *u(re)daka, u(ri)daka* amount of sales
値 *urine* selling price
残 *u(re)-noko(ru)* remain unsold, remain unmarried. *u(re)noko(ri)* goods left unsold; unmarried woman
流 *u(ri)-naga(su)* sell to a distant customer
家 *u(ri)ya, u(ri)ie* house for sale
留 *u(ri)da(me)* banking the sales money; sales receipts
捌 *u(ri)sabaki* sale; selling. *u(ri)-saba(ku)* sell, deal in, dispose of; sell widely
捌人 *u(ri)sabakinin* agent, dealer
笑 *baishō* prostitution
笑婦 *baishōfu* prostitute, streetwalker
11 過 *u(ri)su(gi)* overselling
惜 *u(ri)-oshi(mu)* be indisposed to sell, hoard, restrict sales
控 *u(ri)-hika(eru)* refrain from selling
掛 *u(ri)ka(ke)* credit sales
渋 *u(ri)-shibu(ru)* be indisposed to sell, hoard, restrict sales
得金 *baitokukin* proceeds of a sale
淫 *baiin* social evil, prostitution
淫婦 *baiimpu* prostitute
12 越 *u(ri)ko(shi)* selling more than you own
渡 *u(ri)-wata(su)* sell, negotiate, sign away. *uriwata(shi)* sale and delivery
減 *u(ri)-hera(su)* sell off inventories
勝 *u(ri)-ka(tsu)* sell higher than anyone else
買 *baibai, u(ri)ka(i)* trading, buying and selling; sale
焦 *u(ri)-a(seru)* push the sale, be anxious to sell
場 *uriba* counter, salesroom, shop, store
場係 *uribagakari* sales clerk
場監督 *uriba kantoku* floorwalker
13 僧 *maisu* miscreant priest
損 *u(ri)-sokona(u)* lose a sale, fail to find a market
溜 *u(ri)dame* proceeds; cash on hand
15 勲 *baikun* selling decorations, selling medals
16 薬 *baiyaku, u(ri)gusuri* patent medicine, drugs

5

坔 991 / J5432 / M-X (国字) *nuta* muddy fields.

垉 992 / J5435 / M-X Hō *kuzu(reru)* crumble, collapse.

坿 993 / J5434 / M5009 Fu attach; increase; crystal. *tsu(ku)* adhere, be attached to. *tsu(keru)* affix, attach, fasten.

坡 994 / J5433 / M4966 Ha dike; dam; slope; bank.

坩 995 / J5430 / M4975 Kan jar, pot.
12 堝 *rutsubo, kanka* crucible, melting pot

坤 996 / J3a25 / M4969 Kon divination sign; land, earth.
14 徳 *kontoku* virtues of the empress

坦 997 / J4333 / M4971 Tan level; wide.
8 坦 *tantan(taru)* level, even; peaceful
16 懐 *tankai* frankness

B **坪** 998 / J445a / M4976 Hei. Hyō. *tsubo* area about 36 square feet.
4 刈 *tsuboga(ri)* crop estimate per tsubo
6 当 *tsuboa(tari)* per *tsubo*
10 庭 *tsuboniwa* a small court garden
13 数 *tsubosū* area in *tsubo*, floor space

A **垂** 999 / J3f62 / M5012 Sui *ta(rasu)* suspend, hang down; slouch. *ta(reru), shida(reru) vt* and *vi* hang, droop, drop, lower, pull down; dangle; sag; drip, ooze, trickle; leave behind (at death); give, confer. *tare* hanging; straw curtain; lapel; pocket flap; skirts of a coat; gravy; soy sauce. *nannan to suru* be on the verge of (doing), be close to.

³下 *suika suru* be pendent, hang down. *ta(re)-sa(garu) vi* hang, dangle. *ta(re)-sa(geru) vt* hang (a curtain); droop (a tail); lower (a blind)
⁴込 *ta(rashi)-ko(mu) vt* drop into drop by drop
木 *taruki* rafter
⁵示 *suishi* instruction
⁸直 *suichoku* vertical, perpendicular
直線 *suichokusen* perpendicular line
⁹迹 *suijaku* appearances of Buddha to save people
¹⁰涎 *suizen* watering at the mouth
¹¹教 *suikyō* information, instruction
¹³楊 *suiyō* weeping willow
飾 *tarekaza(ri)* pendant
幕 *taremaku* hanging screen, curtain
準 *suijun* plummet, plumb line
¹⁴髪 *suberakashi* hair tied in back and hanging down. *taregami* long flowing hair
¹⁵穂 *ta(ri)ho* drooping ears (of grain)
線 *suisen* perpendicular line
範 *suihan suru* set an example
²²籠 *ta(re)-ko(meru)* lie over, hang over; stay indoors

6

垳 1000 / J5438 / M-X (国字) *gake* cliff.

垰 1001 / J543b / M-X (国字) *tao, tōge* mountain pass.

垓 1002 / J5436 / M5040 GAI, KAI limit, border; stairs; large number (either 100 quintillion or 100 billion).

垤 1003 / J5439 / M5061 TETSU hill, anthill. *arizuka* anthill.

垪 1004 / J543a / M5086 (国字) *ha* used in proper names.

垜 1005 / J-X / M5049 **垛** 1006 / J-X / M5048 TA, DA firing mound.

垠 1007 / J5437 / M5054 GIN. GON limit, edge; border.

垢 1008 / J3924 / M5058 KŌ. KU. *aka* dirt, grime, scale.
⁵付 *akazu(ku)* be soiled, get dirty
⁷抜 *akanu(ke)* refined, elegant, urbane
⁹染 *akaji(miru)* become grimy
¹⁹離 *kori* purification, lustration

B **垣** 1009 / J3340 / M5060 EN. *kaki* fence, hedge, wall.
³下 *kakimoto* at the bottom of the fence
⁵本 *kakimoto* at the bottom of the fence
¹⁰根 *kakine* fence, hedge
¹²越 *kakigo(shi)* over or through the fence
間見 *kaimami(ru)* peep at, glimpse

A **型** 1010 / J373f / M5030 KEI *kata* model, mold, matrix, impression; style, type, pattern, make; set form; usage.
⁵打機 *kata-u(chi)ki* stamping machine
⁸板 *kataita* die plate
⁹砂 *katasuna* sand for casting
削盤 *katakezu(ri)ban* shaper
¹⁰破 *katayabu(ri) no* unusual, queer, novel
紙 *katagami* sewing pattern
¹⁶録 *katarogu* catalog

A **城** 1011 / J3e6b / M5086′ **城** 1013 / J-X / M5120 JŌ castle. SEI. *shiro* castle, citadel.
³下 *jōka* castle town; feudal capital; the area around a castle
下町 *jōkamachi* castle town, the town around a castle
下盟 *jōka (no) mei* surrender, capitulation
⁴戸 *kido* outer castle gate
内 *jōnai* inside the castle
中 *jōchū* within the castle
⁵代 *jōdai* castle warden
外 *jōgai* outside the castle
市 *jōshi* castle town, fortified town
主 *jōshu* lord of a castle
⁶池 *jōchi* castle and moat; castle moat
守 *jōshu* lord of a castle
⁷址 *jōshi* castle ruins
兵 *jōhei* castle garrison
邑 *jōyū* castle town
⁸門 *jōmon* castle gate
府 *jōfu* town wall; town; capital; barrier
⁹柵 *jōsaku* castle, fort
¹⁰将 *jōshō* castle commander
郭 *jōkaku* castle, citadel

[11] 砦 *jōsai* fort, stronghold, citadel
[12] 塁 *jōrui* fort
[13] 楼 *jōrō* castle tower, watchtower
跡 *shiro ato* castle ruins, castle site
塞 *jōsai* fort, stronghold, castle
[16] 壁 *jōheki* castle wall, rampart 「wall
壁伝 *jōhekizuta(i) ni* along the castle

7

乖 1012 / J5431 / M5104 See 垂 999.

城 1013 / J-X / M5120 See 城 1011.

埖 1014 / J5442 / M-X （国字） *gomi* dust, dirt. used in proper names.

埆 1015 / J543d / M3111 Kaku, Gaku barren land, worn-out land, poor land

埔 1016 / J543e / M5149 Ho used in Chinese place names.

埃 1017 / J543c / M5107 Ai. *hokori* dust. *hokori(ppoi)* dusty.

埒 1018 / J543f / M5123 **埓** 1019 / J5440 / M5124 Retsu. Ratsu. Rachi pale, picket; picket fence; limits. *rachi (ga aku)* be settled, come to an end.
[5] 外 *rachigai* beyond bounds, beyond the pale
[12] 無 *rachi (mo) na(i)* absurd, foolish

B **埋** 1020 / J4b64 / M5116 Mai. *uzu(maru), u(maru)* be filled up, be buried, be imbedded in. *uzu(meru), u(meru)* bury, inter, fill up, pour in, plug up, inlay; make up for. *i(keru)* bury (in the ground); band (a fire). *uzu(moreru), u(moreru)* be buried, be covered; live in obscurity.
[4] 火 *uzu(mi)bi* banked fire
込 *u(me)-ko(mu)* bury in the ground
木 *u(me)ki* wood inlay; wooden plug; filling crack or hole with wood. *u(more)gi* lignite, bogwood, fossil wood
木細工 *u(me)ki zaiku* mosaic in wood
[5] 穴 *u(me)ana* hole for burying things; a loss to be made up
立 *u(me)-ta(teru)* reclaim, fill in, fill up. *umeta(te)* reclamation, filling in
立地 *umetatechi* reclaimed land
[6] 合 *u(me)-a(waseru)* make amends, compensate for
伏 *maifuku suru* lie concealed, lie in ambuscade
伏歯 *maifukushi* impacted tooth
[7] 没 *maibotsu suru* be buried, be entombed; remain obscure
[9] 炭 *ikezumi* banked charcoal fire
草 *u(me)kusa* padding, stuffing, filler
[10] 骨 *maikotsu* interring the bones
[11] 設 *maisetsu suru vt* lay underground
[12] 湯 *u(me)yu* bath which has been cooled down
葬 *maisō* burial, interment
替 *u(me)-ka(eru)* rebury, reinter
[13] 溝 *u(me)mizo* underground sewer
[14] 樋 *umedoi* underground drain
蔵 *maizō suru* burying or hiding underground
蔵地帯 *maizō chitai* mine field
蔵物 *maizōbutsu* buried treasure
蔵量 *maizōryō* amount of underground deposits

8

堵 1021 / J4548 / M-X See 堵 1053.

埜 1022 / J4738 / M5154 See 野 6208.

埣 1023 / J5443 / M5166 Sai. Sotsu dry land; crumbling land. *sone* rocky, barren land.

堋 1024 / J5444 / M5217 Hō bury; archery target. *uzu(meru)* bury.

堊 1025 / J5441 / M5215 A. Aku wall.

埦 1026 / J-X / M5171 Wan bowl.

埵 1027 / J-X / M5190 Ta hard soil.

埼 1028 J3a6b M5201 KI. *saki* cape, spit, promontory.

埠 1029 J4956 M5161 FU wharf.
16 頭 *futō* wharf, pier, quay

A **域** 1030 J3068 M5158 IKI region; limits; stage, level.
4 内 *ikinai* inside the area
5 外 *ikigai* outside the area

埴 1031 J3e7d M5188 SHOKU. *hani, hena* clay.
3 土 *henatsuchi, hanitsuchi* clay
5 生宿 *hanyū (no) yado* a humble house
15 輪 *haniwa* ancient clay images buried with the dead

B **培** 1032 J475d M5195 BAI. HŌ. *tsuchika(u)* cultivate, foster.
6 地 *baichi* bacteria culture medium
11 強 *tsuchika(i)-tsuyo(meru)* foster, develop and strengthen
15 養 *baiyō* cultivation, nurture, culture

B **堕** 1033 J4244 M-X **墮** 1078 J5458 M5481 DA. *da(suru)* descend to, lapse into, degenerate.
9 胎 *datai* miscarriage, abortion
12 落 *daraku* depravity, corruption, degradation, delinquency, apostasy, degeneration
落的 *darakuteki* depraved, corrupt, degenerate, apostatized
13 罪 *dazai* the fall of man

壷 1034 J445b M5657 **壺** 1043 J5464 M5662 KO. *tsubo* jar, pot; hinge knuckle; one's aim. [士]
3 口 *tsuboguchi* jar mouth
8 金 *tsubogane* hinge knuckle
11 瓶 *tsubogame* night-soil receptacle
12 焼 *tsuboyaki* shellfish cooked in the shell
28 鑿 *tsubonomi* hollow chisel

堆 1035 J424f M5211 TAI. *uzutaka(i)* piled high.
3 土 *taido* mound
5 石 *taiseki* moraine
8 肥 *taihi, tsumigoe* compost, barnyard manure
11 雪 *taisetsu* snowdrift
16 積 *taiseki* accumulation, pile, heap

B **掘** 1036 J4b59 M5205 KUTSU. *hori* moat, canal, ditch.
3 川 *horigawa* canal
4 井戸 *horiido* bored well
5 出物 *horida(shi)mono* a rare find; a bargain; a treasure trove
6 江 *horie* canal
10 留 *horido(me)* ditch end
12 割 *horiwa(ri)* canal, dock, ditch
14 端 *horibata* edge of a moat

A **堂** 1037 J4632 M5207 DŌ temple; shrine; hall; reception room; firm; state chamber. *-dō* temple, shrine; shop, store.
3 上 *dōjō* on the roof; court nobles
上人 *tōshōnin, dōjōbito* court noble
4 内 *dōnai* in the temple
6 守 *dōmori* building guard
宇 *dōu* temple, hall, building
8 房 *dōbō* the inside of a house
11 堂 *dōdō(taru)* imposing, majestic, grand, magnificent, stately; fair, square
堂巡 *dōdōmegu(ri)* roll-call vote; vicious circle; going round and round (in an argument); circling a shrine or temple in worship
堂回 *dōdōmegu(ri)* roll-call vote; vicious circle; going round and round (in an argument); circling a shrine or temple in worship
12 塔 *dōtō* temple buildings; temple
奥 *dōō* interior of a hall or temple; secret knowledge

B **堅** 1038 J3778 M5210 KEN. *kata(i)* hard, solid; tough, rigid; tight; steady, firm; strict; safe, reliable, upright; chaste, constant; stiff; bookish; classical; stubborn. *tate no* longitudinal; lengthwise; vertical, perpendicular.
2 人 *katajin* steady person, honest man
4 木 *katagi* hardwood, oak
太 *katabuto(ri)* solidly built (person)
5 田 *katada* hard dry rice field
穴 *tateana* pit; mine shaft; mine pit; ancient dwelling site
甲利兵 *kenkō-rihei* strong armor and sharp weapons

6 気 *katagi na* honest, upright, steady
守 *kenshu* strong defense; strict observation (of rules)
缶 *tategama* vertical cylindrical boiler
7 志 *kenshi* iron purpose
牢 *kenrō* solidity, stability, durability
忍 *kennin* perseverance, fortitude
忍不抜 *kennin fubatsu* perseverance, fortitude
忍持久 *kennin jikyū* untiring perseverance
8 固 *kengo na* strong, solid, secure, firm
肥 *katabuto(ri)* solidly built (person)
実 *kenjitsu na* steady, sound, reliable
岩 *kengan* solid rock
苦 *katakuru(shii)* formal; punctilious; awkward
果 *kenka* nut
果油 *kenkayu* nut oil
9 城 *kenjō* strong fortress
持 *kenji suru* hold on to, stick to
陣 *kenjin* stronghold
炭 *katazumi* hard charcoal
信礼 *kenshinrei* (Christian) confirmation
10 框 *tategamachi* vertical door frame
11 魚 *katsuo* bonito
12 桟 *tatesan* vertical framework
塁 *kenrui* stronghold
13 塩 *katashio* rock salt
塞 *kensai* strong fort
14 樋 *tatedoi* vertical drainpipe
15 蔵 *katazō* honest man, steady person
20 艦 *kenkun* powerful battleship

B **執** 1039 / J3c39 / M5193 SHITSU. SHŪ. *to(ru)* take, hold, seize, catch, capture; fetch; receive, procure, obtain; adopt (a measure); engage (graduates); choose; order (foodstuffs); pick, pluck; make, produce; eat; set up (camp); charge; administer; transact; take (pains); make out (the meaning); remove; take off (one's hat); take out (spots); strike out (words); weed, catch (fish); deprive of; steal; capture (territory), annex; need, require; reserve (rooms); subscribe to; press (a point home); take (a picture); possess. *shi(ssuru)* take, hold, grasp; take to heart; form an attachment; persist in.
2 刀 *shittō* operating (in a hospital)
刀者 *shittōsha* operating surgeon
4 心 *shūshin* devotion, attachment, infatuation
6 成 *to(ri)-na(su)* mediate, intervene, intercede for, recommend. *to(ri)-na(shi)* arrangement; influence; mediation, intercession; good offices
成人 *to(ri)na(shi)bito* intercessor, mediator
成手 *to(ri)na(shi)te* intercessor, mediator
行 *to(ri)-okona(u)* do, act, conduct oneself; carry out; perform, conduct (school); exercise (control); hold (a ceremony). *shikkō* performance
行吏 *shikkōri* bailiff, process server
行委員 *shikkō iin* executive committee; executive officer
行委員会 *shikkō iinkai* executive committee
行停止 *shikkō teishi* stay of execution; stopping operations
行猶予 *shikkō yūyo* stay of execution, suspended sentence
行権 *shikkōken* executive authority
行機関 *shikkō kikan* executive organ
8 拗 *shitsuyō* obstinacy, persistence
念 *shūnen* tenacity; implacability
念深 *shūnembuka(i)* unforgiving, revengeful, vindictive; tenacious
事 *shitsuji* steward, deacon
事職 *shitsujishoku* office of deacon
9 政 *shissei* government, ruler, minister of state
奏 *shissō suru* transmit to the emperor
11 著 *shūchaku* attachment, adhesion, tenacity
達 *shittatsu* relaying a superior's words
達吏 *shittatsuri* bailiff, process server
務 *shitsumu* discharging one's office duties
務心得 *shitsumu kokoroe* office rules
務時間 *shitsumu jikan* office hours
12 着 *shūchaku, shūjaku* attachment, adhesion, tenacity
着心 *shūchakushin* persistence
筆 *shippitsu* writing
筆中 *shippitsuchū* now being written
筆者 *shippitsusha* writer, author
筆料 *shippitsuryō* writing fee
13 意 *shitsui* obstinacy, persistence in opinions
15 権 *shikken* regent

権職 *shikkenshoku* regency

A **基** 1040 J3470 M5197 Kɪ radical (in chemistry); counter for lanterns, wreaths, motors, silos, and heavy machines; foundation; fundamentals; basis. *motoi, moto* basis, foundation, origin. *motozu(ku)* be based on, be founded on.

5 石 *kiseki* cornerstone, foundation stone
本 *kihon* basis, standard
本代謝 *kihon taisha* basic metabolism
本金 *kihonkin* foundation, endowment fund
本的 *kihonteki* basic, fundamental, standard
本的人権 *kihonteki jinken* basic human rights
本協定 *kihon kyōtei* basic agreement, a formula
本英語 *Kihon Eigo* Basic English
本科目 *kihon kamoku* basic subjects
本単位 *kihon tan'i* official standards for weights and measures
本原理 *kihon genri* basic principles
本財産 *kihon zaisan* endowment, permanent property
本産業 *kihon sangyō* basic industries
本給 *kihonkyū* basic salary or wages
本賃金 *kihon chingin* basic wage
6 色 *kishoku* ground color
因 *kiin* cause
地 *kichi* base
7 形 *kikei* basic type
8 金 *kikin* fund, endowment, foundation
底 *kitei* base, basis, foundation
肥 *kihi, motogoe* initial fertilizing
岩 *kigan* bedrock
性岩 *kiseigan* basic rocks
9 音 *kion* fundamental tone
点 *kiten* cardinal point
型 *kikei* basic type
10 部 *kibu* base, pedestal, foundation
11 脚 *kikyaku* base
13 数 *kisū* cardinal number
幹 *kikan* mainstay, nucleus
準 *kijun* standard, basis, norm, criterion
準化 *kijunka* normalization standardization
督 *Kirisuto* Christ, Messiah
督者 *Kirisutosha* a Christian
督教 *Kirisutokyō* Christianity
督教化 *Kirisutokyōka suru* Christianize, evangelize
督教国 *Kirisutokyōkoku* a Christian country
15 線 *kisen* base line; base of a triangle
盤 *kiban* base, foundation, basis
調 *kichō* keynote, basis
調演説 *kichō enzetsu* keynote speech
18 礎 *kiso* foundation
礎工事 *kiso kōji* foundation work
礎代謝 *kiso taisha* basic metabolism
礎杭 *kisogui* foundation piling
礎的 *kisoteki* fundamental, basic
礎音 *kisoon* fundamental tone
礎科学 *kiso kagaku* basic science
礎原価 *kiso genka* first cost
礎控除 *kiso kōjo* basic exemption
礎産業 *kiso sangyō* basic industry

9

堯 1041 J7421 M5272 See 尭 614.

堽 1042 J544e M5298 See 岡 1460.

壺 1043 J5464 M5662 See 壷 1034. [士]

壹 1044 J5465 M5661 See 壱 983. [士]

堺 1045 J3a66 M5289 See 界 3739.

壻 1046 J5466 M5664 See 婿 1246. [士]

堝 1047 J5446 M5247 Kᴀ crucible, melting pot.

B **塚** 1048 J444d M-X **冢** 403 J514f M1585 **塚** 1060 J-X M5345
Chō *tsuka* mound, hillock, tumulus.
5 穴 *tsukaana* grave

堙 1049 J5445 M5239 Iɴ close up, stop up.
13 滅 *immetsu* extinction, destruction, suppression

堡 1050 / J5448 / M5254 Hō, Ho fort.
12 塁 *hōrui, horui* fort, stronghold

B **塀** 1051 / J4a3d / M5316 **塀** 1079 / J-X / M-X (国字) Hei wall, fence.
12 越 *heigo(shi) ni* over the fence
13 際 *heigiwa de* by the fence

B **塔** 1052 / J4563 / M5332 Tō tower, pagoda, steeple, obelisk, monument.
9 型 *tōgata* tower or steeple type
11 婆 *tōba* wooden grave tablet; stupa; pagoda

堵 1053 / J-X / M5279 To fence, railing, enclosure; dwelling.
6 列 *toretsu* line (of men)
列兵 *toretsuhei* soldiers drawn up

B **堤** 1054 / J4469 / M5259 Tei *tsutsumi* dike, bank, embankment.
3 上 *teijō* on the bank
6 防 *teibō* bank, dike, levee
防伝 *teibōzuta(i)* along the dike

堰 1055 / J3161 / M5274 En. *se(ku)* dam up; check, stop, prevent. *seki* dam, embankment.
4 止 *se(ki)-to(meru)* intercept, check; dam up
止湖 *sekito(me)ko* dammed-up lake
12 堤 *entei* dike, weir

B **塁** 1056 / J4e5d / M5316′ **壘** 1109 / J545e / M5574 Rui fort, rampart, walls; base (in baseball).
4 手 *ruishu* baseman
5 打 *ruida* a base hit, a single
打数 *ruidasū* number of extra-base hits
15 摩 *rui (o) ma(su)* attack a fort; catch up with (someone)
審 *ruishin* umpire on bases
16 壁 *ruiheki* rampart, walls

B **堪** 1057 / J342e / M5266 Kan. *ta(eru)* endure; support; withstand, resist, brave, weather; be fit for, be equal to. *ko(raeru)* endure; tolerate; control, stifle; pardon. *kota(eru)* endure. *tama(ranai)* be unbearable; be "dying" to (do something).
4 切 *ta(e)-ki(reru), kora(e)-ki(reru)* endure to the end, bear up. *kora(e)-ki(renai), ta(e)-ki(renai)* be unable to stand it any longer
7 忍 *kannin* pardon; patience, patient endurance. *ta(e)-shino(bu)* endure, bear patiently
忍袋 *kannimbukuro* patience
8 性 *kora(e)shō* patience
10 兼 *tama(ri)-ka(neru), ta(e)-ka(neru), kora(e)-ka(neru)* be unable to endure, lose one's patience; give way
能 *tannō, kannō* skill, mastery; sufficiency
航能力 *tankō nōryoku* navigability
18 難 *ta(e)gata(i), kora(e)gata(i)* unbearable, intolerable

A **場** 1058 / J3e6c / M5278 **塲** 1076 / J5447 / M5385 Jō place, grounds, links, range, course, track, ring. *ba* place, site; space; seat; scene; occasion, situation.
4 内 *jōnai* within the grounds or hall
5 代 *badai* admission fee
末 *basue* outskirts, suburbs
外 *jōgai* outside the premises; outside the market, on the curb; over the fence
外本塁打 *jōgai honruida* home run over the fence
外取引所 *jōgai torihikisho* curb market
6 合 *baai* occasion, circumstances, case
当 *baa(tari)* applause-seeking, sensational (speech)
8 所 *basho* place, area, locality, quarter; position, location; seat, site; scene; room, space; experiences; sumo tournament
所柄 *bashogara* character of a place, location, situation; occasion
所塞 *bashofusa(gi)* an obstacle
所踏 *basho (o) fu(mu)* gain experience
9 面 *bamen* place, scene, spectacle
後 *baoku(re)* stage fright; nervousness
10 席 *baseki* room, space; seat, place
12 裡 *-jōri* arena (of a competition)
違 *bachiga(i)* wrong place, different place
13 馴 *banare* experience
数 *bakazu* experience; many places
塞 *bafusa(gi)* stopgap, space filler; useless thing
14 磁石 *bajishaku* field magnet

9

A **報** 1059 / J4a73 / M5275 HŌ news, report; reward, retribution. *hō(jiru), hō(zuru)* repay, requite; report, inform, disseminate. *muku(iru)* reward, compensate; repay; revenge. *muku(i)* reward; retribution. *shirase* information, report, news; omen.

5 本反始 *hōhonhanshi* repaying our debt of gratitude to our ancestors
6 返 *muku(i)-kae(su)* requite
7 告 *hōkoku* report, information, returns, statement
告者 *hōkokusha* reporter, informer
告書 *hōkokusho* written statement, written report
告簿 *hōkokubo* report book
8 国 *hōkoku* patriotism, national service
知 *hōchi* news, report, intelligence, information
知機 *hōchiki* alarm, communicator
10 恩 *hōon* repaying kindness, gratitude
11 捨 *hōsha* recompense, requital of a favor
道 *hōdō* news, report, intelligence, information
道陣 *hōdōjin* a camp of reporters waiting for news; the news front
12 復 *hōfuku* retaliation, revenge
答 *hōtō* answer, reply
13 酬 *hōshū* remuneration, reward, honorarium, fee, pay, salary
酬目当 *hōshū mea(te)* desire for gain
奨 *hōshō* compensation
奨金 *hōshōkin* cash bonus, reward, bounty
奨物資 *hōshō busshi* grant to encourage production
14 徳 *hōtoku* requital of kindness
15 賞 *hōshō* prize, reward
17 謝 *hōsha* recompense, requital of a favor
償 *hōshō* reward, compensation, remuneration
償物資 *hōshō busshi* grant to encourage production

10

塚 1060 / J-X / M5345 See 塚 1048.

塢 1061 / J5449 / M5357 O. U. embankment; fort; redoubt; village.

塰 1062 / J544b / M-X （国字） *ama* fisherman, shellfish diver.

塙 1063 / J4839 / M5341 KAKU. KŌ. *hanawa* projecting tableland, projecting mountain.

塒 1064 / J544d / M5329 SHI. JI. *negura* roost. *toya* hen coop; roost; actor's rest room. *toguro* coil, spiral.

壼 1065 / J5467 / M5667 KON road within the palace grounds; apartment of court lady. [士]

12 奥 *kon'ō* room deep in palace; secret teachings

塘 1066 / J4564 / M5340 TŌ dike, embankment.

塋 1067 / J544a / M5320 EI cemetery.

11 域 *eiiki* cemetery

B **塑** 1068 / J413a / M5328 SO modeling, molding.

9 造 *sozō* modeling, molding
造芸術 *sozō geijutsu* plastic arts
14 像 *sozō* plaster image, clay figure, plastic image

塞 1069 / J3a49 / M5349 SOKU. SAI. *fusa(gu), fusa(geru) vt* close, shut, cover, block, wall up obstruct, fill; occupy. *fusa(garu)* be closed, be blocked, be obstructed, be clogged, be shut; be occupied. *se(ku)* dam up; check, stop, prevent.

2 入 *se(ki)-i(reru)* stop, check
7 余 *se(ki)-ama(ru)* be unable to hold back
10 栓 *sokusen* an embolism

B **塊** 1070 / J3274 / M5319 KAI lump, chunk, clod, mass, clot, ingot. *katamari* lump, chunk, clod, mass; clump, cluster, group; flock; bigotry; personification (of). *-kure* lump, clod.

3 土 *kaido* lump of earth
7 状 *kaijō no* massive
8 茎 *kaikei* tuber
9 炭 *kaitan* lump coal

10 根 *kaikon* tuberous root
13 鉱 *kaikō* lump ore
16 鋼 *kaikō* steel ingot

塡 1071 J-X M5355 **填** 1072 J4536 M-X TEN. *ha(maru)* go into, fit into; fall into, plunge into; be deceived. *ha(meru)* put on, pull on; inlay, set in; fit in; fill in; throw into; ensnare, cheat.

4 込 *ha(me)-ko(mu)* go into, fit into; fall into, plunge into; be deceived. *hama(ri) ko(mu)* telescope, fall into, get into (trouble), be infatuated with; be addicted to
6 充 *tenjū suru* fill up, plug, stuff, tamp, calk
7 材 *tenzai* filler, filling matter
12 湯 *umeyu* bath which has been cooled down
補 *tempo suru* fill up; compensate for, make good; replenish, complete
隙 *tengeki* calking, filling
13 塞 *tensoku suru* fill up, stop up

A **墓** 1073 J4a68 M5431 BO. *haka* grave, tomb.

5 石 *boseki, hakaishi* tombstone
穴 *boketsu* grave hole
6 地 *bochi* cemetery
守 *hakamori* grave keeper
8 所 *bosho, hakadokoro, hakasho* cemetery
参 *bosan, hakamai(ri)* visit to a grave
表 *bohyō* grave marker, epitaph
9 前 *bozen* before the grave
10 原 *hakawara* cemetery
畔 *bohan de* at the grave
11 掘 *hakaho(ri)* grave-digging; gravedigger
12 場 *hakaba* cemetery
14 銘 *bomei* epitaph
碑 *bohi* tombstone
碑銘 *bohimei* epitaph
誌 *boshi* epitaph
誌銘 *boshimei* epitaph
15 標 *bohyō* grave marker, tombstone
20 籍 *boseki* cemetery register

B **塗** 1074 J4549 M5338 TO. *nu(ru)* paint; plaster; daub, lacquer. *mabu(su)* smear, sprinkle or cover with. *mabu(reru), mami(reru)* be covered or smeared with. *nu(ri)* coating, lacquering, varnishing, painting; lacquered.

3 工 *tokō* painter, plasterer
上 *nu(ri)-a(geru)* finish painting or lacquering
4 方 *nu(ri)kata* way to paint
5 立 *nu(ri)-ta(teru)* put on thick makeup. *nu(ri)ta(te) no* newly painted or plastered
付 *nu(ri)-tsu(keru)* daub, smear
布 *tofu suru* apply (ointment)
6 机 *nu(ri)zukue* lacquered table
8 板 *nu(ri)ita* blackboard
油 *toyu* unction, act of anointing
物 *nurimono* lacquerware
抹 *tomatsu suru* paint over, smear, paint out
抹剤 *tomatsuzai* liniment, ointment
9 屋 *nu(ri)ya* lacquerer
柄 *nu(ri)e* lacquered handle
盆 *nu(ri)bon* lacquered tray
炭 *totan* misery, distress
炭苦 *totan (no) kuru(shimi)* very sad situation
10 師 *nu(ri)shi* lacquerer
消 *nu(ri)-ke(su)* paint out
料 *toryō* paints
12 椀 *nu(ri)wan* lacquered bowl
絵 *nu(ri)e* picture-card for coloring
散 *nu(ri)-chi(rasu)* besmear, daub all over
替 *nu(ri)-ka(eru)* repaint
装 *tosō* painting, coating
装店 *tosōten* painter's shop
装屋 *tosōya* painter
13 隠 *nu(ri)-kaku(su)* cover up
15 潰 *nu(ri)-tsubu(su)* paint out
箸 *nu(ri)bashi* lacquered chopsticks
16 薬 *nu(ri)gusuri* liniment, ointment
壁 *nu(ri)kabe* plastered wall
17 擦 *tosatsu* rubbing and smearing
擦剤 *tosatsuzai* liniment
22 籠 *nu(ri)-ko(meru)* hide and plaster over

A **塩** 1075 J3176 M5382 **壏** 7012 J-X M47550 **鹽** 7015 J7345 M47579 EN salt. *shio* salt; seasoning.

2 入 *shioi(re)* salt shaker
4 引 *shiobi(ki)* salt-cured; salted fish
分 *embun* salt, salinity
水 *ensui, shiomizu* brine, salt water
水風呂 *shiomizuburo* salt-water bath

5 田 *enden* salt field, salt farm
圧 *shioo(shi)* pickling salted vegetables under a weight
汁 *shiojiru* salt water, brine
出 *shioda(shi) suru* steep out the salt
加減 *shiokagen* seasoning
6 米 *embei* salt and rice; the necessities of life
気 *shioke* saltiness
地 *shiochi, shioji* salty wasteland
7 豆 *shiomame* salted beans
辛 *shiokara* salted fish; salted fish entrails. *shiokara(i)* salty, brackish
辛声 *shiokaragoe* hoarse voice
8 味 *shioaji* seasoning
性 *ensei* salinity, saltiness
物 *shiomono* salted fish
9 海 *Shio (no) Umi* the Salt Sea, the Dead Sea
泉 *ensen* salt spring
10 梅 *ambai* seasoning; condition; manner; state of health
浜 *shiohama* salt farm
釜 *shiogama* salt pan
害 *engai* salt-air damage
素 *enso* chlorine
素酸 *ensosan* chloric acid
11 魚 *shiozakana* salted fish
豚 *shiobuta* salt pork
断 *shioda(chi)* salt-free diet
基 *enki* base (in chemistry)
乾 *shioboshi, enkan* salted and dried
12 揉 *shiomomi* squeezing vegetables limp in salt
湯 *shioyu* hot salt water; hot salt-water bath
焼 *shioyaki* fish broiled with salt; boiling off sea water to make salt
税 *enzei* salt tax
蒸 *shiomu(shi)* salting and steaming
煮 *shioni* boiled salted fish
13 煙 *shiokemuri* smoke from the salt furnaces
鉱 *enkō* salt mine
塩梅 *shioambai* seasoning
14 漬 *shiozuke* pickling in salt
酸 *ensan* hydrochloric acid
蔵 *enzō suru* preserve in salt
17 餡 *shioan* salty bean jam
鮭 *shiozake, shiojake* salted salmon
18 類 *enrui* salts

11

塲 1076 J5447 M5385 See **場** 1058.

壽 1077 J5468 M5672 See **寿** 1374. [士]

墮 1078 J5458 M5481 See **堕** 1033.

塀 1079 J-X M-X See **塀** 1051.

墟 1080 J-X M-X **墟** 1090 J5452 M5457 Kyo, Ko ruins.

墅 1081 J5450 M5412 Sho barn, granery. *shimoyashiki* villa.

B **墜** 1082 J4446 M5451 Tsui fall.
3 下 *tsuika* fall
6 死 *tsuishi suru* fall to one's death
12 落 *tsuiraku suru* fall, crash

B **塾** 1083 J3d4e M5402 Juku private school; boarding school; gate house.
5 生 *jukusei* private-school student
8 長 *jukuchō* private-school principal
16 頭 *jukutō* private-school principal; private-school student leader

塹 1084 J544f M5394 Zan moat, ditch.
17 壕 *zangō* trench, dugout
壕工事 *zangō kōji* trench building
壕生活 *zangō seikatsu* trench warfare
壕戦 *zangōsen* trench warfare
壕熱 *zangō netsu* trench fever

A **境** 1085 J362d M5409 Kyō, Kei boundary; region; condition; stage. *sakai* boundary, border, frontier; place.
3 土 *kyōdo* compound, grounds, precincts
4 内 *keidai* compound, grounds, precincts
5 目 *sakaime* border, boundary line; crisis
9 界 *kyōkai* boundary, limits, frontier; environment determined by karma; environment; rank. *keikai* border
界標 *kyōkaihyō* landmark, boundary stone

界線 *kyōkaisen* boundary line
11 遇 *kyōgū* environment, circumstances
域 *kyōiki* boundary; precincts
涯 *kyōgai* environment, circumstances, one's lot, in life

B **墨** 1086 J4b4f M-X **墨** 1091 J-X M5469 BOKU. *sumi* India ink, Chinese ink; ink stick; inked marking string; ink (of a squid).
5 付 *sumitsu(ke)* blackening the face. *sumitsu(ki)* handwriting, autograph; black (not red) seal
汁 *bokujū* India ink
6 糸 *sumiito* inked marking string
色 *sumi iro* India-ink color
池 *bokuchi* inkstone well, inkhorn
刑 *bokukei* punishment by tattooing
守 *bokushu* strict adherence
8 画 *bokuga* India-ink drawing
9 客 *bokkaku, bokkyaku* artist; writer
染 *sumizo(me)* dying black; dyed black; dark
染衣 *sumizo(me)goromo, sumizo(me) no koromo* black robe of a priest
10 消 *sumike(shi)* blotting out characters with ink
書 *sumiga(ki)* inking the outlines of a picture. *bokusho* writing in India ink
11 魚 *ika* squid, cuttlefish
痕 *bokkon* ink marks; handwriting
描 *sumiga(ki)* inking the outlines of a picture
壷 *sumitsubo* ink bottle; carpenter's inking device
12 堤 *bokutei* banks of the Sumida river
絵 *sumie* India-ink drawing, black-and-white drawing
15 縄 *suminawa* inked marking string

塵 1087 J3f50 M5388 CHIN. JIN dust. *chiri, gomi* dust, trash, rubbish. *chiri(bamu)* be covered with dust.
4 心 *jinshin* one contaminated with worldly interests
中 *jinchū ni* in the dust, in the world
5 外 *jingai ni* aloof from the world
払 *chirihara(i), chirihata(ki)* duster
世 *chiri (no) yo, jinsei* this contaminating world
6 灰 *jinkai* dust and ashes
7 劫 *jingō* forever
芥 *chiriakuta, jinkai* rubbish, garbage
8 取 *chirito(ri)* dustpan
事 *jinji* earthly things
9 垢 *jinkō, chiriaka* rubbish, dust, worldly affairs
除 *chiriyo(ke)* dust cloth; dust coat, duster
界 *jinkai* this mundane life
点劫 *jindengō* forever
10 埃 *jin'ai, chirihokori* dust, dirt; this drab world
紙 *chirigami* coarse toilet paper
12 葉 *chiri(p)pa* dust; a tiny bit
塚 *chirizuka* dust heap, dump
13 溜 *chirida(me)* dust box, garbage can, ash can
煙 *chiri kemuri, jin'en* cloud of dust
14 境 *jinkyō* this mundane life
15 箱 *gomibako* garbage box
19 霧 *jimmu* dust haze

A **増** 1088 J417d M5448′ **增** 1089 J-X M5454 ZŌ increase. *masa(ru), ma(su) vt* increase, add to, augment, gain; promote (health); enlarge, extend; *vi* increase. *fu(yasu) vt* increase. *fu(eru) vi* increase. *ma(shi)* increase, extra; every (day). *ma(shi) na* better.
3 上慢 *zōjōman* bragging about one's strength
大 *zōdai suru* increase, enlarge, enhance
大号 *zōdaigō* enlarged issue (of a magazine)
4 水 *ma(shi)mizu* increase in the volume of water. *zōsui suru* rise, swell, flood
5 加 *zōka suru, ma(shi)-kuwa(waru) vi* increase, add, multiply. *ma(shi)-kuwa(eru) vt* increase, add, multiply. *zōka* increase, addition
収 *zōshū* increased yield, increased income
刊 *zōkan* special number
刊号 *zōkangō* special number (of a magazine)
6 血 *zōketsu suru* make blood
7 兵 *zōhei* reinforcements
8 長 *zōchō suru* grow presumptuous, get puffed up
刷 *zōsatsu* additional printing
注 *zōchū* additional notes
版 *zōhan* enlarged edition

9 派 *zōha* reinforcements
音 *zōon* sound amplification
音器 *zōonki* sound amplifier
発 *zōhatsu suru* increase (a bond) issue; put on an extra train
発列車 *zōhatsu ressha* extra train
10 進 *zōshin suru* promote, increase, advance
俸 *zōhō* salary increase
配 *zōhai* increased ration; bonus; increased dividends
員 *zōin* personnel increase
11 強 *zōkyō suru* augment, reinforce, increase
設 *zōsetsu* building enlargement, additional installations
産 *zōsan* production increase
12 殖 *zōshoku suru* increase, multiply, propagate
減 *zōgen* increase and decrease, rise and fall
税 *zōzei* tax increase
結 *zōketsu* adding extra (coaches)
給 *zōkyū* wage increase
補 *zōho* enlargement, supplement
量 *zōryō* quantity increase
援 *zōen* reinforcement
援部隊 *zōen butai* reinforcements
幅 *zōfuku* amplification (in electricity)
幅装置 *zōfuku sōchi* amplifier
幅器 *zōfukuki* amplifier
13 置 *zōchi suru* establish more (offices)
資 *zōshi* capital increase
14 徴 *zōchō* imposition of extra taxes
16 築 *zōchiku suru* extend (a building)
18 額 *zōgaku* increased amount

12

增 1089 J-X M5454 See **増** 1088.

墟 1090 J5452 M5457 See **墟** 1080.

墨 1091 J-X M5469 See **墨** 1086.

墹 1092 J5451 M-X （国字） *mama* steep slope; cliff. *ma* used in proper names.

堵 1093 J5457 M-X CHO.

墫 1094 J5453 M5472 SHUN dancing. Also variant of 樽 2874.

B **墳** 1095 J4a2f M5488 FUN mound; tomb.
13 墓 *fumbo* grave, tomb
墓地 *fumbo (no) chi* native country

13

壅 1096 J5459 M5524 YŌ. *fusa(gu) vt* plug up, shut up. *fusa(garu) vi* be plugged up, be shut up.

B **墾** 1097 J3a26 M5509 KON *ha(ru)* open up farmland.
5 田 *konden, harita* new rice fields

B **壌** 1098 J3e6d M-X **壤** 1116 J5461 M5608 JŌ earth, soil.
3 土 *jōdo* soil

墻 1099 J5456 M5505 **牆** 3524 J602f M19806 SHŌ. *kaki* fence, hedge, wall.
16 壁 *shōheki* fence and wall; fence; wall

墺 1100 J5454 M5504 Ō land, shore; Austria.
4 太利 *Ōsutoria* Austria
6 匈国 *Ōkyōkoku* Austria-Hungary
8 国 *Ōkoku* Austria

B **壇** 1101 J4345 M5528 DAN stage, rostrum, dais; terrace; altar; world (of literature, etc.).
3 上 *danjō* on the platform; on the stage; on the altar
10 家 *danka* families which are temple supporters
12 場 *danjō* stage

B **壊** 1102 J3275 M5541' **壞** 1111 J5455 M5590 E. KAI break. *kowa(su)* break; destroy; tear up; crack; smack; mar. *kowa(reru)* be broken; be demolished; fall into ruin.
6 血病 *kaiketsubyō* scurvy
7 乱 *kairan* corruption, demoralization, subversion, disturbance, destruction

[9] 変 *kaihen* disintegration (of elements)
[10] 疽 *eso* gangrene
残 *kaizan* being broken up and ruined
[12] 廃 *kaihai* ruin, decay
[13] 滅 *kaimetsu* destruction, annihilation

B **壁** 1103 / J4a49 / M5516 HEKI wall; lining (of the stomach); fence; partition. *kabe* wall.
[1] 重 *kabehitoe* neighbor with just a wall between
[3] 土 *kabetsuchi* wall mud, plaster, stucco
[5] 立 *hekiritsu* precipitous; nothing but four empty walls
[7] 床 *kabedoko* ornamental alcove
[8] 板 *kabeita* wainscoting
画 *hekiga* fresco, wall painting; picture hanging on a wall
[10] 紙 *kabegami* wallpaper
書 *kabega(ki), hekisho* ancient laws posted on walls
[11] 掛 *kabeka(ke)* tapestry
寄 *kabeyo(ri) ni* by the wall
[12] 間 *hekikan* between the walls; on the wall
越 *kabego(shi) ni* with a wall between
訴訟 *kabesoshō* grumbling to oneself
[13] 際 *kabegiwa ni* near the wall
塗 *kabenu(ri)* plastering
新聞 *kabe shimbun* wall newssheet (often handwritten)
[14] 隣 *kabedonari* neighbor with just a wall between
[22] 龕 *hekigan* niche, recess

14

壓 1104 / J545a / M5557 See 圧 970.

壗 1105 / J545c / M-X （国字） *mama* steep slope; cliff.

壔 1106 / J-X / M5558 TŌ cylinder; fort.

壑 1107 / J545b / M5554 GAKU, KAKU valley.

壕 1108 / J3968 / M5559 KŌ. GŌ trench, dugout, air-raid shelter. *hori* moat; ditch; canal.

15

壘 1109 / J545e / M5574 See 塁 1056.

壙 1110 / J545d / M5576 KŌ hole.
[5] 穴 *kōketsu* grave, tomb

16

壞 1111 / J5455 / M5590 See 壊 1102.

壟 1112 / J5462 / M5591 **壠** 1113 / J-X / M5592 RŌ mound; grave; rice field division dikes. *oka* hill.
[11] 断 *rōdan suru* monopolize

壜 1114 / J5460 / M5588 **罎** 4631 / J6624 / M28189 DON. *bin* bottle, vial, jar.
[2] 入 *bin'i(ri) no* bottled
[5] 代 *bindai* charge for a bottle
[13] 詰 *binzume* bottled

17

壥 1115 / J545f / M-X See 廛 1644.

壤 1116 / J5461 / M5608 See 壌 1098.

RAD. 士 33

Samurai warrior. Except for the radical character itself, entered below, this radical is treated herein as a variant of Rad. 32. Nickname: Samurai.

A **士** 1117 / J3b4e / M5638 SHI samurai; man, gentleman; scholar. *samurai* samurai, knight. *-shi* suffix for academic degrees.

3 口囗土士【夂夊】夕大女子宀寸小⺌尢尸屮山川巛工己巾干幺广廴廾弋弓ヨ彑彡彳

²人 *shijin* samurai
³女 *shijo* men and women
⁴分 *shibun* samurai status, samurai class
⁵民 *shimin* all classes of people; the people
⁶気 *shiki* morale; martial spirit
⁷君子 *shikunshi* gentleman, man of honor
⁸卒 *shisotsu* private, soldier
官 *shikan* (military or naval) officer
官学校 *shikan gakkō* military academy
⁹風 *shifū* samurai discipline; samurai customs
¹⁰師 *shishi* (ancient) judge
師記 *Shishiki* the Book of Judges
¹¹道 *shidō* chivalry, knighthood, samurai code
族 *shizoku* descendants of samurai
規 *shiki* rules for samurai
¹³農工商 *shi-nō-kō-shō* warriors-farmers-artisans-tradesmen; class distinction
¹⁴魂商才 *shikon-shōsai* gentlemanly spirit and business acumen

RAD. 夂 34

At top: *fuyugashira* (like crown of *fuyu* "winter"). At bottom: *natsuashi* (like legs of *natsu* "summer"). As enclosure: 夊 *suinyō*. This variant and some of the foregoing terms are actually Rad. 35 but are treated herein as Rad. 34. Nickname: Winter.

0

夂 1118 J5469 M5691 Chi *oku(reru)* be late, be delayed.

3

A **変** 1119 J4a51 M5703 **變** 5718 J-X M36112 **變** 5721 J5a4e M36117

Hen change; accident, calamity; uprising; something strange. *hen(jiru), hen(zuru)* *vi* change into, be transformed, be transfigured. *vt* transform, alter, convert. *ka(waru)* change, vary; be revised; be different; be queer; move; be transferred. *ka(eru)* change, vary convert; revise, amend. *kawa(ri)* change, alteration; difference. *kawa(tta)* another, different; various; particular; unusual, novel; peculiar. *kawa(ranu)* constant, unchangeable. *kawa(rinaku)* unchangeably, constantly; eternally; uneventfully. *hen na* strange, suspicious-looking; queer, eccentric, funny. *hen ni* curiously, strangely.

²人 *henjin* eccentric person
⁴心 *henshin* change of mind, inconstancy, apostasy
化 *henka* change, variation, alteration, mutation, transition; transformation, transfiguration, metamorphosis; variety, diversity; infection, declension, conjugation. *henge* goblin, ghost, apparition, bugbear
化球 *henkakyū* ball with a change of speed
幻 *hengen* transformation
幻自在 *hengenjizai* ever-changing
⁵目 *kawa(ri)me* change, turning point, transition, new program
圧 *hen'atsu* transformation (of a current)
圧所 *hen'atsujo* transformer substation
圧器 *hen'atsuki* transformer
⁶色 *henshoku* change of color; fading, discoloration
名 *hemmei* assumed name, alias
光星 *henkōsei* variable star
成 *hensei* metamorphosis
成岩 *henseigan* metamorphic rock
死 *henshi* accidental death
死者 *henshisha* person accidentally killed
⁷身 *henshin* disguise
位 *hen'i* change of position
改 *henkai suru* revise (rules)
乱 *henran* disturbance, uprising, war
声期 *henseiki* puberty in boys, change in voice
体 *hentai* abnormality
体仮名 *hentaigana* anomalous cursive syllabary
形 *henkei* transformation, metamorphosis, modification, variation, deformation; variety, deformity, monster

形虫 *henkeichū* an amoeba
更 *henkō* change, modification, alteration
更不能 *henkō funō* unchangeable
8 性 *hensei suru vt* and *vi* denature; degenerate
法 *hempō* law revision; revised law
物 *hembutsu* eccentric person
易 *kawa(ri)-yasu(i)* changeable, unsettled; inconstant
果 *kawa(ri)-ha(teru)* be completely changed
者 *kawa(ri)mono* an eccentric
事 *henji* accident, emergency, calamity
9 革 *henkaku* change, reform
造 *henzō* alteration, defacement, debasement, falsification, forgery
通 *hentsū* resourcefulness, adaptability
則 *hensoku* irregularity
奏曲 *hensōkyoku* variation (in music)
速 *hensoku* shifting gears
速機 *hensokuki* transmission
10 症 *henshō suru* take a turn, develop into
格 *henkaku* irregularity, irregular conjugation
容 *hen'yō* changed appearance
哲無 *hentetsu (mo) na(i)* usual, mediocre, monotonous
流器 *henryūki* transformer
11 移 *hen'i* change, alteration; transmutation, mutation
転 *henten* mutation, change, vicissitude
動 *hendo* change, fluctuation
異 *hen'i* accident; variation, mutation
12 換 *henkan* change, conversion, diversion, transformation
装 *hensō* disguise, masquerade
13 数 *hensū* variable (in math)
節 *hensetsu* apostasy, betrayal
電所 *hendensho* transformer substation
14 遷 *hensen* transition, vicissitudes, change
種 *henshu, kawa(ri)dane* novelty, exception; hybrid, mutation, variety, freak; eccentric personality
貌 *hembō* transfiguration
模様 *kawa(ri) moyō* fancy pattern
態 *hentai* transformation, metamorphosis; abnormality
態心理 *hentai shinri* abnormal mentality
態心理学 *hentai shinrigaku* abnormal psychology
態的 *hentaiteki* abnormal
態性欲 *hentai seiyoku* abnormal sexuality, sexual perversion
15 調 *henchō* change of tone, variation (in music); irregularity, anomaly, abnormality; modulation (in radio)
質 *henshitsu* deterioration, degeneration
質者 *henshitsusha* a degenerate

7

A **夏** 1120 / J3246 / M5720 GE KA *natsu* summer

3 山 *natsuyama* mountains in summer
大根 *natsudaikon* summer daikon
4 日 *kajitsu, natsubi* summer day
木立 *natsukodachi* a grove in summer
6 衣 *natsugoromo* summer clothes
向 *natsumu(ki)* suitable for summer
休 *natsuyasu(mi)* summer vacation
羽織 *natsubaori* summer *haori* (coat)
至 *geshi* summer solstice
至点 *geshiten* summer solstice
至線 *Geshisen* Tropic of Cancer
8 物 *natsumono* summer goods
服 *natsufuku* summer clothes
季 *kaki* summer season
炉冬扇 *karo-tōsen* summer fires and winter fans; useless things
9 枯 *natsuga(re)* summer slump
前 *natsumae ni* before summer
草 *natsukusa* summer grass | heat
負 *natsuma(ke)* suffering from summer
10 蚕 *natsugo* summer silkworms
時 *natsudoki, kaji* summertime
時刻 *natsu jikoku* daylight-saving time
時間 *natsu jikan* daylight-saving time
11 野 *natsuno* summer fields
菊 *natsugiku* early chrysanthemums
祭 *natsumatsu(ri)* summer festival
12 越 *natsugo(shi)* keeping over the summer
着 *natsugi* summer clothes
帽子 *natsubōshi* summer hat, straw hat
場 *natsuba* summertime
場所 *natsu basho* summer sumo tournament
期 *kaki* summer season
期大学 *kaki daigaku* college summer school
期学校 *kaki gakkō* summer school
期時間 *kaki jikan* summer daylight-saving time

期講座 *kaki kōza* summer school, summer course of study
14 蜜柑 *natsu mikan* bitter summer orange, Chinese citron
15 痩 *natsuyase* summer loss of weight
18 蟬 *natsuzemi* summer cicadas

11

夐 1121 J546b M5731 KEI *haru(ka)* far, distant.
5 古 *keiko* distant past
12 遠 *keien* distant

RAD. 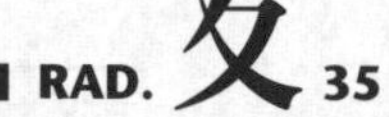 35

Sui or *yuku* to go. This radical is treated herein as a variant of Rad. 34. Nickname: Winter Variant.

夊 1122 J546a M5708 SUI *oso(i)* late, slow.

RAD. 夕 36

Yūbe evening or *ta* (the katakana). Nickname: *Kana Ta.*

A **夕** 1123 J4d3c M5749 SEKI. *yū, yū(be)* evening.
3 山 *yūyama* mountains at evening
4 方 *yūgata* evening
日 *yūhi* setting sun
化粧 *yūgeshō* one's evening toilet
月 *yūzuki* evening moon
月夜 *yūzukiyo* moonlit evening
5 立 *yūdachi* sudden shower, evening shower
立雲 *yūdachigumo* a shower cloud
刊 *yūkan* evening paper
刊紙 *yūkanshi* evening paper
6 凪 *yūnagi* evening calm
8 拝 *yūhai* vespers, evening worship
泊 *yūdoma(ri)* stopping for the night
波 *yūnami* evening waves
刻 *yūkoku* evening
空 *yūzora* evening sky
河岸 *yūgashi* evening fish market
9 風 *yūkaze* evening breeze
映 *yūbae* sunset glow
虹 *yūniji* evening rainbow
星 *yūzutsu* evening star, Venus
栄 *yūba(e)* sunset glow
食 *yūge, yūshoku* supper, evening meal
食会 *yūshokukai* supper party
食後 *yūshokugo* after supper
10 時雨 *yūshigure* evening shower
11 涼 *yūsuzu(mi)* enjoying the evening cool
陽 *sekiyō, yūhi* setting sun
12 晴 *yūba(re)* clearing up in the evening
焼 *yūya(ke)* sunset colors
嵐 *yūarashi* evening storm
雲 *yūgumo* evening clouds
間暮 *yūmagu(re)* evening
景 *yūkei* evenings
景色 *yūgeshiki* evening scene
飯 *yūhan, yūmeshi* evening meal
飯後 *yūhango* after supper
飯時 *yūhandoki* supper time
13 煙 *yūkemuri, yūkeburi* evening hearth smoke
照 *sekishō* evening glow, after glow
14 暮 *yūgu(re)* evening
15 餉 *yūge* evening meal
影 *yūkage* evening light; evening shadows
16 曇 *yūgumori* evening cloudiness
17 闇 *yūyami* dusk, twilight
霞 *yūgasumi* evening mist
18 顔 *yūgao* moonflower; bottle gourd
19 禱 *yūtō* vespers, evening prayers
霧 *yūgiri* evening mist
21 轟 *yūtodoroki* evening noise
24 靄 *yūmoya* evening haze

2

夗 1124 J5249 M5753 EN roll over and lie down.

A 外 1125 / J3330 / M5750 GE. GAI outside, without, beside, beyond the scope of. *hazu(su)* take off, remove, unfasten, undo, detach, disconnect, put out off gear; miss, fail; avoid, evade, dodge. *hazu(reru)* be off, come off, be or get out of place, be out of gear, run off the track, slip out or off, be dislocated, be disconnected, be off the hook (a phone), be unbuttoned, be unzipped. *soto* outside, exterior, open air. *hazu(re)* end, verge, extremity, tip; outskirts; miss, failure. *hoka* some other place; outside; the rest. *hoka no* other, another, different. *no hoka ni* with the exception of. *hoka naranu* none other than, nothing but.

2 力 *gairyoku* external force
人 *gaijin* foreigner, alien
人社会 *gaijin shakai* foreign community
人部隊 *gaijimbutai* foreign legion
3 土 *gedo, gaido* foreign country; rural area
山 *toyama* the last mountain in a chain; foothills
4 心 *gaishin* double mindedness
方 *gaihō* outward. *soppo, soppō* the other way, outside, another direction, off to the side
辺 *gaihen* environs, outskirts
5 皮 *gaihi* outer cover, crust, shell, husk, shuck, hull, cuticle, skin
圧 *gaiatsu* external pressure, outside pressure
史 *gaishi* unofficial history
用 *gaiyō* external use
用薬 *gaiyōyaku* external medicine
出 *gaishutsu, sotode* going out, outting, airing
出日 *gaishutsubi* leave day, day off
出中 *gaishutsuchū* while away, while out; out of the office
出好 *gaishutsuzu(ki)* gadabout
出時間 *gaishutsu jikan* leave time
出着 *gaishutsugi* street wear
出嫌 *gaishutsugira(i)* a stay-at-home
出禁止令 *gaishutsu kinshirei* curfew
6 米 *gaimai* foreign rice
衣 *gaii* outer garment
因 *gaiin* the surface reason
回 *sotomawa(ri)* circumference, perimeter; outside work; circumferential line
気 *gaiki* the air, the open air
伝 *gaiden* a traditional biography
地 *gaichi* overseas territory, outlying territory
灯 *gaitō* outside light
邦 *gaihō* foreign country
夷 *gaii* foreign barbarians
向性 *gaikōsei* extroversion
曲球 *gaikyokkyū* outcurve (baseball)
耳 *gaiji* external ear
耳炎 *gaijien* external otitis
字 *gaiji* characters not among the Jōyō Kanji; foreign letters, foreign language
字紙 *gaijishi* foreign-language newspaper
字新聞 *gaiji shimbun* foreign-language newspaper
交 *gaikō* diplomacy, foreign relations
交上 *gaikōjō* diplomatic
交手段 *gaikō shudan* diplomatic measures
交方針 *gaikō hōshin* diplomatic policy
交文書 *gaikō bunsho* diplomatic document
交白書 *gaikō hakusho* diplomatic white paper
交的 *gaikōteki* diplomatic
交官 *gaikōkan* diplomat, diplomatic official
交使節団 *gaikō shisetsudan* diplomatic mission
交界 *gaikōkai* diplomatic circles
交政策 *gaikō seisaku* diplomatic policy, diplomacy
交員 *gaikōin* canvasser, traveling salesman
交家 *gaikōka* diplomat
交術 *gaikōjutsu* diplomacy
交筋 *gaikō suji* foreign-office sources
交辞令 *gaikō jirei* diplomacy; flattery
交関係 *gaikō kankei* foreign relations
交談判 *gaikō dampan* diplomatic negotiations
交機関 *gaikō kikan* diplomatic channels
7 見 *gaiken, sotomi* external appearance
車 *gaisha* foreign automobile
囲 *sotogako(i)* outer fence
局 *gaikyoku* external bureau
廷 *gaitei* emperor's offices; foreign royal court
役 *gaieki* overseas military service
形 *gaikei* external form, externals, appearance

角 *gaikaku* external angle; outside corner (in baseball)
角高目 *gaikaku takame* high on the outside corner of the plate (baseball)
来 *gairai no* foreign, imported
来者 *gairaisha* person from abroad
来患者 *gairai kanja* outpatient
来語 *gairaigo* word of foreign origin
8 侮 *gaibu* ridicule by foreign countries; outside ridicule
使 *gaishi* foreign envoy
姓 *gaisei* mother's family name
姉 *gaishi* wife's elder sister
征 *gaisei* foreign campaigns
泊 *gaihaku* overnight stay
法 *sotonori* outside measurements
物 *gaibutsu* the externals, material things; external object, foreign matter
的 *gaiteki* external, exterior, outside
歩 *sotoaru(ki)* going out for a walk
炎 *gaien* outer flame
苑 *gaien* outer garden, outer park
典 *Gaiten* Apocrypha
事 *gaiji* foreign affairs
国 *gaikoku, totsukuni* foreign country; foreign
国人 *gaikokujin* foreigner, alien
国行 *gaikokuyu(ki), gaikokui(ki)* going abroad
国伝道 *gaikoku dendō* foreign missions
国使臣 *gaikoku shishin* foreign envoy
国風 *gaikokufū* foreign style
国為替 *gaikoku kawase* foreign exchange
国租界 *gaikoku sokai* foreign concession
国船 *gaikokusen* foreign ship
国債 *gaikokusai* foreign loan
国語 *gaikokugo* foreign language
9 面 *gaimen* exterior, surface, outside, outward appearance. *tonomo* outside the house
信 *gaishin* foreign letter
相 *Gaishō* the Foreign Minister
海 *gaikai, sotoumi* open sea, the high seas
洋 *gaiyō* ocean, open sea
陣 *gejin, gaijin* transept, room just outside of the inner sanctuary of a shrine or temple
政 *gaisei* diplomatic affairs, foreign policies
客 *gaikaku, gaikyaku* tourist, foreign visitor
界 *gaikai* outside world; physical world; the externals
食 *gaishoku* eating out
食券 *gaishokuken* (post-war) rationed meal ticket
祖 *gaiso* mother's parents
祖父 *gaisofu* maternal grandfather
祖母 *gaisobo* maternal grandmother
科 *geka* surgery
科医 *gekai* surgeon
科的 *gekateki* surgical
科学 *gekagaku* surgery
科結 *geka musu(bi)* surgeon's knot
10 庭 *gaitei, soto niwa* outer court
孫 *gaison* child of a daughter who enters another home
紙 *gaishi* foreign-language newspaper
部 *gaibu* exterior, outside world
套 *gaitō* overcoat, cloak
宮 *Gekū, Gegū* Outer Shrine of Ise
郭 *gaikaku* outer wall; outline; contour
郭団体 *gaikaku dantai* auxiliary organization
11 戚 *gaiseki* maternal relative
道 *gedō* heresy, paganism; heretic, pagan (from the Buddhist standpoint); wicked person
側 *gaisoku, sotogawa* exterior outside
族 *gaizoku* mother's or wife's relatives
経 *gaikei* outside diameter
船 *gaisen* foreign ship
教 *gaikyō* Confucianism and other non-Buddhist religions
殻 *gaikaku* shell, crust
商 *gaishō* foreign merchant
寇 *gaikō* foreign invasion
患 *gaikan* foreign troubles, outside troubles
斜視 *gaishashi* walleyed, strabismus
遊 *gaiyū* foreign travel
遊星 *gaiyūsei* outer planet
接 *gaisetsu suru* be circumscribed (in geometry)
接円 *gaisetsuen* circumscribed circle
貨 *gaika* imported goods; foreign money
貨予算 *gaika yosan* foreign-currency control
貨債 *gaikasai* foreign-currency bond
務 *gaimu* foreign affairs
務大臣 *Gaimu Daijin* the Foreign Minister

務省 *Gaimushō* Foreign Affairs Ministry
務員 *gaimuin* canvasser, commercial traveler
野 *gaiya* outfield
野手 *gaiyashu* outfielder
野席 *gaiyaseki* outfield bleachers
野飛球 *gaiya hikyū* fly ball to the outfield
12 塀 *sotobei* outer wall
港 *gaikō* outer port
焰 *gaien* outer flame
甥 *gaisei* the wife's brothers
勤 *gaikin* outside duty, canvassing
殼 *gaikaku* shell, crust
塁 *gairui* an outwork (in castle fortifications)
惑星 *gaiwakusei* major planet, outer planet
13 廓 *gaikaku* outer wall; outline, contour
債 *gaisai* foreign loan, foreign bond, foreign debt
傷 *gaishō* external wound
電 *gaiden* foreign cable
業 *gaigyō* outside work (in surveying)
蒙 *Gaimō* Outer Mongolia
蒙古 *Soto Mōko* Outer Mongolia
資 *gaishi* foreign capital, foreign money
資導入 *gaishi dōnyū* introduction of foreign capital
14 層 *gaisō* outer layers
聞 *gaibun* reputation, honor; respectability
構 *sotogama(e)* outward structure, external appearance
語 *gaigo* foreign language
貌 *gaibō* one's looks, external appearance, externals, exterior
様 *tozama* outside the group; non-Tokugawa daimyo
様大名 *tozama daimyō* non-Tokugawa daimyo
15 線 *gaisen* outside telephone line; outer circle; outside wire
敵 *gaiteki* foreign enemy
賓 *gaihin* foreign visitor
篇 *gaihen* introductory part of a book
輪 *gairin* paddlewheel
輪山 *gairinzan* the outer crater
輪船 *gairinsen* paddle-wheel steamer
16 壁 *gaiheki* outer wall
17 濠 *sotobori* outer moat
18 観 *gaikan* external appearance, outside view
題 *gedai* title (of a play or book); a play, a piece
20 艦 *gaikan* foreign warship
鰐 *sotowa, sotowani* walking with the feet pointed out

3

夙 1126 / J3d48 / M5755 SHUKU. *tsuto ni* bright and early; early in life; long ago; for a long time. *madoki ni* earlier, already, beforehand.
6 成 *shukusei* precocity
7 志 *shukushi* long-cherished desire
8 夜 *shukuya* from morning till night; day and night; always

∧ **多** 1127 / J423f / M5756 **夛** 1128 / J546c / M5759 TA much. *ō(i)* many; copious, abundant; much; frequent. *ta-* many-(sided); multi-; poly-. *ta to suru* appreciate, thank.
2 人数 *taninzu* multitude
3 大 *tadai* great quantity, great number
小 *tashō* a little, somewhat, any, some, slightly, more or less
才 *tasai na* talented
士 *tashi* many talented men
士済済 *tashiseisei* galaxy of able men
4 毛 *tamō* hairiness
孔 *takō no* porous; cavernous; open (weave)
孔性 *takōsei* porosity
孔管 *takōkan* perforated pipe
分 *tabun* probably, maybe; very likely, presumably; a great deal, a great many
方面 *tahōmen no* various, different, manysided, versatile
辺形 *tahenkei* polygon
辺的 *tahenteki* multilateral
少 *tashō* a little, somewhat, any, some, slightly, more or less
少縁 *tashō (no) en* some karma from a previous existence
元 *tagen* pluralism
元描写 *tagembyōsha* descriptions from different viewpoints
元論 *tagenron* pluralism
5 用 *tayō* pressure of business
弁 *taben* talkativeness, verbosity

3 口 囗 土 士 夂 夊 【夕】3 大 女 子 宀 寸 小 ⺌ 尢 尸 屮 山 川 巛 工 己 巾 干 幺 广 廴 廾 弋 弓 彐 彑 彡 彳

収穫 *tashūkaku* abundant harvest
生 *tashō* transmigration of souls
生縁 *tashō (no) en* karma from a previous existence
6 伐 *tabatsu* overcutting (forests)
忙 *tabō* pressure of work
多 *tata* very many, very much; more and more
汗症 *takanshō* excessive sweating
血 *taketsu na* hasty
血質 *taketsushitsu no* hasty
年 *tanen* many years
年生 *tanensei* perennial
肉 *taniku* fleshy
肉性 *tanikusei* fleshy, pulpy, succulent
肉果 *tanikuka* pulpy fruit
肉質 *tanikushitsu* fleshy, pulpy, succulent
7 言 *tagen, tagon* loquacity, verbosity; many words
足 *tasoku* multiped
岐 *taki* digression; many branches (of a road); many divergences
技 *tagi* many skills
売 *tabai* large sale, large turnover
芸 *tagei* versatility
作 *tasaku* being prolific in writing
作家 *tasakuka* voluminous writer
形 *takei* multiformity
形性 *takeisei no* multiform
角 *takaku* many-sided, multiple, multilateral, diversified
角形 *takakkei* polygon
角的 *takakuteki* many-sided, versatile, diversified, multilateral
角経営 *takaku keiei* many-sided enterprise
角農業 *takaku nōgyō* diversified farming
8 雨 *tau* a heavy rain
幸 *takō* great happiness, good fortune
妻 *tasai* plurality of wives
肢選択法 *tashisentakuhō* multiple-choice (test)
事 *taji* eventfulness; storm and stress; press of business
事多端 *taji-tatan no* busy, eventful (life)
9 恨 *takon* many regrets; great discontent
相 *tasō* multiphase
段式 *tadanshiki* multistage (rocket)
型性 *takeisei no* multiform
連装 *tarensō* multibarreled (gun)
面 *tamen* many sides, many phases
面体 *tamentai* polyhedron
音節 *taonsetsu* polysyllablic
音節語 *taonsetsugo* polysyllablic word
重 *tajū* multiplex, multiple
重星 *tajūsei* multiple star
重処理 *tajū shori* multiprocessing
重電信法 *tajū denshinhō* multiplex telegraphy
発式 *tahatsushiki* multiengined
発性 *tahatsusei* multiple (sclerosis)
発機 *tahatsuki* multiengined plane
神教 *tashinkyō* polytheism
神教国 *tashinkyōkoku* pagan countries
神教的 *tashinkyōteki* polytheistic
神教徒 *tashikyōto* polytheist
神論 *tashinron* polytheism
10 病 *tabyō* frail health
能 *tanō* versatility
座機 *tazaki* multiseated plane
11 過 *ōsu(giru)* be too many, be too much
淫 *tain* lasciviousness, lust
彩 *tasai no* colorful, varicolored
望 *tabō* great promise, bright prospects
産 *tasan* fecundity, bearing more than one offspring at a time; productivity
産系 *tasankei* prolific woman
情 *tajō* inconstancy, licentiousness; sentimentalism
情仏心 *tajō-busshin* tenderheartedness
情多恨 *tajō-takon* sentimentality; ardent loves and deep sorrows
情多感 *tajō-takan na* passionate, sentimental
12 量 *taryō* large quantity, a great deal
衆 *tashū* a crowd
項式 *takōshiki* polynomial expression
項選択 *takō-sentaku* multiple-choice (test)
葉飛行機 *tayō hikōki* multiplane
葉機 *tayōki* multiplane
13 勢 *tazei* a crowd of people, numerical superiority
感 *takan* sensibility, susceptibility, sentimentality
義 *tagi* various meanings
義選択法 *tagi-sentakuhō* multiple-choice (test)
福 *(o)tafuku* plain woman, homely woman
福豆 *(o)tafuku mame* a big broad bean

福風 *(o)tafuku kaze* mumps
数 *tasū* large number, multitude; majority
数人 *tasūnin* many persons
数決 *tasūketsu* decision by the majority
数国間 *tasūkokukan no* multilateral
数党 *tasūtō* majority party
数票 *tasūhyō* majority vote, plurality
14 聞 *tabun* much information. *tabun no* well-informed
端 *tatan* many items; pressure of business
寡 *taka* quantity, number, amount
様 *tayō* diversity, variety
様性 *tayōsei* diversity, variety
種 *tashu* various kinds, many kinds
種多様 *tashu-tayō na* various, multifarious, diversified
読 *tadoku* extensive reading
読家 *tadokuka* wide reader, well-read man
15 慾 *tayoku* greed, covetousness
趣 *tashu* wide interests (in art, etc.)
趣味 *tashumi* many-sided interests
16 頭 *tatō no* many-headed
17 謝 *tasha* many thanks; a thousand apologies
18 難 *tanan na* full of difficulties, thorny, tumultuous
額 *tagaku* large sum
19 識 *tashiki* extensive knowledge

5

A **夜** 1129 夕 M5763 YA night. *yo* evening, night. *yoru* night, nighttime, evening; at night. *yo(nabe)* night work. *yo(mosugara)* all night.

3 上 *yoa(gari)* weather clearing at night
叉 *yasha* female demon
4 中 *yachū, yojū* all night, the whole night. *yonaka* midnight, dead of night
分 *yabun* evening, night, nighttime
5 立 *yoda(chi)* setting out at night
市 *yoichi* night market
半 *yowa, yahan* midnight, dead of night
仕事 *yoshigoto* night work
6 色 *yashoku* shades of night; night scene
行 *yakō* night travel, night train. *yagyō* walking around at night
凪 *yonagi* evening calm
回 *yomawa(ri)* night watch; night watchman
気 *yaki* night air, stillness of night, cool evening
曲 *yakyoku* a nocturne
毎 *yogoto* every night
会 *yakai* evening party
会服 *yakaifuku* evening dress
光 *yakō* nocturnal luminescence
光虫 *yakōchū* phosphorescent animalcule
光時計 *yakōdokei* luminous watch
光塗料 *yakō toryō* luminous paint
7 伽 *yotogi* watching, vigil; watcher
攻 *yoze(me)* night attack
更 *yofuka(shi)* staying up late, nightowl. *yofuke ni, yofuke(te)* late at night
来 *yarai* overnight; since last night
汽車 *yogisha* night train
尿症 *yanyōshō* bed-wetting
見世 *yomise* night shop, night fair
見国 *yomi (no) kuni* Hades, the next world
8 長 *yonaga* long night
雨 *yau* night rain
店 *yomise* night stall, night booth; night fair
逃 *yoni(ge)* night flight
泊 *yahaku* night mooring
歩 *yoaru(ki)* walking around at night
具 *yagu* bedding
空 *yozora* night sky
盲症 *yamōshō* night blindness
明 *yoa(kashi)* staying up all night, all-night vigil. *yoa(ke)* dawn, daybreak
明明星 *yoake (no) myōjō* morning star
夜 *yoyo, yo(na)yo(na)* every evening, night after night
夜中 *yoruyonaka* midnight
学 *yagaku* night class, night school
学校 *yagakkō* night school
9 風 *yokaze* night wind
食 *yashoku* supper, night meal
通 *yodō(shi)* all night
昼 *yoruhiru* day and night
10 晒 *yozara(shi)* leaving things exposed outside all night
桜 *yozakura* cherry trees at evening
航 *yakō* night travel
討 *you(chi)* night attack
陰 *yain* shades of evening, dead of night
11 烏 *yogarasu* night crow
宮 *yomiya* eve of a festival vigil

鳥 *yachō* nocturnal bird
道 *yomichi* going out at night, night trip, road at night
遊 *yoaso(bi)* night amusements
深 *yobuka(i)* (staying) up late at night. *yofuke ni, yofu(ke), yofu(kete)* late at night
船 *yofune* night boat
釣 *yozu(ri)* night angling
商 *yoakina(i)* night trading
商人 *yoakindo* night shopkeeper
盗 *yatō* night burglar
12 啼 *yonaki* crying at night
勤 *yakin* night duty, night shift
寒 *yosamu, yozamu* night cold; cold night
嵐 *yoarashi* night storm
景 *yakei* night view
着 *yogi* nightclothes; heavy kimono-like quilt
番 *yoban, yaban* night watch, night sentry
営 *yaei* encamping at night
間 *yakan* night, nighttime
間中学 *yakan chūgaku* evening middle school
間部 *yakambu* night-school session
間勤務 *yakan kimmu* night work
間営業 *yakan eigyō* open at night
間預金金庫 *yakan yokin kinko* night-deposit safe
13 働 *yobatara(ki)* night work
詰 *yozu(me)* night watch
話 *yawa, yobanashi* night talks; evening tea parties
戦 *yasen* night warfare
業 *yagyō* night work, night shift
想曲 *yasōkyoku* a nocturne
14 鳴 *yona(ki)* crying at night
15 稼 *yokasegi* night work; burglary
19 霧 *yogiri* night fog
警 *yakei* night watchman
21 露 *yotsuyu* evening dew, night dew
22 籠 *yogomo(ri)* night of prayer in a temple
襲 *yashū* night attack
24 鷹 *yotaka* nighthawk, prostitute

8

梦 1130 / J546d / M5784 See  1131.

10

A **夢** 1131 / J4c34 / M5801' **梦** 1130 / J546d / M5784 Mu. *yume* dream; vision; illusion, delusion; reverie.
4 幻 *mugen* dreams, visions. *yume-maboroshi* dreams and visions; something visionary
心 *yumegokoro* trance, ecstasy
心地 *yumegokochi* trance, ecstasy
中 *muchū* unconscious; ecstasy; absorption; abstraction
中歩行 *muchū hokō* walking in one's sleep
5 占 *yume urana(i)* fortunetelling by dreams
6 死 *mushi suru* die without accomplishing anything
合 *yumea(wase)* interpretation of dreams
7 判断 *yume handan* interpretation of dreams
見 *yumemi(ru)* dream, fancy. *yumemi* a dream
見者 *yumemi(ru)mono* dreamer
8 枕 *yume makura ni* in a dream
物語 *yume monogatari* story of a dream; fantastic story
11 現 *yumeutsutsu* trance, ecstasy; dream and reality
遊 *muyū* walking in one's sleep
遊病 *muyūbyō* sleepwalking
12 寐 *mubi* awake or asleep
13 解 *yumeto(ki)* interpretation of a dream
路 *yumeji* traveling in a dream; Land of Nod
想 *musō* dream, vision, reverie
想家 *musōka* dreamer
14 語 *yumegata(ri)* story of a dream; fantastic story
21 魔 *muma* a fearful disturbing dream

11

夥 1132 / J546e / M5808 Ka. *obitada(shii)* immense, tremendous. *obitada(shiku)* abundantly, innumerably.
6 多 *kata* many, plentiful

RAD. 大 37

Dai large. At top: *dai kashira.* Variant: 𡗗. Nickname: Big.

A **大** 1133 / J4267 / M5831 TAI, DAI large, huge, grand; the greater; size; very; inveterate (smoker); severe (damage); success. *ō(kii)* large, great, grand, mighty, immense; severe; heavy. *ō(inaru)* big, large, great. *ō(i) ni* very, much, greatly, exceedingly. *ō(zappana)* rough (estimate); loose (talk); generous. *ō(makana)* rough (estimate); general, generous. *tai-* big, huge, grand, major. *tai(shita)* many, much, enormous; great, grand; important; serious; severe, intense; very; what a lot of. *ō(ki)ni* greatly, very much. *ō(isa), ō(kisa)* size, dimensions, volume. *tai(shite)* very, much, greatly, seriously. *ō(bira) ni* openly, publicly. *dai(soreta)* ambitious; daring; outrageous, atrocious. *-dai* the size of.... *dai-* great, prominent, large-scale, serious, severe, gross. *ō-* large, great; heavy (rain); loud (voice); full-size, life-size.

1 一座 *ōichiza* large troupe
2 刀 *daitō, tachi* long sword
力 *dairiki, tairiki* great strength
〆 *ōshime* grand total
八車 *daihachiguruma* large wagon, dray
八洲 *Ōyashima* the Eight Great Islands (of Japan)
八島 *Ōyashima* the Eight Great Islands (of Japan)
入 *ōi(ri)* full house
入道 *ōnyūdō* giant, monster, spectre
入袋 *ōiribukuro* full-house bonus
人 *otona* adult. *otona(buru)* act like an adult. *otona(biru)* look grown up; become precocious. *taijin* giant; adult; man of virtue. *taijin, ushi* polite term used in addressing an important person. *otona(shii)* gentle, quiet, good-tempered.
人気無 *otonagena(i)* childish; mean
人物 *daijimbutsu* great person, person of great character
人並 *otonana(mi) no* like an adult, full-fledged
人染 *otonaji(miru)* become adult-like
人振 *otonabu(ru)* act like an adult
3 巾 *ōhaba* full width; big scale
弓 *ōyumi, taikyū* crossbow, longbow. *daikyū* longbow; archery
凡 *ōyoso* approximately
丈夫 *daijōbu* safe, secure, all right; sure; infallible. *daijōfu* a man, a great man, a brave man
大的 *daidaiteki* great, grand, immense; sweeping (victory), wholesale, large-scale
上段 *daijōdan* raising a sword (to kill)
下馬 *ōgeba* large dismounting signs
三角帆 *daisankakuho* lateen sail
川 *ōkawa, taisen* large river
川端 *ōkawabata* Sumida riverside
工 *daiku* carpenter
工店 *daikuten* carpenter shop
山 *ōyama, taizan* large mountain
山猫 *ōyama neko* lynx
山鳴動 *taizan-meidō* great trouble
口 *ōguchi* large mouth; bragging; exaggeration; large amount. *ōkuchi* large mouth; large amount, large opening
口物 *ōguchimono* big lot (of goods)
口径砲 *daikōkeihō* large cannon
口需要者 *ōguchi juyōsha* large user
小 *daishō* great and small (people); size; large and small sizes; long and short sword. *dai(nari)-shō(nari)* whether large or small
小便 *daishōben* urination and defecation
小問 *daishō (o) to(wazu)* whether large or small
小論 *daishō (o) ron(zezu)* whether large or small
4 戸 *ōdo* main gate
方 *ōkata* probably; almost, mostly; the public. *taihō* in general; broad-mindedness; the public
月 *dai (no) tsuki* the long months
水 *ōmizu* flood, inundation
王 *daiō* the great king
円 *daien* large circle; great circle
凶 *daikyō* very bad luck; atrocity, brutality
厄 *taiyaku* great calamity, great misfortune
切 *taisetsu* important, momentous,

significant. *ōgi(ri)* large cut; last scene of a drama; catastrophe; end

分 *daibu, daibun* greatly, considerably

少 *daishō* great and small (people); size, large and small sizes

夫 *tayū, taifu* main actor. *taifu, daifu* high steward

日本 *Dai Nippon, Dai Nihon, Ōyamato* Japan

文字 *daimonji* large characters; the character 大; *ōmoji* capital letters

反対 *daihantai* intense opposition

元帥 *daigensui* generalissimo

太鼓 *ōdaiko* bass drum, large drum

木 *taiboku, ōki* large tree

木戸 *ōkido* big wooden gate; big town gate

欠 *ōakubi* big yawn

欠伸 *ōakubi* big yawn

火 *taika* big fire, conflagration, holocaust

火傷 *ōyakedo* bad burn

内 *ōuchi* the court, the palace

内山 *ōuchiyama* the palace

仏 *daibutsu* large image of a Buddha

仏殿 *daibutsuden* temple of a huge Buddha

手 *ōte* front castle gate; unit attacking front castle gate. *ōde* both arms; arms spread out

手門 *ōtemon* front castle gate

手柄 *ōtegara* great exploit

手筋 *ōtesuji* large operators, big traders

公 *taikō* ruler

公国 *taikōkoku* grand duchy

公使 *taikōshi* ambassadors and ministers

公望 *taikōbō* sports fisherman

5 白 *taihaku* large cup

皿 *ōzara* large plate, platter, charger

矢 *ōya* large arrow

石 *ōishi, taiseki* big stone

穴 *ōana* big hole; huge deficit; (make) a killing; a big upset (at the races)

尼 *ōama* an old nun

外 *ōhazu(re)* utter failure; big mistake; wild guess

巧 *taikō* great skill, dexterity

功 *taikō* great merit, distinguished services

正 *Taishō* Taisho era (1912-1925)

写 *ōutsu(shi)* a close-up

古 *taiko* ancient times

兄 *ōani* eldest brother. *taikei* polite word for elder brother or someone a little older

半 *taihan* majority, greater part; mostly, nearly all, generally

冊 *taisatsu* bulky volume

旦那 *ōdanna* proprietor, man of the house

出来 *ōdeki* huge success; brilliant move

芝居 *ōshibai* a great drama

打物 *ōu(chi)mono* long weapons

主教 *daishukyō* archbishop (Protestant)

司教 *daishikyō* archbishop (Catholic)

広間 *ōhiroma* grand hall; rotunda

代裏 *daidairi* (ancient) imperial palace

立回 *ōta(chi)mawa(ri)* serious quarrel

立物 *ōda(te)mono* principal actor; prominent figure

仕事 *ōshigoto* big business

仕掛 *ōshika(ke)* large scale

礼 *tairei* state ceremony, enthronement

礼服 *taireifuku* court dress, full-dress uniform

平 *taihei* peace, tranquility

平洋 *Taiheiyō* Pacific Ocean

目 *ōme* generous supervision; winking at, conniving with

目玉 *ōmedama* big eyes; scolding

目見 *ōme(ni)mi(ru)* overlook, let go, connive at

本 *ōmoto* foundation, base, source, fountainhead; fundamentals. *taihon* cardinal principles, great foundation

本山 *daihonzan* important sectarian-headquarters temple

本営 *Daihon'ei* Imperial Headquarters

6 老 *tairō* senior minister

耳 *ōmimi* large ears; being slow of hearing; carelessness

臣 *daijin* cabinet minister; high government official

凪 *ōnagi* flat calm

回 *ōmawa(ri)* circuitous route

成 *taisei* completion, accomplishment; compilation; attainment of greatness, success

向 *ōmuko(u)* standing section, the gallery, the masses

曲 *ōma(gari)* large bend in the road. *ōwada* inlet, creek

任 *tainin* great task, important position, important mission

仰 *ōgyō* exaggeration

奸 *daikan* great wickedness
汗 *ōase* copious sweating
邦 *taihō* great country
全 *taizen* encyclopedia, complete works
旨 *ōmune, taishi* the main idea
吉 *daikichi* excellent luck
字 *ōaza* major section of a village. *taiji* large characters. *dai (no) ji* spread-eagle form like the character 大
当 *oata(ri)* good luck; great success, a killing; bumper crop
兇 *daikyō* notorious scoundrel
江戸 *Ōedo* the great city of Edo
休止 *daikyūshi* (soldier's) long rest period
団円 *daidan'en* end, grand finale; catastrophe
宇宙 *daiuchū* the great universe
西洋 *Taiseiyō* Atlantic Ocean
肌脱 *ōhadanu(gi)* stripping to the waist
臼歯 *daikyūshi* molar
自然 *daishizen* Mother Nature
多数 *daitasū* the great majority
地 *daichi* ground, earth, the solid earth
地主 *ōjinushi* large landowner
好 *daisu(ki)* very fond of
好物 *daikōbutsu* favorite dish
会 *taikai* large meeting, mass meeting, rally, general meeting, conference, convention; tournament, meet
会堂 *daikaidō* cathedral
寺 *ōdera* large temple
寺院 *daijiin* large temple
年 *ōtoshi* last day of the year
年増 *ōtoshima* a beautiful mature woman
行 *taikō* great deeds
行天皇 *taikō tennō* the late emperor
行李 *daikōri* heavy baggage; field train
同 *daidō* general resemblance; combination, union
同小異 *daidō-shōi* substantial identity
同団結 *daidō-danketsu* merger, combination
尽 *daijin* rich man, millionaire, magnate
尽風 *daijinkaze* air of a millionaire
尽遊 *daijin aso(bi)* riotous pleasures
気 *taiki* atmosphere, the air
気圧 *taikiatsu* atmospheric pressure
気汚染 *taiki osen* atmospheric pollution
気圏外 *taikikengai* above the atmosphere
安 *taian* lucky day
安日 *taiannichi* lucky day
安売 *ōyasuu(ri)* big bargain sale
名 *daimyō* feudal lord, daimyo. *taimei* great honor
名旅行 *daimyō ryokō* junket, spendthrift tour
名領 *daimyōryō* fief
7 豆 *daizu, ōmame* soy bean
足 *ōashi* large feet; long stride
医 *taii* great physician
尾 *taibi* end
序 *daijo* prologue, opening act
佐 *taisa* colonel; (navy) captain
作 *taisaku* masterpiece, monumental work
体 *daitai* outline, summary; generally, on the whole; in substance; originally
役 *taiyaku* important task, important role
村 *ōmura, taison* large village
社 *taisha* grand shrine; Izumo Shrine
利 *tairi* huge profit
乱 *tairan* great disturbance, rebellion
別 *taibetsu* general classification
判 *ōban* large old Japanese gold coin; large size (paper of book), folio
助 *ōtasu(kari), ōdasu(kari)* a big help
形 *ōgata* large size, large pattern. *ōgyō* exaggeration, bombast
系 *taikei* outline (of a subject)
兵 *taihei* large army. *taihyō* great stature, large body
志 *taishi* great ambition, aspiration
牢 *tairō* emperor's sacrifice to the gods; splendid feast; Edo jail
旱 *taikan* serious drought
男 *ōotoko* giant. *dai (no) otoko* a real man, a big man
我 *daiga, taiga* the absolute ego, the higher self
君 *ōkimi, ōgimi* sovereign. *taikun* tycoon
束 *ōtaba* large bundle
花火 *ōhanabi* great fireworks display
売出 *ōu(ri)da(shi)* large sale
角豆 *sasage* cowpea
伽藍 *daigaran* huge temple; cathedral
見出 *ōmida(shi)* big headline
見得 *ōmie* magnificent gesture
言 *taigen* grand words; excellent ideas; exaggeration; words of boasting

言壮語 *taigen-sōgo* bragging; exaggeration
身 *taishin* man of rank; man of wealth
身槍 *ōmi (no) yari* long-handled spear
車 *ōguruma* wagon, truck
車輪 *daisharin* large wheel; giant swing; feverishly at work
伯父 *ōoji* great-uncle, granduncle
伯母 *ōoba* great-aunt, grandaunt
声 *ōgoe* loud voice. *taisei* stentorian voice, sonorous tone
声疾呼 *taisei-shikko suru* harangue
麦 *ōmugi* barley
麦刈 *omugika(ri)* barley harvest
局 *taikyoku* the general situation; the issue
局的 *taikyokuteki* general, the whole (situation)
局論 *taikyokuron* a broad view (of the situation)
8 門 *daimon* large outer gate of a Buddhist temple. *ōmon* front gate
雨 *ōame, taiu* heavy rainfall, downpour
国 *taikoku* large country; major power
店 *ōmise, ōdana* large store
供 *ōdomo* young grown-ups
呼 *taiko* loud shout, cry
味 *ōaji no* tasteless, insipid
姉 *ōane, taishi* eldest sister
所 *ōdokoro, ōdoko* powerful family, great house
抵 *taitei* generally, usually, probably; nearly, almost
杯 *taihai* large cup
枚 *taimai* large sum
波 *ōnami* large wave, billow, swell
河 *taiga, ōkawa* large river
知 *taichi* supreme wisdom; sage, a Solomon
股 *ōmata* straddle; long stride
刹 *taisetsu, taisatsu* large temple
効 *taikō* efficacy
命 *taimei* a ruler's command
参 *ōmai(ri)* large crowds of worshippers
官 *taikan* high official, dignitary
宗 *taisō* fundamentals; foundation
受 *ōu(ke)* great popularity, a hit
空 *ōzora, taikū* sky, firmament, space
典 *taiten* state ceremony; important law; excellent publication
昔 *ōmukashi* great antiquity
往生 *daiōjō* peaceful death; the death of a priest; euthanasia
牧者 *Daibokusha* Christ, the Great Shepherd
明神 *daimyōjin* title of a Shinto god
使 *taishi* ambassador
使館 *taishikan* embassy
物 *ōmono* big thing; big shot; big game
物食 *ōmonogu(i)* defeating one's superior
叔父 *ōoji* great-uncle, granduncle
叔母 *ōoba* great-aunt, grandaunt
事 *daiji, taiji* great thing, great undertaking; serious affair, emergency; importance, significance. *daiji ni suru* value, prize, esteem, be careful of. *Daiji(nai)* It matters little. *ōgoto* serious matter
事取 *daiji (o) to(ru)* act carefully
金 *taikin, ōgane* enormous sum, great cost
金持 *ōganemochi* very rich man
金儲 *ōganemōke* making a fortune
逆 *taigyaku* hideous wickedness; treason; patricide
逆無道 *daigyaku-mudō* high treason
逆罪 *taigyakuzai* treason; patricide
法 *taihō* fundamental law
法会 *taihōe* high Buddhist memorial service
法輪 *daihōrin* great wheel of (the Buddhist) law
英国 *Dai Eikoku* British Commonwealth
英帝国 *Daiei Teikoku* British Empire
英断 *daieidan* resolute step
東亜 *Daitōa* Greater East Asia
東亜共栄圏 *Daitōa Kyōeiken* Greater East Asia Coprosperity Sphere
東亜省 *Daitōashō* Ministry for Greater East Asia Affairs
東亜戦争 *Daitōa Sensō* the Greater East Asia War
学 *daigaku* college, university
学生 *daigakusei* university or college student
学出 *daigakude* college graduate
学出身者 *daigaku shusshinsha* college graduate
学自由 *daigaku (no) jiyū* academic freedom
学町 *daigaku machi* college town
学院 *daigakuin* graduate school

学帽 *daigakubō* college cap
学総長 *daigaku sōchō* university president
和 *Yamato* ancient Japan
和心 *Yamatogokoro* Japanese spirit
和火燵 *Yamatogotatsu* foot warmer
和民族 *Yamato minzoku* Japanese race
和言葉 *Yamato kotoba* classical Japanese, native Japanese vocabulary
和島根 *Yamato shimane* Japanese islands
和絵 *Yamatoe* pictures of ancient Japanese life
和琴 *Yamatogoto* ancient koto
和綴 *Yamato toji* Japanese-style bookbinding
和歌 *Yamato uta* 31 syllable poem, tanka
和魂 *Yamatodamashii* Japanese spirit
和撫子 *Yamato nadeshiko* women of Japan
9 食 *taishoku, ōgu(i)* gluttony, voracity; glutton
度 *taido* magnanimity, generosity
廻 *ōmawari* circuitous route
虐 *taigyaku* great cruelty; very bad government
通 *ōdō(ri)* main street, highway, thoroughfare. *daitsū* man of accomplishment
盾 *ōdate* large shield
便 *daiben* feces, excrement
垣 *ōgaki* large enclosing fence
指 *ōyubi* thumb
括 *ōguku(ri)* wrapping up in one bundle
持 *ōmo(te)* big welcome
柄 *ōhei* arrogance. *ōgara* large build; large pattern (in kimonos)
約 *taiyaku* summary, outline; great plan; approximately
計 *taikei* far-reaching policy, long-range plan, great plan
郡 *taigun* a great county
盃 *taihai, ōsakazuki* a large cup
帝 *taitei* a great emperor
軍 *taigun* large army, large force, mighty host. *ōikusa* a big battle; a great war
姦 *taikan* great villainy
荒 *ōa(re)* severe storm; great violence
要 *taiyō* summary, outline
型 *ōgata* large size, large pattern
急 *ōiso(gi)* great haste
負 *ōma(ke)* crushing defeat; great bargain
為 *ō(i)na(rashimeru)* magnify (in the sight of)
速力 *daisokuryoku* high speed
洪水 *daikōzui* deluge
胡坐 *ōagura* careless cross-legged squatting
威張 *ōiba(ri)* great bragging; great braggart
飛球 *daihikyū* a long fly (in baseball)
活躍 *daikatsuyaku* vigorous personal activity
屋 *ōya* landlord
屋根 *ōyane* main roof
相 *taisō* very, very much. *taisō na* a great deal, plenty; exaggerated, extravagant
相撲 *ōzumō* annual sumo matches; exciting sumo match
海 *taikai, daikai, ōumi* the ocean, the open sea
海原 *ōunabara* the ocean, the mighty deep
祖父 *daisofu* great-grandfather
祖母 *daisobo* great-grandmother
胆 *daitan* boldness, intrepidity, hardihood; audacity
胆不敵 *daitan-futeki na* bold and willful; daredevil; audacious; undaunted
降 *ōbu(ri)* heavy precipitation
降霜 *daikōsō* heavy frost
政 *taisei* administration of a country; imperial rule
政奉還 *taiseihōkan* restoration of imperial rule
乗的 *daijōteki* broad-minded
乗仏教 *Daijō Bukkyō* Mahayana Buddhism, Greater-Vehicle Buddhism
変 *taihen* serious, terrible; innumerable; immense; What!; a great change
変安上 *taihen yasua(gari)* very cheap
前 *ōmae* the presence of a god or ruler
前提 *daizentei* the major premise
勇 *taiyū* great courage
勇士 *daiyūshi* great warrior
音 *daion* great noise, loud voice
音声 *daionsei* stentorian voice
音響 *daionkyō* a great noise
風 *ōkaze, taifū* strong wind, storm, hurricane, typhoon. *ōbu(ri)* big things; large size. *ōfū* arrogance

風子油 *daifūshiyu* chaulmoogra oil
風呂敷 *ōburoshiki* big cloth wrapper; bragging
風雨 *daifūu* big rainstorm
神 *ōkami* god
神宮 *Daijingū* the Ise Shrine
神楽 *daikagura* street dance and jugglery performance; sacred shrine music and dancing
洋 *taiyō* ocean
洋州 *Taiyōshū* Oceania
洋性 *taiyōsei* oceanic (climate)
洋学 *taiyōgaku* oceanography
洋島 *taiyōtō* oceanic islands
洋航路船 *taiyō kōrosen* ocean liner
10 庭 *ōniwa* the great court
病 *taibyō* serious illness
師 *daishi* a great Buddhist teacher
剛 *daigō* great strength; very strong man
倭 *Ōyamato* Japan
振 *ōbu(ri)* big things; large size
旆 *taihai* standard, banner; imperial standard
浪 *tairō, ōnami* surge (of waves)
砲 *taihō* gun, cannon, artillery
破 *taiha* dilapidation, run, havoc, serious damage
蚊 *gagambo* daddy longlegs
袖 *ōsode* wide sleeves
釘 *ōkugi* big nail, spike
島 *ōshima* large island
宮 *ōmiya* grand shrine
害 *taigai* great harm, big damage
釜 *ōgama* large kettle, cauldron
笑 *ōwara(i), taishō* loud laughter
差 *taisa* wide difference, great discrepancy, striking contrast
書 *taisho suru* write in large letters
息 *ōiki, taisoku* sigh, long breath
恩 *daion, taion* great kindness; great obligation
挙 *taikyo* great enterprise; united effort
秦 *Taishin* the Great Roman Empire
時代 *ōjidai* great antiquity. *ōjidai na* old-fashioned
株主 *ōkabunushi* large stockholder
流行 *dairyūkō, ōhayari* the fashion, the rage
殉教 *Daijunkyō* the Great Martyrdom
馬鹿 *ōbaka* big fool
恐慌 *daikyōkō* great panic
陰暦 *taiinreki* lunar calendar
真面目 *ōmajime* great earnestness
修道院 *daishūdōin* abbey
原 *taigen* origin, foundation
原則 *daigensoku* broad principle
悟 *taigo, daigo* great wisdom; (Buddhist) enlightenment. *daigo* spiritual awakening, dawn of truth, attainment of a philosophy of life
悟徹底 *daigo-tettei, taigo-tettei* spiritual awakening, dawn of truth, attainment of a philosophy of life
酒 *ōzake, taishu* heavy drinking
酒飲 *ōzakeno(mi)* heavy drinker
将 *taishō* general; admiral; head, leader, boss
将軍 *daishōgun* generalissimo; boss, head
祓 *ōharai, ōbarai* Shinto purification ceremony (June 30 and Dec. 31); exorcism
祓詞 *ōharai (no) kotoba* Shinto purification prayer
都 *taito* great city
都会 *daitokai* big city
家 *taika* mansion, large building; rich or illustrious family; great master, authority. *taike* wealthy family, aristocratic family; an authority, a scholar. *ōya* main building, main house; landlord
家族 *daikazoku* a big family; a big circle of relatives
能 *tainō* great might
能者 *Tainōsha* the Omnipotent God
部 *daibu, taibu* the larger part; a many-volume set. *taibu no, daibu no* voluminous, copious, bulky
部分 *daibubun* greater part, majority; mostly, largely
部屋 *ōbeya* large room; actors' room; utility man; lesser stars
宮司 *daigūji* chief priest of the Ise shrine
宮御所 *Ōmiyagosho* Empress Dowager's Palace
宮様 *Ōmiyasama* Empress Dowager
根 *daikon* the huge white radish, daikon
根役 *daikon'yaku* poor actor, ham (actor)
根卸 *daikon'oro(shi)* grated daikon; daikon grater
根漬 *daikonzuke* pickled daikon

陸 *tairiku* continent; the Continent (of Asia)
陸系 *tairikukei no* continental
陸性 *tairikusei* continental (climate)
陸的 *tairikuteki* continental
陸島 *tairikutō* continental island
陸棚 *tairikubō, tairikuhō, tairikudana* continental shelf
11 喝 *daikatsu suru, taikatsu suru* thunder, roar, yell at
魚 *taigyo* large fish; large catch
鳥 *otori* large bird
鹿 *ōjika, ōshika* elk; moose
麻 *ōasa, taima* hemp. *asa* hemp; flax; ramie; jute; linen. *taima* Shinto paper offerings
虚 *taikyo* the sky, the great void
尉 *taii* captain; lieutenant junior grade
婚 *taikon* imperial wedding
掛 *ōgaka(ri)* large-scale
捷 *taishō* great victory
晦 *ōtsugomori* last day of the year
猟 *tairyō, dairyō* a large catch
略 *tairyaku* summary, outline; great plan; approximately
粒 *ōtsubu* a large drop; a large grain
組 *ōgu(mi)* making up (a newspaper)
脳 *dainō* brain, cerebrum
船 *ōbune, taisen* big ship, ocean liner
蛇 *daija, orochi* monster serpent, boa; large snake
欲 *daiyoku, taiyoku* greed, covetousness; greedy person; great desire
敗 *taihai* crushing defeat, complete rout
赦 *taisha* amnesty; plenary indulgence
釣 *ōzuri* big catch (of fish)
陽 *taiyō* sun
隊 *daitai* battalion
瓶 *ōbin* magnum, two-quart wine bottle
著 *taicho* great work, voluminous work
雪 *ōyuki, taisetsu* heavy snow; heavy snow season
患 *taikan, ōwazura(i)* serious illness; disaster; great trial
梁 *ōhari, ōbari* large beam, crossbeam
望 *taibō, taimō* aspiration, ambition
盗 *daitō* notorious robber
盛 *ōmo(ri)* heaping measure, large serving
匙 *ōsaji* tablespoon
晦日 *Ōmisoka* December 31; New Year's Eve
理石 *dairiseki* marble
兜虫 *ōkabutomushi* Atlas beetle
執事 *daishitsuji* archdeacon
強風 *daikyōfū* strong gale
旋風 *daisempū* tornado
掃除 *ōsōji* semiannual house cleaning
流星 *dairyūsei* major planet
経師 *daikyōji* (ancient) paperhanger
動脈 *daidōmyaku* aorta, main artery
袈裟 *ōgesa* exaggeration; grandiosity; large-scale
規模 *daikibo no* large scale
野 *ōno* big field
野貝 *ōnogai* soft-shelled clam
過 *taika* serious error, grave fault
過去 *daikako* past-perfect tense
酔 *taisui* drunken stupor
酔者 *taisuisha* drunkard
商店 *daishōten* emporium
商人 *daishōnin, ōakindo* a great merchant
斎 *Taisai* Lent
斎節 *Taisaisetsu* Lent
黒 *Daikoku* a god of wealth
黒柱 *daikokubashira* central pillar, king post; pillar, mainstay; family head
黒頭巾 *daikoku zukin* tam-o'shanter, round Scots cap, beret
悪 *daiaku* atrocity, outrage
悪人 *daiakunin* consummate villain, thorough-going rascal
悪者 *ōwarumono* notorious scoundrel
祭 *taisai, ōmatsu(ri)* grand festival
祭日 *taisaibi, taisaijitsu* national holiday
祭司 *daisaishi* high priest
道 *daidō, taidō* highway, street; great moral principle. *ōdō(ri)* main street
道具 *ōdōgu* stage setting, scene; large stage equipment
道商 *daidō akina(i)* hawking, street sale
道商人 *daidō shōnin* street vendor
12 慌 *ōawate* great excitement
淵 *ōfuchi* the great deep
違 *ōchiga(i)* great difference
絎 *ōguke* large stitch; long needle
詔 *taishō* imperial rescript
飯 *ōmeshi* hearty meal
傘 *ōgasa* large umbrella
喜 *ōyoroko(bi)* great joy
寒 *daikan, taikan* midwinter, coldest period
嵐 *ōarashi* severe storm

暑 *taisho* midsummer day (about July 23)
童 *ōwarawa ni* with all one's might
筋 *ōsuji* outline, summary
筒 *ōzutsu* cannon
葬 *taisō* imperial funeral
智 *taichi* great wisdom; sage
覚 *daikaku* great wisdom; (Buddhist) enlightenment
喪 *taimo, taisō* imperial mourning, national mourning
策 *taisaku* fundamental policy, long range features
痛手 *ōitade* severe wound; hard blow; great loss
割引 *ōwaribiki* big discount
評判 *daihyōban, ōhyōban* sensation
場所 *ōbasho* (regular) sumo tournament
惑星 *daiwakusei* major planet
間違 *ōmachiga(i)* big mistake
募集 *daiboshū* wholesale call (for workers)
喧嘩 *ōgenka* big quarrel
厦高楼 *taika-kōrō* large and imposing buildings
勝 *taishō* great victory
勝利 *daishōri* great victory
圏 *taiken* great circle
圏航路 *taiken kōro* great-circle route
幅 *ōhaba* full width; big scale
幅物 *ōhabamono* broadcloth, wide goods
極 *Taikyoku* the Absolute, the First Cause, the Imperial Throne; the maximum
極殿 *Daigokuden* (ancient) Palace Council Hall
奥 *ōoku* inner palace; harem
奥様 *ōokusama* your grandmother
量 *tairyō, dairyō* large quantity
量生産 *tairyō seisan* mass production
量点 *tairyōten* large score
量虐殺 *tairyō gyakusatsu* mass murder, genocide
量得点 *tairyō tokuten* large score
統 *daitō* imperial line
統領 *daitōryō* president
統領夫人 *daitōryō fujin* the first lady
統領令 *daitōryōrei* presidential decree
統領官邸 *Daitōryō Kantei* Executive Mansion
統領教書 *daitōryō kyōsho* president's message
御 *ōmi-, omi-* honorific prefix
御心 *ōmikokoro* imperial heart or will
御世 *ōmiyo* imperial reign
御位 *ōmikurai* imperial throne
御国 *ōmikuni* great august country
御神 *Ōmikami* the Sun Goddess
御所 *ōgosho* retired shogun; boss
御稜威 *ōmiitsu* imperial prestige
衆 *taishū* a crowd, the masses; general public
衆文学 *taishū bungaku* popular literature
衆化 *taishūka* popularization
衆向 *taishūmu(ki)* for everybody, popular
衆伝道 *taishū dendō* public evangelist
衆作家 *taishū sakka* popular writer
衆性 *taishūsei* popularity
衆物 *taishūmono* popular story
衆食堂 *taishū shokudō* (cheap) restaurant, eating place
衆政策 *taishū seisaku* policy toward the masses
衆娯楽 *taishū goraku* mass entertainment
衆教育 *taishū kyōiku* popular education
衆課税 *taishū kazei* taxing the public
衆獲得運動 *taishū-kakutoku undō* public-sympathy drive
13 廈 *taika* large house, grand building, skyscraper
痴 *taichi* a great fool
傷 *ōkizu* serious injury, deep gash
塊 *taikai* great mass, hunk, chunk
嫌 *daikira(i)* abhorrence, great aversion
損 *ōzon* heavy loss
滝 *ōdaki* large waterfall
禍 *taika* great disaster
禄 *tairoku* large fief
話 *ōbanashi* indecent talk
賊 *taizoku* notorious robber
路 *ōji* highway, main street, thoroughfare
胯 *ōmatagi* large strides
鉈 *ōnata* ax
隠 *taiin* great hermit
数 *taisū* great number; round numbers
盞 *taisan* a large cup
節 *taisetsu* great principle; higher law
蒜 *ninniku* garlic
零 *ōkoboshi* loud complaining

意 *taii* gist, outline, summary
勢 *taizei, ōzei* crowd, multitude. *taisei* general trend, current thought
愚 *taigu* a great fool
禁 *taikin* strict prohibition
農 *dainō* large-scale farming; wealthy farmer
憎正 *daisōjō* high priest of a Buddhist sect
椿事 *daichinji* tragic or disastrous accident
楓子油 *taifūshiyu* chaulmoogra oil
慈大悲 *daiji-daihi* great mercy and compassion
預言者 *Daiyogensha* the Major Prophets
殿 *ōtono, ōdono* (polite) palace; daimyo
殿様 *ōtonosama* senior feudal lord
福 *daifuku* great fortune, good luck
福帳 *daifukuchō* old-fashioned account book
腿 *daitai* thigh, femur
腿部 *daitaibu* thigh
腸 *daichō* colon, large intestine
腸炎 *daichōen* colitis
群 *taigun* large crowd, large herd, large flock, large school (of fish)
群衆 *daigunshū* a great multitude
罪 *daizai* terrible crime, grave sin
罪人 *daizainin* desperate criminal
聖 *taisei* a great sage
聖堂 *daiseidō* cathedral
業 *taigyo* great undertaking, noble work, great achievement
業物 *ōwazamono* a sharp sword
戦 *taisen* great war, world war
戦車 *daisensha* super tank
戦前 *taisenzen, taisemmae* before the great war
義 *taigi* law of justice; moral obligation; righteousness; loyalty and patriotism; a great cause
義名分 *taigi-meibun* true sovereign-subject relations; justice
義明文 *taigi-meibun* true sovereign-subject relations; justice
鼓 *taiko, ōtsuzumi* large drum
鼓判 *taikoban* oversized personal seal
鼓持 *taikomo(chi)* male restaurant entertainer; flatterer
鼓腹 *taikobara* fat stomach
鼓橋 *taikobashi* arched bridge
14 層 *taisō* very, very much. *taisō na* a great deal, plenty; exaggerated, extravagant
閤 *taikō* father of the *kampaku* (ancient chief advisor to the emperor)
関 *ōzeki* champion sumo wrestler
徳 *daitoku* virtuous priest; priest; man of wealth
摑 *ōzukami* big handful; the whole (of a problem), outline; summary
概 *taigai* in general; mostly, principally, almost; probably; about, roughly.
taigai ni moderately, reasonably
様 *ōyō na* easygoing, generous; haughty
獄 *taigoku, daigoku* roundup, wholesale arrest
綱 *ōzuna* hawser, cable. *taikō* general rules, fundamental principles; outline, general features
豪 *daigō* great man; rich man
暮 *ōgu(re)* end of the year
雑把 *ōzappa* rough (estimate); loose (talk); generous
熊星 *Daiyūsei* the Big Dipper, Ursa Major
静脈 *daijōmyaku* the main vein, vena 「cava
演習 *daienshū* grand maneuvers
綬章 *daijushō* grand cordon
嘗祭 *Daijōsai* the Great Thanksgiving Festival following the enthronement ceremony
監督 *daikantoku* archbishop, primate
歌劇 *daikageki* grand opera
漁 *tairyō, dairyō* large catch
漁旗 *tairyōki* flag signalling a big catch of fish
蔵 *ōkura* big storehouse
蔵大臣 *Ōkura Daijin* Finance Minister
蔵省 *Ōkurashō* Finance Ministry
蔵経 *Daizōkyō* complete Buddhist scriptures
15 廟 *taibyō* imperial mausoleum; Ise Shrines
慶 *taikei* great happiness
儀 *taigi* national ceremony. *taigi na* laborious; troublesome; wearisome; languid
嘘 *ōuso* big lie
権 *taiken* supreme power, sovereignty
潮 *ōshio* spring tide, flood tide
編 *taihen* a masterpiece, a great work
慾 *daiyoku, taiyoku* greed, covetousness; greedy person; great desire

賢 *taiken* sage, man of great wisdom
磐石 *daibanjaku* large stone, huge crag
熱熱 *ōatsuatsu* keenly enthusiastic; infatuated with
震 *taishin* big earthquake
震災 *daishinsai* a great earthquake; the 1923 Tokyo earthquake
器 *taiki* large receptacle; great genius
器晩成 *taikibansei* Great talents mature late.
[16] 儒 *daiju, taiju* great scholar; great Confucian scholar
橋 *ōhashi* large bridge
樹 *taiju* large tree
積 *ōzu(mori)* rough estimate
頭 *ōatama* large head; leader, boss
錐 *ōgiri* auger
鮃 *ohyō* northern halibut
憲章 *Daikenshō* Magna Carta, Great Charter
鋸 *ōnokogiri, oga* felling saw, pit saw
鋸屑 *ogakuzu* sawdust
[17] 闇 *ōyami* wholesale blackmarketing
鼾 *ōibiki* loud snoring
霜 *ōshimo* heavy frost
檀那 *ōdanna* proprietor, man of the house
檣 *taishō* mainmast
檣帆 *taishōhan* mainsail
[18] 儲 *ōmōke* large profit
鎌 *ōgama* scythe
韓民国 *Daikamminkoku, Taikamminkoku* Republic of Korea
騒 *ōsawa(gi)* clamor, uproar, tumult
観 *taikan* general view, general survey; philosophical view
難 *tainan, dainan* great disaster, great misfortune, dire distress
顔 *ōki (na) kao* arrogant countenance
繭 *ōmayu* large cocoon
藩 *taihan* clan of the first degree
[19] 願 *daigan, taigan* ambition, aspiration; earnest prayer; the heart's desire
鯛 *ōdai* large seabream
蟻 *ōari* army ant
蟻喰 *ōarikui* ant bear, great anteater
[20] 艦 *taikan* big warship

1

央 1134 J546f M5836 KAI. KETSU decide; divide; discriminate; archery glove.

夭 1135 J5470 M5838 YŌ early death; calamity.
[6] 死 *yōshi* premature death
[7] 折 *yōsetsu* premature death
[10] 逝 *yōsei* premature death

A **夫** 1136 J4957 M5835 FŪ, FU husband; man. *otto, tsuma* husband, spouse. *se* a woman's familiar call for her husband or elder brother. *so(re)* that.
[2] 人 *fujin* wife, married lady, Mrs.
[4] 夫 *soresore, sorezore* each, severally, respectively
[7] 役 *buyaku, bueki* forced labor; exacted service
君 *fukun, se(no)kimi* one's husband (honorific)
[8] 妻 *fusai* husband and wife; Mr. and Mrs.
[11] 婦 *fūfu, meoto, myōto* husband and wife; couple; pair
婦生活 *fūfu seikatsu* married life
婦仲 *fūfunaka* conjugal relations, conjugal affection
婦共稼 *fūfu-tomokasegi* dual income, husband and wife both working
婦別 *fūfu waka(re)* divorce, separation
婦連 *myōtozu(re)* husband and wife traveling together
婦約束 *fūfu yakusoku* engagement, betrothal, marriage contract
婦喧嘩 *fūfugenka* matrimonial quarrel
[15] 権 *fuken* husband's marital rights

A **太** 1137 J4240 M5834 TAI. TA. *futo(ru)* get fat, gain, fill out. *futo(rasu), futo(raseru)* fatten, feed up; enrich. *futo(i)* big, thick, burly, fat; deep, sonorous (voice); shameless, audacious, insolent. *futo-* big, fat, noble. *hanaha(da)* extreme, excessive, intense severe, serious, terrible, tremendous, heavy (damage).
[2] 刀 *tachi* long sword
刀打 *tachiu(chi)* crossing swords; opposition, contention
刀先 *tachisaki* sword tip; force of the tongue
刀取 *tachito(ri)* harakiri assistant; head cutter
刀音 *tachioto* clash of swords
刀風 *tachikaze* sword swish; brave fight
刀持 *tachimo(chi)* swordbearer
刀捌 *tachisabaki* wielding the sword

刀筋 *tachisuji* swordsmanship
刀影 *tachikage* sword flash
刀懸 *tachikake* sword rack
3 子 *taishi* crown prince; prince
山 *taisan* large mountain
4 夫 *tayū, taifu* chief actor in a Noh play; entertainer; courtesan; kabuki female-role actor; main actor
公 *taikō* grand duke, prince
公望 *taikōbō* sports fisherman
5 古 *taiko* ancient times
白 *taihaku* refined sugar; thick silk thread; a sweet potato; Venus
白星 *yūzutsu, taihakusei* evening star; Venus
平 *taihei* peace, tranquility
平洋 *Taiheiyō* Pacific Ocean
平洋戦争 *Taiheiyō Sensō* the Pacific War
平楽 *taiheiraku* irresponsible talk
6 糸 *futoito* coarse thread, low-count yarn
后 *taikō* empress dowager, queen dowager
守 *taishu* governor, viceroy, governor-general
字 *futoji* bold-faced type
早計 *taisōkei* making mistakes by hurrying too much
西洋 *Taiseiyō* Atlantic Ocean
7 初 *taisho* the beginning of the world
牢 *tairō* emperor's sacrifice to the gods; splendid feast; Edo jail
8 物 *futomono* dry goods, piece goods
股 *futomomo* thigh
宗 *taisō* dynasty, founder, progenitor, imperial ancestor; origin (of all things)
9 祖 *taiso* founder, progenitor, first emperor (of a dynasty)
巻 *futoma(ki)* thick sushi roll; thick cigarette
神宮 *Daijingū* Ise Shrine
皇太后 *taikō taikō* the empress dowager
10 書 *futoga(ki)* bold stroke
宰府 *Dazaifu* (ancient) Kyūshū government headquarters
陰 *taiin* moon
陰暦 *taiinreki* lunar calendar
11 虚 *taikyo* the sky; the origin of the universe
脛 *futohagi* calf of the leg
陽 *taiyō* sun
陽日 *taiyōjitsu* solar day
陽月 *taiyōgetsu* solar month
陽灯 *taiyōtō* artificial sunlight, sun lamp
陽年 *taiyōnen* solar year
陽系 *taiyōkei* solar system
陽神 *taiyōshin* sun god
陽神経叢 *taiyō shinkeisō* solar plexus
陽神話 *taiyō shinwa* sun myths
陽時 *taiyōji* solar time
陽崇拝 *taiyō sūhai* sun worship
陽黒点 *taiyō kokuten* sunspot
陽暦 *taiyōreki* solar calendar, Julian calendar
陽熱 *taiyōnetsu* solar heat
12 傅 *taifu* tutor to the imperial family
軸 *futojiku* thick-bodied (pen)
筋 *futosuji* thick line, bar
13 腹 *futo(p)para no* generous, magnanimous
鼓 *taiko* a big drum; professional jester; flatterer; big obi bow
鼓判 *taikoban* large seal
鼓形 *taikokei* barrel shape
鼓持 *taikomo(chi)* professional jester; flatterer
鼓結 *taikomusu(bi)* big obi bow
鼓腹 *taikobara* paunch, potbelly, big with child
鼓橋 *taikobashi* arched bridge
14 閤 *taikō* the father of an imperial adviser; Toyotomi Hideyoshi
綱 *futozuna* cable, hawser
18 織 *futoo(ri)* coarse silk

A 天 1138 J4597 M5833 TEN sky, air, heavens, celestial sphere, firmament; heaven, Providence, God, Nature; destiny; weather; top; beginning. *ame* sky, heaven. *ama-* heavenly. *amatsu-* heavenly, imperial.

2 人 *tenjin* nature and man; God and man; celestial being. *tennin* heavenly being; celestial maiden
3 女 *tennyo* heavenly maiden; goddess
子 *tenshi* son of Heaven; the (Chinese) emperor
川 *Ama(no)gawa* Milky Way
工 *tenkō* a work of nature
与 *ten'yo* heaven's gift, a godsend
才 *tensai* genius, prodigy; natural gift
才児 *tensaiji* child prodigy
上 *tenjō* the heavens
下 *amakuda(ri)* descent from heaven;

appointment through influence; top-down decision making. *amakuda(ru)* descend from heaven. *tenka, tenga, ame(ga)shita, ame(no)shita* the whole country; the public, the world; the ruling power; having one's own way; the shogun

下一 *tenkaichi* matchless; best on earth

下一品 *tenka ippin* best article under heaven

下分目 *tenkawa(ke)me* fateful, decisive (war)

下晴 *tenka ha(rete)* right and proper, legal

下無双 *tenkamusō* peerless, unequaled

下無比 *tenkamuhi* peerless, unequaled

4 心 *tenshin* zenith; divine will, providence

火 *tempi* oven. *tenka* fire caused by lightning

父 *Tempu* Heavenly Father

牛 *kamikirimushi, tengyū* long-horned beetle

辺 *teppen* top, summit, apex, pate. *tempen ni* high up in the sky

引 *tembi(ki)* lending money and taking out the interest in advance; payroll deduction

分 *tembun* one's nature, talents, sphere of activity, mission, destiny

手子舞 *tentekomai* whirl of business; have an extremely busy time

水 *tensui* rain water

水桶 *tensui oke* rain barrel

王山 *Tennōzan* Tennozan Hill; strategic point

王星 *Tennōsei, Ten'ōsei* Uranus

文 *temmon* astronomy

文台 *temmondai* astronomical observatory

文学 *temmongaku* astronomy

文学者 *temmongakusha* astronomer

日 *tenjitsu* the sun. *tempi* sun, sunlight

日法 *tempihō* solar-evaporation process (in salt making)

日塩 *tenjitsuen, tempijio* sun-dried salt

日嗣 *ama(tsu)hitsugi* imperial throne; imperial succession (accession)

井 *tenjō* ceiling

井川 *tenjōgawa* a river raised above the surrounding land

井灯 *tenjōtō* ceiling light

井抜 *tenjōnu(ke)* unbounded, limitless; free and indiscreet

井板 *tenjō ita* ceiling boards

井知 *tenjōshirazu* skyrocketing (prices)

井桟敷 *tenjō sajiki* gallery

井裏 *tenjō ura* above the ceiling

5 生 *tensei* nature, disposition; naturally coming into being

外 *tengai* beyond the heavens; farthest regions

平 *Tempyō* era name during Emperor Shōmu's reign (8th c.)

台 *Tendai* Buddhist sect introduced into Japan in the eighth century

丼 *tendon* bowl of rice topped with tempura

瓜粉 *tenkafun* baby powder made from the tuber of the yellow snake gourd

主 *Tenshu* Lord of Heaven, God

主教 *Tenshukyō* Roman Catholicism

6 色 *tenshoku* weather; sky color

年 *tennen* the natural span of life

衣 *ten'i, ten'e* heavenly garment; garment of bodhisattva's statue

衣無縫 *ten'i-muhō* perfect beauty with no trace of artifice; artless and endearing (person)

成 *tensei* nature; product of nature. *tensei no* natural, born (musician)

成美 *tensei (no) bi* natural beauty

刑 *tenkei* divine punishment

刑病 *tenkeibyō* leprosy

守 *tenshu* castle tower

守教 *Tenshukyō* Roman Catholicism

守閣 *tenshukaku* castle tower

地 *tenchi, amatsuchi* heaven and earth, the universe, nature; top and bottom; world, realm, sphere

地人 *tenchijin* heaven, earth, and man; all things in the universe; three-part hierarchical categorization

地万物 *tenchi-bambutsu* the whole creation, everything in heaven and earth

地神命 *tenchi shimmei* the heavenly and earthly gods

地無用 *tenchimuyō* this side up; Do not turn over.

地創造 *Tenchi Sōzō* the Creation

地開闢 *tenchi kaibyaku* creation of heaven and earth

気 *tenki* weather; the elements; fine weather. *(o)tenki* weather; the elements; fine weather; temper, mood

気予報 *tenki yohō* weather forecast
気図 *tenkizu* weather map
気具合 *tenki guai* weather conditions
気屋 *tenkiya* moody person
気相談所 *tenki sōdanjo* weather bureau
気都合 *tenki tsugō* weather conditions
気運 *tenkiun* one's luck with the weather
気模様 *tenki moyō* weather conditions
7 位 *ten'i* imperial throne
佑 *ten'yū* divine aid
助 *tenjo* divine aid
兵 *Tempei* the Imperial Army, heaven-sent army
災 *tensai* natural calamity
来 *tenrai no* heavenly, divine, inspired, heaven-sent
寿 *tenju* natural life span
邪鬼 *amanojaku* a perverse person; a devil in folklore; the devil beneath temple guardian deities' statues
花 *tenka* snow. *tenge, tenke* exquisite heavenly flowers; paper flowers scattered before the Buddha's image
花粉 *tenkafun* baby powder made from the tuber of the yellow snake gourd
休 *tentai* celestial bodies
体力学 *tentai rikigaku* celestial mechanics
体分光術 *tentai bunkōjutsu* astronomical spectroscopy
体写真術 *tentai shashinjutsu* astrophotography
体図 *tentaizu* star map
体学 *tentaigaku* uranography
体物理学 *tentai butsurigaku* astrophysics
体崇拝 *tentai sūhai* star worship, astrolatry
8 金 *tenkin* gilt-top (book)
国 *tengoku* Kingdom of Heaven, paradise, heaven
府 *tempu* nature's storehouse; fertile land; deep scholarship; imperial storehouse; a part of timepiece mechanism
底 *tentei* nadir
使 *tenshi, ten (no) tsuka(i)* angel; imperial messenger
性 *tensei* nature; innate disposition. *tensei no* natural, born (musician)
明 *temmei* dawn, daybreak
杯 *tempai* cup of wine bestowed by the emperor
泣 *tenkyū* rain from a cloudless sky
河 *Ama(no)gawa, Tenga* the Milky Way
命 *temmei* God's will, Heaven's decree; destiny, karma; one's life
岩戸 *Ama (no) Iwato* Gate of the Celestial Rock
長地久 *tenchō-chikyū* lasting forever as do heaven and earth
長節 *Tenchōsetsu* Emperor's Birthday (term used 1868-1945)
空 *tenkū* sky, air, firmament, space
空海濶 *tenkū-kaikatsu* magnanimous and broad-minded as the wide sky and the sea
狗 *tengu* long-nosed goblin, boaster
狗風 *tengu kaze* sudden gust
狗話 *tengubanashi* boastful story
竺 *Tenjiku* (old term for) India
竺牡丹 *tenjiku botan* dahlia
竺浪人 *tenjiku rōnin* wandering lordless samurai
竺鼠 *tenjiku nezumi* guinea pig
9 威 *ten'i* imperial authority, imperial majesty
柱 *tenchū* pillars supporting heaven; morals supporting society
祖 *Tenso* the ancestral Sun Goddess
則 *tensoku* natural law, rule of heaven
降 *amakuda(ru)* descend from heaven. *amakuda(ri)* descent from heaven; top-down decision making; appointment through influence
盃 *tempai* cup of wine bestowed by the emperor
帝 *Tentei* Lord, God, Creator, Heavenly King
草 *tengusa* agar-agar
為 *ten'i* providential, natural
変 *tempen* striking phenomena in heaven; natural calamity
変地異 *tempen-chii* striking phenomena in heaven and earth; natural disaster
神 *tenjin* heavenly gods; Michizane's deified spirit. *tenshin, amatsukami* heavenly gods
神地祇 *tenjin-chigi* gods of heaven and earth
神髭 *tenjin hige* drooping mustache
津乙女 *amatsuotome* celestial maiden

津日嗣 *amatsuhitsugi* imperial throne; imperial succession (accession)
津神 *amatsukami* heavenly gods
津御子 *amatsumiko* emperor
津御祖 *amatsumioya* imperial ancestor
皇 *Tennō, Sumeragi, Sumerogi, Sumeramikoto* Emperor of Japan
皇杯 *Tennōhai* Emperor's Trophy
皇制 *Tennōsei* Emperor system
皇陛下 *Tennō Heika* His Majesty the Emperor
皇家 *Tennōke* the Imperial Family
皇崇拝 *tennō sūhai* emperor worship
皇旗 *Tennōki* Imperial Standard
皇誕生日 *Tennō Tanjōbi* Emperor's Birthday
10 原 *ama(no)hara* the sky, the heavens
候 *tenkō* weather
孫 *tenson* descendant of the heavenly gods; grandson of the Sun Goddess
祐 *ten'yū* divine gracc, providential help
険 *tenken* natural stronghold; rugged place
恵 *tenkei* heaven's blessings
恩 *ten'on* blessings of heaven; blessing of nature; favor of the emperor; divination's luckiest day
宮図 *tenkyūzu* horoscope
狼星 *Tenrōsei* the Dog Star, Sirius
馬 *temba* flying horse, Pegasus; a fine steed
馬空行 *tembakū o i(ku)* advance unobstructed; bold and free flight of imagination
秤 *tembin* (balance) scales, steelyard; shoulder carrying pole
秤棒 *tembimbō* shoulder carrying pole
蚕 *tensan* wild silkworm
蚕糸 *tegusu* silkworm gut. *tensanshi* silk from wild silkworm; silkworm gut
真 *tenshin* natural and unaffected
真爛漫 *tenshin-ramman* naivete, guilelessness, innocence
11 運 *ten'un* destiny, will of Heaven, luck; movement of celestial bodies
授 *tenju* natural gifts; endowed by heaven
涯 *tengai* horizon, skyline; remote region; the whole wide world
理 *tenri* rule of heaven, natural laws
堂 *tendō* heaven, paradise, palace of heaven
窓 *temmado* skylight. *tensō* skylight; head
啓 *tenkei* divine revelation
動説 *tendōsetsu* Ptolemaic theory
産 *tensan* natural products
産物 *tensambutsu* natural products
球 *tenkyū* celestial sphere
球図 *tenkyūzu* celestial map
球儀 *tenkyūgi* celestial globe
眼 *tengan* clairvoyant eyes; rolling back the eyes in convulsions. *tengen* clairvoyant eyes
眼通 *tengantsū, tengentsū* clairvoyance
眼鏡 *tengankyō* physiognomist's magnifying glass; old term for telescope
頂 *tenchō* zenith
頂点 *tenchōten* zenith
頂儀 *tenchōgi* zenith telescope
道 *tentō* Providence, heaven; the sun. *tendō* the way of heaven; Providence; orbits of celestial bodies
道干 *tentōbo(shi) no* sun-dried
道虫 *tentōmushi* ladybug
道乾 *tentōboshi no* sun-dried
道様 *tentōsama* the sun
12 晴 *appa(re)* splendid, praiseworthy; well done
極 *tenkyoku* celestial poles; the North Star
測 *tensoku* astronomical observation; observing heavenly bodies in celestial navigation
朝 *tenchō* imperial court (polite); emperor
童 *tendō* cherub; gods disguised as children; children parading as cherubs
雲 *amagumo* clouds in the sky
象 *tenshō* astronomical phenomenon; weather
象儀 *tenshōgi* planetarium
然 *tennen* nature; spontaneity. *tennen ni* naturally, spontaneously
然色 *tennenshoku* natural color; technicolor
然色写真 *tennenshoku shashin* color photo
然記念物 *tennen kinembutsu* natural monument
然港 *tennenkō* natural harbor
然痘 *tennentō* smallpox
然硝子 *tennen garasu* natural glass
然資源 *tennen shigen* natural resources

13 漢 *Tenkan* the Milky Way
福 *tempuku* heavenly blessing
誅 *tenchū* Heaven's punishment; punishing (someone) in Heaven's name
際 *tensai* horizon
稟 *tempin* natural talents
蓋 *tengai* canopy; dome; priestly minstrel's reed hood
雷 *tenrai* thunder; artificial thunder in the theater
意 *ten'i* divine will, providence; natural laws; emperor's will
業 *tengyō* work of Heaven; emperor's work
路歴程 *Tenro Rekitei* Pilgrim's Progress
照大神 *Amaterasu Ōmikami* the Sun Goddess
照皇大神 *Tenshō Kōdaijin* the Sun Goddess
資 *tenshi* nature; natural talents
資英邁 *tenshi-eimai* highly gifted
幕 *temmaku* curtain hung from the ceiling; tent, pavilion; (ship's) awning
幕造 *temmakuzuku(ri)* tentmaker
幕製造人 *temmaku seizōnin* tentmaker
14 聞 *tembun* emperor's knowledge
網 *temmō* heaven's net, heaven's justice
領 *tenryō* imperial fief; shogunate control
爾遠波 *te-ni-o-ha* the particles
罰 *tembatsu* divine wrath, divine punishment
罰覿面 *tembatsu-tekimen* the swiftness of divine punishment
15 摩 *ten (o) ma(suru)* (a building) soars high
賜 *tenshi* heavenly gift, imperial gift
敵 *tenteki* natural enemy
質 *tenshitsu* innate disposition; natural talents
麩羅 *tempura* (Japanese) deep-fat fried food; plating; sham
賦 *tempu* innate quality, endowment
賦人権 *tempu jinken* natural rights of man
16 壌 *tenjō* heaven and earth
機 *tenki* nature's secret, profound secret; innate qualities; emperor's health
覧 *tenran* imperial inspection
17 聴 *tenchō* emperor's knowledge

爵 *tenshaku* natural nobility, nobility of character
18 職 *tenshoku* one's divinely appointed work in life; emperor's work of ruling; vocation, calling
顔 *tengan* emperor's countenance
鵞絨 *birōdo* velvet
19 警 *tenkei* heaven-sent warning
20 譴 *tenken* divine punishment
21 魔 *temma* demon, evil spirit
22 鷚 *hibari, tenryū* skylark
籟 *tenrai* sound of the wind; beautiful poetry

2

夲 1139 / J5471 / M5845 Tō advance rapidly. Also used as variant of 本 2536.

A 央 1140 / J317b / M5840 Ō middle.

A 失 1141 / J3c3a / M5844 Shitsu error; fault; disadvantage; loss; demerit. *na(kunaru)* be lost; run short, be used up; disappear; die. *na(ku) nasu, na(ku) suru, na(kusu) vt* lose; run out of; remove; absorb. *shis(suru)* lose, miss; forget; be excessive. *u(seru)* disappear, vanish. *ushina(u)* lose, miss (a chance).
4 心 *shisshin* trance, stupefaction, faint
火 *shikka* accidental fire
5 礼 *shitsurei* discourtesy, impoliteness, rudeness
去 *u(se)-sa(ru)* disappear, be gone
6 血 *shikketsu* loss of blood
地 *shitchi* lost territory
当 *shittō* injustice; impropriety; unreasonableness
考 *shikkō* misunderstanding
名 *shitsumei* name unknown
名氏 *shitsumeishi* unknown person
7 言 *shitsugen* improper language, a slip
体 *shittai* mismanagement, fault, error, failure; disgrace, discredit
8 物 *u(se)mono* lost article
効 *shikkō* lapse, abatement, invalidation
命 *shitsumei* losing one's life, dying
念 *shitsunen* lapse of memory, forgetting; oblivion
明 *shitsumei* loss of eyesight
明者 *shitsumeisha* blind person
9 速 *shissoku* a stall (in flying)

透 *shittō suru* devitrify
神 *shisshin* trance, stupefaction, faint
陥 *shikkan* surrender, fall
政 *shissei* misgovernment
点 *shitten* a run charged to the pitcher
10 恋 *shitsuren* unrequited love
笑 *shisshō* spontaneous laughter
格 *shikkaku* disqualification, elimination; incapacity (legal)
格者 *shikkakusha* disqualified person
11 脚 *shikkyaku suru* lose one's standing, fall, be overthrown, stumble
敗 *shippai* failure, mistake, blunder
望 *shitsubō* disappointment, despair
12 敬 *shikkei* rudeness, impoliteness, disrespect. *shikkei suru* say goodbye; act impolitely; steal
策 *shissaku* blunder, slip, error
着 *shitchaku* mistake, negligence
費 *shippi* expenses
13 跡 *shisseki* abscondence, disappearance
意 *shitsui* despair, disappointment; adversity
禁 *shikkin* incontinence (of urine or feces)
業 *shitsugyō* unemployment
業手当 *shitsugyō teate* unemployment allowance
業者 *shitsugyōsha* unemployed person
業保険 *shitsugyō hoken* unemployment insurance
14 墜 *shittsui suru* lose, forfeit, fall, sink (in a person's estimation)
態 *shittai* mismanagement, fault, error, failure; disgrace, discredit
語 *shitsugo* forgetting the words, inability to pronounce a word correctly
語症 *shitsugoshō* loss of speech; agnosia
15 権 *shikken* loss of rights, disenfranchisement
調 *shitchō* lack of harmony
踪 *shissō* abscondence, disappearance
16 錯 *shissaku* blunder, slip, error
18 職 *shisshoku* unemployment
職者 *shisshokusha* unemployed person

3

夸 1142 / J5472 / M5854 KA. KE. KO be extravagant; treat. *hoko(ru)* boast; exaggerate.

夷 1143 / J3050 / M5852 I barbarian. *ebisu* barbarian, savage; Ainu.
7 狄 *iteki* barbarians, aliens
8 国 *ikoku* land of the barbarians
9 俗 *izoku* customs of the barbarians

4

夾 1144 / J5473 / M5867 KYŌ insert between.
14 雑物 *kyōzatsubutsu* foreign element, impurity, admixture

5

臭 1145 / J-X / M5909 Nonstandard for 点 3412.

奄 1146 / J3162 / M5881 EN cover
8 奄 *en'en* breath; breathing

奈 1147 / J4660 / M5893 **柰** 2598 / J-X / M14659 NA What?
7 何 *ikan* what, how
良朝 *Narachō* Nara period (710–794)
良漬 *narazuke* pickles seasoned in saké lees
12 落 *naraku* hell, hades; eternity; theater basement

B **奔** 1148 / J4b5b / M-X **奔** 1151 / J-X / M5921 HON *hashi(ru)* run.
7 走 *honsō* bustle; activity, good offices
8 放 *hompō na* wild, incorrigible, extravagant
命 *hommei* bustle; activity, good offices
10 馬 *homba* galloping horse; runaway horse
逸 *hon'itsu* run away, scamper off
流 *honryū* torrent, rapids
20 騰 *hontō* price jump, boom

B **奉** 1149 / J4a74 / M5894 HŌ. BU. *hō(zuru)* present, dedicate; obey, follow, believe in, serve. *matsu(ru), tatematsu(ru)* offer, present; revere; do respectfully.
4 公 *hōkō* public service; apprenticeship
公人 *hōkōnin* servant, employee
公口 *hōkōguchi* place of employment
公先 *hōkōsaki* place of employment
5 加 *hōga* donation

加帳 *hōgachō* subscription list
仕 *hōshi* service, serving
仕者 *hōshisha* servant (of the people)
6 行 *bugyō* shogunate administrator
灯 *hōtō* votive lantern
安 *hōan suru* enshrine
迎 *hōgei* welcome
迎門 *hōgeimon* welcome arch
7 伺 *hōshi suru* inquire about (one's health)
体 *hōtai suru* carry out the will of one's lord
呈 *hōtei* dedication, presentation
8 送 *hoso suru* see an emperor off
拝 *hōhai* worship
祀 *hōshi suru* enshrine
9 持 *hōji* bear, present, hold up (the emperor's picture)
祝 *hōshuku* celebration
10 書 *hōsho* high-quality paper
納 *hōnō* dedication, offering, oblation
納物 *hōnōbutsu* votive offering
納額 *hōnōgaku* votive tablet
11 唱 *hōshō* singing
12 答 *hōtō* reply to the throne
賀 *hōga* respectful congratulations
賀帳 *hōgachō* subscription list
13 献 *hōken suru* offer (to a shrine)
献式 *hōkenshiki* dedicatory ceremony
献物 *hōkenbutsu* votive offering
献頌 *hōkenshō* offertory; offertory music
14 読 *hōdoku* respectful reading
15 還 *hōkan suru* restore to the emperor
弊 *hōhei* offering
17 戴 *hōtai suru* have (a prince for a president); be the recipient of (an imperial favor); reverently accept
18 職 *hōshoku suru* be in the service of

B **奇** 1150 / J3471 / M5892 KI strangeness, curiosity, eccentricity. *kusu(shiki), ku(shiki)* strange, mysterious. *kusu(shiku) mo, ku(shiku) mo* strangely, mysteriously, ironically. *ki (to) suru* regard as wonderful.

2 人 *kijin* eccentric person
3 才 *kisai* genius, wizard, prodigy
5 功 *kikō* signal success; remarkable effect
6 行 *kikō* eccentric conduct
7 言 *kigen* paradox
妙 *kimyō na* strange, queer, wonderful
抜 *kibatsu na* novel, original, striking, extraordinary, strange
形 *kikei* deformity, abnormality
兵 *kihei* storm troopers, flying corps, commandos
声 *kisei* strange voice, squeaky voice
8 物 *kibutsu, kimotsu* curio; curiosity; eccentric person
知 *kichi* genius
効 *kikō* signal success; remarkable effect
岩 *kigan* fantastic crag
怪 *kikai na, ki(k)kai na* strange, wonderful; weird; outrageous, scandalous, insolent
怪千万 *kikai-semban* very strange
奇 *kiki* something very strange
奇妙妙 *kiki-myōmyō* something very strange
奇怪怪 *kiki-kaikai* something very strange
9 計 *kikei* ingenuity, clever plan
10 骨 *kikotsu na* eccentric; outstanding (person)
病 *kibyō* strange disease
特 *kitoku* miracle. *kitoku na, kidoku na* commendable; charitable
書 *kisho* strange book
11 遇 *kigū* chance meeting
道 *kidō* strange plan; unusual plan
偶 *kigū* odd and even numbers
異 *kii na* odd, strange, wonderful
習 *kishū* strange custom
貨 *kika* curiosity; good opportunity (to make a profit)
術 *kijutsu* jugglery; magic
術師 *kijutsushi* juggler; magician
12 傑 *kiketsu* remarkable man
絶 *kizetsu* very strange
勝 *kishō* surprise victory; successful execution; beauty spot
童 *kidō* prodigy; remarkable child
智 *kichi* genius
策 *kisaku* clever plan
策縦横 *kisaku-jūō* clever planning
13 瑞 *kizui* good omen
禍 *kika* accident, disaster, misfortune
話 *kiwa* strange talk
跡 *kiseki* miracle, wonder, mystery
数 *kisū* odd number; masculine number
想 *kisō* original idea, strange notion
想天外 *kisō-tengai* original idea
14 聞 *kibun* strange news, revelation; anecdote

算 *kisan* strange resources; expedient
態 *kitai* queer, strange, fantastic
15 縁 *kien* irony of fate, strange coincidence
談 *kidan* strange story, adventure story
論 *kiron* strange argument, different idea
16 謀 *kibō* clever stratagem
獣 *kijū* strange animal
薬 *kiyaku* very effective medicine
17 矯 *kikyō* eccentric conduct
18 癖 *kiheki* eccentric habit
観 *kikan* strange sight
蹟 *kiseki* miracle, wonder, mystery
蹟的 *kisekiteki* miraculous
19 警 *kikei na* witty, original, smart
麗 *kirei na* beautiful, lively; clean, neat. *kirei ni* completely, beautifully
麗好 *kireizu(ki)* love of cleanliness
麗所 *kireidokoro* beautiful women; geisha
麗事 *kireigoto* fine skill; simplicity
22 襲 *kishū* surprise attack
襲攻撃 *kishū kōgeki* surprise attack
襲部隊 *kishū butai* shock troops
襲戦 *kishūsen* surprise attack; guerrilla warfare

6

奔 1151 / J-X / M5921 See 奔 1148.

奎 1152 / J5477 / M5911 KEI. KI star, god of literature. *mata* crotch.

奐 1153 / J5476 / M5916 KAN exchange; be large. *saka(n)* be plentiful, be abundant. *aki(raka)* clear; apparent.

奕 1154 / J5475 / M5922 EKI large.
5 世 *ekisei* many generations

B **契** 1155 / J3740 / M5917 KEI *chigi(ru)* pledge, vow, swear, promise.
6 印 *keiin* a seal over the edges of two sheets
合 *keigō* coincidence, agreement
9 約 *keiyaku* contract, agreement, covenant, testament
約者 *keiyakusha* contracting parties
約書 *keiyakusho* contract
約箱 *Keiyaku (no) Hako* Ark of the Covenant
16 機 *keiki* opportunity, chance

A **奏** 1156 / J4155 / M5915 SŌ. *kanade(ru)* play (an instrument). *sō(suru)* play on; speak to a ruler; report to (the emperor); complete.
3 上 *sōjō* report to the emperor
5 功 *sōkō* fruition, success, efficacy
6 任 *sōnin* emperor-approved appointment
任官 *sōninkan* official whose appointment is emperor-approved
8 法 *sōhō* playing (an instrument); touch
効 *sōkō* fruition, success, efficacy
12 弾 *sōdan* reporting (a miscreant official) to the emperor
13 楽 *sōgaku* instrumental music
楽者 *sōgakusha* instrumentalist
楽席 *sōgakuseki* orchestra seats
楽堂 *sōgakudō* concert hall
14 聞 *sōmon* report to the emperor
鳴曲 *sōmeikyoku* sonata (in music)
15 請 *sōsei* petitioning the emperor
16 覧 *sōran* submitting (a document) to the emperor; imperial inspection

7

奐 1157 / J-X / M45958 Nonstandard for 魚 6845.

奙 1158 / J-X / M5931 See 奙 3745.

奘 1159 / J5479 / M5928 SŌ. JŌ. ZŌ large; plentiful, abundant; healthy.

奚 1160 / J5478 / M5930 KEI. GEI maidservant, female slave. *nan(zo)* something; anything; why, how, what. *izu(re)* where, which, who.

套 1161 / J4565 / M5926 TŌ hackneyed.

8

器 1162 / J-X / M-X Nonstandard for 器 898.

9

奠 1163 J547b M5960 TEN decision.
10 都 *tento suru* transfer the capital

奢 1164 J547a M5964 SHA. *ogo(ru)* be extravagant; treat. *ogo(ri)* luxury, extravagance; (my) treat.
8 侈 *shashi* luxury, extravagance
10 恣 *shashi* pride and self-will
13 肆 *shashi* pride and self-will

B 奧 1165 J317c M5981 奥 1166 J547c M5985 Ō. OKU heart, interior. *oku(maru)* lie deep in, extend far back. *oku(matte)* secluded, innermost.
3 山 *okuyama* remote mountain, mountain recesses
4 手 *okute* late crops. *oku(no)te* left hand; upper hand; secret skills; secret, mystery; last resort, trump card
方 *okugata* lady, nobleman's wife
5 付 *okuzuke* colophon
6 行 *okuyuki* depth, length, in depth
印 *okuin* official seal
向 *okumu(ki)* inner part of the house
地 *okuchi, ōchi* interior, backwoods, hinterland
州 *ōshū* interior province; the interior; northern part of Japan
7 床 *okuyuka(shii)* refined, graceful, modest
妙 *ōmyō* secret
8 底 *okusoko, okuzoko* depth, bottom (of one's heart)
9 院 *oku(no)in* inner sanctuary
津城 *okutsuki* tomb, grave
津城所 *okutsukidokoro* tomb, grave
10 庭 *oku niwa* inner garden, back yard
書 *okugaki* postscript (to a book); verification; publication data (in a book)
座敷 *oku zashiki* inner parlor
11 深 *okubuka(i)* deep, profound
許 *okuyuru(shi)* secret; initiation; diploma
12 歯 *okuba* molars, back teeth
間 *oku(no)ma* inner room
勤 *okuzuto(me)* working as a lady's maid
御殿 *okugoten* noble's private quarters
13 義 *okugi, ōgi* mystery, secret, hidden, purpose
意 *okui* true intention
14 様 *okusama, okusan* your or his wife; married lady; madam
様孝行 *okusan kōkō* devoted to one's wife

10

奥 1166 J547c M5985 See 奧 1165.

B 奬 1167 J3e29 M5990′ 奨 1169 J547d M5997 獎 3601 J6052 M20637
SHŌ *susu(meru)* urge, encourage.
7 励 *shōrei* encouragement, promotion, exhortation; message, address
励金 *shōreikin* incentive pay, subsidy
励者 *shōreisha* promoter, supporter
8 学 *shōgaku* encouragement of learning
学金 *shōgakukin* scholarship (grant)
学資金 *shōgaku shikin* scholarship fund
14 導 *shōdō suru* encourage and lead

11

奭 1168 J-X M6000 See 傘 282.

奨 1169 J547d M5997 See 奬 1167.

奩 1170 J547e M5991 REN box; comb box; incense box; incense burner. *hako* box.

B 奪 1171 J4325 M5994 DATSU. *uba(u)* take by force, snatch away, oust, dispossess, deprive of, plunder, usurp; absorb (attention); fascinate.
5 去 *uba(i)-sa(ru)* take away
6 回 *dakkai* recovery, recapture, rescue
返 *uba(i)-kae(su)* take back, recapture
合 *uba(i)-a(u)* scramble for, struggle for
8 取 *uba(i)-to(ru), dasshu suru* plunder. *dasshu* capture, seizure, occupation
9 胎 *dattai* plagiarism
11 掠 *datsuryaku* pillage, plunder, looting
略 *datsuryaku* pillage, plunder, looting
15 還 *dakkan* recovery, recapture, rescue

A 奮 1172 J4a33 M6012 FUN. *furu(u)* be invigorated, be spirited, flourish. *furu(tte)* energetically, heartily.
[5] 立 *furu(i)-ta(tsu)* rouse oneself, be inspired. *furu(i)-ta(taseru)* stir up, arouse
迅 *funjin* dashing forward impetuously
[7] 励 *funrei* strenuous efforts, push, hustle
[9] 発 *fumpatsu* strenuous, effort, spurt
[10] 起 *furu(i)-oki(ru), funki suru* rouse oneself
進 *funshin* dashing forward impetuously
[12] 然 *funzen* resolutely, courageously
[13] 戦 *funsen* hard fighting
[15] 撃 *fungeki* fierce attack
[16] 激 *fungeki* animation, inspiration, excitement
[18] 闘 *funtō* hard struggle, desperate fight, strenuous effort

RAD. 女 38

Onna woman. At left: *onna hen.* Nickname: Woman.

A 女 1173 J3d77 M6036 JO, NYO, NYŌ woman, girl, daughter. *onna, omina* woman, female, sweetheart, girl. *onna(rashii)* womanly, ladylike; effeminate. *onna(datera) ni* unladylike. *me-* female.
[2] 人 *nyonin, jonin* woman
人禁制 *nyonin kinsei* no admittance to women
[3] 女 *meme(shii)* effeminate, unmanly
工 *jokō* woman factory worker
丈夫 *jojōfu* heroine; outstanding woman
大学 *onna daigaku* cultural books for women
三昧 *onnazammi* indulging in lewdness
子 *joshi, nyoshi* woman, female, girl. *onna (no) ko* girl; daughter; baby girl. *onago* girl, woman, maid.
子大学 *joshi daigaku* women's college
子供 *onna kodomo* a woman and her child; a nonentity; a man of straw; an encumbrance
子青年会 *joshi seinenkai* young women's association
子青年団 *joshi seinendan* young women's association
子部 *joshibu* girl's section
[4] 心 *onnagokoro* a woman's heart
手 *onnade* the cursive (*hiragana*) syllabary; a woman's handwriting; the work of women
夫 *meoto, myōto* husband and wife, pair, couple
天下 *onnadenka* a woman who rules the home
戸主 *onna koshu* female head of house
文字 *onna moji* the cursive (*hiragana*) syllabary; a woman's handwriting
王 *joō, nyoō* queen; belle; princess
王蜂 *joōbachi* queen bee
中 *jochū* servant, maid; waitress, barmaid
中入用 *jochū iriyō* servant wanted
中奉公 *jochūbōkō* domestic service
中部屋 *jochūbeya* maid's room
中難 *jochūnan* scarcity or servants
[5] 囚 *joshū* female prisoner
史 *joshi* Mrs., Miss
付 *onnatsu(ki)* a woman's countenance
犯 *nyobon* (priest's) clandestine romance
礼 *jorei* etiquette for ladies
主 *onna aruji* mistress, hostess, landlady
出入 *onnadei(ri)* troubles concerning women
正月 *Onna Shōgatsu* January 15, Ladies' New Year
芝居 *onna shibai* a play by actresses only
白波 *onna shiranami* woman robber
世帯 *onnajotai* household of women
生 *josei* schoolgirl; coed
生徒 *joseito* schoolgirl; coed
[6] 色 *joshoku* feminine charms; sensuality
気 *onnagi* a woman's heart. *onnake, onnakke* signs of a woman around
伊達 *onnadate* a woman who champions the underdog (a female Robin Hood)
任 *onnama(kase)* committing one's work to a woman
好 *onnazu(ki)* woman admirer; one admired by women; a lustful man

仮名 *onnagana* the cursive (*hiragana*) syllabary
7 医 *joi* woman doctor
戒 *jokai* (Buddhist) commandment against lewdness
体 *jotai, nyotai* a woman's body
坂 *onnazaka* the gentler of two slopes
狂 *onnaguru(i)* philandering
形 *onnagata, oyama* female impersonator
兵 *johei* woman soldier (WAC, WAVE, etc.)
系 *jokei* female line
声 *josei* female voice
旱 *onna hideri* shortage of women
児 *joji* baby girl, primary schoolgirl
8 松 *mematsu* red pine
波 *menami* receding wave, backwash
官 *jokan, nyokan* court lady, maid of honor
店員 *joten'in* saleswoman
郎 *jorō* prostitute, geisha
郎屋 *jorōya* brothel
郎買 *jorōka(i)* patronizing prostitutes
郎衆 *jorōshu* prostitute
房 *nyobō, nyōbō* court lady; wife
房役 *nyōbōyaku* righthand man
房言葉 *nyōbō kotoba* court language of the ladies
房持 *nyōbōmo(chi)* a married man
学 *jogaku* women's lessons
学生 *jogakusei* girl student
学院 *jogakuin* girls' school
学校 *jogakkō* girls' school
性 *josei* woman; womanhood; feminine gender
性化 *joseika* feminization, feminism
性的 *joseiteki* feminine, effeminate
性美 *joseibi* womanly beauty
性解放論 *josei kaihōron* feminism
9 食 *onnaku(i)* philanderer, lady-killer
持 *onnamo(chi)* for ladies
神 *megami, joshin* goddess
院 *nyōin, nyoin* a (Buddhist) nun from the Imperial Family
帝 *jotei* empress
客 *onna kyaku* female visitor
皇 *jokō* empress, queen
姿 *onna sugata* the guise of a woman; a womanish pose
10 振 *onnabu(ri)* a woman's charms, a woman's looks
訓 *jokun* women's lessons
殺 *onnagoro(shi)* the killing of a woman; a handsome man
帯 *onna obi* a woman's obi
冥利 *onna myōri* the advantage of being a woman
部屋 *onnabeya* maids' quarters, women's apartment
将 *okami, joshō* landlady, hostess (of a restaurant)
将軍 *joshōgun* an Amazon
流 *joryū* accomplished woman; fair sex; female
流文学 *joryū bungaku* feminine literature
流作家 *joryū sakka* women novelist
流歌手 *joryū kashu* woman singer
11 達 *onnatachi* women. *onnadate* woman outlaw who champions the underdog
盛 *onnazaka(ri)* the prime of womanhood
執事 *onna shitsuji* woman deaconess
道楽 *onna dōraku* sensual pleasures, debauchery
教員 *jokyōin* woman teacher
教師 *jokyōshi* woman teacher
12 傑 *joketsu* heroine; outstanding woman
婿 *josei* son-in-law
御 *nyōgo* court lady; the concubine of an emperor
湯 *onnayu* ladies' bath
装 *josō* female attire; dressing in female attire
給 *jokyū* waitress
給仕 *onna kyūji* waitress
尊 *joson* respect for women
尊男卑 *josondampi* putting women above men
13 僧 *nyosō* Buddhist nun
嫌 *onnagira(i)* woman-hater
業 *onna waza* the work of women
14 誑 *onnatarashi* philanderer, lady-killer
誡 *jokai* instructions for women
監 *jokan* female-prisoner's ward
15 権 *joken* women's rights; woman suffrage
16 親 *onna oya* mother
17 優 *joyū* actress
優劇 *joyūgeki* a play in which female parts are played by women and not men
優髷 *joyūmage* an actress's coiffure
18 難 *jonan* trouble with women

20 護島 *nyogo(ga)shima* isle of women
22 鑑 *jokan* model for women

2

B **奴** 1174 / J455b / M6039 Do manservant, slave; fellow. Nu manservant. *yakko* servant, valet, footman; clown; the fellow, the guy. *yatsu* fellow, guy. *-me* suffix indicating ridicule or despite.
5 凧 *yakkodako* kites shaped like ancient footmen
7 豆腐 *yakkodōfu* tofu cut in cubes
9 姿 *yakko sugata* disguised footman
10 原 *yatsubara* fellows, guys
11 婢 *dohi, nuhi* servant; male or female slaves
12 等 *yatsura* fellows, guys
14 僕 *nuboku* manservant; slave
様 *yakkosan* that guy
鳴 *dona(ru)* roar, shout, yell, growl
鳴込 *dona(ri)-ko(mu)* storm into
鳴立 *dona(ri)-ta(teru)* roar, rave, rage
鳴附 *dona(ri)-tsu(keru)* scold, call down
鳴散 *dona(ri)-chi(rasu)* rant right and left
15 輩 *dohai* we; servants; those fellows
16 隷 *dorei* slave, servant
隷化 *doreika* enslaving
隷所有者 *dorei shoyūsha* slaveholder
隷制 *doreisei* slavery
隷制度 *dorei seido* slavery
隷視 *doreishi suru* treat as slaves, look down on
隷略奪者 *dorei ryakudatsusha* slave raider
隷廃止主義 *dorei haishi shugi* abolitionism
隷廃止論 *dorei haishiron* abolitionism
隷解放 *dorei kaihō* emancipation of slaves

3

妁 1175 / J5522 / M6058 Shaku go-between.

B **妃** 1176 / J485e / M6061 Hi queen; princess. *kisaki* queen.
13 殿下 *Hidenka* Her Imperial Highness (a princess or consort)

B **妄** 1177 / J4c51 / M6063 Bō. Mō. *mida(ri) ni* without authority, without reason, arbitrarily, unnecessarily, indiscriminately, recklessly. *mida(rigamashii)* morally corrupt.
5 用 *bōyō* misuse, abuse
弁 *bōben* incoherent talk
7 言 *bōgen, mōgen* reckless remark, abusive language
8 念 *mōnen* distracting ideas, irrelevant thoughts
9 信 *mōshin, bōshin* blind belief, credulity
10 挙 *bōkyo* unreasonable actions, lack of discrimination
11 動 *mōdō suru, bōdō suru* act blindly
執 *mōshū* deep-rooted delusion
12 評 *bōhyō, mōhyō* unfair criticism, abusive remarks
13 想 *mōsō, bōsō* wild idea, delusion
14 説 *bōsetsu, mōsetsu* fallacy, false report
語 *mōgo, bōgo* reckless remark, abusive language
15 誕 *bōtan* falsehood

B **如** 1178 / J4721 / M6060 Jo. Nyo. *-goto(ki)* like, such as, as if. *shi(kazu)* be better, be best. *shi(ku)* be equal to, be like. *-goto(ku)* like, as, as if. *-goto(shi)* seem to be, be like.
3 上 *jojō* the above-mentioned
才無 *josaina(i), josai (no) na(i)* clever, shrewd, smart, adroit, tactful; sociable
4 月 *Kisaragi* second lunar month
7 来 *Nyorai* Buddha
何 *ikaga* How (about it)? How (are you)? What (do you think)? *ikan* what, how. *ikaga(washi)* unreliable; questionable. *ika(na), ika(naru)* what (kind), anybody, everybody; nobody (with neg.). *ika ni* how. *ika ni mo* indeed, really, certainly; apparently, as if. *ikan nimo shite* by all means
何物 *ikamono* spurious article
何許 *ikabaka(ri)* about how much
何程 *ikahodo* how much, how many, no matter how much
何様 *ikayō* how; what kind. *ikasama* how; what kind; fraud, swindle; I see; to be sure
何様師 *ikasamashi* cheater, deceiver
8 法 *nyohō* pious, faithful, honest
実 *nyojitsu ni* truly, realistically

雨露 *jōro* watering can
13 意 *nyoi* priest's staff; ease, comfort
21 露 *joro* watering can

奸 1179 / J5521 / M6045 KAN wickedness, mischief, rudeness.
2 人 *kanjin* knave, scoundrel
3 才 *kansai* craftiness, cunning
4 凶 *kankyō* wickedness, wicked people
手段 *kanshudan* underhanded trick
6 臣 *kanshin* traitor
曲 *kankyoku* wickedness, wicked scheming
吏 *kanri* corrupt official
7 佞 *kannei* craftiness, wickedness
邪 *kanja* wicked person; wickedness
8 物 *kambutsu* rascal, villain, crook
9 計 *kankei* trick, evil design, sharp practice
10 徒 *kanto* wicked people
11 婦 *kampu* wicked woman
悪 *kan'aku* wickedness, treachery
商 *kanshō* dishonest merchant
12 詐 *kansa* craft, guile, deceit
策 *kansaku* sinister scheme
智 *kanchi* cunning, subtlety
13 賊 *kanzoku* villain, traitor, ruffian
16 謀 *kambō* wicked scheming
18 黠 *kankatsu* craftiness; crafty person
19 譎 *kanketsu* perverseness and prevarication

A **好** 1180 / J3925 / M6053 KŌ. *kono(mu)* like, be fond of. *su(ku)* like, love, be fond of. *kono(mi)* taste, fondness, bent, choice, wish; fashion, mode. *kono(mashii)* desirable, pleasant, enviable. *kono(nde)* by choice, willingly; often. *suki* liking, love, taste, bent. *yo(shi)* good, all right, well, so. *yo(shimi)* friendship, intimacy, good will. *su(kanai)* odious, disagreeable. *i(i), yo(i)* good, good-natured; pleasing; precious; noble; lovely, beautiful, fine; lucky; efficacious; right; suitable; justifiable; appropriate, satisfactory; better; all right; unnecessary; no objection; intimate, friendly; easy; well; desirous. *su(itarashii)* lovable, charming, nice. *-zu(ki)* lover of, fan, enthusiast, maniac.
1 一対 *kōittsui* well-matched couple
2 人物 *kōjimbutsu* good-natured man
3 士 *kōshi* fine man, gentleman
子 *i(i) ko, yo(i) ko* good child, nice boy, nice girl
下物 *kōkabutsu* favorite dish, relish
4 手 *kōshu* good move (in a game)
化 *kōka* getting better
天気 *kōtenki* fine weather
不好 *su(ki)-busu(ki)* taste, likes and dislikes
5 加減 *i(i) kagen no, yo(i) kagen no* moderate, temperate, proper; haphazard; unconvincing, halfhearted. *i(i) kagen* quite, rather (old)
古 *kōko* love of antiquities
古癖 *kōkoheki* antiquarianism, love of antiquities
打 *kōda* a good hit
打者 *kōdasha* (baseball) slugger
打順 *kōdajun* good batting order
6 仲 *i(i) naka, yo(i) naka* intimacy; being in love
在 *kōzai* a good living
地位 *kōchii* advantageous position
印象 *kōinshō* good impression
成績 *kōseiseki* good results
気 *i(i)ki na* easygoing, optimistic; conceited
気味 *i(i)kimi, i(i)kibi, yo(i)kimi* Serves you right.
好 *su(ki)kono(mu)* like, be fond of. *su(ki)zu(ki)* a matter of taste
好翁 *kōkōō* an old man of character
好爺 *kōkōya* a good-natured old man
色 *kōshoku* sensuality, lewdness, lust
色文学 *kōshoku bungaku* pornographic literature
色本 *kōshokubon* suggestive story
色家 *kōshokuka* sensual person
色漢 *kōshokukan* sensual person
7 技 *kōgi* fine play, nice game, good acting
投 *kōtō* nice pitching
男子 *kōdanshi* handsome man
角家 *kōkakuka* wrestling fan
材料 *kōzairyō* good data, good news
位置 *kōichi* good location
8 例 *kōrei* good illustration
味 *kōmi* sweet taste; delicacies
況 *kōkyō* prosperity, boom
物 *i(i) mono, yo(i) mono* a good thing. *kōbutsu* something good; a favorite dish
尚 *kōshō* taste, fashion

3 口囗土士夂夊夕大【女】子宀寸小⺌尢尸屮山川巛工己巾干幺广廴廾弋弓ヨ彑彡彳

者 *su(ki)mono* lover of, person with a taste for; lecherous person
取組 *kōtorikumi* good game, good match
放題 *su(ki)hōdai* doing just as one pleases
奇 *kōki* curiosity, inquisitiveness
奇心 *kōkishin* curiosity, inquisitiveness
学 *kōgaku* love of learning
事 *kōji* happy event; good act; curiosity. *kōzu* curiosity, amateurism, dilettantism
事者 *kōjisha* amateur, dilettante
事家 *kōzuka* dilettante, amateur
9 音 *kōin* good news
発 *kōhatsu* frequent occurrence
10 個 *kōko* propriety. *kōko no* ideal, excellent
都合 *kōtsugō na* favorable, fortunate
時季 *kōjiki* good season for
時期 *kōjiki* good season for
時節 *kōjisetsu* good season for
時機 *kōjiki* opportune moment, nick of time
11 運 *kōun* good fortune, lucky break
情 *kōjō* good feeling, friendliness
転 *kōten* favorable turn, improvement
悪 *kōo* likes and dislikes; fancy; partiality
望 *kōbō* promising future
球 *kōkyū* a fine pitch (to hit)
球家 *kōkyūka* a baseball fan
12 順 *kōjun na* favorable
晴 *kōsei* fine weather
期 *kōki* right time
景気 *kōkeiki* boom, good times
結果 *kōkekka* good results, success
評 *kōhyō* public favor, favorable criticism
評嘖嘖 *kōhyō-sakusaku* very popular
13 適 *kōteki* very suitable, ideal
嫌 *su(ki)-kira(i)* likes and dislikes, taste
漢 *kōkan* fine fellow
愛 *kōai* love, care for, be fond of
感 *kōkan* good feeling, good impression
楽家 *kōgakuka* music lover
意 *kōi* good will, friendliness, favor, kindness, courtesy, good offices
意上 *kōijō* as a favor
戦 *kōsen* pro-war; bellicosity; belligerence
戦的 *kōsenteki* warlike
戦国 *kōsenkoku* warlike nation
戦国民 *kōsen kokumin* warlike nation
14 演 *kōen* good acting
箇 *kōko* propriety. *kōko no* ideal, excellent
15 誼 *kōgi* friendship, intimacy, your kindness
調 *kōchō no* favorable, promising, satisfactory
餌 *kōji* bait, decoy; lure, temptation
劇家 *kōgekika* theatergoer
影響 *kōeikyō* favorable influence
敵 *kōteki* worthy opponent
敵手 *kōtekishu* worthy opponent
16 機 *kōki* good chance, psychological moment
機会 *kōkikai* good chance, psychological moment
18 顔 *i(i) kao, yo(i) kao* good looks; good humor; smiling face; influential person
題目 *kōdaimoku* good topic

4

妒 1181 / J-X / M6082 See **妬** 1197.

㚷 1182 / J562c / M6094 SHI foolish; lewd, salacious; ugly; ridicule.

妝 1183 / J5523 / M6096 SŌ. SHŌ *yosō(u)* dress up; wear; adorn oneself; pretend, feign. *yosō(i)* dress; equipment.

妣 1184 / J5526 / M6103 HI mother.

妓 1185 / J3538 / M6083 GI singing girl, geisha, courtesan, prostitute.
13 楼 *girō* brothel
16 館 *gikan* brothel

妍 1186 / J552b / M6075 **姸** 1206 / J-X / M6247 KEN beauty, splendor, grace.
19 艶 *ken'en* charm, beauty
麗 *kenrei* beauty of facial features

B **妨** 1187 / J4b38 / M6111 BŌ. HŌ. *samata(geru)* disturb, prevent, hamper, hinder, obstruct. *samata(ge)* hindrance, obstacle, barrier, disturbance, inconvenience, encumbrance, interference.

10 害 *bōgai* interference, obstruction, disturbance
害物 *bōgaibutsu* obstacle, impediment
害放送 *bōgai hōsō* radio jamming
13 碍 *bōgai* interference, obstruction, disturbance
19 礙 *bōgai* interference, obstruction, disturbance

B **妥** 1188 / J4245 / M6107 DA peace; depravity.
6 当 *datō* appropriateness, propriety
当性 *datōsei* propriety, adequacy, pertinence, soundness
8 協 *dakyō* compromise, understanding, agreement
協的 *dakyōteki* compromising
協案 *dakyōan* compromise plan
協策 *dakyōsaku* compromise plan
12 結 *daketsu* an agreement

B **妊** 1189 / J4725 / M6072 **姙** 1205 / J552c / M6200 NIN. *hara(mu), migomo(ru)* become pregnant; be pregnant; be filled with.
3 女 *hara(mi) onna* pregnant woman
10 娠 *ninshin* pregnancy, conception
娠中 *ninshinchū* during pregnancy
娠中絶 *ninshin chūzetsu* artificial abortion
娠調節 *ninshin chōsetsu* birth control
11 産婦 *ninsampu* expectant and nursing mothers
婦 *nimpu* pregnant woman
婦服 *nimpufuku* maternity dress

妖 1190 / J4d45 / M6086 YŌ attractive, bewitching; calamity.
3 女 *yōjo* fairy, witch, enchantress, vampire
6 気 *yōki* ghostly, spooky
8 怪 *yōkai* ghost, apparition
怪談 *yōkaidan* ghost story
9 星 *yōsei* unlucky star; comet
美 *yōbi* bewitching beauty
11 婦 *yōfu* enchantress, a Jezebel
術 *yōjutsu* magic, sorcery, witchcraft
婆 *yōba* witch, hag
12 雲 *yōun* ominous cloud
14 精 *yōsei* elf, sprite, fairy
19 艶 *yōen* voluptuous charm
21 魔 *yōma* ghost, apparition

B **妙** 1191 / J4c2f / M6090 MYŌ strange, queer; mystery, miracle; cleverness. *tae(naru)* exquisite, excellent; melodious; delicate; charming; marvelous. *myō(chikirin)* strange, queer.
4 手 *myōshu* excellent skill; expert; good move
5 用 *myōyō* wonderful effect
句 *myōku* clever expression; fine verse
6 曲 *myōkyoku* sweet melody, fine piece of music
7 技 *myōgi* outstanding skill, splendid feat, stunt
8 味 *myōmi* charms, exquisite beauty
所 *myōsho* point of beauty, beauty
法 *myōhō* clever method; marvelous law of Buddha; mystery
法蓮華経 *Myōhō Rengekyō* the Lotus Sutra
典 *myōten* sacred book
9 音 *myōon* beautiful sound
計 *myōkei* wise plan, clever trick
10 致 *myōchi* charms, exquisite beauty
案 *myōan* bright idea, excellent plan
11 理 *myōri* wonderful truths
12 絶 *myōzetsu no* superb, exquisite
策 *myōsaku* clever plan
筆 *myōhitsu* excellent calligraphy or painting
13 適 *myōteki* strange; natural
14 境 *myōkyō* wonderful place
算 *myōsan* clever plan
15 趣 *myōshu* beauties, charms
16 機 *myōki* delicate shift in trends
薬 *myōyaku* miracle drug
17 齢 *myōrei* youth
19 麗 *myōrei* beautiful face

5

妲 1192 / J5527 / M6129 TATSU. TACHI female proper name.

姆 1193 / J5528 / M6159 BO wet nurse.

姑 1194 / J3848 / M6174 KO. *shūtome, shūto* mother-in-law.
10 息 *kosoku* makeshift

B **姐** 1195/J3039/M6172 So girl; elder sister; maidservant.
12 御 *anego* elder sister (polite)

B **姓** 1196/J402b/M6178 Shō. Sei surname, family name. *kabane* new name conferred by the emperor.
4 氏 *seishi* surname
6 名 *seimei* name

妬 1197/J454a/M6121 **妒** 1181/J-X/M6082 To. *neta(mu)* be jealous of, be envious of. *neta(mi)* jealousy. *neta(mashii)* jealous of, envious of; enviable.
4 心 *toshin* jealousy
7 見 *neta(mi)-mi(ru)* look upon with envy

妾 1198/J3e2a/M6147 Shō *mekake, sobame* concubine. *warawa* I.
5 出 *shōshutsu* illegitimate birth
6 宅 *shōtaku* concubine's house
13 腹 *shōfuku* illegitimate birth. *mekakebara* illegitimate child

A **妹** 1199/J4b65/M6138 Mai. *imōto, imoto, imo* younger sister.
4 分 *imōtobun* sworn sister
8 姑 *imoshūtome* sisters of a wife
9 背 *imose* man and wife; elder brother and younger sister; elder sister and younger brother
10 娘 *imōtomusume* younger daughter
脊 *imose* man and wife; elder brother and younger sister; elder sister and younger brother
12 婿 *imōtomuko* husband of a younger sister
御 *imōtogo* your sister

A **妻** 1200/J3a4a/M6140 Sai (my) wife. *tsuma* wife, spouse.
3 女 *saijo* wife; wife and daughters
子 *saishi, tsumako* wife and children, one's family
4 戸 *tsumado* side door; paneled door
6 合 *mea(waseru)* arrange a marriage (for a girl)
7 君 *saikun* wife
8 妾 *saishō* wife and concubines
9 室 *saishitsu* wife
10 恋 *tsumagoi* love for one's spouse
格子 *tsumagōshi* latticework
帯 *saitai* marriage, matrimony
帯者 *saitaisha* married man
12 鈍 *sainoro* being henpecked

A **姉** 1201/J3b50/M6165 **姊** 1202/J-X/M6164 Shi. *ane* elder sister. *nē(san)* elder sister; waitress; girl. *nē(ya)* maid. *-shi* Miss, Mrs.
3 上 *aneue* elder sister
女房 *ane-nyōbō* a wife who is older
4 分 *anebun* elder sister
7 君 *anegimi* elder sister
8 妹 *shimai, ane-imōto* sisters
妹会社 *shimaigaisha* affiliated companies
妹品 *shimaihin* companion product
妹船 *shimaisen* sister ship
10 娘 *anemusume* elder daughter
12 婿 *anemuko* elder sister's husband
御 *anego* elder sister (polite)
貴 *aneki* elder sister
14 様 *nēsan, nēsama* elder sister
様冠 *anesankabu(ri)* female workers' head towels

A **始** 1203/J3b4f/M6166 Shi beginning. *haji(maru) vi* begin, start, open; date from; (season) sets in; arise, break out; originate in. *haji(maranai)* be of no avail, accomplish nothing. *haji(meru) vt* begin, open, start, originate, inaugurate, initiate. *haji(mari)* beginning, inception, opening, start, origin. *haji(me)* beginning, origin. *haji(mete)* (for) the first time; not until. *haji(memashite)* for the first time (I greet you).
5 末 *shimatsu* circumstances; management; disposal, settlement; control
末屋 *shimatsuya* thrifty person
末書 *shimatsusho* written explanation, written apology
5 祖 *shiso* founder, originator, pioneer, progenitor
発 *shihatsu* first train, first bus; starting (station)
発駅 *shihatsu eki* starting station
10 原 *shigen* origin, inception
11 終 *shijū, shotchū* all the time, always, constantly. *shijū no* the whole, all
球 *shikyū* the first ball, opening of the ball game

球式 *shikyūshiki* throwing the first ball, opening of the ball game
動 *shidō* starting (in machines)
動機 *shidōki* starter
12 期 *shiki* beginning date; initial stage
13 業 *shigyō* commencement of work; beginning of a class
業式 *shigyōshiki* opening ceremony
15 審 *shishin* first trial

A **委** 1204 / J3051 / M6181 I. *i(suru)* entrust to, discard. *yuda(neru)* entrust to, devote (oneself) to. *maka(su)*, *maka(seru)* entrust to, leave to. *kuwa(shii)* full, detailed, minute, accurate; versed in, well-informed on.
3 女 *obako* lass
5 付 *ifu* abandonment (of rights or property)
6 曲 *ikyoku* details, circumstances
任 *inin* trust, delegation, authorization, charge, commission, mandate
任状 *ininjō* power of attorney
任統治 *inin tōchi* mandate
任統治権 *inin tōchiken* mandate
10 託 *itaku* trust, consignment, commission
託加工 *itaku kakō* processing materials brought in
託金 *itakukin* money in trust
託保証金 *itaku hoshōkin* consignment, guarantee money
託販売 *itaku hambai* sale on consignment
員 *iin* committeeman, committee, commission
員付託 *iin-futaku* referring to a committee
員会 *iinkai* committee (meeting), board
員長 *iinchō* chairman
11 細 *isai* details, particulars
細面談 *isai mendan* details when I see you
13 棄 *iki* abandonment, desertion, relinquishment
15 嘱 *ishoku suru* entrust with
20 譲 *ijō suru* transfer to

6

姙 1205 / J552c / M6200 See 妊 1189.

姸 1206 / J-X / M6247 See 妍 1186.

姚 1207 / J552d / M6202 Yō beautiful; far, distant.

姶 1208 / J3028 / M6242 Ō attractive; quiet.

姪 1209 / J4c45 / M6226 TETSU. *mei* niece.

姜 1210 / J552a / M6205 KYŌ. KŌ. used in family and river names.

娜 1211 / J5531 / M6311 DA graceful.

姥 1212 / J3138 / M6216 BO. MO. *uba* aged woman.
10 桜 *ubazakura* a faded beauty

娃 1213 / J3023 / M6262 AI, A beautiful, attractive, beautiful woman. *utsuku(shii)* beautiful, attractive.
23 鬟 *aikan* beautiful woman

姨 1214 / J5529 / M6222 I mother's sister, aunt; wife's sister. *oba* mother's sister.
4 父 *ifu* mother's sister's husband
5 母 *ibo* mother's sister

B **姻** 1215 / J3079 / M6250 IN marry.
10 家 *inka* a family related by marriage
11 戚 *inseki* in-laws
族 *inzoku* relative by remarriage
族閥 *inzokubatsu* nepotism

A **姿** 1216 / J3b51 / M6257 SHI. *sugata* figure, form, shape; appearance, attire; posture; oneself; portrait; aspect.
7 見 *sugatami* dresser, full-length mirror
10 容 *shiyō* form, appearance, countenance
11 盛 *sugatazaka(ri)* the charming beauty of young womanhood
12 絵 *sugatae* portrait
13 勢 *shisei* posture, pose
14 態 *shitai* figure, form, style

B **姫** 1217 / J4931 / M6229 **姬** 1220 / J-X / M6230 KI. *hime* princess; young lady of birth. *hime-* little, pretty.
3 小松 *hime komatsu* a small pine
7 君 *himegimi* princess, young lady of birth
9 垣 *himegaki* low fence
10 宮 *himemiya* princess
12 御前 *himegoze, himegozen* princess; young lady of birth; a sweet little girl
14 様 *hiisama* daughter of a noble
15 糊 *himenori* rice paste, rice starch
22 鑑 *hime kagami* a model woman; a model for young women

姦 1218 / J342f / M6217 KAN wickedness, mischief. *kan(suru)* seduce, assault, rape. *kashima(shii)* noisy, boisterous.
2 人 *kanjin* villain, scoundrel
3 才 *kansai* craftiness, cunning
4 凶 *kankyō* wickedness, wicked person
夫 *kampu* adulterer, paramour
6 曲 *kankyoku* wickedness; wicked scheming
吏 *kanri* corrupt official
7 佞 *kannei* wickedness
邪 *kanja* wickedness; wicked person
8 物 *kambutsu* rascal, villain, crook
9 計 *kankei* trick, evil design, sharp practice
通 *kantsū* adultery
通者 *kantsūsha* adulterer, adulteress
通罪 *kantsūzai* crime of adultery
10 徒 *kanto* wicked people
11 婦 *kampu* adulteress
淫 *kan'in* adultery
悪 *kan'aku* wickedness, treachery
12 詐 *kansa* craft, guile, deceit
雄 *kan'yū* great traitor, great villain
富 *kampu* ill-gotten gain
13 賊 *kanzoku* traitor, villain, ruffian
16 謀 *kambō* wicked scheming
18 黠 *kankatsu* craftiness; crafty person
19 譎 *kanketsu* perverseness and prevarication

B **威** 1219 / J3052 / M6259 I dignity, majesty, authority. *odo(su)* threaten; frighten; intimidate. *odoshi* menace, threat; scarecrow.
2 力 *iryoku* power, might, authority, influence
力半径 *iryoku hankei* destructive range
力偵察 *iryoku teisatsu* reconnaissance in force
3 丈高 *itakedaka ni* angrily
4 文句 *odoshi monku* bluff, threatening language
5 付 *odo(shi)-tsu(keru)* to be threatening
令 *irei* authority
圧 *iatsu* coercion
圧的 *iatsuteki* domineering, coercive
6 光 *ikō* power, authority, influence
名 *imei* fame, prestige
7 迫 *ihaku* menace, threat
8 服 *ifuku suru* awe into submission
武 *ibu* authority and force
9 風 *ifū* majesty, dignity
信 *ishin* prestige, authority, honor
10 容 *iyō* dignity, majestic appearance
烈 *iretsu* majesty
11 望 *ibō* influence and popularity
張 *iba(ru), eba(ru)* be proud, swagger
張屋 *iba(ri)ya* braggart, boaster
13 勢 *isei* power, might, authority, influence; high spirits
14 徳 *itoku* virtue and influence
15 儀 *igi* dignity, majesty; dignified manner
権 *iken* authority, power
17 厳 *igen* dignity, majesty
嚇 *ikaku* menace, threat
嚇的 *ikakuteki* threatening, menacing

7

姬 1220 / J-X / M6230 See **姫** 1217.

娉 1221 / J5532 / M6282 HEI, HYŌ question, summon; take a wife. *to(u)* ask, question. HŌ beautiful.

娚 1222 / J5533 / M6306 NAN *meoto* used in proper names. SŌ. DŌ. NŌ *tawamu(reru)* dally, flirt, take liberties.

娥 1223 / J552e / M6331 GA beautiful; a beauty; the moon.

B **娠** 1224 / J3f31 / M6322 SHIN pregnancy.

娟 1225 / J552f / M6321 EN, KEN facial beauty.

娣 1226 J-X M6329 TEI. *imoto, imōto* younger sister.

婀 1227 J5534 M6382 娿 1228 J-X M6381 A. *ada, ada(ppoi)* flirtatious, bewitching.

[9] 娜 *ada(meku)* (women) charm, bewitch

娑 1229 J5530 M6294 SHA old woman.

[11] 婆 *shaba* this corrupt world

婆気 *shabaki, shabake* worldly desires or ambitions

B 娘 1230 J4c3c M6304 JŌ. *musume* daughter, girl, young woman.

[3] 子 *jōshi* girl, woman

子軍 *jōshigun* Amazonian troops

[4] 心 *musumegokoro* girlish innocence

[6] 気質 *musume katagi* the nature of a young woman

[10] 師 *musumeshi* burglarizing a storehouse

[11] 盛 *musumezaka(ri)* the prime of young womanhood

[12] 婿 *musumemuko* adopted son-in-law

B 娯 1231 J3864 M6307′ GO pleasure.

[13] 楽 *goraku* pleasure, amusement, recreation, entertainment

楽用 *gorakuyō* for amusement

楽品 *gorakuhin* plaything

楽室 *gorakushitsu* recreation room

楽場 *gorakujō* amusement place

楽街 *gorakugai* amusement quarter

楽機関 *goraku kikan* recreational facilities

8

婬 1232 J5535 M6440 See 淫 3203.

娩 1233 J4a5a M6337 BEN bear (children).

婪 1234 J553a M6436 RAN covet.

婁 1235 J4f2c M6383 RU, RO frequently; tie.

娶 1236 J5538 M6365 SHU. *meto(ru)* marry (a woman). *meawa(seru)* arrange a marriage (for a woman), give one's daughter in marriage.

娵 1237 J5537 M6364 SHU. SHŪ. SU. *yome* bride, young wife, daughter-in-law.

[2] 入 *yomei(ri)* marriage, wedding

婢 1238 J8839 M6428 HI, *hashitame* maidservant.

[14] 僕 *hiboku* servants, menials

婉 1239 J5536 M6396 EN graceful.

[6] 曲 *enkyoku na* euphemistic, circumloculatory, roundabout, indirect, insinuating

[9] 美 *embi* beauty, charm

B 婆 1240 J474c M6390 BA. *baba* old woman; grandmother. *baba, babā* old woman; wet nurse. *bā(ya)* wet nurse; old maid; old housekeeper.

[4] 心 *bashin* grandmotherly solicitude

[14] 様 *bāsan* old woman; grandmother

[19] 羅門 *Baramon* Brahman

娼 1241 J3e2b M6376 倡 247 J5069 M783 SHŌ prostitute.

[7] 妓 *shogi* prostitute, harlot

[10] 家 *shōka* brothel

[11] 婦 *shōfu* prostitute, harlot

[13] 楼 *shōrō* brothel

B 婚 1242 J3a27 M6418 KON marriage.

[5] 礼 *konrei* wedding ceremony

[9] 姻 *kon'in* marriage

姻届 *kon'in todoke* marriage registration

約 *kon'yaku* engagement, betrothal

約者 *kon'yakusha* fiancé, fiancée

[10] 家 *konka* one's husband's family

宴 *kon'en* wedding feast

[12] 期 *konki* marriageable age

[13] 嫁 *konka* marriage

[15] 儀 *kongi* wedding ceremony

A 婦 1243 J4958 M6432′ FU woman; wife; bride.

[2] 人 *fujin* lady, woman, female

人用 *fujin'yō* for ladies

3 口 囗 土 士 夂 夊 夕 大 9【女】子 宀 寸 小 ⺌ 尢 尸 屮 山 川 巛 工 己 巾 干 幺 广 廴 廾 弋 弓 ヨ 彑 彡 彳

人会 *fujinkai* ladies' society
人参政権 *fujin sanseiken* woman suffrage
人科 *fujinka* gynecology
人科学 *fujinkagaku* gynecology
人病 *fujinbyō* women's diseases
人解放 *fujin kaihō* emancipation of women
人警官 *fujin keikan* policewoman
3 女 *fujo* woman, womankind
女子 *fujoshi* woman and child
8 長 *fuchō* head nurse
10 容 *fuyō* etiquette for women
11 道 *fudō* womanhood, duties of women
14 選 *fusen* woman suffrage
徳 *futoku* womanly virtues
15 権 *fuken* woman's rights
19 警 *fukei* policewoman

9

媛 1244 / J4932 / M6516 EN. *hime* princess; young lady of noble birth.

媚 1245 / J553b / M6513 BI. *ko(biru)* flatter, humor, flirt (by a woman), curry favor. *kobi* flattery, cajolery, flirtation.
14 態 *bitai* coquetry
16 薬 *biyaku* an aphrodisiac
17 諂 *ko(bi)-hetsura(i)* adulation, flattery

B **婿** 1246 / J4c3b / M6470 **壻** 1046 / J5466 / M5664 **聟** 4728 / J665d / M29106
SEI. *muko* son-in-law.
2 入 *mukoi(ri) suru* become the heir of one's wife's family
8 取 *mukoto(ri)* adopting a son-in-law
取娘 *mukoto(ri) musume* a daughter whose husband is adopted into her family
11 探 *mukosaga(shi)* hunting a husband for one's daughter
15 養子 *mukoyōshi* son-in-law adopted as an heir

B **媒** 1247 / J475e / M6498 BAI. *nakadachi* go-between.
4 介 *baikai* mediation, intervention, agency
介物 *baikaibutsu* medium, agency; carrier (of germs), vehicle
6 妁 *baishaku* matchmaking
妁人 *baishakunin* matchmaker, go-between
7 体 *baitai* medium (in biology)
材 *baizai* a catalytic agent
9 染 *baisen* color fixing
10 酌 *baishaku* matchmaking
酌人 *baishakunin* matchmaker, go-between
11 鳥 *otori* a lure, decoy, stool pigeon. *baichō* decoy bird
15 質 *baishitsu* medium (of transmission)

10

嬲 1248 / J554c / M6626 DŌ. NŌ. *tawamu(reru)* dally, flirt, take liberties. *nabu(ru)* play with, mock.

媽 1249 / J5540 / M6590 BO mother; mare.

媼 1250 / J553c / M6588 Ō mother; grandmother; woman. *ōna* old woman.

媳 1251 / J-X / M6573 SEKI. *yome* bride, young wife, daughter-in-law.

嫂 1252 / J553f / M6603 SŌ. *aniyome* elder brother's wife.

媾 1253 / J553d / M6597 KŌ association, intimacy.
6 曳 *aibiki* date, rendezvous, clandestine courting
8 和 *kōwa suru* make peace

嫋 1254 / J553e / M6614 JŌ. *nayo(yakana)* supple, pliant, delicate, slender. *shina(yakana)* pliant, flexible, limber, lithe, graceful. *tao(yakana)* graceful.
6 竹 *nayotake* pliant bamboo
13 嫋 *nayonayo to* feebly, languidly. *nayonayo toshita* feeble, delicate, slender. *jōjō* blowing (of a wind); soft, pliant; resounding

嫉 1255 / J3c3b / M6611 SHITSU. *sone(mu)* be jealous, envy. *neta(mu)* be jealous of, be envious of. *sone(mi), neta(mi)* jealousy, envy.
8 妬 *shitto* jealousy, envy
妬心 *shittoshin* jealousy, envy

[11] 深 *sone(mi)buka(i), neta(mi)buka(i)* envious, jealous
視 *shisshi* jealousy; glaring at; envy

B **嫁** 1256 / J3247 / M6602 KA. *ka(suru), ka(su)* marry (a man); be married to; blame. *totsu(gu)* marry off; get married. *yome* bride, young wife, daughter-in-law.
[2] 入 *yomei(ri)* marriage, wedding
入支度 *yomei(ri)jitaku* trousseau
入衣裳 *yomei(ri)isho* trousseau
[3] 女 *yomejo* bride
[8] 取 *yometo(ri)* taking a wife
[11] 笠 *yome(ga)kasa* limpet, tent shell
[12] 期 *kaki* marriageable age
御 *yomego* bride (polite)
御寮 *yomegoryō* bride (polite)
[13] 資 *kashi* dowry

B **嫌** 1257 / J3779 / M6618 KEN. *iya(garu)* dislike, hate; be unwilling (to do something). *kira(u)* hate, detest, dislike. *kira(i)* dislike, disinclination, abhorrence, prejudice; tinge, touch, suspicion. *kira(i) na* distasteful, disagreeable, repugnant. *iya na* disagreeable. *iya(garase)* a disagreeable thing *iya(rashii)* unpleasant, offensive *iya ni* disagreeably, offensively.
[6] 気 *iyaki, iyake* aversion, repugnance
[7] 忌 *kenki* dislike, aversion
[8] 味 *iyami* disagreeableness; gaudiness; mannerism; sarcasm
[11] 悪 *ken'o* dislike, hatred, abhorrence
悪感 *ken'okan* dislike, hatred
[13] 嫌 *iyaiya* reluctantly
嫌乍 *iyaiyanagara* reluctantly
[14] 厭 *ken'en* dislike, hate, loathing
疑 *kengi* suspicion; accusation
疑者 *kengisha* suspected person

11

嫖 1258 / J5545 / M6637 HYŌ lewd, salacious; amorous; light. *karu(i)* light.

嫗 1259 / J5542 / M6640 U. Ō *ōna* an old woman. *atata(meru)* heat; warm by holding in arms.

嫦 1260 / J5543 / M6663 KŌ moon, girl's name. JŌ good; desirable.
[10] 娥 *jōga* the moon

嫣 1261 / J5541 / M6659 EN beauty.
[12] 然 *enzen(taru)* graceful, smiling, polite

嫩 1262 / J5544 / M6666 DON young; weak.
[9] 草 *wakakusa* young grass
[12] 葉 *don'yō, wakaba* young foliage

B **嫡** 1263 / J4364 / M6656 CHAKU, TEKI legitimacy; legitimate child; legitimate wife; direct descent.
[3] 子 *chakushi* legitimate child
[5] 出 *chakushutsu* legitimacy (of birth)
出子 *chakushutsushi* legitimate child
[7] 男 *chakunan* heir, eldest son
[8] 妻 *chakusai* legitimate wife
[9] 室 *chakushitsu* legitimate wife
[10] 孫 *chakuson* eldest son of one's son and heir; eldest son's descendants
流 *chakuryū* lineage of the eldest son
[14] 嫡 *chakuchaku* direct succession

12

嫺 1264 / J5546 / M6710 — **嫻** 1265 / J5547 / M6711 KAN. GEN graceful; elegant; learn, attain proficiency.

嬋 1266 / J5549 / M6738 SEN beautiful.
[10] 娟 *senken(taru)* graceful, charming, beautiful

嬉 1267 / J3472 / M6736 KI. *ure(shigaru)* be glad, be pleased, rejoice. *ure(shigaraseru)* please, delight, flatter. *ure(shisōna), ure(shigena)* delightful, joyful, happy. *ure(shii)* glad, happy, delightful, pleasant.
[8] 泣 *ure(shi)na(ki)* crying for joy
[10] 涙 *ure(shi)namida* tears of joy
笑 *kishō* happy laughter
[11] 遊 *kiyū* playing happily
[15] 戯 *kigi suru* frolic
嬉 *kiki(taru)* gleeful, joyful

嬌 1268 / J5548 / M6739 KYŌ attractive.
6 名 *kyōmei* reputation for beauty
7 声 *kyōsei* lovely voice
9 姿 *kyōshi* lovely figure
10 笑 *kyōshō* charming smile
11 羞 *kyōshū* charming and coy
14 態 *kyōtai, shina* coquetry
19 艶 *kyōen* fascinating beauty

13

嬖 1269 / J554a / M6770 HEI agreeable person.
6 臣 *heishin* favorite retainer

B **嬢** 1270 / J3e6e / M6807′ **孃** 1277 / J5550 / M6891 JŌ girl, daughter, young lady; Miss.
3 子 *jōshi* a young woman
14 様 *jōsan, (o)jōsan* young lady; your daughter

14

嬬 1271 / J445c / M6821 JU. NYU wife; mistress; weak.

嬪 1272 / J554d / M6819 HIN bride; marriage.

嬰 1273 / J3145 / M6828 EI sharp (in music); baby.
7 児 *eiji, midorigo* infant, baby

嬶 1274 / J554e / M6849 (国字) *kakā, kaka* wife (vulgar).
4 天下 *kakā denka* government by women, petticoat government

嬲 1275 / J554b / M6831 DŌ. JŌ. *nabu(ru)* sport with; ridicule; tease.
8 物 *nabu(ri)mono* laughingstock
10 殺 *nabu(ri)goro(shi)* torturing

16

嬾 1276 / J554f / M6872 RAN be neglectful; be lazy, be tardy; languid; recline.
9 架 *ranka* reading stand
12 惰 *randa* lazy; neglectful

17

孃 1277 / J5550 / M6891 See **嬢** 1270.

孅 1278 / J5551 / M6893 SEN fine, delicate; thin, weak; graceful, elegant.

孀 1279 / J5552 / M6885 SŌ. *yamome* widow.

RAD. 子 39

Ko child. At left: *ko hen.* Nickname: Child.

孑 1280 / J5553 / M6931 KETSU mosquito larva.
3 孒 *bōfura, bōfuri* mosquito larva

A **子** 1281 / J3b52 / M6930 SHI viscount, master; child; male; fruit; seed. SU. *ko* child, offspring; the young (of animals). *ne* 11 p.m. to 1 a.m.; first zodiac sign, rat; north. *ko-* small.
3 女 *shijo* children
山羊 *koyagi* kid
子孫孫 *shishi-sonson* descendants, posterity
4 牛 *koushi* calf
犬 *koinu* puppy
分 *kobun* follower, protégé, apprentice; adopted son; bad elements
午線 *shigosen* the meridian
午線経過 *shigosen keika* crossing the meridian
午環 *shigokan* meridian circle
6 羊 *kohitsuji* lamb
早 *kobaya(i)* easily becoming pregnant
芋 *koimo* young taro tubers
会社 *kogaisha* subsidiary company
安貝 *koyasugai* cowrie
守 *komori* amah; baby tending; baby sitter
守歌 *komori uta* lullaby, nursery rhyme
7 役 *koyaku* child actor, child actress; child's role

弟 *shitei* children
沢山 *kodakusan* many children (in the family)
8 宝 *kodakara* treasure of children
供 *kodomo* child *kodomo(rashii)* childlike
供心 *kodomogokoro* childish mind
供日 *Kodomo (no) Hi* Children's Day, May 5
供気 *kodomogi* the feelings of a child
供好 *kodomozu(ki)* love of children
供向 *kodomomu(ki)* for children
供扱 *kodomoatsuka(i)* treating like a child
供臭 *kodomokusa(i)* childish
供染 *kodomoji(mita)* childish
供時代 *kodomo jidai* childhood
供部屋 *kodomobeya* nursery, children's room
供銀行 *kodomo ginkō* children's bank (in schools)
供騙 *kodomodama(shi)* fooling a child; childish trick
9 音 *shiin, shion* consonant
星 *koboshi* minor star in a binary or multiple star
持 *komo(chi)* a mother; maternity; pregnancy
持甘藍 *komo(chi) kanran* Brussels sprouts
持石 *komo(chi) ishi* conglomerate
持魚 *komo(chi) uo* fish carrying roe
10 孫 *shison* posterity, descendants
株 *kokabu* new shares of stock
殺 *kogoro(shi)* infanticide
息 *shisoku* son
宮 *shikyū* womb
宮口 *shikyūkō* cervix of the uterus
宮炎 *shikyūen* uteritis
宮病 *shikyūbyō* uterine disease
宮癌 *shikyūgan* uterine cancer
11 鹿 *kojika* fawn, young deer
猫 *koneko* kitten
細 *shisai* reasons, circumstances; significance; particulars; hindrance, obstruction, interference
豚 *kobuta* young pig, shoat
規 *hototogisu* cuckoo
12 等 *kora* children
葉 *shiyō* the first leaves of a sprouting seed
13 僧 *kozō* young Buddhist priest; errand boy, shop boy; youngster
獅子 *kojishi* lion cub
煩悩 *kobonnō* fondness for children
福 *kofuku* many children (in the family)
福者 *kobukusha, kofukusha* a person blessed with a large family
飼 *koga(i)* raising from infancy; raising animals from birth
飼者 *kogaimono* an apprentice
14 種 *kodane* issue, offspring, descendants
17 癇 *shikan* eclampsia, puerperal convulsions
爵 *shishaku* viscount
爵夫人 *shishaku fujin* viscountess
22 嚢 *shinō* seed bag

1

B 孔 1282 / J3926 / M6933 Kō. Ku. *ana* hole, aperture, slit; gap, stop (of musical instrument); eyelet; cavity; socket; cave; den; hiding place; pit; fault, defect; deficit; grave; dark horse. *hanaha(da)* very, greatly, exceedingly.
3 子 *Kōshi* Confucius
子廟 *Kōshibyō* Confucian shrine
4 夫子 *Kōfūshi* Confucius
5 穴 *kōketsu* hole, crack, space
8 門 *Kōmon* Confucian School
孟 *Kō-Mō* Confucius and Mencius
孟学 *Komogaku* Confucianism
11 教 *Kōkyō* Confucianism
雀 *kujaku* peacock
雀石 *kujakuseki* malachite
雀草 *kujakusō* maidenhair fern
雀歯朶 *kujaku shida* maidenhair fern
13 聖 *Kōsei* Confucius; a talented man

2

孕 1283 / J5554 / M6938 Yō. *hara(mu)* become pregnant; be pregnant; be filled with.
3 女 *hara(mi) onna* pregnant woman
子 *hara(mi)go* fetus

3

A 存 1284 / J4238 / M6943 Son. Zon. *zon(jiru), zon(zuru)* know, be aware of, be acquainted with; think, believe, feel. *son(suru)* exist, be extant, remain, live; retain, maintain, preserve; consist of; depend on. *nagara(eru)* live on, live long.

3亡 *sombō* life or death, existence, fate
上 *zon(ji)-a(geru)* know, be aware of, be acquainted with
4分 *zombun ni* to one's heart's content, freely, without reserve
5立 *sonritsu* existence, subsistence
外 *zongai* contrary to expectations; beyond expectations
生 *zonjō suru* live
生中 *zonjōchū* during life
6在 *sonzai* existence, subsistence, being
在論 *sonzairon* ontology
7否 *sompi* existence, life or death
8知 *zonchi* knowledge of
念 *zonnen* thought, idea, concept
命 *zommei* alive, living; existence
命中 *zommeichū* during life, while living
11寄 *zon(ji)-yo(ru)* remember, recall. *zon(ji)yo(ri)* one's views; one's acquaintances
掛無 *zon(ji)ga(ke)na(i)* unexpected
12廃 *sompai* continuance or abolition; existence
13置 *sonchi suru* maintain, retain, continue
意 *zon'i* thought; idea
続 *sonzoku* continuance, continued existence, duration
続期間 *sonzoku kikan* the duration

A **字** 1285 J3b7a M6942 JI character, letter, word, handwriting. *aza* section of a village. *azana* nickname, alias, pseudonym.

4引 *jibiki* dictionary
5母 *jibo* letter, alphabet, syllabic character; matrix; type
句 *jiku* terms, wording
号 *jigō* name; nickname; size of type
7体 *jitai* form or style of a character
余 *jiama(ri)* too many characters (for the meter)
8画 *jikaku* character strokes
突 *jitsu(ki)* a pointer
典 *jiten* character dictionary
9面 *jimen, jizura* the appearance of the writing
音 *jion* Chinese *(on)* pronunciation of a character
音語 *jiongo* words formed from Chinese *(on)* sounds
10消 *jike(shi)* eraser
訓 *jikun* the Japanese *(kun)* reading of a character
書 *jisho* character dictionary
11探 *jisaga(shi)* word puzzle
13源 *jigen* construction of a character
解 *jikai* explanation of a passage
数 *jisū* number of characters
彙 *jii* glossary, dictionary
幕 *jimaku* title, caption
義 *jigi* meaning of a word
義的 *jigiteki* literal
義通 *jigidō(ri)* literally

4

孚 1286 J5555 M6948 FU hatch an egg; egg, seed; seed cover; sincerity. *makoto* truth; sincerity, honesty.

9信 *fushin* truth; sincerity

孜 1287 J3b5a M6951 SHI industriousness.

7孜 *shishi to shite* untiringly, diligently

孛 1288 J5556 M6949 HAI comet; dark, obscure. BOTSU be offended, take offense; thick growth.

9星 *haisei* comet
11彗 *haisui* comet

A **孝** 1289 J3927 M6952 KŌ filial piety.

3女 *kōjo* filial daughter
子 *kōshi* filial child
4心 *kōshin* filial devotion
6行 *kōkō* filial piety
7弟 *kōtei* filial piety
10悌 *kōtei* filial piety
11道 *kōdō* filial piety
経 *Kōkyō* the Book of Filial Piety
12順 *kōjun* obedience, filial piety
敬 *kōkei* filial piety
15養 *kōyō* discharge of filial duties

5

孥 1290 J5557 M6967 DO. NU. child; grandchild; servant, slave; captive; wife and children.

15 戮 *doriku* punish wife and children along with the offender

孟 1291 / J4c52 / M6960 Mō chief; beginning.

3 子 *Mōshi* Mencius
10 夏 *mōka* early summer

A **季** 1292 / J3528 / M6965 Ki season. *sue* end.

3 子 *sueko, kishi* the last child
4 月 *Kigetsu* December
父 *kifu* youngest uncle
5 末 *kimatsu* term end
世 *kisei* the last age; the last degenerate age
刊 *kikan* quarterly publication
刊誌 *kikanshi* quarterly magazine
9 後 *kioku(re)* late in the season
春 *kishun* late spring
10 候 *kikō* season
候病 *kikōbyō* seasonal disease
夏 *kika* late summer; sixth lunar month
12 報 *kihō* quarterly report or bulletin
違 *kichiga(i)* off-season
13 節 *kisetsu* the seasons, the time of year
節的 *kisetsuteki* seasonal
節物 *kisetsumono* things in season
節風 *kisetsufū* seasonal wind, monsoon
14 語 *kigo* word referring to seasons (in poetry)
18 題 *kidai* seasonal theme (in poetry)

B **孤** 1293 / J3849 / M6966 Ko orphan. *minashigo* orphan. *hitori de* alone.

3 山 *kozan* a lone mountain
5 立 *koritsu* isolation; helplessness
立主義 *koritsu shugi* isolationism
立政策 *koritsu seisaku* isolationist policy
6 舟 *koshū* a lone boat
帆 *kohan* solitary sailboat
灯 *kotō* solitary light
7 身 *koshin* lonely person
村 *koson* isolated village
児 *koji, minashigo* orphan
児院 *kojiin* orphanage
8 松 *koshō* a lone pine tree
忠 *kochū* undying devotion
9 城 *kojō* an isolated castle
独 *kodoku* solitude, isolation, loneliness
軍 *kogun* isolated force
客 *kokaku* a lone traveler
10 高 *kokō* splendid isolation, proud loneliness; nobility of character
剣 *koken* a sword; only a sword
島 *kotō* a solitary island
12 雁 *kogan* a solitary wild goose
13 愁 *koshū* lonely contemplation
15 蝶 *kochō* a lone butterfly
影 *koei* a lone figure; lonesome person
影悄然 *koei shōzen toshite* forlorn and crestfallen

A **学** 1294 / J3358 / M6974 **學** 1302 / J555c / M7033 Gaku learning, study, science, scholarship, erudition. *mana(bu)* learn, study. *mana(bi)* learning, knowledge; study.

2 力 *gakuryoku* scholarship, knowledge, literary ability
力考査 *gakuryoku kōsa* achievement test
3 才 *gakusai* scholastic ability
士 *Gakushi* Bachelor of Arts; college graduate
士院 *Gakushi'in* the Academy
4 区 *gakku* school district
方 *mana(bi)kata* way to study
内 *gakunai* within the campus
友 *gakuyū* schoolmate, classmate, alumnus
友会 *gakuyūkai* alumni association
5 外 *gakugai* off-campus, outside the school
兄 *gakkei* older student
用品 *gakuyōhin* school supplies
生 *gakusei* student
生主事 *gakusei shuji* dean of students
生用語 *gakusei yōgo* schoolboy slang
生帽 *gakuseibō* school cap
生監 *gakuseikan* dean of students
6 会 *gakkai* institute, academy, learned society, literary society
年 *gakunen* school year
名 *gakumei* technical name
7 位 *gakui* academic degree
究 *gakkyū* scholar, student
究的 *gakkyūteki* scholastic, academic
芸 *gakugei* art and science, literary attainments, culture
芸会 *gakugeikai* a student literary program

8 長 *gakuchō* college president, rector
府 *gakufu* educational institution, seat of learning
取 *mana(bi)-to(ru)* apply a lesson to oneself
制 *gakusei* educational system
舎 *gakusha* school building
事 *gakuji* educational affairs; learning, studies
者 *gakusha* scholar, learned man, scribe
者間 *gakushakan* among scholars
9 風 *gakufū* academic traditions, school character, method of study, a school (of thought)
海 *gakkai* the world of knowledge
派 *gakuha* school, sect
級 *gakkyū* school class, grade, form, standard
則 *gakusoku* school regulations
院 *gakuin* school, academy, seminary
政 *gakusei* government educational administration
界 *gakkai* academic or scientific world
科 *gakka* curriculum, course
科目 *gakkamoku* school subjects
10 修 *gakushū* learning, study
徒 *gakuto* scholar, student, disciple, follower
部 *gakubu* faculty, department, college, school
部長 *gakubuchō* dean of a university department
校 *gakkō* school, educational institution
校一覧 *gakkō ichiran* school catalog
校区 *gakkōku* school district
校出 *gakkōde* educated person, college graduate
校用品 *gakkō yōhin* school supplies
校医 *gakkōi* school doctor
校長 *gakkōchō* school principal
校法人 *gakkō hōjin* educational foundation
校差 *gakkōsa* scholastic disparity among schools
校給食 *gakkō kyūshoku* school lunch
校園 *gakkōen* school garden
校構内 *gakkō kōnai* campus
11 務 *gakumu* educational affairs
堂 *gakudō* educational institution, academy
窓 *gakusō* school
問 *gakumon* learning, studies, scholarship, knowledge, education, culture, science
問的 *gakumonteki* scholarly
理 *gakuri* scientific principle, a theory
理的 *gakuriteki* theoretical
習 *gakushū* learning, study
習法 *gakushūhō* study methods
習場 *gakushūjō* a school
術 *gakujutsu* science, learning, scholarship, art and science
術用語 *gakujutsu yōgo* technical term
術的 *gakujutsuteki* scientific
術語 *gakujutsugo* technical term
12 帽 *gakubō* school cap
殖 *gakushoku* scholarship, learning
童 *gakudō* school child, pupil
費 *gakuhi* school expenses
期 *gakki* school term
期末 *gakkimatsu* end of a school term
期試験 *gakki shiken* term examinations
13 園 *gakuen* school, educational institution; campus
僧 *gakusō* a learned priest pursuing his studies
資 *gakushi* school expenses, educational fund, endowment
業 *gakugyō* studies, schoolwork, classwork, scholarship
際的 *gakusaiteki* interdisciplinary
14 歴 *gakureki* school career, academic record
閥 *gakubatsu* academic clique, school fraternity
僕 *gakuboku* a teacher's student helper
徳 *gakutoku* learning and virtue
説 *gakusetsu* theory
監 *gakkan* college dean
15 課 *gakka* lesson, schoolwork, classwork, subject
寮 *gakuryō* school dormitory
16 館 *gakkan* academy, school
17 績 *gakuseki* student's record
齢 *gakurei* school age
19 識 *gakushiki* scholarship, learning, scientific attainments
20 籍 *gakuseki* school register
籍簿 *gakusekibo* school register

6

孩 1295 / J5558 / M6977 GAI baby; infancy.

[7]児 *gaiji* baby, infant
[8]所 *gaisho* (Catholic) limbo of infants

7

A 孫 1296 / J4239 / M6987 Son descendants. *mago, hiko* grandchild.
[3]子 *magoko* children and grandchildren, descendants
[4]手 *mago(no)te* back scratcher
引 *magobi(ki)* reference to secondary sources
[7]弟子 *mago deshi* disciples of one's disciples
[10]娘 *mago musume* granddaughter
株 *mago kabu* second issue of new shares

8

孰 1297 / J5559 / M6995 Juku. *izu(re)* where, which, who.

9

孱 1298 / J5623 / M7000 Sen. Zen. San weak; suffer; narrow; cry; dangerous. *yowa(i)* weak.

孳 1299 / J555a / M-X 孶 1300 / J-X / M7011 Ji. Shi increase; bear children.

[12]孳 *shishi toshite* untiringly, diligently

10

孶 1300 / J-X / M7011 See 孳 1299.

11

孵 1301 / J555b / M7021 Fu. *kae(su)* hatch, incubate.
[4]化 *fuka* incubation, hatching
化器 *fukaki* incubator
[7]卵 *furan* incubation, hatching
卵器 *furanki* incubator

13

學 1302 / J555c / M7033 See 学 1294.

14

孺 1303 / J555e / M7042 Ju child.
[3]子 *jushi* child, lad, youngster

宀 RAD. 40

U kammuri (crown like the katakana *u*). Note that the crown 穴 is Rad. 116.
Nickname: *Kana U.*

宀 1304 / J555f / M7054 Ben. Men *yane* roof.

2

宂 1305 / J-X / M7056 See 冗 399.

它 1306 / J5560 / M7057 Ta other. *hebi* snake, serpent.

3

宊 1307 / J-X / M7076 See 写 400.

A 宅 1308 / J4270 / M7064 Taku home, house, residence; our home; my husband.
[6]地 *takuchi* building lot, residential land; homestead
扱 *takuatsuka(i)* delivery to the house
[9]急便 *takkyūbin* parcel delivery service
[10]配便 *takuhaibin* parcel delivery service
[12]診 *takushin* home consultation
診時間 *takushin jikan* home office hours

3 口 囗 土 士 夂 夊 夕 大 女 子 【宀】 寸 小 ⺌ 尢 尸 屮 山 川 巛 工 己 巾 干 幺 广 廴 廾 弋 弓 彐 彑 彡 彳

A **宇** 1309 / J3127 / M7067 U eaves; roof; house; heaven.

[4]内 *udai* the whole world. *udai ni* in the whole world, under the sun
[8]宙 *uchū* universe, cosmos
宙人 *uchūjin* alien
宙万物 *uchū-bambutsu* all the universe
宙引力 *uchū inryoku* universal gravitation
宙的 *uchūteki* universal
宙服 *uchūfuku* space suit
宙学 *uchūgaku* cosmology
宙発生論 *uchū hasseiron* cosmogony
宙飛行機 *uchū hikōki* space ship
宙時代 *uchū jidai* space age
宙旅行 *uchū ryokō* space travel
宙船 *uchūsen* space ship
宙雲 *uchūun* cosmic clouds
宙塵 *uchūjin* cosmic dust
宙線 *uchūsen* cosmic rays
宙論 *uchūron* cosmology

A **守** 1310 / J3c69 / M7071 SHU. SU. *mamo(ru)* defend, protect; keep, observe, obey; abide by; stick to; be true to. *mo(ru)* observe. *mamo(ri)* defense; guarding. *mori* nursemaid, baby sitter; baby sitting; (lighthouse) keeper. *(o)mamo(ri)* charm, amulet. *kami* feudal lord.

[2]刀 *mamo(ri)gatana* self-defense sword
[5]立 *mo(ri)-ta(teru)* bring up; support, rally
旧 *shukyū* conservatism
札 *mamo(ri)fuda* paper charm
本尊 *mamo(ri) honzon* guardian deity, patron deity
[6]行 *mamo(ri)-okona(u)* keep, obey
成 *shusei* preservation, maintenance
[7]役 *moriyaku* guardian
抜 *mamo(ri)-nu(ku)* hold fast, protect to the end
兵 *shuhei* guards
[8]卒 *shusotsu* soldiers on guard
[9]神 *mamo(ri)gami, shushin* guardian deity
[10]唄 *moriuta* lullaby; nursery rhyme
宮 *yamori* gecko, wall lizard
[11]袋 *mamo(ri)bukuro* amulet case
[12]備 *shubi* garrison, defense; fielding (baseball)
備兵 *shubihei* garrison, guard
備隊 *shubitai* garrison
備率 *shubiritsu* fielding average (baseball)
[13]節 *shusetsu* constancy, integrity
勢 *shusei* the defensive; defensive attitude; passive attitude
戦 *shusen* defensive war, defensive fight
戦同盟 *shusen dōmei* defensive alliance
[14]歌 *moriuta* lullaby, nursery rhyme
銭奴 *shusendo* a miser, a niggard
[15]衛 *shuei* a guard; a watchman, a doorkeeper
衛長 *shueichō* captain of the guard
[20]護 *shugo* protection; guard; safeguard
護天使 *shugo tenshi* guardian angel
護役 *shugoyaku* guardian
護神 *shugoshin* guardian deity

A **安** 1311 / J3042 / M7072 AN. *yasu(maru)* be rested, feel at ease, be relieved, repose. *yasu(njiru), yasu(nzuru)* be contented, be at ease. *yasura(u)* rest, relax. *yasu(i)* cheap, inexpensive; peaceful, quiet; gossipy, thoughtless. *yasu* cheap, low; drop (in prices). *yasu(ppoi)* cheap-looking, tawdry, insignificant. *yasu(rakana)* peaceful, tranquil, calm, restful. *yasu(pika)* knickknack, cheap finery.

[3]上 *yasua(gari)* economy. *yasua(gari) no* cheap, economical
小説 *yasushōsetsu* cheap fiction
[4]手 *yasude* cheap kind
月給 *yasugekkyū* meager salary
月給取 *yasugekkyūto(ri)* low-salaried man
心 *anshin* peace of mind, freedom from care; (sense of) relief or security; reassurance
心立命 *anjin-ryūmei, anshin-ritsumei* spiritual peace, enlightenment; calm resignation to fate; philosophy
心感 *anshinkan* sense of security
[5]打 *anda* safe hit
本丹 *ampontan* simpleton, dunce
芝居 *yasushibai* cheap theater
石榴 *zakuro* pomegranate
[6]安 *yasuyasu* very peaceful. *yasuyasu to* very easily, without trouble
危 *anki* fate, safety, welfare
死術 *anshijutsu* euthanasia
気 *anki* ease, comfort, feeling at home
気配 *yasukihai* bearish tone, weak tone (on the stock market)

全 *anzen* safety, security
全弁 *anzemben* safety valve
全灯 *anzentō* safety lamp
全地帯 *anzen chitai* safety zone, safety island
全系数 *anzen keisū* safety coefficient
全剃刀 *anzen kamisori* safety razor
全保障 *anzen hoshō* security
全保障理事会 *Anzen Hoshō Rijikai* Security Council
全帯 *anzentai* safety belt
全率 *anzenritsu* safety factor
全第一 *Anzen Daiichi* Safety First
全策 *anzensaku* safe plan
全硝子 *anzen garasu* safety glass
全装置 *anzen sōchi* safety device
全感 *anzenkan* sense of security
全器 *anzenki* safety device
7 住 *anjū suru* live peaceably
佚 *an'itsu* ease, idleness
利 *yasuri* low interest
否 *ampi* safety, welfare, well-being
売 *yasuu(ri)* selling cheap
坐 *anza* sitting at ease; leisure
材料 *yasuzairyō* bearish factor
8 国 *yasukuni, ankoku* a peacefully ruled country
固 *anko* security, firmness, stability
居 *ankyo* an easy life
価 *anka* low price
泊 *yasudoma(ri)* cheap inn
物 *yasumono* cheap article, bargain
臥 *anga* quiet rest
直 *anchoku* cheapness, low price
易 *an'i* ease
定 *antei* stability, equilibrium, stabilization, composure. *an(no)jō* as expected
定性 *anteisei* inclined to be stable or composed
定板 *anteiban* stabilizing fin
定度 *anteido* stability
定感 *anteikan* sense of security
9 保 *ampo* security
10 逸 *an'itsu* ease, idleness
値 *yasune* low price
眠 *ammin* quiet sleep
泰 *antai* peace, security, tranquility
料理屋 *yasuryōriya* cheap restaurant
酒 *yasuzake* cheap saké
酒場 *yasusakaba* cheap saloon
息 *ansoku* rest, repose
息日 *ansokubi, ansokunichi, ansokujitsu* the Sabbath; a sabbath; a day of rest
息日学校 *Ansokunichi Gakkō* Sabbath School
息所 *ansokujo* resting place
息香酸 *ansokkōsan* benzoic acid
11 悪 *yasu(karō)-waru(karō)* You get what you pay for.
宿 *yasuyado* cheap hotel
産 *anzan* easy delivery
12 閑 *ankan to* idly, indolently
堵 *ando* relief, reassurance
惰 *anda* shiftlessness; laziness
着 *anchaku* safe arrival
普請 *yasubushin* cheap structure
13 寝 *yasui* quiet sleep
置 *anchi* enshrinement, installation (of an image)
意 *an'i* peace of mind, freedom from care; (sense of) relief or security; reassurance
楽 *anraku* ease, comfort
楽死 *anrakushi* euthanasia, mercy killing
楽椅子 *anraku isu* easy chair
14 銭 *yasuzeni* small amount of money
雑誌 *yasuzasshi* cheap magazine
静 *ansei* rest, quiet, tranquility
静度 *anseido* degree of quiet (required in a patient)
寧 *annei* public peace, tranquility
寧秩序 *annei-chitsujo* peace and order
15 慮 *anryo* peace of mind, freedom from care; (sense of) relief or security; reassurance
請合 *yasuu(ke)a(i)* rash promise, lightly undertaking (something)
16 穏 *annon, an'on* peace, quiet, tranquility

4

宍 1312 J3c35 M7084 See 肉 4753.

宋 1313 J4157 M7078 Sō Sung (dynasty); dwell.

8 学 *Sōgaku* the learning of the Sungs
9 音 *Sōon* Sung-dynasty pronunciation
12 朝 *Sōchō* Sung dynasty
14 銭 *Sōsen* Sung currency

宏 1314 / J3928 / M7086 Kō wide, large.

3 大 *kōdai na* vast, extensive, magnificent
6 壮 *kōsō na* grand, imposing
7 図 *kōto* large plans
9 荘 *kōsō* splendor, grandeur
12 遠 *kōen na* vast and far-reaching
量 *kōryō* generosity, broadmindedness
13 業 *kōgyō* large extensive enterprise
17 謨 *kōbo* broad national-development plan

A **完** 1315 / J3430 / M7079 Kan completion, end. *mattō(suru)* accomplish, fulfill, complete, preserve (life). *matta(ku)* entirely, completely, wholly, perfectly; truly, indeed.

2 了 *kanryō* completion, conclusion
了形 *kanryōkei* perfect tense
了時制 *kanryō jisei* perfect tense
3 工 *kankō* completion
5 本 *kampon* complete works
6 成 *kansei suru* finish; be finished
成法 *kanseihō* completion (test)
成者 *kanseisha* one who completes
成品 *kanseihin* finished goods
全 *kanzen* perfection, completeness
全主義 *kanzen shugi* perfectionism
全性 *kanzensei* state of perfection
全無欠 *kanzen-muketsu* absolute perfection
全雇用 *kanzen koyō* full employment
全雇傭 *kanzen koyō* full employment
全数 *kanzensū* integer, whole number
7 投 *kantō* full-game pitcher
9 封 *kampū* complete blockade
10 納 *kannō* full payment; full delivery
11 遂 *kansui* completion
済 *kansai* full payment, liquidation
訳 *kan'yaku* complete translation
敗 *kampai* complete defeat
12 備 *kambi* perfection, completion
結 *kanketsu* conclusion, completion
勝 *kanshō* complete victory
13 数 *kansū* integer, whole number
15 徹 *kantetsu* accomplishment, realization, fulfillment; penetration
膚 *kampu* whole skin, uninjured skin
膚無迄 *kampuna(ki) made* thoroughly, completely; scathingly
18 璧 *kampeki* perfect gem, flawlessness; perfection, completeness

— 5 —

宕 1316 / J4566 / M7103 Tō cave.

B **宜** 1317 / J3539 / M7111 Gi. *yo(i), i(i)* good, good-natured; pleasing; precious; noble; lovely, beautiful, fine; lucky; efficacious; right; suitable, justifiable; appropriate, satisfactory; better; all right; unnecessary; no objection; intimate, friendly; easy; well; desirous. *yoro(shiku)* regards, greetings; well, properly, at your own discretion. *yo(shi)* good, all right, well, so. *mube, ube* truly.

10 候 *yōsōrō, yōsoro* Hold her steady (a ship).
15 敷 *yoroshiku* regards, greetings; well, properly, at your own discretion

A **宙** 1318 / J4368 / M7108 Chū air, space, mid-air, sky, heaven; memorization; interval of time.

6 返 *chūgae(ri)* somersault; looping the loop
9 乗 *chūno(ri)* aerial stunts

宛 1319 / J3038 / M7110 En. *a(teru)* address (a letter). *sanaga(ra)* just like. *-zutsu* apiece; each. *ataka(mo)* just as; as it were; fortunately. *-ate* addressed to.

6 行 *atega(u)* allot, fasten to, supply with, choose (a wife for); match with; patch; cover; apply to
先 *atesaki* address
名 *atena* address
名印刷機 *atena insatsuki* addressing machine
7 扶持 *a(tegai)buchi* discretionary allowance
8 金 *ategane* metal patch
11 転 *enten(taru)* smoothly rolling
12 然 *enzen* just as, as though; fortunately.

A **宝** 1320 / J4a75 / M7122 **寶** 1369 / J5570 / M7366 **寳** 1371 / J556f / M7376

Hō treasure. *takara* treasure, valuables; wealth; jewels; mammon.
2 刀 *hōtō* sacred sword; treasured sword
5 玉 *hōgyoku* gem, jewel, precious stone
石 *hōseki* gem, jewel
6 舟 *takarabune* treasure-ship picture
7 貝 *takaragai* cowrie, porcelain shell
8 典 *hōten* thesaurus, treasury of words; manual; precious book
物 *hōmotsu, takaramono* a treasure
物殿 *hōmotsuden* museum, treasury
物館 *hōmotsukan* treasure house
9 冠 *hōkan* crown, diadem
持腐 *takara (no) mo(chi)gusa(re)* wasting talents
10 庫 *hōko* treasure house, treasury
珠 *hōshu* gem, jewel
祚 *hōso* imperial throne; imperial reign
剣 *hōken* sacred sword
島 *takarajima* treasure island
11 探 *takarasaga(shi)* treasure hunt
船 *takarabune* treasure-ship picture
14 算 *hōsan* emperor's age
蔵 *hōzō* the treasury; treasure house
15 箱 *takarabako* strongbox
器 *hōki* treasured article
21 籤 *takarakuji* raffle, lottery
22 鑑 *hōkan* handbook, thesaurus, dictionary

A **宗** 1321 / J3d21 / M7106 Sō. SHŪ religion, sect, denomination. *mune* main point, essence; origin.
5 主 *sōshu* suzerain
6 匠 *sōshō* master (in an art), teacher
旨 *shūshi* doctrine, creed; sect, religion, a faith; one's line, one's taste
旨変 *shūshiga(e)* conversion; proselytism
7 社 *sōsha* the state; the world
8 国 *sōkoku* the home country (in contrast to colonies)
法 *shūhō* (Buddhist) sectarian regulations
制 *shūsei* religious institutions
典 *shūten* scriptures of a Buddhist sect
門 *shūmon* doctrine, creed; sect, religion, a faith; one's line, one's taste
門改 *shūmon-arata(me)* religious investigation
9 風 *shūfū* customs of a religious sect
祖 *shūso* sect founder
派 *shūha* sect, denomination
派的 *shūhateki* sectarian, denominational
派学校 *shūha gakkō* denominational school
派神道 *Shūha Shintō* Sectarian Shinto
10 徒 *shūto* believer, devotee, follower. *muneto* principal vassal; important people
家 *sōka, sōke* head family, main stock; originator
11 族 *sōzoku* relative; one's whole family
規 *shūki* religious rules
務 *shūmu* (Buddhist) sectarian affairs
務所 *shūmusho* temple office
務総長 *shūmu sōchō* head of a Buddhist sect
教 *shūkyō* religion, a faith, creed, cult
教上 *shūkyōjō* from the standpoint of religion
教心 *shūkyōshin* religious sentiment, piety
教史 *shūkyōshi* history of religion
教史家 *shūkyōshika* a historian of religions
教自由 *shūkyō (no) jiyū* religious liberty
教団体 *shūkyō dantai* religious organization
教狂 *shūkyōkyō* religious fanaticism; fanatic
教改革 *Shukyō Kaikaku* Protestant Reformation
教改革者 *shūkyō kaikakusha* religious reformer
教的 *shūkyōteki* religious
教画 *shūkyōga* religious picture
教学 *shūkyōgaku* the study of religion
教性 *shūkyōsei* religious character
教法人 *shūkyō hōjin* registered religious organization
教界 *shūkyōkai* the religious world
教家 *shūkyōka* religious teacher, minister; religious man
教哲学 *shūkyō tetsugaku* philosophy of religion
教教育 *shūkyō kyōiku* religious education
教裁判 *Shūkyō Saiban* the Inquisition
教戦争 *shūkyō sensō* religious war
教暦 *shūkyōreki* religious calendar
教劇 *shūkyōgeki* religious drama, passion play, mystery play, miracle play

教観 *shūkyōkan* religious view
14 閥 *shūbatsu* sectarianism
15 廟 *sōbyō* ancestral mausoleum
論 *shūron* sectarian arguments

5 A **官** 1322 / J3431 / M7107 KAN the Government, the authorities; the Court.
tsukasa office, government office; director, head official.

2 人 *kanjin* officials
3 女 *kanjo* court lady. *kannyo* women workers in the palace of the shogun or emperor
4 氏名 *kanshimei* official title and name
辺 *kampen* government circles, officialdom
辺筋 *kampen suji* government circles, officialdom
公庁 *kankōchō* government and public agencies
公吏 *kankōri* public officials
公私立 *kankō-shiritsu* public and private
公署 *kankōsho* public offices
5 用 *kan'yō* government business; official use
立 *kanritsu* government-operated
仕 *kanshi* government service
本 *kampon* government publication; book belonging to the government
司 *kanshi* government official; government office
民 *kammin* government and people
庁 *kanchō* government office; authorities
庁用語 *kanchō yōgo* official terminology
庁前 *kanchōmae* in front of the government office
6 印 *kan'in* government seal
地 *kanchi* government land
宅 *kantaku* official residence
名 *kammei, kammyō* official title
吏 *kanri* government official or clerk
有 *kan'yū* government ownership
有地 *kan'yūchi* government land
有林 *kan'yūrin* national forest
7 位 *kan'i* office and rank; official rank
社 *kansha* central-government shrine
私 *kanshi* public and private; government and citizenry
邸 *kantei* official residence
兵 *kampei* government forces
8 金 *kankin* government funds
長 *kanchō* chief of a government office
林 *kanrin* government forest
治 *kanchi* nonrepresentative government
物 *kambutsu, kammotsu* government property
服 *kampuku* official uniform
制 *kansei* government organization
命 *kammei* official orders, official business
舎 *kansha* official residence
学 *kangaku* government school; official teaching
事 *kanji* government business
房 *kambō* secretariat
房長官 *Kambō Chōkan* Chief Secretary of the Cabinet
9 食 *kanshoku* meals furnished by the government
威 *kan'i* authority of the office
途 *kanto* government service
海 *kankai* officialdom
紀 *kanki* official discipline
軍 *kangun* government forces, imperial army
品 *kampin* government property
界 *kankai* officialdom
臭 *kanshū* bureaucratic trend, red-tapism
省 *kanshō* government office, department
10 庫 *kanko* government storehouse
修 *kanshū* government editing
記 *kanki* written appointment (to an office)
員 *kan'in* officials
能 *kannō* body functions; carnal desire
能小説 *kannō shōsetsu* sex novel
能主義 *kannō shugi* sensualism
能的 *kannōteki* sensual
11 道 *kandō* government road
務 *kammu* official business
船 *kansen* government ship
許 *kankyo* government license
設 *kansetsu* established by the government
12 等 *kantō* official rank, civil-service grade
営 *kan'ei* government operation
報 *kampō* official telegram; official gazette
尊民卑 *kanson-mimpi* overemphasis on

government at the expense of the people
禄 *kanroku* government salary
給 *kankyū* government supply
給品 *kankyūhin* government issues
費 *kampi* government expense
費生 *kampisei* government student
13 衙 *kanga* government office
話 *Kanwa* the Mandarin language
署 *kansho* government office
業 *kangyō* government enterprise
14 歴 *kanreki* one's official career
選 *kansen* government-appointed (official)
銀 *kangin* government funds
製 *kansei* government manufacture
僚 *kanryō* bureaucracy, officialdom
僚化 *kanryōka* bureaucratization
僚主義 *kanryō shugi* bureaucracy
僚的 *kanryōteki* bureaucratic
僚制 *kanryōsei* bureaucracy
僚政治 *kanryō seiji* bureaucratic government
15 撰 *kansen* government compilation
権 *kanken* government authority
線 *kansen* government railway line
幣 *kampei* government offerings to certain shrines
幣社 *kampeisha* second highest class of prewar shrines
16 憲 *kanken* officials, authorities
17 爵 *kanshaku* office and title
18 職 *kanshoku* government service

A 定 1323 / J446a / M7109 TEI deciding. JŌ. *sada(maru)* be decided, be settled, quiet down. *sada(meru)* establish, lay down, stipulate; decide, determine; appoint, set (a date); pacify. *kima(ru)* be decided, be settled, be arranged; be certain to, be doomed to. *sada(me)* law, rule, regulation, provision; decision; appointment, arrangements; destiny, fate, karma. *sada(mari)* usage, custom, routine, rule; tranquility. *sada(kana)* sure, positive; accurate; reliable; sound, firm; clear, evident; genuine; able, competent; sober, sane; I think; if I remember right. *sada(mete), sada(meshi)* presumably, surely. *ki(matte)* usually, always, invariably. *jō-* regular, permanent.

4 日 *teijitsu* fixed date, appointed date; ordinary times
木 *jōgi* ruler, square; standard
文句 *kima(ri) monku* stereotyped expression
5 石 *jōseki* formula, rules
立 *teiritsu* thesis
圧 *teiatsu* constant pressure
本 *teihon* authentic book or manuscript
収 *teishū* fixed income
収入 *teishūnyū* fixed income
6 式 *jōshiki, teishiki* prescribed form; formula, formality. *teishiki no* regular, formal
年 *teinen* age limit, retirement age
休 *teikyū* regular holiday
休日 *teikyūbi* regular holiday
7 見 *teiken* definite opinion
位 *teii* orientation; fixed position
役 *teieki* prescribed (prison) labor
形 *teikei* fixed form, regular shape
足数 *teisokusū* quorum
角軌道 *teikaku kidō* trajectory
住 *teijū suru* settle down
住地 *teijūchi* permanent abode
住者 *teijūsha* permanent resident
8 店 *jōmise* permanent store
例 *jōrei, teirei* usage, precedent; standing orders; regular (meeting)
法 *jōhō* fixed rule, formula
限 *teigen suru* limit, confine, restrict
刻 *teikoku* regular time, appointed time
性分析 *teisei bunseki* qualitative analysis
価 *teika* fixed price
価表 *teikahyō* price list
命 *jōmyō* normal life span. *teimei* fate; predetermined length of life
命論 *teimeiron* fatalism
命論者 *teimeironsha* fatalist
9 食 *teishoku* regular meal; table d'hôte
連 *jōren* regular customers, frequenters, patrons
律 *teiritsu* fixed law, fixed rhythm
則 *teisoku* established rule, law
点 *teiten* fixed point
客 *jōkyaku* regular customer, frequent visitor
省 *teisei* kindness to parents
冠詞 *teikanshi* definite article
型 *teikei* definite form, type
型化 *teikeika* standardization

型的 *teikeiteki* typical
型詩 *teikeishi* rhymed verse or poems with fixed forms (such as tanka, haiku, sonnets, etc.)
10 席 *jōseki* variety hall; regular seats
紋 *jōmon* family crest
案 *teian* proposal, suggestion, plan
員 *teiin* regular staff, full number; seating capacity; quorum; full complement
員外 *teiingai* supernumerary
時 *teiji* regular time, stated period. *jōtoki* ancient gun or drum time signal; the signaler
時外 *teijigai* overtime
時制 *teijisei* part-time (school system)
11 道 *teidō* natural way, destiny
理 *teiri* theorem, proposition. *jōri* accepted truth
規 *teiki* prescribed, regular. *jōgi* a ruler; a (carpenter's) square; a standard
率 *teiritsu* fixed rate
宿 *jōyado* regular hotel
常 *teijō no* regular; stationary
12 植 *teishoku* the transplantation of seedlings
給 *teikyū* fixed allowance, fixed salary
評 *teihyō* public acknowledgment, general opinion
款 *teikan* articles of incorporation
無 *sada(me)na(ki)* fickle, uncertain, changeable, transient
温 *teion* fixed temperature
温器 *teionki* thermostat
量 *teiryō* fixed quantity; calculation; dose
量分析 *teiryō bunseki* quantitative analysis
着 *teichaku* fixing, fastening, fixation; stationed (at)
着物 *teichakubutsu* fixtures
着液 *teichaku eki* fixing solution
着網 *teichaku ami* fixed offshore fish trap
期 *teiki* stated period; season (train) ticket; rice sold on time; time transaction; time deposit; regular
期払 *teikibara(i)* payment on terms
期刊行物 *teiki kankōbutsu* periodicals
期米 *teikimai* rice sold on time
期列車 *teiki ressha* regular train
期的 *teikiteki* periodic
期券 *teikiken* season (train) ticket, commuter pass
期取引 *teiki torihiki* time transaction
期風 *teikifū* periodic wind, monsoon
期乗車券 *teiki jōshaken* season (train) ticket
期航空路 *teiki kōkūro* air route
期航空機 *teiki kōkūki* commercial plane, airliner
期航路 *teiki kōro* regular air service
期旅客機 *teiki ryokakki* regular plane
期船 *teikisen* regular ship
期預金 *teiki yokin* time deposit
期調査 *teiki chōsa* routine checkup
13 数 *teisū* fixed number, full number, quorum; constant; destiny
置 *teichi* stationary, fixed
業 *teigyō* regular occupation. *jōgō* fixed fate, karma
滑車 *teikassha* fixed pulley
詰 *jōzu(me)* permanent staff
詰員 *jōzu(me)in* permanent man
義 *teigi* definition
義論 *teigiron* dogmatics
14 説 *teisetsu* definite opinion, established theory
15 論 *teiron* fixed opinion, established theory
質分析 *teishitsu bunseki* quantitative analysis
16 積 *teiseki* fixed area
18 礎式 *teisoshiki* cornerstone ceremony
職 *teishoku* regular occupation, steady job
職者 *teishokusha* regular worker
額 *teigaku* fixed amount, flat sum
額税 *teigakuzei* fixed-amount tax
額量 *teigakuryō* ration
額預金 *teigaku yokin* fixed deposit
19 繫場 *teikeijō* anchorage area

A 実 1324/J3c42/M7124 實 1356/J5569/M7294 JITSU truth, reality; sincerity, fidelity; kindness; faith; substance, essence. *mino(ru)* ripen; bear fruit. *jitsu ni, ge ni* truly, really, in truth, surely, in fact. *jitsu wa* really, in fact. *mi* seed, berry, nut, fruit; substance, contents; ingredients; (soup) stock. *makoto* sincerity, honesty, fidelity; truth. *sane* fruit stone, kernel; nucleus.

[2] 入 *mii(ri)* crop; earnings, gains
力 *jitsuryoku* real ability, merit, efficiency; arms, force
力行使 *jitsuryoku kōshi* use of force, wildcat strike
力者 *jitsuryokusha* powerful person
力派 *jitsuryokuha* powerful group
[3] 子 *jisshi* one's own child
[4] 父 *jippu* one's real father
尺 *jisshaku* true measure
[5] 母 *jitsubo* one's real mother
写 *jissha* on-the-spot photograph
兄 *jikkei* one's own elder brother
包 *jippō* real cartridge
生 *miba(e), mishō* seedling
生活 *jisseikatsu* real life
収 *jisshū* actual income, take-home pay
収入 *jisshūnyū* actual income, take-home pay
世界 *jissekai* the outside world
世間 *jisseken* the everyday world
用 *jitsuyō* utility; practical use
用主義 *jitsuyō shugi* pragmatism
用向 *jitsuyōmuki* for practical use
用的 *jitsuyōteki* practical
用品 *jitsuyōhin* utility article
用新案 *jitsuyō shin'an* utility model; practical design
[6] 印 *jitsuin* registered seal
刑 *jikkei* prompt corporal punishment
名 *jitsumei, jitsumyō* real name
有 *jitsuu* reality
存 *jitsuzon* existence
存主義 *jitsuzon shugi* existentialism
在 *jitsuzai* real existence, reality
在論 *jitsuzairon* realism
地 *jitchi* practice; the actual site
地教育 *jitchi kyōiku* workshop
地経験 *jitchi keiken* practical experience
地試験 *jitchi shiken* practical examination, driving test
行 *jikkō* practice, performance, action, execution, realization
行力 *jikkōryoku* executive ability
行予算 *jikkō yosan* operating budget
行委員 *jikkōiin* executive committee; action committee
行者 *jikkōsha* executor, performer, a man of action, one who carries out (plans or principles)
行家 *jikkōka* man of action, practical man
行難 *jikkōnan* impracticability
[7] 見 *jikken* actual observation
状 *jitsujō* actual state of affairs
形 *jikkei* actual size
否 *jippi* fact and falsehood, accuracy, the truth
弟 *jittei* one's real younger brother
兵力 *jitsuheiryoku* effective strength
社会 *jisshakai* the real world, actual society
労働 *jitsurōdō* actual labor
芭蕉 *mibashō* banana tree
利 *jitsuri* utility, benefit, profit
利主義 *jitsuri shugi* materialism, utilitarianism
体 *jittai* substance, entity; antitype
体化 *jittaika suru* substantiate
体的 *jittaiteki* antitypical
体画 *jittaiga* stereograph
体変化 *jittai henka* transubstantiation
体論 *jittairon* substantialism, ontology, noumenalism
体鏡 *jittaikyō* stereoscope
[8] 例 *jitsurei* example, illustration
価 *jikka* true value; sterling worth; actual price; cost; market value
妹 *jitsumai* one's real younger sister
姉 *jisshi* one's real elder sister
効 *jikkō* efficacy, efficiency
直 *jitchoku* steadfastness; seriousness
学 *jitsugaku* practical learning, realism
念論 *jitsunenron* realism
況 *jikkyō* real condition
況放送 *jikkyō hōsō* on-the-spot broadcast
物 *jitsubutsu* substance; the real thing, genuine article, the original
物大 *jitsubutsudai* life-size
物教訓 *jitsubutsu kyōkun* object lesson
物教授 *jitsubutsu kyōju* object-lesson teaching
[9] 施 *jisshi* execution, enforcement
相 *jissō* actual facts; reality
科 *jikka* practical course
[10] 株 *jitsukabu* real stocks
記 *jikki* authentic record
益 *jitsueki* net profit
員 *jitsuin* effectives
家 *jikka* one's original family
[11] 現 *jitsugen* realization, fruition, materialization

3 口囗土士夂夊夕大女子【宀】5 寸小⺌尢尸屮山川巛工己巾干幺广廴廾弋弓彐彑彡彳

理 *jitsuri* principles actually practiced
情 *jitsujō* actual state of affairs
情調査 *jitsujō chōsa* fact-finding
動 *jitsudō* actual work
動時間 *jitsudō jikan* actual work hours
習 *jisshū* practice
習生 *jisshūsei* student apprentice, student assistant
務 *jitsumu* business affairs, business practice
務委員 *jitsumu iin* executive committee
務家 *jitsumuka* businessman
12 検 *jikken* inspection, identification
景 *jikkei* actual view
量 *jitsuryō* real quantity
費 *jippi* actual expense; cost price
弾 *jitsudan* real cartridge, live shell; solid shot; money
弾射撃 *jitsudan shageki* live-ammunition practice
測 *jissoku* actual survey
測図 *jissokuzu* accurate ordnance map
証 *jisshō* actual proof
証主義 *jisshō shugi* positivism
証哲学 *jisshō tetsugaku* positivism, positive philosophy
証論 *jisshōron* positivism
13 話 *jitsuwa* true story
跡 *jisseki* actual traces, evidence
戦 *jissen* actual fighting
数 *jissū* actual number
意 *jitsui* sincerity, faithfulness, kindness; true heart
感 *jikkan* actual sensation, realization, low passions
豊 *mino(ri)yuta(kana)* fruitful
勢力 *jisseiryoku* actual power; effectives
働 *jitsudō* actual work
働時間 *jitsudō jikan* actual work hours
践 *jissen* practice
践的 *jissenteki* practical
践躬行 *jissen-kyūkō* practicing what you preach
業 *jitsugyō* industry, business
業学校 *jitsugyō gakkō* vocational school
業界 *jitsugyōkai* industrial circles, business world
業家 *jitsugyōka* industrialist, businessman
際 *jissai* truth, fact, practice, reality, actual situation; actually; indeed. *jissai no* real, actual
際上 *jissaijō no* effective, real, actual, substantial. *jissaijō* as a matter of fact
際化 *jissaika* making practical
際生活 *jissai seikatsu* real life, practical life
際的 *jissaiteki* practical
際家 *jissaika* practical man, expert
際教育 *jissai kyōiku* practical education
際感 *jissaikan* sense of reality
14 歴 *jitsureki* career; actual experiences
聞 *jitsubun* something one has heard directly; hearing directly
像 *jitsuzō* real image
演 *jitsuen* stage show; exhibition, demonstration
説 *jissetsu* true account, real fact
態 *jittai* actual condition, realities
15 権 *jikken* real power
線 *jissen* solid line
質 *jisshitsu* substance, essence, quality; material, contents
質上 *jisshitsujō* in substance, substantially
質的 *jisshitsuteki* substantial, essential, material, real
質賃金 *jisshitsu chingin* real wages, take-home pay
16 積 *jisseki* capacity, actual size
録 *jitsuroku* authentic account
録物 *jitsurokumono* historical novel
17 績 *jisseki* actual results
18 蹟 *jisseki* actual traces, evidence
験 *jikken* experimentation; experience
験心理学 *jikken shinrigaku* experimental psychology
験所 *jikkenjo* experiment station
験的 *jikkenteki* experimental, empirical
験室 *jikkenshitsu* laboratory
験場 *jikkenjō* proving ground
19 爆弾 *jitsubakudan* live bomb

6

宦 1325 / J5561 / M7138 KAN official.

8 官 *kangan* eunuch
者 *kanja* eunuch

宥 1326 / J4d28 / M7137 YŪ. *nada(meru)* soothe, calm, pacify. *nada(me)* expiation, atonement, reconciliation.

8 免 *yūmen* forgiveness, pardon
和 *yūwa* appeasement
和政策 *yūwa seisaku* appeasement policy
和論者 *yūwaronsha* appeaser
10 恕 *yūjo suru* forgive, excuse
17 賺 *nada(me)-suka(su)* coax, soothe and humor

A **室** 1327 / J3c3c / M7136 SHITSU room, apartment, compartment, chamber. *muro* greenhouse; (ice) house; cellar.
4 内 *shitsunai* indoor, indoors, interior of a room
内灯 *shitsunaitō* inside lights (of a train)
内音楽 *shitsunai ongaku* chamber music
内遊戯 *shitsunai yūgi* indoor games
内場面 *shitsunai bamen* interior scene
内装飾 *shitsunai sōshoku* interior decorating; upholstering
内装飾師 *shitsunai sōshokushi* interior decorator; upholsterer
内楽 *shitsunaigaku* chamber music
内電話 *shitsunai denwa* interphone
内劇 *shitsunaigeki* a play suitable for a small room
5 外 *shitsugai* outdoors
7 町 *Muromachi* Muromachi era (1392–1573)
8 長 *shitsuchō* room monitor
9 咲 *muroza(ki)* blooming under glass
12 温 *shitsuon* room temperature

A **宣** 1328 / J406b / M7132 SEN. *notama(u)* be pleased to say, say. *sen(suru), no(ru)* proclaim, announce. *nobe(ru)* state, speak, recite, relate, mention.
3 下 *senge* imperial proclamation
5 布 *sempu* proclamation, promulgation
6 旨 *senji* imperial command
伝 *no(be)-tsuta(eru)* proclaim, preach. *senden* propaganda, publicity
伝者 *sendensha* herald, propagandist
伝屋 *senden'ya* propagandist, publicity man
伝係 *sendengakari* publicity man
伝部 *sendembu* publicity department
伝隊 *sendentai* propaganda squad
伝費 *sendenhi* publicity expense; advertising expense
伝戦 *sendensen* propaganda war; advertising campaign
伝業 *sendengyō* publicity business
伝業者 *senden gyōsha* publicity agent
伝機関 *senden kikan* propaganda machinery
7 告 *senkoku* sentence, verdict, pronouncement
言 *sengen* declaration, proclamation, profession, statement
言書 *sengensho* (written) declaration, manifesto, statement
8 明 *semmei* enunciation
命 *semmyō* (ancient) imperial proclamation (re-enthronement, succession, marriages, new era names, etc.)
10 託 *sentaku* oracle
11 教 *senkyō* missionary work; preaching; evangelism
教者 *senkyōsha* evangelist, preacher
教師 *senkyōshi* missionary
12 揚 *sen'yō suru* enhance, increase, exalt
13 義 *sengi* justification
戦 *sensen* declaration of war
戦布告 *sensen-fukoku* declaration of war
14 誓 *sensei* vowing, swearing
誓式 *senseishiki* administering an oath
誓書 *senseisho* written oath, deposit
15 撫 *sembu* placation, pacification

A **客** 1329 / J3332 / M7128 KAKU, KYAKU visitor, guest, customer, client; passenger. *kaku-* last (month).
2 人 *kyakujin, marōdo* visitor, guest
3 土 *kyakudo, kakudo* bringing in topsoil; journey; destination
4 月 *kakugetsu* last month
止 *kyakudo(me)* turning away customers; full house
引 *kyakuhi(ki)* soliciting patronage; barker; hotel runner; procurer
分 *kyakubun* guest, honorary member
5 用 *kyakuyō* for guests
礼 *kyakurei* courtesies toward guests
冬 *kakutō* last winter
布団 *kyakubuton* guest bedding
6 死 *kakushi, kyakushi* dying abroad
気 *kakki* youthful ardor; rashness
地 *kakuchi* foreign country
好 *kyakuzu(ki), kyakugono(mi)* choosy (in accepting guests or taxi passengers)

扱 *kyakuatsuka(i)* entertainment of guests
年 *kakunen* last year
7 足 *kyakuashi* customers, clientele
車 *kyakusha, kakusha* railway passenger coach
体 *kakutai, kyakutai* object (in law and philosophy)
位 *kakui* secondary place
択 *kyakuera(mi)* choosy in accepting guests
兵 *kyakuhei* mercenary soldier, volunteer
来 *kyakurai* visitor, caller
8 取 *kyakuto(ri)* men who guide visitors to a hotel; prostitutes hunting for patrons
舎 *kakusha* hotel, inn
受 *kyakuu(ke)* reception of guests
9 待 *kyakuma(chi)* waiting for passengers
亭 *kyakutei* inn
室 *kyakushitsu, kakushitsu* stateroom; guest room; parlor
室係 *kyakushitsugakari* room clerk
10 座 *kyakuza* seats for the guests
席 *kyakuseki* seats for guests
旅 *kakuryo* traveler; travel
員 *kakuin, kyakuin* associate or honorary member; guest (editor)
員教授 *kyakuin kyōju* visiting professor
11 遊 *kakuyū* traveling abroad
情 *kakujō* feelings of a stranger or traveler
船 *kyakusen, kakusen* passenger boat
商売 *kyaku shōbai* hotel, restaurant, or entertainment business
12 間 *kyakuma* parlor, guest room
勤 *kyakuzutome* travelers' guide
寓 *kakugū suru* sojourn, reside temporarily
筋 *kyaku suji* character of a customer
13 殿 *kyakuden* guest's reception room in a temple or a noble's home
僧 *kyakusō* traveling priest
戦 *kyakusen* fighting in a foreign or enemy country
歳 *kakusai* last year
意 *kakui* traveler's homesickness
14 種 *kyakudane* character of customers
語 *kakugo, kyakugo* object (in grammar)
16 膳 *kyakuzen* guest's dinner tray
18 観 *kyakkan, kakkan* the object; the material world
観性 *kyakkansei, kakkansei* objectivity
観法 *kyakkanhō, kakkanhō* objective method
観的 *kyakkanteki, kakkanteki* objective
観視 *kyakkanshi suru* look at objectively
観描写 *kakkan byōsha* objective description
19 臘 *kakurō* last December

— 7 —

B **宰** 1330 / J3a4b / M7160 SAI manager; rule.
9 相 *saishō* prime minister; councilor
12 卿 *saikei* minister; prime minister
14 領 *sairyō* management, supervision; manager, supervisor

宸 1331 / J5562 / M7171 SHIN eaves; palace; imperial courtesy.
12 筆 *shimpitsu* emperor's autograph
15 慮 *shinryo* emperor's heart, emperor's mind
憂 *shin'yū* emperor's anxiety
16 翰 *shinkan* imperial letter
18 襟 *shinkin* emperor's heart, emperor's mind

B **宴** 1332 / J3163 / M7166 EN feast, banquet, party, entertainment. *utage* party, banquet.
6 会 *enkai* feast, banquet, party, entertainment
会場 *enkaijō* banquet hall
10 席 *enseki* banquet, dinner party; banquet
11 遊 *en'yū* drinking party hall; banquet seat
12 飲 *en'in* drinking bout
13 楽 *enraku* revelry, festivities, merrymaking

A **害** 1333 / J3332 / M7165 GAI injury, harm, damage, mischief, interference. *gai(suru), sokona(u)* injure, harm, mar, spoil, damage, impair.
4 心 *gaishin* evil intention, malice, ill will
6 虫 *gaichū* harmful insect, blight, vermin
8 物 *gaibutsu* evil; pest, plague; nuisance
毒 *gaidoku* evil, harm; mischief; virus; poison; evil influence; blight
11 鳥 *gaichō* injurious bird
悪 *gaiaku* harm, injury, evil, mischief, evil influence
13 意 *gaii* malice, ill will, murderous intent

宵 1334 J3e2c M7168 B SHŌ. *yoi* evening, early night hours.

3 口 *yoi (no) kuchi* nightfall, early evening
4 月 *yoizuki* evening moon
月夜 *yoizukiyo* moonlit evening
8 明星 *yoi (no) myōjō* evening star, Venus
10 宵 *yoiyoi* every evening
11 張 *yoi(p)pa(ri)* sitting up late; nighthawk
祭 *yoimatsu(ri)* eve of a festival, vigil
12 越 *yoigo(shi)* (kept) overnight
13 寝朝起 *yoine-asao(ki)* early to bed and early to rise
14 鳴 *yoina(ki)* cockcrowing in the evening
17 闇 *yoiyami* moonless night, dark evening

容 1335 J4d46 M7172 A YŌ form; looks. *i(reru)* put into; permit; accept (advice). *katachi* form, shape; personal appearance.

3 子 *yōsu* situation, aspect, circumstances, movements; appearance; behavior, signs
6 色 *yōshoku* looks, personal appearance
気 *katagi* spirit, character, trait
共 *yōkyō* pro-Communist
共派 *yōkyōha* pro-Communist faction
7 体 *yōtai, yōdai* state of health, condition (of a patient). *yōdai(buru)* put on airs, act important
体書 *yōdaiga(ki), yōdaisho* diagnosis, medical bulletin, medical certificate
8 物 *iremono* receptacle, container
易 *tayasu(i)* easy, simple, light. *yōi na* easy, simple. *yōi(narazu), yōi(naranu)* serious, dangerous, important
9 相 *yōsō* features, looks, physiognomy
姿 *yōshi* form, figure, appearance
11 赦 *yōsha* pardon, forgiveness, mercy
赦無 *yōshana(ku)* mercilessly
12 喙 *yōkai* meddling, interference, interrupting a conversation
量 *yōryō* capacity, content, volume
14 認 *yōnin suru* tolerate, approve of, admit
貌 *yōbō* looks, personal appearance
態 *yōtai, yōdai* state of health, condition (of a patient)
疑 *yōgi* suspicion
疑者 *yōgisha* suspected person
15 儀 *yōgi* deportment, demeanor
器 *yōki* container, receptacle, capsule
16 積 *yōseki* capacity, volume, bulk, measurement, content
積量 *yōsekiryō* volume
積噸数 *yōseki tonsū* displacement tonnage

宮 1336 J355c M7156 A KU. KYŪ, GŪ constellations (of the zodiac); palace. *miya* Shinto shrine; Imperial Palace; prince, princess.

2 人 *miyabito, kyūjin* courtier
3 女 *kyujo* court lady
4 内庁 *Kunaichō* Imperial Household Agency
内官 *kunaikan* imperial household official
内省 *Kunaishō* the former Imperial Household Department
内卿 *kunaikyō* (ancient) imperial household minister
中 *kyūchū, kujū* imperial court
中三殿 *Kyūchū Sanden* the Three Palace Shrines
中礼服 *kyūchū reifuku* court dress
中席次 *kyūchū sekiji* order of court precedence
中喪 *kyūchūmo* court mourning
5 巡 *miyamegu(ri)* pilgrimage to shrines
仕 *miyazuka(e)* court or temple service
司 *gūji* chief priest of a Shinto shrine
6 刑 *kyūkei* castration (of men)
守 *miyamori* guarding a shrine; the temple watcher
守頭 *miyamorigashira* captain of the temple watcher
7 作 *miyazuku(ri)* palace construction, shrine construction
廷 *kyūtei* the Court, the Palace
廷列車 *kyūtei ressha* imperial or royal train
8 居 *miyai* shrine compound; imperial palace
門 *kyūmon* palace gate
参 *miyamai(ri)* shrine visit
9 造 *miyazuku(ri)* palace construction; shrine construction
相 *Kyūshō* Imperial Household Minister
柱 *miyabashira* palace pillars; shrine pillars
室 *kyūshitsu* palace
城 *Kyūjō* the Imperial Palace
城前広場 *Kyūjōmae Hiroba* Imperial Palace Plaza

3 口 囗 土 士 夂 夊 夕 大 女 子 【宀】7 寸 小 ⺌ 尢 尸 屮 山 川 巛 工 己 巾 干 幺 广 廴 廾 弋 弓 ヨ 彑 彡 彳

10 師 *miyashi* miniature-shrine maker
家 *miyake* imperial prince's home or family
11 道 *miyaji* road to a palace; road to a shrine
域 *kyūiki* shrine grounds; palace area
13 殿 *kyūden* palace
路 *miyaji* road to a palace; road to a shrine
14 様 *miyasama* prince; princess
18 闕 *kyūketsu* imperial palace

A **家** 1337 / J3248 / M7169 KA, KE house. *ie, uchi* house, home, residence; housing; family, household; family name; fortune. *-ya* house, shop, store, seller; dealer. *-ke* family. *-ka* person, profession.

2 人 *iebito* people living in the house. *kajin* the family, one's folks. *kenin* retainer, follower
3 女 *kajo* heiress, daughter of the home
子 *ie(no)ko* retainer
子郎党 *ie(no)ko rōtō* family followers, clansmen, adherents
4 中 *uchijū, kachū, iejū* the whole family; all over the house. *kachū* retainer
什 *kajū* furniture, fixtures
元 *iemoto* main family; wife's home
父 *kafu* my father
父長権 *kafuchōken* patriarchal authority
内 *kanai* family, household; one's wife. *yauchi* family; inside the house
内工業 *kanai kōgyō* home industry
内手工業 *kanai shukōgyō* home handicrafts
5 付 *ietsu(ki)* heiress; daughter who brings in a husband as joint heir
号 *yagō* store name, house name, hereditary family name, a stage-family name
奴 *kado* male servant
主 *yanushi, ienushi, iearuji* head of the house, houseowner, landlord
令 *karei* steward, butler
兄 *kakei* my elder brother
出 *iede* leaving home; abscondence
6 老 *karō* chief retainer, daimyo's minister
臣 *kashin* vassal, retainer
守 *iemori, yamori* caretaker, houseowner
毎 *iegoto ni* at every door
名 *iena, kamei* the name of the house, the family name. *kamei, kamyō, kemyō* family name, family honor
伝 *kaden* family history; family (secret) formula; family tradition
伝宝物 *kaden hōmotsu* family heirloom
宅 *kataku* domicile; premises
宅侵入 *kataku shinnyū* trespassing
宅捜索 *kataku sōsaku* domiciliary search
7 見 *iemi* coming to see a house
作 *kasaku* house for rent; building. *ietsuku(ri)* style of house. *iezuku(ri)* house building
扶 *kafu* steward
兎 *kato* tame rabbit
声 *kasei* honor of the family
君 *kakun, iegimi* head of the house
来 *kerai* retainer, retinue, servant
系 *kakei* family lineage
系図 *kakeizu* family tree
8 長 *kachō* family head, patriarch
門 *kamon* one's family or clan
居 *kakyo suru* stay at home
例 *karei* family custom
法 *kahō* family code
並 *iena(mi), yana(mi)* row of houses, every door
宝 *kahō* heirloom
苞 *iezuto* souvenir brought home
学 *kagaku* hereditary learning
具 *kagu* furniture, fixtures
具屋 *kaguya* furniture shop
具師 *kagushi* furniture man
事 *kaji* household affairs; housework; household economy
事向 *kajimu(ki)* household affairs; for the household
事科 *kajika* domestic-science course
事経済 *kaji keizai* household economy
事費 *kajihi* household expenses
9 風 *kafū* family tradition
信 *kashin* word from home
持 *iemo(chi)* homeowner; owner of houses; housekeeping
相 *kasō* the construction of a house (of importance in divination)
柄 *iegara* parentage, pedigree; a good family
乗 *kajō* family history
計 *kakei* household economy, family finances; livelihood

計費 *kakeihi* household expenses
計簿 *kakeibo* household account book
屋 *kaoku* house; building
屋台帳 *kaoku daichō* house register
屋税 *kaokuzei* house tax
屋敷 *ieyashiki* houses and lands, estate, homestead
政 *kasei* household economy
政学 *kaseigaku* domestic science
政科 *kaseika* domestic-science course
政婦 *kaseifu* housekeeper
10 借 *kashaku, ieka(ri)* renting a house
従 *kajū* steward, butler, attendant
桜 *iezakura* cherry tree in the garden
格 *kakaku* family status
紋 *kamon* family crest
訓 *kakun* family precepts
郷 *kakyō* one's old home; one's homeland, one's birthplace
家 *ieie* every house or family
宰 *ietsukasa, iezukasa, kasai* steward of a household
畜 *kachiku* domestic animals
書 *kasho* letter from home
財 *kazai* household goods; family wealth
財道具 *kazai dōgu* household goods
庭 *katei* home; family
庭工業 *katei kōgyō* family industry
庭用 *kateiyō* for home use
庭用品 *katei yōhin* household goods
庭礼拝 *katei reihai* family worship
庭向 *kateimu(ki)* for the home
庭的 *kateiteki* domestic or family (affairs)
庭経済 *katei keizai* household economy
庭訪問 *katei hōmon* visit to a home, home visitation
庭教育 *katei kyōiku* home education
庭教師 *katei kyōshi* private tutor; governess
庭常備薬 *katei jōbiyaku* household medicines
庭着 *kateigi* clothing worn at home
庭裁判所 *katei saibansho* domestic-affairs court
庭欄 *katei ran* family column
11 運 *kaun* family fortunes
婦 *kafu* housewife
探 *iesaga(shi), yasaga(shi)* searching a house (for something); domiciliary search; house hunting
移 *yautsu(ri)* moving
常 *kajō* family custom
累 *karui* family troubles
産 *kasan* family property
族 *kazoku* family, household
族手当 *kazoku teate* family allowance
族向 *kazokumu(ki)* family style
族会議 *kazoku kaigi* family council
族扶養義務 *kazoku fuyō gimu* family responsibility
族法 *kazokuhō* family-rights law
族的 *kazokuteki ni* like a member of the family
族制度 *kazoku seido* family system
族連 *kazokuzure* taking the family along
族風呂 *kazokuburo* family bath (in a hotel)
族席 *kazoku seki* family box seats
族員 *kazokuin* members of the family
族数 *kazokusū* size of a family
族歴 *kazokureki* family history
12 筋 *iesuji* lineage, pedigree, family line
集 *kashū* a poet's poetical works
無 *iena(shi)* homeless
普請 *yabushin* house building
13 禄 *karoku* hereditary stipend
続 *ietsuzu(ki)* row of houses
路 *ieji* the road home
跡 *ieato* remains of a home; family name
数 *yakazu, iekazu* number of houses
鳩 *iebato* dove, domestic pigeon
賃 *yachin* house rent
業 *kagyō* one's occupation or business
禽 *kakin* poultry, fowls
禽商 *kakinshō* poultryman
資 *kashi* family estate
資分散 *kashi bunsan* bankruptcy
督 *katoku* family headship; inheritance; family estate
督相続 *katoku sōzoku* succession to a family headship
督権 *katoku (no) ken* birthright
14 僮 *kadō* house servant
僕 *kaboku* house boy, manservant
鳴 *yana(ri)* rattling of a house
構 *iegama(e)* house structure, style, or appearance
蔵 *iekura* house and storeroom; storeroom within the house. *kazō* household possessions
塾 *kajuku* private school
裹 *iezuto* souvenir brought home

16 鴨 *ahiru* domestic duck
親 *kashin* one's parents
憲 *kaken* family constitution
18 職 *kashoku* one's trade or profession
難 *kanan* family misfortune
19 蠅 *iebae* housefly
蟻 *ieari* house ant
譜 *kafu* genealogy, pedigree
鶏 *kakei* chickens
20 醸 *kajō* home brew

8

寃 1338 / J5563 / M7202 See **冤** 404.

寇 1339 / J5564 / M7209 **寇** 1340 / J-X / M7208 **冦** 402 / J514e / M1590
Kō. *ada* foe, enemy; revenge; enmity, grudge, feud; harm, evil; ruin; invasion.

寅 1341 / J4652 / M7204 In. *tora* 3–5 a.m.; third zodiac sign; tiger.

B **寂** 1342 / J3c64 / M7200 Jaku death of a priest; quietly. Seki quietly. *sa(biru)* mellow, mature. *sabi(shigaru)* feel lonely, miss someone. *sabi* patina, antique look; elegant simplicity; trained reciter's voice. *sami(shii), sabi(shii)* lonely, lonesome; solitary, deserted, desolate. *seki to shita* hushed, still, silent.
6 光浄土 *jakkō-jōdo* Buddhist paradise
7 声 *sa(bi)goe* quiet and impressive voice
12 然 *sekizen(taru)* lonely, lonesome, desolate
13 寞 *sekibaku(taru)* lonely, lonesome, desolate
滅 *jakumetsu* Nirvana, death, annihilation
滅為楽 *jakumetsu-iraku* the joy of entering Nirvana
14 寥 *sekiryō* loneliness, desolateness

A **密** 1343 / J4c29 / M7205 Mitsu secrecy; denseness (of population); minuteness; carefulness; fineness. *hiso(kana), hiso(yakana)* secret, private, stealthy, hushed, still. *misoka* secret.
2 入国 *mitsunyūgoku* smuggling oneself into a country
入国団 *mitsunyūgokudan* smuggling ring
4 夫 *maotoko, mippu* adulterer
5 生 *missei suru* grow luxuriantly
令 *mitsurei* secret orders
6 会 *mikkai* clandestine meeting
旨 *misshi* secret orders
行 *mikkō suru* prowl about
行巡査 *mikkō junsa* plain-clothes police
7 告 *mikkoku* secret information
告者 *mikkokusha* informer, betrayer
売 *mitsubai* smuggling, bootlegging, illicit sale
売者 *mitsubaisha* smuggler, bootlegger
売淫 *mitsubaiin* unlicensed prostitution
8 送 *missō suru* send secretly
使 *misshi* secret messenger, secret agent
林 *mitsurin* thicket, jungle, dense forest
法 *mippō* Buddhist mystery
画 *mitsuga* detailed drawing, carefully finished picture
事 *mitsuji* secret
9 度 *mitsudo* density
造 *mitsuzō* illicit manufacture, moonshining
約 *mitsuyaku* secret agreement
計 *mikkei* secret plan
勅 *mitchoku* secret decree
封 *mippū suru* seal tight
室 *misshitsu* secret room
通 *mittsū* misconduct, adultery; intrigue; criminal connection
通者 *mittsūsha* adulterer
10 書 *missho* secret message
航 *mikkō* stowing away (on a ship)
航団 *mikkōdan* smuggling ring
航者 *mikkōsha* stowaway
11 閉 *mippei suru* seal tight
偵 *mittei* spy
婦 *mippu* adulteress
接 *missetsu na* close, intimate. *missetsu suru* stand close together; stick together
猟 *mitsuryō* poaching (in hunting)
教 *mikkyō* esoteric Buddhism; mysterious religion; the mysteries
密 *mitsumitsu ni* privately, secretly. *hisohiso* secretly, in confidence
12 着 *mitchaku suru* adhere to, be glued to
葬 *missō* private funeral
雲 *mitsuun* thick clouds

集 misshū suru swarm, crowd together
集部隊 misshū butai massed troops
貿易 mitsubōeki smuggling, contraband trade
貿易者 mitsubōekisha smuggler
14 漁 mitsuryō, mitsugyo secret unlicensed fishing
語 mitsugo whispers, confidential talk
15 談 mitsudan secret or confidential talk
儀 mitsugi secrets held within a certain group; initiation to such a group
儀教 mitsugikyō mystery religions
16 謀 mitsubō plot, intrigue, conspiracy
輸 mitsuyu smuggling; contraband
輸入 mitsuyunyū smuggling; contraband
輸入品 mitsuyunyūhin smuggled goods
輸入船 mitsuyunyūsen smuggling vessel
輸出 mitsuyushutsu suru smuggle abroad
輸出入 mitsuyushutsunyū smuggling
輸団 mitsuyudan smuggling ring
輸船 mitsuyusen smuggling vessel
20 議 mitsugi secret conference; private consultation
醸 mitsujō bootlegging

A 宿 1344 J3d49 M7195 SHUKU lodging; inn; post town, relay station, stage. *yado(ru)* lodge, dwell, live in; roost, be pregnant. *yado(su)* keep (a guest); carry (a virus); conceive (a child). *yado* house, home, dwelling; address; inn, lodgings, shelter. *yado(ri)* shelter, taking shelter, lodging.

3 下 *yadosa(gari)* short leave from work
4 引 *yadohi(ki)* hotel runner
六 *yadoroku* my hubby, my old man (the husband)
5 外 *shukuhazu(re)* edge of a stage town
主 *yadonushi* landlord, host. *shukushu* host (in biology)
世 *sukuse, shukuse* previous existence; karma; fate
世因縁 *sukuse innen* karma
6 老 *shukurō* old men, elders, seniors
年 *shukunen* many years
7 坊 *shukubō* temple lodgings
志 *shukushi* long-cherished desire
8 雨 *shukuu* long rain (spell)
舎 *shukusha* lodging, quarters, billet
直 *shukuchoku, tonoi* night duty, night watch
所 *shukusho* address, quarters, lodgings
所氏名 *shukusho-shimei* name and address
泊 *shukuhaku* lodging
泊人 *shukuhakunin* lodger, boarder, guest
泊所 *shukuhakujo* lodgings
泊料 *shukuhakuryō* room-and-board charge
命 *shukumei* fate, destiny, predestination
命的 *shukumeiteki* fatal
命論 *shukumeiron* fatalism
命論者 *shukumeironsha* fatalist
命観 *shukumeikan* fatalism
9 恨 *shukkon* long-standing hatred
陣 *shukujin* encampment
怨 *shukuen* old grudge
屋 *yadoya* inn, hotel, lodginghouse
屋業 *yadoyagyō* hotel business
屋業者 *yadoya gyōsha* hotel man
10 病 *shukubyō* chronic illness
借 *yadoka(ri)* renting a house
将 *shukushō* veteran general
料 *shukuryō* room-and-board charge
根草 *shukkonsō* perennial plant
11 運 *shukuun* fate, destiny
帳 *yadochō* hotel register
許 *yadomoto* one's lodgings, one's residence
酔 *shukusui, futsukayo(i)* a hangover
悪 *shukuaku* past sins, old crimes
患 *shukukan, shukkan* chronic illness; a long-standing grief
望 *shukubō* a long-cherished desire
12 痾 *shukua* chronic disease
割 *yadowa(ri)* billeting, quartering
善 *shukuzen* virtues of a previous arrangement
営 *shukuei* billeting; camp
替 *yadoga(e)* change of quarters
場 *shukuba* post town, relay station, stage
場町 *shukuba machi* hotel town (on the old post roads)
無 *yadona(shi)* homeless person, tramp
無子 *yadona(shi)go* homeless child
13 継 *shukutsu(gi)* (relayed) from post station to post station
罪 *shukuzai* sins of previous existence; original sin
意 *shukui* cherished opinion
賃 *shukuchin, yadochin* hotel charges, lodging expenses

業 *shukugyō* karma's reward
14 銭 *yadosen* hotel charges
駅 *shukueki* post town, relay station; stage
15 縁 *shukuen* karma; destiny, fate
敵 *shukuteki* old enemy
弊 *shukuhei* deep-rooted evil
16 謀 *shukubō* premeditated plan
18 題 *shukudai* homework, lessons; pending questions
題帳 *shukudaichō* workbook
19 願 *shukugan* long-cherished desire

A **寄** 1345 / J3473 / M7203 Ki. *yo(seru)* let approach, bring near; gather, collect, summon, muster; add up; push aside; attack; send a letter; contribute to; become dependent on, take refuge with. *yo(kosu)* send, forward, deliver. *yori* attendance, gathering; collection (of money). *yo(ru)* approach; assemble; call at; come; lean toward; obey; lean on, depend on; conclude; be possessed (by devils); present (offerings). *yo(tte-takatte)* in a crowd. *-yori* from (the north).

3 与 *kiyo* contribution; service
与過失 *kiyo kashitsu* contributory negligence
4 辺 *yo(ru)be* friend; protector, helper
手 *yo(se)te* enemy, attacking force, onset
木 *yo(ri)ki* driftwood. *yo(se)gi* wooden mosaic
切 *yo(se)gi(re)* remnants, scraps of cloth
切細工 *yo(se)ki(re)zaiku* patchwork
5 出 *yo(ri)-da(su)* pick out, sort out, single out
付 *yo(se)-tsu(keru)* let come near. *yo(ri)-tsu(ku)* approach; open (the stock market). *yo(ri)tsu(ki)* opening session (of a stock market). *kifu* donation, endowment
付行為 *kifu kōi* act of endowment, donation
付金 *kifukin* donation, endowment
付者 *kifusha* donor
付財産 *kifu zaisan* endowment
生 *kisei* parasitism
生木 *yadorigi* mistletoe; parasite
生火山 *kisei kazan* parasite volcano
生虫 *kiseichū* parasite, parasitic insects
生虫学 *kiseichūgaku* parasitology
生体学 *kiseitaigaku* parasitology
生物 *kiseibutsu* parasite
6 返 *yo(se)-kae(ru)* approach and return
年波 *yo(ru) toshinami* oncoming age, old age
合 *yo(ri)-a(u) vi* assemble, meet, grow together. *yo(ri)-a(waseru) vt* intertwine. *yoriai* meeting, assembly, party. *yo(se)-a(waseru)* get (people or things) together
合所帯 *yoria(i)jotai* heterogeneous group (of people)
7 住 *kijū* temporary residence
8 泊 *kihaku* anchoring
波 *yosenami* surf
居 *kikyo* temporary dwelling; staying with someone else
居虫 *yadokari* hermit crab
9 食 *kishoku* parasitism, dependency, sponging
10 席 *yose* variety hall, storytellers' hall, music hall, vaudeville
進 *kishin* contribution, donation
値 *yorine* opening price
航 *kikō suru* call at a port, anchor
託 *kitaku* deposition
書 *yosega(ki)* collection of autographs. *kisho* contributed article
留 *kiryū* temporary residence, sojourn
留地 *kiryūchi* place of sojourn
留届 *kiryū todoke* registry of a temporary residence
留者 *kiryūsha* temporary resident, sojourner
11 道 *yo(ri)michi suru* call on the way; detour; stop over
掛 *yo(ri)-ka(karu) vi*, *yo(se)-ka(keru) vt* lean against. *yosekake* leaning; lean-to
添 *yo(ri)-so(u)* draw near; snuggle against
寄 *yo(ri)yo(ri)* occasionally
宿 *kishuku* lodging, board
宿人 *kishukunin* boarder
宿生 *kishukusei* dormitory student
宿舎 *kishukusha* boarding house; school dormitory
宿舎生 *kishukushasei* dormitory student
宿料 *kishukuryō* boarding expenses
12 場 *yo(ri)ba* rendezvous, meeting place
越 *yoko(su)* send, forward; deliver

港 *kikō suru* call at a port
寓 *kigū* lodger, paying guest
棟造 *yo(se)munezuku(ri)* hip roof
集 *yo(se)-atsu(meru)* gather, collect, glean, scrape together; rally (soldiers). *yo(ri)-atsu(maru)* assemble, meet
集人 *yo(ri)atsu(mari)bito* rabble
14 語 *kigo* send word by
算 *yo(se)zan* addition (in math)
15 縋 *yo(ri)-suga(ru)* cling to, rely on
稿 *kikō suru* contribute (to a newspaper)
稿者 *kikōsha* contributor of articles
稿家 *kikōka* contributor of articles
16 頼 *yo(ri)-tano(mu)* depend on, take refuge in
17 鍋 *yo(se)nabe* chowder
18 贈 *kizō, kisō* donation, presentation
贈本 *kizōbon, kisōbon* complimentary copy
贈者 *kizōsha, kisōsha* donor, contributor
贈品 *kizōhin, kisōhin* present, donation
贈書 *kizōsho* books received

— 9 —

寔 1346 / J5566 / M7244 SHOKU. JIKI truth; this; merely. *makoto ni* really, truly.

寐 1347 / J5567 / M7236 BI. *ne(ru)* sleep.

寓 1348 / J3677 / M7243 GŪ temporary abode. *gu(suru)* reside temporarily; keep; imply, suggest.
7 言 *gūgen* allegory, parable
8 居 *gūkyo* temporary residence
所 *gūsho* temporary residence
舎 *gūsha* inn, temporary lodging place
13 話 *gūwa* allegory, fable, parable
意 *gūi* hidden meaning; symbolism; implication; moral

A 富 1349 / J4959 / M7230 富 406 / J495a / M1592 FU. FŪ. *to(masu)* enrich. *to(meru)* wealthy; abundant. *to(mu)* be rich, become wealthy; teem with, abound in; be fruitful; be rife; be replete. *tomi* wealth, mammon, fortune; resources; lottery.
2 力 *furyoku* wealth, resources
3 士山形 *fujisangata* shape of Mt. Fuji
士形 *fujigata* shape of Mt. Fuji
士絹 *fujiginu* fuji silk
士額 *fujibitai* a Mt. Fuji brow
5 札 *tomi fuda* lottery ticket
6 有 *fuyū* wealth, affluence
8 岳 *Fugaku* Mt. Fuji
者 *fūsha, fusha* rich person, millionaire
国 *fukoku* rich country, national resources, national enrichment
国強兵 *fukoku-kyōhei* national wealth and military strength
9 祐 *fuyū* wealth, affluence
栄 *to(mi)-saka(eru)* prosper
10 家 *fūka* wealthy family
11 強 *fukyō* wealth and power
商 *fushō* rich merchant
12 裕 *fuyū* wealth, affluence
裕化 *fuyūka suru* enrich, make wealthy
貴 *fuki, fūki, fukki* wealth and honor
貴利達 *fūki-ritatsu* wealth and success
13 源 *fugen* source of wealth, natural resources
鉱 *fukō* rich ore
農 *funō* rich farmer
14 豪 *fugō* wealthy man, millionaire
16 興業 *tomi kōgyō* lottery enterprise
17 嶽 *Fugaku* Mount Fuji
23 籤 *tomikuji* lottery, lottery ticket

A 寒 1350 / J3428 / M7239 KAN midwinter, coldest season. *samu(garu)* be sensitive to cold. *samu(gari)* a person sensitive to cold. *samu(i)* cold, chilly.
3 土 *kando* lonesome place; poor place
士 *kanshi* a poverty-stricken and helpless person
4 心 *kanshin suru* shudder at, be alarmed
月 *kangetsu* wintry moon
水 *kansui* cold water
中 *kanchū* midwinter, cold season
天 *kanten* agar-agar, vegetable gelatin; freezing weather; wintry sky
天版 *kantemban* hectograph
5 生 *kansei* poverty-stricken student; this (humble) student
玉子 *kantamago* winter eggs
6 竹 *kanchiku* solid bamboo
色 *kanshoku* cold color
行 *kangyō* midwinter religious austerities
衣 *kan'i* winter clothing
地 *kanchi* cold region
灯 *kantō* a light on a cold night; the light of a flame

光 *kankō* solitary light
気 *kanki, samuke* cold, cold weather; chill
気立 *samukeda(tsu)* feel cold, have a chill; feel afraid
7 村 *kanson* deserted village, poor village, out-of-the-way village
声 *kansei* a cold voice. *kangoe* midwinter voice training
花 *kanka* winter flowers; the snow
卵 *kantamago* winter eggs
冷 *kanrei* cold, chilliness
冷地 *kanreichi* cold district
冷前線 *kanrei zensen* cold front
冷紗 *kanreisha* cheesecloth
8 雨 *kan'u* cold rain
国 *kankoku* cold country, cold region
明 *kan'a(ke)* end of the cold season
波 *kampa* cold wave
肥 *kangoe, kangoyashi* winter fertilizing, midwinter manuring
夜 *kan'ya* cold night, winter night
参 *kammai(ri)* midwinter pilgrimage
空 *samuzora* wintry sky, cold weather
苦 *kanku* suffering from the cold
9 風 *kampū, samukaze* cold wind, winter wind
屋 *samu(gari)ya* cold-sensitive person
威 *kan'i* intense cold
点 *kanten* points on the skin sensitive to temperature
室 *kanshitsu* cold house for raising frigid-zone plants
草 *kansō* winter grass
負 *samu(sa)make, kammake* fearful of the cold, weakening in cold weather
紅梅 *kankōbai* winter red-blossom plum tree
垢離 *kangori* mid winter cold-water ablutions
10 庭 *kantei* winter garden
疾 *kanshitsu* a cold
凌 *samu(sa)-shino(gi)* getting through the winter; means of weathering the winter
晒 *kanzara(shi)* exposure to cold weather
梅 *kambai* early plum blossoms
流 *kanryū* cold current
剤 *kanzai* freezing mixture
郷 *kankyō* poor isolated village
烏 *kangarasu* winter crows
害 *kangai* damage from cold
帯 *kantai* frigid zone
烈 *kanretsu* severe cold weather
素 *kanso* poor and simple
修業 *kanshugyō* (Buddhist) winter austerities
11 鳥 *kanchō* winter bird
菊 *kangiku* winter chrysanthemums
貧 *kampin* very poor, indigent
雀 *kansuzume* winter sparrow
12 極 *kankyoku* polar regions
湿 *kanshitsu* cold and moisture
暑 *kansho* hot and cold; temperature; summer and winter
雲 *kan'un* wintry clouds
13 椿 *kantsubaki* winter camellia
詣 *kammai(ri), kammōde* midwinter pilgrimage
暖 *kandan* heat and cold, temperature
暖計 *kandankei* thermometer
14 酸 *kansan* poverty and weakness; loneliness
製 *kansei* made in the cold season
15 餅 *kammochi* midwinter rice cake
熱 *kannetsu* heat and cold; chills and fever
16 稽古 *kangeiko* winter exercise

10

寞 1351 / J556b / M7282 BAKU lonely, quiet.

B **寛** 1352 / J3432 / M7276 **寬** 1355 / J-X / M-X KAN leniency, generosity.

kutsuro(gu) relax, feel at home. *kutsuro(geru)* loosen, ease, relax. *yutta(ri) suru* make oneself at home. *yutta(ri) toshite* at ease, composed. *yutta(ri) shita* quiet, calm, leisurely, composed. *kutsuro(gi)* ease; room, space. *hiro(i)* broad-minded. *yuru(yakana)* loose; easy (slope); gentle, lenient, generous; slow (stream).

3 大 *kandai* magnanimity, liberality; tolerance, leniency
4 仁 *kanjin* magnanimity, generosity
6 衣 *kan'i* lounging clothes
仮 *kanka suru* forgive; tolerate
刑 *kankei* lenient sentence
8 典 *kanten* leniency, clemency

9 厚 *kankō* kindness and largeheartedness
宥 *kan'yū* forgiveness
10 恕 *kanjo* generosity; forgiveness, mercy, leniency
容 *kan'yō* forbearance, tolerance, generosity. *kan'yō no* generous, lenient, long-suffering, broad-minded, tolerant, liberal
容主義 *kan'yō shugi* (religious) toleration
容性 *kan'yōsei* generosity, magnanimity, lenience, tolerance, forbearance
12 裕 *kan'yu* generosity, leniency
17 濶 *kankatsu na* loose (garments); generous
厳 *kangen* lenity and severity

B **寢** 1353 J3f32 M7278′ **寝** 1354 J556a M7289 SHIN sleeping; resting; bed. *ne(ru)* sleep; retire; be bedridden; lie down; lie idle; remain unsold. *ne(kasu), ne(kaseru), ne(seru)* put to sleep; send to bed; lay down, let lie idle. *ne(soberu)* sprawl, lie sprawled. *ne(sobireru)* be wakeful, fail to sleep. *i(nu)* sleep. *ne* sleep. *ne(shina) ni* on retiring *ne(zu) ni* sleeplessly.

2 入 *ne-i(ru)* fall asleep; be dull (the stock market)
入込 *ne-i(ri)-ko(mu)* sleep in, sleep soundly
入端 *nei(ri)bana* first part of a night's sleep
3 刃 *netaba* dull blade, blunt sword
小便 *neshōben* bedwetting
4 込 *neko(mi), nego(mi)* asleep; in bed. *neko(mu)* fall asleep; oversleep; be sick in bed
仏 *nebotoke* recumbent Buddha
不足 *nebusoku* lack of sleep
化粧 *negeshō* removal of makeup before retiring
心 *negokoro* sleeping comfort
心地 *negokochi* sleeping comfort
心地心 *negokochigokoro* sleeping comfort
5 圧 *neo(shi)* pressing clothes under bedding
付 *shin (ni) tsu(ku)* retire, go to bed. *ne-tsu(ku)* fall asleep, be confined to bed. *ne-tsu(kaseru)* put to sleep. *ne(kashi)-tsu(keru)* put to sleep, send to bed
白粉 *neoshiroi* makeup before retiring
台 *shindai, nedai* bed, bedstead, bunk, berth, couch, crib, cot
台虫 *shindai mushi* bedbug
台車 *shindaisha* sleeping car
台券 *shindaiken* sleepingcar ticket
6 衣 *shin'i* night clothes
返 *negaeri* tossing or turning in bed; changing sides; betrayal. *negae(ru)* change sides; betray
汗 *neuse* night sweat
耳水 *nemimi (ni) mizu* great surprise, thunderbolt
耳開 *nemimi (ni) ki(ku)* hear while asleep
7 言 *negoto* talking in sleep, nonsense
床 *nedoko* bed, cot, berth
冷 *nebi(e)* catching cold while sleeping
坊 *nebō* oversleeping, late rising
抉 *ne-koji(reru)* be unable to sleep
忘 *ne-wasu(reru)* oversleep
乱髪 *nemida(re)gami* hair mussed up in sleep
8 房 *shimbō* bedroom
所 *nedoko, shinjo* bedroom
泊 *netoma(ri) suru* stay with, lodge
取 *ne-to(ru)* steal another's lover
直 *ne-nao(su)* go back to bed
具 *shingu* bedding
苦 *neguru(shu)* unable to sleep well
物 *ne(kashi)mono* unsold goods
物語 *nemonogatari* bedtime story
9 首 *nekubi* head of a sleeping person
食 *shinshoku* food and sleep. *negu(i)* living in idleness
相 *nezō* sleeping posture
室 *shinshitsu* bedroom
臭 *negusa(i)* smelling as if someone slept here
姿 *nesugata* sleeping form
巻 *nemaki* night clothes
10 起 *neoki* lying down and arising; waking; daily living
酒 *nezake* a nightcap, a drink at bedtime
息 *neiki* a sleeper's breathing
莫蓙 *negoza* sleeping mat
11 鳥 *nedori, netori* birds at roost
過 *ne-su(giru), ne-su(gosu)* oversleep
惚 *ne-bo(keru), ne-tobo(keru)* be half asleep

寂 *ne-sabi(shii)* missing a sleeping companion
道具 *nedōgu* bedding
転 *ne-koro(bu)* lie down, throw oneself down
転椅子 *nekoro(bi) isu* deck chair
12 棺 *nekan, negan* coffin
覚 *neza(meru)* awake. *nezato(i)* light sleeper
違 *ne-chiga(eru)* strain (the back) in sleep
椅子 *neisu* couch, lounge
間 *nema* bedroom
間着 *nemaki* night clothes
13 損 *ne-sokona(u)* miss a chance to sleep; be wakeful
際 *negiwa ni* just before retiring
飽 *ne-a(kiru)* be tired of sleeping
殿 *shinden* Heian noble's residence
殿造 *shindenzuku(ri)* Heian residential architecture
14 厭 *ne-a(kiru)* be tired of sleeping
腐 *ne-kusa(ru)* oversleep
様 *nezama* sleeping posture
静 *ne-shizu(maru)* fall asleep
17 藁 *newara* (stable) litter, straw
18 穢 *igitana(i)* always sleepy; oversleeping
顔 *negao* sleeping face

11

寢 1354 / J556a / M7289 See **寝** 1353.

寬 1355 / J-X / M-X See **寛** 1352.

實 1356 / J5569 / M7294 See **実** 1324.

寨 1357 / J5c4d / M7298 SAI fort.

寤 1358 / J5568 / M7291 Go awake; understand.
12 寐 *gobi nimo* whether awake or asleep

寥 1359 / J556c / M7292 RYŌ lonely.
14 寥 *ryōryō(taru)* few, rare; lonely, lonesome

A **察** 1360 / J3b21 / M7283 SATSU. *sas(suru), sas(shiru)* presume, surmise; judge; realize, understand; imagine, suppose; sympathize with. *sas(shi)* conjecture; judgment; understanding, consideration, sympathy.
8 知 *satchi* inference

B **寧** 1361 / J472b / M7296′ **寗** 1362 / J-X / M7296 NEI. *mushi(ro* preferably.
4 日 *neijitsu* peaceful day, quiet day
20 馨児 *neikeiji* child prodigy

B **寡** 1363 / J3249 / M7286 KA minority, few, minimum; widow. *yamome* widow. *sukuna(i)* few, a little, scarce, insufficient, seldom.
2 人 *kajin* my humble self (used by royalty)
4 少 *kashō no* little, few, scanty
夫 *yamome* widower
7 言 *kagen* taciturnity, reticence
作 *kasaku* low production
兵 *kahei* small army force
男 *yamome, yamome otoko, yamoo* widower
8 居 *kakyo* widowhood
11 婦 *kafu, yamome* widow
欲 *kayoku* unselfishness
13 勢 *kazei* small military force
14 聞 *kabun* limited information
15 慾 *kayoku* unselfishness
黙 *kamoku* taciturnity, reticence
16 頭政治 *katō seiji* oligarchy

12

寫 1364 / J556d / M7320 See **写** 400.

B **賓** 1365 / J4950 / M-X **賓** 5804 / J-X / M36788 [貝] HIN guest.
9 待 *hintai suru* treating as an honored guest
客 *hinkyaku* guest, guest of honor
10 格 *hinkaku* objective case
13 辞 *hinji* object of a verb

B **寮** 1366 / J4e40 / M7325 RYŌ hostel, dormitory; villa; tea pavilion. *tsukasa* office, government office; director, head official.

⁵母 *ryōbo* matron (of a dormitory)
生 *ryōsei* boarding student
⁸長 *ryōchō* one in charge of a dormitory
¹⁴歌 *ryōka* dormitory song

B 審 1367 / J3f33 / M7316 SHIN hearing, trial, investigation.
saba(ku) judge. *saba(ki)* judgment. *tsumabira(ka)* full, detailed, minute, accurate; versed in, well-informed on.
⁷判 *shimpan, shimban* refereeing, umpireship; trial, judgment
判役 *shimpan'yaku* umpire, referee, judge
判官 *shimpankan* umpire, referee, judge
判者 *shimpansha* umpire, referee, judge
⁹査 *shinsa* judgment, examination, inspection, investigation, screening, auditing (of salaries)
査員 *shinsain* judges, examiners
美 *shimbi* appreciation of the beautiful
美学 *shimbigaku* aesthetics
美眼 *shimbigan* aesthetic sense
¹¹問 *shimmon* interrogation, hearing, trial
理 *shinri* trial, hearing, examination
²⁰議 *shingi* deliberation, discussion, review
議会 *shingikai* deliberative assembly; inquiry commission

13

寰 1368 / J556e / M7344 KAN domain under direct imperial rule; hedge surrounding palace.

16

賓 1369 / J5570 / M7366 See 宝 1320.

寵 1370 / J437e / M7368 CHŌ favor, affection, love, patronage.
⁵用 *chōyō suru* show favor to
⁶臣 *chōshin* favorite retainer; court favorite
⁷児 *chōji* favorite child, pet
⁹姫 *chōki* favorite imperial concubine
¹⁰恩 *choon* great favor
¹¹遇 *chōgū* patronage, special favor
¹³愛 *chōai* favor, affection, love, patronage

17

寶 1371 / J556f / M7376 See 宝 1320.

RAD. 寸 41

Sun (the Japanese inch). At right: *sunzukuri*. Nickname: Inch.

A 寸 1372 / J4023 / M7411 SUN one-tenth of a foot; measure.
³土 *sundo* an inch of land
⁴切 *sungi(ri)* a straight cut
分 *sumbun* a bit, a little
不足 *suntarazu* short person
⁶地 *sunchi* an inch of land
⁷言 *sungen* short but significant words
足 *sunta(razu)* short person
余 *sun'yo* a small amount remaining, a small remnant
志 *sunshi* small token of appreciation
⁸忠 *sunchū* my loyalty (humble)
法 *sumpō* measure, dimension; plan, program, arrangement
法通 *sumpōdō(ri)* to measure; as specified
⁹前 *sunzen* just before
衷 *sunchū* somewhat of a desire; my desire
¹⁰進 *sunshin* inching along
時 *sunji* a moment, a minute
陰 *sun'in* a moment, a minute
書 *sunsho* note, short letter
¹¹描 *sumbyō* thumbnail sketch
断 *sundan suru* cut to pieces, tear to pieces
毫 *sungō* (not) a bit
¹²評 *sumpyō* brief review, thumbnail sketch
¹³暇 *sunka* a moment's leisure
楮 *suncho* note, short letter
鉄 *suntetsu* small weapon; pithy saying
隙 *sungeki* moment of leisure

15 劇 *sungeki* dramatic sketch
18 簡 *sunkan* brief note, short letter

3

A **寺** 1373 / J3b7b / M7414 JI *-ji, tera* temple.

2 入 *terai(ri)* admission to a temple school
3 上 *teraa(gari)* admission to a temple school
子 *terako* temple-school pupil
子屋 *terakoya* temple primary school
小屋 *terakoya* temple primary school
4 内 *jinai* in the temple compound
5 巡 *teramegu(ri)* temple-pilgrimage journey
号 *jigō* Buddhist temple name
6 回 *teramegu(ri)* temple-pilgrimage journey
守 *teramori* temple sexton
7 社 *jisha* temples and shrines
兵 *jihei* monk-soldiers
男 *teraotoko* temple sexton
8 門 *jimon* temple gate; temple
参 *teramai(ri)* temple visit
9 廻 *teramegu(ri)* temple-pilgrimage journey
院 *jiin* temple
10 格 *jikaku* temple rank
11 務 *jimu* temple affairs
務所 *jimusho* temple office
12 塔 *jitō* a temple pagoda
禄 *jiroku* benefice
13 僧 *jisō* temple priest
詣 *teramō(de), teramai(ri)* visiting a temple
預 *teraazu(ke)* confinement in a temple
14 様 *(o)terasama* temple priest
銭 *terasen* charge for the temporary use of land or buildings
領 *jiryō* temple estate, glebe
15 請 *terau(ke)* Buddhist conversion certificate
請状 *terau(ke)jō* Buddhist conversion certificate

4

B **寿** 1374 / J3c77 / M7419′ **壽** 1077 / J5468 / M5672 SU. JU age; one's natural life; longevity; congratulations. *kotobu(ku)* congratulate; wish one well. *kotoho(gu)* congratulate. *kotobuki* long life; congratulations.

5 司 *sushi* sushi, rice mixed with other foods
6 老人 *Jurōjin* a god of longevity
8 命 *jumyō* life, life span
9 盃 *juhai* toasting, drinking to someone's health
12 賀 *juga* long-life celebrations, particulary the 61st, 77th, and 88th birthdays
14 像 *juzō* statue (of a living person)
17 齢 *jurei* long life; age; life

A **対** 1375 / J4250 / M7419 **對** 1387 / J5574 / M7457 TAI the opposite; antonym; even, equal; versus; (score of three) to (one); counter-, anti-, versus. *tai(suru)* face, confront, be opposite; receive (visitors); subtend. *(ni) tai(suru)* toward, to, in, by, against, in answer to; in contrast to; compared with. *tai(shi), tai(shite)* against, opposite, face to face; before; at; contrary to; in preparation for; toward; in return for; as compared with, in contrast to. *tsui* pair, couple, set.

2 人 *taijin* personal, personnel (affairs)
4 支 *tai-Shi* toward China, with China
比 *taihi* contrast, comparison, opposition, dissimilitude, analogy
辺 *taihen* opposite side (in geometry)
手 *aite, taishu* opponent, adversary; the other party
手国 *aitekoku, taishukoku* rival country; enemy country
内 *tainai* internal or domestic (affairs)
内的 *tainaiteki* internal, domestic
中 *tai-Chū* toward China, with China
中共 *tai-Chūkyō* toward Red China, with Red China
日 *tai-Nichi* toward Japan, with Japan
日援助 *tai-Nichi enjo* aid to Japan
日感情 *tai-Nichi kanjō* feeling toward Japan
5 生 *taisei* opposition, symmetry
句 *tsuiku* couplet, distich; antithesis
処 *taisho suru* deal with, cope with
立 *tairitsu* opposition, antagonism; correlation, coordination
立者 *tairitsusha* opponent
外 *taigai* international (problems), foreign (relations), overseas

外的 *taigaiteki* external (affairs)
外援助 *taigai enjo* foreign aid
外貿易 *taigai bōeki* overseas trade
外硬派 *taigai kōha* vigorous foreign policy
外関係 *taigai kankei* foreign relations
6 米 *tai-Bei* with America, toward America
地速度 *taichi sokudo* ground speed
当 *taitō no* corresponding, equivalent, homologous
当額 *taitōgaku* corresponding amount
7 局 *taikyoku* facing a situation
対 *taitai* evenness, equality, a tie
決 *taiketsu* showdown, confrontation
別 *taibetsu* contradistinction
坐 *taiza suru* sit facing each other, sit opposite to
位法 *taiihō* counterpoint
角 *taikaku* opposite angle
角線 *taikakusen* diagonal line
応 *taiō* correspondence, equivalence, opposition
応策 *taiōsaku* countermeasure
抗 *taikō* opposition, antagonism, rivalry; counteraction
抗攻撃 *taikō kōgeki* counterattack
抗馬 *taikōba* rival horse; rival candidate
抗策 *taikōsaku* countermeasure
8 価 *taika* compensation; equivalent; consideration; prices
欧 *tai-Ō* with Europe, toward Europe
岸 *taigan* opposite shore
英 *tai-Ei* toward England, with England
者 *taisha* opponent, rival
物鏡 *taibutsukyō* objective lens
空 *taikū* antiaircraft
空砲火 *taikū hōka* antiaircraft fire, flak
9 連 *tairen* couplet
峙 *taiji suru* confront each other, keep up rivalry, hold one's own against
独 *tai-Doku* toward Germany, with Germany
陣 *taijin suru* encamp opposite the enemy, confront each other
面 *taimen* interview, meeting, facing (someone)
面交通 *taimen kōtsū* facing traffic, walking on the right side
面的 *taimenteki* face to face
10 席 *taiseki suru* sit facing each other, attend together
座 *taiza suru* sit facing each other, sit opposite to
流 *tairyū* convection current
酌 *taishaku* two drinking together
案 *taian* counterproposal
華 *tai-Ka* toward China, with China
称 *taishō* symmetry (in math); second person
称的 *taishōteki* symmetrical
症 *taishō* specific (treatment)
症剤 *taishōzai* allopathic or specific medicine
症薬 *taishōyaku* allopathic or specific medicine
校 *taikō* interschool, intercollegiate
校試合 *taikōjiai* interschool match
校競技 *taikō kyōgi* interschool match
11 偶 *taigū* spouse; pair; antithesis
眼 *taigan (renzu)* eyepiece
訳 *taiyaku* parallel versions
幅 *tsuifuku* pair of hanging pictures
策 *taisaku* countermeasure
等 *taitō* equality, par, parity, equivalent
象 *taishō* object (of worship); subject (of taxation); concern
象物 *taishōbutsu* subject, object (of worship)
13 置 *taichi suru* set opposite or against
戦 *taisen* waging war, competition
戦車砲 *taisenshaho* antitank gun
数 *taisū* logarithms
数表 *taisūhyō* logarithm tables
照 *taishō* contrast, antithesis, comparison
照的 *taishōteki* diametrically opposite
話 *taiwa* conversation, dialogue
話体 *taiwatai* conversational style
話者 *taiwasha* interviewer, interlocutor
15 論 *tairon* arguing face to face; arguing against a proposition
敵 *taiteki* hostile; (trade) with the enemy
質 *taishitsu suru* confront; confront with another witness
談 *taidan* conversation, interview, dialogue
談者 *taidansha* interviewer
18 顔 *taigan* interview, meeting, facing (someone)
蹠 *taiseki, taisho* diametrical opposition
蹠地 *taisekichi, taishochi* the antipodes

蹠的 *taisekiteki, taishoteki* diametrically opposite
蹠点 *taisekiten, taishoten* nadir
19 蘇 *tai-So* toward the Soviet Union, with the Soviet Union
21 露 *tai-Ro* toward Russia, with Russia

6

B **封** 1376 / J4975 / M7426 Fū seal; sealing; closing. Hō fief. *fū(jiru), fū(zuru)* seal, close up, confine, blockade. *hō(zuru)* appoint; invest with a fief; erect a mound.

2 入 *fūnyū* enclosure (in a letter)
3 土 *hōdo* feudal estate; mound of worship
4 込 *fū(ji)-ko(meru), fū(ji)-ko(mu)* enclose, confine, contain, seal up
切 *fūkiri* release of the first run (of a film); beginning
切館 *fūkirikan* a first-run theater
5 目 *fū(ji)me* sealed edge
冊 *hōsaku* imperial order to invest with a fief
6 印 *fūin* seal
地 *hōchi* fief, daimiate
9 建 *hōken* feudalism
建社会 *hōken shakai* feudal society
建体制 *hōken taisei* feudal system
建的 *hōkenteki* feudal
建制 *hōkensei* feudalism
建制度 *hōken seido* feudalism
建思想 *hōken shisō* feudal ideas
建時代 *hōken jidai* the feudal period (1185–1867)
建道徳 *hōken dōtoku* feudal morality
建領主 *hōken ryōshu* feudal lord
10 殺 *fūsatsu* forced out (baseball)
書 *fūsho* sealed letter, sealed document
12 筒 *fūtō* envelope
15 糊 *fū(ji) nori* sealing paste
緘 *fūkan* seal
緘葉書 *fūkan hagaki* letter card
18 鎖 *fūsa* blockade; freezing (funds)
21 蠟 *fūrō, fū(ji)rō* sealing wax

A **専** 1377 / J406c / M-X **專** 1382 / J5573 / M7439 Sen. *moppa(ra)* mainly, solely.

1 一 *sen'itsu, sen'ichi* concentration; best care; primary importance. *sen'itsu no* special, exclusive, principal
4 心 *senshin* undivided attention, concentration; singleness of purpose
5 用 *sen'yō* private use, personal use, exclusive use
用車 *sen'yōsha* personal car
用機 *sen'yōki* personal plane
6 行 *senkō* arbitrary action
任 *sennin* full-time service
有 *sen'yū* exclusive possession
有物 *sen'yūbutsu* exclusive possession
有権 *sen'yūken* monopoly, exclusive right
7 攻 *senkō* special research
決 *senketsu* arbitrariness
売 *sembai* monopoly
売公社 *Sembai Kōsha* Monopoly Corporation
売局 *Sembaikyoku* Monopoly Bureau
売制 *sembaisei* trade monopoly
売品 *sembaihin* monopoly goods, specialty
売特許 *sembai tokkyo* patent
売権 *sembaiken* monopoly
8 念 *sennen* close attention
制 *sensei* despotism, autocracy
制主義 *sensei shugi* despotism, autocracy
制君主 *sensei kunshu* autocrat, tyrant
制君主政体 *sensei kunshu seitai* absolute monarchy
制国 *senseikoku* absolute monarchy
制的 *senseiteki* despotic, autocratic, arbitrary
制政体 *sensei seitai* autocratic government
制政治 *sensei seiji* absolute government
門 *semmon* specialty, line, profession
門化 *semmonka* specialization
門外 *semmongai* layman, outsider
門用語 *semmon yōgo* technical term
門団体 *semmon dantai* professional organization
門医 *semmon'i* medical specialty
門店 *semmonten* specialty store
門的 *semmonteki* professional, technical
門委員 *semmon iin* technical expert
門学校 *semmon gakkō* professional school
門家 *semmonka* specialist, professional, expert
門書 *semmonsho* books in special fields
門教育 *semmon kyōiku* technical or professional education

門語 *semmongo* technical term
9 科 *senka* special course
政 *sensei* despotism, autocracy
10 恣 *senshi* arbitrariness; despotism, tyranny
修 *senshū* specialization
修科 *senshūka* special course
従 *senjū suru* specialize
従者 *senjūsha* full-time worker
従員 *senjūin* full-time union officer
11 断 *sendan* arbitrary action
務 *semmu* special duty; main business; (train) conductor, managing director
務取締役 *semmu torishimariyaku* managing director
12 属 *senzoku* attached to; exclusive; specialization; specialist
13 意 *sen'i* undivided attention, concentration; singleness of purpose
業 *sengyō* specialty, monopoly, main occupation
業者 *sengyōsha* specialist
15 権 *senken* exclusive right; despotism, arbitrary power
横 *sen'ō* arbitrariness; despotism, tyranny
横的 *sen'ōteki* arbitrary

7

尅 1378 / J5571 / M7435 See **剋** 486.

A **将** 1379 / J3e2d / M7437 **將** 1381 / J5572 / M7438 SHŌ commander, general, admiral. *hutu* or, and again. *masa ni* soon, from now on; just about.
2 几 *shōgi* camp stool, folding stool
3 士 *shōshi* officers and men
7 兵 *shōhei* officers and men
来 *shōrai* future, prospects
来有望 *shōrai-yūbō na* promising
来性 *shōraisei* future, possibilities, prospects
8 卒 *shōsotsu* officers and men
官 *shōkan* general, admiral
9 帥 *shōsui* commander
星 *shōsei* a general
軍 *shōgun* general, commander, shogun
軍家 *shōgunke* the shogunate family
軍職 *shōgunshoku* shogunate, office of the shogun
10 校 *shōkō* commissioned officer
11 略 *shōryaku* generalship
12 棋 *shōgi* Japanese chess game
棋指 *shōgisashi* chess player
棋倒 *shōgidao(re)* falling one after another in a row
棋盤 *shōgiban* Japanese chessboard
15 器 *shōki* capacity for generalship

A **射** 1380 / J3c4d / M7434 SHA archery; shooting. *i(ru)* shoot. *sa(su)* shine into, shine upon.
3 干玉 *nubatama* pitch black
4 止 *i-to(meru)* shoot (an animal) to death; win (a girl)
込 *sa(shi)-ko(mu)* shine into. *i-ko(mu)* hit the mark
手 *ite, shashu* archer, bowman, shooter
手船 *itebune* archer's boat (in a battle)
5 出 *i-da(su)* shoot. *shashutsu suru* emit, project, shoot out, catapult, radiate, be radiant
6 尽 *i-tsuku(su)* shoot all arrows
返 *i-kae(su)* shoot back, reflect
合 *i-a(u)* exchange shooting
当 *i-a(teru)* hit the target, shoot
7 角 *shakaku* angle of fire
抜 *i-nu(ku)* shoot through
利 *shari* commercialism, love of gain, moneymaking
利心 *sharishin* mercenary spirit
8 法 *shahō* archery
取 *i-to(ru)* shoot (something)
的 *shateki* target practice
的場 *shatekijō* rifle range
幸 *shakō* speculative spirit
幸心 *shakōshin* speculative spirit
9 通 *i-tō(su)* shoot through
垜 *shada, azuchi* firing mound (in target practice)
界 *shakai* field of fire
10 倒 *i-tao(su)* shoot down, kill by a shot
流 *i-naga(su)* miss the mark
殺 *i-koro(su), shasatsu suru* shoot to death
倖 *shakō* speculative spirit
倖心 *shakōshin* speculative spirit
11 掛 *i-ka(keru)* attack with arrows
貫 *i-nu(ku)* shoot through
距離 *shakyori* rifle range
12 場 *shajō* firing range; target practice; archery ground
竦 *i-suku(meru)* shoot and make the enemy take cover

割 *i-wa(ru)* shoot and split with an arrow
散 *i-chi(rasu)* scatter the enemy (in a volley of arrows)
落 *i-oto(su)* shoot down
程 *shatei* rifle range
程距離 *shatei kyori* range of fire, sphere of interest
13 損 *i-sokona(u), i-son(zuru), i-son(jiru)* miss the mark
14 精 *shasei* ejaculation, emission
15 影 *shaei* projection (in math.)
撃 *shageki* shooting; gunshot; marksmanship
撃場 *shagekijō* target range, rifle range

8

將 1381 / J5572 / M7438 See **将** 1379.

專 1382 / J5573 / M7439 See **専** 1377.

B **尉** 1383 / J3053 / M7440 I. *jō* jailer; old man; rank; company officer.
8 官 *ikan* company officer

9

尌 1384 / J-X / M7448 Ju standing (something) up.

B **尋** 1385 / J3f52 / M7447 Jin fathom. *tazu(neru)* look for, inquire for, ask (someone) a question. *hiro* fathom. *tsu(ide)* next, secondly, subsequently.
2 人 *tazu(ne)bito* missing person, wanted person
5 出 *tazu(ne)-ida(su), tazu(ne)-da(su)* search out; hunt up, hunt down
6 合 *tazu(ne)-a(waseru)* question one another
7 求 *tazu(ne)-moto(meru)* inquire of ; seek for
8 物 *tazu(ne)mono* lost article
者 *tazu(ne)mono* fugitive from justice, man wanted by the police
11 問 *jimmon* questioning
常 *jinjō no* common, usual
常一様 *jinjō-ichiyō* mediocrity; ordinary type
常小学校 *jinjō shōgakkō* elementary school
常科 *jinjōka* elementary course
12 極 *tazu(ne)-kiwa(meru)* search out, inquire in detail
15 窮 *tazu(ne)-kiwa(meru)* search out, inquire in detail

A **尊** 1386 / J423a / M7445 Son. *tatto(bu), tōto(bu), tatto(mu), tōto(mu)* value, prize, esteem; respect, honor, revere. *tatto(i), tōto(i)* precious, valuable, priceless; noble, exalted, sacred. *mikoto* lord, prince.
3 大 *sondai* haughtiness, pomposity, self-sufficiency
下 *sonka* Obediently yours
上 *sonjō* one's superior
4 父 *sompu* your father
公 *sonkō* you (polite); your father
王 *sonnō* reverence for the emperor, advocate of imperial rule
王家 *Sonnōka* Royalists
王党 *Sonnōtō* Imperialists
王討幕 *sonnō-tōbaku* reverence for the emperor and the overthrow of the shogunate
王攘夷 *sonnō-jōi* reverence for the emperor and expulsion of the barbarians
5 台 *sondai* you (ancient or literary)
兄 *sonkei* (polite) an elder brother; an elderly person
号 *songō* honorary title
6 宅 *sontaku* your house
名 *sommei* your name
7 体 *sontai* your health; (Buddhist) image
君 *sonkun* (polite) someone's father; one's companion
来 *sonrai* your visit
8 長 *sonchō* one's superiors, one's seniors
命 *sommei* your order
者 *sonja* Buddhist saint; man of high repute; guest of honor
9 信 *sonshin suru* revere
重 *sonchō* respect, esteem, regard
卑 *sompi* high and low, aristocrat and plebeian
皇 *sonnō* reverence for the emperor, advocate of imperial rule
皇攘夷 *sonnō-jōi* reverence for the emperor and expulsion of the barbarians
10 称 *sonshō* honorary title

家 *sonka* your house
容 *son'yō* your countenance
書 *sonsho* (polite) someone's letter
11 族 *sonzoku* direct ancestors
堂 *sondō* your family; your mother
崇 *sonsū* reverence, veneration
12 属 *sonzoku* direct ancestors; noble ancestors
敬 *sonkei* respect, esteem, honor, reverence
貴 *sonki* noble (person)
13 意 *son'i* your idea
14 像 *sonzō* statue of a noble character; your picture
15 慮 *sonryo* your will, your idea
影 *son'ei* portrait (polite)
17 厳 *songen* dignity, majesty, sanctity
18 顔 *songan* your countenance

11

對 1387 / J5574 / M7457 See **対** 1375.

A **導** 1388 / J4633 / M7463' Dō leading. *michibi(ku)* guide, lead, conduct, usher. *michibi(ki)* guidance. *shirube* guide; guiding; road sign.

2 入 *michibi(ki)-i(reru), dōnyū suru* lead into, bring into; induce; invite; import; introduce
3 下 *michibi(ki)-kuda(ru)* bring down
上 *michibi(ki)-nobo(ru)* bring up, lead up
4 手 *michibi(ki)te* a guide
水 *dōsui* conducting water; hydraulic
水圧力 *dōsui atsuryoku* hydraulic pressure
水学 *dōsuigaku* hydraulics, hydrodynamics
水路 *dōsuiro* raceway, canal
火 *dōka, michibi* fuse, powder train
火索 *dōkasaku* fuse, powder hose
火管 *dōkakan* fuse
火線 *dōkasen* fuse; cause, agency, incentive, impetus, occasion
火縄 *michibi nawa* powder hose
5 出 *michibi(ki)-da(su)* bring out, bring forth, lead out
6 因 *dōin* inducement, incentive, motive, cause, contributing factor
返 *michibi(ki)-kae(su)* bring back, win back, restore
7 体 *dōtai* conductor; medium
尿 *dōnyō suru* catheterize
尿管 *dōnyōkan* ureter
8 者 *dōsha* guide
9 通 *michibi(ki)-tō(ru)* lead through
10 師 *dōshi* officiating (Buddhist) priest
帰 *michibi(ki)-kae(ru)* bring back, lead back
11 教 *michibi(ki)-oshi(eru)* instruct
13 電体 *dōdentai* conductor of electricity
電性 *dōdensei* conductivity
電度 *dōdendo* conductivity
電率 *dōdenritsu* conductivity
14 管 *dōkan* conduit, pipe, aqueduct; standpipe; duct
15 線 *dōsen* leading wire

RAD. 小 42

Shō small. Variant: ⺌. Nickname: Little.

A **小** 1389 / J3e2e / M7473 SHŌ smallness; minor; small. *chii(sai), chii(sana), chi(sai)* small, little, diminutive, minute, fine, trivial. *isasa* small. *ko-* small; short; pretty; petty; nearly. *o-* little; nice, pretty. *shō-* humility prefix; small. *sa-* honorary prefix.

2 力 *kojikara* a little strength
刀 *shōtō* the shorter sword. *kogatana* knife, pocket knife
刀細工 *kogatanazaiku* wood carving; makeshift; cheap trick
人 *shōjin* small person, dwarf; child; mean person; person of small caliber. *shōnin* child. *kobito* dwarf, Lilliputian, pygmy, manikin
人国 *shōjinkoku* land of pygmies, Lilliput
人物 *shōjimbutsu* ungenerous person; low-charactered person
人数 *koninzū* small number of people
3 女 *shōjo* girl, little daughter. *koonna* a young servant; a little girl
川 *ogawa, kogawa* brook, creek

巾 *kohaba* single or narrow width
弓 *koyumi* toy bow
口 *koguchi* end, edge; clue; beginning; small lots; small sum
口扱 *koguchiatsuka(i)* small railway-express shipments
小 *shōshō* a little, a few, slightly
小姓 *kogoshō* young page to a noble
山 *koyama* hill, mound
山羊 *koyagi* kid
才 *kosai, shōsai* quite clever
才子 *kozaishi* clever man
才覚 *kosaikaku* cleverness
4 月 *shō (no) tsuki* short months
止 *koyami* lull, break, let-up
水 *shōsui* urine, urination
爪 *kozume* root of a fingernail
片 *shōhen* piece, fragment
牛 *koushi* calf
犬 *koinu* puppy
円 *shōen* small circle
仏 *kobotoke* small image of Buddha
孔 *shōkō, koana* small hole
引 *shōin* short introduction
分 *shōbun, kowa(ke)* subdivision, breakdown
文字 *komoji* small letters, lower-case letters
火 *boya, shōka* blaze, small fire
火器 *shōkaki* light weapons
天地 *shōtenchi* a small world
天狗 *kotengu* a small but skillful man (in the military arts)
六 *komuzuka(shii)* bothersome, troublesome, finicky, peevish
六ヶ敷 *komuzukashi(i)* bothersome, troublesome, finicky, peevish
心 *shōshin* timidity, cowardice; prudence
心者 *shōshimmono* coward, timid person
心翼翼 *shōshin-yokuyoku* infinite care; trembling
手 *kote* fencing gloves, gauntlet; forearm
手先 *kotesaki* (a good) hand (at)
手調 *koteshira(be)* tryout, rehearsal, workout, preliminary examination
切 *kogi(re)* pieces of cloth, rags. *kogi(ru)* cut up small; haggle, bargain
切手 *kogitte* check
切手帳 *kogittechō* checkbook
太 *kobuto(ri)* plump, buxom; pudgy
太刀 *kodachi* small short sword
太鼓 *kodaiko* small drum; side drum
5 用 *shōyō, koyō* small matter; urination
皿 *kozara* saucer, small plate
石 *sazareishi* small stone. *koishi* pebble, gravel, small stone
穴 *koana* little hole; small groove
尻 *kojiri* end of the sheath of a sword
史 *shōshi* short history
払 *kobara(i)* paying in small installments; small installments
札 *kofuda* a one-act ticket; a small tag. *kozane* small piece of iron or leather (for armor)
丘 *shōkyū* hillock
出 *koda(shi)* passing out a small quantity; frugal use; choosing some out of many; articles so chosen
本 *kohon* small-sized book
正月 *Koshōgatsu* Little New Year's, 15th and 16th days of first lunar month
市民 *shōshimin* lower middle class
旦那 *kodanna* young master
世界 *shōsekai* small world
主観 *shōshukan* narrow personal views
母 *oba* aunt
母様 *obasan, obasama* aunt; lady
生 *shōsei* I
生意気 *konamaiki* impertinence, conceit, impudence
包 *kozutsumi* parcel, package
包郵便 *kozutsumi yūbin* parcel post
冊 *shōsatsu* booklet
冊子 *shōsasshi* booklet, pamphlet, tract, brochure
半日 *kohannichi* almost a half day
半年 *kohannen* nearly half a year
半時 *kohantoki* quarter hour; nearly half an hour
田 *oda* rice field
田原提灯 *odawarajōchin* collapsible cylindrical paper lantern
田原評定 *odawara hyōjō* endless talk, fruitless debate
田原評議 *odawara hyōgi* endless talk, fruitless debate
6 米 *kogome* broken rice
羊 *kohitsuji* lamb
耳 *komimi* little ears (that happen to overhear)
臣 *shōshin* lower-rank retainer; this humble retainer
舟 *obune, kobune* boat, lighter, small craft
回 *komawa(ri)* sharp turn
成 *shōsei* small success

曲 *shōkyoku* short musical piece
伝 *shōden* short biography
弛 *odayu(mu), odaya(mu)* let up briefly (rain, etc.)
安 *shōan* somewhat at ease; satisfaction with minor accomplishments
字 *shōji* small characters, small type; one's baby name. *koaza* small village subsection
当 *koata(ri)* a feeler
早 *kobaya(ku)* somewhat in a hurry; earlier than usual
名 *shōmyō* lesser feudal lord
吏 *shōri* petty official
地主 *shōjinushi* small landowner
臼歯 *shōkyūshi* bicuspid
企業 *shōkigyō* small industries
気 *shōki* timidity, cowardice, prudence
気味 *kokimi, kokibi* sentiment, feeling
休 *koyasu(mi)* short rest, breather
休止 *shōkyūshi* short rest
百合 *sayuri* lily
百姓 *kobyakushō* petty farmer, tenant, peasant
会 *shōkai* small gathering
会派 *shōkaiha* the minor parties
会堂 *shōkaidō* chapel
7 言 *kogoto* scolding, faultfinding
谷 *shōkoku* ravine
豆 *azuki* red bean
貝 *kogai* little shell
走 *kobashi(ri)* hurrying along with small steps
足 *koashi* mincing steps
車 *oguruma* little cart; wheel
序 *shōjo* short introduction
伜 *kosegare* one's little son, little fellow, kid
村 *shōson* hamlet, small village
社 *shōsha* little shrine; low-rank shrine; my company
別 *kowake* subdivision
形 *kogata* small size, small design
兵 *kohyō* small stature; weak soldier
弟 *shōtei* the younger of two younger brothers; (humble) my younger brother
声 *kogoe* low voice, whisper
男 *kootoko* young man; short man
我 *shōga* the ego, one's private self
束 *kotaba* small bundle
役人 *koyakunin* minor official
沢山 *kodakusan* quite a few; not too many
坊主 *kobōzu* young priest, acolyte, novicc
見出 *komida(shi)* subtitle, subheading
角材 *shōkakuzai* scantling
亜細亜 *Shōajiya* Asia Minor
身 *shōshin* humble position; persons of low rank. *komi* tang (of a sword)
身者 *shōshimmono* person of low rank
町 *komachi* beauty, belle, queen
町娘 *komachi musumc* beauty, belle, queen
判 *koban* small size (in printing); small Edo gold coin
判形 *kobangata* oval, elliptical
利 *shōri* small profit
利口 *korikō* somewhat talented, cleverness
利巧 *korikō* somewhat talented, cleverness
売 *kouri* retail sale
売店 *kouriten* retail store
売商 *kourishō* retail trade
麦 *komugi* wheat
麦色 *komugi iro* cocoa brown
麦刈 *komugika(ri)* wheat harvest
麦粉 *komugiko* wheat flour
児 *shōni* little child, infant
児科 *shōnika* pediatrics
児科医 *shōnikai* pediatrician
児科学 *shōnikagaku* pediatrics
児病 *shōnibyō* children's diseases
児時代 *shōni jidai* infancy, childhood
児麻痺 *shōni mahi* infantile paralysis
作 *kosaku* (firm) tenancy. *kozuku(ri)* small size; small stature; small physique
作人 *kosakunin* tenant farmer
作米 *kosakumai* rent paid in rice
作地 *kosakuchi* tenant farm land
作争議 *kosaku sōgi* tenant uprising
作料 *kosakuryō* farm rent
作農 *kosakunō* tenant farming
作農民 *kosaku nōmin* tenant farmers
作権 *kosakuken* tenant rights
8 金 *kogane* small fortune; small sum
門 *komon* small gate
雨 *kosame, koame* light rain, drizzle
供 *kodomo* child
使 *kozukai* janitor; errand boy, servant; spending money

咄 *kobanashi* short story
姓 *koshō* child, youth; page to a noble
姑 *kojūto, kojūtome* sister-in-law
径 *shōkei* lane, path
性 *koshō* child, youth; page to a noble
林 *obayashi* forest. *kobayashi, shōrin* small forest
枝 *koeda* twig; spray
板 *koita* slat
波 *sazanami, sasanami, konami* ripples
知 *shōchi* shallow brains, little knowledge
股 *komata* short steps; crotch, thigh, groin
肥 *kobuto(ri)* somewhat fat
刻 *kokiza(mi)* mincing, chopping fine
舎 *koya* cottage, hut, booth, cabin, shed; theater
官 *shōkan* petty official
者 *komono* menial, servant; small fry
事 *shōji* small matter
奇麗 *kogirei na* trim, neat, snug
委員会 *shōiinkai* subcommittee
国 *shōkoku* small country, weak nation
国民 *shōkokumin* small nation; rising generation
店 *shōten* my little shop. *komise* little store
店員 *shōten'in* young shop clerk
松 *komatsu* young pine tree
松原 *komatsubara* young pine grove
物 *komono* small articles, a little thing
物印刷 *komono insatsu* job printing
突 *kozu(ku)* prod, poke, thrust, push, shake; swing; irritate; thrash
突回 *kozu(ki)-mawa(su)* manhandle, shake; tease; find fault with
学 *shōgaku* elementary education
学生 *shōgakusei* elementary pupil
学校 *shōgakkō* elementary school
夜 *sayo* night
夜中 *sayonaka* midnight
夜曲 *sayokyoku* serenade
夜更 *sayofu(keru)* The night deepens.
夜時雨 *sayo shigure* rain at night, night drizzle
夜嵐 *sayo arashi* night wind, night storm
9 風 *kokaze* light breeze
食 *shōshoku, kogu(i)* light eating, spare diet
盾 *kodate* small shield; screen; cover
柱 *kobashira* small pillar
柄 *kogara* short stature. *kozuka* knife attached to a sword sheath
派 *shōha* a small faction, a small party
胞 *shōhō* vesicle
胆 *shōtan* timidity; cowardice; prudence
計 *shōkei* subtotal
降 *koburi* light snow, light rain, drizzle
変 *shōhen* a slight change
亭 *shōtei* small pavilion, arbor
泉 *koizumi* a little spring
草 *ogusa* small grasses, small weeds
昼 *kohiru* a little before noon; mid-morning snack
勇 *shōyū* a little courage
急 *koiso(gi) ni* somewhat in a hurry
冠者 *kokanja* youth
海峡 *shōkaikyō* narrow channel
飛球 *shōhikyū* pop fly
前提 *shōzentei* minor premise
為替 *kogawase* small money order
要塞 *shōyōsai* blockhouse
首 *kokubi* neck; head
首傾 *kokubi (o) katamu(keru)* tilt the head in curiosity
便 *shōben, shomben* urine, urination
便所 *shōbenjo* urinal
指 *koyubi, shōshi* little finger
指頭大 *shōshitōdai* the size of the end of the little finger
乗仏教 *Shōjō Bukkyō* Hinayana or Lesser-Vehicle Buddhism
乗的 *shōjōteki* narrow-minded
品 *shōhin* something very small; an essay, a literary sketch
品文 *shōhimbun* essay, literary sketch
型 *kogata* small size, small design
型映画 *kogata eiga* small-size movie
面 *kozura* face (impolite)
面倒 *komendō na* annoying, troublesome
面憎 *kozuraniku(i)* impudent; disgusting
春 *koharu* tenth lunar month; Indian summer
春日 *koharubi* Indian-summer day, balmy autumn day
春日和 *koharubiyori* Indian-summer day, balmy autumn day
屋 *shōoku, koya* cottage, hut, booth, cabin, shed. *koya* theater
屋代 *koyadai* theater rent
屋掛 *koyaga(ke) suru* pitch camp. *koyaga(ke)* building a temporary hut; temporary hut, shack

屋組 *koyagu(mi)* framework
10 高 *kodaka(i)* slightly elevated
鬼 *kooni* imp, little devil
庭 *koniwa* small garden
逕 *shōkei* path, lane
俵 *kohyō* small sack; small bag
哨 *shōshō* picket
唄 *kouta* ditty, ballad
娘 *komusume* girl in her early teens; young woman before reaching maturity
振 *kobu(ri)* small size
破 *shōha* slight damage
紋 *komon* fine pattern
恥 *kohazu(kashii)* ashamed, embarrassed, shy
脇 *kowaki* side (of the body)
袖 *kosode* padded silk garment
針 *kobari* short needle, short stitches
家 *shōka, koie, oya* little house; poor home
宴 *shōen* small dinner party
差 *shōsa* small difference, narrow margin
書 *koga(ki)* writing in details; adding marginal notes
息 *koiki* short breaths
株主 *shōkabunushi* small stockholder
浮動 *shōfudō* moderate (stock-market) fluctuations
陪審 *shōbaishin* petty jury
馬 *kouma* pony, colt
馬鹿 *kobaka* somewhat of a fool. *kobaka ni suru* treat with contempt
骨 *kobone* small bones
骨折 *koboneo(ru)* make a little effort. *shōkossetsu* minor bone fracture
料理店 *koryōriten* small restaurant
料理屋 *koryōriya* small restaurant
都市 *shōtoshi* small town
都会 *shōtokai* small town
島 *kojima, shōtō* small island, islet
島田 *ojimada* rice field on a small island
倉 *kokura* duck (cloth)
倉服 *kokurafuku* schoolboy's school uniform
党 *shōtō* minor political party
党分立 *shōtō bunritsu* division into small political parties
荷物 *konimotsu* parcel, package
荷駄馬 *konida uma* pack horse
11 魚 *kozakana, kouo* small fish, fingerling
康 *shōkō* lull, respite, some improvement (in a patient)
過 *shōka* minor error
桶 *kooke* pail, small tub
猫 *koneko* kitten
球 *shōkyū* small ball, small globe
脳 *shōnō* cerebellum
船 *kobune* boat, lighter, small craft
欲 *shōyoku* a slight covetousness
敗 *shōhai* a minor defeat
野 *ono* field
隊 *shōtai* platoon, troop
瓶 *kobin* small bottle
悪 *shōaku* a little sin, a minor crime
宿 *koyado* simple lodging
異 *shōi* minor differences
窓 *komado* small window
雪 *koyuki* light snowfall
運送 *kounsō* parcel transportation
遊星 *shōyūsei* asteroid
規模 *shōkibo* small scale
鳥 *kotori* small bird
鳥屋 *kotoriya* bird shop
道 *komichi* path, lane, alley, byway
道具 *kodōgu* small pieces of equipment; small tools; small stage properties
細工 *kozaiku* handiwork; tricks; tinkering
細工師 *kozaikushi* a man with a handicraft; a tricky person
商 *koakina(i)* retail business, small trade
商人 *koakindo, koshōnin, koakyūdo* small businessman
盗 *shōto* petty thief. *konusu(mi)* petty theft
盗人 *konusubito* petty thief
粒 *kotsubu, shōryū* grain, fine particle
粒金 *kotsubukin* one-fourth *ryō*
粒真珠 *kotsubu shinju* seed pearl
12 喧 *koyakama(shii)* fastidious, faultfinding, fussy about everything
揚 *koa(ge)* unloading (ships)
腕 *koude, kokaina* forearm; weak arm; lack of skill
飲 *shōin* small dinner party
善 *shōzen* a small kindness
寒 *shōkan* winter's milder period
景 *shōkei* a beautiful scene; a small picture of a landscape
量 *shōryō* small quantity, small dose; narrowmindedness

童 *kowarabe, kowarawa, kowappa* youngster, stripling
策 *shōsaku* petty trick
筒 *kozutsu* rifle; small arms
買 *koga(i) suru* buy in small quantities
落 *shōraku* slight (stock-market) decline
葉 *shōyō* lobule, appendage
雲 *shōun* small cloud
智 *shōchi* shallow brains, little knowledge
琴 *ogoto* harp, koto
景気 *shōkeiki* a little boom
集会 *shōshūkai* small gathering
惑星 *shōwakusei* asteroid
幅 *kohaba* single-width (cloth)
幅物 *kohabamono* single-width cloth
蒸気 *kojōki* steam launch
蒸気船 *kojōkisen* steam launch
割 *kowa(ri)* slat, piece of wood
割材 *kowa(ri)zai* scantling
割板 *kowa(ri)ita* slat, piece of wood
遣 *kozukai* spending money, incidental expenses
遣取 *kozukaito(ri)* side job, odd jobs
遣帳 *kozukaichō* petty cashbook
遣銭 *kozukaisen, kozukai zeni* spending money, incidental expenses
間 *koma* small room; brief interval
間切 *komagi(re)* small pieces of cloth; chopped meat
間使 *komazukai* maid
間物 *komamono* notions, knickknacks, sundry wares
間物屋 *komamonoya* haberdashery
間結 *koma musu(bi)* square knot
13 鼓 *kotsuzumi* hand drum
鼠 *konezumi* small rat
僧 *kozō* young Buddhist priest; errand boy, shop boy; youngster
暗 *kogura(i), ogura(i)* dusky; shady
暇 *shōka* a brief leisure
楯 *kodate* small shield; screen; cover
槌 *kozuchi* small mallet; gavel; wand
禄 *shōroku* small stipend
腸 *shōchō* small intestines
腰 *kogoshi* hips; a slight genuflection, a slight bow
艇 *shōtei* small boat
話 *shōwa, kobanashi* anecdote, yarn, small talk
路 *komichi, kōji* path, lane, alley, byway, narrow street
鉢 *kobachi* small bowl
鈴 *osuzu, kosuzu* a little bell
隙 *shōgeki* crevice, small gap; minor discord
歇 *koyami* discontinuance for a short time
禽 *shōkin* small birds
節 *shōsetsu* a small knot (in wood); bar (in music); faithfulness in small matters
罪 *shōzai* minor sin, minor crime
舅 *kojūto* brother-in-law
勢 *kozei* small force, small family
楊子 *koyōji* toothpick
資本 *shōshihon* small capital
意気 *koiki na* stylish, chic, neat, tasteful
預言書 *Shōyogensho* Minor Prophets
腹 *kobara* abdomen
腹立 *koharada(tsu)* become irritated
数 *shōsū* a fraction; a comparatively small number
数点 *shōsūten* decimal point
農 *shōnō* small farmer, peasant, landowner
農民 *shōnōmin* the small farmers
農地 *shōnōchi* small farm holdings
農階級 *shōnō kaikyū* peasantry
14 鼻 *kobana* wings of the nose
像 *shōzō* figurine, statuette
鳴 *sasana(ki)* low twittering
憎 *koniku(rashii)* hateful, horrible, provoking
旗 *kobata* little flag
碑 *shōhi* this (humble) monument
踊 *koodori* dancing for joy
酷 *ko(p)pido(ku)* severely, harshly
銭 *kozeni* small change, loose coins
歌 *kouta* ballad, ditty, little song
管 *shōkan* small pipe
綺麗 *kogirei na* trim, neat, snug
熊星 *Shōyūsei* Ursa Minor
熊座 *Kogumaza* Little Bear, Ursa Minor
説 *shōsetsu* novel, romance, story, fiction
説体 *shōsetsutai* the fictional form
説家 *shōsetsuka* novelist, fiction writer
銃 *shōjū* rifle, small arms
銃射程 *shōjū shatei* range of rifle fire
銃弾 *shōjūdan* bullet
15 潮 *koshio* neap tide
編 *shōhen* short article
縁 *koen* small veranda

膝 *kohiza* the knee
影 *shōei* a small-size photograph
敵 *shōteki* weak opponent, weak enemy
皺 *kojiwa* little wrinkles, crow's feet
箱 *kobako* small box
篇 *shōhen* short article
蕪 *kokabu* small turnip
慧 *kozaka(shii)* smart, conceited; tricky, shrewd
賢 *kozaka(shii), kogashiko(i)* smart, conceited; tricky, shrewd
劇場 *shōgekijō* little theater
器 *shōki* small receptacle; man of small caliber
器用 *kogiyō na* smart, clever
衝 *kozu(ku)* prod, shake, swing; irritate
衝回 *kozu(ki)-mawa(su)* grab by the chest and shake
衝突 *shōshōtotsu* skirmish
16 鴨 *kogamo* duckling
樽 *kodaru* keg
頭 *kogashira* foreman
鮑 *tokobushi* abalone, ear shell
頸 *kokubi* neck of a garment
憩 *shōkei* short rest, recess
機転 *kokiten* being smart; being tricky
17 糠 *konuka* rice bran
糠雨 *konuka ame* drizzling rain
18 難 *komuzuka(shii)* bothersome, troublesome, finicky, peevish. *shōnan* small misfortune; minor fault
額 *shōgaku* small amount
題 *shōdai* subtitle, subhead; trivial subject
藩 *shōhan* the smaller clans
19 鯨 *kokujira* gray whale
20 騰 *shōtō* slight (stock-market) advances
競合 *kozeria(i)* skirmish, bickering; wrangle
艦隊 *shōkantai* flotilla, small fleet
21 癪 *koshaku na* impertinent, impudent
躍 *koodo(ri)* dancing or jumping for joy
22 嚢 *shōnō* small bag, vesicle
24 鬢 *kobin* side lock (of hair)

—— 1 ——

A 少 1390 / J3e2f / M7475 SHŌ small; few; young. *suko(shi)* a small quantity, a little; a few; something; a little while; a short distance. *suko(shimo)* (not) at all. *suku(nai), suke(nai)* few, a little, scarce, insufficient, seldom. *suku(nakarazu)* not a little, in no small numbers. *suku(nage)* scarcity. *suku(nakutomo), suku(nakumo)* at least.

3 女 *shōjo, otome* daughter, young lady, virgin
4 少 *shōshō* a little, a few, slightly
6 安 *shōan* somewhat at ease; satisfaction with minor accomplishments
壮 *shōsō* youth
壮士官 *shōsō shikan* young officer
壮有為 *shōsōyūi no* energetic
年 *shōnen* boy, juvenile
年少女 *shōnen-shōjo* boys and girls
年文学 *shōnen bungaku* juvenile literature
年犯罪 *shōnen hanzai* juvenile delinquency
年団 *Shōnendan* Boy Scouts
年会 *shōnenkai* junior society
年労働 *shōnen rōdō* child labor
年法 *shōnenhō* juvenile law
年院 *shōnen'in* reform school
年感化院 *shōnen kankain* reform school
年審判所 *shōnen shimpanjo* juvenile court
7 佐 *shōsa* major; lieutenant commander; wing commander
弟 *shōtei* young brother
8 者 *shōsha* young person
国民 *shokokumin* the rising generation, children
9 食 *shōshoku* light eating, spare diet
食家 *shōshokuka* light eater
10 将 *shōshō* major general, rear admiral; air commodore
恩 *shōon* small favors
11 康 *shōkō* small improvement (in a patient)
欲 *shōyoku* a little covetousness
尉 *shōi* second lieutenant; ensign
12 閑 *shōkan* short interval of leisure
量 *shōryō* small quantity, small dose
13 資本 *shōshihon* small capital
数 *shōsū* few; minority
数民族 *shōsū minzoku* minority peoples
数者 *shōsūsha* the minority
数党 *shōsūtō* minority party
15 敵 *shōteki* weak opponent, weak enemy
16 憩 *shōkei* short rest, recess
18 額 *shōgaku* small amount

2

尒 1391 J-X M7477 尓 1392 J5575 M7478 See 爾 3521.

3

尖 1393 J406d M7480 SEN. *toga(ru), tonga(ru)* be pointed, be sharp, taper off; be displeased, get angry. *toga(rasu), tonga(rasu), toga(rakasu)* sharpen, point; raise (one's voice); put (one's nerves) on edge. *tonga(ru), tonga(rakaru)* get cross. *toga(ri), tongar(i)* point, tip, peak.

7 兵 *sempei* advance guard
12 塔 *sentō* pinnacle, spire, steeple
14 鼻 *toga(ri)bana* hawk nose
端 *sentan* pointed end, tip; fine point; cusp; spearhead, vanguard
端行 *sentan (o) i(ku)* be in style
15 鋒 *sempō* point
鋭 *sen'ei* radical; acute
鋭化 *sen'eika suru* become acute, be aggravated
鋭分子 *sen'ei bunshi* radical elements
16 頭 *sentō* pinnacle, spire, steeple

5

鼡 1394 J736b M-X Nonstandard for 鼠 7078.

B 尚 1395 J3e30 M7493 SHŌ. *nao* further, furthermore, still, still more, yet; just like. *tatto(bu)* value, prize, esteem; respect, honor, revere. *hisa(shii)* long, long-continued, an old (story).

2 又 *naomata* further, besides
4 以 *naomo(tte)* still more, all the more
友 *shōyū* becoming intimate with the ancients (by reading their works)
5 且 *naokatsu* and yet
古 *shōko* worship of ancient civilizations
古主義 *shōko shugi* worship of ancient civilizations
6 早 *shōsō* prematurity
7 更 *naosara* still, still more, all the more
8 尚 *naonao* still more, all the more
武 *shōbu* militarism, warlike spirit

10

尠 1396 J5576 M7523 尟 1397 J-X M7522 SEN. *sukuna(kumo), sukuna(kutomo)* at least. *sukuna(karazu)* not a little, in no small numbers. *sukuna(i)* few, a little, scarce, insufficient, seldom.

RAD. 尢 43

Dai no mageashi crooked-leg *dai* (large). *Mottomo* just, right, reasonable, natural. Nickname: Crooked Big (cf. 37).

尢 1398 J5577 M7538 Ō crooked leg; hunchback.

1

尤 1399 J4c60 M7543 YŪ superb, outstanding. *motto(morashii)* plausible. *yū(naru)* superb, outstanding. *motto(mo)* reasonable, right, just, natural; of course; although.

8 物 *yūbutsu* something superior; beautiful woman

4

尨 1400 J5578 M7554 BŌ shaggy hair; shaggy dog.

3 大 *bōdai* bulky, enormous, extensive
4 毛 *mukuge* shaggy hair
犬 *mukuinu* shaggy dog

9

A 就 1401 J3d22 M7599 SHŪ. JU. *tsu(ku)* settle in (place); take (a seat); take (a position); depart; study (under a teacher). *(ni) tsu(ite)* concerning; along;

under; per. *tsu(ite) wa, tsu(kimashite) wa* concerning. *-zu(ku)* to become.
4 中 *nakanzuku* especially, above all, among other things
6 任 *shūnin* assumption of office, inauguration
任式 *shūninshiki* inauguration ceremony, installation
7 床 *shūshō* bedridden
役 *shūeki suru* be placed in commission; enter servitude
労 *shūrō* actual work
8 学 *shūgaku* entering school; school attendance
学年齢 *shūgaku nenrei* school age
学児童 *shūgaku jidō* school child
学義務 *shūgaku gimu* compulsory school attendance
10 眠 *shūmin* retiring, going to sleep
航 *shūkō* commissioning a ship
13 寝 *shūshin suru* go to bed, retire
寝前 *shūshinzen* before retiring
業 *shūgyō* employment, starting work
業日数 *shūgyō nissū* days worked
業地 *shūgyōchi* place of work
業時間 *shōgyō jikan* work hours
業率 *shūgyōritsu* percentage of employment
業規則 *shūgyō kisoku* work regulations
15 褥 *shūjoku suru* retire, go to bed
16 縛 *shūbaku* arrest
18 職 *shūshoku* finding employment
職口 *shūshokuguchi* position, opening, employment
職先 *shūshokusaki* place of employment
職時 *shūshokuji* time of employment
職運動 *shūshoku undō* job hunting
職斡旋 *shūshoku assen* placement
職難 *shūshokunan* scarcity of employment

RAD. 尸 44

Shikabane or *kabane* corpse. Nickname: Flag.

尸 1402 J5579 M7630 SHI corpse. *shikabane, kabane* corpse, the remains.
16 諌 *shikan* protest by suicide
骸 *shigai* corpse, remains
9 度 *shakudo* linear measure, scale, gauge, standard
10 骨 *shakkotsu* ulna
11 貫法 *shakkanhō* Japanese system of weights and measures

1

尹 1403 J337a M7631 IN an official rank.

A **尺** 1404 J3c5c M7632 SEKI. SHAKU Japanese foot (1 *shaku* = .994 foot); rule; measure, scale; length. *sashi* measure, rule.
2 八 *shakuhachi* bamboo flute
〆 *shakujime* a unit of timber measurement (1×1×12 feet)
3 寸 *shakusun, sekisun* a bit, a little; a strip (of land); short length
6 地 *shakuchi, sekichi* a single square foot of land; a small strip of land
7 余 *shakuyo* over a foot
8 取 *shakuto(ri)* measuring worm
取虫 *shakuto(ri)mushi* measuring worm

2

B **尼** 1405 J4e74 M7635 **尼** 1406 J-X M-X JI. NI *ama* nun.
6 寺 *amadera* convent
7 君 *amagimi* a lady who becomes a nun
8 法師 *ama hōshi* (Buddhist) nun
10 将軍 *ama shōgun* female shogun
13 僧 *nisō* (Buddhist) priestess
僧院 *nisōin* convent
18 顔 *amagao* a face with no make-up

尻 1407 J3f2c M7634 KŌ. *shiri* buttocks, hips; rear or back of a person; bottom (of a kettle); tail end, tag end.
3 下 *shirisa(gari)* a drop in the back part of anything; lowering the voice at the end of a sentence
上 *shiria(gari)* rising intonation; head over heels; rising market

4 込 *shirigo(mu)* flinch, shrink back, hesitate
切 *shiriki(re)* half-finished
切蜻蛉 *shiriki(re) tombo* something half-finished
5 目 *shirime ni* looking askance
6 当 *shiria(te)* trouser-seat lining
7 尾 *shirio, shippo* tail; end
抜 *shirinu(ke)* forgetfulness
8 長 *shiri (ga) naga(i)* overstaying (guest)
押 *shirio(shi)* boosting, pushing; incitement; instigator; wirepuller
9 拭 *shirinugu(i)* taking the blame or loss for another
重 *shiriomo, shiri (ga) omo(i)* slow-moving
10 馬 *shiriuma* blindly following, indiscriminate imitation
窄 *shirisubo(mari), shirisubo(mi)* tapering; anticlimax, weak ending
11 紮 *shirikara(ge)* tucking up the kimono behind
12 絡 *shirikara(ge)* tucking up the kimono behind
軽 *shirigaru ni* lightly. *shirigaru na* wanton, loose
割 *shiri (ga) wa(reru)* (a secret) is exposed
14 端折 *shiri(p)pasho(ri), shirihasho(ri)* tucking up the kimono behind
15 餅 *shirimochi* falling on one's buttocks

3

B **尽** 1408 / J3f54 / M7642 **盡** 3900 / J6238 / M23029 JIN. *tsu(kusu)* use up, run out of, exhaust; serve, befriend, work for, endeavor, do (one's duty). *tsu(kiru)* become exhausted, be consumed, spend, end. *kotogoto(ku)* all, entirely, completely. *-zu(ku) de* for the sake of, by means of, by force of. *-zu(kushi)* a full enumeration of. *-jin* last day of the month.
2 力 *jinryoku* efforts; assistance
4 日 *jinjitsu* the whole day
5 未来 *jimmirai* forever, eternity
8 果 *tsu(ki)-ha(teru)* be exhausted
忠 *jinchū* loyalty
忠報国 *jinchū-hōkoku* loyalty and patriotism
13 瘁 *jinsui* strenuous efforts; assistance

4

屁 1409 / J557b / M7654 HI. *he, onara* breaking wind, passing gas.
11 理窟 *herikutsu* quibbling
理窟屋 *herikutsuya* quibbler

B **尿** 1410 / J4722 / M7651 NYŌ *shito, yubari, ibari* urine.
5 石 *nyōseki* urinary calculus
8 毒症 *nyōdokushō* uremia
9 砂 *nyōsa* urinary sand
10 素 *nyōso* urea
11 道 *nyōdō* urethra
瓶 *shibin* urinal, pot
12 量 *nyōryō* amount of urination
検査 *nyō kensa* urinalysis
13 意 *nyōi* the urge to urinate
14 酸 *nyōsan* uric acid
管 *nyōkan* ureter
15 器 *nyōki* bed pan, urinal

B **尾** 1411 / J4878 / M7650 BI tail; end; counter for fish. *o* tail; trail (of a meteor); lower slope (of a mountain).
3 上 *onoe* mountain ridge
6 羽 *oha* tail feather
行 *bikō* following, trailing, shadowing
灯 *bitō* taillight; stop light
7 花 *obana* Japanese pampas grass
8 使 *ozuka(i)* tail wagging
長猿 *onagazaru* long-tailed monkey
9 風 *bifū* tail wind
10 骨 *bikotsu* coccyx
根 *one* a mountain ridge
部 *bibu* tail
12 無猿 *ona(shi)zaru* ape
14 端 *bitan* tail tip
15 骶骨 *biteikotsu* coccyx
16 橇 *bisori* tail skid
頭付 *okashiratsu(ki)* whole fish
錠 *bijō* buckle, clasp
錠金 *bijōgane* buckle, clasp
17 翼 *biyoku* tail, tail plane
21 鰭 *obire* caudal fin. *ohire* tail and fin; exaggeration ⌈(language)
22 籠 *birō* indelicate, indecent, vulgar

A **局** 1412 / J3649 / M7653 KYOKU bureau, board, office; central; post office; affair; duty; situation; conclusion. *tsubone* court lady; her apartment; lady-in-waiting.

4 区 *kyokku* postal-zone number
5 外 *kyokugai* the outside; an independent position; irrelevance
外中立 *kyokugai chūritsu* neutrality, indifference
外者 *kyokugaisha* outsider
6 名 *kyokumei* call sign, station name
地 *kyokuchi* locality, the site (of the occurrence)
地化 *kyokuchika* localization
地風 *kyokuchifū* local wind
地戦争 *kyokuchi sensō* limited war
8 長 *kyokuchō* bureau chief, director, postmaster
限 *kyokugen suru* limit, localize
所 *kyokusho* part, section; local
所時 *kyokushoji* local time
所麻酔 *kyokusho masui* local anesthetic
9 面 *kyokumen* checkerboard; aspect, situation
待 *kyokuma(chi)* to be called for, waiting at the (telegraph) office
10 紙 *kyokushi* Japanese vellum
員 *kyokuin* clerk; bureau staff; post-office staff
留 *kyokudo(me)* general delivery
部 *kyokubu* part, section; affected region; privates
部麻酔 *kyokubu masui* local anesthetic
部麻痺 *kyokubu mahi* partial paralysis
部露出 *kyokubu roshutsu* indecent exposure
11 務 *kyokumu* departmental business
12 渡 *kyokuwata(shi)* telegrams to be called for at the post office
番 *kyokuban* telephone-exchange number
報 *kyokuhō* service telegram; official bulletin

5

A 届 1413 J464f M7667 屆 1414 J557c M7666 KAI. *todo(ku)* reach, arrive, be received; be attentive, be realized. *todo(keru)* report, notify; forward. *todoke* report, notice; forwarding, delivery.
5 出 *todo(ke)-de(ru)* report. *todokeide, todokede* report, notice; forwarding, delivery
6 先 *todo(ke)saki* destination, address, consignee
10 書 *todo(ke)sho, todo(ke)ga(ki)* notice, written report
11 済 *todo(ke)zu(mi)* filed

B 屈 1415 J367e M7669 KUTSU. *kus(suru)* bend, bend over; give in, submit to, yield to; flinch. *kaga(mu), kaga(maru), kogo(meru)* stop, lean over, crouch. *kago(mu)* bow, stoop, bend over. *kaga(meru)* bow (the knee); bend (the legs).
4 込 *kaga(mi)-ko(mu)* bend over
6 曲 *kukkyoku suru* be crooked, bend, wind; be indented; be refracted
伏 *kuppuku* surrender, submission
托 *kuttaku* anxiety; trouble, boredom
7 伸 *kusshin* extension and contraction; bending and stretching; flexibility
折 *kussetsu* bending; indentation; refraction
折望遠鏡 *kussetsu bōenkyō* refracting telescope
8 服 *kuppuku* surrender, submission
9 指 *kusshi* counting on the fingers; prominence
10 従 *kutsujū* submission, servitude
託 *kuttaku* worry, trouble; preoccupation; boredom, ennui
辱 *kutsujoku* humiliation, insult; defeat
辱的 *kutsujokuteki* disgraceful, humiliating
11 強 *kukkyō* robust health; obstinacy
12 筋 *kukkin* flexor muscle
15 撓 *kuttō* bending
撓性 *kuttōsei* flexibility

A 居 1416 J356f M7663 KO. KYO residence. *i(ru), o(ru)* be, exist; be found in, stay in; inhabit; live with, reside; be present; remain (sitting).
3 士 *koji* active (Buddhist) layman
丈 *itake* one's sitting height
丈高 *itakedaka ni, idakedaka ni* domineeringly
4 心地 *igokochi* relaxation (at home)
心地良 *igokochiyo(i)* feeling at home, being comfortable. *igokochi (no) yo(i)* cozy, comfortable
中 *kyochū* standing between two people; usual situation
中調停 *kyochū chōtei* mediation, arbitration

5 立 *i(temo)-ta(ttemo)* restless, impatient, itching (to tell)
乍 *inaga(ra)* at home, as one sits
民 *kyomin* residents, inhabitants
6 回 *imawa(ri)* vicinity, neighborhood
宅 *kyotaku* a residence
合 *i-a(wasu), i-a(waseru)* happen to be present
合抜 *ia(i)nu(ki)* swordplay, swordplayer
7 抜 *inu(ki)* a going concern
邸 *kyotei* dwelling place
坐 *i-suwa(ru)* stay on, settle down, remain (in office). *isuwa(ri) no* stationary, permanent
住 *kyojū suru* reside. *izuma(i)* sitting position. *kyojū* residence; address
住地 *kyojūchi* residence; address
住者 *kyojūsha* resident, inhabitant
住費 *kyojūhi* housing expenses
住証明書 *kyojū shōmeisho* residence certificate
住権 *kyojūken* right of residence
8 所 *idokoro, kyosho* residence, whereabouts, address. *o(ri)dokoro* the place where one is
並 *i-nara(bu)* sit in a row, be arrayed
直 *i-nao(ru)* sit straight; change one's attitude; come out strong; turn into a robber; resort to threat
直強盗 *inao(ri) gōtō* burglar who becomes violent when detected
9 食 *igu(i)* living in idleness
廻 *imawa(ri)* vicinity, neighborhood
城 *kyojō* daimyo's residential castle
室 *kyoshitsu* living room; private room, den
相撲 *izumō* wrestling in a sitting posture
待 *ima(chi)* sitting and waiting
待月 *ima(chi)zuki* 18-day-old moon
10 候 *isōrō* hanger-on, dependent, parasite
残 *i-noko(ru)* work overtime; remain behind
浸 *ibita(ru)* move in to stay, camp (in a bar)
眠 *inemu(ri)* doze, nap
酒屋 *izakaya* saloon, pub
留 *kyoryū* residence
留民 *kyoryūmin* residents
留地 *kyoryūchi* settlement, concession
留守 *irusu* "not at home" (said when someone does not want to see the callers)
11 据 *i-su(waru)* stay on, settle down, remain (in office)
12 間 *ima* living room, private room
堪 *i(ta)tama(renai)* too warm; unable to remain
竦 *i-suku(mu), i-suku(maru)* cower, crouch
着 *i-tsu(ku)* settle down
集 *i-atsu(maru)* be gathered together
然 *kyozen* standing firm, steadiness; tranquility; status quo
場 *o(ri)ba* the place where one is
場所 *ibasho* residence; whereabouts
13 睡 *inemu(ri)* nap, doze
続 *i-tsuzu(keru)* stay on
催促 *izaisoku suru* hang on till paid
15 敷当 *ishikia(te)* kimono seat lining
18 職 *ijoku* sedentary occupation
職人 *ijokunin* sedentary artisan

6

屏 1417 J5622 M7692 See  1427.

[illegible] 1418 J-X M-X Nonstandard for 属 1430.

屎 1419 J557d M7689 Shi. Ki. *kuso* excrement, droppings.
7 尿 *shinyō* excreta

屍 1420 J3b53 M7688 Shi corpse. *shikabane* corpse, remains.
7 体 *shitai* corpse
体遺棄罪 *shitai ikizai* crime of abandoning a corpse
9 姦 *shikan* violating a corpse; necrophelia
臭 *shishū* smell of death, putrid smell
16 諫 *shikan* admonishing a ruler by one's death
骸 *shigai* corpse, remains

A 屋 1421 J3230 M7684 Oku roof; house. *-ya* shop, store; seller, dealer; business.
3 上 *okujō* housetop, roof
上庭園 *okujō teien* roof garden
4 内 *okunai* indoors
5 外 *okugai* open air, outdoors
号 *yagō* store name, house name,

hereditary family name, a stage-family name
台 *yatai* a float; a stall
台店 *yatai mise* street stall, stand, booth
台骨 *yataibone* framework, foundation; means, property
7 体 *yatai* a float; a stall
形 *yakata* house, mansion, boat cabin
形船 *yakatabune* houseboat, barge, pleasure boat
8 舎 *okusha* house, building
並 *yana(mi)* row of houses
10 根 *yane* roof, roofing, housetop
根伝 *yanezuta(i)* running from roof to roof
根屋 *yaneya* roofer, thatcher
根葺 *yanefuki* thatching a roof; roof thatcher
根裏 *yaneura* attic; loft
15 敷 *yashiki* mansion, residence, premises; residential site
敷町 *yashiki machi* exclusive residential section

7

屐 1422 / J5621 / M7708 GEKI clog.

屓 1423 / J557e / M7713 **屭** 1436 / J-X / M7823 KI exerting strength.

屑 1424 / J367d / M7709 SETSU. *kuzu* rubbish, junk, trash, waste, scraps, rags, crumbs, waste paper; the scum of society.
2 入 *kuzui(re)* garbage can
6 米 *kuzugome, kuzumai* broken rice
糸 *kuzu ito* waste silk
肉 *kuzu niku* meat scraps, dog meat
羊毛 *kuzu yōmō* shoddy, reclaimed wool
8 物 *kuzumono* trash, junk
9 屋 *kuzuya* junk man
拾 *kuzuhiro(i)* ragpicking; ragpicker
10 値 *kuzune* scrap value
13 鉄 *kuzu tetsu* scrap iron
14 綿 *kuzu wata* waste cotton
18 繭 *kuzu mayu* waste cocoon
22 籠 *kuzu kago* wastebasket

A **展** 1425 / J4538 / M7715 TEN expand.
5 示 *tenji* exhibition, display
示会 *tenjikai* exhibition
示場 *tenjijō* (place of) an exhibition
8 性 *tensei* malleability
11 転 *tenten* rolling
転反側 *tenten-hansoku* tossing in bed, sleeplessness
望 *tembō* view, outlook, prospect
望台 *tembōdai* observatory; observation platform
望車 *tembōsha* observation car
望哨 *tembōshō* observation post, lookout
望鏡 *tembokyo* periscope; field glass
12 開 *tenkai suru* unfold, develop, evolve; deploy
13 墓 *tembo* visiting a grave
16 覧 *tenran* exhibition
覧会 *tenrankai* exhibition, exhibit
覧物 *tenrambutsu* exhibit
覧室 *tenranshitsu* showroom
18 観 *tenkan* exhibition

8

屠 1426 / J454b / M-X Nonstandard for **屠** 1429.

屏 1427 / J X / M7734 **屛** 1417 / J5622 / M7692 HEI, BYŌ wall, fence, screen.
8 居 *heikyo suru* live in retirement
9 風 *byobu* folding screen
風岩 *byōbu iwa* sheer cliff
10 息 *heisoku suru* bate one's breath; be cowed into silence

9

屡 1428 / J3c48 / M7770 Nonstandard for **屢** 1431.

屠 1429 / J-X / M7761 To. *hofu(ru)* slaughter, butcher, massacre, slay.
4 牛 *togyū* slaughtering; butchering
牛場 *togyūjō* slaughterhouse
6 肉 *toniku* butcher's meat
8 所 *tosho* slaughterhouse
10 畜 *tochiku* butchering, slaughtering
殺 *tosatsu* slaughter, butchering; massacre
殺夫 *tosatsufu* butcher, slaughterer
殺場 *tosatsujō* slaughterhouse
殺業 *tosatsugyō* butchering business

12 場 *tojō* slaughterhouse
13 腹 *tofuku* disembowelment
19 蘇 *toso* spiced saké
蘇機嫌 *toso kigen* drunk with New Year's saké

A **属** 1430 J4230 M7754 **屬** 1435 J5624 M7821 ZOKU genus; subordinate official. SHOKU. *zoku(suru), zoku(su)* belong to, be among; fall under; be affiliated with; be subject to; be vested in, be inherent in.
5 目 *shokumoku* attention, observation
6 地 *zokuchi* dependency, territory
州 *zokushū* province
邦 *zokuhō* vassal state, dependency
名 *zokumei* generic name
吏 *zokuri* subordinate official
8 国 *zokkoku* vassal state, dependency
性 *zokusei* attribute
官 *zokkan* government clerk, subordinate official
具 *zokugu* accessories, equipment, appliances
11 望 *shokubō* expectation
14 僚 *zokuryō* subordinate
領 *zokuryō* possession, dependency, dominion

11

屢 1431 J-X M7787 RU. *shibashiba* often, frequently.
6 次 *ruji ni* successively, repeatedly
14 屢 *shibashiba* often, frequently
鳴 *shibana(ku)* sing unceasingly

A **層** 1432 J4158 M-X **層** 1433 J-X M7798 SŌ (social) class; stratum, layer, seam, bed, formation; story, floor; course (of stones).
7 位学 *sōigaku* stratigraphy
状 *sōjō* stratified
状岩 *sōjōgan* stratified rock
12 雲 *sōun* stratus clouds
13 楼 *sōrō* tall building
14 閣 *sōkaku* many-storied building
16 積雲 *sōsekiun* strato-cumulus clouds

12

層 1433 J-X M7798 See **層** 1432.

B **履** 1434 J4d7a M7799 RI. *fu(mu)* step on, trample on, stamp on; carry through, practice; appraise; set foot on; evade payment. *ha(ku)* put on (the feet). *kutsu* shoes, boots.
6 行 *rikō* performance, fulfillment, execution, observance
8 物 *hakimono* footwear
物店 *hakimonoten* footwear store
10 修 *rishū suru* study, complete (a course)
12 違 *ha(ki)-chiga(eru)* to put on someone else's footwear; be mistaken
14 歴 *rireki* personal history, career
歴書 *rirekisho* personal history, vita, resumé

18

屬 1435 J5624 M7821 See **属** 1430.

21

屭 1436 J-X M7823 See **屓** 1423.

屮 RAD. 45

Furukusa old "grass" (i.e., the less complicated "grass," as distinguished from Rad. 140). Variants: 屮, 屮. Nickname: Old Grass.

屮 1437 J5625 M7826 SA *hidarite* left hand.

1

B **屯** 1438 J4656 M7828 TON ton. CHUN. *tamuro* police station; camp, barracks.
5 田 *tonden* colonization
田兵 *tondenhei* agricultural soldiers, colonizers
8 所 *tonsho* post, quarters, military station; police station
12 営 *ton'ei* military camp, barracks, camping

RAD. 山 46

Yama mountain. At left: *yamahen*. Nickname: Mountain.

A 山 1439 / J3b33 / M7869 SAN mount, mountain. *yama* mountain, hill, height, knoll; heap, pile; crown (of a hat); seam (of an obi); speculation, adventure; climax, acme, crisis; forest; mine.

2 刀 *yamagatana* woodman's hatchet
又山 *yamamatayama* mountain upon mountain
人 *yamabito* mountain people; hermit
人蔘 *yama ninjin* wild carrot
3 口 *yamaguchi* start of a climb
女 *yamame* trout, young salmon
山 *yamayama* mountains; very much
川 *yamagawa* mountain stream. *sansen, yama-kawa* mountains and rivers
下 *yamashita, yamamoto, sanka* foot of a mountain
小屋 *yamagoya* mountain hut
上 *sanjō* mountain top
上垂訓 *Sanjō (no) Suikun* Sermon on the Mount
4 手 *yamate, yama(no)te* hilly section of Tokyo; bluff; uptown
方 *yamakata* mountainous area
月 *sangetsu* the moon above a mountain
木 *yamagi* mountain trees
犬 *yama inu* wild dog, wolf, coyote, jackal
辺 *yamabe* the vicinity of a mountain
中 *yamanaka, sanchū* in the mountains
内 *sannai* in the mountains; in a temple compound
元 *yamamoto* colliery, mine; base of a mountain; owner of a mountain
分 *yamawa(ke)* halving, equal division
火事 *yama kaji* forest fire
毛欅 *buna* beech tree
水 *yama mizu* mountain spring water. *sansui* hills and water; landscape, scenery; landscape painting; landscape garden
水画 *sansuiga* landscape painting; a landscape
水画家 *sansui gaka* landscape painter
5 田 *yamada* rice fields in the hills
号 *sangō* temple name
巡 *yamamegu(ri)* mountain trip; mountain pilgrimage; drizzling rain
主 *yamanushi* owner of a mountain area, mountain watchman
出 *yamada(shi)* a rustic
6 色 *sanshoku* mountain scenery; color of the mountains
行 *sankō, yamayu(ki), yamai(ki)* trip into the mountains
気 *sanki* mountain air. *yamaki, yamake, yamagi* speculative spirit; enterprise; pretension
向 *yamamu(kō)* across the mountain
伏 *yamabushi* mountain priest, itinerant priest, hermit
伝 *yamazuta(i)* along the mountains, following a mountain road
地 *yamachi, sanchi* hilly country, mountain area
肌 *yamahada* mountain surface
寺 *yamadera* mountain temple
守 *yamamori* forest ranger
光 *sankō* mountain scenery
羊 *yagi* goat
羊肉 *yagi niku* goat meat
羊鬚 *yagi hige* goatee
7 里 *yamazato* mountain village, hilly district
住 *yamazuma(i)* living in the mountains
抜 *yamanu(ke)* landslide
村 *sanson* mountain village
系 *sankei* mountain system
男 *yama otoko* wild man; woodsman; hillbilly; mountaineer
吹 *yamabuki* yellow rose
吹色 *yamabuki iro* bright yellow, golden; gold
形 *yamagata* chevron
形歯車 *yamagata haguruma* herringbone gears
8 門 *sammon* main (two-story) temple gate
雨 *san'u* rain from the mountains
国 *yamaguni* mountainous province
房 *sambō* a mountain villa; a home in the mountains
径 *sankei* mountain path
河 *sanga, sanka* mountains and rivers; stronghold
育 *yamasoda(chi)* bred in the mountains
幸 *yama (no) sachi, yama sachi* mountain food products

沿 *yamazo(i)* along the foot of a mountain
苞 *yamazuto* mountain souvenirs
岳 *sangaku* mountains
岳病 *sangakubyō* altitude sickness
林 *sanrin* mountains and forests; mountain forest
林官 *sanrinkan* forester
林学 *sanringaku* forestry
林保護 *sanrin hogo* forest conservation
林開拓 *sanrin kaitaku* deforestation
林業 *sanringyō* industry
林檎 *yama ringo* crab apple
林濫伐 *sanrin rambatsu* reckless deforestation
9 面 *yamazura* mountain surface
風 *sampū, yama kaze* mountain wind
廻 *yamamegu(ri)* mountain trip; mountain pilgrimage; drizzling rain
途 *santo* mountain road
城 *yama shiro* a mountain castle
姫 *yama hime* mountain goddess
姥 *yama uba* mountain witch
峡 *yamagai, yamakai, sankyō* gorge, ravine, gap, vale
相 *sansō* the form of a mountain
海 *sankai* mountains and seas; land and sea
狩 *yamaga(ri)* hunting in the mountains
神 *yama (no) kami* god of the mountain; a wife
亭 *santei* mountain villa; mountain inn
彦 *yamabiko* mountain echo; mountain god
荒 *yamaara(shi)* porcupine
茶 *tsubaki* camellia
荘 *sansō* mountain villa, mountain retreat
草 *yama kusa* mountain grass
津浪 *yama tsunami* landslide
背 *sampai* mountain ridge; the back side of the mountain. *yamase* mountain ridge; wind blowing from mountains to the sea
背風 *yamase kaze* wind blowing from mountains to the sea
10 骨 *sankotsu* a large rock
師 *yamashi* speculator; adventurer; impostor, swindler; miner; lumber dealer
桜 *yamazakura* a wild cherry tree, prunus serrulata
砲 *sampō* mountain gun, mountain artillery
祇 *yamatsumi* mountain god
脈 *sammyaku* mountain range
陰 *yama kage, san'in* shelter of the mountains; northern slopes
陵 *sanryō* mountains and hills; imperial tomb
容 *san'yō* the form of a mountain
高 *yamataka* derby hat
高帽 *yamatakabō* derby hat
家 *sanka, yamaga* mountain home, chalet. *yama (no) ie* mountaineers' hut
家住 *yamagazuma(i)* mountain life
家育 *yamagasoda(chi)* country-bred
11 鳥 *yamadori* pheasant; mountain bird
疵 *yama kizu* pottery firing flaw
道 *sandō* mountain pass, mountain path. *yama michi* mountain path
側 *sansoku* mountainside, hillside
掛 *yamaka(ke)* piled high
梔子 *kuchinashi* gardenia
脚 *sankyaku* the foot of a mountain
野 *san'ya* fields and mountains
陽 *san'yō* the southern face of a mountain; the sunny slopes
勘 *yamakan* speculation in business
頂 *sanchō* mountain top
崩 *yamakuzure* landslide
窓 *sansō* window in a mountain villa; mountain villa
梨 *yama nashi* wild pear
盛 *yamamo(ri)* heap, pile; full measure
砦 *sansai* mountain fortifications; bandit den
猫 *yamaneko* wildcat, lynx
猫争議 *yamaneko sōgi* wildcat strike
12 越 *yamago(e), yamago(shi)* crossing a mountain
開 *yamabira(ki)* opening of the mountain-climbing season
湯 *yama(no)yu* mountain hot springs
焼 *yamaya(ki)* burning of dead grass
勝 *yamaga(chi) no* hilly, mountainous
蛙 *yamagaeru* brown frog
蛭 *yamabiru* land leech
颪 *yama oroshi* a wind blowing down off the mountains
奥 *yamaoku* mountain recesses
嵐 *yama arashi* mountain storm

登 *yamanobo(ri)* mountain climbing
番 *yamaban* forest ranger
葡萄 *yama budō* wild grapes
紫水明 *sanshi-suimei* scenic beauty
間 *sankan* in the mountains. *yamaai* glen, ravine, gorge
間僻地 *sankan-hekichi* deep mountain recesses
椒 *sanshō* black pepper
椒魚 *sanshō uo* salamander
葵 *wasabi* Japanese horseradish
葵大根 *wasabi daikon* foreign horseradish
葵目鑢 *wasabime yasuri* rasp
葵卸 *wasabioro(shi)* grater
葵漬 *wasabizu(ke)* pickled horseradish
13 鼠 *yama nezumi* woodchuck; groundhog
僧 *sansō* (Buddhist) priest
塊 *sankai* isolated mountains; mountain range
楼 *sanrō* high mountain building
猿 *yamazaru* wild monkey; a rustic
稜 *sanryo* mountain ridge
続 *yamatsuzu(ki)* mountain chain
腹 *sampuku* hillside, mountainside
蜂 *yamabachi* hornet
裾 *yama suso, yamazuso* foot of a mountain
賊 *sanzoku* mountain bandit
路 *yamaji, sanro* mountain road
際 *yamagiwa* mountain ridge, skyline, base of a mountain
群 *sangun* mountain range
塞 *sansai* mountain fortress; den of bandits
勢 *sansei* condition in the mountains; shape of the mountains
鳩 *yamabato* turtledove
鳩色 *yamabato iro* yellowish blue
14 鳴 *yamana(ri)* rumbling in the mountains. *yamana(rashi)* poplar
端 *yama(no)ha* mountain ridge
駅 *san'eki* stage town in the mountains
寨 *sansai* mountain fortification; bandit den
窩 *sanka* roving mountainous tribes; nomads; outcast tribe; ancient hermit people
15 膚 *yamahada* the face of a mountain
稼 *yamakasegi* work in the mountains
賤 *yamagatsu, yamashizu* mountain dwellers
霊 *sanrei* mountain deity
駕籠 *yama kago* mountain palanquin
16 懐 *yamabutokoro* mountain valley, heart of the mountains
積 *yamazu(mi), sanseki* mountainous pile, big pile
17 嶽 *sangaku* mountains
18 鼬 *yama itachi* ermine
繭 *yama mayu* wild cocoon
19 鯨 *yama kujira* wild-boar meat
霧 *yamagiri* fog in the mountains
麓 *sanroku* the foot of a mountain
21 躑躅 *yama tsutsuji* rhododendron
22 巓 *santen* mountain top
籟 *sanrai* the sound of a mountain breeze in the trees
籠 *yamagomo(ri)* retiring in the mountains; retiring to a mountain temple

1

屾 1440 / J5626 / M-X （国字） *tawa* a col, a saddle.

2

岃 1441 / J5627 / M-X （国字） *nata* hatchet.

3

岁 1442 / J-X / M-X Nonstandard for **出** 445.

屹 1443 / J5628 / M7889 Kitsu towering (mountains).
5 立 *kitsuritsu suru* tower, rise, soar
9 度 *kitto* surely
12 然 *kitsuzen(taru)* towering

4

岌 1444 / J5629 / M7929 Kyū. Gyō. Gō high; dangerous.

岑 1445 / J562a / M7937 Shin. Jin high; dangerous; sharp. *mine* peak, ridge.

岔 1446 / J562b / M7944 Ta branch in road; branch in mountain range.

B **岐** 1447 / J3474 / M7936 KI. *chimata* forking road; street; scene; quarters; arena, theater.
- 5 出 *waka(re)-de(ru)* branch out, diverge, radiate
- 13 路 *kiro* forked road, branch road, crossroad

5

岼 1448 / J5630 / M-X （国字） *yuri* level spot created by sand or dirt deposited by wind or water.

峅 1449 / J5632 / M-X （国字） *kura* valley.

岾 1450 / J5633 / M-X （国字） *yama* mountain.

岫 1451 / J562d / M7991 SHŪ. SHU. *kuki* cave in cliff. *mine* peak; ridge.

岱 1452 / J4252 / M7997 TAI. DAI. name of mountain in China.

岶 1453 / J562f / M8005 HAKU. HYAKU mountain covered by dense growth.

岷 1454 / J5631 / M8007 BIN. MIN name of mountain in China.

岻 1455 / J562e / M8017 JI. NI. name of mountain in China.

岨 1456 / J413b / M7984 SO a rocky mountain.

B **岳** 1457 / J3359 / M8001 **嶽** 1516 / J5656 / M8566 GAKU. *take* peak, mountain.
- 4 父 *gakufu* father-in-law

B **岬** 1458 / J4c28 / M7992 KŌ. *misaki, saki* cape, spit, promontory.
- 12 湾 *kōwan* indentations, capes

A **岸** 1459 / J345f / M8009 GAN. *kishi* bank, shore, coast, brink.
- 4 辺 *kishibe* shore
- 6 向 *kishimu(kō)* opposite bank
- 10 根 *kishine* base of the riverbank
- 11 道 *kishi michi* riverbank road, cliff road
- 16 頭 *gantō* top of a riverbank
- 壁 *gampeki* wharf, breakwater; steep coastal cliff

岡 1460 / J322c / M7962 KŌ. *oka* hill, knoll, rising ground.
- 4 辺 *okabe* vicinity of a hill
- 5 目 *okame* onlooker, bystander
- 目八目 *okamehachimoku* The onlooker sees better than the players.
- 9 持 *okamo(chi)* wooden carrying box
- 11 惚 *okabore* unrequited love, secret affections
- 12 湯 *okayu* tank of clean hot water (in a bath house)
- 焼 *okaya(ki)* jealousy, envy
- 場所 *okabasho* red-light district

A **岩** 1461 / J3464 / M7985 GAN. *iwa* rock, crag; reef.
- 3 山 *iwayama* rocky mountain (large or small)
- 4 戸 *iwato* cave door; grotto; cave home
- 水 *iwamizu* water flowing from the rocks
- 5 石 *ganseki* rock, crag
- 穴 *iwa ana* rocky cave
- 本 *iwa moto* base of a rock
- 7 床 *ganshō* bedrock
- 8 波 *iwanami* waves breaking against the rocks
- 苔 *iwagoke* rock moss
- 9 飛 *iwato(bi)* diving from a high rock; such a diver
- 屋 *iwaya* cavern, grotto, rocky cave
- 峡 *iwa hazama* cleft in the rocks
- 洞 *gantō* rocky grotto
- 乗 *ganjō na* solid, firm, stout. *ganjō* excellent horse; 5-to-15-year-old horse
- 室 *iwamuro* stone hut
- 10 根 *iwane, iwagane* rock, crag; base of a rock
- 11 魚 *iwana* bull trout
- 道 *iwa michi* road along the top of a rocky cliff
- 組 *iwagu(mi)* arrangement of garden rocks
- 清水 *iwa shimizu* spring water among rocks
- 12 間 *iwama* cleft in the rocks; among the rocks or crags
- 棚 *iwatana* ledge

淵 *iwabuchi* deep water at the foot of a rocky cliff
壺 *iwatsubo* rocky cave
13 塩 *gan'en, iwashio* rock salt
隠 *iwagaku(re)* the shadow of a rock
窟 *gankutsu* rocky cave
14 層 *gansō* rock formation
16 橋 *iwabashi* natural rock bridge; stones forming a crossing over rapids
17 礁 *ganshō* reef
19 瀬 *iwase* rocky rapids

6

峇 1462 / J5634 / M8020 Kō cave in mountain; shape of mountain. *horaana* cave.

峙 1463 / J5635 / M8053 Ji. *sobadu(tsu)* tower, soar.

B **峠** 1464 / J463d / M8068 （国字） *tōge* mountain pass; crisis, crest, climax.
11 道 *tōge michi* a road over a mountain pass

B **峡** 1465 / J362e / M8068′ **峽** 1466 / J5637 / M8122 Kyō gorge, ravine.
hazama interval, interstice; ravine, glen; loophole (in a castle).
7 谷 *kyōkoku* glen, ravine, gorge, canyon
12 間 *kyokan* between the mountains; ravine, defile
湾 *kyowan* fjord

7

峽 1466 / J5637 / M8122 See **峡** 1465.

峪 1467 / J563b / M8073 Yoku *tani* vally; ravine.

峺 1468 / J5638 / M8115 Kō *saegi(ru)* obstruct, interrupt, block.

崋 1469 / J563c / M8161 Ka, Ge name of mountain in China.

峭 1470 / J5639 / M8085 Shō high and steep.
5 立 *shōritsu* steep and soaring (mountains)

峨 1471 / J3265 / M8071 **峩** 1472 / J5636 / M8072 Ga high mountain.
10 峨 *gaga(taru)* rugged, craggy

B **峰** 1473 / J4a76 / M8094 **峯** 1474 / J4a77 / M8093 Hō. *mine, ne* peak, summit, top; back (of a sword).
5 打 *mineu(chi)* striking with the back of a sword
10 峰 *minemine* peaks
13 続 *minetsuzu(ki)* succession of peaks
16 頭 *hōtō* the summit of a peak
22 巒 *hōran* mountain range

峻 1475 / J3d54 / M8116 Shun high; steep.
3 下剤 *shungezai* strong purgative
7 坂 *shumpan* steep slope
拒 *shunkyo* positive refusal
別 *shumbetsu* sharp distinction
8 刻 *shunkoku* heartlessness
命 *shummei* strict order; your orders
10 峰 *shumpō* steep peak
烈 *shunretsu na* unrelenting, severity, sternness
13 路 *shunro* steep road
14 酷 *shunkoku* heartlessness
17 厳 *shungen na* strict, harsh, severe
嶺 *shunrei* steep peak

A **島** 1476 / J4567 / M8108 **嶋** 1503 / J4568 / M8434 **嶌** 1504 / J563a / M8435 **嶹** 1505 / J-X / M8433 Tō *shima* island.
2 人 *tōjin, shimabito* islanders
3 山 *shimayama* island mountain
4 中 *tōchū* all over the island
内 *tōnai* on the island
5 田 *shimada* a hairdo
巡 *shimamegu(ri)* island tour
主 *tōshu* island chief
民 *tōmin* islanders
6 伝 *shimazuta(i)* island-hopping
守 *tōshu, shimamori* island chief
8 育 *shimasoda(chi)* brought up on an island
国 *shimaguni, tōgoku* island country
国根性 *shimaguni konjō* insularism
9 風 *shimakaze* island wind
帝国 *tōteikoku* island empire
10 流 *shimanaga(shi)* exile, banishment

3 口囗土士夊夂夕大女子宀寸小⺌尢尸屮【山】7 川巛工己巾干幺广廴廾弋弓ヨ彑彡彳

破 *shimayabu(ri)* escaping from an island exile
陰 *shimakage* the other side of the island
島 *shimajima* islands
16 嶼 *tōsho* islands

8

崔 1477 J5643 M8178 SAI high, big (mountain).

崙 1478 J5646 M8183 **崘** 1479 J5647 M8182 RON used in name of legendary mountain in China.

崚 1480 J5645 M8184 RYŌ towering (mountain).

崟 1481 J5640 M8199 GIN. GON peak, ridge; immense, soaring; steep.

崢 1482 J5644 M8203 SŌ. SHŌ high, steep (mountain); peak.

崗 1483 J563e M8221 KŌ hill.

崑 1484 J5642 M8173 KON used in name of legendary mountain in China.
11 崙 *Konron* name of legendary mountain in China

B **崎** 1485 J3a6a M8169 KI steep. *misaki, saki* cape, spit, promontory.
14 嶇 *kiku* steepness of a road; life's trials

崛 1486 J5641 M8185 **崫** 1487 J-X M8186 KUTSU high and lofty (mountains).
10 起 *kukki suru* rise abruptly, tower high

B **崖** 1488 J3333 M8180 **崕** 1489 J563d M8179 **厓** 648 J-X M2930 GAI. *gake* cliff, bluff, precipice.
11 崩 *gakekuzu(re)* landslide
13 路 *gakeji, gake michi* narrow cliff road; steep stony road
14 端 *gakebata* edge of a cliff

B **崇** 1490 J3f72 M8152 SŪ, SHŪ high. *aga(meru)* respect, revere, adore, worship.
4 仏 *sūbutsu* revering the Buddhas
仏派 *sūbutsuha* (ancient) pro-Buddhist faction
8 拝 *sūhai* worship; admiration, adoration; cult
拝者 *sūhaisha* worshiper, admirer, idolater, devotee
10 高 *sūkō na* lofty, noble, sublime
高美 *sūkōbi* subline beauty, the sublime
12 敬 *sūkei* reverence, adoration, veneration

B **崩** 1491 J4a78 M8212 HŌ. *hō(jiru), hō(zuru)* die. *kuzu(su)* demolish, destroy; level (a hill); crumble (bread); change (money); simplify; put in disorder; cut (prices). *kuzu(reru)* crumble, collapse, cave in , be destroyed, get out of shape; be routed; worsen (weather). *kuzu(shi)* simplified form. *-kuzu(re)* delinquent, degenerate.
5 去 *kuzu(re)-sa(ru)* collapse, crumble away
6 字 *kuzu(shi)ji* abbreviated character
7 売 *kuzu(shi)u(ri)* selling separately
10 書 *kuzu(shi)ga(ki)* grass-hand penmanship
12 御 *hōgyo* demise, death of an emperor
落 *kuzu(re)-o(chiru)* fall down flat; dissolve. *hōraku* collapse, cave-in; slump, crash, heavy decline
13 滅 *kuzu(re)-horo(biru)* crumble to ruins
15 潰 *hōkai* collapse, cave-in
16 壊 *hōkai* collapse, cave-in

9

嵜 1492 J563f M-X See **崎** 1485.

嵋 1493 J564b M8278 BI used in proper names.

嵎 1494 J564a M8281 GŪ. GU mountain recesses; bend in mountain range; corner.

嵒 1495 J5649 M8294 GAN rock, crag; steep; soar (above). *iwa* rock, crag.

嵐 1496 / J4d72 / M8289 RAN. *arashi* storm, tempest.
[6]気 *ranki* mountain air

嵌 1497 / J5648 / M8279 KAN. *ha(maru)* go into, fit into; fall into, plunge into; be deceived. *ha(meru)* put on, pull on; inlay, set in; fit in; fill in; throw into; ensnare, cheat.
[2]入 *kannyū suru, ha(me)-i(reru)* inlay, insert, fit in, dovetail, telescope
[4]込 *ha(me)-ko(mu)* put on, pull on; inlay, set in; fit in; fill in; throw into; ensnare, cheat.
木細工 *hamekizaiku* inlaid woodwork
[7]役 *hama(ri)yaku* fitting role
[11]細工 *hamezaiku* inlaid work; inlay worker
[12]替 *ha(me)-kae(ru)* change (buttons or the cords of wooden clogs, etc.)
[13]頓 *kanton* strangulation (as in hernia)

10

峪 1498 / J564e / M-X （国字） *tao*, *tawa* col, saddle, mountain pass.

嵬 1499 / J564c / M8355 KAI. GAI high, steep; dangerous; rugged.

嵯 1500 / J3a37 / M8363 **嵳** 1501 / J564d / M8361 SA. SHI craggy; steeply towering mountain; boulders scattered on mountain.

嵩 1502 / J3f73 / M8348 SŪ. *ko(zuru), ko(jiru)* be aggravated, grow worse. *kasa(mu)* grow bulky, rise, swell, increase in volume; mount up. *kasa* bulk, volume, quantity, size.
[10]高 *kasadaka na* bulky, voluminous; high-handed
[11]張 *kasaba(ru)* be bulky
掛 *kasa (ni) ka(karu)* take a high-handed attitude

11

嶋 1503 / J4568 / M8434 **嶌** 1504 / J563a / M8435 **㠀** 1505 / J-X / M8433
See **島** 1476.

嶂 1506 / J5651 / M8410 SHŌ high steep mountain; linked ridgelines.

嶇 1507 / J564f / M8426 KU steep.

嶐 1508 / J5657 / M8447 RYŪ shape of mountain.

嶄 1509 / J5650 / M8413 **嶃** 1510 / J-X / M8412 ZAN steep (mountain), high.
[12]然 *zanzen(taru)* prominent, conspicuous, unrivaled

12

嶝 1511 / J5653 / M8482 TŌ slope; sloping road.

嶢 1512 / J5652 / M8491 GYŌ steep, dangerous; high.

13

嶮 1513 / J5655 / M8520 See **険** 6456.

嶬 1514 / J5654 / M8510 GI steep.

嶼 1515 / J5659 / M8561 SHO island.

14

嶽 1516 / J5656 / M8566 See **岳** 1457.

嶺 1517 / J4e66 / M8553 REI. RYŌ. *mine, ne* peak, summit, top; back (of a sword).

嶷 1518 / J5658 / M8545 GYOKU wise.
[5]立 *gyokuritsu* rising, towering

3 口 囗 土 士 夂 夊 夕 大 女 子 宀 寸 小 ⺌ 尢 尸 屮 17【山】 川 巛 工 己 巾 干 幺 广 廴 廾 弋 弓 ヨ 彑 彡 彳

3 — 17

巇 1519 / J-X / M8614 Ki, Gi steep.

巉 1520 / J565a / M8618 Zan. San high, steep, towering (mountain).

11 崖 *zangai* cliff
20 巌 *zangan* soaring crag

巌 1521 / J3460 / M8624′ **巖** 1525 / J565e / M8649 Gan. *iwa* rock, crag, reef. *iwao* (massive) rock.

9 洞 *gantō* cave
乗 *ganjō na* solid, firm, stout. *ganjō* excellent horse; 5-to-15-year-old horse
12 棲 *gansei* cave dwelling; living in the mountains; hermit
13 窟 *gankutsu* cave, cavern, grotto
15 質 *ganshitsu* properties of stone
16 頭 *gantō* top of a rock
壁 *gampeki* cliff

18

巍 1522 / J565b / M8626 Gi high.

10 峨 *giga(taru)* lofty, towering
12 然 *gizen(taru)* lofty, towering
21 巍 *gigi(taru)* lofty, towering

19

巒 1523 / J565d / M8640 Ran small peak.

巓 1524 / J565c / M8644 Ten. *itadaki* summit.

20

巖 1525 / J565e / M8649 See **巌** 1521.

RAD. 川 47

Kawa river or *sambon kawa* 3-stroke "river" (to distinguish it from the 8-stroke river 河). Variant: 巛 *magari kawa* curving "river." Nickname: River.

A **川** 1526 / J406e / M8673 **巛** 1527 / J565f / M8669 Sen. *kawa* river, stream, brook.

3 口 *kawaguchi* mouth of a river
川 *kawagawa* rivers
下 *kawashimo* downstream. *kawakuda(ri)* going down a river
上 *kawakami* upper stream; upstream. *kawanobo(ri)* going up a river
4 心 *senshin* the middle of the river
手 *kawate* riverside; tax on travelers crossing a river
止 *kawado(me)* no ferry service
辺 *kawabe* riverside
5 尻 *kawajiri* river mouth; lower stream
付 *kawatsu(ki)* along the river
6 竹 *kawatake* river bamboo
向 *kawamuka(i)*, *kawamu(kō)* the opposite side of the river
伝 *kawazuta(i) ni* along the river
州 *kawasu* sandbank in a river
合 *kawaa(i)* confluence
守 *kawamori* guard at the ford
7 床 *kawadoko*, *kawatoko* riverbed
8 沿 *kawazo(i) ni* along the river
波 *kawa nami* waves on a stream
股 *kawamata* river fork
岸 *kawagishi* riverbank
9 面 *kawazura*, *kawamo*, *kawa(no)omo* river surface
音 *kawa oto* sound of a flowing river
風 *kawa kaze* river breeze
柱 *kawabashira* bridge pillar
柳 *kawa yanagi* purple willow, river willow. *senryū* comic haiku poem
洲 *kawasu* river sandbar
狩 *kawaga(ri)* river fishing
施餓鬼 *kawa segaki* memorial service for the drowned
10 原 *kawara*, *kawahara* dry riverbed; river beach
流 *kawanaga(re)* river drowning

[11] 魚 *kawauo, kawazakana* river fish
遊 *kawaaso(bi)* boating, rowing
淀 *kawa yodo* river pool
猟 *kawaryō* river fishing
船 *kawabune, kawa fune* river boat, barge, ferry
釣 *kawatsuri* river fishing
[12] 遠 *kawaochi* opposite river bank
開 *kawabira(ki)* river festival
幅 *kawa haba* river width
揚 *kawaa(ge)* unloading (a ship) at the riverside; raising water out of a river
渡 *kawawata(shi)* crossing a river
颪 *kawa oroshi* wind blowing down the river
筋 *kawa suji* river course
越 *kawago(e), kawago(shi)* crossing a river
越人足 *kawago(shi) ninsoku* coolies that carry people across a river
蒸気 *kawajōki* river steamer
蒸汽船 *kawajōkisen* river steamer
[13] 路 *kawaji* watercourses
[14] 端 *kawabata* riverside
[15] 縁 *kawabuchi, kawaberi* riverside
蝦 *kawa ebi* crayfish
論 *kawa ron* struggle over water rights
[19] 瀬 *kawase* rapids, shallows
獺 *kawa uso, kawa oso* otter
藻 *kawamo* plants of the river shallows
霧 *kawagiri* river mist
[28] 鑿 *kawaseseri* river fishing

2

B 巡 1528 / J3d64 / M8680 JUN going around; circumference.
megu(ru) go around; in connection with, concering. *megu(ri)* girth, circumference; tour, round, pilgrimage; flow, circulation; menstruation. *megu(rasu)* surround, make (someone) go around.
(o)mawa(ri)san policeman.
[5] 礼 *junrei* pilgrimage; pilgrim
礼者 *junreisha* pilgrim
[6] 行 *junkō* patrol, beat, round, tour
合 *megu(ri)-a(u)* meet by chance, come across
回 *junkai* tour, round, patrol
回文庫 *junkai bunko* traveling library
回図書館 *junkai toshokan* traveling library
回裁判 *junkai saiban* circuit court
回路 *junkairo* circuit
回講演 *junkai kōen* lecture tour
回講演者 *junkai kōensha* circuit rider, traveling lecturer
[7] 囲 *megu(ri)-kako(mu)* encircle
[8] 拝 *jumpai* circuit pilgrimage
幸 *junkō* imperial tour
歩 *megu(ri)-aru(ku)* walk around, travel around
[9] 廻 *junkai* tour, round, patrol
洋 *jun'yō* cruise; cruising
洋艦 *jun'yōkan* (navy) cruiser
査 *junsa* police, patrolman
査駐在所 *junsa chūzaisho* police substation
[10] 航 *junkō* cruise; cruising
航船 *junkōsen* cruiser
航艦 *junkōkan* cruiser
[11] 遊 *jun'yū* tour
視 *junshi* inspection tour
視人 *junshinin* patrolman; floorwalker
[12] 検 *junken* tour of inspection
[13] 業 *jungyō* provincial tour
[14] 歴 *junreki* tour, trip
察 *junsatsu* patrol, inspection round; visitation
[15] 閲 *jun'etsu* tour of inspection
[16] 錫 *junshaku* (Buddhist) teaching tour
覧 *junran* tour, sightseeing
[19] 警 *junkei* patrolman
[22] 邏 *junra* patrol, round, beat
邏船 *junrasen* patrol boat, revenue cutter

3

A 州 1529 / J3d23 / M8678 SHŪ province, state; continent. SU sandbar, shallows.
[5] 立 *shūritsu* state-owned, state-operated
[8] 法 *shūhō* state law
知事 *shūchiji* state or provincial governor
[9] 俗 *shūzoku* local customs
[12] 税 *shūzei* state tax
[14] 境 *shūkyō* state boundary, provincial boundary

4

巠 1530 J-X M8681 KYŌ. KEI ground water; vertical wave; broad expanse of water.

8

巢 1531 J-X M8696 See 巣 2705.

RAD. 工 48

E (the katakana). At left: エ *takumi hen* (left-side "carpenter's square"). Nickname: *Kana E.*

A 工 1532 J3929 M8714 KU. KŌ artisan, mechanic; manufacture; work.
takumi artisan, mechanic; carpenter.
taku(mu) plan; scheme.
2 人 *kōjin* workman, craftsman
3 女 *kōjo* factory girl
大 *kōdai* engineering college
4 夫 *kufū* device, invention, scheme, means. *kōfu* coolie, workman, laborer
手 *kōshu* workman, trackman
手学校 *kōshu gakkō* trade school
6 匠 *kōshō* mechanic, artisan, craftsman
合 *guai, guwai* fitness, order, condition; way, style; convenience; decency, propriety; state of health; situation; arrangements
7 兵 *kōhei* army engineers
作 *kōsaku* building, engineering; handicraft; maneuvering (in politics)
作物 *kōsakubutsu* building; manufactured articles
作品 *kōsakuhin* handicrafts
作船 *kōsakusen* factory ship
作機械 *kōsaku kikai* machine tools
芸 *kōgei* industrial arts, technology
芸学 *kōgeigaku* technology
芸学校 *kōgei gakkō* technological school
芸品 *kōgeihin* industrial-art objects
芸美術 *kōgei bijutsu* mechanical art
8 房 *kōbō* (artisan's) studio
具 *kōgu* tool, implement
学 *kōgaku* engineering
学士 *Kōgakushi* Bachelor of Engineering
学博士 *Kōgaku Hakase, Kōgaku Hakushi* Doctor of Engineering
事 *kōji* construction
事中 *kōjichū* under construction
事場 *kōjiba* construction site
9 面 *kumen* contriving, managing, raising (funds); circumstances, pecuniary status
科 *kōka* engineering course
科大学 *kōka daigaku* engineering college
10 員 *kōin* factory worker, artisan
11 率 *kōritsu* rate of production
商 *kōshō* industry and commerce; workmen and businessmen
務 *kōmu* engineering
務店 *kōmuten* engineering firm
務所 *kōmusho* engineering office
12 程 *kōtei* process; work progress
費 *kōhi* construction costs
場 *kōjō, kōba* factory, workshop, mill
場主 *kōjōshu* factory owner
場生産 *kōjō seisan* prefabrication
場地 *kōjōchi* factory district
場長 *kōjōchō* factory manager
場制 *kōjōsei, kōbasei* factory system
場街 *kōjōgai* factory town
場渡 *kōjōwata(shi)* factory delivery
場疎開 *kōjō sokai* factory dispersion
13 賃 *kōchin* wages, pay, labor cost
業 *kōgyō* industry
業大学 *kōgyō daigaku* technical college
業化 *kōgyōka* industrialization
業化学 *kōgyō kagaku* industrial chemistry
業用 *kōgyōyō* for industrial use
業史 *kōgyōshi* history of industry
業地 *kōgyōchi* industrial area
業地帯 *kōgyō chitai* industrial area
業国 *kōgyōkoku* industrial nation
業界 *kōgyōkai* industrial circles
業家 *kōgyōka* manufacturer
業塩 *kōgyōen* industrial salt
14 銀 *kōgin* wages, pay
銭 *kōsen* wages, pay
15 廠 *kōshō* arsenal

2

B **巧** 1533 / J392a / M8721 KŌ. *taku(mi) na* skilled. *taku(manai), taku(manu)* artless, natural, unintentional. *taku(mi)* skill, ingenuity.

4 手 *kōshu* a skillful workman
5 弁 *kōben* quibbling
6 舌 *kōzetsu* a clever speaker
匠 *kōshō* skilled carpenter; skilled workman
7 妙 *kōmyō* skill, cleverness, ingenuity
技 *kōgi* skilled workmanship
言 *kōgen* flattery
言令色 *kōgen-reishoku* ingratiating geniality
8 拙 *kōsetsu* tact, skill, performance, workmanship
知 *kōchi* cleverness, tact
者 *kōsha* cleverness, skill, tact
11 遅 *kōchi* slow but sure
12 智 *kōchi* cleverness, tact
16 緻 *kōchi na* elaborate, finely wrought

B **巨** 1534 / J3570 / M8722 KYO. KO. *ōki(i), ōi(naru)* big, large, great.

2 人 *kyojin* giant; great person
人国 *kyojinkoku* land of giants
3 口 *kyokō* big mouth
万 *kyoman* huge fortune, millions
大 *kyodai na* huge, enormous
5 石 *kyoseki* megalith
石記念物 *kyoseki kinembutsu* megalith
6 匠 *kyoshō* master, masterhand, maestro
7 体 *kyotai* large build
材 *kyozai* big timber; big caliber (man)
利 *kyori* huge profit
8 波 *kyoha* billow, large wave
刹 *kyosatsu* large temple
岩 *kyogan* huge rock, crag
歩 *kyoho* long strides
9 星 *kyosei* giant sun; great man, big shot
10 峰 *kyohō* gigantic peak
砲 *kyohō* huge gun
財 *kyozai* huge fortune
11 細 *kyosai* large and small matters; particulars, details. *kosai* greatness and smallness; details, particulars, circumstances
船 *kyosen* ocean liner
舶 *kyohaku* ocean liner
商 *kyoshō* wealthy merchant
盗 *kyotō* big-time robber
視的 *kyoshiteki* macroscopic
12 弾 *kyodan* huge projectile
富 *kyofu* great riches
費 *kyohi* great cost
13 漢 *kyokan* giant
賊 *kyozoku* big-time bandit, big-time pirate
資 *kyoshi* large capital, enormous fund
14 魁 *kyokai* ringleader, chief
像 *kyozō* huge image
16 頭 *kyotō* leader, magnate, big name
17 擘 *kyohaku* an authority, a big shot, a star
18 軀 *kyoku* big frame
額 *kyogaku* enormous sum
20 艦 *kyokan* large warship
鐘 *kyoshō* large hanging bell

A **左** 1535 / J3a38 / M8720 SA left; the following. *hidari* left; the left; leftist. *hidari suru* turn to the left.

3 大臣 *Sadaijin* (ancient) Minister of the Left
4 手 *hidarite* left hand; the left
方 *sahō* the left
辺 *sahen* left side
分 *hidariwa(ke)* parting (the hair) at the left
中間 *sachukan* between left field and center
心房 *sashimbō* left auricle (of the heart)
心室 *sashinshitsu* left ventricle (of the heart)
5 右 *sayū suru* command, dominate, control, sway. *sayū* left and right; one's side; one's attendants. *tokō* this or that. *sau* left and right; news; condition; criticism; command. *to(ni)kaku(ni)* anyway. *to(mo)kaku (mo), to(mo)kaku* anyhow, in any case. *hidari-migi* left and right
打者 *hidaridasha* left-handed batter
6 回 *hidarimawa(ri)* counterclockwise
向 *hidarimu(ki)* turning to the left
団扇 *hidari uchiwa* living in comfort
7 折 *sasetsu suru* turn to the left
社 *sasha* left-wing socialist party
利 *hidarikiki* left-handedness; left-hander; saké drinker. *hidarigitcho* left-handedness; left-hander
邪飛 *sajahi* foul to the left
見右見 *tomikōmi* viewing from all directions

8 注 *sachū* left marginal notes
岸 *sagan* left bank (of a river)
表 *sahyō* chart at the left
官 *sakan, shakan* plasterer
官職 *sakanshoku, shakanshoku* plasterer
9 廻 *hidarimawa(ri)* counterclockwise
派 *saha* left wing; left faction; leftist
歪 *hidariyuga(mi)* inclining to the left
前 *hidarimae* the wrong way, folding left side of a kimono under the right; adversity. *sazen* front of left field
室 *sashitsu* left ventricle (of the heart)
巻 *hidarima(ki)* counterclockwise; perverse; mentally off
10 記 *saki* the following
党 *satō* the opposition party, the Opposition; leftists, the left; drinker, wine lover
書 *hidariga(ki)* writing from the left
袒 *satan* support, alliance
袒者 *satansha* supporter
11 眼 *sagan* left eye
舷 *sagen* port, port side
寄 *hidariyo(ri)* leaning toward the left; leftist
側 *hidarigawa, sasoku* left side; the left
側通行 *hidarigawa tsūkō* Keep to the Left
12 越 *sago(shi)* over left field
程 *sahodo* so much, much, very
証 *sashō* proof
勝手 *hidari katte* left-handedness; left-hander; saké drinker
腕 *hidari ude* left arm
腕投手 *sawan tōshu* left-handed pitcher
13 傾 *sakei* leftist, radical, inclination to the left
褄 *hidarizuma* geisha
14 遷 *sasen* demotion, degradation
様 *sayō* such, like that; yes, indeed; well, let me see. *sayo(nara), sayō(nara)* goodbye. *sonna* that kind of. *hidarizama* wicked way
端 *satan* left edge; left end; left lane
15 縄 *hidarinawa* the wrong way; adversity
器用 *hidarigitcho* left-handedness; left-hander
17 犠飛 *sagihi* left-field sacrifice fly
翼 *sayoku* left flank; left wing, leftist, radical movement; left field
翼手 *sayokushu* left fielder
21 顧 *sako* turning toward the left
顧右見 *sako-uken* indecision
顧右眄 *sako-uben* irresolution, vacillation

4

巫 1536 / J5660 / M8728 FU sorcerer, sorceress. *miko* medium, shrine maiden. *kannagi, kan, kanko* medium, diviner, shrine maiden.
3 女 *miko* medium, sorceress; shrine maiden
山戯 *fuzake(ru)* romp, gambol, frolic; joke, make fun of; flirt

7

A **差** 1537 / J3a39 / M8732 SHI, SA difference, variation; discrepancy; margin; balance; remainder (in subtraction). *sa(su) vt* raise (the hands); stretch out (the hands in dancing); put up (an umbrella); carry (on the shoulder); build (a hut); stretch (a rope); graft (trees); carry (in the belt); lift up; offer. *vi* (the sun) shines; appear on the surface. *sa(shi)* sharpened tube for testing rice in bags; ruler (for measuring); face to face; hindrance; sharing a load. *sa(shi) de* between two persons. *sa(shi)-* emphatic verbal prefix.
2 入 *sa(shi)-i(reru)* insert; send to a prisoner. *sa(shi)i(re)* insertion; something sent to a prisoner
入品 *sashiirehin* something sent to a prisoner
3 口 *sa(shi)guchi* suggestion from the outside
上 *sa(shi)-a(geru)* lift up, raise; give, present, offer; let (a person) have
上物 *sa(shi)a(ge)mono* gift
4 止 *sa(shi)-to(meru)* prohibit, forbid, ban
込 *sa(shi)-ko(mu)* insert, thrust in; flow into; plug in; have a sharp pain. *sashiko(mi)* thrusting; insertion; socket; plug; cap; sharp pain
支 *sa(shi)-tsuka(eru)* be hindered, be interrupted, be prevented; be engaged; suffer inconvenience, have difficulty (in doing); be unable to; be hard up. *sa(shi)tsuka(e)* hindrance,

impediment, interference, interruption; previous engagement

支無 *sa(shi)tsuka(e)na(i)* OK, no trouble, no objection, justifiable, allowable

引 *sa(shi)-hi(ku), sa(p)pi(ku)* deduct. *sashihi(ki)* deduction, subtraction; balance; ebb and flow, rise and fall; intermittence

引勘定 *sashihiki kanjō* account balance

5 立 *sa(shi)-ta(teru)* send, forward, dispatch

付 *sa(shi)-tsu(keru)* point (a gun at); put right under one's nose

加 *sa(shi)-kuwa(eru)* add to

古 *sa(shi)-furu(su)* wear out (a comb or a sword)

出 *sa(shi)-da(su), sa(shi)-ida(su)* present, submit, tender; send in (a card); produce (evidence); file (a petition); send; forward; reach out; extend; mail (a letter). *sa(shi)de(gamashii)* forward, intrusive, impertinent. *sa(shi)-de(ru)* push oneself forward. *sa(shi)ide, sa(shi)de* impertinence

出人 *sashidashinin* sender; addresser

出口 *sa(shi)deguchi* uncalled-for remark

出者 *sa(shi)demono* intruder, meddler, busybody

6 回 *sa(shi)-mawa(su)* send (a car) around

向 *sa(shi)-mu(keru)* send around; direct; turn (the light) toward; cover (with a gun). *sashimu(ki)* for the time being. *sashimuka(i)* face to face

仰 *sa(shi)-ao(gu)* respect, look up to

汐 *sa(shi)shio, sa(shi)jio* rising tide

合 *sa(shi)a(i)* hindrance, impediment, interference, interruption; previous engagement; obstacle; offense

当 *sa(shi)ata(ri)* for the time being. *sa(shi)-ata(ru)* happen to meet; (the sun) shines in

7 足 *sa(shi)ashi* stealthy steps

戻 *sa(shi)-modo(su)* send back, refer back

迫 *sa(shi)-sema(ru)* be imminent, be impending

伸 *sa(shi)-no(beru)* hold out (the hand), extend (the arm), reach out for; thrust (a javelin)

別 *sabetsu* discrimination, distinction, differentiation

別的 *sabetsuteki* discriminatory

別界 *sabetsukai* world of inequality

別待遇 *sabetsu taigū* discriminatory treatment

別関税 *sabetsu kanzei* differential tariff

8 金 *sakin, sa(shi)kin* difference; margin; balance. *sa(shi)gane* carpenter's square; metal foot rule; tip; suggestion; inspiration; instigation

固 *sa(shi)-kata(meru)* shut; warn sternly

送 *sa(shi)-oku(ru)* send, ship; transmit; remit; see off, see home, escort; spend (one's time), live (a life)

担 *sa(shi)-nina(i)* shouldering a load

枝 *sa(shi)eda* graft, slip, scion

油 *sa(shi)abura* lamp oil

知恵 *sa(shi)jie* suggestion, hint

押 *sa(shi)-osa(eru)* seize, attach, garnishee, impound

押品 *sashiosa(e)hin* seized goods

物屋 *sashimonoya* cabinetmaker

物師 *sashimonoshi* cabinetmaker

9 廻 *sa(shi)-mawa(su)* send (a car) around

挟 *sa(shi)-hasa(mu)* insert, put between; interrupt (a conversation); harbor, entertain

10 俯 *sa(shi)-utsumu(ku)* look down, hang the head

紙 *sa(shi)gami* summons, official order

益 *saeki* marginal profit

差 *sa(shitsu)-sa(saretsu)* exchanging saké cups

配 *sahai* conduct of business; management; agency, agent

配人 *sahainin* landlord's agent

11 控 *sa(shi)-hika(eru)* be temperate, use moderation; withhold, refrain from

添 *sa(shi)-so(eru)* present in addition to. *sa(shi)zo(e)* the shorter sword; assistant, auxiliary, second. *sa(shi)zo(i)* assistance, auxiliary, second

許 *sa(shi)-yuru(su)* permit, approve; authorize; acknowledge; confide in; forgive, pardon; release; acquit; overlook

寄 *sa(shi)-yo(ru)* approach; assemble; call at; come; lean toward; obey; lean on; depend on; conclude; be possessed (by devils); present (offerings). *sa(shi)-yo(seru)* let approach, bring near; gather, collect, summon, muster;

add up; push aside; attack; send (a letter); contribute to; become dependent on; take refuge with

異 *sai* difference, disparity

率税 *saritsuzei* graduated tax

掛 *sa(shi)-ka(keru)* hold (an umbrella) over (someone). *sa(shi)-ka(karu)* approach, come near, arrive, hang over, overhang; be urgent, be imminent; be on the point of; be covered; pass by. *sa(shi)ka(ke)* penthouse, lean-to

掛小屋 *sa(shi)ka(ke)goya, sakka(ke)goya* penthouse, lean-to

12 遣 *saken suru* dispatch

渡 *sa(shi)-wata(ru)* cross in a boat. *sa(shi)wata(shi)* diameter, caliber, distance across

違 *sa(shi)-chiga(eru)* misplace. *sai* difference

隔 *sa(shi)-heda(teru)* separate, interpose; screen, shield, estrange

覗 *sa(shi)-nozo(ku)* peep, peek; come into sight

登 *sa(shi)-nobo(ru)* rise, ascend, go up, climb; go to (the capital); add up to; be promoted; advance (in price); sail up; come up (on the agenda)

等 *satō* difference in rank, grade, or class

替 *sa(shi)-ka(eru)* replace, substitute, change

13 詰 *sa(shi)zu(me)* for the time being

障 *sa(shi)-sawa(ru)* be obstructed, be hindered. *sa(shi)sawa(ri)* obstacle, hindrance; offense

置 *sa(shi)-o(ku)* leave, let alone; ignore, neglect, slight

15 潮 *sa(shi)shio, sa(shi)jio* rising tide

16 薬 *sa(shi)gusuri* eye drops, subcutaneous injection

17 翳 *sa(shi)-kaza(su)* hold aloft; shade (the eyes); stick (something) in the hair

18 額 *sagaku* balance, difference, margin

19 繰 *sa(shi)-ku(ru)* manage skillfully

響 *sa(shi)-hibi(ku)* affect, influence

RAD. 己 49

Onore self. Variants: 已 *sude ni* already, 巳 *mi* snake. Nickname: Snake.

巳 1538 / J4c26 / M8744 SHI. *mi* 9–11 a.m.; sixth zodiac sign; serpent.

已 1539 / J5661 / M8743 I. *sude ni* previously; already, long ago; on the point of; actually. *ya(mu) vi* end, stop, cease; subside, calm down, pass; die out, be extinguished; leave, go off; be abandoned. *ya(meru) vt* end, discontinue; give up, abandon; abolish; resign, retire.

3 下 *ika* less than, under, below; and downward; not exceeding; the following; the rest

A **己** 1540 / J384a / M8742 KO. KI F, sixth. *onore, ono* oneself, myself, yourself. *ono(gajishi)* as one pleases. *tsuchinoto* sixth calendar sign.

5 奴 *unu* you rascal

12 等 *oira, onorera* we

1

巴 1541 / J4743 / M8745 HA. *tomoe* huge comma design.

5 瓦 *tomoegawara* comma-pattern tile

旦杏 *hatankyō* plum

4

卮 1542 / J5662 / M8751 SHI large wine bowl; scattered; adapt to the situation.

6

巷 1543 / J392b / M-X **巷** 1544 / J-X / M8756 KŌ. *chimata* forking road; street; scene; quarters; arena, theater.

12 間 *kōkan* the world

14 説 *kōsetsu* rumor, talk of the town

A **巻** 1545 / J342c / M8759′ **卷** 635 / J524b / M2860 KEN, KAN volume, book, part; reel. *ma(ku)* roll up; wind,

coil; tie around; wind up. *maki* roll (of silk); volume, book; winding (of a clock).
3 土重来 *kendo-jūrai* making a success after a failure
上 *ma(ki)-a(geru) vt* roll up; hoist, hoist, heave up; take away, rob; blow up (dust). *ma(ki)-a(garu) vi* curl up into the air (smoke); roll up. *ma(ki)a(ge)* lifting, hoisting
4 毛 *ma(ki)ge* curl, ringlet
尺 *makijaku* measuring tape
込 *ma(ki) ko(mu) vt* roll up, enfold; engulf, swallow up, drag into, involve in
内 *kannai* in this volume
5 付 *ma(ki)-tsu(keru)* wind or tie around, coil. *ma(ki)-tsu(ku)* coil or wind around; twist about
末 *kammatsu* end of a book
6 舌 *ma(ki)jita* trill, rolling the tongue
返 *makikae(shi)* bickering; give and take; fighting back and forth
7 尾 *kambi* end of a book
8 帙 *kanchitsu* a book and its case; books; number of volumes
枠 *ma(ki)waku* spool, bobbin, reel
物 *makimono* a (horizontal) scroll
直 *ma(ki)nao(shi)* rebinding (a scroll); rewinding
取紙 *ma(ki)to(ri)shi* roll of paper
9 首 *kanshu* first page of a book
狩 *ma(ki)ga(ri)* grand hunt
10 起 *ma(ki)-o(kosu)* stir up
紙 *makigami* rolled paper
11 添 *ma(ki)zo(e)* involvement, entanglement
12 結 *ma(ki) musu(bi)* clove hitch
雲 *ma(ki)gumo, ken'un* cirrus clouds
軸 *ma(ki)jiku* scroll
軸帯 *ma(ki)jikutai* roller bandage
揚 *ma(ki)-a(geru) vt* roll up; hoist, heave up; take away, rob; blow up (dust). *ma(ki)-a(garu) vi* curl up into the air (smoke); roll up. *ma(ki)a(ge)* lifting, hoisting
揚機 *ma(ki)a(ge)ki* hoist, winch, windlass
揚轆轤 *ma(ki)a(ge) rokuro* capstan
13 煙草 *ma(ki)tabako* cigarette
14 管 *ma(ki)kan* coiled pipe
髪 *ma(ki)gami* tress, curl
層雲 *kensōun* cirro-stratus clouds
15 線 *ma(ki)sen* winding (in electricity)
16 頭 *kantō* beginning of a book
積雲 *kensekiun* cirro-cumulus clouds
17 鮨 *ma(ki)zushi* sushi rolled in seaweed or egg-omelet strips
藁 *ma(ki)wara* bundle of straw (used as an archery target)
22 鬚 *kenshu* tendril

9

巽 1546 / J1327 / M8765 SON. *tatsumi* southeast.

RAD. 巾 50

Haba width or *kin, kire* cloth. At left: *haba hen* or *kimben.* Nickname: Cloth.

巾 1547 / J3652 / M8771 KIN towel. *haba* width, breadth, range; difference (in price); power, influence.
4 木 *habaki* baseboard
5 広 *hababiro no* wider than usual
7 車 *kinsha* decorated vehicle
12 着 *kinchaku* purse, money bag
着切 *kinchakuki(ri)* pickpocket

2

A **布** 1548 / J495b / M8778 HO. FU. *nuno* cloth.
3 子 *nunoko* padded cotton clothes
巾 *fukin* dish cloth; napkin
4 片 *fuhen* piece of cloth
引 *nunobi(ki)* stretched cloth; cloth lining
切 *nunogi(re)* piece of cloth
5 目 *nunome* texture
石 *fuseki* arrange stones (in a *go* game); place party members in strategic government positions
令 *furei* official notice, proclamation, announcement
6 衣 *fui, hoi* common people; ordinary dress, cotton clothing
団 *futon* bedding, mattress

3 口 囗 土 士 夂 夊 夕 大 女 子 宀 寸 小 ⺌ 尢 尸 屮 山 川 巛 工 己 【巾】 干 幺 广 廴 廾 弋 弓 彐 彑 彡 彳

地 *nunoji* cloth
7 局 *fukyoku* arrangement, composition
告 *fukoku* proclamation, declaration, notification, decree, edict
告書 *fukokusho* proclamation, declaration, notification, decree, edict
8 表紙 *nunobyōshi* cloth binding
9 施 *fuse* alms, charity; temple offering
陣 *fujin* lineup. *fujin suru* take up a position
染 *nunozo(me), nunoso(me)* piece dyeing
海苔 *funori* laundry starch
10 晒 *nunozara(shi)* bleaching cloth; fuller
11 達 *futatsu* proclamation, notification
設 *fusetsu* construction, laying (a railroad, mine, etc.)
袋 *Hotei* a god of fortune
袋腹 *hoteibara* protuberant abdomen
教 *fukyō* missionary work, propaganda, proselytism
教所 *fukyōjo* small chapel
教師 *fukyōshi* missionary, chaplain, propagandist
13 置 *fuchi* arrangement, composition, design

A **市** 1549 / J3b54 / M8775 SHI city, town; market. *ichi* market; fair.
2 人 *shijin* resident, townfolk; merchant. *ichibito* market people
3 子 *ichiko* sorceress, medium, female fortuneteller
上 *shijō* in the town, in the street
4 日 *ichibi* market day
区 *shiku* municipal district; streets
中 *shichū* in the city
内 *shinai* the city, within the city limits
井 *shisei* the street; the town
井人 *shisei (no) hito* townspeople
5 庁 *shichō* municipal office
立 *shiritsu* municipal, city
立学校 *shiritsu gakkō* municipal school
外 *shigai* outside the city limits; suburbs
外電話 *shigai denwa* long distance
民 *shimin* citizen, townspeople
民法 *shiminhō* civil law
民権 *shiminken* citizenship
6 吏員 *shiriin* city employee, city official
会 *shikai* city council
会議員 *shikai giin* city councilman
有 *shiyū* owned by the city
有地 *shiyūchi* city land
有物 *shiyūbutsu* municipal property
有財産 *shiyū zaisan* municipal property
7 役所 *shiyakusho* city hall
町 *shichō* cities and towns
町村 *shichōson* cities, towns, and villages; municipalities
8 門 *shimon* city gate
長 *shichō* mayor
価 *shika* market price, current price
松 *ichimatsu* checked (pattern)
況 *shikyō* market conditions
制 *shisei* municipal organization, municipality
参事会 *shisanjikai* city council
9 政 *shisei* municipal government
10 部 *shibu* urban areas
11 販 *shihan* marketing
12 場 *ichiba, shijō* market
税 *shizei* city tax
葬 *shisō* municipal funeral
費 *shihi* municipal expenditure
営 *shiei* municipal operation
営住宅 *shiei jūtaku* municipal housing
街 *shigai* the streets; town, city
街地 *shigaichi* town areas
街戦 *shigaisen* street fighting
13 債 *shisai* municipal bond.
肆 *shishi* store; market storehouse
電 *shiden* municipal railway; city streetcar
勢 *shisei* city conditions; municipal census
勢調査 *shisei chōsa* municipal census
14 塵 *shijin* city dust; city confusion
20 議 *shigi* city assemblyman

—— **3** ——

师 1550 / J-X / M8800 See **師** 1562.

B **帆** 1551 / J4841 / M8787 HAN. *ho* sail.
4 木綿 *homomen* sailcloth, canvas
5 布 *honuno, hampu* sailcloth, canvas
立貝 *hotategai* scallop (shell)
7 走 *hobashi(ru)* sail, be under sail. *hansō* sailing; gliding
9 柱 *hobashira* mast
前船 *homaesen* sailing vessel
10 桁 *hogeta* (sail) boom, yard
莚 *homushiro* sail matting

11 船 *hansen, hobune* sailing vessel
掛 *hoka(keru)* sail, set sail
掛船 *hoka(ke)bune* sailboat
15 影 *hokage* a sail
17 檣 *hanshō* mast

4

帋 1552 J5663 M8809 See 紙 4455.

A **希** 1553 J3475 M8813 KI. KE. *-Gi-* Greece. *koinega(u)* beg, request, pray, beseech; hope, desire. *mare na* rare, few, phenomenal. *ki-* dilute (acid).
4 少 *kishō* scarcity
元素 *kigenso* rare element
5 代 *kidai, kitai* uncommon, remarkable, matchless
世 *kisei* rare
6 有 *keu* rare, extraordinary
有金属 *keu kinzoku* rare metals
7 求 *kikyū suru* aspire to, seek, demand, ask for
10 書 *kisho* rare book
11 釈 *kishaku* dilution
望 *kibō* hope, desire, aspiration, anticipation; request
望者 *kibōsha* candidate, applicant, aspirant, one who desires
望的観測 *kibōteki kansoku* wishful thinking
望配給 *kibō haikyū* optional extra ration
16 薄 *kihaku na* thin, dilute, sparse, weak

5

帑 1554 J5666 M8838 TŌ. DO money depository.

帚 1555 J5664 M8854 SHŪ. SŌ. *hōki* broom.

帛 1556 J5667 M8855 HAKU cloth.

帙 1557 J5665 M8852 CHITSU Japanese book cover.
2 入 *chitsui(ri)* a book kept in a Japanese book cover

帖 1558 J4421 M8849 CHŌ. JŌ quire (of paper); bundle of seaweed; screen counter; notebook. Also used for 畳 3763.
9 面 *chōmen* notebook
面面 *chōmenzura* accounts; appearance
19 簿 *chōbo* account book

6

B **帥** 1559 J3f63 M8886 SOCHI, SOTSU, SHUTSU, SUI leading (troops). *sotsu, sochi* (ancient) governor.
6 先 *sossen* taking the initiative

B **帝** 1560 J446b M8865 TEI emperor; the god of heaven; the creator. *mikado* emperor (of Japan).
4 日 *teijitsu* lucky day
王 *teiō* sovereign, emperor
王切開術 *teiō sekkaijutsu* Caesarian section
王神権説 *teiō shinkensetsu* theory of the divine right of kings
7 位 *teii* the throne, the crown
8 制 *teisei* imperial government, imperialism
京 *teikyō* the capital
命 *teimei* imperial order
国 *teikoku* empire; imperial
国主義 *teikoku shugi* imperialism
国主義的 *teikokushugiteki* imperialistic
9 威 *teii* imperial majesty
城 *teijō* palace
政 *teisei* imperial government; imperialism; monarchical rule
冠 *teikan* imperial crown, diadem
室 *teishitsu* Imperial Family; Imperial Household
10 座 *teiza* imperial throne
陵 *teiryō* imperial mausoleum
都 *teito* imperial capital
11 道 *teidō* the imperial way, principles of imperial rule
13 業 *teigyō* imperial task
14 徳 *teitoku* emperor's virtue
15 廟 *teibyō* imperial mausoleum
18 闕 *teiketsu* imperial palace gate; imperial palace

7

A **席** 1561 J404a M8926 SEKI seat; mat; a place, room, occasion. *mushiro* straw mat, matting.

3 上 *sekijō* in the seat, in the assembly. *sekijō de* at the meeting , on the occasion
上演説 *sekijō enzetsu* impromptu speech
5 代 *sekidai* room charge; cover charge; admission fee, price of a seat
6 次 *sekiji* seating order, precedence
次札 *sekiji fuda* place card
8 画 *sekiga* offhand drawing
9 亭 *sekitei* variety hall, storytellers' hall, music hall, vaudeville
巻 *sekken suru* conquer everything
10 借 *sekiga(ri)* renting a room or hall
料 *sekiryō* room charge; cover charge; admission fee, price of a seat
書 *sekiga(ki)* offhand writing
11 捲 *sekken suru* sweep over and completely subdue
12 順 *sekijun* seating order, precedence
貸 *sekiga(shi)* renting seats

A **師** 1562 / J3b55 / M8916 SHI teacher, master; exemplary person; army; war.
4 父 *shifu* fatherly master
友 *shiyū* master and friends
6 匠 *shishō* master, teacher
伝 *shiden* instruction from a master
団 *shidan* army division
団長 *shidanchō* division commander
7 走 *shiwasu, shihasu* 12th lunar month, December
弟 *shitei* teacher and student
承 *shishō* learning from a master
8 長 *shichō* teachers, superiors, and men of prominence
門 *shimon* tutelage
事 *shiji suru* study under; look up to; apprentice oneself to
表 *shihyō* model, pattern, paragon, leader, teacher
10 訓 *shikun* the instruction of a teacher
家 *shika* the teacher's home
恩 *shion* the kindness of a teacher
11 道 *shidō* duty of a teacher
13 僧 *shisō* a priestly teacher
14 説 *shisetsu* the teacher's theory
15 範 *shihan* model; teacher; fencing teacher
範学校 *shihan gakkō* normal school
16 儒 *shiju* teacher, scholar

A **帯** 1563 / J4253 / M8929 **帶** 1565 / J5668 / M8950 TAI belt; zone. *obi* obi, belt, sash, girdle, band; belting. *obi(ru), tai(suru)* wear (at the belt), carry, be armed with; be entrusted with; assume, take on (the character of), be tinged with; gird up (one's loins). *-tai* zone, region.
2 刀 *taitō* the sword at one's side
4 止 *obidome* obi clip, obi band
5 皮 *obikawa* leather belt
6 同 *taidō suru* be accompanied by
式 *obishiki* belt (conveyor)
地 *obiji* sash material, obi cloth
7 芯 *obishin* obi padding
状 *obijō* long narrow strip
状地 *taijōchi* strip of land
8 金 *obigane* banding iron
9 革 *obikawa* leather belt
封 *obifū* a half-wrapper (used in mailing)
10 紙 *obigami* wrapper
剣 *taiken* sword at one's side
11 側 *obikawa* obi cloth
12 揚 *obia(ge)* sash to hold obi in place
13 解 *obito(ki)* untying an obi
鉄 *obitetsu* band iron
電 *taiden* electric charge
電体 *taidentai* charged body
14 緑 *tairyoku* greenish
緑色 *tairyokushoku* greenish
15 締 *obiji(me)* band for an obi
線 *taisen* tie (in music)
勲 *taikun* wearing a decoration
16 鋼 *obikō* band steel, hoop
鋸 *obi nokogiri, obi noko* band saw
18 鎖 *obigusari* chain belt

A **帰** 1564 / J3522 / M8930 **歸** 2966 / J5d45 / M16349 **皈** 3868 / J6227 / M22705
KI. *kae(ru)* return; take one's leave; come again; come around (time). *kae(su)* send (someone) back. *ki(suru)* come to, arrive at, result in, end in, lead to; belong to, ascribe to; put down to; impute; be due to; fall into (one's power); (his blood) be upon (him). *kae(ri)* return; return trip. *kae(rigake) ni, kae(rishina) ni, kae(rusa) ni* on returning. *(o)kae(ri)nasai* welcome home, welcome back.
1 一 *kiitsu* unity, unification. *kiitsu suru* be united into one, be reduced to one
2 人 *kae(ranu) hito* dead person
4 心 *kishin* longing for home

支度 *kae(ri)jitaku* preparations to return
化 *kika* naturalization
化人 *kikajin* naturalized person
5 田 *kiden* (an official) returning to the farm
立 *kae(ri)ta(te)* returnee
去 *kae(shi)-sa(ru)* send away
6 米 *kibei* nisei who spend their childhood in Japan; returning to America
向 *kikō suru* proceed to
伏 *kifuku* surrender, submission
任 *kinin* returning to one's post
帆 *kihan* returning sailing ship
宅 *kitaku* homecoming, returning home
休 *kikyū* soldier's early release
休兵 *kikyūhei* soldier on leave
7 足 *kae(ri)ashi ni* on the return journey
車 *kae(ri)guruma* returning conveyance
村 *kison* returning to one's village
邸 *kitei* returning home
来 *kirai* coming back
8 国 *kikoku* returning to one's country
府 *kifu* returning to one's government post
依 *kie* conversion. *kie suru* believe (in Buddhism)
服 *kifuku* surrender, submission
臥 *kiga* retirement from public service
京 *kikyō, kikei* returning to the capital
参 *kisan* returning to a former service
空 *kae(ru) sora* an inclination to return
昔 *kae(ranu) mukashi* the past
9 途 *kito* homeward journey
洛 *kiraku* returning to Kyoto
陣 *kijin* returning from the war
降 *kikō* surrender, submission
品 *kae(ri)hin* returned goods
省 *kisei* homecoming
10 従 *kijū* surrender
旅 *kae(ranu) tabi* the journey to the next world
校 *kikō suru* return to school
耕 *kikō suru* return to the soil
航 *kikō* homeward passage
郷 *kikyō* returning home
荷 *kae(ri)ni* return cargo
家本能 *kika honnō* homing instinct
納 *kinō* induction (in argumentation)
納的 *kinōteki* inductive
納法 *kinōhō* inductive method
11 道 *kae(ri)michi* the way back, return trip
掛 *kaeriga(ke) ni* on the return journey
船 *kisen* returning to one's ship; a ship that has returned
隊 *kitai* returning to one's unit
巣性 *kisōsei* homing instinct
巣本能 *kisō honnō* homing instinct
12 雁 *kigan* returning wild geese
属 *kizoku suru* revert to, be returned to, be restored to
順 *kijun* submission, return to allegiance
港 *kikō suru* return to port
程 *kitei* distance back, the road back
結 *kiketsu* conclusion, end, result
期 *kiki* time of return
着 *kichaku* return, conclusion
営 *kiei* returning to barracks
朝 *kichō* returning from abroad
朝後 *kichōgo* after returning from abroad
13 路 *kiro* homeward journey, return circuit. *kae(ri)michi* the way back, return trip
農 *kinō* going back to the soil
新参 *kae(ri)shinzan* a person who has come back
15 趣 *kishu* conclusion
還 *kikan* return, repatriation; feedback
還兵 *kikanhei* returned soldiers
還者 *kikansha* a repatriate
17 趨 *kishu* conclusion. *kisū* trend, tendency; direction
20 艦 *kikan* returning to one's warship

8

帯 1565 / J5668 / M8950 See **帯** 1563.

帽 1566 / J-X / M8967 See **帽** 1573.

帷 1567 / J5669 / M8954 I curtain, screen.
3 子 *katabira* thin morning kimono
11 帳 *ichō* curtain
12 幄 *iaku* headquarters, general staff
幄上奏 *iaku jōsō* direct appeal to the throne by the military
幄臣 *iaku(no)shin* close adviser
13 幕 *ibaku* curtain; field staff headquarters; secret meeting place

A **帳** 1568 / J4422 / M8939 CHŌ notebook; account book; register; album; curtain dividing a room. *tobari* curtain.

3 口 囗 土 士 夂 夊 夕 大 女 子 宀 寸 小 ⺌ 尢 尸 屮 山 川 巛 工 己 8【巾】 干 幺 广 廴 廾 弋 弓 ヨ 彑 彡 彳

4 元 *chōmoto* manager, promoter, bookmaker
5 尻 *chōjiri* footings, account balance
付 *chōtsu(ke)* bookkeeping; bookkeeper
6 合 *chōa(i)* balance of accounts; keeping accounts; comparison
9 面 *chōmen* notebook, account book, register
面面 *chōmenzura* accounts; appearance
10 消 *chōke(shi)* cancellation, writing off
12 場 *chōba* counter, desk; office; jinricksha pool
19 簿 *chōbo* account book, register

A **常** 1569 / J3e6f / M8955 JŌ. SHŌ. *tsune* normal conditions, regular course of events; one's habit. *tsune no* ordinary, normal, continual. *tsune ni* always, continually. *towa* eternity. *tada* ordinarily. *tsune(naranu)* in vain. *toko-* ever-, endless.

1 乙女 *tokootome* ever-youthful maiden
2 人 *tadabito, tsunebito, jōjin* common man, ordinary person, plain individual
4 心 *jōshin* a sincere heart
日頃 *tsunehigoro* always, usually
5 世国 *tokoyo (no) kuni* distant country; heaven; hades
平倉 *jōheisō* grain reserve
用 *jōyō* common use; addition
用手段 *jōyō shudan* regular means
用者 *jōyōsha* constant user; addict
用漢字 *jōyō kanji* commonly used characters
6 灯 *jōtō* an all-night light
会 *jōkai* regular meeting
任 *jōnin* permanent (post)
任委員 *jōnin iin* standing committee
任委員会 *jōnin iinkai* standing committee
7 住 *jōjū* constancy, continuity; always; usually
住坐臥 *jōjūzaga ni* always
8 供 *jōku* continual offering
例 *jōrei* custom, usual practice
法 *jōhō* usual method
服 *jōfuku* ordinary clothes
事 *jōji* everyday affair
夜 *tokoyo* endless night
夜灯 *jōyatō* light kept lit through the night
9 食 *jōshoku* daily diet, staple food
連 *jōren* regular companions
軌 *jōki* proper course; beaten track
客 *jōkyaku* regular customer; frequent visitor
春 *tokoharu* eternal spring
10 員 *jōin* regular personnel
素祭 *jōsosai* continual meal offering
時 *jōji* usually, habitually, ordinarily
時運転 *jōji unten* regular service
夏 *tokonatsu* perennial summer; a wild pink (flower)
夏国 *tokonatsu no kuni* land of perpetual summer
套 *jōtō no* commonplace, conventional
套手段 *jōtō shudan* old trick, usual practice, regular means
套句 *jōtōku* stock phrase
套語 *jōtōgo* hackneyed expression, household word
11 道 *jōdō* ordinary way, universal practice
経 *jōkei* unchanging moral principles
規 *jōki* established usage; common standard
宿 *jōyado* regular hotel
常 *tsunezune* always, usually
得意 *jōtokui* regular customer
務 *jōmu* regular business; executive director
務委員会 *jōmu iinkai* executive committee
務取締役 *jōmu torishimariyaku* executive director
設 *jōsetsu* permanent; standing (committee)
設小売店舗 *jōsetsu kouri tempo* permanent retail store
設館 *jōsetsukan* cinema
習 *jōshū* usage, custom, common practice
習犯 *jōshūhan* habitual crime; habitual criminal
習的 *jōshūteki* habitual, regular
習者 *jōshūsha* habitual offender
習飲酒者 *jōshū inshusha* habitual drunkard
12 雇 *jōyatoi* regular employee
温 *jōon* normal temperature
勤 *jōkin no* full-time (official)
勝 *jōshō* ever-victorious
勝軍 *jōshōgun* ever-victorious army

備 *jōbi no* standing, permanent, regular
備兵 *jōbihei* regular army
備金 *jōbikin* reserve fund
備軍 *jōbigun* standing army
備薬 *jōbiyaku* household remedy
13 数 *jōsū* constant (in math); fate
節 *tokobushi* abalone, ear shell
置 *jōchi* permanent, standing (committee)
置委員 *jōchi iin* standing committee
14 態 *jōtai* normalcy
緑 *jōryoku* evergreen
緑樹 *jōryokuju* evergreen tree
15 駐 *jōchū* staying permanently
磐 *tokiwa, towa* eternity
磐木 *tokiwagi* evergreen tree
磐津 *tokiwazu* a type of ballad
16 衡 *jōkō* avoirdupois
燔祭 *jōhansai* continual burnt offering
17 闇 *tokoyami* perpetual darkness
19 識 *jōshiki* common sense
識的 *jōshikiteki* sensible, practical
20 議委員会 *jōgi iinkai* executive board
議員 *jōgiin* standing committee

9

幀 1570 / J566c / M8982 TEI making books or scrolls.

幄 1571 / J566a / M8994 AKU curtain. *tobari* curtain.
8 舎 *akusha* pavilion

幇 1572 / J5673 / M8999 HŌ help.
7 助 *hōjo* assistance, backing
12 間 *hōkan, taikomochi* professional jester; flatterer

B **帽** 1573 / J4b39 / M8971 **帽** 1566 / J-X / M8967 BŌ cap, headgear.
3 子 *bōshi* cap, hat, headgear
子屋 *bōshiya* hat shop
11 章 *bōshō* badge

B **幅** 1574 / J497d / M8995 FUKU hanging scroll, picture; width; counter for scrolls. *haba* width, breadth, range; difference (in price); power, influence.
5 広 *hababiro* wide width; wide obi
7 利 *habaki(ki)* man of influence
9 飛 *habato(bi)* broad jump
10 員 *fukuin* width, beam, breadth, extend
13 跳 *habato(bi)* broad jump

10

幃 1575 / J566b / M8993 KI, I bag.

幎 1576 / J566d / M9024 BEKI. MYAKU cover, hide; cloth covering; face cover for dead person; blinds.

幌 1577 / J4b5a / M9022 KŌ. *horo* awning, hood, (folding) top. *tobari* curtain.
9 型自動車 *horogata jidōsha* sedan
10 馬車 *horo basha* covered wagon, covered carriage
蚊帳 *horogaya* mosquito net

A **幕** 1578 / J4b6b / M9051 BAKU, MAKU curtain; bunting; an act (in a play); end; first rank (in sumo); a matter, a case. *tobari* curtain.
3 下 *bakka* shogun; shogun's staff; vassal, feudatory, follower. *makushita* second-class Japanese wrestler
4 切 *makugi(re)* fall of the curtain
内 *makuuchi* first-class wrestler. *maku(no)uchi* first-class wrestler. *maku(no)uchi* a Japanese lunch
5 末 *bakumatsu* latter days of the Tokugawas
6 臣 *bakushin* shogun's vassal
吏 *bakuri* shogunate official
7 兵 *bakuhei* shogunate soldiers
8 府 *bakufu* shogunate
舎 *bakusha* barracks; camp
命 *bakumei* shogunate orders
9 屋 *makuya* tent, tabernacle
政 *bakusei* shogunate government
軍 *bakugun* shogunate army
10 将 *bakushō* shogunate general
12 間 *makuai* interval between acts
開 *makuaki* opening of a play; beginning
無 *makuna(shi)* always
13 電 *makuden* sheet lightning
10 閣 *bakkaku* shogunate cabinet
僚 *bakuryō* staff; staff officer; brain trust; brain truster; adviser

3 口 囗 土 士 夂 夊 夕 大 女 子 宀 寸 小 ⺌ 尢 尸 屮 山 川 巛 工 己 11【巾】 干 幺 广 廴 廾 弋 弓 彐 彑 彡 彳

11

幗 1579 / J566e / M9057 KAKU, KYAKU woman's hair ornament; woman's head covering (for mourning).

幔 1580 / J566f / M9050 MAN curtain.
13 幕 *mammaku* curtain, drapery

12

幮 1581 / J-X / M-X See 幮 1588.

幢 1582 / J5671 / M9087 TŌ. JŌ flag, banner; flagstaff.

幟 1583 / J5670 / M9080 SHI. *nobori* flag, banner, streamer.

幡 1584 / J4828 / M9086 HAN. HON. *hata* flag.

B **幣** 1585 / J4a3e / M9088 **幤** 1586 / J5672 / M-X HEI Shinto zigzag paper offerings; bad habit; humble prefix; gift. *nusa* Shinto offerings of cloth, rope, or cut paper.
5 束 *heisoku* Shinto offerings of cloth, rope, or cut paper
8 物 *heimotsu*, *heibutsu* offering to a god; a present
制 *heisei* monetary system
帛 *heihaku* Shinto offerings of cloth or cut paper
13 殿 *heiden* the room between the hall of worship and the inner sanctuary of a shrine

14

幮 1587 / J-X / M-X See 幮 1588.

15

幮 1588 / J-X / M9134 **幮** 1581 / J-X / M-X **幮** 1587 / J-X / M-X
JU, CHU, CHŪ curtain.

干 RAD. 51

Kan dry or *ichi-jū* (*ichi* "one" plus *jū* "ten"). Nickname: One Ten.

A **干** 1589 / J3433 / M9165 KAN. *hi(ru)* parch, get dry; ebb, recede. *ho(su) vt* dry; desiccate; drain (off); drink up; dry up. *tate* shield. *hidaru(i)* hungry.
3 上 *hiaga(ru)* dry up, parch; ebb away
与 *kan'yo* participation
大根 *hoshidaikon* dried daikon
4 戈 *kanka* shield and spear; weapons; war
支 *kanshi* sexagenary cycle
天 *kanten* drought, dry weather
5 付 *hi-tsu(ku)* dry up
犯 *kampan* infringement, violation
6 肉 *ho(shi)niku* dried meat, pemmican
8 固 *ho(shi)-kata(meru) vt ho(shi)-kata(maru) vi* dry up, harden by drying. *hi-kata(maru) vi* dry and harden
物 *himono*, *karamono* dried fish. *ho(shi)mono* laundry on the line
拓 *kantaku suru* reclaim by drainage
拓地 *kantakuchi* reclaimed land
9 城 *kanjō* bulwark, defender, safeguard
柿 *ho(shi)gaki* dried persimmons
草 *ho(shi)gusa*, *hoshikusa*, *kansō* hay, dry grass
海苔 *ho(shi)nori* dried laver, edible seaweed sheets
10 殺 *ho(shi)-koro(su)* starve (an animal) to death
害 *kangai* drought damage
11 魚 *hiuo*, *kangyo*, *hizakana*, *ho(shi)uo*, *ho(shi)zakana* dried fish
涸 *hi-kara(biru) vi* completely dry up. *ho(shi)-ka(rasu) vt* dry up (a river)
渉 *kanshō* interference, intervention
菜 *ho(shi)na* dried rape, dried greens
乾 *hiboshi ni suru vt* starve to death. *hiboshi ni na(ru) vi* starve to death
菓子 *higashi* candy; cookies
12 場 *ho(shi)ba* drying ground

満 *kamman* ebb and flow, tide
飯 *hoshii* cooked and dried (for preservation) rice
割 *hiwa(re)* cracking due to drying
葉 *hiba* dried daikon leaves
葡萄 *ho(shi) budō* raisins
13 預 *kan'yo* participation
15 魃 *kambatsu* drought
潮 *kanchō, hikishio, hishio* ebb tide
潟 *higata, hikata* tideland; dry beach
16 瓢 *kampyō* dried gourd strings
21 鰯 *hoshika, hiiwashi, ho(shi) iwashi* dried sardines
22 鱈 *hidara* dried codfish

2

A **平** 1590 J4a3f M9167 HYŌ. BYŌ. HEI level, peaceful. *taira(geru)* subjugate; put down (trouble); consume (food), eat up. *taira(gu)* be suppressed. *hei(tsukubaru)* make a deep bow. *hira ni* earnestly, humbly. *hira(tai)* flat, even, level; simple, plain. *tai(ra) na* flat, smooth; calm; a plain; sitting tailor fashion. *tai(rakana)* level; just; peaceful. *hira-* common, ordinary.

3 凡 *heibon na* common, commonplace, ordinary, mediocre
4 日 *heijitsu* weekday, ordinary days
氏 *Heishi* the Tairas
水 *heisui* the usual amount of water; calm water
仄 *hyōsoku* meter (in Chinese poetry); consistency
分 *heibun suru* bisect, divide equally
手 *hirate* palm; equality
手打 *hirateu(chi)* a slap, spanking
方 *heihō* square (of a number); square
方形 *heihōkei* square
方根 *heihōkon* square root
5 芝 *hirashiba* sod
台型貨車 *hiradaigata kasha* flatcar
生 *heizei no* usual, ordinary
生着 *heizeigi* usually worn
平 *heihei* level; ordinary
平凡凡 *heihei-bombon(taru)* ordinary, mediocre
民 *heimin* commoner, plebeian
民主義 *heimin shugi* democracy
6 臼 *hirausu* horizontal stone hand mill
気 *heiki* composure; unconcern

伏 *hirefu(su)* prostrate oneself before. *heifuku suru* fall prostrate
地 *heichi, hirachi* level ground, plain
成 *Heisei* the era beginning 1989
仮名 *hiragana* the cursive syllabary
年 *heinen* normal year, civil year
年作 *heinensaku* normal crop
年並 *heinennami* the same (harvest, rain fall, etc.) as in an average year
安 *heian* peace, tranquility; Heian era (794-1185)
安京 *Heiankyō* ancient Kyoto
安朝 *Heianchō* Heian period
行 *heikō* parallelism, parallel
行四辺形 *heikōshihenkei* parallelogram
行棒 *heikōbō* parallel bars
行線 *heikōsen* parallel line
7 角 *heikaku* straight angle
作 *heisaku* normal crop
身低頭 *heishin teitō suru* prostrate oneself
均 *heikin, narashi* equilibrium, balance, average, mean
均余命 *heikin yomei* life expectancy
均寿命 *heikin jumyō* average life span
均点 *heikinten* average mark, mean point
均値 *heikinchi* average value, mean value
8 坦 *heitan na* even, flat, level
明 *heimei na* clear, simple
泳 *hiraoyo(gi)* breast stroke
版 *heihan* lithography
服 *heifuku* civilian clothes, plain clothes, ordinary clothes
臥 *heiga suru* lie down; be laid up
定 *heitei* suppression, repression, subjugation
底 *hirazoko* flat bottom
底船 *hirazokobune* flat-bottomed boat, scow
価 *heika* normal prices; par; parity
価切下 *heika kirisa(ge)* devaluation
板 *heiban* slab, flat board; monotony; lithography
板測量 *heiban sokuryō* plane-table surveying
炉 *heiro, hiraro* open-hearth furnace
炉法 *heirohō* open-hearth process
易 *heii* easiness; simplicity
易化 *heiika* simplification
和 *heiwa* peace, harmony

和主義 *heiwa shugi* pacifism
和主義者 *heiwa shugisha* pacifist
和共存 *heiwa kyōzon* peaceful coexistence
和会議 *heiwa kaigi* peace conference
和条約 *heiwa jōyaku* peace treaty
和攻勢 *heiwa kōsei* peace offensive
和的 *heiwateki* peaceful
和国 *heiwakoku* a peaceful country
和国家 *heiwa kokka* peace-loving nation
和産業 *heiwa sangyō* peace-time industries
和論者 *heiwa ronsha* pacifist
9 城京 *Heijōkyō* ancient Nara
屋 *hiraya* bungalow, one-story house
屋根 *hirayane* flat roof
信 *heishin* peaceful news
信徒 *hirashinto* layman, laity
面 *heimen* level surface, plane
面図 *heimenzu* ground plan; plane figure
面形 *heimenkei* plane figure
面幾何学 *heimen kikagaku* plane geometry
面鏡 *heimenkyō* plane mirror
10 原 *heigen* plain, moor, prairie
時 *heiji* normal times, peace time
脈 *heimyaku* normal pulse
袖 *hirasode* wide sleeve
家 *hiraya* one-story house. *Heike* the Taira family
素 *heiso* ordinarily, in the past
11 淡 *heitan na* simple, quiet
野 *heiya* a plain, open field
常 *heijō* normal; normally, usually
常通 *heijōdō(ri)* as usual
12 復 *heifuku* restoration to health
温 *heion* the usual temperature
然 *heizen(taru)* calm, composed
等 *byōdō* equality, impartiality
等雇用 *byōdō koyō* equal employment
等観 *byōdōkan* considering all people as equals
13 滑 *heikatsu na* smooth, even, level, flat
絹 *hiraginu* plain silk
14 静 *heisei* tranquility, calm, equanimity
15 熱 *heinetsu* normal (body) temperature
16 穏 *heion* tranquility, calmness, rest
衡 *heikō* equilibrium, balance; equalization
衡感覚 *heikō kankaku* sense of balance
17 謝 *hiraayama(ri)* earnest apology
鍋 *hiranabe* pan, griddle
18 癒 *heiyu* convalescence
織 *hirao(ri)* plain fabrics

3

幵 1591 / J5674 / M9169 KEN *taira* flat, level, smooth.

并 1592 / J5675 / M9170 **幷** 1594 / J-X / M-X HEI put together.

7 呑 *heidon* annexation, merger, swallowing up

A **年** 1593 / J472f / M9168 NEN year; term of service. *toshi* year; age, time of life.

3 子 *toshigo* second child born within a year
下 *toshishita* younger, junior
上 *toshiue* older, senior
久 *toshihisa(shiku)* for many years, anciently
4 内 *nennai* within the year
分 *nembun* yearly amount
月 *nengetsu, toshitsuki* months and years, time
月日 *nengappi* date
中 *nenjū* throughout the year
中行事 *nenjū gyōji* annual functions or events
少 *nenshō* youth
少者 *nenshōsha* youth, minor, young people
5 玉 *(o)toshidama* New Year's gift
収 *nenshū* annual income
市 *toshi (no) ichi* year-end fair
令 *nenrei* age
号 *nengō* era name
末 *nemmatsu* year end
甲斐無 *toshigai (mo) na(i)* unbecoming, unsuitable; disgraceful
功 *nenkō* long service, long experience
功序列 *nenkō joretsu* seniority system
功制度 *nenkō seido* seniority system
代 *nendai* age, era, period; date
代記 *nendaiki* chronicle, chronology
代順 *nendaijun* chronological order
6 回 *toshimawa(ri)* age relationship, luck concerning age. *nenkai* anniversary service (in Buddhism)
次 *nenji* annual; dates
毎 *toshigoto (ni)* annually, yearly

百年中 *nembyaku-nenjū* all year round; year after year
会 *nenkai* conference; annual convention
会費 *nenkaihi* annual fee
年 *toshidoshi, nennen* years, year by year, annually. *toshi (ga) toshi* considering his age
年中 *nen(gara)-nenjū, nen(ga)-nenjū* all year round; year by year
年歳歳 *nennen-saisai* annually, every year
7 豆 *toshi (no) mame* beans of the bean-scattering ceremony
改 *toshiarata(maru)* the New Year dawns
利 *nenri* annual interest rate
初 *nensho* beginning of the year; New Year's greetings
別 *nembetsu* by years
忘 *toshiwasu(re)* year-end drinking party
忌 *nenki* death anniversary, Buddhist anniversary ceremony
男 *toshiotoko* bean scatterer
甫 *nempo* beginning of the year
来 *nenrai* for some years
8 金 *nenkin* annuity, pension
延 *toshiba(e)* approximate age
明 *nen'ake* expiration of a term of service. *toshia(keru)* the New Year dawns
波 *toshinami* old age, oncoming age
取 *toshito(ru), toshi (o) to(ru)* grow old, age
限 *nengen* length of time, term
若 *toshiwaka(i), toshiwaka ni* young, youthful
表 *nempyō* chronological tables, chronology
長 *nenchō* seniority
長者 *nenchōsha* a senior, elderly people
始 *nenshi* beginning of the year; New Year's greetings, New Year's calls
季 *nenki* one's term of service; apprenticeship
季奉公 *nenki bōkō* apprenticeship, indenture
9 度 *nendo* year; fiscal year; school year; term
拾 *toshi (o) hiro(u)* grow old
格好 *toshi kakkō, toshigakkō* approximate age
10 俸 *nempō* annual salary
租 *nenso* annual tax
益 *nen'eki* annual profit
差 *nensa* annual variation
配 *nempai* age
配者 *nempaisha* elderly person
貢 *nengu* land tax (in kind); tribute; ground rent
貢米 *nengumai* annual rice tax
11 掛 *toshiga(ke)* yearly payment
盛 *toshizaka(ri)* prime of life
祭 *toshi matsu(ri)* annual festival. *nensai* anniversary
頃 *toshigoro* age; marriageable age; age of puberty; adolescence; for some years
頃日頃 *toshigoro-higoro* these days
産 *nensan* annual production
産額 *nensangaku* annual production
寄 *toshiyo(ru), toshi (ga) yoru* grow old. *toshiyo(ri)* old person, an elder; older councillor
寄子 *toshiyo(ri)go* child of one's old age
寄役 *toshiyo(ri)yaku* a senior's role
寄臭 *toshiyo(ri)kusa(i)* slovenly like an old man
寄染 *toshiyo(ri)ji(mita)* characteristic of the aging
12 歯 *nenshi* age
越 *toshiko(shi)* year end, New Year's Eve. *toshi (o) ko(su)* the year ends
間 *nenkan* era, period of a year; for the year
税 *nenzei* annual tax
級 *nenkyū* annual salary
割 *nenwa(ri)* annual rate
報 *nempō* annual report
期 *nenki* term of service; apprenticeship
期明 *nenkia(ke)* expiration of a term of service
期者 *nenkimono* apprentice
期奉公 *nenki bōkō* apprenticeship, indenture
賀 *nenga* New Year's greetings; New Year's call
賀状 *nengajō* New Year's card
賀郵便 *nenga yūbin* New Year's mail
賀葉書 *nenga hagaki* New Year's postcard
13 数 *nensū* number of years
嵩 *toshikasa* senior, older, elderly
14 増 *toshima* mature woman, middle-aged woman

3 口 囗 土 士 夂 夊 夕 大 女 子 宀 寸 小 ⺌ 尢 尸 屮 山 川 巛 工 己 巾 5 【干】 幺 广 廴 廾 弋 弓 ヨ 彑 彡 彳

端 *toshiha* age; years
暮 *toshi (no) kure* year end. *toshiku(reru)* the year ends
15 賦 *nempu* annual installment
輪 *nenrin* annual tree ring
輪史学 *nenrin shigaku* dendrochronology
輩 *nempai* age, age of experience
輩者 *nempaisha* elderly person
16 頭 *toshigashira* the oldest person; beginning of the year. *nentō* beginning of the year
17 齢 *nenrei* age
18 額 *nengaku* yearly amount
19 瀬 *toshi (no) se* New Year's Eve, the year end
譜 *nempu* personal chronological history
22 鑑 *nenkan* yearbook

— 5 —

幷 1594 / J-X / M-X See **并** 1592.

A **幸** 1595 / J392c / M9176 Kō happiness, fortune. *sachi, saiwa(i)* happiness; blessing; good fortune. *shiawase* good fortune, happiness, blessing, mercy. *kō(su)* (the emperor) travels.
4 不幸 *kōfukō* weal or woe, good or evil, sunshine and shadow
6 先 *saisaki* good omen; good beginning
9 便 *kōbin* favorable opportunity
甚 *kōjin* a favor; supreme happiness
11 運 *kōun* good fortune
運児 *kōunji* child of fortune
12 無 *sachinashi* no luck, bad luck
13 福 *kōfuku* happiness, welfare

— 10 —

A **幹** 1596 / J3434 / M9183 Kan. *miki* (tree) trunk.
6 竹割 *karatakewa(ri)* cutting straight down; cleaving (a person) in two
8 事 *kanji* manager, secretary
事長 *kanjichō* chief secretary (of a party)
10 流 *kanryū* main current
部 *kambu* management, the executives, the leaders
部会 *kambukai* board of directors
15 線 *kansen* main line, trunk line

RAD. 幺 52

At top: *itogashira* "thread" top. At left: *yō hen* left-side "young."
Nickname: Short Thread (cf. Rad. 120).

幺 1597 / J5676 / M9189 Yō small; young; dark, obscure.

— 1 —

B **幻** 1598 / J3838 / M9190 Gen. *maboroshi* vision, dream; illusion, apparition.
4 日 *genjitsu* mock sun
月 *gengetsu* mock moon
5 世 *gensei* this fleeting world
出 *genshutsu suru* appear as a phantom, appear dimly
6 灯 *gentō* stereopticon, magic lantern
灯会 *gentōkai* stereopticon meetings
灯器 *gentōki* stereopticon projector
灯機械 *gentō kikai* stereopticon projector
8 怪 *genkai* strange, mysterious
11 術 *genjutsu* magic, witchcraft, sorcery
視 *genshi* visual hallucination
12 惑 *genwaku* fascination, bewitching
覚 *genkaku* illusion, hallucination
13 滅 *gemmetsu* disillusionment
夢 *gemmu* dreams, visions
想 *gensō* illusions
想曲 *gensōkyoku* fantasy
14 像 *genzō* phantom, vision, illusion
15 影 *gen'ei* phantom, vision, illusion
影的 *gen'eiteki* illusionary
17 聴 *genchō* auditory hallucination

— 2 —

A **幼** 1599 / J4d44 / M9193 Yō infancy, childhood; infants, children. *osana(i), itokena(i)* infant. *ito* very young.

3 女 *yōjo* baby girl, little girl
子 *osanago* baby, infant, child
4 心 *osanagokoro* child's mind; innocent heart
木 *yōboku* young tree
友達 *osanatomodachi* childhood friend
少 *yōshō* infancy, childhood
少児 *yōshōji* infant, child
5 生 *yōsei* *larva*
主 *yōshu* young master
6 虫 *yōchū* larva
名 *yōmei, yōmyō* one's infant name
年 *yōnen* infancy, childhood
年工 *yōnenkō* child laborer
年労働 *yōnen rōdō* child labor
年学校 *yōnen gakkō* military preparatory school
年時代 *yōnen jidai* childhood
年期 *yōnenki* childhood
7 君 *yōkun* young master
児 *yōji* infant, baby, little child
児死亡率 *yōji shibōritsu* infant mortality rate
児食 *yōjishoku* baby food
児洗礼 *yōji senrei* infant baptism
児預所 *yōji azu(kari)jo* nursery
8 芽 *yōga* germ (in grains)
者 *yōsha* infant, child
9 帝 *yōtei* child emperor
10 時 *yoji* infancy, childhood
恋 *osanagoi* puppy love
宮 *itomiya* infant prince
弱 *yōjaku* young and weak
11 魚 *yōgyo* young fish
鳥 *yōchō* young bird, fledgling
12 童 *yōdō* a small child
13 禽 *yōkin* chick, young bird
愚 *yōgu* childish innocence
馴染 *osananajimi* childhood playmate
稚 *yōchi* infancy, babyhood; crudeness
稚園 *yōchien* kindergarten, preschool
16 樹 *yōju* young tree
17 齢 *yōrei* tender age
齢児 *yōreiji* young child
18 顔 *osanagao* one's baby features

6

B 幽 1600 / J4d29 / M9205 Yū. *yū(suru)* confine to a room. *kasu(kana)* faint, dim, weak, indistinct, hazy; poor, wretched.

5 玄 *yūgen* mystery, the occult
囚 *yūshū* imprisonment
7 谷 *yūkoku* ravine, glen
8 門 *yūmon* pyloris
居 *yūkyo* hermitage, retreat; retirement, seclusion
林 *yūrin* deep forest
明 *yūmei* the present and the other world; dark and light
明相隔 *yūmei-aiheda(teru)* die
9 香 *yūkō* fragrance
室 *yūshitsu* darkened room; quiet room
客 *yūkyaku* a quiet guest; an orchid
界 *yūkai* Hades, realm of the dead
契 *yūkei* secret promise
幽 *yūyū(taru)* deep; dark; quiet
10 冥 *yūmei* semidarkness; deep and strange; Hades
冥界 *yūmeikai* Hades, realm of the dead
11 鳥 *yūcho* mountain bird
閉 *yūhei* house arrest, confinement, imprisonment; depressed feeling
窓 *yūsō* quiet window
寂 *yūjaku* quiet, sequestered
寂味 *yujakumi* solitude, quiet
12 閑 *yūkan na* quiet and secluded
絶 *yūzetsu* a quiet and secluded place
勝 *yūshō* a beautiful and quiet scene
景 *yūkei* a quiet sequestered scene
然 *yūzen na* quiet and secluded
13 微 *yūbi na* dim, indistinct
暗 *yūan na* dark and secluded
雅 *yūga* refinement
愁 *yūshū* deep contemplation
14 境 *yūkyō* solitude; secluded place
魂 *yūkon* spirits of the dead
15 趣 *yūshu* a quiet, natural setting
霊 *yūrei* ghost, apparition, spirit
霊人口 *yūrei jinkō* ghost population
霊会社 *yūreigaisha* bogus company
霊屋敷 *yūrei yashiki* haunted house
霊株 *yūrei kabu* watered stock, bogus shares
霊船 *yūreisen* ghost ship
霊話 *yūreibanashi* ghost story
17 邃 *yūsui na* retired and quiet
邃境 *yūsuikyō* secluded place
26 鬱 *yūutsu* melancholy, dejection, gloom

—— 9 ——

B **幾** 1601 / J3476 / M9208 KI. *iku(ra)* how many, how much; how far, how long; so much per; however (difficult). *iku(raka)* some, something, anything; somewhat, a little, to some extent, partly; in a way. *iku(ra)mo* any amount, any number; (neg.) not many, not much. *iku(tsu)* how many; how old. *hotohoto* almost, quite, really. *iku-* some, several, many; how many, how much.

2 人 *ikunin, ikutari* how many people. *ikunin ka* several people. *ikunin demo* any number of people
3 久 *ikuhisa(shiku)* eternally, forever
万 *ikuman* many tens of thousands
千 *ikusen* thousands (of people)
才 *ikusai* how old, what age
4 月 *ikutsuki* how many months
分 *ikubun* some, something, a part. *ikubun ka* somewhat, partly
日 *ikunichi, ikka* how many days; what day (of the month). *ikunichi ni* what day. *ikunichi demo* for any number of days
日後 *ikunichi(ka) (no) nochi* after some days
日幾日 *ikunichi (mo) ikunichi (mo)* for many days
5 目 *ikume* what weight
世 *ikuyo* many generations
6 年 *ikutose, ikunen* how many years. *ikunen mo* for many years
多 *ikuta no* many
7 何 *ikubaku* how much, how many. *kika* geometry
何学 *kikagaku* geometry
何学的 *kikagakuteki* geometric
何画法 *kika gahō* descriptive geometry
何級数 *kika kyūsū* geometrical series, geometrical progression
8 夜 *ikuyo* how many nights; night after night
昔 *ikumukashi* how ancient
9 度 *ikudo, ikutabi* how often, how many times. *ikudo mo* frequently, many times
通 *ikutō(ri)* how many kinds. *ikutsū* how many copies; how many letters
秋 *ikuaki* many autumns; many years
重 *ikue nimo* again and again; earnestly
10 時 *ikuji* what time
11 許 *ikubaku* how much, how many
望 *kibō* 14th night of the lunar month
12 程 *ikuhodo* about how much
程無 *ikuhodo (mo) na(ku)* not much

RAD. 广 53

Madare trailing *ma* (i.e., the enclosure of Rad. 200 *ma* "hemp"). Also called *ten'ichi-dare* (i.e., a trailing Rad.8). Nickname: Dotted Cliff (cf. Rad. 27).

广 1602 / J5678 / M9221 GEN house; house built high on cliff.

—— 2 ——

A **庁** 1603 / J4423 / M9223 **廳** 1651 / J572c / M9562 CHŌ government office.

4 令 *chōrei* government order
8 舎 *chōsha* government office building

A **広** 1604 / J392d / M9224′ **廣** 1640 / J5722 / M9493 KŌ. *hiro(garu)* vi spread out, extend, reach to. *hiro(geru)* vt expand, enlarge, widen; unfurl; open (arms or a package), stretch, spread. *hiro(maru)* spread, be diffused, prevail, be propagated, pervade, be circulated, become popular. *hiro(meru)* extend, widen, enlarge; spread, disseminate; popularize; advertise, introduce, announce. *hiro(me)* announcement, advertisement. *hiro(i), hiro(yakana)* wide, broad, extensive, spacious.

3 口 *hirokuchi* broad mouth; large-mouthed bottle
小路 *hirokōji* thoroughfare
大 *kōdai na* vast, extensive, magnificent
大無辺 *kōdai-muhen na* boundless, immeasurable, infinite
5 広 *hirobiro toshita* extensive, spacious, roomy

目見 *hiro(i) me (de) mi(ru)* treat magnanimously
6 汎 *kōhan na* wide, extensive, widespread, comprehensive
壮 *kōsō na* grand, imposing
7 角 *kōkaku* wide angle
言 *kōgen* boastful speech
告 *kōkoku* advertisement; public notice; poster, handbill; publicity
告主 *kōkokunushi* (radio) sponsor
告灯 *kōkokutō* advertising lights
告気球 *kōkoku kikyū* advertising balloon
告社 *kōkokusha* advertising agency; publicity bureau
告取 *kōkokuto(ri)* advertising solicitor
告取次店 *kōkoku toritsugiten* advertising agency
告放送 *kōkoku hōsō* commercial radio
告屋 *kōkokuya* advertising agency
告料 *kōkokuryō* advertising rates
告部 *kōkokubu* publicity department
告書 *kōkokuka(ki)* ad writer
告税 *kokokuzei* advertising tax
告業 *kōkokugyo* advertising business
告欄 *kōkokuran* advertising columns
8 居 *kōkyo* spacious residence
9 屋 *hiro(me)ya* town crier, sandwich (advertising) man
狭 *kōkyō* width; area
軌 *kōki* wide gauge
10 原 *kōgen* wide plain, open country
袖 *hirosode* wide sleeve
11 野 *kōya, hirono* open field, open country, wilderness, moorland, plain, prairie
袤 *kōbō* extent, area, expanse
域 *kōiki* wide area
12 遠 *kōen na* vast and far-reaching
間 *hiroma* hall, saloon (on a ship)
場 *hiroba* open field, public square, plaza
幅 *hirohaba* double width
量 *kōryō* largeheartedness, generosity
葉樹 *kōyōju* broad-leafed tree
報 *kōhō* publicity
報部 *kōhōbu* public relations department
13 漠 *kōbaku(taru)* vast, wide, boundless
義 *kōgi* broad sense, broad application
蓋 *hirobuta* large tray; cover for a kimono chest
15 縁 *hiroen* broad veranda; eaves
範 *kōhan* wide, extensive, widespread, comprehensive
範囲 *kōhan'i* wide scope, vast range
17 闊 *kōkatsu na* spacious, wide, extensive
濶 *kōkatsu na* spacious, wide, extensive

3

庄 1605 / J3e31 / M9234 SHŌ level.
9 屋 *shōya* village headman
13 園 *shōen* manor

4

庇 1606 / J485f / M9239 II. *kaba(u)* protect, shield; defend, plead for; harbor (criminals). *hisashi* waves; canopy; penthouse; visor.
5 立 *kaba(i)-ta(te) suru* protect, shield; defend, plead for; harbor (criminals)
14 髪 *hisashigami* low pompadour
20 護 *higo* protection, patronage
護物 *higobutsu* a shelter
護者 *higosha* patron, guardian

A **序** 1607 / J3d78 / M9253 Jo beginning; preface; order, precedence; farewell address; curtain raiser. *tsuide* order; occasion, chance. *tsuide ni* while, on the way, incidentally, while you're about it.
4 文 *jobun* preface, foreword, introduction
6 曲 *jokyoku* prelude, overture
次 *joji* order, sequence
列 *joretsu* rank, grade, order
7 言 *jogen* preface, foreword
9 奏 *josō* introduction (in music)
12 開 *jobira(ki)* beginning (of a celebration)
詞 *joshi* preface
13 数 *josū* ordinal number; numbering
幕 *jomaku* curtain raiser
楽 *jogaku* prelude, overture
14 説 *josetsu* introduction
15 論 *joron* introduction, preface
盤 *joban* opening a game of chess or *go*
盤戦 *jobansen* the beginning of a campaign

B **床** 1608 / J3e32 / M9242 SHŌ floor; bed. *toko* bed; sickbed; floor; alcove; padding. *yuka* floor. *yuka(shii)* admirable, respectable; sweet, charming; interesting; tasteful, mysterious. *-shō* counter for beds.

2 入 *tokoi(ri)* consummation of marriage
几 *shōgi* camp stool, folding stool
3 山 *tokoyama* wrestler's hairdresser; wig maker; a theatrical coiffeur
下 *yukashita* under the floor
上 *tokoa(ge)* recovery from a long illness. *shōjō* on the bed. *yukaue* on the floor, above the floor, floor (lamp).
5 払 *tokobara(i)* recovery from illness
6 机 *shōgi* camp stool, folding stool
8 店 *tokomise* booth, stall
板 *tokoita* alcove floor board. *yukaita* floor boards
虱 *tokojirami* bedbug
9 屋 *tokoya* barber; barber shop
柱 *tokobashira* ornamental alcove post
11 張 *tokoba(ri)* flooring
12 間 *toko(no)ma* large ornamental livingroom alcove
換 *tokoga(e)* transplanting saplings
就 *toko(ni) tsu(ku)* go to bed
13 置 *tokoo(ki)* alcove ornament
置物 *toko okimono* alcove ornamental
15 蝨 *tokojirami* bedbug
17 擦 *tokozure* bedsore
19 離 *tokobana(re)* getting out of bed

5

庚 1609 / J392e / M9278 Kō G, seventh. *kanoe* seventh calendar sign.
5 申塚 *kōshinzuka* stone image of travelers' guardian deity

庖 1610 / J4a79 / M9266 Hō kitchen.
2 丁 *hōchō* kitchen knife; cooking; cook
丁人 *hōchōnin* cook
丁師 *hōchōshi* cook
12 厨 *hōchū* kitchen

A **府** 1611 / J495c / M9283 Fu urban prefecture; government office; representative body; storehouse. *tsukasa* office, government office; director, head official.
3 下 *fuka* metropolitan suburban districts
5 立 *furitsu* managed by an urban prefecture
庁 *fuchō* urban prefectural office
令 *furei* urban prefectural ordinance
6 会 *fukai* urban prefectural assembly
会議員 *fukai giin* urban prefectural assemblyman
8 知事 *fu chiji* urban prefectural governor
9 県 *fuken* prefectures
12 税 *fuzei* urban prefectural tax
営 *fuei* urban prefectural enterprise
20 議会 *fugikai* urban prefectural assembly
議会議員 *fugikai giin* urban prefectural assemblyman

A **底** 1612 / J446c / M9262 Tei bottom, base; kind, sort. *soko* bottom; sole; depth, bowels (of the earth); bottom price.
2 入 *sokoi(re)* touching bottom (stock market)
力 *sokojikara* latent energy, reserve strength
3 土 *sokotsuchi* subsoil
4 辺 *teihen* base (in geometry)
止 *teishi suru* stop
引網 *sokobi(ki)ami* dragnet; dragnet fishing
5 石 *soko ishi* hard core
叩 *soko (o) tata(ku)* empty completely
払 *soko (o) hara(u)* empty completely
本 *teihon* original text
6 光 *sokobika(ri)* lurking luster, latent light
気味悪 *sokokimiwaru(i)* uncanny, ominous
7 角 *teikaku* base angle
豆 *sokomame* blister
冷 *sokobi(e)* chilling to the bone
抜 *sokonu(ke)* bottomless; unbounded; extreme; self-indulgent; indiscreet
抜上戸 *sokonu(ke) jōgo* heavy drinker
抜騒 *sokonu(ke) sawa(gi)* boisterous merrymaking
8 波 *sokonami* ground swell (the wave)
知 *sokoshi(ranu)*, *sokoshi(renu)* bottomless
9 革 *sokogawa* sole; sole leather
10 値 *sokone* bottom price
流 *teiryū* bottom current, undercurrent
荷 *sokoni* ballast
11 釣 *sokozuri* bottom fishing
12 開 *sokobira(ki)* hopper (car)
無 *sokona(shi)* bottomless
13 意 *sokoi* innermost thoughts; secret intention; ulterior motive; undertone (in stock market)
意地 *sokoiji* bottom of one's heart

[16]積 *sokozu(mi)* goods stowed at the bottom, (ship's) ballast

A 店 1613 / J4539 / M9267 TEN shop, store. *mise, tana* shop, store, booth. *tana* house (for rent).
[3]子 *tanako* tenant
[5]立 *tanada(te)* eviction notice
主 *tenshu* storekeeper, shopkeeper
古 *tamburu(shi)* shopworn goods
台 *misedai* counter in a store
仕舞 *misejimai* closing a business
[6]先 *misesaki* shop front
[7]売 *miseu(ri)* sale at a store
[8]者 *tanamono, mise (no) mono* shop clerks
[9]則 *tensoku* store rules
卸 *tanaoro(shi)* inventory taking; faultfinding; comments
前 *tanasaki* shop front
屋 *ten'ya* store, caterer
屋物 *ten'yamono* caterer's dishes
[10]借 *tanaga(ri)* renting a house (from someone), tenancy
晒 *tanazara(shi)* shopworn goods
浚 *tanazarae* clearance (sale)
員 *ten'in* clerk
振舞 *tanaburumai* shop celebration
[11]商 *tanaakina(i)* storekeeping
[12]開 *misebira(ki)* opening a store
番 *miseban* tending a shop, salesperson
貸 *tanaga(shi)* renting a house (to someone)
[13]飾 *misekaza(ri)* window dressing
賃 *tanachin* house rent
[15]舗 *tempo* shop, store
請 *tanau(ke)* security for a tenant
請人 *tanau(ke)nin* guarantor for a tenant
[16]頭 *tentō* shop front, shop window; counter; store

6

庲 1614 / J-X / M-X Nonstandard for 鹿 7017.

庠 1615 / J5679 / M9298 SHŌ. JŌ school; village school.

A 度 1616 / J4559 / M9313 DO degree; extent, measure, limit; a time; graduation, scale; composure. TAKU. TO. *do(suru)* save, redeem, reclaim. *wata(su)* carry across, ferry over, bring over; hand over, deliver; deal (cards); transfer (a business); pay (wages); bridge; stretch (something) across, lay across. *tabi* time, occasion; repetition. *-tai* desiderative verbal suffix.
[5]失 *do (o) ushina(u)* wander aimlessly
外 *dohazu(re), dogai* out of one's consideration, extraordinary, excessive
外視 *dogaishi suru* disregard, neglect, overlook
[6]合 *doa(i)* degree, extent, rate
[7]忘 *dowasu(re)* memory slip, forgetting for the moment
[9]度 *tabitabi, dodo* often, frequently
重 *tabikasa(naru)* occur repeatedly; repeated
胆 *dogimo* heart, spirit
胆抜 *dogimo (o) nu(ku)* startle (someone)
[10]胸 *dokyō* courage, pluck, nerve, bravery
[11]盛 *domo(ri)* graduation, scale
[12]量 *doryō* magnanimity, generosity
量法 *doryōhō* measurement
量原器 *doryō genki* standard of measurement (in a bureau of standards)
量衡 *doryōkō* weights and measures
[13]数 *dosu* frequency, number of times
[18]難 *do(shi)gata(i)* incorrigible, inveterate, hopeless, beyond saving

7

A 庫 1617 / J384b / M9330 KU. KO storehouse. *kura* warehouse, godown; cellar; depository, treasury; granary, elevator.
[2]入 *kurai(re)* warehousing
[5]出 *kurada(shi)* releasing stored goods
[8]官 *kokan* treasurer
[11]移 *kurautsushi* transporting to another storehouse
[13]裏 *kuri* priests' quarters; monastery kitchen

A 庭 1618 / J446d / M9337 TEI. *niwa* yard, courtyard, garden.
[3]口 *niwaguchi* garden entrance
上 *teijō* in the garden
下駄 *niwa geta* garden geta

3 口 囗 土 士 夂 夊 夕 大 女 子 宀 寸 小 ⺌ 尢 尸 屮 山 川 巛 工 己 巾 干 幺 7【广】 廴 廾 弋 弓 ヨ 彑 彡 彳

4 火 *niwabi* bonfire
中 *teichū* in the garden
内 *teinai* in the garden
木 *niwaki* garden tree, shrub, shrubbery
木戸 *niwa kido* garden gate
5 石 *niwa ishi* decorative garden stones; steppingstones; flagstones
6 回 *niwamawa(ri)* around the garden; things concerning the garden
伝 *niwazuta(i)* passing through the yard
先 *niwasaki de* in the garden
7 作 *niwatsuku(ri)* gardening
9 前 *teizen, niwasaki de* in the garden
10 師 *niwashi* landscape gardener
訓 *teikin* home precepts, parental discipline, home education
11 掃 *niwaha(ki)* sweeping the garden
雀 *niwa suzume* garden sparrow
球 *teikyū* tennis
球界 *teikyūkai* tennis world
球選手 *teikyū senshu* tennis player
12 番 *niwaban* guard of the inner garden
13 園 *teien* garden, park
園地 *teienchi* garden plot
園師 *teienshi* gardener, landscape architect
園術 *teienjutsu* landscape gardening
16 樹 *teiju* shrubbery, shrub
燎 *niwabi, teiryō* bonfire

A **座** 1619 / J3a42 / M9319 **坐** 978 / J3a41 / M4931 ZA seat, cushion; throne; a gathering; stand, pedestal, platform; (metal) washer; theater; troupe; constellation. *suwa(ru)* squat down, sit down, (eyes) are fixed on. *za(suru)* be involved in; squat; sit down. *i(masu)* be, go, come (polite). *suwa(ri)* stability. *-za* (ancient) guild.

3 下 *zaka* polite letter ending
4 中 *zachū* in the room; member of the troupe
元 *zamoto* theater manager, producer
込 *suwa(ri)-ko(mu)* sit down, plant oneself down
込罷業 *suwa(ri)-ko(mi) higyō* sit-down strike
5 白 *za (ga) shira(keru)* a chill falls over the gathering
付 *zatsu(ki)* regular actor attached to a theater
礼 *zarei* bow from kneeling position
主 *zasu, zashu* head priest of a temple. *zashu* theater owner
右 *zayū ni* at one's right; at one's side
右銘 *zayū (no) mei* desk motto
6 州 *zasu suru* run aground
7 位 *zai* seating order, precedence
8 金 *zagane* metal washer
長 *zachō* chairman, president, moderator; troupe owner-leader
所 *zasho* one's seat; one's location; emperor's residence
臥 *zaga* sitting and lying down
9 食 *zashoku suru* live in idleness
持 *za (o) mo(tsu)* act as hostess or master of ceremonies
洲 *zasu suru* run aground
乗 *zajō suru* be on board
10 高 *zakō* sitting height
浴 *zayoku* sitz bath
剤 *zazai* suppository
員 *zain* troupe personnel
胼胝 *suwa(ri)dako* foot callous due to sedentary habits
席 *zaseki* seat, pew; cockpit
席満員 *zaseki man'in* Standing Room Only
骨 *zakotsu* hip bone
骨神経 *zakotsu shinkei* sciatic nerve
骨神経痛 *zakotsu shinkeitsū* sciatic neuralgia
11 視 *zashi suru* look on indifferently, be a mere spectator
13 禅 *zazen* meditation (in Zen Buddhism)
蒲団 *zabuton* cushion
業 *zagyō* sedentary work
業者 *zagyōsha* sedentary work
14 像 *zazō* seated image
15 標 *zahyō* coordinates (in math)
談 *zadan* discussion, talking things over
談会 *zadankai* round-table talk, discussion group
敷 *zashiki* room, apartment, drawing room; giving a banquet; entertainer's evening engagement
敷牢 *zashikirō* room for confining people
敷着 *zashikigi* geisha's costume worn while entertaining
16 薬 *zayaku* suppository
興 *zakyō* amusement, entertainment, fun, party games
頭 *zagashira* theater-troupe leader; leading man. *zatō* ancient blind

official; blind masseur; blind man; blind musician
頭鯨 *zatō kujira* humpback whale
17 礁 *zashō* running aground
18 職 *zashoku* sedentary work
職者 *zashokusha* sedentary worker
19 繰 *zagu(ri)* hand reeling

8

座 1620 / J-X / M-X Nonstandard for **座** 1619.

A **康** 1621 / J392f / M9376 Kō peace.
14 寧 *kōnei* a peaceful world

B **廊** 1622 / J4f2d / M-X **廊** 1628 / J-X / M9437 Rō corridor, hall, lobby; tower; watchtower.
3 下 *rōka* corridor, hall, lobby, vestibule

庵 1623 / J3043 / M9369 **菴** 5063 / J683f / M31227 An hermitage, retreat. *io, iori* hermitage; living in a hermitage.
5 主 *anshu* owner of a hermitage
6 守 *iomori* guard of a hermitage
7 住 *anju, anjū* owner of a hermitage; living in a hermitage
9 室 *anshitsu* hermit's cell, sylvan retreat

B **庸** 1624 / J4d47 / M9378 Yō tax paid in labor; ordinary; employment.
2 人 *yōjin* ordinary people. *yōnin* employee
3 才 *yōsai* mediocre talent
6 劣 *yōretsu na* mediocre, commonplace; stupid
7 君 *yōkun* stupid ruler
13 愚 *yōgu* mediocrity; imbecility
14 徳 *yōtoku* common morality
15 器 *yōki* an ordinary individual
16 儒 *yōju* an ordinary Confucianist; an ordinary scholar

B **庶** 1625 / J3d6e / M9373 **庶** 1626 / J-X / M-X Sho all; illegitimate child.
2 人 *shonin, shojin* masses, (common) people
3 子 *shoshi* illegitimate child
5 兄 *shokei* illegitimate elder brother
出 *shoshutsu* illegitimate birth
民 *shomin* masses, the common people
7 系 *shokei* illegitimate line
8 事 *shoji* various matters, everything
9 政 *shosei* all phases of government
10 流 *shoryū* illegitimate family branch
11 務 *shomu* general affairs, miscellaneous affairs
12 幾 *shoki suru* desire, hope. *koinega(u)* beg, request, pray, beseech; hope, desire.

9

廁 1627 / J567a / M9410 See **厠** 654.

廊 1628 / J-X / M9437 See **廊** 1622.

廂 1629 / J567b / M9416 Shō. Sō. *hisashi* eaves; canopy; penthouse; vizor.

B **廃** 1630 / J4751 / M9425 **廢** 1639 / J5726 / M9492 Hai obsolescence; cessation; discarding. *hai(suru)* abolish, abandon; repeal, annul; depose; discontinue. *suta(reru), suta(ru)* become useless, get out of date, die out; be abolished; decline(in prosperity). *ya(meru) vt* end, discontinue; give up, abandon; abolish; resign, retire. *suta(ri)* waste. *ya(me)* end, discontinuance, stop.
2 人 *haijin* invalid, cripple; useless person; abandoned person
刀 *haito suru* abolish the wearing of swords
4 止 *haishi* abolition, discontinuance, abrogation
5 立 *hairitsu* enthronement and dethronement
刊 *haikan* discontinuance of publication
6 気 *haiki* exhaust, ventilation
寺 *haiji* ruined temple
字 *haiji* obsolete character
宅 *haitaku* deserted house
合 *haigō* abolition and amalgamation
合整理 *haigō seiri* reorganization, rearrangement
7 位 *haii* dethronement
坑 *haikō* abandoned mine
址 *haishi* ruins

3 口 囗 土 士 夂 夊 夕 大 女 子 宀 寸 小 ⺌ 尢 尸 屮 山 川 巛 工 己 巾 干 幺 10【广】 廴 廾 弋 弓 ヨ 彑 彡 彳

材 *haizai* scrap wood
兵 *haihei* disabled soldier
8 官 *haikan* abolition of a post
苑 *haien* superannuated plantation
典 *haiten* a discarded organization
学 *haigaku* leave school, stop one's studies
物 *haibutsu* scrap, waste, refuse. *suta(ri)mono* useless thing, obsolete thing
物利用 *haibutsu riyō* the utilization of waste products
9 屋 *haioku* deserted house
除 *haijo suru* remove, take away
帝 *haitei* deposed emperor
品 *haihin* scrap, waste
10 馬 *haiba* superannuated horse
疾 *haishitsu* disablement, deformity
校 *haikō* discontinuing a school
残 *haizan* survival after defeat; decline; ruin
家 *haike* ending a family line; an extinct family. *haika* an extinct or abandoned family
案 *haian* rejected measure, discarded draft
11 娼 *haishō* abolition of prostitution
船 *haisen* scrapped vessel, superannuated ship
12 税 *haizei* abolition of a tax
絶 *haizetsu* extinction
朝 *haichō suru* depose (a ruler)
13 園 *haien* superannuated plantation
滅 *haimetsu* ruin, decay
鉱 *haikō* abandoned mine
棄 *haiki* abandonment, repeal, annulment, abrogation
置 *haichi* abolition and establishment
業 *haigyō* closing up shop, quitting the business
14 嫡 *haichaku* disinheritance
語 *haigo* obsolete word
15 墟 *haikyo* ruins
16 頽 *haitai* decay, deterioration, decadence
18 藩 *haihan* abolition of clans
藩置県 *haihan-chiken* the abolition of the clans and the setting up of prefectures
20 艦 *haikan* superannuated warship

10

廚 1631 / J-X / M-X See 厨 657.

廈 1632 / J567c / M9435 KA. *ie* house.

廓 1633 / J3347 / M9461 KAKU enclosure; quarter. *kuruwa* enclosure, quarter; red-light district.
3 大 *kakudai suru* enlarge
11 清 *kakusei* purification, purge, clean-up

B 廉 1634 / J4e77 / M9436 REN purity; honesty; low price; corner. *yasu(i)* cheap, inexpensive; peaceful, quiet; gossipy, thoughtless. *kado* reason, charge, suspicion; point, account.
3 士 *renshi* a pure uncovetous person
6 吏 *renri* an honest official
7 売 *rembai* bargain sale, dumping
8 直 *renchoku* integrity, honor, uprightness
価 *renka* low price
価版 *renkaban* popular edition
価品 *renkahin* low-priced goods
10 恥 *renchi* honor, integrity
恥心 *renchishin* sense of shame; sense of honor
13 際 *kado(aru)sai* special occasion
15 潔 *renketsu* honesty, integrity, uprightness

11

廏 1635 / J567e / M9453 廐 1636 / J567d / M9454 See 厩 660.

廖 1637 / J5721 / M9464 RYŌ empty, vacant.

12

廚 1638 / J5724 / M9479 See 厨 657.

廢 1639 / J5726 / M9492 See 廃 1630.

廣 1640 / J5722 / M9493 See 広 1604.

廝 1641 J5723 M9487 Shi low-born; servant.

廡 1642 J5727 M9491 Bu. Mu caves; house; corridor, hallway.

廠 1643 J3e33 M9490 Shō workshop.
8 舎 *shōsha* barracks

廛 1644 J5725 M9483 Ten fine residence; shop, store.
15 舗 *tempo* shop

廟 1645 J4940 M9489 Byō mausoleum; shrine; palace.
6 宇 *byōu* mausoleum, shrine
11 堂 *byōdō* the court, cabinet, ministry
20 議 *byōgi* cabinet council; cabinet decision

13

廨 1646 J5728 M9510 Kai. Ge. Ke government office.

廩 1647 J5729 M9515 Rin rice storehouse.

16

廬 1648 J572a M9535 Ro. *io, iori* hermitage; living in a hermitage.

17

廰 1649 J572d M9552 See 庁 1603.

18

廱 1650 J572b M9554 Yo soften, moderate; close, cover; block; ancient Chinese university.

22

廳 1651 J572c M9562 See 庁 1603.

RAD. 廴 54

Ennyō (Enclosure for 延 *en, nobiru* "stretch, lengthen"). Also *innyo* or *innyū*, the "long stride" radical. Nickname. Stretching.

廴 1652 J572e M9566 In walk far; extend.

4

廸 1656 J3772 M-X Teki path, way; morality; advance; lead, instruct. *michi* path, way, road.

4

延 1653 J-X M9569 See 延 1657.

A 延 1657 J3164 M-X 延 1653 J-X M9569 En stretching. *no(biru)* extend, lengthen, stretch, spread; be postponed; increase; grow; progress, develop; be straightened, be flattened, be smoothed; be exhausted. *no(bi)* stretching (the body); excess, surplus; postponement; growth; spread. *no(basu)* lengthen, stretch, extend; let (nails) grow; straighten; uncoil; spread out; reach out; postpone; dilute; smooth out; develop (talents); amass (riches). *no(beru)* make (a bed); stretch, widen, lengthen. *no(be)* futures, credit (buying); stretching; total.
2 人員 *no(be) jin'in* total personnel

B 廷 1654 J446e M9571 Tei imperial court; government office.
2 丁 *teitei* court attendant
4 内 *teinai* in the court
6 臣 *teishin* courtier, court official
吏 *teiri* lesser court official

5

廻 1655 J-X M9573 See 廻 1659.

4 引 *en'in, ennin* delay, postponement, procrastination
日数 *no(be) nissū* total days
5 広 *no(bi)-hiro(garu)* stretch, extend
払 *no(be)bara(i)* deferred payment
6 会 *enkai* postponement or adjournment (of a meeting)
年 *ennen* longevity
7 寿 *enju* prolongation of life
8 金 *no(be)gane* sheet metal; hammered-out sheets; sword, dagger
延 *no(bi)no(bi)* stretching. *no(bi)no(bi) ni naru* be delayed. *en'en(taru)* meandering, serpentine
坪 *no(be) tsubo* total floor space
性 *ensei* malleability
板 *no(be) ita* hammered-out plates
命 *emmei* prolongation of life; long life, longevity
取引 *no(be) torihiki* dealing in futures
長 *enchō* extension, elongation, prolongation; continuation; extent, length
長戦 *enchōsen* extra-inning game
9 音 *en'on* long vowel sound
10 紙 *no(be)gami* paper handkerchief
納 *ennō* deferred payment
時間 *no(be) jikan* total hours
11 袤 *embō* size (of the land)
12 棒 *no(be) bō* (metal) bar
渡 *no(be)wata(shi)* forward delivery
焼 *enshō* spread of a fire
期 *enki* postponement, adjournment, deferment, respite
着 *enchaku* delayed arrival
13 滞 *entai* delay, procrastination, arrearage
17 齢 *enrei* prolongation of life
18 髄 *enzui* afterbrain

6

迺 1658 J4736 M9576 DAI. NAI namely; you; go; arrive; far; this. *sunawa(chi)* namely. *nanji* you. *no* used phonetically.

廻 1659 J3276 M9575 **迴** 1655 J-X M9573 KAI. *mawa(su)* turn, revolve, rotate; circularize; pass around; forward, transmit; refer to; transfer; lend money. *mawa(ru)* turn, go around; revolve, rotate, spin, gyrate; patrol, tour; take effect (medicine); be distributed; be past (time); be transferred. *megu(ru)* go around. *megu(ri)* girth, circumference; tour, round, pilgrimage; flow, circulation; menstruation. (See 回 941 for other related compounds.)
4 文 *kaibun, kaimon* circular letter
天 *kaiten no* epoch-making, stupendous
6 米 *kaimai* rice arrivals
合 *megu(ri)-a(u)* meet by chance
7 折 *kaisetsu* diffraction
状 *kaijō* circular letter
8 国 *kaikoku* pilgrimage, tour
送 *kaisō* forwarding, transportation
10 航 *kaikō* navigation, cruise
11 廊 *kairō* corridor
旋 *kaisen* rotation, revolution
章 *kaishō* a circular
転 *kaiten* revolution, rotation
転椅子 *kaiten isu* swivel chair
14 漕 *kaisō* marine transportation
漕業 *kaisōgyō* marine-transportation business
16 覧 *kairan* circulation of letter or document

A **建** 1660 J377a M9574 KON, KEN build, raise. *ta(tsu)* stand, rise; rouse oneself; be built, be established; go up (smoke); burn out; depart; take flight; run high (waves); stick into; be worked out; be maintained; save (face); establish oneself, begin life; spread (rumors); shut (doors); be active; open (markets); be excited; come (seasons); makes (a total of thirty). *ta(teru)* stand something up, set up, raise; put up; set on edge; prick up (one's ears); build, erect; close (a door); establish; institute, enact; lay (plans); map out; set forth, lay down (a proposition); formulate; render (services), perform; look up to, respect; be loyal to; do justice to; circulate (rumors); have (an aim); establish (oneself), make (a success); support (oneself), make (an oath); sharpen, set (a saw); put up (a candidate); make (tea); save (face).
4 方 *ta(te)kata* architectural style; how to build
込 *ta(te)-ko(mu)* be closely built up
5 立 *konryū* building, erection
白 *kempaku* memorial, petition
白書 *kempakusho* memorial, petition

6 回 *ta(te)-megu(rasu)* build around
地 *ta(te)chi* building plot
7 言 *kengen* memorial, petition, proposal
材 *kenzai* building materials
売 *ta(te)u(ri)* ready-built (house)
8 国 *kenkoku, kengoku* establishing a nation
坪 *tatetsubo* floor space
物 *tatemono* building; architecture
直 *ta(te)-nao(ru)* be rebuilt. *ta(te)-nao(su)* rebuild
具 *tategu* house fittings (doors and windows)
具屋 *tateguya* cabinetmaker
9 連 *ta(te)-tsura(neru)* build house after house
前 *tatemae* framework-erection ceremony; framing a house; fundamental principles
造 *kenzō* building, construction
造物 *kenzōbutsu* building, edifice
10 値 *tatene* official quotations; exchange rates; prices
株 *ta(te)kabu* listed stocks
11 掛 *ta(te)ka(ke)* under construction
設 *kensetsu* building, establishment
設工事 *kensetsu kōji* construction work
設的 *kensetsuteki* constructive
設者 *kensetsusha* builder, founder
設省 *Kensetsushō* Construction Ministry
12 策 *kensaku* recommendation, suggestion
替 *ta(te)-ka(eru)* rebuild
13 業 *kengyō* starting an enterprise
14 増 *ta(te)-ma(su)* build on. *tatema(shi)* extension, annex
網 *ta(te)ami* dragnet, set net, seine
碑式 *kempishiki* dedication of a monument
16 築 *kenchiku* building, architecture
築用材 *kenchiku yōzai* building materials
築技師 *kenchiku gishi* architect
築材料 *kenchiku zairyō* building materials
築物 *kenchikubutsu* building, edifice
築学 *kenchikugaku* architecture
築者 *kenchikusha* builder
築師 *kenchikushi* builder
築家 *kenchikuka* architect
築術 *kenchikujutsu* architecture
築許可 *kenchiku kyoka* building permit
築税 *kenchikuzei* tax on construction
築費 *kenchikuhi* construction costs
築資材 *kenchiku shizai* building materials
築業 *kenchikugyō* building industry
築業者 *kenchikugyōsha* builder
築線 *kenchikusen* building line
築請負 *kenchiku ukeoi* building contract
築請負業者 *kenchiku ukeoi gyōsha* contractor
20 艦 *kenkan* naval construction
議 *kengi* proposal, petition, recommendation
議者 *kengisha* mover, proposer
議案 *kengian* motion, proposition

RAD. 廾 55

Nijū-ashi "twenty" legs (i.e. legs resembling *nijū* "twenty").
Variant: 卄. Nickname: Letter H.

廾 1661 J5730 M9583 Kyō offer; fold one's arms.

1

廿 1662 J467b M9586 Jū. *nijū* twenty.
4 日 *hatsuka* twenty days; twentieth day (of the month)

2

A 弁 1663 J4a5b M9588 辮 4604 J6570 M27991 Ben braid. (See also 1664, 1665, 1666)
14 髪 *bempatsu* pigtail, queue

A 弁 1664 J4a5b M9588 瓣 3689 J6122 M21425 Ben petal, valve. (See also 1663, 1665, 1666)
14 膜 *bemmaku* valve (in internal organs)
20 鰓類 *bensairui* bivalves

A 弁 1665 J4a5b M9588 辨 6002 J517e M38657 辦 6003 J5221 M38656 Ben discrimination. *ben(jiru), ben(zuru)*

3 口 囗 土 士 夂 夊 夕 大 女 子 宀 寸 小 ⺌ 尢 尸 屮 山 川 巛 工 己 巾 干 幺 广 廴 【廾】 弋 弓 ヨ 彑 彡 彳

manage, dispose of, carry through; distinguish, discriminate. *wakima(eru)* discern, discriminate, know, understand, bear in mind. (See also 1663, 1664, 1666)

4 天 *Benten* god of wealth, music, eloquence, and water
6 当 *bentō* lunch, box lunch, lunch box
当屋 *bentōya* lunch vendor
当箱 *bentōbako* lunch box
7 別 *bembetsu* discrimination
10 財天 *Benzaiten* god of wealth, music, eloquence, and water
11 済 *bensai* settlement, payment
理 *benri* management
理士 *benrishi* patent attorney
務官 *bemmukan* commissioner
12 証 *benshō* demonstration, proof
証法 *benshōhō* dialectic, dialectics
証論 *benshōron* apologetics; dialectics
15 慶格子 *benkeigōshi* checked pattern, plaid
慶縞 *benkeijima* plaid, checked pattern
17 償 *benshō* reparation, indemnity, compensation, reimbursement
償金 *benshōkin* reparation, indemnity, compensation, reimbursement

A **弁** 1666 / J4a5b / M9588 **辯** 6005 / J6d67 / M38677 BEN speech, dialect; oratory. *ben(jiru), ben(zuru)* speak, talk, argue. (See also 1663, 1664, 1665)

3 口 *benkō* speech, manner of speaking
士 *benshi* speaker, orator
才 *bensai* eloquence, oratorical talent
5 立 *ben(ji)-ta(teru)* speak eloquently, talk volubly
6 舌 *benzetsu* speech
8 明 *bemmei* explanation, defense, justification
者 *bensha* speaker, orator
12 疏 *benso* excuse, plea, defense
13 解 *benkai* explanation, justification, defense, excuse, apology
14 駁 *bembaku, bempaku* refutation, contradiction, rebuttal, disproof, disputation
15 論 *benron* discussion, argument, debate; oral proceedings, pleading
論大会 *benron taikai* oratorical contest
18 難 *bennan* denunciation, criticism
20 護 *bengo* defense, vindication, explanation, pleading
護人 *bengonin* counsel, defender, advocate
護士 *bengoshi* lawyer, attorney
護士会 *bengoshikai* bar association
護団 *bengodan* defense counsel
護者 *bengosha* defender, advocate
護依頼人 *bengo irainin* client
護料 *bengoryō* lawyer's fee

4

弃 1667 / J5731 / M9594 See **棄** 2787.

弄 1668 / J4f2e / M9596 RŌ. *ijiku(ru), rō(suru)* play with, trifle with. *iji(ru)* touch, tamper with, play with. *moteaso(bu)* play; take pleasure in; play (on an instrument); play with; make sport of; trifle with (affections).

4 火 *rōka* playing with fire
6 舌 *rōzetsu* tongue wagging
回 *iji(ri)-mawa(su), hineku(ri)-mawa(su)* twist up, tinker with
7 言 *rōgen* tongue wagging
9 廻 *hineku(ri)-mawa(su)* twist up, tinker with
12 筆 *rōhitsu* writing and twisting the truth

7

弈 1669 / J5732 / M-X See **奘** 1159.

12

B **弊** 1670 / J4a40 / M9644 HEI evil, abuse, vice, bad custom; breakage; our (humble); Shinto zigzag paper offering; tribute. *tsuie* expenses. *hei-* our (humble).

6 宅 *heitaku* shack; my humble home
衣 *heii* shabby clothes
衣破帽 *heii habō* shabby clothes and an old hat
7 村 *heison* impoverished village; my poor village
社 *heisha* our firm
8 店 *heiten* our shop
制 *heisei* a poor system, a poor organization

[9] 風 *heifū* evil habit, bad custom, abuse
政 *heisei* maladministration
[10] 家 *heika* my humble home
害 *heigai* evil, vice, abuse; harmful influence; bad effect
[11] 習 *heishū* corrupt custom, bad habit
[15] 履 *heiri* worn-out sandals or shoes

弋 RAD. 56

Shikigamae (enclosure for 式 *shiki* "ceremony"). Nickname: Ceremony.

弋 1671 / J5735 / M9656 YOKU piling.

— 1 —

弌 1672 / J5021 / M9658 ICHI one.

— 2 —

弍 1673 / J5031 / M9661 See 弐 1675.

— 3 —

弎 1674 / J-X / M9662 SAN three.

B 弐 1675 / J4675 / M-X 弍 1673 / J5031 / M9661 貳 5783 / J6c48 / M36703
JI. NI two; second. *futa(tsu)* two.
[4] 心 *futagokoro, nishin* duplicity, treachery, double-dealing

A 式 1676 / J3c30 / M9663 SHIKI ceremony, rite, function; method, system; style, form, type, plan; formula, expression (in math); model; law; standard. *-shiki* style, type.
[4] 文 *shikibun* liturgy, ritual, worship manual
日 *shikijitsu* ceremonial occasion
[5] 目 *shikimoku* feudal law code
台 *shikidai* step or platform in an entranceway; slatted removable floor in an entrance hall
[6] 次 *shikiji* the order of a ceremony
年 *shikinen* year of special festivals
[8] 服 *shikifuku* ceremonial dress
典 *shikiten* ceremony, celebration, rites
[9] 後 *shikigo* after the ceremony
[10] 部長 *Shikibuchō* Grand Master of Court Ceremonies
部官 *shikibukan* master of court ceremonies
[12] 場 *shikijō* place of the ceremony; ceremonial hall
[13] 微 *shikibi* decline (in royal fortunes)
辞 *shikiji* address, speech

— 9 —

弑 1677 / J5736 / M9680 SHI. *shii(suru)* murder one's lord, assassinate, kill (one's father).
[8] 逆 *shiigyaku, shigyaku* regicide, murder of one's lord

弓 RAD. 57

Yumi bow (for arrows). At left: *yumi hen*. Nickname: Bow.

A 弓 1678 / J355d / M9692 KYŪ bow; violin bow. *yumi* bow; archery; violin bow; bow shape.
[2] 人 *kyūjin* maker of archery bows
[4] 手 *yunde* archer's hand; the left hand
引 *yumi (o) hi(ku)* draw the bow; rebel
[5] 矢 *yumiya* bow and arrow
矢八幡 *yumiya hachiman* god of war
[7] 状 *kyūjō* arch. *kyūjō no* arched, crescent shaped
形 *kyūkei* crescent form, circle segment. *yuminari, yumigata* arch, arc, curve

8 弦 *yumizuru, yuzuru* bowstring
取 *yumito(ri)* archer, warrior, samurai; famous archer; archery
10 師 *yumishi* bow maker
馬 *kyūba* bow and horse; archery and horsemanship
馬家 *kyūba (no) ie* a samurai family
馬道 *kyūba (no) michi* the way of the samurai
11 道 *kyūdō* archery
術 *kyūjutsu* archery
術師 *kyūjutsushi* archer
張 *yumiha(ri)* bow-handled paper lantern
張月 *yumiha(ri)zuki* crescent moon; waxing moon; waning moon
張提灯 *yumiha(ri)jōchin* bow-handled paper lantern
12 場 *yumiba* archery ground, archery gallery. *yuba* archery ground, archery gallery; house of ill fame
13 勢 *yunzei* the power of a bow; the archer's strength
15 箭 *kyūsen* bows and arrows; arms; war
箭家 *kyūsen (no) ie* a samurai family
箭道 *kyūsen (no) michi* samurai spirit; the way of the samurai
20 懸 *yugake* archer's glove

1

弖 1679 / J5737 / M9703 TE (used phonetically).
14 爾乎波 *te-ni-o-ha* the particles
爾遠波 *te-ni-o-ha* the particles

B **弔** 1680 / J4424 / M9698 CHŌ mourning. *chō(suru)* mourn, condole with. *tomura(u), tobura(u)* mourn for; hold a memorial service for; condole. *tomura(i), tobura(i)* funeral, burial, condolence.
4 文 *chōbun* funeral address
6 合戦 *tomura(i) gassen* battle of revenge
9 客 *chōkaku, chōkyaku* people attending a funeral or offering condolences
10 砲 *chōhō* artillery funeral salute
11 問 *chōmon* condolence call
祭 *chōsai* memorial service
祭料 *chōsairyō* gift at a memorial service
12 詞 *chōshi* message of condolence, memorial address
13 辞 *chōji* message of condolence, memorial address
電 *chōden* telegram of condolence
意 *chōi* condolence, sympathy, mourning
14 旗 *chōki* flag at half-mast
銃 *chōjū* volley of rifles at a funeral
歌 *chōka* elegy, dirge
15 慰 *chōi* condolence, sympathy
慰金 *chōikin* condolence money
20 鐘 *chōshō* funeral bell

A **引** 1681 / J307a / M9699 IN. *hi(ku)* *vt* draw, pull, haul, tug, jerk, drag, trail, bend, attract; lead (horses or captives); draw (lines); admit; install (utilities); quote, refer to; look up (words); subtract, reduce; apply, daub on; blunt (a sword); patronize; choose; draw (a line); catch (a cold). *vi* retreat, withdraw, retire; subside. *hi(kaseru)* redeem, ransom. *hi(keru)* close, be over; can discount; slink away. *hi(ke)* closing (of office, school, etc.); leaving (work); retiring; defeat, reverse; loss. *hi(ki)* flattery, patronage, pull, backing; discount. *-bi(ki)* coated with, plated with. *hi(ki)-* emphatic verbal prefix.
2 入 *hi(ki)-i(reru)* drag in, bring into; win over, interest, entice; pull in, pull back
力 *inryoku* gravitation, attraction
3 下 *hi(ki)-sa(garu)* *vi* retire, withdraw. *hi(ki)-sa(geru)* pull down, lower, reduce. *hi(ki)-oro(su)* pull down; drag off (the rocks), refloat
上 *hi(ki)-a(geru)* *vi* withdraw, retire, leave; be repatriated. *vt* pull up; increase (fares); evacuate; refloat, salvage; recover (a body); promote
上作業 *hikia(ge) sagyō* salvage operations
4 戸 *hi(ki)do* sliding door
比 *hi(ki)-kura(beru)* compare
水 *hi(ki)mizu* irrigation
分 *hi(ki)-wa(keru)* pull apart, separate. *hikiwake* a drawn game
手 *hi(ki)te* knob, handle, catch; patron, admirer. *hi(ku)te* admirer; inducer
手繰 *hi(t)taku(ru)* snatch away, wrest from
止 *hi(ki)-to(meru)* restrain, check; detain, keep back, hold, stop
止策 *hikito(me) saku* measures to induce a person to desist

切 *hi(ki)-ki(ru)* pull and cut; saw off. *hi(kimo)-ki(ranu), hi(kimo)-ki(razu)* uninterrupted. *hi(kimo)-ki(razu) ni* uninterruptedly
切無 *hi(k)ki(ri)na(shi) ni* incessantly, continuously, in rapid succession
火 *inka suru* ignite, catch fire
火性 *inkasei* inflammability
火点 *inkaten* ignition point
込 *hi(ki)-ko(mu)* drag in, bring into; win over, interest, entice; pull in, pull back *hi(k)ko(mu)* draw back, retire; sink, cave in; keep behind; disappear. *hi(k)ko(masu), hi(k)ko(meru), hi(k)ko(mu) vt* draw in, take in; withdraw, retract, pull inside. *hikko(mi), hikiko(mi)* retreat, withdrawal; retirement; depression (a hole)
込車輪 *hikiko(mi) sharin* retractable wheel
込性 *hikko(mi)shō* retiring disposition; conservatism
込思案 *hikko(mi)jian* conservatism
込勝 *hikko(mi)ga(chi) no* retiring (disposition)
込管 *hikiko(mi)kan, hi(k)ko(mi)kan* service pipe
込線 *hikikomisen* service wire; railway siding
5 目 *hi(ke)me* weakness; drawing back
付 *hi(t)tsu(keru), hi(ki)-tsu(keru)* fascinate; pull up (at a gate); have a convulsion. *hi(t)tsu(ku)* stick to , cling to. *hi(ki)tsu(ke)* fit, convulsion
叩 *hi(p)pata(ku)* thrash, box, slap, strike
外 *hi(ki)-hazu(su), hi(p)pazu(su)* pull down, take off, unfasten. *hi(p)pazu(su)* dodge, parry off
払 *hi(ki)-hara(u)* evacuate, vacate
札 *hi(ki)fuda* handbill; lottery ticket
写 *hi(ki)utsu(shi)* copy, tracing
去 *hi(ki)-sa(ru)* retreat, withdraw; subside; deduct
立 *hi(t)ta(teru), hi(ki)-ta(teru)* favor; patronize; support; promote; rouse; enhance; emphasize; shut; escort (a prisoner), march (a person) off. *hi(ki)-ta(tsu)* become active; be inspired; become brisk; set off (to advantage), look better
立役 *hikita(te)yaku* a front; supporter, a friend (in court)
出 *hi(ki)-da(su)* take out, extract; drag out; draw out, lead out, entice out, bring out. *hikida(shi)* (desk) drawer; withdrawal
出物 *hi(ki)demono* gift, souvenir
用 *in'yō* a quotation
用文 *in'yōbun* a quotation
用句 *in'yōku* a quotation
用符 *in'yōfu* quotation marks
6 回 *hi(ki)-mawa(su)* draw (a curtain); parade about; guide
返 *hi(ki)-kae(su)* repeat; send back, reverse; bring back; turn back, retrace (steps)
汐 *hi(ki)shio* ebb tide
合 *hi(ki)-a(u)* be profitable, pay; pull against each other. *hi(ki)-a(waseru)* introduce; compare, collate, check. *hi(ki)a(i)* reference, comparison; witness; a deal
当 *hi(ki)-a(teru)* apply, compare. *hi(ki)a(te)* mortgage, security
7 見 *inken* audience, interview
戻 *hi(ki)-modo(su)* bring back, restore; improve (business); turn back, retrace (steps)
伸 *hi(ki)-noba(su), hi(ki)-no(beru)* stretch out, prolong; elongate; extend; beat out; spin out; enlarge; postpone; filibuster. *hikinoba(shi)* photographic enlargement
抜 *hi(ki)-nu(ku), hi(kko)nu(ku)* extract; uproot; select, pull out
8 金 *hi(ki)gane* trigger
延 *hi(ki) no(beru), hi(ki) noba(su)* stretch out, prolong; elongate; extend; beat out; spin out; enlarge; postpone; filibuster
退 *intai suru, hi(ki)-shirizo(ku)* draw back, retreat. *hi(ki)-no(keru)* drag out of the way. *intai* retirement
例 *inrei* quotation, referring to precedent
放 *hi(ki)-hana(tsu), hi(ki)-hana(su)* pull apart
明 *hi(ki)a(ke)* daybreak
波 *hi(ki)nami* backwash
物 *hi(ki)mono* gift, souvenir
直 *hi(ki)-nao(su)* restore, bring back, redraw (lines, etc.)
毟 *hi(ki)-mushi(ru)* pluck, pick, tear
者 *hi(kare)mono* man under arrest

取 *hi(ki)-to(ru)* take charge of, respond to; take delivery of; claim (a body); retire; die
取人 *hikitorinin* claimer, caretaker, guarantor (of a parolee)
取手 *hikitorite* claimer, caretaker, guarantor (of a parolee)
受 *hi(ki)-u(keru)* be responsible for; take charge of, undertake; consent to; accept, guarantee; contract (a disease). *hikiu(ke)* undertaking; acceptance, underwriting; guarantee, guarantor
受人 *hikiukenin* guarantor; acceptor (of a draft); underwriter
受手 *hikiukete* guarantor; acceptor (of a draft); underwriter
9 連 *hi(ki)-tsu(reru)* bring along
眉 *hi(ki)mayu* painted eyebrows
括 *hi(k)kuru(meru), hi(ki)-kuru(meru)* bring to a conclusion
降 *hi(ki)-o(rosu)* pull down, bring down
10 起 *hi(ki)-oko(su)* raise up, pull up; cause, bring about; raise (questions); create (trouble), provoke, stir up
値 *hi(ki)ne* reduced price
倒 *hi(ki)-tao(su)* pull down, drag down
捕 *hi(ki)-tora(eru), hi(t)tora(eru)* capture, seize, arrest
時 *hi(ke)doki* closing time
浚 *hi(s)sara(u)* snatch, grab, take away
破 *hi(ki)-yabu(ru)* tear, tear up, tear away
致 *inchi* arrest, custody
被 *hi(k)kabu(ru)* pull (bedclothes) over the head
剝 *hi(ki)-ha(gu), hi(ki)-ha(gasu)* tear off, peel off, rip off, strip off; skin, flay; disrobe; deprive of. *hi(ki)-mu(ku)* peel, pare, hull
殺 *hi(ki)-koro(su)* run over and kill
留 *hi(ki)-to(meru)* restrain, check; detain, keep back, hold, stop
11 掛 *hi(k)ka(karu)* be caught in, get stuck; be involved; be cheated. *hi(k)ka(keru)* hang on, hook, throw on; ensnare; defraud, evade (payment); drink (saké). *hi(ki)-ka(keru)* hang up (something); pull (something) over one; request; make connections with. *hi(k)ka(kari)* a hold; connection, complicity, involvement; affair; unsettled account. *hi(k)ka(ke)* hook
据 *hi(ki)-su(eru)* set (a table); lay (a foundation); place (a gun); install, equip; appoint (to a position)
移 *hi(ki)-utsu(ru)* move to. *hi(ki)-utsu(su)* move, transfer; pour into, divert (attention), give (a disease to someone)
船 *hi(ki)fune* tugboat
釣 *hi(t)tsuri* scar, mark of a burn
動 *hi(ki)-ugo(kasu)* pull and move around; tempt and lead around
寄 *hi(ki)-yo(seru)* draw nearer, drag in; attract
窓 *hi(ki)mado* skylight, trap door
責 *inseki suru* take the responsibility
菓子 *hi(ki)gashi* ornamental gift cakes
率 *insotsu suru* lead, command
率者 *insotsusha* leader
張 *hi(p)pa(ru)* pull, draw, jerk, drag, tug at; stretch over; take (someone) to; entice, invite; delay (payment)
張上 *hi(p)pa(ri)-a(geru) vi* withdraw, retire, leave; be repatriated. *vt* pull up; increase (fares); evacuate; refloat, salvage; recover (a body); promote
張込 *hi(p)pa(ri)-ko(mu)* pull in, drag into
張凧 *hi(p)pa(ri)dako* socialite
張出 *hi(p)pa(ri)-da(su)* take out, drag out, bring out, lead out, pull out
張回 *hi(p)pa(ri)-mawa(su)* pull around
12 喩 *in'yu* allusion
換 *hi(ki)-ka(eru)* exchange, change, convert. *hikika(ete), hikika(e)* on the contrary, on the other hand; while, when
渡 *hi(ki)-wata(su)* deliver, transfer, hand over; extradite; stretch across. *hikiwata(shi)* delivery, turning over to, extradition
絞 *hi(ki)-shibo(ru)* wring, squeeze, press, extract; milk; close tight; extort; scold; draw a bow to the limit; draw aside (curtains); tuck up; strain (the voice)
証 *inshō* quotation, citation
着 *hi(ki)-tsu(keru), hi(t)tsu(keru)* fascinate; pull up (at a gate); have a convulsion
落 *hi(ki)-oto(su)* pull down
裂 *hi(s)sa(ku), hi(ki)-sa(ku)* tear off, tear up, rip open; split; separate

割燕麦 *hikiwa(ri) embaku* oatmeal, rolled oats
越 *hi(k)ko(su), hi(ki)-ko(su)* move, change quarters
越先 *hikko(shi) saki* destination in moving
揚 *hi(ki)-a(geru) vi* withdraw, retire, leave; be repatriated. *vt* pull up; increase (fares); evacuate; refloat, salvage; recover (a body); promote
揚者 *hikiagesha* returnee
替 *hi(ki)-kae(ru), hi(k)kae(ru)* exchange (things); change from; reverse
替券 *hikikaeken* cloakroom check
13 継 *hi(ki)-tsu(gu)* take over or hand over (duties); inherit
続 *hi(ki)-tsuzu(ku)* continue, occur in succession. *hi(ki)tsuzu(ki)* continually
詰 *hi(ki)-tsu(meru)* shorten; tighten; economize
置 *inchi* arrest
幕 *hi(ki)maku* a draw curtain
照 *inshō* reference
搔 *hi(k)ka(ku)* scratch, claw, maul
搔回 *hi(k)ka(ki)-mawa(su)* ransack, mess up, carry on high-handedly
14 摑 *hi(t)tsuka(mu)* grab at
綱 *hi(ki)zuna* tow rope; bell rope
算 *hi(ki)zan* subtraction
導 *indō* guidance; address to the departed soul
摺 *hi(ki)-zu(ru)* drag along; seduce; prolong. *hi(ki)zuri* train (of a dress); a low woman
摺込 *hi(ki)-zu(ri)-ko(mu)* drag in
摺出 *hi(ki)-zu(ri)-da(su)* drag out
摺回 *hi(ki)-zu(ri)-mawa(su)* drag around
15 潮 *hi(ki)shio* ebb tide
緩 *hi(ki)-yuru(mu)* weaken the stock market
縄結 *hi(ki)nawa musu(bi)* carrick bend (a knot)
締 *hi(ki)-shi(maru)* become tense; be tightened. *hi(ki)-shi(meru)* tighten; stiffen; strain, brace
19 離 *hi(ki)-hana(su), hi(p)pana(su)* pull apart, separate; outdistance
繰返 *hi(k)ku(ri)-kae(ru)* capsize; collapse; lie on one's back; be reversed; betray. *hi(k)ku(ri)-kae(su)* capsize; knock down; turn over; turn inside out; turn up (a card). *hi(k)ku(ri)kae(shi)* topsy-turvy, upside down, inside out
20 懸 *hi(k)ka(karu)* be caught in, get stuck; be involved; be cheated. *hi(k)ka(keru)* hang on, hook, throw on; ensnare; defraud, evade (payment); drink (saké). *hi(k)ka(kari)* a hold; connection, complicity, involvement; affair; unsettled account. *hi(k)ka(ke)* hook
22 纏 *hi(ki)-mato(meru)* settle, complete, agree upon, arrange; collect; put in order; unify, coordinate
籠 *hi(ki)-komo(ru), hi(k)komo(ru)* stay indoors; be confined indoors
23 攫 *hi(s)sara(u)* snatch, grab, take away
攣 *hi(ki)-tsu(ru)* have a cramp or spasm; twitch; strain (a ligament); have a convulsion. *hikitsuri* scar; spasm, cramp, twitch, convulsion

2

弘 1682 / J3930 / M9709 Ku. Kō. *hiro(i)* broad, wide.
11 済会 *kōsaikai* benefit association
12 報 *kōhō* publicity
報部 *kōhōbu* public relations department

弗 1683 / J4a26 / M9708 Futsu. *doru* dollar.
9 相場 *doru sōba* dollar exchange
10 素 *fusso* fluorine
素酸 *fussosan* fluoric acid
12 箱 *dorubako* cashbox; backer, patron

3

弛 1684 / J4350 / M9724 Chi. Shi. *taru(mu) vi* slacken, loosen, relax. *tayu(mu)* slacken one's efforts. *taru(meru) vt* loosen slack up on. *tayu(i)* tired and weak, listless; without any ambition. *yuru(mu) vi* loosen, lessen; relax; be unguarded; be moderate. *yuru(meru) vt* loosen, unbend, unfasten; relax, ease, slacken; mitigate. *yuru(i)* loose, slack; lenient, generous, slow.
11 張 *shichō* stretching and releasing; alternation of firmness and laxity
張熱 *shichōnetsu, chichōnetsu* remittent fever

12 廃 *shihai suru* relax, slacken
15 緩 *chikan, shikan* relaxation; getting careless

A **弟** 1685 J446f M9737 DAI. TEI younger brother, faithful service to those older; brotherly affection. *otōto, ototo, oto* younger brother.
3 子 *deshi, teishi* pupil, disciple, adherent, follower; apprentice. *teishi* young person; teacher's student-helper
子入 *deshii(ri)* apprenticeship; enrolling
4 分 *otōtobun* a friend treated as a younger brother
7 弟子 *otōto deshi* new pupil; new disciple
8 妹 *teimai* younger brothers and sisters
12 御 *otōtogo* your young brother
13 嫁 *otōtoyome, otoyome* younger brother's wife

5

弩 1686 J5738 M9760 DO. *ōyumi* crossbow, long bow.
3 弓 *dokyū* catapult
9 級艦 *dokyūkan* dreadnaught

B **弧** 1687 J384c M9757 KO arc; arch; bow.
6 灯 *kotō* arc light
光 *kokō* arc light
7 状 *kojō no* arc-shaped
形 *kokei* an arc
15 線 *kosen* an arc

B **弦** 1688 J3639 M9754 GEN bowstring; chord (in geometry); hypotenuse; crescent (moon); bowstring; string (of an instrument). *tsuru* bowstring; teakettle handle made of bamboo or vines.
4 月 *gengetsu* crescent moon
7 声 *gensei* sound of the strings
9 音 *tsuru oto* sound of a vibrating bowstring
13 楽 *gengaku* singing accompanied by stringed instruments
楽隊 *gengakutai* string band
楽器 *gengakki* stringed instruments
14 歌 *genka* singing
管 *genkan* wind and string instruments
15 線 *gensen* catgut

弥 1689 J4c6f M9753 **彌** 1703 J573d M9877 BI. MI. *iya* all the more, increasingly.
3 久 *bikyū suru* stretch out, lengthen (said of time)
上 *iya(ga)ue ni mo* all the more, to cap it all
5 生 *yayoi* spring; third lunar month
立 *yoda(tsu)* quiver with horror
6 次 *yaji(ru)* cheer, support, root for; hoot at, obstruct; jeer at. *yaji* cheering, rooting; heckling, jeering; rooters, hecklers, mob; spectators; busybody; intruder
次馬 *yajiuma* rabble, mob; spectators; busybody; intruder
8 弥 *iyoiyo* more and more
果 *iyaha(te)* away off in the distance
9 栄 *iyasaka(eru)* prosper more and more. *iyasaka* increasing prosperity
11 猛 *yatake ni* impetuously, courageously
猛心 *yatakegokoro* brave heart
14 増 *iyamashi ni* more and more; *iyama(su)* go on increasing
15 撒 *misa* Catholic mass
縫 *bihō* stopgap, temporizing, patching up, glossing over
縫策 *bihōsaku* makeshift, stopgap policy

6

弯 1690 J573f M-X Nonstandard for 彎 1704.

弭 1691 J5739 M9768 BI. MI archery bow made with horn; stop, cease. *yuhazu* notches at ends of bow for string.

7

A **弱** 1692 J3c65 M-X JAKU weakness; the weak. *yowa(maru), yowa(ru) vi* weaken, be emaciated; be dejected; be perplexed. *yowa(meru) vt* weaken. *yowa(ru) vt* impair, weaken, enfeeble. *yowa(i)* weak, feeble, frail, tender; unskilled; weak (alcoholic beverage). *(ka)yowa(i)* frail, feeble. *(hi)yowa(i)* weak, sickly. *-jaku* a little less than.
3 小 *jakushō* puniness; youth
小国 *jakushōkoku* minor power

4 込 *yowa(ri)-ko(mu)* weaken, be at wits' end
切 *yowa(ri)-ki(ru)* faint, be exhausted
5 目 *yowa(ri)me* a time of weakness
祟目 *yowa(ri)me (ni) tata(ri)me* misfortunes never come singly
6 虫 *yowamushi* weakling, coward
行 *jakkō* weakness in execution
気 *yowaki* faintheartedness; bearish sentiment
肉強食 *jakuniku-kyōshoku* survival of the fittest
年 *jakunen* youth
年者 *jakunemmono, jakunensha* youngster
弟 *jakutei* young brother
志 *jakushi* weak will
材料 *yowazairyō* bearish factor
体 *jakutai* weak (organization)
体化 *jakutaika* weakening
8 国 *jakkoku* weak country
卒 *jakusotsu* cowardly soldier
者 *yowa(i)mono, yowa(ki)mono* weak person, the weak *jakusha* the weak, the underdog
味 *yowami* weakness
味噌 *yowamiso* weakling, coward
9 冠 *jakkan* age 20; youth
点 *jakuten* weak point
保合 *yowamochia(i)* (stock market) barely holding steady
音 *yowane* complaints. *jakuon* soft sound
音器 *jakuonki* damper, mute (on musical instruments)
10 衰 *yowa(ri)-otoro(eru)* languish
弱 *yowayowa(shii)* frail, slender, feminine
11 視 *jakushi* weak sight
13 腰 *yowagoshi* weak attitude
15 敵 *jakuteki* weak enemy
震 *jakushin* weak earthquake shock, a minor tremor
輩 *jakuhai* young person; inexperienced person, a novice
17 齢 *jakurei* youth

8

弸 1693 / J573a / M9817 Hō strong bow. *michiru* fill.

A **張** 1694 / J4425 / M9812 Chō counter for bows and stringed instruments.
ha(ru) *vt* put up (a tent); stretch, spread, string, tighten; cover, line; strain; square (elbows); give (a banquet); run (a store); stake (money); display; slap, box, spank; lay (flooring); insist on (one's own way); guard; run after (a girl); fill (with water). *vi* swell, be full; form (ice); be expensive; increase; be heavy; grow stiff; brace up. *ha(ri)* tension; will power, pluck, pride; expansion steadiness. *-ba(ri)* fashion.

2 力 *chōryoku* tension, tensile strength
3 子 *ha(ri)ko* papier-mâché
上 *ha(ri)-a(geru)* raise or strain (the voice)
上綱 *ha(ri)a(ge)zuna* halyard
4 手 *ha(ri)te* slapping (someone)
込 *ha(ri)-ko(mu)* keep watch; be eager for; invest in
切 *ha(ri)-ki(reru)* burst out. *ha(ri)-ki(ru)* string up, stretch tight; be tense, be enthusiastic
5 目 *ha(ri)me* the edge of a piece pasted onto another
巡 *ha(ri)-megu(rasu)* ramify
付 *ha(ri)-tsu(keru)* stick on, paste up (a notice), affix (stamps)
札 *ha(ri)fuda* placard, bill, poster; tag
札無用 *Ha(ri)fuda Muyō* Post No Bills
出 *ha(ri)-da(su)* put up a notice, project, jut out. *harida(shi)* bill, poster, notice; overhang
出窓 *harida(shi) mado* bay window
本 *chōhon* cause; originator; ringleader, perpetrator
本人 *chōhonnin, chōbonnin* originator, ringleader, perpetrator
6 合 *ha(ri)-a(u)* vie with, emulate, compete with. *haria(i)* rivalry, competition; responsiveness; inducement
7 抜 *ha(ri)nu(ki)* papier-mâché
8 板 *ha(ri)ita* fulling board; kimono drying board
物 *ha(ri)mono* cloth-fulling
10 倒 *ha(ri)-tao(su)* knock down, floor (a man)
紋 *ha(ri)mon* pasted crest
紙 *ha(ri)gami* sticker, bills, label, tag
紙禁止 *Ha(ri)gami Kinshi* Post No Bills

番 *ha(ri)ban* watch, guard; watchman, sentinel
替 *ha(ri)-ka(eru)* repaper, replaster, reupholster, recover
裂 *ha(ri)-sa(keru)* burst open; split, break, splinter
13 詰 *ha(ri)-tsu(meru)* strain, stretch, string up, make tense, cover over, freeze over
14 網 *ha(ri)ami* stretched net, set net
綱 *ha(ri)zuna* guy rope

A **強** 1695 / J362f / M9815 **强** 1696 / J-X / M9822 KYŌ, GŌ strength, might; strong person. *tsuyo(i)* strong, powerful, mighty, robust, vigorous, healthy; brave, courageous; severe, intense; durable, solid. *tsuyo(maru)* get strong. *tsuyo(meru) vt* strengthen, intensify, invigorate; confirm; emphasize, increase, redouble. *tsuyo(garu)* show one's toughness. *tsuyo(gari)* bluff, show of strength. *shi(iru)* force, coerce, constrain, compel. *shi(ite)* forcibly, against one's will. *anaga(chi)* necessarily, wholly. *kowa(i)* tough, hard, stiff. *-kyō* a little over, and a fraction. *-zuyo(i)* very.

2 力 *kyōryoku* power, might. *gōriki* Herculean strength; mountain carrier-guide
力犯 *gōrikihan* crime of violence
3 大 *kyōdai na* mighty, powerful
弓 *gōkyū* strong bow
4 火 *tsuyobi* a good (cooking) fire
化米 *kyōkamai* enriched rice
引 *gōin ni* by main force, forcibly
心剤 *kyōshinzai* heart stimulant
5 圧 *kyōatsu* pressure, oppression, coercion
弁 *kyōben suru* quibble, sophisticate
半 *kyōhan* more than half, the greater part
打 *kyōda* hard blow; heavy hit (in baseball); drive (in tennis)
打者 *kyōdasha* heavy hitter
6 気 *tsuyoki* strong spirit. *gōgi na* great, powerful, grand
壮 *kyōsō na* robust, sturdy, strong, vigorous
壮剤 *kyōsōzai* tonic
行 *kyōkō* forcing; enforcement
行軍 *kyōkōgun* forced march
行偵察 *kyōkō teisatsu* reconnaissance in force
7 言 *shiigoto* forcefully dominating the conversation
兵 *kyōhei* good soldier; powerful army
迫 *kyōhaku suru* compel, use duress
迫観念 *kyōhaku kannen* persecution complex
8 雨 *kyōu* heavy rain
固 *kyōko* firmness, stability, security, strength
国 *kyōkoku* strong nation, powerful country
肩 *kyōken* strong-armed (player)
味 *tsuyomi* strength, strong point
直 *kyōchoku, gōchoku* integrity; rigidity
弩 *kyōdo* strong bow
者 *kyōsha* strong person. *gō(no)mono* very strong person; brave warrior
突張 *gōtsu(ku)ba(ri)* hardheartedness; headstrong person
制 *kyōsei* coercion, compulsion, enforcement
制力 *kyōseiryoku* authority, legal power
制天引 *kyōsei tembi(ki)* compulsory check-off
制処分 *kyōsei shobun* legal disposition
制労動 *kyōsei rōdō* forced labor, slave labor, hard labor (in prison)
制作業 *kyōsei sagyō* reform work
制的 *kyōseiteki* compulsory, forced
制結婚 *kyōsei kekkon* forced marriage
制疎開 *kyōsei sokai* forced evacuation, eviction, dismantling, demolishing
制徴募 *kyōsei chōbo* forced enlistment, labor levy
制調停 *kyōsei chōtei* compulsory mediation
制競売 *kyōsei kyōbai* forced auction sale
9 音 *kyōon* accent, stress
風 *kyōfū* moderate gale, strong wind
度 *kyōdo* intensity, strength
持 *kowamo(te)* fear-motivated respect
胆 *gōtan* boldness, hardihood
姦 *gōkan* rape, violation, assault
要 *kyōyō* coercion, enforcement, extortion, persistent demand. *shi(i)-sema(ru)* coerce

10 剛 *kyōgō* strong man
振 *kyōshin* strong swing (on a ball)
酒 *gōshu* heavy drinking
将 *kyōshō* strong general, brave general
記 *kyōki* excellent memory, good memory
烈 *kyōretsu na* strong, intense; gaudy
弱 *kyōjaku* strength, power
11 健 *kyōken* robust health
強 *kowagowa* sound of stiff materials rustling
張 *kowaba(ru) vi* stiffen; become fearful. *kowaba(ruseru), kowaba(rasu) vt* starch
情 *gōjō* obstinacy, stubbornness
球 *gōkyū* fast ball
悪 *gōaku* wickedness
盗 *gōto* burglar, robber; burglary, robbery
欲 *gōyoku* greed, avarice
欲非道 *gōyokuhidō na* insatiable, relentless, rapacious
12 訴 *gōso* direct petition
靭 *kyōjin na* tough, tenacious, stiff
飲 *gōin* heavy drinking, carousing
飯 *kowameshi* rice cooked with red beans
硬 *kyōkō na* firm, vigorous, unbending
硬派 *kyōkōha* diehards, tough elements
13 腰 *tsuyogoshi* firm attitude
腹 *gōfuku* obstinacy, stubbornness
勢 *gōsei na* splendid, great, magnificent
意見 *kowaiken* warning, severe reproof; positive ideas
14 豪 *kyōgō* strong man; champion
奪 *gōdatsu* pillage, plunder, extortion; violence
奪物 *gōdatsubutsu* plunder, loot
奪者 *gōdatsusha* plunderer, robber
15 劇 *kyōgeki na* strong and violent
談 *gōdan* vigorous negotiations, peremptory
調 *kyōchō* emphasis
敵 *gōteki, kyōteki* formidable enemy
暴 *kyōbō* strong and rough, violent
震 *kyōshin* severe earthquake
慾 *gōyoku* greed, avarice
請 *sega(mu), sebi(ru)* tease, press for, tap for (money). *yusu(ru)* extort, blackmail. *neda(ru)* tease, coax, solicit, demand. *gōsei* blackmail, extortion; importunity
請取 *neda(ri)-to(ru), sebi(ri)-to(ru)* tease for and take. *yusu(ri)-to(ru)* wring money out of a person
権 *kyōken* the power of the state
権主義 *kyōken shugi* authoritarianism
権政治 *kyōken seiji* power politics
権発動 *kyōken hatsudō* invoking legal action
16 激 *kyōgeki na* strong and violent
諫 *kyōkan* strong argument (against)
19 識 *kyōshiki* excellent memory
22 襲 *kyōshū* assault, storming; terrific hitting
襲隊 *kyōshūtai* assault unit

9

強 1696 / J-X / M9822 See **強** 1694.

彌 1697 / J492b / M9826 **彍** 1698 / J-X / M9825 HITSU help.

B **弾** 1699 / J4346 / M9836' **彈** 1700 / J573c / M9865 DAN bullet. *dan(jiru), dan(zuru), tan(zuru)* play or twang on a stringed instrument. *hi(ku)* play on. *haji(ku)* fillip, flip, snap; repel, shed (water); use (an abacus). *haji(keru)* split open; spring off. *hazu(mu)* spring, bound, rebound; be inspired, be spurred on; invest in; be generous (in tipping); breathe with difficulty. *hajiki* (metal) spring; marbles. *tama* bullet, shot, shell.

2 力 *danryoku* elasticity, flexibility
力性 *danryokusei* elasticity, resilience, flexibility; adaptability
3 子 *danshi* shot, bullet
丸 *dangan, tama* bullet, shot, shell, cannon ball, projectile
丸切手 *dangan kitte* postal-savings coupons
丸列車 *dangan ressha* super-express, flier
丸除 *dangan'yo(ke)* protection against bullets
丸黒子 *dangan-kokushi* tiny piece (of land)
丸衝撃 *dangan shōgeki* shell shock
4 手 *hi(ki)te* player, performer
片 *dampen* shell splinter
込 *tamago(me)* loading a gun

5 玉 *haji(ki)dama* marbles
圧 *dan'atsu* pressure, oppression, suppression
出 *haji(ki)-da(su)* snap out; expel; calculate; squeeze out (the money needed)
6 返 *haji(ki)-kae(ru)* spring back, rebound, boomerang
7 豆 *haji(ke)mame* pop beans; parched peas
初 *hi(ki)zome* first New Year's playing of an instrument
8 金 *haji(ki)gane* spring; hammer (of a gun)
雨 *dan'u* hail of bullets
性 *dansei* elasticity
劾 *dangai* impeachment, accusation, censure, criticism
9 指 *danshi* fillip, a snap; a moment
除 *tamayoke* protection against bullets, bulletproof
奏 *dansō* playing on stringed instruments
奏法 *dansōhō* touch (on a stringed instrument)
奏者 *dansōsha* stringed-instrument player
11 痕 *dankon* bullet hole, bullet mark
道 *dandō* trajectory, line of fire
道学 *dandōgaku* ballistics
12 程 *dantei* range, gunshot
着 *danchaku* hit, impact
着距離 *danchaku kyori* range, gunshot
13 傷 *tama kizu* bullet wound
幕 *dammaku* barrage
鉄砲 *haji(ki)deppō* air gun
14 語 *hi(ki)gata(ri)* reciting with one's own stringed accompaniment
16 機 *bane, danki* (metal) spring
頭 *dantō* warhead
薬 *dan'yaku* ammunition
薬車 *dan'yakusha* ammunition car or cart
薬匣 *dan'yakukō* ammunition box
薬庫 *dan'yakuko* powder magazine
薬帯 *dan'yakutai* ammunition belt
薬盒 *dan'yakugō* ammunition pouch
薬筒 *dan'yakutō* cartridge, rounds

12

彈 1700 / J573c / M9865 See **弾** 1699.

彁 1701 / J573b / M-X KA used phonetically.

13

彊 1702 / J3630 / M9872 KYŌ, GŌ strong.
8 国 *kyōkoku* a strong country
弩 *kyōdo* strong bow
15 敵 *kyōteki* strong enemy

14

彌 1703 / J573d / M9877 See **弥** 1689.

19

彎 1704 / J573e / M9904 WAN curve; stretching a bow.
2 入 *wannyū* gulf
4 月 *wangetsu* crescent
月状 *wangetsujō* crescent shape
6 曲 *wankyoku* curve, crook, bend

RAD. 彐 58

Kei-gashira or *ino-kashira* pig's head. Also called *yo* (the katakana).
Variants: ヨ, ⺕, 彑. Nickname: Pig's Head.

彑 1705 / J5740 / M9909 KEI pig's head.

3

A **当** 1706 / J4576 / M9913 **當** 3765 / J6144 / M21890 TŌ right; appropriateness, fairness; himself; itself; at the time. *a(taru) vi* and *vt* hit, strike, dash into; touch; shine on; guess right, be fulfilled; succeed; confront; lie (to the south); treat; feel out; undertake; be worth; correspond to; be related to; apply to; draw (a prize); be assigned to; be affected by; be spoiling; be exposed to; warm oneself; shave; grind; this coming (15th); turn out well; take well; be punished (by heaven); stand to reason; deal with; engage (the enemy); need not to (with negative); have (one's turn); be charged with. *a(teru)* apply, place, put; hit (the mark); guess; succeed; expose to; sit (on a cushion); assign, allocate; call on (a pupil). *a(terareru)* be affected (by), suffer (from); be bored, be annoyed. *masa ni* properly, naturally. *a(taranai)* do not deserve, be not justifiable, be not proper. *a(tari)* bruise; bite; exposure (to wind); success, hit; clue, trail, scent; batting average; on this (occasion); in the direction (of). *a(te)* aim; hopes, reckoning; dependence, confidence, clue, pad; blow, stroke. *a(tezuppō)* guesswork, haphazard work. *a(tekko)* guesswork, guessing game. *tō no* the said (person or thing). *-a(tari)* per. *tō-* this (city, etc.).

2 人 *tōnin* the one concerned, the said person, the man himself
3 口 *a(te)kuchi* insinuation
山 *tōzan* this mountain, this temple
千 *tōsen* a matchless warrior
4 手 *tōte* we; our group
日 *tōjitsu* the appointed day, the occasion
月 *tōgetsu* this month
木 *a(te)gi* batten, scantling
込 *a(te)-ko(mu)* count on, anticipate, expect
切 *a(te)gi(re)* patch
今 *tōkon* the present, these days
分 *tōbun* for the present, temporarily
方 *tōhō* I; our part
方側 *tōhōgawa* we
5 石 *a(te)ishi* touchstone
処 *a(te)do* aim
付 *a(te)-tsu(keru)* insinuate
代 *tōdai* the present generation; those days; the present family head
外 *a(tari)hazu(re)* success or failure, risk. *a(te)hazu(re)* disappointment
札 *a(tari)fuda* the winning ticket
主 *tōshu* the present head of the family
用 *tōyō* current use; the business in hand
用日記 *tōyō nikki* diary
用漢字 *Tōyō Kanji* the official 1850 "Current Characters" used till 1981
世 *tōsei* the present time
世向 *tōseimu(ki)* the latest fashion
世風 *tōseifū* the latest fashion, the fashionable style
6 地 *tōchi* this locality
寺 *tōji* this temple
字 *a(te)ji* a phonetic-equivalent character; a substitute character
年 *tōnen* the current year; that year. *a(tari)doshi* bumper year
7 言 *a(te)koto* insinuation
身 *a(te)mi* body blow, knockout punch
住 *tōjū* the present chief priest of a temple
役 *a(tari)yaku* successful role. *tōyaku* this role; this officer
社 *tōsha* this shrine, this firm
初 *tōsho* original; at the beginning
否 *tōhi* right or wrong; justice; propriety, suitability
芸 *a(tari)gei* successful role
狂言 *a(tari)kyōgen* successful play, a hit
局 *tōkyoku* the authorities concerned, the powers that be, the one in authority; an insider
局者 *tōkyokusha* the authorities concerned, the powers that be, the one in authority; an insider
8 金 *tōkin* cash; paying in cash
国 *tōkoku* our country
店 *tōten* this shop, this store, we
所 *tōsho* this place. *a(te)do* aim
物 *a(te)mono* riddle, guessing; covering
夜 *tōya* that night
季 *tōki* present period, this term
直 *tōchoku* on duty
直室 *tōchokushitsu* night-duty room
事 *tōji* related matters *a(te)goto* hopes, reckoning; inference, guessing
事国 *tōjikoku* the country concerned
事者 *tōjisha* the person concerned
9 面 *tōmen suru* face, confront. *tōmen no* immediate, urgent.
風 *tōfū* the present fashion
屋 *a(tari)ya* a lucky person; a good hitter
度 *tōdo* now, this time
前 *a(tari)mae* proper, just, fair, reasonable, natural, ordinary, normal, usual
為 *tōi* what should be
10 馬 *a(te)uma* confronting a mare with a stallion to test readiness to mate; preparatory move

時 *tōji* in these days; in those days; time
流 *tōryū* the style
家 *tōke* this house, this family
座 *tōza* the present; for some time; current; temporary; immediate; current checking account
座逃 *tōzanoga(re)* an excuse; an elusion; makeshift
座凌 *tōzashino(gi) ni* as a temporary measure
座預金 *tōza yokin* current checking account
11 得 *tō (o) e(ta)* accurate, correct
推量 *a(te)zuiryō, a(te)suiryō* guess, guesswork, conjecture
12 散 *a(tari)-chi(rasu)* find fault with everybody
朝 *tōchō* the present imperial court
期 *tōki* the present period, this term
嵌 *a(te)-ha(meru) vt* apply to; assign to. *a(te)-ha(maru) vi* apply to; be true of; conform to
落 *tōraku* election result
然 *tōzen* justly, properly, naturally, necessarily, of course
番 *tōban* being on duty or on guard; man on duty
番号 *a(tari) bangō* winning number
惑 *tōwaku* perplexity, embarrassment; doubt; confusion
惑顔 *tōwakugao* puzzled look
13 該 *tōgai* the appropriate (authorities)
鉢 *a(tari)bachi* earthenware mortar
節 *tōsetsu* these times
障無 *a(tari)sawa(ri) ga na(i)* be harmless; be noncommittal, be neutral
意即妙 *tōi-sokumyō* ready wit
路 *tōro* the authorities, the authorities concerned
路者 *tōrosha* the authorities

4

歳 *tōsai* this year; a yearling
歳児 *tōsaiji* a yearling
14 選 *tōsen* election to office; winning (a lottery)
選者 *tōsensha* successful candidate
17 擦 *a(te)-kosu(ru) vt* insinuate, satirize, take a dig at
18 職 *tōshoku* this occupation; the present occupation; present duties
20 競 *a(te)kura(be)* guess; guessing game; drawing lots
21 籤 *tōsen, a(tari) kuji* the winning ticket
籤者 *tōsensha* prizewinner

6

彖 1707 / J5741 / M9920 TAN (pigs) run; divination.

8

彗 1708 / J5742 / M9927 SUI comet.
9 星 *suisei, hōkiboshi* comet

10

彙 1709 / J5743 / M9936 I same kind.
12 報 *ihō* bulletin, collection of reports

13

彝 1710 / J5734 / M9948 彞 1711 / J5733 / M9950 I moral principle.
10 訓 *ikun* moral principles

15

彞 1711 / J5733 / M9950 See 彝 1710.

RAD. 彡 59

Kami kazari hair ornament. On right: *sanzukuri* right-hand "hair ornament" or right-hand "three." Nickname: Short Hair (cf. Rad. 190)

彡 1712 / J5744 / M9962 SAN long-haired.

4

形 1713 / J3741 / M9969 A GYŌ. KEI shape. *kata* shape, form, make, size, format, mark; pattern, design. *katachi* form, shape; personal appearance. *nari* form, figure, appearance, dress.

4 木 *katagi* wooden model; woodcut printing block
5 代 *katashiro* paper image used in a purification ceremony
付 *katatsu(ki)* a print (cloth)
6 成 *keisei* formation
気 *katagi* spirit, character, trait
似 *keiji* similarity in form
而下 *keijika no* physical, material
而下学 *keijikagaku* the physical sciences
而上 *keijijō no* metaphysical
而上学 *keijijōgaku* metaphysics
式 *keishiki* form; formality
式化 *keishikika* formalization
式主義 *keishiki shugi* formalism, red-tapism
式的 *keishikiteki* formal
式美 *keishikibi* beauty of form
式論 *keishikiron* formalism
7 体 *keitai* shape, form. *narikatachi* appearance
作 *katachizuku(ru)* form, shape, make, mold; buildup
状 *keijō* shape, form
声 *keisei* a type of character one part of which suggests the meaning and one the pronunciation (e.g. 河 and 悶)
見 *katami* memento, souvenir
見分 *katamiwa(ke)* distribution of mementos
9 造 *katachizuku(ru)* form, shape, make, mold; buildup
相 *gyōsō* features, expression; aspect. *keisō* phase, form
姿 *narisugata* appearance, form, costume
10 振 *narifu(ri)* appearance, costume
容 *keiyō* form, figure, appearance; qualification, description; modifying; figure of speech
容詞 *keiyōshi* adjective
11 許 *katabaka(ri)* only a formality, just a small token
12 勝 *keishō* picturesque scenery; advantageous position
無 *katana(shi)* all knocked out of shape, worthless
象 *keishō* shape, figure; appearance; phenomenon
13 跡 *keiseki* traces, evidences, indications
勢 *keisei* condition, situation, prospects
14 貌 *keibō* form, figure, looks
態 *keitai* shape, form, structure
態学 *keitaigaku* morphology
態論 *keitairon* morphology
15 影 *keiei* the form and its shadow; things inseparable
16 鋼 *katakō* shaped steel
骸 *keigai* framework; wreck

6

彦 1714 / J4927 / M9981 **彥** 1715 / J X / M9980 Gen. *hiko* (ancient) boy.

8

彪 1716 / J4937 / M9993 Hyō. Hyū spots; a tiger's spots; small tiger; *aya* figure, design.

彬 1717 / J493b / M9996 Hin harmony; pleasing balance between figure and background.

B **彩** 1718 / J3a4c / M9992 Sai. *irodo(ru)* color, paint, makeup.
6 色 *saishiki, saishoku* coloring, painting
色画 *saishikiga* colored painting
8 画 *saiga* painting, colored picture
12 雲 *saiun* cloudscape; glowing clouds
14 層 *saisō* chromosphere (of the sun)
管 *saikan* artist's brush
管振 *saikan (o) furu(u)* paint or draw

B **彫** 1719 / J4126 / M9995 Chō carving. *ho(ru)* carve, engrave, chisel, sculpture, inscribe.
3 工 *chōkō* carver, engraver, sculptor
上 *ho(ri)-a(geru)* emboss, carve in relief; finish carving or engraving
上細工 *ho(ri)a(ge)zaiku* relief work, embossing
4 心鏤骨 *chōshin-rukotsu* excellent literary work
5 付 *ho(ri)-tsu(keru)* carve (designs)
8 金 *chōkin* metal carving
物 *ho(ri)mono* carving; engraving; sculpture; tattooing
刻 *ho(ri)kiza(mu)* engrave, carve. *chōkoku* carving, engraving, sculpture
刻刀 *chōkokutō* graver, chisel

3 口 囗 土 士 夂 夊 夕 大 女 子 宀 寸 小 ⺌ 尢 尸 屮 山 川 巛 工 己 巾 干 幺 广 廴 廾 弋 弓 ヨ 彑 9【彡】 彳

刻版 *chōkokuban* an engraving
刻物 *chōkokubutsu* an engraving; a carving; a statue
刻界 *chōkokukai* sculpture circles
刻師 *chōkokushi* engraver; carver
刻家 *chōkokuka* engraver; carver
刻術 *chōkokujutsu* sculpture; engraving; the plastic art
12 琢 *chōtaku* carving and polishing
13 塑 *chōso* carving and modeling
塑術 *chōjutsu* the plastic art
14 像 *chōzō* sculpture; carved statue, graven image

9

彭 1720 / J5745 / M10003 Hō swelling; sound of a drum; vigorous; prosperous.
12 湃 *hōhai(taru)* surging

11

B **彰** 1721 / J3e34 / M10015 SHŌ. *aki(rakana)* clear.
14 徳 *shōtoku suru* publicly praise

12

B **影** 1722 / J3146 / M10019 EI shadow. *kage* light; shadow; silhouette; phantom; reflection; figure; trace.
7 身 *kagemi ni* (in) a person's shadow
8 画 *kagee* silhouette
武者 *kagemusha* general's double; wirepuller; man behind the scenes
法師 *kagebōshi* shadow, shadowy figure, silhouette
12 絵 *kagee* silhouette
富士 *kage Fuji* Mt. Fuji's reflection; a cloud over Fuji's summit
14 像 *eizō* shadow, image, phantom
像崇拝 *eizō sūhai* image worship; iconolatry
16 薄 *kage (ga) usu(i)* emaciated
19 響 *eikyō* influence, effect, consequences
響力 *eikyōryoku* influence, effect, consequences
響下 *eikyōka ni* under the influence of

RAD. 彳 60

Gyōnimben (a left-hand element like the first part of Rad. 144 *gyō,* the "going" radical, but used only at the left like Rad. 9 *nimben* left-hand "man"; hence, the "going man" radical). All characters historically treated under Rad. 144 行 are, with the exception of the radical character itself, treated herein as Rad. 60. Nickname: Going Man.

彳 1723 / J5746 / M10037 TEKI. *tatazu(mu)* stop, linger, loiter.

3

征 1724 / J-X / M-X Nonstandard for 衛 1776.

4

彷 1725 / J5747 / M10052 Hō. *samayo(u)* wander around, stray, loiter.
8 彿 *hōfutsu suru* closely resemble
12 徨 *hōkō* wandering, fluctuation, variation. *urotsu(ku)* loiter, putter, prowl, knock around. *urouro* loiteringly, in confusion

A **役** 1726 / J4c72 / M10057 EKI war, campaign, battle, expedition; exacted unpaid labor. YAKU office, post, position, appointment, duty; role; use, service, help. *eki(suru)* employ, enlist the services of, press into service.
2 人 *yakunin* official, officer, office holder
人風 *yakunin kaze* official bearing, official dignity
人根性 *yakunin konjō* official bearing
4 牛 *ekigyū* work cattle
夫 *ekifu* laborer, coolie
不足 *yakubusoku* dissatisfaction with one's lot
5 立 *yakuda(teru), yakuda(tsu), yaku (ni) ta(tsu)* be useful, be helpful, serve the purpose
付 *yakuzu(ke)* allotment of duties; role.

yakuzu(ki) responsible person; assuming office
目 *yakume* duty, office, business, role
目柄 *yakumegara de* by virtue of office
6 回 *yakumawa(ri)* part, burden, responsibility
向 *yakumu(ki)* nature of one's office, one's position
宅 *yakutaku* official residence
名 *yakumei* official title
8 者 *ekisha* servant, emissary; church worker, minister. *yakusha* actor, actress, performer, official
所 *yakusho* government office
所仕事 *yakusho shigoto* bureaucracy, red tape
所式 *yakushoshiki* red tape, departmentalism
所風 *yakushofū* red tape, departmentalism
9 柄 *yakugara* nature of one's office, one's position
10 員 *yakuin* officer, official, person in charge; board, staff
員会 *yakuinkai* board meeting
11 得 *yakutoku* the extra emoluments of office
務 *ekimu* labor, service
12 場 *yakuba* city hall, a public office
割 *yakuwa(ri)* allotment of duties; role
替 *yakuga(e)* change of post
13 僧 *yakusō* temple sexton; officiating priest; assistant priest
14 徳 *yakutoku* emolument, excess remuneration, privileges incidental to an office
15 儀 *yakugi* duty, office, business, role

5

祇 1727 / J-X / M10069 See **低** 166.

徂 1728 / J5749 / M10078 So go.

彿 1729 / J574a / M10071 **髴** 6806 / J717c / M45414 Futsu dimly.

A **径** 1730 / J3742 / M10080′ **徑** 1743 / J574d / M10118 Kei path; diameter; method. *michi* road, path, lane, way, street, highway, route; journey; distance; course, way, means; duty, morality, moral doctrine; teachings; specialty; an art; reason, justice.
6 行 *keikō* going around; developments
10 庭 *keitei* the great difference between individuals
13 路 *keiro* course, route, channel

B **征** 1731 / J402c / M10077 Sei. *sei(suru)* attack the rebellious; collect taxes.
5 圧 *seiatsu* control, conquest
6 衣 *seii* military uniform; traveling garb
伏 *seifuku* conquest, subjugation; mastery, overcoming
伐 *seibatsu* subjection, conquest; chastisement, punishment, extermination
夷 *seii* pacifying the barbarians
夷大将軍 *Seii Taishogun* Commander-in-Chief of the Expeditionary Force Against the Barbarians
8 服 *seifuku* conquest, subjugation; mastery, overcoming
服者 *seifukusha* conqueror, overcomer
服欲 *seifukuyoku* an ambition to have others carry out one's ideas
9 途 *seito* military expedition; journey, travel
客 *seikaku* traveler
10 馬 *seiba* steed; war horse; traveler's horse
討 *seitō* subjection, conquest; chastisement, punishment, extermination
討軍 *seitōgun* expeditionary force
11 略 *seiryaku* conquest, subjugation
13 戦 *seisen* going off to war
14 塵 *seijin* cavalry dust; road dust; travel
18 韓 *seikan* invasion of Korea

B **彼** 1732 / J4860 / M10066 Hi he; that. *kare* he. *ka(no), a(no)* that, the. *are* that, that time. *are(demo)* in a way, in spite of appearances, as it is.
3 女 *kanojo* she; girl friend
丈 *aredake* that much
4 氏 *kareshi* he; beau, lover
切 *are(k)ki(ri), aregi(ri), areki(ri)* since that time; only that much
方 *anata, kanata, achi, atchi, achira* that; the other; the other side; there,

3 口囗土士夂夊夕大女子宀寸小⺌尢尸屮山川巛工已巾干幺广廴廾弋弓⺕彑彡【彳】5

yonder; foreign country. *atchi* Get out of here.
方任 *anatamaka(se)* letting things slide
方此方 *anata-konata, achikochi, achira-kochira* here and there, to and fro, fore and aft
5 処 *asuko, asoko, kashiko* yonder, over there, that place
奴 *aitsu, ayatsu, kyatsu, kayatsu* that fellow, that guy
世 *a(no)yo* the next world
6 地 *ka(no)chi* that land
此 *are kore, kare kore, are(ya)-kore(ya)* this and that, one thing or another
7 我 *higa* oneself and others, each other
8 者誰時 *kawataredoki* dawn
岸 *higan* equinoctial week; Buddhist services during equinoctial week; the other shore; goal
岸桜 *higanzakura* early-flowering ⌈cherry
9 是 *are-kore* this or that
12 程 *arehodo* so much, to that extent
等 *karera* they

A **往** 1733 / J317d / M10073 **徃** 1734 / J5748 / M10074 Ō. *ina(su)* let go; chase away. *yuki* going; travel. *yu(ku)* go; run (water).
4 日 *ōjitsu* ancient times
5 古 *ōko* ancient times
生 *ōjō* death, submission. *ōjō suru* be at one's wit's end
生際 *ōjōgiwa* the point of death
6 返 *yu(ki)kae(ri)* round trip
交 *yukikai* coming and going; street traffic; swing (of a pendulum); social intercourse
年 *ōnen* years ago, formerly, the years past
7 来 *yukiki, ōrai* coming and going; street traffic; road, street, highway, boulevard; fluctuations; correspondence, association; occurring to the mind
来止 *ōraido(me)* No Thoroughfare, Road Closed
8 往 *ōō* sometimes, occasionally, often
券 *ōken* the going half of a round-trip ticket
昔 *ōjaku, ōseki* ancient times
者 *ōsha* the past
事 *ōji* the past, past events
9 信 *ōshin* first half of a reply card
10 時 *ōji* ancient times
航 *ōkō* outward voyage
帰 *yu(ki)kae(ri)* round trip
11 訪 *ōhō* visit, interview
12 診 *ōshin* doctor's visit, house call
復 *ōfuku* round trip; correspondence; association
復切符 *ōfuku kippu* return ticket
復運動 *ōfuku undō* reciprocating motion
復葉書 *ōfuku hagaki* return postcard
復爆撃 *ōfuku bakugeki* shuttle raid
13 路 *ōro* outward journey
15 還 *yu(ki)kae(ri), ōkan* traffic, coming and going, round trip; highway

6

徇 1735 / J574e / M10091 JUN. SHUN proclaim; manage; seek; broad; submit. *tona(eru)* proclaim, announce widely. *shitaga(u)* follow, obey; observe (regulations; submit).

很 1736 / J574c / M10093 KON. GON go against; dispute; very. *moto(ru)* go against, run contrary to.

徉 1737 / J-X / M10094 YŌ wander.

徊 1738 / J574b / M10095 KAI wandering.

衍 1739 / J5e27 / M34033 EN overflowing. [行]
4 文 *embun* pleonasm, redundancy
6 字 *enji* superfluous character
13 義 *engi* expansion, amplification; commentary, adaptation

A **律** 1740 / J4e27 / M10097 RICHI, RITSU law, regulation; rhythm. *ris(suru)* judge, settle, gauge, control. *Ritsu* Buddhist sect originating in the eighth century.
4 文 *ritsubun* the provisions of law; poetry
5 令 *ritsuryō* ancient laws. *ritsurei* national laws
8 例 *ritsurei* ordinance, criminal law

法 *rippō* law, rule, legislation; Law of God
法主義 *rippō shugi* legalism
法学者 *rippō gakusha* scribe, lawyer
10 格 *ritsukaku* a rule, versification, metrical scheme
11 動 *ritsudō* rhythm, rhythmic movement, periodic motion
13 義 *richigi* honesty, integrity, simplicity, sincerity, loyalty
義者 *richigimono* honest and industrious man
14 語 *ritsugo* poetic verse
15 儀者 *richigimono* honest and industrious man

A **待** 1741 / J4254 / M10085 TAI waiting. *ma(tsu) vi* and *vt* wait, wait for; expect, watch for; depend on; treat, deal with. *ma(chiagumu)* be tired of waiting. *ma(tta)* hold on, not ready. *ma(taseru)* detain, keep waiting.
2 人 *ma(chi)bito* expected visitor
4 伏 *ma(chi)bu(seru)* lie in wait for
合 *ma(chi)-a(u)* wait for each other. *ma(chi)-a(waseru)* waiting at a set time. *machiai* tea-ceremony waiting room; geisha entertainment place
合所 *machiaijo* rendezvous; waiting booth
合室 *machiaishitsu* waiting room
8 侘 *ma(chi)-wa(biru)* be tired of waiting
明 *ma(chi) a(kasu)* wait all night
命 *taimei* awaiting orders; being put on the waiting list
受 *ma(chi)-u(keru)* await, expect
9 草臥 *ma(chi)-kutabi(reru)* be tired of waiting
10 倦 *ma(chi)-agu(mu), ma(chi)-a(kiru)* be tired of waiting
針 *ma(chi)bari* marking pin
兼 *ma(chi)-ka(neru)* wait impatiently for
時間 *ma(chi)jikan* waiting time
11 遇 *taigū* treatment, reception, entertainment, (hotel) service; salary, remuneration; rank
惚 *ma(chi)-bo(ke), ma(chi)-bō(ke)* wait in vain
設 *ma(chi)-mō(keru)* expect, wait expectantly for
望 *ma(chi)-nozo(mu)* look for, wait eagerly for. *taibō* expectant waiting
12 遠 *ma(chi)dō(shii), machidō(i)* being long in coming; waiting anxiously for
焦 *ma(chi)-ko(gareru)* wait eagerly for
無 *ma(tta)na(shi)de* without waiting
14 厭 *ma(chi)-agu(mu)* be tired of waiting
構 *ma(chi)-kama(eru)* watch for, wait eagerly for, be prepared for
網 *ma(chi)ami* set net
暮 *ma(chi)-ku(rasu)* wait all day for
15 避 *taihi* shunting (in railroading); taking shelter; escaping
避線 *taihisen* siding, sidetrack
避壕 *taihigō* dugout, shelter, trench
機 *taiki suru* watch and wait, stand by, wait for a chance

A **後** 1742 / J3865 / M10098 GO, KŌ back, rear, behind. *ato* back, rear; results; remainder, sequel; posterity; successor; survivor; effect, influence; estate. *ato no* back, rear, posterior; previous, last; later, subsequent; next, following; future. *ato ni* after, behind, back, backward; ago; next. *oku(rasu), oku(raseru)* retard, delay, defer. *oku(re)* failure, defeat; backwardness, shyness, fear. *oku(reru)* be late, be delayed, be overdue; lag behind; (clocks) lose. *ushi(ro)* back, rear, behind. *ushiro(metai)* underhanded, suspicious. *nochi* after, since then; future; after one's death. *go* after, afterwards, later on, since, hence.
2 人 *kōjin* posterity, future generations
3 口 *atokuchi* aftertaste; remainder; a later turn, engagement, or appointment
山 *atoyama* miner's helper
千両 *ushi(ro) senryō* the beauty of a woman seen from the back
4 手 *ushi(ro)de* (tied with) hands behind the back. *gote* passivity
厄 *atoyaku* year following one's critical year
片付 *atokatazu(ke)* clearing up, putting things in order
日 *gojitsu, gonichi* later on, some other day later on
日談 *gojitsudan* reminiscences, recollections

方 *kōhō, shirie, atokata* rear, back. *nochikata* later
方部隊 *kōhō butai* rear guards
方勤務 *kōhō kimmu* the home front
天 *kōten* results of environment
天性 *kōtensei* characteristics acquired from one's environment
天性免疫不全症候群 *kōtensei men'eki fuzen shōkōgun* acquired immune deficiency syndrome
天的 *kōtenteki* acquired, cultivated
5 代 *kōdai* future generations, posterity
払 *atobara(i)* deferred payment
半 *kōhan* latter half
世 *kōsei, nochi (no) yo* coming age; last days, posterity. *gose, nochi (no) yo* the next world, the future life
弁天 *ushiro benten* beauty of a woman seen from the back
仕舞 *atojimai* clearing up, winding up, selling out
生 *kōsei* being born later; younger people. *goshō* the future life
生大事 *goshō daiji ni* religiously, earnestly, carefully
半生 *kōhansei* latter half of life
半期 *kōhanki* latter half of a year
半戦 *kōhansen* latter half of a game
6 回 *atomawa(shi)* postponement
向 *ushi(ro)mu(ki)* looking backward
列 *kōretsu* rear, back row
灯 *kōtō* taillight
合 *ushi(ro)a(wase) ni* back to back
光 *gokō* halo, corona
先 *atosaki* front and rear; first and last; both ends; context; circumstances, consequences. *atosaki ni suru* reverse, invert
年 *kōnen* in later years, afterward
任 *kōnin* successor
任難 *kōninnan* difficulty in finding an heir
7 足 *atoashi, ushi(ro) ashi* hind leg
身 *kōshin* one's future rebirth; a successor organization
図 *kōto* plans for the future
序 *kōjo* postscript to a book
戻 *atomodo(ri)* going backward, retrogression
述 *kōjutsu suru* state hereafter
作 *atosaku* second crop
役 *atoyaku* successor
来 *kōrai* the future
見 *kōken, ushi(ro)mi* guardianship; assistance
見人 *kōkennin* guardian, tutor, assistant
車 *kōsha* rear car; rear wheel; gun carriage
車軸 *kōshajiku* rear axle
尾 *kōbi* rear, tail
尾灯 *kōbitō* taillight
8 金 *atokin, atogane* balance of payment
門 *kōmon* back gate; back door
送 *kōsō suru* send to the rear; send later
退 *atozusa(ri), atoshiza(ri), atojisa(ri)* falling back, drawing back. *kōtai* retreat
味 *atoaji* aftertaste
押 *atoo(shi)* pushing, backing, boosting
明 *ushi(ro) aka(ri)* a light from the back
板 *ushi(ro) ita* backboard (of a wagon)
肢 *kōshi* hind legs
刻 *gokoku* later on, afterward
夜 *goya* from midnight to morning
命 *kōmei* further instructions
昆 *kōkon* descendants, posterity
妻 *gosai* second wife
学 *kōgaku* younger scholars; younger generation; knowledge to be available in the future
者 *kōsha* the latter
始末 *atoshimatsu* settlement, liquidation, clearing up
知恵 *atojie* hindsight
事 *kōji* future affairs; affairs after one's death
事託 *kōji (o) taku(su)* entrust all to someone when dying
9 面 *kōmen* back side (of something)
首 *ushiro kubi* the back of the head
胤 *kōin* descendant, scion
便 *kōbin* next mail
後 *atoato* distant future. *nochinochi* distant future; future life
咲 *oku(re)za(ki)* late blossoms
悔 *kōkai* repentance, remorse
指 *ushi(ro) yubi* bird's hind toe; finger of scorn
陣 *gojin, kōjin* rear guard
段 *kōdan* latter part (of a story)
前 *ushi(ro)-mae* with front side back
軍 *kōgun* rear guard
室 *kōshitsu* widow; widow of a noble
姿 *ushi(ro) sugata* retreating figure, appearance from the back

架 *kōka* toilet
思案 *atojian* afterthought
奏 *kōsō* postlude
奏曲 *kōsōkyoku* postlude
10 庭 *kōtei* back yard or garden
逸 *kōitsu suru* fumble (a ball)
流 *kōryū* slip stream
祓 *atobarai* cleansing a room after the coffin has left
記 *kōki* postscript
宮 *kōkyū* imperial consort; harem; palace
家 *goke* the bereaved family, widow, widowhood
害 *kōgai* later damage
釜 *atogama* successor
窄 *atosuboma(ri)* narrower and smaller at the end
書 *atoga(ki)* postscript. *kōsho* sequel to a book
部 *kōbu* rear, stern, back part
部灯 *kōbutō* taillight
進 *kōshin* retreat, moving backward; younger generation
進地域 *kōshin chiiki* undeveloped areas
進性 *kōshinsei no* backward
進国 *kōshinkoku* backward country
進諸国 *kōshin shokoku* backward nations
11 清 *atogiyo(me)* cleansing a room after the coffin has left
添 *nochizo(i)* second wife
略 *kōryaku* omitting the last part of an article
脚 *atoashi* hind legs
産 *kōsan, atozan, nochizan* afterbirth, placenta
患 *kokan* seeds of trouble; a future worry
祭 *ato (no) matsu(ri)* too late for the fair, too late for the doctor
12 場 *goba* afternoon market session
項 *kōkō* following clause
棒 *atobō* rear palanquin bearer
程 *nochihodo* later on
期 *kōki* latter period; late (Nara); latter half year; second semester
景 *kōkei* setting, background
葉 *kōyō* posterity, future generations; the latter days of an era
替 *atogawa(ri)* successor
装 *kōsō* breech-loading
報 *kōhō* later report, further information
援 *kōen* assistance, support, backing
援会 *kōenkai* supporters' association
援者 *kōensha* backer, supporter, patron, sponsor
13 園 *kōen* back yard
暗 *ushi(ro)gura(i)* shady, underhanded, suspicious, secretive
楯 *ushi(ro)date* backing, support, protection; backer, supporter
腹 *atobara* afterpains; child by second wife
詰 *gozu(me)* rear guard
馳 *oku(re)base* eleventh hour, last minute
幕 *atomaku* next; next job
裔 *kōei* descendants
嗣 *kōshi* heir, successor
鉢巻 *ushi(ro) hachimaki* head band tied behind
置詞 *kōchishi* postposition
続 *kōzoku no* succeeding, following
続年度 *kōzoku nendo* the following fiscal year
継 *kōkei* succession; successor, heir
継内閣 *kōkei naikaku* incoming cabinet
継者 *kōkeisha* successor, heir
14 腐 *atokusa(re)* trouble afterward
聞 *kōbun* later information
塵 *kōjin* second best; subordination; second best; second fiddle; dust raised after vehicles
髪 *ushi(ro)gami* the hair at the back of the head
15 衛 *kōei* rear guard
編 *kōhen* later volume
輪 *atowa, kōrin* back wheel
影 *ushi(ro) kage* retreating figure, appearance from the back
憂 *kōyū* future worry
篇 *kōhen* last volume, later volumes, last part of the book; sequel
輩 *kōhai* younger men; younger generation; one's juniors
賢 *kōken* wise men of the future
16 頭 *kōtō* back of the head
頭部 *kōtōbu* back of the head
頸部 *kōkeibu* nape of the neck
17 輿 *atogashi* rear palanquin bearer
療法 *kōryōhō* after treatment
18 難 *gonan, kōnan* future trouble, consequences
21 顧 *kōko* looking back; anxiety

口 囗 土 士 夂 夊 夕 大 女 子 宀 寸 小 ⺌ 尢 尸 屮 山 川 巛 工 己 巾 干 幺 广 廴 廾 弋 弓 ヨ 彑 彡 【彳】7

徑 1743 / J574d / M10118 See 径 1730.

B 徐 1744 / J3d79 / M10110 Jo. *omomu(ro) ni* slowly, deliberately, gently.
[3] 行 *jokō suru* go slowly
[8] 歩 *joho* walking slowly
[10] 徐 *jojo ni*, *sorosoro* gradually, steadily, slowly; quietly
[14] 漕 *josō suru* paddle, row slowly

A 従 1745 / J3d3e / M10133 從 1747 / J574f / M10152 Shō. Ju. Jū secondary, incidental, subordinate, accessory, junior; retainer; follow. *shitaga(u)* obey, submit to, comply with, observe (a law); follow; accompany. *shitaga(eru)* be accompanied by, take (someone) with you; subjugate, subdue. *shitaga(tte)* consequently, therefore; in accordance with, in proportion to, as. *ju-* junior or second (in court ranks).
[3] 士 *jūshi* attendant, retainer
[5] 犯 *jūhan* accomplice; complicity
兄 *jūkei* elder male cousin
兄弟 *itoko*, *jūkeitei* male cousin
[6] 行 *shitaga(i)-yu(ku)* go after, follow after
因 *jūin* secondary cause
[7] 兵 *jūhei* guards
弟 *jūtei* younger male cousin
来 *jūrai* heretofore; existing
[8] 妹 *jūmai* younger female cousin
物 *jūbutsu* accessory (in law)
卒 *jūsotsu* servant of a soldier
者 *jūsha* follower, attendant, valet, retinue, servant
事 *jūji suru* engage in, carry on, practice medicine
姉 *jūshi* elder female cousin
姉妹 *jūshimai*, *itoko* female cousin
[9] 前 *jūzen ni* heretofore. *jūzen no* previous, former
軍 *jūgun suru* follow the army; join the colors
軍記者 *jūgun kisha* war correspondent
軍記章 *jūgun kishō* war medal
[10] 容 *shōyō(taru)* composed, calm, tranquil
[11] 婢 *jūhi* servant woman
[12] 順 *jūjun na* submissive, obedient, docile, gentle, meek, tame, pliant, amenable
量税 *jūryōzei* specific duty
属 *jūzoku* subordination; dependency
属文 *jūzoku bun* subordinate clause
属的 *jūzokuteki* subordinate, dependent
属節 *jūzoku setsu* subordinate clause
[13] 業 *jūgyō suru* be employed; resume work
業者 *jūgyōsha* employee
業員 *jūgyōin* employee, working force
[14] 僕 *jūboku* attendant male servant
[15] 横 *jūō* length and breadth; every direction; right and left; warp and woof
[18] 騎 *jūki* followers on horseback

A 徒 1746 / J454c / M10121 To party, set, gang, companions; people. *ada* emptiness, vanity, futility, uselessness, faithlessness, ephemeral thing. *itazura* vanity; uselessness. *itazu(ra)ni* in vain, uselessly, aimlessly. *tada*, *tadano* free, gratis. *tada(naranu)* unusual, extraordinary, serious. *tada* ordinarily. *ada(shi)* fickle, vain; another. *kachi* walking. *muda* futility, uselessness, waste. *kachi de* on foot.
[2] 人 *tadabito* common man. *adabito* fickle person. *kachibito* foot traveler
[3] 口 *adaguchi* unnecessary words. *mudaguchi* idle talk, nonsense
士 *kachi* foot soldier
[4] 心 *adagokoro* fickle heart
手 *toshu* empty-handed, penniless
手体操 *toshu taisō* calisthenics
手空拳 *toshukūken de* empty-handed; without capital
[5] 矢 *adaya* futile arrow shot
立 *kachida(chi)* setting out on foot
広 *dada(p)piro(i)*, *dadabiro(i)* tremendously broad
[6] 行 *tokō* going afoot
死 *toshi suru* die in vain. *toshi* a dog's death
刑 *tokei* penal servitude, prison term
名 *adana* rumor about a romance
[7] 言 *mudagoto* useless words
走 *kachibashi(ri)* running on foot
足 *mudaashi suru* go on a fruitless errand
身 *tada(naranu) mi* pregnant woman
花 *adabana* an abortive flower
労 *torō* wasted effort, lost labor

弟 *totei* apprenticeship; apprentice; errand boy
弟制度 *totei seido* apprentice system
弟学校 *totei gakkō* apprentice school
弟教育 *totei kyōiku* education of apprentices
弟期間 *totei kikan* apprenticeship term
弟養成 *totei yōsei* apprenticeship training
8 波 *adanami* noisy wave
物 *adamono* useless thing, fleeting thing
者 *tadamono* ordinary person
事 *tadagoto, adagoto* useless thing, fleeting thing, trivial matter
武者 *kachimusha* foot soldier
歩 *toho, kachi* walking
歩兵 *tohohei* foot soldier
歩者 *tohosha* pedestrian
歩連絡 *toho renraku* a transfer involving a walk
歩旅行 *toho ryokō* hiko, hiking, walking tour
歩旅行者 *toho ryokōsha* foot traveler
歩競走 *toho kyōsō* walking race
9 食 *toshoku* life of idleness
10 骨 *mudabone* fruitless effort, useless endeavor
桜 *adazakura* ephemeral cherry flowers
党 *totō* conspirators; conspiracy; faction, junta
荷 *kachini* foot traveler's baggage
11 渉 *kachiwata(ri), toshō* fording
12 疎 *adaorosoka ni* (think) light (of).
adaorosoka na careless
雲 *adagumo* fleeting cloud
然 *tsurezure, tozen* tedium, leisure hours
費 *tohi* waste
13 路 *kachiji* going afoot; the road one travels afoot
跣 *kachihadashi* going barefooted
夢 *adayume* idle dream
業 *adawaza* some other thing; useless thing
14 爾 *toji* something worthless or meaningless
15 論 *toron* worthless argument
輩 *tohai* group, set, fellows

8

從 1747 J574f M10152 See **従** 1745.

徠 1748 J5752 M10155 See **来** 2565.

徙 1749 J5750 M10142 SHI *utsu(ru)* move; change, shift; spread. *utsu(su)* transfer, move.

徛 1750 J-X M10148 KI cross over.

徜 1751 J-X M10149 SHŌ wander.
9 徉 *shōyō* wandering

徘 1752 J5751 M10141 HAI wander.
9 徊 *haikai* loitering, sauntering

衒 1753 J6a4a M34045 GEN. *tera(u)* show off, parade, display; pretend, feign. [行]
6 気 *genki* affectation, ostentation, vanity
8 学 *gengaku* pedantry, display of learning

A **術** 1754 J3d51 M34046' JUTSU art, technique, skill; means; artifice, trick, stratagem; resources; magic, conjury. *sube* way, means, resource. [行]
4 中 *jutchū* trick, trap
8 知 *jutchi* wisdom and accomplishments
者 *jutsusha* witch, magician, conjuror
9 計 *jukkei* stratagem, ruse, trick
12 策 *jussaku* artifice, stratagem, trick, intrigue, policy
無 *subena(shi), jutsuna(i)* nothing can be done
13 数 *jussū* artifice, stratagem, trick, intrigue, policy
14 語 *jutsugo* technical term, terminology

A **得** 1755 J4640 M10137 TOKU profit, advantage, benefit. *e(ru), u(ru)* get, acquire, find, earn, win, gain, receive; can, be able to, may; commit (sin). *e(tagaru)* covet, have a desire for. *toku(suru)* gain, save; benefit. *e(tari)* fine, excellent. *e(te)* being apt to.
4 分 *tokubun* profits, winnings, one's share
心 *tokushin* consent; conviction; satisfaction
心尽 *tokushinzu(ku)* mutual consent

手 *ete* strong point, specialty, forte
手物 *etemono* one's specialty
手勝手 *etegatte, etekatte* selfishness, wilfulness
5 失 *tokushitsu* pros and cons, gains and losses, desirability
7 言 *e(mo)-i(warenu)* indescribable, unspeakable, indefinable, exquisite
体 *etai* nature, character
8 物 *emono* weapon
易 *eyasu(i)* easily obtainable
9 度 *tokudo suru* enter the (Buddhist) priesthood
点 *tokuten* marks, score, runs
点掲示板 *tokuten keijiban* scoreboard
11 道 *tokudō* attainment of (Buddhist) salvation.
得 *tokutoku(toshite)* proudly, triumphantly
票 *tokuhyō* votes obtained
票数 *tokuhyōsū* votes obtained
12 策 *tokusaku* profitable plan, good plan. *tokusaku na* advisable, wise, expedient
喪 *tokusō* gaining and losing
13 業士 *tokugyōshi* special-school graduate
意 *tokui(garu)* be elated. *tokui* prosperity; triumph, elation; strong point; customer, client
意回 *tokuimawa(ri)* calling on customers; traveling salesman
意気 *tokuige na* proud, elated
意先 *tokuisaki* customer, client; credit customer
意顔 *tokuigao* triumphant air
意満面 *tokui-mammen* pride
15 賢 *e(tari) kashiko(shi)* That's it! Wonderful! Just what I had hoped for. I was just waiting for this.
18 難 *egata(i)* rare, hard to get
顔 *e(tari)gao* look of triumph, proud face

9

徨 1756 / J5753 / M10178 Kō wandering.

徧 1757 / J-X / M10174 HEN revolve; everywhere.

B **循** 1758 / J3d5b / M10187 JUN follow.
4 吏 *junri* faithful official
15 環 *junkan* circulation, rotation, cycle
17 環期 *junkanki* cycle
環線 *junkansen* loop line
環論 *junkanron* circular reasoning, begging the question, vicious circle
環論証 *junkan ronshō* circular reasoning, begging the question, vicious circle

A **街** 1759 / J3339 / M34051 KAI. GAI street, avenue; town. *machi* town; quarters; street. [行]
3 上 *gaijō* street
6 灯 *gaitō* street light, road lamp
7 角 *machi kado* street corner
10 郭 *gaikaku* area between streets, a block
11 道 *kaidō, gaidō* highway
13 路 *gairo* road, street, avenue, arcade
路樹 *gairoju* shade tree, roadside tree
16 録 *gairoku* recorded street interview
頭 *gaitō* street
頭写真師 *gaitō shashinshi* pavement photographer
頭募金 *gaitō bokin* street solicitation
頭演説 *gaitō enzetsu* street speech
頭録音 *gaitō rokuon* recorded street interview

A **復** 1760 / J497c / M10183 FUKU. *fuku(suru)* return to, revert to, be restored to, resume (one's duties); revenge; reward. *mata, mata to* again.
4 文 *fukubun* translating classical Japanese back into classical Chinese
氏 *fukushi* resumption of former name
円 *fukuen* end of an eclipse
仇 *fukkyū, fukukyū* revenge, reprisal
元 *fukugen* restoration to original state
5 旧 *fukkyū, fukukyū* recovery, restoration, restitution, rehabilitation
申 *fukushin* report
刊 *fukkan* reissue, revived publication
写 *matautsu(shi)* a recopy; copying again
古 *fukko* restoration, revival (of a former regime), reaction

古調 *fukkochō* trend toward old styles
6 任 *fukunin* reappointment, reinstatement
交 *fukkō* restoration of diplomatic relations
7 位 *fukui* restoration, rehabilitation, reinstatement, reinstallment
役 *fukueki* rejoining the colors
8 刻 *fukkoku* reproducing a book from identical plates
命 *fukumei* report
9 奏 *fukusō suru* reinvestigate and report to the throne
活 *fukkatsu* revival, rebirth, resuscitation, regeneration, resurrection
活祭 *Fukkatsusai* Easter
10 原 *fukugen* restoration (to original state)
校 *fukkō, fukukō* return to school, readmittance
祚 *fukuso* restoration to the throne
航 *fukkō* return voyage
配 *fukuhai* resumption of dividends
党 *fukutō* reinstatement in a party
書 *fukusho* a written answer
帰 *fukki* return, comeback, reinstatement, reversion
員 *fukuin* demobilization
員兵 *fukuinhei* demobilized soldier
員者 *fukuinsha* demobilized persons
11 唱 *fukushō suru* recite, rehearse; repeat (a command)
習 *fukushū* review. *sarai* review; rehearsal
12 復 *matamata* again, repeatedly
答 *fukutō* reply, response
13 辟 *fukuheki* restoration of a ruler
路 *fukuro* return trip
業 *fukugyō suru* return to work
14 読 *fukudoku* review
誦 *fukushō suru* recite, rehearse; repeat (a command)
15 権 *fukken, fukuken* reinstatement, rehabilitation, restoration of rights
縁 *fukuen* restoring marital or other relations
調 *fukuchō* a comeback
16 興 *fukkō* revival, resuscitation, resurgence, restoration, rehabilitation, a comeback, renaissance
18 職 *fukushoku* reinstatement, resumption of office, reappointment
20 籍 *fukuseki* reinstating as a member; returning to original domicile
23 讎 *fukushū* revenge, reprisal, retaliation
讐 *fukushū* revenge, reprisal, retaliation

B 御 1761 / J3866 / M10157 Go honorific prefix. Gyo imperial honorary prefix. prefix. *gyo(suru)* control, manage, manipulate, govern; handle; drive (a cart). *o-, on-, mi-* honorific prefixes.
1 一新 *goisshin* Meiji restoration
2 八 *oyatsu* eating between meals
力 *michikara* power of God
人好 *ohitoyo(shi)* easily duped
七夜 *oshichiya* seventh day after birth
3 子 *miko* children of the king; Son of God, Christ
三家 *Gosanke* Three Tokugawa Branches
大 *ontai* boss, governor, general
大葬 *gotaisō* imperial funeral
下 *osa(ge)* hair hanging down the back
下問 *gokamon* emperor's question
上 *okami* emperor, government, authorities; a noble; hostess at a restaurant
上様 *okamisan* wife, madame. *onobo(ri)san* visitor from the country
4 心 *mikokoro* God's will, God's purpose
方 *mikata* friend, ally, supporter. *onkata* person (polite)
水 *omizu* water; holy water
中 *onchū* and Company; Messrs.
互 *otagai ni* mutually, together
尤 *gomotto(mo)* quite right, reasonable
不浄 *gofujō* lavatory, toilet, latrine, comfort station
太鼓 *otaiko* professional jester; drum; the puffed-out bow (of an obi); flattery
日様 *ohisama* the sun
月様 *otsukisama* the moon
父様 *otōsama, otōsan* father

引摺 *ohikizuri* trailing skirt; immoral woman
手 *mite* the hand of God
手玉 *otedama* jackstones; bean bags
手打 *oteu(chi)* a lord killing his retainer
手洗 *mitarashi* holy water at a shrine. *oteara(i)* toilet, lavatory; washstand
手許金 *otemotokin* privy purse
5 代 *miyo* reign, period
札 *ofuda* Shinto talisman
汁 *otsuke* the broth of cooked dishes
礼 *orei* salutation, salute, bow, courtesy, propriety, ceremony, thanks, appreciation, remuneration, return present
包 *okuru(mi), otsutsu(mi)* child's quilt
民 *mitami* people of the king
世 *miyo* reign, period
台所 *midaidokoro* nobleman's wife
付武官 *otsuki bukan* aide, military attache
玉 *otama* egg; tadpole
玉杓子 *otamajakushi* tadpole, wooden tablespoon
生大事 *goshōdaiji ni* zealously
生憎様 *oainikusama* I am sorry.
出 *oide* (polite) coming; going; being
出来 *odeki* rash, eruption
出座 *odemashi* going out, visiting; presence
出御出 *oide-oide* said beckoning to a person to come
召 *ome(shi) ni naru* ride; call (someone); wear
召列車 *ome(shi) ressha* train for royalty
召物 *ome(shi)mono* clothes
召替 *ome(shi)ka(e)* changing cars; changing clothes
召縮緬 *ome(shi) chirimen* striped crepe
召艦 *ome(shi)kan* imperial flagship
目文字 *omemoji* meeting someone
目玉 *omedama* scolding, reprimand
目目 *omeme* the eye (child's word)
目出度 *omedeta(i)* happy, auspicious. *omedetō* congratulations
目通 *omedō(ri)* an audience (with), interview; presence
目掛 *ome(ni)ka(karu)* meet (someone). *ome(ni)ka(keru)* show someone (something)
用 *goyō* your order; your business; official business; king's business
用地 *goyōchi* imperial estate
用邸 *goyōtei* detached palace, imperial villa
用始 *goyō haji(me)* reopening of offices after New Year's
用納 *goyō osa(me)* year-end office closing
用達 *goyōtashi* purveyors to the government
用掛 *goyōgakari* Imperial Household official
用商人 *goyō shōnin* purveyor to the government
用組合 *goyō kumiai* company union
用新聞 *goyō shimbun* government newspaper
6 血 *onchi* blood (polite); the blood of Christ
衣 *gyoi* imperial clothes
好 *okono(mi) no* favorite, requested
旨 *mimune* nobleman's will; God's will
字 *on(no)ji* enough
守 *omamori* a charm
宇 *gyou* imperial reign
先 *osaki* the future. *osaki e, osaki ni* (go) ahead of me; first. *onsaki* one who walked before a noble
存 *gozon(ji)* your acknowledgment; your knowledge; your acquaintance, your awareness
自身 *gojishin* himself, herself
百度 *ohyakudo* circling a shrine 100 times
当家 *gotōke* your house, your family
気色 *mikeshiki* view (polite)
気毒様 *oki(no)dokusama* I am sorry.
朱印 *goshuin* shogun's sealed letter
朱印船 *goshuinsen* shogunate-licensed ship
多分 *gotabun* friend of the majority
多忙中 *gotabōchū* while you were so busy
名 *mina* God's name. *gyomei* emperor's name, imperial signature
名御爾 *gyomeigyoji* imperial seal, privy seal
7 言 *mikotoba* God's Word, the Bible. *mikoto* words of a ruler
身 *omi, ommi* you (familiar)
位 *mikurai* the throne
決 *okima(ri)* usage, custom, routine
社 *miyashiro* shrine

告 *mitsuge, otsuge* oracle, message
忍 *oshino(bi)* traveling incognito
陀仏 *odabutsu* dead person
来光 *goraikō* mountain-top sunrise viewing; mountain-top sunrise
沙汰 *gosata* words of a ruler
杓文字 *oshamoji* ladle, dipper, scoop
足労様 *Gosokurōsama* You have gone to much trouble.
見外 *omiso(re)* failure to recognize
見知置 *omishi(ri)o(ki)* meeting you
伽 *otogi* keeping (a person) company; nursing (a patient)
伽国 *otogi(no)kuni* fairyland
声 *mikoe* your voice; the voice of God
声掛 *okoega(kari)* command, recommendation
8 金 *okane* money
門 *mikado* emperor, palace gate
使 *mitsuka(i)* angel; messenger
抱 *okaka(e)* one's personal attendant (chauffeur, doctor, etc.)
杯 *gyohai* cup (polite); emperor's cup
物 *gyobutsu* imperial property
参 *omai(ri)* visiting a shrine or temple
幸 *miyuki, gokō* visit or attendance of an emperor
苑 *gyoen* imperial garden
免 *gomen* your pardon; declining (something); dismissal; permission; licensed, chartered. *gomen nasai* Pardon me.
者 *gyosha* driver, coachman, bus driver
事 *onkoto* thing (honorific); you
虎子 *omaru* bedpan, pot (familiar)
乳母 *omba* wet nurse
法度 *gohatto* law, ordinance; prohibition
国 *mikuni* heavenly kingdom; our country
国風 *mikuniburi* Japanese manners; Japanese literature
供 *otomo suru* accompany. *osona(e)* *goku, gokū* an offering
供料 *gokuryō* votive offering
所 *gosho* an old imperial palace
所車 *goshoguruma* (ancient) ox carriage
9 拾 *ohiro(i)* walking, hiking
柳 *gyoryū* tamarisk
冠 *okammuri* displeasure
負 *oma(ke)* something extra, embellishment, exaggeration. *oma(ke) ni* furthermore
通夜 *otsuya, otsūya* a wake
為倒 *otamegoka(shi)* cheating under pretense of kindness
星様 *ohoshisama* the stars
持 *omo(tase)* gift
持物 *omota(se)mono* gift
神火 *gojinka* the fires of the gods (in volcanoes)
神酒 *omiki* sacred wine, wine offering
前 *mimae* before (God). *omae* you; Hey there you. *gozen* before a noble; you (polite); (an ancient) term of address for a titled lady
前会議 *gozen kaigi* imperial conference
10 悩 *gonō* your illness; the emperor's illness
株 *okabu* one's position; favorite trick; forte; characteristic
酒 *miki* sacred wine, wine offering. *goshu, osake* saké
酌 *oshaku* serving saké
陵 *goryō* imperial tomb
剣 *gyoken* emperor's sword
宴 *gyoen* court banquet
旅所 *otabisho* resting place for the sacred palanquin
宸筆 *goshimpitsu* imperial autograph
破算 *gohasan* recalculation; fresh start
真影 *goshin'ei* imperial portrait
蚕纏 *okaikoguru(mi)* silk attire
託 *gotaku* tedious talk; impertinent talk; oracle; stating something trivial as if important
託宣 *gotakusen* oracle; stating something trivial as if important
都合 *gotsugō* your convenience
都合主義 *gotsugō shugi* opportunism, time-serving
座 *mikura, mikurai, miza* imperial throne, God's throne. *gozaru, owashimasu* polite for *a(ru)*
座形 *ozanari* mere formality; a commonplace. *ozanari ni* in a perfunctory manner
座所 *gozasho* throne, imperial chamber, imperial seat
料 *goryō* imperial property
料地 *goryōchi* imperial estate
料林 *goryōrin* imperial forest
家人 *gokenin* a lower-grade retainer
家芸 *oiegei* specialty, monopoly

3 口 囗 土 士 夂 夊 夕 大 女 子 宀 寸 小 ⺌ 尢 尸 屮 山 川 巛 工 己 巾 干 幺 广 廴 廾 弋 弓 ヨ 彑 彡 9【彳】

家騒動 *oie sōdō* family quarrel
11 厠 *okawa* bedchamber
捻 *ohine(ri)* wrapped coin offering
経 *okyō* sutras
堂 *midō* main temple of a monastery
菜 *okazu* side dish
袋 *ofukuro* mama
曹子 *onzōshi* son of noble
転婆 *otemba* tomboy, flapper
猟場 *goryōba* imperial forest
遍路 *ohenro* pilgrimage
眼鏡 *omegane* (your) glasses; (your) judgment, discernment
12 裁可 *gosaika* imperial sanction
筆先 *ofudesaki* oracle
勤品 *otsuto(me)hin* bargain goods
無沙汰 *gobusata* neglect to get in touch with
偉方 *oeragata* dignitary
開 *ohira(ki)* adjournment, close
開山 *gokaisan* temple founder
詠 *gyoei* imperial poem
詠歌 *goeika* Buddhist pilgrimage hymn
飯 *gohan, omamma* boiled rice; a meal
飯炊 *gohantaki* rice cooking
飯時 *gohandoki* mealtime
飯蒸 *gohammu(shi)* warming up rice; rice steamer
13 飾 *okaza(ri)* divine ornaments; New Year's decorations; figurehead
数 *okazu* side dish
預 *oazu(ke)* wait (command to a dog); postponement
寝 *oyo(ru)* sleep. *gyoshin* the emperor's going to bed, going to sleep, or sleeping
感 *gyokan* imperial approval
業 *miwaza* the works of God
福分 *ofukuwa(ke)* sharing a gift
裾分 *osusowa(ke)* sharing a gift
馳走 *gochisō* entertainment, treat, feast, dinner, banquet, hospitality
新造 *goshinzō, goshinzo* wife of a prominent person; wife
稜威 *miitsu* virtue of the emperor, glory of the throne
愛想 *oaisō* hospitality; cuteness; (restaurant) bill; attachment
殿 *goten* palace; court; mansion, home of a noble
殿医 *goten'i* shogunate doctor
辞儀 *ojigi* bow, greeting; refusal, hesitation
辞儀戦術 *ojigi senjutsu* kowtowing strategy
跳 *oha(ne)* tomboy, flapper
跳様 *oha(ne)san* tomboy, flapper
陰 *okage* indebtedness, favor, help, support
陰様 *okagesama de* thanks to you
意 *gyoi* your will, your pleasure
意入 *gyoi (ni) i(ru)* to please
意得 *gyoi (o) e(tai)* want to meet; want someone's opinion
14 製 *gyosei* an emperor's poem or song
誓 *michika(i)* God's promises
歌会 *Outakai* Imperial Poetry Party
歌所 *Outadokoro* Imperial Poetry Bureau
髪 *ogushi* the hair (polite)
髪上 *ogushia(ge)* hairdressing (polite)
15 調 *mitsugi* tribute
諚 *gojō* command of a noble; emperor's message
慶 *gyokei* greetings, congratulations; joy
慶事 *gokeiji* imperial wedding, imperial birth
影 *gyoei* portrait of a noble
影石 *mikage ishi* granite
幣 *gohei* Shinto offerings of cloth, rope, or cut paper
幣担 *gohei-katsugi* superstitious person
霊 *mitama* departed spirit; Holy Spirit
霊代 *mitamashiro* symbol of the spirit of the deceased
霊屋 *mitamaya, otamaya* ancestral tomb, mausoleum
16 膳 *gozen* meal, rice, tray, low table
薦 *okomo* beggar
薩 *osatsu* sweet potato
覧 *goran ni naru* see, look, inspect; try (to do). *gorō(jiru)* see (polite)
親父 *goshimpu* your father
嬢様 *ojōsama, ojōsan* young lady, (your) daughter
17 講 *okō* Buddhist service
輿 *mikoshi* palanquin of a Shinto god
18 難 *gonan* calamity, misfortune
雛様 *ohinasama* festival dolls
題 *gyodai* theme of Imperial Poetry Contest
題目 *odaimoku* Nichiren prayer
19 鏡 *mikagami* sacred mirror (in a shrine)
璽 *gyoji* imperial seal, privy seal

簾 *misu* bamboo screen
21 饌 *gyosen, mike* offering to a god; food present to an emperor
22 籠 *okomo(ri)* praying all night in a shrine or temple
27 鬮 *mikuji* sacred lot, written oracle, divination

10

衕 1762 J-X M-X Nonstandard for **術** 1754.

徭 1763 J5754 M10201 Yō corvee, compulsory service, statute labor.

衙 1764 J6a4b M34061 GA government office. [行]

B **微** 1765 J4879 M10203 **微** 1766 J-X M-X BI, MI minuteness; insignificance; vagueness; fewness. *kasu(kana)* faint, dim, weak, indistinct, hazy, poor, wretched.
2 力 *biryoku* poor ability; the little one can do; slender means; little influence
3 才 *bisai* minor talent; my talents (humble)
小 *bishō* minuteness
小体 *bishōtai* granule, minute particle
4 少 *bishō* minute quantity
分 *bibun* differential calculus
分子 *bibunshi* atom; molecule; tiny particle
分学 *bibungaku* differential calculus
分積分学 *bibun-sekibungaku* differential and integral calculus
5 功 *bikō* minor achievement
生物 *biseibutsu* microscopic organism, microbe, germ
生物学 *biseibutsugaku* microbiology
6 行 *bikō* traveling incognito
光 *bikō* faint light, shimmer
7 吟 *bigin suru* hum
妙 *bimyō* delicacy, subtlety, nicety
志 *bishi* small ambition, my ambition
8 雨 *biu* light rain
服 *bifuku* incognito
苦笑 *bikushō* wry smile, faint forced smile
9 音 *bion* a faint sound
風 *bifū* breeze, zephyr
衷 *bichū* true heart, innermost thoughts, sincerity
10 笑 *bishō, hohoe(mi)* smile. *hohoe(mu)* smile; begin to bloom
恙 *biyō* indisposition, slight illness
弱 *bijaku* feebleness
粉炭 *bifuntan* pulverized coal
11 細 *bisai* minuteness, fineness; details
酔 *bisui, horoyo(i)* slight intoxication
粒子 *biryūshi* a very tiny particle
視的 *bishiteki* microscopic
動 *bidō* tremor, quiver
動計 *bidōkei* microseismograph
12 量 *biryō* very small amount
測計 *bisokukei* micrometer
温 *bion* lukewarmness, low temperature
温的 *bionteki* indifferent, lukewarm
温浴 *bion'yoku* tepid bath
温湯 *biontō, nurumayu* lukewarm water
13 傷 *bishō* slight wound, minor injury, scratch
微 *bibi(taru)* slight, small, tiny, petty, feeble, insignificant
睡 *bisui* short sleep, *madoro(mu)* drowse, doze off, nap
禄 *biroku* small stipend, pittance
罪 *bizai* minor offense
意 *bii* small token (of gratitude), my (humble) feelings
14 塵 *mijin* particle, bit, atom
塵計 *mijinkei* micrometer
15 賎 *bisen* low rank, humble station, obscurity
熱 *binetsu* slight fever
震 *bishin* slight earthquake
震計 *bishinkei* microseismograph
16 積分 *bisekibun* differential and integral calculus
穏的 *bionteki* indifferent, lukewarm
20 騰 *bitō* fractional advance (in prices)
21 醺 *bikun* slight intoxication

11

A **徳** 1767 J4641 M10237′ **德** 1770 J-X M10243 TOKU virtue, goodness; good; gain; power to command respect.
4 化 *tokka* moral influence, moral reform
分 *tokubun* profits, winnings, one's share
5 目 *tokumoku* virtues
用 *tokuyō na* economical
用品 *tokuyōhin* bargain goods

6 行 *tokkō* virtuous deeds, goodness
7 沢 *tokutaku* grace, blessing
利 *tokkuri, tokuri* bottle
8 性 *tokusei* morality, moral nature
育 *tokuiku* spiritual education, moral training
9 風 *tokufū* nobility of character
政 *tokusei* benevolent government; moratorium
11 教 *tokkyō* moral teachings
望 *tokubō* moral influence
望家 *tokubōka* man of high repute
13 義 *tokugi* morality, integrity, sincerity
義上 *tokugijō* morally, in honor
義心 *tokugishin* sense of honor, moral sense
15 器 *tokki* talent and virtue; virtuous person
16 操 *tokusō* morality, chastity, virtue

B **徴** 1768 / J4427 / M10238′ **徵** 1769 / J-X / M10239 CHŌ sign, symptom, omen. *chō(suru)* collect, solicit, seek; judge by; question; refer to; call for (someone); demand. *shirushi* sign, indication, omen.
5 用 *chōyō* commandeering, drafting, requisitioning, expropriating
収 *chōshū* collection, levy, assessment
収料 *chōshūryō* collection fee
7 兵 *chōhei* conscription, recruitment, enlistment
兵令 *chōheirei* conscription decree
兵忌避 *chōhei kihi* draft evasion
兵免除 *chōhei menjo* draft exemption
兵制 *chōheisei* conscription system
兵制度 *chōhei seido* conscription system
兵猶予 *chōhei yūyo* temporary draft exemption
兵検査 *chōhei kensa* physical exam for conscription
兵適齢 *chōhei tekirei* draft age
9 発 *chōhatsu* levy, forage, requisition, commandeering
発令 *chōhatsurei* requisition order
発船 *chōhatsusen* requisitioned ship
発隊 *chōhatsutai* foraging party
発権 *chōhatsuken* right of requisition
10 候 *chōkō* sign, indication, omen, symptom
12 証 *chōshō* token, sign
税 *chōzei* tax collection, taxation
税令書 *chōzei reisho* tax bill
募 *chōbo* enlistment, recruitment
募人 *chōbonin* labor service; forced labor
集 *chōshū* levy, enlistment, recruiting
集令 *chōshūrei* order calling up draftees

12

徵 1769 / J-X / M10239 See **徴** 1768.

德 1770 / J-X / M10243 See **徳** 1767.

B **徹** 1771 / J4530 / M10245 TETSU clear. *tes(suru)* pierce, penetrate, strike home; go through, sit up (all night). *tō(ru)* penetrate, permeate. *tō(su)* walk along, pass by; pass through; pass (exams); be known as; be admissible; come in; be understood; reach; draw (on a pipe); drain (as a sink); be consistent.
5 収 *tesshū* withdrawal
6 退 *tettai* withdrawal, evacuation
8 夜 *tetsuya* all night; all-night vigil; sleepless night
底 *tettei* thoroughness, completion
底的 *tetteiteki* thorough, exhaustive, complete
底爆撃 *tettei bakugeki* saturation 「bombing
10 宵 *tesshō* all night, without sleep
12 廃 *teppai* abolition, removal
16 頭徹尾 *tettō-tetsubi* thoroughly, through and through, completely, from start to finish

B **衝** 1772 / J3e57 / M34069 SHŌ brunt; opposition (in astronomy); highway; collision; important point. *tsu(ku)* thrust, pierce, spear, stab, prick; gore; lunge at; push, poke; strike (a bell); attack, strike (at the heart); brave (a storm); be pungent; strike against; (words) rush (to one' s lips). [行]
3 丈 *tsuitake* body length
4 心 *shōshin* heart failure
天 *shōten* high spirits
5 立 *tsuita(te)* single-leaf screen
6 当 *shō (ni) a(taru)* be appointed to a most important position

[8]突 *shōtotsu* collision, bump, impact; conflict, discord, quarrel; encounter, clash
[9]風 *shōfū* air blast
[11]動 *shōdō* shock; impulse, impetus
動的 *shōdōteki* impulsive
[15]撃 *shōgeki* shock, crash, impact; bombardment (in physics); (emotional) shock; trauma
撃療法 *shōgeki ryōhō* shock treatment

— 13 —

徼 1773 / J352b / M-X Nonstandard for 徽 1778.

徼 1774 / J5755 / M10261 KYŌ look around, go around; seek, ask; road; border. *moto(meru)* seek, ask. *megu(ru)* look around, go around.

B 衡 1775 / J3953 / M34078 KŌ measuring rod; scales. *kubiki* yoke. [行]
[5]平 *kōhei na* equitable
[9]度 *kōdo* weights and measures
[15]器 *kōki* scales; weighing

A 衛 1776 / J3152 / M34073 衞 1777 / J6a4c / M34074 EI protection. [行]
[3]士 *eji, eishi* ancient imperial guard; soldiers on guard
[5]生 *eisei* health, hygiene, sanitation
生兵 *eiseihei* medic, medical corpsman
生材料 *eisei zairyō* medical supplies
生法 *eiseihō* hygiene, hygienics
生的 *eiseiteki* hygienic, sanitary
生官 *eiseikan* health officer
生学 *eiseigaku* hygiene, hygienics
生係 *eiseigakari* health officer
生院 *eiseiin* sanitarium
生施設 *eisei shisetsu* sanitary facilities
生思想 *eisei shisō* sanitary knowledge
生班 *eiseihan* a sanitation detail
生家 *eiseika* one who cautiously watches his health
生病院 *eisei byōin* sanitarium, hospital
生隊 *eiseitai* medical corps
[6]戍 *eiju* garrisoning
戍地 *eijuchi* garrison town
[7]兵 *eihei* palace guards; guard, sentinel; garrison
兵勤務 *eihei kimmu* guard duty
[8]所 *eisho* place guarded by soldiers; torpedo room (of a battleship)
[9]星 *eisei* satellite
星国 *eiseikoku* satellite country
星都市 *eisei toshi* satellite towns
[11]視 *eishi* guards at a parliament

— 14 —

徽 1778 / J-X / M10267 徽 1773 / J352b / M-X KI good; beautiful; badge.
[6]号 *kigō* flag emblem, banner, crest
[15]章 *kishō* badge, emblem, ensign

— 21 —

衢 1779 / J6a4d / M34090 KU crossroads. [行]

4-STROKE RADICALS

RAD. 心 61

Kokoro heart. At left: 忄 (3 strokes) *risshimben* left-side standing "heart." At bottom: 心 or ⺗ *shitagokoro* bottom "heart." Nickname: Heart.

A 心 1780 / J3f34 / M10295 SHIN heart, mind, spirit; motive, sense (of duty); padding; wick; core; marrow; vitality. *kokoro* mind, spirit; mentality; idea, thought; heart, feeling; wholeheartedness, sincerity, sympathy; attention; interest, care; will; intention; taste, mood; true meaning (of a poem). *kokoro kara, shin kara* wholeheartedly, sincerely, cordially. *kokoro(narazumo)* unwillingly, reluctantly. *kokoro suru* attend to, care for, mind, notice, pay attention to; take heed.

2 入 *kokoroi(re), kokoroi(ri)* preparation, concern, anxiety

力 *shinryoku* mental power

3 土 *shindo* subsoil

上 *kokoroa(gari)* arrogance

丈 *kokoro (no) take* one's mind, inner thoughts

丈夫 *kokorojōbu na* courageous, secure

4 木 *shingi* axletree

火 *shinka* fire of anger or jealousy

支度 *kokorojitaku* mental attitude

中 *shinjū* double suicide, lover's suicide. *shinchū* heart, mind, inmost thoughts, true motive; at heart

中立 *shinjūda(te)* fidelity

切 *shinki(ri)* snuffers

切鋏 *shinki(ri)basami* snuffer

5 立 *kokoroda(te)* disposition, personality, temperament

付 *kokorozu(ku)* notice, realize, sense; exercise care. *kokorozu(ke)* tip, gratuity; suggestion

外 *shingai* unexpected, regrettable, mortifying

幼 *kokoroosana(i)* childish

失 *kokorou(seru)* faint away

6 耳 *shinji* mind and ears

血 *shinketsu* sincerity

尽 *kokorozu(kushi)* earnest work, kindness, solicitude, efforts

休 *kokoroyasu(me)* consolation

任 *kokoromaka(se)* one's own way, as one desires

好 *kokoroyo(i)* happy, feeling good

忙 *kokorozewa(shii)* rushed (feeling)

扱 *kokoroatsuka(i)* consideration (for others); worry; care; anxiety; solicitude

汲 *kokoro (o) ku(mu)* guess

当 *kokoroa(tari)* knowledge, idea, clue; guess. *kokoroa(te)* hope, expectation, reliance; guess

早 *kokorobaya na* quick-tempered

有気 *kokoroa(ri)ge na* significant, meaningful

次第 *kokoro shidai* depending on how one feels

気 *shinki* mind

安 *kokoroyasu(i)* intimate, friendly, feeling at ease

安立 *kokoroyasuda(te) ni* out of familiarity; as a mark of friendship

行 *kokoroyu(ku)* be satisfied, be lighthearted

行迄 *kokoroyu(ku) made* to one's heart's content

行許 *kokoroyu(ku) baka(ri)* to your heart's content, as much as you please

地 *kokochi, shinchi* feeling, sensation, mood; idea; mental attitude, mental state

地好 *kokochiyo(ku)* pleasantly; willingly

地良 *kokochiyo(ku)* pleasantly; willingly, agreeably

7 足 *kokorota(ru)* be satisfied

床 *kokoroyuka(shii)* refined

材 *shinzai* heartwood, duramen

利 *kokoroki(ku), kokoro (ga) ki(ku)* have good sense; be clever

肝 *shinkan, kokorogimo* heart

乱 *kokoromida(re)* lack of prudence

附 *kokorozu(ke)* tip, gratuity; suggestion

忘 *kokorowasu(re)* sudden failure of memory

余 *kokoro ni ama(ru)* be at one's wit's end

労 *shinrō* anxiety, worry, fear, suspense; trouble, care; good offices

身 *shinshin* mind and body

身喪失 *shinshin sōshitsu* mental derangement

8 底 *kokoro (no) soko, shinsoko, shintei* bottom of one's heart, real intention, motive

延 *kokorobae* mind, heart

房 *shimbō* auricle, atrium

易 *kokoroyasu(i)* intimate, friendly, feeling at ease

疚 *kokoroyama(shii)* conscience-stricken

迷 *kokoro (no) mayo(i)* illusion

性 *shinsei* mind, mentality; nature, disposition

泣 *urana(ku)* weeping within

的 *shinteki* mental, psychological, psychical

服 *shimpuku* admiration and devotion, hearty submission

命 *shimmei* the heart and life
苦 *kokoroguru(shii)* regrettable, sorry, conscience-stricken, unfortunate
学 *shingaku* ethics, moral philosophy
事 *shinji* one's thoughts
取皿 *shinto(ri)zara* fire pan
苛立 *kokoroirada(tsu)* be irritated
長閑 *kokoronodoka na* peaceful, calm in heart, at ease
9 音 *shin'on* heart tone
通 *shintsū* understanding the deeper meaning. *kokoro (ga) kayo(u)* be understood by
便 *kokorodayori* dependence
待 *kokoroma(chi)* anticipation, expectation
後 *kokorookure* timidity
持 *kokoromo(chi)* feeling, sensation, mood; somewhat, a little
柄 *kokorogara* frame of mind
浅 *kokoroasa(i)* (person) with little sympathy; shallow
砕 *kokoro (o) kuda(ku)* worry
祝 *kokoroiwa(i)* wholehearted congratulations
胆 *shintan* one's heart
重 *kokoroomo(i)* distressing
変 *kokorogawa(ri)* change of mind; inconstancy
室 *shinshitsu* ventricle of the heart
急 *kokoroiso(gi), kokorose(ku)* rushed feeling
染 *kokoro (ni) soma(nu)* uncongenial (work)
神 *shinshin* mind
神喪失 *shinshin soshitsu* mental derangement
10 鬼 *kokoro (no) oni* alarmed conscience. *kokoro (o) oni ni suru* determine not to give in
根 *kokorone* inner feelings; motive; disposition; character
残 *kokoronoko(ri)* regret, reluctance
浮 *kokoro (ni) uka(bu)* think about
粉 *kokoro (o) ko ni suru* apply oneself to
恥 *kokoroha(zukashii)* shameful
致 *kokoro (o) ita(su)* apply one's mind to
留 *kokoro (o) to(meru)* pay attention to
弱 *kokoroyowa(i)* weak-willed, fickle
配 *shimpai, kokorokuba(ri)* anxiety, worry, fear, suspense; trouble, care; good offices
配性 *shimpaishō* worry habit
配事 *shimpaigoto* cares, worries, troubles
11 遊 *kokorosusa(bi)* comfort
強 *kokorozuyo(i)* feeling reassured, confident; heartening (news). *kokorogowa(i)* stout-hearted; headstrong
情 *shinjō* one's heart, feelings. *kokoronasake* kind heart
惜 *kokoroo(shii)* regrettable
掛 *kokoroga(keru), kokoro (ni) ka(keru)* intend, lean, aim; look forward to; bear in mind; be careful to provide for. *kokoroga(kari)* worry, anxiety. *kokoroga(ke)* readiness, intention, aim; study, effort; attention, care
清 *kokorogiyo(i)* pure in heart
添 *kokorozo(e)* advice, suggestion
淋 *kokorosabi(shii)* somewhat lonely. *urasabi(shii)* lonely, lonesome
深 *kokorobuka(i)* thoughtful, prudent
眼 *shingan* mind's eye, mental vision
移 *kokoroutsu(ri)* inconstancy, change of heart
細 *kokoroboso(i)* lonely, depressed, disheartening, helpless, forlorn
組 *kokorogu(mi)* intention
動 *kokoro (o) ugo(kasu)* be stirred up; apply one's mind to. *kokoro (ga) ugo(ku)* worry
悪 *kokorowaru(i), kokoroa(shii)* evil hearted; feeling bad
密 *kokorohiso(kani)* inwardly, secretly
寂 *kokorosabi(shii)* somewhat lonely
羞 *kokoroha(zukashii)* shameful
黒 *kokoroguro(i)* evil-hearted
悸亢進 *shinki kōshin* palpitation of the heart
悸昂進 *shinki kōshin* heart acceleration
許 *kokorobaka(ri)* just a little, mere token
許無 *kokoromotona(i)* uneasy, apprehensive; insecure; unreliable
酔 *shinsui* fascination, admiration, devotion
酔者 *shinsuisha* enthusiast, admirer, fan
得 *kokoroe(ru)* know, understand, be aware of; regard as; give consent. *kokoroe* rules, instructions, information; acting (principal); understanding

得違 *kokoroechiga(i)* mistake, misunderstanding; indiscretion
得難 *kokoroegata(i)* strange, inexplicable, hard to understand
得顔 *kokoroegao* proud face
理 *shinri* mentality, psychology
理的 *shinriteki* mental, psychological, psychical
理学 *shinrigaku* psychology, mental philosophy
理学上 *shinrigakujō* psychologically
理学的 *shinrigakuteki* psychological
理戦争 *shinri sensō* psychological warfare
12 痛 *shintsū* anxiety, worry, fear, suspense; trouble, care; good offices
遣 *kokoroya(ri)* relaxation, recreation; sympathy; comfort. *kokorozuka(i)* solicitude, anxiety, regard for
晴 *kokoroba(rashi)* diversion; recreation
棒 *shimbō* axle, shaft, mandrel, piston rod
短 *kokoromijika(i)* short-tempered, restless
程 *kokoro (no) hodo* true heart, true feeling
粧 *kokoroyosooi* preparation
勝 *kokoromasa(ri)* firm character
裡 *shinri* mind, heart
証 *shinshō* a judge's conviction of a prisoner's guilt or innocence; one's impression of a person
軽 *kokorogaru(i)* rash; hasty
隔 *kokoroheda(te)* closing one's heart
寒 *kokorosamu(i)* deeply impressed
悲 *uragana(shii), kokorogana(shii)* sad, sorrowful
惑 *kokoromado(i)* delusion. *kokoromado(u)* be confused
覚 *kokoroobo(e)* remembrance; memo
象 *shinshō* mental image
筋 *shinkin* heart muscle
筋炎 *shinkin'en* myocarditis
無 *kokoro (nimo) na(i)* insincere; unintentional. *kokorona(i)* without ideas, unsympathetic; unrefined; heartless, thoughtless, indiscreet; cruel
無気 *kokoronage* heartlessness
13 腹 *shimpuku* sincerity; the heart; most loyal retainer
障 *kokorozawa(ri)* anxiety, solicitude, worry
裏 *shinri* mind, heart
楽 *kokorodano(shii)* happy
豊 *kokoroyuta(kani)* without fear
置 *kokoroo(ku)* be careful; hesitate
置無 *kokoroo(ki)na(ku)* frankly; confidentially; without anxiety; heartily; without hesitation
電図 *shindenzu* electrocardiogram
電計 *shindenkei* electrocardiograph
意 *shin'i, kokorobae* mind, heart. *kokorobase* mind, heart; thoughtfulness
意気 *kokoroiki* disposition, spirit, feeling
意地 *kokoroiji* stubbornness
14 像 *shinzō* mental image
境 *shinkyō* mental state; mental attitude
憎 *kokoroniku(i)* detestable; refined, graceful, excellent; reticent
構 *kokorogama(e)* mental attitude, preparation
緒 *shinsho, shincho* the mind, emotion
読 *shindoku* reading between the lines
静 *kokoroshizu(kani)* calmly, serenely. *kokoroshizu(ka)* at peace
魂 *shinkon* heart, soul; the bottom of one's heart
算 *shinsan, tsumori* intention, purpose; belief; motive; expectation; idea; estimate
15 憂 *kokorou(i)* heartless
慰 *kokoronagusa(me)* a comfort
賢 *kokorokashiko(i)* wise in heart
器用 *kokorokiyō na* wise
霊 *shinrei* the spirit, soul
霊学 *shinreigaku* occultism, spiritism
霊術 *shinreijutsu* spiritualism
霊教 *shinreikyō* occult science, spiritualism
霊現象 *shinrei genshō* spiritualistic phenomena
霊論 *shinreiron* occult science, spiritualism
16 儘 *kokoro (no) mama* as one pleases
懐 *kokoroyukashi(i)* refined
積 *kokorozumo(ri)* expectation
頭 *shintō* mind, heart
頼 *kokorodano(mi)* dependence, hope, expectation
覧 *kokoroobo(e)* remembrance; reminder; notes
機 *shinki* mind, mental attitude

機一転 *shinki itten* changing one's mind
17 闇 *kokoro (no) yami* darkness of the heart
優 *kokoroyasa(shii)* kindhearted
18 穢 *kokorogitana(i)* foul-minded, evil-minded
糧 *kokoro (no) kate* food for thought
騒 *kokorosawa(gi)* uneasiness. *kokoro (ga) sawa(gu)* be stirred up
髄 *shinzui* essence, pith, spirit, soul, essentials, core, kernel, the life blood
臓 *shinzō* heart; nerve, cheek
臓弁膜症 *shinzō bemmakushō* valvular disease of the heart
臓炎 *shinzōen* inflammation of the heart
臓病 *shinzōbyō* heart disease
臓部 *shinzōbu* the heart of, the core of
臓麻痺 *shinzō mahi* heart failure, heart attack
19 願 *shingan* heart's desire; prayer
鏡 *shinkyō* the heart; a heart clearly differentiating between good and evil; pure heart
20 懸 *kokoroga(ke)* readiness, intention, aim; study, effort; attention, care
22 驕 *kokoroogo(ru)* become proud

1

A 必 $\frac{1781}{\text{J492c}}$ M10299 HITSU certainly. *kanara(zu)* certainly, positively, invariably. *kanara(zushimo)* (not) always, (not) necessarily, (not) all, (not) entirely.
4 中 *hitchū* hitting the target
5 用 *hitsuyō* need, necessity
6 至 *hisshi no* inevitable, necessary
死 *hisshi* inevitable death; desperation. *hisshi no* frantic, desperate
8 定 *hitsujō* certainly, inevitably
治 *hitchi* certain cure
治薬 *hitchiyaku* a necessity guaranteed to cure
9 要 *hitsuyō* need, necessity
要応 *hitsuyō (ni) ō(jite)* as necessary
要条件 *hitsuyō jōken* necessary conditions, requirements
要物 *hitsuyōbutsu* necessities
要事 *hitsuyōji* necessities
要品 *hitsuyōhin* necessities
10 衰 *hissui* bound to decline, decay, or collapse
修 *hisshū* required (subject)
修科目 *hisshū kamoku* required subjects
12 勝 *hisshō* certain victory
須 *hissu* indispensable, necessary, mandatory
須科目 *hissu kamoku* required subjects
然 *hitsuzen* necessity
然性 *hitsuzensei* necessity, inevitability
然的 *hitsuzenteki ni* inevitably, necessarily
13 携 *hikkei* indispensability; manual, handbook
滅 *hitsumetsu* annihilation; death; doomed to perish
14 読 *hitsudoku* required reading
罰 *hitsubatsu* inevitability of punishment
需 *hitsuju* necessary
需品 *hitsujuhin* necessities, essentials

3

忖 $\frac{1782}{\text{J3736}}$ M10326 SON conjecture.
9 度 *sontaku* conjecture, surmise, judgment

B 忙 $\frac{1783}{\text{J4b3b}}$ M10334 BŌ. *isoga(shii), sewa(shii)* busy, occupied. *sewa(shinai)* restless, fidgety, in a hurry.
4 中 *bōchū* during pressure of business
10 殺 *bōsatsu* being worked to death, being pressed with work

A 忘 $\frac{1784}{\text{J4b3a}}$ M10333 BŌ. *wasu(reru)* forget; be forgetful of; forget about; forget (an article). *wasu(reppoi)* forgetful.
6 年 *bōnen* forgetting the hardships of the old year
年会 *bōnenkai* year-end party
7 却 *bōkyaku* memory lapse, forgetfulness
我 *bōga* selflessness, trance, ecstasy; enthusiasm
形身 *wasu(re)gatami* memento, souvenir, keepsake; posthumous child
8 物 *wasu(re)mono* something forgotten
10 恩 *bōon* ingratitude
12 勝 *wasu(re)ga(chi) no* forgetful, oblivious of, negligent

4 【心 忄 ⺗】 戈 戸 手 扌 支 攴 攵 文 斗 斤 方 无 日 曰 月 木 欠 止 歹 殳 毋 比 毛 氏 气 水 氵 氺 火 灬 爪 爫 父 爻 爿 丬 片 牙 牛 犬 犭

A **志** 1785 / J3b56 / M10331 SHI record; shilling; will, intention, motive; determination; aim; ambition, hopes; gift; kindness; offering (Buddhist). *kokoroza(su)* plan, intend, aim at, aspire to, resolve, determine. *kokorozashi* will, intention, motive; determination; aim; ambition, hopes; gift; kindness; offering (Buddhist). *shiringu* shilling.

3 士 *shishi* patriot, public-spirited man
6 気 *shiki* spirit, sentiment, morale
向 *shikō* intention, aim
8 尚 *shishō* will, intention
11 望 *shibō* desire, ambition, choice
望者 *shibōsha* aspirant; applicant
13 節 *shisetsu* constant fidelity
15 趣 *shishu* heart, mind
16 操 *shisō* constancy, purpose, integrity
19 願 *shigan* desire, aspiration; application, volunteering
願兵 *shiganhei* volunteer soldier
願者 *shigansha* applicant, volunteer, aspirant, candidate
願書 *shigansho* written application

B **忌** 1786 / J3477 / M10310 KI mourning; death anniversary; something detestable. *i(mu)* abhor, have an aversion for, avoid, shun; taboo; abstain from. *ima(washii)* objectionable, abominable, offensive; ominous, unlucky. *i(mi)* mourning; taboo.

4 日 *i(mi)bi* unlucky day; death anniversary; purification and fast day. *kijitsu*, *kinichi* death anniversary
月 *kigetsu* month of mourning
中 *kichū* in mourning
引 *kibi(ki)* absence from work due to mourning
5 可 *i(mu)be(ki)* detestable, abominable
6 名 *i(mi)na* posthumous name, canonical name, real name
7 忌 *i(ma)i(mashii)* annoying, provoking
言葉 *i(mi)kotoba* tabooed word
8 明 *kimei*, *i(mi)a(ke)*, *i(mi)a(ki)*, *kia(ke)* end of mourning ; end of childbirth-purification period
物 *i(mi)mono* tabooed thing; thing abstained from
服 *kibuku* mourning clothes
10 部 *Imbe*, *Imibe* ancient (Shinto) priestly family
12 詞 *i(mi)kotoba* tabooed word
13 嫌 *i(mi)-kira(u)* detest, hate
15 避 *kihi* evasion, shirking; challenge (in law)
憚 *kitan* reserve, scruples
憚無 *kitanna(ku)* frankly, without reserve
17 諱 *kii*, *kiki* offense displeasure

B **忍** 1787 / J4726 / M10312′ **忍** 1788 / J-X / M10312 NIN. *shino(bu)* bear, endure, put up with; hide (oneself). *shino(baseru)*, *shino(basu)* conceal, secrete. *shino(bi)* stealing (into); spy; sneak thief; surreptitious visit to a house of ill fame. *shino(biyakani)* stealthily, secretly.

2 入 *shino(bi)-i(ru)* slip in, sneak in, steal into
4 込 *shino(bi)-ko(mu)* slip in, sneak in, steal into
5 冬 *nindō, suikazura* honeysuckle
出 *shino(bi)-de(ru)* slip out, sneak out
6 返 *shino(bi)gae(shi)* sharp-pointed wooden or metal prongs atop fences or walls
7 足 *shino(bi) ashi* tiptoeing, stealthy steps
声 *shino(bi)goe* whisper, suppressed voice
8 泣 *shino(bi)na(ki)* subdued sobbing
歩 *shino(bi)-aru(ku)* sneak around. *shino(bi)aru(ki)* traveling incognito
苦 *ninku* endurance, stoicism
者 *ninja* (ancient) spy, a ninja. *shino(bi) mono* spy, scout
9 音 *shino(bi) ne* weak voice; tearful voice
姿 *shino(bi) sugata* disguise, incognito
耐 *nintai* patience, perseverance, fortitude
耐強 *nintaizuyo(i)* persevering, patient, stoical
10 逢 *shino(bi)ai* secret meeting. *shino(bi)-a(u)* meet clandestinely
従 *ninjū* submission, resignation, meekness
笑 *shinobiwara(i)* stifled laugh, giggle, chuckle
辱 *ninjoku* forbearance, fortitude, resignation, forgiveness
11 術 *ninjutsu* occult art; art of the *ninja*
寄 *shino(bi)-yo(ru)* steal up to, steal upon
13 寝 *shino(bi) ne* slipping away to sleep

18 難 *shino(bi)gata(i)* unbearable, intolerable, insupportable

A 応 1789 J317e M10347' 應 1991 J5866 M11330 Ō yes, all right. *ō(jiru), ō(zuru)* answer, reply to; respond to, accept, obey, comply with, accede to, agree to; subscribe for; apply for (admission); meet, supply; fulfill, satisfy. *kota(eru)* respond, answer; be affected by (pain or stimulation); be effective. *(ni) ō(jite)* in proportion to, in answer to, in obedience to. *irae* answer. *masa(ni)* in the act of, on the point of.

2 力 *ōryoku* stress
4 分 *ōbun* appropriate, reasonable
5 召 *ōshō suru* be drafted
召兵 *ōshōhei* draftee
召者 *ōshōsha* draftee
用 *ōyō* practical application; practice; adaptation; improvement; applied (physics)
用化学 *ōyō kagaku* applied chemistry
用科学 *ōyō kagaku* applied science
用問題 *ōyō mondai* supplementary question
7 対 *ōtai suru* receive, deal with, grant an interview
対振 *ōtaibu(ri)* manner of meeting people
9 信 *ōshin* answer signal
変 *ōhen* expediency
急 *ōkyū* temporary, emergency
急手当 *ōkyū teate* first aid
急手段 *okyu shudan* emergency measures
急策 *ōkyūsaku* emergency measures
10 砲 *ōhō* return fire
射 *ōsha* return the fire
11 問 *ōmon* responding to the question
接 *ōsetsu* reception
接室 *ōsetsushitsu* drawing room, reception room
接間 *ōsetsuma* drawing room, parlor
12 訴 *ōso* countersuit
答 *ōtō* answer, reply, response
報 *ōhō* retribution
募 *ōbo* subscription; application; enlistment, enrollment, entry; response
募者 *ōbosha* subscriber, applicant, entrant, volunteer; buyer (of bonds)
援 *ōen* aid; reinforcement; rescue; backing; cheering
援団 *ōendan* rooting section, rooting group
援歌 *ōenka* rooters' song
13 酬 *ōshū* reply
戦 *ōsen suru* accept a challenge, return the fire
15 諾 *ōdaku* consent; compliance

4

忰 1790 J582d M10381 See 悴 1884.

悩 1791 J-X M10392 See 惱 1833.

忩 1792 J-X M10366 See 怱 1815.

忤 1793 J5758 M10358 GO *sakara(u)* oppose, go against; offend.

忱 1794 J575a M10382 SHIN *makoto* sincerity; truth.

忻 1795 J5757 M10401 KIN. KON be pleased; enjoy.

忝 1796 J575b M10348 TEN. *katajikena(i)* grateful, indebted. *katajikena(kumo)* graciously.

10 涙 *katajike numida* tears of gratitude

忸 1797 J5759 M10397 JIKU shame.

8 怩 *jikuji(taru)* bashful, shameful

忿 1798 J575d M10408 FUN. *ika(ru)* be angry.

9 怒 *funnu, fundo* anger, rage, resentment, indignation, exasperation
12 然 *funzen to* indignantly, in a rage
18 懣 *fumman* anger, resentment, indignation, chagrin, irritation

忽 1799 J397a M10405 KOTSU. *tachima(chi)* in a moment, instantly, immediately, all of a sudden. *yuruga(se)* neglect, disregard.

5 布 *hoppu* hops

11 焉 *kotsuen* suddenly
12 然 *kotsuzen, kotsunen* suddenly
15 諸 *kossho* neglect, disregard; sudden destruction

A **念** 1800 / J4730 / M10390 NEN sense, idea, thought; feeling; desire; concern, attention, care. *nen(jiru), nen(zuru)* pray silently; have in mind, be anxious about. *omo(u)* think, believe, judge, esteem; consider, realize; feel like; regard as; anticipate; imagine, suppose, guess; mistake for; recall; intend; desire; love, care for, yearn after; wonder; suspect.

2 力 *nenriki, nenryoku* will power; faith
入 *nen'i(ri), nen'i(re)* care, scrupulousness, conscientiousness
入方 *nen (no) i(re)kata* caution
4 仏 *Nembutsu* the Buddhist prayer formula; Hail Amida
5 写 *nensha* spirit photography
8 念 *nennen* continually thinking about something
9 為 *nen (no) tame* just to be sure
10 校 *nenkō* the very final proof (printing)
珠 *nenju* rosary
書 *nensho* memorandum
14 誦 *nenju* Buddhist invocation
15 慮 *nenryo* sense, idea, thought; feeling; desire; concern, attention, care
16 頭 *nentō* mind
19 願 *nengan* one's heart's desire; an earnest petition

A **忠** 1801 / J4369 / M10353 CHŪ loyalty, devotion, fidelity, faithfulness.

4 犬 *chūken* faithful dog
6 臣 *chūshin* loyal subject, faithful retainer
7 言 *chūgen* good advice
告 *chūkoku* advice, warning
良 *chūryō* loyalty
孝 *chūkō* loyalty and filial piety
君 *chūkun* loyalty to the ruler
君愛国 *chūkun-aikoku* loyalty and patriotism
8 実 *chūjitsu, mame, mame(yaka)* faithfulness, devotion, honesty, fidelity
実忠実 *mamemame(shii)* honest and devoted, energetic, assiduous
実度 *chūjitsudo* fidelity (in radio)
9 信 *chūshin* faithfulness, devotion, loyalty
貞 *chūtei* constant loyalty
勇 *chūyū* loyalty and bravery
10 純 *chūjun* loyalty, obedience
恕 *chūjo* sincerity and sympathy
烈 *chūretsu* unswerving loyalty
11 婢 *chūhi* faithful maidservant
12 順 *chūjun* allegiance, loyalty, obedience
勤 *chūkin* faithful service, devotion
13 愛 *chūai* loyalty, devotion
節 *chūsetsu* loyalty, devotion
誠 *chūsei* loyalty, sincerity, integrity
誠心 *chūseishin* loyalty, sincerity, devotion
義 *chūgi* loyalty, devotion
義立 *chūgida(te)* act of loyalty
義顔 *chūgigao* loyal-appearing
14 僕 *chūboku* faithful manservant
魂 *chūkon* the loyal dead, faithful spirit
魂碑 *chūkonhi* monument to the war dead
15 霊塔 *chūreitō* monument to the war dead
16 諫 *chūkan* loyal remonstrance

A **快** 1802 / J3277 / M10369 KAI pleasure, enjoyment. *kokoroyo(i)* pleasant, agreeable, comfortable, refreshing, delightful; well (from illness). *kokoroyo(ku)* cheerfully, comfortably, gladly. *kokoroyo(shi)* willing, happy. *kokoroyo(ge) na* cheerful, pleasant, comfortable.

2 刀 *kaitō* sharp sword
4 心 *kaishin no* agreeable, congenial
方 *kaihō* convalescence
5 打 *kaida* clean hit; good drive (baseball)
弁 *kaiben* fluency, eloquence
7 技 *kaigi* superb skill
足調 *kaisokuchō* allegro
男子 *kaidanshi* an agreeable man
男児 *kaidanji* a fine fellow
走 *kaisō* fast sailing, fast running
走船 *kaisōsen* yacht, clipper
走艇 *kaisōtei* yacht, clipper
8 雨 *kaiu* refreshing rain
味 *kaimi* pleasure, delight
事 *kaiji* pleasure, joyful event
9 活 *kaikatsu na* cheery, jovial
哉 *kaisai* shout of joy

美 *kaibi* good feeling
美感 *kaibikan* good feeling
速 *kaisoku* high speed; celerity; mobility
速船 *kaisokusen* high-speed ship
速調 *kaisokuchō* allegro
10 眠 *kaimin* pleasant sleep
挙 *kaikyo* brilliant achievement
記録 *kaikiroku* fine record
12 傑 *kaiketsu* a handsome man
晴 *kaisei* fine weather
絶 *kaizetsu no* exceedingly pleasant
勝 *kulshō* easy victory
腕 *kaiwan* shrewdness, remarkable ability
報 *kaihō* good news
13 適 *kaiteki na* comfortable, pleasant, agreeable
漢 *kaikan* jolly fellow
艇 *kaitei* speed boat
感 *kaikan* agreeable sensation, comfort
楽 *kairaku, keraku* pleasure, enjoyment
楽主義 *Kairaku Shugi* Epicureanism
楽説 *Kairakusetsu* Epicureanism
15 談 *kaidan* pleasant chat
諾 *kaidaku* ready consent
調 *kaichō* harmony; excellent condition
17 闊 *kaikatsu na* fine (spirit), frank
18 癒 *kaiyu* recovery from illness

5

怎 1803 / J5763 / M10431 Sō. Shin *ika(de)* how. *nan(zo)* why, how, what.

怐 1804 / J5761 / M10435 Kō. Ku *oro(ka)* foolish, stupid.

怕 1805 / J5766 / M10448 Ha *oso(reru)* fear, be fearful of.

怙 1806 / J5760 / M10454 Ko rely on, depend on; parent. *tano(mu)* depend on, trust in; ask, request.

怛 1807 / J5765 / M10458 Tan. Tatsu. Tachi *ita(mu)* be sad, feel sorrowful, grieve over.

怦 1808 / J5768 / M10476 Hō be impatient, be dissatisfied; correct, straight.

怩 1809 / J5762 / M10481 Ji shame.

怺 1810 / J576a / M10513 （国字） *kora(eru)* endure; tolerate; control, stifle; pardon.

怏 1811 / J5769 / M10434 Ō dissatisfaction; have a grudge.
8 怏 *ōō toshite* despondently, moodily

怜 1012 / J4e67 / M10461 Rei wise.
10 悧 *reiri* cleverness, sagacity

怫 1813 / J5767 / M10486 Futsu anger.
12 然 *futsuzen to* indignantly, in a rage

怡 1814 / J575e / M10470 I *yoroko(bu)* be pleased, enjoy.
8 怡 *ii* relax and enjoy
9 衎 *ien* enjoy

怱 1815 / J5764 / M10494 **悤** 1854 / J-X / M10693 **匆** 570 / J-X / M-X

忩 1792 / J-X / M10366 Sō rush, be flustered.
6 忙 *sōbō* hurry, being busy
8 卒 *sōsotsu na* sudden, abrupt; hurrying; precipitous
9 怱 *sōsō* hurry, bustle

怯 1816 / J3631 / M10491 Kyō cowardice. *hiru(mu)* wince, flinch, hesitate, waver, fear. *obi(eru)* get frightened; be intimidated; feel shy; have a nightmare.
10 恐 *obi(e)-oso(reru)* fear and tremble
弱 *kyōjaku* cowardice
17 懦 *kyōda* cowardice, timidity
臆 *o(mezu)-oku(sezu)* fearlessly, boldly, courageously

B **怖** 1817 / J495d / M10450 Fu. *o(jiru), oji(keru)* fear, be frightened; be timid; get nervous. *oso(reru)* fear, be overawed, be apprehensive. *kowa(garu)* fear, be afraid of. *kowa(i)* fearful, frightful, terrible, weird. *kowa(garaseru)* frighten, terrorize. *kowa(gari)* timidity, cowardice.
6 気 *ojike, ozoke* fear; awe; timidity; nervousness

8 怖 *ozuozu, odoodo, ojioji, kowagowa* timidly; nervously, gingerly
10 恐 *o(ji)-oso(reru)* fear
12 惑 *o(ji)-mado(u)* be terrified
18 顔 *kowa(i) kao* angry look, grim face

B 怠 1818 / J4255 / M10469 TAI laziness, neglect. *okota(ru)* neglect; be off guard; be feeling better. *nama(keru)* be lazy, be idle; neglect. *okota(rinaku)* diligently. *okota(razu) ni* carefully.
8 屈 *taikutsu* tedium, boredom
者 *nama(ke)mono* sloth; a lazy person
10 納 *tainō* nonpayment, default, delinquency; back taxes
12 惰 *taida* laziness, idleness
勝 *okota(ri)ga(chi)* neglectful
13 業 *taigyō* slowdown tactics, sabotage
14 慢 *taiman* negligence; procrastination; carelessness

怨 1819 / J3165 / M10479 EN. ON. *ura(mu), en(zuru)* bear a grudge, show resentment; be jealous. *ura(meshii), ura(migamashii)* hateful, bitter. *urami* grudge, hatred, malice, bitterness.
6 色 *enshoku* a hostile look
7 言 *engen, uramigoto* grudge, complaint, murmuring
声 *ensei* complaint, murmur
8 府 *empu* object of hatred
念 *onnen* grudge, malice, hatred
9 恨 *enkon* enmity, grudge
13 嗟 *ensa* grudge, resentment
15 敵 *onteki* sworn enemy
霊 *onryō* revengeful ghost; apparition
23 讐 *enshū, onshū* grudge, revenge

B 怒 1820 / J455c / M10439 DO. NU. *ika(ru), oko(ru)* become angry, be offended, become excited. *ika(ri)* anger, indignation, rage, wrath. *ika(raseru), oko(raseru)* offend, anger, irritate. *oko(rippoi)* touchy, excitable, hot-tempered.
3 上戸 *oko(ri) jōgo* quarrelsome drinker
5 付 *oko(ri)-tsu(keru)* scold, storm at
出 *oko(ri)-da(su)* fly into a rage
号 *dogō* roar, outcry, howl
6 色 *doshoku* anger, angry countenance
気 *doki* anger; indignation, resentment
叫 *ika(ri)-sake(bu)* rage
争 *ika(ri)-araso(u)* quarrel
7 坊 *oko(rim)bō* hotheaded person
狂 *ika(ri)-kuru(u)* be terribly angry
声 *dosei* harsh words; angry voice; excited voice
8 肩 *ika(ri)kata* square shoulders
易 *ika(ri)yasu(i)* easily angered
11 唸 *ika(ri)-una(ru)* growl
14 鳴 *dona(ru)* shout at
髪 *dohatsu* anger; hair standing on end
17 濤 *dotō* raging billows, high waves

B 怪 1821 / J3278 / M10483 KE, KAI mystery; apparition. *aya(shimu)* doubt; be suspicious of; wonder at. *aya(shigena), aya(shii)* undependable, strange, mysterious. *ke(shikaran), ke(shikaranu)* rude, disgraceful, indecent, unpardonable, outrageous, absurd.
2 力 *kairiki, kairyoku* superhuman strength
人物 *kaijimbutsu* mystery man
4 火 *kaika* mysterious fire, will-o'-the-wisp
文書 *kaibunsho* objectionable literature
6 死 *kaishi* mysterious death
気 *aya(shi)ge na* questionable, shady, suspicious; unsteady; threatening (rain); broken (English)
光 *kaikō* weird light, will-o'-the-wisp
7 我 *kega* wound, injury; accident, error; casualty
我人 *keganin* injured or wounded person
我負 *kegama(ke)* accidental defeat
我勝 *kegaga(chi)* accidental victory
8 怪 *kaikai* great danger
物 *kaibutsu* monster, apparition
奇 *kaiki na* strange, wonderful; weird; outrageous, scandalous, insolent
奇小説 *kaiki shōsetsu* mystery story
事 *kaiji* mystery, wonder, scandal
事件 *kaijiken* mystery case
11 魚 *kaigyo* a strange fish
鳥 *kechō, kaichō* ominous bird
捷 *kaishō* agility, promptness, shrewdness
異 *kaii* monster. *kaii na* mysterious; marvelous; grotesque
盗 *kaitō* mysterious thief
12 傑 *kaiketsu* prodigy, extraordinary man

腕 *kaiwan* unusual ability, shrewdness
訝 *kegen na, kaiga na* suspicious, puzzled, dubious
童 *kaidō* problem child; prodigy
13 漢 *kaikan* suspicious-looking person
14 聞 *kaibun* strange rumor; scandal
説 *kaisetsu* strange rumor
15 談 *kaidan* ghost story
16 獣 *kaijū* monster

A **性** 1822 / J402d / M10478 SEI sex, gender; nature, attribute. SHŌ nature, disposition; quality; purity. *saga* one's nature; custom.

4 分 *shōbun* nature, disposition
5 生活 *sei seikatsu* sex life
犯罪 *sei hanzai* sex crime
6 向 *seikō* inclination, disposition
行 *seikō* character and conduct
行為 *sei koi* sexual act
交 *seikō* sexual intercourse
交不能 *seikō funō* sexual impotency
7 状 *seijō* characteristics
別 *seibetsu* distinction by sex, sex (male or female)
来 *seirai* by nature, naturally, by birth
8 知識 *sei chishiki* sex information, sexual knowledge
的 *seiteki* sexual
的犯罪 *seiteki hanzai* sex crime
9 急 *seikyū* quick temper, impatience
10 骨 *seikotsu* one's natural constitution; ones natural skills
病 *seibyō* sexually transmitted disease
根 *shōne* nature, disposition, spirit, mind
能 *seinō* performance, efficiency
格 *seikaku* character, personality
格破綻者 *seikaku hatansha* abnormal character
格俳優 *seikaku haiyū* actor expert in character portrayal
格描写 *seikaku byōsha* character portrayal
格異常 *seikaku ijō* abnormal personality
格劇 *seikakugeki* character drama
11 情 *seijō* character, disposition, nature
理 *seiri* inherent characteristics, natural endowments
教育 *sei kyōiku* sex education, sex information
道徳 *sei dōtoku* sexual morality
問題 *sei mondai* sexual problem
悪 *seiaku, shōwaru* evil disposition
悪説 *seiakusetsu* doctrine of original sin
欲 *seiyoku* sexual desire
欲倒錯 *seiyoku tōsaku* sexual perversion
欲倒錯者 *seiyoku tōsakusha* sexual pervert
転換 *sei tenkan* sex change
12 善説 *seizensetsu* doctrine of man's innate goodness
13 愛 *seiai* sexual love
感 *seikan* sexual emotion, sexual sensibility
15 慾 *seiyoku* sexual desire
質 *seishitsu* nature, disposition, temperament; qualities, properties; nature (of an undertaking)
衛生 *sei eisei* sexual hygiene, social hygiene
器 *seiki* reproductive organs
器崇拝 *seiki sūhai* phallicism
18 癖 *seiheki* disposition, inclination, characteristic, idiosyncrasy
懲無 *shōko(ri) (mo) na(i)* unrepentant, untaught by experience, incorrigible

A **急** 1823 / J355e / M10475 KYŪ emergency; suddenness; danger; haste; steep. *iso(gu)* hurry, hasten. *se(kasu)* rush, hurry, expedite. *se(ku) vi* and *vt* hurry, make haste; be impatient; press, urge, hurry up. *a(seru)* be hasty, be in a hurry, be impatient. *kyu na* urgent, sudden; precipitous; sharp (turn); swift. *kyū ni* in a hurry, promptly; suddenly; at a moment's notice.

4 火 *kyūka* a nearby fire, a sudden fire
込 *se(ki)-ko(mu), se(k)ko(mu)* become excited, be agitated, be in a hurry, become impatient
勾配 *kyūkōbai* steep slope
5 用 *kyūyō* urgent business
立 *se(ki)-ta(teru)* hurry, urge, speed up, urge on
6 死 *kyūshi* sudden death
先峰 *kyūsempō* leader, champion, forerunner, vanguard
行 *kyūkō* express train; going in a hurry
行券 *kyūkōken* express ticket
行便 *kyūkōbin* express mail
行軍 *kyūkōgun* quick march, double-quick
7 走 *iso(gi)-hashi(ru)* run quickly

4 【心忄⺗】戈戸手扌支攴攵文斗斤方无日曰月木欠止歹殳毋比毛氏气水氵氺火灬爪爫父爻爿丬片牙牛犬犭

足 *iso(gi)ashi* fast pace. *iso(gi)ashi de* at a quick pace
迫 *kyūhaku* urgency; imminence
告 *kyūkoku* urgent notice
5 坂 *kyūhan* steep hill
坂道 *kyūsakamichi* steep road
8 雨 *kyūu* sudden shower
送 *kyūsō suru* rush (something), dispatch
追 *kyūtsui* hot pursuit
使 *kyūshi* courier, express messenger
所 *kyūsho* vital point, vitals, tender spot, vulnerable spot; secret, key (to)
物 *iso(gi)mono* a rush order; urgent business
命 *kyūmei* urgent orders
昇 *kyūshō* sudden rise (in temperature)
歩 *kyūho* fast walking. *iso(gi)-aru(ku)* hurry along
事 *kyūji* urgent matter, sudden development
性 *kyūsei* acute (illness)
性灰白髄炎 *kyūsei kaihakuzuien* poliomyelitis
性病 *kyūseibyō* acute illness
9 風 *kyūfū* squall
信 *kyūshin* urgent message
派 *kyūha suru* dispatch, expedite
変 *kyūhen* sudden turn; emergency, accident
逝 *kyūsei* sudden death
造 *kyūzō* hurried construction
造家屋 *kyūzō kaoku* prefabricated house; Quonset hut
降 *kyūkō suru* drop rapidly; dive
降下 *kyūkōka* swoop, nose dive
降下爆撃 *kyūkōka bakugeki* dive bombing
速 *kyūsoku na* swift, prompt
速冷凍 *kyūsoku reitō* quick freeze
速度 *kyūsokudo* high speed
速潜航 *kyūsoku senkō* crash dive (of a submarine)
10 症 *kyūshō* sudden illness; emergency case
峻 *kyūshun na* steep
流 *kyūryū* swift current; rapids
配 *kyūhai* special delivery
書 *kyūsho* urgent letter
病 *kyūbyō* sudden illness
病人 *kyūbyōnin* emergency case
進 *kyūshin* rapid progress; going to extremes; radicalism
進化 *kyūshinka suru* become radical
進主義 *kyūshin shugi* radicalism
進的 *kyūshinteki* radical, extreme
進派 *kyūshinha* radicals
進党 *kyūshintō* radical party
11 務 *kyūmu* urgent business, pressing need
設 *kyūsetsu* speedy installation
患 *kyūkan* emergency patient
停車 *kyūteisha* sudden stop
斜面 *kyūshamen* steep slope
転 *kyūten* sudden change
転回 *kyūtenkai* sudden turn, doubling back
転直下 *kyūtenchokka suru* fall headlong; take a sudden turn
転換 *kyūtenkan* sudden change
12 場 *kyūba* emergency, crisis
須 *kyūsu, kibisho* teapot
勝 *sekkachi* hot-tempered person. *sekkachi na* restless, impatient, quick-tempered
募 *kyūbo* recruiting (workers) in a hurry
落 *kyūraku* slump (in prices)
報 *kyūhō* urgent message, alarm
13 雷 *kyūrai* thunder, thunderclap
電 *kyūden* urgent telegram
傾斜 *kyūkeisha* steep slope; heavy list
14 増 *kyūzō* surge, sudden increase
15 劇 *kyūgeki na* sudden, precipitous; radical
談 *kyūdan* fast talking, urgent conversation
撃 *kyūgeki* surprise attack
16 遽 *kyūkyo* hastily, hurriedly
激 *kyūgeki na* sudden, precipitous; radical
18 騎 *kyūki* fast horse
難 *kyūnan* imminent danger; sudden calamity
20 騰 *kyūtō* sudden jump in prices
霰 *kyūsan* sudden hailstorm
22 襲 *kyūshū* surprise attack; raid

A **思** 1824 / J3b57 / M10462 SHI. *omo(u)* think, believe, judge, esteem; consider, realize; feel like; regard as; anticipate; imagine, suppose, guess; mistake for; recall; intend; desire; love, care for, yearn after; wonder; suspect. *omo(wareru)* seem, appear. *omo(waseru)* give the impression that. *omo(eba)* come to think about it. *omo(eraku)* it seems to me.

omo(i) thought, idea, mind, heart, sense; feeling, emotion; affection; desire, wish; expectation; intention, will; pleasure; care, worry; experience. *omo(inashi)* fancy, imagination. *omo(wanu)* unexpected, inconceivable. *omo(washii)* satisfactory, desirable. *omo(wazu)* unintentionally, spontaneously, unconsciously.

2 人 *omo(i)bito* lover, sweetheart

入 *omo(i)-i(ru)* consider, ponder *omo(i)i(re)* one's pleasure, heart's desire; meditation, reverie. *omoi(re)* one's pleasure, heart's desire, meditation, reverie; supposition

3 子 *omo(i)go* favorite child

及 *omo(i)-oyo(bu)* think up, remember, hit upon, think of

上 *omo(i)-a(garu)* be conceited

4 止 *omo(i)-to(maru), omo(i)-todo(maru)* drop (the idea) ⌈consider

比 *omo(i)-kura(beru)* compare and

込 *omo(i)-ko(mu)* be impressed with (an idea); set one's heart on; imagine (something)

切 *omo(i)-ki(ru)* resign to fate; get over (a loss); give up, despair of; resolve. *omo(i)ki(ri)* resignation, determination, decision; vehemently, vigorously; terribly; to heart's content; with all one's might; thoroughly, completely. *omo(i)ki(tta)* drastic, radical

5 立 *omo(i)-ta(tsu)* plan, resolve. *omo(i)ta(chi)* resolve, intention, idea, plan, whim, impulse

巡 *omo(i)-megu(rasu), omo(i)-mawa(su)* recall, ponder over

付 *omo(i)-tsu(kaseru)* remind of, suggest. *omo(i)-tsu(ku)* hit upon, think up (ideas). *omo(i)tsu(ki)* plan, suggestion, casual idea

外 *omo(i) (no) hoka* unexpectedly, beyond expectations

召 *obo(shi)-me(su), omōshi-me(su)* think, believe, judge, esteem; consider, realize; feel like; regard as; anticipate; imagine, suppose, guess; mistake for; recall; intend; desire; love, care for, yearn after; wonder; suspect. *obo(shi)me(shi)* your opinion; your desire; token of gratitude; liking, fancy

弁 *shiben* discrimination, speculation

出 *omo(i)-da(su)* recall, remember. *omo(i)de* memories, recollections

出笑 *omo(i)-da(shi)-wara(u)* laugh at some recollection

出話 *omo(i)debanashi* reminiscences

6 回 *omo(i)-megu(rasu), omo(i)-mawa(su)* recall, ponder over

返 *omo(i)-kae(su)* think over, reconsider

交 *omo(i)-ka(wasu)* love each other

合 *omo(i)-a(u)* love each other. *omo(i)-a(waseru)* consider together. *omo(i)a(i)* mutual love

当 *omo(i)-a(taru), omo(i)-a(teru)* occur to one, think of; suspect

存分 *omo(u)zombun* as one pleases

考 *shikō* thought, consideration, contemplation

考力 *shikōryoku* mental faculties

7 迫 *omo(i)-se(maru)* be driven to despair, be at one's wit's end

侘 *omo(i)-wa(biru)* feel lonely, be sick of

沈 *omo(i)-shizu(mu)* worry

乱 *omo(i)-mida(reru)* be distracted with the thought of

初 *omo(i)-so(meru)* fall in love with

余 *omo(i)-ama(ru)* be overcome with emotion

8 固 *omo(i)-kata(meru)* resolve

迷 *omo(i)-mayo(u)* be unable to decide

知 *omo(i)-shi(ru)* perceive, realize; repent of. *omo(i)-shi(raseru)* teach (someone a lesson). *omo(wazu)-shi(razu)* unintentionally, unconsciously

念 *shinen* thought

直 *omo(i)-nao(su)* reconsider, change one's mind

定 *omo(i)-sada(meru)* resolve

者 *omo(i)mono* sweetheart

事 *omo(i)goto* one's desire, one's prayer

9 通 *omo(i)dō(ri) ni* to one's satisfaction, as much as one likes

計 *omo(i)-haka(ru)* think up

思 *omo(i)omo(i) ni* as one pleases

春期 *shishunki* puberty

10 起 *omo(i)-oko(su)* remember, recall

悩 *omo(i)-naya(mu)* be depressed, be dejected, worry

振 *omo(wase)bu(ri)* coquetry; mystification

残 *omo(i)-noko(su)* leave with regret
浮 *omo(i)-u(kaberu)* recall, remember, hit upon, think up. *omo(i)-u(kabu)* occur to, remind of
料 *shiryō* consideration
索 *shisaku* speculation, thinking, meditation
索的 *shisakuteki* meditative, speculative
索家 *shisakuka* thinker, philosopher
案 *shian* thought, consideration, meditation; plan, resources
案投首 *shian na(ge)kubi* tilting the head in deep thought
案沈 *shian (ni) shizu(mu)* be in deep thought
案余 *shian (ni) a(maru)* be perplexed even after much pondering
案暮 *shian (ni) ku(reru)* be perplexed even after much pondering
11 過 *omo(i)-su(gosu)* worry too much, be over-anxious
惟 *shii* speculation, thinking
設 *omo(i)-mō(keru)* anticipate, think of beforehand, expect
寄 *omo(i)-yo(ru)* recall, remember. *omo(i) (mo) yo(ranai)* unexpected, inconceivable
掛無 *omo(i)ga(ke)na(i)* unexpected
12 遣 *omo(i)-ya(ru)* sympathize with, have consideration for. *omo(i)ya(ri)* sympathy, consideration, compassion
違 *omo(i)chiga(i)* misunderstanding
壷 *omo(u) tsubo* one's wishes or expectations
量 *shiryō* consideration
募 *omo(i)-tsuno(ru)* think more and more of
焦 *omo(i)-koga(reru)* pine for, be deeply in love
惑 *omo(i)-mado(u)* be unable to decide. *omowaku* thought, opinion; intention; expectation; ulterior aim; rumor
惑師 *omowakushi* speculator, plunger, operator
惑違 *omowakuchiga(i)* disappointment, miscalculation
惑買 *omowakuga(i)* speculative purchase
13 煩 *omo(i)-wazura(u)* worry about, be concerned about
詰 *omo(i)-tsu(meru)* think hard, brood over
想 *shisō* thought, idea
想力 *shisōryoku* power of thought
想内容 *shisō naiyō* thought content
想犯 *shisōhan* thought crime
想団体 *shisō dantai* radicalist association
想取締 *shisō torishima(ri)* thought control
想界 *shisōkai* world of thought, realm of ideas
想家 *shisōka* thinker
想問題 *shisō mondai* thought problem
想善道 *shisō zendō* guidance of public thought
想戦 *shisōsen* ideological warfare
想感情 *shisō-kanjō* thoughts and feelings
14 様 *omo(u)sama, omo(u) yō ni* as one pleases
慕 *shibo* yearning, deep affection
暮 *omo(i)-ku(rasu)* live with one dominating thought
15 潮 *shichō* trend of thought
澄 *omo(i)-su(masu)* meditate; lead a life of austerity
慮 *shiryo* discretion, thought, consideration
慮周密 *shiryoshūmitsu ni* discreetly, prudently, judiciously, sensibly
慮深 *shiryobuka(ku)* discreetly, prudently, judiciously, sensibly
16 儘 *omo(u)mama, omo(i) (no) mama* as one pleases

6

恆 1825 / J5771 / M10528 See **恒** 1849.

恠 1826 / J575f / M10574 See **怪** 1821.

恷 1827 / J576e / M-X KYŪ *moto(ru)* go against, conflict with.

恁 1828 / J576c / M10518 JIN. NIN. IN think; thus, in this way.

恂 1829 / J5776 / M10520 JUN. SHUN sincerity; fear, refrain. *makoto* sincerity, truth.

恊 1830 / J5770 / M10535 KYŌ fear; be afraid of. Also used as variant of 協 617.

恚 1831 / J576b / M10566 I anger.

恃 1832 / J5774 / M10521 JI *tano(mu)* depend on.

恟 1833 / J576f / M10573 **忷** 1791 / J-X / M10392 KYŌ fear.

恕 1834 / J3d7a / M10560 JO. *jo(suru)* excuse, tolerate, forgive.

恙 1835 / J5779 / M10565 YŌ. *tsutsuga* illness. *tsutsuga(naku)* safely; in good health.

恪 1836 / J576d / M10592 KAKU carefulness.
6 守 *kukushu suru* adhere to, cling to, be loyal to
12 勤 *kakugon, kakkin* working earnestly

恫 1837 / J5778 / M10594 DŌ, TŌ painful; fearful.
11 喝 *dōkatsu* intimidation, threat, bluster
12 愒 *dōkatsu* intimidation, threat, bluster

恰 1838 / J3366 / M10603 KŌ *ataka(mo), adaka(mo)* just as, as though; fortunately.
6 好 *kakkō* shape, form, appearance; pose, posture; manner; approximately.
kakkō na suitable, reasonable
12 幅 *kappuku* build, physique

恤 1839 / J5775 / M10583 JUTSU relieve. *megu(mu)* bless; show mercy to, render benevolence to. *awa(remu)* have mercy on.
7 兵 *juppei* soldiers' relief
兵資金 *juppei shikin* war-relief fund

恍 1840 / J5772 / M10546 KŌ unclear. *tobo(keru)* grow senile; be stupid; joke; pretend not to know. *ho(reru)* fall in love with, admire, be entranced with.
9 面 *tobo(ke)zura* a stupid look
11 惚 *kōkotsu* rapture, ecstasy, trance
18 顔 *tobo(ke)gao* a stupid look

恣 1841 / J5773 / M10580 SHI. *hoshiimama* self-indulgent, wayward, selfish, arbitrary.
13 肆 *shishi* self-indulgent, wayward, selfish, arbitrary.
意 *shii* selfishness, arbitrariness
意的 *shiiteki* selfish, arbitrary

B **恨** 1842 / J3a28 / M10588 KON. *ura(mu)* bear a grudge, show resentment. *ura(mi)* grudge, hatred, malice. *ura(meshii)* hateful, bitter.
7 言 *ura(mi)goto* grudge, grievance, complaint
8 事 *konji* regrettable matter
10 殺 *konsatsu* intense bitterness

恢 1843 / J327a / M10577 KAI wide; large; enlarge.
7 宏 *kaikō suru* amplify, spread, extend
9 恢 *kaikai* expansiveness, extensiveness, wideness
12 復 *kaifuku* recovery, restoration, rehabilitation
復期 *kaifukuki* convalescence

恬 1844 / J5777 / M10595 TEN composure. *ten toshite* coolly, nonchalantly, indifferently.
11 淡 *tentan na* unselfish, disinterested
12 然 *tenzen toshite* coolly, indifferently
16 澹 *tentan na* unselfish, disinterested

B **恭** 1845 / J3633 / M10596 KYŌ *uyauya(shii)* respectful, reverent.
10 倹 *kyōken* modesty, humility; courtesy, respect
12 順 *kyōjun* allegiance
敬 *kyōkei* respect, reverence, veneration
賀 *kyōga* respectful congratulations
賀新年 *Kyōga Shinnen* Happy New Year
17 謙 *kyōken* modesty, humility

B **恥** 1846 / J4351 / M10585 **耻** 4717 / J6657 / M29019 CHI. *haji* shame, dishonor, disgrace, humiliation, insult. *ha(jiru), ha(zuru)* feel ashamed. *ha(zubeki)* disgraceful, unbecoming. *ha(jirau)* feel shy, be coy, be bashful, blush. *ha(zukashigaru)* be shy, be bashful, be ashamed. *ha(zukashii)* bashful, ashamed, coy; disgraceful, shameful. *ha(zukashikaranu)* worthy, decent, honorable.

[2] 入 *ha(ji)-i(ru)* feel ashamed
[8] 知 *hajishi(razu)* shameless. *haji (o) shi(ru)* refrain from shameful acts
[10] 骨 *chikotsu* pubic bone
晒 *hajisara(shi)* disgrace, shame
辱 *chijoku* disgrace, shame, insult
[11] 雪 *haji (o) susu(gu)* restore face
[12] 慌 *ha(ji)-awa(teru)* put to shame
[18] 曝 *hajisara(shi)* shame, disgrace

B **恵** 1847/J3743/M10618′ **惠** 1876/J582a/M10822 KEI. E. *megu(mi)* blessing, grace, favor; kindness, mercy, benevolence, charity. *megu(mu)* bless; show mercy to, render benevolence to.

[3] 与 *keiyo suru* present, give, bestow
[4] 方 *ehō* lucky direction
方参 *ehōmai(ri)* New Year's visit to a shrine or temple in a lucky direction
比須 *Ebisu* a god of wealth
比須顔 *ebisugao* smiling face
[7] 投 *keitō* presentation
沢 *keitaku* blessing; pity; favor; benefit
[18] 贈 *keizō* presentation

B **悔** 1848/J3279/M10617′ **悔** 1855/J-X/M10659 KAI. GE. *ku(iru)* repent, regret. *ku(yamu)* regret, repent of; mourn for, condole with. *ku(i)* regret, repentance. *ku(yami)* condolence visit; regret, repentance. *ku(yashigaru)* be chagrined (at one's failure); regret (a circumstance); resent (an insult). *kuya(shii)* vexing, regrettable, mortifying.

[7] 言 *kuya(mi)goto* words of condolence
坊 *kuya(shim)bō* person who quickly regrets (something)
改 *ku(i)-arata(meru)* repent of. *ku(i)arata(me)* repentance, penitence
状 *ku(yami)jō* condolence letter
[8] 泣 *ku(yashi)naki* cry of remorse
[9] 恨 *kaikon* remorse; regret; contrition, repentance
[10] 悛 *kaishun* penitence, repentance (Catholic)
涙 *ku(yashi) namida* tears of regret or remorse
紛 *ku(yashi)magi(re) ni* out of spite
悟 *kaigo* repentance, penitence, contrition, remorse
悟者 *kaigosha* a penitent, a contrite sinner
[16] 頽 *ku(i)-kuzuo(reru)* be discouraged and remorseful

B **恒** 1849/J3931/M10527 **恆** 1825/J5771/M10528 KŌ always. *tsune ni* always.

[3] 久 *kōkyū* perpetuity, permanency
久化 *kōkyūka* perpetuation
久性 *kōkyūsei* permanency
久的 *kōkyūteki* permanent
[4] 心 *kōshin* steadiness, constancy
[5] 圧 *kōatsu* constant pressure
[6] 存 *kōzon* conservation (of energy)
[8] 例 *kōrei* regular ceremony; established custom, common usage
性 *kōsei* permanency, constancy
[9] 風 *kōfū* constant wind, trade wind
星 *kōsei* fixed star
[11] 産 *kōsan* fixed property
常 *kōjō* constancy
常的 *kōjōteki* constant
[12] 温線 *kōonsen* isotherm
[13] 数 *kōsū* constant (in science)
[15] 儀 *kōgi* traditional rites

A **息** 1850/J4229/M10601 SOKU son; interest (on money). *iki* breath, respiration. *iki(mu)* strain, bear up, exert one's strength; swagger, bluff, boast. *iki(ru)* be hot with anger. *iko(u)* rest, relax, repose.

[3] 女 *sokujo* daughter
子 *musuko* son, boy, young man
[4] 切 *iki-gi(re)* breathlessness
[5] 付 *ikitsu(ku)* have a respite. *iki (mo) tsu(kasezu)* without giving any respite. *iki (mo) tsu(kazu) ni* holding one's breath
出 *ikida(shi)* air vent; bunghole
[6] 休 *ikiyasu(me)* breathing spell
[7] 吹 *ibu(ki)* breath
抜 *ikinu(ki)* ventilator; breathing space; diversion. *iki-nu(ku)* live through, survive
杖 *ikizue* (palanquin bearer's) resting staff

災 *sokusai* safety, security; peace, tranquility; good health; boredom
男 *sokunan* son
8 苦 *ikiguru(shii)* stuffy, suffocating
9 臭 *iki-kusa(i)* having offensive breath
巻 *iki-ma(ku)* fume, be enraged
急 *iki-se(ku)* breathe hard
急切 *iki-se(ki)-ki(ru)* gasp, pant
10 根 *ikine* breathing; breath; voice. *iki(no)ne* life
11 張 *ikiba(ru)* strain, bear up, exert one's strength; swagger, bluff, boast
12 遣 *ikizu(kai)* breathing
絶 *iki-ta(eru)* die
絶絶 *ikita(e)da(e)* on the verge of death
13 継 *ikitsu(gi)* breathing spell
詰 *ikizu(maru)* be choked, be stifled
15 衝 *ikizu(ku)* heave a sigh
22 籠 *ikigomo(ru)* breathe with difficulty

A **恩** 1851 / J3238 / M10591 ON kindness, goodness, favor, mercy, blessing, benefit.
2 人 *onjin* benefactor, patron
5 主 *onshu* benefactor, patron
6 返 *ongae(shi)* requital of a favor
光 *onkō* the blessing of sunlight; the favor of one's lord
7 沢 *ontaku* favor, benefit
8 知 *onshi(razu)* ingratitude; ungrateful person
命 *ommei* gracious words; gracious command
典 *onten* favor, act of grace, special privilege
9 威 *on'i* justice and mercy; kindness and dignity
恤 *onjutsu* pity, mercy, charity
宥 *on'yū* forgiveness
10 師 *onshi* one's honored teacher
借 *onshaku* loan, borrowing
恵 *onkei* grace, favor, benefit, blessings
恵日 *onkeibi* days of grace
恵期間 *onkei kikan* period of probation, probationary time
11 情 *onjō* compassion; affection
赦 *onsha* amnesty, general pardon
12 給 *onkyū* pension
13 愛 *on'ai, onnai* kindness and affection, love
義 *ongi* favor, obligation, debt of gratitude
14 徳 *ontoku* sympathy, mercy, grace
15 誼 *ongi* favor, obligation, debt of gratitude
賜 *onshi* imperial gift; gracious gift
賞 *onshō* reward
18 顔 *ongan* compassionate face
簡 *onkan* your letter
19 寵 *onchō* grace, favor
21 顧 *onko* favor, patronage
23 讐 *onshū* love and hate

B **恋** 1852 / J4e78 / M10537 **戀** 2017 / J5878 / M11504 REN. *ko(u)* be in love.
koi(suru) love, fall in love with. *koi(shigaru)* yearn for, miss. *koi* love, tender sentiment. *koi(shii)* dear, beloved, darling.
2 人 *koibito* lover, sweetheart
4 心 *koigokoro* love, love's awakening
文 *koibumi* love letter
水 *koi mizu* tears of love
仇 *koigataki* one's rival in love
6 死 *koijini* dying of love
仲 *koinaka* love, love relationship
7 侘 *ko(i)-wa(biru)* be lovesick
乱 *ko(i)-mida(reru)* be lovesick
初 *ko(i)-so(meru)* begin to love
8 妻 *koizuma* loving wife
9 風 *koikaze* love's zephyr
10 疲 *koizuka(re)* haggard from love
病 *koi yami, koi yamai* lovesickness
恋 *renren toshite* fondly, longingly
11 情 *renjō* love, attachment. *koinasake* lovesickness
盛 *koizaka(ri)* lovesick period
12 着 *renchaku* attachment, love
焦 *ko(i)-ko(gareru)* yearn for, be deeply in love with
13 煩 *koiwazura(i)* lovesickness
路 *koiji* romance, love's pathway
愛 *ren'ai* love, lovemaking, passion, emotion, affections
愛至上主義 *ren'aishijō shugi* love for love's sake
愛遊戯 *ren'ai yūgi* trifling with love
愛結婚 *ren'ai kekkon* love marriage
愛関係 *ren'ai kankei* love affair, love relationship
愛観 *ren'aikan* philosophy of love
14 歌 *koiuta, koika, renka* love song, love poem
暮 *ko(i)-ku(rasu)* live deeply in love
慕 *ko(i)-shita(u)* miss, yearn for. *rembo suru* love, fall in love with

15 敵 *koigataki* love rival
慰 *koinagusa(me)* comforting the lovelorn
22 籠 *ko(i)-komo(ru)* be deeply in love

恐 1853 / J3632 / M10552 B Kyō. *oso(reru), oso(roshigaru)* fear, dread, be afraid; be overawed; be apprehensive. *oso(raku)* perhaps, possibly. *oso(re)* fear, dread; consternation; anxiety; reverence, awe; danger, risk; chance, signs. *oso(renagara)* most respectfully. *oso(roshii)* terrible, awful, fierce; tremendous, marvelous. *kowa(i)* fearful, dreadful.
2 入 *oso(re)-i(ru)* be awestruck; be overwhelmed; be humiliated; be astonished, be sorry to trouble, beg pardon; be disconcerted; plead guilty, stand corrected
4 日病 *kyō-Nichibyō* Japanophobia
水病 *kyōsuibyō* rabies
5 乍 *oso(re)naga(ra)* most humbly, most respectfully
6 気 *osoro(shi)ge na* frightening, awful
多 *oso(re)-ō(i)* august, gracious, awe-inspiring, awful
米病 *kyō-Beibyō* fear of America
7 迫 *kyōhaku suru* threaten
8 英病 *kyō-Eibyō* Anglophobia
妻病 *kyōsaibyō* fear of one's wife
怖 *kyōfu* fear, terror, panic
怖心 *kyōfushin* feeling of terror
怖症 *kyōfushō* morbid fear
怖時代 *Kyōfu Jidai* the Reign of Terror
怖感 *kyōfukan* sense of fear
怖観念 *kyōfu kannen* fear complex
9 独病 *kyō-Dokubyō* Germanophobia
10 従 *oso(re)-shitaga(u)* cringe and follow
悦 *kyōetsu* delight, pleasure
悚 *kyōshō* crouching in fear
恐 *oso(ru)-oso(ru)* nervously, timidly, cautiously, reverently. *kowagowa* fearfully. *kyōkyō* respect (in letters)
竜 *kyōryū* dinosaur
11 喝 *kyōkatsu* threat, blackmail
喝取材 *kyōkatsu-shuzai* blackmail, extortion, shakedown
喝罪 *kyōkatsuzai* blackmail
12 慌 *kyōkō* panic, scare, consternation
惑 *oso(re)-mado(u)* be terrified
惶 *kyōkō* fear and trembling; your humble servant
惶敬白 *kyōkō keihaku* respectfully yours
惶謹言 *kyōkō kingen* respectfully yours
13 慎 *oso(re)-tsutsu(shimu)* fear and respect
戦 *oso(re)-onono(ku)* tremble, shudder
14 察 *kyōsatsu suru* respectfully appreciate another's feelings
16 龍 *kyōryū* dinosaur
17 縮 *kyōshuku* obligation, appreciation; regret; shame
謹 *oso(re)-tsutsu(shimu)* fear and respect
21 懼 *kyōku* fear, awe, dread
露病 *kyō-Robyō* Russophobia

7

悤 1854 / J-X / M10693 See **怱** 1815.

悔 1855 / J-X / M10659 See **悔** 1848.

悧 1856 / J5826 / M10689 See **俐** 208.

悁 1857 / J577a / M10623 Ken. En get angry; grow impatient.

悛 1858 / J5822 / M10674 Shun amend.

悒 1859 / J5825 / M10655 Yū. *fusa(gu)* be depressed, have the blues.

悚 1860 / J577e / M10672 Shō fear.
12 然 *shōzen* horror; shuddering

悌 1861 / J4470 / M10642 Tei serving our elders.
12 順 *teijun* obedience

悍 1862 / J577b / M10643 Kan rough, clumsy; violent.
10 馬 *kamba* unruly horse

悃 1863 / J577d / M10625 Kon sincerity.
16 篤 *kontoku* kindness, cordiality

悉 1864 / J3c3d / M10635 SHITSU. *tsu(kusu)* use up, run out of, exhaust; serve, befriend, work for, endeavor, do (one's duty). *kotogoto(ku)* all, entirely, altogether, completely. *tsubusa ni* minutely, fully.
9 皆 *shikkai* entirely, without exception

悋 1865 / J5827 / M10640 RIN stingy.
6 気 *rinki* jealousy, envy
13 嗇家 *rinshokuka* miserly person

悄 1866 / J5821 / M10627 SHŌ anxiety.
10 悄 *shioshio, sugosugo* all alone, despondent, crestfallen, heavy-hearted, weak
12 然 *shōzen(taru)* despondent, crestfallen

B **悩** 1867 / J473a / M10716′ **惱** 1899 / J583d / M10856 NŌ distress, illness. *naya(mu)* worry, be troubled, be afflicted, be in pain. *naya(masu)* annoy, embarrass, afflict, worry, oppress, torment. *naya(mi)* anguish, worry, distress, pain. *naya(mashii)* painful, distressing; melancholy; teasing.
8 苦 *naya(mi)-kuru(shimu)* be sorely troubled
10 殺 *nōsatsu suru* captivate, charm, fascinate

B **悦** 6868 / J3159 / M10629′ ETSU joy, rapture, ecstasy, amusement. *yoroko(bashu)* joyful, glad, pleasant. *yoroko(bi)* joy, delight, pleasure. *yoroko(bu)* rejoice, be glad, be pleased.
8 服 *eppuku* willing submission
13 楽 *etsuraku* enjoyment, pleasure

悖 1869 / J5823 / M10663 HAI. *moto(ru)* be contrary (to), go against, deviate from.
4 反 *haihan suru* be contrary to, go against, violate
8 逆 *haigyaku* unlawfulness, criminality
11 理 *hairi* absurdity
14 徳 *haitoku* immorality, corruption

B **悟** 1870 / J3867 / M10680 GO. *sato(ru)* perceive, discern, realize, understand, comprehend; attain enlightenment, find one's philosophy. *sato(ri)* understanding, comprehension; Buddhist enlightenment; philosophy.
2 入 *gonyū suru* enter (Buddhist) enlightenment
了 *goryō* complete comprehension
4 方 *sato(ri)kata* way of understanding
8 性 *gosei* wisdom, reason
11 道 *godō* (Buddhist) enlightenment
18 難 *sato(ri)gata(i)* hard to understand

B **患** 1871 / J3435 / M10691 GEN. KAN disease. *wazura(u)* be ill, suffer from; be afflicted. *ure(e), ure(i)* distress, sorrow, trouble, anxiety, grief.
8 泣 *wazura(i)-na(ku)* weep
者 *kanja* patient, victim (of a disease)
10 部 *kambu* diseased part, the affected area
家 *kanka* (doctor's) patient
13 禍 *kanka* disaster, misfortune, sorrow
18 難 *kannan* tribulation

B **悠** 1872 / J4d2a / M10681 YU. YŪ distant, longtime; leisure.
3 久 *yūkyū* eternity, permanence
8 長 *yūchō na* slow, tedious, deliberate, leisurely
10 容 *yūyō* repose, composure, serenity
11 悠 *yūyū(taru)* quiet, calm, composed, leisurely, deliberate; eternal, boundless, vast
悠自適 *yūyūjiteki* easy comfortable retirement
12 遠 *yūen* remoteness; eternity; repose
揚 *yūyō* repose, composure, serenity; easy climbing (in a plane)
然 *yūzen(taru)* quiet, calm, composed, leisurely, deliberate; eternal, boundless, vast

A **悪** 1873 / J302d / M10717 **惡** 1875 / J5828 / M10824 O. AKU evil, wrong, vice, wickedness, lawlessness. *a(shikarazu)* do not take offense. *waru(i), a(shii)* bad, evil, wrong; immoral; malicious; blamable; injurious; detrimental, malignant; be indisposed; inferior; homely; poor (memory); inclement; unlucky; out of order; unsavory. *niku(mu)* hate, detest. *niku(i)* hateful, abominable, poor-looking. *waru(bireru)* be timid, be ashamed. *aku(tareru)* be mischievous.

aku(tare) rowdiness; a rowdy. *waru* rascal, ruffian; wickedness. *niku(shimi)* hatred, enmity. *aku-* bad, wrong, evil, vicious, wicked; unfavorable, false; perverted; treacherous. *-niku(i)* difficult, awkward.

2 人 *akunin* bad man, villain
3 女 *akujo* wicked woman, ugly woman
口 *akkō, warukuchi, waruguchi, aku(tare)guchi* verbal abuse, insult, slander, evil speaking
口雑言 *akkō-zōgon* all kinds of malicious gossip
4 心 *akushin* evil thought, malicious motive. *oshin* nausea, urge to vomit
文 *akubun* poor writing, bad style, bad sentence
方 *akugata* villain's part
日 *akubi, akunichi* unlucky day
水 *akusui* undrinkable water
化 *akka* worsening, deterioration, aggravation, degeneration, corruption
友 *akuyū* bad companion
太郎 *akutarō* bad boy, mischievous boy, imp
天使 *akutenshi* evil angels
天候 *akutenkō* bad weather
5 玉 *akudama* bad character, bad person; the villain
用 *akuyō* misuse, abuse, perversion
処 *akusho* dangerous place; house of ill-fame, bad place
巧 *warudaku(mi)* wiles, sinister design, trick, conspiracy, intrigue
令 *akurei* a bad decree
平等 *akubyōdō* leaning over backwards to be impartial
6 舌 *akuzetsu* an evil tongue, gossip
血 *akuchi, oketsu* impure blood
行 *akugyō, akkō* misdeed, wrongdoing, wickedness
気 *warugi* ill will, evil intent, ill feeling, distrust
因悪果 *akuin-akka* sowing evil and reaping evil
因縁 *akuinnen* evil destiny
名 *akumei, akumyō* bad reputation, notoriety, bad name
名高 *akumyōdaka(i)* infamous
7 言 *akugen* uncomplimentary remarks, slander
役 *akuyaku* the villain, the villain's part
投 *akutō* wild pitch
阻 *tsuwari, oso* morning sickness
声 *akusei* bad voice; evil speaking
条件 *akujōken* unfavorable conditions
材料 *akuzairyō* adverse stock-market factors
足掻 *waruagaki* wicked mischief, wicked play
巫山戯 *warufuzake* prank, practical joke, horseplay
8 例 *akurei* bad example
性 *akusei* virulence; malignant (cancer); pernicious (anemia). *akushō* evil nature; licentiousness, lewdness
所 *akusho* dangerous place; house of ill-fame, bad place
法 *akuhō* a bad law
念 *akunen* evil thought, malicious motive, spite
妻 *akusai* a bad wife
果 *akka* bad results
者 *warumono* rascal, ruffian, scoundrel
事 *akuji* evil deed, crime, wickedness
知恵 *warujie* cunning, guile
逆 *akugyaku* treason, treachery, atrocity
逆無道 *akugyaku-mudō* treason, treachery, atrocity
9 風 *akufū* vice, evil manners, bad custom
食 *akujiki suru* eat repulsive things, eat poor food, eat meat. *akushoku suru* eat poor food
疫 *akueki* a plague, pestilence, epidemic
相 *akusō* evil countenance
神 *akujin* evil god
計 *akkei, akukei* plot, trick, evil scheme
政 *akusei* misgovernment
臭 *akushū* bad odor, stench 「underworld
巷 *aku (no) chimata* skid row,
10 鬼 *akki* evil spirit, demon, devil
馬 *akuba, akume* wild horse, unmanageable horse
疾 *akushitsu* malignant or virulent disease
症 *akushō* malignant or virulent disease
徒 *akuto* rascal, scoundrel, villain
党 *akutō* rascal, scoundrel, villain
酒 *akushu* cheap liquor
洒落 *warujare* offensive joke
11 道 *akudō* evil course, wrong course
運 *akuun* bad luck
遊 *waruaso(bi)* prank, evil pleasures, gambling

婦 *akufu* wicked woman
球 *akkyū* hard ball to hit; bad pitch
酔 *waruyo(i)* drunken sickness, drunken frenzy
婆 *akuba* a mean old woman
貨 *akka* bad money
達者 *warudassha* fast slipshod work
推量 *waruzuiryō* distrust, unjust suspicion
悪戯 *waruitazura* mischief
習 *akushū* bad habit, vice
習慣 *akushūkan* bad habit, evil practices
12 税 *akuzei* irrational tax
評 *akuhyō* ill repute, bad reputation, unfavorable criticism
寒 *okan* chill
童 *akudō* bad boy, naughty boy
筆 *akuhitsu* poor handwriting
策 *akusaku* poor policy, poor plan
循環 *akujunkan* vicious circle
13 僧 *akusō* dissolute priest
漢 *akkan* rascal, villain, scoundrel, ruffian, crook
路 *akuro* bad road
夢 *akumu* nightmare, bad dream
意 *akui* ill will, malice
業 *akugyō* evil, sinful deeds. *akugō* evil karma
戦 *akusen* hard fighting
戦苦闘 *akusen-kutō* hard fighting
感 *akkan* ill feeling, unhappy feeling. *okan* feeling feverish and chilly
感化 *akkanka* evil influence
感情 *akkanjō* ill feeling, ill will, animosity, bad impression
14 様 *a(shi)zama ni* unfavorably, slanderously
辣 *akuratsu* craftiness
銭 *akusen* ill-gotten money; bad coin
態 *akutai* abusive language
徳 *akutoku* vices, corruption, immorality
徳新聞 *akutoku shimbun* irresponsible newspaper
15 縁 *akuen* evil destiny, evil connection, unfortunate marriage
罵 *akuba* cursing, vilification
霊 *akurei, akuryō, akurō* evil spirit
弊 *akuhei* vice, abuse, evil
熱 *onetsu* fever following a chill
賢 *warugashiko(i)* cunning, crafty, wily, sly

質 *akushitsu* poor quality, malignancy; viciousness
質化 *akushitsuka* worsening
戯 *itazura, warusa, waruitazura* mean mischief. *akugi* practical joke
戯子 *itazurakko* mischievous boy
戯小僧 *itazura kozō* mischievous boy
戯坊主 *itazura bōzu* mischievous boy
戯者 *itazuramono* loose woman; useless fellow, mischief maker
戯書 *itazuraga(ki)* scribbling, doodling
戯盛 *itazurazaka(ri)* mischievous age
戯着 *itazuragi* rompers, play suit
17 擦 *waruzure* oversophistication. *waruzu(reru)* get worse and worse
18 癖 *akuheki, waruguse* bad habit, vice
騒 *warusawa(gi)* disorderly merrymaking
21 魔 *akuma* Satan; devil, demon, evil spirit; fiend
魔払い *akumahara(i)* exorcism

8

悳 1874 / J575c / M10724 See **徳** 1767.

惡 1875 / J5828 / M10824 See **悪** 1873.

惠 1876 / J582a / M10822 See **恵** 1847.

[illegible] 1877 / J-X / M-X **惧** 1878 / J577c / M10848 See **懼** 2016.

惋 1879 / J5824 / M10664 BON *wasu(reru)* forget. BAN *mado(u)* get lost; be perplexed, be in doubt.

悽 1880 / J582e / M10744 SEI *ita(mu)* be sad; sorrowful; grieve over.

惆 1881 / J582f / M10757 CHŪ *ura(mu)* feel bitter; regret; lose hope.

惓 1882 / J582b / M10795 KEN be respectful; kind; cordial.

惘 1883 / J5831 / M10809 BŌ. MŌ be depressed; lose hope; be shocked. *aki(reru)* be aghast, be disgusted, be shocked.

悴 1884 / J582c / M10726 **忰** 1790 / J582d / M10381 SUI becoming emaciated. *segare* son.

悸 1885 / J5829 / M10733 KI pulsate; shudder.

惹 1886 / J3c66 / M10866 JAKU attract, captivate.
10 起 *jakki suru* bring about, cause, provoke (discussion)

惇 1887 / J4657 / M10759 TON. JUN *atsu(i)* thick; warm hearted; sincere.
9 信 *tonshin* firmly believe
10 恵 *tonkei* rich blessing

悵 1888 / J5830 / M10727 CHŌ be sad.
9 恨 *chōkon* deep regret; bitter resentment
12 然 *chōzen to* sadly, sorrowfully

惣 1889 / J415a / M10829 SŌ all.
7 社 *sōsha* a shrine enshrining several gods
11 菜 *sōzai* side dish

惟 1890 / J3054 / M10820 I. *omom(miru)* consider, reflect. *omo(u)* think, believe, judge, esteem; consider, realize; feel like; regard as; anticipate; imagine, suppose, guess; mistake for; recall; intend; desire; love, care for, yearn after; wonder; suspect.
9 神 *kannagara* as of old
神道 *Kannagara (no) Michi* Shinto, Way of Gods

B **悼** 1891 / J4569 / M10738 TŌ. *ita(mu)* grieve over.
11 惜 *tōseki* lamentation
12 詞 *tōshi* grieving over a bereavement
13 辞 *tōji* message of condolence, funeral oration
14 歌 *tōka* an elegy

B **惑** 1892 / J4f47 / M10789 WAKU. *mado(u)* be perplexed, be in doubt, hesitate, vacillate, go astray, err; be tempted; be infatuated; be misguided. *mado(wasu), mado(wakasu)* perplex; mislead, deceive; tempt; seduce; charm, infatuate. *mado(i)* delusion; perplexity.
7 乱 *wakuran* bewilderment, confusion
8 者 *mado(i)mono* wanderer
9 星 *wakusei* planet
星間 *wakuseikan no* interplanetary
13 溺 *wakudeki* indulgence, addiction; infatuation

惚 1893 / J397b / M10811 KOTSU. *ho(reru)* fall in love with, admire, be entranced with. *boke(ru)* grow senile; become mentally weak; fade, discolor. *hoke(ru)* grow senile; become mentally weak; become enthusiastic; be beside oneself. *hoke, boke* dull; dull-headedness.
4 込 *ho(re)-ko(mu)* fall deeply in love
6 色 *bo(ke) iro* dull color
気 *noroke(ru)* boast of love conquests. *noroke* love affair
気話 *norokebanashi* talking about romance
11 惚 *horebore to* fondly. *horebore suru* be charmed
16 薬 *ho(re)gusuri* love charm, love potion

B **惜** 1894 / J404b / M10814 SEKI. SHAKU. *o(shimu), o(shigaru)* be sparing of; be frugal with; be stingy with; regret; value, prize; be reluctant. *o(shii)* regrettable, pitiful, disappointing; precious; wasteful. *o(shimazu)* without regret, ungrudgingly; generously. *o(shiminaku)* freely, regardless of expenses. *o(shisō) ni* grudgingly, reluctantly.
6 気 *o(shi)ge* regret
無 *o(shi)ge(mo)na(ku)* without regret, ungrudgingly; generously
7 別 *sekibetsu* parting regrets
10 陰 *sekiin* extremely careful use of time
11 敗 *sekihai* regrettable defeat; defeat by a narrow margin
13 歳 *sekisai* lamenting the departing of the old year

悶 1895 / J4c65 / M10729 MON. *moda(eru)* be in agony, be worried.
6 死 *monshi* agonizing death
8 苦 *moda(e)-kuru(shimu)* writhe in pain

[12]悶 *mommon(taru)* discontented
絶 *monzetsu suru* faint; fall in convulsions
着 *monchaku* trouble; dispute

B 惨 1896 J3b34 M10850 慘 1949 J584e M11094 SAN. ZAN disaster; cruelty; wretchedness. *mugo(i)* cruel, merciless, harsh. *mugo(tarashii)* cruel; horrible; tragic. *san(taru)* disastrous, appalling. *mijime na* sad, pitiful, wretched.

[6]死 *zanshi, sanshi* tragic death, violent death
死体 *zanshitai* mangled body
死者 *zanshisha* mangled body
[7]状 *sanjō* pitiful situation
[8]事 *sanji* disaster, tragedy, terrible accident
[9]胆 *santan(taru)* pitiable, wretched
[10]害 *sangai* ravages, havoc, heavy damage
殺 *zansatsu* slaughter, massacre, murder
殺死体 *zansatsu shitai* mangled body
殺者 *zansatsusha* murderer, slayer
殺事件 *zansatsu jiken* murder case
[11]敗 *zampai, sampai* overwhelming defeat, crushing defeat
[12]絶 *sanzetsu* great cruelty
落 *sanraku* slump, sudden fall
[13]禍 *sanka* terrible disaster, calamity, horrors (of war)
[14]酷 *zankoku* cruelty, atrocity, brutality
[15]劇 *sangeki* tragedy, tragic event
[16]憺 *santan(taru)* pitiable, wretched, tragic
澹 *santan(taru)* pitiable, wretched, tragic

A 悲 1897 J4861 M10720 HI. *kana(shimu), kana(shigaru)* grieve, be sad, deplore, mourn for, regret. *kana(shimi)* sorrow, grief. *kana(shige) na* sad, sorrowful, plaintive. *kana(shii)* sad, pathetic, plaintive.

[6]曲 *hikyoku* plaintive melody
壮 *hisō na* pathetic, tragic
[8]泣 *kana(shimi)-na(ku)* mourn and weep. *hikyū* wailing
況 *hikyō* distress, adversity 「mourning
歩 *kana(shimi)-aru(ku)* go around
[9]風 *hifū* a sighing wind; a late-fall wind; the tragedy of life
哀 *hiai* sorrow, grief, misery, pathos
[10]涙 *hirui* tears of sadness
恋 *hiren* disappointed love
[11]運 *hiun* bad luck, misfortune, sad fate
惨 *hisan* misery, wretchedness
望 *hibō* wicked ambition
[12]痛 *hitsū* bitterness, pathos
報 *hihō* sad news, news of a death
喜 *hiki* joy and sorrow
喜劇 *hikigeki* tragicomedy
[13]傷 *hishō* misery, wretchedness
嘆 *kana(shimi)-nage(ku)* weep and wail. *hitan* grief, sorrow
愴 *hisō* pathetic, sad
話 *hiwa* sad story
愁 *hishū* pathos, sorrow
業 *higō* misfortune
[14]鳴 *himei* shriek, scream
境 *hikyō* adversity, distress
酸 *hisan* misery, wretchedness
歌 *hika* elegy, dirge
[15]憤 *hifun* indignation, resentment
憤慷慨 *hifun-kōgai* give vent to a jeremiad
調 *hichō* plaintive note, mournful melody, touch of sadness
歎 *hitan* grief, sorrow
劇 *higeki* tragedy, tragic drama
劇的 *higekiteki* tragic
[18]観 *hikan* pessimism, disappointment
観主義 *hikan shugi* pessimism
観主義者 *hikan shugisha* pessimist
観的 *hikanteki* pessimistic
観説 *hikansetsu* pessimism
観論 *hikanron* pessimism
観論者 *hikanronsha* pessimist
[19]願 *higan* Buddhist prayer for mankind

A 情 1898 J3e70 M10756′ SEI. JŌ feeling, emotion; passion; affection; heart; human nature; sympathy; sincerity; circumstances, facts; obstinacy. *nasake* sympathy, compassion.

[2]人 *jōnin, jōjin* sweetheart, lover
[4]心 *nasakegokoro* sympathy, compassion
火 *jōka* flame of love
夫 *jōfu* adulterer, paramour
[5]史 *jōshi* love story
[6]死 *jōshi* double love suicide
交 *jōkō* intimacy; illicit relations. *nasake (o) kawa(su)* have illicit relations with
合 *jōa(i)* unity of sentiment, sympathy

7 状 *jōjō* circumstances, conditions
状酌量 *jōjō shakuryō* sentence reduction due to commiserative circumstances
8 味 *jōmi* charm, glamor, attraction; warm-heartedness
知 *nasakeshi(razu)* pitiless
念 *jōnen* sentiment
実 *jōjitsu* personal considerations; favoritism; actual circumstances
炎 *jōen* fierce passion
事 *jōji* love affair, liaison
況 *jōkyō* circumstances
況証拠 *jōkyō shōko* circumstantial evidence
10 致 *jōchi* mood, sentiment, artistic effect
11 婦 *jōfu* adulteress
張 *jō (o) ha(ru)* be stubborn
深 *nasakebuka(i)* tenderhearted, compassionate
理 *jōri* heart and mind; reason and sentiment
移 *jō (ga) utsu(ru)* become fond of
欲 *jōyoku* passions, carnal desire
12 景 *jōkei* scene; nature and sentiment
無 *nasakena(i)* heartless, cruel; pitiful, shameful, regrettable
報 *jōhō* information, news, intelligence report
報屋 *jōhōya* sports dopester
報部 *jōhōbu* information bureau
報公開 *jōhō kōkai* making information public
報経路 *jōhō keiro* pipeline, information channel
報機関 *jōhō kikan* counterintelligence corps, information gathering machinery
13 痴 *jōchi* illicit lovemaking
話 *jōwa* lover's talk; love story
愛 *jōai* affection, love
義 *jōgi* friendship
勢 *jōsei* state of affairs, condition, indication, appearance
感 *jōkan* emotion, feeling
意 *jōi* emotion and will; sentiment
意投合 *jōi-tōgō* mutual understanding
14 歌 *jōka* love song
態 *jōtai* situation, state of affairs
緒 *jōcho, jōsho* emotion, feeling
緒主義 *jōsho shugi* emotionalism
15 趣 *jōshu* mood, sentiment; artistic effect
縁 *jōen* love affair
誼 *jōgi* friendship
調 *jōchō* atmosphere, tone, mood, spirit
弊 *jōhei* abuses, favoritism
慾 *jōyoku* passions, carnal desire
熱 *jōnetsu* passion; enthusiasm
16 懐 *jōkai* heart, thoughts, feelings
操 *jōsō* sentiment

9

惱 1899 / J583d / M10856 See 悩 1867.

惴 1900 / J5838 / M10859 ZUI. SUI fear; tremble with fear.

惷 1901 / J5836 / M10864 SHUN be disordered, be in disarray, be confused. *oro(ka)* foolish. *ugome(ku)* wriggle, squirm.

惺 1902 / J5839 / M10868 SEI *sato(ru)* perceive, discern, realize; attain enlightenment.

愃 1903 / J583a / M10891 KEN. SEN rich; pleasant, agreeable; forget. *yutaka na* rich, abundant.

愎 1904 / J583f / M10920 FUKU. HYOKU *moto(ru)* go against, not conform to, resist; be obstinate.

愡 1905 / J583b / M10956 SŌ *sewa(shii)* busy, occupied.

愒 1906 / J-X / M10933 KATSU, KEI, KETSU, KAI covet; threaten.

愠 1907 / J-X / M10954 **慍** 1930 / J5832 / M11059 UN. ON. *ika(ru)* be angry, get excited, be offended.

惼 1908 / J-X / M10872 HEN narrow-minded.

愈 1909 / J-X / M10904 **愈** 1910 / J4c7c / M-X YU. *iyoiyo* more and more, increasingly; at last; beyond doubt.

13 愈 *iyoiyo* more and more, increasingly; at last; beyond doubt

愆 1911 J5834 M10900 KEN mistake, fault, offense.

惶 1912 J5835 M10863 KŌ fear.
21 懼 *kōku* reverence; epistolary closing

愀 1913 J5837 M10884 SHŪ respect.
12 然 *shūzen* change in the color of the face; grief

愕 1914 J5833 M10939 GAKU. *odoro(ku)* be surprised; be frightened.
12 然 *gakuzen to* in terror, in amazement

愍 1915 J583e M10919 BIN. MIN. *awa(remu)* pity, have mercy on, sympathize with. *awa(remi)* pity, compassion.
12 然 *binzen(taru)* pitiable

惻 1916 J583c M10869 SOKU be sad.
12 惻 *sokusoku* pitiful condition
13 隠 *sokuin* pity, sympathy

B 慌 1917 J3932 M11057 慌 1918 J-X M-X 慌 1919 J-X M-X
KŌ. *awa(teru)* be confused, lose one's head, be hurried, be hasty. *awa(tefutameku)* be confused, be disconcerted, be panicked. *awatada(shii)* busy, bustling, hurried, confused.
6 者 *awa(te)mono* absent-minded person, blunderer, scatterbrain, careless person
12 惑 *awa(te)-mado(u)* be flurried and perplexed

B 愉 1920 J4c7b M10905' YU rejoice. *tano(shimu)* enjoy, amuse oneself; anticipate. *tano(shii)* merry, pleasant, cheerful, joyful.
7 快 *yukai na* happy, pleasant, delightful; cheerful
10 悦 *yuetsu* joy
13 楽 *yuraku* pleasure, joy

B 惰 1921 J4246 M10855 DA laziness. *okota(ru)* neglect; be off guard; be feeling better.
2 力 *daryoku* inertia, momentum, force of habit
6 気 *daki* indolence, listlessness
8 性 *dasei* inertia, momentum, force of habit
10 眠 *damin* indolence, inactivity, idle slumber
弱 *dajaku* effeminacy, emasculation, laziness
13 勢 *dasei* inertia, momentum, force of habit

A 想 1922 J415b M10858 SŌ idea, conception, thought. *omo(u)* think, believe, judge, esteem; consider, realize; feel like; regard as; anticipate; imagine, suppose, guess; mistake for; recall; intend; desire; love, care for, yearn after; wonder; suspect.
8 到 *sōtō suru* think of, consider, hit upon
念 *sōnen* idea, conception
定 *sōtei* hypothesis, assumption
9 思 *sōshi* mutual love
10 起 *sōki* recollection, remembrances
11 望 *sōbō* admiration; yearning; anticipation
14 像 *sōzō* imagination, supposition, conjecture
像力 *sōzōryoku* imagination, imaginative power
像上 *sōzōjō no* imaginary
像化 *sōzōka* idealization
像境 *sōzōkyō* dream world, Utopia
像説 *sōzōsetsu* hypothesis

B 愁 1923 J3d25 M10885 SHU. *ure(u), ure(eru)* grieve, lament, be anxious. *ure(i), ure(e)* sad, unhappy, gloomy.
4 心 *shūshin* a sad heart, distress of mind
6 色 *shūshoku* melancholy air, anxious look, traces of sorrow, gloom
7 吟 *shūgin* grieving and worrying
9 思 *shūshi* a sad heart, distress of mind
眉 *shūbi* worried look, knitted brows, anxiety
眉開 *shūbi (o) hira(ku)* be relieved of worry
12 悶 *shūmon* sadness and agony
訴 *shūso* appeal, petition, supplication
雲 *shūun* clouds of sorrow; gloom
然 *shūzen toshite* sorrowfully
13 嘆 *shūtan* lamentation, sorrow

腸 *shūchō* grieving

傷 *shūshō* grief, lamentation; condolence

傷様 *(go)shūshōsama* an expression of condolence

15 歎 *shūtan* grief, lamentation

歎場 *shūtamba* tragic scene

歎話 *shūtambanashi* tale of woe

B **慈** 1924 J3b7c M10980′ **慈** 1929 J-X M11048 Jɪ. *itsuku(shimu)* love, be affectionate to; pity. *itsuku(shimi)* affection, love.

4 心 *jishin* benevolence, mercy

父 *jifu* affectionate father

5 母 *jibo* affectionate mother

兄 *jikei* affectionate elder brother

8 雨 *jiu* beneficial or welcome rain

10 訓 *jikun* kind counsel; mother's advice

恵 *jikei* mercy and love

11 眼 *jigen* merciful eye

12 悲 *jihi* compassion, benevolence, charity, mercy

悲心 *jihishin* benevolence

善 *jizen* charity, philanthropy

善心 *jizenshin* benevolence, liberality

善市 *jizen'ichi* charity bazaar

善会 *jizenkai* philanthropic society

善事業 *jizen jigyō* philanthropic work

善家 *jizenka* charitable person, philanthropist

善箱 *jizembako* charity box

善鍋 *jizennabe* charity pot

13 愛 *jiai* affection, kindness, love, benevolence

B **愚** 1925 J3672 M10946 Gᴜ folly, foolishness, absurdity; fool. *oro(kana), oro(kashii)* foolish, stupid, dull. *gu-* my humble (opinion).

2 人 *gujin* fool, dunce

3 女 *gujo* my (foolish) daughter (humble)

才 *gusai* poor ability, my poor intelligence

4 父 *gufu* my (foolish) father (humble)

夫 *gufu* foolish man

5 母 *gubo* my (foolish) mother (humble)

生 *gusei* I (humble)

付 *gu(nimo)tsu(kanu)* ridiculous, absurd

札 *gusatsu* my letter

兄 *gukei* my (foolish) elder brother (humble)

民 *gumin* ignorant people

6 老 *gurō* my old self

臣 *gushin* foolish retainer

行 *gukō* folly, foolish move

劣 *guretsu* foolishness, stupidity, absurdity

考 *gukō* my humble opinion

7 見 *guken* my humble opinion

言 *gugen* my (foolish) words (humble)

作 *gusaku* poor piece of writing

弟 *gutei* my (foolish) younger brother (humble)

弄 *gurō* mockery, ridicule

図 *guzu(ru)* grumble, criticize; tease; charge falsely; be cloudy. *guzu* dullard

図付 *guzutsu(ku)* dally, loiter, loaf, dawdle, hesitate, be irresolute

図愚図 *guzuguzu* slowly, lazily, leisurely, hesitatingly

8 妹 *gumai* my (foolish) younger sister (humble)

姉 *gushi* my (foolish) elder sister (humble)

拙 *gusetsu* foolish and clumsy; I (humble)

物 *gubutsu* fool, bonehead

陋 *gurō* foolish and mean

直 *guchoku* simple honesty; tactless frankness

妻 *gusai* my (foolish) wife (humble)

忠 *guchū* my loyalty

者 *gusha, oro(ka)mono* fool, dunce

9 昧 *gumai* stupidity, ignorance

計 *gukei* a foolish plan; my (foolish) plan (humble)

衷 *guchū* my feelings

連隊 *gurentai* gang of young toughs

10 将 *gushō* foolish general; stupid commander

案 *guan* my humble opinion, my (foolish) plan (humble); a foolish plan

書 *gusho* trashy book; my humble work

息 *gusoku* my (foolish) son (humble)

挙 *gukyo* foolish undertaking

11 問 *gumon* foolish question

婦 *gufu* foolish woman; my (foolish) wife (humble)

12 鈍 *gudon* stupidity, silliness

策 *gusaku* my (foolish) plan (humble); foolish plan, poor policy

13 僧 *gusō* foolish priest; I (humble, used by a priest)

蒙 *gumō* stupidity

意 *gui* my humble idea
痴 *guchi* grumbling; folly, foolishness *guchi(ru)* complain
痴言 *guchigoto* foolish talk
痴話 *guchibanashi* tedious grumbling
14 説 *gusetsu* foolish view; my humble opinion
察 *gusatsu* my guess, my observation
15 慮 *guryo* my (foolish) idea
稿 *gukō* my poem, my manuscript
論 *guron* foolish argument, absurd opinion; my humble opinion
19 癡 *guchi* grumbling, complaining. *guchi(ru)* complain

A 意 1926 / J3055 / M10921 I mind, heart; care; liking, taste; inclination, will, intention; thought, idea; desire.
2 力 *iryoku* will, will power
4 中 *ichū* intention
中人 *ichū (no) hito* lovers
5 外 *igai na* unexpected, surprising
6 向 *ikō* intention, idea, inclination
匠 *ishō* design, idea
匠権 *ishōken* design right
地 *iji* temper; disposition; will power; obstinacy
地汚 *ijikitana(i)* greedy, gluttonous
地張 *ijiba(ru)* persist in, be obstinate. *iji(p)pa(ri)* obstinacy; obstinate person
地悪 *ijiwaru(i)* ill-tempered, unfortunate
地穢 *ijikitana(i)* greedy, gluttonous
気 *iki* spirit, heart; disposition
気込 *ikigo(mu)* be enthusiastic about
気地 *ikuji, ikiji* self-respect, honor, pride
気投合 *ikitōgō* sympathy, mutual understanding
気阻喪 *ikisosō* depression, dejection
気沮喪 *ikisosō* depression, dejection
気消沈 *ikishōchin* depression, dejection
気軒昂 *ikikenkō* high spirits, high morale
気盛 *ikisaka(n)* high spirits
気筋 *ikisuji* flirting
気揚揚 *iki-yōyō(taru)* triumphant, exultant
気銷沈 *ikishōchin* depression, dejection
気衝天 *ikishōten* high spirits, high morale
7 図 *ito* intention, aim
見 *iken* opinion, idea, suggestion; remonstrance, admonition
見広告 *iken kōkoku* opinion advertising
見書 *ikensho* written opinion
志 *ishi* will, mind, volition
志力 *ishiryoku* will power
志薄弱 *ishi-hakujaku* weak will, lacking a purpose
志薄弱者 *ishi-hakujakusha* weak-willed person
8 表 *ihyō* surprise, something unexpected
味 *imi* meaning, significance
味合 *imia(i)* meaning, reason
味深長 *imishinchō ni* significantly
味論 *imiron* semantics
9 恨 *ikon* grudge, ill-will, enmity
相 *isō* thoughts
思 *ishi* intention, purpose, mind
思表示 *ishi hyōji* declaration of intent
思能力 *ishi nōryoku* mental capacity
10 馬心猿 *iba-shin'en* uncontrollable passions
11 訳 *iyaku* free translation, broad translation
欲 *iyoku* volition, will
13 想 *isō* thoughts
想外 *isōgai no* unexpected, unsuspected
義 *igi* meaning, significance
義深 *igibuka(i)* full of meaning; of great value
15 趣 *ishu* grudge, malice, spite; thoughts; intention
趣返 *ishugae(shi)* revenge
趣斬 *ishugi(ri)* killing (someone) because of a grudge
18 嚮 *ikō* intention, idea, inclination
19 識 *ishiki* consciousness
識不明 *ishiki fumei* unconsciousness
識的 *ishikiteki ni* consciously
識野 *ishikiya* field of consciousness

A 愛 1927 / J3026 / M10947 AI love, affection, favorite. *ai(suru), me(zuru), me(deru)* love; admire, appreciate. *ai(rashii)* lovely, pretty, sweet. *ito(shii)* beloved, dear, loving, pitiable. *mana-* love.
2 人 *aijin* lover; lover of mankind
3 子 *ito(shi)go, aishi* favorite child; beloved child
4 犬 *aiken* pet dog
犬家 *aikenka* dog lover
5 用 *aiyō* habitual use; favorite
他 *aita* altruism

他主義 *aita shugi* altruism
6 好 *aikō* love for, liking for
好者 *aikōsha* lover of
好家 *aikōka* lover of
7 吟 *aigin* favorite poem or song; lover of poetry and song
児 *aiji* beloved child
弟子 *manadeshi* favorite pupil
8 育 *aiiku* tender nurture
妾 *aishō* prostitute
苦 *aikuru(shii)* charming, sweet, cute
妻 *aisai* beloved wife
妻家 *aisaika* devoted husband
国 *aikoku* patriotism
国心 *aikokushin* patriotism
国主義 *aikoku shugi* patriotism
国者 *aikokusha* patriot
玩 *aigan suru* be fond of
玩物 *aigambutsu* prized article; pet
玩者 *aigansha* lover, admirer, fancier
玩動物 *aigan dōbutsu* animal pet
10 娘 *manamusume* favorite daughter
孫 *aison* beloved grandchild
称 *aishō* pet name, term of endearment
息 *aisoku* cute boy, beloved son; your son
校心 *aikōshin* love of one's school
党心 *aitōshin* party loyalty; party spirit
書家 *aishoka* booklover
馬 *aiba* favorite horse
馬家 *aibaka* horse lover
郷 *aikyō* local patriotism
郷心 *aikyōshin* local patriotism
11 唱 *aishō suru* love to read
情 *aijō* love, affection
惜 *aiseki suru* miss (someone); be loathe to part
猫 *aibyō* pet cat
欲 *aiyoku* passion, love and lust
執 *aishū* attachment, covetous affection
鳥家 *aichōka* bird lover
球家 *aikyūka* baseball fan
12 婿 *aisei* favorite son-in-law
着 *aichaku, aijaku* attachment, covetous affection
飲家 *aiinka* habitual drinker
敬 *aikei, aikyō* love and respect; charm, winsomenes, attractiveness, courtesy
敬笑 *aikyōwara(i)* flattering smile
13 煙家 *aienka* habitual smoker
禽 *aikin* pet bird
禽家 *aikinka* bird lover
想 *aiso, aisō* civility, amiability, courtesy, compliments, entertainment, hospitality, sociability
想尽 *aisozu(kashi), aisōzu(kashi)* alienating (someone)
14 徳 *aitoku* practicing charity
憎 *aizō* likes and dislikes, love and hatred, partiality
誦 *aishō suru* love to read
慕 *aibo* love, attachment, adoration
読 *aidoku* reading with pleasure
読者 *aidokusha* reader, subscriber, admirer (of a writer)
読書 *aidokusho* favorite book
15 憫 *aibin* pity, compassion
撫 *aibu suru* love dearly. *aibu* caress
慾 *aiyoku* passion; love; lust
嬌 *aikyō* charm, winsomeness, attractiveness, courtesy
嬌者 *aikyōmono* amicable fellow, funny little fellow
16 嬢 *aijō* beloved daughter
機 *aiki* one's personal plane; one's own camera
餐 *aisan* (Christian) love feast, communion
餐会 *aisankai* (Christian) love feast
20 護 *aigo* protection, tender care
21 顧 *aiko* patronage, favor

A **感** 1928 / J3436 / M10953 KAN feeling, sensation, sentiment; sense; emotion; impression; intuition. *kan(jiru), kan(zuru)* feel, experience, be conscious of; be impressed by; respond to. *kan(ji)* feeling, sense, sensation; perception; sensibility; impression; sentiment; effect, influence; touch, the feel.

2 入 *kan(ji)-i(ru)* be deeply impressed
4 心 *kanshin* admiration, wonder
方 *kan(ji)kata* way of feeling (about something)
化 *kanka* influence, inspiration; reform, correction
化事業 *kanka jigyō* reformatory work
化院 *kankain* reformatory
5 付 *kanzu(ku)* suspect, sense, scent
6 光 *kankō* exposure to light; sensitization
光板 *kankōban* sensitized plate, dry plate
光度 *kankōdo* photosensitivity
光紙 *kankōshi* photographic printing paper

7 応 *kannō* inspiration; divine response; sympathy; effect, efficacy; influence; induction (in electricity)
吟 *kangin* reciting with emotion
状 *kanjō* letter of commendation; letter of approval
声 *kansei* voice of admiration
8 佩 *kampai* deep impression
性 *kansei* sensitivity, sensitiveness, sense
泣 *kankyū suru* be deeply affected, be touched. *kankyu* crying for joy
知 *kanchi* perception
取 *kan(ji)-to(ru)* take in; appreciate (a poem)
服 *kampuku* admiration, wonder
官 *kankan* sense organ
易 *kan(ji)yasu(i)* sensitive to, excitable, nervous, emotional; impressionable
受 *kanju* impression; (radio) reception
受性 *kanjusei* receptivity, sensitivity, susceptibility; irritability
9 度 *kando* sensitivity; severity (of a quake)
冒 *kambō, kaze* a cold, influenza
染 *kansen* infection
10 悟 *kango* feeling and understanding
恩 *kan'on* gratitude
涙 *kanrui* tears of gratitude
11 得 *kantoku suru* get wind of, become aware of, realize
動 *kandō* impression, inspiration, emotion, excitement
動詞 *kandoshi* interjection
情 *kanjō* feelings; emotion; sentiment; impulse; passion
情的 *kanjōteki* emotional, impulsive
情家 *kanjōka* emotional person
情論 *kanjōron* heated argument
12 喜 *kanki* joy, delight, ecstasy
覚 *kankaku* feeling, sensation; senses
覚主義 *kankaku shugi* sensualism
覚神経 *kankaku shinkei* sensory nerves
覚論 *kankakuron* sensationalism; sensualism; esthetics
覚器官 *kankaku kikan* sensory organs
13 嘆 *kantan* admiration, wonder
嘆詞 *kantanshi* interjection
触 *kanshoku* sense of touch, feeling, sensation
電 *kanden* electric shock
傷 *kanshō* sentimentality
傷的 *kanshōteki* sentimental
慨 *kangai* deep emotion
慨無量 *kangai-muryō* full of deep emotion
話 *kanwa* testimony (in church)
話会 *kanwakai* testimony meeting
想 *kansō* thoughts, impressions, sentiments, feelings
想文 *kansōbun* description of impressions
14 銘 *kammei* deep impression
銘的 *kammeiteki* impressive
銘深 *kammeifuka(i)* impressive
15 憤 *kampun suru* be inspired to action
賞 *kanshō* appreciation and praise; reward for merit
潮河川 *kanchō kasen* tidal river
歎 *kantan* admiration; wonder
歎文 *kantambun* exclamatory sentence
歎符 *kantanfu* exclamation point
歎詞 *kantanshi* interjection
16 懐 *kankai* deep impression
激 *kangeki* deep emotion, inspiration, impression
興 *kankyō* interest; fun ⌈inspiration
奮 *kampun* deep emotion, impression,
奮興起 *kampun-kōki* inspired and aroused to action
17 謝 *kansha* thanks; appreciation; thanksgiving; grace
謝状 *kanshajō* letter of thanks, testimonial, citation
謝祭 *kanshasai* Thanksgiving Day, thanks offering

10

慈 1929 / J-X / M11048 See 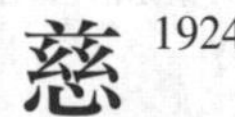 1924.

慍 1930 / J5832 / M11059 See 慍 1907.

慤 1931 / J5842 / M10983 KAKU discreet, prudent; sincere, honest; good. *tsutsu(shimu)* be discreet, be prudent.

愬 1932 / J5847 / M10988 SŌ *oso(reru)* fear, be afraid of. SAKU *utta(eru)* complain of; sue, litigate; appeal to.

10

慱 1933 / J5849 / M11028 TAN. SEN grieve, lament; be round.

愿 1934 / J5845 / M11030 GEN prudent; honest; forthright; serious. *tsutsu(shimu)* be discreet, be prudent.

慂 1935 / J584a / M11039 YŌ direct (someone), advise.

愾 1936 / J5841 / M11029 GAI, KI, KE breathlessness; anger.

慥 1937 / J5854 / M11114 ZŌ. *tashi(kani)* certainly, doubtless.

慝 1938 / J5857 / M11100 TOKU *waru(i)* bad, wicked, evil.

慊 1939 / J5844 / M11051 KEN satisfaction.

[11] 焉 *ken'en(taru)* discontented, dissatisfied

慄 1940 / J584b / M11042 RITSU fear; shudder.

[12] 然 *ritsuzen* horror, shudder, trembling

愧 1941 / J5843 / M10982 KI. *haji(ru)* feel ashamed. *haji(rau)* feel shy, be coy, be bashful, blush.

[6] 死 *kishi suru* die of shame, be mortally ashamed

慇 1942 / J5840 / M11045 IN courtesy.

[17] 懃 *ingin* courtesy; intimacy, friendship

懃無礼 *ingin-burei* hypocritical courtesy

愴 1943 / J5848 / M11008 SŌ be sad. *itama(shii)* pathetic, sad.

[12] 然 *sōzen* deep sorrow

[13] 愴 *sōsō* sadness

B **慨** 1944 / J3334 / M-X **慨** 1974 / J-X / M11122 **慨** 1975 / J-X / M-X

GAI be sad. *nage(ku)* sigh, lament.

[5] 世 *gaisei* concern for the public welfare

[12] 然 *gaizen to* indignantly, with deep regret

[13] 嘆 *gaitan* deploring, regret

B **慎** 1945 / J3f35 / M11024′ **愼** 1946 / J5846 / M11024 SHIN. *tsutsu(shimu)* be discreet, be careful, be prudent, be cautious; restrain oneself, be moderate. *tsutsu(mashige) ni* reverently, respectfully, humbly, modestly. *tsutsu(mashii), tsutsu(mashiyaka) na* modest, reserved, humble, bashful. *tsutsu(shimi)* prudence, modesty, discretion, self-control.

[9] 重 *shinchō* caution, prudence, discretion

[11] 深 *tsutsu(shimi)buka(i)* discreet, prudent, cautious, modest, self-denying

[15] 慮 *shinryo* courteously careful

A **態** 1947 / J4256 / M11052 TAI condition, figure, appearance; voice (of verbs). *waza to* intentionally, deliberately, knowingly. *zama* plight, state, appearance, spectacle.

[7] 見 *zama (o) mi(ro)* Just look at your blunder.

[9] 度 *taido* attitude; posture, bearing, manner

[13] 勢 *taisei* attitude; arrangements

[14] 様 *taiyō* situation, terms

態 *wazawaza* purposely, expressly

B **慕** 1948 / J4a69 / M11088 BO. *shita(u)* yearn for, love dearly, adore, follow. *shita(washii)* dear, beloved, fond of.

[4] 心 *boshin* yearning (for someone)

[7] 求 *shita(i)-moto(meru)* desire, long for

[11] 情 *bojō* longing, affection

[12] 喘 *shita(i)-ae(gu)* long for

喜 *shita(i)-yoroko(bu)* hold dear

焦 *shita(i)-koga(reru)* yearn for

11

慘 1949 / J584e / M11094 See 惨 1896.

憇 1950 / J585c / M11187 See 憩 1980.

慾 1951 / J4d5d / M11163 See 欲 2936.

傷 1952 / J5853 / M11133 SHŌ *ure(eru)* grieve; lament; be sorrowful.

慱 1953 / J5855 / M11137 TAN. SEN grieve, lament; be round.

慵 1954 / J5859 / M11144 YŌ. SHŌ *monou(i)* languid, listless; gloomy.

慼 1955 / J-X / M11158 **慽** 1956 / J-X / M11159 SEKI grieve.

慓 1957 / J5858 / M11084 HYŌ fast, quick, rapid, agile.

慫 1958 / J5851 / M11127 SHŌ advise; persuade.

14 慂 *shōyō* suggestion, persuasion, advice, inducement

慟 1959 / J5856 / M11103 DŌ be sad, grieve.

10 哭 *dōkoku* wailing, lamentation

慳 1960 / J584c / M11140 KEN regret; stinginess.

11 貪 *kendon na* hardhearted, blunt, greedy

慴 1961 / J5852 / M11143 SHŪ, SHŌ fear; threaten.

6 伏 *shūfuku suru* crouch in fear; be overpowered

B **慮** 1962 / J4e38 / M11132 RYO thought, concern, agreement. *omombaka(ru), omompaka(ru)* consider, deliberate, fear. *omombaka(ri), omompaka(ri)* thought, consideration, prudence; fears, apprehension, strategy.

5 外 *ryogai* emergency; unexpectedness; impoliteness

慷 1963 / J584d / M11146 KŌ weep, grieve.

13 慨 *kōgai* resentment, indignation

慨家 *kōgaika* deplorer of existing evils

慧 1964 / J3745 / M11116 KEI wise.

10 悟 *keigo* cleverness

敏 *keibin na* clever, astute

11 眼 *keigan* keen eye

慚 1965 / J5850 / M11096 **慙** 1966 / J584f / M11095 ZAN. *haji(ru)* feel ashamed.

6 色 *zanshoku* blushing with shame

死 *zanshi suru* die of shame; feel very much ashamed

13 愧 *zanki* compunction, shame, humiliation

B **慶** 1967 / J3744 / M11145 KYŌ. KEI. *kei(suru)* congratulate. *yoroko(bu)* rejoice, be happy over.

4 弔 *keichō* congratulations and condolences

弔電報 *keichō dempō* special telegram for congratulations or condolences

6 兆 *keichō* herald of happiness

8 事 *keiji* auspicious event

9 祝 *keishuku* congratulation, celebration

12 賀 *keiga* congratulation

13 福 *keifuku* happiness, well-being

B **慢** 1968 / J4b7d / M11110 MAN laziness; ridicule.

4 心 *manshin* self-conceit, pride

7 言 *mangen* boasting

8 性 *mansei* chronic

性化 *manseika* become chronic

性病 *manseibyō* chronic disease

14 語 *mango* boasting

15 罵 *mamba* scorn, derision

B **憎** 1969 / J417e / M11188′ **憎** 1973 / J-X / M11202 ZŌ *niku(mu)* hate, detest. *niku(garu)* hate. *niku(i)* hateful, abominable; poor-looking. *niku(rashii)* hateful, horrible, provoking. *niku(shimi)* hatred, enmity. *niku(rashige) ni* hatefully, maliciously.

3 口 *niku(mare)guchi* abusive language

子 *niku(mare)ko, niku(marek)ko* bad boy

6 合 *niku(mi)-a(u)* hate one another

気 *nikuge* hate

気無 *nikuge (no) na(i)* innocent, artless, harmless

7 体 *nikutei na* impudent, insolent, hateful

役 *niku(mare)yaku* unpopular role

8 物 *niku(mare)mono* object of hatred

9 思 *niku(karazu) omo(u)* care for, have a fancy for

11 悪 *zōo* malice, hatred, abhorrence

悪心 *zōoshin* malice, hatred, abhorrence

13 嫌 *niku(mi)-kira(u)* detest

14 憎 *nikuniku(shii)* hateful, detestable, loathsome

11 A **慣** 1970 / J3437 / M11111 KAN. *nara(u)* experience; become a habit. *na(rasu)* tame, charm (animals); train, exercise, drill; habituate, accustom to. *na(reru)* get used to, become experienced; be tamed; get too familiar, mature. *na(re)* practice, habit, skill, experience.

5 用 *kan'yō no* common, customary, conventional; colloquial

用上 *kan'yōjō* by usage

用手段 *kan'yō shudan* favorite trick; usual practice

用句 *kan'yōku* an idiom; a common expression

用的 *kan'yōteki* common, colloquial, customary

用音 *kan'yōon* popular pronunciation of a character

用語 *kan'yōgo* idiom; colloquial ⌈expression

6 行 *kankō* usual practice, routine

行犯 *kankōhan* habitual criminal

8 性 *kansei* inertia

例 *kanrei* custom, usage, precedent

例上 *kanreijō* traditionally, conventionally

11 習 *kanshū* custom, common practice

習法 *kanshūhō* common law

16 親 *na(re)-shita(shimu)* get used to

B **憂** 1971 / J4d2b / M11170 YŪ. *ure(u), ure(eru)* grieve, lament, be anxious. *u(ki), u(i)* sad, unhappy, gloomy. *ure(e), ure(i)* distress, sorrow, trouble, anxiety, grief. *usa* gloom, sorrow, melancholy.

4 心 *yūshin* grieving heart

5 目 *ukime* bitter experience, misery, distress, grief, sad thoughts

世 *ukiyo* sad world. *yūsei* worrying about world conditions

6 色 *yūshoku* melancholy air, anxious look, traces of sorrow, gloom

7 身 *ukimi* life of misery

8 国 *yūkoku* patriotism

苦 *yūku* trouble, distress, sorrow

事 *ure(i)goto, ukiji* bitter experience, misery, distress, grief, sad thoughts

9 思 *yūshi suru* grieve

10 悩 *ure(i)-naya(mu)* be grievously troubled

哭 *ukine* sobbing

11 戚 *yūseki* grief

患 *yūkan* sorrow, worry, distress

12 悶 *yūmon* anguish, mortification

晴 *usabara(shi)* diversion, distraction

13 愁 *yūshū* grief, melancholy, gloom

15 慮 *yūryo* anxiety, dread, cares, solicitude

憤 *yūfun* grief and anger

18 顔 *ure(i)gao* anxious look, sad countenance

21 懼 *yūku* fear, apprehension, dread

26 鬱 *yūutsu* melancholy, dejection, gloom

鬱症 *yūutsushō* melancholia, hypochondria

B **慰** 1972 / J3056 / M11135 I. *nagusa(mu) vt* and *vi* amuse oneself; make sport of; seduce. *nagusa(meru), i(suru)* comfort, console, cheer. *nagusa(me)* comfort, consolation, diversion. *nagusa(mi)* amusement, pleasure.

5 主 *Nagusa(me)nushi* the Comforter, the Holy Spirit

半分 *nagusa(mi)-hambun* partly for pleasure

6 合 *nagusa(me)-a(u)* comfort one another

安 *ian* solace, comfort; relaxation, recreation

安会 *iankai* recreational get-together

安所 *ianjo* army brothel

安婦 *ianfu* army prostitute, comfort woman

7 労 *irō suru* recognize (a person's) services

労会 *irōkai* banquet in honor of someone's services

労金 *irōkin* bonus for special services

8 物 *nagusa(mi)mono* object of pleasure; plaything, laughingstock

10 留 *iryū suru* dissuade from resigning

11 問 *imon* condolences; a sympathy call

問状 *imonjō* condolence letter

問使 *imonshi* condolence bearer

問品 *imonhin* comfort articles

問旅行 *imon ryokō* goodwill tour

問婦 *imonfu* army prostitute, comfort woman

問船 *imonsen* ship sent to comfort the soldiers

問袋 *imombukuro* soldiers' comfort bags

13 楽 *iraku* comfort, pleasure
15 撫 *ibu* pacification, soothing
霊祭 *ireisai* memorial service
霊塔 *ireitō* memorial tower
17 謝 *isha* consolation
謝料 *isharyō* consolation money
藉 *isha, iseki* consolation
藉料 *isharyō* consolation money

12

憎 1973 / J-X / M11202 See **憎** 1969.

慨 1974 / J-X / M11122 **概** 1975 / J-X / M-X See **慨** 1944.

憙 1976 / J585a / M11219 Ki *yoroko(bu)* be pleased, rejoice. *kono(mu)* prefer, like. *ā* exclamation.

憊 1977 / J5860 / M11195 Hai fatigue.

憬 1978 / J585d / M11256 Kei. *akoga(reru)* long for.

憖 1979 / J585b / M11215 Gin. *namaji, namaji(i) ni, namaji(kka)* thoughtlessly, rashly, halfheartedly, imperfectly, unsatisfactorily.

B **憩** 1980 / J3746 / M11216 **憇** 1950 / J585c / M11187 Kei. Katsu. *iko(u)* rest, relax, repose.
12 場 *iko(i) (no) ba* place for relaxation

憮 1981 / J5863 / M11259 Bu disappointment.
12 然 *buzen* discouraged, disappointed, astonished

憧 1982 / J4634 / M11242 Shō. Tō. Dō. *akoga(reru)* yearn after, long for; thirst for; aspire to; admire, adore.
15 憬 *dōkei, shōkei, akoga(re)* longing, aspiration

憔 1983 / J585e / M11213 Shō get thin.
7 悴 *shōsui* emaciation, haggardness
11 悴 *shōsui* emaciation, haggardness

憑 1984 / J5861 / M11210 Hyō be possessed. *tsu(ku)* possess, obsess, haunt. *tsuka(reru)* be devil-possessed, be haunted by.
8 拠 *hyōkyo* authority
物 *tsukimono* devil possession; curse

憚 1985 / J585f / M11222 Tan. *habaka(ru)* be afraid of; hesitate; have scruples about, shrink from; pay deference to, stand in awe of; spread (clouds). *habaka(ri)* fear, awe; hesitation; compunction, scruple; reserve, deference; comfort station.
5 乍 *habaka(ri)naga(ra)* with deference, with hesitancy, I'm sorry but...
14 様 *habaka(ri)sama* Thanks for your trouble.

憫 1986 / J5862 / M11252 Bin anxiety. *aware(mu)* have mercy on.
10 笑 *binshō suru* smile with pity
12 然 *binzen(taru)* pitiable
14 察 *binsatsu* compassion, sympathy

憐 1987 / J4e79 / M11206 Ren. *awa(remu)* pity, have mercy on, sympathize with. *awa(remi)* pity, compassion.
11 情 *renjō* pity, compassion
深 *awa(remi)buka(i)* compassionate
13 愍 *remmin* compassion, pity, mercy
15 憫 *rembin* compassion, pity, mercy

A **憲** 1988 / J377b / M11269′ **憲** 1989 / J-X / M11269 Ken law.
7 兵 *kempei* military police
8 法 *kempō* constitution; constitutional law
法記念日 *Kempō Kinembi* Constitution Day (May 3)
法違反 *kempō-ihan* unconstitutionality
9 政 *kensei* constitutional government
政国 *kenseikoku* a country with a constitutional government

B **憤** 1990 / J4a30 / M11239 Fun. *ikidō(ru)* resent, be indignant, become angry. *mutsuka(ru)* be angry (because of being unhappy); be always crying. *ikidōri* resentment, indignation.
6 死 *funshi suru* die in a fit of anger; be unfortunately put out (in baseball)

4 【心忄⺗】12 戈戸手扌支攴攵文斗斤方无日曰月木欠止歹殳毋比毛氏气水氵氺火灬爪爫父爻爿丬片牙牛犬犭

9 怒 *fundo, funnu* anger, rage, resentment, indignation, exasperation
10 起 *funki suru* rouse oneself, be stirred up
12 然 *funzen to* indignantly, in a rage
13 慨 *fungai* resentment, indignation
16 激 *fungeki* resentment; indignation
18 懣 *fumman* anger, resentment, indignation, chagrin, irritation

13

應 1991 / J5866 / M11330 See **応** 1789.

懆 1992 / J586a / M11325 SŌ *ure(eru)* grieve over, lament, be sorrowful.

懋 1993 / J586c / M11333 BŌ. MŌ *tsuto(meru)* serve, be employed. *saka(n)* be plentiful, be abundant. *shige(ru)* flourish.

懍 1994 / J586e / M11335 RIN *oso(reru)* fear, be afraid. *samu(i)* be cold.

懃 1995 / J5869 / M11321 KIN courtesy.

懌 1996 / J5864 / M11334 EKI rejoice.

憺 1997 / J586b / M11305 TAN calm, quiet; move.

懊 1998 / J5865 / M11332 Ō sorrow, be in distress. *jiretta(i)* provoking, irritating; impatient, vexed.
10 悩 *ōnō* agony, worry, trouble

B **憾** 1999 / J3438 / M11312 KAN. *ura(mu)* regret, be sorry for. *ura(mi)* regret. *ura(murakuwa)* regrettably.
7 言 *ura(mi)goto* grudge, grievance, complaint

懈 2000 / J5868 / M11328 KAI, KE laziness. *tayu(i)* tired and weak, listless; without any ambition.
9 怠 *ketai, kaitai* laziness; negligence
15 緩 *kekan* laziness, negligence

B **憶** 2001 / J3231 / M11295 OKU think, remember. *omo(u)* think.
8 念 *okunen* something one always remembers
10 病 *okubyō* cowardice, timidity
11 断 *okudan* deciding without the facts
12 測 *okusoku* guess, speculation, supposition
14 説 *okusetsu* hypothesis, speculation, surmise

B **懇** 2002 / J3a29 / M11326 KON. *nengo(ro) na* kind, courteous, hospitable, cordial.
4 切 *konsetsu* kindness, cordiality, exhaustiveness
7 求 *konkyū* earnest desire
8 命 *kommei* kind words, kind advice
10 書 *konsho* your kind letter
11 情 *konjō* kindliness
望 *kombō, kommō* entreaty
13 意 *kon'i* kindness, intimacy, friendship
話 *konwa* friendly chat
話会 *konwakai* social gathering
15 請 *konsei* entreaty, request
談 *kondan* chat; consultation
談会 *kondankai* social gathering; roundtable discussion
16 篤 *kontoku* kindness, cordiality
親 *konshin* friendship, intimacy
親会 *konshinkai* social gathering
17 懇 *konkon to* earnestly, repeatedly
19 願 *kongan* entreaty, supplication, petition
願的 *konganteki ni* appealingly, imploringly
願者 *kongansha* petitioner, suppliant

B **懐** 2003 / J327b / M11351 **懷** 2009 / J5867 / M11456 KAI heart, feeling. *natsu(kashimu), natsu(kashigaru)* yearn for, miss someone. *natsu(keru)* win over, win another's heart. *natsu(ku)* become attached to. *omo(u)* think, believe, judge, esteem; consider, realize; feel like; regard as; anticipate; imagine, suppose, guess; mistake for; recall; intend; desire; love, care for, yearn after; wonder; suspect. *futokoro* bosom, breast, heart; pocket, purse. *natsu(kkoi)* affectionate, affable, tame. *natsu(kashii)* dear, longed-for; yearning for. *natsu(kashimi)* yearning, nostalgia, kindly feeling.

2 刀 *futokorogatana* dagger; confidant
4 手 *futokorode* hands in pockets, folded arms
中 *kaichū* one's pocket
中物 *kaichūmono* pocketbook; contents of the pocket
中時計 *kaichūdokei* watch
中電燈 *kaichū dentō* flashlight
中鏡 *kaichū kagami* pocket mirror
5 旧 *kaikyū* longing for the old days
古 *kaiko* recalling the old days
古談 *kaikodan* reminiscences
7 妊 *kainin* conception, pregnancy
8 抱 *kaihō suru* entertain, harbor. *da(ki)-kaka(eru)* embrace; hold in the arms
具合 *futokoro-guai* one's financial situation
炉 *kairo* pocket heater
炉灰 *kairobai* pocket-heater fuel
9 胎 *kaitai* conception, becoming pregnant
柔 *kaijū* conciliation, pacification, appeasement
春 *kaishun* arrival at puberty
10 紙 *futokorogami, kaishi* handkerchief paper; paper used in lieu of plate in tea ceremony; paper to be used for writing poetry
都合 *futokoro-tsugō* one's financial situation
剣 *kaiken* dagger (for self-defense)
郷 *kaikyō* nostalgic reminiscence
郷病 *kaikyōbyō* nostalgia, homesickness
11 勘定 *futokoro-kanjō* counting one's pocket money; one's financial position
14 銭 *futokoro zeni* pocket money
慕 *kaibo suru* yearn for
疑 *kaigi* disbelief, skepticism, doubt
疑心 *kaigishin* disbelief, skepticism, doubt
疑主義者 *kaigi shugisha* atheist, skeptic, freethinker
疑説 *kaigisetsu* skepticism
疑論 *kaigiron* skepticism

14

懣 2004 / J5870 / M11384 MAN worry, agony, anger.

懦 2005 / J586f / M11390 DA weakness, cowardice.

4 夫 *dafu* coward, weakling
10 弱 *dajaku* effeminacy, emasculation, laziness

B **懲** 2006 / J4428 / M11399′ **懲** 2007 / J-X / M11424 CHŌ. *ko(rasu), ko(rashimeru), chō(zuru)* chastise, punish, discipline. *ko(riru)* learn by experience; be disgusted with.
7 役 *chōeki* penal servitude
戒 *chōkai* disciplinary punishment, official reprimand
戒処分 *chōkai shobun* disciplinary action
8 治 *chōji* chastisement, punishment
治監 *chōjikan* reformatory, penitentiary
11 悪 *chōaku* chastisement, punishment
14 罰 *chōbatsu* discipline, punishment
罰的 *chōbatsuteki* punitive, disciplinary
17 膺 *chōyō* discipline, punishment
18 懲 *korigori suru, korikori suru* learn from experience; have had enough

15

懲 2007 / J-X / M11424 See **懲** 2006.

懺 2008 / J5873 / M-X **懺** 2012 / J5872 / M11478 ZAN, SAN remorse.
9 悔 *zange, sange* repentance, confession, penitence

16

懷 2009 / J5867 / M11456 See **懐** 2003.

懶 2010 / J5871 / M11455 RAI. *monou(i)* languid, weary, lazy; melancholy, gloomy, dull. *nama(keru)* be lazy, be idle; neglect. *monogusa(i)* lazy.
8 者 *nama(ke)mono* lazy person, idle person
12 惰 *randa, raida* laziness, idleness

B **懸** 2011 / J377c / M11462 KEN. KE. *ka(keru) vt* hang; set up (a ladder); cover; construct, install; sit down; sprinkle, pour on; put on; ring up; weigh; multiply; levy; pay (in installments); anchor; start (a machine); wind; turn on (radio); spend on; offer (prizes); put (under treatment); set (on fire). *ka(karu) vi* hang on, be suspended from, be caught, be trapped; be built; begin; arrive at; require, cost; play against, oppose; be splashed; weigh (a pound); be levied; (the instrument or tool) works; attack, fall on; is now showing at; consult; depend (on a son).

4 引 *kakehi(ki)* bargaining, maneuvering
5 氷 *kempyō* icicle
6 吊式 *kakezurishiki* underslung
7 車 *kensha* retiring from public office on account of age; age 70
8 念 *kenen* fear, anxiety, concern
命 *kemmei* eagerness, earnestness; risking one's life
河 *kenga* rushing stream
河弁 *kenga (no) ben* eloquence, eloquent speech
垂 *kensui* chinning
垂運動 *kensui undō* chinning exercises
9 造 *kakezuku(ri)* hut built out over a valley or river
軍 *kengun* flying corps column; expeditionary army
10 釘 *kakekugi* peg
案 *ken'an* pending question or problem
11 崖 *kengai* overhanging cliff, precipice
章 *kenshō* military sash
12 絶 *kenzetsu* great difference
隔 *ka(ke)-heda(taru)* be remote from; be different from. *ka(ke)-heda(teru)* estrange (people). *kenkaku* difference, discrepancy, gap
替 *kakeka(e)* substitute
腕直筆 *kenwan-chokuhitsu* holding the brush vertically and the arm above the table (in writing large characters)
13 想 *kesō* falling in love, attachment
想文 *kesōbun, kesōbumi* love letter
14 樋 *kakehi* water pipe, conduit, flume
15 賞 *kenshō* offering prizes; prize winning; prize, reward
賞当選者 *kenshō tōsensha* prizewinner
賞金 *kenshōkin* prize money, reward
賞募集 *kenshō boshū* prize contest
賞論文 *kenshō rombun* prize essay
16 橋 *kakehashi* viaduct; suspension bridge; intermediary
壅垂 *ken'yōsui* uvula
19 離 *ka(ke)-hana(reru)* be far from; be different from

17

懺 2012 / J5872 / M11478 See **懺** 2008.

懽 2013 / J5875 / M11497 KAN *yoroko(bu)* be pleased, take pleasure in, rejoice.

18

懾 2014 / J5877 / M11498 SHŌ *oso(reru)* fear, be afraid.

懿 2015 / J5874 / M11501 I *yo(i)* good; pleasing; lovely; right. *uruwa(shii)* lovely, beautiful, fine.

懼 2016 / J5876 / M11488 **惧** 1877 / J-X / M-X **俱** 1878 / J577c / M10848
KU. *oso(reru)* fear, be overawed, be apprehensive.

19

戀 2017 / J5878 / M11504 See **恋** 1852.

RAD. 戈 62

Hoko tasseled spear. At right: *hokozukuri* or *hokogamae*. Variant, at right: 戈. Nickname: Tasseled Spear (cf. Rads. 56 and 110).

戈 2018 / J5879 / M11530 KA. *hoko* halberd; arms; festival car, float.

1

戉 2019 / J587a / M11531 ETSU name of star. *masakari* broadaxe, battle-axe.

戊 2020 / J4a6a / M11532 BO E, fifth. *tsuchinoe* fifth calendar sign.

2

戋 2021 / J-X / M11542 Nonstandard for **銭** 6264.

戌 2022 / J587c / M11535 JUTSU. *inu* 7–9 p.m.; 11th zodiac sign; dog.

戍 2023 / J587B / M11537 JU protection.

8 卒 *jusotsu* border guard

戎 2024 / J3d3f / M11539 JŪ warrior; arms. *ebisu* barbarian, savage; Ainu.

3 士 *jūshi* warrior, soldier
6 衣 *jūi* armor; military uniform
夷 *jūi* barbarians
7 兵 *jūhei* soldiers
15 器 *jūki* arms, weapons of war

A **成** 2025 / J402e / M11542′ **成** 2026 / J-X / M11544 SEI. JŌ. *na(ru)* become, get or grow (old), form (a part of); set in, come (time or seasons); turn into; be reduced to; consist of; be accomplished; result in; prove (fatal); amount to; play the part of; elapse; reach (a certain age); bear, stand; be promoted; be pleased to. *na(su)* do, perform, accomplish; form, make, accomplish. *(o)na(ri)* departure of a high personage; visit of a high personage.

2 人 *seijin* adult. *seijin suru* come of age
人日 *Seijin (no) Hi* Coming-of-Age Day (January 15)
人学校 *seijin gakkō* school for adults
人教育 *seijin kyōiku* adult education
3 下 *na(ri)-sa(garu)* stoop to, be reduced to
丈 *na(ru)take* as…as possible; whenever practicable
上 *na(ri)-a(garu)* rise from the ranks, rise suddenly. *na(ri)a(gari)* upstart
上者 *na(ri)a(gari)mono* upstart; one suddenly rich
4 心 *seishin* nature, disposition
仏 *jōbutsu* attaining Buddhahood, entering Nirvana; death
分 *seibun* ingredient; component; contents
文 *seibun* writing a document; a document
文化 *seibunka* legalization, codification
文法 *seibunhō* statute law, written law
文律 *seibunritsu* statute law, written law
文契約 *seibun keiyaku* written contract
5 立 *na(ri)-ta(tsu)* consist of; materialize; be concluded, be valid. *seiritsu* materialization, realization, formation, organization, completion. *na(ri)ta(chi)* origin, history
句 *seiku* set phrase, idiomatic phrase
代 *na(ri)-ka(waru)* replace (someone)
可 *na(ru)be(ku)* as...as possible, whenever possible
功 *seikō* success, achievement, prosperity
功者 *seikōsha* successful man
6 竹 *seichiku* liquidation, settlement
虫 *seichū* adult insect; adult invertebrate animal
行 *na(ri)-yu(ku)* turn out, become of (a person). *nariyu(ki)* developments, course of events; outcome, consequences, destiny
因 *seiin* origin, cause
合 *na(ri)-a(u)* be nicely finished, be perfected, be completed; go together; become one; become intimate
年 *seinen* majority, adult age, legal age, man's estate
年式 *seinenshiki* coming of age ceremony
年期 *seinenki* adulthood
7 体 *seitai* adult form. *na(ri)katachi* appearance, costume
形 *seikei* plastic surgery
否 *seihi* success or failure
余 *na(ri)-ama(ru)* to make more than enough
8 金 *narikin* the newly rich
長 *seichō* growth
育 *seiiku* growth, development; birth and breeding
実 *Jōjitsu* Buddhist sect originating in the seventh century
典 *seiten* code of laws; established rites
果 *na(ri)-ha(teru)* be reduced to, become. *seika* results, outcome. *na(re) (no) ha(te)* shadow of one's former self
事 *na(rō) koto (nara), na(ru) koto (nara)* if possible

9 約 *seiyaku* promise
10 員 *seiin* charter members
案 *seian* definite plan
11 道 *jōdō suru* attain Buddhahood
婚 *seikon* marriage
掛 *na(ri)-ka(keru), na(ri)-ka(karu)* be coming down with (an illness)
済 *na(ri)-su(masu)* (completely) become
敗 *seibai suru* punish, judge, bring to justice, deal with (a culprit). *seihai* success or failure
規 *seiki no* regular, formal, official, prescribed
12 歯 *seishi* permanent teeth
程 *na(ru)hodo* I see, well, really, to be sure
策 *seisaku* previous strategy; prospects of success
就 *jōju* fulfillment; completion, realization, consummation
13 損 *na(ri)-sokona(u)* fail to become, be unsuccessful in
義 *seigi* justification (Catholic)
業 *seigyō* completion of one's work or study
14 語 *seigo* a set phrase, an idiom
算 *seisan* prospects of success
層 *seisō* stratification
層岩 *seisōgan* sedimentary rock
層圏 *seisōken* stratosphere
層圏飛行 *seisōken hikō* stratosphere flight
層圏飛行機 *seisōken hikōki* stratoplane
15 熟 *seijuku* ripeness; maturity, maturation, attainment of skill
熟児 *seijukuji* fully-developed baby
熟期 *seijukuki* puberty; adolescence; maturity
17 績 *seiseki* results, marks, rating, score
績順 *seisekijun* student rank

3

成 2026 J-X M11544 See **成** 2025.

B **戒** 2027 J327c M11548 KAI commandment; admonition. *imashi(meru)* admonish, warn, prohibit. *imashi(me)* precept, exhortation, instruction, commandment.

4 心 *kaishin* caution, vigilance, discretion
6 行 *kaigyō* penance, austerities
名 *kaimyō, kaimei* Buddhist initiation name; posthumous name
7 告 *kaikoku* warning, caution
9 律 *kairitsu* precepts, commandments
10 師 *kaishi* Buddhist teacher
13 慎 *kaishin suru* be discreet, take care, be cautious
飭 *kaichoku* caution, reprimand
16 壇 *kaidan* temple ordination platform
17 厳 *kaigen* guarding against danger
厳令 *kaigenrei* martial law
20 護 *kaigo* safe custody

A **我** 2028 J3266 M11545 GA ego, self, selfishness, egotism. *waga* my, our, one's own. *ware* I, oneself, self, ego.

2 人 *warehito* myself and others
4 心 *waga kokoro* my heart
方 *wagahō* our side, we
5 立 *ga (o) ta(teru)* insist on one's own ideas
出 *ga (o) da(su)* insist on one's own ideas
乍 *warenaga(ra)* for me (to do such a thing)
田引水 *gaden insui* drawing water for one's own field, promoting one's own interests
6 先 *waresaki ni* self first
7 身 *wagami* myself, oneself
折 *ga (o) o(ru)* defer to another
我 *wareware* we. *ware(mo)ware(mo)* vying with one another
君 *waga kimi* my lord
利 *gari* self-interest
利我利 *garigari* selfishness, selfish person
8 国 *wa(ga) kuni* our country
知 *wareshi(razu)* involuntarily, instinctively
事 *waga koto* personal affair
武者羅 *gamushara na* reckless, daredevil
物 *wagamono* one's own property
物顔 *wagamonogao* like one's own. *waga monogao ni* in a lordly manner
9 通 *ga (o) tō(su)* insist on one's own ideas
10 流 *garyū* self-taught; one's own way
家 *wagaya* our home, our house

党 *wa(ga) tō* our party
11 張 *ga (o) ha(ru)* insist on one's own ideas
情 *gajō* selfishness; bias; personal feelings
欲 *gayoku* selfishness
執 *gashū* egotism; obstinacy
12 勝 *warega(chi)* everybody for himself
等 *warera* we
13 意 *gai* self-will, obstinacy
意得 *wagai (o) e(ru)* approve of
14 慢 *gaman* patience, perseverance, endurance, tolerance, self-control, self-denial
15 褒 *warebome* self-praise
輩 *wagahai* I
16 儘 *wagamama* selfishness, egoism; willfulness, disobedience; whim

4

戔 2029 / J587d / M11559 SEN. SAN harm, injure; lose; be few; be small.

或 2030 / J303f / M11563 WAKU. KOKU. *a(ru)* some, one, a certain, a. *arui(wa)* or; possibly.

7

戝 2031 / J6c43 / M11603 See 賊 5801. Also used as variant of 財 5773.

戚 2032 / J404c / M11594 SOKU. SEKI relative; sadness.

戛 2033 / J587e / M11598 戞 2034 / J5921 / M11605 KATSU halbert.
9 飛 *katto(basu)* knock out (a homer)
12 然 *katsuzen* the sound of striking something hard

8

戞 2034 / J5921 / M11605 See 戛 2033.

戟 2035 / J3761 / M11606 GEKI. *hoko* halberd; arms.

9

戡 2036 / J5922 / M11616 KAN victory.
8 定 *kantei* military suppression of disorder

A 戦 2037 / J406f / M11631′ 戰 2042 / J5925 / M11667 SEN war; battle; game, match. *tataka(u)* wage war; fight; engage in a contest; struggle against. *onono(ku)* tremble, shudder. *wanana(ku)* tremble. *tataka(wasu)* cause a quarrel; bring about a war between other nations; argue hotly; compete. *soyo(gu)* rustle, tremble, quiver, sway, stir. *tataka(i)* war, fight; battle, encounter, strife, conflict; contest (in athletics). *ikusa* war, fight, battle, encounter.
2 力 *senryoku* war potential
3 士 *senshi* soldier, combatant, warrior
4 斗 *sentō* battle, combat, action
火 *senka* war conflagration; war disasters; sword and fire
中 *senchū* during the war
友 *sen'yū* comrade-in-arms
5 史 *senshi* military history; history of the war
功 *senkō* distinguished war service, military merit
犯 *sempan* war crime; war criminal
犯者 *sempansha* war criminal
6 地 *senchi* battlefield, war front
好 *tataka(i)zu(ki)* warlike, bellicose
列 *senretsu* line of battle; line (of ships)
死 *senshi* death in action
死者 *senshisha* a person killed in action
争 *sensō* war, warfare, campaign; battle
争中 *sensōchū* during the war
争未亡人 *sensō mibōjin* war widow
争犯罪 *sensō hanzai* war crime
争犯罪人 *sensō hanzainin* war criminal
争行為 *sensō kōi* act of war
争呆 *sensōboke* combat fatigue
争状態 *sensō jōtai* belligerency, state of war
争法規 *sensō hōki* the rules of war
争放棄 *sensō hōki* war renunciation
争能力 *sensō nōryoku* war potential
争景気 *sensō keiki* war prosperity
争裁判 *sensō saiban* war-crimes trial
争裁判所 *sensō saibansho* war-crimes court

争犠牲者 *sensō giseisha* war victim
7 局 *senkyoku* war situation
役 *sen'eki* war, battle, campaign
抜 *tataka(i)-nu(ku)* fight to a finish
乱 *senran* wars, disturbances
利品 *senrihin* war spoils, trophies
没 *sembotsu* death in battle, killed in action
没者 *sembotsusha* the war dead
車 *sensha* tank; chariot
車長 *senshachō* tank commander
車砲 *senshahō* tank gun
車隊 *senshatai* tank corps
車戦 *senshasen* tank battle, tank warfare
車壕 *senshagō* tank trap
災 *sensai* war damage
災地 *sensaichi* war-stricken area
災者 *sensaisha* war victim
災孤児 *sensai koji* war orphan
災後 *sensaigo* after the war
災流民 *sensai ryūmin* displaced persons
災家族 *sensai kazoku* bombed-out family
8 法 *sempō* strategy, tactics, campaign plan
況 *senkyō* war situation
果 *senka* war results
国 *sengoku* belligerent country; country in civil war
国時代 *sengoku jidai* era of civil wars; turbulent period
歿 *sembotsu* death in battle; killed in action
歿者 *sembotsusha* the war dead
歿勇士 *sembotsu yūshi* the war dead
9 陣 *senjin* war preparations; battlefield
後 *sengo* after the war
後派 *sengoha* postwar generation
前 *senzen* prewar days, before the war
前派 *senzenha* prewar generation
10 記 *senki* military history
病死 *sembyōshi* death from war-contracted disease
時 *senji* wartime, war period
時工場 *senji kōjō* munitions plant
時中 *senjichū* during the war, in wartime
時手当 *senji teate* war bonus
時公債 *senji kōsai* war loan
時功労章 *senji kōrōshō* distinguished-service medal
時色 *senjishoku* wartime look
時体制 *senji taisei* war organization, war footing
時利得税 *senji ritokuzei* war-profits tax
時状態 *senji jōtai* state of war, belligerency, war conditions
時服 *senjifuku* field-service uniform; utility suit
時定員 *senji teiin* war establishment, war footing
時国債 *senji kokusai* war bonds
時保険 *senji hoken* war-risk insurance
時産業 *senji sangyō* war industry
時景気 *senji keiki* war boom
時禁制品 *senji kinseihin* wartime contraband
時補償 *senji hoshō* war indemnity
時編成 *senji hensei* war establishment, war footing
11 域 *sen'iki* war area, theater of war
捷 *senshō* victory, triumph
隊 *sentai* corps; squadron
敗 *sempai* defeat in war
敗国 *sempaikoku* defeated nation
術 *senjutsu* tactics, strategy, art of war, campaign plan
術家 *senjutsuka* tactician
術用 *senjutsuyō no* tactical
略 *senryaku* strategy, tactics
略上 *senryakujō* strategically, from the viewpoint of strategy
略的 *senryakuteki* strategic
略物資 *senryaku busshi* strategic goods
略家 *senryakuka* strategist
略爆撃 *senryaku bakugeki* strategic bombing
12 備 *sembi* war preparations; war preparedness
場 *senjō* battlefield, the front, war theater
渦 *senka* the confusion of war
評 *sempyō* criticism of the game
雲 *sen'un* war clouds
費 *sempi* war expenditures
報 *sempō* war news, war intelligence
勝 *senshō* victory, triumph
勝国 *senshōkoku* victor nation
勝者 *senshōsha* victor
13 債 *sensai* war debts, war bonds
慄 *senritsu* shuddering; frightfulness; shivering
禍 *senka* war damage, ravages of war
跡 *senseki* old battlefield; aftermath of war

意 *sen'i* fighting spirit, hostile intention
戦恐恐 *sensen-kyōkyō toshite* nervously, gingerly
戦兢兢 *sensen-kyōkyō toshite* nervously, gingerly
傷 *senshō* war wound
傷病 *senshōbyō* war injury or illness
傷病者 *senshōbyōsha* war invalid
14 歴 *senreki* war experience, war service
塵 *senjin* dust of battle
端 *sentan* hostilities
15 線 *sensen* battle line, front
16 機 *senki* time to strike; military secret
17 績 *senseki* war record; score
18 鬪 *sentō* battle, action, combat
鬪力 *sentōryoku* combat strength
鬪的 *sentōteki* active; fighting
鬪服 *sentōfuku* combat uniform
鬪員 *sentōin* fighter, combatant
鬪教会 *sentō (no) kyokai* the church militant
鬪隊形 *sentō taikei* line of battle, battle array
鬪帽 *sentōbō* army field cap
鬪靴 *sentōgutsu* combat shoes
鬪旗 *sentōki* battle flag
鬪機 *sentōki* fighter plane
鬪艦 *sentōkan* battleship
20 艦 *senkan* battleship

10

戩 2038 / J-X / M11637 Sen be destroyed.

截 2039 / J5923 / M11639 Setsu. *ta(tsu)* sever, cut off; shut off; interrupt; abstain from; eradicate; suppress. *ki(ru)* cut, chop, hash; carve; saw, clip, shear; slice, strip; fell, cut down; punch; sever (connections); pause, break off; disconnect; turn off; hang up; cross (a street); discount, sell below cost; shake (water) off.

4 切 *ta(chi)-ki(ru)* cut off; block; disconnect
11 断 *setsudan* cutting off
断面 *setsudammen* transverse section
断機 *setsudanki* cutting machine; guillotine
12 然 *setsuzen(taru)* clear, sharp, distinct

11

戮 2040 / J5924 / M11655 Riku kill.

2 力 *rikuryoku* cooperation

B **戯** 2041 / J353a / M11665 **戲** 2043 / J-X / M11668 **戲** 2044 / J5926 / M11681

Gi. Ge. *tawamu(reru)* play, sport, frolic, joke; flirt with. *tawa(keru)* fool, play the fool, act indecently; be silly over; talk foolishly. *ja(reru), za(reru)* be playful, gambol. *jara(kasu)* calling for jokes. *odo(keru)* joke. *soba(eru)* play pranks, be spoiled.

3 口 *odo(ke)guchi* joke
4 文 *gibun* humorous writing
5 芝居 *odoke shibai* comedy, burlesque
6 曲 *gikyoku* drama, play
交 *zarekawa(su)* exchange jokes
7 言 *zaregoto, gigen* joke
作 *gesaku, gisaku* cheap literature, fiction; writing for amusement
作者 *gesakusha* fiction writer, dime novelist
8 画 *giga* cartoon, comics
者 *tawa(ke)mono* fool. *odo(ke)mono* joker, humorist
事 *zaregoto, tawamu(re)goto* wanton sporting
10 笑 *gishō* playful laughter
書 *gisho* rambling writings
12 絵 *zaree* a picture drawn in fun
13 話 *odo(ke)banashi* funny story
14 語 *tawakoto* foolish talk; delirious utterances
歌 *zareuta* limerick, funny song, comic song

12

戰 2042 / J5925 / M11667 See 戦 2037.

13

戲 2043 / J-X / M11668 See 戯 2041.

戲 2044 / J5926 / M11681 See 戯 2041.

戴 2045 / J4257 / M11685 TAI. *itada(ku) vi* and *vt* be crowned with, wear; live under (a ruler); install (a president); receive, accept; buy; take, eat, drink (humble).

8 物 *itada(ki)mono* gift

9 冠式 *taikanshiki* coronation

— 14 —

戳 2046 / J5927 / M11684 TAKU *sa(su)* stab, pierce. *tsu(ku)* thrust, pierce, strike, push.

— 18 —

戵 2047 / J-X / M11695 GU halberd.

RAD. 戸 63

To door. Also called *togashira, to kammuri,* or *todare*. Variant: 戶. Nickname: Door.

A **戸** 2048 / J384d / M11696 **戶** 2049 / J-X / M -X **户** 2050 / J-X / M-X

Ko house; door; family; counter for houses. *to* door.

3 口 *toguchi* door, doorway. *kokō* number of houses; population

4 戸 *koko* houses; *koko ni* at each door, from door to door

5 外 *kogai* open-air, outdoors

付警報器 *totsu(ke)keihōki* door alarm

主 *koshu* head of a family

主権 *koshuken* family headship

6 毎 *kogoto ni* at every door; from door to door

7 別 *kobetsu* each house, house to house

別訪問 *kobetsu hōmon* house-to-house visit

別割 *kobetsuwa(ri)* house taxation rate

8 板 *toita* rain shutter (when used for carrying)

枠 *towaku* door frame

9 前 *tomae* warehouse door; warehouse front

10 框 *togamachi* door frame

11 袋 *tobukuro* built-in box for shutters

12 棚 *todana* locker, cabinet, closet, sideboard, cupboard

惑 *tomado(u)* be at sea, lose one's bearings

13 障子 *toshōji* wooden and translucent doors

数 *kosū* number of houses

数割 *kosūwa(ri)* household tax

15 締 *tojima(ri)* fastening the doors, closing up. *tojime* shutting a door

18 襖 *tobusuma* a door with paper on one side and wood on the other

20 籍 *koseki* census; family register

籍抄本 *koseki shōhon* copy of a family register

籍役場 *koseki yakuba* family-registration office

籍法 *kosekihō* family-registration law

籍証明書 *koseki shōmeisho* family-registry certificate

籍調 *koseki shirabe* census taking

籍謄本 *koseki tōhon* copy of a family register

籍簿 *kosekibo* family register

— 3 —

B **戻** 2051 / J4c61 / M11707 **戾** 2052 / J-X / M11712 REI. *modo(ru)* return, turn back; revert to, resume, return to; be returned; go backward. *modo(su)* return, restore; turn back (a clock); reject; vomit. *moto(ru)* be contrary (to), go against, deviate from.

2 入 *modo(shi)-i(re)* reimbursement

8 金 *modo(shi)kin* refund

9 品 *modo(ri)hin* returned goods

10 荷 *modo(shi)ni* return cargo

11 道 *modo(ri)michi* the way back, return journey

— 4 —

戾 2052 / J-X / M11712 See 戻 2051.

B**房** 2053 J4b3c M11714 Bō house, room; tassel. *fusa* tuft, tassel, fringe; lock (of hair); cluster, bunch, segment (of an orange).

4 毛 *fusage* lock, tuft, tassel
中 *bōchū* in the room; in the bedroom
8 房 *fusafusa* tufty, fringy, bushy (tail), fleecy
事 *bōji* sexual intercourse
事過度 *bōji kudo* sexual excess
9 室 *bōshitsu* a room

A**所** 2054 J3d6a M11715 So. Sho place. *tokoro* place, spot, scene, site, seat; locality, district; room; distance; address; point, feature; passage (in a book), part; thing; time, moment; extent; matter of course. *tokoro ga* but, however, on the contrary. *toko* place. *tokoro de* well, by the way. *-sho, -jo* place, office, bureau.

4 化 *shoke* acolyte, priestling
以 *yuen* reason, the reason why
5 生 *shosei* one's child; one's parents; one's birthplace
用 *shoyō* errand, business, appointment
由 *shoyū* reason
払 *tokorobara(i)* exile to the country
6 行 *shogyō* acts, works
存 *shozon* thought, opinion
自慢 *tokoro jiman* boasting of one's place
在 *shozai* whereabouts, site, position, location, place where something is kept
在地 *shozaichi* seat, location
在無 *shozaina(i)* be bored, have nothing to do
有 *shoyū* possession, ownership; property
有主 *shoyūnushi* owner, proprietor
有地 *shoyūchi* the land one owns
有物 *shoyūbutsu* one's possessions
有者 *shoyūsha* owner, proprietor
有格 *shoyūkaku* possessive case
有権 *shoyūken* ownership
7 見 *shoken* view, opinion, impressions, findings
労 *shorō* illness, indisposition
作 *shosa* conduct; gesture
作事 *shosagoto* dance drama, posture dance
8 長 *shochō* office head, factory head, institute head
念 *shonen* thought, deep thought
定 *shotei no* fixed, prescribed
所 *shosho, tokorodokoro* here and there, several places
所方方 *shosho-hōbō* here and there
9 信 *shoshin* belief, conviction, opinion
柄 *tokorogara* locality, neighborhood, situation; the place being what it is
狭 *tokorosema(i)* crowded; littered up; small (quarters)
思 *shoshi* thought, idea, opinion
要 *shoyō* need
為 *shoi* results; influence, effect; fault. *sei, shoi* act, action, deed, results, results of one's actions
持 *shoji suru* possess, have, own; carry
持人 *shojinin* bearer, holder
持金 *shojikin* funds, money in hand
持者 *shojisha* bearer, holder, possessor
持品 *shojihin* one's personal effects
10 員 *shoin* staff, personnel; staff member
書 *tokoroga(ki)* address
帯 *shotai* household, home
帯主 *shotainushi* head of a household, householder
帯持 *shotaimo(chi)* housekeeping; householder
帯染 *shotaiji(miru)* be domesticated
帯道具 *shotai dōgu* household goods
帯数 *shotaisu* number of households
11 産 *shosan* result, outcome
望 *shomō* desire, request, wish
得 *shotoku* income, earnings; possessions. *tokoro (o) e(ru)* secure a position exactly to one's liking
得者 *shotokusha* income earner
得税 *shotokuzei* income tax
得層 *shotokusō* income group
得顔 *tokoroegao ni* triumphantly
得額 *shotokugaku* amount of income
12 属 *shozoku* attached to; one's post
期 *shoki* anticipation, expectation
違 *tokorochiga(i)* mistaking the place
替 *tokoroga(e)* moving to a new address
番地 *tokorobanchi* address
13 嫌 *tokorokira(wazu)* anywhere, everywhere; indiscriminately
詮 *shosen* after all
置 *shochi* disposal, management; action, measure; treatment
感 *shokan* impressions

業 *shogyō* acts, works
載 *shosai no* printed, published, reported
14 説 *shosetsu* statement, assertion
領 *shoryō* territory, dominion, possession; fief
罰 *shobatsu* penalty, punishment
蔵 *shozō* possession
管 *shokan* jurisdiction
管庁 *shokanchō* the authorities concerned
15 論 *shoron* argument
16 懐 *shokai* impressions, opinions
謂 *iwayuru* the so-called
17 轄 *shokatsu* jurisdiction
19 願 *shogan* desire, wish, request

5

扁 2055 / J5928 / M11724 HEN level, small. *hira(tai)* flat, even, level; simple, plain.
5 平 *hempei* flatness
平足 *hempeisoku* flatfoot
6 舟 *henshū* skiff, little boat
8 青石 *henseiseki* lapis lazuli
10 桃 *hentō* almond
桃油 *hentōyu* almond oil
桃腺 *hentōsen* tonsils
桃腺炎 *hentōsen'en* tonsillitis; quinsy
18 額 *hengaku* framed picture or motto

6

B **扇** 2056 / J4070 / M11743′ SEN. *ao(gu)* fan. *ōgi* folding fan.
3 子 *sensu* folding fan
4 分 *ao(gi)-wa(keru)* winnow
7 形 *senkei, ōgigata* fan shape
状 *senjō* fan-shaped
状地 *senjōchi* alluvial delta
9 面 *semmen* fan paper; folding fan
屋 *ōgiya* fan maker
風機 *sempūki* electric fan
11 情 *senjō* lasciviousness
情的 *senjōteki* lascivious, sensational, suggestive
動 *sendō* instigation, agitation
動者 *sendōsha* instigator, agitator

7

扈 2057 / J6e3d / M11746 KO follow.
10 従 *kojū suru* be in attendance on. *koshō, kojū* follower

8

B **扉** 2058 / J4862 / M11750 HI. *tobira* door; title page, front page.

手 RAD. 64

Te hand. At left: 手, 龵, and 扌 (3 strokes) *tehen*. Nickname: Hand.

A **才** 2059 / J3a4d / M11769 SAI ability, talent, aptitude, genius, acumen, intelligence, wit; cubic foot; year, age; time; occasion; opportunity; limit; vicinity. *-sai* years old, age, year. *zae* intelligence, ability, talent.
2 人 *saijin* talented person, clever person
力 *sairyoku* ability, talent
3 女 *saijo* talented woman
子 *saishi* talented man, clever man
4 分 *saibun* disposition
6 色 *saishoku* wit and beauty
名 *saimei* fame; reputation for ability
気 *saiki* wisdom
気煥発 *saiki kampatsu* great wisdom
気縦横 *saiki jūō* great wisdom
7 走 *saibashi(ru)* be clever, be quick-witted, be precocious
芸 *saigei* talent and accomplishments; wisdom and works
8 物 *saibutsu* talented person, clever person
知 *saichi* wit and intelligence
学 *saigaku* talent and education
10 能 *sainō* talent, ability
11 略 *sairyaku* wise planning
略有 *sairyaku (no) a(ru)* resourceful
12 媛 *saien* literary woman; talented woman
弾 *saihaji(keru)* be presumptuous, be clever and forward
腕 *saiwan* skill, ability
量 *sairyō* measurement
筆 *saihitsu* literary talent, clever style

智 *saichi* wit and intelligence
覚 *saikaku* ready wit; raising (money); plan, device
13 幹 *saikan* ability
槌 *saizuchi* small wooden mallet
槌頭 *saizuchi atama* head like a hammer head
14 徳 *saitoku* intelligence and virtue
15 器 *saiki* talent
19 藻 *saisō* poetic talent

Λ 手 2060 / J3c6a / M11768 SHU. *te* hand, arm; help; handwriting, handle, means; trick, snare; skill; kind; direction, side; trouble, care; control, management; possession; connection; injury. *te ni suru* carry. *te(bura) de* empty-handed. *te(zukara)* personally, with one's own hands. *te(gusune)* prepared and waiting. *-te* person; kind; direction; money.

1 一束 *te-issoku* length of a hand
一杯 *te-ippai* hands full; barely making ends meet; full operation
2 入 *te (o) i(reru)* reach into; correct, retouch, repair; raid; interfere. *tei(razu)* requiring little trouble; untouched, virgin (forest). *tei(re)* repair, remodeling; care, trimming; raid, round-up
力 *shuryoku* hand power
八丁口八丁 *tehatchō-kuchihatchō no* very skilled (person)
3 口 *teguchi* style of work; method employed
下 *te (o) kuda(su)* set to work; do in person; participate; murder. *teshita* subordinate, follower
丈夫 *tejōbu na* strong
土産 *temiyage* visitor's present
小荷物 *tekonimotsu* luggage, hand baggage
工 *shukō* manual work, handicraft
工芸 *shukōgei* handicraft
工教育 *shukō kyōiku* manual training
工業 *shukōgyō* manual labor, handicrafts
4 心 *tegokoro* discretion, consideration, allowance
手 *tete* hands (child's word). *te(ni)te(ni)* in everyone's hands
爪 *tezuma* work at hand; sleight of hand, tricks, juggling
込 *tego(me)* rape, violation, outrage. *te (no) ko(nda)* complicated, laborious, elaborate
中 *shuchū ni* in the hand
元 *temoto* money on hand, one's purse; usual skill
分 *tewa(ke)* division of work. *te (o) wa(katsu)* break off relations with
文庫 *tebunko* small bookcase
内 *te(no)uchi* palm; skill, capacity; gift, alms; scope of one's ability
内職 *tenaishoku* piecework at home
引 *te (o) hi(ku)* lead by the hand; sever connections with. *tebi(ki)* guidance; introduction, primer; good offices, pull; introducer, backer; guide; spinning (silk) by hand
引書 *tebi(ki)sho* guidebook
不入 *teirazu* requiring little work; untouched, virgin (forest)
不足 *tebusoku* shorthanded
水 *temizu, chōzu* water for washing the hands
水場 *chōzuba* toilet, lavatory
水鉢 *chōzubachi* washbasin
切 *te (o) ki(ru)* cut the hand; sever connections with. *tegi(re)* severance of connections
切金 *tegirekin* alimony, heart balm
切話 *tegi(re)banashi* talk of separation
5 玉 *tedama* jackstones; bean bags. *tedama ni* (leading) by the nose
立 *teda(te)* method, means
広 *te (o) hiro(geru)* extend operations. *tebiro(i)* roomy, spacious, large (practice); extensive (trade)
甲 *te(no)kō, tekkō* covering for the back of the hand. *tekkō* old-style Japanese glove
代 *tedai* clerk, salesperson (in a store)
外 *te (no) hoka* beyond expectation
打 *te (o) u(tsu)* clap hands; adopt (a measure); strike a bargain. *teu(chi)* striking a bargain; reconciliation, handmade; killing by one's own hands
払 *tebara(i) suru* have nothing left
平 *te(no)hira* palm
写 *shusha* copying by hand
占 *teura* palmistry
出 *teda(shi)* interference; striking the first blow

本 *tehon* model, pattern, copy, standard
加減 *tekagen* allowance, discretion; tact; skill; measuring in the hand
古摺 *tekozu(ru)* be at wit's end, have a hard time with
付 *te (o) tsu(keru)* touch, lay hands on; attempt, have carnal connections with. *te (ni) tsu(kanai)* unable to settle down (to anything). *tetsu(ke)* way of doing; earnest money, deposit. *tetsu(ki)* way of using the hand
付金 *tezukekin, tetsukekin* earnest money, deposit
弁 *teben de* furnishing one's own lunch
弁当 *tebentō de* furnishing one's own lunch
仕事 *teshigoto* manual labor, hand work
仕舞 *tejimai* clearance (of goods); covering (of shorts) or liquidation (of longs) (stock market)
仕舞売 *tejimai u(ri)* clearance sale
札 *tefuda* name card; a hand (in card playing)
札形 *tefudagata* card-size photo, quarter plate
札判 *tefudaban* card-size photo, quarter plate
6 尽 *te (o) tsu(kusu)* take pains, do everything possible
返 *tegae(shi)* working on something over and over, resewing a kimono; resistance
近 *tejika (na), tejika(i)* near, handy, familiar
休 *teyasu(mi), teyasu(me)* rest, pause
交 *shukō (suru)* hand over, deliver
合 *tea(i)* fellow, chap; party, company, set (of people). *tea(wase)* game, contest, sale, transaction
早 *tebaya(i)* quick, nimble, agile
先 *tesaki* fingers; cat's-paw, tool, agent
向 *tamu(keru)* offer, pay tribute (to the dead). *temu(kau)* resist, oppose, lift one's hand against. *tamu(ke)* offering, parting gift, tribute (to the dead)
向草 *tamu(ke)gusa* Shinto offering; tribute (to the dead)
伝 *tetsuda(u)* help, take part in. *tetsuda(i)* help; helper, assistant
伝手 *tetsuda(i)te* helper, assistant
当 *tea(tari)* the feel; within reach. *tea(tari-battari)* hit-and-miss manner. *teate* allowance, compensation, tip, bonus. *tea(te)* (police) search; treatment, dressing, medical care
当次第 *tea(tari) shidai ni* at random, haphazardly
回 *temawa(shi)* preparation. *te (o) mawa(su)* send out agents, use spies. *temawa(ri)* personal effects; personal surroundings; bodyguard. *te (ga) mawa(ru)* be attentive to, attend to everything
回兼 *temawa(shi)-ka(neru)* be unable to prepare
回品 *temawa(ri)hin* personal effects
7 車 *teguruma* handcart, gocart, wheelbarrow; personal jinricksha
序 *tetsuide ni* as opportunity presents itself
応 *tegotae* resistance, response; effect, result
作 *tezuku(ri) no* handmade, homemade, homegrown. *tesaku* land cultivated for oneself
走 *tabashi(ru)* fly about, scatter
折 *tao(ru)* break off, pluck; deflower
技 *shugi* technique, procedure
抜 *te (o) nu(ku)* eliminate steps, save labor; drop out (of a project); do slipshod work. *tenu(kari)* omission, oversight, error, slip. *tenu(ki)* omission; intentional negligence
利 *tekiki* expert, master hand, one clever with the hands
助 *tedasu(ke)* help, assistance
兵 *shuhei* soldiers under direct command
弄 *temasaguri* searching with the fingers; fumbling
投弾 *tena(ge)dan* hand grenade
足 *teashi* hands and feet, limbs. *shusoku* hands and feet; subordinates
足纏 *teashimato(i)* encumbrance
沢 *shutaku* soil from handling
沢本 *shutakubon* one's favorite books; books from the library of ...
余 *teama(su), te (ni) ama(ru)* be beyond one's power; incorrigible
余者 *teama(shi)mono* someone difficult to handle
芸 *shugei* handicrafts, manual arts, useful arts
芸品 *shugeihin* handicrafts

形 *tegata* draft, promissory note
形交換所 *tegata kōkanjo* clearinghouse
形振出 *tegata furida(shi)* bank draft
形割引 *tegata waribiki* discounting a note
8 金 *tekin* key money, earnest money, deposit. *tegane* ready money
届 *te (ga) todo(ku)* reach (a goal)
底 *tanasoko* palm (of the hand)
刷 *tezu(ri)* hand printing
始 *tehajime* beginning, outset
帖 *techō* notebook
性 *teshō* skill
招 *temane(ku)* beckon
放 *tebana(su)* let go, release; part with, dispose of, send away; leave uncared for; leave off work. *tebana(shi)* hands off (in driving); leaving alone. *tebana(shi) de* freely, uncritically
明 *tea(ki)* leisure, spare time
枕 *temakura suru* use the arm for a pillow
法 *shuhō* technique, technical skill; execution
物 *te(no)mono* specialty, strong point, forte; something in the hand
並 *tena(mi)* skill, performance
斧 *chōna, teono* adze
直 *tenao(shi)* later adjustment
実 *temame na* diligent; skillful
妻 *tezuma* finger tips; sleight of hand, tricks, juggling
者 *te(no)mono* one's men. *tesha* skilled person
押車 *teo(shi)guruma* handcart; wheelbarrow
忠実 *temame na* faithful in one's work
長 *tenaga* long-armed person; kleptomaniac
長猿 *tenagazaru* gibbon
拍 *tebata(ki)* hand clapping
拍子 *tebyōshi* beating time; careless move
取 *teto(ri)* skillful wrestler, good manager. *tedo(ri)* net profit; net income; take-home pay
取早 *te(t)to(ri)bayai* quick; rough and ready
取足取 *teto(ri)-ashito(ri), te(o)to(ri)-ashi(o)to(ri)* by main force, by the hands and feet, bodily
取金 *tedo(ri)kin* take-home pay
9 首 *tekubi* wrist
厚 *teatsu(i)* cordial, courteous, hospitable; liberal (gift)
透 *tesu(ki)* leisure, spare time
垢 *teaka* soil from handling
後 *teoku(re)* too late, belated treatment
拱 *te (o) komanu(ku)* fold the arms; do nothing to help; meditate
拭 *tenugui, tefuki* towel
拵 *tegoshira(e) no* handmade
挟 *tabasa(mu)* carry under the arm; wear, gird on
枷 *tekase* handcuffs, manacles
狭 *tezema na, tezema(i)* narrow, cramped, small
段 *shudan, tedate* resources, way, means, device, expedient, measures
重 *teomo(i)* serious; cordial, hospitable, liberal
柔 *teyawa(rakani)* gently, kindly, leniently
荒 *teara(i), teara na* rough, rude, harsh; violent; outrageous. *teara(ku), teara ni* roughly, violently, rudely
巻 *tema(ki)* hand-rolled; hand-wound
染 *tezo(me)* hand dyed
背 *shuhai* back of the hand
変品変 *te(o)ka(e)-shina(o)ka(ete)* by all possible means
風琴 *tefūkin* accordion, hand organ
活 *teike* personal flower arrangement; personal attendant; redemption of a geisha or prostitute and providing a home for her
活花 *teike (no) hana* a redeemed geisha
品 *tejina* sleight of hand, tricks, juggling
品師 *tejinashi* magician, juggler
洗 *teara(i)* washing the hands; washbasin; washstand; lavatory, toilet
洗所 *teara(i)jo* lavatory
洗鉢 *teara(i)bachi* washbowl
前 *temae* I; you; this side of; this way, toward you; living, livelihood; due to; for the sake of, tea-ceremony procedures; self, ones' own. *(o)temae* tea-serving skill
前味噌 *temae miso* self-praise; bean paste of one's own making
前勝手 *temaegatte* selfishness
負 *te (o) o(u)* hurt yourself. *te(ni)o(enai)* unmanageable, incorrigible. *teo(i)* wound; wounded person

負猪 *teo(i)jishi* wounded boar; desperado
負獅子 *teo(i)jishi* wounded lion; desperado
持 *temo(chi)* holdings, goods on hand
持不沙汰 *temo(chi)busata* idleness, suspense; ennui
持無沙汰 *temo(chi)busata* idleness, suspense; ennui
持品 *temochihin* holdings, goods on hand
持商品 *temo(chi) shōhin* goods on hand
柄 *tegara* merit, feat, exploit
柄者 *tegaramono* meritorious person
柄話 *tegarabanashi* bragging about exploits
柄顔 *tegaragao* triumphant look
相 *tesō* lines of the palm
相占 *tesō uranai* palmistry
相見 *tesōmi* palmist, palm reader
相学 *tesōgaku* palmistry
相術 *tesōjutsu* palmistry
10 振 *te (o) fu(ru)* shake one's hand. *tebu(ri)* gesture
捕 *tedo(ri)* capturing
捌 *tesaba(ki)* processing, maneuvering
酒 *tezake* homemade saké
紋 *shumon* lines in the palm
紙 *tegami* letter, note, epistle
記 *shuki* taking notes; memo
討 *teu(chi)* killing with one's own sword
配 *tekuba(ri), tehai* arrangements; disposition (of men); preparations
酌 *tejaku* drinking alone
部 *shubu* the hand
書 *shusho* autograph; autographed letter. *teka(ki)* good penman. *tega(ki)* hand-written
挙 *te (o) a(geru)* raise a hand; show one's hand; give up
弱女 *tawayame, taoyame* graceful maiden
真似 *temane* gesture, signs; dumb show, pantomime
都合 *tetsugō* circumstances, conditions, reasons; convenience; opportunity, occasion; arrangement, management; accommodation; in all
荷物 *tenimotsu* luggage, baggage, personal effects
料理 *teryōri* home cooking
紡績 *tebōseki* hand spinning
11 疵 *tekizu* wound (on the battlefield)
遊 *teaso(bi)* playing; plaything; gambling. *tesusabi* patting to comfort; play with
遅 *teoku(re)* too late, belated treatment
彫 *tebo(ri)* hand carving
頃 *tegoro na* handy, suitable, moderate
帳 *techō* notebook
強 *tezuyo(i)* strong, firm; severe. *tegowa(i)* stiff, unyielding, stubborn
張 *teba(ru)* be beyond one's power. *teba(ri)* hand-glued
掛 *tega(keru)* handle, manage, work with; rear, look after; have experience with. *te (o) ka(keru)* touch, handle. *te (ni) ka(karu)* fall into another's hand. *te (ga) ka(karu)* require a lot of care. *te (ni) ka(keru)* kill by one's hand; take care of, bring up. *tega(kari)* contact, trail, scent; on hand; hand hold; clue, key
控 *tebika(eru)* hold back, hold off, refrain from. *tebika(e)* note, memorandum; holding back
捷 *tebashiko(i)* quick, nimble, agile
掘 *tebori* digging by hand
探 *tesagu(ri)* fumbling, groping
械 *tegase, tekase* manacles, handcuffs
桶 *teoke* wooden bucket
淫 *shuin* masturbation
理 *shuri* lines in the palms
球 *tedama* cue ball
組 *tegu(mi)* hand composition (in printing); folding one's arms
脱 *tenu(kari)* a slip (in procedure), oversight
船 *tebune* one's own ship
釣 *tezu(ri)* line fishing (with no pole)
堅 *tegata(i)* steady, firm; solid, secure
盛 *temo(ri)* helping oneself, self-service; managing for one's own convenience; trap, trick; self-approved
袋 *tebukuro* gloves, mittens; gauntlet; mitt
細工 *tezaiku* handiwork, handicraft, handmade goods
許 *temoto* money on hand, one's purse; usual skill. *temoto ni* at hand, under one's care
許金 *temotokin* money on hand
毬 *temari* handball

毬唄 *temari uta* a handball song
毬歌 *temari uta* a handball song
習 *tenara(i)* penmanship; practice; learning
習草紙 *tenara(i)zōshi* copybook
習師匠 *tenara(i) shishō* writing master
動 *shudō* hand-operated
動式 *shudōshiki* hand-operated
動車 *shudōsha* handcar
動具 *tedōgu* hand tool; utensil; one's things
術 *shujutsu* surgical operation
術台 *shujutsudai* operating table
術衣 *shujutsui* operating gown
術的 *shujutsuteki* surgical
術室 *shujutsushitsu* surgery, operating room
術料 *shujutsuryō* operating fee
12 痛 *teita(i)* severe, serious, hard (blow)
遣 *tezuka(i)* arrangements; dispositions (of men); subordinate
違 *techiga(i)* hitch, something wrong
勝手 *tegatte* allowance; discretion; tact; skill
順 *tejun* process, routine, procedure
幅 *tehaba* handbreadth
揃 *tezoroi* full number
握 *te (o) nigi(ru)* shake hands; clasp hands (in fear); make up with
植 *teu(e)* personal planting
棒 *tembō* man whose arms are useless; armless man
渡 *tewata(shi)* personal delivery
焼 *te (o) ya(ku)* burn one's fingers, have a bitter experience with. *teya(ki) no* home-baked
焙 *teaburi* hand warmer, small brazier
短 *temiji(kana)* short, brief
絡 *tegara* hair decoration
証 *teshō* evidence
創 *tekizu* wound (on the battlefield)
掌 *shushō, te(no)hira* the palm of the hand
筋 *tesuji, te (no) suji* palm lines; skill (in writing, painting, etc.); means, method; connections. *te (no) suji* veins on the hand
筈 *tehazu* program, plan
答 *tegota(e)* resistance; response; effect; result
筆 *shuhitsu* one's own handwriting
筒 *tezutsu* pistol
着 *te (o) tsu(keru)* begin, start work on
落 *teo(chi)* omission, slip, oversight, neglect
惑 *temadoi* fluster, confusion
替 *tega(wari)* substitute worker
無 *te(mo)na(ku)* easily
覚 *teobo(e)* memory of skills
貸 *te (o) ka(su)* lend a hand
軽 *tegaru na* easy, ready; simple, informal, offhand; cheap. *tegaru(i)* easy (to do)
軽料理 *tegaru ryōri* refreshments, light lunch
腕 *shuwan* ability, skill
腕家 *shuwanka* man of ability
提 *tesage* handbag
提灯 *tejōchin* hand lantern
提金庫 *tesage kinko* cash box, portable safe
提袋 *tesagebukuro* handbag
提鞄 *tesage kaban* briefcase, grip
提籠 *tesage kago* hand basket
間 *tema* time; labor; trouble; wages
間代 *temadai* labor charge
間仕事 *tema shigoto* piecework, odd jobs
間取 *temado(ru)* take time, be delayed
間損 *temazon* wasted labor
間隙 *temahima* labor and time
間賃 *temachin* wages
間潰 *tematsubu(shi)* waste of time
13 鼓 *tetsuzumi* tambourine
傷 *tekizu* wound (on the battlefield)
煩 *te (o) wazura(wasu)* trouble someone
触 *te (o) fu(reru)* touch, lay hands on. *tezawa(ri)* feel, touch
解 *tehodo(ki)* introduction, primer, rudiments
話 *shuwa* sign language
詰 *tezu(maru)* be hard up, be driven to the wall. *tezu(me)* forced liquidation. *tezu(mari)* hard up; stalemate
跡 *shuseki* handwriting (specimen)
鉤 *tekagi* hook
隙 *tesuki* leisure, spare time
障 *tezawari* the feel
飼 *tega(i)* rearing (animals)
馴 *tena(rasu)* tame; train (a person). *tena(reru)* get used to; become skilled in
勢 *tezei* troops under one's command
業 *tewaza* manual work; skill; art

続 *tetsuzu(ki)* procedure, process (of laws), formalities
続上 *tetsuzu(ki)jō* procedurally
際 *tegiwa* performance, execution; skill; tact
際良 *tegiwayo(ku)* skillfully, neatly, cleverly, tactfully
数 *tekazu* trouble; number of moves (in a game). *tesū* trouble, pains, care
数料 *tesūryō* handling charge, commission
裏 *shuri* in the hand. *te (no) ura* palm
裏剣 *shuriken* dart, dirk, throwing knife
塩 *teshio* table salt; small dish
塩皿 *teshiozara* small dish, saucer
塩掛 *teshio (ni) ka(keru)* rear, raise, tame; train (flower)
14 選 *shusen, tesen* handpicking (in mining)
鳴 *te (o) na(rasu)* call by clapping
慣 *tena(reru)* get used to; become skilled in
摑 *tezukami* taking with the fingers
摺 *tesuri* railing, balustrade
槍 *teyari* javelin
種 *tegusa* fingering; gambling; plaything
綱 *tazuna* bridle, reins
踊 *teodo(ri)* posture dancing
酷 *tehido(i)* severe, cruel, merciless
銃 *tezutsu* pistol
窪 *te(no)kubo* hollow of the hand
箒 *tebōki* small broom
管 *tekuda* art, technique; guile, wiles, coquetry; deceit
蔓 *tezuru* interest, influence, connections, good offices, medium
製 *tesei* handmade, homespun
榴弾 *shuryūdan, teryūdan* hand grenade
綺麗 *tegirei na* neat, clean, dexterous
鼻 *tebana* blowing the nose with the fingers
鼻擤 *tebana (o) ka(mu)* blow the nose with the fingers
旗 *tebata* hand flag
旗信号 *tebata shingō* flag signalling
漉 *tesuki* handmade paper
漉紙 *tesukigami* handmade paper
練 *shuren* manual skill. *teren* methods of deception
練手管 *teren-tekuda* method of deception
15 編 *tea(mi)* hand knitting
縫 *tenu(i) no* hand-sewn, hand-tailored
緩 *tenuru(i)* mild, lenient; relaxed; lukewarm; slow, dilatory
縄 *tenawa* curtain rope; rope binding a criminal; halter rope
駒 *tegoma* person kept in reserve
箱 *tebako* hand box, toilet case
慰 *tenagusa(mi)* fingering; gambling
16 懐 *tenazu(keru)* tame, domesticate; win over; win one's heart
機 *tebata* hand loom
積 *tezumo(ri)* rough measurement
錠 *tejō* handcuffs, manacles
録 *shuroku* personal record
鋸 *tenoko* hand saw
頸 *tekubi* wrist
薄 *teusu* weakness, shortage; inadequate preparations. *teusu(i)* scarce, short of; slender (means)
翰 *shukan* letter
17 厳 *tekibi(shii)* severe, scathing, cruel
濡 *te (o) nu(rasazu) ni* without getting wet; without lifting a finger
燭 *teshoku* portable candlestick
鍋 *tenabe* pan
翳 *te (o) kaza(su)* shading (the eyes) with the hand
療治 *teryōji* self-treatment, home treatment
鞠 *temari* handball
鞠唄 *temari uta* handball song
18 癖 *tekuse* kleptomania; hand mannerisms
織 *teo(ri)* hand weaving
職 *teshoku* handicraft
蹟 *shuseki* handwriting (specimen)
簡 *shukan* letter
簞笥 *tedansu* chest of drawers
19 鏡 *tekagami* hand mirror; copybook; model
鞴 *tefuigo* a hand bellows
離 *tebana(reru)* to not need constant care; be finished and ready to deliver
繰 *tagu(ru)* haul in, reel in; trace; unravel. *teguri* spinning by hand; dragnet; arrangement; management
繰上 *taku(shi)-a(geru)* tuck up. *tagu(shi)-a(geru)* haul in
繰込 *tagu(ri)-ko(mu)* haul in
繰出 *tagu(ri)-da(su)* pay out (a line); trace (a clue)

繰揚 *tagu(ri)-a(geru)* haul in
繰網 *tegu(ri) ami* dragnet
20 懸 *tekake* handling something; concubine. *tega(kari)* contact, trail, scent; on hand; hand hold; clue, key
21 纏 *temadoi, tematoi* encumbrance, hindrance to one's work
22 鑑 *tekagami* model; copy; paragon
籠 *tekago* hand basket. *tegome* rape, violation; outrage

— 1 —

扎 2061 / J5929 / M11771 SATSU remove, pull out; get ready; build.

— 2 —

B 払 2062 / J1a27 / M11784 拂 2097 / J5944 / M11936 FUTSU. *hara(u)* clear out, sweep away, wipe off, brush off, drive away, banish; prune; parry; pay; dispose of; wield (a sword) sideways; show interest in. *(o)hara(i)* payment; unneeded things for sale.
3 下 *hara(i)-sa(geru)* sell, dispose of
下品 *haraisagehin* articles sold by the government
4 手 *hara(i)te* payer
込 *hara(i)-ko(mu)* pay in, pay up, pay an installment *haraiko(mi)* payment, installment, subscription
込資本 *haraiko(mi) shihon* paid-up capital
5 出 *hara(i)-da(su)* disburse, pay out; drive away
6 返 *hara(i)-kae(su)* pay back
7 戻 *hara(i)-modo(su)* refund, reimburse
8 底 *futtei* shortage, scarcity, famine
退 *hara(i)-no(keru)* brush aside, ward off, drive away
物 *hara(i)mono* discarded article; article to be disposed of
9 拭 *fusshoku suru* wipe out, sweep away
除 *hara(i)-nozo(ku)* remove, sweep away
10 残 *hara(i)noko(ri)* arrears, balance due
11 過 *hara(i)-su(giru)* overpay
捨 *hara(i)-su(teru)* cast off
済 *hara(i)zu(mi)* paid up, settled
12 暁 *futsugyō* dawn
渡 *hara(i)-wata(su)* pay, pay out, pay over; cash (a check)
落 *hara(i)-oto(su)* shake off, brush off
15 箱 *(o)hara(i)bako* dismissal

A 打 2063 / J4247 / M11781 CHō, DA striking. *u(tsu)* strike, hit, beat, knock, slap, punch, thrash, smite; clap (one's hands); beat (a drum); ring (a bell); (clocks) strike; impress, touch; shoot; pound in (a nail); water, sprinkle; braid; play (checkers); till (the soil); temper (a sword); prepare (buckwheat noodles); present (a play); cast (a net); pay (earnest money). *bu(tsu)* strike, beat; tell, speak; address (an audience). *dāsu* dozen. *u(chi-nomesu)* knock down, beat up. *u(chi)-* emphatic verbal prefix.
2 力 *daryoku* batting power
3 下 *u(chi)-o(rosu)* strike on the head, strike down on, bring an ax down on
上 *u(chi)-a(geru)* shoot up, send up, set off (fireworks); dash against; cast up on shore, wash ashore; finish, end (a performance)
上花火 *uchiage hanabi* skyrocket
4 手 *dashu* (cricket) bowler. *u(chi)te, u(t)te* attacking party, punitive force, pursuers; shooter, murderer
方 *u(chi)kata* how to shoot; batting, stroking (in tennis); how to punctuate
止 *u(chi)-ya(mu) vi* end, stop, cease; subside, calm down, pass; die out, be extinguished; leave, go off; be abandoned. *u(chi)-to(meru)* kill, bring down (a bird). *u(chi)do(me)* end of an entertainment or match
水 *u(chi)mizu* watering, sprinkling
火 *u(chi)bi* five struck from flintstone
込 *u(chi)-ko(mu)* drive in, pound in, shoot into, fall deeply in love, be thrown into, be absorbed in
切 *bu(t)tagi(ru)* cut off, chop off. *u(chi)-ki(ru) vt* end, close, discontinue. *bu(k)ki(ru)* chop, mangle
切棒 *bukkirabō* abruptness, brusqueness
5 立 *u(chi)-ta(teru)* establish
付 *u(chi)-tsu(keru)* strike, knock; pound in (a nail); throw at. *u(chi)tsu(ke) ni* bluntly, directly, flatly. *u(tte)-tsu(ke)* appropriateness of work
叩 *u(chi)-tata(ku), bu(t)tata(ku)* bruise, pound, strike

4 心 忄 ⺗ 戈 戸 【手 2 扌】 支 攴 攵 文 斗 斤 方 无 日 曰 月 木 欠 止 歹 殳 毋 比 毛 氏 气 水 氵 氺 火 灬 爪 爫 父 爻 爿 片 牙 牛 犬 犭

払 *u(chi)-hara(u)* beat off, shake off, sweep off, brush off, drive off, repel, rout

打 *chōchō* clashing of swords; felling of trees

出 *u(chi)-da(su)* begin to beat; open fire; emboss; end, be over. *u(chi)-de(ru), u(tte)-de(ru)* sally out, come forward, be a candidate; fire. *u(chi)da(shi)* close of a performance; embossing; delivery (of a ball)

出小槌 *u(chi)de (no) kozuchi* mallet of luck (Aladdin's lamp)

出後 *u(chi)da(shi)go* after the show

6 回 *u(chi)-mawa(su)* beat about

尽 *u(chi)-tsu(kusu)* shoot up all (ammunition)

返 *u(chi)-kae(su)* strike back; return (the ball); rally; repeat; plow up; renovate (old cotton). *u(chi)kae(shi)* striking back; change of scene

向 *u(chi)-mu(kau)* face, be opposite, meet, confront; oppose, defy; proceed to; get, tend toward; approach

伏 *u(chi)-fu(seru)* overpower, have power over. *u(chi)-fu(su)* humble oneself

当 *u(chi)-a(teru)* dash against

合 *u(chi)-a(u)* fight, exchange blows. *u(chi)-a(waseru)* strike (a thing) against (another). *uchi-a(wase)* previous arrangement; preliminaries, appointment

合会 *uchiawa(se)kai* caucus, consultation, preliminary meeting

7 身 *u(chi)mi* bruise, contusion

抜 *u(chi)-nu(ku)* punch, perforate; stamp out (coins); penetrate, pierce; shoot through

沈 *u(chi)-shizu(mu)* be completely discouraged

克 *u(chi)-ka(tsu)* defeat, conquer, overcome, surmount, recover from (illnesses)

見所 *u(chi)mi(taru) tokoro* to all appearances

8 金 *u(chi)gane* (gun) hammer, cock. *u(chi)kin* extra money paid in a trade

固 *u(chi)-kata(meru)* harden by tamping

延 *u(chi)-no(basu), u(chi)-no(beru)* hammer out

退 *u(chi)-shirizo(ku)* repulse

拉 *u(chi)-hishi(gu)* batter, smite

取 *u(chi)-to(ru)* catch, arrest; take possession of; kill

殴 *bu(n)nagu(ru)* (emphatic) strike, beat

者 *dasha* batter, hitter

垂髪 *u(chi)taregami* letting the hair hang down

明 *u(chi)-a(keru), u(chi)-a(kasu)* reveal, confide in

明話 *u(chi)a(ke)banashi* confidential talk, confession, revealing a secret

物 *u(chi)mono* forged work; sword, weapon; molded cake

物造 *u(chi)monozuku(ri)* hammered work

物師 *u(chi)monoshi* toolmaker, swordsmith

9 飛 *bu(t)to(basu)* (emphatic), beat, strike, knock; let go off. *bu(t)to(bu)* (emphatic) jump

首 *u(chi)kubi* decapitation

建 *u(chi)-ta(teru)* erect, build

廻 *u(chi)-mawa(su)* build an enclosure

連 *u(chi)-tsu(reru)* take (someone) along

砕 *u(chi)-kuda(ku), bu(chi)-kuda(ku)* smash, crush

乗 *u(chi)-no(ru)* ride (a horse)

変 *u(tte)-kawa(ru)* change completely

点 *daten* runs batted in

負 *u(chi)-ma(kasu)* overcome, outrival, defeat

10 倒 *bu(t)tao(su)* knock down. *bu(t)tao(reru)* fall down, be knocked down. *u(chi)-tao(reru)* fall, collapse, drop; break down, die, succumb to; fall senseless; be ruined; have a bad debt. *u(chi)-tao(su)* knock down; overthrow. *datō* knockout; overthrowing

従 *u(chi)-shitaga(eru)* subjugate

悩 *u(chi)-naya(masu)* harass. *u(chi)-naya(mu)* be troubled with

振 *u(chi)-fu(ru)* wave, wag, swing, shake; sprinkle; brandish; jilt, reject; attach, allot

残 *u(chi)-noko(su)* leave unhurt

消 *u(chi)-ke(su)* deny, contradict. *uchike(shi)* denial, negation; negative (in grammar)

破 *u(chi)-yabu(ru)* *vt* tear, rip, rend; break, crush, destroy; violate, transgress; defeat; baffle, frustrate.

daha breaking, destruction, defeat, conquest, overthrow
粉 *u(chi)ko* blade-sharpening powder; flour put on the surface when kneading dough
紐 *u(chi)himo* braid, braided cord
殺 *bu(chi)-koro(su)* club to death. *u(chi)-koro(su)* club to death, stone to death, shoot to death, slay
笑 *u(chi)-e(mu)* smile slightly
荷 *u(chi)ni* jetsam, jettisoned cargo
留 *u(chi)-to(meru)* kill, bring down (a bird). *u(chi)do(me)* end of a match or an entertainment
11 毬 *dakyū* (ancient) Japanese polo
過 *u(chi)-su(giru)* pass by (time)
掛 *u(tte)-kaka(ru)* attack a person. *u(chi)-ka(karu), bu(chi)-ka(karu)* strike at (someone). *u(chi)ka(ke)* long outer robe
据 *u(chi)-su(eru)* whip (a horse)
捨 *u(chi)-su(teru)* throw away, discard, abandon, desert, discard, give up, abandon; renounce, relinquish; resign; lay down (one's life); part with; sacrifice; reject, condemn
捲 *u(chi)-maku(ru)* pound a pitcher (in baseball)
球 *dakyū* batting; batted ball
眺 *u(chi)-naga(meru)* watch, look at, see; scrutinize
敗 *u(chi)-yabu(ru)* defeat, crush
率 *daritsu* batting average
寄 *u(chi)-yo(seru)* break upon (the shore), beat upon
貫 *u(chi)-nu(ku), u(chi)-tsuranu(ku)* pierce
萎 *u(chi)-shio(reru)* droop, wither, wilt, fade; be downcast
菓子 *u(chi)gashi* molded confectionery
12 遣 *utcha(ru), utcha(rakasu)* throw away, throw down, abandon, neglect, leave alone, leave a (person) out
開 *u(chi)hira(ku)* open, unfold, unroll, uncover, unpack, unite, unseal; establish; clear (land); pioneer; clear the way; convene; enlighten (a country); bloom; differ, have a margin; widen (the space between). *dakai* break, development, new turn, solution
場 *u(chi)ba* threshing floor
順 *dajun* batting order
棒 *dabō* batting; bat
勝 *u(chi)-ka(tsu)* defeat, conquer, overcome, surmount, recover from (illnesses)
診 *dashin* percussion, tapping (in medicine)
割 *u(chi)-wa(ru)* divide, cut, halve; separate; split, rip; break, crack, smash; dilute
散 *u(chi)-chi(rasu)* scatter violently
落 *u(chi)-o(tosu)* knock down; shoot down; knock out (a tooth); thresh out; lop off (branches)
集 *u(chi)-tsudo(u)* meet, assemble, congregate; swarm, flock or gather together; be collected, be gathered together; converge
13 傷 *u(chi)kizu* bruise, contusion
損 *u(chi)-sokona(u)* miss, fail to hit
続 *u(chi)-tsuzu(keru)* give repeated blows; fire in succession; batter; continue. *u(chi)-tsuzu(ku)* long, long-continued
数 *dasū* times at bat
毀 *u(chi)-kowa(su), bu(chi)-kowa(su)* break, smash, destroy; take to pieces; frustrate
寛 *uchi-kutsu(rogu)* relax, feel at home
置 *u(chi)-o(ku)* place (emphatic)
電 *daden suru* send a telegram
楽器 *dagakki* percussion instrument
解 *u(chi)-to(keru)* open one's heart, be frank, throw aside reserve
解話 *u(chi)to(ke)banashi* friendly chat, heart-to-heart talk
14 鳴 *u(chi)-na(rasu) vt* ring, sound, blow (a whistle), beat (drums), clank, clink, clap, crack (a whip), smack (lips), cluck (one's tongue), honk; air (grievances); attain (celebrity)
網 *u(chi)ami* casting net
魂消 *bu(t)tamage(ru)* be terribly startled
綿機 *u(chi)wataki* cotton gin
穀 *dakoku* flailing
穀機 *dakokki* threshing instrument, threshing machine
算 *dasan* calculation, self-interest, selfishness
算的 *dasanteki* calculating, mercenary, self-centered
15 線 *dasen* batting lineup

敷 *u(chi)shi(ki)* a spread, an altar cloth
撲 *daboku* contusion, blow
撲傷 *dabokushō* bruise, contusion
撃 *dageki* blow, hit, shock; batting, hitting
撃王 *dagekiō* leading batter
撃率 *dagekiritsu* batting average
撃賞 *dagekishō* batting award
16 壊 *bu(chi)-kowa(su)* break, shatter, smash; upset (a plan), ruin, spoil, frustrate; bungle
17 擲 *bu(n)nagu(ru)* strike, beat, hit. *chōchaku* thrashing, spanking, slapping, striking, beating
18 懲 *u(chi)-ko(rasu)* discipline, chasten, punish by whipping
21 囃 *u(chi)-haya(su)* make a loud (musical) noise

3

扨 2064 J592e M11824 (国字) *sate* well, now.

扛 2065 J592c M11798 Kō raise.
10 秤 *chikiri* large beam balance

扞 2066 J592a M11802 KAN restrain.
10 格 *kankaku* incompatibility, divergence (of views), inconsistency, antagonism

扣 2067 J592b M11807 Kō. *hika(e)* memo; duplicate; waiting; prop; reserve. *hika(eru)* draw in; hold back, suspend (judgment); refrain from; be moderate; write, make notes; wait; have; moderate (a report).
9 除 *kōjo* subtraction, deduction

扠 2068 J592d M11804 SA. *sate* well, now.
2 又 *sate mata* and again
13 置 *sateo(ku)* leave as is

托 2069 J4271 M11793 TAKU. *taku(suru)* entrust with, charge with; pretend; hint.
7 身 *takushin* (Catholic) incarnation
13 鉢 *takuhatsu* religious mendicancy; begging priest

B **扱** 2070 J3037 M-X **扱** 2071 J-X M11835 Sō. KYŪ. *atsuka(u)* treat; entertain; manage, deal with, conduct, work on; handle; manipulate. *shigo(ku)* squeeze through the hand, strip off. *ko(ku)* thresh, strip. *shigoki* woman's undergirdle, waistband; squeezing through.
2 人 *atsuka(i)nin* person in charge
3 下 *ko(ki)-oro(su)* thresh; strip off; criticize meanly
8 使 *ko(ki)-tsuka(u)* work (a person) hard
11 混 *ko(ki)-ma(zeru)* mix together
寄 *ko(ki)-yo(seru)* rake together
12 落 *ko(ki)-o(tosu)* thresh, strip off

4

扱 2071 J-X M11835 See **扱** 2070.

拋 2072 J5946 M11901 See **拋** 2117.

找 2073 J5932 M11851 KA row a boat. Sō *saga(su)* search for.

抂 2074 J5930 M11859 KYŌ. GŌ *mida(reru)* be in disarray, be disorganized, be disordered.

抖 2075 J5935 M11888 TŌ. To wave, brandish (a weapon); take up.

抔 2076 J5938 M11886 HŌ. *nado* and so forth.

抃 2077 J5937 M11860 BEN strike with the hand.
14 舞 *bembu* dancing for joy

抉 2078 J5931 M11873 KETSU. *egu(ru)* gouge, hollow out, bore, excavate. *koji(ru)* gouge; wrench, pry. *kuji(ru)* pick, scoop.
8 取 *egu(ri)-to(ru)* gouge out

扼 2079 J592f M11848 YAKU. *yaku(suru)* command, dominate; prevent, obstruct; hold, grip; crush, defeat.
10 殺 *yakusatsu suru* choke to death

12 腕 *yakuwan suru* clench the fists, roll up the sleeves in anger

扮 2080 / J4a31 / M11830 FUN. *fun(suru), yatsu(su)* impersonate, dress up (as), disguise oneself (as)

12 装 *funsō suru* impersonate. *funsō* garb, style of dress

13 飾 *funshoku* makeup, showy ornaments; embellishment

抓 2081 / J5934 / M11885 SŌ. *tsu(neru), tsu(meru), tsu(mu), tsuma(mu)* pick, pinch; hold in the fingers; summarize.

5 出 *tsuma(mi)-da(su)* pick up and throw out

8 物 *tsuma(mi)mono* crackers, etc., to munch on while drinking

9 食 *tsumamigu(i)* picking and eating; eating stealthily

洗 *tsumamiara(i)* washing out spots

B **択** 2082 / J4272 / M11902′ **擇** 2285 / J5a24 / M12796 TAKU. *yo(ru), era(bu), e(ru)* choose, select; cull out; elect; prefer; decide on.

1 一 *takuitsu* choosing an alternative

一的 *takuitsuteki* alternative

4 分 *yo(ri)-wa(keru)* set apart, sort out, sift, cull, separate, pick out

7 抜 *takubatsu* choosing from among many

10 屑 *yorikuzu* waste, trash, refuse

B **把** 2083 / J4744 / M11874 HA bundle, bunch, sheaf, coil. *to(ru)* take, hold, seize, catch, capture; fetch; receive, procure, obtain; adopt (a measure); engage (graduates); choose; order (foodstuffs); pick, pluck; make, produce; eat; set up (camp); charge; administer; transact; take (pains); make out (the meaning); remove; take off (one's hat); take out (spots); strike out (words); weed, catch (fish); deprive of ; steal; capture (territory), annex; need, require; reserve (rooms); subscribe to; press (a point home); take (a picture); possess. *wa* bundle, faggot, sheaf.

4 手 *totte, torite, hashu* handle, knob, grip. *hashu* grasping the hand

7 住 *hajū suru* retain, keep in mind

住力 *hajūryoku* retentive power

9 持 *haji suru* grasp, hold, clasp

12 握 *haaku* grasp, hold, grip

B **拒** 2084 / J3571 / M-X KYO *koba(mu)* refuse, reject, decline; repudiate; resist, oppose, prevent; deny. *fuse(gu)* defend, protect; resist; keep away, shut out, ward off; prevent.

4 止 *kyoshi suru* refuse, decline, check

7 否 *kyohi* denial, veto, rejection

否権 *kyohiken* veto right

食症 *kyosyokushō* anorexia

12 絶 *kyozetsu* refusal, rejection, rebuff

絶品 *kyozetsuhin* rejected articles

抒 2085 / J5933 / M11884 CHO, SHO, JO tell.

11 情 *jojō* expression of one's feelings; lyricism

情的 *jojōteki* lyrical

情詩 *jojōshi* lyric poetry; lyric poem

情詩人 *jojō shijin* lyric poet

情詩風 *jojōshifū* lyricism

情歌 *jojōka* lyric poetry; lyric poem

A **批** 2086 / J4863 / M11845 HI strike.

5 正 *hisei suru* criticize and correct

7 判 *hihan* criticism, comment

判的 *hihanteki* critical

9 点 *hiten* correction marks (in a manuscript); emphasis marks; points to be criticized

10 准 *hijun* ratification

准書 *hijunsho* instrument of ratification

12 評 *hihyō* criticism, comment

評家 *hihyōka* critic, reviewer

評眼 *hihyōgan* critical eye

18 難 *hinan* criticism, denunciation

20 議 *higi suru* blame, criticize

B **抄** 2087 / J3e36 / M11863 SHŌ selection, summary; one tenth of a *shaku* (勺). *shō(suru)* copy; copy out. *su(ku)* spread out thin; manufacture (paper).

3 上 *suku(i)-a(geru)* scoop up, dip up

5 写 *shōsha* excerpt, quotation

出 *shōshutsu suru* take excerpts

本 *shōhon* excerpt, abridgment, book of selections

[8]物 *shōmono* a printed digest of a book; a copied book; (ancient) Japanese commentary on a Chinese book
[10]書 *shōsho* excerpt, abridgment, book of selections
紙 *shōshi* paper making
紙機 *shōshiki* paper-making machine
[11]掠 *shōryaku* robbery
略 *shōryaku* robbery
訳 *shōyaku* abridged translation
[16]録 *shōroku* quotation, selection; summary

A **承** 2088 / J3e35 / M11852 Jō. Shō. *u(keru)* receive, accept, take, get, obtain; catch (a ball); stop (a blow), parry; answer (the phone); undergo (an operation); take (an exam); sustain (a loss); be exposed to (ridicule); face, front on; inherit; catch the public fancy. *uketamawa(ru)* hear, listen to, be informed.
[4]引 *shōin* consent, acceptance, agreement
允 *shōin* consent, acceptance, agreement
[6]伏 *shōfuku* compliance, consent, submission
[8]服 *shōfuku* compliance, consent, submission
知 *shōchi* consent, assent, admitting, acknowledgment, compliance, agreement
知助 *shōchi(no)suke* agreement
[9]前 *shōzen* continued (from)
[13]継 *shōkei* succession, accession, inheritance
[14]認 *shōnin* approval, consent, agreement, recognition, acknowledgment
認状 *shōninjō* certificate of approval
[15]諾 *shōdaku* acquiescence, consent, agreement

B **扶** 2089 / J495e / M11840 Fu. *tasu(keru)* help; save, rescue; give relief to; spare (life); reinforce; promote; abet.
[6]合 *tasu(ke)-a(u)* cooperate, help each other
[7]助 *fujo* aid, help, support, relief
助料 *fujoryō* pension
[8]育 *fuiku* bringing up (children)
育料 *fuikuryō* charge for rearing others' children
[9]持 *fuchi* stipend, allowance, sustenance
持米 *fuchimai* rice allowance
[10]桑 *Fusō* Japan
[11]掖 *fueki* help, support
[12]植 *fushoku* implantation; establishment, extension
[15]養 *fuyō* support, maintenance
養家族 *fuyō kazoku* family dependents
[17]翼 *fuyoku suru* aid, support

B **抑** 2090 / J4d5e / M11883 Yoku *osa(eru)* stop, check, restrain, pin down; suppress, subdue, control; catch, arrest; govern; stop (the ears); withhold; attach, seize; secure (evidence), estimate conservatively. *osa(e)* weight, paperweight; rear guard; defense; pressure, suppression; control. *somosomo* well, now; in the first place.
[4]止 *yokushi suru* check, checkmate, stave off
切 *osa(e)ki(renai)* uncontrollable, irresistible, irrepressible
[5]圧 *yokuatsu* oppression, repression, pressure, suppression, restraint
付 *osa(e)-tsu(keru)* hold down, curb, control
[7]抑 *somosomo* well, now; in the first place. *yokuyoku* discreet, careful, cautious
[8]物 *osa(e)mono* the last (special) course (of a banquet)
制 *yokusei suru* control, restrain, suppress
制力 *yokuseiryoku* restraining power
制均衡 *yokusei (to) kinkō* system of checks and balances
[10]留 *yokuryū* internment
留国 *yokuryūkoku* detaining country
留所 *yokuryūjo* internment camp
留者 *yokuryūsha* internee
留船 *yokuryūsen* interned ship
[12]揚 *yokuyō* modulation, intonation, accent, rhythm, cadence
[18]難 *osa(e)gata(i)* uncontrollable, irresistible, irrepressible
[26]鬱 *yokuutsu* depression (in psychiatry)

B **抗** 2091 / J3933 / M11889 Kō. *kō(suru)* resist, defy, oppose, antagonize.
[4]日 *kō-Nichi* anti-Japanese
[5]弁 *kōben* plea, defense, protest, refutation, contradiction, answer
生 *kōsei no* antibiotic

生物質 *kōsei busshitsu* an antibiotic
生物質学 *kōsei busshitsugaku* science of antibiotics
6 争 *kōsō* dispute; resistance
7 言 *kōgen* protest, retort
拒 *kōkyo* resistance
告 *kōkoku* protest, appeal
8 毒素 *kōdokuso* antitoxin, antivenom
命 *kōmei* disobedience
命罪 *kōmeizai* the crime of military disobedience
10 病力 *kōbyōryoku* resistance to disease
11 張力 *kōchōryoku* tensile strength
13 戦 *kōsen* resistance
15 敵 *kōteki* resistance to the enemy
20 議 *kōgi* protest, objection
議文 *kōgibun* written protest

A **技** 2092 / J3331 / M11855 GI art, craft; ability, skill, feat, performance. *waza* deed, act, work, art, performance, trick.
3 工 *gikō* artisan, craftsman
4 手 *gishu, gite* assistant engineer; (telegraph) operator
5 巧 *gikō* art, craftmanship, skill, technique; trick
巧的 *gikōteki* skillful, clever; ornate
7 芸 *gigei* arts, crafts, accomplishments
8 法 *gihō* technique
官 *gikan* technical official
10 師 *gishi* engineer, technician
倒 *gitō* technical knockout
倆 *giryō* skill
能 *ginō* ability, capacity, skill, talent
能賞 *ginōshō* technique award (in sumo)
11 術 *gijutsu* art, technique, skill
術士 *gijutsushi* engineer, technician
術官 *gijutsukan* technical official
術者 *gijutsusha* technician, engineer
術家 *gijutsuka* technician, specialist, expert
術賠償 *gijutsu baishō* reparations in technical help
12 量 *giryō* skill
14 監 *gikan* chief engineer

B **拔** 2093 / J4834 / M11901′ **抜** 2099 / J5936 / M11959 BATSU. *nu(ku)* extract, uncork, pull out; root up; unsheathe; pilfer; quote; remove; omit; capture; outrun; shoot through. *nu(keru)* come off, fall out, slip out; be omitted; be missing; be rid of; pass through; escape; be captured; withdraw; be less than. *nu(kasu)* omit, skip over. *nuki(nderu)* excel in, surpass. *nu(karu)* be careless; slip, make a mistake. *nu(kari)* negligence; carelessness. *nu(ki)* omission, removal; defeating. *nu(karanu)* shrewd, on one's guard.
2 入 *nu(ke)-i(ru)* crawl into
刀 *battō* drawing a sword; drawn sword
3 上 *nu(ke)-a(garu)* be bald in front
小路 *nu(ke) kōji* a through passage
4 手 *nu(ki)te, nu(ki)de* overhand stroke
毛 *nu(ke)ge* falling hair, combings, molt
切 *nu(ke)-ki(ru)* get rid of, get free from
5 目 *nu(ke)me* imprudence. *nu(ke)me(nai)* shrewd, alert, careful, tactful, clever
穴 *nu(ke)ana* secret passage, underground exit; loophole; way of escape
代 *nu(ke)-kawa(ru)* shed, molt
写 *nu(ki)utsu(shi)* selection, excerpt
去 *nu(ke)-sa(ru)* lose all (strength). *nu(ki)-sa(ru)* pull out. *bakkyo* extraction (of teeth)
出 *nu(ki)-da(su), nu(ki)-ida(su)* select, extract, pull out. *nu(ke)-da(su), nu(ke)-de(ru)* slip out, sneak away, break out, get loose; excel, surpass, choose the best. *nu(ki) de(ru)* be outstanding
本 *bappon* eradication
打 *nukiu(chi)* sudden attack
打的 *nukiu(chi)teki ni* without notice
6 糸 *basshi* removal of stitches. *nu(ki)ito* drawn thread
合 *nu(ki)-a(waseru)* unsheathe together
衣紋 *nu(ki)emon de* with kimono collar pulled back
7 身 *nu(ki)mi* drawn sword
作 *nu(ke)saku* dunce, simpleton
抜 *nu(ke)nu(ke) to* unashamedly
足 *nu(ki)ashi de* stealthily, gingerly
足差足 *nu(ki)ashi-sa(shi)ashi de* stealthily, gingerly
8 刷 *nu(ki)zu(ri)* a publication of the important parts of a book
放 *nu(ki)-hana(su), nu(ki)-hana(tsu)* unsheathe, draw out, take out
参 *nu(ke)mai(ri)* secret pilgrimage
取 *nu(ki)-to(ru)* pilfer, steal; pull out, extract, take out, tear off

取検査 *nukito(ri) kensa* inspection of (grain) samples

9 首 *nu(ke)kubi* long-necked monster

連 *nu(ki)-tsu(reru), nu(ki)-tsura(neru)* draw swords together

砕 *nu(ki)-kuda(ku)* break (teeth)

10 粋 *bassui* quotation, selection, excerpt; abstract, summary

剣 *bakken* drawing a sword

差 *nu(ki)sa(shi)* slipping off and on; taking on and off.

nu(ki)sa(shinaranu) impossible; being in a dilemma

書 *nukiga(ki)* selection, excerpt

荷 *nu(ki)ni* pilfered goods. *nukeni* smuggled goods

11 道 *nu(ke)michi* bypass; secret path; way of escape, loophole; last resources; excuse

捨 *nu(ki)-su(teru)* cut off from, uproot and throw away

殻 *nu(ke)gara* the shed skin (of a snake or cicada); a person whose mind is elsewhere

商 *nu(ke)akina(i)* smuggling

萃 *bassui* quotation, selection, excerpt; abstract, summary

萃帳 *bassuichō* scrapbook

12 歯 *basshi* extraction of teeth

落 *nu(ke)-o(chiru)* fall out. *nu(ki)-oto(su)* let fall

集 *nu(ki)-atsu(meru)* pull out and gather up. *nukiatsu(me)* quotation; summary

替 *nu(ke)-ka(waru)* shed, molt

13 路 *nu(ke)michi* bypass; secret path; way of escape, loophole; last resources; excuse

群 *batsugun, bakkun* pre-eminence

裏 *nu(ke)ura* bypass; way of escape

14 読 *nukiyo(mi) suru* read or tell part of a story

駆 *nu(ke)ga(ke)* stealing a march on; forestalling; scoop

15 撃 *nukiu(chi)* sudden attack

16 錨 *batsubyō* weighing anchor

17 擢 *batteki* selection, choice

翳 *nu(ki)-kaza(su)* draw a sword and hold it up over one's forehead

18 襟 *nu(ki)eri* pulled-back collar

顔 *nu(karanu) kao* a watchful eye

A 折 2094 / J405e / M11890 SETSU. *o(ru) vt* break, snap, fracture, knock out (teeth); fold, turn down; bend; make (a paper toy); yield (oneself), give in. *o(reru)* snap, break; be folded; give in, submit; turn (to the left or right). *o(re)* fragment, broken piece. *o(ri)* breaking; small food box; time, occasion, juncture; opportunity. *ori(shimo)* just then. *o(ri) kara* just at that time. *-ori-* folding; signature (of a book).

2 入 *o(ri)-i(reru)* fold and insert; tuck in; turn in; read into. *o(ri)-i(tte)* earnestly

3 口 *o(re)kuchi* a split, a break

子 *o(ri)ko* folder (the person)

山 *o(ri)yama* the outside edge of a fold

4 戸 *o(ri)do* folding doors

方 *o(ri)kata* how to fold

木 *o(re)gi* broken tree

尺 *o(ri)jaku* folded ruler

込 *o(ri)-ko(mu)* tuck, turn in; insert. *o(re)-ko(mu)* fold and insert. *o(ri)ko(mi)* insert

中 *setchū* compromise; cross, blending, eclecticism

木戸 *o(ri)kido* folding wooden doors

手本 *o(ri)dehon* folding copybook

5 句 *o(ri)ku* acrostic verse

半 *seppan* halving

本 *o(ri)bon, o(ri)hon* a folding book, a folder

目 *o(re)me, o(ri)me* fold, crease, dog-ear

目切目 *o(ri)me-ki(ri)me* methodical, punctual, steady

目正 *o(ri)metada(shii)* well-mannered; ceremonious

6 曲 *o(ri)-ma(geru)* bend, turn up, turn down

好 *o(ri)yo(ki)* timely, opportune; lucky. *o(ri)yo(ku)* fortunately, just in time

合 *o(ri)-a(u), o(re)-a(u)* come to an agreement. *o(ri)a(i), o(re)a(i)* mutual relations; compromise, agreement, understanding

地図 *o(ri)chizu* folding map

返 *o(re)-kae(ru)* tell again and again. *o(ri)-kae(su)* turn up, turn down, fold back; repeat. *o(ri)kae(shi)* lapel, cuffs, flap; chorus, refrain; repetition

返点 *o(ri)kae(shi)ten* turn-back point
返運転 *o(ri)kae(shi) unten* shuttle service
7 角 *sekkaku* at great pains; on purpose, expressly; kindly. *sekkaku no* valuable, long-awaited
折 *o(ri)o(ri)* occasionally
助 *o(ri)suke* footman, flunkey
8 屈 *o(re)-kaga(mu)* bend. *o(ri)kaga(mi)* bend, curtsy
取 *o(ri)-to(ru)* break off a branch, pick (flowers)
9 柄 *o(ri)kara* just then, at that time. *orie* broken handle
砕 *o(ri)-kuda(ku)* strike down, break down. *o(re)-kuda(keru)* be broken
重 *o(ri)-kasa(naru) vi* overlap; telescope. *o(ri)-kasa(neru) vt* fold back, turn down
衷 *setchū* compromise; cross, blending, eclecticism
衷主義 *setchū shugi* syncretism
10 紙 *o(ri)gami* folded paper; colored folding paper, origami; affidavit, testimonial
紙付 *o(ri)gamizu(ki)* certified, guaranteed; notorious
釘 *o(re)kugi, o(ri)kugi* hooked nail; broken nail
釘流 *o(re)kugiryū* scrawl
11 掛 *o(ri) ka(keru)* bend and hang up
脚 *o(ri)ashi* folding table
悪 *o(ri)a(shiku)* inopportunely, unfortunately
崩 *o(ri)-kuzu(reru)* collapse
12 椅子 *o(ri)isu* folding chair
畳 *o(ri)-tata(mu)* fold up
畳式 *o(ri)tatamishiki* collapsible, folding 「folding
畳自在 *o(ri)tatamijizai* collapsible,
畳椅子 *o(ri)tatami isu* folding chair
畳機 *o(ri)tatamiki* folding machine
13 詰 *orizume* food packed in a small box
節 *o(ri)fushi* chance, occasion; just then; occasionally; opportunity, time
電 *setsuden* zigzag lightning
14 鞄 *o(ri)kaban* folding brief case
15 衝 *sesshō* negotiation
敷 *o(ri)-shi(ku)* kneel. *o(ri)shi(ki)* kneeling (position)
箱 *o(ri)bako* small box made of cardboard or thin wood
18 檻 *sekkan* chastisement, correction; whipping, spanking
襟 *o(ri)eri* turned-down collar; sack coat

A **投** 2095 / J456a / M11887 Tō throw. *tō(jiru), tō(zuru)* throw, throw away, throw into; abandon; launch into, embark on; join (a party); invest in; seize (an opportunity); agree with; catch (the public eye). *na(geru)* throw, hurl; give up; sell at a loss. *na(ge)* a throw, a spill, a fall.

2 入 *na(ge)-i(reru)* throw into; dump in together. *tōnyū suru* throw into; invest. *na(ge)-i(re)* free-style flower arrangement
3 下 *tōka suru* throw down, drop; invest
上 *na(ge)-a(geru)* throw up (in the air)
与 *tōyo suru, na(ge)-ata(eru)* throw to (the dogs)
4 込 *na(ge)-ko(mu)* throw into, dump into. *na(ge)ko(mi)* free-style flower arrangement
手 *tōshu* pitcher, bowler (in cricket)
手力 *tōshuryoku* pitching power
手団 *tōshudan* pitching staff
手位置 *tōshu ichi* pitcher's box
手板 *tōshuban* pitcher's box
手陣 *tōshujin* pitching staff
手戦 *tōshusen* pitching duel
5 付 *na(ge)-tsu(keru)* throw at; throw (someone) down
出 *na(ge)-da(su)* throw out, throw down; stretch out (legs); give up, renounce
仕事 *na(ge)shigoto* slipshod work
石 *tōseki* throwing stones
石機 *tōsekiki* stone catapult
6 返 *na(ge)-kae(su)* throw back
合 *tōgō* agreement, coincidence
光器 *tōkōki* floodlight projector
7 足 *na(ge)ashi* sitting with legs stretched out
身 *tōshin* suicide by drowning
売 *nageu(ri)* bargain sale
売品 *nageurihin* articles on special sale
8 物 *na(ge)mono* sacrifice goods
函 *tōkan suru* mail (a letter). *tōkan* throwing into a box
9 飛 *na(ge)-to(basu)* throw away
首 *na(ge)kubi* dropping the head (in thought)

4 心 忄 小 戈 戸 【手 扌】4 支 攴 攵 文 斗 斤 方 无 日 曰 月 木 欠 止 歹 殳 毋 比 毛 氏 气 水 氵 氺 火 灬 爪 爫 父 爻 爿 丬 片 牙 牛 犬 犭

砕 *na(ge)-kuda(ku)* dash to pieces
降 *tōkō* surrender
係蹄 *na(ge)wana* a lasso
10 倒 *na(ge)-tao(su)* throw (someone) down
射 *tōsha* projection (in math); incidence (in physics); throwing (spears)
殺 *na(ge)-koro(su)* throw and kill
索 *na(ge)nawa* a lasso
罠 *na(ge)wana* a lasso
荷 *na(ge)ni* jetsam, jettisoned cargo
捕手 *tōhoshu* the battery (in baseball)
書 *tōsho* correspondence, contribution
書家 *tōshoka* correspondent, contributor
11 掛 *na(ge)-ka(keru)* throw at; cast over, throw around
捨 *na(ge)-su(teru)* throw away
球 *tōkyū* throwing a ball, pitching, bowling (in cricket); a pitched ball
宿 *tōshuku suru* put up at a hotel
宿者 *tōshukusha* hotel guest
票 *tōhyō* vote, voting, ballot, suffrage
票日 *tōhyōbi* voting day
票区 *tōhyōku* voting precinct
票用紙 *tōhyō yōshi* ballot
票所 *tōhyōjo* polling place, the polls
票函 *tōhyōbako, tōhyōkan* ballot box
票者 *tōhyōsha* voter
票偽造 *tōhyō gizō* vote forgery
票集 *tōhyōatsu(me)* gathering votes
票数 *tōhyōsū* the number of votes
票棄権 *tōhyō kiken* nonvoting
票棄権者 *tōhyō kikensha* nonvoter
票権 *tōhyōken* right to vote, suffrage, voice
票箱 *tōhyōbako* ballot box
票締切 *tōhyō shimeki(ri)* closing of the polls
票録 *tōhyōroku* voting record
12 遣 *na(ge)-ya(ru)* throw away, leave to chance. *na(ge)ya(ri)* negligence, irresponsibility
弾 *tōdan* dropping a bomb
落 *na(ge)-oto(su)* throw down, drop
13 棄 *na(ge)-su(teru)* throw away. *tōki suru* abandon, give up
業 *na(ge)waza* throwing technique
資 *tōshi* investment
資信託 *tōshi shintaku* investment trust
14 槍 *na(ge)yari* dart, javelin, lance; javelin throw
網 *na(ge)ami, toami* casting net
獄 *tōgoku* imprisonment
獄者 *tōgokusha* prisoner
15 縄 *na(ge)nawa* a lasso
影 *tōei suru* reflect, project (an image)
影図法 *tōei zuhō* projection in drawing
稿 *tōkō* contribution (to a magazine)
稿者 *tōkōsha* contributor (to a magazine)
稿欄 *tōkōran* readers' column
16 錨 *tōbyō* anchoring, anchorage
薬 *tōyaku* medication, prescription, dosage
機 *tōki* speculation
機心 *tōkishin* spirit of speculation
機的 *tōkiteki* speculative, risky, adventurous
機熱 *tōki netsu* speculation fever
17 環 *na(ge)wa* quoits
擲 *tōteki suru* throw
擲競技 *tōteki kyōgi* weight-throwing competition
19 離 *na(ge)-hana(su)* throw away

5

抬 2096 / J5a2d / M11912 Nonstandard for **擡** 2302.

拂 2097 / J5944 / M11936 See **払** 2062.

拒 2098 / J-X / M11957 See **拒** 2085.

拔 2099 / J5936 / M11959 See **抜** 2093.

抻 2100 / J593b / M11928 SHIN. CHIN *noba(su)* stretch, extend, lengthen.

拆 2101 / J593e / M11943 TAKU open.

拌 2102 / J5942 / M11951 HAN stir and mix.

拏 2103 / J593c / M11954 DA catch, arrest.

拊 2104 / J5943 / M11947 FU. *ha(ru)* slap, strike.

拑 2105 / J593a / M11956 KAN. KEN *tsugu(mu)* close the mouth, be silent.
3 口 *kankō* closed mouth

拈 2106 / J5940 / M11945 NEN. *hine(ru)* twirl, twist, twiddle; wring, wrench; bend (the body); incline (the head); pinch, defeat. *hine(ri)* pinch (of salt); small gift of money; a twist.
5 出 *nenshutsu suru, hine(ri)-da(su), hine(ri)-ida(su)* think up, propose

B **拐** 2107 / J327d / M11955 **拐** 2108 / J-X / M-X KAI falsify; kidnap.
10 帯 *kaitai* absconding with money
帯者 *kaitaisha* absconder

拉 2109 / J5947 / M11946 RATSU. *ras(suru)* drag along; kidnap. *Ra* Latin. *hishi(geru)* be flattened, be crushed, collapse, give way; be discouraged. *hishi(gu)* crush, smash, overpower.
2 丁 *Raten* Latin
丁語 *Ratengo* Latin
10 致 *ratchi suru, rachi suru* carry away, take captive, kidnap

拇 2110 / J5945 / M11944 BO thumb.
6 印 *boin* thumb print
9 指 *boshi* thumb
指大 *boshidai* thumb size
指頭大 *boshitōdai* the size of the end of the thumb
11 趾 *boshi* big toe

拗 2111 / J5939 / M11962 Ō. YŌ. *ne(jiru)* screw, twist, wrench, distort, wring, turn (a faucet); make capital out of someone's slip of the tongue. *neji(reru)* be twisted, be distorted, kink, twist, be awry; be perverse. *kune(ru), neji(keru)* be crooked, be twisted, be distorted; perverse, cross. *neji(kureru)* be twisted, be distorted, kink, twist, be awry; be perverse. *koji(rasu)* aggravate (a cold). *koji(reru)* be twisted; go wrong, get out of order; become complicated; become cross; become aggravated; mark time. *su(neru)* pout.
7 言葉 *su(ne)kotoba* grumbling
8 者 *neji(ke)mono, su(ne)mono* perverse person
9 音 *yōon* a palatalized or labio-velarized syllable; a Japanese syllable with a palatal or labio-velar semivowel between the (initial) consonant and the vowel

B **抹** 2112 / J4b75 / M11926 MATSU paint, erase, rub.
8 油 *matsuyu* extreme unction
9 茶 *matcha* powdered green tea
香 *makkō* incense; incense powder
香鯨 *makkō kujira* sperm whale
10 消 *masshō* erasure, obliteration; denial; ignoring (an opinion); execution, liquidation
殺 *massatsu* erasure, obliteration; denial; ignoring (an opinion); execution, liquidation

B **拠** 2113 / J3572 / M11985 **㨿** 2257 / J-X / M12674 **據** 2284 / J5a21 / M12839
KYO. KO. *yo(ru)* be based on, follow. *yo(tte)* therefore, consequently.
5 可 *yo(ru)be(ki)* authoritative
出 *kyoshutsu* contribution, donation
6 有 *kyoyū suru* appropriate as one's own
8 所 *yo(ri)dokoro* source, authority
所無 *yondokorona(i)* unavoidable, urgent, necessary
9 城 *kyojō* one's own entrenched castle
点 *kyoten* position, point, base

B **拍** 2114 / J476f / M11952 **𢫦** 2129 / J-X / M11999 HYŌ, HAKU beat (in music). *u(tsu)* strike, hit, beat, knock, slap, punch, thrash, smite; clap (one's hands); beat (a drum); ring (a bell); (clocks) strike; impress, touch; shoot; pound in (a nail); water, sprinkle; braid; play (checkers); till (the soil); temper (a sword); prepare (buckwheat noodles); present (a play); cast (a net); pay (earnest money).
3 子 *hyōshi* time, rhythm, beat, measure, number; tact; chance, the moment
子木 *hyōshigi* wooden clappers, bones
子抜 *hyōshinu(ke)* disappointment
4 手 *hakushu* applause, handclapping. *kashiwade* handclapping (at a shrine)
7 車 *hakusha* spur (on boots)
車加 *hakusha (o) kuwa(eru)* spur on a horse; encourage fast action

B **拓** 2115 / J4273 / M11958 TAKU *hira(ku)* open, clear, break up (land).

3 士 *takushi* settler, colonizer
5 本 *takuhon* rubbed copy; folio of rubbings
6 地 *takuchi* opening up land
12 植 *takushoku* colonization, exploitation
殖 *takushoku* colonization, exploitation
殖者 *takushokusha* colonist

B **披** 2116 / J4864 / M11909 HI open.

7 見 *hiken suru* peruse (a letter)
14 歴 *hireki suru* express (opinions)
17 講 *hikō suru* recite poems
19 瀝 *hireki suru* express (opinions)
21 露 *hirō* announcement
露目 *hirome* announcement, advertisement
露会 *hirōkai* reception (wedding, etc.)
露宴 *hirōen* reception (wedding, etc.)

抛 2117 / J-X / M11948 **拋** 2072 / J5946 / M11901 HŌ. *hō(ru)* hurl. *nageu(tsu)* give up, abandon; relinquish; resign, renounce; lay aside; lay down.

3 上 *hō(ri)-a(geru)* hurl up
4 込 *hō(ri)-ko(mu)* throw into
5 出 *hō(ri)-da(su)* throw out; dismiss, fire; throw up (a job)
7 投 *hō(ri)-na(geru)* throw, heave, toss
8 物線 *hōbutsusen* parabola
10 射 *hōsha suru* shoot
射線 *hōshasen* parabola
13 棄 *hōki suru, na(ge)-su(teru)* waive, resign, abandon, renounce
17 擲 *hōteki suru* abandon, give up; throw away; neglect

A **拡** 2118 / J3348 / M11985′ **擴** 2309 / J5a32 / M12895 KAKU. *hiro(geru) vt* expand, enlarge, widen; unfurl; open (arms or a package), stretch, spread. *hiro(garu) vi* spread out, extend, reach to.

3 大 *kakudai* magnification, enlargement
大率 *kakudairitsu* magnifying power
大鏡 *kakudaikyō* magnifying glass, magnifier
6 充 *kakujū* expansion; amplification; ⌈generalization
7 声器 *kakuseiki* loudspeaker
声装置 *kakuseisōchi* public address system
声機 *kakuseiki* loudspeaker
11 張 *kakuchō* extension, expansion, increase, enlargement, aggrandizement, increase, dilation
12 散 *kakusan* scattering, diffusion

B **抽** 2119 / J436a / M11930 CHŪ pull; extract; excel. *nuki(nderu)* excel in, surpass; choose the best. *nu(ku)* extract, uncork, pull out; root up; unsheathe; pilfer; quote; remove; omit; capture; outrun; shoot through. *hi(ku)* pull.

4 斗 *hikidashi* (desk) drawer
5 出 *chūshutsu suru* educe, abstract, extract. *hikidashi* (desk) drawer; withdrawal
12 象 *chūshō* abstraction
象名詞 *chūshō meishi* abstract noun
象的 *chūshōteki* abstract
象論 *chūshōron* abstract argument, generalities
14 選 *chūsen* lottery, raffle, drawing
21 籤 *chūsen* lottery, raffle, drawing
籤券 *chūsenken* lottery ticket
籤器 *chūsenki* lottery wheel

B **抵** 2120 / J4471 / M11921 TEI touch, reach, resist.

6 当 *teitō* mortgage, hypothec, security
当物 *teitōbutsu* security, pawn, collateral
当流 *teitōnaga(re)* foreclosure
当権 *teitōken* mortgage
7 抗 *teikō* resistance, opposition, defiance; (electrical) resistance
抗力 *teikōryoku* power of resistance; resisting force
抗罪 *teikōzai* mutiny
抗箱 *teikōbako* resistance box
抗器 *teikōki* resistor, rheostat
13 触 *teishoku* conflict, contradiction, infringement

A **担** 2121 / J4334 / M11941 **擔** 2286 / J593f / M12828 TAN carry; raise. *katsu(gu)* shoulder (a load). *kata(geru)* shoulder, carry on the shoulder. *nina(u)* carry on the shoulder; bear a burden. *katsugi* carrier, coolie.

2 入 *katsu(gi)-i(reru)* carry in
人足 *katsugi ninsoku* carrier, coolie

3 上 *katsu(gi)-a(geru), katsu(gi)-nobo(ru)* carry up
4 手 *ninaite* bearer, carrier
夫 *tampu* porter
6 任 *tannin* charge (of something)
当 *tantō* charge (of something)
当者 *tantōsha* the one in charge
9 屋 *katsu(gi)ya* superstitious person; black market peddler
保 *tampo* mortgage, security, guarantee
保付 *tampozu(ki)* secured (loan)
架 *tanka* stretcher, litter
架卒 *tankasotsu* stretcher bearer
10 荷 *tanka* stretcher, litter
11 商 *katsugiakina(i)* peddling; peddler

B **拙** 2122 / J405b / M11965 SETSU clumsy, unskillful. *tsutana(i), mazu(i)* clumsy, bungling, unskillful.
3 工 *sekkō* poor workman
4 文 *setsubun* poor writing, my writing
6 宅 *settaku* my humble home
劣 *setsuretsu na* clumsy, unskillful
7 作 *sessaku* poor work; my humble work
技 *setsugi* clumsy work; my humble efforts
8 者 *sessha* I (humble); an untalented person; an ignorant person
9 速 *sessoku* rough-and-ready, hasty
10 家 *sekka* my humble home
11 訳 *setsuyaku* (my) poor translation
悪 *setsuaku* clumsiness, lack of skill
著 *setcho* my (humble) production
12 策 *sessaku* poor policy, poor plan
筆 *seppitsu* bad handwriting
13 僧 *sessō* your humble priest; a foolish priest
15 稿 *sekkō* poor manuscript; my manuscript

B **拘** 2123 / J3934 / M11963 KŌ seize, arrest. *kakawa(ru)* be concerned with; adhere to; be wedded to one's opinion. *kakawa(razu)* in spite of, regardless of.
4 引 *kōin* arrest, custody
引状 *kōinjō* summons, warrant of arrest
7 束 *kōsoku* restriction, binding, duress
束力 *kōsokuryoku* binding power (of rules)
束者 *kōsokusha* restrainer
束時間 *kōsoku jikan* actual working hours; portal-to-portal time
束時間払賃金 *kōsoku jikambara(i) chingin* portal-to-portal pay
8 泥 *kōdei suru* adhere to, be a stickler for
10 留 *kōryū* detention, arrest, custody
留状 *kōryūjō* arrest warrant
留所 *kōryūjo* detention room
13 禁 *kōkin* confinement, detention, imprisonment
置 *kōchi* detention, confinement, arrest
置所 *kōchisho* detention house, prison

A **招** 2124 / J3e37 / M11968 SHŌ. *mane(ku)* beckon to, invite, summon; engage (someone), call (a doctor); incur, cause. *mane(ki)* invitation.
4 引 *shōin suru* call someone to come
7 声 *shōsei* call (of God)
来 *shōrai suru* lead to, invite, incur, cause
8 命 *shōmei* call (of God)
9 降 *shōkō* urging surrender
客 *shōkyaku* invitation; invited guest
待 *shōtai, shōdai* invitation
待日 *shōtaibi* preview date; invitation date
待会 *shōtaikai* reception
待状 *shōtaijō* letter of invitation
待券 *shōtaiken* complimentary ticket
待客 *shōtaikyaku* invited guest
待席 *shōtaiseki* reserved seat for a guest
10 致 *shōchi* summons, invitation
宴 *shōen* giving an invitation to a banquet
11 寄 *mane(ki)-yo(seru)* call from, bring from
12 雇 *shōko suru* call and employ
集 *shōshū suru, mane(ki)-atsu(meru)* call together
13 聘 *shōhei* engagement, employment
電 *shōden* summons by wire
14 魂 *shōkon* invocation of spirits of the dead
魂社 *shōkonsha* shrine to the war dead
魂祭 *Shōkonsai* Memorial Day
15 請 *shōsei* invitation, call
請国 *shōseikoku* inviting power, host nation

B **抱** 2125 / J4a7a / M11917′ HŌ. *da(ku)* hug, embrace, hold in the arms; sit (on eggs). *ida(ku)* hug, embrace, hold in

4 心忄⺗戈戸 5【手扌】支攴攵文斗斤方无日曰月木欠止歹殳毋比毛氏气水氵氺火灬爪爫父爻爿丬片牙牛犬犭

the arms; entertain (hope); cherish (a desire); harbor (malice); hold, have. *da(kasu)* set a hen. *da(kko) suru* hug, embrace, hold in the arms. *kaka(eru)* hold or carry under or in the arms. *kaka(e)* armful; employee.

2 入 *kaka(e)-i(reru)* hold or carry under or in the arms
3 上 *da(ki)-a(geru)* take up in one's arms
4 止 *da(ki)-to(meru)* hold (a person) back, restrain, catch
込 *da(ki)-ko(mu)* win over, carry in the arms. *kaka(e)-ko(mu)* hold or carry under or in the arms
5 付 *da(ki)-tsu(ku)* embrace; hold forcibly
主 *kaka(e)nushi* employer
6 合 *da(ki)-a(u)* hug, embrace. *da(ki)-a(waseru)* cause to embrace; pawn off poor articles. *hōgō* combination; embrace
合心中 *da(ki)a(i) shinjū* double suicide
合売 *da(ki)a(wase) u(ri)* combination sale
合法 *da(ki)a(wase)hō* contact printing (in photography)
合物 *hōgōbutsu* compound
7 車 *kaka(e)guruma* private jinricksha
卵 *hōran* incubation
卵期 *hōranki* incubation period
8 抱 *da(ki)-kaka(eru)* hold, carry, or embrace (in one's arms)
9 括 *hōkatsu* inclusion, comprehension
負 *hōfu* aspiration, ambition, pretension
10 起 *da(ki)-oko(su)* lift (a person) up, help (a person) to his feet or to sit up (in bed)
留 *da(ki)-to(meru)* hug to restrain
11 寄 *da(ki)-yo(seru)* embrace
著 *da(ki)-tsu(ku)* embrace; hold forcibly
12 竦 *da(ki)-suku(meru)* hug tight
着 *da(ki)-tsu(ku)* embrace; hold forcibly
13 寝 *da(ki)ne* sleeping with a baby
腹 *hōfuku* convulsed with laughter
腹絶倒 *hōfuku-zettō* convulsed with laughter
14 緊 *da(ki)-shi(meru), ida(ki)-shi(meru)* embrace closely, cuddle, hug
15 締 *da(ki)-shi(meru), ida(ki)-shi(meru)* embrace closely, cuddle, hug
16 懐 *hōkai* harboring, cherishing, entertaining
擁 *hōyō* a hug, an embrace

A **拜** 2126 / J4752 / M11969′ **拜** 2127 / J5941 / M11969 HAI worship. *hai(suru)* worship, bow in veneration, pay respects to; receive (an imperial command); see (the emperor). *oga(mu), oroga(mu)* worship, pray to, adore, reverence; look at (with reverence).

1 一神教 *haiitsushinkyō* henotheism
4 火教 *Haikakyō* Zoroastrianism
5 礼 *hairei* worship
6 伏 *haifuku* bowing; bowing and worshiping
7 見 *haiken suru* see, look at, inspect
呈 *haitei* presentation; Dear Sir
承 *haishō suru* I hear that …
8 送 *haisō* (humble) seeing someone off
披 *haihi* (humble) opening (a letter)
命 *haimei* receiving an official appointment
受 *haiju suru* receive, accept
具 *haigu* Faithfully yours
物教 *haibutsukyō* fetishism
金 *haikin* worship of mammon
金主義 *haikin shugi* mammonism
金宗 *haikinshū* mammonism
9 屋 *oga(mi)ya* medicine man, charmer
眉 *haibi* personal meeting
星教 *haiseikyō* star worship
10 借 *haishaku* loan, borrowing
倒 *oga(mi)-tao(su)* entreat into consenting
11 啓 *haikei* Dear Sir, Dear Madam
12 復 *haifuku* in reply to your esteemed letter; Dear Sir, Dear Madam
診 *haishin* medical examination (polite)
賀 *haiga* greetings, congratulations
13 殿 *haiden* outer shrine, hall of worship; holy place; nave
辞 *haiji suru* resign, decline
跪 *haiki suru* kneel reverently
14 聞 *haibun* (humble) listening, hearing
塵 *haijin* flattering a superior
誦 *haishō suru* read, note
読 *haidoku suru* read, note. *haidoku* reverent reading
察 *haisatsu* guess
領 *hairyō suru* receive (from a superior)
領物 *hairyōbutsu* a gift (from a superior)
15 謁 *haietsu* an audience (with the emperor)
16 覧 *hairan* (humble) looking at, examining

[17]趨 *haisū suru* call on, visit
聴 *haichō suru* listen attentively
謝 *haisha suru* thank
戴 *haitai* (humble) receiving (something)
[18]顔 *haigan* personal meeting
観 *haikan* inspection, visit
観料 *haikanryō* (museum) admission charge

B **押** 2128 / J3221 / M11929 Ō. *o(su)* push, shove; press, squash, compress; stamp, seal; do in spite of. *osa(eru)* stop, check, restrain, pin down; suppress, subdue, control; catch, arrest; govern; stop (the ears); withhold; attach, seize; secure (evidence), estimate conservatively. *oshi* weight; authority, influence; self-confidence; a fall (in the stock market). *osa(e)* weight, paperweight; rear guard; defense, pressure, suppression; control. *o(shite)* forcibly; importunately; in spite of. *o(shi)-* emphatic verbal prefix.
[2]入 *o(shi)-i(reru)* push in, force in, squeeze in. *oshi-i(ru)* break im *oshii(re)* clothes closet. *o(shi)i(ri)* burglar, robber
[3]下 *o(shi) sa(geru)* depress, force down. *o(shi)-o(rosu)* take down, lower, pull down, lift down, let down, drop; launch; let off (passengers); wear (for the first time); cause (abortion); grate; invoke; exercise; borrow (in subtraction); lock
上 *o(shi)-a(geru)* force up, push up, boost
[4]止 *o(shi)-to(meru), o(shi)-todo(meru)* stop, prevent, restrain
引 *o(shi)hi(ki)* pushing and pulling
切 *o(shi)-ki(ru)* have one's own way, push through, push and cut. *osa(e)-ki(ru)* shutout (in baseball). *o(shi)ki(tte)* boldly, daringly. *o(shi)ki(ri)* straw cutter; short mane
分 *o(shi)-wa(keru)* push apart, elbow through
込 *o(shi)-ko(mu) vi* push in, crowd into, herd into. *o(shi)-ko(meru) vt* shut up, imprison. *o(shi)ko(mi)* clothes closet; burglar
込強盗 *o(shi)ko(mi) gōtō* burglar
[5]立 *o(shi)-ta(teru), o(t)ta(teru)* raise, set up, erect; hoist
広 *o(shi)-hiro(geru), o(p)piro(geru) vt* expand, enlarge, widen; unfurl; open (arms or a package), stretch, spread
付 *o(shi)-tsu(keru), o(t)tsu(keru)* push against, press down, thrust on; compel, urge; force on, intrude on, impose on. *o(shi)tsu(kegamashii)* unreasonable
弘 *o(shi)-hiro(meru)* extend, spread, amplify; propagate
収 *ōshū* seizure, confiscation
出 *oshida(shi)* presence, appearance; forced (run); pushing out of. *o(shi)-da(su), o(shi)-ida(su)* push out; squeeze out; crowd out; set out all together. *o(shi)-de(ru)* force one's way out
出絵具 *oshida(shi) enogu* tube paint
[6]返 *o(shi)-kae(su)* force back, jostle
印 *ōin* affixing one's seal
伏 *o(shi)-fu(saseru)* force to lie down
当 *o(shi)-a(teru)* push (something) against
気味 *o(shi)gimi* the upper hand, the ascendancy
合 *o(shi)-a(u), o(shi)a(i) suru* jostle, crowd; haggle
合圧合 *o(shi)a(i)-he(shi)a(i)* pushing and jostling
[7]走 *o(p)pashi(ru)* run (emphatic)
戻 *o(shi)-modo(su)* force back; reject, turn down
迫 *o(shi)-sema(ru)* press hard, crowd against
均 *o(shi)-nara(su)* average, generalize
折 *o(shi)-o(ru)* break by pushing
売 *o(shi)u(ri)* high-pressure salesmanship
花 *o(shi)bana* pressed flowers
抜機 *o(shi)nu(ki)ki* punch press
[8]固 *o(shi)-kata(meru)* press together
退 *o(shi)-no(keru)* push away, brush aside, elbow through, crowd out
送 *ōsō* escort
拡 *o(shi)-hiro(geru), o(p)piro(geru) vt* expand, enlarge, widen; unfurl; open (arms or a package), stretch, spread
押 *o(shimo)-o(saremo) shinai* (a man) of established reputation
板 *o(shi)ita* pressing board

4 心忄⺗戈戸【手扌】[5] 支攴攵文斗斤方无日曰月木欠止歹殳毋比毛氏气水氵氺火灬爪爫父爻爿丬片牙牛犬犭

並 *o(shi)na(bete)* generally
直 *o(shi)-nao(su)* restore, correct. *o(shi)-nao(ru)* sit correctly
取 *o(t)to(ru)* seize, snatch
取巻 *o(t)to(ri)ma(ku)* surround, encircle, enclose
9 通 *o(shi)-tō(ru)* force one's way through. *o(shi)-tō(su)* carry through, accomplish, persevere; insist on
型 *o(shi)gata* impression taken by pressing
10 進 *o(shi)-susu(meru)* push, push through, expedite. *o(shi)-susu(mu)* push on, press onward
借 *o(shi)ga(ri)* out of money or supplies, having to borrow
倒 *o(shi)-tao(su)* push down; overwhelm
流 *o(shi)-naga(su)* wash away, sweep away; (waves) drive on
破 *o(shi)-yabu(ru)* break through
11 捺 *ōnatsu* sealing (a document)
捲 *o(shi)-maku(ru)* press on to the end
頂 *o(shi)-itada(ku)* raise reverently to one's head
寄 *o(shi)-yo(seru)* push aside; advance on; besiege (an office); bear down upon; make for the door. *o(shi)-yo(ru)* press together, come close
問答 *o(shi)mondō* heated questioning and answering, dispute
掛 *o(shi)-ka(karu)* lean on, rely on. *o(shi)-ka(keru)* intrude on, throng into
掛客 *o(shi)ka(ke) kyaku* uninvited guest
12 遣 *o(shi)-ya(ru)* push away
開 *o(shi)-hira(ku), o(shi)-a(keru)* force open, push open
渡 *o(shi)-wata(su)* cross over; force one's way across
絵 *o(shi)e* raised cloth pictures
隔 *o(shi)-heda(teru)* be distant from, be separated from, become estranged
葉 *o(shi)ba* pressed leaves
割麦 *o(shi)wa(ri) mugi* rolled barley
13 詰 *o(shi)-tsu(maru)* approach the year end; be jammed, be tight. *o(shi)-tsu(meru)* pack (in a box); drive to the wall
15 潰 *o(shi)-tsubu(su)* smash, crush
縁 *o(shi)buchi* strips to hold something down
黙 *o(shi)-dama(ru)* keep silent
16 錠 *o(shi)jō* thumb latch
17 戴 *o(shi)-itada(ku)* raise reverently to one's head
18 鎮 *o(shi)-shizu(meru)* quiet (someone)
19 離 *o(p)pana(su)* emphatic for *hana(su)*; separate, disconnect, sever; detach; keep apart; alienate; isolate; let go, release, set free.
韻 *ōin* rhyme, rhyming
韻詩 *ōinshi* rhymed verse

6

拓 2129 / J-X / M11999 See 拍 2114.

挛 2130 / J-X / M-X Nonstandard for 攣 2320.

挧 2131 / J594b / M-X U.

拯 2132 / J594e / M11991 SHŌ, JŌ help. *suku(u)* save, help, rescue, relieve (suffering), redeem, reclaim.

挈 2133 / J594d / M12035 KEI carry by hand.

拶 2134 / J3b22 / M12004 SATSU be imminent.

挌 2135 / J5948 / M12047 KAKU strike, hit, fight.
18 闘 *kakutō* scuffle; wrestling; fist fight

挂 2136 / J594c / M12020 KEI, KAI hang.
9 冠 *keikan, kaikan* resignation

拶 2137 / J-X / M12081 (国字) *mushi(ru)* pluck, pick, tear.
8 取 *mushi(ri)-to(ru)* tear off, pluck off

拿 2138 / J593d / M12015 DA arrest, capture.
10 捕 *daho* capture, seizure

拱 2139 / J594a / M11994 KYŌ arch. *kyō(suru), komanu(ku), komane(ku)* fold (the arms).
4 手 *kyōshu* folding the arms

手傍観 *kyōshu-bōkan suru* look on with folded arms, let things go

拵 2140/J594f/M12001 SON. *koshira(eru)* make, prepare, manufacture. *koshira(e)* make, workmanship; mounting; arrangement; attire; makeup. *koshira(etate)* newly made.
8 物 *koshira(e)mono* counterfeit, imitation
直 *koshira(e)-nao(su)* remake, remodel
事 *koshira(e)goto* fabrication

拮 2141/J5949/M11990 KATSU, KETSU, KITSU be imminent.
7 抗 *kikkō* rivalry, competition, antagonism
11 据 *kikkyo* diligence

B 拷 2142/J3969/M12006 KŌ, GŌ beat, torture.
10 訊 *gōjin* torture
11 問 *gōmon* torture, the rack, third degree
問台 *gōmondai* the rack, instrument of torture
15 器 *gōki* instruments of torture

B 括 2143/J3367/M11988 KATSU. *kuku(ru)* tie up, hang (someone); arrest; fasten. *kuru(mu)* wrap up, tuck in. *kuru(meru)* lump together, include, sum up; quibble. *kubi(ru)* constrict. *kubi(reru)* be constricted, contracted, or compressed. *ko(ru)* pack, tie up. *kuku(ri)* tying; bundle; knot; management; conclusion; trap. *kubi(re)* constriction, compression.
5 付 *kuku(ri)-tsu(keru)* tie up, hang (someone); arrest; fasten
8 弧 *kakko* parentheses; brackets
枕 *kuku(ri) makura* stuffed pillow

拭 2144/J3f21/M11989 SHOKU. *fu(ku)* wipe, mop, swab. *nugu(u)* wipe, mop.
4 込 *fu(ki)-ko(mu)* polish, shine, wipe thoroughly
5 去 *nugu(i)-sa(ru)* put off, wipe off, wipe away
8 取 *fu(ki)-to(ru)* wipe off, wipe out, mop up. *nugu(i)-to(ru)* wipe away
10 消 *fu(ki)-ke(su)* wipe out, wipe off, erase
11 掃除 *fuki sōji* wiping; scrubbing
12 落 *nugu(i)-oto(su)* wipe off, wipe away. *fu(ki)-oto(su)* rub out (a stain)

B 挑 2145/J4429/M12055 CHŌ. *ido(mu)* challenge; contend for; make love to.
9 発 *chōhatsu* provocation, excitement, encouragement, suggestion
発的 *chōhatsuteki* provocative, suggestive, lascivious, seditious
13 戦 *chōsen* challenge, defiance
戦状 *chōsenjō* written challenge
戦的 *chōsenteki* defiant, aggressive, provocative, challenging
戦者 *chōsensha* challenger
15 撥 *chōhatsu* provocation, excitement, encouragement, suggestion

B 挟 2146/J3634/M-X 挾 2153/J5951/M12118 KYŌ. *hasa(mu), sashihasu(mu)* put between, hold between; insert, jam into; nip; interpose. *hasa(maru)* get between, be caught in, be jammed in, be hemmed in, be sandwiched between, be pinned under, lie between.
4 込 *hasa(mi)-ko(mu)* insert
5 出 *hasa(mi)-da(su)* clamp onto and take away
6 虫 *hasami mushi* earwig
10 討 *hasamiu(chi)* pincer operation; squeeze
殺 *kyōsatsu suru* run down (a runner in baseball)
将棋 *hasami shōgi* Japanese board game
15 箱 *hasamibako* carrying-pole boxes
撃 *kyogeki* pincer operation. *hasamiuchi* pincer attack

按 2147/J3044/M12038 AN. *an(zuru)* hold; consider, investigate.
4 分 *ambun* proportional division
分比例 *ambun hirei* proportional allotment
手 *anshu* ordination, laying on of hands
手礼 *anshurei* ordination
手礼式 *anshureishiki* ordination ceremony
10 配 *ambai* arrangement, assignment; adjustment, modification, tempering
11 排 *ambai* arrangement, assignment; adjustment, modification, tempering
13 腹 *ampuku* abdominal massage
14 察 *ansatsu* scrutiny

15 摩 *amma* massage; masseur

拳 2148 / J377d / M11996 GEN. KEN *kobushi* fist.
5 玉 *kendama* cup-and-ball toy
8 固 *genko* fists and knuckles
10 骨 *genkotsu* fists and knuckles
拳 *kenken* respectful attitude
匪 *Kempi* Boxers
匪乱 *Kempi (no) Ran* Boxer Rebellion
14 銃 *kenjū* pistol, revolver
18 闘 *kentō* boxing, prizefighting
闘界 *kentōkai* boxing circles
闘家 *kentōka* pugilist
闘場 *kentōjō* boxing ring
闘選手 *kentō senshu* pugilist

A **拾** 2149 / J3d26 / M12014 SHŪ. JŪ ten. *hiro(u)* pick up, gather; find; set (type); go on foot.
3 上 *hiro(i)-a(geru)* pick up, pick out
4 方 *hiro(i)kata* way of picking up (something)
5 収 *shūshū suru* get under control, save
主 *hiro(i)nushi* finder
出 *hiro(i)-da(su)* pick out, select
8 取 *shūshu suru* pick up, gather
物 *hiro(i)mono* something picked up, a find; a bargain; a windfall
歩 *hiro(i)-aru(ku)* picking one's way
11 得 *shūtoku suru* pick up, find
得物 *shūtokubutsu* found article
得者 *shūtokusha* finder
12 集 *hiro(i)-atsu(meru), shūshū suru* gather up, collect; glean
14 遺 *shūi* gleanings
読 *hiro(i)yo(mi)* skimming (a book)
16 録 *shūroku suru* select and record

A **挙** 2150 / J3573 / M[illegible] **舉** 2288 / J5a29 / M[illegible] **擧** 4915 / J-X / M[illegible]
KYO plan, project; behavior; actions; step. *a(geru)* celebrate (a ceremony); join (hands in an effort); have (a child); arrest. *a(garu)* become prosperous; be captured. *kozo(ru)* meet all together. *a(gete)* all, whole, in a body. *kozo(tte)* all, all together.
4 手 *kyoshu* show of hands, raising the hand; salute, touching the cap
止 *kyoshi* bearing, deportment
5 用 *kyoyō suru* appoint, promote
示 *kyoshi suru* cite
句 *ageku* in the end, finally
世 *kyosei* all the people of the world
6 行 *kyokō* performance, celebration, solemnization
式 *kyoshiki* holding a ceremony
7 足 *ageashi* faultfinding
兵 *kyohei* raising an army
8 国 *kyokoku* the whole nation
国一致 *kyokoku-itchi* national unity
国皆兵制度 *kyokokukaihei seido* universal conscription
10 家 *kyoka* the whole family
11 族 *kyozoku* the whole family
動 *kyodō* deportment, conduct
祭 *kyosai* presentation of offerings
措 *kyoso* deportment, conduct
措失 *kyoso (o) ushina(u)* lose one's composure
12 証 *kyoshō* presentation of proof

A **持** 2151 / J3b7d / M12019 JI. *ji(suru)* hold, entertain, maintain; observe (principles). *mo(tsu) vi* and *vt* hold, take, have, possess; carry; maintain; have charge of; wear, last long; pay; bear (a grudge). *mo(teru)* be warmly welcomed; can hold, can carry; propertied, wealthy. *mo(taseru)* let (a person) have, give; get (a wife) for; give to carry; send by; keep, preserve; lean or set against; make (someone) pay. *mo(tanu), mo(tanai)* propertyless, have-not. *mo(chi)* wear, durability; (my) charge; (ladies') wear.
3 上 *mo(chi)-a(geru)* raise, lift, jack up; flatter, praise. *mo(chi)-a(garu)* be raised, be lifted; happen; be promoted with one's class; teaching the same group through the years
久 *jikyū* endurance, persistence
久力 *jikyūryoku* endurance, persistence
久策 *jikyūsaku* dilatory tactics ⌈action
久戦 *jikyūsen* delaying action, holding
4 方 *mo(chi)kata* way to hold; attitude
込 *mo(chi)-ko(mu)* bring in; lodge (a protest); bring to (a decision)
切 *mo(chi)-ki(ru)* keep, continue to hold; hold all; maintain; talk of nothing else.
mo(chi)ki(ri) sole topic (of conversation)
分 *mo(chi)bun* share (of costs); interest in (a business)

5 主 *mo(chi)nushi* proprietor, owner, possessor
古 *mo(chi)-furu(su)* be long in use
去 *mo(chi)-sa(ru)* carry away; make off with
出 *mo(chi)-da(su)* take out; rescue; embezzle; offer (a plan)
6 舟 *mo(chi)bune* one's own ship
行 *mo(tte)-yu(ku), mo(tte)-i(ku)* take along
回 *mo(tte)-mawa(ru), mo(chi)-mawa(ru), mo(chi) mawa(su)* carry around. *mo(tte)-mawa(tta)* circuitous. *mochimawa(ri)* securing decisions by circularizing members
成 *mo(te)na(shi)* treatment, service, reception, hospitality, entertainment. *mo(te)-na(su)* welcome, entertain, treat
扱 *mo(chi)-atsuka(u)* handle
合 *mo(chi)-a(waseru)* have on hand. *mo(chi)-a(u)* maintain equilibrium; share expenses. *mo(chi)a(wase)* things on hand; money on hand. *mo(chi)a(i)* interdependence; steadiness (of the market)
合品 *mo(chi)a(wase)hin* goods on hand
7 戒 *jikai* observance of the Buddhist commandments
役 *mo(chi)yaku* one's role
来 *mo(tte)-ku(ru)* bring, fetch. *mo(chi)-ki(tasu)* take, bring; bring about. *mo(tte)ko(i)* ideal, excellent, just right
余 *mo(te)ama(su)* be embarrassed with; find unmanageable; have too much of
余者 *mo(te)ama(shi)mono* scamp; nuisance, white elephant
8 送 *mo(chi)oku(ri)* bracket, truss
逃 *mochini(ge) suru* make off with, abscond with
味 *mo(chi)aji* natural flavor, characteristic quality
物 *mochimono* property, belongings
直 *mo(chi)-nao(su) vi* and *vt* change one's hold; improve, rally, recover
歩 *mo(chi)-aru(ku)* carry about
参 *jisan suru* bring, take along. *jisan* (by the) kindness of
参人 *jisannin* bearer
参金 *jisankin* dowry
9 持 *mo(chitsu)-mo(taretsu)* helping one another
映 *mo(te)-ha(yasu)* praise, extol
前 *mo(chi)mae* nature, property; share
10 病 *jibyō* chronic illness
料 *mo(chi)ryō* private use
家 *mo(chi)ie* one's own house
荷 *mo(chi)ni* stock, holdings; load
帰 *mo(chi)-kae(ru), mo(tte)-kae(ru)* carry back
株 *mo(chi)kabu* one's stock holdings
株会社 *mo(chi)kabugaisha* holding company
11 過 *mo(chi)-su(giru)* have too much of
運 *mo(chi)-hako(bu)* carry, transport. *mo(chi)hako(bi)* portable, carrying
掛 *mo(chi)-ka(keru)* offer, propose. *mo(tase)-ka(keru)* lean against
寄 *mo(chi)-yo(ru)* (each) contributes
崩 *mo(chi)-kuzu(su)* ruin oneself by dissipation 「hold over
12 越 *mo(chi)-ko(su)* defer; carry forward;
場 *mo(chi)ba* place of duty, one's post, one's beat; jurisdiction
堪 *mo(chi)-kota(eru)* maintain, keep; hold out (longer)
替 *mo(chi)-ka(eru)* shift from one hand to the other; marry again
13 続 *mo(chi)-tsuzu(keru)* persist in. *jizoku* continuation
続的 *jizokuteki* continuous, lasting
14 厭 *mo(chi)-agu(mu)* be tired of holding
腐 *mo(chi)gusa(re)* useless possession
説 *jisetsu* pet theory
15 論 *jiron* pet theory
16 薬 *jiyaku* favorite medicine

A **指** 2152 / J3b58 / M12034 Shi finger. *sa(su)* point to, indicate; name, designate; insert, put into; fill, pour into, drop into (eyes); hold up (an umbrella); wear (a sword); offer (a cup); play; move (in games); rise, flow; be tinged with; point to; proceed to; fix (a day); measure (with a ruler); measure and make (a box); play (chess or checkers). *yubi* finger. *sa(shite)* for, to, toward.

2 人形 *yubi ningyō* fingertip doll
3 小辞 *shishōji* a diminutive (in grammar)
4 手 *sashite* a move; a hand (in playing)
孔 *yubi ana* finger hole (on an instrument)

4 心 忄 ⺌ 戈 戸 【手 6 扌】 支 攴 攵 文 斗 斤 方 无 日 曰 月 木 欠 止 歹 殳 毋 比 毛 氏 气 水 氵 氺 火 灬 爪 爫 父 爻 爿 丬 片 牙 牛 犬 犭

切 *yubiki(ri)* a pledge by hooking each other's little fingers
5 令 *shirei* order, notice, instructions, directive
圧療法 *shiatsu ryōhō* finger-pressure treatment
示 *sa(shi)-shime(su), shishi suru* indicate, point out. *shiji, shishi* indication, instructions, directions. *shiji* a type of character depicting numerals or directions (e.g. 三 and 上)
示代名詞 *shiji daimeishi* demonstrative pronoun
示灯 *shijitō* pilot light, indicator light
示板 *shijiban* notice board
示器 *shijiki* indicator
6 印 *shiin* fingerprint
先 *yubisaki* fingertip
先仕事 *yubisaki shigoto* finger work
名 *shimei suru* name, mention, designate, nominate
名者 *shimeisha* nominator, designator
向 *shikō* directional (antenna)
向性 *shikōsei* directional (antenna)
向電波 *shikō dempa* directional beam
7 折 *yubio(ri)* counting on the fingers; prominence
折数 *yubio(ri)-kazo(eru)* count on one's fingers
図 *sashizu* instructions, orders
図人 *sashizunin* director, instructor; designated person
図書 *sashizusho* (written) orders, directions
8 担 *sa(shi)-nina(u)* shouldering (a load) between carriers
板 *yubi ita* finger board (on a stringed instrument); (door) finger plate
命 *shimei suru* issue specific orders
定 *shitei* appointment, designation, authorization
定席 *shiteiseki* reserved seat
事 *shiji* numeral characters or characters indicating direction (e.g. 三 and 上)
呼 *shiko* beckoning, hailing
呼間 *shiko (no) aida, shiko (no) kan* hailing distance
物 *sashimono* cabinet work, joinery; armor ornament
物屋 *sashimonoya* cabinet maker
物師 *sashimonoshi* cabinet maker
9 相撲 *yubizumō* thumb wrestling
南 *shinan* instruction, guidance
南役 *shinan'yaku* instructor, teacher, master
南所 *shinansho* school, institute
南番 *shinamban* instructor, teacher, master
10 値 *sashine* buying-price limits
紋 *shimon* fingerprint, thumb print
差 *yubisa(shi)* pointing with the finger; index tabs. *yubisa(su)* point to
荷 *sa(shi)ni* a load shouldered between two carriers
針 *shishin* compass needle; guide, manual
針面 *shishimmen* dial (of an instrument)
11 痕 *shikon* fingerprints. *yubi ato* finger mark
宿 *sa(shi)yado* recommending a traveler's next hotel; the recommended hotel
貫 *yubinuki* thimble
12 弾 *yubihaji(ki)* flip, fillip. *shidan, shitan* flip, fillip; rejection; disdain
嵌 *yubihame* thimble, ring thimble
揮 *shiki* command, supervision, instructions, direction, leading
揮刀 *shikitō* saber, parade sword
揮下 *shikika* under one's command
揮官 *shikikan* commander
揮者 *shikisha* commander, director; conductor (of a band), leader
揮棒 *shikibō* baton
13 話 *shiwa* finger language
触 *yubizawa(ri)* fingering, touching
数 *shisū* index, index number; exponent
14 銜 *yubi (o) kuwa(eru)* hold the finger in the mouth; be unable to participate
摘 *shiteki* pointing out, indication
導 *shidō* guidance, leadership, coaching
導主事 *shidō shuji* supervisor
導性 *shidōsei* leadership
導法 *shidōhō* guidance plan
導者 *shidōsha* leader
導委員 *shidō iin* steering committee
導要録 *shidō yōroku* cumulative guidance record
導員 *shidōin* instructor, advisor, supervisor
導案 *shidōan* teaching plan
導原理 *shidō genri* guiding principle
導精神 *shidō seishin* guiding spirit
導権 *shidōken* leadership

15 麾 *shiki* command, supervision, instructions, direction, leading
標 *shihyō* indication, index
輪 *yubiwa* finger ring
16 頭 *shitō* fingertip
頭大 *shitōdai* the size of the end of the little finger
17 環 *yubiwa* finger ring
18 覆 *yubiō(i)* finger shield
21 顧 *shiko* pointing to, taking notice of

7

挾 2153 J5951 M12118 See **挟** 2146.

捩 2154 J5960 M-X See **捩** 2203.

捍 2155 J5952 M12143 KAN *fuse(gu)* ward off; resist; defend. *yugote* archer's arm guard.

捐 2156 J5950 M12150 EN throw away.

捋 2157 J-X M12140 RATSU. RACHI exercise field (for horses).

挵 2158 J-X M12101 RŌ. *moteaso(bu)* play with, handle things.

捉 2159 J422a M12136 SOKU. SAKU. *tora(eru)* catch, arrest, capture. *tsukama(eru), tsura(maeru), torama(eru)* catch, seize, arrest, capture. *tsuka(maru), tsura(maru)* be caught, be arrested; cling to.

挨 2160 J3027 M12082 AI push open.
9 拶 *aisatsu* greeting, salutation; address, reply, response; notice

捗 2161 J-X M12160 **捗** 2173 J443d M-X CHOKU. HO. *hakado(ru)* make progress.
8 取 *hakado(ru)* advance, make headway
10 捗 *hakabaka(shii)* rapid, expeditious, active; favorable

捌 2162 J3b2b M12141 HACHI, HATSU. *saba(ku)* sell; dispose of, deal with; handle, manipulate; loosen (the hair). *saba(keru)* sell, be in demand; be worldly wise; be disentangled; tear, break. *ha(keru)* drain, flow off, run out; sell, be in demand. *ha(ke)* drainage; draining; sale, demand. *saba(keta)* sociable, frank.
3 口 *hakeguchi, sabakiguchi* outlet, market; vent
4 方 *saba(ki)kata* marketing
14 髪 *saba(ki)gami* loosened hair

挫 2163 J3d43 M12087 ZA. *kuji(ku)* crush, break, sprain, dislocate; frustrate; unnerve; dampen (spirits). *kuji(keru)* be broken, crushed, or sprained; be discouraged.
7 折 *zasetsu* frustration, collapse, setback, reverses, discouragement
12 創 *zasō* bruise, sprain, strain, contusion
13 傷 *zashō* bruise, sprain, strain, contusion

挺 2164 J4472 M12106 TEI. CHŌ counter for guns, tools, inksticks, oars, candles, palanquins, and jinrickshas. *tei(suru)* bravely volunteer.
3 子 *teko* lever
子台 *tekodai* fulcrum
7 身 *teishin* volunteer
身隊 *teishintai* volunteer corps
10 進 *teishin suru* go ahead of, dash forward
進隊 *teishintai* advance corps

捏 2165 J5954 M12149 **捏** 2166 J-X M-X **揑** 2215 J-X M12345 NETSU falsify. *ko(neru)* knead, mix; argue. *ne(ru)* gloss, soften; train, drill; polish; refine. *tsuku(neru)* knead, mold.
3 上 *de(tchi)-a(geru)* invent, fabricate, frame up
6 回 *ko(ne)-mawa(su)* knead, mix; be muddy
返 *ko(ne)-kae(su)* knead, mix; be muddy
合機 *konea(wase)ki* kneading machine
9 造 *netsuzō* fabrication, forgery, falsehood
10 粉 *koneko* dough
13 鉢 *konebachi* kneading trough

B **挿** 2167 J415e M12119 **插** 2218 J5967 M12346 **挿** 2219 J-X M12346′ SŌ. *sa(su)* insert, put in; graft (a branch); wear (a sword); carry (in the belt).

hasa(mu), sashihasa(mu) put between, hold between; insert, jam into; nip; interpose. *hasa(maru)* get between, be caught in, be jammed in, be hemmed in, be sandwiched between, be pinned under, lie between.

2 入 *sōnyū* insertion, incorporation, interpolation
4 木 *sashiki* a cutting; planting
5 句 *sōku* parenthetical expression
旧 *sa(shi)-furu(su)* wear out (a comb or sword)
7 図 *sōzu* illustration (in a book)
花 *sōka, sashibana* flower arrangement
8 画 *sashie, sōga* illustration (in a book)
12 絵 *sashie* illustration (in a book)
弾子 *sōdanshi* cartridge clip
13 話 *sōwa* episode

B **搜** 2168/J415c/M12179 **搜** 2238/J5953/M12486 Sō. *saga(su)* search, look for, locate; glean.

5 出 *saga(shi)-da(su)* find out, discover, detect, locate, search out, hunt up
6 回 *saga(shi)-mawa(ru)* hunt around
当 *saga(shi)-a(teru)* find out, discover, detect, locate, search out, hunt up
7 求 *saga(shi)-moto(meru)* seek for
8 物 *saga(shi)mono* something one is looking for
9 査 *sōsa* investigation, search
10 射 *sōsha* searching gunfire
索 *sōsaku* search, investigation; dragging (a river)
索令状 *sōsaku reijō* search warrant
索兵 *sōsakuhei* scout
索隊 *sōsakutai* search party
索権 *sōsakuken* right of search
索機 *sōsakuki* search plane
12 絵 *saga(shi)e* picture puzzle

挽 2169/J-X/M12111 BAN. *hi(ku)* saw; turn (on a lathe); pull (a cart); grind (in a mill).

4 切 *hi(ki)-ki(ru)* saw off
5 台 *hikidai* sawhorse
6 肉 *hikiniku* ground meat, minced meat
回 *bankai* recovery, restoration, retrieval
7 材 *hikizai* lumber
材工場 *hikizai kōjō* lumber mill
8 物 *hikimono* lathe work
物師 *hikimonoshi* a turner
9 茶 *hikicha* powdered tea
10 馬 *bamba* work horse
屑 *hikikuzu* sawdust
12 割 *hi(ki)-wa(ru)* saw. *hikiwa(ri)* lumber
割材 *hikiwa(ri)zai* lumber
14 歌 *banka* elegy, dirge

B **捕** 2170/J4a61/M12157 BU. HO. *tora(eru), torama(eru), tsukama(eru), to(ru)* catch, arrest, capture. *tsukama(ru)* be caught, be captured. *to(reru)* can be held, can take; come off, come apart, be off, be removed; be relieved (of pain); be obtained, be produced; be caught; be earned; come out (well) (a photo); require (time); be interpreted as; can get; let (light) in; take (one's measure); can feel (the pulse); take (a pen and write). *tora(wareru)* be caught, be captured, be arrested; be a slave to; be seized with.

2 人 *tora(ware)bito* captive, exiles
4 手 *hoshu* catcher. *torite* (ancient) policeman
5 囚 *hoshū* prisoner, captive, captivity
去 *tora(e)-sa(ru)* take away, carry away
6 行 *tora(e)-yu(ku)* carry into captivity, lead away
伏 *to(ri)-fu(seru)* bring down (a thief)
吏 *hori* (ancient) policeman
7 身 *torawa(re) (no) mi* a captive
8 物 *torimono* a capture, an arrest
者 *torimono* a capture, an arrest
所 *tora(e)dokoro* the point, meaning. *tsuka(mae)dokoro* grip, hold
所無 *tsuka(mae)dokoro (no) na(i)* slippery; sly; vague
9 食 *hoshoku suru* prey upon
10 逸 *hoitsu* catcher's letting a ball go through
捉 *hosoku* capture, seizure
殺 *hosatsu suru* catch and kill; assist (in baseball)
拿 *hoda* capture, seizure
11 球 *hokyū* a catch (in baseball)
移 *tora(e)-utsu(su)* carry away captive
13 虜 *horyo* prisoner, captive; captivity
15 縄 *torinawa, hojō* rope for tying criminals
16 獲 *hokaku* capture, seizure
縛 *hobaku* arrest, seizure
鯨 *hogei* whaling

鯨船 *hogeisen* whaling ship

B**振** 2171 J3f36 M12093 SHIN *fu(ru)* wave, wag, swing, shake; sprinkle; brandish; jilt, reject; attach, allot. *fu(reru)* lean toward, deflect, tend; shake, swing, oscillate. *furu(u)* shake, wield, brandish; be invigorated, be spirited, flourish. *fu(rareru)* be jilted, be rejected. *fu(ri)* appearance, manners, air, dress, form, posture; pretense, affectation; discipline; custom; swing, shaking; (dance) postures; slant, inclination, deviation, deflection; casual customer; sword counter. *fu(re)* deflection, deviation. *fu(rutta)* splendid, extraordinary, striking, original. *-bu(ri)* lapse of -, after (two years, etc.); for (three days, etc.); manner, style.

3 子 *fu(ri)ko, shinshi* pendulum, bob
上 *fu(ri)-a(geru)* fling up, swing up, whip out, brandish, toss (the head)
4 方 *fu(ri)kata* (my) plans
込 *fu(ri)-ko(mu)* pay in, pay up, pay an installment
切 *fu(ri)-ki(ru)* sever, shake off, free oneself
分 *fu(ri)-wa(keru)* divide in half, distribute. *furiwa(ke)* hair parted and hanging down; carrying packages on a strap over the shoulders
分荷物 *furiwa(ke) nimotsu* a joined pair of bundles slung over the shoulder
分髪 *furiwa(ke)gami* hair parted and hanging down
5 立 *fu(ri)-ta(teru)* shake up, toss (one's head); dishevel; raise (one's voice). *fu(ri)-ta(tsu)* rouse oneself, be inspired
付 *furitsu(ke)* Japanese dance composition; dance coaching
払 *fu(ri)-hara(u)* shake off, whisk off
出 *fu(ri)-da(su)* shake out; infuse, decoct; write (a check). *furida(shi)* start; drawing or issuing (a draft)
出人 *furidashinin* remitter, writer (of a check)
出局 *furidashikyoku* the post office issuing a money order
6 回 *fu(ri)-mawa(su)* brandish, wave, flourish, wave about, swing; display, show off
返 *fu(ri)-kae(ru)* turn the head, look over one's shoulder, turn around, look back
向 *fu(ri)-mu(keru)* turn toward; apply toward, appropriate to. *fu(ri)-mu(ku)* turn toward, look back
合 *fu(ri)a(i)* consideration, comparison, balancing; usage, practice, custom
当 *fu(ri)-a(teru)* assign (work)
仮名 *fu(ri)gana* side *kana* (to show the pronunciation of characters)
7 作 *shinsaku* prosperity
乱 *fu(ri)-midа(su)* shake (one's hair) loose, dishevel
売 *fu(ri)u(ri)* hawking, peddling
8 放 *fu(ri)-hana(su), fu(ri)-hana(tsu)* shake oneself loose, tear away from
受人 *fu(ri)u(ke)nin* drawee
9 飛 *fu(ri)-to(basu)* swing and throw
客 *fu(ri) (no) kyaku* chance customer
10 袖 *fu(ri) sode* long sleeves, long-sleeved kimono
被 *fu(ri)-kabu(ru)* hold aloft, brandish
起 *furu(i)-oko(su)* arouse, awaken, promote. *shinki* encouragement, stimulation
起日 *shinkibi* rally day
11 捨 *fu(ri)-su(teru)* shake off; discard, forsake, abandon, desert, leave off
掛 *fu(ri)-ka(keru)* sprinkle over, splash on. *fu(ri)-ka(karu)* be splashed. *furika(ke)* flakes of fish, seaweed, or other seasonings sprinkled over rice
動 *fu(ri)-ugo(kasu) vt* swing, shake, wag. *fu(ri)-ugo(ku) vi* swing, shake, oscillate. *shindō* oscillation, swing, vibration
粛 *shinshuku* strict enforcement
12 幅 *shimpuku* amplitude (of vibrations); the swing of a pendulum
落 *fu(ri)-oto(su), furu(i)-oto(su)* shake off, throw off, spill, sift out, eliminate
替 *fu(ri)-ka(eru)* transfer (funds). *furikae* change, transfer, postal-transfer account
替貯金 *furikae chokin* postal-transfer account
13 解 *fu(ri)-hodo(ku)* shake and untangle
鈴 *shinrei* ringing a bell; hand bell
14 撒 *fu(ri)-ma(ku)* sprinkle, scatter, diffuse, disperse; lavish
舞 *furuma(u)* behave oneself, entertain, treat. *furumai* behavior, deportment,

demeanor, conduct, manners; entertainment, feast

舞酒 *furumaizake* a saké treat

16 興 *shinkō* promotion, encouragement, arousing

17 盪 *shintō* concussion, shock, impact

翳 *fu(ri)-kaza(su)* fling up, swing up, whip out, brandish, toss (the head)

19 離 *fu(ri)-hana(su)* shake oneself loose, tear away from

22 顫 *shinsen* tremor

顫譫妄症 *shinsen semmōshō* delirium tremens

8

挽 2172 / J4854 / M-X Nonstandard for 挽 2169.

捗 2173 / J443d / M-X Nonstandard for 捗 2161.

掴 2174 / J444f / M-X Nonstandard for 摑 2263.

掻 2175 / J415f / M-X See 搔 2256.

掵 2176 / J595e / M-X （国字） *haba* embankment; cliff.

捶 2177 / J5959 / M12215 SUI take a whip to; strike, beat; pound. *muchiu(tsu)* whip, strike.

掀 2178 / J5957 / M12230 KIN. KEN lift, raise; offer; soar above.

掫 2179 / J5958 / M12287 SŌ. SHU night watch, night watchman. *sarae* rake.

掟 2180 / J595d / M12272 TŌ. CHŌ. JŌ *okite* law, commandments, regulations.

捫 2181 / J595f / M12197 MON to stroke.

12 着 *monchaku* trouble; dispute

掎 2182 / J5956 / M12250 KI *hi(ku)* pull, draw, drag.

4 止 *kishi suru* drag to a halt

掣 2183 / J595a / M12277 SEI pull; pull back; restrain.

7 肘 *seichū* restraint, check, restriction, control, interference

揶 2184 / J5968 / M12437 YA tease, play with.

12 揄 *yayu suru, karaka(u)* ridicule, tease, banter with

掖 2185 / J5955 / M12262 EKI side (of the body); carry under the arm.

8 門 *ekimon* small gate at the side of a large one

掉 2186 / J595c / M12243 TŌ, CHŌ shake and move.

7 尾 *tōbi no, chōbi no* crowning, final finishing

掏 2187 / J595b / M12251 TŌ. *su(ru)* pick a pocket.

13 摸 *suri* pickpocket; pickpocketing

捥 2188 / J-X / M12181 WAN arm. *mogi(ru), mo(gu)* wrest from, snatch from; tear off, break off. *mo(geru)* come off, be broken off. *ude* arm; talent, ability.

8 取 *mo(gi)-to(ru)* wrest from, snatch from; tear off, break off

捺 2189 / J4668 / M12221 NATSU press, print. *o(su), sa(su)* affix a seal, stamp.

6 印 *natsuin* sealing (a document)

9 染 *nassen, oshizome, nasen* (textile) printing

B 措 2190 / J413c / M12286 SO. *o(ku)* give up, suspend, discontinue, lay aside, set apart; except.

13 置 *sochi* measure, step, move, action

辞 *soji* phraseology, wording, diction

辞法 *sojihō* syntax

掠 2191 / J4e2b / M12273 RYAKU. *kasu(meru)* rob, pillage; graze (in passing), skim, sweep over; cheat; hint, suggest. *kasu(ru)* graze (one's leg); squeeze, exploit. *kasu(reru)* be grazed, touch, chip; become hoarse. *kasuri* grazing (something); squeeze, percentage,. kickback.

8 取 *kasu(me)-to(ru), ryakushu suru* rob, cheat, despoil; seize, capture
13 傷 *kasu(ri) kizu* scratch, bruise; slight damage; slight (business) failure
14 奪 *kasu(me)-uba(u)* plunder. *ryakudatsu* pillage, plunder, looting

掩 2192 / J3166 / M12285 EN *ō(u)* cover, shade, conceal, shelter
13 蓋 *engai* cover, covering
15 蔽 *empei* cover, obscuration, occultation, blanketing
撃 *engeki* surprise attack
20 護 *engo* covering, protection, aegis, backing, relief

捲 2193 / J377e / M12208 KEN. *ma(ku)* roll, wind, coil; tie around, wind up. *maku(ru), meku(ru)* turn over (pages); turn up (a card); tear off, take up, rip off; tuck up, bare (one's arm), roll up (one's sleeves). *maku(reru) vi* turn over, turn up; tear off, rip; be rolled up. *makure* burr, snag, catch.
3 上 *maku(ri)-a(geru), maku(shi)-a(geru), ma(ki)-a(geru) vt* roll up; hoist, heave up; take away, rob; blow up (dust)
土重来 *kendochōrai, kendojūrai* making a success after failure
5 立 *maku(shi)-ta(teru)* talk volubly, rattle on
12 落 *maku(re)-o(chiru)* tear off and fall

B **掲** 2194 / J3747 / M12311, **揭** 2216 / J-X / M12389 KEI. KETSU. *kaka(geru)* put up, hang out, hoist, display; publish, insert; describe; mention.
5 示 *keiji* bulletin, notice
示板 *keijiban* bulletin board
示場 *keijiba* notice wall
12 揚 *keiyō suru* hoist, fly, display
13 載 *keisai* publication, insertion

B **据** 2195 / J3f78 / M12204 KYO. *su(eru)* set (a table); lay (a foundation); place (a gun); install, equip; appoint (to a position). *su(waru)* squat down, sit down, (eyes) are fixed on.
5 石 *sueishi* garden flagstones
付 *su(e)-tsu(keru)* install, equip; set up; mount, place in position; set (a charge)
8 物 *suemono* alcove ornament
9 風呂 *suefuro* wooden bath tub
13 置 *su(e)-o(ku)* leave as it is, defer; leave (a loan) unredeemed; establish
16 膳 *suezen* an individually served meal

B **描** 2196 / J4941 / M12339 BYŌ. *ka(ku)* write, compose; draw, paint. *ega(ku)* paint, sketch, draw, describe.
4 切 *ega(ki)-ki(ru)* draw exactly
5 写 *byōsha* description; portrayal; drawing, painting, picture
出 *ega(ki)-da(su)* portray, delineate, depict. *byōshutsu* description; portrayal; drawing, painting, picture
8 画 *byōga* drawing, painting
15 線 *byōsen* a drawn line. *byōsen suru* draw a line

掬 2197 / J3545 / M12290 KIKU. *kiku(su), musu(bu)* scoop up water with the hand. *suku(u)* scoop, dip, ladle.
3 上 *suku(i)-a(geru)* dip up, scoop up
5 出 *suku(i)-da(su)* bail out
7 投 *suku(i)na(ge)* tripping up (someone)
8 取 *suku(i)-to(ru)* dip up, scoop up
14 網 *suku(i)ami* scoop net, dip net

捷 2198 / J3e39 / M12216 SHŌ victory; fast.
7 利 *shōri* victory
8 径 *shōkei* short cut; expedient
9 勁 *shōkei* nimble and strong
急 *shōkyū* speed, urgency
12 報 *shōhō* news of victory
13 戦 *kachiikusa* victory

捧 2199 / J4a7b / M12189 HŌ. *sasa(geru)* lift up; give; offer, consecrate, devote, sacrifice, dedicate.
2 刀 *hōtō* sword salute. *hōtō suru* present (credentials), submit, offer
7 呈 *hōtei* dedication, presentation; gift
8 物 *sasa(ge)mono* offering, sacrifice
9 持 *hōji suru* bear, present, hold up (the emperor's picture)
13 腹 *hōfuku* convulsed with laughter
腹絶倒 *hōfuku-zettō* convulsed with laughter
14 読 *hōdoku suru* read reverently
銃 *sasa(ge)tsutsu* presenting arms

4 心忄⺗戈戸【手扌】支攴攵文斗斤方无日曰月木欠止歹殳毋比毛氏气水氵氺火灬爪爫父爻爿丬片牙牛犬犭 8

B **掌** 2200 / J3e38 / M12248 SHŌ. *tsukasado(ru)* rule, administer, conduct. *tanagokoro* palm, hollow of the hand.
3 大 *shōdai* palm size, small patch (of land)
4 中 *shōchū* in the hand; (something) very small; (something) easily manipulated
中珠 *shōchū (no) tama* the apple of one's eye
中本 *shōchūbon* pocket edition
7 状 *shōjō* palmate, hand-shaped
8 典 *shōten* ritualist
12 握 *shōaku suru* grasp, seize, hold, command
14 管 *shōkan* handling, managing, manipulating

捻 2201 / J4731 / M12222 NEN. *hine(ri)* pinch (of salt); small gift of money; a twist. *hine(ru)* twirl, twist, twiddle; wring, wrench; bend (the body); incline (the head); pinch; defeat. *ne(jiru)* screw, twist, wrench, distort, wring, turn (a faucet); make capital out of someone's slip of the tongue. *neji(reru)* be twisted, be distorted, kink, twist, be awry; be perverse. *hineku(ru)* twirl, twist, play with; twist (the truth in reasoning).
3 子 *neji* screw, faucet, watch spring
4 込栓 *nejiko(mi)sen* plug, attachment
5 出 *hine(ri)-da(su)* squeeze out; work out a plan. *nenshutsu suru* contrive, devise (means), raise (money)
6 回 *hineku(ri)-mawa(su), hine(ri)-mawa(su)* tinker with, twist up, twirl
8 取 *hine(ri)-to(ru)* pinch (something) from
9 廻 *hineku(ri)-mawa(su)* twist up, tinker with
10 挫 *nenza* sprain
11 転 *nenten* twisting, torsion
15 潰 *hine(ri)-tsubu(su)* crush between fingers
16 錐 *neji(re)giri* a twist drill

B **控** 2202 / J3935 / M12283 KŌ. *hika(eru)* draw in; hold back, suspend (judgment); refrain from; be moderate; write, make notes; wait; have; moderate (a report). *hika(e)* memo; duplicate; waiting; prop; reserve.
5 目 *hika(e)me no* moderate, temperate, reserved, conservative
7 邸 *hika(e)tei* villa, retreat
8 所 *hika(e)jo* waiting room
制 *kōsei* checking, controlling
9 除 *kōjo* subtraction, deduction
室 *hika(e)shitsu* waiting room
屋敷 *hika(e) yashiki* villa, retreat
10 書 *hika(e)ga(ki)* notes, memo
11 帳 *hika(e)chō* notebook
12 訴 *kōso* (legal) appeal
訴状 *kōsojō* petition of appeal
訴院 *kōsoin* court of appeal
訴裁判所 *kōso saibansho* appellate court
訴権 *kōsoken* right of appeal
訴審 *kōsoshin* appeal trial

捩 2203 / J-X / M12192 **捩** 2154 / J5960 / M-X REI. RETSU. *yoji(ru), ne(jiru)* screw, twist, wrench, distort, wring, turn (a faucet); make capital out of someone's slip of the tongue. *yoji(reru), neji(reru)* be twisted, be distorted, kink, twist, be awry; be perverse. *moji(ru)* twist, distort; parody. *mojiri* Japanese overcoat; parody. *nejiri, nejire* torsion.
3 上 *ne(ji)-a(geru)* screw upwards
子 *neji* screw, faucet, watch spring
子錐 *nejigiri* gimlet, drill
4 込 *ne(ji)-ko(mu)* screw in; thrust into; protest to
切 *ne(ji)-ki(ru)* wrench off, twist off
6 向 *ne(ji)-mu(keru)* twist, toward
曲 *ne(ji)-ma(geru)* bend by twisting
伏 *ne(ji)-fu(seru)* overpower, get (someone) down
合 *ne(ji)-a(u)* struggle with
7 折 *ne(ji)-o(ru)* twist off
折釘 *nejio(re)kugi* screw hook
8 取 *ne(ji)-to(ru), neji(ri)-to(ru)* wring off, wrest from
11 寄 *ne(ji)-yo(ru)* wind one's way along
12 開 *ne(ji)-a(keru)* wrench open, pry open
13 鉢巻 *neji(ri) hachimaki, neji hachimaki* twisted towel worn around the head
14 網 *moji ami* minnow net

B **掘** 2204 / J3721 / M12264 KUTSU. *ho(ru)* dig, delve; core; excavate; sink (wells); dig up; scoop out; pick (the ear); probe.
3 下 *ho(ri)-sa(geru)* dig down; delve, investigate
上 *ho(ri)-a(geru)* dig up, dig out

4 込 ho(ri)-ko(mu) dig in, dig into
井戸 ho(ri)ido artesian well, bored well
5 出 ho(ri)-da(su) dig out, unearth, exhume, extricate, excavate; pick up (a rare book)
出物 horida(shi)mono treasure trove; lucky find; bargain
6 返 ho(ri)-kae(su) turn up (the soil); tear up (a road)
池 ho(ri)ike an artificial pool
当 ho(ri)-a(teru) find, dig up, strike (oil)
7 抜 ho(ri)-nu(ku) bore through, bore into
抜井戸 horinuki ido bored well
9 削 kussaku excavation
建小屋 ho(t)ta(te)goya hut, shack, cabin
10 起 ho(ri)-o(kosu) dig up; plow up
進 kusshin suru excavate, tunnel
11 崩 ho(ri)-kuzu(su) demolish
12 開 ho(ri)-hira(ku) excavate
割 horiwa(ri) canal
28 鑿 kussaku excavation

A **捨** 2205 / J3c4e / M12191′ **捨** 2206 / J-X / M12191 SHA. su(teru) throw away, discard, abandon, desert, give up; renounce, relinquish; resign; lay down (one's life); part with; sacrifice; reject, condemn.
3 子 su(te)go foundling
小舟 su(te)obune drifting boat; deserted person
4 犬 su(te)inu stray dog
切 su(te)-ki(ru) renounce, give up
5 石 su(te)ishi ornamental garden rocks; road ballast; preparatory work
去 su(te)-sa(ru) forsake; send away; throw away
台詞 su(te)zerifu sharp parting remark
6 仮名 su(te)gana connective kana to assist in reading or to indicate inflection (in Chinese classics)
7 身 su(te)mi self-abandonment. shashin becoming a priest
売 su(te)u(ri) sacrifice sale
児 su(te)go foundling
8 金 su(te)gane wasted money
所 su(te)dokoro dumping ground
10 値 su(te)ne sacrifice price
書 su(te)ga(ki) rambling writing
11 猫 su(te)neko stray cat
12 場 su(te)ba dumping ground, dump
詞 su(te)kotoba sharp parting remark
13 鉢 su(te)bachi despair, desperation
置 su(te)-o(ku) let alone, let pass, overlook

B **掃** 2207 / J415d / M12237′ SŌ. ha(ku) sweep; brush; gather up.
5 立 hakita(te) newly swept
出 ha(ki)-da(su) sweep out
7 初 ha(ki)zome first sweeping of the year
8 取 ha(ki)-to(ru) sweep away, sweep off
9 海 sōkai mine sweeping
海船 sōkaisen mine sweeper
海艇 sōkaitei mine sweeper
除 sōji cleaning, sweeping; cleanup, purge
除人 sōjinin cleaner, janitor
除屋 sōjiya night-soil man
除婦 sōjifu cleaning woman
除器 sōjiki vacuum cleaner
除機 sōjiki vacuum cleaner
10 討 sōtō cleaning up, sweeping, mopping up
射 sōsha sweeping fire
留 ha(ki)da(me) dust heap, rubbish heap
11 捨 ha(ki)-su(teru) sweep away, sweep out
寄 ha(ki)-yo(seru) sweep up
掃除 ha(ki)sōji sweeping and cleaning
12 集 ha(ki)-atsu(meru) sweep up
13 滅 sōmetsu clean sweep, annihilation
溜 ha(ki)da(me) sweepings, rubbish heap, dump
15 蕩 sōtō clearing up, sweeping, mopping up

A **授** 2208 / J3c78 / M12242 JU give, grant. sazu(keru) grant, confer, award, invest (with authority); impart, teach.
sazu(karu), sazu(keraru) be gifted with, be granted, be awarded, be accorded, be blessed with; be taught.
3 与 juyo awarding, conferring
与式 juyoshiki presentation ceremony
7 戒 jukai Buddhist initiation ceremony
8 物 sazu(kari)mono godsend, windfall, gift, boon, blessing
受 juju suru give and receive, deliver and receive
乳 junyū lactation, suckling
乳婦 junyūfu wet nurse
乳期 junyūki lactation period
9 洗 jusen suru baptize (by sprinkling)

洗者 *jusensha* baptizer (by sprinkling)
10 粉 *jufun* pollinization, fertilization
浸 *jushin suru* baptize by immersion
浸者 *jushinsha* baptizer (by immersion)
11 経 *jukyō* teaching the sutras
産 *jusan* placement, employment
産所 *jusanjo* vocational institute (to help the unemployed)
産施設 *jusan shisetsu* vocational-aid center
産場 *jusanjō* employment office
13 業 *jugyō* teaching, instruction, classwork
業料 *jugyōryō* tuition fees
業時間 *jugyō jikan* school hours
14 精 *jusei* fertilization, pollination
15 権 *juken* authorization
賞 *jushō* awarding a prize
17 爵 *jushaku suru* elevate to the peerage

A **採** 2209 / J3a4e / M12274 SAI. *to(ru)* take, hold, seize, catch, capture; fetch; receive, procure, obtain; adopt (a measure); engage (graduates); choose; order (foodstuffs); pick, pluck; make, produce; eat; set up (camp); charge; administer; transact; take (pains); make out (the meaning); remove; take off (one's hat); take out (spots); strike out (words); weed, catch (fish); deprive of; steal; capture (territory), annex; need, require; reserve (rooms); subscribe to; press (a point home); take (a picture); possess. *to(reru)* can be held, can take; come off, come apart, be off, be removed; be relieved (of pain); be obtained, be produced; be caught; be earned; come out (well) (a photo); require (time); be interpreted as; can get; let (light) in; take (one's measure); can feel (the pulse); take (a pen and write).

2 入 *to(ri)-i(reru)* take in, gather in, harvest; accept, adopt, introduce (customs)
3 上 *to(ri)-a(geru)* take up, pick up; deal with; adopt, accept, listen to; dispossess, expropriate, confiscate, revoke; deliver (a baby)
4 方 *to(ri)kata* way of taking (a photo)
5 用 *saiyō suru* use, adopt, employ. *saiyō* introduction, adoption, acceptance; appointment, employment
石 *saiseki* quarrying
出 *saishutsu suru, to(ri)-da(su)* take out
6 血 *saiketsu suru* take a blood sample
伐 *saibatsu* felling (trees)
光 *saikō* lighting
7 択 *saitaku suru* adopt, select
決 *saiketsu* vote, roll call, ballot taking
否 *saihi* adoption or rejection; employment or rejection
8 金 *saikin* gold mining; gold extraction
取 *saishu* picking, gathering, collecting, harvesting; extracting (alcohol)
油 *saiyu* oil drilling
油権 *saiyuken* oil concession
9 点 *saiten* marking, grading
点者 *saitensha* marker, scorer
炭 *saitan* coal mining
炭所 *saitanjo* coal mine, colliery
10 残 *to(ri)noko(ri)* gleaning
11 掘 *saikutsu* mining
12 量 *sairyō* discretion
集 *saishū* collecting, gathering
13 鉱 *saikō* mining
14 綿器 *saimenki* cotton picker
種圃 *saishuho* seed garden
種園 *saishuen* seed garden
算 *saisan* profit
算制 *saisansei* (institutional) financial independence
16 録 *sairoku suru* transcribe, record

B **排** 2210 / J4753 / M12256 HAI *hai(suru)* exclude, expel, reject; push aside, push open; defy; disregard; anti-(Japanese, etc.).

4 日 *hai-Nichi* anti-Japanese
仏派 *haibutsuha* (ancient) anti-Buddhist faction
水 *haisui* drainage; draining; bailing; displacement
水渠 *haisuikyo* drain, culvert
水量 *haisuiryō* displacement
水路 *haisuiro* sewer system
水管 *haisuikan* drainpipe
水噸数 *haisui tonsū* displacement tonnage
5 斥 *haiseki* rejection, exclusion, ostracism, expulsion
外 *haigai* antiforeign
他 *haita* exclusion
他的 *haitateki* exclusive
出 *haishutsu* discharge, exhaust, evacuation

出物 *haishutsubutsu* excreta
6 米 *hai-Bei* anti-American
列 *hairetsu* arrangement, grouping, disposition
気 *haiki* exhaust, ventilation
気坑 *haikikō* ventilation
気鐘 *haikishō* air pump, bell jar
7 尿 *hainyō* urination
卵 *hairan* ovulation
8 英 *hai-Ei* anti-British
泄 *haisetsu* evacuation, discharge, exhaust
泄物 *haisetsubutsu* excrement, excretion
9 便 *haiben* evacuation, bowel movement
除 *haijo* exclusion, removal
臭管 *haishūkan* stench pipe
11 液 *haieki* drainage (in surgery)
球 *haikyū* volleyball
雪 *haisetsu* snow removal
貨 *haika* boycott
13 置 *haichi* arrangement, disposition (of troops)
15 撃 *haigeki* denouncement, rejection
17 擠 *haisei suru* exclude, reject, expel
膿 *hainō* drainage of pus

A **探** 2211 / J4335 / M12276 TAN. *sagu(ru)* search, look for; explore; spy upon, sound out; probe (a wound). *saga(su)* search. *sagu(ri)* sounding out; spy; probe.
3 下 *sagu(ri) sa(geru)* dig for
上 *sagu(ri)-a(geru)* examine by touch
5 出 *sagu(ri) da(su)* spy out, worm out, smell out, search out
6 回 *sagu(ri)-mawa(su), sagu(ri)-mawa(ru)* grope for, fumble for
合 *sagu(ri)a(i)* testing each other's feelings
当 *sagu(ri)-a(teru)* grope and find, discover, locate
7 足 *sagu(ri)ashi* groping (one's way)
求 *saga(shi)-moto(meru)* search for. *tankyū* quest, pursuit, research
究 *tankyū* search, research, inquiry
究心 *tankyūshin* spirit of inquiry
究物 *tankyūbutsu* quest
究者 *tankyūsha* investigator
8 知 *tanchi* detection
知器 *tanchiki* detector
9 査 *tansa* inquiry, investigation
海灯 *tankaitō* searchlight
10 梅 *tambai* plum-blossom viewing
険 *tanken* exploration, expedition
索 *tansaku* search; inquiry, investigation
索的 *tansakuteki* searching (inquiry)
11 訪 *tambō* searching; hunting a news story; journalist
訪記者 *tambō kisha* reporter, interviewer
偵 *tantei* detective work; espionage; detective, spy, investigator, agent
偵小説 *tantei shōsetsu* detective story
偵犬 *tanteiken* police dog
偵物 *tanteimono* detective story
12 測 *tansoku* search, observation
湯 *kukatachi* hot-water ordeal
勝 *tanshō* sightseeing
検 *tanken* exploration, expedition
検記 *tankenki* exploration record
検家 *tankenka* explorer
検船 *tankensen* explorers' vessel
検隊 *tankentai* exploration party
13 照灯 *tanshōtō* searchlight
鉱 *tankō* prospecting
鉱者 *tankōsha* prospector
14 聞 *tambun* detection
15 賞 *tanshō* sightseeing
18 題 *tandai* (ancient) army headquarters

A **推** 2212 / J3f64 / M12284 SUI conjecture. *o(su)* infer, conclude; guess, suppose; recommend, support. *o(shite)* by conjecture, by deduction.
2 力 *suiryoku* thrust, driving power
5 弘 *o(shi)-hiro(meru)* extend, spread, amplify; propagate
6 当 *o(shi)-a(teru)* guess
考 *suikō* inference, deduction, deliberation
7 究 *suikyū* inference
8 知 *suichi* inference, deduction, conjecture
服 *suifuku suru* admire and respect
参 *suisan* visiting; discourtesy
定 *suitei* presumption, conclusion, estimation
9 計 *suikei* estimate
10 称 *suishō* praise; admiration
挙 *suikyo suru* propose (for office)
挙式 *suikyoshiki* installation ceremony
進 *suishin* propulsion, drive, promotion
進力 *suishinryoku* impulse, propulsion
進機 *suishinki* propeller

11 問 *suimon* questioning; investigating (a crime)
移 *suii* transition, change. *o(shi)-utsu(ru)* (times) change, (months) pass
断 *suidan* inference, deduction, conclusion
理 *suiri* reasoning, inference, presumption
理小説 *suiri shōsetsu* detective story
12 測 *suisoku* conjecture, supposition. *o(shi)-haka(ru)* enter into another's feelings
量 *suiryō* guess, inference, imagination; consideration, sympathy
13 奨 *suishō* recommendation, commendation
14 選 *suisen* recommendation
輓 *suiban* recommendation
敲 *suikō* polish, elaboration, choice of diction
察 *suisatsu* guess, inference, imagination; consideration, sympathy
算 *suisan* calculation, reckoning
15 賞 *suishō* recommendation, commendation
論 *suiron* reasoning, inference, deduction
論式 *suironshiki* syllogism
16 薦 *suisen* recommendation, nomination
薦状 *suisenjō* letter of recommendation
薦者 *suisensha* recommender, proposer
薦委員会 *suisen iinkai* nominating committee
17 戴式 *suitaishiki* installation ceremony

A **接** 2213 / J405c / M12280 SETSU. *ses(suru)* touch, contact; adjoin; receive (visitors); be in receipt of; encounter, experience; draw near. *tsu(gu)* join, piece together, splice, cement, set (broken bones); graft (trees). *ha(gu)* patch. *ha(gi)* patch, patches; patching; seam, joint.

4 手 *tsugite* joint, pipe coupling
木 *tsugiki* grafting; grafted tree
木法 *tsugikihō* grafting
5 目 *tsugime, hagime* joint, seam, suture
収 *sesshū* seizure, requisition
6 近 *sekkin* proximity, approach; intimate relations
地 *setchi* ground (connection)
合 *ha(gi)-a(waseru)* sew together; join. *setsugō* union, joining
合剤 *setsugōzai* glue
7 角 *sekkaku* adjacent angle
迫 *seppaku* pressure, urgency; imminence; acuteness, tenseness
伴 *seppan* reception, welcome; serving (food)
吻 *seppun* kiss, kissing
見 *sekken* interview, reception
見日 *sekkembi* reception day, at-home day
尾辞 *setsubiji* suffix
尾語 *setsubigo* suffix
8 受 *setsuju suru* receive, intercept
9 待 *settai* reception, welcome; serving (food)
待室 *settaishitsu* reception room
客 *sekkyaku* receiving visitors
客用 *sekkyakuyō* for customers
客係 *sekkyakugakari* receptionist
客婦 *sekkyakufu* (restaurant) hostess; waitress
客業 *sekkyakugyō* hotel and restaurant business
10 骨 *sekkotsu* bonesetting
骨医 *sekkotsui* bonesetter
骨術 *sekkotsujutsu* bonesetting
11 眼鏡 *setsugankyō* eyepiece
12 着剤 *setchakuzai* binding agent, glue
13 辞 *setsuji* prefixes and suffixes
戦 *sessen* hand-to-hand fighting; close game
続 *setsuzoku* connection, junction, joining
続詞 *setsuzokushi* conjunction
触 *sesshoku* contact, touch, tangency
触反応 *sesshoku hannō* catalysis
触作用 *sesshoku sayō* catalytic action
触面 *sesshokumen* contact surface, contacts (with people)
触点 *sesshokuten* point of contact; point of tangency
触感染 *sesshoku kansen* contagion
14 種 *sesshu* inoculation, vaccination
15 穂 *tsugiho* graft, slip; scion
16 頭辞 *settōji* prefix
頭語 *settōgo* prefix
20 攘 *setsujō* contiguity

B **掛** 2214 / J335d / M12267 KAI. KEI. *ka(karu)* *vi* hang on, be suspended from, be caught, be trapped; be built; begin; arrive at; require, cost; play against, oppose; be splashed; weigh (a pound); be levied; (the instrument or tool) works; attack, fall on; is now showing at; consult; depend (on a son). *ka(keru)* *vt* hang, set up (a ladder); cover; construct, install; sit down; sprinkle, pour on; put on; ring up; weigh; multiply; levy; pay (in installments); anchor; start (a machine); wind; turn on (radio); spend on; offer (prizes); put (under treatment); set (on fire). *kakari* duty; person in charge; expenses, charges; tax; dependence (on someone); scale; outward appearance, construction; beginning; bite (of a tool). *ka(ke)* buckwheat noodles in soup; credit; overcharge; installment. *-ka(keru)* begin, start to. *-ka(ketewa)* (in) the matter of, in. *-ga(ke)* wearing; on (the way); ten percent; times (as large). *-ka(ke)* half finished; (clothes) hook; (table) cover.

2 人 *ka(kari)bito, ka(kari)udo* dependent, hanger-on
3 子 *ka(kari)go* one's support in old age
小屋 *ka(ke)goya* lean-to, temporary hut
4 込 *ka(ke)-ko(mu)* lock with a key
引 *ka(ke)hi(ki)* bargaining; maneuvering
心地 *ka(ke)gokochi* the feel (of a chair)
5 目 *ka(ke)me* weight
矢 *ka(ke)ya* mallet
付 *ka(kari)tsu(ke)no* one's regular (physician)
外 *ka(ke)hazu(shi)* putting on and off; disengaging (gear)
札 *ka(ke)fuda* small hanging plaque for notices; nameplate
払 *ka(ke)bara(i)* settlement of accounts
汁 *ka(ke)shiru, ka(ke)jiru* dressing (on food)
出 *ka(ke)da(shi)* penthouse
代金 *ka(ke)daikin* bill, amount to pay
布 *ka(ke)fu* cloth cover
布団 *ka(ke)buton* covering quilt
6 回 *ka(ke)-megu(rasu)* surround, enclose
字 *ka(ke)ji* hanging scroll
先 *ka(ke)saki* credit customers
行灯 *ka(ke)andon* paper lantern at the entrance
合 *ka(ke)-a(u)* negotiate with, bargain with. *ka(ke)-a(wasu)* *vt* multiply; cross, interbreed. *ka(kari)-a(u)* have dealings with; be involved in. *ka(kari)a(i)* implication, involvement. *kakea(i)* negotiations; dialogue
合話 *kakea(i)banashi* storytelling in dialogue
合漫才 *ka(ke)ai manzai* comic dialogue
7 図 *kakezu* wall map, wall picture
声 *ka(ke)goe* shouting encouragement; shouting in unison to aid effort
売 *kakeu(ri)* selling on credit
8 金 *kakekin* installment payments; credit sales. *ka(ke)gane* hatch, hasp, latch
物 *ka(ke)mono* hanging picture or scroll; (food) dressing; coverlet
肥 *ka(ke)goe* liquid manure
直 *ka(ke)-nao(su)* reweigh; rehang
取 *kaketo(ri)* bill collection; collector
取引 *kaketo(ri)hiki* doing business on credit
9 持 *ka(ke)mo(chi)* holding positions concurrently
冠 *keikan* resignation
竿 *ka(ke)zao* clothes-drying pole
負 *ka(kari)ma(ke)* earnings not covering expenses
看板 *ka(ke)kamban* hanging sign
茶屋 *ka(ke)jaya* wayside teahouse
10 倒 *ka(ke)dao(re)* bad debt; earnings not covering expenses
値 *ka(ke)ne* overcharge; exaggeration
紙 *ka(ke)gami* wrapper, (book) jacket
時計 *ka(ke)dokei* wall clock
11 帳 *ka(ke)cho* charge-account book
捨 *kakezu(te)* abandoning an installment contract
商 *ka(ke)akinai* selling on credit
12 減 *ka(ke)be(ri)* weight loss
湯 *ka(kari)yu* clean hot bath water for rinsing off
絵 *ka(ke)e* hanging picture
詞 *ka(ke)kotoba* play on words
軸 *kakejiku* hanging scroll
買 *ka(ke)ga(i)* credit purchase
違 *ka(ke)-chiga(u)* cross (on the way)
集 *ka(ke)atsu(me)* bill collecting
替 *ka(ke)-ka(eru)* replace, rebuild, substitute. *kakeka(e)* rebuilding (a bridge); rehanging (a scroll). *kakega(e)* substitute
13 鉤 *ka(ke)kagi, ka(ke)bari* long hook
筵 *ka(ke)mushiro* mat curtain
幕 *ka(ke)maku* hangings
蒲団 *ka(ke)buton* covering quilt
14 暦 *ka(ke)goyomi* wall calendar
樋 *ka(ke)hi, ka(ke)doi* water pipe, conduit, flume

銭 *ka(ke)sen* stakes, bet
算 *ka(ke)zan* multiplication
15 蕎麦 *ka(ke)soba* buckwheat noodles in seasoned broth
16 橋 *ka(ke)hashi* viaduct, suspension bridge
18 額 *ka(ke)gaku* hanging framed picture
襟 *ka(ke)eri* changeable kimono collar
醤油 *ka(ke)jōyu* diluted *shōyu* for seasoning
22 籠 *ka(ke)-komo(ru)* lock oneself in

9

揑 2215 / J-X / M12345 See 捏 2165.

揭 2216 / J-X / M12389 See 掲 2194.

揵 2217 / J-X / M-X Nonstandard for 撥 2283.

插 2218 / J5967 / M12346 **揷** 2219 / J-X / M12346′ See 挿 2167.

掾 2220 / J5961 / M12313 EN aid, assist; lower ranking official; edge, border. *jō* provincial official of the third rank.

揀 2221 / J5963 / M12315 KAN, KEN *era(bu)* choose, select; discern.

揖 2222 / J4d2c / M12351 YŪ bow with hands clasped at breast; give way; advance; scoop up. SHŪ gather, assemble.

揩 2223 / J5962 / M12383 KAI wipe.

揄 2224 / J5969 / M12320 YŌ. YU pull; tease, play with.

揆 2225 / J5964 / M12326 KI category; principle; plot; way of doing; plan; road; uprising. *bachi* drumstick.

揃 2226 / J4237 / M12319 SEN. *soro(u)* be complete; be equal; be even, be uniform; be all present. *soro(eru)* arrange; make even; complete, get ready. *soroi* all, both, together; uniform; uniformity; attendance. *soro(tte)* in a body, en masse; all alike. *-soroi* set; suit.

揣 2227 / J5965 / M12371 SHI. SUI. *haka(ru)* conjecture.
15 摩 *shima* guess, conjecture
摩臆測 *shima-okusoku* conjecture, speculation

B **搭** 2228 / J456b / M12508 TŌ load (a vehicle); ride.
9 乗 *tōjō suru* board, get on
乗者 *tōjōsha* passenger, occupant
13 載 *tōsai suru* load; entrain; embark

A **揮** 2229 / J3478 / M12394 KI. *furu(u)* shake, wield, brandish; be invigorated, be spirited, flourish.
9 発 *kihatsu* volatilization
発油 *kihatsuyu* gasoline
発油税 *kihatsuyuzei* gasoline tax
11 毫 *kigō* writing, painting, drawing

B **援** 2230 / J3167 / M12407 EN *tasu(keru)* help, save.
4 引 *en'in* reference
5 用 *en'yō suru* claim, quote, invoke
7 兵 *empei* relief, reinforcements
助 *enjo* assistance, help, pay, support
助額 *enjogaku* amount of aid
8 例 *enrei* illustration
9 軍 *engun* relief, reinforcements
11 隊 *entai* reinforcements
20 護 *engo* covering, protection, aegis, backing, relief

揉 2231 / J5966 / M12332 JŪ. *mo(mu)* rub; massage, shampoo; debate vigorously; train, coach; worry; shove and carry (a portable shrine). *mo(meru)* get into trouble, trouble arises; be rumpled, get out of shape. *mo(mareru)* be tried, be buffeted. *mo(me)* trouble.
2 下 *mo(mi)-o(rosu)* to massage
3 上 *mo(mi)-a(geru)* massage. *momia(ge)* tuft of hair under the temples
4 手 *momide* rubbing one's hands
5 立 *mo(mi)-ta(teru)* rub vigorously; stir up, exasperate
出 *mo(mi)-da(su)* squeeze out
6 合 *mo(mi)-a(u)* jostle, shove and push, have friction

8 事 *momegoto* trouble
9 革 *momigawa* buff, polisher
10 消 *mo(mi)-ke(su)* hush up, suppress; smother (a fire); rub out; crush out; stifle
17 療治 *momiryōji* shampoo, massage

B **握** 2232 / J302e / M12366 AKU. *nigi(ru)* grasp, hold; make (sushi balls); assume (power); make (money); get (proof). *nigi(rasu)* let (someone) take hold of your hand; slip money to, bribe. *nigi(ri)* grasp, grip; handful; handle; rice ball, sushi ball.
2 力 *akuryoku* grasping power
4 手 *akushu* handshaking; reconciliation; harmony
9 屋 *nigi(ri)ya* miser, grasping fellow
10 索 *nigi(ri)zuna* grab line
拳 *nigi(ri)kobushi* clenched fist
12 飯 *nigi(ri)meshi, musubi* rice ball
13 詰 *nigi(ri)-tsu(meru)* grasp and squeeze together
15 潰 *nigi(ri)-tsubu(su)* crush, crumple; shelve, table
締 *nigi(ri)-shi(meru)* squeeze, wring, clasp, hold tightly
17 鮨 *nigi(ri)zushi* sushi ball

B **換** 2233 / J3439 / M12358 **換** 2234 / J-X / M-X KAN. *ka(eru)* change, turn, convert, exchange, renew, substitute, replace. *ka(waru)* replace, relieve.
3 刃 *ka(e)ba* extra blades
5 玉 *ka(e)dama* a substitute, a double
6 衣 *kan'i* changing clothes
地 *ka(e)chi* substitute land
刑 *kankei* change of a sentence from a fine to hard labor
気 *kanki* ventilation
気筒 *kankitō* ventilator
7 言 *kangen (sureba)* in other words
8 金 *kankin suru* realize, turn into money
価 *kanka suru* convert into money
物 *ka(e)mono* exchanging; something exchanged
10 骨奪胎 *kankotsu-dattai* adaptation, modification; plagiarism
11 乾 *ka(e)-ho(su)* drain, empty (a well)
12 喩 *kan'yu* metonymy
着 *ka(e)gi* spare suit
14 算 *kansan* conversion, change, exchange
算表 *kansanhyō* conversion table

B **揺** 2235 / J4d49 / M12445′ **搖** 2239 / J596a / M12479 YŌ. *yu(reru), yu(rameku), yu(ratsuku), yu(ragu), yu(rugu) vi* shake, sway, rock, roll, pitch, tremble, quake, flicker, vibrate, jolt. *yu(suru), yu(suburu), yu(saburu) vt* swing, shake, rock. *yu(rugasu)* shake, wave, swing, sway. *yu(re)* vibration; shock; variety.
3 下 *yu(ri)-sa(geru)* shake down
上 *yu(ri)-a(geru)* swing up, jiggle (a baby on one's back)
5 立 *yu(rugi)-ta(tsu)* stand shaking
6 返 *yu(ri)kae(shi)* an aftershock
曳 *yōei suru* flutter, tremble; trail, linger
10 起 *yu(ri)-oko(su), yu(suri)-oko(su)* wake (someone) up
11 動 *yu(ri)-ugo(ku) vi* quake; swing. *yu(ri)-ugo(kasu) vt* shake, wave, swing, sway. *yu(re)-ugo(ku)* tremble
祭 *yōsai* wave offering
12 揺 *yu(ra)yu(ra), yōyō* wavering, unsettled
落 *yu(ri)-oto(su)* shake off, shake down
無 *yu(rugi)na(i)* firm, steady, secure
椅子 *yu(ri)isu* rocking chair
15 震 *yu(rugi)-furu(eru)* quake and tremble
20 籃 *yōran, yu(ri)kago* cradle
籃地 *yōran (no) chi* the home of, the cradle of, birthplace
籃時代 *yōran jidai* infancy, babyhood
籃期 *yōranki* infancy, babyhood
22 籠 *yu(ri)kago* cradle

B **揚** 2236 / J4d48 / M12355 YŌ praise. *a(garu)* rise, go up; climb up; advance, appreciate; be promoted; improve; enter, call on; be offered; accrue; be finished; (expenses) come to; go bankrupt; begin spinning (cocoons); be caught; get ruffled; eat, drink; die; weaken (as a battery); let up (rain). *a(geru)* raise, elevate; fly (kites); praise; increase, advance; promote, elevate; vomit; usher in, admit; send (to school); offer; present, leave with; finish; arrange (expenses); observe, perform; quote, mention, give (examples); bear (a child); improve (talents); do up (the hair); arrest; engage; fry; (rains) stop; fry in deep fat. *a(ge)* tuck; fried tofu; fried food.
2 力 *yōryoku* lifting power
3 子江 *Yōsukō* Yangtze River

4 戸 *a(ge)do* push-up door
水 *yōsui* pumping water
水所 *yōsuijo* pumping plant
水装置 *yōsui sōchi* pumping equipment
5 句 *a(ge)ku* in the end, finally
7 言 *yōgen* declare, assert, profess
足 *a(ge)ashi* faultfinding
8 板 *a(ge)ita* removable floor boards, trap door
物 *a(ge)mono* fried food
油 *a(ge)abura* frying oil
9 屋 *a(ge)ya* brothel
10 荷 *a(ge)ni* cargo being unloaded
陸 *yōriku* disembarkation; unloading
陸料 *yōrikuryō* landing charge
11 窓 *a(ge)mado* push-up window
12 場 *a(ge)ba* wharf, landing (place)
揚 *yōyō(taru)* triumphant, exultant
雲雀 *a(ge)hibari* skylark
13 幕 *a(ge)maku* noh theater-entrance curtain
15 餅 *a(ge)mochi* fried rice-cake
16 錨機 *yōbyōki* anchor windlass
17 鍋 *a(ge)nabe* frying pan
20 饅頭 *a(ge)manjū* fried bean-jam bun

A **提** 2237 / J4473 / M12344 TEI. CHŌ. *sa(geru)* take along, carry in the hand. *hissa(geru)* carry.
5 示 *teiji suru, teishi suru* present; exhibit; suggest
出 *teishutsu suru* present, introduce (a bill), tender (a resignation), lodge (a petition)
出者 *teishutsusha* proposer, mover
6 灯 *chōchin* paper lantern
灯行列 *chōchin gyōretsu* lantern procession
灯屋 *chōchin'ya* lantern maker
灯持 *chōchimmo(chi)* lantern carrier; exaggerated propaganda
7 言 *teigen* proposal, motion
8 供 *teikyō* offer, tender
9 要 *teiyō* summary
香炉 *teikōro, sa(ge)kōro* censer
10 起 *teiki suru* bring suit; raise a question; file a claim
案 *teian* proposition, suggestion, overture, proposal
案者 *teiansha* proposer, proponent
案家 *teianka* proposer, proponent
11 唱 *teishō* (Buddhist) lecture; advocacy
婆 *Daiba* Deva
12 訴 *teiso suru* sue
琴 *teikin* violin
琴家 *teikinka* violinist
13 携 *teikei* concert, cooperation
督 *teitoku* admiral, commodore
15 論 *teiron* premise
20 議 *teigi* proposal, motion

10

搜 2238 / J5953 / M12486 See **搜** 2168.

搖 2239 / J596a / M12479 See **揺** 2235.

搏 2240 / J5973 / M12466 HAKU. *u(tsu)* strike, hit, beat, knock, slap, punch, thrash, smite; clap (one's hands); beat (a drum); ring (a bell); (clocks) strike; impress, touch; shoot; pound in (a nail); water, sprinkle; braid; play (checkers); till (the soil); temper (a sword); prepare (buckwheat noodles); present (a play); cast (a net); pay (earnest money).

摹 2241 / J-X / M12645 BO. *mo(suru)* imitate.

搆 2242 / J596c / M12447 KŌ pull, draw, drag; build.

搓 2243 / J596d / M12476 SA strike, hit; cut; rub; braid.

搨 2244 / J5972 / M12503 TŌ rub; restrain; cover; transfer. *su(ru)* rub, rub a copy of a stone inscription.

搶 2245 / J596f / M12525 SŌ. SHŌ stab; resist, refuse; rob, cheat; assemble.

搴 2246 / J596b / M12519 KEN pull, pull out; wrap; hoist. *kaka(geru)* put up, hoist.

搢 2247 / J-X / M12494 SHIN put between, insert.
11 紳 *shinshin* rank; high-ranking person, nobles

搦 2248 / J596e / M12500 JAKU. JOKU. DAKU. *kara(meru)* bind, tie up, arrest. *-gara(mi)* the whole (basket); around (30 years old).

4 手 *karamete* rear; back entrance; one who arrests; force attacking the rear of a castle
8 取 *kara(me)-to(ru)* arrest, capture

B **搬** 2249 / J4842 / M12507 HAN carry, transport.

2 入 *hannyū suru* carry in
5 出 *hanshutsu suru* carry out
8 送 *hansō suru* convey
送帯 *hansōtai* conveyor belt

摸 2250 / J4c4e / M12644 MO. search. *mo(suru)* imitate; copy.

5 写 *mosha* copying; copy, replica
10 倣 *mohō* copy, imitation
索 *mosaku* groping
17 擬 *mogi* imitation
擬投票 *mogi tōhyō* straw vote
擬店 *mogiten* refreshment booths (at a party)
擬戦 *mogisen* sham fight
擬試験 *mogi shiken* trial examination

B **搾** 2251 / J3a71 / M12553 SAKU *shibo(ru)* wring, squeeze, press, extract; milk; close tight; extort; scold. *shi(meru)* strangle, constrict, wring.

4 木 *shimegi* oil press
5 汁 *shibo(ri)jiru* juices
出 *shiborida(shi)* (toothpaste) tube
8 油 *sakuyu* expressing oil (from seeds or nuts)
取 *shibo(ri)-to(ru)* wring, squeeze, press, extract; milk; close tight; extort; scold. *sakushu* exploitation; squeezing; sweating
乳 *sakunyū* milking
11 粕 *shibo(ri)kasu, shimekasu* strained lees; oil cake
13 滓 *shibo(ri)kasu, shimekasu* strained lees
17 糟 *shimekasu* oil cake, strained lees

B **摂** 2252 / J405d / M12557′ **攝** 2317 / J5970 / M13010 SETSU. *ses(suru)* act in place of; carry on in addition to. *to(ru)* take, hold, seize, catch, capture; fetch; receive, procure, obtain; adopt (a measure); engage (graduates); choose; order (foodstuffs); pick, pluck; make, produce; eat; set up (camp); charge, administer; transact; take (pains); make out (the meaning); remove; take off (one's hat); take out (spots); strike out (words); weed, catch (fish); deprive of; steal; capture (territory), annex; need, require, reserve (rooms); subscribe to; press (a point home); take (a picture); possess.

4 氏 *sesshi* centigrade
5 生 *sessei* health preservation, hygiene
6 行 *sekkō* performing for another; performing simultaneously
8 取 *sesshu* intake, absorption; adoption
9 政 *sesshō, sessei* regency; regent
政皇后 *sesshō kōgō* empress regent, queen regent
政宮 *sesshō (no) miya* prince regent
10 家 *sekke* the line of regents
11 理 *setsuri* providence
理的 *setsuriteki* providential
14 関 *sekkan* (ancient) regents
関家 *sekkanke* the line of regents
15 養 *setsuyō* care of health, recuperation
20 護腺 *setsugosen* prostate gland
護腺炎 *setsugosen'en* prostatitis

B **携** 2253 / J3748 / M12529 **擕** 2318 / J5a58 / M13008 **攜** 2308 / J-X / M12924

KEI *tazusa(eru)* carry (in the hand); be armed with; carry along, bring (someone) along. *tazusa(waru)* participate in, be concerned in.

2 入 *tazusa(e)-i(ru), tazusa(e)-i(reru)* carry into, bring into
3 下 *tazusa(e)-kuda(ru)* carry down, take down
上 *tazusa(e)-nobo(ru), tazusa(e)-a(geru)* carry up out of, bring up
5 出 *tazusa(e)-da(su)* carry out
6 行 *keikō suru* carry along, bring. *tazusa(e)-yu(ku)* carry to, bring to, carry away
10 帰 *tazusa(e)-kae(ru)* bring back
帯 *keitai* portable. *keitai suru* carry along
帯口糧 *keitai kōryō* field rations
帯兇器 *keitai kyōki* concealed weapons; a criminal's weapons
帯兵器 *keitai heiki* small arms
帯物件 *keitai bukken* personal and household effects

帯品 *keitaihin* personal effects, luggage
帯食糧 *keitai shokuryō* portable army rations
帯電話 *keitai denwa* portable phone

搗 2254 / J5971 / M12480 Tō. *tsu(ku), ka(tsu)* pound, hull, husk; stamp (ore).
3 上 *tsu(ki)-a(geru)* finish pounding (rice)
4 手 *tsukite* pounder (of grain)
5 立 *tsukita(te)* freshly pounded *mochi* (glutinous rice)
6 臼 *tsukiusu* grain mortar
衣 *tōi* pounding cloth (to bring out the gloss)
合 *ka(chi)-a(u)* clash, collide, conflict, interfere with; fall on (a certain day), coincide with
米 *tsukigome* polished rice
米屋 *tsukigomeya* rice-polishing mill
9 砕 *tsu(ki)-kuda(ku)* smash, grind
10 栗 *kachiguri* dried chestnut
11 混 *tsu(ki)-ma(zeru)* mix together, pound together, roll into one
12 減 *tsukibe(ri)* grain-pounding loss
14 精 *tsu(ki)-shira(geru)* polish by pounding
15 潰 *tsu(ki)-tsubu(su)* pound to a jelly

A **損** 2255 / J423b / M12459 Son loss; disadvantage, handicap. *son(suru)* lose, suffer loss. *sokona(u), sokone(ru), son(zuru), son(jiru)* harm, hurt, injure, damage, mar; lose, oppress. *-son(jiru), -sokona(u)* fail in (doing), fail to (do), miss, err in. *-son(ji), -sokona(i)* slip, error, failure.
3 亡 *sombō, sommō* loss
4 友 *son'yū* unprofitable friend
5 失 *sonshitsu* loss
8 金 *sonkin* money loss
所 *sonsho* damaged place
10 耗 *sommō* loss
益 *son'eki* loss and gain; advantage and disadvantage
料 *sonryō* charge for the use of certain articles
料貸 *sonryōga(shi)* letting out for hire
害 *songai* damage, injury, loss; casualties; prejudice
害保険 *songai hoken* insurance against loss
害高 *songaidaka* damages
害賠償 *songai baishō* restitution, compensation for damages or injuries
11 得 *sontoku* loss and gain; advantages and disadvantages
12 量 *sonryō* ullage
13 傷 *sonshō* damage, injury, casualty

搔 2256 / J-X / M12477 **掻** 2175 / J415f / M-X Sō. *ka(ku)* scratch; clear away; rake; comb; paddle; cut off (a head). *ka(ki)-* emphatic prefix.
2 入 *ka(ki)-ire(ru)* rake in, gather in
3 干 *ka(i)-ho(su)* drain dry
上 *ka(ki)-a(geru)* comb upward
口説 *ka(ki)-kudo(ku)* complain of
4 込 *ka(ki)-ko(mu)* carry under the arm, rake in. *kakko(mu)* eat fast
切 *ka(ki)-ki(ru)* cut; cut off; cut and take
分 *ka(ki)-wa(keru)* push or shove aside
5 玉 *kakitama* egg soup
立 *ka(ki)-ta(teru)* stir; rake (the fire); beat, whip; turn up (a wick); arouse (interest), stir up (trouble)
払 *kappara(u)* pilfer, filch. *kappara(i)* sneak thief; shoplifter
出 *ka(i)-da(su)* bail out (a boat); drain out. *ka(ki)-da(su)* scrape out, rake out
6 回 *ka(ki)-mawa(su)* stir, churn, beat, whip; ransack; have one's own way
灯 *ka(i)-tomo(shi)* trim lamps
合 *ka(ki)-a(waseru)* adjust, arrange
7 均 *ka(ki)-nara(su)* adjust, smooth, level out
乱 *ka(ki)-mida(su)* disturb, ruffle, disarrange
卵 *kakitama* egg soup
8 爬 *sōha* curetting, scraping, scooping out
退 *ka(ki)-noke(ru)* push or thrust aside
抱 *ka(ki)-ida(ku)* emphatic for *idaku*: hug, embrace, hold in the arms; entertain (hope); cherish (a desire); harbor (malice); hold, have
取 *ka(i)-do(ru)* take; tuck up. *ka(ki)-to(ru)* scrape off, scrape out
毟 *ka(ki)-mushi(ru)* rend, tear, scratch off
9 巻 *kaima(ki)* sleeved quilt
挟 *ka(ki)-hasa(mu)* carry under the arm
10 消 *ka(ki)-ke(su)* wipe out, efface

流 *ka(ki)-naga(su)* dash, pour, sluice, let run out, flush; float, set adrift; spill; shed (tears); wash away, wash off; forfeit, forclose; exile; cruise (taxis)
破 *ka(ki)-ya(ru), ka(ki)-ka(buru)* tear up
11 疵 *kakikizu* scratch
痒 *sōyō* scratching an itchy place
掘 *kaibo(ri) suru* drain (a pond)
掃 *ka(ki)-ha(ku)* sweep, brush, gather up
探 *ka(ki)-sagu(ru)* scratch around (for something). *ka(ki)-saga(su), ka(ki)-sagu(ru), ka(i)-sagu(ru)* forage, ransack
細 *ka(i)-hoso(ru)* become thin (people)
寄 *ka(ki)-yo(seru)* rake up, gather up
崩 *ka(ki)-kuzu(su)* scratch raw, scratch out
混 *ka(ki)-ma(zeru)* mix, mix up
混機 *kakima(ze)ki* mixer
12 揚 *kakia(ge)* fritters; combing upward
落 *ka(ki)-oto(su)* scrape off (mud); cut off (a head)
集 *ka(ki)-atsu(meru)* rake up, gather up
裂 *ka(ki)-sa(ku)* rend, tear up, scratch and tear up
14 鳴 *ka(ki)-na(rasu)* thrum, strum
摑 *ka(i)-tsuka(mu)* grasp firmly
摘 *ka(i)-tsuma(mu)* summarize
暮 *kaikure* (not) at all
雑 *ka(ki)-ma(zeru)* mix by stirring, mix up
15 撫 *ka(ki)-na(deru)* comb, smooth down
kainade no poor, indifferent
潜 *ka(i)-kugu(ru)* pass through, pass under
16 壊 *ka(ki)-kowa(su)* scratch and ruin
操 *ka(i)-gu(ru)* haul in (a rope); handle (reins)
曇 *ka(ki)-kumo(ru)* be overcast
18 繕 *ka(i)-tsukuro(u)* adjust; put in order; gloss over
23 攫 *kassara(u)* pilfer, filch

11

擄 2257 / J-X / M12674 See **抛** 2113.

摎 2258 / J5977 / M12564 Kō. Kyū. Ryū bind, tie; choke, strangle.

摶 2259 / J5976 / M12642 Tan roll into a ball; strike. *maru(i)* round, circular, spherical. Sen willful; grip. Ten bundle.

摯 2260 / J5975 / M12632 Shi gift, seriousness.

摧 2261 / J5974 / M12609 Sai. *kuda(keru)* break, crumble, be crushed, go to pieces; become familiar. *kuda(ku)* break, smash, crush; pulverize; tax (one's ingenuity); explain simply.

摺 2262 / J4022 / M12647 Shō, Shū fold; rub. *su(ru)* rub; print (on cloth).
4 込 *su(ri)-ko(mu)* rub in
5 本 *surihon* printed book
付 *su(ri)-tsu(keru)* print colors (on cloth, etc.)
付木 *suritsu(ke)gi* (early word for) matches
7 足 *suriashi* shuffling feet, dragging feet
13 鉢 *suribachi* mortar, grinding bowl

摑 2263 / J-X / M12572 Kaku. *tsuka(mu)* catch, seize, grasp, hold, lay hands on. *tsuka(maru)* hang onto, grab onto. *tsuka(maeru)* catch, seize, arrest, capture. *tsuka(maseru)* make (a person) catch hold of, let (a person) grasp; bribe; palm off; impose upon. *tsuka(mi)* handful, grip.
5 出 *tsuka(mi)-da(su)* take out by handfuls
6 合 *tsuka(mi)-a(u)* tussle, grapple
8 取 *tsuka(mi)-to(ru)* snatch off, grasp
拉 *tsuka(mi)-hishi(gu)* crush
所 *tsuka(mi)dokoro* hold, grip
所無 *tsuka(mi)dokoro (no) na(i)* vague, evasive
10 殺 *tsuka(mi)-koro(su)* squeeze to death
11 掛 *tsuka(mi)-ka(karu)* grab at
15 潰 *tsuka(mi)-tsubu(su)* grasp and crush

B **摩** 2264 / J4b60 / M12613′ Ma. *ma(suru)* rub; rub off; polish; grind; graze; scrape; be equal to; be about to reach. *sa(suru)* pat, stroke. *su(ru)* rub, chafe; strike (a match); frost (glass). *su(reru)* rub, chafe, wear; become sophisticated.
4 込 *su(ri)-ko(mu)* rub in
切 *su(ri)-ki(ru) vt* wear out; spend all. *su(ri)-ki(reru) vi* wear out
天楼 *matenrō* skyscraper

5 付 *su(ri)-tsu(keru)* scratch (a match); (dogs) nose (people)
7 利支天 *Marishiten* Buddhist god of war
9 枯 *su(ri)ka(rashi)* serious abrasion, wearing out (of clothes)
11 寄 *su(ri)-yo(ru)* draw near, snuggle up to
12 替 *su(ri)-ka(eru)* secretly substitute
13 滅 *mametsu* wear away, rub down, abrade
17 擦 *masatsu* rubbing, chafing; friction; discord
擦音 *masatsuon* fricative sound

B **擊** 2265/J3762/M12674′ **撃** 2287/J-X/M12800 GEKI. *u(tsu)* attack, defeat, destroy, conquer. *uchi-*, *u(tsu)* strike, hit, beat, knock, slap, punch, thrash, smite; clap (one's hands); beat (a drum); ring (a bell); (clocks) strike; impress, touch; shoot; pound in (a nail); water, sprinkle; braid; play (checkers); till (the soil); temper (a sword); prepare (buckwheat noodles); present (a play); cast (a net); pay (earnest money). *bu(tsu)* strike, beat; tell, speak; address (an audience).
4 方 *u(chi)kata* how to fire (a gun)
止 *u(chi)-to(meru)* kill, bring down (a bird)
7 沈 *gekichin suru* sink a ship
8 退 *gekitai suru* repulse, dislodge, reject, refuse, rebuff
取 *u(chi)-to(ru)* catch, arrest; take possession of; kill
9 柝 *gekitaku* stroke of the clappers
砕 *gekisai suru* defeat (the enemy)
発 *gekihatsu* percussion
10 破 *gekiha suru*, *u(chi)-yabu(ru)* defeat, crush, rout, overthrow; refute
剣 *gekken* fencing
殺 *gekisatsu suru* kill (a person) by shooting
留 *u(chi)-to(meru)* kill, bring down (a bird)
13 滅 *gekimetsu* destruction, annihilation, extermination
鉄 *gekitetsu*, *u(chi)gane* gun hammer
14 摧 *gekisai* crushing, destruction
墜 *gekitsui suru* shoot down
18 懲 *u(chi)-ko(rasu)* punish by whipping
20 攘 *gekijō suru*, repulse, dislodge, reject, refuse, rebuff. *u(chi)-hara(u)* beat off, shake off, sweep off, brush off, drive off, repel, rout

B **摘** 2266/J4526/M12582 TEKI. *tsuma(mu)* pick, pinch; hold in the fingers; summarize. *tsu(mu)* pick, pluck, pull out; trim, clip, nip; gather.
4 切 *tsu(mi)-ki(ru)* pick off; pick all, strip
5 示 *tekishi suru, tekiji suru* point out, give the gist
出 *tekishutsu suru* pick out, take out, extract; expose, point out
7 花 *tekika* thinning out fruit blossoms
8 芽 *tekiga* thinning out buds
果 *tekika* thinning fruit
取 *tsu(mi)-to(ru)* pick, pluck.
tsu(mi)to(ri) picking
取人 *tsu(mi)to(ri)nin* picker
取期 *tsu(mi)to(ri)ki* picking season
9 食 *tsumamigu(i)* picking and eating; eating stealthily
洗 *tsumamiara(i)* washing out spots
草 *tsu(mi)kusa* gathering wild greens
要 *tekiyō* summary, outline
発 *tekihatsu suru* expose, unmask, lay bare, point out
発者 *tekihatsusha* informer, exposer, denunciator
10 破 *tsu(mi)-yabu(ru)* wring off
記 *tekki suru* sum up, summarize
13 載 *tekisai suru* summarize, print an extract
16 録 *tekiroku* summary

12

攪 2267/J3349/M-X See **攪** 2323.

擒 2268/J-X/M12728 See **偣** 265.

撕 2269/J5979/M12705 SHI burst, rend, tear. SEI take in hand, carry.

撈 2270/J597d/M12679 RŌ catch fish.

撻 2271/J5a25/M12774 TATSU whip (someone), strike.

撩 2272/J597c/M12741 RYŌ disorder.

7 乱 *ryōran* profuse blooming

播 2273 J4745 M12747 HA. BAN. HAN. *ma(ku)* plant, sow.

14 種 *hashu* sowing, planting

種期 *hashuki* planting time

B **撲** 2274 J4b50 M12755 BOKU. *u(tsu)* strike, hit, beat, knock, slap, punch, thrash, smite; clap (one's hands); beat (a drum); ring (a bell); (clocks) strike; impress, touch; shoot; pound in (a nail); water, sprinkle; braid; play (checkers); till (the soil); temper (a sword); prepare (buckwheat noodles); present (a play); cast (a net); pay (earnest money). *bu(tsu)* strike, beat; tell, speak; address (an audience). *ha(ru)* slap, strike.

10 倒 *ha(ri)-tao(su)* knock down, floor (a man)

殺 *bokusatsu* clubbing to death

13 滅 *bokumetsu* eradication, destruction, extermination

撓 2275 J597a M12698 TŌ. *tawa(mu) vi* be bent, bend. *tawa(meru) vt* curb, bend. *shina(u)* bend, be pliant, be flexible, be supple; sag. *shiwa(ru)* bend, be pliant. *shio(ru) vt* bend. *ta(meru)* bend, train (branches). *tayu(mu)* slacken one's efforts. *shina(yakana)* pliant, flexible, limber, lithe, graceful. *tawa(wa) ni* heavily. *tawa(yakana)* pliable, flexible, limber.

8 垂 *shinada(reru)* droop, snuggle up to

垂掛 *shinada(re)-ka(karu)* snuggle up to

15 撓 *tawatawa* bending low

撞 2276 J4635 M12717 DŌ. TŌ. *tsu(ku)* thrust, pierce, spear, stab, prick; gore; lunge at; push, poke; strike (a bell); attack; strike (at the heart); brave (a storm); be pungent; strike against; (words) rush (to one's lips).

4 木 *shumoku* wooden bell hammer

木杖 *shumokuzue* crutch; T-headed staff

木形 *shumokugata* T-shape

木鮫 *shumokuzame* hammerhead shark

11 球 *tamatsuki, dōkyū* billiards

12 着 *dōchaku* conflict, inconsistency, contradiction

撰 2277 J4071 M12753 SAN. SEN composing, editing, compiling, selecting. *sen(suru)* write, compose. *era(bu), era(mu)* choose, select; cull out; elect; prefer; decide on.

7 述 *senjutsu* editing, compilation

8 定 *sentei* choice

者 *senja* author

9 食 *e(ri)gu(i)* being choosy in eating

10 修 *senshū* writing, editing

12 集 *senshū* compiling writings; compilation

撚 2278 J4732 M12713 NEN. *yo(ru) vt* twist, twine. *yo(reru)* get twisted, be kinky. *yori* twist, strand. *hine(ru)* twirl, twist, twiddle; wring, wrench; bend (the body); incline (the head); pinch; defeat.

6 糸 *yoriito* twisted thread, twine, yarn

7 戻 *yori (o) modo(su)* untwist, untwine; reunite, be reconciled

10 索 *yorisaku* stranded cable

11 掛 *yori (o) ka(keru)* twist, twine; brace oneself

15 線 *yorisen* stranded wire

撒 2279 J3b35 M12697 SATSU. *ma(ku)* scatter; sprinkle; give (someone) the slip.

4 水 *ma(ki)mizu, sassui, sansui* watering, sprinkling

水夫 *sansuifu* one who sprinkles the streets

水自動車 *sansui jidōsha* water cart, street sprinkler

水車 *sansuisha* water cart, street sprinkler

5 布 *sappu suru* spread, scatter, sprinkle. *sampu* scattering; sprinkling; dispersion

布剤 *sampuzai* disinfecting powder

布薬 *sampuyaku* disinfecting powder

12 散 *ma(ki)-chi(rasu)* scatter about; squander

15 餌 *makie* scattered food; ground bait

B **撤** 2280 J4531 M12726 TETSU. *tes(suru)* withdraw; disarm (a ship); dismantle (a fort); remove, reject, exclude.

5 収 *tesshū* withdrawal

去 *tekkyo* withdrawal, evacuation, removal

6 回 *tekkai suru* withdraw, revoke, retract, relinquish, forgo, repeal
7 却 *tekkyaku* withdrawal, evacuation, removal
兵 *teppei suru* evacuate troops
8 底 *tettei* thoroughness, completion
退 *tettai* withdrawal, evacuation
12 廃 *teppai* abolition, removal

撫 2281 / J496f / M12743 BU. *na(deru)* stroke, pat, smooth down.
3 子 *nadeshiko* a pink
下 *na(de)-o(rosu)* stroke down
上 *na(de)-a(geru)* comb back
4 切 *nadegi(ri)* killing several with one sweep of the sword; a clean sweep
5 付 *na(de)-tsu(keru)* comb down, smooth down. *nadetsu(ke)* smooth hair, flowing hair
付髪 *nadetsu(ke)gami* smooth hair, flowing hair
8 肩 *nadegata* sloping shoulders
育 *buiku* care, tending
9 恤 *bujutsu* relief, aid
11 斬 *nadegi(ri)* killing several with one sweep of the sword; a clean sweep
15 養 *buyō* care, tending

B **撮** 2282 / J3b23 / M12748 SATSU. *tsuma(mu)* pick, pinch; hold in the fingers; summarize. *to(ru)* take (pictures). *tsuma(mi)* knob, (bell) button; pinch (of salt).
4 方 *torikata* way of taking (a photo)
5 出 *tsuma(mi)-da(su)* pick out, drag out, throw out
8 物 *tsumamimono* a relish
取 *tsuma(mi)-to(ru)* pick (apples), pinch off
直 *to(ri)-nao(su)* retake (in photography)
9 食 *tsumamigu(i)* eating with the fingers; eating stealthily; corruption, graft
洗 *tsumamiara(i)* washing out spots
要 *satsuyō* summary, outline, compendium
15 影 *satsuei* photographing
影所 *satsueijo* studio; movie lot

撥 2283 / J597b / M12727 **撓** 2217 / J-X / M-X HATSU. BACHI bone plectrum. *hane(ru)* brush up; reject, exclude, eliminate, skip over; jettison. *hane(kasu)* splash, bespatter.
5 付 *hane-tsu(keru)* refuse, reject, repel, rebuff, turn down
出 *hane-da(su)* eliminate, reject, strike out
6 返 *hane-kae(su)* repulse
7 条 *bane* metal spring
8 物 *hanemono* rejected goods
9 音 *hatsuon* the sound of the *kana* "*n*"
飛 *hane-to(basu)* send (something) flying; spatter, splash
除 *hane-no(keru)* push aside, brush aside
10 荷 *haneni* jetsam; jettisoned cargo; eliminated cargo
11 掛 *hane-ka(keru)* splash, bespatter
釣瓶 *hanetsurube* a well sweep
12 散 *hane-chi(rasu)* splash, splatter
14 銭 *hanesen* commision, squeeze

13

據 2284 / J5a21 / M12839 See 拠 2113.

擇 2285 / J5a24 / M12796 See 択 2082.

擔 2286 / J593f / M12828 See 担 2121.

擊 2287 / J-X / M12800 See 撃 2265.

擧 2288 / J5a29 / M12863 See 挙 2150.

擒 2289 / J5a22 / M12816 KIN *toriko* captive.

擘 2290 / J5a26 / M12835 HAKU tear up.

撼 2291 / J597e / M12775 KAN move.

撿 2292 / J-X / M12779 KEN inspect, check, bind, consider.

擅 2293 / J5a23 / M12790 SEN. *hoshiimama* self-indulgent, wayward, selfish, arbitrary.
11 断 *sendan* arbitrary action
15 権 *senken* exclusive right; despotism

B **擁** 2294 / J4d4a / M12781 YŌ. *yō(suru)* embrace, hug; possess; protect; lead.
5 立 *yōritsu suru* back, support
20 護 *yōgo* protection, defense, assistance; indication
護者 *yōgosha* defender, supporter, advocate

擂 2295 / J5a27 / M12783 RAI. *su(ru)* grind, mash, grate.
5 半 *suriban* fire gong warning of a nearby fire
半鐘 *suribanshō* fire gong warning of a nearby fire
7 身 *surimi* minced meat or fish
9 砕 *su(ri)-kuda(ku)* grind fine, pulverize
10 粉木 *surikogi* pestle
13 鉢 *suribachi* mortar, grinding bowl
15 餌 *surie* ground food

A **操** 2296 / J4160 / M12806 SŌ. *ayatsu(ru)* manipulate, operate, steer; pull strings. *ayado(ru)* tie across (the back). *misao* chastity, virginity, constancy, fidelity, honor.
2 人形 *ayatsu(ri) ningyō* puppet, marionette
6 守 *soshu* constancy, fidelity
行 *sōkō* conduct, deportment
行点 *sōkōten* conduct, deportment
7 作 *sōsa* operation, handling, managing
車 *sōsha* operation (of trains)
車係 *sōshagakari* train dispatcher
車場 *sōshujō* switchyard
8 典 *sōten* drill manual
10 砲 *sōhō* handling of a gun
11 船余地 *sōsen yochi* sea room
舵 *sōda* steering (of a ship)
舵手 *sōdashu* quartermaster
舵室 *sōdashitsu* pilothouse
12 短 *sōtan* curtailed operation
短罷業 *sōtan higyō* slowdown strike
觚 *sōko* literary pursuits
觚会 *sōkokai* literary world
觚者 *sōkosha* journalist, writer
觚界 *sōkokai* literary world
13 業 *sōgyō* operation, work
業率 *sōgyōritsu* percentage of capacity production
業費 *sōgyōhi* operating expenses
業短縮 *sōgyō tanshuku* curtailment of operations
14 練 *sōren* military exercises, drill
16 縦 *sōjū* management, manipulation, piloting, operation, control, maneuvering, driving, steering
縦士 *sōjūshi* pilot; manipulator; wirepuller; manager
縦法 *sōjūhō* manipulation, control
縦者 *sōjūsha* pilot; manipulator; wirepuller; manager

14

擠 2297 / J5a2b / M12848 SEI push aside.

擤 2298 / J-X / M12857 KŌ. KYŌ. *ka(mu)* blow the nose.

擿 2299 / J-X / M12922 TEKI expose, reveal.
9 発 *tekihatsu* expose, unmask, lay bare, point out

擯 2300 / J5a2f / M12880 HIN push (people) back, reject.
5 斥 *hinseki* rejection, exclusion, ostracism; contempt

擣 2301 / J5a2e / M12853 TŌ. *u(tsu)* pound.
6 衣 *toi* pounding cloth to bring out the gloss

擡 2302 / J5a2c / M12851 TAI. DAI *mota(geru)* lift, raise.
16 頭 *taitō suru* raise one's head, come to the fore, become influential, gain power, become famous

擢 2303 / J4527 / M12852 TEKI. TAKU. *nuki(nderu)* excel in, surpass. *nu(ku)* pull out, select.
5 用 *tekiyō suru, takuyō suru* select, choose

擲 2304 / J5a33 / M12893 TEKI. CHAKU. *nagu(ru)* hit, beat, thrash. *nageu(tsu)* give up, abandon; relinquish; resign, renounce; lay aside; lay down.
10 書 *nagu(ri)ga(ki)* scribble
12 弾 *tekidan* grenade

4 心 忄 ⺗ 戈 戶 【手 扌】 14 支 攴 攵 文 斗 斤 方 无 日 曰 月 木 欠 止 歹 殳 毋 比 毛 氏 气 水 氵 ⺢ 火 灬 爪 ⺥ 父 爻 爿 丬 片 牙 牛 犬 犭

擱 2305 / J5a28 / M12892 KAKU lay down, put down.

7 坐 *kakuza* running aground
8 岸 *kakugan suru* run aground
岩 *kakugan suru* run on a sunken rock, run aground
12 筆 *kakuhitsu suru* finish (a letter, article, or book)

B **擦** 2306 / J3b24 / M12862 SATSU. *kosu(ru)* rub, scour, scrub, scratch, scrape, brush. *kosu(reru)* be rubbed. *su(ru)* rub, chafe; strike (a match); frost (glass). *su(reru)* rub, chafe, wear; become sophisticated. *nasu(ru)* rub on, smear; blame another. *kasu(reru), kasu(ru)* graze; squeeze; exploit. *suri* frosted, ground. *-zure* bedsores; sophistication.

4 火 *suribi* fire made by striking a flint; match
込 *su(ri)-ko(mu)* rub in, grind and mix
切 *su(ri)-ki(reru)* wear out. *su(ri)-ki(ru)* cut by rubbing; spend all
5 付 *kosu(ri)-tsu(keru), su(ri)-tsu(keru)* rub on, rub against; strike (a match), rub hard. *nasu(ri)-tsu(keru)* blame another; rub on, smear
半 *suriban* gong fire alarm
6 合 *su(re)-a(u)* rub against, chafe, jostle with, be at variance with, quarrel
8 者 *suremono* sophisticated person
9 枯 *sure(k)ka(rashi), sureka(rashi)* sophisticated person
10 消 *su(ri)-ke(su)* erase, efface
剤 *satsuzai* liniment
剝 *su(ri)-mu(keru) vi* be grazed, be abraded; be chafed. *su(ri)-mu(ku) vt* graze, abrade, chafe
11 疵 *surikizu* marring caused by rubbing
過傷 *sakkashō* abrasion, scratch
12 揉 *su(tta)mo(nda)* quarrel
減 *su(ri)-he(rasu)* wear down, rub off, abrade
落 *su(ri)-oto(su)* rub off, scrape off, file off
違 *su(ri)-chiga(u), su(re)-chiga(u)* pass each other
13 傷 *surikizu* scratch, graze, abrasion. *surekizu* marring caused by rubbing
17 擦 *suresure ni* close by; by a shave; barely. *suresure* unfriendly

B **擬** 2307 / J353c / M12870 GI. *gi(suru)* aim (a gun) at; nominate for office; imitate, mimic; compare. *nazora(eru)* pattern after, imitate, liken to. *ni(seru), nise* sham, counterfeit, forgery, imitation. *magai* imitation, sham.

2 人 *gijin* personification
人化 *gijinka* personification
人法 *gijinhō* personification
4 毛 *gimō* imitation wool
5 古 *giko* imitate the classical styles
古文 *gikobun* classical style
古主義 *giko shugi* classicism
古的 *gikoteki* classical
6 色 *gishoku* protective coloring
死 *gishi* feigning death
似 *giji-* suspected, quasi-, pseudo-, sham
羊皮紙 *giyōhishi* parchment paper
7 作 *gisaku* copying; a copy
兵 *gihei* dummy troops
声 *gisei* onomotopoeia (for sounds)
声法 *giseihō* onomatopoeia
声語 *giseigo* onomatopoetic word
8 物 *magaimono* imitation
宝珠 *giboshi, gibōshu* stone-leek flower, bridge railing-post knob
制 *gisei* legal fiction
制的 *giseiteki* fictitious
制資本 *gisei shihon* fictitious capital
9 革紙 *gikakushi* imitation leather
音 *gion* sound effects, imitation sound, background
音効果 *gion kōka* sound effects, imitation sound, background
10 砲 *gihō* dummy gun
12 装 *gisō* camouflage, disguise
13 戦 *gisen* sham battle
勢 *gisei* bluff, (enemy) deception
14 態 *gitai* onomotopoeia (for actions). *gitai suru* simulate, imitate
態語 *gitaigo* onomotopoetic word
製 *gisei* imitation, forgery, a copy; copying
製弾 *giseidan* blank cartridge
17 壕 *gigō* dummy trench
19 爆弾 *gibakudan* dummy bomb

15

攜 2308 / J-X / M12924 See **携** 2253.

擴 2309 / J5a32 / M12895 See **拡** 2118.

揃 2310 / J5a31 / M12898 SEN *tada(su)* straighten (arrows). *tamo, tama* used in place names.

攅 2311 / J5a39 / M12933 SAN *atsu(maru)* gather, come together, assemble.

擽 2312 / J5a36 / M12919 RYAKU. RAKU. REKI. *kusu(guru)* tickle. *kusugu(ttai)* ticklish; funny.

擺 2313 / J5a34 / M12910 HAI push open.
[11]動 *haidō* oscillation

擾 2314 / J3e71 / M12920 JŌ disturb, throw into confusion.
[7]乱 *jōran* riot, commotion

攀 2315 / J5a35 / M12926 HAN. *yo(jiru)* climb, scale.
[11]梯 *hantei* scaling ladder
[12]登 *yo(ji)-nobo(ru), hanto suru* climb, scale

17

攘 2316 / J5a37 / M12989 JŌ chase away; reject; steal.
[6]夷 *jōi* expulsion of the foreigners
夷論 *jōiron* exclusion policy

18

攝 2317 / J5970 / M13010 See **摂** 2252.

攜 2318 / J5a38 / M13008 See **携** 2253.

19

攤 2319 / J5a3a / M13033 TAN. DAN open; divide; gentle; gamble. *hira(ku)* open.

攣 2320 / J5a3b / M13032 REN crooked, bent.

20

攫 2321 / J5a3c / M13043 KAKU. *sara(u)* carry off, snatch; sweep away, wash away; abduct. *tsuka(mu)* catch, seize, grasp, hold, lay hands on.
[8]取 *kakushu suru* grasp

攪 2322 / J5978 / M13041 KAKU, KŌ disturb, throw into confusion.
[7]乱 *kōran, kakuran* disturbance, agitation
[8]拌 *kōhan suru, kakuhan suru* agitate, stir, whip, beat, churn, mix
拌器 *kakuhanki* agitator, beater, shaker
乳 *kakunyū* churning
乳棒 *kakunyūbō* churn dasher
乳器 *kakunyūki* churn

21

攬 2323 / J5a30 / M13046 RAN hold (in the hand).

RAD. 支 65

Shi or *eda* branch. Also called *jū-mata* (*jū* "ten" plus *mata* "also"). As enclosure: ⻎ *shinyō* or *edanyō*. Nickname: Branch.

A **支** 2324 / J3b59 / M13061 SHI branch. *sasa(eru)* support, maintain, sustain, hold; prop, bolster; check, stem. *tsuka(eru)* be obstructed, be blocked, be stopped up, break down, be choked. *ka(u)* prop up. *sasae* prop, fulcrum. *-Shi-* China.
[3]口 *sasaeguchi* mean criticism of friends
[5]庁 *shichō* government branch office
弁 *shiben* payment, disbursement
出 *shishutsu* expenditure, disbursement
出額 *shishutsugaku* expenditure, disbursement

払 *shihara(u)* pay. *shiharai* payment
払人 *shiharainin* payer
払日 *shiharaibi* payday
払地 *shiharaichi* place of payment
払猶予 *shiharai yūyo* payment postponement
6 那 *Shina* China
那人 *Shinajin* a Chinese
那服 *Shinafuku* Chinese dress
那学 *Shinagaku* Sinology
那事変 *Shina Jihen* the China Incident
那海 *Shinakai* China Sea
那酒 *Shinashu* Chinese wines
那料理 *Shina ryōri* Chinese food
那語 *Shinago* Chinese language
7 言 *sasaegoto* mean criticism
材 *shizai* support, stay, prop
社 *shisha* branch office
局 *shikyoku* branch office
局長 *shikyokuchō* branch manager
8 店 *shiten* branch store, branch office
所 *shisho* branch office, substation
9 度 *shitaku* preparation, arrangements; costume, dress; trousseau
途 *shito* account for the money spent
柱 *shichū* prop, brace, support, fulcrum, underpinning
点 *shiten* fulcrum, bearing
持 *shiji* support, maintenance
持層 *shijisō* supporters
10 流 *shiryū* tributary, branch
脈 *shimyaku* spur, branch, feeder
索 *shisaku* a stay (supporting a mast)
部 *shibu* branch office
部長 *shibuchō* branch manager
配 *shihai* management, control, rule, guidance
配人 *shihainin* manager
配力 *shihairyoku* controlling power, ruling power
配下 *shihaika* under subjection
配民族 *shihai minzoku* master race
配的 *shihaiteki* controlling, dominant
配者 *shihaisha* ruler, administrator
配階級 *shihai kaikyū* ruling class
配層 *shihaisō* the ruling class
配権 *shihaiken* control, supremacy
11 族 *shizoku* branch family; tribe
12 援 *shien* aid, support
給 *shikyū* supply, allowance, payment
13 障 *shishō* obstacle, hindrance; trouble
署 *shisho* branch office, substation
15 廠 *shishō* government branch office
線 *shisen* branch line, spur
19 離滅裂 *shirimetsuretsu* incoherence, inconsistency, disruption

8

攲 2325 / J-X / M13086 Kɪ. *sobada(teru)* prick up (one's ears).

RAD. 支 66

Boku strike. Generally called *to-mata* (the katakana *to* plus *mata* "again"). At right: 攵 *bokunyō, bokuzukuri*, or *no-bun* (like Rad. 67 *bun* but with first stroke changed to katakana *no*). Nickname: Folding Chair.

攴 2326 / J5a3d / M13108 **攵** 2327 / J5a3e / M13109 Boku. Hoku *u(tsu)* hit, strike.

2

攷 2328 / J5a3f / M13111 See **考** 4697.

攸 2329 / J5a40 / M13110 See **收** 675.

3

攸 2330 / J5a41 / M13113 Yū location; far; calm, composed. *tokoro* location, place, circumstances.

B **攻** 2331 / J3936 / M13120 Kō. *se(meru)* attack, assault. *se(me)* attack, offensive.
2 入 *se(me)-i(ru)* invade, raid, rush in to attack, penetrate into
3 口 *se(me)guchi* point of attack
下 *se(me)-kuda(ru)* go down and attack

4 上 *se(me)-nobo(ru)* go up against, attack
手 *se(me)te* assailant, assaulter; attacking force; offensive
込 *se(me)-ko(mu)* attack and invade
太鼓 *se(me)daiko* drum signal for a charge
5 立 *se(me)-ta(teru)* attack incessantly
付 *se(me)-tsu(keru)* fiercely attack
6 伐 *kōbatsu* punitive exhibition
伏 *se(me)-fu(seru)* subdue
防 *kōbō* offense and defense
合 *se(me)-a(u)* attack each other
守 *kōshu* offense and defense; batting and fielding
守同盟 *kōshu dōmei* defensive and offensive alliance
7 囲 *se(me)-kako(mu)* besiege. *kōi* siege
抜 *se(me)-nu(ku)* successfully storm a castle; attack fiercely
究 *kōkyū* investigation, research
8 取 *se(me)-to(ru), kōshu suru* take by storm, capture
具 *semegu* siege engines
9 城 *kōjō* siege
城砲 *kōjōhō* siege gun, siege artillery
10 倦 *se(me)-agu(mu)* become disheartened in conducting a siege
悩 *se(me)-naya(mu)* afflict
11 略 *kōryaku* capture, occupation, invasion
寄 *se(me)-yo(ru), se(me)-yo(seru)* overtake and attack
道具 *se(me)dōgu* weapons of attack, military engines, instrument of warfare
12 落 *se(me)-o(tosu)* take by storm. *kōraku* capturing (a castle)
13 滅 *se(me)-horo(bosu)* attack and overthrow; utterly destroy; subdue
戦 *se(me)-tataka(u)* assault
勢 *kōsei* offensive, aggression
15 撃 *kōgeki suru, se(me)-u(tsu)* attack and crush, cut down. *kōgeki* attack, assault, raid; criticism, denunciation
撃力 *kōgekiryoku* striking power
撃的 *kōgekiteki* aggressive, offensive
撃者 *kōgekisha* invader, aggressor, assailant
撃軍 *kōgekigun* attacking army
撃開始時間 *kōgeki kaishi jikan* zero hour
撃戦 *kōgekisen* aggressive war
撃機 *kōgekiki* attack plane
20 懸 *se(me)-ka(keru), se(me)-ka(karu)* approach to attack

A 改 2332 / J327e / M13114 KAI. *arata(meru)* change, modify, convert; renew, renovate; reform, mend, rectify; amend, revise, improve; examine, inspect, search. *arata(maru)* be renewed, be renovated; change, be modified, be revised; be improved, be reformed; be ceremonious. *arata(mete)* again, anew, formally.

4 元 *kaigen* change of the era
心 *kaishin* conversion; reform
心者 *kaishinsha* convert
5 令 *kairei suru* countermand an order
号 *kaigō* changing a title; changing an era name
札 *kaisatsu* ticket examination
札口 *kaisatsuguchi* ticket gate
正 *arata(me)-tada(su)* revise. *kaisei* revision, amendment; improvement, amelioration
正標準訳 *Kaisei Hyōjun'yaku* Revised Standard Version
6 行 *kaigyō suru* begin new line
印 *kaiin* changing seals
任 *kainin* replacement
名 *kaimei* changing a name
7 作 *kaisaku* adaptation (of a story)
良 *kairyō* improvement, reform
良服 *kairyōfuku* utility suit
良者 *kairyōsha* reformer
8 姓 *kaisei* changing a family name
版 *kaihan* revised edition
定 *kaitei* reform
易 *kaieki* renewing | proselytism
宗 *kaishū* conversion (to another faith);
宗者 *kaishūsha* convert; proselyte
9 変 *kaihen* change, innovation, reformation, transformation
頁 *kaipēji, kaiketsu* new page break
革 *kaikaku* reform, reformation
革案 *kaikakuan* reform measure
造 *kaizō* remodeling, reconstruction
造説 *kaizōsetsu* cataclysm theory
訂 *kaitei* revision
訂版 *kaiteiban* revised edition
訂訳 *Kaiteiyaku* Revised Version
訂増補 *kaitei-zōho* revision and enlargement
10 修 *kaishū* repair, improvement, (riparian) works

悛 *kaishun* penitence, repentance
悟 *kaigo* repentance
称 *kaishō suru* rename, retitle
党 *kaitō* changing sides (in politics)
進 *kaishin* reform; progress
進的 *kaishinteki* progressive
進党 *kaishintō* progressive party
11 組 *kaiso* reorganization
悪 *kaiaku* change for the worse, deterioration
過 *kaika* correcting a mistake
過遷善 *kaika-senzen* correcting a mistake and doing good
訳 *kaiyaku* retranslation, revision
訳者 *kaiyakusha* revisers
12 廃 *kaihai* reorganization, change
善 *kaizen* reform, improvement, amelioration
葬 *kaisō* reburial
装 *kaisō* remodeling, modernization
13 新 *kaishin* renovation, innovation, reformation
14 選 *kaisen* re-election
暦 *kaireki* new year; calendar reform
15 編 *kaihen* reorganization
鋳 *kaichū* reminting; recasting
16 築 *kaichiku* rebuilding, remodeling
18 竄 *kaizan* falsification, mutilation, alteration; correction, amendment, revision
題 *kaidai* retitling

5

A **放** 2333 / J4a7c / M13133 Hō. *hana(tsu)* set free, release, fire, shoot; circulate (rumors); emit, give out; set fire to; banish. *hana(su)* let go, release, disengage; liberate. *hana(reru)* free oneself from. *hō(ru)* throw, hurl, toss; give up; neglect; let alone. *ho(ttarakasu)* neglect, leave undone, lay aside.

2 入 *hana(shi)-i(reru)* let loose in, turn loose in
3 下 *hōka* throwing down; juggling
上 *hō(ri)-a(geru)* hurl up
4 心 *hōshin* absentmindedness; peace of mind
水 *hōsui* drainage, discharge
水路 *hōsuiro* drainage canal
水管 *hōsuikan* drainpipe
火 *hōka* arson, incendiarism
火犯 *hōkahan* arson, incendiarism
火狂 *hōkakyō* pyromaniac
5 生 *hōjō* setting (birds) free
付 *hō(ri)-tsu(keru)* hurl against
去 *hana(chi)-sa(ru)* set free
出 *hō(ri)-da(su)* throw out; dismiss, fire; throw up (a job). *hōshutsu* release, discharge, exhaust
6 血 *hōketsu* bloodletting
任 *hōnin* nonintervention
光 *hōkō* emission of light
7 言 *hōgen* irresponsible talk
尿 *hōnyō* urination
屁 *hōhi* breaking wind, passing gas
佚 *hōitsu* self-indulgence, debauchery
吟 *hōgin suru* sing loudly
技 *hana(re)waza* a grand work
8 念 *hōnen* relaxation, ease
免 *hōmen* release, acquittal
物線 *hōbutsusen* parabola
牧 *hōboku* grazing, pasturage
牧地 *hōbokuchi* pasture, grazing land
送 *hōsō* broadcasting
送局 *hōsōkyoku* broadcasting station
送員 *hōsōin* radio or TV announcer
送記者 *hōsō kisha* radio or TV newsman
9 逐 *hōchiku suru* expel, banish, deport; dismiss
神 *hōshin* freedom from care. *hōshin suru* be dumbfounded
胆 *hōtan* fearlessness
10 馬 *hana(re)uma* runaway horse
逸 *hōitsu* self-indulgence, debauchery
埒 *hōratsu* dissipation, debauchery
校 *hōkō* expulsion from school
恣 *hōshi* self-indulgence
帰 *hana(shi)-kae(raseru)* release and send back
流 *hōryū suru* stock (with fish), let loose
流瓶 *hōryūbin* drift bottle
浪 *hōrō* wandering
浪者 *hōrōsha* wanderer
浪罪 *hōrōzai* vagrancy
浪癖 *hōrōheki* wanderlust
射 *hōsha* emanation, radiation, emission, discharge
射学 *hōshagaku* radiology
射性 *hōshasei* radioactive
射性物質 *hōshasei busshitsu* radioactive materials
射性同位元素 *hōshasei dōi genso* radioisotope

射能 *hōshanō* radioactivity, radiation
射道路 *hōsha dōro* radial roads
射雲 *hōshaun* radioactive cloud
射線 *hōshasen* radiation
11 鳥 *hōchō* setting birds free; birds to be set free
12 遣 *hana(chi)-ya(ru)* let loose; banish, purge
散 *hōsan* radiation; emanation; diffusion; evaporation
13 痰 *hōtan* spitting around
肆 *hōshi* self-indulgence
飼 *hana(chi)ga(i), hana(shi)ga(i)* grazing, pasturage
棄 *hōki* abandonment, resignation, renunciation, waiving
置 *hōchi suru* leave alone, neglect, let lie
電 *hōden* electric discharge
資 *hōshi* investment
14 漫 *hōman* recklessness, laxity, indiscretion
歌 *hōka* loud singing
歌高吟 *hōka kōgin* loud singing
15 論 *hōron* harrangue
談 *hōdan* irresponsible talk; chat
養 *hōyō* outdoor feeding, turning loose
課 *hōka* class dismissal
課後 *hōkago* after school
熱 *hōnetsu* radiation; radiant heat
熱器 *hōnetsuki* radiator
蕩 *hōtō* dissipation, prodigality
蕩者 *hōtōsha* a prodigal, a profligate
蕩家 *hōtōka* a prodigal, a profligate
蕩息子 *hōtō musuko* prodigal son
16 縦 *hōjū, hōshō* self-indulgence, debauchery
17 擲 *hōteki suru* abandon, give up, neglect
18 題 *-hōdai* at will, to one's heart's content
24 鷹 *hōyō* falconry, hawking

5

A **故** 2334 / J384e / M13161 Ko. *yue* reason, cause; circumstances. *yue ni* therefore, consequently. *kotosara ni* especially, intentionally. *furu(i)* old, aged, ancient, antiquated; stale, threadbare; outmoded, obsolete article. *ko-* the late.
2 人 *kojin* the deceased; an old friend. *furubito* the ancients; elderly persons; longtime residents
3 山 *kozan* birthplace, one's old home
5 旧 *kokyū* old acquaintance
主 *koshu* former master
6 老 *korō* old people, seniors
宅 *kotaku* old home, former home
7 里 *furusato, kori* hometown, birthplace
8 国 *kokoku* one's native land; an old country
物 *kobutsu* old article, secondhand article; old tradition
知 *kochi* an old acquaintance; an old intimacy
制 *kosei* former laws; the old system
京 *kokyō* old capital
実 *kojitsu* ancient customs
事 *koji* origin; historical fact; tradition
事来歴 *koji-raireki* origin and history; particulars
9 俗 *kozoku* old customs
10 紙 *koshi* wastepaper
殺 *kosatsu* premeditated murder
郷 *kokyō* birthplace, homeland, hometown
家 *koka* an old family
11 道 *kodō* the old morality; an old road
習 *koshū* old custom
12 買 *kobai* buying stolen goods
智 *kochi* predecessor's wisdom
13 意 *koi* intention, purpose; bad faith
障 *koshō* hindrance, obstacle; difficulty; breakdown; accident; objection
障車 *koshōsha* disabled car
15 縁 *koen* old relationships, old acquaintences
16 親 *koshin* deceased parent; old friend

A **政** 2335 / J402f / M13135 Shō. Sei. *matsurigoto* government, rule.
4 友 *seiyū* political friend
5 庁 *seichō* government office
令 *seirei* government ordinance, cabinet order
6 争 *seisō* political controversy
7 見 *seiken* political views
局 *seikyoku* political situation
体 *seitai* form of government, polity

4 心忄⺗戈戸手扌支【支攵】5 文斗斤方无日曰月木欠止歹殳毋比毛氏气水氵氺火灬爪爫父爻爿丬片牙牛犬犭

社 *seisha* political association
8 所 *Mandokoro* shogunate offices
況 *seikyō* political situation
事 *seiji* political affairs; administrative business
府 *seifu* the government, the administration
府当局 *seifu tōkyoku* government authorities
府案 *seifuan* administration measure
府党 *seifutō* government party
府側 *seifugawa* the administration
府間 *seifukan no* intergovernmental
府筋 *seifu suji* government circles
治 *seiji* government, administration, politics
治力 *seijiryoku* political power, political influence
治上 *seijijō no* political
治史 *seijishi* political history
治犯 *seijihan* political offense; political offender
治犯人 *seiji hannin* political offender
治地理 *seiji chiri* political geography
治休戦 *seiji kyūsen* political truce
治的 *seijiteki* political
治学 *seijigaku* political science, politics
治屋 *seijiya* professional politician, small politician
治革命 *seiji kakumei* political revolution
治家 *seijika* politician, statesman
治哲学 *seiji tetsugaku* political philosophy
治運動 *seiji undō* political campaign, political agitation
治道徳 *seiji dōtoku* political morality
治結社 *seiji kessha* political organization
治熱 *seiji netsu* political excitement
治警察 *seiji keisatsu* political police
9 派 *seiha* political faction, political party
変 *seihen* political change, change of government
客 *seikyaku, seikaku* politician
界 *seikai* political world, political circles
10 党 *seitō* political party
党内閣 *seitō naikaku* party cabinet
党史 *seitōshi* history of political parties
党政治 *seitō seiji* party government
党員 *seitōin* members of a political party
11 道 *seidō* administration, government, rule
情 *seijō* political conditions
商 *seishō* businessman with political ties
経学 *seikeigaku* politics and economics
経科 *seikeika* department of economics and political science
務 *seimu* political affairs, affairs of state
務次官 *seimu-jikan* parliamentary vice-minister
務官 *seimukan* parliamentary official
教 *seikyō* government and education; Church and State
教分離 *seikyō bunri* separation of Church and State, disestablishment of a church
教条約 *seikyōjōyaku* concordat, treaty between Church and State
略 *seiryaku* statecraft, political strategy; expedient
略家 *seiryakuka* political tactician
略婚 *seiryakukon* marriage of expedience
略結婚 *seiryaku kekkon* marriage of expedience
12 策 *seisaku* policy; political measures
13 戦 *seisen* political campaign
14 綱 *seikō* political creed; political platform
15 論 *seiron* politics, political discussion
敵 *seiteki* political opponent
弊 *seihei* political evils
権 *seiken* political power; reins of government, administration
権欲 *seiken'yoku* ambition for political power
談 *seidan* a talk on politics or a law case
談演説 *seidan enzetsu* political speech, campaign speech

6

效 2336 / J5a43 / M13186 See **効** 535.

B **敏** 2337 / J4952 / M13202′ **敏** 2339 / J-X / M13217 BIN agility; alertness.
hashiko(i), hashi(k)ko(i) clever; agile.
3 才 *binsai* outstanding talent
9 速 *binsoku* quickness, agility, activity
活 *binkatsu* quickness, agility, activity

11 達 *bintatsu* wisdom
捷 *binshō* agility, promptness, shrewdness
12 腕 *binwan* ability, capacity
腕家 *binwanka* able person
13 感 *binkan* sensitivity, susceptibility
感性 *binkansei* sensitivity, susceptibility

7

敕 2338 / J5a45 / M13225 See **勅** 540.

敏 2339 / J-X / M13217 See **敏** 2337.

敍 2340 / J5a46 / M13205 **敘** 2341 / J5a47 / M13206 See **叙** 681.

敖 2342 / J5a44 / M13226 Gō play; proud, arrogant. *aso(bu)* amuse oneself, play.

A **敗** 2343 / J4754 / M13227 HAI defeat, reversal. *yabu(ru) vt* defeat. *yabu(reru) vi* be defeated.
3 亡 *haibō* defeat, reversal, rout
5 北 *haiboku* defeat, reversal, rout
6 色 *haishoku* omens of defeat
因 *haiin* cause of defeat
死 *haishi suru* be defeated and killed
兆 *haichō* sign of defeat, signs of failure
血症 *haiketsushō* blood poisoning
7 走 *haisō* rout, flight
兵 *haihei* routed troops
8 退 *haitai* defeat, retreat
者 *haisha* the defeated
9 屋 *haioku* dilapidated cottage
軍 *haigun* defeated army
10 将 *haishō* defeated general
衄 *haijiku* defeat in war
残 *haizan* survival after defeat; decline; ruin. *haizan no* defeated, vanquished
残兵 *haizanhei* troop remnants, deserting troops
12 訴 *haiso* lost case; losing a case
報 *haihō* news of defeat
13 滅 *haimetsu* crushing defeat
戦 *haisen* defeat, a lost battle
戦投手 *haisen tōshu* losing pitcher
15 敵 *haiteki* vanquished enemy

A **救** 2344 / J355f / M13221 KYŪ. *suku(u)* save, help, rescue, relieve (suffering); redeem, reclaim. *suku(i)* salvation, help, rescue, relief.
3 上 *suku(i)-a(geru)* pick up and rescue, save from
与 *kyūyo* granting salvation
4 手 *suku(i) (no) te* helping hand
5 主 *suku(i)nushi* rescuer; Saviour
民 *kyūmin* helping and saving the people
出 *suku(i)-da(su)* help out of (trouble), extricate, rescue from, reclaim (from a life of sin). *kyūshutsu* deliverance, rescue
出者 *kyūshutsusha* deliverer
世 *kyūsei* salvation of the world
世主 *Kyūseishu* the Saviour, the Messiah
世軍 *Kyūseigun* Salvation Army
6 米 *kyūmai, suku(i)mai* relief rice
7 助 *kyūjo* rescue, relief, aid
助米 *kyūjomai* relief rice
助法 *kyujoho* lifesaving
助者 *kyūjosha* rescuer, deliverer, saviour
助信号 *kyūjo shingō* SOS, distress signal
助船 *kyūjosen* lifeboat, rescue boat, salvage boat
助隊 *kyujotai* rescue party
助網 *kyūjoami* streetcar fender; safety net
8 国 *kyūkoku* national salvation
治 *kyūji* cure, remedy
治策 *kyūjisaku* a cure
命 *kyūmei* lifesaving
命服 *kyūmeifuku* life preserver
命具 *kyūmeigu* life preserver
命帯 *kyūmeitai* life belt
命浮標 *kyūmei fuhyō* life buoy
命索 *kyūmeisaku* lifeline
命袋 *kyūmeibukuro* life buoy
命艇 *kyūmeitei* lifeboat
命網 *kyūmeimō* life net
9 神 *suku(i) (no) kami* a special providence
荒 *kyūkō* famine relief
恤 *kyūjutsu* relief, aid
恤金 *kyūjutsukin* relief fund
急 *kyūkyū* deliverance in an emergency
急処置 *kyūkyū shochi* applying first aid
急車 *kyūkyūsha* ambulance
急法 *kyūkyūhō* first aid
急策 *kyūkyūsaku* emergency measures

急箱 *kyūkyūbako* first-aid kit
急薬 *kyūkyūyaku* first-aid medicines
11 船 *suku(i)bune* rescue vessel; lifeboat
貧 *kyūhin* poor relief
貧院 *kyūhin'in* poorhouse
済 *kyūsai* relief, aid; emancipation; salvation; rescue
済金 *kyūsaikin* relief fund
済者 *kyūsaisha* deliverer, savior
済事業 *kyūsai jigyō* relief work
済策 *kyūsaisaku* relief measure
済資金 *kyūsai shikin* relief fund
済論 *kyūsairon* soteriology
12 援 *kyūen* relief, rescue, reinforcement
援米 *kyūemmai* relief rice
援投手 *kyūen tōshu* relief pitcher
援金 *kyūenkin* contribution
15 霊 *kyūrei* salvation, soulwinning
霊者 *kyūreisha* soulwinner
18 難 *kyūnan* rescue, salvage
難作業 *kyūnan sagyō* relief or salvage work
20 護 *kyūgo* relief, rescue
護米 *kyūgomai* relief rice
護所 *kyūgosho* first-aid station
護事業 *kyūgo jigyō* relief work
護班 *kyūgohan* relief squad, rescue party

A **教** 2345 / J3635 / M13213 **教** 2346 / J-X / M13212 KYŌ faith. *oshi(eru)* teach, give lessons; inform; coach. *oso(waru)* learn, be taught, take lessons in. *oshi(e)* teaching; lesson, precept; doctrine, tenet; creed, faith; religion; philosophy.

3 子 *oshi(e)go* pupil, disciple
4 方 *oshi(e)kata* method of teaching
父 *kyōfu* godfather, sponsor; church fathers
込 *oshi(e)-ko(mu)* inculcate, implant
区 *kyōku* parish, district, diocese
区民 *kyōkumin* parishioner
化 *kyōka* culture, education; civilization; evangelization
化団体 *kyōka dantai* social service or religious organization
化事業 *kyōka jigyō* cultural or educational work
5 母 *kyōbo* godmother, sponsor
生 *kyōsei* student teacher
示 *kyōji* instruction, teaching
主 *kyōshu* founder of a religion; spiritual ⌈head
本 *kyōhon* textbook
外別伝 *kyōge betsuden* Buddhist esoteric teaching
令 *kyōrei* teaching and commanding; teaching; rules
令集 *kyōreishū* papal decretals
6 団 *kyōdan* religious body, a religious order
旨 *kyōshi* tenets, doctrine
会 *kyōkai* church; church building
会外 *kyōkaigai* outside the church
会史 *kyōkaishi* church history
会合同 *kyōkai gōdō* church union
会法 *kyōkaihō* canon law
会員 *kyōkaiin* church member
会堂 *kyōkaidō* church, chapel, cathedral, tabernacle
会暦 *kyōkaireki* church calendar
7 材 *kyōzai* teaching materials
役者 *kyōekisha* clergy, pastor, minister
戒 *kyōkai* exhortation, preaching
戒師 *kyōkaishi* prison chaplain, prison missionary
8 知 *oshi(e)-shi(raseru)* inform, teach
官 *kyōkan* educational official; public school teacher; national university professor
具 *kyōgu* teaching tools, teaching aids
典 *kyōten* canon, sacred scriptures of a religion; teaching guide
学 *kyōgaku* education, educational affairs
法 *kyōhō* religion, cult
法師 *kyōhōshi* religious teacher, scribe, rabbi
育 *kyōiku* education
育上 *kyōikujō* educationally speaking
育会 *kyōikukai* educational association
育年齢 *kyōiku nenrei* educational age
育法 *kyōikuhō* teaching methods
育的 *kyōikuteki* educational, cultural
育学 *kyōikugaku* pedagogy, education
育者 *kyōikusha* educator
育制度 *kyōiku seido* educational system
育委員 *kyōiku iin* school-board member
育委員会 *kyōiku iinkai* school board; board of education
育使節団 *kyōiku shisetsudan* educational mission
育界 *kyōikukai* educational circles
育映画 *kyōiku eiga* educational film

育勅語 *Kyōiku Chokugo* Imperial Rescript on Education
育家 *kyōikuka* educator
育費 *kyōikuhi* school expenses; educational fund
育測定 *kyōiku sokutei* educational measurements
育程度 *kyōiku teido* educational standards
育漢字 *kyōiku kanji* the characters required to be learned by elementary-school students
育総監 *Kyōiku Sōkan* Inspector-General of Military Education
育課程 *kyōiku katei* course, curriculum
育機関 *kyōiku kikan* educational institutions
9 祖 *kyōso* founder or head of a sect
室 *kyōshitsu* classroom
草 *oshi(e)gusa* lesson, moral
派 *kyoha* sect, denomination
派神道 *Kyōhu Shintō* Sectarian Shintō
則 *kyōsoku* teaching rules; school rules
則本 *kyōsokubon* music practice book, technical textbook
科 *kyōka* lesson; course, curriculum
科目 *kyōkamoku* studies in school
科用図書 *kyōkayō tosho* textbooks, schoolbooks
科書 *kyōkasho* textbook
皇 *kyōō, kyōkō* pope
皇大使 *kyōkō taishi* papal nuncio
皇公使 *kyōkō kōshi* papal nuncio
皇庁 *Kyōkōchō* Vatican
皇令 *kyōkōrei* papal decretals
皇制度 *Kyōkō Seido* Papacy
皇冠 *kyōkōkan* the Pope's tiara
皇無謬説 *kyōkō mubyūsetsu* papal infallibility
皇領 *Kyōkōryō* the Papal states
皇職位 *kyōkō shokui* the Papacy
10 徒 *kyōto* believer, adherent
案 *kyōan* teaching program, teaching plan
書 *kyōsho* (presidential) message
師 *kyōshi* teacher, minister, rabbi, missionary
師用 *kyōshiyō* for the teacher
唆 *kyōsa* instigation
唆者 *kyōsasha* instigator
唆罪 *kyōsazai* crime of instigation
訓 *kyōkun* lesson, precept, moral, instruction
訓的 *kyōkunteki* instructive, edifying
訓書 *kyōkunsho* books of instruction
員 *kyōin* teacher; faculty
員免許状 *kyōin menkyojō* teacher's certificate
員検定 *kyōin kentei* teacher certification
員養成所 *kyōin yōseijo* teacher training school
11 規 *kyōki* church regulations, church discipline
務 *kyōmu* school affairs; religious affairs
務係 *kyōmugakari* registrar
習 *kyōshū* training, instruction
習所 *kyōshūjo* training institution
授 *kyōju* teaching; professor
授団 *kyōjudan* faculty
授会 *kyōjukai* faculty meeting
授法 *kyōjuhō* teaching methods
理 *kyōri* doctrine, tenet, creed, dogma
理上 *kyōrijō (no)* doctrinal
理学 *kyōrigaku* dogmatics
理要綱 *kyōri yōkō* catechism
理問答 *kyōri mondō* catechism
理問答書 *kyōri mondōsho* catechism
理論 *kyōriron* dogmatics
12 場 *kyōjō* classroom
程 *kyōtei* teaching method
13 義 *kyōgi* doctrine, tenet, creed, dogma
義的 *kyōgiteki* doctrinal
義学 *kyōgigaku* dogmatics
14 練 *kyōren* military drill
説 *kyōsetsu* dogma
導 *oshi(e)-michibi(ku)* instruct and guide. *kyōdō* instruction, training
誨 *kyōkai* exhortation, preaching
誨師 *kyōkaishi* prison chaplain, prison missionary
15 権 *kyōken* educational authority; ecclesiastical authority; the church
課 *kyōka* a course; a textbook
範 *kyōhan* teaching methods; model teaching; textbooks
養 *kyōyō* culture, education, refinement
養学科 *kyōyō gakka* liberal arts
養学部 *kyōyō gakubu* liberal arts school
養費 *kyōyōhi* cultural expenses
16 壇 *kyōdan* rostrum, platform
諭 *oshi(e)-sato(su)* instruct. *kyōyu* instruction; instructor, teacher
頭 *kyōtō* head teacher; vice principal

憲 *kyōken* church constitution
18 鞭 *kyōben* a teacher's whip; teaching school
職 *kyōshoku* teaching; ministry, priesthood, clergy
職者 *kyōshokusha* minister, clergyman, teacher
職員 *kyōshokuin* faculty, teachers
20 籍 *kyōseki* church membership

8

敝 2347 / J5a49 / M13245 HEI. BEI tear; break; tire; lose; humble prefix. *yabu(reru)* tear, rip.

敞 2348 / J5a48 / M13246 SHŌ high (building or site); high and flat.

敦 2349 / J4658 / M13276 TON industry; kindliness.
6 朴 *tomboku na* honest and homely
9 厚 *tonkō* simplicity, naïveté
16 樸 *tomboku na* honest and homely

B **敢** 2350 / J343a / M13260 KAN. *ae(nai)* sad, tragic, pitiful; frail, feeble; fleeting; unkind. *ae(te)* positively, daringly.
6 行 *kankō* execution, decisive action
死 *kanshi* determination to die
争 *kansō* courageous fight
9 為 *kan'i* daring, bravery
12 然 *kanzen to* boldly, fearlessly, bravely
13 戦 *kansen suru* fight to the death
18 闘 *kantō suru* fight bravely. *kantō* determined fighting
闘賞 *Kantōshō* Fighting Spirit Award in sumo

A **敬** 2351 / J3749 / M13285' KEI. KYŌ. *kei(suru)* respect, honor, revere. *uyama(u)* respect, honor, revere, venerate.
4 天 *keiten* reverence of heaven
弔 *keichō* condolence
5 白 *Keihaku* Sincerely yours
礼 *keirei* bow, salutation, salute
6 仰 *keigyō suru* respect, revere
老 *keirō* respect for the aged
7 承 *keishō suru* hear, listen reverently
8 拝 *keihai* reverent worship
服 *keifuku suru* admire and respect
具 *keigu* Sincerely yours
忠 *keichū* loyal service
事 *keiji* respectful service
9 昵 *keijitsu* respect and intimacy
神 *keishin* godliness, reverence, piety
重 *keichō suru* respect, revere
10 称 *keishō* title of honor
虔 *keiken* piety, devotion, reverence
虔主義 *keiken shugi* pietism
12 遠 *keien suru* keep (a person) at a distance; give (a batter) a walk; kick (a person) upstairs
13 愛 *keiai* respect and affection
意 *keii* respect, honor
14 語 *keigo* honorific word
慕 *keibo* love and respect
17 謙 *keiken* piety, devotion
20 譲 *keijō suru* respect; take a humble attitude

A **散** 2352 / J3b36 / M13265 SAN. *san(jiru), san(zuru)* scatter, disperse; spend, squander; dispel, dissipate, chase away. *bara(su)* pull down; take apart; sell (to get rid of); liquidate; defeat; expose. *chi(ru)* fall, scatter, be scattered, be shed; disperse; (rumor) spreads; run, spread, blur. *chi(rasu)* scatter; disperse; dissipate (fog); dispel; take down or loosen (the hair); rout; distribute (handbills); distract (attention); splash on (a pattern). *chi(rakasu)* scatter (around), disarrange, leave untidy. *chi(rakaru)* lie scattered around, be in disorder. *chi(rabaru)* scatter, be scattered (about), lie around. *chi(rashi)* handbill, leaflet. *bara* bulk. *-san* (medicinal) powder.
3 大 *sandai* dilation
4 太鼓 *chi(rashi)daiko* the drum signalling the end of a play
水 *sansui* water sprinkling
水車 *sansuisha* street sprinkler
切 *zangiri* regular haircut (in contrast to the topknot style)
切頭 *zangiri atama* cropped head
文 *sambun* prose
文的 *sambunteki* prosaic
文詩 *sambunshi* poetry in prose
5 去 *chi(ri)-sa(ru)* scatter, be scattered
失 *sanshitsu suru* be scattered and lost
布 *sampu* scattering; sprinkling; dispersion
広告 *chi(rashi) kōkoku* handbill, leaflet

6 会 *sankai* adjournment
光 *sankō* diffused light
在 *sanzai suru* be scattered, straggle, be dotted with
7 見 *sanken suru* be seen here and there
佚 *san'itsu suru* get scattered and lost
乱 *chi(ri)-mida(reru)* disperse in all directions, be scattered around. *sanran* dispersion, scattering
兵 *sampei* skirmisher
兵壕 *sampeigō* trench (in warfare)
8 歩 *sampo* walk, stroll
9 発 *sampatsu* scattered shots; scattered hits
発的 *sampatsuteki* sporadic
10 逸 *san'itsu suru* get scattered and lost
紛 *chi(ri)-maga(u)* scatter around
財 *sanzai* expense, wasted of money, extravagance, spree
剤 *sanzai* powdered medicine
書 *chi(rashi)ga(ki)* irregular writing; writing on alternate lines; writing on odds and ends of paper
荷 *barani* bulk cargo
華 *sange* Buddhist flower-scattering ceremony. *sange suru* die a heroic death
11 娼 *sanshō* scattered prostitution, streetwalker
掛 *chi(ri)-ka(karu)* begin to fall; fall on (something)
票 *sampyō* scattered votes
12 開 *sankai* deployment (of skirmishers)
弾 *sandan, baradama* shot, case shot
散 *sanzan, sanza(ppara)* severely, harshly, terribly; thoroughly, utterly. *chi(ri)chi(ri), chi(ri)ji(ri)* sporadically, separately
策 *sansaku* walk, stroll
落 *sanraku suru* fall and scatter, fall and disappear
13 蓮華 *chi(ri)renge* porcelain spoon
14 漫 *samman na* vague, desultory, distracted
銭 *barasen* small change
模様 *chi(rashi) moyō* scattered pattern
髪 *chi(rashi)gami* hair disheveled or let down. *sampatsu* disheveled hair; hair-cutting
髪屋 *sampatsuya* barber
15 敷 *chi(ri)-shi(ku)* lie scattered
16 積 *barazu(mi)* bulk shipment
薬 *san'yaku* powdered medicine. *chi(rashi)gusuri* a cure-all medicine

9

A 数 2353 / J3f74 / M13319 數 2356 / J5a4b / M13363 SAKU. SOKU. SU. SŪ

strength; fate; law; numbers, figures; numerical. *kazo(eru)* count, calculate, enumerate. *kazu* number, figure. *kazu(naranu)* insignificant, humble. *shibashiba* often, frequently. *sū-* several.

2 人 *sūnin* several people
十 *sūjū* scores (of people)
丁 *sūchō* several blocks
3 子 *kazu(no)ko* herring roe
万 *sūman* tens of thousands
千 *sūsen* thousands
上 *kazo(e)-a(geru)* count up, enumerate
ヶ所 *sūkasho* several places
4 込 *kazo(e)-ko(mu)* number among
切 *kazo(e)-ki(renai), kazo(e)-ki(renu)* countless, incalculable
分間 *sūfunkan* a few minutes
日 *sūjitsu* a few days, several days
日中 *sūjitsuchū* within a few days
日来 *sūjitsurai* for the last few days
日後 *sūjitsugo* after several days
日間 *sūjitsukan* several days
5 立 *kazo(e)-ta(teru)* count up, enumerate
犯 *sūhan* several offenses
占 *kazuurana(i)* divining with numbers
台 *sūdai* several vehicles
6 行 *sūgyō, sūkō* several lines
回 *sūkai* several times
次 *sūji* again and again
列 *sūretsu* progression, series (in math)
百 *sūhyaku* several hundred
年 *sūnen* several years. *kazo(e)doshi* Japanese age
名 *sūmei* several people
多 *amata, sūta* many, multitude. *kazu ō(ku)* in great numbers
地点 *sūchiten* several places
字 *sūji* figure, numeral; tabular matter
字上 *sūjijō* numerically, arithmetically
8 知 *kazushi(renu)* numberless
取 *kazuto(ri)* counting game; tally; scorer
刻 *sūkoku* several hours
直 *kazo(e)-nao(su)* recount
限無 *kazukagi(ri)na(ku)* numberless

4 心 忄 小 戈 戸 手 扌 支 【攴 攵】9 文 斗 斤 方 无 日 曰 月 木 欠 止 歹 殳 毋 比 毛 氏 气 水 氵 氺 火 灬 爪 爫 父 爻 爿 丬 片 牙 牛 犬 犭

4 心忄⺗戈戸手扌支【支攵】文斗斤方无日曰月木欠止歹殳毋比毛氏气水氵氺火灬爪⺥父爻爿丬片牙牛犬犭

奇 *suki* fancy, artistic taste; refined arts. colorfulness; varied fortunes. *sūki na* unlucky
奇屋 *sukiya* tea-ceremony arbor
学 *sūgaku* mathematics
学上 *sūgakujō* mathematically
学的 *sūgakuteki* mathematical
学者 *sūgakusha* mathematician
学家 *sūgakuka* mathematician
9 度 *sūdo* several times
秒 *sūbyō* several seconds
10 個 *sūko* several (objects)
倍 *sūbai* several times as (large)
値 *sūchi* numerical value
珠 *juzu, zuzu* a string of beads; a (Buddhist) rosary
11 章 *sūshō* several chapters
寄 *suki* fancy, artistic taste; refined arts.
寄者 *sukisha* lover of, person with a taste for; lecherous person
寄屋 *sukiya* tea-ceremony parlor; detached tea-ceremony house
理 *sūri* mathematical principle; mathematics
理上 *sūrijō* mathematically
理的 *sūriteki* mathematical
理派経済学 *sūriha keizaigaku* mathematical economics
12 渡 *kazo(e)-wata(su)* count out (things)
詞 *sūshi* numeral
違 *kazo(e)-chiga(eru)* count wrong, miscalculate
量 *sūryō* quantity, volume
等 *sūtō* very, much, exceedingly
葉 *sūyō* several (sheets, photos, etc.)
13 損 *kazo(e)-soko(nau)* count wrong
数 *kazukazu* many
14 滴 *sūteki* a few drops
語 *sūgo* a few words
歌 *kazo(e)uta* a number song
箇 *sūko* several (objects)
種 *sūshu* several kinds
種類 *sūshurui* several kinds
15 億 *sūoku* hundreds of millions
16 頭 *sūtō* several head (of cattle)
18 難 *kazo(e)gata(i)* countless

10

敲 2354 J5a4a M13337 敲 2355 J-X M13338 Kō. *tata(ku)* strike, beat, hit, knock, slap, thrash, rap, pat, pound, maul; clap (the hands); sound out (views); criticize.

11

數 2356 J5a4b M13363 See 数 2353.

B敷 2357 J495f M13359′ 敷 2358 J-X M13359 Fu. *shi(ku)* spread; pave; sit (on a cushion); lay (a railway); gravel (a road); promulgate; draw up. *shi(ki)* (flower) stand; deposit money.
5 瓦 *shi(ki)gawara* floor tile
皮 *shi(ki)gawa* fur cushion, bearskin, etc.
石 *shi(ki)ishi* paving stone, flagstone, pavement
写 *shi(ki)utsu(shi)* tracing
台 *shi(ki)dai* step or platform in an entranceway; slatted removable floor in an entrance hall
布 *shikifu* (bed) sheet, sheeting
布団 *shikibuton* the lower futon
6 地 *shikichi* site
8 金 *shikikin* deposit money
居 *shikii* threshold, doorsill
延 *fuen* amplification, development, enlargement
板 *shi(ki)ita* floor boards
物 *shikimono* carpet, rug, matting, cushion
9 革 *shi(ki)gawa* inner sole
衍 *fuen* amplification, development, enlargement
砂 *shi(ki)zuna* sand for spreading (on the yard)
10 島 *Shikishima* (ancient) Japan
島道 *Shikishima (no) michi* the art of Japanese poetry
11 設 *fusetsu* construction, laying (a railroad, mine, etc.)
設水雷 *fusetsu suirai* submarine mine
設権 *fusetsuken* construction rights
設機雷 *fusetsu kirai* submarine mine
13 詰 *shi(ki)-tsu(meru)* cover over, spread all over
煉瓦 *shi(ki)renga* paving bricks
蒲団 *shi(ki)buton* the lower futon
14 網 *shi(ki)ami* a square fish net lowered on a pivoted pole
銀 *shi(ki)gin* deposit money
17 藁 *shi(ki)wara* litter, stall straw

A **敵** 2359 / J4528 / M13354 TEKI enemy, foe, opponent. *teki(suru)* turn against, fight against, antagonize, be a match for. *kataki* enemy; competitor; revenge.

4 手 *tekishu* opponent, adversary; the hand of the enemy
中 *tekichū* midst of the enemy
5 本主義 *tekihonshugi* make-believe, feint, pretense
6 地 *tekichi* enemy territory
同士 *katakidōshi* mutual enemies
7 役 *katakiyaku, tekiyaku* villain's role
状 *tekijō* the condition of the enemy
兵 *tekihei* enemy troops
対 *tekitai* hostility, antagonism, contention
対心 *tekitaishin* hostility, enmity, animosity
対行為 *tekitai kōi* hostilities, hostile act
対行動 *tekitai kōdō* hostilities, hostile act
対的 *tekitaiteki* hostile
8 味方 *teki-mikata* friend or foe; opposing forces
国 *tekikoku, tekkoku* enemy's country
国語 *tekikokugo* the enemy's language
性 *tekisei* enemy character
性国 *tekiseikoku* hostile country
性者 *tekiseisha* person of enemy character
性貨物 *tekisei kamotsu* goods destined for the enemy
9 城 *tekijō* enemy castle
陣 *tekijin* enemy camp, enemy position
持 *katakimo(chi)* a person subject to revenge
軍 *tekigun* enemy army
背 *tekihai* the enemy's rear
前 *tekizen* before the enemy
前上陸 *tekizen jōriku* landing in face of the enemy
10 匪 *tekihi* enemy bandit
将 *tekishō* enemy general
討 *katakiu(chi)* vengeance, revenge
11 側 *tekigawa* enemy side
状 *tekijō* enemy movements
視 *tekishi suru* regard with hostility; show enmity toward. *tekishi* hostility, enmity
船 *tekisen* enemy ship
産 *tekisan* enemy property
貨 *tekika* enemy goods
12 弾 *tekidan* enemy bullets
塁 *tekirui* enemy fort
営 *tekiei* enemy camp
13 意 *tekii* hostility, animosity
勢 *tekizei* enemy strength
愾 *tekigai* hostility, enmity, animosity
愾心 *tekigaishin* hostility, enmity, animosity
14 旗 *tekiki, tekki* enemy flag
15 影 *tekiei* signs of the enemy
16 機 *tekiki, tekki* enemy plane
18 騎 *tekiki, tekki* enemy cavalry
20 艦 *tekikan, tekkan* enemy ship
艦隊 *tekikantai* enemy fleet
22 襲 *tekishū* enemy attack

12

A **整** 2360 / J4030 / M13394 **整** 2361 / J X / M13393 SEI arranging. *totono(eru)* prepare, arrange; fill (orders); supply; raise (money); put in order, tidy up, adjust (clothes); regulate; settle; purchase. *totono(u)* be prepared, be arranged, be in order, be adjusted, be well regulated; be settled.

6 地 *seichi* land readjustment; soil preparation
列 *seiretsu* array, lineup, parade
合 *seigo* adjustment, coordination; integration; consolidation; conformity (in geology)
7 形 *seikei* plastic surgery
形手術 *seikei shujutsu* plastic surgery operation
形外科 *seikei geka* plastic surgery
8 枝 *seishi* pruning
版 *seihan* composing type
直 *totono(e)-nao(su)* rearrange, prepare again
9 除 *seijo* divisibility
10 骨 *seikotsu* osteopathy, bone-setting
流 *seiryū* rectification, commutation; detection
流子 *seiryūshi* commutator
流器 *seiryūki* rectifier (in electricity)
11 理 *seiri* arrangement, adjustment, regulation, consolidation; liquidation, reorganization; retrenchment, curtailment, shake-up, abridgement
理部 *seiribu* (newspaper) make-up department

4 心忄⺌戈戸手扌支【攴 11 攵】文斗斤方无日曰月木欠止歹殳毋比毛氏气水氵氺火灬爪⺥父爻爿丬片牙牛犬犭

理箱 *seiribako* filing cabinet; card file
理箪笥 *seiridansu* filing cabinet
[12] 備 *seibi* complete equipment; consolidation
然 *seizen(taru)* orderly, regular, systematic, trim, accurate, well-organized
[13] 数 *seisū* integer, whole number
頓 *seiton* (good) order, arrangement, regulation
[15] 調 *seichō* head oarsman, stroke

13

斂 2362 / J5a4c / M13407 REN tighten, stiffen.

14

斃 2363 / J5a4d / M13417 HEI. *tao(reru), tao(su)* fall, collapse, drop; break down, die, succumb to; fall senseless; be ruined; have a bad debt.
[6] 死 *heishi suru* fall dead, die

RAD. 文 67

Bun literature. Nickname: Literary.

A 文 2364 / J4a38 / M13450 MON $\frac{1}{100}$ of a *hyakume*; crest; figures; = BUN. BUN literary text, production, composition; sentence; style; literature, art; the pen; civil affairs; decoration; characters; elegance. *aya* design; figure of speech; plan, plot. *fumi* letter, note. *-mon* size (of tabi).
[2] 人 *bunjin* a writer, the literati
[3] 才 *bunsai* literary talent
士 *bunshi* a writer, the literati
士連 *bunshiren* the literati
[4] 月 *fuzuki, fumizuki* seventh lunar month
中 *bunchū* in the document
化 *bunka* culture, civilization
化人 *bunkajin* cultured person
化日 *Bunka (no) Hi* Culture Day, November 3
化史 *bunkashi* cultural history
化生活 *bunka seikatsu* cultural life
化村 *bunka mura* modern village
化住宅 *bunka jūtaku* modern dwelling
化的 *bunkateki* cultural
化国 *bunkakoku* civilized country
化国家 *bunka kokka* cultured nation
化映画 *bunka eiga* cultural film
化財 *bunkazai* cultural assets
化祭 *bunkasai* cultural festival
化遺産 *bunka isan* cultural inheritance
化勲章 *bunka kunshō* culture medal
[5] 目 *ayame* designs, patterns; distinction
民 *bummin* civilian
句 *monku* phrase, expression; complaint; objection; excuse
句無 *monkuna(shi)* perfect, satisfactory
[6] 臣 *bunshin* civil official
机 *fuzukue* book table
名 *bummei* literary fame
字 *moji, monji* letter, character; writings
字板 *mojiban* dial, clock face
字通 *mojidō(ri) no* literal
字盤 *mojiban* dial, clock face
[7] 言 *bungen, mongon* phrase, expression
身 *irezumi, bunshin* tattooing
体 *buntai* literary style
芸 *bungei* liberal arts, literary arts, learning
芸批評 *bungei hihyō* literary criticism
芸的 *bungeiteki* literary
芸界 *bungeikai* art and literary circles
芸家 *bungeika* literary man
芸復興 *bungei fukkō* renaissance, revival of learning
芸欄 *bungeiran* literary column
[8] 例 *bunrei* model sentence; model for writing
林 *bunrin* literary circle; collection of literary works
物 *bumbutsu* civilization
盲 *mommō* ignorance, illiteracy
采 *bunsai* rhetorical flourishes; beautiful coloring
具 *bungu* writing materials, stationery
苑 *bun'en* literary world; anthology
典 *bunten* grammar book
事 *bunji* civil affairs, literary matters
房具 *bumbōgu* writing materials, stationery

房具屋 *bumbōguya* stationer
治 *bunchi, bunji* civilian administration
治的 *bunchiteki* civilian
官 *bunkan* civil official
官優位 *bunkan yūi* superiority of civil (to military) service
武 *bumbu* literary and military arts, the sword and the pen
武百官 *bumbu hyakkan* civil and military officials
法 *bumpō* grammar
法上 *bumpōjō* grammatically
法家 *bumpōka* grammarian
明 *bummei* civilization, culture
明人 *bummeijin* civilized people
明史 *bummeishi* history of civilization
明国 *bummeikoku* civilized country
明病 *bummeibyō* diseases of civilization, sexually transmitted disease
明開化 *bummei-kaika* civilization and enlightenment
学 *bungaku* literature
学士 *Bungakushi* Bachelor of Arts
学上 *bungakujō no* literary
学史 *bungakushi* history of literature
学会 *bungakukai* literary society
学作品 *bungaku sakuhin* literary production
学的 *bungakuteki* literary
学者 *bungakusha* a member of the literati, scholar
学界 *bungakukai* literary world
学書 *bungakusho* a literary work
学博士 *Bungaku Hakushi* Doctor of Literature, PhD
学賞 *bungakushō* literary award
9 面 *bummen* contents of a letter
通 *buntsū* correspondence, communication
相 *Bunshō* Education Minister
科 *bunka* department of literature; literary course
政 *bunsei* cultural administration
段 *bundan* paragraph
10 庫 *bunko* hand box, bookcase; library, archives
脈 *bummyaku* context
案 *bun'an* draft
華 *bunka* glory of civilization; beauty in prose
弱 *bunjaku* frivolity, effeminacy
書 *bunsho, monjo* document, writing, letter, note, archives, literature, correspondence, records
書伝道 *bunshō dendō* literature evangelism
部 *mombu* education
部大臣 *Mombu Daijin* Education Minister
部省 *Mombushō* Ministry of Education
11 鳥 *bunchō* Java sparrow, paddy bird
道 *bundō* learning
運 *bun'un* cultural progress, enlightenment
彩 *bunsai* rhetorical flourishes
責 *bunseki* responsibility for the wording of an article
理 *bunri* context, line of thought; science and literature
理学 *bunrigaku* liberal arts and science
教 *bunkyō* education, culture
教府 *bunkyō (no) fu* office of education
章 *bunshō* sentence; article, composition; style
章体 *bunshōtai* literary style
章家 *bunshōka* good writer
章道 *bunshōdō* art of writing
章語 *bunshōgo* literary language
12 博 *Bunhaku* Doctor of Literature
棚 *fudana* bookshelf
詞 *bunshi* the words of a sentence
集 *bunshū* anthology, prose collection
無 *monna(shi) no* penniless
筆 *bumpitsu* writing, literary art
筆家 *bumpitsuka* member of the literati
筆業 *bumpitsugyō* literary profession
13 雅 *bunga* elegance, grace (in literature)
辞 *bunji* the words of a sentence
飾 *bunshoku* rhetorical flourishes
義 *bungi* meaning (of a passage)
意 *bun'i* meaning (of a passage)
勢 *bunsei* force (in writing)
楽 *bunraku* puppet theatre, *Bunraku*
献 *bunken* literature; records, documents; bibliography
献学 *bunkengaku* bibliography
14 様 *mon'yō* design; figure of speech; plan, plot
豪 *bungō* literary master
墨 *bumboku* literature; documents; (written) characters
選 *bunsen* anthology; typesetting
選工 *bunsenkō* typesetter

4 心 忄 ⺗ 戈 戸 手 扌 支 攵 攴 【文】 斗 斤 方 无 日 曰 月 木 欠 止 歹 殳 毋 比 毛 氏 气 水 氵 氺 火 灬 爪 爫 父 爻 爿 丬 片 牙 牛 犬 犭

語 *bungo* literary language
語文 *bungobun* literary language
語体 *bungotai* literary style
15 談 *bundan* literary talk
箱 *fubako* letter box, dispatch box
範 *bumpan* model composition
勲 *bunkun* distinguished civil services
16 壇 *bundan* literary circles; literary column
18 鎮 *bunchin* paperweight
題 *bundai* theme, subject
19 藻 *bunsō* rhetorical flourishes; literary talent

3

孝 2365 / J555d / M13453 Nonstandard for 学 1294.

4

B 斉 2366 / J4046 / M13454 齊 7084 / J736e / M48560 SEI. *hito(shii)* equal, similar. *totono(eru)* prepare, arrange, fill (orders); supply; raise (money); put in order, tidy up, adjust (clothes); regulate; settle; purchase.

1 一 *seiitsu* equality; good order
6 列 *seiretsu* array, lineup, parade
10 射 *seisha* volley, fusillade
11 唱 *seishō suru* sing in unison

6

斎 2367 / J-X / M13460 See 斎 2368.

7

B 斎 2368 / J3a58 / M13467 齋 7085 / J6637 / M48565 斎 2367 / J-X / M13460

SAI, SEI Buddhist food; room. *imi* religious purification. *itsu(ku)* worship, enshrine. *i(mu)* abhor, avoid, taboo, shun. *toki* meals exchanged by parishioners and priests. *hito(shii)* equal, similar, like, equivalent.

4 日 *saijitsu* fast day. *i(mi)bi* unlucky day; death anniversary; purification and fast day
5 主 *saishu* master of (religious) ceremonies; chief priestess of Ise
7 戒 *saikai* purification
8 服 *saifuku* priestly vestments
9 垣 *igaki, i(mi)gaki* shrine fence
10 部 *Imbe, Imibe* ancient (Shinto) priestly family
宮 *saigū* the (ancient) imperial princesses serving at the Ise shrine
11 祭 *itsu(ki)-matsu(ru)* deify and worship
12 場 *saijō* place of ceremony, place of a funeral service

8

斌 2369 / J494c / M13468 HIN pleasing balance between figure and background. *uruwa(shii)* beautiful, lively, fine.

斐 2370 / J4865 / M13469 HI beautiful; patterned.

斑 2371 / J4843 / M13470 HAN spot. *buchi, madara, hadare* spots, specks, patches. *fu* spot, speck, speckle, stripe, streak. *mura* unevenness, inequality; blemishes; capriciousness.

2 入 *fui(ri)* spotted, mottled, variegated
4 犬 *madara inu, buchi inu* a spotted dog
5 白 *hampaku* grayish color
6 気 *muraki* uneven temper; whim
7 条 *hanjō* mottled streaks
8 岩 *hangan* porphyry
9 点 *hanten* spot, speck
10 馬 *shimauma* zebra
消 *muragi(e)* show remaining in spots
紋 *hammon* spot, speck
11 雪 *madara yuki, hadare yuki* snow remaining in spots
15 蝶 *madarachō* monarch butterfly

11

齋 2372 / J-X / M-X See 齋 7086.

RAD. 斗 68

To or *to masu* (a unit of measure). Also, at right, *tozukuri*. Nickname: Dots and Cross.

B **斗** 2373 / J454d / M13489 To ten *shō* (1 *to* = 4.8 gallons (U.S.) = 18 liters); a one-*to* measure; saké ladle; the Big Dipper. *-bakari* approximately; only, merely, alone; degree; almost, practically; absorbed in; continue doing; just now; be about to do; be ready for; have no alternative; now or never. (Also non-standard for 鬪 6418 and pronounced Tō.)

9 南 *tonan* south of the Big Dipper; the whole world
10 酒 *toshu* a *to* of saké; a big supply of saké

6

A **料** 2374 / J4e41 / M13501 Ryō charge, rate, fee; allowance; materials; measuring.

6 地 *ryōchi* preserve, estate
8 金 *ryōkin* charge, rate, fee, fare
9 亭 *ryōtei* restaurant
10 紙 *ryōshi* paper, writing paper
11 率 *ryōritsu* tariff, rates
理 *ryōri* cooking, cuisine, dish, food; fare; management; administration
理人 *ryōrinin* cook
理役 *ryōriyaku* chef
理店 *ryōriten* restaurant
理屋 *ryōriya* restaurant
理室 *ryōrishitsu* kitchen
理番 *ryōriban* cook
12 飲 *ryōin* food and drink
18 簡 *ryōken* idea, thought, intention, inclination, motive, decision; discretion; forgiveness; toleration

7

斛 2375 / J5a4f / M13508 Koku a measure, 10 *to* (see Weights and Measures).

B **斜** 2376 / J3c50 / M13509 Sha slanting, oblique. *hasu, hasukai* slanting, diagonal, oblique. *nana(me)* slanting, diagonal, oblique, askew; unpleasant, disagreeable. *nana(menarazu)* exceedingly.

4 日 *shajitsu* westering sun
辺 *shahen* oblique side, leg (of a triangle), hypotenuse
方形 *shahōkei* rhombus
5 平面 *shaheimen* oblique plane
6 向 *nana(me)-mu(kō) ni* diagonally across
交 *hasukai* diagonal, oblique
列駐車 *sharetsuchūsha* angle parking
7 角 *shakaku* oblique angle, bevel
9 面 *shamen* slope, inclined plane
前 *nana(me)mae* advancing obliquely
巷 *shakō* red-light district
11 眼 *shagan* strabismus, squint (cross-eye or walleye)
視 *shashi, yabunira(mi)* strabismus, squint (cross-eye or walleye)
視眼 *shashigan* squint eye (cross-eye or walleye)
陽 *shayō* setting sun
陽族 *shayōzoku* declining upper class
陽階級 *shayō kaikyū* declining upper class
12 塔 *shatō* Leaning Tower (of Pisa)
堤 *shatei* sloping bank
歯車 *nana(me)haguruma* bevel gear
13 照 *shashō* rays of the setting sun
14 構 *sha(ni)kama(eru)* take one's stance
15 線 *shasen* oblique line
影 *shaei* slanting shadow
16 頸 *shakei* wryneck

9

斟 2377 / J5a50 / M13517 Shin dip (water); estimate.

10 酌 *shinshaku suru* consider, allow for, guess; dip (water); add some and cut out some
12 量 *shinryō* conjecture

10

斡 2378 / J3036 / M13522 Atsu go around; rule, administer.

11 旋 *assen* kind offices, mediation

斡人 *assennin* mediator, agent, go-between

斡料 *assenryō* agent's charge

斡業 *assengyō* agency; intermediary

RAD. 斤 69

Kin (a Japanese pound) or *ono* axe. On right: *onozukuri*. Nickname: Axe.

B **斤** 2379 / J3654 / M13534 KIN *kin* 1 $\frac{1}{3}$ pounds, catty; axe.

5 目 *kimme* weight in *kin* or catties

12 量 *kinryō* weight

1

B **斥** 2380 / J404d / M13535 **斥** 2381 / J-X / M-X SEKI. *shirizo(ku)* *vi* retreat, recede, withdraw. *shirizo(keru)* *vt* repel, repulse, reject.

2 力 *sekiryoku* repulsion, repulsive force

10 候 *sekkō* scout, patrol, spy

候兵 *sekkōhei* reconnoitering party

候隊 *sekkōtai* reconnoitering party

4

斧 2382 / J4960 / M13539 FU. *ono* axe, hatchet.

5 正 *fusei* correction, revision

7 足類 *fusokurui* bivalves

13 鉞 *fuetsu* axe; battle-axe; curtailment

5

斫 2383 / J5a51 / M13548 SHAKU strike; cut; large gap; foolish. *ki(ru)* cut, slice.

7

斬 2384 / J3b42 / M13555 ZAN beheading. *ki(ru)* kill; cut. *-kiri* murder.

5 処 *zan (ni) sho(suru)* behead

6 死 *kiriji(ni)* fighting to death (with swords)

合 *kiria(i)* crossing swords, fighting with swords

奸 *zankan* slaying the wicked

奸状 *zankanjō* assassin's written vindication

8 苛 *ki(ri)-saina(mu)* hack to pieces

9 首 *zanshu* decapitation. *ki(ri)kubi* decapitation; a severed head

首刑 *zanshukei* execution by decapitation

10 殺 *zansatsu suru* slay, kill

11 得 *ki(ri)doku* no retribution for a samurai killing a commoner

据 *ki(ri)-su(eru)* cut down an enemy

掛 *ki(ri)-ka(karu)* stab at, attack (with a sword)

笥 *ki(ri)-saina(mu)* hack to pieces

12 割 *ki(ri)-sa(ku), ki(ri)-wa(ru)* cut up

13 新 *zanshin* novelty, originality, newness

罪 *zanzai* sword execution, beheading

14 嘖 *ki(ri)-saina(mu)* hack to pieces

髪 *zampatsu* cutting off the topknot

A **断** 2385 / J4347 / M13557 **斷** 2388 / J5a52 / M13611 DAN decision, judgment; cutting. *dan(jiru), dan(zuru)* conclude, judge. *ta(tsu)* sever, cut off; shut off, interrupt; abstain from; eradicate; suppress. *kotowa(ru)* decline, refuse; apologize; give notice; warn; dismiss; prohibit. *dan(jite)* positively, decidedly; by no means. *kotowa(ri)* refusal; excuse, apology; notice, warning; permission; prohibition. *(o)kotowa(ri)* not allowed.

3 口 *dankō* fracture (in gems)

4 日 *ta(chi)bi* fast day; Lent

水 *dansui* suspension of water supply, no water

切 *ta(chi)-ki(ru)* cut off; disconnect; ⌈block

片 *dampen* fragment, piece, bit, crumb, odds and ends, shred, scrap

片的 *dampenteki* fragmentary, piecemeal

5 乎 *danko* firm, decisive, resolute, determined, drastic, conclusive

去 *ta(chi)-sa(ru)* cut off, do away with

末魔 *dammatsuma* the hour of death

6 行 *dankō* decisive action, resolute enforcement

交 *dankō* rupture of relations
7 言 *dangen* (positive) assertion, declaration, affirmation
状 *kotowa(ri)jō* a letter turning down a proposition
8 金 *dankin* warm friendship
固 *danko* firm, decisive, resolute, determined, drastic, conclusive
物 *ta(chi)mono* food abstained from, forbidden food
念 *dannen* abandomment, relinquishment, despairing of
定 *dantei* decision, conclusion
岸 *dangan* rugged beach, sea cliff
郊競走 *dankōkyōsō* cross-country race
9 食 *danjiki* fast, fasting
除 *ta(chi)-nozo(ku)* cut off, do away with
面 *dammen* section; cross section
面図 *dammenzu* cross-section drawing
10 案 *dan'an* decision, conclusion
書 *kotowa(ri)ga(ki)* proviso, explanatory note
酒 *danshu* giving up alcohol
酒友会 *Danshu Tomo (no) Kai* Alcoholics Anonymous
11 崖 *dangai* precipice, cliff
章 *danshō* literary fragment
断呼 *dandanko* firm, decisive, resolute, determined, drastic, conclusive
12 絶 *danzetsu* extinction, rupture, severance
割 *ta(chi)-wa(ru)* cut open, cut apart
落 *ta(chi)-oto(su)* snap off
雲 *dan'un* scattered clouds
然 *danzen* resolutely, decisively, positively, absolutely
裁 *dansai* cutting (paper, etc.)
裁機 *dansaiki* printer's paper cutter
13 滅 *ta(chi)-horo(bosu)* put to death, cut off, consume
腸 *danchō* heartbreak
罪 *danzai* conviction, condemnation; decapitation
想 *dansō* random thoughts
続 *danzoku* stopping and starting
続的 *danzokuteki* intermittent, fitful, off and on
続器 *danzokuki* a make-and-break device
14 層 *dansō* (geological) fault, shift, slip
種 *danshu* castration, sterilization
髪 *dampatsu* haircutting; bobbed hair
截 *dansetsu suru* cut
15 線 *dansen* disconection, broken wire
篇 *dampen* short piece of writing, unfinished book
16 頭 *dantō* decapitation
頭台 *dantōdai* guillotine
18 簡 *dankan* fragmentary documents

8

斯 2386 / J3b5b / M13563 SHI this. *ka(karu)* such. *ka(ku), ka(kute), ka(kushite)* thus, in this way. *kō* thus, so, like this, in this way. *kō to* a word filling in awkward spaces in conversation. *ka(no)* that.
6 如 *ka(ku) no goto(ku)* thus. *ka(ku) no goto(ki)* such (a)
7 言 *kō i(u)* this kind of, such
9 界 *shikai* this field (of medicine), this circle (of experts), this society
11 道 *shido* profession, line, craft; field
許 *kakubaka(ri), kabaka(ri)* this much, so much, (not) more
12 程 *kahodo* this much, so much, (not) more
斯 *kōkō, kakukaku, kakkaku* so and so, such and such
14 様 *kayō na* such
様斯様 *kayōkayō no* such and such

9

A **新** 2387 / J3f37 / M13572 SHIN newness, novelty. *atara(shii)* new, novel, fresh, recent, modern. *atara(shigaru)* be fond of. *ara(ta) ni suru* make new. *ara-, ara(tana)* new, fresh, novel. *ara, sara* newness; something new. *nii-* new. *shin-* new, modern, novel, fresh, neo-.
2 人 *shinjin* new face; new star; man of advanced ideas
人類 *shinjinrui* new breed (of young person)
刀 *shintō* new sword; modern sword
入 *shinnyū* new, incoming, entering
入生 *shinnyūsei* new student
入者 *shinnyūsha* newcomer
3 工夫 *shinkufū* new device, new gadget
大陸 *shintairiku* new continent; New World
4 手 *arate* new move, new form, new trick; reinforcements

4 心忄⺗戈戸手扌支攴攵文斗【斤】9 方无日曰月木欠止歹殳毋比毛氏气水氵氺火灬爪爫父爻爿丬片牙牛犬犭

月 *shingetsu* new moon, crescent moon
毛 *shimmō* virgin wool
天地 *shintenchi* the new world
中間層 *shinchūkansō* the new middle class
仏 *arabotoke, shimbotoke* recently buried person
仏教 *Shimbukkyō* the New Buddhism
[5]田 *arata, shinden* new rice field
札 *shinsatsu* new paper money
主 *shinshu* new ruler
令 *shinrei* new decree
古 *shinko* new and old
出 *shinshutsu* new appearance
本 *shimpon* a new publication; a brand-new book
平民 *shinheimin* the former *eta* class
旧 *shinkyū* new and old; incoming and outgoing
旧両約聖書 *Shinkyū Ryōyaku Seisho* the Old and New Testaments, the full Bible
刊 *shinkan* new publication
刊書 *shinkansho* new publication
刊紹介 *shinkan shōkai* book review
世代 *shinsedai* new era
世界 *shinsekai* new world; the New World
世帯 *shinjotai, arajotai* a new home
生 *shinsei* new life; new birth, rebirth, regeneration; reincarnation
生児 *shinseiji* newborn baby
生命 *shinseimei* new life
生面 *shinseimen* new phase
生活 *shinseikatsu* new life
生活運動 *shinseikatsu undō* new-life movement
生涯 *shinshōgai* new life, new career
[6]米 *shimmai* new rice; novice, beginner, newcomer
式 *shinshiki* a new form; a new formula
曲 *shinkyoku* new tune, new musical composition
任 *shinnin* new appointment
地 *shinchi* reclaimed land; newly-laid-out land; red light district
宅 *shintaku* new residence; a new branch family
安値 *shin'yasune* new low, all-time low
仮名遣 *shinkanazukai* the new *kana* spelling
字 *shinji* characters made in Japan
字体 *shinjitai* a new form of a character
年 *Shinnen* New Year
年御歌会 *Shinnen Outakai* New Year's Imperial Poetry Party
[7]車 *shinsha* new car
作 *shinsaku* a new production, a new book
役 *shin'yaku* new post
村 *shinson* new village
形 *shingata* new style
邸 *shintei* new residence
兵 *shimpei* raw recruit, new conscript
声 *shinsei* a new note
来 *shinrai* newcomer
局面 *shinkyokumen* new aspect
体 *shintai* new style
体制 *shintaisei* new system, new structure
体詩 *shintaishi* new poetic style; new-style poem
[8]居 *shinkyo* new residence, new home
店 *shimmise* new store
例 *shinrei* new example, new precedent
味 *shimmi* fresh taste, freshness; novelty
宗教 *shinshūkyo* new religion
所帯 *shinjotai, arajotai* a new home
枕 *niimakura* the bridal bed
法 *shimpō* new method; new law
注 *shinchū* new commentary
服 *shimpuku* new clothes
奇 *shinki* novelty, originality
芽 *shimme* sprout, bud, shoot
妻 *niizuma* bride, young wife
学期 *shingakki* new school term
知識 *shinchishiki* up-to-date knowledge, advanced ideas
版 *shimpan* new publication
郎 *shinrō* bridegroom
郎新婦 *shinrō shimpu* the bride and bridegroom
参 *shinzan* newcomer, novice
参者 *shinzanmono* newcomer, novice
事実 *shinjijitsu* new facts
事業 *shinjigyō* new enterprise
制 *shinsei* new system
制大学 *shinsei daigaku* new-system university
制中学校 *shinsei chūgakkō* new-system junior high school
制高等学校 *shinsei kōtōgakkō* new-system senior high school

9 風 *shimpū* new style
香 *shinko, shinkō* pickled vegetables, (Japanese) pickles
柄 *shingara* new pattern
派 *shimpa* new school (of thought); new-style kabuki
秋 *shinshū* early autumn
院 *shin'in* a newly abdicated emperor
盆 *niibon* first *Bon* festival after death
前 *shimmae, shimmai* novice, beginner, newcomer
客 *shinkyaku* new visitor; new customer
星 *shinsei* a nova; a new star; a new movie star
茶 *shincha* first tea of the season
草 *niikusa* new grass growth
型 *shingata* new style
紀元 *shinkigen* new era, new stage
面目 *shimmemmoku* new phase, new aspect
思想 *shinshisō* new idea
造 *shinzō* new construction; new wife; single young lady
造語 *shinzōgo* newly coined word
約 *Shin'yaku* New Testament
約聖書 *Shin'yaku Seisho* the New Testament
訂 *shintei* new revision
訂版 *shinteiban* newly revised edition
政 *shinsei* new government regime
政権 *shinseiken* the new administration
春 *Shinshun* the New Year
春早早 *shinshun sōsō* early in the New Year
品 *shimpin* new article
品同様 *shimpin dōyō* looking like new
発見 *shinhakken* new discovery
発足 *shinhossoku* new start
発明 *shinhatsumei* recent invention
発意 *shimbochi, shimbotchi* novice, neophyte
10 馬 *shimba* new horse, unbroken horse
進 *shinshin no* rising (scholar), up-and-coming (leader)
造 *shinzō, shinzo* new construction; new wife; single young lady
値 *shinne* new price
修 *shinshū* new compilation
涼 *shinryō* beginning of the cool season
株 *shinkabu* new stock, new shares
酒 *shinshu* new saké, new brew
都 *shinto* new capital
家 *shinke* newly established family
案 *shin'an* new idea, new design, novelty, new departure
党 *shintō* new political party
書 *shinsho* new book
荷 *shinni* new supply, fresh goods
時代 *shinjidai* new era
秩序 *shinchitsujo* new order
高値 *shintakane* new high, all-time high
記録 *shinkiroku* new record
陳代謝 *shinchintaisha* renewal, replacement, regeneration; metabolism
帰朝者 *shinkichōsha* Japanese just returned from abroad
11 道 *shindō* new road
婦 *shimpu* bride
粧 *shinshō* new garb; new equipment; new binding; new finish
訳 *shin'yaku* new translation, new version
設 *shinsetsu* new organization
釈 *shinshaku* new interpretation
著 *shincho* new book
雪 *shinsetsu* fresh snow
患者 *shinkanja* a new case, a new patient
規 *shinki* novelty, originality, new, newly created
規蒔直 *shinki makinao(shi)* starting afresh
教 *Shinkyō* Protestantism
教国 *Shinkyōkoku* Protestant countries
教徒 *Shinkyōto* a Protestant
婚 *shinkon* new marriage; newly married
婚夫婦 *shinkon fūfu* newlyweds
婚生活 *shinkon seikatsu* early married life
婚旅行 *shinkon ryokō* honeymoon
12 装 *shinsō* new garb; new equipment; new binding; new finish
報 *shimpō* new information, news
開 *shinkai* newly opened, reclaimed
開地 *shinkaichi* reclaimed land, newly opened land
着 *shinchaku* new arrivals
着荷 *shinchakuni* newly arrived goods
13 殿 *shinden* new palace; new mansion
解 *shinkai* new interpretation
路 *shinro* new road
義 *shingi* new meaning
傾向 *shinkeikō* new trend
14 暦 *shinreki* new calendar; solar calendar
選 *shinsen* newly elected; newly compiled

4 心 忄 ⺗ 戈 戸 手 扌 支 攴 攵 文 斗 14【斤】 方 无 日 曰 月 木 欠 止 歹 殳 毋 比 毛 氏 气 水 氵 氺 火 灬 爪 爫 父 爻 爿 丬 片 牙 牛 犬 犭

種 *shinshu* new species
緑 *shinryoku* fresh verdure
説 *shinsetsu* new theory
語 *shingo* new word
穀 *shinkoku* new rice, new grain
境地 *shinkyōchi* a new area; a new field of endeavor
嘗祭 *Niinamesai* Shinto Harvest Festival (Nov. 23)
製 *shinsei* new, newfangled
製品 *shinseihin* new products
聞 *shimbun* newspaper
聞口調 *shimbun kuchō* newspaper style
聞代 *shimbundai* newspaper monthly subscription charge
聞広告 *shimbun kōkoku* newspaper advertising
聞用紙 *shimbun yōshi* newsprint
聞体 *shimbuntai* newspaper style
聞社 *shimbunsha* newspaper company
聞売 *shimbun'u(ri)* news dealer
聞売店 *shimbun baiten* newsstand
聞条例 *shimbun jōrei* press law
聞屋 *shimbun'ya* newspaper delivery center; newspaperman; newsboy
聞科 *shimbunka* journalism (course)
聞界 *shimbunkai* the newspaper world
聞通信社 *shimbun tsūshinsha* news agency
聞班 *shimbunhan* press section
聞紙 *shimbunshi* newspapers
聞紙上 *shimbunshijō ni* in a newspaper
聞記者 *shimbun kisha* journalist, reporter
聞記事 *shimbun kiji* newspaper article
聞配達 *shimbun haitatsu* newspaper delivery
聞配達夫 *shimbun haitatsufu* newspaper delivery boy
聞倫理規程 *shimbun rinri kitei* newspaper code of ethics
聞業 *shimbungyō* journalism
聞種 *shimbundane* news; news source
聞購読者 *shimbun kōdokusha* newspaper subscriber
15 劇 *shingeki* new drama; new school of acting
編 *shimpen* new edition
調 *shinchō suru* have (some clothes) made
鋳 *shinchū* new minting
鋭 *shin'ei* freshly picked, newly produced; newly built
趣向 *shinshukō* new idea; novel device; novelty; originality
16 館 *shinkan* new building, annex
薬 *shin'yaku* new medicine
憲法 *Shinkempō* the New Constitution (of 1946)
機軸 *shinkijiku* new device; new departure; new idea
築 *shinchiku* new building, new construction
築祝 *shinchiku iwa(i)* housewarming
興 *shinkō* new, rising, newly established, newly awakened
興国 *shinkōkoku* rising nation
興宗教 *shinkō shūkyō* new religions
興勢力 *shinkō seiryoku* resurgence of power
17 講 *shinkō* new lecture
鮮 *shinsen* freshness
鮮味 *shinsemmi* freshness
18 顔 *shingao* newcomer, new face
19 羅 *Shiragi* the ancient Korean kingdom of Silla

14

斷 2388 / J5a52 / M13611 See 断 2385.

RAD. 方 70

Hō direction or *kata* side, person. On left: *hōhen* or *kata hen*. Nickname: Direction.

A 方 2389 / J4a7d / M13620 Hō direction, way; side; part; square; way, method, means, scheme, process. *kata* direction; settlement; person. *masa(ni)* right now. *-gata* type, style. *-kata* manner, method, fashion; side, party; toward (evening); person in charge; care of. *-e* direction; location; time. *(ni) ata(ri)* at the time of.
3 丈 *hōjō* ten feet square; superior priest's quarters; chief priest of a temple

土 *hōdo* country
寸 *hōsun* square *sun*; one's ideas; one's object
4 方 *katagata* people, persons; everywhere; this and that; any way. *hōbō* every direction, everywhere
円 *hōen* squares and circles
今 *hōkon* the present time
5 処 *hōsho* location
正 *hōsei* contract, behavior, moral character
6 舟 *hakobune* an ark; (Noah's) ark; the ark (of the covenant)
式 *hōshiki* formula; form; method, system; formalities, usage
尖碑 *hōsenhi* obelisk
向 *hōkō* direction, bearings, course, line, destination, aim
向板 *hōkōban* destination sign
向舵 *hōkōda* rudder
向探知機 *hōkō tanchiki* radar
向転換 *hōkō tenkan* change of direction; change of one's aim in life
向音痴 *hōkō onchi* no sense of direction
7 角 *hōgaku* direction, quarter
言 *hōgen* dialect; provincialism
里 *hōri* a square *ri* (see Weights and Measures)
形 *hōkei* square
図無 *hōzu (no) na(i)* endless, limitless
位 *hōi* direction, course
位基点 *hōi kiten* cardinal points of the compass
8 所 *hōsho* location
法 *hōhō* way, method, means, scheme, process
法論 *hōhōron* methodology
9 面 *hōmen* direction, way; side; district; sphere; line; phase
途 *hōto* means, way
便 *hōben* expedient, means, instrument
陣 *hōjin* square formation, phalanx
10 針 *hōshin* magnetic needle; course, policy, plan, principle, purpose
剤 *hōzai* prescription
案 *hōan* plan, program
11 術 *hōjutsu* art, method, magic
略 *hōryaku* plan, scheme, program
眼紙 *hōganshi* graph paper
12 策 *hōsaku* plan, policy
程式 *hōteishiki* equation
16 錐 *hōsui* square drill; square pyramid
錐形 *hōsuikei* square pyramid

4

於 2390 / J3177 / M13628 O. *(ni) oi(te)* at, in, on, as for, as to. *(ni) o(keru)* at, in.

5

B **施** 2391 / J3b5c / M13629 SHI. SE. *hodoko(su)* give alms; conduct (educational work); carry out; administer (first aid); apply (bandages); perform (an operation). *hodoko(shi)* alms, almsgiving.
3 工 *shikō suru, sekō suru* carry out, execute, operate
与 *hodoko(shi)-ata(eru)* give alms. *seyo* charity
5 主 *seshu* chief mourner; donor, benefactor
6 米 *semai* relief rice
行 *shikō suru* execute, carry out. *segyō suru* give alms
7 条 *shijō* making lines; rifling a gun barrel
8 物 *hodoko(shi)mono* alms, almsgiving
肥 *sehi* fertilization, manuring
9 政 *shisei* government, administration, statesmanship
政方針 *shisei hōshin* party line; the administration program
11 術 *shijutsu* surgical operation
設 *shisetsu* institution, establishment; equipment, facilities
12 散 *hodoko(shi)-chi(rasu)* give alms freely
策 *shisaku* a policy, a measure
13 業 *shigyō, segyō* management, operation
業林 *segyōrin* commercial forest
15 餓鬼 *segaki* service for the unmourned dead
16 薬 *seyaku* free medicine
17 療 *seryō* free medical tratment
療病院 *seryō byōin* charity hospital
療患者 *seryō kanja* charity patient

6

旄 2392 / J5a56 / M13642 BŌ. MŌ flag; tassel; long-haired cow. *hata* flag, banner.

旆 2393 / J5a54 / M13646 HAI flag.

旃 2394 / J5a53 / M13640 SEN woolen cloth.
6 那 *senna* senna

旁 2395 / J5a55 / M13637 BŌ. *tsukuri* a radical appearing on the right side of a character. *katawa(ra)* side; besides; while. *katagata* at the same time.
10 旁 *katagata* incidentally, at the same time

A**旅** 2396 / J4e39 / M-X **旅** 2397 / J-X / M13644 RYO journey; go around. *tabi* journey. *tabi suru* make a trip.
2 人 *tabibito, ryojin* traveler, wayfarer
人宿 *ryojin yado* inn
4 心 *tabigokoro* the tedium of a journey
中 *ryochū* on a journey
支度 *tabijitaku* journey preparation; traveling outfit
日記 *tabi nikki* travel diary
5 用 *ryoyō* traveling expenses
立 *tabida(tsu)* set out on a trip. *tabida(chi)* departure
出 *tabide* departure
芝居 *tabi shibai* performance by traveling troupe
6 衣 *tabigoromo* traveling clothes
回 *tabimawa(ri)* touring
団 *ryodan* brigade
先 *tabisaki* destination; place of sojourn. *tabisaki de* while traveling
行 *ryokō* travel, trip, journey
行先 *ryokōsaki* destination
行券 *ryokōken* passport
行者 *ryokōsha* traveler, tourist
行免状 *ryokō menjō* passport
行記 *ryokōki* travelog, itinerary
行家 *ryokōka* traveler, tourist
行案内 *ryokō annai* guidebook; itinerary
行傷害保険 *ryokō shōgai hoken* travel-accident insurance
7 戻 *tabimodo(ri)* return from a trip
住 *tabizuma(i)* one's stopping place on a trip
役者 *tabi yakusha* traveling player
芸人 *tabi geinin* itinerant player
芸者 *tabi geisha* itinerant geisha
8 所 *tabisho* resting place for a *mikoshi*
枕 *tabimakura* sleeping away from home; journey
舎 *ryosha* hotel, inn
歩 *tabiaru(ki)* traveling
空 *tabi (no) sora* strange land
券 *ryoken* passport
者 *tabi (no) mono* traveler
9 連 *tabizu(re)* traveling companion
亭 *ryotei* inn, hotel
姿 *tabi sugata* traveling outfit
客 *ryokaku, ryokyaku* traveler, passenger, tourist
客列車 *ryokaku ressha* passenger train
客運輸 *ryokaku un'yu* passenger traffic
客業 *ryokakugyō* tourist trade
客機 *ryokakki* passenger plane
10 疲 *tabitsuka(re)* travel fatigue
烏 *tabigarasu* one who is always traveling
11 情 *ryojō* travel weariness
宿 *tabiyado, ryoshuku* hotel
商 *ryoshō* commercial traveler
商人 *tabi shōnin* peddler, commercial traveler
12 順 *Ryojun* Port Arthur, Lü Shun
程 *ryotei* distance, journey
費 *ryohi* traveling expenses
装 *ryosō* traveling outfit
装束 *tabi shōzoku* traveling outfit
13 僧 *tabisō* itinerant priest
路 *tabiji* journey
寝 *tabine* staying at an inn
愁 *ryoshū* lonesomeness on a journey
15 痩 *tabiyase* losing weight from traveling
稼 *tabikase(gi)* itinerant work
16 窶 *tabiyatsu(re)* travel fatigue
興行 *tabi kōgyō* traveling show
館 *ryokan* hotel
館業 *ryokangyō* hotel business
22 嚢 *ryonō* traveling bag
籠 *hatago* inn
籠屋 *hatagoya* inn

— 7 —

旌 2398 / J5a57 / M13658 SEI flag; praise.
14 旗 *seiki* flag, banner

A 族 2399 / J4232 / M13661 ZOKU family, relatives, clan, tribe, race. *yakara* family, relatives; party, colleagues, gang.
5 生 *zokusei suru* (plants) grow in clusters; (animals) live in herds or flocks
8 長 *zokuchō* patriarch, chief, family head
制 *zokusei* patriarchal family system
制政治 *zokusei seiji* patriarchal government
10 称 *zokushō* family-rank designation
党 *zokuto* companions
14 閥主義 *zokubatsu shugi* nepotism
15 縁 *zokuen* family ties
20 籍 *zokuseki* social status and domicile

B 旋 2400 / J407b / M13656 SEN go around.
4 毛 *tsumuji, semmō* a whirl of hair on the head; a cowlick
毛曲 *tsumujima(gari)* cranky person; perverse person, screwball
6 回 *senkai* revolution, rotation, turning, circling
回砲 *senkaihō* swivel gun
7 条銃 *senjōjū* rifle
9 風 *sempū, tsumujikaze* whirlwind
律 *senritsu* melody
11 転 *senten* turning, rotation
15 盤 *semban* lathe
盤工 *sembankō* turner, lathe man

9

旒 2401 / J5a58 / M13676 RYŪ counter for flags.

10

A 旗 2402 / J347a / M13687 KI. *hata* flag, banner, standard, ensign, pennant, streamer.
3 下 *kika, hatashita* beneath the banner.
4 手 *kishu* standard bearer
号 *kigō* flag emblem
日 *hatabi* national holiday
5 本 *hatamoto* a vassal directly under the shogun
6 色 *hatairo* tide of war; outlook. *kishoku* flag, banner; one's attitude, one's stand
印 *hatajirushi* flag, banner; one's attitude, one's stand
行列 *hata gyōretsu* flag parade
8 取 *hatato(ri)* flag race
9 持 *hatamo(chi)* standard bearer
亭 *kitei* inn, restaurant
竿 *hatazao* flagstaff, flagpole
巻 *hata (o) ma(ku)* surrender, give up
10 振 *hatafu(ri)* flagman; starter; flag wagging
挙 *hataage* raising an army; launching a business
11 章 *hatajirushi, kishō* flag mark, ensign; slogan
魚 *kajiki* marlin, swordfish
魚鮪 *kajiki maguro* mole
12 揚 *hataa(ge)* raising an army; launching a business
13 鼓 *kiko* colors and drums; army
鼓堂堂 *kiko-dōdō to* triumphantly, with colors flying
15 幟 *kishi* flag, banner; one's attitude, one's stand
標 *hatajirushi* flag mark, ensign; slogan
16 頭 *hatagashira* top of the flagpole; chief
20 艦 *kikan* flagship

12

旛 2403 / J5a5a / M-X See 旛 2404.

14

旛 2404 / J5a59 / M13700 HEN flag.

RAD. 无 71

Mu or *nashi* nothing. Also *munyō*. Variants: 无 and 旡 or 旡 (5 strokes). Do not confuse with Rad. 92. Nickname: Crooked Heaven (cf. 天 *ten* heaven).

无 2405 / J5a5b / M13716 BU. MU *na(i)* not exist, nothing.

旡 2406 / J5a5c / M13717 KI. KE sob, choke.

5

B 既 2407 / J347b / M13721 旣 2408 / J-X / M13724 既 2409 / J-X / M13725

KI. *sude ni, sunde ni* previously; already, long ago; on the point of; actually. *sude ni shite* meanwhile.

5 刊 *kikan* already published
刊号 *kikangō* back numbers
6 存 *kizon* existing
成 *kisei* existing, accomplished, completed, established
成作家 *kisei sakka* established writer
成事実 *kisei jijitsu* accomplished fact
成宗教 *kisei shūkyō* the old established religions
成品 *kiseihin* finished articles
成訳 *kiseiyaku* existing translations
7 決 *kiketsu* settled, decided; convicted
決因 *kiketsushū* convict, convicted person
8 定 *kitei* fixed, prearranged
事 *sunde (no) koto ni* previously; already, long ago; on the point of; actually
知 *kichi* (already) known, well-known
知数 *kichisū* known quantity
往 *kiō* the past
往症 *kiōshō* patient's history
往歴 *kiōreki* patient's history
10 記 *kiki no* the above-mentioned
耕地 *kikōchi* land under cultivation
11 遂 *kisui* consummated, perpetrated
済 *kisai* already paid up
習 *kishū* already learned
望 *kibō* 16th night of a lunar month
婚 *kikon* already married
婚者 *kikonsha* married person
得 *kitoku* already acquired
得権 *kitokuken* vested interests
設 *kisetsu* already constructed, established, existing
設線 *kisetsusen* lines in operation
12 報 *kihō* previous report
13 電 *kiden* previous message
14 製 *kisei* ready-made
製服 *kiseifuku* ready-made clothing
製品 *kiseihin* manufactured goods, ready-made goods

7

旣 2408 / J-X / M13724 既 2409 / J-X / M13725 See 既 2407.

RAD. 日 72

Hi or *nichi* day. At left: *hi hen* or *nichi hen*. Variant: 曰. This variant is actually Rad. 73 but, with the exception of the radical character itself, is treated herein as a variant of Rad. 72. Nickname: Sun.

A 日 2410 / J467c / M13733 JITSU, NICHI, NITSU day; Sunday. *hi* sun; time; day, date. *hi(narazu)* before long, in a few days. *hi niwa* if, in case. *hi(mosugara)* all day long. *-ka* day. *-Nichi-* Japanese.

1 一日 *hihitohi, hiichinichi, hi(gana)ichinichi* all day long, day by day
2 入 *hi(no)i(ri)* sunset
入方 *hi (no) i(ru) hō* west
3 夕 *nisseki* day and night
子 *nisshi* number of days, time
干 *hibo(shi)* sun-dried, sun-baked
久 *hihisa(shiku)* for a long time, for some time

下 *hi (no) shita ni* under the sun, in the whole world
丸 *Hi(no)maru* the Japanese flag, the ball of the sun, sun flag
4 日 *hi(ni)hi(ni)* daily. *hibi* daily; days. *nichinichi* daily, every day
比 *Nippi* Japan and the Philippines
迫 *Hi (ga) ko(mu)* The day is fast approaching.
中 *nitchū* during the day. *hinaka* broad daylight, daytime. *Nitchū* Japan and China
仏 *Nichi-Futsu* Japan and France
切 *higi(ri)* fixed day; setting the day
支 *Nisshi* Japan and China
支事変 *Nisshi Jihen* Sino-Japanese War (1937–45)
月 *jitsugetsu* sun and moon; time, days, years
月星辰 *jitsugetsu seishin* heavenly bodies
5 目 *hi(no)me* sun, sunlight
立 *hida(tsu)* grow up; get well. *hida(chi)* convalescence after childbirth; growth of an infant
加 *Nikka* Japan and Canada; Japan and California
外 *itsuzoya, jitsugai* When was it?; recently, once, some time ago
収 *nisshū* one day's income
永 *hinaga* long spring days
用 *nichiyō* daily use, of daily necessity
用品 *nichiyōhin* daily necessities
付 *hizuke* date, dating
付変更線 *hizuke henkōsen* the international date line
刊 *nikkan* daily publication, a daily
刊新聞 *nikkan shimbun* daily newspaper
出 *hi(no)de, nisshutsu* sunrise
本 *Nihon, Nippon* Japan. *Hi(no)moto* Land of the Rising Sun
本一 *Nihon'ichi, Nippon'ichi* Japan's best
本人 *Nihonjin, Nipponjin* Japanese
本刀 *Nihontō* Japanese sword
本三景 *Nihon Sankei* Japan's three noted scenic sights (Matsushima, Miyajima, and Amanohashidate)
本犬 *Nihonken, Nihon inu* Japanese dog
本史 *Nihonshi* Japanese history
本化 *Nihonka* Japanization
本主義 *Nihon shugi* Japanism
本交通公社 *Nihon Kōtsū Kōsha* Japan Travel Bureau
本男子 *Nihon danshi* sons of Japan
本的 *Nihonteki* Japanese (art)
本国 *Nipponkoku* Japan
本画 *Nihonga* Japanese painting or drawing
本画界 *Nihongakai* Japanese art circles
本帝国 *Nippon Teikoku* the Empire of Japan
本鉄道 *Nihon Tetsudō* Japan Railways; JR
本風 *Nihonfū* Japanese style
本海 *Nihonkai* the Japan Sea
本海流 *Nihon Kairyū* Japan Current
本専売公社 *Nihon Sembai Kōsha* Japan Monopoly Corporation
本酒 *Nihonshu* saké
本紙 *Nihonshi* Japanese paper
本書紀 *Nihonshoki* an ancient Japan chronicle
本訳 *Nihon yaku* Japanese translation
本脳炎 *Nihon nōen* Japanese encephalitis, sleeping sickness
本間 *Nihomma* Japanese-style room
本晴 *Nihomba(re)* ideal weather, clear sky, glorious weather
本電信電話 *Nihon Denshin Denwa* Nippon Telephone and Telegraph Corporation, NTT
本語 *Nihongo, Nippongo* Japanese language
本髪 *Nihongami* Japanese hairdo
本製 *Nihonsei* Japanese make
本銀行 *Nippon Ginkō* Bank of Japan
本贔屓 *Nippombiiki* pro-Japanese
6 米 *Nichi-Bei* Japan and America
印 *Nichi-In* Japan and India
伊 *Nichi-I* Japan and Italy
次 *nichiji* the date
当 *hiata(ri)* sunny place; exposure to the sun. *nittō* daily allowance, a day's pay
共 *Nikkyō* Japan Communist Party
毎 *higoto ni* daily
向 *hinata* sunny place, sunshine. *hinata(bokko)* basking in the sun
向水 *hinata mizu* sun-warmed water
向臭 *hinatakusa(i)* the fresh smell of sundrying; countrified
光 *nikkō* sunshine, sunlight, sun
光石 *nikkōseki* sunstone

光信号 *nikkō shingō* heliogram
光浴 *nikkōyoku* sun-bath
光消毒 *nikkō shōdoku* disinfection by sunning
光療法 *nikkō ryōhō* heliotherapy, sun cure
7 赤 *Nisseki* Japan Red Cross
足 *hiashi* daytime; sun's position
決 *higi(me) de* by the day
宋 *Nissō* Sino (Sung)-Japanese
系 *Nikkei* Japanese descent
系米人 *Nikkei Beijin* Japanese-American
没 *nichibotsu* sunset
没後 *nichibotsugo* after sunset
没前 *nichibotsuzen* before sunset
没時 *nichibotsuji* time of sunset
没頃 *nichibotsugoro* about sunset
8 延 *hino(be)* postponement
明 *Nichi-Min* Sino(Ming)-Japanese
送 *hioku(ri)* passing the time (days)
限 *nichigen* time limit, date, term
取 *hido(ri)* setting a date; the date
夜 *nichiya* day and night; always
直 *nitchoku* a day shift; the day's work
参 *nissan* daily visits (to a shrine, etc.)
歩 *hibu* daily interest
英 *Nichi-Ei* Japan and England
東 *Nittō* Japan, Land of the Rising Sun
長 *hinaga* a long day
長石 *nitchōseki* sunstone
和 *hiyori* weather conditions; fair weather; situation
和下駄 *hiyori geta* fair weather geta
和見 *hiyorimi* weather forecasting; weather vane; opportunism; marking time; wait-and-see (policy)
周運動 *nisshū undō* diurnal motion
9 食 *nisshoku* solar eclipse
遂 *hi (o) o(tte)* day by day
柄 *higara* kind of day (lucky or unlucky)
計 *nikkei* daily account, daily expenses; the day's total
除 *hiyoke* sunshade, awning, blind
独 *Nichi-Doku* Japan and Germany
独伊防共協定 *Nichi-Doku-I Bōkyō Kyōtei* The Tripartite Pact among Japan, Germany, and Italy
10 差 *hiza(shi)* sunlight; sun's height
華 *Nikka* Japan and Nationalist China
帰 *higae(ri)* a one-day (trip)
進 *nisshin* advancing daily
進月歩 *nisshin geppo* steady advance
時 *nichiji* date; time; date and hour
時計 *hidokei* sundial
記 *nikki* diary, journal
記帳 *nikkichō* a diary
射 *nissha, hizashi* sunlight; height of the sun
射病 *nisshabyō* heatstroke; sunstroke
陰 *hikage* shade
陰者 *hikagemono* one who stays out of the public eye, an obscure person; a concubine
11 頃 *higoro* normally, habitually, always; for a long time
捲 *himeku(ri)* calendar pad
掛 *higake* daily intallment
済 *hinashi* daily intallment
脚 *hiashi* daytime; sun's position
産 *nissan* daily output
盛 *hizakari* high noon
貨 *nikka* Japanese goods; Japanese money
乾 *hiboshi* sun-dried, sun-baked
章旗 *Nisshōki* Rising Sun Flag
清 *Nisshin* Sino (Manchu)-Japanese
清戦争 *Nisshin Sensō* Sino-Japanese War (1894–95)
清戦役 *Nisshin Sen'eki* Sino-Japanese War (1894–95)
常 *nichijō* everyday, usually, always; daily; ordinary
常用品 *nichijō yōhin* daily necessities
常茶飯事 *nichijō sahanji* an everyday occurrence
12 雇 *hiyatoi* day-to-day employment
間 *hiai* time; daily interest rate
満 *Nichi-Man* Japan and Manchuria
焼 *hiya(ke)* sunburn
短 *himijika* shortening of the days
程 *nittei* day's schedule
給 *nikkyū* day wages, daily wages
割 *hiwa(ri)* daily rate, daily quota. *hiwari de* by the day
勤 *nikkin* daily work
傘 *higasa* parasol
貸 *higa(shi)* lending by the day
報 *nippō* daily news, daily report
13 蓮宗 *Nichirenshū* Buddhist sect originating in the thirteenth century
溜 *hidama(ri)* sunny place; exposure to the sun
数 *nissū* number of days, time. *hikazu* number of days; the kind of day (lucky or unlucky)
暈 *nichiun* halo, ring around the sun

新 *nisshin* starting each day anew
蔭 *hikage* shade
蔭者 *hikagemono* one who stays out of the public eye
照 *hide(ri), nisshō* sunshine, drought, dry weather
照計 *nisshōkei* heliograph, sunshine recorder
嗣 *hitsugi* imperial throne
嗣御子 *hitsugi (no) miko* crown prince
傭 *hiyō, hiyatoi* day-to-day employment
傭取 *hiyōto(ri)* day laborer
傭稼 *hiyōkasegi* working by the day; day laborer
14 読 *hiyo(mi)* day-by-day calendar
誌 *nisshi* diary, journal
語 *Nichigo* Japanese language
銀 *Nichigin* Bank of Japan
銭 *hizeni* daily receipts; a loan to be repaid in daily installments
増 *hima(shi) ni* daily, day by day, gradually
増物 *hima(shi)mono* things left over
暮 *higu(re), hi (no) ku(re)* twilight; sunset, dusk, evening. *higu(rashi)* a day's living
暮方 *higu(re)gata* sunset, twilight, dusk, evening
15 稼 *hikasegi* day labor
課 *nikka* daily lesson; one's regular work
賦 *hibu* daily installments
輪 *nichirin* sun, orb of day
蝕 *nisshoku* solar eclipse
影 *hikage* sunlight; sun's shadow
16 録 *nichiroku* journal
17 濠 *Nichi-Go* Japan and Australia
鮮 *Nissen* Japan and Korea
18 韓 *Nikkan* Japan and Korea
曝 *hizarashi* bleaching; exposure to the sun
覆 *hiōi, hioi* sunshade, awning, curtain, blind
曜 *Nichiyō* Sunday
曜日 *Nichiyōbi* Sunday
曜日休業令 *Nichiyōbi Kyūgyōrei* Sunday laws
曜版 *Nichiyōban* Sunday Edition
曜学校 *Nichiyō Gakkō* Sunday School
19 蘇 *Nisso* Japan and the Soviet Union
蘭 *Nichi-Ran* Japan and Holland
21 露 *Nichi-Ro* Japan and Russia
露戦役 *Nichi-Ro Sen'eki* Russo-Japanese War
露戦争 *Nichi-Ro Sensō* Russo-Japanese War

1

旦 2411 / J4336 / M13734 TAN dawn, early morning.

3 夕 *tanseki* morning and evening, day and night
6 那 *danna* master; husband; gentleman
那方 *dannagata* the gentlemen, Messrs.
那様 *dannasan, dannasama* master; husband; gentleman
14 暮 *tambo* morning and evening

A **旧** 2412 / J356c / M13737 **舊** 4916 / J6751 / M30249 KYŪ old things; old times; old friend; old calendar; former, ex-. *furu-* used article, secondhand. *furu(i)* old, aged, ancient, antiquated; stale, threadbare; outmoded, obsolete article.

3 土 *kyūdo* former property, former territory
大陸 *Kyūtairiku* the Old World
4 友 *kyūyū* an old friend
5 刊 *kyūkan* back number; old edition
正月 *Kyūshōgatsu* New Year's Day in the lunar calendar
世界 *Kyūsekai* the Old World
市街 *kyūshigai* old town
主 *kyūshu* a former lord
6 臣 *kyūshin* an old retainer
式 *kyūshiki* old type, old style
地 *kyūchi* former property, former territory
邦 *kyūhō* an old country
交 *kyūkō* an old friendship
号 *kyūgō* old name; back number
宅 *kyūtaku* former residence
年 *kyūnen* the old year, last year
7 址 *kyūshi* historic ruins
来 *kyūrai* from ancient times, formerly. *kyūrai no* traditional
体制 *kyūtaisei* old regime
8 居 *kyūkyo* former residence
例 *kyūrei* old custom, tradition
姓 *kyūsei* former name, maiden name
知 *kyūchi* an old friend; an old friendship
官 *kyūkan* former government official
典 *kyūten* tradition; a classic
事 *kyūji, kuji* past events, bygones

制 *kyūsei* old system, old order
制度 *kyūseido* old system, old order
9 風 *kyūfū* old customs
俗 *kyūzoku* old customs
恨 *kyūkon* an old grudge
派 *kyūha* old school; old style; conservative people
封 *kyūhō* a former fief
故 *kyūko* antiquity; an old acquaintance
型 *kyūgata, kyūkei* old style, old type
怨 *kyūen* old grudge
思想 *kyūshisō* old-fashioned idea
約 *kyūyaku* an old promise; the old covenant; the Old Testament
約聖書 *Kyūyaku Seisho* Old Testament
10 師 *kyūshi* one's old teacher; one's old master
株 *kyūkabu* old stock (in a firm)
記 *kyūki* an old chronicle, an old record
都 *kyūto* the old capital
家 *kyūka* an old family
恩 *kyūon* old favors
11 道 *kyūdō* an old road
教 *Kyūkyō* Roman Catholicism
13 債 *kyūsai* old debt
跡 *kyūseki* historic ruins
新訳聖書 *Kyūshin'yaku Seisho* Old and New Testaments
14 暦 *kyūreki* the old lunar calendar
聞 *kyūbun* old news
態 *kyūtai* old state of affairs
15 墟 *kyūkyo* ruins, remains
稿 *kyūkō* old manuscript
縁 *kyūen* old relationship; old acquaintance
誼 *kyūgi* old friendship
敵 *kyūteki* old enemy
歓 *kyūkan* an old joy
弊 *kyūhei* standing evil; conservatism; the old school. *kyūhei na* old-fashioned, antiquated, conservative
16 懐 *kyūkai* love of antiquity
18 蹟 *kyūseki* historic ruins
観 *kyūkan* former state, former appearance
藩 *kyūhan* former clan
藩主 *kyūhanshu* former feudal lord

2

臾 2413 / J-X / M14281 See **舁** 4908. [曰]

旨 B 2414 / J3b5d / M13738 SHI. *uma(garu)* relish, show a liking for. *mune* purport; principle; instructions; will, thinking. *uma(i)* delicious, appetizing; skillful, clever, expert; wise; successful; fortunate; splendid; promising.
5 汁 *uma(i) shiru* the lion's share, the cream
6 旨 *umauma to* successfully, nicely
15 趣 *shishu* opinion, idea; meaning, gist, tenor; aim, motive, purpose

旬 B 2415 / J3d5c / M13746 JUN ten-day period. SHUN season (for specific products).
4 日 *junjitsu* ten-day period
月 *jungetsu* a month and ten days; ten months; a short time
5 外 *shunhazu(re)* off-season
刊 *junkan* published every ten days
7 余 *jun'yo* over ten days
12 報 *jumpō* ten-day report

旭 2416 / J3030 / M13747 KYOKU. *asahi* the morning sun, the rising sun.
4 日 *kyokujitsu* the rising sun
日昇天 *kyokujitsu-shōten* the rising sun
日旗 *Kyokujitsuki* Rising Sun Flag
6 光 *kyokkō* rays of the rising sun
13 暉 *kyokki* rays of the rising sun
14 旗 *Kyokki* Rising Sun Flag

曳 2417 / J3148 / M14282 **曵** 2420 / J5b2a / M14284 EI. *hi(ku)* draw, pull, haul, tug, jerk, drag, trail, bend, attract; lead (horses or captives); draw (lines); admit; install (utilities); quote, refer to; look up (words); subtract, reduce; apply, daub on; blunt (a sword); patronize; choose; catch (a cold). [曰]
4 火弾 *eikadan* tracer bullet
6 曳 *eiei* heaving, pulling
光弾 *eikōdan* tracer bullet, star shell, flare bomb
10 馬 *hikiuma* draft horse
11 船 *hikifune, hikibune, eisen* tug boat
14 網 *hikiami* seine, dragnet

曲 A 2418 / J364a / M14280 KYOKU music, tone, melody, composition; fault. *ma(garu) vi* bend, curve, swerve; be crooked; turn; be awry; be perverse; lean; decline. *ma(geru) vt* bend, curve; lean, bow; distort; depart from (principles); pawn. *ma(gari-kuneru)* curve, meander, wind. *kuma* corner, nook, recess; indentation, bend, turn; shade, shading; make-up. *ma(gatta)* leaning, bent, curved, crooked; winding, meandering, zigzag; perverse, wicked; distorted. *kune(ri)* bend, twist. *ma(garinari) ni* some way or other. [日]

4 水 *kyokusui* meandering stream
尺 *kanejaku, kyokushaku, maga(ri)jaku, kanezashi* common Japanese foot; carpenter's square
5 玉 *magatama* (ancient) comma-shaped jewels
目 *maga(ri)me* turn, bend, curve. *kyokumoku* musical selection, program; tunes
7 角 *maga(ri)kado* street corner, road turn
技 *kyokugi* acrobatic feats
折 *kyokusetsu* winding, meandering; indentations; vicissitudes, complications
芸 *kyokugei* tricks, acrobatic stunts
芸師 *kyokugeishi* acrobat, tumbler
8 物 *ma(ge)mono* circular box
直 *kyokuchoku* merits (of a case); right or wrong
易 *ma(ge)yasu(i)* pliant, supple, flexible
突 *kudo* flute hole; cooking stove
者 *kusemono* ruffian, villain, knave; thief; suspicious fellow
事 *kyokuji* wickedness, injustice. *kusegoto* crookedness, something not right; something out of the ordinary; something unpleasant, something disgusting; unlawfulness; something unhappy, calamity
学 *kyokugaku* inferior scholarship
学阿世 *kyokugaku-asei* twisting the truth and catering to the public
9 飛 *kyokuto(bi)* fancy diving
度 *kyokudo* curvature
乗 *kyokuno(ri)* trick riding
独楽 *kyokugoma* top-spinning tricks
10 流 *kyokuryū* meandering stream
射 *kyokusha* high-angle fire
射砲 *kyokushahō* howitzer; high-angle gun
馬 *kyokuba* circus; equestrian feats
馬団 *kyokubadan* circus troupe
馬師 *kyokubashi* circus stunt rider
11 道 *maga(ri)michi* roundabout road; curving road
率 *kyokuritsu* curvature
12 弾 *kyokubi(ki)* trick playing (on an instrument)
飲 *kyokuno(mi)* drinking while doing an acrobatic stunt
筆 *kyokuhitsu* misrepresentation, falsification
13 路 *kyokuro* winding road. *maga(ri)michi* roundabout road; curving road
解 *kyokkai* misconstruction, distortion
節 *kyokusetsu* tune
14 説 *kyokusetsu* false theory
15 舞 *kusemai* recitative dance
調 *kyokuchō* melody, tune
論 *kyokuron* biased argument
線 *kyokusen* curve, curved line
線美 *kyokusembi* linear beauty
19 譜 *kyokufu* musical composition; notes

A **早** 2419 / J4161 / M13742 SA. SŌ. SATSU. *haya(i)* quick, fast, speedy; brisk; prompt; early; premature. *haya(meru) vt* hasten, precipitate, accelerate, expedite; advance (the date). *haya(maru)* be hasty, be rash. *haya(ru)* be hasty, be rash. *(O)ha(yō)* Good Morning. *haya(sa)* swiftness; being early; speed. *ha(ya)* already, now, so soon.

3 川 *hayakawa* swift river
口 *hayakuchi, hayaguchi* fast talking; tongue twister
口言葉 *hayakuchi kotoba* tongue twister
4 引 *hayabi(ki)* leaving early
天 *sōten* dawn, early morning
分 *hayawa(kari)* quick understanding; easy guide
少女 *saotome* rice-planting girl
手 *hayate* squall
手回 *hayatemawa(shi)* early precipitation
手雲 *hayategumo* hurricane clouds
5 目 *hayame ni* early, ahead of time
立 *hayada(chi)* early morning departure
打 *hayauchi* dispatch by horse
出 *hayade* early arrival at the office
世 *sōsei* early death

4 心忄⺗戈戸手扌支攴攵文斗斤方无【日曰】2 月木欠止歹殳毋比毛氏气水氵氺火灬爪爫父爻爿丬片牙牛犬犭

仕舞 *hayajimai* early closing
生 *hayauma(re)* born between January 1 and March 31. *hayana(ri)* early crop, early fruit. *wase* early ripening; a precocious child
生児 *sōseiji* premature baby
生種 *waseshu* an early variety
6 老 *sōrō* premature old age
耳 *hayamimi* insider; keen of hearing
回 *hayamawa(ri)* a dash around (the world)
成 *sōsei* early maturity
死 *hayaji(ni), sōshi* premature death
早 *sōsō, hayahaya* Hurry up. *hayabaya* early, immediately. *sōsō* Hurriedly yours.
年 *sōnen* youth, early years
合点 *hayaga(t)ten, hayagaten* hasty conclusion, premature judgment
7 足 *hayaashi* quick pace, quick march, trot, fast walking
技 *hayawaza* quick work; sleight of hand
呑込 *hayanomiko(mi)* hasty conclusion
見表 *hayamihyō* chart, table
言葉 *hayakotoba* fast speaking
8 退 *sōtai, hayabiki* leaving early
所 *haya(i) tokoro* promptly
参 *sōsan* early arrival (at a meeting); early morning visit (to a shrine or temple)
事 *haya(i) koto* promptness
者勝 *haya(i)monoga(chi)* first-come-first-served
取 *hayato(ri)* snapshot
苗 *sanae* rice seedlings
苗取 *sanaeto(ru)* transplant rice
苗歌 *sanae uta* rice-planting song
9 速 *sassoku* immediately, speedily
咲 *hayaza(ki)* early blooming; precocious
秋 *sōshū* early fall
計 *sōkei na* rash, premature, hasty
変 *hayagawa(ri)* quick change of costume, sudden transformation
春 *sōshun* early spring
急 *sōkyū, sakkyū* urgent, pressing; great speed
逝 *sōsei* early death
飛脚 *hayabikyaku* courier, running messenger
発性痴呆症 *sōhatsusei chihōsyō* dementia praecox
10 馬 *hayauma* post horse, steed
起 *hayao(ki)* early rising
書 *hayaga(ki)* writing in a hurry
11 道 *hayamichi* shortcut
婚 *sōkon* early marriage
掘 *hayabo(ri)* early crop
桶 *hayaoke* (cheap) coffin
船 *hayafune* clipper, fast boat
雪 *sōsetsu* early snow
教育 *sōkyōiku* early education
産 *sōzan* premature birth
産児 *sōzanji* premature baby
12 間 *hayama ni* early
晩 *sōban* early and late; sometime or other; finally, after all
暁 *sōgyō* daybreak, dawn
飯 *hayameshi* early meal; fast eating
朝 *sōchō* early morning
場米 *hayabamai* early rice
期 *sōki* early stage
期診断 *sōki shindan* early diagnosis
13 業 *hayawaza* quick work; sleight of hand
寝 *hayane* retiring early
14 稲 *wase* early rice. *wase no* early ripening; precocious
15 蕨 *sawarabi* early bracken
熟 *sōjuku* precocity; premature development
駕籠 *hayakago* express palanquin
19 瀬 *hayase* swift current, rapids
禱 *sōtō* morning prayers, matins
20 鐘 *hayagane* fire bell

3

曳 2420 / J5b2a / M14284 See **曳** 2417. [日]

旱 2421 / J5a5d / M13752 KAN. *hideri* drought, dry weather; shortage.
4 水 *kansui* drought and floods
天 *kanten* drought, dry weather
7 災 *kansai* drought disaster
9 荒 *kankō* land ruined by drought
10 害 *kangai* drought damage
12 雲 *kan'un* dry cloud
13 損 *kanson* drought damage fields
15 魃 *kambatsu* drought

B **更** 2422 / J3939 / M14283 KŌ a watch of the night. *fu(kasu)* sit up late. *fu(keru)* get late; grow old; reach the height of the season. *arata(maru)* be renewed, be renovated; change, be modified, be revised; be improved, be reformed; be ceremonious. *sara ni* again; after all; more and more. *sara(nari)* of course. [日]

5 代 *kōtai suru* exchange (something)
正 *kōsei* correction, revision, rectification
生 *kōsei* rebirth, resuscitation, rehabilitation, reorganization, regeneration
生期 *kōseiki* change of life, menopause
6 年期 *kōnenki* menopause, change of life
衣 *kōi* seasonal changing of clothes; lady court attendant; second lunar month. *koromogae* seasonal changing of clothes
衣室 *kōishitsu* dressing room
7 迭 *kōtetsu* change, shake-up, reshuffle, exchanging places
位 *kōi* second accession of the same emperor
改 *kōkai* renewal, renovation, reform
更 *sarasara* (not) all
8 始 *kōshi* renewal, reform
9 訂 *kōtei* revision
10 紗 *sarasa* cotton print, calico
13 新 *kōshin* renewal, innovation, renovation

4

冐 2423 / J-X / M-X See **冒** 3915.

昻 2424 / J3937 / M13783 See **昂** 2447.

昃 2425 / J5a60 / M13785 SHOKU. SHIKI *katamu(ku)* lean, slant, tilt; (sun) go down.

昊 2426 / J5a5f / M13799 KŌ sky; heavens; immense.

旺 2427 / J3222 / M13774 Ō. *sakan* flourishing, successful; beautiful; vigorous.

11 盛 *ōsei na* excellent, flourishing, prosperous

昌 2428 / J3e3b / M13803 SHŌ proseperous; bright, clear.

5 平 *shōhei* peace, tranquility

旻 2429 / J5a61 / M13775 BIN autumn sky; sky, heavens.

4 天 *binten* sky, heavens
7 序 *binjo* autumn

B **昆** 2430 / J3a2b / M13792 KON descendants; elder brother.

5 布 *kombu, kobu* kombu, tangle, kelp, sea tang, devil's apron
布茶 *kobucha, kombucha* kelp tea
6 虫 *konchū* insect, bug
虫学 *konchūgaku* entomology

昏 2431 / J3a2a / M13806 KON dark; evening, dusk.

7 乱 *konran* derangement, muddle, bewilderment
8 迷 *kommei* confusion, bewilderment, stupor, unconsciousness
昏 *konkon to* unconsciously
10 倒 *kontō* swoon, faint
冥 *kommei* complete darkness
11 酔 *konsui* dead drunk
12 惑 *konwaku* ignorance of the truth and lack of judgment
13 睡 *konsui* coma, stupor, dead sleep
睡病 *konsuibyō* sleeping sickness

A **易** 2432 / J3057 / M13814 EKI divination, augury, fortunetelling. I easiness. *yasu(i)* easy, simple, light; habitual. *-yasu(i)* be liable to, be ready to, be easy to.

6 行 *igyō* easy way of salvation, Buddhist salvation by faith
8 易 *ii(taru)* simple, easy. *yasuyasu* very easy
学 *ekigaku* study of divination
者 *ekisha* fortuneteller, diviner
事 *kaegoto* swapping, exchanging
11 道 *ekidō* divination, fortunetelling
術 *ekijutsu* art of divination
経 *Ekikyō* the Book of Divination, Yi Jing
断 *ekidan* divination, fortunetelling
17 簀 *ekisaku* death, demise of sages

A **昔** 2433 / J404e / M13816 SHAKU. SEKI. *mukashi* antiquity, old times.

心 忄 㣺 戈 戸 手 扌 支 攴 攵 文 斗 斤 方 无 【日 曰】4 月 木 欠 止 歹 殳 毋 比 毛 氏 气 水 氵 氺 火 灬 爪 爫 父 爻 爿 丬 片 牙 牛 犬 犭

4 日 *sekijitsu* old times
5 乍 *mukashinaga(ra)* as of yore
6 年 *sekinen* antiquity; formerly; years ago
気質 *mukashi-katagi* old-time spirit
8 昔 *mukashimukashi* long ago
者 *mukashimono* old folks
9 風 *mukashifū no* old-fashioned
10 時 *sekiji* old times
13 話 *mukashibanashi* folklore, legend; reminiscences
馴染 *mukashinajimi* old friend, crony
14 様 *mukashiyō* old-fashioned
語 *mukashigata(ri)* an ancient tale

B **昇** 2434 / J3e3a / M13794 SHŌ. *nobo(ru)* rise, ascend, go up, climb; go to (the capital); add up to; be promoted; advance (in price); sail up; come up (on the agenda). *nobo(ri)* ascent; up train (toward the capital).

3 口 *nobo(ri)kuchi, nobo(ri)guchi* way up (to trains)
4 天 *shōten* ascension; the Ascension (of Christ)
6 任 *shōnin* promotion
9 級 *shōkyū* promotion, advancement
叙 *shōjo* promotion (of officials), advancement
段 *shōdan* promotion
降 *shōkō* rise and fall; ascent and descent; fluctuations
降口 *shōkōguchi* companionway, hatchway, (ship) entrance
降場 *shōkōjō* (station) platform
降機 *shōkōki* elevator, hoist, dumbwaiter
10 進 *shōshin* promotion, advancement
格 *shōkaku* raising of status
華 *shōka* sublimation (in chemistry)
12 給 *shōkyū* salary raise
13 殿 *shōden* the privilege of attending the imperial court
16 龍 *nobo(ri)ryū* rising dragon
20 騰 *shōtō suru* rise, go up, soar

A **明** 2435 / J4c40 / M13805 **明** 3909 / J-X / M23178 MEI clearness, shining; eyesight; discernment. MYŌ next (week), tomorrow (morning). MIN Ming (Dynasty). *a(keru)* open; empty, vacate; leave (a space); clear (the table); make (a hole); reserve (a seat), stay away from; dawn; end, expire, be over; open, begin. *a(ku)* open, be opened; start, begin, commence; become vacant, become empty, be disengaged, be free; expire, be over. *a(kasu)* spend, pass the time; reveal, divulge. *a(ke)* expiration, end; dawn. *akashi* proof. *aka(ri)* light, lamp; vindication. *aka(rui)* bright, light; cheerful, sunny; clear, clean; conversant with. *aki(raka)* bright; clear, plain, distinct, definite, obvious, indisputable, evident. *a(kuru)* next, following. *saya(keshi)* clear; refreshing; pure. *a(ki)-* empty, vacant, unoccupied, spare (time).

4 方 *a(ke)gata* dawn
月 *meigetsu* bright moon, bright moonlight
分 *meibun* moral duty; justice
天子 *meitenshi* wise ruler
文 *meibun* express provision
文化 *meibunka suru* stipulate
日 *myōnichi, ashita, asu* tomorrow. *a(keno)hi* the next day; tomorrow
日明後日 *asu-asatte* tomorrow or the next day
5 白 *meihaku na* clear, unmistakable
示 *meiji, meishi* clear statement
払 *a(ke)-hara(u)* leave open (a house or window); throw open
主 *meishu* wise ruler
弁 *meiben* clear understanding
6 色 *meishoku* bright color
地 *a(ki)chi* vacant lot, vacant land
先 *aka(ri)saki ni* in (a person's) light
年 *myōnen* next year
7 言 *meigen* declaration, assertion
快 *meikai* clear, explicit
君 *meikun* wise ruler
8 国 *Minkoku* China of the Mings
店 *a(ki)dana, a(ki)mise* vacant store
放 *a(ke)-hana(su)* throw open, open wide; leave open. *a(ke)-hana(reru)* grow light, dawn. *a(kep)pana(shi)* leaving (a door) open; blunt, frank, openhearted
取 *aka(ri)to(ri)* skylight, dormer
盲 *a(ki)mekura* illiterate
治神宮 *Meiji Jingū* Meiji Shrine
治節 *Meijisetsu* Emperor Meiji's birthday anniversary
治維新 *Meiji Ishin* Meiji Restoration
明 *akaaka to* brightly. *meimei* very clear

明白白 *meimei-hakuhaku* very clear
明星 *a(ke) (no) myōjō* morning star, Venus
明後日 *myōmyōgonichi, shiasatte, yanoasatte, yanaasatte* two days after tomorrow
9 屋 *a(ki)ya* vacant house
度 *meido* brightness
城 *a(ki)jiro* vacant castle
神 *myōjin* gracious deity
星 *myōjō* morning star; Venus; Lucifer; (literary) star
春 *myōshun* next spring
後日 *myōgonichi, asatte* day after tomorrow
後年 *myōgonen* year after next
10 倫 *meirin* making clear the moral obligations of man
残 *a(ke)-noko(ru)* lingering (night)
記 *meiki suru* specify
敏 *meibin* intelligence, discernment
烏 *a(ke)garasu* crows cawing at dawn
家 *a(ki)ya, a(ki)ie* vacant house, empty house
哲 *meitetsu* wise man, sage
部屋 *a(ki)beya* vacant room
朗 *meirō na* clear, bright, cheerful
朗化 *meirōka suru* cheer up, brighten
11 達 *meitatsu* wisdom, intelligence
視 *meishi* clear vision
断 *meidan* wise judgment
窓 *aka(ri)mado* window
笛 *meiteki* a good flute
巣 *a(ki)su* empty nest; vacant house; pilferer
細 *meisai* details, particulars. *meisai na* obvious
細書 *meisaisho* detailed statement, specifications
眸 *meibō* bright eyes
眸皓歯 *meibō-kōshi* beautiful face
眸禍 *meibōka* ruin brought about by one's beauty
12 間 *a(ki)ma* vacant room. *a(kezuno)ma, a(kazuno)ma* forbidden or haunted room
媚 *meibi na* picturesque, beautiful
晩 *myōban* tomorrow night
晰 *meiseki na* clear, distinct
渡 *a(ke)-wata(ru)* dawn, become light. *a(ke)-wata(su)* vacate; evacuate; surrender
答 *meitō* definite answer
番 *a(ke)ban* off duty
智 *meichi* wisdom, intelligence
御目出 *A(kemashite) Omede(tō) (Gozaimasu)* Happy New Year.
朝 *myōchō, myōasa* tomorrow morning. *Minchō* Ming Dynasty; Ming style
朝活字 *Minchō katsuji* Ming-dynasty-style characters
13 解 *meikai* clear understanding
障子 *a(kari) shōji* translucent paper doors
滅 *meimetsu suru* appear and disappear, flicker, glimmer
滅灯 *meimetsutō* occulting light
暗 *meian* light and darkness
暗灯 *meiantō* occulting light
暗度 *meiando* brightness
14 徳 *meitoku* illustrious virtue
徴 *meichō* clarification
察 *meisatsu* discernment, insight
暮 *aka(shi)-ku(rasu), a(ke)-ku(rasu)* live. *a(ketemo)-ku(retemo)* always. *a(ke)-ku(re)* day and night, morning and evening; day in and day out, all the time, early and late
15 澈 *meitetsu* the clearness of water
澄 *meichō na* clear
確 *meikaku na* clear, distinctive, definite
17 瞭 *meiryō* clearness
19 離 *a(ke)-hana(reru)* become light, dawn
鏡 *meikyō* clear mirror
鏡止水 *meikyō shisui* serene frame of mind
20 鐘 *a(keno) kane* a bell at dawn
礬 *myōban* alum

5

昿 2436 / J5b26 / M-X — Nonstandard for **曠** 2525.

昜 2437 / J5a66 / M13832 — See **陽** 6470.

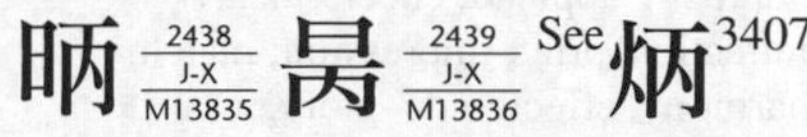

晒 2438 / J-X / M13835 **昺** 2439 / J-X / M13836 — See **炳** 3407.

旺 2440 / J-X / M-X — Nonstandard for **曜** 2522.

昴 2441 / J5a65 / M13865 Bō. Myō *Subaru* the Pleiades.

昶 2442 / J5a64 / M13867 Chō long; long time; clear; stretch.

曷 2443 / J5b2b / M14290 [曰] Katsu. Kachi *nan(zo), izuku(nzo)* what, why, how.

昧 2444 / J4b66 / M13846 Mai dark; foolish.

11 爽 *maisō* daybreak, dawn

昵 2445 / J5a63 / M13866 Jitsu reconcile, approach; become intimate.

6 近 *jikkin* intimacy

17 懇 *jikkon* intimacy

A **昭** 2446 / J3e3c / M13855 Shō clear, bright.

5 示 *shōshi suru* show clearly

代 *shōdai* enlightened era, glorious reign

8 和 *Shōwa* the name of the era from 1926 to 1989

和天皇 *Shōwa Tennō* the Shōwa Emperor

9 昭 *shōshō* clearness

昻 2447 / J-X / M13885 **昂** 2424 / J3937 / M13783 Kō rise.

10 進 *kōshin* rise; acceleration; exasperation

12 揚 *kōyō suru* exalt, promote, enhance

然 *kōzen(taru)* elated, triumphant

16 奮 *kōfun* excitement, agitation, stimulation

20 騰 *kōtō* sudden price jump

A **映** 2448 / J3147 / M13838 Ei reflecting; projection. *ei(jiru), ei(zuru)* be reflected in, shine on; impress, appear to. *ha(eru)* shine, be brilliant; look attractive. *utsu(ru)* be reflected; match, harmonize, be becoming; be taken (a photo). *utsu(su)* copy, transcribe, duplicate, reproduce, trace; describe, picture, photograph. *ha(yasu)* applaud, cheer. *utsu(ri)* reflection, print, impression; match, harmony, effect. *hae* glory.

5 写 *eisha* projection

写幕 *eisha maku* screen (for pictures)

写機 *eishaki* projector

8 画 *eiga* cinema, movie, moving picture, film

画化 *eigaka* filming, making a film version

画界 *eigakai* screen world, filmdom

画劇 *eigageki* screenplay

画館 *eigakan* movie theater

12 渡 *ha(e)-wata(ru)* shine all over

14 像 *eizō* reflection, image, silhouette

A **昨** 2449 / J3a72 / M13847 Saku the past; yesterday, last (year). *saku-* last (year); yesterday.

3 夕 *sakuyū* last evening

4 今 *sakkon* nowadays, recently

日 *sakujitsu, kinō* yesterday

日今日 *kinō (no) kyō* just now

5 冬 *sakutō* last winter

6 年 *sakunen* last year

年末 *sakunemmatsu* end of last year

8 夜 *sakuya, yūbe* last night, last evening

非今是 *sakuhikonze* vacillation, fickleness

9 秋 *sakushū* last fall

春 *sakushun* last spring

10 紙 *sakushi* yesterday's paper

夏 *sakka* last summer

12 晩 *sakuban* last night, last evening

暁 *sakugyō* at daybreak yesterday

朝 *sakuchō* yesterday morning

A **昼** 2450 / J436b / M13886 **晝** 2465 / J5a6c / M13948 Chū daytime, midday. *hiru* midday, daytime, noon.

3 下 *hirusa(gari)* early afternoon

4 日中 *hiruhinaka* daytime; noon

6 休 *hiruyasu(mi)* noon recess, noon rest period

行灯 *hiruandon* (useless as) a lantern at noon day

光色電球 *chūkōshoku denkyū* daylight lamp

8 夜 *chūya, hiru (mo) yoru (mo)* day and night

夜舎 *chūya (o) o(kazu)* continuing day and night

夜兼行 *chūya kenkō* working day and night

9 食 *chūshoku, chūjiki, hiruge* lunch, midday meal

前 *hirumae* forenoon; just before noon

10 時 *hirudoki* noon, lunch time

11 過 *hirusu(gi)* afternoon
頃 *hirugoro* about noon
12 間 *hiruma, chūkan* daytime; during the day
飯 *hirumeshi, chūhan* lunch, midday meal
13 寝 *hirune* siesta, nap
14 鳶 *hirutombi* sneak thief
15 餉 *hiruge* lunch, midday meal
16 餐 *chūsan* luncheon
興行 *hirukōgyō* matinee

B 是 2451 / J4027 / M13859 ZE right, justice. *kore* this. *kore de* with this. *kore demo* such as I am. *koko ni* here. *kore kara* now, from now on, from here.
3 丈 *kore dake* only this much, this much, so much
4 切 *koregi(ri), koreki(ri), kore(k)ki(ri)* just this time, never again; This is all.
以 *kore (o) motte* with this
以上 *kore ijō* better than this
5 正 *zesei* correction, revision
6 式 *koreshiki* such a trifle; just this much
先 *kore (yori) saki* previously, meanwhile; farther on
迄 *kore made* until now; before now; no more hope
7 見 *kore-mi(yogashi) ni* ostentatiously
位 *koregurai* only this much, this much, so much
8 於 *koko (ni) oi(te)* then
限 *korekagi(ri)* just this time, never again; This is all.
非 *zehi* right or wrong, pro and con; surely, by all means. *zehi suru* comment on, criticize
非共 *zehitomo* surely; please
非曲直 *zehi-kyokuchoku* good and bad; right and wrong
非無 *zehina(i)* inevitable; necessary, unavoidable
9 是 *korekore* this and that; etc.
kore(wa)kore(wa) an exclamation of surprise
是非非 *zeze-hihi* fair and just, clear-cut (policy)
是非非主義 *zeze-hihi shugi* fair and just, clear-cut (policy)
11 許 *korebaka(ri)* only this, so little
12 程 *korehodo* this much, so much, (not) more

等 *korera* these
14 認 *zenin* approval

A 星 2452 / J4031 / M13837 SEI, SHŌ star. *hoshi* star; spot, dot, mark; bull's eye; one's fortune; point, score.
4 斗 *seito* stars
月夜 *hoshizukiyo* starlit night
5 占 *hoshi urana(i), seisen* astrology, horoscope
6 行 *seikō* great speed
回 *hoshimawa(ri)* one's fortune
団 *seidan* star cluster
合 *hoshia(i)* July Seventh meeting of the Cowherd Star (Altair) and the Weaver Star (Vega)
7 図 *seizu* star map
形 *hoshigata* star shape
条旗 *Seijōki* the Stars and Stripes
辰 *seishin* stars, heavenly bodies
辰崇拝 *seishin sūhai* astrolatry, star worship
8 雨 *seiu* meteoric showers
明 *hoshi aka(ri)* starlight
河 *Seika* the Milky Way
夜 *seiya* starry night
学 *seigaku* astronomy
学家 *seigakuka* astronomer; astrologer
9 食 *seishoku* occultation; cover, obscuration, blanketing
型 *hoshigata* star shape
珊瑚 *hoshi sango* bloodstone
10 座 *seiza* constellation
座早見図 *seiza hayamizu* planisphere
11 宿 *seishuku* constellation
章 *seishō* badge, star
祭 *Hoshi Matsu(ri)* Tanabata Weaver Star Festival (July 7)
12 雲 *seiun* nebula
雲説 *seiunsetsu* nebular hypothesis
13 群 *seigun* star cluster
15 標 *seihyō* asterisk, star
影 *hoshikage* starlight
17 霜 *seisō* years, time

A 春 2453 / J3d55 / M13844 SHUN spring. *haru* spring, springtime. *haru(meku)* become springlike.
2 七草 *haru (no) nanakusa* the seven herbs of spring
3 山 *haruyama* mountains in the spring
4 心 *shunshin* thoughts of spring; air of spring; sexual passion

方 *harube* springtime
日 *haruhi, shunjitsu* spring day
分 *shumbun* vernal equinox
分日 *Shumbun (no) Hi* the Vernal Equinox (holiday, March 21)
分点 *shumbunten* the vernal equinoctial point
5 立 *haruta(tsu)* Spring is coming on.
本 *shumpon* pornographic book
6 色 *shunshoku* spring scenery
気 *shunki* atmosphere of spring, spring fever, spring landscape
帆 *shumpan* a boat floating on the water in spring; spring sailing
光 *shunkō* spring scenery
先 *harusaki* early spring
7 売 *haru (o) u(ru)* sell one's virtue, prostitute oneself
告鳥 *harutsu(ge)dori* nightingale
8 雨 *harusame, shun'u* spring rain; bean-jelly sticks
物 *harumono* spring goods
郊 *shunkō* spring countryside
画 *shunga* erotic *ukiyoe* print; pornography
季 *shunki* spring, springtime
季皇霊祭 *Shunki Kōreisai* Shinto Festival of the Vernal Equinox
9 風 *harukaze, shumpū* spring breeze
信 *shunshin* signs of spring, tidings of flowers
思 *shunshi* thoughts of spring
草 *haru kusa* new spring grass
秋 *haru-aki, shunjū* spring and fall; months and years
秋富 *shunjū (ni) to(mu)* be young
10 時 *shunji* springtime
眠 *shummin* morning sleep in spring
蚕 *haruko, harugo, shunsan* spring silkworms
宵 *shunshō* spring evening, spring night
宮 *tōgū, haru (no) miya* the crown prince. *shunkyū* palace of the crown prince
容 *shun'yō* spring scene
夏秋冬 *shun-ka-shū-tō* the four seasons; the year round
11 情 *shunjō* sexual passion
野 *haruno* fields in spring
陽 *shun'yō* springtime; spring sunshine
雪 *shunsetsu* spring snow
12 暁 *shungyō* spring dawn
寒 *shunkan* late cold spell
嵐 *shunran* spring storm; spring mists
着 *harugi* spring wear; New Year's clothes
場所 *haru basho* spring sumo tournament
景 *shunkei* spring scene
景色 *harugeshiki* spring scenery
13 暖 *shundan* warm spring weather
蒔 *harumaki* spring sowing
夢 *shummu* a dream of a spring evening; something fleeting
雷 *shunrai* spring thunder
愁 *shunshū* gloom in spring
15 駒 *harugoma* spring colt; pony dance; pep
16 機発動期 *shunki hatsudōki* age of puberty
17 霞 *harugasumi* spring haze
18 蟬 *haruzemi* spring cicada

6

晦 2454 / J3322 / M-X Nonstandard for **晦** 2478.

晋 2455 / J3f38 / M13899 **晉** 2456 / J5a69 / M13898 SHIN advance.

晁 2457 / J5a6a / M13889 CHŌ. JŌ morning.

晃 2458 / J3938 / M13891 **晄** 2459 / J5a68 / M13892 KŌ clear.
10 晃 *kōkō(taru)* brilliant, light

晏 2460 / J5a67 / M13914 AN late; (the sun) sets; quiet.
6 如 *anjo* being at ease, comfort, peace
12 然 *anzen to* peacefully

晒 2461 / J3b2f / M13924 **曬** 2528 / J-X / M14266 SAI. *sara(su)* bleach, refine; expose, air. *sarashi* bleaching; bleached cotton.
4 木綿 *sarashimomen* bleached cotton cloth
5 台 *sarashidai* pillory, stocks
8 者 *sarashimono* exposed criminal
9 首 *sarashikubi* unburied severed head
10 粉 *sarashiko* bleaching powder, chloride of lime

14 飴 *sarashiame* thick rice syrup

A 時 2462 J3b7e M13890 JI hour, o'clock, time; Buddhist sect originating in the thirteenth century. *toki* time, hour, moment; occasion; season; opportunity; the times; tense. *toki(meku)* prosper, flourish, be influential; prosperous, influential. *toki ni* now, by the way, in passing. *toki(naranu)* unseasonable, untimely, inopportune; sudden, unexpected. *toki ni totte* on the occasion, for the occasion. *toki niwa, toki(tama), toki toshite* occasionally. *toki(shimo), toki(shimoare)* just then. *toki to shite* sometimes, in some cases. *-ji* time, period.

2 人 *jijin* contemporaries. *toki (no) hito* a person in the public eye
3 下 *jika* at present
4 文 *jibun* modern writing
日 *jijitsu* the date, the time; days
化 *shike(ru)* be stormy; be gloomy. *shike* stormy weather, heavy sea; scarcity of fish; business depression
分 *jibun* time, hour, season, time of year; (proper) time, opportunity; those days
分時 *jibundoki* mealtime
5 外 *tokihazu(re)* unseasonable, untimely, inopportune
世 *jisei* the times, the era. *tokiyo* era, age; current trends
世時節 *tokiyo-jisetsu* the times and seasons; this world's constant changes
代 *jidai* period, age, stage, antiquity
代色 *jidaishoku* era color
代行列 *jidai gyōretsu* historic pageant
代性 *jidaisei* characteristic of the age
代物 *jidaimono* an antique, historical object; historical play
代後 *jidaioku(re)* out-of-date
代相 *jidaisō* trend of the times
代思想 *jidai shisō* current thinking
代思潮 *jidai shichō* trend of the times
代病 *jidaibyō* morbid idea of the times
代遅 *jidaioku(re)* out-of-date
代精神 *jidai seishin* spirit of the times
代劇 *jidaigeki* historic costume play; historical play
代錯誤 *jidai sakugo* anachronism; being behind the times
代寵児 *jidai (no) chōji* a man of the times
6 至 *toki-ita(ranu)* unappreciated. *toki-ita(tte)* timely
好 *jikō* fashion, fad, vogue
7 局 *jikyoku* situation
折 *tokio(ri)* at times, occasionally
余 *jiyo* over an hour
辰儀 *jishingi* chronometer
8 雨 *shigu(reru)* the late rains fall; tears fall. *shigure, jiu* late fall or early winter rain; shedding tears
価 *jika* current price
服 *jifuku* appropriate clothing
制 *jisei* tense (in grammar)
効 *jikō* statute of limitations
宜 *jigi* the right time; season's greetings; bowing
宗 *Jishū* a Buddhist sect
刻 *jikoku* time, hour, the time
刻表 *jikokuhyō* time table, schedule
事 *jiji* current events
事問題 *jiji mondai* current topics
事解説 *jiji kaisetsu* comment on current events
限 *jigen* time limit; period; limited
限装置 *jigen sōchi* timing mechanism
限錠 *jigenjō* time lock
限爆弾 *jigen-bakudan* time bomb
9 風 *jifū* fashion of the day
疫 *jieki* epidemic, pestilence, plague
速 *jisoku* speed per hour
俗 *jizoku* ways of the age; current trends; conventionality
相 *jisō* tense (in grammar)
点 *jiten* occasion
計 *tokei* clock, watch, timepiece
計工 *tokeikō* watchmaker
計台 *tokeidai* clock stand, clock tower
計仕掛 *tokeijika(ke)* clockwork
計仕掛爆弾 *tokeijika(ke) bakudan* time bomb
計回 *tokeimawa(ri)* clockwise
計店 *tokeiten* watchmaker, jewelry store
計屋 *tokeiya* watchmaker, jeweler
計信管 *tokei shinkan* clockwork fuse
計師 *tokeishi* watchmaker, jeweler
計番 *tokeiban* clock master
計爆弾 *tokei bakudan* time bomb
10 借 *tokiga(ri)* temporary loan
流 *jiryū* trend of the times
砲 *jihō* time gun

時 *tokidoki* sometimes, occasionally, frequently; each time, each season. *tokidoki no* seasonal, occasional, recurrent. *jiji* from time to time
時刻刻 *jiji-kokkoku* hourly; momentarily
差 *jisa* time difference
差惚 *jisaboke* jetlag
差出勤 *jisa shukkin* staggered office hours, flexible worktime
候 *jikō* season, time of year; climate
候中 *jikōata(ri)* under the weather
候外 *jikōhazu(re)* unseasonable
11 鳥 *hototogisu* cuckoo
運 *jiun* tide of fortune
偶 *tokitama* at times, infrequently, occasionally
球 *jikyū* time ball
務 *jimu* current affairs
移 *toki (o) utsu(sazu)* immediately
習 *jishū* periodic reviewing
得 *toki (o) e(ru)* be prosperous
得顔 *toki(o)egao ni* proudly, triumphantly
12 給 *jikyū* payment by the hour
評 *jihyō* editorial comment
期 *jiki* time, the times, season
無 *tokina(shi)* no settled time; atmosphere of failure
貸 *tokiga(shi)* temporary loan, call money, trust credit
報 *jihō* review; time siren
場合 *toki (to) baai de* according to time and place
間 *jikan* an hour; time; period
間外 *jikangai* late; overtime; outside of hours
間表 *jikanhyō* timetable, schedule
間制賃金 *jikansei chingin* hour-pay system
間記録器 *jikan kirokuki* time clock
間割 *jikanwari* timetable, schedule
間給 *jikankyū* payment by the hour
間給水 *jikan-kyūsui* hour-restricted water supply
間塞 *jikanfusagi* stopgap
間厲行 *jikan reikō* promptness in appointments
13 勢 *jisei* spirit of the age, trend of the times, conditions
節 *jisetsu* season; the times; opportunity
節柄 *jisetsugara* in these times
14 様 *jiyō* latest fashion
15 儀 *jigi* season's greetings; bowing
論 *jiron* contemporary opinion, comment on current events
弊 *jihei* evils of the times
16 機 *jiki* opportunity, time, occasion
20 鐘 *jishō* hour bells, (ship's) time bells

A **書** 2463 / J3d71 / M14294 SHO handwriting; letter, note; book. *sho(suru)* write. *ka(ku)* write, compose; draw, paint. *fumi* letter, note. [曰]
2 入 *ka(ki)-i(reru)* enter, write in, mortgage
入日 *kakii(re)bi* red-letter day, a day to look forward to
入時 *kakii(re)doki* best season (for profits)
3 及 *ka(ki)-oyo(bu)* be able to write (a certain amount)
下 *ka(ki)-kuda(su)* write down. *ka(ki)-oro(su)* write a new play
上 *ka(ki)-a(geru)* finish writing; write out
4 手 *ka(ki)te* calligrapher, copyist; painter
方 *ka(ki)kata* manner of writing; penmanship, (prescribed) form
止 *ka(ki)-todo(meru)* record, chronicle. *ka(ki)-sa(su)* leave off writing, leave unfinished
込 *ka(ki)-ko(mu)* enter, write in; mortgage
中 *shochū* within the letter, the book, or the document
分 *ka(ki)-wa(keru)* classify and write up
5 目 *shomoku* catalog of books
立 *ka(ki)-ta(teru)* write up; feature; write against; enumerate
史 *shoshi* books; history of books; history of calligraphy
付 *ka(ki)-tsu(keru)* make a note of. *kakitsuke* note; bill
加 *ka(ki)-kuwa(eru)* add; add a postscript
写 *ka(ki)-utsu(su)* copy, transcribe. *shosha* copying
出 *ka(ki)-da(su)* begin to write; make an excerpt; make out a bill; present in writing. *ka(ki)da(shi)* opening paragraph; bill
冊 *shosatsu* books
生 *shosei* student; one studying while working in a teacher's home
生論 *shoseiron* impractical argument

6 尽 *ka(ki)-tsuku(su)* write exhaustively
式 *shoshiki* blank form
伝 *ka(ki)-tsuta(eru)* hand down to posterity (in writing)
交 *ka(ki)-ka(wasu)* exchange notes. *ka(ki)-ma(zeru)* write a medley of ideas
名 *shomei* title of a book
7 見 *shoken* reading
足 *ka(ki) ta(su)* add, write a postscript
体 *shotai* penmanship style; style of one's characters
改 *ka(ki)-arata(meru)* rewrite
役 *ka(ki)yaku* copyist, scribe
抜 *ka(ki)-nu(ku)* abstract, copy out, take an excerpt. *kakinu(ki)* quotation, excerpt
状 *shojō* letter
狂 *shokyō* bibliomania; bibliomaniac
乱 *ka(ki)-mida(su)* scribble, scrawl
初 *ka(ki)zo(me)* first writing of the new year
判 *ka(ki)han* written seal, monogram, signature
言葉 *ka(ki)kotoba* written language
8 店 *shoten* bookstore; publisher
房 *shobō* library; bookstore
送 *ka(ki)-oku(ru)* write a letter, send a letter
林 *shorin* bookstore
板 *ka(ki)ita* writing tablet
法 *shohō* calligraphy, penmanship
取 *ka(ki)-to(ru)* take down, write from dictation. *kakito(ri)* dictation
画 *shoga* pictures and writings
並 *ka(ki)-nara(beru)* line up points in a speech
直 *ka(ki)-nao(su)* rewrite
表 *ka(ki)-ara(wasu)* write out, express, publish
具合 *ka(ki)guai* style of writing
物 *shomotsu* books. *ka(ki)mono* something written, papers
物道楽 *shomotsu dōraku* bibliomania; booklover
9 面 *shomen* letter, document, contents
風 *shofū* style of calligraphy
信 *shoshin* letter, message, correspondence
洩 *ka(ki)-mo(rasu)* omit, leave out (words)
巻 *shokan* book
架 *shoka* bookshelf, bookcase
院 *shoin* window writing alcove; drawing room; study; school; publishing house
院造 *shoinzuku(ri)* palatial Momoyama residential architecture
10 庫 *shoko* book room, library
起 *ka(ki)oko(shi)* opening paragraph
振 *kakibu(ri)* style of writing
残 *ka(ki)-noko(su)* omit (something) in writing; leave a will behind; leave a history behind
流 *ka(ki)-naga(su)* write with ease
消 *ka(ki)-ke(su)* erase and rewrite
破 *ka(ki)-yabu(ru)* write and tear up
紋 *ka(ki)mon* hand-drawn family crest
家 *shoka* good penman, calligrapher
留 *ka(ki)-to(meru)* write down; make a note of; jot down. *kakitome* registered mail
留料 *kakitomeryō* registration fee
留郵便 *kakitome yūbin* registered mail
記 *ka(ki)-shiru(su)* write down, record. *shoki* clerk, secretary, scribe
記会計 *shoki-kaikei* secretary-treasurer
記長 *shokichō* chief clerk, chief secretary
記官 *shokikan* secretary
記官長 *shokikanchō* chief secretary
記補 *shokiho* assistant clerk
11 道 *shodo* calligraphy
過 *ka(ki)su(gi)* writing too much
添 *ka(ki)-so(eru)* add, write a postscript
淫 *shoin* booklover, bookworm
渋 *ka(ki)-shibu(ru)* hesitate to write or sign
混 *ka(ki)-ma(zeru)* write a medley of ideas
経 *Shokyō* Shu Jing, Shu Ching (a Chinese classic)
終 *ka(ki)-owa(ru)* finish writing
崩 *ka(ki)-kuzu(su)* write in slurred characters
著 *ka(ki)-arawa(su)* publish
斎 *shosai* study, library, den
12 越 *ka(ki)-ko(su)* write and send hither
遣 *ka(ki)-ya(ru)* send a note
違 *ka(ki)-chiga(eru)* miswrite. *ka(ki)chiga(i)* clerical error, slip of the pen
換 *ka(ki)-kae(ru)* rewrite; renew (a bond); transfer, convey. *kakika(e)* writing over again

棚 *shodana* bookshelf
絵 *ka(ki)e* original picture; hand-drawn picture
証 *shoshō* documentary evidence
割 *kakiwa(ri)* background, scenery (on a stage)
散 *ka(ki)-chi(rasu)* scribble, scrawl
落 *ka(ki)-oto(su)* omit, leave out (words)
集 *ka(ki)-atsu(meru)* compile, collect
替 *ka(ki)-ka(eru)* rewrite; renew (a bond); transfer, convey
評 *shohyō* book review
評家 *shohyōka* book reviewer
13 損 *ka(ki)-sokona(u), ka(ki)-son(jiru)* miswrite
続 *ka(ki)-tsuzu(keru)* continue to write
辞 *shoji* the words of a letter
肆 *shoshi* bookstore
置 *kakio(ki)* farewell note, will
賈 *shoko* bookseller
聖 *shosei* master calligrapher
賃 *ka(ki)chin* writing charge
載 *ka(ki)-no(seru)* publish, print; register, enroll, enter
14 慣 *ka(ki)-na(reru)* get used to writing
様 *ka(ki)zama* manner of writing
漏 *ka(ki)-mo(rasu)* omit in writing, leave out
誤 *ka(ki)-aya(maru)* miswrite
算 *shosan* writing and arithmetic
誌学 *shoshigaku* bibliography
16 翰 *shokan* letter, note, epistle
翰文 *shokambun* letter-writing style
翰箋 *shokansen* letter paper
17 擲 *ka(ki)-nagu(ru)* dash off (articles)
18 難 *ka(ki)niku(i)* difficult to write or draw
類 *shorui* documents, papers
類箱 *shoruibako* filing cabinet
簡 *shokan* letter, note, epistle
簡文 *shokambun* letter-writing style, epistolary style
簡紙 *shokanshi* stationery
簡集 *shokanshū* collected letters
簡箋 *shokansen* letter paper
20 籍 *shoseki, shojaku* books, publication
籍商 *shosekishō* bookseller, bookstore
籍業 *shosekigyō* publishing business

7

曽 2464 J413e M-X Nonstandard for  2483.

晝 2465 J5a6c M13948 See 昼 2450.

晩 2466 J-X M13940 **晚** 2467 J-X M-X See 晩 2491.

晃 2468 J-X M-X Nonstandard for 晃 397.

晢 2469 J5a71 M13953 **晣** 2470 J-X M13954 SEI. SETSU bright, clear.

晞 2471 J5a6b M13949 KI dry; hang out to dry; sunrise.

晟 2472 J5a70 M13950 SEI. JŌ bright, clear; abundant.

晧 2473 J5a6e M13961 KŌ sunrise; bright, brilliant.

晤 2474 J5a6d M13956 GO clear.

曼 2475 J5258 M14298 MAN wide; beautiful. [曰]
7 陀羅 *mandara* mandala, picture of Buddhas
10 荼羅 *mandara* mandala, picture of Buddhas

晨 2476 J5a6f M13962 SHIN morning, early.
8 明 *shimmei* morning star
9 星 *shinsei* morning star

曹 2477 J4162 M14297 B SŌ, ZŌ friend. [曰]
5 司 *zōshi* cadet, young son
8 長 *sōchō* sergeant-major
11 達 *sōda* soda
達水 *sōdasui* soda water

晦 2478 J-X M13960 **晦** 2454 J3322 M-X KAI dark. *kura(masu)* give the slip to, disappear. *tsugomori* month end, last day of the month; the dark of the moon.
4 日 *misoka* the last day of the month
8 明 *kaimei* day and night, night and darkness

10 朔 *kaisaku* last and first days of successive months
冥 *kaimei* darkness
11 渋 *kaijū* ambiguity, obscurity

8

暎 2479 J5a75 M14048 See 映 2448.

昮 2480 J5a73 M-X HI separate, go away.

晰 2481 J5a72 M13990 SHAKU. SEKI clear.

B 晶 2482 J3e3d M14000 SHŌ clear; crystal.
4 化 *shōka* crystallization

曾 2483 J412d M14299 SŌ. SO. *katsu(te), kat(te)* once, before, formerly; ever, never (neg.); former, ex-. [曰]
9 祖父 *sōsofu, hiijiji, hiōji* great-grandfather
祖母 *sōsobo, hiibaba, hiōba* great-grandmother
10 孫 *hiimago, sōson, hiko, himago* great-grandchild

A 暑 2484 J3d6b M14031' 暑 2496 J-X M14031 SHO summer heat. *atsu(garu)* feel the heat, swelter. *atsu(gari)* sensitivity to heat; a person sensitive to hot weather. *atsu(i)* hot, warm, sultry. *atsu(sa)* heat, hot weather.
4 中 *shochū* midsummer, hot season. *atsusaata(ri)* heatstroke, sunstroke.
中見舞 *shochū mima(i)* summer health inquiry
中休暇 *shochū kyūka* summer vacation
6 気 *atsuke, shoki* hot weather; heatstroke, sunstroke
気中 *shokiata(ri)* heatstroke, sunstroke
8 苦 *atsuguru(shii), atsukuru(shii)* sultry, sweltering
9 屋 *atsu(gari)ya* person sensitive to hot weather
10 凌 *atsu(sa)shino(gi)* relief from the heat
12 寒 *shokan* heat and cold; a year
15 熱 *shonetsu* summer heat

B 暁 2485 J3647 M14031 曉 2513 J5a7c M14176 暁 2495 J-X M-X GYŌ. *akatsuki* dawn, daybreak; in the event (of).
4 天 *gyōten* dawn
天星 *gyōten (no) hoshi* morning star; a few
5 旦 *gyōtan* dawn, daybreak
6 光 *gyōkō* light at dawn
色 *gyoshoku* scene at dawn
7 更 *akatsuki(no)kō* early morning, 4–6 a.m.
8 明星 *ake (no) myōjō* morning star, Venus; Lucifer
9 通 *gyōtsū* thorough knowledge
紅 *gyōkō* rosy dawn
星 *gyōsei* morning star, Venus; rarity
10 起 *gyōki* arising early
11 達 *gyōtatsu* thorough knowledge
12 智 *gyōchi* great wisdom
20 鐘 *gyosho* a bell at daybreak

B 替 2486 J4258 M14300 TAI. TEI. *ka(eru)* change, turn, convert, exchange, renew, substitute, replace. *kawa(ru)* replace, relieve. *kawa(ri)* substitute, deputy, proxy, alternate, relief; compensation; second helping. *ka(e)-* spare, substitute, exchange. *kae(de)* at, for, per. [曰]
3 刃 *ka(e)ba* extra blades
5 玉 *ka(e)dama* substitute, a double
6 地 *ka(e)chi* substitute land
字 *ka(e)ji* a substitute character of the same pronunciation
名 *ka(e)na* alias
7 狂言 *kawa(ri) kyōgen* new play, new program
8 肩 *ka(e)gata* spare palanquin carrier
事 *ka(e)goto* swapping, exchanging
10 馬 *ka(e)uma* spare horse
11 得 *ka(e)doku* gain in exchanging (something)
12 着 *ka(e)gi* a change of clothing
13 損 *ka(e)zon* a loss in exchanging (something)
蓋 *ka(e)buta* extra lid
14 歌 *ka(e)uta* parody in song

A 景 2487 J374a M13983 KEI view, scene.
6 色 *keshiki, keishoku* scenery, landscape

仰 *keikō* love of virtue. *keigyō* adoration, admiration; a love of virtue
気 *keiki* the times, business conditions; liveliness
気付 *keikizu(ku)* boom, become active. *keikizu(ke)* promotion stunt
気良 *keikiyo(ku)* briskly, prosperously
8 況 *keikyō* situation; outlook
物 *keibutsu* (seasonal) scenery; premium, present
9 品 *keihin* premium, present, bonus
品券 *keihinken* premium lottery ticket
10 致 *keichi* beauty of nature
11 教 *Keikyō* Nestorianism
教徒 *Keikyōto* a Nestorian
12 勝 *keishō* picturesque scenery; advantageous position
雲 *keiun* an auspicious cloud
13 福 *keifuku* great happiness
14 慕 *keibo suru* honor, worship
15 趣 *keishu* scenery, landscape
18 観 *keikan* spectacle,view

A **晴** 2488 / J4032 / M13994 SEI. *ha(reru)* clear up; (doubts) vanish; be refreshed. *ha(rasu)* dispel, clear away (gloom); refresh (oneself). *ha(re)* fine weather. *ha(reyakana)* clear, bright; radiant, cheerful. *ha(rete)* openly, publicly. *ha(regamashii)* openhearted, frank.
3 上 *ha(re)-a(garu)* clear up
4 天 *seiten* fine weather, clear sky
天白日 *seiten-hakujitsu* innocence; clear weather
6 好 *seikō* beautiful clear skies
衣 *haregi, hareginu* one's best clothes
衣装 *hareishō* one's best clothes
8 雨 *seiu* rain or shine; weather conditions
雨計 *seiukei* barometer
9 姿 *ha(re)sugata* wearing one's best clothes
10 陰 *seiin* sunlight and shadow
朗 *seirō* clear, fair, fine, bright
耕雨読 *seikō-udoku* working in fair weather and reading in wet
12 間 *ha(re)ma* clear interval
晴 *ha(re)ba(reshii), harebare(shita)* clear, cloudless; cheerful, refreshing; splendid
渡 *ha(re)-wata(ru)* clear up
着 *ha(re)gi* one's best clothes
場所 *ha(re) (no) basho* a large gathering
勝負 *ha(re) shōbu* public contests
14 模様 *ha(re) moyō* clearing weather
16 曇 *seidon* fine weather and cloudy

B **普** 2489 / J4961 / M13982 **普** 2494 / J-X / M-X FU. *amane(ku)* widely, generally.
3 及 *fukyū* diffusion, dissemination
及版 *fukyūban* cheap popular edition
9 段 *fudan* usually, habitually, continually; constantly; indecision, irresolution
段着 *fudangi* ordinary clothes
通 *futsū* ordinary, common, usual, mediocre
通人 *futsūjin* ordinary person
通名詞 *futsū meishi* common noun
通法 *futsūhō* common law
通科 *futsūka* regular or general course
通株 *futsū kabu* common stock
通選挙 *futsū senkyo* universal suffrage
11 遍 *fuhen* universality, ubiquity, omnipresence
遍妥当性 *fuhen-datōsei* ability to fit into any situation
遍性 *fuhensei* universality, ubiquity, omnipresence
遍的 *fuhenteki* universal, omnipresent
14 選 *fusen* universal suffrage
15 請 *fushin* building, construction
請場 *fushimba* building plot

智 2490 / J4352 / M14010 CHI wisdom, intellect; intelligence, reason; strategem.
2 力 *chiryoku* wisdom, intellectual power, mental capacity, intellect, mentality, brains
4 仁勇 *chi-jin-yū* wisdom, benevolence, and courage
8 育 *chiiku* mental education
者 *chisha* wise person, sage
9 勇 *chiyū* intelligence and courage; wise and courageous person

10 将 *chishō* resourceful general
能 *chinō* knowledge and ability
能犯 *chinōhan* intellectual crime, crime of deception
能指数 *chinō shisū* IQ, intelligence quotient
能商 *chinōshō* IQ, intelligence quotient
能検査 *chinō kensa* mental test
恵 *chie* wisdom, sense, sagacity, intelligence, resourcefulness
恵者 *chiesha* wise person
恵袋 *chiebukuro* one's close advisor; brain trust
恵歯 *chieba* wisdom tooth
恵輪 *chie (no) wa* puzzle ring
恵熱 *chie netsu* fever accompanying dentition
恵競 *chie kurabe* quiz contest
11 略 *chiryaku* ingenuity, talents
12 歯 *chishi* wisdom tooth
13 愚 *chigu* wisdom and foolishness; wise men and fools
15 慮 *chiryo* wise idea; planning ability
慧 *chie* wisdom, sense, sagacity, intelligence, resourcefulness
16 謀 *chibō* ingenuity, resourcefulness
19 識 *chishiki* wisdom
22 嚢 *chinō* brains, wits

A **晩** 2491 / J4855 / M14030' **晚** 2466 / I-X / M13940 **晩** 2467 / I-X / M-ẋ

BAN evening, night; the end of all things; late.
4 方 *bangata* toward evening
5 生 *okute, bansei* late rice; late crops
冬 *bantō* late winter
6 成 *bansei* late success; late development
年 *bannen* late in life
7 花 *banka* late-blooming flowers
8 刻 *bankoku* toward evening
学 *bangaku* late education
9 秋 *banshū* late fall
春 *banshun* late spring
10 酌 *banshaku* an evening drink of saké
夏 *banka* late summer
蚕 *bansan* late cocoons
11 遅 *ban'oso(ku)* late at night
婚 *bankon* late marriage
涼 *banryō* the cool of the evening
12 飯 *bammeshi* evening meal, supper
景 *bankei* evening; an evening scene
13 節 *bansetsu* life's closing years
照 *banshō* setting sun
14 稲 *bantō, okute* late rice
16 餐 *bansan* supper, dinner
餐式 *Bansanshiki* the Lord's Supper, Eucharist, Holy Communion
餐会 *bansankai* dinner party, banquet
17 霜 *bansō* late frost
霞 *banka* evening afterglow
19 禱 *bantō* evening prayer
20 鐘 *banshō* curfew; evening bell

A **最** 2492 / J3a47 / M14301 SAI. *motto(mo)* most. *sai-* ultra, most, maximum, extreme. *ito-* extremely, greatly. [曰]
3 小 *saishō* the smallest, the minimum
小限 *saishōgen* minimum
小限度 *saishō gendo* minimum
上 *saijō* the best; the highest
上級 *saijōkyū* superlative degree; highest class
上等 *saijōtō* top quality, super
上権 *saijōken* supreme power, supremacy
大 *saidai* maximum, greatest, largest
大限 *saidaigen* maximum
大限度 *saidai gendo* maximum
大級 *saidaikyū* superlative degree; highest class
大速力 *saidai sokuryoku* maximum speed
下 *saika* lowest; worst
下位 *saikai* lowest position, lowest rank
下級 *saikakyū* lowest class, lowest grade
下等 *saikatō* lowest grade
下層 *saikasō* the lowest class (of people)
4 中 *saichū ni, sanaka ni* in the midst of, at the height of. *monaka* middle; bean-jam wafer
少 *saishō* the fewest, the least, the minimum; the youngest
5 北 *saihoku* northernmost
古 *saiko* the oldest
右翼 *saiuyoku* extreme right wing
左翼 *saisayoku* extreme left wing
6 西 *saisei* westernmost
早 *mohaya* now, soon, already, by now
多数 *saitasū* the largest number
尖端 *saisentan* the lead, foremost, forefront
好調 *saikōchō* perfect (pitching) form
近 *saikin* recently; latest, newest

近親 *saikinshin* nearest relative
近親者 *saikinshinsha* nearest relative
7 尾 *saibi* the end, the very last
初 *saisho* the first, the beginning
良 *sairyō* the best, the ideal
良種 *sairyōshu* best variety
低 *saitei* lowest, minimum
低温度計 *saitei ondokei* minimum thermometer
低寒暖計 *saitei kandankei* minimum thermometer
8 長 *saichō no* longest
底 *saitei* lowest, minimum
果 *saiha(te)* farthest limit; farthest land
東 *saitō* easternmost
9 南 *sainan* southernmost
前 *saizen* foremost; short time ago; just now
前列 *saizenretsu* forefront, very front line
前線 *saizensen* spearhead, front, first line
後 *saigo, iyahate* the last, the end. *saigo no* last, final. *saigo ni* in conclusion; in the long run
後的 *saigoteki* final
後通告 *saigo tsūkoku* ultimatum
後通牒 *saigo tsūchō* ultimatum
10 徐行 *saijokō* dead slow, very slow
恵国 *saikeikoku* most-favored nation
恵国条欵 *saikeikoku jōkan* most-favored-nation clause
恵国待遇 *saikeikoku taigū* most-favored-nation treatment
高 *saikō* maximum, supreme, highest, best
高司令官 *saikō shireikan* commander-in-chief
高司令部 *saikō shireibu* supreme command
高位 *saikōi* highest place
高学府 *saikō gakufu* highest seat of learning
高価格 *saikō kakaku* ceiling price
高法規 *saikō hōki* supreme law
高点 *saikōten* highest point; highest mark
高品 *saikōhin* articles of highest quality
高峰 *saikōhō* highest peak; highest point reached
高善 *saikōzen* the highest good
高裁 *Saikōsai* Supreme Court
高裁判所 *Saikō Saibansho* Supreme Court
高最低寒暖計 *saikō-saitei kandankei* maximum-and-minimum thermometer
高温度計 *saikō ondokei* maximum thermometer
高寒暖計 *saikō kandankei* maximum thermometer
高権 *saikōken* supreme power, absolute supremacy
高潮 *saikōchō* highwater mark; high tide; climax, peak, acme
11 深 *saishin* greatest depth
悪 *saiaku* the worst
寄 *moyo(ri) no* neighboring, nearest
盛期 *saiseiki* golden age, height of prosperity; the season, the best time (for)
強 *saikyō* strongest
強調 *saikyōchō* re-emphasis
終 *saishū* the last, the end; final
終日 *saishūbi* the last day
終回 *saishūkai* the last inning
終的 *saishūteki* ultimate
終段階 *saishū dankai* the final step
終案 *saishūan* the final plan
12 勝 *saishō* the supreme thing, the best
期 *saigo* one's last moments; death; fate
善 *saizen* the very best
最 *itodo* more and more
敬礼 *saikeirei* profound obeisance, deep respect
短 *saitan* shortest
短距離 *saitan kyori* shortest distance
13 愛 *saiai no* dearest, beloved
適 *saiteki* optimum
適地 *saitekichi* the most suitable site
適任者 *saitekininsha* the best qualified person
新 *saishin* newest, latest, up-to-date
新式 *saishinshiki* latest style
新版 *saishimpan* latest edition
新流行 *saishin ryūkō* latest fashion

9

會 2493 / J5072 / M14306 See **会** 143. [曰]

普 2494 / J-X / M-X See **普** 2489.

曉 2495 J-X M-X See 暁 2485.

暑 2496 J-X M14051 See 暑 2484.

暄 2497 J5a77 M14033 KEN warm; end of spring.

暘 2498 J5a78 M14066 YŌ dawn; bright; clear; dry.

暉 2499 J5a76 M14038 KI shine, light.

13 暉 *kiki* brilliance

暈 2500 J5a74 M14037 UN halo, ring, corona. *boka(su) vt* shade off; obscure. *bo(keru) vi* fade, become dim. *kasa* halo, ring, corona.

6 色 *unshoku* iridescence
8 取 *kumado(ri)* shading; makeup
17 翳 *un'ei* halation (in photography)

B 暇 2501 J324b M14036 KA rest, leisure. *hima* time; leisure; poor business; leave of absence; dismissal; divorce. *itoma* leisure, spare time; dismissal; divorce; leave; leave-taking.

3 乞 *itomagoi* farewell visit
4 日 *kajitsu* holiday, day off
8 取 *himado(ru)* take time; be delayed
15 潰 *himatsubu(shi)* waste of time, killing time

A 暖 2502 J4348 M14064 DAN warmth. *atata(meru), atta(meru) vt* warm, heat. *atata(maru), atta(maru)* warm oneself, sun oneself, get warm. *atataka(i), attaka(i)* warm, mild, genial, cordial.

5 冬 *dantō* mild winter
冬異変 *dantō-ihen* an unusually mild winter
6 色 *danshoku* warm-looking (clothes)
気 *danki* heat, warmth, warm weather
地 *danchi* warm region
衣 *dan'i* warm clothes; dressing warmly
衣飽食 *dan'i hōshoku* warm clothing and plenty to eat, luxury
8 国 *dankoku, dangoku* warm country
房 *dambō* heating
波 *dampa* warm wave
炉 *danro* fireplace, hearth, stove
9 室 *danshitsu* heated room, greenhouse, hothouse
10 流 *danryū* warm current
帯 *dantai* subtropics
13 戦争 *atataka(i) sensō* warm war
19 簾 *noren* shop curtain, sign curtain; reputation, goodwill
簾師 *norenshi* swindler, crook

A 暗 2503 J3045 M14065 AN dark. *kura(mu)* grow dark; be dazzled; be blinded. *kura(masu)* disappear, give (a person) the slip. *kura(ku) suru* darken, shade, make dim. *kura(gari)* darkness, gloom. *kura(i)* dark, gloomy, somber; dim, faint; ignorant. *yami* darkness; grief, gloom; disorder; black market. *kura(me)* gathering darkness. *an(ni)* tacitly, implicity, informally, indirectly, obscurely.

4 中 *anchū* in the dark
中飛躍 *anchū hiyaku* secret maneuvers
中模索 *anchū mosaku* groping in the dark
5 示 *anji* hint, suggestion
号 *angō* code, password
号文 *angōbun* coded message
6 色 *anshoku* dark color
合 *angō* coincidence
灰色 *ankaishoku* dark gray, taupe
7 車 *ansha* propeller, screw
町 *kura(i) machi* the underworld
君 *ankun* foolish ruler
赤色 *ansekishoku* dark red
8 所 *ansho* dark place
夜 *an'ya* dark night
事 *kuragoto* secret acts
9 香 *ankō* a fragrance from somewhere; the fragrance of flowers at night
室 *anshitsu* dark room
紅 *ankō* dark red
紅色 *ankōshoku* dark red
10 流 *anryū* undercurrent
涙 *anrui* silent tears
紛 *kuramagi(re) ni* under cover of darkness
弱 *anjaku* weak-mindedness
記 *anki* memorization
記物 *ankimono* something to be memorized
殺 *ansatsu* assassination
殺者 *ansatsusha* assassin
11 唱 *anshō* memorization, recitation

転 *anten* sudden darkening of the stage (to change scenery)
黒 *ankoku* darkness
黒日 *Ankokubi* the Dark Day
黒面 *ankokumen* seamy side, gloomy side
黒界 *ankokukai* the underworld
黒時代 *Ankoku Jidai* the Dark Ages
黒街 *ankokugai* the underworld
12 喩 *an'yu* metaphor
雲 *an'un* dark clouds
渠 *ankyo* drain, culvert
惑 *ku(re)-mado(u)* be nonplussed
然 *anzen* discouraged, disappointed, astonished
紫色 *anshishoku* dark purple
13 溝 *ankō* buried drain-tile sewer
路 *anro* dark road; underground passage
愚 *angu* weak-mindedness, stupidity
褐色 *ankasshoku* dark brown
暗 *an'an* darkness; stillness in the depths
暗裏 *an'anri(ni)* tacitly, implicitly, obscurely, by implication, secretly
14 誦 *anshō* memorization, recitation
算 *anzan* mental arithmetic
緑色 *anryokushoku* dark green
15 潮 *anchō* undercurrent
影 *an'ei* shadow, gloom
黙 *ammoku* silence
黙了解 *ammoku (no) ryōkai* tacit understanding
16 澹 *antan* darkness, gloom
17 闇 *kurayami, kureyami* darkness; dark place; privacy; lawlessness
礁 *anshō* reef, sunken rock
翳 *an'ei* shadow, gloom
18 闘 *antō* secret feud
21 躍 *an'yaku* secret maneuvers
26 欝 *an'utsu* gloom, melancholy

10

曄 2504 / J5b21 / M14169 Yō sparkle, shine; clear; flash. *kagaya(ku)* glitter, shine.

暝 2505 / J5a79 / M14083 Mei dark.

暢 2506 / J442a / M14095 Chō stretch.

6 気 *nonki* optimistic; carefree; careless, reckless

B **暦** 2507 / J4e71 / M14111' **曆** 2512 / J-X / M14171 Ryaku. Reki.
koyomi calendar, almanac.
4 日 *rekijitsu* calendar day; time
月 *rekigetsu* calendar month
6 年 *rekinen* calendar year, civil year; time
年度 *rekinendo* calendar year
7 改正 *koyomi kaisei* calendar reform
8 学 *rekigaku* the study of the calendar
法 *rekihō* calendar making
法改正 *rekihō no kaisei* calendar reform
11 術 *rekijutsu* calendar-construction rules
13 数 *rekisū* calendar making; number of years; one's fate; the year

A **暮** 2508 / J4a6b / M14128 Bo. *kura(su)* live, make a living; spend (one's time). *ku(reru)* get dark; (the sun) sets; (the season) ends; (time) passes; be overwhelmed. *kura(shi)* living, livelihood; circumstances. *ku(re)* sunset, nightfall; year-end; end.
4 方 *ku(rashi)kata* manner of living. *ku(re)gata, kure(tsu)kata* nightfall
5 払 *ku(re)bara(i)* paying at the year end; year-end payment
6 色 *boshoku* twilight scene
行 *ku(re)-yu(ku)* get dark
向 *ku(rashi)mu(ki)* circumstances, livelihood
合 *ku(re)a(i)* about sunset
年 *bonen* one's later years
8 雨 *bou* an evening shower
夜 *boya* evening, night
果 *ku(re)-ha(teru)* get completely dark
9 秋 *boshū* late fall
春 *boshun* late spring
10 紛 *ku(re)magi(re)* being benighted
11 移 *ku(re)-utsu(ru)* get dark
雪 *bosetsu* evening snowfall
12 渡 *ku(re)-wata(ru)* the whole landscape darkens
景 *bokei* twilight, evening scene
雲 *boun* evening clouds
13 塞 *ku(re)-fusaga(ru)* get completely dark
愁 *boshū* the loneliness of evening
14 様 *ku(rashi)yō* manner of living
暮 *ku(re)gu(re)* nightfall

11

暹 2509 / J5a7b / M14150 SEN dawn; advance.

B **暫** 2510 / J3b43 / M14120 ZAN *shibara(ku)* for a while, a moment; for a long time.

8 定 *zantei* provisional, tentative
定条約 *zantei jōyaku* provisional treaty
定的 *zanteiteki* provisional, tentative
定案 *zanteian* tentative plan
10 時 *zanji, shibushi* a short while, for some time. *zanji no* transient, momentary

A **暴** 2511 / J4b3d / M14137 BAKU, BŌ violence, force, outrage, cruelty. *aba(reru)* rage, rave, fret; buck. *aba(ku)* unearth, disclose, rave, divulge, reveal; open (a grave).

2 力 *bōryoku* violence, force, terrorism
力団 *boryokudan* terrorist organization, gangster group
力沙汰 *bōryokuzata* acts of violence
3 子 *aba(rek)ko* unruly child
4 込 *aba(re)-ko(mu)* storm into, burst into
5 令 *bōrei* wicked decree
出 *aba(re)-da(su)* grow restive, begin to act violently; begin to buck
民 *bōmin* mob, insurgents
6 行 *bōkō* act of violence, assault, outrage
回 *aba(re)-mawa(ru)* rampage, tear around, run riot
吏 *bōri* dishonest official
7 言 *bōgen* harsh or abusive language
走 *bōsō* running wildly
戻 *bōrei* tyranny, atrocity
投 *bōtō* wild pitch; wild throw
状 *bōjō* atrocity, violence
狂 *aba(re)-kuru(u)* rage, run amuck, tear around
利 *bōri* excessive profits, usury
君 *bōkun* tyrant
坊 *aba(rem)bō* rascal
8 逆 *bōgyaku* violence, lawlessness
者 *aba(re)mono* rowdy
若無人 *bōjaku-bujin* arrogance, defiance
虎憑河 *bōko-hyōka* perilous venture, risky attempt
9 廻 *aba(re)-mawa(ru)* rampage, tear around, run riot
威 *bōi* tyranny, great violence, havoc
虐 *bōgyaku* tyranny, atrocity
政 *bōsei* tyrannical government
発 *bōhatsu* accidental gun discharge
勇 *bōyū* brute strength
食 *bōshoku* gluttony, intemperance in eating
食家 *bōshokuka* glutton, excessive eater
風 *bōfū* storm
風雨 *bōfuu* rainstorm
風信号 *bōfūshingō* storm warning
風進路 *bōfu shinro* storm path
風雪 *bōfūsetsu* blizzard, snowstorm
風圏 *bōfūken* storm area
風警報 *bōfū keihō* storm warning
10 馬 *aba(re) uma* restive horse, runaway
進 *bōshin* rushing recklessly; presumption
徒 *bōto* mob, rioters, insurgents, mutineers
挙 *bōkyo* violence, outrage; riot
11 悪 *bōaku* violence, tyranny, atrocity
動 *bōdō* riot, uprising
動者 *bōdōsha* rioter, insurgent, rebel, mutineer
動罪 *bōdōzai* rioting charge
12 評 *bōhyō* fierce criticism
落 *bōraku* slump, sharp break, crash, heavy decline (in prices)
飲 *bōin* heavy drinking, carousing
13 漢 *bōkan* ruffian, desperado
14 慢 *bōman* insolence, arrogance
説 *bōsetsu* preposterous theory
15 論 *bōron* irrational argument
20 騰 *bōtō* sudden (price) rise
21 露 *bakuro* exposure, disclosure

12

曆 2512 / J-X / M14171 See 暦 2507.

曉 2513 / J5a7c / M14176 See 暁 2485.

暼 2514 / J5a7e / M14155 HETSU. HECHI sunset.

暾 2515 / J5a7d / M14160 TON sunrise; warm; sunshine.

4 心 忄 小 戈 戸 手 扌 支 攴 攵 文 斗 斤 方 无 【日 12 曰】 月 木 欠 止 歹 殳 毋 比 毛 氏 气 水 氵 氺 火 灬 爪 爫 父 爻 爿 丬 片 牙 牛 犬 犭

曁 2516 / J5a7a / M14165 KI extend; arrive; together.

暸 2517 / J5b22 / M14148 RYŌ clear.

B **曇** 2518 / J465e / M14172 DON. *kumo(ru) vi* cloud up; fog up, become dim, be blurred; be gloomy. *kumo(rasu) vt* cloud up, dim, blur, fog, dull (the color); tarnish; shade (one's face); darken. *kumo(ri)* cloudiness, shadow, blur, dimness; gloom; suspicion; slur, stain; frosted (glass).

4 日 *kumo(ri)bi* cloudy day; the sun covered with clouds

天 *donten* cloudy weather, overcast sky

12 勝 *kumo(ri)ga(chi) na* cloudy

13

曙 2519 / J3d6c / M-X See 曙 2523.

曚 2520 / J5b24 / M14223 BŌ. MŌ *kura(i)* dark, obscure; dim.

曖 2521 / J5b23 / M14206 AI dark; not clear.

9 昧 *aimai* vagueness, ambiguity, obscurity

14

A **曜** 2522 / J4d4b / M14227' YŌ day of the week; light; shining.

4 日 *yōbi* weekday

曙 2523 / J-X / M14220 **曙** 2519 / J3d6c / M-X SHO. *akebono* dawn, daybreak.

6 光 *shokō* dawn; prospects

15

曝 2524 / J4778 / M14239 BAKU. *sara(su)* bleach; refine; expose, air.

9 首 *sharekōbe, sarekōbe* skull

10 書 *bakusho* airing of books

11 涼 *bakuryō* airing clothes

21 露 *bakuro* exposure, disclosure

曠 2525 / J5b25 / M14245 KŌ wide; worthless.

3 久 *kōkyū* wasting time

4 日 *kōjitsu* wasting time

日弥久 *kōjitsu-bikyū* procrastination

5 古 *kōko no* historic, unprecedented

世 *kōsei no* unparalleled, epoch-making

10 原 *kōgen* wide plain, open country

11 野 *kōya, hirono* wilderness, moorland, prairie

18 職 *kōshoku* neglect of official duty

16

曦 2526 / J5b27 / M14253 KI. GI sunlight; color of the sun.

17

曩 2527 / J5b28 / M14258 NŌ *saki ni* before, earlier than; ahead, beyond, away; previously; recently.

19

曬 2528 / J-X / M14266 See 晒 2461.

RAD. 曰 73

Iwaku to speak or *hirabi* (a flattened Rad. 72 *hi*). With the exception of the radical itself, which follows, this radical is treated herein as a variant of Rad. 72.

Nickname: Flat Sun.

曰 2529 / J5b29 / M14278 ETSU. OCHI. *iwa(ku)* say; reason; pretext; a history, a past, a story. *notama(u)* say, be pleased to say.

5 付 *iwa(ku)tsu(ki) no* (someone) with a history

RAD. 月 74

Tsuki moon. At left: *tsuki hen.* With the exception of the radical character itself, which follows, this radical is herein treated as a variant of Rad. 130.
Nickname: Moon.

A 月 2530 / J376e / M14330 GETSU moon; month; Monday. GATSU month (of the year). *tsuki* moon; month.
3 下 *gekka ni* on a moonlit night, in the moonlight
下氷人 *gekka hyōjin* go-between, matchmaker, Cupid
下美人 *gekka bijin* night-blooming cereus
4 日 *gappi* date. *tsukihi* months and days, time and tide; one's star
月 *tsukizuki* every month
水 *gessui* menstruation
5 石 *gesseki* moonstone
立 *tsuita(chi)* first day of the month
代 *sakayaki* shaven part of the head
刊 *gekkan* monthly publication
払 *tsukibarai* monthly installments
収 *gesshū* monthly income
旦 *gettan* first day of the month; criticism; comment
末 *getsumatsu, tsukizue* end of the month
世界 *gessekai* lunar world, the moon
仕舞 *tsukijimai* month's end
6 色 *gesshoku* moonlight
回 *tsukimawa(ri)* one's luck for the month
毎 *tsukigoto ni* monthly
次 *getsuji* monthly. *tsukinami* every month; common
次的 *tsukinamiteki* formal, conventional
光 *gekkō* moonlight, moonbeam
光冠 *gekkōkan* lunar corona
7 足 *tsukita(razu), tsukita(ranu)* premature birth
迫 *geppaku* month's end; end of December
役 *tsukiyaku* menstruation
決 *tsukigi(me)* monthly contract. *tsukigi(me) no* monthly
利 *getsuri* monthly interest
別 *tsukibetsu* by months
形 *gekkei, tsukigata* half-moon shape
余 *getsuyo* over a month
来 *getsurai* a few months ago

見 *tsukimi* viewing the moon; moonlight party
見玉子 *tsukimi tamago* fried egg
見団子 *tsukimi dango* dumplings offered to the moon
見卵 *tsukimi tamago* fried egg
見草 *tsukimisō* moon flower
見宴 *tsukimi (no) en* moon-viewing party
8 送 *tsukioku(ri)* putting off from month to month
例 *getsurei* monthly
始 *tsukihaji(me)* beginning of the month
明 *getsumei, tsukiaka(ri)* moonlight
物 *tsuki (no) mono* menstruation
並 *tsukina(mi)* every month; common
参 *tsukimai(ri)* monthly visit (to a shrine or temple)
表 *geppyō* monthly list
事 *getsuji* menstruation
長石 *getchōseki* moonstone
夜 *tsukiyo, getsuya* moonlit night
夜見 *tsukiyomi, tsukuyomi* the moon
9 面 *getsumen* the moon's surface
食 *gesshoku* eclipse of the moon
眉 *tsuki (no) mayu* pretty arched eyebrows
待 *tsukima(chi)* waiting for the moonrise
後 *tsukioku(re)* back numbers (of a monthly)
10 俸 *geppō* monthly salary
都 *tsuki (no) miyako* city in the moon
華 *gekka* moonlight
桂 *gekkei* laurel; moon; moonlight
桂冠 *gekkeikan* crown of laurel
桂樹 *gekkeiju* laurel tree, bay tree
11 遅 *tsukioku(re)* a month or more older
頃 *tsukigoro* these past months
掛 *tsukigake* monthly installments
産 *gessan* monthly output
雫 *tsuki (no) shizuku* dewdrops
雪花 *tsuki-yuki-hana* moon, snow, and flowers; the beauty of the four seasons; elegance
経 *gekkei* menstruation
経帯 *gekkeitai* hygenic band, sanitary napkin

12 雇 *tsukiyato(i)* hiring by the month
越 *tsukigo(shi) no* (bill) hanging over from last month
極 *tsukigime* monthly contract. *tsukigime no* monthly
割 *tsukiwari* monthly allocation
番 *tsukiban* monthly duty, monthly shift
替 *tsukiga(e)* every other month
報 *geppō* monthly report, monthly review
卿雲客 *gekkei unkaku* court nobles
評 *geppyō* monthly review
評子 *geppyōshi* monthly reviewer
給 *gekkyū* monthly salary
給日 *gekkyūbi* payday
給取 *gekkyūto(ri)* white-collar worker
給袋 *gekkyūbukuro* pay envelope
13 詣 *tsukimōde* monthly visit (to a shrine or temple)
跨 *tsuki (o) mata(gu)* extend into the next month
障 *tsuki (no) sawari* menstruation
暈 *getsuun, tsukigasa* a halo, a ring
14 読 *tsukiyomi* the moon
15 輪 *tsuki(no)wa, getsurin* ring around the moon. *gachirin, getsurin, gatsurin* round moon
蝕 *gesshoku* eclipse of the moon
影 *tsukikage, getsuei* moonlight, moonbeams
賦 *geppu* monthly installment
賦払 *geppubara(i)* monthly payments
17 謝 *gessha* monthly tuition
齢 *getsurei* age of the moon
18 額 *getsugaku* monthly amount
曜 *Getsuyō* Monday
曜日 *Getsuyōbi* Monday
21 露 *getsuro* the moon and dew; moonlight reflected from the dew

RAD. 木 75

Ki tree. At left: *ki hen.* Nickname: Tree.

A **木** 2531 / J4c5a / M14415 BOKU tree. MOKU tree; Thursday. *ki, ko* tree; wood; timber; lumber; wooden clappers.

2 刀 *bokutō* wooden sword
乃伊 *miira* mummy
3 口 *koguchi* cut end, butt end. *kiguchi* cross section of wood; lumber quality
下 *ki (no) shita, ko (no) shita* under a tree
工 *mokkō* woodworking; woodworker
工所 *mokkōjo* woodworking shop; sawmill
工場 *mokkōjō* woodworking shop; sawmill
4 木 *kigi* every tree; many trees; all kinds of trees
毛 *mokumō, mokumo* excelsior
片 *mokuhen* block; chip; splinter
仏 *kibotoke, kibutsu* wooden Buddha; insensible person
切 *kigi(re)* piece of wood, chip, chunk, splinter
太刀 *kidachi* wooden sword
戸 *kido* gate, wicket, wooden door, wooden gate; entrance; castle gate
戸札 *kido fuda* wooden admission ticket
戸番 *kidoban* doorman, gatekeeper
戸御免 *kido gomen* admission free
戸銭 *kidosen* admission fee
5 瓦 *kigawara, kogawara* wooden roof tiles
皮 *mokuhi* bark
皿 *kizara* wooden dish
目 *mokume* wood grain. *kime* wood grain; texture
立 *kodachi* clump of trees, thicket, grove, standing trees
札 *kifuda* wooden tag or ticket
末 *konure* twig, tree top
石 *bokuseki* trees and stones, inanimate objects
石漢 *bokusekikan* unsusceptible person
6 羽 *koba* shingles
舟 *kibune* wooden ship
匠 *mokushō* carpenter
灰 *kibai* wood ashes
印 *kijirushi, mokuin* woodcutter's mark
地 *kiji* grain of wood; plain wood
肌 *kohada, kihada* bark of a tree
竹継 *ki (ni) take (o) tsu(gu)* lack harmony
7 材 *mokuzai* wood, timber, lumber

杓 *kisaku* wooden ladle
8 杯 *mokuhai* wooden cup
枕 *kimakura* wooden pillow
取 *kido(ri)* lumber dressing
実 *ko(no)mi, ki(no)mi* fruit, nut, berry
沓 *kigutsu* wooden shoes
芽 *ko(no)me, ki(no)me* leaf buds; roasted tea leaves
苺 *kiichigo* raspberry
版 *mokuhan* wood-block printing; wood-block print
版画 *mokuhanga* wood block print
版摺 *mokuhanzuri* wood engraving
9 食 *mokujiki* fruit diet
香 *kiga, ki(no)ka* smell of fresh wood
屋 *kiya* lumber shed, lumber merchant
拾 *kihiro(i)* gathering wood; wood gatherer
枯 *koga(rashi)* wintry wind
柵 *mokusaku* wooden barricade, fence
盃 *mokuhai* wooden cup
星 *Mokusei* Jupiter
型 *kigata* wooden pattern
造 *mokuzō, kizuku(ri)* sawmilling. *mokuzō* wooden
造船 *mokuzōsen* wooden ship
炭 *mokutan, kizumi* charcoal
炭画 *mokutanga* charcoal drawing
10 骨 *mokkotsu* wooden frame (of a building)
屑 *kikuzu* shavings, chips
晒 *kizarashi* tree-ripened persimmons
振 *kibu(ri)* tree shape
栓 *mokusen* wooden plug
釘 *kikugi* wooden peg
陰 *kokage* tree shade, bower
剣 *bokken* wooden sword
莓 *kiichigo* raspberry
納屋 *kinaya* woodshed
馬 *mokuba* rocking horse
馬飛 *mokubato(bi)* horse vaulting (in a gym)
挽 *kobiki* sawyer
挽小屋 *kobikigoya* small sawmill
挽所 *kobikisho* sawmill
11 魚 *mokugyo* wooden temple drum
彫 *kibo(ri), mokuchō* wood carving
深 *kobuka(i)* deep in the forest
理 *mokuri* tree rings; the grain of wood
船 *mokusen* wooden ship
訥 *bokutotsu* rugged honesty
菟 *mimizuku, zuku* horned owl
細工 *kizaiku* woodwork
蛋白石 *mokutampakuseki* wood opal
偶 *deku, mokugū, bokugū* wooden figure, dummy, puppet
偶坊 *dekunobō* puppet (doll); blockhead
12 間 *ko(no)ma* through the trees; among the trees
場 *kiba* lumberyard
割 *kiwa(ri)* allotment of lumber
登 *kinobo(ri)* tree climbing
琴 *mokkin* marimba, xylophone
喰虫 *kikuimushi* wood borer
遣 *kiyari* workmen's chant; carrying a big load together
遣音頭 *kiyari ondo* workmen's chant
遣唄 *kiyari uta* workmen's chant
葉 *ko(no)ha, ki(no)ha* foliage of trees
葉石 *ko(no)haishi* fossil leaf
葉微塵 *ko(p)pa-mijin* to fragments, into atoms
13 鼠 *kinezumi* squirrel
蓮 *mokuren* magnolia
暗 *kogura(i)* dark (in a forest). *kogu(re)* darkness of a forest
槌 *kizuchi, saizuchi* mallet, gavel
槌頭 *saizuchi atama* head like a hammer head
鉢 *kibachi* wooden bowl
隠 *kogaku(re)* hiding behind trees
靴 *kigutsu* wooden shoes
煉瓦 *kirenga, mokurenga* wooden bricks
賃宿 *kichin'yado* cheap lodging house
賊 *tokusa* horsetail
賊色 *tokusa iro* blackish green
14 像 *mokuzō* wooden image; figurehead
摺 *kizuri* lath
精 *mokusei* wood alcohol, methyl alcohol; an echo
銃 *mokujū* wooden gun
蔦 *kizuta* ivy
暮 *kogu(re), ko(no)ku(re)* darkness of a forest
瑪瑙 *mokumenō* wood agate
端 *ki(no)hashi, koppa, koba* block, chip (of wood); worthless thing; worthless person
端微塵 *koppa-mijin* smithereens
管 *mokkan* wooden pipe; bobbin
管楽器 *mokkan gakki* wind instruments of wood
製 *mokusei no* wooden, made of wood

製品 *mokuseihin* woodenware
綿 *momen* cotton, cotton cloth. *kiwata* cotton plant
綿糸 *momen ito* cotton thread
綿物 *momemmono* cotton goods; cotton clothes
綿織物 *momen orimono* cotton fabrics
15 履 *pokkuri, bokkuri, bokuri* girls' flat geta
瘤 *kikobu* knot (on a tree)
膚 *kihada* bark of a tree
槿 *mukuge* rose of Sharon
醂 *kizawa(shi)* ripe persimmon
鋏 *kibasami* pruning shears
箱 *kibako* wooden box
霊 *kodama* spirit of a tree; echo. *kodama suru* echo, resound
質 *mokushitsu* lignum, woody tissue, woody fiber
舞 *komai* laths
舞掻 *komaikaki* lathing; lather
17 螺子 *mokuneji* wood screw
18 叢 *komura* clump of trees; shade of dense trees
曜 *Mokuyō* Thursday
曜日 *Mokuyōbi* Thursday
19 蘭 *mokuran* magnolia
髄 *mokuzui* pith
21 蠟 *mokurō* vegetable wax
鐸 *bokutaku* bell with a wooden clapper; a leader; a great teacher

1

朮 2532 / J5b32 / M14423 JUTSU *mochiawa* a kind of millet. *okera* a kind of herb.

A **札** 2533 / J3b25 / M14422 SATSU paper money; counter for bonds, etc. *fuda* tag, placard; name plate; check; charm, (playing) card; tender, bid.
2 入 *satsui(re)* billfold, wallet
4 止 *fudado(me)* full house
5 付 *fudatsu(ki)* branded, marked (with prices); notorious; ex-convict
7 束 *satsu taba* bundle of paper money
8 所 *fudasho* amulet-issuing office

A **末** 2534 / J4b76 / M14420 BATSU. MATSU end; powder. *sue* end, close; tip, top; the future; posterity; youngest child. *sue ni* finally. *ura* top end, tip. *ure* new shoots, new growth (of a tree). *-matsu* the end of; powder.
3 女 *matsujo* youngest daughter
子 *basshi, masshi, sueko, sue(k)ko* youngest child
4 方 *sue(tsu)kata* end of a period; end of the world
日 *matsujitsu* last day (of the month)
5 広 *suehiro* folding fan. *suehiro(gari)* spreading out like an open fan
代 *matsudai* eternity
末 *suezue* distant future; descendants; lower classes. *sue(no)sue* the last
世 *sue(no)yo, masse* last days
6 成 *uranari* fruit at the end of the vine; weak-looking fellow
寺 *matsuji* branch temple
年 *matsunen* the last years, the final years, the last generation
7 尾 *matsubi* end, close
技 *matsugi* poor workmanship
社 *massha* subordinate shrine; professional jester
弟 *mattei, battei* youngest brother; last disciple
男 *batsunan* youngest son
8 長 *suenaga(ku)* long, forever
季 *makki* closing years, last stage
若 *urawaka(i)* youthful
始終 *sueshijū* forever, for life
法 *mappō* latter days (in Buddhism), age of decadence
法思想 *mappō-shisō* pessimism due to decadent-age theory
9 香 *makkō* incense, incense powder
枯 *uraga(re)* dying of the little twigs and branches
派 *mappa* sect; underling
10 座 *matsuza* lowest seat
流 *matsuryū, batsuryū* descendants
恐 *sueoso(roshii)* ominous, uncertain of the future
席 *masseki, basseki* lowest seat
席汚 *masseki (o) kega(su)* attend a meeting (humble)
11 梢 *masshō* tree top, tip; periphery; minor details, nonessentials
梢的 *masshōteki* trivial, minor, insignificant
梢神経 *masshō shinkei* peripheral nerves
12 項 *makkō* the last paragraph
期 *makki* closing years, last stage. *matsugo* deathbed, hour of death

葉 *batsuyō* the last descendant; the last days of any age. *matsuyō* end, close. *uraba, ureba* end leaves, top leaves, last leaves
筆乍 *mappitsunaga(ra)* a letter-closing phrase expressing regret for a delay
13 路 *matsuro, batsuro* last days, end, fate
節 *massetsu* minor details, nonessentials
裔 *matsuei, batsuei* descendants
14 僚 *batsuryō* low-ranking official
端 *mattan* end, tip, extremities
15 輩 *mappai* underling, rank and file
16 頼 *suetano(moshii)* promising (future)

Λ **未** 2535 / J4c24 / M14419 MI not yet. *ima(da)* as yet, hitherto; not yet (with neg.). *ima(dani)* still, even now, until this very day. *mada* not yet; still; so far; more, besides; only. *ima(dashi)* something to be desired. *hitsuji* 1–3 p.m.; eighth zodiac sign; sheep. *mi-* un-, not yet.
2 了 *miryō no* unfinished, unfilled (order), unexecuted
3 亡人 *mibōjin* widow
4 公表 *mikōhyō* not yet officially announced
5 刊 *mikan no* unpublished
未 *madamada* still, still more, much more
処分 *mishobun* unsettled, unfinished, undivided (profits)
処置 *mishochi* untreated
払 *mihara(i)* unpaid
払込 *miharaiko(mi)* not paid up (capital)
収 *mishū* accrued, outstanding
収入金 *mishūnyūkin* accounts receivable
6 成 *misei* uncompleted, unfinished, crude
成年 *miseinen* minority, not of age
成年者 *miseinensha* a minor
成品 *miseihin* unfinished goods; a person not grown up
7 見 *miken no* unacquainted, unknown
改心者 *mikaishinsha* unconverted person
完 *mikan no* incomplete, unfinished
完成 *mikansei no* incomplete
来 *mirai* future; future life; future tense
来完了 *mirai kanryō* future perfect
来派 *miraiha* futurism
決 *miketsu* pending, unsettled
決囚 *miketsushū* unconvicted prisoner
決済 *mikessai* outstanding (account)
決算 *mikessan* outstanding (account)
決監 *miketsukan* detention prison
8 届 *mitodo(ke)* failing to report
明 *mimei* early dawn
到 *mitō* untrodden, unexplored
青年 *miseinen* minority, not of age
知 *michi* unknown, strange
知数 *michisū* unknown number
定 *mitei* undecided, pending
定稿 *miteikō* unfinished manuscript
9 信者 *mishinja* unbeliever; inquirer
発 *mihatsu ni* before anything happens, previously
発行 *mihakkō* unissued
発見 *mihakken* undiscovered, unexplored
発表 *mihappyō* not yet announced
発達 *mihattatsu* undeveloped
10 進 *mishin* nonpayment of tribute
納 *minō* payment default
記入 *mikinyū* blank (book)
消化 *mishōka* unfulfilled (orders)
耕地 *mikōchi* uncultivated land
配当 *mihaitō* undivided (profits)
帰還者 *mikikansha* unrepatriated person
11 済 *misai no* unpaid
設 *misetsu* uninstalled, projected
教育 *mikyōiku no* untrained
組織 *misoshiki* unorganized
遂 *misui* attempted (crime)
遂罪 *misuizai* attempted crime
婚 *mikon* unmarried
婚者 *mikonsha* unmarried person
経過 *mikeika* unexpired
経験 *mikeiken no* inexperienced
経験者 *mikeikensha* inexperienced person
12 満 *miman* less than, below
然 *mizen ni* before anything happens, previously
曾有 *mizou, misou* unprecedented, unheard of
復員 *mifukuin no* not yet demobilized
登記 *mitōki* unregistered
就学児童 *mishūgaku jidō* preschool child
着 *michaku* nonarrival
着手 *michakushu* (work) not yet started
開 *mikai* uncivilized, barbarous; not blooming

開拓 *mikaitaku* undeveloped, wild (areas)
開拓地 *mikaitakuchi* undeveloped area
開発 *mikaihatsu* undeveloped (countries), backward, unentered
開墾 *mikaikon* uncultivated
開墾地 *mikaikonchi* virgin soil, uncultivated land
13 詳 *mishō no* unknown, unidentified
解決 *mikaiketsu no* unsettled, pending
14 聞 *mimon* having not yet heard
練 *miren* unskilled; lingering affection
製品 *miseihin* unfinished article
15 確定 *mikakutei* unsettled, pending
踏 *mitō* untrodden, unexplored
踏査 *mitōsa* unexplored
熟 *mijuku na* unripe, raw; unskilled, immature, inexperienced
熟者 *mijukumono* a green hand, a novice
16 墾 *mikon* uncultivated
墾地 *mikonchi* uncultivated land

1 A **本** 2536 / J4b5c / M14421 HON book; this, the same, the present, the current; main; true; real; regular, normal; counter for long things. *moto* beginning, origin; foundation, basis, source; cause; root (of a tree); (raw) material, base; capital; principal; cost; forebears; formerly.

2 人 *honnin* the person himself; the said person; the principal
人次第 *honnin shidai* It depends on him.
3 土 *hondo* mainland; Japan proper
山 *honzan* head temple; this temple
丸 *hommaru* inner citadel
4 心 *honshin* one's right mind, real motive, true sentiment, real intention, conscience
手 *honte* regular way, trump card
日 *honjitsu* today
分 *hombun* one's duty; original position
文 *hombun, hommon* text (of a treaty); body (of a letter)
文批評 *hommon hihyō* textual criticism
5 田 *honden* old rice field
立 *hontate* bookrack, book ends
号 *hongō* current number
庁 *honchō* head government office
代 *hondai* money for books
令 *honrei* this law
本 *motomoto* from the first, originally; by nature, naturally
末 *hommatsu* cause and effect; the means and the end; root and branch; substance and shadow; beginning and end
末転倒 *hommatsu-tentō* overturning plans
6 色 *honshoku* one's real character; true quality
式 *honshiki* orthodox style. *honshiki no* formal, regular
件 *honken* this case
好 *honzu(ki)* a bookworm, bibliophile; fondness for books
州 *Honshū* Japan proper, Main Island
刑 *honkei* regular penalty
邦 *hompō* this country, our country
旨 *honshi* the main purpose; the true aim; the true reason
宅 *hontaku* principal residence
当 *hontō, hontō no* true, real, actual, proper, genuine; natural; veritable, substantial. *hontō ni* in earnest; very; really. *hontō(rashii)* probable, plausible, likely.
名 *hommyō, hommei* real name, family name
有観念 *hon'yū kannen* innate idea
気 *honki* earnestness, seriousness, soberness
気違 *honkichiga(i)* bibliomania; bibliomaniac; raving, madness
会員 *honkaiin* regular member
会議 *honkaigi* plenary session, regular session
年 *honnen* this year
年度 *honnendo* the current year
7 局 *honkyoku* main office; telephone central
決 *hongima(ri)* final decision
社 *honsha* main shrine; this shrine; main office; our firm
条 *honjō* this article (of a document)
芸 *hongei* main forte
来 *honrai* originally, primarily, essentially, naturally; properly speaking; just, proper
攻撃 *honkōgeki* main attack
初子午線 *honsho shigosen* Greenwich Meridian
位 *hon'i* standard, basis, principle; system

位貨幣 *hon'i kahei* legal tender
体 *hontai* substance, entity, the thing itself; true form; antitype; object of worship; main part (of a book)
体論 *hontairon* ontology
8 店 *honten* head office; main store; this store
房 *hombō* main quarters of a temple
姓 *honsei* original surname
性 *honshō, honsei* original nature, real character, oneself
物 *hommono* real article, real thing; expert performance
命 *hommei* prospective winner, favorite in a contest
官 *honkan* former post; permanent appointment; principal assignment; permanent official; the present official; I, me
妻 *honsai* legal wife
金庫 *honkinko* main depository
国 *hongoku* one's own country
国人 *hongokujin* native, citizen
拠 *honkyo* stronghold, inner citadel; base, headquarters
拠地 *honkyochi* stronghold, inner citadel; base, headquarters
9 音 *honne* real intention, motive
屋 *hon'ya* bookstore; publisher; main building. *hon'oku* principal residence
通 *hondō(ri)* main street, boulevard
城 *honjō* this castle; inner citadel
科 *honka* regular course; this lesson
則 *honsoku* rules; original rules
降 *hombu(ri)* regular rainfall
陣 *honjin* troop headquarters; daimyo's inn; stronghold
省 *honshō* this ministry; the home office
食虫 *honku(i)-mushi* bookworm (literal and figurative)
契約 *honkeiyaku* formal contract
建築 *honkenchiku* permanent construction
草学 *honzōgaku* study of medicinal herbs
10 症 *honshō* this sickness
俸 *hompō* regular salary; basic salary; full pay
校 *honkō* main school; this school
流 *honryū* main current; main current (of thought)
部 *hombu* headquarters
員 *hon'in* this member (of an assembly), I, me
案 *hon'an* this plan
書 *honsho* the text, the script; this book
能 *honnō* instinct
家 *honke* main family; originator
家本元 *honke-hommoto* original home, birthplace; originator
格 *honkaku* propriety
格化 *honkakuka suru* regularize; get up speed, proceed at full tilt
格的 *honkakuteki* full-dress, regular; real, genuine, earnest; normal, typical; fundamental
11 道 *hondō* highway, main road; the right road
務 *hommu* duty; regular business
隊 *hontai* main body (of an army)
堂 *hondō* main temple building; nave
章 *honshō* this chapter
望 *hommō* long-cherished ambition; satisfaction
船 *honsen* mother ship; this ship
船渡 *honsenwata(shi)* F.O.B., free on board
12 復 *hompuku* complete recovery
棚 *hondana* bookshelf
極 *hongima(ri)* final decision
統 *hontō* true; the main stream in a lineage
結 *hommusu(bi)* square knot
訴 *honso* original (legal) suit
朝 *honchō* this land; our country; Imperial Court
尊 *honzon* main image, the idol; the main image one worships; object of adoration; the man himself; the master of the house
筋 *honsuji* main thread (of a story)
葬 *honsō* formal funeral
番 *homban* the actual performance
営 *hon'ei* headquarters
然 *honnen* disposition, nature. *honzen no* natural, inborn, inherent
街道 *honkaidō* main road
塁 *honrui* base, stronghold, main fort; home plate
塁打 *honruida* home run
場 *homba* home, habitat, center
場所 *hombasho* sumo pavilion
場物 *hombamono* genuine article

13 殿 *honden* main shrine; inner sanctuary
源 *hongen* origin, root, cause; principle
絹 *honken* pure silk
腰 *hongoshi* earnestness, seriousness
署 *honsho* police headquarters; main office; this office
義 *hongi* true meaning, underlying principle
意 *hon'i* motive, will, real intention, hopes
業 *hongyō* principal occupation
試験 *honshiken* final examination
14 読 *hon'yo(mi)* good reader; scenario reading
誌 *honshi* this magazine
領 *honryō* characteristic; specialty; duty; proper function; original fief
15 線 *honsen* main (railway) line
論 *honron* main discourse; this subject; body (of a speech)
影 *hon'ei* umbra
箱 *hombako* bookcase
舗 *hompo* head office; main store; this store
調子 *honchōshi* proper key; keynote; normal condition
舞台 *hombutai* main stage, public place
質 *honshitsu* essence, reality
質的 *honshitsuteki ni* essentially, substantially
16 懐 *honkai* long-cherished ambition; satisfaction
膳 *honzen* regular dinner
館 *honkan* main building; this building
曇 *hongumo(ri)* low-cloud overcast
18 職 *honshoku* principal occupation; an expert; I
題 *hondai* the main question
19 願 *hongan* Amida Buddha's original vow; long-cherished desire
20 籍 *honseki* permanent domicile
籍地 *honsekichi* permanent domicile
23 籤 *honkuji* first prize in a private lottery

2

权 2537 / J-X / M-X Nonstandard for **權** 2853.

杁 2538 / J5b35 / M-X （国字） *iri* sluice-gate.

朷 2539 / J5b37 / M14432 Tō heartwood; name of tree.

朸 2540 / J5b36 / M14433 Ryoku. Riki wood grain; annular rings; corner. *mokume* wood grain. *ōgo* shoulder yoke.

朿 2541 / J5b33 / M14441 Shi *toge* thorn.

朶 2542 / J5b34 / M14430 Da branch.

A **机** 2543 / J3479 / M14435 Ki. *tsukue* desk, table.
3 下 *kika* under the desk
上 *kijō* top of a desk. *kijō no* academic, theoretical, impractical
4 辺 *kihen* around the table

B **朴** 2544 / J4b51 / M14428 Boku simple, plain; docile. *hō* tree used for the legs of geta, magnolia hypoleuca
8 直 *bokuchoku* simplicity, naïveté, honesty
念仁 *bokunenjin* a quiet unsociable person; blockhead
11 訥 *bokutotsu* rugged honesty
12 歯 *hōba* heavy geta
16 樹 *enoki* nettle tree

B **朽** 2545 / J3560 / M14439 Kyū. *ku(chiru)* decay, rot; remain in seclusion.
4 木 *kuchiki* decayed wood. *kyūboku* decayed wood; an old person
8 果 *ku(chi)-ha(teru)* rust away, rot away, completely decay
10 残 *ku(chi)-noko(ru)* decay and remain
12 廃 *kyūhai* decay
葉 *kuchiba* dead leaves
16 壊 *kyūkai* rotten and easily broken

B **朱** 2546 / J3c6b / M14424 Shu cinnabar; vermilion. *aka* scarlet, red, bloody.
3 子学 *Shushigaku* Neo-Confucianism
6 肉 *shuniku* red ink pad
印 *shuin* red seal
印状 *shuinjō* license with a red seal; shogunate license to trade
印船 *shuinsen* shogunate-licensed trading ship
8 門 *shumon* red-lacquered gate

泥 *shudei* red pottery
9 点 *shuten* red mark
10 唇 *shushin* red lips
書 *shusho, shuga(ki)* writing in red
12 筆 *shuhitsu* red-ink brush
13 塗 *shunu(ri)* red (lacquer)
14 墨 *shuboku, shuzumi* red-ink stick. *shuboku* red and black
16 鞘 *shuzaya* red-lacquered sword sheath

3

朸 2547 / J5b3d / M14488' （国字） See **朸** 2613.

杢 2548 / J4c5d / M14487 （国字） MOKU woodworker.

李 2549 / J4d7b / M14459 RI. *sumomo* plum.

杌 2550 / J-X / M14457 GOTSU. KOTSU. *kirikui* stump, stubble.

杠 2551 / J5b3a / M14481 KŌ carry on the shoulder.

杞 2552 / J5b39 / M14479 KO, KI river willow.
15 憂 *kiyū* absurd fear, needless anxiety

杙 2553 / J5b3b / M14473 YOKU. *kui* stake, post, picket, piling.
5 打 *kuiu(chi)* driving a pile

杏 2554 / J3049 / M14461 KYŌ. *anzu* apricot.
3 子 *anzu* apricot

杖 2555 / J3e73 / M14469 JŌ. *tsue* staff, cane.
6 曳 *tsue (o) hi(ku)* take a walk; travel
9 柱 *tsue-hashira* a cane and a pillar; a person one banks on

杣 2556 / J5b3c / M14488 （国字） *soma* timber forest; timber, lumber; woodcutter.
2 人 *somabito* woodsman, woodcutter
3 山 *somayama* timber forest

杆 2557 / J5b38 / M14449 **桿** 2674 / J5b65 / M14823 KAN shield; pole.
7 状 *kanjō* rodlike
状菌 *kanjōkin* bacillus
11 菌 *kankin* bacillus

杓 2558 / J3c5d / M14466 SHAKU ladle, scoop.
3 子 *shakushi* dipper, ladle, scoop
子定規 *shakushi-jōgi* hard-and-fast rule, formalism, officialism
4 文字 *shamoji* dipper, ladle, scoop

Λ **束** 2559 / J422b / M14480 SOKU bundle, sheaf, ream (of paper). *taba(neru)* bundle, tie in a bundle; govern, manage, control. *tsuka(neru)* tie in bundles; fold (one's arms); administer. *taba* bundle, bunch, sheaf, coil. *tabane* bundle; control, management. *tsuka* handbreadth; bundle.
10 帯 *sokutai* old ceremonial court dress
12 間 *tsuka (no) ma* brief time, a moment
14 髪 *sokuhatsu* Western hairstyle
16 積 *taba(ne)-tsu(mu)* shock (grain)
縛 *sokubaku* restraint, restriction, shackles

杜 2560 / J454e / M14477 TO. ZU. *mori* woods, grove.
4 氏 *tōji* saké brewer
8 松 *toshō* juniper tree
12 絶 *tozetsu* suspension, interruption
14 漏 *zurō na* careless, negligent
15 撰 *zusan na* slovenly, careless, inaccurate
18 鵑 *token, hototogisu* cuckoo
鵑花 *tokenka, satsuki* an early small azalea

A **材** 2561 / J3a60 / M14463 ZAI log; timber, lumber, wood; material; talent.
4 木 *zaimoku* logs, timber, lumber
木屋 *zaimokuya* lumberyard, lumber dealer
木商 *zaimokushō* lumber business; lumber dealer
木問屋 *zaimokudon'ya* lumber wholesaler
木結 *zaimoku musu(bi)* timber hitch
木置場 *zaimoku o(ki)ba* lumberyard
10 料 *zairyō* materials; factor; data

[13] 幹 *zaikan* ability
[15] 質 *zaishitsu* lumber quality
器 *zaiki* talent, ability

B **杉** 2562 / J3f79 / M14452 SAN. *sugi* cryptomeria, sugi, Japan cedar.
[3] 下駄 *sugi geta* geta of cryptomeria wood
[4] 戸 *sugido* cryptomeria door
[5] 生 *sugifu* cryptomeria forest
皮 *sugikawa* cryptomeria bark
[7] 形 *suginari no* cone-shaped
[8] 板 *sugi ita* cryptomeria boards
並木 *sugi namiki* an avenue of cryptomerias
[9] 垣 *sugigaki* a cryptomeria hedge
柱 *sugibashira* cryptomeria posts
[11] 菜 *sugina* horsetail (plant)
[12] 葉 *sugiba* cryptomeria leaves
[15] 箸 *sugibashi* cryptomeria chopsticks

A **条** 2563 / J3e72 / M14486 **條** 2675 / J5b6a / M14859 JŌ article, clause, item; line, stripe, streak; column (of smoke); ray (of light). *kudari* article, clause, paragraph. *-jō* since, because, although, though; article (of a document).
[4] 文 *jōbun* text, provisions
[5] 目 *jōmoku* articles, stipulations
令 *jōrei* law, ordinance, bylaw, rule, regulation
[6] 件 *jōken* proviso, stipulation, condition
件付 *jōkentsu(ki)* conditional
[7] 条 *jōjō* every item
[8] 例 *jōrei* law, ordinance, bylaw, rule
法 *jōhō* itemized regulations
[9] 約 *jōyaku* treaty, pact
約国 *jōyakukoku* treaty signatory
約港 *jōyakukō* treaty port
[11] 痕 *jōkon* streak
理 *jōri* logic, reason
規 *jōki* provisions, rules
章 *jōshō* provisions, clauses
[12] 項 *jōkō* clause, article, stipulations
款 *jōkan* stipulation, provision, article, clause
[13] 鉄 *jōtetsu* bar iron, rod iron
蒔 *sujimaki* drilling, sowing in rows

A **村** 2564 / J423c / M14464 SON *mura* village, hamlet.
[2] 人 *murabito* villager
八分 *murahachibu* ostracism
[4] 内 *sonnai* within the village
夫子 *sompūshi* village schoolmaster; an educated person in the country
[5] 立 *sonritsu* established by the village
民 *sommin* villagers
芝居 *mura shibai* village show
[6] 老 *sonrō* old people of the village
会 *sonkai* village assembly
名 *sommei* village name
吏 *sonri* village official
有 *son'yū* village ownership
有林 *son'yūrin* village forest
[7] 邑 *son'yū* village
里 *murazato* villages
村 *muramura* villages
社 *sonsha* village shrine
役場 *mura yakuba* village office
[8] 長 *sonchō* village mayor
雨 *murasame* passing shower
制 *sonsei* village organization
舎 *sonsha* a village home
学究 *songakkyū* village schoolmaster
[9] 政 *sonsei* village government
[10] 翁 *son'ō* an old villager
時雨 *murashigure* autumn shower
[11] 道 *sondō* village road
祭 *mura matsuri* village festival
[12] 税 *sonzei* village tax
童 *sondō* village child
落 *sonraku* village, hamlet
営 *son'ei* operated by the village
費 *sompi* village expenses
[14] 境 *murazakai* edge of the village

A **来** 2565 / J4d68 / M14489 **來** 173 / J5054 / M581 **徠** 1748 / J5752 / M10155 **耒** 4706 / J6650 / M28898 RAI coming. *ki(taru)* come, arrive; be due to; next, forthcoming. *ki(tasu)* cause, bring about, produce. *ku(ru)* come, come to hand, arrive, approach; call on; come on (rain); set in, be due; become, grow, get; come from; be caused by; derive from. *-rai* since (last month); for (ten days). *rai-* next (year).
[4] 方 *kikata* your coming. *ki(shi)kata, ko(shi)kata* the past
月 *raigetsu* next month
日 *rainichi* arrival in Japan; coming to Japan. *ku(ru)hi* the coming days
日来日 *ku(ru)hi(mo)-ku(ru)hi(mo)* every day

5 立 *kita(te)* new arrival
由 *raiyū* reason; origin, destiny; history; derivation, source; originally, naturally
付 *kitsu(keru)* call frequently
可 *ki(taru)be(ki)* the coming, the next
世 *raisei* the future, posterity. *raise* the next world
6 迎 *raigō* the coming of Amida Buddha to welcome the spirits of the dead; mountaintop sunrise
向 *ki-mu(kau)* come facing (us)
任 *rainin* arrival at one's post
合 *ki-a(waseru)* happen to come along
宅 *raitaku* coming of a visitor to one's home
年 *rainen, ku(ru)toshi* the coming year
会 *raikai* attendance
会者 *raikaisha* attendance, those present
7 車 *raisha* your coming, your visiting me
攻 *raikō* invasion
状 *raijō* letter received
社 *raisha* visit to a company
邸 *raitei* visiting someone's residence
来週 *rairaishū* week after next
8 店 *raiten* coming to the store
往 *raiō* going and coming, next year
9 信 *raishin* letter received
院 *raiin* coming to the hospital
春 *raishun, raiharu* next spring
客 *raikyaku, raikaku* visitor, caller
客攻会 *raikyakuzeme (ni) a(u)* be besieged with visitors
客筋 *raikyaku suji* customers, clients
10 週 *raishū* next week
航 *raikō* arrival of ships; arrival by ship
貢 *raikō suru* come to pay tribute
書 *raisho* letter received
11 掛 *ki-ka(karu)* happen to come. *kiga(ke) ni* on the way here
寇 *raikō* invasion, raid
遊 *raiyū* visit
遊者 *raiyūsha* visitor, tourist
訪 *raihō* visit, call
訪者 *raihōsha* visitor, caller
12 復 *raifuku* return, coming back
援 *raien* assistance, support
診 *raishin* doctor's visit
朝 *raichō* arrival in Japan, visiting Japan
着 *raichaku* arrival
賀 *raiga* your coming; coming with happy news
場 *raijō* attendance
場者 *raijōsha* those attending
13 電 *raiden* incoming telegram
意 *raii* purpose of a visit
14 歴 *raireki* history, career
15 談 *raidan* interview
駕 *raiga* your coming, your presence
賓 *raihin* guest, visitor; visitor's arrival
賓席 *raihinseki* visitors' seats
17 聴 *raichō* attendance
臨 *rairin* attendance, presence; visit, coming, advent
18 難 *kiniku(i)* difficult to come
観 *raikan* inspection visit
観者 *raikansha* visitor (to an exhibit)
22 襲 *raishū* attack, invasion, raid

4

柯 2566 / J-X / M-X — Nonstandard for 柯 2611.

栈 2567 / J-X / M-X — Nonstandard for 材 2561.

枦 2568 / J5b45 / M-X — (国字) Nonstandard for 櫨 2910.

杰 2569 / J5b3f / M14498 — KETSU excellence.

杲 2570 / J5a5e / M14500 — KŌ. GŌ bright; high.

枅 2571 / J5b47 / M14525 — KEI. KEN *hijiki* cross-beam, rafter.

枋 2572 / J5b44 / M14532 — HŌ weir, fish trap. *mayumi* spindle tree.

枌 2573 / J5b43 / M14534 — FUN. BUN white elm. *sogi* thin-sawed slats for roofing.

B **析** 2574 / J404f / M14538 — SEKI divide; tear; analyze.

杷 2575 / J4747 / M14505 — HA a kind of rake.

杼 2576 J5b41 M14513 CHO. *hi* shuttle.

杳 2577 J5a62 M14501 YŌ darkness, indistinctness. *yō to shite* dimly; (not) in the least.

杪 2578 J5b42 M14490 BYŌ. *kozue* twig; treetop.

枘 2579 J-X M14552 ZEI. NEI. *hozo* tenon, cog.

枇 2580 J487a M14528 BI spoon.
8 杷 *biwa* loquat

杵 2581 J354f M14503 SHO. SO. *kine* wooden pestle, pounder.
9 柄 *kinezuka* long-handled pestle
14 歌 *kine uta* grain pounder's song

A **枚** 2582 J4b67 M14554 BAI. MAI counter for thin flat things. *-mai* page, leaf (of a book), sheet.
10 挙 *maikyo suru* enumerate, mention
13 数 *maisū* the number of flat things

杭 2583 J393a M14494 KŌ. GŌ. *kui* stake, post, picket, piling.
5 打 *kuiu(chi)* driving a pile
打機 *kuiu(chi)ki* pile driver

枉 2584 J5b3e M14530 Ō. *ma(geru) vt* bend, curve; lean, bow; distort; depart from (principles); pawn. *ma(gete)* forcibly, against one's will.
8 易 *ma(ge)-yasu(i)* pliant, supple, flexible
15 駕 *ōga* your visit

B **枠** 2585 J4f48 M14576 （国字） *waku* frame, framework; reel, spindle, spool; rim; box (in printing); limit.
4 内 *wakunai* within the limits
5 外 *wakugai* beyond the limits
7 形空中線 *wakugata kūchūsen* loop antenna, frame aerial
11 組 *wakugu(mi)* frame, framework, framing

B **杯** 2586 J4755 M14497 **盃** 3387 J4756 M22955 HAI cup, glass; toast, congratulatory cup; counter for cupfuls. *sakazuki* wine glass, saké cup; chalice, cup.
8 事 *sakazukigoto* drinking feast; exchange of nuptial cups; pledging over winecups
9 洗 *haisen* a sink
15 盤 *haiban* glasses and plates
盤狼藉 *haiban-rōzeki* disorderly drinking party

枡 2587 J5b46 M14577 **桝** 2673 J4b71 M-X （国字） *masu* measuring box.
5 目 *masume* measure
7 形 *masugata* square shape
売 *masuu(ri)* sale by measure
11 組 *masugu(mi)* temple bracket assemblies
12 落 *masuoto(shi)* rattrap
13 搔 *masukaki* stick for leveling the contents of a measuring box

B **枢** 2588 J3f75 M14577' **樞** 2828 J5c64 M15450 SŪ. *toboso* pivot; door.
8 府 *Sūfu* Privy Council
9 要 *sūyō* importance
11 務 *sūmu* important business; secret business
密 *sūmitsu* secret government affairs
密院 *Sūmitsuin* Privy Council
密顧問官 *Sūmitsu Komonkan* Privy Counselor
12 軸 *sūjiku* pivot; axle; center
軸国 *Sūjikukoku* the Axis Powers
16 機 *sūki* important state affairs
機卿 *sūkikyō, sūkikei* (Catholic) cardinal

枕 2589 J4b6d M14546 CHIN. *makura* pillow.
2 刀 *makuragatana* bedside sword
3 上 *chinjō* bedside
4 木 *makuragi* railroad tie
辺 *makurabe, chimpen* bedside
元 *makuramoto* bedside
6 当 *makuraa(te)* pillow slip
合戦 *makura kassen* pillow fight
10 席 *chinseki* pillow and rug; bed; bedroom; night entertainer
捜 *makurasaga(shi)* bedroom theft; bedroom thief
紙 *makuragami* toilet paper

時計 *makuradokei* alarm clock
11 探 *makurasaga(shi)* bedroom theft; bedroom thief
掛 *makuraka(ke)* pillow slip
許 *makuramoto* bedside
屏風 *makura byōbu* bed screen
12 詞 *makura kotoba* a 'pillow word'; a conventional epithet
16 頭 *chintō* bedside
18 覆 *makuraōi* pillow slip

A **林** 2590 J4e53 M14551 Rɪɴ. *hayashi* forest.
4 木 *rimboku* forest tree
5 立 *rinritsu* forest (of chimneys)
8 学 *ringaku* forestry
学士 *Ringakushi* Bachelor of Forestry
学者 *ringakusha* forestry expert
学博士 *Ringaku Hakushi* a Doctor of Forestry
9 政 *rinsei* forestry management
泉 *rinsen* landscape garden
11 道 *rindō* forest road
務官 *rimmukan* (government) forester
産 *rinsan* forestry products
産物 *rinsambutsu* forest products
野 *rin'ya* woodland, forests
野庁 *rin'yachō* forestry agency
野局 *rin'yakyoku* forestry bureau
12 間 *rinkan* in the forest
間学校 *rinkan gakkō* outdoor school, camping school
13 業 *ringyō* forestry
15 縁 *rin'en* forest edge
17 檎 *ringo* apple
檎酒 *ringoshu* cider
檎酸 *ringosan* malic acid

A **枝** 2591 J3b5e M14557 Sʜɪ. Kɪ. *eda, e* branch, bow, twig, limb.
3 川 *edagawa* branch of a river
4 切 *edaki(ri)* pruning
5 付 *edatsu(ki)* ramifications; shape (of a tree)
7 角 *edazuno* antlers
豆 *edamame* green soybeans
折 *edao(ri)* breaking branches (to mark a mountain trail). *shio(ri)* guide book
折戸 *shio(ri)do* garden gate, gate of branches
8 垂柳 *shidare yanagi* weeping willow
垂桜 *shidarezakura* weeping cherry
9 城 *edajiro* branch castle
柿 *edagaki* persimmons on the branch; persimmons drying on a skewer
枯病 *edaga(re)byō* twig blight
10 振 *edabu(ri)* ramifications; shape (of a tree)
11 道 *edamichi* branch road
族 *shizoku* tribe; branch family
移 *edautsu(ri)* moving from branch to branch
隊 *shitai* detachment (of troops)
接 *edatsugi* cleft grafting
接法 *edatsugihō* cleft grafting
12 結 *edamusu(bi)* rolling hitch
葉 *edaha, shiyō* leaves and branches, foliage; ramifications; side issues; digression; minor details
葉末節 *shiyō-massetsu* branches and leaves; unimportant details
13 話 *edabanashi* digression
幹 *shikan* trunk and branches
継 *edatsu(gi)* cleft grafting
継法 *edatsu(gi)hō* cleft grafting

A **松** 2592 J3e3e M14516 **枩** 2593 J5b40 M-X Sʜō. *matsu* pine.
3 山 *matsuyama* pine-covered hill
4 木 *matsu(no)ki* pine tree
内 *matsu(no)uchi* New Year's season
6 虫 *matsumushi* a cricket
竹 *matsutake* New Year's pine-and-bamboo decorations
竹梅 *shō-chiku-bai* pine-bamboo-plum; congratulatory tree decorations
8 明 *taimatsu* pine torch, torchlight, firebrand
林 *matsubayashi* pine forest
板 *matsuita* pine board
並木 *matsu namiki* an avenue or row of pines
9 風 *matsukaze, shōfū* wind through the pines
柏 *shōhaku* pines and oaks; faithfulness
茸 *matsutake, matsudake* a kind of edible mushroom
10 原 *matsubara* pine grove
脂 *matsuyani, shōshi* rosin, pine resin
根油 *shōkon'yu* turpentine
11 魚 *katsuo, shōgyo* bonito
毬 *matsukasa* pine cone
12 傘 *matsukasa* pine cone
葉 *matsuba* pine needles

葉杖 *matsubazue* crutches
[13] 飾 *matsukaza(ri)* New Year's pine decorations
[19] 韻 *shōin* music of the pines
[21] 露 *shōro* a kind of edible mushroom
[22] 籟 *shōrai* sighing of the pine trees

A **果** 2594 / J324c / M14556 Ka fruit; reward. *ha(tasu)* carry out, achieve, complete; realize, perform, fulfill. *ha(teru)* end, be finished, be exhausted; die, perish. *ōse(ru)* succeed in doing. *hatashite* as was expected; really. *ha(teshi), ha(te)* end, limit, bounds, extremity, result; fate. *-ha(teru)* be tired out; be used up.

[5] 皮 *kahi* fruit peeling
汁 *kajū* fruit juice
[6] 肉 *kaniku* the flesh of fruit
合 *ha(tashi)a(i)* duel
[7] 状 *hata(shi)jō* (fighter's) letter of challenge
[8] 取 *hakado(ru)* move right ahead (with the work)
果 *hakabaka(shii)* rapid, expeditious, active; favorable
物 *kudamono* fruit
物屋 *kudamonoya* fruit store
実 *kajitsu* fruit; nut; berry
実店 *kajitsuten* fruit store
実酒 *kajitsushu* cider, wine, plum liquor
[9] 食 *kashoku* living on fruit
[11] 断 *kadan na* decisive, resolute, drastic
菜 *kasai* fruits and vegetables
[12] 敢 *hakana(i)* fleeting, momentary, ephemeral; vain, empty, hopeless; fickle, inconstant, unstable; fragile, frail; pitiful, poor, sad, miserable. *kakan na* resolute, determined, bold
然 *kazen* as was expected
無 *hakana(i)* fleeting, transitory, ephemeral. *ha(teshi)na(ku)* eternally, interminably. *ha(teshi) (ga) na(i)* endless, boundless, fathomless, eternal
報 *kahō* good fortune, luck; happiness
報者 *kahōmono* lucky fellow
[16] 糖 *katō* fruit sugar
樹 *kaju* fruit tree
樹園 *kajuen* orchard

A **板** 2595 / J4844 / M14518 Han. Ban. *ita* board, plank; planking; plate, sheet; the stage.

[3] 子 *itago* a board on which to practice swimming strokes (in water); floor planks in a small Japanese boat
[4] 戸 *itado* wooden door
木 *hangi* (printing) block, woodcut, engraving block
切 *itaki(re)* piece of wood, scrap lumber
元 *hammoto* publisher
[5] 石 *itaishi* slate; slab; flagstone
本 *hampon* a book printed from wood blocks; a printed book
仕切 *itajikiri* wooden partition
付草履 *itazu(ki) zōri* wooden-soled sandals
目 *itame* grain (in wood)
目紙 *itamegami* paper made of several pasted sheets
[6] 行 *hankō* wood-block printing
[7] 囲 *itagako(i)* board fence, wooden fence
庇 *itabisashi* eaves
床 *itadoko* wooden-floored *tokonoma* alcove
材 *itazai* boards
車輪 *itasharin* disk wheel
[8] 金 *itagane* metal plate, sheet metal; sheet gold or sheet silver. *bankin* sheet gold; sheet silver
画 *hanga* woodcut print
表紙 *itabyōshi* wooden book covers
[9] 垣 *itagaki* wooden fence
前 *itamae* a cook
挟 *itabasami* dilemma, predicament
屋 *itaya* a board roof; a house roofed with boards
屋貝 *itayagai* scallop (shell)
屋根 *itayane* wooden roof
[10] 扇 *itaōgi* fan made of wooden strips
挽 *itahiki* sawing lumber
紙 *itagami* cardboard
書 *bansho* writing on a blackboard
[11] 張 *itaba(ri)* boarding; planking; boarded-up place
[12] 場 *itaba* a cook (in a restaurant)
塀 *itabei* wooden wall, board fence
割 *itawa(ri)* splitting into boards; boards so formed
葺 *itabuki* roofing of boards
硝子 *itagarasu* plate glass
間 *ita(no)ma* wooden floor
間稼 *ita(no)ma kase(gi)* bathhouse thief
[14] 摺 *hansuri* wood-block printing

[15]縁 *itaen* floored veranda
敷 *itaji(ki)* wooden floor; removable slatted floor
[16]橋 *itabashi* wooden bridge
壁 *itakabe* wooden wall
[19]簾 *itasudare* Venetian blind

A **東** 2596 / J456c / M14499 Tō *higashi* east. *azuma* east; Eastern Japan.
[3]上 *tōjō* going to Tokyo; going east
[4]方 *tōhō, tōbō* east, eastward; eastern; the Orient
方教会 *Tōhō Kyōkai* The Eastern Church
天 *tōten* the eastern sky
天紅 *tōtenkō* crowing in the morning
[5]北 *tōhoku, higashikita* northeast. *Tōhoku* the Northeast
北人 *Tōhokujin* Northeasterner
半 *tōhan* the eastern half
半球 *Higashi Hankyū* Eastern Hemisphere
[6]行 *tōkō* eastbound
向 *higashimu(ki)* facing east
邦 *Tōhō* Oriental country, the Orient, an eastern country
夷 *tōi* eastern barbarians
印度 *Higashi Indo* East Indies
印度会社 *Higashi Indo Gaisha* East India Company
西 *tōzai* east and west; Orient and Occident; Your attention please.
西屋 *tōzaiya* town crier
西南北 *tōzainamboku* east, west, south, and north, all directions
[7]男 *azuma otoko* a man from East Japan
亜 *Tōa* East Asia, the Orient
亜諸民族 *Tōa shominzoku* East-Asian peoples
亜諸国 *Tōa shokoku* East-Asian countries
[8]門 *tōmon* eastern gate
国 *tōgoku* eastern country; eastern provinces; Kanto Provinces
征 *tōsei* eastern expedition
欧 *Tōō* Eastern Europe
郊 *tōkō* eastern suburbs
京都 *Tōkyōto* Tokyo Metropolis
奔西走 *tōhon-seisō suru* busy oneself, bestir oneself, be on the go, take an active interest
岸 *tōgan* eastern coast; east bank
岸沿 *tōganzo(i) ni* along the east coast; along the eastern seashore
[9]面 *tōmen* facing the east; east face, east side; the east
風 *tōfū, kochi, kochi kaze* east wind; spring wind
屋 *azumaya* arbor, bower, summer house
独 *Tōdoku* East Germany
軍 *tōgun* the eastern army
南 *tōnan, higashiminami* southeast
南亜 *Tōnan'a* Southeast Asia
海 *tōkai* eastern sea
海地方 *Tōkai Chihō* Eastern-Sea Area
海道 *Tōkaidō* Eastern Sea Road
洋 *Tōyō* Orient
洋人 *Tōyōjin* Orientals
洋主義 *Tōyō shugi* the Orient for the Orientals
洋風 *tōyōfū no* Oriental
洋通 *Tōyōtsū* Orientalist
[10]進 *tōshin suru* proceed east
航 *tōkō* sailing east, eastbound
部 *tōbu* eastern part
都 *Tōto* the Eastern Capital, Yedo, Edo; Tokyo
宮 *tōgū, haru(no)miya* crown prince
[11]側 *higashigawa* east side, east bank. *tōsoku* east side
経 *tōkei* east longitude
寄 *higashiyo(ri)* easterly (wind)
[12]雲 *shinonome* daybreak, dawn
[14]遷 *tōsen suru* move (the capital) east
漸 *tōzen* eastward advance
端 *tōtan* east end, eastern tip
歌 *tōka* the old Kanto-area folk songs

5

柁 2597 / J4248 / M14599 See **舵** 4937.

柰 2598 / J-X / M14659 See **奈** 1147.

梻 2599 / J-X / M-X Nonstandard for **様** 2821.

枳 2600 / J5b4c / M14583 Kɪ. Sʜɪ *karatachi* a trifoliate orange.

枴 2601 / J5b4a / M14584 Kᴀɪ *tsue* cane.

4 心忄⺗戈戸手扌支攴攵文斗斤方无日曰月【木】5 欠止歹殳毋比毛氏气水氵氺火灬爪爫父爻爿丬片牙牛犬犭

枹 2602 / J5b54 / M14589 Fu. Ho *bachi* drumstick. *naranoki* Japanese oak, type of wood used for charcoal.

柆 2603 / J5b56 / M14606 Rō broken tree.

柎 2604 / J5b55 / M14616 Fu flower calyx; raft; grip on bow or sword. *utena* calyx; pedestal.

柞 2605 / J5b50 / M14636 Saku. Sa large trees. *hahaso* a kind of oak.

柤 2606 / J5b4f / M14642 Sa handrail; dam. So *manaita* cutting board.

柧 2607 / J5b57 / M14645 Ko corner; wine cup.

柬 2608 / J5b4b / M14655 Kan. Ken choose; letter; name card. *era(bu)* choose, select.

柮 2609 / J5b53 / M14657 Totsu to cut; a stump.

柝 2610 / J5b51 / M14633 Taku sounding sticks.

柯 2611 / J5b49 / M14658 **柯** 2566 / J-X / M-X Ka a handle.

柢 2612 / J5b52 / M14640 Tei root; be founded on.

栃 2613 / J464a / M14687 （国字） *tochi* horse chestnut.

柊 2614 / J4922 / M14610 Shu. Shū. *hiiragi* holly.

枷 2615 / J5b48 / M14587 Ka. *kase* shackles, irons, handcuffs, bonds.

枸 2616 / J5b4e / M14588 Ku quince tree.
[19]櫞酸 *kuensan* citric acid

柩 2617 / J5b4d / M14650 Kyū bier. *hitsugi* coffin, hearse, casket.
[7]車 *kyūsha* hearse

栂 2618 / J444e / M14686 （国字） *tsuga* hemlock, hemlock-spruce.
[8]松 *tsuga-matsu* hemlock-spruce

柾 2619 / J4b6f / M14675 （国字） *masa, masame* straight grain. *masaki* spindle tree.
[5]目 *masame* straight grain

柵 2620 / J3a74 / M14665 Saku stockade, fence, palisade. *shigara(mu)* entwine around; check (a current) with a weir. *shigarami* weir.
[9]垣 *sakugaki* fence

柑 2621 / J343b / M14619 Kon. Kan citrus fruit; orange.
[3]子類 *kōjirui* citrus fruits
[16]橘類 *kankitsurui* citrus fruits

柚 2622 / J4d2e / M14629 Yu. Yū. Jiku. *yuzu* citron.
[3]子 *yuzu* citron
子湯 *yuzuyu* hot citron bath
[12]湯 *yuzuyu* hot citron bath

柏 2623 / J4770 / M14617 Haku. Hyaku. *kashiwa* oak.
[4]手 *kashiwade* handclapping in worship at a shrine
[14]槙 *byakushin* juniper tree
[15]餅 *kashiwa mochi* rice cake wrapped in ⌈oak leaf

柿 2624 / J3341 / M14681 **柹** 2625 / J-X / M14596 Shi. Ji *kaki* persimmon. *kokera* shingle.
[6]色 *kaki iro* yellowish brown
[8]板 *kokera ita* thin shingles
[11]渋 *kakishibu* persimmon juice

柘 2626 / J4453 / M14626 Sha, So wild mulberry.
[14]榴 *zakuro* pomegranate
榴子 *zakuroshi* garnet
榴石 *zakuroishi* garnet
榴珠 *zakuroshu* garnet

B **柄** 2627 / J4a41 / M14603 Hei. *e* handle, crank, grip, hilt, shaft, knob, spoke (of steering wheel on a ship). *gara* pattern, design; build; character, nature. *tsuka* hilt, grip, handle (of a knife).

7 杓 *hishaku* dipper, ladle, scoop
9 染 *garazo(me)* dyeing in designs
11 袋 *tsukabukuro* sword-hilt cover
16 樽 *edaru* fancy two-handled (saké) barrel

B **某** 2628 / J4b3f / M14618 Bō one, a certain; that person; that thing.
nanigashi somebody, a certain person; a certain amount. *soregashi* somebody, a certain person; I.
4 月 *bōgetsu* a certain month
氏 *bōshi* a certain person
6 地 *bōchi* a certain piece of land
8 所 *bōsho* a certain place

B **柳** 2629 / J4c78 / M14662 Ryū. *yanagi* willow.
6 糸 *ryūshi* graceful willow branches
行李 *yanagigōri* wicker trunk
7 条 *ryūjō* willow branches
9 眉 *ryūbi* beautiful eyebrows
13 腰 *yanagigoshi* slender figure, slim waist; willowy
暗花明 *ryūan-kamei* bright flowers under dark willows; rural springtime; red-light district

A **査** 2630 / J3a3a / M14643 Sa investigate.
5 収 *sashū suru* investigate and confiscate
8 定 *satei* assessment; revision; audit (of salaries); investigation and decision
11 問 *samon* inquiry, hearing
問会 *samonkai* court of inquiry
12 証 *sashō* visa; investigation and attestation
13 照 *sashō* a checkup
14 察 *sasatsu* inspection, investigation
15 閲 *saetsu* inspection, investigation

A **柱** 2631 / J436c / M14660 Chū cylinder, supports for strings on a lute; pillar, post.
hashira pillar, column, post, pole; support, prop, stay; sole support; counter for Shinto gods. *ji* bridge (of a stringed instrument).
5 石 *chūseki* pillar, mainstay, cornerstone
6 式 *chūshiki* column type
7 体 *chūtai* column shaft
状 *chūjō* columnar, pillar-like
10 時計 *hashiradokei* wall clock
11 廊 *chūrō* colonnade, portico
掛 *hashiraka(ke)* a motto or picture hanging on a post
14 暦 *hashiragoyomi* wall calendar
16 頭 *chūtō* capital of a column

B **架** 2632 / J324d / M14586 Ka frame, mount, stand, support; hang up; shelf.
ka(suru) build (a bridge), construct.
ka(keru) vt hang.
3 上 *kajō* on the shelf
工歯 *kakōshi* dental bridge
工義歯 *kakō gishi* dental bridge
5 台 *kadai* abutment; stand, frame, holder
8 空 *kakū* aerial, overhead, trolley; fiction.
kakū no fanciful, fictitious, Utopian
空索道 *kakū sakudō* aerial cableway
空線 *kakūsen* aerial cable, overhead wire, trolley wire
11 設 *kasetsu* construction, building
道橋 *kadōkyō* road overpass
15 線 *kasen* aerial wiring
16 橋 *kakyō* bridge building
橋工事 *kakyō kōji* bridge-construction work

B **柔** 2633 / J3d40 / M14622 Jū, Nyū weakness; gentleness; softness.
yawa(ragu) vi soften, be reconciled; lessen; calm down. *yawara(geru) vt* soften, moderate, ease, alleviate, mitigate, relax; appease; dilute (wine); tone down (colors); comfort; pacify, quiet.
yawa(rakai), yawa(rakana), yawa(i) soft, tender, plastic, limp, gentle, mellow.
yawa(ra) jujitsu.
4 毛 *jūmō* soft hair
5 皮 *jūhi* tanned leather
6 肌 *yawahada* soft skin
8 物 *yawa(raka)mono* silks
和 *nyūwa* gentleness, meekness, mildness
9 柔 *yawayawa* softly, pliantly; gently, mildly; gradually
10 弱 *jūjaku, nyūjaku* weakness, effeminacy, enervation
11 魚 *ika* squid, cuttlefish
婉 *jūen na* gentle and graceful
術 *jūjutsu* jujitsu, jujutsu
道 *jūdō* jujitsu, jujutsu, judo
道家 *jūdōka* judo expert
軟 *jūnan na* soft, pliable, flexible, elastic

軟体操 *jūnan taisō* calisthenics

軟性 *jūnansei* pliability, softness, elasticity, suppleness

12 順 *jūjun* obedience, meekness, docility

靭 *jūjin* elasticity, flexibility

靭性 *jūjinsei* elasticity, flexibility

15 膚 *yawahada* soft skin

17 懦 *jūda* effeminacy

B **枯** 2634 / J384f / M14579 Ko. *ka(reru)* wither, die, be dead; age; be seasoned; fog up. *ka(rasu)* kill (vegetation); let dry; season (lumber). *ka(rebamu)* wither. *ka(re)-, ka(ra)-* dead.

3 山 *ka(re)yama* a hill covered with dead vegetation

4 方 *ka(re)gata* time for the leaves to fall

木 *ka(re)ki, ka(ra)ki, koboku* dead tree

5 生 *ka(re)fu* area of dead grass

芝 *ka(re)shiba* dry lawn, dry grass

6 色 *ka(re) iro* dead color

死 *koshi* withering, dying

亙 *ka(re)-wata(ru)* die completely, die all over the area

7 花 *ka(re)bana* faded flowers

8 枝 *ka(re)eda, ka(ra)eda, ka(re)e* dead branch

林 *korin* the bare woods in winter

果 *ka(re)-ha(teru)* waste away

9 枯 *ka(re)ga(re)* the dying of the leaves, beginning to wither

草 *ka(re)gusa, ka(re)kusa* dry grass, hay

10 骨 *kokotsu* decomposed bones; buried person; deceased person

凋 *kochō suru* wither, decay

11 淡 *kotan* elegant simplicity

渇 *kokatsu suru* dry up; be exhausted; become poverty-stricken

野 *ka(re)no* desolate field

12 葉 *ka(re)ha, ka(re)ba, koyō* dead leaf

14 増 *ka(re)-masa(ru)* go on withering

竭 *koketsu suru* dry up

槁 *kokō* withering, emaciation

20 礬 *koban* burnt alum

21 露柿 *korogaki* dried persimmons

A **栄** 2635 / J3149 / M14687 **榮** 2791 / J5c46 / M15273 Ei prosperity, glory, splendor, honor. *saka(eru)* prosper, flourish, thrive. *ha(eru)* shine, be brilliant; look attractive. *saka(e)* glory, prosperity. *hae* glory. *hae(aru)* glorious.

4 化 *eika suru* glorify

6 行 *saka(e)-yu(ku)* become more and more prosperous or glorious

光 *eikō* glory

7 位 *eii* exalted position

利 *eiri* wealth and fame

8 典 *eiten* honors; ceremony, exercises

9 冠 *eikan* laurels, garland

枯 *eiko* ups and downs, rise and fall, vicissitudes

枯盛衰 *eiko seisui* prosperity and decline, vicissitudes of fortune

10 進 *eishin* promotion, advancement

称 *eishō* honorable title

華 *eiga* glory, splendor, prosperity; luxury; majesty

辱 *eijoku* honor and disgrace; prestige, dignity, honor, reputation

11 達 *eitatsu* fame, distinction, rise, advancement

転 *eiten* promotion

12 落 *eiraku* flourishing and declining

13 誉 *eiyo* honor, fame, glory

15 養 *eiyō* nutrition, nourishment, sustenance

養士 *eiyōshi* nutritionist

養分 *eiyōbun* nutrient

養不足 *eiyō fusoku* undernourishment, malnutrition

養不良 *eiyō furyō* undernourishment, malnutrition

養生理学 *eiyō seirigaku* nutritional physiology

養失調 *eiyō shitchō* undernourishment, malnutrition

養価 *eiyōka* food value

養物 *eiyōbutsu* nutriment, nourishing food

養学 *eiyōgaku* dietetics

養素 *eiyōso* nutrient

養障害 *eiyō shōgai* nutritional disorder

17 爵 *eishaku* peerage, title

20 耀 *eyō, eiyō* luxury, splendor, prosperity

A **染** 2636 / J4077 / M14621 Sen. *so(mu), so(maru)* be dyed, be imbued with, be tainted with. *so(meru)* dye, color, paint. *shi(miru)* soak in, permeate, infiltrate; pierce (as a wind); be imbued with, be influenced by; smart; be sensitive to pain. *shi(mi)* stain, blot, spot, smudge. *so(me)* dyeing, printing. *-zo(me)* dyed.

[2]入 *shi(mi)-i(ru)* soak into, permeate, infiltrate; be impressed with
[3]工 *senkō* dyer
上 *so(me)-a(garu)* be completely dyed. *so(me)-a(geru)* finish dyeing
[4]方 *so(me)kata* dyeing process
込 *so(me)-ko(mu)* dye in designs. *shi(mi)-ko(mu)* soak into, permeate, infiltrate; be impressed with
分 *so(me)-wa(keru)* dye in different colors
毛 *semmō* dyeing the hair
毛剤 *semmōzai* hair dye
[5]付 *shi(mi)-tsu(ku)* be dyed in deeply, be stained. *so(me)-tsu(keru)* dye in (patterns)
出 *so(me)-da(su)* dye (patterns)
[6]糸 *so(me)ito* dyed thread
返 *so(me)-kae(su)* redye. *so(me)-kae(ru)* soak into, permeate, infiltrate; be impressed with
地 *so(me)ji* dyed cloth
色 *senshoku* dyeing
色体 *senshokutai* chromosome
[7]抜 *so(me)-nu(ku)* dye in the grain. *shi(mi)-nu(ki)* removal of stains
更 *so(me)-kae(ru)* redye
[8]直 *so(me)-nao(su)* redye
物 *somemono* dyeing; dyed goods
物屋 *somemonoya* dyer
物師 *somemonoshi* dyer
[9]革 *so(me)kawa* dyed leather
通 *shi(mi)-tō(ru)* soak through, penetrate, permeate, infiltrate
柄 *so(me)gara* dyed designs
型 *so(me)gata* dyed pattern
染 *shimijimi* keenly, seriously, heartily, thoroughly
飛白 *so(me)gasuri* a cotton cloth with printed patterns
[10]料 *senryō* dyes, dyestuffs
粉 *so(me)ko* dyestuff
[12]渡 *shi(mi)-wata(ru)* penetrate, spread, pervade
着 *shi(mi)-tsu(ku)* be deeply dyed
替 *so(me)ka(e)* redyeing
筆 *sempitsu* writing; painting
筆料 *sempitsuryō* writing fee
[14]髪剤 *sempatsuzai* hair dye
模様 *so(me)-moyō* printed pattern
[16]薬 *so(me)gusuri* dye, dyestuff
[18]織 *senshoku* dyeing and weaving

6

桧 2637 / J4930 / M-X Nonstandard for 檜 2894.

栢 2638 / J337c / M14714 See 柏 2623.

档 2639 / J5b63 / M-X Tō seat; wooden frame; document.

栩 2640 / J5b5b / M14721 KU *kunugi* a kind of oak.

栫 2641 / J5b61 / M14724 SEN. SON close off with branches; weir, fish trap.

栲 2642 / J5b5e / M14734 Kō *nurude* a sumac. *tae* fabric woven from bark fibers.

栲 2643 / J5b5d / M14767 Ko name of a tree.

桙 2644 / J5b62 / M14784 Bō *hoko* halbert.

栞 2645 / J5b59 / M14708 KAN. *shiori* bookmark; guidebook.

框 2646 / J5b5a / M14780 KYō. *kamachi* frame, framework

桎 2647 / J5b5f / M14768 SHITSU fetters.
[11]梏 *shikkoku* fetters, bonds, yoke

桛 2648 / J-X / M14796 (国字) *kase* reel, hank, skein.
[6]糸 *kase ito* reeled thread

B **栓** 2649 / J4072 / M14689 SEN bolt, stopper, cork, plug, ear plug, bung, faucet, peg.
[7]抜 *sennu(ki)* corkscrew, bottle opener

栖 2650 / J4034 / M14693 SEI. *su* nest, rookery, breeding place, beehive, cobweb; den, haunt.
[10]息 *seisoku suru* inhabit, live in, lodge in

梅 2651 / J4073 / M14737 SEN Japanese bead tree.

17 檀 *sendan* Japanese bead tree

桓 2652 / J343c / M14774 KAN marking post.

8 表 *kambyō* entrance post; *torii*
10 桓 *kankan* strong, valiant

桔 2653 / J354b / M14777 KETSU, KITSU a sweep-well bucket; used in plant names.

11 梗 *kikyō* a root used in making cough medicine
15 槔 *kikkō* a sweep-well bucket

B **栽** 2654 / J3a4f / M14750 SAI planting.

11 培 *saibai* cultivation (of plants)
培所 *saibaijo* plantation
培種 *saibaishu* agricultural species

桐 2655 / J364d / M14770 TŌ. *kiri* the paulownia tree.

3 下駄 *kiri geta* geta made of paulownia wood
8 油 *kiriyu, kiri abura, tōyu* wood oil, tung oil, nut oil, China wood oil
18 簞笥 *kiri tansu* chest of drawers of paulownia wood

桁 2656 / J3765 / M14754 KŌ. *keta* beam, girder, spar, yard; unit or column (in figures).

3 下 *ketashita* clearance (under overpass)
5 外 *ketahazu(re)* wide difference; extraordinary
12 違 *ketachiga(i)* off on the decimal point; wide difference
16 橋 *ketahashi* girder bridge

柴 2657 / J3c46 / M14664 SHI. SAI. *shiba* brushwood, firewood.

4 木 *shibaki* brushwood
刈 *shibaka(ri)* gathering firewood; firewood gatherer
8 門 *saimon* brushwood gate, humble cottage
10 栗 *shibaguri* small chestnut
11 笛 *shibabue* leaf flute

B **桟** 2658 / J3b37 / M14796 **棧** 2708 / J5c22 / M14963 SAN crosspiece, cleat, frame, door bolt; shelf; jetty; suspension bridge.

5 瓦 *sangawara* pantile, common roof tile
10 俵 *sandawara* round straw cover
俵法師 *sandawarabōshi* round straw cover
11 道 *sandō* plank road
15 敷 *sajiki* reviewing stand, box, gallery
16 橋 *sambashi* wharf, jetty. *sankyō* wharf; bridge

桂 2659 / J374b / M14755 KEI. *katsura* Judas tree, katsura tree, cinnamon tree.

5 皮 *keihi* cassia bark, cinnamon
皮油 *keihiyu* cinnamon oil
7 男 *katsurao, katsura otoko* man in the moon
9 冠 *keikan* crown of laurel
冠詩人 *keikan shijin* poet laureate
11 庵 *keian* servant's registry

B **核** 2660 / J334b / M14743 KAKU nucleus, core, seed, kernel. *kaku no* nuclear. *sane* fruit stone, kernel, nucleus.

4 心 *kakushin* core, kernel
反応 *kaku hannō* nuclear reaction
分裂 *kaku bunretsu* nuclear fission
分裂質 *kaku bunretsushitsu* fissionable materials
7 兵器 *kaku heiki* nuclear weapons
8 武装 *kaku busō* nuclear arms
実験 *kaku jikken* nuclear experiments
物理学 *kaku butsurigaku* nuclear physics
12 弾頭 *kaku dantō* nuclear warhead

B **桑** 2661 / J372c / M14772 SŌ. *kuwa* mulberry.

5 田 *sōden* mulberry plantation
6 色 *kuwa iro* light yellow
8 門 *sōmon* priesthood; Buddhism
苗 *sōbyō* mulberry seedling
苺 *kuwa ichigo* fruit of the mulberry
9 海 *sōkai* this world's sudden changes
畑 *kuwabatake* mulberry field
13 園 *sōen* mulberry plantation
14 摘 *kuwatsu(mi)* picking mulberry leaves; mulberry-leaf pickers

栗 2662 / J372a / M14695 RITSU. *kuri* chestnut.

4 毛 *kurige* chestnut color; bay horse, sorrel

5 石 *kuri ishi* chestnut-size stone, pebble
6 色 *kuri iro* chestnut color
名月 *kuri meigetsu* hunters' moon
羊羹 *kuri yōkan* chestnut bean-jelly
11 毬 *iga* burr
12 飯 *kuri meshi* chestnut rice
13 鼠 *risu* squirrel
17 餡 *kurian* chestnut bean jam
20 饅頭 *kuri manjū* chestnut-jam steamed dumpling

B **桃** 2663 / J456d / M14757 Tō. *momo* peach.
3 山 *Momoyama* era (1576～1598)
6 色 *momo iro* rose, pink
色遊戯 *momo-iro yūgi* love affair
色雑誌 *momo iro zasshi* yellow journal
7 李 *tōri* peaches and plums
花 *tōka* peach blossom
12 割 *momowa(re)* a popular hairstyle among young women during the Meiji and Taisho period
13 園 *momozono* peach orchard
節句 *Momo (no) Sekku* the Doll Festival
源 *tōgen* quiet country garden; heaven on earth; Shangri-La
源郷 *tōgenkyō* quiet country garden; heaven on earth; Shangri-La

A **桜** 2664 / J3a79 / M14796 **櫻** 2917 / J5d2f / M15888 Ō. *sakura* flowering cherry; cherry blossoms; pink color; horse meat.
4 月 *sakurazuki* third lunar month
木 *sakuragi* cherry tree
6 肉 *sakuraniku* horse meat
色 *sakura iro* the color of cherry blossoms; pink, cerise
7 坊 *sakurambō* edible cherry
花 *ōka, sakurabana* cherry-blossom season
貝 *sakuragai* a cherry shell
9 狩 *sakuraga(ri)* looking for cherry blossoms
草 *sakurasō* primrose
10 時 *sakuradoki* cherry-blossom season
桃 *sakurambō, ōtō* edible cherry
紙 *sakuragami* handkerchief paper, toilet paper
12 湯 *sakurayu* cherry-blossom drink
雲 *ōun* clouds of cherry blossoms
飯 *sakurameshi* rice cooked with soy sauce and saké
14 漬 *sakurazuke* pickled cherry blossoms
15 餅 *sakura mochi* a round glutenous-rice cake filled with sweet bean paste covered with a salted cherry leaf
16 樹 *ōju* cherry tree

A **株** 2665 / J3374 / M14723 SHU. *kabu* stump; shares, stocks; connections; business; counter for small plants.
4 分 *kabuwa(ke)* dividing roots
5 主 *kabunushi* shareholder
主総会 *kabunushi sōkai* stockholders' general meeting
6 式 *kabushiki* shares, stocks
式市場 *kabushiki shijō* stock market
式会社 *kabushiki kaisha* joint-stock corporation
式仲買 *kabushiki nakagai* stock brokerage
式仲買人 *kabushiki nakagainin* stockbroker
式合資会社 *kabushiki gōshi kaisha* jointstock limited partnership
式取引所 *kabushiki torihikijo* stock exchange
式相場 *kabushiki sōba* stock quotations
8 金 *kabukin* a share, stock
価 *kabuka* price of stocks
券 *kabuken* stock certificate
9 屋 *kabuya* stockbroker
11 張 *kabuha(ri)* a root sprouting profusely

A **梅** 2666 / J475f / M14795' **梅** 2676 / J-X / M14830 BAI. *ume* plum, plum tree.
3 干 *umeboshi* pickled plums
7 見 *umemi* plum-blossom viewing
花 *baika* plum blossoms
8 枝 *ume(ga)e* plum branch
林 *bairin* plum orchard
毒 *baidoku* syphilis
毒性 *baidokusei* syphilitic
雨 *baiu, tsuyu* rainy season
雨明 *tsuyua(ke), baiua(ke)* end of the rainy season
雨型 *tsuyugata* rainy-season meteorological conditions
雨時 *tsuyudoki* rainy season
雨晴 *tsuyuba(re)* end of the rainy season

4 心 忄 㣺 戈 戸 手 扌 支 攴 攵 文 斗 斤 方 无 日 曰 月 【木】6 欠 止 歹 殳 毋 比 毛 氏 气 水 氵 氺 火 灬 爪 爫 父 爻 爿 丬 片 牙 牛 犬 犭

9 香 *ume(ga)ka* plum-blossom fragrance
畑 *umebatake* plum orchard
10 酒 *umeshu, baishu* plum brandy
12 酢 *umezu* plum juice, plum vinegar
13 園 *baien* plum orchard
14 暦 *umegoyomi* harbingers of spring (plum blossoms)
漬 *umezuke* pickled plums

A **案** 2667 / J3046 / M14762 AN proposition, suggestion, plan, idea; opinion; expectation; bill, draft, measure; table. *an(jiru), an(zuru)* worry, be anxious, be afraid, ponder, fear. *an(zuru) ni* it seems to me that.

3 上 *anjō* on the table
山子 *kakashi, kagashi* scarecrow; figurehead
4 文 *ambun* draft
分 *ambun* proportional division
内 *annai* guidance; guide; announcement, invitation, notice; familiarity (with)
内広告 *annai kōkoku* classified advertisements
内図 *annaizu* information map
内状 *annaijō* letter of invitation
内所 *annaijo* information office
内者 *annaisha* guide
内記 *annaiki* guidebook
内書 *annaisho* guidebook
内業者 *annai gyōsha* guide
内標 *annaihyō* direction sign
内嬢 *annaijō* girl guide
5 外 *angai* surprisingly; disappointingly; unexpectedly
出 *anshutsu* contrivance, invention, studying out (something)
6 件 *anken* item, case, matter
8 定 *an(no)jō* as feared, as expected
18 顔 *an(ji)gao* worried look

A **格** 2668 / J334a / M14749 KŌ. KAKU status, rank; capacity, character; standard; a rule; a case (in law); case (in grammar).

3 下 *kakusa(ge)* demotion, downgrading
上 *kakua(ge)* status elevation
子 *kōshi* lattice, coffer, grating, fretwork
子戸 *kōshido* lattice door
子窓 *kōshimado* latticed window
子細工 *kōshizaiku* latticework
子縞 *kōshijima* checkered pattern
子織 *kōshio(ri)* checkered-patterned cloth
4 天井 *gōtenjō* coffered ceiling
5 付 *kakuzu(ke), kakutsu(ke)* rating, classification, allocation, conditioning
外 *kakuhazu(re)* inferior, ungraded (goods). *kakugai* special, exceptional
外品 *kakugaihin* inferior goods
6 好 *kakkō* shape, form, appearance; pose, posture; manner; approximately. *kakkō na* suitable, reasonable
式 *kakushiki* status, rank, social standing; rules of etiquette
式張 *kakushikiba(ru)* be overly formal
安 *kakuyasu na* cheap, reasonable
安品 *kakuyasuhin* bargain goods
7 言 *kakugen* maxim, proverb
別 *kakubetsu ni* especially, exceptionally
8 例 *kakurei* precedent; ruling
9 段 *kakudan no* special, exceptional, remarkable, appreciable
10 差 *kakusa* difference in quality
納 *kakunō* housing for equipment or machines
納庫 *kakunōko* hangar
15 調 *kakuchō* the style and meter of a poem
18 闘 *kakutō* fist fight; scuffle; wrestling

A **校** 2669 / J393b / M14713 KYŌ. KŌ school; (printing) proof; comparison; correction; investigation. *kō(su)* test, correct, proofread. *-kō* school; proof.

2 了 *kōryō, kyōryō* proofreading completed
4 内 *kōnai* school grounds
友 *kōyū* schoolmate, alumnus
友会 *kōyūkai* alumni association
5 主 *kōshu* school owner
本 *kōhon* perfected text
外 *kōgai* outside the school; extension
外生 *kōgaisei* extension student
外教授 *kōgai kyōju* extra-curricular teaching
正 *kōsei* proofreading
正刷 *kōseizu(ri)* galley proofs
正係 *kōseigakari* proofreader
正済 *kōseizu(mi)* corrected proof, corrected
6 合 *kyōgō, kogō* proofreading

7 医 *kōi* school doctor
8 長 *kōchō* principal, schoolmaster, rector
門 *kōmon* school gate
服 *kōfuku* school uniform
舎 *kōsha* school building
定 *kōtei* revision
具 *kōgu* school equipment
9 風 *kōfū* school spirit; school customs
紀 *kōki* school rules
則 *kōsoku* school regulations
訂 *kōtei* revision
訂版 *koteiban* revised edition
10 庭 *kōtei* campus, school playground
訓 *kōkun* school rules; school mottos
倉 *azekura* a storehouse built of square logs; a log house
書 *kōsho* correcting the characters in books; collating old books
11 務 *kōmu* school affairs
勘 *kōkan suru* compare and consider; compare with the original and correct
章 *kōshō* school pin
12 葬 *kōsō* school funeral
14 僕 *kōboku* school janitor
旗 *kōki* school flag
歌 *kōka* school song
15 閲 *kōetsu* revision

A **根** 2670 / J3a2c / M14745 KON root (of a plant); root, radical (in science and math); stamina *ne* root; base (of a hill); head (of a boil); origin; foundation; peak. *ne(kosogi), ne(kosoge)* all, completely, thoroughly. *ne(kkara)* (not) at all, (not) in the least.

3 子 *nekko* root, stump, stub
上 *nea(gari)* roots above ground
4 方 *nekata* the lower part; the root
比 *konkura(be)* endurance contest
引 *nebi(ki)* uprooting; redemption, ransom
元 *kongen* root, origin, cause, source. *nemoto* part near the root; base, bottom
分 *newa(ke)* dividing plants (roots)
太 *neda* joints, sills. *nebuto* (skin) boil
切 *negi(ri)* radical cure; excavation
切虫 *neki(ri)mushi* cutworm
切葉切 *neki(ri)-haki(ri)* everything; completely
5 付 *nezu(ku), netsu(ku)* take root. *netsu(ke)* toggle for suspending a pouch from belt
号 *kongō* radical sign (in math)
本 *kompon* root, origin, cause; basis. *nemoto* part near the root; base, bottom
本主義 *kompon shugi* fundamentalism
本主義者 *kompon shugisha* fundamentalist
本法 *komponhō* fundamental law
本的 *komponteki na* fundamental, basic, drastic
6 回 *nemawa(ri)* circumference of the root. *nemawa(shi)* digging around the root, negotiating with all concerned parties before making a formal decision
扱 *neko(gi)* uprooting
気 *konki* patience, perseverance, energy
気負 *konkima(ke)* being overcome in perseverance
8 底 *kontei* root; basis, foundation
治 *konchi, konji* complete cure
肥 *negoe* initial fertilizer, root fertilizer
限 *konkagi(ri)* with all one's might
茎 *konkei* root stalk, rhizome
性 *konjō* disposition, nature
拠 *konkyo* basis, foundation; authority
拠地 *konkyochi* base, headquarters
9 城 *nejiro* stronghold, citadel; headquarters, base of operations
持 *ne (ni) mo(tsu)* resent, bear a grudge
柢 *kontei* root; basis, foundation
負 *komma(ke)* losing stamina; losing in a test of strength; losing patience
10 原 *kongen* root, origin, cause
差 *neza(su)* take root; originate in; show signs of. *neza(shi)* taking root; breeding, birth
11 問 *nedo(i) suru* be inquisitive
強 *nezuyo(i)* firmly rooted; deep-seated. *nezuyo(ku)* firmly, steadfastly, tenaciously
張 *neba(ri)* deep spreading roots
接 *netsugi* root grafting
深 *nebuka(i)* deep-rooted, ingrained
雪 *neyuki* lingering snow
基 *konki* origin, cause
菜類 *konsairui* root crops
掘葉掘 *neho(ri)-haho(ri)* inquisitively; completely
12 絶 *konzetsu, nedaya(shi)* eradication
葉 *kon'yō* leaves near the base of a plant

葉無 *ne (mo) ha (mo) na(i)* without foundation
無 *nena(shi)* without root; an arrow without an arrowhead; groundless
無言 *nena(shi)goto* unfounded report
無草 *nena(shi)gusa* duckweed; something unsettled
13 源 *kongen* root, origin, cause, source
継 *netsu(gi)* splicing rotten underpinning
際 *negiwa* root of a tree
幹 *konkan* root and trunk; basis; nucleus; keynote
15 瘤 *konryū* root tubercles
締 *neji(me)* tamping down the soil around the roots
18 覆 *neōi* mulch
20 競 *konkura(be)* endurance contest

7

梠 2671 J5b71 M14862 See 櫚 2905.

梼 2672 J456e M14911 See 檮 2897.

桝 2673 J4b71 M-X Nonstandard for 枡 2587.

桿 2674 J5b65 M14823 See 杆 2557.

條 2675 J5b6a M14859 See 条 2563.

梅 2676 J-X M14830 See 梅 2666.

梹 2677 J5b6e M14909 See 檳 2901.

桀 2678 J5b5c M14753 KETSU coarse; bear, carry; excel; bird roosting tree. *ara(i)* coarse, crude.

桾 2679 J5b75 M14821 KUN. *sarugaki* a kind of persimmon. *kunugi* a kind of oak.

梍 2680 J5b74 M14839 SŌ *saikachi* honey locust tree.

梛 2681 J5b6b M14856 DA. NA. *nagi* a kind of tall evergreen tree.

梺 2682 J5b72 M14910 （国字） *fumoto* foothills.

椛 2683 J3371 M15065 （国字） *momiji* autumn foliage. Used also as a variant of 樺 2817.

梏 2684 J5b67 M14841 KOKU manacles.

A **械** 2685 J3323 M14882 KAI fetters; machine; instrument.

桷 2686 J5b64 M14813 KAKU rafter.

梻 2687 J-X M14911 （国字） *shikimi* a tree whose branches are placed on Buddhist graves, an aniseed tree.

梓 2688 J3034 M14845 SHI. *azusa* catalpa tree.

梮 2689 J-X M14879 KIKU. *kanjiki* snowshoes.

桴 2690 J5b6f M14807 FU. *bachi* drumstick. *ikada* raft.

梃 2691 J5b6c M14827 CHŌ. TEI. *teko* lever.
3 子 *teko* lever

梔 2692 J5b69 M14846 SHI gardenia.
3 子 *kuchinashi* gardenia

梭 2693 J5b68 M14878 SA. *hi* shuttle.
11 魚 *kamasu* barracuda

桶 2694 J3233 M14811 YŌ. TŌ. *oke* tub, bucket.
9 屋 *okeya* cooper

梢 2695 J3e3f M14866 SHŌ. *kozue* twig; treetop.
12 葉 *ureba* the end leaves

梱 2696 / J3a2d / M14883 **梱** 2707 / J-X / M14947 KON. *kō(ru)* pack, tie up. *kōri* bale (of silk or thread). *kori* bale, pack, package.
5 包 *kompō* packing, crating; package

梨 2697 / J4d7c / M14873 RI. *nashi* pear, Japanese pear; pear tree.
13 園 *rien* theatrical world; pear orchard
20 礫 *nashi (no) tsubute* no communication

梗 2698 / J393c / M14849 KŌ, KYŌ for the most part; close up.
13 塞 *kōsoku* stoppage, blocking; infarction; (money) stringency
14 概 *kōgai* outline, summary

梶 2699 / J3361 / M14889 BI. *kaji* oar, sculling oar, shaft.
4 木 *kaji(no)ki* paper mulberry
12 棒 *kajibō* (wagon) shafts

梧 2700 / J3868 / M14872 GO desk. *aogiri* Chinese parasol tree; phoenix tree. *sasa(eru)* support.
3 下 *goka* under a desk
10 桐 *godō* Chinese parasol tree; phoenix tree
12 葉 *goyō* leaf of Chinese parasol tree

梵 2701 / J5b70 / M14888 BON Sanskrit; purity; Buddhist believer.
4 天王 *Bonten'ō* Brahma, the Creator
6 字 *Bonji* Sanskrit characters
14 語 *Bongo* Sanskrit
20 鐘 *bonshō* temple bell

梁 2702 / J4e42 / M14825 RYŌ bridge beams. *hari, utsubari, uchibari* beam, girder. *yana* weir, fish trap, fish pond.
3 山泊 *ryōzampaku* center of operations; gathering of kindred spirits
上君子 *ryōjō (no) kunshi* robber; rat
4 木 *ryōboku* beam
7 材 *harizai* beam, girder
12 間 *harima* span (in construction)

梟 2703 / J5b66 / M14861 KYŌ. *fukurō* owl. *kyō(suru)* expose (a severed head).
10 将 *kyōshō* brave general
11 猛 *kyōmō* fierce
悪 *kyōaku* great treachery; very atrocious person
12 雄 *kyōyū* ringleader, accomplished villain
13 罪 *kyōzai* crime of exposing a severed head
15 敵 *kyōteki* treacherous enemy

梳 2704 / J5b60 / M14886 SO. *su(ku)* comb (the hair); card (wool). *kushikezu(ru)* comb.
3 子 *sukiko* hairdresser's assistant
4 手 *sukite* hairdresser's assistent
毛 *sukige* combings
8 油 *sukiabura* pomade
取 *su(ki)-to(ru)* comb (the hair) out clean
14 綿 *sukimen* cotton carding
19 櫛 *sukigushi* fine-toothed comb

A **巣** 2705 / J4163 / M8696 **巢** 1531 / J-X / M8696 SŌ. *su* nest, rookery, breeding place, beehive, cobweb; den, haunt. *suku(u)* build (a nest).
5 立 *suda(chi)* leaving the nest; becoming independent; leaving one's confinement; graduation
13 隠 *sugaku(re)* hiding in the nest
窟 *sōkutsu* den, haunt, hangout, home
15 箱 *subako* nest box, hive
18 雛 *suhina* nestling
19 鶏 *sudori* setting hen
22 籠 *sugomo(ru)* to nest

梯 2706 / J4474 / M14881 TEI. *hashigo* ladder, stairs; insatiable drinking.
3 子 *hashigo, teishi* ladder, stairs; insatiable drinking.
子段 *hashigodan* step, stair, stairway
子乗 *hashigono(ri)* ladder stunts
子酒 *hashigozake* insatiable drinking; heaver drinker
子飲 *hashigono(mi)* insatiable drinking; heaver drinker
子登 *hashigonobo(ri)* ladder climbing; by leaps and bounds
4 尺 *teishaku* map scale
7 状 *teijō* echelon formation; trapezoid
形 *hashigogata, teikei* echelon formation; trapezoid
9 陣 *teijin* echelon
11 隊 *teitai* echelon

棞 2707 / J-X / M14947 See 梱 2696.

棧 2708 / J5c22 / M14963 See 桟 2658.

槌 2709 / J4448 / M-X Nonstandard for 槌 2769.

椢 2710 / J5b7a / M-X KAI bottom; box. *kunugi* a kind of oak.

椦 2711 / J5b7b / M-X KEN.

椥 2712 / J5c29 / M-X (国字) *nagi* a kind of large evergreen tree.

椨 2713 / J5c2d / M-X (国字) *tafu, tabu, tabunoki* a kind of camphor tree.

椡 2714 / J5c31 / M-X (国字) *kunugi* a kind of oak.

椣 2715 / J5c30 / M-X (国字) *shide, shidenoki* a kind of birch.

棆 2716 / J5c32 / M14916 RIN *kusunoki* camphor tree.

棔 2717 / J5c21 / M14931 KON *nemunoki* a silk tree.

棠 2718 / J5c2b / M14953 TŌ. DŌ *yamanashi* wild pear.

棡 2719 / J5b7c / M14955 KŌ crossbeams of a fence; a kind of large tree.

棣 2720 / J5c28 / M14957 TEI. DAI *niwaume* a flowering almond.

棯 2721 / J5c2c / M14977 NEN. NIN. JIN a kind of fruit.

椁 2722 / J5b76 / M15003 KAKU. *hitsugi* coffin. *uwahitsugi* outer coffin.

椄 2723 / J5c26 / M15008 SHŌ. SETSU *tsugiki* grafting; a grafted tree.

椈 2724 / J5b78 / M15014 KIKU *buna* Japanese beech tree.

椋 2725 / J4c3a / M15020 RYŌ *muku* a kind of elm.

椌 2726 / J5b7d / M15021 KŌ name of a box-like ancient musical instrument.

椏 2727 / J5b73 / M15025 A. *mata* crotch of tree.

椙 2728 / J3f7a / M15063 (国字) *sugi* Japanese cedar; cryptomeria.

棘 2729 / J5b79 / M14938 KYOKU thorn. *toge* thorn, splinter; spine; biting words. *odoro* briers, thicket, the bush.

棱 2730 / J-X / M14979 RYŌ. RO sharp place.

椒 2731 / J5c25 / M15029 SHŌ mountain ash.

椀 2732 / J4f50 / M15001 WAN wooden bowl, lacquered bowl.

椚 2733 / J5c2f / M15064 (国字) *kunugi* a kind of oak used for charcoal.

椪 2734 / J5c2e / M-X PON Poona, a city in India.

9 柑 *ponkan* a kind of *mikan*

棍 2735 / J5b7e / M14924 KON a cane.

12 棒 *kombō* club, nightstick; lever

棗 2736 / J5c27 / M14937 SŌ. *natsume* jujube.

12 椰子 *natsume yashi* date (palm).

椅 2737 / J3058 / M15009 I chair.

3 子 *isu* chair, seat, couch; office, position

棹 2738 / J5c2a / M14992 TŌ. *sao* pole, rod; beam (of scales); (well) sweep; neck

(of violin). *saosa(su)* pole (a boat).
14 歌 *tōka* boat song, boatmen's song

椰 2739 / J5c3f / M15069 YA coconut tree.
3 子 *yashi* palm tree, coconut tree
子油 *yashiyu* palm oil, coconut oil

棕 2740 / J5c23 / M14933 **椶** 2755 / J5c24 / M15070 SHU the hemp palm
19 櫚 *shuro* the hemp palm
櫚油 *shuroyu* palm oil

棉 2741 / J4c49 / M14919 MEN. *wata* cotton.
7 花 *menka* raw cotton
18 織機 *men'o(ri)ki* cotton loom

椎 2742 / J4447 / M15024 TSUI. *tsuchi* hammer, mallet. *shii* an oak.
9 茸 *shiitake* a kind of edible mushroom
10 骨 *tsuikotsu* vertebra

棲 2743 / J4033 / M14980 SEI. *su(mu)* live, dwell.
5 処 *sumika* dwelling; nest; den (of robbers)
10 息 *seisoku suru* inhabit, dwell in, lodge in
息地 *seisokuchi* habitat

B **棋** 2744 / J347a / M14922 **棊** 2745 / J5b77 / M14921 KI *go*; Japanese chess.
3 士 *kishi* a *go* player
7 局 *kikyoku* the game of *go*; the *go* board
9 客 *kikyaku, kikaku* chess player; *go* player
15 敵 *kiteki* one's opponent in a chess game

B **棺** 2746 / J343d / M14993 KAN *hitsugi* casket, coffin.
7 車 *kansha* hearse
9 舁 *kanka(ki)* pallbearer
11 側 *kansoku ni* beside the coffin
掛 *kanka(ke)* coffin drape, pall
桶 *kan'oke* casket, coffin

B **棟** 2747 / J456f / M14949 TŌ. *mune* ridge, ridgepole; counter for buildings.
3 上 *munea(ge)* ridgepole raising
上式 *munea(ge)shiki* ridgepole-raising ceremony
4 木 *munagi* ridgepole
5 瓦 *munegawara* ridge tile
11 梁 *tōryō* chief support, pillar (in a nation); chief, leader, foreman
12 割長屋 *munewa(ri) nagaya* duplex; a long partitioned house

B **棚** 2748 / J432a / M14941 HŌ. BYŌ. *tana* shelf, ledge, rack, mount, mantelpiece; trellis, lattice.
3 上 *tanaa(ge) suru* shelve, pigeonhole, table (a motion), sidetrack
4 引 *tanabi(ku)* trail, hang over (fog or smoke)
7 状 *hōjō* shelf formation
8 承 *tanau(ke)* shelf bracket
牡丹 *tanabota* windfall
10 晒 *tanazarashi* shopworn stock

A **森** 2749 / J3f39 / M14974 SHIN. *mori* woods, grove.
8 林 *shinrin* forest, wood
林学 *shinringaku* forestry
林限界 *shinrin genkai* timber line
林帯 *shinrintai* forest zone
林開墾 *shinrin kaikon* clearing a forest
林愛護 *shinrin aigo* forest conservation
12 閑 *shinkan to shita* silent, hushed, deserted
森 *shinshin* deeply forested; towering
17 厳 *shingen na* solemn, grave, awe-inspiring
19 羅 *shinra* luxurious growth; crowds of people
羅万象 *shinra-banshō* all creation, the universe

A **棒** 2750 / J4b40 / M14929 BŌ stick, cane, rod, pole, stake, pile, club, bar; line, dash.
3 口紅 *bō kuchibeni* lipstick
4 引 *bōbi(ki)* cancellation, writing off
切 *bōki(re)* a piece of wood; a piece of a broken pole
手振 *botefu(ri)* peddler
5 立 *bōda(chi)* standing up straight (because of surprise)
7 杙 *bōgui* stake, pile
状 *bōjō* cylindrical shape
8 使 *bōtsuka(i)* stick, fighting, stick fighter
押 *bōo(shi)* pole-pushing (game)
杭 *bōgui* pile, stake

乳切 *bōchigi(ri), bōchigi(re)* broken stick
9 紅 *bōbeni* lipstick
10 倒 *bōtao(shi)* pole-fighting game
振 *bō (ni) fu(ru)* fail, come to naught
高跳 *bōtakato(bi)* pole vault
11 術 *bōjutsu* stick fighting
組 *bōgu(mi)* setting type in a galley; one's pal
13 鉄 *bōtetsu* bar iron
暗記 *bōanki* rote memorization
14 鼻 *bōbana* tip of a pole
読 *bōyo(mi)* accentless reading; reading Chinese in the Chinese order
銀 *bōgin* bar silver
磁石 *bōjishaku* bar magnet
16 縞 *bōjima* stripes
鋼 *bōkō* bar steel
諳記 *bō anki* rote memorization
22 鱈 *bōdara* dried cod

A **植** 2751 / J3f22 / M15023 SHOKU planting. *u(eru)* plant, set out, raise, sow; set type. *u(waru)* be planted.
2 人 *u(e)bito* planters
4 込 *u(e)-ko(mu)* plant (trees). *u(e)ko(mi)* shrubbery, thick growth of plants
木 *ueki* garden plant, shrub, tree
木屋 *uekiya* gardener, nurseryman
木鉢 *uekibachi* flowerpot
5 付 *u(e)-tsu(keru)* plant, set out, transplant; implant
付機 *uetsu(ke)ki* seed-planting machine
皮 *shokuhi* skin grafting
皮法 *shokuhihō* skin grafting
皮術 *shokuhijutsu* skin grafting
民 *shokumin* colonization, settlement; colonist, settler
民地 *shokuminchi* colony, settlement
民地化 *shokuminchika* colonization
民政策 *shokumin seisaku* colonialism
民時代 *shokumin jidai* colonial period
民都市 *shokumin toshi* (Roman) colony
6 字 *shokuji* typesetting, composition
字機 *shokujiki* linotype
8 林 *shokurin* afforestation
物 *shokubutsu* plant, vegetation, flora
物人間 *shokubutu ningen* human vegetable
物性 *shokubutsusei* vegetable property
物学 *shokubutsugaku* botany
物界 *shokubutsukai* vegetable kingdom
物病 *shokubutsubyō* plant disease
物崇拝 *shokubutsu sūhai* plant worship
物採集 *shokubutsu saishū* plant collecting
物園 *shokubutsuen* botanical garden
物誌 *shokubutsushi* flora
物質 *shokubutsushitsu* vegetable matter
10 疱瘡 *u(e)bōsō* vaccination, inoculation
12 替 *u(e)-ka(eru)* transplant, replant
16 樹 *shokuju* tree planting
樹祭 *Shokujusai* Arbor Day

A **検** 2752 / J3821 / M15065' **檢** 2883 / J5c7d / M15684 KEN investigation. *ken(suru)* investigate.
4 水 *kensui* examination of water
尺 *kenjaku suru* scale timber
分 *kembun* inspection, examination
5 札 *kensatsu* examination of tickets
出 *kenshutsu* search; (chemical) detection
圧 *ken'atsu* measuring pressure
圧器 *ken'atsuki* pressure gauge
6 死 *kenshi* investigating a death; autopsy
印 *ken'in* stamp of approval
地 *kenchi* land survey
字 *kenji* list of characters (by total strokes) whose radicals are obscure
糸器 *kenshiki* yarn-testing machine
7 車 *kensha* vehicle inspection
尿 *kennyō* urine examination
束 *kensoku* restraint, restriction; arrest, custody
8 使 *kenshi* official who verifies the facts
波 *kempa* detection (in electricity)
乳 *kennyū* milk examination
事 *kenji* prosecuting attorney
事局 *kenjikyoku* prosecutor's office
定 *kentei* official certification, approval, authorization; examination, inspection; license
定料 *kenteiryō* examination fee
定済 *kenteizu(mi)* inspected (by the government)
定試験 *kentei shiken* licensing examination
9 便 *kemben* stool examination
音器 *ken'onki* sonometer
屍 *kenshi* investigating a death; autopsy
屍官 *kenshikan* coroner
疫 *ken'eki* quarantine
疫所 *ken'ekisho* quarantine station

疫官 *ken'ekikan* quarantine doctor
査 *kensa* inspection, examination
査役 *kensayaku* inspector, auditor
査所 *kensajo* inspection station
査官 *kensakan* inspector, auditor
査済 *kensazu(mi)* examined, passed
10 校 *kengyō* blind court musician
梅 *kembai* syphilis test
討 *kentō* investigation, examination, study, test
針 *kenshin* inspection of a meter or a gauge
索 *kensaku suru* refer to, look up (a word); make a laboratory test
案 *ken'an* postmortem examination
挙 *kenkyo* arrest, roundup
流計 *kenryūkei* galvanometer, ammeter
流器 *kenryūki* galvanometer, ammeter
11 視 *kenshi* investigation of the facts
問 *kemmon* inspection, examination
問所 *kemmonjo* checkpoint
眼 *kengan* optometry, eye examination
眼医 *kengan'i* optometrist
12 証 *kenshō* verification, inspection
番 *kemban* geisha exchange
湿器 *kenshitsuki* hygrometer
温 *ken'on* thermometry
温器 *ken'onki* clinical thermometer
診 *kenshin* medical examination
診日 *kenshimbi* medical-examination day
14 算 *kenzan* verification of accounts, checking figures
察 *kensatsu* investigation and prosecution
察庁 *kensatsuchō* prosecuting attorney's office
察官 *kensatsukan* prosecuting attorney
15 震器 *kenshinki* seismograph
閲 *ken'etsu* inspection, censorship
閲官 *ken'etsukan* inspector, censor
潮 *kenchō* tidal observation
潮器 *kenchōki* tide gauge
16 糖計 *kentōkei* saccharimeter
19 鏡 *kenkyō* microscopic examination
覈 *kenkaku* strict inverstigation
23 黴 *kembai* syphilis test

A **極** 2753 / J364b / M15181 KYOKU end; highest rank; the poles; (electric) poles. GOKU very, extremely, highly, most, quite. *kiwa(maru)* terminate; reach an extreme; be in a dilemma. *kiwa(meru)* investigate thoroughly, master; carry to extremes. *ki(meru)* fix, decide, agree upon; appoint, choose; resolve. *ki(maru)* be decided, be settled, be arranged; be certain to, be doomed to. *kime* agreement, contract. *kima(ri)* settlement, conclusion, agreement; system, regularity; rule; habit. *kiwa(marinai)* endless, eternal. *kiwa(mete)* very, exceedingly. *kiwa(mi)* height, acme, extremity. *-gime* by (the month).

2 力 *kyokuryoku* with all one's might
3 大 *kyokudai* the greatest, maximum
上 *gokujō* first-rate, finest quality, the best
小 *kyokushō, gokushō* the smallest, minimum
小型写真機 *gokushōgata shashinki* miniature camera
4 手 *kimete* winning move, deciding factor
月 *gokugetsu* December; the last month of the year
内 *gokunai* top-secret, confidential
切 *kima(ri)ki(tta)* fixed, definite, stereotyped; self-evident, clear
文句 *kima(ri) monku* stereotyped phrase
込 *ki(me)-ko(mu)* take for granted, assume, pretend
込人形 *kimeko(mi) ningyō* kimono-dressed doll pasted on wood
5 玉 *ki(me)dama* winning pitch
付 *ki(me)-tsu(keru)* scold, reprimand. *kiwa(me)tsu(ki)* guaranteed
北 *kyokuhoku* extreme north, North Pole
右 *kyokuu* extreme right
左 *kyokusa* extreme left
6 尽 *kiwa(me)-tsuku(su)* know thoroughly; measure the full extent
印 *gokuin* seal, stamp die, hallmark, impression; proof of genuineness
地 *kyokuchi* the pole, polar regions
刑 *kyokkei* capital punishment; extreme penalty
光 *kyokkō* northern lights, aurora borealis; southern lights, aurora australis
7 言 *kyokugen* extreme criticism
位 *kyokui* highest position (of a retainer)
8 所 *kyokusho* end, conclusion
限 *kyokugen* limit, extremity
東 *Kyokutō* Far East

9 度 *kyokudo* highest degree, the extreme, maximum
洋 *kyokuyō* polar seas
点 *kyokuten* highest point, climax, summit, zenith; nadir, bottom
美 *kyokubi* surpassing beauty
前線 *kyokuzensen* polar front
10 流 *kyokuryū* polar current
秘 *gokuhi* top-secret, confidential
致 *kyokuchi* culmination, perfection
11 球 *ki(me)dama* forte; mainstay; winning shot (in sports)
貧 *gokuhin* destitution
彩色 *gokusaishiki* brilliant coloring, full color (illustrations)
道 *gokudō na* wicked, villainous, brutal, dissipated
道者 *gokudōmono* scoundrel, villain, profligate
悪 *gokuaku* brutality, atrocity. *kima(ri) waru(i) awkward, embarrassed*
悪人 *gokuakunin* confirmed criminal, very wicked person
12 圏 *kyokken, kyokuken* polar circle
極 *gokugoku* very, severely
寒 *gokkan* intense cold, midwinter
量 *kyokuryō* maximum dose
暑 *gokusho* severe heat
13 微 *kyokubi, gokubi* infinitesimal, microscopic
意 *gokui* mystery; the secrets (of the art)
楽 *gokuraku* paradise
楽往生 *gokurakuōjō* easy death; euthanasia
楽浄土 *gokuraku jōdo* (Buddhist) paradise
楽鳥 *gokurakuchō* bird of paradise
14 製 *gokusei* the best make
端 *kyokutan* an extreme, extremity
端主義 *kyokutan shugi* radicalism, extremism
端家 *kyokutanka* extremist, radical
端論 *kyokutanron* extreme view, radical view
端論者 *kyokutan ronsha* extremist
15 論 *kyokuron* extreme argument; extreme criticism
熱 *gokunetsu* high fever, intense heat

9

楳 2754 / J4760 / M15178 See **梅** 2666.

椶 2755 / J5c24 / M15078 See **棕** 2740.

梻 2756 / J3a67 / M-X Nonstandard for **榊** 2808.

樋 2757 / J4875 / M-X Nonstandard for **樋** 2816.

椹 2758 / J5c3b / M15082 CHIN. JIN. *sawara* a kind of cedar. *ategi* cutting block, chopping block.

楙 2759 / J5c3e / M15140 BŌ. MU *shige(ru)* grow thickly. *boke* Japanese flowering quince.

楝 2760 / J5c42 / M15148 REN *ōchi* Japanese bead tree.

楞 2761 / J5c41 / M15149 RŌ. RYŌ corner; square piece of lumber.

楴 2762 / J5c3c / M15179 TEI *kanzashi* ornamental hairpin.

楸 2763 / J5c36 / M15186 SHŪ. SHU *hisagi* a kind of oak. *kisasage* a Japanese catalpa.

椋 2764 / J5c39 / M15214 （国字） *hazō, hanzō, hanizō* a kind of container for pouring liquids.

榁 2765 / J5c43 / M15217 （国字） *muro, muronoki* a kind of evergreen tree.

楖 2766 / J4f31 / M15226 RŌ.

槌 2767 / J-X / M15318 **槌** 2709 / J4448 / M-X TSUI. *tsuchi* hammer, mallet.

楡 2768 / J5c40 / M15153 YU. *nire* elm.

楢 2769 / J466a / M15154 SHŪ. YŪ. *nara* oak.

楮 2770 / J5c3a / M15172 CHO. *kōzo* paper mulberry.

楚 2771 / J413f / M15141 SO whip; cane.
13 楚 *soso(taru)* graceful, neat

椴 2772 / J464e / M15075 TAN fir.
8 松 *todomatsu* fir, white fir

椒 2773 / J5c35 / M15147 KO pepper. *kurumi* walnut.
12 椒 *koshō* pepper

楪 2774 / J5c44 / M15167 CHA. YŌ. CHŌ lacquered dish.
3 子 *chatsu, chasu* round, shallow red dish

楹 2775 / J5c33 / M15188 EI. YŌ *hashira* thick, round pillar, column.
12 棟 *eitō* pillar and ridge beam; important person

楯 2776 / J3d5d / M15173 JUN. *tate* shield, buckler, escutcheon; pretext.
8 突 *tatetsu(ku)* oppose, defy

楓 2777 / J4976 / M15126 FŪ. FU. *kaede* maple tree.
3 子香 *fūshikō* galbanum

椽 2778 / J5c3d / M15087 TEN. *en* veranda, porch, balcony, margin, edge. *taruki* rafter
3 大 *tendai* rafter size; powerful writing

楠 2779 / J466f / M15152 NAN. *kusu, kusunoki* camphor tree.
4 木 *kusunoki* camphor tree

楕 2780 / J424a / M15133 **橢** 2829 / J5c73 / M15565 DA ellipse.
4 円 *daen* oval, ellipse
円形 *daenkei* oval ellipse

楷 2781 / J5c34 / M15185 KAI square-character style; straight tree; correctness, rule, model.
6 行草 *kai-gyō-sō* square, cursive, and grass characters
10 書 *kaisho* square character, printed style

椿 2782 / J4458 / M15090 CHIN. *tsubaki* camellia.
8 油 *tsubaki yu; tsubaki abura* camellia oil
事 *chinji* accident; sudden occurrence

楫 2783 / J5c37 / M15168 SHŪ. *kai, kaji* oar, sculling oar, rudder.
8 取 *kajito(ri)* helmsman
9 音 *kaji oto* the sound of oars

楊 2784 / J4d4c / M15112 YŌ. *kawa yanagi* willow.
3 子江 *Yōsukō* Yangtze River
8 枝 *yoji* toothpick; toothbrush
9 柳 *yanagi, kawa yanagi, yōryū* riverside willows

B **楼** 2785 / J4f30 / M15212 **樓** 2830 / J5c6c / M15430 RŌ tower, turret, lookout, high building. *takadono* stately mansion.
3 上 *rōjō* upper story; balcony; roof garden
5 主 *rōshu* brothel proprietor
8 門 *rōmon* tower gate, two-story gate
14 閣 *rōkaku* many-storied building

楔 2786 / J5c38 / M15131 KETSU. SETSU. *kusabi* wedge; arrowhead; cleat; chock; tie, pledge; dovetail.
5 石 *kusabiishi* keystone
7 状文字 *ketsujō moji* cuneiform writing
形 *kusabigata, kekkei* wedge-shaped, V-shaped; cuneiform
形文字 *kusabigata moji* cuneiform writing
10 栓 *kusabisen* cotter pin, key

B **棄** 2787 / J347e / M14913 **棄** 2788 / J-X / M-X KI. *su(teru)* throw away, discard, abandon, desert, give up; renounce, relinquish; resign; lay down (one's life); part with; sacrifice; reject, condemn.
3 子 *sutego* foundling
5 石 *suteishi* ornamental garden rocks; road ballast; preparatory work
世 *kisei* death
6 老 *kirō* an old person thrown away in the mountains
死 *kishi* exposing a corpse in the city
7 却 *kikyaku suru* reject, dismiss; abandon, renounce waive
児 *kiji* abandoned child

9 約 *kiyaku* breaking a promise
背 *kihai* giving up and turning back
10 捐 *kien* donation; abandonment
15 権 *kiken suru* abstain from voting; renounce one's rights
権者 *kikensha* nonvoter

A **業** 2789 / J3648 / M15170 Gyō vocation, occupation, business, trade, profession; industry; undertaking; studies; arts; conduct, act; service; achievement. Gō karma. *waza* deed, act, work, art, performance, trick.

4 火 *gōka* hell fire
6 因 *gōin* karma
8 物 *wazamono* sharp sword
果 *gōka* effects of karma
者 *gyōsha* the trade, businessperson concerned
突張 *gōtsukuba(ri)* boasting, pride
9 界 *gyōkai* the business world, industry, the trade
界紙 *gyōkaishi* trade journal
10 病 *gōbyō* incurable disease
11 務 *gyōmu* business, affairs, duties, work, service, operations
12 報 *gōhō* karma effects, fate, inevitable retribution
13 腹 *gōhara* spite, resentment
14 種 *gyōshu* business category
態 *gyōtai* business conditions
17 績 *gyōseki* achievement, performance, results, work, contribution
19 曝 *gōzara(shi)* disgrace, shame

A **楽** 2790 / J335a / M15213 **樂** 2832 / J5c5b / M15399 Raku comfort, ease, relief; pleasure; concluding program. Gaku music. *tano(shimu), tano(shibu)* enjoy; amuse oneself; anticipate. *tano(shimi), tano(shibi)* pleasure, enjoyment, happiness; amusement; anticipation. *tano(shii)* merry, pleasant, cheerful, joyful. *tano(shige) na* merry, pleasant, happy, gay. *raku na* easy.

2 人 *gakujin* musician, minstrel. *rakujin* person living at ease
3 土 *rakudo* paradise, a pleasant land
士 *gakushi* bandsman, musician
弓 *gakkyū* bow (of a violin)
才 *gakusai* musical talent
4 手 *gakushu* musician, bandsman
天 *rakuten* optimism
天主義 *rakuten shugi* optimism
天主義者 *rakuten shugisha* optimist
天地 *rakutenchi* paradise; amusement park
天的 *rakutenteki* optimistic, cheerful, happy-go-lucky
天家 *rakutenka* optimist, easygoing person
5 台 *gakudai* music stand
6 団 *gakudan* band, orchestra
曲 *gakkyoku* musical composition, tune
地 *rakuchi* pleasant circumstances
8 長 *gakuchō* bandmaster, conductor, musical director
典 *gakuten* musical grammar
9 音 *gakuon* musical tone
界 *gakkai* musical circles, the world of music
屋 *gakuya* dressing room, greenroom; behind the scenes
屋落 *gakuyao(chi)* a matter not understand by the outside, inside information, shop talk
屋話 *gakuyabanashi* backstage talk
10 員 *gakuin* bandsman
書 *rakuga(ki)* scribbling in public places, graffiti
11 隊 *gakutai* band, orchestra
章 *gakushō* a movement (in music)
12 焼 *rakuya(ki)* hand-molded pottery; *raku* ware
勝 *rakushō* easy victory
13 園 *rakuen* pleasure garden, paradise
殿 *gakuden* hall of music
寝 *rakune* nap, rest
楽 *rakuraku to* comfortably; very easily. *rakuraku suru* feel relieved
聖 *gakusei* celebrated musician
隠居 *rakuinkyo* comfortable retirement
15 劇 *gakugeki* opera, musical drama
調 *gakuchō* musical tone
器 *gakki* musical instrument
器伴奏 *gakki bansō* instrumental accompaniment
器店 *gakkiten* music shop
16 壇 *gakudan* music circles
18 観 *rakkan* optimism
観主義 *rakkan shugi* optimism

観的 *rakkanteki* optimistic, hopeful
19 譜 *gakufu* sheet music, music book, musical notation, the score

10

滎 2791 / J5c46 / M15273 See 栄 2635.

樅 2792 / J-X / M-X Nonstandard for 樅 2838.

槝 2793 / J5c4f / M-X （国字） *kashi* mooring pole.

榾 2794 / J5c53 / M-X （国字） *hokuso* punk; touchwood.

榔 2795 / J5c59 / M-X Rō cage; room, house; window.

榑 2796 / J5c54 / M15222 Fu *kure* a bark-covered log.

榠 2797 / J5c55 / M15244 Myō. Bei. Mei a kind of quince; late-picked tea.

榧 2798 / J5c52 / M15258 Hi *kaya* Japanese evergreen nutmeg, a *kaya* tree.

榱 2799 / J5c63 / M15276 Sui *taruki* rafter.

榲 2800 / J5c45 / M15277 Otsu quince. On. *sugi* Japanese cedar, cryptomeria. *ne* root.

榿 2801 / J5c48 / M15298 Ki. Kai *hannoki* an alder, a black alder.

槎 2802 / J5c4c / M15320 Sa. Ja. Sha *ikada* raft, float. *ki(ru)* slice, cut.

槐 2803 / J5c47 / M15323 Kai. E. *enju* a Japanese pagoda tree; a Chinese scholar tree.

榜 2804 / J5c56 / M15241 Bō rudder; oar; nameplate.

槃 2805 / J5c51 / M15303 Han tub.

槁 2806 / J5c49 / M15300 Kō die (vegetation).

搨 2807 / J5c50 / M15292 Tō chair.

榊 2808 / J-X / M15352 榊 2756 / J3a67 / M-X （国字） *sakaki* sacred Shinto tree, *cleyera ochnacea*.

榾 2809 / J5c4b / M15297 Kotsu. *hota* chip, piece of wood.

榎 2810 / J315d / M15219 Ka. *enoki* hackberry; nettle tree; lotus tree.

榛 2811 / J3f3a / M15240 Shin. *hashibami* hazel, filbert. *han* black alder.
4 木 *han(no)ki* black alder

槊 2812 / J-X / M15325 槊 2813 / J5c4e / M15316 Saku halberd.
7 杖 *sakujō* ramrod, cleaning rod

槓 2814 / J5c4a / M15343 Kō lever.
7 杆 *kōkan* lever

榕 2815 / J5c57 / M15228 Yō. *akō* an evergreen mulberry.
16 樹 *yōju* banyan

樋 2816 / J-X / M15415 樋 2757 / J4875 / M-X Tō. *hi, toi* water pipe, gutter, downspout; aqueduct, flume; conduit; trough.
8 門 *himon* sluice

樺 2817 / J3372 / M15497 Ka. *kaba, kamba* birch.
4 太 *Karafuto* Sakhalin
6 色 *kaba iro* reddish yellow

槙 2818 / J7422 / M15310 槇 2819 / J4b6a / M-X Shin twig. *maki* an ornamental evergreen.
5 皮 *maihada, makihada* oakum, calking
6 肌 *maihada, makihada* oakum, calking

榴 2820 / J5c58 / M15280 **橊** 2859 / J-X / M15525 Ru, Ryu pomegranate.
12 散弾 *ryūsandan* shrapnel shell
弾 *ryūdan* shell
弾砲 *ryūdampō* howitzer
20 霰弾 *ryūsandan* shrapnel shell

A **様** 2821 / J4d4d / M15352' **樣** 2827 / J-X / M-X **樣** 2831 / J5c6b / M15457

様 2856 / J-X / M-X Yō way, manner, method; kind, class; (to that) effect. *sama* situation, circumstances, condition. *sama* Mr., Mrs., Messrs., Mme., Miss, Master. *yō na* like, such as. *yō ni* in order to; in such a way, in such a manner. *zama* plight, state, appearance, spectacle.
3 子 *yōsu* situation, aspect, circumstances, movements; appearance, behavior, signs
子振 *yōsubu(ru)* put on airs, pose for effect
5 付 *samazu(ke) suru* address everyone with the title "sama"
6 式 *yōshiki* style, form, pattern
7 見 *Zama (o) mi(ro).* Just look at your blunder.
9 相 *yōsō* aspect, phase, condition
14 様 *samazama na* various, varied, sundry
態 *yōtai* form, situation; condition of the patient

槍 2822 / J4164 / M15319 Sō. *yari* spear, lance, javelin.
5 玉 *yaridama* victim, sacrifice
6 先 *yarisaki* spearhead
7 投 *yarina(ge)* javelin throwing, javelin contest
兵 *sōhei* spearman, lanceman
8 法 *sōhō* drilling with spears
9 持 *yarimo(chi)* spearman; spear carrier
10 衾 *yaribusuma* ring of steel
11 術 *sōjutsu* drilling with spears
術家 *sōjutsuka* spearman
18 騎兵 *sōkihei* lancer

A **構** 2823 / J393d / M15317 Kō. *kama(eru)* build; keep house; take a posture; assume an attitude; pose as; be ready for; feign, pretend; set up (camp). *kama(u)* mind, care about; pay attention to; interfere with; be hospitable; tease, molest; expel, banish. *ku(u)* build (a nest). *kama(e)* construction, architecture, style, appearance; posture; attitude; enclosure radical. *kama(i)* meddling, concern; entertainment, hospitality; banishment. *(o)kama(i nashi ni)* regardless of.
4 手 *kama(i)te* companion, protector
文 *kōbun* sentence construction, syntax
内 *kōnai, kama(e)uchi* compound, grounds, premises
5 外 *kōgai* outside the premises
6 成 *kōsei suru* comprise. *kōsei* composition, organization, construction, line-up
成分子 *kōsei bunshi* components
成団体 *kōsei dantai* affiliated organizations
成員 *kōseiin* member
7 図 *kōzu* plot (of a novel); plan (of a life); composition (of a painting); design; sketch
材 *kōzai* construction materials
9 造 *kōzō* construction, framework, structure; setup, organization
造上 *kōzōjō* structurally
造力学 *kōzō rikigaku* structural mechanics; theory of structure
造不況 *kōzōfukyō* structural depression
造主義 *kōzō shugi* structuralism
造調整 *kōzō chōsei* structural adjustment
造鋼 *kōzōkō* strural steel
13 想 *kōsō* plan, idea, conception, plot
16 築 *kōchiku suru* build, construct
築物 *kōchikubutsu* a structure

B **概** 2824 / J3335 / M15217' **槪** 2860 / J-X / M15364 **槩** 2861 / J-X / M15364' Gai condition, situation; approximation. *gai(shite)* generally, as a rule, on the whole. *ōmu(ne)* in general; mostly, principally, almost; probably; about, roughly.
7 見 *gaiken* general view, outline
言 *gaigen* summary, general remarks
8 況 *gaikyō* outlook, over-all condition, general situation
念 *gainen* general idea, concept
念化 *gainenka* generalization
念芸術 *gainen geijutsu* conceptual art
念的 *gainenteki ni* roughly, generally

[9]括 *gaikatsu* summary, generalization
計 *gaikei* rough estimate
則 *gaisoku* general rules, general principles
要 *gaiyō* summary, outline, synopsis, résumé
[11]略 *gairyaku* outline, summary, gist, résumé; roughly, approximately, in brief
[12]報 *gaihō* summary
[13]数 *gaisū* round numbers
[14]説 *gaisetsu* general statement, outline
貌 *gaibō* outline (of an event)
算 *gaisan* approximation, rough estimate
[15]論 *gairon* introduction, outline, general remarks
[18]観 *gaikan* general view, outline

A 模 2825 / J4c4f / M15453 Mo. Bo. *mo(suru)* copy, imitate, mock. *katado(ru)* pattern after, imitate, symbolize.
[5]写 *mosha* copying; copy, replica
写器 *moshaki* mimeograph
[9]型 *mokei* model, pattern
造 *mozō* imitation, copy, reproduction; counterfeit
造宝石 *mozō hōseki* imitation gem
造品 *mozōhin* imitation
造紙 *mozōshi* vellum paper
造真珠 *mozō shinju* imitation pearls
[10]倣 *mohō* copy, imitation
索 *mosaku* groping
[14]様 *moyō* pattern, design; appearance; circumstances
様入 *moyōi(ri) no* figured
様替 *moyōga(e)* remodeling, alteration, change
[15]糊 *moko* dimness, vagueness, stupidity
範 *mohan* model, pattern, example
範生 *mohansei* model student
範的 *mohanteki* exemplary
範試合 *mohanjiai* exhibition game
[17]擬 *mogi* imitation
擬店 *mogiten* buffet, refreshment booth (at a party)
擬戦 *mogisen* sham fight
擬試験 *mogi shiken* trial examination

11

槨 2826 / J5c5a / M15362 See 椁 2723.

樣 2827 / J-X / M-X See 様 2821.

樞 2828 / J5c64 / M15450 See 枢 2588.

槝 2829 / J5c73 / M15565 See 椙 2780.

樓 2830 / J5c6c / M15430 See 楼 2785.

樣 2831 / J5c6b / M15457 See 様 2821.

樂 2832 / J5c5b / M15399 See 楽 2790.

槧 2833 / J5c61 / M15359 Zan. Sen. Zen placard; printing block; letter; book. *fuda* tag, placard; notice board.

槫 2834 / J5c67 / M15366 Tan. Sen hearse; round. *maru(i)* round, circular; spherical.

槭 2835 / J5c65 / M15369 Seki. Shuku *kaede* maple tree.

槲 2836 / J5c60 / M15375 Kaku. Gaku *kashiwa* oak.

槹 2837 / J5c5f / M15385 Kō *hanetsurube* sweep-well bucket.

樅 2838 / J5c62 / M15404 Shō. *momi* fir, white fir, silver fir.

槶 2839 / J5c6e / M15416 Kan thick growth of trees.

樔 2840 / J5c66 / M15433 Sō dip; net, fish net; watchtower. *yagura* watchtower.

樗 2841 / J4374 / M15438 Cho. *gonzui* a sumac. *ōchi* Japanese bead tree.

樛 2842 / J5c5c / M15445 Kyū. Ku bend; undulate; tie. *tsuki* a kind of Zelkova tree.

梼 2843 / J5c78 / M15455 CHŌ kind of bird; kind of plant. *tsuta* ivy.

B **槽** 2844 / J4165 / M15393 SŌ tub, tank, vat.

槻 2845 / J4450 / M15390 KI. *tsuki* a kind of Zelkova tree.

樒 2846 / J5c69 / M15428 MITSU. *shikimi* a tree whose branches are placed on Buddhist graves, an aniseed tree.

樏 2847 / J-X / M15425 RUI. *kanjiki* snowshoes.

槿 2848 / J5c5d / M15395 KIN rose of Sharon.

7 花 *kinka* rose of Sharon

樫 2849 / J335f / M15485 （国字） *kashi* evergreen oak.

12 棒 *kashibō* oak club, oak stick

樊 2850 / J5c68 / M15414 HAN. BON cage; fence; edge; enclosure. *magaki* rough-woven fence.

22 籠 *hanrō* cage; confinement
25 籬 *hanri* rough-woven fence; opening to study or document

樟 2851 / J3e40 / M15451 SHŌ. *kusu* camphor tree; camphor.

4 木 *kusu(no)ki* camphor tree
11 脳 *shōnō* camphor
脳油 *shōnōyu* camphor oil
脳精 *shōnōsei* spirits of camphor

A **標** 2852 / J4938 / M15442 HYŌ signpost; mark; target; designate. *shirushi* sign, mark; symbol, emblem; badge; evidence; souvenir; token; brand, trademark; signs, indications; omen; seal.

4 木 *hyōboku* signpost, grave post
5 石 *hyōseki* boundary stone; milestone
号 *hyōgō* symbol, emblem, sign
示 *hyōji* indication, expression; marking
札 *hyōsatsu* nameplate, door plate
本 *hyōhon* specimen
6 灯 *hyōtō* signal light, pilot light
8 注 *hyōchū* top marginal notes
的 *hyōteki* mark, target
定 *hyōtei suru* orientate; range (a telescope)
9 柱 *hyōchū* pylon, guidepost
10 高 *hyōkō* height above sea level
記 *hyōki* a mark; marking
11 章 *hyōshō* ensign, emblem, badge, mark
12 註 *hyōchū* top marginal notes
13 準 *hyōjun* standard, norm, level, criterion, canon, measure
準化 *hyōjunka* standardization
準米 *hyōjummai* standard rice
準的 *hyōjunteki* standard, normal, regular, average
準型 *hyōjungata* standard type
準軌間 *hyōjun kikan* standard railway gauge
準時 *hyōjunji* standard time, Greenwich time
準時計 *hyōjundokei* chronometer
準液 *hyōjun'eki* standard solution (liquid)
準偏差 *hyōjun hensa* standard deviation
準語 *hyōjungo* standard language
14 旗 *hyōki* flag marker
榜 *hyōbō suru* profess, advocate. *hyōbō* sign, signboard, doorplate; poster, billboard; appearance; figurehead; policy; attraction; closing time
語 *hyōgo* slogan, motto
15 縄 *shimenawa* sacred shrine rope
18 題 *hyōdai* title (of a book)
19 識 *hyōshiki* landmark; sign, signal, beacon; criterion

A **権** 2853 / J3822 / M15484 **權** 2916 / J5c5e / M15926 GON, KEN authority, power; rights, concession. *gon-* assistant (in the Shinto hierarchy).

2 力 *kenryoku* power, authority, influence
力争 *kenryoku araso(i)* struggle for supremacy
力者 *kenryokusha* man of power
力政治 *kenryoku seiji* power politics
力関係 *kenryoku kankei* power relation
力闘争 *kenryoku tōsō* power struggle
4 内 *kennai* within one's authority
化 *gonge* (Buddhist) incarnation, avatar, embodiment, personification
5 外 *kengai* outside the jurisdiction (of)
6 臣 *kenshin* influential retainer
7 助 *gonsuke* manservant
利 *kenri* rights, claim, privilege, title;

authority, powers; goodwill; franchise; agency
利付 *kenritsu(ki)* rights attached
利金 *kenrikin* key money
8 門 *kemmon* man of influence
限 *kengen* power, authority, jurisdiction
官 *kenkan* influential official
妻 *gonsai* concubine
9 変 *kempen* expediency
要 *ken'yō* important and influential (position or person)
柄 *kempei* authority, power
柄尽 *kempeizu(ku)* authoritative, dictatorial
威 *ken'i* authority, power, dignity, prestige
威的 *ken'iteki* authoratative
威主義 *ken'i shugi* authoritarianism
威者 *ken'isha* an authority
威筋 *ken'i suji* authoritative sources
威誌 *ken'ishi* authoritative magazine
10 原 *kengen* title (to territory)
益 *ken'eki* rights, interests
家 *kenka* influential house
能 *kennō* authority, power; function, faculty
11 道 *kendō* policy, expediency, trick, makeshift
現 *gongen* incarnation of Buddha; avatar; Tokugawa Ieyasu
12 詐 *kensa* deceptive plan
貴 *kenki* rank and influence; a man of rank and influence
13 勢 *kensei* power, influence
勢家 *kenseika* a powerful man
16 衡 *kenkō* balance, equilibrium
謀 *kembō* scheme, stratagem, plot
謀家 *kembōka* schemer
謀術数 *kembō-jussū* trickery, diplomacy, Machiavellism
17 輿 *ken'yo* origin, beginning

A **横** 2854 / J3223 / M15484' **横** 2857 / J-X / M15594 Ō horizontal. *yoko* side, flank; horizontal direction; width, breadth, beam; woof. *yoko(taeru)* lay (oneself) down, lie down; place across. *yoko(tawaru)* lie down, stretch out on.
2 丁 *yokochō* lane, alley, side street
4 手 *yokode* hand clapping. *yokote ni* at one side, at one's side
木 *yokogi* crosspiece, bar, crossbar, crosstree, singletree, rail
辷 *yokosuberi* skid, slip, sideslip
切 *yokogi(ru)* intersect, cross
太 *yokobuto(ri)* plumpness, pudginess
文 *ōbun* horizontal writing, Western writing
文字 *yokomoji* European writing, crosswise writing
引 *yokobi(ki)* crosscut
引鋸 *yokobi(ki) nokogiri* crosscut saw
5 目 *yokome* side glance; amorous glance; crosscut saw
穴 *yokoana* cave, tunnel
付 *yokozu(ke)* coming alongside
6 糸 *yokoito* woof
死 *ōshi* violent, tragic, accidental, or unnatural death; a dog's death
向 *yokomu(ki)* turning sideways
好 *yokozu(ki)* immoderately fond of
帆 *ōhan* square sail
合 *yokoa(i)* side, flank
行 *ōkō suru* walk sideways; swagger; stride
行闊歩 *ōkō-kappo* swaggering around
7 見 *yokomi* side glance
谷 *ōkoku* transverse valley
位 *ōi* transverse position of the fetus
投 *yokonu(ge)* throwing sideways, side throw
町 *yokochō* lane, alley, side street
車 *yokoguruma* perverseness
車押 *yokoguruma (o) o(su)* be perverse
8 長 *yokonaga* oblong
雨 *yokoame, yokosame* driving rain
逆 *ōgyaku* boisterous, wild, unreasonable
抱 *yokoda(ki)* carrying (a child) under the arm
泳 *yokooyo(gi)* side stroke
波 *yokonami* side wave, broadside sea, transverse wave
取 *yokodo(ri)* usurpation; seizure; snatching; intercepting
肥 *yokobuto(ri)* fat, plumpness, pudginess
臥 *ōga* lying on the side
殴 *yokonagu(ri)* side blow, sideswipe
歩 *yokoaru(ki) suru* walk sideways
9 面 *yokotsura, yoko(t)tsura, yokozura* side of the face
風 *yokokaze, ōfū* crosswind
飛 *yokoto(bi)* scurrying away
柄 *ōhei* arrogance
降 *yokobu(ri)* driving rain

這 *yokoba(i)* crawl sideways
乗 *yokono(ri)* riding sideways
封筒 *yokobūtō, yoko fūtō* Western-style envelope
10 倒 *yokodao(re)* lying sideways along (the track). *yokodao(shi), yokotao(shi)* skidding and tumbling
桁 *yokogeta* crossbeam
流 *yokonaga(re)* flowing into blackmarket channels. *yokonaga(shi)* diversion into illegal channels
書 *yokoga(ki)* writing horizontally
紙破 *yokogamiyabu(ri)* perverseness, waywardness
恋慕 *yoko rembo* illicit love
座標 *ōzahyō* abscissa
11 道 *yokomichi* side street; crossroad; wrong way; side issue; evil course. *ōdō* wickedness, wrong, injustice; crossroad
舵 *ōda* diving rudder
転 *ōten* lateral turn; barrel roll (of a plane)
隊 *ōtai* rank, line
貫 *ōkan* running across; east and west
笛 *yokobue, ōteki* flute, fife
笛吹 *yokobuefu(ki)* flutist
断 *ōdan* crossing, intersection
断者 *ōdansha* street-crossing pedestrian
断歩道 *ōdan hodō* pedestrian crossing
断面 *ōdammen* cross section
断線 *ōdansen* transverse line
12 幅 *yokohaba* breadth, width
揺 *yokoyu(re)* rolling, a roll
棒 *yokobō* bar, horizontal bar; dash; horizontal line
軸 *yokojiku* horizontal shaft, cross axle
筋 *yokosuji* transversal; lateral stripes
着 *ōchaku* dishonesty; cunning; impudence; laziness; selfishness
雲 *yokogumo* bank of clouds
裂 *yokoza(ki), yokoza(ke)* a horizontal tear
隔膜 *ōkakumaku* the diaphragm
13 溢 *ōitsu* overflowing, inundation
睨 *yokonira(mi)* a sharp sidelong glance
腹 *yoko(p)para, yokohara, yokobara* side, flank
罫 *yokokei* horizontal lines
意地 *yokoiji* perverseness, obstinacy
14 槍 *yokoyari* interruption
様 *yokozama* wickedness. *yokozama ni* sideways, laterally, askance
綱 *yokozuna* champion sumo wrestler; top in the class
綴 *yokotoji* side stitch
隣 *yokodonari* next door
領 *ōryō* usurpation, seizure, dispossession; embezzlement, misappropriation
奪 *ōdatsu* usurpation, seizure, dispossession; embezzlement, misappropriation
15 暴 *ōbō* violence, oppression, high-handedness
震 *ōshin* lateral shock (quake)
線 *ōsen* horizontal line, abscissa
線小切手 *ōsen kogitte* crossed check
16 縞 *yokojima* lateral stripes
縦 *yokotate* length and breadth
薙 *yokonagi* side sweep; sweeping from side to side
18 額 *yokogaku* framed horizontal scroll
顔 *yokogao* profile, side view, silhouette
19 櫛 *yokogushi* side comb
20 議 *ōgi* arguing persistently
25 鬢 *yokobin* side locks; cheek

12

橤 2855 / J-X / M15569 See 惢 5188.

樣 2856 / J-X / M-X See 様 2821.

橫 2857 / J-X / M15594 See 横 2854.

𣝁 2858 / J-X / M15501 See 榻 2807.

檑 2859 / J-X / M15525 See 榴 2820.

槪 2860 / J-X / M15364 **槪** 2861 / J-X / M15364' See 概 2824.

榀 2862 / J5c71 / M-X See 柾 2619.

橡 2863 / J464b / M15564 **橡** 2864 / J-X / M-X SHŌ. *tochi* horse chestnut.

樶 2865 / J5c70 / M15491 SAI *fushi* knot in wood; joint.

橲 2866 / J5c6f / M15623 （国字）*zusa* Japanese storax; used in proper names.

橅 2867 / J-X / M15513 BO. MO. *buna* beech tree.

橘 2868 / J354c / M15551 KITSU. *tachibana* mandarin orange; orange crest.

橦 2869 / J5c75 / M15578 SHU pole.

檠 2870 / J5c7b / M15681 KEI. KYŌ *yudame* instrument to rebend bow.

樵 2871 / J3e41 / M15489 SHŌ. *kiko(ru), ko(ru)* cut wood. *kikori* woodcutting; woodcutter, lumberjack.

4 夫 *kikori, shōfu* woodcutter, lumberjack

橈 2872 / J5c76 / M15521 DŌ. *kai* oar, scull, paddle.

8 受 *kaiu(ke)* oarlock
10 座 *kaiza* oarlock

樸 2873 / J5c77 / M15495 BOKU. *kohada* bark of a tree.

8 直 *bokuchoku* simplicity, naïveté, honesty
念仁 *bokunenjin* a quiet unsociable person; one not too bright

橇 2874 / J5c72 / M15517 KYŌ. ZEI. *sori* sled, sleigh, sledge, skid. *kanjiki* snowshoes.

4 犬 *sori inu* sled dog
13 滑 *sorisuberi* sleighing

樽 2875 / J432e / M15500 SON. *taru* barrel, cask, keg, tub.

2 入 *tarui(ri)* barreled (liquor)
9 柿 *tarugaki* persimmons seasoned in saké barrels (to remove astringency)
13 詰 *taruzume* barreled, casked

橄 2876 / J5c6d / M15512 KAN.

25 欖 *kanran* olive
欖山 *Kanranzan* Mount of Olives
欖石 *kanranseki* chrysolite, olivine
欖油 *kanran'yu* olive oil

橙 2877 / J5c74 / M15552 TŌ. *daidai* bitter orange.

5 皮 *tōhi* orange peeling
6 色 *daidai iro* orange color
7 花 *tōka* orange blossom
花油 *tōkayu* neroli oil
12 酢 *daidaizu* bitter-orange juice

A **樹** 2878 / J3c79 / M15496 JU *ki* tree, wood. *ta(teru)* stand something up, set up, raise; put up; set on edge; prick up (one's ears); build, erect; close (a door); establish; institute, enact; lay (plans); map out; set forth, lay down (a proposition); formulate; render (services), perform; look up to, respect; be loyal to; do justice to; circulate (rumors); have (an aim); establish (oneself), make (a success); support (oneself); make (an oath); sharpen, set (a saw); put up (a candidate); make (tea); save (face).

3 下 *juka ni* under a tree
上 *jujō no, jujō ni* on a tree
4 木 *jumoku* trees and shrubs, ardor
木学 *jumokugaku* dendrology
木限界線 *jumoku genkaisen* timber line
5 皮 *juhi* bark
立 *juritsu* establishment, setting (a record)
氷 *juhyō* silver frost (on trees)
7 身 *jushin* tree trunk
8 林 *jurin* forest
9 海 *jukai* a sea of foliage, a sea of forests
10 脂 *jushi* resin, rosin
陰 *juin* shade of a tree
11 液 *jueki* sap
頂 *juchō* top of a tree
12 間 *jukan* among the trees; between the trees
葉 *juyō* leaves of a tree
13 幹 *jukan* trunk of a tree
17 齢 *jurei* a tree's age

A **橋** 2879 / J3636 / M15526 KYŌ. *hashi* bridge.

4 爪 *hashizume* bridge approach
5 台 *kyōdai* bridge abutment
6 守 *hashimori* bridge watchman
7 杙 *hashigui* bridge pile
8 杭 *hashigui* bridge pile
9 架 *kyōka* bridge girder
10 桁 *hashigeta* bridge girder
畔 *kyōhan* bridge approach
11 脚 *kyōkyaku* bridge pier
梁 *kyōryō* bridge
12 渡 *hashiwata(shi)* building a bridge; mediation, good offices
普請 *hashibushin* bridge construction
13 詰 *hashizume* bridge approach
14 銭 *hashisen* bridge toll
16 頭 *kyōtō* vicinity of a bridge
頭陣地 *kyōtō jinchi* bridgehead
頭堡 *kyōtōhō* bridgehead, beachhead
20 懸 *hashigaka(ri)* bridge-type passageway

A **機** 2880 / J3521 / M15561 KI opportunity; occasion, time; machine, airplane. *hata* loom.

3 女 *kijo* female weaver
才 *kisai* promptness, quick wit, superior talent
上 *kijō* aboard a plane
4 内 *kinai* within the plane
内通信 *kinai tsūshin* intercom
5 巧 *kikō* contrivance; means; clever thinking
失 *ki (o) ushina(u)* lose a chance
甲 *kikō* armored
甲車両 *kikō sharyō* armored vehicles
甲部隊 *kikō butai* armored corps
6 先 *kisen* before the occurrence
帆船 *kihansen* steam-and-sail ships
会 *kikai* opportunity, chance
会主義 *kikai shugi* opportunism
会均等 *kikai kintō* equal opportunity
7 見 *ki (o) mi(ru)* watch for an opportunity
尾 *kibi* airplane tail
体 *kitai* fuselage
材 *kizai* machine parts, machinery, equipment
8 知 *kichi* wit, resources, tact
宜 *kigi* opportunity, occasion
9 首 *kishu* nose of a plane
屋 *hataya* weaver
乗 *ki (ni) no(ru)* take advantage of an opportunity
変 *kihen* opportunism; deceptive power
要 *kiyō* important considerations
10 根 *kikon* talent, gift
敏 *kibin* shrewdness, alertness, astuteness
能 *kinō* faculty, function, process
能主義 *kinō shugi* functionalism
能的 *kinōteki* functional
11 運 *kiun* luck; tendency; opportunity
略 *kiryaku* resources; expedient; tact
務 *kimu* important state affairs
船 *kisen* motorboat
転 *kiten* tact, ready wit
密 *kimitsu* secrecy, secret
密費 *kimitsuhi* secret funds
動 *kidō* mobile
動力 *kidōryoku* mobile power, motive force; maneuverability
動化 *kidōka* mechanization
動部隊 *kidō butai* mechanized unit
動演習 *kidō enshū* maneuvers
械 *kikai* machine, mechanism, gear
械工 *kikaikō* mechanic, machinist
械工具 *kikai kōgu* machine tools
械工学 *kikai kōgaku* mechanical engineering
械工場 *kikai kōjō* machine shop, engineering works
械工業 *kikai kōgyō* machine industry
械化 *kikaika* mechanization; mechanized
械刈 *kikaiga(ri)* haircutting with clippers
械文明 *kikai bummei* machine civilization
械仕掛 *kikaijika(ke)* mechanism, machinery
械糸 *kikai ito* filatures
械体操 *kikai taisō* calisthenics using equipment
械的 *kikaiteki* mechanical
械油 *kikai abura, kikaiyu* machine oil, lubricating oil
械学 *kikaigaku* mechanics
械屋 *kikaiya* machinist
械製 *kikaisei no* machine-made
械製作所 *kikai seisakujo* machine shop
械語 *kikaigo* machine language
械編 *kikaia(mi)* machine knitting
械縫 *kikainu(i)* machine-sewed
械機 *kikaibata* power loom

[12] 軸 *kijiku* axis; axle; plan; contrivance
智 *kichi* wit, resources, tact
[13] 微 *kibi* secrets, inner workings, delicate turn
雷 *kirai* (sea) mine
雷原 *kiraigen* minefield
業 *kigyō* the textile industry
業界 *kigyōkai* textile world
業家 *kigyōka* weaver, textile manufacturer
嫌 *kigen* health; cheer; temper, mood
嫌気褄 *kigenkizuma* another's whim
嫌伺 *kigen'ukaga(i)* inquiry about someone's health
嫌良 *kigen'yo(ku)* cheerfully, with good grace
嫌取 *kigento(ri)* humoring; flatterer
嫌買 *kigenka(i)* a man of moods
嫌顔 *kigengao* joyful face
[14] 構 *kikō* mechanism, structure, organization, setup
種 *kishu* the type of plane
銃 *kijū* machine gun
銃掃射 *kijū sōsha* machine-gunning
関 *kikan* engine, machine; means, instrument; agency, organization, facilities, institution; organ
関士 *kikanshi* engineer
関手 *kikanshu* locomotive engineer
関化現象 *kikanka genshō* institutionalization
関車 *kikansha* locomotive
関兵 *kikanhei* fireman, stoker; machinist
関助手 *kikan joshu* railway fireman
関長 *kikanchō* chief engineer
関投資家 *kikan tōshika* institutional investor
関室 *kikanshitsu* engine room
関庫 *kikanko* roundhouse
関砲 *kikanhō* machine gun
関紙 *kikanshi* bulletin, organ
関部 *kikambu* ship's engineers
関誌 *kikanshi* bulletin, regular publication of a society
関銃 *kikanjū* machine gun
関雑誌 *kikan zasshi* bulletin, regular publication of a society
[15] 縁 *kien* opportunity
鋒 *kihō* point, brunt (of an attack)
影 *kiei* (sight of) a plane
器 *kiki* machinery and tools
[16] 謀 *kibō* plan, scheme, plot
[17] 翼 *kiyoku* airplane wings
[18] 織 *hatao(ri)* weaving; weaver; grasshopper
織虫 *hatao(ri) mushi* grasshopper

13

橥 2881 / J5d2c / M-X — Nonstandard for 櫟 2906.

檥 2882 / J-X / M15690 — See 艤 4949.

檢 2883 / J5c7d / M15684 — See 検 2752.

櫛 2884 / J367b / M-X — Nonstandard for 櫛 2909.

檍 2885 / J5c7a / M15656 — OKU *mochi, mochinoki* ilex, birdlime tree.

檗 2886 / J5d21 / M15669 — BAKU. HAKU *kihada* Amur or Chinese cork tree.

檬 2887 / J5d28 / M15710 — MŌ mango.

檎 2888 / J3869 / M15657 — KIN, GON pear; apple; Pyrus.

橿 2889 / J3360 / M15629 — KYŌ a kind of oak.

檞 2890 / J-X / M15679 — KAI. *kashiwa* oak.

檄 2891 / J5c7c / M15639 — GEKI written appeal, manifesto, declaration, summons. *geki(suru)* appeal to, send a manifesto.
[4] 文 *gekibun* written appeal, manifesto

檐 2892 / J5c79 / M15659 — EN *noki* eaves.
[8] 雨 *en'u* rain pouring from eaves
[13] 鈴 *enrin* wind chimes hanging from eaves

檣 2893 / J5c7e / M15687 SHŌ. *hobashira* mast.
3 上 *shōjō* top of the mast
6 灯 *shōtō* front-mast light
9 竿 *shōkan* mast
16 頭 *shōtō* masthead

檜 2894 / J5b58 / M15676 **桧** 2637 / J4930 / M-X KAI. *hinoki, hi* Japanese cypress.
5 皮 *hiwada* cypress bark
皮葺 *hiwadabuki* cypress-bark roof
12 葉 *hiba* cedar-like shrub
14 舞台 *hinoki butai* cypress-floored stage, high-class stage

檀 2895 / J4349 / M15632 DAN, TAN a kind of cedar, sandalwood. *mayumi* spindletree.
6 那 *danna* master; husband; gentleman
那寺 *dannadera* one's family temple
10 徒 *danto* temple supporter
紙 *danshi* fine crepe paper
家 *danka* families supporting a temple

14

檯 2896 / J5c6a / M15754 See **枱** 2846.

檮 2897 / J5b6d / M15713 TŌ. DŌ tree stump; foolish, ignorant.

櫃 2898 / J5d24 / M15757 KI. *hitsu* chest, coffer; rice tub.

檸 2899 / J5d26 / M15742 DŌ. NEI lemon.
17 檬 *dōmō, remon* lemon

櫂 2900 / J5d25 / M15756 TŌ. *kai* oar, scull, paddle.
8 拍子 *kaibyōshi* rowing stroke

檳 2901 / J5d27 / M15734 BIN betel-nut palm.
13 榔 *binrō* betel nut, betel-nut palm
榔子 *binrōji* betel nut

檻 2902 / J5d23 / M15745 KAN. *ori* cage, pen, corral, fold; cell, jail.
8 房 *kambō* cell, ward
9 穽 *kansei* corrals and traps

15

櫑 2903 / J5d2a / M15796 RAI. RE *sakadaru* wine cask.

櫞 2904 / J5d29 / M15822 EN a kind of lemon tree.

櫚 2905 / J5d2d / M15815 RO, RYO a kind of quince.

櫟 2906 / J5d2b / M15823 **檪** 2881 / J5d2c / M-X REKI. *kunugi* a kind of oak used for charcoal.

櫝 2907 / J-X / M15821 TOKU. *hitsu* chest, coffer; rice tub.

櫓 2908 / J4f26 / M15798 **艪** 4951 / J6762 / M30580 RO sculling oar; oar; tower. *yagura* tower, turret; scaffolding.
18 櫂 *rokai* oars
臍 *robeso* sculling-oar pivot; oarlock

櫛 2909 / J-X / M15817 **櫛** 2884 / J367b / M-X SHITSU. *kushi* comb.
4 比 *shippi suru* stand in a long row
5 払 *kushihara(i)* comb-cleaning brush
7 形 *kushigata* comb-like; arch-shaped; arched window
9 風沐雨 *shippū mokuu* hard toil, hardships
10 挽 *kushibiki* comb making

16

櫨 2910 / J4827 / M15844 RO (carpenter's) square. *haze* wax tree; sumac.

櫪 2911 / J5d2e / M15846 REKI feed trough; crib; horse barn. *kunugi* a kind of oak used for charcoal.

欖 2912 / J-X / M15905 **欖** 2923 / J5d34 / M15964 RAN Chinese olive.

櫧 2913 / J-X / M15843 SHO. SO. *kashi* oak.

B欄 2914 J4d73 M15880' 欄 2915 J-X M15904 RAN column (in a newspaper); blank; space; railing. *obashima* handrail.
3 干 *rankan* railing, balustrade
5 外 *rangai* margin (of a page)
12 間 *ramma* transom; transom work

17

欄 2915 J-X M15904 See 欄 2914.

權 2916 J5c5e M15926 See 権 2853.

櫻 2917 J5d2f M15888 See 桜 2664.

欅 2918 J-X M-X 櫸 2919 J5d30 M15883 KYO. *keyaki* Zelkova tree.

櫺 2920 J5d32 M15887 REI. RYŌ latticework; grip; name of star.
3 子 *renji* latticework

19

欛 2921 J-X M15945 See 欛 2925.

欒 2922 J5d33 M15947 RAN chinaberry tree; round; harmonious.

21

欖 2923 J5d34 M15964 See 欖 2912.

鬱 2924 J3135 M-X See 鬱 2926.

欛 2925 J-X M15971 欛 2921 J-X M15945 HA. *tsuka* hilt, grip, handle (of a knife).

22

鬱 2926 J-X M15978 鬱 6830 J5d35 M45671 UTSU gloom, depression, melancholy. *us(suru), fusa(gu)* be depressed, have the blues.
4 込 *fusa(gi)-ko(mu)* be depressed, have the blues
6 血 *ukketsu* blood congestion
気 *ukki* close air; gloom, melancholy
8 林 *utsurin* dense forest
金色 *ukon iro* saffron color
金香 *ukkonkō* tulip
9 勃 *utsubotsu(taru)* pent up, stored; energetic, irresistible
10 陶 *uttō* sultriness, stuffiness; unpleasantness; bother. *uttō(shii)* gloomy, depressing; dull, cloudy
12 散 *ussan* recreation, diversion, distraction
葱 *ussō* luxurious foliage; energetic spirits
13 蒼 *ussō(taru)* thick, dense, luxuriant
15 憤 *uppun* resentment, grudge, anger
16 積 *usseki* congestion, stagnation
26 鬱 *utsuutsu to* gloomily, cheerlessly

24

欟 2927 J5d36 M15986 （国字） *tsuki* a kind of zelkova tree.

RAD. 欠 76

Akubi yawn; also *ken, ketsu,* or *kakeru* lacking. Nickname: Yawning.

A欠 2928 J3767 M15991 缺 4626 J657e M28122 KETSU lack, gap. *ka(ku)* lack; break, crack, chip; neglect; fail in; omit. *ka(keru)* be broken (off), be chipped; lack, be missing; wane; be vacant (a position). *ka(kasu)* miss (a meeting). *ka(ke)* broken piece (of glass, etc.). *akubi* yawn (欠 only).
3 乏 *ketsubō* want; dearth, famine; scarcity, shortage
乏症 *ketsubōshō* deficiency disease
4 文 *ketsubun* missing part (of a manuscript)
片 *kakera* fragment, splinter, chunk
5 目 *ka(ke)me* break; rupture; short weight
礼 *ketsurei* neglect of courtesies

4 心忄⺗戈戸手扌支攴攵文斗斤方无日曰月木【欠】0 止歹殳毋比毛氏气水氵氺火灬爪爫父爻爿丬片牙牛犬犭

4 心 忄 ⺗ 戈 戸 手 扌 支 攴 攵 文 斗 斤 方 无 日 曰 月 木 2【欠】 止 歹 殳 毋 比 毛 氏 气 水 氵 氺 火 灬 爪 爫 父 爻 爿 丬 片 牙 牛 犬 犭

可 *ka(ku)be(karazu)* indispensable
本 *keppon* missing volume
号 *ketsugō* missing number (of a magazine)
6 如 *ketsujo* lack, privation, deficiency
字 *ketsuji* omitted word; courtesy spaces left above famous names
7 伸 *akubi* yawn
9 除 *ketsujo* removal, omission
点 *ketten* faults, defect, weakness
盈 *ketsuei* lack and plenty
食 *kesshoku* going without a meal
食児童 *kesshoku jidō* pupils going to school without lunch
陥 *kekkan* defect, fault, deficiency
陥児 *kekkanji* defective child
10 唇 *iguchi, kesshin* harelip
航 *kekkō* steamship-service suspension
配 *keppai* curtailment of rations
員 *ketsuin* vacant position
格 *kekkaku* lack of qualifications
格者 *kekkakusha* unqualified person
席 *kesseki* absence; default
席届 *kesseki todoke* report of a school absence
席者 *kessekisha* absentee
席裁判 *kesseki saiban* court sentence of an absent criminal
12 場 *ketsujō* not in the lineup
量 *ketsuryō* ullage
落 *ketsuraku* lack, absence
番 *ketsuban* missing number
勤 *kekkin* absence
勤届 *kekkin todoke* report of an absence
勤者 *kekkinsha* absentee
勤率 *kekkinritsu* absenteeism rate
13 損 *kesson* deficit, shortage, loss; damage
14 漏 *ketsurō* omission
16 壊 *kekkai suru* collapse

2

A 次 2929 / J3c21 / M15992' SHI. JI order, sequence; times; next; below. *tsu(gu)* rank next to, come after. *tsugi* next; stage station, stage. *tsugi ni* then, subsequently. *tsu(ide)* next, secondly, subsequently. *-ji* order.

3 女 *jijo* second daughter
4 元 *jigen* dimension (in math)
5 代 *jidai* the next era
兄 *jikei* second elder brother
号 *jigō* next issue
打者 *jidasha* the batter on deck
6 回 *jikai* next time
次 *tsugitsugi ni* one by one, one after another, successively
会 *jikai* the next meeting
年 *jinen* the next year
7 序 *jijo* order, system
位 *jii* second rank, second place
亜 *jia-* hypo- (in chemicals)
条 *jijō* the next article, the next entry
男 *jinan* second son
男坊 *jinambō* second son
8 長 *jichō* vice- or assistant executive
官 *jikan* vice-minister, under-secretary, assistant secretary
表 *jihyō* the following table
9 点 *jiten* runner-up
点者 *jitensha* runner-up
10 席 *jiseki* associate, junior, assistant; runner-up
将 *jishō* second in command
11 第 *shidai* order, precedence; circumstances, occasion; reason, cause; as soon as; at one's pleasure; according to. *shidai ni* gradually
第書 *shidaiga(ki)* printed program
12 間 *tsugi(no)ma* antechamber; next room
期 *jiki* next term
善 *jizen no* second best
13 数 *jisū* degree (in math)

4

欣 2930 / J3655 / M16008 KIN rejoice. *yoroko(bu)* rejoice, be glad, be pleased. *yoroko(bashii)* joyful, glad, pleasant.

7 快 *kinkai na* pleasant, delightful
8 欣 *kinkin* joy, delight
10 悦 *kin'etsu* joy, gladness
12 喜 *kinki* joy, delight
然 *kinzen(taru)* joyful, cheerful
14 慕 *kimbo* admiration, adoration
15 舞 *kimbu* dancing with joy
16 懐 *kinkai suru* think happily of

B 欧 2931 / J3224 / M16024' 歐 2946 / J5d3f / M16185 Ō Europe.

2 人 *Ōjin* a European
4 文 *ōbun* European language, foreign text
化 *ōka* Europeanization, Westernization
氏管 *ōshikan* eustachian tube

[6]米 *Ō-Bei* Europe and America
州 *Ōshū* Europe
州共同市場 *Ōshū Kyōdō Shijō* European Common Market
州連合軍 *Ōshū Rengōgun* Allied Powers in Europe
州経済共同体 *Ōshū Keizai Kyōdōtai* European Economic Community
[7]亜 *Ō-A* Europe and Asia
[9]風 *Ōfū* European style, Occidental
洲 *Ōshū* Europe
[19]羅巴 *Yōroppa* Europe
[21]露 *Ō-Ro* European Russia

6

欬 2932 / J-X / M16061 See 咳 789.

7

欵 2933 / J-X / M16085 See 款 2938.

欸 2934 / J5d37 / M16090 Ai scold; bemoan; moan; get angry.

欷 2935 / J5d38 / M16087 Ki cry.
[8]泣 *kikyū* sobbing
[16]歔 *kikyo* sobbing

A欲 2936 / J4d5f / M16080 慾 1951 / J4d5d / M11163 Yoku covetousness; greed, passion, desire, craving, appetite. *hos(suru)* desire, want. *ho(shigaru)* desire, want, covet. *ho(shii)* desire, want.
[4]心 *yokushin* selfishness, acquisitiveness
[5]目 *yokume* partial view; partiality; sanguine hope
[7]求 *yokkyū* desire, craving, aspiration
[8]念 *yokunen* desire, wish, appetite, passions
[9]相 *yokusō* acquisitiveness
界 *yokukai* this greedy world
[11]張 *yokuba(ru)* be greedy, be covetous. *yokuba(ri)* greed, covetousness
得 *yokutoku* self-interest, selfishness. *yokutoku(zuku) no* selfish, mercenary
情 *yokujō* desire, craving, passion
深 *yokufuka* greed, covetousness. *yokufuka(i)* greedy; covetous
望 *yokubō* desire, craving; wants; ambition

8

欹 2937 / J5d3a / M16093 I. *sobada(teru)* prick up (one's ears).

B款 2938 / J343e / M16107 欵 2941 / J-X / M16125 欵 2933 / J-X / M16085
Kan article, section; goodwill, friendship; collusion.
[9]通 *kan (o) tsū(jiru)* collusion with the enemy
待 *kantai* entertainment, hospitality
[14]語 *kango* pleasant chat

B欺 2939 / J353d / M16097 Ki, Gi *azamu(ku), dama(su)* deceive, cheat, delude.
[8]取 *azamu(ki)-to(ru)* take by deceit, defraud
[12]惑 *azamu(ki)-mado(wasu)* deceive and lead astray
[16]瞞 *giman* deception, imposition
瞞的 *gimanteki* deceptive, false
瞞者 *gimansha* deceiver

欽 2940 / J3656 / M16104 Kin respect, revere; long for.
[6]仰 *kingyō suru* revere and honor
[8]定 *kintei* authorized, appointed
定訳聖書 *Kinteiyaku Seisho* Authorized Version; King James Version
定詩人 *kintei shijin* poet laureate
定憲法 *kintei kempō* constitution granted by the emperor
[14]慕 *kimbo suru* revere and long for

9

欵 2941 / J-X / M16125 See 款 2938.

歃 2942 / J5d3d / M16131 Sō *susu(ru)* sip, suck up, slurp.

歇 2943 / J5d3c / M16141 Ketsu out of (food, etc.), be exhausted; stop; rest.

歉 2944 / J5d3e / M16159 Ken dissatisfied, unsatisfying; insufficiency, shortage.

10

A **歌** 2945 / J324e / M16167 KA. *uta(u)* sing, recite, chant, carol. *uta* poem, tanka, ballad, poetry; singing.

2 人 *kajin, utabito* poet
3 口 *utaguchi* mouthpiece (of a flute); poetic style; poetic skill
女 *utame* singer, songstress
上 *uta(i)-a(geru)* write poetry
4 心 *utagokoro* poetic sentiment
手 *kashu, uta(i)te* singer, vocal soloist
5 仙 *kasen* great poet
出 *uta(i)-da(su)* break out in song
6 曲 *kakyoku* melody, tune, song
交 *uta(i)-ka(wasu)* sing responsively
合 *uta(i)-a(u)* sing responsively. *uta(i) awa(se)* poetry contest
会 *kakai, utakai* poetry party, poetry competition
会始 *utakaihaji(me)* Imperial Poetry Contest
7 吹 *kasui* singing and playing the flute
妓 *kagi* geisha, singing girl
沢 *utazawa* popular ballad
声 *utagoe* singing; singing voice. *uta(i)goe* singing voice. *kasei* singing
言葉 *utakotoba* poetic diction
8 枕 *utamakura* oft-repeated descriptive epithets in poetry
学 *kagaku* poetry, versification
9 風 *kafū* poetic style
垣 *utagaki* (ancient) dancing-and-singing party
姫 *utahime* songstress
神 *kashin* muse, goddess of poetry
10 屑 *utakuzu* doggerel, trivial poetry
格 *kakaku* poetry style; poetry rules
書 *kasho* book of poems
留多 *karuta* playing cards
11 道 *kadō* versification; tanka poetry
唱 *kashō* song; singing. *utauta(i)* singer; prostitute
崇 *uta(i)-aga(meru)* extol in song
12 詞 *utakotoba* poetic diction. *kashi* the words of a song, lyrics
詠 *utayo(mi)* poet, tanka composer
集 *kashū* anthology; a book of poetry
13 話 *kawa* poetry talk
聖 *kasei* a great poet
14 碑 *kahi* a tanka inscription
誦 *kashō* singing loudly
歌者 *utauta(u) mono* singer
15 劇 *kageki* opera
稿 *kakō* manuscript of a poem
調 *kachō* tune, melody, air, aria
論 *karon* poetry review
舞 *kabu* singing and dancing, entertainment
舞伎 *kabuki* popular drama, kabuki
舞妓 *kabuki* popular drama, kabuki
16 壇 *kadan* poetry circles
謡 *kayō* song, ballad
謡曲 *kayōkyoku* popular song
18 題 *kadai* name of a poem
20 競 *utakura(be)* poetry contest

11

歐 2946 / J5d3f / M16185 See **欧** 2931.

歎 2947 / J4337 / M16182 TAN grief, lamentation. *nage(ku)* sigh, lament, moan, grieve; regret, deplore, sorrow. *nageka(shii), nagekawa(shii)* sad, wretched, deplorable.

7 声 *tansei* sign, lamentation; sigh of admiration
9 美 *tambi* admiration, adoration
10 称 *tanshō* praise, admiration, applause
息 *tansoku* sigh, grief, deploring
13 嗟 *tansa* groan, sigh of despair
15 賞 *tanshō* praise, admiration, applause
19 願 *tangan* entreaty, petition, appeal, suit
願書 *tangansho* written petition

B **歓** 2948 / J343f / M16197 **歡** 2953 / J5d44 / M16242 KAN joy, pleasure. *yoroko(bi)* joy, delight, pleasure. *yoroko(bu)* rejoice, be glad, be pleased.

4 心 *kanshin* favor
6 会 *kankai* a happy party
迎 *kangei* welcome
迎会 *kangeikai* welcome meeting, reception
迎攻 *kangeize(me)* lionization
迎門 *kangeimon* welcome arch
迎辞 *kangei (no) ji* welcome address
7 声 *kansei* cheers, shout of joy
8 送 *kansō* hearty send-off

送会 *kansōkai* farewell meeting
呼 *kanko* ovation, a cheer
呼声 *kanko (no) koe* shout of joy, a cheer
[9] 待 *kantai* entertainment, hospitality, warm reception
[12] 喜 *kanki, kangi* joy, gladness
[13] 楽 *kanraku* pleasure, enjoyment
楽街 *kanrakugai* amusement center; red-light district
楽郷 *kanrakukyō* amusement district
[15] 談 *kandan* pleasant chat

12

歙 2949 / J5d40 / M16204 KYŪ. SHŌ suck; inhale; suppress; meet, join; threaten. *su(u)* suck, sip, inhale.

歔 2950 / J5d41 / M16198 KYO cry.
[11] 欷 *kyoki, susurina(ki)* sobbing, weeping

13

歛 2951 / J5d42 / M16210 See 斂 2362.

歟 2952 / J5d43 / M16226 YO *ya, ka* an interrogative particle.

17

歡 2953 / J5d44 / M16242 See 歓 2948.

RAD. 止 77

Tomeru to stop. At left: 𣥂 *tome hen.* Nickname: Stopping.

A **止** 2954 / J3b5f / M16253 SHI. *to(maru)* stop, halt, stand still, pull up; cease, be interrupted, be discontinued; be choked; alight on, perch, roost; be held in position. *to(meru)* stop; check; allay (pain); fasten; turn off; detain; forbid to do; dissuade. *todo(maru)* stop, halt, stay, remain, stay behind, be limited to. *todo(meru)* stop, cease, detain, put an end to; leave; fix; remain in (a certain condition); content oneself with. *ya(mu) vi* end, stop, cease; subside, calm down, pass; die out, be extinguished; leave, go off; be abandoned. *ya(meru) vt* end, discontinue; give up, abandon; abolish; resign, retire. *yo(su)* stop, discontinue, give up. *sa(su)* stop; leave something unfinished. *to(me)* stopping; prohibition; end; a stop. *to(mare)* halt, stop. *ya(mi), ya(me)* end, discontinuance, stop. *yoshi* stop, discontinue. *todo(me)* finishing blow. *to(mari)* stop, stoppage; end, termination. *-sa(shi)* stopping.
[4] 木 *to(mari)gi* roost, perch
水 *shisui* still water
手 *to(me)te* peacemaker (in a quarrel)
[5] 立 *to(me)da(te) suru* check, stop, prevent; dissuade
処 *to(me)do* termination, end
[6] 血 *shiketsu* stopping of bleeding, stanching
血法 *shiketsuhō* stanching blood
血剤 *shiketsuzai* a hemostatic drug
[7] 役 *to(me)yaku* peacemaker (in a quarrel)
男 *to(me)otoko* peacemaker (in a quarrel)
[9] 音器 *shionki* (piano) damper; damping
[10] 息 *shisoku* stopping to rest
[11] 得 *ya(mu) (o) e(zu)* unavoidably, inevitably, necessarily. *ya(mu) (o) e(nai)* unavoidable, necessary, inevitable, obligatory
宿 *shishuku* lodging
宿人 *shishukunin* lodger, boarder
宿所 *shishukusho* lodgings
[12] 間 *ya(mi)ma* lull (in a storm)
結 *to(me)musu(bi)* overhand knot
痛剤 *shitsūzai* painkiller
[13] 置 *todo(me)-o(ku)* keep here
[17] 螺旋 *to(me)neji* lock nut
[18] 難 *ya(mi)gatai* compelling

1

A **正** 2955 / J4035 / M16255 SEI right, righteousness, justice; original; plus, positive; genuine. SHŌ just; punctual; senior; right, righteousness, justice. *tada(su)* correct; adjust; reform; redress, straighten; amend. *masa(ni)* correctly, surely. *masa(shiku)* surely, no doubt, evidently. *tada(shii)* right, righteous, just; honest, truthful, proper, correct; lawful; healthy; moral; straight; straightforward; perfect. *sei-* regular.

3 大 *seidai* fairness, justice
子 *shōshi* twelve midnight
三角形 *seisankakukei* equilateral triangle
4 文 *seibun* the official text
月 *Shōgatsu* the first month; January; the New Year
切 *seisetsu* tangent (in trigonometry)
午 *shōgo* noon, midday
反対 *seihantai* exactly opposite
比例 *seihirei* direct proportion, direct ratio
中 *seichū* the exact middle
中線 *seichūsen* median line
方 *seihō* square
方形 *seihōkei* square
5 目 *masame* straight grain
北 *seihoku* due north
史 *seishi* authentic history
号 *seigō* plus sign
出 *seishutsu no* legitimate (child)
本 *shōhon* book of registration; text of a play. *seihon* text, original, facsimile
甲板 *seikampan* main deck
正 *seisei to* accurately, exactly; punctually; neatly, nicely
正堂堂 *seisei-dōdō(taru)* fair and square, open and aboveboard
犯 *seihan* principal offense; principal offender
犯者 *seihansha* principal offender
札 *shōfuda* correct-price tag
札付 *shōfudatsu(ki)* plainly marked; notorious person
札値段 *shōfuda nedan* fixed price
6 色 *seishoku* primary colors
西 *seisei* due west
式 *seishiki* proper form, formality
気 *shōki* consciousness; sanity, reason; soberness. *seiki* true heart, true spirit, true character
伝 *seiden* authentic biography
会員 *seikaiin* regular member
字 *seiji* correct characters
字法 *seijihō* correct orthography
当 *seitō na* just, justifiable, right, due, proper, equitable, reasonable, legitimate, lawful
当化 *seitōka suru* justify, warrant
当防衛 *seitō bōei* legitimate self-defense
7 体 *shōtai* natural shape; one's true colors, true character; consciousness; senses
位 *seii* correct location, correct position
邪 *seija* right and wrong
否 *seihi* right and wrong
系 *seikei* legitimate line; direct descent
兵 *seihei* regular soldiers
坐 *seiza suru* sit (or squat) straight
投手 *seitōshu* regular pitcher
攻法 *seikōhō* frontal attack
社員 *seishain* regular member, staff member
角定木 *seikaku jōgi* a try square
8 門 *seimon* main gate, main entrance
価 *seika* net price, regular price
使 *seishi* senior envoy, chief delegate
弦 *seigen* sine (in trigonometry)
物 *shōbutsu* genuine article
服 *seifuku* uniform, regulation dress
宗 *masamune* sword blade by Masamune
妻 *seisai* legal wife
東 *seitō* due east
金 *shōkin* specie, bullion, cash
金銀行 *shōkin ginkō* specie bank
直 *shōjiki* honesty, integrity, frankness
直者 *shōjikimono* honest person
味 *shōmi* net
味重量 *shōmi jūryō* net weight
味値段 *shōmi nedan* net price
9 風 *shōfū* right style
則 *seisoku no* correct, proper, formal, regular, systematic, normal
南 *seinan* due south
客 *shōkyaku, seikaku* guest of honor
負 *seifu* positive and negative, plus and minus
面 *matomo* the front; honesty. *shōmen* front, frontage, facade
面向 *shōmemmu(ki)* front view
面図 *shōmenzu* front elevation
面衝突 *shōmen shōtotsu* head-on collision
10 座 *seiza suru* sit (or squat) straight. *shōza* seat of honor

格 *seikaku* correct rules
訓 *seikun* correct *kun* reading
朔 *seisaku* beginning of the month or the year; New Year's Day; the calendar
員 *seiin* regular member
真正銘 *shōshin-shōmei* the genuine article
書 *seisho* square characters, printed style
書法 *seishohō* correct orthography
11 道 *seido* righteousness; path of righteousness, path of duty, the right track
眼 *seigan* aiming at the eye (with a sword)
経 *seikyō* canon of Scripture
副 *seifuku* original and copy; chief and vice-chief
貨 *seika* specie, metallic currency
視 *seishi* looking straight ahead; viewing sincerely
視眼 *seishigan* correct vision
常 *seijō* normalcy, normality, normal
常化 *seijōka* normalization
教 *seikyō* orthodoxy; Greek Orthodox Church
教会 *Seikyōkai* Greek Orthodox Church
教員 *seikyōin* regular teacher, licensed teacher
教師 *seikyōshi* ordained minister, regular teacher
規 *seiki no* regular, legal, formal, established, legitimate
規曲線 *seiki kyokusen* probability curve, normal curve
規兵 *seikihei* regulars, regular soldiers
規軍 *seikigun* regular army
12 閏 *seijun* normal and leap (years); legitimate and illegitimate (dynasties)
帽 *seibō* cap of a uniform
割 *seikatsu* secant (in trigonometry)
朝 *seichō* legitimate dynasty
装 *seisō* uniform, full dress
覚 *shōgaku* (Buddhist) perfect enlightenment
覚坊 *shōgakubō* large sea turtle
統 *seitō no* legitimate, orthodox, traditional
統派 *seitōha* orthodox school
統信教 *seitō shinkyō* orthodoxy
13 殿 *seiden* main temple; state chamber
絹 *shōken* pure silk
続 *seizoku* a book or document and its supplement
腹 *seifuku* legitimacy
解 *seikai* correct interpretation, correct answer, correct solution
路 *seiro* righteousness; path of righteousness, path of duty, the right track
数 *seisū* positive number
夢 *masayume* a dream that comes true
意 *seii* true heart; correct meaning
業 *seigyō* legitimate occupation, honest business
電気 *seidenki* positive electricity
義 *seigi* righteousness, justice, right, correct meaning
義感 *seigikan* sense of justice
14 嫡 *seiteki, seichaku* legal wife; her child; main family
銘 *shōmei* genuine autograph; genuine article
訳 *seigo* correction
誤表 *seigohyō* errata
15 編 *seihen* main part of a book
論 *seiron* sound argument
調 *seichō* traditional tune
賓 *seihin* guest of honor
確 *seikaku* exactness, authenticity, veracity
確爆撃 *seikaku bakugeki* pinpoint bombing | subject
課 *seika* regular curriculum, required
課外 *seikagai* extracurricular
16 餐 *seisan* formal dinner, banquet
18 鵠 *seikoku* the mark, the point, the bull's eye

2

此 2956 / J3a21 / M16259 Shi. *ko(no)* this, current; next, coming; last, past. *kore* this. *koko ni* here.
2 人 *ko(no) hito* this person
3 上 *ko(no)ue* furthermore, besides; any longer. *ko(no)ue wa* now. *ko(no)ue(monai)* best, greatest, matchless. *ko(no)ue tomo* furthermore
丈 *koredake* only this much, this little
4 月 *ko(no) tsuki* this month
辺 *ko(no) hen, ko(no) atari, kokora* in this area, around here

分 *ko(no) bun dewa* at this rate
方 *ko(no)hō* this one; I, we. *kochira, konata, kotchi* here, this side. *ko(no) kata* since; this person
方面 *ko(no) hōmen* this direction; this field (of activity)
5 外 *ko(no) hoka* besides this; moreover; except this
奴 *koitsu* this guy, this fellow
世 *ko(no) yo* this world, this life
処 *koko* here, this place. *koko(ira)* around here
処迄 *koko made* to this point; up till now
処先途 *koko (o) sendo to* making a last stand
処彼処 *koko-kashiko* here and there, far and wide, everywhere
処暫 *koko shiba(raku)* recently
6 次 *ko(no) tsugi* next
此 *kore-kore* this and that; etc.; so and so, such and such
先 *ko(no) saki* hereafter, up ahead, further on
年 *ko(no) toshi* this year
年頃 *ko(no) toshigoro* for years, in recent years
7 位 *ko(no) kurai* about so much, so many, so large, so wide, etc.
8 所 *ko(no) tokoro* now, lately. *koko* here
限 *kore kagi(ri)* only this much
9 度 *ko(no) tabi* at this time
通 *ko(no) tō(ri)* like this; as you see
後 *ko(no)go, ko(no) nochi* hereafter
故 *ko(no) yue ni* for this reason
段 *ko(no) dan* at this time
前 *ko(no) mae* last time, previously
点 *ko(no) ten* this point of view, this angle
10 時 *ko(no) toki* at this time, then
11 道 *ko(no) michi* the art, the line, the trade, the profession
頃 *ko(no)goro, ko(no) koro* these days, recently, now
許 *kore baka(ri), kore(p)paka(ri), kore(p)paka(shi)* only this, only this much
12 間 *ko(no) aida, konaida* the other day, recently
程 *ko(no) hodo* the other day, recently
等 *korera* these
13 際 *ko(no) sai* now, on this occasion
節 *ko(no) setsu* now at present
14 様 *ko(no) yō na* such, this kind of. *ko(no) yō ni* in this way
種 *ko(no) shu* this kind
16 儘 *ko(no) mama* as it is

3

歩 2957 / J-X / M16264 See **歩** 2958.

4

A **歩** 2958 / J4a62 / M16284 **歩** 2957 / J-X / M16264 Ho step, pace; foot soldier. Bu rate, six feet square, *tsubo*; chance of winning. *aru(ku)* walk, hike, step. *ayu(mu)* walk, step. *fu* pawn (in Japanese chess).

1 一歩 *hoippo* step by step
4 方 *aru(ki)kata* pace, gait, way of walking
引 *bubi(ki)* discount, reduction, rebate
5 付 *aru(ki)tsu(ki)* manner of walking
6 回 *aru(ki)-mawa(ru)* walk around, gad about
行 *hokō* walking
行可能 *hokō-kanō na* ambulatory (patient)
行者 *hokōsha* pedestrian
合 *ayu(mi)-a(u)* step up to, compromise. *buai* rate, ratio, percentage; commission
合高 *buaidaka* percentage
合算 *buaizan* percentage calculation
7 初 *aru(ki)zo(me)* a baby's first steps
兵 *hohei* infantry, foot soldier
8 板 *ayu(mi)ita* footboard; running board; gangplank
卒 *hosotsu* infantryman
武 *hobu* a short distance; walking
9 度 *hodo* pace, cadence
度計 *hodokei* pedometer
10 哨 *hoshō* sentinel, sentry
振 *aru(ki)bu(ri)* pace, gait, way of walking
11 廊 *horō* connecting corridor
道 *hodō* footpath, sidewalk
寄 *ayu(mi)-yo(ru)* step up to, approach; compromise
12 測 *hosoku* pacing (a distance)
割 *buwa(ri)* proportion; commission
程記録計 *hoteikirokukei* pedometer

13 数 *hosū* number of steps
数計 *hosūkei* pedometer
15 調 *hochō* pace, step, cadence, acting in unison
16 橋 *hokyo* footbridge

A 武 2959 / J4970 / M16273 MU. BU military affairs, military arts, chivalry, military glory, military power, arms. *take(shi)* brave.

2 人 *bujin* military man
力 *buryoku* armed might, the sword, force
力外交 *buryoku gaikō* armed diplomacy
力政治 *buryoku seiji* power politics
力戦 *buryokusen* armed conflict
3 士 *bushi, mononofu* samurai, warrior
士気質 *bushi katagi, bushi kishitsu* samurai spirit
士道 *bushidō* Bushido, samurai code of chivalry
士階級 *bushi kaikyū* warrior class
4 辺 *buhen* military affairs; military people
5 功 *bukō* military exploits
弁 *buben* soldier
6 臣 *bushin* military retainer
名 *bumei* military fame
7 技 *bugi* military arts
芸 *bugei* martial arts
8 門 *bumon* military family, warrior class
官 *bukan* military or naval officer
具 *bugu* arms, armor
学 *bugaku* military science
事 *buji* military affairs; martial arts
者 *musha* warrior
者振 *mushabu(ri)* prowess, gallantry. *mushaburu(i)* shaking with excitement
者振付 *mushabu(ri)tsu(ku)* jump into the fray
者修業 *musha shugyō* samurai drill, knight errantry
者絵 *mushae* warrior picture
者慄 *mushaburu(i)* shaking with excitement
者震 *mushaburu(i)* shaking with excitement
9 威 *bui* military power
侠 *bukyō* chivalry, gallantry, heroism
神 *bushin* god of military arts
勇 *buyū* bravery, valor, military prowess
勇伝 *buyūden* martial story; a heroic episode
10 庫 *buko* armory
将 *bushō* military commander
烈 *buretsu* military merit
陵桃源 *Buryotōgen* Utopia
骨 *bukotsu* uncouth, clumsy, brusque
骨者 *bukotsumono* boor, rustic
家 *buke* samurai; warrior
家物 *bukemono* samurai romance
家政治 *buke seiji* feudal government
家時代 *buke jidai* the feudal period (1185–1867)
11 道 *budō* military arts; Bushido
運 *buun* the fortunes of war
術 *bujutsu* military arts
張 *buba(ru)* be soldierly, be martial
略 *buryaku* strategy, military tactics
教 *bukyō* the teachings of Bushido
断 *budan* militarism
断主義 *budan shugi* militarism
断的 *budanteki* militaristic
断政治 *budan seiji* military government
12 備 *bubi* military preparation, armaments, defenses
装 *busō* arms, armament; armed. *busō suru* arm
装中立 *busō chūritsu* armed neutrality
装平和 *busō heiwa* armed peace
装具 *busōgu* accouterments
装都市 *busō toshi* fortified city
装船 *busōsen* armed ship
装解除 *busō kaijo* disarmament
装警官 *busō keikan* armed police
14 徳 *butoku* martial arts
15 勲 *bukun* deeds of arms
器 *buki* weapon, arms, ordnance
器倉 *bukigura* armory, arsenal
器庫 *bukiko* armory, ordnance department
器貸与 *bukitaiyo* lend-lease
22 鑑 *bukan* book of heraldry

5

歪 2960 / J4f44 / M16286 WAI. E. *hizu(mu)* warp, be crooked, get bent, be strained. *yuga(mu), iga(mu)* warp, swerve, deflect, be crooked, be distorted, be bent, incline, slant; be perverted, be cross-grained. *iga(meru), yuga(meru) vt* bend, curve, warp, distort. *ibitsu no* oval,

4 心 忄 ⺗ 戈 戸 手 扌 支 攴 攵 文 斗 斤 方 无 日 曰 月 木 欠 8【止】歹 殳 毋 比 毛 氏 气 水 氵 氺 火 灬 爪 ⺤ 父 爻 爿 丬 片 牙 牛 犬 犭

elliptical; distorted, crooked, irregular, warped. *iga(mi), yuga(mi)* strain, distortion, bend.

2 力 *wairyoku* stress

6 曲 *waikyoku* distortion, falsification, perversion

8

A **歯** 2961 / J3b75 / M16323 **齒** 7088 / J736f / M48583 SHI tooth; age. *ha* tooth, cog, dent.

2 入 *hai(re)* repairing clogs

4 止 *hado(me)* brake

切 *hagi(ri)* gnashing the teeth; cutting cogs. *hagi(re)* the feel when biting; manner of enunciation

切良 *hagi(re) (no) yo(i)* crisp, staccato

5 石 *shiseki* hard tooth tartar, calculus deposit

立 *ha (ga) ta(tanai)* hard to chew; unable to compete with

牙 *shiga* teeth; teeth and tusks

牙状 *shigajō* dentation

牙疾患 *shiga shikkan* dental disease

牙掛 *shiga (ni) ka(kenai)* no argument necessary

牙萠出 *shigahōshutsu* dentition, teething

牙矯正術 *shiga kyōseijutsu* orthodontia

6 肉 *haniku, shiniku* gums, tooth ridge

向 *hamu(kau)* strike at; bite back; turn on, rise against, oppose, defy

列 *shiretsu* row of teeth

列矯正 *shiretsu kyōsei* orthodontia

7 車 *haguruma* cogwheel, gear

応 *hagota(e)* hard to chew; tough; crisp

状 *shijō* dentation; tooth shape

形 *hagata* tooth mark, impression of the teeth

医者 *haisha* dentist

8 固 *hagata(me)* tooth-hardening meal; New Year's feast

軋 *hagishi(ri)* involuntary nocturnal tooth grinding

並 *hanara(bi), hana(mi)* row of teeth; set of teeth; dentition

芽 *shiga* tooth germ

茎 *haguki* gum, tooth ridge

9 面 *shimen* surface of a tooth

音 *shion* dental (consonant)

食 *ha (o) ku(i-shibaru)* bear up in tragedy; stand pain well; hold one's temper

垢 *shikō* tooth tartar

冠 *shikan* crown of a tooth

軌条 *shikijō* cograil

神経 *shishinkei* dental nerve

科 *shika* dentistry

科大学 *shika daigaku* dental college

科医 *shikai* dentist

科医学 *shikaigaku* dentistry

科医院 *shikaiin* dentist's office

科医師 *shikaishi* dentist

科医術 *shikaijutsu* dentistry

科病院 *shika byōin* dental hospital

10 根 *shikon, ha(no)ne* root of a tooth; fang

浮 *ha (ga) u(ku)* teeth get loose; to tire of someone's bragging

11 黒 *(o)haguro* tooth blackening

痒 *hagayu(i)* impatient, tantalized, chagrined, vexed

脱 *hanu(ke)* falling out of teeth; a person with missing teeth. *hanu(ke) no* toothless

12 痛 *haita, shitsū* toothache

15 質 *shishitsu* quality of teeth

槽 *shisō* tooth socket, alveolar bone

槽膿漏 *shisō nōrō* pyorrhea

16 磨 *hamiga(ki)* toothpaste; dentifrice

磨粉 *hamigakiko* tooth powder

磨揚子 *hamigakiyōji* toothbrush

18 噛 *haga(mi)* gnashing of teeth

髄 *shizui* pulp of a tooth, the nerve

21 齦 *shigin* the gums

齦炎 *shigin'en* gingivitis

9

B **歳** 2962 / J3a50 / M16326' **歲** 2963 / J-X / M16326 SEI, SAI year, age; time; occasion; opportunity; limit; vicinity. *toshi* age. *-sai* years old, age, year.

2 入 *sainyū* annual revenue

4 月 *saigetsu* time

5 市 *toshi (no) ichi* year-end market

旦 *saitan* the New Year

出 *saishutsu* annual expenditures

末 *saimatsu* year-end

6 次 *saiji* year

7 余 *saiyo* over a year

8 事 *saiji* the year's events

9 首 *saishu* beginning of the year

10 時記 *saijiki* almanac

12 晩 *saiban* year end
費 *saihi* annual expenditure
13 歳 *saisai* yearly, every year
14 暮 *seibo* year-end; year-end present
徳神 *toshitokujin* goddess of lucky directions
19 瀬 *toshi (no) se* New Year's Eve

10

A 歴 2964 / J4e72 / M16334' 歷 2965 / J-X / M16340 REKI history; continuation; passing (of time). *rekki to shita* clear, plain, unmistakable.

5 代 *rekidai* successive generations, successive emperors
代史 *rekidaishi* chronicles, annals
史 *rekishi* history
史上 *rekishijō* historically
史小説 *rekishi shōsetsu* historical novel
史地図 *rekishi chizu* historical map; atlas
史地理 *rekishi chiri* historical geography
史的 *rekishiteki* historic, historical, traditional
史画 *rekishiga* historical picture
史学 *rekishigaku* history
史学派 *rekishigakuha* historical school
史家 *rekishika* historian
史哲学 *rekishi tetsugaku* historical philosophy
史劇 *rekishigeki* historical drama
史観 *rekishikan* historical viewpoint
6 伝 *rekiden* tradition
任 *rekinin suru* successively fill several posts
年 *rekinen* year after year
年齢 *rekinenrei* chronological age
11 遊 *rekiyū suru* tour, itinerate
訪 *rekiho* round of calls; tour of visitation
12 然 *rekizen(taru)* plain, distinct, clear
13 戦 *rekisen* long military service
14 歴 *rekireki* notables, dignitaries; illustrious families. *rekireki(taru)* clear
16 覧 *rekiran* looking around

12

歷 2965 / J-X / M16340 See 歴 2964.

14

歸 2966 / J5d15 / M16349 See 帰 1564.

RAD. 歹 78

Ichi-ta (*ichi* "one" plus the katakana *ta*) or *gatsu* dried bones. At left: *ichi-ta hen* or *gatsu hen*. As enclosure: 歹 *shinigamae* (enclosure like that of *shinu* "die") or *ichi-ta*. Nickname: Death.

歹 2967 / J5d46 / M16359 GATSU. GACHI. TAI bare bones; bad, wrong.

2

A 死 2968 / J3b60 / M16365 SHI death. *shi(nu), shi(suru)* die. *shi(nareru)* be bereaved, have (someone) die.

2 人 *shinin, shibito, shi(ni)bito* dead person, the killed
力 *shiryoku* desperate effort
3 亡 *shibō* death
亡広告 *shibō kōkoku* obituary notice
亡届 *shibō todoke* report of death
亡表 *shibōhyō* mortality tables
亡者 *shibōsha* the deceased; persons killed, deaths
亡者欄 *shibōsharan* obituary column
亡率 *shibōritsu* mortality, death rate
亡診断書 *shibō shindansho* death certificate
亡数 *shibōsū* number of deaths
亡欄 *shibōran* obituary column
4 文 *shibun* a document no longer of any value
方 *shi(ni)kata* manner of death; way to commit suicide
水 *shi(ni)mizu* water given to the dying
中 *shichū* fatal situation
切 *shi(ni)-ki(ru)* die

分 *shi(ni)-waka(reru)* be separated by death
火山 *shikazan* extinct volcano
支度 *shi(ni)jitaku* preparation for death
5 生 *shishō, shisei* life and death
目 *shi(ni)me* the moment of death
囚 *shishū* condemned criminal
処 *shi(ni)dokoro, shisho* place to die; place of death
去 *shikyo* death
出 *shide* dying and proceeding to the next world
出山 *shide (no) yama* the next world
出旅 *shide (no) tabi* journey to the next world
6 肉 *shiniku* dead flesh, carrion
色 *shishoku* pallor of death
灰 *shikai* cinders, ashes; lack of liveliness. *shi(no)kai* ashes of a nuclear bomb
地 *shichi* jaws of death, fatal situation; battlefield
守 *shishu* stubborn defense
行進 *shi (no) kōshin* death march
因 *shiin* cause of death
因統計 *shiin tōkei* statistics on death; causes of death
刑 *shikei* capital punishment
刑囚 *shikeishū* criminals condemned to death
刑執行 *shikei shikkō* execution of a criminal
刑場 *shikeijō* place of execution
刑罪 *shikeizai* capital offense
7 角 *shikaku* dead space (in firing)
決 *shi (o) kes(suru)* resign to die
没 *shibotsu* death
別 *shibetsu* bereavement
花 *shi(ni)bana* a glorious death
児 *shiji* dead child; stillborn child
体 *shitai* corpse, remains
体検案 *shitai ken'an* autopsy
体解剖 *shitai kaibō* autopsy
体置場 *shitai o(ki)ba* morgue
体遺棄罪 *shitai ikizai* crime of abandoning a corpse
8 金 *shi(ni)gane* wasted money; idle capital; money saved for death
所 *shisho, shi(ni)dokoro* place of death; place to die
歿 *shibotsu* death
法 *shihō* a dead law
命 *shimei* life and death; fate
苦 *shiku* death pangs, agony of death
果 *shi(ni)-ha(teru)* die (out), become extinct
学問 *shi(ni)gakumon* unprofitable knowledge
物 *shibutsu* dead thing, inanimate object
物狂 *shi(ni)monoguru(i)* death struggle; desperation, frantic efforts
者 *shisha* dead person
者達 *shishatachi* the dead
9 面 *shimen* death mask
屍 *shishi* corpse
相 *shisō* shadow of death
神 *shi(ni)gami* god of death; death
胎 *shitai* dead fetus
重 *shi(ni)-kasa(naru)* die in swift succession. *shijū* dead weight
変 *shi(ni)-ka(waru)* be reborn in another existence
軍 *shi(ni)ikusa* a fight to the death; soldiers who so fight
後 *shi(ni)-oku(reru)* outlive, survive. *shigo* after death, posthumously
後硬直 *shigo kōchoku* rigor mortis
海 *Shikai* Dead Sea
海写本 *Shikai Shahon* Dead Sea Scrolls
活 *shikatsu* life and death
活問題 *shikatsu mondai* a matter of life and death
10 馬 *shiba* dead horse
病 *shibyō* fatal disease
時 *shi(ni)doki* the time to die; the time of death
恥 *shi(ni)haji* shameful death
脈 *shimyaku* fatal pulse; exhausted ore vein
致 *shi (o) itasu* die
11 掛 *shi(ni)-ka(karu), shi(ni)-ka(keru)* be dying
球 *shikyū* dead ball (in baseball)
許 *shi(nu)bakari* about to die
産 *shizan, shisan* stillbirth
産児 *shisanji* stillborn baby
12 絶 *shi(ni)-ta(eru)* die out, become extinct. *shizetsu* extinction, destruction
期 *shiki, shigo* time of death, the last hour
装束 *shi(ni)shōzoku* burial clothes

覚悟 *shi(no)kakugo* readiness to die
場 *shi(ni)ba* place of death; place to die
場所 *shi(ni)basho* place of death; place to die
13 損 *shi(ni)-sokona(u)* fail in suicide attempt; outlive one's time
滅 *shimetsu* extinction, destruction
際 *shi(ni)giwa* dying hour
戦 *shisen* death struggle
罪 *shizai* capital punishment
傷 *shishō* casualties, killed and wounded
傷者 *shishōsha* casualties, killed and wounded
14 様 *shi(ni)zama* manner of death
語 *shigo* dead language; obsolete word
蔵 *shizō* hoarding
15 線 *shisen* the death line; dead wire (in electricity); crisis; the brink of death
賜 *shi (o) tama(u)* permit one to commit *harakiri*
霊 *shiryō* departed spirits
16 骸 *shigai* corpse, remains
18 闘 *shitō* life-and-death struggle
顔 *shi(ni)gao* the face of a dead person
20 懸 *shi(ni)-ka(karu)* to be dying.
shi(ni)kake on the verge of death

4

殁 2969 / J5d47 / M16385 See **没** 3066.

殀 2970 / J5d48 / M16390 Yō death at a young age.

5

殄 2971 / J5d49 / M16413 Ten *ta(eru)* cease; cease to exist, die out.

殆 2972 / J4b58 / M16430 Tai. Dai. *hoton(do), hotohoto* almost, quite, really.

殃 2973 / J5d4a / M16410 Ō. *wazawai* calamity, misfortune, woe, evil, curse.
7 災 *ōsai* calamity
13 禍 *ōka* calamity

6

B **殉** 2974 / J3d5e / M16448 Jun. *jun(jiru), jun(zuru)* die a martyr, follow (someone) by committing suicide; follow in resigning.
6 死 *junshi suru* die a martyr, follow (someone) by committing suicide; follow in resigning
8 国 *junkoku* dying for one's country
11 教 *junkyō* martyrdom
教者 *junkyosha* martyr
18 職 *junshoku* dying at one's post
難 *junnan* martyrdom
難者 *junnansha* martyr, victim

B **殊** 2975 / J3c6c / M16451 Shu. *koto ni* especially, exceptionally, above all.
5 外 *koto (no) hoka* exceedingly, unusually; unexpectedly
功 *shukō* meritorious deeds
7 更 *kotosara ni* especially, intentionally
9 珍 *shuchin* something very strange
10 恩 *shuon* a special kindness
11 遇 *shugū* cordial treatment, special favor
12 勝 *shushō na* laudable, admirable, commendable
15 勲 *shukun* meritorious deeds
勲賞 *shukunshō* the outstanding performance award (in sumo)
19 寵 *shuchō* special favor

A **残** 2976 / J3b44 / M16459 **殘** 2978 / J5d4c / M16506 Zan remainder; balance. *noko(ru)* remain, be left over; stay, linger; survive. *noko(su)* leave behind; keep back; leave undone; reserve; save, amass; bequeath. *sokona(u)* harm, hurt, injure, damage, mar; lose, oppress. *noko(razu)* all, entirely, without exception. *noko(ri)* remainder, remnant, residue.
3 亡 *zambō* defeat and flight
4 日 *zanjitsu* the setting sun; the remaining days
月 *zangetsu* waning moon, morning moon
火 *zanka* embers, remaining fire
片 *zampen* remaining piece
5 生 *zansei* one's remaining years
冬 *zantō* the remaining days of winter
本 *zampon* books in stock, books unsold

6 灯 *zantō* the lights still burning
光 *zankō* afterglow
多 *noko(ri)ō(i)* regrettable; reluctant to part
年 *zannen* one's remaining years
存 *zanzon suru, zanson suru* survive, remain
存物 *zanzombutsu* things remaining
存者 *zansonsha* survivor, holdover
7 兵 *zampei* remnant troops, survivors
花 *zanka* the remaining flowers
忍 *zannin* cruelty, atrocity, brutality
忍性 *zanninsei* brutal nature, bloodthirstiness
余 *zan'yo* remainder, residue, remnant, balance
余財産 *zan'yo zaisan* remaining assets
余額 *zan'yogaku* balance
8 金 *zankin* balance, surplus
物 *zambutsu, noko(ri)mono* remnants; scraps, leftovers, remains
刻 *zankoku* cruelty, atrocity, brutality
夜 *zan'ya* daybreak
肴 *zankō* the fish left over from a meal
念 *zannen* regret, disappointment, chagrin
念乍 *zannennaga(ra)* although regrettable
念賞 *zannenshō* consolation prize
9 香 *zankō* lingering scent
虐 *zangyaku* cruelty, atrocity, brutality
秋 *zanshū* the last days of autumn
紅 *zankō* the scattered flowers remaining
星 *zansei* the morning star
春 *zanshun* the last days of spring
品 *zampin* remnant sale
品整理 *zampin seiri* clearance sale
10 高 *zandaka, noko(ri)daka* balance, remainder
涙 *zanrui* traces of tears
殺 *zansatsu* slaughter, massacre, murder
部 *zambu* remainder, remnant
夏 *zanka* the last days of summer
党 *zantō* remnants of a defeated party
留 *zanryū suru* remain behind
11 惜 *noko(ri)o(shii)* regrettable; reluctant to part
陽 *zan'yō* the setting sun
隈 *noko(ru)-kuma(naku)* throughout; thoroughly; everywhere
菊 *zangiku* chrysanthemums blooming on to early winter
雪 *zansetsu* lingering snow
盗 *zantō* bandits still at large
務 *zammu* unfinished business
務整理 *zammu seiri* winding up business
12 渣 *zansa* residue, dregs, leavings
飯 *zampan* left-over rice; leavings from a meal
殽 *zankō* the fish left over from a meal
期 *zanki* unexpired period
寒 *zankan* cold spell in spring
暑 *zansho* lingering summer heat
塁 *zanrui* runners left on bases; remaining forts
13 滓 *zanshi* residue, dregs, leavings
煙 *zan'en* lingering smoke
賊 *zanzoku* inflicting damage; one who does so; bandits still at large
夢 *zammu* a lingering dream
照 *zanshō* afterglow
業 *zangyō* overtime
業手当 *zangyō teate* overtime pay
14 像 *zanzō* afterimage
酷 *zankoku* cruelty, atrocity, brutality
15 編 *zampen* the books still in existence; the books on the shelves
影 *zan'ei* traces, relics
敵 *zanteki* enemy stragglers
熱 *zannetsu* lingering summer heat
16 骸 *zangai* corpse, carcass; ruins, debris, wreck, remains of
18 額 *zangaku* balance (of an account)
類 *zanrui* those who remain; those not killed
簡 *zankan* fragmentary copy of a book

7

殍 2977 / J5d4b / M16464 HYŌ. FU *uejini* death by starvation.

8

殘 2978 / J5d4c / M16506 See 残 2976.

殕 2979 / J5d4d / M16498 BOKU. FU collapse; spoil, grow moldy; tear. *tao(reru)* fall down, collapse.

殛 2980 / J-X / M16517 KYOKU punish.

6 刑 *kyokkei* capital punishment; extreme penalty

B **殖** 2981 / J3f23 / M16502 SHOKU increasing. *fu(eru)* increase, multiply, accrue; (water) rises. *fu(yasu)* increase, add to, raise, multiply, augment.

5 広 *fu(e)-hiro(garu)* increase and spread abroad, multiply

民 *shokumin* colonization, settlement; colonist, settler

10 高 *fuedaka* increase, increment

財 *shokuzai* saving money; money-making; increasing one's wealth

11 産 *shokusan* increase in production; industry; production

14 増 *fu(e) ma(su)* multiply

10

殞 2982 / J5d4e / M16535 IN. *o(chiru)* fall, drop down. *shi(nu)* die.

11

殤 2983 / J5d4f / M16557 SHŌ death at an early age (under 12 years old).

12

殪 2984 / J5d50 / M16578 EI. *tao(su)* topple, fell, kill. *tao(reru)* fall down, collapse; die.

殫 2985 / J5d51 / M16581 TAN. *tsu(kiru)* run out, expire, be used up. *tsu(kasu)* use up, exhaust.

14

殯 2986 / J5d52 / M16596 HIN lying in state, unburied coffin.

10 宮 *hinkyū* temporary imperial mortuary

15

殱 2987 / J5d54 / M-X See 殲 2988.

17

殲 2988 / J5d53 / M16608 **殱** 2987 / J5d54 / M-X SEN massacre.

13 滅 *semmetsu* annihilation

RAD. 殳 79

Ru-mata (the katakana *ru* plus *mata* "again").

Nickname: Windy Again (cf. Rads. 16 and 29).

殳 2989 / J5d55 / M16613 SHU. JU pike.

13 傷 *ōshō* striking and injuring; a bruise

4

B **殴** 2990 / J3225 / M16618' **毆** 3002 / J5d58 / M16674 Ō. *nagu(ru)* hit, beat, thrash.

4 込 *nagu(ri)-ko(mu)* attack, assault, break into

5 付 *nagu(ri)-tsu(keru)* strike, beat, thrash

打 *ōda* blow, assault (and battery)

6 返 *nagu(ri)-kae(su)* strike back

合 *nagu(ri)-a(u)* fight, exchange blows

9 飛 *nagu(ri)-to(basu)* knock over, strike (someone) hard

10 倒 *nagu(ri)-tao(su)* knock down

殺 *nagu(ri)-koro(su), ōsatsu suru* strike dead, beat to death

5

A **段** 2991 / J434a / M16619 DAN steps, stair, flight of stairs; column; paragraph; act, scene; case, question; grade, class, rank, level; degree, extent. TAN a measure of land. *kiza* scratches, mutilation (of furniture).

5 平 *dambira* broadsword, sword

丘 *dankyū* terrace, bench

7 別 *tambetsu* acreage, land area

8 物 *dammono* many-act musical drama. *tammono* cloth; textiles, drapery; dry goods, piece goods

取 *dando(ri)* program, plan, arrangements

歩 *tambu* one-tenth hectare
9 通 *dantsū* rug, carpet
畑 *dambata* terraced farm
段 *dandan* steps, staircase, terrace; gradually, increasingly, one after another. *gizagiza* notches, indentation; ruggedness; fringes
段畑 *dandambatake* terraced fields
11 階 *dankai* grade, rank, step, phase, stage. *kizahashi* steps; arrangements
袋 *dambukuro* large sack; baggy trousers
梯子 *dambashigo* staircase
12 落 *danraku* period, stop, section, end of a paragraph; conclusion, settlement
違 *danchiga(i)* different class, different level
14 鼻 *dambana* aquiline nose

6

㱾 2992 / J-X / M16625 KAI laughing voice.

殷 2993 / J5d56 / M16627 IN flourishing.
10 殷 *in'in(taru)* roaring, booming, bellowing, pealing, reverberating
11 盛 *insei* prosperity
12 富 *impu* wealth, prosperity
14 賑 *inshin* prosperity

A **殺** 2994 / J3b26 / M16629 **殺** 2995 / J-X / M16638 SATSU. SAI. SETSU. *koro(su)* kill, murder, butcher; waste (money); suppress (anger); hold (breath); put out, strike out. *so(gu) vt* chip, slice off, cut aslant, split off; diminish, reduce; dampen, spoil, mar. *so(geru) vi* split, splinter; be sunken; be sharpened; miss the mark.
2 人 *satsujin* murder, homicide, manslaughter
人犯 *satsujinhan* the crime of murder
人光 *satsujinkō* death ray
人光線 *satsujin kōsen* death ray
人的 *satsujinteki* murderous; deadly (heat); hectic (situation); cutthroat (competition)
人鬼 *satsujinki* cutthroat, bloodthirsty felon
人罪 *satsujinzai* murder, competition
4 文句 *koro(shi) monku* a "killing" expression; cooing words
5 生 *sesshō suru* destroy life, kill animals. *sesshō na* cruel
生戒 *sesshōkai* Buddhist precept against killing
生禁断 *sesshō kindan* hunting and fishing prohibited
6 竹 *so(gi)take* sharp bamboo sticks
伐 *satsubatsu na* bloodthirsty, brutal, savage, warlike, fierce
合 *koro(shi)-a(u)* kill one another
虫剤 *satchūzai* insecticide
気 *sakki* bloodthirstiness; fury; wild excitement
気立 *sakkida(tsu)* get excited; be bloodthirsty
8 到 *sattō suru* rush in, pour in, throng to; descend on, storm, swoop down on
9 屋 *koro(shi)ya* a hired assassin
風景 *sappūkei* inelegance, vulgarity, lack of taste; dreariness
10 害 *satsugai, setsugai* murder, killing, manslaughter, assassination
害人 *satsugaijin* murderer, slayer
害者 *satsugaisha* murderer, slayer
11 掠 *satsuryaku* killing and robbing
略 *satsuryaku* killing and robbing
菌 *sakkin* sterilization, disinfection, pasteurization
菌力 *sakkinryoku* germicidal effect
菌剤 *sakkinzai* germicide, disinfectant
13 傷 *sasshō* bloodshed; casualties
意 *satsui* murderous intent
鼠剤 *sassozai* rat poison
15 戮 *satsuriku* massacre, slaughter

7

殺 2995 / J-X / M16638 See **殺** 2994.

B **殻** 2996 / J334c / M-X **殼** 2997 / J5d57 / M16646 KAKU. *kara* husk, hull, nutshell; cast-off skin; tofu refuse; corpse; earth's crust.
7 麦 *karamugi* unhulled wheat or barley
9 竿 *karazao, karasao* flail

— 8 —

殼 2997 / J5d57 / M16646 See 殻 2996.

殽 2998 / J-X / M16647 Kō mix.

𣪘 2999 / J-X / M16645 Kyū surrender.

— 9 —

毀 3000 / J544c / M16654 Ki. *kobo(tsu)* break, destroy, demolish. *kobo(reru)* be nicked, be broken, go to pieces. *kowa(su)* break, smash, destroy; take to pieces; frustrate. *kowa(reru)* break, be broken, be wrecked, be ruined, go to pieces, be damaged, be destroyed; break down; miscarry, be broken off. *kowa(re)* breakage, wreckage, fragment.

[8] 物 *kowa(re)mono* fragile article
[11] 敗 *kihai suru* destroy
[13] 傷 *kishō* injury, damage
損 *kison* injury, damage
棄 *kiki* damage, destruction
誉 *kiyo* praise and censure, criticism
誉褒貶 *kiyo-hōhen* praise and censure, criticism

B 殿 3001 / J4542 / M16651 Ten. Den hall, mansion, palace, temple, rear guard. *dono* mister. *shingari* rear. *tono* lord; mansion, place. *-dono* Mr.

[3] 下 *Denka* Highness
上 *tenjō, denjō* the court; palace circles; palace floor
上人 *tenjōbito, denjōbito* courtier, court official
上間 *tenjō(no)ma* palace floor
[4] 方 *tonogata* men, gentlemen
中 *denchū* in the palace
[6] 宇 *den'u* a shrine building
[8] 舎 *densha* a palace
[10] 原 *tonobara* the nobility; (polite for) man
[11] 達 *tonotachi* the nobility; (polite for) visitors
堂 *dendō* palatial building
[12] 御 *tonogo* gentlemen
[14] 閣 *denkaku* palace
様 *tonosama* feudal lord
様仕事 *tonosama shigoto* dilettante work, amateur work (in art)
様芸 *tonosamagei* dilettantism; amateurism (in art)
様育 *tonosamasoda(chi)* brought up in luxury
様風 *tonosamafū* lordly air
様蛙 *tonosamagaeru* bullfrog

— 11 —

毆 3002 / J5d58 / M16674 See 殴 2990.

毅 3003 / J3523 / M16673 Ki strong.

[12] 然 *kizen(taru)* dauntless, firm, resolute

RAD. 毋 80

Haha mother, *kan no haha* (like the top element of *kan*, a unit of weight), or *nakare* not. Variant: 母 (5 strokes) *haha*. Nickname: Mother.

毋 3004 / J5d59 / M16721 Bu. Mu *naka(re)* be not; do not; must not.

A 母 3005 / J4a6c / M16723 Bo. *haha* mother; cause; motive. *(o)kā(san)* mother, mama.

[3] 上 *hahaue* my dear mother
子 *boshi, hahako* mother and child. *boshi* principal and interest
子家庭 *boshi katei* fatherless home
子寮 *boshiryō* mother's home; home for mothers and children
[4] 方 *hahakata* the mother's side (of the family)
日 *Haha (no) Hi* Mother's Day (the second Sunday of May)
[6] 后 *bokō* empress dowager
[7] 体 *botai* mother's body; parent organization
系 *bokei* maternal line

系制度 *bokei seido* matriarchal system
系家族 *bokei kazoku* matriarchal family
8 乳 *bonyū* mother's milk
国 *bokoku* mother country
国語 *bokokugo* mother tongue
性 *bosei* motherhood
性愛 *boseiai* a mother's love
9 音 *boin, boon* vowel
屋 *omoya, moya* main building (of a noble's home)
指 *boshi* thumb
胎 *botai* mother's womb
型 *bokei* matrix (in printing)
10 校 *bokō* one's alma mater
殺 *hahakoro(shi), hahagoro(shi)* matricide
11 鳥 *hahadori* mother bird
船 *bosen* mother ship
堂 *bodō* your mother
教会 *bokyōkai* mother church
12 港 *bokō* home port
斑 *bohan* pigmentation
違 *hahachiga(i)* stepbrother, stepsister
御 *hahago* (polite for) mother
御前 *hahagozen* (polite for) mother
14 様 *kāsama, kāsan* mother, mama
語 *bogo* mother tongue
15 権 *boken* maternal authority
権制度 *boken seido* matriarchal system
16 親 *hahaoya* mother
親似 *hahaoyani* taking after one's mother
20 艦 *bokan* mother ship, tender, carrier

2

A **每** 3006 / J4b68 / M16724' MAI. *-goto ni* each, every, at an interval of, whenever. *mai-* every, each, apiece.

3 夕 *maiyū* every evening
4 日 *mainichi* every day, daily
月 *maitsuki, maigetsu* monthly, every month
5 号 *maigō* each issue
6 回 *maikai* every time
次 *maiji* every time
年 *maitoshi, mainen* every year, annually
每 *maimai* each time; frequently; always
8 夜 *maiyo* every evening, every night
9 度 *maido* each time, frequently; always
10 週 *maishū* every week, weekly
時 *maiji* every hour, per hour
12 晚 *maiban* every evening, every night
朝 *maiasa, maichō* every morning
期 *maiki* every term, every quarter

4

A **毒** 3007 / J4647 / M16730 **毒** 3008 / J-X / M-X DOKU poison; virus, venom, germ, toxin; harm, injury; malice, spite. *doku(suru)* poison, harm, corrupt, spoil. *doku(zuku)* curse, revile, abuse.

2 人参 *dokuninjin* poison hemlock
3 口 *dokuguchi* abuse, foul tongue
刃 *dokujin* assassin's dagger
4 心 *dokushin* malice, spite
手 *dokushu* the clutches (of a usurer, a villain, etc.)
中 *dokuata(ri)* poisoning
5 牙 *dokuga* poison fang
矢 *dokuya* poisoned arrow
汁 *dokujū* poisonous juices
6 舌 *dokuzetsu* wicked tongue; abusive language
虫 *dokumushi, dokuchū* poisonous insect
気 *dokuke, dokki, dokke* noxious air, poisonous air, virulence, poisonous breath; malice, spite
気抜 *dokki (o) nu(ku)* startle someone
7 言 *dokugen* abusive language
麦 *dokumugi* darnel, tares
見 *dokumi* tasting for poison
見役 *dokumiyaku* taster for poison
8 性 *dokusei* virulence, poisonous character
物 *dokubutsu* poisonous substance, toxicant
念 *dokunen* intention to hurt others
炎 *dokuen* poisonous flame
突 *dokuzu(ku)* gossip, spread rumors
毒 *dokudoku(shii)* poisonous; venomous, malicious, acrimonious; heavy, gross, disagreeable
味 *dokumi* tasting for poison
味役 *dokumiyaku* taster for poison
9 除 *dokuyoke* protection against poisoning
草 *dokusō* poisonous plant
10 消 *dokuke(shi)* antidote
酒 *dokushu* poisoned saké
殺 *dokusatsu* poisoning
害 *dokugai* poisoning
素 *dokuso* toxin, ptomaine, poison

11 婦 *dokufu* wicked woman, vampire
液 *dokueki* poisonous liquid
蛇 *dokuja, dokuhebi* venomous serpent
断 *dokuda(chi)* abstaining from certain foods
悪 *dokuaku* great wickedness
焔 *dokuen* poisonous flame
12 筆 *dokuhitsu* stinging pen
13 腺 *dokusen* poison gland
蛾 *dokuga* poisonous moth
14 説 *dokusetsu* wicked tongue; abusive language
蜥蜴 *dokutokage* venomous lizard
15 質 *dokushitsu* poisonous element, poisonous nature
16 薬 *dokuyaku* poison, poisonous drug

— 9 —

毓 3009/J5d5a/M16740 See 育 4773.

RAD. 比 81

Kuraberu to compare. Nickname: Comparing.

A 比 3010/J4866/M16743 Hɪ ratio; comparison; an equal, a match. *hi(suru)* compare. *kura(beru)* compare, balance, contrast. *tagu(eru)* compare with. *kura(bekko)* race. *tagui* kind, sort, class. *koro* time; about, toward. *-Hi-* Philippines. *-kura(be)* contest, trial (of strength).
4 比 *hihi* all, one and all
5 目魚 *hirame* flounder, flatfish, halibut
丘 *biku* Buddhist priest
丘尼 *bikuni* Buddhist nun
6 年 *hinen* every year, year by year
色計 *hishokukei* colorimeter
8 肩 *hiken suru* rank with
価 *hika* parity
況 *hikyo* comparison
物 *kura(be)mono* comparison, match
例 *hirei* proportion; ratio
例代表 *hirei daihyō* proportional representation
例代表制 *hirei daihyōsei* proportional representation
例配分 *hirei haibun* proportional allotment
9 重 *hijū* specific gravity; density; priority, relative importance
10 倫 *hirin* a peer, an equal
島 *Hitō* Philippines
11 率 *hiritsu* ratio; percentage
12 喩 *hiyu* simile, metaphor; allegory, parable, fable
喩的 *hiyuteki* figurative, allegorical
13 適 *hiteki suru* compare with, match, rival, be equal to
較 *hikaku* comparison; comparative (anatomy)
較史 *hikakushi* comparative history
較言語学 *hikaku gengogaku* comparative linguistics
較的 *hikakuteki* relative, comparative
較宗教学 *hikaku shūkyōgaku* comparative religions
較級 *hikakukyū* comparative degree
15 隣 *hirin* vicinity
論 *hiron* analogy; comparative study
敵 *hiteki suru* compare with, match, rival, be equal to
熱 *hinetsu* specific heat
17 翼 *hiyoku* wings abreast; congenial couple; single garment made to look double
翼塚 *hiyokuzuka* lover's double grave
18 類 *hirui* a parallel, an equal
類無 *hiruina(i)* unparalleled, incomparable

— 5 —

毘 3011/J487b/M16753 毗 3012/J-X/M16752 Hɪ help, assist.
7 沙門 *Bishamon* a God of Wealth

RAD. 毛 82

Ke hair (of animals). Nickname: Fur.

A **毛** 3013 / J4c53 / M16772 Mō hair, tenth of a *rin*. *ke* hair, fur, feather, down. *ke(darake)* hairy.

4 孔 *keana* pores
切 *kegi(re)* abrasion from wearing wool
5 穴 *keana* pores
叩 *kebataki* feather duster
布 *mōfu* blanket, steamer rug
生液 *mōseieki* hair grower
生薬 *kehaegusuri* hair restorer
皮 *kegawa, mōhi* fur, skin, pelt
皮商 *kegawashō* furrier
皮製品 *kegawa seihin* fur products
6 糸 *keito* wool yarn, worsted
羽 *keba* nap, fuzz, pile
色 *keiro* color of the hair; disposition
虫 *kemushi* caterpillar
衣 *kegoromo* fur coat
7 抜 *kenu(ki)* hair tweezers
更 *kegawari* shedding, molting
8 並 *kena(mi)* the lie of the hair; color of the hair; disposition; lineage
9 染 *kezo(me)* dyeing the hair
染薬 *kezo(me)gusuri* hair dye
10 根 *mōkon* hair root
莨 *kimpōge* buttercup
留 *kedo(me)* the nut of a violin bow
唐 *ketō* foreigner
唐人 *ketōjin* foreigner
11 彫 *kebo(ri)* engraving lines
深 *kebuka(i)* hairy
脛 *kezune* hairy legs
細血管 *mōsai kekkan* capillaries
細管 *mōsaikan* capillaries
12 焼 *keya(ki)* singeing
程 *kehodo mo* (not) a bit
筋 *kesuji* a hair
筆 *mōhitsu* writing or painting brush
替 *kega(wari)* shedding, molting
無山 *kena(shi)yama* bald hill
13 嫌 *kegira(i)* antipathy, prejudice
鉤 *kebari* fishing fly
際 *kegiwa* the hairline
裏 *keura* fur lining
14 箒 *kebōki* feather brush
管 *mōkan* capillaries
髪 *mōhatsu* hair
製品 *mōseihin* woolen goods
15 編 *keami* knitting; knitted
16 頭 *mōtō* (not) at all
17 氈 *mōsen* rug, carpet
18 織 *keo(ri)* woolen goods
織物 *keorimono* woolen goods
22 嚢 *mōnō* hair follicle

4

毟 3014 / J5d5b / M16790 (国字) *mushi(ru)* pluck, pick, tear.

8 取 *mushi(ri)-to(ru)* tear off, pluck off

7

毫 3015 / J5d5d / M16831 Gō a fine hair; brush. *gō(mo)* (not) in the least, (not) at all.

5 末 *gōmatsu* a small quantity, a little; a few; something; a little while; a short distance; (not) in the least; (not) at all
18 釐 *gōri* very small quantity

毬 3016 / J5d5c / M16837 Kyū. *iga* burr. *mari* ball.

7 投 *marina(ge)* playing catch
8 果 *kyūka* tree cone
果植物 *kyūka shokubutsu* conifer
10 栗 *igaguri* chestnuts in burrs; close-cropped head
19 藻 *marimo* ball-shaped duckweed; an aegagropila

8

毯 3017 / J5d5f / M16858 Tan wool rug.

毳 3018 / J5d5e / M16872 Zei. *keba* nap, fuzz, pile. *mukuge* down, fluff.

5 立 *kebada(tsu)* be fluffy, be plushy

13

氈 3019 / J5d61 / M16982 Sen woolen cloth, rug.

RAD. 氏 83

Uji surname, clan. Nickname: Clan.

A **氏** 3020 / J3b61 / M17026 SHI Mr.; family, clan. *uji* clan; lineage, birth; surname.

2 人 *ujibito* clansman
3 子 *ujiko* shrine parishioner
6 寺 *ujidera* clan temple
名 *shimei, ujina* surname
名点呼 *shimei tenko* roll call
9 神 *ujigami* Shinto clan god, patron deity. *uji (no) kami* clan chieftain
11 族 *shizoku* family, clan
族制度 *shizoku seido* family system, clan system
19 譜 *shifu* genealogy

1

A **民** 3021 / J4c31 / M17028 MIN *tami* people, nation, subjects.

2 力 *minryoku* national manpower
4 心 *minshin* popular sentiment
5 生 *minsei* people's livelihood, people's welfare
生委員 *minsei iin* district welfare officer
主 *minshu* democracy
主化 *minshuka* democratization
主主義 *minshu shugi* democracy
主国 *minshukoku* democratic state
主的 *minshuteki* democratic
主政体 *minshu seitai* democratic form of government
主政治 *minshu seiji* democratic government
主党 *minshutō* democratic party
6 団 *mindan* a foreign-settlement corporation
有 *min'yū* private ownership
7 利 *minri* people's interests
兵 *mimpei* militia
芸 *mingei* folk craft, folk art
8 国 *Minkoku* The Republic of China
法 *mimpō* civil law, civil code
事 *minji* civil affairs; civil case
事上 *minjijō no* civil
事的 *minjiteki* civil
事事件 *minji jiken* civil case
事裁判 *minji saiban* civil trial
事訴訟 *minji soshō* civil suit
9 風 *mimpū* national customs
度 *mindo* cultural standard
草 *tamigusa* people, populace
俗 *minzoku* ethnic customs, folk customs
俗学 *minzokugaku* folklore
政 *minsei* civil government, democracy
政長官 *minsei chōkan* civil governor
10 家 *minka* private house
11 宿 *minshuku* a private house providing lodging and meals to transient guests
情 *minjō* condition of the people; the sentiment of the people
望 *mimbō* hopes of the people
族 *minzoku* race, people, ethnic group
族史 *minzokushi* history of a people
族主義 *minzoku shugi* nationalism
族芸術 *minzoku geijutsu* ethnic crafts
族的 *minzokuteki* racial, ethnic
族性 *minzokusei* racial trait, ethnic character
族学 *minzokugaku* ethnology
族学者 *minzokugakusha* ethnologist
族宗教 *minzoku shūkyō* ethnic religions
族移動 *minzoku idō* racial migration
族解放 *minzoku kaihō* ethnic liberation
族意識 *minzoku ishiki* national consciousness
族精神 *minzoku seishin* ethnic spirit, national spirit
12 営 *min'ei* private management
間 *minkan no* private, civilian, civil, popular, folk, unofficial
間人 *minkanjin* nongovernment person
間飛行 *minkan hikō* civil aviation
衆 *minshū* people, populace, masses
衆化 *minshūka* popularization
衆的 *minshūteki* democratic
衆駅 *minshū eki* a railway station built with government and popular support
13 話 *minwa* folklore
意 *min'i* popular will
業 *mingyō* private enterprise
数記 *Minsūki* the Book of Numbers (in the Bible)
14 選 *minsen* popular election
徳 *mintoku* national morality

4 心 忄 㣺 戈 戸 手 扌 支 攴 攵 文 斗 斤 方 无 日 曰 月 木 欠 止 歹 殳 毋 比 毛 4【氏】 气 水 氵 氺 火 灬 爪 爫 父 爻 爿 丬 片 牙 牛 犬 犭

需 *minju* civilian requirements
需品 *minjuhin* consumer goods
15 権 *minken* civil rights
論 *minron* public opinion
16 謡 *min'yō* popular song, ballad, folk song

4

氓 3022 J5d62 M17030 Bō people.

气 RAD. 84

Kigamae "vapor" enclosure. Nickname: Steam.

气 3023 J5d63 M17043 Ki air; gas; breath; spirit; steam.

1

気 3024 J-X M-X See 気 3025.

2

A 気 3025 J3524 M17046 氣 3028 J5d66 M17059 氛 3026 J-X M17052

気 3024 J-X M-X Ki, Ke spirit, mind, soul, heart; intention; bent, interest; mood, feeling; temper, disposition, nature; care, attention; air, atmosphere; flavor; odor; energy, essence; air, indications, symptoms; taste; touch, dash, shade, trace; spark, flash; suspicion. *ki (ni) suru* mind, care, take to heart, be nervous about. *ki (ni) naru* weigh on the mind, get on one's nerves; take a fancy to; feel inclined to. *ki (ga) suru* think, feel. *ki (ga) aru* have the intention (of doing something). *-ke, -ge* feeling; taste.

2 入 *ki (ni) i(ru)* be pleased with, be satisfactory. *ki(ni)i(ri)* favorite, pet
力 *kiryoku* energy, vigor, vitality, mettle, push
3 丈 *kijō na* stouthearted
丈夫 *kijōbu* reassurance
丈者 *kijōmono* stouthearted person
4 心 *kigokoro* temper, disposition
込 *kigo(mi)* ardor, enthusiasm, ambition
孔 *kikō* pore; (whale's) blowhole
引 *ki (o) hi(ku)* analyze a person's thinking
化 *kika* evaporation; vaporization
化器 *kikaki* carburetor
分 *kibun* feeling, mood, spirit
分転換 *kibun tenkan* mental diversion; change of environment
5 立 *ki (ga) ta(tsu)* get excited, be aroused. *kida(te)* disposition, temperament
弁 *kiben* air valve
失 *ki (o) ushina(u)* faint
付 *ki (ga) tsu(ku)* be aware of, notice, realize. *ki (o) tsu(keru)* take care of, be careful, be attentive to, take note of; be on the lookout. *kizu(ku)* notice, perceive, find out, think of, get wind of. *kitsu(ke)* encouragement; restorative, stimulant, smelling salts; reviving. *ki (o) tsu(ke)* Attention! *-kitsuke, -kizuke* in care of.
付薬 *kizukegusuri* a stimulant
圧 *kiatsu* atmospheric pressure. *keo(sareru)* be overpowered, be overawed
圧計 *kiatsukei* barometer
圧谷 *kiatsu (no) tani* trough
圧配置 *kiatsu haichi* the weather picture
6 色 *keshiki(bamu)* look hurt; get excited; get angry. *kishoku* mood, feeling; expression; countenance; feelings. *kewai, kehai* sign, indication. *keshiki* signs, indications; feelings; popularity; your will, your pleasure; reason; getting excited, getting angry
回 *ki (o) ma(wasu), ki (ga) mawa(ru)* give play to imagination; make a suspicious conjecture
団 *kidan* air mass
尽 *kizu(kushi)* earnest exertion
気 *ki (ga) ki (denai)* be always worrying
向 *ki (ga) mu(ku)* feel inclined
任 *kimaka(se) ni* one's pleasure, free will
休 *kiyasu(me) ni* for peace of mind
忙 *kizewa(shii)* restless, bustling, fidgety
扱 *kiatsuka(i)* solicitude, anxiety, worry
早 *kibaya na, ki (no) haya(i)* quick-tempered

多 *ki (ga) ō(i)* wavering, vacillating
宇 *kiu* magnanimity; feeling
宇快闊 *kiu-kaikatsu na* magnanimous
合 *kia(i)* feeling, temper, disposition; a puff of breath; yell. *ki (ga) a(u)* congenial
合入 *kia(i) (o) i(reru)* encourage
合負 *kia(i)ma(ke) suru* be outdone by another's will power
合術 *kia(i)jutsu* hypnotism
7 迫 *kihaku* soul; great energy, great mental power
抜 *ki (ga) nu(keru)* be discouraged. *ki (ga) nu(keta), ki (no) nu(keta)* insipid, stale. *kinu(ke)* absentmindedeness, dejection
折 *kio(re)* depression, dejection
沈 *ki (ga) shizu(mu)* be discouraged
状 *kijō na* gaseous
狂 *ki (ga) kuru(u)* go insane; lose one's head; run amuck, rave; be madly in love; go haywire. *kiguru(i)* out of one's senses, out of season (flowering)
利 *ki (ga) ki(ku)* have good judgment, be clever. *ki (o) ki(kasu)* use one's head, be sensible. *ki (no) ki(ita)* sensible, intelligent, clever, respectable, in good taste. *ki (no) ki(kanai)* dull, awkward, unrefined
位 *kigurai* feelings
位高 *kigurai (no) taka(i)* noble, proud, dignified
体 *kitai* gas, vapor, gaseous body
体力学 *kitai rikigaku* aerodynamics, aeromechanics
体化 *kitaika* vaporization
体動力学 *kitai dōrikigaku* aerodynamics
体爆薬 *kitai bakuyaku* fuel air explosive
8 長 *kinaga na* leisurely, patient
送 *kisō* pneumatic-tube dispatch
迷 *kimayo(i)* hesitation, uneasiness
性 *kishō* disposition, temperament
拙 *kimazu(i)* disagreeable, unpleasant
易 *kiyasu(ku)* freely, with a light heart
受 *kiu(ke)* popularity, favor, reception, reputation
苦労 *kigurō* worry, anxiety
所為 *ki (no) sei* fancy, imagination
泡 *kihō* air bubble
泡水準器 *kihō suijunki* spirit level
取 *kedo(ru)* suspect, sense. *kido(ru)* be affected, assume airs, pose as. *kido(ri)* affectation
取屋 *kido(ri)ya* affected person, dandy, dude
炎 *kien* flame; bombast, tall talk
炎万丈 *kienbanjō* high spirits
毒 *ki (no) doku* pitiable, miserable; regrettable; too bad
毒様 *(o)ki(no)dokusan, (o)ki (no) dokusama* That's too bad.
味 *kimi, kibi* feeling; touch, dash, shade, tinge; taste and savor; suspicion. *-kimi, -gimi* tendency
味好 *kimiyo(i)* good feeling
味合 *kimia(i)* touch, dash, shade, tinge; suspicion
味悪 *kimiwaru(i), kibiwaru(i)* uncanny, weird, lurid, gruesome, ominous, repulsive, eerie, creepy
9 音 *kion* aspirate
風 *kippu, kifū* character, disposition, temper; morale, spirit
食 *ki (ni) ku(wanu)* go against the grain, be unsatisfactory, be disagreeable, dislike
後 *kioku(re)* timidity
持 *kimochi* feeling, mood. *kimochi(yoku)* agreeably, cheerfully
相 *kissō* look, expression
海 *kikai* atmosphere
重 *kiomo(i)* heavyhearted, depressed
乗 *kino(ri) suru, ki (ga) no(ru)* be interested in
変 *kigawa(ri)* change of mind; fickleness
前 *kimae* temperament; generosity
品 *kihin* (moral) tone, dignity, grace, nobility, refinement
室 *kishitsu* air chamber
荒 *kiara na* hot-tempered
急 *kizewa(shii)* restless, bustling, fidgety
保養 *kihoyō* recreation, relaxation
負 *kio(u)* brace oneself; stir up one's fighting spirit
負立 *kio(i)-ta(tsu)* rouse against, nerve (for a struggle), brace up; be enthusiastic
10 高 *kedaka(i)* noble, exalted, graceful
疲 *kizuka(re)* mental fatigue, worry, boredom
病 *ki (ni) ya(mu)* worry about, be sensitive about. *kiya(mi), kibyō* blues, depression. *ki (no) ya(mai)* anxiety, illness; nervous breakdown

進 *ki (ga) susu(mu)* feel inclined
振 *kebu(ri)* air, appearance; behavior; bearing; indications
根 *kikon* aerial root; energy, perseverance
格 *kikaku* grace, dignity
流 *kiryū* air current
紛 *kimagure* caprice, whim, uneven temper
恥 *kihazu(kashii)* ashamed, bashful, shy, embarrassed
胸 *kikyō* pneumothorax
脈 *kimyaku* connection; collusion; communication
配 *kehai, kewai* sign, indication. *kikuba(ri)* vigilance; worry. *kihai* market trend
兼 *kiga(ne)* constraint, deference, scruple, hesitation
差 *ki (ga) sa(su)* be concerned
留 *ki (ni) to(meru)* give heed to, take notice of
弱 *kiyowa(i)* timid, fainthearted
骨 *kikotsu* spirit, soul, mettle, backbone. *kibone* mental effort
骨折 *kibone (ga) o(reru)* be ever worrying
随 *kizui* willfulness, selfishness, self-indulgence
随気儘 *kizui-kimama na* willful
息 *kisoku* breathing; breath
息奄奄 *kisoku-en'en* gasping for breath, dying
候 *kikō* climate; weather; season
候学 *kikōgaku* climatology
候風 *kikōfū* seasonal wind, monsoon
候順応 *kikō junnō* acclimatization
候療法 *kikō ryōhō* climatotherapy
11 運 *kiun* luck; tendency, opportunity
遅 *kioku(re) no* afraid
強 *kizuyo(i)* brave, resolute; reassuring; hardhearted. *kizuyo(ku)* resolutely, cheerfully, confidently
掛 *kiga(kari)* anxiety
済 *ki (ga) su(mu)* be satisfied, be appeased
移 *kiutsu(ri)* fickleness; sympathy
組 *kigu(mi)* attitude, ardor, preparation
細 *ki (ga) hoso(i)* cowardly
転 *kiten* tact; ready wit
悪 *ki (o) waru(ku) suru* hurt one's feelings
崩 *kikuzu(re)* slump, depression
動車 *kidōsha* diesel train
張 *kiba(ru)* exert oneself, make an effort; be extravagant, make a show. *kiba(ri)* exertion, effort. *ki (ga) ha(ru)* be under tension
張屋 *kiba(ri)ya* one who shows off
密 *kimitsu* airtight
密室 *kimitsushitsu* airtight chamber
球 *kikyū* balloon
球庫 *kikyūko* balloon hangar
球隊 *kikyūtai* balloon corps
12 圏 *kiken* atmosphere
遣 *kizuka(u)* be anxious about, worry about. *kizuka(i)* fear, worry, solicitude. *kizuka(washii)* anxious
遠 *ki (ga) tō(ku) naru* feel dizzy
揉 *ki (o) mo(mu)* worry, be anxious
晴 *kiba(rashi)* diversion, recreation, relaxation, amusement. *ki(o)harasu* clear one's mind
温 *kion* air temperature
短 *kimijika na; ki (ga) mijika(i)* hot-tempered, impatient, touchy
絶 *kizetsu* fainting
散 *kisan(ji)* relaxation, diversion, amusement, recreation
筒 *kitō* steam cylinder
落 *kio(chi)* discouragement, despondency. *ki (o) oto(su)* be discouraged
換 *ki (o) ka(eru)* change one's mind
焔 *kien* flame; bombast, tall talk
焔家 *kienka* big talker
軽 *kigaru na* cheerful; buoyant, lighthearted
軽者 *kigarumono* jolly fellow
無 *ki (no) na(i)* indifferent, lukewarm, uninterested
無性 *kibushō* laziness
無精 *kibushō* laziness
違 *kichiga(i)* insanity; mania, fanaticism; lunatic; fanatic, enthusiast, fan
違日和 *kichiga(i)biyori* unsettled weather
違水 *kichiga(i)mizu* alcoholic liquor
違花 *kichiga(i)bana* flower blooming out of season
違雨 *kichiga(i)ame* fitful rain
違染 *kichiga(i)ji(miru)* resemble a lunatic

違病院 *kichiga(i) byōin* mental hospital
象 *kishō* climate, weather, weather conditions; meteorology (of a place); disposition, temperament; characteristics
象庁 *Kishōchō* Weather Bureau
象台 *kishōdai* weather observatory
象学 *kishōgaku* meteorology
象注意報 *kishō chūihō* weather warning
象特報 *kishō tokuhō* storm warning
象衛星 *kisho eisei* meteorological satellite
象観測 *kishō kansoku* meteorological observations
象観測船 *kishō kansokusen* weather observation ship
象警報 *kishō keihō* weather warning
13 働 *kibatara(ki)* quick wit, tact; quick-witted person
褄 *kizuma* feelings
触 *kabu(reru)* have a skin eruption; be influenced by, become infected with (communism). *kabure* skin eruption, boils from poisonous plants; students influenced by socialism or communism
詰 *kizuma(ri)* constraint, embarrassment
障 *ki (ni) sawa(ru)* offend; get offended. *kiza* affectation. *kizawa(ri)* disagreeable feeling
稟 *kihin* hereditary traits
塞 *kifusa(gi)* gloom, depression
嵩 *kigasa* determination to win
節 *kisetsu* courage and integrity; weather
置 *ki (ga) o(kenai)* feel at home
勢 *kisei* energy, enthusiasm, spirit
楽 *kiraku* feeling at home, ease, comfort
14 構 *kigama(e)* anticipation, readiness
概 *kigai* spirit, pep, pluck; backbone; self-respect; courage
魂 *kikon* spirits of the dead
管 *kikan* windpipe, trachea
管支 *kikanshi* bronchial tube
管支炎 *kikanshien* bronchitis
管支肺炎 *kikanshi haien* bronchial pneumonia
管炎 *kikan'en* tracheitis
15 魄 *kihaku* soul; great energy, great mental power
鋭 *kiei* spirit, impetuosity, energy
慰 *kinagusa(mi)* diversion, recreation, relaxation, amusement
熱 *kinetsu* steam heat
質 *kishitsu* temperament, disposition. *katagi* spirit, character, trait
16 纏 *kimotsu(re)* confused feelings
儘 *kimama, ki(no)mama* willfulness, selfishness, self-indulgence
儘放題 *kimama-hōdai* behaving as one pleases
18 難 *kimuzuka(shii)* hard to please, moody
難屋 *kimuzuka(shi)ya* a person hard to please, moody person
19 韻 *kiin* refinement, taste, tone
20 懸 *ki (ni) ka(karu)* be anxious about. *ki (ni) ka(kenai)* take no notice of; take it easy. *kigaka(ri)* anxiety
22 嚢 *kinō* air sac, air bladder, gas bag
26 鬱 *kiutsu* gloom, melancholy

4

[illegible] 3026 / J-X / M17052 See 気 3025.

氛 3027 / J5d64 / M17048 FUN air; atmosphere; portent.
7 囲気 *fun'iki* atmosphere, ambience

6

氣 3028 / J5d66 / M17059 See 気 3025.

氤 3029 / J5d65 / M17060 IN spirited, full of spirit.

RAD. 水 85

Sui or *mizu* water. At left: 氵 (3 strokes) *sanzui* (3-stroke "water," as distinguished from Rad. 15). At bottom: 氺 (5 strokes) *shita mizu*. Nickname: Water.

A 水 3030 / J3f65 / M17083 SUI water; ice water; Wednesday. *mizu* water. *mizu(ppoi)* watery.

2 入 *mizu-i(razu) de* privately, among ourselves. *mizui(re)* water jug, pitcher
入話 *mizu-i(razu) (no) hanashi* heart-to-heart talk
力 *suiryoku* water power
力工学 *suiryoku kōgaku* hydraulic engineering
力学 *suirikigaku, suiryokugaku* hydraulics
力発電所 *suiryoku hatsudensho* hydroelectric plant
力電気 *suiryoku denki* hydroelectricity
3 口 *mizukuchi* faucet; dam inlet, dam outlet. *minakuchi* irrigation water gate
上 *suijō* water (transportation); aquatic; floating. *minakami* headwater, source
上小学校 *suijō shōgakkō* primary schools for children living on the water
上水車 *mizua(ge) suisha* scoop water wheel
上生活 *suijō seikatsu* life on the water
上生活者 *suijō seikatsusha* seafarer
上飛行機 *suijō hikōki* hydroplane, seaplane
上機 *suijōki* hydroplane, seaplane
上警察 *suijō keisatsu* water police
上競技 *suijō kyōgi* water sports
4 心 *mizugokoro* advice on swimming; readiness to follow
手 *kako* pilot, sailor. *mizu (no) te* castle water supply
月 *suigetsu* water and moon; reflection of the moon
火 *suika* fire and water
牛 *suigyū* water buffalo
辺 *suihen* water's edge, beach
引 *mizuhiki* two-color strings for tying gifts
切 *mizugi(re)* water shortage
天 *suiten* sea and sky
分 *suibun* moisture, water, humidity; juice; water content
不入 *mizu-i(razu) de* privately, among ourselves
化物 *suikabutsu* hydrate
夫 *suifu, kako* sailor, mariner
夫仲間 *suifu nakama* shipmate
夫長 *suifuchō* boatswain
中 *suichū* submarine, aquatic, underwater; in water. *mizuata(ri)* illness from water
中速力 *suichū sokuryoku* submerged speed
中爆弾 *suichū bakudan* depth bomb
中爆雷 *suichū bakurai* depth charge
5 母 *kurage* jellyfish
玉 *mizutama* a drop of water; a drop of dew
生 *suisei* aquatic (plant)
仙 *suisen* daffodil; narcissus
仕事 *mizu shigoto* washing and scrubbing
白粉 *mizu oshiroi* liquid face paint
加減 *mizu kagen* amount of water
石鹼 *mizu sekken* soft soap
田 *suiden, mizuta* paddy field
田作 *suidensaku* working the rice fields
圧 *suiatsu* hydraulic pressure
圧計 *suiatsukei* water-pressure gauge
圧管 *suiatsukan* penstock
圧機 *suiatsuki* hydraulic press
平 *suihei* water level; horizontal
平的分業 *suiheiteki bungyō* horizontal international specialization
平社 *Suiheisha* an organization to restore the eta class to full social privileges
平面 *suiheimen* water level, level surface
平動 *suiheidō* horizontal earthquake vibration
平運動 *suihei undō* social-equality movement
平距離 *suihei kyori* horizontal distance
平棒 *suihei bō* horizontal bar
平線 *suiheisen* horizon
平器 *suiheiki* a level
6 色 *mizuiro* light blue, water green

虫 *mizumushi* water insect; athlete's foot
気 *mizuke* dampness, moisture, juice. *suiki* dropsy; moisture, humidity, vapor
汲 *mizuku(mi)* drawing water
防 *suibō* flood prevention
争 *mizu araso(i)* irrigation dispute
成岩 *suiseigan* sedimentary rock
死 *suishi* drowning
死人 *suishinin* drowned person
先 *mizusaki* course; current direction; pilot; piloting
先人 *mizusakinin* ship's pilot
先案内 *mizusaki-annai* pilot; piloting
7 車 *suisha, mizuguruma* water wheel
攻 *mizuze(me)* cutting off the water supply from a castle; flooding a castle compound (in warfare); flooding through broken dikes
利 *suiri* water utilization; water supply; irrigation
系 *suikei* mountain drainage system, water system
声 *suisei* sound of flowing water
牢 *mizurō* dungeon using water torment
災 *suisai* flood
芸 *mizugei* water stunts
冷式 *suireishiki* water-cooled
見舞 *mizu mima(i)* visit to flood victims
吹雪 *mizu fubuki* spray
芭蕉 *mizubashō* a skunk cabbage
位 *suii* water level
位標 *suiihyō* watermark
兵 *suihei* (navy) sailor
兵服 *suiheifuku* naval sailor's suit; girl's sailor suit
呑 *mizunomi* drinking glass
呑百姓 *mizunomibyakushō* poor farmer
呑場所 *mizunomibasho* drinking fountain
呑器 *mizunomiki* drinking fountain
8 門 *suimon* floodgate, penstock, sluice
明 *suimei* shimmering of clear water
枕 *mizu makura* water pillow
杯 *mizu sakazuki* farewell cups of water
沫 *suimatsu* spray, splash
泡 *minawa* foam, bubbles. *mizu(no)awa, suihō* foam, bubbles; nothing; failure
油 *mizu abura* hair oil; lamp oil
炊 *mizutaki* boiling without seasoning
物 *mizumono* matter of chance; liquid; fruit

肥 *mizugoe, suihi* liquid manure
苔 *mizugoke* bog moss; incrustation
取舟 *mizuto(ri)bune* water-carrying boat
治療法 *suichiryōhō* hydrotherapy
底 *minasoko, suitei* sea bottom, river bottom
底荷 *mizu sokoni* water ballast
性 *mizushō* light, flirtatious, wanton. *suisei* of water
性塗料 *suisei toryō* water colors; distemper
茎 *mizuguki* writing brush
茎跡 *mizuguki (no) ato* beautiful calligraphy
泳 *suiei, mizuoyo(gi)* swimming
泳大会 *suiei taikai* swimming meet
泳場 *suieijō* swimming place; swimming pool
泳帽 *suieibō* swimming cap
泳着 *suieigi* swimming suit
9 面 *suimen, minomo* surface of the water
音 *mizuoto, mizu (no) oto* the sound of water
屋 *mizuya* water carrier; water font at shrine or temple; dish cupboard, washing area in tea ceremony room
指 *mizusashi* water jug, pitcher
柱 *mizubashira* column of water, waterspout. *suichū* column of water
枯 *mizuga(re)* drought
洟 *mizu(p)pana, mizubana* watery nasal discharge
神 *suijin* water god, water nymph
盃 *mizu sakazuki* farewell cups of water
軍 *suigun* (old word for) navy
星 *Suisei* Mercury
臭 *mizukusa(i)* watery; reserved, formal, distant
草 *suisō, mizukusa* aquatic plant
風呂 *mizuburo* cold bath
俣病 *minamatabyō* disease caused by mercury poisoning
飛沫 *mizushibuki* water spray
茶屋 *mizujaya* a busy shop selling tea and drinks
浅黄 *mizuasagi* light blue
垢 *mizuaka* incrustation, slime
垢離 *mizugori* cold-water ablutions
洗 *mizuara(i), suisen* washing
洗式 *suisenshiki* flush type
洗式便所 *suisenshiki benjo* flush toilet

洗便所 *suisembenjo* flush toilet
10 馬 *suiba* fording a river on horseback
師 *suishi* (old word for) navy
捌 *mizuhake* drainage
流 *suiryū* current, stream, watercourse
浴 *suiyoku* bathing, cold bath. *mizua(bi)* bathing
浸 *mizubita(shi)* flooded out, submersion
紋 *suimon* wavelet, water rings
脈 *suimyaku* water vein
陸 *suiriku* land and water
郷 *suikyō, suigō* riverside district
都 *suito* town on the water's edge
差 *mizusa(shi)* water jug, pitcher. *mizu (o) sa(su)* cause trouble between people
時計 *mizudokei* water clock
疱 *suihō* blister
疱瘡 *mizubōsō* chicken pox
耕 *suikō* hydroponics
耕法 *suikōhō* hydroponics
素 *suiso* hydrogen
素爆弾 *suiso bakudan* hydrogen bomb
害 *suigai* flood damage, inundation
害地 *suigaichi* flooded area
害防止 *suigai bōshi* flood control
害対策 *suigai taisaku* flood-control measures
害保険 *suigai hoken* flood insurance
害家屋 *suigai kaoku* flooded homes
害救済 *suigai kyūsai* flood relief
害罹災民 *suigai risaimin* flood victims
11 鳥 *mizudori, mizutori, suichō* waterfowl
運 *suiun* water transportation
遊 *mizuaso(bi)* wading, playing in water
域 *suiiki* river basin; an area of the ocean
張 *mizuba(ri)* fulling
桶 *mizuoke* pail, bucket, cistern
深 *suishin* water depth
球 *suikyū* water polo
船 *mizubune* cistern, water trough; water boat; water-logged boat
瓶 *mizugame* water jar
密 *suimitsu* watertight
萍 *suihyō* floating waterweed
菜 *mizuna* a variety of greens with slender leaves
盛 *mizumo(ri)* a carpenter's level
責 *mizuze(me)* water torture (to secure confessions)
菓子 *mizugashi* fruit
商売 *mizu shōbai* the entertainment business
理学 *suirigaku* hydrography
悪戯 *mizu itazura* playing in water
掛論 *mizuka(ke)ron* futile argument
眼鏡 *mizu megane* diver's goggles
魚 *suigyo* fish and water
魚交 *suigyo (no) majiwa(ri)* intimate friendship
族 *suizoku* aquatic animals
族館 *suizokukan* aquarium
彩画 *suisaiga* watercolor painting
彩画家 *suisai gaka* watercolor painter
彩絵具 *suisai enogu* watercolors
道 *suidō* waterworks; water pipes; aqueduct; waterway, channel; city water
道工事 *suidō kōji* water works
道局 *suidōkyoku* water bureau
道栓 *suidōsen* hydrant, faucet
道料 *suidōryō* water charge
道部 *suidōbu* water department
道橋 *suidōkyō* aqueduct bridge
産 *suisan* marine products
産大学 *suisan daigaku* fisheries college
産庁 *Suisanchō* the Fisheries Agency
産技師 *suisan gishi* marine-products expert
産物 *suisambutsu* marine products
産学 *suisangaku* fishery science
産学校 *suisan gakkō* fisheries school
産業 *suisangyō* fisheries, marine products industry
12 圏 *suiken* the hydrosphere
痘 *suitō* chicken pox
棲 *suisei* aquatic (animal)
温 *suion* water temperature
程 *suitei* water route
絵 *mizue* watercolor painting
脹 *mizubukure* water blister
筒 *suitō* water bottle, canteen
着 *mizugi* swimming suit
落 *mizuo(chi)* solar plexus, pit of the stomach
葬 *suisō* burial at sea
番 *mizuban* irrigation watchman
煮 *mizuni* boiled in unsalted water
無月 *minazuki* sixth lunar month
蒸気 *suijōki* water vapor
疏通 *mizuhake* drainage
揚 *mizua(ge)* landing (goods); earnings; defloration; preservation (of cut flowers)

揚機 *mizua(ge)ki* irrigation wheel
割 *mizuwa(ri)* diluting with water; packing inferior goods beneath a high-quality layer
割株 *mizuwa(ri)kabu* watered stock
晶 *suishō* quartz
晶体 *suishōtai* crystalline lens
量 *suiryō* water volume
量計 *suiryōkei* water meter
飲 *mizuno(mi)* drinking glass
飲百姓 *mizino(mi)byakushō* poor tenant farmers
飲器 *mizino(mi)ki* drinking fountain
13 閘 *suikō* canal lock
搔 *mizukaki* webfoot, web
楊 *suiyō* riverside willows
楢 *mizu nara* an oak
溜 *mizutamari* pool, puddle. *mizutame* reservoir, cistern
煙 *mizu kemuri, suien* spray, splashes
腫 *suishu* dropsy
路 *suiro* waterway, channel; aqueduct
飼 *mizuka(u)* water (a horse)
禽 *suikin* waterfowl
嵩 *mizu kasa* water volume
勢 *suisei* force of water
鉄砲 *mizudeppō* squirt gun
溶性 *suiyōsei* water-soluble
溶液 *suiyōeki* a solution
源 *suigen* river source, fountainhead
源地 *suigenchi* catchment basin, reservoir
際 *mizugiwa, migiwa* water's edge, beach
際立 *mizugiwada(tte)* splendid (performance); neat (job); clean (hit)
準 *suijun* water level; standard
準器 *suijunki* a level (the tool)
雷 *suirai* torpedo
雷母艦 *suirai bokan* torpedo-boat depot ship
雷防禦網 *suirai bōgyomō* torpedo net
雷艇 *suiraitei* torpedo boat
雷敷設 *suirai fusetsu* mine laying
雷敷設艦 *suirai fusetsukan* mine layer
14 増 *mizuma(shi)* dilution, watering
漉 *mizuko(shi)* filter, strainer, percolator
滴 *suiteki* drop of water
漬 *mizuzu(ku)* soak or stand in water
漏 *mizumo(ri), mizumo(re)* leaking
稲 *suitō* wet-land rice
精 *suisyō* quartz
練 *suiren* swimming practice; art of swimming
飴 *mizuame* millet jelly
管 *suikan* water pipe, hose
酸化物 *suisanka butsu* hydroxide
様便 *suiyōben* watery stools
様液 *suiyōeki* aqueous humor
蜜 *suimitsu* (a quality) peach
蜜桃 *suimitsutō* (a quality) peach
墨 *suiboku* India-ink painting; India ink for painting
墨画 *suibokuga* India-ink painting
銀 *suigin* mercury
銀灯 *suiginto* mercury-vapor lamp
銀柱 *suiginchū* column of mercury
銀電池 *suigin denchi* mercury cell
銀寒暖計 *suigin kandankei* mercury thermometer
15 撒 *mizumaki* street sprinkling
槽 *suisō* water tank, water trough, cistern
澄 *mizusu(mashi)* water spider
線 *suisen* water line
論 *suiron* water dispute
蝕 *suishoku* erosion
盤 *suiban* flower basin
質 *suishitsu* water quality
16 樽 *mizudaru* (ship's) water tub
膨 *mizubukure* water blister
頭 *suitō* near the water
薬 *mizugusuri, suiyaku* liquid medicine
18 翻 *mizukobo(shi)* slop bucket
甕 *mizugame* water jar
曜 *Suiyō* Wednesday
曜日 *Suiyōbi* Wednesday
難 *suinan* sea disaster; flood
難除 *suinan'yoke* charm against drowning
難救助 *suinan kyūjo* sea rescue
難救済 *suinan kyūsai* sea rescue
19 瀬 *mizuse* swift current; a fording place
爆 *suibaku* hydrogen bomb
獺 *kawa uso* otter
鏡 *mizukagami* reflecting water
20 蘚 *mizugoke* bog moss; incrustation
礬土 *suibando* bauxite
礬土鉱 *suibandokō* bauxite deposit
22 嚢 *suinō* water bag, filter, percolator

1

A 永 3031 / J314a / M17088 EI. *naga(i)* long, lengthy. *towa* eternity. *naga(raku)* a long time.
3 小作 *eikosaku* perpetual land lease

4 心忄⺗戈戸手扌支攴攵文斗斤方无日曰月木欠止歹殳毋比毛氏气【水氵氺】火灬爪爫父爻爿丬片牙牛犬犭

小作権 *eikosakuken* perpetual land lease
久 *eikyū, tokoshie* eternity, perpetuity, immortality. *eikyū ni, tokoshie ni* everlastingly
久性 *eikyūsei* permanency
久歯 *eikyūshi* permanent tooth
4 日 *eijitsu* a long spring day
5 生 *eisei* eternal life, immortality
永 *eiei to, naganaga to* very long, at great length; tediously; forever
代 *eitai* permanence, eternity
代借地 *eitai shakuchi* perpetual lease
世 *eisei* eternity, perpetuity, immortality, permanence
世中立 *eisei chūritsu* permanent neutrality
世中立国 *eisei chūritsukoku* a permanent neutral
6 存 *eizon, eison* durability, permanence, perpetuity
年 *einen* many years, a long time
年間 *naganenkan* a long period of time
7 別 *eibetsu* last farewell
劫 *eigō* eternity, perpetuity
牢 *eirō* life imprisonment
寿 *eijū* long life
住 *eijū* permanent residence
住者 *eijūsha* permanent resident
住権 *eijūken* denizenship; permanent residence
10 眠 *eimin* eternal sleep, death
11 訣 *eiketsu* last farewell
12 遠 *eien* eternity, immortality, perpetuity, permanence
13 続 *eizoku, nagatsuzu(ki)* permanence, continuation
続性 *eizokusei* permanence

A **氷** 3032 / J4939 / M17087 **冰** 412 / J5156 / M1612 HYŌ. *kō(ru)* freeze; be frozen over; congeal. *kōri* ice; shaved ice. *hi* ice; hail.
2 人 *hyōjin* a go-between (in marriage)
3 山 *hyōzan* iceberg
刃 *hyōjin* a sharp, glistening sword
4 水 *kōri mizu, kōrisui* shaved ice, ice water
5 田 *hyōden* a field of eternal snow
7 床 *hyōshō* ice sheet
8 枕 *kōri makura* ice pillow
河 *hyōga* glacier
河時代 *hyōga jidai* glacial period
河期 *hyōgaki* glacial period
9 面 *hyōmen* ice surface
屋 *kōriya* ice vendor, ice shop
挟 *kōribasami* ice tongs
柱 *hyōchū, tsurara* icicle, ice pillar
海 *hyōkai* frozen sea; icy waters
室 *himuro, hyōshitsu, kōri muro* ice house, ice room, cold room
炭 *hyōtan* ice and charcoal; contradiction
砂糖 *kōrizatō* rock candy, sugar candy
削機 *hyōsakuki, hyōsakki* ice-shaving machine
点 *hyōten* freezing point
点下 *hyōtenka* below freezing
10 原 *hyōgen* ice field; ice floe; snow field
11 釈 *hyōshaku* melting like ice; dispelling doubts
雪 *hyōsetsu* ice and snow
袋 *kōribukuro* ice bag
菓 *hyōka* ices
菓子 *kōrigashi* a frozen sweet; sherbert
12 結 *hyōketsu* freezing
期 *hyōki* ice age
晶 *hyōshō* ice crystals
酢酸 *hyōsakusan* glacial acetic acid
13 塊 *hyōkai* lump of ice, block of ice; ice floe
滑 *kōrisube(ri)* ice skating
解 *hyōkai* melting, thawing
詰 *kōrizume* packing in ice
14 漬 *kōrizuke* putting down in ice
15 輪 *hyōrin* the moon
蝕 *hyōshoku* glacial scouring
震 *hyōshin* ice quake
醋酸 *hyōsakusan* glacial acetic acid
18 瀑 *hyōbaku* ice fall
19 霧 *hyōmu* ice fog
22 嚢 *hyōnō* ice bag, ice pack

2

氾 3033 / J4845 / M17101 HAN spread out; wide.
17 濫 *hanran* flooding

汀 3034 / J4475 / M17103 TEI. *migiwa* water's edge, shore.
15 線 *teisen* beach line

B **汁** 3035 / J3d41 / M17104 JŪ, SHŪ juice. *shiru* juice; sap; soup, broth; gravy; pus. *tsuyu* juice; sap; soup, broth; gravy.

8 物 *shirumono* soups
11 液 *jūeki* juice
12 椀 *shiru wan* bowl of soup; soup bowl

A 求 3036 / J3561 / M17105 KYŪ. GU. *moto(meru)* want, wish for, request, demand; seek, search for; pursue (pleasure); hunt (a job); buy.
2 人 *kyūjin* help wanted
人口 *kyūjinguchi* job vacancy
人広告 *kyūjin kōkoku* help-wanted ad
人者 *kyūjinsha* employer, someone seeking workers
4 心力 *kyūshinryoku* centripetal force
6 刑 *kyūkei suru* prosecute
8 法者 *guhōsha* (Buddhist) inquirer
妻広告 *kyūsai kōkoku* ad for a wife
11 道 *kyudo, gudō* seeking for truth
道者 *kyūdōsha, gudōsha* inquirer, truth seeker, catechumen
婚 *kyūkon* proposal, courtship
婚広告 *kyūkon kōkoku* matrimonial ad
婚者 *kyūkonsha* suitor
13 愛 *kyuai* courtship
15 縁 *kyūen* courtship
16 積 *kyūseki* mensuration
17 償 *kyūshō* claim for damages
18 職 *kyūshoku* job hunting, seeking employment
職広告 *kyūshoku kōkoku* situation-wanted ad
職者 *kyūshokusha* job applicant
職係 *kyūshokugakari* applicant interviewer

3

汢 3037 / J5d69 / M-X TO （国字） *nuta* muddy fields.

汕 3038 / J5d68 / M17128 SAN. SEN fish swimming; fishing with a dip net; net.

汞 3039 / J5d67 / M17139 KŌ mercury.

汝 3040 / J4672 / M17138 JO. *nanji, nare* you, thou.
12 等 *nanjira* you (classical plural)

汐 3041 / J3c2e / M17122 SEKI. SHAKU. *shio* tide; salt water; opportunity.
3 干狩 *shiohiga(ri)* low-tide shell gathering
12 焼 *shioya(ke)* tanned by salt air

A 池 3042 / J4353 / M17141 CHI. *ike* pond, pool, cistern, basin, reservoir.
4 心 *chishin* center of a pond, bottom of a pond
辺 *chihen* edge of a pond
8 沼 *chishō* ponds and swamps
9 神 *ikegami* god of the pond
10 畔 *chihan* edge of a pond
11 魚 *chigyo* pond fish
16 頭 *chitō* edge of a pond

汎 3043 / J4846 / M17120 氾 3044 / J-X / M-X HAN pan-.
4 太平洋 *hantaiheiyō* Pan-Pacific
6 米 *ham-Bei* Pan-American
9 独 *han-Doku* Pan-German
神教 *hanshinkyō* pantheism
神論 *hanshinron* pantheism
13 愛 *han'ai* philanthropy, humanity
意語 *han'igo* ambiguous term
15 論 *hanron* outline, summary

B 江 3045 / J393e / M17140 KŌ. *e* inlet, bay.
3 口 *kōkō* large estuary
山 *kōzan* rivers and mountains
上 *kōjō* riverside; the banks of the Yangzi
4 心 *kōshin* the middle of the river
月 *kōgetsu* the moon over a river; the moon reflected in a river
水 *kōsui* river water; the Yangzi
戸 *Edo* Edo, Tokyo, Edo era (1603-1867)
戸子 *Edo(k)ko* true Tokyoite
戸前 *Edomae* Edo-style (cooking)
5 北 *kōhoku* north of the Yangzi
6 西 *kōsei* the western part of the lower Yangzi area
7 村 *kōson* river village
8 河 *kōga* the Yangzi and Yellow rivers
東 *kōtō* east of a river
9 風 *kōfū* river wind
海 *kōkai* rivers and seas; a place separated from the mundane world
南 *kōnan* south of the Yangzi
10 畔 *kōhan* riverside, river bank

12 湖 *kōko* the public, the world; rivers and lakes

B **汗** 3046 J3440 M17130 KAN. *ase(bamu), ase suru* be sweaty. *ase* perspiration. *ase(daku)* dripping with sweat. *ase(mizuku)* dripping with sweat.
4 水 *asemizu* copious sweating
不知 *aseshirazu* prickly-heat powder
牛充棟 *kangyū-jūtō* a superabundance of books
6 血 *kanketsu* sweat and blood
衣 *kan'i* undershorts; clothes wet with perspiration
7 含 *asegu(mu)* perspire
8 性 *aseshō* tendency to perspire
知 *aseshi(razu)* prickly-heat powder
取 *aseto(ri)* underwear
9 拭 *asefuki* cloth for wiping off the sweat
臭 *asekusa(i)* smelling of sweat
染 *aseji(miru)* be stained with sweat
10 疹 *asemo, asebo* prickly heat, heat rash
流 *asenaga(shi)* washing off the sweat
13 掻 *ase(k)kaki, asekaki* heavy perspirer
腺 *kansen* sweat gland
塗 *asemidoro* dripping with sweat
15 瘡 *asemo, asebo* prickly heat, heat rash
18 顔 *kangan* sweating from shame
顔至 *kangan (no) ita(ri)* deeply ashamed, feeling awkward
19 襦袢 *asejiban* underwear

B **汚** 3047 J3178 M17133 **汙** 3048 J-X M17132 O. *kega(su)* make dirty, stain, pollute, defile, contaminate; disgrace, dishonor; rape. *kega(reru)* get dirty; be defiled; be contaminated. *yogo(su) vt* stain, soil, pollute; defile, debauch. *yogo(reru) vi* get dirty, be stained, be contaminated, tarnish. *yogo(reta)* loathsome; obscene. *kega(re)* uncleanness, impurity, disgrace. *yogo(re)* dirt, spot, stain, filth. *kitana(i)* dirt, filthy, unclean, soiled; shabby; indecent, obscene; base, sordid; stingy; foul. *kega(rawashii)* filthy; unfair.
4 水 *osui* filthy water, sewage
6 行 *okō* disgraceful conduct, scandal, immoral relations
名 *omei* stigma, dishonor, disgrace, slur, infamy
吏 *ori* corrupt official
8 物 *obutsu* dust, dirt, filth, garbage, ashes; impurities; sewage. *yogo(re)mono* the washing, laundry
事 *kega(shi)goto* blasphemy
9 俗 *ozoku* bad custom, evil habit
垢 *okō* dirt, uncleanliness
臭 *oshū* evil odor
染 *osen* stain, blot, spot, smudge, disgrace
点 *oten* stain, blot, spot, smudge, blur; flaw; disgrace
点抜 *shimi-nu(ki)* removal of stains
10 辱 *ojoku* disgrace, humiliation, insult
11 習 *oshū* evil habit
13 損 *oson* stain
14 塵 *ojin* filthy dust, rubbish
16 濁 *odaku* corruption, graft
18 穢 *owai, oai* night soil, muck, filth, uncleanliness, squalor. *oe* filth, dirt
穢屋 *owaiya* night-soil collector
職 *oshoku* graft, bribery
職罪 *oshokuzai* graft, bribery

4

汨 3049 J5d71 M17152 BEKI. MYAKU used in proper names. KATSU. KOCHI sink, subside.

汳 3050 J5d72 M17164 HEN. BEN used in proper names.

汾 3051 J5d70 M17178 FUN. BUN used in proper names.

沂 3052 J5d6b M17183 KI. KIN. GIN used in proper names; edge, border; a kind of flute.

沚 3053 J5d6d M17213 SHI small river island; water's edge.

沌 3054 J4659 M17193 TON primeval chaos.

汰 3055 J4241 M17160 DA. TA luxury; select.

沁 3056 J5d6e M17182 SHIN. *shi(miru)* penetrate, soak in.

汪 3057 J5d6a M17154 Ō flowing full; expanse of water; wide; deep; large.

[9] 洋 *ōyō* great expanse of water, leisure

冱 3058 / J5d6c / M17194 Gō close up; freeze, freeze over; congeal.
[12] 寒 *gokan* intense cold

沐 3059 / J5d74 / M17201 Moku. *moku(suru)* wash; bathe; moisten.
[8] 雨 *mokuu* getting soaked in the rain
[10] 浴 *mokuyoku* washing the hair and bathing; cleansing the body, ablutions
[12] 猴 *mokkō* monkey

沓 3060 / J3723 / M17206 Tō. *kutsu* shoes, boots.
[3] 下 *kutsushita* socks, stockings
[5] 石 *kutsuishi* pillar or post foundation stones
[10] 師 *kutsushi* shoemaker
[11] 脱 *kutsunu(gi)* bootjack

沃 3061 / J4d60 / M17184 Yoku pour; fertility.
[3] 土 *yokudo* fertile soil; mold
[6] 地 *yokuchi* fertile land
[9] 度 *yōdo* iodine
[10] 素 *yōso* iodine
[11] 野 *yokuya* fertile field
[21] 饒 *yokujō na* fertilc, rich, fruitful

B **沢** 3062 / J4274 / M17234 **澤** 3338 / J5f37 / M18383 Taku swamp; blessing. *sawa* swamp, marsh, dale, valley.
[3] 山 *takusan* a great many, a large quantity, abundance, plenty
[4] 水 *sawamizu* swamp water
辺 *sawabe* edge of a swamp
[5] 田 *sawada* flooded rice fields; rice fields near a swamp
[6] 地 *sawachi* marshy land
[11] 庵 *takuan* pickled daikon
庵漬 *takuanzuke* pickled daikon

沙 3063 / J3a3b / M17212 Sa. Sha. *isago, suna* sand.
[3] 土 *sado* sandy soil
[7] 汰 *sata* instructions, directions, orders; notice, information message; report, rumor; affair
汰止 *sataya(mi)* calling off; dropping
汰限 *sata (no) kagi(ri)* absurd, preposterous
汰書 *satasho* written instructions; written message
[8] 門 *shamon* Buddhist priest
弥 *shami* Buddhist acolyte, novice
[9] 洲 *sasu* sand bar, sandbank, reef
[10] 蚕 *gokai* lugworm
[13] 漠 *sabaku* desert
[16] 嘴 *sashi, shashi* sandbar, sandspit

汲 3064 / J3562 / M17163 Kyū. *ku(mu)* draw (water), ladle, dip, scoop, pump, consider; sympathize with; drink; think.
[2] 入 *ku(mi)-i(reru)* draw in
[3] 干 *ku(mi)-ho(su)* pump out, bail out
上 *ku(mi)-a(geru)* pump up, scoop up
[4] 水 *ku(mi)mizu, kyūsui* pumping water
込 *ku(mi)-ko(mu)* fill with water
[5] 立 *kumita(te) no* fresh from the well
出 *ku(mi)-da(su)* pump out, dip out, bail out
[7] 汲 *kyūkyū toshite* diligently, industriously
[8] 取 *ku(mi)-to(ru)* draw (water), dip, ladle, drain, bail out; take into consideration, make allowance for
取屋 *kumito(ri)ya* night-soil collector
[11] 乾 *ku(mi)-ho(su)* pump out, bail out
[12] 替 *ku(mi)-ka(eru)* pumping out a well

B **沖** 3065 / J322d / M17209 **冲** 413 / J5155 / M1616 Chū. *okitsu, oki* offing, open sea. *chū(suru)* rise high in the sky.
[4] 辺 *okibe* the offing
天 *chūten* rising into the heavens
[5] 出 *okida(shi)* bearing off the coast
白波 *oki(tsu)shiranami* white waves at sea
[6] 合 *okia(i)* offshore, offing
合漁業 *okia(i) gyogyō* offshore fisheries
仲仕 *okinakashi* longshoreman
[8] 取 *okito(ri)* offshore fishing
取値段 *okito(ri) nedan* cost including freight, C.I.F.
[10] 値 *okine* free-overside price
島 *oki(tsu) shima* an offshore island
[11] 釣 *okizuri* offshore fishing
[12] 渡 *okiwata(shi)* free overside
[14] 漁 *okiryō* offshore fishing
[15] 縄開発庁 *Okinawa Kaihatsuchō* Okinawa Development Agency

16 積土 *chūsekido* alluvial soil
19 繋 *okigakari* anchoring in the offing

B 没 3066 / J4b57 / M17233 沒 3067 / J5d73 / M17204 歿 2969 / J5d47 / M16385

BOTSU. MOTSU. *bos(suru)* sink, set, go down; hide, be hidden, fall into; disappear; die. *botsu* rejection of manuscript; deceased. (Some scholars limit the meaning of 歿 to dying).

2 入 *botsunyū suru, motsunyū suru* be absorbed in
人格的 *botsujinkakuteki* poor personality
4 分暁漢 *botsubungyōkan, wakarazuya* a fool, a person who does not understand anything
5 収 *bosshū* confiscation
6 年 *botsunen* year of death
交渉 *bokkōshō, botsukōshō* no connection (with), no relation to
7 却 *bokkyaku suru* discard and ignore
我 *botsuga* selflessness
9 前 *botsuzen* before death
後 *botsugo* after death, posthumously
食子 *mosshokushi, bosshokushi* gallnut
食子酸 *mosshokushisan* gallic acid
10 書 *bossho* rejected manuscript
11 理想 *botsurisō* lack of ideals; realism (in literature)
常識 *botsujōshiki* lack of common sense
12 落 *botsuraku* ruin, downfall, bankruptcy
落者 *botsurakusha* a bankrupt person; a ruined people
13 義道 *mogidō na* cruel, brutal, heartless
15 趣味 *bosshumi na* insipid, prosaic, dull
16 頭 *bottō suru* be absorbed in, be devoted to

A 汽 3068 / J3525 / M17177 滊 3252 / J-X / M18019 KI vapor; steam.

5 圧 *kiatsu* steam pressure
圧計 *kiatsukei* steam gauge
6 缶 *kikan* boiler, steam generator
缶夫 *kikanfu* boilerman
缶室 *kikanshitsu* boiler room
缶管 *kikankan* boiler tube
7 車 *kisha* train; steam train
車弁 *kishaben* railway lunch
車弁当 *kisha bentō* railway lunch
車便 *kishabin de* by rail, by express, by freight
車道 *kishamichi* railway line
車賃 *kishachin* railway fare
11 笛 *kiteki* steam whistle, siren
船 *kisen* steamship
船会社 *kisengaisha* steamship company
13 艇 *kitei* steam launch
14 管 *kikan* steam pipe
16 嘴 *kishi* steam nozzle

B 沈 3069 / J4440 / M17189 CHIN. SHIN. JIN aloes. *shizu(mu) vi* sink, be submerged; subside, cave in; feel depressed, be overcome with. *shizu(meru) vt* sink, submerge, immerse. *shizu(me)* immersion.

2 丁花 *jinchōge, chinchōge* sweet-smelling daphne
3 下 *chinka* sinking, subsidence, settlement, dip
4 水 *chinsui* sink in water
7 吟 *chingin suru* meditate, muse
沈 *chinchin, shinshin* getting later; getting quiet; deep interior; feeling (the cold)
没 *chimbotsu* sinking, foundering, submersion
没船 *chimbotsusen* sunken vessel
8 泥 *chindei* silt
金彫 *chinkimbo(ri)* lacquer ware inlaid with gold
金塗 *chinkinnu(ri)* lacquer ware inlaid with gold
9 重 *chinchō* composure and dignity
思 *chinshi* contemplation, meditation
勇 *chin'yū* self-possession, cool courage
香 *chinkō, jinkō* aloes
香樹 *chinkōju* aloes
降 *chinkō* sedimentation, settling, subsidence, sinking
降速度 *chinkō sokudo* (blood) sedimentation rate
10 荷 *shizu(me)ni* jetsam, jettison
11 淪 *chinrin suru* sink into obscurity, lose caste, be ruined
船 *chinsen* sunken ship
設 *chinsetsu suru* lay in water
12 痛 *chintsū* pathetic, sad
渣 *chinsa* sediment, dregs
着 *chinchaku* composure, calmness
13 殿 *chinden* precipitation, sedimentation, subsidence

溺 *chindeki* indulgence, addiction, dissipation
滞 *chintai* stagnation, inactivity
14 静 *chinsei* stillness, tranquility, placidity; slackness, dullness, stagnation, inactivity
15 潜 *chinsen suru* be engrossed in
毅 *chinki* composure
黙 *chimmoku* silence, reticence
黙家 *chimmokuka* a silent person, reticent person
16 積 *chinseki* sedimentation, deposition
澱 *odo(mu)* precipitate, settle. *chinden* precipitation, sedimentation, subsidence
澱池 *chindenchi* settling reservoir
澱物 *chindembutsu* deposit, precipitate
澱槽 *chindensō* settling tank
26 欝 *chin'utsu* melancholy, gloom

A 決 3070 / J3768 / M17174 KETSU decision, vote. *kes(suru) vt* settle, vote on, judge, decide. *vi* be settled, be decided; collapse, give way. *ki(maru)* be decided, be settled, be arranged; be certain to, be doomed to. *ki(meru)* fix, decide, agree upon; appoint, choose; resolve. *ki(me)* arrangement, contract. *(o)ki(mari)* usage, custom, routine; fixed charge. *kes(shite)* (with neg.) never, by no means.
4 心 *kesshin* determination, resolution
手 *ki(me)te* deciding factor, winning move
水 *kessui* water breaking through a dike or water gate
込 *ki(me)-ko(mu)* take for granted, assume, pretend
文句 *ki(mari) monku* favorite phrase, cliché
5 付 *ki(me)-tsu(keru)* scold, reprimand
6 行 *kekkō* decisive action
死 *kesshi* preparedness for death, do-or-die spirit
死隊 *kesshitai* suicide corps
7 別 *ketsubetsu* separation, farewell
8 所 *ki(me)dokoro, ki(me)doko* the time to decide; important time
河 *kekka* river flooding through broken dikes
定 *kettei* decision, determination, conclusion, settlement
定投票 *kettei tōhyō* deciding vote
定版 *ketteiban* final edition (of a book)
定的 *ketteiteki* definite, final, decisive, conclusive, peremptory
定書 *ketteisho* written decision or findings
定権 *ketteiken* right of decision, decisive power
定論 *ketteiron* determinism
10 起 *kekki suru* rise, spring to one's feet
11 済 *kessai* settlement, liquidation
断 *ketsudan* decision, determination
断力 *ketsudanryoku* resolution, determination, decision
12 答 *kettō* definite answer
着 *ketchaku* conclusion, settlement
然 *ketsuzen(taru)* firm, decisive, determined
裂 *ketsuretsu* breakdown, rupture
裁 *kessai* sanction, approval
勝 *kesshō* decision (in a contest)
勝者 *kesshōsha* finalist
勝点 *kesshōten* goal, finishing line
勝戦 *kesshōsen* finals
勝線 *kesshōsen* goal, finishing line
13 意 *ketsui* resolution, determination
戦 *kessen* decisive battle; deciding match, finals
戦投票 *kessen tōhyō* final election
14 疑論 *ketsugiron* casuistry
選 *kessen* final election
選投票 *kessen tōhyō* final vote, run-off primary
算 *kessan* settlement, liquidation
算日 *kessambi* settlement day
算期 *kessanki* financial settlement period
算報告 *kessan hōkoku* financial reports
15 潰 *kekkai* rip, break
16 壊 *kekkai* rip, break
18 闘 *kettō* duel
20 議 *ketsugi* resolution, decision, vote
議文 *ketsugibun* written resolution
議事項 *ketsugi jikō* actions taken, resolutions
議案 *ketsugian* resolution, proposal
議権 *ketsugiken* right of voting
議録 *ketsugiroku* minutes of a meeting
議機関 *ketsugi kikan* party machine, caucus, voting organ

泪 3071 / J5e25 / M17318 See **淚** 3154.

沾 3072 / J5d7e / M17259 See **霑** 6536.

沺 3073 / J5e21 / M17254 DEN. TEN vast spreading water; broad, vast, expansive.

泅 3074 / J5d7a / M17270 SHŪ. JU *oyo(gu)* swim.

泓 3075 / J5d77 / M17288 Ō. KŌ deep clear water.

泗 3076 / J5d79 / M17294 SHI used in proper names. *namida* tears.

泙 3077 / J5e24 / M17296 HŌ surging water. HEI valley.

泝 3078 / J5d7b / M17300 SO *sakanobo(ru)* go upstream.

泯 3079 / J5e23 / M17324 BIN. MIN *horo(biru)* become extinct, die out; be exhausted.

泱 3080 / J5d76 / M17326 Ō. EI broad deep flowing water; billowing clouds.

泛 3081 / J5e22 / M17298 HAN. *uka(bu)* float, refloat, surface; flit across (the face), occur to; play (about the lips, as a smile); rise in the world; rest in peace.

沱 3082 / J5d7d / M17243 TA, DA flowing of tears.

泄 3083 / J5d75 / M17267 SETSU, EI leak.

泔 3084 / J-X / M17289 KAN. *yusu(ru)* rinse and comb (the hair).

沫 3085 / J4b77 / M17235 MATSU. *awa* bubble, foam, froth, scum, suds. *shibuki* spray, splash.

B **況** 3086 / J3637 / M17264 **况** 416 / J5157 / M1620 KYŌ. *ma(shite)* still more, still less (neg.). *iwa(n'ya)* still more; (neg.) much less.

沽 3087 / J5d78 / M17258 KO buying and selling; price.
8 券 *koken* bill of sale; a person's character; face
13 聖 *kosei* simony

沛 3088 / J5d6f / M17216 HAI big rain; swamp.
8 雨 *haiu* downpour, cloudburst
12 然 *haizen* downpour, cloudburst

沮 3089 / J5d7c / M17238 SO. *haba(mu)* obstruct, prevent, impede, deter, hinder, thwart, resist, frustrate.
4 止 *soshi* obstruction, check, hindrance, interference
12 喪 *sosō* loss of energy, loss of power, dejection

A **泳** 3090 / J314b / M17328 EI. *oyo(gu)* swim; totter; keep afloat, get along. *oyo(gi)* swim, swimming.
4 手 *oyo(gi)te* swimmer
5 出 *oyo(gi)-da(su)* set out swimming
6 回 *oyo(gi)-mawa(ru)* swim around
8 法 *eihō* swimming style
者 *eisha* swimmer

B **沼** 3091 / J3e42 / M17257 SHŌ swamp, lake. *numa* swamp, bog, pond, lake.
5 田 *numata* marshy rice field
6 気 *shōki* marsh gas, methane
地 *numachi, shōchi* marsh land
7 沢 *shōtaku* marsh, swamp
12 湖 *shōko* swamps and lakes

B **泌** 3092 / J4867 / M17279 HITSU, HI flow; soak in; penetrate; secrete.
7 尿 *hinyō, hitsunyō* urinary
尿科学 *hinyō kagaku* urology
尿器 *hinyōki* urinary organs
尿器科学 *hinyōki kagaku* urology

B **泡** 3093 / J4b22 / M17307 HŌ. *awa, abuku* bubble, foam, froth, scum, suds.

5 立 *awada(teru)* bubble, foam, lather
立器 *awada(te)ki* eggbeater
立機 *awada(te)ki* eggbeater
8 沫 *hōmatsu, utakata* bubble, foam, froth
沫会社 *hōmatsugaisha* industrial bubble
11 粒 *awatsubu* a bubble
雪 *awayuki* light snow
14 銭 *abukuzeni* easy money, ill-gotten money

B **沸** 3094 / J4a28 / M17251 FUTSU. *wa(ku) vi* boil, get hot; ferment; seethe; be in an uproar; gush out; grow, breed, be hatched. *wa(kasu) vt* boil; heat up (the bath); melt.
3 上 *wa(ki)-a(garu)* boil up; well up
5 立 *wa(ki)-ta(tsu)* boil up, seethe, ferment, stir
6 返 *wa(ki)-kae(ru)* seethe, boil up; be in an uproar
9 点 *futten* boiling point
12 湯 *futtō* boiling water
20 騰 *futtō* boiling, seething, bubbling; agitation
騰点 *futtōten* boiling point

A **泉** 3095 / J4074 / M17274 SEN. *izumi* spring, fountain(head), source.
3 下 *senka* hades; the next world
4 水 *sensui* fountain, miniature lake
5 石 *senseki* ponds, streams, and rocks (in a garden)
9 亭 *sentei* garden-pond arbor
11 貨紙 *senkashi* reclaimed paper
13 殿 *izumidono* ancient garden pavilion
源 *sengen* source of a stream
15 熱 *izumi netsu* a type of scarlet fever

A **沿** 3096 / J3168 / M17260 **沿** 3097 / J-X / M17261 EN following along. *so(u)* run along; lie along; be situated on.
8 岸 *engan* coast, shore
岸国 *engankoku* coastal nation
岸漁業 *engan gyogyō* offshore fishing
9 革 *enkaku* history, development
海 *enkai* coast, shore, sea, inshore, coastal waters
海州 *Enkaishū* Maritime Provinces
11 道 *endō* route, course; roadside
13 路 *enro* route
15 線 *ensen no* along the railway line

B **泰** 3098 / J4259 / M17325 TAI calm, peace; easy; large, wide. *Tai* Thai, Thailand, Siam.
3 山 *taizan* high mountain; Mt. Taishan (in China)
山鳴動 *taizan-meidō* great trouble
4 斗 *taito* an authority
5 平 *taihei* peace, tranquility
平期 *taiheiki* a period of peace
6 西 *Taisei* the Occident
安 *taian* peace, tranquility
8 国 *Taikoku* Thailand, Siam
12 然 *taizen(taru)* calm, composed; firm
然自若 *taizen-jijaku* imperturbability, presence of mind

B **泊** 3099 / J4771 / M17275 HAKU (three-day) stay. *to(maru)* stay at, put up at; ride at anchor. *to(meru)* lodge a person. *toma(ri)* anchorage; stopping (for the night); night duty.
4 込 *toma(ri)-ko(mu)* stop at, live in, stay overnight
6 地 *hakuchi* anchorage, berth
合 *toma(ri)-a(waseru)* stop at the same inn
9 客 *toma(ri)kyaku* overnight guest
11 掛 *toma(ri)ga(ke)* visiting over night
船 *hakusen* anchoring
船渠 *hakusenkyo* wet dock
12 番 *toma(ri)ban* night duty
渠 *hakkyo* wet dock, a dock where water is held when the tide ebbs
13 賃 *toma(ri)chin* hotel charges

A **治** 3100 / J3c23 / M17256 JI. CHI peace; government. *ji(suru)* cure, heal; rule; conserve (resources). *osa(meru), chi(suru)* govern, manage, regulate; quell, subdue; patch up; heal. *osa(maru)* be at peace; calm down; be settled, be ruled. *nao(ru)* be mended; get well; be restored; return to normal; be installed (as a legal wife); change (from third to second class). *nao(su)* mend, repair, put in order, reform, correct; revise, amend; re-do, alter; cure; restore; adjust, regulate; convert (money).
3 山 *chisan* flood-control tree planting on a watershed
下 *chika no* under the rule of
4 水 *chisui* riparian works, flood control

水工学 *chisui kōgaku* hydraulic engineering
水工事 *chisui kōji* riparian works
5 平 *chihei* peace and tranquility
世 *chisei, jisei* reign, rule, regime, dynasty
外法権 *chigai-hōken* extraterritoriality
6 安 *chian* public peace and order
安条例 *chian jōrei* peace regulations
安維持 *chian iji* maintenance of public peace
安維持法 *chian ijihō* peace-preservation law
安警察 *chian keisatsu* peace-preservation police
7 乱 *chiran* war and peace
8 国 *chikoku* government
者 *chisha* ruler, governor
9 要 *chiyō* principles of government
11 略 *chiryaku* statesmanship
産 *chisan* property management
13 跡 *chiseki* administration's record
罪 *chizai* criminal procedure
17 績 *chiseki* administration's record
療 *chiryō* medical treatment
療代 *chiryōdai* doctor's fee
療所 *chiryōsho* infirmary, treatment rooms
療法 *chiryōhō* therapeutics, cure, remedy
療学 *chiryōgaku* therapeutics
療師 *chiryōshi* one who gives treatments
18 癒 *chiyu* healing, cure, recovery
癒力 *chiyuryoku* healing power

5 A **波** 3101 / J4748 / M17308 HA wave. *nami* wave, billows.
3 及 *hakyū suru* be propagated; extend, spread; affect, influence
4 止場 *hatoba* wharf, quay, jetty, pier
5 立 *namida(tsu)* be choppy, be wavy, be rolling (with billows); boil up; ripple
打 *namiu(tsu)* dash against; undulate
打際 *namiu(chi)giwa* beach
打髪 *namiu(tsu)kami* wavy hair
布 *habu* a poisonous Okinawa snake
布茶 *habucha* stinkweed-seed tea
布草 *habusō* stinkweed
7 状 *hajō* wave, undulation
乱 *haran* waves, billows; commotion; wide fluctations
形 *namigata* ripple mark
花 *nami (no) hana* salt
8 長 *hachō* wave length
枕 *namimakura* sea voyage
沫 *namishibuki* spray, spindrift
9 面 *hamen* wave surface; wave front
風 *namikaze* wind and waves; discord, trouble
除 *namiyoke* breakwater, sea wall
乗 *namino(ri)* surf riding. *nami (ni) no(ru)* ride on a wave (of success)
10 高 *hakō* wave height
浪 *harō* waves, billows
紋 *hamon* ripple, wave ring
11 動 *hadō* wave motion, undulatory motion
頂 *hachō* wave crest
寄 *namiyo(ru)* be wavy
12 間 *namima ni* on the waves
颪 *namioroshi* a strong wind at sea
13 路 *namiji* sea route; sea voyage
跡 *namiato* ripple marks
際 *namigiwa* the ocean beach
15 穂 *nami (no) ho, namiho* whitecaps
線 *hasen* wavy line
16 頭 *hatō* on the waves; wave crest; on the sea; whitecaps. *namigashira* whitecaps
17 濤 *hatō* billows, rough seas, large waves
磯際 *nami-isogiwa* the water's edge (on a beach)
20 瀾 *haran* waves, billows; commotion; wide fluctuations
瀾万丈 *haran-banjō* great changes

A **河** 3102 / J324f / M17245 KA. *kawa* river, stream.
3 上 *kajō* on the river; by the river; upper reaches
口 *kakō* river mouth, estuary
口港 *kakōkō* estuary harbor
川 *kasen* rivers
川工学 *kasen kōgaku* riparian engineering
川工事 *kasen kōji* riparian works
4 心 *kashin* middle of the river
水 *kasui* river water; river, stream
公 *kakō* river god
5 北 *kahoku* north of the Yellow River
7 身 *kashin* current of the river
床 *kashō, kawadoko* river bed
系 *kakei* river system
8 底 *kawazoko , katei* river bed, river bottom; channel

東 *katō* east of the river
岸 *kashi* riverside, waterfront; fish market; scene, place; one's trade or field. *kawagishi, kagan* riverside, river bank
岸通 *kashidō(ri)* river road
岸揚 *kashia(ge)* riverfront unloading
岸端 *kashibata* riverside
9 峡 *kakyō* swift-river canyon
津 *kashin* ford; river port
神 *kashin* river god
南 *kanan* south of the Yellow River
10 馬 *kuba* hippopotamus
流 *karyū* stream
畔 *kahan* riverside
原 *kawara, kawahara* river beach, dry river bed
原乞食 *kawara kojiki* Edo actors (a term of opprobrium)
原物 *kawaramono* beggar, outcast; actor
11 魚 *kagyo, kawa uo* river fish,
鹿 *kajika* singing frog
豚 *fugu, katon* puffer, globefish pufferfish, blowfish
12 港 *kakō* river port
湾 *kawan* estuary
童 *kappa, kawa(p)pa* a waterinp; a river monster; expert swimmer
13 戦 *kasen* fighting in a river (not in boats)
跡湖 *kasekiko* river-bed lake
19 獺 *kuwu uso* otter
23 鱒 *kawa masu* brook trout

A 注 3103 / J436d / M17316 CHŪ notes, comment; N.B. *chū(suru)* comment on; annotate. *soso(gu) vt* pour into, pour on, irrigate, sprinkle; shed (tears). *vi* (rain) falls; flow into; pay attention to, concentrate on. *tsu(gu)* pour in, fill, put in (more coal). *sa(su)* pour (a drink), serve (drinks); mix into.
2 入 *chūnyū suru* pour into, put into, inject, impregnate, infuse, instill, implant, imbue
4 水 *chūsui* flooding; douche
込 *soso(gi)-ko(mu)* pour into, flow into. *tsu(gi)-ko(mu)* pour into; invest, sink (money) into
文 *chūmon* an order
文用紙 *chūmon yōshi* order blank
文先 *chūmonsaki* where you place your order
文帖 *chūmonchō* order book
文取 *chūmonto(ri)* taking orders
文品 *chūmonhin* goods ordered
文流 *chūmonnaga(re)* canceled order
文書 *chūmonsho, chūmonga(ki)* order form
文帳 *chūmonchō* order book
文聞 *chūmonki(ki)* taking orders
5 目 *chūmoku* attention, observation, notice
出 *soso(gi)-da(su)* pour out
7 足 *tsu(gi)-ta(su)* pour more into
8 油 *chūyu* oiling, lubrication. *soso(gi) abura* anointing oil
油器 *chūyuki* oiler, lubricator
9 連 *shime* sacred Shinto rope
連飾 *shimekaza(ri)* sacred Shinto rope
連縄 *shimenawa* sacred Shinto rope
10 進 *chūshin* information, warning
記 *chūki suru* make entries, write down
射 *chūsha* injection, shot
射針 *chūshabari* hypodermic needle
射液 *chūsha eki* hypodermic injection
射器 *chūshaki* hypodermic syringe
11 掛 *soso(gi)-ka(karu)* flow into, flow against. *soso(gi)-ka(keru)* pour out upon
視 *chūshi* close observation, attention, scrutiny
釈 *chūshaku* notes, comment, exegesis
13 解 *chūkai* notes; comment; commentary
解者 *chūkaisha* commentator
解書 *chūkaisho* commentary
意 *chūi* attention, care, heed; warning, advice, hint; interest
意力 *chūiryoku* power of attention
意人物 *chūi jimbutsu* suspicious character
意事項 *chūi jikō* N.B.; suggestions; matters requiring attention
意書 *chūiga(ki)* notes, instructions
意報 *chūihō* storm warning

A 泣 3104 / J3563 / M17309 KYŪ. *na(ku)* cry, weep, wail, moan. *na(kasu), na(kaseru)* let cry, make cry; grieve, worry. *na(keru)* shed tears, be moved to tears.
2 入 *na(ki)-i(ru)* weep silently or bitterly
3 上戸 *na(ki)jōgo* drunkard

心 忄 小 戈 戸 手 扌 支 攴 攵 文 斗 斤 方 无 日 曰 月 木 欠 止 歹 殳 毋 比 毛 氏 气 【水 氵 氺】 火 灬 爪 爫 父 爻 爿 丬 片 牙 牛 犬 犭

5

4 止 *na(ki)-ya(mu)* stop crying
5 付 *na(ki)-tsu(ku)* implore, entreat
出 *na(ki)-da(su)* burst into tears, begin to cry
6 虫 *na(ki)mushi* crybaby
血 *kyūketsu* shedding tears of blood
伏 *na(ki)-fu(su)* throw oneself down crying; break down
叫 *na(ki)-sake(bu)* cry, yell, scream, wail
7 言 *na(ki)goto* complaint, grievance
沈 *na(ki)-shizu(mu)* break down and cry
別 *na(ki)waka(re)* tearful parting
声 *na(ki)goe* a cry, a crying voice
男 *na(ki)otoko* men hired as mourners; a man who often cries
8 明 *na(ki)-a(kasu)* cry all night
泣 *na(ki)na(ki)* between sobs, with an aching heart; barely. *na(ku)na(ku)* tearfully, with an aching heart
味噌 *na(ki)miso* crybaby, one who cries easily
9 面 *na(ki)tsura, na(kit)tsura* tear-stained face
10 倒 *na(ki)-tao(reru)* fall down crying
涙 *na(ki) (no) namida (de)* in tears
涕 *kyūtei* crying in tears
笑 *na(ki)wara(i)* tearful smile, tragicomedy
真似 *na(ki)mane* crocodile tears, weeping in mimicry
11 寄 *na(ki)yo(ri)* getting together to comfort one another
崩 *na(ki)-kuzu(reru)* break down and cry
12 喚 *na(ki)-wame(ku)* cry, scream, wail
場 *na(kase)ba* pathetic scene
訴 *kyūso* appeal (to authorities)
落 *na(ki)-o(tosu)* persuade in tears
悲 *na(ki)-kana(shimu)* cry and grieve
13 嗄 *na(ki)-ka(rasu)* cry oneself hoarse
腫 *na(ki)-ha(rasu)* cry one's eyes out
寝入 *na(ki)nei(ri)* crying oneself to sleep
14 暮 *na(ki)-ku(rasu)* live in sorrow
17 頻 *na(ki)-shiki(ru)* wail, sob bitterly
濡 *na(ki)-nu(reru)* be tearstained
噦 *na(ki)-jaku(ru)* sob
18 顔 *na(ki)gao* tear-stained face

B 泥 3105 / J4525 / M17311 DEI mud, mire. *nazu(mu)* adhere to, be attached to. *doro, hiji* mud, mire, dirt, slush; disgrace.
3 土 *deido* mud, mire
4 中 *deichū* in the mire
火山 *deikazan* mud volcano
水 *deisui, doromizu* muddy road
水生活 *doromizu seikatsu* life of shame
水社会 *doromizu shakai* red-light districts
水稼業 *doromizu kagyō* life of vice
5 玉 *dorodama* dead pearl, a dark and imperfect pearl
田 *dorota* muddy rice field
仕合 *dorojiai* corrupt campaign, mudslinging
6 地 *deichi* swamp, marsh, bog, morass
7 足 *doroashi* muddy feet
坊 *dorobō* thief, burglar, robber
状 *deijō no* muddy, pasty
弄 *doroiji(ri)* playing in the mud
8 金 *deikin* alluvial gold
泥 *dorodoro* all muddied up
沼 *doronuma* bog, slough, quagmire
板岩 *deibangan* shale
9 海 *doroumi* muddy ocean
臭 *dorokusa(i)* smelling of mud
炭 *deitan, sukumo* peat
炭地 *deitanchi* peat bog, peat moss
炭沼 *deitanshō* peat bog
炭苔 *deitangoke* peat moss
10 浚 *dorosara(i)* mud dredging
浚機 *dorosaraiki* dredger
11 道 *doromichi* muddy road
掬 *dorosuku(i)* mud scoop
酔 *deisui* dead drunk
12 棒 *dorobō* thief, burglar, robber
落 *dorooto(shi)* mud scraper
絵具 *doroenogu* distemper (in painting)
13 滓 *deisai* sludge
鉱 *deikō* slime ore
靴 *dorogutsu* muddy shoes
塗 *doromami(re)* covered with mud
試合 *dorojiai* corrupt campaign, mudslinging
搔 *dorokaki* door scraper
搔器 *dorokakiki* door scraper
15 縄 *doronawa* unpreparedness, last-minute preparations; locking the barn after the horse is gone
17 濘 *nuka(ru), nukaru(mu)* get muddy, be muddy, be slushy. *nukarumi, nukari, deinei* mud, slush, mire; muddy road

A 油 3106 / J4c7d / M17253 YU. YŪ. *abura* oil. *abura(giru)* be excessively fat.

[2]入 *aburai(ri)* oiled
[4]手 *aburade, aburatte* greasy hands
井 *yusei* oil well
井戸 *aburaido* oil well; oil spring
[5]田 *yuden* oil field, oil well, oil land
圧 *yuatsu* oil pressure; hydraulic
布 *yufu* oilcloth, oiled cloth
母頁岩 *yuboketsugan* oil shale
[6]虫 *aburamushi* cockroach; plant louse; hanger-on
団 *yuton* waxed cloth; oiled-paper cushion
気 *aburake, abura(k)ke* greasiness, oiliness
汗 *aburaase* perspiration from pain
[7]足 *aburaashi* sweaty feet
身 *aburami* fat (of meat)
冷 *yurei* oil cooling
状 *yujō no* oily
[8]性 *yusei no* oily
性塗料 *yusei toryō* oil paint
洋 *abura(o)soso(gu)* anoint with oil
注者 *abura(o)soso(gareta)mono* anointed one
送船 *yusōsen* oil tanker
送管路 *yusōkanro* pipeline
送管線 *yusōkansen* pipeline
[9]染 *aburaji(miru)* become oily or oil stained
単 *yutan* oilcloth, tarpaulin
[10]庫 *yuko* oil bunker
紙 *aburagami, yushi* oil paper, oiled paper
脂 *yushi* fat, fats and oils
差 *aburasa(shi)* oiler, oil cup, oil can
砥石 *abura toishi* oil stone
[11]断 *yudan* negligence, unpreparedness, carelessness
菜 *aburana* a rape (plant)
[12]揚 *aburaa(ge), aburage* fried tofu
壺 *aburatsubo* oil cup, oil can, oil bottle
然 *yūzen toshite* freely, copiously, abundantly
量計 *yuryōkei* oil gauge
絵 *aburae* oil painting
絵具 *abura enogu* oil paints
[13]煙 *yuen* lampblack, carbon black
煠 *aburaitame* frying
照 *aburade(ri)* sultry sun
障子 *aburashōji* translucent oiled-paper doors
搾 *aburashibo(ri)* oil press
搾具 *abura shiborigu* oil press
搾器 *abura shiboriki* oil press
[14]層 *yusō* oil strata
管 *yukan* oil pipe
墨 *aburazumi* marking ink
[15]締木 *aburashi(me)gi* oil press
槽 *yusō* oil tank
槽車 *yusōsha* tank car
槽船 *yusōsen* oil tanker
[16]濃 *abura(k)ko(i), aburako(i)* greasy, fatty, oily
薬 *aburagusuri* ointment, liniment, salve
[17]糟 *aburakasu* oil cake, the soy-bean waste after the oil is expressed
[18]蟬 *aburazemi* common locust
[20]灌 *abura(o)soso(gu)* anoint with oil
灌者 *abura(o)soso(gareta) mono* anointed one

A 法 3107 / J4b21 / M17290 Hō law, rule, principle; legislation, regulation; code; method, way, model, manner, system, process, art, technique; rites, religion, doctrine; reason; mood (of verbs). *nori* law, rule; model; doctrine.

[2]力 *hōriki* the merits of Buddhism
人 *hōjin* legal person, corporation
人税 *hōjinzei* corporation tax
[4]文 *hōbun* the law; letter of the law; law and literature
文化 *hōbunka suru* legalize, enact into a law
王 *Hōō* Pope; Gautama; famous priest
王庁 *Hōōchō* Vatican
王令 *Hōōrei* Papal decretals
王制度 *Hōō seido* Papal system, the Papacy
王使節 *Hōō shisetsu* Papal delegate
王政治 *Hōō seiji* Papacy
王無謬説 *Hōō mubyūsetsu* Papal infallibility
王権 *Hōōken* Papacy
王職 *Hōōshoku* Papacy
[5]外 *hōgai* exorbitant, unreasonable; extraordinary
主 *hossu, hosshu* high priest (of a Buddhist sect)
号 *hōgō* (Buddhist) posthumous name
令 *hōrei* laws and ordinances
[6]衣 *hōi, hōe* robes of (Buddhist) priests
式 *hōshiki* formula; form; method, system; formalities, usage

印 *hōin* the highest rank in the Buddhist priesthood; (Edo) scholar; (Edo) artist
灯 *hōtō* the light of Buddhism; religious tradition
会 *hōe* (Buddhist) memorial service
名 *hōmyō* (Buddhist) priest's name; posthumous name
7 身 *hosshin* immortal soul (in Buddhism)
医学 *hōigaku* medical jurisprudence
廷 *hōtei* law court, courtroom
廷侮辱 *hōtei bujoku* contempt of court
廷侮辱罪 *hōtei bujokuzai* contempt of court
8 例 *hōrei* regulations for carrying out laws
帖 *hōjō* folding copybook
的 *hōteki* legal, legalistic
服 *hōfuku* judge's robe, barrister's robe, clerical robe
官 *hōkan* judge; judiciary
典 *hōten* code of laws, statute
事 *hōji* (Buddhist) memorial service
治 *hōchi* constitutional government
治国 *hōchikoku* constitutional state
制 *hōsei* laws, legislation
制局 *Hōseikyoku* Legislative Bureau
制経済 *hōsei-keizai* law and economics
学 *hōgaku* law, jurisprudence
学士 *Hōgakushi* LL.B., Bachelor of Laws
学博士 *Hōgaku Hakushi* LL.D., Doctor of Laws
定 *hōtei* legal, designated by law
定伝染病 *hōtei densembyō* contagious disease designated by law
定相続人 *hōtei sōzokunin* an heir-at-law
定選挙費用 *hōtei senkyo hiyō* legal election fund
定貨幣 *hōtei kahei* legal tender
定猶予期間 *hōtei yūyo kikan* days of grace
9 度 *hatto* law, ordinance; prohibition
相 *Hōshō* Minister of Justice. *Hossō* Buddhist sect originating in the seventh century
科 *hōka* law course, law department
則 *hōsoku* law, rule
政 *hōsei* law and government
界 *hōkai* (Buddhism's) universe
皇 *hōō* tonsured emperor; Pope
要 *hōyō* (Buddhist) memorial service
律 *hōritsu* law
律上 *hōritsujō* legally
律学 *hōritsugaku* jurisprudence
律学者 *hōritsu gakusha* lawyer
律屋 *hōritsuya* lawyer
律家 *hōritsuka* lawyer, jurist
律案 *hōritsuan* proposed law
律書 *hōritsusho* law book
律語 *hōritsugo* legal term
10 師 *hōshi* (Buddhist) priest
悦 *hōetsu* religious exaltation, ecstasy, rapture
被 *happi* worker's livery coat
案 *hōan* bill, measure
華経 *Hokekyō* the Lotus Sutra
益剝奪 *hōeki hakudatsu* outlawry
11 眼 *hōgen* next to the highest priestly rank in Buddhism
経 *hōkei* law and economics
貨 *hōka* legal tender
術師 *hōjutsushi* magician
理 *hōri* principle of law
理学 *hōrigaku* jurisprudence
曹 *hōsō* judge, judiciary
曹界 *hōsōkai* legal circles
規 *hōki* regulations, laws; legislation
規典令 *hōki-tenrei* laws and regulations
規典例 *hōki-tenrei* laws and regulations
務 *hōmu* judicial affairs
務大臣 *Hōmu Daijin* Minister of Justice
務官 *hōmukan* judiciary, judge advocate
務省 *Hōmushō* Ministry of Justice
12 博 *Hōhaku* Doctor of Laws
統 *hōtō* the succession of (Buddhist) teachings
13 話 *hōwa* (Buddhist) sermon
楽 *hōraku* pleasure of a virtuous (Buddhist) life; entertainment; entertainment for the gods
14 網 *hōmō* justice, meshes of the law
語 *hōgo* (Buddhist) sermon
15 権 *hōken* legal right
談 *hōdan* (Buddhist) sermon
論 *hōron* (Buddhist) doctrinal discussion
幣 *hōhei* fapi, Chinese legal tender; legal currency
17 螺 *hora* trumpet shell; boast
螺吹 *horafu(ki)* boaster

螺貝 *horagai* conch, trumpet shell; boast
18 難 *hōnan* (Buddhist) religious persecution

6

浊 3108 / J-X / M-X Nonstandard for 濁 3348.

洙 3109 / J5e2c / M17381 SHU. JU. SU used in proper names.

洫 3110 / J5e29 / M17403 KYOKU. KEKI ditch, moat. *mizo* irrigation ditch.

洳 3111 / J5e2e / M17414 JO. NYO soak; wet, humid.

洶 3112 / J5e28 / M17417 KYŌ. KU *wa(ku)* gush forth, flow out.

洸 3113 / J5e2b / M17419 KŌ. Ō bubbling water sparkling in the sun; brave.

洽 3114 / J5e2a / M17426 KŌ. KYŌ *amane(ku)* widely, extensively; universally.

洌 3115 / J5e30 / M17361 RETSU pure.

洵 3116 / J5e2d / M17416 JUN alike. *makoto* truth.

洄 3117 / J-X / M17353 KAI flowing water.
12 游 *kaiyū* run of fish

洩 3118 / J314c / M17401 EI. SETSU. *mo(ru), mo(reru)* leak, escape; shine through; find expression; be disclosed; be omitted, be excluded. *mo(rasu)* spill, let leak; omit, miss, leave out; divulge; betray; give vent to, express; let go. *mo(ri)* leak, leakage.
14 聞 *mo(re)-ki(ku)* overhear

洛 3119 / J4d6c / M17383 RAKU Kyoto, the capital.
4 中 *rakuchū* in Kyoto
5 外 *rakugai* suburbs of Kyoto; metropolitan suburbs

洲 3120 / J3d27 / M17413 SHŪ continent. SU sand bar, shallows. *shima* island. *kuni* country.
4 内 *shūnai* inside the state; inside the country
5 外 *shūgai* outside the state; outside the country
11 崎 *susaki* sandspit

洟 3121 / J5e26 / M17387 I. TEI tear; nasal discharge. *hana, hanashiru* nasal discharge.
4 水 *hanamizu* watery nasal discharge
8 垂 *hanatare, hanatara(shi), hana(t)tare, hana(t)tara(shi)* dirty nose; sniveler
垂小僧 *hanatare kozō* dirty-nosed youngster; urchin

津 3122 / J4445 / M17396 B SHIN. *tsu* port, harbor; ferry. *tsuyu* juice; sap; soup, broth; gravy.
8 波 *tsunami* tsunami, tidal wave
9 津 *shinshin* brim full of
津浦浦 *tsutsu-uraura ni* throughout the land, in every nook and corner
10 浪 *tsunami* tsunami, tidal wave
11 液 *shin'eki* sputum, saliva

洪 3123 / J393f / M17402 B KŌ flood; vast.
3 大 *kōdai* great size
4 水 *kōzui, ōmizu* inundation, flood, deluge
7 図 *kōto* ambitious scheme
10 恩 *kōon* great blessings, great benevolence
11 基 *kōki* foundation of a great enterprise
13 業 *kōgyō* great achievement

洒 3124 / J5e2f / M17374 SHA. SON. SAI. SEN wash, rinse, sprinkle. *susu(gu)* wash, pour on, rinse.
9 洒落落 *shasha-rakuraku na* unconventional, frank, unconstrained
11 掃 *saisō* cleaning
脱 *shadatsu na* unconventional, unconstrained
12 落 *share(ru)* joke, play on words, dress stylishly, try to look smart. *sharaku na* unconventional, frank, unconstrained. *share* sense of humor; witticism, joke, pun, play on words, pun; personal adornment. *(o)share* personal adornment

4 心忄⺗戈戸手扌支攴攵文斗斤方无日曰月木欠止歹殳毋比毛氏气【水氵氺】6 火灬爪爫父爻爿丬片牙牛犬犭

4 心 忄 ⺗ 戈 戸 手 扌 支 攴 攵 文 斗 斤 方 无 日 曰 月 木 欠 止 歹 殳 毋 比 毛 氏 气 【水 6 氵 氺】 火 灬 爪 爫 父 爻 爿 丬 片 牙 牛 犬 犭

落気 *shareke, share(k)ke* a bent for joking; sense of humor; vanity in dress
落臭 *sharekusa(i)* knowing, smart, impudent

B **洞** 3125 / J4636 / M17386 Dō cavity. Tō cave. *hora* cave, den, excavation.
5 穴 *horaana dōketsu* cave, den, excavation
7 見 *dōken* insight, penetration
8 門 *dōmon* tunnel
9 峠 *hora(ga)tōge* sitting on the fence
11 視 *dōshi* insight, discernment
13 窟 *dōkutsu* cave
14 察 *dōsatsu, tōsatsu* insight, discernment
察力 *dōsatsuryoku* insight
察眼 *dōsatsugan* insight
18 観 *dōkan* insight, penetration

A **派** 3126 / J4749 / M17428 **派** 3127 / J-X / M17427 Ha group, party, clique; faction, sect; school (of art, etc.). *ha(suru)* dispatch, send.
4 手 *hade* flashiness, gaudiness, gaiety. *hade(yakana)* flashy, gaudy
手好 *hadezu(ki) na* fond of display
手者 *hadesha* man of fashion, a dandy
手姿 *hadesugata* flashy appearance
5 生 *hasei* derivation; dividing and growing
生的 *haseiteki* derivative, secondary
生語 *haseigo* a derivative
出 *hashutsu suru vi* and *vt* send out, dispatch; be derived from
出所 *hashutsujo* branch office; police box
出婦 *hashutsufu* housekeeper working by the day
7 別 *habetsu* division (by sects, etc.)
兵 *hahei* dispatch of troops
12 遣 *haken suru* send, dispatch
遣軍 *hakengun* expeditionary army
遣隊 *hakentai* detachment (of troops)
14 閥 *habatsu* clique, faction

B **浄** 3128 / J3e74 / M17451 **淨** 3163 / J5e46 / M17669 Jō. *kiyo(i)* clean, clear; pure, innocent, noble. *kiyo(meru)* purify, cleanse; consecrate; exorcise. *kiyo(maru), kiyo(mawaru)* be purified, be cleansed.
3 土 *jōdo* pure land, (Buddhist) paradise
土宗 *Jōdoshū* a Buddhist sect originating in the 12th century
土真宗 *Jōdo Shinshū* a Buddhist sect originating in *Jōdoshū*.
土教 *Jōdokyō* Buddhist teaching concerning paradise
4 火 *jōka* sacred fire
化 *jōka* purification, cleanup
水 *jōsui* clean water
水池 *jōsuichi* filter bed
5 写 *jōsha* clean copy
6 衣 *jōi, jōe* pure white robe; Shinto priest's robe
地 *jōchi* sacred area, temple area, temple food storehouse
7 戒 *jōkai* (Buddhist) commandments
9 界 *jōkai* sacred place, (Buddhist) paradise
玻璃 *jōhari* clear crystal
10 財 *jōzai* money offering, votive offering, collection
書 *jōsho* clean copy
11 域 *jōiki* sacred precincts
菌槽 *jōkinsō* septic tank
13 罪 *jōzai* purgation (from sins)
14 瑠璃 *jōruri* a ballad-drama
18 穢 *jōe* pure things and sordid; the world of the Buddhas and that of ordinary men

A **浅** 3129 / J4075 / M17452 **淺** 3162 / J5e49 / M17697 Sen. *asa(i)* shallow; superficial; short (time); slight (connection); pale, light (color). *asa(hakana)* frivolous, shallow, rash, foolish. *asa(mashii)* wretched, miserable, pitiable; despicable, base, shameful. *asa-* light (color); slight (wound).
3 才 *sensai* lack of ability, incompetence
4 手 *asade* slight wound
5 田 *asada* shallow rice field
7 見 *senken* superficial idea, shallow view
8 学 *sengaku* superficial knowledge, superficiality
知恵 *asajie* shallow wit
9 紅 *senkō* light red
海 *senkai* shallow sea
海魚 *senkaigyo* shallow-sea fish
草海苔 *asakusa nori* laver, sheets of dried seaweed
草紙 *asakusagami* coarse toilet paper
11 黄 *asagi* light blue, pale blue

黒 *asaguro(i)* dark, dusky, swarthy, brunet, dark-complexioned, dark-skinned
12 葱 *asagi* light blue, pale blue
13 蜊 *asari* short-necked clam
墓 *asahaka na* frivolous, shallow, rash, foolish
14 聞 *sembun* a narrow view
緑 *asamidori* light green
15 慮 *senryo* indiscretion, thoughtlessness
16 薄 *sempaku* shallowness; superficiality, flimsiness, frivolity
17 鍋 *usunube* shallow pan
19 瀬 *asase* shoal, shallows, sand bar, ford

A **洋** 3130 / J4d4e / M17363 Yō ocean, sea, channel. *yō-* foreign, Western, European.

2 刀 *yōtō* saber
3 上 *yōjō* on the ocean, in mid-ocean
4 犬 *yōken* Western dog
5 本 *yōhon* a Western book; a book bound in Western style
6 行 *yōkō* foreign travel; company, firm
灰 *yōkai* cement
式 *yōshiki* Western style
灯 *yōtō* lamp
8 服 *yōfuku* Western clothes
服屋 *yōfukuya* clothing store, tailor shop; tailor
学 *yōgaku* Western learning
学者 *yōgakusha* students of Western learning
画 *yōga* Western painting; Western film
画界 *yōgakai* Western art circles (in Japan)
画家 *yōgaka* painter of Western pictures
9 風 *yōfū* Western style
洋 *yōyō(taru)* vast, broad, wide
紅 *yōkō* carmine, crimson
盃 *koppu* tumbler, glass
室 *yōshitsu* Western-style room
食 *yōshoku* Western food
食屋 *yōshokuya* Western-style restaurant
食器 *yōshokuki* Western dishes
品 *yōhin* haberdashery
品店 *yōhinten* haberdasher's store
品屋 *yōhin'ya* haberdasher's store
10 酒 *yōshu* Western liquor
紙 *yōshi* Western paper
書 *yōsho* Western book
家具 *yōkagu* Western furniture
11 梨 *yōnashi* Western pear
貨 *yōka* Western money
菓子 *yōgashi* Western confectionery
12 間 *yōma* Western-style room
傘 *yōgasa* Western umbrella
装 *yōsō* Western dress
琴 *yōkin* piano
裁 *yōsai* Western dressmaking
裁学校 *yōsai gakkō* Western dressmaking school
裁師 *yōsaishi* Western-style dressmaker
13 楽 *yōgaku* Western music
楽器 *yōgakki* Western musical instruments
14 種 *yōshu* foreign breed
綴 *yōtoji* Western-style binding
銀 *yōgin* nickel silver, German silver
算 *yōzan* Western arithmetic
髪 *yōhatsu* Western hairdo
16 館 *yōkan* Western-style building

A **洗** 3131 / J4076 / M17379 SEN. *ara(u)* wash; inquire into, probe. *ara(i)* wash; washing.

3 上 *ara(i)-a(geru)* finish washing; wash well
4 分 *ara(i)-wa(keru)* separate by washing
5 立 *ara(i)da(teru), ara(i)-ta(teru)* examine closely, ferret out, check up on. *ara(i)ta(te)* just washed
去 *ara(i)-sa(ru)* wash away
礼 *senrei* baptism by sprinkling
礼式 *senreishiki* baptism by sprinkling
礼名 *senrelmel* name given at baptism
礼室 *senreishitsu* baptistry
礼場 *senreijō* baptistry
礼盤 *senreiban* baptismal font
6 米 *semmai* cleaned rice
7 足 *sensoku* washing the feet; foot bath
足式 *sensokushiki* foot-washing ceremony
車 *sensha* car wash
車場 *senshajō* car-washing place
8 物 *ara(i)mono* the washing, laundry
9 砂利 *ara(i)jari* washed gravel
浄 *senjō* washing, cleaning, rinsing; ablution
浄式 *senjōshiki* ablutions
面 *semmen* washing the face
面台 *semmendai* washstand
面所 *semmenjo* washroom, lavatory

面器 *semmenki* washbasin, washbowl
10 晒 *ara(i)zara(shi)* laundry-worn garment
浚 *ara(i)zara(i)* everything, the whole thing; completely
流 *ara(i)-naga(su)* wash away
粉 *ara(i)ko* powdered soap
剤 *senzai* cleansing agent, detergent
11 張 *ara(i)ha(ri)* fulling; washing and stretching
清 *ara(i)-kiyo(meru)* wash clean, cleanse
眼 *sengan* eye washing
脳 *sennō* brainwashing
12 場 *ara(i)ba* place to do laundry
湯 *sentō* bathhouse, public bath
落 *ara(i)-oto(su)* wash off, wash out (stain), rinse out (soap)
13 煉 *senren* refining; polishing
鉱 *senkō* ore washing
鉱夫 *senkōfu* ore washer (the workman)
14 滌 *sendeki, senjō* washing, rinsing
練 *senren* refining; polishing
髪 *sempatsu* washing the hair, shampoo. *ara(i)gami* washed hair
15 盤 *semban* washbasin, laver
16 薬 *ara(i)gusuri* lotion
17 濯 *ara(i)susu(gi)* washing, laundry. *sentaku* laundering. *susugi* rinsing, washing; water for washing the feet
濯石鹸 *sentaku sekken* laundry soap
濯板 *sentaku ita* washboard
濯物 *sentakumono* the washing, laundry
濯屋 *sentakuya* laundry; laundryman
濯挟 *sentakubasami* clothespins
濯機 *sentakuki* washing machine
濯盥 *sentakudarai* washtub

6 A **活** 3132 / J3368 / M17423 KATSU resuscitation; living; being helped. *i(kiru)* live, subsist, exist; be enlivened; stet; be safe (on first). *i(kasu)* revive, resuscitate; restore to life; let live, spare a life; make the most of; give life to; stet. *hatara(ku)* work, labor; do, act, commit, practice, work on; come into play; be conjugated; reduce the price. *i(keru)* keep alive; arrange flowers (in a vase). *iki* freshness; stet.
2 力 *katsuryoku* vitality
人 *katsujin* a living person
人形 *ikiningyō* living doll; lifelike doll
人画 *katsujinga* picture formed of living people
4 仏 *katsubutsu, ikibotoke* living Buddha; Grand Lama
火山 *kakkazan* active volcano
5 写 *kassha* candid photography
弁 *katsuben* silent-film interpreter
用 *katsuyō* practical use; declension, conjugation, inflection
用形 *katsuyōkei* conjugation
用例 *katsuyōrei* paradigm
用語 *katsuyōgo* inflected words
6 気 *kakki* liveliness, vigor, activity
気付 *kakkizu(keru)* invigorate, animate. *kakkizu(ku)* become active, become animated
字 *katsuji* type
字本 *katsujibon* books printed from movable type
字地金 *katsujijigane* type metal
字合金 *katsuji gōkin* type metal
字盤 *katsujiban* type case
字鋳造 *katsuji chūzō* type casting
字鋳造所 *katsuji chūzōsho* type foundry
字鋳造機 *katsuji chūzōki* type caster
7 作 *ikezuku(ri)* slicing live fish
花 *ikebana* flower arrangement
8 例 *katsurei* living example
法 *kappō* practical plan
況 *kakkyō* vigor, activity, liveliness
物 *katsubutsu* living being
性 *kassei* activated, active (oxygen)
性炭 *kasseitan* activated carbon
版 *kappan* type, printing
版本 *kappambon* printed book
版所 *kappanjo* print shop
版刷 *kappanzuri* type printing; printed matter
版屋 *kappan'ya* printer; print shop
9 活 *ikiiki* lively
胆 *ikigimo* liver from a living animal
計 *kakkei* livelihood, living
炭 *ikezumi* banked charcoal fire
発 *kappatsu* vigor, vivacity, activity
10 栓 *kassen* faucet
殺 *kassatsu* life and death
殺自在 *kassatsu-jizai* power of life and death
11 魚 *ikeuo* fish kept in tank for food
眼 *katsugan* open eyes, penetrating eye; insight
船 *ikebune* live-fish tank

断層 *katsudansō* active fault
動 *katsudō* activity, action, operations; energy; service; function; movies
動力 *katsudōryoku* activity, vitality
動的 *katsudōteki* active, dynamic
動写真 *katsudō shashin* moving picture
動家 *katsudōka* energetic person
12 喩法 *katsuyuhō* personification
13 路 *katsuro* way of escape, last resort
塞 *kassoku* piston
塞桿 *kassokukan* piston rod
14 歴 *katsureki* historical drama
語 *katsugo* living words, living language
15 劇 *katsugeki* action picture; riotous scene
潑 *kappatsu* vigor, vivacity, activity
線 *kassen* live wire
舞台 *katsubutai* living stage, arena, sphere of activity
16 嘴 *kasshi* faucet
21 躍 *katsuyaku suru* be active in, jump into action

A **海** 3133 / J3324 / M17450 **海** 3137 / J-X / M17503 KAI *umi* sea, ocean.

2 人 *ama, kaijin* fisherman; salt maker
人小舟 *ama obune* fisherman's boat
3 口 *kaikō* harbor entrance
士 *ama* fisherman; salt maker
女 *ama* woman shell diver
山 *umiyama* sea and mountains; height and depth
千山千 *umisen-yamasen* an old codger
上 *kaijō* maritime, seafaring, seaborne, overseas
上自衛隊 *Kaijō Jieitai* Maritime Self-Defense Force
上保安 *kaijō hoan* maritime safety
上保安庁 *Kaijō Hoanchō* Maritime Safety Agency
上保安官 *Kaijō Hoankan* Marine Police
上保安部 *Kaijō Hoambu* Marine Police headquarters
上保険 *kaijō hoken* maritime insurance
上権 *kaijōken* sea power
4 手 *umite* near the sea
月 *kurage* jellyfish. *kaigetsu* a clear moon over the sea
牛 *kaigyū, umiushi* sea cow, dugong
辺 *kaihen, umibe, unabata, umibeta* seashore, beach, coast, seaside
内 *kaidai* the whole (island) country
中 *kaichū* in the sea; marine. *watanaka* in the ocean; on the ocean
王星 *Kaiōsei* Neptune
水 *kaisui* sea water
水浴 *kaisuiyoku* sea bathing
水浴場 *kaisuiyokujō* bathing beach
水帽 *kaisuibō* bathing cap
水着 *kaisuigi* bathing suit
5 氷 *kaihyō* coastal sea ice
外 *kaigai* overseas, foreign; abroad
外版 *kaigaiban* overseas edition
外放送 *kaigai hōsō* overseas broadcasting
外事情 *kaigai jijō* overseas news
外派兵 *kaigai hahei* sending troops overseas
外発展 *kaigai hatten* overseas expansion
外進出 *kaigai shinshutsu* overseas expansion
外渡航 *kaigai tokō* foreign voyage
外電報 *kaigai dempō* overseas cable
6 気 *kaiki* sea air, sea breeze
防 *kaibō* coast defense
防艦 *kaibōkan* coast-defense ship
老 *ebi* lobster; shrimp, prawn
老色 *ebiiro* reddish brown
老茶 *ebicha* maroon
老錠 *ebijō* padlock
7 角 *kaikaku* headland, cape
里 *kairi* knot, nautical mile
図 *kaizu* marine chart
技 *kaigi* seamanship
抜 *kaibatsu* height above sea level
坊主 *umibōzu* sea monster
兵 *kaihei* (U.S.) marines
兵隊 *kaiheitai* (U.S.) marines
8 門 *kaimon* straits, channel, sound
国 *kaikoku* maritime nation, sea-girt country
松 *umimatsu* seacoast pines
法 *kaihō* maritime law
沿 *umizo(i)* coastlands
苔 *nori* laver (an edible seaweed)
苔巻 *norima(ki)* rice wrapped in seaweed
事 *kaiji* maritime affairs
事思想 *kaiji shisō* knowledge of the sea
事裁判所 *kaiji saibansho* maritime court
底 *kaitei* ocean floor; submarine
底火山 *kaitei kazan* submarine volcano

底地震 *kaitei jishin* submarine earthquake
底電信 *kaitei denshin* submarine telegram
底電線 *kaitei densen* submarine cable
岸 *kaigan* seashore, coast, beach, waterfront. *umigishi* beach, seaside
岸防備 *kaigam-bōbi* coast defense
岸沿 *kaiganzo(i) ni* along the coast; along the seashore
岸通 *kaigandō(ri)* bund
岸線 *kaigansen* coastline; coastal railway
9 面 *kaimen* (surface of) the sea, sea level. *umizura* surface of the sea
風 *kaifū, umikaze* sea breeze
相 *Kaishō* Navy Minister
神 *kaijin, kaishin, watatsumi* sea god, Neptune
胆 *uni* sea urchin
南 *kainan* southern coasts
星 *hitode* starfish
峡 *kaikyō* straits, channel, sound
峡植民地 *Kaikyō Shokuminchi* Straits Settlements
草 *kaisō, umikusa* seaweeds, marine plants
草麺 *kaisōmen* seaweed noodles
洋 *kaiyō* ocean
洋気候 *kaiyō kikō* marine climate
洋汚染 *kaiyō osen* marine contamination
洋学 *kaiyōgaku* oceanography
洋牧場 *kaiyō bokujō* marine ranching
洋観測衛星 *kaiyō kansoku eisei* marine observation satellite
軍 *kaigun* navy
軍力 *kaigunryoku* naval strength
軍大臣 *Kaigun Daijin* Navy Minister
軍工廠 *kaigun kōshō* naval dockyard
軍兵学校 *Kaigun Heigakkō* Naval Academy
軍国 *kaigunkoku* a naval power
軍省 *Kaigunshō* Admiralty, Navy Department
軍葬 *kaigunsō* navy funeral
軍旗 *kaigunki* navy flag
軍機 *kaigunki* navy plane
10 馬 *kaiba, seiuchi* walrus. *todo* sea lion
原 *unabara, wata(no)hara* ocean, sea, the deep
浜 *kaihin* seashore, beach, coast
流 *kairyū* ocean current
狸 *kairi* beaver
豹 *azarashi, kaihyō* seal
家 *umi (no) ie* beach pavilion
容 *kaiyō* magnanimous forgiveness
竜王 *kairyūō* dragon king, dragon god
員 *kaiin* sailor, seaman, crew
員審判所 *kaiin shimpanjo* marine court
陸 *kairiku* land and sea
陸空 *kairikukū* land, sea, and air
陸風 *kairikufū* land and sea breezes
11 魚 *kaigyo* sea fish
鳥 *kaichō, umidori* sea bird
亀 *umigame* sea turtle
道 *kaidō* coastal highway
域 *kaiiki* an area of the ocean
深 *kaishin* ocean depth
猫 *umi neko* sea gull
豚 *iruka* dolphin, porpoise
船 *umibune* seagoing vessel
蛇 *kaida, umi hebi* sea snake
商 *kaishō* marine commerce
運 *kaiun* marine transportation, maritime
運業 *kaiungyō* shipping business; merchant marine
産 *kaisan* marine products
産物 *kaisambutsu* marine products
産業 *kaisangyō* marine-products industry
12 湾 *kaiwan* gulf, bay
港 *kaikō* ocean port
淵 *kaien* ocean depths, ocean deep
程 *kaitei* distance by sea, nautical mileage
葬 *kaisō* burial at sea
堡 *kaihō* coastal battery
象 *seiuchi, kaizō* walrus
13 鼠 *namako* sea cucumber; sea slug
塩 *kaien* salt made from sea water
損 *kaison* sea damage
溝 *kaikō* an ocean deep
路 *kairo, umiji* ocean route, sea paths
際 *umigiwa* seaside, beach
戦 *kaisen* naval battle
跡湖 *kaisekiko* inland salt lake
賊 *kaizoku* pirate
賊版 *kaizokuban* pirated edition/version
賊船 *kaizokusen* pirate ship
14 鳴 *umina(ri), kaimei* roar of the ocean
端 *umibata* beach seashore, coast
精 *umi(no)sei* mermaid
綿 *kaimen* sponge

関 *kaikan* maritime customs
関税 *kaikanzei* import duties
15 蝕 *kaishoku* sea erosion
盤車 *hitode* starfish
潮 *kaichō* tide, current
潮音 *kaichōon* sound of the sea
16 鴨 *umigamo* sea duck
嘯 *kaishō* tidal bore
錨 *kaibyō* drag anchor
獣 *kaijū* marine animal
燕 *umi tsubame* stormy petrel
壁 *kaiheki* sea wall, breakwater
18 難 *kainan* sea disaster
難救護所 *kainan kyūgosho* life-saving station
難審判庁 *Kainan Shimpanchō* Marine Accidents Inquiry Agency
19 獺 *rakko* sea otter
藻 *kaisō* sea weeds, marine plants
霧 *kaimu* sea fog
20 鯽 *umi tanago* surf perch
21 魔 *Kaima* Davy Jones
22 鰻 *anago, umi unagi* sea eel
鷗 *umi kamome* sea gull
23 鱒 *umi masu* sea trout
26 驢 *ashika* sea lion, hair seal

7

涜 3134/J4642/M-X Nonstandard for **瀆** 3373.

溲 3135/J-X/M-X See **溲** 3265.

涉 3136/J-X/M17530 See **渉** 3190.

海 3137/J-X/M17503 See **海** 3133.

涛 3138/J4573/M-X Nonstandard for **濤** 3361.

浙 3139/J5e36/M17458 SETSU used in proper names; wash (rice).

浤 3140/J5e33/M17471 KŌ. GYŌ water gushing forth; clear deep water.

浹 3141/J5e35/M17506 SHŌ far and wide; period. *amane(ku)* widely, extensively; universally.

浬 3142/J333d/M17485 RI nautical mile, knot. *kairi* knot, nautical mile.

涕 3143/J5e38/M17543 TEI. *namida* tears; sympathy.
8 泣 *teikyū* weeping

涎 3144/J5e37/M17536 SEN. EN. *yodare* slobber, saliva.
11 掛 *yodareka(ke)* bib

涓 3145/J5e32/M17541 KEN a drop; pure.
10 埃 *ken'ai* something very small
14 滴 *kenteki* a drop of water

浣 3146/J5e31/M17470 KAN wash.
6 衣 *kan'i* washing clothes; laundered clothes
13 腸 *kanchō* enema
14 熊 *araiguma* raccoon

浩 3147/J3940/M17479′ **澔** 3315/J-X/M18338 KŌ wide expanse; abundance; vigorous.
12 然 *kōzen taru* great and prosperous; broad-minded
然気 *kōzen (no) ki* energy, vigor
19 瀚 *kōkan na* bulky, voluminous

涅 3148/J5e3a/M17521 **湼** 3149/J-X/M17574 NETSU black soil.
6 色 *kuri iro* black
14 槃 *nehan* nirvana
槃会 *nehan'e* anniversary of the Buddha's death

涌 3150/J4d30/M17534 **湧** 3207/J4d2f/M17862 YŌ. YU. *wa(ku) vi* boil, get hot; ferment; seethe; be in an uproar; gush out; grow, breed, be hatched. *wa(kasu) vt* boil; heat up (the bath); melt.
5 立 *wa(ki)-ta(tsu)* bubble up, well up
出 *wa(ki)-de(ru), yōshutsu suru, yūshutsu suru* gush forth or out, spout, flow out, well up, bubble up. *wa(ki)-da(su)* cause to gush out
10 起 *wa(ki)-oko(ru)* arise

浚 3151 / J5e34 / M17460 SHUN. *sara(eru), sara(u)* clean, dredge, drag.
8 泥機 *shundeiki* mud dredge
12 渫 *shunsetsu* dredging
渫船 *shunsetsusen* dredger
渫機 *shunsetsuki* dredger

B **浜** 3152 / J494d / M17462 **濱** 3355 / J5f40 / M18537 HIN. *hama* beach, seashore; fishing village.
4 手 *hamate* near the beach
辺 *hamabe* beach, seashore
9 面 *hamazura* the open beach
風 *hamakaze* beach wind
12 焼 *hamayaki* sea bream broiled whole
街道 *hamakaidō* beach road
13 路 *hamaji* beach road

A **浴** 3153 / J4d61 / M17496 YOKU. *yoku(suru)* bathe, be favored with; bask in. *a(biru)* bathe in, pour on oneself, bask in, be flooded with, be under (fire); be accused of, be charged with, expose oneself to, be subjected to, receive (applause). *a(biseru)* pour on; subject to, impute to, deluge with.
5 用 *yokuyō* for the bath
用石鹸 *yokuyō sekken* bath soap
6 衣 *yokui, yukata* unlined cotton kimono, bathrobe, dressing gown
衣掛 *yukataga(ke) de* wearing an unlined summer kimono
9 後 *yokugo* after the bath
客 *yokkaku, yokkyaku* bathing guest
室 *yokushitsu* bathroom
11 掛 *a(bise)-ka(keru)* pour on; subject to, impute to, deluge with
12 場 *yokujō* bathroom, bathhouse
場主 *yokujōshu* bathhouse keeper
15 槽 *yokusō* bathtub

B **涙** 3154 / J4e5e / M17573′ **淚** 3161 / J-X / M17644 **泪** 3071 / J5e25 / M17318
RUI. *namida* tear; sympathy. *namida(ppoi)* easily shedding tears.
5 乍 *namidanaga(ra) ni* in tears
7 含 *namidagu(mu)* be moved to tears. *namidagu(mashii)* tearful, sad, pathetic
声 *namidagoe* tearful voice
8 金 *namidakin* consolation money
雨 *namidaame* a light rain
10 脆 *namidamoro(i)* given to weeping
11 眼 *ruigan* eyes welling with tears
13 腺 *ruisen* tear gland
14 管 *ruikan* tear duct
18 顔 *namidagao* tearful face
22 嚢 *ruinō* tear sac

B **浪** 3155 / J4f32 / M17482 RŌ. *nami* waves, billows.
2 人 *rōnin* lordless samurai, adventurer; unsuccessful examinee, jobless person
人組 *rōningumi* students who failed in entrance examinations
3 士 *rōshi* lordless samurai, adventurer
6 宅 *rōtaku* home of a lordless samurai
曲 *rōkyoku* musical recital of ancient tales
曲師 *rōkyokushi* minstrels
7 花節 *naniwabushi* minstrels; musical recital of ancient tales
花節語 *naniwabushikata(ri)* minstrels
9 速 *Naniwa* ancient Osaka
10 浪 *rōrō* wandering
華 *Naniwa* ancient Osaka
12 費 *rōhi* waste, extravagance
費癖 *rōhiheki* spendthrift habits
14 漫主義 *rōman shugi* romanticism
漫的 *rōmanteki* romantic (school)
漫派 *rōmanha* romantic school, romanticism

B **浦** 3156 / J313a / M17475 HO. *ura* creek, inlet; bay, gulf; beach, seacoast.
2 人 *urabito* seaside dweller
4 辺 *urabe* seacoast
6 舟 *urabune, urafune* ships at anchor in the bay
凪 *uranagi* calm on the bay
回 *urawa, urami* coastal indentations
曲 *urawa, urami* coastal indentations
伝 *urazuta(i)* following the seacoast
安国 *Urayasu (no) Kuni* (ancient name for) Japan
7 里 *urazato* seaside village
8 波 *uranami* breakers
和 *uranagi* calm on the bay
9 風 *urakaze* sea breeze
洲 *urasu* sandspit
12 越 *urako(shi)* crossing the bay; sea breeze
13 路 *uraji* road leading to the beach

15 潮 *urashio* bay tides
17 磯 *uraiso* sea beach

B 浸 3157 / J3f3b / M17505′ SHIN. *hita(su)* soak, dip, steep, immerse, moisten, wet, dunk, drench. *hita(ru)* be soaked in, be immersed in, be flooded, be submerged; be bathed in; be addicted to. *tsuka(ru)* be soaked in; be submerged; be flooded; take a dip; be seasoned. *(o)hita(shi)* boiled greens with dressing.

2 入 *shinnyū suru* seep in, flow in
4 水 *shinsui* inundation, flood, submersion; leaking
水家屋 *shinsui kaoku* houses under water
5 出 *shinshutsu* exudation, percolation, effusion; extraction (in chemistry)
礼 *shinrei* baptism by immersion
礼水槽 *shinrei (no) suisō* baptistry
礼式 *shinreishiki* an immersion baptism
礼派 *Shinreiha* Baptists
礼教会 *Shinrei Kyōkai* Baptist Church
礼場 *shinreijō* baptistry
9 食 *shinshoku* erosion; corrosion
染 *shinsen* permeation, infiltration, saturation
透 *shintō* permeation, infiltration, osmosis
透作戦 *shintō sakusen* infiltration operations
10 害 *shingai* infringement, violation, trespass, impairment
15 潤 *shinjun* permeation, infiltration, saturation
蝕 *shinshoku* erosion; corrosion

A 消 3158 / J3e43 / M17529′ SHŌ. *ke(su)* extinguish, blow out; turn off, erase, cross out; neutralize (odors or poisons); deaden (noise); cancel (in fractions). *ki(eru), ki(yuru)* be extinguished; melt away; disappear, die out; wear away; burst (as a bubble).

2 入 *ki(e)-i(ru)* vanish
3 口 *ke(shi)guchi* fire-fighting front
4 方 *ki(e)gata* about to go out or disappear
止 *ke(shi)-to(meru)* extinguish, get under control
火 *shōka* fire fighting
火水管 *shōka suikan* fire hose
火用 *shōkayō* for fire
火用水 *shōka yōsui* water for fires
火栓 *shōkasen* fire hydrant
火器 *shōkaki* fire extinguisher
化 *shōka* digestion, assimilation
化力 *shōkaryoku* digestive power
化不良 *shōka furyō* indigestion
化作用 *shōka sayō* digestive process
化剤 *shōkazai* aid to digestion
化液 *shōka eki* digestive fluid
化管 *shōkakan* digestive tract
化器 *shōkaki* digestive organs
5 去 *ke(shi) sa(ru)* erase, blot out. *ki(e)-sa(ru)* disappear, die out, melt away. *shōkyo* elimination
失 *ki(e)-u(seru)* die out, disappear, fail. *shōshitsu* disappearance, vanishing
石灰 *shōsekkai* slacked lime, calcium hydroxide
6 印 *keshiin* postmark, cancellation stamp
灯 *shōtō* putting out the lights
光 *shōkō* passing time, getting along
防 *shōbō* fire fighting
防手 *shōbōshu* fire fighter
防夫 *shōbōfu* fireman
防庁 *Shōbōchō* The Fire Defense Agency
防自動車 *shōbō jidōsha* fire engine
防官 *shōbōkan* fire-department officer
防栓 *shōbōsen* fire hydrant
防部 *shōbōbu* fire department
防組 *shōbōgumi* company of fire fighters
防隊 *shōbōtai* fire brigade
防署 *shōbōsho* fire station
7 沈 *shōchin* dejection, depression
却 *shōkyaku* erasure, effacement; expenditure; repayment, redemption, amortization
8 長 *shōchō* ebb and flow, prosperity and decay
果 *ki(e)-ha(teru)* disappear, vanish
炎剤 *shōenzai* an antiphlogistic
毒 *shōdoku* disinfection, sterilization, fumigation, pasteurization
毒衣 *shōdokui* disinfected garment
毒液 *shōdoku eki* antiseptic solution
毒済 *shōdokuzu(mi)* disinfected
毒器 *shōdokuki* sterilizer
毒薬 *shōdokuyaku* disinfectant
9 飛 *ke(shi)-to(bu)* fly off
除 *shōjo* deletion
炭 *ke(shi)zumi* extinguished charcoal

音 *shōon* silencing (a machine)
音器 *shōonki* silencer, muffler, mute, damper
10 残 *ki(e)-noko(ru), ke-noko(ru)* remain unmelted; linger (snow)
消 *ki(e)gi(e)* (a fire) just about out; absentmindedness
夏 *shōka* summering, going away for the summer
耗 *shōkō suru, shōmō suru* consume, exhaust, dissipate, use up
耗品 *shōmōhin* supplies, consumer goods
耗症 *shōmōshō* atrophy, a wasting disease
耗戦 *shōmōsen* war of attrition
息 *shōsoku* news, letter, circumstances
息子 *shōsokushi* doctor's probe
息文 *shōsokubun* personal letter
息通 *shōsokutsū* informed person
息筋 *shōsoku suji* informed circles
11 掛 *ki(e)-ka(karu)* about to go out, about to disappear
12 閑 *shōkan* killing time
散 *shōsan* dissipation, dispersion, disappearance
壺 *ke(shi)tsubo* charcoal extinguishing jar
寒 *shōkan* getting through the winter
然 *shōzen(taru)* despondent, crestfallen
極 *shōkyoku* negative pole; conservatism
極主義 *shōkyoku shugi* negativism
極性 *shōkyokusei* passiveness
極的 *shōkyokuteki* passive, negative, conservative, destructive
費 *shōhi* consumption; expenditure
費力 *shōhiryoku* consumer buying power
費市場 *shōhi shijō* consumers' market
費地 *shōhichi* consumer area
費材 *shōhizai* consumer goods
費者 *shōhisha* consumer
費者物価 *shōhisha bukka* consumer price
費者物価指数 *shōhisha bukka shisū* consumer price index
費物資 *shōhi busshi* consumer goods
費高 *shōhidaka* (amount of) consumption
費財 *shōhizai* consumer goods
費組合 *shōhi kumiai* cooperative society
費税 *shōhizei* excise tax, consumption tax
13 滅 *ke(shi)-horo(bosu)* destroy, consume. *shōmetsu suru* be destroyed. *shōmetsu* extinction, disappearance, nullification
煙機 *shōenki* smoke consumer
14 磁 *shōji* demagnetization
15 憂 *shōyū* dispelling grief
16 磨 *shōma* abrasion, wearing down
18 難 *ki(e)ga(te) no* lingering (snow)
20 護謨 *keshigomu* rubber eraser

B **浮** 3159 / J4962 / M17487 FU. *u(ku)* float, be floated, rise to the surface; be cheered up; be set on edge, feel loose (teeth); be left over, be saved. *u(kasu), u(kaberu) vt* float, launch, sail (a toy ship), refloat; waft; express (feelings in the face); recall. *u(kabu) vi* float, refloat, surface; flit across (the face), occur to; play (about the lips, as a smile); rise in the world; rest in peace. *u(kareru)* be in high spirits, go on a spree. *u(kasareru)* be carried off, be captivated, be exhilarated. *u(kanu)* gloomy. *u(ki)* cork, float, buoy, lifebuoy, life belt. *u(ita)* gay, cheerful, frivolous. *u(ki)-* floating.
2 力 *furyoku* buoyancy, lift
3 土 *u(ki)tsuchi* light floating soil
女 *u(kare)me* prostitute
上 *u(ki)-a(geru)* come to the surface, surface, float, refloat, be refloated; be lifted out of the water; come out in relief. *fujō suru, u(ki)-a(garu), u(kabi)-a(garu)* float, refloat, surface
上彫 *u(ki)a(ge)bo(ri)* relief, embossed carving
4 心 *fushin* center of buoyancy
木 *fuboku* driftwood
5 立 *u(ki)-ta(tsu)* be buoyant, be cheered up, be exhilarated
付 *u(wa)tsu(ku)* be fickle, be flippant, be restless
氷 *fuhyō* ice floe, drift ice
出 *u(ki)-de(ru)* come to the surface; loom. *u(ki)da(shi)* embossed
石 *fuseki, karuishi, u(ki)ishi* pumice stone
石鹸 *u(ki)sekken* floating soap
世 *ukiyo* this transitory world, the earth
世波 *ukiyo (no) nami* this world's troubles

世風 *ukiyo (no) kaze* this world's troubles
世草子 *ukiyozōshi* realistic Edo novel
世絵 *ukiyoe* genre picture, ukiyoe
世絵派 *ukiyoeha* the ukiyoe school
世絵師 *ukiyoeshi* an ukiyoe artist
6 舟 *u(ki)bune* pontoon
名 *u(ki)na* romance, scandal, rumor, love affair
灯台 *u(ki)tōdai* lightship
気 *u(wa)ki* inconstancy, faithless love, wantonness, affair
気分 *u(kare) kibun* sportive spirit, mirth, gaiety
気者 *u(wa)kimono* inconstant lover, licentious person
7 言 *fugen* wild rumor, unfounded report
身 *u(ki)mi* floating on one's back
体 *futai* floating body
沈 *fuchin, u(ki)shizu(mi)* rise and fall, ebb and flow, ups and downs, vicissitudes
男 *u(kare) otoko* dissolute man
足 *u(ki)ashi* wavering
足立 *u(ki)ashida(tte)* ready to run away
足場 *u(ki)ashiba* floating work platform
8 沼 *u(ki)numa, u(ki)nu* muddy swamp
歩 *u(kare)-aru(ku)* gad around. *u(ki)ayu(mi)* walking lightly, tiptoeing
具 *u(ki)gu* water wings
9 垢 *u(ki)aka* scum
城 *fujō, u(ki)shiro* floating castle, giant battleship
洲 *u(ki)su* floating grass plot (in a muddy lake)
草 *u(ki) kusa* floating weed, duckweed; precarious business
10 根 *u(ki) ne* roots of water plants
浮 *u(ki)u(ki) to* buoyantly, cheerfully, jauntily
秤 *u(ki)bakari* hydrometer
脂 *u(ki) abura* floating oil
烏 *u(kare)garasu* crow crying by moonlight
島 *u(ki) shima* floating island
荷 *u(ki)ni* flotsam, flotage
華 *fuka* display, ostentation, vanity, frivolity
起重機 *u(ki) kijūki* floating crane
流 *furyū* floating, drifting
流水雷 *furyū suirai* floating mine
流機雷 *furyū kirai* floating mine, drifting mine
浪 *furō* vagrancy, wandering
浪人 *furōnin* a vagrant
浪児 *furōji* juvenile vagrant, waif
浪者 *furōsha* hobo, tramp, vagabond
11 魚 *u(ki) uo* surface fish
彫 *ukibori* relief, embossed carving
萍 *u(ki) kusa* floating plants
袋 *u(ki)bukuro* air bladder; water wings, life preserver, float, tire
巣 *u(ki)su* floating nest
船渠 *u(ki)dokku* floating dock
遊 *fuyū* floating, suspension
遊生物 *fuyū seibutsu* plankton
動 *fudō suru* float; be wafted; fluctuate; be unsettled
動人口 *fudō jinkō* floating population
12 揚 *fuyō* floating, flotage, flotation
渣 *u(ki)kasu* scum
游 *fuyū* floating, suspension
葉 *fuyō, u(ki)ha* floating leaf
雲 *fuun, u(ki)gumo* floating cloud; something unsettled
貸 *u(ki)ga(shi)* illegal loan
棧橋 *u(ki)sambashi* floating pier
13 腰 *u(ki)goshi no* wavering, unsteady, faltering
腫 *muku(mu)* swell, bloat. *fushu, mukumi* edema, dropsy
寝 *u(ki)ne* sleeping in a ship, uneasy sleep; sleeping adulterously
14 漂 *fuhyo* floating, flotage
説 *fusetsu* wild rumor, speculation
塵子 *unka* leaf hopper, a rice insect
15 標 *fuhyō* buoy
潮 *u(ki)shio* tidal current
輪 *u(ki)wa* buoyant water ring
16 橋 *fukyō, u(ki)hashi* floating bridge, pontoon bridge
錨 *fubyō* floating anchor, drift anchor
薄 *fuhaku* frivolity, levity
18 織 *u(ke)o(ri), u(ki)o(ri)* weaving with raised figures; brocade
騒 *u(kare)sawa(gi)* merrymaking; noisy party
19 瀬 *u(kabu)se* chances in life
22 嚢 *u(ki)bukuro* air bladder; water wings, life preserver, float, tire

A **流** 3160 / J4e2e / M17572′ RU. RYŪ current; counter for flags. *naga(reru)* flow, trickle, ooze, drain, run down; be washed away; float, drift; wander; be forfeited, be foreclosed; lapse; incline to; be swayed by; (years) pass. *naga(su)* dash, pour, sluice, let run out, flush; float, set adrift; spill; shed (tears); wash away, wash off; forfeit, foreclose; exile; cruise (taxis). *naga(re)* flow, stream, waters, current; passage (of time), descent; school; abandonment; foreclosure; tendency. *naga(shi)* sink; bath-attendant service; cruising (taxi); strolling musician. *(o)naga(re)* suspension, adjournment, calling off. *-ryū* style, fashion, type, form, manner; school, system; class, order, rate, rank, grade.

2 人 *runin* exile
入 *ryūnyū suru, naga(re)-i(ru)* flow into
3 川 *naga(re)gawa* running stream
下 *naga(re)-kuda(ru)* flow down; drink down; descend
亡 *ryūbō* having no settled abode
丸 *naga(re)dama* stray bullet
4 木 *ryūboku, naga(re)gi* driftwood
水 *naga(re) mizu, ryūsui* running water
元 *naga(shi)moto* kitchen sink and work area
込 *naga(re)-ko(mu)* flow into, run into, drift into. *naga(shi)-ko(mu)* wash down, pour into
込担保 *naga(re)ko(mi) tampo* foreclosure
5 用 *ryūyō* diversion, misappropriation
目 *naga(shi)me* sidelong glance
矢 *naga(re)ya* stray arrow
石 *sasuga ni* as might be expected
去 *naga(re)-sa(ru)* flow past
氷 *ryūhyō* drift ice, ice drift
失 *ryūshitsu suru* be washed away
出 *naga(re)-de(ru), naga(re)-da(su)* flow out, flow on, gush forth; drain out, drift away; shed water. *ryūshutsu* discharge, outward flow, drain (of gold)
民 *ryūmin* drifting people, displaced persons
布 *rufu* circulation, diffusing, dissemination
布本 *rufubon* popular edition
6 血 *ryūketsu* bloodshed
返 *naga(re)-kae(ru)* flow back
汗 *ryūkan* perspiration
灯 *ryūtō* setting paper lanterns adrift; a drifting lantern
合 *naga(re)-a(waseru)* flow together
会 *ryūkai* adjournment for lack of a quorum
年 *ryūnen* the stream of time
刑 *ryūkei, rukei* deportation, banishment, exile; transportation of a criminal
刑地 *ryūkeichi* penal colony
刑者 *ryūkeisha* an exile
行 *naga(re)-yu(ku)* flow along. *haya(ru)* be fashionable, be popular, be prevalent; flourish, prosper, have a large practice. *ryūkō, hayari* fashion, popularity, prevalence
行文句 *hayari monku* cant phrase
行地 *ryūkōchi* infected area
行児 *ryūkōji, hayari(k)ko* popular person; popular geisha
行言葉 *hayari kotoba* popular expression
行性感冒 *ryūkōsei kambō* flu, influenza
行風 *hayari kaze* influenza
行後 *ryūkōoku(re)* going out of fashion
行病 *ryūkōbyō, hayari yamai* epidemic, pestilence
行眼 *hayarime* conjunctivitis
行感冒 *ryūkō kambō* flu, influenza
行語 *ryūkōgo* a word on everybody's lips
行歌 *hayari uta, ryūkōka* popular song
7 作 *naga(re)zuku(ri)* wave style of shrine roof
作業 *naga(re) sagyō* assembly-line operation
体 *ryūtai* fluid
体力学 *ryūtai rikigaku* hydrodynamics
言 *ryūgen, rugen* false rumor
言飛語 *ryūgenhigo* rumor, gossip
言蜚語 *ryūgenhigo* rumor, gossip
8 歩 *naga(re)-aru(ku)* wander around
者 *naga(re)mono* vagrant; stranger; bird of passage
9 連 *ryūren* staying on
通 *ryūtsū* circulation of money; flow of water; ventilation
速 *ryūsoku* speed of a current
俗 *ryūzoku* convention, the beaten track
派 *ryūha* a school of thought; a system
眄 *ryūben, naga(shi)me* sidelong glance, looking askance

砂 *ryūsa, ryūsha* river sand; sandy area, desert
星 *ryūsei, naga(re)boshi* falling star, meteor; skyrocket
星雨 *ryūseiu* meteoric shower
星群 *ryūseigun* meteoric shower
10 涎 *ryūzen suru* (the mouth) waters for something; greatly desire
浪 *rurō* vagrancy, wandering, exile
涕 *ryūtei suru* shed tears, weep
11 過 *naga(re)-su(giru)* flow past, flow over
域 *ryūiki* river basin
捨 *naga(shi)-su(teru)* throw out (a liquid)
転 *ruten* perpetual motion; vicissitudes; wandering, vagrancy; transmigration
寄 *naga(re)-yo(ru)* drift in
産 *ryūzan* abortion; miscarriage, failure
動 *ryūdō* flow, flowing, floating, circulation, fluidity, mobility; liquid (assets); current (liabilities)
動体 *ryūdōtai* a fluid
動物 *ryūdōbutsu* fluid, liquid, liquid food
動性預金 *ryūdōsei yokin* floating deposit
動食 *ryūdōshoku* liquid diet, liquid food
動資本 *ryūdō shihon* liquid capital
12 弾 *ryūdan, naga(re)dama* stray bullet
渡 *naga(re)-wata(ru)* wander about
寓 *ryūgū* a roaming life
筋 *naga(re) suji* course (of a river)
着 *naga(re)-tsu(ku)* drift to, be washed ashore
落 *ryūraku* drift, driftage
量 *ryūryō* amount of flow
量計 *ryūryōkei* flow meter
13 罪 *ruzai* exile, banishment; transportation (of a criminal)
感 *ryūkan* flu, influenza
14 暢 *ryūchō* fluency, facility
網 *naga(shi) ami* drift net
説 *ryūsetsu* false rumor
15 儀 *ryūgi* a school of thought; style; system; method, form, way
弊 *ryūhei* current evil, abuse
質 *ryūshichi, naga(re)jichi* forfeited pawned article
線型 *ryūsenkei* streamlined
18 謫 *rutaku, ryūteki* exile, banishment
竄 *ryūzan* deportation, banishment, exile
19 離 *ryūri suru, sasura(u)* wander, roam
麗 *ryūrei na* fluent, flowing, smooth
鏑馬 *yabusame* horseback archery
21 露 *ryūro suru* disclose, reveal, express

8

涙 3161 / J-X / M17644 See 淚 3154.

淺 3162 / J5e19 / M17697 See 浅 3129.

淨 3163 / J5e46 / M17669 See 浄 3128.

渚 3164 / J3d6d / M-X See 渚 3228.

渕 3165 / J5e3c / M-X Nonstandard for 淵 3237.

淵 3166 / J5e3d / M17750 Nonstandard for 淵 3237.

渗 3167 / J-X / M-X Nonstandard for 滲 3302.

港 3168 / J-X / M-X See 港 3242.

淅 3169 / J5e48 / M17617 SEKI. SHAKU wash (rice); sound of rain

淇 3170 / J5e3f / M17620 KI. GI used in proper names.

淌 3171 / J5e45 / M17629 SHŌ. TŌ large waves.

淒 3172 / J5e47 / M17635 SEI. SAI *samu(i)* cold, cool. also nonstandard for 凄 425.

淕 3173 / J5e4c / M17638 RIKU. ROKU sleet, slush; sparkle of snow.

淞 3174 / J5e44 / M17651 SHŌ. SHU used in proper names.

淤 3175 / J5e4b / M17665 YO. O mud; clog up; obstruct. *doro* mud.

淬 3176 / J5e43 / M17679 SAI. SE *nira(gu)* temper (a sword); anneal; quench.

淮 3177 / J5e4e / M17682 KAI. E. WAI used in proper names.

淹 3178 / J5e3b / M17696 EN soak; linger; a long time; cover.

渮 3179 / J5e51 / M17782 KA used in proper names.

淆 3180 / J5e42 / M17619 KŌ turbidity; mixing.

B **涯** 3181 / J3336 / M17582 GAI shore.

淀 3182 / J4d64 / M17610 TEN. DEN. *yodo(mu)* stagnate, be stagnant; settle, deposit; be sluggish; hesitate; stammer. *yodo* pool (in a river), eddy.

涵 3183 / J-X / M17595 **涵** 3184 / J5e3e / M-X KAN steep (in water), dip; put into.
[15] 養 *kan'yō* cultivation, training, fostering

淼 3185 / J-X / M17699 BYŌ wide expanse of water.
[12] 淼 *byōbyō* endless expanse of water

淪 3186 / J5e4d / M17675 RIN sink; ripple.
[12] 落 *rinraku* ruin, misery, fall

淘 3187 / J4571 / M17642 TŌ select.
[7] 汰 *tōta* selection; weeding out, reducing, retrenchment; dismissal, shake-up

淙 3188 / J5e4a / M17643 SŌ sound of flowing water.
[11] 淙 *sōsō(taru)* murmuring, babbling

淳 3189 / J3d5f / M17690 JUN pure.
[6] 朴 *jumboku* simplicity and honesty
[7] 良 *junryō* simple goodness

B **渉** 3190 / J3e44 / M17749′ **涉** 3136 / J-X / M17530 SHŌ. *wata(ru)* cross, ford, ferry; be imported; change hands; make one's way through life; sweep across; migrate; be provided.
[5] 外 *shōgai* public relations, liaison
[11] 猟 *shōryō* extensive reading

B **淑** 3191 / J3d4a / M17634 SHUKU. *shito(yakana)* graceful, polite, gentle; pure.
[3] 女 *shukujo* lady
[14] 徳 *shukutoku* womanly virtues

涸 3192 / J5e41 / M17601 KO. *ka(reru) vi* dry up, go dry; be exhausted; mature, mellow. *ka(rasu) vt* dry up, exhaust.
[11] 渇 *kokatsu suru* dry up; be exhausted; become poverty-stricken
[14] 竭 *koketsu suru* dry up

淦 3193 / J5e40 / M17667 KAN. KON. *aka* bilge water.
[4] 水 *kansui* bilge water
[6] 汲 *akakumi* bailing equipment
[8] 取 *akato(ri)* bailing equipment

淋 3194 / J4e54 / M17626 RIN lonely. *sabi(reru)* become deserted, decline in prosperity. *sabi(shii), sami(shii), samu(shii)* lonely, lonesome, solitary, deserted, desolate.
[4] 巴液 *rimpa eki* lymph
巴腺 *rimpasen* lymph gland
[10] 疾性 *rinshitsusei* gonorrheal
[14] 漓 *rinri(taru)* profuse

B **渇** 3195 / J3369 / M17748 **渴** 3208 / J-X / M17788 KATSU thirst. *kas(suru)* be thirsty; dry (up); long for. *kawa(ku)* be thirsty; feel dry; dry up, be parched. *kawa(ki)* thirst.
[4] 水 *kassui* water shortage
水期 *kassuiki* water-shortage period
[6] 仰 *katsugō, katsugyō* adoration, admiration
[10] 衰 *kawa(ki)-otoro(eru)* be dry and dreary
[11] 望 *kawa(ki)-nozo(mu)* long for. *katsubō* craving, longing, thirsting for

B **渓** 3196 / J374c / M-X **溪** 3253 / J5e64 / M17967 KEI valley. *tani* valley.

⁴水 *keisui* mountain stream
⁷谷 *keikoku* valley, ravine, canyon
声 *keisei* sound of a valley stream
⁹泉 *keisen* valley spring
¹⁰流 *keiryū* mountain stream
¹²間 *keikan* ravine

A **済** 3197 / J3a51 / M17749 **濟** 3354 / J5f3b / M18498 SAI. SEI. *su(mu)* end; do without; avoid; be excusable; need not. *su(masu), su(maseru)* finish up; settle (one's account); make do. *na(su)* pay back. *suku(u)* save, help, rescue, relieve (suffering), redeem, reclaim. *su(manai)* inexcusable, unjustifiable, regrettable, repentant. *su(mimasen)* Excuse me; I'm sorry. *su(mi)* settled, O.K.. *-zu(mi)* finished.
³口 *su(mi)kuchi* the end of an incident
⁵生 *saisei* life saving
民 *saimin* relieving the sufferings of the people
世 *saisei* social reform
世事業 *saisei jigyo* public-welfare work
⁹度 *saido* (Buddhist) redemption, salvation (from pain)
¹¹済 *seisei, saisai* many
崩 *na(shi)-kuzu(su)* pay little by little; finish little by little. *na(shi)kuzu(shi)* payment by installments

B **涼** 3198 / J4e43 / M17606 **凉** 421 / J515a / M1665 RYŌ cool. *suzu(mu)* cool oneself, enjoy the evening air. *suzu(shii), suzu(yaka) na* cool, refreshing.
⁵台 *suzu(mi)dai* bench for enjoying the evening cool
⁶舟 *suzu(mi)bune* barge for enjoying the evening cool
気 *ryōki* the cool air
⁸雨 *ryōu* cooling rain
味 *ryōmi* coolness, cool
夜 *ryōya* cool evening
⁹風 *suzukaze, ryōfū* cool breeze
秋 *ryōshū* cool fall; ninth lunar month
客 *suzu(mi)kyaku* people enjoying the cool evening

A **液** 3199 / J3155 / M17586 EKI liquid, fluid, juice, sap, secretion. *tsuyu* juice; sap; soup, broth; gravy.
⁴化 *ekika* liquefaction
⁵圧 *ekiatsu* fluid pressure
汁 *ekijū, tsuyu* juice; sap
⁷冷 *ekirei* liquid-cooling
状 *ekijō* liquid state
体 *ekitai* liquid, fluid
体比重計 *ekitai hijūkei* hydrometer
体圧力 *ekitai atsuryoku* fluid pressure
体空気 *ekitai kūki* liquid air
体燃料 *ekitai nenryō* liquid fuel
⁸肥 *ekihi* liquid fertilizer
⁹面 *ekimen* surface of a liquid
¹⁰浸 *ekishin* immersion
剤 *ekizai* liquid medicine
¹²量 *ekiryō* liquid measure
晶 *ekishō* liquid crystal

B **渋** 3200 / J3d42 / M17750′ **澁** 3314 / J5f27 / M18312 JŪ. SHŪ. *shibu(ru)* hesitate, be reluctant; have loose painful bowel movements. *shibu* puckery taste (of persimmons); sobriety, quietness. *shibu(i)* puckery, astringent; sullen; quiet, sober; tasteful (in dress).
⁵皮 *shibukawa* astringent skin (of a chestnut); discolored skin
⁶色 *shibu iro* tan color
⁷抜 *shibunu(ki)* removing puckery taste
⁸味 *shibumi* puckery taste, astringency; good taste, sobriety, refinement
苦 *jūku* bitter puckery taste; disharmony
⁹面 *jūmen, shibuzura, shibutsura* sullen face, grimace
柿 *shibugaki* puckery persimmon
茶 *shibucha* coarse tea
¹⁰紙 *shibukami, shibugami* paper treated with astringent persimmon juice
¹¹渋 *shibushibu, shibujibu, shibu(ri)-shibu(ri)* reluctantly, grudgingly
¹³滞 *jūtai* stagnation, retardation
腹 *shibu(ri)bara* painful loose bowels

B **添** 3201 / J453a / M17698 TEN. *so(u) vi* accompany; marry; be added to; suit, meet, satisfy, be adjusted to. *so(eru) vt* add to, attach, append; accompany; garnish; imitate.
⁴文 *so(e)bumi* accompanying letter
木 *so(e)gi* splint, splice, brace
手紙 *so(e)tegami* accompanying letter
⁵付 *tempu suru* append, accompany
加 *tenka suru* annex, append, add

加物 *tenkabutsu* an annex; an appendix; an addition; an additive
7 役 *so(e)yaku* secondary post, assistant
状 *so(e)jō* accompanying letter
言葉 *so(e)kotoba* advice, support, good offices
8 物 *so(e)mono* addition, supplement, premium
臥 *so(i)bu(shi)* (mother and child) sleeping together
乳 *so(e)ji suru* suckle (a child)
9 削 *tensaku* correction
10 書 *tensho, so(e)ga(ki)* postscript, additional writing, letter of introduction; accompanying letter
11 遂 *so(i)-to(geru)* be faithful till death
12 景 *tenkei* human interest (in pictures)
13 寝 *so(i)ne* sleeping with one's child

B **淡** 3202 / J4338 / M17660 TAN. *awa(i)* light, faint, pale, fleeting; a little.
4 水 *tansui* fresh water
水魚 *tansuigyo* fresh-water fish
水湖 *tansuiko* fresh-water lake
5 白 *tampaku na* light; frank; indifferent to
6 色 *tanshoku* light color
7 赤色 *tansekishoku* rose color
8 泊 *tampaku na* light; frank; indifferent to
9 紅 *tankō* pink, rose pink
紅色 *tankōshoku* pink, rose pink
11 淡 *tantan(taru)* unconcerned, disinterested; plain, light
彩 *tansai* light coloring
菜 *tansai* sea mussel
雪 *awayuki* a light snowfall
黒色 *tankokushoku* gray
黄 *tankō* lemon yellow, buff, straw color
黄色 *tankōshoku* lemon yellow, buff, straw color
12 紫色 *tanshishoku* light purple
13 褐色 *tankasshoku* light brown
14 墨 *tamboku* pale India ink
緑色 *tanryokushoku* light green
15 影 *tan'ei* adumbration
17 藍色 *tanranshoku* light blue

淫 3203 / J307c / M17678 **婬** 1232 / J5535 / M6440 IN lewdness, licentiousness. *in(suru)* indulge in, go to excess. *mida(rana), mida(rigawashii)* licentious, indecent, lewd.
4 心 *inshin* sexual passion
6 行 *inkō* obscenity, harlotry
7 佚 *in'itsu* profligacy
乱 *inran* debauchery, lewdness, lasciviousness
声 *insei* cheap music
売 *imbai* prostitution
売婦 *imbaifu* prostitute
売宿 *imbai yado* brothel
8 雨 *in'u* prolonged rain, long damaging rain
奔 *impon* lewdness, lasciviousness
事 *inji* lascivious act
9 風 *impū* lewd manners, immorality
10 祠 *inshi* shrine of an evil deity
書 *insho* pornographic book
11 婦 *impu* harlot
欲 *in'yoku* lust
12 猥 *inwai* indecency, obscenity
13 楽 *inraku* carnal pleasure
15 蕩 *intō* dissipation, lewdness
慾 *in'yoku* lust
19 靡 *imbi* impurity, obscenity

A **混** 3204 / J3a2e / M17694 KON. *kon(jiru), kon(zuru) vi* and *vt* mix; blend; adulterate; confound, confuse. *ma(zeru)* mix, blend, mingle; include, let in on. *ma(zaru), ma(jiru) vi* be mixed, be blended; mingle with.
2 入 *konnyū suru vi* and *vt* mingle, adulterate; get mixed
5 用 *kon'yō suru vt* mix, mingle
6 色 *konshoku* compound color, hue
同 *kondō* confusion; mixing; merger
気 *ma(jiri)ke* mixture, impurities
返 *ma(ze)-kae(su), ma(zek)kae(su)* stir up; interrupt, interfere with
交 *konkō* confusion, jumble, mixture
在 *konzai* mixture
血 *konketsu* racial mixture
血児 *konketsuji* half-breed, mulatto, Eurasian
成 *konsei* mixture, composition
成酒 *konseishu* mixed liquor
合 *ma(ze)-a(waseru) vt* mix, blend, compound. *maji(ri)-a(u) vi* mix. *kongō* mixing; mixture
合列車 *kongō ressha* mixed freight-and-passenger train
合体 *kongōtai* a mixture
合物 *kongōbutsu* mixture, compound, amalgam

合酒 *kongōshu* mixed liquors
合機 *kongōki* mixing machine
7 作 *konsaku* mixed crops
沌 *konton* chaos, nebulosity, confusion
乱 *konran* disorder, chaos, confusion
声 *konsei* mixed voices
声合唱 *konsei gasshō* mixed chorus
8 迷 *kommei* confusion, bewilderment; stupor, unconsciousness
物 *ma(jiri)mono* mixture, something impure. *ma(ze)mono* adulteration, mixture
和 *konwa* mixture, mingling
和物 *konwabutsu* mixture
和機 *konwaki* mixing machine
9 信 *konshin* jamming, interference
10 浴 *kon'yoku* mixed bathing (in a bath house)
流 *konryū* crosscurrents
紡 *kombō* mixed spinning; mixed yarn
11 淆 *konkō* mixture, confusion, jumble
混 *konkon toshite* copious (flow); confused
12 然 *konzen(taru)* whole, entire, harmonious
13 戦 *konsen* free-for-all fight
載 *konsai* mixed loading; mixed freight
14 雑 *konzatsu* confusion, disorder, congestion
雑時 *konzatsuji* rush hour
15 線 *konsen* entanglement of wires; confusion
16 濁 *kondaku* turbidity, muddiness

Λ **清** 3205/J4036/M17695, SHŌ. SEI. SHIN China, Manchu (dynasty). *kiyo(meru)* purify, cleanse; consecrate; exorcise. *kiyo(maru), kiyo(mawaru)* be purified, be cleansed. *su(masu)* clear, clarify, settle; strain (one's ears); look grave. *kiyo(i)* clean, clear; pure, innocent; noble. *kiyo(me)* purification, sanctification; cleansing, purgation; exorcism; ablution. *kiyo(rakana)* clear.
1 一票 *kiyo(ki) ippyō* honest vote
3 子音 *seishiin* voiceless sound
4 水 *shimizu, seisui* clear water, pure water
元 *kiyomoto* a ballad-drama
友 *seiyū* refined friend
8 例 *seiretsu na* clear, limpid
所 *kiyodokoro* kitchen in a noble's home
明 *seimei* pure and clear
事 *kiyo(me)goto* purification
国 *Shinkoku* China under the Manchus
国人 *Shinkokujin* the Chinese people (under the Manchus)
9 音 *seion* unvoiced sound
香 *seikō* fragrance, perfume
冽 *seiretsu na* clear (water)
秋 *seishū* clear fall (weather)
剃 *kiyozori* second time over in shaving
泉 *seisen* crystal spring
栄 *seiei* your health and prosperity
風 *seifū* a cool refreshing breeze
風明月 *seifū-meigetsu* pure as the wind and clear as the moon; purity of heart
浄 *seijō, shōjō* purity, spotlessness
浄無垢 *shōjōmuku* perfect purity, innocence
10 流 *seiryū* clear stream
酒 *seishu, sumizake* refined saké
祥 *seishō* spirit, energy
純 *seijun* purity
陰 *seiin* cool shadows
党 *seito* clearing a political party (of undesirable elements)
書 *seisho, kiyoga(ki)* clean copy
素 *seiso* neatness
11 遊 *seiyū* excursion, outing
清 *seisei suru* feel refreshed, feel relieved. *sugasuga(shii)* refreshing, soothing
貧 *seihin* honorable poverty
掃 *seisō* cleaning
掃夫 *seisōfu* garbage man
教 *Seikyō* Puritanism
教徒 *Seikyōto* Puritans
涼 *seiryō na* cool, refreshing
涼剤 *seiryōzai* refrigerant
涼飲料水 *seiryō inryōsui* cooling drink
12 閑 *seikan* quiet, tranquility
朝 *Shinchō* Manchu dynasty. *seichō* square character with thin horizontal strokes
朝活字 *seichō katsuji* square character with thin horizontal strokes
13 適 *seiteki* health, prosperity, comfort
福 *seifuku* happiness, welfare
節 *seisetsu* integrity
楚 *seiso* neatness
廉 *seiren* purity and unselfishness, honesty, integrity
廉潔白 *seiren-keppaku* uprightness
新 *seishin na* fresh, new

新味 *seishimmi* freshness
14 算 *seisan* liquidation, settlement
15 澄 *seichō na* clear; serene
談 *seidan* elevated conversation
潔 *seiketsu* cleanliness, neatness, purity
潔法 *seiketsuhō* general housecleaning
16 濁 *seidaku* purity and impurity; good and evil
興 *seikyō* innocent amusement
17 聴 *seichō* your kind attention (to my talk)

A **深** 3206 / J3f3c / M17687 SHIN deep. *fuka(meru) vt, fuka(maru) vi* deepen, heighten, intensify, strengthen. *fuka(mi)* a depth, deep place; profundity. *fuka(su)* sit up late. *fuke(ru)* get late; grow old; reach the height of the season. *fuka(i)* deep; thick, dense; profound, intense; intimate.

2 入 *fukai(ri) suru* be engrossed in, be taken up with, go too far into
3 山 *miyama, shinzan* mountain recesses, remote mountains
山木 *miyamagi* deep-forest trees
山幽谷 *shinzan-yūkoku* distant mountains and solitary valleys
山桜 *miyamazakura* wild flowering cherry
山鴉 *miyamagarasu* mountain crow
山躑躅 *miyama tsutsuji* wild azalea
4 手 *fukade* deep wound, severe injury, mortal wound
爪 *fukazume* the quick of a fingernail
化 *shinka* deepening
切 *shinsetsu* kindness
5 玄 *shingen* mystery
6 仲 *fuka(i) naka* intimacy
交 *shinkō* close friendship
宇宙 *shin'uchū* deep space
7 谷 *shinkoku* deep valley, ravine
更 *shinkō* midnight, dead of night
8 長 *shinchō na* profound, deep
追 *fukao(i)* chasing (the enemy) too far
味 *fukami* depth; deep place
沓 *fukagutsu* long boots or shoes
呼吸 *shinkokyū* deep breathing, deep breath
夜 *shin'ya* dead of night, midnight
夜放送 *shin'ya hōsō* late-night broadcasts
刻 *shinkoku na* serious, keen, acute, significant
刻化 *shinkokuka* intensification, aggravation
9 厚 *shinkō na* deep (sympathy), close (relations)
度 *shindo* depth
浅 *shinsen* depth
重 *shinchō na, shinjū na* relaxed and dignified
思 *shinshi* deep thinking
怨 *shin'en* deep resentment
甚 *shinjin no* profound, deep
紅 *shinku* deep crimson
紅色 *shinkōshoku* deep ruby red
海 *shinkai* deep sea. *shinkai no* abysmal
海作業 *shinkai sagyō* deep-sea salvage
海波 *shinkaiha* deep-sea wave
海魚 *shinkaigyo* deep-sea fish
海漁業 *shinkai gyogyō* deep-sea fisheries
海線 *shinkaisen* deep-sea cable
海爆弾 *shinkai bakudan* depth charge
10 酒 *fukazake* heavy drinking
耕 *shinkō* deep plowing
11 彫 *fukabo(ri)* deep carving
情 *fukanasake* inordinate show of affection
深 *fukabuka to* very deeply. *shinshin* getting later; getting quiet; deep interior; feeling (the cold)
酔 *fukayo(i)* deep drunkenness
窓 *shinsō* a secluded inner room. *shinsō ni* very carefully
雪 *shinsetsu, miyuki* deep snow
12 痛 *shintsū* deep sorrow
遠 *shin'en na* profound, deep, unfathomable
間 *fukama* depth, deep place; intimacy
閑 *shinkan toshita* silent, hushed, deserted
淵 *shin'en* abyss, ravine
奥 *shin'ō* abstruse principles, esoteric doctrines, mysteries
13 傷 *fukade* deep wound, severe injury
靴 *fukagutsu* long boots
意 *shin'i* deep meaning
14 閨 *shinkei* inner bedroom
緑 *shinryoku* dark green. *fukamidori* dark green, verdure
酷 *shinkoku na* serious, keen, acute
15 履 *fukagutsu* long boots; high shoes
慮 *shinryo* thoughtfulness, foresight, prudence

潭 *shintan* abyss, ravine
憂 *shin'yū* deep anxiety, great fear; deep grief
16 謀 *shimbō* deeply laid plan
謀遠慮 *shimbōenryo* careful plans for the future
17 邃 *shinsui na* profound, abstruse
謝 *shinsha* deep gratitude, sincere apology
鍋 *fukanabe* deep pan, pot

9

湧 3207 / J4d2f / M17862 See **涌** 3150.

渇 3208 / J-X / M17788 See **渴** 3195.

浇 3209 / J482e / M-X See **澆** 3325.

漣 3210 / J4e7a / M-X See **漣** 3259.

溂 3211 / J5e63 / M-X See **刺** 484.

渝 3212 / J5e61 / M17761 YU. *ka(waru)* change, vary; be revised; be different; move; be transferred. *ka(eru)* change, vary, convert; revise, amend.

渤 3213 / J5e5f / M17769 BOTSU. BOCHI water gushing forth.

渭 3214 / J5e4f / M17781 I used in proper names.

湎 3215 / J5e5e / M17826 MEN. BEN drown, sink, flounder; become obsessed with.

湘 3216 / J3e45 / M17842 SHŌ used in proper names; boil.

湟 3217 / J5e54 / M17850 KŌ *hori* moat, ditch, canal.

湫 3218 / J5e57 / M17867 SHŪ. SHŌ. SHU cramped swamp land; pond; lament. *kute, kude* marsh, marshland.

湶 3219 / J5e59 / M17892 SEN. *izumi* spring, fountain (head), source. *awara* wet meadowland.

湲 3220 / J5e53 / M17877 KAN the sound of running water.

渟 3221 / J5e5b / M17763 TEI stop.

湃 3222 / J5e5c / M17808 HAI sound of waves.

渣 3223 / J5e56 / M17767 SA dregs.

渥 3224 / J302f / M17770 AKU kindness.

渫 3225 / J5e58 / M17778 SETSU dredging; cleaning out.

湊 3226 / J4c2b / M17822 SŌ. *minato* harbor, port.

湑 3227 / J-X / M17829 SHO. *shitami* dregs, lees.

渚 3228 / J-X / M17750 **渚** 3164 / J3d6d / M-X SHO. *nagisa* beach, shore, strand.

湍 3229 / J5e5a / M17825 TAN rapids; rushing stream; seething. *se* current, rapids, shallows, shoal.

渠 3230 / J3574 / M17764 KYO ditch, canal, dock.
14 魁 *kyokai* ringleader, boss, chief

渙 3231 / J5e52 / M17757 KAN scatter.
9 発 *kampatsu* proclamation

游 3232 / J5e62 / M17792 YŪ float. *oyo(gu)* swim.
9 侠 *yūkyō* chivalrous man; gangster

湮 3233 / J5e50 / M17873 IN sink; plug up.
7 没 *imbotsu suru* fall into ruins; sink into oblivion, disappear

13 滅 *immetsu* destruction, suppression

湛 3234 / J4339 / M17846 TAN. *tata(eru)* fill; wear (a smile).
12 湛 *tantan(taru)* overflowing; deep, abysmal
然 *tanzen(taru)* overflowing; deep, abysmal

渺 3235 / J5e5d / M17794 BYŌ minuteness; boundless, far, wide. *byō(taru)* little, tiny, insignificant.
9 茫 *byōbō(taru)* boundless, vast
12 渺 *byōbyō(taru)* boundless, vast
然 *byōzen(taru)* boundless, vast
13 漠 *byōbaku(taru)* boundless, vast

渾 3236 / J5e55 / M17800 KON large; all; turbidity. *sube(te)* all, the whole; entirely; in general.
4 天儀 *kontengi* celestial globe
7 身 *konshin* the whole body
沌 *konton* chaos, confusion, nebulosity
12 渾 *konkon* copious (flow); confused
然 *konzen(taru)* whole, entire; harmonious

淵 3237 / J4a25 / M17692 EN edge. *fuchi* deep pool, deep water, abyss, the depths.
8 底 *entei* bottom of the abyss
12 淵 *fuchibuchi* depths (of the sea)
13 源 *engen* origin, source, fountainhead
18 藪 *ensō* center, seat, home, cradle of
叢 *ensō* center, seat, home, cradle of
19 瀬 *fuchise* pools and shoals; vicissitudes

B **滋** 3238 / J3c22 / M17919' **滋** 3250 / J-X / M18021 JI more and more; be luxuriant; planting; turbidity.
8 雨 *jiu* beneficial rain, welcome rain
味 *jimi no* dainty, delicious, nourishing
11 強飲料 *jikyō inryō* tonic drink
15 養 *jiyō* nourishment
養分 *jiyōbun* nutritious element, nutrient
養物 *jiyōbutsu* nourishing food
養剤 *jiyōzai* nutrient medicine (as vitamins)
養過多 *jiyōkata* hypertrophy
養灌腸 *jiyō kanchō* rectal alimentation

B **湾** 3239 / J4f51 / M17920 **灣** 3393 / J5f54 / M18823 WAN gulf, bay, inlet.
2 入 *wannyū* inlet, gulf
3 口 *wankō* bay entrance
4 内 *wannai* inside the bay
6 曲 *wankyoku* curve, crook, bend
7 形 *wankei* bay formation
8 屈 *wankutsu* curve, crook, bend
10 流 *Wanryū* Gulf Stream
12 奥 *wan'ō* bay bottom
16 頭 *wantō* head of a bay

A **湖** 3240 / J3850 / M17836 KO *mizuumi* lake.
3 上 *kojō* on the lake
4 心 *koshin* center of a lake
水 *kosui* lake
辺 *kohen* the vicinity of a lake
8 底 *kotei* lake bottom
岸 *kogan* lake shore
沼 *koshō* lakes and marshes
沼学 *koshōgaku* limnology
9 面 *komen* lake surface
風 *kofū* lake breeze
10 畔 *kohan* lake shore, lakeside
12 港 *kokō* lake harbor

B **渦** 3241 / J3132 / M17771 KA. *uzumaki, uzu* eddy, whirlpool, vortex.
4 中 *kachū* in the whirlpool
7 状星雲 *kajō seiun* spiral nebula
状星雲説 *kajō seiunsetsu* nebular hypothesis
9 巻 *uzumaki* eddy, whirlpool, vortex; coil. *uzuma(ku)* eddy, whirl, swirl, curl (smoke)
巻発条 *uzumaki hatsujō* coiled spring
10 流 *karyū* eddy, whirlpool, maelstrom
紋 *kamon* whirlpool design
11 動 *kadō* vortex
12 雲説 *kaunsetsu* nebular hypothesis
15 潮 *uzushio* whirling tides
線 *uzusen* spiral line
輪 *uzuwa* whirlpool form

A **港** 3242 / J3941 / M17783' **港** 3168 / J-X / M-X KŌ *minato, -kō* port, harbor.
3 口 *kōkō, minatoguchi* harbor entrance
4 内 *kōnai* inside the harbor
5 外 *kōgai* outside the harbor
市 *kōshi* port city

[7] 図 *kōzu* harbor map
町 *minatomachi* harbor town
[8] 門 *kōmon* harbor entrance
[10] 都 *kōto* port city
[11] 務 *kōmu* harbor service
務部 *kōmubu* harbor office
務部長 *kōmu buchō* harbormaster
[12] 税 *kōzei* harbor dues
湾 *kōwan* harbors
湾労働者 *kōwan rōdōsha* longshoreman
[16] 頭 *kōtō* waterfront

B **湿** 3243 / J3c3e / M17920' **濕** 3353 / J5f3c / M18483 SHITSU dampness, moisture; itch. *shime(ru)* get damp, get moist, get wet. *shime(su), shime(rasu)* wet, moisten, dampen. *shito(ru)* get damp, become moist. *shime(ppoi)* damp, moist, humid, wet; gloomy, depressing. *shime(ri)* dampness, humidity, moisture; a sprinkle. *shime(yakana)* quiet, gentle; gloomy, dismal.
[5] 田 *shitsuden* rice fields that always have standing water
布 *shippu* compress, fomentation
[6] 気 *shike(ru), shikke(ru)* get damp, be moist, be wet. *shikke, shikki, shime(ri)ke* moisture, humidity, dampness. *shike* moisture
地 *shitchi* swampy land, damp ground
[7] 声 *shime(ri)goe* tearful voice
[8] 板 *shitsuban* wet plate (photography)
性 *shissei* wet (pleurisy)
性肋膜炎 *shissei rokumakuen* wet pleurisy
[9] 度 *shitsudo* humidity
度計 *shitsudokei* hygrometer
[10] 疹 *shisshin* eczema, rash
[11] 船渠 *shitsusenkyo, shitsudokku* wet dock
[12] 量 *shitsuryō* wet weight
[15] 潤 *shitsujun* moisture, humidity, dampness
潤気候 *shitsujun kikō* humid climate
潤空気 *shitsujun kūki* moist air, humid air
[19] 霧 *shitsumu* wet fog

A **測** 3244 / J422c / M17780 SOKU. *haka(ru)* measure, gauge, weigh; fathom, sound; compute, estimate.
[6] 地 *sokuchi* land survey, geodetic survey
地学 *sokuchigaku* geodesy
[8] 知 *haka(ri)-shi(ru), sokuchi suru* infer, understand, fathom, determine
定 *sokutei* measurement, survey, sounding, calibration, determination, test
定法 *sokuteihō* mensuration
[9] 度 *sokudo* measurement
音器 *sokuonki* sonometer
[10] 候 *sokkō* meteorological observation
候所 *sokkōjo* weather station
[11] 深 *sokushin* sounding
距儀 *sokkyogi* range finder
[12] 程器 *sokuteiki* (ship's) log
遠機 *sokuenki* range finder
量 *sokuryō* survey; surveying; sounding; measurement
量士 *sokuryōshi* surveyor
量術 *sokuryōjutsu* the science of surveying
量船 *sokuryōsen* surveying ship
[13] 鉛 *sokuen* plummet, sounding lead
微尺 *sokubishaku* micrometer
微計 *sokubikei* micrometer
[15] 線 *sokusen* measuring line
縄 *haka(ri)nawa* measuring line
熱 *sokunetsu* calorimetry
熱器 *sokunetsuki* calorimeter
[16] 錘 *sokusui* sounding lead
[18] 難 *haka(ri)gata(i)* immeasurable, inestimable, unfathomable, inscrutable, hard to foresee

A **湯** 3245 / J4572 / M17874 TŌ hot water *yu* hot water, hot bath, hot spring.
[3] 口 *yuguchi* source of a hot spring
女 *yuna* hot-springs prostitute
上 *yua(gari)* just after the bath; bathrobe
[4] 水 *yumizu* hot and cold water; plenty of everything
中 *yuata(ri) suru* be affected by hot springs
引 *yubi(ku)* parboil
元 *yumoto* the source of a hot spring
文字 *yumoji* loincloth
[5] 玉 *yudama* boiling-water bubbles
札 *yufuda* bath ticket
加減 *yukagen* bath temperature
[6] 気 *yuge* steam, vapor
[7] 冷 *yuza(mashi)* boiled water, cooled hot water; water cooler. *yuza(me)* after-bath chill

4 心 忄 㣺 戈 戸 手 扌 支 攴 攵 文 斗 斤 方 无 日 曰 月 木 欠 止 歹 殳 毋 比 毛 氏 气 【水 氵 氺】 9 火 灬 爪 爫 父 爻 爿 丬 片 牙 牛 犬 犭

4 心 忄 ⺗ 戈 戸 手 扌 支 攴 攵 文 斗 斤 方 无 日 曰 月 木 欠 止 歹 殳 毋 比 毛 氏 气 【水 氵 氺】 火 灬 爪 爫 父 爻 爿 丬 片 牙 牛 犬 犭

呑 *yunomi* teacup
花 *yu (no) hana, yubana* hot-springs incrustations
豆腐 *yudōfu* boiled tofu
8 沸 *yuwa(kashi)* teakettle
治 *tōji suru* take healing baths
治場 *tōjiba* health resort
9 屋 *yuya* public bathhouse
通 *yudō(shi)* steaming
垢 *yuaka* incrustation, boiler scale
巻 *yuma(ki)* loincloth
10 釜 *yugama* kettle, cauldron
浴 *yuami* bath
浴海綿 *yuami kaimen* bath sponge
11 船 *yubune* bathtub
責 *yuze(me)* boiling-water ordeal
桶 *yuoke* bathtub
桶読 *yutōyo(mi)* mixing a *kun* and an *on* reading in the same word
12 場 *yuba* hot-springs bathroom, home bathroom
葉 *yuba* dried tofu skin of boiled soy milk
煮 *yuni* boiling, seething
湯婆 *yutampo* hot-water bottle
13 殿 *yudono* bathroom
滝 *yudaki* hot falls, hot shower
煎 *yusen* decoction, boiling (in a double boiler)
14 銭 *yusen* bath charge
15 槽 *yubune* bathtub
熨斗 *yunoshi* steam ironing
16 薬 *tōyaku* infusion
20 灌 *yukan* washing a body for burial

9 A 温 $\frac{3246}{J3239}$ M17774 溫 $\frac{3251}{J\text{-}X}$ M17968 On. *atata(meru), atta(meru)* warm, heat. *atata(maru), atta(maru), nuku(maru)* warm oneself, sun oneself, get warm. *nukumo(ru)* warm oneself, get warm. *nuku(meru)* warm slightly. *nukumo(ri), nuku(mi)* (slight) warmth. *nukuto(i), nuku(i)* warm, mild, genial. *atataka(i), attaka(i)* warm, mild, genial, cordial.

4 水 *onsui* warm water
5 石 *onjaku* heated warming stone; pocket warmer
布 *ompu* hot compress
6 色 *onshoku* warm color; angry countenance
気 *onki* warmth, sultriness, heat
存 *onzon suru, onson suru* preserve, retain
血動物 *onketsu dōbutsu* warm-blooded animal
7 言 *ongen* kind word
床 *onshō, ondoko* hotbed
良 *onryō na* gentle, amiable
灸 *onkyū* moxa cautery
8 和 *onwa na* gentle, mild, temperate
突 *ondoru* Korean floor heater, hypocaust
9 厚 *onkō na* gentle
室 *onshitsu* greenhouse
室効果 *onshitsu kōka* greenhouse effect
故 *onko* looking into the past; checking into history
故知新 *onkochishin* learning from the past
度 *ondo* temperature
度計 *ondokei* thermometer
度感覚 *ondo kankaku* sense of temperature
泉 *onsen, ideyu* hot spring
泉郷 *onsenkyō* hot-springs town
泉場 *onsemba, onsenjō* spa, hot-springs resort
10 座 *onza* sitting peacefully
容 *on'yō* kindly face
帯 *ontai* temperate zone
浴 *on'yoku* hot bath, warm bath
浴療法 *on'yoku ryōhō* hot-water treatments
11 健 *onken na* quiet, dependable, uniform
情 *onjō* warm heart; kindliness
情主義 *onjō shugi* kind treatment (of employees)
習 *sara(eru), sara(u)* review, rehearse, practice. *onshū, sarai* review, rehearsal
習会 *onshūkai* (Japanese) music-and-dance recital
12 順 *onjun* gentleness, docility, obedience
湯 *ontō* comfortably hot bath; hot spring
温 *nukunuku* comfortably warm
湿布 *onshippu* hot fomentations
13 雅 *onga na* graceful, affable
感 *onkan* sense of heat
罨法 *on'ampō* hot fomentations
暖 *ondan* warmth
暖前線 *ondan zensen* warm front
15 熱療法 *onnetsu ryōhō* thermo therapy
18 顔 *ongan* kindly face

B **渡** 3247 / J454f / M17765 To. *wata(ru)* cross, ford, ferry; be imported; change hands; make one's way through life; sweep across; migrate; be provided. *wata(su)* carry across, ferry over, bring over; hand over, deliver; deal (cards); transfer (a business); pay (wages); bridge; stretch (something) across; lay across. *wata(ri)* passage, transit; gangplank; length, diameter; negotiations; migration (of birds); payable at. *wata(shi)* ferry; delivery; transfer; ford. *watarai* one's occupation.

2 人 *wata(ri)bito, wata(ri)nin* migratory worker; hobo; stranger
3 川 *Wata(ri)gawa* River Styx
4 仏 *to-Futsu* going to France
5 台 *to-Dai* going to Taiwan
世 *tosei* living, livelihood, subsistence; business, trade, profession
世人 *toseinin* chivalrous man; gangster
6 舟 *wata(shi)bune, wata(ri)bune* ferryboat
合 *wata(ri)-a(u)* cross swords, exchange blows; argue
守 *wata(shi)mori* ferryman
米 *to-Bei* going to the United States
米中 *to-Beichū* while in the United States
7 初 *wata(ri)zo(me)* bridge dedication
来 *torai suru* visit; come across the sea. *torai* importation, influx, entrance (of a new religion)
8 板 *wata(ri)ita* gangplank, board crosswalk
物 *wata(ri)mono* imported goods; heirloom; wages
欧 *to-Ō* going to Europe
歩 *wata(ri)-aru(ku)* wander from place to place, walk across. *toho* walking
英 *to-Ei* going to England
者 *wata(ri)mono* migratory worker; hobo; stranger
奉公 *wata(ri)bōkō* working here and there as a servant
河 *toka* river crossing
河地帯 *toka chitai* bridgehead
9 海 *tokai* crossing the ocean; passage
洋 *toyō* transoceanic
洋爆撃 *toyō bakugeki* overseas bombing
10 唐 *to-Tō* going to Tang China
航 *tokō* voyage, tour; a sailing, a crossing
航地 *tokōchi* the land of one's sojourn
航者 *tokōsha* foreign traveler, passenger
航免状 *tokō menjō* passport
航費 *tokōhi* traveling expenses
11 鳥 *wata(ri)dori* migratory bird, bird of passage
過 *toka* crossing a strait
廊 *wata(ri)rō* covered passageway
廊下 *wata(ri) rōka* covered passageway
船 *wata(shi)bune, wata(ri)bune, tosen* ferry
船場 *tosemba, tosenjō* ferrying place
船賃 *tosenchin* ferry charge
12 場 *wata(shi)ba* ferrying place, ford
御 *togyo suru* proceed to, repair to
13 賃 *wata(shi)chin* ferrying charge
14 銭 *wata(shi)sen* ferry charge
15 稼 *wata(ri) kase(gi)* migratory work
16 鴉 *wata(ri)garasu* a large Hokkaido crow
頭 *totō* ferry
橋式 *tokyōshiki* bridge-opening ceremony
17 鮮 *to-Sen* going to Korea

A **満** 3248 / J4b7e / M17921′ **滿** 3283 / J5e60 / M18099 MAN fullness, enough; pride. *mi(tsuru), mi(chiru)* be full; rise (tides); mature, expire. *mi(tasu)* fill; supply, make good; satisfy, appease, answer (the need), meet (the demand). *man-* full, fully, fulfillment; a full (year); a full (five years).

2 人 *Manjin* a Manchurian
了 *manryō* expiration
3 山 *manzan* the whole hill, the whole mountain
干 *michihi, mankan* ebb and flow
4 月 *mangetsu* full moon
水 *mansui* full to the brim
天 *manten* the whole sky
天下 *mantenka* the whole world
5 目 *mammoku* whole view; as far as the eye can see
目蕭条 *mammokushōjō(taru)* bleak, dreary
6 州 *Manshū* Manchuria
州国 *Manshūkoku* Manchukuo
州事変 *Manshū Jihen* The Manchurian Incident

州語 *Manshūgo* the Manchurian language
7 足 *manzoku* satisfaction, contentment. *manzoku na* satisfactory, complete, proper, sound (health). *mi(chi)-ta(riru)* fulfill, fill up
身 *manshin* the whole body
作 *mansaku* bumper crop
更 *manzara* (not) wholly, (not) altogether
9 面 *mammen* the whole face
洲 *Manshū* Manchuria
点 *manten* perfect, perfect score
10 座 *manza* the whole assembly
悦 *man'etsu* great joy, rapture
株 *mankabu* full subscription (for shares)
配 *mampai* full delivery of rationed goods
員 *man'in* no vacancy, full house
11 堂 *mandō* the whole audience
遍無 *mambenna(ku)* equally, uniformly, without exception, all around
12 開 *mankai* full bloom
喫 *mankitsu suru* have enough of; fully enjoy
幅 *mampuku* full width; full area
満 *mi(chi)-mi(chiru)* fill up. *mamman(taru)* full of (vigor, etc.)
渡 *mi(chi)-wata(ru)* be prevalent
腔 *mankō no* wholehearted
期 *manki* expiration (of a period)
塁 *manrui* full bases
場 *manjō* the whole assembly
場一致 *manjō-itchi de* unanimously
13 溢 *mi(chi)-afu(reru)* be full of
腹 *mampuku* satiety
鉄 *Mantetsu* South Manchurian Railway
蒙 *Mammō* Manchuria and Mongolia
載 *mansai* full load
15 潮 *manchō, michishio* high tide
17 鮮 *Man-Sen* Manchuria and Korea
18 額 *mangaku* full amount
19 願 *mangan* fulfillment of a vow
20 艦飾 *mankanshoku* dressed-up (ship); dolled-up (person)

A **減** 3249 / J383a / M17759 GEN decrease, decline. *gen(jiru), gen(zuru)* decrease; mitigate, appease; dwindle; subtract, deduct. *he(ru), me(ru)* decrease, dwindle, subside; wear and tear; get hungry. *he(su), he(rasu)* reduce, decrease, shorten, curtail; be hungry. *me(ri), he(ri)* decrease, wear, loss, waste.
3 口 *he(razu)guchi* the last word, talking back to
4 水 *gensui* low water; subsiding water; reduced water supply
反 *gentan* acreage reduction
込 *me(ri)-ko(mu)* sink into, stick into
少 *genshō* decrease, reduction, decline
5 圧 *gen'atsu* lowering the pressure
収 *genshū* decrease in income or production
号 *gengō* sign of subtraction
6 刑 *genkei* reduction of penalty
光 *genkō suru* extinguish; dim
7 車 *gensha* reduction in transportation service
作 *gensaku* short crop, diminished yield
却 *genkyaku* reduction
身法 *genshinhō* weight-reducing program
8 退 *gentai* decline, ebb, waning, subsiding; loss (of appetite); failing (eyesight)
価 *genka* discount, price reduction
法 *gempō* subtraction
物 *he(razu)mono* worthless person
免 *gemmen* reduction and exemption; mitigation and remission
9 食 *genshoku* cutting down on food; reduced rations
封 *gempō* cutting down the size of a fief
段 *gentan* acreage reduction
点 *genten* demerit mark
削 *gensaku* reduction
速 *gensoku* speed reduction
速度 *gensokudo* speed reduction
10 高 *he(ri)daka* ullage, loss in weight
俸 *gempō* salary reduction
租 *genso* tax reduction
耗 *gemmō, genkō* decrease
配 *gempai* dividend reduction
殺 *gensatsu suru, gensai suru* diminish, reduce, attenuate, deaden, impair, detract from
衰 *gensui* decrease
員 *gen'in* personnel reduction
11 張 *me(ri)ha(ri)* loosening and tightening
産 *gensan* decreased production
12 税 *genzei* reduction of taxes

給 *genkyū* wage cut, salary reduction
軽 *genkei* reduction (of a penalty)
量 *genryō* loss in quantity
筆 *gempitsu* writing briefly
等 *gentō* reduction, mitigation, commutation; lowering the class
13 債 *gensai* partial payment of a debt
損 *genson* decrease; loss, wear, depreciation
資 *genshi* reduction of capital
14 磁 *genji* demagnetization
算 *genzan* subtraction
15 摩 *gemmu* lubrication
16 磨性 *gemmasei* antifriction, lubricating
17 縮 *genshuku* reduction, retrenchment
18 額 *gengaku* reduction, cut

10

滋 3250 / J-X / M18021 See **滋** 3238.

溫 3251 / J-X / M17968 See **温** 3246.

滊 3252 / J-X / M18019 See **汽** 3068.

溪 3253 / J5e64 / M17967 See **渓** 3196.

溏 3254 / J5e6f / M17925 Tō. Dō pond; mud, muddy. *ike* pond.

溘 3255 / J5e65 / M17936 Kō *tachimachi* in an instant. *niwaka* sudden, abrupt.

溽 3256 / J5e69 / M17996 Joku hot and humid, steamy; moisten.

滉 3257 / J5e66 / M18017 Kō. Ō deep, wide expanse (of water).

溟 3258 / J5e72 / M17947 Mei dark; ocean.

漣 3259 / J-X / M18155 Ren. *sazanami* ripples.

滓 3260 / J5e68 / M18034 Shi. *ori* dregs, sediment, grounds. *kasu* dregs, grounds, refuse, sediment, scum, dross.

滕 3261 / J5e6e / M18036 Tō. Dō gush forth, flow out.

溍 3262 / J-X / M17922 Shin water.
9 神 *shinshin* court nobles

溷 3263 / J5e67 / M17986 Kon get muddy.
16 濁 *kondaku* turbidity, muddiness

滂 3264 / J5e71 / M18003 Bō, Hō flow.
8 沱 *bōda to* copiously, abundantly

溲 3265 / J5e6c / M17979 **溲** 3135 / J-X / M-X Shu, Shū, Sō urine.
11 瓶 *shubin* chamber pot

溥 3266 / J5e70 / M17957 Fu. Ho big, immense; universal
4 天 *futen* the whole world

滄 3267 / J5e6b / M18007 Sō ocean.
9 海 *sōkai* blue sea
13 溟 *sōmei* blue sky

漠 3268 / J4779 / M18149 B Baku vague, obscure; desert; wide.
12 然 *bakuzen* vague, obscure
13 漠 *bakubaku* vague, obscure; vast, boundless

滔 3269 / J5e6d / M18035 Tō overflowing.
4 天 *tōten* spreading all over the sky
天勢 *tōten (no) ikioi* irresistible power
13 滔 *tōtō(taru)* rushing, swift; eloquent; universal

溢 3270 / J306e / M17951 Itsu. *afu(reru)* overflow, flow over, inundate. *kobo(reru) vi* spill, overflow, be scattered. *kobo(su) vt* spill; grumble over.
4 水 *issui* inundation, overflow
5 出 *isshutsu* overflowing, effusion, gushing out
6 血 *ikketsu* effusion of blood, internal hemorrhage

溺 3271 / J452e / M17990 DEKI *obo(reru)* drown, indulge in. *obo(rasu), obo(rakasu)* drown (a person); cause to indulge in.
6 死 *dekishi, obo(re)ji(ni), obo(re)shi(ni)* drowning
死体 *dekishitai* drowned body
死者 *dekishisha* drowned person
13 愛 *dekiai* dotage, infatuation

溯 3272 / J5e6a / M17975 **遡** 6094 / J414c / M39048 SAKU. SO. *sakanobo(ru)* go upstream; retrace the past.
3 上 *sojō suru* go upstream
及 *sakkyū, sokyū* tracing back
及的 *sokyūteki* retrospective
6 行 *sokō* going upstream
9 洄 *sokai* going upstream
10 航 *sokō* going up against a stream

B **滝** 3273 / J426c / M18067 **瀧** 3376 / J426d / M18671 RŌ. SŌ. *taki* waterfall; rapids, cascade.
3 口 *takiguchi* top of a waterfall
川 *takigawa* rapids
12 飲 *takino(mi)* gulping down a drink
壺 *takitsubo* pool below a waterfall
登 *takinobo(ri)* (fish) climbing a waterfall
19 瀬 *taki(tsu)se* rapids; waterfall

A **源** 3274 / J383b / M17926 GEN. *gen-, minamoto* source, origin. *Minamoto* Genji family, the Minamotos.
4 氏 *Genji* Genji, the Minamoto family
5 平 *Gempei* Genji and Heike, the Minamoto and Taira clans
9 泉 *gensen* fountainhead, wellspring, source, origin
泉所得税 *gensen shotokuzei* withholding income tax
泉徴収 *gensen chōshū* collecting (taxes) at the source
泉課税 *gensen kazei* taxation at source
10 流 *genryū* source, origin

B **溝** 3275 / J3942 / M17944 KŌ. *dobu* ditch, gutter, sewer, drain. *mizo* ditch, gutter, drain; groove, slot; gulf, gap.
3 川 *mizogawa* a moat of running water
4 水 *dobu mizu* ditch water
切 *mizoki(ri)* grooving, fluting
8 板 *dobu ita* boards covering a ditch
泥 *dobu doro* silt, muck
10 浚 *mizosara(i)* ditch cleaning
11 渠 *kōkyo* ditch, sewer, canal, aqueduct; rift, gulf
17 壑 *kōgaku* ditches and valleys

溜 3276 / J4e2f / M17943 RYŪ. *tama(ru) vi* collect, gather, accumulate; be saved (money); be in arrears. *ta(meru) vt* accumulate, pile up, store, save, collect. *tama(ri)* waiting room, rendezvous, taxi stand, parking place; (stair) landing; (baseball) dugout; soy sauce. *tame* sink, sump, manure vat.
4 水 *tama(ri) mizu* standing water, stagnant water
込 *ta(me)-ko(mu)* save up; hoard, amass; store up
6 池 *tameike* reservoir, irrigation pond, tank, cistern
9 食 *tamegu(i) suru* eat enough to last a long time
10 涙 *tame namida* pent-up tears
息 *tameiki* sigh, deep breath
11 桶 *tameoke* tub; manure bucket
12 飲 *ryūin* gastric disturbance
飲下 *ryūin (ga) sa(garu)* feel at ease again
13 置 *ta(me)-o(ku)* store, lay by

B **溶** 3277 / J4d4f / M17983 YŌ. *to(keru) vi* melt, dissolve, thaw. *to(kasu) vt* melt, dissolve, liquefy. *to(ku) vt* dissolve, melt.
4 化 *yōka* melting
5 去 *to(ke)-sa(ru) vt* melt away. *to(kashi)-sa(ru) vt* melt (something) away
6 合 *to(ke)-a(u)* melt into, fade into
8 性 *yōsei* soluble
明 *yōmei* fade-in (in movies)
岩 *yōgan* lava
10 剤 *yōzai* solvent, solution; flux (in metallurgy)
11 接 *yōsetsu* welding
液 *yōeki* solution, solvent
12 媒 *yōbai* a solvent
13 暗 *yōan* fade-out, dissolving (in movies)
鉱炉 *yōkōro* blast furnace

解 *yōkai* melting; solution; liquefaction
解力 *yōkairyoku* solvency
解状態 *yōkai jōtai* in solution
解性 *yōkaisei* solubility
解度 *yōkaido* solubility
解点 *yōkaiten* melting point

A 準 3278 J3d60 M17934 準 428 J5245 M1695 JUN. *jun(jiru), jun(zuru)* apply correspondingly, correspond to, be proportionate to, conform to. *nazora(eru)* pattern after, liken to, imitate. *jun-* semi-, quasi-, associate; standard; rule; level; aim. *(ni) jun(jite)* in proportion to.

4 尺 *junshaku* surveyor's leveling pole
5 用 *jun'yō suru* apply
6 会員 *junkaiin* associate member
7 社員 *junshain* associate member; junior employee
決勝 *junkesshō* semifinals
決勝戦 *junkesshōsen* semifinals
8 拠 *junkyo* conformity; authority (of); standard
9 則 *junsoku* regulations; standard
急 *junkyū* local express
11 教員 *junkyōin* assistant teacher
教授 *junkyōju* associate professor
12 備 *jumbi* preparation; provision, reserve
備日 *jumbi (no) hi* preparation day
備中 *jumbichū* in preparation; not open for business
備金 *jumbikin* reserve fund
備資金 *jumbi shikin* reserve funds
備銀行 *jumbi ginko* reserve bank
備管制 *jumbi kansei* preliminary control of lights
13 禁治産 *junkinchisan* quasi-incompetence (in law)
15 縄 *junjō* a level and an inked string; norm, rule, standard

B 滅 3279 J4c47 M18008 METSU. *horo(biru)* be ruined; perish. *horo(bosu)* ruin, destroy, overthrow. *mes(suru) vi* die, be destroyed, be extinguished. *mes(suru) vt* destroy, exterminate; extinguish. *meri* loss, waste, leakage.

2 入 *me-i(ru)* feel depressed
3 亡 *metsubō* downfall, destruction
5 去 *horo(boshi)-sa(ru)* destroy and obliterate. *horo(bi)-sa(ru)* perish from
失 *horo(bi)-u(seru), messhitsu suru* perish
6 尽 *horo(boshi)-tsuku(su)* completely destroy
多 *metta na* reckless, careless. *metta ni* seldom, rarely
多打 *mettau(chi)* random shooting
多矢鱈 *mettayatara ni* recklessly, frantically, indiscriminately
多斬 *mettagiri* hacking to pieces
7 却 *mekkyaku* destruction, extinction
私奉公 *messhihōkō* selfless patriotic service
8 金 *mekki* gilt; gilding, plating
法 *meppō na* absurd, unreasonable, exorbitant; extraordinary; awful, horrible
9 度 *metsudo* nirvana, final emancipation, complete annihilation of self
相 *messō na* extraordinary, unreasonable
茶 *mecha na* absurd, unreasonable, unjust
茶苦茶 *mechakucha* confusion; absurdity, mess, wreck, ruin
茶滅茶 *mechamecha* mess, wreck, ruin, confusion
11 菌 *mekkin* sterilization, disinfection, pasteurization
12 絶 *horo(boshi)-ta(yasu)* destroy. *horo(bi)-ta(eru), metsuzetsu* be destroyed
散 *horo(boshi)-chi(rasu)* scatter and destroy
裂 *metsuretsu* incoherence, inconsistency; disruption

B 滞 3280 J425a M18067' 滯 3285 J5e7c M18075 TAI stopping. *todokō(ru)* stagnate; be delayed, be left undone; be overdue, fall into arrears. *nazu(mu)* lose heart; be in pain; be in earnest, adhere to, be attached to. *todokō(ri)* stagnation; hitch, hindrance, delay; arrearage, indebtedness. *tai-* staying in (a certain country).

4 支 *tai-Shi* staying in China
日 *tai-Nichi* staying in Japan
仏 *tai-Futsu* staying in France
6 米 *tai-Bei* staying in the United States
伊 *tai-I* staying in Italy
在 *taizai* stay, sojourn
在中 *taizaichū* during one's stay
在地 *taizaichi* place of sojourn
在者 *taizaisha* visitor, sojourner

在客 *taizaikyaku* guest, sojourner
在費 *taizaihi* hotel expenses
8 欧 *tai-Ō* staying in Europe
英 *tai-Ei* staying in England
京 *taikyō* staying in the capital
京中 *taikyōchū* while in Tokyo
空 *taikū* staying in the air
空飛行 *taikū hikō* endurance flight
空時間 *taikū jikan* flight duration
9 独 *tai-Doku* staying in Germany
陣 *taijin* encampment
10 郷 *taikyō* living in one's native place
荷 *taika* freight congestion; accumulation of stocks
留 *tairyū* stay, sojourn
納 *tainō* nonpayment, default, delinquency; back taxes
納処分 *tainō shobun* coercive collection
納者 *tainōsha* defaulter; delinquent taxpayer
11 貨 *taika* freight congestion; accumulation of stocks
12 勝 *todokō(ri)ga(chi)* tendency to leave undone; tendency to stagnate
21 露 *tai-Ro* staying in Russia

A **漢** 3281/J3441/M18068′ **漢** 3284/J-X/M18153 KAN Han (Dynasty); (old name for) China; masculine suffix.
2 人 *Kanjin* a Chinese
3 口 *Kankō* Hankow
土 *Kando* China
才 *Kanzai, Kansai* mastery of Chinese literature
子 *kanshi* male, man
4 文 *kambun* Chinese writing, Chinese composition
文学 *kambungaku* Chinese literature
方 *kampō* Chinese medicinal art
方医 *kampōi* Chinese herb doctor
方医学 *kampō igaku* Chinese medicinal art
方薬 *kampōyaku* Chinese medicine
5 民族 *Kamminzoku* Chinese people
6 竹 *kanchiku* solid bamboo
奸 *kankan* traitor, betrayer
字 *kanji* the Chinese characters
名 *kammei* Chinese name
8 学 *kangaku* Chinese literature
学者 *kangakusha* Sinologue
法 *kampō* Chinese medicinal art
法医 *kampōi* Chinese herb doctor
法薬 *kampōyaku* Chinese medicine
和 *Kan-Wa* China and Japan, Chinese and Japanese (languages)
和字典 *Kan-Wa jiten* Chinese-Japanese character dictionary
和辞典 *Kan-Wa jiten* Chinese-Japanese character dictionary
9 音 *kan'on* Han-dynasty pronunciation
10 家 *kanka* Han dynasty; Chinese herb doctor
書 *kansho, karabumi* Chinese book, Chinese classics
11 族 *Kanzoku* Han (Chinese) race
訳 *kan'yaku* translation into Chinese
12 朝 *kanchō* Han dynasty
13 詩 *kanshi* Chinese poetry
詩文 *kanshibun* Chinese poetry and literature
14 語 *kango* Chinese word
16 儒 *kanju* Chinese Confucian scholar
薬 *kan'yaku* Chinese medicine
20 籍 *kanseki* Chinese book, Chinese classics

B **滑** 3282/J336a/M18032 KATSU. KOTSU. *sube(ru)* slide, glide, skate; be slippery; slip; fail in exams. *nume(rakasu), sube(rasu), sube(rakasu)* let slip, make slip. *nume(ru)* be lazy, play all the time. *sube(ri)* sliding, slipping; slippage; slide; slip; skid. *sube(rakana)* smooth. *name(rakana)* smooth. *nume(ri)* slime, slipperiness. *sube(kkoi)* smooth, slippery, velvety, slick.
2 入 *sube(ri)-i(ru)* slide into
3 下 *sube(ri)-kuda(ru)* slide down
4 止 *suberido(me)* tire chains; nonskid heels
尺 *suberijaku* slide rule
込 *sube(ri)-ko(mu)* slide into (a base); slip into (a ditch)
5 皮 *suberikawa, suberigawa* sweatband
弁 *katsuben, sube(ri)ben* slide valve
台 *suberidai* launching platform, ways; (children's) slide; sliding bed
出 *sube(ri)-de(ru)* slide out of. *sube(ri)da(shi)* start, beginning. *sube(ri)-da(su)* start sliding; start out
石 *kasseki* talc
石粉 *kassekiko* talcum powder
7 車 *kassha, sube(ri)guruma, semi* pulley, block, tackle

走 *kassō* gliding, planning, sliding, skating, coasting, taxiing
走路 *kassōro* runway
走輪 *kassōrin* landing gear
8 板 *suberiita* runner (on a sled)
易 *sube(ri)yasu(i)* greasy, slimy, slippery
歩 *nume(ri)-aru(ku)* saunter around
空 *kakkū suru* glide, volplane
空士 *kakkūshi* glider pilot
空機 *kakkūki* glider, sailplane
9 降 *kakkō* descent (by ski, glider, etc.)
10 席 *kasseki* sliding seat
剤 *katsuzai* lubricant
11 脱 *katsudatsu* slipperiness
寄 *sube(ri)-yo(ru)* slide up to
12 結 *suberimusu(bi)* slip knot
落 *sube(ri)-o(chiru)* slip off
16 稽 *kokkei* joke, pleasantry, humor. *odoke* joke
稽口 *odokeguchi* joke
稽本 *kokkeibon* comic books
稽芝居 *odoke shibai* comedy, burlesque
稽者 *odokemono* joker, humorist
稽家 *kokkeika* humorist, joker
稽話 *odokebanashi* funny story

11

滿 3283 / J5e60 / M18099 See **満** 3248.

漢 3284 / J-X / M18153 See **漢** 3281.

滯 3285 / J5e7c / M18075 See **滞** 3280.

澙 3286 / J-X / M-X Nonstandard for **潟** 3328.

潅 3287 / J3443 / M18216 See **灌** 3390.

滬 3288 / J5e76 / M18072 Ko used in proper names; Shanghai.

滷 3289 / J5f23 / M18088 Ro salty (water).

漾 3290 / J5f21 / M18184 Yō *tadayo(u)* drift about, be adrift; float on the waves.

滸 3291 / J5e77 / M18089 Ko vicinity.

漓 3292 / J5f22 / M18127 Ri dropping; soak in.

漱 3293 / J5e7b / M18171 Sō. *kuchisusu(gu), kuchisoso(gu)* gargle, rinse the mouth.

漲 3294 / J5e7d / M18173 Chō. *minagi(ru)* overflow, be swollen; overflow (with sympathy).

潁 3295 / J5e73 / M18188 Ei. Yō used in proper names.

滌 3296 / J5e7e / M18069 Teki. Deki. *susu(gu)* rinse, pour on. *ara(u)* wash.

滾 3297 / J5e78 / M18098 Kon flow. *tagi(ru) vi* boil, seethe, foam. *tagi(rakasu) vt* boil up.
14 滾 *konkon to* copiously (flowing)

漿 3298 / J5e79 / M18185 Shō a drink.
8 果 *shōka* berry
11 液 *shōeki* juice, sap; blood serum

B **滴** 3299 / J4529 / M18084 Teki *shizuku* drop. *shitata(ru)* drip, drop; trickle. *shitatari* drop; trickle.
3 下 *tekika suru* drop, drip, distill, trickle
4 水 *tekisui* water dripping
16 薬 *tekiyaku* (medicine) drops

漉 3300 / J3977 / M18112 Roku. *su(ku)* manufacture paper; spread out thin. *ko(su)* strain, filter, percolate.
2 入 *sukii(re)* watermarking
6 返 *su(ki)gae(su)* remanufacture, remake (paper)
10 紙 *koshigami* filter paper
14 網 *koshiami* strainer

B **漬** 3301 / J4452 / M18167 Shi. *tsu(keru)* soak, moisten, steep; pickle, preserve, add (salt) to. *tsuka(ru)* be soaked in; be submerged; be flooded; take a dip; be seasoned. *hita(su)* soak, dip, steep, immerse, moisten, wet, dunk,

drench. *hita(ru)* be soaked in, be immersed in, be flooded, be submerged; be bathed in; be addicted to.
4 込 *tsu(ke)-ko(mu)* pickling a large amount
8 物 *tsukemono* Japanese pickles
10 梅 *tsukeume* pickling plums
11 菜 *tsukena* greens for pickling

11 **滲** 3302 / J5e7a / M18081 SHIN. *shi(miru)* soak in, permeate, infiltrate; pierce (as a wind); be imbued with, be influenced by; smart; be sensitive to pain. *niji(mu)* blot, spread, run, blur, ooze.
2 入 *shinnyū* permeation, infiltration, percolation
5 出 *shi(mi)-de(ru)* ooze, exude, percolate, soak through. *shinshutsu* exudation, percolation, effusion; extraction (in chemistry)
出性 *shinshutsusei* wet (pleurisy)
出性体質 *shinshutsusei taishitsu* allergic constitution
9 通 *shi(mi)-tō(ru)* soak through, penetrate, permeate, infiltrate
透 *shintō* permeation, infiltration, osmosis
12 渡 *shi(mi)-wata(ru)* penetrate, spread, pervade

B **漂** 3303 / J493a / M18102 HYŌ. *tadayo(u)* float (on the water).
5 白 *hyōhaku* bleaching
失 *hyōshitsu suru* drift away
8 泊 *hyōhaku* wandering, vagabondage; drifting
9 砂 *hyōsa* drift sand
10 浪 *hyōrō* wandering, vagabondage
流 *hyōryū* drifting
流木 *hyōryūboku* driftwood
流民 *hyōryūmin* persons adrift; castaways
流者 *hyōryūsha* a person adrift; a castaway
流物 *hyōryūbutsu* flotsam
流船 *hyōryūsen* a drifting ship; a derelict
12 着 *hyōchaku* drifting ashore

B **漆** 3304 / J3c3f / M18108 SHITSU. *urushi* lacquer, varnish.
3 工 *shikkō* lacquer work; lacquer worker
6 気触 *urushikabure* lacquer poisoning
9 革 *urushi kawa* enameled leather
屋 *urushiya* lacquer shop
11 黒 *shikkoku* jet black
細工 *urushizaiku* lacquer ware
12 喰 *shikkui* plaster, mortar, stucco, whitewash
絵 *urushie* lacquer painting
13 塗 *urushinu(ri)* lacquering; lacquer ware
14 蔦 *urushizuta* poison ivy
15 器 *shikki* lacquer ware

B **漸** 3305 / J4132 / M18179 ZEN gradually advancing. *yōya(ku), yōyō* gradually; finally; barely.
5 加 *zenka* gradual increase
6 次 *zenji* gradually
8 追 *zen (o) ō(te)* gradually
9 持 *zen (o) mo(tte)* gradually
降 *zenkō* gradual decrease
10 時 *zenji* gradually
進 *zenshin* gradual progress, steady advance
進主義 *zenshin shugi* moderatism
進的 *zenshinteki* gradual, moderate
12 減 *zengen* gradual decrease
落 *zenraku* gradual decline
13 滅 *zemmetsu* gradual destruction
14 漸 *yakuyaku* gradually
増 *zenzō* gradual increase
増的 *zenzōteki* increasingly
20 騰 *zentō* gradual rise (in prices)

漕 3306 / J4166 / M18131 SŌ. *ko(gu)* row, scull, paddle.
2 入 *ko(gi)-i(ru)* row in. *ko(gi)-i(reru)* row (a boat) in
4 手 *kogite, sōshu* rower, oarsman
5 付 *ko(gi)-tsu(keru)* row up to, reach
出 *ko(gi)-da(su), ko(gi)-ida(su)* begin to row
6 回 *ko(gi)-mawa(ru)* row around
7 戻 *ko(gi)-modo(su)* row back
別 *ko(gi)-waka(reru)* row away
9 通 *ko(gi)-kayo(u)* travel by rowboat
11 船 *kogibune* rowboat
寄 *ko(gi)-yo(ru), ko(gi)-yo(seru)* row up to

12 渡 *ko(gi)-wata(ru)* row across
程 *sōtei* boat-race distance
着 *ko(gi)-tsu(keru), ko(gi)-tsu(ku)* row up to, reach
13 損 *ko(gi)-sokona(u)* run into a boat; strike the shore
艇 *sōtei* rowing, boating
14 暮 *ko(gi)-kura(su)* row all day long

B **漏** 3307 / J4f33 / M18120 Rō leaking; water clock; time. *mo(ru), mo(reru)* leak, escape, shine through; find expression; be disclosed; be omitted, be excluded. *mo(rasu)* spill, let leak; omit, miss, leave out; divulge; betray; give vent to, express; let go. *mo(ri)* leak, leakage.
3 口 *rōkō* vent, leak
4 水 *rōsui* water leakage
斗 *jōgo, rōto* funnel
斗状 *rōtojō* funnel-shaped
斗雲 *rōtoun* funnel cloud
5 出 *rōshutsu* leak, leakage, seepage
7 告 *rōkoku* letting secrets leak out
8 泄 *rōei, rōsetsu* leakage; disclosure
刻 *rōkoku* water clock
9 屋 *rōoku* leaky house
洩 *rōei* leakage; disclosure
12 無 *mo(re)na(ku)* without exception
13 損 *rōson* leakage, ullage
電 *rōden* short circuit, leakage of electricity
14 聞 *rōbun suru* overhear

B **漫** 3308 / J4c21 / M18166 Man. *suzu(ro), sozo(ro)* involuntarily, in spite of oneself. *mida(ri) ni* without authority, without reason, arbitrarily, unnecessarily, indiscriminately, recklessly. *midari(gamashii)* morally corrupt.
3 才 *manzai* comic dialogue
4 文 *mambun* random notes
7 言 *mangen, sozo(ro)goto* rambling talk
8 雨 *sozo(ro) ame* a drizzle
歩 *mampo, sozo(ro)aru(ki), suzu(ro)aru(ki)* a ramble, a stroll, a walk
画 *manga* comics, cartoon, caricature
画家 *mangaka* cartoonist
10 涙 *sozo(ro) namida* involuntary tears
11 遊 *man'yū* trip, tour, travel
遊客 *man'yū kyaku* tourist, sightseer
12 評 *mampyō* literary gossip, rambling criticism
寒 *sozo(ro) samu(i)* rather cold
筆 *mampitsu* random notes
然 *manzen(taru)* random, rambling, desultory
14 読 *mandoku* desultory reading
漫 *mamman(taru)* vast, boundless
漫的 *mammandē* slow, slow-going
15 罵 *mamba* abuse, irresponsible criticism
談 *mandan* idle talk, comic chat
談家 *mandanka* humorist
16 録 *manroku* random comments

A **漁** 3309 / J3579 / M18101 Gyo, Ryō fishing; fishery; catch, haul. *sunado(ru), isa(ru)* to fish. *asa(ru)* fish, forage, browse, hunt for; gather (news).
4 戸 *gyoko* fisher's hut
火 *gyoka, isaribi* fisher's fire lure
父利 *gyofu(no)ri* running off with a prize while others are fighting for it
区 *gyoku* fishing area
夫 *gyofu* fisherman
夫利 *gyofu(no)ri* running off with a prize while others are fighting for it
5 民 *gyomin* fishers
6 舟 *gyoshū, isaribune* fishing boat
色 *gyoshoku* debauchery
回 *asa(ri)-mawa(ru)* forage around, hunt around
7 村 *gyoson* fishing village
利 *gyori* fishing interests
労 *gyorō* fishing
8 法 *gyohō* fishing method
具 *gyogu* fishing tackle
者 *gyosha* fisher
10 師 *ryōshi* fisher
翁 *gyoō* old fisherman
家 *gyoka* fisher's home
書 *gyosho* book hunting
11 猟 *gyoryō* fishing and hunting
船 *gyosen, ryōsen* fishing boat
12 場 *gyojō, ryōba* fishing grounds
港 *gyokō* fishing port
期 *gyoki, ryōki* fishing season
13 業 *gyogyō* fishing industry
業法 *gyogyōhō* fishing law
業権 *gyogyōken* fishing rights

4 心 忄 小 戈 戸 手 扌 支 攴 攵 文 斗 斤 方 无 日 曰 月 木 欠 止 歹 殳 毋 比 毛 氏 气 【水 氵 氺】 火 灬 爪 爫 父 爻 爿 丬 片 牙 牛 犬 犭

14 網 *gyomō* fishing net
歌 *gyoka* fisher's song
15 撈 *gyorō* fishing
16 獲 *gyokaku* fishing; catch, haul
獲物 *gyokakubutsu* a catch of fish
17 礁 *gyoshō* artifically-made fishing grounds

A **演** 3310 / J3169 / M18130 EN. *en(jiru), en(zuru)* perform, play, act, enact, render, stage, put on.
5 出 *enshutsu* production, performance, rendition, presentation; a play
出者 *enshutsusha* producer, director
出家 *enshutsuka* producer, director
7 技 *engi* acting, performance
技場 *engijō* entertainment hall
芸 *engei* entertainment, performance
芸会 *engeikai* an entertainment
芸者 *engeisha* performer, artiste
8 武 *embu* military exercises, fencing and judo
9 奏 *ensō* (musical) performance, recital
奏会 *ensōkai* concert, recital
奏曲目 *ensō kyokumoku* musical program
奏法 *ensōhō* execution, technique, interpretation
11 習 *enshū* practice, exercises; maneuvers, sham battle; seminar
習林 *enshūrin* experimental forest
習場 *enshūjō* parade ground
13 義 *engi* expansion, amplification; commentary, adaptation
14 説 *enzetsu* speech, lecture, address, oration
説法 *enzetsuhō* eloquence, oratory
説家 *enzetsuka* speaker, orator
15 舞場 *embujō* theater, playhouse
劇 *engeki* drama, play
劇的 *engekiteki* dramatic, theatrical
劇界 *engekikai* the theatrical world
劇術 *engekijutsu* dramatics
劇場 *engekijō* the stage, the theater
16 壇 *endan* rostrum, platform
17 戯 *engi* play, theatricals; drama; dramatics
18 題 *endai* subject of an address
19 繹 *en'eki* deductive reasoning
繹法 *en'ekihō* deductive method

12

潴 3311 / J5f4c / M18287 See 瀦 3377.

潡 3312 / J5f2d / M18313 See 澄 3333.

澑 3313 / J5f31 / M18335 See 溜 3276.

澁 3314 / J5f27 / M18312 See 渋 3200.

澔 3315 / J-X / M18338 See 浩 3147.

潘 3316 / J5f2f / M18236 HAN water in which rice has been washed.

潦 3317 / J5f33 / M18259 RŌ garden pond; rain water; long rain.

潯 3318 / J5f29 / M18280 JIN water's edge; pool near water's edge.

潸 3319 / J5f26 / M18293 SAN tears flowing; rain coming down.

潼 3320 / J5f2e / M18302 DŌ. TŌ used in proper names.

澈 3321 / J-X / M18319 TETSU become clear.

潅 3322 / J5e74 / M18123 GAI pour.

濆 3323 / J5f39 / M-X **濆** 3339 / J-X / M18446 FUN gush forth.

潭 3324 / J5f2c / M18271 TAN pool; abyss; deep. *fuchi* deep pool, deep water, abyss, the depths.

潑 3325 / J-X / M18225 HATSU leap; pour on.
9 剌 *hatsuratsu(taru)* lively, animated

潺 3326 / J5f25 / M18298 SEN sound of flowing water.
12 湲 *senkan(taru)* babbling (brook)

澆 3327 / J5f24 / M18317 GYŌ frivolity.
8 季 *gyōki* decadence, degeneration

B **潟** 3328 / J3363 / M18247 SEKI. *kata* lagoon.
12 湖 *sekiko* salt-water lagoon

澗 3329 / J3442 / M-X **㵎** 3330 / J-X / M18253 KAN valley river.
4 水 *kansui* water of a valley stream
7 声 *kansei* the sound of a valley stream

澎 3331 / J5f30 / M18332 HŌ, HYŌ sound of flowing water.
12 湃 *hōhai(taru)* surging
湖島 *Hōkotō* Pescadores

A **潔** 3332 / J3769 / M18231 KETSU. *isagiyo(i)* pure, clean, righteous; manly, gallant, sportsmanlike.
5 白 *keppaku* purity, innocence, integrity
11 斎 *kessai* abstinence, purification
18 癖 *keppeki* fastidiousness

B **澄** 3333 / J4021 / M18315 CHŌ. *su(mu)* be clear, become clear, clarify. *su(masu)* clear, clarify, settle; strain (one's ears); look grave.
5 汁 *suma(shi)jiru* clear broth or stock (seasoned with shaved dried bonito, certain seaweeds, etc.)
6 亙 *su(mi)-wata(ru)* be perfectly clear
8 明 *chomei* lucidity, serenity, clearness, clarity
9 屋 *su(mashi)ya* self-composed person, prim-looking girl
12 渡 *su(mi)-wata(ru)* be perfectly clear
15 徹 *chōtetsu na* transparent

B **潤** 3334 / J3d61 / M18255 JUN. *uruo(u) vi* be watered; profit by, receive benefits, become rich. *uruo(wasu), uruo(su) vt* moisten, water, irrigate, dip; enrich, profit. *uru(mu)* be dimmed, be clouded, get muddy; be wet. *fuya(kasu)* steep, soak. *fuya(keru)* swell up, become soaked. *uruo(i)* dampness, rain; gain; favor; charm. *uru(mi)* dimness, cloudiness, opacity, blur; moisture.
6 色 *junshoku* rhetorical flourishes
7 沢 *juntaku* gloss, luster; moisture, abundance; profit, favor
12 筆 *jumpitsu* painting and writing
筆料 *jumpitsuryō* writing fee, painting fee
13 飾 *junshoku* rhetorical flourishes
滑 *junkatsu* lubrication
滑油 *junkatsuyu* lubricating oil

潰 3335 / J4459 / M18281 KAI. *tsubu(su)* crush, smash, break; dissipate; waste (time); kill, butcher; demolish; melt down. *tsubu(reru)* be smashed, break, be destroyed, collapse; be defaced (type); be ruined; be worn down. *tsui(eru)* be routed, collapse.
7 走 *kaisō* rout, stampede
決 *kaiketsu* rip, break, cleavage, crevasse
利 *tsubushi (ga) ki(ku)* be clever at any task
乱 *kairan* rout
10 値 *tsubu(shi)ne* scrap value
家 *tsubu(re)ie* demolished house; tumble-down house
11 敗 *kaihai* complete defeat
12 散 *kaisan* being broken up and scattered
落 *tsubu(re)-o(chiru)* collapse
13 滅 *kaimetsu* destruction, annihilation
14 瘍 *kaiyō* ulcer

A **潮** 3336 / J442c / M18277' CHŌ. *shio* tide; salt water; opportunity. *ushio* tide, sea water
2 入 *shioi(ri)* coming in of the tide
3 干 *shiohi* low tide
干狩 *shiohiga(ri)* shell gathering at low tide
4 水 *chōsui* tidewater. *shio mizu* sea water
6 気 *shioke* salt air
汲 *shiokumi* flooding salt beds
合 *shioa(i)* between tides
先 *shiosaki* rising of the tide; time to begin
汐 *chōseki* ebb and flow, tide
汐風 *chōsekifū* tidal wind
8 門 *chōmon* tide gate
9 音 *chōon* sound of waves
風 *shio kaze* sea breeze, salt air
待 *shioma(chi)* waiting for the tide
海 *shio umi* the sea

4 心 忄 ⺗ 戈 戸 手 扌 支 攴 攵 文 斗 斤 方 无 日 曰 月 木 欠 止 歹 殳 毋 比 毛 氏 气 【水 氵 12 氺】 火 灬 爪 ⺤ 父 爻 爿 丬 片 牙 牛 犬 犭

紅 *chōkō suru* redden, flush, color up
津波 *shio tsunami* tidal bore
10 候 *chōkō* tide period
時 *shiodoki* tidal hour; favorable opportunity, psychological moment
流 *chōryū* tide, current; trend
害 *chōgai* tidewater damage
差 *chōsa* tide range
12 湯 *shioyu* sea-water bath
焼 *shioya(ke)* tanned by salt air. *shioya(ki)* broiling fish with salt
嵐 *shio arashi* strong sea breeze
13 閘 *chōkō* tide lock
煙 *shio kemuri* salt spray
解 *chōkai* diliquescence
路 *shioji* the sea, the deep
15 標 *chōhyō* tide mark
18 騒 *shiosai* roar of the sea

B 潜 3337 J4078 M18241 潛 3352 J5f2a M18240 SEN. *hiso(meru)* conceal, hide; lower (the voice). *hiso(maru)* be hushed. *hiso(mu)* lurk, lie dormant, be hidden. *kazu(ku)* dive, submerge. *kugu(ru)* pass through, pass under. *mogu(ru)* dive; get into, crawl into. *kugu(ri)* wicket gate, side gate. *hisoka ni* secretly.

2 入 *sennyū* infiltration, sneaking in
4 心 *senshin* meditation
戸 *kugu(ri)do* side door, side gate, wicket gate, private door
込 *mogu(ri)-ko(mu)* get in, crawl in, slip in; hide
水 *sensui* diving
水夫 *sensuifu* diver
水母艦 *sensui bokan* submarine tender
水服 *sensuifuku* diving suit
水病 *sensuibyō* submarine sickness, bends
水業 *sensuigyō* diving business
水業者 *sensuigyōsha* diver, diving contractor
水器 *sensuiki* diving bell, diving apparatus
水艦 *sensuikan* submarine
6 行 *senkō* traveling in disguise; submarine voyage
行運動 *senkō undō* underground movement
伏 *sempuku* concealment, hiding, ambush; incubation
伏性 *sempukusei no* latent (disease)
伏期 *sempukuki* incubation period
在 *senzai* potentiality, latency, dormancy
在失業 *senzai shitsugyō* potential unemployment
在意識 *senzai ishiki* subconsciousness, subliminal self
7 没 *sembotsu suru* be submerged, dive
8 幸 *senkō* emperor's secret visit
函 *senkan* construction caisson
函病 *senkambyō* bends, caisson sickness
9 待 *hiso(mi)-ma(tsu)* lie in ambush, lurk around
10 流 *senryū* undercurrent
航 *senkō* submarine voyage
航水雷 *senkō suirai* submarine torpedo
航艇 *senkōtei* submarine, U-boat
11 望鏡 *sembōkyō* periscope
13 隠 *hiso(mi)-kaku(reru)* lie in wait
勢力 *senseiryoku* potential energy, latent power

13

澤 3338 J5f37 M18383 See 沢 3062.

瀆 3339 J-X M18446 See 瀆 3323.

澡 3340 J5f36 M18379 Sō. *ara(u)* wash. *susu(gu)* wash, pour on, rinse.

澣 3341 J5f35 M18382 KAN. *ara(u)* wash. *susu(gu)* wash, pour on, rinse.

澪 3342 J5f3a M18398 REI, RYŌ *mio* water route, navigable channel.

濂 3343 J5f32 M18441 REN water flowing at intervals.

澳 3344 J5f34 M18412 IKU, Ō curving shoreline; bend in a river; offing.

8 門 *Makao* Macao

濛 3345 J5f42 M18491 Mō dark.

6 気 *mōki* fog, mist, vapor
16 濛 *mōmō(taru)* dense, thick, dim, vague

濬 3346 J5f38 M18421 TAN frankly, simply.
8 泊 *tampaku* light; frank; indifferent to
16 濬 *tantan* unconcerned, disinterested; plain, light

澱 3347 J4543 M18410 DEN. *ori* dregs, sediment, grounds. *yodo(mu)* stagnate, be stagnant; settle, deposit; be sluggish; hesitate; stammer. *yodo* pool (of a river).
10 粉 *dempun* starch
粉質 *dempunshitsu* starchiness

B 濁 3348 J4279 M18440 JOKU, DAKU. *nigo(ri)* uncleanness; wrong; muddiness, impurity; voicing marks; voiced sound, voiced consonant; unrefined saké. *nigo(ru)* be muddy, be impure; be voiced; be vague. *nigo(su), nigo(rasu)* make muddy, make cloudy; quibble; prevaricate.
3 子音 *dakushiin* voiced consonant
4 水 *dakusui* muddy water
5 世 *dakusei, jokuse* corrupt world
6 江 *nigo(ri)e* muddy stream
7 声 *nigo(ri)goe, damigoe, dakusei* hoarse voice, thick voice
9 音 *dakuon* voiced sound
点 *dakuten, nigo(ri)ten* voiced consonant marks
10 流 *dakuryū* muddy stream
酒 *dakushu, nigo(ri)zake, doburoku* unrefined saké, raw saké

B 濃 3349 J473b M18442 NŌ dark, thick, undiluted. *ko(i)* dark, deep; saturated; strong (drink); intimate; thick. *koma(yakana)* ardent.
4 化 *nōka* thickening, concentration
化粧 *ko(i)geshō* heavy makeup
8 青色 *nōseishoku* deep blue
9 厚 *nōkō* thickness, density, concentration; richness; elaborateness; ardency; tenseness
度 *nōdo* density, thickness, consistency, concentration
茶 *ko(i) cha* dark brown, umber color
紅色 *nōkōshoku* crimson
11 淡 *nōtan* light and shade
紺 *nōkon* dark blue, navy blue
密 *nōmitsu na* thick; crowded
黄土 *nōkōdo* sienna
12 紫 *komurasaki* dark purple
紫色 *nōshishoku* deep purple
13 溶液 *nōyōeki* concentrated solution
褐色 *nōkasshoku* dark brown
14 緑 *nōryoku* dark green
緑色 *nōryokushoku* dark green
17 縮 *nōshuku* concentration
19 艶 *nōen na* charming, bewitching
霧 *nōmu* dense fog

A 激 3350 J3763 M18438 GEKI. *geki(suru)* get excited, be agitated, be enraged, be exasperated, chafe; urge, encourage, incite. *hage(shii)* violent, vehement, furious, severe, acute, intense, extreme, passionate, heated, stormy (applause); tempestuous (temperament); mighty.
4 化 *gekka, gekika* intensification, aggravation
6 成 *gekisei suru* aggravate, intensify, accelerate, precipitate
7 励 *gekirei* urging, encouragement, incitement
声 *gekisei* gruff voice
8 突 *gekitotsu* crash, collision
9 変 *gekihen* sudden change, upheaval, convulsion, cataclysm
昂 *gekkō, gekikō* excitement, exasperation, indignation, resentment
発 *gekihatsu* fit, spasm; outburst, explosion of anger
臭 *gekishū* strong odor
怒 *gekido* rage, indignation, exasperation
甚 *gekijin* violence, severity
10 高 *gekikō, gekkō* excitement, agitation
浪 *gekirō* high waves, high seas; raging waves
流 *gekiryū* swift current, raging stream, rapids
烈 *gekiretsu* violence, severity, vehemence, fierceness
11 情 *gekijō* violent emotion, passion, fury, outburst
務 *gekimu* exhausting work
動 *gekidō* terrible shock, concussion, upheaval; agitation
12 痛 *gekitsū* sharp pain
越 *gekietsu na* violent, vehement, fiery
減 *gekigen* marked decrease, sharp decline
湍 *gekitan* rapids, torrent
暑 *gekisho* severe heat

4 心 忄 小 戈 戸 手 扌 支 攴 攵 文 斗 斤 方 无 日 曰 月 木 欠 止 歹 殳 毋 比 毛 氏 气 【水 氵 氺】 火 灬 爪 爫 父 爻 爿 丬 片 牙 牛 犬 犭

落 *gekiraku* slump, crash, heavy decline
13 戦 *gekisen* severe fight
14 増 *gekizō* sudden increase; heavy swell
語 *gekigo* harsh language
15 憤 *gekifun* terrible anger; resentment
痩 *gekiyase* anorexic weight loss
論 *gekiron* heated argument
賞 *gekishō* high praise
震 *gekishin* severe earthquake
賛 *gekisan* great praise
18 闘 *gekitō* fierce fighting
職 *gekishoku* exhausting work

14

澀 3351 / J5f28 / M18311 See 渋 3200.

濳 3352 / J5f2a / M18240 See 潜 3337.

濕 3353 / J5f3c / M18483 See 湿 3243.

濟 3354 / J5f3b / M18498 See 済 3197.

濱 3355 / J5f40 / M18537 See 浜 3152.

濔 3356 / J4654 / M-X See 瀞 3380.

濔 3357 / J5f3e / M18482 DEI *mi(chiru)* be full; rise (tides); fill up.

濮 3358 / J5f41 / M18526 BOKU, HOKU used in proper names.

濘 3359 / J5f3f / M18487 NEI muddiness. *nuka(ru)* be muddy.

B **濯** 3360 / J4275 / M18532 TAKU. *soso(gu), susu(gu), yusu(gu), isu(gu)* wash, pour on, rinse.

濤 3361 / J5e39 / M18508 TŌ. *nami* waves, billows.
7 声 *tōsei* sound of the waves.

濬 3362 / J5f3d / M18524 SHUN deep; dredge. *sara(u)* dredge.

10 哲 *shuntetsu* person with deep knowledge

濠 3363 / J396a / M18502 GŌ. *hori* moat, ditch, canal. *Gō-* Australia.
6 州 *Gōshū* Australia

濶 3364 / J6f69 / M18547 **闊** 6409 / J6f68 / M41429 KATSU wide.
8 歩 *kappo suru* stride, strut, swagger
11 達 *kattatsu* magnanimity, generosity
12 葉樹 *katsuyōju* deciduous or broad-leafed tree

濡 3365 / J4728 / M18504 JU. *nure(ru)* be wet, get wet, be damp, be soaked; make love. *nura(su)* wet, soak, dip, dampen.
4 手 *nurete* wet hand
文 *nurebumi* love letter
仏 *nurebotoke* Buddhist image out in the open
6 米 *nuregome* water-damaged rice
色 *nureiro* (glossy) wet color
衣 *nureginu, nuregoromo* wet clothes; false charge
衣着 *nureginu (o) ki(ru)* accept the guilt of another
8 事 *nuregoto* love affair
10 紙 *nuregami* damp paper
荷 *nureni* sea-damaged goods
11 雪 *nureyuki* damp snow
12 場 *nureba* love scene
渡 *nu(re)-wata(ru)* get wet all over
13 鼠 *nurenezumi* drowned rat; a person soaked to the skin
14 髪 *nuregami* newly-washed hair; glossy hair
15 縁 *nureen* open veranda

B **濫** 3366 / J4d74 / M18521 RAN overflow; spread over. *mida(ri) ni* without authority, without reason, arbitrarily, unnecessarily, indiscriminately, recklessly. *midari(gamashii)* morally corrupt.
2 入 *rannyū* discourteous running in and out
5 用 *ran'yō* abuse, misuse, misappropriation
立 *ranritsu* standing in disorder; (candidates) coming forward in great numbers; confusion, turmoil

出 *ranshutsu suru* publish (in great quantity), flood the market
6 伐 *rambatsu* indiscriminate deforestation
7 作 *ransaku* overproduction; excessive writing
9 造 *ranzō* overproduction, careless manufacture
発 *rampatsu* excessive money issue
11 設 *ransetsu suru* establish too many (schools)
12 飲 *ran'in* drinking excessively
費 *rampi* waste, extravagance
14 読 *randoku* indiscriminate reading
製 *ransei* overproduction; careless manufacture
15 賞 *ranshō suru* lavish honors and rewards upon
16 獲 *rankaku* indiscriminate fishing or hunting
靛 *ranten* indigo
18 觴 *ranshō* origin, source, beginning

15

濺 3367 / J5f45 / M18557 Sen *soso(gu)* pour on, sprinkle; irrigate.

瀁 3368 / J5f47 / M18573 Yō vast expanse of water.

瀋 3369 / J5f44 / M18600 Shin juice, sap; soup, broth.

瀏 3370 / J5f48 / M18607 Ryū clean, clear; deep, cool.

瀑 3371 / J5f46 / M18609 Baku. *taki* waterfall; rapids, cascade.
5 布 *bakufu* waterfall

濾 3372 / J5f49 / M18565 Ro. *ko(su)* strain, filter, percolate.
4 水機 *rosuiki* filter
5 布 *koshi nuno* filter cloth
7 床 *roshō* filter bed
10 紙 *roshi, koshigami* filter paper
11 液 *roeki* filtrate
過 *roka* filtering, percolation
過池 *rokachi* filter bed
過紙 *rokashi* filter paper
過器 *rokaki* filter, strainer, percolator

瀆 3373 / J-X / M18591 Toku, Doku blaspheme. *kega(su) vt* defile, pollute, stain. *kega(reru) vi* be defiled, be polluted, be soiled.
9 神 *tokushin* blasphemy, sacrilege, profanity
神罪 *tokushinzai* blasphemy, sacrilege, profanity
18 職 *tokushoku* bribery, graft
職罪 *tokushokuzai* bribery, graft

瀉 3374 / J5f43 / M18596 Sha, *kuda(shi)* purgation, evacuation.
3 下剤 *shagezai* a cathartic
6 血 *shaketsu* bloodletting
7 利塩 *sharien* Epsom salt, magnesium sulfate
12 痢 *shari* diarrhea
13 腹 *kudaribara* diarrhea

16

濳 3375 / J5f2b / M18683 See 潜 3337.

瀧 3376 / J426d / M18671 See 滝 3273.

瀦 3377 / J4375 / M-X Cho puddle; pool; swamp.

瀛 3378 / J5f4a / M18656 Ei. Yō ocean; pond; swamp. *umi* ocean.

瀚 3379 / J5f4b / M18652 Kan wide and large.

瀞 3380 / J-X / M18659 Sei. Shō. *toro* pool (in a river).

瀕 3381 / J494e / M18636 Hin shore, brink; near. *hin(suru)* be on the verge of.
6 死 *hinshi* on the verge of death

瀝 3382 / J5f4d / M18658 Reki dropping.
8 青 *rekisei, chan* asphalt, bitumen, (mineral) pitch
青炭 *rekiseitan* bituminous coal

瀟 3383 / J5f4f / M18660 Shō pure, clean.

9 洒 *shōsha na* elegant, trim, neat, refined
19 瀟 *shōshō* heavy rain and wind
22 灑 *shōsha na* elegant, trim, neat, refined

B **瀬** 3384 / J4025 / M18672′ **瀨** 3385 / J-X / M18672 RAI. *se* current, torrent, rapids, shallows, shoal.
4 戸 *seto* strait, channel
戸口 *setoguchi* the entrance to a strait
戸欠 *setoka(ke)* potsherd
戸引 *setobi(ki), setohi(ki)* enameled
戸内海 *Setonaikai* Inland Sea
戸物 *setomono* porcelain; pottery
戸物屋 *setomonoya* dish store
戸際 *setogiwa* crucial moment, crisis, threshold, brink, eleventh hour
15 踏 *sebu(mi)* wading to test depth; first trial, trial balloon, making inquiries

瀘 3386 / J5f4e / M18646 RO. name of the river (in China)

17

瀲 3387 / J5f52 / M18693 REN water overflowing; float; soak; water's edge.

瀾 3388 / J5f51 / M18722 RAN large waves.

瀰 3389 / J5f50 / M18690 BI wide.

14 漫 *biman* diffusion, permeation

灌 3390 / J5e75 / M18759 KAN. *soso(gu) vt* pour into, pour on, irrigate, sprinkle; shed (tears). *soso(gu) vi* (rain) falls; flow into; pay attention to, concentrate on.
4 木 *kamboku* shrub, shrubbery
水 *kansui* sprinkling, irrigation
仏 *kambutsu* Buddha's birthday celebration
仏会 *kambutsue* Buddha's birthday celebration
10 流 *kanryū suru* irrigate
11 域 *kan'iki* drainage basin
祭 *kansai* drink offering, libation
13 腸 *kanchō* enema
15 漑 *kangai* irrigation, watering
漑地 *kangaichi* irrigated land

19

灘 3391 / J4667 / M18784 TAN. *nada* open sea.

灑 3392 / J5f53 / M18774 SHA, SAI pour.
12 落 *sharaku* clear-cut personality

22

灣 3393 / J5f54 / M18823 See **湾** 3239.

RAD. 火 86

Hi or *ka* fire. At left: *hi hen*. At bottom: 灬 *yotsu ten* four dots or *renga* or *rekka* (*ka* "fire" in a *retsu* "row"). Nickname: Fire.

A **火** 3394 / J3250 / M18850 KA fire; Tuesday. *hi* fire, flame, blaze. *(toro)bi* low fire. *ho* fire.
2 入 *hii(re)* fire pan; first lighting (of a furnace); heating
力 *karyoku* steam power; heating power; force of the flames
力電気 *karyoku denki* steam-generated electricity
3 干 *hibo(shi)* fire-dried; drying by the fire
口 *hokuchi* tinder. *kakō* crater. *higuchi* burner; muzzle (of a gun); origin of a fire
口丘 *kakōkyū* volcanic cone
口金 *hokuchigane* metal fire-striking rod
口原 *kakōgen* crater basin
口原湖 *kakōgenko* crater lake
口湖 *kakōko* crater lake
口箱 *hokuchibako* tinderbox
口壁 *kakōheki* crater wall
山 *kazan* volcano

山口 *kazankō* crater
山灰 *kazambai* volcanic ash
山国 *kazankoku* volcanic country
山性微動 *kazansei bidō* volcanic tremor
山泥 *kazandei* volcanic mud
山岩 *kazangan* lava, igneous rock
山学 *kazangaku* volcanology
山活動 *kazan katsudō* volcanic activity
山脈 *kazammyaku* volcanic range
山島 *kazantō* volcanic island
山帯 *kazantai* volcanic zone
山弾 *kazandan* volcanic boulders
山錐 *kazansui* volcanic cone
山礫 *kazanreki* volcanic ash
4 手 *hi(no)te* flames, blaze, fire. *kashu* stoker
水 *himizu* fire and water; discord
片 *kahen* sparks
中 *kachū* in the fire
元 *himoto, hi (no) moto* origin of a fire
夫 *kafu* fireman, stoker
切 *hiki(ri)* rubbing sticks to make a fire
切臼 *hiki(ri) usu* fire stone
5 玉 *hidama, hi (no) tama* fireball, falling star
皿 *hizara* chafing dish; fire grate; bowl of a pipe
矢 *hiya* fire arrow
付 *hitsu(ke)* arson; an incendiary. *hitsu(ki)* kindling
失 *kashitsu* accidental fire
加減 *hikagen* condition of the fire
打 *hiu(chi)* striking fire with steel on stone; or the equipment used
打石 *hiu(chi)ishi* flint stone
打金 *hiu(chi)gane* the steel (of a flint-and-steel set)
打道具 *hiu(chi) dōgu* flint and steel
打箱 *hiu(chi)bako* tinderbox
6 色 *hi iro* color of red-hot metal; dark crimson
刑 *kakei* burning at the stake
宅 *kataku* burning house; this world of suffering
先 *hisaki* flames; forefront of the fire. *hosaki* flame tips
成岩 *kaseigan* igneous rocks
気 *kaki* fire. *hi(no)ke* heat of fire
気厳禁 *Kaki-Genkin* Inflammable—Keep Out.
7 車 *hi (no) kuruma* fiery chariot; extreme poverty

床 *kashō, hidoko* fire bed, fire grate
攻 *hize(me)* fire attack
吹竹 *hifu(ki)dake* bamboo blowpipe for charcoal fires
見 *hi(no)mi* fire tower
見櫓 *hi(no)mi yagura* fire tower
花 *hibana* spark
花散 *hibana (o) chi(rasu)* quarrel incessantly
災 *kasai* conflagration, fire
災保険 *kasai hoken* fire insurance
災報知器 *kasai hōchiki* fire-alarm box
災警報 *kasai keihō* fire alarm
8 門 *kamon* cannon mouth
明 *hiaka(ri)* firelight
炉 *karo* hearth; furnace; stove
炙 *hiaburi* burning to death; the stake
炎 *kaen* flames, blazes
炎放射器 *kaen hōshaki* flame thrower
炎瓶 *kaembin* Molotov cocktail
事 *kaji* conflagration, fire
事見舞 *kaji mima(i)* sympathy call after a fire
事泥 *kajidoro* thief at a fire
事場 *kajiba* scene of the fire
事場泥棒 *kajiba dorobō* thief at a fire
9 風 *kafū* fire and wind
食 *kashoku* eating cooked food
屋 *hoya* lamp chimney
持 *himo(chi)* fire-holding qualities
柱 *hibashira* pillar of fire; blazing column
海 *hi (no) umi* a lake of fire; the Lake of Fire
除 *hiyoke* protection from fire
室 *kashitsu* firebox
急 *kakyū* urgency, emergency
点頃 *hitobo(shi) koro* evening
砕流 *kasairyū* pyroclastic flow
星 *Kasei* Mars
星人 *Kaseijin* Martian
10 酒 *kashu* strong drink
粉 *hi(no)ko* sparks
砲 *kahō* gun, cannon
砲攻撃 *kahō kōgeki* gunfire
消 *hike(shi)* fireman; fire brigade; fire extinguisher
消役 *hike(shi)yaku* troubleshooter
消壺 *hike(shi) tsubo* charcoal extinguisher
11 遊 *hiaso(bi)* playing with fire; playing with love

桶 *hioke* round wooden brazier
移 *hiutsu(ri)* catching fire, igniting
脚 *hiashi* spreading of a fire
祭 *kasai* offering by fire
責 *hize(me)* ordeal by fire
乾 *hiboshi* fire-dried; drying by the fire
悪戯 *hi itazura* playing with fire
達磨 *hidaruma* mass of flames
12 渡 *hiwata(ri)* fire walking
焚 *hitaki* building a fire
焙 *hiaburi* burning to death, the stake
脹 *hibukure* burn blister
番 *hi(no)ban* night watch, fire watchman
無焜炉 *hina(shi) konro* fireless cooker
焔 *kaen* flame, blaze
焔放射器 *kaen hōshaki* flame thrower
葬 *kasō* cremation
葬炉 *kasōro* crematory
葬場 *kasōba* crematory
13 傷 *yakedo, kashō* burn, scald
掻 *hikaki* poker, fire rake
煙 *kaen* fire and smoke
鉢 *hibachi* brazier
戦 *kasen* shooting battle
勢 *kasei* force of the flames
照 *hote(ru)* feel hot, flush, burn. *hote(ri)* glow, heat; burning sensation
蓋 *hibuta* cover for a gun barrel
蓋切 *hibuta (o) ki(ru)* open fire
14 種 *hidane* live coals (for starting a fire); remains of a fire
綿 *kamen* gun cotton
15 線 *kasen* firing line
影 *hokage* firelight; fire; shadows of the firelight; forms moving in the firelight
箸 *hibashi* tongs
箭 *kasen* fire arrow
熱 *kanetsu* heat
器 *kaki* firearms
熨斗 *hinoshi* flatiron
縄 *hinawa* fuse cord
縄銃 *hinawajū, hinawazutsu* matchlock, harquebus
16 燵 *kotatsu* charcoal brazier in a floor well; heat source under a table and quilt
薬 *kayaku* gunpowder
薬庫 *kayakuko* powder magazine
燄 *kaen* flame, blaze
燄放射器 *kaen hōshaki* flame thrower
18 曜 *Kayō* Tuesday
曜日 *Kayōbi* Tuesday
難 *kanan* fire calamity
難除 *kanan'yoke* charm against fire
23 鑽 *hikiri* rubbing sticks to make a fire
鑽臼 *hikiri usu* fire stone

2

A **灯** 3395/J4574/M18855 **燈** 3476/J4575/M19402 TEI. CHŌ. TŌ lamp, light; counter for lights. *akari, akashi, tomoshibi, hi* a light.

3 下 *tōka* beneath the lamp
4 心 *tōshin* wick
心油 *tōshin'yu* kerosene
火 *tōka* a light, lamplight. *tōka ni* by lamplight
火管制 *tōka kansei* light control, brownout, blackout
火親 *tōka shitashi(mu)* study earnestly
5 用 *tōyō* for illumination
用石油 *tōyō sekiyu* kerosene
台 *tōdai* lighthouse, beacon; lampstand
台守 *tōdaimori* lighthouse keeper
6 光 *tōkō* light, lamplight
光信号 *tōkō shingō* flashlight signaling
7 芯 *tōshin* wick
8 油 *tōyu, toboshi abura* lamp oil
明 *tōmyō* light offered to a god
明台 *tōmyōdai* stand for an offering of a light
11 船 *tōsen* lightship
15 標 *tōhyō* light buoy
影 *hokage, tōei* flicker of light
22 籠 *tōrō* garden lantern, votive lantern
籠流 *tōrōnaga(shi)* setting afloat the *Bon* Festival lanterns

A **灰** 3396/J3325/M18859 **灰** 3397/J-X/M18858 KAI. *hai* ashes. *aku* puckery juice. *hai ni suru* burn up; cremate. *hai ni naru* be reduced to ashes; be cremated.

3 土 *haitsuchi* ashes and earth; poor volcanic soil
5 皿 *haizara* ash tray
白 *kaihaku* ash color, light gray
白質 *kaihakushitsu* gray matter
汁 *aku* lye; harsh taste
汁抜 *akunu(ki)* removal of the harsh taste in vegetables. *akunu(ke), akunu(keta)* refined, elegant, urbane

6 色 *hai iro* ashen, ash color, gray
成 *hai ni na(ru)* be reduced to ashes; be cremated
7 吹 *haifu(ki)* bamboo (tobacco) ash receptacle
均 *hainarashi* ash leveler
8 押 *haiosa(e), haio(shi)* ash leveler (used in a brazier)
受 *haiu(ke)* ash pan, ash tray
青色 *kaiseishoku* grayish blue
9 洗 *akuara(i)* scour, washing vegetables in lye
神楽 *haikagura* raising a cloud of ashes
12 殻 *haigara* ashes
13 掻 *haika(ki)* poker, ash rake
塗 *haimami(re)* covered with ashes
14 塵 *kaijin* ashes and dust
緑色 *kairyokushoku* greenish gray
16 篩 *haifurui* ash strainer
18 燼 *kaijin* complete destruction

3

灼 3398 J3c5e M18878 SHAKU. *arata(kana)* miraculous.
15 熱 *shakunetsu* incandescence, red heat, scorching heat

灸 3399 J3564 M18872 KYŪ moxa cautery, chastisement. *yaito* moxa cautery.
8 所 *kyusho* moxa treatment points (scars)
治 *kyūji* moxa cautery
9 点 *kyuten* moxa treatment points (scars)
11 術 *kyūjutsu* moxa cautery

A **災** 3400 J3a52 M18879 SAI. *wazawai* calamity, misfortune, woe, evil, curse.
4 厄 *saiyaku* calamity, disaster, accident
5 民 *saimin* calamity sufferers
10 害 *saigai* disaster, calamity, accident
害地 *saigaichi* stricken area
害保険 *saigai hoken* accident-and-sickness insurance
害救助 *saigai kyūjo* disaster relief
11 異 *saii* natural calamity
患 *saikan* misfortune, calamity
13 禍 *saika* accident, calamity, disaster, misfortune
18 難 *sainan* calamity, disaster, accident, misfortune

4

炙 3401 J5f55 M18922 SHA. *abu(ru)* roast, toast, broil, grill; warm; dry.

炒 3402 J5f56 M18915 SŌ. SHŌ. *i(ru)* broil; parch; roast (in a pan); fire (tea); fry. *iri* parching, roasting, popping.
5 玉子 *iritamago* scrambled eggs
6 米 *irigome* parched rice
7 豆 *irimame* parched beans
8 物 *irimono* parched grains or beans
13 塩 *irijio* parched salt

B **炉** 3403 J4f27 M18902 **爐** 3506 J6024 M19566 RO furnace, kiln, hearth; (nuclear) reactor.
4 火 *roka* hearth fire
辺 *robata, rohen* fireside, hearth
7 床 *roshō* hearth
10 格子 *rogōshi* furnace grate
12 棚 *rodana* mantlepiece
13 滓 *rokasu* slag, refuse metals
14 端 *robata* fireside, hearth
16 頭 *rotō* around the hearth

B **炎** 3404 J316a M18910 EN inflammation. *honō, honoho, homura* flame, blaze.
3 上 *enjō* blazing up; destruction (of a large building) by fire
4 天 *enten* blazing heat, scorching sun
8 炎 *en'en(taru)* blazing, fiery
9 威 *en'i* extreme heat, sultriness
10 症 *enshō* inflammation
12 暑 *ensho* intense heat, heat wave
15 熱 *ennetsu* sweltering heat

B **炊** 3405 J3f66 M18904 SUI. *ta(ku), kashi(gu)* cook, boil.
4 夫 *suifu* a male cook
5 出 *takida(shi)* emergency rice feeding
8 具 *suigu* cooking utensils
事 *suiji* cooking, culinary affairs
事係 *suijigakari* cook, chef
事場 *suijiba* kitchen, cookhouse, field kitchen, galley
11 婦 *suifu* a female cook, kitchen maid
12 飯 *suihan* cooking rice

飯器 *suihanki* electric rice cooker
29 爨 *suisan* cooking

5

炮 3406 / J5f5c / M18954 Hō burn; roast.

炳 3407 / J5f5b / M18960 **昞** 2438 / J-X / M13835 **昺** 2439 / J-X / M13836
HEI clear and bright.
5 乎 *heiko* very clear

炯 3408 / J5f57 / M18956 **烱** 3422 / J5f58 / M19040 KEI light; clear.
9 炯 *keikei(taru)* glaring, penetrating
11 眼 *keigan* keen eye

炬 3409 / J5f59 / M18949 KO. KYO torch, signal fire.
4 火 *kyoka* pine torch, torchlight, firebrand
11 眼 *kyogan* penetrating eye
16 燵 *kotatsu* charcoal brazier in a floor well; heat source under a table or quilt

炸 3410 / J5f5a / M18979 SAKU frying; explosion.
9 発 *sakuhatsu* explosion
12 裂 *sakuretsu* explosion
裂弾 *sakuretsudan* explosive
16 薬 *sakuyaku* explosives

B **為** 3411 / J3059 / M18981 **爲** 3513 / J602a / M19686 I. *na(ru)* change; be of use; reach to. *na(su)* do. *su(ru)* do; try; play; practice; cost; serve as; pass, elapse. *ni su(ru)* make (something) of (a person); turn into (money). *tame* good, advantage, benefit, welfare, sake; to, in order to; because of, as a result of. *tame ni* for, for the sake of, to one's advantage, in favor of, on behalf of.
2 人 *hitotonari* temperament
4 手 *narite* candidate; suitable person
5 出来 *shi-deka(su)* finish up
6 尽 *shi-tsuku(su)* do everything possible
合 *shi-a(u)* do together
7 体 *teitaraku* state of affairs, predicament. *etai* nature, character
初 *shi-so(meru)* begin to do. *shiso(me)* outset, beginning
来 *shikita(ri)* customs
8 果 *shi-ō(seru)* accomplish
放題 *shihōdai* having one's own way
9 政者 *iseisha* statesman
政家 *iseika* politician
10 残 *shi-noko(su)* leave unfinished
納 *shiosa(me)* finishing up
11 遂 *na(shi)-to(geru), shi-to(geru)* accomplish, finish, fulfill
過 *shi-su(giru)* overdo, do too much
術 *se(n)sube* proper methods
終 *na(shi)-o(eru) vt* accomplish, finish. *na(shi)-o(waru) vi* finish
悪 *shiniku(i)* hard to do
12 遣 *shi(te) ya(ru)* do for (someone); deceive, hoodwink
筋 *tamesuji* patron; effective means
落 *shio(chi), shioto(shi)* omission, oversight. *shi-oto(su)* fail to do; make light of, neglect
替 *kawase* money order; exchange
替手形 *kawase tegata* draft
替尻 *kawasejiri* balance of exchange
替相場 *kawase sōba* exchange rates
替銀行 *kawase ginkō* exchange bank
替管理 *kawase kanri* exchange control
13 損 *shi-sokona(u), shi-son(jiru)* fail, blunder, make a mistake
続 *shi-tsuzu(keru)* continue to do, persist in doing

A **点** 3412 / J4540 / M18980 **點** 7057 / J735a / M48083 **奌** 3492 / J-X / M-X
TEN point; mark; score, run; speck; stain; defect; a detail; standpoint; items, pieces; decimal point; vote. *ten(jiru), ten(zuru)* drop; light, kindle; make tea. *tomo(ru), tobo(ru)* burn, be lighted. *tomo(su), tobo(su)* light, turn on. *tsu(ku)* (electricity) comes on. *tsu(keru)* turn on (electricity), light up. *sa(su)* light (a fire); apply moxa cautery.
4 心 *tenshin, tenjin* Zen monk's snack; Chinese dessert; dim sum
火 *tenka* lighting, ignition
火栓 *tenkasen* spark plug
火薬 *tenkayaku* priming powders
5 示 *tenji* pointing out
付 *tentsu(ke)* marking, grading
6 灯 *tentō* lighting
字 *tenji* Braille
光 *tenkō* spotlight
在 *tenzai suru* be dotted with

[8] 呼 *tenko* roll call, muster
画 *tenga* stippling. *tenkaku* the strokes of a character
者 *tenja* critic of haiku poetry
取 *tento(ri)* competition for school marks; keeping score; score
取虫 *tento(ri)mushi* derisive term for a diligent student
[9] 点 *tenten* here and there, sporadically, scattered; in drops; little by little; dot, spot
茶 *tencha* boiling tea (for a tea ceremony)
[11] 描 *tembyō* sketch
眼 *tengan suru* drop medicine in the eyes
[12] 検 *tenken* inspection, examination; roll calling
景 *tenkei* the incidental details of a picture
[13] 睛 *tensei* adding eyes and other finishing touches to an animal painting
滅 *temmetsu* turning a light on and off
滅器 *temmetsuki* electric switch
数 *tensū* marks, credits, points; score, runs; number of items
数切符 *tensū kippu* ration-point coupon
数制 *tensūsei* point rationing system
[14] 綴 *tentei, tentetsu* a line (of mountains, islands, houses, etc.)
滴 *tenteki* falling drops, raindrops; intravenous drip, IV
滴器 *tentekiki* dropper
[15] 播 *tempa* sowing spaced seeds
線 *tensen* dotted line; perforated line
[16] 頭 *tentō suru* nod

A **炭** 3413 / J433a / M18953 TAN charcoal; coal. *sumi* charcoal.
[2] 入 *sumii(re)* charcoal container
[3] 山 *tanzan* coal mine
[4] 木 *sumigi* charcoal wood
火 *sumibi, tanka* charcoal fire; coals of fire
化 *tanka* carbonization
化水素 *tanka suiso* hydrocarbon
化物 *tankabutsu* carbide
水 *tansui* coal and water; carbon and hydrogen
水化物 *tansuikabutsu* carbohydrates
水車 *tansuisha* engine tender
水船 *tansuisen* supply ship
[5] 田 *tanden* coal field
[6] 団 *tadon* charcoal ball
[7] 車 *tansha* coal wagon, coal truck, coal car (of a locomotive)
坑 *tankō* coal mine
坑夫 *tankōfu* coal miner
[8] 取 *sumito(ri)* charcoal scuttle
[9] 屋 *sumiya* charcoal dealer
[10] 庫 *tanko* coal bin, coal bunker
俵 *sumidawara* charcoal sack
挾 *sumibasa(mi)* charcoal tongs
消 *sumike(shi)* covered jar for putting out burning coals
脈 *tammyaku* coal vein
疽病 *tansobyō* anthrax
素 *tanso* carbon
素紙 *tansoshi* carbon paper
素棒 *tansobō* carbon rod; carbon points
素線 *tansosen* carbon filament
[12] 焼 *sumiya(ki)* charcoal making; charcoal maker
焼竈 *sumiya(ki)gama* charcoal kiln
[13] 継 *sumitsu(gi)* replenishing charcoal
鉱 *tankō* coal mine
鉱業 *tankōgyō* coal-mining industry
[14] 層 *tansō* coal seam
塵 *tanjin* coal dust
酸 *tansan* carbonic acid
酸水 *tansansui* carbonated water
酸孔 *tansankō* a mofette
酸瓦斯 *tansan gasu* carbon dioxide
酸泉 *tansansen* carbonated spring
酸紙 *tansanshi* carbon paper
酸曹達 *tansan sōda* sodium carbonate
[15] 窯 *sumigama* charcoal kiln
質 *tanshitsu* coal quality
[20] 礦 *tankō* coal mine
[21] 竈 *sumigama* charcoal kiln

6

烟 3414 / J5f5d / M19022 See 煙 3456.

烛 3415 / J-X / M19017 Nonstandard for 燭 3496.

烋 3416 / J5f5e / M18991 KYŪ. GŌ boasting; fortunate; pleasant, pleasing; good; softening.

烝 3417 / J5f5f / M19019 Jō. Shō steam; encourage; many, plentiful. *mu(su)* steam.

烘 3418 / J-X / M19012 Kō. *abu(ru)* roast, toast, broil, grill; warm; dry.

烙 3419 / J5f60 / M19014 Raku burn.

6 印 *rakuin* mark, brand, stigma, branding iron

B **烈** 3420 / J4e75 / M18987 Retsu. *hage(shii)* violent, vehement, furious, severe, acute, intense, extreme, passionate, heated, stormy (applause); tempestuous (temperament); mighty.

3 士 *resshi* patriot, hero
女 *retsujo* heroine
4 日 *retsujitsu* a hot day
火 *rekka* raging fire
夫 *reppu* patriot; hero
9 風 *reppū* violent wind, hurricane, gale
10 烈 *retsuretsu(taru)* ardent, intense, vehement
11 婦 *reppu* a virtuous woman; heroine
15 震 *resshin* violent earthquake

烏 3421 / J3128 / M18998 U. O. *karasu* crow, raven.

3 口 *karasuguchi* ruling pen
4 木 *uboku* ebony
6 行水 *karasu (no) gyōzui* a quick bath
合衆 *ugō(no)shū* disorderly crowd, mob
羽玉 *ubatama no* jet black; pitch dark
羽色 *karasuba iro* glossy black
7 貝 *karasugai* fresh-water mussel
8 金 *karasugane* money lent at daily interest
10 竜茶 *ūroncha* oolong tea
紙 *karasugami* coarse dark-brown paper
11 蛇 *karasu hebi* a black snake
12 帽子 *eboshi* noble's court headgear
犀角 *usaikaku* black rhinoceros horn
13 賊 *ika* squid, cuttlefish
14 鳴 *karasuna(ki)* cry of the crow
滸 *oko(gamashii)* presumptuous, impertinent; ridiculous, absurd
17 濡羽色 *karasu no nureba iro* glossy black (hair)

7

烱 3422 / J5f58 / M19040 See **炯** 3408.

焔 3423 / J316b / M-X Nonstandard for **燄** 3485.

焉 3424 / J5f61 / M19076 En. *izuku(nzo)* how, why. *koko ni* then.

烹 3425 / J4b23 / M19049 Hō. *ni(ru) vt* boil, cook.

烽 3426 / J5f62 / M19059 Hō signal fire.

4 火 *hōka, noroshi* signal fire, rocket, beacon

8

焰 3427 / J-X / M19141 Nonstandard for **燄** 3485.

煉 3428 / J4e7b / M-X Nonstandard for **煉** 3455.

焙 3429 / J-X / M19130 Ō. *uzumibi* banked fire, ash fire.

焠 3430 / J-X / M19111 Sai. *nama(su)* anneal.

焱 3431 / J-X / M19142 En. *honō* flame, blaze.

焜 3432 / J5f63 / M19103 Kon shine.

8 炉 *konro* portable cooking stove. *shichirin* small charcoal stove

焙 3433 / J5f64 / M19099 Hō. Hai. *hō(jiru)* fire, heat, roast. *abu(ru)* roast, toast, broil, grill; warm; dry.

5 出 *aburida(shi)* invisible (ink)
9 茶 *hōjicha* roasted tea
10 烙 *hōraku* baking pan
22 籠 *aburiko* grill; basket for drying over a fire

焚 3434 / J4a32 / M19100 Fun. *ta(ku)* burn, kindle, build (a fire); boil, cook.

ya(ku) vt set fire to, burn, fire; bake, roast (over a fire), toast, broil, parch; char, scorch, singe; cremate; print (photos); be envious of.

3 口 *takiguchi* fuel-feed hole
4 火 *takibi* blazing fire, bonfire
5 付 *ta(ki)-tsu(keru)* light, kindle, build (a fire); instigate, stir up. *takitsu(ke)* kindling, fire lighter
出 *takida(shi)* emergency rice feeding
6 尽 *ta(ki)-tsu(kusu)* burn up; run out of fuel
8 物 *takimono* firewood, kindling, fuel
10 書 *funsho* burning of books
11 捨 *ta(ki)-su(teru)* leave a fire to burn out
12 落 *takioto(shi)* embers, charred firewood

A **然** 3435 J4133 M19149 Zen. Nen. *sō, sa* so. *shika(rashimeru)* to decree. *sō(shite), so(shite)* and. *sa(ri) towa* if so, well. *sa(ru)* a certain, such. *shika(ruba)* if so, in that case. *shika(razu)* no, it is not so. *shika(redomo)* but. *shika(ri)* yes, you are right. *shika(rubeki)* due, proper, reasonable, respectable, justifiable. *shika(ru) ni* however, nevertheless, on the contrary. *shika(shi), sare(do)* but, however. *shika(mo)* moreover, nevertheless. *shika* so, in that way. *-zen* resembling.

5 可 *shika(ru)be(ku)* as you think best, appropriately, reasonably
乍 *shikashinagara* but, however. *sanaga(ra)* as if; just like
6 迄 *samade* to that extent, so much
気無 *sa(rige)na(i)* unconcerned, nonchalant
7 体 *sa(aranu)tei* an unconcerned air
12 程 *sahodo* very much, much, very. *saruhodo ni* well, now
斯 *sōkō* this and that; hesitatingly
然 *shikajika* and so on. *so(u)so(u)* again and again
14 様 *sayō na* such, of that kind, like that
15 諾 *zendaku* word of honor

B **焦** 3436 J3e47 M19119 Shō. *ko(geru) vi* burn, scorch, singe, char. *ko(gasu) vt* burn, scorch, char, singe; pine for. *koga(reru)* pine for, yearn for; be deeply in love with; be scorched. *ase(ru)* be in a hurry, be hasty, be impatient, be overzealous. *ji(reru)* be irritated. *ji(rasu)* irritate. *ji(rettagaru)* be impatient. *ko(gashi)* parched-barley flour. *ji(rettai)* irritating, provoking; impatient, vexed.

3 土 *shōdo* burnt ground; scorched earth
土戦術 *shōdo senjutsu* scorched-earth strategy
4 心 *shōshin* impatience, worry, excitement
5 付 *ko(ge)-tsu(ku)* get charred, get burnt
6 死 *koga(re)jini suru* die of love for
9 眉 *shōbi* emergency, urgency, imminence
点 *shōten* focus
臭 *kogekusa(i), kinakusa(i)* smelling burnt
茶 *kogecha* dark brown
茶色 *kogecha iro* dark brown
15 慮 *shōryo* impatience, worry
熱 *shōnetsu* scorching heat; scorching
熱地獄 *shōnetsu jigoku* burning hell
17 燥 *shōsō* impatience, irritation, uneasiness
20 躁 *shōsō* impatience, irritation, uneasiness

B **煮** 3437 J3c51 M19165′ **煑** 3441 J-X M19188 **𤎩** 3442 J-X M19187 Sha. *ni(eru)* boil, cook, be cooked, be boiled. *ni(ru) vt* boil, cook. *ni* cooking.

2 〆 *ni-shi(meru)* boil up thoroughly
3 干 *nibo(shi)* small dried sardines
上 *ni(e)-a(garu)* be thoroughly boiled. *ni-a(geru)* boil thoroughly
4 方 *nikata* cookery; cook
込 *ni-ko(mu)* cook together. *niko(mi)* meat and vegetable stew
切 *ni(e)-ki(ranai)* be half-cooked; vague, halfhearted, vacillating
5 立 *ni-ta(teru)* boil up, bring to a boil. *ni-ta(tsu)* boil up, bring to a boil; begin to boil
付 *ni-tsu(keru)* boil hard
汁 *nijiru, nitsuyu, nishiru* gravy, stock, broth
加減 *niekagen* amount of boiling
出 *ni-da(su) vt* boil down, decoct, extract. *nida(shi)* stock, broth
出汁 *nida(shi)jiru* soup stock, broth
6 色 *niiro* color of well-cooked food; broth
返 *ni(e)-kae(ru), ni(ekuri)-kae(ru)* boil over, seethe, ferment, come to a boil

合 *ni-a(waseru)* boil together
7 豆 *nimame* boiled beans
冷 *ni-sa(masu)* let cool after boiling
花 *ni(e)bana* fresh tea
抜 *ninu(ki)* paste made from boiled rice flour
抜玉子 *ninu(ki) tamago* boiled egg
8 炊 *nita(ki)* boiling
物 *nimono* cooking; cooked food
直 *ni-nao(su)* boil again, recook
沸 *shafutsu suru, ni(e)-ta(giru)* boil up
沸消毒 *shafutsu shōdoku* sterilization by boiling
9 染 *ni-shi(meru)* boil hard
10 凍 *nikogo(ri)* boiled-down food
殺 *nikoro(shi)* death by boiling
11 魚 *nizakana* boiled fish
過 *ni-su(giru), ni-su(gosu)* overdo, overboil
頃 *nigoro* the time the cooking is done
崩 *ni(e)-kuzu(reru)* be cooked to pieces
12 湯 *ni(e)yu* boiling water
焼 *niya(ki)* cooking
焚 *nitaki* cooking
13 溢 *ni(e)-kobo(reru)* boil over
詰 *ni-tsu(maru)* be boiled down. *ni-tsu(meru) vt* boil down
14 滾 *ni(e)-ta(giru) vi* boil up, seethe, ferment
15 蕩 *ni-toro(kasu)* simmer until dissolved
16 凝 *nikogori* boiled-down food; jelly
麺 *nyūmen* boiled vermicelli
19 繰返 *ni(e)-ku(ri)-kae(ru)* boil up

A **焼** 3438 / J3e46 / M19166′ **燒** 3475 / J5f76 / M19420 **焼** 3440 / J-X / M-X

SHŌ burning. *ya(ku) vt* set fire to, burn, fire; bake, roast (over a fire), toast, broil, parch; char, scorch, singe; cremate; print (photos); be envious of. *ya(keru) vi* be burnt, be burnt down; be roasted, be toasted, be grilled, be broiled; be scorched; be sunburnt; warm up, heat up (as a motor); be tarnished, fade; have heartburn; be jealous of; glow, be illuminated. *ya(ki)* baking, toasting, roasting, broiling; roast; porcelain; tempering; discipline.

2 入 *ya(ki)i(re)* hardening, tempering. *ya(ki) (o) i(reru)* torture
3 土 *shōdo, ya(ke)tsuchi* baked clay, parched ground
山 *ya(ke)yama* burning mountain; burnt-over mountain
刃 *ya(ki)ba* tempered blade
4 切 *ya(ke)-ki(ru)* burn itself out
太 *ya(ke)buto(ri)* getting richer after a fire
木杭 *ya(ke)bokkui* charred posts; firebrand
火箸 *ya(ke)hibashi* hot tongs
5 瓦 *ya(ke)gawara* burnt tile
穴 *ya(ke)ana* hole made by burning
立 *ya(ki)-ta(teru)* burn fiercely. *ya(ki)ta(te)* piping hot, freshly baked; freshly roasted, freshly broiled
処 *ya(ke)do* burn; scald
付 *ya(ki)-tsu(keru)* join by baking; bake (porcelain); enamel; glaze; plate; stain (glass); fuse together; print (pictures). *ya(ki)-tsu(ku)* scorch. *yakitsu(ke)* baking; enamelling; plating; annealing; (photographic) printing
払 *ya(ki)-hara(u)* burn up, consume. *ya(ki)hara(i)* violent burning of unwanted goods
打 *yakiu(chi)* setting on fire, attacking and burning
失 *ya(ke)-u(seru), shōshitsu suru* destroy by fire
出 *ya(ke)-da(sareru)* be burnt out. *ya(ke)da(sare)* people burnt out
玉機関 *ya(ki)dama kikan* semi-diesel engine
石 *ya(ke)ishi* hot stone; pumice stone, lava
石膏 *ya(ki)sekkō* plaster of Paris
6 米 *ya(ki)gome* parched rice, burnt rice
肉 *ya(ki)niku* roast meat, roast fowl
回 *ya(ki) (ga) mawa(ru)* lose one's energy
尽 *ya(ki)-tsuku(su)* burn up, consume, reduce to ashes. *ya(ke)-tsu(kiru)* burn out
印 *ya(ki)in* brand, branding iron; stigma
芋 *ya(ki)imo* baked or roasted sweet potato
団子 *ya(ki)dango* toasted dumpling
夷 *shōi* burning up
夷弾 *shōidan* incendiary bomb, incendiary shell
死 *shōshi, ya(ke)ji(ni)* death by fire
死体 *shōshitai* charred body
死者 *shōshisha* person burnt to death

7 足 *ya(ke)ta(ranai)* rare, underdone
灼 *shōshaku suru* cauterize
判 *ya(ki)han, ya(ki)ban* branding iron, brand; stigma
却 *shōkyaku* destruction by fire, incineration
麦 *ya(ki)mugi* parched barley
串 *ya(ki)gushi* skewer, spit
豆腐 *ya(ki)dōfu* broiled bean curd
戻 *ya(ki)-modo(su)* anneal, temper
戻鋼 *ya(ki)modo(shi)kō* tempered steel
8 金 *ya(ki)gane* branding iron, marking iron
板 *ya(ki)ita* hot plate
枠 *ya(ki)waku* photographic printing frame
物 *ya(ki)mono* pottery, porcelain
直 *ya(ki)-nao(su)* rebake; warm over; overbake; rehash; adapt; imitate; overprint (in photography)
林檎 *ya(ki)ringo* baked apple
9 香 *shōkō* incense offering
畑 *ya(ki)bata, ya(ke)bata, ya(ki)batake, ya(ke)batake* burnt-over fields
砂 *ya(ke)zuna* hot sandbag (for treatments)
型 *ya(ki)gata* dry-sand mold
海苔 *ya(ki)nori* toasted seaweed
10 残 *ya(ke)-noko(ru)* remain unburnt, escape a fire. *ya(ke)noko(ri)* articles saved from a fire; remains after a fire
酒 *ya(ke)zake* drowning one's cares in saké
討 *ya(ki)u(chi)* an attack with fire
酎 *shōchū* a low-grade alcoholic drink
殺 *ya(ki)-koro(su)* *vt* burn to death, burn alive
畠 *ya(ki)bata, ya(ke)bata, ya(ki)batake, ya(ke)batake* burnt-over fields
栗 *ya(ki)guri* roasted chestnut
11 魚 *ya(ki)zakana* broiled fish
鳥 *ya(ki)tori* fried chicken, roast fowl, yakitori
痕 *shōkon* scar from a burn
過 *ya(ki)-su(giru)* overcook; overprint (photography)
捨 *ya(ki)-su(teru)* burn up, incinerate
接 *ya(ki)tsu(gi) suru* cement broken porcelain together by baking
豚 *ya(ki)buta* roast pork
野 *ya(ke)no* burnt field, burnt prairie
野原 *ya(ke)nohara, ya(ke)no(ga)hara* burnt-out area
12 場 *ya(ki)ba* crematory
渣 *ya(ke)kasu* cinders
絵 *ya(ki)e* pyrography; pyrograph
蛤 *ya(ki)hamaguri* baked clams
鈍 *ya(ki)-nama(su)* anneal
飯 *ya(ki)meshi* fried rice
落 *ya(ke)-o(chiru)* be burnt down
焦 *ya(ke)ko(ge), ya(ke)koga(shi)* hole made by burning
13 傷 *ya(ke)kizu* a burn
塊 *shōkai* clinker
塩 *ya(ki)shio* baked salt, table salt
滅 *shōmetsu sasu, ya(ki)-horobo(su)* *vt* destroy by fire. *shōmetsu suru* *vi* be destroyed by fire
腹 *ya(ke)bara* despair, desperation
跡 *ya(ke)ato* fire ruins
棄 *ya(ki)-su(teru)* destroy by fire. *shōki* destruction by fire
14 増 *yakima(shi)* an extra print
網 *ya(ki)ami* toasting grill, broiling grill
餅 *ya(ki)mochi* toasted rice cake
15 麸 *ya(ki)fu* baked wheat-gluten bread
窯 *ya(ki)gama* kiln, oven
蕎麦 *ya(ki)soba* fried noodles
17 鍋 *ya(ki)nabe* frying pan
19 鏝 *ya(ki)gote* hot iron; flatiron; soldering; iron, cautering iron; pyrographic iron

A **無** 3439 / J1e35 / M19113 MU, BU nothing, nil, negation. *na(i), na(shi)* none. *na(kattara)* if there were none; were it not for; unless. *mu ni suru* make worthless. *na(ku) naru* be lost; run short, be used up; disappear; die. *naku(su), na(ku) suru* lose; run out of; remove; absorb. *na(kute)* without; for want of; in the absence of. *na(sasōna)* unlikely, improbable. *na(kumogana)* needless, useless. *na(shi) ni, na(shi) de* without.
1 一文 *muichimon* penniless
一物 *muichibutsu, muichimotsu* penniless
2 二 *muni* matchless, unparalleled
二無三 *munimusan* recklessly, furiously, desperately, forcibly
力 *muryoku* helpless, incompetent; lack of funds
力化 *muryokka suru* become powerless
人 *bunin, mujin* shortage of help; unmanned. *mujin, munin* uninhabited

人地帯 *mujin chitai* no-man's land
人飛行機 *mujin hikōki* pilotless plane
人島 *mujintō* uninhabited island
人電車 *mujin densha* runaway tram
人境 *mujin(no)kyō* uninhabited region
3 口 *mukuchi* reticence
下 *muge ni* flatly, squarely, point-blank
才 *musai* incompetence, lack of ability
干渉 *mukanshō* nonintervention
上 *mujō no* supreme, best, greatest
上光栄 *mujō (no) kōei* great fame
上権 *mujōken* supremacy
4 心 *mushin* request. *mushin no* innocent; insentient; involuntary
手 *mute de* empty-handed; with bare hands; unarmed; without funds
比 *muhi no* peerless, unparalleled
毛 *mumō* hairless
水 *musui* anhydrous
双 *musō* peerless, unparalleled
日付 *muhizuke* undated
分別 *mufumbetsu* rashness, indiscretion
方針 *muhōshin* without a plan
月謝 *mugessha* free tuition
欠 *muketsu* perfection
欠席 *mukesseki* perfect attendance
辺 *muhen na* limitless, boundless, infinite
辺際 *muhensai* infinity
5 代 *mudai* free, no charge
功 *mukō* void, invalid; ineffective
生 *musei* lifeless
生物 *museibutsu* inanimate object; lifeless thing
札 *musatsu* without tickets
札乗車 *musatsu jōsha* riding without tickets
主 *mushu* ownerless
主義 *mushugi* unprincipled, lacking a fixed purpose
礼 *burei* discourtesy, rudeness
礼者 *bureimono, bureisha* rude person
礼講 *bureikō* informal party, unrestrained revelry
用 *muyō* useless; unwanted; unnecessary; prohibited; without business
用心 *buyōjin* insecurity, carelessness
用心配 *muyō (no) shimpai* needless worry
用長物 *muyō (no) chōbutsu* useless thing
6 色 *mushoku* colorless, achromatic
休 *mukyū* no holiday
地 *muji* solid color
灯 *mutō* no light (at night)
考 *mukanga(e)* thoughtlessness
自覚 *mujikaku na* apathetic, blind to, unconscious of
任所大臣 *muninsho daijin* minister of state without portfolio
字幕映画 *mujimaku eiga* film without subtitles
血 *muketsu* bloodless
血革命 *muketsu kakumei* bloodless revolution
尽 *mujin* infinity, endless, unfathomable; lottery savings system
尽蔵 *mujinzō* inexhaustible supply
死 *mushi* no outs (in baseball)
死満塁 *mushi-manrui* no outs and bases full
気力 *mukiryoku* lethargy, enervation
気味 *bukimi* ill-feeling
防備 *mubōbi* unfortified, open, defenseless
防備都市 *mubōbi toshi* open city
安打 *muanda* no hits
安打無得点 *muanda-mutokuten* a no-hit and no-run (game)
名 *mumei* unnamed, anonymity, obscurity; unjustifiable
名氏 *mumeishi* anonymous person
名兵士 *mumei heishi* the unknown soldier
名指 *mumeishi* ring finger
名骨 *mumeikotsu* hipbone
名戦士 *mumei senshi* the unknown soldier
7 住 *mujū* (temple) without a resident priest
位 *mui* without rank
私 *mushi* unselfishness, impartiality
芸 *mugei no* uncultured, unaccomplished
邪気 *mujaki* innocence, artlessness
沙汰 *busata* silence, neglect to write or call
作法 *busahō* bad manners, discourtesy, rudeness
花果 *ichijiku, ichijuku* fig
材料 *muzairyō* no new factors (on the stock market)
投票 *mutōhyō* elected without opposition

批判的 *muhihanteki* uncritical
医地域 *muichiiki* doctorless area
医村 *muison* doctorless village
尾 *mubi* tailless
尾翼機 *mubiyokuki* flying wing, tailless plane
体 *mutai* forcibly
体財産 *mutai zaisan* intangible assets
技巧 *mugikō* artless
技能 *muginō no* unskilled (job)
利子 *murishi* non-interest-bearing
利息 *murisoku* non-interest-bearing
形 *mukei no* abstract, incorporeal, immaterial; moral, spiritual; invisible, intangible
形文化財 *mukei-bunkazai* intangible cultural asset
言 *mugon* silence
言行 *mugon (no) gyō* silent austerities
言劇 *mugongeki* pantomime
我 *muga* selflessness; ecstasy
我夢中 *muga-muchū* unconsciousness; ecstasy
我境 *muga(no)kyō* self-effacement
条件 *mujōken* unconditional
条件降伏 *mujōken kōfuku* unconditional surrender
条件降服 *mujōken kōfuku* unconditional surrender
条約 *mujōyaku* treatyless
声 *musei* voiceless, noiseless, silent
声子音 *musei shiin* voiceless sound
声音 *museion* voiceless sound
声映画 *musei eigu* silent film
声銃 *museijū* noiseless gun
8 届 *mutodo(ke)* without permission; without notice
性 *musei* asexual. *bushō* laziness, indolence. *mushō* thoughtless, rash, indiscreet; immoderate; unnecessary
明 *mumyō* darkness, illusion
効 *mukō* void, invalid; ineffective
官 *mukan* without office
毒 *mudoku* nonpoisonous
拘束 *mukōsoku* nonrestraint
制限 *museigen* unlimited, unrestricted
担保 *mutampo* unsecured, without collateral
表情 *muhyōjō na* expressionless
免許 *mumenkyo* unlicensed
価 *muka* priceless; valueless
価値 *mukachi no* worthless
味 *mumi* tasteless, flat, insipid
味乾燥 *mumi-kansō na* dry as dust, uninteresting
抵当 *muteitō* (borrowing) without security
抵抗 *muteikō* nonresistance, passive resistance
法 *muhō* injustice; wrong; unlawfulness; outrage; violence
法者 *muhōmono* outlaw, outrageous fellow
知 *muchi* ignorance, illiteracy, stupidity
知蒙昧 *muchi-mōmai* unenlightenment
念 *munen* regret; resentment; chagrin; impassive state of mind
念無想 *munen-musō* impassive state of mind
定見 *muteiken* lack of principle, inconstant
定形 *muteikei* amorphous
実 *mujitsu* falsehood; innocence
実罪 *mujitsu (no) tsumi* false charge
学 *mugaku* ignorance; illiteracy
学者 *mugakusha* an ignorant person
事 *buji* safety, security; peace, tranquility; good health; boredom
事故 *mujiko* no accident, no trouble; safety (week)
所得 *mushotoku* without income
所属 *mushozoku* free, independent, nonaffiliated, nonpartisan
所属地帯 *mushozoku chitai* no-man's land
妻 *musai* celibacy
妻主義 *musai shugi* celibacy
妻者 *musaisha* single person
限 *mugen* infinite, endless, unfathomable; infinity, eternity
限大 *mugendai* infinity. *mugendai no* infinitely great
限小 *mugenshō* the infinitesimal
限地獄 *mugen jigoku* a Buddhist hell
限軌道 *mugen kidō* endless track, caterpillar
限責任 *mugen sekinin* unlimited liability
9 音 *buin* long silence, neglect (to write)
垢 *muku* purity, innocence; plain-colored suit; an all-white garb
冠 *mukan* uncrowned
臭 *mushū* odorless

要 *muyō* useless; unwanted; unnecessary; prohibited; without business
信心 *mushinjin* impiety, unbelief, infidelity
恰好 *bukakkō* unshapeliness, clumsiness
造作 *muzōsa* easiness; simplicity; artlessness
計画 *mukeikaku na* haphazard, unplanned
思慮 *mushiryo* thoughtlessness, indiscretion
封書状 *mufū shojō* unsealed letter
神経 *mushinkei* callousness, apathy, stolidity
神論 *mushinron* atheism
茶 *mucha na* absurd, unreasonable; reckless, wanton; excessive, immoderate
茶苦茶 *muchakucha* confused; absurd, unreasonable; reckless, mad
為 *bui, mui* idleness, inaction
為替 *mukawase, mugawase* no draft, no exchange involved
風 *mufū* dead calm
風帯 *mufūtai* doldrums
風流 *mufūryū* lack of refinement
軌道 *mukidō* trackless
軌道生活 *mukidō seikatsu* dissipated life
軌道電車 *mukidō densha* trolley bus
政府 *museifu* anarchy
政府主義 *museifu shugi* anarchism
政府主義者 *museifu shugisha* anarchist
10 根 *mukon* groundless, unfounded, false
残 *muzan* cruel, merciless, pitiful
粋 *busui na* inelegant, unromantic, lacking in polish
恥 *muchi* shamelessness, impudence
益 *mueki* futility, uselessness, carelessness
害 *mugai* harmless, innocent, inoffensive
記名 *mukimei* blank (endorsement), unregistered, uninscribed (shares)
症状 *mushōjō* no symptoms
格社 *mukakusha* an ungraded shrine
秩序 *muchitsujo* disorder, confusion, chaos
差別 *musabetsu, mushabetsu* indifference; making no discrimination
挨拶 *buaisatsu* impoliteness, incivility
酒精 *mushusei* nonalcoholic
脊椎動物 *musekitsui dōbutsu* invertebrate animal
病 *mubyō* no illness
病息災 *mubyō-sokusai* perfect health
配 *muhai* nondividend
配当 *muhaitō* nondividend
骨 *bukotsu* uncouth, clumsy, brusque
骨者 *bukotsumono* uncouth person
料 *muryō* no charge, free
料図書館 *muryō toshokan* free library
料貸出図書館 *muryō kashidashi toshokan* free circulating library
能 *munō* inefficiency, incompetence
能力 *munōryoku* incompetence, impotence
能力者 *munōryokusha* incompetent or inefficient person
能者 *munōsha* incompetent of inefficient person
11 疵 *mukizu* flawless, faultless, sound, without blemish
道 *budō, mudō* tyranny; atrocity; ⌈wickedness
偏 *muhen* justice, impartiality
惨 *muzan* cruel, merciless; pitiful
情 *mujō* heartlessness, cruelty
視 *mushi suru* disregard; defy, set aside, ignore
聊 *buryō, muryō* boredom, tediousness
欲 *muyoku* not covetous
常 *mujō no* uncertain, evanescent, transient
異 *bui* safety, security; peace, tranquility; good health; boredom
菌 *mukin* pasteurized, sterilized, aseptic, germfree
責任 *musekinin* irresponsibility
停車 *muteisha* nonstop
得点 *mutokuten* scoreless (game)
規律 *mukiritsu* disorderliness, negligence
経験 *mukeiken* inexperience
教会主義 *mukyōkai shugi* nondenominationalism
教育 *mukyōiku na* uneducated, uncultured
断 *mudan* unannounced; unauthorized
断欠勤 *mudan kekkin* absent without permission, AWOL
宿 *mushuku* homeless
宿者 *mushukusha* vagrant, homeless person

産 *musan* without property
産者 *musansha* proletarian, have-nots
産政党 *musan seitō* proletarian party
産党 *musantō* proletarian party
産階級 *musan kaikyū* proletarians, property-less class
理 *muri* unreasonable, unjustifiable, unnatural; impossible, beyond one's strength; overwork; extravagance. *muri(karanu)* reasonable, natural. *muri ni* forcibly, against one's will
理矢理 *muriyari ni* forcibly, against one's will
理心中 *muri shinjū* forced double suicide
理押 *murio(shi)* pushing things too far
理取 *murido(ri)* exaction, extortion
埋往生 *muriōjō* forced obedience
理強 *murijii* coercion
理無体 *muri-mutai* forcibly
理解 *murikai* lack of understanding or sympathy
理遣 *muriyari ni* forcibly, against one's will
理算段 *murisandan* proceeding in spite of difficulties; straining to raise money
理難題 *murinandai* unreasonable demand
12 帽 *mubō de* hatless
税 *muzei* duty-free, tax-free
給 *mukyū* unpaid, nonsalaried
辜 *muko no* innocent, harmless
筆 *muhitsu* illiteracy
筋 *mukin* nonreinforced
策 *musaku* resourcelessness
智 *muchi* ignorance, illiteracy, stupidity
無 *na(ke)na(shi)* the little one has. *na(i)na(i) suru* hide
割礼 *mukatsurei* uncircumcision
証拠 *mushōko* lack of evidence
統制 *mutōsei* uncontrolled
結果 *mukekka* negative result
勝負 *mushōbu* a tie, a draw
着陸 *muchakuriku* nonstop (flight)
報酬 *muhōshū no* nonsalaried
遠慮 *buenryo* forwardness, impertinence, audacity, boldness, frankness
間地獄 *muken jigoku* a Buddhist hell
痛 *mutsū* painless
痛分娩 *mutsū bumben* painless childbirth
量 *muryō* infinite, immeasurable
量寿 *muryōju* immeasurable bliss
期 *muki* unlimited, perpetual, indefinite
期刑 *mukikei* life imprisonment
期限 *mukigen* unlimited, perpetual, indefinite
期延期 *muki enki* postponed without setting another date
期懲役 *muki chōeki* life imprisonment
13 傷 *mukizu* flawless, faultless, sound, without blemish
嗜 *butashinami* poor preparation
碍 *muge* freedom from obstacle
数 *musū* innumerable
鉄砲 *muteppō na* reckless, thoughtless
義道 *mogidō na* cruel, brutal, heartless
頓着 *mutonchaku, mutonjaku* nonchalance, indifference
慈悲 *mujihi na* cruel, merciless
感覚 *mukankaku* insensibility, numbness, apathy, callousness
試験 *mushiken de* without examination
鉛白粉 *muen-oshiroi* non-lead face paint
想無念 *musō-munen* Zen meditation
暗 *muyami na, muyami(yatarana)* thoughtless, rash, indiscreet; immoderate; unnecessary
暗矢鱈 *muyami-yatara na* thoughtless, rash, indiscreet; immoderate; unnecessary
節制 *musessei* intemperance, profligacy
節操 *musessō* unchastity, inconstancy
電 *muden* wireless, radio
電放送 *muden hōsō* radio broadcast
勢 *buzei, muzei* shortage of people, numerical inferiority
勢力 *museiryoku* powerless, without influence
賃 *muchin* no charge
賃乗車 *muchin jōsha* free ride, stolen ride
煙 *muen* smokeless
煙火薬 *muen kayaku* smokeless powder
煙炭 *muentan* anthracite coal
愛敬 *buaikyō* rudeness; unsociability
愛想 *buaisō* rudeness; unsociability
愛嬌 *buaikyō* rudeness; unsociability
罪 *muzai* innocent, not guilty
罪判決 *muzai hanketsu* acquittal
罪放免 *muzai-hōmen* innocent and acquitted

蓋 *mugai no* open, uncovered
蓋車 *mugaisha* open freight car
蓋貨車 *mugai kasha* open freight car
意味 *muimi* meaningless, nonsensical, to no purpose
意義 *muigi* meaningless, nonsensical, to no purpose
意識 *muishiki* unconsciousness; involuntariness
意識的 *muishikiteki* unconscious; involuntary
資力 *mushiryoku* lack of funds
資本 *mushihon* without funds
資格 *mushikaku* disqualification; incapacity
資格者 *mushikakusha* disqualified person
14 慚 *muzan* cruel, merciless; pitiful
様 *buzama na* unshapely, unsightly, unpresentable; uncouth, clumsy
精 *bushō* sloth, laziness
銘 *mumei* unsigned, no signature
雑作 *muzōsa* easiness; simplicity; artlessness
関心 *mukanshin* unconcern, indifference, apathy
関係 *mukankei no* unconcerned, unrelated
銭 *musen* without money; no need for money
銭旅行 *musen ryokō* a penniless journey; traveling with no money
銭遊興 *musen yūkyō* merrymaking without paying
銭飲食 *musen inshoku* leaving a restaurant without paying
駄 *muda* futility, uselessness, waste
駄口 *mudaguchi* idle talk, nonsense
駄死 *mudaji(ni)* useless death
駄言 *mudagoto* useless words
駄足 *mudaashi suru* make a fruitless call
駄骨 *mudabone* fruitless effort
駄書 *mudaga(ki)* idle scribbling
駄遣 *mudazukai* squandering
駄話 *mudabanashi* idle talk, gossip
15 慮 *muryo* approximately
論 *muron* of course, naturally
敵 *muteki* invincible, unrivaled
暴 *mubō* recklessness, thoughtlessness
窮 *mukyū* eternity, immortality
慾 *muyoku* not covetous
慙 *muzan* cruel, merciless; pitiful
器用 *bukiyō* clumsiness, unskillfulness
趣味 *mushumi* lack of taste, vulgarity; prosaic
調法 *buchōhō* discourtesy
縁 *muen* no surviving relatives
縁仏 *muembotoke* a deceased without relatives
縁墓地 *muembochi* cemetery for the unclaimed
線 *musen* wireless; no electricity service; no need for electricity
線工学 *musen kōgaku* radio engineering
線中継 *musen chūkei* radio relay
線灯台 *musen tōdai* radio beacon
線周波数 *musen shūhasū* a radio frequency
線通信 *musen tsūshin* radio communication
線航路標識 *musen kōro hyōshiki* radio beacon
線電信 *musen denshin* wireless telegraphy
線電報 *musen dempō* radiogram
線電話 *musen denwa* radio telephone
線標識 *musen hyōshiki* radio beacon
線操縦 *musen sōjū* radio-controlled (plane)
16 稽 *mukei* absurdity, nonsense
糖 *mutō* unsweetened
謀 *mubō na* reckless, thoughtless
頭 *mutō* headless
頼 *burai* villainy
頼漢 *buraikan* villain, scoundrel, outlaw
機 *muki* inorganic, mineral
機化学 *muki kagaku* inorganic chemistry
機物 *mukibutsu* inorganic substance; minerals (in food)
17 償 *mushō* free, no charge
償行為 *mushō (no) kōi* volunteer service
爵 *mushaku* untitled
18 難 *bunan* safety, security; faultlessness; no difficulty
類 *murui* choicest, finest
題 *mudai* no title
謬性 *mubyūsei* infallibility
職 *mushoku* unemployed, no occupation
職者 *mushokusha* unemployed person
職業 *mushokugyō* unemployed, no occupation

19 礙 *muge* freedom from obstacles
識 *mushiki* ignorance, illiteracy
韻詩 *muinshi* blank verse, unrhymed poem
警告 *mukeikoku de* without warning
警察 *mukeisatsu* anarchy, lawlessness
20 競争 *mukyōsō* without a rival
籍者 *musekimono* person without registered domicile; vagrant; outlaw
22 鑑札 *mukansatsu* without a license

9

焼 3440 J-X M-X See 焼 3438.

煑 3441 J-X M19188 **煮** 3442 J-X M19187 See 煮 3437.

熘 3443 J-X M19221 See 燄 3485.

煢 3444 J5f69 M19217 KEI. KYŌ alone; single; only child; widow; widower.

煦 3445 J5f68 M19225 KU *atata(meru)* heat, warm up.

煬 3446 J5f6c M19235 YŌ *abu(ru)* broil, roast, grill.

煨 3447 J-X M19228 WAI banked fire

煥 3448 J5f65 M19224 KAN shine.
9 発 *kampatsu suru* glitter, brighten

煌 3449 J5f6a M19181 KŌ. *kirame(ku)* glitter, gleam, twinkle. *kira(rakana), kirabi(yakana)* glittering, bright and beautiful; clear speech.
13 煌 *kōkō(taru)* bright, brilliant

煠 3450 J-X M19213 YŌ. CHŌ. SŌ. SHŌ. *ita(meru)* to sauté. *yu(deru) vt* boil, seethe. *yu(daru) vi* boil, seethe.
3 上 *yu(de)-a(geru)* finish boiling
5 汁 *yudejiru* broth
7 卵 *yudetamago* boiled eggs
13 溢 *yu(de)-kobo(su)* scald, parboil

煖 3451 J5f6b M19196 DAN warm.
6 衣 *dan'i* warm clothes; dress warmly
8 炉 *danro* fireplace, hearth, stove
房 *dambō* heating
房車 *dambōsha* heated automobile
房装置 *dambō sōchi* heating system

煤 3452 J4761 M19220 BAI. *susu* soot. *susu(keru), susuba(mu), susu(buru)* get sooty, be sooty, get smoked up; be smoke-dried.
5 田 *baiden* coal field
払 *susuhara(i)* housecleaning
6 竹 *susudake* smoked bamboo
色 *susu iro* sooty color, grayish black
10 埃 *susu-hokori* soot and dust
11 掃 *susuhaki* housecleaning
13 煙 *baien* soot and smoke, smoke

煎 3453 J4079 M19184 SEN. *i(ru)* broil, parch, roast, fire (tea), boil down (in oil). *sen(jiru)* boil, decoct, infuse.
5 立 *i(ri)ta(te)* freshly parched.
sen(ji)ta(te) no freshly drawn (tea)
付 *i(ri)-tsu(keru)* parch, roast, broil, scorch. *i(ri)-tsu(ku)* be scorched; boil down
汁 *senji* broth
出 *sen(ji)-da(su)* extract by boiling, prepare an infusion of, decoct
玉子 *iritamago* scrambled eggs
7 豆腐 *iridōfu* dry seasoned tofu
9 茶 *sencha* green tea
10 剤 *senzai* decoction
13 詰 *sen(ji)-tsu(meru)* boil down, condense
15 餅 *sembei* Japanese rice cracker; wafer
餅蒲団 *sembeibuton* thin bedding; hard bed
16 薬 *sen(ji)gusuri, sen'yaku* (medical) decoction, infusion
17 鍋 *irinabe* roasting pan

B **煩** 3454 J4851 M19229 BON. HAN trouble, worry. *wazura(u)* be ill; worry, be afflicted, be in pain, be troubled. *wazura(wasu), wazura(waseru)* trouble, keep (someone) busy, disturb, annoy. *uru(sagaru)* feel annoyed by, regard as a nuisance. *uru(sai)* annoying, troublesome, irksome, inquisitive, importunate. *wazura(i)* agony, anxiety;

illness; involvement, trouble. *wazura(washii)* troublesome, complicated, confused.

4 方 *urusagata* disagreeable disposition; disagreeable person
6 忙 *hambō* pressure of business
多 *hanta* so many as to be a nuisance
7 労 *hanrō* worry, annoyance
9 型 *urusagata* disagreeable disposition; disagreeable person
10 悩 *bonnō* evil passions, carnal desire
11 務 *hammu* troublesome work
累 *hanrui* cares, annoyances
12 悶 *hammon* anguish, worry, trouble
14 瑣 *hansa na* troublesome; complicated; minute; subtle; delicate
語 *hango* tedious language
雑 *hanzatsu* complexity, trouble, complication, intricacy
18 簡 *hankan* rush and leisure; complication and simplicity

煉 3455 / J-X / M19178 REN. *ne(ru)* refine (metals). *neri* kneading over fire.

5 白粉 *nerioshiroi* liquid face-powder
瓦 *renga* brick
瓦屋 *rengaya* brickmaker
瓦師 *rengashi* bricklayer
瓦粘土 *renga nendo* brick clay
瓦場 *rengajō* brickyard
瓦塀 *rengabei* brick wall
瓦製造所 *renga seizōjo* brickyard
瓦舗道 *renga hodō* brick pavement
瓦職 *rengashoku* bricklayer
6 合 *ne(ri)-a(waseru)* knead together; compound
羊羹 *neriyōkan* bean jelly
8 固 *ne(ri)-kata(meru)* harden by kneading
物 *nerimono* paste, bean jelly, pastry
乳 *rennyū* condensed milk
9 炭 *rentan* briquette
10 粉 *neriko* dough
12 歯磨 *nerihamigaki* toothpaste
14 獄 *rengoku* purgatory
15 餌 *nerie* moist feed for birds
16 薬 *nerigusuri, neriyaku* ointment
17 鍛 *ne(ri)-kita(eru)* temper; drill, train

B **煙** 3456 / J316c / M19203 **烟** 3414 / J5f5d / M19022 EN smoke. *kemu(ru), kebu(ru)* smoke, smolder, be smoky, appear dim. *kemu(rasu)* smoke up, fumigate. *kemu(i), kebu(i)* smoky. *kemuri, kemu, kebu, keburi* smoke; fumes; spray. *kemu(tagaru)* be sensitive to smoke; feel awkward. *kebu(tai), kemu(tai)* smoky; feeling awkward.

4 火 *enka* rocket, beacon. *hanabi* fireworks, firecrackers
水晶 *kemuri suishō* smoky quartz
5 出 *kemurida(shi), kemuda(shi)* chimney, funnel
8 雨 *en'u* misty, fine, or drizzling rain
波 *empa* hazy sea, spray
毒 *endoku* smoke pollution
突 *entotsu* chimney, smokestack, funnel, stovepipe
突男 *entotsu otoko* chimney sitter
9 草 *tabako* tobacco, cigar, cigarette
草入 *tabako-i(re)* cigarette case; tobacco pouch; cigar box
草盆 *tabako bon* tobacco brazier
草飲 *tabakono(mi)* a smoker
草銭 *tabakosen* spending money
10 害 *engai* smoke pollution
11 道 *endō* flue
12 弾 *endan* smoke bomb
筒 *entō* chimney, smokestack, funnel, stovepipe
13 路 *enro* flue
幕 *emmaku* smoke screen
14 塵 *engin* cloud of dust; worldly affairs
管 *enkan* chimney. *kiseru* (tobacco) pipe; stolen train ride
管乗 *kiseruno(ri)* stolen train ride
17 霞 *enka* smoke and mist; a view
19 霧 *emmu* haze, mist, smog

A **照** 3457 / J3e48 / M19226 SHŌ. *te(ru)* shine. *te(rasu)* shine on, shed light on, illuminate; compare with. *te(reru)* be bashful. *te(ri)* sunshine; dry weather, drought; gloss, luster.

3 上 *te(ri)-a(garu)* clear up after a rain
4 尺 *shōshaku* backsight (of a gun)
込 *te(ri)-ko(mu)* shine into; shine for a long period. *te(ri)ko(mi)* sunshine, long dry spell
5 付 *te(ri)-tsu(keru)* shine down on, beat down on
出 *te(rashi)-da(su)* shed light on
6 返 *te(ri)-kae(su)* reflect

合 *te(ri)-a(waseru), te(rashi)-a(waseru), te(rashi)-a(wasu), shōgō (suru)* verify, check, compare
会 *shōkai* inquiry
会中 *shōkaichū* in communication (with)
7 応 *shōō* balance (in writing); accordance
8 明 *shōmei* illumination, lighting, flare
明弾 *shōmeidan* flare, star shell
9 度 *shōdo* (intensity of) illumination
降 *te(ri)fu(ri)* sunshine and rain; changing moods
星 *shōsei* muzzle sight
査 *shōsa* verification
10 射 *shōsha* shining
12 渡 *te(ri)-wata(ru)* shine all over
葉 *te(ri)ha* glossy leaves
13 隠 *te(re)kaku(shi)* covering up one's shame
照坊主 *te(ru)te(ru)bōzu* paper doll used in praying for good weather
準 *shōjun* aim, aiming, sight
準爆撃 *shōjumbakugeki* precision bombing
15 影 *shōei* portrait
輝 *te(ri)-kagaya(ku)* shine brightly
16 覧 *shōran suru* see clearly
17 臨 *shōrin suru* rule; come (polite)

10

熔 3458 / J4d50 / M19319 See 鎔 6327.

煿 3459 / J-X / M19277 See 爆 3505.

焰 3460 / J-X / M-X See 燄 3485.

熏 3461 / J5f6d / M19300 See 燻 3503.

熕 3462 / J5f70 / M19321 Kō（国字）*ōzutu* cannon.

熄 3463 / J5f6f / M19287 Soku cessation.

煕 3464 / J7426 / M-X **熙** 3465 / J5f66 / M19192 **凞** 3466 / J5f67 / M19292
Ki shine.

熅 3467 / J-X / M19288 Un. On. *iki(re)* sultriness, stuffiness.

熊 3468 / J3727 / M19294 Yū. *kuma* bear.
4 手 *kumade* rake, fork
9 狩 *kumaga(ri)* bear hunting
11 祭 *kuma matsu(ri)* bear-sacrifice festival
13 蜂 *kumabachi* hornet
22 襲 *Kumaso* (ancient) Kyushu tribe

煽 3469 / J407a / M19272 Sen. *ao(ru)* fan, flap; instigate, agitate; bolster up; gulp down, quaff. *ao(gu)* fan; instigate. *oda(teru)* stir up, instigate; flatter.
4 止 *ao(ri)do(me)* door stop
5 石 *senseki* natural coke
立 *ao(ri)-ta(teru), ao(gi)-ta(teru)* instigate, stir up
11 動 *sendō* instigation, agitation
情 *senjō* lasciviousness
情的 *senjōteki* lascivious, sensational, suggestive

11

熬 3470 / J5f72 / M19352 Gō *i(ru)* parch (beans), roast (coffee).

熨 3471 / J5f71 / M19346 I. Utsu. *noshi* flatiron. *no(su)* smooth out, straighten out.
4 斗 *noshi* label attached to gifts; a paper imitation of *noshi awabi*
斗鮑 *noshi awabi* strip of dried abalone marking a present

A **熟** 3472 / J3d4f / M19332 Juku. *u(reru), juku(suru), juku(su)* ripen, mellow, mature; acquire skill; be ripe for; become popular (as a word). *u(mu)* ripen. *kona(reru)* be digested; combine; be skilled; be pulverized. *na(reru)* get used to, become experienced; be tamed; get too familiar, mature. *jit(to)* firmly, intently, patiently.
6 成 *jukusei suru* ripen, mature; cure; ferment
字 *jukuji* a word of two or more characters; a set phrase
考 *jukukō, jukkō* due consideration, deliberation, mature reflection

年 *jukunen* middle age
8 知 *jukuchi* thorough knowledge
9 音 *jukuon* the syllabary syllables
思 *jukushi* careful consideration
柿 *jukushi* ripe persimmon
柿主義 *jukushi shugi* waiting quietly for things to develop
柿臭 *jukushikusa(i)* drunk
10 眠 *jukumin* sound sleep
蚕 *jukusan* mature silkworm
11 達 *jukutatsu* mastery, proficiency
視 *jukushi* steady gaze, scrutiny
酔 *jukusui* dead drunk
13 睡 *jukusui* sound sleep
路 *jukuro* familiar road
14 語 *jukugo* a word of two or more characters; a set phrase
読 *jukudoku* careful reading
練 *jukuren* skill, mastery, practice
練工 *jukurenkō* skilled worker
練者 *jukurensha* skilled individual
15 談 *jukudan* due deliberation, careful consultation
蕃 *jukuban* friendly tribes
熟 *tsukuzuku to* thoroughly, entirely, really, wistfully, earnestly, attentively, greatly, profoundly, keenly. *tsuratsura* attentively, carefully, deeply
慮 *jukuryo* mature deliberation
慮断行 *jukuryo-dankō* deliberate and decisive
16 覧 *jukuran* scrutiny
20 議 *jukugi* due deliberation, careful consultation

A 11 **熱** 3473 / J472e / M19360 **熱** 3474 / J-X / M-X NETSU heat, warmth; temperature; fever; mania, fad; enthusiasm; passion. *nes(suru) vt* heat, make hot; burn, boil. *vi* become warm; become excited; become earnest. *atsu(garu)* feel the heat, swelter. *iki(ru)* be hot and sultry. *hotō(ru), hotobo(ru)* get heated; get angry. *atsu(i)* hot. *hotobo(ri)* warmth, heat; sensation, furore; enthusiasm, energy, momentum; reputation. *atsu(gari)* person sensitive to heat.

2 力学 *netsurikigaku* thermodynamics
3 上 *netsu (o) a(geru)* become earnest
4 火 *nekka* intense heat. *atsubi* hot fire
中 *netchū* enthusiasm, zeal, mania
中性子 *netsu chūseishi* thermal neutron
中性子炉 *netsu chūseishiro* thermal neutron reactor
心 *nesshin* earnestness, enthusiasm
心家 *nesshinka* enthusiast, devotee, fan
心党 *nesshintō* zealots
5 弁 *netsuben* fervent speech
6 灰 *atsubai* hot ashes
気 *netsuke* feverishness. *nekki* heat, hot air; enthusiasm
気消毒 *nekki shōdoku* heat (hot-air) sterilization
気球 *nekkikyū* hot-air balloon
血 *nekketsu* hot blood, fiery spirit, zeal
血児 *nekketsuji* a hot-blooded man
血漢 *nekketsukan* a hot-blooded man
7 位 *netsui* thermal unit
冷 *netsusa(mashi)* antipyretic
狂 *nekkyō* enthusiasm, frenzy, rage, mania, excitement
8 国 *nekkoku* hot country
性 *nessei* earnestness; accompanied by high fever
波 *neppa* heat wave
苦 *atsukuru(shii)* sultry, sweltering
9 風 *neppū* fiery-hot wind
屋 *atsu(gari)ya* person sensitive to heat
度 *netsudo* degree of temperature or enthusiasm
発 *neppatsu* attack of fever; generation of heat
単位 *netsu tan'i* heat unit
10 涙 *netsurui* hot tears
烈 *netsuretsu na* ardent, passionate, vehement
射病 *nesshabyō* sunstroke, heat prostration
核 *netsukaku* thermonuclear
核反応 *netsu kakuhannō* nuclear fusion
病 *netsubyō* fever
病的 *netsubyōteki* feverish
帯 *nettai* torrid zone, tropics
帯低気圧 *nettai teikiatsu* tropical cyclone
帯性 *nettaisei* tropical
帯林 *nettairin* tropical forest
帯雨林 *nettai urin* tropical rain forest
帯夜 *nettaiya* hot and muggy night
帯魚 *nettaigyo* tropical fish
11 情 *netsujō* fervor, warmth, ardent love, passion

球 *nekkyū* hot pitch (baseball)
望 *netsubō* fervent hope, longing
12 湯 *nettō* boiling water
量 *netsuryō* heat value, caloric value
13 鬧 *nettō* din, hustle and bustle
源 *netsugen* heat source
誠 *nessei* earnestness, warmth, enthusiasm, devotion, sincerity
愛 *netsuai* ardent love, devotion
意 *netsui* zeal, enthusiasm
感 *nekkan* feverish feeling
戦 *nessen* hot fight, close game
戦争 *atsu(i) sensō* hot war
雷 *netsurai* heat thunderstorm
電発電 *netsuden hatsuden* thermal electric power generation
14 演 *netsuen* enthusiastic performance
15 線 *netsusen, nessen* heat rays; hot wire, infrared (rays)
罵 *netsuba* vehement reproach
16 燗 *atsukan* hot saké
17 療法 *netsu ryōhō* heat therapy
19 願 *netsugan* earnest entreaty
禱 *nettō* fervent prayer

12

燒 3475 / J5f76 / M19420 See 焼 3438.

燈 3476 / J4575 / M19402 See 灯 3395.

燵 3477 / J5f7d / M19504 （国字） Tatsu a foot-warmer.

熹 3478 / J5f74 / M19380 Ki heat, boil, steam; faint light.

燉 3479 / J5f77 / M19403 Ton, Don fiery.

熾 3480 / J5f75 / M19385 Shi burning; flourishing. *oko(ru)* be kindled. *oko(su)* build a fire.
10 烈 *shiretsu* violence, severity, fierceness

燔 3481 / J5f78 / M19426 Han burn.
6 刑 *hankei* burning to death, the stake
11 祭 *hansai* burnt offering

燋 3482 / J-X / M19410 Shō scorch; bonfire.
15 熱 *shōnetsu* scorching heat; scorching
熱地獄 *shōnetsu jigoku* burning hell

燎 3483 / J5f79 / M19414 Ryō burn, bonfire.
4 火 *ryōka* signal fire, bonfire
10 原火 *ryōgen (no) hi* prairie fire, wildfire

燧 3484 / J5f7c / M19469 Sui signal fire. *hiuchi* tinder, making a fire (with flint and iron). *hikiri* making a fire (with wood).
5 石 *suiseki, hiuchi ishi* flint
6 臼 *hikiri usu* fire stone
8 杵 *hikirigine* rubbing stick (for making a fire)

燄 3485 / J-X / M19395 **燄** 3486 / J-X / M-X **焰** 3427 / J-X / M19141

焔 3460 / J-X / M-X En *honoo, homura* flame, blaze.
6 色 *enshoku* flame color, flame scarlet, bright reddish orange
12 硝 *enshō* gunpowder, niter
16 *en'en(taru)* blazing, fiery

燗 3487 / J-X / M-X **燗** 3488 / J5f73 / M19431 Ran. Kan warming saké. *kan(suru)* heat saké.
7 冷 *kanza(mashi)* leftover warmed saké
10 酒 *kanzake, kanshu* warmed saké
14 徳利 *kandokuri* saké-warming bottle
17 鍋 *kannabe* saké-warming pan

燕 3489 / J316d / M19429 En *tsubame, tsubakura, tsubakuro* the swallow.
7 麦 *karasu mugi, embaku* oats
尾服 *embifuku* swallow-tailed coat
11 雀 *enjaku* small birds
巣 *enzu* swallow's nest; edible bird's-nest

A **燃** 3490 / J4733 / M19394 Nen. *mo(su), mo(yasu)* burn. *mo(yuru), mo(eru)* burn, blaze, glow.
3 上 *mo(e)-a(garu)* blaze up, burn up
4 木 *mo(e)gi* firebrand
切 *mo(e)-ki(ru)* burn out, burn up
5 立 *mo(e)-ta(tsu)* blaze up, burn up

付 *mo(e)-tsu(ku)* ignite
出 *mo(e)-da(su)* ignite, begin to burn. *mo(e)-de(ru)* blaze out
6 行 *mo(e)-yu(ku)* burn along, burn up to
8 拡 *mo(e)-hiro(garu)* (fires) spread
杭 *mo(e)gui* half-burnt post
易 *mo(e)yasu(i)* inflammable
9 思 *mo(eru) omo(i)* burning passion
10 残 *mo(e)noko(ri)* embers, something half-burnt
差 *mo(e)sa(shi)* embers, something half-burnt
料 *nenryō* fuel
料電池 *nenryō denchi* fuel cell
料廠 *nenryōshō* fuel depot
11 移 *mo(e)-utsu(ru)* catch fire, ignite
崩 *mo(e)-kuzu(reru)* burn up
殻 *mo(e)gara* embers, cinders
盛 *mo(e)-saka(ru)* burn fiercely
12 焼 *nenshō* combustion
焦 *mo(e)-koge(ru)* be charred in a fire
13 滓 *mo(e)kasu* cinders
15 質 *nenshitsu* combustibility
18 難 *mo(e)niku(i)* noninflammable

13

營 3491 J535b M19457 See **営** 857.

點 3492 J-X M-X See **点** 3412.

B **燥** 3493 J4167 M19467 SŌ dry up. *kawa(ku), hasha(gu) vi* dry up, parch.

燬 3494 J5f7b M19478 KI fire; burn. *ya(ku)* burn, set afire.

燮 3495 J5259 M19481 SHŌ moderate, soften; boil; finally. *yawa(ragu)* soften, moderate, lessen.

燭 3496 J3f24 M19480 SOKU, SHOKU light; candle power.
5 台 *shokudai* candlestick, candlestand
6 光 *shokkō* candle power; candlelight

燠 3497 J5f7a M19458 U. IKU. Ō. *oki* embers, live coals.
4 火 *okibi* blazing fire
13 搔 *okikaki* poker, fire shovel

燦 3490 J3b38 M19468 SAN brilliance. *san(taru)* brilliant.
12 然 *sanzen* brilliance, radiance
17 燦 *sansan(taru)* brilliant, bright
21 爛 *sanran(taru)* brilliant, bright, radiant

燐 3499 J4e55 M19417 RIN phosphorus.
3 寸 *matchi* match
4 火 *rinka* phosphorescence
6 光 *rinkō* phosphorescence
8 肥 *rimpi* phosphate manure
14 酸 *rinsan* phosphoric acid

14

燿 3500 J6022 M19520 YŌ shine.

燹 3501 J6021 M19508 SEN prairie fire; signal fire.

燼 3502 J5f7e M19515 JIN embers.
7 余 *jin'yo* embers; survival

燻 3503 J5f6e M19513 **熏** 3461 J5f6d M19300 KUN. *ibu(ru)* smolder, fume, smoke. *ibu(su)* fumigate; oxidize; smoke (meat). *kusu(beru), fusu(boru), kusu(boru), kuyu(ru)* smoke, smolder; get sooty; stay indoors; remain in obscurity. *kusu(beru), fusu(beru), kuyu(raseru)* smoke, smoke out, fumigate. *ibu(shi)* fumigation; oxidation; smoking (meat).
5 出 *ibu(shi)-da(su)* smoke out
6 肉 *kunniku* smoked meat
12 蒸 *kunjō* fumigation
蒸剤 *kunjōzai* fumigant
14 銀 *ibu(shi)gin* oxidized silver
製 *kunsei* smoking (fish or pork)
製品 *kunseihin* smoked products

15

爍 3504 J6023 M19549 SHAKU shine; hot; disappear. *hika(ru)* shine, gleam.

B **爆** 3505 J477a M19540 BAKU. *ha(zeru)* burst open, pop, split.

4心 *bakushin* center of the explosion, epicenter
心地 *bakushinchi* center of the explosion
6竹 *bakuchiku* firecracker
死 *bakushi* death from bombing
7沈 *bakuchin* blowing up and sinking
9音 *bakuon* buzzing, whirr; explosion, detonation
風 *bakufū* bomb blast, shell blast, explosion blast
砕 *bakusai* blasting
発 *bakuhatsu* explosion, blasting
発力 *bakuhatsuryoku* explosive power
発物 *bakuhatsubutsu* explosives
発的 *bakuhatsuteki* explosive
発室 *bakuhatsushitsu* combustion chamber ⌈fuse
発信管 *bakuhatsu shinkan* detonating
発管 *bakuhatsukan* detonator
発薬 *bakuhatsuyaku* blasting power, explosive compound
10粉 *bakufun* explosive powder
笑 *bakushō* roar of laughter
破 *bakuha* explosion, blasting
破薬 *bakuhayaku* blasting charge
12弾 *bakudan* bomb
弾投下 *bakudan tōka* bombing
裂 *bakuretsu* explosion, blasting
裂弾 *bakuretsudan* bomb, explosive shell
13傷 *bakushō* damage from explosion
煙 *bakuen* the smoke of an explosion
雷 *bakurai* depth bomb
14鳴 *bakumei* detonation
15撃 *bakugeki* bombing
撃手 *bakugekishu* bombardier
撃行 *bakugekikō* bombing mission
撃照準器 *bakugeki shōjunki* bombsight
撃機 *bakugekiki* bombing plane
16薬 *bakuyaku* blasting power, explosive compound

16

爐 3506 / J6024 / M19566 See 炉 3403.

17

爛 3507 / J6025 / M19604 RAN. *tada(reru)* be sore, be inflamed, be bleary; fester. *tada(rakasu)* cause to be inflamed.
5日 *tada(re)me* sore eyes, bleary eyes
6死 *ranshi* burning to death
14漫 *ramman(taru)* glorious, luxuriant, splendid
15熟 *ranjuku* overripeness; overmaturity; full maturity; mellow ripeness
21爛 *ranran(taru)* fiery, glaring, piercing; blazing, flaming; glittering

25

爨 3508 / J6026 / M19648 SAN. *kashi(gu)* cook, boil.

RAD. 爪 87

Tsume nail, claw. At top: ⺥ or ⺤ *tsume kammuri* or *no-tsu* (the katakana *no* plus the katakana *tsu*). Nickname: Claw.

爪 3509 / J445e / M19653 SŌ. *tsume* nail, claw, talon, hoof; hook, catch; plectrum.
4木 *tsumaki* twigs for fuel, brushwood
切 *tsumeki(ri)* nail clipper
5牙 *sōga* teeth and claws; clutches; cat's paw, tool
立 *tsumada(teru)* stand on tiptoe; stretch
6印 *tsumein* thumbprint
先 *tsumasaki* tiptoe, tip of the toe
9革 *tsumakawa* leather toe covers on geta
音 *tsumaoto* sound of drumming fingers; sound of a koto; sound of hoofs
紅 *tsumabeni* fingernail polish
11痕 *tsume ato* scratch; pinch mark
掛 *tsumaga(ke)* toe covers on geta
12弾 *tsumebi(ki), tsumabi(ki)* playing a stringed instrument with fingers. *tsumahajiki* flip, fillip; elbowing; ostracism; black sheep
13跡 *tsume ato* scratch; pinch mark
楊子 *tsumayōji* toothpick

4 心忄⺗戈戸手扌支攵文斗斤方无日曰月木欠止歹殳毋比毛氏气水氵氺火灬 4【爪】爫父爻爿丬片牙牛犬犭

楊枝 *tsumayōji* toothpick
16 磨 *tsumemigaki* nail file; manicure
19 繰 *tsumagu(ru)* to finger

4

爭 3510 / J6027 / M19663 See 争 69.

爬 3511 / J6028 / M19662 HA scratch.
6 虫 *hachū* reptile
行 *hakō* creeping, crawling

5

爰 3512 / J6029 / M19672 EN. *koko ni* here.

8

爲 3513 / J602a / M19686 See 為 3411.

13

B **爵** 3514 / J3c5f / M19710' **爵** 3515 / J-X / M19711 SHAKU peerage, court rank.
7 位 *shakui* peerage, court rank

14

爵 3515 / J-X / M19711 See 爵 3514.

RAD. 父 88

Chichi father. Nickname: Father.

A **父** 3516 / J4963 / M19721 FU. *chichi* father. *(o)tō(chan)* papa, daddy (juvenile).
3 子 *fushi* father and child
上様 *chichiuesama* your father; my dear father
4 方 *chichikata, tetekata* father's side, male line
日 *Chichi (no) Hi* Father's Day
5 母 *chichihaha, fubo, tete-haha* father and mother
兄 *fukei* parents and older brothers; guardians
兄会 *fukeikai* parents' association
6 老 *furō* elders, the aged
7 君 *chichigimi, fukun* father (polite)
系 *fukei* male line, father's side
系家族 *fukei kazoku* paternal family
9 音 *fuin, fuon* consonant
祖 *fuso* ancestors, forefathers
10 殺 *chichigoro(shi)* patricide
12 御 *tetego, chichigo* your father
無子 *chichina(shi)go* fatherless child
無児 *tetena(shi)go* illegitimate child
14 様 *tōsan, tōsama* papa, daddy, father
15 権 *fuken* paternal rights, paternity
16 親 *chichi oya, tete oya* father
親似 *chichioyani* taking after one's father

8

爺 3517 / J4c6c / M19734 YA. *jii, jii(ya)* old man. *jijii* old man, grandpa.
9 臭 *jijikusa(i)* old-mannish

爻 RAD. 89

Majiwaru to mix. Variant: 㐅. Nickname: Double X.

爻 3518 / J602b / M19737 Kō. Gyō *maji(waru)* mix with, associate with; join.

5

爼 3519 / J602c / M19743 See 俎 209.

7

爽 3520 / J4156 / M19746 Sō. *sawa(yakana)* refreshing, bracing; clear, resonant, sweet (voice); fluent.

[7] 快 *sōkai na* refreshing, exhilarating
[10] 涼 *sōryō na* cool and refreshing
[11] 爽 *sawasawa toshite* refreshingly

10

爾 3521 / J3c24 / M19750 尒 1391 / J-X / M7477 尔 1392 / J5575 / M7478

Ji. Ni. *nanji* thou, you. *shika* so, in that way.

[7] 来 *jirai* since then
[9] 後 *jigo* thereafter

爿 RAD. 90

Hidari kata (a left-hand *kata* "side," to distinguish it from Rad. 91). Variant: 丬 (3 strokes) *shō hen*. Nickname: Left Side.

爿 3522 / J602d / M19758 Shō piece of wood; left half of split tree.

4

牀 3523 / J602e / M19763 See 床 1608.

13

牆 3524 / J602f / M19806 See 墻 1099.

片 RAD. 91

Migi kata (a right-hand *kata* "side," to distinguish it from Rad. 90) or *kata hen*. Nickname: Right Side.

A 片 3525 / J4a52 / M19813 Hen *hira* leaf, sheet, petal, flake. *kata-* one (eye, etc.); single (shift, etc.); one-way; one-sided.

[1] 一方 *kataippō* one side; one party; the other side; the other party; mate to (a shoe)
[3] 口 *katakuchi* lipped bowl; one side of a story
下 *katasa(gari)* uneven (hem); wrong slant (in writing)
刃 *kataha* single-edged (sword)
[4] 戸 *katado* one-leaf door
方 *katappō, katahō, katakata* one side; one party; the other side; the other party; mate to (a shoe)
片 *hempen* pieces, scraps
辺 *katahoto(ri)* corner, remote rural location
引 *katahi(ki)* flattering some people only
手 *katate* one hand. *katate no* single-handed, one-handed
手仕事 *katate shigoto* side job
手桶 *katate oke* pail
手間 *katadema, katatema* spare time
手落 *katateo(chi)* partiality, unfairness
手業 *katate waza* side job

5 目 *katame* one eye. *mekkachi* one-eyed person

付 *katazu(keru)* put in order; put away; dispose of, solve, finish; marry off, get married. *katazu(ku)* be put in order; be settled, be disposed of; marry (a man)

田舎 *katainaka* backwoods

6 糸 *kataito* single-strand thread

耳 *katamimi* one ear

帆 *kataho* close-hauled sail

仮名 *katakana, katakanna* the square syllabary

合掌 *kata gasshō* a one-handed gesture of respect

肌 *katahada* one shoulder bared

肌脱 *katahada nu(gu)* bare one shoulder; assist

7 角 *katakado* one corner

貝 *katagai* univalve

足 *kataashi* one leg; one foot

身 *katami* one side of the body or dress; sliver; slice (of bonito); half (a beef carcass)

里 *katazato* out-of-the-way village

町 *katamachi* town on one side of a road only

言 *hengen* a word, a few words. *katakoto* lisp, babble; one side of a story

言交 *katakotoma(jiri)* lisping, babbling; broken (English)

言隻句 *hengen-sekku* just a word

8 岡 *kataoka* a hill steeper on one side

孤 *kataminashigo* child who has lost one parent

押 *katao(shi)* shoulder-pushing game; pushing from one side only

枝 *kataeda, katae* branches on one side

泣 *katana(ki)* weeping alone

盲 *katameshii* one-eyed person

岩 *hengan* schist

岸 *katagishi* one bank (of a river)

空 *katazora* one part of the sky

9 便 *katadayori, katabin* one-way correspondence

恨 *kataura(mi)* hated by one group only

思 *kataomo(i)* unrequited love

為替 *katagawase* unbalanced exchange

面 *katamen, katatsura, kataomote* one side, one face

面物 *katamemmono* cloth with pattern on only one side; single-faced phonograph record

10 時 *henji, katatoki* moment, instant. *katatoki mo* even for a moment

流 *katanaga(re)* a shed roof

眠 *katanemu(ri)* nap; light sleeping

脇 *katawaki* the side of the chest; one side, the side; aside

陰 *katakage* shade (of a tree or building); shelter

恋 *katakoi* unrequited love

荷 *katani* one-sided load

息 *kataiki* gasping for breath

栗粉 *katakuriko* an edible starch (from dogtooth violet)

11 道 *katamichi* one way

掛 *kataka(ke)* hanging on one side; sailing with one sail

眼 *katame* one eye

脚 *kataashi* one leg; one foot

隅 *katasumi* nook, corner

務的 *hemmuteki* unilateral

務契約 *hemmu keiyaku* one-sided or unilateral contract

脳 *hennō* (refined) camphor

脳油 *hennōyu* camphor oil

寄 *katayo(ri)* inclination; offset; polarization. *katayo(ru)* lean, incline; be biased

寄見 *katayo(ri)-mi(ru)* show partiality

側 *katagawa, katakawa* one side

側町 *katakawa machi* one-sided street, one-way street

側通行 *katagawa tsūkō* one-way traffic

側街 *katagawa machi* a road with houses on one side only

12 廂 *katabisashi, katahisashi* single-sloped roof

結 *katamusu(bi)* overhand knot

腕 *kataude* one arm; right-hand man

跛 *katachimba* one side; one party; the other side; the other party; mate to (a shoe)

落 *kataoto(shi)* pushing down one side; partiality. *katao(chi)* heavy on one side; preponderance; partiality; one part cut off

番 *kataban* single shift

雲 *hen'un, katagumo* scattered clouds
貿易 *katabōeki* one-way trade, unbalanced trade
割 *katawa(ri)* half. *katawa(re)* fragment; one of the group; the other half; the accomplice
割月 *katawa(re)zuki* crescent moon, half-moon
13 寝 *katane* sleeping on the side
意地 *kataiji na* narrow-minded, uncompromising, stubborn
腹 *katahara* one side (of the body)
腹痛 *katahara-ita(i)* absurd, ridiculous, contemptible
14 聞 *katagi(ki)* one-sided information
端 *kata(p)pashi, katahashi* an end, an edge, a side; smattering; fag end; petty official
端者 *katawamono* a cripple, a disabled person
15 膝 *katahiza* one knee
輪 *katawa* one wheel
影 *hen'ei* glimpse; shadow, sign, speck (of cloud)
膚 *katahada* one side of the body bared
膚脱 *katahada nu(gu)* bare one shoulder; assist
16 親 *kataoya* one parent
頬 *katahō, katahoo, katahoho* one cheek
17 躄 *kataizari* crippled in one knee
臂 *katahiji* one elbow
18 顔 *katagao* one side of the face, one face
19 靡 *katanabi(ki)* being swayed by one side only
21 贔屓 *katahiiki* flattering some people only
22 聾 *katatsumbo* deaf in one ear
24 鱗 *henrin* a (fish) scale; a part, a particle; a glimpse

4

A **版** 3526 / J4847 / M19817 HAN printing block or plate; printing; edition, impression; board; label.
4 木 *hangi* (printing) block, woodcut, engraving block
元 *hammoto* publisher
5 本 *hampon* wood-block book; printed book
6 行 *hankō* printing block; publication; stamp
7 図 *hanto* dominion, territory
8 画 *hanga* woodcut print
9 屋 *han'ya* block cutter, stamp or seal engraver
14 摺 *hansuri* printing from plates
15 権 *hanken* copyright
権法 *hankenhō* copyright law
権侵害 *hanken shingai* copyright infringement
20 籍 *hanseki* register of land and people; land and people

8

牋 3527 / J6030 / M19849 See **箋** 4304.

牌 3528 / J4757 / M19854 HAI label, signboard; medal. *pai* mahjong playing tiles.

9

牒 3529 / J4428 / M19871 CHŌ label; genealogy; circular. *chō(zu)* circularize, notify.

15

牘 3530 / J6031 / M19906 TOKU letter.

4
心忄⺗戈戸手扌支攴攵文斗斤方无日曰月木欠止歹殳毋比毛氏气水氵氺火灬爪爫父爻爿丬【片】5 牙牛犬犭

RAD. 牙 92

Kiba tusk or *kiba hen*. Variant: 牙 (5 strokes). Do not confuse with Rad. 71. Nickname: Tusk.

牙 3531 / J3267 / M19909 GA. GE. *kiba* tusk, fang, canine tooth, eyetooth.
9 保 *gaho* brokerage
城 *gajō* stronghold, inner citadel
12 営 *gaei* headquarters camp
15 儈 *gakai* broker, agent

RAD. 牛 93

Ushi cow. At left: 牜 *ushi hen*. Nickname: Cow.

A **牛** 3532 / J356d / M19922 GO. GYŪ beef, cow. *ushi* cattle, cow, bull, ox.
2 刀 *gyūtō* butcher knife
3 小屋 *ushigoya* cattle barn
4 方 *ushikata* cattle herder
5 皮 *gyūhi* cowhide
6 缶 *gyūkan* canned beef
羊 *gyūyō* cattle and sheep
耳 *gyūji(ru)* control, lead, command; direct. *gyūji* ox ears
肉 *gyūniku* beef
肉屋 *gyūnikuya* butcher; butcher shop
7 車 *gyūsha, ushiguruma* oxcart. *gissha* (ancient) cow carriage
8 追 *ushio(i)* cattle herder
使 *ushitsuka(i)* cattle herder
舎 *gyūsha* cow barn, cow shed
歩 *gyūho, ushi (no) ayumi* snail's pace
乳 *gyūnyū* (cow's) milk
乳屋 *gyūnyūya* milkman, milk dealer
9 屋 *gyūya* butcher shop, beef restaurant
疫 *gyūeki* rinderpest, cattle plague
10 馬 *gyūba* horses and cattle
脂 *gyūshi* beef tallow, beef suet
殺 *ushikoro(shi)* slaughterer
部屋 *ushibeya* cow stall
12 痘 *gyūtō* cowpox, vaccine
蛙 *ushigaeru* bullfrog
飯 *gyūmeshi* stewed beef and rice
飲 *gyūin* drinking like a cow
飲馬食 *gyūin-bashoku* gluttony
13 酪 *gyūraku* butter
飼 *ushika(i)* raising cattle; cowboy, cowherd; cattleman
蒡 *gobō* burdock
17 鍋 *gyūnabe* popular Japanese beef-and-vegetable dish, sukiyaki
糞 *gyūfun* cow manure
19 蠅 *ushibae* warble fly

2

牟 3533 / J4c36 / M19928 BŌ. MU pupil of the eye; mooing of a cow.

牝 3534 / J4c46 / M19925 HIN *mesu, men, me-* female.
4 牛 *meushi* cow
犬 *mesu inu, meinu* female dog, bitch
6 羊 *mehitsuji* ewe
7 牡 *mesu-osu* male and female
8 狐 *megitsune* female fox
11 鹿 *mejika* doe, hind
13 獅子 *mejishi* lioness
19 鶏 *hinkei* hen

3

牢 3535 / J4f34 / M19934 RŌ prison, jail; hardness.
2 人 *rōnin* lordless samurai, adventurer; unsuccessful examinee; jobless person
入 *rōi(ri)* entering prison
5 乎 *rōko(taru)* firm, strong, inflexible, steadfast
6 死 *rōshi* death in prison
7 囲 *rōgako(i)* prison wall
役人 *rōyakunin* jailer
8 固 *rōko(taru)* firm, strong, inflexible, steadfast
9 屋 *rōya* prison, jail
10 破 *rōyabu(ri)* jailbreak

記 *rōki suru* fix in the memory
12 番 *rōban* jailer
14 獄 *rōgoku* prison, jail

牡 3536/J3234/M19933 Bo. *osu, on-, o-* male.
3 山羊 *oyagi* billy goat, he-goat
4 牛 *oushi* bull, ox, steer
丹 *botan* tree peony
丹杏 *botankyō* plum
丹刷毛 *botambake* powder puff
丹雪 *botan yuki* large snowflakes
丹餅 *botamochi* glutenous rice cake enclosed in bean jam
6 羊 *ohitsuji* ram
10 馬 *ouma* stallion, horse
11 鹿 *ojika* stag, buck
猫 *oneko* tomcat
20 蠣 *kaki* edible oyster
蠣田 *kakida* oyster bed
蠣床 *kakidoko* oyster bed, oyster farm
蠣船 *kakibune* oyster boat
蠣殻 *kakigara* oyster shell

4

A 牧 3537/J4b52/M19950 Boku. *boku(suru)* care for, shepherd, feed. *maki* pasture.
2 人 *bokujin* shepherd, herdsman
4 牛 *bokugyū* grazing cattle; pasturing cattle
大 *bokufu* ranch hand
5 民 *bokumin* governing the people
民官 *bokuminkan* governor of the people
6 地 *bokuchi* pasture land, grazing land
羊 *bokuyō* sheep raising
羊地 *bokuyōchi* pastoral land
羊者 *bokuyōsha* shepherd
羊歌 *bokuyōka* pastoral poem
会 *bokkai* pastoral care
会学 *bokkaigaku* pastoral theology
会祈禱 *bokkai kitō* pastoral prayer
会書簡 *Bokkai Shokan* the Pastoral Epistles
8 者 *bokusha* shepherd, herder
9 草 *bokusō, makigusa* grass, pasture
草類 *bokusōrui* pasture grasses
10 馬 *bokuba* grazing horse
畜 *bokuchiku* cattle raising
畜業 *bokuchikugyō* cattle raising
師 *bokushi* pastor, minister, priest
師補 *bokushiho* assistant pastor
師管轄区 *bokushi kankatsuku* parish
師館 *bokushikan* parsonage
師職 *bokushishoku* the ministry; orders; pastorate
11 野 *bokuya* pasture land, ranch
笛 *bokuteki* shepherd's flute
12 場 *bokujō* stock farm, pasture. *makiba* pasture, grazing land
童 *bokudō* cowboy, shepherd
14 歌 *bokka* pastoral song

A 物 3538/J4a2a/M19959 Butsu. Motsu. *mono* thing, object, matter; somebody, something, success; reason. *mono no* about, nearly, a matter of. *mono(suru)* do, perform; write (poetry).
2 入 *monoi(ri)* expenses
力 *butsuryoku* the power of material things; the power of wealth
3 乞 *monogoi* begging
上担保 *butsujō tampo* secured mortgage
干 *monoho(shi)* a frame for drying clothes
干竿 *monoho(shi)zao* clothes-drying pole
干場 *monoho(shi)ba* drying place
4 心 *monogokoro* judgment, discretion. *busshin* matter and mind
分 *monowaka(ri)* understanding
5 申 *monomō(su)* I say; Hello.
6 色 *busshoku suru* look for; select
件 *bukken* thing, article
好 *monogono(mi)* fastidiousness. *monozu(ki)* curiosity, eccentricity, whim
交 *bukkō, butsukō* barter
争 *monoaraso(i)* quarreling, rivalry
7 足 *monota(razu), monota(rinai)* unsatisfying; unsatisfactory; something missing
侘 *monowabi(shii)* lonely, comfortless
体 *buttai* body, solid, object, substance. *mottai* overemphasis
狂 *monoguru(i)* insanity; mad person (in plays). *monoguru(oshii), monoguru(shii), monoguru(washii)* crazy, wild, desperate
別 *monowaka(re)* rupture (of relations)
忘 *monowasu(re)* forgetfulness
売 *monou(ri)* peddler, vendor; peddling

忌 *monoimi* fast, abstinence
言 *mono-i(u)* speak; talk. *mono-i(wazu)* saying nothing; a quiet person; a dumb person. *mono-i(i)* way of speaking; speech, language; dispute; objection
言事 *monoi(u) koto* speaking
見 *monomi* sightseeing; watchtower; scout; patrol
見事 *mono(no)migoto ni* splendidly
見高 *monomidaka(i)* burning with curiosity
見遊山 *monomi yusan* pleasure-seeking
見櫓 *monomi yagura* watchtower
8 取 *monoto(ri)* thief
怪 *mokke* something unexpected. *mono(no)ke* specter, evil spirit
性 *bussei* property of matter
怖 *monooji* timidity
知 *monoshi(razu)* ignorant person. *monoshi(ri)* extensive knowledge; well-informed person, scholar
具 *mono(no)gu* weapons, armor
学 *monomana(bi)* learning
事 *monogoto* things, matters
物 *monomono(shii)* showy, pompous, pretentious
物交換 *butsubutsu-kōkan* barter
的 *butteki* material, physical
的損害 *butteki songai* property damage
的資源 *butteki shigen* material resources
価 *bukka* prices
価水準 *bukka suijun* price level
価安定 *bukka antei* price stabilization
価表 *bukkahyō* price list
価指数 *bukka shisū* price index
価釘付 *bukka kugizu(ke)* pegging of prices
価騰貴 *bukka tōki* rise in prices
9 音 *monooto* sound, noise
持 *monomo(chi)* wealthy person
指 *monosashi* ruler, measure, yardstick
珍 *monomezu(rashii)* curious
故 *bukko suru* die; be dead
哀 *mono (no) awa(re)* pathos; esthetic sense. *monoawa(re)* a pity
思 *monoomo(u)* worry; be buried in grief. *monoomo(i)* reverie, meditation; anxiety.
monoomo(washige) na pensive, meditative
柔 *monoyawa(rakana)* mild, gentle
臭 *monogusa* laziness; idler. *monogusa(na), monogusa(i)* lazy
相飯 *mossōmeshi* prison rations
活論 *bukkatsuron* animism
品 *buppin* goods, article, commodity
品保険 *buppin hoken* property insurance
品税 *buppinzei* commodity tax
10 凄 *monosugo(i)* ghastly, lurid, weird; terrible, tremendous. *monosusama(jii)* dreadful, alarming
恥 *monohazuka(shii)* shy, bashful
陰 *monokage* cover, hiding
案 *monoan(ji)* worry, anxiety
笑 *monowara(i)* laughingstock, joke
差 *monosa(shi)* ruler, measure, yardstick
真似 *monomane, monomanebi* imitating (sounds or gestures)
納 *butsunō* payment in kind
納税 *butsunōzei* tax payment in kind
11 情 *butsujō* public feeling; state of affairs
惜 *monoo(shimi)* stinginess
淋 *monosabi(shii)* lonely, lonesome, dreary
欲 *butsuyoku* worldly desire
断 *monoda(chi)* fast, abstinence
堅 *monogata(i)* firm, honest, faithful
貨 *bukka* commodities
捨場 *monosuteba* garbage dump
産 *bussan* produce, product
産地 *bussanchi* place of production
産取引所 *bussan torihikijo* commodity exchange
理 *butsuri* natural law; physics
理化学 *butsuri kagaku* physical chemistry; physics and chemistry
理的 *butsuriteki* physical (properties, etc.)
理学 *butsurigaku* physics
理学者 *butsurigakusha* physicist
理論 *butsuriron* materialism
理療法 *butsuri ryōhō* physiotherapy
12 越 *monogo(shi) ni* indirectly
税 *butsuzei* tax on goods and possessions
量 *butsuryō* material resources
悲 *monogana(shii)* sad, plaintive, melancholy
覚 *monoobo(e)* memory

象 *busshō* an object; material phenomena
貰 *monomora(i)* beggar; sty (on the eyelid)
13 暗 *monogura(i)* fairly dark
腰 *monogoshi* manner, bearing, demeanor
馴 *monona(reru)* be used to; be skilled; be sophisticated
数 *mono (no) kazu* something of value
新 *monoatara(shii)* something new
置 *monooki* storeroom
羨 *monouraya(mi)* envy, jealousy
資 *busshi* commodities, resources
14 慣 *monona(reru)* be used to; be skilled; be sophisticated
種 *monodane* the fundamental thing
静 *monoshizu(kana)* quiet, still; serene
語 *monogatari* story, legend, romance, narrative. *monogata(ru)* tell, narrate
語劇 *monogatarigeki* melodrama
15 論 *butsuron* public discussion, public criticism
憂 *monou(i)* languid, weary, lazy; melancholy, gloomy, dull
慾 *butsuyoku* worldly desire
質 *busshitsu* matter, substance
質文明 *busshitsu bummei* material civilization
質主義 *busshitsu shugi* materialism
質主義的 *busshitsushugiteki* materialistic
質的 *busshitsuteki* material (things)
質偏重 *busshitsu henchō* materialism
18 騒 *bussō na* disturbed, troublous, unsettled, dangerous. *monosawaga(shii)* noisy, boisterous
19 識 *monoshi(ri)* extensive knowledge; well-informed person, scholar
20 議 *butsugi* public discussion, public criticism

5

B **牲** 3539 / J4037 / M19986 SEI. *ikenie, nie* sacrifice, offering, gift.

牴 3540 / J6032 / M19988 TEI touch.
13 触 *teishoku* conflict, contradiction, infringement

6

A **特** 3541 / J4643 / M20013 TOKU special. *toku ni* especially, particularly.
3 大 *tokudai* oversize
上 *tokujō no* finest, highest grade
4 火点 *tokkaten* pillbox
5 示 *tokuji suru* be distinguished by
功 *tokkō* special efficacy
6 色 *tokushoku* characteristic, peculiarity, idiosyncrasy
旨 *tokushi* special consideration
有 *tokuyū* characteristic of, peculiar to
有性 *tokuyūsei* peculiarity
有財産 *tokuyū zaisan* one's separate property
7 技 *tokugi* special skill, specialty
志 *tokushi* volunteering; zeal; benevolence
志家 *tokushika* volunteer, self-sacrificing person
売 *tokubai* special sale
売日 *tokubaibi* bargain day
別 *tokubetsu* special, extraordinary
別号 *tokubetsugō* special number
別扱 *tokubetsu atsuka(i)* special handling
別列車 *tokubetsu ressha* special train
別急行 *tokubetsu kyūko* limited express
別席 *tokubetsu seki* reserved seat
8 例 *tokurei* special case, exception
使 *tokushi* special envoy, special messenger
性 *tokusei* characteristic, peculiarity
典 *tokuten* special favor, privilege
長 *tokuchō* distinctive feature; strong point, forte, merit
長的 *tokuchōteki* characteristic
効 *tokkō* special efficacy
効薬 *tokkōyaku* specific remedy
命 *tokumei* special appointment
命全権大使 *tokumei zenken taishi* envoy extraordinary and ambassador plenipotentiary
命全権公使 *tokumei zenken kōshi* envoy extraordinary and minister plenipotentiary
定 *tokutei suru* specify
定局 *tokuteikyoku* privately-owned post office
定税 *tokuteizei* differential tax
価 *tokka* special price

価品 *tokkahin* bargain goods
価品売場 *tokkahin uriba* bargain counter
価販売 *tokka hambai* bargain sale
9 級 *tokkyū* extra-special class or grade
点 *tokuten* special favor, privilege
発 *tokuhatsu* special (train)
急 *tokkyū* limited express
科兵 *tokkahei* technical soldier
科隊 *tokkatai* technical corps
約 *tokuyaku* special contract
約店 *tokuyakuten* special agent, chain store
待 *tokutai* special treatment, distinction
待生 *tokutaisei* scholarship student
待券 *tokutaiken* complimentary ticket
派 *tokuha suru* dispatch
派大使 *tokuha taishi* ambassador extraordinary
派使節 *tokuha shisetsu* special envoy, special mission
派員 *tokuhain* delegate; special correspondent
10 進 *tokushin* special promotion in rank
記 *tokki* special mention
配 *tokuhai* special ration, special dividend, bonus
高 *tokkō* thought-control police
高課 *tokkōka* thought-control police
恵 *tokukei, tokkei* special favor, privilege
恵待遇 *tokkei taigū* preferential treatment
恵税率 *tokkei zeiritsu* preferential tariff
恵関税 *tokkei kanzei* preferential duties
殊 *tokushu na* special, characteristic, typical, individual, unique
殊性 *tokushusei* peculiarity, characteristic
殊学校 *tokushu gakkō* special school
殊飛行 *tokushu hikō* acrobatic flight
殊病 *tokushubyō* peculiar disease
殊部落 *tokushu buraku* an eta community
殊教育 *tokushu kyōiku* education for the handicapped
殊喫茶 *tokushu kissa* cabaret, night club
殊銀行 *tokushu ginkō* chartered bank
殊鋼 *tokushukō* special steel
11 設 *tokusetsu* special installation
務 *tokumu* special duty
務兵 *tokumuhei* special-service soldier
務機関 *tokumu kikan* spying organization
務艦 *tokumukan* special-service vessel
赦 *tokusha* amnesty, special pardon
赦令 *tokusharei* act of amnesty
産 *tokusan* specialty, special product
産地 *tokusanchi* special-product area
産物 *tokusambutsu* special products
産品 *tokusanhin* specialties, special products
異 *tokui* peculiar, unique
異体質 *tokui taishitsu* allergy, idiosyncrasy
異性 *tokuisei* singularity, special characteristics
異質 *tokuishitsu* idiosyncrasy
許 *tokkyo* patent, (company) charter, concession, license, special permission
許庁 *Tokkyochō* Patent Agency
許状 *tokkyojō* charter, special license
許品 *tokkyohin* patented article
許証 *tokkyoshō* letters patent
許権 *tokkyoken* patent
許権使用料 *tokkyoken shiyōryō* royalty
12 等 *tokutō* special grade
報 *tokuhō* news flash
飲街 *tokuingai* red-light district
筆 *tokuhitsu* special mention
筆大書 *tokuhitsu-taisho suru* write in large or red letters
集 *tokushū* special edition; special collection
集号 *tokushūgō* special issue
13 電 *tokuden* special telegram
14 選 *tokusen* special selection; recognition; special make
徴 *tokuchō* distinctive feature
種 *tokudane* exclusive news, scoop. *tokushu* special kind
需 *tokuju* emergency demand
製 *tokusei* special make
15 賞 *tokushō* special commendation; special reward
質 *tokushitsu* characteristic, special quality
権 *tokken* privilege, special rights, prerogative; (civil) liberties; chartered rights
権者 *tokkensha* privileged person
権階級 *tokken kaikyū* privileged classes
16 輯 *tokushū* special edition
薦 *tokusen* specially recommended

7

犁 3542 J6035 M20037 See 犂 3547.

牾 3543 J6033 M20028 Go *saka(rau)* oppose, act contrary to.

牽 3544 J3823 M20025 KEN. *hi(ku) vt* draw, pull, haul, tug, jerk, drag, trail, bend, attract; lead (horses or captives); draw (lines); admit; install (utilities); quote, refer to; look up (words); subtract, reduce; apply, daub on; blunt (a sword); patronize; choose; catch (a cold). *vi* retreat, withdraw, retire; subside.

4 引 *ken'in suru* haul, tow, pull, drag

引力 *ken'inryoku* pulling power

引車 *ken'insha* tractor

8 制 *kensei* check, restraint, constraint; diversion, feint, screen

制球 *kenseikyū* a throw to check a runner

9 連 *kenren suru* be related to

11 強 *kenkyō* distortion of facts

強付会 *kenkyō-fukai no* farfetched, distorted

8

犇 3545 J6036 M20058 HON. *hishi(meku)* clamor; jostle; squeak. *hishi to* firmly, tightly

12 犇 *hishihishi* tightly, firmly; thick and fast; crowded

犀 3546 J3a54 M20045 SAI rhinoceros.

7 角 *saikaku* a rhinoceros horn

利 *sairi na* keen, acute, penetrating

犂 3547 J6034 M20048 犁 3542 J6035 M20037 RI. REI. RYŪ. *suki* plow.

4 牛 *rigyū* cow spotted with black and white

6 先 *sukizaki* plowshare

16 篦 *sukibera* plowshare

10

犖 3548 J6038 M20126 RAKU brindled ox; clear; superior.

犒 3549 J6037 M20114 KŌ. *negira(u)* thank for, reward for.

13

B 犠 3550 J353e M20190' 犧 3552 J603a M20209 GI sacrifice.

5 打 *gida* sacrifice hit

9 牲 *gisei* (animal) sacrifice, offering; self-sacrifice

牲打 *giseida* sacrifice hit

牲的 *giseiteki* self-sacrificing

牲者 *giseisha* victim, prey

牲制度 *gisei seido* sacrificial system

15

犢 3551 J6039 M20196 TOKU. *koushi* calf.

14 鼻褌 *fundoshi* loincloth

16

犧 3552 J603a M20209 See 犠 3550.

RAD. 犬 94

Inu dog. At left: 犭 (3 strokes) *kemono hen* left-hand "animal." Nickname: Dog.

A 犬 3553 J3824 M20234 KEN dog. *inu* dog; spy. *inu(koro)* puppy.

3 小屋 *inugoya* kennel

6 死 *inuji(ni) suru* die a dog's death; die in vain

合 *inua(wase)* dog fight; sicking dogs on each other

7 芸 *inugei* dog trick

8 侍 *inuzamurai* depraved samurai

泳 *inuoyogi* dog paddle

舎 *kensha* kennel, doghouse

9 狩 *inuga(ri)* mad-dog hunt; wild-dog hunt
10 馬 *kemba* dog and horse; my humble self
釘 *inukugi* spike
殺 *inukoro(shi)* dog catcher
骨折 *inuboneo(ri)* fruitless effort
11 猫 *inu-neko* dogs and cats
商 *inushō* dog fancier
12 歯 *kenshi* cuspid, eyetooth, canine tooth
13 搔 *inukaki* dog paddle
猿 *ken'en* dog and monkey; loggerheads
15 潜 *inukuguri* dog's hole in a fence
16 儒 *kenju* a highbrow scholar
儒学派 *kenjugakuha* the Cynics
23 鷲 *inuwashi* golden eagle

2

A 犯 3554 / J4848 / M20238 BON. HAN offense, crime; counter for criminal offenses. *oka(su)* commit, sin against; violate, break; defy, disregard; attack, assault; seduce, rape.

2 人 *hannin* criminal, offender
6 行 *hankō* crime, offense
8 逆 *hangyaku* defiance of law and morality
9 則 *hansoku* transgression; default
則者 *hansokusha* transgressor; defaulter
13 跡 *hanseki* evidences of a crime
意 *han'i* criminal intent; malice
罪 *hanzai* crime, offense
罪人 *hanzainin* offender, criminal, convict
罪心理 *hanzai shinri* criminal psychology
罪心理学 *hanzai shinrigaku* criminal psychology
罪学 *hanzaigaku* criminology
罪者 *hanzaisha* offender, criminal, convict
罪型 *hanzaigata* criminal type
罪容疑者 *hanzai yōgisha* suspected criminal
罪捜査 *hanzai sōsa* criminal investigation
罪嫌疑者 *hanzai kengisha* suspected criminal

3

犲 3555 / J603c / M20248 See 豺 5754.

A 状 3556 / J3e75 / M20257 狀 3557 / J-X / M20280 JŌ condition, circumstances; form, appearances; letter.

8 況 *jōkyō* circumstances
9 挟 *jōbasami* letter file
10 挿 *jōsa(shi)* simple letter file, letter rack
差 *jōsa(shi)* simple letter file, letter rack
11 袋 *jōbukuro* envelope
12 景 *jōkei* scene; nature and sentiment
13 勢 *jōsei* state of affairs, condition, indication, appearance
14 態 *jōtai* state of affairs, situation
15 箱 *jōbako* message case

4

狀 3557 / J-X / M20280 See 状 3556.

犹 3558 / J603b / M20259 Nonstandard for 猶 3593.

狃 3559 / J603d / M20289 JŪ. NYU *na(reru)* become used to; become tame; mature. *nara(u)* learn.

狄 3560 / J603f / M20290 TEKI barbarian.

狆 3561 / J603e / M20293 CHŪ. *chin* Pekinese dog, lap dog, Japanese pug, Japanese spaniel. *chin(koro)* puppy.

B 狂 3562 / J3638 / M20287 KYŌ lunatic. *kyō(suru)* go insane; be beside oneself with. *kuru(u)* go insane; lose one's head; run amuck, rave; be madly in love; go haywire, break down; be upset; warp; fluctuate; miss the mark; (winds) howl. *kuru(waseru), kuru(wakasu), kuru(wasu)* derange, dislocate; drive mad; upset, discomfit, disturb. *fu(reru)* go mad, be crazy. *kuru(i)* madness, insanity; confusion; warp; going wide of the mark; fluctuations. *kuruo(shi)* about crazy. *kuru(washii)* appearing to be crazy. *-kyō* maniac, enthusiast, fan.

2 人 *kyōjin* lunatic, maniac
3 女 *kyōjo* madwoman
4 文 *kyōbun* humorous composition
犬 *kyōken* mad dog
犬病 *kyōkembyō* rabies
5 句 *kyōku* comic 17-syllable haiku poem
6 回 *kuru(i)-mawa(ru)* rave, run amuck
死 *kyōshi, kuru(i)ji(ni)* death from madness
気 *kyōki* madness, insanity
妄 *kyōbō, kyōmō* crazy
7 乱 *kyōran* fury, frenzy, madness
言 *kyōgen* play, drama; program; noh comedy; trick, make-believe
言自殺 *kyōgen jisatsu* faked suicide
言作者 *kyōgen sakusha* dramatist, playwright
言師 *kyōgenshi* noh comedian
8 的 *kyōteki* insane; frantic; fanatic
奔 *kyōhon suru* rush around, run wild; bestir oneself
炎 *kyōen* fierce flames
者 *kyōsha* lunatic, maniac
9 風 *kyōfū* fierce wind
咲 *kuru(i)za(ki)* off-season flowering
信 *kyōshin* fanaticism
信性 *kyōshinsei* fanaticism
信的 *kyōshinteki* fanatical
信者 *kyōshinsha* fanatic, faddist
12 喚 *kuru(i)-wame(ku)* rave
焔 *kyōen* fierce flames
喜 *kyōki* wild joy, ecstasy
13 痴 *kyōchi* madness and foolishness
漢 *kyōkan* madman
詩 *kyōshi* humorous Edo poems
夢 *kyōmu* a crazy dream
愚 *kyōgu* madness and foolishness
想 *kyōsō* fantasy, daydream
想曲 *kyōsōkyoku* rhapsody
14 歌 *kyōka* comic tanka poem
態 *kyōtai* disgraceful conduct
15 暴 *kyōbō* rage, frenzy
17 濤 *kyōtō* raging billows
20 瀾 *kyōran* raging billows
騰 *kyōtō* sudden jump in stock-market prices
躁 *kyōsō* fury, frenzy; clamor

5

狎 3563 / J6040 / M20329 Ō. *na(reru)* get used to, become experienced; be tamed; get too familiar, mature.

狒 3564 / J6041 / M20338 Hɪ baboon.
8 狒 *hihi* baboon

狗 3565 / J3669 / M20345 Kᴜ pup, dog.
6 肉 *kuniku* dog flesh

狛 3566 / J397d / M20349 Hᴀᴋᴜ lion-dog shrine guardians. *koma* part of ancient Korea.
4 犬 *koma inu* lion-dog (stone) shrine guardians

狙 3567 / J4140 / M20347 So. *nera(u)* aim at, sight; watch for, shadow, stalk. *nera(i)* aim.
8 所 *nera(i)dokoro* target; objective
15 澄 *nera(i)-su(masu)* take careful aim
撃 *neraiu(chi), sogeki* shooting, sniping
撃兵 *sogekihei* sniper; marksman

狐 3568 / J3851 / M20333 Ko. *kitsune* fox.
4 火 *kitsunebi* St. Elmo's fire, will-o'-the-wisp
5 付 *kitsunetsu(ki)* spirit possession; one possessed by spirits
6 色 *kitsune iro* tan, light brown
8 狗狸 *kokkuri* Ouija board; table tapping, table tipping
9 臭 *wakiga* abnormal underarm odor
10 狸 *kori* foxes and badgers, sly fellow; enchantment
格子 *kitsunegōshi* lattice work
12 提灯 *kitsune (no) chōchin* St. Elmo's Fire, will-o'-the-wisp; Jack-o'-lantern
13 嫁入 *kitsune (no) yomei(ri)* a line of will-o'-the-wisps; sudden shower during sunshine
14 疑 *kogi* doubt, hesitation, indecision

6

猪 3569 / J6042 / M20366 See 豬 5759.

狠 3570 / J6043 / M20362 Kᴀɴ, Kᴏɴ sound of dogs fighting; bite; extreme.

4 心忄⺗戈戸手扌支攴攵文斗斤方无日曰月木欠止歹殳毋比毛氏气水氵氺火灬爪爫父爻爿丬片牙牛【犬犭】6

狡 3571 / J6044 / M20365 Kō. *zuru(i), kosu(i)* cunning, sly, crafty; niggardly.

6 吏 *kōri* crafty official
7 兎 *kōto* sly rabbit; swift rabbit
12 智 *kōchi* craft, cunning
13 猾 *kōkatsu* cunning
15 賢 *zurugashiko(i)* crafty, cunning
16 獪 *kōkai* cunning, craftiness; sophistication

B **狭** 3572 / J3639 / M20406′ **狹** 3575 / J6045 / M20428 Kyō. *seba(meru) vt* narrow, contract, reduce. *seba(maru) vi* narrow, become narrow, contract. *sema(i)* narrow, small (area), limited, tight. *sa-* honorary prefix.

3 小 *kyōshō na* narrow, cramped, limited
山 *sayama* a small mountain
4 心症 *kyōshinshō* heart attack, angina pectoris
8 門 *sema(ki)mon* narrow gate
苦 *semakuru(shii)* cramped
9 軌 *kyōki* narrow gauge
巷 *kyōkō* narrow streets
10 殺 *kyōsatsu suru* run down and put out (in baseball)
窄 *kyōsaku* constriction, strangulation
11 過 *semasu(giru)* be too narrow
斜 *kyōsha* red-light district
斜巷 *kyōsha (no) chimata* red-light district
12 間 *hazama* interval; interstice; ravine, glen; loophole (in a castle)
隘 *kyōai na* narrow, cramped; narrow-minded
量 *kyōryō* narrow-mindedness
13 義 *kyōgi* narrow sense
19 霧 *sagiri* light fog, mist, haze

B **狩** 3573 / J3c6d / M20390 Shu. *ka(ru)* hunt. *ka(ri)* hunting; raiding; gathering (mushrooms); viewing (maples).

2 人 *kariudo, karyūdo* hunter
3 小屋 *ka(ri)goya* hunting lodge
4 犬 *ka(ri)inu* hunting dog
込 *ka(ri)ko(mi)* round-up, arrest
5 矢 *ka(ri)ya* hunter's arrow
立 *ka(ri)-ta(teru)* chase away, hunt out
出 *ka(ri)-da(su)* hunt out, round up
6 衣 *ka(ri)ginu* hunting suit; (ancient) official garb
7 声 *ka(ri)goe* hunters' shouts
11 猟 *shuryō* hunting
猟小屋 *shuryō goya* shooting lodge
猟地 *shuryōchi* hunting grounds
猟会 *shuryōkai* hunting party
猟法 *shuryōhō* game laws
猟免状 *shuryō menjō* hunting license
猟家 *shuryōka* hunter
猟期 *shuryōki* hunting season
猟場 *shuryōjō* game preserve
12 場 *ka(ri)ba* hunting preserve
14 暮 *ka(ri)-kura(su)* spend (one's day) hunting
20 競 *ka(ri)kura(be), ka(ri)kura* hunting chase

A **独** 3574 / J4648 / M20406 **獨** 3607 / J6057 / M20725 Doku alone. *hitori, hitori(botchi)* alone, on one's own. *hitori(deni)* of itself, spontaneously, automatically. *-Doku-* Germany.

1 乙 *Doitsu* Germany
2 力 *dokuryoku* one's own effort
3 口 *hito(ri)guchi* monologue, soliloquy
4 仏 *Doku-Futsu* Germany and France
天下 *hitoritenka, hitoridenka* sole figure, boss of the show, without a rival
天狗 *hitori tengu* conceited person
5 白 *dokuhaku* monologue, soliloquy
占 *dokusen, hitoriji(me)* exclusive possession; monopoly; brushing everyone else aside
占企業 *dokusen kigyō* monopolistic enterprise, a trust
占的 *dokusenteki* monopolistic
占事業 *dokusen jigyō* monopolistic enterprise, a trust
占禁止法 *dokusen-kinshihō* antitrust law
立 *dokuritsu* independence, freedom; self-support; separation, isolation. *hitorida(chi)* standing alone, independence
立心 *dokuritsushin* spirit of independence
立主義 *dokuritsu shugi* secessionism, separatism
立自尊 *dokuritsu-jison* independence and self-respect
立自営 *dokuritsu-jiei* independence and self-support
立国 *dokuritsukoku* independent country

立性 *dokuritsusei* inclination toward independence
立独行 *dokuritsu-dokkō* independence, self-reliance
立独歩 *dokuritsu-doppo* independence, self-reliance
立祭 *Dokuritsusai* Independence Day
立戦争 *Dokuritsu Sensō* Revolutionary War
立語 *dokuritsugo* an independent word (in a sentence)
立権 *dokuritsuken* autonomy
6 自 *dokuji no* original, peculiar, characteristic; personal, individual
行 *dokkō* self-reliance; traveling alone
伊 *Doku-I* Germany and Italy
合点 *hitorigatten, hitorigaten* hasty conclusion
7 見 *dokken* private views
言 *dokugen, hitorigoto* soliloquy; monologue
走 *dokusō* running alone; sailing alone (ships)
住居 *hitorizumai* living alone
吟 *dokugin* solo poem-recitation
決 *hitorigi(me)* on one's own authority
坐 *dokuza* sitting alone
身 *dokushin, hitorimi* single life, celibacy
身者 *dokushinsha* single person
身寮 *dokushinryō* bachelor's quarters
8 居 *dokkyo* solitude, solitary life
往 *dokuō* going one's own way
歩 *hitoriaru(ki)* walking alone; going it alone. *doppo* ambulatory
英 *Doku-Ei* Germany and England
学 *dokugaku* self study
房 *dokubō* solitary cell
房監禁 *dokubō kankin* solitary confinement
9 活 *udo* edible-stem vegetable plant resembling rhubarb
相撲 *hitorizumō* fighting windmills; one-sided contest
奏 *dokusō* instrumental solo
奏会 *dokusōkai* instrumental recital
10 逸 *Doitsu* Germany
修 *dokushū* studying by oneself
特 *dokutoku* peculiarity, uniqueness
酌 *dokushaku* drinking alone
案内 *hitori annai, dokuannai* self-instruction book, key
11 得 *dokutoku* peculiarity, uniqueness
唱 *dokushō* vocal solo
唱会 *dokushōkai* vocal recital
眼 *dokugan no* one-eyed
眼竜 *dokuganryū* one-eyed hero
断 *dokudan* arbitrary decision; dogmatism
断専行 *dokudan-senkō* arbitrary action
習 *dokushū* studying by oneself
習書 *dokushūsho* crib, pony
12 善 *hitoriyo(gari), dokuzen* self-importance, self-conceit, self-complacency, self-gratification
善主義 *dokuzen shugi* a feeling that only oneself is right; self-righteousness
善的 *dokuzenteki* self-righteous, self-complacent
創 *dokusō* originality, invention
創力 *dokusōryoku* creative talent, inventive power, originality initiative
創性 *dokusōsei* originality
創的 *dokusōteki* original, creative
裁 *dokusai* autocracy, dictatorship
裁者 *dokusaisha* autocrat, dictator
裁的 *dokusaiteki* autocratic, dictatorial
裁制 *dokusaisei* dictatorship, autocracy
裁政治 *dokusai seiji* autocracy, dictatorship
13 寝 *hitorine* sleeping alone
禁法 *dokkinhō* antitrust law
楽 *koma* top
楽鼠 *komanezumi* dancing mouse
14 漕 *dokusō* running alone; (ship) sailing alone
語 *dokugo* talking to oneself, monologue, soliloquy. *Dokugo* German language
領 *Dokuryō* German possessions
暮 *hitorigu(rashi)* single life, celibacy, living alone
演 *dokuen* solo recital; solo performance
演会 *dokuenkai* solo recital, solo performance
15 舞台 *hitoributai* alone on the stage; monopolizing the stage; one-man show
16 稽古 *hitorigeiko* self-education
壇場 *dokudanjō* one's unrivaled field, unchallenged position
擅 *dokusen* doing as one pleases
擅場 *dokusenjō* one's unrivaled field, unchallenged position

20 艦 *Dokukan* German warship

7

狹 3575 / J6045 / M20428 See 狭 3572.

狽 3576 / J4762 / M20433 Bai wolf; be flurried.

狷 3577 / J6046 / M20426 Ken short-tempered.
4 介 *kenkai na* narrow-minded, uncompromising
9 狭 *kenkyō na* narrow-minded, uncompromising

狸 3578 / J432c / M20427 **貍** 5761 / J6c3e / M36561 Ri. *tanuki* badger; cunning person.
10 眠 *tanuki nemu(ri)* feigned sleep
11 婆 *tanuki baba* witch, cunning hag
13 寝 *tanukine* feigned sleep
寝入 *tanuki ne-i(ri)* feigned sleep
16 親父 *tanuki oyaji* cunning old man

狼 3579 / J4f35 / M20432 Rō. *ōkami* wolf.
4 火 *rōka* beacon fire
9 星 *Rōsei* Sirius, Dog Star
10 狽 *urota(eru)* get confused, lose one's head. *rōbai* consternation, dismay, panic
狽者 *urotaemono* one easily flustered
13 煙 *rōen, noroshi* signal fire, beacon, rocket
16 燧 *rōsui* beacon fire
17 藉 *rōzeki* confusion, disorder, violence, riot
藉者 *rōzekimono* rioter, ruffian

8

猗 3580 / J6048 / M20493 I beautiful; long; thick growth; add. *ā* exclamation.

猝 3581 / J604c / M20500 Sotsu, Sochi *niwa(ka)* sudden, abrupt.

猊 3582 / J6049 / M20468 **貎** 5763 / J6c3f / M36572 Gei lion; the seat of a famous priest.
3 下 *geika* your highness, your grace, your eminence

猖 3583 / J604b / M20490 Shō storm around; be insane; severe; violence.
15 獗 *shōketsu* rage, violence, fury

猜 3584 / J604a / M20499 Sai jealousy; doubt.
7 忌 *saiki* envy, jealousy
忌心 *saikishin* envy, jealousy
14 疑 *saigi* suspicion, jealousy and doubt
疑心 *saigishin* suspicion, jealousy and doubt

猪 3585 / J4376 / M20511 **豬** 3589 / J-X / M20534 Cho. *i, inoshishi, shishi* wild boar.
3 口 *choko, choku* saké cup
口才 *chokozai na, chokusai na* impertinent, impudent
5 牙 *choki* light flat-bottomed rowboat
牙船 *chokibune* light flat-bottomed rowboat
8 突 *chototsu* recklessness
武者 *inoshishi musha* daredevil, foolhardy warrior
9 首 *ikubi* bull neck (short and thick)
勇 *choyū* foolhardiness, desperate courage
13 飼 *inoshishika(i)* keeper of wild boars
16 頸 *ikubi* bull neck (short and thick)

B **猫** 3586 / J472d / M20535 Byō. *neko* cat.
2 入 *neko-i(razu)* rat poison
5 可愛 *nekokawai(garu)* dote on (children)
6 舌 *nekojita* aversion to hot food
7 車 *nekoguruma* wheelbarrow
足結 *nekoashi musu(bi)* cat's-paw knot
9 背 *nekoze* stoop, round shoulders
10 被 *nekokaburi* hypocrisy, false modesty, feigned innocence; hypocrite; wolf in sheep's clothing
11 族 *byōzoku* cat family
脚 *nekoashi* carved table leg
15 撫声 *nekonadegoe* coaxing voice, insinuating voice
17 糞 *nekobaba* embezzlement, misappropriation

B 猟 3587 J4e44 M20512′ 獵 3613 J605a M20768 獦 3610 J-X M20759

RYŌ shooting, hunting; game, take, bag. *kari* hunting; raiding.

2 人 *kariudo, karyūdo, ryōjin* hunter, sportsman
刀 *ryōtō* hunting knife
4 犬 *ryōken, kari inu* hunting dog
6 色 *ryōshoku* lewdness, debauchery
色家 *ryōshokuka* philanderer, lewd person
8 虎 *rakko* sea otter
狗 *ryōku* hunting dog
具 *ryōgu* hunting equipment
季 *ryōki* hunting season
官 *ryōkan* office-seeking
官運動 *ryōkan undō* office-seeking
奇 *ryōki* hunting for the bizarre
奇文学 *ryōki bungaku* bizarre literature
10 師 *ryōshi* hunter
12 場 *ryōba, ryōjō* game preserve, hunting grounds
期 *ryōki* hunting season
14 銃 *ryōjū* shotgun, hunting gun

B 猛 3588 J4c54 M20498 MŌ wildness, fierceness; strength. *take(ru)* become furious, rush, rage, rave. *take(ku), mō ni* valiantly, bravely, fiercely.

4 火 *mōka* raging flames; heavy gunfire
犬 *moken* fierce dog
反撃 *mōhangeki* fierce counterattack
5 打 *mōda* slugging (in baseball)
打者 *mōdasha* slugger (in baseball)
打球 *mōdakyū* a hard-hit ball
7 攻 *moko* fierce attack
攻撃 *mōkōgeki* fierce attack
8 雨 *mōu* heavy rain, downpour, cloudburst
虎 *mōko* fierce tiger
毒 *mōdoku* deadly poison
者 *mosa* veteran; man of valor
9 威 *mōi* violence, fierceness
勇 *mōyū* bravery
省 *mōsei* serious reflection
10 進 *mōshin suru* dash forward, drive on
将 *mōshō* brave general, brave warrior
射 *mōsha* heavy fire; severe fighting
烈 *mōretsu na* violent, furious, fierce, keen (competition), intense, awful
訓練 *mōkunren* hard training
11 鳥 *mōchō* bird of prey
猛 *takedake(shii)* fierce, ferocious; audacious
悪 *mōaku na* savage, ferocious
運動 *mōundō* frantic efforts; strong lobby
12 然 *mōzen to* fiercely, resolutely, savagely
13 禽 *mōkin* bird of prey
勢 *mōsei* great strength; military strength
14 練習 *mōrenshū* intensive practice
15 撃 *mōgeki* severe blow, fierce attack
16 獣 *mōjū* fierce animal
獣使 *mōjūzuka(i)* wild-animal trainer
獣狩 *mōjūga(ri)* big-game hunting
19 爆 *mōbaku* heavy bombing
22 襲 *mōshū* fierce attack

9

猪 3589 J-X M20534 See 猪 3585.

猷 3590 J4d32 M20558 YŪ measure; plan, scheme.

猯 3591 J604e M20540 TAN *inoshishi* wild boar.

猴 3592 J604d M20553 KŌ monkey.

B 猶 3593 J4d31 M20557 獝 3603 J-X M-X YŪ. YU. *nao* further, furthermore, still, still more, yet, just like.

3 子 *yūshi* nephew; another's child considered as one's own
4 予 *yūyo* postponement, grace, extension (of time); reprieve, stay; delay; slackness
予期間 *yūyo kikan* renewal period, period of grace, legal delay, cooling-off period

猥 3594 J6050 M20519 WAI obscene. *mida(ra) na* licentious, indecent, lewd. *mida(ri) ni* without authority, without reason, arbitrarily, unnecessarily, indiscriminately, recklessly. *midari(gamashii)* morally corrupt.

5 本 *waihon* pornographic book
14 雑 *waizatsu* confusion, disorder
15 談 *waidan* indecent talk

[17] 褻 *waisetsu* obscenity, indecency, licentiousness

猩 3595 / J604f / M20528 SHŌ orangutan.
[9] 紅熱 *shōkōnetsu* scarlet fever
[12] 猩 *shōjō* orangutan; heavy drinker
猩木 *shōjōboku* poinsettia
猩草 *shōjōsō* poinsettia
猩緋 *shōjōhi* scarlet

B 献 3596 / J3825 / M20539 獻 3614 / J605b / M20783 KEN, KON counter for drinks. *sasa(geru), ken(jiru), ken(zuru), tatematsu(ru)* present, dedicate, offer.
[3] 上 *kenjō suru* present to
[4] 木 *kemboku* donating lumber to a shrine or temple; such donated lumber
[5] 本 *kempon* presentation (copy)
立 *kondate* menu, program, schedule
立表 *kondatehyō* menu
[6] 灯 *kentō* votive light or lantern
[7] 言 *kengen* memorial, petition, proposal
呈 *kentei* presentation
身 *kenshin* devotion, dedication
身的 *kenshinteki* self-sacrificing, devoted
身者 *kenshinsha* dedicated person
[8] 杯 *kempai suru* drink to someone's health
物 *kemmotsu* a present. *sasagemono* offering
金 *kenkin* offering, donation, collection
金者 *kenkinsha* donor
金袋 *kenkimbukuro* offering bags
金箱 *kenkimbako* offertory box
[9] 盃 *kempai suru* drink to someone's health
茶 *kencha* powdered-tea offering
[10] 酌 *kenshaku* offering a drink
貢 *kenkō* paying tribute
納 *kennō* presentation, donation
納地 *kennōchi* dedicated land
納者 *kennōsha* donor
納品 *kennōhin* gift
[11] 堂 *kendō* dedication of a temple or church
堂式 *kendōshiki* dedication ceremony
[12] 詠 *ken'ei* dedication of a poem
策 *kensaku* suggestion, recommendation
替 *kentai suru* assisting a ruler in suppressing evil and upholding good
[13] 酬 *kenshū* exchange of winecups
[21] 饌 *kensen* offering to a god

10

獏 3597 / J6053 / M20638 貘 5765 / J6c42 / M36621 BAKU tapir.

猾 3598 / J6051 / M20583 KATSU crafty.

獅 3599 / J3b62 / M20609 SHI lion. *shishi* lion.
[3] 子 *shishi* lion
子王 *shishiō* king of beasts
子吼 *shishiku* lion's roar; a denouncing speech; oratorical skill
子使 *shishizuka(i)* lion tamer
子鼻 *shishibana, shishi(p)pana* pug nose
子舞 *shishimai* lion-mask dance
子奮迅 *shishi funjin* rushing ahead at full tilt

B 猿 3600 / J316e / M20584 EN monkey. *mashira* monkey. *saru* monkey, ape; mimic; sly person; door bolt; fastener.
[2] 人 *enjin* ape man
[5] 芝居 *saru shibai* monkey show
[6] 回 *sarumawa(shi)* monkey trainer
似 *saruni* accidental personal resemblance
[8] 股 *sarumata* undershorts
知恵 *sarujie* shallow cleverness
[9] 面 *sarumen* monkey face
廻 *sarumawa(shi)* monkey trainer
[10] 真似 *sarumane* indiscriminate imitation
[11] 眼 *sarumanako* large sunken eyes
[12] 猴 *enkō* long-armed monkey
[13] 楽 *sarugaku* noh-drama prototype
[15] 賢 *sarugashiko(i)* cunning
[17] 臂 *empi* a long arm
[18] 類 *enrui* the apes
[22] 轡 *sarugutsuwa* (mouth) gag

11

奬 3601 / J6052 / M20637 See 奨 1167.

B 獄 3602 / J3976 / M20603 GOKU prison, jail. *hitoya* prison, jail.
[4] 内 *gokunai* prison interior

4 心忄⺗戈戸手扌支攴攵文斗斤方无日曰月木欠止歹殳毋比毛氏气水氵⺢火灬爪⺤父爻爿丬片牙牛【犬 9 犭】

中 *gokuchū* in prison, imprisoned
5 囚 *gokushū* prisoner
6 衣 *gokui* prison uniform
死 *gokushi* death in prison
吏 *gokuri* jailor
8 門 *gokumon* prison gates
房 *gokubō* prison cell
卒 *gokusotsu* prison guards; hell's tormenting devils
舎 *gokusha* prison house, jail
9 屋 *gokuya* prison, jail
則 *gokusoku* prison regulations
11 窓 *gokusō* prison window; prison
道 *gokudō na* brutal, villainous, wicked, dissipated
道者 *gokudōmono* scoundrel, villain, profligate
13 裏 *gokuri* inside the prison

12

獐 3603 / J-X / M•X See 猶 3593.

獠 3604 / J-X / M20692 Ryō hunting; night hunting.

獗 3605 / J6055 / M20671 Ketsu storm around; be crazy.

B **獣** 3606 / J3d43 / M20714' **獸** 3612 / J6059 / M20775 Jū. *kedamono, kemono* animal, beast.
4 心 *jūshin* brutal heart
毛 *jūmō* animal hair
5 皮 *jūhi* animal skin, hide
6 肉 *jūniku* meat, flesh of animals
行 *jūkō* bestiality, assault (on a woman)
7 医 *jūi* veterinarian
医学 *jūigaku* veterinary science
医学校 *jūi gakkō* veterinary college
医業 *jūigyō* veterinary practice
8 性 *jūsei* animal nature, bestiality, brutality
的 *jūteki* brutal, beastly
9 疫 *jūeki* cattle disease
姦 *jūkan* bestiality
炭 *jūtan* animal charcoal
10 脂 *jūshi* animal fat, tallow
帯 *jūtai* zodiac
11 欲 *jūyoku* carnal desire, lust, bestiality
15 慾 *jūyoku* carnal desire, lust, bestiality
18 類 *jūrui* beasts, animals

13

獨 3607 / J6057 / M20725 See 独 3574.

獪 3608 / J6056 / M20729 Kai crafty.

B **獲** 3609 / J334d / M20758 Kaku. *e(ru), u(ru)* get, acquire, find, earn, win, gain, receive; can, be able to, may; commit (sin).
8 物 *emono* game, bag, catch, spoils, prize, trophy, booty, prey
11 得 *kakutoku* acquisition, possession

14

獵 3610 / J-X / M20759 See 猟 3587.

獰 3611 / J6058 / M20755 Dō. Nei bad.
11 悪 *dōaku* wickedness, perverseness
猛 *dōmō, neimō* ferocity

15

獸 3612 / J6059 / M20775 See 獣 3606.

獵 3613 / J605a / M20768 See 猟 3587.

16

獻 3614 / J605b / M20783 See 献 3596.

獺 3615 / J605c / M20782 Datsu. *uso, kawa uso* otter.

5-STROKE RADICALS

RAD. 玄 95

Gen blackness. Nickname: Dark (cf. Rad. 203).

B 玄 3616 / J383c / M20814 GEN occultness, mystery, black.
2 人 *kurōto* professional, expert; geisha, prostitute
人筋 *kurōto suji* professionals, the initiated
5 玄 *gengen* profundity
冬 *gentō* winter
6 米 *gemmai* unpolished rice, whole-grained rice, brown rice
米食 *gemmaishoku* unpolished-rice diet
7 妙 *gemmyō na* abstruse, occult, mysterious, miraculous
9 風 *gempū* impressiveness, deep feeling, solemnity
10 孫 *yashago, genson* great-great-grandchild
能 *gennō* large hammer
11 黄 *genkō* black and yellow; heaven and earth
理 *genri* abstruse theory, profound mystery
12 雲 *gen'un* black clouds; India ink
13 義 *gengi* (Catholic) mystery
14 徳 *gentoku* mysterious virtue, profound virtue
関 *genkan* porch, entranceway, vestibule, front door
関払 *genkambara(i)* refusing a visitor saying no one is at home
関先 *genkansaki* front door, entrance
関番 *genkamban* doorkeeper, janitor

5

茲 3617 / J-X / M20816 兹 380 / J-X / M-X 玆 5011 / J6824 / M30911
SHI. *koko ni* here.

6

A 率 3618 / J4e28 / M20817′ SOTSU. RITSU rate, percentage; proportion; coefficient, factor; constant; index. *hiki(iru)* lead, spearhead (a group), command (troops).
6 先 *sossen* taking the initiative
8 直 *sotchoku* frankness, openheartedness
10 倒 *sottō* fainting, swooning
12 然 *sotsuzen* suddenly, unexpectedly
14 爾 *sotsuji na* abrupt, sudden

RAD. 玉 96

Tama jewel. Variant: 王 (4 strokes) *ō* king. At left: 𤣩 (4 strokes) *tama hen* or *ō hen*. At bottom: 𤣩 (4 strokes). Nickname: Jewel.

A 王 3619 / J3226 / M20823 Ō *kimi* king, rule, magnate, baron.
3 土 *ōdo* royal or imperial domain
女 *ōjo* princess
子 *ōji* prince
4 手 *ōte* check, checkmate
水 *ōsui* aqua regia
化 *ōka* imperial influence; assimilation (of new territory)
公 *ōkō* king and princes; noble rank
5 母 *ōbo* king's mother, queen mother; grandmother (polite)
立 *ōritsu* royal
民 *ōmin* king's subject
6 衣 *ōi* royal robes
后 *ōkō* queen
妃 *ōhi* queen
7 佐 *ōsa* helping the king
位 *ōi* the throne, the crown
位回復 *ōi kaifuku* restoration of a ruler

位継承 *ōi keishō* succession to the throne
位継承者 *ōi keishōsha* successor to the throne
8 国 *ōkoku* kingdom, monarchy
法 *ōhō* king's decree
制 *ōsei* monarchical system
命 *ōmei* king's command
者 *ōja, ōsha* king, ruler, monarch, sovereign; royalty
事 *ōji* imperial or royal cause
9 威 *ōi* royal majesty
侯 *ōkō* princes, royalty, crowned heads
城 *ōjō* royal castle
冠 *ōkan* crown, diadem; bottle cap
室 *ōshitsu* ruling family
政 *ōsei* imperial rule, monarchy
政復古 *Ōsei Fukko* Imperial Restoration
政維新 *Ōsei Ishin* Imperial Restoration
10 座 *ōza* throne; God's throne; championship
師 *ōshi* emperor's teacher; imperial army
孫 *ōson* royal grandchild
旅 *ōryo* troops under the emperor's command
都 *ōto* royal capital
家 *ōke* royal family
宮 *ōkyū* royal palace
党 *ōtō* Tories, Royalists
11 道 *ōdō* rule of right; principles of royalty
族 *ōzoku* royalty; royal (family); member of a royal family
12 統 *ōtō* royal line, royal descendants
朝 *ōchō* dynasty
13 業 *ōgyō* rule, rulership
14 旗 *ōki* royal standard
15 権 *ōken* ruling authority, the State
19 覇 *ōha* rulers and usurpers

A 玉 3620 / J364c / M20821 GYOKU gem, jewel, precious stone, jade. *tama* ball, bowl, sphere, bulb; lens; gem, jewel, bullet, shot, shell; billiards; tool, cat's-paw; pretty girl; person; margin (in stocks); testicles. *tama-* beautiful; round.
3 子 *tamago* egg; spawn, roe; (an expert) in the making
子泡立器 *tamago-awada(te)ki* eggbeater
子巻 *tamagomaki* meat rolled in thin omelet
子焼 *tamagoyaki* fried eggs; omelet
4 戸 *tamado* a beautiful door; the door of a shrine
什 *gyokujū* your poem
手箱 *tamatebako* Pandora's box; treasured casket
5 目 *tamamoku* pretty (wood) grain
台 *tamadai* billiard table
石 *gyokuseki* gems and stones; wheat and tares. *tamaishi* pebble, boulder
石混淆 *gyokuseki-konkō* a mixture of good and bad
6 成 *gyokusei suru* attain perfection
印 *gyokuin* jewel seal
汗 *tama (no) ase* beads of perspiration
虫 *tamamushi* an insect with iridescent wings
虫甲斐絹 *tamamushi kaiki* iridescent silk cloth
虫色 *tamamushi iro* iridescence
7 体 *gyokutai* imperial presence, emperor's person
声 *tama (no) koe* sweet voice, silvery voice; beautiful words
条 *gyokujō* beautiful branches; important rules
串 *tamagushi, tamakushi* Shinto sacred paper-decked *sakaki* branch offering
8 杯 *gyokuhai* jade cup
垂 *tamadare* bamboo curtain; palace
歩 *gyokuho* walking (polite)
突 *tamatsu(ki)* billiards
苗 *tamanae* rice sprouts
9 屋 *tamaya* jeweler, lapidary
垣 *tamagaki* shrine fence
砕 *gyokusai* honorable death, honorable defeat
冠 *gyokukan* jeweled crown; beautiful crown, ceremonial crown
姿 *gyokushi* beautiful figure
砂利 *tamajari* pebbles, gravel
音 *gyokuon* emperor's voice. *gyokuin* voice or sound as clear as a bell
音放送 *gyokuon hōsō* the emperor's broadcast
10 屑 *gyokusetsu* pulverized jewels; snow; beautiful literature
座 *gyokuza* imperial throne, throne
容 *gyokuyō* beautiful features
11 疵 *tama (ni) kizu* a flaw in the jewel
転 *tamakoroga(shi)* bowling; roulette; pinball

5 玄【玉王】瓜瓦甘生用田疋疒癶白皮皿目矛矢石示ネ内禾穴立

章 *gyokushō* excellent composition; your letter. *tamazusa* your letter
細工 *tamazaiku* jewelry
12 詠 *gyokuei* your poem
筆 *gyokuhitsu* your handwriting
葱 *tamanegi* onion
葉 *gyokuyō* beautiful leaf; the Imperial Family
無 *tamana(shi)* total loss, spoiling
13 殿 *gyokuden* jeweled palace; beautiful mansion
楼 *gyokurō* a magnificent structure
飾 *tamakaza(ri)* jewelry
蜀黍 *tōmorokoshi* corn, maize
14 摧 *gyokusai* brave death
緒 *tama(no)o* bead string; thread of life
15 稿 *gyokkō* your manuscript
盤 *gyokuban* jade dish, beautiful dish
質 *gyokushitsu* beautiful disposition
輦 *gyokuren* imperial carriage
器 *gyokki* jeweled utensil
17 輿 *tama (no) koshi* jeweled palanquin
18 髄 *gyokuzui* chalcedony
繭 *tama mayu* dupion cocoon
顔 *gyokugan* beautiful face; emperor's face
顔容 *tama (no) kambase* beautiful face
19 韻 *gyokuin* your poem
璽 *gyokuji* the seal of a sovereign
簾 *gyokuren* beautiful jeweled blind; blind (polite). *tama sudare* a blind decorated with beads
藻 *tamamo* seaweed
20 霰 *tamaarare* hail
21 露 *gyokuro* refined green tea

3

玖 3621 / J366a / M20846 KYŪ. KU beautiful black gem; nine.

4

玩 3622 / J3461 / M20872 GAN. *mochiaso(bu), moteaso(bu)* play; take pleasure in; play (on an instrument); play with; make sport of; trifle with (affections).
7 弄 *ganrō suru* make sport of, toy with, play with
弄物 *ganrōbutsu* plaything, toy
8 味 *gammi suru* taste, enjoy, appreciate
物 *gambutsu, moteaso(bi)mono* toy, plaything
具 *gangu, omocha* toy
具屋 *omochaya* toy shop
具商 *gangushō* toy shop

5

珎 3623 / J605f / M20921 Nonstandard for 珍 3631.

珀 3624 / J6061 / M20904 HAKU amber.

珂 3625 / J3251 / M20906 KA jewel.

玲 3626 / J4e68 / M20888 REI sound of jewels.

玳 3627 / J605e / M20889 **瑇** 3655 / J-X / M21102 TAI tortoise shell.
13 瑁 *taimai* tortoise shell

玻 3628 / J6060 / M20899 HA glass.
15 璃 *hari* crystal, glass

珈 3629 / J605d / M20915 KA ornamental hairpin.
12 琲 *kōhii* coffee
琲沸 *kōhiiwaka(shi)* coffeepot
琲挽 *kōhiihiki* coffee grinder; coffee grinding

珊 3630 / J3b39 / M20917 SAN stagger; loneliness. *senchi* centimeter.
13 瑚 *sango* coral
瑚虫 *sangochū* coral insect
瑚海 *Sangokai* Coral Sea
瑚島 *sangotō* coral island
瑚礁 *sangoshō* coral reef

B **珍** 3631 / J4441 / M20920 CHIN rare, curious, strange. *mezura(shigaru)* think (something is) strange. *mezura(shigatte)* out of curiosity. *mezura(shii)* new, novel, rare, strange, curious, unusual; nice (gift).
4 什 *chinjū* rare article, rare utensil
5 本 *chimpon* rare book
6 気 *mezu(rashi)ge ni* with curiosity

[7]妙 *chimmyō* queerness, oddity
[8]味 *chimmi* delicacy
物 *chimbutsu* curiosity
奇 *chinki* novelty, curiosity
宝 *chimpō* valuables, treasure
果 *chinka* rare fruit
肴 *chinkō* rare dish
事 *chinji* marvel, rare event
[9]柄 *chingara* rare pattern
重 *chinchō suru* prize, value highly
品 *chimpin* curio, rare article
客 *chinkyaku, chinkaku* welcome visitor
[10]書 *chinsho* rare book
[11]菓 *chinka* rare sweets
現象 *chingenshō* strange phenomenon
[12]稀 *chinki* something strange, something rare
貴 *chinki na* curious, valuable
無類 *chimmurui no* queer, singular, unique; phenomenal
[14]聞 *chimbun* news, revelation
説 *chinsetsu* novel idea, strange theory
蔵 *chinzō no* treasured (book, etc.)
[15]談 *chindan* funny story, anecdote, news, episode, gossip
器 *chinki* rare article
[17]糞漢 *chimpunkan* gibberish, jargon, nonsense

6

瑛 3632 / J607e / M-X Nonstandard for 瓔 3685.

珮 3633 / J6063 / M20977 See 佩 186.

珥 3634 / J6062 / M20964 JI. NI stone in earring; sword guard.

珞 3635 / J6064 / M20953 RAKU necklace.

A **班** 3636 / J4849 / M20976 HAN corps, unit, squad; party, companions, group; order.
[5]田 *handen* ancient farmland allotment
田収授 *handen-shūju* (ancient) government distribution of land
[8]長 *hanchō* group leader

B **珠** 3637 / J3c6e / M20956 SHU. JU. *tama* gem, jewel.
[5]玉 *shugyoku* gem, jewel, jewelry
[13]数 *juzu, zuzu* a string of beads; a (Buddhist) rosary
数玉 *juzudama* rosary bead
数繫 *juzutsuna(gi)* tying in a row
数繫囚人 *juzutsuna(gi) (no) shūjin* chain gang
[14]算 *shuzan* abacus calculation

珪 3638 / J373e / M20972 **硅** 4001 / J626b / M24151 KEI jade tablet or scepter (as symbol of authority); silicon.
[3]土 *keido* silica, silicon dioxide
[4]化木 *keikaboku* petrified wood
木石 *keibokuseki* petrified wood
[5]石 *keiseki* silica
[8]岩 *keigan* quartzite
[9]砂 *keisha* silica; quartz
肺症 *keihaishō* silicosis of the lungs
[10]素 *keiso* silicon
[14]酸 *keisan* silicic acid

7

琅 3639 / J6066 / M21013 See 瑯 3657.

琢 3640 / J4276 / M-X Nonstandard for 琢 3650.

珸 3641 / J6069 / M20993 GO a kind of jewel.

琉 3642 / J4e30 / M20978 RYŪ, RU lapis lazuli.
[11]球 *Ryūkyū* the Ryukyu islands
[15]璃 *ruri* emerald; lapis lazuli

A **球** 3643 / J3565 / M21011 KYŪ globe, sphere, ball; bulb; (radio) tube. *tama* ball, bowl, sphere, bulb.
[2]入軸承 *tamai(re) jikuu(ke)* ball bearing
[4]心 *kyūshin* center of a sphere
孔 *kyūkō* golf-green cup
[6]団 *kyūdan* baseball team
[7]体 *kyūtai* sphere, globe
技 *kyūgi* any game where a ball is used
投 *tamana(ge)* playing ball, playing catch
状 *kyūjō* globular shape

形 *kyūkei* globular form
8 茎 *kyūkei* (plant) bulb
9 速 *kyūsoku* speed of the ball
拾 *tamahiro(i)* caddy; poor ball player
乗 *tamano(ri)* balancing or running on a ball
界 *kyūkai* baseball world
面 *kyūmen* spherical surface
面三角 *kyūmen sankaku* spherical triangle
面三角法 *kyūmen sankakuhō* spherical trigonometry
面幾何学 *kyūmen kikagaku* spherical geometry
10 根 *kyūkon* tuber, bulb, rhizome
11 菜 *tamana* cabbage
12 場 *kyūjō* baseball field, a ballpark
13 電 *kyūden* ball lightning
碍子 *tamagaishi* globe insulator
14 窩関節 *kyūka kansetsu* ball-and-socket joint
15 戯 *kyūgi* billiards
審 *kyūshin* baseball umpire

A **理** 3644 / J4d7d / M21014 Ri reason, justice, truth, principle. *kotowari* reason.

4 不尽 *rifujin na* unreasonable, unfair, absurd
化学 *rikagaku* physics and chemistry
5 由 *riyū* reason, cause; pretext, excuse; consideration, motive
外 *rigai no* supernatural; transcendental
6 合 *ria(i)* reason
会 *rikai* understanding
8 非 *rihi* relative, merits. *ri(ga)hi(demo)* no matter what happens
屈 *rikutsu* theory; reason, logic; argument; pretext. *rikutsu(ppoi)* argumentative
法 *rihō* law
念 *rinen* idea; ideology
性 *risei* reason, reasoning power
性的 *riseiteki* reasonable
知 *richi* intellect, intelligence
知的 *richiteki* intellectual
事 *riji* director, trustee
事会 *rijikai* board of directors; UN Security Council
事長 *rijichō* board chair
事国 *rijikoku* member nation (of the United Nations Security Council)
学 *rigaku* physics, physical sciences
学士 *Rigakushi* Bachelor of Science
学者 *rigakusha* physicist, scientist
学会 *rigakukai, rigakkai* scientific world
学博士 *Rigaku Hakushi* Doctor of Science
学療法士 *rigaku ryōhōshi* physical therapist
9 科 *rika* science
神論 *rishinron* deism
10 財 *rizai* economy, finance
財学 *rizaigaku* political economy
財家 *rizaika* financier, economist
容 *riyō* tonsorial art
容学校 *riyō gakkō* barber school
容師 *riyōshi* barber, hairdresser
容業 *riyōgyō* barber and beauty parlor business
12 博 *Rihaku* Doctor of Science
無 *kotowarina(i)* no reason for it, nothing can be done about it; terrific
智 *richi* intellect, intelligence
智的 *richiteki na* intellectual
13 詰 *rizu(me)* persuasion, reasoning. *ri (ni) tsu(maru)* be pushed to the wall in an argument
義 *rigi* truth
解 *rikai* understanding, comprehension; appreciation
解力 *rikairyoku* comprehension, understanding
路 *riro* reason, argument
路整然 *riro-seizen toshita* logical
窟 *rikutsu* theory; reason, logic; argument; pretext. *rikutsu(ppoi)* argumentative
窟屋 *rikutsuya* argumentative person
窟責 *rikutsuze(me)* stern and unsympathetic criticism
想 *risō* ideal
想化 *risōka* idealization
想主義 *risō shugi* idealism
想的 *risōteki* ideal
想型 *risōgata* ideal type
想郷 *risōkyō* earthly paradise, utopia
想家 *risōka* idealist
14 髪 *rihatsu* haircutting
髪店 *rihatsuten* barbershop
髪師 *rihatsushi* barber, hairdresser
15 論 *riron* theory
論的 *rironteki* theoretical; argumentative

論家 *rironka* theorist
論闘争 *riron tōsō* public debate

A **現** 3645 / J383d / M21004 GEN present, existing, actual. *gen(zu)* reveal; be revealed. *ara(wasu)* show, indicate, display, prove, disclose, express; represent; distinguish oneself. *ara(wareru)* appear, emerge, come in sight, show up; be revealed, be discovered; be mentioned; become famous. *gen ni* actually, really. *utsutsu* reality; reverie; ecstasy, absent-mindedness; vision. *ara(ware)* manifestation, expression. *ara(wa) ni* openly, publicly; frankly, clearly.

2 人神 *arahitogami* the divine present emperor
3 下 *genka* the present time
4 尺 *genshaku* full size
今 *genkon* the present time, today
5 生 *gennama* hard cash
出 *ara(ware)-de(ru)* appear. *genshutsu* appearance, revelation, emergence
用語 *gen'yōgo* living language
世 *gensei, gense, genze, utsu(shi)yo* this present world, this life, this transient world
世的 *genseiteki, genseteki* worldly, secular
世紀 *genseiki* this century
代 *gendai* present age, today, modern times
代人 *gendaijin* moderns
代文 *gendaibun* current style
代化 *gendaika* modernization
代主義 *gendai shugi* modernism
代主義者 *gendai shugisha* modernist
代式 *gendaishiki* modern style
代版 *gendaiban* modern edition
代風 *gendaifū* modern style
代臭 *gendaishū* modernity
代語 *gendaigo* living language, present-day language
代劇 *gendaigeki* modern play
6 米 *gemmai* rice on hand
任 *gennin* present post; incumbent
存 *genson, genzon* living, existing, extant; the Real Presence
有 *gen'yū* existing, present, in actual possession
年度 *gennendo* the present fiscal year
地 *genchi* the actual place. *genchi no* local
地法人 *genchi hōjin* local subsidiary
地調査 *genchi chōsa* on-the-spot investigation
行 *genkō no* present, existing, current, in force, in operation
行犯 *genkōhan* flagrant crime, crime seen by a police officer
行犯人 *genkō hannin* criminal taken in the act
行法 *genkōhō* existing legislation, present law
行訳 *genkōyaku* the translation now in use
在 *genzai* the present time, now; present tense; actually; the Real Presence.
在地 *genzaichi* place where one is now located
在完了 *genzai kanryō* present-perfect tense
在品 *genzaihin* stock on hand
在高 *genzaidaka* amount on hand
在員 *genzaiin* present members
7 身 *genshin, utsu(shi)mi* this mortal body; this present existence. *utsusemi* this mortal body
利 *genri* present profits
兵 *gempei* soldiers at hand
状 *genjō* existing state of affairs, present situation, status quo
状維持 *genjō-iji* preserving the status quo
住 *genjū* present residence; present head priest of a temple
住地 *genjūchi* present address
住所 *genjūsho* present address
役 *gen'eki* active service; commissioned (battleship)
役兵 *gen'ekihei* soldier on active duty
役選手 *gen'eki senshu* active player
8 送 *gensō* sending cash, shipping gold
価 *genka* current price
況 *genkyō* present condition
制 *gensei* present system
官 *genkan* present post
物 *gembutsu* the actual article

5 物取引| *gembutsu torihiki* cash transaction
金 *genkin* cash, specie, money in hand, down payment. *genkin na* mercenary
7 金化 *genkinka* cashing (in), converting to cash, liquidating assets
金出納帳 *genkin suitōchō* cashbook
金出納簿 *genkin suitōbo* cashbook
金主義 *genkin shugi* cash policy, mercenariness
金売買 *genkim-baibai* cash sale
実 *genjitsu* actuality, reality
実化 *genjitsuka* realization, materialization
実主義 *genjitsu shugi* realism
実性 *genjitsusei* possibility of being realized
実的 *genjitsuteki* realistic, materialistic, pragmatic, actual, real
実派 *genjitsuha* realists
実界 *genjitsukai* the real world
実暴露 *genjitsu bakuro* disillusionment
9 神 *aragami* present living deity, the present emperor
前 *genzen* before one's eyes
政府 *genseifu* the present government
品 *gempin* the actual articles, stock on hand
品給与 *gempin kyūyo* wages in kind
10 高 *gendaka* present amount
症 *genshō* present symptoms
俸 *gempō* present salary
員 *gen'in* present members
時 *genji* the present time
時代 *genjidai* the present time
11 務 *gemmu* present business
12 然 *genzen to* plainly, distinctly
象 *genshō* phenomenon, occurrence, appearance
象学 *genshōgaku* phenomenology
場 *gemba, genjō* the scene, the spot. *gemba* the construction site
場不在 *genjō fuzai* absence
場不在証明 *genjō fuzai shōmei* alibi
13 数 *gensū* actual number; effectives
勢 *gensei* present state; present strength
業 *gengyō* outdoor service, field work
業員 *gengyōin* outdoor worker, field worker, operative
14 像 *genzō* developing (a film)
像液 *genzōeki* developing solution
18 職 *genshoku* present position

玄【玉王】瓜瓦甘生用田疋疒癶白皮皿目矛矢石示礻禸禾穴立

8

琳 3646 / J4e56 / M21077 RIN a kind of jewel; blue jewel; ringing sound of gems when struck.

瑛 3647 / J314d / M21127 EI. YŌ jewel's sparkle; a kind of quartz.

琲 3648 / J606a / M21075 HAI string of many pearls.

琶 3649 / J474a / M21081 HA, BE lute.

琢 3650 / J-X / M21058 TAKU polish.
16 磨 *takuma* diligent application

琥 3651 / J6068 / M21061 KO jeweled utensil.
9 珀 *kohaku* amber

琺 3652 / J606b / M21088 HŌ enamel.
13 瑯 *hōrō* enameled ware
瑯質 *hōrōshitsu* (tooth) enamel

琵 3653 / J487c / M21080 BI glissando on strings; a lute.
12 琶 *biwa* lute
琵法師 *biwa hōshi* lute-playing itinerant priest
琵湖 *Biwako* Lake Biwa

B **琴** 3654 / J3657 / M21079 GON. KIN harp. *koto* long horizontal Japanese harp, a koto; lyre. *kinnokoto* a seven-stringed koto.
4 爪 *kotozume* plectrum
6 曲 *kinkyoku* playing on the koto
9 柱 *kotoji* stop, bridge (on musical instruments)
13 瑟 *kinshitsu, kinhitsu* large and small Japanese harp
瑟相和 *kinshitsu aiwa(su)* be happily married

15 線 *kinsen* heartstrings

9

瑇 3655 J-X M21102 See 玳 3627.

瑶 3656 J6076 M-X Nonstandard for 瑤 3666.

瑯 3657 J6067 M21163 **琅** 3639 J6066 M21013 RŌ a jewel.

琿 3658 J606d M21093 KON. GUN used in proper names.

瑙 3659 J606f M21125 NŌ agate, onyx.

瑟 3660 J606e M21133 SHITSU large koto.

瑁 3661 J6070 M21096 MAI ancient Chinese imperial jewels.

瑚 3662 J386a M21126 KO. GO ancestral-offering receptacle.

瑜 3663 J6071 M21129 YU a jewel.

7 伽 *Yuga* Yoga
伽行者 *Yuga gyōsha* a Yogi

瑕 3664 J606c M21120 KA *kizu* flaw; weak point *ara* defect, flaw, blemish.

11 疵 *kashi* flaw, defect, blemish
15 瑾 *kakin* flaw, defect, blemish, stain

瑞 3665 J3f70 M21131 ZUI congratulations.

6 気 *zuiki* good omen
兆 *zuichō* good omen
9 相 *zuisō* good omen
10 祥 *zuishō* good omen
11 鳥 *zuichō* bird of good omen
12 雲 *zuiun* auspicious clouds
13 瑞 *mizumizu(shii)* young and vivacious
夢 *zuimu* auspicious dream
15 穂 *mizuho* young heads of rice
穂国 *Mizuho(no)kuni* Japan, the Land of Abundant Rice

10

瑤 3666 J7424 M21149 YŌ beautiful; jewel-like.

瑳 3667 J3a3c M21170 SA polish.

瑱 3668 J-X M21167 TEN ear decoration.

璃 3669 J4d7e M21196 RI lapis lazuli.

瑩 3670 J6072 M21155 EI. YŌ clear, bright; light; shine. *akira(ka)* clear.

瑪 3671 J6075 M21156 ME agate, onyx.

13 瑙 *menō* agate

瑰 3672 J6073 M21164 KAI strange.

11 偉 *kaii na* brawny, muscular, impressive

瑠 3673 J4e5c M21143 RU lapis lazuli.

14 璃 *ruri* lapis lazuli
璃色 *ruri iro* ultramarine, bright blue

瑣 3674 J6074 M21147 SA small; chain.

5 末 *samatsu na* trivial, trifling
8 事 *saji* a trifle; something petty
11 細 *sasai na* trivial, small, petty
14 瑣 *sasa(taru)* trivial, insignificant; tedious

11

璋 3675 J6078 M21211 SHŌ a jewel; jeweled implement with rounded top and squared bottom.

5 玄 12【玉王】瓜瓦甘生用田疋疒癶白皮皿目矛矢石示ネ内禾穴立

瑾 3676 J6077 M21187 KIN a jewel.

12

瑠 3677 J6065 M21249 See 瑠 3672.

璞 3678 J6079 M21245 HAKU unpolished gem; unadorned. *aratama* unpolished gem.

13

璧 3679 J607a M21269 HEKI. *tama* ball, bowl, sphere, bulb.

B 環 3680 J3444 M-X 環 3681 J-X M21287 KAN ring. *wa* circle, ring, link, wheel, hoop, loop. *tamaki* circle, ring.

7 状 *kanjō* ring, loop, circle
状線 *kanjōsen* loop line, belt line
9 指 *kanshi* ring finger
海 *kankai* surrounding seas. *kankai no seagirt*
11 視 *kanshi* concentrated attention
13 節 *kansetsu* segment (of a worm)
14 境 *kankyō* environment, circumstances
境芸術 *kankyō geijutsu* environmental art
境科学 *kankyō kagaku* environmental science
境倫理 *kankyō rinri* environmental ethics
境悪 *kankyōaku* unfavorable external developments
境権 *kankyōken* environmental right
境難民 *kankyō nammin* environmental refugees
17 礁 *kanshō* atoll

14

瓊 3682 J607b M21328 KEI. GYŌ a jewel; red gemstone.

B 璽 3683 J3c25 M21309 JI emperor's seal.

16

瓏 3684 J607c M21340 RŌ clarity; sound of jewels.

17

瓔 3685 J607d M21347 YŌ, EI jeweled necklace.
10 珞 *yōraku* necklace; hanging temple

RAD. 瓜 97

Uri melon. Nickname: Melon.

瓜 3686 J313b M21371 KA. *uri* melon.
5 田 *kaden* melon patch
8 実顔 *urizanegao* oval face; classic face
10 核顔 *urizanegao* oval face; classic face
6 虫 *tentōmushi* ladybug
18 箪 *hyōtan* gourd, bottle gourd
箪鯰 *hyōtan namazu* slippery fellow

6

瓠 3687 J6121 M21392 KO. *hisago* gourd.

11

瓢 3688 J493b M21419 BYŌ. HYŌ *hisago* gourd.

14

瓣 3689 J6122 M21425 See 弁 1664.

RAD. 瓦 98

Kawara tile. As enclosure: 瓦. Nickname: Tile.

瓦 3690 / J3424 / M21438 GA. *kawara* tile. *guramu* gram.
5 石 *gaseki* tiles and stones; worthless things; rubble; rubbish
6 全 *gazen* mediocre life
8 版 *kawaraban* printing from impressions on baked tiles
9 屋 *kawaraya* tiler; tilemaker
屋根 *kawara yane* tiled roof
10 家 *kawaraya* tile-roofed house
12 焼 *kawaraya(ki)* tilemaking; tilemaker
斯 *gasu* gas
葺 *kawarabuki* tile roofing
落 *gara* stock-market slump
落落 *garao(chi)* stock-market slump; crash
13 解 *gukai* collapse, overthrow, fall, breakdown
18 職 *kawarashoku* tiler; tilemaker
20 礫 *gareki* rubble; rubbish

2

瓧 3691 / J6123 / M21442 （国字） *dekaguramu* decagram, ten grams.

3

瓩 3692 / J6124 / M21450 （国字） *kiroguramu* kilogram, 1000 grams.

4

瓮 3693 / J6125 / M21461 See 甕 3709.

瓲 3694 / J6126 / M21467 （国字） *ton, kiroton* ton, 1000 kilograms.

瓰 3695 / J6127 / M21465 （国字） *deshiguramu* decigram, $\frac{1}{10}$ gram.

瓱 3696 / J6128 / M21466 （国字） *miriguramu* milligram, $\frac{1}{1000}$ gram.

6

瓷 3697 / J612a / M21491 SHI. JI high-quality porcelain.

瓸 3698 / J6129 / M21499 （国字） *hekutoguramu* hectogram, 100 grams.

B **瓶** 3699 / J4953 / M21486 **甁** 3700 / J-X / M21537 HEI, BIN bottle, vial, jar, flask. *kame* jar, jug, vat, urn, vase.
13 詰 *binzume* bottling; canning in jars

8

甁 3700 / J-X / M21537 See 瓶 3699.

9

甄 3701 / J612b / M21557 KEN. SHIN porcelain; implements used in making pottery; decern, discriminate; make clear. *sue* porcelian.

甅 3702 / J612d / M21561 （国字） *senchiguramu* centigram, $\frac{1}{100}$ gram.

甃 3703 / J612c / M21554 SHŪ. *shikigawara* floor tile.
5 石 *shikiishi* paving stone, flagstone, pavement

10

甍 3704 / J6130 / M21587 BŌ. MYŌ. *iraka* roof tile; tiled roof.

11

甎 3705 / J612f / M21589 See 磚 4043.

甑 3706 / J3979 / M-X SŌ *koshiki* pottery rice steamer.

甌 3707/J612e/M21586 Ō. O small bowl; jar, urn; deep cup. *kame* jar, urn, vase, jug.

甕 3709/J6131/M21617 Ō. *kame, mika* jar, jug, vat, urn, vase.

13

甓 3708/J6132/M21609 HEKI. BYAKU *kawara* tile, floor tile.

RAD. 甘 99

Amai sweet. Nickname: Sweet.

B 甘 3710/J3445/M21643 KAN. *ama(eru), ama(ttareru)* presume upon, take advantage of; coax. *ama(nzuru), ama(njiru)* be content with, be resigned to. *ama(yakasu)* pamper, be indulgent, coddle. *ama(i)* sweet; honeyed (words); lenient; half-witted; easy-going; soft, mild; loose; trashy, sentimental. *ama(ttarui)* sugary, sentimental. *uma(i)* delicious, appetizing; skillful, clever, expert; wise; successful; fortunate; splendid; promising. *ama-* sugared, sweet; slightly salted.

3 口 *amakuchi* sweet flavor; mildness; sweet tooth; flattery; stupidity. *umakuchi* clever talking
子 *ama(ttarek)ko* spoiled child
4 心 *kanshin* satisfaction
井 *kansei* excellent well
6 死 *kanshi suru* die happily
7 言 *kangen* flattery, blarney
汞 *kankō* calomel, mercurous chloride
8 雨 *kan'u* refreshing rain
受 *kanju suru* submit to, put up with
苦 *kanku* joys and sorrows, ups and downs
味 *kammi, amami* sweetness, lusciousness
味料 *kammiryō* sweetening ingredients
9 泉 *kansen* spring of excellent water
美 *kambi* sweetness
草 *kanzō* licorice
茶 *amacha* hydrangea tea
海苔 *amanori* purple laver, an edible seaweed
10 酒 *amazake* sweet saké
党 *amatō* person with a sweet tooth
栗 *amaguri* broiled sweet chestnuts
納豆 *amanattō* sweet red-bean candy
12 煮 *amani* sweet cooking
13 塩 *amajio* slightly salted
辞 *kanji* clever speech; flattery
夢 *kammu* pleasant dreams
14 酸 *kansan* sweets and bitters, pains and pleasures
蔗 *kansho, kansha, satōkibi* sugar cane
蔗糖 *kanshotō* cane sugar, sucrose
17 藍 *kanran* cabbage
薯 *kansho* sweet potato
19 藷 *satsuma imo, kansho* sweet potato
21 露 *kanro* nectar, sweetness
露水 *kanrosui* syrup, nectar, sweetened water

4

B 甚 3711/J3f53/M21648 JIN exceedingly. *hanaha(da)* very, greatly, exceedingly. *hanaha(dashii)* extreme, excessive, intense, severe, serious, terrible, tremendous, heavy (damage). *ita(ku)* exceedingly.

3 大 *jindai na* very great, enormous; serious
4 以 *hanaha(da) mot(te)* exceedingly
5 句 *jinku* lively song; lively dance

6

甜 3712/J453c/M21656 甛 3713/J-X/M21655 TEN sweet.

5 瓜 *makuwa uri* muskmelon
11 菜 *tensai, satō daikon* sugar beet
菜糖 *tensaitō* beet sugar

— 8 —

甞 3714 / J6133 / M21659 See 嘗 878.

RAD. 生 100

Umareru to be born. Nickname: Birth.

A 生 3715 / J4038 / M21670 SHŌ, SEI birth; life, existence, living; subsistence; student. *ha(eru)* grow, spring up; cut (teeth). *ha(yasu)* grow, cultivate, wear (a beard). *i(kasu)* revive, resuscitate; restore to life; let live, spare a life; make the most of; give life to; stet. *i(keru)* keep alive; arrange flowers (in a vase); living (adj.). *i(kiru)* live, subsist, exist; be enlivened; stet; be safe (on first). *na(rasu)* cause to bear (fruit). *na(ru)* grow (on a plant), bear (fruit). *na(su)* bear (a child). *o(u)* grow. *shō(jiru), shō(zuru)* produce, yield, create, give rise to, bear, breed; happen, result from. *u(mareru)* be born. *u(mu)* bear, give birth to, breed, spawn; produce, yield (interest). *nama* raw, uncooked, fresh; unripe, half-boiled, rare, hard cash, impertinent, conceited; inexperienced; (beer) on tap; crude (rubber), unprocessed. *i(ki)* living; freshness; stetting. *u(mare)* birth, origin, lineage; birthplace. *u(mi)* childbirth, bearing a child. *-fu* grassy place; woods. *ki-* pure, undiluted, genuine; raw, crude.

1 一本 *kiippon no* pure, unadulterated; simple, honest
2 人形 *i(ki) ningyō* lifelike doll, living doll
3 子 *namako* ore, bullion, pig, corrugated sheet iron. *u(mino)ko* a mother's own child. *na(sanu)ko* stepchild; adopted child
干 *namabi, namabo(shi)* half-dried
上 *o(i)-nobo(ru), ha(e)-a(garu), o(i)-a(garu)* grow
4 方 *i(ki)kata* way of life, how to live
水 *nama mizu* unboiled water
火 *i(ke)bi* banked fire
爪 *namazume* the quick (of the fingernails)
仏 *i(ki)botoke* a living Buddha; an incarnation of Buddha; a virtuous priest
欠伸 *nama akubi* slight yawn
化学 *seikagaku* biochemistry
木 *nama ki* a living tree; unseasoned wood
木綿 *kimomen* unbleached cotton cloth
5 母 *seibo* one's real mother
生 *seisei* lively, vividly. *namanama(shii)* green, raw, fresh; unripe; still warm (game birds, etc.); reeking (of blood). *i(ki)i(ki) toshita* lively, vivid, graphic
白 *namajiro(i), namatchiro(i)* pale, wan
皮 *kigawa, nama kawa* raw hides, pelts
目 *i(ki)me* hope of living
付 *u(mare)-tsu(ku)* be endowed with. *u(mi)-tsu(keru)* give birth to, lay, deposit, spawn. *u(maremo)tsu(kanu)* not congenital. *u(mare)tsu(ki)* nature, character, disposition; by nature, naturally
写 *i(ki)utsu(shi), shōutsu(shi)* close resemblance
台 *u(mi)dai* birthstool
乍 *i(ki)naga(ra)* alive. *u(mare)naga(ra)* by nature, naturally
出 *u(mi)-da(su)* bring forth, yield, produce; give birth to. *u(mi)-de(ru)* be born. *ha(e)-de(ru)* sprout, come up. *u(mare)-de(ru)* be born. *o(i)-ide(ru)* grow up
民 *seimin* the people, subjects
半可 *namahanka na* superficial, half-baked
石灰 *seisekkai* quicklime
甲斐 *i(ki)gai* (something) worth living (for)
立 *u(mi)ta(te)* newly laid, fresh (eggs).

uma(re)-ta(te) newborn. *oita(chi)* early days, childhood; antecedents; personal history, growing up

立地 *oita(chi) (no) chi* birthplace

6 米 *namagome* uncooked rice

糸 *kiito* raw silk thread

肉 *seiniku* fresh meat

色 *seishoku* animated look, energetic appearance

血 *ikichi* lifeblood

行 *o(i)-yu(ku)* grow gradually

成 *seisei* creation, formation, generation

気 *seiki* animation, life, spirit, vitality

仲 *na(sanu)naka* no blood relationship

先 *o(i)saki* future career, remaining years

字引 *i(ki) jibiki* walking dictionary, living dictionary

如来 *i(ki) nyorai* living Buddha

地 *seichi* birthplace. *kiji* one's true colors; ground; body (of porcelain); cloth, suiting

地獄 *i(ki) jigoku* hell on earth, living hell

合 *u(mare)-a(waseru)* be born at the same time

合点 *namagaten* premature judgment, hasty conclusion

年 *u(mare)doshi, seinen* year of birth; age. *shōnen* the years of one's life, age.

年月日 *seinengappi* date of birth

死 *seishi, i(ki)shi(ni), shōshi, shōji* life or death, life and death

死問題 *seishi mondai* life-and-death matter

死統計 *seishi tōkei* vital statistics

返 *i(ki)-kae(rasu)* revive, resuscitate; bring to life. *i(ki)-kae(ru)* revive, be resuscitated, come to life

返事 *nama henji* vague answer

返辞 *nama henji* vague answer

存 *i(ki)-naga(raeru)* live on, enjoy longevity; survive (a disaster); outlive (someone). *seizon* existence, being, life, survival

存中 *seizonchū* during one's lifetime

存者 *seizonsha* survivor

存権 *seizonken* right to live

存競争 *seizon kyōsō* struggle for existence

7 身 *i(ki)mi, namami* living flesh, flesh and blood, the quick; raw meat, raw fish

抜 *ha(e)nu(ki)* native-born

肝 *i(ki)gimo* liver of a living animal

別 *i(ki)waka(re), seibetsu* lifelong separation

更 *o(i)-kawa(ru)* change as one gets older

花 *i(ke)bana* flower arrangement. *seika* flower arrangement; natural flower

良 *iki (no) i(i)* lively, fresh

来 *shōrai no, seirai no* natural, innate, inborn. *seirai* by nature, naturally, by birth

呑込 *namanomiko(mi)* incomplete understanding

兵法 *nama byōhō* crude tactics; smattering of knowledge

体 *seitai* living body

体学 *seitaigaku* somatology

体解剖 *seitai kaibō* vivisection

8 長 *i(ki)-naga(raeru)* live on, enjoy longevity; survive (a disaster); outlive (someone). *seichō* growth (usually of plant)

国 *shōkoku, shōgoku* one's native country or province

延 *i(ki)-no(biru)* live long, outlive (someone), survive (a disaster)

拡 *i(ki)-hiro(garu)* grow luxuriantly

限 *i(kiru) kagi(ri)* as long as life continues

育 *ha(e)-soda(tsu)* (flowers) spring up. *seiiku* growth, development; birth and breeding

直 *kisugu na* gentle and straightforward

易 *namayasa(shii)* easy, simple

若 *namawaka(i)* young, green

苦 *u(mi) (no) kuru(shimi)* birth pangs, travail

茂 *o(i)-shi(geru)* grow luxuriantly

者 *shōja* living beings. *seisha* living person

味噌 *nama miso* uncooked bean paste

学者 *nama gakusha* dilettante, smatterer

学問 *nama gakumon* superficial knowledge

命 *seimei* life; soul

命工学 *seimei kōgaku* biotechnology

命保険 *seimei hoken* life insurance

命科学 *seimei kagaku* bioscience

命線 *seimeisen* lifeline

物 *i(ki)mono, seibutsu* living creature, life. *na(ri)mono* farm products.

namamono uncooked food, raw fish, unbaked pastry
物地理学 *seibutsu chirigaku* biological geography
物学 *seibutsugaku* biology
物物理学 *seibutsu butsurigaku* biophysics
物界 *seibutsukai* plants and animals, animate creation, life
物兵器 *seibutsu heiki* biological weapon
物指標 *seibutsu shihyō* biological indicator
物時計 *seibutsu dokei* biological clock
9 面 *seimen* new field; first meeting
首 *nama kubi* freshly-severed head
保 *seiho* life insurance
垣 *i(ke)gaki* hedge
後 *seigo* after birth
枯 *namaga(re)* not quite dead (vegetation)
胆 *i(ki)gimo* liver of a living animal
変 *ha(e)-ka(waru)* grow up in place of previous vegetation; molt. *u(mare)-ka(waru)* be born again; be regenerated; transmigrate, be reincarnated; start life anew. *u(mare)ka(wari)* new birth; rebirth, transmigration, incarnation, reincarnation
前 *seizen* during one's lifetime; lifetime
茹 *namayu(de)* half-boiled
故郷 *u(mare) kokyō* birthplace, ancestral home
神 *i(ki)gami* a god in human form, a living god
神様 *i(ki)gamisama* a god in human form, a living god
計 *seikei* livelihood, living
計費 *seikeihi* living expenses
臭 *namagusa(i)* smelling of fish; bloody
臭坊主 *namagusa bōzu* corrupt or worldly priest
臭物 *namagusamono* raw things (like fish and meat)
活 *seikatsu* life, livelihood
活力 *seikatsuryoku* vitality, resourcefulness
活水準 *seikatsu suijun* standard of living
活史 *seikatsushi* life history (in biology)
活必需品 *seikatsu hitsujuhin* necessities
活困窮者 *seikatsu konkyūsha* needy person
活改善 *seikatsu kaizen* improvement of living conditions
活法 *seikatsuhō* way of life
活苦 *seikatsuku* hard life, economic distress
活物資 *seikatsu busshi* necessities
活科学 *seikatsu kagaku* domestic science
活給 *seikatsukyū* living wage, subsistence pay
活費 *seikatsuhi* living expenses
活賃金 *seikatsu chingin* living wage, subsistence pay
活戦線 *seikatsu sensen* battle of life
活様式 *seikatsu yōshiki* mode of living
活難 *seikatsunan* hard life, economic distress
10 馬 *i(ki)uma* living horse; shrewd fellow
起 *seiki* occurrence of phenomena
埋 *i(ki)u(me)* burying alive
娘 *kimusume* maiden, virgin, innocent girl
徒 *seito* student, pupil
捕 *i(ke)do(ru)* capture alive
酒 *kizake* pure saké
粋 *kissui* purity
紙 *kigami* unsized paper
恥 *i(ki)haji* living in dishonor, lifelong shame
家 *seika* the house of one's birth
害 *shōgai* suicide
素性 *uma(re)sujō* circumstances of birth
真面目 *kimajime* too serious; a person who is too serious; honesty, sincerity
残 *i(ki)-noko(ru)* survive, outlive. *i(ki)noko(ri), seizon* survival
残者 *seizansha, i(ki)noko(ri)mono* survivor
殺 *seisatsu* life and death. *namagoro(shi) suru* half-kill; keep in suspense; leave unfinished
殺与奪 *seisatsu-yodatsu* killing and letting live; giving and taking away
息 *seisoku suru* live, subsist; multiply
息子 *kimusuko* unsophisticated young man
11 魚 *namazakana, seigyo, nama uo* raw fish, fresh fish, live fish
麻 *kiasa* raw hemp

唾 *nama tsuba* sour spittle
得 *seitoku, shōtoku* nature; naturally; capturing alive. *shōtoku no* natural, inborn, inherent, congenital
涯 *shōgai* life, career, lifetime; for life
渋 *kishibu* puckery persimmon juice
酔 *namaei, namayo(i)* half-drunk
動 *seidō* being full of life
彩 *seisai* beautiful light, luster
菜 *namana* salad
乾 *namakawa(ki)* not fully dry
菓子 *namagashi* unbaked cakes
菩薩 *i(ki) bosatsu* living Buddha; a great person
理 *seiri* physiology, menstruation
理休暇 *seiri kyūka* a special menstrual leave for women
理学 *seirigaku* physiology
理的 *seiriteki* physiological
理的食塩水 *seiriteki shokuensui* saline solution
理的現象 *seiriteki genshō* a physiological phenomenon
理衛生 *seiri-eisei* physiology and hygiene
産 *seisan* production
産力 *seisanryoku* productive capacity, productivity
産手段 *seisan shudan* means of production
産地 *seisanchi* producing area
産年度 *seisan nendo* production year
産物 *seisambutsu* produce, product
産者 *seisansha* producer
産高 *seisandaka* yield, production, output
産財 *seisanzai* producer's goods
産過剰 *seisan kajō* overproduction
産費 *seisanhi* production cost
産機関 *seisan kikan* means of production
産額 *seisangaku* amount of production
12 揚 *namaa(ge)* fried tofu
検 *seiken* biopsy
温 *namanuru(i)* lukewarm; half-hearted; mild
焼 *namaya(ke), namaya(ki)* (food) not thoroughly cooked. *namaya(ki)* poorly tempered sword
硬 *seikō* crudeness, immaturity
落 *u(mare)o(chiru)* be born. *u(mi)-o(tosu)* give birth to (animals)
替 *ha(e)-ka(waru)* grow up in place of. *haekawa(ri)* second dentition
煮 *namani(e)* half-cooked, rare; vague
覚 *namaobo(e)* smattering
証文 *i(ki)jōmon* living witness
殖 *seishoku* reproduction, procreation, generation
殖不能 *seishoku funō* impotence
殖器 *seishokki* reproductive organs
殖器崇拝 *seishokki sūhai* phallicism, phallic worship
13 傷 *nama kizu* sore, unhealed wound
損 *u(mi)-sokona(u), u(mi)-soko(neru)* miscarry. *u(mare)-sokona(i)* an unfortunate birth; a good-for-nothing
暖 *namaatataka(i)* lukewarm
滅 *shōmetsu* birth and death; appearance and disappearance
猿 *kizaru* wild monkey
絹 *kiginu* raw silk cloth
腥 *namagusa(i)* smelling of fish; bloody
際 *ha(e)giwa* the hairline
新 *namaatara(shii)* brand new
節 *namabushi, namaribushi* half-dried bonito
業 *seigyō, sugiwai, nariwai* occupation, calling, living, livelihood
意気 *namaiki* conceit, impertinence
14 聞 *namagi(ki)* smattering of knowledge
憎 *ainiku, ayaniku* unfortunately, unluckily; too bad, a pity
様 *o(i)zama* condition of growing plants
餌 *i(ki)e, namae* live bait, raw bait
態 *seitai* mode of life, ecology
態系 *seitaikei* ecosystem
態学 *seitaigaku* ecology
15 誕 *seitan* birth, nativity
麩 *shōfu* wheat starch
麺 *seimen* raw noodles
蕃 *seiban* aborigines, wild tribesmen
霊 *i(ki)ryō* apparition of a living person. *seirei* life; people; the public
熟 *seijuku* ripeness, maturity
蕎麦 *kisoba* buckwheat noodles
還 *seikan* returning alive; scoring a run
還者 *seikansha* survivor
16 獲 *seikaku* capturing alive
親 *u(mi) (no) oya* one's real parent; originator, creator
薑 *shōga* ginger
壁 *nama kabe* undried wall

薬 *i(ki)gusuri* the elixir of youth. *kigusuri* a natural drug
薬屋 *kigusuriya* drugstore, apothecary
17 優 *o(i)-masa(ru)* grow older and more beautiful
簀 *i(ke)su* (restaurant) fish tank
鮮 *seisen na* fresh
鮮果物 *seisen kabutsu* perishable foods
18 噛 *namaka(jiri)* superficial knowledge
類 *shorui, seirui* living creatures
顔 *i(ki)gao* the face of a living person
繭 *nama mayu* raw cocoon
贄 *i(ke)nie* (animal) sacrifice
醤油 *kijōyu* raw *shoyu*, raw soy
織物 *kiorimono* raw silk
21 蠟 *kirō* crude wax

6

A 産 3716 J3b3a M21684′ 產 3717 J-X M21684 SAN childbirth; product; native (of a place); fortune, property *san(suru) vi* and *vt* produce, yield, bring up, bear (a child); appear; be born; be brought up. *u(mu)* bear, give birth to, breed, spawn; produce, yield (interest). *u(mareru)* be born. *u(mi)* childbirth, bearing a child.

3 土 *ubusuna* tutelary deity, guardian god
土神 *ubusunagami* tutelary deity, guardian god
4 月 *u(mi)zuki* last month of pregnancy
毛 *ubuge* downy, hairy; down, fluff, pin feathers
5 出 *sanshutsu* output, yield, production
出物 *sanshutsubutsu* product, production, produce; result
出高 *sanshutsudaka* output, yield, production
6 米 *sammai* the rice production
衣 *san'i, ubugi, ubuginu* clothes for a newborn baby
地 *sanchi* producing area
気 *sanke, san(no)ke* labor pains
気付 *sankezu(ki)* premonition of labor pains
7 別 *sambetsu* industrial union
声 *ubugoe* baby's first cry
児 *sanji* newborn baby; the baby about to be born
児制限 *sanji seigen* birth control
卵 *sanran* egg-laying, spawning
卵期 *sanranki* breeding season, spawning season
8 物 *sambutsu* product, production, produce; result
具 *sangu* obstetrical supplies
金 *sankin* gold mining
金地 *sankinchi* gold-producing area
金地帯 *sankin chitai* gold field
金高 *sankindaka* gold output
金業 *sankingyō* gold mining industry
金熱 *sankin netsu* gold rush
9 屋 *ubuya* maternity room
後 *sango* after childbirth
院 *san'in* maternity hospital
室 *sanshitsu* maternity ward, delivery room
前 *sanzen* before delivery (of the baby)
前産後 *sanzen-sango* before and after childbirth
科 *sanka* obstetrics
科医 *sankai* obstetrician
科学 *sankagaku* obstetrics
科病院 *sanka byōin* maternity hospital
10 馬 *samba* horse breeding
破 *san (o) yabu(ru)* use up all one's property
11 婦 *sampu* woman in childbirth
婦人科 *sanfujinka* obstetrics and gynecology
婆 *samba* midwife
婆役 *sambayaku* sponsor
12 殖 *sanshoku* breeding, propagation
湯 *ubuyu* baby's first bath
落 *u(mi) oto(su)* give birth to
13 傾 *san (o) katamu(keru)* use up all one's property
業 *sangyō* industry
業人 *sangyōjin* industrialist
業立国 *sangyō-rikkoku* national economy based on industry
業合理化 *sangyō gōrika* well-regulated industry
業住宅 *sangyō jūtaku* industrial worker's housing
業国 *sangyōkoku* industrial nation
業国営 *sangyō kokuei* nationalization of industry
業界 *sangyōkai* industrial world
業革命 *Sangyō Kakumei* the Industrial Revolution
業婦人 *sangyō fujin* women in industry
業組合 *sangyō kumiai* industrial guild, industrial association

業転換 *sangyō tenkan* industrial conversion
15 褥 *sanjoku* confinement; labor bed
褥期 *sanjokuki* lying-in period
褥熱 *sanjoku netsu* puerperal fever
16 親 *u(mi) (no) oya* one's true parent
18 額 *sangaku* production, yield, output

7

甦 3718 J6134 M21691 甦 3720 J-X M-X So. Su *yomigae(ru)* be resurrected, be revived, be resuscitated, be rehabilitated.
5 生 *sosei* rebirth; resuscitation; rehabilitation, reorganization, regeneration

甥 3719 J3179 M21689 Sei. Sō. *oi* nephew.
12 御 *oigo* nephew (polite)

9

甦 3720 J-X M-X See 甦 3718.

RAD. 用 101

Mochiiru to use. Nickname: Using.

A 用 3721 J4d51 M21703 Yō business, work; function; errand; engagement; use, service; expenses; call of nature. *yō(zuru), mochi(iru)* use; adopt (a method); employ. *-yō* for, used for.
2 人 *yōnin* steward, factotum
4 方 *mochi(i)kata* directions, way to use
不用 *yōfuyō* needed or not; useful or not
心 *yōjin* care, caution, discretion
心深 *yōjimbuka(i)* careful, thoughtful, cautious, scrupulous, alert
心棒 *yōjimbō* cudgel; bodyguard, protector
水 *yōsui* city water; water for fire; irrigation water; cistern water
水池 *yōsuichi, yōsui ike* reservoir
水桶 *yōsui oke* water barrel
水路 *yōsuiro* flume; water system
水権 *yōsuiken* water rights
5 弁 *yōben* errand, business
立 *yōda(teru)* lend, advance (money). *yōda(te)* accommodation (in business). *yō (ni) ta(tsu)* be useful
立金 *yōda(te)kin* a loan, an advance
6 向 *yōmu(ki)* business, errand, commission
件 *yōken* business, matter, items
地 *yōchi* required land, reservation, lot, site
字 *yōji* the use of the characters
7 言 *yōgen* declinable word
足 *yōta(shi)* performing an errand; taking care of nature's call
役 *yōeki* service
兵 *yōhei* tactics, troop manipulation
材 *yōzai* materials; lumber, timber
材林 *yōzairin* timber forest
8 金 *yōkin* money wanted, extraordinary levy; public money
例 *yōrei* example, illustration
所 *mochi(i)dokoro* use
法 *yōhō* directions, how to use
命 *yōmei* command, order, request
事 *yōji* errand, business, appointment
具 *yōgu* tool, instrument; machinery; apparatus; utensils; appliances; (sporting) goods; (teaching) aids
具類 *yōgurui* furnishings
9 度 *yōdo* expenses; supplies
途 *yōto* use, service
品 *yōhin* supplies
便 *yōben* defecation
便後 *yōbengo* after stool
10 紙 *yōshi* blank form; stationery, writing paper
益権 *yōekiken* usufruct
11 達 *yōtashi* transactions of business, running errands; purveyor
捨 *yōsha* forgiveness, hesitation
済 *yōzu(mi)* business finished, affairs settled
船 *yōsen* chartered ship
務 *yōmu* business, cares, routine
務員 *yōmuin* clerks

12 量 *yōryō* dosage, dose
筆 *yōhitsu* use of a brush
無 *yōna(shi) no* idle, leisurely, useless
13 意 *yōi* preparation, arrangement
意周到 *yōi-shūtō* prudence, cautiousness, thorough preparation
14 聞 *yōki(ki)* taking orders
箋 *yōsen* form, blank, stationery, writing pad
語 *yōgo* term, terminology, vocabulary, diction
語例 *yōgorei* examples of word use
語索引 *yōgo sakuin* (Bible) concordance
語解 *yōgokai* glossary
語癖 *yōgoheki* one's idiom
15 談 *yōdan* business talk
器 *yōki* tool, instrument; chamber pot; using tools
器画 *yōkiga* mechanical drawing
18 簞笥 *yōdansu* chest of drawers

2

甫 3722 / J4a63 / M21706 Ho. Fu. *haji(mete)* for the first time; not until.

甬 3723 / J6135 / M21707 Yō. Yu road; road on palace grounds.
11 道 *yōdō* road bordered by high walls; road on palace grounds

田 RAD. 102

Ta rice paddy. At left: *ta hen.* Nickname: Rice Field.

A **由** 3724 / J4d33 / M21724 Yū, Yu. *yo(ru)* depend on. *yoshi* reason, cause, significance; means, way; effect; point; intent. *yo(tte)* therefore, consequently.
5 由 *yuyu(shii)* grave, serious, alarming
7 来 *yurai suru* derive from, originate in. *yurai* reason; origin, destiny; history; derivation, source; originally, naturally
来書 *yuraisho* history, memoirs
12 無事 *yoshina(shi)goto* trivial thing, nonsense
11 緒 *yuisho* history, lineage
15 縁 *yuen* acquaintance; relation; affinity; reason

B **甲** 3725 / J3943 / M21725 Kan high (voice). Kō A, first class; former; back (of the hand); instep; armor; shell, tortoise shell, carapace. *kōra* shell (of turtle or crab). *yoroi* suit of armor. *kinoe* first calendar sign.
1 乙 *kōotsu* A and B, excellent and good; discrimination
5 巡 *kōjun* heavy cruiser
6 虫 *kōchū, kabutomushi* a beetle
7 兵 *kōhei* arms; war; armed warrior
状腺 *kōjōsen* thyroid gland
8 所 *kandokoro* finger board (of a musical instrument); vital point
卒 *kōsotsu* armored warrior
夜 *kōya* 8 p.m.
板 *kampan* deck
板渡 *kampan watashi* free on board, F.O.B
9 冑 *katchū, kōchū* armor and helmet
10 高 *kōdaka na* high-backed; high in the instep. *kandaka(i)* shrill, high-pitched
11 掛 *kōga(ke)* gauntlet; spats
殻 *kōkaku* carapace, shell, crust
12 鈑 *kōhan* steel plates
斐 *kai* effect, result; use, avail, worth
斐甲斐 *kaigai(shii)* gallant, heroic, brave
斐性 *kaishō* resourcefulness, ability
斐無 *kaina(shi)* worthless, useless, hopeless
13 鉄 *kōtetsu* armor plate
鉄板 *kōtetsuban* armor plate
鉄艦 *kōtetsukan* armored ship
14 種 *kōshu* grade A, first grade
15 論乙駁 *kōron-otsubaku* pros and cons
19 羅 *kōra* shell, carapace

A **申** 3726 / J3f3d / M21726 Shin. *mō(su)* have the honor to; say, tell, talk, speak, declare; call, term, name. *saru* 3–5 p.m; ninth zodiac sign; monkey.
2 入 *mō(shi)-i(reru)* propose, suggest. *mō(shi)i(re)* proposal, offer; notice, report

[3]子 *mō(shi)go* a heaven-sent child (in answer to a Shinto or Buddhist prayer)
上 *mō(shi)-a(geru)* say, tell, state (humble)
[4]分 *mō(shi)bun* objection; shortcomings
込 *mō(shi)-ko(mu)* propose (marriage); offer (mediation); make an overture (of peace); challenge; lodge (objections); request (an interview); apply for (a job); subscribe for; book, reserve. *mōshiko(mi)* proposal, offer, overture; challenge
込書 *mōshikomisho* application blank; written application
込順 *mōshiko(mi)jun* order of applications
[5]立 *mō(shi)ta(teru)* declare; plead
付 *mō(shi)-tsu(keru)* order, instruct
出 *mō(shi)-de(ru)* report to, tell; suggest, submit; request. *mō(shi)-i(de), mōshide* proposal; request, claim; report, notice
[6]合 *mō(shi)-a(waseru)* arrange; appoint; agree upon
[7]述 *mō(shi)-no(beru)* say, tell, state
告 *shinkoku* report, statement, notification; filing a return
告箱 *shinkokubako* suggestion box
[8]送 *mō(shi)-oku(ru)* write to; send word to; hand over (official business)
受 *mō(shi)-u(keru)* accept; ask for; charge (a price)
命記 *Shimmeiki* Deuteronomy
[10]兼 *mō(shi)-ka(neru)* I'm sorry to trouble you.
[11]遅 *mō(shi)-oku(reru)* be slow in saying
添 *mō(shi)-so(eru)* add to what has been said.
訳 *mō(shi)wake* excuse, apology
[12]越 *mō(shi)-ko(su)* send word to, write to
遣 *mō(shi)-tsuka(wasu)* write to; send word to; hand over (official business)
開 *mō(shi)-hira(ku)* explain, justify
渡 *mō(shi)-wata(su)* tell, announce, declare, order
[14]聞 *mō(shi)-ki(kaseru)* tell, talk to
様 *mō(shi)yō* words, expression
[15]請 *shinsei* application, petition
請書 *shinseisho* written application
[18]難 *mō(shi)-niku(i)* I'm sorry to trouble you.

A 田 3727 / J4544 / M21723 DEN *ta* rice field, paddy field.

[3]子 *tago* peasant, rustic
[4]井 *tai* rice-field well
五作 *tagosaku* peasant, rustic
夫 *dempu* peasant
夫野人 *dempu-yajin* rustic, boor
[5]打 *tau(chi)* rice-field tilling
[6]舟 *tabune* small flat-bottomed boat
虫 *tamushi* ringworm
地 *denchi, denji* land, farm, rice fields
毎月 *tagoto (no) tsuki* moon reflected in many paddy fields
[7]作 *tazuku(ri)* rice-field tilling
吾作 *tagosaku* peasant, rustic
[8]舎 *inaka* the country, the provinces, rural areas. *inaka(meku)* wear a rustic air
舎人 *inakajin, inakabito* a person from the country
舎大尽 *inaka daijin* provincial millionaire
舎生 *inakau(mare)* country-born
舎弁 *inakaben* provincial dialect
舎出 *inakade* from the country
舎回 *inakamawa(ri)* provincial tour
舎気質 *inaka katagi, inaka kishitsu* rusticity, provincialism
舎住 *inakazuma(i)* country life
舎侍 *inakazamurai* boorish samurai
舎育 *inakasoda(chi)* country-bred
舎者 *inakamono* a rustic
舎風 *inakafū* rustic manners, country style
舎臭 *inakakusa(i)* rustic, countrified
舎染 *inakajimi(ru)* wear a rustic air
舎家 *inakaya* rural cottage
[9]面 *tazura* surface of the rice field
畑 *tahata, dempata, tahatake* fields and rice paddies
草 *tagusa* rice-field weeds
[10]圃 *tambo* rice field
租 *denso* rice-field tax
家 *denka* rural cottage, the country
畠 *dempata, tahatake* fields and rice paddies
[11]野 *den'ya* cultivated fields
紳 *denshin* country gentleman
[12]植 *taue* rice transplanting
植歌 *taue uta* rice-planting song
[13]鼠 *tanezumi* field rat
楽 *dengaku* ancient music and dancing; tofu baked with miso

園 *den'en* fields and gardens; rural districts
園都市 *den'en toshi* garden city; suburbs
園詩 *den'en shi* pastoral poem
園詩人 *den'en shijin* pastoral poet
[16] 鴫 *tashigi* snipe
[17] 螺 *tanishi* fresh-water snail

2

甸 3728 / J5231 / M21732 TEN. DEN area surrounding the imperial capital.

A **町** 3729 / J442e / M21735 **甼** 3730 / J6136 / M-X CHŌ town; block; street; 2.45 acres; 119 yards. *machi* town; quarters; street.
[2] 人 *chōnin* merchant
人町 *chōnimmachi* the merchants' district
[4] 内 *chōnai* in the town; in the block; the neighborhood
中 *machijū* throughout the town, the whole town. *machinaka de* on the streets
[5] 立 *chōritsu* established by the town
外 *machihazu(re)* outskirts
民 *chōmin* townspeople
[6] 会 *chōkai* town council, town-block association
名 *chōmei* town name, block name, street name
[7] 角 *machikado* street corner
住 *machizuma(i)* town or city life
町 *machimachi* towns, cities
役場 *machi yakuba* town office
医 *machii* the local doctor
医者 *machi isha* practicing physician
村 *chōson* towns and villages
村会 *chōsonkai* town and village assemblies
村長 *chōsonchō* town and village mayors
村制 *chōsonsei* municipal organizations
[8] 長 *chōchō* town mayor
制 *chōsei* town organization
育 *machisoda(chi)* brought up in a town
並 *machina(mi)* row of houses along the street
歩 *chōbu* hectare (2.45 acres)
[9] 政 *chōsei* town government
[10] 家 *chōka* town house, merchant's house
[11] 道場 *machi dōjō* small town temple; small martial-arts institute
[12] 税 *chōzei* town tax
筋 *machisuji* street
費 *chōhi* town expenses
[13] 続 *machitsuzu(ki)* continuation of the town
[20] 議 *chōgi* town councilmember

A **男** 3731 / J434b / M21730 DAN baron; man, male. NAN counter for sons. *otoko, onoko* man, male; fellow; adult; manhood; male servant; paramour. *otoko(rashii)* manly, manful. *otoko(datera) ni* unmanly.
[1] 一匹 *otoko-ippiki* a full-grown man
[3] 工 *dankō* male worker
子 *danshi* man, male, boy, son. *o(no)ko, otoko (no) ko* boy, boy baby, son
子用 *danshiyō* for men
女 *danjo, nannyo* men and women, both sexes. *otoko-onna* hermaphrodite
女共学 *danjo kyōgaku* coeducation
女合唱 *danjo gasshō* mixed chorus
女同権 *danjo dōken* equality of the sexes
女組 *danjogumi* coeducational class
[4] 心 *otokogokoro* a man's heart
手 *otokode* man's hand; man's strength; Chinese characters
木 *ogi* tenon
文字 *otoko moji* male handwriting; Chinese characters
[5] 生 *dansei* male student
立 *otokodate* one who champions the underdog
囚 *danshū* male prisoner
世帯 *otokojotai* household of men
[6] 色 *danshoku, nanshoku, okama* sodomy, male homosexual
気 *otokogi* chivalry, manhood, gallantry. *otoko(k)ke* a male, a man
向 *otokomu(ki)* for men
好 *otokozu(ki)* men's favorite; amorous woman
同士 *otokodōshi* men companions
伊達 *otokodate* one who champions the underdog
[7] 体 *nantai* a man's body
坂 *otokozaka* the steeper slope

5

玄玉王瓜瓦甘生用 3【田】疋疒癶白皮皿目矛矢石示ネ内禾穴立

狂 *otokoguru(i)* wantonness, running after men
系 *dankei* male line, father's side
声 *dansei* male voice
旱 *otoko hideri* dearth of men
児 *danji* boy, son
芸者 *otoko geisha* male entertainer; professional jester
8 松 *otoko matsu* black (male) pine
泣 *otokona(ki)* unmanly weeping
波 *onami* advancing wave
物 *otokomono* men's wear
妾 *otoko mekake* paramour
所帯 *otokojotai* household of men
性 *dansei* male, male sex; masculinity, manliness
性的 *danseiteki* manly
性美 *danseibi* masculine beauty
9 持 *otokomo(chi)* for gentlemen
神 *ogami, o(no)kami* male god
前 *otokomae* man's looks; good bearing
10 振 *otoko(p)pu(ri), otokobu(ri)* a man's bearing
殺 *otokokoro(shi), otokogoro(shi)* vampire, unscrupulous flirt
帯 *otoko obi* man's belt
根 *dankon, nankon* penis; phallus
根崇拝 *dankon sūhai* phallicism
冥加 *otoko myōga* blessing of being a man
冥利 *otoko myōri* the advantage of being a man
11 達 *otokotachi* men. *otokodate* one who champions the underdog
娼 *danshō* male prostitute
盛 *otokozaka(ri), osaka(ri)* prime of manhood
12 湯 *otokoyu* men's bath
勝 *otokomasa(ri)* spirited, strong-minded
衆 *otokoshū* manservant
装 *dansō* male attire
尊女卑 *danson-johi* subjection of women
13 嫌 *otokogira(i)* manhater
滝 *odaki* the greater of two waterfalls
節句 *Otoko (no) Sekku* Boy's Festival (May Fifth)
14 監 *dankan* male prisoners' ward
16 親 *otoko oya* father
17 優 *dan'yū* actor
爵 *danshaku* baron
21 鰥 *otoko yamome* widower

3

甾 3732 / J6137 / M21760 Nonstandard for **留** 3750.

A **画** 3733 / J3268 / M21739′ **画** 3734 / J-X / M21739 **畫** 3759 / J6141 / M21859 **畵** 3764 / J-X / M21877 GA, E picture, drawing, painting, sketch. KAKU stroke (in a character). *kaku(suru)* draw, demarcate, mark, divide, map out. *ega(ku)* draw, paint, sketch, describe.
1 一 *kakuitsu* uniformity, standardization
一主義 *kakuitsu shugi* standardization
2 人 *gajin* painter, artist
3 工 *gakō, edakumi* painter, artist
才 *gasai* artistic talent
4 心 *gashin* artistic instinct
引 *kakubi(ki)* arranged by strokes
5 布 *gafu* canvas for oil painting
本 *gahon* picture copybook
世的 *kakuseiteki* epoch-making
仙紙 *gasenshi* drawing paper
用紙 *gayōshi* drawing paper
6 匠 *gashō* painter, artist
因 *gain* art motif
会 *gakai* artists' patrons' association
7 伯 *gahaku* artist, master painter
8 帖 *gajō* picture album
板 *gaban* drawing board, drafting board
法 *gahō* art of drawing and painting
学 *gagaku* drawing
学紙 *gagakushi* drawing paper
9 面 *gamen* scene, picture, the screen (in TV); photo
風 *gafū* style of painting
室 *gashitsu* art studio
架 *gaka* easel
10 師 *gashi* painter, artist
紙 *gashi* drawing paper
家 *gaka* painter, artist
竜点睛 *garyō-tensei* adding the eyes to the dragon; the finishing touch
11 廊 *garō* picture gallery
道 *gadō* art of painting
帳 *gachō* picture album
商 *gashō* picture dealer
12 幅 *gafuku* picture scroll
筆 *gahitsu* artist's brush
策 *kakusaku suru* plan, scheme, formulate a program, maneuver
然 *kakuzen(taru)* distinct, clear-cut

報 *gahō* illustrated news magazine, pictorial
期的 *kakkiteki* epoch-making
13 楼 *garō* high decorated building
障 *gashō* pictured paper doors
意 *gai* meaning of a picture
聖 *gasei* master painter
14 像 *gazō* portrait, picture
餅 *gahei, gabei* failure, fiasco, collapse; something of little valuc
15 稿 *gakō* sketch
談 *gadan* discussions on art and painting
鋲 *gabyo* thumbtack, drawing pin
賛 *gasan* legend over a picture
16 壇 *gadan* artists' world, painting circles
龍点睛 *garyō-tensei* adding the eyes to the dragon; the finishing touch
18 題 *gadai* subject of a painting, motif, theme
19 譜 *gafu* picture book, picture album
22 讃 *gasan* legend over picture

4

畆 3735 / J613c / M21763 See **畝** 3748.

畊 3736 / J6139 / M21773 See **耕** 4710.

畉 3737 / J613a / M21768 FU, BU *tagaya(su)* plow, cultivate.

畋 3738 / J5a42 / M21774 TEN, DEN prepare a field for planting; hunt.

A **界** 3739 / J3326 / M21775 **畍** 3740 / J6138 / M21776 **堺** 1045 / J3a66 / M5289
KAI circle, world, boundary, limits. *sakai* boundary, border, frontier; place.
11 隈 *kaiwai* neighborhood; district
15 標 *kaihyō* boundary marker

A **畑** 3741 / J482a / M21797 (国字) *hata, hatake* field, farm, plantation, garden; one's specialty.
4 水練 *hatake suiren* learning how to swim on dry land, book learning
5 打 *hatau(chi)* plowing up ground
6 地 *hatachi* farmland
7 作 *hatasaku* upland farming
8 物 *hatakemono, hatamono* products of the field
12 違 *hatakechiga(i)* out of one's line
13 鼠 *hata nezumi* field mouse
14 稲 *hataine* = 陸稲 *okabo* rice grown in a dry field

畏 3742 / J305a / M21778 **[illegible]** 3743 / J-X / M21785 I. *oso(reru)* fear, be overawed, be apprehensive. *kashiko(mu)* fear. *kashiko(maru)* obey respectfully; sit respectfully *kashiko(i)* august, majestic. *kashiko(kumo)* graciously.
4 友 *iyū* honored friend
6 多 *oso(re)ō(i)* gracious, august; awe-inspiring, awful
8 怖 *ifu* awe, fear, fright
服 *ifuku suru* submit from fear
12 敬 *ikei* reverence, awe, respect
17 縮 *ishuku suru* wince, cower, recoil (from), be awestruck, shrink (from a difficulty)
21 懼 *iku* reverence, awe, fear

5

畛 3744 / J613b / M21810 SHIN road between paddies; border, boundary; edge.

畚 3745 / J613d / M21809 **畚** 1158 / J-X / M5931 HON. *mokko* earth-carrying basket *fugo* hamper, bamboo basket.

B **畔** 3746 / J101a / M21801 HAN. *aze, kuro* rice-paddy ridge, levee.

畠 3747 / J482b / M21827 (国字) *hatake, hata* garden, field, farm, plantation.
8 物 *hatamono* field crop

B **畝** 3748 / J4026 / M21815 BŌ. HO ridge, furrow, rib (in cloth). *se* thirty *tsubo*. *une* ridge (in a field), furrow, rib or cord (in cloth). *u(neru)* undulate, meander, surge, swell, roll.
5 立 *uneda(te)* building rice-field ridges
13 溝 *unemizo* furrow ridges

B **畜** 3749 / J435c / M21814 CHIKU domesticated fowl and animals.
4 犬 *chikken* keeping a dog

5 生 *chikushō* beast, brute; angry exclamation of disgust
生道 *chikushōdō* incest
8 肥 *chikuhi* animal fertilizer
舎 *chikusha* barns and poultry sheds
10 殺 *chikusatsu* slaughtering
11 産 *chikusan* animal husbandry
産業者 *chikusangyōsha* rancher, stock-raiser
18 類 *chikurui* domestic animals, livestock

A **留** 3750 / J4e31 / M21808 **畱** 3758 / J-X / M21867 RYŪ. RU. *to(maru)* stop, halt, stand still, pull up; cease, be interrupted, be discontinued; be choked; alight on, perch, roost; be held in position. *to(meru)* stop; check; allay (pain); fasten; turn off; detain; forbid to do; dissuade. *todo(maru)* stop, halt, stay, remain, stay behind; be limited to. *todo(meru)* stop, cease, detain, put an end to; leave; fix; remain in (a certain condition); content oneself with. *to(me)* stopping; prohibition; end; a stop.
3 山 *to(me)yama* mountain preserve
5 処 *to(me)do* termination, end
6 任 *ryūnin* remaining in office
年 *ryūnen suru* (student) stay back a year, be held back a year
年者 *ryūnensha* a student remaining in the same class; a repeater
守 *rusu* absence, being away from home; watching a house; neglecting (responsibilities)
守中 *rusuchū* during one's absence
守宅 *rusutaku* absent master's home
守居 *rusui* caretaker; watching a house
守師団 *rusu shidan* reserve division
守家族 *rusu kazoku* family of an internee
守隊 *rusutai* the force remaining behind
守番 *rusuban* caretaker; watching a house
守番電話 *rusuban denwa* a telephone answering machine
7 別 *ryūbetsu* farewell to those staying on
8 金 *to(me)gane* clasp
学 *ryūgaku* studying abroad
学生 *ryūgakusei* overseas student
学者 *ryūgakusha* a person studying abroad
9 保 *ryūho* reserving, withholding, saving, protection
10 針 *to(me)bari* pin, safety pin; broach; hairpin
11 鳥 *ryūchō* nonmigratory bird
桶 *tomeoke* oval wooden bucket
12 場 *tomeba* fish or forest preserve; usher's quarters
13 意 *ryūi* attention, heed, consideration
置 *to(me)-o(ku)* lock up, detain, retain; leave till called for, quarantine. *ryūchi* detention, custody, retention
置郵便 *tomeoki yūbin* mail left until called for, general delivery
置場 *ryūchijō* house of detention; police cell; guardhouse
置電報 *tomeoki dempō* telegram to be called for
置権 *ryūchiken* lien
15 鋲 *to(me)byō* thumbtack
18 職 *ryūshoku* remaining in one's position

6

畩 3751 / J613e / M-X (国字) *kesa* sash, surplice.

畤 3752 / J613f / M21837 JI, SHI festival grounds.

畦 3753 / J674d / M21842 KEI. *aze* rice-paddy ridge. *une* ridge (in a field), furrow, rib or cord (in cloth).
7 豆 *azemame* soybeans grown on rice-field ridges
11 道 *azemichi* path between rice fields
13 溝 *azemizo* furrow

畢 3754 / J492d / M21829 HITSU. *owa(ru)* end, terminate, adjourn, be over, die, finish, complete. *owa(ri)* end, conclusion, expiration.
5 生 *hissei* lifelong
生作 *hissei (no) saku* one's masterpiece
生業 *hissei (no) gyō* lifework
11 竟 *hikkyō* after all, in short, virtually

A **略** 3755 / J4e2c / M21839 **畧** 3756 / J6140 / M21840 RYAKU abbreviation, abridgment; omission; outline. *ryaku(su), ryaku(suru)* abridge, omit, shorten, abbreviate; capture, seize, plunder. *hobo* almost, nearly.

4 文 *ryakubun* abridged sentence
5 史 *ryakushi* brief history
号 *ryakugō* short address, abbreviated form
6 式 *ryakushiki* informality
伝 *ryakuden* brief biography
字 *ryakuji* simplified characters; abbreviation
名 *ryakumei* initials; initialing
7 言 *ryakugen* brief statement, summary
図 *ryakuzu* outline map; rough plan
述 *ryakujutsu* brief account
体 *ryakutai* short form
8 取 *ryakushu* capture, occupation, plunder
服 *ryakufuku* ordinary dress, informal attire; dishabille
画 *ryakuga* rough sketch
9 則 *ryakusoku* regulations in brief
10 称 *ryakushō* abbreviation; abbreviated name
記 *ryakki* brief account, outline
11 章 *ryakushō* miniature decoration
12 帽 *ryakubō* ordinary cap
筆 *ryakuhitsu* abbreviating characters; shortening sentences
装 *ryakusō* ordinary dress, informal attire; dishabille
13 解 *ryakkai* brief explanation
意 *ryakui* the general meaning, the main reason
14 歴 *ryakureki* brief personal history, brief biography
綬 *ryakuju* miniature decoration
説 *ryakusetsu* brief explanation, outline
語 *ryakugo* abbreviation
奪 *ryakudatsu* pillage, plunder, looting, depredation
奪隊 *ryakudatsutai* raiding party
15 儀 *ryakugi* informality

A **異** 3757 / J305b / M21854 I uncommonness, strangeness, queerness; difference. *i na* strange, wonderful, curious. *koto(naru)* differ, vary; be unusual. *koto (ni) suru* differ, vary.

2 人 *ijin* foreigner; different person
人種 *ijinshu* alien race
3 才 *isai* genius, prodigy
口同音 *ikudōon ni* with one accord, by common consent, unanimously
4 心 *ishin* treachery, intrigue
文 *ibun* variant (reading); strange report, strange tales
日 *ijitsu* another day; a day in the past; a day in the future
火 *kotobi* strange or unsacred fire
父 *ifu* different father
分子 *ibunshi* alien elements, outsider
5 母 *ibo* different mother
本 *ihon* a different edition; another book; a strange book
6 色 *ishoku* different color; novelty
名 *imyō, imei* another name, nickname, alias
存 *izon* objection
同 *idō* difference
同識別 *idō shikibetsu* identification
邦 *ihō* foreign country
邦人 *ihōjin* foreigner, stranger, gentile
7 見 *iken* different opinion; objection
言 *igen* languages, tongues
図 *ito* sinister design, ulterior motive
状 *ijō* something wrong, accident, change, abnormality
形 *igyō na, ikei na* fantastic, grotesque
花受精 *ikajusei* cross-pollinization
体 *itai* different shape or form; a nonstandard character form
体同心 *itai dōshin* perfect accord
8 例 *irei* exception; illness
姓 *isei* a different name
性 *isei* the opposite sex
物 *ibutsu* foreign substance, foreign body
宗 *ishū* different religion or sect
国 *ikoku, kotokuni* foreign country. *ikoku no* foreign
国風 *ikokufū* foreign customs
国情調 *ikoku jōchō* exotic mood, foreign sentiments
国語 *ikokugo* foreign language
9 風 *ifū* unusual customs
俗 *izoku* strange custom
変 *ihen* accident, disaster
臭 *ishū* offensive smell
10 称 *ishō* another name, alias, pseudonym
郷 *ikyō* foreign country
書 *isho* rare book, strange book
11 域 *iiki* foreign lands
動 *idō* change, shifting
彩 *isai* conspicuous color. *isai(aru)* conspicuous, brilliant, resplendent
教 *ikyō* heathenism, paganism, heresy

教主義 *ikyō shugi* paganism
教徒 *ikyōto* heathen, pagans, heretics
常 *ijō* anything unusual; abnormality
常人格 *ijō jinkaku* abnormal personality
常反応 *ijō hannō* allergy
常感 *ijōkan* a strange feeling
12 朝 *ichō* a foreign court; foreign country
象 *ishō* strange phenomenon; vision
13 腹 *ifuku, kotohara* child of a different mother
数 *isū no* exceptional, unusual, phenomenal
義 *igi* different meaning
意 *ii* different idea; idea of rebellion
14 聞 *ibun* another story; a strange tale
境 *ikyō* foreign country
様 *iyō na* strange, quaint, outlandish
説 *isetsu* different opinion
種 *ishu* different kind, different species; variety
種繁殖 *ishu hanshoku* crossbreeding
端 *itan* heresy
端者 *itansha* heretic
端糾問 *itan kyūmon* inquisition
端排斥 *itan haiseki* anathema
15 論 *iron* different opinion; objection
質 *ishitsu* heterogeneity
18 類 *irui* varieties, different kinds
20 議 *igi* objection, protest
議無 *igina(shi)* no objection

7

畱 3758 / J-X / M21867 See **留** 3750.

畫 3759 / J6141 / M21859 See **画** 3733.

畤 3760 / J6147 / M-X Nonstandard for **疇** 3771.

畭 3761 / J6142 / M21861 Yo cultivate new land; fresh field.

A **番** 3762 / J4856 / M21858 BAN watch, guard; duty; number; order; size, game, round, turn, bout. *ban(suru)* keep watch, guard. *tsuga(u)* pair, mate, join, copulate. *tsuga(eru)* mate; pair; notch (an arrow); exchange (promises). *tsugai* pair, couple, brace (of ducks); joint.

2 人 *bannin* watchman, guard; caretaker, janitor
3 小屋 *bangoya* watcher's hut
4 手 *bante* (thread) count (size)
犬 *banken* watchdog
5 目 *tsugaime* joint, hinge
代 *bangawa(ri)* shift, relief, alternation
付 *banzuke* graded list; program
台 *bandai* watcher's seat
号 *bangō* number
号付 *bangōtsuke* numbering
外 *bangai* outside; extra
外物 *bangaimono* oversize item
6 地 *banchi* number
7 狂 *bankuru(wase)* program change; upset; surprise
兵 *bampei* sentry, guard, sentinel
8 所 *bansho* guard box
卒 *bansotsu* sentinel, sentry
9 茶 *bancha* coarse tea
11 組 *bangumi* program
12 傘 *bangasa* coarse oilpaper umbrella
16 頭 *bantō* clerk, secretary, attendant; steward, manager

B **畳** 3763 / J3e76 / M21875′ **疊** 3772 / J6148 / M21983 CHŌ. JŌ mat counter. *tata(mu)* fold, fold up, furl, shut up, shut; wind up (affairs); do away with, kill; bear in mind. *tata(maru)* be folded (up). *tatami* straw mat, straw matting. *tata(mi)*-folding, collapsible.

2 入 *tata(mi)-i(reru)* fold up, fold in
3 上 *tata(mi)-a(geru)* fold up
小刀 *tata(mi) kogatana* pocket knife
4 尺 *tata(mi)jaku* folding rule
込 *tata(mi)-ko(mu)* fold in; fold up; bear in mind
水練 *tatami suiren* "swimming" on tatami; useless effort
5 用 *jōyō suru* use over again
目 *tata(mi)me* crease, fold. *tatamime* the mesh in the face of a straw mat
句 *jōku* repetition, burden, refrain
付 *tatamizu(ki)* covered with matting
叩 *tatamitata(ki)* beating a straw mat
6 返 *tata(mi)-kae(su)* fold back
8 直 *tata(mi)-nao(su)* refold
表 *tata(mi) omote* facing for a straw mat
9 音 *jōon* repetition of the same sound in a word
建具 *tatami-tategu* mats and fixtures

屋 *tatamiya* straw mat dealer, straw mat maker
屋台 *tata(mi)yatai* folding dancing stage
10 紙 *tatōgami, tata(mi)gami, tatō* paper handkerchief; kimono wrapping paper
針 *tatamibari* a *tatami* needle
11 掛 *tata(mi)-ka(keru)* press (someone), ply (with questions), follow up
梯子 *tata(mi)bashigo* folding ladder
12 替 *tatamiga(e)* refacing straw mats, renewing straw mats ⌈cot
13 寝台 *tata(mi) shindai* folding bed, camp
14 語 *jōgo* syllable repetition to indicate plurals, etc. ⌈meshes
算 *tatamizan* fortunetelling by straw mat
15 縁 *tatamiberi* straw mat border
18 職 *tatamishoku* straw mat maker

8

畫 3764 / J X / M21877 See 画 3733.

當 3765 / J6144 / M21890 See 当 1706.

畷 3766 / J466d / M21892 Tetsu. Tei. Sei. *nawate* rice-field ridge path.

畸 3767 / J6143 / M21893 Ki difference; strange; cripple.

7 形 *kikei* deformity, abnormality
形足 *kikeisoku* clubfoot
形児 *kikeiji* deformed child

10

畿 3768 / J3526 / M21925 Ki capital; capital suburbs.
4 内 *Kinai* the Five Capital Provinces around Kyoto

11

畳 3769 / J614a / M-X Nonstandard for 畳 3763.

14

疆 3770 / J6145 / M21961 Kyō boundary.

疇 3771 / J6146 / M21967 Chū before; companion; same kind.

17

疊 3772 / J6148 / M21983 See 畳 3763.

疉 3773 / J6149 / M21982 Nonstandard for 畳 3763.

RAD. 疋 103

Hiki (counter for animals). At left: 𤴔 *hiki hen.* Nickname: Animal Counter.

疋 3774 / J4925 / M21994 Hitsu. *hiki* head (animal counter); roll of cloth.

7

NOTE: Characters 3775 and 3776 are sometimes used interchangeably. It is therefore necessary to look under both for definitions and compounds.

疏 3775 / J4141 / M22000 So estrangement; sparseness; neglect. (See note above.)
4 水 *sosui* drainage; canal
7 状 *sojō* written explanation
8 明 *somei* evidence for credibility
注 *sochū* notes and comments
9 通 *sotsū* drainage; mutual understanding
11 略 *soryaku na* crude, rough, plain, humble, shabby; careless, rude
12 註 *sochū* notes and comments

B **疎** 3776 / J4142 / M22002 So rough; sparseness; estrangement. *uto(mu), uto(njiru), uto(nzuru)* neglect, shun, alienate. *maba(ra) na* sparse, thin (hair); scattered, sporadic, straggling (village). *oro(ka)* making light of; ...to say nothing

玄 玉 王 瓜 瓦 甘 生 用 田 9【疋】 疒 癶 白 皮 皿 目 矛 矢 石 示 ネ 内 禾 穴 立

of ... *orosu(ku) na* negligent, careless. *uto(i)* distant, estranged; disinterested, ignorant of. *uto(mashii)* disagreeable. (See note above.)

4 水 *sosui* drainage; canal
5 外 *sogai* estrangement, indifference, neglect
7 抜 *oronu(ku)* thin out (plants)
8 放 *sohō* carelessness, fault, oversight
明 *somei* evidence for credibility
林 *sorin* sparse woods
画 *soga* rough sketch
9 音 *soon, soin* estrangement, neglect, long silence
通 *sotsū* drainage; mutual understanding
11 略 *soryaku na* crude, rough, plain, humble, shabby; careless, rude
密 *somitsu* sparseness and luxuriant growth
12 遠 *soen* estrangement, neglect (to write), long silence
疎 *utouto(shii)* estranged
隔 *sokaku* alienation, estrangement
開 *sokai* dispersal, evacuation, deployment
開先 *sokaisaki* reception area, place of refuge
14 漏 *sorō* carelessness, negligence
雑 *sozatsu na* coarse, rough, crude

9

A 疑 3777 / J353f / M22007 GI. *utaga(u), utagu(ru)* doubt; distrust; be suspicious of. *utaga(i), utagu(ri)* doubt, question, uncertainty, skepticism; suspicion; distrust. *utaga(washii)* doubtful, questionable, uncertain, disputable; suspicious.

4 心 *gishin* doubt, suspicion, fear, apprehension
6 似 *giji-* suspected, quasi-, pseudo-, sham
字 *giji* a character of questionable form
8 念 *ginen* doubt, suspicion, misgivings, scruples
9 点 *giten* doubtful point
11 惧 *gigu* apprehension, uneasiness
深 *utaga(i)buka(i)* doubting, distrustful, incredulous; suspicious
問 *gimon* question, problem, doubt
問文 *gimombun* interrogative sentence
問代名詞 *gimon daimeishi* interrogative pronoun
問符 *gimonfu* question mark
問詞 *gimonshi* interrogative word
12 雲 *giun* cloud of suspicion
惑 *giwaku* doubt, misgivings, distrust, suspicion
13 辞 *giji* a questionable word
義 *gigi* doubt
14 獄 *gigoku* scandal, graft case
21 懼 *giku* apprehension, uneasiness

RAD. 疒 104

Yamaidare trailing "sickness." Nickname: Sick.

2

疔 3778 / J614b / M22019 TEI. CHŌ carbuncle.

6 気 *senki* colic, abdominal pain
12 痛 *sentsū* colic, abdominal pain

3

疚 3779 / J614c / M22033 KYŪ. *yama(shii)* ashamed, painful, having a guilty conscience, sickly.

疝 3780 / J614d / M22040 SEN colic, abdominal pain.

4

疥 3781 / J614e / M22057 KAI. *hatake* scabby eruption, scabs.

22 癬 *kaisen* itch, scabies, mange

疣 3782 / J614f / M22050 YŪ. YU. *ibo* wart.

11 痔 *iboji* hemorrhoids
12 蛙 *ibogaeru* toad

B 疫 3783 / J3156 / M22069 YAKU, EKI epidemic.
9 神 *ekijin* sickness-producing god
10 鬼 *ekiki* god of sickness
病 *ekibyō, yakubyō* pestilence, plague, epidemic
病神 *yakubyōgami* god of the plague
12 痢 *ekiri* children's dysentery
17 癘 *ekirei* pestilence, epidemic, plague

5

痓 3784 / J-X / M-X Nonstandard for 痙 3812.

痐 3785 / J-X / M22088 痐 3807 / J615e / M22289 A chronic illness.

疸 3786 / J6155 / M22094 TAN jaundice.

疽 3787 / J6154 / M22106 SO carbuncle.

疹 3788 / J3f3e / M22097 SHIN, CHIN measles; sickness

疳 3789 / J6151 / M22085 KAN children's diseases.
10 高 *kandaka(i)* shrill, high pitched

痃 3790 / J6152 / M22124 GEN cramps.
18 癖 *kempeki* stiff shoulders; massage

疱 3791 / J6157 / M22082 HŌ smallpox; blister.
15 瘡 *hōsō* smallpox

疼 3792 / J6156 / M22105 TŌ pain. *uzu(ku)* ache, pain; tingle; fester.
12 痛 *tōtsū* pain

痂 3793 / J6150 / M22122 KA. KE. *kasa* scab. *ka(seru)* dry up, scab, slough.
5 皮 *kahi* scab

痀 3794 / J-X / M22120 KU crouch, hunchback.
16 瘻 *kuru* rickets
瘻病 *kurubyō* rickets

B 症 3795 / J3e49 / M22140 SHŌ illness; condition of a patient; nature of a disease, symptoms.
7 状 *shōjō* symptoms; condition of the illness
8 例 *shōrei* a case (a patient)
10 候 *shōkō* symptoms

B 疲 3796 / J4868 / M22084 HI. *tsuka(reru)* get tired, grow weary. *tsuka(rakasu), tsuka(rasu)* tire (a horse), weary (one's mind), exhaust (one's energy)
4 切 *tsuka(re)-ki(ru)* be tired out
5 目 *tsuka(re)me* eyestrain
乍 *tsuka(re)naga(ra)* even though tired
7 労 *hirō* fatigue
8 果 *tsuka(re) ha(teru)* be tired out
10 衰 *tsuka(re)-otoro(eru)* languish
15 弊 *hihei* impoverishment, exhaustion
16 憊 *hihai* being tired out

B 疾 3797 / J3c40 / M22112 SHITSU illness, disease. *to(ku)* fast, swiftly; early. *to(kku) kara* since long ago. *to(u) ni, to(kku) ni* long ago; already. *to(u) kara* for a long time. *haya(i)* fast. *yama(shii)* ashamed, painful, having a guilty conscience, sickly.
6 行 *shikkō suru* hasten, hurry
7 走 *shissō suru* scamper, dash along. *shissō* a sprint, a dash
8 呼 *shikko* shout, yell
苦 *shikku* affliction, distress, suffering
9 風 *shippu, hayate* squall, gale, hurricane, fresh breeze
風迅雷的 *shippū-jinraiteki ni* swiftly, with lightning speed
風雲 *hayategumo* hurricane clouds
10 病 *shippei* sickness
疾 *to(ku)to(ku)* in a great hurry
11 患 *shikkan* disease, ailment
強風 *shikkyōfū* gale
14 駆 *shikku suru* scamper, speed, dash along

A 病 3798 / J4942 / M22127 痡 3799 / J-X / M-X BYŌ. HEI. *ya(mu)* get sick, be sick, suffer from. *ya(meru)* be sick, be in ill health. *yamai* illness; bad habit; weakness; passion. *-ya(mi)* sufferer of (a disease). *ya(mi)-* diseased.
2 人 *byōnin* patient, invalid

3 上 *ya(mi)a(gari)* convalescence
4 犬 *byōken* sick dog
中 *byōchū* during an illness
夫 *byōfu* sick husband
5 付 *ya(mi)-tsu(ku)* get sick; be absorbed in; fall into in a habit. *ya(mi)tsu(ki)* becoming sick; infatuation; falling into a bad habit
6 因 *byōin* cause of the disease, etiology
死 *byōshi* natural death, death from illness
返 *ya(mi)kae(shi)* relapse
名 *byōmei* name of a disease
虫害 *byōchūgai* insect damage
気 *byōki* sickness, disease, ailment; fault; infirmity
気中 *byōkichū* during illness
気見舞 *byōki mima(i)* calling on the sick
7 足 *ya(mi)ashi* diseased foot
身 *byōshin* weak constitution, ill health
体 *byōtai* weak constitution, ill health
没 *byōbotsu* death from illness, natural death
状 *byōjō* patient's condition
兵 *byōhei* sick soldier
児 *byōji* sick child
床 *byōshō* sickbed
床日誌 *byōshō nisshi* clinical report, nurse's report
床録 *byōshōroku* clinical record; nurse's report
8 性 *byōsei* nature of the disease
所 *byōsho* patient's location; the ailing part
歿 *byōbotsu* death from illness, natural death
牀 *byōshō* sickbed
舎 *byōsha* infirmary, hospital
苦 *byōku* suffering from illness
妻 *byōsai* sick wife
者 *byōsha* sick person
臥 *byōga suru* be sick in bed, be bedridden
臥中 *byōgachū* bedridden
毒 *byōdoku* virus, germ
毒保有者 *byōdoku hoyūsha* germ carrier
的 *byōteki* morbid, abnormal, unsound
的窃盗 *byōteki settō* kleptomaniac
的盗癖 *byōteki tōheki* kleptomania
9 後 *byōgo* convalescence; after an illness
変 *byōhen* pathological change
室 *byōshitsu* sickroom, ward, sick bay, infirmary
院 *byōin* hospital, infirmary
院列車 *byōin ressha* hospital train
院船 *byōinsen* hospital ship
10 骨 *byōkotsu* weak constitution
症 *byōshō* nature of a disease
根 *byōkon* cause of the disease; root of an evil
衰 *byōsui* weakness from illness
害 *byōgai* health impairment from illness; crop damage due to disease
家 *byōka* patient's home
耄 *ya(mi)-hō(keru)* become emaciated
弱 *byōjaku* delicate constitution
原 *byōgen* cause of a disease
原体 *byōgentai* pathogenic agent
原菌 *byōgenkin* virus, germ
11 婦 *byōfu* sick wife
眼 *byōgan* sore eye
菌 *byōkin* bacteria
患 *byōkan, ya(mi)wazura(i)* sickness
巣 *byōsō* focus (of an infection)
理 *byōri* cause and extent of a disease
理学 *byōrigaku* pathology
理解剖学 *byōrikaibōgaku* pathological anatomy
12 間 *byōkan* during illness
棟 *byōtō* ward
13 煩 *ya(mi)-wazura(u)* be sick
蓐 *byōjoku* sickbed
勢 *byōsei* progress of the disease
源 *byōgen* cause of a disease
14 歴 *byōreki* patient's case history
態 *byōtai* patient's condition
15 褥 *byōjoku* sickbed
弊 *byōhei* evil, vice, abuse; harmful influence; bad effect
18 癖 *byōheki* peculiarity, weakness, bad habit
軀 *byōku* ill health, sickly constitution
21 魔 *byōma* disease, demon of ill health
竈 *byōsō* focus of infection, disease center

6

痊 3800 / J6159 / M22141 SEN *i(eru)* recover, be healed. *i(yasu)* heal, cure.

痍 3801 / J6158 / M22148 I injury.

痒 3802 / J615a / M22163 Yō. *kayu(garu)* itch. *kayu(i), kai(i)* itchy.

痕 3803 / J3a2f / M22171 Kon. *ato* mark; footprint.

13 跡 *konseki* traces, vestiges, evidences

跡器官 *konseki kikan* vestigial organ

痔 3804 / J3c26 / M22167 Ji piles, hemorrhoids.

5 出血 *jishukketsu* bleeding of piles

10 疾 *jishitsu* hemorrhoids

核 *jikaku* hemorrhoids

16 瘻 *jirō* anal fistula, piles

疵 3805 / J6153 / M22089 Shi. *kizu* crack, flaw; scratch; speck; (fruit) bruise; fault; blemish, stain; weakness.

5 付 *kizutsu(ku)* get injured, be wounded; be damaged; be disgraced. *kizutsu(keru)* wound, injure; mar, damage; disgrace

8 咎 *kizutogame* irritate a wound

10 病 *kizuyami* illness from an injury

11 痕 *kizuato* scar from a wound

13 瑕 *shika* defect, fault, weakness

跡 *kizuato* scar from a wound

16 薬 *kizugusuri* salve, ointment

7

瘦 3806 / J4169 / M-X See 瘦 3832.

痾 3807 / J615e / M22289 See 疴 3785.

痞 3808 / J615d / M22206 Hi, Bi. *tsukae* abdominal or chest congestion; constipation.

痣 3809 / J615c / M22218 Shi. *aza* birthmark, mole.

B **痢** 3810 / J4e21 / M22213 Ri diarrhea.

10 病 *ribyō* diarrhea

痤 3811 / J-X / M22221 Za. *enogo* swelling of the lymph glands.

15 瘡 *zasō* acne

痙 3812 / J615b / M22186 Kei. *tsu(ru)* have a cramp.

23 攣 *keiren, hikitsuri* scar; cramp, spasm, twitch, convulsion

B **痘** 3813 / J4577 / M22185 Tō smallpox.

8 苗 *tobyō* vaccine

9 面 *tōmen* pockmarked face

11 痕 *abata, tōkon* pockmark

痕面 *abatazura* pitted face

15 瘡 *tōsō* smallpox

A **痛** 3814 / J444b / M22195 Tsū pain. *ita(mu)* feel a pain, hurt; be hurt, be damaged, be spoiled, be bruised, wear out, be worn out. *ita(meru)* hurt, injure, impair, spoil, worry, bother, afflict, cause pain. *ita(mi)* pain, ache. *ita(garu)* complain of pain. *ita(i)* painful, sore; trying. *ita(mashii), ita(washii)* sad, pitiful, wretched, pathetic.

2 入 *ita(mi)-i(ru)* be grateful for

4 心 *tsūshin* anxiety, worry, fear, suspense; trouble, care

手 *itade* serious wound; hard blow

切 *tsūsetsu ni* keenly, acutely

5 日 *ita(i)me* hard experience

付 *ita(me)-tsu(keru)* rebuke, reprove, scold severely

打 *tsuda* painful blow; grand-slam hit

7 言 *tsūgen* bitter criticism

快 *tsūkai* thrill, keen pleasure. *tsūkai na* extremely delightful, very gratifying; merciless incisive

8 苦 *ita(mi)-kuru(shimu)* suffer. *tsūku* pain, pang, anguish

事 *itagoto* severe blow, pain

9 悔 *tsūkai* deep remorse, penitence

点 *tsūten* point of pain

恨 *tsūkon* great sorrow, bitterness

恨事 *tsūkonji* sad incident

10 烈 *tsūretsu na* severe, bitter, scathing

哭 *tsūkoku* lamentation

11 痒 *tsūyō* interest, concern; pain and tickling. *ita(shi)kayu(shi) no* delicate, ticklish (question)

惜 *tsūseki* great sorrow, deep regret, lamentation
責 *tsūseki suru* denounce vigorously
12 痛 *itaita(shii)* pitiful, pathetic
棒 *tsūbō* harsh criticism
飲 *tsūin* carousal
覚 *tsūkaku* sense of pain
13 嘆 *tsūtan* bitter grief, deep regret
感 *tsūkan suru* feel keenly; fully realize
14 歎 *tsūtan* bitter grief, deep regret
15 憤 *tsūfun* great indignation
論 *tsūron* vehement argument
罵 *tsūba* condemnation, denunciation
撃 *tsūgeki* hard blow, severe attack
20 癢 *tsūyō* interest, concern; pain and tickling

8

痿 3815 / J615f / M22290 I become numb; wither; become weak.

瘁 3816 / J6161 / M22294 ZUI, SUI fatigue; take sick.

痼 3817 / J6160 / M22285 KO chronic illness.
10 疾 *koshitsu* chronic disease

痲 3818 / J6164 / M22254 MA measles; paralysis.
11 酔 *masui* anesthetic
13 痺 *mahi* paralysis, palsy, numbness, stupor
16 薬 *mayaku* anesthetic, narcotic

痳 3819 / J6165 / M22255 RIN gonorrhea.
8 毒 *rindoku* gonorrhea, clap
10 病 *rimbyō* gonorrhea, clap
疾 *rinshitsu* gonorrhea, clap
11 菌 *rinkin* gonococcus; gonorrhea, clap

痺 3820 / J6163 / M22280 **痹** 3821 / J-X / M22279 HI palsy. *shibi(reru)* become numb, be paralyzed.
16 薬 *shibiregusuri* anesthetic
19 鯰 *shibire namazu* electric catfish
22 鰻 *shibire unagi* electric eel
23 鱏 *shibire ei* electric ray

痰 3822 / J6162 / M22251 DAN, TAN sputum, phlegm.
4 切飴 *tanki(ri) ame* cough syrup
6 吐 *tanha(ki)* spittoon, cuspidor
9 咳 *tanseki* mucous cough
11 唾 *tantsuba* expectoration, spittle
12 壺 *tantsubo* spittoon, cuspidor

B **痴** 3823 / J4354 / M22257 **癡** 3849 / J6177 / M22591 CHI foolish.
2 人 *chijin* dunce, fool, idiot
7 言 *shiregoto* foolish speaking
呆 *chihō* imbecility; dementia
呆症 *chihōshō* dementia
8 者 *chisha, shiremono* fool; rascal
事 *shiregoto* foolish thing
11 情 *chijō* blind love
12 鈍 *chidon* stupidity, dullness
13 漢 *chikan* a pervert, a molester
愚 *chigu* stupidity, imbecility
話 *chiwa* lovers' talk
話言 *chiwagoto* love-talk vocabulary
話狂 *chiwaguru(i)* petting, dalliance
話喧嘩 *chiwagenka* lovers' quarrel
14 態 *chitai* silliness

9

瘉 3824 / J6168 / M22318 YU *i(eru)* recover, be healed. *i(yasu)* heal, cure.

瘍 3825 / J6167 / M22327 YŌ boil, carbuncle.

瘧 3826 / J616a / M22419 GYAKU ague, intermittent fever. *okori* fever and ague.

瘋 3827 / J6166 / M22322 FŪ insanity; headache.
24 癲 *fūten* insanity

10

瘟 3828 / J6169 / M22396 ON contagious disease.

瘡 3829 / J616c / M22404 SŌ wound; boil. *kasa* syphilis.

瘢 3830 / J616d / M22405 HAN scar.
11 痕 *hankon* scar, cicatrix.

瘤 3831 / J616e / M22408 RYŪ. *kobu* wen, lump, bump, swelling.
5 付 *kobutsu(ki)* wen; nuisance; having a child along
8 取 *kobuto(ri)* (story of the) removal of the wen
9 胃 *kobui* rumen, paunch
10 起 *ryūki* swelling like a boil

瘦 3832 / J-X / M22415 SŌ. SHŪ. SHU. *yase(ru)* get thin.
3 女 *yaseonna* thin woman
4 犬 *yaseinu* skinny dog
7 男 *yaseotoko* thin man
我慢 *yasegaman* enduring to the breaking point
身 *sōshin* slender body, thin body
身法 *sōshinhō* slenderizing
10 衰 *ya(se)-otoro(eru)* become emaciated, waste away; be blighted
11 細 *ya(se)-hoso(ru)* get thin; become just skin and bones
脛 *yasezune* thin legs
18 軀 *sōku* a lean figure
19 羸 *sōrui* fatigue

瘠 3833 / J616b / M22401 SEKI. JAKU. *yase(ru)* get thin, lose weight; pine away; get sterile. *yase(gisu) no* slim, slender, thin. *yase(ppochi)* mere skeleton; rawboned
3 土 *yasetsuchi* barren soil
5 世帯 *yasejotai* poor household, straitened circumstances
6 地 *yasechi, sekichi* barren land, acid soil
7 形 *yasegata* slender figure
身代 *yaseshindai* scanty means
我慢 *yasegaman* strained endurance; feeble resistance
9 面 *yaseomote* thin face
10 馬 *yaseuma* scrawny horse
衰 *ya(se)-otoro(eru)* become emaciated, waste away; be blighted
11 細 *ya(se)-hoso(ru)* get thin, lose weight
12 腕 *yaseude* weak arm; feeble strength, poor ability
落 *ya(se)-o(chiru)* get thin, lose weight
16 薬 *yasegusuri* reducing medicine, weight-loss medicine

11

瘻 3834 / J6171 / M22467 RU, RŌ fistula.

瘭 3835 / J-X / M22440 HYŌ a whitlow.
5 疽 *hyōso* felon, whitlow

瘴 3836 / J616f / M22455 SHŌ miasma.
6 気 *shōki* miasma, poison, pestilential vapor; malice, evil; a cold

瘰 3837 / J6170 / M22447 RUI swollen neck glands.

12

癆 3838 / J6174 / M22512 RŌ grow progressively weaker; addiction; pain.

癘 3839 / J6176 / M22556 REI contagious disease; leprosy.

癌 3840 / J3462 / M22538 GAN cancer; cancerous evil; stumbling block.
13 腫 *ganshu* cancer, cancerous growth

癈 3841 / J6173 / M22520 HAI chronic illness; getting crippled.
2 人 *haijin* invalid, cripple; useless person; abandoned person
10 疾 *haishitsu* disablement, deformity

B 療 3842 / J4e45 / M22500 RYŌ heal, cure.
8 法 *ryōhō* medical treatment, remedy
治 *ryōji* medical treatment, remedy
15 養 *ryōyō* recuperation, medical care
養中 *ryōyōchū* under medical care
養所 *ryōyōjo* sanitorium

癇 3843 / J6172 / M22518 癎 3844 / J-X / M-X KAN hot temper, irritability, nervousness, sensitiveness.
7 声 *kangoe* angry voice
9 持 *kammo(chi)* hot-tempered person
10 症 *kanshō* irritability, hot temper
18 癖 *kampeki* hot temper, irritability

[21]癪 *kanshaku* passion, temper, irritability
癪玉 *kanshakudama* anger
癪持 *kanshakumo(chi)* hot-tempered person

13

癜 3845 / J6175 / M22570 TEN *namazu* leucoderma; vitiligo; piebald skin.

癕 3846 / J-X / M22549 **癰** 3856 / J617e / M22638 YŌ carbuncle.

B **癒** 3847 / J4c7e / M22545 YU. *i(yasu)* heal, cure; quench (thirst); wreak (vengeance). *i(eru), nao(ru)* recover, be healed, heal.
[6]合 *yugō* agglutination, adhesion, knitting
[12]着 *yuchaku suru* adhere, knit, unite, heal up. *yuchaku* adhesion
[18]難 *iegata(i)* hard to cure

B **癖** 3848 / J4a4a / M22550 HEKI habit. *kuse* habit, peculiarity, vice, trait, fault; curl, kink; mannerism. *-kuse ni* and yet, when, though.
[4]毛 *kusege* curly hair, kinky hair
[5]付 *kusezu(ku)* become a habit; develop a strange reading tone; snarl up (hair)
[8]直 *kusenao(shi)* straightening out one's hair
事 *kusegoto* characteristic habit

14

癡 3849 / J6177 / M22591 See 痴 3823.

15

癢 3850 / J6178 / M22602 YŌ itchy. *kayu(i), kai(i)* itchy, itching.

16

癧 3851 / J617c / M22617 REKI swollen neck glands.

癨 3852 / J6179 / M22618 KAKU heatstroke, sunstroke.

癪 3853 / J617b / M22626 (国字) *shaku* spasms, convulsions, hysteria, sharp pain.
[6]虫 *shaku (no) mushi* feeling of intense anger
[13]触 *shaku (ni) sawa(ru)* irritate, exasperate
[14]種 *shaku (no) tane* reason for an outburst of anger

癩 3854 / J617a / M22622 RAI leprosy, Hansen's disease.
[8]者 *raisha* leprosy victim
[10]病 *raibyō, kattai* leprosy, Hansen's disease
病人 *raibyōnin* leprosy victim
[11]菌 *raikin* the germ of leprosy
患者 *raikanja* victims of leprosy
[17]療養所 *rairyōyōsho* leprosarium

17

癬 3855 / J617d / M22629 SEN ringworm.

18

癰 3856 / J617e / M22638 See 癕 3846.

19

癲 3857 / J6221 / M22643 TEN insanity.
[7]狂 *tenkyō* insanity
[17]癇 *tenkan* epilepsy; epileptic fit
癇持 *tenkammo(chi)* an epileptic

癶 RAD. 105

Hatsugashira (crown like that on *hatsu* "to depart"). Nickname: Dotted Tent.

癶 3858 / J6222 / M22657 HATSU. HACHI oppose; open; go. *somu(ku)* go against, oppose, run contrary to.

4

癸 3859 / J6223 / M22660 KI tenth, J. *mizunoto* tenth calendar sign.

A **発** 3860 / J482f / M22662′ **發** 3861 / J6224 / M22669 HOTSU, HATSU departure; discharge (of a gun). *has(suru)* discharge, fire; emit, emanate, radiate, give out; publish; utter, give vent to; give rise to; originate in, spring from, emanate from; start from; flow from; send out, dispatch, forward; leave, start, take off, announce; break out (a disease). *aba(ku)* unearth, disclose, divulge, reveal; open (a grave). *-hatsu* departure; round, shot; dated.

4 心 *hosshin* new intention; (Buddhist) religious awakening
火 *hakka* ignition, combustion; discharge, firing
火点 *hakkaten* combustion point
火演習 *hakka enshū* firing practice
5 句 *hokku* 17-syllable poem in three lines of five, seven, and five syllables; a haiku
刊 *hakkan* publication
令 *hatsurei* official announcement
布 *happu* proclamation; issuance; promulgation
生 *hassei* occurrence, outbreak; genesis; production, growth, development, rise
生学 *hasseigaku* genetics, embryology
6 向 *hakkō* departure
汗 *hakkan* perspiring
企 *hokki* promotion of a plan
会 *hakkai suru* open a meeting
会式 *hakkaishiki* opening ceremony
光 *hakkō* radiation, luminescence
光体 *hakkōtai* luminous stellar bodies
行 *hakkō* publication; flotation; issue
行人 *hakkōnin* publisher
行日 *hakkōbi* date of issue
行元 *hakkō moto* place of publication
行所 *hakkōsho* publishing house
行者 *hakkōsha* publisher
行高 *hakkōdaka* the amount of an issue
行部数 *hakkō busū* circulation (of a magazine)
行停止 *hakkō teishi* ceasing publication
7 見 *hakken* discovery, detection, revelation
赤 *hosseki* redness
走 *hassō* starting; first race
足 *hossoku, hassoku* starting, inauguration
車 *hassha* departure of a vehicle
狂 *hakkyo* madness, insanity
兌 *hatsuda* issue, publication
作 *hossa* fit, spasm, an attack of
作的 *hossateki* spasmodic, fitful
売 *hatsubai* sale
売部数 *hatsubai busū* circulation
条 *hatsujō, bane, zemmai* (metal) spring
条仕掛 *banejikake* spring mechanism, clockwork
条秤 *zemmaibakari* spring balances
言 *hatsugen* speaking, speech, proposal
言力 *hatsugenryoku* the authority behind a speech
言投票 *hatsugen tōhyō* voice vote
言者 *hatsugensha* speaker
言権 *hatsugenken* right to speak, a voice in
声 *hassei* utterance, exclamation, speaking
声法 *hasseihō* vocalization, enunciation; elocution
声映画 *hassei eiga* sound picture
声帯 *hasseitai* vocal cords
声器 *hasseiki* vocal organs
声爆弾 *hassei bakudan* scream bomb
8 送 *hassō* sending, forwarding, shipping
明 *hatsumei* invention, contrivance; cleverness
泡 *happō, hatsubō* blister
注 *hatchū* ordering (goods)
効 *hakkō* coming into effect
芽 *hatsuga* germination, sprouting
券 *hakken* note issuing
表 *happyō* announcement, communique

明 *hatsumei* invention, innovation
明者 *hatsumeisha* inventor
明品 *hatsumeihin* invention, contrivance
明家 *hatsumeika* inventor
育 *hatsuiku* growth, development, progress
育不全 *hatsuikufuzen na* abortive; underdeveloped
育時代 *hatsuiku jidai* formative years
育時期 *hatsuiku jiki* formative years
9 信 *hasshin* sending a letter or telegram
信音 *hasshinon* dial tone
音 *hatsuon* pronunciation, enunciation, articulation
音学 *hatsuongaku* pronunciation, enunciation, articulation
音符号 *hatsuon fugō* phonetic symbols
10 病 *hatsubyō* onset of a disease, stroke
疹 *hasshin, hosshin* eruption, rash
破 *happa* blasting
航 *hakkō* departure, sailing
振器 *hasshinki* oscillator
祥 *hasshō* ancestral origin; appearance of a good omen
祥地 *hasshōchi* cradle, birthplace
射 *hassha* discharge, firing; emanation, radiation
射管 *hasshakan* torpedo tube
案 *hatsuan* suggestion, proposition, motion
案者 *hatsuansha* proposer
起 *hokki* promotion (of a plan); proposition, suggestion
起人 *hokkinin* originator, promoter, sponsor
起者 *hokkisha* originator
砲 *happō* firing, discharge
砲事件 *happō jiken* a shooting affair
砲戦 *happōsen* shooting war
展 *hatten* expansion, extension, development, growth; dissipation
展性 *hattensei* possibilities for growth
展的 *hattenteki* expanding, growing
展途上国 *hatten tojōkoku* developing countries
展家 *hattenka* a man about town; fast liver, playboy
展期 *hattenki* period of expansion
11 達 *hattatsu* growth, development, progress, advancement
掘 *hakkutsu* excavation; disinterring, exhuming
現 *hatsugen* revelation, manifestation
情 *hatsujō* sexual excitement, heat (in animals)
情期 *hatsujōki* puberty; mating season
動 *hatsudō* motion, activity; exercise (of power)
動力 *hatsudōryoku* motive power
動的 *hatsudōteki* active
動機 *hatsudōki* motor, engine
動機船 *hatsudōkisen* motorboat, motor ship
12 揚 *hatsuyō* exaltation, promotion
揮 *hakki* exhibition, demonstration
港 *hakkō* leaving port
程 *hattei* start of journey
給 *hakkyū suru* issue (passports, etc.)
註 *hatchū* ordering (goods)
散 *hassan* exhalation; emanation; diffusion; radiation; evaporation; divergence
着 *hatchaku* departure and arrival
覚 *hakkaku* detection, disclosure
喪 *hatsumo* death announcement
13 源 *hatsugen* source of water, origins
煙 *hatsuen* fuming, emitting smoke
艇 *hattei* start of boat race
意 *hatsui, hotsui* initiative, suggestion, original idea
想 *hassō* expression (in music); conception (of an idea)
禁 *hakkin* banned, sale prohibited
電 *hatsuden* generation of electricity; dispatch of a telegram
電子 *hatsudenshi* armature
電用原子炉 *hatsudenyō genshiro* power reactor
電体 *hatsudentai* charged body
電所 *hatsudensho* powerhouse, generating plant
電機 *hatsudenki* dynamo, generator
14 端 *hottan, hattan* origin, commencement
語 *hatsugo* speech, utterance; introductory word to a sentence such as "well"
駅 *hatsueki* starting station
酵 *hakkō* fermentation
酵素 *hakkōso* ferment, yeast, leaven
15 憤 *happun suru* be enraged; be inspired

熱 *hatsunetsu* attack of fever; generation of heat
輦 *hatsuren* departure of imperial carriage
16 奮 *happun suru* be enraged; be inspired
頭人 *hottōnin* ringleader, originator, promoter
17 癌性 *hatsugansei* carcinogenic
癌物質 *hatsugan busshitsu* carcinogen
20 議 *hatsugi, hotsugi* proposal, motion
21 露 *hatsuro* expression, manifestation, revelation

7

發 3861 / J6224 / M22669 See **発** 3860.

A **登** 3862 / J4550 / M22668 Tō. To. *nobo(ru)* rise, ascend, go up, climb; go to (the capital); add up to; be promoted; advance (in price); sail up; come up (on the agenda). *nobo(ri)* ascent; up train (toward the capital).

3 山 *tozan* mountain climbing, mountain ascent
山者 *tozansha* mountain climber
山家 *tozanka* mountaineer, alpinist
山隊 *tozantai* mountain-climbing party
山期 *tozanki* mountain-climbing season
5 用 *tōyō* appointment; promotion
庁 *tōchō* attendance at the office
仙 *tōsen suru* die; become a deathless saint
6 行 *tōkō* hill climbing
7 坂 *nobo(ri)zaka* ascent, upgrade
8 板 *tōban suru* step into the pitcher's box
9 城 *tōjō* attendance at the castle
院 *tōin* attendance at the diet
省 *tōshō* attendance at the ministry
10 高 *tōkō suru* climb up, ascend
祚 *tōso* accession to the throne
竜門 *tōryūmon* the only gateway to eminence
校 *tōkō* attending school
校拒否 *tōkōkyohi* refusal to attend school
校拒否症 *tōkōkyohishō* school refusal syndrome
記 *tōki* registry, registration
記所 *tōkisho* registration place
記料 *tōkiryō* registration fee
11 庸 *tōyō* appointment; promotion
道 *nobo(ri)michi* uphill road, road up a mountain
頂 *tochō, tōchō* ascent (of a mountain)
第 *tōdai suru* pass an exam
舷礼 *tōgenrei* salute from the deck
12 遐 *tōka* death of an emperor
極 *tōkyoku* accession, enthronement
場 *tōjō suru* enter the stage; appear on the scene
場人物 *tōjō jimbutsu* cast of a play
13 楼 *tōrō* going up a tower; visiting a brothel
載 *tōsai suru* register, record, enter
14 閣 *tōkaku* climbing a tower; entering the cabinet
16 壇 *tōdan* ascending the platform
録 *tōroku* registration, entry, record, enrollment
録済 *tōrokuzu(mi)* registered
録商標 *tōroku shōhyō* registered trademark
録簿 *tōrokubo* register
17 臨 *tōrin suru* mount an eminence; ascend the throne
19 簿 *tōbo* registration
攀 *tōhan suru* climb up, ascend
攀者 *tōhansha* climber
攀隊 *tōhantai* climbing party

RAD. 白 106

Shiroi white. Nickname: White.

A **白** 3863 / J4772 / M22678 HAKU, BYAKU white. *shiro(mu), shira(mu)* grow light; turn gray, whiten; weaken. *shiro* white; innocence. *shiro(i)* white; fair (skin); gray (hair); blank (paper); spotless; innocent. *shiro(ppoi)* whitish. *shiro* feigned ignorance. *serifu* speech, words, lines, remarks. *shiro(meru)* vt. whiten. *shira(keru)* become cheerless; become chilled; be spoiled (as a child). *shira-* white.

2 十字 *hakujūji* white cross
人 *hakujin* white person, Caucasian
人種 *hakujinshu* white race

3 土 *shiratsuchi* kaolin; mortar
下 *shiroshita* treacle, molasses
刃 *hakujin, shiraha* naked sword, drawn sword
小豆 *shiroazuki* small white bean
子 *shirako* milt, roe; albino. *shiro(k)ko* albino
子鳩 *shirakobato* turtledove
川夜船 *shirakawa-yofune* sound sleep
4 文 *hakubun* old unpunctuated Chinese text
水 *shiromizu* white water left after washing rice
太 *shirata* sapwood
内障 *hakunaishō* white cataract
日 *hakujitsu* daytime, broad daylight
日夢 *hakujitsumu* daydream
木 *shiraki* plain wood, unfinished woodwork
木綿 *shiro momen* white cotton cloth
切 *shira (o) ki(ru)* pretend not to know
切符 *shirogippu* first-class ticket
5 目 *shirome* whites of the eyes
生地 *shirokiji* white cloth; white ground
白 *shirojiro* pure, white. *shirajira* dawning. *hakuhaku* very clear. *shirajira(shii)* barefaced (lie). *shirajira(shiku)* with feigned ignorance; under false premises
白明 *shirashiraa(ke)* dawn, daybreak
玉 *hakugyoku* white jade. *shiratama* white gem, pearl; rice-flour dumplings
玉粉 *shiratamako* rice flower
玉椿 *shiratama tsubaki* white camellia
6 糸 *shiraito* white thread
衣 *byakui, byakue, hakui* white robe
地 *shiroji* white cloth; white ground
地図 *hakuchizu* outline map, contour map
帆 *shiraho* white sail; boat with a white sail
光 *hakkō* white light, corona
百合 *shirayuri* Easter lily, white lily
灯油 *hakutōyu* kerosene
米 *hakumai* polished rice
米食 *hakumaishoku* white-rice diet
羽 *shiraha* white feather
羽矢立 *shiraha(no)ya (o) ta(teru)* choose a human sacrifice; select someone
血病 *hakketsubyō* leukemia
血球 *hakkekkyū* white corpuscles
色 *hakushoku* white
色人種 *hakushoku jinshu* white race, Caucasian
色金 *hakushokukin* white gold
7 身 *shiromi* white of an egg; white meat; sap; sapwood
妙 *shirotae* white; white cloth
状 *hakujō* confession, acknowledgment
兎 *shiro usagi* white rabbit
系露人 *Hakkei Rojin* White Russian
亜 *hakua* chalk, chalkstone
亜館 *Hakuakan* White House
兵 *hakuhei* naked sword, drawn sword
兵戦 *hakuheisen* hand-to-hand fight
8 金 *hakkin* platinum
雨 *hakuu* shower
味 *shiromi* whiteness; white of an egg
波 *shiranami* white-capped waves; thief
泡 *shiraawa* white bubbles, foam
狐 *byakko, shirogitsune* white fox
夜 *hakuya, byakuya* white (arctic) night, short night
苔 *hakutai* fur on the tongue
拍子 *shirabyōshi* medieval female dancer, a hetaera, a courtesan
虎隊 *Byakkotai* the White Tiger Brigade
9 面 *hakumen* unpainted face; pale face; fair skin; inexperience. *shirafu* sobriety, soberness
眉 *hakubi* prominence, excellence, best example, the pick of
洲 *shirasu* sand bar; court, the bar
虹 *shironiji* fog bow, white rainbow
星 *shiroboshi* white dot; victory mark
茶 *shiracha* straw color, light brown
昼 *hakuchū* daytime, broad daylight, midday
飛白 *shiro kasuri* white cloth with black splashed patterns
胡麻 *shirogoma* white sesame seed
砂 *hakusha, shirosuna, hakusa* white sand
砂青松 *hakusa-seishō* white sand and green pines; beautiful seashore scene
砂糖 *shirozatō* white sugar
10 馬 *hakuba, shirouma, shirauma* white horse
骨 *hakkotsu* skeleton, bleached bones
扇 *hakusen* white fan
閃 *hakusen* white flash (on TV)
梅 *shiraume* white plum blossoms; white-blossom plum tree
浜 *shirahama* white beach
酒 *shirozake* white saké

書 *hakusho* a white paper, a white book
陶土 *hakutōdo* kaolin
栗毛 *shirakurige* light-chestnut-colored horse
紙 *shirakami, hakushi* white paper; blank paper; flyleaf; clean slate
紙委任状 *hakushi ininjō* a blank power of attorney
粉 *oshiroi* face powder, face paint
粉下 *oshiroishita* powder base, face cream, beauty wash
粉気無 *oshiroike (no) na(i)* without make-up
粉刷毛 *oshiroibake* powder puff
粉臭 *oshiroikusa(i)* makeup overdone
粉焼 *oshiroiya(ke)* (cosmetic) powder burn
粉箱 *oshiroibako* face-powder box
11 魚 *shirauo* whitebait
鳥 *hakuchō* swan
黒 *shirokuro* black and white; good and bad; right or wrong; guilty or innocent
描 *hakubyō* plain sketch
菜 *hakusai* Chinese cabbage; celery cabbage
菊 *shiragiku* white chrysanthemum
票 *hakuhyō* white (affirmative) vote; blank vote; favorable vote
雪 *hakusetsu, shirayuki* (white) snow
粘土 *hakunendo* alumina, argil
鹿毛 *shirakage* light-fawn-colored horse
張提灯 *shiraha(ri)jōchin* white paper lantern
眼 *shirome, hakugan* the whites of the eyes
眼視 *hakuganshi suru* look coldly at, look askance at, frown upon
堊 *hakua* chalk; chalkstone; white wall
堊館 *Hakuakan* White House
12 歯 *shiraha* white teeth
晰 *hakuseki* white
湯 *sayu* plain hot water
焼 *shiraya(ki)* broiling fish unseasoned
斑 *shirafu, shirobuchi* white spot
絣 *shiro kasuri* white cloth with black splashed patterns
貂 *shiroten* ermine
皙 *hakuseki* white (race), white complexion
煮 *shirani* boiled salted fish
葦毛 *shiroashige* gray horse
装束 *shiroshōzoku* white dress
無垢 *shiromuku* white silk kimono
葡萄酒 *shiro budōshu* white wine
雲 *hakuun, shirakumo* white clouds, fleecy clouds
雲母 *shiro ummo* muscovite, mica
13 鼠 *shironezumi* white rat
痴 *hakuchi* imbecility
蓮 *byakuren* white lotus
滝 *shirataki* a sheet-like waterfall
絹 *shiroginu* white silk
鉛 *hakuen* white lead
戦 *hakusen* hand-to-hand fight; bare-handed fight
塗 *shironu(ri)* whitewashed, white-painted, white-plastered
詰草 *shirotsumekusa* white clover
鉢巻 *shirohachimaki* white headband
話 *hakuwa* colloquial Chinese
話文学 *hakuwa bungaku* colloquial Chinese literature
14 旗 *hakki, shirahata* white flag; flag of truce
樺 *shirakaba, shirakamba* white birch
磁 *hakuji* white chinaware
綾 *shiraaya* figured white silk
銀 *shirogane* silver
墨 *hakuboku* chalk
熊 *shirokuma* polar bear
綿布 *shiromempu* white cotton
銅 *hakudō* nickel
銅貨 *hakudōka* nickel coins
髪 *hakuhatsu, shiraga* white hair, gray hair
髪染 *shiragazo(me)* dyeing gray hair black
髪頭 *shiraga atama* gray head
15 線 *hakusen* white line, white tape
蝶 *shirochō* white butterfly
熱 *hakunetsu* white heat, incandescence; climax
熱化 *hakunetsuka suru* approach the climax
熱灯 *hakunetsutō* incandescent lamp
熱戦 *hakunetsusen* an exciting game
16 糖 *hakutō* white sugar
鞘 *shirasaya* a plain wood scabbard
髭 *shirahige* gray mustache
壁 *shirakabe, hakuheki* white wall, whitewashed wall
頭翁 *hakutōō* white haired old man
17 濠 *Hakugō* White-Australia
鍵 *hakken* the white keys

5 玄玉王瓜瓦甘生用田疋疒癶 0【白】皮皿目矛矢石示ネ内禾穴立

檀 *byakudan* sandalwood, almug wood
檀油 *byakudan'yu* sandalwood oil
18 襟 *shiroeri* white collar
璧 *hakuheki* white gem; a treasure
19 蟻 *shiroari* white ant, termite
20 蘭 *byakuran, hakuran* white orchid
21 魔 *hakuma* white devil, the snow
蠟 *hakurō* white refined wax
露 *Hakuro* White Russia; white dew
23 鑞 *byakurō, shirome* pewter, solder
24 鷺 *shirasagi* snowy heron

1

A 百 3864 / J4934 / M22679 佰 174 / J5051 / M553 BYAKU. HYAKU hundred; a great number; all. *momo* hundred; a great number, great amount.

2 八鐘 *hyakuhachi (no) kane* bells tolling out the old year
人一首 *hyakunin'isshu* 100 poems by 100 famous poets; the poem card game
3 万 *hyakuman* million
万長者 *hyakumanchōja* millionaire; multimillionaire
万遍 *hyakumamben* a million times; praying a million times
4 方 *hyappō* in every way
匁 *hyakume* five-sixths of a pound
分比 *hyakubunhi* percentage
分率 *hyakubunritsu* percentage
日咳 *hyakunichizeki* whooping cough
日紅 *sarusuberi* crape myrtle
日草 *hyakunichisō* zinnia
5 出 *hyakushutsu suru* arise in great numbers
世 *hyakusei* a long era
6 行 *hyakkō* all acts
舌鳥 *mozu* shrike
年祭 *hyakunensai* centennial celebration
色眼鏡 *hyakuiro megane* kaleidoscope
合 *yuri* lily
合木 *yuri (no) ki* tulip tree
合根 *yurine* lily bulb
合樹 *yuri (no) ki* tulip tree
7 足 *mukade* centipede
芸 *hyakugei* Jack-of-all-trades
花 *hyakka* all varieties of flowers; many flowers
花繚乱 *hyakka-ryōran* blooming in profusion; a gathering of many beautiful women
8 味 *hyakumi* all kinds (of food)
官 *hyakkan* all the officials
事 *hyakuji* all, everything
卒長 *hyakusotsuchō* centurion
姓 *hyakushō* farmer, peasant. *hyakusei* the common people
姓一揆 *hyakushō ikki* peasants' revolt
9 計 *hyakkei* all means
点 *hyakuten* hundred points, perfect mark
面相 *hyakumensō* life's many phases
発百中 *hyappatsu-hyakuchū* always hitting the bull's-eye; infallibility
科 *hyakka* many subjects (for study)
科全書 *hyakka zensho* encyclopedia
科事典 *hyakka jiten* encyclopedia
10 倍 *hyakubai* a hundredfold
般 *hyappan no* all, every, all kinds of
害 *hyakugai* great damage
鬼夜行 *hyakki-yagyō, hyakki-yakō* pandemonium, scandalous scene
11 済 *Kudara* an ancient Korean kingdom, Paekche
貨 *hyakka* all kinds of goods
貨店 *hyakkaten* department store
12 景 *hyakkei* 100 famous views
13 雷 *hyakurai* a hundred thunderclaps
戦百勝 *hyakusen-hyakushō* ever-victorious; many successful campaigns; invincibility
14 聞 *hyakubun* hearing a hundred times
態 *hyakutai* various phases
15 弊 *hyakuhei* all evils
16 錬 *hyakuren* well-tempered; well drilled; well trained
獣 *hyakujū* all kinds of animals
薬 *hyakuyaku* sundry remedies
薬長 *hyakuyaku (no) chō* the best medicine, i.e., saké
18 難 *hyakunan* all obstacles, all sorts of trouble

2

皃 3865 / J6226 / M22686 See 貌 5762.

皀 3866 / J6225 / M22683 KYŪ. KYŌ fragrance of grain.

3

A **的** 3867 / J452a / M22692 TEKI. *mato* mark, target; object; the point. *-teki* adjective ending.

[4] 中 *tekichū suru* hit the mark, come true, guess right
[5] 外 *matohazu(re)* wide of the mark; out of focus
[9] 屋 *tekiya* racketeer, faker; stall keeper
[15] 確 *tekkaku, tekikaku* precision, accuracy, infallibility

4

皈 3868 / J6227 / M22705 See 帰 1564.

B **皆** 3869 / J3327 / M22699 KAI. *mina, minna* all, everybody, everything.

[5] 目 *kaimoku* altogether; (not) at all
[6] 伝 *kaiden* initiation
伐 *kaibatsu* clearing (land)
伐地 *kaibatsuchi* cleared land
[9] 皆 *minamina* all (people)
皆様 *minaminasama* all the people, all of you
[10] 納 *kainō* full (tax) payment
殺 *minagoro(shi)* massacre, annihilation
既 *kaiki* total eclipse, totality
既日食 *kaiki nisshoku* total solar eclipse
既日蝕 *kaiki nisshoku* total solar eclipse
既月食 *kaiki gesshoku* total lunar eclipse
既月蝕 *kaiki gesshoku* total lunar eclipse
既食 *kaikishoku* total eclipse, totality
既蝕 *kaikishoku* total eclipse, totality
[11] 済 *kaisai* full payment, settlement
[12] 無 *kaimu* nothing
勤 *kaikin* perfect attendance
勤賞 *kaikinshō* reward for perfect attendance
[14] 様 *minasama, minasan* all of you, all the people

A **皇** 3870 / J3944 / M22701 KŌ. Ō. *sumeragi, sumera* emperor.

[3] 土 *kōdo* the emperor's domain
女 *kōjo, ōjo* imperial princess
子 *ōji, kōshi* imperial prince
上 *kōjō* emperor
[4] 化 *kōka* imperial authority
天 *kōten* heaven, providence
太子 *kōtaishi* crown prince
太子妃 *kōtaishihi* the crown princess
太子殿下 *Kōtaishi Denka* His Highness the Crown Prince
太后 *kōtaikō, kōtaigō* empress dowager, queen mother
太后陛下 *Kōtaigō Heika* Her Imperial Majesty the Empress Dowager
太弟 *kōtaitei* emperor's younger brother
太神宮 *Kōtai Jingū* the Ise Shrine
太孫 *kōtaison* emperor's eldest direct-line grandson
[5] 兄 *kōkei* the emperor's elder brother
礼砲 *kōreihō* imperial salute, 21 guns
[6] 妃 *kōhi* empress, queen
考 *kōkō* the late emperor
后 *kōgō* empress, queen
后陛下 *Kōgō Heika* Her Majesty the Empress
[7] 図 *kōto* the emperor's plan
位 *kōi* imperial throne
沢 *kōtaku* imperial favors
系 *kōkei* imperial line
弟 *kōtei* emperor's younger brother
君 *sumeragimi* (the Japanese) emperor
[8] 国 *kōkoku* the (Japanese) Empire
妹 *kōmai* the emperor's younger sister
姉 *kōshi* the emperor's elder sister
宗 *kōsō* emperor's ancestors
典 *koten* Japanese classics
居 *kōkyo* Imperial Palace
居前広場 *Kōkyomae Hiroba* Palace Plaza
[9] 威 *kōi* imperial power or prestige
胤 *kōin* imperial descendant
城 *kōjō* imperial palace
祖 *kōso* founder of the Imperial Family, Emperor Jimmu; the Sun Goddess
軍 *kōgun* imperial army
室 *Kōshitsu* the Imperial Household, the reigning line
紀 *Kōki* Imperial Era
紀紀元 *Kōki Kigen* Imperial Era
帝 *kōtei* emperor
帝礼拝 *kōtei reihai* emperor worship
[10] 孫 *kōson* imperial grandchild, imperial descendant
祚 *kōso* imperial throne

5 玄玉王瓜瓦甘生用田疋疒癶【白】皮皿目矛矢石示ネ内禾穴立

陵 *kōryō* imperial mausoleum
都 *kōto* imperial capital
恩 *kōon* imperial favor
宮 *kōgū* imperial palace
宮警察 *Kōgū Keisatsu* Imperial Guards
11 道 *kōdō* the imperial way
運 *kōun* prosperity of the imperial throne
基 *kōki* foundation of the imperial rule
族 *kōzoku* member of the Imperial Family
族会議 *Kōzoku Kaigi* Imperial Family Council
族旗 *kōzokuki* imperial standard
12 統 *kōtō* imperial line
朝 *kōchō* imperial court; Japan
御国 *Sumeramikuni* Japan
13 継 *kōkei* emperor's successor
嗣 *kōshi* imperial heir, crown prince
漢薬 *kōkan'yaku* Chinese herb remedies
14 旗 *kōki* imperial standard
15 霊 *kōrei* spirits of the emperors
17 謨 *kōbo* imperial policy
18 闕 *kōketsu* Imperial Palace
儲 *kōcho* heir apparent, crown prince

5

皋 3871 / J6228 / M22714 See **皐** 3873.

6

皎 3872 / J6229 / M22724 KYŌ. KŌ white; shining.
15 潔 *kyōketsu, kōketsu* purity, innocence, integrity, bravery

皐 3873 / J3b29 / M22727 **皋** 3871 / J6228 / M22714 KO swamp, shore.
4 月 *satsuki* lunar fifth month

7

皖 3874 / J622a / M22736 KAN morning star; clear.

皓 3875 / J622b / M22732 KŌ white, clear.
12 歯 *kōshi* white teeth

8

晳 3876 / J622c / M22748 SEKI white; pale skin.

10

皚 3877 / J622d / M22765 GAI white.
15 皚 *gaigai(taru)* snowy, silver white.

RAD. 皮 107

Kegawa animal hide or *hi no kawa* (*kawa* "leather" or "skin" written with the character read *hi*) as distinguished from Rad. 177. Nickname: Skin.

A **皮** 3878 / J4869 / M22823 HI. *kawa* skin; hide; leather; fur, pelt; bark; peeling, husk, shell; film, cream.
3 工場 *kawa kōba* tannery
下 *hika no* subcutaneous
下注射 *hika chūsha* hypodermic injection
4 切 *kawaki(ri)* leather cutter; beginning; originator
5 付 *kawatsu(ki)* unskinned
6 衣 *kawagoromo, kawaginu* fur coat, leather coat
肉 *hiniku(ru)* be sarcastic. *hiniku* sarcasm, irony
肉屋 *hinikuya* cynic, a sarcastic person
8 具 *kawagu* leather goods
9 革 *hikaku* hides, leather
屋 *kawaya* furrier, tanner
相 *hisō na* apparent, outward, surface, superficial
10 被 *kawakabu(ri)* leather headgear; wearing leather headgear
針 *kawabari* leather needle
剥 *kawaha(gi)* skinner. *kawamu(ki)* paring, peeling

11 笛 *kawabue* whistling with the lips
袋 *kawabukuro* leather bag, wineskin
12 殻 *hikaku* shell, crust
14 層 *hisō* cortex
製 *kawasei* made of leather
算用 *kawazan'yō, kawasan'yō* counting one's unhatched chickens
15 膚 *hifu* skin
膚炎 *hifuen* dermatitis
膚科 *hifuka* dermatology
膚科学 *hifukagaku* dermatology
膚骨 *hifu (to) hone* skin and bone
膚病 *hifubyō* skin disease
膚感覚 *hifu kankaku* sense of touch
22 癬 *hizen* itch, scabies, mange

—— 5 ——

皰 3879 / J622e / M22844 Hō. Byō *nikibi* pimple.

—— 7 ——

皴 3880 / J622f / M22866 SHUN *shiwa* wrinkle, crease. *hibi* crack.

8 法 *shumpō* rendering of stones and mountains in Chinese painting

—— 9 ——

皷 3881 / J7369 / M22887 See **鼓** 7076.

皸 3882 / J6230 / M22888 **皹** 3883 / J6231 / M-X KUN. *hibi* skin cracks or roughness (due to cold or wind).

—— 10 ——

皺 3884 / J6232 / M22899 SHŪ. *shiwa* wrinkles, lines (on the face); creases, rumples, folds. *shiwa(darake)* wrinkled.
5 立 *shiwada(tsu)* wrinkle up
6 曲 *shūkyoku* a fold (in geology)
7 伸 *shiwano(bashi)* smoothing; recreation, amusement
8 苦茶 *shiwakucha* wrinkled, crumpled, withered
11 寄 *shiwayo(ru)* become wrinkled. *shiwayo(se)* shifting (the loss) to
13 腹 *shiwabara* wrinkled abdomen

RAD. 皿 108

Sara dish or *shitazara* bottom "dish." Nickname: Dish.

A **皿** 3885 / J3b2e / M22941 BEI. MYō. *sara* dish; a helping; a course.
6 回 *saramawa(shi)* dish-spinning trick
9 洗 *saraara(i)* dishwashing; dishwasher
10 秤 *sarabakari* balances

—— 3 ——

盂 3886 / J6233 / M22949 U bowl.
20 蘭盆 *Urabon* Feast of Lanterns. *Obon* Feast of the Dead
蘭盆会 *Urabon'e* Feast of Lanterns

—— 4 ——

盃 3887 / J4756 / M22955 See **杯** 2586.

盈 3888 / J314e / M22961 EI. *mi(chiru), mi(tsuru)* be full; rise (tides); mature, expire.
4 月 *eigetsu* waxing moon
11 虚 *eikyo suru* wax and wane
17 虧 *eiki, michikake* waxing and waning phases (of the moon)

B **盆** 3889 / J4b5f / M22959 BON Lantern Festival, Festival of the Dead; tray.
5 石 *bonseki* tray-landscape foundation stone
6 地 *bonchi* round valley, hollow, basin
灯籠 *Bondōrō, Bon tōrō* a *Bon*-Festival lantern
8 画 *bonga* tray landscape
10 栽 *bonsai* miniature tray landscape
11 祭 *Bon Matsu(ri)* the *Bon* Festival
12 景 *bonkei* tray landscape
提灯 *bonjōchin* the *Bon* Festival lantern

14 踊 *Bon Odo(ri)* the *Bon* Festival Dance
暮 *Bon-ku(re)* *Bon* and year-end seasons

5

盍 3890 / J6234 / M22980 Kō. Gō cover; meet, congregate. *nanzo...-zaru* why not ...?

A **益** 3891 / J3157 / M22972′ Eki, Yaku gain, benefit, profit, use, advantage. *eki(suru)* be beneficial, useful, profitable, or valuable. *ma(su)* *vt* increase, add to, augment, gain; promote (health); enlarge, extend. *vi* increase.
4 友 *ekiyū* good friend, useful friend
6 虫 *eikichū* beneficial insect
8 金 *ekikin* profit
9 荒男 *masurao* warrior; manly person
10 益 *masumasu* increasingly, more and more
11 鳥 *ekichō* beneficial bird

6

盖 3892 / J6235 / M22996 See **蓋** 5155.

盒 3893 / J6236 / M22988 Kō covered utensil.

B **盗** 3894 / J4570 / M23000 **盜** 3896 / J5d39 / M23006 Tō thief. *nusu(mu)* steal, rob, pilfer.
2 人 *nusubito, nusutto* thief
人根性 *nusubito konjō* thievish propensity
人猛猛 *nusubito-takedake(shii)* brazen (robber)
4 心 *tōshin, nusu(mi)gokoro* impulse to steal, thieving propensity
5 用 *tōyō* embezzlement; surreptitious use
犯 *tōhan* burglary, theft
去 *nusu(mi)-sa(ru)* run away with, kidnap
出 *nusu(mi)-da(su)* steal
6 伐 *tōbatsu* secret felling (of trees)
汗 *tōkan, nease* night sweat
7 見 *nusu(mi)-mi(ru)* steal a glance
足 *nusu(mi)ashi* walking stealthily
作 *tōsaku* plagiarism
8 取 *nusu(mi)-to(ru)* steal
9 食 *nusu(mi)gu(i)* stealing and eating
品 *tōhin* stolen article, stolen goods
10 笑 *nusu(mi)wara(i)* laughing up one's sleeve
11 視 *tōshi suru* peek unseen
12 塁 *tōrui* stolen base
13 賊 *tōzoku* thief, robber, burglar
電 *tōden* stealing electricity by wire tapping
載 *tōsai* plagiarism
14 聞 *nusu(mi)gi(ki)* eavesdropping, wire tapping
読 *nusu(mi)yo(mi)* surreptitious reading
17 聴 *tōchō* wire tapping; unlicensed radio listening
18 癖 *tōheki* kleptomania
難 *tōnan* robbery, burglary, theft
難品 *tōnanhin* stolen goods
難保険 *tōnan hoken* theft insurance

A **盛** 3895 / J4039 / M23001′ **盛** 3897 / J-X / M23005 Shō. Sei. Jō. *sakae(ru)* prosper, flourish; copulate (animals). *mo(ru)* serve, fill; heap up; prescribe or give (medicine); poison; mark out, graduate. *mo(ri)* quantity; good measure, liberal serving. *saka(n) na* prosperous; successful (meeting); energetic; enthusiastic; popular; furious (attack); keen (competition); extensive, large. *saka(ri)* height, peak; prime, bloom; heat (in animals).
3 土 *mo(ri)tsuchi* raising the ground level
大 *seidai na* prosperous, grand, magnificent, successful (meeting), enthusiastic (welcome)
上 *mo(ri)-a(garu)* rise, swell. *mo(ri)-a(geru)* pile up, heap up
4 込 *mo(ri)-ko(mu)* incorporate in
切 *mo(ri)ki(ri)* single helping
5 代 *seidai* prosperous age
6 返 *mo(ri)-kae(su)* rally, recover
会 *seikai* successful meeting
年 *seinen* prime of life
名 *seimei* fame, reputation
7 花 *mo(ri)bana* flowers arranged in a basin or tray
沢山 *moridakusan* many, a lot of, all kinds of; crowded (program)
8 況 *seikyō* prosperity, success, boom
典 *seiten* grand ceremony
者 *shōja* prosperous person

事 *seiji* grand event; splendid enterprise
9 砂 *mo(ri)zuna* a pile of sand
10 時 *seiji* prime of life; prosperous age. *saka(ri)doki* prosperous time; crowded time; season or heat (in animals)
殺 *mo(ri)-koro(su)* kill by poisoning
夏 *seika* midsummer
衰 *seisui* rise and fall, ups and downs, vicissitudes; welfare
宴 *seien* grand banquet
挙 *seikyo* an excellent plan; a prosperous enterprise
11 運 *seiun* prosperity, good fortune
菓子 *mo(ri)gashi* cakes arranged in a basket
12 場 *saka(ri)ba* pleasure resort; busiest quarters (of a town), crowded place
粧 *seisō* heavy elegant make-up
装 *seisō* best clothes, beautiful attire, full regalia, full armor
14 徳 *seitoku* illustrious virtues
15 儀 *seigi* grand ceremony
潰 *mo(ri)-tsubu(su)* get a person drunk
蕎麦 *mo(ri)soba* buckwheat noodles served on a draining receptacle
18 観 *seikan* grand spectacle

7

盗 3896 / J5d39 / M23006 See 盗 3894.

盛 3897 / J-X / M23005 See 盛 3895.

8

盞 3898 / J6237 / M23020 SAN wine cup. *sakazuki* wine glass, saké cup.

A 盟 3899 / J4c41 / M23024 MEI oath; alliance.
4 友 *meiyū* staunch friend
5 主 *meishu* leader, leading power (of an alliance)
兄 *meikei* an honored friend
6 休 *meikyū* student strike
邦 *meihō* ally
9 約 *meiyaku* pledge, pact, alliance

9

盡 3900 / J6238 / M23029 See 尽 1408.

B 監 3901 / J3446 / M23032 KAN *asa* office, government office; director, head official.
6 守 *kanshu* custody, surveillance
守人 *kanshunin* custodian, (forest) ranger
8 房 *kambō* cell, ward ⌈supervisor, auditor
事 *kanji* inspector, superintendent,
9 軍 *kangun* command of an army
査 *kansa* inspection; auditing; auditor
査役 *kansayaku* inspector, controller, auditor
10 修 *kanshū* (editorial) supervision
11 埋下 *kanrika* under the supervision of
視 *kanshi* guarding, observation, inspection, supervision, surveillance
視所 *kanshisho* observation post, guard box, lookout
視者 *kanshisha* superintendent, watchman, caretaker
視班 *kanshihan* inspection team
視船 *kanshisen* police boat
視線 *kanshisen* picket line
13 禁 *kankin* imprisonment
督 *kantoku* supervision, surveillance, jurisdiction; inspector, superintendent; direction; (film) director; manager; bishop
督下 *kantokuka* under the jurisdiction of
督者 *kantokusha* overseer, superintendent, inspector
督官 *kantokukan* inspector, superintendent ⌈authorities
督官庁 *kantoku kanchō* competent
14 獄 *kangoku* prison, jail, penitentiary, place of detention
製 *kansei* controlled manufacturing
察 *kansatsu* inspection; inspector
察官 *kansatsukan* police supervisor
20 護 *kango* custody

10

B 盤 3902 / J4857 / M23036 BAN, HAN shallow bowl, platter, tray, tub; board; phonograph record.
5 石 *banjaku* huge rock. *banseki* the *go* board and its stones

台 *bandai* shallow fish tray
7 陀 *handa* solder; pewter
9 面 *bammen* face of a record or board
10 秤 *sarabakari* balances
根 *bankon* coiled root; obstacle; hardship
根錯節 *bankon-sakusetsu* severe trials, hardships
15 踞 *bankyo suru* lurk in the way; proudly occupy (territory), be dominant, hold sway

11

盧 3903 J623a M23050 Ro hut.

盥 3904 J6239 M23041 KAN. *tarai* tub, washbasin.
6 回 *taraimawa(shi)* balancing a spinning wash tub; monopolizing power in a clique; working through a profitable deal; holding (a suspect) at one police station after another

12

盪 3905 J623b M23062 Tō *toro(keru)* *vi* melt, be charmed, be captivated. *toro(kasu)* *vt* melt, fuse; charm, captivate.

RAD.  109

Me eye. At left: *me hen*. Nickname: Eye.

A **目** 3906 J4c5c M23105 MOKU item, division, class; order (of plants or animals). *me* eye; look, gaze; notice, attention; viewpoint; discrimination, insight; experience; treatment; care, favor, pity; texture, weave; mesh; grain, square; sight, vision; tooth (of a saw); weight; momme (0.1325 oz.); eye (of a needle). *moku(suru)* regard as. *me(boshii)* attractive, conspicuous, notable; valuable. *me(magurushii)* dizzy, bewildering; bustling. *ma* eye. *-me* ordinal ending, -st, -nd, -rd, -th; point; degree, extent.
2 八分 *mehachibu* a little below the eyes; most respectfully; a little less than full
3 下 *meshita* subordinate, junior, inferior
上 *meue* seniors, superiors
子勘定 *me(no)ko kanjō* measuring with the eye; mental arithmetic
子算 *me(no)kozan* measuring with the eye; mental arithmetic
4 方 *mekata* weight
止 *me (o) to(meru)* examine carefully
辺 *ma(no)ata(ri)* in one's presence, before one's eyes
切 *me(k)ki(ri)* considerably, noticeably
元 *memoto* the eyes
今 *mokkon* now, at the present
分量 *mebunryō* eye measurement
引袖引 *mehi(ki)-sodehi(ki)* calling attention by winking or sleeve pulling
5 立 *meda(tsu)* be conspicuous. *me (ni) ta(tsu)* be prominent. *meta(te)* setting (a saw)
処 *medo* aim, goal; outlook; eye (of a needle)
尻 *mejiri* the outside corner of the eye
打 *meu(chi)* perforation
礼 *mokurei* nod (in greeting)
白押 *mejiroo(shi)* jostling, milling
出度 *medeta(i)* happy, auspicious; stupid, half-witted. *(o)medeto(u) (gozaimasu)* congratulations. *medeta(ku)* happily, successfully, auspiciously
玉 *me (no) tama, medama* eyeball; scolding
玉焼 *medamaya(ki)* eggs sunny side up
付 *metsu(ki)* look, eye expression. *metsu(karu), me(kkaru)* be found; be found out, be discovered. *me(kkeru)* find; find out; discover; locate; catch sight of; notice; recognize; hunt for, get used to seeing, be familiar to. *metsu(ke)* feudal overseer, public censor
付役 *metsu(ke)yaku* feudal overseer, public censor

付物 *metsu(ke)mono* a find, acquisition
6 色 *me (no) iro, meiro* expression of the eyes, one's countenance
近 *mejika* nearness
印 *mejirushi* landmark, pylon, guide, mark
次 *mokuji* table of contents
安 *meyasu* standard, criterion; aim
当 *mea(te)* guide (as a star); aim. *ma(no)a(tari)* face to face, on the spot, in one's presence, with ones own eyes
早 *mebaya(i)* sharp-eyed, shrewd, easily awakened
先 *mesaki* before one's eyes, under one's nose; immediate future; foresight, acumen; appearance
7 見 *memi(e)* audience, interview; stage debut; service on-trial (of a servant)
角 *mekado* corner of the eye, a sharp look
庇 *mabisashi* visor, eyeshade
利 *meki(ki)* judging; judge, connoisseur, virtuoso. *me (ga) ki(ku)* have good judgement; be a good superintendent
余 *me (ni) ama(ru)* scandalous, intolerable
呉 *me (o) ku(reru)* examine carefully
医者 *meisha* oculist
抜 *menu(ki) no* main; important
抜通 *menu(ki)do(ri)* principal street
8 送 *mokusō suru* gaze after
明 *mea(ki)* one who can see, educated person. *mea(kashi)* detective, (police) spy
注 *me (o) soso(gu)* examine carefully
肥 *me (ga) koe(ru)* have good judgement
刺 *meza(shi)* dried sardines tied through their eyes
毒 *me(no)doku* something tempting
的 *mokuteki* aim, purpose, intention
的地 *mokutekichi* destination
的物 *mokutekibutsu* objective
的格 *mokutekikaku* objective case
的税 *mokutekizei* special-purpose tax
的補語 *mokuteki hogo* objective complement
9 面 *mezura* appearance, outward show
屎 *mekuso* eye mucus, eye discharge
途 *mokuto* aim, goal
通 *medō(ri)* an audience (with); height of the eyes. *me (o) tō(su)* glance through
垢 *meaka* eye mucus
指 *meza(su)* aim at; spot or eye (someone)
映 *mabayu(i)* glaring; dazzling, blinding
前 *me (no) mae* in one's presence, close at hand. *mokuzen* under one's nose, before one's eyes; immediate (gain). *mesaki* before one's eyes, under one's nose; immediate future; foresight, acumen; appearance
星 *meboshi* objective
10 高 *me (ga) taka(i)* have good judgement
病 *meyami* eye trouble; person with eye trouble
眩 *mekurume(ku)* be dazzled. *me (ga) kura(mu)* be dizzy. *memai* dizziness.
紛 *memaguru(shii)* dizzy, bewildering, dazzled, confused
脂 *meyani* eye mucus, eye secretion
配 *mekuba(se) suru* wink significantly at. *mekuba(ri)* vigilance, surveillance
敏 *mezato(i), mebashiko(i)* quick-eyed, sharp-eyed
笑 *mokushō* laughing with the eyes
差 *meza(su)* aim at; spot (someone). *manaza(shi)* a glance, a look
11 張 *meba(ri) suru* paste paper over, seal up (a window)
掛 *mega(keru)* aim at
深 *mabuka ni, mebuka ni* down over the eyes
移 *meutsu(ri)* distraction, difficulty in choosing
許 *memoto* the eyes
盛 *memo(ri)* scale, graduation
12 減 *mebe(ri)* weight loss
測 *mokusoku* measuring with the eye
違 *mechiga(i)* mistaken observation
覚 *meza(masu) vt* rouse, awaken. *meza(meru) vi* wake up, awake to (reality). *meza(me)* waking, awakening, conversion. *meza(mashii)* remarkable, conspicuous, brilliant. *meza(mashi)* eye-opener (a drink)
覚時計 *meza(mashi)dokei* alarm clock
13 溢 *mekobo(re)* overlooking, oversight. *mekobo(shi)* connivance, overlooking
隠 *mekaku(shi)* eye bandage, blindfold; blinkers; a (board) screen
障 *mezawa(ri)* eyesore, disfigurement, unsightly object, unsightly area

馴 *mena(reru)* get used to seeing
新 *meatara(shii)* novel, original
蓋 *mabuta* eyelid
睫 *mokushō* eyes and eyebrows; something very close
睫間 *mokushō (no) kan ni* imminently
塗 *menu(ri)* sealing, plastering up
14 端 *mehashi* tact
語 *mokugo suru* wink at
算 *mokusan* anticipation, calculation
旗魚 *mekajiki* swordfish
鼻 *mehana* eyes and nose
鼻立 *mehanada(chi)* looks, features
腐 *mekusa(re)* bleary-eyed person (not alcoholic)
腐金 *mekusa(re)gane* pittance
15 標 *mokuhyō* sign, mark; target; objective; standard
潰 *metsubu(shi)* powder thrown to blind the eyes
縁 *mabuchi* eyelid
論 *mokuro(mu)* plan, scheme, contemplate
論見 *mokuromi* plan, scheme; aim, intention; frame up.
敵 *me (no) kataki* enmity, hostility
撃 *mokugeki* observation
撃者 *mokugekisha* eyewitness
16 積 *mezumo(ri)* estimating by eye
賭 *mokuto suru* see, observe, witness
醒 *meza(masu)* rouse, awaken
録 *mokuroku* contents, list, inventory, catalog
薬 *megusuri* eye medicine. *me (no) kusuri* a treatment for sore eyes
17 瞽 *meshii* blindness; a blind person
糞 *mekuso* eye mucus, eye discharge
18 癖 *mekuse* twitching of the eye
顔 *megao* a look
19 鏡 *megane* eye glasses
20 懸 *me (ni) kake(ru)* show; help
22 籠 *mekago* openwork basket

3

B **盲** 3907 / J4c55 / M23132 Bō. Mō blindness. *mekura, meshii* blindness; blind person; ignorance, ignoramus.
2 人 *mōjin* blind person
5 打 *mekurau(chi)* hitting blindly; random firing
目 *mōmoku* blindness
目的 *mōmokuteki* blind (devotion)
目飛行 *mōmoku hikō* instrument flying
7 判 *mekuraban* blindly stamping one's seal
8 学校 *mōgakkō* school for the blind
9 信 *mōshin* blind belief, credulity
点 *mōten* blind spot
10 進 *mōshin* rushing recklessly; presumption
従 *mōjū* blind obedience
射 *mōsha* shooting blindly
11 探 *mekurasagu(ri)* blindly groping
動 *mōdō, bōdō* acting blindly
断 *mōdan* hasty conclusion
唖 *mōa* blind and dumb
唖学校 *mōa gakkō* school for the blind and dumb
12 買 *mekuraga(i)* buying blindly
13 愛 *mōai* blind love
滅法 *mekura meppō* recklessness
腸 *mōchō* appendix; caecum
腸炎 *mōchōen* appendicitis
14 暦 *mekuragoyomi* picture calendar for illiterates
導犬 *mōdōken* seeing-eye dog
管銃創 *mōkan jūsō* lodged-bullet wound
15 撃 *mekurau(chi)* random shooting
16 壁 *mekura kabe* windowless wall
19 爆 *mōbaku* indiscriminate bombing

A **直** 3908 / J443e / M23136 JIKI, CHOKU honesty, frankness; simplicity; correctness; being straight; night duty. *nao(ru)* be mended; get well; be restored; return to normal; be installed (as a legal wife); change (from third to second class). *nao(su)* mend, repair, put in order, reform, correct; revise, amend; re-do, alter; cure; restore; adjust, regulate; convert (money). *jika ni* directly, firsthand, in person. *jiki* direct, in person; soon; at once; just; near by. *jiki ni* soon; immediately; easily. *ne* price, cost, value. *su(gu)* immediately; easily; right (near). *su(gu) na* honest, upright. *tada(chi) ni* immediately, directly, in person. *hita to* close to. *nao(ki)* straight, upright. *nao(shi)* correction; repair; person making repair. *tada* direct; close; straight; immediately. *nao* straight; mischief; ordinary, common. *hita* earnestly; immediately; exactly.

2 刀 *chokutō* straight sword
3 上 *chokujō* directly above; going steadily upward
下 *chokka* directly under. *chokka suru* fall perpendicularly
下型地震 *chokkagata jishin* earthquake involving vertical displacement
4 中 *tadanaka* middle
方体 *chokuhōtai* right-angled parallelepiped
5 払 *jikibara(i)* cash payment
出 *chokushutsu suru* shoot straight out; grow straight down
立 *chokuritsu* vertical, perpendicular, upright, erect. *chokuritsu suru* stand erect, rise perpendicularly
立不動 *chokuritsu-fudō* standing at attention
立茎 *chokuritsukei* erect stem
6 行 *chokkō* through, non-stop
伝 *jikiden* direct transmission (of mysteries or skill); initiation
列 *chokuretsu* series wiring
7 角 *chokkaku* right angle
言 *chokugen* plain speaking
走 *hitabashi(ri)* running swiftly
系 *chokkei* lineal descendant, direct line
売 *chokubai suru* sell directly
弟子 *jiki deshi* personal pupil
足袋 *jika tabi* work *tabi*
8 送 *chokusō* direct delivery
往 *chokuō suru* go unhesitatingly forward
径 *chokkei* diameter
押 *hitao(shi) ni* steadily
物 *nao(shi)mono* mending
垂 *hitatare* ancient ceremonial court robe
直 *jikijiki no* personal, direct
参 *jikisan* immediate follower (of the shogun)
取引 *jiki torihiki* spot transaction, cash transaction
9 面 *chokumen suru* face, confront, be confronted by
通 *chokutsū* direct communication, through service
後 *chokugo* immediately after, right behind
前 *chokuzen* just before
奏 *jikisō* direct report to the throne
映館 *chokueikan* chain movie theaters
10 進 *chokushin suru* go right on, go straight ahead
流 *chokuryū* direct current
航 *chokkō* direct voyage, direct service
射 *chokusha* direct fire, frontal fire; direct rays
11 達 *jikitatsu* direct delivery
球 *chokkyū* straight ball
視 *chokushi suru* look straight at, face squarely
訳 *chokuyaku* literal translation
情 *chokujō* frankness, impulsiveness
情径行 *chokujokeikō* frankness; impulsiveness
接 *chokusetsu* direct, immediate, personal, firsthand
接伝染 *chokusetsu densen* direct infection
接行動 *chokusetsu kōdō* direct action
接法 *chokusetsuhō* direct method; indicative mood
接的 *chokusetsuteki* direct
接教授法 *chokusetsu kyōjuhō* direct method of teaching
接税 *chokusetsuzei* direct tax
接費 *chokusetsuhi* direct cost
接話法 *chokusetsu wahō* direct quotation
12 属 *chokuzoku* direct control
喩 *chokuyu* simile
渡 *jikawata(shi)* direct delivery
焼 *jikaya(ki)* broiling over an open fire
税 *chokuzei* direct tax
結 *chokketsu* direct connection
訴 *jikiso* direct appeal
筆 *jikihitsu* one's own handwriting. *chokuhitsu* writing with an upright brush; frank writing
答 *chokutō, jikitō* prompt answer, direct personal answer
営 *chokuei* direct management

覚 *chokkaku* intuition, insight
間比率 *chokkan hiritsu* ratio of direct to indirect taxes
覚的 *chokkakuteki ni* intuitively
13 腸 *chokuchō* rectum
話 *jikiwa* one's own account (of something)
路 *chokuro, sugumichi* straight road, short cut
感 *chokkan* intuition
感的 *chokkanteki* intuitive
14 様 *su(gu)sama* immediately
説法 *chokusetsuhō* indicative mood
截 *chokusetsu na* frank, straightforward
截簡明 *chokusetsu-kammei* simple and plain
15 線 *chokusen* straight line, air line, beeline
線形 *chokusenkei* rectangular figures
談 *jikidan, jikadan* personal account (of); direct talks
談判 *jika dampan* direct talks
撃 *chokugeki* direct hit
撃弾 *chokugekidan* direct hit
16 諫 *chokkan* personal admonition
覧 *jikiran* respectfully looking at (something)
積出 *jiki tsumidashi* immediate shipment
輸入 *chokuyunyū, jiki yunyū* direct import
輸出 *chokuyushutsu, jiki yushutsu* direct export
17 謝 *hitaayama(ri)* earnest apology
轄 *chokkatsu* direct control
轄地 *chokkatsuchi* area under direct control (of the shogun)
轄植民地 *chokkatsu shokuminchi* crown colony
18 観 *chokkan* intuition, insight
観的 *chokkanteki* intuitive

4

明 3909 / J-X / M23178 See 明 2435.

盻 3910 / J623d / M23166 Kei, Gei glare at; reflect upon, look back, reminisce.

眈 3911 / J623e / M23189 Tan look; glare at, stare at.

B **盾** 3912 / J3d62 / M23171 Jun. *tate* shield, buckler, escutcheon; pretext.

眄 3913 / J6240 / M23182 Ben looking askance.

眇 3914 / J623f / M23188 Byō minuteness. *byō(taru)* little, tiny, insignificant. *sugame* squint, cross-eyes, walleyes.
9 眇 *byōbyō(taru)* trifling, slight

B **冒** 3915 / J4b41 / M-X **冐** 393 / J666e / M1534 Bō. *oka(su)* risk, face, defy, dare; (diseases) attack; damage; desecrate; assume (a name).
10 険 *bōken* risk, venture, adventure
険的 *bōkenteki* adventurous, risky
険談 *bōkendan* adventure story
16 頭 *bōtō* opening paragraph or statement
18 瀆 *bōtoku* blasphemy, profanity, desecration, sacrilige

A **省** 3916 / J3e4a / M23179 Sei. Shō ministry, department; province (in China). *habu(ku)* omit, eliminate; curtail, economize. *kaeri(miru)* look back; turn around, look back upon, review; examine oneself; take notice of. *tsukasa* office, government office; director, head official.
5 令 *shōrei* ministerial ordinance
11 略 *shōryaku* abbreviation, abridgment, omission
12 筆 *shōhitsu* abbreviation; simplified form of a character. *seihitsu* cutting out some strokes in a character; omitting some passages
14 察 *seisatsu, shōsatsu* reflection, consideration

眉 3917 / J487d / M23190 Bi. Mi. *mayu* eyebrow.
4 毛 mayuge eyebrows
5 目 *bimoku* face, looks, features
尻 *mayujiri* end of an eyebrow
7 庇 *mabisashi* visor; eyeshade
11 唾物 *mayutsubamono* fake
12 間 *miken* brow, middle forehead
14 墨 *mayuzumi* blackened eyebrows; eyebrow pencil

A **県** 3918 / J3829 / M23210′ **縣** 4555 / J6551 / M27784 KEN prefecture; district (in China). *agata* ancient demarcated cultivated areas.

2 人 *kenjin* native of a prefecture
人会 *kenjinkai* an association of people from the same province
3 下 *kenka* in or under the prefecture, throughout the prefecture
5 立 *kenritsu* prefectural (institution)
庁 *kenchō* prefectural office
外 *kengai* outside the prefecture
令 *kenrei* prefectural ordinance
6 会 *kenkai* prefectural assembly
有 *ken'yū* owned by the prefecture
7 社 *kensha* prefectural shrine
8 治 *kenchi* prefectural administration
知事 *ken chiji* prefectural governor
11 道 *kendō* prefectural road
視学 *kenshigaku* prefectural school inspector
12 税 *kenzei* prefectural tax
営 *ken'ei* prefectural operation
13 債 *kensai* prefectural loan
勢調査 *kensei chōsa* prefectural census
20 議 *kengi* prefectural assembly member
議会 *kengikai* prefectural assembly
議会議員 *kengikai giin* prefectural assembly member

A **看** 3919 / J3447 / M23196 **看** 3921 / J X / M-X KAN. *mi(ru)* see.

6 守 *kanshu* jailer
守者 *kanshusha* jailer
8 取 *mi-to(ru)* care for the sick. *kanshu suru* see through, perceive, notice, get wind of
板 *kamban* sign, signboard, doorplate; poster, billboard; appearance; figurehead; policy; attraction; closing time
板屋 *kamban'ya* sign maker
板倒 *kambandao(re)* ostentatious
板娘 *kamban musume* show girl
板描 *kambanka(ki)* sign painter
9 点 *kanten* viewpoint
客 *kankyaku* spectators, visitors, audience
10 破 *mi-yabu(ru), kampa suru* see through, penetrate, fathom
病 *kambyō* nursing (a patient)
病人 *kambyōnin* nurse
病疲 *kambyōzuka(re)* nursing fatigue
11 過 *kanka* connivance, shutting one's eyes to
做 *mi-na(su)* consider as
経 *kankin* silent sutra reading
貫 *kankan* weighing; platform scales
20 護 *kango* nursing
護兵 *kangohei* army nurse, medic
護士 *kangoshi* (male) nurse
護長 *kangochō* chief nurse (in the army)
護法 *kangohō* nursing art
護卒 *kangosotsu* army nurse, medic
護学 *kangogaku* nursing science
護疲 *kangotsuka(re)* nursing fatigue
護婦 *kangofu* (female) nurse
護婦長 *kangofuchō* head nurse
護婦学院 *kangofu gakuin* nurses' training school
護婦養成所 *kangofu yōseijo* nurses' training school

A **相** 3920 / J416a / M23151 SŌ aspect, phase, physiognomy. SHŌ minister of state, councilor. *ai-* together, each other; mutually, reciprocally; fellow-; emphatic verbal prefix.

4 反 *aihan suru* be contrary to, disagree with
引 *aibi(ki) suru* pull apart, pull against each other
手 *aite* companion, mate, date, partner; the other party, opponent, adversary; object
手方 *aitekata* the other party, opponent
手役 *aiteyaku* partner, opposite player or actor, companion
手国 *aitekoku* the country we are dealing with
手取 *aitedo(ru)* take on (opponents); sue
互 *sōgo* mutual, reciprocal. *aitagai ni* mutually, each other, one another
互安全保障 *sōgo anzen hoshō* mutual security
互会社 *sōgogaisha* mutual insurance company
互作用 *sōgo sayō* reciprocal action, interaction
互扶助 *sōgo fujo* mutual aid
互条約 *sōgo jōyaku* bilateral treaty, treaty of reciprocity
互依存 *sōgo izon* interdependence

互保険会社 *sōgo hokengaisha* mutual insurance company
互組合 *sōgo kumiai* cooperative society, mutual-aid association
互援助 *sōgo enjo* mutual assistance
互援助条約 *sōgo enjo jōyaku* mutual-assistance treaty
互貿易 *sōgo bōeki* mutual trade
互貯蓄銀行 *sōgo chochiku ginkō* mutual savings bank
互銀行 *sōgo ginkō* mutual-financing bank
互関係 *sōgo kankei* reciprocity, interrelationship
5 仕 *aishi* companion, associate
打 *aiu(chi)* striking each other simultaneously
加平均 *sōka heikin* arithmetical mean
生 *aioi* growing up together
生松 *aioi (no) matsu* twin pines; double pine
6 老 *aio(i)* a couple growing older together
成 *aina(ru)* emphatic for *na(ru)*: become, get or grow (old), form (a part of); set in, come (time or seasons); turn into; be reduced to; consist of; be accomplished; result in; prove (fatal); amount to; play the part of; elapse; reach (a certain age); bear, stand; be promoted; be pleased to
曳 *aibiki* lovers' secret meeting, a date
次 *aitsu(gu)* follow in succession. *aitsu(ide)* in succession
好 *sōgō* looks, features, countenance
交 *aimaji(waru)* associate with. *tsuru(mu)* mate, copulate
会 *aikai suru* assemble
共 *aitomo ni* together
年 *aidoshi* the same age
争 *aiaraso(u)* quarrel, dispute
合傘 *aia(i)gasa de* under the same umbrella
似 *sōji* resemblance, similarity, analogy
似形 *sōjikei* similar figures (in math)
似点 *sōjiten* points of agreement
伝 *sōden* inheritance, heirship; conferring of priestly orders
伝不動産 *sōden fudōsan* family estate
伝動産 *sōden dōsan* heirloom
当 *sōtō na* suitable, proper, corresponding, reasonable; respectable; sufficient, adequate, passable. *sōtō suru* befit, be worthy of; deserve, merit; correspond to; be proportionate to
当品 *sōtōhin* articles of similar value
当数 *sōtōsū* quite a number
当欄 *sōtōran* corresponding column
7 見 *sōmi* physiognomist
図 *aihaka(ru)* counsel together. *aizu* sign, signal
床 *aidoko* sleeping in the same room
応 *fusawa(shii)* suitable, becoming, fitting, worthy of, proper, adequate, appropriate. *sōō* suitability, fitness
励 *aihage(mu)* encourage each other
伴 *aitomona(u)* accompany. *shōban* participation
作 *aisaku* intercrop
住 *aizu(mi)* living together
役 *aiyaku* colleague
扶 *aitasu(keru)* help each other
克 *sōkoku* rivalry
弟子 *aideshi* fellow pupil, fellow apprentice
身互 *aimitaga(i)* mutual assistance
対 *aitai suru* face each other, lie opposite. *sōtai* relativity, reciprocity, symmetry. *aitai de* personally, directly
対立 *aitairitsu suru* oppose; face each other
対尽 *aitaizu(ku) de* by common consent
対的 *sōtaiteki* relative, reciprocal
対性 *sōtaisei* relativity
対性原理 *sōtaisei genri* theory of relativity
対原理 *sōtai genri* theory of relativity
対湿度 *sōtai shitsudo* relative humidity
対義務 *sōtai gimu* reciprocal obligations
8 退 *aibiki suru* mutually retreat
性 *aishō* affinity, compatibility
並 *ainara(bu)* line up with
定 *aisada(meru)* ordain, decide on
9 連 *aitsurana(ru)* be joined
俟 *aima(tte)* coupled with, in cooperation with
持 *aimo(chi)* cooperation, interdependence, mutual help; common possession; sharing (expenses)
計 *aihaka(ru)* plan together

客 *aikyaku* roommate; fellow passenger; one sharing a seat
乗 *aino(ri)* riding together. *sōjō* multiplication
変 *aikawa(razu)* as usual
剋 *sōkoku* rivalry
前後 *aizengo* about the same time
思 *sōshi* mutual love
思仲 *sōshi (no) naka* courtship
思相愛 *sōshisōai* mutual love
10 孫 *aimago* persons with the same grandparents
称 *sōshō* symmetry
討 *aiu(chi)* two or more pouncing on one enemy
殺 *sōsatsu, sōsai* offset, cancellation (of obligations)
容 *aiu(renai)* contrary, incompatible
11 惚 *aibo(re)* mutual love
接 *aises(suru)* meet, get together
済 *aisu(mimasen)* I'm sorry.
添 *aiso(u)* marry and live together
宿 *aiyado(ri), aiyado* lodging together
12 間 *aima* interval; leisure. *ai(no)ma* a room between; low central room in certain shrines
婿 *aimuko* husbands of sisters
棒 *aibō* pal, partner, accomplice
結 *aimusu(bu)* join together with
傘 *aigasa de* under the same umbrella
喜 *aiyoroko(bu)* rejoice together
等 *sōtō* equality
集 *aiatsu(maru), aitsudo(u)* *vi* gather together
場 *sōba* market price; speculation; estimation
場師 *sōbashi* speculator, operator, plunger
違 *sōi* difference, disparity, gap, discrepancy, disagreement, variation, contrast
違点 *sōiten* point of difference
違無 *sōina(i)* no doubt that. *sōina(ku)* without fail, surely
13 嫁 *aiyome* women whose husbands are brothers
携 *aitazusa(ete)* together with, hand-in-hand, in couples
煌 *aikira(meku)* flash together
継 *aitsu(gu)* continue
触 *aifu(reru)* touch each other
戦 *aitataka(u)* fight
愛 *sōai* mutual love
槌 *aizuchi, ai (no) tsuchi* chiming in with another's conversation
槌打 *aizuchi (o) u(tsu)* chime in with, echo (someone)
続 *sōzoku* succession, inheritance, descent
続人 *sōzokunin* heir
続争 *sōzoku araso(i)* succession quarrels
続者 *sōzokusha* heir
続財産 *sōzoku zaisan* inheritance
続税 *sōzokuzei* inheritance tax
続権 *sōzokuken* heirship, right of inheritance
14 構 *aikama(ete)* certainly, beyond doubt
貌 *sōbō* features, looks, physiognomy
関 *sōkan* mutual relationship, interdependence
関的 *sōkanteki* correlative
関係数 *sōkan keisū* coefficient of correlation
関関係 *sōkan kankei* reciprocity, interrelation, correlation
15 輪 *sōrin* pagoda finial
撃 *aiu(chi)* striking each other simultaneously
器 *shōki* capacity for premiership
撲 *sumō* sumo, wrestling; wrestling match; sumo wrestler
撲取 *sumōto(ri)* sumo wrestler
談 *sōdan* consultation, conversation, talk; bargain; offer, proposal; agreement, arrangement. *sōdan(zuku)* mutual agreement
談会 *sōdankai* consultation, conference
談役 *sōdan'yaku* counselor, consultant
談所 *sōdanjo* information bureau, consultation bureau
談相手 *sōdan aite* adviser, confidant
16 謀 *aihaka(ru)* plan together; plot together
整 *aitotono(u)* be prepared, be arranged. *aitotono(eru)* prepare, arrange
17 償 *aitsuguna(u)* recompense each other
19 識 *sōshiki* acquaintance

5

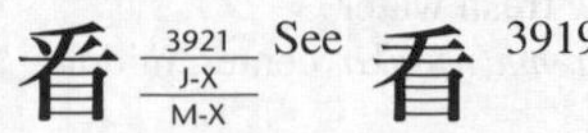
看 3921 J-X M-X See 看 3919.

眤 3922 / J6242 / M23247 See **睇** 3937.

昧 3923 / J6246 / M23230 MAI dark.

眩 3924 / J6241 / M23254 GEN faint. *gen(su)* get dizzy; dazzle. *kurume(ku)* go round and round, get dizzy. *mabu(shii)* dazzling, glaring, blinding. *mabayu(i)* glaring, dazzling, blinding.

11 彩 *gensai* camouflage
12 惑 *genwaku suru* dazzle, daze, blind
然 *genzen* dizziness; dazzling
13 暈 *gen'un, memai* dizziness

B **眠** 3925 / J4c32 / M23240 MIN sleep. *nebu(ru), nemu(ru)* sleep, die. *nemu(tagaru)* feel sleepy. *nemu(ri-kokeru)* sleep soundly. *nemu(i), nebu(tai), nemu(tai), nemu(ge) ni, nemu(tage) ni, nemu(sō) ni, nemu(tasō) ni* sleepy, drowsy, lethargic.

6 気 *nemuke* sleepiness, drowsiness
気覚 *nemukeza(mashi)* cure for drowsiness
9 草 *nemu(ri)gusa* mimosa, sensitive plant
10 病 *nemu(ri)byō* sleeping sickness
16 薬 *nemu(ri)gusuri* sleeping medicine; narcotics

A **真** 3926 / J3f3f / M23236 **眞** 3927 / J6243 / M23235 SHIN truth; reality; genuineness; Buddhist sect originating in the thirteenth century. *makoto* sincerity, honesty, fidelity; truth. *shin ni, hon ni* truly, actually, really. *ma-* just, right, due (east); pure, genuine, true.

1 一文字 *maichimonji* straight, as the crow flies
2 二 *ma(p)puta(tsu) ni, mafuta(tsu) ni* right in half
人 *shinjin* true man
人間 *maningen* an honest man, a good citizen
3 下 *mashita* right under, directly below
上 *maue* right above
丸 *ma(m)maru* perfect circle. *ma(m)maru(i)* perfectly round
4 心 *magokoro* sincerity, devotion
水 *mamizu* fresh water
中 *manaka, ma(n)naka* center, middle, midway
円 *ma(m)maru* perfect circle. *ma(m)maru(i)* perfectly round
円真珠 *shin'en shinju* cultured pearls
5 打 *shin'u(chi)* star performer
北 *makita* due north
平 *ma(t)taira na* perfectly level. *ma(p)pira* (not) by any means; humbly, sincerely
冬 *mafuyu* dead of winter
只中 *ma(t)tadanaka* right in the midst of, right at the height of
四角 *mashikaku, ma(s)shikaku* square
白 *ma(s)shiro, mashiro* pure white
正 *shinsei* genuine, authentic, true, pure
正直 *mashōjiki, ma(s)shōjiki* perfectly honest
正面 *mashōmen, ma(s)shōmen* directly opposite, right in front
田 *sanada* plait; braid
田虫 *sanada mushi* tapeworm
田紐 *sanada himo* braid
田編 *sanada a(mi)* plait
6 竹 *madake* a long-jointed bamboo
西 *manishi* due west
因 *shin'in* true reason, true motive
近 *maji(ka) ni* nearness, proximity. *majika(i)* near at hand
向 *ma(k)kō* brow; front. *mamuka(i), mamu(ki)* face to face, straight ahead, just in front of. *hitamu(ki) na* earnest; single-handed
如 *shinnyo* the absolute, absolute reality
帆 *maho* full sail
先 *ma(s)saki* the head, the foremost; beginning
似 *mane(ru)* imitate, mimic, mock, follow suit. *mane* mimicry, imitation; behavior, pretense
似事 *manegoto* sham, make-believe, mere form
7 言 *Shingon* Buddhist sect originating in the eighth century
赤 *ma(k)ka* deep red, crimson
否 *shimpi* true or false
8 青 *ma(s)sao na* deep blue; ghastly pale
底 *shintei* bottom of one's heart, real intention, motive
価 *shinka* true value
味 *shimmi* true meaning
性 *shinsei* inborn nature, genuine
物 *shimbutsu* genuine article
直 *ma(s)sugu na* straight, direct, upright, erect; honest; frank

東 *mahigashi* due east

夜中 *mayonaka* dead of night, midnight

逆 *masaka* by no means

逆様 *ma(s)sakasama ni* headlong, head over heels

実 *shinjitsu* truth, reality, fact; in reality, truly

実一路 *shinjitsu ichiro* path of sincerity

実性 *shinjitsusei* fidelity, truth, authenticity, credibility

空 *shinkū* vacuum. *shinkū no* hollow, empty

空帯 *shinkūtai* air pocket

空掃除器 *shinkū sōjiki* vacuum cleaner

空電球 *shinkū denkyū* vacuum bulb

空管 *shinkūkan* vacuum tube

9 迹 *shinseki* true autograph

後 *maushi(ro)* right behind

砂 *masago* sand

紅 *shinku* crimson

前 *ma(m)mae ni* right in front of, just opposite

南 *maminami* due south

美 *shimbi* true beauty

勇 *shin'yū* true courage, true heroism

海豚 *mairuka* porpoise, dolphin

面目 *majime* serious, earnest, honest. *shimmemmoku* one's true character, oneself; seriousness, earnestness

面目腐 *majimekusa(ru)* pretend to be serious

相 *shinsō* the truth, the facts, the real situation

相調査 *shinso chosa* fact finding

昼 *mahiru* broad daylight, midday

昼間 *ma(p)piruma* broad daylight

10 症 *shinshō* genuine case (of a disease)

個 *shinko no* real, true

夏 *manatsu* midsummer

剣 *shinken* real sword; earnestness

剣勝負 *shinkenshōbu* fighting with real swords; game played in real earnest

珠 *shinju* pearl

珠母 *shinjubo* mother-of-pearl

珠色 *shinju iro* pearl gray

珠光 *shinjukō* pearl iridescence

珠貝 *shinjugai* pearl oyster

珠取 *shinjuto(ri)* pearl fishing; pearl diver

珠細工 *shinju zaiku* pearl work

珠湾 *Shinju Wan* Pearl Harbor

珠層 *shinjusō* mother-of-peart

珠質 *shinjushitsu* mother-of-pearl

珠養殖 *shinju yōshoku* pearl cultivation

珠養殖場 *shinju yōshokujō* pearl-oyster beds

珠擬 *shinjumaga(i)* imitation pearl

11 黒 *ma(k)kuro na* jet black

偽 *shingi* truth or error, authenticity

情 *shinjō* true feeling

深 *mabuka ni* down over the eyes

理 *shinri* truth

率 *shinsotsu* honesty, sincerity, frankness

盛 *ma(s)saka(ri), masaka(ri)* height of, middle of; full bloom

清水 *mashimizu* pure water, clear water

唯中 *ma(t)tadanaka* right in the midst of

魚板 *manaita* chopping board

12 筆 *shimpitsu* autograph; one's own handwriting; personal note

最中 *ma(s)saichū* midst; height

善美 *shin-zen-bi* the true, the good, and the beautiful

13 裸 *ma(p)padaka* totally naked

跡 *shinseki* true autograph

際 *magiwa ni* just before, on the verge of

新 *maatara(shii)* brand new

義 *shingi* true meaning

蒼 *massao* very pale

暗 *makkura* total darkness; shortsightedness

暗闇 *makkurayami* total darkness

意 *shin'i* real intention, true motive; true meaning

意義 *shin'igi* true meaning

14 綿 *mawata* silk floss, silk wadding

箇 *shinko no* real, true

疑 *shingi* truth or error, authenticity

15 摯 *shinshi* sincerity, earnestness

16 鴨 *magamo* mallard duck

諦 *shintei, shintai* ultimate truth, essence (in Buddhism)

17 鍮 *shinchū* brass

18 蹟 *shinseki* true autograph

髄 *shinzui* essence, pith, spirit, soul, essentials, core, kernel, the life blood

鯉 *magoi* black carp

顔 *magao* serious look

19 贋 *shingan* the genuine and the spurious

鯛 *madai* red sea bream

6

眶 3928 J-X M23310 KYŌ eyelid.

眥 3929 J6244 M23250 **眦** 3930 J6245 M23251 SEI. SHI. SAI. *manajiri, mejiri* outside corner of the eye.

眴 3931 J-X M23307 SHUN. JUN. KEN. GEN. *mekuwa(su), mekuwa(seru)* signal with the eyes.

眸 3932 J6248 M23312 BŌ pupil (of the eye). *manazashi* a look (at someone). *hitomi* pupil of the eye.
3 子 *bōshi* pupil of the eye.

B **眺** 3933 J442f M23314 CHŌ. *naga(meru)* watch, look at, see; scrutinize. *naga(me)* view, scene.
11 望 *chōbō* prospect, view, outlook

眷 3934 J6247 M23311 KEN look around, consider, regard affectionately.
10 恋 *kenren* attachment, love, yearning
11 族 *kenzoku* family, dependents, household
12 属 *kenzoku* family, dependents, household
13 愛 *ken'ai suru* love, be fond of
21 顧 *kenko* favor, patronage

A **眼** 3935 J3463 M23318 GAN. GEN. *me* eye; look, gaze; notice, attention; viewpoint; discrimination, insight; experience; treatment; care, favor, pity; texture, weave; mesh; grain, square; sight, vision; tooth (of a saw); weight; eye (of a needle). *manako* eye.
2 力 *ganriki, ganryoku* insight, power of observation
3 下 *ganka* (a view) below one's eyes
4 辺 *ma (no) ata(ri)* in one's presence, before one's eyes
孔 *gankō* eye socket
中 *ganchū ni* in one's eyes; in one's view
中置 *ganchū (ni) o(kanai)* disregard, ⌜ignore
5 玉 *medama* eyeball
目 *gammoku* core, point, gist, essence, main object
6 気 *ganki* eye disease
光 *gankō* glint of the eye; discernment, insight
7 医者 *meisha* oculist
8 底出血 *gantei shukketsu* eye hemorrhage
9 前 *ganzen* before one's eyes
界 *gankai* field of range of vision
科 *ganka* ophthalmology
科医 *gankai* ophthalmologist
10 病 *gambyō, meya(mi)* eye disease; person with sore eyes
疾 *ganshitsu* eye disease
差 *manaza(shi)* a look (at someone)
帯 *gantai* eye bandage
11 深 *mabuka ni* down over the eyes
球 *gankyū* eyeball. *medama, me (no) tama* eyeball; scolding
球銀行 *gankyū ginkō* eye bank
12 筋 *gankin* eye muscles
13 窠 *ganka* eye socket
勢 *gansei* expression of the eyes
14 窩 *ganwa, ganka* eye socket
精疲労 *gansei hirō* eyestrain
18 瞼 *ganken, mabuta* eyelid
19 識 *ganshiki* insight, discrimination, discernment
鏡 *gankyō, megane* spectacles, glasses
鏡屋 *meganeya* optician
鏡蛇 *megane hebi* cobra
鏡越 *meganego(shi) ni* over one's spectacles
鏡橋 *meganebashi* arched bridge

7

眖 3936 J-X M-X Nonstandard for **睍** 3947.

睇 3937 J6249 M23360 TEI looking askance at.
11 視 *teishi suru* look askance at

A **着** 3938 J4365 M23339 CHAKU arrival, finish (in a race); suit counter. *ki(ru), chaku(suru)* put on, wear. *ki(seru)* clothe, dress, put on; cover, plate, coat, gild; veneer; blame for, impute a crime to. *ki(konasu)* wear, dress. *tsu(ku), chaku(suru)* arrive at, reach, attain to. *ki(se)* dish cover. *ki(gonashi)* style of dress. *ki(nikui)* uncomfortable or awkward to wear. *-ki* wearing; clothes.

3 工 *chakkō* starting construction

丈 *kitake* dress length

4 手 *chakushu* start, commencement

火 *chakka* igniting

水 *chakusui* alighting on water

尺 *kijaku* suit measurement; dress length; kimono-length bolt

込 *ki-ko(mu)* wear extra clothes. *kigo(mi)* underwear

心 *kigokoro* the feeling of clothes

心地 *kigokochi* fit and feel (of clothes)

切 *ki-ki(ru)* wear to rags, wear out completely. *ki(ta)ki(ri)* wearing all one owns

切雀 *ki(ta)ki(ri) suzume* a person with only one kimono

5 用 *chakuyō suru* wear, have on

目 *chakumoku* viewpoint, observation

付 *kitsu(ke)* dressing (someone); attire

古 *ki-furu(su), kiburu(su)* wear out. *kifuru(shi), kiburu(shi)* old clothes

6 衣 *chakui* dressing (oneself); one's clothes

任 *chakunin* arrival at one's post

色 *chakushoku* color, coloration, coloring; embellishment

色写真 *chakushoku shashin* color photograph

7 車 *chakusha* train arrival

初 *kiso(me)* first wearing (of a suit)

良 *kiyo(i)* comfortable to wear

身着儘 *ki(no)mi-ki(no)mama de* (sleep) in one's clothes; without changing one's clothes; with only the clothes on one's back

8 逃 *kini(ge)* running off wearing someone else's clothes

物 *kimono* clothes, kimono

服 *chakufuku* dressing (oneself); embezzlement, misappropriation

直 *ki-nao(su)* change clothes

実 *chakujitsu na* trustworthy, sober-minded, steady

9 通 *kidō(shi)* wearing continuously

重 *ki-kasa(neru)* wear layers of clothes

発 *chakuhatsu* arrival and departure

草臥 *ki-kutabi(reru)* be worn out, wear out

信 *chakushin* arrival of mail

信局 *chakushinkyoku* destination post office

10 席 *chakuseki* taking a seat

座 *chakuza* taking a seat

倒 *kidao(re)* extravagance in dress

値 *chakune* C.I.F. (cost, insurance, and freight)

時 *kidoki* the proper time to wear (certain clothes)

流 *kinaga(shi)* not dressed up

破 *ki-yabu(ru)* wear out (clothes)

料 *kiryō* clothing materials

剣 *chakken, tsu(ke)ken* fixed bayonet

殺 *ki-koro(su)* wear out (clothes) without repairing

荷 *chakuni, chakka* goods arrived

帯 *chakutai* wearing a maternity belt

陸 *chakuriku* landing, alighting

陸地 *chakurikuchi* landing zone

陸車輪 *chakuriku sharin* landing wheel

陸料 *chakurikuryō* (airplane) landing charges

陸場 *chakurikujō* landing field, airstrip

11 添 *ki-so(u)* put on extra clothing

船 *chakusen* ship arrival

道楽 *kidōraku* love of dress; lover of fine clothes

眼 *chakugan* viewpoint, observation

眼点 *chakuganten* point observed or aimed at; viewpoint

12 御 *chakugyo suru* (the emperor) takes his seat

換 *ki-ka(eru), kigae(ru)* change clothes

港 *chakkō* arrival at port

脹 *ki buku(reru)* be fat with extra winter clothes

筆 *chakuhitsu* beginning to write; manner of writing

着 *chakuchaku* steadily

弾距離 *chakudan kyori* range (of a gun)

替 *kiga(e)* changing clothes; change of clothes

替所 *kiga(e)jo* dressing room

13 腹 *chakufuku* embezzlement, misappropriation

際 *kigiwa* being about to wear; one's appearance in (certain clothes)

飾 *ki-kaza(ru)* dress up; wear fine clothes

馴 *ki-na(rasu)* get used to wearing

電 *chakuden* telegram received

意 *chakui* conception, caution

想 *chakusō* conception, idea

14 慣 *ki-na(rasu)* get used to wearing
駅 *chakueki* destination station
18 癖 *kiguse* dressing habits
類 *kirui* clothing
20 艦 *chakkan* deck landing
22 籠 *kigomi, kigome* underwear

—— 8 ——

睚 3939 / J624a / M23437 GAI, GE eyelid, corner of eye; glare, angry stare. *manajiri* corner of eye.

睛 3940 / J624d / M23438 SEI. *hitomi* pupil of the eye.

睢 3941 / J-X / M23450 KI. SUI open the eyes wide.

睥 3942 / J624e / M23459 **睤** 3943 / J-X / M23458 HEI glare at.
13 睨 *heigei suru* glare at, scowl at, frown on, look askance at, leer at

睫 3944 / J624c / M23469 SHŌ. *matsuge* eyelashes.
4 毛 *matsuge* eyelashes; cilia

睦 3945 / J4b53 / M23460 BOKU. *mutsu(majii)* friendly, intimate, harmonious. *mutsu(mu), mutsu(bu)* get along well together.
4 月 *mutsuki* first lunar month
7 言 *mutsugoto* lovers' talk, words of friendship

B **督** 3946 / J4644 / M23457 TOKU. *toku(suru)* command, lead, supervise; urge.
7 励 *tokurei* encouragement
9 促 *tokusoku suru* urge, dun, press (a person for action)
13 戦 *tokusen suru* urge on to victory
戦隊 *tokusentai* front-line disciplinary corps

睨 3947 / J624b / M23464 GEI. *nira(mi)* glaring at; authority, power. *nira(mu), nira(meru)* glare at, scowl at; keep an eye on; suspect (of a crime); estimate.
5 付 *nira(mi)-tsu(keru), ne(me)-tsu(keru)* glare at, scowl at
6 回 *ne(me)-mawa(su)* glare around
返 *nira(mi)-kae(su)* glare back
合 *nira(mi)-a(u)* glare at each other, be at odds. *nira(mi)-a(waseru)* take (something) for comparison

B **睡** 3948 / J3f67 / M23448 SUI. *nemu(ru), nebu(ru)* sleep, die. *nemu(garu)* feel sleepy. *nemu(gari), nemu(gariya)* sleepyhead.
6 気 *nemuke, suike* sleepiness, drowsiness
7 余 *suiyo* after awakening
10 眠 *suimin* sleep
眠中 *suiminchū* while sleeping
眠不足 *suimimbusoku, suimin fusoku* lack of sleep
眠剤 *suiminzai* sleeping drug, narcotic
眠時間 *suimin jikan* hours of sleep
13 蓮 *suiren* water lily
21 魔 *suima* sleepiness, drowsiness; sandman

—— 9 ——

睿 3949 / J624f / M23536 See 叡 683.

睹 3950 / J6251 / M23519 TO see; examine closely; show.

睾 3951 / J6250 / M23535 KŌ testicles.
3 丸 *kōgan* testicles

—— 10 ——

瞎 3952 / J6252 / M23586 KATSU, KECHI blind; one-eyed.

瞋 3953 / J6253 / M23568 SHIN. *ika(ru)* be angry, get excited, be offended.
10 恚 *shin'i* wrath, indignation

瞑 3954 / J6254 / M23600 MEI sleep, dark. *mei(suru)* close (one's eyes); sleep in peace. *tsubu(ru)* close (one's eyes).
5 目 *meimoku suru* close one's eyes; die
13 想 *meisō* meditation, contemplation

—— 11 ——

瞟 3955 / J-X / M23650 HYŌ, BYŌ scrutinizing search.

[5] 目 *higarame* eyes out of line

瞞 3956 / J6256 / M23649 MAN, MON deception; coaxing; imposition; obscuring.

[12] 着 *manchaku* imposture, deception

瞠 3957 / J6255 / M23651 DŌ stare intently.

[5] 目 *dōmoku suru* stare in wonder
[8] 若 *dōjaku* amazement
[12] 然 *dōzen* eye-popping surprise

12

瞶 3958 / J6258 / M23713 KI lacking the pupil of the eye.

瞥 3959 / J4a4d / M23672 BETSU glance at.

[7] 見 *bekken* glance, glimpse

瞭 3960 / J4e46 / M23697 RYŌ clear.

[12] 然 *ryōzen(taru)* obvious, clear, plain

瞳 3961 / J4637 / M23707 DŌ. *hitomi* pupil of the eye.

[4] 孔 *dōkō* pupil of the eye

瞰 3962 / J6257 / M23704 KAN look, see.

[3] 下 *kanka suru* overlook, command a bird's-eye view of
[10] 射 *kansha suru* fire down on
[11] 視 *kanshi* overlooking; bird's-eye view

13

瞹 3963 / J6259 / M23727 See 曖 2521.

瞻 3964 / J625d / M23742 SEN. *mi(ru)* see, look at, witness, observe, examine.

瞿 3965 / J625a / M23747 KU stare at; peer at; surprised look; angry look.

瞼 3966 / J625b / M23744 KEN. *mabuta* eyelids.

矇 3967 / J625e / M23774 MŌ blind.

[9] 昧 *mōmai* ignorance

瞽 3968 / J625c / M23745 KO blind person.

[8] 者 *kosha* blind person

B 瞬 3969 / J3d56 / M23694 SHUN. *mabata(ku), majiro(gu)* wink, blink. *matata(ku)* wink, twinkle, flicker. *shibatata(ku), shibata(ku)* wink, blink. *mebata(ki), mabata(ki)* wink, blink. *matata(ki)* wink; twinkling (of stars).

[8] 刻 *shunkoku* moment, instant
[10] 時 *shunji* instant, moment, second, minute
息 *shunsoku* instant, moment, second
[12] 間 *shunkan* instant, moment, second. *mabata(ku)ma ni, matata(ku)ma ni* in the twinkling of an eye

15

矍 3970 / J625f / M23792 KAKU surprise and confusion.

[23] 鑠 *kakushaku* vigorous old age. *kakushaku(taru)* hale and hearty

19

矗 3971 / J6260 / M23836 CHOKU luxuriance.

矕 3972 / J-X / M23834 BAN. *misona(wasu)* see, witness, inspect.

21

矚 3973 / J6261 / M23841 SHOKU look intently.

[5] 目 *shokumoku* attention, observation

矛 RAD. 110

Hoko spear. At left: *hoko hen.* Nickname: Spear (cf. Rad. 62).

B **矛** 3974 / J4c37 / M23846 **鉾** 6255 / J4b48 / M40353 MU. BŌ. *hoko* halberd; arms; festival car, float.

6 先 *hokosaki* the point of a sword; spearhead; the brunt (of an argument); the aim (of an attack)

9 盾 *mujun* contradiction

13 楯 *mujun* contradiction

4

矜 3975 / J6262 / M23852 KIN, KYŌ pride, respect.

9 恃 *kyōji* dignity, pride

持 *kyōji, kinji* dignity, pride

矢 RAD. 111

Ya arrow. At left: *ya hen.* Nickname: Arrow.

A **矢** 3976 / J4c70 / M23929 SHI. *ya* arrow.

4 文 *yabumi* letter tied to an arrow, a succession of letters

木 *ya(no)ki* arrowwood

5 玉 *yadama* arrows and bullets, missiles

立 *yata(te)* inkhorn; ink-and-pen case

6 竹 *yadake, yatake* arrow bamboo, arrow shaft

印 *yajirushi* a direction arrow

叫 *yasake(bi)* archers' cries, din of battle

先 *yasaki* arrowhead; the point; the moment

羽 *yabane* arrow feathers

羽根 *yabane* weather vane

7 来 *yarai* picket fence, palisade, stockade, barrier

8 表 *yaomote* thick of the fight; front line of archers; face of the enemy

9 面 *yaomote* thick of the fight; front line of archers; face of the enemy

音 *yaoto* hum of an arrow

柄 *yagara* arrow shaft

飛白 *yagasuri* arrow patterns

狭間 *yazama* loophole, crenel

矧 *yahagi* arrow making

矧師 *yahagishi* arrow maker

10 庭 *yaniwa* archery grounds. *yaniwa ni* suddenly, instantly

師 *yashi* arrow maker

衾 *yabusuma* shower of arrows

根 *ya(no)ne* arrowhead

根石 *ya(no)ne ishi* flint arrowhead

11 頃 *yagoro* bowshot

張 *ya(p)pari, yahari* too, also, as well, likewise, like the rest, still, just the same, after all, nevertheless

12 場 *yaba* archery ground, archery gallery; house of ill fame

軸 *yajiku* arrow shaft

壺 *yatsubo* aim of an arrow

筒 *yazutsu* quiver

筈 *yahazu* notch of an arrow

筈模様 *yahazu moyō* herringbone pattern

13 傷 *yakizu* arrow wound

継早 *yatsu(gi)baya ni* rapidly, in quick succession

催促 *ya (no) saisoku* urgent demand

14 種 *yadane* remaining arrows (in the quiver)

22 鱈 *yatara ni* indiscriminately, blindly, recklessly

鱈書 *yataraga(ki)* scribbling

2

矣 3977 / J6263 / M23931 I euphonic particle.

3

A **知** 3978 / J434e / M23935 CHI knowledge, acquaintance, sense. *shi(ru)* know; understand; appreciate recognize; realize; notice, sense, feel; remember; infer, gather; be concerned with. *shi(reru)*

become known, be disclosed, be found out, turn out to be. *shi(rasu)* rule (a country). *shi(raseru)* inform, give notice. *shi(rase)* information, report, news; omen. *shi(reta)* obvious; negligible. *-(kamo)shi(renai)* maybe, perhaps, one can't tell. *-(ka)shi(ra)* I wonder if ... *-shi(razu)* unconsciously, unknowingly; free from (hot weather).

2 人 *chijin, shiryūdo, shi(ri)bito* acquaintance
力 *chiryoku* wisdom, intellectual power, mental capacity, intellect, mentality, brains
3 己 *chiki* acquaintance, appreciative friend
4 日 *chinichi* pro Japanese
辺 *shi(ru)be* acquaintance, friend
切 *shi(re)ki(tta)* obvious
友 *chiyū* intimate acquaintance
5 召 *shi(roshi)me(su)* know; rule, reign
6 合 *shi(ri)-a(u)* know each other. *shiria(i)* an acquaintance
名 *chimei no* noted, well-known
行 *chigyō* fief, stipend, land tenure, daimyo's estate. *chikō* knowledge and action
行地 *chigyōchi* a fief
行取 *chigyōto(ri)* feudal vassal, daimyo
7 見 *chiken* knowledge, information; view, opinion
抜 *shi(ri)-nu(ku)* know thoroughly
8 性 *chisei* intellect, intelligence, mentality
知 *shi(razu)-shi(razu)* unconsciously, unknowingly
育 *chiiku* mental training
命 *chimei* age fifty; knowing life
者 *chisha* wise man, sage
事 *chiji* governor
的 *chiteki* mental, intellectual
的労働 *chiteki rōdō* brain work; intelligent service
9 勇 *chiyū* wisdom and valor
10 振 *shi(ranu)fu(ri)* feigned ignorance; indifference. *shi(tta)fu(ri)* pretending to know
恵 *chie* wisdom, sense, sagacity, intelligence, resourcefulness
恵者 *chiesha* wise man
恵袋 *chiebukuro* brain trust, close advisers
恵歯 *chieba* wisdom tooth
恵熱 *chie netsu* fever accompanying dentition
能 *chinō* intellect, intelligence, mental faculties
能犯 *chinōhan* the crimes of forgery, deception, etc.
能的 *chinōteki* intellectual
能指数 *chinō shisū* intelligence quotient, I.Q.
能商 *chinōshō* intelligence quotient, I.Q.
能検査 *chinō kensa* mental test
11 遇 *chigū* favor, friendship, appreciation
略 *chiryaku* ingenuity, talents
悉 *chishitsu* complete knowledge of
過程知 *shi(ri)-su(giru) hodo shi(ru)* know full well
12 歯 *chishi* wisdom tooth
渡 *shi(re)-wata(ru)* become widely known
覚 *chikaku* perception, sensation
覚力 *chikakuryoku* perceptibility, sensibility
覚神経 *chikaku shinkei* sensory nerves
14 徳 *chitoku* knowledge and virtue; erudition and character
徳体 *chi-toku-tai* mental, spiritual, and physical
15 慮 *chiryo* wise idea; planning ability
16 謀 *chibō* ingenuity, resourcefulness
18 顔 *shi(ri)gao* knowing look. *shi(ranu)kao, shi(ran)kao* unconcerned air, indifference
19 識 *chishiki* knowledge, information, learning, attainments, understanding
識人 *chishikijin* a highbrow, an intellectual
識欲 *chishikiyoku* love of learning
識階級 *chishiki kaikyū* intelligentsia
識階層 *chishiki kaisō* intelligentsia
識慾 *chishikiyoku* love of learning

4

矧 3979 / J476a / M23938 SHIN. *ha(gu)* feather (an arrow), fletch.

矩 3980 / J366b / M23947 KU. *kane* ruler, carpenter's square.
4 手 *kane(no)te* right angle
尺 *kanejaku* common Japanese foot; carpenter's square
勾配 *kane kōbai* 45-degree slope

7 折 *kaneo(ri)* bent into a right angle
形 *kukei* rectangle

7

覘 3981 / J-X / M23979 See 規 5524.

短 3982 / J433b / M23978 A TAN shortness, brevity; fault, defect, demerit, weak point. *mijika(i)* short, brief.

2 刀 *tantō* short sword, dagger
刀直入 *tantō-chokunyū* getting right into the subject; frankness
3 小 *tanshō na* small, stunted
才 *tansai* little talent
4 文 *tambun* short sentence; short composition
尺 *tanzaku, tanjaku* small vertical poem card
水路 *tansuiro* 25-meter swim
日 *tanjitsu* short days; a short time
日月 *tanjitsugetsu* short period of time
5 打 *tanda* chopping (in baseball)
冊 *tanzaku, tanjaku* small vertical poem card
句 *tanku* short phrase
句集 *tankushū* phrase book
6 衣 *tan'i* waistcoat, jacket
気 *tanki* quick temper, irritability, impatience
曲 *tankyoku* short musical piece
7 見 *tanken* shortsightedness, narrow view
身 *tanshin* small stature
兵急 *tampeikyū na* impetuous; sudden
兵戦 *tampeisen* hand-to-hand fight
8 所 *tansho* shortcoming, defect, fault
夜 *miji(ka)yo, tan'ya* short (summer) night
命 *tammei* short life
波 *tampa* short-wave (length)
波長 *tanhachō* short wave
9 信 *tanshin* brief note, news brief
音 *tan'on* short sound
音階 *tan'onkai* minor scale
10 針 *tanshin* hour hand
剣 *tanken* dagger; hour hand
時日 *tanjijitsu* short time
時間 *tanjikan* short time
11 脚 *tankyaku* short leg
距離 *tankyori* short distance, short range; short-distance race, dash, sprint
距離競争 *tankyori kyōsō* short-distance race, dash, sprint
12 絡 *tanraku* short circuit
評 *tampyō* short criticism, brief review
軸 *tanjiku* minor axis
期 *tanki* short term, short time
期大学 *tanki daigaku* junior college
期間 *tankikan* short time
期戦 *tankisen* short war
期興行 *tanki kōgyō* a play with a short run
期講習 *tanki kōshū* short course
13 路 *tanro* short circuit
靴 *tangutsu* low shoes
資 *tanshi* short-term loan, call loan
詩 *tanshi* short poem
詩形 *tanshikei* short-poem forms
艇 *tantei* boat
艇操練 *tantei sōren* lifeboat drill
艇競漕 *tantei kyōsō* boat race, regatta
14 銃 *tanjū* pistol, revolver
歌 *tanka* 31-syllable poem, tanka
髪 *tampatsu* short hair
15 慮 *tanryo* hot temper; shallowness; narrow-mindedness
編 *tampen* short story, short novel
調 *tanchō* minor key
篇 *tampen* short story, short novel
篇小説 *tampen shōsetsu* short story, short novel
篇集 *tampenshū* sketch book, collection of short stories or essays; short novel
17 縮 *tanshuku* shortening, curtailment, reduction, abridgment, abbreviation
縮形 *tanshukukei* shortened form
18 軀 *tanku* short stature
簡 *tankan* brevity, simplicity
20 籍 *tanzaku, tanjaku* small vertical poem card

8

矮 3983 / J6264 / M23995 WAI, AI low; short.

2 人 *waijin* dwarf, manikin, pygmy
3 小 *waishō na* diminutive, pygmy, Lilliputian; stunted
8 林 *wairin* brushwood
9 屋 *waioku* humble cottage; my house
16 樹 *waiju* dwarf tree

[18] 軀 *waiku* small stature
[19] 鶏 *chabo* bantam; midget

12

B 矯 3984 / J363a / M24015 KYŌ. *ta(meru)* straighten; correct, reform, cure; control (one's feelings); pretend, falsify; aim.
[5] 正 *kyōsei* reform, correction, training
正院 *kyōseiin* reform school
正保護 *kyōsei-hogo* correction and rehabilitation
正教育 *kyōsei kyōiku* corrective education 「reform, cure
[8] 直 *ta(me)-nao(su)* set up again; correct,
[9] 風 *kyōfū* moral reform
眇 *ta(metsu)-suga(metsu)* with scrutinizing eyes
[15] 弊 *kyōhei* reform of evil habits; correction of abuses
[16] 激 *kyōgeki na* radical, extreme, eccentric

RAD. 石 112

Ishi stone. At left: *ishi hen*. Nickname: Stone.

A 石 3985 / J4050 / M24024 石 3986 / J-X / M24026 SEKI. SHAKU. *ishi* stone, pebble, rock; jewel; the go playing stones. *koku* 4.96 bushels; 10 cubic feet (of lumber).
[3] 女 *sekijo, umazume* barren woman
山 *ishiyama* quarry, stony mountain
川 *ishikawa* river with a stony bottom
工 *ishiku, sekkō* stonemason, stonecutter
弓 *ishiyumi* crossbow, catapult
小屋 *ishigoya* stone hut
[4] 文 *ishibumi* stone monument
火 *sekka* flint fire; flash
片 *sekihen* piece of stone, stone chip
化 *sekka* petrifaction
仏 *ishibotoke, sekibutsu* stone Buddha; stony-hearted person; taciturn person
引 *ishihi(ki)* hauling large stones
切 *ishiki(ri)* stonecutting, quarrying; stonecutter
切場 *ishiki(ri)ba* quarry, stone pit
[5] 目 *ishime* crack in a rock; grain in stone
打 *ishiu(chi)* stoning
[6] 臼 *ishi usu* stone mortar, stone mill
匠 *sekishō* stonemason
合戦 *ishi gassen* a fight with stones
灯籠 *ishidōrō* stone lantern
竹 *sekichiku* a pink
竹色 *sekichiku iro* pink color
地 *ishiji* stony ground
地蔵 *ishi Jizō* stone image of Jizo
灰 *ishibai, sekkai* lime
灰水 *sekkaisui* limewater
灰石 *sekkaiseki* limestone
灰泥 *sekkaidei* lime mortar
灰岩 *sekkaigan* limestone
灰窯 *ishibaigama* limekiln
[7] 床 *ishidoko* masonry river bed
投 *ishina(ge)* stone throwing; sling; catapult
花菜 *sekkasai* agar-agar, Ceylon moss
材 *sekizai* stone, building stone
材商 *sekizaishō* stone merchant
[8] 門 *ishimon* stone gate
径 *ishimichi* stony road
刻 *sekkoku* stone carving; carved stone
斧 *sekifu, ishi ono* stone ax
突 *ishizu(ki)* the point of a sword scabbard; a cover for a spear handle
版 *sekiban* lithography; lithograph
版刷 *sekibanzu(ri)* lithography
英 *sekiei* quartz
英灯 *sekieitō* quartz light
英岩 *sekieigan* quartzite
油 *sekiyu* kerosene, petroleum
油王 *sekiyuō* oil king
油井戸 *sekiyu ido* oil well
油危機 *sekiyu kiki* oil crisis
油坑 *sekiyukō* oil well
油埋蔵量 *sekiyu maizōryō* oil reserves
油焜炉 *sekiyu konro* kerosene stove
油鉱床 *sekiyu kōshō* oil deposit
油資源 *sekiyu shigen* oil resources
油槽 *sekiyusō* oil tank
[9] 屋 *ishiya* stone merchant, stonemason
造 *ishizuku(ri), sekizō* masonry; made of stone

垢 *ishi aka* vegetation clinging to river-bottom rocks
垣 *ishigaki* stone wall
柱 *sekichū* stone pillar
神 *ishigami, shakujin* a stone that is worshipped, a stone god
段 *ishidan* stone step, stone steps
風呂 *ishiburo* stone bath
炭 *sekitan* coal; carboniferous
炭粉 *sekitanko* coal dust
炭船 *sekitansen* coal ship
炭液化 *sekitan ekika* coal liquefaction
炭産地 *sekitan sanchi* coal field
炭殻 *sekitangara* cinders
炭鉱業 *sekitan kōgyō* coal-mining industry
炭層 *sekitansō* coal bed, coal seam
炭酸 *sekitansan* carbolic acid, phenol
炭積込 *sekitan tsu(mi)ko(mi)* loading coal
10 高 *kokudaka* crop, yield; stipend, salary; amount of rice
原 *ishiwara* stony field
屑 *ishi kuzu* stone chips, rubble
挽 *ishihiki* hauling large stones
剣 *sekken* stone sword
竜子 *tokage* lizard
部金吉 *ishibekinkichi* man of incorruptible character, a Joseph
11 道 *ishimichi* stony road
婦 *sekifu* barren woman
組 *ishigu(mi)* arrangements of stones in a garden
船 *ishibune* stone-carrying boat
崖 *ishigake* cliff, stone wall
細工 *ishi zaiku* masonry
脳油 *sekinōyu* crude oil
12 間 *ishi(no)ma* stone-floored room (in certain shrines)
塀 *ishibei* stone wall
塔 *sekitō* tombstone, stone slab, stone monument
塚 *ishizuka* pile of stones, cairn
弾 *ishihaji(ki)* marbles (the game)
棺 *sekkan, sekikan* sarcophagus, stone coffin
焼 *ishiya(ki)* roasting on hot stones
割 *ishiwa(ri)* breaking up stones
畳 *ishidatami* stone pavement, stone flooring; checkered pattern
筆 *sekihitsu* slate pencil
筍 *sekijun* stalagmite
13 塊 *sekkai, ishikoro, ishikure* stones, pebbles, piece of stone
槌 *ishizuchi* stone hammer; tamper
鉢 *ishibachi* stone bowl
窟 *sekkutsu* stone cave
楠花 *shakunage* rhododendron
14 像 *sekizō* stone image; stone statue
摺 *ishizuri* a rubbing of a carved inscription
榻 *ishizuri* a rubbing of a carved inscription
碑 *sekihi* tombstone, stone slab, stone monument
綿 *ishiwata, sekimen* asbestos
膏 *sekkō* gypsum, satin spar, alabaster, plaster of Paris
墨 *sekiboku* graphite, black lead
製 *ishisei* made of stone
榴 *zakuro* pomegranate
榴石 *sekiryūseki, zakuro ishi* garnet
15 盤 *sekiban* a slate
器 *sekki* stonework; stone implement
器時代 *Sekki Jidai* Stone Age
16 橋 *ishibashi, sekkyō* stone bridge
積 *ishizu(mi)* masonry
頭 *ishi atama* hardhead, obstinate person
19 蹴 *ishikeri* hopscotch
鏃 *sekizoku* flint arrowhead
21 蠟 *sekiro* paraffin
24 鹼 *sekken* soap
鹼石 *sekkenseki* soapstone
25 鼈 *hizaragai* a chiton, a coat-of-mail (a shell)

1

石 3986 / J-X / M24026 See 石 3985.

3

矼 3987 / J6265 / M24044 Kō stepping stones; stone bridge; hard; certain.

4

砌 3988 / J6266 / M24062 SAI. SEI. *migiri* time, occasion.

砒 3989 / J6267 / M24068 HI arsenic.
10 素 *hiso* arsenic
14 酸 *hisan* arsenic acid

B 砕 3990 / J3a55 / M24080' 碎 4009 / J626c / M24284 SAI. *kuda(ku)* break, smash, crush; pulverize; tax (one's ingenuity); explain simply. *kudake(ru)* break, crumble, be crushed, go to pieces; become familiar. *kuda(keta)* broken, crushed; familiar, popular, friendly.

4 片 *saihen* fragment, splinter
5 石 *saiseki* broken stone, rubble; something worthless; crushing rock
氷 *saihyō* rubble ice, fragmentary ice
氷船 *saihyōsen* icebreaker
6 米 *kuda(ke)mai, kuda(ke)gome* broken rice
7 身 *saishin* extreme hardship
8 波 *kuda(ke)nami* breakers, surf
岩機 *saiganki* rock crusher
9 炭器 *saitanki* coal crusher
10 屑 *saisetsu* fragments, splinters, smashed up scrap materials
13 鉱 *saiko* ore crushing
鉱機 *saikōki* ore crusher
19 離 *kuda(ki)-hana(su)* break off from

A 研 3991 / J3826 / M24080 硏 4000 / J-X / M24177 KEN. *to(gu)* sharpen, grind, scour, hone, polish; wash (rice).

3 上 *to(gi)-a(geru)* sharpen up
4 水 *to(gi)mizu* whetstone water; water rice has been washed in
5 立 *to(gi)ta(te)* just sharpened
7 究 *kenkyū* study, research, investigation
究心 *kenkyūshin* inquiring mind
究生 *kenkyusei* research student
究会 *kenkyūkai* research society
究所 *kenkyūjo, kenkyūsho* laboratory, research institute
究科 *kenkyūka* postgraduate course, seminar
究室 *kenkyūshitsu* laboratory, seminar room
究員 *kenkyūin* researcher
究家 *kenkyūka* researcher
8 歩 *kempo* a lady's graceful walk
学 *kengaku* study
物師 *togimonoshi* tool grinder; polisher of swords and mirrors
9 革 *to(gi)kawa* strop
屋 *togiya* polisher, grinder, sharpener
10 修 *kenshū* study and training
修所 *kenshūjo* training institute
15 摩 *kemma* grinding, polishing; studying
澄 *to(gi)-su(masu)* polish well; sharpen well
16 磨 *kemma* grinding, polishing; studying
磨機 *kemmaki* grinder, polisher
23 鑽 *kensan* study

A 砂 3992 / J3a3d / M24046 SA. SHA. *isago, suna* sand.

3 土 *sado, shado* sandy soil
子 *sunago* sand; paper speckled with gold; gold dust; silver dust
山 *sunayama* sand hill, sand bank
上 *sajō* on the sand
5 丘 *sakyū* sand dune, sand hill
丘林 *sakyūrin* forest on a sand dune
6 色 *suna iro* sand color
地 *sunaji* sandy soil
防 *sabō* erosion control
州 *sasu* sandbar, sandbank, reef
7 吹 *sunafu(ki)* sandblast
利 *jari, zari* gravel, ballast, pebbles
利土 *jarido* gravelly soil
利道 *jari michi* gravel road
8 岩 *sagan, shagan* sandstone
岸 *sagan* sandy river bank
金 *sakin, shakin* gold dust, alluvial gold, placer gold
金採集 *sakin saishū* placer mining
9 洲 *sasu* sandbar, sandbank, reef
型 *sunagata* (foundry) sandbox
風 *safū* sandstorm
風呂 *sunaburo* sand bath
10 原 *sunahara* desert, sandy plain
埃 *sunabokori* dust, dust storm
浜 *sunahama, sahin* sandy beach
留 *sunado(me)* sand-erosion barrier
蚤 *suna nomi* sand flea
時計 *sunadokei* sand clock, hourglass
11 遊 *sunaaso(bi)* playing in the sand
粒 *suna tsubu* grain of sand
12 場 *sunaba* sand pit
絵 *sunae* sand picture
13 漠 *sabaku* desert
煙 *suna kemuri* dust clouds
路 *suna michi* sandy road
鉄 *satetsu, shatetsu* iron sand, magnetic sand
14 塵 *sajin* dust storm
漉 *sunago(shi)* sand filtering
15 箱 *sunabako* sandbox; sander (on an engine)
16 嘴 *shashi, sashi* sandbar; sandspit

篩 *sunaburui* sand strainer
糖 *satō* sugar
糖大根 *satō daikon* sugar beet
糖黍 *satō kibi* sugar cane 「sugar
糖煮 *satōni* preserving by boiling with
糖楓 *satō kaede* sugar maple
糖漬 *satōzuke* food preserved in sugar; sweetmeats
20 礫 *sareki, shareki* gravel, pebbles
22 嚢 *sanō, shanō, sunabukuro* sandbag

5

砺 3993 / J4557 / M-X Nonstandard for **礪** 4056.

砿 3994 / J395c / M-X See **鉱** 6252.

砠 3995 / J6269 / M24084 So stone-capped mountain; dirt-capped mountain.

砧 3996 / J354e / M24099 **碪** 4022 / J6274 / M24339 CHIN. *kinuta* fulling block.

砥 3997 / J4556 / M24093 SHI. *to* whetstone, grindstone.
5 石 *toishi* whetstone, grindstone, hone
9 革 *to(gi)kawa* strop, strap
10 粉 *tonoko* polishing powder

B **砲** 3998 / J4b24 / M24120 HŌ gun, cannon, battery; gunnery, ordnance, artillery. *tsutsu* gun.
3 口 *hōkō* caliber, muzzle (of gun)
工 *hōkō* artillery and engineers
丸 *hōgan* cannonball
丸投 *hōganna(ge)* shot-put
4 手 *hōshu* gunner
火 *hōka* gunfire, shellfire
5 台 *hōdai* battery, fort
6 列 *hōretsu* gun emplacement
7 身 *hōshin* gun barrel
車 *hōsha* gun carriage
尾 *hōbi* breech (of gun or cannon)
床 *hōshō* gun platform
声 *hōsei* sound of firing, roar of a gun
兵 *hōhei* artillery; gunner
兵工廠 *hōhei kōshō* arsenal, armory
8 金 *hōkin* gun metal
門 *hōmon* embrasure; battleship porthole; gun
卒 *hōsotsu* artilleryman
10 座 *hōza* gun platform
11 術 *hōjutsu* gunnery, artillery
12 塔 *hōtō* turret, cupola
弾 *hōdan* projectile
塁 *hōrui* battery, fort
13 戦 *hōsen* artillery duel
煙 *hōen* cannon smoke
煙弾雨 *hōen-dan'u* the smoke of guns and a hail of bullets
14 銅 *hōdō* gun metal
15 撃 *hōgeki* bombardment, cannonade
20 艦 *hōkan* gunboat

A **破** 3999 / J474b / M24124 HA. *ya(buru) vt* tear, rip, rend; break, crush, destroy; violate, transgress; defeat; baffle, frustrate. *yabu(ku) vt* tear, rip, rend. *yabu(reru), yabu(keru) vi* be torn, tear, rip open; be broken, burst; rupture, collapse; be worn out; be defeated; be frustrated. *yabu(re)* rupture, breach, rent, tear, breakdown, collapse. *yabu(rekabure)* desperation.
3 口 *yabu(re)guchi* breach (in a wall)
4 片 *hahen* fragment, splinter; scrap, broken piece
太鼓 *yabu(re)daiko* drum with a broken cover; human wreck
天荒 *hatenkō* unprecedented, record-breaking
5 目 *yabu(re)me, ya(re)me* tear, rent, split, breach
出 *yabu(ri)-de(ru)* bursting out (of water)
瓜 *haka* girls at 16; men at 64
瓜期 *hakaki* pubescence (in girls)
甲弾 *hakōdan* armor-piercing shell
甲爆弾 *hakō bakudan* armor-piercing bomb
6 防法 *Habōhō* Subversion Prevention Law
竹 *hachiku* splitting bamboo
竹勢 *hachiku (no) ikio(i)* violent force
7 戒 *hakai* breaking the Buddhist commandments
却 *hakyaku* destruction, demolition
牢 *harō* jailbreak
邪顕正 *haja-kenshō* the destruction of wickedness and the establishment of righteousness

局 *hakyoku* catastrophe, cataclysm, collapse
局的 *hakyokuteki* catastrophic, cataclysmic
8 門 *hamon* excommunication, expulsion
取 *yabu(ri)-to(ru)* conquer
物 *wa(re)mono* broken article; fragile article
9 風 *hafu* gable
屋 *haoku* dilapidated house
垣 *yaregaki* broken fence or hedge
砕 *hasai* crushing, smashing, splintering
約 *hayaku* breach of contract
10 倫 *harin* immorality
格 *hakaku* exception
浪 *harō* breakers, surf
11 船 *hasen* shipwreck
産 *hasan* bankruptcy
産者 *hasansha* bankrupt person
12 裂 *haretsu* explosion, bursting, rupture, eruption
落戸 *narazumono* shiftless person
gorotsuki bully, ruffian, desperado
13 損 *hason* damage, breakage, breach
滅 *hametsu* ruin, destruction, collapse
毀 *haki* destruction; reversal (by a court)
棄 *haki* breaking (a treaty), revocation, annulment, downfall
傷風 *hashōfū* tetanus, lockjaw
廉恥 *harenchi* shamelessness, infamy
14 摧 *hasai* crushing, smashing, splintering
獄 *hagoku* jailbreak
綻 *hatan* failure, ruin, bankruptcy (of business or character)
算 *hasan* checking, refiguring; doing over again
15 談 *hadan* cancellation, annulment, rupture, breaking off, rejection
16 壊 *hakai* destruction, demolition, collapse
壊力 *hakairyoku* destructive power
壊分子 *hakai bunshi* subversive elements
壊主義 *hakai shugi* vandalism
壊的 *hakaiteki* destructive
壊者 *hakaisha* destroyer, desolator
壊消防 *hakai shōbō* wrecking
壊消防隊 *hakai shōbōtai* wrecking crew
17 鍋 *warenabe* cracked pot
18 顔 *hagan* broad smile
顔一笑 *hagan-isshō* broad smile
19 鏡 *hakyō* broken mirror; divorce
20 鐘 *waregane* cracked bell
21 魔弓 *hamayumi* exorcising bow (used in ridgepole-raising ceremony); toy bow and arrow

6

研 4000 / J-X / M24177 See 研 3991.

硅 4001 / J626b / M24151 See 珪 3638.

砦 4002 / J3a56 / M24098 SAI. *toride* fort, stronghold, entrenchments.

7

硴 4003 / J626d / M-X （国字） *kaki* oyster.

硲 4004 / J4823 / M24243 （国字） *hazama* gorge, ravine, gap, valley. *sako* valley, ravine.

硯 4005 / J3827 / M24233 KEN. *suzuri* inkstone.
5 石 *suzuri ishi* inkstone
9 海 *suzuri (no) umi* well of the inkstone
15 箱 *suzuribako* inkstone case

B **硫** 4006 / J4e32 / M24229 RYŪ sulphur.
6 安 *ryūan* ammonium sulphate
11 黄 *iō, yuō* sulphur, brimstone
黄泉 *iōsen* sulphur spring
黄華 *iōka* flowers of sulphur
14 酸 *ryūsan* sulphuric acid
酸紙 *ryūsanshi* parchment paper

B **硝** 4007 / J3e4b / M24201 SHŌ saltpeter.
3 子 *garasu* glass, pane
子戸 *garasudo* glass door
子切 *garasuki(ri)* glass cutter
子糸 *garasu ito* spun glass
子板 *garasu ita* plate glass; pane
子屋 *garasuya* glass shop
子張 *garasuba(ri)* glazing
子商 *garasushō* glass shop

5 玄 玉 王 瓜 瓦 甘 生 用 田 疋 疒 癶 白 皮 皿 目 矛 矢 8【石】示 ネ 内 禾 穴 立

子窓 *garasu mado* glazed window
子細工 *garasuzaiku* glasswork
子棒 *garasubō* glass rod
子綿 *garasumen* glass wool
子管 *garasukan* glass tube
子器 *garasuki* glassware
子職工 *garasu shokkō* glass blower
4 化 *shōka* nitrification
化綿 *shōkamen* guncotton
13 煙 *shōen* gunpowder smoke
14 酸 *shōsan* nitric acid
酸銀 *shōsangin* silver nitrate
16 薬 *shōyaku* gunpowder

B **硬** 4008 / J3945 / M24230 Kō. *kata(i)* hard, solid; tough, rigid; tight; steady, firm; strict; safe, reliable, upright; chaste, constant; stiff; bookish; classical; stubborn.
3 口蓋 *kōkōgai* hard palate
4 木 *kōboku* hardwood
水 *kōsui* hard water
文学 *kōbungaku* solid reading
化 *kōka* hardening; vulcanization; sclerosis; stiffening
化病 *kōkabyō* sclerosis, hardening
化症 *kōkashō* sclerosis, hardening
5 玉 *kōgyoku* jadeite
石鹼 *kōsekken* hard soap
6 式 *kōshiki* hard, rigid
式飛行船 *kōshiki hikōsen* rigid dirigible
式庭球 *kōshiki teikyū* hardball tennis
8 直 *kōchoku na* sturdy, stout, inflexible
性 *kōsei* hardness
性下疳 *kōsei gekan* hard (syphilitic) canker
9 派 *kōha* tough elements
度 *kōdo* hardness, solidity
度計 *kōdokei* hardness tester
10 骨 *kōkotsu* hard bone; firmness, inflexibility, stubbornness
骨漢 *kōkotsukan* sturdy individual, man of will power
11 球 *kōkyū* hard (tennis) ball
軟 *kōnan* (relative) hardness
貨 *kōka* metallic money, coin
教育 *kōkyōiku* Spartan discipline
12 筆 *kōhitsu* hard writing instruments (pen and pencil)
14 膏 *kōkō* ointment, salve
15 質 *kōshitsu* hardness; firmness of disposition
質護謨 *kōshitsu gomu* hard rubber

8

碎 4009 / J626c / M24284 See 砕 3990.

碑 4010 / J-X / M24289 See 碑 4028.

碆 4011 / J626e / M24273 HA arrowhead; stone attached by a cord or net to an arrow.

碓 4012 / J3130 / M24294 TAI, TE a foot-driven mortar, a foot-driven mill.

碚 4013 / J6270 / M24309 BAI, HAI bud; mound; cultivate, foster.

碗 4014 / J4f52 / M24306 WAN porcelain bowl, teacup.

碕 4015 / J3a6c / M24296 KI. *saki* cape, spit, promontory.

碍 4016 / J3337 / M24283 **礙** 4055 / J6328 / M24542 GE. GAI obstacle.
3 子 *gaishi* insulator

碌 4017 / J6271 / M24282 ROKU. *roku na* satisfactory, proper, respectable, right, good, worth mentioning; many, much; enough. *roku ni* well, properly, satisfactorily; sufficiently, enough.
12 無 *roku(demo)na(i)* useless
13 碌 *rokuroku* well, properly, satisfactorily; sufficiently, enough; to no purpose, in idleness

硼 4018 / J626f / M24254 HŌ sound of two stones struck together.
9 砂 *hōsha* borax
10 素 *hōso* boron
14 酸 *hōsan* boric acid

碇 4019 / J4476 / M24275 TEI. *ikari* anchor, grapnel.
8 泊 *teihaku* anchorage, moorings
泊地 *teihakuchi* anchorage, moorings, berth
泊灯 *teihakutō* anchor light

泊所 *teihakujo* anchorage, moorings, berth
泊料 *teihakuryō* anchorage fees
泊船 *teihakusen* ship at anchor
泊港 *teihakukō* anchorage harbor
13 置 *teichi* anchorage, moorings

B 碁 4020 / J386b / M24261 Go go, Japanese checkers.
5 石 *goishi* a go stone, a checker
打 *gou(chi)* a go player
6 会 *gokai* commercial go-playing parlor
会所 *gokaijo* commercial go-playing parlor
9 客 *gokyaku* a go player
15 盤 *goban* checkerboard, go board
盤乗 *gobanno(ri)* standing on a checkerboard
盤割 *gobanwa(ri)* laid out like a checkerboard
盤縞 *gobanjima* checkered pattern

9

磖 4021 / J6275 / M24350 See 瑙 3659.

碄 4022 / J6271 / M24339 See 砧 3996.

碵 4023 / J6273 / M-X Seki. Tei.

碬 4024 / J-X / M24341 Ka, Ke tool grinder.

碣 4025 / J6272 / M24326 Ketsu round stone monument.

碩 4026 / J4059 / M24338 Seki large; eminent; great.
8 学 *sekigaku* profound scholar
14 徳 *sekitoku* man of great virtue
16 儒 *sekiju* Confucian scholar; scholar

碧 4027 / J4a4b / M24334 Heki blue; green.
4 水 *hekisui* blue water
5 玉 *hekigyoku* jasper
8 空 *hekikū, aozora* azure sky
11 眼 *hekigan* blue eyes
15 潭 *hekitan* blue expanse (of water)

B 碑 4028 / J486a / M24364′ Hi monument, tombstone. *ishibumi* stone monument.
4 文 *hibun* epitaph, inscription
5 石 *hiseki* tombstone, stone slab, stone monument
8 帖 *hijō* a rubbing of a stone monument
9 面 *himen* the face of a monument or its inscription
14 誌 *hishi* epitaph, inscription
銘 *himei* epitaph, inscription

A 磁 4029 / J3c27 / M24364 磁 4031 / J-X / M24382 Ji magnetism; porcelain.
2 力 *jiryoku* magnetism
3 土 *jido* kaolin, clay for making chinaware
4 化 *jika* magnetization
5 北 *jihoku* magnetic north
石 *jishaku, jiseki* magnet, compass
石盤 *jishakuban* mariner's compass
6 気 *jiki* magnetism
気学 *jikigaku* magnetics
気嵐 *jiki arashi* magnetic storm
8 性 *jisei* magnetism
9 界 *jikai* magnetic field
南極 *jinankyoku* south magnetic pole
10 針 *jishin* magnetic needle
荷 *jika* magnetic charge
12 場 *jijō, jiba* magnetic field
極 *jikyoku* magnetic pole
13 鉄 *jitetsu* magnetic iron
鉄鉱 *jitekkō* lodestone, magnetite
15 器 *jiki* porcelain

10

碼 4030 / J627b / M24368 See 瑪 3671. Also *yādo* English yard (distance).

磁 4031 / J-X / M24382 See 磁 4029.

磅 4032 / J627c / M24386 Hō sound of stone falling; become obstructed. *pondo* pound (weight, sterling).

5 玄玉王瓜瓦甘生用田疋疒癶白皮皿目矛矢【石】示ネ禸禾穴立

碣 4033 / J6277 / M24389 KATSU talc.

磋 4034 / J6278 / M24395 SA polish.

磑 4035 / J6276 / M24402 GAI mortar, hand mill.

磊 4036 / J627d / M24394 RAI many stones.
12 落 *rairaku* frankness, openheartedness

磐 4037 / J4858 / M24401 HAN, BAN wall (in a mine). *iwa* rock, crag; reef.
5 石 *banjaku* huge rock

碾 4038 / J627a / M24370 TEN, DEN mortar, hand mill. *hi(ku)* grind (grain).
6 臼 *hikiusu* hand grinding mill
12 割 *hi(ki)-wa(ru)* grind. *hikiwa(ri)* cracked or ground barley
割麦 *hikiwa(ri) mugi* cracked or ground barley
15 磑 *atsuusu* stone hand mill

10 [石]

A 確 4039 / J334e / M24366 碻 4040 / J-X / M-X KAKU firm, tight, hard, solid. *tashi(kameru)* ascertain, confirm, verify. *kaku(taru), tashi(ka) na* sure, positive; accurate; reliable; sound, firm; clear, evident; genuine; able, competent; sober, sane; I think; if I remember right. *tashi(ka) ni* certainly, doubtless. *tashi(ka) niwa* for certain. *shika to* certainly, definitely, exactly, firmly, fully.
5 立 *kakuritsu* establishment
乎 *kakko(taru)* firm, determined, indomitable
乎不抜 *kakko-fubatsu* invincible, indefatigable
乎不動 *kakko-fudō* invincible, indefatigable
6 守 *kakushu suru* adhere to, cling to, be loyal to
7 言 *kakugen* positive statement
8 固 *kakko(taru)* sure, firm
実 *kakujitsu* certainly, authenticity, reliability
実性 *kakujitsusei* reliability, certainty, validity
定 *kakutei* decision, confirmation
定的 *kakuteiteki* definite
定期限 *kakutei kigen* definite period
9 保 *kakuho suru* secure, ensure, assure, guarantee, maintain
信 *kakushin* conviction, confidence, assurance
約 *kakuyaku* definite promise
11 率 *kakuritsu* probability 「antagonism
執 *kakushitsu, kakushū* discord,
12 答 *kakutō* definite answer
然 *kakuzen(taru)* definite, positive
報 *kakuhō* definite news, authentic report
証 *kakushō* conclusive evidence, assurance, confirmation, corroboration
証的 *kakushōteki* corroborative
14 聞 *kakubun suru* learn reliably
徴 *kakuchō* positive proof
認 *kakunin suru* verify, certify, confirm, validate
説 *kakusetsu* established theory
15 論 *kakuron* sound reasoning, incontrovertible argument

11

碻 4040 / J-X / M-X See 確 4039.

磧 4041 / J6321 / M24448 SEKI rocky beach; riverbank.

磬 4042 / J627e / M24454 KEI. KYŌ upside-down V-shaped stone gong; skillful horse-handling; strangle.

甎 4043 / J6322 / M24418 甎 3705 / J612f / M21589 SEN tile.
9 茶 *tancha, dancha* (cheap) brick tea

磔 4044 / J6279 / M24406 TAKU crucifixion; pulling limb from limb; exposing a corpse. *haritsuke* crucifixion.
6 刑 *takkei, haritsuke* crucifixion
刑柱 *takkeibashira* stake, cross
10 殺 *takusatsu* crucifixion by lance thrusts

B 磨 4045 / J4b61 / M24449' MA. *miga(ku)* polish, scour; shine (shoes); brush (teeth); improve (skill), cultivate (character), train (the mind). *su(ru)* rub,

chafe, file; lose. *su(reru)* rub, chafe, wear; become sophisticated. *to(gu)* sharpen, grind, scour, hone, polish; wash (rice).
4 込 *su(ri)-ko(mu)* grind and mix
切 *su(ri)-ki(ru)* cut by rubbing; spend all (one's money)
5 石 *togiishi* whetstone, grindstone
出 *su(ri)-da(su)* polish
6 合 *su(ri)-a(waseru)* fit by rubbing together
9 砂 *miga(ki)zuna* polishing sand
砕 *su(ri)-kuda(ku)* rub to pieces
研紙 *makenshi* emery paper
10 消 *su(ri)-ke(su)* erase, efface
粉 *miga(ki)ko* polishing powder
紙 *miga(ki)gami* emery paper
耗 *mamō* abrasion, wear
11 崩 *su(ri)-kuzu(su)* rub to pieces
12 揉 *sut(ta)mon(da) suru* be confused
減 *su(ri)-he(rasu)* wear away, rub down, abrade
13 損 *mason* wear and tear
滅 *mametsu* wear and tear; defacement; crushing (a nerve)
15 潰 *su(ri)-tsubu(su)* pulverize; mash; deface; lose (a fortune)

12

磴 4046 / J6324 / M24178 Tō stony slope; stone steps; stone bridge.

磽 4047 / J6323 / M24494 Kō, Kyō barren, rocky land.

B **礁** 4048 / J3e4c / M24502 Shō sunken rock.

磯 4049 / J306b / M24465 Ke. Ki. *iso* seashore, beach.
4 辺 *isobe* seashore, beach
6 伝 *isozuta(i)* following the beach
8 松 *isomatsu* seashore pines
波 *isonami* breakers
9 臭 *isokusa(i)* smelling of the beach (fish and shells)
10 浪 *isonami* breaker, surf
11 釣 *isozuri* beach fishing
13 路 *isoji* beach road; vicinity of the beach
19 蟹 *isogani* sand crab

13

磔 4050 / J-X / M-X Nonstandard for 礫 4059.

礇 4051 / J2325 / M34505 Iku jade-like jewel.

礑 4052 / J6327 / M24526 Tō bottom, sole, depth. *hata to, hatta to* slapping sound; suddenly.

礒 4053 / J6326 / M24527 Gi stone, crag; beach. *iso* beach, sand.

B **礎** 4054 / J4143 / M24522 So. *ishizue* foundation stone, cornerstone.
5 石 *soseki* cornerstone, foundation stone, footstone
7 材 *sozai* foundation materials

14

礙 4055 / J6328 / M24542 See 碍 4016.

礪 4056 / J626a / M24571 Rei whetstone; polish.

15

礦 4057 / J6268 / M24564 See 鉱 6252.

礬 4058 / J6329 / M24573 Ban alum.
3 土 *hando, bando* alumina, aluminum oxide
4 水 *dōsa* sizing, glaze

礫 4059 / J632a / M24572 Reki *tsubute* small stones.
3 土 *rekido* gravelly soil
8 岩 *rekigan* conglomerate

5
玄 玉 王 瓜 瓦 甘 生 用 田 疋 疒 癶 白 皮 皿 目 矛 矢 石 0【示 ネ】 禸 禾 穴 立

RAD. 示 113

Shimesu to show. At left: 礻 or ネ (4 strokes) *shimesu hen*. Nickname: Showing.

A **示** 4060 / J3c28 / M24623 JI. SHI indication. *shime(su)* show, indicate, point out, give (an example), signify, display, express. *shime(shi)* (parental) discipline; revelation.

5 圧計 *shiatsukei* pressure gauge
6 合 *shime(shi)-a(u)* inform one another; show one another. *shime(shi)-a(waseru), shime(shi)-a(wasu)* inform one another; plan together; plot together
9 威 *jii* demonstration (against something)
威的 *jiiteki* demonstrative, threatening
威運動 *jii undō* demonstration (against something)
10 唆 *shisa* suggestion
11 達 *shitatsu* directions, instructions
現 *jigen* divine revelation; divine miracles (in Buddhism or Shinto)
教 *shikyō* instruction, information
15 談 *jidan* settlement out of court

1

A **礼** 4061 / J4e69 / M24626′ **礼** 4062 / J-X / M24626 **禮** 4113 / J6339 / M24844

RAI, REI salutation, salute, bow, courtesy, propriety, ceremony, thanks, appreciation, remuneration, return present. *uya* courtesy.

6 回 *reimawa(ri)* round of thank-you visits
式 *reishiki* etiquette, manners
7 状 *reijō* letter of thanks
8 金 *reikin* honorarium, remuneration, reward, fee
法 *reihō* courtesy, propriety, manners, decorum
物 *reimotsu, reibutsu* present, gift
服 *reifuku* full dress, dress suit, ceremonial dress, evening dress, dress uniform, vestments
参 *reimai(ri)* thanksgiving visit to a shrine
奉公 *reibōkō* unremunerated post-apprenticeship service
典 *reiten* ceremony, ritual, rite, sacraments
典律 *reitenritsu* ceremonial law
拝 *reihai, raihai* worship; adoration; church service
拝式 *reihaishiki* church services
拝学 *reihaigaku* liturgics
拝者 *reihaisha* worshipper
拝堂 *reihaidō* chapel, church, tabernacle, worship hall
10 砲 *reihō* gun salute
11 遇 *reigū* cordial reception; honors, privileges
12 帽 *reibō* ceremonial hat, silk hat
装 *reisō* ceremonial dress, full dress
13 節 *reisetsu* courtesy, etiquette, propriety, manners
義 *reigi* courtesy, propriety, manners, decorum
楽 *reigaku* etiquette and music
15 賛 *raisan* worship, adoration, admiration, praise
儀 *reigi* courtesy, propriety, manners, decorum
儀正 *reigitada(shii)* courteous
儀作法 *reigisahō* courtesy, propriety, manners, decorum
20 譲 *reijō* politeness, courtesy
22 讃 *raisan* worship, adoration, admiration, praise

2

祁 4063 / J3737 / M24634 KI. GI big, large; excessive; quiet; plentiful.

6 祁 *kiki* silence; plentiful
12 寒 *kikan* terribly cold

3

祀 4064 / J632b / M24633 SHI. *matsu(ru)* enshrine, worship.

A **社** 4065 / J3c52 / M24631′ **社** 4066 / J-X / M24631 SHA Shinto shrine; association; firm, company, office. *yashiro* Shinto shrine.

2 人 *shajin* shrine priests; villagers
4 中 *shachū* office staff; clique, troupe

友 *shayū* friend of the firm; colleague
内 *shanai* in the shrine; in the company
内電話 *shanai denwa* office telephone system
5 主 *shashu* the head of a company
司 *shashi* a Shinto priest
号 *shagō* shrine category; company name
用 *shayō* for company business
用族 *shayōzoku* persons living high on their firm's expense account
外 *shagai* outside the company
外船 *shagaisen* tramp steamer
6 寺 *shaji* shrines and temples
宅 *shataku* company living quarters
名 *shamei* company name
団 *shadan* corporation, association
団法人 *shadan hōjin* corporate person
交 *shakō* society; social life
交性 *shakōsei* sociability
交的 *shakōteki* social, sociable
交服 *shakōfuku* party clothes, evening dress
交室 *shakōshitsu* social hall
交界 *shakōkai* society circles
交家 *shakōka* a social person
交場 *shakōjō* social hall
交場裏 *shakōjōri ni* in fashionable society
会 *shakai* society, community, the world; social (service)
会人 *shakaijin* a member of society
会化 *shakaika* socialization
会不安 *shakai fuan* social unrest
会史 *shakaishi* social history
会民主主義 *shakai minshu shugi* social democracy
会主義 *shakai shugi* socialism
会主義者 *shakai shugisha* socialist
会生活 *shakai seikatsu* social life, community life
会生物学 *shakai seibutsugaku* sociobiology
会生態学 *shakai seitaigaku* ecology
会改良 *shakai kairyō* social reform
会状勢 *shakai jōsei* social conditions
会言語学 *shakai gengogaku* sociolinguistics
会性 *shakaisei* social nature
会的 *shakaiteki* social
会学 *shakaigaku* sociology
会奉仕 *shakai hōshi* social service
会制度 *shakai seido* social system
会事情 *shakai jijō* social conditions
会事業 *shakai jigyō* social service, public-welfare work
会面 *shakaimen* society page, local news page
会相 *shakaisō* phase of life
会科 *shakaika* social studies
会科学 *shakai kagaku* social science
会革命 *shakai kakumei* social revolution
会連帯 *shakai rentai* social solidarity
会政策 *shakai seisaku* social policy
会保険庁 *Shakai Hokenchō* Social Insurance Agency
会保障 *shakai hoshō* social security
会党 *Shakaitō* Socialist Party
会部 *shakaibu* city editor's section
会部長 *shakai buchō* city editor
会悪 *shakaiaku* social crime
会教育 *shakai kyōiku* social education
会探訪 *shakai tambō* local-news reporter
会運動 *shakai undō* social movement; public campaign
会組織 *shakai soshiki* social structure
会問題 *shakai mondai* social problem
会資本 *shakai shihon* social overhead capital
会福祉 *shakai fukushi* social welfare
会意識 *shakai ishiki* social consciousness
会層 *shakaisō* social strata
会鍋 *shakai nabe* charity kettle
会観 *shakaikan* one's view of society
7 告 *shakoku* public announcement
8 長 *shachō* company (firm) president
命 *shamei* company orders
参 *shasan* visiting a shrine
9 屋 *shaoku* company building
則 *shasoku* company regulations
是 *shaze* company policy
風 *shafū* company customs
10 格 *shakaku* shrine rank
員 *shain* company personnel, clerk
家 *shake* hereditary family of Shinto priests
11 運 *shaun* company fortunes
船 *shasen* company boat
務 *shamu* shrine affairs
務所 *shamusho* shrine office
12 葬 *shasō* company funeral

5 玄玉王瓜瓦甘生用田疋疒癶白皮皿目矛矢石【示 4 礻】禸禾穴立

費 *shahi* company expenses
13 殿 *shaden* main shrine building
業 *shagyō* company business
債 *shasai* company bonds
債発行 *shasai hakkō* bond issue
14 旗 *shaki* company flag
説 *shasetsu* an editorial
領 *sharyō* shrine land
15 稷 *shashoku* the sovereign family, the state
線 *shasen* private railroad line
16 頭 *shatō* shrine precincts

4

祇 4067 / J-X / M24639 **祇** 4068 / J3540 / M-X GI national god, local god; peaceful; great.

B **祉** 4069 / J3b63 / M24641′ **祉** 4070 / J-X / M24641 SHI happiness.

B **祈** 4071 / J3527 / M24640′ **祈** 4072 / J-X / M24640 KI. *ino(ru)* pray; wish. *ino(ri)* prayer, grace.
6 合 *ino(ri)-a(u)* pray together
7 求 *ino(ri)-moto(meru)* pray for
8 雨 *kiu* praying for rain
念 *kinen* prayer
奉 *ino(ri)-tatematsu(ru)* pray (polite)
事 *negigoto* prayer
10 殺 *ino(ri)-koro(su)* pray for someone's death
14 誓 *kisei* vow, oath, pledge
15 請 *kisei* praying (to Shinto or Buddhist deities)
19 願 *kigan suru, ino(ri)-nega(u)* pray, implore. *kigan* prayer, supplication
願文 *kigambun* optative sentence
禱 *kitō* prayer; devotions; grace; exorcism
禱会 *kitōkai* prayer meeting
禱者 *kitōsha* suppliant
禱週 *kitōshū* week of prayer
禱師 *kitōshi* faith healer, medicine man, shaman
禱料 *kitōryō* gift in return for prayers
禱書 *kitōsho* prayer book
禱僧 *kitōsō* a praying priest

5

祢 4073 / J-X / M24679 **祢** 4074 / J472a / M-X See **禰** 4115.

祕 4075 / J6330 / M24663 See **秘** 4140.

祚 4076 / J632f / M24668 SO imperial throne; happiness.

祇 4077 / J632d / M24665 SHI be respectful.

祟 4078 / J632e / M24674 SUI curse. *tata(ru)* bring evil upon, curse, haunt, torment.

祐 4079 / J4d34 / M24652′ **祐** 4080 / J-X / M24652 YŪ help.
12 筆 *yūhitsu* private secretary

祠 4081 / J632c / M24676 SHI small shrine; worship, deify; festival. *hokora* small shrine.
11 堂 *shidō* mortuary temple

祓 4082 / J6331 / M24658 FUTSU. *hara(u)* purify, exorcise, drive out (spirits). *hara(i)* Shinto prayer; purification; exorcism.
11 清 *hara(i)-kiyo(meru)* purify, exorcise

A **祖** 4083 / J4144 / M24664′ **祖** 4084 / J-X / M24664 SO ancestor, founder, originator, pioneer.
4 父 *sofu* grandfather. *ōji* an old man
父母 *sofubo* grandparents
父祖母 *jiji-baba* grandparents; old people
5 母 *sobo, baba, ōba, oba* grandmother
6 考 *sokō* deceased father and grandfather
先 *sosen* ancestors
先崇拝 *sosen sūhai* ancestor worship
7 述 *sojutsu* exposition, propagation
述者 *sojutsusha* expounder, exponent
8 宗 *sosō* ancestors, ancestry
国 *sokoku* fatherland, native country
国愛 *sokokuai* love of one's fatherland
9 神 *soshin* ancestral gods
10 師 *soshi* sect founder
13 業 *sogyō* a business kept in the family for many generations

15 廟 *sobyō* ancestral tomb

A **祝** 4085 J3d4b M24672′ **祝** 4086 J-X M24672 SHUKU, SHŪ celebration, congratulations. *shuku(suru)* celebrate, congratulate, bless. *iwa(u)* congratulate, celebrate, commemorate. *iwa(i)* celebration, festival, congratulations.

4 文 *shukubun* congratulatory address
日 *iwa(i)bi, shukujitsu* holiday, festival day, feast day
火 *iwa(i)bi* festival bonfire
7 言 *shūgen* congratulations; celebration; wedding
言客 *shūgenkyaku* wedding guest
8 杯 *shukuhai* congratulatory cup, a toast
物 *iwa(i)mono* congratulatory gift
典 *shukuten* celebration, festival
事 *iwa(i)goto, hogigoto* auspicious occasion, celebration
10 砲 *shukuhō* artillery salute
宴 *shukuen* congratulatory banquet, feast
11 祭 *shukusai* festivals, feasts
祭日 *shukusaijitsu* festivals, feasts
12 勝 *shukushō* victory celebration
詞 *norito, shukushi* Shinto ritual prayer, congratulatory address
着 *shūchaku* felicitations
賀 *shukuga* celebration, congratulations
賀会 *shukugakai* congratulatory party
13 福 *shukufuku* blessing; benediction
辞 *shukuji* congratulatory address
電 *shukuden* congratulatory telegram
意 *shukui* congratulations
14 歌 *shukuka* festive song
15 儀 *shūgi* congratulations; celebration; congratulatory gift; tip
19 禱 *shukutō* benediction, blessing

A **神** 4087 J3f40 M24673′ **神** 4088 J-X M24673 JIN, SHIN god, deity; mind, soul. *kami* God, god, Allah. *kami(sabita), kan(sabita)* venerable, hallowed. *kan-, kamu-* god.

2 人 *kami bito* Shinto priest. *shinjin* god and man; man of god; Shinto priest
力 *shinryoku* divine power
4 文 *shimmon* written vow to a god
木 *shimboku* sacred tree
火 *shinka* sacred fire
父 *shimpu* priest, father
化 *shinka* deification
少女 *kami otome* shrine maidens
仏 *shimbutsu, kami-hotoke* gods and Buddhas
仏基 *Shin-Butsu-Ki* Shinto, Buddhism, and Christianity
仏混淆 *Shin-Butsu konkō* Shinto-Buddhist amalgamation
5 田 *kamita* shrine rice field
矢 *kamiya* the arrows of the gods
主 *kannushi* Shinto priest
占 *shinsen* divination
去 *kamisa(ru), kansa(ru)* decease of a noble
功皇后 *Jingū Kōgō* Empress Jingu
出鬼没 *shinshutsu-kibotsu* elusiveness
代 *jindai, shindai, kamiyo* age of the gods
代杉 *jindai sugi* lignitized cryptomeria
仙 *shinsen* wizard, Taoist hermit-wizard
仙境 *shinsenkyō* fairyland, unearthly place
6 式 *shinshiki* Shinto rites
気 *shinki* energy, spirits; a feeling of veneration
曲 *Shinkyoku* (Dante's) Divine Comedy
托 *shintaku* an oracle
灯 *shintō* sacred lantern, festival lantern
州 *shinshū* divine land, land of the gods
色 *shinshoku* the heart and the countenance; attitude
色自若 *shinshoku-jijaku* perfect composure, presence of mind
7 身 *kami(naranu) mi* not a god
佑 *shin'yū* providence, divine help
体 *shintai* god body in a Shinto shrine
妙 *shimmyō na, shimbyō na* mysterious, marvelous; admirable; docile, tame, meek; faithful
技 *shingi* consummate skill
杉 *kamisugi* a sacred cryptomeria; ancient cryptomeria on shrine grounds
助 *shinjo* divine aid
兵 *shimpei* soldiers of the gods, soldiers protected by the gods
来 *shinrai* divine inspiration
社 *jinja, jinsha* Shinto shrine
社局 *Jinjakyoku* Shrine Bureau
社参拝問題 *Jinja Sampai Mondai* The Shrine Question
社神道 *Jinja Shintō* Shrine Shinto
8 国 *shinkoku, kamiguni* the land of the gods

性 *shinsei* divinity, divine nature, godliness
明 *shimmei* deity
命 *shimmei* divine command
参 *kamimai(ri)* visiting shrines
宝 *shimpō* sacred treasure
官 *shinkan* Shinto priest
苑 *shin'en* shrine garden
事 *shinji, jinji* Shinto ceremonies. *kamigoto* work of the gods; religious rites
知学 *shinchigaku* theosophy
武天皇祭 *Jimmu Tennō Sai* Emperor Jimmu's death anniversary
学 *shingaku* theology
学的 *shingakuteki* theological
学校 *shingakkō* theological seminary
9 威 *shin'i* power or majesty of the gods
速 *shinsoku* speed, promptness, quickness
垣 *kamigaki* Shinto shrine fence
神 *kōgō(shii)* divine, solemn, awe-inspiring. *kamigami* gods, idols
勅 *shinchoku* oracle
品 *shimpin* inspired work, masterpiece
泉 *shinsen* spring on shrine grounds
通力 *jintsūriki, shintsūriki* occult, supernatural, or divine power
信心 *kamishinjin* (Shinto) piety
風 *kamikaze* providential wind; suicide plane. *shimpū* providential wind
風特攻隊員 *kamikaze tokkōtaiin* suicide pilot
前 *shinzen* at the shrine, before the god
前結婚 *shinzen kekkon* Shinto wedding
降 *kamio(roshi)* spiritism, spiritualism, necromancy
降会 *kamio(roshi) (no) kai* séance
政 *shinsei* theocracy
政国 *shinseikoku* a theocracy
変 *shimpen* a tremendous change
変化 *shimpenka* a strange change
変不思議 *shimpen-fushigi* marvel, miracle
祇 *jingi* deities of heaven and earth
祇局 *Jingikyoku* Shrine Bureau
祇歌 *jingika* Shinto hymn
10 馬 *shimme* sacred horse
酒 *miki, shinshu* sacred wine, wine offering
託 *shintaku* divine message, oracle
剣 *shinken* divine sword, sacred sword
都 *shinto* holy town
宮 *jingū* Shinto shrine; Ise Shrines
恩 *shin'on* God's goodness
格 *shinkaku* Godhead, divinity, fatherhood of God
格化 *shinkakuka* deification
秘 *shimpi* mystery
秘小説 *shimpi shōsetsu* mystery novel
秘主義 *shimpi shugi* mysticism
秘的 *shimpiteki* mystic, mysterious, miraculous
秘派 *shimpiha* mystic school
秘家 *shimpika* a mystic
秘哲学 *shimpi tetsugaku* mystic philosophy, esoterics
秘説 *shimpisetsu* mysticism
秘境 *shimpikyō* land of mystery
秘劇 *shimpigeki* mystery drama
11 遊 *kamiaso(bi)* dancing before the gods
道 *Shintō, Kami (no) Michi, Kan(nagara) (no) Michi, Shindō* Shinto
域 *shin'iki* shrine precincts
術 *shinjutsu* a strange act
掛 *kamika(kete)* swearing by a god; positively
授 *shinju* divine gift
略 *shinryaku* a strange plan
寄 *kamiyo(se)* oracle of a god
異 *shin'i* miracle, marvel
符 *shimpu* talisman, amulet, charm
経 *shinkei* nerves
経中枢 *shinkei chūsū* nerve center
経系 *shinkeikei* nervous system
経学 *shinkeigaku* neurology
経病 *shinkeibyō* nervous disease
経症 *shinkeishō* nervous disease, neurosis
経家 *shinkeika* nervous person
経衰弱 *shinkei suijaku* nervous exhaustion
経細胞 *shinkei saibō* nerve cell
経過敏 *shinkei-kabin* oversensitiveness
経痛 *shinkeitsū* neuralgia
経戦 *shinkeisen* war of nerves, psychological warfare
経節 *shinkeisetsu* ganglion
経質 *shinkeishitsu* nervousness, nervous temperament
12 棚 *kamidana* Shinto household shrine
童 *shindō* prodigy, child wonder
葬 *shinsō* Shinto funeral

智 *shinchi* divine wisdom
無月 *kannazuki, kaminazuki, kamina(shi)zuki* tenth lunar month (the month the gods are all away at the Izumo shrine)
13 詣 *kami mōde* shrine visitation
隠 *kamikaku(shi), kamigaku(shi)* hidden by the gods. *kamigaku(re)* hiding of the gods; hiding from everyone
意 *shin'i* divine will, divine decree, providence
感 *shinkan* inspiration, intuition
業 *kamiwaza* providence; act of God; superhuman feat
殿 *shinden* temple, shrine, sanctuary
話 *shinwa* myth; mythology
話学 *shinwagaku* mythology
話劇 *shinwageki* mythological play
楽 *kagura* Shinto dance
楽堂 *kaguradō* Shinto dance pavilion
楽殿 *kaguraden* Shinto dance pavilion
楽獅子 *kagurajishi* lion mask festival
聖 *shinsei* divine nature; sacredness, sanctity, holiness; godliness; dignity. *shinsei na* sacred, divine
聖同盟 *Shinsei Dōmei* the Holy Alliance
聖冒瀆 *shinsei bōtoku* blasphemy
聖視 *shinseishi suru* regard as sacred
聖羅馬帝国 *Shinsei Rōma Teikoku* Holy Roman Empire
14 像 *shinzō* (rare) Shinto image; Shinto picture
僕 *shimboku* (Christian) believer
徳 *shintoku* divine virtues
様 *kamisama* god; God
語 *kamigata(ri)* oracle of a god
魂 *shinkon* heart, soul
罰 *shimbatsu* divine punishment
嘗祭 *Kannamesai* Shinto Festival of New Rice (Oct. 17)
15 廟 *shimbyō* Shinto shrine
慮 *shinryo* divine will, divine decree, providence
箭 *kamiya* arrows of the gods
器 *jingi, shinki* the sacred treasures

権 *shinken* divine right
権政治 *shinken seiji* theocracy
霊 *shinrei* divine spirit
霊界 *shinreikai* spirit world
16 橋 *shinkyō* sacred bridge
頼 *kamidano(mi)* calling on a god in distress
薬 *shin'yaku* wonder drug
憑 *kamigaka(ri)* spirit possession
17 輿 *mikoshi, shin'yo* palanquin of a Shinto god, portable shrine
18 癒 *shin'yu* divine healing, faith healing
職 *shinshoku* Shinto priest
髄 *shinzui* true meaning, mystery
19 鏡 *shinkyō* divine mirror; the Mirror of the Three Imperial Treasures
韻 *shin'in* superb spirit
璽 *shinji* sacred jewels; emperor's seal
20 懸 *kamigaka(ri), kangaka(ri)* spirit possession
21 饌 *shinsen* offering, oblation
23 籤 *mikuji* sacred lot, written oracle, divination
25 籬 *himorogi* offerings to the gods

6

A 票 4089 / [illegible] / M24694 Hyō label; ballot; ticket; sign.
5 札 *hyōsatsu* name plate, doorplate
7 決 *hyōketsu* vote, voting
13 数 *hyōsū* number of votes

B 祥 4090 / J3e4d / M24689′ 祥 4091 / J-X / M24689 Jō, Shō happiness. *saga* good omen.
4 月 *shōtsuki* death month
12 雲 *shōun* auspicious clouds
13 瑞 *shōzui* good omen

A 祭 4092 / J3a57 / M24700 Sai. *matsu(ru)* offer prayers; celebrate; deify; enshrine; worship. *matsu(ri)* festival, feast. *-sai* festival.
3 上 *matsu(ri)-a(geru)* exalt (someone)
4 文 *saimon* Shinto funeral prayer; address to the gods
日 *saijitsu* national holiday, festival day, feast day

5 玄玉王瓜瓦甘生用田疋疒癶白皮皿目矛矢石【示 7 ネ】内禾穴立

込 *matsu(ri)-ko(mu)* kick upstairs, move some to a sinecure
5 礼 *sairei* festival, feast, rituals
主 *saishu* master of (religious) ceremonies; high priestess of Ise
司 *saishi* priest
司長 *saishichō* (Jewish) high priest
司長達 *saishichōtachi* high priests (of the Jews)
司職 *saishishoku* priesthood
6 式 *saishiki* rites, ritual, ceremony
8 具 *saigu* equipment used in ceremonies
典 *saiten* festival, rite
事 *saiji* sacred rites, festival
祀 *saishi* Shinto ceremony, religious ceremony
祀料 *saishiryō* funeral expense grant
服 *saifuku* vestments
服室 *saifukushitsu* vestry
9 神 *saijin, saishin* the enshrined deity
政 *saisei* church and state, ceremonies and government
政一致 *saisei-itchi* union of Religion and the State
10 酒 *saishu* (ancient) master of ceremonies; college president; education minister
12 場 *saijō* place of a ceremony
詞 *saishi* Shinto priest's address
13 殿 *saiden* shrine, sanctuary
15 儀 *saigi* festival
器 *saiki* ceremonial equipment
16 壇 *saidan* altar
18 騒 *matsu(ri)sawa(gi)* festivities, merrymaking

7

祷 4093 / J4578 / M-X Nonstandard for **禱** 4114.

8

禀 4094 / J6349 / M24742 See **稟** 4153.

祺 4095 / J6332 / M24733 Ki, Gi fortunate, happy; auspicious omen.

禄 4096 / J4f3d / M24741′ **祿** 4097 / J6333 / M24741 Roku fief, allowance, pension, grant; happiness.

9 食 *roku (o) ha(mu)* receive salary (from a daimyo)
10 高 *rokudaka* fief, allowance, pension, grant, happiness
11 盗人 *rokunusubito* a person drawing a salary though performing little of importance

A **禁** 4098 / J3658 / M24743 Kin prohibition, ban, embargo; law. *kin(jiru), kin(zuru)* prohibit, ban, forbid, repress, restrain; abstain from.

4 方 *kimpō* secret formula
中 *kinchū* the Court, Imperial Palace, Imperial Household
内 *kindai* palace
止 *kinshi* prohibition, ban, taboo, embargo
止令 *kinshirei* prohibition decree; injunction
止命令 *kinshi meirei* prohibition decree; injunction
5 穴 *kinketsu* important parts of the body; important places
句 *kinku* tabooed word
圧 *kin'atsu* prohibition, suppression, ban
処 *kinsho* place of confinement; a place of no admittance
札 *kinsatsu* prohibition notice board
令 *kinrei* ban, embargo, interdict, prohibition
6 伐 *kimbatsu* prohibition of tree cutting
7 足 *kinsoku* confinement
廷 *kintei* imperial court, imperial palace
戒 *kinkai* commandment
忌 *kinki* taboo, contraindication
8 固 *kinko* imprisonment
所 *kinsho* place of confinement; a place of no admittance
法 *kimpō* prohibitory law
物 *kimmotsu* taboo, forbidden thing, injurious thing, something to avoid
苑 *kin'en* imperial garden
治産 *kinchisan, kinjisan* incompetency (in law)
治産者 *kinchisansha* a person adjudged incompetent
制 *kinsei* prohibition, ban, embargo
制品 *kinseihin* contraband articles
9 城 *kinjō* palace
軍 *kingun* palace guard

10 秘 *kimpi* palace secret; top secret
殺 *kinsatsu* imprisonment and execution
書 *kinsho* prohibited literature; proscribed book
酒 *kinshu* prohibition, temperance, abstinence
酒令 *kinshurei* prohibition law
酒州 *kinshushū* prohibition state
酒会 *kinshukai* temperance society
酒国 *kinshukoku* a country prohibiting liquors
酒法 *kinshuhō* prohibition law
酒家 *kinshuka* total abstainer
酒党 *kinshutō* prohibition party
酒薬 *kinshuyaku* medicines to break alcohol habit
11 鳥 *kinchō* protected birds
教 *kinkyō* prohibition of a religion
転載 *kintensai* reprinting forbidden, all rights reserved
断 *kindan* prohibition
断木実 *kindan (no) ko(no)mi* the forbidden fruit
欲 *kin'yoku* self-denial, asceticism; abstinence, continence, mortification
欲主義 *kin'yoku shugi* asceticism, stoicism
欲主義者 *kin'yoku shugisha* ascetics
猟 *kinryō* prohibition of hunting; No Hunting
猟区 *kinryōku* no-hunting area
猟地 *kinryochi* no-hunting area
猟期 *kinryōki* closed hunting season
12 遏 *kin'atsu* forcible prohibition
絶 *kinzetsu* prohibition
裡 *kinri* imperial court, imperial palace
13 煙 *kin'en* prohibition of smoking; No Smoking
裏 *kinri* imperial court, imperial palace
裏様 *kinrisama* the (Japanese) emperor
14 厭 *majinai, kin'en* spell, charm, enchantment
獄 *kingoku* imprisonment
漁 *kinryō, kingyo* prohibition of fishing; No Fishing
漁区 *kinryōku* no-fishing area
漁期 *kinryōki* out of season for fishing
15 慾 *kin'yoku* abstinence, self-denial, asceticism
慾主義 *kin'yoku shugi* asceticism, stoicism
16 衛 *kin'ei* imperial guards
錮 *kinko* imprisonment
輸 *kin'yu* embargo on shipments
輸品 *kin'yuhin* contraband
18 闕 *kinketsu* imperial palace

9

禎 4099 / J4477 / M24767′ **禎** 4100 / J-X / M24767 TEI happiness.

禊 4101 / J6334 / M24760 **禊** 4107 / J-X / M-X KEI. KATSU. *misogi* Shinto purification ceremony.
8 事 *keiji* Shinto purification

B **禍** 4102 / J3252 / M24766′ **禍** 4103 / J-X / M24766 KA calamity, misfortune. *maga, wazawai* calamity, misfortune, woe, evil, curse.
4 心 *kashin* treachery, malice
6 因 *kain* cause of trouble
7 言 *magagoto* unlucky words
乱 *karan* disturbances; disasters
災 *kasai* disaster, misfortune
8 幸 *magasachi* fortunes
事 *magagoto* evil, mishap, disaster
10 根 *kakon* root of evil
害 *kagai* evil, harm, mischief
11 患 *kakan* disaster, calamity, evil
13 福 *kafuku* weal or woe; ups and downs
16 機 *kaki* root of evil
18 難 *kanan* calamity, disaster, accident, misfortune

B **禅** 4104 / J4135 / M24787′ **禪** 4110 / J6338 / M24835 ZEN silent meditation; Buddhist sect originating in the twelfth century.
5 尼 *zenni* Zen nun
6 寺 *zendera* Zen temple
7 杖 *zenjō* stick to keep Zen meditators awake
8 門 *zemmon* entering the Zen priesthood
房 *zembō* Zen temple; Zen priest's cell
味 *zemmi* Zen flavor, mysticism
林 *zenrin* Zen temple
宗 *zenshū* Zen sect
学 *zengaku* Zen doctrines
10 師 *zenji* high priest in a Zen sect
家 *zenka, zenke* Zen sect; Zen temple; Zen priest
11 堂 *zendō* Zen study temple

[13] 僧 *zensō* Zen priest
話 *zenwa* Zen talk
[14] 閣 *zenkaku* Zen temple
[20] 譲 *zenjō* abdication

A 福 4105/J4a21/M24768′ 福 4106/J-X/M24768 FUKU fortune, blessing, luck, wealth; food which has been offered to gods.
[2] 人 *fukujin* fortunate person
[3] 千年 *fukusennen* the millennium
[4] 引 *fukubiki* lottery
引券 *fukubikiken* lottery ticket
[7] 沢 *fukutaku* happiness and blessings
利 *fukuri* prosperity, welfare, well-being
助 *fukusuke* a large-headed male doll which brings good luck; a large-headed person
寿 *fukuju* prosperity and longevity
[8] 祉 *fukushi* prosperity, welfare, well-being
祉国家 *fukushi kokka* a welfare state
[9] 相 *fukusō* happy look, radiant face
神 *fukujin, fuku (no) kami* god of wealth, god of good fortune
神漬 *fukujinzuke* pickles preserved in soy
音 *fukuin* gospel, good news, glad tidings
音主義 *fukuin shugi no* evangelical
音的 *fukuinteki* evangelical
音書 *Fukuinsho* The Gospels
音書対観 *Fukuinsho taikan* a harmony of the Gospels
[11] 運 *fukuun* happiness and good fortune
[13] 福 *fukubuku(shii)* radiant, genial
禄寿 *Fukurokuju* a god of wealth
[14] 徳 *fukutoku* good fortune, happiness and prosperity; good deeds and the resultant prosperity

10

禊 4107/J-X/M-X See 禊 4101.

禝 4108/J6335/M24792 SHOKU used in personal names.

11

頴 4109/J3150/M24824 See 穎 4173.

12

禪 4110/J6338/M24835 See 禅 4104.

禦 4111/J357a/M24820 GYO. *fuse(gu)* defend, protect; resist; keep away, shut out, ward off; prevent.

禧 4112/J6336/M24828 KI fortunate; auspicious; joyful.

13

禮 4113/J6339/M24844 See 礼 4061.

14

禱 4114/J-X/M24852 TŌ. *ino(ru)* pray.

禰 4115/J-X/M24851 祢 4116/J4729/M-X NE ancestral shrine.
[8] 宜 *negi* Shinto priest of lower rank

17

禳 4117/J633a/M24868 JŌ. *hara(u)* purify, exorcise, drive out (spirits).
(o)hara(i) Shinto prayer; purification; exorcism.

RAD. 禸 114

Jū or *ashiato* footprint. Note that this is a 5-stroke radical and is so counted whenever it appears. Nickname: Footprint.

4

禹 4118 J633b M24885 U name of a Chinese emperor.

禺 4119 J633c M24886 GU long-tailed monkey; separation; appear.

8

禽 4120 J3659 M24893 KIN bird; captive; capture. *tori* bird.
8 舎 *kinsha* poultry shed
11 鳥 *kinchō* birds
16 獣 *kinjū* birds and animals

RAD. 禾 115

Nogi the katakana *no* plus *ki* "tree." At left: *nogi hen*. Nickname: 2-Branch Tree (cf. Rads. 75 and 127).

禾 4121 J3253 M24906 KA rice; grain; sprouts; straw

2

禿 4122 J4645 M24910 TOKU. *ha(geru)* become bald; become bare. *chibi(ru)* wear out, waste away. *hage* baldness, bald person. *kaburo* baldhead. *kamuro* little girl employed in a brothel as an attendant.
3 山 *hageyama* bare mountain
上 *ha(ge) a(garu)* (one's hair) recedes
9 茶瓶 *hage chabin* baldheaded man
12 筆 *chibi fude, tokuhitsu* worn-down writing brush
14 髪 *tokuhatsu* baldness
16 頭 *hageatama, tokutō* baldness, bald head; baldheaded person
頭病 *tokutōbyō* pathological baldness, alopecia

B 秀 4123 J3d28 M24911 SHŪ excellence; beauty. *hii(deru), sugu(reru)* surpass, excel, tower above, rise to eminence.
3 才 *shūsai* genius, person of great talents, prodigy
5 句 *shūku* excellent haiku poem; wisecrack
7 吟 *shūgin* excellent poem
抜 *shūbatsu* excellence, pre-eminence
8 英 *shūei* excelling
9 眉 *shūbi* prominent eyebrows; beautiful eyebrows
美 *shūbi* superb beauty
10 逸 *shūitsu* supreme excellence; masterpiece
12 絶 *shūzetsu* supreme excellence
14 歌 *shūka* gems of poetry
19 麗 *shūrei na* graceful, beautiful

A 私 4124 J3b64 M24913 SHI I; private affairs. *watakushi, watashi, washi* I, myself, private (affairs). *watakushi suru* think only of one's own gain. *hiso(ka) na* secret, private, stealthy, hushed.
2 人 *shijin* private individual
3 大 *shidai* private college
子 *shishi* illegitimate child
小説 *watakushi shōsetsu, shishōsetsu* a first-person novel; an "I" novel
4 心 *shishin* selfishness, private interest
方 *watakushikata* I; on my part
文書 *shibunsho* private document
5 用 *shiyō* personal use; private business, misappropriation, embezzlement
田 *shiden* private rice land
立 *shiritsu* private, nongovernment
立学校 *shiritsu gakkō* private school
生子 *shiseishi, shiseiji* illegitimate child
生児 *shiseiji* illegitimate child

生活 *shiseikatsu* one's private life
6 行 *shikō* private conduct
印 *shiin* personal seal
曲 *shikyoku* unfair dealings, irregularities, graft
刑 *shikei* lynching
交 *shikō* private relations
宅 *shitaku* private house
考 *shikō* personal opinion
自身 *watakushi jishin* myself
有 *shiyū* private ownership
有地 *shiyūchi* private land
有物 *shiyūbutsu* private property
有財産 *shiyū zaisan* private property
有権 *shiyūken* right of private property
7 見 *shiken* personal opinion
利 *shiri* self-interest, personal gain
邸 *shitei* private residence
兵 *shihei* private army
8 法 *shihō* private law
版 *shihan* private publication
物 *shibutsu* private property, personal effects
的 *shiteki* private, personal
事 *shiji, watakushigoto* personal affairs
学 *shigaku* private school; one's personal theory
学校 *shigakkō* private school
服 *shifuku* ordinary clothes; plain-clothes police officer
服刑事 *shifuku keiji* plain-clothes police officer
服警官 *shifuku keikan* plain-clothes police officer
9 通 *shitsū* illicit intercourse
信 *shishin* private message
恨 *shikon* personal grudge
室 *shishitsu* private room
怨 *shien* grudge, enmity
10 消 *shishō* embezzlement, misappropriation
流 *watakushiryū* one's personal method
称 *shishō* pretension, assumption (of a title)
記 *shiki* private record
財 *shizai* private means, private property
益 *shieki* self-interest, personal gain
案 *shian* one's personal plan
党 *shitō* faction, junta
恩 *shion* personal obligations
書 *shisho* private document, private letter
書函 *shishokan, shishobako* post-office box
書箱 *shishobako* post-office box
11 道 *shidō* private road, private path
達 *watakushitachi* we
情 *shijō* personal feelings, bias
淑 *shishuku suru* adore, look up to, pattern after
設 *shisetsu* private
欲 *shiyoku* self-interest, selfish desire
娼 *shishō* streetwalker, unlicensed prostitute
娼窟 *shishōkutsu* a brothel
12 訴 *shiso* civil suit
費 *shihi* private expense, one's own expense
報 *shihō* private message, private report
貿易 *shibōeki* private trade
営 *shiei* private operation
営事業 *shiei jigyō* private enterprise
13 腹 *shifuku* one's own pocket
腹肥 *shifuku (o) ko(yasu)* line one's own pockets
話 *shiwa* whispered conversation
鉄 *shitetsu* private railway line
罪 *shizai* personal injury
意 *shii* selfishness; bias; one's own idea
14 選 *shisen* personal choice, personal appointment
語 *sasaya(ku)* whisper, murmur. *sasayakigoto, shigo* secret talk, whispering
説 *shisetsu* privately held theory
蔵 *shizō suru* possess
塾 *shijuku* private school
製 *shisei* privately manufactured
15 憤 *shifun* enmity, grudge
撰 *shisen* personal choice
権 *shiken* private rights
線 *shisen* private railway line
談 *shidan* private conversation
論 *shiron* private opinion
慾 *shiyoku* self-interest, selfish desire
鋳 *shichū* secret minting
鋳銭 *shichūsen* counterfeit coins
18 闘 *shitō* private strife
20 議 *shigi* personal view; private discussion; backbiting
23 讐 *shishū* personal enemy

3

秉 4125 / J633d / M24932 HEI. HYŌ sheaf. *to(ru)* take in the hand, take.

4

秕 4126 / J633e / M24958 See **粃** 4388.

秔 4127 / J-X / M24954 See **粳** 4408.

秬 4128 / J6340 / M25002 Kyo, Go a kind of millet.

A **秒** 4129 / J4943 / M24952 Byō one-sixtieth of a minute (of time, latitude, degree, etc.).
9 速 *byōsoku* speed per second
10 針 *byōshin* second hand (of a watch)
時計 *byōdokei* stopwatch

A **科** 4130 / J324a / M24950 Ka course, branch, department, faculty, school, college; arm (of defense); family (in biology). *ka(suru), ka(su)* inflict (punishment), fine. *toga* fault, blame; charge, offense, sin, transgressions, trespasses. *shina* actions, deportment. *shigusa* acting, gestures.
2 人 *toganin* criminal, offender
5 白 *serifu, kahaku* speech, words, lines, remarks
目 *kamoku* subdivision (in scientific classification)
6 名 *kamei* family name (in biology)
7 条 *kajō* laws; assortment, category
8 長 *kachō* department head
学 *kagaku* science
学小説 *kagaku shōsetsu* science fiction
学用語 *kagaku yōgo* scientific term
学技術 *kagaku gijutsu* scientific technique
学的 *kagakuteki* scientific
学者 *kagakusha* scientist
学書 *kagakusho* scientific book
学哲学 *kagaku tetsugaku* scientific philosophy
学戦 *kagakusen* scientific warfare
学語 *kagakugo* scientific term
9 怠 *katai* inexcusable error, carelessness, fault
10 料 *karyō* minor fine
挙 *kakyo* the (ancient) Chinese higher civil-service examinations
12 程 *katei* circumstances; order; degree

A **秋** 4131 / J3d29 / M24940 Shū *aki* autumn. *aki(meku), aki(sabu)* feel like fall.
2 七草 *aki (no) nanakusa* fall flowers
刀魚 *samma* saury, skipper, mackerel, pike
3 口 *akiguchi* early fall
山 *akiyama* mountains in the fall
4 水 *shūsui* clear river water in autumn
日 *shūjitsu* autumn day
日和 *akibiyori* clear fall weather
分 *shūbun* fall equinox
分日 *Shūbun (no) Hi* the Fall Equinox
5 田 *akita* ripened rice fields, fall rice fields
立 *akita(tsu)* fall arrives
収 *akiosa(me)* fall crops
6 色 *shūshoku, aki (no) iro* autumn scenery, fall colors
気 *shūki* fall air
7 作 *akisaku* fall-sown crops; fall-harvested crops
冷 *shūrei* autumn chill, cool fall weather
声 *shūsei* sound of the autumn wind
8 雨 *shūu, akisame* autumn rain
波 *shūha* amorous glance, wink
郊 *shūkō* autumn fields
空 *akizora* autumn sky
季 *shūki* autumn
季皇霊祭 *Shūki Kōreisai* Shinto Festival of the Autumnal Equinox
9 風 *shūfū, aki kaze* autumn breeze
咲 *akisa(ki)* fall blooming
思 *shūshi* the lonely feeling of fall
草 *akigusa* fall flowers
10 蚕 *akiko, akigo, shūsan* fall silkworms
時雨 *akishigure* a shower in late autumn
12 晴 *akiba(re)* clear fall weather
植 *akiue* fall planting
湿 *akijime(ri)* long fall rain
期 *shūki* autumn
買 *akiga(i)* buying up in the fall
落 *akio(chi)* poor rice crop
場 *akiba* autumn time
場所 *akibasho* fall sumo tournament
13 蒔 *akimaki* fall sowing
16 曇 *akigumo(ri)* cloudy fall weather
17 闌 *akita(keru)* autumn ends
霜 *shūsō* autumn frost
霜烈日 *shūsō-retsujitsu* withering frost and scorching sun; severe punishment

18 穫 *shūkaku* fall crop
繭 *aki mayu* fall cocoon crop
19 霧 *akigiri* autumn mists
21 露 *shūro* autumn dew

5

秡 4132 J6341 M24990 HATSU, BACHI damaged rice plants.

秦 4133 J3f41 M24995 SHIN Qin dynasty. *hata* name given anciently to naturalized foreigners.

秤 4134 J4769 M24993 SHŌ. *hakari* balances, scales, steelyard.
12 量 *hyōryō* estimation, weighing

B **秩** 4135 J4361 M24998 CHITSU salary; order.
7 序 *chitsujo* order, system, discipline, regularity, method
序正 *chitsujo-tada(shii)* in good order

秣 4136 J6342 M24992 MATSU. *magusa* fodder, feed, hay.
4 切 *magusaki(ri)* hay cutter
11 桶 *magusaoke* manger

秧 4137 J633f M24996 Ō. *sanae* rice seedlings.
8 取 *sanaeto(ru)* transplant rice
14 歌 *sanae uta* rice-planting song

B **租** 4138 J4145 M24988 So crop tax; borrowing.
9 界 *sokai* concession, settlement
10 借 *soshaku suru* lease
借地 *soshakuchi* leased territory, leasehold
借権 *soshakuken* lease, leasehold
12 税 *sozei* taxes, taxation

B **称** 4139 J3e4e M25016′ **稱** 4155 J634a M25180 SHŌ name, title; fame; praise. *tona(eru), shō(suru)* name, entitle; claim, plead, pretend to be; praise, admire. *tona(eru)* recite, chant; call upon; cry, yell *(banzai)*; advocate, preach; quote (prices). *tata(eru)* praise, admire.
5 号 *shōgō* title, degree
6 名 *shōmyō* reciting the Buddha Amida's name
8 呼 *shōko* appellation, name, title
9 美 *shōbi* praise, admiration
11 道 *shōdō* advocacy
12 揚 *shōyō* praise, admiration
15 賛 *shōsan* praise, admiration
22 讃 *shōsan* praise, admiration

A **秘** 4140 J486b M24977 **祕** 4075 J6330 M24663 HI secret. *hi(meru), hi(suru)* conceal, keep a secret. *hisoka ni* secretly.
4 文 *himon* magic formula, incantation, curse, spell, charm
方 *hihō* secret formula, secret process
中 *hichū* in secret
仏 *hibutsu* a Buddhist idol kept hidden
5 史 *hishi* secret history
本 *hihon* treasured book, tabooed book
6 曲 *hikyoku* secret or esoteric music
伝 *hiden* secret, mystery, secret formula
8 法 *hihō* secret formula, secret process
宝 *hihō* treasure, treasured article
事 *hiji* secret; mystery; private affairs. *hi(me)goto* secret. *misokagoto* secret; clandestine relationship
9 計 *hikei* secret plan, deep plot
封 *hifū* carefully sealing (a letter)
要 *hiyō* mystery, secret
10 匿 *hitoku suru* hide, conceal
書 *hisho* private secretary
書官 *hishokan* private secretary
書科 *hishoka* a secretarial course
書室 *hishoshitsu* secretarial office
書課 *hishoka* a secretarial section, secretariat
11 術 *hijutsu* secret art; the mysteries
訣 *hiketsu* secret; the mysteries; the key to
密 *himitsu* secrecy, privacy, mystery, secret
密外交 *himitsu gaikō* secret diplomacy
密会 *himitsukai* secret meeting
密教 *himitsukyō* esoteric Buddhism
密探偵 *himitsu tantei* secret agent
密結社 *himitsu kessha* secret society
密話 *himitsubanashi* confidential talk
12 結 *hiketsu* constipation
奥 *hiō* secrets, mysteries
策 *hisaku* a secret plan
13 話 *hiwa* secret story; secret history

置 *hi(me)-o(ku)* hide
義 *higi* mystery
14 語 *higo* secret words
蔵 *hizō* treasuring
16 謀 *hibō* clandestine plan
録 *hiroku* confidential document, secret memoirs
薬 *hiyaku* nostrum, secret medicine
18 蹟 *hiseki* (Catholic) sacraments
19 願 *higan* unspoken prayer
25 鑰 *hiyaku* secret, key

6

A **移** 4141 / J305c / M25045 I. *utsu(ru)* move, change, shift, pass into, drift; soak in; be infected, catch (a cold); catch fire, spread. *utsu(su)* move, transfer; pour into, divert (attention), give (a disease to someone). *utsu(rou)* change, shift, fade, decline.

2 入 *inyū* import
5 民 *imin* immigration; emigration; immigrant; emigrant; settler, colonist
出 *ishutsu suru* ship out; export
出入 *ishutsunyū* trade with colonies
6 行 *ikō suru* veer to, shift to, switch over to. *utsu(ri)-yu(ku)* change, shift, come and go
気 *utsu(ri)gi* whim, frivolity, fickleness
安 *utsu(ri)ya(sui)* changeable, fickle; transient; infectious, contagious
7 住 *ijū* migration; emigration; immigration; moving
住民 *ijūmin* emigrant; immigrant; settler; colonist
住者 *ijūsha* emigrant; immigrant
8 送 *isō* transfer, transport, remove
9 香 *utsu(ri)ga* lingering scent
乗 *ijō suru* transfer to
変 *utsu(ri)-kawa(ru)* change, shift, come and go. *utsu(ri)kawa(ri)* change, transition
10 記 *iki* transfer of entry
11 転 *iten* moving; transfer; demise
動 *idō* movement, transfer, migration, turnover, locomotion
動大使 *idō taishi* roving ambassador
動図書館 *idō toshokan* mobile library
動警察 *idō keisatsu* mobile police
12 棲 *isei* migration (of birds)
植 *ishoku* transplanting; naturalization (of plants); (skin) grafting
絵 *utsushie* decalcomania, process of transferring pictures to china, etc.
13 牒 *ichō* notification to the authorities
14 管 *ikan* transfer of control
15 調 *ichō* transposition
駐 *ichū suru* move, transfer
20 譲 *ijō* transfer, assignment
籍 *iseki* changing one's domiciliary registry

7

稈 4142 / J6343 / M25074 KAN hollow jointed stem; straw.

稍 4143 / J6344 / M25083 SŌ. *yaya* a little, slightly, somewhat.

3 久 *yayahisa(shiku)* for some time
12 稍 *yaya* a little, slightly, somewhat

A **程** 4144 / J4478 / M25081' TEI degree; law; formula; distance. *hodo* limits, limit, extent, degree; moderation; social status; distance; time; amount. *-hodo* about, more or less, as, to the degree.

6 近 *hodochika(i)* near
好 *hodoyo(ku)* properly, judiciously, moderately
合 *hodoa(i)* limit, limits
7 良 *hodoyo(i)* good, favorable, proper; moderate, temperate; vague (answer)
9 度 *teido* degree, extent, limit, level, standard
11 経 *hodohe(te)* after a while
12 遠 *hodotō(karanu)* not too far
程 *hodohodo ni* properly, judiciously, temperately, moderately
無 *hodona(ku)* soon afterward

稀 4145 / J3529 / M25058 KI. KE. *mare na* rare, phenomenal, few. *ki-* dilute (acid).

3 土類元素 *kidorui genso* rare earth elements
4 元素 *kigenso* rare element
少 *kishō* scarcity
少物資 *kishō busshi* scarce materials
5 代 *kidai no, kitai no* uncommon, rare; remarkable, matchless; notorious
世 *kisei no* extraordinary, unique. *kisei* rare

5 玄玉王瓜瓦甘生用田疋疒癶白皮皿目矛矢石示ネ内 7【禾】穴立

⁶有 *keu* rare, extraordinary
⁸金属 *kikinzoku* rare metals
¹⁰書 *kisho* rare book
¹¹釈 *kishaku* dilution
¹²稀 *maremare* very few; very strange
¹⁴酸 *kisan* dilute acid
¹⁶薄 *kihaku na* thin, lean, rare, diluted, sparse, weak
¹⁷覯 *kikō* accidental meeting; infrequent meeting; something strange
覯本 *kikōbon* rare book
覯書 *kikōsho* rare book

A **税** 4146 / J4047 / M25070′ ZEI tax, duty.
⁴込 *zeiko(mi)* (salary) before tax is taken out
引 *zeibi(ki)* after taxes
引給与 *zeibi(ki) kyūyo* take-home pay
⁵目 *zeimoku* tariff items
収 *zeishū* tax revenue
⁶吏 *zeiri* tax officer
吏長 *zeirichō* head tax collector
⁸金 *zeikin* tax, duty
法 *zeihō* tax law, taxation scheme
制 *zeisei* tax system
表 *zeihyō* tariff
¹¹率 *zeiritsu* tax rates; tariff
務 *zeimu* tax business
務官吏 *zeimu kanri* tax collector, revenue officer
務署 *zeimusho* tax office
¹²期 *zeiki* tax period
¹³源 *zeigen* tax source
¹⁴関 *zeikan* customs; customs house
関司 *zeikanshi* customs inspector
関吏 *zeikanri* customs inspector
関長 *zeikanchō* superintendent of customs
¹⁸額 *zeigaku* tax amount

8

稘 4147 / J6345 / M25118 See 期 4836.

稙 4148 / J6346 / M25119 CHOKU early-planting rice.

稔 4149 / J4c2d / M25107 JIN, NIN, NEN harvest; ripen.

稠 4150 / J6347 / M25130 CHŪ density.
¹¹密 *chūmitsu na, chōmitsu na* dense, thick, crowded

稗 4151 / J-X / M25113 **稗** 4156 / J4923 / M-X HAI humble. *hie* deccan grass, a barnyard grass.
⁵史 *haishi* legend, fiction, romance
¹⁰益 *hieki* usefulness

稜 4152 / J4e47 / M25123 RYŌ angle, edge, corner; power, majesty.
⁹威 *ryōi, miitsu* imperial majesty
¹³稜 *ryōryō(taru)* rugged
¹⁵線 *ryōsen* mountain-ridge line

稟 4153 / J6348 / M25127 **禀** 4094 / J6349 / M24742 HIN, RIN salary in rice.
⁷告 *hinkoku, rinkoku* notice, notification
⁸性 *hinsei, rinsei* nature, character
¹⁵質 *hinshitsu* natural disposition
請 *rinsei* petition
請書 *rinseisho* petition
²⁰議 *ringi, hingi* reaching a decision by circulating a letter

B **稚** 4154 / J4355 / M25120 CHI young. *itokena(i)* young (child).
³子 *chishi* a little child; a seedling, a bud, a sprout
⁴心 *chishin* a childish mind
⁶気 *chiki* childishness
⁷児 *chigo* baby, child; page; festive children
⁸拙 *chisetsu na* unskillful, childish
拙美 *chisetsubi* beauty of artlessness
¹¹魚 *chigyo* young fish

9

稱 4155 / J634a / M25180 See 称 4139.

稗 4156 / J4923 / M-X See 稗 4151.

A **穀** 4157 / J3972 / M25188′ **穀** 4160 / J-X / M25221 **穀** 4417 / J-X / M27067 KOKU cereals, grain.
⁸物 *kokumotsu* cereals, grain
⁹食 *kokushoku* cereal diet; grain-eating
¹⁰粉 *kokufun* grain or rice flour

倉 *kokugura, kokusō* granary, grain
11 粒 *kokuryū* kernel, grain ⌊a sprout
断 *kokuda(chi)* abstinence from grains
12 減 *kokube(ri)* volume loss in stored grain
象虫 *kokuzōmushi* grain weevil
15 潰 *gokutsubu(shi)* idler, drone
18 類 *kokurui* grains

B **稲** 4158 / J3070 / M25187′ **稻** 4161 / J634b / M25216 Tō. *ine, ina-* rice plant.
3 子 *inago* locust
4 木 *inagi* rice-drying rack
刈 *ineka(ri)* rice reaping
5 田 *inada* rice field
6 舟 *inabune* boats that carry rice sheaves
扱 *ineko(ki)* threshing; threshing machine
光 *inabikari* lightning
7 作 *inasaku* rice crop; rice cultivation
8 苗 *tōbyō* rice seedlings
妻 *inazuma* lightning
9 架 *hasa, tōka* rice-drying rack
10 株 *inakabu, ine kabu* rice stubble
荷 *Inari* harvest god; fox god
荷鮨 *inarizushi* fried tofu stuffed with seasoned rice
11 掛 *ineka(ke)* rice-drying rack
粒 *inatsubu* a grain of rice
13 幹 *inagara* grain stems
15 穂 *inaho, inabo* heads of rice
熱 *imochi* rice blight
熱病 *imochibyo* rice blight
17 藁 *inawara* rice straw
18 叢 *inamura* stack of rice straw

A **種** 4159 / J3c6f / M25174 Shu kind, class, variety; seed; species. *tane* seed, kernel; kind, species; quality, tone; material; breed; topic; cause, source; trick; data; inside story; secret; leaven. *kusa* materials, origins.
2 入 *tanei(renu)* unleavened
3 下 *taneoro(shi)* sowing, seeding
子 *shushi* seed, pit, stone
子島 *tanegashima* matchlock gun, arquebus
4 牛 *taneushi* bull
切 *tanegi(re)* exhaustion of seed; exhaustion of materials
5 皮 *shuhi* seed coat
目 *shumoku* item; lot; event (as a race)
付 *tanetsu(ke)* mating
本 *tanehon* source book; original; manual
仕掛 *tanejika(ke)* secret; secret device
6 牝 *tanemesu* a breeding mare
芋 *tane imo* seed potatoes
名 *shumei* species name
7 別 *shubetsu* classification, assortment
芸 *shugei* planting trees and plants
卵 *tanetamago* nest egg
牡 *taneosu* a stud horse
牡蠣 *tanegaki* seed oyster
8 明 *taneaka(shi)* exposure of a trick; exposing a secret
板 *taneita* negative
油 *taneabura* vegetable oil, rapeseed oil
取 *taneto(ri)* plants grown for seeds; seed raising; breeding; reporting, reporter
苗園 *shubyōen* nursery company
物 *tanemono* seeds; buckwheat noodle dish; shaved ice with fruit syrup
物屋 *tanemonoya* seed store
9 畑 *tanebatake* seed garden
籾 *tanemomi* seed rice
変 *tanegawa(ri)* half-brother; half-sister; variety (of plant)
10 馬 *taneuma, shuba* stud horse, stallion
紙 *tanegami* (silkworm) egg card
起原 *shu (no) kigen* the origin of species
畜 *shuchiku* breeding stock
畜農業 *shuchiku nōgyō* animal husbandry
11 掛 *tane (o) ka(keru)* breed
粒 *tanetsubu* kernel, a grain
族 *shuzoku* race, tribe, family, caste; genus, species
族的 *shuzokuteki* racial, tribal
12 属 *shuzoku* kind, genus, species
無 *tanena(shi)* seedless
違 *tanechiga(i)* half-brother, half-sister
痘 *shutō* vaccination, inoculation
痘料 *shutōryō* vaccination fee
痘証明書 *shutō shōmeisho* vaccination certificate
13 蒔 *tanemaki* sowing, seeding, planting
14 種 *shuju* variety. *kusagusa* various
種相 *shujusō* various phases
種雑多 *shuju-zatta* various kinds
種様様 *shuju-samazama* great variety
18 類 *shurui* kind, variety, class, species
類分 *shuruiwa(ke)* classification, assortment

類別 *shuruibetsu* classification, assortment

10

穀 4160 / J-X / M25221 See **穀** 4157.

稲 4161 / J634b / M25216 See **稻** 4158.

稺 4162 / J-X / M25213 See **穉** 4178.

稭 4163 / J374e / M25218 Nonstandard for **稽** 4174.

槦 4164 / J634e / M-X Yō.

稷 4165 / J634d / M25207 Shoku. *kibi* millet.

B **稿** 4166 / J3946 / M25220 **稾** 4167 / J634c / M25219 Kō copy, manuscript, draft; straw.

5 本 *kōhon* manuscript
10 料 *kōryō* payment for a manuscript

B **穂** 4168 / J4a66 / M25236′ **穗** 4177 / J634f / M25298 Sui. *ho* ear, head (of grain); crest (of waves).

6 先 *hosaki* beard of grain; head of grain; spearhead
7 状 *suijō* a shape like a head of grain
8 波 *honami* waving grain
11 掛 *hoka(ke)* offering of heads of grain

B **稼** 4169 / J3254 / M25217 Ka. *kase(gu)* work; earn money. *kasegi* work; income.

2 人 *kaseginin* breadwinner, hard worker
4 手 *kasegite* breadwinner, hard worker
6 行 *kakō* operation (of a factory)
8 取 *kase(gi)-to(ru)* earn by working
10 高 *kasegidaka* earnings
11 動 *kadō* operation, actual work
18 穡 *kashoku* farming

11

穐 4170 / J302c / M25281 Nonstandard for **穐** 4184.

穆 4171 / J4b54 / M25251 Boku, Moku respect; sincerety; politeness; beauty; gentleness.

穇 4172 / J-X / M25256 San. *hie* deccan grass, a barnyard grass.

穎 4173 / J314f / M25267 **頴** 4109 / J3150 / M24824 Ei heads of grain; point (of an instrument); cleverness.

3 才 *eisai* brilliant intellect, talent, genius
10 悟 *eigo* intelligent, shrewd
11 脱 *eidatsu suru* gain recognition

稽 4174 / J-X / M-X Kei think, consider; quarrel.

5 古 *keiko* practice, training, study, instruction
古所 *keikojo* practice room
古着 *keikogi* gym suit, practice suit
9 首 *keishu* bowing to the floor and worshipping
10 留 *keiryū* stopping

B **穏** 4175 / J323a / M25280′ **穩** 4183 / J6353 / M25344 On. *oda(yaka)* calm, quiet, peace; moderation. *oda (yakanaranu)* disquieting, alarming, serious, threatening.

6 当 *ontō na* proper, reasonable, just, right, moderate
8 和 *onwa* moderation
和派 *onwaha* moderate party
和論者 *onwaronsha* a moderate
9 便 *ombin na* gentle, quiet, peaceable; private, out of court
11 健 *onken na* quiet, dependable, uniform
健派 *onkenha* moderate party

A **積** 4176 / J4051 / M25266 Seki product (in math); acreage, contents, measurement. *tsu(mu) vt* pile up, stack, lay; load, ship, take on; accumulate, amass, save. *tsu(moru) vi* accumulate, be piled up, be amassed; lie on, be covered (with snow); amount to; estimate, calculate, measure. *tsu(mori)* intention, purpose; belief; motive; expectation; idea; estimate. *tsu(mi)* loading; shipment; capacity. *-zu(mi)* shipment, loading, burden, capacity.

2 入 *tsu(mi)-i(reru)* ship, take on

3 上 *tsu(mi)-a(geru)* pile up, accumulate
4 方 *tsu(mi)kata* manner of loading
木 *tsu(mi)ki* toy blocks; piled timber
切 *tsu(mi)-ki(ru)* ship completely
込 *tsu(mi)-ko(mu)* load, take on, ship. *tsu(mi)ko(mi)* shipping, loading; shipment
込値段 *tsumiko(mi) nedan* price F.O.B.
分 *sekibun* integral calculus
分学 *sekibungaku* integral calculus
5 石 *tsu(mi)ishi* pile of stones; cornerstone
立 *tsu(mi)-ta(teru)* save, reserve, amass. *tsu(mi)ta(te)* reserve funds
立金 *tsumitatekin* reserve fund
出 *tsu(mi)-da(su)* send, ship, forward. *tsu(mi)da(shi)* shipment, forwarding
出人 *tsu(mi)da(shi)nin* shipper
出費 *tsu(mi)da(shi)hi* shipping expenses
6 返 *tsu(mi)-kae(su)* ship back
年 *sekinen* (many) years
7 戻 *tsu(mi)-mo(dosu)* re-export, reship, send back
乱雲 *sekiran'un* cumulo-nimbus clouds
8 金 *tsu(mi)gane, tsu(mi)kin* reserve funds, savings
取 *tsu(mi)-to(ru)* take on, load
肥 *tsu(mi)goe* compost, barnyard manure
直 *tsu(mi)-nao(su)* reload, pile over again
送 *sekisō, tsu(mi)oku(ri)* consignment, shipment. *tsu(mi)-oku(ru)* consign, ship
送品 *sekisōhin* consignment, shipment
9 恨 *tsu(moru) ura(mi)* growing hatred, suppressed hatred
卸 *tsu(mi)oro(shi)* loading and unloading; unloading; cargo handling
重 *tsu(mi)-kasa(naru) vi* be piled up, accumulate. *tsu(mi)-kasa(neru) vt* pile up, accumulate
怨 *sekien* a succession of grudges
10 残 *tsu(mi)-noko(su)* leave out of shipment. *tsu(mi)noko(ri), tsu(mi)noko(shi)* short shipment, goods left behind
財 *sekizai* building up wealth; accumulated wealth
荷 *tsu(mi)ni* load, freight, cargo, shipment
書 *tsu(mori)ga(ki)* written estimate
11 過 *tsu(mi)-su(giru)* overload. *tsu(mori)-su(giru)* overestimate, overvalue
悪 *sekiaku* accumulated wickedness, series of evil deeds
雪 *sekisetsu* drifted snow, deep snow, snowdrift
12 貯 *tsu(mi)-takuwa(eru)* store up
善 *sekizen* accumulation of good deeds
量 *sekiryō* carrying capacity, tonnage
雲 *sekiun* cumulus clouds
違 *tsu(mori)chiga(i)* miscalculation
替 *tsu(mi)-ka(eru)* transship, reship. *tsu(mori)ga(e)* recalculation
極 *sekkyoku* the positive
極外交 *sekkyoku gaikō* positive foreign policy
極性 *sekkyokusei* positiveness
極的 *sekkyokuteki* positive, active, constructive, progressive
13 置場 *tsu(mi)o(ki)ba* freight yard
載 *sekisai* lading, loading, carrying
載量 *sekisairyō* carrying capacity, load
載噸数 *sekisai tonsū* freight capacity
14 読 *tsundo(ku)* pile up on the desk without reading
算 *sekisan* addition, estimate
15 憤 *sekifun* grudge, resentment
弊 *sekihei* deep-seated evil
16 積 *tsu(mori)-tsu(moru)* go on, pile up, accumulate

12

穂 4177 / J634f / M25298 See 穂 4168.

穉 4178 / J6350 / M25282 稚 4162 / J-X / M25213 CHI infancy.

6 気 *chiki* childishness

13

穣 4179 / J3e77 / M25335′ 穰 4185 / J6355 / M25383 JŌ good crops; prosperity.

B 穫 4180 / J334f / M25334′ KAKU harvest; reap. *to(ru)* to harvest.

穡 4181 / J6351 / M25325 SHOKU harvest.

穢 4182 / J6352 / M25331 AI, E. *kega(su)* make dirty, stain, pollute, defile, contaminate; disgrace, dishonor; rape.

kega(reru) get dirty; be defiled; be contaminated. *kega(re)* uncleanness, impurity, disgrace.

6 多 *eta* outcasts, the *eta* class
8 苦 *musakuru(shii)* filthy, shabby, untidy

— 14 —

穩 4183 / J6353 / M25344 See **穏** 4175.

— 16 —

穐 4184 / J6354 / M25381 See **秋** 4131.

— 17 —

穰 4185 / J6355 / M25383 See **穣** 4179.

RAD. 穴 116

Ana kammuri "hole" crown. Variants: 穴, 宂. Nickname: Cave.

A **穴** 4186 / J-X / M-X **穴** 4187 / J376a / M25406 **宂** 4188 / J-X / M-X

KETSU, *ana* hole, aperture, slit; gap, stop (of musical instrument); eyelet; cavity; socket; cave; den; hiding place; pit; fault, defect; deficit; grave; dark horse.

3 子 *anago* sea eel, conger eel
8 居 *kekkyo* cave dwelling
居人 *kekkyojin* cave dweller, cave man
明 *anaa(ki)* perforated; drilled (pearls)
明真珠 *anaa(ki) shinju* drilled pearls
10 埋 *anau(me)* filling a hole; stopgap; covering a deficit
11 痔 *anaji* anal fistula
道 *anamichi* tunnel, gallery
探 *anasaga(shi)* faultfinding
掘 *anaho(ri)* excavation, digging a hole; novice, bungler
釣 *anazu(ri)* sniggling for eels
12 植 *anau(e)* dibbling
開工具 *anaa(ke) kōgu* drill bit
開器 *anaa(ke)ki* punch, stiletto
13 隙 *ketsugeki* aperture, crevice
塞 *anafusa(gi)* stopgap; plugging a hole
煉瓦 *ana renga* perforated brick
14 蔵 *anagura* cellar
熊 *anaguma* badger
15 播 *anamaki* dibbling
16 縢 *anakaga(ri)* buttonhole sewing

— 2 —

A **究** 4189 / J3566 / M25409 KYŪ. *kiwa(meru)* investigate thoroughly, master; carry to extremes.

7 局 *kyūkyoku* eventuality, extremity
8 明 *kyūmei* investigation, inquiry
11 理 *kyūri* study of natural laws
竟 *kyūkyō* end, extremity. *kukyō na, kukkyō na* superb, best, ideal
12 極 *kyūkyoku* eventuality, extremity, desperate situation

— 3 —

穹 4190 / J6356 / M25414 KYŪ sky.

13 蒼 *kyūsō* blue vault of heaven
15 窿 *kyūryū* the vault of heaven

B **突** 4191 / J464d / M25424 **突** 4193 / J-X / M25439 TOTSU protruding, thrusting. *tsu(ku)* thrust, pierce, spear, stab, prick; gore; lunge at; push, poke; strike (a bell); attack; strike (at the heart); brave (a storm); be pungent; strike against; (words) rush (to one's lips). *tsutsu(ku)* poke, pick at, peck, elbow. *tsun-, tsu(ki)-* prefix meaning *tsu(ku)*.

2 入 *totsunyū suru* plunge into, rush in, cut in between. *tsu(ki)-i(ru)* rush into. *tsu(ki)-i(reru)* thrust into
3 上 *tsu(ki)-a(geru)* push up; toss up; nauseate
上戸 *tsu(ki)a(ge)do* overhung door
4 止 *tsu(ki)-to(meru)* make sure of
込 *tsu(ki)-ko(mu), tsu(k)ko(mu)* thrust into, poke into; plunge into, dip; penetrate, pierce; ram in; close in on; give (one) a thrust
切 *tsu(ki)-ki(ru)* break through, go right across

支 *tsukkai* prop, stay, support, brace
支棒 *tsukkaibō* prop, stay, support, brace
5 目 *tsukime* hitting the eye on some projection
付 *tsu(ki)-tsu(keru)* point (a gun at); put right under one's nose
出 *tsu(ki)-da(su), tsunda(su)* push out, stick out, stretch out, jut out. *tsu(ki)-de(ru)* project, stick out, jut, bulge out. *tsu(ki)da(shi)* protrusion; start; newcomer; hors d'oeuvre. *tosshutsu* projection, protrusion, prominence
立 *tsu(t)ta(tsu)* stand, stand up straight. *tsu(ki)-ta(teru)* stab, thrust violently, set a stake. *tsu(ki)-ta(tsu) vi* stick in; rise sharply
立上 *tsu(t)ta(chi)-a(garu)* jump to one's feet
6 返 *tsu(ki)-kae(su)* thrust in return; refuse to accept
回 *tsutsu(ki)-mawa(su)* poke around
如 *totsujo, totsujo toshite* suddenly, unexpectedly
合 *tsu(ki)-a(u)* poke each other, thrust each other. *tsu(ki)-a(waseru), tsu(ki)-a(wasu)* confront (someone) with, bring face to face; compare with. *tsu(ki)a(i)* thrusting one another
当 *tsu(ki)-atu(ru)* collide; come to the end of a street. *tsu(ki) a(toru)* dash against, run against. *tsu(ki)ata(ri)* collision; dead end of a street or hallway
先 *tossaki* tip (of something)
7 角 *tokkaku* convex angle
走 *tsu(p)pashi(ru)* run swiftly
戻 *tsu(ki)-modo(su)* give a thrust in return; thrust back; refuse to accept
抜 *tsu(ki)-nu(keru) vi* pierce through, break through. *tsu(ki)-nu(ku) vt* pierce, shoot through, penetrate
8 放 *tsu(p)pana(su), tsu(ki)-hana(su)* throw off, forsake
明 *tsu(ki)-a(keru)* push open
刺 *tsu(ki)-sa(saru) vi* stick, pierce. *tsu(ki)-sa(su) vt* pierce, penetrate
突 *tsu(t)tsu(ku)* prompt (someone)
拍子無 *toppyōshi (mo) na(i)* out of tune; exorbitant
9 風 *toppū* squall, sudden gust
飛 *tsu(ki)-to(basu)* knock (a person) down; push away. *toppi na* wild, extraordinary, fantastic, risky, reckless, eccentric
通 *tsu(ki)-tō(ru) vi* pierce, penetrate, stick into. *tsu(ki)-tō(su) vt* pierce, penetrate
指 *tsu(ki)yubi* sprained finger
除 *tsu(ki)-no(keru)* push aside, elbow out
発 *toppatsu* burst, gust, outbreak
10 起 *tokki* protuberance, prominence, projection
進 *tosshin* rush, onrush, dash, charge
倒 *tsu(ki)-tao(su)* knock (a person) down
破 *toppa suru* break through; overcome. *tsu(ki)-yabu(ru)* break through, pierce, pass (an exam); exceed, go over (a goal)
殺 *tsu(ki)-koro(su)* stab to death; gore to death
11 張 *tsu(p)pa(ru)* stretch (an arm) against, plant (one's foot) on; insist on. *tsu(p)pa(ri)* prop, brace, support, bolster, strut, buttress, (door) bar
眼 *tsu(ki)me* hitting the eye on some projection
転 *tsu(k)koro(basu), tsu(ki)-koro(basu)* knock (a person) down
崩 *tsu(ki)-kuzu(su)* level, rout
掛 *tsu(ki)-ka(karu)* thrust at (with a knife)
掛草履 *tsukka(ke) zōri* slipper-type zori
貫 *tokkan* a charge (in war)
貫作業 *tokkan sagyō* rush work
12 遣 *tsu(ki)-ya(ru)* push away
堤 *tottei* pier, breakwater
棒 *tsu(ki)bō* goad
落 *tsu(ki)-o(tosu)* push off, thrust down. *tsu(ki)oto(shi)* sag (in the stock market)
然 *totsuzen* suddenly, unexpectedly
然変異 *totsuzen hen'i* mutation
13 傷 *tsu(ki)kizu* stab wound
詰 *tsu(ki)-tsu(meru)* investigate; think hard; brood over
14 端 *toppana, tottan* tip of a headland. *toppashi* extreme end
慳貪 *tsu(k)kendon na* sharp, blunt, harsh
15 撥 *tsu(p)pa(neru)* reject, spurn, refuse
撃 *totsugeki* charge, assault
撃兵 *totsugekihei* shock troops
撃隊 *totsugekitai* shock troops
撃路 *totsugekiro* a breach
16 錐 *tsu(ki)giri* awl
28 鑿 *tsu(ki)nomi* scraper (the tool)

5 玄 玉 王 瓜 瓦 甘 生 用 田 疋 疒 癶 白 皮 皿 目 矛 矢 石 示 礻 内 禾 [3]【穴】 立

A **空** 4192 / J3675 / M25415 Kū air, sky; emptiness; vanity, unreality; hollow; void. *su(ku), a(ku) vi* become empty, be less crowded. *a(keru) vt* empty. *a(ita)* open; empty, vacant. *a(ki)* gap, opening, aperture; space, blank, vacancy. *kara* emptiness, vacancy, hollowness, vacuum. *kara, kara(ppo)* empty. *muna(shii)* void, empty, vain; ineffective; lifeless. *sora* sky, heavens, air, weather, memory, absent-mindedness. *utsu(ro)* hollow, cavity, void; emptiness. *utsuke, ukke* emptiness; dumbness. *kū ni* vainly, ineffectively. *a(ki)-* empty, vacant, unoccupied, spare (hours). *sora-* pretended, sham, mock.

[4]文 *kūbun* dead letter, scrap of paper
井 *karai* empty well
元気 *kara genki* mere bravado
手 *karate de, kūshu de* empty-handed; with bare fists. *karate* barehanded fighting, karate
手形 *kara tegata* bad check; empty promise
中 *kūchū* air, sky, space. *kūchū no* aerial, air
中分解 *kūchū bunkai* disintegration of a plane in flight
中広告 *kūchū kōkoku* skywriting
中写真 *kūchū shashin* air photo; aerial photography
中征服 *kūchū seifuku* mastery of the air
中飛行 *kūchū hikō* aviation
中窒素 *kūchū chisso* atmospheric nitrogen
中魚雷 *kūchū gyorai* aerial torpedo
中偵察 *kūchū teisatsu* air reconnaissance
中戦 *kūchūsen* air battle; aerial warfare
中滑走 *kūchū kassō* gliding
中滑走機 *kūchū kassōki* glider, sailplane
中楼閣 *kūchū rōkaku* castle in the air; mirage
中線 *kūchūsen* antenna
中権 *kūchūken* air right
中輸送 *kūchū yusō* air transportation
中優越 *kūchū yūetsu* air superiority
[5]母 *kūbo* aircraft carrier
白 *kūhaku* blank space, vacuum, void
目 *sorame* misperception, mistake; pretending not to see; upward look
尻 *kara(k)ketsu no* penniless
世辞 *kara seji* flattery, empty compliments
[6]耳 *soramimi* mishearing; feigned deafness
舟 *karabune, karafune* empty ship
色 *sora iro* sky blue; weather
回 *karamawa(ri)* racing (of a propeller); skidding (of a car); profitless business activity; fruitless effort
死 *soraji(ni)* feigned death
似 *sorani* accidental resemblance
地 *akichi, kūchi* vacant lot, open space, room
合 *soraa(i)* looks of the sky, weather
名 *kūmei* empty name; false reputation
缶 *akikan* empty can
返事 *sora henji* random answer
自慢 *karajiman* vain boast, braggadocio
気 *kūki* air, atmosphere
気力学 *kūki rikigaku* aerodynamics
気弁 *kūkiben* air valve
気伝染 *kūki densen* infection
気抜 *kūkinu(ki)* ventilator
気冷却 *kūki reikyaku* air cooling
気枕 *kūki makura* air pillow
気制動機 *kūki seidōki* air brake
気浴 *kūkiyoku* air bath
気袋 *kūkibukuro* air sac
気電池 *kūki denchi* air cell
気銃 *kūkijū* air gun
気療法 *kūki ryōhō* air cure
[7]言 *kūgen* idle talk. *soragoto* falsehood, lie
谷 *kūkoku* lonely valley
身 *karami* light luggage
豆 *soramame* broad bean; horse bean
車 *karaguruma, kūsha* empty conveyance
位 *kūi* vacant post, post in name only
冷 *kūrei* air cooled
冷式 *kūreishiki* air-cooled
[8]店 *akidana, aki mise* vacant store
房 *kūbō* vacant room
送 *kūsō* air transportation
所 *kūsho* space, open space, blank space
明 *kūmei* moon's reflection in clear water
泣 *sorana(ki)* crocodile tears
取引 *kara torihiki* bogus transaction
念仏 *kara nembutsu* formal Buddhist prayer; empty phrases, fruitless talk. *sora nembutsu* pretending to pray

空 *kūkū* vanity, nothing; absent-mindedness; lack of tenacity; evil passions. *sorazora(shii)* feigned, false, empty, obvious, transparent
空寂寂 *kūkū-jakujaku* absent-minded; null and void
空漠漠 *kūkū-bakubaku(taru)* vast and empty
9 音 *sorane* false cry, falsehood
屋 *akiya* vacant house
咳 *karazeki, karaseki* dry or hacking cough
恍 *soratobo(keru)* feign innocence; feign ignorance
洞 *kūdō* cave, hollow, cavity
軍 *kūgun* air force
室 *kūshitsu* vacant room
茶 *karacha* tea without cakes
勇気 *kara yūki* mere bravado
威張 *kara ibari* bluff; mock dignity
相場 *karasōba, kūsōba* speculation, fictitious transaction
要塞 *sora (no) yōsai* flying fortress
飛円盤 *sorato(bu) emban* flying saucer
海作戦 *kūkai sakusen* air-sea operations
風 *kara(k)kaze, karakaze* dry wind
風呂 *karaburo* steam bath, Turkish bath
前 *kūzen no* unprecedented, record-breaking
前絶後 *kūzen-zetsugo* unparalleled
10 馬 *karauma* unloaded horse
席 *kūseki* vacant seats, vacancy
悦 *sorayoroko(bi)* premature joy
振 *karabu(ri)* missing a ball, strike
涙 *soranamida* crocodile tears
眠 *soranemu(ri)* feigned sleep
砲 *kūhō* blank shot
紙 *kūshi* blank paper
恥 *sorahazu(kashii)* feeling strangely ashamed
冥 *kūmei* sky, empty sky, the heavens
家 *akiya* vacant house
笑 *sorawara(i)* forced laugh, feigned smile
荷 *karani* no load, empty, unloaded
恐 *soraosoro(shii)* having vague fears
拳 *kūken* empty hand; one's own efforts
梅雨 *kara tsuyu* dry rainy season
部屋 *akibeya* vacant room
時間 *akijikan* open period, spare time
挺隊 *kūteitai* airborne unit
11 唾 *karatsubaki* spittle
堀 *karabori* dry moat
惚 *soratobo(keru)* feign innocence; feign ignorance
殼 *akigara* empty sea shell
理 *kūri* abstract or impracticable theory
脛 *karahagi* bare shins
船 *kūsen, karabune* empty ship
転 *kūten, karamawa(ri)* racing (an engine)
釣 *karazu(ri)* fishing without bait
瓶 *akibin* empty bottle
虚 *kūkyo* emptiness; hollow; without content; fruitlessness. *kūkyo na* empty, vacant, hollow; inane
虚感 *kūkyokan* feeling of emptiness
巣 *akisu* sneak thief, prowler
巣狙 *akisunera(i)* sneak thief, prowler
12 間 *akima* vacant room. *kūkan* space; room; air space
弾 *kūdan* blank shot
港 *kūkō* airfield, airport
疎 *kūso na* vain, groundless, futile
寐 *sorane* feigned sleep
蒸 *karamushi* steaming, sultriness
覚 *soraobo(e)* memorization. *uroobo(e)* faint memory
費 *kūhi* wastefulness
閑地 *kūkanchi* an open (unused) field
景気 *karageiki* false boom; false show of activity
13 漠 *kūbaku(taru)* vast; boundless; vague, dreamy
渓 *kūkei* dry valley; lonely valley
路 *kūro* air lane
隙 *kūgeki* vacant space, aperture, gap
際 *kūsai* the distant sky
夢 *sorayume* false dream
雷 *kūrai* aerial torpedo
電 *kūden* static
鉄砲 *karadeppō* empty gun; empty cartridge; falsehood
腹 *kūfuku, sukihara, suki(p)para* hunger, empty stomach
腹時 *kūfukuji* time when the stomach is empty
寝 *sorane* feigned sleep
寝入 *soranei(ri)* feigned sleep
想 *kūsō* daydream, air castle, fancy, imagination, vision
想的 *kūsōteki* visionary, Utopian
想家 *kūsōka* dreamer, idealist, visionary

想論 *kūsōron* idle theory, pipe dream
14 閨 *kūkei* deserted wife's chamber
嘔 *karaezuki* nausea (without being able to vomit)
模様 *sora moyō* looks of the sky, weather
説 *kūsetsu* empty theorizing; baseless rumor
説法 *karaseppō* empty preaching (in Buddhism)
15 嘘 *karauso* barefaced lie
穂 *utsubo, utsuo* quiver
談 *kūdan* gossip, idle talk
論 *kūron* abstract or impracticable theory
褒 *sorabo(me)* empty praise
箱 *karabako* empty box
16 嘯 *sorausobu(ku)* feign unconcern
濛 *kūmō* drizzly murkiness
錠 *karajō* worthless lock
頼 *soradano(mi)* vain hopes, hoping against hope
輸 *kūyu* air transportation
輸作業 *kūyu sagyō* airlift operation
輸部隊 *kūyu butai* airborne unit
17 壕 *kūgō, karabori* dry moat
鼾 *soraibiki* sham snoring
18 臑 *karasune* bare shins
蟬 *utsusemi* cicada's discarded skin
騒 *karasawa(gi)* much ado about nothing
19 壜 *akibin* empty bottle
爆 *kūbaku* bombing
22 聾 *soratsumbo* feigned deafness
襲 *kūshū* air raid
襲警戒 *kūshū keikai* air-raid precaution
襲警報 *kūshū keihō* air-raid alarm
23 籤 *karakuji* a blank (in lottery)

4

突 4193 / J-X / M25439 See **突** 4191.

穽 4194 / J6357 / M25433 Sei sunken trap.

B **窃** 4195 / J4060 / M25453 **竊** 4222 / J6366 / M25713 Setsu. *nusu(mu)* steal. *hiso(ka) na* secret, private, stealthy, hushed.

5 用 *setsuyō suru* use secretly
8 取 *sesshu* theft, stealing
11 盗 *settō* theft, larceny
盗罪 *settōzai* theft, larceny

5

窈 4196 / J6358 / M25463 Yō quiet.
11 窕 *yōchō na* refined, attractive, charming; wide and quiet; deep and significant

窄 4197 / J3a75 / M25455 Saku narrow. *subo(mu), subo(maru)* narrow, get narrower. *subo(meru)* make narrower; shut (an umbrella); fold, furl; shrug; pucker up. *tsubo(mu), tsubo(maru) vi* shut, close, get narrower. *tsubo(meru) vt* shut, close; fold; make narrower; gather up (skirts); shrug; pucker up.

穿 4198 / J407c / M25436 Sen. *ha(ku)* put on (the feet or legs). *uga(tsu)* dig, cut through, pierce, drill, penetrate; put on, wear. *hojiku(ru), hoji(ru)* dig up; pick (ears or teeth); examine closely; worm out; pick at (a person). *uga(tta)* happy (expression), witty (remark).
4 孔 *senkō* perforation; punching; rupture
心地 *ha(ki)gokochi* comfortable on the feet
5 古 *ha(ki)furu(shi)* worn-out shoes
出 *hojiku(ri)-da(su)* dig up; pick (ears or teeth); examine closely; worm out; pick at (a person)
7 初 *ha(ki)zo(me)* first wearing of footwear
8 刺 *senshi* puncturing a body cavity
9 屋 *hojiku(ri)ya* inquisitive person
11 掘 *senkutsu* excavation
捨 *ha(ki)-su(teru)* wear out (footwear)
12 替 *ha(ki)-ka(eru)* change socks or footwear
違 *ha(ki)-chiga(eru)* put on someone else's footwear; be mistaken. *hakichiga(e)* misunderstanding, misconception
28 鑿 *sensaku* excavation, boring, search, inquiry, investigation

6

窕 4199 / J635a / M25496 CHŌ quiet.

窒 4200 / J4362 / M25493 B CHITSU plug up, obstruct.
6 死 *chisshi* death from suffocation
10 息 *chissoku* suffocation, asphyxiation
素 *chisso* nitrogen
素肥料 *chisso hiryō* nitrogenous fertilizer

窓 4201 / J416b / M25494 **窗** 4202 / J6359 / M25517 A SŌ window. *mado* window, windowpane.
3 口 *madoguchi* window
5 外 *sōgai* out of the window; outside the window
台 *madodai* window sill
付封筒 *madozu(ki) fūtō* window envelope
8 明 *madoaka(ri)* window light
枠 *madowaku* window frame or sash
9 前 *sōzen* in front of the window
11 掛 *madoka(ke)* window curtain
12 越 *madogo(shi) ni* over the window sill
割 *madowa(ri)* fenestration
硝子 *madogarasu* window pane
13 際 *madogiwa ni* at the window
飾 *madokaza(ri)* window display

7

窗 4202 / J6359 / M25517 See **窓** 4201.

窘 4203 / J635b / M25519 KIN. *tashina(meru)* rebuke, reprove.

窖 4204 / J635c / M25516 KŌ. KYŌ. *anagura* cellar.
10 倉 *kōsō* cellar

8

窠 4205 / J-X / M25556 KA nest, hole. *su* nest, rookery, breeding place, beehive, cobweb; den, haunt.

窟 4206 / J3722 / M25552 KUTSU. *iwaya* cavern.

9

窬 4207 / J-X / M25582 YU dig (a hole); bore (a hole).

窩 4208 / J635d / M25579 KA, WA cave; pouch.

窪 4209 / J3726 / M25580 A. *kubo(mu)* cave in, sink, become hollow. *kubo(mi)* hollow, cavity, dent, pit. *kubo* depression, hollow.
5 田 *kubota* a rice field in a low place
6 地 *kubochi* hollow, depression, low ground

10

窯 4210 / J4d52 / M25594 **窰** 4211 / J635f / M25595 B YŌ. *kama* kiln, oven, furnace, stove.
13 業 *yōgyō* ceramics, brickmaking, glassmaking, and cement manufacture
業美術 *yōgyō bijutsu* ceramic art
業家 *yōgyōka* ceramist

窮 4212 / J3587 / M25593 **竆** 4219 / J-X / M25686 B KYŪ. *kyū(suru)* be destitute; suffer; be perplexed; be cornered. *kiwa(maru)* terminate; reach an extreme; be in a dilemma. *kiwa(meru)* investigate thoroughly, master; carry to extremes.
2 人 *kyūjin* poor people
3 乏 *kyūbō* poverty
5 冬 *kyūtō* end of winter; year end
民 *kyūmin* poor people
6 死 *kyūshi* dying of distress and poverty
地 *kyūchi* dilemma, predicament
7 困 *kyūkon* distress, pain, poverty
局 *kyūkyoku* eventuality, extremity
迫 *kyūhaku* financial difficulty, distress
状 *kyūjō* distress, sad plight
余 *kyūyo* desperation
余一策 *kyūyo (no) issaku* the last resort
8 屈 *kyūkutsu* narrowness; being cramped; formality, strictness; restraint, oppressiveness
追 *kyūtsui suru* drive into a corner; corner with questions

11 鳥 *kyūchō* a cornered bird
達 *kyūtatsu* poverty and fame
理 *kyūri* mastery of truth
訳 *kyūyaku* strained translation
12 極 *kyūkyoku* eventuality, extremity
策 *kyūsaku* last resort
無 *kiwama(ri)na(ku)* endless
13 鼠 *kyūso* a cornered mouse
14 境 *kyūkyō* dilemma, predicament, extremity

11

窿 4213 / J6363 / M25660 RYŪ vault (of the sky), dome.

窶 4214 / J6360 / M25628 RŌ. KU. RU. *yatsu(su)* disguise oneself as; adorn oneself; pine away; act shamefully; abbreviate (a character). *yatsu(reru)* become emaciated, be worn out.

窺 4215 / J312e / M25633 KI. *ukaga(u)* watch for (a chance), lie in wait, spy on, reconnoiter; see, discover.

7 見 *kiken suru* peek
8 知 *kichi suru, ukaga(i)-shi(ru)* perceive, understand
11 探 *ukaga(i)-sagu(ru)* spy out
14 窬 *kiyu* maliciously looking for a break

12

竃 4216 / J3376 / M-X See **竈** 4221.

13

竅 4217 / J6361 / M25680 KYŌ hole; dig a hole; pressure. *ana* hole, cave.

竄 4218 / J6362 / M25679 ZAN, SAN flee; hide; renew.

2 入 *zannyū suru* take refuge in, enter by mistake
入者 *zannyūsha* refugee, fugitive
6 伏 *zampuku* running off and hiding
7 走 *zansō* fleeing

14

竆 4219 / J-X / M25686 See **窮** 4212.

15

竇 4220 / J6365 / M25695 TŌ hole, round hole; ditch. *ana* hole, cave, pit.

16

竈 4221 / J635e / M25703 SŌ. *kamado, kama* kitchen stove, furnace, oven; household. *hettsui* hearth; kitchen stove.

4 元 *kamamoto* kitchen
9 神 *kamadogami* god of the hearth

17

竊 4222 / J6366 / M25713 See **窃** 4195.

RAD. 立 117

Tatsu to stand. At left: 立 *tatsu hen.* Nickname: Standing.

A **立** 4223 / J4e29 / M25721 RYŪ, RITSU standing. *ta(tsu)* stand, rise; rouse oneself; be built, be established; go up (smoke); burn out; depart; take flight; run high (waves); stick into; be worked out; be maintained; save (face); establish oneself, begin life; spread (rumors); shut (doors); be active; open (markets); be excited; come (seasons); makes (a total of thirty). *ta(teru)* stand something up, set up, raise; put up; set on edge; prick up (one's ears); build, erect; close (a door); establish; institute, enact; lay (plans); map out; set forth, lay down (a proposition); formulate; render (services), perform; look up to, respect; be loyal to; do justice to; circulate (rumors); have (an aim); establish (oneself), make (a success); support (oneself); make (an oath); sharpen, set (a saw); put up (a candidate); make (tea);

save (face). *ta(taseru)* make stand, set upright, raise, lift up; rouse (to activity). *ta(chi)* start, departure; (a charcoal fire) burning out. *ta(tchi)* standing up (juvenile). *ta(te)* leading part; leading actor. *ta(chi-hadakaru)* stand in one's way, confront. *rittoru* liter. *-ta(teru)* up (as in stir up noise). *ta(chi)-* standing; emphatic prefix.

2 入 *ta(chi)-i(ru)* enter, penetrate; interfere in, be inquisitive

入検査 *tachii(ri) kensa* spot inspection

入禁止 *Tachiiri Kinshi* Keep Out

3 上 *ta(chi)-a(garu)* stand up, rise, spring up, regain one's feet, stand erect. *ta(chi)-nobo(ru)* rise, ascend. *ta(chi)-a(gari)* starting; beginning. *ta(chi)-a(ge)* initialization process

女形 *ta(te)oyama* leading female-role actor

小便 *ta(chi)shōben* urinating in public

巾跳 *ta(chi)habatobi* standing broad jump

4 日 *ta(chi)bi* anniversary of a death

木 *ta(chi)ki* standing tree, standing timber

止 *ta(chi)-do(maru)* stop, halt, stand still

毛 *ta(chi)ke, ta(chi)ge* crops yet to be harvested

込 *ta(chi)-ko(mu)* be crowded. *ta(te)-ko(meru)* shut (the doors of a room). *ta(chi)-ko(meru)* (smoke or fog) spreads all over

切 *ta(te)-ki(ru)* close up, shut up

太子 *rittaishi* investiture of the crown prince

方 *rippō* cube

方体 *rippōtai* a cube

方根 *rippōkon* cube root

方容積 *rippō yōseki* cubic capacity

5 石 *ta(te)ishi* stone signpost, milestone, standing stone

代 *ta(chi)ka(wari)* taking turns. *ta(chi)ka(watte)* in place of

付 *ta(te)tsu(ke)* the movement of doors; doing (something) continuously

札 *ta(te)fuda* notice board, signboard

礼 *ritsurei* deciding on ceremony; standing courtesies; rising courtesy; passing courtesies

去 *ta(chi)-sa(ru)* leave, depart

冬 *rittō* setting in of winter

出 *ta(chi)-ide(ru)* emphatic for *de(ru)*; appear, come out, emerge; haunt, infest; be found, get back; be served (meals); lead to, enter; find (oneself) at; come out (as a result); leave, go out, get out; attend, appear; work (at); participate; launch (into); run (for an office); be published; sell; depart; graduate; break out, originate; be raised, be produced; issue from, be traced to, be derived from, stem from; protrude, stick out; exceed, interfere, intrude

正安国 *risshō-ankoku* establishment of national peace and security

6 至 *ta(chi)-ita(ru)* come to this pass

尽 *ta(chi)-tsuku(su)* continue standing

返 *ta(chi)-kae(ru)* return; recover (one's senses)

向 *ta(chi)-mu(kau)* face, confront; fight against; head for

地 *ritchi* location of industry

交 *ta(chi)-ma(jiru)* join

行 *ta(chi)-yu(ku)* maintain itself, last, stand, make itself pay; get along, making a living

行司 *ta(te)gyōji* the chief umpire in sumo

回 *ta(chi)-megu(ru)* walk around. *ta(te)-mawa(su)* surround with. *ta(chi)-mawa(ru)* move around; act, conduct oneself, maneuver, go to; haunt; enact (a fighting scene)

回先 *ta(chi)mawa(ri)saki* a criminal's hangout

合 *ta(chi)-a(u)* attend, be present at, take part in, witness; be pitted against. *tachia(i)* presence, attendance; conference, session; witnessing

会 *tachia(i)* attendance, presence, witnessing

会人 *tachiainin* witness, teller (in voting), observer

会演説 *tachiai enzetsu* competitive speech; debate

7 言 *ritsugen* expression of opinion

戻 *ta(chi)-modo(ru)* return to, fall back on

坊 *ta(chim)bō* casual laborer; tramp, loafer, loiterer; standing around

坑 *ta(te)kō* mine shaft
別 *ta(chi)-waka(reru)* part (company)
彷徨 *ta(chi)-samayo(u)* wander, roam
身 *risshin* success in life
身出世 *risshin-shusse* success in life
役 *ta(chi)yaku* leading role. *ta(te)yaku* leading actor
役者 *ta(te)yakusha* leading actor; protagonist; leading spirit
売 *tachiu(ri)* street peddling; street peddler
売人 *tachiurinin* street peddler
志 *risshi* fixing one's aim and pressing on
志伝 *risshiden* success story
見 *ta(chi)mi* viewing from the gallery while standing
見客 *ta(chi)mikyaku* the gallery; standee
見席 *ta(chi)miseki* gallery, standing room
体 *rittai* solid, solid body
体交叉点 *rittai kōsaten* overhead pass
体図形 *rittai zukei* solid figure
体的 *rittaiteki* three-dimensional
体美 *rittaibi* beauty of solid objects (sculpture, buildings)
体映画 *rittai eiga* three-dimensional movie; 3-D movie
体幾何学 *rittai kikagaku* solid geometry
体戦 *rittaisen* three-dimensional warfare
8 国 *rikkoku* rebuilding a country
居 *ta(chi)i* standing and sitting; deportment
迷 *ta(chi)-mayo(u)* (clouds) float along, drift
坪 *ta(te)tsubo, ryūtsubo* a cubic *ken*, 6x6x6 feet
所 *ta(chi)dokoro ni* immediately, in an instant, on the spur of the moment, in no time; impromptu
板 *ta(te)ita* standing board
枠 *ta(te)waku* upright frame
泳 *tachioyo(gi)* treading water
物 *ta(te)mono* leading actor; protagonist
並 *ta(chi)-nara(bu)* stand in a row, line up; be equal to
命 *ritsumei* quietness of spirit
直 *ta(te)-nao(ru) vi* recover, rally, pick up. *ta(te)-nao(su) vt* recover, rally; make over; recover (one's energy); reorganize, reshuffle. *ta(chi)nao(shi)* rebuilding as before. *tachinao(ri)* recovery, restoration
歩 *ta(chi)aru(ki)* toddling, walking
往生 *ta(chi)ōjō suru* make a last stand; be stalled, be stranded; be nonplused; be at a standstill
退 *ta(chi)-no(ku)* leave, depart, vacate, evacuate; take refuge
退人 *ta(chi)no(ki)nin* one who quits the premises
退料 *ta(chi)no(ki)ryō* compensation for removal
法 *rippō* legislation, lawmaking
法上 *rippōjō no* legislative
法者 *rippōsha* lawgiver, lawmaker
法権 *rippōken* legislative power
法機関 *rippō kikan* legislative body
9 飛 *ta(chi)to(bi)* standing plunge
食 *tachigu(i), risshoku* eating while standing
通 *ta(chi)-dō(su)* stand all the way. *ta(te)-tō(su)* maintain to the last
後 *ta(chi)-oku(reru)* be slow in jumping into (the fray); make a belated start; be too late; allow (someone) to get a head start
枯 *ta(chi)ga(rashi), tachiga(re)* blight
派 *rippa na* fine, handsome, excellent, grand; imposing, commanding, honorable, respectable; commendable, noble; prominent; honest; legal, legitimate; sufficient, justifiable
秋 *risshū* setting in of fall
前 *ta(te)mae* principle, policy, rule, basis, system
姿 *ta(chi)sugata* standing pose, standing position
春 *risshun* setting in of spring
待月 *ta(chi)ma(chi)zuki* 17-day-old moon
看板 *ta(te)kamban* standing signboard
草臥 *ta(chi)-kutabi(reru)* get tired standing
10 席 *ta(chi)seki* standing room (at a performance)
疲 *ta(chi)-tsuka(reru)* be tired of standing
哨 *risshō* standing guard
悩 *ta(chi)-naya(mu)* hesitate, come to a standstill, be held up
消 *tachigi(e)* going out, dying out, flickering out

眩 *ta(chi)kura(mi), ta(chi)gura(mi)* dizziness

射 *rissha* firing from a standing position

夏 *rikka* the official first day of summer

党 *rittō* formation of a new party

帰 *ta(chi)-kae(ru)* return, go back to, come back to (the subject)

候補 *rikkōho* announcing one's candidacy

高跳 *ta(chi)takatobi* standing high jump

振舞 *ta(chi)burumai* farewell dinner. *ta(chi)furumai* deportment

烏帽子 *ta(te)eboshi* noble's high headgear

案 *ritsuan* plan, design, draft

案者 *ritsuansha* planner, designer, drafter

11 遅 *ta(chi)oku(re)* losing an opportunity

掛 *ta(chi)-ka(keru), ta(chi)-ka(karu)* begin to rise

添 *ta(chi)-so(u)* stand close

寄 *ta(chi)-yo(ru)* get near; call at, drop in, look (someone) up; stop over

脚 *rikkyaku suru* be based on

脚地 *rikkyakuchi* position, standpoint, viewpoint

脚点 *rikkyakuten* position, standpoint, viewpoint

12 越 *ta(chi)-ko(eru)* surpass, be superior to; go

喰 *ta(chi)gui* eating while standing

場 *tachiba* standpoint, position, footing, station; attitude; situation; viewpoint; standing room. *ta(te)bu* stopping place, stage; cab stand; wholesaler

竦 *ta(chi)-suku(mu)* be petrified

勝 *ta(chi)-masa(ru)* excel, surpass, outrival

証 *risshō* proof, demonstration, substantiation

飲 *ta(chi)no(mi)* drinking while standing

葵 *ta(chi)aoi* hollyhock

番 *ta(chi)ban* watch, guarding; guard, sentry, picket

替 *ta(te)-ka(eru)* advance money; pay for another; lend

替金 *tatekaekin* advance money

13 働 *ta(chi)-hatara(ku)* work, go about one's work

続 *ta(te)tsuzu(ke)* succession, continuation

腹 *rippuku* anger, indignation

話 *ta(chi)banashi* standing and chatting

詰 *ta(chi)zu(me)* being kept standing

塞 *ta(chi)-fusa(garu)* stand in the way, block the way, confront, head off

罩 *ta(chi)-ko(meru)* hang over, envelop, shroud

14 腐 *ta(chi)gusa(re)* dilapidation

聞 *ta(chi)gi(ku)* overhear, eavesdrop. *ta(chi)gi(ki)* eavesdropping, overhearing

像 *ritsuzō* a standing image

構 *ta(chi)-kama(eru)* take an attitude; be ready for a fight

網 *ta(te)ami* dragnet, set net, seine

15 穂 *ta(chi)ho* standing grain

膝 *ta(te)hiza* drawn-up knee

論 *ritsuron* argument; argumentation

撃 *ta(chi)u(chi)* firing from a standing position

16 篭 *ta(te)-komo(ru)* remain in seclusion; entrench oneself in a castle

稽古 *ta(chi)geiko* rehearsal

錐 *rissui* a standing drill (the tool)

錐地 *rissui (no) chi* a small plot of ground

錐余地 *rissui (no) yochi* standing room

憲 *rikken* adopting a constitution

憲民主政体 *rikken minshu seitai* constitutional democracy

憲君主政体 *rikken kunshu seitai* constitutional monarchy

憲国 *rikkenkoku* a country with a constitution

憲的 *rikkenteki* constitutional

憲政体 *rikken seitai* constitutional form of government

憲政治 *rikken seiji* constitutional government

18 襟 *ta(chi)eri* stand-up collar

騒 *ta(chi)-sawa(gu)* make a noise, be boisterous, shout, clamor; raise an uproar; be excited, be agitated; bustle around; make a fuss about; make merry, go on a spree

19 願 *ritsugan* praying to a god

離 *ta(chi)-hana(reru)* be away from

瀬 *ta(tsu)se* standpoint, position

瀬無 *ta(tsu)se (ga) na(i)* be in a dilemma

22 籠 *ta(te)-komo(ru)* remain in seclusion; entrench oneself in a castle

2

竍 4224 / J6367 / M25726 （国字） *dekarittoru* decaliter, ten liters.

3

竏 4225 / J6368 / M25731 （国字） *kirorittoru* kiloliter, 1000 liters.

4

竒 4226 / J5474 / M25736 See 奇 1150.

竕 4227 / J6369 / M25740 （国字） *deshirittoru* deciliter.

竓 4228 / J636a / M25738 （国字） *miririttoru* milliliter.

5

竚 4229 / J636c / M25744 See 佇 152.

竝 4230 / J636d / M25752 See 並 24.

站 4231 / J636b / M25742 TAN stop, halt.

B **竜** 4232 / J4e35 / M25751 **龍** 7103 / J4e36 / M48818 RYŪ, RYŌ dragon; imperial. *tatsu* dragon.

3 口 *tatsu(no)kuchi* dragon-head gargoyle; spout of a gutter
4 王 *ryūō* dragon god, dragon king
5 田姫 *tatsutahime* goddess of autumn
6 舌蘭 *ryūzetsuran* century plant
7 車 *ryūsha* imperial carriage
8 虎 *ryūko, ryōko* dragon and tiger; hero; clever writing; good writer
9 神 *ryūjin* dragon god, dragon king
胆 *rindō* gentian, bellflower
巻 *tatsuma(ki)* waterspout
10 骨 *ryūkotsu* keel
宮 *ryūgū* sea god's dragon palace
涎香 *ryūzenkō* ambergris
12 落子 *tatsu (no) oto(shi)go* sea horse
15 蝦 *Ise ebi* spiny lobster
駕 *ryōga* imperial carriage
16 頭 *ryūzu* watch stem
頭蛇尾 *ryūtōdabi* fast start and slow finish; ending in an anticlimax
18 顔 *ryōgan, ryūgan* imperial countenance
20 攘虎搏 *ryūjōkohaku* fierce fighting

6

竡 4233 / J636e / M25767 （国字） *hekutorittoru* hectoliter, 100 liters.

竟 4234 / J706f / M25757 KYŌ. *owa(ru)* end, terminate, adjourn, be over; die. *owa(ri)* end, conclusion, expiration. *tsui ni* finally, after all.

A **章** 4235 / J3e4f / M25761 SHŌ chapter; composition; poem; badge, mark, sign; design.

5 句 *shōku* passage, chapter and verse
11 魚 *tako* octopus
13 数 *shōsū* number of chapters
節 *shōsetsu* chapter and verse

7

竢 4236 / J636f / M25770 See 俟 203.

竦 4237 / J6370 / M25776 SHŌ revere, fear. *suku(mu) vi* crouch, cower, lie quiet; be cramped; get wrinkled. *suku(meru) vt* duck (one's head); shrug (one's shoulders); make (someone) crouch.

12 然 *shōzen* horror; shuddering

竣 4238 / J3d57 / M25773 SHUN end, finish.

3 工 *shunkō* completion
工式 *shunkōshiki* ceremony of completion
工期 *shunkōki* time of completion
5 功 *shunkō* completion
6 成 *shunsei* completion

A **童** 4239 / J4638 / M25775 DŌ child. *warawa, warabe* child.

3 女 *dōjo, dōnyo* girl, maiden, lass
子 *dōji* child, boy
4 心 *dōshin* child's mind, naïveté
5 幼 *dōyō* child, infant
7 児 *dōji* a child

8 画 *dōga* pictures drawn by a child; pictures for children
9 貞 *dōtei* chastity; (Catholic) nun
13 蒙 *dōmō* child
話 *dōwa* nursery tale, fairy tale, juvenile tale
話劇 *dōwageki* juvenile play
14 歌 *warabe uta* children's folk songs
16 謡 *dōyō* children's song, nursery rhyme
18 顔 *dōgan* boyish face

8

豎 4240 / J4328 / M25790 Ju. *tate* length; height; warp.
5 穴 *tateana* pit, hole; mine shaft; site of ancient pit dwelling
6 缶 *tategama* vertical boiler
7 坑 *tatekō* mine shaft
8 物 *tatemono* vertical scroll
10 框 *tategamachi* door frame
挽大鋸 *tatebiki onokogiri* pit saw
11 笛 *tatebue* clarinet
12 棺 *tatekan* upright coffin
琴 *tategoto* harp; lyre
14 樋 *tatedoi, tatetoyo* downspout
21 鰭 *tatebire* vertical fin
23 罐 *tategama* vertical boiler

9

竰 4241 / J6372 / M25808 (国字) *senchirittoru* centiliter.

竭 4242 / J6371 / M25803 Ketsu end, exhaust. *tsu(kusu)* use up, run out of, exhaust; serve, befriend, work for, endeavor, do (one's duty).
6 尽 *ketsujin* used up

B 端 4243 / J433c / M25806 Tan origin; end; point. *hashi, haji, ha* end, tip; edge, border, one side; corner; beginning; scrap of cloth. *hana* beginning, inception; end, edge, verge, point, extremity, cape. *hashita* fraction, odd sum, fragment, scrap. *hashitana(i)* uncouth, rude. *hata* side, edge. *tsuma* end. *hashi kara* one after another. *hashi(kure), hashi(kkure)* scrap, piece, bit. *-tan* tip, extremity.
3 女 *hashitame* maidservant
子 *tanshi* terminal (in electricity)
山 *hayama* foothill
4 切 *hashigi(re)* cloth scraps, odds and ends
午 *Tango* Boy's Festival (May 5)
5 正 *tansei* correct, just, orderly, proper
本 *hahon* odd volume
末機 *tammatsuki* computer terminal
末装置 *tammatsu sōchi* computer terminal
6 近 *hashijika ni* near the edge; just at the threshold
7 役 *hayaku* minor post; minor role
折 *hasho(ru), hashio(ru)* tuck up; abridge
坐 *tanza suru* sit erect
8 金 *hashitagane* small change; pittance
居 *hashii* being at the end of the house or on the veranda
物 *hamono* incomplete set; odds and ends
的 *tanteki na* direct, blunt, frank
武者 *hamusha* private, common soldier
9 乗 *hashinori* climbing on the end; just riding a bit
10 座 *tanza suru* sit erect
倪 *tangei* limit; from beginning to end; mountain tops and river banks; guess, conjecture
唄 *hauta* ditty, short popular song
書 *hagaki* postcard. *hashiga(ki)* preface, introduction; postscript
12 喰 *hashibami* clamp (in building)
無 *hashitana(i)* rude. *hashina(ku) mo* suddenly, unexpectedly, accidentally
然 *tanzen(taru)* correct, proper
13 艇 *tantei* boat
数 *hasū* fraction, odd sum
14 端 *hashibashi* parts, odds and ends
綱 *hazuna* halter
緒 *tansho, tancho* beginning, first step, clue
銭 *hasen* small change; pittance
境 *hazakai* between harvests, lean period
境期 *hazakaiki* between harvests, lean period
16 整 *tansei na* correct, just, orderly, proper
17 厳 *tangen na* solemn and serene
19 麗 *tanrei* grace, beauty

15

A 競 4244 / J3625 / M25831 競 4245 / J513f / M25840 Kyō. Kei. *kiso(u), kio(u)*

5 玄玉王瓜瓦甘生用田疋疒癶白皮皿目矛矢石示礻禸禾穴 17【立】

emulate, compete with. *se(ru)* compete, vie, bid; sell at auction. *seri* auction. *-kura* race, bout, contest.
3上 *se(ri)-a(geru)* auction off
4手 *serite* bidder
5市 *seriichi* auction house
6肌 *kio(i)hada* gallantry
合 *se(ri)-a(u)* compete with, vie for. *araso(i)-a(u)* contend with, quarrel. *kyōgō* concurrence, conflict, competition
争 *kyōsō* rivalry, contest, competition
争入札 *kyōsō nyūsatsu* sealed bidding
争心 *kyōsōshin* competitive or fighting spirit
争車 *kyōsōsha* racing car
争者 *kyōsōsha* contestant, competitor, rival
争価格 *kyōsō kakaku* competitive price
争相手 *kyōsō aite* competitor, rival
争場裡 *kyōsō jōri* area of competition
争試験 *kyōsō shiken* competitive examination
7走 *kiso(i)-hashi(ru)* to race. *kyōsō* race
走者 *kyōsōsha* runner, racer
技 *kyōgi* contest, sporting event, tournament, race
技会 *kyōgikai* athletic meet, contest
技場 *kyōgijō* stadium
売 *seriu(ri)* auction; auctioneer. *kyōbai* auction
売人 *kyōbainin* auctioneer
売台 *kyōbaidai* auction block
売場 *kyōbaijō* auction house, auction room
8泳 *kyōei* swimming race
歩 *kyōho* walking race
9映 *kyōei* competitive film exhibition
10射 *kyōsha* shooting contest
馬 *keiba* horse race; horse racing
馬馬 *keibauma* racehorse
馬場 *keibajō* racetrack
馬騎手 *keiba kishu* jockey
11掛 *kio(i)-ka(karu)* be determined to win
12落 *se(ri)-o(tosu)* bid successfully, knock down. *kyōraku* auctioning, bidding
買人 *kyōbainin* bidder
13艇 *keitei, kyōtei* boat race
業 *kyōgyō* business competition
14漕 *kyōsō* regatta, boat race
演 *kyōen* recital contest
演会 *kyōenkai* recital contest
15輪 *keirin* bicycle race

17

競 4245 / J513f / M25840 See 競 4244.

6-STROKE RADICALS

RAD. 竹 118

Take bamboo. Variant: ⺮ *take kammuri* "bamboo" crown. Nickname: Bamboo.

A 竹 4246 / J435d / M25841 CHIKU bamboo. *take* bamboo; bamboo wind instrument.
2刀 *chikutō, shinai* fencing stick
3子 *take (no) ko* bamboo shoots
下駄 *takegeta* bamboo clogs
5皮 *take (no) kawa* bamboo sheath
矢来 *take yarai* bamboo palisade
6光 *takemitsu* bamboo sword; a blunt sword
7材 *chikuzai* bamboo
8林 *chikurin, takebayashi* bamboo grove
帛 *chikuhaku* history
9屋 *takeya* bamboo dealer
垣 *takegaki* bamboo fence, bamboo hedge
柱 *takebashira* bamboo pole, bamboo post
竿 *takezao* bamboo pole
柄杓 *takebishaku* bamboo ladle
10原 *takehara* bamboo grove
釘 *take kugi* bamboo peg
格子 *takegōshi* bamboo lattice
馬 *takeuma, chikuba* bamboo horse; stilts
馬友 *chikuba (no) tomo* a small child's playmate

11 梯子 *takebashigo* bamboo ladder
細工 *takezaiku* bamboo work, bamboo ware
12 筒 *takezutsu* bamboo pipe
13 楊子 *take yōji* bamboo-handled toothbrush
園生 *take (no) sonoo* bamboo garden; the Imperial Family
14 槍 *take yari* bamboo spear
箒 *takebōki* bamboo broom
製 *takesei* made of bamboo
15 縁 *takeen* bamboo-floored veranda
器 *chikki* bamboo ware
16 篦 *takebera* bamboo spatula. *shippei* slapping opponent's wrist with first two fingers, a fillip
篦返 *shippeigae(shi)* retaliation
17 簀 *takesu* removable bamboo floor
18 藪 *take yabu* bamboo grove
叢 *takamura* bamboo grove
22 籠 *take kago* bamboo basket

2

竺 4247 / J3c33 / M25842 JIKU, CHIKU bamboo.

3

笂 4248 / J6373 / M-X (国字) *utsubo* quiver.

笈 4249 / J3568 / M25869 KYŪ portable bookcase carried on the back.
9 負 *kyū (o) o(u)* depart for an education

竿 4250 / J3448 / M25854 KAN. *sao* pole, rod; beam (of scales); (well) sweep; neck (of a violin).
6 竹 *saodake* bamboo pole
10 秤 *saobakari* steelyard, beam balance
11 掛 *saoka(ke)* fishpole holder
釣 *saozuri* pole fishing
16 頭 *kantō* top of a pole

4

笋 4251 / J6424 / M25873 See 筍 4281.

笆 4252 / J6376 / M25865 HA, HE thorny bamboo; thorny bamboo hedge.

笊 4253 / J6375 / M25872 SŌ. *zaru* bamboo basket.

笏 4254 / J6374 / M25882 KOTSU. *shaku* mace, baton, scepter.

笄 4255 / J6422 / M25862 — **筓** 4274 / J-X / M26005 KEI. *kōgai* ornamental hairpin; metal rod attached to sword sheath; crossbar of an anchor; ancient comb.

A **笑** 4256 / J3e50 / M25885 SHŌ laughter. *wara(u)* laugh, smile; ridicule; be in full bloom. *e(mu)* smile, bloom; split, open, crack. *emi* smile. *wara(i)* laughing, smile; derision.
3 上戸 *wara(i) jōgo* a merry drinker; one who is always laughing
4 止 *shōshi na* laughable, ridiculous; pitiful; contemptible
止千万 *shōshi-semban* extremely funny
5 出 *wara(i)-da(su)* burst out laughing
6 気 *shōki* laughing gas, nitrous oxide
7 声 *wara(i)goe, shōsei* laughter, laugh; laughing voice
8 物 *wara(i)mono* object of ridicule
者 *wara(ware)mono* laughingstock
事 *wara(i)goto* laughing matter
9 柄 *shōhei* laughingstock
草 *wara(i)gusa* laughingstock
10 納 *shōno* your acceptance; receiving
殺 *shōsatsu suru* laugh off; laugh to scorn
12 絵 *wara(i)e* comic picture; pornographic picture
割 *e(mi)-wa(reru)* crack, split open
壺 *etsubo* smile of satisfaction
13 話 *wara(i)banashi, shōwa* humorous story
14 種 *wara(i)gusa, wara(i)dane* laughingstock
語 *shōgo* laughing and talking at the same time
15 劇 *shōgeki* farce (in dramatics)
談 *shōdan* jolly talk
16 覧 *shōran* your inspection
18 顔 *egao, wara(i)gao* smiling face, radiant look

笑 4257 / J637d / M25954 See 矢 3976.

筑 4258 / J-X / M25918 See 筑 4280.

笘 4259 / J6378 / M25911 SEN bamboo whip; wooden writing tablet.

笳 4260 / J6377 / M25950 KA reed flute.

笵 4261 / J637b / M25952 HAN, BON law, regulation; model, pattern; bamboo frame.

笨 4262 / J637c / M25939 HON coarse (not fine).

笴 4263 / J-X / M24951 KA arrow shaft.

笙 4264 / J6379 / M25913 SHŌ a reed instrument used in *Gagaku*.

笥 4265 / J3f5a / M25934 SU, SHI *ke* lunch box; food box; clothes chest.

笧 4266 / J-X / M25938 SAKU. *shigara(mu)* entwine around; check (a current) with a weir. *shigarami* weir.

笞 4267 / J637a / M25921 CHI whip; crime punishable by flogging. *shimoto* whip, scourge. *muchi* whip, rod.
6 刑 *chikei* whipping, flogging; the lash
13 罪 *chizai* crime punishable by flogging

A **笛** 4268 / J452b / M25917 TEKI flute. *fue* flute, pipe, clarinet, whistle, fife, pitch pipe, bagpipe, piccolo.
4 手 *tekishu* flutist
7 吹 *fue-fu(ku)* play a flute. *fuefu(ki)* flute player, clarinetist
声 *tekisei* sound of a flute, piping; (train) whistle

笠 4269 / J335e / M25924 RYŪ. *kasa* bamboo hat; one's influence; lampshade; (chimney) hood.
3 子 *kasago* rock cod, rockfish
4 切 *kasa (ni) ki(ru)* brag
5 石 *kasaishi* capstone
8 松 *kasamatsu* umbrella-like pine

B **符** 4270 / J4964 / M25935 FU sign, mark, tally; charm, amulet.
2 丁 *fuchō* sign, mark, token, symbol; code; secret (price) mark; password, countersign
5 号 *fugō* mark, sign, symbol, code
6 合 *fugō* agreement, coincidence, correspondence, conformity
9 点 *futen* dot (in music)
13 牒 *fuchō* sign, mark, token, symbol; code; secret (price) mark; password, countersign
節 *fusetsu* tally, check

笹 4271 / J3a7b / M25968 (国字) *sasa* bamboo grass.
6 舟 *sasabune* toy bamboo-leaf boat
10 原 *sasawara* field of bamboo grass
12 葉 *sasaba, sasa(p)pa* bamboo leaf
14 飴 *sasaame* glutinous rice jelly wrapped in bamboo-grass leaves
15 縁 *sasaberi* lace, frill, edging
18 藪 *sasayabu* bamboo-grass brush

A **第** 4272 / J4268 / M25943 TEI, DAI residence. DAI- number (1, 2, 3, etc.).
1 一 *dai-ichi ni* first, in the first place. *dai-ichi no* first, foremost, primary, initial, principal, chief. *dai-ichi* the first, the best, number one, the greatest
一人者 *dai-ichininsha* an authority, tops (in one's field)
一人称 *dai-ichininshō* first person (in grammar)
一次 *dai-ichiji* first
一次世界大戦 *Dai Ichiji Sekai Taisen* the First World War
一印象 *dai-ichi inshō* first impression
一位 *dai-ichii* first rank
一声 *dai-issei* first talk (on returning from abroad)
一歩 *dai-ippo* first step, initial step
一担保 *dai-ichi tampo* first mortgage
一流 *dai-ichiryū no* first-rate, topnotch, foremost, gilt-edged
一党 *dai-ittō* dominant party

一着 *dai-itchaku* first arrival; first step (to take)
一義 *dai-ichigi* original meaning; first principal, essential point, first consideration
一種 *dai-isshu* first class (mail, etc.)
一線 *dai-issen* front line
一審 *dai-isshin* first trial, first instance
2 二人称 *dai-nininshō* second person (in grammar)
二次 *dai-niji* second
二次世界大戦 *Dai Niji Sekai Taisen* the Second World War
二次的 *dai-nijiteki* secondary
二義 *dai-nigi* secondary meaning
3 三人称 *dai-sanninshō* third person (in grammar)
三者 *dai-sansha* third party, disinterested person
三国 *dai-sangoku* third power
三国人 *dai-sangokujin* third power national
三帝国 *Dai-San Teikoku* the Third Reich
三階級 *dai-san kaikyū* bourgeoisie, middle class
4 六感 *dai-rokkan* the sixth sense
五列 *dai-goretsu* fifth column
五部隊 *dai-go butai* fifth column
5 四階級 *dai-shi kaikyū* proletariat

6

箏 4273 / J6438 / M-X Nonstandard for 箏 4313.

笄 4274 / J-X / M26005 See 笄 4255.

筅 4275 / J6426 / M25986 SEN bamboo whisk; tea whisk.

筐 4276 / J637e / M26001 KYŌ. *katami* bamboo basket.

筈 4277 / J4826 / M25990 KATSU. *hazu* notch of an arrow; something that ought to, must, or should be; something to be expected; be due to.

筌 4278 / J6425 / M25995 SEN fish trap. *uke, ue* weir, fish trap.

筬 4279 / J642d / M26067 SEI, JŌ kind of bamboo; yarn guide, reed (in weaving).

筑 4280 / J435e / M26002 **筑** 4258 / J-X / M25918 CHIKU an ancient musical instrument.
12 紫 *Tsukushi* Kyūshū

筍 4281 / J6423 / M25997 **笋** 4251 / J6424 / M25873 JUN. *takenoko* bamboo shoots.
5 生活 *takenoko seikatsu* red-ink living, living by selling personal effects
7 医者 *takenoko isha* quack doctor

筏 4282 / J4835 / M26000 BATSU. *ikada* raft.
3 士 *ikadashi* raftsman
9 乗 *ikadano(ri)* raftsman
10 師 *ikadashi* raftsman

B **筒** 4283 / J457b / M26004 TŌ pipette, tube. *tsutsu* pipe, tube, case, gun barrel, sleeve, well curb.
3 口 *tsutsuguchi* tube end; nozzle
4 井 *tsutsui* round well
6 先 *tsutsusaki* pipe end, hose nozzle, gun muzzle; the fireman holding the nozzle
7 抜 *tsutsunu(ke) ni* directly, clearly, just as told
形 *tsutsugata* cylindrical shape, barrel shape
10 袖 *tsutsusode* tight sleeve, tight-sleeved dress

A **策** 4284 / J3a76 / M26009 SAKU plan, scheme, policy; step, means; whip. *saku(suru)* plan.
3 士 *sakushi* schemer, tactician, man of resources
7 応 *sakuō* cooperation, concert, collusion
11 略 *sakuryaku* stratagem, scheme, plan, policy, frame-up
動 *sakudō* scheming, maneuvering, manipulation
動家 *sakudōka* schemer, mischief-maker, a Machiavellian
13 戦 *sakusen* military or naval operations
源 *sakugen* base of operations
源地 *sakugenchi* base of operations
16 謀 *sakubō* artifice, stratagem, frame-up

6 【竹】米糸缶网罒羊羽老耂而耒耳聿肉月臣自至臼舌舛舟艮色艸艹虍虫血行衣衤西

A 答 4285 / J457a / M26006 Tō answer. *kota(eru)* answer; respond; solve. *kota(e)* answer; solution.
[5] 弁 *tōben* reply, explanation, defense
申 *tōshin* a report
申案 *tōshin'an* draft of a report
申書 *tōshinsho* findings, report, draft
礼 *tōrei* return salute, return courtesy
礼使節 *tōrei shisetsu* goodwill envoy
礼砲 *tōreihō* return gun salute
[6] 返 *kota(e)-kae(su)* return an answer
[10] 砲 *tōhō* return salute
案 *tōan* examination paper
[11] 訪 *tōhō* return visit
[13] 辞 *tōji* formal reply, response
酬 *tōshū* answer
電 *tōden* reply telegram
[17] 謝 *tōsha* acknowledgment

A 筋 4286 / J365a / M25994 Kin muscle, sinew, tendon. *suji* muscle; sinew, tendon; vein; fiber; string; line; stripe, streak; plot, plan; reason, logic; circumstances; thread, sequence; quarters, sources, authorities; lineage, strain, stock, descent; grain, texture. *suji(darake)* sinewy; stringy.
[2] 力 *kinryoku* physical strength
[3] 子 *sujiko* salmon roe
[5] 目 *sujime* fold, crease; lineage, pedigree; reason, logic, thread, chain (of reasoning); method, system
[6] 向 *sujimu(kai), sujimu(kō)* diagonally opposite
交 *sujika(i)* diagonal, oblique; brace
合 *sujiai* reason
肉 *kinniku* muscles, sinews
肉労働 *kinniku rōdō* physical labor
[8] 金 *sujigane* metal reinforcement
[10] 骨 *kinkotsu, sujibone* sinews and bones
書 *sujiga(ki)* synopsis, outline; scenario, plot, story; plan, program, schedule
[11] 道 *sujimichi* reason, logic, thread, chain (of reasoning); method, system
張 *sujiba(ru)* become stringy, become brawny; stand on ceremony
[12] 揉 *sujimomi* muscle massage
筋 *sujisuji* lines
違 *sujichiga(i)* cramp, sprain, absurdity; intersection. *sujikai* diagonal, oblique; brace
[14] 膜 *kimmaku* the fascia

A 等 4287 / J4579 / M25992 Tō class, grade, degree; and so forth; equality. *hito(shii)* equal, similar, alike, equivalent. *-nado* and so forth. *-ra* and others, and the like; a plural ending.
[4] 分 *tōbun* division into equal parts; equal parts
比 *tōhi* proportion
比級数 *tōhi kyūsū* geometrical progression, geometrical series
辺 *tōhen* equal sides
辺三角形 *tōhen sankakukei* equilateral triangle
[5] 外 *tōgai* inferior grades
号 *tōgō* the sign of addition
圧線 *tōatsusen* isobar
[6] 式 *tōshiki* equality
[7] 角 *tōkaku* equal angles
位 *tōi* rank, grade, class, scale
身 *tōshin* life-size
身像 *tōshinzō* life-size statue
[8] 並 *hito(shi)nami* same, ordinary
雨線図 *tōusenzu* rainfall map
価 *tōka* equivalence, parity
価量 *tōkaryō* equivalent amount
[9] 級 *tōkyū* class, grade, order, rank, magnitude, rating, classification
[10] 値 *tōchi* equal value
高耕作 *tōkō kōsaku* contour plowing
高線 *tōkōsen* contour line
差 *tōsa* difference; equal difference
差中項 *tōsa chūkō* arithmetical mean
差級数 *tōsa kyūsū* arithmetical series, progression
[11] 距離 *tōkyori* equal distances; equidistance
脚三角形 *tōkyaku sankakukei* isosceles triangle
[12] 間 *tōkan* neglect, disregard
閑 *naozari, tōkan* neglect, disregard
量 *tōryō no* equivalent
等 *tōtō* etc., and so forth
温 *tōon* equal temperature
温線 *tōonsen* isotherm
[15] 輩 *tōhai* companions
質 *tōshitsu* homogeneity
[16] 親 *tōshin* degree of kinship

A 筆 4288 / J492e / M25987 Hitsu. *fude* writing brush, paintbrush; writing, drawing, painting; the pen; handwriting, penmanship; literary work.

2 入 *fudei(re)* writing-brush holder. *fude (o) i(reru)* correct a document
力 *hitsuryoku* power of the pen
3 工 *hikkō* writing-brush maker
才 *hissai* literary talent
4 太 *fudebuto ni* in bold strokes, in a bold hand, in bold lettering
不精 *fudebushō* poor correspondent
5 生 *hissei* copyist, amanuensis
立 *fudeta(te)* writing-brush holder. *fude (ga) ta(tsu)* be clever and fast in writing
写 *hissha* copying
6 舌 *hitsuzetsu* the pen and the tongue
先 *fudesaki* brush tip; handling the brush; writing. *(o)fudesaki* prophecy, oracle
名 *hitsumei* pen name, pseudonym
8 使 *fudezuka(i)* penmanship; writing technique, stroke of the pen
法 *hippō* penmanship style; manner
者 *hissha* writer, author
忠実 *fudemame* ready writer, good correspondent
9 洗 *hissen* brush-washing receptacle
硏 *hikken* pen and ink; literary work
陣 *hitsujin* composing sentences, writing
架 *hikka* pen rack
10 紙 *hisshi* pen and paper
致 *hitchi* stroke of the brush; style
耕 *hikkō suru* copy, stencil
耕料 *hikkōryō* copying fee
記 *hikki* taking notes; notes, copying
記者 *hikkisha* copyist
記帳 *hikkichō* notebook
記試験 *hikki shiken* written examination
12 順 *hitsujun* stroke order
硯 *hikken* pen and ink; literary work
答 *hittō* written reply
13 禍 *hikka* serious slip of the pen
触 *hisshoku* touch of the pen
誅 *hitchū* an attack in the press
跡 *hisseki* holograph; handwriting (specimen)
馴 *fudena(rashi)* writing exercise
戦 *hissen* the war of the pen
置 *fude (o) o(ku)* leaving off writing
意 *hitsui* one's feeling when writing; writing style; the meaning
勢 *hissei* power of the pen; penmanship
14 端 *hittan* brush or pen tip; stroke of the pen
算 *hissan* calculation
管 *hikkan* handle of a writing brush; a writing brush
罰 *hitsubatsu* an attack in the press
墨 *hitsuboku* pen and ink
墨紙 *hitsubokushi* pen, ink, and paper
15 談 *hitsudan* conversation by writing
調 *hitchō* penmanship, calligraphy
鋒 *hippō* literary style
16 録 *hitsuroku* recording
頭 *hittō* head of a brush; first in the list
頭者 *hittōsha* head of the house (in a government registry)
18 蹟 *hisseki* holograph; handwriting (specimen)

7

[illegible] 4289 / J-X / M-X Nonstandard for 簿 4364.

筺 4290 / J6421 / M-X Nonstandard for 筐 4276.

筥 4291 / J6428 / M26051 KYO box; rice container; a four-handful sheaf.

筰 4292 / J642b / M26074 SAKU, SHAKU bamboo rope.

筱 4293 / J642c / M26076 SHŌ. *shinodake* a small bamboo.

筴 4294 / J6429 / M26079 SAKU divining sticks. KYŌ chopsticks; hold (something) between.

筩 4295 / J-X / M26062 TŌ bamboo tube.

筧 4296 / J642a / M26059 KEN. *kakehi* water pipe, conduit, flume.

筵 4297 / J6427 / M26080 莚 5040 / J682f / M31059 EN mat, matting; feast, banquet, party, entertainment; seat. *mushiro* straw mat, matting.

筮 4298 / J642e / M26070 ZEI divining; diviner's equipment.
2 卜 *zeiboku* divining with divining rods
6 竹 *zeichiku* divining rods

6 【竹】 米糸缶网罒羊羽老耂而耒耳聿肉月臣自至臼舌舛舟艮色艸艹虍虫血行衣衤西

A 節 4299/J4061/M26102 節 4319/J-X/M-X 節 4320/J-X/M26243

SETSU season, period, occasion, time; verse, clause, paragraph, section, stanza; integrity, honor. *ses(suru)* be temperate, be moderate; control, restrain; save, be sparing. *fushi* joint, knuckle; knob, lump, knot; tune, melody; point (in a talk). *notto* knot, nautical mile.

2 刀 *settō* sword given by the emperor to the commander-in-chief
4 水 *sessui* water economy
介 *sekkai* untimely interference
分 *setsubun* last day of winter
5 用 *setsuyō* frugality, economy
目 *fushime* knots in lumber
穴 *fushiana* knothole
立 *fushi(kure)da(tsu)* be knotty; be bony
句 *sekku* annual festival
付 *fushizu(ke)* setting to music
6 米 *setsumai* rice economy
回 *fushimawa(shi)* melody, intonation
会 *sechie* court banquet
8 供 *sekku* annual festival
制 *sessei* temperance, moderation, self-restraint
季 *sekki* year end
9 食 *sesshoku* moderation in eating, spare diet
度 *setsudo* rule, standard; instructions; moderation
約 *setsuyaku* economy
奏 *sessō* rhythm
10 倹 *sekken* economy, thrift
酒 *sesshu* temperance, sobriety; moderation in drinking
11 婦 *seppu* virtuous wife
欲 *setsuyoku* curbing desires
12 減 *setsugen* curtailment, economy, retrenchment
期 *sekki* time, chance
13 煙 *setsuen* moderation in smoking
節 *fushibushi* joints; points (in a talk)
義 *setsugi* fidelity to principle, constancy; honor
電 *setsuden* economy of electricity
16 操 *sessō* constancy, integrity, honor, chastity
18 織 *fushio(ri)* pongee, coarse silk

8

筓 4300/J-X/M-X Nonstandard for 笄 4255.

箸 4301/J4824/M-X Nonstandard for 箸 4328.

箘 4302/J6430/M26147 簵 4303/J6431/M26157 KIN, GON small bamboo used for arrow shafts; arrow; bamboo sprout; dice.

箋 4304/J6435/M26122 牋 3527/J6030/M19849 SEN paper; label; letter; composition.

箚 4305/J6434/M26149 剳 511/J-X/M-X SATSU a retainer's written report to his lord.

箙 4306/J6439/M26148 FUKU. *ebira* quiver.

箕 4307/J4c27/M26143 KI winnowing device. *mi* winnow, winnowing fan, winnowing fork.

箒 4308/J6436/M26139 SŌ. *hōki* broom.

箜 4309/J6433/M26151 KŌ, KU. *kugo, kūgo* harp-like musical instrument.
15 篌 *kugo, kūgo* harp-like musical instrument

箆 4310/J4a4f/M26114 篦 4333/J6444/M26356 HEI. HAI. *hera* spatula. *no* arrow shaft; arrow-shaft bamboo.
12 棒 *berabō na* absurd, unreasonable, exorbitant; awful, terrible

箍 4311/J6432/M26130 KO. *taga* barrel hoop.
6 回 *tagamawa(shi)* rolling a hoop
15 緩 *taga (ga) yuru(mu)* weaken; lose interest (in a task)

箔 4312/J4773/M26142 BAKU, HAKU foil, leaf, tinsel, gilt.
5 打 *hakuu(chi)* goldbeater; the work of a goldbeater

9 屋 *hakuya* goldbeater, gilder

箏 4313 / J6437 / M26133 Sō a koto. *koto* long horizontal Japanese zither, a harp with 13 strings, a koto; lyre. *sōnokoto* a koto.

6 曲 *sōkyoku* koto music

12 琴 *sō (no) koto* a koto

箝 4314 / J642f / M26152 Kan. Ken. *su(geru)* insert (in a tube or hole); fit into; attach (a geta thong).

3 口 *kankō suru* muzzle, hush up, restrict liberty of speech. *kankō, kenkō* gagging, silencing

12 替 *su(ge)-kae(ru)* change (buttons, geta cords, etc.)

B **箇** 4315 / J3255 / M26116 Ka, Ko counter for things.

7 条 *kajō* items; errors; articles

条書 *kajōgaki* itemization, items

8 所 *kasho* place, spot, point, section, part, passage (in a book)

13 数 *kosū* number of articles

14 箇 *koko* one by one; individuals. *koko ni* individually, separately

箇別別 *koko-betsubetsu* each one separately

A **算** 4316 / J3b3b / M26146 San divining (block); calculation; number; abacus; plan; probability. *kazo(eru), san(suru)* number, count, calculate.

2 入 *sannyū* inclusion in the calculation

4 木 *sangi* divining block; calculating device

5 出 *sanshutsu* computation, calculation

用 *san'yō, sannyō* calculation, computation

用高 *san'yōdakai* stingy, close (in figuring)

用数字 *san'yō sūji* Arabic numerals

7 乱 *san (o) mida(su)* scatter in all directions

8 法 *sampō* arithmetic

定 *santei* calculation, estimate, assessment, amount

9 段 *sandan suru* try, contrive, manage

11 術 *sanjutsu* arithmetic

術平均 *sanjutsu heikin* arithmetical mean

術級数 *sanjutsu kyūsū* arithmetical progression

術家 *sanjutsuka* arithmetician

12 散 *san (o) chi(rasu)* scatter in all directions

筆 *sampitsu* writing and arithmetic

無 *sanna(shi)* countless

13 数 *sansū* calculation, computation; arithmetic, mathematics

置 *san (o) o(ku)* divine, foretell; calculate

14 暦 *sanreki* arithmetic and calendar studies

15 盤 *soroban* abacus; account

盤珠 *sorobandama* abacus beads; counting beads; account

盤勘定 *soroban kanjō* calculation on an abacus

A **管** 4317 / J3449 / M26162 Kan pipe, tube; (brush) holder; wind instrument. *kuda* pipe, tube; drunken talk.

3 下 *kanka* jurisdiction, control

4 区 *kanku* jurisdictional area; parish

内 *kannai* within the jurisdiction of

切器 *kanki(ri)ki* pipe cutter

5 玉 *kudatama* ancient cylindrical jewels

外 *kangai* outside the jurisdiction

主 *kanshu* head priest

6 守 *kanshu* custody and protection

7 見 *kanken* narrow view; view; personal views

状 *kanjō* tubular

8 長 *kanchō* superintendent priest (in shrines and temples)

制 *kansei* control

弦 *kangen* wind and string instruments; music

弦楽 *kangengaku* orchestra; orchestral music

弦楽器 *kangen gakki* wind and string instruments

10 流 *kudanaga(shi)* shooting logs down a stream

財人 *kanzainin* trustee, custodian, administrator, receiver

11 絃 *kangen* wind and string instruments; music

絃楽 *kangengaku* orchestra; orchestral music

絃楽器 *kangen gakki* wind and string instruments

理 *kanri* managing, administration, supervision, control
理人 *kanrinin* steward, manager, supervisor, executor, caretaker, trustee, steward
理下 *kanrika* under the supervision of
理図 *kanrizu* control chart
理法 *kanrihō* methods of administration, management
理価格 *kanri kakaku* managed price
理費 *kanrihi* administrative expense
理貿易 *kanri bōeki* government-managed trade
理職 *kanrishoku* management
12 掌 *kanshō* management, charge
13 楽 *kangaku* the music of wind instruments
楽器 *kangakki* wind instruments
14 領 *kanrei* governor-general. *kanryō* governor-general in the Muromachi period
管 *kudakuda(shii)* tedious, verbose; detailed
17 轄 *kankatsu* jurisdiction, control
轄官庁 *kankatsu kanchō* competent authorities
轄違 *kankatsuchiga(i)* lack of jurisdiction
轄権 *kankatsuken* jurisdiction

9

篏 4318 / J643d / M-X See 嵌 1497.

節 4319 / J-X / M-X **節** 4320 / J-X / M26243 See 節 4299.

箪 4321 / J433d / M-X Nonstandard for 簞 4357.

篌 4322 / J643c / M26272 Go.

篋 4323 / J643a / M26271 Kyō *hako* box, bamboo container.

篇 4324 / J4a53 / M26257 Hen volume, book; chapter, section, part; compilation, editing.

箭 4325 / J407d / M26193 Sen. *ya* arrow.

篁 4326 / J643b / M26249 Kō. *takamura* bamboo grove.

箴 4327 / J643e / M26214 Shin warning, counsel, precept; needle.
7 言 *shingen* proverb, maxim, warning

箸 4328 / J-X / M26224 **箸** 4301 / J4824 / M-X Do. Cho. Jaku. Chaku. *hashi* chopsticks.
13 置 *hashio(ki)* chopstick rest

篆 4329 / J643f / M26256 Ten seal-style characters.
6 字 *tenji* seal character
8 刻 *tenkoku* seal engraving
10 書 *tensho* seal characters (ancient forms)

B **範** 4330 / J484f / M26253 Han example, model, pattern; limit.
7 囲 *han'i* extent, scope, limits, sphere, range; purview
囲内 *han'inai* within the bounds
囲外 *han'igai* beyond the pale, beyond bounds
8 例 *hanrei* example
9 型 *hankei* (iron) mold
19 疇 *hanchū* category

A **箱** 4331 / J4822 / M26209 Sō. *hako* box, case, chest, bin, coffer, railway car.
2 入 *hakoi(ri)* boxed
入娘 *hakoi(ri) musume* innocent maiden, well-protected daughter
4 火鉢 *hako hibachi* boxed brazier
5 代 *hakodai* charge for a box
6 舟 *hakobune* an ark; (Noah's) ark
8 枕 *hako makura* box pillow
9 屋 *hakoya* boxmaker
型 *hakogata* coupé, limousine, closed car
10 庭 *hako niwa* miniature garden
師 *hakoshi* train thief
書 *hakoga(ki)* painter's or calligrapher's autograph on the box
馬車 *hako basha* closed carriage
根草 *hakonesō* maidenhair fern
11 梯子 *hakobashigo* staircase-cupboard combination

[13]詰 *hakozume* boxed, cased

10

篭 4332 / J4f36 / M26371 See 籠 4376.

篦 4333 / J6444 / M26356 See 箆 4310.

篢 4334 / J6442 / M26387 See 蓑 5143.

篠 4335 / J-X / M26328 See 篠 4352.

篥 4336 / J6445 / M26352 RIKI, RITSU, RICHI horn, flageolet.

篷 4337 / J644b / M26404 HŌ, BO. *toma* bamboo or reed awning. *fune* boat.

篳 4338 / J644a / M26393 HICHI, HITSU fence.

[16]篥 *hichiriki* double-reed instrument used in *Gagaku*

篩 4339 / J6441 / M26359 SHI. *furu(u)* sieve, sift, screen. *furui* sieve, sifter.

[4]分 *furu(i)-wa(keru)* screen, sieve, sift out

篝 4340 / J6440 / M26320 KŌ basket. *kagari* camp fire, fishing fire, beacon fire.

[4]火 *kagaribi* camp fire, fishing fire, beacon fire

[11]船 *kagaribune* boats fishing with lights

篡 4341 / J-X / M26330 **簒** 4345 / J5255 / M26490 SAN rob.

[5]立 *sanritsu suru* usurp the throne

[12]弑 *sanshii, sanshi* killing a ruler and usurping the throne

[14]奪 *sandatsu* usurpation

B **篤** 4342 / J4646 / M26344 TOKU. *atsu(i)* kind, cordial, fervent, affectionate; serious (illness). *toku to* deliberately, carefully, seriously.

[6]行 *tokkō* good deeds, goodness

[7]志 *tokushi* benevolence; zeal; volunteering

志家 *tokushika* volunteer, self-sacrificing person

[8]実 *tokujitsu* sincerity, faithfulness

学 *tokugaku* love of learning

[9]厚 *tokkō na* sincere, warmhearted

信 *tokushin* devotion

[13]農 *tokunō* conscientious farmer

A **築** 4343 / J435b / M26298 CHIKU. *kizu(ku)* build, construct.

[3]山 *tsukiyama* artificial miniature hill

上 *kizu(ki)-a(geru)* build up

[5]立 *kizu(ki)-ta(teru)* build up

[6]地 *tsukiji* reclaimed land. *tsuiji* a roofed mud wall

地塀 *tsuijibei* a roofed mud wall

[8]直 *kizu(ki)-nao(su)* repair, rebuild

[9]造 *chikuzō* building, construction

城 *chikujō* fortification; castle construction

[12]堤 *chikutei* embankment, banking

港 *chikkō, chikukō* harbor construction

[13]園 *chikuen* construction of a park or garden

[14]増 *kizu(ki)-ma(su)* build on to

11

簑 4344 / J6443 / M-X See 蓑 5143.

簒 4345 / J5255 / M26490 See 篡 4341.

篶 4346 / J644e / M26403 EN. *kurodake* black bamboo.

簍 4347 / J644d / M26456 RŌ coarsely woven bamboo basket.

簗 4348 / J644c / M-X (国字) *yana* weir, fish trap, fishpond.

簓 4349 / J6449 / M26494 (国字) *sasara* bamboo whisk; broken end of a bamboo stalk.

簀 4350 / J6447 / M26419 SAKU. *su* rough mat (of bamboo or reeds).

[3]子 *sunoko* portable slatted floor piece

6

[竹] 米糸缶网罒羊羽老耂而耒耳聿肉月臣自至臼舌舛舟艮色艸艹虍虫血行衣衤西

11

簇 4351 / J6448 / M26437 ZOKU. *muraga(ru)* crowd, flock, swarm.

5 生 *zokusei suru* (plants) grow in clusters; (animals) live in herds or flocks

出 *zokushutsu suru* spring up like mushrooms

篠 4352 / J3c44 / M-X **篠** 4335 / J-X / M26328 ZŌ. *shino* a small bamboo. *sasa* bamboo grass.

6 竹 *shinodake* small bamboo

8 突雨 *shinotsu(ku) ame* driving rain, cloudburst

11 笛 *shinobue* bamboo flute

12

簟 4353 / J6452 / M26510 TEN, DEN. *takemushiro* woven bamboo mat.

簣 4354 / J644f / M26524 KI, GI. *mokko, ajika* bamboo basket (for carrying earth).

簫 4355 / J6454 / M26560 SHŌ a *shō no fue*, a panpipe-like wind instrument.

簧 4356 / J6450 / M26541 KŌ flute reed.

簞 4357 / J-X / M26509 TAN bamboo rice basket.

11 笥 *tansu* chest of drawers, dresser, buffet, cupboard

笥預金 *tansu yokin* hoarded cash

A **簡** 4358 / J344a / M26520' **簡** 4359 / J-X / M26520 KEN, KAN brevity, simplicity. *fuda* tag, placard; nameplate; check; charm, (playing) card; tender, bid.

5 札 *kansatsu* wooden tag

古 *kanko na* simple and antique

6 朴 *kamboku* simplicity

7 抜 *kambatsu* selection

8 明 *kammei* brevity, conciseness

法 *kampō* simple method

易 *kan'i* simplicity, easiness

易化 *kan'ika* simplification

易住宅 *kan'i jūtaku* simple house, prefabricated house, Quonset hut

易保険 *kan'i hoken* post-office life insurance

易食堂 *kan'i shokudō* quick lunch

易旅館 *kan'i ryokan* cheap lodging house

易書簡 *kan'i shokan* letter card

易宿泊所 *kan'i shukuhakujo* cheap lodging house

易裁判所 *kan'i saibansho* police court

9 便 *kamben* simplicity; convenience; expediency

約 *kan'yaku* conciseness, brevity, simplification, abbreviation

勁 *kankei* strength in spite of small stature

要 *kan'yō na* brief and to the point

単 *kantan* brevity, simplicity

単服 *kantanfuku* women's light summer wear; utility dress

単着 *kantangi* women's light summer wear; utility dress

10 素 *kanso* simplicity

素化 *kansoka* simplification

11 略 *kanryaku* simplicity; brevity, conciseness; informality

12 短 *kantan* brevity, simplicity

15 潔 *kanketsu* brevity, conciseness, simplicity

閲 *kan'etsu suru* investigate; choose

閲点呼 *kan'etsu tenko* (ancient) periodic roll call of veterans

16 樸 *kamboku* simplicity

19 牘 *kandoku, kantoku* document, letter

13

籀 4360 / J645a / M26646 CHŪ, JU read; a style of calligraphy.

簷 4361 / J6453 / M26607 EN eaves.

簽 4362 / J6455 / M26614 SEN label; signature.

簸 4363 / J4876 / M26609 HA. *hi(ru)* winnow, fan.

B **簿** 4364 / J4a6d / M26623' BO. HAKU. *-bo* record book.

[10] 記 *boki* bookkeeping

簾 4365 / J4e7c / M26616 REN a screen. *sudare, su* bamboo screen, rattan blind.
[4] 戸 *sudo* reed door
[11] 屏風 *sudare byōbu* bamboo folding screen

14

旗 4366 / J6459 / M-X KI. *hata* flag, banner, pennant.

簪 4367 / J6451 / M26558 SHIN. *kanzashi* ornamental hairpin.

B 籍 4368 / J4052 / M26676 SEKI domiciliary register; membership.

籃 4369 / J6457 / M26640 RAN basket.
[11] 球 *rankyū* basketball

籌 4370 / J6456 / M26675 CHŪ plan.
[11] 略 *chūryaku* plan, scheme, policy, stratagem, plot, trick

15

籤 4371 / J645f / M-X See 籤 4378.

籔 4372 / J6458 / M26708 See 藪 5240.

籐 4373 / J645b / M26693 TŌ rattan, cane.
[11] 細工 *tōzaiku* rattan work
[12] 椅子 *tōisu* cane chair, rattan chair
[13] 蓆 *tōmushiro* rattan mat

16

籐 4374 / J645c / M26733 See 籐 4373.

籟 4375 / J645d / M26751 RAI rustling of the wind.

籠 4376 / J6446 / M26752 RŌ. *ko(mu)* be crowded; requiring (a lot of work). *ko(meru)* include; load (a gun); concentrate on; devote oneself to. *komo(ru)* seclude oneself, be confined in; be implied; be stuffy; be filled with (smoke). *kago* cage, coop; basket. *ko* basket, bamboo containers.
[4] 手 *kote* fencing gloves, gauntlet, forearm
[5] 目 *kagome* basket interstices; woven bamboo pattern
[6] 耳 *kagomimi* poor memory
[7] 抜 *kagonu(ke)* defrauding, swindling
[8] 居 *rōkyo* confinement (indoors)
枕 *kago makura* basket pillow
[9] 屋 *kagoya* basketmaker; basket shop
城 *rōjō* siege, confinement (indoors). *rōjō suru* be besieged
[11] 球 *rōkyū* basketball
[12] 絡 *rōraku suru* cajole, inveigle, entice

17

籥 4377 / J6460 / M26771 YAKU bamboo practice brush; three- or six- hole flute; lock.

籤 4378 / J645e / M26769 籤 4371 / J645f / M-X SEN *kuji* lottery, lot, raffle.
[4] 中 *kujiatu(ri)* winning in a lottery
引 *kujibi(ki)* drawing lots
[5] 札 *kuji fuda* lottery tickets
[8] 逃 *kujinoga(re)* elimination by lottery
[10] 弱 *kujiyowa(i)* unlucky in lotteries
[11] 運 *kujiun* one's luck in lotteries
強 *kujizuyo(i)* lucky in lotteries

19

籬 4379 / J6461 / M26803 RI. *magaki* rough-woven fence; bamboo hedge.

RAD. 米 119

Kome rice. At left: *kome hen*. Nickname: Rice.

A **米** 4380 J4a46 M26832 BEI. MAI *kome, yone* rice. *-Bei-* U.S.A. *bei-* rice. *mētoru* meter.

2 人 *Beijin* an American
4 仏 *Bei-Futsu* America and France
5 代 *komedai* rice money
加 *Bei-Ka* America and Canada
本土 *Beihondo* Stateside, the States, the American mainland
6 虫 *kome no mushi* rice weevil
州 *Beishū* the Americas
7 麦 *beibaku* rice and barley; grain
作 *beisaku* rice culture, rice crop
杉 *beisugi* cedar
材 *beizai* American timber
兵 *beihei* U.S. soldier; U.S. sailor
寿 *beiju* 88th birthday
利堅 *Meriken* American
利堅粉 *merikenko* wheat flour
8 国 *Beikoku* U.S.A.
使 *beishi* an American envoy
価 *beika* the price of rice
所 *komedokoro* rice-producing area
松 *beimatsu* Oregon pine, Douglas fir
英 *Bei-Ei* America and Britain
9 屋 *komeya* rice merchant
栂 *beitsuga* hemlock, hemlock spruce
独 *Bei-Doku* America and Germany
軍 *Beigun* U.S. armed forces
食 *beishoku* rice diet
食虫 *komeku(i)mushi* drone, idler
食鳥 *komeku(i)dori* bobolink
10 俵 *komedawara* straw rice bag
粉 *komeko, kome(no)ko* rice flour
納 *beinō* payment of taxes in rice
紙 *beishi* American paper; the American press
倉 *komegura* rice granary
案 *beian* American proposal
華 *Bei-Ka* America and China
11 粒 *kome tsubu, beiryū* a grain of rice
貨 *beika* American currency, U.S. dollar
商 *beishō* rice dealer
問屋 *komedonya* rice wholesaler
産 *beisan* rice production
産地 *kome (no) sanchi* rice-producing district
12 飯 *beihan, kome (no) meshi* boiled rice
13 塩 *beien* rice and salt; livelihood
搗 *kometsuki* polishing rice
資 *beishi* American capital
14 綿 *beimen* American (raw) cotton
語 *Beigo* Americanism, American English, American
誌 *beishi* American magazine
穀 *beikoku* rice
16 磨 *kometo(gi)* washing rice
噸 *beiton* short ton
17 檜 *beihinoki* spruce
糠 *kome nuka* rice bran
18 櫃 *komebitsu* rice bin; one's source of a living; breadwinner
騒動 *kome sōdō* rice riot
19 蘇 *Bei-So* America and the Soviet Union
20 艦 *beikan* American warship

2

籵 4381 J6462 M26837 (国字) *dekamētoru* decameter, 10 meters.

3

粂 4382 J3729 M26860 (国字) *kume* used in proper names.

粁 4383 J364e M26858 (国字) *kiromētoru* kilometer, 1000 meters.

籾 4384 J4c62 M26857 **籾** 4385 J-X M26853 (国字) *momi* unhulled rice.
11 殻 *momigara* chaff
14 摺 *momisuri* hulling rice

4

粔 4386 J6464 M-X Ko.

粍 4387 J4c30 M26881 (国字) *mirimētoru* millimeter, one-thousandth of a meter.

粃 4388 J6463 M26861 **秕** 4126 J633e M24958 HI. *shiina* empty grain husk; desiccated, unripe fruit

9 政 *hisei* misgovernment

B 粋 4389/J3f68/M26875 粹 4409/J646f/M26987 SUI purity, essence, pith, cream, pick, elite, choice; elegance; fashion; taste; gracefulness; considerateness. SAI. *iki* chic, style.

2 人 *suijin* refined man, romantic man, man about town
7 狂 *suikyō* raving drunkenness
8 事 *ikigoto* love intrigue, romance
9 美 *suibi* exquisite beauty

A 粉 4390/J4a34/M26872 FUN dust, powder. *ko, kona* flour, meal, powder. *deshimētoru* decimeter, $\frac{1}{10}$ meter.

5 末 *fummatsu* powder, dust
本 *fumpon* copy, reproduction
白粉 *kona oshiroi* face powder
石鹼 *kona sekken* powdered soap
6 米 *kogome* broken rice
7 状 *funjō* powder
8 乳 *funnyū* powdered milk
味噌 *kona miso* powdered bean paste
9 食 *funshoku* powdered food
屋 *konaya* flour mill, flour dealer
糾 *funkyū* disorder, entanglement, confusion
炭 *funtan* pulverized coal. *konazumi* pulverized charcoal
茶 *konacha* pulverized tea, powdered tea
砕 *funsai* pulverization, smashing, crushing
砕機 *funsaiki* crusher, pulverizer
10 粉 *konagona* in very small pieces
骨 *funkotsu* earnestness, diligence
骨砕身 *funkotsu-saishin suru* do one's very best
11 雪 *kona yuki* powder snow
13 飾 *funshoku* makeup, showy ornaments; embellishment
微塵 *kona mijin, komijin* smithereens, fragments
14 塵 *funjin* flour and dust; inconsequential things; mundane things
16 薬 *konagusuri, kogusuri* medicine powder
篩機 *konafuruiki* flour bolter
17 黛 *funtai* cosmetics

5

粕 4391/J4774/M26891 HAKU. *kasu* scrap, waste.

8 取 *kasuto(ri)* low-grade liquor
取雑誌 *kasuto(ri) zasshi* cheap magazine
14 漬 *kasuzuke* vegetables pickled in saké lees

B 粒 4392/J4e33/M26884 RYŪ grain; drop. *tsubu* grain, drop; counter for tiny particles.

3 子 *ryūshi* particle (of matter); corpuscle
7 状 *ryūjō no* granular
形 *tsubugata* a tablet (in medicine)
9 食 *ryūshoku* eating rice, rice diet
11 粒 *ryūryū to* assiduously, painstakingly, strenuously. *tsubutsubu no* lumpy, granulated
粒辛苦 *ryūryū-shinku no* strenuous, painstaking, assiduous
12 揃 *tsubuzoroi* uniformly good
14 選 *tsubuyori* the pick of the lot

B 粘 4393/J4734/M26901 黏 7050/J7356/M48007 NEN. *neba(ru)* be sticky, be glutinous, be greasy; persevere. *ne(ru)* knead. *neba(ri)* stickiness, viscosity; tenacity, perseverance. *neba(i), neba(tta)* sticky.

2 力 *nenryoku* tenacity, viscosity
3 土 *nendo, nebatsuchi* clay, slime
5 付 *nebatsu(ku)* be sticky, adhere to
6 気 *neba(ri)ke, neba(rik)ke* stickiness, viscosity; tenacity, perseverance
7 体 *nentai* waxy substance
8 性 *nensei* viscosity
泥 *nendei* slime
9 度 *nendo* viscosity
11 強 *neba(ri)zuyo(i)* tenacious, persevering
粘 *nebaneba suru* sticky, syrupy, gummy
液 *nen'eki* mucus, phlegm; slime
液質 *nen'ekishitsu no* phlegmatic
12 結 *nenketsu* coking, caking
着 *neba(ri)-tsu(ku)* be sticky, adhere to. *nenchaku* adhesion
着力 *nenchakuryoku* adhesive power, tenacity
13 滑 *nenkatsu na* greasy and slippery

稠 *nenchū* stickiness
14 膜 *nemmaku* mucous membrane
15 質 *nenshitsu* viscosity

5 B **粗** 4394 / J4146 / M26898 So roughness, coarseness; not fine; neglect; carelessness. *ara(i), ara(ppoi)* coarse, rough, rugged; loose (fabric); large (meshes). *ara* defect, flaw, blemish. *ara-* rough, coarse, natural, sparse, crude.

3 大 *sodai na* coarse, rough
大塵芥 *sodai gomi* large pieces of trash
4 方 *arakata* mostly, almost, roughly
毛布 *somōfu* duffel blanket
5 皮 *arakawa* raw hide, bark, husk
布 *sofu* coarse cloth, canvas, sackcloth. *aranuno* gunny, sacking, sackcloth
末 *somatsu na* crude, rough, plain, humble, shabby; careless, rude. *somatsu ni suru* waste
仕上 *arashiage* rough work, roughing
目 *zarame* coarse, brown crystallized sugar
目鑢 *arame yasuri* rasp
6 衣 *soi* coarse clothing, poor garb
朶 *soda* faggot, brushwood
8 金 *aragane* ore
放 *sohō* carelessness, fault, oversight
板 *araita* rough lumber
服 *sofuku* plain dress, poor clothing
肴 *sokō* simple food
忽 *sokotsu* carelessness, rashness, absent-mindedness; blunder, fault, error
忽者 *sokotsumono* careless person, absent-mindedness
9 食 *soshoku* coarse fare, plain food, poor diet
造 *sozō* crude manufacture; crude articles
拵 *aragoshira(e)* spadework, preliminary work
拭 *arabuki* rough wiping
研 *aratogi* rough grinding
品 *soshina, sohin* trifling gift; inferior goods
茶 *socha* coarse tea
相 *sosō* carelessness, oversight
相火 *sosōbi* accidental fire
10 起 *araoko(shi)* rough ground-breaking
酒 *soshu* cheap saké
砥 *arato* grindstone, coarse whetstone
莚 *aramushiro* loosely-woven mat
11 彫 *arabori* rough carving
探 *arasaga(shi)* faultfinding
略 *soryaku na, zonzai na* crude, rough, plain, humble, shabby; careless, rude
野 *soya na* rustic, rude, vulgar
密 *somitsu* roughness and fineness
笨 *sohon* crudeness, roughness
菓 *soka* cakes, refreshments
悪 *soaku na* coarse, crude, inferior
悪品 *soakuhin* crude articles, inferior goods
12 遠 *soen* estrangement, neglect (to write), long silence
飯 *sohan* plain meal
筋 *arasuji* outline, summary, synopsis
13 鉋 *araganna* jack plane
鉱 *sokō* unprocessed ore
塗 *aranu(ri)* first plaster coat, roughly plastered walls
14 漉 *aragoshi* rough filter; rough filtering
銅 *sodō* unrefined copper
雑 *sozatsu na* coarse, rough, rude
製 *sosei* crude manufacture
製品 *soseihin* crude articles
製塩 *soseien* coarse salt
製糖 *soseitō* unrefined sugar
製濫造 *sosei-ranzō* mass production of poor articles
15 縫 *aranu(i)* basting, tacking
暴 *sobō na* wild, rude, violent, hard, fierce
16 積 *arazu(mori)* rough estimate
糖 *sotō* raw sugar
餐 *sosan* plain meal

6

粭 4395 / J6466 / M-X (国字) *sukumo* chaff, rice hulls.

糀 4396 / J6468 / M-X Jɪ.

粡 4397 / J6469 / M26928 Tō unpolished rice. *chimaki* rice dumpling wrapped in bamboo leaves.

粢 4398 / J6467 / M26932 SHI (cereal) grain; millet.

粤 4399 / J6465 / M26935 ETSU alas.

B **粧** 4400 / J3e51 / M26945 SHŌ *yosōu* adorn (one's person).

粨 4101 / J646a / M26949 (国字) *hekutomētoru* hectometer, 100 meters.

粥 4402 / J3421 / M26938 IKU. JUKU. *kayu, kai* rice gruel.

9 食 *kayushoku* a meal of rice gruel
13 腹 *kayubara* living on rice gruel

粟 4403 / J3040 / M26922 ZOKU. *awa* millet.

5 立 *awada(tsu)* have goose flesh (from cold or horror)
9 畑 *awabata* millet field
11 粒 *awatsubu, zokuryū* millet grain
12 粥 *awagayu* millet gruel
14 餅 *awamochi* millet *mochi,* millet rice-cake
15 穂 *awabo* heads of millet

7

粮 4404 / J646e / M26952 See **糧** 4426.

粱 4405 / J646d / M26962 RYŌ a kind of large-grained millet.

糀 4406 / J6471 / M27013 (国字) *kōji* koji, malted rice, yeast.

粲 4407 / J646c / M26966 SAN bright.

12 然 *sanzen* brilliance; smiling with rows of white teeth showing

粳 4408 / J646b / M26967 **秔** 4127 / J-X / M24954 KŌ. *uruchi* ordinary rice.

12 黍 *urukibi* nonglutinous millet

8

粹 4409 / J646f / M26987 See **粋** 4389.

粽 4410 / J6470 / M26993 SŌ. *chimaki* rice dumpling wrapped in bamboo leaves.

A **精** 4411 / J403a / M26997' SHŌ. SEI spirit, ghost, fairy; energy, vitality; white rice; details; excellence; purity; skill. *shira(geru)* refine, polish. *kuwa(shii)* full, detailed, minute, accurate; versed in, well informed.

1 一 *seiitsu* purity
一杯 *seiippai* with all one's might
2 入 *sei (o) i(reru)* work earnestly
力 *seiryoku* energy, vigor, vitality
力家 *seiryokka, seiryokuka* energetic person, go-getter
3 子 *seishi* sperm
4 分 *seibun* nourishment; energy, strength
5 巧 *seikō na* elaborate, exquisite, delicate
出 *seida(su)* exert oneself, be diligent, work hard
白 *seihaku* refining, polishing
白米 *seihakumai* polished rice
白所 *seihakusho* rice mill
白糖 *seihakutō* refined sugar
6 肉 *seiniku* fresh meat
虫 *seichū* spermatozoa
気 *seiki* energy, spirit; essence
米 *seimai* white rice
米所 *seimaisho* rice mill
7 麦 *seibaku* cleaning; cleaned wheat or barley
励 *seirei* diligence; industry
妙 *seimyō na* fine, exquisite; subtle
兵 *seihei, seibyo* picked troops
8 金 *seikin* refined gold
舎 *shōja* temple, monastery, convent
限根限 *seikagi(ri)-konkagi(ri)* with all one's might
油 *seiyu* refined oil
油所 *seiyujo* oil refinery
9 通 *seitsū suru* be versed in, be conversant with, be posted on
洗 *seisen* scouring
査 *seisa* careful investigation
度 *seido* accuracy
神 *seishin* mind, spirit, soul, heart; intention, motive; the spirit (of the thing)
神力 *seishinryoku* mental power
神文化 *seishin bunka* moral culture
神主義 *seishin shugi* idealism, spiritualism

神主義者 *seishin shugisha* idealist, spiritualist
神分析 *seishin bunseki* psychoanalysis
神分析学 *seishin bunsekigaku* psychoanalysis
神分裂症 *seishin bunretsushō* schizophrenia
神外科 *seishingeka* psychosurgery
神生物学 *seishin seibutsugaku* psychobiology
神生理学 *seishin seirigaku* psychophysiology
神年齢 *seishin nenrei* mental age
神身体医学 *seishin shintai igaku* psychosomatic medicine
神医学 *seishin igaku* psychiatry
神労働 *seishin rōdō* mental work
神状態 *seishin jōtai* mental condition
神的 *seishinteki* mental, spiritual
神的援助 *seishinteki enjo* moral support
神物理学 *seishin butsurigaku* psychophysics
神界 *seishinkai* mental world
神科 *seishinka* psychiatry
神科学 *seishin kagaku* mental science
神病 *seishimbyō* insanity, mental disease
神病学 *seishimbyōgaku* psychiatry
神病学者 *seishinbyō gakusha* psychiatrist
神病院 *seishin byōin* mental hospital, insane asylum
神病理学 *seishin byōrigaku* psychopathology
神修養 *seishin shūyō* mental training
神異状 *seishin ijō* mental derangement
神感応 *seishin kannō* telepathy
神障害 *seishin shōgai* mental derangement
神衛生 *seishin eisei* mental therapy
神論 *seishinron* idealism; spiritualism
神論者 *seishinronja* idealist; spiritualist
神錯乱 *seishin sakuran* delirium
神薄弱 *seishin hakujaku* weak-mindedness
神薄弱児 *seishin hakujakuji* mentally handicapped child
神療法 *seishin ryōhō* psychotherapy
神療養所 *seishin ryōyōjo* mental hospital
10 悍 *seikan na* intrepid, fierce
根 *seikon* energy, vitality
酒 *seishu* refined saké
粉 *seifun* fine powder
粋 *seisui* purity; unselfishness; clear weather
華 *seika* essence; brilliance
進 *shōjin* concentration, diligence, devotion; purification; abstinence
進日 *shōjimbi* day of abstinence from flesh food
進料理 *shōjin ryōri* vegetarian diet, vegetarian food
進揚 *shōjin'a(ge)* vegetable tempura, deep-fried vegetables
進落 *shōjin'o(chi), shōjin'oto(shi)* first meat after fasting
11 液 *seieki* semen, sperm
粗 *seiso* fineness or coarseness
細 *seisai* minuteness, precision, accuracy
彩 *seisai* luster, brilliance; vividness
巣 *seisō* seminal glands
密 *seimitsu* precision, accuracy; minuteness
密工業 *seimitsu kōgyō* precision-machine industry
密科学 *seimitsu kagaku* exact sciences
密計器 *seimitsu keiki* precision gauge
密機械 *seimitsu kikai* precision instruments
密爆撃 *seimitsu bakugeki* precision bombing
12 勤 *seikin* diligence, good attendance
13 解 *seikai* detailed commentary
鉄 *seitetsu* refined iron
義 *seigi* exact meaning; detailed exposition
農 *seinō* industrious farmer
14 精 *seizei* to the utmost, as far as possible; at most; at best
読 *seidoku* careful reading, discriminate reading
銀 *seigin* refined silver
銅 *seidō* refined copper
管 *seikan* seminal duct
魂尽 *seikontsu(kiru)* lose all one's energy
選 *seisen* careful selection
選品 *seisenhin* select goods
練 *seiren* refining, smelting, tempering
練剤 *seirenzai* scouring agent
算 *seisan* exact calculation, accurate

account; adjustment; settlement of accounts
算所 *seisanjo* fare-adjustment office
製 *seisei* careful manufacture; refining
製所 *seiseijo* refinery
製油 *seiseiyu* refined oil
製法 *seiseihō* refining process
製品 *seiseihin* refined article; finished goods
製糖 *seiseitō* refined sugar
15 撰 *seisen* careful preparation
確 *seikaku* accuracy, precision
鋭 *seiei na* very powerful; highly efficient (weapons). *seiei* picked (troops)
霊 *seirei* spirit, soul (of the deceased). *shōryō* spirits of the dead, spirit visitor
霊崇拝 *seirei sūhai* animism
霊崇拝者 *seirei sūhaisha* animist
霊説 *seireisetsu* animism
16 緻 *seichi na* nice, fine, minute, subtle, delicate, exquisite, elaborate
糖 *seitō* sugar refining; refined sugar
糖所 *seitōjo* sugar refinery
錬 *seiren* refining, smelting
錬所 *seirenjo* refinery, smelter
18 髄 *seizui* essence, pith, spirit, soul, essentials, core, kernel, the lifeblood
22 嚢 *seinō* seminal vesicle

9

粯 4412 / J6473 / M27014 JIN a dish of rice mixed with hot soup.

糎 4413 / J4138 / M27057 (国字) *senchimētoru* centimeter, one-hundredth of a meter.

粽 4414 / J6472 / M27023 JŪ mix.
12 飯 *katemeshi* rice mixed with whatever is available

糊 4415 / J3852 / M27037 KO. KOTSU. *nori* paste, glue; starch; sizing.
2 入 *norii(re)* paste container
3 口 *kokō* bare existence, livelihood, living on others
5 目 *norime* starching
付 *noritsu(ke)* starching; pasting
8 板 *noriita* paste-making board
刷毛 *noribake* paste brush
11 張 *noriba(ri)* pasting, starching
12 壺 *nori tsubo* paste pot
13 塗 *koto suru* patch up, gloss over

10

糢 4416 / J6477 / M27116 See 模 2825.

糓 4417 / J-X / M27067 See 穀 4157.

糘 4418 / J6474 / M-X (国字) *sukumo* chaff, rice hulls.

糒 4419 / J6475 / M27065 BI. HAI. *hoshii, hoshiii* dried boiled rice.

糖 4420 / J457c / M27070 TŌ sugar.
A
4 化 *tōka* turning to sugar
分 *tōbun* sugar content
6 衣 *tōi* sugar coating
衣錠 *tōijō* sugar-coated pill
7 尿病 *tōnyōbyō* diabetes
8 乳 *tōnyū* sweetened condensed milk
11 菓 *tōka* sweets, candy
13 楓 *tōfū* sugar maple
業 *tōgyō* sugar industry
14 蜜 *tōmitsu* molasses
15 質 *toshitsu* sugariness, saccharinity
18 類 *tōrui* sugars

11

糝 4421 / J-X / M27101 SHIN, SAN rice grain.
10 粉 *shinko* rice flour, rice-flour dough

糜 4422 / J6476 / M27097 BI be inflamed.
21 爛 *biran* inflammation, erosion of skin or mucous membranes
爛性 *biransei* irritating, poisonous (gas)

糟 4423 / J416c / M27104 SŌ. *kasu* dregs, grounds, refuse, sediment, scum, dross.
8 取 *kasuto(ri)* low-grade liquor
11 粕 *sōhaku* lees, dregs, leavings
17 糠 *sōkō* humble living

糠妻 *sōkō (no) tsuma* a wife married in poverty, a faithful companion

糠 4424 / J3947 / M27105 Kō. *nuka* rice bran.

4 中 *kōchū* in rice bran
8 雨 *nukaame* drizzle
油 *nuka abura* rice-bran oil
味噌 *nuka miso* salted rice bran paste (for pickling)
味噌漬 *nukamisozuke* vegetables pickled in rice-bran paste
10 悦 *nuka yoroko(bi)* premature rejoicing
12 喜 *nuka yoroko(bi)* premature rejoicing
13 働 *nukabatara(ki)* fruitless effort

糞 4425 / J4a35 / M27102 Fun excrement. *kuso* feces, excrement, droppings.

2 力 *kusojikara* brute force, great strength
3 土 *fundo* loose dirt, black earth; dirt, filth
7 尿 *funnyō* excreta, feces and urine
8 味噌 *kusomiso* sweeping condemnation
9 便 *fumben* excrement, night soil, stools
度胸 *kusodokyō* foolhardiness, reckless bravery
10 骨 *kusobone* needless exertion
勉強 *kusobenkyō* cramming
真面目 *kusomajime* absurd seriousness
12 壺 *kuso tsubo* night-soil receptacle
塚 *funzuka* dunghill
落着 *kusoo(chi)tsu(ki) no* provokingly calm
13 塊 *funkai* stools
溜 *kusodame* manure tank
詰 *funzuma(ri)* constipation

12

B **糧** 4426 / J4e48 / M27132 **粮** 4404 / J646e / M26952 Ryō. Rō. *kate* food, provisions, bread.

9 食 *ryōshoku* provisions, food, victuals, rations
10 秣 *ryōmatsu* provisions and fodder
11 道 *ryōdō* supply of provisions

14

糲 4427 / J647a / M27181 Rei unpolished rice.

糯 4428 / J6479 / M27173 Da. *mochigome* glutinous rice.

6 米 *mochigome* glutinous rice

16

糴 4429 / J647b / M27191 Teki, Jaku buy (grains). *kaiyone* purchased grain.

19

糶 4430 / J647c / M27207 Chō. *seri* auction.

3 下 *serisa(ge)* an auction in which the price is gradually lowered until a buyer is found
7 売 *seriu(ri)* auction

RAD. 糸 120

Ito thread. At left: *ito hen.* Nickname: Long Thread (cf. Rad. 52).

A **糸** 4431 / J3b65 / M27221 **絲** 4474 / J652f / M27448 Shi thread; one ten-thousandth of a hair. *ito* thread, yarn; gut; string (of a violin); (fish) line.

2 入 *itoi(ri)* cotton-silk mixture
3 口 *itoguchi* thread end; beginning; clue
4 切歯 *itoki(ri)ba* eyetooth, canine tooth
5 瓜 *hechima* snake gourd
目 *itome* fine line; kite string; thread weight
6 竹 *itotake, shichiku* musical instruments; music
7 車 *itoguruma* spinning wheel
杉 *itosugi* cypress
状 *shijō no* thready
8 雨 *itosame* fine rain
底 *itozoko* bottom rim line (of porcelain)
価 *shika* price of thread; price of raw silk
物 *itomono* haberdashery
取 *itoto(ri)* silk reeling, silk spinning
9 屋 *itoya* thread and yarn shop; raw silk merchant
柳 *itoyanagi* weeping willow
巻 *itomaki* spool, bobbin, reel; beam (in weaving); turning peg

巻鱏 *itomaki ei* manta ray
10 屑 *itokuzu* waste thread, ravelings
捌 *itosabaki* playing a stringed instrument
桜 *itozakura* drooping cherry
11 遊 *itoyū* shimmering of heated air
釣 *itozu(ri)* line fishing
毫 *shigō* infinitesimal quantity, a hair, a thread, a tiny bit
偏景気 *itohen keiki* textile boom
12 硝子 *itogarasu* spun glass
道 *itomichi* samisen training; fishline or thread guide
13 蒟蒻 *itogonnyaku* devil's-tongue noodles
15 撚 *itoyori* twining
16 鋸 *itonoko* scroll saw; jeweler's saw
19 繰 *itoku(ri)* reeling, filature; spinner; reel
20 蘭 *itoran* thready orchid

1

糺 4432 / J647d / M27222 See **糾** 4438.

A **系** 4433 / J374f / M27223 Kei system; lineage; faction, group; zone; corollary; connection.
6 列 *keiretsu* order, succession
列化 *keiretsuka suru* put in order, systematize
7 図 *keizu* genealogy, pedigree
図学 *keizugaku* genealogy (the study)
12 統 *keitō* system; geological formation; lineage, ancestry
統的 *keitōteki* systematic
統神学 *keitō shingaku* systematic theology
統樹 *keitōju* genealogical tree
19 譜 *keifu* genealogy, lineage

2

糾 4434 / J-X / M27227 See **糾** 4438.

3

紂 4435 / J6521 / M27239 Chū. Jū a crupper.

紆 4436 / J647e / M27244 U crouch.

6 曲 *ukyoku suru* meander
7 余 *uyo* meandering; beating around the bush; abundant talent
余曲折 *uyo-kyokusetsu* meandering; complications; vicissitudes

A **級** 4437 / J3569 / M27258' **級** 4442 / J-X / M27294 Kyū grade, class, rank; steps; decapitated head.
4 友 *kyūyu* classmate
5 外 *kyūgai* offgrade; below par
7 別 *kyūbetsu* grading
8 長 *kyūchō* head of the class, monitor
13 数 *kyūsū* series or progression (in math)

B **糾** 4438 / J356a / M-X **糾** 4434 / J-X / M27227 **糺** 4432 / J647d / M27222
Kyū. *tada(su)* ask, demand, question; investigate, ascertain, verify. *azana(u)* twist (rope).
6 合 *kyūgō suru* rally, muster
8 明 *kyūmei* arraignment; searching examination
11 問 *kyūmon* cross-examination; arraignment
12 弾 *kyūdan* impeachment, censure
13 罪 *kyūzai* investigating a crime

A **紀** 4439 / J352a / M27234 Ki account, narrative, history, annals, geological period.
4 元 *kigen* era, epoch; imperial era; A.D., C.E.
元前 *kigenzen* B.C., B.C.E
元後 *kigengo* A.D., C.E.
元節 *Kigensetsu* Empire Day, anniversary of Emperor Jimmu's Accession (Feb. 11)
6 伝体 *kidentai* biographical history
行 *kikō* travelogue
行文 *kikōbun* travelogue
8 念 *kinen* commemoration, remembrance
9 律 *kiritsu* regulations; order; discipline; system; regularity
要 *kiyō* memoirs, bulletin

A **約** 4440 / J4c73 / M27242 Yaku promise, vow; approximately; abridgment. *yaku(suru)* promise; economize. *tsuzu(maru)* shrink; be summarized. *tsuzu(meru)* condense, reduce, shorten, curtail, abridge; economize. *tsuzu(mari)* conclusion. *tsuzu(mayakana)* neat and small, modest, unpretentious; concise; frugal.

4 手 *yakute* promissory note
日 *yakujitsu* appointment day
文 *yakubun suru* summarize, condense
分 *yakubun* reduction of a fraction to lowest terms
7 言 *yakugen* contraction; summary
束 *yakusoku* pledge, promise; appointment, date; contract, agreement, bargain, betrothal, covenant; condition; convention, rule, destiny
束手形 *yakusoku tegata* promissory note
束事 *yakusokugoto* promise, engagement, pledge
8 定 *yakujō* promise, agreement, contract
定書 *yakujōsho* written contract, agreement
定済 *yakujōzu(mi)* sold; promised; engaged
12 款 *yakkan* stipulation, agreement, article
13 数 *yakusū* a measure; a divisor
14 説 *yakusetsu* summary
15 諾 *yakudaku suru* promise and be responsible for
論 *yakuron* summary

A **紅** 4441 / J3948 / M27243 Gu. Ku. Kō red, crimson. *beni* red, crimson; rouge, lipstick. *kurenai* deep red, crimson. *momi* red silk cloth.

1 一点 *kōitten* one red flower in the foliage; sole woman in a men's party; a touch of color
4 毛 *kōmō* red hair
毛人 *kōmōjin* European, foreigner
5 生姜 *beni shōga* red pickled ginger
玉 *kōgyoku* ruby, carbuncle (gem); Jonathan apple
玉髄 *kōgyokuzui, benigyokuzui* carnelian, sardius, sard
白 *kōhaku* red and white
白粉 *beni-oshiroi* rouge and powder
6 色 *kōshoku* red
血 *kōketsu* blood, red blood
灯 *kōtō* red light; red lantern
灯巷 *kōtō (no) chimata* red-light district
8 炎 *kōen* red blazes
宝玉 *kōhōgyoku* ruby
9 革 *benigawa* red leather
海 *Kōkai* Red Sea
茶 *kōcha* black tea
染 *benizo(me)* red cloth
10 唇 *kōshin* red lips
梅 *kōbai* red-blossom plum tree
涙 *kōrui* tears of blood; tears of a beautiful woman; dew on the flowers
粉 *beniko* powdered rouge. *kōfun* rouge and powder
脂 *kōshi* rouge
差指 *benisa(shi)yubi* ring finger, third finger
11 殻 *benigara* Indian red, red-ocher rouge, red oxide of iron
12 斑 *kōhan* red spots (on the skin), erythema
裙 *kōkun* scarlet border; beautiful geisha
葉 *kōyō* fall colors. *momiji* maple; autumnal foliage; venison
葉狩 *momijiga(ri)* viewing autumn leaves
葉葉 *momijiba* scarlet maple leaves
13 楼 *kōrō* red-lacquered building; brothel
煙 *kōen* scarlet smoke
絹 *momi* red silk (cloth)
蓮 *guren* red lotus flower
蓮焔 *guren (no) honō* roaring flames
14 塵 *kōjin* clouds of dust; the dust of a busy city; this world's troubles
閨 *kōkei* bedroom of a beautiful woman
榴石 *kōryūseki* carbuncle (gem)
15 潮 *kōchō suru* blush, redden, be rosy; be flushed with drink; menstruate
熱 *kōnetsu* red hot temperature
16 燄 *kōen* red blazes, solar prominences
縞瑪瑙 *beni shimamenō* sardonyx
17 鮭 *benizake* red salmon, sockeye
18 顔 *kōgan* rosy cheeks, ruddy face
23 鱒 *beni masu* red trout, blueback salmon, sockeye

4

級 4442 / J-X / M27294 See 級 4437.

紕 4443 / J6523 / M27279 Hi edge decoration; decorate; mistake.

紜 4444 / J6522 / M27296 Un disarray, disorder, confusion.

紘 4445 J3949 M27289 Kō large.

紗 4446 J3c53 M27287 SA. SHA gauze, gossamer.

紊 4447 J6524 M27261 BIN, BUN disturb, throw into confusion.
7 乱 *bunran, binran* disorder, confusion

紐 4448 J4933 M27268 CHŪ. JŪ. *himo* string, cord, braid, lace, band, tape, strap, thong, ribbon; restrictions, conditions.
5 付 *himotsu(ki)* encumbrance, strings, conditions
7 状 *chūjō* string shape
9 革 *himokawa* strap, flat thong
10 帯 *jūtai, chūtai* band, bond, tie
13 解 *himoto(ku)* read, peruse

B **索** 4449 J3a77 M27306 SAKU rope, cord. *tsuna* rope, cord, string, line, hawser, cable; morality. *moto(meru)* search for.
4 引 *sakuin* index
7 条 *sakujō* cable, rope
条鉄道 *sakujō tetsudō* cable railway
8 具 *sakugu* rigging, gear, tackle
10 莫 *sakubaku(taru)* desolate, bleak, dreary
11 道 *sakudō* overhead freight-carrying cable
12 然 *sakuzen(taru)* dry, desolate
15 敵 *sakuteki* searching for the enemy

B **紡** 4450 J4b42 M27305 Bō. *tsumu(gu)* spin, make yarn.
4 毛 *bōmō* carded wool
16 機 *bōki* spinning machine
錘 *bōsui, tsumu* spindle
17 績 *bōseki* spinning
績工 *bōsekikō* spinner
績工場 *bōseki kōjō* spinning mill
績業 *bōsekigyō* spinning industry
18 織 *bōshoku* spinning and weaving
織機 *bōshokuki* spinning and weaving machinery

B **紋** 4451 J4c66 M27262 MON crest; (textile) figures.
4 日 *mombi* holiday
切型 *monki(ri)gata no* conventional, hackneyed, stereotyped
5 付 *montsu(ki)* crested kimono
6 羽二重 *mon habutae* figured habutae silk
7 形 *mongata* crest design
8 所 *mondokoro* crest
服 *mompuku* crested kimono
11 章 *monshō* crest; coat of arms
章学 *monshōgaku* heraldry
14 様 *mon'yō* crest pattern
15 標 *monjirushi* armorial bearings
17 縮緬 *mon chirimen* figured crepe
18 織 *mon'o(ri)* figured textiles

B **紛** 4452 J4a36 M27295 FUN. *magi(reru), magu(reru)* be mistaken for, be confused with; go astray; be diverted from. *magi(rawasu), magi(rasu)* divert, distract; beguile; evade; conceal. *maga(u)* be mistaken for; become confused. *magi(rawashii)* misleading, ambiguous. *magi(remonai)* obvious, certain. *-magi(re) ni* in a fit of (anger); under the influence of (alcohol).
4 込 *magi(re)-ko(mu), magu(re)-ko(mu)* get lost with; disappear in (the crowd)
方無 *mago(u)katana(ki)* unmistakable, evident, authentic
5 失 *funshitsu* loss
6 当 *magu(re)ata(ri)* lucky hit
争 *funsō* dispute, quarrel, complications
7 乱 *funran* disorder, confusion, entanglement
8 易 *magi(re)yasu(i)* ambiguous, misleading
9 糾 *funkyū* complication, entanglement, confusion
10 紛 *funpun* confusedly, pell-mell
12 然 *funzen* confusion, complications
13 飾 *funshoku* makeup, showy ornaments; embellishment
18 擾 *funjō* disorder, uproar, agitation, complications, trouble
20 議 *fungi* dissension, controversy, dispute

A **納** 4453 J473c M27264 Nō. Tō. NA. *osa(meru)* obtain, reap; dedicate, consecrate; pay; supply; store; finish;

collect; restore; replace; accept (a present); bury; gather; rally (troops); sheathe (the sword). *osa(maru)* be paid; be restored; stay (in the stomach); look composed; be contented; be satisfied; be settled. *osa(mari)* end, settlement, conclusion. *osa(me)* tax; the end.

2 入 *nōnyū* payment; delivery
入後 *nōnyūgo* after payment
4 戸 *nando* closet, back room, storeroom
戸色 *nando iro* grayish blue
5 札 *nōsatsu* pilgrim's card (left at temple)
本 *nōhon* presentation copy; censor's copy
付 *nōfu* payment, delivery
付金 *nōfukin* contribution
6 返 *osa(mari)-kae(ru)* be satisfied with; be in one's element; be unmoved, be cool
会 *nōkai* the last meeting (of the period)
7 豆 *nattō* fermented soy beans
8 金 *nōkin* payment; money due; money paid
所 *nassho* tax office, temple office
杯 *nōhai* the last cup
受 *nōju* receipt, acceptance
采 *nōsai* betrothal gift
9 屋 *naya* shed, barn
品 *nōhin* delivery; delivered goods
10 骨 *nōkotsu* depositing the ashes (of the dead)
骨堂 *nōkotsudō* ossuary, crypt
11 得 *nattoku* assent, agreement, consent, compliance
涼 *nōryō* enjoying the cool of the evening
12 棺 *nōkan* placing in the coffin
期 *nōki* payment date, delivery date
税 *nōzei* tax payment
税者 *nōzeisha* taxpayer
税額 *nōzeigaku* amount of one's taxes

A **純** 4454 / J3d63 / M27277 JUN purity, innocence; net (profit). *jun na* pure, innocent, chaste, natural, genuine.

1 一 *jun'itsu* purity, genuineness, homogeneity, uniformity
4 心 *junshin* purity, sincerity
毛 *jummō* all-wool
化 *junka* purification
文学 *jumbungaku* pure literature
日本風 *jun-Nihonfū* pure Japanese style
分 *jumbun* fineness
分度 *jumbundo* fineness
5 白 *jumpaku* pure white
乎 *junko no* pure, sheer, unalloyed
正 *junsei na* pure, genuine
正科学 *junsei kagaku* pure science
6 朴 *jumboku* simplicity and honesty
血 *junketsu no* purebred, thoroughbred
血種 *junkesshu* pure breed
7 利 *junri* net profit
良 *junryō* pure, genuine
8 金 *junkin* pure gold, solid gold
忠 *junchū* unselfish loyalty
国産 *junkokusan* an all-Japanese product
所得 *junshotoku* net income
9 度 *jundo* purity
美 *jumbi* unalloyed beauty
重量 *junjūryō* net weight
10 真 *junshin* purity, sincerity
粋 *junsui* purity, genuineness
粋主義 *junsui shugi* purism (in art)
益 *jun'eki* clear profit
益金 *jun'ekikin* clear profit
11 黒 *junkoku* jet black
情 *junjō* pure heart; naïveté; self-sacrificing devotion
理 *junri* pure reason, scientific principle
理論 *junriron* rationalism
12 然 *junzen(taru)* pure, sheer, veritable, absolute, perfect
13 損 *junson* complete loss
絹 *junken* pure silk
鉄 *juntetsu* malleable iron
14 種 *junshu* thoroughbred
綿 *jummen* all-cotton
銀 *jungin* pure silver, solid silver
15 潔 *junketsu* purity, integrity, innocence
潔教育 *junketsu kyōiku* education in sexual morality

A **紙** 4455 / J3b66 / M27293 SHI *kami* paper.

1 一重 *kami hitoe* tiny crack; something very thin; very slight difference
2 入 *kamii(re)* purse, wallet
3 子 *kamiko* paper garment
上 *shijō de* on paper; by letter; in the newspaper or magazine
上投票 *shijō tōhyō* straw vote
4 片 *shihen* piece of paper
切 *kamiki(re)*, *kamigi(re)* piece of paper. *kamiki(ri)* paper knife; paper cutter

5 札 *kami fuda* tag, label
包 *kamizutsumi* paper package
芝居 *kami shibai* picture-story show
白粉 *kami oshiroi* face-powder paper
石盤 *kami sekiban* paper slate
石鹸 *kami sekken* soap paper
6 灯 *shitō* paper-enclosed light
7 折 *kamio(ri)* paper folding
花 *kamibana* paper flowers
8 函 *kamibako* carton
価 *shika* price of paper
表紙 *kamibyōshi* paper cover
9 面 *shimen* (newspaper) space; letter; newspaper
屋 *kamiya* paper store, paper mill
挟 *kamibasami* paper clip
草 *kamigusa* papyrus
型 *shikei* stereotype
背 *shihai* back of the paper; (reading) between the lines
巻 *kamimaki* cigarette
巻煙草 *kamimaki tabako* cigarette
10 紐 *kami himo* paper twine
差 *kamisashi* paper feeding (in printing)
屑 *kamikuzu* waste paper
屑拾 *kamikuzuhiro(i)* ragpicker
屑買 *kamikuzuka(i)* ragman
屑籠 *kamikuzu kago* wastebasket
11 魚 *shimi, shigyo* clothes moth, silverfish, bookworm
帳 *shichō* paper mosquito net
張 *kamiha(ri)* papering
捻 *koyori* twisted-paper string
袋 *kamibukuro, kambukuro* paper sack or bag
細工 *kamizaiku* making articles out of paper (by hand)
12 幅 *shifuku* paper width
絵 *kamie* picture drawn on paper
13 数 *shisū* number of pages
障子 *kami shōji, kami sōji* translucent paper door
鉄砲 *kamideppō* popgun
14 漉 *kamisu(ki)* papermaking
製 *kamisei* made of paper
鳶 *ikanobo(ri), ika* (flying) kite
15 撚 *koyori* twisted-paper string
箱 *kamibako* carton
幣 *shihei* paper money
質 *shishitsu* quality of paper
器 *shiki* paper articles, paper container
縄 *kami nawa* paper string
16 縒 *koyori, kamiyori* twisted-paper string
18 雛 *kamibina* paper doll
23 鑢 *kami yasuri* sandpaper; emery paper

A **素** 4456 / J4147 / M27300 So principle; element. Su naked, uncovered, simple. *moto* beginning, origin; foundation, basis, source; cause; root (of a tree); (raw) material, base, capital; principal; cost; forebears; formerly. *moto(yori)* from the beginning; of course.

2 人 *shirōto, shiroto* amateur; layman; novice; outsider; unskilled hand; decent woman
人女 *shirōto onna* a respectable (nonprofessional) woman
人下宿 *shirōto geshuku* lodging in a private home
人目 *shirōtome* untrained eye
人芝居 *shirōto shibai* amateur theatricals
人臭 *shirōtokusa(i)* amateurish, untrained
人劇 *shirōtogeki* amateur dramatics
3 子 *soshi* device
4 手 *sude* empty hands, bare hands. *sude de* barehanded, unarmed, with naked fists
5 生 *sujō* birth, parentage, lineage; identity, personal history
6 行 *sokō* conduct, behavior
因 *soin* basic factor; predisposition
地 *sochi, soji* grain of wood; plain wood; foundation, groundwork
朴 *soboku* simplicity, artlessness
肌 *suhada* bare skin; stark naked
早 *subaya(i)* quick, agile
気無 *sokkena(i)* curt, blunt, brusque
7 見 *hiyaka(su)* only pretend to be buying
足 *suashi* bare feet
材 *sozai* raw materials; matter, material, subject matter
志 *soshi* original purpose
町人 *suchōnin* ordinary townsmen
8 姓 *sujō* birth, parentage, lineage; identity, personal history
性 *sujō* birth, parentage, lineage; identity, personal history
的 *suteki* grand, cute, fine, big, splendid, remarkable, superb
服 *sofuku* plain white clothes; mourning clothes

直 *sunao na* gentle, meek; obedient; tame; honest, frank
知顔 *soshi(ranu) kao* innocent look
9 面 *shirafu* sobriety, soberness. *sumen* sober face, unmasked face
首 *sokubi, so(k)kubi* one's head, one's "block" (head)
通 *sudō(ri)* passing through without stopping
透 *sudō(shi) no* transparent; plain glass (spectacles)
封 *sohō* rich family; rich person
封家 *sohōka* rich family; rich person
10 振 *sobu(ri)* manner, behavior, attitude, bearing, look
浪人 *surōnin* (derogatory word for) lordless retainer
破抜 *suppanu(ku)* expose, disclose
11 描 *sobyō, sugaki* rough sketch
瓶 *sugame* unglazed pottery
祭 *sosai* cereal offering
乾 *subo(shi)* drying in the shade
粒子 *soryūshi* the tiniest particle of matter, elemental (subatomic) particles
12 晴 *suba(rashii)* splendid, magnificent, glorious, excellent, superb, remarkable
焼 *suya(ki)* unglazed pottery
寒貧 *sukampin* poverty; pauper; beggar
13 絹 *soken* coarse silk
裸 *suhadaka* nudity
跣 *suhadashi* going barefooted
数 *sosū* indivisible numbers
意 *soi* original purpose
14 語 *sugata(ri)* recital without samisen accompaniment
読 *sodoku* reading without getting the meaning
15 膚 *suhada* stark naked
敵 *suteki* grand, cute, fine, big, splendid, remarkable, superb
養 *soyō* elementary attainments
質 *soshitsu* temperament, character, nature; constitution; quality; predisposition
16 懐 *sokai* cherished desire
樸 *soboku* simplicity, artlessness
餐 *sosan* a sinecure
麺 *sōmen* somen, vermicelli
18 顔 *sugao* unpainted face; sober face

5

紘 4457 / J6526 / M-X Kō. *wata* cotton, cotton wadding.

紵 4458 / J652a / M27353 CHO. JO. *ichibi* a kind of flax.

紿 4459 / J6529 / M27369 TAI. *azamu(ku)* deceive, cheat, delude.

絅 4460 / J6525 / M27375 KEI, GYŌ light overrobe, light cape; type of veil.

絏 4461 / J6528 / M27347 SETSU. *kizuna* fetters, yoke, encumbrance.

紬 4462 / J445d / M27338 CHŪ. *tsumugi* pongee.
6 糸 *tsumugi ito* silk thread from waste cocoons

紮 4463 / J6527 / M27341 SATSU. *kara(geru)* tie up, pack up; tuck up.
3 上 *kara(ge)-a(geru)* tie tightly, bind up
5 付 *kara(ge)-tsu(keru)* tie tightly, bind up

絆 4464 / J652b / M27376 HAN. *hoda(su)* tie. *kizuna* bonds, fetters; yoke; encumbrance; ties.
12 創膏 *bansōkō* adhesive plaster

B **紹** 4465 / J3e52 / M27361 SHŌ inherit; help.
4 介 *shōkai* introduction, presentation
介状 *shōkaijō* letter of introduction
介者 *shōkaisha* introducer
7 述 *shōjutsu* a further explanation by someone else

B **紺** 4466 / J3a30 / M27362 KON dark blue, navy blue.
6 地 *konji* dark blue ground (cloth)
8 青 *konjō* Prussian blue, deep blue
9 屋 *kon'ya, kōya* dyer
14 碧 *kompeki* dark blue

B **紳** 4467 / J3f42 / M27348 SHIN good belt; gentleman.
3 士 *shinshi* gentleman
士的 *shinshiteki* gentlemanly

士服 *shinshifuku* men's wear
士協定 *shinshi kyōtei* gentlemen's agreement
士録 *shinshiroku* who's who, directory
11 商 *shinshō* merchant prince

紘 4468 / J383e / M27373 GEN string, chord. *ito* string (on a violin); samisen music.
7 声 *gensei* sound of the strings
13 楽 *gengaku* string music
楽器 *gengakki* stringed instruments
14 歌 *genka* singing accompanied by stringed instruments
管 *genkan* wind and stringed instruments
15 線 *gensen* catgut, string for musical instrument

B **累** 4469 / J4e5f / M27343 RUI involvement, trouble; tie up; pile up; continually.
4 日 *ruijitsu* many days
5 代 *ruidai* successive generations; from generation to generation
加 *ruika* acceleration; accumulation
世 *ruisei* successive generations; from generation to generation
犯 *ruihan* repeated offense
犯者 *ruihansha* repeat offender
6 次 *ruiji ni* successively, repeatedly
年 *ruinen* successive years, every year
年統計 *ruinen tōkei* annual statistics
7 卵危 *ruiran (no) ayau(ki)* imminent danger
9 計 *ruikei* total
乗 *ruijō* involution, raising to a higher power (in math)
10 進 *ruishin* successive promotions; graduated increase
進税 *ruishinzei* graduated tax
進課税 *ruishin kazei* graduated tax
11 累 *ruirui(taru)* piled up; in heaps
14 増 *ruizō* gradual increase
算 *ruisan* total
16 積 *ruiseki* accumulation, pile, heap

A **組** 4470 / J4148 / M27374 So. *kumi(suru)* take part in; be implicated in; side with; support. *ku(mu)* braid, plait; construct; assemble; cross (legs); fold (arms); unite with, cooperate with; grapple with. *kumi* class, party, group; set; pack (of cards); suit; assortment; typesetting. *-gumi* group, gang; company.
2 入 *ku(mi)-i(reru)* include, insert, enroll
3 子 *ku(mi)ko* member of a squad (of firemen, etc.)
下 *kumishita* subordinates; privates
上 *ku(mi)-a(geru)* compose; build up. *ku(mi)-a(garu)* be composed (in printing); be framed (in construction)
4 戸 *ku(mi)do* lattice door
方 *ku(mi)kata* way of constructing, etc.
込 *ku(mi)-ko(mu)* cut in (in printing); insert, include
分 *kumiwu(ke)* sorting, separation into groups
5 付 *ku(mi)-tsu(ku)* grapple with, clinch, pounce on
打 *kumiu(chi)* grapple, scrimmage
立 *ku(mi)-ta(teru)* construct, erect, frame, assemble. *kumita(te)* construction, framework, organization, composition, assembly, erection
立工 *kumita(te)kō* assembler, fitter
立工場 *kumita(te) kōjō* assembly plant
立式 *kumitateshiki* prefabricated, collapsible, convertible (car)
立住宅 *kumita(te) jūtaku* prefabricated house, Quonset
6 糸 *ku(mi)ito* braid
成 *sosei* composition, formation, constitution
曲 *kumikyoku* suite, selection (in music)
伏 *ku(mi)-fu(seru)* get or hold (a person) down
会 *kumikai* class meeting, group meeting
合 *ku(mi)-a(u)* form a partnership; grapple with; be pitted against. *ku(mi)-a(wasu), ku(mi)-a(waseru)* combine; intertwine; dovetail. *kumiai* association, league, fraternity, union, partnership, guild, trust, cartel, syndicate. *ku(mi)a(i)* grapple, scrimmage. *kumiawa(se)* combination; assortment; braid; matching, pairing; schedule
合工場 *kumiai kōjō* union shop
合主義 *kumiai shugi* unionism
合役員 *kumiai yakuin* union official
合法 *kumiawa(se)hō* matching test
合員 *kumiaiin* partner, union member
合教会 *Kumiai Kyōkai* Congregational Church

合教会制 *Kumiai-Kyōkaisei* Congregationalism
合組織 *kumiai soshiki* union organization
合組織化 *kumiai soshikika* unionization
合組織者 *kumiai soshikisha* union organizer
合費 *kumiaihi* union dues
8 長 *kumichō* group leader, foreman
版 *ku(mi)han* typesetting, composition
物 *ku(mi)mono* plaiting, braiding, knitting
直 *ku(mi)-nao(su)* recompose; rebraid; reknit
9 重 *ku(mi)jū* tier of boxes
10 紐 *ku(mi)himo* braid
討 *kumiu(chi)* grappling; scrimmage
11 掛 *ku(mi)ka(ke)* partly completed
12 換 *ku(mi)-ka(eru)* rearrange
替 *ku(mi)-ka(eru)* rearrange
違 *ku(mi)-chiga(eru)* make a mistake in construction
14 閣 *sokaku* formation of a cabinet
15 敷 *ku(mi)-shi(ku)* get or hold (a person) down
縄 *ku(mi)nawa* plaited rope
16 頭 *kumigashira* group leader, foreman
18 織 *soshiki* organization, inauguration, composition, structure, setup; anatomy, texture, tissue, organism; system
織立 *soshikida(tta)* systematic
織化 *soshikika* systematization, organization ⌈labor
織労働者 *soshiki rōdōsha* organized
織的 *soshikiteki* systematic, methodical
織学 *soshikigaku* histology
織神学 *soshiki shingaku* systematic theology

A **終** $\frac{4471}{\frac{J3d2a}{M27372}}$ SHŪ end. *owa(ru) vi* end, terminate, adjourn, be over; die. *vt* end, finish, complete. *o(eru) vt* end, finish, complete. *owa(ri)* end, conclusion, expiration. *tsui ni* finally, after all.

2 了 *shūryō* end, termination, signing off, expiration, conclusion, completion
了後 *shūryōgo* after the termination of
3 夕 *shūseki* all night
4 日 *shūjitsu, hinemosu, himosugara, hisugara* all day
止 *shūshi* termination, cessation, stop
止符 *shūshifu* full stop, period, end
5 生 *shūsei* all through life; a lifetime
世 *shūsei* all through life, lifelong
刊 *shūkan* ceasing publication
刊号 *shūkangō* final issue
末 *shūmatsu* end, conclusion, termination, settlement, result
末時代 *shūmatsu jidai* last days
末論 *shūmatsuron* eschatology
末観 *shūmatsukan* eschatology
6 曲 *shūkyoku* the final musical number
年 *shūnen* the whole year; the whole life
列車 *shūressha* last train
7 車 *shūsha* last train or streetcar for the day
尾 *shūbi* end
局 *shūkyoku* end, conclusion, finale
決 *shūketsu* settlement
身 *shūshin* the whole life
身刑 *shūshinkei* life sentence
身年金 *shūshin nenkin* life annuity
身会員 *shūshin kaiin* life membership
身官 *shūshinkan* life appointment; official appointed for life
身保険 *shūshin hoken* life insurance
身恩給 *shūshin onkyū* life pension
身雇用 *shūshin koyō* lifetime employment
身禁錮 *shūshin kinko* life imprisonment
身懲役 *shūshin chōeki* life imprisonment
8 油 *shūyu* extreme unction
夜 *shūya, yomosugara* all night
始 *shūshi* beginning and end; from first to last; always
始一貫 *shūshi-ikkan shita* constant, consistent
9 点 *shūten* terminus
10 航 *shūkō* last voyage
宵 *shūshō* all night
息 *shūsoku* cessation, eradication
11 焉 *shūen* last moments, death
雪 *shūsetsu* the last snow
12 極 *shūkyoku* finality, extremity
結 *shūketsu* conclusion, termination
期 *shūki* expiration, termination
着駅 *shūchaku eki* terminal station
13 幕 *shūmaku* end, close, curtain; closing scene, closing drama
電 *shūden* the last train or streetcar for the day

電車 *shūdensha* the last train or streetcar for the day
業 *shūgyō* close of work, end of a school term
業式 *shūgyōshiki* closing ceremony
戦 *shūsen* end of the war, termination of hostilities
戦処理費 *shūsen shorihi* occupation expenses
戦直後 *shūsen chokugo* right after the war
戦後 *shūsengo* after the war
戦前後 *shūsen zengo* before and after the war
14 演 *shūen* end of a performance
熄 *shūsoku* cessation, eradication
端 *shūtan* terminus, terminal
駅 *shūeki* terminal station
15 審 *shūshin* final trial
盤 *shūban* nearing the end of the (chess or checker) game
盤戦 *shūbansen* the ending of a campaign
17 霜 *shūsō* the last frost
19 禱 *shūtō* closing prayer, benediction

A **細** 4472 / J3a59 / M27344 SAI. *hoso(ru)* get thin; taper off. *hoso(meru)* make narrow. *hoso(i)* fine (line); thin (voice); slender; narrow (trousers). *koma(ka) na, koma(kai), koma(i)* small, fine; detailed; minor, trifling; elaborate, delicate; stingy, frugal; small (change). *koma(kashii)* very small. *koma(yakana)* warm, tender, close; minute; deep (color). *(ka)boso(i)* slender, slim, feeble, delicate. *sasa(yakana)* small. *isasa* small. *sazare-* small. *sasa-* small; a few.
3 小 *saishō* the finest, the minute, the infinitesimal. *sasayaka na* small; poor, humble
大 *saidai* great and small
大洩 *saidaimo(rasazu)* absolutely everything
工 *saiku* work, craftsmanship, ware; artifice, device, tactics, trick
工人 *saikunin* craftsman, artisan, workman
工物 *saikumono* handiwork
4 心 *saishin* carefulness, discretion
手 *hosode no* thin, fine
毛 *saimō* cilia
片 *saihen* fragment, piece, splinter
孔 *saikō* small cavity; pore; small hole
切 *komagi(re)* small pieces of cloth; chopped meat. *komagi(ri)* chopped meat
分 *saibun suru* divide into small parts
5 目 *saimoku* details, specifications, items. *hosome* narrow eyes; narrow openings
石 *sazareishi* pebble, gravel
末 *saimatsu* a trifle; powder
民 *saimin* the poor, paupers
民窟 *suiminkutsu* slums
6 糸 *hosoito* fine thread, fine-yarn count
行 *saiko* small acts
字 *saiji* small characters, small type
7 見 *saiken* close inspection
身 *hosomi* narrow blade
別 *saibetsu* itemization, subdivision
声 *hosogoe* weak voice
君 *saikun* wife; my wife
8 長 *hosonaga(i)* slender, lanky, linear, long and narrow
雨 *saiu* misty rain, drizzle
波 *sasanami, sazanami* ripples
事 *saiji* minor affair; trifle; details
9 面 *hosoomote* slender face
革 *hosokawa* shoe welt
首 *hosokubi* slender neck
則 *saisoku* bylaws, detailed rules
胞 *saibō, saihō* cell
胞工学 *saibō kōgaku* cell technology
胞学 *saibōgaku* cytology
胞診 *saibōshin* cytodiagnosis
胞融合 *saibō yūgō* cell fusion
10 流 *sairyū* brook, rivulet
記 *saiki* minute description, full account
部 *saibu* details
書 *hosoga(ki), saisho* small writing, fine writing
帯 *hosoobi* undersash, girdle
11 道 *hosomichi* path, narrow lane
粒 *sairyū* granule, infinitesimal grains
細 *komagoma* in pieces, in detail. *hosoboso(shita)* slender, delicate, scanty (living). *sasayaka na* small; poor, humble
密 *saimitsu* minuteness
雪 *sasameyuki* light snow
菌 *saikin* germ, microbe, bacteria, bacillus
菌学 *saikingaku* bacteriology, microbiology

6 竹米【糸】缶网罒羊羽老耂而耒耳聿肉月臣自至臼舌舛舟艮色艸艹虍虫血行衣衤西

菌戦 *saikinsen* germ warfare
菌爆弾 *saikinbakudan* germ bomb
12 腕 *hosoude* thin arm; slender means; poor ability
評 *saihyō* detailed criticism
筆 *saihitsu* fine brush; writing fine
13 微 *saibi* minuteness
腰 *saiyō, hosogoshi* slender hips, slender waist
隙 *saigeki* slit
節 *saisetsu* minor details
14 塵 *saijin* dust in the atmosphere
説 *saisetsu* detailed explanation
15 瑾 *saikin* small defect
論 *sairon* full treatment, detailed explanation
緻 *saichi na* minute, detailed
16 濁 *sasanigo(ri)* somewhat muddy
17 螺 *kishigo, kishago, kisago* periwinkle
謹 *saikin* small defect

A **経** 4473 J3750 M27392 **經** 4493 J6534 M27508 KEI longitude; sutra; warp. KYŌ sutra. *he(ru)* pass, elapse; pass through; experience. *ta(tsu)* pass, elapse, expire. *he(te)* through, by way of, via. *tate* length; height; warp. *ta(teba)* (a few days) hence. *tateito* warp (in weaving).

3 上 *he-a(garu)* rise to fame
口的 *keikōteki* oral (medication)
口感染 *keikō kansen* infection via the mouth
4 文 *kyōmon* sutras
木 *kyōgi* thin sheets of wood
水 *keisui* menstruation
5 由 *keiyu* via. *keiyu suru* go by way of
史 *keishi* ethics and history books
札 *kyōfuda* phylactery
外典 *Keigaiten* the Apocrypha
外聖書 *Keigai Seisho* the Apocrypha
世 *keisei* government, administration; statesmanship, statecraft
世家 *keiseika* statesman, administrator
6 糸 *tateito* warp
血 *keiketsu* menstrual flow
伝 *keiden* scriptures and commentary
7 声 *kyōgoe* sutra-reading voice
8 国 *keikoku* administration, government
帙 *kyōchitsu* sutra covers
函 *kyōkan* sutra box
学 *Keigaku* Confucianism
典 *kyōten, keiten* sacred books; sutras; the Bible; the canon; the Scriptures
典外 *Keitengai* the Apocrypha
9 度 *keido* longitude
廻 *he-megu(ru)* travel about, wander about
界 *keikai* boundary, border
10 差 *keisa* longitudinal difference
書 *keisho* Chinese classics
師 *kyōji* paperhanger
師屋 *kyōjiya* paperhanger; philanderer
11 過 *keika* progress, course, development; interim; lapse; expiration; transit (of a moon)
略 *keiryaku* governing (a country)
堂 *kyōdō* sutra library
帷子 *kyōkatabira* shroud, grave clothes
常 *keijō* ordinary, current (budget)
常収支 *keijōshūshi* balance of current account
常利益 *keijōrieki* ordinary profit
常費 *keijōhi* current expenditures
理 *keiri* management, accounting
理士 *keirishi* public accountant
理学 *keirigaku* accounting
理学校 *keiri gakkō* paymasters' school
済 *keizai* economy; economics; finance; thrift
済人 *keizaijin* financial expert
済力 *keizairyoku* economic strength
済上 *keizaijō* economically, financially
済水域 *keizai suiiki* economic zone
済不快指数 *keizai fukaishisū* economic misery index
済成長率 *keizai seichōritsu* rate of economic growth
済企画庁 *Keizai Kikakuchō* Economic Planning Agency
済状態 *keizai jōtai* financial condition
済的 *keizaiteki* financial; economic; economical
済学 *keizaigaku* economics; political economy
済面 *keizaimen* economic situation
済界 *keizaikai* financial circles
済封鎖 *keizai fūsa* economic blockade
済家 *keizaika* economist, thrifty person
済違犯 *keizai ihan* violation of commercial laws (price control, etc.)
済博 *Keizaihaku* Doctor of Economics
済圏 *keizaiken* international economic block

済戦 *keizaisen* economic war
済網 *keizaimō* unified economic area
済欄 *keizairan* financial column
12 費 *keihi* expenses, cost, outlay
営 *keiei* construction; management, operation; development; project
営法 *keieihō* management
営学 *keieigaku* business management
営者 *keieisha* operator, manager
営参加 *keiei sanka* management participation
営経済学 *keiei keizaigaku* business economics
営費 *keieihi* operating expenses
営権 *keieiken* rights of management
営難 *keieinan* financial difficulties
13 路 *keiro* the road one has traveled; channel; circumstances
14 綸 *keirin* government, administration, statesmanship
読 *kyōyo(mi)* reading sutras, Buddhist priest
歴 *keireki* personal history, career; pilgrimage
歴公報 *keireki kōhō* bulletin of candidates' careers
歴放送 *keireki hōsō* broadcast of candidates' careers
15 線 *keisen* meridian
16 緯 *keii* longitude and latitude, position; warp and woof; particulars. *ikisatsu* complication, troubles. *tateyoko* length and breadth; every direction; right and left; warp and woof
緯儀 *keiigi* theodolite; altazimuth
18 櫃 *kyōbitsu* large sutra box
験 *keiken* experience
験上 *keikenjō* from experience
験主義 *keiken shugi* empiricism
験死亡表 *keiken shibōhyō* mortality tables
験的 *keikenteki* experiential, empirical
験者 *keikensha* experienced person
験表 *keikenhyō* mortality tables
験学派 *keikengakuha* empiric school
験科学 *keiken kagaku* experimental science
験家 *keikenka* experienced person
験談 *keikendan* personal-experience narrative
験論 *keikenron* empiricism

6

綌 4474 / J652f / M27448 See **糸** 4431.

絳 4475 / J652c / M27449 Kō. *aka* deep red.

紲 4476 / J6532 / M27397 Setsu tie.

絖 4477 / J652d / M27409 Kō. *nume* white satin.

絣 4478 / J6533 / M27429 **絣** 4502 / J-X / M27571 Hō. *kasuri* splashed pattern; cloth with a splashed pattern.

絮 4479 / J6531 / M27443 Jo cotton.
14 説 *josetsu* detailed explanation

絓 4480 / J-X / M27403 Kai catch on something.
6 糸 *shike ito, suga ito* raw silk thread

絢 4481 / J303c / M27427 Ken kimono design.
21 爛 *kenran(taru)* dazzling, gorgeous, flowery, gaudy

絎 4482 / J652e / M27396 Kō. *ku(keru)* to blindstitch.
15 縫 *kukenu(i)* blind stitch

絨 4483 / J6530 / M27435 Jū wool cloth.
4 毛 *jūmō* wool
12 毯 *jūtan* rug, carpet
15 緞 *jūtan* rug, carpet

B **絡** 4484 / J4d6d / M27426 Raku. *kara(mu) vi* coil around, get twisted; stick to; pick a quarrel. *kara(meru) vt* twine around. *shigara(mu)*, *kara(maru)* twist around; get caught in; be urged on by. *mato(u)* wear; wind around.
5 付 *kara(mi)-tsu(ku)* twist about, entwine; cling to; be caught in
6 合 *kara(mi)-a(u)* get or be intertwined, be in gear with
19 繹 *rakueki* ceaseless traffic

繰 *karaku(ri)* mechanism, contrivance, scheme, makeshift
繰人形 *karaku(ri) ningyō* marionette, puppet

B **絞** 4485 / J394a / M27421 Kō. *shi(meru)* strangle, constrict, wring. *shibo(ru)* wring, squeeze, press, extract; milk; close tight; extort; scold. *shibo(ri)* dapple, white-spotted cloth; stop, diaphragm.

3 上 *shibo(ri)-a(geru)* gather up (a curtain); squeeze (money) out of
5 弁 *shibo(ri)ben* throttle valve
出 *shibo(ri)-da(su)* press out, squeeze out, drain out. *shibo(ri)da(shi)* (toothpaste) tube
6 刑 *kōkei* death by hanging
7 扼 *kōyaku* strangulation
9 染 *shibo(ri)zo(me)* a dyeing process where the designs are formed by tightly tying small places here and there, tie-dyeing
首 *kōshu* hanging, strangulation
首台 *kōshudai* gallows
首刑 *kōshukei* death by hanging
10 殺 *kōsatsu* hanging, strangulation. *shi(me)-koro(su)* strangle to death
13 罪 *kōzai* hanging (criminals)
15 盤 *kōban* capstan

B **紫** 4486 / J3b67 / M27337 Shi purple, violet. *murasaki* purple, violet; soy sauce.

4 水晶 *murasaki suishō, murasakizuishō* amethyst
5 布 *murasaki nuno* (ancient) purple cloth
外線 *shigaisen* ultraviolet rays
石 *shiseki* an inkstone
石英 *shisekiei, murasaki sekiei* amethyst
8 金 *shikin* gold-copper alloy
11 紺 *shikon* purplish blue
陽花 *ajisai* hydrangea
12 斑病 *shihambyō* purpura
雲 *shiun* purple congratulatory clouds
雲英 *rengesō* a purple vetch
13 煙 *shien* tobacco smoke; purple smoke; purple haze
電 *shiden* flashes of lightning
17 檀 *shitan* red sandalwood, rosewood
19 蘇 *shiso* beefsteak plant
蘇湯 *shisoyu* beefsteak-plant tea

A **統** 4487 / J457d / M27447 Tō relationship; lineage; beginning. *su(beru)* control, supervise, govern. *sube(te)* all, the whole; entirely; in general.

1 一 *tōitsu* unity, unification, consolidation, uniformity, coherence; standardization; rule, dominance; concentration
一力 *tōitsuryoku* unifying power
一性 *tōitsusei* unity, uniformity
一的 *tōitsuteki* unified
一国 *tōitsukoku* a unified country
一戦線 *tōitsu sensen* united front
6 合 *tōgō suru* integrate, combine, unify
合参謀本部 *Tōgō Sambō Hombu* Joint Chiefs of Staff
8 治 *tōchi suru, tōji suru, su(be)-osa(meru)* reign over, rule
治者 *tōchisha, tōjisha* ruler, sovereign
治権 *tōchiken* sovereignty
制 *tōsei* control, regulation
制下 *tōseika* under the control of
制品 *tōseihin* controlled goods
9 括 *tōkatsu* generalization. *su(be)kuku(ru)* generalize
帥 *tōsui* high command
帥部 *tōsuibu* the high command
帥権 *tōsuiken* authority of the supreme command
計 *tōkei* statistics
計分析 *tōkei bunseki* statistical analysis
計年鑑 *tōkei nenkan* statistical yearbook
計的 *tōkeiteki* statistical
計学 *tōkeigaku* science of statistics
計表 *tōkeihyō* statistical table, returns
計家 *tōkeika* statistician
計報告 *tōkei hōkoku* statistical report
計調査 *tōkei chōsa* statistical research
11 率 *tōsotsu suru* command, lead
率者 *tōsotsusha* commander, leader
12 御 *tōgyo suru* rule, control, administer
覚 *tōkaku* apperception
14 領 *tōryō* chief, manager, dictator
監 *tōkan* supervision; commander; resident-general
17 轄 *tōkatsu* control
轄者 *tōkatsusha* the one in charge

A **絵** 4488 / J3328 / M27464' **繪** 4597 / J6569 / M27939 Kai. *e* picture, drawing, painting, sketch, illustration, cut, print.

2 入 *ei(ri)* illustrated, pictorial
4 心 *egokoro* artistic taste
手本 *edehon* illustrated copybook
文字 *emoji* picture writing, hieroglyphics
双紙 *ezōshi* picture book
5 凧 *edako* picture kite
札 *efuda* picture card
本 *ehon* picture book
6 羽 *eba* haori coat with continuous pictorial design
羽羽織 *eba haori* haori coat with continuous pictorial design
羽織 *ebaori* haori coat with continuous pictorial design
7 図 *ezu* drawing, illustration, diagram, plan, design, sketch, map, chart
図引 *ezuhi(ki)* drawing; one who draws
図面 *ezumen* plan, design
8 取 *edo(ru)* paint, color, trace
具 *e(no)gu* paints, colors, oils, pigments
事 *kaiji* picture, painting
刷毛 *ebake* artist's brush
空言 *esoragoto* fabrication, unreality
物語 *emonogatari* illustrated book
画 *kaiga* picture, painting, drawing
画界 *kaigakai* painting circles
9 柄 *egara* pattern, design
姿 *esugata* portrait, likeness, picture
看板 *ekamban* billboard
草紙 *ezōshi* picture book
巻 *emaki* picture scroll
巻物 *emakimono* picture scroll
10 師 *eshi* painter, artist
捜 *esaga(shi)* picture puzzle
書 *eka(ki)* painter, artist
馬 *ema, euma* votive picture (originally of a horse)
馬屋 *emaya* votive-picture dealer
馬堂 *emadō* votive-picture gallery
馬殿 *emaden* votive-picture hall
11 探 *esaga(shi)* picture puzzle
描 *eka(ki)* painter, artist; painting
12 詞 *ekotoba* words explaining a picture
筆 *efude* paintbrush
葉書 *ehagaki* picture postcard
13 絹 *eginu* silk canvas, drawing silk
解 *eto(ki)* explanation of a picture, illustration
話 *ebanashi* picture story
14 像 *ezō* portrait, likeness, picture
15 踏 *efu(mi), ebu(mi)* image trampling, trampling on the image of Christ
16 謎 *enazo* picture puzzle

A **給** 4489 / J356b / M27432 KYŪ wage; gift; wage grade. *kyū(suru)* allow, grant, supply; favor. *tama(waru), tama(u), tamo(u)* deign to, grant, give, bestow on, honor with.

3 与 *kyūyo* grant, ration; compensation, allowance
与水準 *kyūyo suijun* wage level
与体系 *kyūyo taikei* wage system
与金 *kyuyokin* allowance, grant, dole
4 分 *kyūbun* salary
水 *kyūsui* water supply, water distribution
水自動車 *kyūsui jidōsha* water wagon
水車 *kyūsuisha* water wagon
水所 *kyūsuijo* water station
水栓 *kyūsuisen* hydrant, faucet
水塔 *kyūsuitō* water tower, tank
水量 *kyūsuiryō* amount of water supplied
水管 *kyūsuikan* water pipe
5 付 *kyūfu suru* present, pay, deliver, furnish
仕 *kyūji* office boy or girl, page, bellhop; waiter, waitress; table service
仕人 *kyūjinin* waiter, waitress
仕役 *kyūjiyaku* butler, cupbearer
6 血者 *kyūketsusha* blood donor
気管 *kyūkikan* air duct
7 助 *kyūjo* charity, alms
8 金 *kyūkin* wages
所 *kyūsho* granted land, territory
油 *kyuyu* supply of oil; refueling
油所 *kyūyusho* filling station
油船 *kyūyusen* tanker
9 食 *kyūshoku* providing with food, supplying (school) lunches
食施設 *kyūshoku shisetsu* cooking facilities
炭 *kyūtan* supply of coal
炭所 *kyūtanjo* coaling station
炭船 *kyūtansen* coal ship, collier
10 料 *kyūryō* wages, salary, payroll
料日 *kyūryōbi* pay day
料支払簿 *kyūryō shiharaibo* pay roll
料生活者 *kyūryō seikatsusha* salaried worker
料取 *kyūryōto(ri)* salaried worker
料袋 *kyūryōbukuro* pay envelope
12 費 *kyūhi* scholarship, student support
費生 *kyūhisei* scholarship student

13 源 *kyūgen* source of supply
電 *kyūden* supply of electricity
15 養 *kyūyō* rations, provisions, allowance
養係 *kyūyōgakari* quartermaster

A **絶** 4490/J4064/M-X **絕** 4491/J-X/M27407 ZETSU. *zes(suru)* be beyond (words). *ta(tsu)* sever, cut off; shut off, interrupt; abstain from; eradicate; suppress. *ta(eru)* become extinct, die out, discontinue, end, fail, peter out. *ta(yasu)* exterminate, eradicate, root out; run out of (stock); let (a fire) go out. *ta(ete)* (with neg.) never. *ta(ezaru)* unceasing, continual. *ta(ezu)* constantly, unceasingly; always.

2 入 *ta(e)-i(ru)* expire, die
3 大 *zetsudai na* tremendous, immense
4 水 *zessui* abstaining from water
5 句 *zekku suru* forget one's lines. *zekku* a style of Chinese poetry
世 *zessei* peerless, unrivaled, unequaled
6 叫 *zekkyō* scream, exclamation
好 *zekkō no* splendid, grand, first-rate
好機 *zekkōki* best chance
交 *zekkō* breaking off friendship; breaking off diplomatic relations
交状 *zekkōjō* letter breaking off relations
7 妙 *zetsumyō no* most admirable, exquisite, superb
体絶命 *zettai-zetsumei* desperate situation, last extremity
対 *zettai no* absolute, positive, categorical, unconditional
対化 *zettaika suru* make absolute
対反対 *zettai hantai* positive opposition
対多数 *zettai tasū* absolute majority
対安静 *zettai ansei* complete rest
対的 *zettaiteki* absolute, positive, imperative
対性 *zettaisei* absoluteness
対者 *zettaisha* God; the Absolute
対所有権 *zettai shoyūken* absolute ownership
対服従 *zettai fukujū* absolute obedience
対音高 *zettai onkō* absolute pitch
対音感 *zettai onkan* absolute pitch
対過半数 *zettai kahansū* absolute majority
対量 *zettairyō* absolute minimum quantity (required)
対温度 *zettai ondo* absolute temperature
対零度 *zettai reido* absolute zero
対禁酒 *zettai kinshu* total abstinence
対権 *zettaiken* absolute authority
対権力 *zettai kenryoku* absolute authority
対優位 *zettai yūi* absolute advantage
8 佳 *zekka no* superb
所 *zessho* steepness and impassability of roads
命 *zetsumei* death
果 *ta(e)-ha(teru)* be extinguished, be exterminated, die out
東 *Zettō* Far East
版 *zeppan* out of print
版書 *zeppansho* a book that is out of print
9 後 *zetsugo* no precedent involved
海 *zekkai* distant seas
品 *zeppin* rare article, masterpiece
美 *zetsubi* exquisiteness, matchless beauty
食 *zesshoku* fasting
食療法 *zesshoku ryōhō* fast treatment
10 倫 *zetsurin* excellence, superiority
倒 *zettō suru* be convulsed with laughter
島 *zettō* lonely island
家 *zekke* extinct family
息 *zessoku suru* expire, die
11 唱 *zesshō* fine poem; excellent song
頂 *zetchō* summit, peak, climax, acme, zenith
望 *zetsubō* hopelessness, despair
望的 *zetsubōteki* hopeless, desperate
12 絶 *ta(e)da(e)* faint, almost exhausted
勝 *zesshō* fine scenery
景 *zekkei* superb view
筆 *zeppitsu* one's last literary work
無 *zetsumu* nothing, naught, nil
間 *ta(e)ma* interval, intermission, pause; break, gap
間無 *ta(e)mana(ku)* continually, unceasingly
13 滅 *ta(e)-horo(bosu)* quench, put out. *zetsumetsu* eradication, extermination
15 賛 *zessan* great praise
縁 *zetsuen* insulation; isolation; breaking off relations; dissociating oneself from
縁体 *zetsuentai* insulator, nonconductor
縁線 *zetsuensen* insulated wire
縁器 *zetsuenki* insulator
16 壁 *zeppeki* precipice, cliff, bluff
22 讃 *zessan* great praise

A **結** 4492 / J376b / M27398 KETSU. *musu(bu)* tie, bind; tie a knot; make (contracts, treaties, and friendships); join; finish, wind up; unite with; organize. *musu(boreru)* tangle, knot, kink, get twisted; get complicated. *yu(u), i(u)* do up (the hair); make (a braided fence). *iwa(eru), yuwa(eru)* bind, fasten, tie, tie up. *su(ku)* make (a net). *musu(bi)* knot; end, conclusion.

2 了 *ketsuryō suru* end, terminate
3 上 *yu(i)-a(geru)* do up (the hair)
4 文 *ketsubun* epilogue, conclusion, complimentary closing
手 *sukite* net maker
方 *yu(i)kata* hairstyle. *musu(bi)kata* hairstyle; way of tying
5 目 *musu(bi)me, shiba(ri)me* knot
石 *kesseki* calculus, stones (in the biliary or urinary tracts)
句 *kekku* conclusion; after all; the last line of a poem
付 *musu(bi)-tsu(keru) vt* tie up, join together, link together. *musu(bi)-tsu(ku) vi* join with, ally with
氷 *keppyō* freezing; frost
末 *ketsumatsu* end, conclusion, termination, settlement, result
6 成 *kessei* formation, organization
托 *kettaku* collusion, complicity, conspiracy
肌帯 *yuwadaobi* maternity belt
合 *ketsugō suru, musu(bi)-a(waseru)* tie together, unite, combine. *musu(bi)-a(u)* unite with, cleave to. *ketsugo* union, fusion, cohesion, joint, coupling, link
合体 *ketsugōtai* a united body
7 尾 *ketsubi* end, conclusion
局 *kekkyoku* after all, in conclusion
社 *kessha* association, society
束 *kessoku* union, unity
8 実 *ketsujitsu* fruit bearing; success
果 *kekka* consequences, result, effect
9 姻 *ketsuin* becoming relatives
神 *Musu(bi) (no) Kami* Cupid
約 *ketsuyaku* making a promise
巻 *kekkan* the last volume (of a sutra)
10 託 *kettaku* conspiracy, collusion, complicity
党 *kettō* formation of a party
納 *yuinō* engagement present
納金 *yuinōkin* engagement gift of money
核 *kekkaku* tubercule; tuberculosis
核菌 *kekkakukin* tuberculosis germ
核療養所 *kekkaku ryōyōjo* tuberculosis sanitarium
11 紮 *kessatsu* ligature
婚 *kekkon* marriage
婚生活 *kekkon seikatsu* married life
婚行進曲 *kekkon kōshinkyoku* wedding march
婚式 *kekkonshiki* wedding
婚式場 *kekkon shikijō* wedding parlor
婚届 *kekkon todoke* marriage registration
婚披露 *kekkon hirō* wedding reception
婚相手 *kekkon (no) aite* person one is to marry
婚相談所 *kekkon sōdanjo* matrimonial agency
婚指輪 *kekkon yubiwa* wedding ring
婚記念日 *kekkon kinembi* wedding anniversary
婚期 *kekkonki* marriageable age
婚媒介人 *kekkon baikainin* matchmaker, go-between
婚媒介所 *kekkon baikaijo* matrimonial agency
婚詐欺 *kekkon sagi* fake marriage
婚観 *kekkonkan* ideas of marriage
12 着 *ketchaku* conclusion, settlement
番 *ketsuban* determining the order of work shifts
集 *kesshū* concentration; regimentation; the editing of Gautama's works by his disciples
晶 *kesshō* crystal; crystallization
晶体 *kesshōtai* crystal
晶学 *kesshōgaku* crystallography
13 滞 *kettai* the rest between heartbeats
腸 *ketchō* the colon
解 *ketsuge* settlement of accounts
節 *kessetsu* knot; tubercule; nodule
盟 *ketsumei* pledging
14 語 *ketsugo* conclusion
髪 *keppatsu* hairdressing; hairstyling
構 *kekkō* structure; architecture; setup; quite sufficient; very well; fairly well. *kekkō na* splendid, excellent
構人 *kekkōjin* good-natured person, an honest person
膜 *ketsumaku* conjunctiva

膜炎 *ketsumakuen* conjunctivitis
15 縁 *ketsuen* accepting Buddhism; forming karma relationships
論 *ketsuron* conclusion
審 *kesshin* conclusion of a hearing
縄 *ketsujō* knotted cord
17 霜 *kessō* formation of frost
19 願 *ketsugan* expiration of a (Buddhist) vow
21 露 *ketsuro* formation of dew
露点 *ketsuroten* dew point

7

經 4493 / J6534 / M27508 See **経** 4473.

絛 4494 / J6536 / M27465 Jū. Tō. *sanada* braid, plait, braided cord.

綉 4495 / J6535 / M27493 Tō. Shū embroidery; piece of cotton cloth; figured cloth.

綏 4496 / J6537 / M27501 Sui rope, strap to hang onto in a vehicle. *yasu(i)* inexpensive; peaceful, quiet.

綛 4497 / J6539 / M27534 (国字) *kasuri* splashed pattern; cloth with splashed pattern. *kase* reel, hank, skein.

絽 4498 / J6538 / M27474 Ro a silk gauze.
18 織 *roo(ri)* gauze fabric
縮緬 *rochirimen* gauze crepe

A **絹** 4499 / J3828 / M27470 Ken silk. *kinu* silk, silk thread.
5 布 *kempu* silk, silk cloth
本 *kempon* silk used for art painting
6 地 *kinuji* silk fabrics
糸 *kinu ito, kenshi* silk thread
糸紡績 *kenshi bōseki* silk reeling, silk spinning
8 物 *kinumono* silk goods
10 紡 *kembō* spun silk
11 張 *kinuba(ri)* silk-covered
紬 *kenchū* pongee
笠 *kinugasa* long-handled silk umbrella
12 絵 *kinue* picture on silk
13 業 *kengyō* silk industry
業者 *kengyōsha* silk dealer
14 綾 *kinu aya* silk damask
綿 *kinu wata* silk floss
17 縮 *kinuchiji(mi)* crinkled silk
18 織物 *kinu orimono* silk goods

A **続** 4500 / J4233 / M27533 **續** 4610 / J6574 / M28037 Zoku continuation, second series. *tsuzu(ku) vi* continue; be contiguous. *tsuzu(keru) vt* continue. *tsuzu(ki)* continuation, succession; another installment, sequel; series; row. *-tsuzu(ki)* row; continuity; succession.
5 生 *zokusei* frequent occurrence, series of events
刊 *zokkan suru* continue publication
出 *zokushutsu* frequent occurrence, series of events
6 行 *zokkō suru* go on, continue, resume
会 *zokkai suru* resume, continue
合 *tsuzu(ki)a(i)* connection, relationship
字 *tsuzu(ke)ji* cursive handwriting
8 物 *tsuzu(ki)mono* serial story
9 映 *zokuei* continued run of a film
柄 *tsuzu(ki)gara* family relationship
発 *zokuhatsu* frequent occurrence, series of events
発症 *zokuhatsushō* secondary disease
10 航 *zokkō suru* continue the voyage; hold the course
書 *tsuzu(ke)ga(ki)* cursive handwriting
12 開 *zokkai suru* resume, continue
飯 *sokui* rice paste
報 *zokuhō* further news
番号 *tsuzu(ki) bangō* serial number
13 続 *zokuzoku* successively, one after another
14 様 *tsuzu(ke)sama ni* successively, consecutively, in a row
演 *zokuen* continued run of a show
15 稿 *zokkō* remaining manuscripts (to be furnished)
審 *zokushin* re-examination, retrial
篇 *zokuhen* sequel, continuation, supplementary volume
20 騰 *zokutō* continued advance in prices

B **継** 4501 / J3751 / M27531 **繼** 4603 / J656b / M27997 Kei. *tsu(gu)* succeed to, inherit; follow; patch; graft (trees); tell. *tsu(gi)* patch. *mama(shii)* fostered (child). *mama-* step- (child, etc.).

3 子 *mamako, keishi* stepchild
子虐 *mamako iji(me)* ill-treatment of a stepchild
4 手 *tsu(gi)te* joint, pipe coupling
木 *tsu(gi)ki* grafting, grafted tree
父 *mamachichi, keifu* stepfather
切 *tsu(gi)gi(re)* patch
夫 *keifu* second husband
5 母 *mamahaha, keibo* stepmother
目 *tsu(gi)me* joint, seam, suture
立 *tsu(gi)ta(te)* relay
兄弟 *mama kyōdai* half brothers from different mothers
6 合 *tsu(gi)-a(wasu), tsu(gi)-a(waseru)* join together, patch, splice, dovetail, glue together
当 *tsugia(te)* patchwork
7 走 *keisō* relay race
足 *tsu(gi)-ta(su)* add to, extend, piece. *tsu(gi)ta(shi)* adding to
述 *keijutsu suru* pass on the word
8 泳 *keiei* relay swimming
物 *tsu(gi)mono* patch
受 *keiju* inheritance
妻 *keisai* second wife
承 *keishō* succession, accession, inheritance
承者 *keishōsha* successor
9 室 *keishitsu* second wife
竿 *tsu(gi)zao* jointed fishing rod; jointed stem
10 紛 *mamako* undissolved powder lump
13 継 *tsu(gi)tsu(gi)* in turn, one after another
嗣 *keishi* successor, heir
電器 *keidenki* (electric) relay
続 *keizoku* continuation
続性 *keizokusei* continuity
続的 *keizokuteki* continuous, habitual
続飛行 *keizoku hikō* endurance flight
16 親 *mamaoya* stepparent

8

絣 4502 / J-X / M27571 See 絣 4478.

緍 4503 / J-X / M27607 See 緡 4541.

緕 4504 / J656e / M-X Nonstandard for 纃 4607.

綟 4505 / J6546 / M27540 REI yellowish-green, grass green. *moji, mojiri* loosely woven linen.

綢 4506 / J6542 / M27546 CHŪ, JU be clothed in, entwine; bundle; woven silk.

綣 4507 / J653c / M27550 KEN coil, wreath; follow about; attachment.

綫 4508 / J6540 / M27564 SEN thread, string, line.

綵 4509 / J653d / M27580 SAI patterned silk. *aya* pattern, design.

綬 4510 / J3c7a / M27565 JU cordon, ribbon (a decoration).

綮 4511 / J653b / M27569 KEI a device or emblem on a flag or banner.

綰 4512 / J6547 / M27575 WAN. *waga(neru)* bend round, bend into a hoop.

綯 4513 / J6543 / M27573 TŌ. *na(u)* twist, twine, make (rope).

綻 4514 / J433e / M27587 TAN. *hokoro(biru)* be rent, be ripped; unravel, run; begin to open; smile. *hokoro(basu), hokoro(baseru)* tear, rip; smile.

緇 4515 / J653e / M27600 SHI black; black clothing, priest's clothing; a priest.
6 衣 *shie, shii* black clothing; priest's clothing; priest

B 維 4516 / J305d / M27568 I tie; rope.
9 持 *iji* upkeep, support, maintenance
13 新 *Ishin* 1868 Imperial Restoration

緋 4517 / J486c / M27604 HI scarlet, cardinal.
6 衣草 *higoromosō* salvia
18 鯉 *higoi* red carp, golden carp

綽 4518 / J653f / M27590 SHAKU loose; lenient.
6 名 *adana* nickname

14 綽 *shakushaku(taru)* ample, leisurely, deliberate

綸 4519/J6545/M27583 RIN thread, silk cloth.
3 子 *rinzu* figured satin
6 旨 *rinshi* imperial order 「mandate
7 言 *ringen* emperor's word, imperial

綜 4520/J416e/M27535 SŌ rule.
6 合 *sōgō* synthesis, coordination, composite
合大学 *sōgō daigaku* university
合的 *sōgōteki* overall, all-around, collective, synthetic, composite, comprehensive
9 括 *sōkatsu* synthesis, summarization, recapitulation

B緒 4521/J3d6f/M27632 緖 4535/J-X/M27633 SHO, CHO beginning, inception; end. *itoguchi* thread end; beginning; clue. *o* cord, strap, thong; clog cord; string.
7 言 *chogen, shogen* forward, preface, introduction
12 就 *sho (ni) tsu(ku)* be started
13 戦 *shosen* beginning of hostilities
業 *shogyō* work undertaken
15 締 *oji(me)* pouch drawstring
論 *choron, shoron* introduction, preface

綺 4522/J653a/M27586 KI figured cloth; beautiful.
14 語 *kigo* flowery language
15 談 *kidan* a strange story; an adventure story
19 羅 *kira* fine clothes. *kira(biyakana)* gorgeous, gaudy, dazzling
羅星 *kiraboshi* glittering stars
羅星如 *kiraboshi (no) gotoku* a galaxy of dignitaries
麗 *kirei na* beautiful, lovely; clean, neat. *kirei ni* completely, beautifully
麗好 *kireizu(ki)* love of cleanliness
麗事 *kireigoto* fine skill, simplicity

綾 4523/J303d/M27591 RYŌ. *aya* design, figured cloth, twill.
5 布 *ayanuno* twill damask and brocade
6 糸 *ayaito* colored thread
地 *ayaji* figured cloth
8 取 *ayato(ru)* tie across (the back). *ayato(ri)* string play (cat's cradle, etc.)
13 絹 *ayaginu* figured silk
15 緞子 *ayadonsu* damask
16 錦 *ayanishiki* twill damask and brocade
18 織 *ayao(ri)* twill

B緊 4524/J365b/M27603 KIN hard, solid; reliable; tight. *shi(maru) vi* be tightened. *shi(meru) vt* tighten.
4 切 *kinsetsu na* urgent, pressing
7 迫 *kimpaku* tension, strain
束 *kinsoku* tying up firmly
9 要 *kin'yō* important, momentous
急 *kinkyū* crisis, emergency; urgency, rush
11 密 *kimmitsu* rigor, closeness; compactness
張 *kinchō* strain, tension, seriousness
張味 *kinchōmi* strain, tension, seriousness
14 緊 *hishihishi* tightly, firmly; thick and fast; crowded
褌一番 *kinkon-ichiban suru* gird oneself for an effort
16 縛 *kimbaku suru* bind tightly
17 縮 *kinshuku* shrinkage, contraction, constriction; strict economy, retrenchment

B綱 4525/J394b/M27576 KŌ class (in zoology). *tsuna* rope, cord, string, line, hawser, cable; morality.
4 手 *tsunade* mooring rope, towing line
引 *tsunahi(ki)* tug-of-war; forward puller
5 目 *kōmoku* gist, outline, main points
打 *tsunau(chi)* ropemaking; ropemaker
8 具 *tsunagu* cordage, rigging, tackle
9 要 *kōyō* outline, summary, essentials
紀 *kōki* ropes; law and order, administration, official discipline
紀粛正 *kōki shukusei* enforcement of official discipline
11 常 *kōjō* morals, morality
梯子 *tsunabashigo* rope ladder
12 渡 *tsunawata(ri)* tightrope walking, tightrope walker; danger. *tsunawata(shi)* rope ferry
14 領 *kōryō* general plan; main points, summary

綴 4526 / J4456 / M27579 TEI. TETSU. SETSU. *tsuzu(ru)* spell; compose, write; bind; patch. *to(jiru)* bind, file, sew up. *tsuzuri* spelling, orthography; binding, patching. *tsuzu(re)* rags, tatters. *to(ji)* binding, sewing.

4 方 *tsuzu(ri)kata* composition, theme; spelling, how to spell. *tojikata* binding, how to bind
込 *to(ji)-ko(mu)* file; interleave, insert. *tojiko(mi)* file
5 目 *tojime* seam. *tsuzu(ri)me* joint, seam
付 *to(ji)-tsu(keru)* sew together
本 *tojihon* bound book
6 糸 *tojiito* binding thread, basting thread
合 *tsuzu(ri)-a(waseru)* sew together, patch; bind together, fasten, file
字 *setsuji, teiji, tsuzuriji* spelling, orthography
8 金 *tojigane* binding strip
直 *to(ji)-nao(su)* rebind
10 釘 *toji kugi* rivet
13 蓋 *tojibuta* mended lid
16 機械 *toji kikai* stitching machine

B **網** 4527 / J4c56 / M27577 MŌ net; network. *ami* net, netting.

3 子 *amiko* netter (one who handles the nets)
4 戸 *amido* screen door
引 *amihi(ki)* net puller; pulling in a net
元 *amimoto* head fisher
5 石 *amiishi* net weights
打 *amiu(chi)* net fishing
目 *amime, ami (no) me* net meshes
目版 *amimeban* halftone (plate)
代 *ajiro* wickerwork; wicker net
代笠 *ajirogasa* wicker hat
7 状 *mōjō* net form
形 *amigata no* reticulated
杓子 *amijakushi* ladle, scoop, skimmer
8 版 *amihan* halftone (plate)
刺 *amisa(shi)* netmaking
10 針 *amibari* netting needle
11 麻 *amiso* net cord
船 *amibune* fishing boat (using nets)
袋 *amibukuro* net bag
細工 *amizaiku* net maker; filigree work
12 棚 *amidana* baggage rack
結 *amisuki* netmaker, netmaking
14 膜 *mōmaku* retina
19 羅 *mōra suru* include, contain; collect

A **緑** 4528 / J4e50 / M27541' **綠** 4529 / J-X / M27541 RYOKU, ROKU. *midori* green; verdure.

3 土 *ryokudo* a verdant area
4 化 *ryokka, ryokuka* tree planting, afforestation
内障 *ryokunaishō* glaucoma
5 石鹼 *ryokusekken* green soap, soft soap
玉 *ryokugyoku* emerald, beryl
玉石 *ryokugyokuseki* emerald, beryl
玉髄 *midori gyokuzui* chrysoprase
6 色 *midori iro* green. *ryokushoku* green, verdure
地 *ryokuchi* green stretch of land; oasis
地化 *ryokuchika* afforestation
地帯 *ryokuchitai* green belt
8 門 *ryokumon* arch of leaves or evergreens
雨 *ryokuu* rain falling on fresh verdure
青 *rokushō* green rust, copper rust
林 *ryokurin* a green forest; a robber
肥 *ryokuhi* green-manure crop
岩 *ryokugan* greenstone
9 便 *ryokuben* child's green bowel movement
茶 *ryokucha* green tea, Japanese tea
草 *ryokusō* green grass
柱石 *ryokuchūseki* beryl
10 陰 *ryokuin* tree shade, shady nook
陰樹 *ryokuinju* shade tree
11 野 *ryokuya* green field
12 葉 *ryokuyō* green leaves
13 煙 *ryokuen* evening haze
16 樹 *ryokuju* green tree, foliage
19 藻 *ryokusō* green algae

A **練** 4530 / J4e7d / M27631' **練** 4534 / J-X / M27689 REN. *ne(ru)* gloss, soften; train, drill; polish; refine. *ne(reru)* be docile, be teachable; become dependable. *ne(reta)* mellowed. *ne(ri)* kneading; glossing (silk).

6 糸 *ne(ri)ito* glossed silk thread
回 *ne(ri)-mawa(ru)* parade, march
成 *rensei* training
7 兵 *rempei* military drill, parade
兵場 *rempeijō* parade ground
8 金 *renkin* refining, smelting, tempering
固 *ne(ri)-kata(meru)* harden by kneading
乳 *rennyū* condensed milk
歩 *ne(ri)-aru(ku)* parade, march
9 炭 *rentan* briquette

6 竹米【糸】缶网罒羊羽老耂而耒耳聿肉月臣自至臼舌舛舟艮色艸艹虍虫血行衣衤西

10 粉 *ne(ri)ko* dough
11 達 *rentatsu* skill, dexterity
習 *renshū* training, practice, rehearsal
習不足 *renshūbusoku* lack of training
習生 *renshūsei* student, trainee, apprentice
習用 *renshūyō* for training purposes
習曲 *renshūkyoku* étude, a study (in music)
習所 *renshūjo* training institute
習帳 *renshūchō* exercise book, workbook
12 塀 *ne(ri)bei* mud or plastered wall
13 絹 *ne(ri)ginu* glossed silk
鉄 *rentetsu* wrought iron
16 磨 *remma* exercise, training, drilling
薬 *ne(ri)gusuri, ne(ri)yaku* ointment

A **綿** 4531 / J4c4a / M27592 **緜** 4533 / J6544 / M27644 MEN cotton; cotton thread; cotton cloth. *wata* cotton, cotton wool.
2 入 *watai(re)* padded clothes; cotton-quilted bedclothes
3 子 *watako* a cape (the wearing apparel)
4 火薬 *menkayaku* guncotton
天鵞絨 *membirōdo* cotton velvet, velveteen
毛 *watage* fluff, nap, fuzz, down, pile, fleece
毛布 *memmōfu* cotton blanket
5 打 *watau(chi)* cotton willowing
布 *mempu* cotton cloth
6 糸 *menshi* cotton thread or yarn
羊 *men'yō* sheep
衣 *men'i* cotton clothing; clothing of a cotton mixture
7 花 *menka* raw cotton
8 服 *mempuku* cotton clothes
実 *menjitsu, wata(no)mi* cotton seed
実虫 *wata(no)mi mushi* bollworm
実油 *menjitsuyu, wata(no)mi abura* cottonseed oil
9 屋 *wataya* cotton dealer
津見 *watatsumi* god of the sea
10 紡 *membō* cotton spinning
11 商 *watashō* cotton dealer
密 *memmitsu na* minute, detailed; careful, meticulous
12 雲 *watagumo* fleecy clouds
帽子 *watabōshi* bride's silk-floss veil
13 業 *mengyō* cotton industry
14 綿 *memmen(taru)* endless, continuous
製品 *menseihin* cotton goods
17 縮 *menchiji(mi)* cotton crepe
18 織物 *men'orimono* cotton goods
19 繰 *wataku(ri)* cotton ginning
繰工 *wataku(ri)kō* cotton ginner
繰機 *wataku(ri)ki* cotton gin
20 繻子 *menjusu* cotton satin, sateen

A **総** 4532 / J416d / M27620 **總** 4575 / J6541 / M27844 SŌ- whole, all, general, gross, total, full. *su(beru)* control, supervise. *fusa* tuft, tassel, fringe, lock (of hair); cluster, bunch, segment (of an orange). *sō(jite)* in general, as a rule. *sato(i)* clever, intelligent; keen, quick. *sube(te)* all, the whole; entirely; in general.
2 二階 *sōnikai* full two-story house
入歯 *sōi(re)ba* full set of false teeth
力 *sōryoku* full strength
力戦 *sōryokusen* total war
3 大将 *sōdaishō* commander-in-chief
4 予算 *sōyosan* complete budget
元締 *sōmotoji(me)* general manager
支出 *sōshishutsu* total expenditure
支配人 *sōshihainin* general manager
毛 *fusage* lock, tuft, tassel. *sōke, sōmō* all wool
毛立 *sōkeda(tsu)* shudder, have goose flesh, feel one's hair standing on end
5 立 *sōda(chi)* all standing up together
代 *sōdai* representative, delegate
出 *sōde* full force
主事 *sōshuji* executive director, general secretary
仕舞 *sōjimai* closing up, selling out
目 *sōmoku* catalog; table of contents
目録 *sōmokuroku* catalog; table of contents
収入 *sōshūnyū* total income
収益 *sōshūeki* gross earnings
司令官 *Sōshireikan* SCAP; Supreme Commander
司令部 *Sōshireibu* SCAP, GHQ; General Headquarters
本山 *sōhonzan* sectarian headquarters temple
本店 *sōhonten* head office
本部 *sōhombu* general headquarters
本家 *sōhonke* head family

6 回診 *sōkaishin* the doctor's rounds (in a hospital)
会 *sōkai* general meeting, annual conference, assembly, synod
会屋 *sōkaiya* a gangster who extorts money in return for not causing trouble at a shareholders' meeting
同盟 *sōdōmei* federation
同盟罷業 *sōdōmei higyō* general strike
合 *sōgō* synthesis, coordination, composite
合大学 *sōgō daigaku* university
合写真 *sōgō shashin* composite photo
合的 *sōgōteki* overall, all-round, collective, synthetic, composite, comprehensive
合計画 *sōgō keikaku* comprehensive plan
合雑誌 *sōgō zasshi* all-purpose magazine
合課税 *sōgō kuzei* taxation on aggregate income
合競技 *sōgō kyōgi* all round games
7 見 *sōken* attending in a large party
身 *sōmi, sōshin* the whole body
局 *sōkyoku* overseas (newspaper) headquarters
社 *sōsha* shrine enshrining several gods
決算 *sōkessan* complete financial statements
攻撃 *sōkōgeki* general attack, general offensive
投票数 *sōtōhyōsū* total votes cast
花 *sōbana* tips to all, rewards for everyone
花的 *sōbanateki* across-the-board, pleasing everyone
体 *sōtai* all, the whole. *sōtai ni* on the whole, in general
体的 *sōtaiteki ni* generally
8 長 *sōchō* (college) president; secretary-general
和 *sōwa* total
画 *sōkaku* complete number of strokes (in a character)
退却 *sōtaikyaku* general retreat
所得 *sōshotoku* gross income
坪数 *sōtsubosū* total area in *tsubo* (see Weights and Measures)
9 帥 *sōsui* commander, leader
計 *sōkei* total
則 *sōsoku* general rules, general provisions
軍 *sōgun* the whole army
点 *sōten* total marks
重量 *sōjūryō* gross weight
革 *sōgawa* full-leather binding
革製 *sōgawasei* leather-bound
指揮 *sōshiki* supreme command; supreme commander
指揮官 *sōshikikan* supreme commander
括 *su(be)-kuku(ru)* generalize. *sōkatsu* synthesis, summarization, recapitulation
括的 *sōkatsuteki* all-inclusive, all-embracing, lump-sum, general
括保険 *sōkatsu hoken* blanket insurance
括運賃 *sokatsu unchin* lump-sum freight
10 高 *sōdaka* total amount
称 *sōshō* general term. *sōshō suru* speak in general terms
益 *sōeki* gross profit
益金 *sōekikin* gross profit
員 *sōin* full force, all hands, the entire staff
員集合 *sōin shūgō* muster
11 捲 *sōmaku(ri)* general survey, sweeping criticism
崩 *sōkuzu(re)* general rout, collapse, stampede
菜 *sōzai* daily fare, plain food, ordinary side dish
勘定 *sōkanjō* full payment, final settlement
動員 *sōdōin* general mobilization
掛 *sōga(kari)* combined efforts
掛費 *sōga(kuri)hi* total expenses
理 *sōri* president, leader, prime minister
理大臣 *sōri daijin* prime minister
理庁 *sōrichō* prime minister's office
理府 *sōrifu* prime minister's office
務 *sōmu* general affairs; manager
務局 *sōmukyoku* general-affairs department
務長官 *sōmu chōkan* director-general
務部長 *sōmu buchō* general manager
12 揚 *sōa(ge)* hiring (calling in) all (the geisha)
統 *sōtō* leader, president, generalissimo
集 *sōshū* an anthology of prose and poetry by many writers
復習 *sōfukushū* complete final review. *sōzarai* rehearsal; complete final review
量 *sōryō* gross weight, gross volume

量噸 *sōryō ton* gross tonnage
裁 *sōsai* president, governor (of a bank)
裁職 *sōsaishoku* the presidency (of an organization)
13 数 *sōsū* total number
意 *sōi* consensus of opinion
勢 *sōzei* the whole army; all members
幹事 *sōkanji* general secretary
義歯 *sōgishi* full set of false teeth
辞職 *sōjishoku* resignation en masse
督 *sōtoku* governorship; governor; governor-general
督府 *sōtokufu* government-general
14 総 *fusafusa* tufty, fringy, bushy (tail), fleecy
説 *sōsetsu* introduction, general remarks
嘗 *sōna(me)* tasting everything; a sweeping victory
選挙 *sōsenkyo* general election
監 *sōkan* inspector general, commissioner, president
監督 *sōkantoku* general manager
領 *sōryō* ruling; heir, eldest son, eldest child, family head
領事 *sōryōji* consul-general
領事館 *sōryōjikan* consulate-general
領娘 *sōryō musume* eldest daughter
領息子 *sōryō musuko* eldest son and heir
15 締 *sōji(me)* total; general manager
論 *sōron* general remarks, introduction
調書 *sōchōsho* summarized statement
罷業 *sōhigyō* general strike
16 噸数 *sōtonsū* gross tonnage
17 轄 *sōkatsu* general control, general supervision
18 額 *sōgaku* total amount
19 蹶起 *sōkekki suru* arouse (people)
24 攬 *sōran* superintendence, control

9

緜 4533 / J6544 / M27644 See 綿 4531.

緤 4534 / J-X / M27689 See 練 4530.

緒 4535 / J-X / M27633 See 緒 4521.

緼 4536 / J-X / M27701 See 縕 4561.

緝 4537 / J6549 / M27645 SHŪ. *tsumu(gu)* spin, make yarn. *atsu(meru)* collect, gather. *nu(u)* sew, stitch. *yawa(ragu)* soften, moderate.

緤 4538 / J654a / M27657 SETSU. SECHI. *kizuna* leash, fetters.

緲 4539 / J654d / M27687 BYŌ, MYŌ faint, vague; distant, vast.

縅 4540 / J654f / M27730 (国字) *odo(su)* threaten; frighten; intimidate.

緡 4541 / J654e / M27652 **緍** 4503 / J-X / M27607 BIN. KON. *sashi* paper string, straw string.

緬 4542 / J4c4b / M27674 MEN fine thread.
6 羊 *men'yō* sheep

緻 4543 / J-X / M27700 **緻** 4557 / J654c / M-X CHI fine (not coarse).
11 密 *chimitsu na* minute, fine, nice, elaborate, delicate, accurate, discriminating

縋 4544 / J6557 / M27740 TSUI. *suga(ru)* cling to, hang on to, lean on; depend on; appeal to.
5 付 *suga(ri)-tsu(ku)* cling to, hang on to, lean on; depend on; appeal to

緘 4545 / J6548 / M27638 KAN. *kan(suru)* shut, close, seal.
3 口 *kankō suru* keep silent
15 黙 *kammoku* silence, reticence

緞 4546 / J654b / M27646 DON, TAN damask.
3 子 *donsu* damask
11 帳 *donchō* drop curtain; second-rate (actor)
帳役者 *donchō yakusha* barnstormer, second-rate actor

B **縄** 4547 / J466c / M27729 **繩** 4598 / J656a / M27937 Jō. *nawa* rope, cord.

4 文 *jōmon* straw-rope pattern
手 *nawate* rope
5 目 *nawame* fetters, chain; arrest; knot
付 *nawatsu(ki)* prisoner in bonds
7 抜 *nawanu(ke)* slipping one's bonds
9 飛 *nawato(bi)* skipping rope
矩 *jōku* marking line and a square
10 帯 *nawa obi* rope belt
11 張 *nawaba(ri)* stretching a rope; cordon; sphere of influence, jurisdiction
規 *jōki* provisions, rules
梯子 *nawabashigo* rope ladder
13 暖簾 *nawa noren* rope curtain; tavern; cheap restaurant
14 墨 *jōboku* inked timber-marking string; standard
19 簾 *nawa sudare* rope curtain; tavern; cheap restaurant

A **線** 4548 / J407e / M27641 Sen line; track, route; wire.

4 分 *sembun* line segment
内球 *sennaikyū* fair ball
引 *sembi(ki)* ruling lines
引小切手 *sembi(ki) kogitte* crossed check
7 材 *senzai* wire rod, wire
形 *senkei* straight alignment
条 *senjō* streak, line
8 画 *senga* line drawing, line engraving
9 香 *senkō* incense stick
香花火 *senkō hanabi* firecracker
12 間 *senkan* spaces (on a musical staff)
量 *senryō* radiation dose
13 路 *senro* railway track
路工手 *senro kōshu* railway section hand
路用地 *senro yōchi* railway right of way
路伝 *senrozuta(i)* along the tracks
15 輪 *senrin* (electric) coil
審 *senshin* linesman (in a game)

B **締** 4549 / J4479 / M27651 Tei. *shi(meru)* tie, tighten; wring, constrict, strangle; shut; total; control strictly; rebuke. *shi(maru)* be shut, be locked, be fastened; be tight, be firm; become sober, reform; be thrifty. *shi(mete)* total.

3 上 *shi(me)-a(geru)* tie up
4 込 *shi(me)-ko(mu)* shut in, lock in
切 *shi(me)-ki(ru)* close, close up, keep closed. *shimeki(ri)* closing, closing up; deadline; cutoff; cofferdam
太鼓 *shi(me)daiko* drum whose heads are tied on with tightening cords
5 付 *shi(me)-tsu(keru)* bind, throttle; strangle, choke; press hard, compress; control strictly
出 *shi(me)-da(su)* shut out, lock out
7 売 *shi(me)u(ri)* cornering the market and making large profits
8 金 *shi(me)gane* clamp
具 *shi(me)gu* clamp, fastener
9 屋 *shi(mari)ya* thrifty person; stingy person
括 *shi(me)-kuku(ru)* hold together, bind; supervise, control. *shi(me)kuku(ri)* supervision, control; completion
約 *teiyaku suru* make a treaty. *teiyaku* treaty, agreement
約国 *teiyakukoku* treaty powers, signatories
10 高 *shi(me)daka* total
12 結 *teiketsu suru* conclude, contract
13 盟 *teimei* conclusion of a treaty
盟国 *teimeikoku* treaty powers, signatories

B **縫** 4550 / J4B25 / M27805 **縫** 4556 / J-X / M27809 Hō. *nu(u)* sew, stitch, embroider. *nu(i)* sewing; embroidery.

3 工 *hōkō* seamstress, tailor
上 *nu(i)a(ge)* tuck
4 反 *nu(i)-kae(su)* sew over, remake
込 *nu(i)-ko(mu)* sew in, tuck
5 目 *nu(i)me* seam, suture
付 *nu(i)-tsu(keru)* sew on
代 *nu(i)shiro* the margin left for a seam; a seam
包 *nu(i)guru(mi)* actors' clothing to imitate animals; stuffed toys
6 糸 *nuiito* sewing thread
合 *nu(i)-a(waseru)* sew up, sew together. *hōgō* suturing, stitching
8 取 *nu(i)to(ri)* embroidery, sewing
直 *nu(i)-nao(su)* sew over, remake
物 *nuimono* sewing, needlework
物台 *nuimonodai* sewing table
10 紋 *nu(i)mon* embroidered crest
針 *nu(i)bari* sewing needle
12 揚 *nu(i)a(ge)* tuck
14 箔 *nu(i)haku* embroidery

模様 *nu(i)moyō* embroidered figures
18 繕 *nu(i)-tsukuro(u)* patch; sew on a patch

B **緩** 4551 / J344b / M27669 KAN. *yuru(mu) vi* loosen, lessen; relax; be unguarded; be moderate. *yuru(meru) vt* loosen, unbend, unfasten; relax, ease, slacken; mitigate. *yuru(yakana)* loose; easy (grade); gentle, lenient, generous; slow (stream). *yukku(ri)* slowly, gently, leisurely. *yuru(i)* loose, slack; lenient, generous, slow.

3 下剤 *kangezai* laxative
6 行 *kankō* going slowly
曲球 *kankyokkyū* slow curve
8 歩 *kampo* slow walk
和 *kanwa* relief; mitigation; alleviation; pacification
和政策 *kanwa seisaku* appeasement policy
9 怠 *kantai* neglect (of duty); rough manners; fault, error
急 *kankyū* high and low speed; tempo; emergency, circumstances
急車 *kankyūsha* caboose
10 流 *kanryū* slow current
11 球 *kankyū* slow ball
12 焼 *kanshō* slow-burning
焼性 *kanshōsei* slow-burning
13 傾斜 *kankeisha* gentle slope
14 慢 *kamman* slow moving; inactivity
15 緩 *yuruyuru* slowly, leisurely, gently
衝 *kanshō* mediation
衝地 *kanshōchi* neutral zone
衝地帯 *kanshō chitai* demilitarized zone
衝国 *kanshōkoku* buffer country
衝帯 *kanshōtai* neutral zone
衝器 *kanshōki* buffer, bumper, shock absorber

A **編** 4552 / J4a54 / M27665 HEN compilation, editing; completed poem; a book; a part of a book. *a(mu)* knit, plait, braid, net, weave, twist, crochet; compile, edit, frame. *a(mi)-* braided, knitted.

2 入 *hennyū* entry, incorporation, enlistment, enrollment
3 上 *amia(ge)* high lace shoes
上靴 *amia(ge)gutsu* high lace shoes
4 戸 *a(mi)do* braided door
5 目 *a(mi)me* knitting stitch
出 *a(mi)-da(su)* invent, devise, originate, work out
6 成 *hensei* formation, organization, composition
曲 *henkyoku* arrangement (in music)
次 *henji* line up
合 *a(mi)-a(wasu), a(mi)-a(waseru)* intertwine, knit together
年史 *hennenshi* annals, chronicle
年体 *hennentai* chronological order
7 述 *henjutsu* gathering materials and writing a book
8 物 *amimono* knitting, crocheting
制 *hensei* formation, organization, composition
者 *hensha* editor, compiler
10 修 *henshū* compilation, editing
針 *a(mi)bari* knitting needle, crochet hook
11 組 *henso* combination; braid
隊 *hentai* formation (flight)
笠 *a(mi)gasa* braided hat
12 棒 *a(mi)bō* knitting needle
集 *henshū* editing, compilation
集局 *henshūkyoku* editorial department
集長 *henshūchō* editor in chief
16 輯 *henshū* editing, compilation
20 纂 *hensan* compilation, editing

B **縁** 4553 / J316f / M27656' **緣** 4554 / J-X / M27656 EN relation, connection, affinity, ties, bond; blood relation; karma relation; fate, destiny; chance; marriage; acquaintance; marriage alliance; veranda, balcony. *fuchido(ru)* add a border. *enishi* relation, connection, affinity, ties, bond; blood relation, karma relation; fate, destiny; chance; marriage; acquaintance; marriage alliance. *fuchi* edge, verge, shore, side, brink, margin, brim, rim, flange, frill, frame, bank, fringe, border. *heri* edge, verge, brink, margin, border, fringe, rim, brim, hem, limb (of the sun). *yukari* acquaintance; relation; affinity. *yosuga* way, means.

3 下 *en(no)shita ni* under the floor; out of sight, in the background
4 日 *ennichi* a fair; temple festival
辺 *empen* connections, relatives, kith and kin
引 *embi(ki)* relation, connection, relative
切 *enki(ri)* separation, divorce, severing of connections

5 石 *fuchiishi* curb, curbstone
由 *en'yū* relationship
付 *enzu(ku)* get married. *enzu(keru)* give in marriage
台 *endai* bench
6 先 *ensaki* edge of the veranda
8 板 *en'ita* veranda flooring
取 *fuchito(ri), herito(ri)* bordering, hemming
定 *ensada(me)* marriage contract
者 *enja* relative
9 柱 *embashira* veranda post
故 *enko* relation, connection, affinity
故者 *enkosha* relative
10 起 *engi* history, origin, legend; omen; luck; portent
家 *enka* related family
11 側 *engawa* veranda, porch, balcony, open corridor
組 *engumi* betrothal, wedding, marriage; alliance; adoption; fraternization, affiliation
12 遠 *endōi* late marriage
結 *emmusu(bi)* marriage, marriage tie, love knot
無 *herina(shi)* unbordered
13 続 *entsuzu(ki)* relationship, connection
飾 *fuchikaza(ri)* frill, edging, fringe
14 端 *embana* edge
語 *engo* associated word
15 縫 *fuchinu(i)* hemming, hemstitching, bordering
談 *endan* marriage proposal, offer of marriage, marriage engagement
16 頭 *fuchigashira* pommel (of a sword)
18 類 *enrui* connections, relatives

10

縣 4555 / J6551 / M27784 See **県** 3918.

縫 4556 / J-X / M27809 See **縫** 4550.

緻 4557 / J654c / M-X See **緻** 4543.

縢 4558 / J6558 / M27783 Tō. Dō. *kaga(ru)* cross-stitch; hemstitch; sew up; darn.

縒 4559 / J6553 / M27751 Shi. Sa. *yo(ru) vt* twist.

縡 4560 / J6552 / M27781 Sai affairs, matters; publish. *koto* breath, life.
4 切 *kotoki(reru)* die

縟 4561 / J6555 / M27779 Joku decoration.
5 礼 *jokurei* officialism, red tape

縉 4562 / J6556 / M27737 **縉** 4563 / J-X / M-X Shin thin red cloth; high officer.
9 紳 *shinshin* rank; high-ranking person, noble

縕 4564 / J-X / M27757 **縕** 4536 / J-X / M27701 On, Un old cotton.

縺 4565 / J6561 / M27838 Ren. *motsu(reru)* tangle, knot, kink, get twisted; get complicated. *motsu(re)* tangle, entanglement, trouble, complication.
4 毛 *motsu(re)ge* matted or tangled hair

B**緯** 4566 / J305e / M27687 I woof; horizontal; left and right; parallels of latitude; latitude. *nuki* woof.
6 糸 *nukiito, yokoito* woof
9 度 *ido* latitude
15 線 *isen* parallel of latitude

B**縛** 4567 / J477b / M27771 Baku arrest, binding. *shiba(ru)* bind, tie, fasten, truss, fetter, restrain, chain; arrest, catch. *imashi(me)* binding, bonds.
3 上 *shiba(ri)-a(geru)* tie up; truss up
5 付 *shiba(ri)-tsu(keru)* tie up, fasten to
9 首 *shiba(ri)kubi* beheading

縊 4568 / J6550 / M27738 I. *kubi(ru)* strangle (a person) to death. *kubi(reru)* strangle oneself, hang oneself.
6 死 *ishi, kubi(re)ji(ni)* death by strangling
刑 *ikei* death by strangling, hanging
10 殺 *kubi(ri)-koro(su)* strangle (a person) to death

6 竹米【糸】缶网罒羊羽老耂而耒耳聿肉月臣自至臼舌舛舟艮色艸艹虍虫血行衣衤襾

10

縞 4569 / J3c4a / M27777 Kō. *shima* stripe.
[3] 大理石 *shima dairiseki* Oriental alabaster
[5] 玉髄 *shima gyokuzui* chalcedony
[8] 物 *shimamono* striped cloth
[9] 柄 *shimagara* striped pattern
[10] 馬 *shima uma* zebra
[11] 蛇 *shima hebi* striped snake
[13] 鼠 *shima nezumi* squirrel
[14] 瑪瑙 *shima menō* onyx, wood agate, sardonyx
模様 *shima moyō* striped pattern
[18] 織 *shimaori* woven in stripes
織物 *shima orimono* striped cloth

B **繁** 4570 / J484b / M27803' **繁** 4574 / J-X / M27849 Han frequency, complexity, trouble. *shige(ru)* grow thick, be overgrown, be luxuriant. *shige(ku)* thickly, densely; frequently. *shige(ri), shige(mi)* thicket, bush.
[4] 文 *hambun* extreme rhetorical flourishes
文縟礼 *hambun jokurei* red tape, officialism
[6] 忙 *hambō* pressure of business
多 *hanta* very numerous; many things to do
[8] 昌 *hanjō* prosperity, success
茂 *hammo* luxuriant growth
[9] 栄 *han'ei* prosperity
[10] 華 *hanka* prosperity, bustle
華街 *hankagai* a busy street
[11] 務 *hammu* exhausting work, an arduous task; pressure of business
盛 *hanjō, hansei* prosperity
[12] 閑 *hankan* rush and leisure
殖 *hanshoku suru* breed, propagate, increase, multiply
[14] 雑 *hanzatsu* complexity, intricacy, trouble
[15] 劇 *hangeki* pressure of business
[18] 簡 *hankan* simplicity and complexity

A **縦** 4571 / J3d44 / M27804' **縱** 4576 / J6554 / M27819 Shō. Jū length, height. *hoshiimama* self-indulgent, wayward, selfish, arbitrary. *tate* length; height; warp. *yoshi* a hesitant OK; if, if by any chance. *tatoe, tatoi* if, even if, though, although.
[4] 引鋸 *tatebi(ki) nokogiri* ripsaw
[6] 糸 *tateito* warp (in weaving)
列 *jūretsu* column, file, queue
列行進 *jūretsu kōshin* a march in a file
[7] 走 *jūsō* following a mountain ridge
坑 *tatekō* mine shaft
[8] 波 *tatenami* longitudinal wave
[9] 陣 *jūjin* column (of soldiers)
[10] 射 *jūsha* raking fire
書 *tatega(ki)* vertical writing
座標 *tatezahyō* ordinate (in math.)
[11] 隊 *jūtai* column (of soldiers)
断 *jūdan* cutting vertically
貫 *jūkan suru* traverse from end to end
[12] 揺 *tateyu(re)* pitch (of a ship)
結 *tatemusu(bi)* vertical knot
軸 *tatejiku* spindle
筋 *tatesuji* vertical line, longitudinal stripe
裂 *tateza(ki)* ripping lengthwise
[14] 様 *tatezama* lengthwise
[15] 線 *jūsen* vertical line
横 *tate-yoko, jūō* length and breadth; every direction; right and left; warp and woof. *jūō ni* vertically and horizontally
横無尽 *jūō-mujin* rush of business
横無礙 *jūō-muge* free, unrestricted
横談 *jūōdan* a talk on miscellaneous subjects
[16] 縞 *tatejima* vertical stripes; striped fabric
覧 *jūran* inspection; reading
覧御随意 *jūran gozuii* admission free, open to the public

11

縺 4572 / J3d2b / M-X See **繍** 4600.

繋 4573 / J3752 / M-X Nonstandard for **繫** 4601.

繁 4574 / J-X / M27849 See **繁** 4570.

總 4575 / J6541 / M27844 See **総** 4532.

縱 4576 / J6554 / M27819 See **縦** 4571.

縵 4577 / J655c / M27829 MAN, BAN unpatterned silk; plain, undecorated.

繆 4578 / J6559 / M27855 BYŪ error; wrap around.

A **績** 4579 / J4053 / M27845 SEKI exploits; unreeling cocoons.

縻 4580 / J655b / M27839 BI. MI rope.

縲 4581 / J6560 / M27821 RUI tie.
12 絏 *ruisetsu* fetters, bonds

繃 4582 / J655e / M27852 HŌ wrap.
10 帯 *hōtai* bandage, dressing

縹 4583 / J655d / M27837 HYŌ. *hanada* light blue.
6 色 *hanada iro, hana iro* light blue
12 渺 *hyōbyō* haziness; vastness

縷 4584 / J655f / M27832 RU thread.
7 述 *rujutsu suru* tell in detail
10 骨 *rukotsu suru* work hard, take great pains
14 説 *rusetsu suru* tell in detail
17 縷 *ruru* minutely. *ruru(taru)* continuous

A **縮** 4585 / J3d4c / M27815 SHUKU. *chiji(kamu), chiji(mu), chiji(komaru)* shrink, contract, shrivel, wrinkle. *chiji(masu), chiji(meru), chiji(komeru)* shorten, contract, shrink, reduce, boil down, simplify, abbreviate, abridge, condense, compress, crumple, wrinkle, withdraw. *chiji(keru), chiji(maru)* be shortened, be contracted, be reduced, be abridged; be abbreviated, shrink, shrivel, wrinkle. *chijiku(reru), chiji(kamaru)* curl up; squeeze into; shrink, shorten, contract, be abridged. *chiji(reru)* be wavy, curl; shrink; be corrugated, be wrinkled. *chiji(rakasu), chiji(rasu), chiji(raseru) vt* curl, crinkle, crimp. *chiji(mi)* crepe, shrunken cloth.
3 小 *shukushō* reduction, retrenchment, cut
上 *chiji(mi)-a(garu)* shrink up; quail, flinch, wince, cower
4 毛 *chiji(re)ge* curly, wavy, or fuzzy hair
尺 *shukushaku* reduced scale
5 写 *shukusha* copying on a small scale; reduced copy
7 図 *shukuzu* reduced drawing, miniature copy; epitome
8 刷 *shukusatsu* small-type edition, pocket edition
刷版 *shukusatsuban* small-type edition, pocket edition
10 留 *chiji(mi)do(me)* shrinkproof
12 減 *shukugen suru* reduce
15 緬 *chirimen* crepe
緬皺 *chirimenjiwa* facial wrinkles
18 織 *chiji(mi)o(ri)* cotton crepe, preshrunk cloth

B **繊** 4586 / J4121 / M27874 **纖** 4618 / J6579 / M28072 **纎** 4611 / J657a / M28042
SEN fine, slender; thin kimono.
4 手 *senshu* slender hand; woman's work
毛 *semmō* cilia, fine hair
5 巧 *senkō* cleverness at fine work
7 条 *senjō* filament
9 指 *senshi* a woman's slender fingers
柔 *senjū na* graceful, lithe; limber
10 弱 *senjaku* weakness, frailty
11 細 *sensai na* fine, nice; delicate; subtle
14 維 *sen'i* fiber, textiles, strand
維工業 *sen'i kōgyō* textile industry
維学 *sen'igaku* (study of) textiles
維性 *sen'isei no* fibrous
維品 *sen'ihin* textiles
維根 *sen'ikon* fibrous roots
維素 *sen'iso* cellulose, fibrin
19 麗 *senrei na* splendid and beautiful

12

繦 4587 / J655a / M-X KYŌ, KŌ knotted silk; knotted string; strap for carrying child. *mutsuki* diaper.

繖 4588 / J6564 / M27896 SAN shade, silk shade; parasol, umbrella.

繝 4589 / J6563 / M27908 KAN, GEN brocade thread.

繞 4590 / J6565 / M27909 JŌ. NYŌ. *megu(ru)* surround; return (seasons). *mawa(ru)* turn, go around; revolve, rotate, spin, gyrate; patrol; tour, take effect (medicine); be distributed; be past (time); be transferred. *motō(ru)* wander around.

繧 4591 / J6562 / M27936 UN brocade thread.
18 繝 *ungen* dyeing technique to create layered effect of dark and light colors

繚 4592 / J6567 / M27904 RYŌ put on; twist around.
7 乱 *ryōran* scattering far and wide

繙 4593 / J6566 / M27901 HAN. *himoto(ku)* read, peruse.
14 読 *handoku* perusal

B **繕** 4594 / J4136 / M27893 ZEN. *tsukuro(u)* repair, mend, darn; trim, tidy up, adjust.
5 立 *tsukuro(i)-ta(teru)* put up a good front
8 直 *tsukuro(i)-nao(su)* repair
13 飾 *tsukuro(i)-kaza(ru)* conceal (a mistake)

B **繭** 4595 / J4b7a / M27944 KEN. *mayu* cocoon.
6 糸 *kenshi* cocoon and silk thread
8 価 *mayuka* the price of cocoons
11 紬 *kenchū* pongee

A **織** 4596 / J3f25 / M27892 SHOKU, SHIKI weaving. *o(ru)* weave. *o(ri)* fabric, weave.
3 女 *o(ri)me, shokujo* woman weaver
子 *o(ri)ko* weaver, textile worker
工 *shokkō* weaver
上 *o(ri)-a(geru)* be completely woven
4 手 *o(ri)te* weaver
文 *shokumon* an inwoven design; figured cloth
方 *o(ri)kata* the weave; how to weave
込 *o(ri)-ko(mu)* weave into
元 *o(ri)moto* weaver, textile manufacturing
5 目 *o(ri)me* texture
出 *o(ri)da(shi)* woven figures; selvage. *o(ri)-da(su)* inweave designs
6 糸 *o(ri)ito* strand; thread for weaving
色 *o(ri)iro* natural-color cloth (undyed after weaving)
返 *o(ri)-kae(su)* reweave
成 *o(ri)-na(su)* weave (something); assemble
地 *o(ri)ji* texture
交 *o(ri)-maji(eru)* weave into
合 *o(ri)-a(waseru)* interweave, inweave
8 物 *orimono* cloth; textiles
物商 *orimonoshō* draper
物業 *orimonogyō* textile manufacturing
9 姫 *o(ri)hime* woman textile worker
10 紋 *o(ri)mon* crest woven into the cloth
14 模様 *o(ri)moyō* woven design
15 縫 *o(ri)nu(i), shokuhō* weaving and sewing
16 機 *shokki* weaving machine, loom

13

繪 4597 / J6569 / M27939 See **絵** 4488.

繩 4598 / J656a / M27937 See **縄** 4547.

繹 4599 / J6568 / M27975 EKI pull out.

繡 4600 / J-X / M27913 SHŪ sew; figured cloth.
6 匠 *shūshō* embroiderer

繫 4601 / J-X / M27940 **繋** 4573 / J3752 / M-X KEI. *tsuna(gu)* tie, fasten, chain, hitch, tether; moor; keep on a leash; connect, join; sustain, preserve (life). *tsuna(garu)* be connected, be tied up, be fastened to; be related to, follow closely. *kaka(ru)* anchor, lie at anchor. *tsuna(gi)* connection, bond, tie; stopgap, substitute.
4 止 *tsuna(gi)-to(meru)* tie, fasten, chain, hitch, tether; moor; keep on a leash; connect, join; sustain, preserve (life)
爪 *ka(ke)zume* plectrum
5 目 *tsuna(gi)me* joint
6 合 *tsuna(gi)-a(waseru)* connect, join
争 *keisō* dispute, contention
7 束 *keisoku* tying up in bundles; depriving of liberty
10 索 *keisaku* mooring ropes
留 *keiryū* mooring, anchorage

留気球 *keiryū kikyū* captive balloon
留船 *keiryūsen* moored ship
留塔 *keiryūtō* mooring mast
留場 *keiryūjō* moorings
11 累 *keirui* encumbrances, dependents
船 *keisen* mooring (a ship)
船所 *keisenjo* moorings, berthage
船料 *keisenryō* mooring charge
12 属 *keizoku* relationship
場 *kaka(ri)ba* anchorage, berth, mooring, roadstead
13 辞 *keiji* copula
16 縛 *keibaku* tying up; destiny

B **繰** 4602 / J372b / M27953 Sō. *ku(ru)* reel (thread); wind; gin (cotton); spin; turn (pages); look up (a word, etc.); refer to; count (the days); open (shutters).
2 入 *ku(ri)-i(reru)* deposit, transfer (money)
入金 *kuriirekin* transfer money, transfer balance, transfer fund
3 下 *ku(ri)-sa(geru)* move ahead (an appointment). *ku(ri)-oro(su)* gradually lower
上 *ku(ri)-a(geru)* advance (a date)
4 戸 *ku(ri)do* sliding door
込 *ku(ri)-ko(mu)* deposit, transfer; assign; march in ; rush in; turn out
5 広 *ku(ri)-hiro(geru)* unroll; spread (a rug)
出 *ku(ri)-da(su)* pay out (rope); call out (troops); go forth; disburse
出梯子 *ku(ri)da(shi)bashigo* extension ladder
出鉛筆 *ku(ri)da(shi) empitsu* mechanical pencil
6 返 *ku(ri)-kae(su)* do over, repeat, duplicate
合 *ku(ri)-a(wasu)* arrange things, manage
糸 *ku(ri)ito* reeling thread; raw silk thread
糸工 *ku(ri)itokō* silk reeler
7 言 *ku(ri)goto* tedious talk; repetition; complaint
戻 *ku(ri)-modo(su)* telescope (a fishing rod); repeat
8 延 *ku(ri)-no(beru)* postpone, defer
取 *ku(ri)-to(ru)* reel off (thread)
11 寄 *ku(ri)-yo(seru)* pull toward one
12 替 *ku(ri)-ka(eru)* change, shift; appropriate
越 *ku(ri)-ko(su)* transfer, carry forward
越金 *kurikoshikin* balance forwarded
14 綿 *ku(ri)wata* ginned cotton
綿機械 *ku(ri)wata kikai* cotton gin

14

繼 4603 / J656b / M27997 See **継** 4501.

辮 4604 / J6570 / M27991 See **弁** 1663.

繿 4605 / J6571 / M28009 See **襤** 5507.

繽 4606 / J656f / M28000 Hɪɴ, Bɪɴ abundant, plentiful; in disarray, disordered.

䌖 4607 / J656d / M28020 (国字) *kasuri* splashed pattern; cloth with splashed pattern.

纂 4608 / J353c / M28012 Sᴀɴ editing, compiling.
7 述 *sanjutsu suru* gather materials and write
10 修 *sanshū* compiling, editing

繻 4609 / J656c / M27996 Sʜᴜ satin, fine silk.
3 子 *shusu* satin
9 珍 *shuchin* figured satin

15

續 4610 / J6574 / M28037 See **続** 4500.

纖 4611 / J657a / M28042 See **繊** 4586.

纏 4612 / J453b / M28043 See **纒** 4617.

纈 4613 / J6572 / M28028 Kᴇᴛsᴜ tie-dyeing.

纘 4614 J6573 M28030 SAN inherit, carry on; continue; collect.

纐 4615 J6576 M28050 (国字) KŌ tie-dyeing.

21 纐 *kōkechi, kōketsu* tie-dyeing

16

纜 4616 J-X M28053 **纜** 4623 J657c M28100 RAN. *tomozuna* hawser.

纏 4617 J6575 M28058 **纏** 4612 J453b M28043 TEN. *mato(u)* wear; wrap up, tie up. *mato(maru), matsu(waru)* coil around; follow about; dangle after. *mato(meru)* settle, complete, agree upon, arrange; collect; put in order; unify, coordinate. *mato(maru)* be settled, be completed; be collected; be in order; be coherent; be united. *kuru(mu)* wrap up, tuck in. *kuru(meru)* lump together, include, sum up; quibble. *mato(matta)* round, large, definite, coherent. *mato(i)* fireman's standard.

3 上 *mato(me)-a(geru)* sum up, unite
5 付 *mato(i)-tsu(ku)* coil around; follow about; dangle after
7 足 *tensoku* foot binding
役 *matomeyaku* mediator
9 持 *matoimo(chi)* standard bearer
14 綿 *temmen* involvement, entanglement
16 頭 *tentō* celebration
18 繞 *tenjō suru* creep, twine around

17

纖 4618 J6579 M28072 See **繊** 4586.

纒 4619 J-X M-X See **纏** 4617.

纓 4620 J6577 M28067 EI, YŌ string; crown string; saddle strap; tie, bind. EI tassle on a crown.

纔 4621 J6578 M28070 SAN. ZAN. SAI. *wazuka* a little, a small quantity.

18

纛 4622 J657b M28093 TŌ, DŌ ceremonial pennant, banner.

21

纜 4623 J657c M28100 See **纜** 4616.

RAD. 缶 121

Mizugame water jar. At left: *hodogi hen* left-side "earthen jar." Nickname: Jar.

B **缶** 4624 J344c M28108 **罐** 4632 J6625 M28194 **鑵** 6370 J6f51 M41064 KAN can. *kama* steam boiler.

4 切 *kanki(ri)* can opener
13 詰 *kanzume* canning, canned goods; confining
詰工 *kanzumekō* canner, packer
詰工場 *kanzume kōjō* cannery
詰屋 *kanzumeya* cannery
詰業 *kanzumegyō* canning business

3

缸 4625 J657d M28112 KŌ. GŌ. *kame* large urn.

4

缺 4626 J657e M28122 See **欠** 2928.

11

罐 4627 J-X M-X Nonstandard for **缶** 4624.

罅 4628 J6621 M28169 KA. *hibi* crack, fissure, hole.

12 焼 *hibiya(ki)* crackleware
割 *hibiwa(re)* crack
裂 *karetsu* tearing; cracking

14

罌 4629 / J6622 / M28185 Ō vase.
12 粟 *keshi* poppy
粟種 *keshidane* poppy seed

15

罍 4630 / J6623 / M28187 RAI liquor container.

16

罎 4631 / J6624 / M28189 See **壜** 1114.

17

罐 4632 / J6625 / M28194 See **缶** 4624.

RAD. 网 122

Amigashira "net" crown. Variant: 罒 (5 strokes) *ami me* ("net" shaped like *me* "eye"), *megashira* "eye" crown, or *yoko me* sideways "eye." Nickname: Net.

网 4633 / J6626 / M28199 BŌ, MŌ *ami* net.

3

罕 4634 / J6627 / M28217 KAN bird net; flag. *mare* rare.

罔 4635 / J6628 / M28211 MŌ, BŌ net. *ami* net.

4

罘 4636 / J6629 / M28224 FU, FŪ net; rabbit net; deer net; bird net.

5

罟 4637 / J662a / M28248 KO net; fish net.
10 師 *koshi* one who fishes

罠 4638 / J662b / M28249 BIN. MIN. *wana* trap, snare.
12 結 *wana musu(bi)* running knot

8

罧 4639 / J662e / M28285 SHIN. RIN. *fushizuke* weir, fish trap made of brush.

罩 4640 / J662d / M28289 TŌ fish basket kept in water.

罨 4641 / J662c / M28288 AN cover.
8 法 *ampō* fomentation, compress, pack, poultice

罫 4642 / J3753 / M28295 KAI. KE, KEI ruled line.
4 引 *keibi(ki)* ruling; ruler; marking gauge; scriber
引紙 *keibi(ki)gami* ruled paper
10 紙 *keishi, keigami, kegami* lined paper
15 線 *keisen* ruled line

A **署** 4643 / J3d70 / M28311 **署** 4646 / J-X / M28319 SHO government office, (police) station. *sho(suru)* sign, write one's name. *tsukasa* office, government office; director, head official.
6 名 *shomei* signature, autograph
名国 *shomeikoku* signatory power
名捺印 *shomei-natsuin* signature and seal
8 長 *shochō* government office chief; police chief
10 員 *shoin* an official attached to an office

A **罪** 4644 / J3a61 / M28293 ZAI. *tsumi* sin, crime, offense, guilt, blame, fault, misconduct. *tsumi suru* charge; sentence; punish.
2 人 *tsumibito* sinner. *zainin* criminal
6 名 *zaimei* the charge, name of the crime
7 作 *tsumitsuku(ri)* sinfulness; sinner
状 *zaijō* nature of an offense, charges

状書 *zaijōga(ki)* (criminal's) superscription
[9]科 *zaika* crime; wickedness; punishment
[11]過 *zaika* offense, sin, fault
得 *tsumi (o) e(ru)* become guilty
深 *tsumibuka(i)* sinful, guilty
祭 *zaisai* sin offering
責 *zaiseki* liability of the accused; guilt, sin, wrongdoing
悪 *zaiaku* crime, sin, vice
悪感 *zaiakukan* sense of wrong, guilty conscience
[12]証 *zaishō* evidence of guilt
[13]滅 *tsumihorobo(shi)* amends, expiation, penance, conscience money
跡 *zaiseki* evidence of guilt
業 *zaigō* sin, iniquity, crime
障 *zaishō* sins, offenses
障消滅 *zaishō shōmetsu* expiation of one's sins
[14]罰 *zaibatsu* crime, offense
[15]質 *zaishitsu* nature of a crime

A **置** 4645 / J4356 / M28298 CHI. *o(ku) vt* place, put, set, deposit, lay; leave behind; keep, have, leave; establish; employ; appoint; post, station; pawn; skip (one day). *vi* be formed (dew). *o(keru)* go on (this way); keep (over night). *o(itekibori), o(itekebori)* leaving behind, giving the slip to. *-o(ki)* every other (day). *o(ki)-* standing, placed.
[3]土産 *o(ki)miyage* souvenir, memento, parting present
[4]文 *o(ki)bumi* a book left to posterity
方 *o(ki)kata* manner of placing
引 *o(ki)bi(ki)* taking someone's luggage and leaving an empty bag
手紙 *o(ki)tegami* letter left behind
戸棚 *o(ki)todana* chest of drawers
火燵 *o(ki)gotatsu* portable brazier
[5]石 *o(ki)ishi* garden landscaping stone
旧 *o(ki)-furu(su)* leave around to deteriorate
去 *o(ki)za(ri)* deserting (someone)
[6]行 *o(ite) yu(ku)* leave behind
返 *o(ki)-kae(ru)* replace
字 *o(ki)ji* characters skipped over in reading Chinese
[7]床 *o(ki)doko* movable *tokonoma* alcove
忘 *o(ki)-wasu(reru)* mislay; leave behind, forget
来 *o(ite) ku(ru)* leave behind
[8]迷 *o(ki)-mayo(u)* be at a loss as to where to put (something)
所 *o(ki)dokoro* storehouse, yard, place to put something
放 *o(kip)pana(shi), o(ki)hana(shi)* leaving things around
物 *okimono* ornament for display (in *tokonoma*), objet d'art
直 *o(ki)-nao(su)* replace, rearrange, transpose, interchange
[9]屋 *o(ki)ya* geisha house; red-light district
炬燵 *o(ki)gotatsu* portable boxed brazier
[10]酒 *chishu* opening a drinking party
時計 *o(ki)dokei* table clock
[11]鳥 *o(ki)tori* decorative bird
道 *o(ki)michi* raised road
違 *o(ki)-chiga(eru)* misplace
据 *o(ki)-su(eru)* lay (a stone)
[12]換 *o(ki)-ka(eru)* replace, rearrange, transpose, interchange. *chikan* substitution, replacement, displacement (in chemistry)
惑 *o(ki)-mado(wasu)* mislay
場 *o(ki)ba* storehouse, yard, place to put something
場所 *o(ki)basho* storehouse, yard, place to put something
[13]路 *o(ki)michi* raised road
[15]潮 *o(ki)shio* a good chance to stop

9

署 4646 / J-X / M28319 See 署 4643.

B **罰** 4647 / J4833 / M28315 **罸** 4648 / J662f / M28343 BATSU punishment, penalty. BACHI retribution, divine punishment. *bas(suru)* punish.
[6]当 *bachia(tari)* the damned, the cursed
[8]金 *bakkin* fine, penalty
杯 *bappai* penalty cup (that the loser has to drink)
[9]則 *bassoku* penal regulations
点 *batten* demerit marks
[10]俸 *bappō* docking of salary

10

罸 4648 / J662f / M28343 See 罰 4647.

罵 4649 / J474d / M28333 BA. *nonoshi(ru)* abuse, insult, speak ill of.
7 言 *bagen* abuse, insult, slander, evil speaking
声 *basei* boos, jeers
10 倒 *batō* denunciation, abuse
12 詈 *bari* abuse, reviling
詈雑言 *barizōgon* abusive language

B 罷 4650 / J486d / M28336 HI *ya(mu) vi* end, stop, cease; subside, calm down, pass; die out, be extinguished; leave, go off; be abandoned. *ya(meru) vt* end, discontinue; give up, abandon; abolish; resign, retire. *maka(ru)* leave, withdraw, go. *ya(me)* end, discontinuance, stop.
3 工 *hikō* strike, walkout
15 市 *hishi* merchants' selling strike
出 *maka(ri)-de(ru)* present oneself; appear before; leave, withdraw
6 成 *maka(ri)-na(ranu)* must not be; be not allowed
8 免 *himen* dismissal
9 通 *maka(ri)-tō(ru)* pass
為 *maka(ri)-na(ranu)* must not be; be not allowed
12 越 *maka(ri)-ko(su)* visit, call on, go
間違 *maka(ri)-machiga(u)* make a mistake. *maka(ri)-machiga(ttemo)* at the worst. *maka(ri)-machiga(eba)* if worse comes to worst
13 業 *higyō* strike, walkout

11

罹 4651 / J586d / M28347 RI. *kaka(ru)* catch, get, contract (illness).
7 災 *risai* suffering (from a calamity), affliction
災民 *risaimin* victims, sufferers
災者 *risaisha* victims, sufferers
10 病 *ribyō* contraction of a disease
11 患 *rikan* contracting a disease

13

羃 4652 / J6632 / M28393 冪 408 / J5151 / M1601 BEKI power (in math); cover.

羂 4653 / J6630 / M28386 KEN. *wana* trap, snare.

14

羆 4654 / J6631 / M28398 HI. *higuma, shiguma* brown bear.

B 羅 4655 / J4d65 / M28397 RA silk gauze, thin silk.
6 列 *raretsu* marshalling; an array. *raretsu suru* arrange, enumerate, itemize.
宇 *rau, rao* bamboo pipestem
宇竹 *raodake* bamboo pipestem
宇替 *raoga(e)* bamboo pipestem seller
7 甸 *Raten* Latin
甸語 *Ratengo* Latin
10 紗 *rasha* woolen cloth
針 *rashin* compass needle
針儀 *rashingi* compass
針盤 *rashimban* compass
馬 *Rōma* Rome
馬加特力 *Rōma Katoriku* Roman Catholic
馬字 *Rōmaji* Roman letters, Roman alphabet
馬字綴 *Rōmajitsuzu(ri)* romanization
馬教 *Rōmakyō* Roman Catholicism
馬数字 *Rōma sūji* Roman numerals
13 漢 *rakan* arhat

17

羇 4656 / J6634 / M28412 See 羈 4657.

19

羈 4657 / J6633 / M28417 羇 4656 / J6634 / M28412 覊 5521 / J6b2b / M34795 覉 5520 / J-X / M34794 KI reins; connection.
7 束 *kisoku* suppression of freedom
10 旅 *kiryo* travel
11 絆 *kihan* restraint, yoke, shackles; ties, bonds

RAD. 羊 123

Hitsuji sheep. At left: ⺶ *hitsuji hen.* At top: ⺷. Nickname: Sheep.

A 羊 4658 / J4d53 / M28425 Yō. *hitsuji* sheep.
3 小屋 *hitsujigoya* sheepfold
4 水 *yōsui* amniotic fluid
毛 *yōmō* wool
5 皮 *yōhi* sheepskin
皮紙 *yōhishi* parchment, sheepskin
皮綴 *yōhi toji* sheepskin binding
6 肉 *yōniku* mutton
7 角 *yōkaku* ram's horns
8 舎 *yōsha* sheep shed
10 脂 *yōshi* mutton tallow
12 歯 *shida* fern
歯類 *shidarui* ferns
13 腸 *yōchō(taru)* meandering, zigzag, winding
飼 *hitsujika(i)* shepherd, shepherdess
群 *yōgun* flock of sheep
酪 *yōraku* sheep's milk
16 頭 *yōtō* (going around in) sheep's clothing
頭狗肉 *yōtō-kuniku* selling inferior goods under a famous name
19 羹 *yōkan* sweet bean jelly
羹色 *yōkan iro* a dull purplish color

2

羌 4659 / J6635 / M28429 Kyō barbarian. *ā* sigh.

3

A 美 4660 / J487e / M28435 Bi beauty, grace, charm. *utsuku(shii)* beautiful, lovely, fine, good-looking; picturesque; sweet (voice); noble, pure.
2 人 *bijin* a beautiful woman
人比 *bijin-kura(be)* beauty contest
人投票 *bijin tōhyō* beauty contest
人画 *bijinga* picture of a beautiful woman
人草 *bijinsō* poppy
3 女 *bijo* beautiful woman
4 文 *bibun* ornate writing
化 *bika* beautification, idealization
少年 *bishōnen* handsome youth
爪術 *bisōjutsu* manicure, pedicure
以教会 *Mii Kyōkai* Methodist Church
5 玉 *bigyoku* gem, precious stone
田 *biden* good rice field
本 *bihon* beautifully bound book
6 色 *bishoku* beautiful color
名 *bimei* good name, fame, high reputation
7 言 *bigen* honeyed words; maxim
妙 *bimyō* elegance, grace, exquisiteness
妓 *bigi* beautiful geisha
技 *bigi* brilliant performance, fine play
形 *bikei* beautiful form; beautiful woman
声 *bisei* beautiful voice
男 *binan, bidan* handsome man
男子 *binanshi, bidanshi* handsome man
男美女 *binan-bijo* beautiful men and women
8 味 *bimi* relish, good flavor, delicacy, rich dishes, deliciousness. *oi(shii)* delicious
服 *bifuku* fine clothes
的 *biteki* esthetic
育 *biiku* esthetic culture
果 *bika* good results
事 *migoto* splendid, beautiful. *biji* commendable act
学 *bigaku* esthetics
学的 *bigakuteki* esthetic
9 音 *bion* beautiful voice
風 *bifū* beautiful custom
俗 *bizoku* beautiful custom
姫 *biki* beautiful girl, beauty
点 *biten* good point, virtue, merit
美 *bibi(shii)* beautiful, splendid
食 *bishoku* dainty food; lavish diet
食主義 *bishoku shugi* epicureanism
食家 *bishokuka* gourmet
10 酒 *bishu, umazake* quality saké
称 *bishō* euphemism
挙 *bikyo* commendable act
容 *biyō* beautiful face; beauty
容体操 *biyō taisō* calisthenics
容的 *biyōteki* beautiful
容学校 *biyō gakkō* beauticians' school
容院 *biyōin* beauty parlor
容室 *biyōshitsu* beauty parlor

容師 *biyōshi* beautician
容術 *biyōjutsu* beauty culture
11 術 *bijutsu* art, fine arts
術工芸 *bijutsu kōgei* industrial art, arts and crafts, artistic handicrafts
術心 *bijutsushin* artistic sense
術史 *bijutsushi* history of art
術的 *bijutsuteki* artistic
術学校 *bijutsu gakkō* school of fine arts
術院 *bijutsuin* academy of art
術品 *bijutsuhin* work of art
術界 *bijutsukai* the world of art
術家 *bijutsuka* artist
術眼 *bijutsugan* artistic eye
術商 *bijutsushō* art dealer
術館 *bijutsukan* art gallery
12 粧 *bishō* beautiful attire; beautiful makeup
景 *bikei* lovely view
装 *bisō* rich attire, fine dress
13 祿 *biroku* handsome stipend
感 *bikan* sense of beauty
意識 *biishiki* art appreciation
辞 *biji* flowery language; clever writing
辞学 *bijigaku* rhetoric
14 徳 *bitoku* virtue, fine trait; good deed
貌 *bibō* good looks
髪 *bihatsu* beautiful hair
15 調 *bichō* harmony, melody
談 *bidan* praiseworthy anecdote, story
髯 *bizen* fine beard; fine mustache
質 *bishitsu* good quality, merit, fine traits
17 醜 *bishū* personal appearance, beauty or ugliness
18 観 *bikan* lovely view, beautiful sight
顔 *bigan* beautiful face
顔水 *bigansui* face lotion
顔術 *biganjutsu* facial treatment, the beautician's art
19 麗 *birei* beautiful; clean, pure

4

羔 4661 / J6636 / M28447 Kō. *kohitsuji* lamb.

5

羚 4662 / J6639 / M28463 Rei antelope.
6 羊 *kamoshika, reiyō* antelope

羝 4663 / J6638 / M28470 Tei. *ohitsuji* ram.
6 羊 *teiyō* ram

羞 4664 / J6637 / M28471 Shū. *haji(ru)* feel ashamed.
10 恥 *shūchi* shyness, bashfulness; dishonor, disgrace
恥心 *shūchishin* sense of shame, shyness, modesty

7

羨 4665 / J4122 / M28503 Sen. *uraya(mu)* be envious, be jealous, covet. *uraya(mashii)* enviable.
11 望 *sembō* envy

A **群** 4666 / J3732 / M28498 **羣** 4667 / J663a / M28497 Gun group, crowd, gang, herd, swarm, flock; common run. *mu(reru), mura(garu)* crowd, flock, swarm. *mu(re)* group, crowd, flock, herd, bevy, school, swarm; cluster (of stars); clump. *mura* crowd; swarming.
3 口 *gunkō* the words of many people
小 *gunshō* the small, the many, the vulgar
山 *gunzan* many mountains; mountain ranges
下 *gunka* many retainers
5 生 *gunsei* all animate creation; many people; gregariousness
立 *murada(tsu)* gather and stand together. *murada(chi)* standing in a group
民 *gummin* masses, populace, multitude
6 羊 *gun'yō* many sheep
臣 *gunshin* the whole body of officials
邦 *gumpō* many countries
7 体 *guntai* colony (in biology)
芳 *gumpō* many beautiful flowers
8 青 *gunjō* ultramarine, navy blue
居 *mure-i(ru)* crowding in, coming together. *gunkyo* gregariousness
牧 *gumboku* many local officials
盲 *gummō* blind populace; illiterates
9 俗 *gunzoku* many people, the public
神 *gunshin* many gods
発地震 *gumpatsu jishin* swarm earthquakes
10 起 *gunki* insurrection
島 *guntō* archipelago, group of islands

党 *guntō* many political parties; organizing a party
書 *gunsho* many books
11 遊 *gun'yū* many swimming together
盗 *guntō* gang of robbers
12 棲 *gunsei* gregariousness
雲 *murakumo* cloud masses
落 *gunraku* many communities; a cluster of plants
衆 *gunshū* crowd, multitude
雄 *gun'yū* rival chiefs
雄割拠 *gun'yū kakkyo* rivalry of local barons
集 *mure-atsu(maru)* gather in large groups. *gunshū* crowd, multitude, group
集心理 *gunshū shinri* mob psychology, mass psychology
集心理学 *gunshū shinrigaku* mob psychology, mass psychology
14 像 *gunzō* sculptured group
疑 *gungi* many doubts; doubts of the people
聚 *gunshū* a herd, a flock
20 議 *gungi* multitudinous opinions

A **義** 4668 / J3541 / M28504 GI justice, righteousness, morality; humanity; integrity, honor, loyalty, chivalry, devotion; meaning, significance. *gi to suru* justify. *gi-* in-law; artificial.
2 人 *gijin* righteous man, noble-hearted man
3 士 *gishi* loyal retainer; righteous person; martyr
子 *gishi* adopted child
4 心 *gishin* chivalrous spirit, public spirit
手 *gishu* artificial arm; artificial hand
父 *gifu* father-in-law; foster father; stepfather
犬 *giken* faithful dog
化 *gika* (Catholic) justification
太夫 *gidayū* ballad-drama music
5 母 *gibo* mother-in-law, foster mother, stepmother
甲 *gikō* plectrum
民 *gimin* public-spirited man
兄 *gikei* elder brother-in-law
兄弟 *gikyōdai* brother-in-law, stepbrother, sworn brother
6 気 *giki* chivalrous spirit, chivalry, heroism
7 足 *gisoku* artificial leg
兵 *gihei* loyal soldier, volunteer corps
弟 *gitei* younger brother-in-law
8 金 *gikin* contribution
枝 *gishi* grafting (plants)
肢 *gishi* artificial limb
者 *gisha* righteous person
和団 *Giwadan* the Boxers
妹 *gimai* younger sister-in-law
姉 *gishi* elder sister-in-law
姉妹 *gishimai* sister-in-law
9 軍 *gigun* righteous army
侠 *gikyō* chivalry, generosity, heroism
侠心 *gikyōshin* chivalrous spirit, public spirit
勇 *giyū* heroism, loyalty and courage
勇団 *giyūdan* patriotic volunteer corps
勇兵 *giyūhei* volunteer soldier
勇軍 *giyūgun* volunteer corps
勇艦隊 *giyū kantai* volunteer fleet
10 徒 *gito* champions of righteousness
倉 *gisō* emergency grain storehouses
挙 *gikyo* worthy undertaking; heroic deed
烈 *giretsu* heroism, nobility of soul
捐 *gien* donation, contribution
捐金 *gienkin* donation, contribution
11 眼 *gigan* artificial eye
脚 *gikyaku* artificial leg
務 *gimu* duty, obligation, responsibility, liability
務心 *gimushin* sense of duty
務年限 *gimu nengen* obligatory term of service
務的 *gimuteki* obligatory, binding, compulsory
務者 *gimusha* debtor, responsible person
務教育 *gimu kyōiku* compulsory education
務観念 *gimu kannen* sense of duty
理 *giri* sense of duty, sense of honor, obligation, justice, courtesy, debt of gratitude
理人情 *giri-ninjō* justice and charity, duty and humanity
理不知 *girishirazu* ignorant of one's duty; a person ignorant of one's duty
理付合 *girizu(ki)a(i)* association based merely on duty
理尽 *girizu(ku) de* out of deference to; as a matter of duty
理合 *giria(i)* association based merely on duty

理知 *girishi(razu)* ungrateful person
理張 *giriba(ru)* be faithful to duty; be overzealous socially
理堅 *girigata(i)* loyal to duty
12 歯 *gishi* artificial tooth, false tooth
絶 *gizetsu suru* disown, break off relationship
援 *gien* donation, contribution
援金 *gienkin* donation, contribution
13 解 *gikai* exposition, commentary
賊 *gizoku* chivalrous robber
戦 *gisen* holy war, crusade
14 僕 *giboku* faithful servant
旗 *giki* flag of loyalty, banner of righteousness
認 *ginin* (Christian) justification
塾 *gijuku* a private school
15 憤 *gifun* righteous indignation

9

羹 4669/J663e/M28536 羮 4672/J663d/M28584 KŌ. *atsumono* hot soup.

羯 4670/J663b/M28537 KATSU, KETSU barbarian.
16 磨 *katsuma* karma

10

羲 4671/J663c/M28552 KI, GI used in proper names.

13

羮 4672/J663d/M28584 See 羹 4669.

羶 4673/J663f/M28581 SEN odor of sheep. *namagusa(i)* smelling of sheep.

羸 4674/J6640/M28583 RUI weak; thin.
10 弱 *ruijaku* weakness, feebleness, imbecility

RAD. 羽 124

Hane feather, wing. At top: *hane kammuri*. Variant: 羽. Nickname: Wing.

A 羽 4675/J3129/M28614 U. *ha* feather. *hane* feather, plumage, wing; blade, paddle, fan. *wa* bird counter.
2 二重 *habutae* habutae silk
3 子 *hago, hane* shuttlecock
子板 *hagoita* battledore
子突 *hanetsu(ki)* battledore and shuttlecock
4 毛 *umō* feathers, plumage, down
化 *uka* emergence (of insects); people sprouting wings and flying
太 *hata* grouper (a fish)
5 目 *hame* panel, wainscoting; predicament, plight
目板 *hameita* wainscoting
6 衣 *hagoromo* robe of feathers
交 *hagai* pinion, wings
団扇 *hauchiwa* feather fan
7 抜 *hanu(ke)* molting
8 突 *hanetsu(ki)* battledore and shuttlecock
9 音 *haoto, hane oto* flapping sound, sound of birds on the wing
風 *hakaze* breeze caused by flapping wings
10 振 *habu(ri)* plumage; influence, power
根突 *hanetsu(ki)* battledore and shuttlecock
13 搏 *habata(ku)* flap, flutter. *habata(ki)* flapping, fluttering
裏 *haura* the underside of a bird's wings
蒲団 *hanebuton* down puff; quilt of down, feather bed
14 箒 *habōki, hanebōki* feather brush
15 撃 *hau(tsu), habata(ku)* flap wings
17 翼 *uyoku* wings; assistance
18 織 *haori* Japanese half-coat. *hao(ru)* put on, slip over
19 蟻 *haari, haneari* winged ant

4

翆 4676/J6643/M28647 Nonstandard for 翠 4685.

6

B 翁 4677 / J3227 / M28635' Ō old man; venerable. *okina* old man.

翅 4678 / J6642 / M28642 SHI *hane* (insect) wings.
7 状 *shijō* wing shape

5

A 翌 4679 / J4d62 / M28657' 翊 4680 / J6644 / M28655 YOKU. *akuru* next, following.
4 日 *yokujitsu* the next day
月 *yokugetsu* the next month
6 年 *yokutoshi, yokunen* the next year
11 翌日 *yokuyokujitsu* two days after
翌年 *yokuyokunen* year after next
12 晩 *yokuban* the next evening, the next night
暁 *yokugyō* at dawn the next day
朝 *yokuchō, yokuasa* the next morning

A 習 4681 / J3d2c / M28672' SHŪ. *nara(u)* learn, be taught, take lessons, practice. *nara(wasu)* have children study or practice. *nara(i)* habit, custom, usage; the way, the lot. *nara(washi)* custom, usage, tradition.
4 込 *nara(i)-ko(mu)* master, be grounded in
6 行 *nara(i)-okona(u)* learn to do, learn to follow
合 *shūgō* reconciling or compromising views
字 *shūji* penmanship, calligraphy
字帳 *shūjichō* copybook
7 作 *shūsaku* a practice project
8 性 *shūsei* habit, second nature
学 *shūgaku* learning, studying
9 俗 *shūzoku* usage, convention
11 得 *shūtoku* learning, acquirement
12 覚 *nara(i)-obo(eru)* learn (a trade)
14 練 *shūren* drill, training
慣 *shūkan* custom, habit, way, usage, practice
慣性 *shūkansei* tendency
慣法 *shūkanhō* common law
15 熟 *shūjuku* mastery, proficiency
18 癖 *shūheki* habit

6

翕 4682 / J6645 / M28691 KYŪ gather.
12 然 *kyūzen* spontaneously, with one accord

翔 4683 / J6646 / M28689 SHŌ. *ka(keru)* soar, fly.
3 上 *ka(ke)-nobo(ru)* fly up, mount up
10 破 *shōha suru* complete a flight

8

翡 4684 / J6647 / M28733 HI a kind of kingfisher.
14 翠 *hisui* jade, chrysoprase; kingfisher. *kawasemi* kingfisher

翠 4685 / J3f69 / M28732 SUI. *midori* green, verdure.
5 玉 *suigyoku* emerald; jade
6 色 *suishoku* verdure, green
8 雨 *suiu* rain falling on green leaves
13 微 *suibi* blue mountains, mountain side
楊 *suiyō* willows in leaf
14 緑玉 *suiryokugyoku* emerald
22 巒 *suiran* green hills, verdant mountains

9

翦 4686 / J6648 / M28752 See 剪 502.

翥 4687 / J-X / M28744 SHO fly up.

翩 4688 / J6649 / M28762 HEN fluttering (of a flag); wave; turn; soar.
15 翩 *hempen(taru)* fluttering; frivolous
18 翻 *hempon(taru)* fluttering; frivolous

翫 4689 / J3465 / M28766 GAN. *moteaso(bu)* play; take pleasure in; play (on an instrument); play with; make sport of; trifle with (affections).
8 味 *gammi suru* taste; enjoy; appreciate
15 賞 *ganshō* appreciation, admiration

10

翰 4690 J344d M28780 KAN letter; writing brush.
8 長 *Kanchō* Cabinet (Chief) Secretary
林 *kanrin* literary circles
林院 *kanrin'in* academy, institute
14 墨 *kamboku* brush and ink; writing; drawing

11

翳 4691 J664a M28796 EI. *kaza(su)* hold aloft; shade (the eyes); stick (something) in the hair. *kasu(mu)* be purblind.
5 目 *kasu(mi)me* blurred eyes

B 翼 4692 J4d63 M28801' YOKU wing; plane; flank. *tsubasa* wings.
7 状 *yokujō* wing shape
10 桁 *yokuketa* spar
12 幅 *yokufuku* wingspread
14 端 *yokutan* wing tip
15 賛 *yokusan* support, approval, countenance
17 翼 *yokuyoku na* careful, prudent

12

翹 4693 J664b M28808 GYŌ excellence.
11 望 *gyōbō* hope, expectancy

B 翻 4694 J4b5d M28814 飜 6673 J664c M44009 HON. HAN. *hirugae(ru) vi* turn over, wave, flutter. *hirugae(su) vt* change (one's mind); turn, reverse; wave, flutter; dodge. *kobo(reru) vi* spill, overflow, be scattered. *kobo(su) vt* spill; grumble over. *hirugae(tte)* on second thought.
7 弄 *honrō suru* toss (a ship) about; flirt with; make fun of
8 刻 *honkoku, hankoku* reprint
10 案 *hon'an* an adaptation
11 訳 *hon'yaku* translation, version
訳官 *hon'yakkan* official translator
訳者 *hon'yakusha* translator
訳物 *hon'yakumono* a translation
訳家 *hon'yakuka* translator
訳書 *hon'yakusho* a translation
訳違 *hon'yakuchiga(i)* mistranslation
訳権 *hon'yakuken* translation rights
12 然 *honzen to* suddenly
筋斗 *mondori* somersault, handspring, tumbling
13 意 *hon'i suru* change one's mind

14

耀 4695 J1d51 M28828 YŌ. *kagaya(ku)* shine, sparkle, gleam, twinkle; brilliant, radiant, bright. *kagaya(kasu) vt* light up, brighten, illumine. *kagaya(kashii)* bright (future); brilliant (achievement).

RAD. 老 125

Rō or *oi* old. Variant: 耂 (4 strokes) *oi kammuri* or *oigashira*. Nickname: Old Man.

A 老 4696 J4f37 M28842 RŌ aging, old age, old people. *o(iru), oiba(mu)* grow old. *fu(keru)* grow old. *o(iraku)* old age. *o(i)* old age; old person. *o(i)-* old, aging.
2 人 *rōjin* old person; old folks
3 女 *rōjo* old woman; senior lady-in-waiting
子 *o(i)go* child of one's old age. *Rōshi* Laozi, founder of Taoism
大 *rōdai* aging
大国 *rōtaikoku, rōdaikoku* decadent nation
大家 *rōtaika* veteran authority
4 手 *rōshu* an old hand, past master, veteran, expert
木 *rōboku, o(i)ki* an old tree
父 *rōfu* one's aged father
込 *o(i)-ko(mu)* grow old, weaken with age

中 *rōjū* councilor of the shogun
公 *rōkō* (polite) old nobleman
友 *rōyū* an old friend
水夫 *rōsuifu* an old sailor
心 *o(i)gokoro* feeling old
心地 *o(i)gokochi* feeling old
少 *rōshō* old and young
少不定 *rōshō-fujō* uncertainty of life
夫 *rōfu* an old man; this old man (oneself)
夫婦 *rōfūfu* an old couple
5 母 *rōbo* an aged mother
生 *rōsei* an old man (referring to himself)
功 *rōkō na* veteran, experienced
巧 *rōkō na* veteran, experienced
幼 *rōyō* old people and children, young and old
台 *rōdai* (polite word in letters) an old person
兄 *rōkei* aging elder brother, respected aging friend
6 臣 *rōshin* senior retainer
行 *o(i)-yu(ku)* gradually grow old
成 *hine(ru)* grow old. *mase(ta)* precocious, forward, sophisticated. *rōsei* maturity, experience, precocity
死 *rōshi suru* die of old age
朽 *rōkyū* superannuation, decrepitude. *o(i)-ku(chiru)* grow old and useless
壮 *rōsō* young and old
吏 *rōri* an experienced official
先 *o(i)saki* an old person's remaining years
先生 *rōsensei* an old teacher
年 *rōnen* old age, declining years
年者 *rōnensha* old people
年期 *rōnenki* old age
7 身 *rōshin* aged body; an old person (polite)
体 *rōtai* old body, an aged person
妓 *rōgi* an old geisha
杉 *rōsan* an old cryptomeria
兵 *rōhei* an old soldier, veteran
来 *rōrai* since growing old
寿 *rōju* longevity, old age
8 松 *o(i)matsu, rōshō* an old pine tree
波 *o(i)nami* growing old and wrinkled
若 *rōjaku, rōnyaku* old and young
苦 *rōku* the troubles of old age
妻 *rōsai* aged wife
果 *o(i)-ha(teru)* weaken with age

者 *rōsha* an old person
9 後 *rōgo* old age, declining years
荘学 *Rōsōgaku* Taoism
10 馬 *rōba, o(i)uma* old horse
骨 *rōkotsu* old bones, old man
病 *oiyami, rōbyō* infirmities of age
師 *rōshi* an aged teacher; aged priest
酒 *rōshu* old wine
将 *rōshō* veteran general
衰 *o(i)-otoro(eru)* grow old and weak. *rōsui* senility, old-age infirmity
翁 *rōō* an old man
耄 *o(i)-bo(reru)* to age and weaken. *rōmō, o(i)bo(re)* second childhood; senile person; age and weakness
叟 *rōsō* an old man
弱 *rōjaku* old-age infirmity; old and young
11 婦 *rōfu* an old woman; this old woman (oneself)
惚 *o(i)bo(reru)* to age and weaken. *o(i)bo(re)* second childhood; senile person; age and weakness
悴 *rōsui* getting old and emaciated
盛 *o(i)-saka(ru)* be vigorous in old age
視眼 *rōshigan* farsightedness
眼 *rōgan* farsightedness
眼鏡 *rōgankyō* glasses for older people
婆 *rōba* an old woman
婆心 *rōbashin* grandmotherly concern, excessive solicitude
12 雄 *rōyū* an old hero
爺 *oyaji, rōya* elderly man, old man
廃 *rōhai* superannuation
廃物 *rōhaibutsu* waste matter, waste products
13 僧 *rōsō* an old priest
媼 *rōō* an old woman
歳 *rōsai* old age
楽 *oiraku* an old man's leisure
農 *rōnō* an old farmer
14 僕 *rōboku* old manservant
境 *rōkyō* old age, declining years
緑 *o(i)midori* dark green
練 *rōren na* experienced, veteran, skilled
練家 *rōrenka* expert, veteran
15 輩 *rōhai* the aged
熟 *rōjuku* mature skill, maturity, mellowness
舗 *rōho, shinise* long-established shop
16 儒 *rōju* an old Confucian scholar; a great teacher

嬢 *rōjō* maiden lady
樹 *rōju* an old tree
獪 *rōkai na* crafty, astute, wily
17 優 *rōyū* an old actor or actress
齢 *rōrei* old age
齢者 *rōreisha* old people
齢艦 *rōreikan* superannuated vessel
18 軀 *rōku* old age; enfeebled body
顔 *rōgan* face of an old person
19 識 *rōshiki* mature ideas
20 艦 *rōkan* superannuated ship
21 鶯 *o(i)ugulsu, rōō* a nightingale still singing when spring is past

2

A 考 4697 / J394d / M28843 Kō thought, consideration; research, treatise.
kanga(eru) think, consider, believe, suspect; be of the opinion; intend; expect, hope, fear; judge, conclude; imagine, suppose; regard as; be discreet; ponder over; reconsider; be prepared for; invent.
kanga(e) thought; idea; opinion; intention; discretion; consideration; deliberation; resolution, plan; expectation; imagination.
4 方 *kanga(e)kata* way of thinking; point of view; solution
込 *kanga(e)-ko(mu)* be absorbed in thought, meditate
5 付 *kanga(e)-tsu(ku)* recall, remember; invent
出 *kanga(e)-da(su)* think out, invent; recall, remember; begin to think
古 *kōko* study of antiquities
古学 *kōkogaku* archeology
古学者 *kōkogakusha* archeologist
6 回 *kanga(e)-megu(rasu)* ponder, think out (a solution)
合 *kanga(e)-a(waseru)* think of together
当 *kanga(e)-a(taru)* occur to one; suspect
7 妣 *kōhi* one's deceased parents
抜 *kanga(e)-nu(ku)* reflect, think over
究 *kōkyū* investigation, research
8 味 *kanga(e)-aji(wau)* carefully think over
物 *kanga(e)mono* puzzle, problem
直 *kanga(e)-nao(su)* reconsider
事 *kanga(e)goto* something to think about; concern, preoccupation, worry
9 計 *kanga(e)-haka(ru)* plan
訂 *kōtei* critical historical research
査 *kōsa* consideration; test; quiz
10 案 *kōan suru* contrive, plan, originate.
kōan idea, plan; project; scheme; device, gadget
11 深 *kanga(e)buka(i)* thoughtful, prudent
12 証 *kōshō* investigation, research
違 *kanga(e)chiga(i)* misconception, mistake
量 *kōryō* consideration
13 試 *kōshi* examination
14 慣 *kanga(e)-na(reru)* be accustomed to think
様 *kanga(e)yō* way of thinking, viewpoint
察 *kōsatsu* consideration, inquiry
15 慮 *kōryo* careful thought, consideration, deliberation
課 *kōka* studying students' or personnel records (for placement purposes)
課表 *kōkahyō* business record; personnel record
18 験 *kōken* investigation
19 覈 *kōkaku* thinking and investigating

4

A 者 4698 / J3c54 / M28852 者 4702 / J-X / M28853 SHA person; thing. *mono* person, somebody. *-sha* agent, actor.

耄 4699 / J664e / M28848 耄 4700 / J-X / M28850 Bō, Mō senility.
12 期 *bōki* age of senility
13 碌 *mōroku* senility, second childhood

耆 4701 / J664d / M28849 KI, SHI senility.
6 老 *kirō* person in his or her sixties or seventies
那教 *Jainakyō* Jainism
11 宿 *kishuku* veteran (educator), authority
14 徳 *kitoku* an old man of character

5

者 4702 / J-X / M28853 See 者 4698.

6

耋 4703 / J664f / M28861 TETSU advanced age, elderly person.

6 竹米糸缶网罒羊羽【老耂】6 而耒耳聿肉月臣自至臼舌舛舟艮色艸艹虍虫血行衣衤西

RAD. 而 126

Shikashite and then. Nickname: Rake.

而 4704 / J3c29 / M28871 Jɪ. *shika(shite)* but, however. *shika(mo)* moreover, nevertheless. *sōshi(te), soshi(te)* and.

— 3 —

B 耐 4705 / J4251 / M28879 Tᴀɪ enduring. *ta(eru)* endure; support; withstand, resist, brave, weather; be fit for, be equal to.

[3] 乏 *taibō* austerity, voluntary privation
乏生活 *taibō seikatsu* life of austerity, hard life
久 *taikyū* endurance, persistence, permanence, durability
久力 *taikyūryoku* durability, persistence, staying power, lasting quality
久性 *taikyūsei* durability, persistence, staying power, lasting quality
[4] 水 *taisui* waterproof, watertight
切 *ta(e)-ki(reru)* be able to endure
火 *taika* fireproof
火材 *taikazai* fireproof material
火性 *taikasei* fire-resistant
火粘土 *taika nendo* fireproof clay
火煉瓦 *taika renga* firebrick
[7] 忍 *ta(e)-shino(bu)* patiently endure. *tainin* patience, perseverance, fortitude
[11] 貧生活 *taihin seikatsu* hard life
[12] 湿 *taishitsu* moistureproof
寒 *taikan* coldproof
寒性 *taikansei* cold-resistant
寒装置 *taikan sōchi* winterizing
[14] 酸 *taisan* acidproof, acid-resistant
[15] 熱 *tainetsu* heat-resisting
震 *taishin* earthquake-proof
震力 *taishinryoku* strength to withstand earthquakes

RAD. 耒 127

Suki hen left-side "plow" or *rai-suki* (*rai* being the *on* both of *suki* "plow" and 來 or 耒 *kuru* "come"). Nickname: 3-Branch Tree (cf. Rads. 75 and 115).

耒 4706 / J6650 / M28898 See 来 2565.

— 4 —

耙 4707 / J6652 / M28911 Hᴀ forked hoe.

耘 4708 / J6651 / M28910 Uɴ. *kusagi(ru)* weed.

B 耗 4709 / J4c57 / M28909' Mō, Kō *he(ru)* decrease.

[10] 高 *he(ri)daka* ullage, loss in weight
[12] 廃 *kōhai* decline (in morality)

A 耕 4710 / J394c / M28907' Kō. *tagaya(su)* plow, cultivate.

[3] 土 *kōdo* rich soil, mold
土機 *kōdoki* farm tractor
[4] 夫 *kōfu* farmer
[6] 地 *kōchi* arable land; farm land
地整理 *kōchi seiri* resurvey of farm lands making certain adjustments
[7] 作 *kōsaku* cultivation, farming
作地 *kōsakuchi* arable or cultivated land
作物 *kōsakubutsu* farm products
作者 *kōsakusha* tiller, farmer
作器械 *kōsaku kikai* farm implements
[8] 牧 *kōboku* farming and dairying
[10] 馬 *kōba* plow horse
耘 *kōun* farming, cultivation
耘機 *kōunki* farm tractor
[11] 野 *kōya* arable land
運機 *kōunki* farm tractor
[13] 農 *kōnō* farming; farmer
[14] 種 *kōshu* (land) cultivation
種学 *kōshugaku* agronomy
[15] 稼 *kōka* farming, agriculture
[18] 織 *kōshoku* farming and weaving

5

耜 4711 / J6653 / M28915 SHI. *suki* plow, plow blade.

7

耡 4712 / J6654 / M28927 SHOKU, JO ancient system of grain tax. *su(ku)* plow, cultivate. *suki* plow.

9

耦 4713 / J-X / M28952 GŪ plowing; a pair.

8 刺 *gūshi* killing each other

10

耨 4714 / J6655 / M28961 DŌ hoe, weed; exclude.

RAD. 耳 128

Mimi ear. At left: *mimi hen*. Enclosure: 耳. Nickname: Ear.

A **耳** 4715 / J3c2a / M28999 JI ear. *mimi* ear; edge, border; loop; selvage; bread crusts.

3 下腺 *jikasen* parotid gland

下腺炎 *jikasen'en* mumps

4 孔 *jikō* ear orifice

元 *mimimoto de* around one's ears

5 目 *jimoku* eye and ear; one's attention; informer

旧 *mimifuru(i)* stale, hackneyed

打 *mimiu(chi) suru* whisper in another's ear

6 早 *mimibaya(i)* quick of hearing

朶 *mimitabu* earlobe. *jida* earlobe, ears

8 門 *jimon* ear orifice

底 *jitei* ears

垂 *mimidare* ear discharge

学問 *mimi gakumon* learning by ear, picked-up knowledge

9 屎 *mimi kuso* earwax

垢 *mimi aka* earwax

科 *jika* otology

10 疾 *jishitsu* ear diseases

11 埵 *mimitabu* earlobe

許 *mimimoto de* around one's ears

殻 *jikaku* auricle, external ear

寄 *mimiyo(ri) na* welcome, encouraging

12 痛 *jitsū* earache

遠 *mimidō(i)* strange, uncommon; deaf. *mimi (ga) tō(i)* to be deaf

順 *jijun* intelligent and understanding heart; sixtieth year of age

13 傾 *mimi (o) katamu(keru)* listen

掻 *mimikaki* earpick

隠 *mimikaku(shi)* ear-covering hairstyle

障 *mimizawa(ri) na* discordant, harsh

飾 *mimikaza(ri)* ear ornament; earring

新 *mimiatara(shii)* new, novel

14 鳴 *jimei, mimina(ri)* ringing in the ears

慣 *mimina(reru)* get used to hearing

漏 *jirō, mimidare* ear discharge, earwax

語 *sasaya(ku)* whisper, murmur. *jigo* whisper

鼻 *jibi* ear and nose

鼻咽喉 *jibiinkō* ear, nose, and throat

鼻咽喉科 *jibiinkōka* otorhinolaryngology

16 盥 *mimidarai* tub with handles

17 聾 *mimishii* deafness; a deaf person

擦 *mimikosuri* whispering

環 *mimiwa, jikan* earring

翼 *jiyoku* auricle, pinna

19 鏡 *jikyō* ear speculum

2

耶 4716 / J4c6d / M29008 YA. JA. *ya, ka* question mark.

19 蘇 *Yaso* Jesus

蘇紀元 *Yaso Kigen* Christian Era

蘇紀元後 *Yaso Kigengo* After Christ, A.D.

蘇紀元前 *Yaso Kigenzen* Before Christ, B.C.

蘇教 *Yasokyō* Christianity

6 竹米糸缶网罒羊羽老耂而耒【耳】聿肉月臣自至臼舌舛舟艮色艸艹虍虫血行衣衤西

4

耻 4717 / J6657 / M29019 See 恥 1846.

聏 4718 / J-X / M29018 Nonstandard for 職 4742.

耾 4719 / J-X / M29025 Kō deafness.

耿 4720 / J6656 / M29026 Kō light.
12 然 *kōzen* clearness; shining

耽 4721 / J433f / M29024 TAN. *fuke(ru)* be addicted to; be absorbed in.
9 美 *tambi* estheticism
美主義 *tambi shugi* estheticism
美的 *tambiteki* esthetic
美派 *tambiha* esthetic school
13 溺 *tandeki* addiction, dissipation
溺生活 *tandeki seikatsu* riotous life
14 読 *tandoku suru* read avidly
読者 *tandokusha* inveterate reader

5

聊 4722 / J6658 / M29049 RYŌ. *isasa(ka)* a little, slightly, somewhat. *isasaka no* scanty, trivial.

聆 4723 / J6659 / M29044 REI hear; follow; realize.

6

聠 4724 / J-X / M29066 Nonstandard for 聯 4737.

聒 4725 / J665a / M29062 KATSU noisy.

7

聘 4726 / J665b / M29079 HEI. *hei(suru)* engage, invite, summon.
5 用 *heiyō suru* engage, hire

A **聖** 4727 / J403b / M29074' SHŌ, SEI saint; sage; great master; holiness, sacredness, holy. *hijiri* high-ranking priest; emperor; sage; saint; a master. *sei(naru)* holy, sacred. *sei (to) suru* keep holy. *sei-* holy.
2 人 *shōnin, seijin* sage, saint, holy man, great religious leader
3 土 *seido* sacred place
山 *seizan* sacred mountain, holy mountain
上 *seijō* the emperor
4 日 *seijitsu* the sacred sun; a holy day; the Sabbath, the Lord's Day
水 *seisui* holy water
火 *seika* sacred fire, sacred torch
王 *seiō* the emperor (polite); a wise and virtuous emperor
化 *seika* sanctification
天子 *seitenshi* wise and virtuous emperor
公会 *Seikōkai* Anglican Church, Episcopalian Church
5 母 *seibo* the emperor's mother; a sage's mother; the Virgin Mary
句 *seiku* Bible verse
史 *seishi* sacred history
代 *seidai* glorious reign
主 *seishu* the emperor (polite); a wise and virtuous emperor
世 *seisei* glorious reign
礼典 *seireiten* sacraments
6 伝 *seiden* (Catholic) tradition
地 *seichi* Holy Land; sacred ground
会 *seikai* sacred assembly, church
旨 *seishi* the imperial will
年 *seinen* holy year
名 *Seimei* (God's) Holy Name
7 体 *seitai* eucharist, host
沢 *seitaku* imperial favor
別 *seibetsu* consecration; sanctification
君 *seikun* a virtuous emperor
寿 *seiju* the emperor's age
8 性 *seisei* sanctity, sacredness
所 *seijo* sanctuary, temple; holy place
明 *seimei* a polite word used in addressing the emperor
油 *seiyu* holy oil
河 *seiga* sacred river
夜 *seiya* the holy night; the night Christ was born, Christmas Eve
典 *seiten* a sage's writings, the sacred books of a religion; the Bible, the Buddhist Scriptures, the Koran; rites, sacraments

学 *seigaku* learning of the sages; Confucianism
者 *shōja, seija* saint, holy man; Holy One
画像 *seigazō* icon
金曜日 *Seikin'yōbi* Good Friday
9 約 *seiyaku* covenant
勅 *seichoku* imperial rescript
帝 *seitei* a virtuous emperor
10 週 *Seishū* Holy Week
峰 *seihō* sacred peak
徒 *seito* saint, disciple
訓 *seikun* sacred teachings
都 *Seito* the Holy City, Jerusalem
哲 *seitetsu* sage, wise man
恩 *seion* imperial favor
座宣言 *seiza sengen* ex-cathedra
骨 *seikotsu* sacred bones
骨匣 *seikotsukō* reliquary
書 *Seisho* Bible, Scriptures
書上 *Seishojō no* Biblical
書朗読 *Seisho rōdoku* Scripture reading
11 運 *seiun* fortunes of the emperor
域 *seiiki* sacred precincts
経 *seikei* cannon of scripture; a sage's writing
教 *seikyō* sacred teachings; Christianity; the teachings of the saints
断 *seidan* imperial decision
堂 *seidō* Confucian temple; temple; sanctuary
道 *shōdō* the holy path (of Buddhism)
道門 *shōdōmon* (Buddhist) doctrine of salvation by works
12 湖 *seiko* sacred lake
詔 *seishō* imperial command
雄 *seiyū* holy man, hero saint
晩餐 *Seibansan* the Lord's Supper, Holy Communion
13 跡 *seiseki* a spot honored by the imperial presence
戦 *seisen* holy war, crusade
意 *seii* the imperial will; the will of a sage; the will of God
楽 *seigaku* sacred music
業 *seigyō* sacred work; imperial achievements
14 聞 *seibun* imperial knowledge
像 *seizō* sacred image; icon; the image of a saint; an image of Confucius
徳 *seitoku* virtues; the emperor's virtues
算 *seisan* the emperor's age
遺物 *seiibutsu* religious relic
歌 *seika* sacred song, hymn, chant
歌隊 *seikatai* choir
歌隊長 *seikataichō* choirmaster
歌集 *seikashū* hymnal
15 廟 *seibyō* Confucian temple
慮 *seiryo* imperial wishes
潔 *seiketsu* holiness, sacredness; purification; sanctification
霊 *Seirei* Holy Spirit
賢 *seiken* the sages and saints
駕 *seiga* imperial carriage
器 *seiki* consecrated utensil, sacred vessel
誕祭 *Seitansai* Christmas
誕節 *Seitansetsu* Christmas
16 壇 *seidan* altar, pulpit
諭 *seiyu* the emperor's wisdom
覧 *seiran suru* (the emperor) observes
餐 *Seisan* Holy Communion; Eucharist
餐式 *Seisanshiki* Holy Communion, Lord's Supper, the Sacrament, Eucharist
17 聴 *seichō* (the emperor) listens
18 蹟 *seiseki* a spot honored by the imperial presence
職 *seishoku* ministry, clergy, holy orders
職者 *seishokusha* minister, clergyman
職席 *seishokuseki* chancel
職授与 *seishoku juyo* investiture
19 寵 *seichō* grace
譚曲 *seitankyoku* oratorio

8

聟 4728 / J665d / M29106 See **婿** 1246.

聢 4729 / J665e / M29113 (国字) *shika to* certainly, definitely, exactly.

聡 4730 / J416f / M29109 **聰** 4735 / J6662 / M29154 Sō. *sato(i)* wise; having a quick memory. *mimizato(i)* excellent hearing; quick understanding.
8 明 *sōmei* wisdom, sagacity
10 敏 *sōbin* sagacity, cleverness

聚 4731 / J665c / M29093 SHU. SHŪ. *atsu(maru)* assemble. *atsu(meru)* gather (people) together.
12 落 *juraku, shūraku* centers of population (towns and villages)

6 竹米糸缶网罒羊羽老耂而耒 8【耳】聿肉月臣自至臼舌舛舟艮色艸艹虍虫血行衣衤西

[17]斂 *shūren* gathering in; heavy taxation

A 聞 4732 / J4a39 / M29104 BUN. MON. *ki(ku)* hear, listen to; learn of; inquire; follow advice. *ki(kasu), ki(kaseru)* inform; secure acquiescence; read to, play for, sing to; give the tune. *ki(koeru)* hear, be heard; sound, ring, seem; be well known; be reasonable. *ki(kareru)* be overheard; be tolerable; be fairly good. *ki(kitagaru)* be inquisitive, be curious. *ki(koenai)* be unreasonable, be cruel. *ki(koe)* reputation, fame, notoriety, publicity. *ki(koegashi) ni* within hearing; wanting to be heard.

[2]入 *ki(ki)-i(reru)* comply with, grant (a request), accept (a resignation), assent to. *ki(ki)-i(ru)* listen attentively

[3]及 *ki(ki)-oyo(bu)* hear of, hear about. *ki(ki)oyo(bi)* hearsay

下手人 *ki(ki)beta (na) hito* a poor listener

上手人 *ki(ki)jōzu na hito* a good listener

[4]手 *ki(ki)te* listener, audience

方 *ki(ki)kata* way of listening

込 *ki(ki)-ko(mu)* be informed of. *kikiko(mi)* tip, hearsay, information

切 *ki(ki)-ki(ru)* learn from hearing just once

分 *ki(ki)-wa(keru)* be reasonable, understand. *ki(ki)wa(ke)* reasonableness; listening to reason

分無 *ki(ki)wa(ke)na(i)* helpless, innocent, naïve

[5]旧 *ki(ki)-fu(ru), ki(ki)-furu(su)* get tired of hearing

付 *ki(ki)-tsu(keru)* hear (the sound of), learn of, overhear, get wind of

外 *ki(ki)-hazu(su)* miss hearing

召 *ki(koshi)-me(su)* hear of, learn of; take a drink

古 *ki(ki)furu(shita)* timeworn, hackneyed

出 *ki(ki)-da(su), ki(ki)-ida(su)* find out, hear

巧者 *ki(ki)gōsha* a good listener

[6]尽 *ki(ki)-tsuku(su)* hear all about

気 *ki(kanu) ki* determination to win

返 *ki(ki)-kae(su)* be told again, inquire again

伝 *ki(ki)-tsuta(eru)* hear secondhand. *ki(ki)tsuta(e)* hearsay

交 *ki(ki)-ka(wasu)* ask here and there, ask among ourselves

合 *ki(ki)-a(waseru)* inquire about. *ki(ki)a(wase)* inquiry

耳 *ki(ki)mimi* attentive ears

耳立 *ki(ki)mimi (o) ta(teru)* listen carefully

[7]見 *ki(ki)-mi(ru)* hear and see

辛 *ki(ki)zura(i)* hard to hear

役 *ki(ki)yaku* official who hears people's complaints

忘 *ki(ki)-wasu(reru)* forget what one hears; forget to inquire about (something)

忌 *ki(ki)i(mi)* mourning for distant relatives

[8]届 *ki(ki)-todo(keru)* grant (a request); hear; accept (a resignation), accede to, comply with; acknowledge

始 *ki(ki)-haji(meru)* begin to hear. *ki(ki)haji(me)* something heard for the first time

所 *ki(ki)dokoro, ki(ki)doko* essential point to listen for

物 *ki(ki)mono* news, highlights

知 *bunchi suru ki(ki)-shi(ru)* hear of, be informed of

直 *ki(ki)-nao(su)* inquire again, listen again

定 *ki(ki)-sada(meru)* check on what one hears

苦 *ki(ki)guru(shii)* offensive to the ear, hard to grasp the meaning of; scandalous; objectionable

咎 *ki(ki)-toga(meru)* challenge (a speaker); rebuke

学 *ki(ki)gaku* learn by being with someone

事 *ki(ki)goto* something worth listening to

取 *ki(ki)-to(ru)* catch, follow, understand. *ki(ki)to(ri)* hearing, audition

取難 *ki(ki)to(ri)gata(i)* hard to understand

[9]通 *ki(ki)-tō(su)* listen clear through

洩 *ki(ki)-mo(rasu)* miss hearing. *ki(ki)-mo(re)* something one missed hearing

栄 *ki(ki)ba(e) no aru* something worth listening to

糾 *ki(ki)-tada(su)* ascertain, verify

[10]従 *ki(ki)-shitaga(u)* hearken unto

挿 *ki(ki)-hasa(mu)* listen and retain

残 *ki(ki)-noko(su)* fail to hear
流 *ki(ki)-naga(su)* pay no attention to
酒 *ki(ki)zake* tasting wine
納 *kikiosa(me)* the last time we heard (him)
差 *ki(ki)-sa(su)* listen only halfway through
書 *kikiga(ki)* verbatim notes
留 *ki(ki)-todo(meru)* listen carefully
11 過 *ki(ki)-sugo(su)* listen without remembering
達 *buntatsu* fame, reputation
惚 *ki(ki)-ho(reru)* listen with rapt interest
捨 *ki(ki)-su(teru)* ignore, overlook
悪 *ki(ki)niku(i)* awkward to ask; hard to hear
12 渡 *ki(koe)-wata(ru)* be noised abroad. *ki(ki)-wata(su), ki(ki)-wata(ru)* keep hearing, hear continually
違 *ki(ki)-chiga(eru), ki(ki)-chiga(u)* mishear, be misinformed. *ki(ki)chiga(i), ki(ki)chiga(e), kikitaga(i), kikitaga(e)* hearing incorrectly
善 *ki(ki)yo(i)* good to hear
落 *ki(ki)-o(tosu)* miss hearing
惑 *ki(ki)-mado(u)* be perplexed by what one hears
覚 *ki(ki)-obo(eru)* learn by ear
13 損 *ki(ki)-sokona(u)* mishear. *ki(ki)zon* hearing about something to one's disadvantage
煩 *ki(ki)-wazura(u)* be pained by what one hears
継 *ki(ki)-tsu(gu)* keep on listening; hear from a line of informants
隠 *ki(ki)-kaku(su)* pretend not to listen
飽 *ki(ki)-a(kiru)* be tired of hearing, get tired of
馴 *ki(ki)-na(reru)* get used to hearing
置 *ki(ki)-o(ku)* hear, keep in mind
業 *ki(ki)waza* the business of listening
寝入 *ki(ki)nei(ri)* listening and falling asleep
14 徳 *ki(ki)doku* worthwhile hearing
慣 *ki(ki)-na(reru)* get used to hearing
漏 *ki(ki)-mo(rasu)* miss hearing. *ki(ki)-mo(re)* something one missed hearing
15 澄 *ki(ki)-su(masu)* listen attentively
質 *ki(ki)-tada(su)* ascertain, verify
16 積 *ki(ki)-tsumo(ru)* listen clear through
18 嚙 *ki(ki)-kaji(ru)* have a smattering of knowledge
21 囃 *ki(ki)-haya(su)* hear and praise

9

聠 4733 / J665f / M29134 Nonstandard for **聯** 4737.

10

聳 4734 / J-X / M-X Nonstandard for **聳** 4739.

11

聽 4735 / J6662 / M29154 See **聡** 4730.

聲 4736 / J6661 / M29166 See **声** 989.

聯 4737 / J4e7e / M29153 Ren set; party, company, gang, clique. See 連 6062 for compounds.

聱 4738 / J-X / M29159 Gō poor sentences.

聳 4739 / J6660 / M29167 Shō. *sobi(eru)* rise, soar, tower. *sobi(yakasu)* throw back (the shoulders and swagger along).
5 立 *sobi(e)-ta(tsu)* tower up. *shōritsu suru* rise precipitously
11 動 *shōdō* shock

B **聴** 4740 / J4430 / M29173 **聽** 4744 / J6665 / M29211 Chō careful inquiry. *ki(kanai)* headstrong, naughty. *ki(ku)* hear, listen to, learn of; inquire; follow advice.
2 力 *chōryoku* hearing ability
力計 *chōryokukei* audiometer
4 込 *ki(ki)-ko(mu)* be informed of. *ki(ki)ko(mi)* tip, hearsay, information
8 官 *chōkan* auditory organ
者 *chōsha* hearer, listener
取 *chōshu* listening, hearing, audition, radio reception
取者 *chōshusha* radio listener
取料 *chōshuryō* radio license fee

6 竹米糸缶网罒羊羽老耂而耒【耳】11 聿肉月臣自至臼舌舛舟艮色艸艹虍虫血行衣衤西

取書 *chōshusho* write-up of a criminal investigation
9 度 *chōdo* audibility
神経 *chōshinkei* auditory nerve
音 *chōon* hearing, sound detection, sound transmission
音器 *chōonki* audiophone, hydrophone, listening instrument
音機 *chōonki* sound detector (for approach of enemy planes)
10 従 *chōjū suru* follow advice
容 *chōyō* compliance, permission
11 許 *chōkyo* permission, approval
問会 *chōmonkai* public hearing
視 *chōshi* viewing and listening (to TV)
視覚 *chōshikaku* audio-visual
視覚教具 *chōshikaku kyōgu* audio-visual aids
12 衆 *chōshū* audience
覚 *chōkaku* sense of hearing
診 *chōshin* stethoscopy
診器 *chōshinki* stethoscope
13 罪師 *chōzaishi* (Catholic) confessor
14 聞 *chōmon* audience, audition. *chōbun* hearing, listening
聞会 *chōmonkai* public hearing
15 器 *chōki* auditory organ
17 講 *chōkō* lecture attendance, auditing
講生 *chōkōsei* auditing student, listener
講券 *chōkōken* lecture admittance ticket
講者 *chōkōsha* a lecture audience

12

聶 4741 / J6663 / M29179 SHŌ whisper.

A **職** 4742 / J3f26 / M29183 SHOKU employment, work, job, office. SHIKI occupation, handicraft. *tsukasa* office, government office; director, head official.
2 人 *shokunin* worker, mechanic, craftsperson
人気質 *shokunin katagi, shokunin kishitsu* artisan spirit
3 工 *shokkō* factory worker
4 分 *shokubun* duties; vocation
6 印 *shokuin* a government seal
安 *shokuan* employment security office
名 *shokumei* occupation name; official title
7 別 *shokubetsu* class of service
8 長 *shokuchō* foreman, overseer
制 *shokusei* office organization; holy orders; ministry
9 級 *shokkyū* position, job grade
10 能 *shokunō* work efficiency
能給 *shokunōkyū* efficiency pay
員 *shokuin* staff, personnel, faculty; staff member, employee
員団 *shokuindan* a staff of assistants
員組合 *shokuin kumiai* employees' union
員録 *shokuinroku* list of government officials; army register, bluebook
11 域 *shokuiki* occupation, one's post
責 *shokuseki* official duties
階 *shokkai* position, job grade
階制 *shokkaisei* civil-service system
務 *shokumu* office, job, duties
務執行 *shokumu shikkō* performance of duties
務質問 *shokumu shitsumon* police check-up (on a criminal)
12 場 *shokuba* place of work, workshop
掌 *shokushō* duties, functions, office
13 群 *shokugun* occupational group
業 *shokugyō* occupation, business, trade, vocation, profession
業安定 *shokugyō antei* employment security
業安定所 *shokugyō anteijo, shokugyō anteisho* employment security office
業別 *shokugyōbetsu* by occupations
業性 *shokugyōsei* occupational
業軍人 *shokugyō gunjin* professional soldier
業病 *shokugyōbyō* occupational diseases
業婦人 *shokugyō fujin* career woman; employed woman
業紹介 *shokugyō shōkai* employment service
業紹介所 *shokugyō shōkaijo* employment agency
業教育 *shokugyō kyōiku* vocational education
業野球 *shokugyō yakyū* professional baseball
業補導 *shokugyō hodō* vocational guidance
業適性 *shokugyō tekisei* vocational aptitudes

業斡旋所 *shokugyō assenjo* employment agency
14 歴 *shokureki* one's occupational history
種 *shokushu* occupation category
種別 *shokushubetsu* by occupations
15 権 *shokken* official authority
権上 *shokkenjō* by virtue of office, ex officio
19 蟻 *shokugi* worker ant

14

聹 4743 / J6664 / M29199 NEI. *mimi aka* earwax.

16

聽 4744 / J6665 / M29211 See 聴 4740.

聾 4745 / J4f38 / M29212 Rō deafness. *rō(suru)* deafen. *tsumbo, mimishii* deafness; deaf person.
8 者 *rōsha* deaf person
学校 *rōgakkō* school for the deaf
11 啞 *rōa* deaf-mute
啞学校 *rōa gakkō* school for the deaf
12 桟敷 *tsumbo sajiki* upper gallery, blind seat

RAD. 聿 129

Fude writing brush. At right: *fudezukuri*. Variant: 聿. Nickname: Brush.

聿 4746 / J6666 / M29215 ITSU brush; finally; self; relate; follow; here; fast.

6

B 粛 4747 / J3d4d / M29223' 肅 4748 / J6669 / M29225 SHUKU. *shuku toshite* quietly, softly, solemnly.
5 白 *shukuhaku* Respectfully yours
正 *shukusei* regulation, enforcement
8 学 *shukugaku* school purge
9 軍 *shukugun* army purge
10 殺 *shukusatsu suru* wither, blight
党 *shukutō suru* clean up the (political) party
11 清 *shukusei* purge, cleanup, liquidation
粛 *shukushuku to* softly, quietly, solemnly
12 然 *shukuzen to* softly, quietly, solemnly

7

肅 4748 / J6669 / M29225 See 粛 4747.

肆 4749 / J6668 / M29226 SHI four.

肄 4750 / J6667 / M29224 I learn; investigate.
11 習 *ishu* learn, practice, train
13 業 *igyo* learning, education

8

肇 4751 / J4825 / M29228 肈 4752 / J-X / M29230 CHŌ beginning.
8 国 *chōkoku* founding a nation

RAD. 肉 130

Niku flesh, meat. Variants: 肉 and 月 or 月 (4 strokes) *nikuzuki* ("flesh" written like character for *tsuki* "moon"). These variants may often belong to Rad. 74, but except for "moon" itself, are treated herein as Rad. 130. Nickname: Meat.

A 肉 4753 / J4679 / M29236 宍 1312 / J3c35 / M7084 NIKU flesh, muscles; meat; the flesh; seal pad, ink pad; thickness, succulence. *shishi* muscles; meat. (Today 宍 is only read *shishi*.)
2 入 *nikui(re)* seal pad, stamp pad.
nikui(ri) container for meat
3 叉 *nikusa, nikusashi* meat fork
4 片 *nikuhen* piece of meat; folds of flesh
牛 *nikugyū* beef cattle

太 *nikubuto* bold-faced (type)
切 *nikuki(re)* slice of meat
切庖丁 *nikuki(ri)bōchō* butcher knife, carver
5 付 *nikuzu(ku)* put on flesh. *nikuzu(ki), nikutsu(ki)* one's build. *nikuzu(ke)* modeling (in clay, etc.)
汁 *nikujū, nikuju* meat juice, broth, soup
6 色 *niku iro, nikushoku* flesh color
池 *nikuchi* seal pad, stamp pad
刑 *nikukei* corporal punishment; the punishment of mutilating the body
交 *nikkō* sexual intercourse
7 迫 *nikuhaku suru* close in on, press hard, compete fiercely
声 *nikusei* natural voice, lifelike tone
豆蔻 *nikuzuku* nutmeg
身 *nikushin* the flesh, the body; kindred, blood relationship
身間 *nikushinkan* among relatives
体 *nikutai* the flesh, the body
体小説 *nikutai shōsetsu* erotic fiction
体文学 *nikutai bungaku* erotic literature
体的 *nikutaiteki* corporal, concerning the body
体美 *nikutaibi* physical beauty
8 刺 *nikusashi* meat fork. *mame* a corn, blister
芽 *nikuga, nikuge* granulation (in medicine)
9 食 *nikushoku, nikujiki* meat diet
屋 *nikuya* butcher shop; butcher
冠 *nikkan* cockscomb, crest (of a bird)
界 *nikukai, nikkai* sensual world, physical world
10 挽 *nikuhi(ki)* meat grinder
桂 *nikkei* cinnamon, cassia bark
11 彫 *nikubori* relief (in sculpture)
情 *nikujō* carnal desire
眼 *nikugan* naked eye
欲 *nikuyoku* animal passions, lusts of the flesh
12 弾 *nikudan* human bullet
筆 *nikuhitsu* autograph, one's own painting, one's own handwriting
筆画 *nikuhitsuga* original painting
13 腫 *nikushu* sarcoma
塊 *nikukai, nikkai* piece of flesh; the flesh, the body
感 *nikkan* animal passion, carnal desire, sexual feeling
感的 *nikukanteki* carnal
14 製品 *niku seihin* meat products
15 縁 *nikuen* blood relative
慾 *nikuyoku* animal passions, lusts of the flesh
質 *nikushitsu* nature of the flesh; composed of flesh
16 親 *nikushin* kindred, blood relationship
薄 *nikuhaku suru* close in on, press hard, compete fiercely
17 鍋 *niku nabe* a pot for cookking meat ; meat boiled with tofu and vegetables
18 類 *nikurui* meats
叢 *shishimura* a piece of flesh
19 襦袢 *niku juban* tights
20 饅頭 *niku manjū* meat bun

2

肋 4754 / J4f3e / M29239 ROKU. *abara* rib.
4 木 *rokuboku* Swedish bars, wall bars (for calisthenics)
7 材 *rokuzai* framing timbers (as in a ship)
10 骨 *rokkotsu, abarabone* ribs
12 間 *rokkan* intercostal, between the ribs
14 膜 *rokumaku* pleura
膜炎 *rokumakuen* pleurisy

B **肌** 4755 / J4829 / M29242 KI. *hada, hadae* skin, body; grain, texture; disposition.
6 色 *hada iro* flesh color
衣 *hadagi* underwear
合 *hadaa(i)* disposition
7 身 *hadami* the body
11 理 *kime* grain; texture
脱 *hadanu(gi)* bare to the waist
12 寒 *hadasamu(i), hadazamu(i)* chilly
着 *hadagi* underwear
13 触 *hadazawa(ri)* the touch, the feel
19 襦袢 *hada juban* underwear

A **有** 4756 / J4d2d / M14332 YŪ possession. U being, existence. *yū(suru)* have, possess. *a(ru)* there is, have, exist; occur; be located, be contained in; (it) measures; happen; be found; be held; consist of. *a(ramashi)* approximately, almost. *a(rayuru), a(ritoarayuru)* all, every. *a(risōna)* probable. *a(rimoshinai)* imaginary, nonexistent. [月]

2 力 *yūryoku na* influential
力者 *yūryokusha* an influential person, a powerful person
力筋 *yūryoku suji* influential quarters
3 士 *yūshi* sympathy, interest
丈 *a(rit)take, a(ri)take* all there is
4 心 *ushin* thoughtful consideration
夫 *yūfu* married (woman)
夫姦 *yūfukan* adultery by a woman
孔材 *yūkōzai* porous wood
孔性 *yūkōsei* porosity, porousness
孔質 *yūkōshitsu* porosity, porousness
孔螺旋 *yūkō rasen* screw eye
5 功 *yūkō* efficient; meritorious
司 *yūshi* authorities, officials
用 *yūyō na* useful, available, serviceable. *yūyō(sa)* usefulness, helpfulness
用性 *yūyōsei* usefulness
史 *yūshi* historical
史以来 *yūshi irai* since the dawn of history
史前 *yūshizen no* prehistoric
史時代 *yūshi jidai* historic period
6 合 *a(ri)-a(u)* happen to be, happen to have on hand. *a(ri)a(wase)* what's on hand
気音 *yūkion* an aspirate
色 *yūshoku* colored (race)
色人種 *yūshoku jinshu* colored race
色星 *yūshokusei* colored star
名 *yūmei na* famous; notorious; proverbial
名人 *yūmeijin* celebrity, person of distinction
名品 *yūmeihin* well-known
名税 *yūmeizei* penalty for greatness
名無実 *yūmei-mujitsu* nominal, titular
7 利 *yūri na* advantageous, profitable, better
余 *a(ri)-ama(ru)* be superfluous, be in excess. *yūyo* excess
位者 *yūisha* holder of court rank
形 *yūkei* material, concrete, visible
形無形 *yūkei-mukei* visible and invisible; material and spiritual
志 *yūshi* sympathy, interest; volunteer
志者 *yūshisha* sympathizer, supporter, volunteer
体 *a(ri)tei* the plain truth
体物 *yūtaibutsu* something material
体動産 *yūtai dōsan* tangible property
体資産 *yūtai shisan* tangible assets
声 *yūsei* voiced, vocal
声子音 *yūsei shion, yūsei shiin* voiced consonant
声音 *yūseion* voiced sound
声音化 *yūseionka* vocalization, voicing
8 金 *a(ri)gane* ready cash
性 *yūsei* sexual; having sex
卦 *uke* period of luck
実 *a(ri)(no)mi* pear
妻 *yūsai* married (man)
毒 *yūdoku* poisonous
事 *yūji* emergency, unusual event
耶無耶 *uyamuya na* noncommital
明 *aria(ke)* daybreak, dawn with the moon shining; all night long
明月 *aria(ke)zuki* the moon shining at dawn
刺鉄条網 *yūshi tetsujōmō* barbed-wire entanglements
刺鉄線 *yūshi tessen* barbed wire
価 *yūka* valuable, negotiable
価物 *yūkabutsu* valuables
価証券 *yūka shōken* valuable securities
価証券取引税 *yūka shōken torihikizei* securities transaction tax
限 *a(ru)kagi(ri)* as long as we have some. *a(ran)kagi(ri)* all, to the utmost. *a(ri)kiri* only that, only that much; as much as possible. *yūgen* limited, finite
限会社 *yūgengaisha* limited company, ltd.
限責任 *yūgen sekinin* limited liability
限責任会社 *yūgen-sekiningaisha* limited liability company, inc.
効 *yūkō* effectiveness, efficiency; validity; availability
効性 *yūkōsei* validity
効期限 *yūkō kigen* term of validity
効期間 *yūkō kikan* term of validity, available period
効適切 *yūkō-tekisetsu* effective and appropriate
効数字 *yūkō sūji* significant figures
効需要 *yūkō juyō* effective demand
9 神論 *yūshinron* deism, theism
為 *ui* vicissitudes of life; perpetual change in destiny caused by karma. *yūi no* capable, efficient, promising
為転変 *ui-tempen* vicissitudes of life

10 高 *a(ri)daka* amount on hand; goods on hand
益 *yūeki na* beneficial, profitable, instructive, edifying
兼 *a(ri)-ka(nenai)* possible, not impossible
能 *yūnō na* capable, efficient
租地 *yūsochi* taxable land
脊動物 *yūseki dōbutsu* vertebrate animal
畜農業 *yūchiku nōgyō* diversified farming
害 *yūgai na* harmful, noxious, destructive
害物 *yūgaibutsu* dangerous substances
料 *yūryō* toll; charge
料入場者 *yūryō nyūjōsha* paid admissions
料図書館 *yūryō toshokan* rental library
料道路 *yūryō dōro* toll road
料橋梁 *yūryō kyōryō* toll bridge
11 得 *a(ri)u(beki)* possible, probable, likely. *a(ri)-u(ru)* possible, probable, likely
理 *yūri* rational
望 *yūbō* good prospects
頂天 *uchōten* exaltation, rapture, ecstacy
袋動物 *yūtai dōbutsu* pouched animal
情 *ujō* sentience, sentient being. *yūjō no, ujō no* sentient, sensitive, animate
情物 *yūjōbutsu* sentient beings
終 *yūshū* a fine conclusion
終美 *yūshū (no) bi* perfection, crowning glory
産 *yūsan* having wealth; millionaire
産階級 *yūsan kaikyū* propertied class
12 勝 *a(ri)ga(chi)* common, frequent, incidental; apt to happen
衆 *yūshū* multitude, people
象無象 *uzō-muzō* riffraff, rabble
閑 *yūkan* leisure
閑階級 *yūkan kaikyū* the leisure class
給 *yūkyū* salaried
給休暇 *yūkyū kyūka* paid vacations
無 *umu, yūmu* existence; presence; yes or no. *a(ri)na(shi)* whether there is any or not
無相通 *umu-aitsū(zuru), umu-aitsū(jiru)* share, help mutually
税 *yūzei* taxable, dutiable
税地 *yūzeichi* taxable land
税品 *yūzeihin* dutiable goods
期 *yūki* a definite period
期刑 *yūkikei* penal servitude for a stated period
期懲役 *yūki chōeki* penal servitude with hard labor for a stated period
13 福 *yūfuku* prosperity, affluence
触 *a(ri)fu(reta)* ordinary, stereotyped
数 *yūsū no* prominent, distinguished; very few
煙炭 *yūentan* soft coal
感地震 *yūkan jishin* an earthquake which is felt
資格者 *yūshikakusha* eligible person, qualified person
蓋 *yūgai* covered
蓋車 *yūgaisha* covered wagon
蓋貨車 *yūgai kasha* box car
意 *yūi no* conscious, voluntary, intentional
意犯 *yūihan* deliberate offense; deliberate offender
意味 *yūimi na* significant
意義 *yūigi na* significant
罪 *yūzai* guilt, criminality
罪人 *yūzainin* guilty person
罪判決 *yūzai hanketsu* conviction
罪者 *yūzaisha* guilty person
罪認定 *yūzai nintei* finding guilty
罪議決 *yūzai giketsu* verdict of conviction
14 徳 *yūtoku* virtuous, good. *utoku* virtuous person
様 *a(ri)sama, a(ri)yō* situation, circumstances; sight; the (naked) truth
髪 *uhatsu* unshorn (nun)
15 勲者 *yūkunsha* the holder of a decoration
権 *yūken* one's rights; voting rights
権者 *yūkensha* qualified person; eligible voter; franchise holder; constituent body, electorate
線 *yūsen* wire (as opposed to wireless)
線電信 *yūsen denshin* wire telegraph
線電話 *yūsen denwa* wire telephone
16 儘 *a(rino)mama, a(ruga)mama* as it is, the simple truth
機 *yūki* organic
機化合物 *yūki kagōbutsu* organic compound
機化学 *yūki kagaku* organic chemistry
機体 *yūkitai* organism
機性 *yūkisei* organic
機物 *yūkibutsu* organic matter, organism
機的 *yūkiteki* organic

機肥料 *yūki hiryō* organic fertilizer
機農業 *yūki nōgyō* organic farming
機酸 *yūkisan* an organic acid
機質 *yūkishitsu* organic matter
機質肥料 *yūkishitsu hiryō* organic fertilizer
17 償 *yūshō* compensation, consideration
鍵楽器 *yūken gakki* keyed musical instrument
爵 *yūshaku* titled
爵者 *yūshakusha* titled person, peer
18 職 *yūshoku* employed; ancient court and military practices
職者 *yūshokusha* employed people
職家 *yūshokuka* person versed in ancient court and military practices
難 *a(ri)gata(garu)* be thankful. *a(ri)gata(i)* thankful, grateful, blessed. *a(ri)gato(u)* thank you
難味 *arigatami* value, virtue, blessing, dignity, sanctity (of)
難迷惑 *a(ri)gatameiwaku* embarrassing favor
難涙 *a(ri)gatanamida* tears of gratitude
19 識 *yūshiki* intellectual (person)
識者 *yūshikisha* intellectual person, learned person

3

肓 4757 / J666b / M29259 Kō area in lower chest (anciently believed to be unreachable by acupuncture or medicine).

肛 4758 / J666a / M29271 Kō anus.
8 門 *kōmon* anus

肚 4759 / J666c / M29270 To. *hara* abdomen, belly, bowels, stomach; heart, mind; intention; courage, spirit, pluck; anger; womb; thickest or widest part.
7 芸 *haragei* composure, wisdom, and steady leadership in crises
13 裏 *tori* in the heart

B **肖** 4760 / J3e53 / M29263 Shō resemble. *ayaka(ru)* resemble.
8 者 *ayaka(ri)mono* lucky fellow; similar person, one who resembles someone
14 像 *shōzō* portrait, picture
像画 *shōzōga* portrait; portrait painting

肘 4761 / J292a / M29268 Chū. *hiji* elbow; arm (of something).
4 木 *hijiki* bracket
8 金 *hijigane* hook, hinge
枕 *hiji makura (o) suru* use the elbow for a pillow
突 *hijitsu(ki)* elbow rest
11 掛 *hijika(ke)* elbow rest; bay window
12 壺 *hijitsubo* socket hinge
13 鉄 *hijitetsu* rebuff
鉄砲 *hijideppō* rebuff

B **肝** 4762 / J344e / M29273 Kan liver. *kimo* liver; pluck, courage, nerve.
2 入 *kimoi(ri)* assisting
3 小 *kimo (ga) chii(sai)* cowardly
4 文 *kammon* important passage (in a text)
太 *kimofuto(i)* courageous
心 *kanjin na* essential, important, fundamental
心要 *kanjin-kaname no* main, basic
5 玉 *kimo(t)tama, kimodama* courage, nerve
7 冷 *kimo (o) hi(yasu)* be startled
8 油 *kan'yu* liver oil, cod-liver oil
炎 *kan'en* hepatitis
9 要 *kan'yō* import; importance, necessity
胆 *kantan* liver and gall; innermost heart
胆相照 *kantan'aite(rasu)* become intimate
11 脳 *kannō* liver and brains
12 腎 *kanjin na* fundamental, important, essential
腎要 *kanjin-kaname no* main, basic
13 煎 *kimoi(ri)* good offices, sponsorship, go-between, promoter, overseer
14 銘 *kammei* deep impression
魂 *kimodama, kimotama, kimodamashii, kimo(t)tama* courage, nerve
15 潰 *kimotsubu(shi)* terrific surprise
18 臓 *kanzō* liver
臓炎 *kanzōen* hepatitis

4

肬 4763 / J666f / M29304 Yū. Yu. *ibo* wart.

肫 4764 J-X M29303 JUN dried meat.

朒 4765 J666d M29305 TOTSU, JIKU new moon.

B **肪** 4766 J4b43 M29302 BŌ fat.

肴 4767 J3a68 M29322 KŌ. *sakana* fish, a side dish.

B **肢** 4768 J3b68 M29285 SHI limbs, arms and legs.

7 体 *shitai* limbs, members; body

体不自由児 *shitaifujiyūji* physically handicapped child

朋 4769 J4a7e M14340' [月] HŌ friend, companion.

4 友 *hōyū* friend, companion

10 党 *hōtō* faction, clique

15 輩 *hōbai* comrade, friend, associate, fellow apprentice

肱 4770 J394f M29315 KŌ. *kaina* arm; ability, talent. *hiji* elbow; arm (of something).

4 木 *hijiki* (temple) bracketing

11 掛 *hijika(ke)* resting the elbows, armrest; bay window

掛窓 *hijika(ke) mado* bay window

B **肯** 4771 J394e M29311 KŌ. *ukega(u), gae(njiru), gae(nzuru)* agree to, consent, comply with, undertake.

8 定 *kōtei suru* affirm, acknowledge

定文 *kōteibun* affirmative sentence

定的 *kōteiteki* affirmative

14 綮 *kōkei* the point, the mark

股 4772 J3854 M29284 KO thigh, crotch; yarn; strand; ply. *mata* crotch, thigh, groin. *momo* thigh, femur.

4 火 *matabi* sitting astride a brazier

引 *momohi(ki)* drawers, underwear

8 肱 *kokō* one's trusted associate

10 骨 *kokotsu* femur, thigh bone

座 *matagura* crotch, thigh, groin

旅 *matatabi* gambler's wandering life

14 関節 *kokansetsu* hip joint

17 擦 *matazu(re)* saddle sore, thigh sore

A **育** 4773 J3069 M29318 IKU. *soda(tsu)* be raised, be brought up, grow, grow up. *soda(teru), haguku(mu)* raise, rear, bring up. *soda(te)* bringing up, raising. *soda(chi)* breeding, growth.

3 上 *soda(te)-a(geru)* raise, rear, bring up, train, educate

4 方 *soda(te)kata* method of bringing up, method of raising

6 行 *soda(chi)-yu(ku)* grow up

成 *ikusei* rearing, training

7 児 *ikuji* care of children

児法 *ikujihō* the rearing of children

児食 *ikujishoku* baby food

児院 *ikujiin* orphanage, nursery school

児室 *ikujishitsu* nursery

児時間 *ikuji jikan* nursing time

8 苗 *ikubyō* raising seedlings

英 *ikuei* education

英会 *ikueikai* scholarship society; educational society

14 種 *ikushu* (plant) breeding

種所 *ikushujo* (plant) nursery

種家 *ikushuka* (plant) breeder

16 親 *soda(te) oya* foster parent

18 雛器 *ikusūki* breeder

A **肥** 4774 J486e M29290 HI. *ko(eru)* get fat; get fertile. *ko(yasu)* fertilize, enrich; fatten; feather one's nest; pamper one's taste. *futo(ru)* get fat, gain, fill out. *koyashi* manure, fertilizer. *koe* night soil; manure.

3 土 *ko(e)tsuchi, hido* rich soil, loam, mold

大 *hidai* corpulence, hypertrophy

4 太 *ko(e)-futo(ru)* grow fat, be well fed

5 立 *hida(tsu)* grow up; get well. *hida(chi)* convalescence after childbirth, growth of an infant

代 *koedai* cost of manuring, cost of getting night soil carried away

6 肉 *hiniku* fat flesh

舟 *koebune* night-soil boats

地 *ko(e)chi* fertile soil

汲 *koyashiku(mi), koeku(mi)* carrying night soil; night-soil carrier

7 車 *koyashiguruma, koeguruma* night-soil cart

沃 *hiyoku* fertility

8 取 *koeto(ri)* emptying night-soil; night-soil man
育 *hiiku* fattening cattle for slaughtering
担桶 *koe tago* night-soil bucket
9 厚 *hikō* thickening (of the skin, etc.)
柄杓 *koebishaku* night-soil dipper
10 馬 *hiba* a fat horse
料 *hiryō* fertilizer, compost, manure
11 桶 *koe oke, koyashi oke* night-soil bucket
船 *koebune* fertilizer boat
12 満 *himan suru* become obese
満症 *himanshō* illness due to obesity
13 溜 *koeda(me)* night-soil vat

A **服** 4775 / J497e / M14345' FUKU dress, costume, clothes, garment, suit, uniform. *fuku(suru)* yield to, obey; abide by; be devoted to, acknowledge, admit; serve (in the army); discharge (duties). *matsuro(u)* obey. [月]
5 用 *fukuyō suru* take (medicine, etc.), use internally; dress (oneself)
用量 *fukuyōryō* dose, dosage
6 地 *fukuji* cloth, suiting, dress materials
刑 *fukukei* servitude
7 役 *fukueki* servitude, military service
忌 *fukuki* mourning
8 制 *fukusei* dress regulations, costume
毒 *fukudoku* taking poison
毒自殺 *fukudoku jisatsu* suicide by poisoning
9 屋 *fukuya* tailor, dressmaker
10 従 *fukujū* obedience, submission
従心 *fukujūshin* obedience, submissive spirit
従的 *fukujūteki* obedient, submissive
11 務 *fukumu* duties, public service
務年限 *fukumu nengen* tenure of office
務時間 *fukumu jikan* office hours
12 属 *fukuzoku suru* become a retainer; yield allegiance to
装 *fukusō* dress, garments, costume, attire
装随意 *fukusō zuii* dress optional, informal attire
喪 *fukumo* mourning
喪者 *fukumosha* mourners
13 飾 *fukushoku* dress and its ornaments, attire, personal appearance
罪 *fukuzai* pleading guilty, confession of guilt, submission
16 薬 *fukuyaku* taking medicine
17 膺 *fukuyō suru* bear in mind, take to heart, treasure

B **肩** 4776 / J382a / M29299 KEN. *kata* shoulder.
2 入 *katai(re)* assistance. *kata (o) i(reru)* assist, sponsor, participate
3 口 *kataguchi* (top of) the shoulder
下 *katasaga(ri)* uneven (hem); wrong slant (in writing)
4 引 *kembi(ki)* stiff shoulders
5 代 *katagawa(ri)* relief palanquin bearer; one who shoulders another's debt or business proposition
甲 *kenkō* shoulder
甲骨 *kenkōkotsu* shoulder blade
甲部 *kenkōbu* shoulder
6 当 *kataa(te)* shoulder pad
先 *katasaki* (top of) the shoulder
7 身 *katami* shoulder and body; face (that one loses), honor
車 *kataguruma* (riding) on the shoulders
8 押 *katao(shi)* shoulder-pushing game; support, assistance
並 *kata (o) nara(beru)* stand or walk in a row; run neck and neck
9 透 *katasuka(shi)* dodging
持 *kata (o) mo(tsu)* assist, flatter
怒 *kata (o) ika(rasu)* strut along
風切 *kata (de) kaze (o) ki(ru)* strut along
胛骨 *kenkōkotsu* shoulder blade
10 骨 *katabone* shoulder blade
部 *kembu* shoulders
息 *kata (de) iki suru* pant
書 *kataga(ki)* title, degree; address (on a letter); criminal record
書付 *kataga(ki)zu(ki)* titled (person); notorious (person)
11 張 *kata (ga) ha(ru)* feel shoulder pains
掛 *kataka(ke)* shawl
脱 *katanu(gu)* partially remove outer garment; strip to the waist
章 *kenshō* shoulder strap, epaulette
袋 *katabukuro* shoulder bag
12 越 *katago(shi)* over the shoulder
幅 *katahaba* breadth of one's shoulders
揚 *kataa(ge)* shoulder tuck
替 *katagawa(ri)* relief palanquin bearer; one who shoulders another's debt or business proposition

竹米糸缶网罒羊羽老耂而耒耳聿【肉月】臣自至臼舌舛舟艮色艸艹虍虫血行衣衤西

6 貸 *kata (o) ka(su)* assist, sponsor, participate
13 馴 *katanara(shi)* light training, warming up, workout
15 摩 *kemma* rubbing shoulders with the crowd
摩轂擊 *kemma-kokugeki* jostling and bustling
18 癖 *kempeki* stiff shoulders; massage

5

冐 4777 / J-X / M-X Nonstandard for 冒 3915.

脉 4778 / J6677 / M29421' See 脈 4805.

朏 4779 / J5b2c / M14351 Hɪ. *mikazuki* new moon, crescent moon. [月]

胖 4780 / J6676 / M29381 Hᴀɴ half of a sacrifice; ribs; abundant, plentiful.

胥 4781 / J6671 / M29406 Sʜᴏ mutual; all; see; aid; lower-ranked official.

胝 4782 / J6673 / M29395 Cʜɪ chap, crack, corn, callus.

胛 4783 / J6670 / M29392 Kō shoulder blade.

胙 4784 / J6672 / M29387 Sᴏ. *himorogi* offering to the gods.

冑 4785 / J6674 / M29349 Cʜū lineage; helmet. *kabuto* helmet, headpiece. *yoroi* armor. *yoro(u)* arm oneself; put on armor.

胤 4786 / J307d / M29405 Iɴ descendant. *tane* issue, offspring; paternal blood.
12 違 *tanechiga(i)* half-brother; half-sister

胚 4787 / J6675 / M29390 Hᴀɪ embryo.
8 芽 *haiga* embryo bud, germ
芽米 *haigamai* rice with the germ remaining
9 胎 *haitai suru* germinate; be pregnant with; originate in, result from

B **胞** 4788 / J4b26 / M29396' Hō theca, sac, sheath, case; placenta.
3 子 *hōshi* spore
6 衣 *ena, hōi* placenta
9 胎 *hōtai* placenta

B **胎** 4789 / J425b / M29369 Tᴀɪ womb, uterus.
4 内 *tainai* interior of the womb. *tainai kara* from the mother's womb
5 生 *taisei* gestation
生学 *taiseigaku* embryology, ontology
7 位 *taii* presentation (in childbirth)
児 *taiji* fetus
児殺 *taijigoro(shi)* aborticide, feticide
8 芽 *taiga* embryo
毒 *taidoku* congenital syphilis
11 教 *taikyō* prenatal care; antenatal training
動 *taidō* quickening, fetal movement; (trouble) fomenting
動期 *taidōki* quickening time
15 盤 *taiban* placenta, afterbirth

B **胆** 4790 / J4340 / M29354 **膽** 4875 / J673c / M29933 Tᴀɴ gall bladder; courage. *i* gall bladder. *kimo* liver; pluck, nerve, courage.
2 力 *tanryoku* courage, nerve, grit
5 汁 *tanjū* bile, gall
汁質 *tanjūshitsu* bilious or choleric temperament
石 *tanseki* gallstones
石病 *tansekibyō* illness due to gallstones
石症 *tansekishō* illness due to gallstones
9 勇 *tan'yū* fearlessness, pluck
11 液 *tan'eki* bile, gall
略 *tanryaku* courage and resourcefulness
12 結石 *tan kesseki* biliary calculus, gallstones
14 管 *tankan* biliary ducts
20 礬 *tamban* blue vitriol; copper sulfate
22 嚢 *tannō* gall bladder
嚢炎 *tannōen* gall bladder inflammation

A **肺** 4791 / J4759 / M29422' Hᴀɪ lung.
5 出血 *hai shukketsu* lung hemorrhage
6 血 *haiketsu* lung hemorrhage
尖 *haisen* lung apex
7 肝 *haikan* lungs and liver; innermost heart

8 門 *haimon* hilum of a lung
炎 *haien* pneumonia
9 活量 *haikatsuryō* lung capacity
10 病 *haibyō* pulmonary tuberculosis, consumption
部 *haibu* lungs
浸潤 *haishinjun* tuberculosis
11 魚 *haigyo* lungfish
患 *haikan* pulmonary tuberculosis
12 葉 *haiyō* lobe of the lung
結核 *hai kekkaku* pulmonary tuberculosis
腑 *haifu* lungs; (one's inmost) heart; important point
腑衝 *haifu (o) tsu(ku)* be deeply impressed
17 癌 *haigan* lung cancer
18 臓 *haizō* lungs
22 嚢 *hainō* lung sac

胡 4792 / J3855 / M29400 U. Go. Ko barbarian, foreign.
5 瓜 *kyūri* cucumber
7 坐 *agura* sitting cross-legged
乱 *uron na* suspicious-looking
8 国 *kokoku* (ancient) North China barbarian nations
9 臭 *wakiga* abnormal underarm odor
10 馬 *koba* northern barbarian's horse
桃 *kurumi* walnut; nut
桃割 *kurumiwa(ri)* nutcracker
11 麻 *goma* sesame, sesame seed
麻油 *goma abura* sesame-seed oil
麻塩 *goma shio* salted, parched sesame seed; gray hair
麻擂 *gomasu(ri)* apple polisher, brown-noser; sycophant
麻蠅 *goma(no)hai* a crook
12 散臭 *usankusa(i)* suspicious-looking
椒 *koshō* pepper
椒入 *koshōi(re)* pepper shaker
14 歌 *koka* songs of the North China peoples
15 蝶 *kochō* butterfly
22 蘿蔔 *ninjin* carrot; ginseng

A **胃** 4793 / J305f / M29348 I stomach; paunch, crop, craw.
8 炎 *ien* gastritis
10 病 *ibyō* stomach trouble
部 *ibu* stomach region
弱 *ijaku* indigestion
11 袋 *ibukuro* stomach; paunch, crop, craw
液 *ieki* gastric juice
液酸度 *ieki sando* gastric acidity
12 痛 *itsū* stomachache
腑 *i(no)fu* stomach
散 *isan* stomach medicine
痙攣 *ikeiren* stomach cramps
13 腸 *ichō* stomach and intestines
腸病 *ichōbyō* gastrointestinal disorder
腸楽 *ichōyaku* stomach and bowel medicine
14 酸 *isan* stomach acid
酸過多 *isankata* gastric hyperacidity
酸過多症 *isankatashō* gastric hyperacidity
15 熱 *inetsu* gastric fever
潰瘍 *ikaiyō* stomach ulcer
16 壁 *iheki* stomach lining
17 癌 *igan* stomach cancer
19 鏡 *ikyō* gastroscope
22 嚢 *ibukuro* stomach

A **背** 4794 / J4758 / M29363 Hai back, behind. *somu(ku)* act contrary to, go back on, disobey, defy, rebel against, turn one's back on. *somu(keru)* look away from, avert. *se* back, back side; stature, height; ridge. *sei* stature, height. *sobira, sena* back.
3 丈 *setake, seitake* height, stature
4 比 *seikura(be)* comparison of statures
反 *haihan suru* contradict, be contrary to, interfere with
水陣 *haisui (no) jin* last stand
戸 *sedo* back door, back gate
戸口 *sedoguchi* back door, back gate
中 *senaka* back
中合 *senakaa(wase)* back to back; discord, feud
5 広 *sebiro* business suit
去 *somu(ki)-sa(ru)* go astray
付鋸 *sezu(ki) noko* backsaw
6 向 *haikō* facing toward the back; obedience and disobedience. *se (o) mu(keru)* turn the back on; pretend not to see; not cooperate with
任 *hainin* breach of trust
汗 *haikan* humiliation; cold sweat (on the back)
7 戻 *hairei suru* disobey, transgress; run counter to, be contrary to

伸 *seno(bi) suru* stretch oneself, stand on tiptoe
8 板 *seita* slab (of a log)
泳 *haiei, seoyo(gi)* backstroke swimming
9 面 *haimen* rear, back, reverse
信 *haishin* breach of faith, betrayal, apostasy
後 *haigo* back, rear; backing
約 *haiyaku* breach of promise, default
叛 *haihan* rebellion, revolt
恰好 *seikakkō* stature, height, size, build, shape of the back
革 *segawa* leatherback (book)
革綴 *segawa toji* half-leather binding
負 *seo(u), sho(u)* carry on the back, shoulder, be burdened with
負子 *sho(i)ko, seo(i)go* pack frame
負込 *sho(i)ko(mi), seo(i)ko(mi)* unsalable goods. *sho(i)-ko(mu), seo(i)-ko(mu)* carry on the back; be saddled with
負投 *sho(i)na(ge), seo(i)na(ge)* throwing over the shoulder; betrayal
負梯子 *sho(i)bashigo, seo(i)bashigo* pack frame
10 骨 *sebone* backbone, spinal column, spine
高 *seitaka no* taller than average
進 *haishin* withdrawal, retreat
峰 *semine* (horse's) back
振 *seburu(i) suru* shake oneself
部 *haibu* back, posterior
恩 *haion* ingratitude
11 理 *hairi* absurdity
教 *haikyō* apostasy
教国 *haikyōkoku* apostate country
教者 *haikyōsha* apostate
12 開 *sebira(ki)* slicing a fish down the back
順 *sejun* order of height
景 *haikei* background; scenery, setting; backing, pull
筋 *sesuji* line of the backbone; seam down the back. *haikin* the muscles of the back
番号 *sebangō* number on a player's back
13 較 *seikura(be)* comparison of statures
馳 *haichi suru* contradict, be contrary to, interfere with
14 徳 *haitoku* immorality, corruption
15 震 *seburu(i) suru* shake oneself
19 離 *hairi* estrangement
21 鰭 *sebire* dorsal fin
22 嚢 *hainō* knapsack, pack

6

胶 4795 / J-X / M29494 Nonstandard for **脇** 4807.

胱 4796 / J6679 / M29432 Kō bladder.

B **朕** 4797 / J443f / M14361 CHIN imperial we. [月]

胼 4798 / J6726 / M29453 **胼** 4823 / J-X / M29586 HEN callus, corn.

胯 4799 / J6678 / M29430 Kō. *mata* crotch.
4 火 *matabi* sitting astride a brazier
10 座 *matagura* crotch, thigh, groin

脆 4800 / J4048 / M29468 ZEI. *moro(i)* brittle, fragile; easy (to beat); sentimental, susceptible. *moro(ku)* easily.
8 性 *zeisei* brittleness; frailty
10 弱 *zeijaku na* fragile, frail, delicate, tender, flimsy, brittle

朔 4801 / J3a73 / M14359 SAKU conjunction (in astronomy). *tsuitachi* first day of the month. [月]
4 日 *tsuitachi* first day of the month
5 北 *sakuhoku* north
9 風 *sakufū* north wind
11 雪 *sakusetsu* northern snows

A **朗** 4802 / J4f2f / M14362' **朗** 4813 / J-X / M14364 RŌ. *hogara(ka) na* clear, bright, serene; melodious; cheerful, sunny. [月]
7 吟 *rōgin suru* recite, sing
10 朗 *rōrō(taru)* sonorous, silvery (voice or moon)
12 詠 *rōei* recitation
報 *rōhō* good news
14 誦 *rōshō* recitation, reading aloud
読 *rōdoku* reading aloud
読演説 *rōdoku enzetsu* a speech that is read

B **脅** 4803 / J363c / M29466 KYŌ. *obiya(kasu)* threaten; coerce.

7 迫 *kyōhaku* threat, menace, terrorism, coercion
迫状 *kyōhakujō* intimidating letter
迫的 *kyōhakuteki* menacing, threatening
迫者 *kyōhakusha* intimidator
迫罪 *kyōhakuzai* intimidation
9 威 *kyōi* threat, menace
12 喝 *kyōkatsu suru* threaten, intimidate, menace

脊 4804 / J4054 / M29472 SEKI. *se, sei* stature, height.
9 柱 *sekichū* spine, spinal column, backbone
10 索 *sekisaku* notochord
11 梁 *sekiryō* spine, spinal column
12 椎 *sekitsui* spinal column, spine; vertebra
椎骨 *sekitsuikotsu* vertebrae
椎動物 *sekitsui dōbutsu* vertebrates
18 髄 *sekizui* spinal cord

A **脈** 4805 / J4e2c / M29470 **脈** 4806 / J-X / M29469 **脉** 4778 / J6677 / M29421'
MYAKU vein (of ore); blood vessel; pulse; pulsation; hope.
5 打 *myakuu(tsu)* (the heart) pounds
圧計 *myakuatsukei* sphygmomanometer
7 状 *myakujō* veinlike
8 所 *myakudokoro* place where the pulse is felt; vital point
拍 *myakuhaku* pulsation
10 脈 *myakumyaku* continuous
11 動 *myakudo* pulsating motion
12 絡 *myakuraku* context, logical connection
13 搏 *myakuhaku* pulsation. *myakuu(tsu)* pulsate
数 *myakusū* pulse rate
14 管 *myakkan* blood vessel; duct

脇 4807 / J4f46 / M29467 KYŌ. *waki* the other way; another place; side, armpit, flank; supporting role.
3 下 *waki (no) shita* armpit; armhole
5 目 *wakime* onlooker's eyes; looking aside
付 *wakizu(ke)* directional words on an envelope
7 見 *wakimi suru* look aside, look off, look away
役 *wakiyaku* supporting role
9 柱 *wakibashira* door post, door jamb
挟 *wakibasa(mu)* hold under the arm
10 師 *wakishi* assistant actor
差 *wakiza(shi)* short sword
息 *kyōsoku* armrest
11 道 *wakimichi* side road, branch road; digression
12 間 *wakima* side room
13 腹 *wakibara* side of the chest, flank

B **脂** 4808 / J3b69 / M29463 SHI fat; rouge. *abura* fat, grease, tallow, blubber, lard, suet. *abura(gitta)* greasy, oily; fleshy. *yani* resin, rosin, gum; nicotine, tar; earwax, eye discharge.
3 下 *yanisa(garu)* assume airs; be complacent; chuckle (to oneself)
4 太 *aburabuto(ri)* obesity
6 気 *aburake* greasiness, oiliness
汗 *abura ase* greasy sweat
7 身 *aburami* fat meat
尾 *aburao* fat tail (of sheep)
8 油 *shiyu* fatty oil
肪 *shibō* fat, grease, blubber, suet, lard
肪症 *shibōshō* adiposity
肪組織 *shibō soshiki* fatty tissue
肪過多 *shibōkata* obesity
肪過多症 *shibōkatashō* obesity
肪腫 *shibōshu* fatty tumor, lipoma
肪酸 *shibōsan* fatty acids
肪質 *shiboshitsu* fats
9 染 *aburaji(miru)* become oily or oil-stained
10 粉 *shifun* cosmetics
14 張 *aburagi(tta)* obese, very fat
15 質 *shishitsu* fats

A **能** 4809 / J473d / M29454 NŌ ability, talent, skill, capacity; noh play, classical drama. *ato(u)* can, be able to; be possible; be done, be finished, be ready; be made of; be established, be set up; be formed; come into being; grow, be produced; break out; be good at; be versed in; become intimate with. *yoku(suru)* be skilled in. *yo(ku)* skillfully, thoroughly.
2 力 *nōryoku* ability, faculty, capacity
4 文 *nōbun* skilled in writing

文家 *nōbunka* skilled writer
5 弁 *nōben* eloquence, oratory
弁家 *nōbenka* orator
6 吏 *nōri* able official
7 狂言 *nō kyōgen* noh farce, noh interlude
役者 *nō yakusha* noh actor
9 面 *nōmen* noh mask
10 書 *nōga(ki)* advertising the excellence of ones's wares; boasting. *nōsho* excellent calligraphy; calligraphy
11 動 *nōdō* activity, actual work
動的 *nōdōteki* active
動免疫 *nōdō men'eki* active immunity
動態 *nōdōtai* active voice
率 *nōritsu* efficiency
率的 *nōritsuteki* efficient
率給 *nōritsukyū* efficiency wages
率賃金 *nōritsu chingin* efficiency wages
12 筆 *nōhitsu* skilled penmanship; skilled calligrapher
無 *nōna(shi)* incompetence; ne'er-do-well
13 楽 *nōgaku* noh drama
楽堂 *nōgakudō* noh theater
15 舞台 *nō butai* noh stage

B **胴** 4810 / J4639 / M29436 Dō torso, trunk (of a body); body armor; body (of a suit); drum (of a machine); barrel (of a horse); cylinder (of a drum); bulge (of a bucket); hull (of a ship); hub (of a wheel).
3 上 *dōa(ge)* tossing (a person); hoisting (a person to the shoulders)
4 中 *dōnaka* torso
6 回 *dōmawa(ri)* girth
7 体 *dōtai* body, torso, trunk; hull; fuselage
乱 *dōran* wallet, grip, collecting case
忘 *dōwasu(re)* memory slip, forgetting for the moment
声 *dōgoe* heavy voice, deep resonant voice
8 金 *dōgane* metal clasp
長 *dōnaga* long-torsoed
9 巻 *dōmaki* bellyband
枯病 *dōga(re)byō* blight
10 部 *dōbu* abdomen (in animals)
11 張声 *dōba(ri)goe* thick voice
欲 *dōyoku* avarice, greed; cruelty, inhumanity
慾者 *dōyokumono* greedy person
12 揚 *dōa(ge)* congratulatory tossing of a person
脹 *dōbuku(re)* swollen abdomen
着 *dōgi* undergarment; vest, waistcoat
間声 *dōmagoe* thick voice; deep resonant voice
13 慄 *dōburu(i)* shivering, trembling
15 締 *dōji(me)* belt, waistband
震 *dōburu(i)* shivering, trembling
慾 *dōyoku* avarice, greed; cruelty; inhumanity
18 鎧 *dōyoroi* body armor

A **胸** 4811 / J363b / M29442 Kyō. *mune* chest, breast, bosom; heart, mind, feelings. *muna-* breast.
3 三寸 *munesanzun* heart, mind, feelings
4 毛 *munage* chest hair, breast down
水 *kyōsui* pleural effusion (the fluid in pleurisy)
中 *kyōchū* one's heart, mind, or intentions
元 *munamoto* breast; pit of the stomach
6 回 *munemawa(ri)* chest measurement
宇 *kyōu* heart
先 *munasaki* breast; pit of the stomach, solar plexus
当 *munea(te)* breastplate, bib, chest-protector
当錐 *munea(te)giri* breast drill
7 囲 *kyōi* chest measurement
8 底 *kyōtei, munazoko* innermost heart
板 *manaita* the breast
泳 *kyōei* breast stroke
苦 *munaguru(shii)* feeling heavy in the chest
9 前 *munasaki* breast; pit of the stomach, solar plexus
背 *kyōhai* chest and back; front and back
10 骨 *kyōkotsu* breastbone, sternum
座 *munagura* the breast
部 *kyōbu* chest, breast
郭 *kyōkaku* the chest wall
倉 *munagura* the breast
11 勘定 *munakanjō* mental arithmetic; expectation
12 痛 *kyōtsū* chest pain
間 *kyōkan* breast, chest
幅 *munehaba, munahaba* chest breadth
椎 *kyōtsui* thoracic vertebrae
焼 *muneya(ke), munaya(ke)* heartburn, sour stomach
腔 *kyōkō, kyōkū* thorax, thoracic cavity

13 飾 *munekaza(ri)* brooch
裏 *kyōri* one's inmost heart, one's bosom
14 像 *kyōzō* bust
膜 *kyōmaku* pleura
膜炎 *kyōmakuen* pleurisy
算 *munazan* mental arithmetic; expectation
算用 *munazan'yō* mental arithmetic; expectation
16 墻 *kyōshō* breastwork, parapet
懐 *kyōkai* heart; in the heart; thoughts
壁 *kyōheki* chest walls; breastworks; parapet
17 糞悪 *munakuso (ga) waru(i)* feel grieved, feel disgusted
18 騒 *munasawa(gi)* uneasiness; (heart) flutter; emotional upset
襟 *kyōkin* heart, bosom
襟開 *kyōkin (o) hira(ite)* frankly

7

朖 4812 / J5b2d / M14363 **朗** 4813 / J-X / M14364 See 朗 4802. [月]

脯 4814 / J667d / M29543 Ho. *hojishi* dried meat.

脩 4815 / J667b / M29535 Shu dried meat; study; dry up.

脰 4816 / J-X / M29544 Tō nape of the neck.

脣 4817 / J667c / M29526 Shin. *kuchibiru* lip.

脛 4818 / J667a / M29504 Kei. *hagi, sune* leg, shin.
3 巾 *habaki* leggings
6 当 *sunea(te)* leggings, shin guards
10 骨 *keikotsu* shinbone, tibia
18 噛 *sunekaji(ri)* hanger-on, sponger, one still dependent on his parents

A **望** 4819 / J4b3e / M14368' Mō. Bō full moon; hope. *nozo(mu)* desire; aspire to; expect, hope for; like, choose; see, command (a view of). *nozo(mashii)* desirable, welcome, advisable. *nozo(mi)* desire, hope, expectation; ambition; prospects; preference. *mochi* full moon. [月]
4 手 *nozo(mi)te* applicant; candidate, aspirant; buyer
月 *mochizuki, bōgetsu* full moon
5 外 *bōgai no* unexpected
6 次第 *nozo(mi) shidai* as desired
7 見 *nozo(mi)-mi(ru)* scan (the scene); look into (the future). *bōken* watching from afar
9 通 *nozo(mi)dō(ri)* as desired
10 郷 *bōkyō* homesickness, nostalgia
12 遠 *bōen-* telescopic
遠写真 *bōenshashin* telephoto
遠鏡 *bōenkyō* telescope; binoculars
13 楼 *bōrō* watchtower
蜀 *bōshoku* insatiability
16 薄 *nozo(mi)usu* little hope

B **脚** 4820 / J3553 / M29502 Kaku, Kyaku leg, skid; undercarriage. *ashi* foot; leg; paw; flipper, tentacles, arms; walk, step, pace, speed; footing; draft (of a ship); foot (of a mountain); trace; deficit, shortage. *-kyaku* chair counter.
2 力 *kyakuryoku, kyakuriki* walking ability
3 下 *kyakka ni* at one's feet
4 元 *ashimoto* gait, pace, step
5 立 *kyatatsu* footstool, stepladder
付 *ashitsu(ki)* something with legs; sole of the foot
半 *kyahan* leggings, gaiters
本 *kyakuhon* play, drama, script
本家 *kyakuhonka* playwright, dramatist
本書 *kyakuhonka(ki)* scriptwriter, playwright
6 光 *kyakkō* footlights
色 *kyakushoku* plot, dramatization; stage or screen version
色者 *kyakushokusha* dramatizer, adapter
気 *kakke* beriberi
気衝心 *kakke shōshin* beriberi heart disease
8 注 *kyakuchū* footnotes
並 *ashina(mi)* pace, step
9 首 *ashikubi* ankle
10 部 *kyakubu* leg
荷 *ashini* ballast
11 絆 *kyahan* leggings, gaiters
12 湯 *kyakutō* hot foot bath
註 *kyakuchū* footnotes

14 榻 *kyatatsu* footstool; stepladder
15 線美 *kyakusembi* beauty of leg lines
19 韻 *kyakuin* rhyme

A 脳 4821 / J473e / M29567' **腦** 4839 / J672a / M29681 Nō brain; memory.
3 下垂体 *nōkasuitai* pituitary gland
4 天 *nōten* scalp, pate, crown of the head; head; brain
中 *nōchū* in one's head
5 出血 *nōshukketsu* apoplexy, cerebral hemorrhage, stroke
6 死 *nōshi* brain death
充血 *nōjūketsu* brain congestion
7 乱 *nōran* worry, anguish
8 炎 *nōen* brain inflammation, encephalitis
卒中 *nōsotchū* apoplexy
垂体 *nōsuitai* pituitary gland
味噌 *nōmiso* gray matter, brains
10 症 *nōshō* brain fever
振盪 *nōshintō* brain concussion
病 *nōbyō* brain fever; nervous disorder, neurosis; mental disease
病院 *nōbyōin* mental hospital, hospital for brain diseases
脊髄 *nōsekizui* brain and spinal cord
脊髄炎 *nōsekizuien* encephalomyelitis
脊髄膜炎 *nōsekizuimakuen* cerebrospinal meningitis
11 貧血 *nōhinketsu* cerebral anemia
軟化症 *nōnankashō* softening of the brain
13 裏 *nōri* brain; mind; memory; in the mind; in the heart
溢血 *nōikketsu* apoplexy, cerebral hemorrhage, stroke
14 膜炎 *nōmakuen* meningitis
15 漿 *nōshō* gray matter, brains
震盪 *nōshintō* concussion of the brain
18 髄 *nōzui* brain

B 脱 4822 / J4326 / M29539' Datsu removing. *das(suru) vi* escape from; get rid of; be omitted, be left out. *vt* take off (clothes); omit; rise above. *nu(gu)* take off (clothes), undress. *nu(geru)* come off, slip off, slip down. *nu(gasu), nu(gaseru)* strip off clothes, undress (someone). *nu(keru)* come off, fall out, slip out; be omitted; be missing; be rid of; pass through; escape; be captured; withdraw; be less than. *to(reru)* can be held, can take; come off, come apart, be off, be removed; be relieved (of pain); be obtained, be produced; be caught; be earned; come out (well) (a photo); require (time); be interpreted as; can get; let (light) in; take (one's measure); can feel (the pulse); take (a pen and write).
2 刀 *dattō* drawing a sword; ceasing to carry a sword
力感 *datsuryokukan* feeling of exhaustion
4 文 *datsubun* missing passage (in a document)
水 *dassui* dehydration, desiccation, evaporation
化 *dakka suru* change plans
毛 *datsumō, nu(ke)ge* falling out of hair; depilation; shed feathers
毛剤 *datsumōzai* a depilatory
5 皮 *dappi* shedding, molting, emergence
出 *dasshutsu* escape, extrication; prolapse. *nu(ke)-da(su)* leave; escape
6 臼 *dakkyū* dislocation
色 *dasshoku* decoloration, bleaching
会 *dakkai* withdrawal (from an organization)
字 *datsuji* omitted character; omitted word
衣 *datsui* undressing
衣所 *datsuijo* dressing room, bathhouse
7 肛 *dakkō* prolapse of the anus
却 *dakkyaku suru* get rid of, extricate oneself from, emerge from
兎 *datto* dashing away; tremendous speed
走 *dassō* escape, flight, desertion, abscondence
走軍 *dassōgun* an army in flight
8 退 *dattai* secession, withdrawal
垂 *dassui* prolapse
法 *dappō* fleeing from the law
法行為 *dappō kōi* law evasion
9 胎 *dattai* plagiarism
臭 *dasshū* deodorization
俗 *datsuzoku* becoming a hermit; separating oneself from the world
俗味 *datsuzokumi* unworldliness
俗的 *datsuzokuteki* unworldly, saintly
10 疽 *dasso* gangrene
党 *dattō* withdrawal from a party

脂 *dasshi* fat removal; nonfat, skim (milk); flesh-reducing
脂粉乳 *dasshi funnyū* powdered skim milk
脂綿 *dasshimen* absorbent cotton
11 捨 *nu(gi)-su(teru)* throw off (clothes), kick off (boots)
掛 *nu(gi)-ka(keru)* take off (garments) and hang up
船 *dassen* desertion from a ship
殻 *dakkaku* shedding, molting, casting off. *nu(ke)gara* cast-off skin
殻機 *dakkakuki* threshing machine
12 帽 *datsubō* removing the headgear; hats off
税 *datsuzei* tax evasion
落 *datsuraku* molting, falling off; omission; defection, desertion, apostasy
営 *datsuei* desertion from barracks
13 棄 *nu(gi)-su(teru)* throw off (clothes), kick off (boots)
腸 *datchō* hernia, rupture
腸帯 *datchōtai* truss
14 漏 *datsurō* omission
獄 *datsugoku* jail-breaking
誤 *datsugo* omissions and errors
監 *dakkan* jailbreak
穀 *dakkoku* threshing
穀機 *dakkokuki* threshing machine
15 稿 *dakkō* completion of writing
線 *dassen* derailment; deviation, aberration, digression
17 糞 *dappun* evacuation (of bowels)
18 藩 *dappan* a samurai leaving his lord and becoming a *rōnin* or lordless samurai
19 離 *datsuri* severing (oneself) from, getting rid of
20 艦 *dakkan* desertion from a warship
籍 *dasseki* omission from the register

8

腁 4823 / J-X / M29586 See 胼 4798.

脐 4824 / J-X / M-X Nonstandard for 臍 4887.

腆 4825 / J6722 / M29602 Ten plentiful; thick; good; complete.

腔 4826 / J3950 / M29630 Kō body cavity.

腊 4827 / J-X / M29614 Seki dried meat.

12 葉 *sakuyō* pressed leaves

朞 4828 / J5b2e / M14377 Ki one period. [月]

6 年 *kinen* one year

腓 4829 / J6724 / M29629 Hi. *fukurahagi, komura, kobura* calf (of the leg).

6 返 *komuragae(ri)* leg cramps

脾 4830 / J6723 / M29579 Hi spleen.

8 炎 *hien* splenitis
13 腹 *hibara* sides (of a person)
18 臓 *hizō* spleen

腑 4831 / J6725 / M29626 Fu viscera, bowels; mind; reason, understanding

5 甲斐無 *fugaina(i)* spiritless, cowardly; worthless
7 抜 *funu(ke)* dunce, fool, idiot, imbecile, simpleton
12 落 *fu (ni) o(chinai)* cannot fathom, cannot understand

B **脹** 4832 / J4431 / M29570 Chō. *fuku(ramu) vi* distend, bulge, fill out, swell, dilate, rise. *fuku(reru) vi* swell, fill out, get big, bulge, expand, dilate, distend, rise, be inflated. *fuku(ramasu), fuku(rakasu), fuku(raseru) vt* dilate, expand, distend, swell, blow up, puff out, inflate, pump up, raise (bread). *fuku(yokana)* plump, fat, well-rounded.

9 面 *fuku(ret)tsura no* sulky, sullen
10 粉 *fuku(rashi)ko* baking powder
13 腫 *chōshu* swelling

腋 4833 / J667e / M29615 Eki. *waki* armpit, side.

3 下 *waki (no) shita, ekika* armpit
4 毛 *wakige, ekimō* underarm hair
8 明 *wakia(ke)* side kimono slits. *wakia(ki)* placket (in a skirt)
9 臭 *wakiga, ekishū* offensive underarm odor
14 窩 *ekika* armpit

8

腎 4834 / J3f55 / M29621 JIN kidney.

5 石 *jinseki* kidney stone
8 炎 *jin'en* nephritis
18 臓 *jinzō* kidney
臓炎 *jinzōen* Bright's disease, nephritis
臓病 *jinzōbyō* kidney disease
臓結石 *jinzō kesseki* kidney stones

B **腐** 4835 / J4965 / M29625 FU. *kusa(ru), kusa(reru)* rot, decay; turn sour; fester; corrode; be corrupted; feel gloomy. *kusa(rasu), kusa(raseru), kusa(rakasu) vt* let spoil, rot, corrode, addle. *kuta(su)* let rot, spoil; slander. *kusa(su)* ridicule. *kusare-* spoiled, decayed, rotten.

4 心 *fushin* pains, trouble, hard work, diligence, intense application
6 肉 *funiku* tainted meat, putrid flesh; carrion; gangrene
朽 *fukyū* decay, decomposition, putrefaction
合 *kusa(re)-a(u)* enter into illicit intimacy. *kusa(re)a(i)* illicit relations; shady connections
7 乱 *furan* inflammation, festering, decomposition
卵 *furan* bad egg
8 刻 *fukoku* etching
果 *kusa(ri)-ha(teru)* be corrupt
9 食 *fushoku* corrosion, erosion, rot, rust
11 敗 *fuhai* decay, decomposition, rottenness, putrefaction; necrosis; corruption, degeneration, depravity
12 葉土 *fuyōdo* leaf mold
植 *fushoku* humus, leaf mold
植土 *fushokudo* humus, leaf mold
植質 *fushokushitsu* humus
15 穂 *kusa(ri)ho* mildew
縁 *kusa(re)en* mismated marriage; unpleasant relationships
蝕 *fushoku* corrosion, erosion, rot, rust
16 儒 *fuju* pedant, worthless scholar
21 爛 *furan* putrefaction

A **期** 4836 / J347c / M14378 KI, GO time, date, period, term; an age; season; session; a stage; opportunity. *ki(suru)* expect, anticipate, hope for, rely on; appoint (a day). *go(suru)* wait expectantly for. *ki(sezu) shite* unexpectedly, accidentally. [月]

4 日 *kijitsu, kinichi* date; time limit
月 *kigetsu* the appointed month; one full month
5 末 *kimatsu* term end
末試験 *kimatsu shiken* final examination
6 米 *kimai* rice for future delivery
年 *kinen* one year
成 *kisei* realization (of a plan)
成同盟 *kisei dōmei* uniting to carry out a plan
先 *kisaki* future stocks, forward merchandising
先物 *kisakimono* future stocks, forward merchandising
8 限 *kigen* term, period, time limit
限経過 *kigen keika* overdue
限満了 *kigen manryō* expiration of a term
9 首 *kishu* beginning of a period
待 *kitai* expectation, hope, anticipation, contemplation
待外 *kitaihazu(re)* disappointment
11 望 *kibō* expectant waiting
12 間 *kikan* term, period
間中 *kikanchū* during the period
間外 *kikangai* between sessions
間満了 *kikam-manryō* maturity, expiration
13 節 *kisetsu* season, opportunity

B **腕** 4837 / J4f53 / M29631 **捥** 2188 / J-X / M12181 WAN arm. *ude* arm; ability, talent. *kaina* arm.

2 力 *wanryoku* muscular strength, brute force, brawn
力沙汰 *wanryokuzata* fist fighting
4 比 *udekura(be)* trial of strength, trial of skill
木 *udegi* bracket, crosspiece, roof truss, armrest
木信号 *udegi shingō* semaphore
5 白 *wampaku* naughtiness, mischief
仕事 *udeshigoto* manual labor
立 *udeda(te) suru* fight, resort to force
立伏 *udeta(te)fu(se)* lie down on one's arms
6 尽 *udezu(ku) de* by main force. *udezu(ku) no* forcible, strong-arm
扱 *udeko(ki)* man of ability
先 *udesaki* the hand. *udesaki de* by one's own strength

次第 *udeshidai de* according to one's ability
[7] 利 *udeki(ki)* man of ability
角力 *udezumō* arm wrestling, hand wrestling
[8] 金 *udegane* outrigger; bracket, bracketing
押 *udeo(shi)* arm wrestling, hand wrestling
限 *udekagi(ri)* with all one's might
[9] 首 *udekubi* wrist
前 *udemae* ability, skill, capacity
相撲 *udezumō* arm wrestling
[10] 骨 *udebone* arm bone, wristbone; strength
時計 *udedokei* wristwatch
[11] 捲 *udemaku(ri) suru* roll up one's arms, bare one's arm
組 *udegu(mi)* folding one's arms
章 *wanshō* armband, arm badge, chevron, stripes
[12] 揃 *udezoro(i)* a lineup of experts
無 *udena(shi)* armless person; weak person; unskilled person
[13] 試 *udedame(shi)* trial of strength
飾 *udekaza(ri)* bracelet
節 *udebushi, ude(p)pushi* arm joint, muscular strength
節強 *ude(p)pushi (no) tsuyo(i)* strong, muscular
[14] 関節 *wankansetsu* wrist joint
[15] 輪 *udewa* bracelet
[20] 競 *udekura(be)* trial of strength, trial of skill

A **朝** 4838 / J442b / M14374' CHŌ dynasty; reign, regime; period, epoch; the court. *asa* morning, forenoon. *ashita* morn, morning. *chō(suru)* proceed to the palace; empty into (the sea). [月]
[3] 夕 *asayū, chōseki* day and night, morning and evening; always; daily. *asa(na)-yū(na)* morning and evening
三暮四 *chōsamboshi* six of one and half a dozen of the other
[4] 方 *asagata* toward morning; during the morning
込 *asago(me)* a morning raid
月夜 *asazukiyo* the moon shining toward morning
日 *asahi* morning sun, rising sun
日影 *asahikage* morning sunshine
[5] 立 *asada(chi)* early-morning departure
刊 *chōkan* morning paper
礼 *chōrei* morning meeting, morning exercises
市 *asa ichi* morning market
出 *asade* morning attendance, morning duty
未来 *asamadaki* before daybreak
令暮改 *chōrei-bokai* the issue of an order in the morning and its repeal in the evening; lack of principle
[6] 臣 *chōshin* courtier; the court. *ason* a high-ranking noble
衣 *chōi* court dress
凪 *asanagi* morning calm (at sea)
早 *asahaya(ku)* early in the morning
[7] 見 *chōken* imperial audience
廷 *chōtei* imperial court
来 *chōrai* since morning
改暮変 *chōkai-bohen* the issue of an order in the morning and its repeal in the evening; lack of principle
[8] 雨 *asaame* morning rain
拝 *chōhai* morning worship; congratulations to the emperor
明 *asaa(ke)* daybreak, dawn
和 *asanagi* morning calm (at sea)
服 *chōfuku* court dress
命 *chōmei* imperial command, government order
参 *asamai(ri)* morning visit to a shrine or temple
典 *chōten* court ceremony
東風 *asakochi* east wind in the morning
[9] 威 *chōi* imperial authority
政 *chōsei* imperial government
星 *asaboshi* morning star
風 *asakaze* morning breeze
風呂 *asaburo* morning bath
食 *chōshoku* breakfast
食後 *chōshokugo* after breakfast
[10] 起 *asao(ki)* early rising
酒 *asazake* a morning saké drink
陰 *asakage* morning shade; shady places in the morning
朗 *asaborake* dawn, daybreak
家 *chōka* imperial court
貢 *chōkō suru* bring tribute
恩 *chōon* favor of a ruler
帰 *asagae(ri)* returning after an overnight stay
[11] 鳥 *asadori* early rooster

涼 *asasuzu, asasuzu(mi)* morning coolness
船 *asabune* boat setting out in the morning
野 *chōya* government and the people; the whole nation
陽 *chōyō, asahi* morning sun
12 間 *asama, asa(no)ma* during the morning
開 *asaa(ke)* dawn, daybreak
晴 *asaba(re)* clear morning
晩 *asaban* morning and evening; always
湿 *asajime(ri)* morning dampness
湯 *asayu* morning bath
焼 *asaya(ke)* sunrise colors
朝 *asa(na)-asa(na)* morning after morning
寒 *asasamu* morning coolness
雲 *asagumo* morning clouds
賀 *chōga* congratulating the emperor
飯 *asameshi, asahan* breakfast
飯前 *asameshimae* before breakfast; something so simple it can be done before breakfast, a piece of cake
13 腹 *asabara, asa(p)para* morning empty feeling; something very easy
意 *chōi* the opinion of the imperial court
寝 *asane* morning sleep, late rising
寝坊 *asanebō* late rising; late riser
14 駆 *asaga(ke)* attack in the morning; departure in the morning
暮 *chōbo* morning and evening
髪 *asagami* hair still uncombed
15 儀 *chōgi* court ceremonies
権 *chōken* imperial authority
潮 *asashio* morning tide
課 *chōka* (Catholic) matins
餉 *asage* breakfast
影 *asakage* morning shadows; morning reflections; morning sunshine
敵 *chōteki* traitor, rebel, enemy of the emperor
16 憲 *chōken* constitution
曇 *asagumo(ri)* cloudy morning
餐 *chōsan* breakfast
稽古 *asageiko* morning exercise
17 霞 *asagasumi* morning mist
鮮 *Chōsen* Korea
鮮人参 *Chōsen ninjin* ginseng
鮮民主主義人民共和国 *Chōsen Minshu Shugi Jimmin Kyōwakoku* (North) Korean Democratic People's Republic
18 顔 *asagao* morning glory
19 禱 *chōtō* (Catholic) matins
霧 *asagiri* morning fog
20 議 *chōgi* imperial court conference
懸 *asaga(ke)* attack in the morning; departure in the morning
21 露 *chōro, asa tsuyu* morning dew
24 靄 *asa moya* morning mist

9

腦 4839 / J672a / M29681 See **脳** 4821.

膀 4840 / J-X / M29700 See **髈** 7100.

腴 4841 / J672b / M29713 YU grow fat; fatty.

腟 4842 / J6735 / M29667 **膣** 4861 / J6734 / M29849 CHITSU vagina.

腱 4843 / J6727 / M29708 KEN tendon.

腮 4844 / J6728 / M29702 **顋** 6642 / J707b / M43576 SAI. *ago* jaw.

腥 4845 / J6729 / M29678 SEI. *namagusa(i)* bloody, smelling of fish, smelling raw.
8 物 *namagusamono* raw things (like fish and meat)

腿 4846 / J425c / M29747 TAI. *momo* thigh, femur.
6 肉 *momoniku* round steak; ham

腺 4847 / J4123 / M29746 SEN gland.
10 病質 *sembyōshitsu* weak constitution
15 熱 *sennetsu* glandular fever

腫 4848 / J3c70 / M29697 SHU tumor, swelling. *ha(reru)* swell, become swollen. *ha(rebottai)* beginning to swell. *ha(rasu)* inflame, cause to swell. *ha(re)* swelling, dropsy.
3 上 *ha(re)-a(garu)* swell up
大症 *shudaishō* bunion

8 物 *shumotsu, haremono* tumor, abscess, boil, swelling
12 脹 *shuchō* swelling, puffiness, protuberance
14 瘍 *shuyō* tumor, neoplasm
瘍学 *shuyōgaku* oncology
15 瘤 *shuryū* tumor

A **腸** 4849/J4432/M29721 **膓** 4862/J6736/M29811 CHŌ intestines, bowels, entrails; digestive system in lower animals. *harawata* intestines, bowels, entrails, viscera; the heart. *wata* entrails.
4 中 *chōchū ni* in the intestines
8 炎 *chōen* enteritis, inflammation of the intestines
9 胃 *chōi* stomach and intestines
10 部 *chōbu* intestinal region
11 閉塞 *chōheisoku* intestinal obstruction
12 満 *chōman* abdominal dropsy
結核 *chōkekkaku* intestinal tuberculosis
13 詰 *chōzume* sausage
15 線 *chōsen* catgut
潰瘍 *chōkaiyō* intestinal ulcer
16 壁 *chōheki* intestinal wall

B **腰** 4850/J3978/M29705 YŌ. *koshi* hips, loins, waist, pelvic region; small of the back; haunch; lower-panel wainscoting (lower wall only); stem (of a wine glass).
3 下 *koshi (o) oro(su)* sit down
巾着 *koshiginchaku* belt purse; one's shadow; a henchman
4 元 *koshimoto* woman working for a noble family; the hips
5 付 *koshitsu(ki)* gait; posture
布 *koshinuno* loincloth
弁 *koshiben* petty official, low-salaried worker
弁当 *koshibentō* lunch tied to the belt; lunch-carrying workers. *koshibentō de* carrying a lunch
6 肉 *koshiniku* loin, sirloin
回 *koshimawa(ri)* hip measurement
当 *koshia(te)* bustle
羽目 *koshihame* panel, wainscoting
7 囲 *yōi* the hip measurement
抜 *koshinu(ke)* cowardice; coward; cripple. *koshi (ga) nu(keru)* be very much surprised
低 *koshi (ga) hiku(i)* humble
折 *koshio(re)* poor poem, doggerel; stooped over (old people). *koshi (o) o(ru)* bow; surrender; interrupt (someone)
8 板 *koshiita* panels; wainscoting (lower wall only)
物 *koshi (no) mono* sword worn at the side
9 砕 *koshikuda(ke)* weakening, hips giving way (and falling)
巻 *koshima(ki)* underskirt; loincloth, flannel waistband
10 骨 *koshibone, yōkotsu* hipbone; perseverance
高 *koshidaka* high wainscoting; long-stemmed goblet. *koshi (ga) taka(i)* proud
部 *yōbu* pelvic region, hips, loins, waist
帯 *koshiobi* waistband; narrow obi used to hold the tucked-up kimono in place
弱 *koshiyowa* lack of persistence. *koshi (ga) yowa(i)* weak, vacillating
11 張 *koshiba(ri)* papering or wainscoting lower part of a wall
強 *koshi (ga) tsuyo(i)* firm (character); strong (paste); stiff (paper)
掛 *koshika(keru)* sit down. *koshikake* seat, chair, bench, stool, pew, bleachers; steppingstone to something higher
掛仕事 *koshikake shigoto* temporary work
12 痛 *yōtsū, koshiita* lumbago, pain in the hip, pain in the back
間 *yokan* the hips
揚 *koshia(ge)* tuck at the waist
椎 *yōtsui* lumbar vertebrae
椎麻酔 *yōtsui masui* spinal anesthesia
湯 *koshiyu* hip bath, sitz bath
15 縄 *koshinawa* waist cord (for tying prisoners)

A **腹** 4851/J4a22/M29722 FUKU. *(o)naka* belly, stomach. *hara* abdomen, belly, bowels, stomach; heart, mind; intention; courage, spirit, pluck; anger; womb; thickest or widest part.
1 一杯 *hara-ippai* full stomach; to one's heart's content
3 子 *harako* fish eggs
下 *harakuda(ri)* diarrhea. *harakuda(shi)* diarrhea; laxative

工合 *haraguai* condition of the bowels
4 心 *fukushin* trusted friend; trusted retainer
水 *fukusui* abdominal dropsy
中 *fukuchū* in the abdomen, in the heart
切 *haraki(ri)* suicide by disembowelment
5 圧 *fukuatsu* muscular abdominal pressure
打 *harau(chi)* bellyflop
立 *harada(tsu)* get angry, take offense. *harada(tashii)* irritating, exasperating
立紛 *harada(chi)magi(re)* beside oneself with anger
6 臣 *fukushin* trusted friend; trusted retainer
虫 *hara (no) mushi* intestinal worms; heart, intention; courage
汚 *haragitana(i)* low-minded
合 *haraa(wase)* facing each other
当 *haraa(te)* chest and stomach armor; belly band
式 *fukushiki no* abdominal
式呼吸 *fukushiki kokyū* abdominal breathing
7 芸人 *haragei (no) hito* a person of strong personality
8 具合 *haraguai* condition of the bowels
9 持 *haramo(chi)* slow digestion; feeling of fullness
拵 *haragoshira(e)* eating
巻 *haramaki* waistband
背 *fukuhai* front and back; close relative
這 *harabai, hara(m)bai* lying on the stomach. *haraba(u)* crawl
10 部 *fukubu* abdomen, belly
案 *fukuan* plan, scheme, idea
帯 *haraobi, fukutai* health band, bellyband, saddle girth
消化 *haragonashi* digestion
11 黒 *haraguro(i)* evilhearted, crafty. *haraguro* schemer
掛 *haraga(ke)* workman's backless pocketed vest
探 *hara (o) sagu(ru)* probe another's feelings
据 *hara (o) su(eru)* make a decision
据兼 *hara (ni) su(e)-ka(neru)* be unable to tolerate
12 痛 *fukutsū, haraita, haraita(mi)* stomachache, colic, abdominal pain
減 *hara (ga) he(ru)* be hungry
腔 *fukkō, fukukō, fukukū* abdominal or peritoneal cavity
割 *hara (o) wa(ru)* make an abdominal incision; tell everything
筋 *hara suji, fukukin* abdominal muscles
違 *harachiga(i)* born of a different mother
13 鼓 *haratsuzumi* drum of the belly
塞 *harafusa(gi)* staying one's hunger
話術 *fukuwajutsu* ventriloquy
14 膜 *fukumaku* peritoneum
膜炎 *fukumakuen* peritonitis
蔵 *fukuzō* keeping things to oneself
蔵無 *fukuzōna(ku)* freely, frankly, plainly
15 稿 *fukkō* plan, scheme, idea
16 壁 *fukuheki* abdominal wall
18 癒 *haraise* retaliation. *hara (ga) i(reru)* be satisfied with one's revenge
穢 *haragitana(i)* base-minded
臓無 *fukuzōna(ku)* frankly, plainly, freely
21 鰭 *harabire* ventral fin

10

膊 4852 / J672e / M29782 HAKU arm.

膌 4853 / J-X / M29794 SEKI become emaciated.

B **膜** 4854 / J4b6c / M29808' MAKU membrane.

膄 4855 / J-X / M29758 SHŪ, SHU become emaciated.

膈 4856 / J672d / M29772 KAKU area between the chest and the abdomen.
14 膜 *kakumaku* diaphragm

膃 4857 / J672c / M29757 OTSU fat, corpulent.
8 肭臍 *ottosei* fur seal

膂 4858 / J6730 / M29755 RYO backbone.
2 力 *ryoryoku* muscular strength

膀 4859 / J672f / M29748 BŌ bladder.

[10]胱 *bōkō* urinary bladder
胱炎 *bōkōen* bladder infection
胱結石 *bōkō kesseki* bladder stones

膏 4860 J3951 M29800 Kō paste, ointment, plaster. *abura* fat, grease, tallow, lard, suet, blubber.
[6]血 *kōketsu* sweat and blood
[8]油 *kōyu* lamp oil
壌 *kōjō* fertile soil
[16]薬 *kōyaku* salve, ointment, plaster
薬張 *kōyakuba(ri)* patchwork, makeshift

11

膣 4861 J6734 M29849 See 腟 4842.

腸 4862 J6736 M29811 See 腸 4849.

鱈 4863 J6733 M-X Setsu. *tara* codfish.

膕 4864 J6732 M29816 Kaku. Koku. Kyoku. *hikagami* hollow of the knee.

膵 4865 J6739 M29920 (国字) Sui pancreas.
[11]液 *suieki* pancreatic juice
[18]臓 *suizō* pancreas

膠 4866 J6731 M29841 Kō. *nikawa* glue. *nibe* fish glue, isinglass.
[4]水 *kōsui* sizing
化 *kōka suru* gelatinize
[11]接 *kōsetsu* sticking
[12]着 *kōchaku* agglutination; stalemate
着剤 *kōchakuzai* glue, binder
[14]漆 *kōshitsu* glue and lacquer; great intimacy
[15]質 *kōshitsu no* gluey, gelatinous, colloidal
[22]嚢 *kōnō* capsule

B膚 4867 J4966 M29829 Fu. *hada, hadae* skin, body; grain, texture; disposition.
[6]色 *hada iro* flesh color
[7]見 *fuken* superficial views
身 *hadami* the body
身離 *hadami-hana(sazu)* (purse and other articles) always carried on one's person
[9]浅 *fusen* superficiality
[11]脱 *hadanu(gi)* bare to the waist
[12]焼 *hadaya(ki)* casehardening
寒 *hadasamu(i), hadazamu(i)* chilly
着 *hadagi* underwear
[13]触 *hadazawa(ri)* the touch, the feel
[19]襦袢 *hada juban* underwear

膝 4868 J4928 M29837 Shitsu. *hiza* knee; lap.
[3]下 *shikka* paternal home; at the knees. *hizamoto* with one's parents; with one's lord close by; ruler's capital city
小僧 *hizakozō* kneecap
[4]元 *hizamoto* with one's parents; with one's lord close by; ruler's capital city
反射 *shitsuhansha* knee jerk
[5]正 *hiza (o) tada(su)* sit (on the floor) correctly
[6]行 *shikkō* going on one's knees
交 *hiza (o) maji(eru)* have a frank talk
[8]送 *hizaoku(ri)* moving closer together (in seats)
枕 *hizamakura* using someone's lap for a pillow
突 *hizatsu(ki)* small knee mat
拍子 *hizabyōshi* beating time on one's knee
[10]株 *hizakabu* kneecap
栗毛 *hizakurige* a hike; traveling on foot, shank's mare
[11]掛 *hizaka(ke)* lap robe
組 *hizagu(mu)* cross the knees. *hizagu(mi)* crossed legs
崩 *hiza (o) kuzu(su)* relax one's squatting position
[13]詰談判 *hizazu(me) dampan* direct negotiations
蓋骨 *shitsugaikotsu* kneecap
蓋腱反射 *shitsugaiken hansha* knee jerk
[14]関節 *shitsukansetsu* knee joint
[16]頭 *hizagashira* kneecap
[19]繰 *hizagu(ri)* sitting closer

6 竹米糸缶网罒羊羽老耂而耒耳聿【肉月】臣自至臼舌舛舟艮色艸艹虍虫血行衣衤襾

12

膸 4869 J673b M29924 See **髓** 6791.

臈 4870 J6745 M29953 See **臘** 4888.

膰 4871 J6738 M29882 HAN. *himorogi* offerings to the gods.

膩 4872 J6737 M29862 JI oil; oily skin; smooth.
13 滑 *jikatsu* slippery, smooth

膳 4873 J4137 M29891 ZEN small low table; tray.
4 夫 *kashiwade* butler
5 立 *zenda(te)* setting the table; preparations, program, scheme
10 部 *zembu* tray of food

B **膨** 4874 J4b44 M29861 BŌ get fat; get thick, swell. *fuku(reru)* swell.
3 大 *bōdai* swelling, expansion
10 粉 *fukura(shi)ko* baking powder
隆 *bōryū suru* swell up
11 張 *bōchō* swelling; inflation; expansion, growth, increase
12 満 *bōman suru* be inflated
脹 *bōchō* swelling; inflation; expansion, growth, increase

13

膽 4875 J673c M29933 See **胆** 4790.

臉 4876 J6740 M29954 KEN area under eyes; face.

臂 4877 J673e M29944 HI. *hiji* elbow; arm (of something).

膺 4878 J673f M29928 YŌ breast; strike, hit.
18 懲 *yōchō* punishment, chastisement

膾 4879 J673a M29937 KAI. *namasu* fish salad, raw fish and vegetables.
8 炙 *kaisha* a household word; universal praise

臀 4880 J673d M29939 **臋** 4881 J-X M29940 DEN. *shiri* buttocks, hips; rear or back of a person; bottom (of a kettle); tail end, tag end.
6 肉 *denniku* rump flesh (of animals)
7 位 *den'i* breech presentation (obstetrics)
10 部 *dembu* buttocks, hips, haunch

朦 4882 J5b2f M14409 MŌ dim, obscure. [月]
6 気 *mōki* fog, mist, vapor
17 朦 *mōmō(taru)* gloomy; depressed
20 朧 *mōrō(taru)* dim, hazy, vague, obscure

臆 4883 J3232 M29951 OKU timidity; breast, heart, mind. *oku(suru)* fear, hesitate, be nervous, be cowardly, be timid.
7 見 *okken* one's own idea, my guess
9 面 *okumen* shy face
10 病 *okubyō* cowardice, timidity
病者 *okubyōmono* coward
病風 *okubyōkaze* panic, loss of nerve
病神 *okubyōgami* god of cowardice
11 断 *okudan* guess, hypothesis, supposition
12 測 *okusoku* guess, hypothesis, supposition
14 説 *okusetsu* conjecture, hypothesis

膿 4884 J473f M29938 NŌ pus, discharge. *u(mu)* form pus, fester, suppurate. *umi* pus, discharge.
5 汁 *nōjū, umishiru* pus, discharge
6 血 *umichi, nōketsu* blood and pus, bloody pus
8 毒症 *nōdokushō* blood poisoning
10 疱 *nōhō* pustule
痂疹 *nōkashin* impetigo
13 腫 *nōshu* abscess
14 漏 *nōrō* pyorrhea
瘍 *nōyō* boil, abscess
瘍歯 *nōyōshi* abscessed tooth
15 潰 *nōkai* suppuration, ulceration

14

臑 4885 J6742 M29986 DŌ. *sune* leg, shin.
6 当 *sunea(te)* leggings, shin guards
18 噛 *sunekaji(ri)* hanger-on, sponger

A臟 4886 / J4221 / M29995' 臟 4892 / J6747 / M30046 Zō viscera, bowels.
[8] 物 *zōmotsu, harawata* entrails, giblets
[12] 腑 *zōfu* intestines, entrails
[15] 器 *zōki* intestines, internal organs, viscera, bowels

臍 4887 / J6741 / M29967 SEI. ZAI. *heso, hozo* navel.
[3] 下 *seika* lower abdomen
下丹田 *seika-tanden* pit of the stomach
[6] 曲 *heso (o) ma(geru)* get cross.
hesomaga(ri) perverse person
[10] 帯 *saitai, seitai* umbilical cord
[14] 緒 *heso (no) o* umbilical cord
[19] 繰 *hesoku(ri)* secret savings, pin money
繰金 *hesoku(ri)gane* secret savings, pin money

— 15 —

臘 4888 / J6744 / M30009 RŌ 12th lunar month.

— 16 —

臚 4889 / J6746 / M30027 RO skin; abdomen; line up; convey (message).

臙 4890 / J6743 / M30018 EN rouge.
[10] 脂 *enji* rouge; lipstick; a dark-red pigment; cochineal
脂色 *enji iro* deep red

朧 4891 / J5b30 / M14411 RŌ. *oboro* haziness, dreaminess, gloom. [月]
[4] 月 *oborozuki* hazy moon
月夜 *oborozukiyo* misty moonlit night
[6] 気 *oboroge na* indistinct, misty, dreamy
[8] 夜 *oboroyo* misty moonlit night
昆布 *oboro kombu* sliced tangle (seaweed)
[20] 朧 *oboro-oboro* haziness, dreaminess

— 17 —

臟 4892 / J6747 / M30046 See 臟 4886

— 19 —

臠 4893 / J6748 / M30049 REN. *misona(wasu)* see, witness, inspect.

RAD. 臣 131

Shin or *kerai* retainer, minister, subject. As a radical this is always counted as 6 strokes even though it often seems to have 7.

Nickname: Minister (of State).

A臣 4894 / J3f43 / M30068 SHIN *omi* retainer, subject.
[3] 子 *shinshi* retainer
下 *shinka* subject, retainer, vassal
[5] 民 *shimmin* subject, national
[8] 服 *shimpuku suru* obey, follow
事 *shinji* allegiance, retainer's service
[10] 従 *shinjū* serving as a retainer; retainer
[11] 庶 *shinsho* retainers and the people
道 *shindō* practice of loyalty
[12] 属 *shinzoku* vassalage, subjection
[13] 節 *shinsetsu* a retainer's integrity
[14] 僚 *shinryō* officials in service
僕 *shimboku* retainer, servant, retinue
[16] 隷 *shinrei* retainer
[20] 籍 *shinseki* status of a subject
籍降下 *shinseki kōka* (royalty) becoming subjects
籍降嫁 *shinseki kōka* (a princess) marrying a commoner

— 2 —

臤 4895 / J-X / M30070 KAN, KEN hard; wise.

臥 4896 / J3269 / M30071 卧 4897 / J-X / M-X GA. *fu(su), ga(su)* bend down, bow down, lie prostrate. *fu(seru)* lie down, retire, go to bed.

7 床 *gashō* confined to bed. *fushido* a bed
8 所 *fushido* bed, cot, place to sleep
10 病 *gabyō* bedridden
竜 *garyō* a reclining dragon; a famous person in obscurity
13 煙 *gaen* ancient firefighter
16 薪嘗胆 *gashin-shōtan* perseverance and determination

8

臧 4898 / J6749 / M30083 Sō, Zō good; thick; conceal; bribe; servant.

11

A **臨** 4899 / J4e57 / M30087 Rin. *nozo(mu)* face, front on, border on; meet; be confronted by; be on the verge of; attend, assist at; deal with; rule over; command a view of; deign to; visit, call on; come upon; come up to.

4 月 *ringetsu* last month of pregnancy
5 写 *rinsha* copying
6 行 *rinkō* proceeding to a place
休 *rinkyū* special holiday
地 *rinchi no* on-the-spot, field
在 *rinzai* presence
死体験 *rinshitaiken* near-death experience
7 床 *rinshō* clinical
床工学技士 *rinshō kōgaku gishi* clinical engineer
床医学 *rinshō igaku* clinical medicine
床的 *rinshōteki* clinical
床家 *rinshōka* clinician
床尋問 *rinshō jimmon* clinical examination
床像 *rinshōzō* clinical picture, clinical findings
床講義 *rinshō kōgi* clinical lecture, clinic, bedside instruction
8 幸 *rinkō* imperial visit
9 界 *rinkai* limit; critical (temperature)
海 *rinkai* marine, seaside
海実験所 *rinkai jikkenjo* marine laboratory
10 席 *rinseki* presence, attendance, those present
書 *rinsho* copying characters from a model book
時 *rinji* temporary, special, extraordinary
時利得税 *rinji-ritokuzei* excess-profits tax
時国会 *rinji kokkai* special session of congress
時費 *rinjihi* emergency expenses
11 終 *rinjū* dying hour, deathbed, one's last hour
船 *rinsen* ship visit, ship search
船権 *rinsenken* right to search a ship
12 場 *rinjō* visit, presence, attendance
御 *ringyo* imperial visit
検 *rinken* inspection visit, raid, domiciliary search
港列車 *rinkō ressha* train to the port
港線 *rinkōsen* railway line to the port
13 戦 *rinsen* going to the battlefield
16 機 *rinki ni* extemporaneously, impromptu
機応変 *rinki-ōhen* adaptation to circumstances

RAD. 自 132

Mizukara oneself. Nickname: Dotted Eye (cf. Rad. 109).

A **自** 4900 / J3c2b / M30095 Shi, Ji oneself. *mizuka(ra)* oneself, personally. *onozuka(ra), ino(zuto)* naturally, of itself.

2 力 *jiryoku* self-reliance, one's own efforts, self-help. *jiriki* (Buddhist) salvation by works
力本願 *jiriki hongan* salvation by works; continence, self-control, self-denial
力更生 *jiriki-kōsei* attaining success by overcoming difficulties
3 大 *jidai* boasting
刃 *jijin* suicide
己 *jiko* oneself, ego. *jiko-* self-, auto-
己中心 *jiko-chūshin no* selfish, self-centered
己反省 *jiko-hansei* introspection
己本位 *jiko-hon'i* egotism, selfishness

己主義 *jiko-shugi* egoism, selfishness
己弁護 *jiko-bengo* self-justification
己批判 *jiko-hihan* self-criticism
己実現 *jiko-jitsugen* self-realization, self-expression
己表現 *jiko-hyōgen* self-expression
己保存 *jiko-hozon* self-preservation
己宣伝 *jiko-senden* self-advertisement
己発展 *jiko-hatten* self-aggrandizement
己流 *jikoryū* one's own style. *jikoryū no* self-styled, self-taught
己訓練 *jiko-kunren* self-discipline
己紹介 *jiko-shōkai* self-introduction
己満足 *jiko-manzoku* self satisfaction
己欺瞞 *jiko-giman* self-deception
己暗示 *jiko-anji* autosuggestion
己催眠 *jiko-saimin* autohypnosis
己解剖 *jiko-kaibō* self-analysis
己感情 *jiko-kanjō* emotional result of one's own estimate of oneself
己嫌悪 *jiko-ken'o* self-abhorrence
己犠牲 *jiko-gisei* self-sacrifice
己犠牲的 *jiko-giseiteki* self-sacrificing
4 火 *jika* a fire starting in one's home
今 *jikon* hereafter
分 *jibun* self, oneself. *jibun no* one's own, personal
分天狗 *jibun tengu* self-conceited person
分自身 *jibun-jishin* oneself (emphatic)
分持 *jibunmo(chi)* paying one's own way, providing for oneself
分勝手 *jibun-katte* selfishness, egoism
5 生 *jisei* spontaneous generation, wild or natural growth
用 *jiyō* for personal use
白 *jihaku* confession, acknowledgment
他 *jita* oneself and others; transitive and intransitive
弁 *jiben* paying one's own expenses
失 *jishitsu* absent-mindedness; stupor, daze; unconsciousness; apathy
立 *jiritsu* independence, self-reliance, self-support
立経済 *jiritsu keizai* economic independence
主 *jishu* independence, autonomy
主化 *jishuka suru* make independent
主的 *jishuteki* independent, autonomous
主番組 *jishubangumi* sustaining program (sponsorless)
主権 *jishuken* independence, autonomy
由 *jiyū* independence, freedom, liberty; liberal; voluntary
由人 *jiyūjin* free people
由民 *jiyūmin* free people
由平等 *jiyū-byōdō* freedom and equality before the law
由市場 *jiyū shijō* free market
由主義 *jiyū shugi* liberalism
由自在 *jiyū-jizai na* free, unrestricted
由行動 *jiyū kōdō* free hand, independent action
由形 *jiyūgata* free style (swimming)
由労働者 *jiyū rōdōsha* casual laborer
由画 *jiyūga* freehand drawing
由国 *jiyūkoku* independent nation
由国家 *jiyū kokka* a free nation
由放任 *jiyū hōnin* noninterference, laissez faire
由型 *jiyūgata* free style
由研究 *jiyū kenkyū* independent investigation
由神学 *jiyū shingaku* liberal theology
由思想 *jiyū shisō* liberal thought
由思想家 *jiyū shisōka* freethinkers
由党 *jiyūtō* liberal party
由都市 *jiyū toshi* free city
由航行権 *jiyū kōkōken* freedom of passage
由恋愛 *jiyū ren'ai* free love
由訳 *jiyūyaku* free translation
由販売 *jiyū hambai* unrestricted trade
由教育 *jiyū kyōiku* liberal education
由経済 *jiyū keizai* free economy
由船舶 *jiyū sempaku* neutral ship
由港 *jiyūkō* free port
由勝手 *jiyū katte* willfulness
由貿易 *jiyū bōeki* free trade
由貿易地域 *jiyū bōeki chiiki* free trade zone
由渡航 *jiyū tokō* unrestricted ship passage
由結婚 *jiyū kekkon* common-law marriage
由裁量 *jiyū sairyō* latitude, discretion
由廃業 *jiyū haigyō* prostitute's self-emancipation
由営業 *jiyū eigyō* nonrestricted business
由詩 *jiyūshi* free verse
由意志 *jiyū ishi* free will; spontaneity
由解放 *jiyū kaihō* setting free
由選択 *jiyū sentaku* free choice
由権 *jiyūken* civil liberties
由諸国 *jiyū shokoku* the free nations

由憲法 *jiyū kempō* flexible constitution
由競争 *jiyū kyōsō* open competition
6 尽 *jijin* suicide
伝 *jiden* autobiography
任 *jinin* pretension, bragging
刎 *jifun suru* decapitate oneself
存 *jizon, jison* self-existence
宅 *jitaku* one's home, private residence
宅教授 *jitaku kyōju* tutoring in the home
在 *jizai ni* freely, at will
在書架 *jizai shoka* expandable bookcase
在梯子 *jizaibashigo* extension ladder
在鉤 *jizaikagi* pot hanger, pot hook
在継手 *jizai tsu(gi)te* universal joint
在錐 *jizaisui* expanding bit
在鍵 *jizaikagi* pot hook, pot hanger
7 足 *jisoku* self-sufficiency, satisfaction with what one possesses
身 *jishin* self, oneself, itself, yourself. *jishin de* by oneself, in person, personally
序 *jijo* author's preface
戒 *jikai* self-discipline
体 *jitai* one's own body, oneself, itself; originally
決 *jiketsu* self-determination; resignation; suicide
沈 *jichin suru* scuttle one's own boat
利 *jiri* self-interest, personal gain
判 *jihan* one's own decision, one's own judgment
助 *jijo* self-help, self-reliance
邸 *jitei* one's residence
余 *jiyo* the others, the rest
花受粉 *jikajufun* self-pollination
作 *jisaku* one's own work
作農 *jisakunō* owner-farmer
作農民 *jisaku nōmin* owner-farmers
我 *jiga* self, the ego
我主義 *jiga shugi* egotism, egoism
我自讃 *jiga-jisan* self-praise
我実現 *jiga-jitsugen* self-realization
8 供 *jikyō* confession
明 *jimei* self-evidence
注 *jichū* annotating one's own writings; such annotations
炊 *jisui* cooking for oneself
知 *jichi* knowing oneself
若 *jijaku* composure, calmness
制力 *jiseiryoku* power of self-control
制心 *jiseishin* self-control
国 *jikoku* one's own country. *jikoku no* native, domestic
国民 *jikokumin* one's countrymen
国語 *jikokugo* one's mother tongue
画 *jiga* picture painted by oneself
画自賛 *jiga-jisan* praising one's own picture
画像 *jigazō* self-portrait
画賛 *jigasan* praising one's own picture
画讃 *jigasan* praising one's own picture
治 *jichi* self-government
治会 *jichikai* student council
治体 *jichitai* self-governing body
治的 *jichiteki* autonomous, self-governing
治制 *jichisei* self-governing system
治植民地 *jichi shokuminchi* dominion, self-governing colony, crown colony
治領 *jichiryō* self-governing dominion
治権 *jichiken* autonomy
9 首 *jishu* surrender (to police)
派 *jiha* one's own party
活 *jikatsu* self-support
科 *jika* one's own sins
刭 *jikei suru* decapitate oneself
剃 *jizo(ri) suru* shave oneself
卑 *jihi* debasing oneself
前 *jimae de* at one's own expense. *jimae no* independent (geisha)
恃 *jiji* self-reliance
省 *jisei* self-examination
浄作用 *jijōsayō* self-purification
信 *jishin* self-confidence
信満満 *jishin-mamman* great self-confidence
叙 *jijo* writing one's story
叙伝 *jijoden* autobiography
乗 *jijō suru* square (a number)
乗根 *jijōkon* square root
重 *jijū* dead weight. *jichō* self-respect, self-love, prudence, circumspection; care of the body
重心 *jichōshin* (proper) pride
負 *jifu* bragging about one's ability; conceit
負心 *jifushin* conceit
発 *jihatsu* spontaneousness
発性 *jihatsusei* spontaneousness
発的 *jihatsuteki* spontaneous, voluntary, free-will
律 *jiritsu* autonomy, self-control, self-determination

律性 *jiritsusei* autonomy
律神経 *jiritsu shinkei* autonomic nerves
律神経失調症 *jiritsu shinkei shitchōshō* autonomic ataxia
律訓練法 *jiritsu kunrenhō* autogenic training
10 修 *jishū* self-study
称 *jishō* self-styled, would-be; first person
害 *jigai* suicide
党 *jitō* one's own party
差 *jisa* deviation
書 *jisho* one's own writing, autograph
記 *jiki* writing personally; self-registering
記晴雨計 *jiki seiukei* recording barometer
記寒暖計 *jiki kandankei* recording thermometer
殺 *jisatsu* suicide
殺未遂 *jisatsu misui* attempted suicide
殺未遂者 *jisatsu misuisha* attempted suicide (the person)
殺的 *jisatsuteki* suicidal
殺者 *jisatsusha* a suicide (the person)
家 *jika* one's own home; one's self
家中毒 *jika chūdoku* autointoxication
家用 *jikayō* private use
家用車 *jikayōsha* private automobile
家広告 *jika kōkoku* self-advertisement, publicity stunt
家本位 *jika hon'i* egotism, selfishness
家伝染 *jika densen* autoinfection
家受精 *jika jusei* self-reproduction
家保存 *jika hozon* self-preservation
家保険 *jika hoken* self-insurance
家製 *jikasei no* home-brewed
家撞着 *jika-dōchaku* self-contradiction
11 得 *jitoku* self-satisfaction; self-acquirement; apprehension, understanding
晦 *jikai* hiding oneself and one's talents
著 *jicho* one's own publication
粛 *jishuku* self-control, self-discipline
堕落 *jidaraku* depravity
販機 *jihanki* vending machine
閉症 *jiheishō* autism
問 *jimon suru* question oneself
問自答 *jimon-jitō* soliloquy, monologue, answering one's own question
惚 *unubo(reru)* be conceited, flatter oneself
惚者 *unubo(re)mono* conceited person
転 *jiten* rotation
転車 *jitensha* bicycle
習 *jishū* studying by oneself
習自学 *jishū-jigaku* studying by oneself
責 *jiseki* self-condemnation
責点 *jisekiten* earned run
動 *jidō* automatic action
動人形 *jidō ningyō* automaton, robot
動小銃 *jidō shōjū* automatic rifle
動火器 *jidō kaki* automatic firearms
動収穫機 *jidō shūkakuki* threshing machine
動自転車 *jidō jitensha* motorcycle
動式 *jidōshiki no* automatic
動式電話機 *jidōshiki denwaki* dial phone
動車 *jidōsha* automobile
動車王 *jidōshaō* automobile king
動車屋 *jidōshaya* garage, auto repair shop
動車速度計 *jidōsha sokudokei* speedometer
動車庫 *jidōshako* garage
動車部隊 *jidōsha butai* motorized unit
動車隊 *jidōshatai* automobile corps
動車強盗 *jidōsha gōtō* automobile thief
動車税 *jidōshazei* automobile tax
動車路 *jidōsharo* driveway, auto road
動車電話 *jidōsha denwa* car telephone
動車置場 *jidōsha okiba* motor pool
動車駐車場 *jidōsha chūshajō* parking place, parking lot
動的 *jidōteki* automatic
動制御 *jidō seigyo* automatic control
動連結機 *jidō renketsuki* automatic coupler
動計算器 *jidō keisanki* taximeter
動消火機 *jidō shōkaki* automatic sprinkler system
動販売食堂 *jidō hambai shokudō* automat
動販売器 *jidō hambaiki* automatic vending machine
動階段 *jidō kaidan* escalator
動扉 *jidō tobira* automatic doors
動詞 *jidōshi* intransitive verb
動艇 *jidōtei* motorboat
動電話 *jidō denwa* public telephone
動橇 *jidō sori* motor sledge

動操縦装置 *jidō sōjū sōchi* automatic pilot
12 廃 *jihai* (prostitute's) voluntary emancipation
評 *jihyō* self-criticism
訴 *jiso* surrender (to police)
証 *jishō* one's own evidence
敬 *jikei* self-respect
筆 *jihitsu* one's own handwriting
営 *jiei* self-management
裁 *jisai* suicide
給 *jikyū* self-support
給自足 *jikyū-jisoku* self-support, self-sufficiency
尊 *jison* self-respect; self-esteem, conceit
尊心 *jisonshin* self-respect; self-esteem, conceit
覚 *jikaku* consciousness; self-consciousness; insight; realization
覚的 *jikakuteki* subjective (symptoms)
覚症 *jikakushō* subjective symptoms, patient's complaints
覚症状 *jikakushōjō* subjective symptoms, patient's complaints
費 *jihi* one's own expense
費出版 *jihi shuppan* publication at one's own expense
費番組 *jihi bangumi* sustaining program (sponsorless)
然 *shizen, jinen* nature. *shizen no* natural; unaffected; spontaneous, automatic
然人 *shizennin* natural person
然力 *shizenryoku* natural agencies
然木 *shizemboku* naturally grown trees
然生 *jinensei* wild growth
然失業率 *shizen shitsugyōritsu* natural rate of unemployment
然本然 *shizen-honnen no* natural
然主義 *shizen shugi* naturalism
然色 *shizenshoku* natural color
然死 *shizenshi* natural death
然言語 *shizen gengo* natural language
然林 *shizenrin* natural forest, virgin forest
然物 *shizembutsu* natural objects
然的 *shizenteki* natural
然法 *shizenhō* natural law, law of nature
然法則 *shizen hōsoku* natural law
然界 *shizenkai* natural world
然食品 *shizen shokuhin* natural food
然美 *shizembi* natural beauty; beauty of nature
然発火 *shizen hakka* spontaneous combustion
然発生 *shizen hassei* spontaneous generation; spontaneity
然科学 *shizen kagaku* natural science
然秩序 *shizen chitsujo* natural order
然教 *shizenkyō* nature worship
然描写 *shizembyōsha* description of nature
然崇拝 *shizen sūhai* nature worship
然淘汰 *shizen tōta* natural selection
然現象 *shizen genshō* natural phenomena
然数 *shizen (no) sū* fate
然増加 *shizen zōka* unearned increment
然増収 *shizen zōshū* natural increase, accretion
然権 *shizenken* natural rights
然論 *shizenron* naturalism
然燃焼 *shizen nenshō* spontaneous combustion
然薯 *jinenjo* a wild mountain potato, a wild yam
然療法 *shizen ryōhō* nature cure, naturopathy; physiotherapy
然観 *shizenkan* view of nature
13 適 *jiteki* easy and comfortable living
働 *jidō* automatic action
滅 *jimetsu* natural decay; self-ruin, suicide, self-destruction
腹 *jibara* one's own pocketbook
愛 *jiai* self-love, selfishness, egoism, self-regard
署 *jisho* autograph, signature
意識 *jiishiki* self-consciousness
業自得 *jigō-jitoku* reaping what one sows
棄 *jiki, yake* despair; desperation
棄八 *yake(noyam)pachi* desperate person
棄酒 *yakezake* drowning one's cares in saké
棄飲 *yakeno(mi)* drinking to forget one's troubles
棄腹 *yakebara, yake(p)para* desperation, despair
棄糞 *yakekuso* desperation; despair
14 選 *jisen* personal choice
像 *jizō* self-bust (sculpture)
説 *jisetsu* one's own view
認 *jinin* admission
製 *jisei* one's own making
堕落 *jidaraku* personal untidiness

慢 *jiman* pride, boasting
慢臭 *jimankusa(i)* boastful
慢話 *jimambanashi* boastful talk
慢顔 *jimangao* boastful look
15 嘲 *jichō* self-scorn
慰 *jii* self-consolation; masturbation
賛 *jisan* self-praise
縄自縛 *jijōjibaku* caught in one's own trap
暴 *jibō* neglecting or injuring one's body
暴自棄 *jibōjiki* despair, desperation
暴酒 *yakezake* drowning one's cares in saké
16 儘 *jimama* selfishness, egoism; willfulness, disobedience; whim
彊 *jikyō* strenuous efforts
燃 *jinen* spontaneous combustion
縛 *jibaku* being circumscribed by one's own words and actions
薦 *jisen* recommending oneself
壊 *jikai* disintegration
壊作用 *jikai sayō* disintegration
衛 *jiei* self defense; bodyguard
衛長 *jieichō* captain of the guard
衛隊 *Jieitai* Self-Defense Force
衛権 *jieiken* right of self-defense
18 瀆 *jitoku* masturbation
瀆行為 *jitoku kōi* masturbation
19 爆 *jibaku* suicide explosion
爆機 *jibakuki* suicide bomber
警 *jikei* self-warning, vigilance
警団 *jikeidan* vigilance committee
22 讃 *jisan* praising oneself

3

B 臭 4901 / J3d2d / M30103' 臭 4902 / J-X / M30108 SHŪ odor, savor, fragrance. *kusa(i)* ill-smelling; suspicious-looking. *nio(i)* smell, odor, scent; stench; fragrance, aroma, perfume. *-kusa(i)* smelling; smacking of; looking (suspicious).
6 名 *shūmei* shameful reputation
気 *shūki* offensive odor, stench
気止 *shūkido(me)* deodorizer
8 味 *kusami, shūmi* offensive odor; savor, flavor, smack; group, faction
物 *kusa(i)mono* scandal
10 素 *shūso* bromine
素酸 *shūsosan* bromic acid
13 跡 *shūseki* scent, trail
14 聞 *shūbun* scandal, ill-fame

4

臭 4902 / J-X / M30108 See 臭 4901.

至 RAD. 133

Itaru to arrive. Nickname: Arriving.

A 至 4903 / J3b6a / M30142 SHI. *ita(ru)* go, proceed, come; arrive, reach, attain; result in, lead to. *ita(ri)* the utmost, the height of, climax; on account of. *ita(ru made)* to, until. *ita(ranai)* imperfect, incompetent, careless. *ita(tte)* very, exceedingly. *ita(tte) wa* as for, as to.
3 大 *shidai no* vast, enormous; remarkable; important
才 *shisai* rare talents; a man of rare talents
上 *shijō* supremacy
上命令 *shijōmeirei* a supreme (inviolable) command; the categorical imperative
上権 *shijōken* supremacy, sovereignty
4 心 *shishin* sincerity
仁 *shijin* great sympathy
公 *shikō* supreme fairness
公至平 *shikō-shihei* very just
6 尽 *ita(reri)-tsu(kuseri)* complete, thorough
当 *shitō* proper, reasonable, fair
近 *shikin* very, very near
近弾 *shikindan* near miss
7 言 *shigen* wise saying
妙 *shimyō na* very strange
材 *shizai* rare talents; a person with rare talents
芸 *shigei* top artistic skill
孝 *shikō* supreme filial piety
8 所 *ita(ru)tokoro* everywhere
幸 *shikō* supreme happiness
宝 *shihō* the greatest treasure

4 【至】

9 便 *shiben* very convenient
点 *shiten* solstice, equinoctial point
要 *shiyō* essence; vital importance
急 *shikyū* urgent
急便 *shikyūbin* express mail
急報 *shikyūhō* urgent telegram, urgent call
10 純 *shijun* purity, sincerity
高 *shikō* supremacy, sublimity
高者 *Shikōsha* the Most High, God
11 情 *shijō* sincerity; natural feelings
理 *shiri* a well-understood truth
軟風 *shinampū* light breeze
12 極 *shigoku* very, quite, exceedingly
尊 *Shison* the Throne, the Emperor
善 *shizen* supreme good
軽風 *shikeifū* light breeze
13 福 *shifuku* beatitude, supreme bliss, highest good
誠 *shisei* sincerity, faith, devotion; one's true heart
愚 *shigu* height of folly; biggest fool
楽 *shiraku* supreme happiness. *shigaku* excellent music
聖 *shisei* highest virtue
14 徳 *shitoku* highest virtue
15 論 *shiron* a very reasonable argument
18 難 *shinan* extreme difficulty
難事 *shinanji* a most difficult problem

4

B 致 4904 / J4357 / M30149 CHI. *ita(su)* do; send, forward; cause, incur; render (assistance); exert (oneself); engage, call in (a doctor).
4 方 *ita(shi)kata* way, method, means, help, course, resource
方無 *ita(shi)katana(ku)* unavoidably
5 仕 *chishi suru* resign
6 死 *chishi no* fatal, deadly, lethal, mortal
7 身 *chishin* sacrificing one's life for one's lord
8 知 *chichi* great wisdom
命的 *chimeiteki* fatal, deadly, lethal, mortal
命傷 *chimeishō* fatal injury
14 様 *ita(shi)yō* way, method, means, help, course, resource

8

臺 4905 / J674a / M30161 See 台 699.

10

臻 4906 / J674b / M30165 SHIN arrive, reach; be delivered; gather.

RAD. 臼 134

Usu mortar. Nickname: Mortar.

臼 4907 / J3131 / M30173 KYŪ. *usu* mortar, hand mill.
5 石 *usuishi* millstone, stone mortar, stone mill, burstone
10 挽 *usuhi(ki)* milling; miller
砲 *kyūhō* mortar
12 歯 *kyūshi, usuba* molar
14 歌 *usuuta* rice pounders' song

2

臾 4908 / J674c / M30178 臾 2413 / J-X / M14281 YU, YO, YŌ a little while; urging.

3

舁 4909 / J674d / M30188 YO. *ka(ku), ka(ki)-a(geru)* bear, carry (a palanquin).
2 入 *ka(ki)-i(reru)* carry in
3 上 *ka(ki)-a(geru)* shoulder (a palanquin). *ka(ki)-nobo(ru)* carry up, bring up
7 戻 *ka(ki)-modo(ru), ka(ki)-modo(su)* carry back

5

舂 4910 / J674e / M30195 SHŌ. *usutsu(ku)* pound (in a mortar); sink, set (the sun).

7

輿 4911 / J6750 / M30212 See 与 6.

舅 4912 / J674f / M30208 KYŪ. *shūto* father-in-law.
8 姑 *kyūko* parents-in-law

9

A 興 4913 / J363d / M30226 KŌ. KYŌ interest, entertainment, pleasure. *kyō(garu)* be amused or interested in. *kyō(jiru), kyō(zuru)* amuse oneself, make merry. *oko(ru)* rise, flourish. *oko(su)* revive, retrieve (fortunes), raise up.
3 亡 *kōbō* rise and fall, ups and downs
6 行 *kōgyō* entertainment industry
行化 *kōgyōka suru* stage or film a story
行主 *kōgyō nushi* promoter, producer
行師 *kōgyōshi* producer, show manager
7 亜 *kōa* the development of Asia
8 国 *kōkoku* making a country prosperous; prosperous country
味 *kyōmi* interest
味本位 *kyōmi hon'i no* popular (literature, etc.)
味津津 *kyōmi-shinshin(taru)* of great interest
味深 *kyōmibuka(i), kyōmifuka(i)* very interesting
9 信所 *kōshinjo* detective agency
信録 *kōshinroku* directory
10 起 *kōki* rise, ascendency; aroused energy; high-spirited action
隆 *kōryū* rise, prosperity
11 敗 *kōhai* rise and fall (of nations)
12 廃 *kōhai* rise and fall; destiny
替 *kōtai* rise and fall (of nations)
13 業 *kōgyō* industrial enterprise
業銀行 *kōgyō ginkō* industrial bank
15 趣 *kyōshu* interest (in something)
16 醒 *kyōza(meru)* lose interest. *kyoza(mashi), kyoza(me)* a killjoy, a wet blanket
奮 *kōfun* excitement, agitation, stimulation
奮剤 *kōfunzai* stimulant

10

擧 4914 / J5a2a / M30238 See 挙 2150.

11

舉 4915 / J-X / M30241 See 挙 2150.

舊 4916 / J6751 / M30249 See 旧 2412.

RAD. 舌 135

Shita tongue. At left: *shita hen.* Nickname: Tongue.

A 舌 4917 / J4065 / M30277 ZETSU. *shita* tongue; reed; clapper. *shita(tarui)* lisping.
3 口 *zekkō* tongue and mouth; lips; way of speaking
上 *shitaue* words
4 不足 *shitatarazu* lisping; one who lisps, tongue-tied person
5 代 *zetsudai, shitadai* notice, announcement
打 *shitau(chi)* smacking one's lips; clicking the tongue; hissing; saying "tut-tut"
圧子 *zetsuatsushi* tongue depressor
6 先 *shitasaki* tongue tip
先三寸 *shitasaki-sanzun* eloquence
7 足 *shitata(razu)* lisp; lisper
車 *shitaguruma* chattering steadily
状 *zetsujō* tongue shape
利 *shitaki(ki)* taster
8 長 *shitanaga* boaster
苔 *zettai* fur on the tongue
9 音 *zetsuon* lingual sound
巻 *shita (o) ma(ku)* be astonished
10 舐 *shitana(mezuri)* licking the lips, licking one's chops
11 強 *shitagowa(i)* unable to speak distinctly

13 鼓 *shitatsuzumi* smacking one's lips
触 *shitazawa(ri)* taste ⌊(when eating)
戦 *zessen* a war of words ⌈tongue
禍 *zekka* an unfortunate slip of the
禍事件 *zekka jiken* incriminating utterance
14 端 *zettan* tip of the tongue
15 鋒 *zeppō* tongue
16 縺 *shitamotsu(re)* lisp; lisper
頭 *zettō* tip of the tongue
17 癌 *zetsugan* tongue cancer

2

舎 4918 / J6752 / M30278 See 舍 189.

4

舐 4919 / J6753 / M30283 **䑛** 4921 / J-X / M30310 SHI. *nebu(ru), na(meru)* lick; lap up; burn up; taste; undergo; underrate, despise. *name(zuru)* lick one's lips.

6

舒 4920 / J5030 / M30300 SHO, JO spread, extend; loose; slow.
9 巻 *joken, jokan* spread out, open (a scroll)

8

䑛 4921 / J-X / M30310 See 舐 4919.

9

舖 4922 / J6754 / M30323 See 舗 322.

10

舘 4923 / J345c / M30326 See 館 6701.

RAD. 舛 136

Mai ashi dancing "legs" (i.e., the lower element in *mau* "to dance") or *masu* (i.e., the right-hand element in the character for *masu* "a measure"). As commonly printed and written, this rather rare element actually has 7 strokes and it is normally so counted herein. Nickname: Dancing.

舛 4924 / J4124 / M30338 SEN. *somu(ku)* go against, disobey; rebel. *masu* a measuring box.

6

舜 4925 / J3d58 / M30339 SHUN morning glory; rose of Sharon, althea.

8

B **舞** 4926 / J4971 / M30342' BU. *ma(u)* dance; flutter about, flit; circle, wheel. *mai* dancing; dance.
3 子 *maiko* dancing girl
下 *ma(i)-sa(garu)* come down dancing
上 *ma(i)-a(garu)* soar, fly high, be ⌊whirled up
4 手 *ma(i)te* dancer
込 *ma(i)-ko(mu)* come in dancing; drop in on, visit; befall; (snow) blows in
5 台 *butai* stage ⌈broadcast
台中継 *butai chūkei* live stage
台生活 *butai seikatsu* stage career
台芸術 *butai geijutsu* theatrical art
台効果 *butai kōka* stage effect
台面 *butaimen* scene
台負 *butaima(ke)* stage fright
台度胸 *butai dokyō* stage nerves
台開 *butaibira(ki)* opening of a new theater
台装置 *butai sōchi* stage setting
台裏 *butaiura* behind the scenes
台劇 *butaigeki* stage drama
台稽古 *butaigeiko* dress rehearsal
台顔 *butaigao* face with heavy makeup
6 衣 *ma(i)ginu* dancing costume
曲 *bukyoku* musical dance, music and dancing

7 戻 *ma(i)-modo(ru)* find one's way back, return
妓 *ma(i)ko, bugi* dancing girl
狂 *ma(i)-kuru(u)* dance wildly, dance in a frenzy
9 姫 *maihime* dancing girl
10 扇 *maiōgi* dancer's fan
納 *ma(i)-osa(meru)* end the dance
容 *buyō* dancing form
11 掛 *ma(i)-ka(keru)* flutter over
13 楽 *bugaku* Court dance and Court music
14 踊 *ma(i)-odo(ru)* dance *buyō* dancing; dance
踊劇 *buyōgeki* dance drama
15 踏 *butō* dancing
踏曲 *butōkyoku* dance music
踏会 *butōkai* ball, dance
踏狂 *butōkyō* dance craze
踏者 *butōsha* dancer
踏病 *butōbyō* St. Vitus' dance, chorea
踏場 *butōjō* dance hall

RAD. 舟 137

Fune hen left-side "ship." Variant: 舟. Nickname: Ship.

B **舟** 4927 / J3d2e / M30350 SHŪ boat. *fune* boat, ship, vessel, steamer, liner, barge; shipping; tank, trough, cistern, vat.
2 人 *funabito, shūjin* a seaman, a ship passenger
3 子 *shūshi* a seaman, a ship passenger
6 行 *shūkō* navigation; going by ship
7 足 *funaashi* draft; speed (of a ship)
車 *shūsha* boats and vehicles; transportation facilities
9 軍 *shūgun* (ancient) navy
10 師 *shūshi* (ancient) navy
航 *shūkō* voyage
11 運 *shūun* ship transportation, freighting by ship
遊 *funaaso(bi), shuyu* boating
脚 *funaashi* draft of a ship; speed of a ship
12 筏 *shūbatsu* boats and rafts; boat
13 艇 *shūtei* boat, craft
路 *shūro, funaji* ship's course
14 歌 *funauta* sailor's song, boat song
端 *funabata* gunwale
16 橋 *shūkyō* pontoon bridge

3

舡 4928 / J-X / M30362 KŌ boat.

4

舮 4929 / J6764 / M-X Nonstandard for 艫 4952.

舩 4930 / J6755 / M30384 See 船 4939.

B **般** 4931 / J484c / M30388 HAN carry; all.
8 若 *hannya* wisdom personified; demoness
若湯 *hannyatō* saké

舫 4932 / J6756 / M30386 HŌ, BŌ. *moya(u)* moor, berth, tie up (a boat). *moya(i)* moorings.
11 船 *moyaibune* moored boat, berthed vessel
12 結 *moyaimusu(bi)* bowline knot

A **航** 4933 / J3952 / M30385 KŌ navigation; cross over. *kō(suru)* sail, cruise, navigate; fly.
6 行 *kōkō* navigation, cruise
8 送 *kōsō suru* send by ship or plane
空 *kōkū* aviation, flight, air navigation
空力学 *kōkū rikigaku* aerodynamics
空士 *kōkūshi* aviator
空写真 *kōkū shashin* air photograph
空母艦 *kōkū bokan* aircraft carrier
空灯台 *kōkū tōdai* aerial lighthouse
空会社 *kōkūgaisha* aviation company
空自衛隊 *kōkū jieitai* Air Self-Defense Force
空服 *kōkūfuku* aviator's uniform
空学 *kōkūgaku* aeronautics
空学校 *kōkū gakkō* aviation school
空事業 *kōkū jigyō* air transportation business

空便 *kōkūbin* airmail
空病 *kōkūbyō* air sickness
空家 *kōkūka* aviator
空時代 *kōkū jidai* air age
空郵便 *kōkū yūbin* airmail
空部 *kōkūbu* air force
空部隊 *kōkū butai* air force
空書簡 *kōkū shokan* air letter
空術 *kōkūjutsu* aviation, aeronautics
空船 *kōkūsen* airship, dirigible, blimp
空隊 *kōkūtai* air force
空基地 *kōkū kichi* air bases
空貨物 *kōkū kamotsu* air freight
空港 *kōkūkō* airport, airfield
空路 *kōkūro* air route, air lane
空機 *kōkūki* airplane, aircraft
空輸送 *kōkū yusō* air transportation
9 海 *kōkai* voyage, ocean navigation
海士 *kōkaishi* mate, navigating officer
海日誌 *kōkai nisshi* ship's log
海者 *kōkaisha* navigator, mariner, seaman
海時 *kōkaiji* ship's time
海術 *kōkaijutsu* navigation, seamanship
海証明書 *kōkai shōmeisho* navicert
海暦 *kōkaireki* nautical almanac
11 船 *kōsen* ocean-going vessel; vessel under way
12 程 *kōtei* ship's run; voyage; lap, leg
13 跡 *kōseki* wake of a ship
続力 *kōzokuryoku* cruising range; flying range
続距離 *kōzoku kyori* cruising range
路 *kōro* sea route, steamer lane, service
路標識 *kōro hyōshiki* navigation aids, lighthouse

5

舸 4934 / J6757 / M30404 KA large boat.

舳 4935 / J6758 / M30397 JIKU. *he, hesaki* bow, prow.
6 先 *hesaki* bow, prow
22 艫 *jikuro* stem to stern, fore and aft

B **舶** 4936 / J4775 / M30402 HAKU ship.
5 用 *hakuyō* marine
用機関 *hakuyō kikan* marine engine
7 来 *hakurai* importation; imported goods
来品 *hakuraihin* imported goods
来種 *hakuraishu* foreign varieties
13 載 *hakusai* ocean transportation; importation; imported goods

舵 4937 / J4249 / M30400 **柁** 2597 / J4248 / M14599 DA rudder. *kaji* rudder, helm, wheel.
3 子 *kajiko* helmsman
4 手 *dashu* helmsman, coxswain
8 取 *kajito(ri)* steering; helmsman; coxswain; guidance, leadership; leader
9 柄 *kajizuka* tiller
15 輪 *darin* steering wheel, helm
16 機 *daki* helm, steering gear, rudder

舷 4938 / J383f / M30403 GEN gunwale. *funaberi, funabata* ship's side, gunwale.
6 灯 *gentō* running light, side light
8 門 *gemmon* gangway (to a ship)
11 梯 *gentei* gangway, gangway ladder
舷 *gengen* gunwale to gunwale
窓 *gensō* porthole
側 *gensoku* ship's side, broadside
側上縁 *gensoku uwabuchi* gunwale
15 縁 *gen'en* gunwale
16 墻 *genshō* ship's bulwarks
頭 *gentō* gunwale, ship's side
17 牆 *genshō* ship's bulwarks

A **船** 4939 / J4125 / M30407 SEN ship. *fune* boat, ship, vessel, steamer, liner, barge; shipping; tank, trough, cistern, vat. *-sen* ship, vessel.
2 人 *funabito* seaman; passenger
3 子 *funako* boatman
大工 *funadaiku* ship carpenter
小屋 *funagoya* boathouse
4 方 *funakata* boatman
中 *senchū* ship's interior
内 *sennai* on the ship
夫 *sempu* seaman
火事 *funakaji* ship fire
5 尻 *funajiri* stern
主 *funanushi, senshu* shipowner
号 *sengō* ship name
台 *sendai* ways, shipbuilding slip
出 *funade* ship's departure
外 *sengai* overboard
外機 *sengaiki* outboard motor
6 匠 *senshō* ship carpenter

团 *sendan* fleet of vessels
曳 *funahi(ki)* towing
灯 *sentō* ship's lamp
守 *funamo(ri)* boat watcher
成金 *funanarikin* shipping magnate
7 貝 *funegai* ark shell
足 *funaashi* draft; speed (of a ship)
医 *sen'i* ship's doctor
尾 *sembi* ship's stern
体 *sentai* hull, ship
材 *senzai* ship timber
形 *funagata* boat-shaped
8 長 *senchō* ship's captain
底 *funazoko, sentei* ship's bottom; bilge
房 *sembō* ship's cabin
価 *senka* cost of a ship
板 *funaita* ship timber
泊 *funadoma(ri)* anchorage; anchoring, calling
具 *funagu, sengu* ship tackle, rigging
具商 *sengushō* ship chandler
9 首 *senshu, miyoshi* bow, prow
便 *funabin, sembin, funadayo(ri)* shipping service, sea mail
卸 *funaoro(shi)* ship launching
乗 *funano(ri)* sailor, seaman, mariner; traveling by ship
軍 *funaikusa* sea battle
客 *senkyaku, senkaku* ship passenger
室 *senshitsu* stateroom, cabin
型 *senkei* boat shape; model of a boat
幽霊 *funayūrei* siren, spirit of the sea
10 骨 *senkotsu* ship's ribs
唄 *funauta* sailor's song; boat-rowing song
旅 *funatabi* voyage
倉 *sensō* hold (of a ship), hatch
員 *sen'in* crew, ship's company, sailors
荷 *funani* ship's cargo, freight
荷証券 *funani shōken* bill of lading
11 淦 *funaaka* bilge water
脚 *funaashi, senkyaku* draft; speed (of a ship)
酔 *funayo(i)* seasickness
隊 *sentai* fleet of ships
宿 *funayado* shipping agent
窓 *funamado, sensō* porthole, cabin window
渠 *senkyo* dock
梯子 *funabashigo* gangplank
道具 *funadōgu* ship's tackle, rigging
問屋 *funadon'ya, funadoiya* shipping agent
遊 *funaaso(bi)* boat ride, boating
遊山 *funayusan* boat ride, excursion
側 *sensoku* ship's side
側渡 *sensokuwata(shi)* free alongside
舶 *sempaku* ship, vessel, bottoms
舶法 *sempakuhō* shipping law
舶業 *sempakugyō* shipping business
12 場 *funaba* harbor, wharf, anchorage
幅 *sempuku* ship's beam
渡 *funawata(shi)* ferry; delivery from ship; free on board, F.O.B.
喰虫 *funakuimushi* shipworm
着 *funatsu(ki)* wharf, anchorage
着場 *funatsukiba* harbor, wharf, anchorage
13 溜 *funadama(ri)* coastal anchorage
腹 *sempuku* shipping, bottoms, cargo space
蛸 *funedako* paper nautilus
路 *funaji, funamichi, senro* course, channel; sea route; voyage; wake
跡 *funaato* wake (of a ship)
賃 *funachin* boat fare; freight rates; charterage
14 端 *funabata* ship's side, gunwale
綱 *funatsuna* ship's tackle
歌 *funauta* sailor's song, boat-rowing song
蔵 *funagura* boathouse
15 縁 *funaberi* ship's side, gunwale
影 *sen'ei* sign of a ship
霊 *funadama* ship's guardian deity
16 橋 *funabashi, senkyō* floating bridge, pontoon bridge
積 *funazu(mi)* shipment, shipping, loading, lading
艙 *sensō* hold (of a ship), hatch
頭 *sendō* boatman, seaman, mariner
17 檣 *senshō* mast
齢 *senrei* ship's age
19 瀬 *funase* coastal anchorage
繰 *funagu(ri), funaku(ri)* shipping schedule
繋 *funagaka(ri)* anchorage; anchoring, calling
20 艦 *senkan* ships
籍 *senseki* ship's registry
籍港 *sensekikō* ship's port of registry

6 竹米糸缶网罒羊羽老耂而耒耳聿肉月臣自至臼舌舛 7【舟】艮色艸艹虍虫血行衣衤西

7

艀 4940 / J6759 / M30431 FU. *hashike* sampan, lighter, barge.

11 船 *hashikebune* sampan, lighter, barge

艇 4941 / J447a / M30440 TEI small boat. B

7 身 *teishin* boat length
体 *teitai* hull
8 長 *teichō* coxswain; captain
9 首 *teishu* bow (of a boat)
10 員 *teiin* boat crew
庫 *teiko* boathouse
庫番 *teikoban* boathouse keeper
11 舳 *teijiku* stern
隊 *teitai* flotilla

10

艘 4942 / J675b / M30511 SHŌ. SHŪ. SŌ ship counter.

艙 4943 / J675a / M30516 SŌ hold (of a ship).

3 口 *sōkō* hatch, hatchway

11

艚 4944 / J675d / M30523 SŌ, ZŌ small boat.

艝 4945 / J675c / M30536 (国字) *sori* sled, sleigh.

12

艟 4946 / J675e / M30549 DŌ fighting ship.

19 艨 *dōmō* warship

13

艢 4947 / J6760 / M30559 See **檣** 2893.

艨 4948 / J6761 / M30574 MŌ.

18 艟 *mōdō* warship

艤 4949 / J675f / M30565 **檥** 2882 / J-X / M15690 GI landing a boat.

6 舟 *gishū* ship's outfit, rigging, preparation for sailing
12 装 *gisō* ship's outfit, rigging
装品 *gisōhin* ship fittings

14

艦 4950 / J344f / M30571 KAN warship. B

3 上 *kanjō* aboard a warship
上機 *kanjōki* carrier-based plane
6 列 *kanretsu* column of warships
7 尾 *kambi* stern (of a warship)
体 *kantai* warship's hull
8 長 *kanchō* captain of a warship
底 *kantei* warship's bottom
9 首 *kanshu* bow of a warship
型 *kankei* warship type
10 砲 *kampō* ship's guns
砲射撃 *kampō shageki* warship bombardment
11 側 *kansoku ni* alongside a warship
隊 *kantai* squadron, fleet
船 *kansen* ships and warships
船使用時 *kansen shiyōji* ship's time
12 幅 *kampuku* the beam of a warship
13 艇 *kantei* naval vessels
載 *kansai* carried on board a warship
載機 *kansaiki* carrier-based plane
14 旗 *kanki* warship's ensign
種 *kanshu* warship class
16 橋 *kankyō* bridge of a warship
17 齢 *kanrei* age or life of a warship

15

艪 4951 / J6762 / M30580 See **櫓** 2908.

16

艫 4952 / J6763 / M30582 RO bow, prow; stern. *tomo* stern.

14 綱 *tomozuna* hawser

RAD. 艮 138

Nezukuri (the right-hand side of *ne* "root"). Variant: 𠂈 (5 strokes).
Nickname: Good (as in 良 *yoi* "good").

艮 4953 / J3a31 / M30596 GON, KON stopping. *ushitora* northeast.

1

A **良** 4954 / J4e49 / M30597 RYŌ good, fine. *i(i), yo(i)* good, good-natured; pleasing; precious, noble; lovely, beautiful, fine; lucky; efficacious; right; suitable; justifiable; appropriate, satisfactory; better; all right; unnecessary; no objection; intimate, friendly; easy; well; desirous. *yo(ku) suru* be skilled in. *yo(sa)* goodness, virtue, merit. *yo(shi)* good, all right, well, so.

2 人 *i(i)hito* good person, good-natured person; sweetheart; a certain person. *ryojin* good person; husband. *otto* husband
3 工 *ryōkō* good worker, skilled artisan
才 *ryōsai* excellent talent
4 心 *ryōshin* conscience
方 *ryōhō* good method; good prescription
日 *ryōjitsu* lucky day, auspicious day
月 *ryōgetsu* a beautiful moon; tenth lunar month
友 *ryōyū* good friend, good company
5 田 *ryōden* fertile rice field
主 *ryōshu* good master; good ruler
民 *ryōmin* good citizens
6 匠 *ryōshō* good carpenter; good worker
好 *ryōkō na* good, favorable, satisfactory
年 *i(i)toshi* good mature age
吏 *ryōri* good official, talented official
7 辰 *ryōshin* good day, good opportunity
医 *ryōi* good doctor
図 *ryōto* good plan
材 *ryōzai* good timber. *ryōsai* excellent talent
否 *ryōhi* good or bad; quality
兵 *ryōhei* good soldier; picked army
良 *yo(ku)yo(ku)* very carefully, exceedingly, heartily
8 性 *ryōsei* benign (tumor)
法 *ryōhō* good method, excellent plan
知 *ryōchi* intuition
夜 *ryōya* moonlit night
果 *ryōka* good results
妻 *ryōsai* good wife
妻賢母 *ryōsai-kembo* good wife and wise mother
9 俗 *ryōzoku* good customs
相 *ryōsō* wise and good cabinet minister
計 *ryōkei* good plan, clever scheme
政 *ryōsei* good government
品 *ryōhin* superior article
風 *ryōfū* good custom
風美俗 *ryōfū-bizoku* good customs
10 馬 *ryōba* fine horse
師 *ryoshi* good teacher
将 *ryōshō* good general
剤 *ryōzai* effective medicine
家 *ryōka* good family
案 *ryōan* good idea
書 *ryōsho* good book
能 *ryōnō* natural ability
11 過 *yosu(giru)* be too good
習 *ryoshu* good customs
貨 *ryōka* good money
12 港 *ryōkō* good harbor
筆 *ryōhitsu* good writing brush; good article; good book; good writer
策 *ryōsaku* good plan, good policy
13 賈 *ryōko* virtuous merchant
農 *ryōnō* good farmer
14 種 *ryōshu* thoroughbred, good breed
導体 *ryōdōtai* good conductor
15 縁 *ryoen* happy (marital) match
質 *ryōshitsu* good quality
器 *ryōki* a good receptacle; excellent talent
16 薬 *ryōyaku* good medicine
19 識 *ryōshiki* good sense

11

艱 4955 / J6765 / M30600 KAN difficult. *naya(mu)* be distressed.

8 苦 *kanku* privation, suffering
18 難 *kannan* privations, hardships, trouble
難辛苦 *kannan-shinku* privations, hardships, trouble

RAD. 色 139

Iro color. Nickname: Color.

A 色 4956 / J3f27 / M30602 SHOKU, SHIKI color. *iro* color, tint, tinge; complexion; countenance, look; sensual pleasure; sweetheart; charms; fall colors; embellishment; slight concession; kind. *iro(meku)* color, be tinged, liven, become active, be stirred; begin to waver (in battle). *iro(zuku)* color, color up. *iro(ppoi)*, *iro(mekashii)* amorous, fascinating, seductive. *iro(nna)* various.

3 女 *iroonna* concubine
4 文 *irobumi* love letter
止 *irodo(me)* color fixing
分 *irowa(ke)* coloring; classification; colored
分地図 *irowa(ke) chizu* colored map
5 白 *irojiro* light complexion; white
目 *irome* amorous glance
付 *irozu(ku)* color, color up; (leaves) redden. *irotsu(ke)* coloring, painting
収差 *iroshūsa* chromatic aberration
写真 *irojashin* color photo
仕掛 *irojika(ke)* feigned love
6 糸 *iroito* colored thread
色 *iroiro na* various
尽 *irozu(kume)* dressing colorfully
好 *irogono(mi)* sensuality, lust
灯 *shikitō* colored lamp
合 *iroa(i)* coloring, tint, shade, tone
合 *iroa(wase)* color matching
気 *iroke* coloring, shade, tone; coquetry; passion; romance; inclination, interest
気付 *irokezu(ku)* arrive at puberty
気違 *irokichiga(i)* sex mania
7 里 *irozato* red-light district
抜 *ironu(ki)* decoloration
沢 *shikitaku* complexion; luster, polish
狂 *iroguru(i)*, *irokichigai* sex mania
町 *iromachi* red-light district
良 *iroyo(i)* favorable (answer)
即是空 *shikisokuzekū* the vanity of all things (a Buddhist concept)
男 *irootoko* paramour, lady-killer
男役 *irootokoyaku* handsome male actor
8 刷 *irozu(ri)* color print; color printing
物 *iromono* colored fabrics
取 *irodo(ru)* color, paint, make up. *irodori* coloring, coloration; color scheme; makeup
盲 *shikimō* color blindness
直 *ironao(shi)* changing wedding garments for ordinary clothes; redyeing
事 *irogoto* love affair; love scene
事師 *irogotoshi* philanderer, lady-killer
9 革 *irogawa* dyed leather
香 *iroka* color and scent; loveliness, charm
変 *irogawa(ri)* discoloration; queer color, different kind
染 *irozo(me)* dyeing; dyed
度測定 *shikidosokutei* colorimetry
10 消 *iroke(shi)* achromatism. *iroke(shina)* unromantic, prosaic
紙 *irogami* colored paper. *shikishi* square drawing paper
恋 *irokoi* love, sentiment
差 *iroza(shi)* coloring, tone, shade
素 *shikiso* coloring matter, pigment
弱 *shikijaku* slight color blindness
配合 *iro (no) haigō* color scheme
11 黒 *iroguro* dark complexion
道 *shikidō* sexual passion
欲 *shikiyoku* sexual passion, lust
彩 *shikisai* color, coloration, hue, tint
盛 *irozaka(ri)* sweet sixteen; female maturity
眼鏡 *iromegane* colored glasses; prejudiced view
情 *shikijō* sexual passion, lust
情狂 *shikijōkyō* sex mania
12 揚 *iroa(ge)* redyeing
絵 *iroe* colored picture

覚 *shikikaku* color sense
硝子 *iro garasu* colored glass
13 絹 *iroginu* colored silk
話 *irobanashi* love story; love talk
感 *shikikan* color vision
鉛筆 *iroempitsu* crayon, colored pencil
14 摺 *irozuri* color printing
褪 *iroza(meru)* fade
褪 *irozame* fading of colors
様様 *irosamazama no* multicolored
15 敵 *irogataki* love rival
慾 *shikiyoku* sexual passion, lust
調 *shikichō* color tone
調和 *iro (no) chōwa* color harmony
19 艶 *iro tsuya* complexion; luster, polish
21 魔 *shikima* masher, libertine, lady-killer

13

艶 4957 / J3170 / M30632 **艷** 4958 / J6766 / M30637 **豔** 5741 / J-X / M36332

En luster, glaze, polish; charm. *tsuya(meku)* be glossy, be charming, be colorful. *nama(meku)* be charming, be colorful, be of excellent quality, be beautiful. *tsuya(yakana)* glossy and beautiful. *nama(mekashii)* charming, captivating. *tsuya* gloss, luster, glaze, polish, brightness; charm, romance, love. *tsuya(ppol)* romantic, spicy, amorous. *ade(yakana)* charming, fascinating.

4 文 *embun* love letter
5 出 *tsuyada(shi)* burnishing, glazing, polishing, mercerizing, calendering
布巾 *tsuyabukin* polishing cloth
6 色 *enshoku* bright countenance
7 言 *engen* love talk
8 物 *tsuyamono* love story
事 *tsuyagoto* love affair, romance
9 拭 *tsuyabu(ki) suru* rub and polish
美 *embi* beauty, charm
姿 *adesugata* charming figure
10 紙 *tsuyagami* glossy paper
殺 *ensatsu* captivate, charm, fascinate
書 *ensho* love letter
消 *tsuyake(shi)* frosted (glass)
消硝子 *tsuyake(shi) garasu* frosted glass
13 福 *empuku* good fortune in love; beau, gallant
話 *enwa, tsuyabanashi* love story, romance
14 聞 *embun* love affair, love rumor
種 *tsuyadane* love affair, love rumor
歌師 *enkashi* street troubadour
16 薬 *tsuyagusuri* a chemical for adding luster
19 艶 *tsuyatsuya shita* glossy, bright, slick
麗 *enrei* beauty, charm

18

艷 4958 / J6766 / M30637 See 艶 4957.

RAD. 艸 140

Kusu grass. At top: 艹 (4 strokes) or 艹 (3 strokes) *kusa kammuri* or *sōkō* "grass" crown. These variants are here always counted as 3 strokes. Do not confuse with 廾 Rad. 55, which has longer verticals. Nickname: Grass.

艸 4959 / J6767 / M30638 Sō. *kusa* grass; plants.

2

艾 4960 / J6768 / M30648 Kai. *mogusa* moxa. *yomogi* sagebrush, wormwood, mugwort; an edible weed.

3

B **芝** 4961 / J3c47 / M30699' Shi. *shiba* lawn, sod, turf.

4 刈機 *shibaka(ri)ki* lawn mower
5 生 *shibafu, shibau* lawn, turf, grass plot
6 地 *shibachi* grass plot, lawn
8 居 *shibai* play, drama, show
居小屋 *shibaigoya* playhouse, theater
居気 *shibaigi* striving for effect; dramatic behavior
居染 *shibaiji(miru)* be stage-minded
9 草 *shibakusa* lawn, sod, turf

芒 4962 / J676a / M30682 Bō beard (of grains). *nogi, noge* beard (of grains).

6 竹米糸缶网罒羊羽老耂而耒耳聿肉月臣自至臼舌舛舟艮色【艸艹】虍虫血行衣衤西

3

susuki Japanese pampas grass.

芍 4963 J6769 M30674 SHAKU peony.

16 薬 *shakuyaku* peony

B **芋** 4964 J3072 M30670' U. *imo* potato.

6 虫 *imomushi* a green caterpillar
8 茎 *zuiki* taro stem
11 掘 *imoho(ri)* digging sweet potatoes
12 焼酎 *imojōchū* sweet-potato liquor
14 種 *imodane* seed potatoes
蔓 *imozuru* sweet-potato vines

4

芽 4965 J-X M30747 See 芽 5002.

芙 4966 J4967 M30694 FU. *hasu* water lily.

芫 4967 J676b M30727 GEN, GAN Japanese lilac.

苡 4968 J676f M30792 I a kind of plantain.

苅 4969 J3423 M30771 KAI cutting (grass).

芹 4970 J365c M30742 KIN. *seri* parsley.

芻 4971 J676d M30744 SŪ grass cutting; hay.

芟 4972 J676c M30701 SEN. SAN. *ka(ru)* cut, clip, trim, harvest, mow.

9 除 *senjo suru, sanjo suru* cut away

芬 4973 J676e M30728 FUN perfume.

7 芬 *fumpun(taru)* fragrant
19 蘭 *Finrando* Finland

芭 4974 J474e M30730 BA banana.

15 蕉 *bashō* banana plant
蕉布 *bashōfu* abaca cloth

芦 4975 J3032 M30716 **蘆** 5244 J6943 M32425 RO. *ashi, yoshi* reed,

11 笛 *roteki* reed flute
16 薈 *rokai* aloes

芯 4976 J3f44 M30732 SHIN wick.

4 切 *shinki(ri)* snuffers
6 地 *shinji* padding
8 取皿 *shinto(ri)zara* snuffer tray

芥 4977 J3329 M30715 KAI. KE. *karashi* mustard. *karashina* mustard (plant), rape. *gomi, akuta* dust, trash, rubbish.

3 子 *karashi* mustard. *keshi* poppy
子人形 *keshi ningyō* miniature doll
子泥 *kaishidei, karashidei* mustard plaster
子油 *karashiyu* mustard oil
子粒 *keshitsubu* poppy seed; something tiny
子菜 *karashina* mustard (plant), rape
子漬 *karashizuke* mustard pickles
子種 *karashidane* mustard seed. *keshidane* poppy seed
子雛 *keshibina* tiny doll
8 取 *gomito(ri)* dustpan; garbage collector
9 屋 *gomiya* garbage collector
10 浚 *gomisarai* garbage collector
11 捨場 *gomisu(te)ba* garbage dump, refuse heap
13 溜 *gomitame* garbage dump, refuse heap
15 箱 *gomibako* garbage box

A **芸** 4978 J375d M30741' **藝** 5235 J693a M32330 GEI art, craft; artistic accomplishment; performance, acting; trick, stunt, feat.

2 人 *geinin* player, performer, entertainer, actor
3 子 *geiko* geisha
才 *geisai* artistic talent
4 文 *geibun* art and literature
6 当 *geitō* an art, trick, feat, stunt, performance
名 *geimei* stage name, screen name
7 妓 *geigi* geisha
8 林 *geirin* art and literary circles
苑 *geien* art and literary circles
事 *geigoto* accomplishments
者 *geisha* geisha, singing girl, entertainer

者屋 *geishaya* geisha house
者買 *geishaka(i)* buying the favors of a geisha
9 風 *geifū* acting; technique (in music, etc.)
10 能 *geinō* public entertainment; accomplishments, attainments
能人 *geinōjin* star, entertainer
能科 *geinōka* art course
能祭 *geinōsai* festival of the entertaining arts
11 道 *geidō* art, accomplishments
術 *geijutsu* art, the arts
術肌 *geijutsuhada* artistic nature
術的 *geijutsuteki* artistic
術院 *Geijutsuin* Academy of Art
術家 *geijutsuka* artist
術祭 *geijutsusai* arts festival
12 無 *geina(shi)* uncultured person
無猿 *geina(shi)zaru* uncultured person
13 園 *geien* art and literary circles
18 題 *geidai* title of a play

B **芳** 4979 / J4b27 / M30736' Hō fragrance. *kōba(shii)*, *kamba(shii)* fragrant; balmy; favorable. *kamba(shikunai)* poor, unfavorable; disgraceful. *hō-* a prefix of respect.
3 山 *Hōzan* Mt. Yoshino
4 心 *hōshin* your good wishes, your kind intentions
5 札 *hōsatsu* your honorable letter
6 気 *hōki* a fragrant scent
年 *hōnen* the years of youth
名 *hōmei* good name, your name; praise
名録 *hōmeiroku* visitors' register, list of acquaintances
7 辰 *hōshin* auspicious day
声 *hōsei* high fame
志 *hōshi* your kindness
8 味 *hōmi* a good taste
枝 *hōshi* a fragrant branch of flowers
郊 *hōkō* a field of fragrant flowers; suburbs in spring
命 *hōmei* your orders
9 香 *hōkō* perfume, fragrance
眉 *hōbi* eyebrows of a beautiful woman
信 *hōshin* your kind letter
紀 *hōki* age (of a young lady)
草 *hōsō* fragrant grass
契 *hōkei* your promise
春 *hōshun* the fragrance of spring flowers
10 書 *hōsho* your kind letter
華 *hōka* the fragrance of flowers
恩 *hōon* people's kindnesses
烈 *hōretsu na* rich, aromatic (wine)
11 情 *hōjō* your good wishes, your kindness
液 *hōeki* delicious-smelling soup
12 景 *hōkei* the flower-decked spring landscape
13 園 *hōen* a park fragrant with beautiful flowers
意 *hōi* a suggestion of spring; your desire
14 墨 *hōboku* scented ink; your esteemed letter
15 慮 *hōryo* your mind
醇 *hōjun na* well-mellowed (saké)
16 翰 *hōkan* your fine letter
18 馥 *hōfuku* spreading of sweet perfume
顔 *hōgan* your beautiful face
20 醸 *hōjō* saké with an enticing aroma

A **花** 4980 / J3256 / M30734' Ke. Ka flower. *hana* flower, blossom; cherry blossoms; essence, spirit, pride; pearl; youth; best days; beautiful woman, flower arrangement; flower-card game. *hana(yakana)* gay, showy, brilliant, gorgeous. *hanaya(gu)* become brilliant.
2 入 *hanai(re)* flower vase
4 月 *kagetsu* flowers and the moon; poetic arts
木 *kaboku* flowers and trees; flowering trees. *hana (no) ki* flowering tree
片 *kahen* petal
王 *kaō* king of flowers, peony
文字 *hanamoji* capital letter
毛氈 *hanamōsen* figured carpet
火 *hanabi* fireworks, firecrackers
火線香 *hanabisenkō* joss-stick fireworks; mere fireworks (nothing to worry about)
5 生 *hanai(ke)* flower vase
立 *hanata(te)* flower vase
甲 *kakō* aged sixty
代 *hanadai* price of the flowers; geisha fee
札 *hanafuda* flower-card game
氷 *hanagōri* flowers frozen in ice
市 *hana ichi* flower market
台 *kadai* stand for a vase

弁 *hanabira, kaben* petal
兄 *kakei* the plum tree
卉 *kaki* flowering plant
卉園芸 *kaki engei* floriculture
6 色 *hana iro* light blue
匠 *kashō* landscape gardener
尽 *hanazu(kushi)* flower enumeration; many-flowered design
合 *hanaa(wase)* flower-card game
会 *kakai* flower-arrangement meeting
守 *hanamori* flower guard (against theft)
自動車 *hanajidōsha* flower-decked automobile
7 作 *hanazukuri* floriculture; florist
形 *hanagata* floral pattern; flourish; ornament; star actor; a popular person
売 *hanau(ri)* flower seller
花 *hanabana(shii)* brilliant, magnificent, spectacular
束 *hanataba* bouquet
吹雪 *hanafubuki* falling cherry blossoms
見 *hanami* flower viewing
見酒 *hanamizake* viewing cherry blossoms and drinking saké
言葉 *hanakotoba* the language of flowers
8 押 *kaō* signature (not a stamp)
実 *kajitsu* flowers and fruit; exterior and interior
季 *kaki* flowering season
9 面 *kamen* a beautiful face
香 *kakō* the fragrance of flowers
信 *kashin* tidings of flowers
咲 *hanasa(kaseru)* cause to bloom. *hanasa(ku)* bloom
垣 *hanagaki* a flowering hedge
持 *hana (o) mo(tasu)* humbly crediting another with one's exploits
活 *hanaike* flower vase
畑 *hanabatake* flower bed, flower garden
神 *kashin* flower goddess; spirit of a flower
冠 *kakan* corolla (of a flower); garland, wreath
品 *kahin* the value of flowers
客 *kakaku* flower-viewing guests; customers
紅葉 *hana-momiji* flowers and maples; fine spring and autumn leaves
相撲 *hanazumō* amateur sumo wrestling
屋 *hanaya* flower store
屋敷 *hanayashiki* flower garden
柳 *karyū* blossoms and willows; geisha; prostitutes; red-light district
柳界 *karyūkai* geisha quarters; red-light district
柳病 *karyūbyō* sexually transmitted disease
10 圃 *kaho* flower garden
唇 *kashin* petals; lips; flower-like lips
候 *kakō* the flowering season
時 *hanadoki* the flowering season; the cherry season
紋 *kamon* flower design
陰 *hanakage* shadow of flowers; shadow of flowering trees
宴 *kaen, hana (no) en* flower-viewing party
容 *kayō* beautiful looks
莚 *hanamushiro* figured mat
茣蓙 *hanagoza* flowered mat
紛 *kafun* pollen
紛症 *kafunshō* hay fever
11 道 *kadō* flower arrangement. *hanamichi* passage through the audience to the stage
野 *hanano* field of flowers
瓶 *kabin, hanagame* vase
笠 *hanagasa* flower-decked hat
梨 *karin* Chinese quince
盛 *hanazaka(ri)* flowers in full bloom
祭 *Hanamatsuri* Buddha's birthday festival (April 8)
崗岩 *kakōgan* granite
菱草 *hanabishisō* California poppy
菖蒲 *hanashōbu, hanaayame* iris, blue flag
鳥 *kachō* flowers and birds
鳥風月 *kachōfūgetsu* beauties of nature; elegant pursuits
12 婿 *hanamuko* bridegroom
街 *kagai, hanamachi* red-light district
結 *hanamusu(bi)* rosette
詞 *hanakotoba* the language of flowers
軸 *kajiku* flower stalk
期 *kaki* the flowering season
傘 *hanagasa* painted paper umbrella
筐 *hanagatami* flower basket
筏 *hanaikada* blossoms floating down a stream
筒 *hanazutsu* flower tube
葵 *hanaaoi* hollyhock
葉 *kayō* floral leaf

椰菜 *hanayasai* cauliflower
13 園 *hanazono, kaen* flower garden
蜂 *hanabachi* bumblebee
鉢 *hanabachi* flowerpot
飾 *hanakaza(ri)* floral decoration
電車 *hana densha* floral streetcar, a streetcar float
嫁 *hanayome* bride
嫁料 *hanayomeryō* marriage present (from the groom)
嫁御 *hanayomego* bride
嫁御寮 *hanayomegoryō* bride
14 魁 *oiran* prostitute, courtesan
暦 *hanagoyomi* a calendar with information about flowers
摘 *hanatsu(mi)* flower picking
綵 *hanazuna* festoons; festoonery
蜜 *kamitsu* nectar
聟 *hanamuko* bridegroom
模様 *hana moyō* floral design
15 輪 *hanawa* wreath
鋏 *hanabasami* pruning shears
影 *kaei* reflection of flowers
器 *kaki* flower vase
16 壇 *kadan* flower bed, flower garden
樹 *kaju* flowering tree
曇 *hanagumo(ri)* hazy weather in spring
17 環 *hanawa* wreath
18 顔 *kagan* a beautiful face
19 櫚 *karin* Chinese quince
譜 *kafu* flower album
20 簪 *hanakanzashi* floral hairpin
22 鰹 *hanagatsuo* dried bonito shavings
籠 *hanakago* flower basket

5

苓 4981 / J4e6a / M30777 REI, RYŌ cocklebur, burrweed.

苙 4982 / J677e / M30783 RYŪ (pig) pen, corral.

苳 4983 / J6774 / M30811 TŌ. *fuki* butterbur, coltsfoot.

苹 4984 / J6779 / M30823 HEI, HYŌ. *ukigusa* floating plants. *yomogi* mugwort.

苻 4985 / J6778 / M30825 FU a kind of vine; sheath, cover.

范 4986 / J6777 / M30834 HAN, BON bee; mold; rule; pattern.

茆 4987 / J677b / M30838 BŌ a watershield.

苣 4988 / J6770 / M30794 KYO torch.

苒 4989 / J6772 / M30776 ZEN flourishing, luxuriant.

苺 4990 / J6775 / M30824 BAI. *ichigo* strawberry.

B **茎** 4991 / J3754 / M30861' **莖** 5037 / J6833 / M31052 KEI, KYŌ *kuki* stem, stalk.

苴 4992 / J6773 / M30813 SO. *tsuto* straw wrapper; souvenir gift.

苜 4993 / J677c / M30787 MOKU, BOKU clover.
14 蓿 *mokushuku* a burr clover, snail clover

茉 4994 / J677d / M30841 MATSU jasmine.
10 莉花 *matsurika* jasmine

茄 4995 / J3258 / M30835 KA eggplant.
3 子 *nasu, nasubi* eggplant

苑 4996 / J3171 / M30774 EN garden, farm, yard. *sono* park, garden.
6 地 *enchi* park

苞 4997 / J677a / M30789 HŌ (corn) husk, bract. *tsuto* straw wrapper; souvenir gift.
8 苴 *tsuto* straw wrapper, souvenir gift. *hōsho, hōso* straw wrapper; gift; bribe. *aramaki* gift of fish wrapped in bamboo leaves, etc.

B **茂** 4998 / J4c50 / M30833' MO. *shige(ru)* grow thick, be overgrown, be luxuriant.
6 合 *shige(ri)-a(u)* grow luxuriantly
8 林 *morin* a luxuriant forest

荀 5000-range entry

荀 4999 J6771 M30790 Kō *iyashiku(mo)* any, at all, in the least, even in the slightest degree.

[5] 且 *kōsho* neglecting, slighting. *karisome* neglecting, slighting; trifling; temporary

[6] 安 *kōan* procratination, momentary ease

苧 5000 J4377 M30798 CHO. *o* hemp, flax; hemp thread. *karamushi* ramie.

[11] 麻 *karamushi, choma* ramie, China grass

殻 *ogara* hemp reed, hemp stalk

苔 5001 J425d M30778 TAI moss. *koke* moss; lichen; incrustation; fur (on the tongue). *kokera* moss.

[5] 生 *kokemu(su)* the moss grows or spreads

[13] 筵 *kokemushiro* moss-covered ground

[20] 蘚 *taisen* moss, lichen

A **芽** 5002 J326a M30860' GA. *me* sprout, spear, germ. *megu(mu)* bud, sprout.

[5] 生 *mebae* bud, sprout, seedling. *meba(eru)* sprout, bud

出度 *medeta(i)* congratulatory, auspicious

[9] 胞 *gahō* spore

[11] 接 *metsu(gi)* bud grafting, inlay graft

苫 5003 J4651 M30802 SEN. *toma* rush matting.

[6] 舟 *tomabune* rush-thatched boat

[9] 屋 *tomaya* a hut roofed and walled with rushes

[11] 船 *tomasen* rush-roofed boat

[12] 葺 *tomabuki* rush thatch

B **苗** 5004 J4944 M30781' BYŌ, MYŌ. *nae* seedling, sapling, shoot.

[4] 木 *naegi* sapling, seedling

[5] 代 *nawashiro, naeshiro* rice-seedling bed

代田 *naeshiroda, nawashiroda* rice seedling bed

[6] 字 *myōji* surname

[7] 床 *naedoko* seedbed, nursery

売 *naeu(ri)* seedling seller

[10] 圃 *byōho* seedbed, nursery

[11] 族 *Byōzoku* south China mountain tribes, the Miao, the Hmong

茅 5005 J337d M30836 BŌ. *kaya, chigaya, chi* miscanthus reed.

[8] 舎 *bōsha* thatched cottage, hovel, my humble cottage

[9] 屋 *bōoku* thatched cottage, hovel, my humble cottage

[11] 船 *kayabune* miscanthus-carrying boat (often set afire in the midst of an enemy fleet)

[12] 場 *kayaba* hayfield; field of miscanthus

葺 *kayabuki* miscanthus-thatched

萱 *chigaya* a kind of grass

[14] 蜩 *higurashi* clear-toned cicada

苛 5006 J3257 M30785 KA. *iji(meru), saina(mu)* torment, scold, chastise.

[3] 小 *kashō* too fine

[5] 立 *irada(teru)* irritate, exasperate. *irada(tsu)* be irritated, be exasperated

令 *karei* harsh orders

[8] 法 *kahō* severe laws

刻 *kakoku* severity, cruelty

苛 *iraira suru* get nervous, be irritated, fret

性 *kasei* caustic

性石灰 *kasei sekkai* quicklime

性曹達 *kasei sōda* caustic soda, sodium hydroxide

[9] 虐 *kagyaku* cruel treatment

政 *kasei* tyranny, despotism

重 *kajū no* burdensome, excessive

[10] 烈 *karetsu na* severe, stern

[11] 責 *kashaku* torture, maltreatment

[12] 税 *kazei* heavy taxation

[14] 酷 *kakoku* rigor, severity, cruelty

[17] 厳 *kagen* severe cruelty

斂 *karen* oppression (by taxation, etc.)

斂誅求 *karen-chūkyū* exaction, extortion

A **若** 5007 J3c63 M30796' JAKU. NYA. *mo(shi), mo(shimo)* if. *moshi (kashitara), moshi(ka) suru to* perhaps, possibly. *mo(shikuwa)* or, otherwise. *mo(shiya)* by any chance, perchance. *waka-, waka(i)* young, juvenile, youthful; younger, junior; immature, inexperienced; low number. *waka(yagu)* grow young again, look young. *shi(ku)* be equal to, compare with.

[2] 人 *wakōdo, waka(i)hito* young person, young man, young woman

3 干 *jakkan, sokobaku, sokubaku* some, a number of
4 手 *wakate* young person; young official
木 *wakagi* sapling, young tree
水 *wakamizu* first water drawn on New Year's Day
夫婦 *wakafūfu* young couple
5 布 *wakame* an edible seaweed
旦那 *wakadanna* young master, young gentleman
白髪 *wakajiraga, wakashiraga* prematurely gray hair
6 竹 *wakatake* young bamboo
死 *wakaji(ni)* premature death
気 *wakage, wakagi* youthful vigor
返 *wakagae(ru)* grow young again
向 *wakamuki* suitable for the young
年 *jakunen* youth
年者 *jakunemmono* youngster
年寄 *wakadoshiyo(ri)* a young person with old characteristics
7 作 *wakazuku(ri)* makeup to look younger
役 *wakuyaku* role for a young actor
禿 *wakahage* premature baldness
君 *wakagimi* young lord
8 松 *wakamatsu* young pine tree; New Year's pine-tree decorations
枝 *wakaeda* shoot, young branch
命 *jakumei* young life
芽 *wakame* young buds, sprouts, shoots
苗 *wakanae* young plants
若 *wakawaka(shii)* youthful, young
者 *wakamono, waka(i)mono* young person; young manservant; young apprentice, young man, lad, youth
事 *mo(shimono) koto* accident, emergency, contingency
武者 *wakamusha* young warrior
9 造 *wakazō* youngster, stripling
草 *wakagusa, wakakusa* tender grass, young grass
後家 *wakagoke* young widow
10 宮 *wakamiya* young prince; newly-built shrine; subshrine to a son of a main deity
党 *wakatō* young servant, attendant
11 菜 *wakana* young greens, herbs
盛 *wakazaka(ri)* bloom of youth, prime of life
紳士 *wakashinshi* young gentleman
12 湯 *wakayu* first water boiled on New Year's Day
葉 *wakaba* new leaves, fresh verdure
衆 *wakashū, waka(i)shū* young person; young manservant; young apprentice, young man, lad, youth
紫 *wakamurasaki* light purple
13 殿 *wakatono* young lord
隠居 *wakainkyo* person who retired early
14 様 *wakasama* young lord, young master
緑 *wakamidori* new foliage
15 輩 *jakuhai* young people; novice
19 鶏 *wakadori* pullet

A **英** 5008 / J3151 / M30808' EI England, Britain; gifted person; wit. *-Ei, Ei-* English.

2 人 *Eijin* Englishman, Englishwoman
3 寸 *eisun* English inch
才 *eisai* brilliant intellect, talent, genius
下院 *Eikain* British House of Commons
4 斤 *eikin* pound
尺 *eishaku* English foot
文 *Eibun* English, English composition
文法 *Eibumpō* English grammar
文学 *Eibungaku* English literature
文典 *Eibunten* English grammar
文和訳 *Eibun-Wayaku* English-to-Japanese translation
5 主 *eishu* wise ruler
本国 *Eihongoku* England
6 米 *Ei-Bei* England and America
気 *eiki* excellent talent
名 *eimei* fame, glory, reputation
会話 *Eikaiwa* English conversation
字 *Eiji* English letter
字新聞 *Eijishimbun* English-language newspaper
7 里 *eiri* English mile
図 *eito* excellent plan
系 *Eikei* British (enterprise)
声 *eisei* fame, glory, reputation
8 法 *Eihō* English law
知 *eichi* wisdom, intelligence; intellect
和 *Ei-Wa* English-Japanese
京 *Eikyō* London, the British capital
武 *eibu* distinguished bravery
果 *eika* decisivenss
明 *eimei na* clever, intelligent, clear-sighted
明果断 *eimei-kadan no* wise and decisive

学 *Eigaku* study of English
学者 *Eigakusha* English scholar
国 *Eikoku* England, Great Britain, United Kingdom
国人 *Eikokujin* Britisher, Englishman, Englishwoman
国風 *Eikokufū* Briticism
9 風 *eifū* eminent virtues
俊 *eishun* genius, prodigy, talented person
軍 *Eigun* British army
発 *eihatsu* great wisdom
姿 *eishi* noble figure
10 書 *Eisho* English book, English Literature
哲 *eitetsu* genius, prodigy, talented person
11 略 *eiryaku* excellent talent
船 *eisen* English ship
訳 *Eiyaku* English translation
断 *eidan* prompt decision, resolution, drastic steps
12 貨 *eika* English currency, sterling; English goods
偉 *eii* outstanding fame
尋 *eihiro* English fathom
雄 *eiyū* hero
雄的 *eiyūteki* heroic
雄崇拝 *eiyū sūhai* hero worship
13 詩 *eishi* English poem
傑 *eiketsu* an outstanding person
聖 *eisei* natural wisdom
誉 *eiyo* fame, great praise
資 *eishi* brilliant qualities, fine character. *Eishi* British capital (money)
14 語 *Eigo* the English language
領 *eiryō* British possession, dominion, or territory
魂 *eikon* departed spirit
15 邁 *eimai* wise and brave, great, talented
霊 *eirei* spirits of the war dead; great men
16 噸 *eiton* British ton, long ton
19 蘭 *Ei-Ran* England and Holland
蘭銀行 *Eiran Ginkō* Bank of England
20 艦 *Eikan* British battleship
21 露 *Ei-Ro* England and Russia

A 苦 5009 / J366c / M30797' KU suffering, trial, worry, trouble, hardship, difficulty, toil. *kuru(shimu), kuru(shigaru)* suffer; groan; be troubled, be worried, be perplexed; strive, try hard. *kuru(shimeru)* torment; harass, worry; persecute, inflict pain. *niga(mu), niga(ru)* feel bitter; scowl. *ku ni suru* worry. *kuru(shii)* painful; distressing, embarrassing, difficult, bitter; straitened; farfetched; stiff (climb). *niga(i)* bitter; hard, trying. *kuru(shimi)* pain, agony, torment, trouble, distress; mortification.

2 力 *kūrī* coolie
3 口 *nigakuchi* gossip, criticism
土 *kudo, ku(no)do* this painful world; magnesia. *nigatsuchi* poor soil
4 心 *kushin* pains, trouble, anxiety; hard work, diligence
手 *nigate* weak point; ugly customer
切 *niga(ri)-ki(ru)* look blue, look disgusted
5 汁 *kujū* bitterness of life; a hard time. *nigari* brine
艾 *nigayomogi* wormwood
6 肉 *kuniku* countermeasure at personal sacrifice
虫 *nigamushi* bitterness
行 *kugyō* penance, austerities, mortification
7 言 *kugen* frank advice, exhortation
走 *niga(mi)bashi(ru)* have a manly bearing
吟 *kugin suru* compose laboriously
役 *kueki* hard labor, drudgery; penal servitude
労 *kurō* hardships, difficulties, trials; toil; anxiety
労人 *kurōnin* world-wise person
労性 *kurōshō* habit of worrying
8 使 *kushi* abuse, exploitation, overworking
杯 *kuhai* bitter cup, ordeal
況 *kukyō* hard circumstances, trouble, predicament, crisis
苦 *niganiga(shii)* unpleasant, disgusting, loathsome, shameful, scandalous
味 *kumi, nigami* bitter taste
味走 *nigamibashi(tta)* sternly handsome
学 *kugaku* studying under adversity
学生 *kugakusei* self-supporting student
9 海 *kukai* this world of suffering
界 *kukai, kugai* this world of suffering; life of prostitution
思 *kushi* pains, trouble, anxiety; hard work, diligence

茗 *kumei* strong tea
衷 *kuchū* distress
10 悩 *kunō* distress, suffering. *kuru(shimi)-naya(mu)* be in distress
紛 *kuru(shi)magi(re) ni* out of desperation, driven by distress, under pressure
笑 *kushō, nigawara(i)* bitter smile, forced smile
11 渋 *kujū* bitter and puckery; drenched; sentences hard to understand
菜 *nigana* bitter herbs
患 *kugen* agony
情 *kujō* complaint, objections, troubles
情処理 *kujō shori* settling grievances
12 痛 *kutsū* pain, suffering, agony
悶 *kumon* agony, anguish
寒 *kukan* suffering from the cold; coldest season; 13th lunar month
無 *ku(mo)na(ku)* easily, without trouble
13 塩 *nigari, nigashio* brine
戦 *kusen* hard fighting; tight game
節 *kusetsu* fidelity in adversity
楽 *kuraku* pleasure and pain
楚 *kuso* hardships, troubles, distress
14 境 *kukyō* hard circumstances, trouble, predicament, crisis
15 慮 *kuryo* pains, trouble, anxiety; hard work, diligence
熱 *kunetsu* oppressive heat
16 諫 *kukan* frank exhortation
18 闘 *kutō suru* fight hard; struggle (for a living)
難 *kunan* suffering, hardship, passion (of Christ)
難者 *kunansha* sufferer

6

荞 5010 / J684f / M31130 See **荞** 5083.

茲 5011 / J6824 / M30911 **玆** 380 / J-X / M-X See **玆** 3617.

茖 5012 / J6823 / M30863 KAKU garlic; a kind of leek.

茯 5013 / J682a / M30906 FUKU medicinal fungus.

荀 5014 / J6826 / M30929 SHUN, JUN used in proper names.

荅 5015 / J6829 / M30937 TŌ azuki beans. *kota(eru)* answer, reply.

荐 5016 / J6828 / M30951 SEN straw mat; weed; frequently.

茨 5017 / J3071 / M30896 SHI. *ibara* thorn, briar.

茵 5018 / J6821 / M30914 IN. *shitone* cushion; mattress.

茜 5019 / J302b / M30871 SEN. *akane* madder, red dye, madder red, Turkey red.

茱 5020 / J6825 / M30910 SHU river ginger tree; oleaster.
12 萸 *shuyu* river ginger tree; oleaster

茴 5021 / J6822 / M30913 KAI, UI fennel.
9 香 *uikyō* fennel

荏 5022 / J3141 / M30950 JIN bean.
8 苒 *jinzen to* procrastinatingly

茗 5023 / J682c / M30864 MYŌ, MEI tea.
10 荷 *myōga* ginger

茘 5024 / J682d / M30866 **荔** 5025 / J-X / M30865 REI scallion, a small onion.
8 枝 *reishi* litchi (nut)

茸 5026 / J427b / M30918 JŌ. *take* mushroom.
9 狩 *takega(ri)* mushroom gathering

荊 5027 / J3755 / M-X **荆** 5028 / J-X / M30940 KEI thorn; whip. *ibara* thorn, briar.

6 竹米糸缶网罒羊羽老耂而耒耳聿肉月臣自至臼舌舛舟艮色【艸艹】6 虍虫血行衣衤西

8 妻 *keisai* my wife
9 冠 *keikan* crown of thorns
12 棘 *bara, keikyoku* brambles, thorns

茫 5029 / J682b / M30900 Bō wide, extensive.
9 洋 *bōyō(taru)* limitless, boundless
茫 *bōbō(taru)* vague, vast, extensive
12 然 *bōzen* absent-mindedly, in a daze
然自失 *bōzen-jishitsu* abstraction, stupefaction, entrancement
13 漠 *bōbaku* vague, vast, extensive

茹 5030 / J6827 / M30921 Jo. *yu(deru), u(deru) vt* boil, seethe. *yu(daru), u(daru) vi* boil, seethe. *yu(de)* boiled.
3 上 *yu(de)-a(geru)* finish boiling
5 汁 *yudejiru* broth
玉子 *yude tamago, ude tamago* boiled egg
7 卵 *yude tamago, ude tamago* boiled egg
13 溢 *yu(de)-kobo(su)* scald, parboil

B **荘** 5031 / J4171 / M30890 **莊** 5038 / J6837 / M31035 Sō villa, inn. Shō villa, cottage, feudal manor.
9 屋 *shōya* village headman
重 *sōchō* solemnity, gravity, impressiveness
13 園 *shōen, sōen* manor
17 厳 *sōgon* solemnity, sublimity, impressiveness, magnificence, majesty
19 麗 *sōrei* splendor, grandeur

A **草** 5032 / J4170 / M30945' Sō. *kusa* grass; grass hand(writing); weeds; herbs, plants; pasture. *sō(suru)* write, draft. *kusa(ikire)* hot and humid feeling when walking through tall summer grass.
3 子 *sōshi* storybook; copybook
4 火 *kusabi* grass fire
分 *kusawa(ke)* going through deep grass; founding a village; village founder; pioneer
双紙 *kusazōshi* picture book
刈 *kusaka(ri)* grass cutting, mowing
刈鎌 *kusaka(ri)gama* sickle
木 *sōmoku, kusaki* vegetation, trees and plants
木灰 *sōmokubai, sōmokukai* ash from burnt vegetation
木靡 *kusaki(mo)nabi(ku)* everyone obeys
5 田 *kusada* weedy rice field; a growing rice field
市 *kusaichi* a special one-night market selling altar equipment for the Buddhist Obon Festival
本 *sōhon* herbs; draft, manuscript
6 色 *kusa iro* dark green, emerald green
衣 *kusagoromo* grass clothes
地 *sōchi* steppes. *kusachi* meadow, grassland
仮名 *sōgana* hiragana, the cursive syllabary
7 村 *kusamura* remote country
花 *sōka, kusabana* flowering plant
8 枕 *kusamakura* traveling
取 *kusato(ri)* weeding; weeding tool; weeder
臥 *kutabi(reru)* be tired, be exhausted. *kusabushi* lying on the grass; sleeping in the field
苺 *kusaichigo* wild strawberry
毟 *kusamushi(ri)* weeding
9 食 *sōshoku no* herbivorous
屋 *kusaya, sōoku* thatched hut, straw hut
昧 *sōmai* primitive state
枯 *kusaga(re)* dying of the grass; the fall
草 *sōsō* brevity; rudeness; hurry; the closing words of a letter
紅葉 *kusamomiji* fall colored grasses
相撲 *kusazumō* local sumo match
10 原 *sōgen* prairie, grassy plain, steppe. *kusawara, kusahara* meadow, grass plot
紙 *sōshi* shadow of the grass
陰 *kusakage* shadow of the grass
案 *sōan* draft (of a law or manuscript)
書 *sōsho* cursive script, grass hand
莚 *kusamushiro* grass rug; grassy field
根 *sōkon* grass roots
根木皮 *sōkombokuhi* roots and bark; Chinese medicinal materials. *sōkommokuhi* medicinal plants
11 庵 *kusa(no)iori, kusa(no)io, sōan* hut, hermitage, thatched cottage
深 *kusabuka(i)* grassy; backwoods; remote
堂 *sōdō* thatched cottage; my humble abode
笛 *kusabue* reed whistle

萌 *kusamoe* sprouting of the grass in spring
野 *kusano* grassy field. *sōya* citizenry; lower strata (of people)
野球 *kusayakyū* grass-lot baseball
12 間 *sōkan* in the grass; deep rural area
場 *kusaba* grass plot, meadow, pasture, turf
葺 *kusabuki* grass thatch
創 *sōsō* inauguration, beginning, origination
創期 *sōsōki* early period
葉 *kusa (no) ha* blade of grass
葉蔭 *kusaba (no) kage (de)* under the sod, in the grave
13 搔 *kusaka(ki)* hoe, rake
隠 *kusagaku(re)* hiding in the grass; retired to the country
飼 *kusaka(i)* raising cattle on grass
蓬蓬 *kusabōbō* rank weed growth
14 箒 *kusabōki* broom ⌈manuscript
15 稿 *sōkō* lecture notes, outline, draft,
履 *zōri* sandals, zori
履掛 *zōrigu(ke) de* wearing zori
鞋 *waraji* straw sandals
鞋虫 *warajimushi* sow bug
鞋銭 *warajisen* trip money
16 薙剣 *Kusanagi (no) Tsurugi* the Sacred Sword (one of the Three Imperial Treasures)
17 藁 *kusuwuru* grass and straw, fodder
18 鎌 *kusagama* sickle
叢 *kusamura* clump of bushes, grassy place, thicket, jungle, the bush
19 廬 *sōro* thatched hut, humble abode
20 競馬 *kusakeibu* local horse race
21 露 *kusa tsuyu, sōro* dewdrops on the grass; fleeting things

A **茶** 5033 / J4363 / M30915 SA, CHA tea; tea plant; tea leaves; light brown. *cha(gakatta)* brownish. *cha (ni) suru* make fun of. *cha(ppoi)* brownish, light brown.

2 人 *chajin, sajin* tea-ceremony expert
入 *chai(re)* tea canister
3 巾 *chakin* tea cloth
4 化 *chaka(su)* laugh away, make fun of
5 代 *chadai* charge for tea; tip
礼 *sarei* tea ceremony
台 *chadai* teacup saucer
出 *chada(shi)* teapot
目 *chame(ru)* play pranks. *chame* playfulness, mischief; urchin; brown eyes
目気 *chameki* mischief, playfulness
6 臼 *chausu* hand tea-grinding mill
色 *cha iro* light brown, tawny
気 *chaki* playfulness, mischievousness; unworldliness
托 *chataku* teacup holder
汲 *chaku(mi)* serving tea
会 *chakai, cha(no)e* tea party, tea ceremony
缶 *chakan* tea canister
7 杓 *chashaku* tea ladle
利 *chaki(ki)* tea tasting; tea taster
呑 *chanomi* teacup; tea lover; tea drinking
坊主 *chabōzu* tea server (to a shogun)
8 店 *chamise* teahouse
房 *sabō* refreshment parlor
所 *chadokoro* tea-growing area
9 柱 *chabashira* tiny tea stalk (in a cup of tea) signifying good luck
畑 *chabatake* tea plantation
亭 *satei* tea pavilion, tea room
盆 *chabon* tea tray
室 *chashitsu* tea arbor; tea cottage; tearoom
茶 *chacha* interruption
柄杓 *chabishaku* tea dipper
屋 *chaya* teahouse; tea dealer
屋酒 *chayazake* saké drunk at a teahouse
10 席 *chaseki* tea arbor, tea cottage; tea-ceremony seat
釜 *chagama* teakettle
11 渋 *chashibu* tea incrustation
断 *chada(chi)* abstinence from tea
商 *chashō* tea merchant
匙 *chasaji* teaspoon ⌈ceremony
道 *chadō, sadō* Way of Tea, tea
道具 *chadōgu* tea ceremony utensils
瓶 *chabin* tea urn, teapot
瓶頭 *chabin-atama* bald head
菓 *chaka, saka* tea and cakes, light refreshments
菓子 *chagashi* teacakes
12 間 *cha(no)ma* family living room
粥 *chagayu* tea gruel
棚 *chadana* tea-service shelf
湯 *cha(no)yu* tea ceremony, Way of Tea
殻 *chagara* tea grounds

壺 *chatsubo* tea canister
筌 *chasen* tea whisk
筒 *chazutsu* tea container
椀 *chawan* teacup; rice bowl
椀蒸 *chawammu(shi)* steamed custard of vegetables, egg, and meat
飯 *chameshi* rice boiled in tea, oil, or saké
飯事 *sahanji* everyday occurrence
番 *chaban* tea-ceremony assistants; burlesque, low comedy
番狂言 *chaban kyōgen* burlesque, low comedy
番劇 *chabangeki* burlesque, low comedy
飲 *chano(mi)* teacup; tea lover; tea drinking
飲友達 *chano(mi)tomodachi* crony, pal
飲茶碗 *chano(mi)jawan* teacup
飲話 *chano(mi)banashi* gossip
13 園 *chaen, saen* tea plantation
滓 *chakasu* tea grounds
腹 *chabara* the bowels after heavy tea drinking; drinking tea to satisfy hunger
業 *chagyō* tea industry
碗 *chawan* rice bowl; teacup
碗蒸 *chawammu(shi)* steamed custard of vegetables, egg, and meat
褐色 *chakasshoku* yellowish brown
話 *chabanashi, chawa, sawa* tea-table talk, gossip
話会 *chawakai, sawakai* tea party
14 摘 *chatsumi* tea picking; tea picker
漉 *chako(shi)* tea strainer
漬 *chazuke* simple meal; tea poured on boiled rice
箒 *chabōki* feather brush used in the tea ceremony
15 磨 *chausu* hand tea-grinding mill
請 *chau(ke)* teacakes
寮 *saryō, charyō* tea-ceremony cottage; tea-ceremony room
箱 *chabako* tea chest, tea caddy
舗 *chaho* tea store
器 *chaki* tea-serving equipment
16 濁 *cha (o) nigo(su)* cover up one's mistakes
18 簞笥 *chadansu* tea cupboard

A **荒** 5034 / J3953 / M30953' Kō. *ara(i)* rough, rude, wild, harsh, violent, gruff, fierce. *ara(ppoi)* rough, rude, violent, wild. *sabi(reru), a(reru)* be ruined, become stormy; tear around; get chapped. *a(rabiru), a(raburu)* get rough, be insolent. *susa(bu), susa(mu)* get desolate, go wild; decline; get rough. *a(rasu)* lay waste. *a(rarageru)* raise voice in anger. *a(rekure)* daredevil, rowdy, a tough. *are* storm, stormy weather; chapping, roughness. *arara(ka) ni* violently, roughly. *ara-* wild, rough, fierce, wild; drastic. *-ara(shi)* robbery, robber.

3 土 *kōdo* barren land
山 *arayama* steep mountain
亡 *kōbō* dissipation
4 日 *a(re)bi, kōjitsu* stormy day
木 *araki* logs in bark
毛 *arage* bristle
牛 *araushi* untamed ox
凶 *kōkyō* famine; poor crops
天 *kōten* stormy weather
5 田 *kōden, a(re)ta, arata* uncultivated rice field
石 *araishi* rough stone
立 *arada(tsu)* be excited, be exasperated, be agitated. *arada(teru)* aggravate, exasperate
外 *kōgai* outside the country, foreign
民 *kōmin* people suffering from famine
仕事 *arashigoto* rough work, hard work; robbery, burglary; a big haul; heavy manual labor
目 *arame* sackcloth
目鑢 *arameyasuri* rasp
布 *aranuno* sackcloth
布衣 *aranuno(no)koromo* sackcloth
6 行 *a(re)-yu(ku)* gradually get rough. *aragyō* religious austerities, asceticism
回 *a(re)-mawa(ru), ara(shi)-mawa(ru)* rampage, tear around, break into
地 *arechi* waste land, wilderness, desert
肌 *arehada* rough skin
年 *kōnen* year of bad crops
夷 *araebisu* barbarians
7 作 *arazuku(ri)* spadework, preliminary arrangements
狂 *a(re)-kuru(u)* get stormy, rage; get angry
肝 *aragimo* liver; pluck, courage
8 波 *aranami* stormy seas, raging waves
育 *arasoda(chi)* careless upbringing; a spoiled child

果 *a(re)-ha(teru)* be dilapidated, be ruined, lie waste, be desolate
者 *ara(kure)mono* a ruffian
事 *aragoto* ruffian's part (in a play)
性人 *a(re)shō(no)hito* person whose skin chaps easily
武者 *aramusha* daredevil, rowdy, a tough
放題 *a(re)hōdai* left to go to ruin
物 *aramono* kitchenware, sundries
物屋 *aramonoya* kitchenware store
9 屋 *ubaraya, kōoku* dilapidated house
造 *arazuku(ri)* spadework, preliminary arrangements
垣 *aragaki* shrine fence
海 *araumi* rough sea
畑 *arahata* a field left uncultivated
研 *aratogi* rough grinding
神 *aragami* fierce deity. *kōjin* kitchen god
胆 *aragimo* courage, nerve
削 *arakezu(ri)* roughing, rough planing, rough hewing, rough turning
怠 *kotai* laziness and pleasure-seeking
荒 *araara(shii)* rough, wild, violent, rude, harsh, gruff, fierce
巻 *aramaki* fresh slightly-salted salmon; a gift of fish wrapped in bamboo leaves
10 馬 *arauma, a(re)uma* untamed horse, restive horse
原 *kōgen* wilderness, desert
涼 *kōryō(taru)* bleak
陬 *kōsū* deep rural areas
都 *kōto* destroyed city
唐 *kōtō* absurdity, nonsense
唐言 *kōtō (no) gen* nonsense, wild talk
唐無稽 *kōtōmukei* absurdity, nonsense
11 涼 *kōryō(taru)* desolate, dreary
淫 *kōin* sexual indulgence
球 *a(re)dama* poor pitching
酔 *kōsui* dead drunk
野 *arano, areno, kōya* wilds, wilderness, desert
菰 *aragomo* coarse straw mat
12 廃 *a(re)-suta(reru)* become desolate, be dilapidate. *kōhai* desolation, ruin, dilapidation
廃地 *kōhaichi* waste land, devastated area
13 働 *arabatara(ki)* rough work, hard work
塚 *a(re)zuka* heap, bare mound
損 *kōson* dilapidation, ruin
滅 *ara(shi)-horo(bosu)* ravage, devastate
跡 *a(re)ato* ruins, desolation
歳 *kōsai* year of bad crops
蒔 *aramaki* sowing untilled soil
14 寥 *kōryō na* desolate and lonely
模様 *a(re)moyō* threatening sky
15 瘠 *kōseki no* waste and worn-out (land)
潮 *arashio* stormy tide
稼 *arakase(gi)* robbery, burglary; a big haul; heavy manual labor
誕 *kōtan* nonsense
縄 *aranawa* rough straw rope
蕪 *kōbu* wilderness, desolation
蕪地 *kōbuchi* deserted and desolate place
16 壁 *arakabe* rough plaster coat
17 磯 *araiso, ariso* a reefy coast, a windswept seashore
療治 *araryōji* drastic treatment; murder
23 鷲 *arawashi* fierce eagle; air ace

7

莵 5035 / J6839 / M-X Nonstandard for 菟 5077.

荳 5036 / J683a / M30989 See 豆 5735.

莖 5037 / J6833 / M31052 See 茎 4991.

莊 5038 / J6837 / M31035 See 荘 5031.

莱 5039 / J4d69 / M-X See 萊 5073.

莚 5040 / J682f / M31059 See 筵 4297.

荵 5041 / J683b / M30994 NIN. JIN. *shinobu(gusa)* hare's-foot fern.

莅 5042 / J682e / M31024 RI view; approach; watch; conduct; take up office.

莇 5043 / J6836 / M31026 CHO, JO. *kuko* a Chinese matrimony vine.

莉 5044 / J683d / M31034 RI jasmine.

莎 5045 J6835 M31040 SA. *hamasuge* nut grass, coco grass.

莠 5046 J683c M31065 YŪ incognito, bad disguised as good. *hagusa* a tare.

莪 5047 J6830 M31077 GA a kind of thistle.

莩 5048 J-X M31076 HYŌ very thin.

莓 5049 J6776 M31047 BAI, MAI wild strawberry.

莟 5050 J6831 M31064 GAN. *tsubomi* bud.

莫 5051 J6834 M31090 GO mat, matting.

13 蓙 *goza* mat, matting

莞 5052 J3450 M31063 KAN reed used for *tatami* covers.

14 爾 *kanji toshite* with a smile

荼 5053 J6838 M31008 TA, ZU, TO, DA a weed.

9 毘 *dabi* cremation

荻 5054 J322e M31005 TEKI. *ogi* reed.

10 原 *ogihara* reedy field

莢 5055 J6832 M31069 KYŌ. *saya* pod, hull, husk, shell, boll, case.

13 隠元 *sayaingen* kidney bean

15 豌豆 *sayaendō* garden pea, field pea

莨 5056 J683e M31075 RŌ. *tabako* tobacco.

2 入 *tabakoi(re)* cigarette case

9 屋 *tabakoya* tobacconist

盆 *tabakobon* tobacco tray

14 銭 *tabakosen* pocket money

莫 5057 J477c M31078 BAKU. BO. *naka(re)* must not, do not, be not.

3 大 *bakudai na* vast, immense, enormous

大小 *meriyasu* knitted goods

8 逆 *bakugeki, bakugyaku* firm friendship

逆友 *bakugeki (no) tomo* an intimate friend

B 華 5058 J325a M31119 GE. KA flower; petal; shining, luster; appearance; ostentation. *hanaya(gu)* become brilliant. *hana* flower. *hana(yakana)* gay, showy, brilliant, gorgeous. *-Ka-* China.

4 中 *Kachū* Central China

氏 *kashi* Fahrenheit

氏寒暖計 *kashi kandankei* Fahrenheit thermometer

5 甲 *kakō* one's 61st birthday

北 *Kahoku* North China

6 名 *kamei* fame, good reputation

字紙 *kajishi* Chinese newspaper

7 言 *kagen* flowery words

押 *kaō* signature

8 京 *kakei* the flowery capital; the beautiful capital

実 *kajitsu* flowers and fruit; appearance; content

表 *kahyō* monument at a cemetery entrance; a torii

9 南 *Kanan* South China

客 *kakyaku, kakaku* special guests

美 *kabi* pomp, splendor; gaudiness, colorfulness

冑 *kachū* aristocracy, nobility

洛 *karaku* capital; Kyoto

10 容 *kayō* a beautiful face

華 *hanabana(shii)* brilliant, magnificent, spectacular

11 道 *kadō* flower arrangement

族 *kazoku* noble, peer

12 奢 *kasha* luxury, pomp, extravagance. *kyasha na* delicate, slender; fragile

14 僑 *Kakyō* overseas Chinese

墨 *kaboku* your beautiful letter

16 翰 *kakan* your publication

17 厳 *Kegon* Buddhist sect originating in the eighth century

燭 *kashoku* bright light

燭典 *kashoku (no) ten* wedding ceremony

18 顔 *kagan* a beautiful face

19 麗 *karei* splendor, magnificence

A 荷 5059 J3259 M31000' KA shoulder-pole load. *nina(u)* carry, bear (a burden), shoulder (a gun). *ni* load, baggage, freight, cargo; burden.
3 下 *nioro(shi)* unloading, discharge. *ni (ga) o(riru)* be freed from responsibility
4 厄介 *niyakkai* encumbrance
5 札 *nifuda* tag, label
主 *ninushi* shipper
6 扱 *niatsuka(i)* freight handling
印 *nijirushi* mark on the baggage
7 車 *niguruma* cart, wagon
作 *nizuku(ri)* packing, baling, crating
抜 *ninu(ki)* pilferage
足 *niashi* sale; ballast; lading. *nita(ri)* barge, lighter
足船 *nita(ri)bune* barge, lighter
役 *niyaku* handling cargo
役人夫 *niyaku nimbu* longshoreman
8 物 *nimotsu* baggage; load
凭 *nimota(reru)* to oversupply, overstock
送 *nioku(ri)* consignment
送人 *nioku(ri)nin* sender
担 *katan* support; conspiracy, complicity. *nikatsu(gi)* carrying; laden
担者 *katansha* participants, supporters; conspirators
受 *niu(ke)* receipt of goods
受人 *niu(ke)nin* consignee
9 拵 *nigoshira(e)* packing, crating
持 *nimo(chi)* porter, carrier
卸 *nioro(shi)* unloading, discharge
重 *kajū* load
姿 *nisugata* type of packing
負 *nio(i)* shouldering a load
造 *nizuku(ri)* packing, baling, crating
造人 *nizuku(ri)nin* packer
造費 *nizuku(ri)hi* packing charges
10 捌 *nisaba(ki)* sale, disposal of goods
馬 *niuma* pack horse
馬車 *nibasha* wagon, dray, cart
11 脚 *niashi* sale; ballast; lading
船 *nibune* freighter; lighter
動 *niugo(ki)* movement of goods
12 渡 *niwata(shi)* delivery
勝 *ni (ga) ka(tsu)* the responsibilities are too heavy
葉 *kayō* lotus leaves
揚 *nia(ge)* unloading, landing
揚人足 *nia(ge) ninsoku* longshoreman
揚料 *nia(ge)ryō* landing charges
揚船 *nia(ge)sen* lighter, barge
揚場 *nia(ge)ba* landing place
13 解 *nihodo(ki)* unpacking
嵩 *nigasa* bulk. *nigasa(mi)* overstocked, glutted
電 *kaden* electric charge
14 駄 *nida* horseload, pack
15 鞍 *nigura* pack saddle
16 積 *nizu(mi)* loading
薄 *niusu* shortage of goods

8

葛 5060 J336b M-X Nonstandard for 葛 5126.

蒴 5061 J684e M-X See 萌 5094.

菷 5062 J6848 M31234 See 帚 1555.

菴 5063 J683f M31227 See 庵 1623.

菔 5064 J-X M31170 See 蔔 5173.

萢 5065 J684d M-X (国字) *yachi* bog land, wetlands

菘 5066 J6845 M31177 SŪ. SHŪ. *tōna* Chinese rape plant.

菻 5067 J6852 M31238 RIN a kind of thistle.

菽 5068 J6843 M31241 SHUKU legumes, beans, peas.

萇 5069 J6849 M31256 CHŌ a kind of fruit called carambola

萋 5070 J6846 M31264 SEI luxurious growth; respectful.

萓 5071 J6840 M31279 GI day lily.

菁 5072 J6847 M31136 SEI turnip.

6 竹米糸缶网罒羊羽老耂而耒耳聿肉月臣自至臼舌舛舟艮色【艸 艹】虍虫血行衣衤西

8

萊 5073 J-X M31262 **莱** 5039 J4d69 M-X RAI goosefoot, pigweed.

菆 5074 J-X M31146 SHU arrow.

萄 5075 J463a M31252 DŌ, TŌ grape vine, wild grape.

萍 5076 J684c M31266 HEI, HYŌ *ukikusa* floating plants.

菟 5077 J-X M31189 TO, TSU dodder (plant).

萃 5078 J6844 M31251 SUI, ZUI, SAI gather, collect, assemble.

菰 5079 J3856 M31217 KO. *komo* a reed used for matting.

萁 5080 J-X M31248 KŌ. *mamegara* bean stalks and pods.

菠 5081 J684a M31190 HA spinach.

16 薐草 *hōrensō* spinach

菲 5082 J684b M31220 HI thin; inferior.

3 才 *hisai* lack of ability, incompetence

莽 5083 J-X M31132 **莾** 5084 J-X M31133 **莽** 5010 J484f M31130

BŌ, MŌ grass, grassy field.

10 莽 *bōbō to* thickly; untrimmed, shaggy; bursting (into flames)

菖 5085 J3e54 M31174 SHŌ iris.

13 蒲 *ayame* Japanese iris. *shōbu* iris, flag

蒲湯 *shōbuyu* bath water with iris leaves

菫 5086 J6841 M31207 KIN. *sumire* violet.

5 外線 *kingaisen* ultraviolet; black light

11 菜 *sumire* violet

萎 5087 J3060 M31269 I. *na(eru)* wither, droop, weaken; be paralyzed, be lame. *shibo(mu), shio(reru), shina(biru)* droop, wither, wilt, fade; be downcast.

17 縮 *ishuku* withering, contraction, atrophy

19 靡 *ibi* decline, decay, drooping

菎 5088 J6842 M31160 **崑** 5089 J-X M-X KON a kind of fragrant herb.

11 麻 *hima, tōgoma* castor oil plant; castor beans

麻子 *himashi* castor bean

麻子油 *himashiyu* castor oil

菅 5090 J3f7b M31142 KAN. *suge* sedge.

10 原 *sugawara* field of sedge

11 笠 *sugegasa* sedge hat

12 畳 *sugedatami* sedge mat

13 筵 *sugemushiro* sedge mat

B **菌** 5091 J365d M31156' KIN fungus, germ, bacteria.

8 毒 *kindoku* mushroom poison

9 保有者 *kinhoyūsha* germ carrier

18 類 *kinrui* fungi

類学 *kinruigaku* study of fungi

菱 5092 J4929 M31219 RYŌ. *hishi* water chestnut; diamond (shape).

7 形 *ryōkei, hishigata* rhombus shape; diamond shape

13 鉄鉱 *ryōtekkō* loadstone

14 模様 *hishi moyō* diamond design

15 餅 *hishimochi* colored rice for the Girls' Festival

菩 5093 J4a6e M31205 BO kind of grass; sacred tree.

12 提 *bodai* Buddhahood; supreme enlightenment; repose; salvation

提心 *bodaishin* aspiration for Buddhahood; devout disposition

提寺 *bodaiji* a family temple

提所 *bodaisho* a family temple

提樹 *bodaiju* bo tree; lime tree; linden tree

16 薩 *bosatsu* bodhisattva; Buddhist saint

萌 5094 J4b28 M31265 HŌ. BŌ. *moe(ru)* sprout, bud. *moya(su)* to malt, cause to sprout artificially. *kiza(su)* show signs or symptoms of. *moya(shi)* malt;

artificially sprouted beans or grains. *kiza(shi)* signs, omen, symptoms; germination.
4 木 *moegi* sprouts; tree coming into leaf
5 立 *moe-ta(tsu)* sprout, bud
出 *moe-de(ru)* sprout, bud
7 豆 *moya(shi)mame* sprouting beans
8 芽 *hōga* germination; germ, sprout
11 黄色 *moegi iro* light green

B **菓** 5095 / J325b / M31168' KA cakes; fruit.
3 子 *kashi* confectionery, pastry, candy
子皿 *kashizara* cake plate
子折 *kashio(ri)* cake box
子屋 *kashiya* confectionery
子重 *kashijū* small tier of cake boxes
子料 *kashiryō* cake money; cake-money tip
子鉢 *kashibachi* cookie jar
子箱 *kashibako* box of sweets
子器 *kashiki* cake-serving bowl

B **菊** 5096 / J3546 / M31153' KIKU chrysanthemum.
2 人形 *kikuningyō* a doll made of a shaped growing chrysanthemum
4 月 *kikuzuki* ninth lunar month
日和 *kikubiyori* fine fall chrysanthemum weather
6 芋 *kikuimo* Jerusalem artichoke
7 見 *kikumi* chrysanthemum viewing
作 *kikuzuku(ri)* chrysanthemum growing; chrysanthemum grower
判 *kikuban* small octavo
花 *kikka* chrysanthemum
9 炭 *kikuzumi* chrysanthemum charcoal
11 細工 *kikuzaiku* skillful chrysanthemum culture
13 節句 *Kiku (no) Sekku* Chrysanthemum Festival

A **菜** 5097 / J3a5a / M31184' SAI side dish; greens; vegetables. *na* greens; vegetables; the rape or mustard plant.
2 刀 *nagatana* kitchen knife
4 切庖丁 *na(k)ki(ri)bōchō* kitchen knife
7 花 *na (no) hana* mustard flowers, rape blossoms
9 食 *saishoku* vegetarian diet; plain food
食主義 *saishoku shugi* vegetarianism
食主義者 *saishoku shugisha* a vegetarian
食動物 *saishoku dōbutsu* herbivorous animal
10 根 *saikon* vegetable roots
12 葉 *na(p)pa* greens
葉服 *na(p)pafuku* overalls
13 園 *saien* vegetable garden
14 漬 *nazuke* pickled vegetables
種 *natane* rapeseed
種油 *natane abura* rapeseed oil
15 箸 *saibashi* chopsticks for cooking

A **著** 5098 / J4378 / M31302 **著** 5104 / J-X / M31410 CHO literary work. *ara(wasu)* write, publish. *ichijiru(shii)* remarkable, phenomenal.
3 大 *chodai na* exceptionally large
6 名 *chomei* eminence, celebrity, fame
7 述 *chojutsu* literary work
述家 *chojutsuka* a writer
述業 *chojutsugyō* literary profession
作 *chosaku* literary work, book; authorship
作物 *chosakubutsu* literary work, book
作者 *chosakusha* author, writer
作家 *chosakuka* author, writer
作権 *chosakuken* copyright
8 明 *chomei na* clear, plain, obvious, conspicuous
者 *chosha* author, writer
9 変 *chohen* a big change
10 書 *chosho* literary work, book
書目録 *chosho mokuroku* bibliography
11 患 *chokan* serious illness

9

蓬 5099 / J4b29 / M-X Nonstandard for **蓬** 5157.

葢 5100 / J6864 / M31432 Nonstandard for **蓋** 5155.

蒂 5101 / J685c / M31495 See **蔕** 5169.

菟 5102 / J4551 / M-X Nonstandard for **菟** 5077.

6 竹米糸缶网罒羊羽老耂而耒耳聿肉月臣自至臼舌舛舟艮色【艸 9 艹】虍虫血行衣衤西

萬 5103 J685f M31339 See 万 7.

著 5104 J-X M31410 See 著 5098.

蓮 5105 J4f21 M-X Nonstandard for 蓮 5158.

萪 5106 J6854 M31334 KA a kind of wisteria.

蔲 5107 J6857 M31342 KAN kind of grass.

萵 5108 J6862 M31351 WA lettuce.

萸 5109 J6850 M31356 YU oleaster.

葆 5110 J685e M31381 HŌ, HO thick growth; roots.

葎 5111 J4e2a M31397 RITSU. *mugura* creeper; trailing plants.

葩 5112 J685d M31441 HA. *hana* flower, petal.

葫 5113 J6859 M31443 KO garlic.

葮 5114 J685b M31450 DAN. *mukuge* rose of Sharon.

葯 5115 J6860 M31451 YAKU pollen packet at end of stamen; a kind of tall grass, angelica.

葷 5116 J6858 M31461 KUN spicy or odoriferous plants (e.g., garlic, leeks, onions).

葹 5117 J6861 M31464 SHI. *onamomi, namomi* cocklebur, burrweed.

董 5118 J4621 M31433 TŌ correct.

萼 5119 J6855 M31361 蕚 5183 J6856 M31970 GAKU calyx, cup.

葵 5120 J302a M31458 KI. *aoi* hollyhock.

萱 5121 J337e M31345 KEN. *kaya* miscanthus reed.

12 葺 *kayabuki* the common miscanthus thatch

萩 5122 J476b M31333 SHŪ. *hagi* bush clover.

10 原 *hagiwara* reedy field

葱 5123 J472c M31454 SŌ. *negi* stone leek, Welsh onion, long onion.

7 坊主 *negi bōzu* flowering onion head

葭 5124 J6853 M31449 KA. *yoshi, ashi* reed.

17 簀 *yoshizu* reed screen

葺 5125 J4978 M31465 SHŪ. *ashi* reed, rush. *fu(ku)* to thatch, cover, shingle, tile.

4 刈 *ashika(ri)* cutting reeds; the cutter
5 石 *fukiishi* slate
8 板 *fukiita* shingles
12 替 *fu(ki)-ka(eru)* rethatch, reroof, retile

葛 5126 J-X M31420 KATSU. *tsuzura* arrowroot, a strong-fiber vine. *kuzu* kudzu, arrowroot; arrowroot starch.

5 布 *kuzufu* grass cloth
6 衣 *katsui* thin coarse hemp kimono
7 折 *tsuzurao(ri)* winding path
折道 *tsuzurao(ri) michi* winding path
10 粉 *kuzuko* arrowroot starch or flour
15 餅 *kuzu mochi* arrowroot-flour cake
18 藤 *kattō* complications, dissension
22 籠 *tsuzura* suitcase, wicker basket, trunk

葡 5127 J4972 M31430 BU, HO wild grape.

11 萄 *budō* grapes, grapevine
萄状菌 *budōjōkin* staphylococcus
萄畑 *budōbatake* vineyard
萄酒 *budōshu* wine
萄液 *budōeki* grape juice

萄園 *budōzono, budōen* vineyard
萄酸 *budōsan* racemic acid
萄糖 *budōtō* grape sugar, dextrose, glucose

B **葬** 5128 / J4172 / M31448' Sō. *hōmu(ru)* bury; shelve. *tomura(u)* mourn for; hold a memorial service for; condole. *tomura(i)* funeral, burial, condolence.

5 礼 *sōrei* funeral service
主 *sōshu* chief mourner
6 式 *sōshiki* funeral ceremony
列 *sōretsu* funeral procession
8 具 *sōgu* funeral accessories
具師 *sōgushi* undertaker
送 *sōsō* attendance at a funeral
送曲 *sōsōkyoku* funeral march
送行進曲 *sōsō kōshinkyoku* funeral march
送歌 *sōsōka* funeral dirge
11 祭 *sōsai* funerals and festivals
14 歌 *sōka* dirge, elegy
15 儀 *sōgi* funeral service
儀社 *sogisha* undertaker
儀屋 *sōgiya* undertaker
儀場 *sōgijō* funeral parlor

A **葉** 5129 / J4d55 / M31387' Yō leaf; plane; lobe; counter for flat things. *ha, ha(ppu)* leaf, foliage, needle, blade, spear, frond.

4 月 *hazuki* eighth lunar month
5 広 *habiro* broadness of leaves
末 *hazue* leaf tip
7 状 *hajō* leaflike
牡丹 *habotan* cabbage
8 物 *hamono* leafy plants and trees
並 *hana(mi)* leaf arrangement
芽 *yōga* leaf bud
9 風 *hakaze* the wind passing through the leaves
柄 *yōhei* leaf stem
茶 *hacha* leaf tea
巻 *hamaki* cigar
10 振 *habu(ri)* leaf arrangement
桜 *hazakura* cherry foliage
脈 *yōmyaku* leaf vein
陰 *hakage ni* under the leaves
書 *hagaki* postcard
12 越 *hago(shi)* (seen) through the leaves
13 鉄 *yōtetsu* sheet iron
隠 *hagaku(reru)* hide in the trees
裏 *haura* underside side of a leaf
14 酸 *yōsan* folic acid
緑素 *yōryokuso* chlorophyll
15 縁 *yōen* margin of a leaf

A **落** 5130 / J4d6e / M31362' Raku. *o(chiru)* fall, drop, come down, go down; drip; collapse, cave in; sink; fail (in exams); be missing; come off, come out; flee; lose popularity; abate; flow into; be inferior; fall unconscious; fade; be captured, be carried away by. *o(tosu)* drop, let fall; throw down; throw (a shadow); miss (a ball), fumble; lose; capture; omit; degrade; depreciate, detract from; decrease; make worse; drive away, exorcise; leave behind; knock down (an article); cause abortion; entrap; end (a story) with a punch; remove (stains). *o(chibureru)* be ruined, sink into poverty. *o(chi)* error, fault, slip; point (of a joke); outcome. *o(toshi)* trap; false bottom; ashpan; chute; brazier. *-o(chi)* off, less, minus; flight. *o(chi)-* lower, low; fallen (fruit); defeated.

2 人 *ochūdo, ochibito, ochiudo* refugee; deserter; fugitive
入 *o(chi)-i(ru)* fall into, get into, slide into, lapse into; cave in, sink; fall (a fort)
丁 *rakuchō* missing pages
3 口 *o(chi)guchi* beginning of the fall of leaves; spout; mouth (of a river); brink (of a waterfall); successful bidder, lottery winner
子 *o(toshi)go* illegitimate child
下 *rakka* falling, descent
下傘 *rakkasan* parachute
下傘兵 *rakkasanhei* paratrooper
4 戸 *o(toshi)do* trapdoor
手 *rakushu* receiving
文 *o(toshi)bumi* letter purposely dropped or left behind
方 *o(chi)kata* weakening, falling
日 *rakujitsu* setting sun
月 *rakugetsu* setting moon
水 *o(toshi)mizu* letting water out of a rice field; such water
毛 *o(chi)ge* falling hair
込 *o(chi)-ko(mu)* fall in; sink, subside; decline (of prices); come in
5 目 *o(chi)me* declining fortune, adversity
穴 *o(toshi)ana* pitfall, trap

付 *o(chi)tsu(ki)* serenity, calmness, stability
主 *o(toshi)nushi* loser (of something)
失 *o(chi)-u(seru)* flee, escape, abscond
札 *rakusatsu* successful bid. *o(chi)fuda* prize-winning ticket
札人 *rakusatsunin* successful bidder
札値 *rakusatsune* contract price
6 行 *o(chi)-yu(ku)* flee
合 *o(chi)-a(u)* meet, come upon, rendezvous. *o(chi)a(i)* meeting; confluence
字 *rakuji* omitted character
成 *rakusei* completion of construction
成式 *rakuseishiki* building-completion ceremony
伍 *rakugo* straggling, dropping out; losing out (in the struggle for existence)
伍者 *rakugosha* straggler
7 足 *o(chi)ashi* flight; time of fleeing; receding of water
車 *rakusha suru* fall off a racing vehicle
体 *rakutai* falling body
卵 *o(toshi)tamago* poached eggs
花 *rakka* falling of blossoms; scattered blossoms
花生 *rakkasei* peanuts
花狼藉 *rakkarōzeki suru* fall off, pass away, scatter
8 延 *o(chi)-no(biru)* make good one's escape
物 *o(toshi)mono* lost article
命 *rakumei* death
英 *rakuei* falling of blossoms; scattered blossoms
武者 *ochimusha* fugitive warrior
9 首 *rakushu* lampoon, satirical poem
胤 *rakuin, o(toshi)dane* illegitimate child
城 *rakujō* fall of a castle
後 *rakugo* straggling, dropping out; losing out in the struggle for existence
胆 *rakutan* discouragement 「heap
重 *o(chi)-kasa(naru)* fall upon; fall in a
度 *o(chi)do* fault, error, slip, lapse, oversight; blame, guilt
度無 *o(chi)dona(ku)* blamelessly
星 *rakusei* falling star, meteor
星雨 *rakuseiu* meteoric shower
10 馬 *rakuba* a fall from a horse. *rakuba suru* fall from a horse, be thrown from a horse

涙 *rakurui suru* shed tears
紙 *o(toshi)gami* toilet paper
差 *rakusa* water level, head, fall
書 *rakuga(ki)* scribbling in public places, graffiti. *rakusho* anonymous critical broadsides
莫 *rakubaku(taru)* dreary, desolate, lonesome
栗 *o(chi)guri* fallen chestnut
11 魚 *o(chi)uo* dead fish
掛 *o(chi)-ka(karu)* fall upon; begin to fall
球 *rakkyū* missing a ball; muffed ball
脱 *rakudatsu* omission
陽 *rakuyō* setting sun
第 *rakudai* failure in an examination
第生 *rakudaisei* student who failed
第点 *rakudaiten* failing mark
12 款 *rakkan* writer's or artist's signature
掌 *rakushō* receiving
筆 *rakuhitsu* beginning to write
落 *o(chi)o(chi)* quietly, peacefully, comfortably
無 *o(chi)na(ku)* without exception, thoroughly
着 *o(chi)-tsu(keru)* calm (oneself). *o(chi)-tsu(ku)* calm down; settle down; keep cool; subside (pain); be steady; harmonize with. *ochitsu(ki)* calmness, serenity; stability. *rakuchaku* settlement, end, conclusion
着払 *o(chi)-tsu(ki)-hara(u)* be perfectly calm
着先 *ochitsu(ki)saki* place where one stays
着所 *ochitsu(ki)dokoro* happy dwelling, haven of rest
葉 *o(chi)ba* fallen leaves. *rakuyō* fall of leaves; fallen leaves
葉松 *karamatsu, rakuyōshō* larch
葉樹 *rakuyōju* deciduous tree
葉籠 *o(chi)bakago* stray notes
13 暉 *rakki* setting sun
話 *o(toshi)banashi* funny story, pointed story
飾 *rakushoku* taking the tonsure
雷 *rakurai suru* be struck by lightning
零 *o(chi)kobo(re)* what's left; things scattered around
勢 *o(chi)zei* fleeing army. *rakusei* declining market

照 *rakushō* setting sun
14 髪 *rakuhatsu* tonsure. *o(chi)gami* falling hair
選 *rakusen* election defeat; rejection
選者 *rakusensha* unsuccessful candidate
語 *rakugo* humorous story
語家 *rakugoka* storyteller; comedian
15 潮 *rakuchō*, *o(chi)shio* low tide, ebb tide
魄 *ochibure(ru)* be ruined, be reduced to poverty, fall low. *ochibure* stricken with adversity. *rakuhaku* straitened circumstances
縁 *o(chi)en* low veranda
盤 *rakuban* cave-in
磐 *rakuban* cave-in
穂 *o(chi)bo* gleanings
穂拾 *o(chi)bohiro(i)* gleaning; gleaner
16 鮎 *o(chi)ayu* sweetfish descending rivers for spawning
17 藉 *rakuseki* buying a geisha her contractual freedom
18 羂 *o(toshi)wana* pit trap
20 籍 *rakuseki* no registration (in the census register); buying a geisha her contractual freedom

10

蒭 5131 / J685a / M31598 See 芻 4971.

蒋 5132 / J3e55 / M-X See 蔣 5177.

蒹 5133 / J6865 / M31621 KEN. *ogi* reed. *himeyoshi* a kind of reed.

蓁 5134 / J686d / M31639 SHIN bushy, verdant; abundant.

蓉 5135 / J4d56 / M31648 YŌ lotus.

蓊 5136 / J6863 / M31650 Ō flower stalk; thick growth, lush.

蓍 5137 / J6869 / M31655 SHI. *medohagi* a sericea.

蔀 5138 / J3c43 / M31748 HŌ. *shitomi* latticed shutters.

蓏 5139 / J-X / M31658 RA fruit growing on low plants.

蒴 5140 / J-X / M31614 SAKU (seed) capsule.

蒻 5141 / J686a / M31623 NYAKU. JAKU a kind of water plant.

蓙 5142 / J6868 / M31709 (国字) ZA. *goza* mat, matting.

蓑 5143 / J4c2c / M31661 **簑** 4334 / J6442 / M26387 SA. *mino* straw raincoat.

蒜 5144 / J4947 / M31562 SAN. *ninniku* garlic.

蒡 5145 / J6870 / M31572 BŌ. HŌ burdock

蓚 5146 / J686b / M-X SHŪ (used only in compounds).
14 酸 *shūsan* oxalic acid

蒿 5147 / J6866 / M31634 KŌ mugwort.
8 苣 *chisha, chisa* lettuce

蓆 5148 / J686e / M31645 SEKI. *mushiro* straw mat, matting.
5 包 *mushirozutsu(mi)* mat-wrapped bundle

蓐 5149 / J686c / M31660 JOKU bed.
13 傷 *jokushō* bedsores
15 瘡 *jokusō* bedsores

蒟 5150 / J6867 / M31566 KU devil's tongue (plant).
13 蒻 *konnyaku* devil's tongue
蒻版 *konnyakuban* hectograph

蔭 5151 / J307e / M31840 IN. *kage* shade; backing, (your) assistance.
5 乍 *kagenaga(ra)* secretly
7 言 *kagegoto* malicious gossip
位 *in'i* hereditary court rank

蓖 5152 / J686f / M31626 HI, HEI caster oil plant.
11 麻 *hima, tōgoma* castor oil plant
麻子 *himashi* castor bean
麻子油 *himashiyu* castor bean oil

蒔 5153 / J3c2c / M31546 SHI. JI. *ma(ku)* sow (seed).
5 付 *ma(ki)tsu(ke)* sowing, seeding
12 絵 *makie* gold or silver lacquer work
22 蘿 *inondo* dill

蒙 5154 / J4c58 / M31555 MŌ ignorance; darkness. *kōmu(ru)* get, receive, be subjected to, sustain (damage), suffer (loss). *kōmu(rasu)* cause (damage); inflict on; subject to.
5 古 *Mōko* Mongolia
古人 *Mōkojin* Mongolian
古襲来 *Mōko Shūrai* Mongolian Invasion
9 昧 *mōmai* ignorance
14 塵 *mōjin suru* flee from the palace (the emperor)

蓋 5155 / J3338 / M31652 GAI cover. *futa* cover, lid, flap, hood. *keda(shi)* probably; after all; in the long run.
7 車 *gaisha* covered wagon
8 明 *futaa(ke)* opening, commencement
物 *futamono* covered dish
12 然 *gaizen* probable
然性 *gaizensei* probability
然的 *gaizenteki* probable

蒲 5156 / J3377 / M31611 FU. BO. HO. BU. *gama* flag, cattail, bulrush. *kaba* bulrush.
4 公英 *tampopo* dandelion
6 色 *kaba iro* reddish-yellow
団 *futon* bedding; mattress; pallet
団蒸 *futommu(shi)* wrapping (someone) in a quilt
9 柳質 *horyū (no) shitsu* delicate health
14 鉾 *kamaboko* boiled fish paste
鉾小屋 *kamabokogoya* a beggar's hut

蓬 5157 / J-X / M31720 HŌ. *yomogi* sagebrush, wormwood, mugwort; an edible weed.
5 生 *yomogifu, yomogiu* wasteland; area overgrown with weeds
11 萊 *hōrai* isle of eternal youth; fairyland; Elysian fields; eternal youth ornament
萊米 *hōraimai* rice from Taiwan
萊豆 *hōrai mame* sugar-coated beans
13 蓬 *hōhō to* thickly; untrimmed, shaggy; bursting (into flames)
14 髪 *hōhatsu* unkempt hair
16 頭 *hōtō* tousled hair

蓮 5158 / J-X / M31722 REN. *hasu, hachisu* lotus.
6 池 *hasuike* lotus pond
10 根 *renkon* lotus root
華 *renge* lotus, lotus flower
華草 *rengesō* a purple vetch
12 葉 *hasuha, hasu(p)pa* lotus leaf. *hasuha na, hasu(p)pa na* wanton, loose, coquettish
葉女 *hasuha onna, hasu(p)pa onna* hussy, flapper
葉者 *hasuhamono, hasu(p)pamono* hussy, flapper
葉娘 *hasuha musume, hasu(p)pa musume* hussy, flapper

蒐 5159 / J3d2f / M31539 SHŪ gather.
10 荷 *shūka* collection of cargo
12 集 *shūshū* collection, accumulation
集品 *shūshūhin* collectors' items
集美術品 *shūshū bijutsuhin* art collection
集家 *shūshūka* collector
集欲 *shūshūyoku* collecting craze
集癖 *shūshūheki* collecting habit
16 輯 *shūshū* collection, gathering up, accumulation

葦 5160 / J3031 / M31437 I. *ashi, yoshi* reed, bulrush.
4 戸 *yoshido* (sliding) reed door
毛 *ashige* a grey horse, a dappled gray
火 *ashibi* torchlight of reeds
5 生 *ashifu* reedy area
6 舟 *ashibune* reed boat
9 垣 *ashigaki* reed fence
11 船 *ashibune* reed-carrying boat; boat used for harvesting reeds
笛 *ashibue* reed flute
17 簀 *yoshizu* reed screen

B **蓄** 5161 / J435f / M31642' CHIKU. *takuwa(e)* store, hoard, savings. *takuwa(eru)* store, lay in stock, save, keep, wear (a mustache).
2 力 *chikuryoku* accumulating power
5 生腹 *chikushōbara* multiple (human) births
8 妾 *chikushō* keeping a concubine
9 音器 *chikuonki* phonograph
音機 *chikuonki* phonograph
10 財 *chikuzai* amassing of wealth
13 電 *chikuden* charging with electricity
電池 *chikudenchi* storage battery
電器 *chikudenki* electric condenser
16 積 *chikuseki* accumulation, amassing
17 膿症 *chikunōshō* sinusitis

蒼 5162 / J4173 / M31627 SŌ. *ao* blue, pale.
4 天 *sōten* blue sky
5 生 *sōsei* the people, the masses
白 *aojiro(i), sōhaku na* pale, pallid, livid
8 穹 *sōkyū* blue sky
空 *sōkū* blue sky
氓 *sōbo* the people
9 海 *sōkai* blue sea
茫 *sōbō taru* dusky, shadowy
10 浪 *sōrō* blue waves
12 惶 *sōkō* bustle, hurry
然 *sōzen(taru)* blue; dim; gloomy, somber
13 鉛 *sōen* bismuth
14 褪 *aoza(meru)* get pale

A **蒸** 5163 / J3e78 / M31618' JŌ. SHŌ. *mu(su)* steam, heat up (with steam); be close, be sultry; foment, poultice. *mu(reru)* be stuffy, get musty; moulder, heat. *mu(rasu)* steam, cook by steam. *fu(kasu)* steam. *fu(keru)* be steamed, be boiled. *mu(shi)-* steamed (dish).
5 立 *mu(shi)ta(te)no* just steamed
6 返 *mu(shi)-kae(su)* reheat, steam over; repeat, bring up again
気 *jōki* steam, vapor; steamship
気力 *jōkiryoku* steam power
気孔 *jōkikō* volcanic vent
気汽缶 *jōki kikan* steam boiler
気室 *jōkishitsu* steam chamber
気風呂 *jōkiburo* steam bath
気釜 *jōkigama* steam boiler
気船 *jōkisen* steamship
気管 *jōkikan* steampipe
気機関 *jōki kikan* steam engine
気機関車 *jōki kikansha* steam locomotive
8 物 *mu(shi)mono* steamed food
9 風呂 *mu(shi)buro* Turkish bath, steam bath
発 *jōhatsu* evaporation, volatilization
発熱 *jōhatsu netsu* heat of evaporation
発器 *jōhatsuki* evaporator
10 釜 *mu(shi)gama* steam kettle
留 *jōryū* distillation
留水 *jōryūsui* distilled water
留酒 *jōryūshu* distilled liquor
留器 *jōryūki* a still
11 菓子 *mu(shi)gashi* steamed cake
12 飯 *mu(shi)meshi* reheated rice
散 *jōsan* evaporation, volatilization
暑 *mu(shi)atsu(i)* sultry, sweltering
焼 *mu(shi)ya(ki)* baking in covered casseroles
焼器 *mushiyakiki* oven
蒸 *mu(shi)mu(shi) suru* be sultry, be close
13 溜 *jōryū* distillation
溜水 *jōryūsui* distilled water
溜器 *jōryūki* a still
14 腐 *mu(re)gusa(re)* dry rot
15 熱 *jōnetsu* stuffiness, sultriness
17 鍋 *mu(shi)nabe* casserole
19 餾 *jōryū* distillation
22 籠 *seiro, seirō* steamer, basket for steaming rice

11

蕁 5164 / J-X / M-X See 蕁 5195.

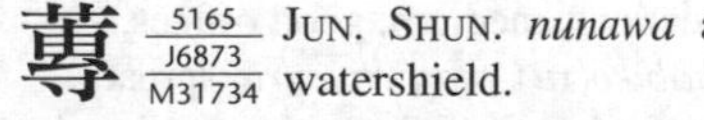
蓴 5165 / J6873 / M31734 JUN. SHUN. *nunawa* a watershield.

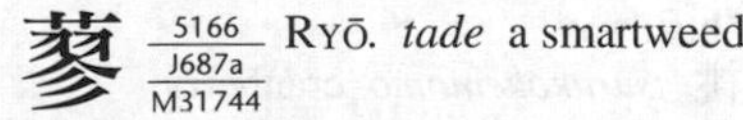
蓼 5166 / J687a / M31744 RYŌ. *tade* a smartweed.

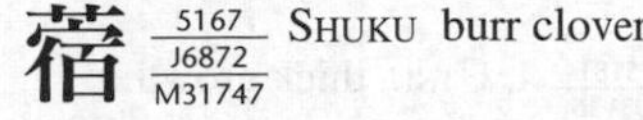
蓿 5167 / J6872 / M31747 SHUKU burr clover.

蔆 5168 / J6851 / M31760 RYŌ. *hishi* water chestnut.

蔕 5169 / J6878 / M31789 TEI. *heta* calyx, stem. TAI thorn, burr.

蔡 5170 / J6871 / M31818 SAI grow like weeds; rules; decline; turtle shell.

蔲 5171 / J-X / M31741 **蔻** 5172 / J-X / M-X KŌ, KU nutmeg.

蔔 5173 / J6879 / M31785 **菔** 5064 / J-X / M31170 FUKU giant radish, daikon.

蔘 5174 / J6875 / M31795 SHIN luxurious growth of grass.

蔟 5175 / J6877 / M31815 ZOKU gather together.

蔗 5176 / J6874 / M31794 SHA, SHO sugar cane.

蔣 5177 / J-X / M31820 SHŌ a reed.

9 政権 *Shōseiken* Chiang (Kai Shek) regime.

蔦 5178 / J4455 / M31828' CHŌ. *tsuta* ivy.

12 葛 *tsutakazura* vines, creepers

蔑 5179 / J4a4e / M31781 BETSU. *naigashiro (ni) suru* ignore, despise, neglect, ridicule. *nami(suru)* set at naught, ridicule. *sagesu(mu), sageshi(mu)* despise, ridicule.

11 視 *besshi* contempt, derision; slight

蔓 5180 / J4c22 / M31784 MAN. *habiko(ru)* spread, sprawl; overgrow; thrive; be rampant, become powerful. *tsuru* vine, tendril, runner; influence, connections, medium, good offices.

8 延 *habiko(ru), man'en suru* spread, diffuse, prevail, be widespread, gain headway

苔桃 *tsurukokemomo* cranberry

9 草 *tsurukusa* creeper, climber, vine

蔚 5181 / J3136 / M31805 I, UTSU thick growth. *otokoyomogi* (a kind of) mugwort; thick growth, thicket.

12 然 *utsuzen* thick growth

14 爾 *iji* thick growth

16 薈 *utsuwai* luxuriant vegetation

A **蔵** 5182 / J4222 / M31885' **藏** 5227 / J6936 / M32264 SŌ. ZŌ. *kura* storehouse, warehouse, godown; cellar; depository, treasury; granary, elevator. *zō(suru)* hide; accumulate; have, own, keep, cherish. *osa(meru)* obtain, reap; dedicate, consecrate; pay; supply; store; finish; collect; restore, replace. *-zō* possession.

2 人 *kurando* imperial-archives keeper

入 *kurai(re)* warehousing

4 方 *kurakata* the one in charge of a storehouse

元 *kuramoto* warehouse superintendent

5 払 *kurabara(i)* clearance (sale)

出 *kurada(shi)* releasing (goods) from a storehouse

本 *zōhon* one's library, one's private collection of books

6 米 *kuramai* stored rice

7 作 *kurazuku(ri)* storehouse style (architecture)

8 版 *zōhan* copyrighted by

9 持 *kuramo(chi)* warehouse owner; warehousing

相 *zōshō, zōsō* finance minister

屋敷 *kura yashiki* daimyo's city storehouse

10 匿 *zōtoku suru vt* and *vi* hide

浚 *kurazara(e)* clearance sale

書 *zōsho* one's library, book collection

書狂 *zōshokyō* bibliomania; bibliomaniac

書家 *zōshoka* book collector, large library owner

11 移 *kurautsu(shi)* transporting to another storehouse

船 *kurabune* ship used for storage

12 開 *kurabira(ki)* first opening of the storehouse in the new year

番 *kuraban* warehouse guard

13 置 *zōchi, kura-o(ki)* storing

12

蕚 5183 / J6856 / M31970 See 萼 5119.

蕀 5184 / J687b / M31898 KYOKU a kind of milkwort.

蕕 5185 J6924 M31961 Yū. Yu. a kind of bunge, a bluebeard.

蕘 5186 J687d M31965 Jō. *takagi* firewood.

蕑 5187 J-X M31954 Kan. *fujibakama* agueweed (a fall flower).

蕊 5188 J3c49 M31939 蕋 5189 J6923 M31940 蘂 5243 J6922 M32410

橤 2855 J-X M15569 Zui. *shibe* pistil; stamen.

蕈 5190 J687e M31928 Jin. *kinoko* mushroom; toadstool; fungus. *take* mushroom.

9 狩 *kinokoga(ri)* hunting mushrooms

蕉 5191 J3e56 M31937 Shō banana.

9 風 *shōfū* correct style in haiku (like Bashō's)

蔬 5192 J6876 M31839 So greens, vegetables.

11 菜 *sosai* vegetables, greens

蔽 5193 J4a43 M31888 Hei. *ō(i)* cover, covering; shade; mantle, coat; hood, bonnet; casing; awning. *ō(u)* cover, veil; hang over; brood over; conceal; overlap; shelter; screen; disguise; wrap; obscure; shade; overshadow.

13 隠 *ō(i)-kaku(su)* cover; conceal

蕨 5194 J4f4f M32001 Ketsu. *warabi* bracken, fernbrake.

9 狩 *warabiga(ri)* bracken gathering

蕁 5195 J6921 M31899 蕁 5164 J-X M-X Jin a kind of grass.

11 麻 *irakusa* nettle

麻疹 *jimmashin* hives, rash

蕪 5196 J4973 M32004 Bu. *kabu, kabura* turnip.

11 菁 *kabura* turnip

13 辞 *buji* my humble remarks

14 雑 *buzatsu na* unpolished, crude

蕎 5197 J363e M31946 Kyō buckwheat.

7 麦 *soba* buckwheat; buckwheat noodles

麦屋 *sobaya* buckwheat-noodle shop

麦粉 *sobako* buckwheat flour

麦殻 *sobagara* buckwheat chaff

蕩 5198 J4622 M32002 Tō. *toro(kasu) vt* melt, fuse; charm, captivate. *toro(keru) vi* melt, fuse; charm, captivate.

3 子 *tōshi* prodigal son; profligate

4 心 *tōshin* debauchery, dissipation

6 尽 *tōjin* squandering

7 児 *tōji* debauchee, libertine

15 蕩 *tōtō(taru)* vast, rushing (water)

蕃 5199 J4859 M31906 Ban, Han grow luxuriously.

2 人 *banjin* aborigine

6 地 *banchi* barbaric region

夷 *ban'i* barbarians, savages

7 社 *bansha* aborigines' village

8 国 *bankoku* backward country; foreign country

11 族 *banzoku* savage tribe

12 椒 *tōgarashi* red pepper

殖 *hanshoku suru* breed, propagate, increase, multiply

14 語 *bango* aboriginal language

13

薗 5200 J3172 M32119 See 園 962.

薮 5201 J4c79 M-X Nonstandard for 藪 5240.

薯 5202 J3d72 M-X Nonstandard for 薯 5230.

蕗 5203 J4979 M31964 Ro. *fuki* a butterbur, a big rhubarb, a coltsfoot.

蕣 5204 J687c M31991 Shun. *mukage* a rose of Sharon. *asagao* morning glory.

薀 5205 J6925 M32071 Un, On water weed; hornwort; load, gather; abundant.

薐 5206 / J6933 / M32108 RO spinach.

薛 5207 / J692d / M32123 SETSU mugwort. *hamasuge* nut grass, coco grass.

薜 5208 / J6930 / M32125 HEI teasel, vine; creeper.

薇 5209 / J692f / M32092 BI an edible fern.

薈 5210 / J6927 / M32093 KAI luxuriant vegetation.

薤 5211 / J6926 / M32141 KAI. *rakkyō* scallion, shallot, a small onion.

薑 5212 / J6928 / M32110 KYŌ. *hajikami* ginger.

薊 5213 / J6929 / M32095 KEI. *azami* thistle.

蕷 5214 / J6931 / M32054 YO. *imo* potato.

蕾 5215 / J6932 / M32067 RAI. *tsubo(mu)* bear buds. *tsubomi* bud.

薨 5216 / J692a / M32147 KŌ. *kō(jiru), kō(zuru)* die.
5 去 *kōkyo* death, demise

薩 5217 / J3b27 / M32189' SATSU Buddha.
15 摩守 *satsuma (no) kami* one who steals ⌈a ride
摩燒 *Satsumayaki* Satsuma ware
摩薯 *satsuma imo* sweet potato

蕭 5218 / J692b / M32012 SHŌ a weed, mugwort; lonely; silent, calm.
7 条 *shōjō(taru)* bleak, desolate, lonely
12 然 *shōzen(taru)* bleak, desolate, lonely
16 蕭 *shōshō(taru)* bleak, desolate

B **薦** 5219 / J4126 / M32143' SEN. *susu(me)* recommendation, advice, encouragement. *susu(meru)* recommend, advise, encourage; offer (wine). *komo* mat.
5 包 *komozutsu(mi)* wrapping in matting; mat-wrapped bundle
7 抜 *sembatsu* recommendation; promoting (someone)
10 骨 *senkotsu* the sacrum
被 *komokaburi* mat-wrapped saké cask
挙 *senkyo* recommendation

薔 5220 / J692c / M32113 SHOKU, SHŌ a kind of grass.
16 薇 *bara, shōbi, ibara* rose, rosebush
薇水晶 *bara suishō* rose quartz
薇石英 *bara sekiei* rose quartz
薇色 *bara iro* rose color, rose pink
薇園 *baraen* rose garden

薙 5221 / J4665 / M32121 TEI. *na(gu)* mow down (the enemy).
2 刀 *naginata* halberd
5 立 *na(gi)-ta(teru)* mow down right and left
6 伏 *na(gi)-fu(seru)* cut down
10 倒 *na(gi)-tao(su)* mow down (the enemy)
射 *chisha* strafing; heavy gunfire
14 髪 *chihatsu, teihatsu* tonsure, cutting off the hair

B **薪** 5222 / J3f45 / M32149' SHIN. *maki* firewood. *takigi* firewood, kindling, fuel.
4 木 *shimboku* firewood
水 *shinsui* fuel and water; cooking; salary; board
7 材 *shinzai* branches for firewood
9 屋 *makiya, takigiya* firewood dealer
炭 *shintan* wood and charcoal, fuel
炭商 *shintanshō* fuel business
12 割 *takigiwa(ri), makiwa(ri)* chopping wood; ax, hatchet

B **薫** 5223 / J3730 / M32173 **薰** 5226 / J-X / M32192 KUN. *kun(zuru)* send forth fragrance, be scented, impregnate with. *kao(ru)* smell, be fragrant. *kuyu(rasu)* smoke (tabacco); burn (incense). *kao(ri)* fragrance, perfume, aroma, odor, scent, smell.
4 化 *kunka* influencing people by one's virtue
8 物 *takimono* incense

育 *kun'iku* moral education
9 風 *kumpū* balmy breeze
香 *kunkō* incense, fragrance
染 *kunsen* being under good influence
10 陶 *kuntō* education, training, instruction, discipline
13 煙 *kun'en* fragrant smoke
14 製 *kunsei* smoking (fish or pork)

A **薬** 5224 / J4c74 / M32188' **藥** 5236 / J693b / M32341 YAKU medicine. *kusuri* medicine; glaze, enamel; chemical; gunpowder; benefit.
2 九層倍 *kusurikusōbai* the high cost of medicine
4 方 *yakuhō* prescription, formula
5 玉 *kusudama* decorative rosette
代 *kusuridai*, *yakudai* medical fee, doctor's fee, charge for medicine
礼 *yakurei* medical charge
用 *yakuyō* medicinal use
用石鹼 *yakuyō sekken* medicated soap
石 *yakuseki* medical treatment
石效無 *yakuseki kō na(ku)* in spite of all medical treatment
包 *yakuhō* gun cartridge; a wrapped dose of medicine
包紙 *yakuhōshi* a paper wrapping for a dose of medicine
6 缶 *yakan* teakettle
7 売 *kusuriu(ri)* medicine salesman
局 *yakkyoku* dispensary, medical office, pharmacy
局方 *yakkyokuhō* pharmacopoeia
8 店 *yakuten* drugstore
価 *yakuka*, *yakka* medical charge
味 *yakumi* spices, flavor, seasoning; the taste of a medicine
効 *yakkō* medicinal value, remedial result
物 *yakubutsu* medicines, drugs, *materia medica*
物学 *yakubutsugaku* pharmacology, *materia medica*
物学者 *yakubutsu gakusha* pharmacologist
物療法 *yakubutsu ryōhō* medication, medicinal therapy
学 *yakugaku* pharmacology
学士 *Yakugakushi* Bachelor of Pharmacology
学者 *yakugakusha* pharmacologist
学博士 *Yakugaku Hakushi* Doctor of Pharmacology
9 屋 *kusuriya* drug store
指 *kusuriyubi* third finger, ring finger
研 *yagen* druggist's mortar
品 *yakuhin* medicines, drugs, chemicals
室 *yakushitsu* dispensary, pharmacy; powder chamber
草 *yakusō* medicinal plants
草学 *yakusōgaku* medicinal botany
草園 *yakusōen* a garden of medicinal plants
10 師 *Yakushi* the Buddha of healing
酒 *yakushu* saké containing medicine
莢 *yakkyō* cartridge, cartridge case
剤 *yakuzai* medicine, drugs, compounded medicines
剤学 *yakuzaigaku* pharmacology
剤師 *yakuzaishi* pharmacist
11 液 *yakueki* liquid medicine
瓶 *kusuribin*, *yakubin* vial, medicine bottle
袋 *yakutai* small paper containers for dispensing medicine
理的 *yakuriteki* pharmacological
12 湯 *kusuriyu*, *yakutō* medicated bath
筒 *yakutō* cartridge
13 園 *yakuen* medicinal-herb garden
14 種 *yakushu* drugs, pharmacopoeia, materia medica
種商 *yakushushō* druggist
15 餌 *yakuji* medicine; medicine and food
箱 *kusuribako* medicine chest
舗 *yakuho* drugstore
22 嚢 *yakunō* medicine bag; cartridge bag
籠 *yakurō* medicine chest
籠中物 *yakurōchū (no) mono* a puppet, a tool (in someone's hand)
25 鑵 *yakan* teakettle
鑵頭 *yakan atama* bald head

B **薄** 5225 / J4776 / M32083' HAKU. *usu(i)* thin, weak (tea), light, pale, faint, scanty, ungenerous. *usu(meru)* dilute, weaken. *usu(ragu)*, *usu(rogu)*, *usu(reru)* thin, thin out, fade, grow pale, be toned down, get dim, cool (emotions), abate, lessen, decline. *usu(ppera) na* thin; shallow-minded, superficial, frivolous. *-usu, usu-* thin, weak, scanty, slightly, light (color).
3 刃 *usuba* thin blade; vegetable knife

才 *hakusai* mediocre ability
4 手 *usude* slight wound, minor injury; a thin article
日 *usubi* soft beams of sunlight
片 *hakuhen* thin leaf, thin layer; splinter, potsherd
切 *usugi(ri)* slicing thin
化粧 *usugeshō* light makeup
5 白 *usushiro(i)* off-white
皮 *hakuhi* thin leather. *usukawa* thin skin, film, thin layer, membrane; scum
目 *usume* rather light, comparatively thin; half-closed eyes
収 *hakushū* a small income
氷 *hakuhyō, usugōri* thin ice; danger
6 色 *usu iro* light color, pale color
行 *hakkō* careless behavior
衣 *usugoromo, hakui* thin garment; shabby garment
地 *usuji* thin cloth; thin metal
汚 *usugitana(i)* filthy, dirty, bedraggled
光 *hakkō* pale light, faint light
肉彫 *usunikubo(ri)* low relief, bas-relief
気味悪 *usukimi (no) waru(i), usukimiwaru(i)* weird, uncanny, eerie, unearthly; ominous
7 赤 *usuaka(i)* light red
利 *hakuri* small profits, narrow margin, low interest
利多売 *hakuri-tabai* small profits and large sales
志 *hakushi* weakness of mind; weakness of purpose; small token of gratitude
志弱行 *hakushi-jakkō* weak purpose and indecision
8 明 *hakumei, usuaka(ri)* twilight, dawn. *usuakaru(i)* dim; gloomy, somber
物 *usumono* thin silk, flimsy dress
盲 *usumekura* gravel-blindness
命 *hakumei* evil fate, misfortune
幸 *hakkō* misfortune, bad luck
板 *hakuhan, usuita* thin plate, sheet
板硝子 *usuita garasu* sheet glass
9 柿 *usugaki* light persimmon color
紅 *usubeni, usukurenai* light crimson; light rouge
茶 *usucha* weak tea
茶色 *usuchairo* light brown, buff
10 俸 *hakuhō* low salary
倖 *hakkō* misfortune, bad luck
桜 *usuzakura* slightly tinted cherry blossoms
紙 *usugami* thin paper, tissue paper
紗 *hakusa* delicate gauze, gossamer
笑 *usuwara(i)* faint smile
弱 *hakujaku* flimsiness, weakness; feebleness, infirmity
桃色 *usumomoiro* peach-blossom pink
馬鹿 *usubaka* fool, simpleton, sluggard, half-wit
荷 *hakka* mint, peppermint
荷水 *hakkasui* peppermint solution
荷油 *hakkayu* peppermint oil
荷脳 *hakkanō* menthol crystals
荷糖 *hakkatō* peppermint
11 黒 *usuguro(i)* dark, dusky, dingy
遇 *hakugū* cold reception
運 *hakuun* evil fate, misfortune
情 *hakujō* poor sense of duty; unkindness; cruelty; coldheartedness
商 *usuakina(i)* light trading
雪 *usuyuki* light snow; sugar-coated cookie
野呂 *usunoro* stupidity
12 給 *hakkyū* meager salary
鈍 *usunoro* simpleton, sluggard, half-wit
寒 *usu(ra)samu(i)* chilly
着 *usugi* thin clothing, scanty clothes
葉 *usuyō* thin paper, tracing paper
雲 *usugumo* thin clouds, fleecy clouds
紫 *usumurasaki* light purple, orchid
痘痕 *usuabata* light pockmarks
13 塩 *usujio* slightly salted
暗 *usugura(i)* dim; gloomy, somber. *usukura(gari)* dim light, gloom, dusk
絹 *usuginu* thin silk, sheer silk
14 層 *hakusō* thin layer, seam (in geology)
徳 *hakutoku* easy virtue
緑 *usumidori* light green
綿 *usuwata* light cotton padding
暮 *hakubo* nightfall, dusk, twilight
墨 *usuzumi* thin India ink
15 縁 *usuberi* bordered matting, thin matting
16 曇 *usugumo(ri)* slightly cloudy
薄 *usu-usu* thinly, slightly, vaguely, a little
髭 *usuhige* thin beard
鋼板 *usukōban* sheet steel
17 謝 *hakusha* small token of gratitude
霞 *usugasumi* light haze
18 織 *usuo(ri)* gauze
藤色 *usufujiiro* lilac color
19 霧 *usugiri* thin mist

14

薰 5226 J-X M32192 See 薫 5223.

藏 5227 J6936 M32264 See 蔵 5182.

薺 5228 J6935 M32208 SEI, ZAI puncture vine, burnut. *nazuna* shepherd's purse, a mother's heart.

薹 5229 J6937 M32204 TAI. *to* seed pod.

薯 5230 J-X M32191 SHO. *imo* potato.

藉 5231 J6934 M32242 SHA, SEKI rug; borrow; lend; make excuses; spread out.

3 口 *shakō* pretense

藐 5232 J6938 M32267 BAKU far, distant. BYŌ small; regard lightly.

11 視 *byōshi suru* regard lightly, treat with contempt

藍 5233 J4d75 M32258 RAN. *ai* indigo (blue); indigo plant.

5 玉 *rangyoku* aquamarine (a gem), *aidama* indigo ball

6 色 *ai iro, ranshoku* dark blue

13 鼠 *ainezumi* bluish gray

16 靛 *ranjō* indigo

藁 5234 J4f4e M32222 KŌ. *wara* straw.

2 人形 *wara ningyō* straw effigy

4 火 *warabi* straw fire

5 半紙 *warabanshi* a low-grade paper

打機 *warau(chi)ki* straw-softening machine

6 灰 *warabai* straw ashes

8 沓 *waragutsu* straw shoes

苞 *warazuto* straw wrapper

9 屋根 *wara yane* straw roof

草履 *wara zōri* straw sandals

10 紙 *waragami* rice paper

家 *waraya* straw-thatched hut

11 細工 *warazaiku* straw work

12 葺 *warabuki* straw thatch

13 靴 *waragutsu* straw shoes

筵 *wara mushiro* straw mat; straw matting

蒲団 *warabuton* straw mattress, straw pallet

15 縄 *wara nawa* straw rope

15

藝 5235 J693a M32330 See 芸 4978.

藥 5236 J693b M32341 See 薬 5224.

藷 5237 J3d73 M-X Nonstandard for 藷 5247.

藜 5238 J693c M32326 REI. *akaza* wild spinach, goosefoot.

藕 5239 J6939 M32298 GŪ carpet; lend; borrow.

7 花 *gūke* lotus

藪 5240 J692e M32348 **籔** 4372 J6458 M26708 SŌ. *yabu* thicket, bush, underbrush, grove.

2 入 *yabui(ri)* servants' day, apprentices' holiday

7 医 *yabui* quack doctor

医者 *yabu isha* quack doctor

11 蛇 *yabuhebi* boomerang, hornet's nest, stirring up unnecessary trouble

13 睨 *yabunira(mi)* squint, cross-eye; wrong view

藤 5241 J4623 M32340' TŌ. *fuji* wisteria.

4 氏 *Tōshi* Fujiwara family

6 色 *fuji iro* light purple, lilac, mauve, lavender

7 花 *tōka* wisteria blossoms

8 波 *fujinami* waves of wisteria flowers

10 浪 *fujinami* waves of wisteria flowers

12 棚 *fujidana* wisteria trellis

壺 *fujitsubo* barnacle

紫 *fuji murasaki* dark lilac, smalt, powder blue

6 竹米糸缶网罒羊羽老耂而耒耳聿肉月臣自至臼舌舛舟艮色【艸艹】虍虫血行衣衤西

15

藩 5242 / J484d / M32346' B HAN feudal clan; enclosure.
3 士 *hanshi* retainer
4 内 *hannai* within the fief
5 札 *hansatsu* a daimyo's paper money
主 *hanshu* feudal lord, daimyo
6 老 *hanrō* head retainer
7 邸 *hantei* daimyo's estate; daimyo's Edo estate
兵 *hampei* a daimyo's soldiers
8 治 *hanchi* government of a fief
学 *hangaku* school for samurai children
9 侯 *hankō* daimyo
政 *hansei* clan government
10 校 *hankō* clan schools
恩 *han'on* the favor of a daimyo
11 屏 *hampei* bulwark, pillar
12 営 *han'ei* operated by the clan
14 閥 *hambatsu* clanship, clannism
境 *hankyō* boundary of a fief
16 儒 *hanju* a daimyo's scholar
20 籍 *hanseki* fief

16

蘂 5243 / J6922 / M32410 See 蕊 5188.

蘆 5244 / J6943 / M32425 See 芦 4975.

藾 5245 / J6941 / M32405 RAI a type of mugwort.

蘢 5246 / J6944 / M32438 RŌ. *ōkedate* smartweed.

藷 5247 / J-X / M32391 SHO. *imo* potato.

蘋 5248 / J6940 / M32435 HIN water weeds; water plants.
11 菜 *hinsai* edible water plants

藹 5249 / J693d / M32397 AI flourishing; be luxuriant; harmonize. *rō(taketa)* graceful, noble, refined.
19 藹 *aiai to* harmoniously, peacefully

蘊 5250 / J693e / M32434 UN pile up.
12 奥 *un'ō, unnō* abstruse principles, esoteric doctrines, mysteries
13 蓄 *unchiku* erudition, learning

藺 5251 / J6942 / M32399 RIN. *i* a rush (used for *tatami* covers).
9 草 *igusa* a rush (used for *tatami* mats)
10 莚 *imushiro* rush mat

蘇 5252 / J4149 / M32427 **穌** 5253 / J693f / M-X SO. SU. *yomigae(ru)* be resurrected, be revived, be resuscitated, be rehabilitated. *yomigae(ri)* resurrection; reviving, resuscitation; rehabilitation. *-So-* Soviet Union.
5 生 *sosei* revival, resuscitation; resurrection
9 連 *Soren* Union of Soviet Socialist Republics
連邦 *Sorempō* Soviet Union
連圏 *Sorenken* Soviet sphere of influence
12 満 *So-Man* Soviet Union and Manchuria

藻 5254 / J4174 / M32401 B SŌ. *mo* duckweed, seaweed.
7 抜 *monu(ke)* cast-off skin
10 屑 *mokuzu* seaweeds
13 塩 *moshio* salt from burning seaweed
塩草 *moshiogusa* seaweed used in making salt; anthology
18 類 *sōrui* seaweeds

蘭 5255 / J4d76 / M32477' **蘭** 5257 / J-X / M32519 RAN orchid; Dutch.
2 人 *Ranjin* Dutch people
4 方 *Rampō* Dutch medicine
方医学 *Rampō igaku* Dutch medicine
6 印 *Ran'in* Netherlands East Indies
7 医 *Ran'i* Dutch physician
8 学 *Rangaku* study of the Dutch language
14 語 *Rango* the Dutch language
領東印度諸島 *Ranryō Higashi Indo Shotō* Netherlands East Indies

17

蘯 5256 / J623c / M32532 See 蕩 5198.

蘭 5257 / J-X / M32519 See 蘭 5255.

蘗 5258 / J5d22 / M32479 Getsu. Haku stump; root.

蘰 5259 / J6946 / M32541 (国字) *katsura, kazura* vine.

蘖 5260 / J5d31 / M32478 Getsu. *hikobae* sprout, offshoot, shoot.

蘞 5261 / J-X / M32490 Ren a kind of weed.

7 辛 *egara(i), egara(ppoi)* acrid, pungent

蘚 5262 / J6945 / M32483 Sen moss.

8 苔学 *sentaigaku* bryology, the study of mosses

18 類 *senrui* moss, lichen

— 19 —

蘿 5263 / J6947 / M32590 Ra ivy.

RAD. 虍 141

Tora kammuri or *toragashira* "tiger" top—really an enclosure. Nickname: Tiger.

虍 5264 / J6948 / M32674 Ko tiger-spots, mottled.

— 2 —

虎 5265 / J3857 / M32675 Ko. *tora* tiger, drunkard.

3 口 *kokō* very dangerous place; tiger's den

子 *omaru* bedpan, pot. *tora (no) ko* tiger cub; one's treasure; one's savings

4 刈 *toraga(ri)* close-cropped (head)

5 穴 *koketsu* tiger's den; dangerous place

9 狩 *toraga(ri)* tiger hunt

巻 *tora (no) maki* pony, answer book; trade secrets; the trump card; the authority; the open sesame

挟 *torabusami* rattrap, steel trap

10 狼 *korō* tiger and wolf; wild beast; cruel man, brute

11 視 *koshi suru* glare at

視眈眈 *koshi-tantan* on the alert; gloatingly; with vigilant hostility

12 斑 *torafu, torabuchi* tiger's stripes

16 嘯 *koshō* tiger's roar; hero's exploits

22 鬚 *torahige* bristly beard

— 4 —

虔 5266 / J694a / M32686 Ken respect; be just.

B **虐** 5267 / J3554 / M32678' Gyaku. *shiita(geru)* oppress, tyrannixe.

3 刃 *gyakujin* a cruel killing

8 使 *gyakushi* driving hard, immoderation, abuse; exploitation

9 待 *gyakutai* mistreatment, abuse, cruelty

政 *gyakusei* tyranny, despotism, oppressive government

10 悩 *shiita(ge)-naya(masu)* oppress and afflict

殺 *gyakusatsu* massacre, butchery, carnage

11 遇 *gyakugū* mistreatment, abuse, cruelty

— 5 —

處 5268 / J313d / M32697 See 処 435.

B **虚** 5269 / J3575 / M32708 **虛** 5270 / J-X / M32709 Kyo, Ko emptiness; unpreparedness; crack, fissure; unguarded position; untruth. *muna(shiku) suru* make empty. *uro* cavity, hollow, hole. *ukke* emptiness. *muna(shii)* void, empty, vain; ineffective; lifeless.

3 士 *kyoshi* careless critic; samurai in name only

4 文 *kyobun* worthless argument; mere surface decoration

日 *kyojitsu* day of leisure

心 *kyoshin* disinterestedness, lack of prejudice

心坦懐 *kyoshin tankai* frankness

5 礼 *kyorei* formalities, empty forms

6 伝 *kyoden* false rumor, false reputation
妄 *kyomō, kyobō* falsehood, something unsubstantiated; delusion, superstition
名 *kyomei* notoriety, false reputation, publicity
仮 *koke* dunce, idiot
仮威 *kokeodo(shi)* empty threat, bluff, imposing display
7 言 *kyogen* falsehood
位 *kyoi* titular post; vacant post
声 *kyosei* threatening voice
労 *kyorō* emaciation
8 実 *kyojitsu* truth and falsehood; preparedness and unpreparedness; the situation
空 *kokū* empty space, empty sky
空摑 *kokū (o) tsuka(mu)* struggle for breath
9 威 *kyoi* empty boasting
乗 *kyo (ni) jō(jiru)* take advantage of someone's negligence
室 *kyoshitsu* an empty house
栄 *kyoei* vanity, vainglory
栄心 *kyoeishin* vanity, vainglory
10 病 *kyobyō* feigned illness
耗 *kyomō* deterioration; disappearance; emaciation
弱 *kyojaku* feebleness, weakness; imbecility
弱児童 *kyojaku jidō* feeble children
弱者 *kyojakusha* feeble person
11 虚実実 *kyokyo-jitsujitsu* clever competition; clever fighting
偽 *kyogi* falsehood, fiction, fallacy
偽申告 *kyogi shinkoku* perjury
脱 *kyodatsu* prostration, collapse
脱状態 *kyodatsu jōtai* despondency
12 報 *kyohō* false alarm
無 *kyomu* nothingness
無主義 *kyomu shugi* nihilism
無党 *kyomutō* nihilists
無僧 *komusō* flute-playing Zen mendicant priests, mendicant flute player
13 辞 *kyoji* a lie, falsehood
飾 *kyoshoku* ostentation, show, affectation
数 *kyosū* imaginary number
勢 *kyosei* bluff
勢張 *kyosei (o) ha(ru)* boast without reason
14 聞 *kyobun* false rumor; false reputation
像 *kyozō* virtual image, ghost image (in optics)
構 *kyokō* fabrication, falsehood
説 *kyosetsu* false report; false theory
静 *kyosei* a calm and carefree heart
15 線 *kyosen* dotted line
談 *kyodan* baseless talk, rumor; false theory; Taoist talk; idle talk
誕 *kyotan* falsehood, fiction, fallacy
論 *kyoron* false argument
器 *kyoki* something in name only; nominal position
16 懐 *kyokai* a carefree heart

6

虛 5270 / J-X / M32709 See **虚** 5269.

7

號 5271 / J694b / M32726 See **号** 692.

B **虞** 5272 / J3673 / M32723' GU. *osore* fear; anxiety; concern; uneasiness.
9 美人草 *gubijinsō* field poppy, red poppy

B **虜** 5273 / J4e3a / M32720' RYO captive; barbarian; low epithet for the enemy.
toriko captive, victim, slave.
5 囚 *ryoshū* captive, prisoner
16 獲 *ryokaku* captive; capturing alive; capturing and killing

11

虧 5274 / J694c / M32770 KI wane. *ka(keru)* (the moon) wanes.
4 月 *kigetsu* waning moon
13 損 *kison suru* break

RAD. 虫 142

Mushi insect. At left: *mushi hen*. Nickname: Bug.

A 虫 5275/J436e/M32804 蟲 5384/J6a35/M33633 CHŪ. *mushi* worm, vermin, bug, insect; temper; nervousness, peevishness; bad company.

3 干 *mushibo(shi)* airing (clothes and books)
下 *mushikuda(shi)* worm medicine
6 気 *mushike* bowel complaint, nervous weakness, trouble with worms
7 良 *mushi(no)i(i)* selfish; arbitrary
売 *mushiu(ri)* insect dealer
声 *chūsei* the humming of insects
8 送 *mushioku(ri)* torch procession to drive away insects
知 *mushi (ga) shi(rasu)* have a premonition
供養 *mushi kuyō* Buddhist memorial service for the bugs killed by the farmers plowing their fields
垂 *chūsui* the appendix
垂切除術 *chūsui setsujojutsu* appendectomy
垂炎 *chūsuien* appendicitis
9 食 *mushiba(mu)* be wormy. *mushiku(i)* worm-eaten spot
除 *mushiyo(ke)* insect powder, charm against insects
封 *mushifū(ji)* exorcism
10 害 *chūgai* insect pests, insect damage, blight
11 唾 *mushizu* sour eructation
眼鏡 *mushimegane* magnifying glass
12 歯 *mushiba* decayed tooth
喰 *mushikui* worm-eaten spot
媒花 *chūbaika* flower fertilized by insects
13 腹 *mushibara* worm pains
14 様垂 *chūyōsui* vermiform appendix
様突起 *chūyō tokki* the appendix
様突起炎 *chūyō tokkien* appendicitis
16 薬 *mushigusuri* worm medicine
17 螻 *mushikera* worm, insect; someone beneath one's notice
18 類 *chūrui* worms and insects
22 籠 *mushikago* insect case

2

虱 5276/J694d/M32812 蝨 5347/J697c/M33303 SHITSU. *shirami* lice, vermin.

15 潰 *shiramitsubu(shi) ni* one by one, individually

3

虻 5277/J303a/M32835 蝱 5278/J-X/M32836 蝱 5346/J-X/M33318 BŌ. *abu* horsefly, gadfly.

虹 5279/J467a/M32830 KŌ. *niji* rainbow.

11 彩 *kōsai* iris (of the eye)
23 鱒 *niji masu* rainbow trout

4

蚜 5280/J-X/M32882 See 蚜 5298.

蚌 5281/J6953/M32851 BŌ. HŌ *dobugai, karasugai* fresh-water mussel. *hamaguri* clam.

蚣 5282/J694f/M32892 SHŌ, KŌ insect.

蚩 5283/J6950/M32902 SHI insect; fool; confused.

蚪 5284/J6951/M32903 To tadpole.

蚓 5285/J694e/M32866 IN earthworm.

蚋 5286/J6952/M32850 蜹 5315/J-X/M33201 ZEI. NEI. ZETSU. NECHI. *buyu, buyo, butto* gnat, sand fly.

3 子 *buyu, buyo* gnat, sand fly

蚤 5287 / J4742 / M32893 Sō. *nomi* flea.
8 取 *nomito(ri)* flea catching; flea powder
取粉 *nomito(ri)ko* flea powder
取眼 *nomito(ri) manako* keen eyes

B **蚊** 5288 / J3263 / M32849 **蚉** 5289 / J-X / M32848 BUN. *ka* mosquito.
8 取線香 *katori senkō* mosquito incense
9 屋 *kaya* mosquito net
姥 *ga(no)uba, kagambo, gagambo* daddy longlegs
柱 *kabashira* column of flying mosquitoes
除 *kayo(ke)* mosquito smudge; mosquito net
10 針 *kabari* fishing fly, fly hook
11 帳 *kaya, kachō* mosquito net
帳地 *kayaji* mosquito netting
12 遣 *kayari* mosquito smudge
遣火 *kayaribi* mosquito smudge
遣線香 *kayari senkō* mosquito incense
13 鉤 *kabari* fishing fly, fly hook
18 燻 *kafusu(be), kaibu(shi)* smoking out mosquitoes

A **蚕** 5290 / J3b3d / M32869 **蠶** 5410 / J6a44 / M33890 SAN. *kaiko* silkworm.
6 糸 *sanshi* silk thread, silk yarn
糸業 *sanshigyō* sericulture industry
糸試験所 *sanshi shikenjo* silk experiment station
7 豆 *soramame* broad bean, horse bean
児 *sanji* silkworm
卵 *sanran* silkworm egg
卵紙 *sanranshi* silkworm-egg card
8 具 *sangu* sericultural equipment
9 食 *sanshoku* encroachment, aggression, inroad, invasion
室 *sanshitsu* silkworm-raising room
10 座 *sanza* silkworm basket
紙 *sanshi* silkworm-egg card
13 業 *sangyō* sericulture
14 種 *sanshu* silkworm-egg card

5

蛎 5291 / J3342 / M-X Nonstandard for 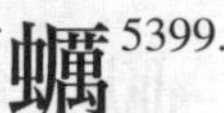 5399.

蚶 5292 / J6954 / M32925 KAN. GAN. *akagai* an ark shell.

蚫 5293 / J695b / M32984 (国字) *awabi* abalone.

蛉 5294 / J6959 / M32969 REI dragonfly; moon moth.

蛄 5295 / J6956 / M32960 KO, KU a mole cricket; cicada.

蛅 5296 / J-X / M32961 SEN larva of a moth; grub.
18 蟖 *kemushi* caterpillar

蚰 5297 / J6958 / M32918 YŪ millipede.
13 蜒 *gejigeji* millipede; wretch

蚜 5298 / J-X / M-X **蚜** 5280 / J-X / M32882 KA plant louse, aphis.
6 虫 *aburamushi* plant louse, aphis

蛆 5299 / J6957 / M32963 SO. *uji* worm, grub, maggot, larva.
6 虫 *ujimushi* worm, grub, maggot, larva

蚯 5300 / J6955 / M32916 KYŪ earthworm.
10 蚓 *mimizu* earthworm
蚓書 *mimizuga(ki)* scrawl
蚓腫 *mimizubare* welt, inflamed scratch

蛋 5301 / J4341 / M32977 TAN barbarian; egg.
5 白 *tampaku* protein; albumen
白石 *tampakuseki* opal
白石映光 *tampakuseki eikō* opalescence
白光 *tampakukō* opalescence
白質 *tampakushitsu* protein; albumen

B **蛍** 5302 / J3756 / M32983 **螢** 5365 / J6a25 / M33434 KEI. *hotaru* firefly.
4 火 *keika* light of a firefly. *hotarubi* the light of a firefly; small banked fire (charcoal)
5 石 *keiseki, hotaru ishi* fluorspar, fluorite
6 光 *keikō* fluorescence. *hotaru (no) hikari* light of a firefly
光灯 *keikōtō* fluorescent light
光体 *keikōtai* fluorescent body
光板 *keikōban* flourescent screen or plate

光物質 *keikō busshitsu* fluorescent body
光染料 *keikō senryō* fluorescent dyes
光透視法 *keikōtōshihō* fluoroscopy
光塗料 *keikō toryō* fluorescent paint
9 狩 *hotaruga(ri)* firefly catching
11 雪 *keisetsu* diligent study
雪功 *keisetsu (no) kō* the fruit of diligent study
雪時代 *keisetsu jidai* school days

B **蛇** 5303 J3c58 M32964 JA, DA (large) snake, serpent; hard drinker. *hebi, kuchinawa* snake.
3 口 *jaguchi* faucet, hydrant; drain
5 皮 *hebikawa* snakeskin
目 *ja (no) me* bulls-eye; umbrella with a bulls-eye design
目傘 *ja(no)megasa* umbrella with a bulls-eye design
6 行 *dakō suru* crawl meanderingly. *dakō* meandering
7 足 *dasoku* superfluity, redundancy, padding
身 *jashin* snakelike body
体 *jatai no* serpentine
状運動 *dajō undō* serpentine motion
8 使 *hebitsuka(i)* snake charmer
毒 *jadoku* snake poison, venom
10 紋石 *jamonseki* serpentine (a gem)
13 腹 *jubaru* bellows; cornice
14 管 *jakan* hose
19 蠍視 *dakatsushi suru* detest, hate like poison
22 籠 *jakago* gabion, rock-filled bamboo embankment basket

6

蛩 5304 J695e M33037 KYŌ *kōrogi* cricket.

蛬 5305 J695f M33047 KYŌ *kōrogi* cricket. *kigirisu* praying mantis.

蛯 5306 J6962 M33061 (国字) *ebi* shrimp, prawn.

蛛 5307 J6961 M33002 CHU spider.

蛭 5308 J4948 M33048 SHITSU. *hiru* leech.

蛞 5309 J695d M33008 KATSU a kind of slug.
15 蝓 *namekuji* slug, dew snail

蛔 5310 J695c M32990 KAI intestinal worms.
6 虫 *kaichū* round intestinal worm

蛟 5311 J6960 M33009 KŌ dragon.
10 竜 *kōryō* rain dragon; hidden genius

蛤 5312 J483a M33023 KŌ. *hamaguri* clam.
17 鍋 *hamanabe, hamagurinabe* clam chowder

蛙 5313 J333f M32997 A. *kaeru, kawazu* frog.
7 足 *kaeruashi* frog kick (in swimming)
8 泳 *kaeruoyo(gi)* breast stroke
9 飛 *kawazuto(bi)* leapfrog, island hopping
11 釣 *kaerutsuri* frog fishing
13 跳 *kaerutobi* leapfrog

B **蛮** 5314 J485a M33044 **蠻** 5409 J6a47 M33914 BAN barbarian.
2 人 *banjin* savage, barbarian
力 *banryoku* brute force
5 民 *bammin* savage people
6 行 *bankō* barbarism, brutality
地 *banchi* barbaric region
7 声 *bansei* rough voice
8 的 *banteki* savage, barbarous, rustic
9 風 *bampū* barbarian customs
勇 *ban'yū* brute courage, reckless valor, foolhardiness
10 骨 *bankotsu* brute courage, recklessness
11 族 *banzoku* savage tribe
習 *banshū* barbarous custom
14 境 *bankyō* land of the barbarians
語 *bango* aboriginal language; language of the barbarians
16 隷 *banrei* slaves of the barbarians
18 襟 *bankara* uncouthness; rough person

7

蛹 5315 J-X M33201 See **蛹** 5286.

6 竹米糸缶网罒羊羽老耂而耒耳聿肉月臣自至臼舌舛舟艮色艸艹虍 7【虫】血行衣衤西

蜑 5316 J6969 M33119 TAN minority ethnic group in China. *ama* diver; fisherman.

蜒 5317 J6963 M33120 EN meandering, serpentine.

蜓 5318 J-X M33121 TEI millipede; lizard.

蜊 5319 J696d M33106 RI a kind of bivalve.

蜍 5320 J696b M33110 SHO toad.

蜋 5321 J-X M33108 — **螂** 5348 J6a27 M33362 RŌ mantis.

蛻 5322 J6968 M33078 ZEI. *monu(keru)* (insects) molt; excel. *monuke* cast-off skin.

蜈 5323 J6965 M33099 GO centipede.
10 蚣 *gokō* centipede

蜉 5324 J696a M33104 FU kind of ant; May fly.
15 蝣 *fuyū* May fly; something ephemeral

蛾 5325 J326b M33082 GI. GA moth.
9 眉 *gabi* arched eyebrows; a beauty

蛹 5326 J696c M33076 YŌ *sanagi* chrysalis, pupa.
6 虫 *yōchū* chrysalis, pupa

蜃 5327 J6967 M33089 SHIN clam.
6 気楼 *shinkirō* mirage

蜆 5328 J6964 M33093 KEN. *shijimi* a fresh-water clam.
5 汁 *shijimijiru* fresh-water-clam soup
7 貝 *shijimigai* a fresh-water clam

蜀 5329 J6966 M33086 SHOKU Szechwan; green caterpillar.
12 葵 *tachiaoi* hollyhock
黍 *morokoshi, shokusho* Indian millet; sorghum, kaoliang
黍粉 *morokoshiko* cornmeal

蛸 5330 J427d M33072 SŌ. SHŌ. *tako* octopus, devilfish; pile driver; dirt tamper.
2 入道 *takonyūdō* octopus; bald-headed man; ram
7 坊主 *tako bōzu* octopus; bald-headed man
10 配当 *tako haitō* bogus dividend (from fictitious profits)
11 船 *takobune* paper nautilus
12 壺 *takotsubo* octopus trap; foxhole

蜂 5331 J4b2a M33088 HŌ. *hachi* bee, wasp, hornet.
8 房 *hōbō* honeycomb; beehive; apiary
10 起 *hōki* insurrection; disturbance
11 鳥 *hachidori* hummingbird
雀 *hachisuzume* hummingbird
巣 *hachi (no) su* beehive, honeycomb
13 腰 *hōyō* slender waist
14 蜜 *hachimitsu* honey
窩 *hōka* beehive
21 蠟 *hachirō* beeswax, bee glue

8

蜡 5332 J4f39 M-X Nonstandard for **蠟** 5403.

蝕 5333 J3f2a M-X Nonstandard for **蝕** 5358.

蜩 5334 J6973 M33166 CHO *higurashi* clear-toned cicada.

蜴 5335 J696e M33190 EKI lizard.

蜱 5336 J-X M33182 *dani* tick, mite.

蜿 5337 J696f M33210 EN meandering.
13 蜒 *en'en taru* meandering, serpentine

蜥 5338 J6972 M33157 SHAKU, SEKI a lizard.
14 蜴 *tokage* lizard

蜷 5339 / J6970 / M33199 KEN. *nina* a small spiral edible river shell.

7 局 *toguro* coil, spiral

蜚 5340 / J6974 / M33138 HI cockroach.

14 語 *higo* rumor, gossip

蜻 5341 / J6971 / M33203 SEI dragonfly.

11 蛉 *tombo* dragonfly

蛉返 *tombogae(ri)* somersault; looping the loop

蛉釣 *tombotsu(ri)* dragonfly catching; dragonfly catcher

13 蜓 *tombo* dragonfly

蜘 5342 / J4358 / M33134 CHI spider.

12 蛛 *kumo* spider

蛛千 *kumode* crossing of many streets, confusion of mind *kumode ni* crosswise; in various directions

蛛巣 *kumo (no) su* spiderweb

蛛蟹 *kumogani* spider crab

蜜 5343 / J4c2a / M33143 MITSU honey, nectar, molasses, honeydew.

4 月 *mitsugetsu* honeymoon

7 豆 *mitsumame* boiled beans with treacle

8 房 *mitsubo* honeycomb

9 柑 *mikan* tangerine, mandarin orange

13 蜂 *mitsubachi* honeybee

21 蠟 *mitsurō* beeswax

9

蝿 5344 / J4768 / M-X Nonstandard for 蠅 5394.

蟒 5345 / J6a3d / M-X Nonstandard for 蟒 5367.

蝱 5346 / J-X / M33318 See 虻 5277.

蝨 5347 / J697c / M33303 See 虱 5276.

蝍 5348 / J6a27 / M33362 See 蜋 5321.

蝉 5349 / J4066 / M-X Nonstandard for 蟬 5388.

蝪 5350 / J6a23 / M33305 TŌ spider.

蝓 5351 / J6a21 / M33261 YU slug, snail.

蝣 5352 / J6a22 / M33292 YŪ May fly.

蝠 5353 / J6975 / M33288 FUKU bat.

蝎 5354 / J6979 / M33254 **蠍** 5389 / J6a38 / M33707 KATSU. *sasori* scorpion.

蝮 5355 / J697d / M33309 FUKU. *mamushi* viper, adder, asp.

蝴 5356 / J697a / M33328 KO butterfly.

15 蝶 *kochō* butterfly

蝌 5357 / J6978 / M33248 KA tadpole.

10 蚪 *otamajakushi, kato* tadpole

蝕 5358 / J-X / M33264 SHOKU eclipse, occultation; be defective. *mushiba(mu)* be wormy.

9 甚 *shokujin* maximum obscuration (in an eclipse)

蝟 5359 / J6976 / M33287 I. *harinezumi* hedgehog.

12 集 *ishū suru* swarm, throng, flock together

蝙 5360 / J697e / M33271 HEN bat.

15 蝠 *kōmori* bat; umbrella, parasol

蝠傘 *kōmorigasa* umbrella, parasol

蝗 5361 / J697b / M33267 KŌ. *inago, batta* locust.

6 虫 *inago* grasshopper

10 害 *kōgai* locust damage

6 竹米糸缶网罒羊羽老耂而耒耳聿肉月臣自至臼舌舛舟艮色艸艹虍【虫】9 血行衣衤襾

蝸 5362 / J6977 / M33338 KA snail.
4 牛 *katatsumuri, katatsuburi, dedemushi, dendemmushi, kagyū* snail
牛殻 *kagyūkaku* snail shell
19 廬 *karo* little house; my humble home

蝶 5363 / J4433 / M33333 CHŌ butterfly.
7 貝 *chōgai* pearl oyster, mother-of-pearl
形 *chōgata* butterfly-shaped
12 結 *chōmusu(bi)* bowknot
番 *chōtsugai, chōban* hinge, hinge joint
15 蝶 *chōchō* butterfly
17 鮫 *chōzame* sturgeon
18 類 *chōrui* butterflies

蝦 5364 / J325c / M33299 KA. GE. *ebi* lobster, shrimp, prawn.
6 夷 *Ezo* Ainu; Hokkaido. *Emishi, Emisu* Ainu
夷地 *Ezochi* Hokkaido
夷松 *ezo matsu* spruce, silver fir
13 腰 *ebigoshi* bent with age
16 錠 *ebijō* padlock
蟇 *gama* toad, bullfrog
蟇口 *gamaguchi* purse
蟇足 *gama ashi* breast stroke
19 蟹 *ebigani* crawfish, crayfish

10

螢 5365 / J6a25 / M33434 See **蛍** 5302.

螕 5366 / J-X / M33410 HEI. *dani* tick, mite.

蟒 5367 / J-X / M33572 **蠎** 5373 / J6a3c / M33724 BŌ. MŌ. *uwabami* anaconda; boa constrictor; python.

螟 5368 / J6a26 / M33429 MEI an injurious parasite.
6 虫 *meichū* rice borer, pearl moth

蟆 5369 / J6a32 / M33542 **蟇** 5370 / J6a31 / M33543 BA. MA. *hiki* toad.
3 孑 *buyo* gnat, sand fly
12 蛙 *hikigaeru* toad

融 5371 / J4d3b / M33384 B YŪ. *to(keru) vi, to(kasu) vt* dissolve, melt.
4 込 *to(ke)-ko(mu)* melt into, merge into
化 *yūka suru* soften, dissolve
6 合 *yūgō* fusion, union
会 *yūkai* melting together; naturally understanding
8 和 *yūwa* melting; softening; conciliation; soothing
9 点 *yūten* melting point
通 *yūzū* accommodation, financing, loan; circulation; transfer; elasticity, adaptability, versatility
通手形 *yūzū tegata* negotiable paper
通念仏 *Yūzūnembutsu* Buddhist sect originating in the 12th century
10 剤 *yūzai* flux
11 雪 *yūsetsu* thaw, melting snow
12 然 *yūzen to shita* quiet, calm, leisurely
13 解 *yūkai* fusing, melting, dissolving
資 *yūshi* financing
15 熱 *yūnetsu* heat of fusion

11

螳 5372 / J6a30 / M33503 See **蟷** 5393.

蠎 5373 / J6a3c / M33724 See **蟒** 5367.

螗 5374 / J6a2c / M-X (国字) JŌ *momu, momi* frog, toad.

螻 5375 / J6a33 / M33515 RŌ. *kera* a mole cricket.

螯 5376 / J6a28 / M33496 GŌ. *hasami* claws, pincers.

螫 5377 / J6a2e / M33491 SEKI. *sa(su)* (bee's) sting.
13 傷 *sashikizu* a bite (injury)

螽 5378 / J6a2a / M33519 SHŪ grasshopper.
12 斯 *kirigirisu* grasshopper, katydid

蟀 5379 / J6a2b / M33531 SHUTSU cricket; grasshopper.
7 谷 *komekami* temple (of the head)

蟋 5380 / J6a29 / M33550 SHITSU cricket; grasshopper.
17 蟀 *kōrogi* cricket *kirigirisu* grasshopper, katydid

蟄 5381 / J6a2f / M33537 CHITSU. *chis(suru)* hibernation of insects.
6 伏 *chippuku* hibernation; concealment
8 居 *chikkyo suru* be cooped up, stay indoors. *chikkyo* house arrest

螺 5382 / J4d66 / M33512 RA. *nina, nishi* a small edible spiral river shell.
3 子 *neji, rashi* screw, faucet, (watch) spring
子切 *nejiki(ri)* threader; thread cutting
子回 *nejimawa(shi)* screwdriver, wrench
7 状 *rajō* screw shape, spiral
11 階 *rakai* winding staircase
旋 *rasen* screw; spiral; spiral spring
旋状 *rasenjō* screw shape, spiral
旋形 *rasenkei* screw shape; spiral
旋降下 *rasen kōka* spiral dive
旋銃 *rasenjū* rifle
13 鈿 *raden* mother-of-pearl

12

蠎 5383 / J-X / M-X See 蟒 5267.

蟲 5384 / J6a35 / M33633 See 虫 5275.

蟖 5385 / J-X / M33578 SHI larva of a moth; grasshopper.

蟯 5386 / J6a34 / M33626 GYŌ an intestinal worm.
6 虫 *gyōchū* pinworm, threadworm

蟠 5387 / J6a36 / M33591 HAN. BAN. *wadakama(ru)* be coiled up; stretch out tortuously; lurk, be harbored. *wadakama(ri)* vexations, cares; ill feeling; reserve.
15 踞 *bankyo suru* possess and dominate a wide area

蟬 5388 / J-X / M33616 SEN. *semi* cicada, locust.
7 吟 *sengin* cry of the cicada
声 *semigoe* voice like a cricket
10 時雨 *semi shigure* an outburst of cricket chirping
11 脱 *sendatsu* a cicada's shell, leaving this world; a shell only
13 蛻 *senzei* a cicada's shell; leaving this world

13

蠍 5389 / J6a38 / M33707 See 蝎 5354.

蟶 5390 / J6a3a / M33664 TEI. *mate, mategai* razor clam.

蠖 5391 / J6a3f / M33752 KAKU, WAKU inchworm.

蟾 5392 / J6a39 / M33676 SEN toad.
13 蜍 *hikigaeru* toad

蟷 5393 / J6a3b / M33665 螳 5372 / J6a30 / M33503 TŌ mantis.
15 螂 *kamakiri, tōrō* praying mantis

蠅 5394 / J6a24 / M33690 YŌ. *hae, hai* fly.
5 叩 *haitataki* flyswatter
打 *haeu(chi)* flyswatter
8 取 *haeto(ri), haito(ri)* flycatcher
取草 *haito(ri)gusa* Venus' flytrap
取粉 *haito(ri)ko* fly powder
取紙 *haito(ri)gami* flypaper

蟹 5395 / J332a / M33668 蠏 5396 / J6a37 / M33669 KAI. *kani* crab.
3 工船 *kanikōsen* crab-canning ship
4 文字 *kani monji, kani moji* horizontal writing, Western writing
6 行 *kaikō* walking sideways
缶 *kanikan* canned crab
行文字 *kaikō monji, kaikō moji* horizontal writing, Western writing
8 股 *ganimata* bowlegged

蟻 5397 / J3542 / M33672 GI. *ari* ant.
6 地獄 *arijigoku* ant lion
7 町 *ari (no) machi* slum

[9] 軍 *gigun* ant army
巻 *arimaki* ant cow
[10] 差 *arisa(shi)* dovetail joint
[12] 塔 *ari (no) tō* anthill
塚 *arizuka* anthill
集 *gishū suru* swarm, crowd together, flock together
[13] 継 *aritsu(gi)* dovetail joint
[14] 酸 *gisan* formic acid

14

蠑 5398 / J6a3e / M33738 EI, YŌ newt; lizard.

蠣 5399 / J695a / M33799 REI oyster.

蠕 5400 / J6a40 / M33749 ZEN crawling (of a worm), squirming, moving.
[11] 動 *zendō suru* creep, worm along. *zendō* peristaltic movement
動運動 *zendō undō* peristaltic movement

15

蠡 5401 / J6a42 / M33796 REI, RA be worm-eaten; clam shell; snail.

蠢 5402 / J6a41 / M33797 SHUN. *ugome(ku)* wriggle, squirm. *ugome(kasu)* be elated with success.
[11] 動 *shundō* wriggling, squirming; despicable acts

蠟 5403 / J-X / M33786 RŌ wax.
[2] 人形 *rō ningyō* wax figure
[4] 引 *rōbi(ki)* waxing
[5] 石 *rōseki* alabaster, pencil stone
付 *rōzu(ke)* soldering
付鏝 *rōzu(ke) kote* soldering iron
[10] 紙 *rōgami* wax paper
[11] 細工 *rōzaiku* waxwork
[14] 様 *rōyō no* waxy, waxen
製 *rōsei* waxen, wax
[17] 燭 *rōsoku* candle

16

蠹 5404 / J6a46 / M33824 **蠧** 5407 / J6a45 / M33896 To worm-eaten; damage; wicked person.
[8] 毒 *todoku suru* demoralize
[11] 魚 *shimi* clothes moth, silverfish, bookworm
[13] 賊 *tozoku suru* smash up

17

蠱 5405 / J6a43 / M33867 KO a destructive rice worm; lead astray.
[12] 惑 *kowaku* fascination, enchantment, glamor; delusion, seduction
惑的 *kowakuteki* fascinating, alluring

18

蠶 5406 / J-X / M33891 See 蚕 5290.

蠧 5407 / J6a45 / M33896 See 蠹 5404.

蠵 5408 / J-X / M33887 KEI, KI a kind of turtle.
[11] 亀 *taimai* hawksbill turtle; tortoise shell

19

蠻 5409 / J6a47 / M33914 See 蛮 5314.

20

蠺 5410 / J6a44 / M33890 See 蚕 5290.

RAD. 血 143

Chi blood. At left: 血 *chi hen*. Nickname: Dotted Dish (cf. Rad. 108).

A 血 5411 / J376c / M33964 KETSU blood. *chi* blood, consanguinity. *chi(bamu)* become bloody. *chi(darake)* bloody, bloodstained.

2 刀 *chigatana* bloodstained blade
4 文 *chibumi* document written in blood
止 *chido(me)* styptic
友病 *ketsuyūbyō* bleeders' affliction, hemophilia
5 石 *kesseki* bloodstone
巡 *chi (no) megu(ri)* circulation of the blood
玉髄 *ketsugyokuzui* bloodstone
圧 *ketsuatsu* blood pressure
圧計 *ketsuatsukei* sphygmomanometer
6 肉 *ketsuniku* flesh and blood
行 *kekkō* circulation of the blood
印 *ketsuin* blood seal
汗 *kekkan* bloody sweat. *chi(to)ase* industry and patience
合 *chia(i)* fish meat of bloody color
色 *kesshoku* complexion
色素 *kesshikiso* hemoglobin
汐 *chishio* blood
汐海 *chishio(no)umi* pool of blood
気 *kekki* youthful vigor, hot blood. *chi(no)ke* blood
気多 *chi(no)ke (no) ō(i)* ruddy, full-blooded, hotheaded
気無 *chi(no)ke (no) na(i)* pale, white as a sheet
気盛 *kekkizaka(ri) no* vigorous, sanguine
7 豆 *chimame* blood blister
走 *chibashi(ru)* become bloodshot
尿 *ketsunyō* blood in the urine
沈 *ketchin* precipitation of blood
判 *keppan* seal of blood
判書 *keppansho* petition sealed in blood
8 雨 *chi(no)ame* bloodshed
迷 *chimayo(u)* lose control of oneself, run wild, be out of one's head
性 *kessei no* bloody
性便 *kesseiben* bloody stools
9 胤 *ketsuin* lineage, descendants
便 *ketsuben* bloody stools
相 *kessō* expression, looks
染 *chizo(me) no* bloodstained
10 振 *chibu(rui)* shaking off the blood; puerperal vertigo
涙 *chi (no) namida, ketsurui* tears of blood; bitter tears
脈 *ketsumyaku* blood vessel; blood relationship
書 *kessho* writing in blood
栓 *kessen* thrombus
栓症 *kessenshō* thrombosis
11 痕 *kekkon* bloodstain
道 *chi (no) michi* (women's) dizziness; hysterics; brain congestion
清 *kessei* blood serum, lymph
眼 *chimanako* bloodshot eye; earnest searching
祭 *chimatsu(ri)* blood offering, offering to the war god
達磨 *chidaruma* covered with blood
族 *ketsuzoku* blood relative
族結婚 *ketsuzoku kekkon* consanguineous marriage, intermarriage
球 *kekkyū* corpuscle
球計算 *kekkyu keisan* blood count
液 *ketsueki* blood
液欠乏 *ketsueki ketsubō* anemia
液型 *ketsuekigata* blood type
液病 *ketsuekibyō* a blood disorder
液移送 *ketsueki isō* blood transfusion
液検査 *ketsueki kensa* blood test
液循環 *ketsueki junkan* blood circulation
液像 *ketsuekizō* differential blood count
液銀行 *ketsueki ginkō* blood bank
液輸送 *ketsueki yusō* blood transfusion
12 斑 *keppan* blood spot
税 *ketsuzei* blood tax, heavy taxation; conscription
統 *kettō* lineage, pedigree, family line
筋 *chisuji* blood relationship, lineage, stock, strain
13 痰 *kettan* bloody phlegm
塊 *kekkai* blood clot, clotted blood
煙 *chikemuri* spray of blood
続 *chitsuzu(ki)* continuous lineage

6 竹米糸缶网罒羊羽老耂而耒耳聿肉月臣自至臼舌舛舟艮色艸艹虍虫 2【血】行衣衤西

腥 *chinamagusa(i)* bloody
路 *ketsuro* a way out, the way through, a way of escape
戦 *kessen* bloody battle
塗 *chinu(ru)* smear with blood. *chimami(re), chimidoro* bloodstained
盟 *ketsumei* blood pledge
盟団 *ketsumeidan* blood brotherhood, daredevil party
14 管 *kekkan* blood vessel
瑪瑙 *ketsumenō* bloodstone
15 潮 *chishio* the blood
糊 *chinori* slimy blood
縁 *ketsuen* blood relative; blood relationship
漿 *kesshō* blood plasma, serum
16 糖 *kettō* blood sugar
17 膿 *chi umi* bloody pus

2

衄 5412 J-X M-X See **衃** 5414.

3

衂 5413 J6a49 M33971 See **衃** 5414.

4

衃 5414 J6a48 M33973 **衄** 5415 J-X M33975 **衂** 5413 J6a49 M33971 **衄** 5412 J-X M-X **衄** 5418 J-X M34021 JIKU nosebleed.
6 血 *hanaji, jinketsu* nosebleed

6

衉 5416 J-X M33985 KAKU vomit.

A **衆** 5417 J3d30 M33981 SHU, SHŪ great numbers, multitude, populace; companions.
2 人 *shūjin* many people; the public
3 口一致 *shūkō-itchi shite* by common consent, unanimously
4 心 *shūshin* public feeling, the feeling of many
5 生 *shujō* mankind, human beings; all living beings
目 *shūmoku* public attention
6 多 *shūta* great numbers
7 芳 *shūhō* all kinds of flowers; many fragrant flowers
8 知 *shūchi* the wisdom of all
苦 *shūku* much distress; the hardships of people
参両院 *Shūsan-ryōin* both Houses of the Diet
9 院 *Shūin* House of Representatives, the Lower House
怨 *shūen* public hatred, public grievance
怒 *shūdo* the wrath of many
10 座 *shūza* large meetinghouse
徒 *shuto, shūto* many priests, priests studying in a large temple; priest soldiers
辱 *shūjoku* being humiliated before many
11 庶 *shūsho* common people, populace, masses
遇 *shūgu* ignorant crowd, mob, unthinking masses
望 *shūbō* the hope of many people; popular sentiment
12 評 *shūhyō* popular opinion
智 *shūchi* the wisdom of many
13 意 *shūi* the ideas of the people
愚 *shūgu* many fools
14 説 *shūsetsu* many theories
寡 *shūka* odds, disparity in numbers
15 慮 *shūryo* the ideas of many
論 *shūron* the argument of many
敵 *shūteki* numerous enemies
20 議 *shūgi* deliberation, public discussion
議一決 *shūgi-ikketsu suru* decide in council
議所 *shūgisho* council
議院 *Shūgiin* Lower House
議院議長 *Shūgiin Gichō* Speaker of the Lower House
議院議員 *Shūgiin giin* member of the Lower House

14

衄 5418 J-X M34021 See **衃** 5414.

RAD. 行 144

Yukigamae or *gyōgamae* "going" enclosure. With the exception of the radical character itself, shown below, all characters historically belonging to this radical are herein treated under Rad. 60. Nickname: Going.

A 行 5419 / J3954 / M34029 AN. KŌ party, suite; journey; expedition; line, row. GYŌ line, row; religious austerities. *i(ku), yu(ku)* go; run (water). *gyō(suru)* act, conduct oneself. *i(keru)* can go; can drink; can speak (a language); good. *oko(nau)* do, act, conduct oneself; carry out; perform, conduct (school); exercise (control); hold (a ceremony). *okona(wareru)* be practiced; become operative; take place; prevail, obtain; come into use; continue. *ya(ru)* give, let have, bestow on, present; send; do, perform, undertake; do for; act; study; row; operate; hold (a meeting), give (a dinner); eat, drink, smoke, find solace in. *yu(ki), i(ki)* going; travel. *i(ttakiri), yu(kikkiri)* gone for good. *oko(nai)* act, action, deed, conduct, behavior, religious austerities. *kudari* column of print; sentence. *-yuki* bound for.

2 人 *kōjin* passerby, pedestrian
4 手 *yukute* destination, route, objective
止 *yu(ki)do(mari), i(ki)do(mari)* no passage, dead end, blind alley
水 *gyōzui* tub bath
火 *anka* bed warmer, foot warmer
文 *kōbun* writing; style; diction; literature
文流麗 *kōbun-ryūrei* clever and speedy writing
方 *yu(ki)gata* the direction one is to go. *yu(ki)kata* way of doing. *yukue* whereabouts
方不明 *yukue-fumei* missing; unaccounted for
方定 *yukue-sada(menu)* aimless, wandering, homeless
5 巡 *yu(ki)-megu(ru), i(ki)-megu(ru)* go around
付 *i(ki)tsu(ke), yu(ki)tsu(ke) no* habitual, regular, favorite
末 *yu(ku)sue* one's future, fate
司 *gyōji* sumo referee
平 *yukihira* casserole, white glazed porcelain pan
平鍋 *yukihira nabe* casserole, white glazed porcelain pan
6 行 *yu(ku)yu(ku)* on the way; go on and on. *yu(ku)yu(ku) wa* in the future, someday
回 *yu(ki)-megu(ru)* go around
返 *yu(ki)-kae(ru)* make a round trip. *i(ki)-kae(ri)* round trip
次 *yu(ki)shina, i(ki)shina* on the way
列 *gyōretsu* procession, parade, queue
灯 *andon* paper-enclosed oil light
交 *yu(ki)-ka(u)* come and go. *yu(ki)kō, yu(ki)ka(i)* coming and going; street traffic; swing (of a pendulum); social intercourse
合 *yu(ki)-a(u)* meet, come across, fall in with
会 *i(ki)-a(u)* meet on the way
当 *yu(ki)-a(taru), i(ki)-a(taru)* come up against, be struck by. *i(ki)a(tari-battari)* haphazard, happy-go-lucky
年 *gyōnen* age at death. *kōnen* age, number of years
先 *yu(ki)saki, yu(ku)saki, i(ki)saki, i(ku)saki* destination, whereabouts, address. *yu(ku)saki* one's future, fate
先先 *yu(ku) sakizaki de* wherever one goes
在 *anzai* emperor's temporary headquarters
在所 *anzaisho* emperor's temporary headquarters
成 *yu(ki)na(ri)* leaving things to chance. *i(ki)na(ri)* suddenly, abruptly
成三宝 *yu(ki)na(ri)-sambō* careless fellow
成放題 *i(ki)na(ri)-hōdai, yu(ki)na(ri)-hōdai* letting things slide; careless and slovenly
7 戻 *yu(ki)modo(ri)* round trip; divorced wife
体 *gyōtai* appearance; cursive characters

状 *gyōjō* behavior, conduct, deportment, manners
別 *yu(ki)-waka(reru)* go separate ways
住坐臥 *gyōjū-zaga* daily life; walking, stopping, sitting and lying down
李 *kōri* wicker telescope trunk; baggage; travel preparations
李詰 *kōrizume* packing in wicker telescope trunks
8 金 *kōkin* bank funds
届 *yu(ki)-todo(ku)* be scrupulous, be attentive, be careful, be prudent, be thorough, be hospitable
迷 *yu(ki)-mayo(u)* miss one's way
使 *kōshi suru* use; exercise (rights); put in circulation
所 *yu(ki)dokoro* destination; whereabouts
幸 *gyōkō, miyuki* journey, visit, or attendance of the emperor
者 *gyōja* devotee, ascetic, pilgrim
事 *gyōji* event, function, observance
9 連 *yu(ki)-tsu(reru)* accompany
通 *yu(ki)-kayo(u), i(ki)-kayo(u)* come and go
客 *kōkaku* passer-by, pedestrian, traveler
星 *kōsei* planet
草 *gyōsō* cursive and grass hand
春 *yu(ku) haru* departing spring
軍 *kōgun* march, marching
軍命令 *kōgun meirei* marching orders
軍路 *kōgunro* line of march, route
為 *kōi* act, deed, conduct, transaction, practices. *yu(ki)na(ri)* leaving things to chance
為者 *kōisha* actor, transactor, offender
政 *gyōsei* administration
政下 *gyōseika* under the jurisdiction of
政学 *gyōseigaku* political science
政部 *gyōseibu* the administration
政改革 *gyōsei kaikaku* administrative reform
政指導 *gyōsei shidō* administrative guidance
政管理庁 *Gyōsei Kanrichō* the Administrative Management Agency
政機関 *gyōsei kikan* adminstrative organ
政権 *gyōseiken* administrative authority
10 逸 *yu(ki)-hagu(reru)* go astray, get lost
逢 *i(ki)-a(u)* meet on the way
倒 *ikidao(re), yukidao(re)* falling ill on the road; falling dead on the road
悩 *yu(ki)-naya(mu)* be deadlocked, be in difficulty
旅 *kōryo* travel; traveler
員 *kōin* bank clerk
宮 *angū* emperor's temporary palace
書 *gyōsho* semicursive writing
進 *kōshin* advance; march; parade
進曲 *kōshinkyoku* (musical) march
11 過 *i(ki)-su(giru), yu(ki)-su(giru)* go too far, go to extremes, go beyond. *yu(ki)su(gi)* going too far, going to extremes; overdoing
務 *kōmu* bank business
啓 *gyōkei* visit or attendance of an empress or a crown prince
掛 *yu(ki)ga(ke), i(ki)ga(ke)* on the way. *yu(ki)-ga(kari)de* by force of circumstances
掛上 *yu(ki)ga(kari)jō* by force of circumstances
脚 *angya* pilgrimage; (a priest's) walking tour; tour
脚僧 *angyasō* itinerant priest
商 *gyōshō* peddling, itinerant trade; peddler
商人 *gyōshōnin* peddler, commercial traveler
動 *kōdō* action, conduct, movements, operations
動力 *kōdōryoku* ability to act
動半径 *kōdō hankei* cruising radius; sphere of activity
動主義 *kōdō shugi* behaviorism
動隊 *kōdōtai* action group
動開始 *kōdō kaishi* deployment
動開始日 *kōdō kaishibi* D-day
動開始時間 *kōdō kaishi jikan* zero hour
動様式 *kōdō yōshiki* behavior pattern
動態型 *kōdō taikei* behavior pattern
動範囲 *kōdō han'i* sphere of action
12 場 *yu(ki)ba* place to go, resort, destination
渡 *yu(ki)-wata(ru), i(ki)-wata(ru)* extend; prevail; spread; penetrate; reach
程 *kōtei* distance; journey; march; itinerary; stroke (of a piston)
着 *i(ki)-tsu(ku), yu(ki)-tsu(ku)* arrive at, reach

惑 *yu(ki)-mayo(u)* miss one's way
装 *kōsō* traveling attire
違 *yu(ki)-chiga(eru)* mistake one's direction. *yu(ki)chiga(i), i(ki)chiga(i)* crossing; missing each other; misunderstanding, disagreement; error
雲 *kōun* moving clouds
雲流水 *kōun-ryūsui* moving clouds and running water; taking life easy
間 *gyōkan* between the lines
間注 *gyōkanchū* interlinear notes
13 殿 *anden* emperor's temporary abode
続 *yu(ki)-tsuzu(keru)* continue to frequent
詰 *yu(ki)-zu(maru), i(ki)-zu(maru), yu(ki)-tsu(maru)* be deadlocked, come to a standstill, be reduced to the last extremity, go to the wall; be tongue-tied
跡 *gyōseki* conduct, behavior
路 *kōro* path, road, course, career
路病者 *kōro byōsha* person taken ill on the road
楽 *kōraku* picnic, excursion; having a good time
楽地 *kōrakuchi* pleasure resort
楽客 *kōrakukyaku* excursionists
14 摺 *yukizuri* passing closely; time of passing; on the way; temporary action
暮 *yu(ki)ku(reta)* belated, benighted
15 摩 *yukizuri* passing closely; time of passing; on the way; temporary action
儀 *gyōgi* behavior, manners, deportment
澄 *okona(i)-su(masu)* follow Buddhist teachings; put on airs; pose (as someone)
賞 *kōshō* conferring of rewards
22 嚢 *kōnō* knapsack; mail bag; wallet

RAD. 衣 145

Koromo clothes. At left: 衤 (5 strokes), *koromo hen*. Nickname: Clothing.

A **衣** 5420 / J3061 / M34091 E, I garment. *koromo* clothes, robe; dressing; frosting; coating. *kinu* clothing, kimono.
4 手 *koromode* sleeve
5 生活 *iseikatsu* clothing habits
8 服 *ifuku* clothes, clothing
服室 *ifukushitsu* wardrobe (room)
9 香 *ikō* perfume on the clothing
架 *ika* clothes rack
食 *ishoku* food and clothes, livelihood
食住 *ishokujū* food, clothing, and shelter; necessities of life
冠 *ikan* kimono and (ancient) headdress
冠束帯 *ikan-sokutai* full traditional ceremonial court dress; Shinto priest's garb
10 桁 *ikō* clothes rack
料 *iryō* clothing
帯 *itai* clothes and obi; full court dress
紋 *emon* dress, clothes, drapery (of a statue)
紋掛 *emonka(ke)* coat hanger
11 魚 *shimi* clothes moth, silverfish, bookworm
12 替 *koromoga(e)* seasonal change of clothes
装 *ishō* clothes, wardrobe, costume
13 鉢 *ihatsu, ehatsu* assuming the mantle of
14 摺 *kinuzure* rustling (of clothes)
裳 *ishō* clothes, costume, wardrobe
裳方 *ishōkata* theatrical dresser
裳屋 *ishōya* costumer
裳持 *ishōmo(chi)* person with a large wardrobe
裳部屋 *ishōbeya* wardrobe
裳道楽 *ishō-dōraku* extravagant in dress
15 摩 *kinuzure* rustling of clothes
18 類 *irui* clothing
22 嚢 *kakushi* pocket

3

衫 5421 / J6a4e / M34111 SAN. clothing; underclothing.

A **表** 5422 / J493d / M34105 HYŌ table, schedule, diagram, chart, list. *ara(wasu), hyō(suru)* express, show, manifest. *arawa(reru)* appear, emerge, come in sight, show up; be revealed, be discovered, be mentioned; become famous. *omote* surface, right side, face;

6 竹米糸缶网罒羊羽老耂而耒耳聿肉月臣自至臼舌舛舟艮色艸艹虍虫血行【衣衤】3 西

exterior, outside; front; the street; mat covers; head (of a coin); first half (of an inning).

2 二階 *omote nikai* second floor front room
3 口 *omoteguchi* front door
土 *hyōdo* topsoil
4 日本 *Omote Nihon* Pacific seaboard of Japan
5 白 *hyōhaku* expression, confession
皮 *hyōhi* epidermis; bark, rind, peel, husk
立 *omoteda(tsu)* become public, be known. *omoteda(tta)* public, open; formal, official. *omoteda(tte)* publicly, openly; ostensibly; formally
付 *omotetsu(ki)* frontage
号 *hyōgō* symbol, emblem, sign
札 *hyōsatsu* nameplate, door plate
出 *hyōshutsu* expression, presentation
玄関 *omote genkan* front door, vestibule
示 *hyōji* indication, expression
示灯 *hyōjitō* signal light
示物 *hyōjibutsu* something indicative of
示書 *hyōjisho* a written statement
6 衣 *hyōi, uwagi* coat, tunic, jacket
向 *omotemu(ki)* publicly, openly; ostensibly; formally
7 芸 *omotegei* main accomplishments
沙汰 *omotezata* publicity, lawsuit
作 *omotesaku* first crop, important crop
決 *hyōketsu* vote, voting
決権 *hyōketsuken* voting rights
8 門 *omotemon* front gate
明 *hyōmei* indication, manifestation, demonstration, expression, announcement
表紙 *omotebyōshi* front cover
忠塔 *hyōchūtō* war-memorial monument
忠碑 *hyōchūhi* war-memorial monument
具 *hyōgu* mounting (a picture)
具屋 *hyōguya* paperer, picture framer
具師 *hyōgushi* paperer, picture framer
9 通 *omotedō(ri)* main street
看板 *omote kamban* sign out in front; a front (for someone)
音文字 *hyōon moji* phonetic symbol
音字母 *hyōon jibo* phonetic alphabet
面 *hyōmen* surface, face, outside; appearance
面上 *hyōmenjō* on the surface
面化 *hyōmenka suru* come to a head, become an issue, break
面的 *hyōmenteki ni* on the surface
面張力 *hyōmen chōryoku* surface tension
10 紙 *hyōshi* cover, binding
記 *hyōki suru* publish (information); list (prices); declare (the value); write; address (a package)
座敷 *omote zashiki* front room, parlor, living room
11 側 *omotegawa* the front
情 *hyōjō* facial expression
現 *hyōgen* expression, presentation
12 着 *uwagi* coat, tunic, jacket
替 *omotega(e)* refacing *(tatami)* mats
装 *hyōsō* mounting
象 *hyōshō* symbol, emblem
13 解 *hyōkai* illustration by tables
裏 *hyōri* inside and outside; two sides
意文字 *hyōi moji* hieroglyph, ideograph
14 徴 *hyōchō* appearing on the surface; a sign
構 *omotegama(e)* the front of a building, facade
彰 *hyōshō* commendation, awarding
15 編 *omoteami* plain knitting
18 題 *hyōdai* title (of a book or lecture); index

4

衮 5423 / J-X / M34121 See **袞** 5441.

衷 5424 / J-X / M34139 See **衷** 31.

衵 5425 / J6a52 / M34135 JITSU, NICHI everyday wear; underclothing. *akome* underclothing, under robe.

袂 5426 / J6a56 / M34154 BEI. *tamoto* sleeve; bag of the sleeve; foot (of a hill); edge; approach.

衽 5427 / J6a53 / M34146 **袵** 5446 / J6a54 / M34237 JIN. *kokubi* neck of a garment. *okumi* gusset, gore.

衾 5428 / J6a50 / M34147 KIN. *fusuma* quilt, bedding.

袁 5429 / J6a4f / M34152 EN long kimono.

9 彦道 *engendō* gambling

衲 5430 / J6a55 / M34130 NŌ, DŌ mend, repair; clothing; priest's robes;

6 衣 *nōi* priest's robes; priest.

衿 5431 / J365e / M34149 KIN. *eri* neck, neckband, collar, lapel.

4 止 *eridome* brooch, breast pin
元 *erimoto* front of neck
6 当 *eria(te)* cloth to protect the back of the collar
7 足 *eriashi* border of the hair in back
9 首 *erikubi* nape of the neck
度 *kindo* magnanimity, generosity
巻 *erimaki* muffler, scarf, neckpiece
10 留 *erido(me)* brooch, breast pin
11 章 *erishō* badge
13 飾 *erikaza(ri)* necktie, cravat, bow
裏 *eriura* cloth to protect the back of the collar
14 髪 *erigami* back hair
16 懐 *kinkai* the heart; thought; magnanimity

B **衰** 5432 / J3f6a / M34127 SUI. *otoro(eru)* decline, wane, weaken, abate, decay, wither, waste away.

3 亡 *suibō* ruin, downfall, collapse
5 世 *suisei* this decadent world
6 色 *suishoku* fading color; fading beauty
死 *suishi suru* become emaciated and die; wither away
兆 *suichō* signs of decline
8 退 *suitai* decline, decadence, waning; ebb tide
果 *otoro(e)-ha(teru)* be utterly spent or crushed
10 残 *suizan na* emaciated, worn out
耗 *suimō suru* weaken and decline
弱 *suijaku* weakness, debility, prostration, breakdown
11 運 *suiun* declining fortunes, decadence
13 微 *suibi* decline, decadence, waning; ebb tide
滅 *suimetsu* decline and fall
勢 *suisei* downward tendency, decay, decline
14 態 *suitai* weakening, decline
15 弊 *suihei* decline
16 頽 *suitai* decline, decadence, waning; ebb tide
18 軀 *suiku* emaciated body

5

袮 5433 / J6a59 / M-X Nonstandard for 禰 7068.

袰 5434 / J6a5e / M-X (国字) *horo* hood.

袹 5435 / J6a5a / M34196 BATSU warrior's headband.

袤 5436 / J6a5d / M34213 BŌ length.

袒 5437 / J6a58 / M34184 TAN baring the shoulder; strip to the waist.

袢 5438 / J6a5b / M34210 HAN summer kimono, short clothing.

袍 5439 / J6a5c / M34174 HŌ coat.

袗 5440 / J6a57 / M34194 SHIN black clothing; formal wear; embroidery.

6 衣 *shin'i* embroidered kimono

衮 5441 / J6a51 / M34203 **袞** 5423 / J-X / M34121 KON imperial robes.

16 龍 *konryō* imperial robes

袈 5442 / J3736 / M34166 KE a coarse camlet.

13 裟 *kesa* Buddhist priest's stoal, sacred shoulder scarf
裟掛 *kesaga(ke)* hanging diagonally from the shoulder; a diagonal sword-cut from the shoulder
裟斬 *kesagi(ri)* cutting (a man) diagonally from the shoulder

B **袋** 5443 / J425e / M34171 TEI. TAI bag; bag counter. *fukuro* bag, sack, pouch. *(o)fukuro* mama.

2 入 *fukuroi(ri)* pouched, sacked
3 小路 *fukurokōji* blind alley
4 戸棚 *fukurotodana* bookshelves

6 竹米糸缶网罒羊羽老耂而耒耳聿肉月臣自至臼舌舛舟艮色艸艹虍虫血行【衣衤】西 5

5 叩 *fukurodataki* sound thrashing, beating
6 耳 *fukuromimi* retentive memory; a person with a good memory
地 *fukurochi* land cut off from access to a road
7 町 *fukuromachi* blind alley
8 物 *fukuromono* bags and pouches
11 道 *fukuromichi* blind road
張 *fukuroha(ri)* paper bagmaking
13 鼠 *fukuro (no) nezumi* trapped mouse; tight box, fine fix
15 縫 *fukuronu(i)* double sewing

袖 5444 / J4235 / M34192 SHŪ. *sode* sleeve; sleeve pocket; wing (of a building); extension (of a table). *sode ni suru* jilt, cold shoulder (someone).
3 口 *sodeguchi* cuff, sleeve band
下 *sode(no)shita* bribe
乞 *sodego(u)* beg. *sodego(i)* beggar; begging
丈 *sode take* sleeve length
4 手 *shūshu* putting one's hands in one's sleeves; detestation of work
手傍観 *shūshu-bōkan* passively looking on
9 垣 *sodegaki* low fence; fence flanking a gate
珍 *shūchin* pocket (edition)
珍本 *shūchimbon* pocket-size book; manual
10 振 *sodebu(ru)* wave the sleeve (in sad parting or in dancing)
時雨 *sode shigure* weeping
11 章 *sodeshō* (soldier's) stripes
12 無 *sodena(shi)* sleeveless coat
13 裏 *sode ura* sleeve lining

B **被** 5445 / J486f / M34222 HI receiving. *kabu(ru) vi* and *vt* wear, put on; take (the blame); pour on; be covered with; ship (a wave); have (labor pains); be accidentally exposed (a film). *kabu(seru)* cover with; put on; pour on, play (a stream of water) on; fix (blame) on; shift (responsibility) on. *kabu(saru)* get covered; overlap; hang over. *ō(u)* cover, veil; hang over; brood over; conceal; overlap; shelter; screen; disguise; wrap, envelop; obscure; shade; overshadow. *hi-* recipient or victim of (an action). *kōmu(ru)* get, receive, sustain (an injury), be subjected to (criticism). *kazu(ku)* put on, wear. *kazu(keru)* blame. *ō(i)* cover, covering; shade; mantle, coat; hood, bonnet; casing; awning.
4 支払人 *hishiharainin* payee
5 圧迫 *hiappaku* oppressed
写体 *hishatai* the one being photographed
用者 *hiyōsha* employee
6 衣 *kazuki, katsugi* lady's veil
7 抑留者 *hiyokuryūsha* internee
災 *hisai* suffering (from a calamity); affliction
災者 *hisaisha* victim, sufferer
告 *hikoku* defendant
告人 *hikokunin* defendant
告席 *hikokuseki* tribunal, the bar, the dock
8 金 *kabu(se)kin* rolled gold, filled gold
物 *kabu(ri)mono* headgear, headdress. *ki(se)mono* clothes
治者 *hichisha* the governed
拘束者 *hikōsokusha* the restrained
服 *hifuku* clothing
服庫 *hifukuko* clothing depot
服廠 *hifukushō* clothing depot
9 造物 *hizōbutsu* creation, creatures
後見者 *hikōkensha* ward, protégé
保険物 *hihokembutsu* insured property
保険者 *hihokensha* insured person
保護国 *hihogokoku* dependency, protectorate
保護者 *hihogosha* ward, protégé
10 害 *higai* damage, harm, casualties, injury
害地 *higaichi* stricken area
害妄想 *higaimōsō* persecution complex
害者 *higaisha* victim, injured party, sufferer
害高 *higaidaka* amount of damage
11 推薦者 *hisuisensha* nominee
12 弾 *hidan* being bombed
13 傭者 *hiyōsha* employee
14 疑者 *higisha* a suspect
選挙人 *hisenkyonin* person eligible for election
選挙資格 *hisenkyo shikaku* qualification for election
選挙権 *hisenkyoken* eligibility for election
18 覆 *hifuku* covering, mantle, insulation
贈与者 *hizōyosha* donee
19 爆 *hibaku* being bombed
爆地 *hibakuchi* bombed area
爆者 *hibakusha* bombing victims

6

袛 5446 / J6a54 / M34237 See **衽** 5427.

裃 5447 / J6a61 / M34282 (国字) *kamishimo* old ceremonial garb; samurai garb.

袴 5448 / J3853 / M34236 KO. *hakama* men's formal divided skirt, women's pleated skirt.

袷 5449 / J3041 / M34240 KŌ. KYŌ. *awase* lined; lined kimono.

袱 5450 / J6a60 / M34232 FUKU a wrapper made of cloth.
10 紗 *fukusa* silk wrapper (for gifts); tea-ceremony dishcloth

裄 5451 / J6a62 / M34283 (国字) *yuki* sleeve length.
3 丈 *yukitake* sleeve and dress length

袿 5452 / J6a5f / M34255 KEI. *uchiki* an ancient ordinary kimono.
11 袴 *keiko* lady's court robe

B **裂** 5453 / J4e76 / M34260 RETSU. *sa(ku) vt* split, rend, tear, burst, rip, crack. *sa(keru) vi* split, rend, tear, burst, rip, crack.
5 目 *sa(ke)me* rent, tear, crack, fissure, split, slit, cleft, rip, rift
8 帛 *reppaku* a woman's wail
10 殺 *sa(ki)-koro(su)* tear to death
11 痔 *sa(ke)ji, ki(re)ji* anal fistula
12 開 *rekkai suru* burst open
13 傷 *resshō* lacerated wound
溝 *rekkō* tooth grooves
19 離 *sa(ki)-hana(su)* rend from, tear (something) away from

A **裁** 5454 / J3a5b / M34258 SAI. *saba(ku)* judge. *ta(tsu)* cut out (a suit); sever, cut off; shut off, interrupt; abstain from; eradicate; suppress. *saba(ki)* judgment, decision, verdict. *ta(chi)* cutting, cut.
3 上 *ta(chi)a(gari)* (tailor's) cutting; styling
4 方 *ta(chi)kata* cutting, cut
5 可 *saika* sanction, approval
7 決 *saiketsu* decision, judgment, ruling
決書 *saiketsusho* written verdict
判 *saiban* trial; adjudication
判人 *saibannin* judge
判上 *saibanjō no* judicial
判沙汰 *saibanzata* lawsuit, litigation
判長 *saibanchō* presiding judge
判所 *saibansho* a court; courthouse
判官 *saibankan* the judge
判権 *saibanken* jurisdiction
8 板 *ta(chi)ita* tailor's cutting board
物 *ta(chi)mono* cuttings (cloth or paper)
定 *saitei* decision, ruling, award, arbitration
庖丁 *ta(chi)bōchō* tailor's knife
10 屑 *ta(chi)kuzu* cuttings, scraps
11 掛 *ta(chi)-ka(keru)* begin to cut
許 *saikyo* sanction, approval
断 *saidan suru* cut off; cut out (clothes); decide, judge
断師 *saidanshi* (tailor's) cutter
12 割 *ta(chi)-wa(ru)* cut open, cut apart; divide
量 *sairyō* discretion
15 縫 *saihō* sewing. *ta(chi)-nu(u)* cut and sew
縫師 *saihōshi* tailor, seamstress

A **装** 5455 / J4175 / M34283' **裝** 5456 / J6a66 / M34321 SŌ. SHŌ. *yoso(u)* dress; spruce up; pretend, disguise; profess. *yosō(i)* array, dress, equipment.
2 丁 *sōtei* binding, format
5 本 *sōhon* binding, format
甲 *sokō* armor, armor plate
甲自動車 *sōkō jidōsha* armored car
甲車 *sōkōsha* armored car
甲艦 *sōkōkan* armored warship
7 束 *sōzoku, shōzoku* costume (of ancient nobles); personal appearance; clothing; interior decoration; landscaping; household furniture
身具 *sōshingu* personal ornaments
8 具 *sōgu* equipment; harness; trappings; furnishings, fittings
10 釘 *sōtei* binding, format
12 備 *sōbi* equipment; outfit, rigging
幀 *sōtei* binding, format
弾 *sōdan suru* load (a gun)
着 *sōchaku suru* equip, fit, install, lay, lay down, place

6 竹米糸缶网罒羊羽老耂而耒耳聿肉月臣自至臼舌舛舟艮色艸艹虍虫血行【衣 7 衤】西

13 塡 *sōten* gun charge
置 *sōchi* equipment, installation, plant, apparatus, device
飾 *sōshoku* ornament, ornamentation, decoration, adornment
飾用 *sōshokuyō* for decoration
飾法 *sōshokuhō* ornamentation, decoration
飾的 *sōshokuteki* ornamental, decorative
飾画 *sōshokuga* decorative painting
飾具 *sōshokugu* jewelry
飾音 *sōshokuon* grace note
飾品 *sōshokuhin* ornaments, decorations, upholstery; trinkets, trimmings
16 薬 *sōyaku* charging with gunpowder
蹄 *sōtei* shoeing (a horse)
蹄師 *sōteishi* horseshoer

7

裝 5456 J6a66 M34321 See 装 5455.

裟 5457 J3a40 M34325 SA surplice (Buddhist).

裘 5458 J6a64 M34312 KYŪ leather clothing.

裔 5459 J6a63 M34303 EI descendant; border.

裙 5460 J6a65 M34314 KUN hem (of a garment); underwear.

B **裕** 5461 J4d35 M34305 YŪ. *yutaka* abundant, rich, fruitful, fertile.
7 余 *yūyo* postponement, grace, extension (of time); reprieve, stay; delay; slackness
12 然 *yūzen* quiet, calm, composed, leisurely, deliberate; eternal, boundless, vast
13 福 *yūfuku* prosperity, affluence

A **裏** 5462 J4e22 M34294 **裡** 5463 J4e23 M34295 RI inside. *uchi ni* amidst, in. *ura* reverse, wrong side; undersurface, inside; palm, sole; opposite; back, rear; lining, last half (of an inning).
3 山 *urayama* the hill back of one's home; a hill back from the seashore
口 *uraguchi* back door, rear entrance
口営業 *uraguchi eigyō* illegal business
4 手 *urate* back of the house
方 *urakata* scene shifter; lady consort (to a high personage)
毛 *urake* fleece lining
反 *uragae(ru)* be turned inside out. *uragae(su)* turn inside out; turn the other way, turn (something) over. *uragae(shi)* inside out; upside down
日本 *Ura-Nippon, Ura-Nihon* Japan Sea coast areas
切 *uragi(ri)* treachery, betrayal, perfidy. *uragi(ru)* betray
切者 *uragirimono* betrayer, traitor, turncoat, informer
5 付 *urazu(keru)* support; endorse; substantiate. *urazu(ke)* backing, security; proof, foundation; lining (something); something lined. *urazu(ki)* lined; something lined
付物資 *urazu(ke)busshi* collateral goods
打 *urau(chi)* lining, backing; vouching for
打紙 *urau(chi)gami* end leaves (of a book), lining paper
6 返 *uragae(su)* turn inside out; turn the other way, turn (something) over. *uragae(ru)* be turned inside out. *uragae(shi)* inside out; upside down
地 *uraji* lining
合 *uraa(wase)* fitting things back to back; agreement of minds
名 *urana* secret name, alias
7 囲 *uragako(i)* back fence
作 *urasaku* second crop, interim crop
町 *uramachi* back street, back alley, slums
声 *uragoe* falsetto
8 門 *uramon* back gate
店 *uradana* house in an alley, rear tenement, slums
板 *uraita* roof boards; ceiling
長屋 *uranagaya* rear tenement
表 *ura-omote* wrong side out; both sides; reverse, opposite; double-dealing
表紙 *urabyōshi* back cover
9 屋 *uraya* alley house, rear tenement, slum
通 *uradō(ri)* back street, side street, alley

背戸 *urasedo* back door
面 *rimen* back, reverse, other side, inside, tails (of coins), background
面史 *rimenshi* hidden historical background
10 庭 *ura niwa* rear garden, backyard
紋 *uramon* informal crest
釘 *urakugi* nails sticking through
鬼門 *urakimon* unlucky quarter (southwest)
書 *uragaki* endorsement; proof; note on back of the scroll
書人 *uragakinin* endorser
書譲渡 *uragaki jōto* endorsing over to
11 道 *ura michi* back street; secret path
問 *urado(u)* ascertain a person's innermost feelings
側 *uragawa* the reverse, the lining
情 *ura nasake* inner affection
12 貸屋 *uragashiya* house in back for rent
13 腹 *urahara* opposite, reverse, contrary
話 *urabanashi* a story not generally known
14 漉 *uragoshi* strainer, colander
18 襟 *uraeri* neckband lining

A **補** 5464 / J4a64 / M34320 HO assistant, learner. *ogina(u)* supply, make good, make up (losses), stop (a gap), offset, piece out; compensate for; supplement. *ho(suru)* appoint, select. *-ho* assistant.
2 力 *horyoku suru* intensify
4 欠 *hoketsu* filling a vacancy; making up a shortage
欠募集 *hoketsu-boshū suru* inviting (students) to fill vacancies
欠選手 *hoketsu senshu* substitute player, pinch hitter
欠選挙 *hoketsu senkyo* by-election, special election
5 正 *hosei* revision; correction; compensation (in machines); supplementary (budget)
6 血 *hoketsu* replenishing a patient's blood supply
回 *hokai* extra innings
任 *honin suru* appoint to office; take up one's duties
充 *hojū* supplement, complement, draft, replacement
充兵 *hojūhei* reservist, recruit
充隊 *hojūtai* draft, reserves
7 角 *hokaku* supplementary angle
完税 *hokanzei* surtax
足 *hosoku* replenishment, complement, amendment
足合 *hosoku(shi)a(u)* complement each other
足語 *hosokugo* complement (in grammar)
佐 *hosa* assistance; assistant; counselor
佐人 *hosanin* assistant
佐役 *hosayaku* adviser
助 *hojo* assistance; subsidy; supplement; auxiliary
助金 *hojokin* subsidy, grant, appropriation, bounty
助貨幣 *hojo kahei* subsidiary coin
8 注 *hochū* supplementary note
肥 *hohi* supplementary fertilizer
乳 *honyū* lactation, suckling
9 則 *hosoku* supplementary rules
10 修 *hoshū* repair, mending; correction
記 *hoki suru* add more to an article
殺 *hosatsu* an assist (in baseball)
11 強 *hokyō suru* strengthen the weak places
習 *hoshū* supplementary study materials
祭 *hosai* (Catholic) deacon
12 遺 *hoi* supplement, appendix
註 *hochū* supplementary note
筆 *hohitsu suru* add to (in writing); finish writing
給 *hokyū* supply, replenishment
給金 *hokyūkin* subsidy, bonus
13 塡 *hoten suru* fill, supply (a deficiency), make up (a loss)
14 綴 *hotei suru* replenish
語 *hogo* complement (in grammar)
箋 *hosen* tag, slip, label
導 *hodō* guidance
16 薬 *ogina(i)gusuri* tonic, restorative
整 *hosei* manipulation
17 講 *hokō* supplementary lecture
翼 *hoyoku* assistance; assistant; counselor
聴器 *hochōki* hearing aid
償 *hoshō* indemnity, compensation, reparation
償金 *hoshōkin* indemnity, compensation money
18 闕 *hoketsu* filling a vacancy
職 *hoshoku* appointment to a position

襃 5465 / J6a6a / M34362 HAI long, dragging (garments).

裼 5466 / J6a69 / M34379 SEKI bare the shoulder, roll up one's sleeves. TEI swaddling clothes; diapers.

褂 5467 / J6a68 / M34401 KAI, KE a long overgarment.

裹 5468 / J6a67 / M34372 KA. *tsutsu(mu)* wrap, pack up; cover with; dress in; conceal.

裲 5469 / J6a6c / M34356 RYŌ ancient robe.

18 襠 *uchikake* long outer robe

褄 5470 / J6a6d / M34410 (国字) *tsuma* skirt.

8 取 *tsumado(ru)* tuck up a skirt

裨 5471 / J6a6b / M34338 HI help.

10 益 *hieki* profit, benefit, good

裳 5472 / J3e58 / M34357 SHŌ. *mo* ancient skirt.

13 裾 *mosuso* cuff (of trousers); hem (of a skirt); foot (of a mountain)

B 褐 5473 / J336c / M-X 褐 5478 / J-X / M34435 KATSU woolen kimono.

4 夫 *kappu* cloth made from waste fibers

6 色 *kasshoku* brown. *kachi iro* dark blue

色人種 *kasshoku jinshu* brown race, Malay race

9 炭 *kattan* brown coal, lignite

裾 5474 / J3f7e / M34382 KYO. *suso* cuff (of trousers); hem (of a skirt); foot (of a mountain).

3 山 *susoyama* foothills

4 分 *susowa(ke)* distribution of a gift; sharing

6 回 *susomawa(shi)* hem line

8 物 *susomono* lower-grade wares

9 持 *susomo(chi)* train bearer

11 野 *susono* foot (of a mountain)

13 裏 *susoura* hem

14 綿 *susowata* cotton skirt padding; kimono with padded skirts

模様 *susomoyō* skirt design

B 裸 5475 / J4d67 / M34371 RA. *hadaka* naked body, nude; uncovered, only partially clothed, undressed; without investing; leafless; unpreparedness (for a wedding); unsaddled; denuded, bare.

1 一貫 *hadaka ikkan* starting from scratch; bankrupt

3 女 *rajo* nude woman

山 *hadaka yama* bare mountain; deforested mountain

4 文 *hadakabumi* folded letter sent without an envelope

火 *hadakabi* open fire

5 出 *rashutsu* exposure, denudation

6 虫 *hadakamushi* caterpillar

7 足 *hadashi* bare feet

坊 *hadakambō* naked person

身 *rashin* nakedness; bareness

麦 *hadaka mugi* a species of rye

形 *ragyō* naked; uncovered

体 *ratai* naked body, nakedness, nudity

体主義 *ratai shugi* nudism

体画 *rataiga* nude picture

8 岩 *hadaka iwa* bare rock

10 馬 *hadaka uma* barebacked horse

11 婦 *rafu* nude woman

眼 *ragan* the naked eye

商売 *hadaka shōbai* wrestling; boxing

14 像 *razō* nude statue

15 線 *hadakasen*, *rasen* bare wire

A 製 5476 / J403d / M34380 SEI. *sei(suru)* make, manufacture. *-sei* make, manufacture.

5 出 *seishutsu* production

氷 *seihyō* ice manufacture

氷所 *seihyōjo* ice plant

本 *seihon* bookbinding

本屋 *seihon'ya* bookbinder

本業 *seihongyō* bookbinding business

6 式 *seishiki* style

缶 *seikan* can manufacturing; boiler manufacturing

糸 *seishi* silk-thread manufacture

糸工場 *seishi kōjō* silk mill

糸学 *seishigaku* filature science

糸業 *seishigyō* silk industry
7 図 *seizu* drafting; cartography, mapmaking; drawing
図家 *seizuka* cartographer
作 *seisaku* manufacture, production
作所 *seisakujo* factory, workshop, plant
作者 *seisakusha* manufacturer, maker; producer
材 *seizai* sawing, lumbering
材工 *seizaikō* sawyer
材所 *seizaisho* sawmill
材業 *seizaigyō* lumber industry
材機 *seizaiki* sawmill machinery
8 法 *seihō* method of manufacture, process, recipe
表 *seihyō* tabulation
油 *seiyu* oil refining
油所 *seiyujo* oil factory; oil refinery
油業 *seiyugyō* oil industry
版 *seihan* platemaking (printing)
版所 *seihanjo* platemaker's shop
版者 *seihansha* platemaker
版屋 *seihan'ya* platemaker's shop
9 品 *seihin* manufactured goods, products
炭 *seitan* charcoal manufacture
茶 *seicha* tea processing
茶業 *seichagyō* tea-processing industry
革 *seikaku* tanning
革所 *seikakujo* tannery
革業 *seikakugyō* tanning industry
造 *seizō* manufacture, production, making
造人 *seizōnin* maker
造元 *seizōmoto* manufacturer
造所 *seizōjo* factory, workshop
造法 *seizōhō* process of manufacture
造者 *seizōsha* maker
造品 *seizōhin* manufactured goods
造場 *seizōjō* factory, mill, workshop
造業 *seizōgyō* manufacturing industry
造権 *seizōken* manufacturing rights
10 釘機 *seiteiki* nail-making machine
粉 *seifun* milling flour
粉所 *seifunjo* flour mill
粉機 *seifunki* flour grinder
陶 *seitō* porcelain manufacturing
陶術 *seitōjutsu* ceramics
陶業 *seitōgyō* porcelain industry
紙 *seishi* paper manufacture
紙工場 *seishi kōjō* paper mill
紙会社 *seishigaisha* paper mill
紙場 *seishijō* paper mill
紙業 *seishigyō* paper-manufacturing industry
11 麻 *seima* flax or jute or hemp spinning
産 *seisan* production
菓 *seika* confectionery
菓業 *seikagyō* confectionery business
12 帽 *seibō* hat manufacture
帽業 *seibōgyō* hat industry
絨 *seijū* wool weaving
絨所 *seijūjo* woolen mills
13 塩 *seien* salt manufacture
塩業 *seiengyō* salt industry
鉄 *seitetsu* iron manufacture
鉄所 *seitetsujo* iron works
鉄業 *seitetsugyō* iron industry
靴 *seika* shoemaking
靴工 *seikakō* shoemaking
靴業 *seikagyō* shoemaking industry
14 銑 *seisen* pig-iron manufacture
16 錬 *seiren* refining, smelting
錬所 *seirenjo* refinery, smelter
麺 *seimen* noodle manufacture
麺機 *seimenki* noodle-making machine
糖 *seitō* sugar manufacture
糖会社 *seitōgaisha* sugar company
糖所 *seitōjo* sugar refinery
糖業 *seitōgyō* sugar industry
鋼 *seikō* steel manufacturing
鋼法 *seikōhō* steelmaking process
鋼所 *seikōjo* steel works
鋼業 *seikōgyō* steel industry
薬 *seiyaku* medicine manufacture; manufactured medicine
薬化学 *seiyaku kagaku* pharmaceutical chemistry
薬会社 *seiyakugaisha* pharmaceutical company
薬業 *seiyakugyō* pharmaceutical industry

9

禪 5477 / J6a7c / M-X — Nonstandard for 禅 5500.

褐 5478 / J-X / M34435 — See 褐 5473.

褓 5479 / J6a70 / M34438 — Hō. Ho diaper.

褌 5480 / J6a6e / M34428 KON. *fundoshi* loincloth.

褊 5481 / J6a6f / M34420 HEN narrow, small.
9 狭 *henkyō* narrow-mindedness

褪 5482 / J6a74 / M34503 TON. TAI *a(seru), sa(meru)* fade, discolor.
6 色 *taishoku* fading; faded color
9 紅色 *taikōshoku* light pink

B **褒** 5483 / J4b2b / M34437 **襃** 5489 / J6a71 / M34552 HŌ. *ho- (mechigiru), ho(mesoyasu)* praise, extol. *ho(meru)* praise, commend.
3 上 *ho(me)-a(geru)* praise, extol
5 立 *ho(me)-ta(teru)* praise, extol
6 合 *ho(me)a(i)* logrolling tactics
7 状 *hōjō* certificate of merit, honorable mention
言葉 *ho(me)kotoba* eulogy, compliment
8 奉 *ho(me)-matsu(ru)* praise; render homage to
9 美 *hōbi* prize, reward
10 称 *ho(me)-tata(eru)* admire, praise, applaud
貶 *hōhen* praise and censure, criticism
11 章 *hōshō* medal
12 詞 *ho(me)kotoba* words of praise
13 辞 *hōji* praise, eulogy
奨 *hōshō* compensation
14 歌 *ho(me)-uta(u)* sing praises to
15 賞 *hōshō* prize, reward

A **複** 5484 / J4a23 / M34417 FUKU double, compound, composite, multiple. *futatabi, mata* again.
4 文 *fukubun* compound sentence
火山 *fukukazan* compound volcano
5 母音 *fukuboin* diphthong
写 *fukusha* copying, duplication; duplicate, copy, facsimile
写写真 *fukusha shashin* photostat, photocopy
本 *fukuhon* duplicate, copy
本位制 *fukuhon'isei* bimetallism
6 式 *fukushiki* double-entry (bookkeeping)
式学級 *fukushiki gakkyū* multiple-grade classroom
合 *fukugō* composite, complex, compound
合名詞 *fukugō meishi* compound noun
合企業 *fukugō kigyō* conglomerate
合動詞 *fukugō dōshi* compound verb
合詞 *fukugōshi* compound word
合語 *fukugōgo* compound word
7 利 *fukuri* compound interest
8 刻 *fukkoku* reproducing book plates
屈折 *fukukussetsu* double refraction
9 星 *fukusei* multiple star
10 座機 *fukuzaki* two-seater plane
11 眼 *fukugan* compound eye (of an insect)
視 *fukushi* double vision
習 *fukushū* review
12 葉 *fukuyō* biplane; compound leaf
13 滑車 *fukukassha* compound pulley
数 *fukusū* plural
数型 *fukusūkei* plural form
試合 *fukushiai* doubles (in tennis)
14 製 *fukusei* reproduction, duplication, reprinting
複線 *fukufukusen* four-track railway
雑 *fukuzatsu* complexity, complication, intricacy; maze, labyrinth
雑化 *fukuzatsuka* complication
雑骨折 *fukuzatsu kossetsu* compound fracture
15 縁 *fukuen* conjugal reconciliation
線 *fukusen* double track

10

樸 5485 / J-X / M-X Nonstandard for 樸 5512.

褞 5486 / J6a72 / M34475 UN, ON robe.

褥 5487 / J6a73 / M34495 JOKU. *shitone* cushion, mattress, bedding.
11 婦 *jokufu* a woman resting after childbirth

褫 5488 / J6a75 / M34504 CHI rob.
14 奪 *chidatsu suru* deprive, degrade, strip

11

襃 5489 / J6a71 / M34552 See 褒 5483.

襄 5490 / J6a77 / M34556 Jō climb; look up; raise (one's voice); high; change; ride.

褻 5491 / J6a78 / M34536 Setsu filthy.

褸 5492 / J6a7a / M34530 Ro, Ru rags.

襀 5493 / J-X / M34544 Seki. *hida* pleat, fold, tuck, crease.

襁 5494 / J6a76 / M34545 襁 5497 / J-X / M-X Kyō diaper.
[14] 褓 *kyōhō, (o)mutsu, oshime, mutsuki* diaper, swaddling clothes

褶 5495 / J6a79 / M34525 Shū pleats.
[6] 曲 *shūkyoku* a fold (in geology)

12

襍 5496 / J7037 / M34596 See 雑 6507.

襁 5497 / J-X / M-X See 襁 5494.

襖 5498 / J3228 / M-X See 襖 5503.

囊 5499 / J4739 / M-X Nonstandard for 囊 933.

襌 5500 / J6a7b / M34593 Tan. *hitoe* an unlined kimono.

13

襞 5501 / J6a7e / M34645 Heki. *hida* pleat, fold, tuck, crease.

襠 5502 / J6a7d / M34649 Tō. *machi* gusset, gore, etc. (in sewing).

襖 5503 / J-X / M34629 襖 5498 / J3228 / M-X Ō. *fusuma* opaque sliding paper door.
[13] 障子 *fusuma shōji* opaque sliding paper door

B 襟 5504 / J365f / M34647 Kin. *eri* neck, neckband, collar, lapel.
[4] 止 *eridome* brooch, breast pin
元 *erimoto* front of neck
[6] 当 *eria(te)* cloth to protect the back of the collar
[7] 足 *eriashi* border of the hair in back
[9] 首 *erikubi* nape of the neck
度 *kindo* magnanimity, generosity
巻 *erimaki* muffler, scarf, neckpiece
[10] 留 *erido(me)* brooch, breast pin
[11] 章 *erishō* badge
[13] 飾 *erikaza(ri)* necktie, cravat, bow
裏 *eriura* cloth to protect the back of the collar
[14] 髪 *erigami* back hair
[16] 懐 *kinkai* the heart; thought; magnanimity

14

襪 5505 / J6b24 / M34696 Batsu tabi, socks.

襦 5506 / J6b21 / M34678 Ju. *shitagi* underwear.
[10] 袢 *juban* underwear

襤 5507 / J6b22 / M34674 Ran rags.
[16] 褸 *boro, ranru* rag, scrap; tattered clothes; fault, defect; shabbiness
褸糞 *borokuso* trash, a word of disparagement

15

襭 5508 / J6b23 / M34702 Ketsu *tsumabasa(mu)* tuck up the skirt of a kimono under the belt to carry things.

16

襯 5509 / J6b25 / M34712 Shin underwear.
[6] 衣 *shin'i, shatsu* underwear

B 襲 5510 / J3d31 / M34717 Shū attack. *oso(u)* attack, advance on; succeed to; call unexpectedly. *kasa(ne)* pile, heap, layer; suits; set; course (of stones).
[5] 用 *shūyō suru* adopt, follow

⁶名 *shūmei* succession to another's professional name
⁷攻 *oso(i)-se(meru)* array against
来 *shūrai* invasion, raid, attack; visitation (of a calamity)
¹¹掛 *oso(i)-ka(karu)* rush on, attack, swoop down on
¹⁵撃 *shūgeki* attack, charge, raid
¹⁷爵 *shūshaku* succession to the peerage

— 17 —

襴 5511 / J6b26 / M34728 RAN a kind of cloth.

襷 5512 / J6b27 / M34737 (国字) *tasuki* cord for holding up sleeves.
¹¹掛 *tasukiga(ke)* holding up sleeves with a cord

RAD. 西 146

Nishi west. Variants: 襾, 覀. Nickname: West.

襾 5513 / J6b28 / M34762 A cover.

A **西** 5514 / J403e / M34763 SEI, SAI *nishi* west.
³土 *seido* western lands
山 *seizan* western hills
下 *saika suru* start for Kansai or western Japan
⁴日 *nishibi* westering sun
天 *seiten* western sky
方 *seihō* west, western, westward; the West. *Saihō* Western Paradise
方浄土 *Saihō Jōdo* Western Paradise
方教会 *Seihō Kyōkai* the Western Church
方極楽 *Saihō Gokuraku* Western Paradise
⁵北 *seihoku, nishikita* northwest
半球 *nishi hankyū* Western Hemisphere
瓜 *suika* watermelon
瓜糖 *suikatō* watermelon sugar
⁶向 *nishimu(ki)* facing west
⁸明 *nishiaka(ri)* twilight
郊 *seikō, saikō* western suburbs
京 *Saikyō* Kyoto, the Western Capital
学 *Seigaku* Western learning
東 *nishi-higashi* east and west; direction
国 *saikoku, saigoku* the western countries; western Japan
国巡礼 *saikoku junrei, saigoku junrei* west Japan 33-temple pilgrimage
岸 *seigan* west coast; west bank
岸沿 *seiganzo(i) ni* along the western coast; along the western seashore
欧 *Seiō* Western Europe; the West, the Occident
欧人 *Seiōjin* Westerner, European
欧化 *Seiōka* Europeanization
欧的 *Seiōteki* Western (style)
⁹面 *seimen, saimen* west side; the west; facing west
風 *nishi kaze, seifū* west wind; autumn wind; zephyr
海 *seikai* the western sea. *saikai* the western sea; the Kyushu seas
独 *Sei-Doku* West Germany
紀 *Seiki* A.D. Current Era, Common Era (C.E.)
軍 *seigun* the western army
南 *seinan, nishiminami* southwest
南役 *Seinan (no) Eki* Satsuma Rebellion
洋 *Seiyō* the West, the Occident; the western ocean
洋人 *Seiyōjin* Westerner, European
洋大根 *Seiyō daikon* radish
洋化 *Seiyōka* Westernization, Europeanization
洋気触 *Seiyō kabure* influence of the West
洋杉 *Seiyō sugi* cedar
洋李 *Seiyō sumomo* prune, plum
洋画 *Seiyōga* Western painting
洋風 *Seiyōfū* Western style
洋造 *Seiyōzuku(ri)* Western-style building
洋紀元 *Seiyō kigen* Christian Era
洋南瓜 *Seiyō kabocha* pumpkin
洋独活 *Seiyō udo* asparagus
洋思想 *Seiyō shisō* Western ideas
洋流 *Seiyōryū* Western ways
洋料理 *Seiyō ryōri* Western cooking
洋菓子 *Seiyōgashi* Western confectionery

洋間 *Seiyōma* Western-style room
洋館 *Seiyōkan* Western-style building
10 進 *seishin suru* proceed west
航 *seikō* sailing west, westbound
哲 *seitetsu* Western philosophy; Western philosopher
部 *seibu* the west, western part
部物 *seibumono* a Western (film)
部前線 *Seibu Zensen* the Western Front
部劇 *seibugeki* a Western (film)
11 遊 *saiyū, seiyū* visiting the west; visiting the Occident
域 *seiiki* India and lands to the west of China
側 *nishigawa* west side, west bank; the Western Powers. *seisoku* west side, west bank
経 *seikei* west longitude
教 *seikyō* Western religion, Christianity
寄 *nishiyo(ri)* westerly
14 漸 *seizen* westward advance
端 *seitan* western extremity
暦 *Seireki* Christian Era, Current Era, Common Era
暦紀元 *Seireki Kigen* Christian Era, Current Era, Common Era
16 諺 *seigen* Western proverb

3

A **要** 5515 / J4d37 / M34768' Yō main point, essence; aim; secret; need. *yō(suru), i(ru)* require, need; waylay, ambush. *yō(suru) ni* in the last analysis, in short. *i(ranu)* unwanted, useless, unnecessary. *kaname* pivot; the main point; the key (to).
2 人 *yōjin* leading personage, important man
4 心 *yōjin* care, caution, discretion
5 用 *yōyō* important matter; necessity; use
目 *yōmoku* principal items
石 *kaname ishi* keystone
処 *yōsho* the important points; the gist
6 因 *yōin* primary factor, main cause, prerequisite
式 *yōshiki* formality
件 *yōken* requisite, important matter; qualification; essentials
地 *yōchi* strategic point, important place
旨 *yōshi* gist, point, essentials; argument; summary; fundamental principles
7 図 *yōzu* rough sketch, sketch map
求 *yōkyū* request, demand, requirement
8 枢 *yōsū* importance
具 *yōgu* necessary tools
注意 *yōchūi* requiring (medical) care
所 *yōsho* important position, strategic point
所要所 *yōsho-yōsho* important places
9 約 *yōyaku* summary, digest
点 *yōten* gist, essentials, substance
10 部 *yōbu* essential part
員 *yōin* necessary personnel
害 *yōgai* fort, stronghold
素 *yōso* element, essential, requisite, constituent
11 略 *yōryaku* choosing the important sections and omitting the rest; digest of an article; gist, summary
務 *yōmu* important business
訣 *yōketsu* secret, key
望 *yōbō suru* cry for, demand, long for
望書 *yōbōsho* written request
12 項 *yōkō* gist, synopsis, important point
港 *yōkō* important port
13 義 *yōgi* essentials, essence, digest
路 *yōro* important road, main artery; responsible position; the authorities
塞 *yōsai* fort, stronghold, fortification
塞地帯 *yōsai chitai* fortified zone
塞戦 *yōsaisen* siege warfare
14 綱 *yōkō* outline, summary; general idea; general plan, prospectus
語 *yōgo* the important words; the summary
説 *yōsetsu* outline, general statement
領 *yōryō* the point, gist, essentials, outline, summary
領良 *yōryōyo(ku)* pointedly, sensibly, practically
15 衝 *yōshō* important place
談 *yōdan* important talks
請 *yōsei* demand, request, requirement
撃 *yōgeki* ambush attack
16 諦 *yōtei* secret (of success)
覧 *yōran* survey, summary, outline; handbook, directory, catalog
17 償 *yōshō* claim for damages
18 職 *yōshoku* responsible post

6

覃 5516 / J6b29 / M34778 Tan delicious; stretch out; long; deep; large; quiet.
3 及 *tankyū* stretch (to)

⁹思 *tanshi* deep thought

12

B覆 5517 / J4a24 / M34789' FUKU. FU. *kutsuga(eru)* overturn, capsize; fall; be ruined. *kutsuga(esu)* overturn, capsize; overthrow; undermine; frustrate; veto; disprove (a theory). *ō(u)* cover, veil; hang over; brood over; conceal; overlap; shelter; screen; disguise; wrap, envelop; obscure; shade; overshadow. *ō(i)* cover, covering; shade; mantle, coat; hood, bonnet; casing; awning.

4 水 *fukusui* spilt water
7 没 *fukubotsu suru* capsize and sink; suffer a serious defeat or a serious reversal in family fortunes
8 刻 *fukkoku* reproducing a book from identical plates
9 奏 *fukusō suru* reinvestigate and report
面 *fukumen* mask, veil, disguise
面子 *fukumenshi* anonymous writer
10 書 *fukusho* an answer by letter
11 啓 *fukukei* my answer (a letter salutation)
13 滅 *fukumetsu* overthrow, destruction
14 墜 *fukutsui* leaning and falling; the destruction of a family
蔵 *fukuzō* keeping things to oneself
蔵無 *fukuzōna(ku)* freely, frankly, plainly
15 輪 *fukurin* ornamental border
審 *fukushin* retrial
19 轍 *fukutetsu* ruts of an overturned carriage; the mistakes of our predecessors

13

覈 5518 / J6b2a / M34791 KAKU investigate.

B覇 5519 / J4746 / M34790 霸 6547 / J5b31 / M42490 HA supremacy, leadership, domination, hegemony; supreme ruler; champion.

6 気 *haki* ambition
8 府 *hafu* shogunate
者 *hasha* supreme ruler; champion
11 道 *hadō* military rule
道政策 *hadō seisaku* plans for world conquest
13 業 *hagyō* exploits; domination
15 権 *haken* domination, supremacy, leadership

17

覊 5520 / J-X / M34794 See 羈 4657.

19

覉 5521 / J6b2b / M34795 See 羈 4657.

7-STROKE RADICALS

RAD. 見 147

Miru to see. Nickname: Seeing.

A見 5522 / J382b / M34796 KEN, GEN hopes, chances; ideas, opinion. *mi(ru)* see, look at, witness, observe; regard as; sightsee; look through; examine; consult (a lexicon); tell (one's future); estimate; care for; try, test. *mi(eru)* see; be seen, be visible, be in sight; look like, seem, appear; come, show up; be found. *mi(seru)* show, let see, display; make look like, pretend. *mami(eru)* see, be presented to, have an audience with. *mi(sebirakasu)* display, flaunt, parade. *mi(seshime)* object lesson, warning, example. *mi(ttomonai)* indecent, unbecoming, scandalous; unsightly, ugly. *mi(e)* ostentation. *mi(tekure)* appearance.

2 入 *mi-i(ru)* gaze intently at, scrutinize; curse; (devils) possess (people)

3 上 *mi-a(geru)* look up at; admire, respect
下 *mi-kuda(su)* command a view of; look down on, despise. *mi-o(rosu)* overlook, command a view of. *mi-sa(geru)* look down over; look down on
下果 *mi-sa(ge)-ha(teru)* look despisingly down on. *misa(ge)ha(teta)* mean, contemptible
4 手 *mite* onlooker
方 *mikata* viewpoint, way of looking
比 *mi-kura(beru)* compare with the eye
込 *mi-ko(mu)* expect, anticipate; estimate; trust; mark (as a victim). *miko(mi)* hope, prospects, possibility, forecast, expectation
込違 *miko(mi)chiga(i)* miscalculation
切 *mi-ki(ru)* see all; abandon; sell at a bargain
切品 *mikirihin* clearance goods
分 *mi-wa(keru)* distinguish, recognize; judge; identify. *miwa(ke)* distinction; discrimination, judgment; identification, recognition
分難 *miwa(ke)gata(i)* indistinguishable, unrecognizable
5 立 *mi-ta(teru)* diagnose; choose; compare to; form an opinion. *mida(te)* appearance. *mita(te)* diagnosis; choice; opinion; seeing off
処 *midokoro* merit, promise
巡 *mi-megu(ru)* inspect, make the rounds
外 *mi-hazu(su)* miss seeing, overlook. *mi-so(reru)* fail to recognize
収 *miosa(me)* farewell look
台 *kendai* rack for holding a book
失 *mi-ushina(u)* lose sight of, miss
付 *mitsu(karu)* be found; be found out, be discovered. *mitsu(keru)* find; find out; discover, locate; catch sight of; notice, recognize; hunt for, get used to seeing, be familiar to. *mitsuke* approach (to a castle gate)
付出 *mitsu(ke)-da(su)* search out, hunt up
出 *mi-ida(su)* discover, detect, select, find out. *mida(shi)* heading, caption, subtitle, index
出語 *mida(shi)go* index word
本 *mihon* sample, pattern, specimen, copy, model, example
本市 *mihon ichi* industrial fair
世 *mise* store, shop, booth, office
世物 *misemono* show, exhibition, circus
世開 *misebira(ki)* opening a new store
目 *mi(ru)me* the sight; power of observation. *mi(ta)me ni* to look at. *mime* looks, features, face, form
目好 *mimeyo(i)* good-looking
目形 *mimekatachi* looks, features, face, form
目良 *mimeyo(i)* good-looking
目姿 *mimesugata* form, figure, appearance
目麗 *mime-uruwa(shii)* beautiful (woman)
6 回 *mi-mawa(ru)* patrol, inspect. *mimawa(ri)* patrol, round of inspection; patrolman, inspector, floorwalker
尽 *mi-tsu(kusu)* see all
向 *mi-mu(ku)* look around, look toward (us)
印 *ken'in* ordinary seal
地 *kenchi* standpoint, viewpoint
交 *mi-ka(wasu)* exchange glances
守 *mi-mamo(ru)* watch over
劣 *mioto(ri)* unfavorable comparison
合 *mi-a(u)* exchange glances; counterbalance. *mi-a(waseru)* exchange glances; postpone. *mia(i)* marriage interview
合結婚 *mia(i) kekkon* marriage after just one interview
当 *mi-ata(ru)* be found. *kentō* aim, mark; estimate, guess; direction; approximation
当違 *kentōchiga(i)* wrong guess, miscalculation
返 *mi-kae(ru)* look back or over the shoulder. *mi-kae(su)* look back, stare back at; triumph over. *mikae(shi)* inside the cover
返物資 *mikaeri busshi* collateral goods
返品 *mikae(ri)hin* returned goods
7 見 *mi(ru)mi(ru)* in an instant. *mi(su)mi(su)* before one's very eyes. *mi(ru)mi(ru) uchi ni* while looking
辛 *mizurai* unbearable to look at; ugly, unattractive
坊 *mi(e)bō* vain person, a fop
抜 *mi-nu(ku)* see through

初 *mi-so(meru)* see for the first time, fall in love at first sight
附 *mitsuke* approach (to a castle gate)
忘 *mi-wasu(reru)* forget, fail to recognize
良 *mi(ttomo)i(i)* respectable, dignified
8 金 *mi(se)gane* show money
届 *mi-todo(keru)* ascertain, verify
逃 *mi-noga(su)* miss, overlook, let pass, wink at, leave at large
送 *mi-oku(ru)* see off, bid farewell; follow with one's eyes; escort (home); care for until death; let pass; wait and see
始 *mihaji(me)* seeing for the first time
所 *midokoro* merit, promise. *mi(ta) tokoro* to all appearances
放 *mi-sa(ku)* look afar. *mi-hana(su)* forsake, abandon
限 *mi-kagi(ru)* forsake, desert, abandon, despair of
直 *mi-nao(su)* look again; take a turn for the better; think better of
参 *genzan, kenzan suru* see, meet
定 *mi-sada(meru)* ascertain, make sure of
易 *miyasu(i)* easy to see; obvious, clear; easy to read (a thermometer)
受 *mi-u(keru)* see, come across, judge by appearances
苦 *miguru(shii)* disgraceful; unsightly; indecent; clumsy
咎 *mi-toga(meru)* question, challenge; find fault with
学 *kengaku* study and observation
者 *kensha* sightseer
果 *mi-ha(teru)* see through to the finish; be seen to the last
事 *migoto* beautiful, splendid
知 *kenchi suru, mi-shi(ru)* know by inspection, knowing by sight. *mishiri* an acquaintance. *mi-shi(ranu), mi(zu)-shi(razu) no* strange, unknown
知越 *mishi(ri)go(shi)* well-acquainted
取 *mi-to(ru)* see and know, notice, discern, recognize; see and copy. *mi(te) to(ru)* realize, understand
取図 *mitorizu* rough sketch, sketch map
物 *mimono* sight, spectacle, attraction. *kembutsu* sightseeing. *mi(se)mono* show, circus
物人 *kembutsunin* sightseer, visitor, spectator
物席 *kembutsuseki* seats at a game or theater
物衆 *kembutsushū* theater audience, crowd at a game
9 透 *mi(e)-su(ku)* be transparent. *mi-su(kasu)* see through. *mi-tō(su)* get an unobstructed view; see through
通 *mi-tō(su)* get an unobstructed view; see through. *mitō(shi)* perspective, unobstructed view; outlook, forecast
映 *miba(e)* outward appearance
神 *kenshin* vision of God; actually perceiving a god
計 *mi-haka(ru), mi-haka(rau)* choose freely; time (a visit)
変 *mi-ka(eru)* prefer; forsake for some other (person or thing)
栄 *mie* appearance; show, display
栄坊 *miebō* fop, coxcomb, vain person
栄張 *mie (o) ha(ru)* show off, be vainglorious. *mie(p)pari* personal display
10 逸 *mi-so(reru)* miss seeing, overlook. *mi-(hagureru)* miss, lose sight of
振 *mi(nu)fu(ri) (o) suru* pretend not to see
残 *mi-noko(su)* leave unseen
破 *mi-yabu(ru)* see through
料 *kenryō* admission fee
納 *miosa(me)* farewell look
紛 *mi-mago(u)* err in observing
殺 *migoro(shi)* letting (someone) die before one's eyes without helping
兼 *mi-ka(neru)* be unable to look on with indifference; can't stand to see
真似 *mimane* seeing and copying
11 過 *mi-su(gosu), mi-su(gusu)* miss, overlook, let pass, wink at, leave at large
做 *mina(su)* regard as, consider, presume
頃 *migoro* the time to see
得 *mie* pose, posture, gesture. *mi(eru)* see, be seen, be visible, be in sight; look like; seem, appear, come, show up; be found
惚 *mi-to(reru), mi-ho(reru)* be charmed by, gaze in rapture
据 *mi-su(eru)* stare at, gaze at
捨 *mi-su(teru)* forsake, desert, abandon, leave desolate

悪 *miniku(i)* hard to see, indistinct; illegible
掛 *mi-ka(keru)* see, meet; perceive, notice. *mika(ke)* appearance; apparent
掛通 *mika(ke)dō(ri)* true to appearances
掛倒 *mika(ke)dao(shi)* mere show, deceptive appearances
習 *mi-nara(u)* receive training; learn by observation; follow an example. *minarai* apprenticeship; apprentice, learner
習工 *minaraikō* apprentice
習士官 *minarai shikan* cadet
習生 *minaraisei* trainee
張 *miha(ru)* watch, stand guard, picket; strain (one's eyes). *miha(ri)* guard, lookout, picket; floorwalker
張人 *miha(ri)bito, miha(ri)nin* watcher, lookout
張台 *miha(ri)dai* watchtower
張所 *miha(ri)sho* lookout, crow's nest, watcher, lookout
張番 *mihariban* guard, picket; floorwalker
12 開 *mi-hira(ku)* open (the eyes) wide. *mihira(ki)* a double page picture or chart
遣 *mi-ya(ru)* look at, glance at
違 *mi-chiga(eru)* mistake, cannot recognize. *michiga(i), michiga(e)* misperception, mistake
逃 *mi-noga(su)* miss, overlook, let pass, wink at, leave at large
場 *miba* looks, appearance. *mi(se)ba* highlight (of a play)
晴 *mi-ha(rasu)* command a view of. *miha(rashi)* view, outlook, visibility
極 *mi-kiwa(meru)* see through, discern, probe, make sure of
渡 *mi-wata(su)* look out over, survey (the scene)
落 *mi-o(tosu)* miss seeing, overlook, lose sight of
番 *kemban* geisha exchange
装 *minari* attire, personal appearance
覚 *mi-obo(eru)* remember, recognize
間 *mi(ru) ma ni* before one's very eyes
間違 *mi-machiga(eru)* mistake, cannot recognize
越 *mi-ko(su)* anticipate, foresee; look across
越松 *miko(shi) (no) matsu* overhanging pine
13 損 *mi-sokona(u)* misjudge, mistake, miss seeing. *mi-son(zuru), mi-son(jiru)* make a mistake in observation
解 *kenkai* opinion, view
詰 *mi-tsu(meru)* gaze at, stare at, behold
較 *mi-kura(beru)* compare with the eye
隠 *mi(e)gaku(re)* appearing and disappearing; visible and invisible
飽 *mi-a(kiru)* be tired of looking at
馴 *mi-na(reru)* get used to seeing, be familiar to
置 *mi(te) o(ku)* count on (an hour)
14 聞 *kemmon, kembun, miki(ki)* information; experience, observation
境 *misakai* distinction, discrimination
慣 *mi-na(reru)* get used to seeing, be familiar to (me)
様 *miyō* viewpoint, way of looking
誤 *mi-aya(maru)* err in observing, mistake a signal
15 澄 *mi-su(masu)* observe carefully; make sure
蕩 *mi-to(reru)* be charmed by, gaze in rapture
影無 *mi(ru)kage(mo)na(i)* wretched, miserable
舞 *mi-ma(u)* inquire about a sick person. *mima(i)* inquiry, expression of sympathy
舞人 *mima(i)nin* sympathizer, visitor
舞状 *mima(i)jō* letter of sympathy
舞金 *mima(i)kin* money gift to a sick person
舞品 *mima(i)hin* gift to a sick person
舞客 *mima(i)kyaku* hospital visitors
16 縊 *mi-kubi(ru)* belittle, underrate
積 *mi-tsu(moru)* estimate at, value at, assess (damage). *mitsumo(ri)* estimate, quotation
積書 *mitsumorisho* written estimate
17 優 *mimasa(ri) suru* look better, compare favorably
18 繕 *mi-tsukuro(u)* choose freely; time (a visit)
顕 *mi-ara(wasu)* reveal
19 離 *mi-hana(su)* desert, abandon, give up (hope)
識 *kenshiki* views, discernment, knowledge; dignity, self-respect
識振 *kenshikibu(ru)* pretend to know it all

識張 *kenshikiba(ru)* pretend to know it all
²¹露 *mi-ara(wasu)* detect, expose, see through
²²霽 *mi-haru(kasu)* see over a broad area

— 4 —

覓 5523 / J6b2c / M34815 BEKI. *moto(meru)* want, request; seek, search for; pursue (pleasure); hunt (a job).

A規 5524 / J352c / M34810 槼 3981 / J-X / M23979 KI standard; measure.
⁵正 *kisei* regulation, control
⁶那 *kina* quinine, cinchona
⁸制 *kisei* regulation, control
定 *kitei* bylaws, provisions, regulations
⁹律 *kiritsu suru* govern (a program). *kiritsu* regulations; order; discipline; system; regularity ⌈criterion, rule
矩 *kiku* compasses and ruler; standard,
約 *kiyaku* agreement, pact, rules, code, bylaws, articles
則 *kisoku* regulation, rule
則立 *kisokuda(tsu)* be perfectly arranged
則尽 *kisokuzu(kume)* bound by rules
則的 *kisokuteki* regular, systematic, orderly
則書 *kisokusho* prospectus, (school) catalog, regulations
則動詞 *kisoku dōshi* regular verb
¹⁰格 *kikaku* standard, norm, gauge, rule
格化 *kikakuka* standardization, normalization; prefabrication; reorientation
格品 *kikakuhin* standardized goods
¹²程 *kitei* bylaws, provisions, regulations
¹³準 *kijun* standard, basis
準化 *kijunka* normalization
¹⁴模 *kibo* scale, scope, plan, structure
¹⁵範 *kihan* standard, norm, criterion

A視 5525 / J3b6b / M34827' 視 5526 / J-X / M34836 SHI regard as. *mi(ru)* see, look at; guard. *-shisuru* regard as, look upon as. *shi-* apparent (in astronomy).
²力 *shiryoku* eyesight, visual power
力検査 *shiryoku kensa* eye test
⁵号通信 *shigō tsūshin* communication by visible signals
⁷角 *shikaku* angle of vision; optic angle; viewpoint
⁸官 *shikan* the organ of sight
学 *shigaku* school inspection; school inspector
学官 *shigakkan* government school inspector
⁹度 *shido* visibility
点 *shiten* viewpoint
界 *shikai* range of vision, visibility
神経 *shishinkei* optic nerve
¹⁰差 *shisa* parallax
¹¹野 *shiya* field of vision
運動 *shiundō* apparent motion
¹²程 *shitei* visibility, visual range
診 *shishin* examination of a patient by inspection
覚 *shikaku* sense of sight, vision
¹³感 *shikan* sense of sight, vision
¹⁴察 *shisatsu* inspection, observation
¹⁵線 *shisen* line of vision
¹⁷聴 *shichō* attention, interest; viewing TV
聴率 *shichōritsu* audience rating
聴覚 *shichōkaku* visual and auditory senses, sight and hearing, audiovisual
聴覚教材 *shichōkaku kyōzai* audio-visual aids
聴覚教育 *shichōkaku kyōiku* audio-visual education

— 5 —

視 5526 / J-X / M34836 See 視 5525.

覘 5527 / J6b2d / M34840 TEN. *nozo(ku)* peep, peek; come in sight.

覗 5528 / J4741 / M34839 SHI. *nozo(ku)* peep, peek; come in sight.
⁴込 *nozo(ki)-ko(mu)* look into, peer into, peep in
⁵穴 *nozoki ana* peephole, sky hole

A覚 5529 / J3350 / M34846 覺 5539 / J6b34 / M34973 KAKU. *obo(eru)* remember, memorize; learn, perceive; feel, experience, know; expect. *sato(ru)* perceive, discern, realize, understand, comprehend; attain enlightenment, find one's philosophy. *sa(masu)* *vt* awake,

wake up. *sa(meru) vi* awake, be disillusioned; sober up. *obo(ezu)* involuntarily, unwittingly, instinctively. *obo(shii)* looking like a, apparently a (foreigner). *obo(e)* feeling, learning; memory, recollection; esteem, memo.

7 束無 *obotsukana(i)* uncertain, dubious, uneasy, precarious (living), unsteady, unreliable, almost hopeless

8 知 *kakuchi* preception

知主義 *kakuchi shugi* gnosticism

10 書 *oboegaki* memo, note; memorial, protocol; book of remembrance

悟 *kakugo* resolution, readiness, expectation, resignation; perception (of truth)

悟前 *kakugo (no) mae* resignation to whatever may happen

11 帳 *obo(e)chō* memorandum, notebook

12 違 *obo(e)chiga(i)* misunderstanding, memory slip

13 際 *sa(me)giwa* on the verge of awakening

16 醒 *kakusei* awakening, disillusionment

醒剤 *kakuseizai* stimulant

19 識 *kakushiki suru* know and understand

7

覡 5530 J6b2e M34875 Geki. *kannagi* medium, diviner.

9

覩 5531 J6b2f M34913 To see.

覦 5532 J6b30 M34904 Yu coveting high rank.

A **覧** 5533 J4d77 M34928 Ran. *mi(ru)* see.

12 勝 *ranshō* beholding a marvelous view

A **親** 5534 J3f46 M34918 Shin intimacy; parents; relative. *oya* parent; dealer (in card games); banker (in gambling). *chika(i)*, *shita(shii)* intimate, familiar, friendly. *shita(shimu)* be intimate with; have a liking for; take habitually. *shita(shimi)* intimacy, familiarity, friendship. *mizukara* oneself, personally. *shin-* pro-(American).

3 子 *oyako* parent and child; bowl of rice topped with chicken and eggs. *shinshi* parent and child

子丼 *oyako domburi* bowl of rice topped with chicken and eggs

4 心 *oyagokoro* parental love, parent's heart

方 *oyakata* boss, foreman

日 *shin-Nichi* pro-Japanese

木 *oyagi* the host plant of a graft

父 *shimpu* father. *oyaji* (in familiar talk) governor, judge, father

犬 *oya inu* mother dog

仏 *shin-Futsu* pro-French

仁 *oyaji* (in familiar talk) governor, judge, father

元 *oyamoto ni* at home, with one's parents

友 *shin'yū* close friend, chum, pal

文字 *oya moji* capital letter

不孝 *oyafukō* lack of filial piety

王 *shinnō* imperial prince

王家 *shinnōke* imperial prince's family

切 *shinsetsu* kindness

切気 *shinsetsugi* kindliness, friendship

分 *oyabun* boss, chief, head

分子分 *oyabun-kobun* leaders and followers

5 母 *shimbo* one's true mother

玉 *oyadama* boss, chief, leader

石 *oya ishi* cornerstone

旧 *shinkyū* relatives and old friends

代代 *oyadaidai no* ancestral

旦那 *oya danna* the old master

兄弟 *oya-kyōdai* parents, brothers, and sisters; nearest relatives

6 米 *shim-Bei* pro-American

好 *shinkō* intimacy, friendship

交 *shinkō* friendship, intimacy

合 *shita(shimi)a(u)* be familiar with

団体 *oya dantai* parent organization

会社 *oyagaisha*, *oya kaisha* parent company; holding corporation; assembly plant

近 *shinkin* familiarity; personal attendants

近性 *shinkinsei* familiarity

近感 *shinkinkan* feeling of familiarity

任 *shinnin* personal imperial appointment

任式 *shinninshiki* imperial investiture ceremony
任官 *shinninkan* official personally appointed by the emperor
7 身 *shimmi* relative. *shimmei no* kind, cordial, sincere
里 *oyazato* hometown
兵 *shimpei* bodyguard, imperial bodyguard
告 *shinkoku* personal statement; personal accusation
孝行 *oya-kōkō* filial piety
8 征 *shinsei* emperor's personal campaign
披 *shimpi* confidential, personal, private
拝 *shimpai* worship (by the emperor)
泣 *oyana(kase)* disappointment to parents
英 *shin-Ei* pro-English
炙 *shinsha* close contact
知 *oyashi(razu)* wisdom tooth; dangerous place; everyone for himself; a child who does not know his parents
和 *shinwa* friendship, fellowship, fraternity
和力 *shinwaryoku* chemical attraction, affinity
9 風 *oyakaze* parental authority
厚 *shinkō* intimacy; kindness
指 *oyayubi* thumb; the boss
昵 *shinjitsu* familiarity
柱 *oyabashira* central pillar
独 *shin-Doku* pro-German
神 *oyagami* clan god, ancestral god
政 *shinsei* direct imperial rule
思 *oyaomo(i)* filial affection
重代 *oyajūdai* successive generations
10 骨 *oyabone* outer rib of a fan
株 *oyakabu* original stock
殺 *oyagoro(shi), oyakoro(shi)* parricide, matricide
書 *shinsho* autographed letter
馬鹿 *oyabaka* parental overindulgence
展 *shinten* confidential, personal (letter)
展書 *shintensho* confidential letter
11 鳥 *oyadori* parent bird, mother bird
掛 *oyaga(kari)* dependence on father
猫 *oya neko* mother cat
船 *oyabune* depot ship; large Chinese junk
許 *oyamoto* parental roof; parents; home; banker for gamblers
密 *shimmitsu* intimacy, close friendship
祭 *shinsai* Shinto rites conducted by the emperor
教会 *oya kyōkai* mother church
戚 *shinseki* relative
戚関係 *shinseki kankei* kinship
族 *shinzoku* relatives
族会議 *shinzoku kaigi* family council
族結婚 *shinzoku kekkon* consanguinous marriage, intermarriage
族閥 *shinzokubatsu* nepotism
12 御 *oyago* (your) parents
椀 *oyawan* large rice bowl
疎 *shinso* degree of intimacy
勝 *oyamasa(ri)* a child surpassing his parents
爺 *oyaji* (in familiar talk) governor, judge, father
等 *shintō* degree of kinship
筆 *shimpitsu* one's own writing
裁 *shinsai* imperial decision
証券 *oya shōken* master (insurance) policy
無 *oyana(shi)* orphaned
無子 *oyana(shi)go* orphan
善 *shinzen* friendship, amity, goodwill
善日 *shinzembi* good-neighbor day
善条約 *shinzen jōyaku* treaty of amity
善使節 *shinzen shisetsu* good-will envoy
善飛行 *shinzen hikō* good-will flight
善関係 *shinzen kankei* friendly relations
13 馴 *shitashi(mi)-na(reru)* become friends
愛 *shin'ai* affection, love
署 *shinsho* personal signature
電 *shinden* ruler's telegram
睦 *shimboku* friendship, reunion
睦会 *shimbokkai, shimbokukai* social gathering
14 銀行 *oyaginkō* parent bank
15 閲 *shin'etsu* personal inspection
権 *shinken* parental authority and responsibility
縁 *shin'en* relative
16 衛 *shin'ei* imperial guards
衛兵 *shin'eihei* bodyguard
衛隊 *shin'eitai* bodyguard troops
17 優 *oyamasa(ri)* a child surpassing his parents
臨 *shinrin* imperial visit, personal presence

鍵 *oya kagi* master key
18 藩 *shimpan* daimyos related to the Tokugawa shoguns
類 *shinrui* relative
類付合 *shinruizu(ki)a(i)* association among relatives; intimate association
19 蘇 *shin-So* pro-Soviet
20 譲 *oyayuzu(ri)* inheritance from a parent
21 露 *shin-Ro* pro-Russian

10

覯 5535 / J6b32 / M34937 Kō happening to meet.

覬 5536 / J6b31 / M34934 Ki coveting high rank.
16 覦 *kiyu suru* have designs on

11

覲 5537 / J6b33 / M34952 Kin. *mami(eru)* meet; have an audience with.

A **観** 5538 / J3451 / M34955 **觀** 5542 / J6b37 / M34993 Kan look, appearance; spectacle; condition; view, outlook. *kan(zuru)* view, contemplate. *mi(ru)* see, look at, witness, observe; regard as; sightsee; look through; examine, consult (a lexicon); tell (one's fortune); estimate; care for; try, test.
4 月 *kangetsu* moon viewing
天喜地 *kanten kichi* ecstasy
5 世音 *Kanzeon* Goddess of Mercy, Kannon
世音菩薩 *Kanzeon Bosatsu* Goddess of Mercy, Kannon
6 光 *kankō* sightseeing
光団 *kankōdan* tourist party
光客 *kankōkyaku* tourist, sightseer
光船 *kankōsen* excursion ship
7 花植物 *kanka shokubutsu* flowering plant
兵 *kampei* show of force
兵式 *kampeishiki* military review, parade
8 取 *kanshu suru* see through, perceive, notice, get wind of
者 *kansha* sightseer
念 *kannen* meditation; idea; intention; sense (of duty); resignation to, preparation; conviction
念主義 *kannen shugi* idealism
念的 *kannenteki* ideal, ideological
念連合 *kannen rengō* association of ideas
念論 *kannenron* idealism, ideology
念闘争 *kannen tōsō* ideological warfare
9 点 *kanten* viewpoint, angle of vision
相学 *kansōgaku* phrenology
相術 *kansōjutsu* phrenology
客 *kankaku, kankyaku* visitors, spectators, audience
客層 *kankakuso, kankyakusō* the audience level
音 *Kannon* Bodhisattva of mercy, Kannon
音堂 *Kannondo* a temple to the Bodhisattva of Mercy (Kannon)
音菩薩 *Kannon Bosatsu* Bodhisattva of Mercy, Kannon
音開 *kannombira(ki)* folding doors
10 梅 *kambai* viewing plum blossoms
桜 *kan'ō* viewing the cherries
桜会 *kan'ōkai* cherry-blossom party
11 菊 *kangiku* chrysanthemum viewing
望 *kambō* observation
12 衆 *kanshū* audience, spectators
象 *kanshō* meteorological observation
葉植物 *kan'yō shokubutsu* foliage plant
測 *kansoku* observation, survey; thinking, opinion
測気球 *kansoku kikyū* observation balloon
測所 *kansokujo* observatory; observation post
13 楓 *kampū* viewing maple leaves
想 *kansō* contemplation, observation
照 *kanshō* contemplation, (esthetic) intuition
戦 *kansen suru* witness a battle or a game
戦武官 *kansembukan* military observer
14 察 *kansatsu* observation, survey, investigation, supervision; view
察力 *kansatsuryoku* power of observation
察者 *kansatsusha* observer
察眼 *kansatsugan* an observing eye
15 劇 *kangeki* theatergoing

潮 *kanchō* watching the tide
賞 *kanshō* admiration, enjoyment
賞植物 *kanshō shokubutsu* ornamental plants
16 覧 *kanran* inspection, viewing
覧券 *kanranken* admission ticket
覧者 *kanransha* spectator, visitor
覧席 *kanranseki* seats, grandstand
覧料 *kanranryō* admission fee
覧税 *kanranzei* entertainment tax
20 艦式 *kankanshiki* naval review

13

覺 5539 / J6b34 / M34973 See 覚 5529.

14

覽 5540 / J6b35 / M34977 See 覧 5533.

15

覿 5541 / J6b36 / M34984 TEKI meet, see.

9 面 *tekimen no* immediate, instantaneous, swift

17

觀 5542 / J6b37 / M34993 See 観 5538.

角 RAD. 148

Tsuno horn. At left: *tsuno hen*. Nickname: Horn.

A 角 5543 / J3351 / M35003 KAKU angle; corner; square; squared timber; target. *kado* corner; angle; edge; angularity; harshness. *kaku(na)* square, four-cornered. *tsuno* horn, antlers; feeler, tentacle. *tsuno(gumu)* sprout. *sumi* corner, nook.

2 力 *sumō* sumo wrestling; wrestler
3 叉 *tsunomata* points on antlers
4 刈 *kakuga(ri)* square-cut hair
5 皿 *kakuzara* square plate
石 *kakuishi* square stone
立 *tsunoda(teru)*, *kadoda(teru)* be sharp, be pointed; be rough; sound harsh. *kado (ga) ta(tsu)* sound harsh
目立 *tsunomeda(teru)* be sharp, be pointed; be rough; sound harsh
6 字 *kakuji* square characters
行灯 *kakuandon* square paper lantern
7 角 *kadokado ni* on every corner. *kadokado(shii)* angularity, stiffness, harshness
材 *kakuzai* squared timber, lumber
形 *kakugata* square shape
8 店 *kado mise* corner store
取 *kado (ga) to(reru)* be tactful
突 *tsunotsu(ki)* bullfight; brushing by; wrangling
突合 *tsunotsu(ki)a(i)* bickering, wrangling
9 革 *kadogawa* corner leather (on a book)
度 *kakudo* angle
通 *kakutsū* an expert on sumo
逐 *kakuchiku suru* compete with, vie with
柱 *kakuchū* square pillar, prism (in math). *kakubashira* square pillar
盆 *kakubon* square tray
背革 *kadosegawa* three-quarter binding
速度 *kaku sokudo* angular velocity
屋敷 *kado yashiki* corner house
砂糖 *kakuzatō* cube sugar
10 帯 *kaku obi* a man's stiff obi
素 *kakuso* keratin
袖 *kakusode* square bag sleeves; civilian clothes; plain-clothes man
袖巡査 *kakusode junsa* plain-clothes man
11 張 *kakuba(ru)* be angular; become formal
距 *kakkyo* angular distance
瓶 *kakubin* square bottle
笛 *tsunobue* bugle, trumpet, horn
細工 *tsunozaiku* horn work
視差 *kaku shisa* angular parallax
12 帽 *kakubō* square college cap
13 隠 *tsunokaku(shi)* bride's wedding hood

14 膜 *kakumaku* cornea 「cornea
膜炎 *kakumakuen* inflammation of the
15 質 *kakushitsu* keratin, horniness
質物 *kakushitsubutsu* horny (keratin) material
16 樽 *tsunodaru* two-handled keg
鋼 *kakkō* square bar steel
錐 *kakusui* pyramid
17 壔 *kakutō* prism
18 襟 *kakueri* square neck (in a garment)
23 鑢 *kaku yasuri* square file

5

觚 5544 J6b38 M35013 Ko cup; piece of wood used before paper for writing letters.

觝 5545 J6b3a M35051 TEI touch, feel.

13 触 *teishoku* touch, feel; feeling

6

觜 5546 J6b39 M35050 See **嘴** 905.

B **触** 5547 J3f28 M35070 **觸** 5551 J6b3d M35181 SHOKU touching. *fu(reru)* touch, feel, hit, strike, graze; announce, proclaim, mention, refer to; conflict with, be contrary to. *sawa(ru)* touch, feel. *fu(re)* touch, contact; official notice. *sawa(ri)* touch, feel; point (of a story); good mixer.

4 手 *shokushu* feeler, tentacle
込 *fu(re)-ko(mu)* announce, pretend to be, pass off for, pose as
太鼓 *fu(re)daiko* drum beating (to announce sumo)
5 目 *shokumoku* seeing
示 *fu(re)-shime(su)* proclaim, announce
出 *fu(re)da(shi)* announcement, advertisement; introduction
6 回 *fu(re)-mawa(su)*, *fu(re)-mawa(ru)* spread (a rumor), noise abroad, broadcast
合 *fu(re)-a(u)* touch, come in contact with
7 角 *shokkaku* feeler, antenna, tentacle
吻 *shokufun* proboscis
8 知 *shokuchi suru* feel, perceive by touching
官 *shokkan* the organ of touch
9 発 *shokuhatsu* contact detonation
発水雷 *shokuhatsu suirai* contact mine
10 書 *fu(re)ga(ki)* circularized official announcement
11 接 *shokusetsu* touching
12 媒 *shokubai* catalyst
渡 *fu(re)-wata(su)* spread (a rumor), noise abroad, broadcast
診 *shokushin* palpation, manipulation, manual examination
覚 *shokkaku* sense of touch
13 感 *shokkan* touch sensation

A **解** 5548 J3272 M35067 **觧** 5549 J6b3b M35074 GE, KAI explanation, notes; key; excuse; understanding. *kai(suru)* understand, comprehend, interpret. *to(ku)* untie, undo, loosen, unpack; unravel, disentangle, unsew; dismantle; solve, answer; dispel; cancel; absolve; release; dismiss (a person); explain. *to(ku)*, *to(kasu)* comb out. *to(keru)* get loose, come untied; relent; be solved, be dispelled; be relieved (of a job). *hodo(ku)* *vi* and *vt* undo, untie, unpack, unfasten, loosen, unlace, unravel, get untied. *hogu(reru)*, *hodo(keru)* get loose, get untied. *hogu(su)*, *hogo(su)* untie, unfasten, loosen, fray, unknit, unravel, disentangle. *hogo(reru)* get loose, get untied; fray, get disentangled. *hotsu(reru)* fray, ravel, stray, become loose. *waka(ru)* understand, comprehend; know, be known, be identified; be open to reason, be sensible; can tell (what will happen); appreciate; be announced; be discovered; recognize. *ge(senai)* (it) passes understanding.

5 付 *to(ki)-tsu(keru)* comb; persuade
氷 *kaihyō* thaw; thawing
6 団 *kaidan* disbanding
式 *kaishiki* solution, key
任 *kainin* dismissal, release
合 *to(ke)-a(u)* be melted together, be reconciled. *to(ke)a(i)* compromise
7 体 *kaitai* dismantling, dissolution, liquidation; autopsy
決 *kaiketsu* solution, settlement
8 明 *to(ki)-a(kasu)*, *kaimei suru* explain, elucidate
法 *kaihō* (key to) a solution

版 *kaihan* type distribution
物 *to(ki)mono* old clothes to be ripped apart
官 *gekan* dismissing an official
毒剤 *gedokuzai* antidote
析 *kaiseki* analysis
析幾何学 *kaiseki kikagaku* analytical geometry
放 *to(ki)-hana(tsu), kaihō suru* release, deliver, liberate, emancipate
放的 *kaihōteki* open-minded, frank
放感 *kaihōkan* the feeling of freedom upon release
9 約 *kaiyaku* cancellation of a contract
除 *kaijo* cancellation, rescinding; release; exoneration
10 悟 *kaigo* enlightenment
消 *kaishō* dissolution, liquidation; cancellation; settlement
党 *kaitō* dissolution of a party
帰 *to(ki)-kae(su)* let go free, release (prisoners)
剖 *kaibō* dissection; autopsy; analysis
剖学 *kaibōgaku* anatomy
剖室 *kaibōshitsu* dissecting room
11 停 *kaitei* removing a ban, releasing from suspension
捨 *to(ki)-su(teru)* break the bonds
脱 *gedatsu* (Buddhist) salvation, emancipation, deliverance
釈 *kaishaku* explanation, interpretation
隊 *kaitai* demobilization
12 雇 *kaiko* discharge, dismissal
散 *kaisan* dispersion, disbanding, dissolution, dismissal
答 *kaitō* answer, solution
13 傭 *kaiyō* dismissal, discharge
解 *to(ki)-hogo(su), to(ki)-hodo(ku) vt* unravel, rip apart
義 *kaigi* explanation
禁 *kaikin* lifting a ban or embargo
14 読 *kaidoku* deciphering, decoding
語 *kaigo* understanding a word
髪 *hotsu(re)gami* uncombed hair, stray hair
説 *kaisetsu* explanation, commentary
説者 *kaisetsusha* commentator, expounder
説欄 *kaisetsuran* commentator's column
15 熱 *genetsu* alleviation of fever
熱剤 *genetsuzai* antipyretic
16 薬 *geyaku* antidote
18 職 *kaishoku* discharge, dismissal
題 *kaidai* synopsis, review of a subject
27 纜 *kairan* sailing, leaving

11

觴 5550 / J6b3c / M35157 Shō cup.

13

觸 5551 / J6b3d / M35181 See **触** 5547.

RAD. 言 149

Kotoba word. At left: *gomben* left-side "speaking." Nickname: Speaking.

A **言** 5552 / J3840 / M35205 Gen, Gon word; phrase; speech; statement. *yu(u), i(u)* say, tell, talk, speak, declare; call, term, name. *kotoba* word, term; phrase; language; a language; dialect; statement. *i(i-konasu)* express correctly. *i(i-sobireru)* fail to tell, miss a chance of telling. *i(waba)* so to speak, in a sense. *(to) i(eba)* speaking of. *(towa) i(u) monono, (towa)i(e)* but, still, however. *i(ikonashi)* an expression. *i(wambakari)* as much as to say. *i(wazumogana)* better left unsaid. *-koto* word.

2 入 *i(i)-i(reru)* propose, suggest
3 及 *i(i)-oyo(bu)* refer to, mention. *genkyū* reference
上 *gonjō suru* relate, inform, report (to a higher person)
丸 *i(i)-maru(meru)* skillfully deceive in talking
下 *genka ni, gonka ni* promptly, readily
下手 *i(i)beta* poor speaker
4 止 *i(i)-ya(meru)* finish speaking
込 *i(i)-ko(meru)* propose, make an overture
中 *i(i)-a(teru)* guess right

切 *i(i)-ki(ru)* declare, say definitely; tell all
分 *i(i)bun* one's say, one's point; objection, complaint; excuse, explanation; case
文 *gembun* words and sentences
文一致 *gembun itchi* unification of the written and spoken languages
方 *i(i)kata* way of saying
方無 *i(wan)katana(shi)* inexpressible, indescribable
5 立 *i(i) ta(teru)* state, maintain, allege
句 *genku* words, phrases
広 *i(i)-hiro(meru)* proclaim, noise about
旧 *i(i)-furu(su)* say the same thing all the time. *i(i)-furu(shita)* hackneyed, stale
外 *gengai no* unexpressed, implied, implicit
古 *i(i)-furu(shita)* hackneyed, stale
去 *i(i)-sa(ru)* leave a message and depart
乍 *-i(i)naga(ra)* even so, granting that
出 *i(i)-da(su), i(i)-ida(su)* start talking; break the ice, speak out; propose
甲斐 *i(i)gai no aru* worth mentioning
付 *i(i)-tsu(karu)* have orders (to do). *i(i)-tsu(keru)* order (to do). *kotozu(karu)* be entrusted with; be asked to send word. *kotozu(ke)* message. *kotozu(keru)* entrust with (a message). *i(i)tsu(ke)* order, instructions
付口 *i(i)tsu(ke)guchi* talebearing
包 *i(i)-kuru(meru)* quibble
6 色 *genshoku* words and facial expression
回 *i(i) mawa(su)* express (well). *iimawa(shi)* an expression; phraseology
尽 *i(i)-tsu(kusu)* tell all, exhaust (a subject)
返 *i(i)-kae(su)* talk back to
伝 *i(i)-tsuta(eru)* hand down, circulate, inform. *iitsuta(e)* tradition, legend. *kotozuta(e), kotozu(te)* declaration, hearsay, message
伏 *i(i)-fu(seru)* argue down, confute
交 *i(i)-kawa(su)* pledge one's love; talk together
合 *i(i)-a(u)* quarrel, argue. *i(i)-a(waseru)* arrange beforehand
当 *i(i)-a(teru)* guess right
争 *i(i)-araso(u)* quarrel, dispute
迄無 *i(u)made(mo)na(i)* a matter of course; it goes without saying

行 *genkō* speech and conduct, profession and practice
行録 *genkōroku* memoirs
成 *i(i)na(ri)* being submissive, saying yes to all
成次第 *i(i)na(ri) shidai* submissive to everyone
成放題 *i(i)na(ri) hōdai* submissive to everyone
7 言 *gengen* every word. *i(u) (ni) i(warenu)* inexpressible, indescribable
足 *i(i)-ta(su)* say something further
改 *i(i)-arata(meru)* correct oneself
抜 *i(i)-nu(keru)* give an evasive answer, excuse oneself, explain away, quibble. *iinu(ke)* evasion, excuse, prevarication
乱 *i(i)-mida(reru)* confuse, refute; interrupt (a conversation); talk confusedly
含 *i(i) fuku(meru)* instruct, inculcate
来 *i(i)ki(tari)* legend, tradition
8 延 *i(i)-no(basu)* postpone with excuses
逆 *i(i)-sakara(u)* speak against
逃 *i(i)noga(re)* evasion, excuse, prevarication
送 *i(i)-oku(ru)* send word
退 *i(i)-no(keru)* argue away, refute
拡 *i(i)-hiro(meru)* proclaim, noise about
明 *i(i)-a(kasu)* talk the whole night through. *gemmei* declaration, announcement, statement
放 *i(i)-hana(tsu), i(i)-hana(su)* declare, assert
知 *i(i)shi(renu)* unspeakable, inexpressible
並 *i(i)-nara(beru)* line up points in a speech
直 *i(i)-nao(su)* restate, correct
歩 *i(i)-aru(ku)* spread tales
表 *i(i)-ara(wasu)* declare, express
事 *i(i)goto* one's remarks; topic of conversation; excuse, pretext; complaint
9 廻 *i(i)-mawa(su)* express well
通 *i(i)-tō(su)* persist in saying
連 *i(i)-tsura(neru)* enumerate, line up
拵 *i(i)-koshira(eru)* make up a story
洩 *i(i)-mo(rasu)* disclose; leave unsaid
祝 *kotoho(gu)* congratulate
前 *i(i)mae* excuse, pretense
草 *i(i)gusa* one's remarks; topic of

conversation; excuse, pretext; complaint
負 *i(i)-ma(keru)* lose out in an argument. *i(i)-ma(kasu)* refute
10 値 *i(i)ne* seller's price
悩 *i(i)-naya(mu)* hesitate to say
振 *i(i)bu(ri), i(ip)pu(ri)* manner of speaking
残 *i(i)-noko(su)* leave word; leave unsaid. *i(i)noko(ri)* something left unsaid
消 *i(i)-ke(su)* deny, retract
破 *i(i)-yabu(ru)* refute
紛 *i(i)-magi(rasu), i(i)-magi(rawasu)* prevaricate, quibble. *i(i)-hagura(su)* deceive (someone) in talking
兼 *i(i)-ka(neru)* hesitate to say, be unable to say
容 *gen'yō* words and facial expression
差 *i(i)-sa(su)* check oneself in speaking, stop short
挙 *kotoa(ge) suru* speak; criticize
11 過 *i(i)-su(giru), i(i)-su(gosu)* overstate, say too much. *i(i)-ayama(tsu)* misstate, make a slip
做 *i(i)-na(su)* state something dubious as a fact; offer excuses; describe
張 *i(i)-ha(ru)* insist on, maintain
掛 *i(i)-ka(keru)* speak to; start talking; accuse. *i(i)ga(kari)* false accusation; pretext; commitment
捲 *i(i)-ma(kuru)* argue down, confute
捨 *i(i)-su(teru)* make a parting remark
淀 *i(i)-yodo(mu)* hesitate in saying
渋 *i(i)-shibu(ru)* hesitate to say, falter
終 *i(i)-owa(ru)* finish talking
訳 *i(i)wake* apology, excuse, explanation, justification
訛 *i(i)nama(ri)* corrupt form. *i(i)-nama(ru)* be corrupted
動 *gendō* speech and conduct
悪 *i(i)niku(i)* awkward to say
寄 *i(i)-yo(ru)* court, woo; approach defiantly. *kotoyo(su)* spread rumors; pass on a message
習 *i(i)-nara(wasu)* be handed down; have a habit of saying. *i(i)nara(washi)* tradition, legend; usage
責 *genseki* responsibility for a statement
12 遣 *i(i)-tsuka(wasu), i(i)-ya(ru)* send a message
開 *i(i)-hira(ku)* justify, explain, vindicate
換 *i(i)-ka(eru)* say in other words
渡 *i(i)-wata(su)* sentence, condemn; order, instruct, announce
竦 *i(i)-suku(meru)* down someone in an argument
散 *i(i)-chi(rasu)* spread (a report)
違 *i(i)-chiga(eru)* misstate, make a slip. *iichiga(i)* misstatement
募 *i(i)-tsuno(ru)* argue vehemently
落 *i(i)-o(tosu)* leave unsaid, neglect to mention
葉 *koto(no)ha* words; a tanka poem. *kotoba* words, language
葉尻 *kotobajiri* end of a word; slip of the tongue
葉付 *kotobatsu(ki)* way of speaking
葉返 *kotoba (o) kae(su)* answer, refute
葉尽 *kotoba (o) tsu(kusu)* explain carefully
葉余 *kotoba (ni) ama(ru)* inexpressible
葉使 *kotobazuka(i)* speech, diction
葉違 *kotobataga(i)* quarreling; breaking a promise; slip of the tongue
葉添 *kotobazo(e)* advise, good offices, support
葉遣 *kotobazuka(i)* speech, diction
葉数 *kotobakazu* words, speech
葉濁 *kotoba (o) nigo(su)* speak ambiguously
13 損 *i(i)-sokona(u), i(i)-son(jiru)* make a slip; fail to tell, misstate
継 *i(i)-tsu(gu)* transmit, inform (someone)
続 *i(i)-tsuzu(keru)* continue to say
辞 *genji* words, speech, language, expression
触 *i(i)-fu(rasu)* spread a report or rumor
詰 *i(i)-tsu(meru)* argue down
詫 *i(i)-wa(biru)* fail to tell, miss a chance to tell
馴 *i(i)-na(reru)* be accustomed to say
置 *i(i)-o(ku)* leave a message
14 腐 *i(i)-kusa(su)* speak evil of
聞 *i(i)-ki(kasu), i(i)-ki(kaseru)* tell (a person to do something), instruct; persuade, admonish
漏 *i(i)-mo(rasu)* disclose; leave unsaid
種 *i(i)gusa* one's remarks
説 *gensetsu* remark, opinion, statement

誤 *i(i)-ayama(ru)* misstate, make a slip
貌 *gembō* words and facial expression
暮 *i(i)-ku(rasu)* pass the time talking
様 *i(i)yō, i(i)zama* way of saying,
様無 *i(i)yō (no) na(i)* indescribable, inexpressible
語 *gengo, gongo* language, speech, words. *i(wazu)-kata(rasu)* tacitly, by implication
語不随 *gengo fuzui* speech impediment
語形態学 *gengo keitaigaku* morphology
語学 *gengogaku* philology; linguistics
語学者 *gengogakusha* linguist, philologist
語道断 *gongo-dōdan* unmentionable, outrageous, unpardonable
語障害 *gengo shōgai* speech impediment
15 談 *gendan* conversation, talk
諍 *i(i)isakai* verbal quarrel
霊 *kotodama* soul or power of language
慰 *i(i)-nagusa(meru)* console
質 *genshitsu, genchi* pledge, commitment, promise
論 *genron* speech, discussion
論自由 *genron no jiyū* freedom of speech
論界 *genronkai* the press
18 繕 *i(i)-tsukuro(u)* gloss over
難 *i(i)gata(i)* difficult to say, unmentionable, inexpressible
顕 *i(i)-ara(wasu)* declare, express
21 囃 *i(i)-haya(su)* praise; spread (a report)
22 籠 *i(i)-ko(meru)* argue down, confute

2

B **訂** 5553 / J447b / M35211 TEI correct; decide.
5 正 *teisei* correction; revision

訃 5554 / J6b3e / M35214 FU obituary, report of a death.
7 告 *fukoku* obituary, report of a death
9 音 *fuin, fuon* report of a death
10 報 *fuhō* report of a death, obituary

A **計** 5555 / J3757 / M35220 KEI plan, scheme, trick; total; meter, gauge. *haka(ru)* measure, gauge, weigh; fathom, sound; compute, estimate. *haka(ru)* plan, devise, scheme; counsel with; have in mind; aim at; deceive, impose on; measure. *haka(rau)* manage, arrange, dispose of, see about, talk over.
3 上 *keijō suru* add up, appropriate
6 吏 *keiri* treasurer
7 売 *haka(ri)u(ri)* selling by measure
8 直 *haka(ri)-nao(su)* reweigh, remeasure
歩器 *keihoki* pedometer
画 *keikaku* plan, scheme, project; intention
画的 *keikakuteki* planned, intentional, premeditated
画者 *keikakusha* planner, promoter
画案 *keikakuan* plan, blueprint, schedule
画経済 *keikaku keizai* planned economy
画線 *keikakusen* projected (railway) line
10 料 *keiryō* estimating
時 *keiji* timing (in races)
時員 *keijiin* timers (at a race)
11 略 *keiryaku* plan, trick, stratagem
理士 *keirishi* public accountant
12 策 *keisaku* plan, stratagem
量 *keiryō* measuring, weighing, computation, measurement
量器 *keiryōki* meter, gauge, scale
13 数 *keisū* calculation, computation
14 算 *keisan* computation, calculation
算尺 *keisanjaku* slide rule
算学 *keisangaku* (science of) accounting
算式 *keisanshiki* formula
算係 *keisangakari* accountant
算高 *keisandaka(i)* mercenary, calculative
算書 *keisansho* statement (of account)
算器 *keisanki* calculator, computer
算簿 *keisambo* account book
15 慮 *keiryo* planning
器 *keiki* meter, gauge

3

訐 5556 / J6b40 / M35234 KETSU reveal; criticize; speak frankly.

訖 5557 / J6b3f / M35242 KITSU. *o(waru)* end, halt. *tsui ni* finally, at last, in the end.

訌 5558 J6b41 M35228 Kō get confused.

[6] 争 *kōsō* confused fighting

訊 5559 J3f56 M35224 JIN request; question, investigate. *ki(ku), tazu(neru)* ask, inquire.

[6] 返 *tazu(ne)-kae(su)* question again

[11] 問 *jimmon* cross-examination, interrogation, inquest

B **託** 5560 J4277 M35243 TAKU requesting, entrusting with. *taku(suru)* entrust with, charge with; pretend; hint. *kotozu(karu)* be requested. *kako(tsu), kakotsu(keru), kotozu(keru)* pretend; plead; make excuses. *kako(chi)* complaining, grumbling.

[7] 言 *kagoto, takugen, kakotsukegoto* excuse, pretext, plea

児所 *takujisho* day nursery; nursery school

[8] 送 *takusō suru* consign, send by (someone), check (baggage)

[9] 宣 *takusen* (Buddhist or Shinto) oracle

A **討** 5561 J4624 M35231 Tō. *u(tsu)* attack, defeat, destroy, conquer.

[2] 入 *u(chi)-i(ru)* break into, raid

[4] 手 *u(chi)te, u(t)te* attacking party, punitive force, pursuers; shooter, murderer

[6] 死 *uchijini* death in battle

伐 *tōbatsu* subjugation, suppression

伐軍 *tōbatsugun* punitive force

伐隊 *tōbatsutai* punitive force

伐戦 *tōbatsusen* punitive expedition

[7] 究 *tōkyū* study, research, investigation

[8] 取 *u(chi)-to(ru)* catch, arrest; take possession of; kill

果 *u(chi)-hata(su)* slay

[9] 洩 *u(chi)-mo(rasu)* let escape, fail to kill

[10] 匪 *tōhi* bandit suppression

[13] 滅 *u(chi)-horo(bosu)* destroy

幕 *tōbaku suru* attack the shogunate

[14] 漏 *u(chi)-mo(rasu)* let escape, fail to kill

[15] 論 *tōron* debate, discussion, contention, argumentation

論会 *tōronkai* forum, debate; debating society

論終結 *tōron shūketsu* closure of debate

[20] 議 *tōgi* debate, discussion

議事項 *tōgi jikō* agenda items

議案 *tōgian* subject for debate

議場 *tōgijō* forum

A **訓** 5562 J3731 M35238 KIN, KUN Japanese reading (of a character); explanation of a character; lesson; regulation; rule. *oshi(eru)* instruct. *yo(mu)* read. *kun(zuru)* read; read in the *kun* .

[4] 化 *kunka* instruction

[5] 示 *kunji* instruction

令 *kunrei* directive, instructions

[7] 言 *kungen* instruction, precept

戒 *kunkai* admonition, warning

状 *kunjō* letter of instruction

告 *kunkoku* instruction

[8] 育 *kun'iku* education, discipline

[9] 点 *kunten* punctuation marks

[10] 陶 *kuntō* education, training, instruction, discipline

[11] 釈 *kunshaku* explaining the meaning of characters

[12] 詁 *kunko* exegesis, interpretation of old words

詁学 *kunkogaku* exegetics

[13] 辞 *kunji* address to students

解 *kunkai* explanation of terms; interpretation of a passage

話 *kunwa* fable, moral tale

義 *kungi* the reading and meaning of a character

蒙 *kummō* enlightenment, instruction

電 *kunden* telegraphic instructions

[14] 読 *kundoku, kun'yo(mi)* reading characters with Japanese sounds

誨 *kunkai suru* instruct, enlighten

誡 *kunkai* admonition, warning

導 *kundō* training

練 *kunren* training, practice, drill, discipline, schooling

練所 *kunrenjo* training institute

[16] 諭 *kun'yu* admonition, exhortation

A **記** 5563 J352d M35244 KI account, narrative, history, annals; remembering; writing; the *Kojiki*. *ki(suru)* write down, record, describe; remember. *shiru(su)* write down; inscribe; mention, give an account of. *shirushi* record.

[2] 入 *kinyū* entry (in a record)

5 号 *kigō* mark, sign, symbol
6 伝 *kiden* history and biography
名 *kimei* signature
名投票 *kimei tōhyō* signed ballot
名株 *kimei kabu* registered stock
名株券 *kimei kabuken* registered stock
名帳 *kimeichō* register
7 述 *kijutsu* description, account
8 法 *kihō* notation
帖 *kichō* registry; entry, posting, bookkeeping; signature
帖係 *kichōgakari* bookkeeper
者 *kisha* journalist, reporter
者団 *kishadan* press group, press association
者会見 *kisha kaiken* news conferences, press interview
者席 *kishaseki* press box, press table
事 *kiji* description, statement, news item, article
事文 *kijibun* descriptive composition
事広告 *kiji kōkoku* article-type advertisement
事体 *kijitai* factual style (of article)
念 *kinen* remembrance, commemoration
念日 *kinembi* memorial day, anniversary
念切手 *kinen kitte* commemorative stamp
念会 *kinenkai* commemorative meeting, memorial service
念号 *kinengō* memorial number (of a magazine)
念物 *kinembutsu* souvenir, keepsake, monument
念品 *kinenhin* souvenir, memento
念章 *kinenshō* commemorative medal
念祭 *kinensai* anniversary
念碑 *kinenhi* monument
念樹 *kinenju* memorial tree
念館 *kinenkan* memorial hall
9 紀 *Kiki* the *Kojiki* and the *Nihonshoki*
11 章 *kishō* medal, badge, insignia
帳 *kichō* registry; entry, posting, bookkeeping; signature
帳所 *kichōsho* place where visitors sign
帳係 *kichōgakari* bookkeeper
13 載 *kisai* statement, publication; entry
数法 *kisūhō* numerical notation
14 聞 *kibun* dictated record
誦 *kishō* memorizing
銘 *kimei* inscription, engraving
16 憶 *kioku* memory, remembrance, recollection
憶力 *kiokuryoku* memory
憶術 *kiokujutsu* mnemonics
憶喪失 *kioku sōshitsu* loss of memory, amnesia
憶喪失症 *kioku sōshitsushō* loss of memory, amnesia
録 *kiroku* record, document, archives, minutes, proceedings, chronicle
録文学 *kiroku bungaku* documentary literature
録的 *kirokuteki* record-making
録係 *kirokugakari* recorder, one in charge of records
録映画 *kiroku eiga* documentary film
録破 *kirokuyabu(ri)* record-breaking; extraordinary
録漏 *kirokumo(re)* omitted from the record

4

訝 5564 / J-X / M35260 **訝** 5573 / J6b43 / M-X Gᴀ. Gᴇ. *ibuka(ru)* doubt, be suspicious of, wonder. *ibuka(shii)* undependable, strange, mysterious.

B **訟** 5565 / J3e39 / M35266 Sʜō accuse.

訥 5566 / J6b44 / M35274 Tᴏᴛsᴜ stutter.
5 弁 *totsuben* slow of speech, defective speech
7 言 *totsugen* slow of speech, defective speech

訣 5567 / J376d / M35272 Kᴇᴛsᴜ separation; part; secret.
7 別 *ketsubetsu* separation, farewell
10 宴 *ketsuen* parting spree
12 飲 *ketsuin* parting cup
13 辞 *ketsuji* farewell words

訛 5568 / J6b42 / M35256 **譌** 5698 / J6b77 / M35951 Kᴀ. *nama(ru)* speak with an accent; be corrupted. *ayama(ri)* mistake. *nama(ri)* dialect, brogue, accent.
6 伝 *kaden* false report, misinformation
7 言 *kagen* dialect, brogue

声 *damigoe* hoarse voice, thick voice
9 音 *kaon* provincialism, brogue
10 称 *kashō* a corruption (in speech)
14 語 *kago* dialect, brogue

A **許** 5569 / J3576 / M35298 KYO. KO. *yuru(su)* permit, approve; authorize; acknowledge; confide in; forgive, pardon; release, acquit; overlook. *moto* (parental) roof, a person's house. *-bakari* approximately; only, merely, alone; degree; almost, practically; absorbed in; continue doing; just now; be about to do; be ready for; have no alternative; now or never.

5 可 *kyoka* permission, approval, license, permit, authorization, admission
可申請 *kyoka shinsei* license application
可制 *kyokasei* license system
可料 *kyokaryō* license fee
可書 *kyokasho* written permission
可証 *kyokashō* permit, license
7 否 *kyohi* permission, sanction
10 容 *kyoyō* permission, approval; pardon
11 婚 *iinazuke* fiance, fiancee
13 嫁 *iinazuke* fiancee
15 諾 *kyodaku* consent, approval, permit

A **設** 5570 / J405f / M35293 SETSU. *mō(keru)* prepare, provide; establish, found, set up, organize; enact, lay down (rules); get (a child).

5 立 *setsuritsu suru* establish, found, organize, promote, incorporate
立者 *setsuritsusha* founder, organizer
8 定 *settei* establishment, creation
9 計 *sekkei* plan, design
計図 *sekkeizu* plan, draft, blueprint
計者 *sekkeisha* planner, designer
11 問 *setsumon* question
12 備 *setsubi* equipment, fixtures, installations, arrangements, accommodations, convenience, facilities
営 *setsuei* construction, arrangements
13 置 *setchi suru* establish, found

A **訪** 5571 / J4b2c / M35284 HŌ. *otozu(reru)* visit, call on. *tazu(neru)* call on, visit, look up. *tobura(u), to(u)* call on, visit, offer sympathy.

4 日 *hō-Nichi* visiting Japan
中 *hō-Chū* visiting China
6 米 *hō-Bei* visiting America
9 客 *hōkyaku, hōkaku* visitor
11 問 *hōmon* visit, interview, call
問先 *hōmonsaki* place visited
問者 *hōmonsha* caller, visitor
問客 *hōmonkyaku* caller, visitor
問飛行 *hōmon hikō* good-will flight
問記者 *hōmon kisha* interviewer
問着 *hōmongi* visiting dress
問談 *hōmondan* interview

A **訳** 5572 / J4c75 / M35324' **譯** 5709 / J6c23 / M36023 YAKU translation. EKI. *yaku(su), yaku(suru)* translate. *wake* meaning, sense; reason, cause; circumstances, the case; understanding (between them). *yaku* translation, version; interpretation.

2 了 *yakuryō suru* finish translating
4 文 *yakubun* translation, version, rendering
方 *yaku(shi)kata* how to translate; method of translation
5 出 *yakushutsu* translation
本 *yakuhon* translated book
6 合 *wakea(i)* meaning; reason; circumstances
7 述 *yakujutsu suru* translate and explain. *yakujutsu* translation
述者 *yakujutsusha* translator
8 注 *yakuchū* translation with notes
知 *wakeshi(razu)* a boor; one who doesn't understand anything. *wakeshi(ri)* one who understands
者 *yakusha* translator
9 柄 *wakegara* meaning, sense; reason, cause; circumstances, the case; understanding (between them)
10 書 *yakusho* a translation, a version, translated book
12 違 *yaku(shi)chiga(i)* mistranslation
無 *wakena(i), wake(no)na(i)* easy, simple
13 解 *yakkai* annotated translation, paraphrase
詩 *yakushi* translated poem
14 語 *yakugo* word used in translation, an equivalent
読 *yakudoku* reading a manuscript and giving explanations
18 難 *yaku(shi)niku(i)* difficult to translate

5

訮 5573 J6b43 M-X See 訮 5564.

詆 5574 J6b49 M35356 TEI criticize; scold; denounce; deceive; coerce.

詒 5575 J6b48 M35376 I. TAI send; leave to (one's successor); entrust; deceive.

詈 5576 J6b4a M35360 RI ridicule.

訶 5577 J6b45 M35328 KA scold.

詁 5578 J6b46 M35347 KO chatter.

詑 5579 J4242 M35374 I. TA deceive, delude. *wa(biru)* apologize. *wa(bi)* apology.

詛 5580 J6b47 M35390 SO. *noro(u)* curse.
8 呪 *noroi* curse

B **詔** 5581 J3e5b M35379 SHŌ imperial edict. *mikotonori* imperial edict, decree.
5 令 *shōrei* imperial edict
9 勅 *shōchoku* imperial proclamation
10 書 *shōsho* imperial edict

A **詞** 5582 J3b6c M35394 SHI words; poetry. *kotoba* words.
8 宗 *shisō* great scholar, literary man
10 致 *shichi* the import of words
書 *kotobaga(ki)* notes; foreword
華 *shika* beautiful phraseology
11 章 *shishō* poetry and prose
19 藻 *shisō* figure of speech, rhetorical flourishes; prose and poetry

註 5583 J4370 M35340 CHŪ notes, comment. *chū(suru)* comment on; annotate.
4 文 *chūmon* an order
10 記 *chūki suru* make entries; write down
11 釈 *chūshaku* notes, comment, exegesis
釈本 *chūshakubon* commentary
釈者 *chūshakusha* commentator, annotator
釈書 *chūshakusho* a commentary
12 疏 *chūso* notes, comment; commentary
13 解 *chūkai* notes, comment; commentary

B **詠** 5584 J3153 M35409 **咏** 748 J5269 M3494 **詠** 5591 J-X M-X
EI poem; song; singing; composing. *yo(mu)* recite, chant. *ei(suru)* write poems; recite poems.
2 入 *yo(mi)-i(reru)* mention (in a poem)
5 史 *eishi* epic, historical poem
出 *eishutsu* writing poetry or songs
7 吟 *eigin* reciting poetry
8 物 *eibutsu* a nature poem
9 草 *eisō* draft of a poem
10 進 *eishin* presentation of a poem (to the Court)
13 嘆 *eitan* exclamation, admiration
14 誦 *eishō* reciting poetry
歌 *eika* composition of a poem or song; poem; song; Buddhist pilgrim's song
15 歎 *eitan* exclamation, admiration

B **詐** 5585 J3a3e M35373 SA. *itsuwa(ru)* lie, falsify; deceive; pretend; deceive, cheat.
8 取 *sashu* fraud, swindle
10 病 *sabyō* feigned illness
称 *sashō* misrepresentation, false statement, impersonation
害 *sagai* prejudice (in law)
11 偽 *sagi* lie, falsehood
術 *sajutsu* deceptive means
略 *saryaku* fraud, swindle
12 欺 *sagi* fraud, swindling
欺投票 *sagi tōhyō* fraudulent voting
欺師 *sagishi* swindler, impostor, crook
16 謀 *sabō* fraud, swindle

B **診** 5586 J3f47 M35337 SHIN seeing; diagnosing. *mi(ru)* diagnose, examine.
11 断 *shindan* diagnosis
断書 *shindansho* medical certificate
14 察 *shinsatsu* medical examination
察日 *shinsatsubi* consultation day
察台 *shinsatsudai* examining table
察券 *shinsatsuken* consultation ticket
察室 *shinsatsushitsu* doctor's examining room
察料 *shinsatsuryō* medical fee, doctor bill

察時間 *shinsatsu jikan* consultation hours
察無料 *shinsatsu muryō* free consultation
17 療 *shinryō* examination and treatment
療中 *Shinryōchū* The doctor is in.
療所 *shinryōjo* clinic, medical office
療時間 *shinryō jikan* consultation hours

A **評** 5587 / J493e / M35383 Hyō criticism, comment. *hyō(suru)* criticize, comment on.
6 伝 *hyōden* critical biography
7 言 *hyōgen* critical remark
決 *hyōketsu* decision, verdict
判 *hyōban* fame, reputation, popularity; sensation; rumor
判物 *hyōbammono* well-known or popular person
8 注 *hyōchū* commentary
定 *hyōjō* conference, consultation. *hyōtei* rating, evaluation
者 *hyōsha* critic, reviewer
価 *hyōka* appraisal, valuation, assessment; appreciation
価額 *hyōkagaku* estimated value
9 点 *hyōten* examination marks
11 釈 *hyōshaku* annotation, commentary
12 註 *hyōchū* commentary
14 語 *hyōgo* critical remark; mark; epithet
15 論 *hyōron* criticism, review, comment, editorial
論界 *hyōronkai* the commentator's circle
論家 *hyōronka* critic, commentator, reviewer
20 議 *hyōgi* consultation, discussion, conference, deliberation
議会 *hyōgikai* council, conference
議所 *hyōgijo* conference room, forum
議員 *hyōgiin* councillor; trustee; board of trustees
議員会 *hyōgiinkai* council, conference, board meeting

B **訴** 5588 / J414a / M35325 So. *utta(eru)* sue; complain of (pain); appeal to; have recourse to. *utta(e)* lawsuit, complaint, accusation, charge, indictment; appeal, petition.
2 人 *sonin* accuser, one who sues
5 出 *utta(e)-de(ru)* lodge a complaint
6 因 *soin* cause of action, charge, count
件 *soken* a case (at law)
7 状 *sojō* petition, written complaint
8 追 *sotsui* legal action, proceedings; prosecution, impeachment; charges
事 *utta(e)goto* a case, legal suit
10 陳 *sochin suru* sue
11 訟 *soshō* lawsuit, litigation
訟人 *soshōnin* plaintiff
訟手続 *soshō tetsuzuki* legal proceedings
訟代理人 *soshō dairinin* counsel, attorney
訟当事者 *soshō tōjisha* litigant
訟法 *soshōhō* legal procedure (code)
訟事件 *soshō jiken* case, lawsuit
訟依頼人 *soshō irainin* client
訟費用 *soshō hiyō* costs (of a lawsuit)
訟関係人 *soshō kankeinin* litigant
15 権 *soken* right to sue
19 願 *sogan* appeal, petition
願人 *sogannin* appellant, petitioner

A **証** 5589 / J3e5a / M35341 **證** 5697 / J6b7a / M35946 Shō proof, evidence; certificate. *shō(suru)* prove, guarantee. *akashi suru* witness. *akashi* proof, evidence, vindication, witnessing.
2 人 *akashibito, shōnin* witness
人台 *shōnindai* witness stand
人席 *shōninseki* witness chair
4 文 *shōmon* deed, bond, promissory note
5 左 *shōsa* proof, evidence, testimony
6 印 *shōin* document seal
会 *akashikai* testimony meeting
7 言 *shōgen* testimony, evidence
8 明 *shōmei* proof, evidence; testimony, witness; certification
明書 *shōmeisho* certificate
明済 *shōmeizu(mi)* already proved
券 *shōken* securities, bonds, deed, certificate
券会社 *shōkengaisha* securities company
券取引所 *shōken torihikijo* securities exchange
券業 *shōkengyō* security business
拠 *shōko* proof, evidence, testimony
拠人 *shōkonin* witness
拠立 *shōkoda(teru)* prove, substantiate, corroborate

拠物 *shōkobutsu* material evidence
拠物件 *shōko bukken* material evidence
10 紙 *shōshi* sticker, tourist stamp, inspection stamp
書 *shōsho* bond, deed, certificate
11 票 *shōhyō* voucher
13 跡 *shōseki* evidence, traces, vestiges
16 憑 *shōhyō* evidence, proof, testimony

6

訣 5590 J-X M35495 See **訣** 5653.

詠 5591 J-X M-X Nonstandard for **詠** 5584.

誨 5592 J-X M-X Nonstandard for **誨** 5616.

詢 5593 J6b4e M35411 JUN consult with.

詣 5594 J3758 M35412 KEI. *kei(suru)* visit a temple or shrine. *mai(ru), mō(deru)* go; come; call, visit; visit a shrine. *mō(de), mai(ri)* temple or shrine visit.

詬 5595 J6b4d M35433 KŌ ridicule, put to shame. *nonoshi(ru)* revile.
10 辱 *kōjoku* disgrace, insult

誂 5596 J6b50 M35469 CHŌ. *atsura(eru)* order.
6 向 *atsura(e)mu(ki)* suitable, satisfactory, ideal
8 物 *atsura(e)mono* goods ordered

詼 5597 J6b4b M35462 KAI joke, jest, play.
10 笑 *kaishō* joke and laugh
15 嘲 *kaichō* joke, jest
16 諧 *kaikai* joke, jest, prank

詫 5598 J4f4d M35431 TA. *wa(biru)* apologize, make an excuse. *wabi* apology, excuse, intercession.
2 入 *wa(bi)-i(ru)* humbly apologize
7 言 *wabigoto* apology
状 *wabijō* written apology

誅 5599 J6b4f M35472 CHŪ death penalty; punishment. *chū(suru)* punish with death.
6 伐 *chūbatsu* punitive expedition
7 求 *chūkyū suru* extort, squeeze, exact tribute
15 戮 *chūriku* death punishment

誄 5600 J6b51 M35471 RUI condolence message.
4 文 *ruibun* funeral address
12 詞 *ruishi* message of sympathy
13 詩 *ruishi* elegy
14 歌 *ruika* dirge

B **該** 5601 J333a M35445 GAI the said.
6 地 *gaichi* the said area
当 *gaitō* pertinence, relevance
当者 *gaitōsha* the person concerned or qualified
10 案 *gaian* the said proposal
12 博 *gaihaku na* profound, extensive (knowledge)

B **誉** 5602 J4d40 M35498 **譽** 5708 J6c25 M36066 YO. *home(ru)* praise. *homa(re)* honor, glory.
5 立 *ho(me)-ta(teru)* praise, praise profusely
7 言葉 *homekotoba* words of praise
8 者 *homemono* someone praised by all
奉 *ho(me)-matsu(ru)* praise (God)
10 高 *homa(re)taka(i)* renowned
称 *ho(me)-soya(su)* praise profusely
11 望 *yobō* fame
14 歌 *ho(me)-uta(u)* praise (God)
21 囃 *ho(me)-haya(su)* praise profusely

詭 5603 J6b4c M35434 KI lie; deceive.
5 弁 *kiben* sophism, sophistry; chicanery; paradox; play on words
弁学派 *Kiben Gakuha* the Sophists
弁家 *kibenka* sophist; quibbler
9 計 *kikei* trick, wiles
11 道 *kidō* deceptive methods, questionable means
偽 *kigi* deception
術 *kijutsu* trickery
12 策 *kisaku* trick, stratagem
16 謀 *kibō* ruse, trick

詮 5604 / J4127 / M35435 SEN discussion; selection; methods called for; result, effect. *sen(zuru)* think over; discuss. *kai* effect, result, use.

4 方 *senkata* resources, means, way
方無 *senkatana(ku)* unavoidably, helplessly
10 索 *sensaku* search, inquiry, investigation
索好 *sensakuzu(ki)* inquisitive, prying, curious
11 術 *sensube* proper methods
12 無 *senna(i)* useless
20 議 *sengi* discussion, investigation, inquiry, examination
議立 *sengida(te)* inquiry, thorough investigation

B **誇** 5605 / J3858 / M35474 KO. *hoko(ru)* boast of, be proud of. *hoko(rakasu)* take a boastful attitude. *hoko(rashii)* proud. *hoko(rashige ni)* proudly, triumphantly. *hoko(ri)* pride.

3 大 *kodai* exaggeration, hyperbole, bombast
大妄想狂 *kodai mōsōkyō* megalomania
5 示 *koshi, koji* ostentation, display
6 色 *koshoku* a proud countenance
10 高 *hoko(ri)taka(i)* proud, lordly. *hoko(ri)-taka(buru)* be boastful, be proud
称 *koshō* exaggeration, boasting
11 張 *kochō* exaggeration
張法 *kochōhō* hyperbole
張的 *kochōteki* exaggerated, bombastic
18 顔 *hoko(ri)gao* triumphant look

A **誠** 5606 / J403f / M35497' **誠** 5612 / J-X / M35537 SEI. *imashi(meru)* admonish, warn; prohibit. *makoto* sincerity, honesty, fidelity; truth. *makoto no* true, genuine, actual. *makoto ni* really; extremely. *makoto(shiyakana)* plausible.

4 心 *seishin* sincerity
心誠意 *seishin-seii* sincerity, wholehearted devotion; sincerely, devotedly
8 直 *seichoku* honest and sincere
実 *seijitsu* sincerity, honesty, truthfulness, faithfulness
忠 *seichū* true loyalty
9 信 *seishin* sincerity
10 恐 *seikyō* fear and reverence
烈 *seiretsu* sincerity and purity
11 情 *seijō* sincerity, a true heart
13 意 *seii* sincerity, good faith

B **詳** 5607 / J3e5c / M35446 SHŌ. *tsumabira(kana), kuwa(shii)* full, detailed, minute, accurate; versed in, well-informed on.

6 伝 *shōden* detailed biography
7 言 *shōgen* detailed explanation
述 *shōjutsu* detailed explanation
10 記 *shōki* minute description, full account
11 略 *shōryaku* details and rough outlines
細 *shōsai* details, particulars
密 *shōmitsu na* detailed
12 註 *shōchū* copious notes
報 *shōhō* particulars, full report
13 解 *shōkai* detailed explanation
14 説 *shōsetsu* detailed explanation
察 *shōsatsu* careful observation
15 論 *shōron* full treatment, detailed explanation
16 録 *shōroku* detailed record
覧 *shōran* looking over in detail

A **話** 5608 / J4f43 / M35441 WA. *hana(su)* talk, speak, converse; tell; explain. *hana(seru)* sensible, intelligent, agreeable. *hanashi tsuide ni* in the course of the conversation. *hanashi* talk, chat, conversation; story; rumor; news; consultation, negotiations; facts, reasons.

3 口 *hana(shi)kuchi* opening up a conversation; way of speaking; one's real meaning
下手 *hanashibeta* poor talker
上手 *hanashijōzu* good conversationalist
4 手 *hana(shi)te* speaker
方 *hana(shi)kata* way of speaking
込 *hana(shi)-ko(mu)* have a long talk with
5 半分 *hanashi-hambun* a statement to be taken at half its face value
甲斐 *hana(shi)gai* effect of a speech
6 好 *hana(shi)zu(ki) na* talkative, gossipy
合 *hana(shi)-a(u)* discuss, talk over, consult with. *hanashia(i)* consultation; agreement

声 *hana(shi)goe* a voice, a whisper
言葉 *hana(shi)kotoba* speech, spoken language
8 法 *wahō* parlance; narration
実入 *hanashi (ni) mi (ga) i(ru)* put one's whole self into a talk
9 柄 *wahei* topic of conversation
相手 *hanashi aite* adviser, someone to talk to
10 振 *hana(shi)buri* manner of speaking
家 *hana(shi)ka* storyteller
11 術 *wajutsu* storyteller's art
掛 *hana(shi)-ka(keru)* accost, speak to
12 替 *hanashika(watte)* not to change the subject but...
13 嫌 *hana(shi)gira(i)* taciturn, reticent
14 種 *hanashi (no) tane* topic of conversation
16 頭 *watō* topic of conversation
18 題 *wadai* topic of conversation

B **詰** 5609 / J354d / M35440 KITSU. *tsu(mu)* be pressed in, be packed, become close; be checkmated. *tsu(meru) vt* stuff, fill, pack, plug; place closely; write closely; sit closely; shorten; curtail; checkmate; keep doing; hold (one's breath). *vi* attend (office). *tsu(maru)* be stopped up, be blocked; be full, be stuffed; be shortened, contract; be hard up; be hold up, be deadlocked. *naji(ru)* reprove, rebuke, blame. *tsu(me)* stuffing, packing, stopper; end, foot of, edge; checkmate; appointment to. *tsu(maranai)* trifling, insignificant, small, of no account, worthless, trashy, foolish, despicable, uninteresting, cheerless, monotonous. *tsu(mari)* after all, eventually; in short, to sum up; in other words. *-zu(me)* packed in, bottled in; boxed in; kept (standing); on duty at.
4 手 *tsu(me)te* packer
木 *tsu(me)ki* wooden plug
込 *tsu(me)-ko(mu)* stuff, pack, jam into; crowd into; tamp
切 *tsu(me)-ki(ru)* be in constant attendance (as a valet); be always on the job
5 旦 *kittan* early morning, tomorrow morning
石 *tsu(me)ishi* foundation stone
6 伏 *tsu(me)-fu(seru)* explain and secure compliance
合 *tsu(me)-a(waseru)* assort, pack an assortment. *tsumeawa(se)* assortment (of cakes). *tsumia(i)* working at the same place; coworker; arguing
8 屈 *kikkutsu* crouching; difficulty in explaining characters or writing
所 *tsumesho* office; guard room; crew room; side room. *tsu(maru)tokoro* after all
物 *tsu(me)mono* stuffing, dressing (a fowl), filling, packing, padding, plugging
11 問 *kitsumon* grilling, cross-examination
掛 *tsu(me)-ka(keru)* crowd into, throng around
寄 *tsu(me)-yo(ru), tsu(me)-yo(seru)* draw near, approach, edge in, press upon
責 *kisseki* reproof, censure
12 番 *tsu(me)ban* one's turn for duty
替 *tsu(me)-ka(eru)* repack, refill, rebottle
朝 *kitchō* tomorrow morning
13 腹 *tsu(me)bara* forced suicide, forced disembowelment; forced resignation
14 綿 *tsu(me)wata* padding, filler; sanitary pad
18 襟 *tsu(me)eri* stand-up collar; close-buttoned collar

A **詩** 5610 / J3b6d / M35427 SHI poem, poetry.
2 人 *shijin* poet; minstrel
3 才 *shisai* poetic genius
4 心 *shishin* poetic sentiment
文 *shibun* prose and poetry, literature
友 *shiyu* poetical friend
5 句 *shiku* verse, stanza
史 *shishi* an epic poem
仙 *shisen* great poet
6 会 *shikai* poetry meeting
7 作 *shisaku suru* write poetry
体 *shitai* poetic form
吟 *shigin* reciting Chinese poems
抄 *shishō* selection of poems
材 *shizai* material for poetry
形 *shikei* poetic form; poetic rhythm
8 味 *shimi* poetic sentiment
的 *shiteki* poetical, poetic
的情緒 *shiteki jōcho* poetic mood
宗 *shisō* great poet
学 *shigaku* study of poetry
9 律 *shiritsu* poetic rhythm
思 *shishi* poetic sentiment; poetic talent

草 *shisō* first draft of a poem
巻 *shikan* an anthology of poetry
10 格 *shikaku* laws of poetry; poetic quality
家 *shika* poet
11 情 *shijō* poetic sentiment, poetic interest
眼 *shigan* poetic understanding
経 *Shikyō* Book of Songs. *Shi Jing* (a Chinese classic)
12 詞 *shishi* poetic diction
集 *shishū* anthology of poetry
13 話 *shiwa* a talk on poetry
意 *shii* meaning of a poem
想 *shisō* thought of a poem
聖 *shisei* great poet
14 選 *shisen* anthology of poems
境 *shikyō* a poetic location
歌 *shika, shiika* Chinese and Japanese poetry
魂 *shikon* poetic sentiment, poetic interest
15 趣 *shishu* poetic beauty, poetic sentiment
劇 *shigeki* dramatic poem
稿 *shikō* draft of a poem
論 *shiron* essay on poetry
篇 *Shihen* Psalms, Psalter
篇記者 *Shihen Kisha* the Psalmist
16 壇 *shidan* poetry circles
興 *shikyō* poetic inspiration
18 題 *shidai* title of a poem; material for a poem
19 藻 *shisō* poetic language, poetic skill; poem; prose composition

A **試** 5611 / J3b6e / M35415 SHI testing. *kokoro(miru)* try, attempt. *tame(su)* attempt, try, experiment, test, sample. *kokoro(mi)* trial, test, attempt, experiment; ordeal, temptation.

5 用 *shiyō* trial
写 *shisha* preview, private showing
6 行錯誤 *shikō-sakugo* trial and error
合 *shiai* contest, match, game, bout, tournament, joust
合場 *shiaijō* ball park, football field, court, ring
7 作 *shisaku* trial manufacture, first production, trial production
売 *shibai* commercial adventure
8 刷 *shisatsu* proof printing
金 *shikin* assaying
金石 *shikinseki* touchstone; test, test case
9 食 *shishoku* sampling food
乗 *shijō* trial ride
10 剤 *shizai* reagent
案 *shian* draft, tentative plan
射 *shisha* test firing
射弾 *shishadan* trial shot
11 問 *shimon* question, interview, test, quiz, examination
斬 *tame(shi)gi(ri)* trying out a new sword (on corpses or prisoners)
毫 *shigō* first writing of the year
球式 *shikyū shiki* the first ball; opening of the first ball game
運転 *shiunten* trial run, test run
掘 *shikutsu* prospecting
掘者 *shikutsusha* prospector
掘権 *shikutsuken* mining claim
12 植 *shishoku* experimental planting
焼 *tame(shi)ya(ki)* photographic proof
補 *shiho* probationer, beginner
飲 *shiin suru* sampling beverages
筆 *shihitsu* first writing of the new year
検官 *shikenkan* inspector
13 煉 *shiren* test, trial, probation, ordeal
14 演 *shien* rehearsal, preview
練 *shiren* test, trial, probation, ordeal
算 *shisan* preliminary calculation; auditing accounts
算表 *shisanhyō* trial balance
15 論 *shiron* preliminary essay, sketch
16 薬 *shiyaku* reagent; a test
17 聴 *shichō* audition
18 験 *shiken* examination; experiment; test, trial; demonstration
験工場 *shiken kōjō* pilot plant
験台 *shikendai* test case, guinea pig, test
験地獄 *shiken jigoku* the hell of (entrance) examinations
験所 *shikensho* laboratory, experimental station
験的 *shikenteki* experimental; tentative
験官 *shikenkan* examiner
験紙 *shikenshi* litmus paper
験勉強 *shiken-benkyō* cramming for examinations
験済 *shikenzu(mi)* tried, proved
験問題 *shiken-mondai* examination questions
験場 *shikenjō* examination hall; laboratory; experimental station
験管 *shikenkan* test tube

7

誡 5612 J-X M35537 See **誡** 5606.

誕 5613 J-X M35516 See **誕** 5640.

誚 5614 J6b57 M35529 SHŌ blame; censure.

誥 5615 J6b55 M35549 KŌ tell, inform; admonish; instruct.

誨 5616 J6b52 M35553 KAI instruct.
16 諭 *kaiyu* enlightenment

誡 5617 J6b53 M35538 KAI commandment, admonition. *imashi(meru)* admonish, caution, reprove. *imashime* admonition, rebuke.
7 告 *kaikoku* warning, caution

誣 5618 J6b58 M35542 FU. BU. *shii(ru)* slander, accuse falsely.
7 言 *bugen, fugen, shiigoto* calumny, slander, false charge
告 *bukoku, fukoku* slander, false charge

誑 5619 J6b54 M35510 KYŌ. *tabura(kasu), tabura (kasu)* deceive, cheat, defraud; bewitch; delude; soothe, calm. *tabaka(ru)* cheat; impose on. *ta(rasu)* coax, cajole; deceive.
4 込 *ta(rashi)-ko(mu)* coax, cajole; deceive
12 詐 *kyōsa* deception

A **誌** 5620 J3b6f M35501 SHI records; document; magazine. *shiru(su)* write down; inscribe; mention, give an account of. *shirushi* record. *-shi* magazine.
3 上 *shijō* in a magazine
4 友 *shiyū* fellow subscriber
5 代 *shidai* price of a magazine
9 面 *shimen* a page of a magazine

誦 5621 J6b56 M35551 SHŌ. JU. ZU *shō(suru)* recite, chant.
10 記 *shōki* reciting from memory
11 経 *zukyō, jukyō* reading the sutras
習 *shōshū suru* learn by memorizing
12 詠 *shōei* reciting poetry

B **誓** 5622 J4040 M35514 SEI. *chika(u)* swear, pledge, vow. *chika(i)* oath, pledge, vow. *chika(tte)* positively, surely.
4 文 *seibun, seimon* written oath
文立 *seimonda(te)* making a vow; delivering a written vow
文払 *seimombara(i)* bargain sale
7 言 *seigon, seigen* oath, vow, pledge, affirmation
9 約 *seiyaku* a written vow
約者 *seiyakusha* party to a covenant
約書 *seiyakusho* written pledge, covenant
10 紙 *seishi* written pledge
12 詞 *seishi* oath, pledge
13 盟 *seimei* a vow
19 願 *seigan* oath, pledge, vow
願者 *seigansha* one who makes a vow

A **認** 5623 J4727 M35502' **認** 5624 J-X M35502 NIN. *mito(meru)* witness; sight; discern, authorize, recognize; appreciate; approve of; judge, conclude; believe; regard as. *shitata(meru)* write, draw up; eat. *mito(me)* approval; private seal.
5 用 *nin'yō* admission, tolerance, acknowledgment
可 *ninka* approval, license, permission
可状 *ninkajō* permit, license
可書 *ninkasho* permit, license, charter
可証 *ninkashō* permit, license, charter
6 印 *mito(me)in, nin'in* personal seal, signet
合 *mito(me)-a(u)* see another's viewpoint
7 否 *nimpi* approval or disapproval
8 知 *ninchi* recognition, acknowledgment
定 *nintei* authorization, recognition, acknowledgment, presumption, permission; identification
10 容 *nin'yō* admission, tolerance, acknowledgment
11 許 *ninkyo* consent, recognition
12 証 *ninshō* approval, validation, confirmation, certification
15 諾 *nindaku* assent, admission, approval
19 識 *ninshiki* recognition, understanding, knowledge

識不足 *ninshiki fusoku* lack of understanding
識票 *ninshikihyō* identification
識論 *ninshikiron* epistemology

7 B 誘 5625 / J4d36 / M35525 Yū. *saso(u)* invite, ask; call for; provoke, cause; bring (tears); allure, tempt, seduce. *izana(u)* invite; lead, tempt. *obi(ku)* decoy, entice, lure.
2 入 *obi(ki)-i(reru)* decoy, entice, lure into
4 水 *saso(i)mizu* pump priming
込 *saso(i)-ko(mu)* entice into
引 *yūin suru* entice, invite, beguile, induce, attract, allure
5 出 *obi(ki)-ida(su), obi(ki)-da(su), saso(i)-da(su), yūshutsu suru* decoy, entice, lure away
6 因 *yūin* immediate cause; incentive, motive
虫灯 *yūchūtō* luring lamp
8 拐 *yūkai* kidnapping, abduction
拐者 *yūkaisha* kidnapper, abductor
拐罪 *yūkaizai* the crime of kidnapping
9 発 *yūhatsu suru* cause, induce, lead up to, give advice to
10 起 *yūki suru* give rise to, lead to, cause
致 *yūchi suru* lure, entice, invite, bring about
殺 *yūsatsu suru* seduce and kill
11 掖 *yūeki suru* lead, guide, help, instruct
寄 *obi(ki)-yo(seru)* lure toward
12 惑 *yūwaku* temptation, seduction
惑物 *yūwakubutsu* temptation, seduction
惑者 *yūwakusha* tempter, seducer
13 蛾灯 *yūgatō* luring lamp
14 導 *yūdō* induction, incitement, inducement, encouragement
導兵器 *yūdō heiki* guided missiles
導訊問 *yūdō jimmon* leading question
導弾 *yūdōdan* guided missile
導爆弾 *yūdō bakudan* guided missile

A 誤 5626 / J386d / M35546' Go. *ayama(ru) vi* and *vt* err, be mistaken; do wrong; mislead. *ayama(ri)* mistake, error. *ayama(tte)* by mistake, accidentally.
5 用 *goyō* misapplication, misuse, abuse
写 *gosha* scribal error, error in copying
6 伝 *goden* misinformation, incorrect report
字 *goji* wrong character, wrong word, misprint
7 判 *gohan* mistrial, miscarriage of justice, misjudgment
8 送 *gosō suru* missend
9 信 *goshin* mistaken belief
10 称 *goshō* misnomer
記 *goki* clerical error, misentry, error in writing
配 *gohai* misdelivery (of letters)
殺 *gosatsu suru* kill by mistake; kill the wrong person
差 *gosa* error, aberration
11 脱 *godatsu* mistakes and omissions
訳 *goyaku* mistranslation
12 植 *goshoku* typographical error, erratum, misprint
診 *goshin* wrong diagnosis
報 *gohō* misinformation, incorrect report
13 解 *gokai* misunderstanding, misconception, delusion
電 *goden* incorrect telegram
載 *gosai* clerical error, misentry, error in writing
14 聞 *gobun* misunderstanding, false report, misinformation
綴 *gotetsu* misspelling
認 *gonin* misunderstanding, misconception, mistake
読 *godoku* misreading
説 *gosetsu* mistaken theory
算 *gosan* miscalculation
15 審 *goshin* wrong refereeing
18 謬 *gobyū* error, fallacy, mistake
21 魔化 *gomaka(su)* cheat, deceive, camouflage, hoodwink, prevaricate; gloss over, cover up; tamper with, doctor up; patch up; quibble; embezzle

A 説 5627 / J4062 / M35556' Zei. Etsu. Setsu opinion, view, assertion; comment; theory; rumor, report; version. *to(ku)* explain, expound, advocate, preach, teach, persuade.
3 及 *to(ki)-oyo(bu)* mention, refer to
4 分 *to(ki)-wa(keru)* explain
5 付 *to(ki)-tsu(keru)* talk into, persuade, prevail upon
去 *to(ki)-sa(ru)* completely explain
出 *to(ki)-ida(su), to(ki)-da(su)* begin to speak; begin to explain
6 伏 *to(ki)-fu(seru), to(ki)-fu(su)* confute, argue down, convince; prevail on,

persuade to do. *seppuku* persuading, persuasion, convincing
7 述 *setsujutsu* explanation, exposition
8 法 *seppō* (Buddhist) sermon
服 *seppuku* persuading, convincing
明 *setsumei suru, to(ki)-aka(su)* explain, interpret, illustrate, solve (a riddle). *setsumei, tokiaka(shi)* explanation, interpretation, description
明文 *setsumeibun* accompanying explanation
明図 *setsumeizu* explanatory diagram
明的 *setsumeiteki* explanatory
明者 *setsumeisha* expositor; exponent
明書 *setsumeisho* explanatory note
10 起 *to(ki)-o(kosu)* begin to explain
破 *to(ki)-yabu(ru)* confute. *seppa* refutation
11 問 *setsumon* investigation of a question; a proposition, a problem
掛 *yo(mi)-ka(keru)* begin to read; stop reading
経 *sekkyō* (Buddhist) sermon
得 *settoku* persuasion
得力 *settokuryoku* persuasive power
得代表 *settoku daihyō* a representative who explains a proposition
教 *to(ki)-oshi(eru)* propound, preach. *sekkyō* sermon; preaching; admonition; scolding
教所 *sekkyōjo* preaching place
教学 *sekkyōgaku* homiletics, sermonology
教者 *sekkyōja, sekkyōsha* preacher
教師 *sekkyōshi* preacher
教壇 *sekkyōdan* pulpit
12 落 *to(ki)-o(tosu)* talk into, win over
13 勧 *to(ki)-susu(meru)* persuade, urge, exhort
話 *setsuwa* story, narrative
話的 *setsuwateki* narrative (form)
14 聞 *to(ki)-ki(kasu)* explain, instruct, reason with
16 諭 *setsuyu suru, to(ki)-sato(su)* convince, persuade; reprove

A **語** 5628 / J386c / M35533 Go word, speech, language, term. Gyo. *kata(ru)* talk, tell, narrate, recite. *kata(rau)* talk, chat; pledge one's troth; invite, entice; win; conspire with. *kata(rai)* talk, chat; lovers' vow. *kata(ri)* narrative (in the noh); reciter. *-go* (technical) term; language.
4 手 *kata(ri)te* speaker, narrator, reciter
5 句 *goku* words, phrases
出 *kata(ri)-da(su)* utter, speak out
6 気 *goki* tone of voice, manner of speaking
伝 *kata(ri)-tsuta(eru)* pass on (traditions)
次 *goji ni* while on the subject
合 *kata(ri)-a(u)* talk together
7 尾 *gobi* word ending, the inflected end of a word
尾変化 *gobi henka* inflection of words
述 *kata(ri)-no(beru)* proclaim, tell
形 *gokei* word form
告 *kata(ri)-tsu(geru)* tell
呂 *goro* the sound, euphony
呂合 *goroa(wase)* rhyming game
8 明 *kata(ri)-aka(su)* talk all night
法 *gohō* diction, phraseology, grammar, syntax
物 *kata(ri)mono* narrative; theme of a folk song
学 *gogaku* language study; linguistics
学者 *gogakusha* linguist
9 草 *kata(ri)gusa* topic, story
10 根 *gokon* stem, root of a word
格 *gokaku* grammar
脈 *gomyaku* interrelationship of words
部 *kataribe* family of professional narrators
原 *gogen* derivation, etymology
原学 *gogengaku* etymology
11 掛 *kata(ri)-ka(keru)* address, speak to
族 *gozoku* a family of languages
釈 *goshaku* explanation of words
13 源 *gogen* derivation, etymology
源学 *gogengaku* etymology
継 *kata(ri)-tsu(gu)* transmit, hand down
数 *gosū* number of words
群 *gogun* a family of languages
彙 *goi* vocabulary, glossary
義 *gogi* meaning of a word
意 *goi* meaning of a word
勢 *gosei* stress, emphasis, tone, accent; the power of words; manner of speaking
感 *gokan* the impression of words
幹 *gokan* stem, root of a word
路 *goro* the sound, euphony
路合 *goroa(wase)* rhyming game
14 聞 *kata(ri)-ki(kaseru), kata(ri)-ki(kasu)* inform, tell

15 調 *gochō* accent, tone, rhythm
幣 *gohei* unhappy expression, faulty expression, misleading statement, misunderstanding
16 頭 *gotō* first part of a word
録 *goroku* analects, book of aphorisms
18 類 *gorui* parts of speech

A **読** 5629/J4649/M35580' **讀** 5719/J6c26/M36088 Tō. Toku, Doku

reading. *yo(mu)* read, peruse; understand, read (one's heart), guess, divine. *yo(meru)* can read; be legible, be readable; read well; be decipherable; understand, perceive, see through. *yo(mi-konasu)* read thoroughly. *yo(mi)* reading; Japanese rendering of a Chinese character. *yo(mide)* worthwhile reading.

2 入 *yo(mi)-i(ru)* read earnestly, be absorbed in reading. *yo(mi)-i(reru)* mention (in a poem)
了 *dokuryō suru* finish reading
人 *yomibito* author of a poem
人知 *yo(mi)bitoshi(razu)* writer of the poem unknown
3 下 *yo(mi)-kuda(su)* read through, peruse
上 *yo(mi)-a(geru)* read aloud, read off, read out (the names)
4 手 *yo(mi)te* reader; composer of a poem
方 *yo(mi)kata* way of reading; lesson; pronunciation
止 *yo(mi)sa(shi)* half-read
切 *yo(mi)-ki(ru)* read through, finish reading
心術 *tokushinjutsu* mind reading, mental telepathy
心術師 *tokushinjutsushi* mind reader
5 本 *tokuhon* reader. *yomihon* reader, storybook
6 尽 *yo(mi)-tsu(kusu)* read everything
返 *yo(mi)-kae(su)* reread
会 *dokkai* reading (of a bill)
合 *yo(mi)-a(waseru), yo(mi)-a(wasu)* read and compare
8 物 *yomimono* reading matter, a reading
取 *yo(mi)-to(ru)* read (someone's) mind, guess, divine
直 *yo(mi)-nao(su)* reread
易 *yo(mi)yasu(i)* easy to read; legible
者 *dokusha* reader, subscriber
者層 *dokushasō* class of readers
9 通 *yo(mi)-tō(su)* read through
点 *tōten* comma
後 *dokugo* after reading
後感 *dokugokan* impression of a book
10 流 *yo(mi)-naga(su)* read fluently; read without thinking
破 *dokuha suru, yo(mi)-yabu(ru)* read through
耽 *yo(mi)-fuke(ru)* be absorbed in reading
唇 *dokushin* lip reading
唇術 *dokushinjutsu* lip reading
書 *yo(mi)ka(ki)* reading and writing. *dokusho, tokusho* reading books
書人 *dokushojin* a reader of books, a scholar; the intelligentsia
書力 *dokushoryoku* reading ability
書三昧 *dokushozammai* only reading all the time
書会 *dokushokai* reading circle, reading club
書狂 *dokushokyō* a bookworm
書室 *dokushoshitsu* reading room
書界 *dokushokai* reading public
書家 *dokushoka* well-read person
11 過 *dokka suru* skim over, miss, overlook
違 *yo(mi)chiga(i)* misreading
頃 *yo(mi)goro no* readable, fit to read
終 *yo(mi)-owa(ru), yo(mi)-o(eru)* finish reading
経 *dokyō, dokkyō* chanting Buddhist sutras
12 落 *yo(mi)-o(tosu)* overlook in reading
13 溜 *yo(mi)-ta(meru)* read and retain
解 *dokukai* reading and explaining a book
話術 *dokuwajutsu* lip reading
14 聞 *yo(mi)-ki(kasu)* read to, read for. *yomiki(ki)* reading and listening
慣 *yo(mi)-na(reru)* get used to reading
誤 *yo(mi)-ayama(ru)* misread, mispronounce
18 癖 *yo(mi)kuse* peculiar pronunciation
難 *yo(mi)niku(i)* hard to read; illegible

8

諌 5630/J3452/M35642 See **諫** 5664.

詑 5631 J6b5c M35682 Jō command.

諏 5632 J3f5b M35648 SHU, SU, Sō consult.

諍 5633 J6b5a M35643 Sō remonstrate. *isaka(u), araso(u)* quarrel, dispute.

誼 5634 J3543 M35605 GI friendship, intimacy, good will. *yoshi(mi)* friendship, intimacy, good will.

諄 5635 J6b59 M35622 JUN. *hichikudo(i)* tedious.
15 諄 *junjun to* earnestly, patiently, repeatedly

諂 5636 J6b5b M35616 TEN. *hetsura(u)* flatter, curry favor.
16 諛 *ten'yu* flattery

B 謁 5637 J315a M35690' 謁 5649 J-X M35757 ETSU audience (with a ruler). *es(suru)* have an audience with.
7 見 *ekken* an audience (with someone)
見室 *ekkenshitsu* audience chamber

B 諾 5638 J427a M35687 DAKU assent, consent, agreement. *daku(suru)* agree to. *ubena(u)* agree to; follow.
7 否 *dakuhi* definite answer, yes or no, acceptance or refusal
15 諾 *dakudaku* yes yes

誹 5639 J4870 M35601 HI ridicule, slander.
13 毀 *hiki* slander, calumny, libel
毀罪 *hikizai* defamation, libel
16 諧 *haikai* 17-syllable poem; a humorous haiku poem
17 謗 *hibō* slander; abuse
20 議 *higi* abusive argument

A 誕 5640 J4342 M35692' 誕 5613 J-X M35516 TAN be born; deceive; lie; be arbitrary.
5 生 *tanjō* birth, nativity
生日 *tanjōbi* birthday
生石 *tanjōseki* birthstone
生祝 *tanjō iwa(i)* birthday party; birthday gift
7 辰 *tanshin* birthday

諒 5641 J4e4a M35653 RYō fact, reality. *ryō (to) suru* understand; appreciate; excuse.
7 承 *ryōshō* acknowledgment
10 陰 *ryōan* national mourning (for an emperor)
13 解 *ryōkai* understanding, comprehension
14 察 *ryōsatsu* understanding, sympathy, consideration
17 闇 *ryoan* national mourning (for an emperor)

誰 5642 J432f M35586 SUI. *dare, tare* who. *dare(ka)* someone, somebody. *dare mo, dare(shimo)* everyone; (neg.) no one.
1 一人 *dare hitori mo* (neg.) no one
4 方 *donata* who
7 何 *suika suru* challenge, question
8 彼 *darekare, tarekare* this or that person; many people; anyone. *dare(mo)-kare(mo)* everyone
彼無 *darekarena(shi)* everybody
9 某 *taresore, taregashi* someone or other

A 談 5643 J434c M35633 譚 5696 J6b7d M35978 DAN conversation, talk. *dan(jiru), dan(zuru)* discuss, talk (with or about); negotiate with.
4 片 *dampen* short talk, occasional talk
込 *dan(ji)-ko(mu)* protest against
6 合 *dan(ji)-a(u)* negotiate with, consult together. *dango* consultation, conference
合尽 *dangōzu(ku)* (not a verb) mutual agreement
7 判 *dampan* negotiation, conference, parley, discussion
余 *dan'yo* after speaking; while speaking
10 笑 *danshō* friendly chat
13 義 *dangi* lecture, lesson, sermon (Buddhist)
話 *danwa* conversation, talk, chat, speaking
話体 *danwatai* conversational style
話室 *danwashitsu* lounge
話管 *danwakan* speaking tube
15 論 *danron* discussion, argument, discourse

論風発 *danron-fūhatsu* eloquence; ready controversialist

20 議 *dangi* lecture, lesson, sermon (Buddhist)

A **課** 5644 / J325d / M35589 KA lesson; section, department; allotment, division. *ka(suru), ka(su)* levy, assess; assign (a task); charge with.

5 目 *kamoku* subject, course, curriculum; items

外 *kagai* extracurricular

外活動 *kagai katsudō* extracurricular activities

外講義 *kagai kōgi* university extension lecture

7 役 *kaeki* taxes; conscripted labor

8 長 *kachō* section head

10 員 *kain* section staff

11 率 *karitsu* tax rate

12 程 *katei* course, curriculum, routine

税 *kazei* taxation, assessment, tax, duty, levy

税所得 *kazei shotoku* taxable income

税品 *kazeihin* taxable or dutiable article

税率 *kazeiritsu* tax rate

13 業 *kagyō* schoolwork, lessons

14 徴金 *kachōkin* charges

18 題 *kadai* subject, theme, problem, homework

B **請** 5645 / J4041 / M35640' SHIN. SHŌ. JŌ. SEI requesting, inviting. *shō(jiru), shō(zuru)* invite, usher in. *ko(u)* ask, request; invite; pray for; beg, solicit. *u(keru)* receive, accept, take, get, obtain; face, front on, inherit; catch the public's fancy.

2 人 *u(ke)nin* guarantor, bondsman

入 *shō(ji)-i(reru)* usher in, ask in

5 出 *u(ke)-da(su)* redeem, ransom, buy out, pay off, take out of pawn

6 托 *seitaku* solicitation, entreaty

合 *u(ke)-a(u)* undertake; promise, guarantee. *u(ke)a(i)* guarantee, assurance

7 判 *u(ke)han* surety seal

売 *u(ke)u(ri)* retailing

求 *ko(i)-moto(meru)* ask for, beg. *seikyū* demand, claim, application

求人 *seikyūnin* claimant, applicant

求者 *seikyūsha* claimant, applicant

求書 *seikyūsho* application, written claim

8 取 *u(ke)-to(ru)* receive, accept; believe, understand. *uketori* receipt, acknowledgment

歩 *ko(i)-aru(ku)* go around begging

受 *ko(i)-u(keru)* ask and receive

9 待 *shōdai* invitation

負 *u(ke)-o(u)* contract for, undertake. *ukeoi* contract

負人 *ukeoinin* contractor

負入札 *ukeoi nyūsatsu* contract bid

負工 *ukeoikō* pieceworker

負仕事 *ukeoi shigoto* job work, piecework, contract work

負契約 *ukeoi keiyaku* contract

負師 *ukeoishi* contractor

負値段 *ukeoi nedan* contract price

負業 *ukeoigyō* contracting business

負賃金 *ukeoi chingin* piecework pay

10 託 *seitaku* request, secret request

訓 *seikun* request for instructions

書 *u(ke)ga(ki), u(ke)sho* written acknowledgment; letter to acceptance; receipt

11 宿 *u(ke)yado* servant's registry

13 暇 *seika* requesting a vacation; a vacation

19 願 *seigan* petition

願者 *seigansha* petitioner

願書 *seigansho* (written) petition

A **論** 5646 / J4f40 / M35658 RON argument; discourse. *agetsura(u), ron(jiru), ron(zuru)* discuss, argue, comment on, deal with, consider.

3 及 *ronkyū suru* touch on, refer to, enter into

4 文 *rombun* dissertation, thesis, article, paper, treatise, essay

5 立 *ron(ji)-ta(teru)* argue eloquently

外 *rongai* beside the point, irrelevant

弁 *romben* argument

功 *ronkō* decision on service merits

功行賞 *ronkō kōshō* distribution of awards

6 尽 *ron(ji)-tsu(kusu)* discuss thoroughly

合 *ron(ji)-a(u)* discuss together, argue with

旨 *ronshi* point of an argument

考 *ronkō* a study
争 *ronsō* dispute, controversy, argument
争点 *ronsōten* point of dispute
7 述 *ronjutsu* statement, enunciation
決 *ronketsu* conclusion, decision
判 *rompan* argument, disputation
究 *ronkyū suru* discuss thoroughly
告 *ronkoku* stating one's belief; prosecution; prosecutor's address
8 拠 *ronkyo* basis of an argument, data
法 *rompō* argument, reasoning, logic
者 *ronsha* disputant; advocate, the present writer
9 陣 *ronjin* argument
点 *ronten* point at issue, disputed point
客 *ronkaku, ronkyaku* disputant, controversialist
10 破 *rompa suru* refute, argue against. *rompa* rebuttal
11 断 *rondan* verdict, conclusion
理 *ronri* logic
理上 *ronrijō* logically (speaking)
理的 *ronriteki* logical
理学 *ronrigaku* logic
理学上 *ronrigakujō* logically (speaking)
12 結 *ronketsu* conclusion of an argument
評 *rompyō* criticism, review, comment
証 *ronshō* proof, demonstration
策 *ronsaku* an article on current problems
13 詰 *ron(ji)-naji(ru), ronkitsu suru* argue and criticize. *ron(ji)-tsu(meru)* drive an argument home
戦 *ronsen* verbal battle, argument
罪 *ronzai suru* prosecute
意 *ron'i* point of an argument
14 語 *Rongo* Confucian Analects
説 *ronsetsu* discourse, dissertation; editorial
駁 *rombaku suru* refute, argue against
15 調 *ronchō* tone of the argument
談 *rondan* arguing
鋒 *rompō* force of an argument, logic
敵 *ronteki* opponent (in debate), adversary
16 壇 *rondan* world of criticism; lecture platform
18 難 *ronnan* denunciation, criticism, censure
題 *rondai* subject, theme, topic for debate
叢 *ronsō* collection of treatises
20 議 *rongi* discussion, controversy, argument

A **調** 5647 / J4434 / M35609' CHŌ tune, tone, meter; key (in music); style of writing; tax in kind. *chō(zuru)* investigate, scrutinize; provide; prepare; make; curse, exorcise; ridicule. *shira(beru)* test, examine, investigate, survey, check up; inspect, overhaul; search for; look up (a word); refer to (a book); interrogate; correct (papers); play (on an instrument). *totono(eru)* prepare, arrange; fill (orders); supply; raise (money); put in order, tidy up, adjust (clothes); regulate; settle; purchase. *totono(u)* be prepared, be arranged, be in order, be adjusted, be well regulated; be settled. *mitsugi* tribute. *shira(be)* melody, tune; notes.

3 上 *shira(be)-a(geru)* investigate thoroughly
子 *chōshi* tune, tone, key, note, pitch; time, rhythm; accent; vein; manner, style; condition, state (of health); trend
子付 *chōshizu(ku)* relax; warm up to; be elated by; be gay-spirited
子外 *chōshihazu(re)* discord, false note, out of tune
子物 *chōshimono* matter of chance; person easily elated
子者 *chōshimono* person easily elated
5 号 *chōgō* key signature (in music)
6 糸 *shira(be)ito* belt lacing
伏 *chōbuku* curse, exorcism
色 *chōshoku* mixing colors; toning (in movies)
色板 *chōshokuban* palette
印 *chōin* signature, signing, sealing
印式 *chōinshiki* ceremony of signing
印国 *chōinkoku* signatory powers
合 *chōgō* mixing, compound
合物 *chōgōbutsu* mixture, compound, concoction
合剤 *chōgōzai* mixture, compound, concoction
8 法 *chōhō* convenience, usefulness. *chōhō(garu)* find useful, think highly of
物 *shira(be)mono* research; matter for investigation

和 *chōwa* harmony, accord, agreement; symphony; symmetry; conformity
直 *shira(be)-nao(su)* reinvestigate, reexamine
定 *chōtei* settlement
味 *chōmi* seasoning, flavor
味料 *chōmiryō* condiments, seasoning, relishes, dressing
9 革 *shira(be)gawa* belt, band, belting
速機 *chōsokuki* governor, speed regulator
度 *chōdo* furniture, appliances, utensils, supplies
度品 *chōdohin* furniture, appliances, utensils, supplies
律 *chōritsu* tuning
律師 *chōritsushi* piano tuner
査 *chōsa* investigation, examination, inquiry, survey, research
査委員 *chōsa iin* examiner, investigator
10 進 *chōshin* preparation
貢 *chōkō* tribute
書 *chōsho* protocol, preliminary memorandum, record
帯 *chōtai* belt, belting
剤 *chōzai* compounding medicines
剤師 *chōzaishi* druggist
馬 *chōba* horsebreaking, horse training
馬師 *chōbashi* horse trainer
馬場 *chōbajō* riding ground
11 達 *chōtatsu, chōdatsu* supply, procurement, provision
略 *chōryaku* plan
教 *chōkyō* breaking or training (animals)
停 *chōtei* arbitration, conciliation, mediation, intercession, intervention
理 *chōri* cooking
理人 *chōrinin* cook
理台 *chōridai* kitchen table
理法 *chōrihō* cookery; recipe
理場 *chōriba* kitchen
13 節 *chōsetsu* regulation, adjustment, control, modulation, governing, tempering, tuning, tuning in
14 練 *chōren* military drill
製 *chōsei* manufacture, preparation
髪 *chōhatsu* barbering
髪室 *chōhatsushitsu* barber shop
16 整 *chōsei* regulation, adjustment, governing, control, coordination, correction, modulation, tuning

A **諸** 5648 J3d74 M35691' **諸** 5650 J-X M35743 SHO- many, several, various, all. *moro-* every; many; two; together.

2 人 *shonin, shojin, morobito* all people, everyone
入費 *shonyūhi* sundry expenses
3 士 *shoshi* many people
子 *shoshi* you; sage, master
刃 *moroha no* double-edged
4 氏 *shoshi* all of you
王 *shoō* all the kings, many kings
仏 *shobutsu* all Buddhas
天 *shoten* the heavens
公 *shokō* government officials; gentlemen
手 *morote, shote* with both hands
手当 *shoteate* sundry allowances
方 *shohō* every direction, all sides, everywhere
方面 *shohōmen* all directions
5 白 *morohaku* quality saké
処 *shosho* many places
兄 *shokei* dear friends
司 *shoshi* many officials
本 *shohon* many kinds of books
外国 *shogaikoku* many foreign countries
民族 *shominzoku* many nations or races
6 色 *shoshiki* commodities
式 *shoshiki* commodities
肌 *morohada* stripped to the waist
州 *shoshū* all the provinces
寺 *shoji* various temples, all temples
共 *morotomo ni* altogether, together
行 *shogyō* all worldly things; all phenomena
行無常 *shogyō-mujō* the vanity of all things (a Buddhist concept)
7 声 *morogoe ni* with one voice, in unison
芸 *shogei* arts, accomplishments
君 *shokun* gentlemen, ladies and gentlemen, my friends, you
車通行止 *Shosha Tsūkōdome* All Vehicles Stop Here.
8 味 *moromi* unrefined saké or soy
姉 *shoshi* all you women
所 *shosho* here and there
宗 *shoshū* all sects; various sects
物価 *shobukka* the prices of commodities
事 *shoji* various matters, everything
事万端 *shoji-bantan* everything

事倹約 *shoji ken'yaku* all-around economy
国 *shokoku* all countries, various countries; all provinces
国民 *shokokumin* all the nations, all peoples
国家 *shokokka* all nations
国語 *shokokugo* all languages
9 侯 *shokō* the princes, the daimyos
相 *shosō* various aspects, all phases
派 *shoha* the minor parties (in a legislature)
神 *shoshin* all the gods; many gods
政 *shosei* all phases of government
点 *shoten* all points
彦 *shogen* many fine people; you (polite)
星 *shosei* leaders, celebrities
10 将 *shoshō* the commanders
般 *shohan no* various, several, all, every
島 *shotō* group of islands, archipelago
家 *shoka* many houses; many people in the area; many schools of thought; many scholars
都市 *shotoshi* all cities
11 道 *shodō* arts, accomplishments
掛 *shoka(kari), shoga(kari)* expenses, charges, costs
経費 *shokeihi* costs, expenses
問題 *shomondai* all questions, various questions
13 聖徒日 *Shoseitobi* All Saints Day
14 種 *shoshu* various kinds, all kinds
説 *shosetsu* various views, various theories
雑費 *shozappi* miscellaneous expenses
15 膝 *morohiza* both knees
諸 *moromoro no* all, all kinds of, various
賢 *shoken* ladies and gentlemen
権利 *shokenri* all rights
膚 *morohada* stripped to the waist
膚脱 *morohadanu(gu)* bare both shoulders; exert supreme effort
18 藩 *shohan* the clans

9

謁 5649 / J-X / M35757 See **謁** 5637.

諸 5650 / J-X / M35743 See **諸** 5648.

諞 5651 / J6b66 / M35703 HEN eloquent speech; flattery; pride.

諡 5652 / J6b6b / M35708 SHI. *okurina* posthumous name.
5 号 *shigō* posthumous name

諛 5653 / J6b67 / M35696 **諛** 5590 / J-X / M35495 YU. *hetsura(u)* flatter.
7 言 *yugen* flattery

諠 5654 / J6b63 / M35706 KEN forget; noisy.
17 譁 *kenka* quarrel, dispute

諤 5655 / J6b60 / M35713 GAKU speaking the truth.
16 諤 *gakugaku no* outspoken

謂 5656 / J3062 / M35759 I. *iwa(re)* reason; origin; a history; oral tradition. *i(i)* meaning. *yu(u), i(u)* say, tell, talk, speak, declare; call, term, name.
6 因縁 *i(ware)-innen* reason; origin; a history; oral tradition

諢 5657 / J6b64 / M35709 KON joke, jest; joker.
6 名 *kommei* nickname

諺 3838 / J-X / M35747 **諺** 5659 / J3841 / M-X GEN. *kotowaza* maxim, proverb
4 文 *ommon, ommun, gemmon, gembun* Korean script
13 解 *genkai* colloquial explanation

B **諮** 5660 / J3b70 / M35728 SHI. *haka(ru)* consult with.
11 問 *shimon* question, inquiry
13 詢 *shijun* question, inquiry

謎 5661 / J4666 / M35800 MEI. *nazo* riddle, puzzle, enigma; hint, tip.
11 掛 *nazoka(ke)* asking riddles
13 解 *nazoto(ki)* riddle solving
16 謎 *nazonazo* riddle, puzzle, enigma; hint, tip

諳 5662 / J6b5e / M35736 AN. *sora(njiru), sora(nzuru)* memorize; recite from memory.

10 記 *anki* memorization
記力 *ankiryoku* memory, retentive power
14 誦 *anshō* recitation, memorization

諦 5663 / J447c / M35716 TEI. TAI. *akira(meru)* abandon, give up, resign to, be reconciled to.
8 念 *teinen* a heart that understands truth
11 視 *teishi suru* stare, watch carefully
18 観 *teikan* clear vision; resignation (to)

諫 5664 / J6b5d / M35724 **諌** 5630 / J3452 / M35642 KAN. *isa(meru)* remonstrate with, admonish, dissuade.
4 止 *kanshi* dissuasion
6 死 *kanshi suru* remonstrate at the risk of one's life
争 *kansō* outspoken remonstrance
7 言 *kangen* remonstrance; admonition

諜 5665 / J4435 / M35697 CHŌ. *chō(zuru)* spy out, reconnoiter.
6 合 *shime(shi)-a(waseru)* arrange previously; conspire with
8 者 *chōja* spy
12 報 *chōhō* intelligence, secret information
報網 *chōhōmō* intelligence network

B **謡** 5666 / J4d58 / M35779' **謠** 5673 / J6b6f / M35832 YŌ. *uta(u)* chant. *utai* chanting of the noh; noh singer.
5 本 *utaibon* text of a noh drama
6 曲 *yōkyoku* noh chant
7 初 *uta(i)zo(me)* first singing of the *utai* in the new year
8 物 *utaimono* an *utai* poem for recitation

諭 5667 / J4d21 / M35727' **諭** 5668 / J-X / M35727 YU. *sato(su)* admonish, charge, remonstrate with, counsel, persuade, warn; make known to. *sato(shi)* advice, reproof, admonition; oracle.
5 示 *yushi* instructions, message, admonition
6 旨 *yushi* explanation, reasoning
7 告 *yukoku* counsel, instruction, warning
11 達 *yutatsu* official instructions, notice

諷 5669 / J6b65 / M35741 FŪ. FU. *fū(suru)* hint, suggest, insinuate; satirize, lampoon.
7 言 *fūgen* allusion, hint, insinuation, sarcasm, innuendo
8 刺 *fūshi* sarcasm, innuendo, irony
刺文 *fūshibun* satirical prose
刺画 *fūshiga* cartoon
16 諫 *fūkan* exhortation by insinuation
諭 *fūyu* hint, insinuation; allegory
諭法 *fūyuhō* allegory

諧 5670 / J6b5f / M35718 KAI harmony, order, suitability.
9 音 *kaion* melody, harmony
15 調 *kaichō* melody, harmony, unity
17 謔 *odoke, kaigyaku* joke
謔口 *odokeguchi* joke, jest
謔芝居 *odoke shibai* comedy, burlesque
謔者 *odokemono* joker, humorist
謔話 *odokebana(shi)* funny story

B **謀** 5671 / J4b45 / M35756 BŌ. MU. *haka(ru)* plan, devise, scheme; counsel with; have in mind; aim at; deceive, impose on. *tabaka(ru)* cheat, impose on. *hakarigoto* plan, scheme, policy, stratagem, plot, trick.
3 士 *bōshi* planner
4 反 *muhon* rebellion, insurrection, treason
5 主 *bōshu* chief plotter
6 臣 *bōshin* strategist, tactician
7 判 *bōhan* forged seal
9 計 *bōkei* plot, plan, scheme, stratagem, ruse
叛 *muhon, bōhan* rebellion, insurrection, treason
叛人 *muhonnin* conspirator, rebel
叛心 *muhonshin* spirit of revolt
叛気 *muhongi* spirit of revolt
10 殺 *bōsatsu* premeditated murder
書 *bōsho* forged document
11 略 *bōryaku* strategy, scheme, plot
20 議 *bōgi* consultation; conspiracy

10

謌 5672 / J6b68 / M35797 See 歌 2945.

謠 5673 / J6b6f / M35832 See 謡 5666.

諢 5674 J6b76 M35928 See **嘩** 861.

謔 5675 J6b62 M35810 **謔** 5676 J-X M-X GYAKU sport with.

諱 5677 J6b61 M35733 KI. *imina* posthumous name; real name.

謇 5678 J6b69 M35791 KEN difficult; speak frankly; truth. *domo(ru)* stammer, stutter.

謚 5679 J6b6a M35823 EKI laughing.

謨 5680 J6b75 M35864 BO plan, deliberate.

謐 5681 J6b6d M35803 HITSU quiet, peaceful.

謟 5682 J-X M35831 TŌ. *utaga(u)* doubt.
11 晦 *tōkai suru* maintain incognito, disappear

謗 5683 J6b6e M35817 BŌ. *soshi(ru)* slander, revile, disparage, censure, criticize.
6 合 *soshi(ri)-a(u)* slander each other
20 議 *bōgi* slander, abuse, criticism

謖 5684 J6b6c M35816 SHOKU arise.
12 然 *shokuzen* fold clothing neatly
17 謖 *shokushoku* soar above; sound of wind

B **謄** 5685 J4625 M35780' TŌ copy.
5 本 *tōhon* certified copy, transcript, duplicate; domiciliary registration copy
写 *tōsha* copy, reproduction; mimeographing
写版 *tōshaban* mimeograph, copying machine
写版刷 *tōshabanzu(ri)* mimeographed copy
写料 *tōsharyō* copying fee
写機 *tōshaki* mimeograph, copying machine
12 貴 *tōki* rise in prices

B **謙** 5686 J382c M35821' KEN. *herikuda(ru)* humble oneself, condescend, be modest.
7 抑 *ken'yoku* humbling oneself
8 退 *kentai* humility
10 称 *kenshō* humble expression
11 虚 *kenkyo* modesty, humility
13 辞 *kenji* humble words
遜 *kenson* humility, modesty
遜家 *kensonka* modest person
14 徳 *kentoku* humility, modesty
20 譲 *kenjō* modesty, humility
譲語 *kenjōgo* humble word

A **謝** 5687 J3c55 M35827 SHA. *sha(suru)* thank; apologize; decline, refuse; take one's leave. *ayama(ru)* apologize; be floored *ayama(ri)* apology, excuse.
5 礼 *sharei* thanks; remuneration, honorarium
6 肉祭 *shanikusai* fiesta, carnival
7 状 *shajō* letter of thanks; letter of apology
8 金 *shakin* monetary gift of thanks
10 恩 *shaon* repaying a kindness, expression of gratitude
恩会 *shaonkai* a party to show gratitude
12 絶 *shazetsu suru* refuse, decline (to see)
13 辞 *shagi* address of thanks; apology
電 *shaden* telegram of thanks
意 *shai* gratitude, thanks; apology
罪 *shazai* apology
罪状 *shazaijō* written apology

B **謹** 5688 J3660 M35850' **謹** 5690 J-X M35900 KIN. *tsutsushi(mu)* be discreet, be careful, be prudent, be cautious; restrain oneself, be moderate. *tsutsushi(mi)* prudence, modesty, discretion, self-control. *tsutsushi(nde)* respectfully, reverently, humbly.
5 白 *Kimpaku* Sincerely yours
写 *kinsha* respectfully copied
7 言 *Kingen* Sincerely yours
告 *kinkoku suru* respectfully inform
承 *kinshō suru* listen respectfully
8 直 *kinchoku* conscientiousness

7 見角【言】谷豆豕豸豸貝赤走足身車辛辰辵辶邑阝酉釆里

奏 *kinsō* reverent report to the emperor
10 書 *kinsho* respectively written
11 啓 *Kinkei* Dear Sirs, Gentlemen
12 賀新年 *Kinga Shinnen* Happy New Year
13 慎 *kinshin* penitence; discipline; domiciliary confinement
話 *kinwa* respectful remarks
飭 *kinchoku* deep reverence
14 選 *kinsen* reverent choice
製 *kinsei* carefully produced by
15 撰 *kinsen* reverent writing
17 厳 *kingen na* stern, serious, solemn, austere
聴 *kinchō suru* listen attentively

A **講** 5689 / J3956 / M35824 Kō club, association; lecture. *kō(jiru), kō(zuru)* read aloud; lecture on; read with; study; practice; conceive, devise.
4 中 *kōchū, kōjū* religious association (of non-Christians)
7 社 *kōsha* religious association (of non-Christians)
究 *kōkyū* research, investigation
8 学 *kōgaku* research, pursuit of study
武 *kōbu* military training
和 *kōwa suru* make peace with
和全権 *kōwa zenken* peace delegate
和会議 *kōwa kaigi* peace conference
和条約 *kōwa jōyaku* peace treaty
和使 *kōwashi* peace emissary
和使節 *kōwa shisetsu* peace mission
和談判 *kōwa dampan* peace negotiations
10 席 *kōseki* lecture hall
座 *kōza* lectureship; correspondence course; course of study
師 *kōshi* speaker, lecturer, instructor
書 *kōsho* interpretation of a book
11 堂 *kōdō* lecture hall, auditorium
釈 *kōshaku* lecture, storytelling
釈師 *kōshakushi* professional storyteller
習 *kōshū* short training course
習会 *kōshūkai* short training course, institute, training school
習所 *kōshūjo* training school
12 評 *kōhyō* criticism, review
13 話 *kōwa* lecture, address, talk
筵 *kōen* lecture, address
解 *kōkai* discourse, expository sermon
解説教 *kōkai sekkyō* discourse, expository sermon
義 *kōgi* lecture, exposition
義録 *kōgiroku* correspondence course; text of lectures
14 説 *kōsetsu* exposition, explanation
読 *kōdoku suru* read and explain
読者 *kōdokusha* one who reads and explains
演 *kōen* lecture, address
演会 *kōenkai* lecture meeting; series of lectures
演者 *kōensha* lecturer, speaker
15 談 *kōdan* storytelling; narrative
談師 *kōdanshi* professional storyteller
16 壇 *kōdan* lecture platform, rostrum, pulpit
壇討論会 *kōdan tōronkai* panel discussion

11

謹 5690 / J-X / M35900 See 謹 5688.

謾 5691 / J6b74 / M35909 Man despise, deceive.

謦 5692 / J6b72 / M35856 Kei coughing, clearing the throat.
9 咳 *keigai* pleasure of meeting

謳 5693 / J6b70 / M35885 Ō. *uta(u)* extol; declare, state expressly. *uta(wareru)* be famous, be notorious.
12 揚 *uta(i)-a(geru)* energetically propagandize
14 歌 *ōka* glorification, eulogy, applause; song of praise

謫 5694 / J6b73 / M35868 **讁** 5717 / J-X / M36091 Taku crime; criticism; blame; dismissal; exile.
8 居 *takkyo* exile, seclusion, confinement
所 *takusho* place of exile
10 流 *takuryū* banishment, exile

謬 5695 / J4935 / M35872 Byū. *ayamari* mistake.
6 伝 *byūden* false report, false rumor

7 見 *byūken* wrong view, mistaken notion, false idea, misconception, misunderstanding 「false report
14 説 *byūsetsu* fallacy, mistaken opinion,
15 論 *byūron* fallacy, fallacious argument

12

譚 5696 / J6b7d / M35978 See **談** 5643.

證 5697 / J6b7a / M35946 See **証** 5589.

A **譌** 5698 / J6b77 / M35951 See **訛** 5568.

譖 5699 / J6b7c / M-X **譛** 5700 / J6b7b / M35972 SHIN slander, falsely accuse.

譎 5701 / J6b79 / M35956 KETSU. *itsuwa(ru)* lie, falsify; deceive; pretend; deceive, cheat.
12 詐 *kissa, kessa* falsehood

譏 5702 / J6b78 / M35958 KI. *soshi(ru)* slander, revile, disparage, censure, criticize.
6 合 *soshi(ri)-a(u)* slander each other
15 誹 *kihi* slander, abuse

B **譜** 5703 / J4968 / M35990 **譜** 5707 / J-X / M-X FU music, note, staff, score; album, record, table; genealogy.
5 代 *fudai* successive generations; hereditary Tokugawa daimyo
代大名 *fudai daimyō* hereditary Tokugawa daimyo
8 表 *fuhyō* staff (in music)
11 第 *fudai* successive generations

A **識** 5704 / J3c31 / M35974 SHIKI know, discriminate, write.
2 力 *shikiryoku* knowledge, judgment, discernment, vision, intelligence
7 見 *shikken* knowledge, judgment, discernment, vision, intelligence
別 *shikibetsu* discrimination, discernment, identification
8 者 *shikisha* intelligent people, thinkers, intelligentsia
9 度 *shikido* intelligence and magnanimity
12 量 *shikiryō* personal appearance, features
16 閾 *shikiiiki* threshold of consciousness

A **警** 5705 / J3759 / M35989 KEI. *imashi(meru)* admonish, warn, prohibit. *imashime* precept, exhortation, instruction, commandment.
5 句 *keiku* aphorism, witticism
巡 *keijun* patrol
世 *keisei* warning to the public; writing on the wall
世家 *keiseika* seer, prophet
6 吏 *keiri* police officer
防 *keibō* preserving order
防団 *keibōdan* civilian guards, air-defense unit
7 抜 *keibatsu* something extraordinary
告 *keikoku* warning, advice
戒 *keikai* warning, admonition; vigilance
戒色 *keikaishoku* warning color
戒網 *keikaimō* police cordon
戒管制 *keikai kansei* air defense dim-out
戒線 *keikaisen* police cordon
戒警報 *keikai keihō* air-raid warning
8 固 *keigo* guard, escort, convoy, patrol
官 *keikan* police officer
官隊 *keikantai* police force, posse
9 急 *keikyū* alarm, emergency
乗警察 *keijō keisatsu* railway police
10 悟 *keigo na* clever and quick to understand
砲 *keihō* warning gun
部 *keibu* police inspector
11 務 *keimu* police affairs
笛 *keiteki* horn, alarm whistle, foghorn
視 *keishi* police superintendent
視庁 *Keishichō* Metropolitan Police Headquarters
12 棒 *keibō* nightstick, truncheon
報 *keihō* warning, alarm
報器 *keihōki* warning bell or siren
備 *keibi* defense, guard, policing
備兵 *keibihei* guard
備隊 *keibitai* garrison, guards; patrol squad
備艦 *keibikan* guard ship
14 語 *keigo* words of admonition
察 *keisatsu* police (force); police station
察犬 *keisatsuken* police dog, bloodhound

察手帳 *keisatsu techō* police blotter
察分署 *keisatsu bunsho* police substation
察庁 *Keisatsuchō* National Police Agency
察犯 *keisatsuhan* police offense
察医 *keisatsui* police doctor
察長 *keisatsuchō* chief of police
察官 *keisatsukan* police officer
察国家 *keisatsu kokka* police state
察隊 *keisatsutai* police force, constabulary
察群 *keisatsugun* police force
察署 *keisatsusho* police station
察署長 *keisatsushochō* chief of police
察権 *keisatsuken* police power
15 衛 *keiei* guard, patrol, escort
標 *keihyō* danger sign
16 醒 *keisei suru* warn, awake, arouse
18 蹕 *keihitsu* heralding, clearing the road
20 鐘 *keishō* fire bell, alarm bell
護 *keigo* guard, escort, convoy, patrol
護者 *keigosha* watcher, guard
22 邏 *keira* patrol officer

13

譱 5706 / J6641 / M36028 See **善** 858.

譜 5707 / J-X / M-X See **譜** 5703.

譽 5708 / J6c25 / M36066 See **誉** 5602.

譯 5709 / J6c23 / M36023 See **訳** 5572.

譟 5710 / J6c21 / M35998 Sō. *sawa(gu)* be boisterous; make noise; cry out.

譴 5711 / J6c24 / M36043 Ken scold. *seme(ru)* reproach.
11 責 *kenseki* rebuke, reprimand, censure

譬 5712 / J6c22 / M36019 Hi. *tato(eru)* compare, illustrate, speak figuratively. *tatoe, tatoi* parable, illustration, figure of speech.
12 喩 *hiyu* simile, metaphor; allegory, parable, fable
13 話 *tatoebanashi* parable, fable, allegory

譫 5713 / J6b7e / M36017 Tō, Sen delirious talk.
6 妄 *semmō* delirium
7 言 *uwakoto, uwagoto* foolish talk; delirious utterances
14 語 *uwagoto* talking in a delirium

B **譲** 5714 / J3e79 / M36037' **讓** 5725 / J6c2a / M36139 Jō. *yuzu(ru)* turn over, hand over, transfer, convey, assign, deed, bequeath, give away, give up; sell, dispose of; yield to; be inferior to; defer, postpone.
3 与 *jōyo* cession, transfer; concession
6 合 *yuzu(ri)-a(u)* compromise, concede
7 位 *jōi* abdication
状 *yuzurijō* deed, grant, assignment
8 歩 *jōho* concession, conciliation, compromise, condescension
受 *yuzu(ri)-u(keru)* inherit, receive, take over, obtain by transfer
12 渡 *yuzu(ri)-wata(su)* turn over, hand over, convey, cede. *jōto* transfer, conveyance, delivery, grant
渡人 *jōtonin, yuzuriwata(shi)nin* grantor, transferor
渡証書 *yuzuriwata(shi) shōsho, jōto shōsho* deed of conveyance, assignment

A **護** 5715 / J386e / M36038' Go. *mamo(ru)* defend, protect; keep, observe, obey; abide by; stick to; be true to.
7 身 *goshin* self-protection, self-defense, self-preservation
身仏 *goshimbutsu* personal guardian 「Buddha
身法 *goshinhō* methods of self-defense
身術 *goshinjutsu* art of self-defense
8 法 *gohō* defense of the constitution; defense of a religion
国 *gokoku* defense of the fatherland
国神社 *gokoku jinja* shrine of the war dead
送 *gosō* convoy, escort
送車 *gosōsha* patrol wagon or car
送船 *gosōsen* convoying vessel
岸 *gogan* sea wall; river dike
岸工事 *gogan kōji* riparian works, embankment, levee

岸基礎 *gogan kiso* riprap
9 持 *goji* defense, protection, maintenance, retention; prayer
11 符 *gofu* charm, amulet, talisman
15 摩 *goma* offering incense and praying
摩灰 *goma(no)hai* highway robber
衛 *goei* guard, convoy, escort
衛巡査 *goei junsa* police escort, police guard
衛兵 *goeihei* military escort, guard, bodyguard
衛者 *goeisha* guard
衛艦 *goeikan* escort ship
16 憲 *goken* safeguarding the constitution
17 謨 *gomu* rubber

A **議** 5716 / J3544 / M36027 GI consultation, deliberation, debate; consideration, proposal, suggestion.
gi(suru) discuss, deliberate on, consider.
2 了 *giryō suru* close a debate, finish deliberation
3 士 *gishi* counselor
6 会 *gikai* deliberative assembly
会政治 *gikai seiji* parliamentary government
7 判 *gihan* deliberation and decision
決 *giketsu* decision, resolution
決権 *giketsuken* voting right
決機関 *giketsu kikan* legislative assembly
8 長 *gichō* chair, speaker, president (of the senate)
官 *gikan* counselor, judge
定 *gitei, gijō* agreement
定書 *giteisho, gijōsho* protocol; written agreement
事 *giji* proceedings
事日程 *giji nittei* agenda
事目録 *giji mokuroku* agenda
事妨害 *giji bōgai* filibuster, obstructive tactics
事堂 *gijidō* assembly hall, capitol, diet building
事項目 *giji kōmoku* agenda
事録 *gijiroku* minutes, proceedings, report, journal
9 院 *giin* the House, the Diet Chamber
院制度 *giin seido* parliamentary system
院政治 *giin seiji* parliamentary government
10 席 *giseki* parliamentary seat, the floor
案 *gian* bill, measure
員 *giin* member of an assembly
員総会 *giin sōkai* party caucus
12 場 *gijō* assembly hall, chamber, the House, the floor
15 論 *giron* argument, discussion, controversy, debate
論好 *gironzu(ki) na* argumentative
論家 *gironka* argumentative person, good debater
18 題 *gidai* topic for discussion, agenda

14

譾 5717 / J-X / M36091 See **譾** 5694.

15

變 5718 / J-X / M36112 See **変** 1119.

讀 5719 / J6c26 / M36088 See **読** 5629.

讃 5720 / J3b3e / M36110 See **讚** 5729.

16

變 5721 / J5a4e / M36117 See **変** 1119.

讐 5722 / J3d32 / M36125 **讎** 5723 / J6c28 / M36124 SHŪ enemy. *ada* enemy; revenge.

讌 5724 / J6c27 / M36121 EN. *utage* party, banquet.
12 飲 *en'in* drinking bout

17

讓 5725 / J6c2a / M36139 See **譲** 5714.

讖 5726 / J6c2b / M36144 SHIN foretelling, presage, omen.

讙 5727 / J6c2c / M36157 KAN noisy, boisterous.

讒 5728 / J6c29 / M36137 ZAN defamation.
2 人 *zanjin* slanderer
3 口 *zankō* false charge, slander, defamation
6 奸 *zankan* wicked slanderer
7 言 *zangen* false charge, slander, defamation
8 者 *zansha* slanderer
9 奏 *zansō* slandering the emperor
12 間 *zankan* separating people by slandering
訴 *zanso* false charge, slander, defamation
17 謗 *zambō* libel, slander, defamation

19

讃 5729 / J6c2d / M36163 **讚** 5720 / J5720 / M3b3e SAN praise; title or brief inscription on a picture.
6 仰 *sangō* praise
9 美 *sambi* praise, adoration
美歌 *sambika* hymn
13 嘆 *santan* praise, admiration
辞 *sanji* eulogy, compliment
14 歌 *sanka* praise, admiration
15 歎 *santan* praise, admiration

RAD. 谷 150

Tani valley. At left: *tani hen*. Nickname: Valley.

A **谷** 5730 / J432b / M36182 KOKU. *tani* valley, dale, ravine; trough (of a wave); trough (in atmospheric pressure). *-ya* valley.
3 口 *taniguchi* mouth of a valley
川 *tanigawa* valley stream, mountain stream
4 水 *tanimizu* valley water, rill
6 地 *yachi* low damp area, swamp
7 谷 *tanidani* valleys
8 底 *tanizoko, tanisoko* bottom of a ravine; valley bottom
9 風 *tanikaze* valley wind
11 道 *tanimichi* pass, defile, notch
12 渡 *taniwata(ri)* flying over the valleys (birds); trees spanning a valley with their branches
間 *tanima, taniai* ravine, chasm, dell, valley
間百合 *tanima (no) yuri* lily of the valley
間姫百合 *tanima (no) hime yuri* lily of the valley

4

谺 5731 / J-X / M36193 See 谺 5732.

5

谺 5732 / J6c2e / M-X KA. *kodama* spirit of a tree; echo.

10

豁 5733 / J6c2f / M36221 KATSU empty, wide.
11 達 *kattatsu* magnanimity, generosity
12 然 *katsuzen to* all of a sudden; extensively

谿 5734 / J6c30 / M36219 KEI valley. *tani* valley.
7 谷 *keikoku* valley, ravine, canyon
10 流 *keiryū* mountain stream
16 壑 *keigaku* deep valley

RAD. 豆 151

Mame bean. At left: 豆 *mame hen*. Nickname: Bean.

A **豆** 5735 / J4626 / M36245 TŌ. ZU. *mame* beans, peas, pulse. *mame-* miniature, midget, pocket (battleship), small.
2 人形 *mame ningyō* miniature doll
5 本 *mame hon* miniature book

台風 *mame taifū* small typhoon
6 名月 *mame meigetsu* moon of 13th day of ninth lunar month
白動車 *mame jidōsha* midget auto
8 油 *mame abura* soybean oil
炒 *mamei(ri)* parched beans
乳 *tōnyū* soybean milk
9 柿 *mamegaki* small persimmon
炭 *mametan* oval briquets
11 粒 *mame tsubu* separate beans
萠 *mame moya(shi)* bean sprouts
12 絞 *mameshibo(ri)* polka-dot pattern
13 幹 *mamegara* beanstalks and pods
戦車 *mame sensha* midget tank
鉄砲 *mamedeppō* popgun, bean shooter
電球 *mame denkyū* miniature light bulb
14 腐 *tōfu* bean curd, tofu
15 撒 *mamema(ki)* bean-scattering ceremony
17 糟 *mamekasu* beancake

3

豈 5736 / J6c31 / M36249 Kai. Gai. *ani* an interjection of surprise.

6

A **豊** 5737 / J1b2d / M36263 **豐** 5740 / J6c34 / M36304 Hō. *yuta(kana)* abundant; rich; fruitful. *toyo-* excellent, rich.
4 凶 *hōkyō* rich or poor harvest, nature of the harvest
水 *hōsui* abundance of water
水期 *hōsuiki* high-water season, rainy season
6 年 *hōnen* fruitful year
年満作 *hōnen-mansaku* a good year and bumper crops
7 作 *hōsaku* abundant harvest
沃 *hōyoku* fertility
9 栄昇 *toyosakanobo(ru)* rise in brilliance (the sun)
12 満 *hōman* stout, corpulent
富 *hōfu* abundance, wealth
葦原 *Toyoashihara* (ancient) Japan
14 漁 *hōryō, hōgyo* big catch (of fish)
旗雲 *toyohatagumo* pretty bank of clouds
15 潤 *hōjun* rich and prosperous; luxurious (fruit)
熟 *hōjuku* abundant harvest. *hōjuku suru* ripen
頬 *hōkyō* plump cheeks
18 穣 *hōjō* abundant harvest; excellent crop
19 艶 *hōen* voluptuous beauty
21 饒 *hōjō* fertility

8

豌 5738 / J6c32 / M36273 En pea.
7 豆 *endō* peas
豆豆 *endō mame* peas

豎 5739 / J6c33 / M36280 Ju vertical; child.
3 子 *jushi* child, lad, youngster; stripling, greenhorn
6 吏 *juri* subordinate official

11

豐 5740 / J6c34 / M36301 See 豊 5737.

21

豔 5741 / J-X / M36332 See 艶 4957.

RAD. 豕 152

Buta or *inoko* pig. At left: *inoko hen*. Variant: 豸 (6 strokes). Nickname: Pig.

豕 5742 / J6c35 / M36334 Shi. *inoko* hog.

4

B **豚** 5743 / J465a / M36352 Ton hog. *buta* pig, hog, swine.

7 見角言谷豆【豕 豸】4 豸貝赤走足身車辛辰辵辶邑阝酉釆里

3 小屋 *butagoya* hogpen; hovel, shack
4 毛 *tommō* hog bristle
犬 *tonken* hogs and dogs; foolish people
汁 *tonjiru, butajiru* pork broth soup
6 肉 *butaniku, tonniku* pork, hog meat
肉商 *tonnikushō* pork butcher
7 尾 *butao, tombi* pigtail, queue
児 *tonji* my son (humble)
8 舎 *tonsha* pigsty
10 脂 *tonshi* lard
15 箱 *butabako* police detention jail

5

A **象** 5744 / J3e5d / M36372 **豫** 5745 / J-X / M36373 Shō image; shape; sign (of the times). Zo elephant. *katado(ru)* pattern after, imitate; symbolize.
5 皮病 *zōhibyō* elephantiasis
牙 *zōge* ivory
牙細工 *zōgezaiku* ivory work
牙塔 *zōge (no) tō* ivory tower
牙質 *zōgeshitsu* dentine
6 虫 *zōmushi* weevil
7 形 *shōkei* copying the form (of something); hieroglyphics
形文字 *shōkei monji, shōkei moji* hieroglyphics, Chinese characters; a type of characters resembling pictures (e.g. 馬, 魚, and 鳥)
11 眼 *zōgan* inlay, damascene work
12 嵌 *zōgan* inlay, damascene work
14 鼻虫 *zōhanamushi* weevil
徴 *shōchō suru* symbolize, foreshadow. *shōchō* symbol, emblem
徴主義 *shōchō shugi* symbolism
徴的 *shōchōteki* symbolic
徴詩 *shōchōshi* symbolic poetry

6

豢 5746 / J6c36 / M36380 Kan, Ken raise domestic livestock on grain.

7

豨 5747 / J-X / M36404 **豬** 5748 / J-X / M-X Ki large hog.

9 勇 *kiyū* fierce courage

B **豪** 5749 / J396b / M36406 Gō great, powerful, excelling.
6 気 *gōki* sturdy spirit
壮 *gōsō* splendor, magnificence, grandeur
7 快 *gōkai na* exciting, stirring, lively; heroic; largehearted; splendid
8 放 *gōhō na* largehearted, frank, unaffected
物 *erabutsu, eramono* great character
者 *gō(no)mono* past master, veteran
雨 *gōu* heavy rain, downpour, cloudburst
雨禍 *gōuka* flood devastation
9 胆 *gōtan* boldness, hardihood
勇 *gōyū* bravery, prowess
10 家 *gōka* wealthy and powerful family
華 *gōka* splendor, pomp, extravagance
華版 *gōkaban* deluxe edition
11 遊 *gōyū* wild merrymaking
族 *gōzoku* powerful family or clan
盛 *gōsei* luxury, magnificence, extravagance
爽 *gōsō* fine disposition
商 *gōshō* wealthy merchant
商層 *gōshōsō* wealthy merchant class
12 傑 *gōketsu* hero, outstanding person
猪 *yamaarashi* porcupine
飲 *gōin* heavy drinking, carousing
奢 *gōsha* luxury, magnificence, extravagance
13 勢 *gōsei* luxury, magnificence, extravagance
農 *gōnō* wealthy farmer
14 語 *gōgo* bombast, boasting, big talk
15 邁 *gōmai* intrepidity, indomitableness

9

豬 5750 / J6c37 / M36432 See 猪 3585.

豫 5751 / J502e / M36425 See 予 68.

RAD. 豸 153

Mujina badger or *ashinakimushi* reptiles. At left: *mujina hen.*
Nickname: Clawed Dog (cf. Rads. 87 & 94).

豸 5752 J6c38 M36496 CHI snake; legless insect.

3

豹 5753 J493f M36499 HYŌ leopard, panther.
[9] 変 *hyōhen* sudden change

豺 5754 J6c39 M36500 SAI jackal.
[10] 狼 *sairō* jackals and wolves; cruel person; wicked person

4

豾 5755 J-X M36509 See 貅 5760.

貔 5756 J6c41 M36504 貔 5764 J6c40 M36606 HI heraldic beast symbolizing bravery.
[13] 貅 *hikyū* brave warrior

5

貂 5757 J6c3a M36528 CHŌ. *ten* marten, sable.

6

貊 5758 J6c3d M36550 BAKU barbarian.

貉 5759 J6c3b M36549 狢 5769 J6042 M20366 KAKU. *mujina* badger.

貅 5760 J6c3c M36542 豾 5755 J-X M36509 KYŪ heraldic beast symbolizing bravery.

7

貍 5761 J6c3e M36561 See 狸 3578.

貌 5762 J4b46 M36556 BŌ form, appearance; countenance.

8

貎 5763 J6c3f M36572 See 猊 3582.

10

貔 5764 J6c40 M36606 See 豼 5756.

貘 5765 J6c42 M36631 See 獏 3597.

RAD. 貝 154

Kai shell or *kogai* small "shell" (to distinguish it from Rad. 181).
At left: *kai hen.* Nickname: Small Shell.

A 貝 5766 J332d M36656 BAI shellfish. *kai* shell; shellfish.
[9] 拾 *kaihiro(i)* shell gathering
柱 *kaibashira* shell ligament
[11] 細工 *kaizaiku* shellwork
[12] 焼 *kaiya(ki)* baking in the shell
殻 *kaigara* sea shell
殻石灰 *kaigara sekkai* shell lime
殻追放 *kaigara tsuihō* ostracism
殻骨 *kaigarabone* shoulder blade
殻細工 *kaigarazaiku* shellwork
[13] 塚 *kaizuka* shell mound, kitchen midden

18 類 *kairui* shellfish
類学 *kairuigaku* conchology

2

貟 5767 J-X M36659 Nonstandard for 員 808.

B 貞 5768 J4467 M36658 Jō. Tei chastity; constancy; righteousness.
3 女 *teijo* virtuous woman, faithful wife
6 臣 *teishin* a faithful retainer
8 実 *teijitsu* fidelity, faithfulness
10 純 *teijun* rectitude
烈 *teiretsu na* very virtuous (woman)
11 婦 *teifu* virtuous woman, faithful wife
淑 *teishuku* chastity, feminine modesty
13 節 *teisetsu* fidelity, constancy, virginity
15 潔 *teiketsu* chastity, purity
16 操 *teisō* chastity, virginity
操蹂躪 *teisō jūrin* violation of chastity, rape
操観念 *teisō kannen* sense of virtue

B 負 5769 J4969 M-X 貭 5770 J-X M36660 Fu negative, minus; minus sign. *ma(keru)* be defeated; get the worst of it; be overcome with; yield to; be inferior to; lower the price; be poisoned with lacquer. *ma(kasu)* overcome, outrival, defeat. *ma(karu)* reduce the price. *ma(kesaseru)* knock the price down. *o(u)* bear, carry on the back; owe; assume, bear (a responsibility); be accused of; sustain (an injury). *o(wasu), o(waseru)* make carry, burden with, entrust with, charge with, blame. *o(mbu), o(buu)* carry on the back. *o(busaru)* ride on the back; rely on, be dependent on. *ma(ke)* defeat. *(o)ma(ke)* a small discount; a little extra thrown in; exaggeration, embellishment. *(o)ma(ke) ni* in addition, besides.
4 心 *ma(keji)kokoro* working to keep ahead of others
方 *ma(ke)kata* extent of a defeat
切 *o(i)-ki(ru)* be able to bear
5 目 *oime* debt
6 色 *ma(ke)iro* signs of defeat
気 *ma(ken)ki* unyielding spirit, competitive spirit
号 *fugō* minus sign
劣 *ma(kezu)-oto(razu)* equally strong; neck and neck
7 投手 *ma(ke) tōshu* losing pitcher
8 退 *ma(ke)-shirizo(ku)* defeat and leave
担 *futan* encumbrance, burden, load, responsibility, obligation, liability
物 *o(i)mono* burden, debt
9 革 *o(i)kawa* shoulder carrying strap
軍 *ma(ke) ikusa* defeat, losing battle
10 馬 *ma(ke) uma* losing horse
紐 *obuihimo* cloth cord tying the baby to the mother's back. *o(i)himo* cloth cord for carrying things on the back
荷 *fuka* burden, load (electricity)
根性 *ma(keji)konjō* working to keep ahead of others
11 運 *o(i)-hako(bu)* carry burdens
惜 *ma(ke)o(shimi)* unwillingness to admit defeat
12 越 *ma(ke)ko(shi)* more losses than wins
13 債 *fusai* debt, liabilities, loan
嫌 *ma(ke)gira(i)* unyielding, unbending. *ma(kezu)gira(i)* having a will to win
数 *fusū* negative number
傷 *fushō* injury, wound, bruise, cut
傷兵 *fushōhei* wounded soldier
傷者 *fushōsha* wounded or injured person
14 魂 *ma(keji)damashii* unyielding spirit; working to keep ahead of others

3

貶 5771 J6c4a M36707 Hen. *hen(suru)* degrade, demote, belittle. *kena(su)* disparage, despise, denounce. *otoshi(meru)* look down on.
7 言 *otoshi(me)goto* insult
14 様 *otoshi(me)zama* insulting way
18 謫 *hentaku suru* degrade, demote, debase

B 貢 5772 J3957 M36665 Kō. Ku. *mitsugi* tribute. *mitsu(gu)* support, finance. *kō(suru)* bear tribute.
6 米 *kōbei, kōmai* tribute rice, tax paid in rice
8 使 *kōshi* tribute bearers
物 *mitsugimono, kōbutsu, kōmotsu* tribute
10 進 *kōshin* bearing tribute
租 *kōso* tribute, annual tax
租米 *kōsomai* tax rice, tribute rice
献 *kōken* contribution, service

[13]調 *kōchō* offering tribute; tribute
[15]賦 *kōfu* tribute; paying tribute

A 財 5773 / J3a62 / M36664 ZAI, SAI money, wealth, assets; property; commodities.
[2]力 *zairyoku* financial ability, competence; resources, assets; solvency
[5]布 *saifu* purse
[6]団 *zaidan* foundation, financial group, consortium, syndicate, endowment
団法人 *zaidan hōjin* incorporated foundation; juridical person
[8]物 *zaibutsu, zaimotsu* property, goods
宝 *zaihō* wealth, treasure, valuables
[9]界 *zaikai* financial world, money market
界人 *zaikaijin* financier, businessman
政 *zaisei* public financial affairs; economy
政学 *zaiseigaku* the science of finance
政学者 *zaiseigakusha* teacher of finance
政的 *zaiseiteki* financial
政的負債 *zaiseiteki fusai* financial obligations
政的援助 *zaiseiteki enjo* financial support
政家 *zaiseika* financier
[11]欲 *zaiyoku* greed for wealth
貨 *zaika* commodities, property, wealth
務 *zaimu* financial affairs
務官 *zaimukan* finance secretary
務顧問 *zaimu komon* financial adviser
産 *zaisan* property, estate, fortune, assets
産没収 *zaisan bosshū* confiscation of property
産家 *zaisanka* wealthy person
産税 *zaisanzei* property tax, capital tax
産管理 *zaisan kanri* property management
産権 *zaisanken* property rights
[13]源 *zaigen* source of funds, resources, finances
[14]閥 *zaibatsu* financial clique, giant family trust
[22]嚢 *zainō* purse, moneybag, riches

4

貳 5774 / J6c49 / M-X See 弐 1675.

質 5775 / J6c44 / M36694 See 質 5817.

賢 5776 / J-X / M36695 Nonstandard for 賢 5816.

貪 5777 / J6c45 / M36680 TAN, DON coveting. *musabo(ru)* covet, indulge in.
[6]汚 *tan'o* greed, corruption
[9]食 *donshoku* voracity, ravenousness. *musabo(ri)-ku(u), musabo(ri) kura(u)* greedily devour
[11]婪 *donran, tanran* covetousness, greed
[15]慾 *don'yoku* covetousness, greed

B 貫 5778 / J3453 / M36681 KAN 8 ⅓ pounds. *tsuranu(ku)* pierce, penetrate, perforate; shoot through; attain (one's object). *nuki* brace.
[7]入 *kannyū suru* penetrate
[4]木 *kannuki, kan(no)ki* gate bar
[5]目 *kamme* 8 ⅓ pounds; weight
主 *kanju, kanzu* (Buddhist) head priest
[8]長 *kanchō* superintendent priest
[9]首 *kanshu* head priest
通 *kantsū suru* pierce, penetrate, perforate, tunnel through
[10]流 *kanryū suru* flow through
[11]頂 *kanchō* superintendent priest
[13]禄 *kanroku* weight, dignity
[15]徹 *kantetsu* accomplishment, realization, fulfillment; penetration
[20]籍 *kanseki* census

B 販 5779 / J484e / M36679 HAN sell, trade.
[7]売 *hambai* sale, selling
売人 *hambainin* seller, agent
売元 *hambaimoto* selling agency
売店 *hambaiten* shop, store
売所 *hambaisho* shop, store
売価格 *hambai kakaku* selling price
売係 *hambaigakari* salesman
売品 *hambaihin* articles for sale
売員 *hambaiin* salesman
売術 *hambaijutsu* salesmanship
売組合 *hambai kumiai* marketing co-operative
売税 *hambaizei* sales tax
売戦 *hambaisen* sales war

売網 *hambaimō* sales network
13 路 *hanro* market, outlet

A **責** 5780 J4055 M36682 SEKI. SHAKU. *se(meru)* condemn, blame, censure, criticize, take to task; torture, persecute; urge, tease (to do something). *se(me)* responsibility, liability, blame, guilt, censure; torture, torment.
5 立 *se(me)-ta(teru)* persecute, torture severely; urge
付 *se(me)-tsu(keru)* vehemently criticize
6 任 *sekinin* responsibility, liability
任者 *sekininsha* person responsible
任感 *sekininkan* sense of responsibility
8 具 *se(me)gu* instruments of torture
苦 *semeku* torture, torment, cruelty
苛 *se(me)-saina(mu)* ill-treat, torment, torture, molest, persecute
11 問 *se(me)do(u)* question critically; question by third-degree
務 *sekimu* duty, obligation
道具 *semedōgu* instruments of torture
12 惑 *se(me)-mado(wasu)* criticize violently and confuse
13 塞 *se(me)-fusa(gi)* fulfillment of one's responsibility

A **貨** 5781 J325f M36678 KA freight; goods, property.
7 車 *kasha* freight car; van
車渡 *kashawata(shi)* F.O.B., free on board
8 物 *kamotsu, kabutsu* freight, cargo, goods
物列車 *kamotsu ressha* freight train
物自動車 *kamotsu jidōsha* truck
物車 *kamotsusha* freight train
物取扱 *kamotsu toriatsukai* forwarding, transportation
物係 *kamotsugakari* freight clerk
物陸揚 *kamotsu rikua(ge)* cargo unloading
物船 *kamotsusen* freighter
物置場 *kamotsu okiba* freight yard
物駅 *kamotsu eki* freight depot
物廠 *kamotsushō* freight depot
9 客車 *kakyakusha* freight and passenger train
客船 *kakakusen, kakyakusen* cargo and passenger ship
10 財 *kazai* wealth, worldly goods
12 殖 *kashoku* money-making
15 幣 *kahei* money, currency, coin, coinage
幣学 *kaheigaku* numismatics

A **貧** 5782 J494f M36677 HIN, BIN poverty. *hin(suru)* become poor, live in poverty. *mazu(shii)* poor, destitute; meager.
3 土 *hindo* poor soil; a poor country
乏 *bimbō* poverty
乏人 *bimbōnin* poor man, the poor
乏性 *bimbōshō* destined to poverty
乏所帯 *bimbōjotai* poor household
乏神 *bimbōgami* god of poverty
乏揺 *bimbōyusu(ri), bimbōyuru(gi)* nervous mannerism, nervous twitch
乏暮 *bimbōgura(shi)* needy circumstances
乏籤 *bimbō kuji* unlucky number, a blank; bad bargain
5 民 *himmin* poor people
民街 *himmingai* slums
民窟 *himminkutsu* slums
6 血 *hinketsu* anemia
血症 *hinketsushō* anemia
7 困 *hinkon* poverty; lack
8 苦 *hinku* hardship, serious poverty
者 *hinja* poor person
9 相 *hinsō na* poor looking
10 家 *hinka* poor home
弱 *hinjaku na* poor, meager, scanty
12 寒 *hinkan* destitution
富 *himpu* rich and poor; wealth and poverty
13 鉱 *hinkō* low-grade ore
農 *hinnō* needy peasant
15 賎 *hinsen na* poor and lowly
窮 *hinkyū* great poverty
窮化 *hinkyūka suru* impoverish

— 5 —

貳 5783 J6c48 M36703 See 弐 1675.

貰 5784 J6c4c M36727 FUN decorate; ornament.

貽 5785 J6c46 M36719 I. leave behind; gift.
7 貝 *igai* mussel (shell)

A **費** 5786 / J4871 / M36717 Hɪ expenses, cost. *tsuiya(su)* spend, consume, waste. *tsui(eru)* become less; be wasted. *tsuie* expenses.

5 用 *hiyō* expenses, cost
目 *himoku* expense item
9 途 *hito* expense item
10 消 *hishō* embezzlement, misappropriation

貼 5787 / J453d / M36718 Cʜō counter for medicine packages. *ha(ru)* stick, paste, affix, post, paper, apply (tile, etc.).

5 用 *chōyō* pasting, affixing
付 *ha(ri)-tsu(keru)* stick on, paste up, affix (stamps). *chōfu suru* affix, stick, attach, apply, paste
札 *ha(ri)fuda* placard, bill, poster; tag
出 *ha(ri)-da(su)* put up a notice. *harida(shi)* bill, poster, notice
10 紙 *ha(ri)gami* sticker, bill, tag, label
紙厳禁 *Harigami Genkin* Post No Bills

A **貿** 5788 / J4b47 / M36721 Bō exchange.

8 易 *bōeki* trade, commerce
易収支 *bōekishūshi* trade balance
易会社 *bōekigaisha* trading firm
易風 *bōekifū* trade wind
易保険 *bōeki hoken* export insurance
易品 *bōekihin* articles of commerce
易船 *bōekisen* trading vessel
易商 *bōekishō* trader, importer, exporter
易商人 *bōeki shōnin* trader
易場 *bōekijō* foreign market
易港 *bōekikō* trading port, commercial port
易業 *bōekigyō* trading business
易摩擦 *bōeki masatsu* trade friction

貰 5789 / J4c63 / M36699 Sᴇɪ. *mora(u)* get, have, obtain, receive, accept; get (him) to do (it). *morai* tip, gratuity; geisha's call from another entertainment. *(o)morai* beggar.

3 子 *moraigo* adoption, adopted child
4 手 *moraite* recipient, receiver
方 *mora(i)kata* manner of receiving
水 *morai mizu* water from a neighbor
火 *moraibi* a neighbor's fire that spreads to one's home
8 泣 *mora(i)na(ki)* weeping in sympathy
物 *moraimono* present, gift
乳 *morai chichi* milk from another's breast
受 *mora(i)-u(keru)* receive (something)
10 涙 *morai namida* tears of sympathy

A **賀** 5790 / J326c / M36725 Gᴀ congratulations, felicitations, compliments, joy of the occasion. *ga(suru)* celebrate, congratulate, compliment, approve of.

5 正 *Gashō* New Year's congratulations, Happy New Year
7 状 *gajō* greeting card
寿 *gaju* congratulations on a long life
8 表 *gahyō* congratulatory card to a high personage
9 客 *gakaku* well-wisher, congratulator
10 宴 *gaen* banquet
席 *gaseki* seat of honor
書 *gasho* congratulatory letter
12 詞 *gashi* greetings, congratulations
13 辞 *gaji* congratulations, felicitations
筵 *gaen* congratulatory banquet
意 *gai* congratulatory feeling

A **貯** 5791 / J4379 / M36698 Cʜō. *takuwa(eru)* store, lay in stock, save, keep, wear (a mustache). *ta(meru) vt* accumulate, pile up, store, save, collect. *takuwa(e)* store, hoard, savings.

4 木池 *chobokuchi* mill pond
木場 *chomokujō* log-storage place
水 *chosui* storage of water
水池 *chosuichi* reservoir
水塔 *chosuitō* water tower
水量 *chosuiryō* amount of stored water
水槽 *chosuisō* water tank
6 米 *chomai* storing rice; stored rice
8 金 *chokin* savings, deposit
金通帳 *chokin tsūchō* bank book
金箱 *chokimbako* savings box, bank
9 炭 *chotan* storing coal; stored coal
炭所 *chotanjo* coal-storage place
13 溜 *choryū* accumulation (of body fluids)
蓄 *chochiku* savings
蓄心 *chochikushin* thriftiness
蓄預金 *chochiku yokin* savings deposit
14 蔵 *chozō* storage, preservation
蔵米 *chozōmai* stored rice
蔵所 *chozōsho* storage place, repository, depot
蔵物 *chozōbutsu* stock, supplies
蔵品 *chozōhin* stock, supplies

蔵者 *chozōsha* hoarder
蔵室 *chozōshitsu* storeroom, stock room
蔵庫 *chozōko* storehouse

A **貸** 5792 / J425f / M36709 TAI. *ka(su)* lend; hire out, rent, lease; give credit to. *ka(shi)* loan, lending; bill, account, debt; hire, renting; for rent, for hire.

3 下 *ka(shi)-sa(geru)* lend; lease. *ka(shi)sa(ge)* government loan or lease
与 *kashi-ata(eru)* let out, lease, lend. *taiyo* loan, lending
4 手 *ka(shi)te* creditor, lender; landlord
方 *kashikata* creditor; how to lend; credit side
元 *ka(shi)moto* banker; boss gambler
切 *kashi-ki(ru)* reserve, book. *kashiki(ri)* reserved; reservation
切扱 *kashiki(ri)atsuka(i)* carload consignment
切車 *kashiki(ri)sha* reserved car
5 主 *kashinushi* lender, creditor; landlord
布団 *ka(shi)buton* bedding for rent
付 *kashi-tsu(keru)* lend, advance. *kashitsu(ke)* lending
付金 *kashitsukekin* loan, advance
付信託 *kashitsukeshintaku* loan trust
本 *kashihon* book for lending
本屋 *kashihon'ya* rental library
出 *ka(shi)-da(su)* lend. *kashida(shi)* loan, lending; advance; credit
出図書館 *kashida(shi) toshokan* lending library
出金 *kashidashikin* a loan
6 舟 *ka(shi)bune* boat for rent
地 *ka(shi)chi* lot or land for rent
衣裳 *ka(shi) ishō* clothes or costumes for rent
自動車 *ka(shi) jidōsha* hired car, taxi
7 売 *ka(shi)u(ri)* sale on credit
8 店 *ka(shi)dana, ka(shi) mise* store for rent
物 *ka(shi)mono* things for rent
金 *kashikin* loan
金庫 *ka(shi) kinko* safety deposit box
金業 *kashikingyō* moneylender
9 室 *kashishitsu* room for rent
10 席 *kashiseki* hall for rent, room for rent
借 *taishaku* loan, debit and credit, lending and borrowing. *ka(shi)ka(ri)* loan; lending and borrowing
料 *ka(shi)ryō* rent, hire; loan charge
馬車 *ka(shi)basha* carriage for hire
部屋 *ka(shi)beya* room for rent
座敷 *ka(shi) zashiki* room for rent; house of ill-fame
倒 *kashidao(re)* bad debts
倒金 *kashidao(re)kin* bad debts
家 *ka(shi)ie, kashiya* house for rent
家札 *kashiya fuda* for-rent sign
家普請 *kashiyabushin* flimsy structure
11 渋 *ka(shi)-shibu(ru)* be unwilling to lend
12 越 *kashiko(shi)* overdraft; outstanding account
間 *kashima* room for rent
証文 *ka(shi) shōmon* promissory note
費 *taihi* loan; scholarship
費生 *taihisei* scholarship student
13 賃 *ka(shi)chin* rent, hire
14 厩 *ka(shi) umaya* livery stable

A **買** 5793 / J4763 / M36708 BAI buying. *ka(u)* buy, invest in; incur; appreciate; call in (geisha). *ka(i)* buying.

2 入 *ka(i)-i(reru)* purchase, lay in
〆 *ka(i)shime* cornering the market
人 *kaite* buyer
人気 *ka(i) ninki* bullish sentiment, buying tone
3 上 *ka(i)-a(geru)* buy, buy up; bid up
上品 *kaiagehin* purchases
4 手 *kaite* buyer
方 *ka(i)kata* purchaser; way to buy
込 *ka(i)-ko(mu)* purchase, buy up
切 *ka(i)-ki(ru)* buy up, reserve, book, charter
5 立 *ka(i)ta(te) no* brand-new
付 *kaitsu(ke)* buying
収 *baishū* buying up, purchasing
主 *kainushi* buyer
占 *ka(i)-shi(meru)* buy up, corner (the market)
出 *ka(tte)-de(ru)* proceed without detailed instructions. *kaida(shi)* wholesale purchasing, laying in (supplies)
弁資本家 *baiben shihonka* a comprador
6 気 *ka(i)ki* bullish sentiment
地 *ka(i)chi* land buying; bought-up land
合 *ka(i)-a(wase)* having (goods) on hand
7 足 *ka(i)-ta(su)* make additional purchases
戻 *ka(i)-modo(su)* buy back, redeem

初 *ka(i)zo(me)* first purchase of the new year
求 *ka(i)-moto(meru)* purchase
言葉 *ka(i) kotoba* a sharp response to a cutting remark
8 価 *ka(i)ka* buying price
物 *kaimono* purchase; shopping; bargain
取 *ka(i)-to(ru)* buy, buy up
注文 *ka(i)chūmon* buying orders
受 *ka(i)-u(keru)* acquire by purchase
受人 *kaiu(ke)nin* buyer
9 食 *ka(i)gui* buying and eating (sweets) between meals
乗 *ka(i)-no(seru)* buy more; make more commitments
相場 *ka(i) sōba* buying rate (of exchange); bull market
為替 *ka(i)gawase* buying exchange
10 進 *ka(i)susu(mi)* active buying
値 *kaine* cost price
埋 *ka(i)-u(meru)* cover (a short sale)
時 *ka(i)doki* time to buy
被 *ka(i)-kabu(ru)* pay too much for; overestimate, overvalue
11 過 *ka(i)-su(giru)* overbuy
唱 *ka(i)tona(e)* bidding (on the stock market)
控 *ka(i)-hika(eru)* refrain from buying
掛 *ka(i)ka(ke)* buying on credit
掛金 *ka(i)ga(ke)kin* debt, accounts payable
12 集 *ka(i)-atsu(meru)* buy up
13 溜 *ka(i)da(meru)* hoard, buy up
置 *ka(i)o(ki)* hoarding
馴染 *ka(i)naji(mi)* being a regular customer
14 徳 *kaidoku* buying at a bargain
漁 *ka(i)-asa(ru)* buy up
煽 *ka(i)-ao(ru)* bid up; corner (the market)

A **貴** 5794 / J352e / M36704 KI. *tōto(bu), tatto(bu), tōto(mu), tatto(mu)* value, prize, esteem; respect, honor, revere. *tōto(i), tatto(i)* valuable, precious; noble, exalted, venerable. *ki-* your.

2 人 *kijin* noble, nobleman, man of rank, dignitary; the nobility
3 女 *kijo, anata* lady, you (feminine)
下 *kika* you
4 方 *anata, anta, kihō* you
公 *kikō* you
公子 *kikōshi* young noble
5 石 *kiseki* gem, precious stone
札 *kisatsu* your letter
台 *kidai* you
兄 *kikei* you
号 *kigō* honorary title; rank of nobility; scholastic degree
6 臣 *kishin* high-ranking retainer, your retainer
地 *kichi* your place, there
邦 *kihō* your country
宅 *kitaku* your home
7 状 *kijō* your letter
社 *kisha* your company
男 *kidan, anata* you (masculine)
君 *kikun* you (classical and masculine)
8 所 *kisho* your place
命 *kimei* your orders
官 *kikan* you (an official)
金属 *kikinzoku* precious metals
国 *kikoku* your country
国語 *kikokugo* your language
9 相 *kisō* noble features
重 *kichō na* precious, priceless
重品 *kichōhin* valuables; treasure
10 紙 *kishi* your magazine, your newspaper; your letter
家 *kika* your home
書 *kisho* your letter
息 *kisoku* your son
11 紳 *kishin* men of rank
著 *kicho* the book you wrote
婦人 *kifujin* lady. *kifujin(rashii)* ladylike
族 *kizoku* nobility
族的 *kizokuteki* aristocratic
族院 *Kizokuin* House of Peers, Upper House, House of Lords
族政治 *kizoku seiji* aristocracy
12 答 *kitō* your answer
報 *kihō* your report
13 殿 *kiden* you (at present a term of ridicule)
僧 *kisō* you (a ranking priest)
酬 *kishū* reply to your letter
意 *kii* your will, your opinion, your pleasure
14 様 *kisama* you (vulgar)
15 慮 *kiryo* your idea
賤 *kisen* high and low, rich and poor
賓 *kihin* a noble visitor
賓室 *kihinshitsu* distinguished visitors' reception room

賓席 *kihinseki* distinguished visitors' gallery
16 覧 *kiran* your observation (of something)
翰 *kikan* your letter
橄欖石 *kikanranseki* chrysolite
18 顕 *kiken* men of distinction, dignitaries
簡 *kikan* your letter

6

賍 5795 J6c5c M36774 See 贓 5835.

賎 5796 J4128 M-X Nonstandard for 賤 5813.

貲 5797 J6c47 M36702 SHI atone, expiate; pay a fine.

賈 5798 J6c4b M36755 KO buy; trader.

賂 5799 J4f28 M36738 RO. *mainai* bribe.

B **賄** 5800 J4f45 M36745 WAI. KAI. *makana(u)* board; supply; finance. *makana(i)* board, meals; catering, feeding.
13 賂 *wairo* bribe, bribery

B **賊** 5801 J4231 M36759 ZOKU rebel; traitor; robber. *zoku(suru)* injure, kill.
3 子 *zokushi* traitor, rebel, conspirator
4 心 *zokushin* planning to steal; defiant spirit, determination to inflict damage
6 臣 *zokushin* traitor, rebel, conspirator
名 *zokumei* name of a rebel
7 兵 *zokuhei* insurgents, rebels
9 軍 *zokugun* insurgents, rebel army
10 徒 *zokuto* rebels, traitors
虐 *zokugyaku* damage and ill-treatment
将 *zokushō* insurgent army leader
党 *zokutō* rebels, traitors
11 船 *zokusen* pirate ship
14 魁 *zokkai* rebel leader

A **賃** 5802 J4442 M36743 CHIN hire, rent, wages, fare, freight, charge, fee.
3 上 *chin'a(ge)* wage increase
5 仕事 *chinshigoto* piecework
7 労働 *chinrōdō* working for wages
8 金 *chingin* wages, pay. *chinkin* wages; fare; (freight) rates
金支払日 *chingin shiharaibi* payday
金労働者 *chingin rōdōsha* those working for wages
金制 *chinginsei* wage system
金表 *chinginhyō* wage table
金指数 *chingin shisū* wage index
金率 *chinginritsu* wage scale
金統制 *chingin tōsei* wage control
10 借 *chinshaku, chinga(ri)* hiring, renting, leasing, hire
借人 *chinshakunin* lessee, leaseholder
借地 *chinshakuchi* leased land
借料 *chinshakuryō* rent
12 貸 *chintai, chingashi* lease, hire
貸人 *chintainin* lessor
貸借 *chintaishaku* leasing, chartering
貸料 *chintairyō* rent
14 銀 *chingin* wages, pay
銭 *chinsen* wages
15 稼 *chinkase(gi)* working for wages
餅 *chimmochi* commercial rice cake

A **資** 5803 J3b71 M36750 SHI resources, capital, funds; materials; data; quality, disposition; help. *shi(suru)* be conducive to, contribute to, assist.
2 力 *shiryoku* means, resources, funds
5 本 *shihon* capital; fund
本力 *shihonryoku* amount of capital
本化 *shihonka* capitalization
本収支 *shihon shūshi* balance of capital account
本主 *shihon nushi* capitalist, financier
本主義 *shihon shugi* capitalism
本金 *shihonkin* capital, capital stock
本逃避 *shihon tōhi* capital flight
本財 *shihonzai* capital goods
本家 *shihonka* capitalist, financier
本準備金 *shihon jumbikin* capital reserve
7 材 *shizai* materials, supplies
8 性 *shisei* nature, disposition
金 *shikin* fund, capital
金化 *shikinka* capitalization, converting (goods) into money
金源 *shikingen* source of funds
10 料 *shiryō* materials, data
財 *shizai* property, means, assets
格 *shikaku* qualifications, requirements, capabilities

格審査 *shikaku shinsa* screening, qualifying examination
11 産 *shisan* property, means, assets
産家 *shisanka* wealthy person
産凍結 *shisan tōketsu* freezing of assets
13 源 *shigen* resources
15 質 *shishitsu* nature, disposition

7

賓 5804 / J-X / M36788 See **賓** 1365.

賍 5805 / J-X / M-X Nonstandard for **贖** 5838.

賑 5806 / J4678 / M36785 SHIN. *nigi(wau)* flourish, be bustling. *nigi(wai)* prosperity, bustle, crowd. *nigi(washii), nigi(yakana)* lively, gay, cheerful; bustling, populous; noisy; prosperous.
9 恤 *shinjutsu* relief, charity, alms
恤金 *shinjutsukin* relief fund, alms
14 賑 *niginigi(shii)* prosperous; merry

8

賓 See 1365.

賭 5807 / J4552 / M-X See **賭** 5819.

賣 5808 / J6c4e / M36025 See **売** 990.

賚 5809 / J6c4f / M36805 RAI give, present; gift.

B **賠** 5810 / J4765 / M36818 BAI indemnify.
17 償 *baishō* reparation, indemnity, compensation
償金 *baishōkin* indemnity, reparations, damages

B **賦** 5811 / J496a / M36800 FU ode, prose poem, poetical prose; tribute, exacted service; installment. *fu(suru)* compose, write; allot.
3 与 *fuyo suru* give
5 払 *bubara(i), fubara(i)* installment plan
7 役 *fueki* forced labor; exacted service
8 金 *fukin* installment
性 *fusei* heredity
10 租 *fuso* tribute, tax
12 税 *fuzei* taxation
13 詩 *fushi* writing poetry
15 課 *fuka* tax, levy, assessment

B **賜** 5812 / J3b72 / M36809 SHI. *tama(waru), tamo(u), tama(u)* deign to, grant, give, bestow on, honor with. *tamamono* gift, boon, results.
8 金 *shikin* government money award
杯 *shihai* trophy from the imperial family
10 宴 *shien* court banquet
書 *shisho* a book gift from the emperor
13 暇 *shika* furlough, leave of absence
15 謁 *shietsu* an audience with the emperor
16 諡 *shishi* posthumous name conferred by the emperor
餐 *shisan* court banquet
21 饌 *shisen* lunch in imperial company

賤 5813 / J6c4d / M36826 **賎** 5796 / J4128 / M-X SEN. *iya(shimu)* despise. *iya(shii)* humble; base, mean, vile, vulgar; greedy. *shizu* low-rank person; poverty.
3 女 *shizu(no)me* woman of humble birth
5 民 *semmin* the lowly, the poor, the outcasts, serfs, peasants
民層 *semminsō* the poor class; the outcasts
6 劣 *senretsu* meanness, foul play
7 坊 *iya(shim)bō* greedy person
役 *sen'eki* menial service
男 *shizu(no)o* man of humble birth
8 金属 *senkinzoku* base metals
10 家 *shizu(ga)ya* humble cottage, hovel
13 業 *sengyō* mean occupation; shameful calling
業婦 *sengyōfu* prostitute

A **賛** 5814 / J3b3f / M36841 **贊** 5829 / J6c55 / M36935 SAN praise; title or brief inscription on a picture; agreement. *san(su)* assist, agree with, support; praise.
6 同 *sandō* approval, endorsement
仰 *sangō* praise
成 *sansei* approval, agreement, support, favor

成者 *sanseisha* approver, supporter, patron
7 助 *sanjo* support, backing, approval
否 *sampi* approval or disapproval, yes and no, for and against
9 美 *sambi* praise, adoration
美歌 *sambika* hymn
12 評 *sampyō* favorable criticism
13 嘆 *santan* praise, admiration
辞 *sanji* eulogy, compliment
意 *san'i* approval
14 歌 *sanka* praise, admiration

A **賞** 5815 / J3e5e / M36813 SHŌ prize, reward; praise. *shō(suru), home(ru)* praise, commend, admire, enjoy (beauty). *me(deru)* love; appreciate.
3 与 *shōyo* reward, prize, bonus
与金 *shōyokin* a bonus
7 状 *shōjō* honorable mention, certificate of merit
8 金 *shōkin* prize, monetary reward
味 *shōmi* relish, gusto, appreciation
杯 *shōhai* trophy, prize cup
玩 *shōgan* admiration, appreciation, enjoyment
9 盃 *shōhai* trophy, prize cup
品 *shōhin* (nonmonetary) prize
美 *shōbi* praise, admiration
12 揚 *shōyō* praise, admiration
牌 *shōhai* medal
詞 *shōshi* commendation, eulogy
13 嘆 *shōtan suru* admire and praise
14 罰 *shōbatsu* rewards and punishments; praise and blame; justice
15 賜 *shōshi* offering a prize; the prize
歎 *shōtan suru* admire and praise
賛 *shōsan* praise, admiration, commendation
翫 *shōgan* admiration, appreciation, enjoyment
22 讃 *shōsan* praise, admiration, commendation
鑑 *shōkan suru* admire and praise

B **賢** 5816 / J382d / M36822 KEN wisdom, cleverness. *kashiko(i)* wise, intelligent. *saka(shirana)* pert, impertinent. *saka(shii)* clever, bright, intelligent, wise.
2 人 *kenjin* wise man
3 女 *kenjo* wise woman
才 *kensai* man of ability
4 夫人 *kempujin* wise lady
5 母 *kembo* wise mother
主 *kenshu* wise lord
兄 *kenkei* elder brother (referring to a friend)
6 臣 *kenshin* wise retainer
7 否 *kempi* wisdom and its lack
良 *kenryō* wisdom and virtue, the wise and virtuous
弟 *kentei* your young son
8 所 *Kashikodokoro* Palace Sanctuary
明 *kemmei* wisdom, intelligence, advisability, prudence
郎 *kenrō* your son
妻 *kensai* intelligent housewife
者 *kenja* wise man
9 相 *kenshō* wise premier; wise minister; wise councilor
10 息 *kensoku* your son
哲 *kentetsu* wise man
能 *kennō* wisdom and talent; a wise and talented person
11 婦 *kempu* wise woman
12 策 *kensaku* wise policy
13 愚 *kengu* wisdom or folly; wisdom; the wise and the foolish
聖 *kensei* wise men and saints
14 察 *kensatsu* your discernment, judgment, understanding, or sympathy
15 慮 *kenryo* wise consideration

A **質** 5817 / J3c41 / M36833 SHITSU substance, matter, quality, temperament. SHICHI hostage, pawn, pledge, hock. *tada(su)* ask, demand, question; investigate, ascertain, verify. *tachi* nature (of a person); quality.
2 入 *shichii(re)* pawning
5 札 *shichifuda* pawn ticket
6 地 *shichichi* pawning land; pawned land
朴 *shitsuboku* simplicity
7 材 *shichizai* pawned article
8 店 *shichiten* pawnshop
物 *shichimono, shichimotsu* pawned article
的 *shitsuteki* qualitative
受 *shichiu(ke)* redeeming a pawned article
券 *shichiken* pawn ticket
実 *shitsujitsu* plainness, simplicity
実剛健 *shitsujitsu-gōken* frugal and courageous

9 屋 *shichiya* pawnshop
草 *shichigusa* article for pawning
10 流 *shichinaga(re)* unredeemed pawn
素 *shisso* simplicity, modesty, frugality
11 商 *shichishō* pawnshop
問 *shitsumon* question; interrogation
問者 *shitsumonsha* questioner, interrogator
問書 *shitsumonsho* written inquiry; questionnaire
問戦 *shitsumonsen* interpellation war (in parliamentary assemblies)
問演説 *shitsumon enzetsu* interpellation speech
問欄 *shitsumon ran* question column
12 量 *shitsuryō* mass (in physics)
13 置 *shichio(ki)* pawning
14 種 *shichigusa* article for pawning
疑 *shitsugi* question, inquiry, interpellation
疑応答 *shitsugi-ōtō* questions and answers
16 樸 *shitsuboku* simplicity

9

賴 5818 / J-X / M36861 See **頼** 6635.

賭 5819 / J-X / M36847 **賭** 5807 / J4552 / M-X To gambling. *to(suru)* wager, bet; risk, stake, hazard. *ka(keru)* wager, place a bet. *kake* a bet, wager, gambling.
4 手 *kakete* one who bets
元 *kakemoto* bookmaker
8 金 *kakekin* stakes, bet
物 *kakemono, tobutsu* wager, bet, stake
事 *kakegoto* wager, gambling
9 屋 *kakeya* bookmaker
10 馬 *kakeuma* race horse; horse race
12 場 *toba* gambling place
博 *tobaku* gambling
博犯 *tobakuhan* gambling (crime)
博場 *tobakujō* gambling house
13 碁 *kakego* playing game of *go* for stakes

10

賻 5820 / J6c52 / M36881 Fu condolence gift.

賺 5821 / J6c51 / M36880 Tan. Ren. *suka(su)* coax, humor, persuade.

賽 5822 / J6c50 / M36886 Sai dice; temple visit.
5 目 *sai (no) me, saime* dots on dice
14 銭 *saisen* offering
銭箱 *saisembako* offering box

B **購** 5823 / J3958 / M36885 Kō. *agana(u)* buy.
2 入 *kōnyū* purchase, buying
入者 *kōnyūsha* purchaser
入通帳 *kōnyū tsūchō* consumer's purchasing book, ration book
7 求 *kōkyū* purchase
10 書 *kōsho* purchasing books; purchased books
12 買 *kōbai* purchasing
買力 *kōbairyoku* purchasing power
買心 *kōbaishin* customer's interest
買者 *kōbaisha* buyer
買部 *kōbaibu* shopping service
買組合 *kōbai kumiai* co-operative society
14 読 *kōdoku* subscription
読者 *kōdokusha* subscriber
読料 *kōdokuryō* subscription charge

11

贓 5824 / J-X / M36904 See **贓** 5835.

贄 5825 / J6c53 / M36907 Shi gift; offering. *nie* sacrifice, offering; gift.

贅 5826 / J6c54 / M36908 Zei luxury, extravagance; wen; uselessness.
6 肉 *zeiniku* superfluous flesh, fat, excrescence; proud flesh
尽 *zei (o) tsu(kusu)* live luxuriously
7 言 *zeigen* redundant words
沢 *zeitaku* luxury, extravagance
沢屋 *zeitakuya* luxury-loving person
沢品 *zeitakuhin* article of luxury
沢税 *zeitakuzei* luxury tax
8 物 *zeibutsu* a luxury, something superfluous
14 語 *zeigo* redundant words

B**贈** 5827 / J4223 / M36920' **贈** 5828 / J-X / M36929 Zō, Sō presenting (something). *oku(ru)* send, give to, award to, confer on.

3 与 *zōyo* donation, presentation
与者 *zōyosha* donor
与物 *zōyobutsu* gift, present
与財産 *zōyo zaisan* donated property
与税 *zōyozei* gift tax
5 本 *zōhon* book gift, complimentary copy
号 *zōgō* posthumous name
収賄 *zōshūwai* corruption, bribery
7 位 *zōi suru* confer a posthumous rank
呈 *zōtei* presentation
呈本 *zōtei hon* presentation copy, gift book
呈式 *zōtei shiki* presentation ceremony
呈者 *zōteisha* giver, donor
呈品 *zōteihin* present, gift
呈株 *zōtei kabu* bonus stock
8 物 *oku(ri)mono* present, gift
10 進 *zōshin* presentation
12 答 *zōtō* exchange of presents
答用 *zōtōyō* for gifts
答品 *zōtōhin* present, gift
13 賄 *zōwai* bribery, corruption, graft
賄罪 *zōwaizai* bribery crime
16 諡 *zōshi* posthumous title

12

贈 5828 / J-X / M36929 See 贈 5827.

贇 5829 / J6c55 / M36935 See 贇 5814.

贋 5830 / J3466 / M36943 **贋** 5837 / J-X / M36972 Gan counterfeit. *nise* sham, counterfeit, forgery, imitation, false (prophet). *ni(seru)* copy, imitate, counterfeit, forge.

4 手紙 *nise tegami* forged letter
5 札 *nise satsu, nise fuda, gansatsu* counterfeit paper money
6 印 *nise in* forged seal
7 作 *gansaku* sham, counterfeit
8 金 *nisegane* counterfeit money
物 *nisemono, gambutsu* imitation, forgery, counterfeit, sham
9 首 *nise kubi* falsified severed head
造 *ganzō* counterfeiting, forgery, fabrication
造紙幣 *ganzō shihei* counterfeit paper money

13

贇 5831 / J6c56 / M36909 In beautiful.

贍 5832 / J6c58 / M36945 Sen add; supplement; be sufficient; abundant.

贏 5833 / J6c57 / M36950 Ei victory; surplus; wrap.

7 余 *eiyo* remainder

14

贐 5834 / J6c59 / M36956 Jin gift. *hanamuke* parting gift, farewell gift.

贓 5835 / J6c5b / M36962 **贜** 5839 / J-X / M36990 **賍** 5824 / J-X / M36904 Zō bribery.

8 物 *zōbutsu* stolen goods
9 品 *zōhin* stolen goods

贔 5836 / J6c5d / M36963 Hi strength, power.

9 負 *hiiki* patronage, partiality, favoritism
10 屓 *hiiki* patronage, partiality, favoritism
屓目 *hiikime* viewing favorably

15

贋 5837 / J-X / M36972 See 贋 5830.

贖 5838 / J6c5e / M36970 Shoku. *agana(u)* redeem, ransom, purchase, expiate. *agana(i)* redemption, atonement.

5 代 *agana(i)shiro* ransom
主 *agana(i)nushi* redeemer
出 *agana(i)-da(su)* rescue, redeem
9 宥 *shokuyū* (Catholic) indulgence, pardon
13 罪 *shokuzai* atonement, redemption, expiation

罪金 *shokuzaikin* ransom
罪所 *shokuzaisho* mercy seat (in the sanctuary)

17

贜 5839 J-X M36990 See 贓 5835.

RAD. 赤 155

Aka red. Nickname: Red.

A **赤** 5840 J4056 M36993 SEKI. SHAKU. *aka, aka(i)* red, crimson, scarlet. *aka* Communist, Red. *aka(bamu)* redden, color up, blush. *aka(ramu)* become red. *aka(rameru), aka(meru), aka(mu)* blush, redden. *aka(chan)* baby. *aka-* complete, entirely.

2 十字 *sekijūji* red cross; Red Cross
十字社 *Sekijūjisha* Red Cross Society
3 土 *akatsuchi, sekido* red clay, red loam
子 *akago* baby. *sekishi* baby; subjects
小豆 *azuki* small red bean
大根 *aka daikon* red radish; lip communist
4 心 *sekishin* sincerity, true heart
手 *sekishu* bare hand, bare fists
日 *sekijitsu* burning sun
化 *sekika, sekka* communization
切符 *akagippu* third-class ticket
毛 *akage* red hair
毛布 *akagetto* red blanket; a rustic
5 玉 *akadama* red ball; wind signal; amber; the red ball (in billiards); a red gem; amber
瓦 *akagawara* red tile
目 *akame* bloodshot eyes. *akambei* turning the eyelids inside out, making faces at someone
札 *akafuda* goods sold; clearance goods
本 *akahon* dime novel
他人 *aka (no) tanin* strangers
広場 *Aka(no) Hiroba* Red Square
外線 *sekigaisen* infrared rays
6 色 *sekishoku, aka iro* red color; Communism
地 *akaji* red cloth; red ground
肌 *akahada* plucked (chicken) skin; abraded skin; nakedness; bareness
字 *akaji* red figures, deficit
合羽 *akagappa* red oil-paper raincoat
血球 *sekkekkyū* red corpuscle
7 貝 *akagai* ark shell, bloody clam
赤 *akaaka to* brightly
身 *akami* heartwood; lean meat
坊 *aka(m)bō, aka(m)bo* baby
沈検査 *sekichin kensa* blood sedimentation test
8 門 *akamon* red gate; Tokyo University
松 *akamatsu* red pine
茄子 *akanasu* tomato, love apple
9 面 *sekimen* a blush, shamefacedness. *akatsura* red face
軍 *Sekigun* Red Army
信号 *aka shingō* red light, red danger signal
砂糖 *akazatō* brown sugar
茶 *akacha(keru)* turn reddish. *akacha* russet, reddish brown
茶色 *akacha iro* russet, reddish brown
10 馬 *aka uma* red horse
鬼 *aka oni* red devil; merciless debt collector
恥 *akahaji* public disgrace, open shame
剥 *akamu(ke)* skin abrasion
11 黒 *akaguro(i)* dark red
道 *sekidō* equator
脚 *sekkyaku no* barefooted
貧 *sekihin* extreme poverty
雪 *sekisetsu* red snow (due to mountain moss)
12 痢 *sekiri* dysentery
帽 *akabō* redcap
蛙 *akagaeru* reddish frog
飯 *akameshi, sekihan* rice and red-bean dish
紫 *aka murasaki* purplish red
13 禍 *sekka* Red Peril
誠 *sekisei* sincerity
靴 *akagutsu* brown shoes
電車 *aka densha* red-lamp car, last street car
新聞 *aka shimbun* yellow journal
褐色 *sekkasshoku* reddish brown

裸 *akahadaka* stark naked. *sekira* stark naked; open, frank
裸裸 *sekirara* nakedness, nudity; frankness
14 旗 *sekki* red flag; the Taira flag; danger flag; revolution flag. *aka hata* red flag; the Red Flag
墨 *akazumi* vermilion stick, red ink
熊 *akaguma* brown bear
瑪瑙 *aka menō* sardius
銅 *shakudō* gold-copper alloy
銅色 *shakudō iro* brown color
15 膚 *akahada* plucked (chicken) skin; abraded skin; nakedness; bareness
嘘 *aka uso* barefaced lie
衛軍 *Sekieigun* the Red Army
樫 *akagashi* red oak, live oak
潮 *aka shio* reddish-brown tide
蕪 *aka kabu* red turnip
熱 *sekinetsu* red heat
線区域 *akasen kuiki* red-light district
16 燐 *sekirin* red phosphorus
髭 *aka hige* red beard
縞瑪瑙 *akashima menō* sardonyx
18 顔 *aka(ra)gao* ruddy face
19 鯛 *akadai* red bream
21 魔 *sekima* Red menace
鰯 *akaiwashi* dried salted sardines
露 *Sekiro* Red Russia

4

B 赦 5841 / J3c4f / M36999 SHA forgiveness. *yuru(su)* permit, approve; authorize; acknowledge; confide in; forgive, pardon; release, acquit; overlook.
5 令 *sharei* amnesty order
7 状 *shajō* an official letter pardoning a criminal
8 免 *shamen* pardon, amnesty, absolution, clemency
免券 *shamenken* (Catholic) indulgence
13 罪 *shazai* pardon, amnesty, absolution

5

赧 5842 / J6c5f / M37001 TAN get red.

7

赫 5843 / J3352 / M37010 KAKU. *kat(to)* suddenly. *kagaya(kasu)* light up, brighten, illumine.
7 灼 *kakushaku(taru)* brilliant, glorious, bright, blazing, glittering
9 怒 *kakudo* fury, burst of temper
14 赫 *kakukaku, kakkaku(taru)* bright, brilliant, distinguished

9

赭 5844 / J6c60 / M37017 SHA red.
3 土 *shado* red soil
9 面 *shamen, akatsura* ruddy face
18 顔 *shagan* ruddy face

RAD. 走 156

Hashiru to run. Variant: 赱 *sōnyō* "running" enclosure. Nickname: Running.

A 走 5845 / J4176 / M37034 赱 5846 / J6c61 / M37034' SŌ. *hashi(ru)* run, rush, flee; turn to, become; go to excess. *hashi(rakasu), hashi(raseru)* make (someone or something) run. *hashi(ri)* first of the season; first supplies.
3 下 *hashi(ri)-o(riru)* run down
上 *hashi(ri)-a(garu)* run up
4 込 *hashi(ri)-ko(mu)* run into (a house)
5 去 *hashi(ri)-sa(ru)* run away
出 *hashi(ri)-de(ru)* pull out (of a station); run toward; run out of (a house)
6 回 *hashi(ri)-mawa(ru)* run around
7 抜 *hashi(ri)-nu(keru)* run through. *hashi(ri)-nu(ku)* outrun; run through till the end
8 使 *hashi(ri)zuka(i)* errand boy, messenger
法 *sōhō* running form
狗 *sōku* hunting dog; tool, cat's paw
卒 *sōsotsu* footman, courier
者 *sōsha* (base) runner, (track) runner
9 査 *sōsa* scanning (in TV)
10 破 *sōha suru* run through

書 *hashi(ri)ga(ki)* cursive writing, scrawl, hasty writing
帰 *hashi(ri)-kae(ru)* run back, run home
馬灯 *sōmatō, sōbatō* revolving lantern; everchanging panorama
高跳 *hashi(ri) takatobi* running high jump
11 道 *hashi(ri) michi* runway
過 *hashi(ri)-su(giru)* run past
寄 *hashi(ri)-yo(ru)* come running, run up to
12 越 *hashi(ri)-ko(su)* outrun, outdistance
幅跳 *hashi(ri) habatobi* running broad jump
程 *sōtei* a drive, a run (in a conveyance)
程計 *sōteikei* taximeter
塁 *sōrui* base running
塁者 *sōruisha* base runner
13 路 *sōro* race track, course; escapee's trail
14 読 *hashi(ri)yo(mi)* reading hurriedly

2

B 赴 5847 / J496b / M37040 FU. *omomu(ku)* proceed to; get, become, tend toward.
6 任 *funin suru* proceed to a new appointment. *funin* (new) appointment
任地 *funinchi* place of appointment
12 援 *fuen suru* come to the rescue, reinforce, help

3

赳 5848 / J6c62 / M37038 KYŪ valiant, strong, brave.

A 起 5849 / J352f / M37048 KI. *o(kiru)* get up, rise, awake; occur; (a fire) is kindled. *oko(su)* raise up, set up, pick up (someone); open, begin; promote, organize; generate; get sick; awaken; establish; plow; kindle (a fire). *oko(ru)* happen; break out; originate in; rise, flourish, spring up; be produced; have an attack of. *ta(tsu)* stand, rise; rouse oneself; be built, be established; go up (smoke); burn out; depart; take flight; run high (waves); stick into; be worked out; be maintained; save (face); establish oneself, begin life; spread (rumors); shut (doors); be active; open (markets); be excited; come (seasons); makes (a total of thirty). *ta(taseru)* make stand, set upright, raise, lift up; rouse (to activity). *oko(ri)* origin, source, beginning; cause.
3 工 *kikō* breaking ground
工式 *kikō shiki* ground-breaking ceremony
上 *ta(chi)-a(garu), o(ki)-a(garu)* get up, rise
上小法師 *o(ki)a(gari)koboshi* tumbler, self righting toy
4 毛 *kimō* nap raising
5 用 *kiyō* appointment, employment
句 *kiku* opening line of a Chinese poem
出 *o(ki)-de(ru)* get up, rise up
立 *oko(ri)-ta(tsu)* rise up. *o(ki)-ta(tsu)* rise, get up. *kiritsu* rising, standing
立投票 *kiritsu tōhyō* standing vote
6 因 *kiin suru* originate in; be attributable to
返 *o(ki)-kae(ru)* turn over in bed; get up; sit up
伏 *kifuku* ups and downs, undulations; relief (map). *o(ki)fu(shi)* getting around; rising and lying down; morning and evening, daily life
死 *kishi* saving from the jaws of death
死回生 *kishi kaisei* revival, resuscitation; entering great happiness
7 床 *kishō* getting up, rising
抜 *o(ki)nu(ke) ni* on arising
承転結 *kishō-tenketsu* rules for composing Chinese poetry
8 明 *o(ki)-a(kasu)* stay up all night
臥 *kiga suru* live, dwell. *kiga* daily life
直 *o(ki)-nao(ru)* sit up
居 *kikyo* state of health; daily life. *tachii* one's movement
居振舞 *tachii furumai* deportment, manners
9 首 *kishu* beginning
点 *kiten* starting point; terminus; home port
重機 *kijūki* crane, derrick
重機船 *kijūkisen* floating crane
草 *kisō* drafting
草者 *kisōsha* draftsman, drafter
10 原 *kigen* origin, beginning
座 *kiza suru* sit up in bed
起 *o(ki)o(ki)* just out of bed
案 *kian suru* draft, draw up

11 掛 *o(ki)ga(ke)* just after getting up
動 *kidō* starting
動機 *kidōki* starter, starting motor
12 結 *kiketsu* beginning and end
筆 *kihitsu* beginning to write
番 *o(ki)ban* night watch
訴 *kiso* prosecution, indictment, accusation, litigation
訴状 *kisojō* written indictment
訴猶予 *kiso yūyo* stay of prosecution
13 債 *kisai* bond issue, loan flotation
源 *kigen* origin, beginning
準 *kijun* starting point
業 *kigyō* starting a business, promotion of an enterprise
電 *kiden* generation of electricity
電力 *kidenryoku* electromotive force
14 端 *tachiha* chance to stand; chance to leave
誓 *kisei* vow, pledge, pact
磁力 *kijiryoku* magnetomotive force
算 *kisan* starting point in reckoning
算日 *kisambi* beginning date
15 稿 *kikō* drafting an article
請 *kishō* written vow, pledge (in Buddhism or Shinto)
請文 *kishōmon* personal contract
19 爆 *kibaku* priming (in explosives)
爆剤 *kibakuzai* detonator, percussion cap
爆薬 *kibakuyaku* detonator, percussion cap

5

趁 5850 / J6c63 / M37083 CHIN reach an impasse; follow.

B **越** 5851 / J315b / M37110 OTSU. ETSU. *ko(su)* cross; pass; spend; tide over; outrun; exceed; surpass; move; go; come. *ko(eru)* cross; go beyond; exceed; clear (an obstacle); overstep (authority). *ko(ezaru)* not more than (two months). *(o)ko(shi)* coming. *-go(shi)* over, across, long-standing, beyond.

5 冬 *ettō* passing the winter
6 次 *etsuji* cutting across a normal process
年 *etsunen suru, otsunen suru* ring out the old year; tide over the year end; pass the winter, hibernate
年生 *etsunensei* biennial (plant)
9 度 *etsudo* exceeding. *ochido* error
11 階 *ekkai* skipping up through court ranks irregularly
14 獄 *etsugoku* jailbreak
境 *ekkyō* border transgression
境事件 *ekkyō jiken* border incident
15 権 *ekken no* unauthorized. *ekken, okken* arrogation, abuse of confidence, going beyond one's authority

B **超** 5852 / J4436 / M37096 CHŌ super-, ultra-. *ko(eru)* cross; go beyond; exceed; clear (an obstacle); overstep (authority).

2 人 *chōjin* superhuman
人的 *chōjinteki* superhuman
人間的 *chōningenteki* superhuman
3 凡 *chōbon* extraordinary, unusual
大型 *chōōgata* supersize
大型爆弾 *chōōgata bakudan* blockbuster bomb
6 自然 *chōshizen* supernaturalness
自然力 *chōshizenryoku* supernatural power
7 克 *chōkoku suru* conquer, overcome, tide over, surmount
8 弩級艦 *chōdokyūkan* superdreadnaught
国家主義 *chōkokka shugi* ultranationalism
国家的 *chōkokkateki* ultranationalistic
9 俗 *chōzoku* unworldliness
重戦車 *chōjū sensha* super tank, mammoth tank
音 *chōon* supersonic
音波 *chōompa* supersonic waves
音速 *chōonsoku* supersonic speed
10 悟 *chōgo* superior wisdom
党派 *chōtōha* bipartisanship
高 *chōkō* ultrahigh
高速度 *chōkōsokudo* super high speed
高速道路 *chōkōsoku dōro* freeway, super highway
特作 *chōtokusaku* super film, feature
特作品 *chōtokusakuhin* super film, feature
特急 *chōtokkyū* super express
11 脱 *chōdatsu suru* transcend, stand aloof, rise above
現実主義 *chōgenjitsu shugi* surrealism
現実派 *chōgenjitsuha* surrealists
過 *chōka* excess. *chōka suru* exceed
過勤務 *chōka kimmu* overtime work

過額 *chōkagaku* excess, surplus, overflow

12 越 *chōetsu suru* be superior, excel, surpass, stand above, stand aloof. *chōetsu* superiority, excellence, preeminence, transcendency

超 *chōchō-* super-, ultra-

短波 *chōtampa* ultrashort wave, ultrahigh frequency

満員 *chōman'in* packed with people

然 *chōzen(taru)* transcendental, standing aloof, with a detached air

然内閣 *chōzen naikaku* supraparty government

絶 *chōzetsu* transcendence; superiority, excellence

絶性 *chōzetsusei* transcendence

絶論 *chōzetsuron* transcendentalism

13 感覚的 *chōkankakuteki* beyond the reach of the senses

18 顕微鏡 *chōkembikyō* ultramicroscope

7

趙 5853 / J6c64 / M37171 Chō, Jō slow gait; cross; extend; nimble; small; few.

8

B **趣** 5854 / J3c71 / M37207 Shu. *omomu(ku)* proceed to; become; tend toward. *omomuki* import, meaning, contents, tenor, gist; tone, touch, sentiment, charm; aspect, appearance.

6 向 *shukō* plan, idea, device, plot

旨 *shushi* opinion, idea; meaning, gist, tenor; aim, motive, purpose

8 味 *shumi* taste, charm; zest, interest, hobby

13 意 *shui* opinion, idea; meaning, gist, tenor; aim, motive, purpose

意書 *shuisho* prospectus

10

趨 5855 / J3f76 / M37238 Sū, Shu run; go; quick; tend toward.

6 向 *sūkō* trend, tendency

8 拝 *sūhai* going out to meet (an important person)

13 勢 *sūsei* trend, tendency

足 RAD. 157

Ashi leg, foot. At left: ⻊ *ashi hen*. Nickname: Foot.

A **足** 5856 / J422d / M37365 Soku foot; leg; counter for pairs of footwear. *ashi* foot; leg; paw; flipper, tentacles, arms; walk, step, pace, speed; footing; draft (of a ship); foot (of a mountain); trace; deficit, shortage. *ashi, (o)ashi* money. *ta(ru), ta(riru)* be sufficient, suffice; serve, answer, will do (for something); be worth, deserve; be satisfied; qualify. *ta(su)* add to, add up; make up for; make good; supply, supplement. *ta(rinai), ta(ranai), ta(ranu), ta(razu)* be insufficient, lack; be missing; be unworthy, be not worth it; be beneath notice; dull, stupid. *ta(rinasa)* insufficiency, shortcomings. *ta(shi)* complement, supplement; making up; supply; help. *-soku* pair (a counter).

3 下 *ashimoto* gait, pace, step. *ashimoto ni, sokka ni* at one's feet. *sokka* you (familiar and polite)

4 止 *ashido(me)* confinement; inducement to stay

元 *ashimoto* gait, pace, step

手 *ashite* hands and feet

手纏 *ashitemato(i), ashidemato(i)* encumbrance, hindrance, impediment

5 付 *ashitsu(ki)* gait; legged (utensil)

代 *ashidai* traveling expenses

台 *ashidai* step, stool, footstool; steppingstone; springboard

6 早 *ashibaya* quick, swift-footed

7 序 *ashitsuide ni* while on one's feet

利 *Ashikaga* Ashikaga Era (1392–1573)

形 *ashigata* footprint

芸 *ashigei* foot tricks

労 *sokurō* trouble of going somewhere

8 長 *ashinaga* long-legged person

固 *ashigata(me)* walking practice

取 *ashido(ri)* gait, manner of swimming or walking; trace, track (of an offender); trend of (prices)

並 *ashina(mi)* pace, step
炙 *ashiabu(ri)* foot warmer
拍子 *ashibyōshi* beating time with feet
忠実 *ashimame na* faithful (in work)
[9] 音 *ashioto* sound of footsteps
首 *ashikubi* ankle
拭 *ashifu(ki)* foot towel, foot wiper
拵 *ashigoshira(e)* footgear
枷 *ashigase, ashi kase* fetters, shackles, irons, hobbles
洗 *ashiara(i)* tub; foot washing
前 *ta(shi)mae* complement, supplement; making up; supply; help
型 *ashigata* shoe last
[10] 高 *ashidaka* long-legged
捌 *ashisaba(ki)* footwork (in sports)
浴 *sokuyoku* foot bath
部 *sokubu* the foot
釜 *ashigama* kettle with legs
弱 *ashiyowa* poor walker
真似 *ashi mane* gesturing with the feet
[11] 掛 *ashiga(kari)* scaffolding; foothold; clue. *ashika(ke)* footing, foothold; pedal, footboard; step; going on (about so many years)
許 *ashimoto* gait, pace, step
萎 *ashina(e)* lame person
袋 *tabi* foot gloves, Japanese socks, tabi
袋屋 *tabiya* dealer in tabi
袋跣足 *tabihadashi* in stocking (tabi) feet
[12] 痛 *sokutsū* footsore, pain in the foot
場 *ashiba* scaffold; footing, foothold; situation
湯 *ashiyu* foot bath
勝 *ta(razu)ga(chi)* unable to make ends meet
軽 *ashigaru* footman, foot soldier; lowest samurai
[13] 鼎 *ashiganae* three-legged kettle
掻 *aga(ku)* paw, struggle, wriggle, flounder
溜 *ashidamari* stand, foothold, footing; stopping place; center of activity
継 *ashitsu(gi)* footstool
腰 *ashikoshi* legs and loins
触 *ashiza(wari)* the feel to the foot
跡 *ashiato, sokuseki* footprint
障 *ashiza(wari)* in the way when walking
馴 *ashina(rashi)* walking practice
裏 *ashiura, ashi(no)ura, anaura* sole of the foot
業 *ashiwaza* footwork (in judo); foot tricks
[14] 摺 *ashizu(ri)* stamping or scraping the feet
駄 *ashida* high clogs
算 *ta(shi)zan* addition
[15] 踏 *ashibu(mi), ashifu(mi)* stepping, stamping; step; stalemate, marking time; treadle machine
[16] 縺 *ashimotsu(re)* faltering walk
頸 *ashikubi* ankle
盥 *ashidarai* foot tub
繁 *ashishige(ku)* frequently
[18] 癖 *ashikuse* gait
[19] 蹴 *ashige* kicking
[20] 競 *ashikura(be)* foot race
[21] 纏 *ashimato(i)* impediment, encumbrance, hindrance

4

跂 5857 / J6c65 / M37416 — KI hyperdactylia; stand on tiptoes.

趾 5858 / J6c66 / M37406 — SHI footprint; feet. *ato* remains.

趺 5859 / J6c67 / M37392 — FU foot; arch of foot; heel; sitting in lotus position.
[7] 坐 *fuza* sitting in lotus position

5

跏 5860 / J6c68 / M37457 — KA sitting cross-legged; sitting in lotus position.

跖 5861 / J6c6a / M37469 — SEKI sole (of foot).

跌 5862 / J6c6b / M37450 — TETSU stumble.

跚 5863 / J6c69 / M37477 — SAN stagger, reel, stumble.

跑 5864 / J-X / M37461 — HŌ. *daku* trotting, trot.

跛 5865 / J6c6c / M37479 — HA. HI. BI. *bikko, chimba* lameness, lame person; an

odd (shoe), one of a pair. *chimba na* odd (pair), odd (shoe).
6 行 *hakō* limping; lack of coordination

B 距 5866 / J3577 / M37481 KYO. *heda(taru)* be distant.
10 骨 *kyokotsu* anklebone
19 離 *kyori* distance, range, interval; gap
離測定器 *kyori sokuteiki* range finder

跋 5867 / J6c6d / M37446 　跋 5868 / J-X / M37447 HATSU, BATSU epilogue, book postscript.
4 文 *batsubun* epilogue, book postscript
11 扈 *bakko* rampancy, prevalence, domination
涉 *basshō* traveling, hiking
14 語 *batsugo* book postscript

— 6 —

跟 5869 / J6c70 / M37491 KON heel.

跫 5870 / J6c6f / M37519 KYŌ sound of footsteps.
9 音 *kyōon, ashioto* footsteps

跣 5871 / J6c71 / M37497 SEN barefooted.
7 足 *hadashi* bare feet

跨 5872 / J3859 / M37504 KO. KA. *mataga(ru)* be, sit, or stand astride; extend over; be laid across. *mata(gu)* straddle, bestride.
15 線橋 *kosenkyō* overpass

B 践 5873 / J4192 / M37547' 　踐 5883 / J6c78 / M37608 SEN. *fu(mu)* step on, trample on, stamp on; carry through, practice; appraise; set foot on; evade payment.
10 祚 *senso* accession to the throne
祚式 *sensoshiki* accession ceremony

跪 5874 / J6c6e / M37516 KI. *hizamazu(ku)* kneel.
6 伏 *kifuku suru* kneel and lie down
7 坐 *kiza suru* kneel down
8 拝 *kihai suru* kneel and worship. *kihai* genuflection

B 跡 5875 / J4057 / M37493 SEKI. *ato* mark, print, impression; trace, track, trail; wake; marks, traces, evidence; scar; ruins, precedent.
4 片付 *atokatazu(ke)* cleaning up, putting things in order
切 *togi(reru)* stop, cease
切跡切 *togi(re)-togi(re) ni* (working) spasmodically
5 白波 *atoshiranami* complete disappearance
目 *atome* heir, successor
目相続 *atome sōzoku* heirship
7 役 *atoyaku* successor
形 *atokata* traces, marks, vestiges, evidence
形無 *atokatana(i)* no traces
8 取 *atoto(ri)* heir, successor
始末 *atoshimatsu* settlement, liquidation, clearing up
12 絶 *toda(eru)* stop, cease
13 継 *atotsu(gi)* heir, successor

A 路 5876 / J4f29 / M37524 RO road, route, path. *-ji* route, road; distance. *michi* road, path, lane, way, street, highway, route; journey; distance; course, way, means; duty, morality, moral doctrine; teachings; specialty; an art; reason, justice
2 人 *rojin* passersby
3 上 *rojō* on the road; road
4 辺 *rohen* roadside
5 用 *royō* traveling expenses
6 次 *roji* road, route; on the way
地 *roji* alley, lane, garden path
7 床 *roshō* roadbed
9 面 *romen* road surface
面電車 *romen densha* streetcar
12 程 *rotei* distance, mileage
費 *rohi* traveling expenses
傍 *robō* roadside, wayside
傍人 *robō (no) hito* a passerby; one with whom one has no connections
傍伝道 *robō dendō* street evangelism
傍演説 *robō enzetsu* wayside speech
傍演説者 *robō enzetsusha* street preacher
14 銀 *rogin* traveling expenses
15 標 *rohyō* road sign
線 *rosen* route, way
盤 *roban* roadbed
16 頭 *rotō* wayside, roadside

B**跳** 5877 / J4437 / M37533 CHŌ. *ha(neru)* leap, spring up, hop; jerk, prance, buck; bound; spatter, splash; snap, crack, sputter; close, be over. *odo(ru)* dance; leap, skip; throb (the heart); act as a cat's-paw; double (the interest on a debt). *to(bu)* jump, leap, spring, bound, vault, hop. *ha(ne)* splashes (of mud).

3 上 *ha(ne)-a(garu)* jump up, spring up
下 *tobio(ri)* jumping off a (moving vehicle)
下自殺 *tobio(ri) jisatsu* suicide by leaping off (a height)
4 手 *to(bi)te* jumper (sport)
反 *ha(ne)-kae(ru) vi* rebound, recoil, bounce, spring back. *ha(ne)-kae(su) vt* kick back, throw off
込台 *tobiko(mi)dai* diving board
5 台 *to(bi)dai* vaulting horse
出 *ha(ne)-da(su), ha(ne)-de(ru), to(bi)-de(ru)* spring out
6 回 *odo(ri)-mawa(ru), ha(ne)-mawa(ru), to(bi)-mawa(ru)* jump around, cut capers, romp, gambol
返 *ha(ne)-kae(su)* bounce back
8 退 *ha(ne)-no(ku), to(bi)-no(ku)* jump back
板 *ha(ne)ita, to(bi)ita* springboard
9 飛 *ha(ne)-to(bu)* leap, spring up, hop; jerk, prance, buck; bound; spatter, splash; snap, crack, sputter; close, be over
10 起 *ha(ne)-o(kiru)* jump up, spring up
11 梁 *chōryō* rampancy, domination
12 越 *to(bi)-ko(eru)* jump over, fly over, fly across
弾 *chōdan* ricocheting bullet
開橋 *chōkaikyō* balanced drawbridge
16 橋 *ha(ne)bashi* drawbridge
20 競 *to(bi)kura, to(bi)kura(be)* jumping match
21 躍 *ha(ne)-odo(ru)* prance around. *chōyaku suru* jump, leap, skip, bounce, spring
躍板 *chōyakuban* springboard, diving board

7

踈 5878 / J6c73 / M37579 See **疎** 3776.

跣 5879 / J6c75 / M37552 TO barefoot.

踉 5880 / J6c74 / M37585 RŌ, RYŌ stagger, falter.

跼 5881 / J6c72 / M37548 KYOKU. *kago(mu) kugu(maru)* bow, stoop, bend over, crouch.
17 蹐 *kyokuseki suru* crouch, stoop; sneak around

B**踊** 5882 / J4d59 / M37587 YŌ. *odo(ru)* dance; leap, skip; throb (the heart); act as a cat's-paw; double (the interest on a debt). *odo(ri)* dance; dancing; step.

3 子 *odo(ri)ko* dancer, dancing girl
6 字 *odo(ri)ji* sign of repetition of characters or kana
7 抜 *odo(ri)-nu(ku)* dance through (the night)
12 場 *odo(ri)ba* dance hall; stair landing
15 戯 *odo(ri)-tawamu(reru)* dance around

8

踐 5883 / J6c78 / M37608 See **践** 5873.

踟 5884 / J6c79 / M37645 CHI hesitate, be undecided.

踞 5885 / J6c77 / M37642 KYO crouch, bend over.

踠 5886 / J-X / M37646 EN. *moga(ku)* writhe, struggle, squirm, wriggle; impatient for.

踪 5887 / J6d29 / M37668 **蹤** 5901 / J6d27 / M37823 SŌ, SHŌ remains (of something); clue, footprint.
13 跡 *sōseki* one's whereabouts

踝 5888 / J6c76 / M37641 KA. *kurubushi* ankle; anklebone.
10 骨 *kakotsu* anklebone

B**踏** 5889 / J4627 / M37602 **蹈** 5895 / J6d25 / M37744 TŌ. *fu(mu)* step on, trample on, stamp on; carry through, practice; appraise; set foot on; evade payment. *fu(maeru)* step on, stand on.

2 入 *fu(mi)-i(reru), fu(mi)-i(ru)* walk in on, step in, tread upon
4 止 *fu(mi)-todo(maru)* stand one's ground, hold one's own; stay in office. *fu(mi)-todo(meru)* bring oneself to a stop
込 *fu(mi)-ko(mu), fu(n)go(mu)* step into; break into, raid
分 *fu(mi)-wa(keru)* push one's way though
反返 *fu(n)zo(ri)-ka(eru)* lean back, fall backward; assume a haughty attitude
切 *fu(mi)-ki(ru)* cross; push off (in jumping). *fungi(ru)* proceed with decision. *fumikiri* railway crossing
切番 *fumikiriban* railway-crossing guard
5 石 *fu(mi)ishi* steppingstone
立 *fu(mi)-ta(teru)* to injure the foot by stepping on something sharp
付 *fu(mi)-tsu(keru), fu(n)-zu(keru)* step on and scatter, tread on, trample; spurn, despise, slight
台 *fu(mi)dai* footstool, step, steppingstone, springboard
外 *fu(mi)-hazu(su)* miss one's footing, make a false step
出 *fu(mi)-da(su)* step forward, advance, tread upon
6 臼 *fu(mi)usu* mortar worked by treading
7 車 *fu(mi)guruma* treadmill
均 *fu(mi)-nara(su)* level by treading
抜 *fu(mi)-nu(ku)* to injure the foot by stepping on something sharp
8 固 *fu(mi) kata(meru)* stamp down, pack down (snow)
退 *fu(mi)-no(ku)* liquidate (stocks)
迷 *fu(mi)-mayo(u)* lose the way, go astray
所 *fu(mi)dokoro* footing, place to step. *fu(mae)dokoro* footing; standpoint
拉 *fu(mi)-shida(ku)* step on and break, crush underfoot
板 *fu(mi)ita* footboard, pedal, treadle, running board
9 砕 *fu(mi)-kuda(ku)* crush, trample to pieces
段 *fu(mi)dan* step, stair, carriage step, footboard
査 *tōsa* survey, exploration, investigation
荒 *fu(mi)-ara(su)* trample down, ravage, devastate
10 進 *fu(mi)-susu(mu)* tread upon
倒 *fu(mi)-tao(su)* evade payment; trample over, kick down
従 *fu(mi)-shitaga(u)* follow in one's footsteps
消 *fu(mi)-ke(su)* stamp out (a fire)
破 *fu(mi)-yabu(ru)* walk across; travel on foot. *tōha suru* crush underfoot; travel on foot
殺 *fu(mi)-koro(su)* trample to death
11 張 *fu(m)ba(ru)* stretch (the legs); straddle; hold out, persist in; exert oneself
涸 *fu(mi)-kara(su)* dry up by treading
貫 *fu(mi)-nu(ku)* to injure the foot by stepping on something sharp
12 越 *fu(mi)-ko(eru), fu(mi)-ko(su)* step over, step across
違 *fu(mi)-chiga(eru)* dislocate, turn, twist, put out of joint
堪 *fu(mi)-kota(eru)* hold one's own, hold one's ground
場 *fu(mi)ba* footing, place to step
幅 *fu(mi)haba* (stair) tread
換 *fu(mi)-ka(eru)* change step, shift from one foot to another
渡 *fu(mi)-wata(ru)* cross over
絵 *fu(mi)e* crucifix plaque to be stepped on as evidence of faith
絞 *fu(mi)-shibo(ru)* tread out (the wine)
割 *fu(mi)-wa(ru)* step on and break
13 継 *fu(mi)tsu(gi)* footstool
跡 *fu(mi)ato* footprint
毀 *fu(mi)-kowa(su)* trample to pieces, crush
14 鳴 *fu(mi)-na(rasu)* stamp noisily
15 潰 *fu(mi)-tsubu(su)* crush under foot
締 *fu(mi)-shi(meru)* step firmly, step cautiously
17 藁 *fu(mi)wara* litter
19 鞴 *tatara* foot bellows
22 襲 *tōshū suru* follow, follow suit
23 躙 *fu(mi)-niji(ru)* trample down

9

踴 5890 J6c7d M37684 See **踊** 5882.

踰 5891 J6c7c M37675 YU cross, go over; pass, go beyond.

7 見角言谷豆豕豸貝赤走 9【足】身車辛辰辵⻌邑阝酉釆里

蹂 5892 J6c7a M37718 JŪ step on.
23 躙 *jūrin* trampling, overrunning, devastation; infringement, violation

踵 5893 J6c7b M37686 SHŌ. *kakato, kubisu, kibisu, kagato* heel.
6 返 *kubisu (o) kae(su)* return, go back
10 骨 *shōkotsu* heel bone
11 接 *kubisu (o) ses(suru)* follow one after another

蹄 5894 J447d M37724 TEI. *hizume* hoof.
7 状 *teijō* horseshoe shape
形 *teikei* U shape, horseshoe shape
形磁石 *teikei jishaku* horseshoe magnet
13 鉄 *teitetsu* horseshoe
鉄工 *teitetsukō* horseshoer
鉄形 *teitetsukei* horseshoe shape
鉄術 *teitetsujutsu* horseshoeing

10

蹈 5895 J6d25 M37744 See 踏 5889.

蹊 5896 J6c7e M37747 KEI path.

蹐 5897 J6d24 M37766 SEKI stealthy footsteps.

蹇 5898 J6d21 M37741 KEN. *iza(ru)* crawl along. *izari* a cripple. *ashinae* lame person, a cripple.
11 脚 *kenkyaku* cripple

蹉 5899 J6d22 M37745 SA stumble.
12 跌 *satetsu* stumbling, failure, setback, reverses, deadlock

蹌 5900 J6d23 M37755 SŌ move; run; stagger.
13 踉 *yorobo(u)* totter along. *yoroyoro to, yoboyobo to, sōrō to* unsteadily, totteringly
17 蹌 *sōsō* moving; dancing; staggering

11

蹤 5901 J6d27 M37823 See 踪 5887.

蹙 5902 J6d26 M37790 **⿰足戚** 5903 J-X M37791 SHUKU a tight place; scowling; approaching, shrinking.

蹕 5904 J6d2b M37783 HITSU one who precedes a king in a procession.

蹟 5905 J4058 M37814 SEKI, SHAKU remains (of something), footprint, traces.

蹠 5906 J6d28 M37815 SEKI. *ashiura, ashi(no)ura, anaura* sole of the foot.

蹣 5907 J6d2a M37822 MAN staggering, tottering.
12 跚 *yoro(keru), yorome(ku), yorobo(u)* stagger, totter along, reel, falter. *mansan(taru)* reeling, staggering. *yoroyoro to* totteringly.

12

躇 5908 J6d30 M37925 CHO hesitate.

蹼 5909 J6d2e M37889 BOKU. *mizukaki* webfoot, web.

蹶 5910 J6d2c M37880 **蹷** 5911 J-X M37881 KETSU stumble;
10 起 *kekki suru* jump to one's feet; stand up against
12 然 *ketsuzen to* resolutely; with a spring

蹲 5912 J6d2d M37874 SON. SHUN. *uzukuma(ru)* crouch, squat down, cower. *tsukuba(u)* crouch, squat. *tsukuba(i)* washbasin in garden.
8 居 *sonkyo* crouching
15 踞 *sonkyo* crouching

蹴 5913 J3d33 M37876 SHUKU. SHŪ. *ke(ru)* kick.
3 上 *ke-aga(ru)* jump up. *ke-age(ru)* kick up. *kea(ge)* step riser
4 爪 *kezume* spur, cockspur

込 ke-ko(mu) kick in
5 立 ke-ta(teru) kick up
出 ke-da(su), ke(ri)-da(su) start kicking, kick off
6 返 ke-kae(su) kick back
合 ke-a(u), ke(ri)-a(u) kick each other. kea(i) cockfight
8 放 ke-hana(su) kick open, kick off
9 飛 ke-to(basu) kick off; kick down; turn down
10 倒 ke-tao(su), ke(ri)-tao(su) kick down, kick over
破 ke-yabu(ru), ke(ri)-yabu(ru) kick open
殺 ke-koro(su), ke(ri)-koro(su) kick to death
11 毬 kemari (ancient) football
転 ke-koro(basu) kick down
球 shūkyū football
球界 shūkyūkai world of football
球場 shūkyūjō football field
12 散 ke-chi(rasu) kick around, rout
違 ke-chiga(eru) dislocate by kicking. kechiga(i) stumble; blunder, failure
落 ke-oto(su) kick down; kick overboard
22 躓 ke-tsumazu(ku) stumble over, trip, fail, bog down

13

躅 5914 J6d31 M37917 躑 5927 J-X M38028 CHOKU, TAKU tap with the feet; ruins.

躄 5915 J6d32 M37913 躃 5916 J-X M37912 HEKI. iza(ru) crawl along. izari, ashinae a cripple.

躁 5917 J6d2f M37906 SŌ noisy.
7 狂 sōkyō frenzy, raving madness, wild excitement.
9 急 sōkyū quick temper, impatience
10 病 sōbyō mania
26 鬱病 sōutsubyō manic-depressive insanity

14

躋 5918 J6d33 M37949 SEI climb.

躊 5919 J6d34 M37941 CHŪ hesitate.
19 躇 chūcho hesitation, vacillation, indecision. tamera(u) hesitate, waver.

躑 5920 J6d36 M37963 TEKI shaga(mu) squat, crouch, sit on the heels.
20 躅 tsutsuji azalea

躍 5921 J4c76 M37955' B YAKU. odo(ru) dance; leap, skip; throb (the heart); act as a cat's-paw; double (the interest on a debt).
3 上 odo(ri)-a(geru) jump up, dance for joy
4 込 odo(ri)-ko(mu) jump into
6 如 yakujo(taru) vivid, graphic, lifelike, true to nature
字 odo(ri)ji sign of repetition
10 起 yakki excitement; jumping up and down; desperation; enthusiasm, zeal
進 yakushin rush, dash; onslaught; prancing, dancing ahead
11 掛 odo(ri)-ka(karu) spring upon, jump, swoop down on
動 yakudō suru move lively
12 越 odo(ri)-ko(su), odo(ri)-ko(eru) jump over
20 懸 odo(ri)-ku(kuru) spring upon, jump, swoop down on

15

躔 5922 J6d37 M37970 TAN step; surround; go around; sign; footprint.

躓 5923 J6d35 M37967 CHI. tsumazu(ku) stumble, trip; falter, be balked.
10 倒 tsumazu(ki)-tao(reru) stumble and fall

16

躙 5924 J6d38 M37983 See 躪 5926.

18

蹞 5925 / J6d3a / M38009 Jō step on.

19

躪 5926 / J6d39 / M38026 **躙** 5924 / J6d38 / M37983 RIN. *niji(ru)* edge forward; trample down.

11 寄 *niji(ri)-yo(ru)* edge up to

21

躧 5927 / J-X / M38028 See **躅** 5914.

RAD. 身 158

Mi body. At left: *mi hen*. Nickname: Body.

A **身** 5928 / J3f48 / M38034 SHIN. *mi, karada* body; person; the quick; one's station in life; self; heart, soul, mind; ability; flesh, meat; life; blade; container; garment width. *mi(jirogu)* stir (oneself) slightly. *mi(gonashi)* deportment.

3 巾 *mihaba* width of a garment
丈 *mitake, mi (no) take* height, stature
上 *shinjō* merit; body; one's fortune, one's history; estate; social position. *shinshō* one's fortune, one's history; one's property; social position. *mi(no)ue* one's fortune, one's future, one's lot; one's history
上判断 *mi(no)ue handan* telling a person's fortune
上持 *shinshōmo(chi)* rich person; housekeeping
上相談 *mi(no)ue sōdan* consultation about personal affairs
上話 *mi(no)uebanashi* life story
4 心 *shinshin* body and mind
方 *mikata* friend, ally, supporter
欠 *mika(ki)* dried herring
辺 *shimpen* one's person
中 *shinchū* in the body; in the bosom; in the camp
内 *miuchi* one's whole body; relatives; friends, followers
支度 *mijitaku* dress, outfit (for a trip)
毛 *mi(no)ke* body hair
毛立 *mi(no)keda(tsu)* (hair) stands on end (because of fear or the cold)
元 *mimoto* one's birth, identity, history, career; character
元保証 *mimoto hoshō* personal references
元保証人 *mimoto hoshōnin* surety, guarantor
分 *mibun* status, social position, identity, birth, circumstances
分不相応 *mibun fusōō* beyond one's means
分制 *mibunsei* caste, social stratification
分相応 *mibun sōō* within one's means
分違 *mibunchiga(i)* difference in social standing
分証明書 *mibun shōmeisho* identification document
5 包 *miguru(mi)* one's belongings
仕度 *mijitaku* preparation
仕舞 *mijimai* clothes; outfit (for a trip)
代 *shindai* property, estate, wealth. *migawa(ri)* vicarious substitute. *mi(no)shiro* ransom money
代金 *mi(no)shirokin* ransom money
代限 *shindaikagi(ri)* bankruptcy
6 近 *miji(ka) ni* near oneself
任 *mimaka(se)* doing as one pleases
共 *midomo* I (familiar)
回 *mi(no)mawa(ri)* personal belongings
回品 *mi(no)mawa(ri)hin, mimawa(ri)hin* personal belongings
7 投 *mina(ge)* drowning oneself; drowned person. *mi (o) na(geru)* drown oneself
抜 *minu(ke)* severing connections
形 *minari* (a person's) appearance

売 *miu(ri)* selling oneself for a term of service
状 *mijō* (a person's) nature; rank; behavior
体 *shintai, karada* the body
体付 *karadatsu(ki)* build, figure
体的 *shintaiteki* physical
体粉 *karada (o) ko ni suru* work hard
体惜 *karada (o) o(shimu)* spare oneself, be lazy
体検査 *shintai kensa* physical examination; searching a person
体障害者 *shintai shōgaisha* the physically handicapped, cripple
体髪膚 *shintai-happu* body, hair, and skin; the whole body
8 長 *mitake, shinchō, mi (no) take* stature, height
固 *migatame* personal preparation
性 *mijō* (a person's) nature; rank; behavior
知 *mishi(razu)* self-conceit
舎 *moya* main building of a noble's home
命 *shimmei* the body and life; life
受 *miu(ke)* buying a geisha; redeeming a geisha
空 *misora* the body; one's fortune
9 首 *shinshu* head and body
屋 *moya* main building of a noble's home
後 *shingo* after one's death
拵 *migoshira(e)* outfit (for a trip); makeup
柄 *migara* one's person
重 *miomo* pregnancy
持 *mimo(chi)* conduct, morals; pregnancy
持女 *mimo(chi) onna* pregnant woman
10 振 *miburu(i)* shivering, shuddering. *mibu(ri)* gesture
粉 *mi (o) ko ni suru* work assiduously
窄 *misubora(shii)* shabby, poor, miserable
11 廊 *shinrō* nave
過 *misu(gi)* living, livelihood
動 *miugo(ki)* moving around
寄 *miyo(ri)* a relative
許 *mimoto* one's birth, identity, history, career; character
許引受人 *mimoto hikiukenin* guarantor, surety
12 悶 *mimoda(eru)* writhe in pain
幅 *mihaba* width of a garment
軽 *migaru na* light, agile
替 *miga(wari)* vicarious substitute
勝手 *migatte* selfishness, egotism
程 *mi(no)hodo* social standing
程知 *mi(no)hodo shi(razu)* not knowing one's place
13 嗜 *midashina(mi)* care of personal appearance, grooming
14 構 *migama(eru), migama(e) suru* stand ready, stand on guard
銭 *mizeni* one's pocket money
15 締 *miji(mari)* preparation; behavior
請 *miu(ke)* ransom, redemption
褒 *mibo(me)* praising oneself; pride
罷 *mimaka(ru)* die, pass away
震 *miburu(i)* shivering, trembling, shuddering
16 儘 *mimama* freedom
18 繕 *mizukuro(i) suru* dress up
21 贔屓 *mibiiki* nepotism, clannishness
22 籠 *migomo(ru)* conceive, become pregnant; hide

3

躬 5929 / J6d3b / M38038 **躳** 5933 / J-X / M38089 KYŪ body; self.

6 行 *kyūkō suru* practice, exemplify, take the initiative

4

躯 5930 / J366d / M-X Nonstandard for **軀** 5935.

5

躰 5931 / J6d3c / M38065 See **体** 165.

6

躱 5932 / J6d3e / M38078 TA avoid, escape; parry.

7

躳 5933 / J-X / M38089 See **躬** 5929.

9

躾 5934 / J6d3f / M38123 (国字) *shitsu(keru)* discipline, train, bring up. *shitsuke* discipline, training, upbringing.
4 方 *shitsukekata* way of training

11

軀 5935 / J-X / M38137 KU body. *mukuro, karada* body; corpse; tree with rotten heart.
13 幹 *kukan* torso; the body proper (without head and appendages)

12

軅 5936 / J6d40 / M-X Nonstandard for 軈 5938.

13

體 5937 / J6d3d / M38157 See 体 405.

17

軈 5938 / J6d41 / M38167 (国字) *yaga(te)* soon after, soon, presently; almost, all but; no more than; after all.

RAD. 車 159

Kuruma vehicle. At left: *kuruma hen*. Nickname: Car.

A **車** 5939 / J3c56 / M38172 SHA vehicle; a vehicle load. *kuruma* wheel; vehicle, carriage, wagon; cart, wheelbarrow; go-cart; jinricksha; van, automobile.
2 力 *shariki* cart coolie; cart
3 上 *shajō* on the train, in the car
大工 *kuruma daiku* wheelwright
4 戸 *kurumado* wheeled sliding door
止 *kurumado(me)* wheel block; railway buffer stop; Closed to Vehicles.
内 *shanai* inside the car
引 *kurumahi(ki)* jinricksha puller
夫 *shafu* jinricksha puller
井戸 *kuruma ido* well provided with pulley and rope
中 *shachū* in a vehicle
中談 *shachūdan* train interview
5 代 *kurumadai* fare, hire; cartage charge; tip
外 *shagai* outside the car
台 *shadai* chassis
付椅子 *kurumatsu(ki) isu* chair on casters
6 地 *shachi* capstan, windlass
両 *sharyō* vehicles, rolling stock
7 体 *shatai* chassis, car body
8 券 *shaken* bicycle-race ticket
9 屋 *kurumaya* jinricksha puller; jinricksha station; wheelwright
室 *shashitsu* (train) compartment
10 座 *kurumaza* sitting in a circle
庫 *shako* carbarn, garage
馬 *shaba* horses and vehicles
馬代 *shabadai* traveling expenses
馬道 *shabadō* road for vehicles and horses
11 道 *shadō* roadway, driveway
寄 *kurumayo(se)* entrance way for vehicles
窓 *shasō* car window
12 軸 *shajiku* axle
裂 *kurumaza(ki)* tearing a body apart with the legs tied to separate carts
検 *shaken* vehicle inspection
掌 *shashō* conductor
掌区 *shashōku* conductor's station
13 賃 *kurumachin* fare, hire; cartage charge; tip
14 塵 *shajin* dust raised by vehicles
15 輪 *sharin* wheel
駕 *shaga* imperial carriage
輛 *sharyō* heavy vehicles; rolling stock
輛連結 *sharyō renketsu* car coupling
19 轍 *shatetsu* rut

1

軋 5940 / J6d42 / M38173 ATSU. *kishi(ru), kishime(ku)* squeak, grate, creak, clash with. *kishi(mu)* squeak, grate, creak.
22 轢 *atsureki* friction, discord, strife

2

B **軌** 5941 / J3530 / M38176 **軌** 5942 / J-X / M-X KI wheel track; railway; orbit; rut; rule; model; road; way of doing.

1 一 *ki (o) itsu (ni) suru* act in the same way (as someone)
7 条 *kijō* rails
11 道 *kidō* railway, tramway; orbit; beaten track
12 間 *kikan* railway-track gauge
13 跡 *kiseki* wagon tracks
15 範 *kihan* model, standard, pattern

A **軍** 5943 / J3733 / M38179 GUN army, force, troops. *ikusa* war; battle; campaign; army.

2 刀 *guntō* saber, side arms, service sword
人 *gunjin* soldier, member of the military
人生活 *gunjin seikatsu* military life
3 士 *gunshi* soldiers
4 手 *gunte* army cotton gloves
夫 *gumpu* military porter
5 功 *gunkō* meritorious war service
礼 *gunrei* military honors
民 *gummin* the military and civilians
令 *gunrei* military command
令部 *Gunreibu* Naval General Staff
司令官 *gunshireikan* military commander
司令部 *gunshireibu* military headquarters
用 *gun'yō* military use
用犬 *gun'yoken* war dog
用地図 *gun'yō chizu* army (topographic) map
用金 *gun'yōkin* war funds, war chest; campaign fund
用品 *gun'yōhin* military stores, munitions of war
用鳩 *gun'yōbato* carrier pigeon
用機 *gun'yōki* warplane
6 衣 *gun'i* military clothes
団 *gundan* army corps
団長 *gundanchō* corps commander
7 役 *gun'eki, gun'yaku* military service
医 *gun'i* military surgeon
医学校 *gun'i gakkō* military medical college
医監 *gun'ikan* surgeon major general
医総監 *gun'i sōkan* surgeon general
8 長 *gunchō* combat commander
門 *gummon* camp gate; a general (polite)
使 *gunshi* truce bearer
服 *gumpuku* military or naval uniform
制 *gunsei* military system military organization
卒 *gunsotsu* soldier
学 *gungaku* military science, strategy, tactics
官憲 *gunkanken* military authorities
拡 *gunkaku* expansion of armaments
拡競争 *gunkaku kyōsō* armaments race
法 *gumpō* military law; martial law; tactics, strategy
法会議 *gumpō kaigi* court-martial
国 *gunkoku* nation at war, militant nation
国主義 *gunkoku shugi* militarism
国色 *gunkokushoku* military character
事 *gunji* naval and military affairs; military
事力 *gunjiryoku* military force, military strength
事上 *gunjijō no* military, strategic
事工場 *gunji kōjō* war plant
事公債 *gunji kōsai* war bond, war loan
事犯 *gunjihan* military offense
事行動 *gunji kōdō* military movements
事同盟 *gunji dōmei* military alliance
事会議 *gunji kaigi* council of war
事的 *gunjiteki* military
事協定 *gunji kyōtei* military pact
事面 *gunjimen* military aspect
事通 *gunjitsū* person versed in military affairs
事通信員 *gunji tsūshin'in* war correspondent
事施設 *gunji shisetsu* military installations
事秘密 *gunji himitsu* military secret
事基地 *gunji kichi* military base
事教練 *gunji kyōren* military training
事費 *gunjihi* war funds, war expenditures
事裁判 *gunji saiban* court martial
事裁判所 *gunji saibansho* military court
事輸送 *gunji yusō* military transport
事諜報 *gunji chōhō* military intelligence
事警察 *gunji keisatsu* military police
事顧問 *gunji komon* military adviser

9 律 *gunritsu* martial law; articles of war; military discipline; military law
神 *gunshin* god of war; war hero
紀 *gunki* military discipline
陣 *gunjin* camp, battlefield
陣医学 *gunjin igaku* military medicine
政 *gunsei* military government
政府 *gunseifu* military government
政部 *gunseibu* military government
10 馬 *gumba* army horse
扇 *gunsen* ancient commander's fan
師 *gunshi* strategist, tactician; schemer
将 *gunshō* army commander
容 *gun'yō* military accouterments; troop formation
書 *gunsho* military book, war history
記 *gunki* war chronicle
記物語 *gunki monogatari* war chronicle
配 *gumbai* stratagem, tactics; (ancient) military leader's fan; sumo umpire's fan
配団扇 *gumbai uchiwa* (ancient) military leader's fan
部 *gumbu* military authorities, army circles
部独裁 *gumbu dokusai* military dictatorship
11 道 *gundō* military road
情 *gunjō* military situation
略 *gunryaku* strategy, tactics
務 *gummu* military and naval affairs; military service
船 *gunsen* warship
規 *gunki* military regulation
票 *gumpyō* military scrip
曹 *gunsō* sergeant
隊 *guntai* army, troops, corps
隊化 *guntaika* militarization
隊生活 *guntai seikatsu* army life
隊式 *guntaishiki* military style, army style
隊行進曲 *guntai kōshinkyoku* military march
隊葬 *guntaisō* military funeral
12 属 *gunzoku* civilian in military employ
帽 *gumbō* military cap
港 *gunkō* naval port, naval station
営 *gun'ei* military camp
装 *gunsō* soldier's equipment
費 *gumpi* war funds, war expenditures
備 *gumbi* armaments, military preparations
備制限 *gumbi seigen* limitation of armaments
備拡張 *gumbi kakuchō* expansion of armaments
備撤廃 *gumbi teppai* complete disarmament
備縮小 *gumbi shukushō* reduction of armaments
13 鼓 *gunko* war drum
路 *gunro* military road
靴 *gunka* military shoes
勢 *gunzei* military forces, host, troops
資 *gunshi* war materiel; military expenses; war fund; campaign funds
資金 *gunshikin* war funds; campaign funds
楽 *gungaku* military music
楽手 *gungakushu* military band member
楽長 *gungakuchō* military band master
楽隊 *gungakutai* military or naval band
14 閥 *gumbatsu* army clique, militarist party
旗 *gunki* battle flag, colors, ensign
歌 *gunka* war song
管区 *gunkanku* military district
需 *gunju* munitions, military stores
需工場 *gunju kōjō* war plant
需工業 *gunju kōgyō* munitions industry
需品 *gunjuhin* munitions of war, military stores
需景気 *gunju keiki* war prosperity
15 談 *gundan* war story
器 *gunki* implements of war
16 機 *gunki* military secret
17 縮 *gunshuku* disarmament, limitation of arms
縮協定 *gunshuku kyōtei* disarmament agreement
18 職 *gunshoku* military profession, military post
19 警 *gunkei* military police
20 議 *gungi* war council
籍 *gunseki* military or naval register, muster roll
艦 *gunkan* warship, battleship
艦鳥 *gunkanchō, gunkandori* frigate bird

3

軒 B 5944 / J382e / M38187 Ken house counter. *noki* eaves.
3 下 *nokishita* under the eaves
6 灯 *kentō* eaves lantern, door light

合 *nokia(i)* chinks in the eaves; the eaves; the sky seen beyond the eaves
先 *nokisaki* edge of the eaves; house frontage
7 別 *kembetsu* house to house
8 並 *nokinara(bi), nokina(mi)* row of houses
9 昂 *kenkō* climbing high; high spirits, full of energy
10 高 *kenkō* high spirits
12 提灯 *nokijōchin* eaves lantern
13 軽 *kenchi* difference, inequality
数 *kensū* number of houses
樋 *nokidoi* eaves gutter
14 端 *nokibata, nokiba* edge of the eaves
16 頭 *kentō* edge of the eaves
18 檻 *kenkan* railing

4

軎 5945 J6d11 M-X Nonstandard for 轟 5991.

軛 5946 J6d43 M38207 YAKU. *kubiki* yoke.

B 軟 5947 J4670 M38213 NAN. *yawaraka(i)* soft.
3 口蓋 *nankōgai* soft palate
4 木 *namboku* soft lumber, softwood
毛 *nammō* pubescence; downy hair
化 *nanka* softening, mollification; weakening (of a market)
文学 *nambungaku* light literature
水 *nansui* soft water
水剤 *nansuizai* water softener
5 打 *nanda* a bunt (in baseball)
6 式飛行船 *nanshiki hikōsen* nonrigid airship
式庭球 *nanshiki teikyū* softball tennis
式野球 *nanshiki yakyū* softball
7 体動物 *nantai dōbutsu* mollusca
8 泥 *nandei* sludge, mud, ooze
性下疳 *nansei gekan* soft chancre
9 風 *nampū* gentle breeze, zephyr
便 *namben* loose bowel movement
派 *nampa* moderate party
炭 *nantan* soft coal
10 骨 *nankotsu* cartilage, gristle
弱 *nanjaku* weakness, effeminacy
11 球 *nankyū* softball
13 絹 *nanken* glossed silk
鉄 *nantetsu* malleable iron, wrought iron
禁 *nankin* internment; house arrest
14 膏 *nankō* soft ointment
15 論 *nanron* weak argument

A 転 5948 J453e M38234' 轉 5984 J6d5b M38507 TEN turn, remove, change. *ten(jiru), ten(zuru)* vt and vi revolve, rotate, turn around; turn, shift; alter, change; move, be transferred. *koro(bu), maro(bu)* fall down, tumble. *koro(geru), koro(garu)* roll over, tumble; lie down (on the lawn); be convulsed (with laughter). *koro(gasu), koro(basu), maro(basu), maro(bakasu)* knock down, roll over. *utata* more and more, increasingly; somehow; indeed.
2 入 *tennyū* transfer into, moving into. *maro(bi)-i(ru)* roll into
入学 *tennyūgaku* transferring from another school
入者 *tennyūsha* members received
4 込 *koro(ge)-ko(mu), koro(gari)-ko(mu)* roll into, come one's way, devolve on, fall heir to
化 *tenka suru* change, be transformed
切支丹 *koro(bi) Kirishitan* Christians who gave in to persecution
5 用 *ten'yō suru* divert, convert
写 *tensha suru* transfer, transcribe, copy
去 *koro(gashi)-sa(ru)* roll away
出 *tenshutsu* transfer, moving out; transfer (of a ration record or church membership)
出先 *tenshutsusaki* new address
出届 *tenshitsu todoke* notification of moving
出者 *tenshutsusha* person transferred
出証明 *tenshutsu shōmei* moving certificate
6 回 *koro(bi)-mawa(ru)* wallow, welter, tumble about. *koro(ge)-mawa(ru)* tumble about; writhe. *tenkai* revolution, rotation
成 *tensei* changing form
任 *tennin* change of post
宅 *tentaku suru* move, change one's address
向 *tenkō* turn, conversion, about-face
向点 *tenkōten* turning point
会 *tenkai* transfer of church membership
会状 *tenkaijō* (church) letter of transfer

地 *tenchi* change of air, change of climate
地療養 *tenchi ryōyō* changing climate for one's health
地療養所 *tenchi ryōyōjo* convalescent rest home
7 身 *tenshin* changing one's status or occupation
位 *ten'i* transposition, dislocation, displacement
住 *tenjū* changing one's residence
売 *tembai* resale
車台 *tenshadai* turntable
8 居 *tenkyo* moving, changing quarters
送 *tensō suru* transmit; refer back (to a committee); translate (a cable); forward (mail)
注 *tenchū* a type of characters which now also represent concepts related to the original (e.g. 金 "money" as well as the original "metal")
官 *tenkan suru* be transferred to another office
免 *temmen* transferring and dismissal
学 *tengaku* changing schools
炉 *tenro* revolving furnace, converter
炉鋼 *tenrokō* converter steel, Bessemer steel
9 音 *ten'on* euphonic change
科 *tenka suru* change one's course
封 *tempū* changing fiefs
変 *tempen* mutation, change, vicissitude
室 *tenshitsu* changing rooms
10 進 *tenshin suru* shift (army) field positions
借 *tenshaku* sublease
倒 *koro(bi)-tao(reru)* fall down. *tentō suru* turn over, turn upside down, fall down violently; invert; reverse
校 *tenkō* changing schools
記 *tenki* posting (in bookkeeping)
帰 *tenki* turning point
11 得 *tentoku* subsequent purchase
移 *ten'i* change, transition
訛 *tenka* corruption (of a word)
転 *tenten suru* pass from hand to hand, change hands often; go rolling along; roam around
宿 *tenshuku suru* change lodgings
婆 *(o)temba* tomboy, flapper
12 属 *tenzoku suru* be transferred
結 *tenketsu* development and conclusion
補 *tempo* transfer, shuffling
勤 *tenkin suru* be transferred to another office
期 *tenki* crisis (in sickness)
落 *maro(bashi)-o(tosu), koro(bashi)-o(tosu)* roll (something) down (a hill). *tenraku suru, koro(ge)-o(chiru)* fall off, tumble down
貸 *tentai* sublease
貸借 *tentaishaku* sublease
換 *tenkan suru* convert; divert, distract; reconvert; switch; transpose
換社債 *tenkan shasai* convertible bond
換炉 *tenkanro* converter
換期 *tenkanki* turning point
換器 *tenkanki* commutator
13 嫁 *tenka* blame another for one's mistake
禍 *tenka* changing calamity into happiness
戦 *tensen suru* take part in various battles, fight here and there
寝 *koro(bi)ne, utatane* nap, doze. *gorone* sleeping with one's clothes on
置 *tenchi suru* transpose, displace, dislocate
義 *tengi* figurative meaning
意 *ten'i* figurative meaning
業 *tengyō suru* change one's employment
載 *tensai* reproduction, reprinting in another publication
路手 *tenroshu* switch operator
路機 *tenroki* railway switch
14 漕 *tensō* water transportation
15 調 *tenchō* changing the key in the midst of a musical piece
輪羅針儀 *tenrin rashingi* gyrocompass
16 機 *tenki* turning point
18 覆 *tempuku* overthrow, overturn; subvert; upset, capsize
職 *tenshoku* change of post; change of occupation
職者 *tenshokusha* newcomer, one who has changed his work
19 鏡儀 *tenkyōgi* transit
轍 *tentetsu* shunting, switching
轍手 *tentetsushu* switch operator, points tender
轍器 *tentetsuki* railway switch
轍機 *tentetsuki* railway switch

20 籍 *tenseki* transfer of domicile, church membership, or school enrollment

5

軻 5949 / J6d46 / M38274 KA difficult progress (as of wheels); Mencius' given name.

軫 5950 / J6d47 / M38243 SHIN be sad; revolve.

8 念 *shinnen* imperial solicitude
15 憂 *shin'yū* deep grief, worry

軼 5951 / J6d45 / M38275 ITSU pass along; rut.

8 事 *itsuji* unknown fact
10 書 *issho* a lost book

B **軸** 5952 / J3c34 / M38769 JIKU axis; axle; spindle; shaft; pivot; stem, stalk; (pen) holder; scroll picture.

4 木 *jikugi* splint; matchstick; scroll rod
8 承 *jikuuke* bearings (in machines)
受 *jikuu(ke)* bearing
物 *jikumono* scroll picture
11 距 *jikukyo* wheelbase

A **軽** 5953 / J375a / M38281 **輕** 5961 / J6d4b / M38346 KEI. *karu(i), karo(i)* light; trifling, unimportant, simple, easy; plain or light (meal); undignified. *karo(njiru), karo(nzuru)* slight, make light of; neglect; belittle; underrate; pay no attention to. *karu(ku) suru* lighten, relieve. *karu(yakana)* light, easy. *kei-* light.

3 口 *karukuchi, karuguchi* joke; talkativeness
子 *karuko* coolie, porter
小 *keishō na* slight, trifling
工業 *keikōgyō* light industry
4 少 *keishō na* trifling, slight
文学 *keibungaku* light literature
水 *keisui* light water
水炉 *keisuiro* light water reactor
5 目 *karume* light weight. *karumi ni* rather lightly
石 *karuishi* pumice stone
打 *keida* light blow; pat; light hit
犯罪 *keihanzai* minor offense
巡 *keijun* light cruiser
巡洋艦 *keijun'yōkan* light cruiser
6 舟 *keishu* fast light boat, skiff
衣 *keii* simple clothing, light clothing
合金 *keigōkin* light alloy
気球 *keikikyū* dirigible balloon
自動車 *keijidōsha* a light car
7 妙 *keimyō na* facile, clever, witty
快 *keikai* nimbleness; lightheartedness; convalescence
兵 *keihei* light-armed soldier
作業 *keisagyō* light work
労働 *keirōdō* light work
8 雨 *keiu* light rain
侮 *keibu* contempt, scorn
油 *keiyu* light fuel oil
物 *karumono* lightweight silks
卒 *keisotsu* rashness, haste
易 *keii* easy, light, simple
忽 *keikotsu* carelessness, indiscretion
金属 *keikinzoku* light metals
佻 *keichō* frivolity, thoughtlessness
佻浮華 *keichō-fuka* display, ostentation, vanity, frivolity
佻浮薄 *keichō-fuhaku* irresponsibility; frivolity
9 風 *keifū* light breeze
食 *keishoku* light meal
度 *keido* slight degree
科 *keika* minor offense, light punishment
重 *keijū, keichō* relative importance; relative seriousness; relative weight
音楽 *keiongaku* light music
飛行機 *keihikōki* light plane
便 *keiben* convenience, simplicity
便食堂 *keiben shokudō* snack bar
便鉄道 *keiben tetsudō* narrow-gauge railway
10 病 *keibyō* slight illness
倢 *keishō* agility
浮 *keifu* frivolity, fickleness
砲 *keihō* light gun
荷 *karuni* light load, ballast
航空機 *keikōkūki* lighter-than-air aircraft
症 *keishō* minor illness
症例 *keishōrei* light cases (of illness)
挙 *keikyo* carelessness; rash undertaking
挙妄動 *keikyo-mōdō* rash behavior
11 視 *keishi suru* despise, slight, ignore, neglect

舸 *keika* a light fast boat
率 *karohazumi, karuhazumi, keisotsu* rashness, hastiness
12 減 *keigen* reduction, alleviation, commutation
焼 *karuya(ki)* wafer
軽 *karugaru(shii)* indiscreet, thoughtless, careless; frivolous. *karugaru to* easily. *keikei ni* carelessly, rashly
寒 *keikan* slightly cold spell; chilly feeling
装 *keisō* lightweight equipment; lightweight dress
喜劇 *keikigeki* light comedy
飲食店 *keiinshokuten* light lunch, diner
量 *keiryō* light weight
量拳闘選手 *keiryō kentō senshu* lightweight boxer
量選手 *keiryō senshu* lightweight-class athlete
13 傷 *keishō* minor injury
微 *keibi na* insignificant, minor, slight, light (illness)
罪 *keizai* minor offense
裘 *keikyū* light fur robe
戦車 *keisensha* light tank
禁錮 *keikinko* minor imprisonment
業 *karuwaza* acrobatics; risky undertaking
業師 *karuwazashi* acrobat, tumbler
14 罰 *keibatsu* light punishment
蔑 *keibetsu* contempt, slight, scorn
演劇 *keiengeki* light theatricals
歌劇 *keikageki* light opera
15 輩 *keihai* underling, small fry
16 薄 *keihaku* insincerity; untruthfulness; frivolity; inconstancy; flattery
機 *keiki* light machine gun
機関銃 *keikikanjū* light machine gun
18 騎兵 *keikihei* light cavalry
19 羅 *keira* gossamer, silk gauze
爆 *keibaku* light bomber
爆撃機 *keibakugekiki* light bomber
20 躁 *keisō na* thoughtless, rash, flighty

6

輀 5954 / J-X / M38287 See 轜 5990.

輌 5955 / J6d52 / M-X Nonstandard for 輛 5969.

軾 5956 / J6d48 / M38285 SHOKU front railing on a cart (for leaning on when bowing to someone outside).

輅 5957 / J6d4a / M38302 RO cart, large cart.

輊 5958 / J6d49 / M38311 CHI low.

B **較** 5959 / J3353 / M38297 KAKU. KŌ. *kura(beru)* compare, balance, contrast. contrast.
12 量 *kōryō* comparison, guessing

B **載** 5960 / J3a5c / M38309 SAI. *no(ru)* ride, board, mount; get up on; spread (paints); be taken in; share in, join; be found in (a dictionary); feel like doing; be mentioned in; be in harmony with. *no(seru)* place, put, lay, set; let (one) take part; impose on; record, mention.
9 炭 *saitan* coaling
11 貨屯数 *saika tonsū* deadweight tonnage
貨吃水 *saika kissui* ship's draft
貨吃水線 *saika kissuisen* Plimsoll mark, the draft line
16 積 *saiseki* carrying; loading
録 *sairoku suru* record

7

輕 5961 / J6b4b / M38346 See 軽 5953.

輒 5962 / J6b4c / M38336 CHŌ easily; repeatedly; soon; rarely; immobile.

輓 5963 / J6d4e / M38337 BAN pull.
6 近 *bankin* recent times

輔 5964 / J4a65 / M38342 HO helping; helper. *tasu(keru)* help.
7 佐 *hosa* assistance; assistant; counselor
12 弼 *hohitsu* assistance, counsel
14 導 *hodō* guidance
17 翼 *hoyoku* assistance

8

輾 5965 J6d4d M38359 See **輒** 5962.

輅 5966 J-X M38381 See **轗** 5989.

輜 5967 J6d4f M38368 SHI canopied cart; baggage cart.

輟 5968 J6d50 M38374 TETSU cease, halt, stop; bind, repair, mend.

輛 5969 J6d51 M38361 RYŌ counter for heavy vehicles and railway cars.

輦 5970 J6d53 M38393 REN palanquin; carriage of a noble.
3 下 *renka* imperial capital
17 轂 *renkoku* imperial carriage

B **輩** 5971 J475a M38398 HAI fellow, people, companion; line. *tomogara, yakara* fellows, companions, set.
3 下 *haika* followers, adherents
5 出 *haishutsu suru* (people with talent) appear successively; come crowding on

B **輝** 5972 J3531 M38372 KI. *kuguyu(ku)* shine, sparkle, gleam, twinkle; brilliant, radiant, bright. *kagaya(kasu) vt* light up, brighten, illumine. *kagaya(ki)* brilliancy, radiance, splendor, glitter. *kagaya(kashii)* bright (future); brilliant (achievement).
5 石 *kiseki* pyroxene; augite
出 *kagaya(ki)-de(ru)* shine out from
12 渡 *kagaya(ki)-wata(ru)* shine out far and wide
15 輝 *kiki* brilliance

A **輪** 5973 J4e58 M38400 RIN ring, circle; wheel; corolla; wheel counter. *wa* circle, ring, link, wheel, hoop, loop.
4 止 *wado(me)* wheel block; railway buffer stop
切 *wagi(ri)* round slices
6 回 *wamawa(shi)* hoop rolling
死 *rinshi suru* run over and kill
伐 *rimbatsu* lumbering area by area (in a permanent forest)
灯 *rintō* a light on a Buddhist altar
7 作 *rinsaku* crop rotation
投 *wana(ge)* quoits
抜 *wanu(ke)* jumping through a hoop
状 *rinjō* ring shape
形 *wanari, wagata, rinkei* circle, ring, ring shape
9 廻 *rinne* transmigration
乗 *wano(ri)* riding in a circle
姦 *rinkan suru* rape by turns, gang rape
10 郭 *rinkaku* outlines, contours, profile, skyline; sketch, outline
索 *wanawa* lasso
差 *wasa* loop
11 唱 *rinshō* a round (in music)
袈裟 *wagesa* simple circular priest's scarf
転 *rinten* rotation
転機 *rintenki* cylinder press; mimeograph
12 軸 *rinjiku* wheel and axle
違 *wachiga(i)* two interlaced circles
番 *rimban* turn, rotation; executive committee chairman (of a Buddhist sect)
番制 *rimbansei* rotation system, job rotation
13 禍 *rinka* traffic accident
廓 *rinkaku* outlines, contours, profile, skyline, sketch, outline
廓地図 *rinkaku chizu* outline map
14 読 *rindoku* reading by turns
蔵 *rinzō* prayer wheel
舞 *rimbu* round dance
15 縁 *wabuchi* rim of a wheel
17 講 *rinkō* several people taking turns reading and explaining (a book)

9

輹 5974 J6d56 M38440 FUKU connection between axle and cart.

輳 5975 J6d54 M38429 SŌ gather.

輯 5976 J3d34 M38420 SHŪ gather, collect, compile.
16 録 *shūroku* compilation, editing

輻 5977 J6d55 M38442 FUKU *ya* spoke (of a wheel).

7 見角言谷豆豕豸貝赤走足身 9【車】辛辰辵辶邑阝酉釆里

10 射 *fukusha* radiation (of heat, light, etc.)
射線 *fukushasen* rays of radiation
射熱 *fukusha netsu* reflected heat, radiant heat
12 湊 *fukusō* convergence
16 輳 *fukusō* convergence

A **輸** 5978 / J4d22 / M38438' YU send, transport. *yu(suru)* be inferior to.
2 入 *yunyū* imports; importation; introduction
入国 *yunyūkoku* importing nation
入品 *yunyūhin* imports
入港 *yunyūkō* an importing port
入超過 *yunyū chōka* unfavorable trade balance
入額 *yunyūgaku* amount of imports
5 出 *yushutsu* exports; exportation
出入 *yushutsunyū* exporting and importing
出入品 *yushutsunyūhin* exports and imports
出入差 *yushutsunyū (no) sa* balance of trade
出国 *yushutsukoku* exporting nation
出品 *yushutsuhin* exports, goods for export
出許可 *yushutsu kyoka* export license
出港 *yushutsukō* an exporting port
出税 *yushutsuzei* export tax
出割当 *yushutsu waria(te)* export quota
出超過 *yushutsu chōka* favorable balance of trade
出業 *yushutsugyō* export business
出禁止 *yushutsu kinshi* export embargo
出額 *yushutsugaku* amount of exports
6 血 *yuketsu* blood transfusion
7 尿管 *yunyōkan* ureter
卵管 *yurankan* oviduct, fallopian tube
8 卒 *yusotsu* transport soldier
乳管 *yunyūkan* milk duct
送 *yusō* transportation
送列車 *yusō ressha* transport train
送船 *yusōsen* transport ship
送路 *yusōro* trucking road
送機 *yusōki* transport plane
送難 *yusōnan* transportation difficulties
9 胆管 *yutankan* bile duct
11 移出入 *yuishutsunyū* exporting and importing
14 精管 *yuseikan* spermaduct
20 贏 *yuei, shuei* gain or loss; victory or defeat

10

轂 5979 / J6d58 / M38479 KOKU hub. *koshiki* hub (of a wheel).

轅 5980 / J6d57 / M38483 EN. *nagae* shaft.

B **轄** 5981 / J336d / M38482' KATSU. *kusabi* wedge.

輾 5982 / J6d59 / M38467 TEN. DEN. *kishi(ru)* squeak, creak, grate.
11 転 *tenten suru* roll
転反側 *tenten-hansoku suru* toss around in bed

輿 5983 / J4d41 / M38468 YO. *kago, koshi* palanquin; bier.
2 入 *koshi-i(re)* wedding; bridal procession; bride's entry to groom's home
6 地 *yochi* earth, world
11 望 *yobō* popularity, esteem, reputation; confidence
15 論 *yoron* public opinion
論調査 *yoron chōsa* public-opinion survey

11

轉 5984 / J6d5b / M38507 See **転** 5948.

轌 5985 / J6d5a / M-X (国字) *sori* sled, sleigh.

轆 5986 / J6d5c / M38502 ROKU pulley. *koro* roller.
23 轤 *rokuro* pulley; lathe; windlass; potter's wheel
轤首 *rokurokubi, rokurokkubi* long-necked monster

12

轎 5987 / J6d5d / M38532 KYŌ small cart; palanquin.

轍 5988 / J4532 / M38524 Tetsu *wadachi* rut, wheel track.
[3] 叉 *tessa* (railway) frog
[15] 踏 *tetsu (o) fu(mu)* follow the footsteps of one's predecessor

13

轗 5989 / J6d5e / M38550 輡 5966 / J-X / M38381 Kan difficulty.
[12] 軻 *kanka* separation from the world

14

轜 5990 / J6d5f / M38571 輀 5954 / J-X / M38287 Ji hearse.
[7] 車 *jisha* hearse

轟 5991 / J396c / M38577 Gō. *todoro(ku)* roar, thunder, boom, resound, ring; become well-known; throb.
[7] 沈 *gōchin* instant sinking
[9] 音 *gōon* deafening roar, loud report
[12] 渡 *todoro(ki)-wata(ru)* roar, boom, thunder
然 *gōzen(taru)* roaring, deafening, thunderous
[21] 轟 *todo(ro)todo(ro) to* with a rumbling sound. *gōgō to* thunderously, with a rumble

15

轡 5992 / J3725 / M38587 Hi. *kutsuwa* (horse's) bit.
[6] 虫 *kutsuwa mushi* a noisy cricket

轢 5993 / J6d60 / M38588 Reki. *hi(ku)* run over (people). *kishi(ru)* creak, squeak, grate.
[6] 死 *rekishi suru* be run over and killed
[8] 逃 *hi(ki)ni(ge)* hit-and-run
[10] 倒 *hi(ki)-tao(su)* run down (someone with a car)
殺 *rekisatsu suru, hi(ki)-koro(su)* run over and kill
[11] 断 *rekidan* (a train) running over and severing a body

16

轣 5994 / J6d61 / M38593 Reki wagon tracks; creaking noise.

轤 5995 / J6d62 / M38596 Ro pulley, capstan.

RAD. 辛 160

Karai bitter. Variant: 𢆵 Nickname: Bitter.

B 辛 5996 / J3f49 / M38630 辛 5997 / J-X / M38630' Shin H. eighth. *kara(i)* hot, acrid, sharp; salty; bitter, trying; harsh, severe. *kara(kumo), karō(jite)* barely. *tsura(i)* painful, trying, bitter, cruel. *kanoto* eighth calendar sign.
[3] 口 *karakuchi* salty tooth; dry (saké); bitterness, acrimony
[5] 目 *kara(i)me, tsura(i)me* hard time, bitter experience. *karame* saltiness
[6] 気 *shinki* ill-feeling, unhappiness
気臭 *shinkikusa(i)* feeling depressed, having the blues
[7] 辛 *karagara* barely, with difficulty
労 *shinrō* hardship, toil, trouble
[8] 抱 *shimbō* patience, perseverance, endurance
苦 *shinku* hardship, toil, trouble
味 *karami* salty, hot, or sharp taste
味噌 *karamiso* salty *miso* (bean paste)
[10] 党 *karatō* drinker
[12] 勝 *shinshō* narrow victory
煮 *karani* cooking with a generous amount of salt
[14] 辣 *shinratsu na* bitter, sharp, acrimonious
酸 *shinsan* hardships, privations

5

辜 5998 / J6d63 / M38636 Ko sin, fault. *tsumi* crime.

6

辟 5999 / J6d64 / M38642 Heki false; punish; crime; law; ruler.

8 易 *hekieki suru* wince; shrink back; succumb to; be frightened; be disconcerted

A **辞** 6000 / J3c2d / M38638 **辭** 6004 / J6d66 / M38671 Ji word, term, expression; sentence; an address. *ji(suru)* resign, leave, decline. *ya(meru)* resign. *ina(mu)* refuse, decline; deny.

5 令 *jirei* written appointment, government order; commission; wording
去 *jikyo suru* leave, quit, retire
世 *jisei* passing away; last words; deathbed poem
6 色 *jishoku* words and looks
任 *jinin* resignation
7 別 *jibetsu* saying farewell
8 退 *jitai* refusal, declining
林 *jirin* dictionary
典 *jiten* dictionary
表 *jihyō* written resignation
9 柄 *jihei* excuse; pretense
10 書 *jisho* dictionary, glossary
11 章 *jishō* a composition, an article
13 彙 *jii* letter of resignation
意 *jii* intention to resign
15 儀 *jigi* bow, greeting; refusal, declining; hesitation
18 職 *jishoku* resignation
職願 *jishoku nega(i)* letter of resignation
20 譲 *jijō suru* give way to another

7

辣 6001 / J6d65 / M38646 Ratsu bitter.

8 油 *rāyu* red-pepper oil (a seasoning)
12 腕 *ratsuwan* shrewdness, sharpness, acumen, great tact

9

辨 6002 / J517e / M38657 **辧** 6003 / J5221 / M38656 See 弁 1665.

12

辭 6004 / J6d66 / M38671 See 辞 6000.

14

辯 6005 / J6d67 / M38677 See 弁 1666.

RAD. 辰 161

Tatsu dragon or, commonly, *shin no tatsu* (the character for "dragon" that is also read *shin*, as distinguished from Rad. 212).

辰 6006 / J4324 / M38682 Shin. *tatsu* 7-9 a.m.; fifth zodiac sign; dragon.

9 砂 *shinsha* cinnabar

3

B **辱** 6007 / J3f2b / M38686 Joku. *hazuka(shimeru)* humiliate, put to shame, disgrace, insult; rape, assault. *katajikena(i)* thankful, indebted. *haji* shame, dishonor, disgrace, humiliation, insult.

8 知 *jokuchi* acquaintance
命 *jokumei* grateful orders
10 涙 *katajike namida* tears of gratitude

6

B **農** 6008 / J4740 / M38688 Nō agriculture; farmers.

3 山村 *nō-san-son* agricultural and mountain villages
山漁村 *nō-san-gyo-son* agricultural, mountain, and fishing villages
工 *nō-kō* agriculture and industry
工商 *nō-kō-shō* agriculture-industry-commerce; farmers-artisans-merchants
工業 *nō-kō-gyō* agriculture and industry

4 父 *nōfu* husbandman
夫 *nōfu* farmer, farmhand
水産 *nō-sui-san* agricultural and marine products
5 奴 *nōdo* serf
民 *nōmin* peasants, farmers
本主義 *nōhon shugi* building a nation on an agricultural economy
6 会 *nōkai* agricultural association
地 *nōchi* farmland
地改革 *nōchi kaikaku* agrarian reform
7 兵 *nohei* agrarian soldiers
作 *nōsaku* land cultivation
作物 *nōsakubutsu* crops, farm produce
村 *nōson* farm village, rural community, agricultural district
村伝道 *nōson dendō* rural evangelism
芸 *nōgei* agricultural technology
芸化学 *nōgei kagaku* agricultural chemistry
8 協 *nōkyō* agricultural cooperative
法 *nōhō* agricultural law; farming methods
牧 *nōboku* general farming (crops and animals)
具 *nōgu* farm implements
事 *nōji* agriculture
事試験所 *nōji shikenjo* agricultural experiment station
学 *nōgaku* agriculture
学校 *nōgakkō* agricultural school
学書 *nōgakusho* agricultural books
林 *nōrin* agriculture and forestry
林大臣 *Nōrin Daijin* Agriculture and Forestry Minister
林学校 *nō-rin gakkō* agriculture and forestry school
林省 *Nōrinshō* Ministry of Agriculture and Forestry
9 相 *Nōshō* Agriculture and Forestry Minister
科 *nōka* agriculture department; agricultural course
科大学 *nōka daigaku* agricultural college
政 *nōsei* agricultural administration
政学 *nōseigaku* agricultural economics
10 時 *nōji* the farmers' busy season
家 *nōka* farmhouse; farmers
耕 *nōkō* farming, farm labor
耕用水 *nōkō yōsui* irrigation water
11 道 *nōdō* agricultural road
婦 *nōfu* woman farmer
務 *nōmu* agricultural affairs
産 *nōsan* agricultural products
産物 *nōsambutsu* agricultural products
12 場 *nōjō* farm, ranch, plantation
期 *nōki* farming season
閑 *nōkan* farmers' slack season
閑期 *nōkanki* farmers' slack season
13 園 *nōen* farm, plantation
業 *nōgyō* agriculture
業大学 *nōgyō daigaku* agricultural college
業国 *nōgyōkoku* agricultural nation
業協同組合 *nōgyō kyōdō kumiai* agricultural cooperative
業組合 *nōgyō kumiai* agricultural association
16 機具 *nōkigu* farm equipment
薬品 *nōyakuhin* agricultural chemicals
繁 *nōhan* farmers' busy season
繁休暇 *nōhan kyūka* school vacation during the busy farming season
繁期 *nōhanki* the farmers' busy season
17 鍛冶 *nōkaji* a farm blacksmith

RAD. 辵 162

Always used as an enclosure in the modified form 辶 (2 strokes) or 辶 (3 strokes).
Shinnyū "advancing" enclosure (like that of *shin, susumu* "to advance").
Nickname: Road (as in 道 *michi* road).

1

辷 6009 / J6d68 / M38703 (国字) *sube(ru)* slide, glide, skate; be slippery; slip; fail in exams.

2

B 込 6010 / J397e / M38712 (国字) *ko(mu)* be crowded; requiring (a lot of work). *ko(meru)* include; load (a gun); concentrate on; devote oneself to. *-ko(mu)* (get) into, (slip) into, (fall) into. *ko(mi)* mixture; a line of plants. *-ko(mi) de* in bulk; included.

2 入 *ko(mi)-i(ru)* be complicated
3 上 *ko(mi)-a(geru)* feel nauseated, feel like vomiting; be filled (with anger)
5 矢 *ko(me)ya, ko(mi)ya* ramrod
6 合 *ko(mi)-a(u)* be crowded, be jammed. *ko(mi)a(i)* a crowd
8 物 *ko(me)mono, ko(mi)mono* stuffing
直 *ko(me)-nao(su)* reload

A **辺** 6011 / J4a55 / M38710′ **邊** 6124 / J6e34 / M39216 HEN side; boundary, border; beach; region, district, rural areas; vicinity; approximation. *ata(ri), hoto(ri), he* vicinity. *-be* vicinity.

3 土 *hendo* remote region
5 民 *hemmin* people in the deep rural areas
6 地 *henchi* remote place
防 *hembō* frontier defenses
9 要 *hen'yō* frontier fort
10 陲 *hensui* remote place
陬 *hensū* deep rural areas
11 涯 *hengai* limit, end, extremity
12 幅 *hempuku* personal appearance
13 鄙 *hempi na* remote, secluded
塞 *hensai* frontier fort
14 境 *henkyō* frontier, remote region
境精神 *henkyō seishin* frontier spirit
19 疆 *henkyō* frontier, remote region

辻 6012 / J4454 / M38711 (国字) *tsuji* crossroad, street crossing, street corners; streets; roadside.

4 辻 *tsujitsuji ni* at every street corner
5 占 *tsujiura* omen, divining papers, fortunetelling strips of paper
6 自動車 *tsuji jidōsha* taxi
7 車 *tsujiguruma* jinricksha for hire
8 店 *tsuji mise* corner store
9 待 *tsujima(chi)* waiting to be hired
便所 *tsuji benjo* public lavatory
10 馬車 *tsuji basha* cab
11 斬 *tsujigi(ri)* street murder
堂 *tsujidō* wayside shrine
商人 *tsuji shōnin* street vendor
強盗 *tsuji gōtō* highway robbery, holdup
12 番 *tsujiban* guard, watchperson
番人 *tsujibannin* guard, watchperson
13 褄 *tsujitsuma* consistency, coherence, reasonableness
14 説法 *tsuji seppō* street preaching
15 談義 *tsuji dangi* street lecture; wayside storytelling
17 講釈 *tsujigōshaku* wayside storyteller

3

迄 6013 / J4b78 / M38724 KITSU. *made* to, till, until, up to; as far as; to the extent of; limited to. *made ni* by, before, not later than.

B **迅** 6014 / J3f57 / M38727′ JIN. *haya(i)* fast.

9 速 *jinsoku* swiftness, promptness
12 雷 *jinrai* thunderclap; suddenness

辿 6015 / J4329 / M38718 TEN. *tado(ru)* follow (a road), pursue (a course), follow up.

10 書 *tado(ri)ga(ki)* poor handwriting
12 着 *tado(ri)-tsu(ku)* grope along to, struggle on to
14 読 *tado(ri)yo(mi)* reading with difficulty

迂 6016 / J312a / M38722 **迃** 6017 / J-X / M38723 U roundabout way.

6 回 *ukai* detour, roundabout way
曲 *ukyoku suru* meander
12 遠 *uen na* roundabout; devious; circumlocutory
13 路 *uro* detour, roundabout way
愚 *ugu* stupidity, silliness
17 闊 *ukatsu* carelessness, stupidity
濶 *ukatsu* carelessness, stupidity

4

迚 6018 / J6d69 / M38773 (国字) *totemo* some way or other; very.

B **迎** 6019 / J375e / M38748′ GEI. *muka(eru)* meet, greet, welcome; invite, engage. *muka(e)* meeting; person sent to meet.

2 入 *muka(e)-i(reru)* usher in, welcome
4 水 *muka(e)mizu* priming
火 *muka(e)bi* fire to welcome returning souls
5 打 *muka(e)-u(tsu)* await and attack an approaching enemy

6 合 *geigō* flattery, ingratiation
7 角 *muka(e)kaku* angle of attack
車 *muka(e)guruma* vehicle sent to meet someone
8 送 *geisō* meeting and seeing off
9 春 *geishun* welcoming the new year
10 酒 *muka(e)zake* drinking again (the next day), hair of the dog
11 接 *geisetsu* meeting and entertaining
15 撃 *geigeki* ambush attack
賓 *geihin* welcoming guests
賓館 *geihinkan* reception hall

A **返** 6020 J4a56 M38758' HEN answer. *kae(ru)* go back; return to former employer; (colors) fade. *kae(su)* return, give back; repay; put back; overturn; requite (favors); take vengeance; turn around; answer; regurgitate. *kae(shi)* return gift; (money) change; return poem; answer; change of scene. *(o)kae(shi)* return; reply.
2 刀 *kae(su) katana de* (killing) with the return blow of the sword
3 上 *henjō suru* send back, return, resign (a rank)
5 付 *hempu suru* give back, return
礼 *henrei* return gift
本 *hempon* books and magazines returned
6 返 *kae(su)gae(su)* repeatedly. *kae(su)gae(su) mo* really, certainly
7 戻 *henrei suru* give back, return
却 *henkyaku* return, repayment
花 *kae(ri)bana* unseasonable flower
8 金 *henkin* repayment
送 *hensō suru* send back, return
忠 *kae(ri)chū* treachery, betrayal
事 *henji* reply
9 咲 *kae(ri)za(ku)* bloom a second time. *kae(ri)za(ki)* second bloom; a comeback (in business)
盃 *hempai suru* offer the cup in return
点 *kae(ri)ten* marks indicating the Japanese order of reading Chinese (*kambun*)
品 *hempin* returned goods
信 *henshin* reply
信料 *henshinryō* return postage
10 納 *hennō* return, restoration
討 *kae(ri)u(chi)* killing a would-be avenger
書 *hensho* reply
11 済 *hensai* payment, refunding, redemption, repayment
12 答 *hentō* reply
着 *kae(ri)-tsu(ku)* get back, return
報 *hempō* requital, retaliation, retort
13 辞 *henji* reply
電 *henden* reply telegram
照 *henshō* evening glow
14 歌 *henka, kae(shi)uta* poem in reply
15 還 *henkan* return, restoration, repayment

A **近** 6021 J3661 M38752' KIN. *chika(i)* early, immediate; near, short (road), close by; akin to; nearby, bordering on, verge of, tantamount to; intimate, friendly. *chika(zuku)* approach, get acquainted with, associate with. *chika(zukeru)* allow to approach, associate with. *chika(zuki)* acquaintance, friendship. *chika(ku)* before long; nearby, neighborhood, vicinity; approximately. *chika(shii)* intimate, friendly.
4 火 *kinka, chikabi* nearby fire
辺 *kimpen* neighborhood, vicinity
日 *kinjitsu* soon, in a few days
日点 *kinjitsuten* perihelion
5 目 *chikame* nearsightedness; short sightedness
付 *chikazu(ki)* acquaintance, friendship
刊 *kinkan* recent issue; forthcoming book
古 *kinko* early modern age
民 *kimmin* nearby peoples
世 *kinsei* recent times
世史 *kinseishi* modern history
代 *kindai* modern times
代人 *kindaijin* modern person, a modern
代化 *kindaika* modernization
代文学 *kindai bungaku* modern literature
代史 *kindaishi* modern history
代主義 *kindai shugi* modernism
代主義者 *kindai shugisha* modernist
代的 *kindaiteki* modern
代味 *kindaimi* modernity
代国家 *kindai kokka* a modern nation
代思想 *kindai shisō* modern thought, modernism
代戦 *kindaisen* modern warfare
代劇 *kindaigeki* modern drama

6 臣 *kinshin* trusted vassal, personal attendant
回 *chikamawa(ri)* neighborhood, vicinity; shortcut
因 *kin'in* immediate cause
近 *chikajika, kinkin* nearness; before long, at an early date
年 *kinnen* in recent years
在 *kinzai* neighboring villages, suburban districts
地点 *kinchiten* perigee
似 *kinji* approximation; very similar
似值 *kinjichi* approximate decimal fraction
7 体 *kintai* recent style
作 *kinsaku* recent literary work
村 *kinson* neighboring villages
状 *kinjō* one's daily life; recent events; present situation
来 *kinrai* recently
8 国 *kingoku* neighboring countries or districts
侍 *kinji* attendant, suite
況 *kinkyō* recent condition
郊 *kinkō* suburbs
東 *Kintō* Near East
事 *kinji* recent events
所 *kinjo* neighborhood, vicinity
所回 *kinjomawa(ri)* formal neighborhood calls
所合壁 *kinjo gappeki* immediate neighborhood
所迷惑 *kinjo meiwaku* neighborhood nuisance
所泣 *kinjona(kase)* troubling the neighbors
所騒 *kinjosawa(gase)* neighborhood disturbance
9 姻 *kin'in* near relative
県 *kinken* neighboring prefectures
海 *kinkai* coastal waters, adjacent seas
海物 *kinkaimono* inshore fish
海航路 *kinkai kōro* coastal service
海魚 *kinkaigyo* inshore fish
海魚業 *kinkaigyogyō* coastwise fisheries
10 時 *kinji* recently
郷 *kingō* neighboring districts, countryside
家 *kinka* neighboring house
11 道 *chikamichi* short cut
頃 *chikagoro* recently, nowadays
情 *kinjō* one's daily life; recent events; present situation
接 *kinsetsu* neighboring, adjacent
寄 *chikayo(ru)* approach. *chikayo(seru)* allow to approach, associate with
習 *kinjū* daimyo's personal retainer
著 *kincho* recent (literary) work
距離 *kinkyori* short distance, close range
視 *kinshi* nearsightedness, shortsightedness
視眼 *kinshigan* nearsightedness, shortsightedness
眼 *chikame, kingan* nearsightedness, shortsightedness
眼的 *kinganteki* nearsighted
眼者 *kingansha* nearsighted person
眼鏡 *kingankyō* glasses for the nearsighted
12 間 *chikama* neighborhood, vicinity
傍 *kimbō* vicinity, neighborhood, environs
詠 *kin'ei* recent poems
着 *kinchaku* recent arrival
13 電 *kinden* recent cable, wire just received
業 *kingyō* recent (literary) work
14 境 *kinkyō* close land
隣 *kinrin* neighborhood, vicinity
15 影 *kin'ei* recent portrait
畿 *Kinki* the Osaka-Kyoto area, the prefectures of Hyogo, Kyoto, Osaka, Mie, Nara, Shiga, and Wakayama
畿地方 *Kinki chihō* the Osaka-Kyoto area, the prefectures of Hyogo, Kyoto, Osaka, Mie, Nara, Shiga, and Wakayama
16 衛 *konoe* imperial guards; bodyguards
衛兵 *konoehei* imperial guards; bodyguards
衛隊 *konoetai* imperial guards; bodyguards
親 *kinshin* near relative
親者 *kinshinsha, kinshinja* near relative
親相姦 *kinshin sōkan* incest
親結婚 *kinshin kekkon* consanguineous marriage

5

迹 6022 / J4676 / M38793 See 邇 6122.

迯 6023 / J6d6d / M38802 See 逃 6038.

迢 6024 J6d6b M38781 CHŌ far; distant; high; tall.

迥 6025 J6d6a M38786 KEI. *haru(ka)* far, distant.

迪 6026 J6d6c M38795 TEKI road, path, way; teach; lead; advance.

迦 6027 J3260 M38789 KA, KE (used phonetically).

迨 6028 J-X M38777 SHŌ. *made* to, till, until, up to, as far as; to the extent of; limited to. *made ni* by, before, not later than.

B 迭 6029 J4533 M38800' TETSU alternation.
5 立 *tetsuritsu suru* alternate

A 述 6030 J3d52 M38803' JUTSU state, speak, relate. *nobe(ru)* state, speak, recite, relate, mention.
7 作 *jutsusaku* writing a book, literary work
10 部 *jutsubu* predicate
14 語 *jutsugo* predicate
16 懐 *jukkai* recollections, reminiscences; *shukkai* lament

B 迫 6031 J4777 M38797' HAKU. *se(maru)* press for, urge, force, spur on; approach; gain on, close in on; be on the verge of; be imminent. *se(ru)* urge on.
2 力 *hakuryoku* force; intensity; appeal
3 上 *se(ri)-a(geru)* push up
5 出 *se(ri)-da(su)* push out, come up through a trap door
9 促 *sema(ri)-unaga(su)* urge and press on
持 *serimo(chi)* arch
持台 *serimo(chi)dai* abutment
10 真 *hakushin* truthfulness to life, verisimilitude
真性 *hakushinsei* truthfulness to life, verisimilitude
害 *hakugai* oppression, persecution
害者 *hakugaisha* persecutor
12 間 *hazama* interval; interstice; ravine, glen; loophole (in a castle)
15 撃 *hakugeki suru* attack at close quarters
撃砲 *hakugekihō* mortar, mine thrower

6

廼 6032 J6d72 M38831 DAI. NAI. *sunawa(chi)* namely, that is to say. *nanji* you. *no* noun modification particle.

迴 6033 J6d6f M38818 KAI go around.

逅 6034 J6d70 M38848 KŌ meet.

迹 6035 J6d71 M38827 SEKI. SHAKU. *ato* mark, print, impression; track, trace, trail; wake; marks, traces, evidence; scar; ruins; precedent.

迸 6036 J6d7e M38867 迸 6066 J-X M38929 HŌ. *hotobashi(ru), tobashi(ru)* gush out, spurt, spout, splash, spray. *tabashi(ru)* flay about, scatter. *tobatchi(ri)* splash, spray; involvement.

A 迷 6037 J4c42 M38825' MEI. *mayo(u)* be perplexed, be in doubt, hesitate, vacillate, go astray, err; be tempted; be infatuated; be misguided. *mayo(wakasu), mayo(wasu)* perplex; mislead, deceive; tempt; seduce; charm, infatuate. *samayo(u)* wander around, stray, loiter. *mayo(i)* perplexity, doubt; ignorance; illusion, delusion, infatuation, skepticism.
2 入 *mayo(i)-i(ru)* wander into
3 子 *maigo, mayo(i)go* lost child
子札 *maigofuda* child's identification tag
4 込 *mayo(i)-ko(mu)* go astray, lose one's way
5 去 *mayo(i)-sa(ru)* wander away
出 *mayo(i)-de(ru)* go astray. *mayo(i)-da(su)* lead astray, cause to wander
6 妄 *meimō* illusion, fallacy, delusion
7 言 *yomaigoto* grumbling, muttering, nonsense
9 信 *meishin* superstition
信家 *meishinka* superstitious person
10 宮 *meikyū* maze, labyrinth; mystery
11 彩 *meisai* camouflage
12 惑 *meiwaku* trouble, annoyance
惑気 *meiwakuge na* bothersome
13 路 *meiro* maze, labyrinth, blind alley

7 見角言谷豆豕豸貝赤走足身車辛辰【辵辶】6 邑阝酉釆里

夢 *meimu* illusion, fallacy, delusion
想 *meisō* fallacy
15 論 *meiron* fallacy, absurd opinion
16 離 *samayo(i)-hana(reru)* stray away, wander away

B **逃** 6038 / J4628 / M38845' Tō. *nige(ru)* flee, run away, escape; shirk, evade, back out. *noga(su), niga(su)* let go, set free, let escape, miss (a chance). *noga(reru)* escape, avoid, evade, shirk.
2 了 *ni(ge)-ō(seru)* escape safely
3 口 *ni(ge)guchi* way of escape, loophole
口上 *ni(ge)kōjō* excuse, evasion, quibbling
亡 *tōbō* flight, escape, abscondence, desertion
亡者 *tōbōsha* absconder, deserter, escapee
4 水 *ni(ge)mizu* mirage of water
込 *ni(ge)-ko(mu)* run into, seek shelter
支度 *ni(ge)jitaku* preparation for flight
5 打 *ni(ge) (o) u(tsu)* flee from responsibility
去 *ni(ge)-sa(ru)* flee away
失 *ni(ge)-u(seru)* flee, run away, disappear
出 *ni(ge)-da(su), noga(re)-de(ru)* flee, run away
6 回 *ni(ge)-mawa(ru)* run around trying to escape
返 *ni(ge)-kae(ru)* flee home
7 足 *ni(ge)ashi* flight; preparation to flee
言葉 *ni(ge)kotoba* excuse, evasion, quibbling
走 *ni(ge)-hashi(ru)* flee, run away. *tōsō* flight, desertion, escape
走者 *tōsōsha* fugitive, deserter
8 延 *ni(ge)-no(biru)* escape safely
迷 *ni(ge)-mayo(u)* flee hither and yon
易 *ni(ge)yasu(i)* evanescent
9 途 *ni(ge)michi* way of escape, loophole
後 *ni(ge)-oku(reru)* fail to escape
10 残 *noga(re)-noko(ru)* escape capture
帰 *ni(ge)-kae(ru)* run back, return safely, flee home
11 道 *ni(ge)michi* way of escape; way out (of a difficulty)
張 *ni(ge) (o) ha(ru)* flee from responsibility
眼 *ni(ge) manako* eyes bent on fleeing
12 場 *ni(ge)ba* place of refuge; means of escape; exit. *noga(re)ba* refuge, shelter, asylum
散 *ni(ge)-chi(ru)* disperse, scatter; be routed
散 *tōsan* flight
落 *ni(ge)-o(chiru)* escape safely
惑 *ni(ge)-mado(u)* flee hither and yon
13 損 *ni(ge)-soko(nau)* fail to escape
腰 *ni(ge)goshi* preparation to flee; evasive attitude
路 *ni(ge)michi* way of escape, loophole
隠 *ni(ge)-kaku(reru)* hide
15 避 *tōhi* escape, evasion, flight
18 竄 *tōzan suru* flee

A **送** 6039 / J4177 / M38842' Sō sending. *oku(ru)* send, ship; transmit; remit; see off; see home, escort; spend (one's time), live (a life); add *okurigana* (*kana* showing inflection).
4 火 *oku(ri)bi* bonfire sending off the spirits
込 *oku(ri)-ko(mu)* see (someone) home; usher in. *oku(ri)ko(mi)* feeding (a machine)
5 付 *sōfu* sending, forwarding, remitting
主 *oku(ri)nushi* sender
出 *oku(ri)-da(su)* forward, send out; see (a person) out, send away
本 *sōhon* delivery of books
本料 *sōhonryō* book delivery charge
6 返 *oku(ri)-kae(su)* send back, repatriate
先 *oku(ri)saki* forwarding address, cosignee
仮名 *oku(ri)gana* suffixed *kana* showing inflection
気管 *sōkikan* air pipe, air duct
迎 *sōgei, oku(ri)muka(e)* seeing (someone) off and meeting upon return
迎者 *sōgeisha* people seeing (someone) off and meeting on return
7 状 *oku(ri)jō* invoice
兵 *sōhei* dispatch of troops
呈 *sōtei* presentation
言葉 *oku(ri) kotoba* cue, catchword
別 *sōbetsu* farewell, send-off
別会 *sōbetsukai* farewell party
8 届 *oku(ri)-todo(keru)* see (a person) home; usher in

油管 *sōyukan* oil pipeline
受信機 *sōjushinki* transceiver
金 *sōkin* remittance; remitting
金人 *sōkinnin* remitter
金先 *sōkinsaki* person to whom remitted
金額 *sōkingaku* amount remitted
9 風 *sōfū* air blast, forced draft, ventilation
風機 *sōfūki* air blower, ventilator
信 *sōshin* transmission of a message
信局 *sōshinkyoku* transmitting station
信機 *sōshinki* transmitter
10 狼 *oku(ri)ōkami* a following wolf; a man who persists in following a woman
料 *sōryō* postage, shipping cost
致 *sōchi* sending, dispatch, commitment
荷 *sōka* consignment, forwarding, delivery
11 達 *sōtatsu* delivery, dispatch
球 *sōkyū* handball; throwing a ball; missing a ball (by catchers)
12 検 *sōken* sending to the prosecuter
葬 *sōsō* funeral
13 賃 *oku(ri)chin* shipping charges
電 *sōden* transmission of electricity
電線 *sōdensen* power line
話 *sōwa* transmission (of a telephone message)
話口 *sōwaguchi* telephone mouthpiece
話料 *sōwaryō* (telephone) charges
話器 *sōwaki* transmitter
15 還 *sōkan* repatriation
還者 *sōkansha* repatriate
20 籍 *sōseki* transfer of domicile

A **退** 6040 / J4260 / M38839' TAI. *shirizo(ku), shisa(ru), shiza(ru), susa(ru)* retreat, withdraw; retire, resign. *shirizo(keru)* repel, drive away, expel; depose; keep away; reject, turn down. *no(ku)* get out of the way; go away. *no(keru), do(keru)* get rid of, remove; finish; omit, exclude. *hi(ku)* retreat, withdraw, retire; subside, abate, ebb. *do(ku)* get out of the way, move aside.
3 下 *taige suru* retire from the imperial presence
4 化 *taika* degeneration, retrogression, depravation, atrophy
引 *no(p)piki(naranu)* unavoidable, inevitable, imperative
5 庁 *taichō* leaving the office
去 *taikyo* evacuation, withdrawal, removal, exodus, departure
出 *taishutsu* leaving, withdrawal
出時間 *taishutsu jikan* closing hour
6 色 *taishoku* fading; faded color
行 *taikō* regression (in psychoanalysis)
任 *tainin* retirement from office
会 *taikai* withdrawal from membership
7 身 *taishin* dropping out of government work
廷 *taitei* leaving the court
却 *taikyaku* retreat, withdrawal
位 *taii* abdication
位説 *taiisetsu* proposed abdication
社 *taisha* retirement from a firm; leaving the office
社時間 *taisha jikan* closing time
役 *taieki* retirement from military service
役後 *taiekigo* after retirement from military service
役軍人 *taieki gunjin* war veteran
役艦 *taiekikan* decommissioned warship
8 治 *taiji* subjugation; extermination; crusade (against); control
京 *taikyō* leaving the capital; leaving Tokyo
官 *taikan* retirement from office
歩 *taiho suru* retrograde, degenerate; deteriorate
学 *taigaku* dropping out of school
屈 *taikutsu* tedium, boredom
屈凌 *taikutsushino(gi)* killing time
9 院 *taiin* leaving the hospital
陣 *taijin* decampment, retirement
軍 *taigun* retreat, withdrawal
紅色 *taikōshoku* pink color
10 席 *taiseki suru* leave one's seat; withdraw, retire
修 *taishū* spiritual retreat
時 *hikedoki* closing time
校 *taikō* expulsion from school; leaving school
耕 *taikō* retirement in the country
11 敗 *taihai* defeat
転 *taiten* distraction. *taiten(naku)* diligently
12 場 *taijō suru* leave, walk out, exit, withdraw
散 *taisan suru* disperse, break up (a crowd)
廃 *taihai* deterioration, degeneration, laxness, corruption, decadence, ruin

廃的 *taihaiteki* corrupt
13 路 *tairo* path of retreat
勢 *taisei* downward tendency, decline, decay
隠 *taiin* retirement
隠料 *taiinryō* retirement allowance
14 蔵 *taizō* hoarding
蔵者 *taizōsha* hoarder
蔵物資 *taizō busshi* hoarded goods
15 避 *taihi* taking refuge, evacuation
潮 *taichō* ebb tide, low tide
17 嬰 *taiei* conservatism; retrogression
嬰的 *taieiteki* conservative, negative, passive, destructive
18 職 *taishoku* retirement (from office)
職手当 *taishoku teate* retirement allowance, severance pay
職年限 *taishoku nengen* age limit
職年齢 *taishoku nenrei* retirement age
職金 *taishokukin* retirement allowance
職者 *taishokusha* retired employee
職資金 *taishoku shikin* retirement allowance
職積立金 *taishoku tsumitatekin* retirement fund
20 譲 *taijō* modesty, humility

A **逆** 6041/J3555/M38849' GYAKU, GEKI reverse, inverse, opposite, unnatural; wicked; traitorous. *saka(rau)* oppose, act contrary to; offend. *gyaku ni* conversely, inversely, contrariwise, on the other hand, vice versa. *saka(sa), saka(sama), saka(shima)* reverse, inversion, upside down.

3 子 *sakago* breech presentation (in obstetrics)
下 *gyakka, gyakuka* nose dive
上 *nobo(seru)* be dizzy, be feverish, get excited, be enthusiastic over. *gyakujō, nobose* rush of blood to the head, dizziness; madness, distraction
叉 *sakamata* killer whale
4 心 *gyakushin* treachery, perfidy, treason
手 *gyakute* foul trick, dirty trick. *sakate ni* with point downward, (holding) upside down
日 *gyakubi* evil day (for fishermen)
水 *gyakusui* water diverted to check a flood
卍 *sakasa manji* reversed swastika, Western swastika
比 *gyakuhi* inverse ratio
比例 *gyakuhirei* inverse proportion
5 用 *gyakuyō* reverse use, perversion
目 *sakame* interlocked grain; against the grain
立 *sakada(teru) vt* stand on end (hair), bristle up, ruffle up (feathers). *sakada(tsu) vi* stand on end, stand up, bristle up, oppose. *saka(rai)-ta(tsu)* rise against. *sakada(chi)* handstand, standing on one's head
6 臣 *gyakushin* rebellious retainer, traitor, insurgent
行 *gyakkō, gyakukō* retrogression, backward movement; countermarch
争 *saka(rai)-araso(u)* rebel against
名 *gyakumyō* posthumous (Buddhist) name
光 *gyakkō* backlighting (in photography)
光線 *gyakkōsen* backlighting (in photography)
7 戻 *gyakumodo(ri)* retrogression, reversal, relapse, reverting to, going back to
乱 *gyakuran* rebellion, insurrection
児 *sakago* breech presentation (in obstetrics)
作用 *gyaku sayō* reaction, adverse effect
攻撃 *gyaku kōgeki* counterattack
8 送 *gyakusō* sending back
追 *sakao(i)* turning to chase one's pursuers
波 *sakanami* choppy sea, head sea
事 *saka(sama)goto* wrong order
宣伝 *gyaku senden* counterpropaganda
効果 *gyakkōka, gyakukōka* reverse effect
性石鹼 *gyakusei sekken* antiseptic soap
9 風 *gyakufū* adverse wind, head wind
恨 *sakaura(mi)* returned hate
剃 *sakazo(ri)* shaving against the "grain"
変 *gyakuhen* adverse change
巻 *sakama(ku)* roll, surge, boil, rage
飛込 *sakato(bi)ko(mi)* headlong plunge
10 進 *gyakushin* backward movement
徒 *gyakuto* rebel, traitor, insurgent
旅 *gekiryo* inn; entertaining travelers
流 *gyakuryū* countercurrent, adverse tide; regurgitation (of blood)
浪 *sakanami* head sea, choppy sea
討 *sakau(chi)* counterattack
剥 *sakamu(ke)* hangnail

[11] 運 *gyakūn* reverse of fortune
捲 *sakama(ku)* roll, surge, boil, rage
理 *gyakuri* paradox
転 *gyakuten* (sudden) change, reversal, retrogression; loop; reverse
産 *gyakuzan* breech presentation
淘汰 *gyaku tōta* reverse selection (in the evolutionary theory)
屏風 *sakasa byōbu* inverted screen (beside a corpse)
捩 *sakane(ji)* twisting contrariwise; retort; turning the tables on
捩食 *sakane(ji) (o) ku(wasu)* criticize in return
[12] 結 *gyaku musu(bi)* granny knot
落 *sakao(toshi)* descending a steep cliff; dropping (something) straight down; steep cliff; storming a castle from the rear; headlong fall; downhill rush
富士 *sakasa Fuji* inverted reflection of Mt Fuji
貸与 *gyaku taiyo* reverse lend-lease
[13] 睫 *sakasa matsuge, sakamatsuge* turned-in eyelashes
賊 *gyakuzoku* rebel, traitor, insurgent
数 *gyakusū* reciprocal number
夢 *sakayume* vain dream
意 *gyakui* treachery, perfidy, treason
[14] 境 *gyakkyō* reverses, adversity, unfavorable circumstances
漕 *gyakusō* backing (with an oar)
睹 *gyakuto* a conjecture
語 *sakasa kotoba* word of opposite meaning
算 *gyakusan* counting backwards
説 *gyakusetsu* paradox
説的 *gyakusetsuteki* paradoxical
[15] 撫 *sakana(de)* rubbing against the grain
潮 *gyakuchō, sakashio* head tide, reverse tide, adverse current, weather tide, cross tide
縁 *gyakuen* irony of fate
撃 *gyakugeki* counterattack
磔 *sakaharitsuke, sakabaritsuke* crucifixion upside down
磔刑 *gyaku haritsuke* crucified upside down
[16] 輸入 *gyaku yunyū* reimportation
輸出 *gyaku yushutsu* re-exportation
[22] 襲 *gyakushū* counterattack, sortie
[23] 鱗 *gekirin* imperial wrath

A **追** 6042 / J4449 / M38836' TSUI. *o(u)* drive away; chase; drive (cattle); follow, pursue (pleasure). *o(tte)* later on, soon after. *o(kkake)* meanwhile, presently. *o(i)-* follow-up. *-o(i)* herder.

[2] 入 *o(i)-i(reru)* chase in
[3] 及 *tsuikyū suru* gain on; overtake, carry out; solve (a crime)
[4] 手 *otte, o(i)te* tail wind; pursuer
込 *o(i)-ko(mu)* corner, drive into; run on (a certain page-in printing); strike inward (a disease)
弔 *tsuichō* mourning
分 *oiwake* forked road, parting of the ways; pack-horse driver's song
分節 *oiwakebushi* pack-horse driver's song
[5] 白 *tsuihaku* postscript
目 *o(i)me* always losing battles
立 *o(i) ta(teru), o(t)ta(teru)* hurry off, urge on, drive away, evict
申 *tsuishin* postscript; additional application
付 *o(i)-tsu(ku), o(t)tsu(ku)* overtake
打 *o(i)u(chi), tsuigeki* pursuit, attack
払 *o(p)para(u), o(i)-hara(u)* drive away, rout. *o(i)bara(i)* later payment
出 *o(i)-da(su)* expel, put out, eject, dismiss
加 *tsuika* addition, appendix, supplement
加予算 *tsuika yosan* additional budget, supplementary estimates
[6] 行 *o(i)-yu(ku)* pursue. *tsuiko* following suit; pursuit
回 *o(i)-mawa(su)* chase around; follow about; order around. *oimawa(shi)* chasing around; factory at-large labor
返 *o(i)-kae(su), o(k)kae(su)* repeal, repulse, send away, turn back
伏 *o(i)-fu(seru)* drive into a corner
羽子 *o(i)hago* playing battledore and shuttlecock
羽根 *o(i)hane* playing battledore and shuttlecock
而 *otte* soon, afterwards
而書 *ottega(ki)* postscript
[7] 走 *o(i)-hashi(rasu)* chase away. *tsuisō* pursuit
尾 *tsuibi* pursuit
迫 *o(i)-sema(ru)* overtake

伸 *tsuishin* postscript
抜 *o(i)-nu(ku)* pass (a car), outdistance, outsail, outstrip
利 *tsuiri* seeking only profit
完 *tsuikan suru* complete subsequently
究 *tsuikyū* investigation, inquiry
求 *o(i)-moto(meru), tsuikyū suru* pursue; follow up, seek for
求者 *tsuikyūsha* pursuer
8 金 *o(i)gane* throwing good money after bad
退 *o(i)-no(keru), o(i)-shirizo(keru)* chase (the enemy) back
追 *o(i)o(i) ni* gradually; in due time
送 *tsuisō suru* send promptly afterwards
使 *o(i)-tsuka(u)* work (someone) hard
炊 *o(i)da(ki)* additional boiling (of rice)
肥 *tsuihi, o(i)goe* supplementary fertilizer
突 *tsuitotsu* rear-end collision, bump
注文 *o(i)chūmon* repeat order
取込 *o(t)to(ri)-ko(mu)* pursue and surround
放 *o(i)-hana(tsu)* chase away. *tsuihō* exile, banishment, excommunication, deportation; purge
放人 *tsuihōnin* an exile
放令 *tsuihōrei* purge directive
放令該当者 *tsuihōrei gaitōsha* persons affected by a purge
放者 *tsuihōsha* purgee
放解除 *tsuihō kaijo* depurging
放解除者 *tsuihō kaijosha* depurgee
9 風 *o(i)kaze, o(i)te* tail wind
悔 *tsuikai* repentance
10 修 *tsuishū* requiem mass, memorial service
従 *tsuijū suru* follow; imitate; be servile to. *tsuishō* flattery
捕 *tsuiho suru, tsuibu suru, o(i)-tora(eru)* pursue and capture, hunt down
納 *tsuinō* supplementary payment
記 *tsuiki* postscript
随 *tsuizui suru* follow in the wake of
剥 *o(i)hagi* highway robber
書 *o(tte)ga(ki)* postscript
起訴 *tsuikiso* supplementary indictment
討 *tsuitō, o(i)u(chi)* subjugation, chastisement
討軍 *tsuitōgun* punitive force
11 惜 *tsuiseki* mourning
掛 *o(i)-ka(keru), o(k)ka(keru)* chase, run after
捲 *o(i)-maku(ru)* drive away, rout
崩 *o(i)-kuzu(su)* pursue and crush
悼 *tsuitō* mourning; memorial (address)
悼会 *tsuitōkai* memorial services
悼歌 *tsuitōka* dirge
12 越 *o(i)-ko(su)* pass (a car), outdistance, outsail, outstrip
遣 *o(i)-ya(ru)* drive away
訴 *tsuiso* supplementary suit
散 *o(i)-chi(rasu)* disperse, scatter, drive away, rout
落 *o(i)-oto(su)* chase away; capture (a castle); pillage
善 *tsuizen* Buddhist memorial service
善供養 *tsuizen-kuyō* Buddhist memorial service
13 福 *tsuifuku* requiem mass; memorial service
腹 *o(i)bara, tsuifuku* suicide to follow one's dead master
詰 *o(i)-tsu(meru)* corner, drive to the wall, run down, track down
想 *tsuisō* recollection, reminiscence
試験 *tsuishiken* supplementary exam
頌 *tsuishō suru* confer posthumous honors
跡 *tsuiseki* pursuit
跡者 *tsuisekisha* pursuer
跡機 *tsuisekiki* pursuit plane
14 増 *tsuizō* addition, supplement
認 *tsuinin* ratification, confirmation
銭 *o(i)sen* throwing good money after bad
罰 *tsuibatsu* additional punishment
慕 *tsuibo suru* cherish the memory of, yearn for
徴 *tsuichō* additional collection, supplementary charge
徴金 *tsuichōkin* additional collection, supplementary charge
徴税 *tsuichōzei* supplementary tax
15 縋 *o(i)-suga(ru)* close in on, tread on the heels of
踪 *tsuishō suru* shadow (someone); recollect
撃 *tsuigeki, o(i)u(chi)* pursuit, attack
撃戦 *tsuigekisen* running fight, pursuit battle
撃機 *tsuigekiki* pursuit plane
16 懐 *tsuikai* recollection, reminiscence
憶 *tsuioku* recollection, reminiscence

録 *tsuiroku* supplement, postscript, addendum
18 贈 *tsuizō* posthumous conferment of court rank
蹤 *tsuishō suru* pursue; recollect
21 儺 *tsuina* exorcism
22 籠 *o(i)-ko(meru)* confine in house arrest
25 躡 *tsuijō* pursuit

7

逎 6043 / J6e25 / M38874 See 遒 6077.

迫 6044 / J6d7a / M-X (国字) *sako* valley, ravine. *seko* alpine valley, narrow valley.

逑 6045 / J6d73 / M38878 Kyū gather, meet. *tsureai* spouse, companion.

逖 6046 / J6d78 / M38886 Teki. *tō(i)* far, distant. *haru(ka)* far, distant.

逋 6047 / J6d79 / M38871 Ho flee.

逞 6048 / J6d77 / M38896 Tei. *takuma(shii)* sturdy, brawny, stalwart, masculine; resolute, bold. *takuma(shiku)* vigorously, powerfully. *takuma(shū) suru* give free play to; stretch one's imagination; rage; be rampant; increase in violence.

逍 6049 / J6d76 / M38873 Shō saunder, loaf.
13 遙 *shōyō* ramble, saunder, walk

逡 6050 / J6d75 / M38899 Shun fall back, go ahead.
5 巡 *shunjun* hesitation, vacillation, indecision

B**逝** 6051 / J4042 / M38895 Sei. *yu(ku)* die, pass away.
5 去 *seikyo* death
9 春 *yu(ku) haru* departing spring

逕 6052 / J6d74 / M38883 Kei path.
10 庭 *keitei* difference, discrepancy
13 路 *keiro* course, channel, route

逗 6053 / J3f60 / M38887 Tō stop.
10 留 *tōryū* stay, sojourn
留客 *tōryūkyaku* guest, visitor, sojourner

逢 6054 / J3029 / M38901 Hō. *a(u)* meet, interview. *a(waseru)* introduce, expose to, subject to.
4 引 *aibi(ki)* date, rendezvous, clandestine courting
6 曳 *aibiki* lovers' secret meeting, a date
12 着 *hōchaku* face, encounter
19 瀬 *ōse* meeting, tryst, date

B**逓** 6055 / J447e / M38881' **遞** 6095 / J6e2a / M39045 Tei in turn; sending (parcels) in feudal times.
5 加 *teika* successive increase, acceleration
6 伝 *teiden* relaying a message; the post horse; the post rider
次 *teiji* in order, successively
8 送 *teisō* forwarding
9 信 *teishin* communications
信省 *Teishinshō* (prewar) Communications Ministry
12 減 *teigen* successive diminution
14 増 *teizō* gradual increase

B**逐** 6056 / J4360 / M38877 Chiku. *o(u)* drive away; chase; drive (cattle); follow, pursue (pleasure). *to(geru)* accomplish, attain; commit (suicide).
1 一 *chikuichi* one by one, in detail, minutely
4 日 *chikujitsu* daily, day after day
6 次 *chikuji* one by one, point by point, in order, in succession, successively, gradually
年 *chikunen* annually, year by year
字的 *chikujiteki* literal, word for word
7 条 *chikujō* section by section, point by point
11 鹿 *chikuroku* competition (in elections)
鹿戦 *chikurokusen* election campaign
13 電 *chikuden* flight, abscondence
14 語的 *chikugoteki* literal, word for word
語訳 *chikugoyaku* literal translation

B **途** 6057 / J4553 / M38882' To, Zu way, road. *michi* road, path, lane, way, street, highway, route; journey; distance; course, way, means.

3 上 *tojō* on the way; on the road
4 切 *togi(reru)* break, pause, be interrupted
切途切 *togi(re)-togi(re)* interruption
方 *tohō* way, destination, direction, reason
方無 *tohō(mo)na(i)* extraordinary, absurd, preposterous, exorbitant, ludicrous
方暮 *tohō (ni) ku(reru)* be at one's wit's end
中 *tochū* on the way, enroute
中下車 *tochū gesha* stopover, getting off before the destination shown on the ticket
中計時 *tochū keiji* lap time (in races)
6 次 *toji* on the way
12 絶 *toda(eru)* cease, stop, end. *tozetsu* suspension, interruption
14 端 *totan ni* in the act of, just as
19 轍無 *totetsu(mo)na(i)* wild, absurd, exorbitant

這 6058 / J4767 / M38889 Sha. *ha(u)* crawl, creep; grovel; trail (vines).

2 入 *hai(ru)* enter, break into; join; enroll; contain, hold; accommodate; have (an income of)
入口 *hairiguchi* entrance
入込 *hai(ri)-ko(mu)* get into, come in
3 下 *ha(i)-o(riru)* crawl down
上 *ha(i)-a(garu)* crawl up, climb up
4 込 *ha(i)-ko(mu)* crawl into
5 出 *ha(i)-de(ru), ha(i)-da(su)* crawl out
6 回 *ha(i)-mawa(ru)* crawl about
8 松 *haimatsu* creeping pine
物 *ha(u)mono* creeping things
歩 *ha(i)-aru(ku)* crawl along
10 般 *shahan no* such, of this type
這 *ha(i)ha(i)* creeping, crawling. *hōhō* confusedly; proceeding with difficulty; perplexity
這体 *hōhō(no)tei* hurriedly, precipitately
12 渡 *ha(i)-wata(ru)* crawl across; walk a short distance
登 *ha(i)-nobo(ru)* crawl up, climb up
21 纏 *ha(i)-matsuwa(ru)* crawl up and cling to

B **透** 6059 / J4729 / M38876' Tō. *tō(ru)* permeate, penetrate. *su(ku)* be transparent; be seen through; be thin; leave a gap. *su(kasu)* leave a space; thin (trees); make transparent; look through. *su(kashi)* watermark; openwork; transparent. *su(ki)* time; leisure; gap, crack; room space; chance; unpreparedness, unguarded moment. *su(kasazu)* at once, right away. *tō(su)* let (light) through, penetrate.

5 目 *sukime* crevice, gap, space
写 *tōsha, su(ki)utsu(shi)* tracing, copy
写紙 *tōshashi* tracing paper
7 見 *su(ki)mi* stealing a glance; casting a furtive glance
8 明 *tōmei* transparency
明体 *tōmeitai* a transparent medium
明度 *tōmeido* transparency, clearness
9 通 *su(ki)-tō(ru)* be transparent
11 彫 *su(kashi)bori* openwork
過 *tōka* permeability
過性 *tōkasei* permeability
視 *tōshi* seeing through; clairvoyance
視力 *tōshiryoku* penetration; psychic powers
視図 *tōshizu* cutaway view
視者 *tōshisha* clairvoyance
視画 *tōshiga* perspective drawing
視画法 *tōshigahō* perspective
12 間 *su(ki)ma* crevice, gap, opening, space
絵 *su(kashi)e* transparency (pictures)
14 察 *tōsatsu* insight, discernment
模様 *su(kashi) moyō* designs in a transparent medium
15 徹 *su(ki)-tō(ru)* be transparent, be clear, be seen through. *tōtetsu suru* penetrate, pierce, permeate; be transparent; prevail; penetrating; coherent. *tōtetsu(shita)* transparent, clear; pure

A **速** 6060 / J422e / M38897' Soku. *haya(i), sumi(yakana)* speedy, prompt, swift. *haya(meru) vt* hasten, precipitate, accelerate, expedite; advance (the date).

2 力 *sokuryoku* speed, velocity, rate
5 写 *sokusha* quick copying; snapshot
6 成 *sokusei* quick training, short course instruction
成科 *sokuseika* short course, intensive course
7 決 *sokketsu* quick decision, snap judgment

[8] 刻 *sokkoku* instantly, immediately
歩 *hayaashi, sokuho* quick march, quick time, fast walking, trot
効 *sokkō* immediate effect
効薬 *sokkōyaku* quick remedy
[9] 度 *sokudo* speed, velocity, pace, rate; tempo (in music), time
度計 *sokudokei* speedometer
[10] 座 *sokuza* prompt, impromptu
射 *sokusha* quick firing, quick fire
射砲 *sokushahō* rapid-firing gun
記 *sokki* shorthand
記者 *sokkisha* shorthand writer
記術 *sokkijutsu* shorthand, stenography
記録 *sokkiroku* shorthand notes
[11] 球 *sokkyū* fast ball
断 *sokudan* prompt decision; hasty conclusion, snap judgment
達 *sokutatsu* special delivery
達郵便 *sokutatsu yūbin* special delivery
[12] 答 *sokutō* prompt answer
報 *sokuhō* urgent message
報板 *sokuhōban* a newspaper bulletin board
[13] 戦即決 *sokusen-sokketsu* blitz warfare
[14] 読 *sokudoku* rapid reading
算 *sokusan* rapid calculation

A **造** 6061 / J4224 / M38898' ZŌ. *tsuku(ru)* make, create, manufacture, prepare, draw up, write, compose; build; coin; cultivate; organize, establish; make up (a face), trim (a tree); fabricate; prepare food; commit (sin). *tsuku(ri)* make, structure, construction; physique, build; workmanship; (a woman's) makeup; cultivation; a mounting. *-zuku(ri)* made of; work; architectural style.
[3] 上 *tsuku(ri)-a(geru)* build up; complete
[4] 方 *tsuku(ri)kata* way of making; recipe, how to grow (something); style of building; construction; workmanship
反 *zōhan* revolution
化 *zōka* creation, nature
仏 *zōbutsu* making (Buddhist) images
[5] 付 *tsuku(ri)-tsu(keru)* fix, fasten firmly. *tsuku(ri)tsu(ke)* fixture, built-in furnishings
主 *tsuku(ri)nushi* creator, maker; the Creator
出 *tsuku(ri)-da(su)* make, manufacture, raise (crops)
本 *zōhon* bookbinding
石税 *zōkokuzei* brewage tax
[6] 血 *zōketsu* blood making
成 *tsuku(ri)-na(su), zōsei* create
返 *tsuku(ri)-kae(su)* make over again
合 *tsuku(ri)-a(waseru)* make two (things) and join (them) together; make a duplicate
寺 *zōji* temple building
[7] 言 *zōgen, tsuku(ri)goto* fabrication, lie, false report
声 *tsuku(ri)goe* unnatural voice; imitating voice
花 *tsuku(ri)bana, zōka* artificial flower
形 *zōkei* modeling, molding
形美術 *zōkei bijutsu* sculpture and the plastic arts
兵 *zōhei* ordnance, arms manufacture
兵廠 *zōheishō* arms factory, arsenal, armory
作 *zōsaku* making; house fixtures; facial features. *zōsa* trouble, difficulty
作付 *zōsakutsu(ki)* furnished (house) with fixtures
作無 *zōsana(i)* easy, simple
[8] 直 *tsuku(ri)-nao(su)* remake, rebuild
事 *tsuku(ri)goto* falsehood, fabrication
林 *zōrin* forestation; reforestation
林法 *zōrinhō* forest management, forestry
林学 *zōringaku* the science of forestry
物 *zōbutsu* God's creation, heaven and earth
物主 *Zōbutsushu* Creator, Maker, God
物者 *Zōbutsusha* Creator, Maker, God
[9] 型 *zōkei* modeling, molding
[10] 修 *zōshū suru* construct
笑 *tsuku(ri)wara(i)* a forced laugh
酒 *zōshu* saké brewing
酒屋 *zōshuya* saké brewer
[11] 船 *zōsen* shipbuilding
船所 *zōsenjo* shipyards
船界 *zōsenkai* shipbuilding world
船業 *zōsengyō* shipbuilding industry
[12] 営 *zōei* building, construction
営地 *zōeichi* building site
営物 *zōeibutsu* buildings
営費 *zōeihi* building expenses

13 詣 *zōkei* scholarship, erudition
話 *tsuku(ri)banashi* fabrication
意 *zōi* inventiveness; planning
園 *zōen* landscape gardening
園術 *zōenjutsu* landscape gardening
14 鼻 *zōbi* nasal plastic surgery
語 *zōgo* coined word
15 幣 *zōhei* minting, coinage
幣局 *zōheikyoku* the mint
16 機 *zōki* engine building
20 艦 *zōkan* naval construction

A **連** 6062 / J4f22 / M38902' REN ream; set; party, company, gang, clique; series counter. *tsura(naru)* range, be connected with, join; stand in a row; attend; join one's people (in death). *tsura(neru)* put in a row, join. *tsu(reru)* take (someone) along. *tsu(re)* companion. *(ni) tsu(rete)* in proportion to; accompanied by; to the accompaniment of.

3 山 *renzan* mountain range
下 *tsu(re)-ku(daru)* lead down, bring down
上 *tsu(re)-no(boru)* bring up out of
子 *tsure(k)ko, tsu(re)ko* child brought by second wife or husband. *renji* lattice work
子窓 *renji mado* lattice window
4 日 *renjitsu* day after day, every day
木 *rengi* pestle
中 *renchū, renjū* party, company, clique
5 用 *ren'yō* continuous use
句 *renku* couplet
打 *renda* succession of hits (in baseball)
去 *tsu(re)-sa(ru)* lead away
出 *tsu(re)-da(su)* lead (someone) out, bring out; entice, abduct
立 *tsu(re)da(tsu)* accompany. *renritsu* alliance, coalition, union
立方程式 *renritsu hōteishiki* simultaneous equations
立内閣 *renritsu naikaku* coalition cabinet
6 行 *tsu(re)-yu(ku)* take (someone) along. *renkō suru* walk a suspect to the police
休 *renkyū* consecutive holidays
年 *rennen* every year; many years
名 *remmei* joint signature
安打 *ren'anda* succession of hits (in baseball)
邦 *rempō* federated states, union, commonwealth, federal state; federation
邦政府 *Rempō Seifu* Federal Government
邦準備銀行 *Rempō Jumbi Ginkō* Federal Reserve Bank
合 *tsu(re)-a(u)* keep company with, get married. *rengō* union, combination, federation, alliance. *tsure(ai)* spouse, mate
合国 *rengōkoku* allied nations, allies
合軍 *rengōgun* allied armies
合責任 *rengō sekinin* joint responsibility
合艦隊 *rengō kantai* combined squadron
7 戻 *tsu(re)-modo(su)* take back, bring back, lead back
作 *rensaku* joint authorship; repeated cultivation of the same field
坐 *renza* implication, complicity; sitting in the same seat
判 *rempan, remban* joint signature; joint seal
判状 *rempanjō, rembanjō* jointly sealed compact
8 枝 *renshi* (polite for) the brother of an important personage
夜 *ren'ya* night after night, nightly
呼 *renko* repeated calls
呼音 *renkoon* repetition of a syllable
9 係 *renkei* connection, liaison, contact
枷 *karazao, renka* flail
星 *rensei* binary star
奏 *rensō* instrumental number
袂 *rembei* en masse, all together, in a body
袂辞職 *rembei jishoku* mass resignation
発 *rempatsu* occurring continually; running fire, volley
発銃 *rempatsujū* magazine rifle
10 座 *renza* implication, complicity; sitting in the same seat
借 *renshaku* joint debt
峰 *rempō* series of peaks, range
珠 *renju* five-in-a-row game
破 *rempa* a succession of victories (in games)
記 *renki suru* list, catalog
帰 *tsu(re)-kae(ru)* bring (someone) back
帯 *rentai* joint responsibility, solidarity

帯責任 *rentai sekinin* joint liability
帯責務 *rentai sekimu* joint liability
11 接 *rensetsu* combination, connection
添 *tsu(re)-so(u)* be married to
敗 *rempai* successive defeats
動 *rendō* gearing, linkage, drive
累 *renrui* implication, involvement, complicity
隊 *rentai* regiment
隊長 *rentaichō* regimental commander
隊旗 *rentaiki* regimental colors
12 弾 *tsu(re)bi(ki)* accompaniment, accompanist. *rendan* two-piano number
勝 *renshō* series of victories
衆 *tsu(re)shu* one's companion, one's party
絡 *renraku* connection, contact, liaison, communication
絡船 *renrakusen* ferryboat, connecting steamer
結 *renketsu* coupling, connection, joint; combination
結器 *renketsuki* coupling
結機 *renketsuki* coupling
13 携 *renkei* cooperation, collaboration, association
続 *renzoku* continuation, succession, sequence, series
署 *rensho* joint signature
想 *rensō* association of ideas
盟 *remmei* league, federation, union
載 *rensai suru* publish serially
戦 *rensen* series of battles; every battle
戦連敗 *rensen-rempai* succession of defeats
戦連勝 *rensen-renshō* succession of victories
14 関 *renkan* connection, relation, association
綿 *remmen(taru)* consecutive, continuous
語 *rengo* compound word, phrase
歌 *renga* linked haiku poems
銀 *Rengin* Federal Reserve Bank
銀券 *renginken* Federal Reserve Bank note
16 濁 *rendaku* a euphonic change of an unvoiced to a voiced sound
17 環 *renkan* chain link
18 類 *renrui* same kind; accomplice
顔 *tsu(renai) kao* an unsympathetic countenance
鎖 *rensa* chain, series, links
鎖反応 *rensa hannō* chain reaction
鎖店 *rensaten* chain store
鎖劇 *rensageki* combination of moving pictures and vaudeville
19 禱 *rentō* litany
覇 *rempa* successive championships
繫 *renkei* connection, liaison, contact

A 通 6063 / I444c / M38892' Tsu. Tō. Tsū pass; expert. *tsu(zuru), tsū(jiru)* pass, run; be opened (to traffic); prevail, pervade, transmit (electricity); be well versed in; be understood; become intimate with; communicate secretly with; send in (one's card). *tō(ru)* walk along, pass by; pass through; pass (exams); be known as; be admissible; come in; be understood; reach; draw (on a pipe); drain (as a sink); be consistent. *tō(su)* let (someone) pass; pass (something) through; make way for; let in, admit; usher in; cut through; pierce; permeate, penetrate; carry one's point; persist in; look over (a book); keep on doing, continue; pose as; pass (a law); order (a meal). *kayo(u)* commute; attend (school); ply between; frequent (a place); go (for treatments); circulate; breathe; be charged with. *kayo(wasu), kayo(waseru)* send (to school); charge (with electricity); circulate. *tsū(guru)* make a show of knowledge. *tō(risugari)* on the way. *tsū(jite)* through, via; throughout, all over; total, together with; in collusion with. *tō(shite)* through, through the medium of, through the good offices of; for (five days). *tō(shi)* consecutive (pages). *tō(tte)* via, by way of. *tsū(ji)* bowel evacuation, stool; effect. *tō(ri)* road, street, thoroughfare; street traffic; drainage; penetration (of a voice); kind; suite, set (of furniture); way, manner; reputation, favor; understanding; like, the same. *kayo(i)* daily attendance; living out; plying; a line, a run; bankbook; chit book. *tō(shi) de* straight through, without stopping. *(o)tō(shi) suru* usher in. *tō(shi)* hors d'oeuvre. *tō(shi)-* through (bill of lading). *-tsū* thorough knowledge of, authority on, expert judge, connoisseur; knowledge of the world; occult powers;

part, copy; counter for cables, letters, or copies. *-dō(ri)* street; in accordance with; according to; just as, as. *-dō(shi)* all through (the night); all the time.

1 一遍 *tō(ri)ippen no* casual, passing, perfunctory, formal

2 人 *tsūjin* man about town; a well-informed person; brothel visitor; a romantic man

力 *tsūriki* supernatural power, occult power

4 分 *tsūbun* reduction of fractions to common denominator

切符 *tō(shi)kippu, tō(shi)gippu* through ticket

5 矢 *tō(shi)ya* long-distance archery

弁 *tsūben* interpreter, interpreting

用 *tsūyō* common use, circulation, currency

用口 *tsūyōguchi* service entrance, side door

用門 *tsūyōmon* service entrance, side door

用期間 *tsūyō kikan* period of (a ticket's) validity

6 好 *tsūkō* friendship; amity, friendly relations

交 *tsūkō* diplomatic relations

合 *tsū(ji)-a(waseru) , tsū(ji)-a(u)* plot together. *tō(ri)-a(waseru)* happen to come along

名 *tō(ri)na* one's popular name; house name

気 *tsūki* ventilation, draft, airing

気孔 *tsūkikō* vent

有 *tsūyū no* common

有性 *tsūyūsei* common trait, common properties

行 *tō(ri)-yu(ku)* pass by. *tsūkō* passing, passage, transit, traffic

行人 *tsūkōnin* passerby, pedestrian, wayfarer

行止 *Tsūkōdo(me)* No Thoroughfare, road blocked

行区分 *tsūkō kubun* traffic lane

行券 *tsūkōken* a pass, safe-conduct, toll-road ticket

行料 *tsūkōryō* passage money, toll

行税 *tsūkōzei* transit duty, traveling tax

行権 *tsūkōken* right-of way

7 見 *tsūken* general view, perusal

坊 *tō(sem)bō suru* bar the way, head off; interrupt (by making a human chain)

抜 *tō(ri)-nu(keru)* pass through

狂言 *tō(shi) kyōgen* presentation of a whole play

言 *tsūgen* popular saying

言葉 *tō(ri) kotoba* catchword; thieves' slang, group jargon; a common phrase

告 *tsūkoku* notification, announcement

告書 *tsūkokusho* written notice

告済 *tsūkokuzu(mi)* notified

8 雨 *tō(ri)ame* passing shower

例 *tsūrei* usually, customarily

性 *tsūsei* common quality; common gender

法 *tsūhō* universal law

念 *tsūnen* common sense, generally accepted idea

宝 *tsūhō* coin, currency

券 *tsūken* ticket, pass

者 *tō(ri)mono* well-known person, popular figure, man about town

事 *tsūji* interpreter; (Dutch) interpreter

夜 *tsuya* deathwatch, wake. *tsūya* all night

夜僧 *tsuyasō* priest engaged for a deathwatch

学 *tsūgaku* attending school

学生 *tsūgakusei* day student

知 *tsūchi* notification, information

知洩 *tsūchimo(re)* uninformed of

知書 *tsūchisho* notice

知簿 *tsūchibo* school report card

9 計 *tsūkei* total

則 *tsūsoku* general rules

院中 *tsūinchū* coming for treatments

相場 *tō(ri)sōba* market price; accepted custom

風 *tsūfū* ventilation, airing, draft

風筒 *tsūfūtō* ventilator

風器 *tsūfūki* ventilator, aerator

俗 *tsūzoku* popularity, conventionality

俗小説 *tsūzoku shōsetsu* popular fiction

俗文 *tsūzokubun* popular writing

俗化 *tsūzokuka* popularization

俗体 *tsūzokutai* colloquial style

俗的 *tsūzokuteki* popular

俗語 *tsūzokugo* colloquialism

信 *tsūshin* correspondence, communication, intelligence, information, news, dispatch, report

信士 *tsūshinshi* telegraph operator
信文 *tsūshimbun* written communication
信伝道 *tsūshin dendō* newspaper evangelism
信社 *tsūshinsha* news agency
信妨害 *tsūshin bōgai* communications jamming
信学校 *tsūshin gakkō* correspondence school
信施設 *tsūshin shisetsu* communications systems
信紙 *tsūshinshi* correspondence card
信員 *tsūshin'in* correspondent, reporter
信隊 *tsūshintai* single corps
信販売 *tsūshin hambai* mail-order business; mail-order sale
信教育 *tsūshin kyōiku* education by correspondence
信教授 *tsūshin kyōju* instruction by correspondence
信筒 *tsūshintō* message tube
信費 *tsūshinhi* postage
信路 *tsūshinro* news channel
信網 *tsūshimmō* news-gathering facilities
信線 *tsūshinsen* lines of communication
信機関 *tsūshin kikan* communication facilities
信衛星 *tsūshin eisei* communication satellite
信講座 *tsūshin kōza* correspondence course
信簿 *tsūshimbo* report card
信欄 *tsūshinran* correspondence column
10 称 *tsūshō* popular name, alias
航 *tsūkō suru* navigate, sail, ply
11 廊 *tsuro* passageway, corridor
道 *tō(ri)michi* passage, path, route; one's way; (cattle) runway
達 *tsūtatsu, tsūdatsu* communication, notification; proficiency, mastery, skill
帳 *kayo(i)chō, tsūchō* bankbook; chit book
掛 *tō(ri)ga(karu), tō(ri)-ka(karu)* happen to come along. *tō(ri)ga(kari) ni* as one passes on the way. *tō(ri)ga(ke)* passing on the way
患 *tsūkan* common evil, universal trouble
過 *tō(ri)-su(giru)* to pass, pass through. *tsūka* passage, transit. *tsūka suru* to pass, pass through
過通行権 *tsūkatsūkōken* right of transit passage
過駅 *tsūka eki* a station at which the train does not stop
運 *tsūun* express, transportation, forwarding
運機関 *tsūun kikan* transportation facilities
産相 *Tsūsanshō* Minister of International Trade and Industry
産省 *Tsūsanshō* Ministry of International Trade and Industry
貨 *tsūka* currency
貨収縮 *tsūka shūshuku* (money) deflation
貨膨張 *tsūka bōchō* (money) inflation
訳 *tsūyaku* interpreting; interpreter
訳生 *tsūyakusei* student interpreter
訳官 *tsūyakukan* official interpreter
訳者 *tsūyakusha* interpreter
商 *tsūshō* commerce, trade
商条約 *tsūshō jōyaku* commercial treaty
商航海条約 *tsūshō kōkai jōyaku* treaty of commerce and navigation
商産業省 *Tsūshō-Sangyōshō* Ministry of International Trade and Industry
常 *tsūjō* normally, generally, ordinarily; regular (meeting)
常日 *tsūjōbi* ordinary day, week day, work day
常礼服 *tsūjō reifuku* dress suit
常会員 *tsūjō kaiin* ordinary member
常服 *tsūjōfuku* everyday clothes, business suit
常国会 *tsūjō kokkai* ordinary Diet session
常郵便物 *tsūjō yūbimbutsu* ordinary mail matter
常総会 *tsūjō sōkai* ordinary general meeting
12 越 *tō(ri)-ko(su)* go beyond; pass through; be more than
暁 *tsūgyō* all night; thorough knowledge
詞 *tsūshi* (ancient) interpreter
違 *tō(ri)-chiga(u)* go past (a person)
款 *tsūkan* treachery
筋 *tō(ri)suji* route, course, road
報 *tsūhō* report, bulletin, news
番号 *tō(shi)bangō* serial number
勤 *tsūkin, kayo(i)zuto(me)* living away from one's work
勤電車 *tsūkin densha* commuter train
13 辞 *tsūji* interpreter, (Dutch) interpreter

解 *tsūkai* a commentary
詰 *kayo(i)zu(me)* frequent visiting. *kayo(i)-tsu(meru)* visit frequently
路 *tō(ri)michi, kayo(i)michi, kayo(i)ji* route, path. *tsūro* passageway, path, thoroughfare, entranceway, aisle, catwalk
義 *tsūgi* general principle; common interpretation
電 *tsūden* circular telegram
牒 *tsūchō* notification
牒者 *tsūchōsha* spy, secret agent
話 *tsūwa* phone call
話口 *tsūwaguchi* mouthpiece
話室 *tsūwashitsu* phone booth
話料 *tsūwaryō* phone-call charge
話量 *tsūwaryō* telephone traffic
話管 *tsūwakan* speaking tube
14 関 *tsūkan* customs clearance
説 *tsūsetsu* common opinion
読 *tsūdoku suru* read through
語 *tsūgo* cant phrase, lingo
算 *tsūsan* totaling
15 論 *tsūron* outline, introduction (to literature)
弊 *tsūhei* common evil
16 謀 *tsūbō suru* conspire with, work in concert
薬 *tsū(ji)gusuri* a laxative
覧 *tsūran* general view, perusal
稽古 *kayo(i)geiko* taking lesson
18 観 *tsūkan* general view
21 魔 *tō(ri)ma* phantom

見角言谷豆豕豸貝赤走足身車辛辰【辵辶】7 邑阝酉釆里

8

達 6064 / J6d7d / M-X Nonstandard for **達** 6088.

遁 6065 / J-X / M-X Nonstandard for **遁** 6087.

迸 6066 / J-X / M38929 See **迸** 6036.

逶 6067 / J6d7b / M38949 I move diagonally.

逵 6068 / J6d7c / M38948 KI broad road.
13 路 *kiro* highway

B **逮** 6069 / J4261 / M38931' TAI chase.
8 夜 *taiya* death anniversary
10 捕 *taiho* arrest, capture
捕令 *taihorei* arrest warrant
捕状 *taihojō* arrest warrant
捕者 *taihosha* captor
捕命令 *taiho meirei* arrest warrant

A **週** 6070 / J3d35 / M38937' SHŪ week.
4 日 *shūjitsu* week day
5 刊 *shūkan* weekly publication
刊新聞 *shūkan shimbun* weekly newspaper
刊誌 *shūkanshi* weekly publication
末 *shūmatsu* weekend
末中 *shūmatsujū* over the weekend
末旅行 *shūmatsu ryokō* weekend trip
6 休 *shūkyū* weekly holiday
7 忌 *shūki* death anniversary
12 間 *shūkan* week
給 *shūkyū* weekly pay
評 *shūhyō* weekly review
番 *shūban* weekly duty
報 *shūhō* weekly bulletin, weekly paper

B **逸** 6071 / J306f / M38951' **逸** 6072 / J-X / M38951 ITSU idleness, leisure. *is(suru)* miss (a chance); let escape; deviate from. *so(reru)* miss the mark, deviate from, diverge, glance off, go astray; be off (the tune). *so(raseru), so(rasu)* look away, evade, elude, parry. *hagu(reru)* go astray, become separated from. *haya(ru)* be hasty, be rash.
4 文 *itsubun* unknown writings, lost writing; excellent writings
5 矢 *so(re)ya* stray arrow
出 *isshutsu* escape; excelling, prominence
民 *itsumin* retired person, hermit
7 走 *issō suru* escape, scud, scamper away
足 *issoku* a fast runner; excellence
材 *itsuzai* outstanding talent
8 居 *ikkyo suru* living a lazy life
物 *itsubutsu* excellent person, superb article. *ichimotsu* excellent animal
事 *itsuji* anecdote; unknown fact
9 速 *ichihaya(ku)* promptly

品 *ippin* superb article
10 書 *issho* a lost book
11 球 *ikkyū* muffed ball
脱 *itsudatsu* deviation, omission
12 弾 *so(re)dama* stray bullet
散 *issan ni* at top speed
13 話 *itsuwa* anecdote
楽 *itsuraku* pleasure
14 聞 *itsubun* something unheard of

A **進** 6073 / J3f4a / M38943' SHIN advancing. *shin(zuru), shin(jiru), shin(zeru)* give, present. *susu(mu) vi* advance, proceed, progress; be promoted; be in an advanced stage; (watches) gain; feel like (doing). *susu(meru) vt* move forward; set (watches) ahead; promote, elevate; stimulate; speed up; present.

2 入 *shinnyū(suru), susu(mi)-i(ru)* go on into, penetrate, enter
3 上 *susu(mi)-nobo(ru)* go up to. *shinjō suru* give, offer, present
4 化 *shinka* evolution; progress
化論 *shinkaron* theory of evolution
化論者 *shinkaronja* evolutionist
水 *shinsui* launching (a ship)
水台 *shinsuidai* launching ways
水式 *shinsuishiki* launching ceremony
5 出 *susu(mi)-de(ru)* step forward. *susu(mi)-da(su)* bring forward. *shinshutsu* advance, march, inroad, push; expansion
6 行 *shinkō suru, susu(mi)-yu(ku)* go forward, advance
行係 *shinkōgakari* steering committee, person directing proceedings
7 言 *shingen* advice, memorial, proposal
攻 *shinkō* attack, drive
来 *susu(mi)-ku(ru)* advance toward
呈 *shintei* presentation
呈本 *shinteibon* complimentary copy
呈者 *shinteisha* presenter
8 物 *shimmotsu* present, gift
取 *shinshu* enterprise
退 *shintai* advance or retreat; movement; course of action; conduct; attitude; resigning or carrying on
退伺 *shintai ukaga(i)* informal resignation (leaving the decision to superiors)
学 *shingaku* entrance to a higher school
学適性検査 *shingaku tekisei kensa* aptitude test, achievement test
歩 *shimpo* advance, progress
歩主義 *shimpo shugi* progressivism
歩派 *shimpoha* progressives
歩党 *shimpotō* progressive party
9 度 *shindo* progress
級 *shinkyū* (school) promotion
発 *shimpatsu suru* march off, start
軍 *shingun* a march, an advance
軍中 *shinguncū* on the march
10 捗 *shinchoku* progress, advance
航 *shinkō suru* proceed, sail ahead
展 *shinten* development, progress
展振 *shintembu(ri)* nature of developments
貢 *shinkō* paying tribute
貢国 *shinkōkoku* tributary nation
貢船 *shinkōsen* tribute-bearing ships; ships trading with the Mings
11 運 *shin'un* progress, advancement
略 *shinryaku suru* advance and capture
寄 *susu(mi)-yo(ru)* approach
12 塁 *shinrui suru* advance a base
13 適 *shinteki* aptitude test, achievement
路 *shinro* course, way, route
14 境 *shinkyō* progress, improvement
15 撃 *shingeki* assault, charge, attack, advance
駐 *shinchū* occupation, stationing
駐兵 *shinchūhei* occupation soldier
駐軍 *shinchūgun* occupation army
17 講 *shinkō* lecturing to the emperor

9

迸 6074 / J-X / M-X Nonstandard for 遷 6114.

遥 6075 / J4d5a / M-X Nonstandard for 遙 6097.

逾 6076 / J6e27 / M38977 YU *ko(eru)* cross, pass over; go beyond, exceed.

遒 6077 / J6e24 / M39008 SHŪ. *sema(ru)* approach, close in on; press for, urge. *tsuyo(i)* strong, powerful.

遖 6078 / J6e28 / M39030 (国字) *appa(re)* exclamation of appreciation.

遏 6079 / J6e21 / M39004 ATSU stop, suppress.

遐 6080 / J6e22 / M39005 KA distant.

遑 6081 / J6e23 / M39006 KAN. *itoma* leisure.

逞 6082 / J6e26 / M38993 TEI. *sasuga ni* as might be expected.

B **遇** 6083 / J3678 / M38991' GŪ. GU. *gū(suru)* treat, entertain, receive, deal with. *ashira(u)* receive, entertain; deal with, treat, manage, manipulate. *a(u)* meet, interview.
4 不遇 *gūfugū* happiness and sorrows

B **遂** 6084 / J3f6b / M38985' SUI. *to(geru)* accomplish, attain, commit (suicide). *tsui ni* finally, after all.
6 行 *suikō* accomplishment, execution, prosecution (of a war)

逼 6085 / J492f / M38973 FUKU. HITSU. *sema(ru)* press for, urge, force, spur on; approach; gain on, close in on; be on the verge of, be imminent.
7 迫 *hippaku* (money) stringency
13 塞 *hissoku* poverty-stricken and slipping into obscurity; house arrest

B **遍** 6086 / J4a57 / M39001' HEN times. *amane(ku)* widely, generally, everywhere.
6 在 *henzai* omnipresence, ubiquity
13 路 *henro* pilgrim
14 歴 *henreki* travels, pilgrimage

遁 6087 / J465b / M38982 **遯** 6102 / J6e2c / M39089 TON. *noga(reru)* escape, avoid, evade, shirk.
2 入 *tonnyū suru* flee to a safe place
5 世 *tonsei* seclusion from the world, escape from life
世主義 *tonsei shugi* monasticism, asceticism
世者 *tonseisha* hermit, recluse
7 走 *tonsō* flight
8 退 *noga(re)-shirizo(ku)* flee back
13 辞 *tonji* excuse, evasion, prevarication

A **達** 6088 / J4323 / M39011' TATSU. *tas(suru)* reach, arrive at, attain; amount to; become expert, be versed in; accomplish; notify. *tat(te)* forcibly, unreasonably. *tas(shinai)* fall short of; be uncompleted. *tas(shi)* government notice. *-tachi* plural ending.
2 人 *tatsujin* expert, master, master mind, great character, philosopher
3 士 *tasshi* expert, master
4 文 *tatsubun* clear composition
5 示 *tasshi* government notice
弁 *tatsuben* eloquence, fluency
6 成 *tassei* achievement, accomplishment
7 見 *takken* clearsightedness, penetration, farsightedness; excellent idea
8 者 *tassha na* healthy, strong; skillful; free (in a language)
10 書 *tas(shi)ga(ki)* government notification
11 眼 *tatsugan* farsightedness, insight
12 筆 *tappitsu* facile pen, skillful hand; speedy writing
13 意 *tatsui* intelligibility, perspicuity
15 摩 *Daruma* Dharma (an Indian priest, the founder of Zen Buddhism in China); tumbler (toy)
16 頼喇嘛 *Darai Rama* Dalai Lama
磨 *Daruma* Dharma (an Indian priest, the founder of Zen Buddhism in China); tumbler (toy)
磨船 *darumabune, darumasen* lighter, barge
18 観 *takkan* farsighted view; philosophic view
19 識 *tasshiki* great insight, farsightedness

B **遅** 6089 / J4359 / M38989' **遲** 6108 / J6e2f / M39113 CHI. *oku(reru)* be late, be delayed, be overdue; lag behind; (clocks) lose. *oku(rasu), oku(raseru)* retard, delay, defer. *oso(nawaru)* be late. *oso(i)* late; slow. *oso(kutomo)* at the latest. *oso-* slow, late.
4 日 *chijitsu* long spring days
5 生 *osouma(re)* born after April 1 (school entrance date)
6 成 *osona(ri)* late crop
早 *oso(kare)-haya(kare)* sooner or later
7 足 *osoashi* slow speed

8 延 *chien* delay, retardation, procrastination
参 *chisan* lateness, tardiness
知恵 *osojie* retarded development of understanding
刻 *chikoku* tardiness, lateness
刻届 *chikoku todoke* excuse for tardiness
刻者 *chikokusha* latecomer
9 速 *chisoku* speed; progress
咲 *osoza(ki)* late blooming; late flower
発 *chihatsu* delayed start, delayed action
発爆弾 *chihatsu bakudan* time bomb
10 桜 *osozakura* late-blooming cherries
脈 *chimyaku* slow pulse
配 *chihai* delay in rationing
11 遅 *chichi* slow, lagging
過 *ososu(giru)* be too late
12 鈍 *chidon* dullness, stupidity
着 *chichaku* late arrival
智慧 *osojie* retarded development of understanding
13 滞 *chitai* delay, procrastination, arrearage
蒔 *osoma(ki)* late planting. *osoma(ki) ni* late, too late
14 疑 *chigi* hesitation, vacillation, indecision

A **過** 6090 / J3261 / M39002' Ka error; excess. *su(giru)* pass, go past; elapse; exceed. *su(gosu)* pass, spend; tide over; go through; live, (eat) too much. *yo(giru)* pass by, cross, go across. *ayamu(tsu)* err. *ayama(chi)* fault, error, indiscretion. *ayama(tte)* by mistake, accidentally. *su(ginai)* nothing more than, merely. *-su(giru)* over-, too; to a fault, in excess. *-su(gi)* past, after; over; too; excessive.
3 大 *kadai na* excessive; unreasonable; too large
大評価 *kadai hyōka* overvaluation
小 *kashō* too small
小評価 *kashō hyōka* undervaluation
4 日 *kajitsu* recently, the other day
分 *kabun na* excessive; unmerited; generous
不及 *kafukyū* excess or deficiency
不足 *kafusoku* excess or deficiency
少 *kashō* too few
少生産 *kashō seisan* underproduction
5 半 *kahan* the greater part
半数 *kahansū* majority, plurality, greater part
去 *su(gi)-sa(ru)* pass. *kako* the past; previous life; previous existence; past tense
去完了 *kako kanryō* past perfect tense
去帳 *kakochō* death registry (in a temple)
失 *kashitsu* error, blunder; accident; negligence
失者 *kashitsusha* party at fault
失致死罪 *kashitsu chishizai* accidental homicide
6 行 *su(gi)-yu(ku)* pass, go past
当 *katō na* excessive, undeserved, unreasonable, exorbitant
多 *kata* excess, superabundance
年度 *kanendo* past financial year
7 言 *kagen, kagon* exaggeration; saying too much
労 *karō* overwork, strain
労死 *karōshi* death due to overwork
9 食 *kashoku* overeating
食症 *kashokushō* binge eating
信 *kashin suru* trust too much; overestimate (ability); be overconfident 「mistake
怠 *katai* negligence, carelessness,
美 *kabi* exceedingly beautiful
負荷 *kafuka* overload (in electricity)
重 *kajū* overweight
重労働 *kajū rōdō* overwork
度 *kado* excess
度緊張 *kadokinchō* hypertension
10 振 *kabu(ri)* overdraft
称 *kashō* undeserved praise
料 *karyō* correctional fine
納 *kanō suru* overpay
員 *kain* supernumerary
般 *kahan* some time ago, recently
般来 *kahanrai* for some time
敏 *kabin* nervousness, oversensitiveness
敏症 *kabinshō* hypersensitiveness
11 剰 *kajō* excess, surplus
剰人口 *kajō jinkō* surplus population
剰生産 *kajō seisan* overproduction
剰流動性 *kajō ryūdōsei* excess liquidity
12 程 *katei* process, course
勤 *kakin* overwork
給器 *kakyūki* supercharger
越 *Sugikoshi* the Passover
越節 *Sugikoshi Setsu* the Passover

越祝 *Sugikoshi no Iwai* the Passover
越祭 *Sugikoshi no Matsuri* the Passover
渡 *kato* crossing; ferry; changing from the old (to the new)
渡時代 *kato jidai* transition period
渡期 *katoki* transition period
14 誤 *kago* mistake, fault
酷 *kakoku* rigor, severity, cruelty
酸化 *kasanka* peroxide
酸化水素 *kasanka suiso* hydrogen peroxide
酸化脂質 *kasankashishitsu* peroxidized lipid
15 褒 *kahō* overpraise
賞 *kashō* undeserved praise
熱 *kanetsu* superheating
16 激 *kageki na* extreme, radical
激主義 *kageki shugi* extremism, radicalism
激派 *kagekiha* extremists, radical party

A **道** 6091 / J463b / M39010' Dō district, province, prefecture; road. *michi* road, path, lane, way, street, highway, route; journey; distance; course, way, means; duty, morality, moral doctrine; teachings; specialty; an art; reason, justice. *michi(naranu)* improper, illicit. *michi(sugara)* on the way.
4 心 *dōshin* moral sense; piety, faith
中 *dōchū* during the journey
中記 *dōchūki* trip record
中駕籠 *dōchū kago* sedan chair
化 *dōke(ru)* jest, clown. *dōke* clowning, antics, tomfoolery, pleasantry
化芝居 *dōkeshibai* farce, low comedy
化役 *dōkeyaku* a clown, fool, mimic
5 庁 *Dōchō* Hokkaido Government Office
民 *Dōmin* the people of Hokkaido
6 行 *michiyu(ki)* going down the road; eloping; Japanese traveling garb
次 *michisugara* on the way
7 床 *dōshō* roadbed
均 *michinara(shi)* road leveling; bulldozer
8 念 *dōnen* moral sense; piety, faith
者 *dōsha, dōja* pilgrim
学 *dōgaku* Confucianism; Taoism; moral philosophy
学者 *dōgakusha* moralist
具 *dōgu* tool, instrument, implement, utensil, appliance; furniture; (stage) scenery; instrumentality, means, vehicle; steppingstone
具方 *dōgukata* scene shifter, stage carpenter
具立 *dōguda(te)* tool layout; preparatory work; preliminary arrangements; one's features
具作 *dōguzuku(ri)* toolmaker
具屋 *dōguya* secondhand furniture dealer
具造 *dōguzuku(ri)* toolmaker
具部屋 *dōgubeya* toolroom; property room
具箱 *dōgubako* toolbox
9 途 *dōto* road, path, lane, way, street, highway, route; journey; distance; course, way, means; duty, morality, moral doctrine; teachings; specialty; an art; reason, justice
連 *michizu(re)* traveling companion
俗 *dōzoku* priests and laity
草 *michikusa* road side grass; playing along the way
祖神 *dōsojin* traveler's guardian deity
10 師 *dōshi* moralist; Taoist
破 *dōha* declaration
家 *Dōka* Taoist scholar
案内 *michi annai* guidance; guide; signpost
11 道 *michimichi* on the way, while walking
教 *Dōkyō* Taoism
断 *dōdan* unreasonable, absurd
理 *dōri* reason, right, truth. *kotowari* reason
理詰 *dōrizu(me)* persuasion, reasoning
12 場 *dōjō* gymnasium, arena; Buddhist seminary
順 *michijun* route, itinerary
程 *dōtei, michinori* distance; journey; process
筋 *michisuji* path, way, route, itinerary; reason
普請 *michi bushin* road repair
13 話 *dōwa* moral discourse, parable
路 *dōro* road, way, street, route, highway, thoroughfare
義 *dōgi* morality, moral principles
義心 *dōgishin* moral sense, moral scruples
楽 *dōraku* dissipation, prodigality, hobby
楽者 *dōrakumono* a profligate, a libertine

楽息子 *dōraku musuko* prodigal son
14 端 *michibata* roadside
歌 *dōka* didactic poem
導 *michi shirube* road marker
徳 *dōtoku* morals, morality, virtue
徳上 *dōtokujō* morally, from a moral standpoint
徳心 *dōtokushin* moral sense
徳主義 *dōtoku shugi* moralism, moralizing
徳的 *dōtokuteki* moral, ethical
徳学 *dōtokuguku* moral philosophy
徳律 *dōtokuritsu* moral law
徳家 *dōtokuka* man of virtue
徳教育 *dōtoku kyōiku* moral education
徳劇 *dōtokugeki* morality play
15 標 *michi shirube, michijirushi, dōhyō* road

A **運** 6092 / J313f / M38998' UN destiny, fate, lot, fortune, luck. *hako(bu)* carry, transport; progress, advance. *megu(ru) vi* and *vt* turn, go around; revolve, rotate, spin, gyrate; patrol, tour; take effect (medicine); be transferred. *megu(rasu)* enclosed, surround; turn, turn around; ponder; devise. *hako(bi)* carrying; arrangements, managing, paving the way; progress; stage; step, pace.

3 上 *hako(bi)-nobo(ru), hako(bi)-a(geru)* carry up, bring up
4 込 *hako(bi)-ko(mu)* carry in, bring in
不運 *unfuun* luck
5 用 *un'yō suru* make use of, employ (capital), enforce (laws); invest, put in practice
去 *hako(bi)-sa(ru)* carry away, carry off
出 *hako(bi)-da(su)* carry out
6 行 *unkō* motion, movement, revolution. *unkō suru* ply between, run
気 *unki* fate, fortune
休 *unkyū* service suspended (trains, etc.)
任 *ummaka(se)* trusting to luck
7 良 *un'yo(ku)* fortunately, luckily
否天賦 *umpu-tempu* trusting to chance
8 性 *unsei* determining one's fate by the sexagenary cycle
河 *unga* canal, waterway
命 *ummei* destiny, fate
命付 *ummeizu(keru)* condemn
命論 *ummeiron* fatalism
命論者 *ummeironsha* fatalist
送 *unsō* shipping, transportation, forwarding
送会社 *unsōgaisha* transportation company
送状 *unsōjō* invoice, waybill
送店 *unsōten* forwarding agency, express company
送屋 *unsōya* forwarding agency, express company
送保険 *unsō hoken* transportation insurance
送料 *unsōryō* transportation charge
送船 *unsōsen* transport ship, freighter
送費 *unsōhi* transportation expense
送業 *unsōgyō* transportation business
送業者 *unsōgyōsha* expressman, forwarding agent
9 指 *unshi* fingering (in music)
炭船 *untansen* coal vessel, collier
炭機 *untanki* coal conveyer
10 座 *unza* a meeting of poets to write and criticize haiku poems
航 *unkō suru* operate (ships or aircraft)
針 *unshin* handling the needle
帰 *hako(bi)-kae(ru)* carry back
11 転 *unten* operation; motion; running, working; driving (a car)
転士 *untenshi* mate, officer (on a ship); driver
転手 *untenshu* driver, engineer, chauffeur, operator (of a machine)
転中 *untenchū* in motion, running
転台 *untendai* driver's platform, driver's cab
転系統 *unten keitō* transportation system, route
転資本 *unten shihon* operating fund, working capital
転資金 *unten shikin* working capital, operating fund, campaign fund
動 *undō* motion, movement; exercise; sports, games; campaign; agitation; lobbying
動用具 *undō yōgu* sporting goods
動失調 *undō shitchō* lack of muscular coordination; locomotor ataxia
動会 *undōkai* athletic meet
動服 *undōfuku* sports clothes, uniform
動具 *undōgu* sporting goods
動屋 *undōya* campaigner (for a candidate)
動界 *undōkai* sporting circles

動神経 *undō shinkei* motor nerves
動施設 *undō shisetsu* sports equipment
動員 *undōin* campaigner
動記者 *undō kisha* sports writer
動記事 *undō kiji* sports news
動家 *undōka* sportsman, athlete
動家的 *undōkateki* sportsmanlike
動家的精神 *undōkateki seishin* sportsmanship
動場 *undōjō* playing field
動帽 *undōbō* sports cap
動量 *undōryō* momentum
動着 *undōgi* athletic suit
動靴 *undōgutsu* sports shoes
動障碍 *undō shōgai* motor disturbance
動選手 *undō senshu* athlete, sportsman
動精神 *undō seishin* sportsmanship
動熱 *undō netsu* love of sports
動器官 *undō kikan* organ of locomotion
動器具 *undō kigu* sporting goods
動療法 *undō ryōhō* exercise cure
動競技 *undō kyōgi* athletic sports
動欄 *undōran* sporting columns
12 筆 *umpitsu* strokes of the brush, handling the brush
営 *un'ei* operation, management, administration
13 試 *undame(shi) suru* try one's luck, take a chance
勢 *unsei* fate, fortune
賃 *unchin* shipping charges
賃込 *unchinko(mi) de* including freight, C.I.F.
搬 *umpan* transportation, transfer
搬人 *umpannin* porter, carrier
搬夫 *umpanfu* porter, carrier
搬車 *umpansha* cart, wagon, truck, lorry
搬費 *umpanhi* transportation charges
搬器 *umpanki* carts
14 漕 *unsō* shipping, marine transportation
算 *unzan* mathematical operation, calculation
16 輸 *un'yu* transportation
輸会社 *un'yugaisha* transportation company
輸省 *Un'yushō* Transportation Ministry
輸業 *un'yugyō* transportation business

A **遊** 6093 / J4d37 / M38994' YŪ. YU. *aso(bu)* play; enjoy oneself; visit; take a holiday; be out of use, be unemployed, be idle; study under; go on a spree. *aso(baseru), aso(basu)* amuse, entertain; let play; be pleased to. *aso(bi)* play, game, sport, amusement, recreation, fun, outing; play (of a wheel); gambling; dissipation; dull business; idle time; light (literature). *susa(bi)* amusement, recreation.

2 人 *aso(bi)nin* gambler; a jobless person
3 士 *yūshi* playboy
子 *yūshi* wanderer, traveler, capital
山 *yusan* excursion, outing, picnic
弋 *yūyoku* cruise
女 *aso(bi)me, yūjo* harlot, prostitute
女町 *yūjo machi* red-light district
女屋 *yūjoya* brothel
4 心 *aso(bi)gokoro, yūshin* a desire to play or have a good time
手 *aso(bi)te* high liver, fast-living person
友達 *aso(bi) tomodachi* playmate, companion in play
5 失 *yūshitsu* shortstop error
民 *yūmin* idle people, idlers; the unemployed; unemployment
半分 *aso(bi)hambun* half in fun
仕事 *aso(bi) shigoto* pastime, diversion. avocation
6 行 *yūkō, yugyō* tour, wandering, movement, revolution
好 *aso(bi)zu(ki)* pleasure seeker
仲間 *aso(bi)nakama* playmate, companion
休 *yūkyū* idle, unused
休施設 *yūkyū shisetsu* idle facilities
休資本 *yūkyū shihon* idle capital
7 車 *aso(bi)guruma* idle pulley
里 *yūri* red-light district
技 *yūgi* commercially licensed games (like mahjong)
冶 *yūya* playboy, classy dresser; person of questionable habits
冶郎 *yūyarō* a profligate, a libertine
芸 *yūgei* the polite accomplishments
芸人 *yūgeinin* actors, singers
芸師 *yūgeishi* entertainer
8 金 *yūkin, aso(bi)gane* idle money
底 *yūtei* breechblock (of a gun)
明 *aso(bi)-a(kasu)* play all night
直 *yūchoku* a short liner that is caught (in baseball)
歩 *yūho* walk, stroll, ramble
学 *yūgaku* traveling to study

事 *aso(bi)goto, susa(bi)goto* game, pastime, diversion
泳 *yūei* swimming
泳術 *yueijutsu* getting along in the world
牧 *yūboku* nomadism
牧民 *yūbokumin* nomads
9 食 *yūshoku suru* live in idleness
俠 *yūkyō* chivalrous man; gangster
軍 *yūgun* reserve corps, flying column
客 *yūkyaku* playboy; tourist; frequenter of brothels
星 *yūsei* planet
相手 *aso(bi) aite* playmate, companion (in amusement)
10 郭 *yūkaku* red-light district
宴 *yūen* banquet
時間 *aso(bi) jikan* recess, playtime
11 道具 *aso(bi) dōgu* plaything, toy
船 *yūsen* yacht, pleasure boat
船宿 *yūsen yado* riverside teahouse
動気球 *yūdō kikyū* dirigible balloon
動隊 *yudotai* mobile corps
猟 *yūryō* hunting
猟地 *yūryōchi* game preserve
猟会 *yūryōkai* hunting party
猟服 *yūryōfuku* hunting suit
猟免状 *yūryō menjō* hunting license
猟家 *yūryōka* hunter
猟期 *yūryōki* hunting season
12 場 *aso(bi)ba* playground
惰 *yūda* laziness, indolence
13 廓 *yūkaku* red-light district
楽 *yūraku* amusement, pleasure, recreation
資 *yūshi* idle capital
園 *yūen* amusement park, recreation area
園地 *yūenchi* amusement park, recreation area, playground
14 歴 *yūreki* tour, pleasure trip
暮 *aso(bi)-ku(rasu)* idle time away
説 *yūzei* electioneering tour, oratorical campaign, agitation tour; campaign speech
説員 *yūzeiin* stump speaker
説旅行 *yūzei ryokō* speaking tour, junket
15 標 *yūhyō* vernier
標尺 *yūhyōshaku* vernier scale
撃 *yūgeki* raid; shortstop
撃手 *yūgekishu* shortstop
戯 *aso(bi)-tawamu(reru)* play, frolic. *yūgi* games, sport, play, entertainment, amusement, pastime
戯的 *yūgiteki* playful, sportive
戯場 *yūgijō* playground
蕩 *yūtō* dissipation, profligacy
蕩文学 *yūtō bungaku* pornographic literature
蕩児 *yūtōji* dissipated person
16 覧 *yūran* excursion, sightseeing
覧地 *yūranchi* excursion, sightseeing
覧客 *yūrankyaku* tourists, sight-seers
覧船 *yūransen* excursion boat
興 *yūkyō* pleasure-seeking, amusement, spree
興者 *yūkyōsha* carouser, reveler
興街 *yūkyōgai* amusement center; red-light district
興税 *yūkyōzei* entertainment tax
興費 *yūkyōhi* amusement expenses, price of a spree
18 癖 *aso(bi)guse* habit of idleness
19 離 *yūri* separation, isolation

10

遡 6094 / J414c / M39048 See **溯** 3272.

遞 6095 / J6e2a / M39045 See **逓** 6055.

遘 6096 / J6e29 / M39031 Kō. *a(u)* meet, run into.

遙 6097 / J7423 / M39035 Yō. *haru(ka) ni* far off, in the distance, a long time ago, by far. *haru(keshi)* distant.
8 拝 *yōhai* worshipping from afar
13 遙 *harubaru* from afar, all the way, far out over (the sea)

遜 6098 / J423d / M39038 SON. *herikuda(ru)* humble oneself, condescend, be modest.
6 色 *sonshoku* inferiority
13 辞 *sonji* modest speech
20 譲 *sonjō* humility, modesty

B **違** 6099 / J3063 / M39067 I. *chiga(u)* differ, vary; disagree with; be mistaken; cross or pass (someone); No (negation). *chiga(eru)* change, alter, vary, disguise; make a mistake; break (a promise); sprain, dislocate; cross (two sticks). *taga(u)* differ from, vary; violate, break, transgress. *taga(eru)* break (a promise or a law), violate. *chiga(i)* difference, divergence, disparity, discrepancy. *chiga(inai)* I am sure.

4 反 *ihan* violation, infringement, breach (of contract)
5 犯 *ihan* violation, transgression
失 *ishitsu* mistake
6 式 *ishiki* informality; breach of etiquette
8 例 *irei* unconventionality
法 *ihō* unlawfulness; foul (play)
法性 *ihōsei* illegality
9 勅 *ichoku* disobeying an imperial decree
背 *ihai* violation, transgression
約 *iyaku* breach of contract, default
約金 *iyakukin* breach of contract penalty
12 棚 *chiga(i)dana* staggered shelves
14 算 *isan* miscalculation
16 憲 *iken* unconstitutionality
19 警罪 *ikeizai* police offense, petty crime

B **遣** 6100 / J382f / M39052' KEN. *tsuka(wasu)* send, dispatch; give, donate, bestow on; do for (someone). *ya(ru)* give, let have, bestow on, present; send; do, perform, undertake; do for; act; study; row; operate; hold (a meeting), give (a dinner); eat, drink, smoke; find solace in. *yoko(su)* send, forward, deliver. *ya(ri-konasu)* manage a difficult task. *tsuka(u)* use; handle, manipulate; employ; need, want; spend, consume; speak (English); practice (fencing); take (one's lunch); circulate (bad money).

3 口 *yarikuchi* procedure, policy, way of doing
上 *ya(ri)-a(geru)* finish; wind up
4 戸 *yarido* sliding door
手 *yarite* person with talent, tactician, performer
水 *ya(ri)mizu* water conduit; stream coursed through a garden
込 *ya(ri)-ko(meru)* snub, refute, corner
方 *ya(ri)kata* way of doing, method, manner of doing means, arrangement, management
方無 *yarukatana(i)* inexpressible (feeling)
切 *ya(ri)-ki(renai)* cannot stand, cannot go on, cannot make ends meet, be intolerable
5 外 *kengai* sent abroad
出 *ya(ri)-da(su)* begin, embark on, take up
付 *ya(ri)-tsu(keru), ya(t)tsu(keru)* be accustomed to; always be giving; defeat
付仕事 *yattsu(ke) shigoto* hurried work
6 米 *kembei* sent to America
尽 *ya(ri)-tsuku(su)* do all in one's power
返 *ya(ri)-kae(su)* try again, make over; refute, answer back
合 *ya(ri)-a(u)* do something) against each other, quarrel, argue
7 抜 *ya(ri)-nu(ku)* carry through, do thoroughly, complete, accomplish
8 放 *ya(rip)pana(shi), ya(ri)bana(shi)* leave in disorder, leave half done; carelessness, negligence
取 *ya(ri)to(ri) suru* give and take, reciprocate, exchange
直 *ya(ri)-nao(su)* do over, remake, resume, begin again
9 通 *ya(ri)-tō(su)* carry out, complete, accomplish
10 時 *ya(ri)doki* proper time to do, convenient time, opportunity; marriageable age
兼 *ya(ri)-ka(neru)* dare not do, hesitate to do
唐使 *kentōshi* envoy to Tang China
11 過 *ya(ri)-su(giru)* overdo, carry too far, drink too much, give too much. *ya(ri)-su(gosu)* let a person go past
遂 *ya(ri)-to(geru)* accomplish, fulfill, finish
掛 *ya(ri)-ka(keru)* begin to do, proceed to make. *ya(ri)ka(ke)* leaving (the work) half done
12 場 *ya(ri)ba* disposal; use; place (to put a thing)
違 *ya(ri)-chiga(eru)* bungle, mismanage, spoil, make a mistake, be unsuccessful
替 *ya(ri)-ka(eru)* do over again, start over
13 損 *ya(ri)-soko(nau)* bungle, mismanage, spoil, make a mistake, be unsuccessful
14 端 *yariha* the method to be followed; the time to deliver; the opportunity
18 難 *ya(ri)niku(i)* hard to do
19 瀬無 *yarusena(i), yaruse (ga) na(i)* uneasy, cheerless, dreary, grief-stricken, wretched

繰 *ya(ri)-ku(ru)* proceed in spite of shortages. *ya(ri)ku(ri)* tiding over, makeshift, manipulation
繰算段 *yariku(ri) sandan* hurrying around to settle a problem

A **遠** 6101 / J3173 / M39047' EN. ON. *tō(i)* far, distant, remote; hard (of hearing). *tō(ku)* far away, in the distance. *tō(zakaru) vi* become more distant, recede; die away; keep away, stand aloof, be estranged. *tō(zakeru) vt* keep away, keep at a distance, shun, abstain from; alienate. *tō(karazu), tō(karazu) shite* soon, in the near future. *tō-* far, distant.

2 人 *enjin* a person from a faraway land
3 大 *endai na* far-reaching, grand, lofty
山 *enzan, tōyama* distant mountain
干潟 *tōhigata* broad lagoon left by a receding tide
4 方 *empō* great distance, long way; distant place
火 *tōbi* building a fire at a distance
心力 *enshinryoku* centrifugal force
心分離法 *enshin bunrihō* centrifuge separation method
日点 *ennichiten, enjitsuten* aphelion
5 目 *tōme* distant view, farsightedness
矢 *tōya* long-distance arrow; long-distance archery
由 *en'yu* remote cause
去 *tōza(karu)* recede into the distance
出 *tōde* going afar; changing a geisha registry to another city
耳 *tōmimi* sharp ear
6 回 *tōmawa(ri)* roundabout way, detour. *tōmawa(shi)* roundabout expression
因 *en'in* remote, underlying, or predisposing
地 *enchi* distant place, remote place
交近攻 *enkō-kinkō* befriending distant states and antagonizing those near
近 *enkin* distance, far and near, perspective. *ochikochi* here and there
近法 *enkinhō* law of perspective
近調節 *enkin chōsetsu* (eye) accommodation
7 走 *to(p)pashi(ri)* long-distance flight
足 *ensoku* trip, hike, picnic, excursion, outing
吠 *tōboe* howling
攻 *tōze(me)* attacking from afar and besieging
声 *tōgoe* distant howl (of a dog)
来 *enrai* foreign visitor, visitor from afar
赤外線 *ensekigaisen* far infrared rays
見 *tōmi* watchtower; distant view; background. *enken* looking into the distance; distant view
見櫓 *tōmi yagura* watchtower
8 国 *engoku, ongoku* distant land
退 *tōno(keru)* keep (someone) at a distance. *tōno(ku)* stay at a distance; recede, fade away
泳 *en'ei* long-distance swim
歩 *tōaru(ki)* long walk
征 *ensei* expedition, invasion, campaign; a tour (by a team of performers)
征軍 *enseigun* invaders, expeditionary force; visiting team
征隊 *enseitai* invaders, expeditionary force; visiting team
9 音 *tōne* distant sound
廻 *tōmawa(ri)* circuitous route. *tōmawa(shi)* roundabout expression
浅 *tōasa* a wide shallow beach; a shoal
祖 *enso, tōtsu oya* forefathers; remote ancestors
乗 *tōno(ri)* a long ride
巻 *tōma(ki)* surrounding at a distance
海 *enkai* deep sea, ocean
海魚 *enkaigyo* deep-sea fish
洋 *en'yō* ocean, deep sea
洋航海 *en'yō kōkai* ocean navigation
洋漁業 *en'yō gyogyō* deep sea fishing
10 馬 *emba* long ride on a horse
流 *onru* exile
阪 *ensū* far country
島 *entō, tōjima* a distant island. *entō* exile to an island
11 戚 *enseki* distant relative
道 *endō* a long walk; a roundabout way
略 *enryaku* farsighted policy or program
野 *tōno* distant field
望 *embō* vista, distant view, perspective
距離 *enkyori* long distance, great distance, long-range
眼 *engan* farsightedness
眼鏡 *tōmegane* (old word for) telescope
視 *enshi* farsightedness
視画 *enshiga* perspective
視眼 *enshigan* farsightedness
12 遠 *tōdō(shii)* distant

景 *enkei* distant view, vista, perspective, background
隔 *enkaku* distant, remote, isolated
隔操縦 *enkaku sōjū* remote control
13 路 *enro* long road, long journey; roundabout way, detour, long distance
裔 *en'ei* remote descendant
雷 *enrai* distant thunder
14 鳴 *tōna(ri)* distant peals (of thunder), distant roar (of the sea)
境 *enkyō* distant borders
15 縁 *tōen* distant relative
慮 *enryo* reserve, modesty, deference, restraint, discretion; forethought, prudence
慮深 *enryobuka(i)* reserved, backward, bashful, shy, modest
慮勝 *enryoga(chi)* modest, reserved, diffident
慮無 *enryona(ku)* unreserved, frankly
16 謀 *embō* forethought, foresight
18 竄 *enzan* exile

11

遯 6102 / J6e2c / M39089 See **遁** 6087.

遷 6103 / J-X / M-X See **遷** 6113.

遨 6104 / J6e2b / M39073 Gō. *aso(bu)* amuse oneself, play.

B **遭** 6105 / J4178 / M39082' Sō. *a(u)* meet, interview. *a(waseru)* introduce, expose to, subject to.
11 遇 *sōgū* an encounter, meeting someone
遇戦 *sōgūsen* encounter, battle action
18 難 *sōnan* disaster, accident, shipwreck, distress
難者 *sōnansha* victim, sufferer, survivor
難信号 *sōnan shingō* distress signal, SOS

B **遮** 6106 / J3c57 / M39086 Sha. *saegi(ru)* interrupt, obstruct, intercept.
2 二無二 *shanimuni* recklessly, furiously, desperately, forcibly
6 光 *shakō suru* shade, darken, cut off the light
11 断 *shadan* interception, isolation
断器 *shadanki* circuit breaker, railroad crossing gate
断機 *shadanki* circuit breaker, railroad crossing gate
15 蔽 *shahei* cover, shelter
蔽物 *shaheibutsu* cover, shelter

A **適** 6107 / J452c / M39076' Teki suitable. *teki(suru)* fit, suit, agree with, be adapted to, be qualified for. *kana(u)* suit, be capable of; measure up to expectations; suit, be capable of; measure up to expectations; match, rival, keep up to expectations; rival, keep up with; stand (the work); bear (the heat). *kana(eru)* grant, hear, answer. *tama no* occasionally, rare. *tamasaka* occasionally. *tamatama* casually, unexpectedly; few.
4 中 *tekichū suru* hit the mark, guess right, come right
切 *tekisetsu na* pertinent, appropriate, adequate, timely
不適 *teki-futeki* fitness, aptitude, propriety
5 用 *tekiyō suru* apply
正 *tekisei na* proper, right, reasonable, normal
6 地 *tekichi* suitable site
合 *tekigō* conformity, compatibility, adaptation
当 *tekitō na* suitable, proper, right; adequate; competent, qualified; reasonable, timely
任 *tekinin* suitability, competence
任者 *tekininsha* well-qualified person
任証 *tekininshō* efficiency certificate
7 役 *tekiyaku* suitable post
否 *tekihi* propriety, fitness, aptitude
材 *tekizai, tekisai* the right person
材適所 *tekizai-tekisho* the right person in the right place
応 *tekiō* adaptation, accommodation, adjustment, conformity
応性 *tekiōsei* adaptability, flexibility
応症 *tekiōshō* diseases for which there is a specific medicine
8 例 *tekirei* good example, typical instance
所 *tekisho* proper place
法 *tekihō* legality, lawfulness
宜 *tekigi* suitableness
性 *tekisei* adaptability

性検査 *tekisei kensa* aptitude test, qualifying examination
者 *tekisha* suitable person
者生存 *tekisha seizon* survival of the fittest
9 度 *tekido ni* moderately, in moderation, temperately
10 従 *tekijū suru* follow
帰 *tekki suru* lead to, follow
時 *tekiji* timely, at any time, at all times
時打 *tekijida* a timely hit
時安打 *tekiji anda* a timely hit
格 *tekikaku, tekkaku* competency, fitness
格性 *tekikakusei* fitness
格者 *tekikakusha* qualified person
11 訳 *tekiyaku* exact translation
12 温 *tekion* correct temperature
評 *tekihyō* just criticism; appropriate comment
量 *tekiryō* proper quantity, proper dose
策 *tekisaku* appropriate countermeasures
13 業 *tekigyō* the right vocation
16 薬 *tekiyaku* specific remedy
17 齢 *tekirei* marriageable age; conscription age
齢期 *tekireiki* marriageable age
18 職 *tekishoku* an appropriate occupation (for a certain person)

12

遲 6108 / J6e2f / M39113 See **遅** 6089.

遶 6109 / J6e2d / M39122 Jō, Nyō go around; surround.

邁 6110 / J6e32 / M39169 Mai. go; excel.
10 進 *maishin suru* push on, press on

遼 6111 / J4e4b / M39137 Ryō distant.
8 東半島 *Ryōtō Hantō* Liaotong Peninsula
12 遠 *ryōen na* distant, remote

B **遵** 6112 / J3d65 / M39118' Jun follow, obey; learn.
6 行 *junkō* obedience
守 *junshu suru* obey, observe
守者 *junshusha* observers (of a law)
8 奉 *jumpō suru* obey, observe
法 *jumpō na* law-abiding
法精神 *jumpō seishin* law-abiding spirit

B **遷** 6113 / J412b / M39123' **遷** 6103 / J-X / M-X Sen. *utsu(ru)* move, change, shift; pass into, drift; soak in; be infected, catch (a cold); catch fire, spread. *utsu(su)* move, transfer; pour into, divert (attention), give (a disease to someone).
4 化 *senge* demise of a dignitary
8 幸 *senkō suru* (the emperor) moves away (from the capital)
延 *sen'en* delay, procrastination, postponement
延策 *sen'ensaku* delaying tactics
10 座 *senza* transfer of a shrine
都 *sento* moving the capital
宮 *sengū* transferring the god-body to a new shrine
11 移 *sen'i* transition, change
12 御 *sengyo* moving (of the emperor or the *shintai* of a shrine)
15 避 *utsu(ri)-sa(keru)* move away from

A **選** 6114 / J412a / M39127' Sen selection, choice. *yo(ru), era(bu), e(ru), era(mu)* choose, select; cull out; elect; prefer; decide on. *sugu(ru)* choose, select, cull out.
3 士 *senshi* select samurai
4 分 *yo(ri)-wa(keru), e(ri)-wa(keru), era(bi)-wa(keru), e(ri)-wa(katsu)* set apart, sort out, sift, cull, separate, pick out
手 *senshu* athlete, player
手団 *senshudan* team, squad
手控場 *senshu hikaejō* players' dugout
手権 *senshuken* championship title
5 出 *e(ri)-da(su), era(bi)-da(su)* select, pick out, cull out. *senshutsu* election
民 *semmin* chosen people, the elect
外 *sengai* left out, not chosen
外佳作 *sengai kasaku* honorable mention
6 任 *sennin suru* select, appoint, assign; nominate; elect
好 *yo(ri)gono(mi), e(ri)gono(mi)* fastidiousness, overnicety in choice
当 *era(bi)-a(teru)* make a happy choice
考 *senkō* selection, evaluation (of people)

7 別 *era(bi)-wa(katsu)* set apart. *sembetsu* selection, separation, concentration (in mining)

良 *senryō* the people's choice; diet member

択 *sentaku* selection, choice, option, selectivity

択権 *sentakuken* right of choice, option

抜 *e(ri)-nu(ku)* choose, select, pick out, sort out. *sembatsu* selection, choice

抜試験 *sembatsu shiken* selective examination

8 取 *era(bi)-to(ru), e(ri)-to(ru), yo(ri)-to(ru), yo(ri)-do(ru)* pick out, select, choose

直 *era(bi)-nao(su)* re-elect

定 *era(bi)-sada(meru)* appoint. *sentei* selection, choice

者 *senja* judge, selector

9 除 *e(ri)-no(keru)* sort out, weed out

炭 *sentan* coal screening

科 *senka* special course

科生 *senkasei* special student

10 屑 *e(ri)kuzu, yo(ri)kuzu* waste, trash, refuse

挙 *senkyo* election

挙人 *senkyonin* elector, voter; electorate

挙干渉 *senkyo kanshō* government election intervention

挙日 *senkyobi* election day

挙区 *senkyoku* election district, precinct, constituency

挙民 *senkyomin* electorate

挙立合人 *senkyo tachiainin* election witness

挙母体 *senkyo botai* electorate; electoral college

挙法 *senkyohō* election law

挙侯 *senkyokō* elector (of Saxony)

挙違反 *senkyo ihan* election irregularity

挙運動 *senkyo undō* election campaign

挙場 *senkyojō* the polls, election booth

挙期日 *senkyo kijitsu* election day

挙戦 *senkyosen* election campaign

挙演説 *senkyo enzetsu* campaign speech

挙権 *senkyoken* suffrage, franchise, right to vote

11 捨 *e(ri)-su(teru)* in choosing leave the bad behind

球眼 *senkyūgan* batting eye

12 集 *senshū* selection, anthology

13 嫌 *erigira(i)* choosing only what suits the fancy

滓 *yo(ri)kasu, e(ri)kasu* remnants, refuse

鉱 *senkō* concentration of ore

14 歌 *senka* selected poem; selection of poems

管 *senkan* election administration

16 衡 *senkō* selection, evaluation

録 *senroku suru* select, gather materials, and write

A **遺** 6115 / J3064 / M39134' I. YUI. *noko(su)* leave behind; bequeath; save, reserve.

3 子 *ishi* posthumous child

4 文 *ibun* literary remains

5 功 *ikō* works following the deceased

令 *irei* dying orders

失 *ishitsu* loss

失物 *ishitsubutsu* lost article

失品 *ishitsuhin* lost article

6 臣 *ishin* surviving retainer

存 *ison* extant, still existing

伝 *iden* heredity

伝子 *idenshi* gene

伝子工学 *idenshi kōgaku* genetic engineering

伝子地図 *idenshi chizu* gene map

伝子治療 *idenshi chiryō* gene therapy

伝子診断 *idenshi shindan* gene diagnosis

伝子操作 *idenshi sōsa* gene manipulation

伝因子 *iden'inshi* gene

伝法 *idenhō* law of heredity

伝学 *idengaku* genetics

伝病 *idembyō* hereditary disease

7 図 *ito* posthumous plan, person's last wishes

尿 *inyō* bed-wetting

作 *isaku* posthumous works

体 *itai* corpse, remains

址 *ishi* (historic) ruins

利 *iri* unexploited source of wealth

志 *ishi* dying wish

芳 *ihō* memory or autograph of the deceased

児 *iji* orphan

言 *yuigon, igen, igon* will, testament, last request

言状 *yuigonjō* will, testament

言者 *yuigonsha* testator

言書 *yuigonsho* will, testament
8 孤 *iko* orphan
法 *ihō* a law established by a deceased ruler
物 *yuimotsu* keepsake; inheritance, bequest. *ibutsu* relic, (old) remains, memento
制 *isei* institutions bequeathed from the past
命 *imei* will, dying instruction
事 *iji* reminiscences, memories
9 風 *ifū* tradition, hereditary custom
香 *ikō* a lingering odor reminding one of the giver (of clothes, etc.)
俗 *izoku* ancient customs which survive
恨 *ikon* grudge, ill-will, enmity
品 *ihin* articles of the deceased
臭 *ishū* scent (in hunting)
草 *isō* posthumous works
10 骨 *ikotsu* remains, ashes of the deceased
訓 *ikun, yuikun* dying instructions
財 *izai* inheritance, bequest, heritage
書 *isho* posthumous work; note left by the dead
烈 *iretsu* distinguished deeds of the departed
家族 *ikazoku* bereaved family
留 *iryū suru* bequeath
留品 *iryūhin* lost articles
11 族 *izoku* bereaved family
脱 *idatsu* omission
著 *icho* posthumous work
産 *isan* inheritance, bequest, heritage
産相続 *isan sōzoku* succession to property
産相続人 *isan sōzokunin* heir
産管理人 *isan kanrinin* administrator of an estate
12 詠 *iei* posthumous song or poem; a song or poem by an ancient composer
詔 *ishō* the last will of an emperor
13 跡 *iseki, yuiseki* (historic) ruins, remains, relics
棄 *iki* abandonment, desertion
愛 *iai* bequest, relic of the dead
業 *igyō* work left at death
腹 *ifuku* posthumous child
腹子 *ifuku (no) ko* posthumous child
14 像 *izō* afterimage
徳 *itoku* benefit from ancestors' virtue
漏 *irō* omission, negligence, oversight
精 *isei* nocturnal emission
誡 *ikai, yuikai* dying instructions
算 *isan* miscalculation
髪 *ihatsu* hair of the deceased
墨 *iboku* autograph of the deceased
15 稿 *ikō* posthumous manuscript
賢 *iken* able people left out of office
16 骸 *igai, yuigai* remains, corpse, (dead) body
薫 *ikun* lingering fragrance
憾 *ikan na* regrettable, unsatisfactory
憾乍 *ikannaga(ra)* regrettably
18 贈 *izō, isō* bequest, legacy
蹟 *iseki* (historic) ruins
類 *irui* surviving animals; party remnants

13

遷 6116 / J6e35 / M-X See **辺** 6011.

遽 6117 / J6e31 / M39161 KYO fear; quick; be agitated. *awa(teru)* be hurried, be confused. *awatada(shii)* busy, bustling, hurried, confused. *niwaka(ni)* suddenly.

邂 6118 / J6e30 / M39173 KAI meet unexpectedly.
9 逅 *kaikō* chance meeting

邀 6119 / J6c33 / M39168 YŌ go to meet; call.
15 撃 *yōgeki suru, muka(e) u(tsu)* ambush, assault, execute a surprise attack

B **避** 6120 / J4872 / M39163' HI. *yo(keru), sa(keru)* avoid, avert, ward off, keep aloof from, stay away from; evade, shirk, shun.
7 妊 *hinin* contraception
妊法 *hininhō* contraceptive method
8 所 *sa(ke)dokoro* refuge, stronghold
泊所 *hihakusho* harborage
10 病院 *hibyōin* isolation hospital
12 寒 *hikan* wintering, hibernation
寒地 *hikanchi* winter resort
暑 *hisho* summering; going to a summer resort
暑地 *hishochi* summer resort
暑客 *hishokyaku* summer residents
13 雷針 *hiraishin* lightning rod

雷器 *hiraiki* lightning arrester
18 難 *hinan* shelter, refuge, evacuation
難民 *hinammin* refugees
難所 *hinanjo* shelter structures
難者 *hinansha* refugees
難場 *hinanjō* shelter area

B **還** 6121 / J3454 / M39174' KAN. GEN. *kae(ru)* return; take one's leave; come again; come around (time). *kae(su)* send (someone) back.
4 元 *kangen* restoration; reduction (chemistry)
元牛乳 *kangen gyūnyū* mixed powdered milk
元米 *kangemmai* requisitioned rice returned to the farmer
5 付 *kampu* return, restitution, restoration
収 *kanshū suru* take back from
6 任 *gennin* return of an official to his former post
7 却 *kankyaku suru* send (something) back
8 幸 *kankō* return to the emperor
9 俗 *genzoku* quitting the priesthood, return to secular life
10 流 *kanryū* a return, flowing back, convection, return current
納 *kannō* repayment
都 *kanto* return to the government
11 啓 *kankei* return to the empress or crown prince
12 御 *kangyo* return of members of the Imperial Family
14 暦 *kanreki* one's 61st birthday
魂 *kankon* resurrection of the dead

14

邇 6122 / J6d6e / M39193 JI approach; near.

邃 6123 / J6364 / M39191 SUI deep in the interior; profound.

15

邊 6124 / J6e34 / M39216 See 辺 6011.

邌 6125 / J-X / M39219 REI. RAI. *ne(ru)* walk slowly, parade.

19

邏 6126 / J6e36 / M39259 RA go around; conceal.
8 卒 *rasotsu* patrolman, policeman

RAD. 邑 163

Ōzato large village (in contradistinction to Rads. 166 & 170). Except for the radical character itself, always used at right in the modified form 阝 (2 strokes) *ōzatozukuri*. Nickname: Right Village.

邑 6127 / J4d38 / M39269 YŪ village, rural community, town; dominion.

4

邨 6128 / J6e37 / M39313 See 村 2564.

那 6129 / J4661 / M39305 NA what?
4 辺 *nahen ni* where, whither

B **邦** 6130 / J4b2e / M39310 HŌ country. *kuni* country.
2 人 *hōjin* fellow countryman; a Japanese
3 土 *hōdo* country, realm
4 文 *hōbun* Japanese language
6 字 *hōji* Japanese characters
字新聞 *hōji shimbun* a Japanese-language newspaper
8 国 *hōkoku* country, nation
画 *hōga* a Japanese movie or painting
10 家 *hōka* one's country
11 域 *hōiki* political boundaries
訳 *hōyaku* translation into Japanese
貨 *hōka* Japanese money or goods; yen
13 楽 *hōgaku* Japanese music
14 語 *hōgo* vernacular; Japanese language

5

邯 6131 / J6e38 / M39330 KAN rich and abundant. used in Chinese place names.

邱 6132 / J6e39 / M39335 KYŪ hill. used in Chinese place names.

邵 6133 / J6e3a / M39343 SHŌ used in Chinese place and proper names.

B **邸** 6134 / J4521 / M39347 TEI *yashiki* mansion, residence.

4 中 *teichū* in the mansion
内 *teinai* grounds, premises
6 宅 *teitaku* mansion, residence
8 門 *teimon* mansion gate

B **邪** 6135 / J3c59 / M39357 SA. JA injustice, unrighteousness, wickedness *yokoshima* wickedness, wrong, injustice.

4 心 *jashin* sinister design
5 正 *jasei* right and wrong, truth and error
6 行 *jakō* going diagonally; wickedness
気 *jaki* miasma, poison, pestilential vapor; malice, evil; a cold
曲 *jakyoku* wickedness, injustice
7 見 *jaken* cruelty, hardheartedness; wrong view
8 佞 *janei* wickedness and flattery; wicked flatterer
法 *jaho* sorcery, witchcraft; heresy
知 *jachi* perverted talent, cunning, guile
念 *janen* sinister design, evil intention
宗 *jashū* heretical sect, heresy, evil (foreign) religion
宗門 *jashūmon* heretical religion
9 神 *jashin* evil deity, false god; demon
飛球 *jahikyū* foul ball
10 鬼 *jaki* a devil, imp, evil spirit
険 *jaken* cruelty, hardheartedness
11 道 *jadō* evil course; heresy
婬 *jain* adultery
推 *jasui* unjust suspicion, distrust
淫 *jain* lewdness, immorality
視 *jashi* an evil eye
球 *jakyū* foul ball
欲 *jayoku* carnal desire
教 *jakyō* heresy, paganism, heathenism
悪 *jaaku* wickedness, viciousness, vice
12 揄 *jayu suru* ridicule, tease
雲 *jaun* ominous clouds
13 想 *jasō* wicked person
14 説 *jasetsu* heresy
慳 *jaken* cruelty, hardheartedness
慳者 *jakemmono* heartless person
15 慾 *jayoku* carnal desire, evil passion
21 魔 *jama* hindrance, obstacle, barrier, inconvenience, encumbrance, interference, disturbance
魔立 *jamada(te)* hindrance, interference, disturbance
魔物 *jamamono* obstacle, hindrance, burden; nuisance, a bore
魔者 *jamamono* a person who is in the way

6

郁 6136 / J306a / M39371 IKU cultural progress; perfume.

B **郊** 6137 / J3959 / M39392 KŌ suburbs; rural area.

5 外 *kōgai* suburbs, outskirts
11 野 *kōya* suburban fields

B **郎** 6138 / J4f3a / M39405 **郞** 6139 / J-X / M39431 RŌ man; husband; counter for sons.

3 女 *iratsume* (familiar word for an ancient) young lady
7 君 *rōkun* young nobleman, young lord
10 従 *rōjū* a samurai's retainer
党 *rōtō, rōdō* retainers, vassals
12 等 *rōdō* retainers, vassals

7

郞 6139 / J-X / M39431 See 郎 6138.

郛 6140 / J6e3e / M39428 FU quarter, district; area inside castle wall.

郢 6141 / J6e3b / M39438 EI used in Chinese place names.

郤 6142 / J6e3c / M39440 GEKI look upward; gap, span, interstice.

A **郡** 6143 / J3734 / M39436 GUN *kōri* county, district.

[6] 会 *gunkai* county assembly
[7] 役所 *gun'yakusho* county office
[8] 長 *gunchō* head county official
制 *gunsei* county system
[9] 県 *gunken* counties and prefectures
県制度 *gunken seido* prefectural system
[10] 部 *gumbu* rural districts; counties

8

B **郭** 6144 / J3354 / M39474 KAKU enclosure; quarters. *kuruwa* enclosure, fortification; quarters; red-light district.

[3] 大 *kakudai* large and wide. *kakudai suru* enlarge
[4] 内 *kakunai* within the enclosure
中 *kakuchū* within the enclosure
公 *kakkō* cuckoo
公鳥 *kakkōdori* cuckoo
[5] 外 *kakugai* outside the enclosure
[11] 清 *kakusei* suru purify

A **郷** 6145 / J363f / M39498' **鄕** 6151 / J-X / M-X KYŌ village, native place. GŌ country, district, village.

[2] 人 *kyōjin* villagers; townmate
[3] 士 *gōshi* a country samurai
土 *kyōdo* one's birthplace, one's old home
土文学 *kyōdo bungaku* local literature
土色 *kyōdoshoku* local color
土芸術 *kyōdo geijutsu* rural crafts
土愛 *kyōdoai* local patriotism
土閥 *kyōdobatsu* group of clansmen
土誌 *kyōdoshi* local history
[5] 民 *gōmin* rural folk
[7] 邑 *kyōyū* village, hamlet
里 *kyōri* one's old home, native place
村 *gōson* villages
社 *gōsha* village shrine, district shrine
[8] 国 *kyōkoku* native land
学 *kyōgaku* village school
[9] 信 *kyōshin* message from home
俗 *kyōzoku* village customs
軍 *gōgun* ex-soldier, reservist, veteran
思 *kyōshi* thoughts of home
[10] 党 *kyōtō* one's fellow villagers; one's village
党心 *kyōtōshin* provincialism
[13] 愁 *kyōshū* nostalgia, homesickness
[14] 関 *kyōkun* the gate of one's home town; home town, birthplace
塾 *kyōjuku* teaching in a rural environment
[15] 閭 *kyōryo* village gate; the village; one's home town
談 *kyōdan* rural talk, rural speech

A **部** 6146 / J4974 / M39460 BU department, bureau, section; faculty; division, class, category; part, portion, region; copy, volume, set. *be* the large ancient family.

[3] 下 *buka* subordinate, follower; under one's command
[4] 内 *bunai* circles; the department; the section; the staff
分 *bubun* part, portion, section. *buwa(ke)* classification
分食 *bubunshoku* partial eclipse
分品 *bubunhin* parts, accessories
分蝕 *bubunshoku* partial eclipse
[5] 民 *bemin* members of the large ancient family
外 *bugai* outside the service
外秘 *bugaihi* restricted to the service
[6] 会 *bukai* sectional meeting
[7] 局 *bukyoku* department, bureau
位 *bui* part (of the body), region
[8] 長 *buchō* head of a division, department, or section
門 *bumon* class, group, department, section, category; branch, line, field; genus, order, type
所 *busho* one's post of duty
[9] 面 *bumen* field, aspect, phase, side
首 *bushu* radical (of a character)
活 *bukatsu* club activities
厚 *buatsu na, buatsu(i)* thick, bulky, massive
品 *buhin* parts, accessories
屋 *heya* room, apartment
屋中 *heyajū* throughout the room
屋代 *heyadai* room rent
屋住 *heyazu(mi)* homeless hanger-on; an heir who has not yet taken over
屋着 *heyagi* house dress
[10] 将 *bushō* a general
員 *buin* staff; staff member, member, club members
[11] 族 *buzoku* tribe
隊 *butai* unit, corps, squad, detachment
隊長 *butaichō* commanding officer
[12] 属 *buzoku* attached to an office

落 *buraku* community, settlement, village
13 数 *busū* number of copies, circulation
署 *busho* one's post of duty
18 類 *burui* class, heading, group, category, order, division
類分 *buruiwa(ke)* classification, grouping

A **郵** 6147 / J4d39 / M39485 YŪ stagecoach stop; mail.
8 券 *yūken* postage stamp
送 *yūsō* mailing
送料 *yūsōryō* postage
送差止 *yūsō sashitome* postal ban
送費 *yūsōhi* postage expense
送無料 *yūsō muryō* postage-free
送禁止 *yūsō kinshi* postal ban
9 政 *yūsei* postal system
政省 *Yūseishō* Ministry of Postal Services
便 *yubin* mail
便小為替 *yūbin kogawase* small money order
便切手 *yūbin kitte* postage stamp
便年金 *yūbin nenkin* post office annuity
便行嚢 *yūbin kōnō* mailbag
便車 *yūbinsha* mail car
便局 *yūbinkyoku* post office
便私書函 *yūbin shishokan* post office box
便物 *yūbimbutsu* mail matter
便函 *yūbimbako* mailbox
便受 *yūbin u(ke)* mailbox
便注文 *yūbin chūmon* mail order
便屋 *yūbin'ya* mail carrier
便為替 *yūbingawase, yūbin kawase* postal money order
便料 *yūbinryō* postage
便馬車 *yūbin basha* mail coach
便配達 *yūbin haitatsu* mail delivery, mail carrier
便振替貯金 *yūbin furikae chokin* postal transfer account
便袋 *yūbimbukuro* mailbag
便落 *yūbin oto(shi)* mail chute
便貯金 *yūbin chokin* postal savings
便葉書 *yūbin hagaki* postcard
便集配人 *yūbin shūhainin* mail carrier
便電信為替 *yūbin denshingawase* postal telegraphic money order
便箱 *yūbimbako* mailbox
10 書 *yūsho* a letter sent by mail
11 船 *yūsen* mail steamer
袋 *yūtai* maibag
12 税 *yūzei* postage; rate of postage
税不足 *yūzei fusoku* postage due

A **都** 6148 / J4554 / M39497' **都** 6149 / J-X / M39509 TO, TSU *miyako* capital, metropolis.
2 人 *miyakobito, tojin* town or city people
人士 *tojinshi* townspeople, a metropolitan, citizens of the capital
3 下 *toka* throughout the capital, in the metropolis
大路 *miyako ōji* main thoroughfare of the metropolis
4 心 *toshin* heart of the city
内 *tonai* within the capital
5 立 *toritsu* metropolitan, municipal
庁 *Tochō* Tokyo Metropolitan Government Office
民 *Tomin* Tokyo citizens
民税 *tominzei* residents' tax
市 *toshi* cities; towns and cities
市生活 *toshi seikatsu* city life
市伝道 *toshi dendō* city evangelism
市対抗 *toshi taikō* intercity match
市計画 *toshi keikaku* town planning
6 合 *tsugō* circumstances, conditions, reasons; convenience; opportunity, occasion; arrangement, management; accommodation; in all
合上 *tsugōjō* for convenience' sake, in view of circumstances
合良 *tsugoyo(ku)* fortunately, successfully, satisfactorily
会 *Tokai* Tokyo Metropolitan Assembly. *tokai* city, town
会人 *tokaijin* townsmen, city residents
会生活 *tokai seikatsu* city life
会地 *tokaichi* urban areas
会風 *tokaifū* urban manners, urbanity
会発達 *tokai hattatsu* urbanization
7 住居 *miyakozumai* city life
8 門 *tomon* city gates; the capital
府 *tofu* cities and towns
制 *tosei* metropolitan government
育 *miyakosoda(chi)* town-bred
長官 *To chōkan* Tokyo governor
知事 *To chiji* Tokyo governor
9 度 *tsudo* each time, whenever, as often as
俗 *tozoku* metropolitan customs

城 *tojō* castle town
11 鳥 *miyakodori* sea gull
道府県 *to-dō-fu-ken* urban and rural prefectures
12 落 *miyakoo(chi)* leaving or fleeing from the capital
営 *Toei* operated by Tokyo
13 雅 *toga* elegance, refinement
詣 *miyakomō(de)* going to the capital
路 *miyakoji* road to the capital; roads in the capital
鄙 *tohi* town and country
20 議会 *To Gikai* Tokyo Metropolitan Assembly

9

都 6149 / J-X / M39509 See **都** 6148.

鄂 6150 / J6e3f / M39520 GAKU used in Chinese place names.

10

鄕 6151 / J-X / M-X See **郷** 6145.

鄒 6152 / J6e40 / M39562 SŪ, SHŪ used in Chinese place names.

11

鄙 6153 / J6e41 / M39597 HI lowliness; countryside. *hina* countryside. *hina(biru)* be countrified.
2 人 *hinabito, hijin* a rustic
6 劣 *hiretsu* meanness, foul play
7 見 *hiken* my humble opinion
言 *higen* slang expression
8 陋 *hirō* low rank; wickedness, vulgarity
9 俗 *hizoku na* rustic, countrified; low-class
12 猥 *hiwai* indecency, obscenity
14 語 *higo* slang
歌 *hinata uta* pastoral song

11

鄲 6154 / J6e42 / M39659 TAN used in Chinese place names.

鄭 6155 / J4522 / M39647 TEI an ancient Chinese province.
9 重 *teichō* courtesy

13

鄰 6156 / J6e43 / M39656 See **隣** 6484.

酉 RAD. 164

Tori or *hiyori no tori* ("the bird of the zodiac," as distinguished from the common bird of Rad. 196). At left: *tori hen.* In combinations this element connotes liquid and hence in any position is generally called *sakezukuri* (i.e., the right-hand element of the character for saké). Nickname: Saké.

酉 6157 / J4653 / M39763 YŪ. *tori* 5-7 p.m., tenth zodiac sign; bird; west.
5 市 *tori (no) ichi* year-end fair

2

酊 6158 / J6e44 / M39764 TEI intoxication.

酋 6159 / J3d36 / M39765 SHŪ chieftain.
8 長 *shūchō* chief, chieftain

A **酒** 6160 / J3c72 / M39776 SHU *sake* saké, rice wine; alcoholic liquor.
4 手 *sakate* drink money, tip
太 *sakabuto(ri)* getting fat from drinking
5 母 *shubo* yeast, ferment
仙 *shusen* heavy drinker
代 *sakadai, sakashiro* price of saké; saké gift to workers; workers' bonus, tip
石酸 *shusekisan* tartaric acid
6 肉 *shuniku* saké and meat
色 *shushoku* wine and women, debauchery
好 *sakezu(ki)* drinker

池肉林 *shuchi-nikurin* sumptuous feast
気 *sakake, shuki* smell of liquor
気違 *sake kichiga(i)* crazed with drink; such a drunk; heavy drinking; heavy drinker
7 狂 *shukyō, sakeguru(i)* drunken frenzy
乱 *shuran* drunken frenzy; vicious drinker
呑 *sakenomi* drinker
男 *sake otoko* brewer
8 店 *saketen, sakamise* saké shop
杯 *shuhai* wine glass
毒 *shudoku* alcoholism
肴 *shukō, sake-sakana* food and drink
肴料 *shukōryō* monetary gift for food
9 屋 *sakaya* wine shop; wine merchant
保 *shuho* canteen, post exchange, PX
後 *shugo* after drinking saké
客 *shukyaku* drinker
臭 *sakekusa(i)* reeking of liquor
食 *shushoku, shushi* revelry; saké and food
食料 *shushokuryō* monetary gift for food
造 *shuzō, sakezuku(ri), sakazuku(ri)* saké brewing
造米 *shuzōmai* rice for saké brewing
造家 *shuzōka* brewer
造税 *shuzōzei* tax on alcoholic liquor
造場 *shuzōjō* brewery, distillery
造業 *shuzōgyō* brewery business
10 席 *shuseki* banquet, feast
徒 *shuto* drinking companion
浸 *sakabita(ri), sakebita(ri)* steeped in liquor; drinking daily. *sakabita(shi)* steeped in liquor
家 *shuka* wine shop; drinker
宴 *shuen* banquet, drinking bout
息 *sakaiki* alcoholic breath
振舞 *sakaburumai* drinking bout
11 淫 *shuin* wine and women
粕 *sake kasu* saké lees
船 *sakabune* wine press, vat
販 *shuhan* sale of liquor
断 *sakada(chi)* swearing off from drinking
盛 *sakamo(ri)* carousal, revelry
12 場 *sakaba* bar, barroom
税 *shuzei* liquor tax
飲 *sakeno(mi)* drinker
壺 *sakatsubo* saké jar
量 *shuryō* drinking capacity
12 塩 *sakeshio* saké seasoning
肆 *shushi* liquor store
戦 *shusen* drinking bout
14 豪 *shugō* heavy drinker
蔵 *sakagura* wine cellar, wineshop
精 *shusei* alcohol, spirits, hard liquor
精飲料 *shusei inryō* alcoholic liquor
15 幟 *shushi* saloon banner
槽 *sakabune* wine press, vat
器 *shuki* saké cup
16 樽 *sakadaru* wine barrel
興 *shukyō* conviviality, merrymaking
機嫌 *sasakigen* tipsiness
17 糟 *sake kasu* saké lees
18 癖 *sake kuse, sakaguse, shuheki* drinking habits
類 *shurui* alcoholic liquors
21 饌 *shusen* food and drink

3

酎 6161 J4371 M39772 CHŪ saké.

B **酌** 6162 J3c60 M39768 SHAKU serving saké; the server. *ku(mu)* draw (water), ladle, dip, scoop, pump; consider; sympathize with; drink; think.
6 交 *ku(mi)-ka(wasu)* rearrange
11 婦 *shakufu* waitress, barmaid
12 量 *shakuryō* consideration, pardon, extenuation

A **配** 6163 J475b M39771 HAI distribute; spouse; exile; rationing. *hai(suru)* allot; arrange; match (a couple); exile; subordinate. *kuba(ru)* distribute; serve (food); allocate; keep (your eyes) on. *ashira(u)* arrange, decorate; garnish; accompany (a singer).
3 下 *haika* subordinates, followers, adherents
4 水 *haisui* water supply; water distribution
分 *haibun* distribution, apportionment
5 付 *haifu* distribution, apportionment

7 見角言谷豆豕豸貝赤走足身車辛辰莽辶邑阝 4【酉】采里

布 *haifu* distribution, apportionment
本 *haihon* distribution, apportionment
6 色 *haishoku* color scheme
列 *hairetsu* arrangement, grouping, disposition
合 *haigō* composition, combination, distribution, arrangement, harmony, match, (color) scheme; mixture
当 *haitō* dividend, share, quota, allotment
当金 *haitōkin* share, dividend
7 車 *haisha* car allocation
役 *haiyaku* cast (of a play)
8 所 *haisho* place of exile
物 *kuba(ri)mono* things to distribute; gifts
祀 *haishi suru* enshrine; dedicate a shrine
9 陣 *haijin* camp layout
炭 *haitan* coal distribution
10 流 *hairyū, hairu* exile, banishment
剤 *haizai* compounding a prescription; correct handling (of a question)
11 船 *haisen* ship allocation
遇 *haigū* combination; spouse; marriage
遇者 *haigūsha* spouse, consort
達 *haitatsu* delivery, distribution; delivery person
達人 *haitatsunin* delivery person, mail carrier, person who delivers milk
達先 *haitatsusaki* destination, receiver
達料 *haitatsuryō* delivery charge
達違 *haitatsuchiga(i)* misdelivery
12 属 *haizoku* attached to, assigned to
備 *haibi* arrangement, disposition, stationing
給 *haikyū* distribution, rationing
給米 *haikyūmai* rationed rice
給所 *haikyūjo* distribution point
給物 *haikyūmono* rationed goods, a ration
給品 *haikyūhin* rationed goods
給量 *haikyūryō* a ration
13 置 *haichi* arrangement, disposition (of troops)
意 *haii* concern, anxiety, worry
電 *haiden* distribution of electricity
電会社 *haidengaisha* power company
電所 *haidensho* power station
電線 *haidensen* service wire
電盤 *haidemban* switchboard
14 管 *haikan* plumbing, piping
15 慮 *hairyo* consideration, solicitation, care, concern, anxiety, trouble
線 *haisen* (electric) wiring
16 餐 *haisan suru* distribute the elements (in the Christian Communion Service)
膳 *haizen suru* set the table
膳室 *haizenshitsu* serving room
18 謫 *haitaku* exile

4

酘 6164 / J6e46 / M39797 Tō ferment twice, referment; refermented saké.

酖 6165 / J6e45 / M39792 TAN addicted to. CHIN poison.
13 溺 *tandeki* addiction, dissipation

B**酔** 6166 / J3f6c / M39807 **醉** 6178 / J6e4d / M39906 SUI. *yo(u)* get drunk; feel sick; be poisoned; be elated, be spellbound. *yo(pparau)* get drunk. *yo(i), ei* intoxication. *yo(idore)* drunkard.
2 人 *suijin* a drunk
4 心地 *yo(i)gokochi, eigokochi* a gloriously drunk feeling
5 払 *yoppara(i)* drunkard
生夢死 *suisei-mushi* dreaming one's life away
7 言 *eigoto* words of a drunkard
狂 *yo(i)-kuru(u)* be raving drunk. *suikyō* raving drunkenness
余 *suiyo* drunken
8 泣 *eina(ki)* crying while drunk
臥 *yo(i)-fu(su), ei-fu(su)* sleep off a drunk
歩 *suiho* staggering gait, grogginess
事 *eigoto* actions of a drunkard
10 倒 *yo(i)-tao(re), eidao(re)* falling down drunk
酒 *suishu* drunkenness
紛 *yo(i)magire, eimagire* hopelessly drunk
11 眼 *suigan* bleary eyes
眼朦朧 *suigammōrō(taru)* (eyes) dimmed with drunk
13 痴 *yo(i)-shi(reru)* be befuddled. *eikurui, eigurui* craze with drink
漢 *suikan* drunkard
14 態 *suitai* intoxication, drunkenness
15 潰 *yo(i)-tsubu(reru)* be dead drunk.

yo(i)-tsubu(su) make someone dead drunk
[16] 醒 *yoiza(me), eiza(me), yoizama(shi)* sobering up
[18] 顔 *suigan* face of a drunkard

5

酥 6167 / J6e48 / M39835 SO beverage made from milk; dairy products.

酣 6168 / J6e47 / M39825 KAN. *takenawa* height of, full swing, thick of.

B 酢 6169 / J3f5d / M39824 SAKU. SO. *su* vinegar. *su(i), su(ppai)* sour, acid, tart.
[8] 物 *su(no)mono* vinegared dish
[14] 漬 *suzuke* pickling
酸 *sakusan* acetic acid

6

酩 6170 / J6e49 / M39846 MEI sweet saké.
[9] 酊 *meitei* drunkenness

B 酬 6171 / J3d37 / M39850 SHŪ. *mukui* reward; retribution.
[10] 恩祭 *shūonsai* peace offering

B 酪 6172 / J4d6f / M39847 RAKU whey; broth; fruit juice.
[13] 農 *rakunō* dairy farming
農家 *rakunoka* dairy farmer
農場 *rakunōjō* dairy farm
[14] 酸 *rakusan* butyric acid
製品 *rakuseihin* dairy products

7

酲 6173 / J6e4b / M39865 TEI be hung over; long; give up.

酳 6174 / J6e4a / M39866 IN rinse; rinse out the mouth with wine, offer wine.

B 酵 6175 / J395a / M39868 KŌ fermentation. *moto* materials for making saké.
[5] 母 *kōbo* yeast, leaven
母菌 *kōbokin* yeast fungus
[10] 素 *kōso* enzyme, ferment
素学 *kōsogaku* enzymology

B 酷 6176 / J3973 / M39870' KOKU severity, cruelty. *hido(i), mugo(i)* cruel, harsh, merciless, atrocious; unjust, unfair; severe, intense, bitter, serious, terrible, outrageous, unreasonable. *hanahada* very, greatly, exceedingly.
[5] 目 *hido(i)me* rough handling, maltreatment
[6] 似 *kokuji* close resemblance
刑 *kokkei* severe punishment
吏 *kokuri* exacting official
[8] 使 *kokushi* hard-driving, abuse, exploitation
[10] 烈 *kokuretsu no* severe, intense, rigorous
[11] 遇 *kokugū* maltreatment
[12] 税 *kokuzei* severe taxes
寒 *kokkan* intense cold; depth of winter
暑 *kokusho* intense heat
評 *kokuhyō* severe criticism
評家 *kokuhyōka* bitter critic
[15] 熱 *kokunetsu* intense heat
[16] 薄 *kokuhaku* brutality, atrocity

B 酸 6177 / J3b40 / M39871 SAN acid; bitterness. *su(i), su(ppai)* sour, acid, tart.
[4] 化 *sanka* oxidation
化物 *sankabutsu* oxide
化窒素 *sanka chisso* nitrous oxide, laughing gas
[8] 味 *su(i)mi, sammi* acidity, sourness
性 *sansei* acidity
性反応 *sansei hannō* acid reaction
性症 *sanseishō* acidosis
[9] 度 *sando* acidity
[10] 素 *sanso* oxygen
素吸入 *sanso kyūnyū* oxygen inhalation
素補給装置 *sanso hokyū sōchi* oxygen equipment
[11] 基 *sanki* acid radical (in chemistry)
敗 *sampai* acidification
敗乳 *sampainyū* sour milk
[14] 鼻 *sambi* extreme pain; deep sorrow
[15] 漿提灯 *hōzukijōchin* small round red lantern
[18] 類 *sanrui* acids

8

醉 6178 / J6e4d / M39906 See 酔 6166.

醋 6179 | J6e4c | M39911 SAKU. *su* vinegar.

14 酸 *sakusan* acetic acid

醂 6180 | J6e4e | M39891 RAN. *awa(su), sawa(su)* remove astringency; bleach in water.

9 柿 *sawa(shi)gaki* persimmon with astringency removed

醇 6181 | J3d66 | M39901 JUN pure saké; purity; affection.

4 化 *junka suru* refine, purify, chasten, sublimate; be refined, be chastened

5 正 *junsei* pure, genuine

乎 *junko no* pure, sheer, unalloyed

6 朴 *jumboku* simplicity and honesty

8 味 *jummi* a pure, rich taste

9 厚 *junkō no* kindhearted, courteous

風 *jumpū* good custom

風美俗 *jumpū bizoku* good customs

15 醇 *junjun to* in a kindly manner

9

醗 6182 | J4830 | M-X Nonstandard for  6194.

醐 6183 | J386f | M39930 GO a kind of cream obtained from boiling butter.

醍 6184 | J4269 | M39924 DAI whey; good Buddhist teaching.

16 醐味 *daigomi* sweet taste; zest for life; Buddha's excellent teachings

醒 6185 | J4043 | M39936 SEI. *sa(meru) vi* awake; be disillusioned; sober up. *sa(masu) vt* wake up, awake.

13 際 *sa(me)giwa ni* on the verge of awakening

10

醤 6186 | J3e5f | M-X Nonstandard for 醬 6192.

醢 6187 | J6e4f | M39981 KAI salted fish guts; salted chopped meat.

醞 6188 | J-X | M39974 UN fermentation.

20 釀 *unjō suru vt* ferment, brew

B **醜** 6189 | J3d39 | M39969 SHŪ ugliness; uncleanness; shame. *miniku(i)* bad-looking, ugly; unsightly; indecent, disgraceful.

3 女 *shūjo, shikome* homely woman, plain-looking woman

6 行 *shūkō* disgraceful conduct, scandal, immoral relations

交 *shūkō* immoral relations, intimacy

名 *shūmei* scandal, ill fame. *shikona* true name; nickname; wrestler's name

7 状 *shūjō* disgraceful state of affairs

声 *shūsei* embarrassing rumor, scandal

男 *buotoko, shikoo* ugly-looking man

9 美 *shūbi* beauty or ugliness, personal appearance

11 婦 *shūfu* homely woman

悪 *shūaku* unsightliness, ugliness, meanness, offensiveness

13 漢 *shūkan* a despicable man; an ugly man

業 *shūgyō* shameful calling, prostitution

業婦 *shūgyōfu* prostitute

14 聞 *shūbun* scandal, ill fame

態 *shūtai* shameful conduct; ugly scene

関係 *shūkankei* immoral relations, intimacy

18 類 *shūrui* "black sheep;" corrupt element

11

醫 6190 | J6e50 | M40006 See 医 590.

醪 6191 | J6e52 | M40004 RŌ. *moromi* unrefined saké or soy.

醬 6192 | J-X | M40011 **醤** 6186 | J3e5f | M-X SHŌ. *hishio* a kind of *miso*.

8 油 *shōyu* soy sauce

12

醯 6193 | J6e51 | M40036 KEI vinegar; pickled in vinegar.

醱 6194 | J-X | M40041 HATSU fermentation, brewing.

[14] 酵 *hakkō* fermentation
酵物 *hakkōbutsu* products of fermentation

13

醴 6195 / J6e54 / M40053 REI sweet drink made from fermented rice; sweet.

醵 6196 / J6e53 / M40055 KYO contribution for a feast.
[5] 出 *kyoshutsu* donation, contribution
[8] 金 *kyokin* raising money

B 醸 6197 / J3e7a / M40064' 釀 6199 / J6e56 / M40099 JŌ. *kamo(su)* brew; cause, give rise to.
[5] 出 *kamo(shi)-da(su)* cause, bring about
[6] 成 *jōsei suru* brew; foment, breed, cause, create
[9] 造 *jōzō* brewing, distilling
造人 *jōzōnin* brewer, distiller
造所 *jōzōsho* brewery
造学 *jōzōgaku* science of brewing
造酒 *jōzōshu* brewage
造家 *jōzōka* brewer, distiller
造業 *jōzōgyō* brewing industry

14

醺 6198 / J6e55 / M40070 KUN hunger.

17

釀 6199 / J6e56 / M40099 See 醸 6197.

18

釁 6200 / J6e57 / M40103 KIN sprinkling blood on the altar.
[14] 端 *kintan* beginning of a war; basis of a misunderstanding

RAD. 釆 165

Nogome (i.e., the katakana *no* plus Rad. 119 *kome* "rice").
At left: *nogome hen*. Nickname: Topped Rice.

采 6201 / J3a53 / M40116 釆 6202 / J4850 / M40115 SAI dice; form, appearance. *to(ru)* take. *irodori* coloring.
[5] 日 *suime, sai(no)me* dots on dice
[6] 地 *saichi* fief, domain
[7] 邑 *saiyū* fief; vassalage
[10] 配 *saihai* baton of command; duster

4

B 釈 6203 / J3c61 / M40120' 釋 6205 / J6e59 / M40129 SHAKU, SEKI explanation. *to(ku)* explain.
[7] 言 *shakugen* excuse
[8] 放 *shakuhō* release, liberation, acquittal
明 *shakumei* explanation; vindication
典 *shakuten* Buddhist literature
迦 *Shaka* Gautama, Sakyamuni
迦牟尼 *Shakamuni* Sakyamuni, Gautama, Buddha
迦如来 *Shaka Nyorai* Sakyamuni
迦像 *Shakazō* an image of Gautama
[11] 教 *Shakkyō* Buddhism
[12] 尊 *Shakuson* Buddha, Gautama
奠 *shakuten, sekiten* a festival to Confucius and his disciples
然 *shakuzen toshite* with sudden awakening, well satisfied with (an explanation)
[13] 義 *shakugi* commentary, exposition
義学 *shakugigaku* exegesis

5

釉 6204 / J6e58 / M40121 YŪ glaze, enamel.
[16] 薬 *uwagusuri, yūyaku* glaze, enamel

13

釋 6205 / J6e59 / M40129 See 釈 6203.

RAD. 里 166

Sato village or *ri* two and a half miles. At left: 里 *sato hen*. Nickname: Village.

A 里 6206 / J4e24 / M40131 RI village; a Japanese league, 2.44 miles. *sato* village, hamlet, the country; parents' home.

2 人 *rijin, satobito* villagers, countryfolk
3 子 *satogo* child put out to nurse, foster child
4 心 *satogokoro* homesickness, nostalgia
方 *satokata* wife's home, wife's folks; childhood home of an adopted son
中 *satonaka* rural town
6 芋 *satoimo* taro
7 扶持 *satobuchi* child-fostering expenses
言葉 *sato kotoba* courtesan's language; rural dialect
9 俗 *rizoku* local customs
神楽 *sato kagura* local shrine pantomime; village dramatic performance
10 帰 *satogae(ri)* bride's first visit to her old home
12 程 *ritei* mileage; distance
程標 *riteihyō* posts marking distances in *ri*
13 数 *risū* mileage, distance
15 標 *rihyō* milestone
16 謡 *riyō* ballad, folk song, popular song
親 *satooya* foster parent

2

A 重 6207 / J3d45 / M40132 CHŌ. JŪ nest of boxes. *kasa(neru)* pile up, heap up, add, repeat. *kasa(naru)* pile up, be piled; lie on one another. *omo(ru)* get heavy; grow serious. *omo(njiru), omo(nzuru)* honor, respect, esteem, prize. *omo(i), omo(tai)* heavy; massive; serious; important; severe; oppressed. *omo(mi)* importance, weight, dignity. *omo(sa)* weight. *kasa(ne)* pile, heap, layer; suits; set; course (of stones). *kasa(nete)* repeatedly, again. *omo(na), omo(naru)* main, principal, important. *jū-* heavy; double. *-e* -fold, ply. *-jū* -fold.

2 力 *jūryoku* gravity
3 工業 *jūkōgyō* heavy industry
大 *jūdai na* important, serious
大化 *jūdaika* aggravation
大性 *jūdaisei* importance, seriousness
大視 *jūdaishi* taking (something) seriously
4 心 *jūshin* center of gravity
火器 *jūkaki* heavy weapons
手 *omode* serious wound or injury
手代 *omotedai* head steward (of an estate)
水 *jūsui* heavy water
水素 *jūsuiso* heavy hydrogen
5 用 *jūyō suru* appoint to a responsible post
目 *omome* a little heavy
石 *omoshi, omo(shi) ishi* stone weights on pickle-tub covers
立 *omoda(tsu), omoda(tta)* main, principal, important, conspicuous, prominent
圧 *jūatsu* pressure
代 *jūdai* successive generations
犯 *jūhan, chōhan* felony; felon; old offender
出 *jūshutsu suru* cite again
母音 *jūboin* diphthong
6 臣 *jūshin* chief vassal; senior statesman
任 *jūnin* heavy responsibility, important post; re-election, reappointment
刑 *jūkei* heavy sentence
合 *kasa(nari)-a(u)* lie on top of each other, overlap; pile up
7 言 *jūgon* a succession of words of similar meaning
囲 *jūi, chōi* close siege
体 *jūtai* seriously ill
役 *omoyaku* heavy responsibilities; director. *jūyaku* director, directorate
利 *jūri* compound interest
労働 *jūrōdō* heavy labor; hard labor (in prison)
8 味 *omomi* weight; importance; emphasis; dignity
油 *jūyu* crude oil; fuel oil
版 *jūhan* additional printing, literary piracy

刻 *jūkoku* reprinting
宝 *chōhō(garu)* find useful; think lightly of. *chōhō* convenience, usefulness. *chōhō, jūhō* priceless treasure
苦 *omokuru(shii)* heavy, cumbrous; gloomy, oppressive, leaden; awkward (expression)
金属 *jūkinzoku* heavy metals
9 厚 *jūkō* thickness; composure and dignity. *chōkō* composure and dignity
科 *jūka* serious crime; heavy punishment
重 *kasa(ne)gasa(ne)* frequently; sincerely; exceedingly. *omoomo(shii)* serious, grave, dignified. *jūjū no* repeated, manifold. *jūjū ni* extremely. *jūjū nimo* repeatedly
星 *jūsei* multiple star
奏 *jūsō* instrumental duet
軌条 *jūkijō* heavy rail
炭酸曹達 *jūtansan sōda* sodium bicarbonate; baking soda
点 *jūten* colon; emphasis, importance
点主義 *jūten shugi* priority system
要 *jūyō na* important, momentous; essential; principal, major
要性 *jūyōsei* importance, gravity
要視 *jūyōshi suru* regard highly
要産業 *jūyō sangyō* key industry
10 病 *jūbyō* serious illness
砲 *jūhō* heavy artillery
荷 *juka* heavy freight; heavy responsibility. *omoni* load, heavy burden, encumbrance
恩 *chōon* special blessing. *jūon* heavy obligation
書用羊皮紙 *kasa(ne)ga(ki)yō yōhishi* palimpsest
症 *jūshō* serious illness
症者 *jūshōsha* the seriously ill
症例 *jūshōrei* serious cases (of illness)
11 過 *omosu(giru)* be too heavy
掛 *kasa(ne)-ka(keru)* lap, overlap
液 *jūeki* heavy liquids
視 *jūshi* serious consideration
訳 *jūyaku* retranslation
陽 *chōyō* Chrysanthemum Festival (the ninth day of the ninth lunar month)
患 *jūkan* serious illness
曹 *jūsō* sodium bicarbonate, baking soda
責 *jūseki* heavy responsibility
商主義 *jūshō shugi* mercantilism
婚 *jūkon* bigamy
婚者 *jūkonsha* bigamist
12 湯 *omoyu* thin rice gruel, rice water
税 *jūzei* heavy taxation
詞 *kasa(ne) kotoba* repeated word or phrase
畳 *chōjō* piled one upon another; excellent, splendid
着 *kasa(ne)gi* wearing one garment over another
量 *jūryō* weight; heavyweight boxer
量挙 *jūryōa(ge)* weight lifting
量拳闘選手 *jūryō kentō senshu* heavyweight champion
量感 *jūryōkan* thick and heavy
量感覚 *jūryō kankaku* sense of weight
量選手 *jūryō senshu* heavyweight champion
量噸 *jūryōton* dead-weight tonnage
量噸数 *jūryō tonsu* dead-weight tonnage
13 詰 *jūzume* food packed in nest of lacquered boxes
愛 *jūai* endearment
罪 *jūzai* felony, serious crime
戦車 *jūsensha* heavy tank
禁錮 *jūkinko* imprisonment with hard labor
農主義 *jūnō shugi* emphasizing agriculture
傷 *jūshō, omode* serious wound or injury
傷者 *jūshōsha* severely wounded person
14 説 *jūsetsu* re-explanation
罰 *jūbatsu* heavy punishment
態 *jūtai* seriously ill
酸素 *jūsanso* heavy oxygen
複 *chōfuku, jūfuku* duplication, overlapping, repetition, redundancy
複保険 *jūfuku hoken* double insurance
15 縁 *jūen* double marriage (in the same family); intermarriage
器 *jūki* a treasure; an invaluable person
箱 *jūbako* nest of boxes
箱読 *jūbako yo(mi)* mixed *on-kun* pronunciation
16 噸 *jūton* long ton
積 *jūseki suru* pile up
篤 *jūtoku na* serious (illness)
機 *jūki* heavy machine gun

機関銃 *jūkikanjū* heavy machine gun
17 聴 *chōtei* hard of hearing
謹慎 *jūkinshin* close confinement (in one's barracks)
18 職 *jūshoku* responsible position
鎮 *jūchin* leader, authority, mainstay
騎兵 *jūkihei* heavy cavalry
19 爆 *jūbaku* heavy bomber
爆撃機 *jūbakugekiki* heavy bomber

4

A **野** 6208 / J4c6e / M40133 Ya field, plain; the Opposition; civilian life; rustic. *no* field, plain. *ya-, no-* wild.
2 人 *yajin* a rustic; a boor; common people
3 山 *noyama* hills and fields
川 *nogawa* stream flowing through a field
下 *ya (ni) kuda(ru)* resign from government service
4 火 *nobi* brush fire, prairie fire
牛 *noushi, yagyū* wild ox, bison, buffalo
犬 *yaken* stray dog
中 *nonaka no, nonaka ni* in the field
天 *noten* open air
分 *nowaki* wintry blast
太 *nobuto(i)* audacious, impudent
夫 *yafu* rural man
手 *yashu* fielder
手選択 *yashu sentaku* fielder's choice
辺 *nobe* fields
辺送 *nobeoku(ri)* funeral
辺煙 *nobe (no) kemuri* the smoke of a crematory
心 *yashin* ambition, aspiration, sinister design, intrigue, treachery
心家 *yashinka* an ambitious person
心満満 *yashin-mamman na* very ambitious
5 立 *noda(chi), noda(te)* (nobles) resting in the field. *noda(te)* an outside bath
史 *yashi* an unauthorized history
末 *nozue* edge of the field, corner of the field
生 *yasei* wildness; wild
生果物 *yasei kudamono* wild fruit
生動物 *yasei dōbutsu* wild animals
生植物 *yasei shokubutsu* wild plants
外 *yagai* the fields, the open air, outdoors; suburbs
外運動 *yagai undō* a field sport, outdoor exercises
外演習 *yagai enshū* field exercises; field work
外劇 *yagaigeki* outdoor drama
外撮影 *yagai satsuei* location (in filming)
外撮影中 *yagai satsueichū* on location
6 羊 *yagi* goat
色 *yashoku* views of fields
伏 *nobushi* mountain priest, itinerant priest, hermit
寺 *nodera* temple in a field
守 *nomori* a field watch
合 *yagō* cohabitation without marriage
合夫婦 *yagō fūfu* common-law couple
7 沢 *nozawa* swampy fields
兎 *nousagi* wild rabbit, hare
良 *nora* the fields; laziness
良犬 *nora inu* stray dog
良仕事 *nora shigoto* farm work, field work
良猫 *nora neko* stray cat
良着 *noragi* farm field smock
8 郎 *yarō* fellow, guy, rogue
育 *nosoda(chi)* wild
武士 *nobushi* wandering samurai, freelance
性 *yasei* wild nature, uncouthness
性児 *yaseiji* wild boy
性的 *yaseiteki* wild, rough, mean, rude
性味 *yaseimi* roughness, wildness, rusticity
放 *nobana(shi)* posturing; pasture; leaving things to themselves
放図 *nohōzu na* haphazard, wild, proud
放途 *nohōzu na* haphazard, wild, proud
放埒 *nohōratsu* unbridled license
9 面 *nozura* the field
陣 *nojin* bivouac
卑 *yahi na* rode, coarse, vulgar
荒 *noara(shi)* theft or damage of crops
草 *yasō* wild grass, wild pants. *nogusa* grass in a field
10 馬 *nouma* wild horse
原 *nohara* plain, field, moor, wilderness, prairie
師 *yashi* showman; quack, charlatan
晒 *nozara(shi) no* weatherworn
致 *yachi* rural beauty, rural air, rusticity
党 *yatō* opposition party
叟 *yasō* elderly rural man
帰 *nogae(ri)* returning from the fields at nightfall

倒 *nota(reru)* fall by the wayside
倒死 *notareji(ni)* dying of exposure
砲 *yahō* field gun; field artillery
砲兵 *yahōhei* field artilleryman; field artillery
11 鳥 *yachō* wild fowl, wild bird
遊 *noaso(bi)* picnic, outing
道 *nomichi* road across a field
帳 *yachō, nochō* field notes; (surveyor's) field notebook
情 *yajō* rural feeling, rural sentiment
猫 *noneko* stray cat
猪 *yacho* wild boar
宿 *nojuku* camping out
菊 *nogiku* wild camomile
望 *yabō* ambition, aspiration, sinister design, intrigue, treachery
菜 *yasai* vegetables
菜物 *yasaimono* vegetables
菜畑 *yasaibatake* vegetable garden
球 *yakyū* baseball
球気違 *yakyū kichiga(i)* baseball fan
球狂 *yakyūkyō* baseball fan
球界 *yakyūkai* baseball world
球連盟 *yakyū remmei* baseball league
球場 *yakyūjō* baseball park
球試合 *yakyū shiai* baseball game
球選手 *yakyū senshu* baseball player
球熱 *yakyū netsu* baseball fever
12 焼 *noya(ki)* winter burning of the fields
景 *yakei* view of open fields; landscape views
葡萄 *nobudo* wild grapes
蛮 *yaban* heathenism, barbarism
蛮人 *yabanjin* barbarian, savage
蛮国 *yabankoku* uncivilized country
営 *yaei* camping, camp, bivouac
営地 *yaeichi* camping ground
営者 *yaeisha* camper
13 鼠 *nonezumi* field mouse
僧 *yasō* rural priest
猿 *yaen* wild monkey
路 *nomichi, noji* road across a field
飼 *noga(i)* pasturing, turning (animals) loose in a field. *noga(i) no* wild
鄙 *yahi na* vulgar, coarse, ill-mannered
禽 *yakin* wild fowl, wild bird
戦 *yasen* open warfare, field operations
戦病院 *yasen byōin* field hospital
14 選 *yasen* fielder's choice
蜜 *nomitsu* wild honey
暮 *yabo na* rustic, unrefined; stupid, unfeeling; stale; conventional
暮天 *yaboten na* rustic, unrefined; stupid, unfeeling; stale; conventional
15 趣 *yashu* rural beauty, rural air, rusticity
16 積 *nozu(mi)* piling up (supplies) outside
薔薇 *nobara, noibara* a wild rose
獣 *yajū* wild animal, wild game
獣狩 *yajūga(ri)* wild animal hunt
18 斃死 *notareji(ni)* dying of cxposure
19 鶏 *yakei* pheasant
26 驢馬 *noroba* wild donkey

5

A **量** 6209 J4e4c M40138 RYŌ quantity, amount, volume; magnanimity; a measure. *haka(ri)* measure, weight. *haka(ru)* measure, gauge, weigh; fathom, sound; compute, cstimate.
2 入 *haka(ri)-i(reru)* measure into
3 子論 *ryōshiron* quantum theory
4 込 *haka(ri)-ko(mu)* measure liberally
水器 *ryōsuiki* water meter
5 目 *ryōme* weight
6 刑 *ryōkei* weighing an offense
7 見 *ryōken* idea, thought, intention, inclination, motive, decision; discretion; forgiveness; toleration
売 *haka(ri)u(ri)* selling by measure
8 的 *ryōteki* quantitative
知 *haka(ri)-shi(ru), ryōchi suru* to measure, to fathom
直 *haka(ri)-nao(su)* reweigh; measure again
11 産 *ryōsan* mass production
12 感 *ryōkan* volume (in a painting)
15 器 *ryōki* a measure for volume

11

釐 6210 J6e5a M40146 RI few; one-tenth of a *bu*.
8 金税 *rikinzei* the *likin*, local Chinese customs charges

8-STROKE RADICALS

RAD. 金 167

Kane metal, money, gold. At left: 金 *kane hen.* Nickname: Metal.

A 金 6211 / J3662 / M40152 KON. KIN gold; money; Friday. *kane* money, metal. *kana-* metal.

[1] 一封 *kin'ippū* a wrapped gift of money
[2] 入 *kanei(re)* purse, wallet; till
力 *kinryoku* the power of wealth
[3] 口 *kinguchi, kinkuchi, kinkō* gold-tipped
子 *kinsu* money, funds
山 *kanayama* metal mine. *kinzan* gold mine; mountain fortress
工 *kinkō* goldsmith; metalworker; metalwork
巾 *kanakin* shirtings, calico, unbleached muslin
才覚 *kane saikaku* raising money
[4] 円 *kin'en* money
仏 *kanabutsu, kanabotoke* metal Buddha; cold person
元 *kanemoto* financial backer
水引 *kimmizuhiki* golden paper cord
文字 *kimmoji* gilt letters
火箸 *kanahibashi* iron tongs
比羅 *Kompira* the seafarer's god
欠 *kinketsu* money stringency
欠病 *kinketsubyō* sick from shortage of money
切 *kinki(ri)* castration
切声 *kanaki(ri)goe* shrill voice, scream
[5] 玉 *kingyoku* jewels, gold and gems. *kintama* gold ball; testicles
瓦 *kanagawara* copper roof tiles
穴 *kinketsu* capitalist, financial backer
句 *kinku* beautiful phrase; beautiful saying
打 *kinchō* sword oath
札 *kinsatsu* golden label
主 *kinshu* financier, capitalist, backer
台 *kindai* gold mounting
氷 *kanakōri* something very cold
包 *kanezutsu(mi)* moneybag, bundle of money
生木 *kane (no) na(ru) ki* the goose that lays the golden egg
目 *kaneme* monetary value
目品 *kaneme no shina* valuable good
本位 *kinhon'i* gold standard
本位制 *kinhon'isei* gold standard
石 *kinseki* metal and rock; monument; solidity
石文 *kinsekibun* stone monument inscription
石交 *kinseki no majiwa(ri)* close friendship
石学 *kinsekigaku* study of stone monument inscriptions
[6] 臼 *kanausu* metal (perfumery) mortar
衣 *kin'i* beautiful clothes
匠 *kinshō* worker in gold and silver
回 *kanemawa(ri)* money circulation; financial condition
尽 *kanezuku de* by the power of money, at any cost
印 *kin'in* gold seal
地 *kinji* ground strewn with gold dust
合金 *kingōkin* gold alloy
米糖 *kompeitō* confetti
灯籠 *kanadōrō* metal lantern
糸 *kinshi* gold thread, spun gold
糸入 *kinshii(ri)* interwoven gold thread
気 *kanake* metallic toast; money
気違 *kane kichiga(i)* miser
字 *kinji* gold letters
字塔 *kinjitō* a pyramid; a monumental work
光 *kimpika* golden luster; that which glitters. *kimpika no* glittering, sparkling
光物 *kimpikamono* tinsel, trinkets
色 *kinshoku, kin iro, konjiki* golden color
色夜叉 *konjiki yasha* usurer, miser
色堂 *konjikidō* the golden pavilion in a temple
[7] 見 *kanemi* testing money; money tester
言 *kingen* maxim, golden rule, aphorism

位 *kin'i* fineness of gold
作 *kinzuku(ri)* made of gold
吹 *kanefu(ki)* assaying
坑 *kinkō* gold mine
利 *kinri* interest rate, bank rate
判 *kanaban* metal stamp, metal seal
声 *kinsei* sound emitted by metal objects
売 *kaneu(ri)* gold-dust dealer
串 *kanagushi* iron skewer
杓子 *kanajakushi* metal ladle, dipper
沙汰 *kanezata* a money problem
8 使 *kanezuka(i)* way of spending
味 *kanaaji* quality of iron; sharpness of edged tools
性 *kinshō* fineness of gold. *kaneshō* quality of metal
所 *kanedokoro* source of funds, metal-mining area
杯 *kimpai* gold cup
泥 *kondei, kindei* gold dust; gold paint
波 *kimpa* golden waves
的 *kinteki* bull's eye; object to long for
肥 *kimpi* commercial fertilizer
帛 *kimpaku* gold and cloth; return gift
具 *kanagu* metal fittings of fixtures
券 *kinken* gold certificate
事 *kanegoto* a matter of money
門海峡 *Kimmon Kaikyō* Golden Gate
枝 *Kinshi* the Imperial Family
枝玉葉 *Kinshi Gyokuyō* the Imperial Family
物 *kanamono* hardware
物屋 *kanamonoya* hardware store
9 風 *kimpū* autumn breeze
食 *kaneku(i)* spendthrift; taking a lot of money
屎 *kanakuso* slag, dross
建 *kinda(te), kinta(te)* gold basis, quotations in gold
廻 *kanemawa(ri)* money circulation; financial condition
造 *kanazuku(ri)* metalworker; metalworking
持 *kanemochi* person of wealth
柑 *kinkan* kumquat
冠 *kinkan* a gold crown (on a tooth)
品 *kimpin* money and valuables
星 *Kinsei* Venus. *kimboshi* splendid victory
臭 *kanakusa(i)* smelling of metal
茶 *kincha* reddish brown
型 *kanegata* metal pattern
巻 *kanema(ki)* metal hoop
相学 *kinsōgaku* metallography
看板 *kin kamban* gilt signboard; a catchy slogan
毘羅 *Kompira* the seafarer's god
科玉条 *kinka-gyokujō* one's watchword; a consuming principle; an excellent law
単本位 *kin tanhon'i* gold standard
砂 *kinsha* gold dust
砂子 *kin sunago* gold dust, gold-sprinkled lacquer
為替 *kinkawase* gold exchange
為替本位制 *kinkawase hon'isei* gold exchange standard
城 *kinjō* an impregnable castle
城湯池 *kinjō-tōchi* a impregnable castle
城鉄壁 *kinjō-teppeki* an impregnable castle
10 高 *kindaka* amount of money
屑 *kanakuzu* scrap metal, scrap iron, metal filings
扇 *kinsen* gilt fan
借 *kanaka(ri)* borrowing money; debt
砧 *kanatoko* anvil
粉 *kimpun, kinko* gold dust
納 *kinnō* cash payment
紛 *kimmaga(i)* imitation gold
紗 *kinsha* high-class kimono cloth
紙 *kingami, kinshi* gold paper, gilt paper
脈 *kimmyaku* gold vein
被 *kinki(se) no* gold-plated
針 *kinshin* needle; golden needle
員 *kin'in* money, cash
容 *kin'yō* image of Buddha
財布 *kane saifu* moneybag
時計 *kindokei* gold watch
庫 *kinko, kanegura* safe, vault; cashbox; depository; treasure house; financier
庫破 *kinkoyabu(ri), kanegurayabu(ri)* safe-breaking
釘 *kanakugi* iron nail
釘流 *kanakugiryū* scrawl
剛 *kongō* diamond; great strength; strong man; emery powder
剛力 *kongōriki* Herculean strength
剛心 *kongōshin* earnest faith
剛不壊 *kongō-fue* adamant
剛石 *kongōseki* diamond
剛杖 *kongōzue* pilgrim staff
剛砂紙 *kongōshashi* emery powder, corundum

11 側 *kingawa no* gold-cased
帳 *kinchō* gold-decorated doors
張 *kimba(ri)* rolled gold, gold-plated, gold-filled
掘 *kaneho(ri)* miner
梃 *kanateko* crowbar
渋 *kanashibu* rusty water
堂 *kondō* main temple structure
章 *kinshō* beautiful writing (literature)
袋 *kanabukuro* moneybag
商人 *kane akindo* gold-dust dealer
婚式 *kinkonshiki* golden wedding
産地 *kinsanchi* gold field
偏 *kanehen* the radical 金
偏景気 *kanehen keiki* a metal (industry) boom
屏 *kimbyō* a screen coated with gold
屏風 *kimbyōbu* a screen coated with gold
細工 *kinzaiku* goldwork, gold ware, gold mounting
細工人 *kinzaikunin* goldsmith
魚 *kingyo* goldfish
魚屋 *kingyoya* goldfish seller
魚草 *kingyosō* snapdragon
魚鉢 *kingyobachi* goldfish bowl
貨 *kinka* gold coin
貨本位 *kinka hon'i* gold standard
貨国 *kinkakoku* gold-standard country
貨制 *kinkasei* gold coinage system
貨幣 *kinkahei* gold coin
12 歯 *kimba* gold tooth
遣 *kanezuka(i)* way of spending
椀 *kanawan, kanamari* metal bowl
焼 *kanaya(ki), kaneya(ki)* branding
創 *kinsō* sword cut
策 *kinsaku suru* raise money, get a loan. *kinsaku* means of raising money
筋 *kinsuji* gold stripes
着 *kinki(se) no* gold-plated
無垢 *kimmuku* pure gold
満家 *kimmanka* wealthy person, millionaire
象眼 *kin zōgan* inlaying with gold, gold inlay
棒 *kanabō* iron rod, metal rod, bar; crowbar; iron club; horizontal bar
棒引 *kanabōhi(ki)* night guard; gossiper
牌 *kimpai* gold medal
牌受領者 *kimpai juryōsha* gold medalist
壺 *kanatsubo* metal jar
壺眼 *kanatsubo manako* eyes glaring with infuriation
貸 *kaneka(shi)* moneylender; moneylending
貸業 *kaneka(shi)gyō* moneylending business
属 *kinzoku* metal
属工業 *kinzoku kōgyō* metalworking industry
属性 *kinzokusei* metal. *kinzokusei no* metallic
属疲労 *kinzoku hirō* metal fatigue
属細工 *kinzokuzaiku* metal working; metalwork
属貨幣 *kinzoku kahei* metallic currency
属製 *kinzokusei* made of metal
属製品 *kinzoku seihin* hardware
13 鼓 *kinko* drum and cymbals
塊 *kinkai* nugget, gold bullion, gold bar
搔 *kanaga(ki)* farmer's hoeing fork
滓 *kanakasu, kanakuso* slang, dross
詰 *kanezuma(ri), kinzuma(ri)* shortage of money
鉄 *kintetsu* metal; firmness
蓮花 *kinrenka* nasturtium
盞花 *kinsenka* marigold
準備 *kin jumbi* gold reserves
蒔絵 *kimmakie* gold lacquer work
解禁 *kin kaikin* lifting the gold embargo
殿 *kinden* golden palace, luxurious palace
殿玉楼 *kinden-gyokurō* palace, mansion
槌 *kanazuchi* hammer, sledge
槌頭 *kanazuchi atama* hardhead; stubborn person
鉱 *kinkō* gold ore
鉱脈 *kinkōmyaku* gold vein
14 閣 *kinkaku* golden building; beautiful building
網 *kanaami* wire netting, screen
酸 *kinsan* auric acid
銅 *kondō* gilt bronze
穀 *kinkoku* money and grain
箍 *kanataga* metal hoop
罰 *kanebachi* the results of foolish spending
蔵 *kanegura* treasure house; financier, backer
蔓 *kanezuru* source of money, a "gold mine"
髪 *kimpatsu* fair hair; blonde; golden hair, auburn hair

製 *kinsei* made of gold
鳳花 *kimpōge* buttercup
管楽器 *kinkan gakki* brass musical instrument
緑玉 *kinryokugyoku* chrysoberyl
緑石 *kinryokuseki* chrysoberyl
銀 *kingin* gold and silver; money
銀複本位制 *kingin fukuhon'isei* bimetallism
箔 *kimpaku* gold leaf, gold foil
箔屋 *kimpakuya* goldbeater
銭 *kinsen* money, cash
銭出納係 *kinsen suitōgakari* cashier, teller, treasurer
銭出納簿 *kinsen suitōbo* cashbook
銭尽 *kinsenzu(ku) de* by the power of money
銭貸付 *kinsen kashitsu(ke)* moneylending
銭登録器 *kinsen tōrokuki* cash register
15 衡 *kinkō* troy weight
線 *kinsen* gold lines
談 *kindan* conference about money; request for a loan
賦 *kanekuba(ri)* passing out money
鋤 *kanesuki* iron plow
鋏 *kanebasami* metal shears
敷 *kanushiki* anvil
箱 *kanebako* cashbox, money chest; capitalist, backer; resources; breadwinner
篦 *kanabera* trowel
箸 *kanahashi, kanabashi* iron tongs
幣 *kimpei* gold coin; gold-colored Shinto offerings
質 *kinshitsu* fineness of gold
器 *kinki* golden furniture, golden vessel
縁 *kimbuchi* gold rims, gilt frame, gilt edges; gold-rimmed (glasses)
縁眼鏡 *kimbuchi megane* gold-rimmed glasses
輪 *kanawa* hoop, ring, or band of metal; dog collar
輪際 *konrinzai* never, by no means
権 *kinken* almighty dollar, financial influence
権政治 *kinken seiji* plutocracy
権貴族 *kinken kizoku* the wealthy
16 縛 *kanashiba(ri)* binding hand and foot
錆 *kanasabi* rust
鋸 *kane nokogiri* hacksaw
親 *kane oya* financier, capitalist, backer
盥 *kanadarai* metal basin, washbowl
甌 *kinnō* gold vase
甌無欠 *kinnō-muketsu* perfect, flawless, ideal
輸出 *kin yushutsu* export of gold
輸出禁止 *kin yushutsu kinshi* gold embargo
輸出解禁 *kin yushutsu kaikin* lifting the gold embargo
融 *kin'yū* money (market), credit situation, money circulation; financial
融市場 *kin'yu shijō* money market
融先物取引 *kin'yū sakimono torihiki* interest-rate futures transaction
融団 *kin'yūdan* syndicate
融界 *kin'yūkai* financial circles
融政策 *kin'yū seisaku* financial policy
融恐慌 *kin'yū kyōkō* financial panic
融梗塞 *kin'yū kōsoku* tight money
融組織 *kin'yū soshiki* banking system
融筋 *kin'yū suji* financial interests
融統制 *kin'yū tōsei* monetary control
融債 *kin'yūsai* bank debenture
融業 *kin'yūgyō* financial operations, banking business
融資本 *kin'yū shihon* financial capital
融機関 *kin'yū kikan* banking facilities
17 糟 *kanakasu* metal dross
鎚 *kanazuchi* hammer, sledge
鍼 *kinshin* needle; golden needle
鍍金 *kimmekki* gilding, gold plating
環 *kinkan* gold ring
環食 *kinkanshoku* annular solar eclipse
環蝕 *kinkanshoku* annular solar eclipse
18 闕 *kinketsu* palace
櫃 *kanebitsu* cashbox, money chest; capitalist, backer; resources; breadwinner
鎖 *kingusari* gold chain
額 *kingaku* amount of money
儲 *kanemōke* money-making
儲主義 *kanemōke shugi* the almighty-dollar principle
曜 *Kin'yō* Friday
曜日 *Kin'yōbi* Friday
19 繰 *kanegu(ri), kaneku(ri)* financing
鯱 *kin (no) shachihoko* golden dolphin
離 *kanebana(re)* spending money freely
鶏 *kinkei* golden pheasant
蘭 *kinran* intimate friendship
20 鐘 *kinshō* gold bell

簪 *kin kanzashi, kinsan* gold hairpin
22 襴 *kinran* gold brocade
聾 *kanatsumbo* stone-deaf
轡 *kanagutsuwa* horse's bit; hush money
嚢 *kinnō* purse, moneybag
23 鑞 *kinrō* solder

2

釖 6212 / J6e5b / M40157 See 刀 448.

釛 6213 / J6e5e / M40163 Koku gold.

釟 6214 / J6e5c / M40167 Hatsu, Hachi assaying, smelting.

釜 6215 / J3378 / M40164 釡 6216 / J6e5d / M40170 Fu. *kama* kettle, cauldron, iron pot; boiler. *kanae* three-legged kettle.
6 糸 *kama ito* floss silk
9 屋 *kamaya* large-kettle installer
茹 *kamaude, kamayude* boiling or roasting in a kettle
12 飯 *kamameshi* rice served in the kettle
焚 *kamataki* stoker, fireman
13 煎 *kamairi* boiling in a kettle; boiling (a criminal) to death
14 鳴 *kamana(ri)* sound of a boiling kettle
15 敷 *kamashi(ki)* kettle rest

釘 6217 / J4523 / M40159 Tei. Chō. *kugi* nail, spike, tack; rivet; peg.
5 目 *kugime* location of the nail
付 *kugitsu(ke)* nailing; pegging; standing transfixed
打 *kugi (o) u(tsu)* pound in a nail; renew a promise
打機 *kugiu(chi)ki* riveting machine
7 応 *kugigota(e)* holding strength of a nail; staying power; effectiveness
抜 *kuginu(ki)* pinchers, nail-puller, claw hammer
12 裂 *kugiza(ki)* tearing clothes on a nail
13 隠 *kugikaku(shi)* decorative cover for a nail head
15 締 *kugiji(me)* nailing shut

A 針 6218 / J3f4b / M40165 Shin needle. *hari* needle, pin; staple; fishhook; stinger; spine (of a fish); thorn; stitch; (watch) hand; (phonograph) needle; (hypodermic) needle; sting; molehill; acupuncture. *(o)hari* needlework, sewing; seamstress.
3 女 *harime* seamstress
山 *hariyama* pincushion
小棒大 *shinshō-bōdai* exaggeration, hyperbole
4 毛 *harige* bristle
孔 *hariana, medo* pinhole
孔写真機 *hariana shashinki* pinhole camera
5 目 *harime* seam
仕事 *hari shigoto* needlework, sewing
6 耳 *hari (no) mimi* the eye of a needle
尖 *harisaki* needle point
7 状 *harijō no* needle-shaped, pointed
8 刺 *harisa(shi)* pincushion
金 *harigane* wire
金綴 *hariganetoji* stapler
10 師 *harishi* needlemaker
11 術 *shinjutsu* acupuncture
12 葉 *shin'yō* evergreen needles
葉樹 *shin'yōju* coniferous tree, needle-leaf tree
13 路 *shinro* direction, compass bearing
15 箱 *haribako* needlecase, sewing box

3

釼 6219 / J6e5f / M-X See 剣 498.

釵 6220 / J6e60 / M40191 Sai, Sa two-pronged ornamental hairpin.

鉇 6221 / J6e61 / M40192 Shi. *hoko* halberd.

釧 6222 / J367c / M40176 Sen bracelet.

釦 6223 / J4b55 / M40175 Kō. *botan* button.

B 釣 6224 / J4460 / M40172 Chō. *tsu(ru)* angle, fish, catch; decoy, allure, *tsu(reru)* be caught; have a cramp. *tsu(ri)* change (for a dollar); (rod) fishing.

³下 *tsu(ri)-sa(geru)* suspend from
上 *tsu(ri)-a(geru)* pull in (a fish); raise (one's eyes); boost (prices). *tsu(ri)-a(garu)* be hung up, be lifted up, turn up
⁴戸 *tsurido* overhead door
手 *tsurite* angler; mosquito-net hanger
込 *tsu(ri)-ko(mu)* decoy into, lure, ensnare, tempt, attract
天井 *tsuri tenjō* suspended ceiling
太鼓 *tsuridaiko* suspended drum
⁵目 *tsurime* slant eyes
台 *tsuridai* stretcher, litter
出 *tsu(ri)-da(su)* pull out (a fish); decoy, lure
⁶糸 *tsuri ito* fishing line
合 *tsu(ri)-a(u)* match, suit, balance, be in harmony, be in proportion. *tsuriai* balance, equilibrium, proportion, symmetry, harmony, match
仲間 *tsuri nakama* fishing companion
灯籠 *tsuridōrō* hanging lantern
⁷床 *tsuridoko* hammock
花 *tsuribana* flowers in a hanging vase
花活 *tsuribanai(ke)* hanging vase
花瓶 *tsuri kabin* hanging vase
⁸具 *tsurigu* fishing tackle
⁹革 *tsurikawa* hand straps on bus, subway, or streetcar
竿 *tsurizao* fishing rod
¹⁰師 *tsurishi* angler
針 *tsuribari* fishhook
¹¹堀 *tsuribori* fishpond
船 *tsuribune* fishing boat, boat-shaped vase
梯子 *tsuribashigo* rope ladder
道具 *tsuri dōgu* fishing tackle
魚 *tsuriuo* game fish. *chōgyo* angling, fishing
魚法 *chōgyohō* angling, fishing
瓶 *tsurube* well bucket
瓶打 *tsurubeu(chi)* volley, firing in succession
瓶落 *tsurubeoto(shi)* volley, firing in succession
¹²場 *tsuriba* fishing place
棚 *tsuridana* hanging shelf
提灯 *tsurijōchin* hanging lantern
¹³殿 *tsuridono* (ancient) pond pavilion
¹⁴銭 *tsurisen* change (for a dollar)
漁具 *tsuri gyogu* fishing tackle
¹⁶橋 *tsuribashi* suspension bridge
鬚 *tsurihige* upturned mustache
²⁰鐘 *tsurigane* hanging bell; temple bell
²²籠 *tsuri kago* fisherman's basket; hanging basket

8 【金】4 長門阜阝隶隹雨青非

4

釟 6225 / J6e65 / M-X Nonstandard for 鐸 6356.

鈎 6226 / J3343 / M40220 See 鉤 6250.

釿 6227 / J6e63 / M40203 KIN edge; chopping; edging; edge of an implement; hatchet.

鈩 6228 / J6f4f / M-X **鑪** 6369 / J6f4e / M41038 RO hearth, fireplace; furnace.

鈞 6229 / J6e62 / M40238 KIN equal; important point; thirty *kin*.

鈕 6230 / J6e66 / M40228 CHŪ. *botan* button.

鈑 6231 / J6e67 / M40224 HAN. *itagane* sheet metal.

鈀 6232 / J-X / M40200 HAKU. *kanaguki* farmer's hoeing fork.

鈔 6233 / J6e64 / M40227 SHŌ selection, summary; one tenth of a *shaku* (勺). *shō(su)* copy; copy out.

鈇 6234 / J-X / M40213 FU axe.
¹³鉞 *fuetsu* ax; battle-ax

B **鈍** 6235 / J465f / M40219 DON dullness, slowness, foolishness. *nibu(ru)* become dull, weaken. *nibu(rasu), nibu(raseru)* dull, blunt, take the edge off, weaken. *nama(ru)* get dull. *nama(kura)* blunt sword, lazy fellow. *noro(i)* slow, dilatory, dull; flirtatious. *nibu(i)* dull, slow; blunt (tool); dim (light); thick (voice). *noro* dullness.
²刀 *dontō, namakuragatana* blunt sword
³才 *donsai* dullness, stupidity

[6]色 *nibu iro, nibi iro* dark gray
行 *donkō* ordinary train
[7]角 *donkaku* obtuse angle
[8]物 *dombutsu* dunce, blockhead. *namakuramono* dull sword
[9]重 *donjū* dull-witted, stolid, phlegmatic
臭 *norokusa(i), donkusa(i)* slow, leisurely, sluggish
[10]根 *donkon* dull, foolish, incapable
[11]麻 *domma* dullness
[12]痛 *dontsū* dull pain
間 *noroma* stupidity
鈍 *noronoro* slowly, leisurely, sluggishly
[13]感 *donkan* stolidity, thickheadedness
[15]調 *donchō* dull (market)
器 *donki* dull weapon, blunt sword

5

鈷 6236 / J385a / M40270 Ko Buddhist weapon; cobalt, sky blue, navy blue. *hinoshi* an iron, a flatiron.

鉅 6237 / J6e6a / M40286 Kyo hard; frightening; big; many; hook; steel.

鉐 6238 / J6e71 / M40298 Seki, Jaku brass; high-quality copper.

鉚 6239 / J6e76 / M40309 Ryū, Ru pure gold.

鈸 6240 / J-X / M40271 Hachi, Hatsu, Bachi cymbals.

鉉 6241 / J6e6b / M40290 Gen. *tsuru* handle.

鉈 6242 / J6e6d / M40289 Sha. *nata* hatchet.

鈿 6243 / J6e6f / M40279 Den. *kanzashi* ornamental hairpin.

鉞 6244 / J6e68 / M40313 Etsu. *masakari* battle-ax, broad-ax.

鉗 6245 / J6e69 / M40306 Ken. Kan. *tsugu(mu)* shut (one's mouth).
[3]子 *kanshi* forceps

鉦 6246 / J3e60 / M40322 Sei, Shō gong. *kane* bell, gong, chimes, carillon.
[5]叩 *kanetata(ki)* rod used in ringing a bell; a man who goes around ringing a bell while reciting sutras and begging, mendicant priest
[13]鼓 *shōko* bell and drum

B **鈴** 6247 / J4e6b / M40267 Rei, Rin bell, hand bell, buzzer. *suzu* bell.
[5]生 *suzuna(ri)* abundance of fruit (on a tree)
[19]蘭 *suzuran* lily-of-the-valley
蘭灯 *suzurantō* an arch of lights

鉋 6248 / J6e70 / M40292 Hō, Byō. *kanna* carpenter's plane.
[10]屑 *kannakuzu* shavings
[11]掛 *kannaka(ke)* planing
[15]盤 *kannaban* planer

B **鉢** 6249 / J482d / M40317 Hatsu, Hachi bowl, rice tub, pot; crown, brainpan.
[4]木 *hachi (no) ki* potted tree
[6]合 *hachia(wase)* bumping of heads, collision
[8]物 *hachimono* food served in bowls; potted plant
[9]巻 *hachimaki* (towel) headband, hatband, frontlet
[12]植 *hachiu(e)* potted plant

鉤 6250 / J6e6c / M40319 **鈎** 6226 / J3343 / M40220 Kō. *kagi* hook, barb, gaff; brackets (in punctuation).
[2]十字 *kagi jūji* swastika
[4]手 *kagi(no)te* right angle; bend; bend in the road; kleptomaniac
[6]虫 *kōchū* hookworm
[7]状 *kōjō* hook-shaped
[10]針 *kagibari* hook, crochet hook
[12]裂 *kagiza(ki)* tear, rent (in one's clothes)
[14]鼻 *kagibana* hooked nose
[15]餌 *kōji* hook and bait
縄 *kagi nawa* hooked rope

B **鉛** 6251 / J3174 / M40310 En. *namari* lead (metal).
[3]山 *enzan* lead mine, lead deposits
工 *enkō* plumber
[4]中毒 *enchūdoku* lead poisoning

5 白 *empaku* white lead
6 色 *namari iro, enshoku* lead color
8 版 *emban* stereotype
直 *enchoku* perpendicular, plumb
毒 *endoku* lead poisoning
10 華 *enka* former word for face paint
12 筆 *empitsu* lead pencil
測線 *ensokusen* sounding line
13 塊 *enkai* lead ingot
鉱 *enkō* lead mine
14 管 *enkan* lead pipe
16 錘 *ensui* plumb bob, plummet

A **鉱** 6252 / J395b / M40340' **鑛** 6363 / J6f4a / M41010 **礦** 4057 / J6268 / M24564 **砿** 3994 / J395c / M-X Kō ore.

3 工業 *kōkōgyō* mining and manufacturing
山 *kōzan, kanayama* mine
山王 *kōzan'ō* mining king
山技師 *kōzan gishi* mining engineer
山学 *kōzangaku* mining engineering
山師 *kōzanshi* mine operator
山業 *kōzangyō* mining industry
4 水 *kōsui* mineral water
夫 *kōfu* miner
区 *kōku* mining area, diggings
区税 *kokuzei* mine-lot tax
5 石 *kōseki* ore, mineral, (radio) crystal
石受信機 *kōseki jushinki* crystal (radio) set
7 床 *kōshō* ore deposits
坑 *kōkō* mine, shaft, pit
8 油 *kōyu* kerosene, mineral oil
毒 *kōdoku* mine pollution; copper poisoning
物 *kōbutsu* minerals, inorganic substances
物油 *kōbutsuyu* mineral oil
物学 *kōbutsugaku* mineralogy
物質 *kōbutsushitsu* mineral matter
9 泉 *kōsen* mineral springs
10 脈 *kōmyaku* vein of ore
員 *kōin* miners
11 産 *kōsan* mineral product
産地 *kōsanchi* district rich in minerals
産物 *kōsambutsu* mineral products
13 滓 *kōsai* slag, dross
業 *kōgyō* mining industry
業地 *kōgyōchi* mining area
業家 *kōgyōka* mine operator
業税 *kōgyōzei* mining tax
業権 *kōgyōken* mining rights
14 層 *kōsō* ore bed
21 蠟 *kōrō* mineral wax
蠟油 *kōrōyu* paraffin oil

A **鉄** 6253 / J4534 / M40285 **鐵** 6354 / J6f44 / M40945 TETSU iron, steel; reddish black, iron blue. *kurogane* iron. *kana-, kane-* metal.

2 人 *tetsujin* a very robust man
十字勲章 *Tetsujūji Kunshō* the Iron Cross
刀 *tettō* steel sword
刀木 *tagayasan, tettōboku* ironwood
3 山 *tetsuzan* iron mountain
叉 *kanamata* forked iron poker
工 *tekkō* ironworker, blacksmith
工場 *tekkōjō* ironworks
4 心 *tesshin* iron core; firm will
片 *teppen* piece of iron
尺 *tetsujaku* common Japanese foot; carpenter's square
分 *tetsubun* iron content
牛 *tetsugyū* army tank
牛部隊 *tetsugyū butai* tank corps
火 *tekka* red-hot iron; ordeal; gunfire; swords and guns; brave heart
火丼 *tekka domburi* a bowl of tuna slices on boiled rice
火巻 *tekkamaki* tuna slices rolled in rice and covered with laver
火場 *tekkaba* gambling room; battlefield
火箸 *kanahibashi* iron tongs
5 甲 *tekkō* iron armor; iron helmet
石 *tesseki* iron and steel. *tesseki no* adamantine, firm
石心 *tessekishin* adamantine will
6 色 *tetsu iro* reddish black, iron blue
血 *tekketsu* blood and iron; war preparations; military strength
衣 *tetsui* armor
合金 *tetsugōkin* ferroalloy
舟 *tesshū* boat, steel pontoon
舟橋 *tesshūkyō* pontoon bridge
7 床 *kanatoko* anvil
坑 *tekkō* iron mine
材 *tetsuzai* iron or steel material
条網 *tetsujōmō* barbed-wire entanglement
8 門 *tetsumon* iron gate

味 *kaneaji* quality of iron
沓 *kanagutsu* horseshoe
炙 *tekkyū* roasting grill
板 *teppan, tetsu ita, tetsuban* steel plate, sheet of iron
板焼 *teppan'yaki* meat roasted on a hot plate
9 柵 *tessaku* iron railing, iron fence
炮 *teppō* gun, firearms; bath fire-pipe
肺 *tetsuhai, tetsu (no) hai* iron lung
則 *tessoku* ironclad rule
軌 *tekki* iron rail
面皮 *tetsumempi* impudence, audacity
10 屑 *tetsu kuzu* scrap iron
扇 *tessen* iron-ribbed fan
挺 *kanateko* crowbar
粉 *teppun* iron filings
剤 *tetsuzai* iron pills (medicine)
索 *tessaku* cable, cableway (for hauling)
案 *tetsuan* irrevocable decision
格子 *tetsugōshi* iron-barred window, iron grating
拳 *tekken* clenched fist
拳制裁 *tekken seisai* the law of the clenched fist
骨 *tekkotsu* steel frame
骨木船 *tekkotsu mokusen* steel-framed wooden ship
骨構造 *tekkotsu kōzō* steel-frame construction
砲 *teppō* gun, firearms; bath fire-pipe
砲玉 *teppōdama* bullet; lost messenger
砲打 *teppōu(chi)* shooting
砲傷 *teppō kizu* bullet wound
砲腹 *teppōbara* suicide by shooting in the abdomen
砲鍛冶 *teppō kaji* gunsmith
11 桶 *tettō* steel vat
渋 *kanashibu* rusty water
脚 *tekkyaku* iron legs
船 *tessen* steel ship; ironclad
瓶 *tetsubin* iron teakettle
窓 *tessō* steel-barred window; prison bars; prison
兜 *tetsu kabuto* steel helmet
道 *tetsudō* railway, railroad
道工手 *tetsudō kōshu* railway trackman
道工学 *tetsudō kōgaku* railway engineering
道公安官 *tetsudō kōankan* railway police
道用地 *tetsudō yōchi* railway land
道自殺 *tetsudō jisatsu* railway suicide
道往生 *tetsudō ōjō* railway suicide
道便 *tetsudōbin* railway express
道馬車 *tetsudō basha* horsecar
道電化 *tetsudō denka* railway electrification
道網 *tetsudōmō* railway network
道敷設権 *tetsudō fusetsuken* railway right-of-way
道線路 *tetsudō senro* railroad track; right-of-way
12 扉 *teppi* iron door
塔 *tettō* steel tower
帽 *tetsubō* steel helmet
弾 *tetsudan* iron ball, shot
棍 *tekkon* iron club
湯 *tettō* molten iron
傘 *tessan* steel dome, steel-roofed stadium
筋 *tekkin* ferro-(concrete), iron bar
筆 *teppitsu* stylus, stencil pen, steel pen; engraving tool; powerful pen
腕投手 *tetsuwan tōshu* cannon-ball pitcher
棒 *kanabō, tetsubō* iron rod, metal rod, bar; crowbar; iron club; horizontal bar
棒曳 *kanabōhiki* night guard; a gossip
13 路 *tetsuro* railroad
鉢 *teppachi, teppatsu* priest's iron begging bowl
褐色 *tekkasshoku* iron gray
槌 *tettsui* iron hammer; large hammer; hammer (in sports)
槌投 *tettsuina(ge)* hammer throw
鉱 *tekkō* iron ore
鉱泉 *tekkōsen, tetsu kōsen* ferruginous springs
14 銭 *tessen* iron coin
管 *tekkan* iron pipe
製 *tessei* made of iron or steel
15 線 *tessen* steel wire
敷 *kanashi(ki)* anvil
箸 *kanabashi* iron tongs
質 *tesshitsu no* ferrous
器 *tekki* ironware, hardware; grill, gridiron; iron tool
器時代 *Tekki Jidai* Iron Age
漿 *kane, tesshō* tooth blackening
漿染 *kanezo(me)* blackening the teeth
漿黒 *kaneguro* blackening the teeth
16 橋 *tekkyō* steel bridge

蹄 *tettei* horseshoe
錆 *tetsu sabi* iron rust; rust color
壁 *teppeki* iron wall; impregnable fortress
鋼 *tekkō* iron and steel
鋼業 *tekkōgyō* iron-and-steel industry
17 環 *tekkan* steel cordon; iron ring. *tetsuwa* iron quoits
鍋 *tetsu nabe, kananabe* iron or copper kettle
鎚 *kanazuchi* hammer
18 鎖 *tessa* iron chain
鞭 *kanabuchi, kanamuchi* metal whip
騎 *tekki* armored cavalry; brave cavalry
20 艦 *tekkan* an ironclad warship

6

銕 6254 / J6e6e / M40382 See 鉄 6253.

鉾 6255 / J4b48 / M40353 See 矛 3974.

銖 6256 / J6e73 / M40383 SHU small amount; unit of money (one quarter of a *bu* 分 = one-sixteenth of a *ryō* 両).

銜 6257 / J6e72 / M40390 KAN. *kutsuwa* horse's bit. *kuwa(eru)* take or hold in the mouth or between the teeth; bite.

鋩 6258 / J6e7a / M40490 **鋩** 6259 / J-X / M40489 BŌ sword point.

銚 6260 / J4438 / M40387 CHŌ saké bottle.
3 子 *chōshi* saké dipper; saké bottle

銛 6261 / J6e75 / M40389 SEN. *mori* harpoon, gaff.
12 筒 *morizutsu* harpoon gun

銓 6262 / J6e74 / M40378 SEN measure; scales; weigh.
16 衡 *senkō* careful selection; careful analysis (of abilities)

B **銑** 6263 / J412d / M40376 SEN. *zuku* pig iron.
13 鉄 *sentetsu, zukutetsu* pig iron
16 鋼 *senkō* pig iron

A **銭** 6264 / J412c / M40413 **錢** 6282 / J6f22 / M40563 **戋** 2021 / J-X / M11542
SEN one-hundredth of a yen; coin. *zeni* money.
2 入 *zenii(re)* purse; till
7 形 *zenigata* shape of a coin; paper money offered to a god
8 金 *zenikane* money
放 *zenibana(re)* spending money freely
取 *zenito(ri)* profiting; expensiveness
9 型 *zenigata* coin casting
11 貨 *senka* coins
12 湯 *sentō* bathhouse, public bath
無 *zenina(shi)* penniless
14 穀 *senkoku* money and grain
15 箱 *zenibako* cashbox, till, money box
18 儲 *zenimō(ke)* money-making
19 離 *zenibana(re)* spending money freely

B **銘** 6265 / J4c43 / M40385 MEI inscription, signature (of an artisan); precept, motto. *mei(jiru), mei(zuru)* engrave, impress upon.
2 刀 *meitō* a sword inscribed by the maker
4 文 *meimon* maker's inscription
5 仙 *meisen* a silk cloth
打 *meiu(tsu)* sign, name, announce
7 肝 *meikan* permanently remembering
8 刻 *meikoku suru* engrave; impress upon
9 柄 *meigara* brand, name, description
茶 *meicha* refined tea
10 記 *meiki suru* impress upon
酒 *meishu* superior saké
酒屋 *meishuya* saloon; brothel
14 旗 *meiki* funeral banner (carrying name of the deceased)
銘 *meimei ni* apiece, to each
銘伝 *meimeiden* lives, biographies

A **銅** 6266 / J463c / M40361 DŌ copper. *aka, akagane* copper.
3 山 *dōzan* copper mine
6 色 *dōshoku* copper-colored
7 坑 *dōkō* copper mine
8 板 *dōban* sheet copper
版 *dōban* copperplate
9 臭 *dōshū* corruption, mercenary spirit

11 貨 *dōka* copper coin
細工 *dōzaiku* copper work
細工人 *dōzaikunin* coppersmith
12 牌 *dōhai* bronze medal
壺 *dōko* copper boiler
13 塊 *dōkai* copper ingot
鉱 *dōkō* copper ore
14 像 *dōzō* bronze statue, bronze image
銭 *dōsen* copper coins
製 *dōsei* made of copper
15 線 *dōsen* copper wire, copper wiring
盤 *dōban* bronze basin
器 *dōki* bronze or copper utensil, copperware
器時代 *Dōki Jidai* Bronze Age
19 鏡 *dōkyō* bronze mirror
21 鐸 *dōtaku* bronze bell
27 鑼 *dora* gong, tom-tom
鑼声 *doragoe* gruff voice

B 銃 6267 / J3d46 / M40359 JŪ gun, arms. *tsutsu* gun.

3 口 *jūkō, tsutsuguchi* gun muzzle
士 *jūshi* musketeer
工 *jūkō* gunsmith, armorer
丸 *jūgan* bullet
4 火 *jūka* gunfire
6 刑 *jūkei* execution by a firing squad
7 身 *jūshin* gun barrel
尾 *jūbi* breech of a small gun
床 *jūshō* gun stock
把 *jūha* grip of a gun
声 *jūsei* a shot, gun report
9 後 *jūgo* home front
架 *jūka* gun rest, gun mount
前哨 *jūzenshō* arms sentry
10 砲 *jūhō* firearms
殺 *jūsatsu* shooting to death, execution by shooting
剣 *jūken* bayonet, side arms
剣道 *jūkendō* bayonet fencing
剣術 *jūkenjutsu* bayonet practice
11 眼 *jūgan* loophole
猟 *jūryō* hunting
猟会 *jūryōkai* hunting party
猟法 *jūryōhō* game laws
猟服 *jūryōfuku* hunting coat
猟免状 *jūryō menjō* hunting license
猟税 *jūryōzei* hunting tax
猟期 *jūryōki* hunting season
猟禁止期 *jūryō kinshiki* closed hunting season
12 弾 *jūdan* bullet
創 *jūsō* bullet wound
13 傷 *jūshō* gunshot wound
14 槍 *jūsō* bayonet
槍突撃 *jūsō totsugeki* bayonet charge
15 撃 *jūgeki* rifle shooting
器 *jūki* small arms

A 銀 6268 / J3664 / M40355 GIN silver. *shirogane* silver. *gim(bura)* a stroll along the Ginza.

2 入 *gin'i(ri)* decorating with silver or silver thread
3 山 *ginzan* silver mine
5 台 *gindai* silver building; beautiful building; a silver ground of an industrial-art piece
世界 *gin sekai* silvery world, vast snowy scene
本位 *gin hon'i* silver standard
本位制 *gin hon'isei* silver standard
6 糸 *ginshi* silver thread, silver cord
色 *gin iro, ginshoku* silver color, silvery
字 *ginji* silver letters
光 *ginkō* silvery light
地 *ginji* silvery ground
地金 *gin jigane* silver bullion
行 *ginkō* bank
行手形 *ginkō tegata* bank draft
行団 *ginkōdan* banking syndicate
行券 *ginkōken* bank note
行取引 *ginkō torihiki* bank account; banking transactions
行界 *ginkōkai* banking circles
行荒 *ginkō a(rashi)* bank robbery, bank robber
行為替 *ginkō kawase* bank draft
行員 *ginōin* bank clerk, bank staff
行家 *ginkōka* banker
7 作 *ginzuku(ri)* made of silver
位 *gin'i* silver quality
坑 *ginkō* silver mine
芦 *shirogane yoshi* pampas grass
杏 *ginnan* gingko nut. *ichō* gingko tree, maidenhair tree
杏返 *ichōgae(shi)* butterfly coiffure
8 性 *ginsei* quality of silver
杯 *gimpai* silver cup
波 *gimpa* silvery waves
泥 *gindei* silver paint
狐 *gingitsune* silver fox
券 *ginken* silver certificate

板写真 *gimban shashin* daguerreotype
河 *Ginga* Milky Way; the Galaxy
河団 *gingadan* cluster of galaxies
河系 *Gingakei* the Galaxy
河系内星雲 *gingakeinai seiun* galactic nebula
河系外星雲 *gingakeigai seiun* extragalactic nebula
9 盃 *gimpai* silver cup
茶色 *ginchairo* silver gray
単本位 *gin tanhon'i* silver standard
砂 *ginsha* silver dust
砂子 *gin sunago* silver dust
10 座 *ginza* silver mint; the Ginza
扇 *ginsen* silver fan
流 *ginnaga(shi)* silvering; a dandy; an impostor
粉 *gimpun* powdered silver
紙 *gingami* silver paper
脈 *gimmyaku* vein of silver ore
被 *ginki(se)* silvering, silver plating
11 側 *gingawa* silver (watch) case
婚式 *ginkonshiki* silver wedding
屏 *gimbyō* screen coated with silver
屏風 *gimbyōbu* screen coated with silver
細工 *ginzaiku* silverwork
細工師 *ginzaikushi* silversmith
貨 *ginka* silver coin
貨幣 *ginkahei* silver coin
12 牌 *gimpai* silver medal
筋 *ginsuji* silver line
着 *ginki(se)* silvering, silver plating
無垢 *gimmuku* pure silver
13 鼠 *ginnezumi, ginnezu* silver grey
漢 *Ginkan* Milky Way
鉱 *ginkō* silver ore, silver mine
鈴 *ginrei* silver bell
幕 *gimmaku* silver screen
塊 *ginkai* silver ingot, silver bullion, bar silver
塊色 *ginkaishoku* silver gray
14 閣 *ginkaku* silver building; beautiful building
箔 *gimpaku* silver foil
髪 *gimpatsu* silver hair
製 *ginsei* made of silver
製品 *ginseihin* silverware, silver utensil
15 縁 *gimbuchi* silver rim
線 *ginsen* silver line
髯 *ginsen* beautiful white beard
幣 *gimpei* silver coin; silver-colored Shinto offerings
盤 *gimban* skating rink; ice surface; large silver platter
器 *ginki* silver utensils
輪 *ginrin* silver ring
輪部隊 *ginrin butai* bicycle unit
16 磨 *gimmiga(ki)* silver polish
17 燭 *ginshoku* silvery light from a candlestick
環 *ginkan* silver ring
翼 *gin'yoku* silvery wings
22 襴 *ginran* silver brocade
23 鑞 *ginrō* silver solder

7

鋪 6269 / J4a5f / M40491 See **舗** 322.

鋜 6270 / J-X / M40469 SAKU. ZAKU. *kanahodashi* fetters, shackles.

銹 6271 / J6c78 / M40426 **鏽** 6353 / J-X / M40857 SHŪ. SHU. *sabi* rust, tarnish.

鋏 6272 / J6e77 / M40450 KYŌ. *hasami* scissors; punch. *yattoko* pinchers, pliers.

錵 6273 / J6f26 / M40591 (国字) *nie* cloudy patterned area between body and edge of a sword; holmium.

鋩 6274 / J6f25 / M40596 (国字) *kazari* metal jewelry.
18 職 *kazarishoku* jeweler

鋒 6275 / J4b2f / M40455 HŌ dagger, sword's point. *hoko* halberd; arms; festival car, float.
6 先 *hokosaki* the point of a sword; spearhead; the brunt (of an argument); the aim (of an attack)
14 鋩 *hōbō* sword's point, sharp disposition

銷 6276 / J6e79 / M40424 SHŌ erase. *sa(su)* shut (the door).
7 沈 *shōchin* dejection, depression
却 *shōkyaku* erasure, effacement; expenditure; repayment, redemption, amortization
10 夏 *shōka* summering, going away for the 「summer

8 【金】長門阜阝隶隹雨青非

鋲 6277 / J4946 / M40503 (国字) *byō* rivet, tack, thumbtack, hobnail.
5 打 *byōu(chi)* riveting
10 釘法 *byōteihō* riveting
15 締 *byōji(me)* riveting

鋤 6278 / J3d7b / M40480 Jo. *su(ku)* spade up, plow. *suki* spade for cultivation, plow.
4 込 *su(ki)-ko(mu)* plow in
6 返 *su(ki)-kae(su)* turn over (soil), plow
10 起 *su(ki)-oko(su)* turn over (soil), plow
12 焼 *sukiyaki* Japanese beef meal, sukiyaki
17 鍬 *suki-kuwa* plows and hoes, farm tools
19 簾 *joren* small hand scoop

B **鋭** 6279 / J3154 / M40418' Ei sharpness; edge; (sharp) weapon; picked men (soldiers), the pick. *surudo(i)* pointed, sharp; violent, scathing; keen (sense); sharp (ear); penetrating (eye); shrewd.
6 気 *eiki* courage, ardor, high spirits
7 角 *eikaku* acute angle
利 *eiri* sharpness, keenness
兵 *eihei* picked troops
9 音 *eion* shrill sound
10 師 *eishi* efficient army corps
敏 *eibin* sharpness, keenness, sensitiveness; mental acumen
13 意 *eii* eagerly, earnestly
傑 *eiketsu* hero, great person, mastermind
感 *eikan* sensitiveness
15 鋒 *eihō* brunt of an attack or argument

B **鋳** 6280 / J4372 / M40503' **鑄** 6360 / J6f49 / M40972 Shu. Shū, Chū casting. *i(ru)* cast, mint, coin.
3 工 *chūkō* caster, cast-iron worker
4 込 *i-ko(mu)* cast in a mold
8 金 *chūkin* casting
物 *imono* cast metal; casting
直 *i-nao(su)* recast, recoin
9 型 *igata* mold; pig bed; matrix; die
造 *chūzō* casting, founding; minting, coining
造所 *chūzōsho* mint; foundry; type foundry
11 貨 *chūka* minting; coinage; coin
掛 *i-ka(keru)* tinker with, mend
掛屋 *ika(ke)ya* tinner
13 塊 *chūkai* ingot
鉄 *itetsu, chūtetsu, igane* cast iron, iron casting
14 像 *chūzō* molten image
15 潰 *i-tsubu(su)* melt down
16 鋼 *chūkō* steel casting; cast steel
鋼所 *chūkōjo* steel mill
鋼塊 *chūkōkai* ingot steel

8

鎚 6281 / J444a / M-X Nonstandard for 鎚 6310.

錢 6282 / J6f22 / M40563 See 銭 6264.

錂 6283 / J6e7d / M-X Ryō used in proper names.

錙 6284 / J6f21 / M40548 Shi scale; unit of weight; small amount; plentiful.

錮 6285 / J6e7e / M40578 Ko to tie.

錣 6286 / J6f24 / M40566 Tetsu. *shikoro* armor neckplates.

鋺 6287 / J6e7c / M40507 En. *kanamari* metal bowl.

錻 6288 / J6f27 / M40597 Bu tin plate.
2 力 *buriki* tin plate

錏 6289 / J6e7b / M40534 A. *shikoro* the neck plates of armor; ammonium.
17 鍜 *aka* the neck plates of armor

錚 6290 / J6f23 / M40553 Sō gong.
16 錚 *sōsō(taru)* prominent, outstanding

B **錘** 6291 / J3f6e / M40547 Sui. *omori* weight, plumb bob, sinker, sounding lead. *tsumu* spindle.
7 状 *suijō* spindle-shaped
9 重 *suijū* plumb bob

錫 6292 / J3c62 / M40573 Seki, Shaku copper; gold-copper alloy. *suzu* tin.

7 杖 *shakujō* priest's staff
14 製 *suzusei* made of tin
製品 *suzu seihin* tinware

B **錠** 6293 / J3e7b / M40559 CHŌ. TEI. JŌ lock, padlock, latch; pill; close up; counter for pills.
9 前 *jōmae* lock
前直 *jōmaenao(shi)* locksmith
前屋 *jōmaeya* locksmith
10 剤 *jōzai* pill, lozenge, tablet

錐 6294 / J3f6d / M40536 SUI pyramid; cone; gimlet. *kiri* auger, drill, awl, gimlet.
5 穴 *kiriana* gimlet hole; bull's-eye
7 体 *suitai* conical form
形 *suikei* pyramidal
12 揉 *kirimo(mi)* drilling, boring; tailspin

錨 6295 / J4945 / M40598 BYŌ. MYŌ. *ikari* anchor, grapnel.
6 地 *byōchi* anchorage
8 泊 *byōhaku* anchorage, anchoring
12 結 *ikarimusu(bi)* fisherman's bend
18 鎖 *byōsa* chain cable

錆 6296 / J3b3c / M40523 SHŌ. *sabi(ru)* get rusty, rust; mature and die (fish). *sabi* rust, tarnish.
2 刀 *sabigatana* rusty sword
4 止 *sabido(me)* rust preventative
5 付 *sabi-tsu(ku)* rust together
6 色 *sabi iro* rust color, reddish brown
16 鮎 *sabi ayu* mature trout

鋸 6297 / J3578 / M40505 KYO. *nokogiri, noko* saw.
10 屑 *nokokuzu* sawdust
12 歯 *nokogiriba, kyoshi* saw tooth; indentation
歯車 *noko haguruma* ratchet wheel
歯状 *kyoshijō* indentation, saw-tooth formation
17 鮫 *nokogirizame* saw shark
23 鱝 *nokogiriei* sawfish

A **録** 6298 / J4f3f / M40519 **錄** 6303 / J-X / M40611 ROKU. *shiru(su), roku(suru)* record.
8 画 *rokuga* television recording
事 *rokuji* recorder, secretary
9 音 *rokuon* sound recording, transcription
音板 *rokuomban* record, transcription
音放送 *rokuon hōsō* broadcast of a transcription
音盤 *rokuomban* recording disk

B **錯** 6299 / J3a78 / M40579 SAKU mix; be in disorder. *ma(zeru)* mix, blend, mingle; include, let in on. *ma(jiru)* be mixed, be blended; mingle with.
7 角 *sakkaku* alternate angles
乱 *sakuran* confusion, distraction, derangement
12 覚 *sakkaku* optical illusion; hallucination
14 綜 *sakusō* complication, intricacy
誤 *sakugo* mistake
雑 *sakuzatsu* complication, intricacy
18 簡 *sakkan* paragraphs or pages out of order

B **錬** 6300 / J4f23 / M40576 **鍊** 6304 / J-X / M40602 REN. *ne(ru)* refine (metals); drill, train; polish (sentences). *ne(ri)* tempering.
6 成 *rensei* training, drilling
8 金 *ne(ri)gane* tempered steel
金術 *renkinjutsu* alchemy
11 達 *rentatsu* skill, dexterity
清 *ne(ri)-kiyo(meru)* test and purify
13 鉄 *rentetsu, ne(ri)kurogane* wrought iron
16 鋼 *renkō* wrought steel

錦 6301 / J3653 / M40569 KIN. *nishiki* brocade; fine dress; honors.
6 地 *kinchi* your place
11 眼鏡 *nishiki megane* kaleidoscope
12 絵 *nishikie* woodblock color print
14 旗 *kinki* gold-brocade flag; imperial standard
19 繍 *kinshū* embroidered brocade; rich autumnal tints
鶏 *kinkei* golden pheasant
22 嚢 *kinnō* brocade bag

A **鋼** 6302 / J395d / M40509 KŌ steel. *hagane* steel.
4 心 *kōshin* steel core
片 *kōhen* steel billet, steel slab
5 玉石 *kōgyokuseki* corundum
6 色 *hagane iro* steel blue
7 材 *kōzai* rolled steel; steel materials

[8] 板 *kōhan, kōban* steel sheet, steel plate
[10] 索 *kōsaku* wire rope or cable
[12] 筆 *kōhitsu* ruling pen
[13] 塊 *kōkai* steel ingot
鉄 *kōtetsu* steel
鉄車 *kōtetsusha* steel (railway) car
鉄板 *kōtetsuban* steel plate
鉄管 *kōtetsukan* steel tubing
鉄製 *kōtetsusei* made of steel
鉄線 *kōtetsusen* steel wire
[14] 管 *kōkan* steel tubing
製 *kōsei* steel manufacture; steel products
[15] 線 *kōsen* steel wire

9

錄 6303 / J-X / M40611 See 録 6298.

錬 6304 / J-X / M40602 See 錬 6300.

錤 6305 / J6f2c / M40620 CHIN soft voice; (railroad) tie, crosstie; cutting board; support.

鍜 6306 / J6f28 / M40626 KA the neck plates of armor.

鍠 6307 / J6f29 / M40630 KŌ, Ō the sound of a bell; a ceremonial weapon.

鍮 6308 / J6f2b / M40645 CHŪ brass.

鎹 6309 / J6f31 / M40766 (国字) *kasugai* clamp.

鎚 6310 / J-X / M40715 TSUI. *tsuchi* hammer, mallet.

鍾 6311 / J3e61 / M40672 SHŌ gather, collect.
[13] 愛 *shōai* deep affection

鍍 6312 / J4555 / M40607 TO plating, gilding.
[8] 金 *mekki, tokin* gilt; gilding, plating; gold plating; gold filled
[14] 銀 *togin* silvering

鍔 6313 / J4457 / M40617 GAKU. *tsuba* sword guard; supporting brim of a kettle.
[7] 迫合 *tsubazeria(i)* close fighting

鍬 6314 / J372d / M40643 SHŌ. *kuwa* hoe with long blade set at an acute angle.
[2] 入 *kuwai(re)* first (ceremonial) plowing of the new year
[6] 先 *kuwasaki* metal blade of the hoe

鍋 6315 / J4669 / M40603 KA. *nabe* pan, pot, kettle.
[8] 金 *nabegane* cast iron
底景気 *nabezoko keiki* economic depression
[12] 焼 *nabeya(ki)* scalloped; cooked in a casserole
[13] 蓋 *nabebuta* kettle lid
[14] 墨 *nabezumi* kettle soot

鍼 6316 / J6f2a / M40667 SHIN needle. *hari* needle.
[7] 灸 *shinkyū* acupuncture and moxibustion
医 *shin'i* acupuncture doctor
医者 *hariisha* needle doctor, acupuncture practitioner
[8] 治 *shinji* acupuncture
[11] 術 *shinjutsu* acupuncture

鍵 6317 / J3830 / M40654 KEN (piano) key. *kagi* key.
[5] 穴 *kagi ana* keyhole
[11] 袋 *kagibukuro* key bag
[13] 楽器 *kengakki* keyed musical instrument
[15] 盤 *kemban* keyboard
[17] 環 *kagiwa* key ring
[25] 鑰 *ken'yaku* key, solution

B **鍛** 6318 / J4343 / M40625 TAN. *kita(eru)* forge, temper; drill, train, practice.
[3] 上 *kita(e)-a(geru)* temper thoroughly; train well
工 *tankō* metalworker
工所 *tankōjo, tankōsho* foundry
[7] 冶 *tan'ya* forging. *kaji* blacksmith
冶工 *kajikō* metalworker, blacksmith
冶屋 *kajiya* blacksmith
[8] 金 *tankin* wrought gold
[9] 造 *tanzō* forging
[11] 接 *tansetsu* welding

13 鉄 *tantetsu* tempering iron; wrought iron, malleable iron
16 鋼 *tankō* forged steel
錬 *tanren* temper, forging; hardening; discipline, training

10

鎰 6319 / J6f2d / M40747 Itsu measure of weight; key; lock.

鎗 6320 / J4179 / M40709 Sō. *yari* spear, lance, javelin.

鎬 6321 / J6f2e / M40741 Kō. *shinogi* sword-blade ridges.
9 削 *shinogi (o) kezu(ru)* fight desperately

鎍 6322 / J-X / M10691 Saku wire; (watch) spring.
7 条 *sakujō* cable, steel rope
条鉄道 *sakujō tetsudō* cable railway

鏈 6323 / J6f3a / M40779 Ren. *kusari* chair; irons; connection. *kusa(ru) vt* and *vi* connect.
11 帷子 *kusari katabira* coat of mail
15 縄 *kusari nawa* chain cable

鎧 6324 / J333b / M40735 Gai. *yoro(u)* put on armor; arm oneself. *yoroi* suit of armor.
4 戸 *yoroido* Venetian blinds
8 板 *yoroiita* louver boards
武者 *yoroi musha* armed warrior
10 袖一触 *gaishū-isshoku* easy victory
11 窓 *yoroimado* louver window
12 装 *gaisō* sheathing, armoring

B **鎖** 6325 / J3a3f / M40708' **鎖** 6325 / J6e79 / M40708 **鏁** 6331 / J-X / M40770
Sa. *kusari* chain; irons; connection. *to(zasu)* shut, close, lock, fasten; plunge (in grief).
4 止 *kusarido(me)* sprocket
7 状 *sajō* chainlike
8 国 *sakoku* national isolation, exclusion of foreigners
10 骨 *sakotsu* clavicle, collarbone
12 港 *sakō* closing the ports
歯車 *kusari haguruma* sprocket wheel

鎌 6326 / J3379 / M40693 Ren. *kama* sickle, scythe; trick.
2 入 *kamai(re)* harvesting
4 止 *kamado(me)* cutting grass and trees prohibited
切 *kamaki(ri)* praying mantis
7 足 *kamaashi* legs bowed in; sitting (on the floor) with heels spread apart
9 首 *kamakubi* gooseneck
10 倉 *Kamakura* Kamakura Era (1185-1333)
差 *kamasa(shi)* sickle sheath
11 脚 *kamaashi* legs bowed in; sitting (on the floor) with heels spread apart
14 槍 *kamayari* forked spear

鎔 6327 / J6f30 / M40704 **熔** 3458 / J4d50 / M19319 Yō. *to(keru) vi* fuse, melt. *to(kasu) vt* fuse, melt, smelt.
4 化 *yōka* melting
8 和 *yōwa* fusion
岩 *yōgan* lava
岩流 *yōganryū* lava flow
9 点 *yōten* melting point
10 剤 *yōzai* flux (in metallurgy)
11 接 *yōsetsu* welding
接工 *yōsetsukō* welder
接剤 *yōsetsuzai* welding flux
接管 *yōsetsukan* welded pipe
接機 *yōsetsuki* welding machine
13 滓 *yōshi* slag
鉱炉 *yōkōro* blast furnace
解 *yōkai* melting, fusing
解性 *yōkaisei* fusibility
鉄 *yōtetsu* ingot iron, ingot steel
鉄場 *yōtetsuba* forge
16 融 *yōyū* fusion, melting, smelting, flux
融点 *yōyūten* melting point

B **鎮** 6328 / J4443 / M40745 **鎭** 6329 / J6f2f / M40744 Chin ancient garrisons for peace-preservation. *shizu(maru) vi* get quiet, calm down, grow still; subside, die down; be suppressed. *shizu(meru) vt* calm, pacify; soothe, alleviate; appease; suppress, quell. *shizu(me)* pillar (of society).
4 止 *chinshi suru* allay pain
火 *chinka suru* be extinguished, be brought under control
5 圧 *chin'atsu* suppression, subjugation
台 *chindai* army camp
6 西 *Chinzei* (old name for) Kyushu

守 *chinju* local Shinto deity, tutelary god
守府 *chinjufu* navy yard, naval station, admiralty port
8 定 *chintei suru* suppress, repress, subdue, pacify
10 座 *chinza suru* be enshrined
12 痛 *chintsū* relieving pain
痛剤 *chintsūzai* painkiller, sedative
痛薬 *chintsūyaku* painkiller, sedative
14 静 *chinsei* calm, quiet, tranquillity; appeasement, pacification
静剤 *chinseizai* sedative, tranquilizer
静期間 *chinsei kikan* cooling-off period
魂 *chinkon* repose of souls
魂曲 *chinkonkyoku* requiem
魂祭 *chinkonsai* Shinto service for the repose of the dead
15 撫 *chimbu* pacification, placating
20 護 *chingo suru* pacify and preserve a country

11

鍜 6330 / J6f35 / M40821 See 銹 6271.

鏁 6331 / J-X / M40770 See 鎖 6325.

鏐 6332 / J6f39 / M40789 RYŪ pure gold; the bow of a catapult.

鏗 6333 / J6f33 / M40801 KŌ ringing sound; strike, hit.

鏑 6334 / J452d / M40790 TEKI. *kabura* arrowhead.

鏨 6335 / J6f34 / M40824 SAN. *tagane* cold chisel, graver.

鏃 6336 / J6f37 / M40772 SOKU. ZOKU. *yajiri* arrowhead; barb of an arrow.

鏘 6337 / J6f36 / M40802 SŌ the tinkling of jade or metal pendants.
12 然 *sōzen* clink, metallic sound

鏖 6338 / J6f32 / M40799 Ō. *minagoro(shi)* massacre, annihilation.
10 殺 *ōsatsu* massacre, annihilation, extermination

鏤 6339 / J6f3b / M40820 RU. *chiriba(meru)* inlay, set, mount.
10 骨 *rukotsu no* painstaking

鏝 6340 / J6f38 / M40807 MAN. *kote* laundry iron; curling iron; soldering iron; trowel.
8 板 *koteita* ironing board

鏡 6341 / J3640 / M40812 A KYŌ. *kagami* mirror; speculum; barrelhead. round rice-cake offering.
4 戸 *kagamido* paneled door
5 玉 *kyōgyoku* objective lens
立 *kagamita(te)* mirror stand
台 *kyōdai* dresser, mirror stand
8 板 *kagamiita* panels
9 面 *kyōmen* surface of a mirror
11 掛 *kagamika(ke)* mirror stand
12 開 *kagamibira(ki)* cutting the New Year's rice cakes
13 裏 *kyōri ni* in the mirror
15 餅 *kagamimochi* round glutenous-rice cakes (often used as offerings)

12

鐵 6342 / J6f45 / M-X See 鉄 6253.

鐄 6343 / J4c7a / M-X Nonstandard for 鐄 6357.

鐇 6344 / J6f40 / M40874 HAN. *tazuki* adze, broad-bladed axe; vanadium.

鐐 6345 / J6f41 / M40886 RYŌ steel; silver; gold; fetters.

鐓 6346 / J6f3e / M40891 TAI butt end; tang; ferrule.

鐔 6347 / J6f3d / M40893 TAN. *tsuba* sword guard; hilt.

鐙 6348 / J462a / M40904 TŌ. *abumi* stirrup.

鐫 6349 / J6f43 / M40924 Sen. *ho(ru)* carve, engrave, chisel, sculpture, inscribe.

鐃 6350 / J6f3f / M40867 Dō. Nyō gong.
13 鉢 *nyōbachi* cymbals

鐚 6351 / J6f3c / M40907 Wa. *bita* coin of smallest value.
14 銭 *bitasen* coin of smallest value

B 鐘 6352 / J3e62 / M40902 Shō. Shu. *kane* bell, gong, chimes, carillon.
7 状 *shōjō* bell-shaped
声 *shōsei* the sound of a bell
8 乳石 *shōnyūseki* stalactite
乳洞 *shōnyūdō* stalactite cave
13 鼓 *shōko* bell and drum
楼 *shōrō, shuro* belfry, bell tower
14 銅 *shōdō* bell metal
銘 *shōmei* a bell inscription
15 樓 *shōrō* belfry, bell tower
鋳 *kanei* bell casting
撞 *kanetsu(ki)* bell ringer; bell ringing
撞堂 *kanetsukidō* bell tower, belfry

13

鏽 6353 / J-X / M40857 See 銹 6271.

鐵 6354 / J6f44 / M40945 See 鉄 6253.

鐺 6355 / J6f46 / M40954 Tō, Sō chain; tripod kettle. *kojiri* the tip of a sheath; the point of a scabbard.

鐸 6356 / J4278 / M40951 Taku large hand bell.

鑓 6357 / J-X / M40998 (国字) *yari* spear, lance, javelin.

鐶 6358 / J6f42 / M40946 Kan metal ring; link; drawer handle. *tamaki* circle, ring.

鏝 6359 / J6f47 / M-X Ban, Man an ornament on a carriage horse.

14

鑄 6360 / J6f49 / M40972 See 鋳 6280.

B 鑑 6361 / J3455 / M40988 鑒 6362 / J6f48 / M40989 Kan. *kanga(miru)* take warning from, learn a lesson from. *kagami* mirror, pattern, example. *kanga(mite)* in view of, learning a lesson from.
5 札 *kansatsu* license, permit
7 別 *kambetsu* discrimination, judgment
8 定 *kantei* judgment, expert opinion, legal advice, appraisal, criticism
定人 *kanteinin* appraiser; connoisseur; expert witness
定者 *kanteisha* appraiser; connoisseur; expert witness
定家 *kanteika* appraiser; connoisseur; expert witness
定料 *kanteiryō* legal fee, expert's fee
定書 *kanteisho* expert's report
9 査 *kansa* inspection; inspector
15 賞 *kanshō* appreciation
賞力 *kanshōryoku* power of appreciation, an eye for (something)
賞眼 *kanshōgan* an eye for; an artist's eye
19 識 *kanshiki* judgment, discernment, discrimination, appreciation
識力 *kanshikiryoku* discernment
識家 *kanshikika* connoisseur, appraiser, discerner
識眼 *kanshikigan* discerning eye

15

鑛 6363 / J6f4a / M41010 See 鉱 6252.

鑣 6364 / J-X / M41022 Hyō. *kutsuwa* (horse's) bit.

鑢 6365 / J6f4c / M41021 Ro. Ryo. *yasuri* file, rasp.

鑠 6366 / J6f4b / M41019 Shaku. *toro(kasu) vi* melt, fuse; charm, captivate.

鑞 6367 / J6f4d / M41014 Rō solder.

[5]付 *rōzu(ke)* soldering

鑽 6368 J6f54 M41009 鑚 6374 J6f53 M41082 SAN. *ki(ru)* make a fire by rubbing sticks together.
[4]孔機 *sankōki* boring machine
[5]出 *ki(ri)-da(su)* rub sticks together to make a fire

16

鑪 6369 J6f4e M41038 See 鈩 6228.

17

鑵 6370 J6f51 M41064 See 缶 4624.

鑰 6371 J6f50 M41051 YAKU lock.

鑲 6372 J-X M41053 JŌ fit into.
[12]嵌 *jōkan* dental inlay

18

鑷 6373 J6f52 M41069 JŌ tweezers; hair ornament. *kenuki* (hair) tweezers.

19

鑚 6374 J6f53 M41082 See 鑽 6368.

鑾 6375 J6f56 M41083 RAN. *suzu* bells on imperial carriage or horse.

鑼 6376 J6f55 M41081 RA gong.

20

钁 6377 J6f57 M41092 KYAKU, KAKU plow; hoe.

鑿 6378 J6f58 M41088 SAKU. *nomi* chisel.
[4]井 *sakusei* well drilling
孔機 *sakkōki* mortising machine
[8]岩機 *sakuganki* rock drill

RAD. 長 168

Nagai long. At left: 镸 (7 strokes) *nagai hen*. Nickname: Long.

A 長 6379 J4439 M41100 镸 6380 J-X M41101 CHŌ head, chief, headman, commander, director, manager; merit, forte, advantage; superiority; length. *chō(jiru), chō(zuru)* grow up; be one's senior; excel in. *naga(raeru)* live long, live on. *naga(meru)* lengthen, prolong. *ta(keru)* excel in, be proficient in; grow older. *naga(i)* long, lengthy. *naga(ki)* length, long period. *naga(ku)* long, a long time, eternally. *naga(sa)* length. *naga(tarashii)* lengthy, long and boring. *osa* chief, head. *naga(no)* long, eternal. *tokoshi(e) ni* forever. *naga(raku)* long, a long time. *chō-* long; deep.
[2]刀 *naginata* halberd. *chōtō* long sword
[3]女 *chōjo* eldest daughter
子 *chōshi* eldest son; first child
弓 *chōkyū* longbow
久 *chōkyū* permanence, endurance; eternity, perpetuity
上 *chōjō* a senior, one's elder, a superior
大 *chōdai na* tall and stout
大息 *chōtaisoku* deep sigh
[4]月 *nagatsuki* ninth lunar month
引 *nagabi(kaseru)* prolong, drag out. *nagabi(ku)* be prolonged, drag out
方形 *chōhōkei* rectangle, oblong
水路 *chōsuiro* 50-meter (swim) course
火鉢 *nagahibachi* oblong brazier
文 *chōbun* long letter, long document
文句 *nagamonku* lengthy speech
円 *chōen* ellipse, oval
円形 *chōenkei* ellipse, oval
日 *chōjitsu* a long period of time, a long day

日月 *chōjitsugetsu* long period of time
5 生 *chōsei, nagaiki* long life, longevity
目 *nagame ni* lengthily, a little longer
石 *chōseki* feldspar
尻 *nagajiri* long visit, overstaying
幼 *chōyō* young and old
打 *chōda* extra-base hit, long drive
汀 *chōtei* long beach
兄 *chōkei* eldest brother
広舌 *chōkōzetsu* eloquence; long-windedness
6 舌 *chōzetsu* eloquence
虫 *nagamushi* snake
江 *chōkō* long river; Yangzi Jiang
芋 *nagaimo* yam
老 *chōrō* an elder, a senior, a superior; priest, presbyter
老教会 *Chōrō Kyōkai* Presbyterian Church
年 *naganen* a long time, many years
年月 *chōnengetsu* a long period of time
7 足 *chōsoku* rapid strides, leaps and bounds
身 *chōshin* great stature
男 *chōnan* eldest son
寿 *chōju* longevity, long life
8 長 *naganaga(shii)* long-drawn-out. *naganaga to* very long, at great length; tediously
雨 *nagaame* a long rain
居 *nagai* a long visit, overstaying
追 *nagaoi* a long pursuit
押 *nageshi* horizontal timbers in a house frame
所 *chōsho* one's forte, strong point; advantages
枕 *nagamakura* bed bolster
泣 *nagana(ki) suru* weep long
夜 *chōya* a long night
命 *chōmei* a long life, longevity
官 *chōkan* magistrate, chief, governor, president, secretary, administrator, director
者 *chōja* millionaire, rich person. *chōsha* one's superior, one's senior
事 *naga(i) koto* for a long time
波 *chōha* a long wave
波長 *chōhachō* long wave length
物 *chōbutsu* useless thing, white elephant
物語 *nagamonogatari* tedious speech
9 屋 *nagaya* tenement building, long apartment house
途 *chōto, nagamichi* a long way, a great distance
逝 *chōsei suru* die, pass away
城 *chōjō* a long castle; the Great Wall of China; a great national leader
恨 *chōkon* long-standing hatred
持 *nagamo(chi)* oblong chest; durability, endurance
柄 *nagae* a long handle; spear
客 *nagakyaku* a guest who stays long
洋袴 *nagazubon* long trousers
音 *choon* a long sound, a long vowel, long tone, dash
音階 *chōonkai* major scale; gamut
音符 *chōompu* macron, long-vowel mark
10 座 *chōza* a long stay (in someone's home)
唄 *nagauta* song accompanied by the samisen
旅 *nagatabi* a long trip
袖 *nagasode, chōshū* long-sleeved kimono or its wearer; courtiers
針 *chōshin* the long hand, the minute hand
剣 *chōken* a long sword; the minute hand
家 *nagaya* tenement building, long apartment house
脇差 *nagawakizashi* long sword; professional gambler
時間 *chōjikan* a long time; long-playing
射程 *chōshatei* a long range
射程砲 *chōshateihō* long range artillery
11 蛇 *chōda* a long snake; a long line, a long queue; a hero
符 *chōfu* dash (in telegraphy)
距離 *chōkyori* a long distance, a long range
距離電話 *chōkyori denwa* long-distance telephone call
12 閑 *nodo(kana), nodo(yakana)* tranquil, mild, peaceful, balmy. *nodo(kesa)* tranquility, serenity, calmness
堤 *chōtei* a long dike
湯 *nagayu* staying in the bath a long time
程 *chōtei* a great distance
軸 *chōjiku* major axis
葱 *naganegi* long, green onions
椅子 *nagaisu* couch, settee
須鯨 *nagasu kujira* razorback whale
短 *chōtan* length; long and short, merits

and demerits. *naga(shi)-mijika(shi)* either too long or too short
短打 *chōtanda* long and short hits
期 *chōki* a long period
期予報 *chōki yohō* long-range forecasting
期戦 *chōkisen* prolonged war
13 煩 *nagawazura(i)* a long illness
話 *nagabanashi* a long talk, tedious talk
路 *nagamichi* a long road
靴 *nagagutsu* boots; high shoes. *chōka* high shoes
寝 *nagane* a long sleep
嘆 *chōtan* a deep sigh
嘆息 *chōtansoku* a deep sigh
14 旗 *chōki* pennant
駆 *chōku suru* ride a long distance; pursue the enemy a long distance
歌 *chōka, nagauta* a long epic poem
髪 *chōhatsu* long hair
髪賊 *Chōhatsuzoku* Taiping Rebellion
調 *chōchō* major key
15 編 *chōhen* a long story; a long poem; a long film
編小説 *chōhen shōsetsu* a long fiction story
談 *chōdan* a long talk
談議 *nagadangi* tedious discourse, a long talk
歎 *chōtan* a deep sigh
歎息 *chōtansoku* a deep sigh
篇 *chōhen* a long story; a long poem; a long film
篇小説 *chōhen shōsetsu* a long fiction story
16 噸 *chōton* a long ton
17 講 *chōkō* a long talk, a long lecture
18 軀 *chōku* tall stature
鞭 *chōben* a long whip
19 襦袢 *nagajuban* long underwear
22 鬚鯨 *nagasu kujira* fin whale, common finback whale

RAD. 門 169

Mon or *kado* gate. As enclosure: *mongamae* or *kadogamae*. Nickname: Gate.

A 門 6381 / J4c67 / M41208 Mon gate, gateway; private school; class; counter for cannon. *kado* gate, door.
2 人 *monjin* disciple, pupil
3 口 *kadoguchi* gateway, entrance, front door
上 *monjō* above the gate
乞食 *kado kojiki* beggar at the gate
下 *monka* vicinity of the gate; disciple, pupil; discipleship
下生 *monkasei* disciple, pupil
4 火 *kadobi* funeral bonfire (at the gate); Lantern Festival fire
辺 *kadobe* gate; door; vicinity
内 *monnai* within the gate
戸 *monko* door, entrance; pedigree, lineage
戸張 *monko (o) ha(ru)* build a house; open an institute
戸開放主義 *monko kaihō shugi* open-door policy
5 生 *monsei* pupil, disciple
田 *kadoda* rice field at the gates
付 *kadozu(ke)* strolling singer, street musician
札 *monsatsu, kado fuda* name plate
出 *kadode, kadoide* departure
外 *mongai* outside the gate; outside one's speciality; another matter
外漢 *mongaikan* outsider, layperson, someone outside the field
6 迎 *kadomuka(e)* standing at the gate waiting for a visitor
地 *monchi* pedigree, lineage
灯 *montō* gate light
守 *kadomori* gatekeeper
先 *kadosaki* front of a house; entrance; the door
毎 *kadogoto ni* at every gate, from door to door
行灯 *kado andon* advertising lantern
百姓 *kadobyakushō* gate attendant who farms nearby
7 弟 *montei* pupil, disciple
8 送 *kadooku(ri)* seeing (someone) off at the gate
松 *kadomatsu* New Year's pine-and-bamboo decorations
臥 *kadobu(shi)* beggar lying at the gate
限 *mongen* closing time, curfew

並 *kadona(mi)* row of houses. *kadona(mi) ni* at every door, from door to door. *kadonara(bi)* row of houses; neighbors. *kadonara(be)* houses whose ridges are continuous

9 屋 *kadoya* gatehouse

柱 *monchū, mombashira* gatepost

院 *mon'in* the mother of an emperor who is not herself an empress

前 *monzen* before the gate

前市 *monzen'ichi* a gate crowed with callers

前払 *monzembara(i)* turning people away at the gate

前町 *monzemmachi* a temple town, a shrine town

前雀羅 *monzen-jakura* deserted, lonely

10 徒 *monto* believer, adherent; student

脇 *kadowaki ni* at the gate

11 涼 *kadosuzu(mi)* cooling off at the gate

12 歯 *monshi* incisors, front teeth

扉 *mompi* leaves of a gate

違 *kadochiga(i), kadochiga(e), kadotaga(i), kadotaga(e)* barking up the wrong tree; the wrong house or person; irrelevant; wrong

開 *kadobira(ki)* opening a store

番 *momban* doorkeeper

13 詰 *kadozu(me)* threshold; house entrance

跡 *monzeki* priest prince; temple whose head is a prince; Honganji Temple

14 閥 *mombatsu* pedigree, lineage

構 *mongama(e), kadogama(e)* gate style. *mongama(e) no* with a stately gate. *mongama(e)* the radical 門

15 標 *mompyō* name plate

16 謡 *kadoutai* beggar singing at the gates

衛 *mon'ei* guard, porter, gatekeeper

19 櫓 *kadoyagura* gate watchtower

22 鑑 *monkan* gate pass

1

閂 6382 / J6f59 / M41211 SAN. SEN. *kannuki* gate bar, gate bolt.

2

閃 6383 / J412e / M41214 SEN. *hirame(kasu)* brandish, flash, display. *hirame(ku)* flash, flicker; flutter, wave.

6 光 *senkō* flash, glint

光写真 *senkō shashin* flash photography

光灯 *senkōtō* flashlight; photoflash, flash bulb

光電球 *senkō denkyu* flashbulb

光器 *senkōki* flash outfit

10 閃 *sensen(taru)* flashing, bright, glistening

12 渡 *hirame(ki)-wata(ru)* flash across, flash continuously

15 輝 *senki* flash, glint

3

閊 6384 / J6f5b / M41229 (国字) *tsuka(eru)* be obstructed, be blocked, be stopped up, break down, be choked.

A **閉** 6385 / J4a44 / M41222 **閇** 6386 / J6f5a / M41220 HEI. *to(jiru), shi(meru)* shut, close. *to(zasu)* shut, close, lock, fasten, plunge (in grief)

3 口 *heikō suru* be dumbfounded, be stumped, be silent

4 込 *to(ji)-ko(meru)* lock up, shut in, confine. *ta(te)-ko(meru)* shut up (the house)

止機 *heishiki* circuit breaker; railway crossing gate

5 出 *shi(me)-da(su)* shut out, lock out

6 会 *heikai* adjournment, closing

7 尿 *heinyō* retention of urine

廷 *heitei* court adjournment

8 門 *heimon* closing the gate; house imprisonment

居 *heikyo suru* stay indoors

店 *heiten* closing the shop; going out of business

9 院 *heiin* adjournment of congress

10 校 *heikō* closing a school

息 *heisoku suru* bate one's breath; be cowed into silence

12 場 *heijō* closing a place

13 塞 *to(ji)-fusa(geru)* close up, cover over. *heisoku* blockade

幕 *heimaku* falling of the curtain

業 *heigyō* closing shop or office

電路 *heidenro* closed circuit

16 館 *heikan suru* close the doors (of a hall)

18 鎖 *heisa* closing, closure, lockout

22 籠 *to(ji)-komo(ru)* confine oneself, remain indoors

4

閔 6387 / J6f5c / M41251 BIN pay a convalescent visit.

閖 6388 / J6f5d / M41260' (国字) *yuri* tidegate. *yu(reru)* sway, rock on the waves.

閏 6389 / J313c / M41244 JUN intercalation; intercalary month; illegitimate throne. *urū* intercalation.

4 日 *junjitsu* leap day
月 *urūzuki, jungetsu* intercalary month
6 年 *urūdoshi, junnen* leap year; intercalary year

B **閑** 6390 / J3457 / M41247 KAN. *hima* leisure.

2 人 *himajin, kanjin* man of leisure
4 月 *kangetsu* farmers' quiet months
中 *kanchū* leisure time
文字 *kammoji, kammonji* idle word; leisurely writing
日 *kanjitsu* holiday
日月 *kanjitsugetsu* long period of leisure
5 田 *kanden* fallow rice field
古鳥 *kankodori* cuckoo
6 地 *kanchi* secluded place; retirement; easy post
宅 *kantaku* quiet home
7 言 *kangen* useless words
住 *kanjū* quiet home
吟 *kangin* leisurely reciting of poems
却 *kankyaku* negligence, oversight
8 居 *kankyo* leisurely life; quiet retreat
所 *kansho* quiet place. *kanjo* lavatory
管 *kankan* a post requiring little work
歩 *kampo* leisurely walk
事 *kanji* idleness
事業 *kanjigyō* work in leisure hours
9 客 *kankaku* person of leisure
10 庭 *kantei* quiet garden
11 寂 *kanjaku* quiet; tranquillity
窓 *kansō* a quiet window
12 閑 *himahima ni* at one's leisure. *kankan* quiet, leisure, rolling quietly along (in a vehicle)
疎 *kanso na* quiet and isolated
散 *kansan* leisure; quiet; inactivity
雲 *kan'un* lazily floating clouds
13 暇 *kanka* leisure
雅 *kanga* refinement; quietude
話 *kanwa* quiet talk; gossip
14 語 *kango* idle talk
静 *kansei* quietness, tranquillity
15 談 *kandan* quiet conversation, idle talk
18 職 *kanshoku* an easy job; a leisurely task

A **間** 6391 / J3456 / M41249 **閒** 6392 / J-X / M41248 KAN interval; space; between; among; discord; favorable opportunity. KEN six feet. *ai* interval; between, medium; crossbred. *aida, awai* space, interval, gap; between, among; midway; on the way; distance; time, period; relationship. *ma* space, room; interval; pause; rest (in music); time; a while; leisure; luck; timing, harmony. *ma(monaku)* soon.

1 一髪 *kan'ippatsu* a hair's breadth
3 口 *maguchi* frontage; width
子 *ai(no)ko* Eurasian, mulatto; crossbreed, hybrid
4 手 *ai(no)te* interlude; accompaniment; sideshow; strain of music
欠 *kanketsu* intermittence; intermittent
尺 *mashaku* measurement; accounting
中 *-aidajū* during
引 *mabi(ku)* thin out. *mabi(ki)* thinning out (plants); killing unwanted children
切 *magi(ri)* tacking (in sailing). *magi(ru)* tack; divide, partition
5 田 *kanden* fallow rice field
代 *madai* room rent
仕切 *majiki(ri)* partition, division
6 色 *kanshoku* intermediary colors
近 *majika* nearness, proximity. *majika(i)* near at hand
伐 *kambatsu* periodic thinning (of a forest)
合 *ma(ni)a(u)* be in time for; serve the purpose; can do without. *ma(ni)a(waseru)* make (something) do; get (something) ready. *ma(ni)a(wase)* makeshift, expedient. *maa(i)* interval
7 作 *kansaku* intercrop, crop planted between rows
判 *aiban* medium size (in printing)
男 *maotoko* adultery; adulterer
投詞 *kantōshi* interjection
抜 *ma (ga) nu(keru)* be stupid; be funny;

be out of harmony. *manu(ke)* disharmony; stupidity; simpleton, moron. *manu(kesa)* stupidity
抜面 *manu(ke)zura* dumb look
8 延 *mano(binoshita)* slow, dull, vacant-looking (face)
性 *kansei no* asexual; having some characteristics of both parents
取 *mado(ri)* plan of the house, room arrangement
服 *aifuku* spring or fall wear
者 *kanja* spy
9 食 *kanshoku, aidagu(i)* eating between meals
柄 *aidagara* relation, relationship
怠 *madaru(i), madaru(kkoi)* slow, dull, tedious
竿 *kenzao* measuring rod
奏曲 *kansōkyoku* interlude
点線 *kantensen* boundary of crosses and dots on a map
10 紙 *aigami* sheets inserted to prevent smudging
借 *maga(ri)* renting a room
借人 *magarinin* roomer
11 道 *kandō* secret path, side road, short cut
脳 *kannō* interbrain
悪 *ma(ga)waru(i)* be embarrassed, feel self conscious
断 *kandan* interruptions; intervals
断無 *kandanna(ki)* incessant, continuous
接 *kansetsu* indirect
接伝染 *kansetsu densen* indirect infection
接税 *kansetsuzei* indirect tax
接費 *kansetsuhi* overhead cost
接照明 *kansetsu shōmei* indirect lighting
接話法 *kansetsu wahō* indirect quotation
接選挙 *kansetsu senkyo* indirect election (e.g., via electors)
12 間 *mama* occasionally, frequently
遠 *madō ni* at long intervals
違 *machiga(u) vi* mistake. *machiga(eru) vt* mistake. *machiga(tta)* wrong, mistaken. *machiga(e), machiga(i)* mistake; fault, failure; indiscretion, dispute
税 *kanzei* indirect tax
隔 *kankaku* space
着 *aigi* spring or fall wear
無 *ma(mo)na(ku)* soon, in a moment
然 *kanzen* subject to criticism
貸 *maga(shi)* renting out a room
13 隙 *kangeki* gap, aperture, opening, space, interstice, crevice. *ma(gana)-suki(gana)* always, constantly
際 *magiwa ni* just before, on the verge of, at the eleventh hour
数 *kensū* number of *ken* in length. *makazu* number of rooms.
歇 *kanketsu* intermittence; intermittent
歇泉 *kanketsusen* geyser, intermittent hot-water service (at hot springs)
歇温泉 *kanketsu onsen* geyser
歇熱 *kanketsu netsu* intermittent fever, ague
14 髪入 *kampatsu (o) i(rezu)* in the twinkling of an eye
15 緩 *manuru(i)* slow, sluggish
16 積 *kenzumo(ri)* measuring land
諜 *kanchō* spy, secret agent

A **開** 6393 / J332b / M41233 Kai opening. *hira(ku)* open, unfold, unroll, uncover, unpack, untie, unseal; establish; clear (land); pioneer; clear the way; convene; enlighten (a country); bloom; differ, have a margin; widen (the space between). *hira(keru)* become civilized, become modernized; become sensible; be opened to traffic; feel relief; be open; grow, develop (a town). *a(keru)* open; empty, vacate; leave (a space); clear (the table); make (a hole); reserve (a seat), stay away from; dawn; end, expire, be over; open, begin. *a(ku)* open, be opened; start, begin, commence; become vacant, become empty, be disengaged, be free; expire, be over. *a(karu) vi* open. *a(ita)* open; empty, vacant. *hira(keta)* open, clear, commodious; civilized, modernized; sociable. *hira(ki)* opening; cupboard; difference; margin; aperture; breaking up (of a meeting).
3 口 *kaikō* opening a speech
山 *kaizan, kaisan* (sect) founder; pioneer
4 戸 *hira(ki)do* hinged door
方 *kaihō* extraction of roots (in math)
化 *kaika* civilization, enlightenment
5 田 *kaiden* making paddy fields
立 *kairyū, kairitsu* extraction of the cube root

広 *a(ke)-hiro(geru)* open wide
庁 *kaichō* opening a government office
札 *kaisatsu* opening of bids
平 *kaihei* extraction of the square root
市 *kaishi* opening a city (to commerce)
6 地 *kaichi* opened-up land
帆 *kaihan suru* set sail
会 *kaikai* opening a meeting
会日 *kaikaibi* opening day
会中 *kaikaichū* during the session
会辞 *kaikai(no)ji* opening address
7 局 *kaikyoku* opening a new telephone exchange, post office, or broadcasting station
廷 *kaitei* court session; trial
作 *kaisaku* opening up land and planting
坑 *kaikō* opening a mine
花 *kaika* flowering, blossoming
8 門 *kaimon* opening of the gate
国 *kaikoku* founding of a country; opening of a country
店 *kaiten* opening of a new shop
始 *kaishi* commencement, inauguration
披 *kaihi suru* open (a letter)
明 *kaimei* civilization, enlightenment
函 *kaikan* emptying a mailbox
直 *hira(ki)-nao(ru)* become defiant; become serious; turn upon
拓 *kaitaku* clearing, reclamation, exploitation, opening up land
拓者 *kaitakusha* cultivator; settler, colonist, pioneer
放 *kaihō suru, hira(ki)-hana(tsu)* open, throw open; leave open. *a(ke)-hana(su)* throw open; leave open. *a(kep)pana(shi) no* frank, openhearted; leaving (a door) wide open
放的 *kaihōteki* frank candid, openhearted
放性結核 *kaihōsei kekkaku* active tuberculosis
放無用 *Kaihō Muyō* Keep the Door Closed.
9 通 *kaitsū* opening to traffic
城 *kaijō* capitulation (of a fort)
祖 *kaiso* (sect) founder; apostle (to the...); originator, author, inventor
院 *kaiin* opening congress; hospital opening
陣 *kaijin* breaking camp
削 *kaisaku* cutting through (a road); digging a canal; clearing (land, for farming)
封 *kaifū suru* break the seal, open. *hira(ki)fū, kaifū* unsealed letter
巻 *kaikan* opening a book and reading; first part of a book
発 *kaihatsu* colonization; development; enlightenment
発途上国 *kaihatsu tojōkoku* developing country
10 進 *kaishin* (military) developments
悟 *kaigo* enlightenment, wisdom
陳 *kaichin suru* express (opinions). *kaichin* statement
校 *kaikō* opening a school
校式 *kaikōshiki* school opening ceremony
11 運 *kaiun* better fortune
帳 *kaichō* exhibiting a Buddhist image; opening a gambling game
設 *kaisetsu* establishment, inauguration, opening; installation (of telephones)
窓 *hira(ki) mado* casement window
基 *kaiki* laying a foundation; founding; a founder
船渠 *kaisenkyo* tidal basin
眼 *kaigan, kaigen* enlightenment, spiritual awakening; opening the eyes (investing a new image with sacred qualities)
眼式 *kaigenshiki* ceremony of opening the eyes (of an image)
票 *kaihyō* counting the ballots
票所 *kaihyōjo* ballot-counting place
閉 *kaihei* opening and shutting; (electrical) make and break. *a(ke)ta(te)* opening and shutting
閉器 *kaiheiki* a make-and-break switch
閉機 *kaiheiki* circuit breaker; railroad-crossing gate
閉橋 *kaiheikyō* drawbridge
12 扉 *kaihi suru* open the door
場 *kaijō* opening
渠 *kaikyo* open ditch
期 *kaiki* session (of congress)
港 *kaikō* opening a port; open port
港場 *kaikōjō* treaty port, open port
13 路 *kairo* open circuit
幕 *kaimaku* rising of the curtain
障子 *hira(ki) shōji* casement translucent doors
電路 *kaidenro* open circuit

催 *kaisai* holding (a meeting)
催中 *kaisaichū* in session
催地 *kaisaichi* site (of an exhibition)
戦 *kaisen* outbreak of war
戦後 *kaisengo* after the opening of hostilities
戦前 *kaisenzen* before the opening of hostilities
業 *kaigyō* opening a business or a practice
業医 *kaigyōi* doctor in private practice
業届 *kaigyō todo(ke)* report of the opening of a business
14 演 *kaien* opening of a play; opening of a lecture
綱 *hira(ki)zuna* ripcord
16 橋 *kaikyō suru* open a new bridge
館 *kaikan* opening of a new hall
墾 *kaikon* cultivating new land
墾可能地 *kaikon-kanōchi* arable land
墾地 *kaikonchi* cultivated land
17 講 *kaikō* opening of a lecture course
豁 *kaikatsu na* open (land); magnanimous
18 襟 *kaikin* open-collared (shirt)
21 闢 *kaibyaku* beginnings, creation, founding (of an empire)
28 鑿 *kaisaku* clearing (land, for farming); cutting through (a road); digging (a canal)

5

閠 6394 / J6f60 / M-X GYOKU.

鬧 6395 / J6f5f / M41264 **閙** 6822 / J7229 / M45639 DŌ noisy.

閘 6396 / J6f5e / M41263 KŌ water gate, lock.
8 門 *kōmon* lock gate (for ships)

6

閤 6397 / J395e / M41301 KŌ small side gate.

B **閥** 6398 / J4836 / M41308 BATSU lineage, pedigree; clique, faction, clan, combine.
11 族 *batsuzoku* clan, clique

閧 6399 / J6f62 / M41311 KŌ. *toki* war cry.
7 声 *toki (no) koe* war cry

閨 6400 / J6f61 / M41312 KEI. *neya* bedroom.
4 中 *keichū* bedroom; family life; harem
7 秀 *keishū* accomplished woman
8 門 *keimon* bedroom; family life
房 *keibō* bedroom; family life; harem
9 室 *keishitsu* bedroom; harem; wife
怨 *keien* the ill feeling of a divorcee; a woman's ill feeling
14 閥 *keibatsu* nepotism

A **閣** 6401 / J3355 / M41300 KAKU tower, tall building, palace; cabinet (of a government).
3 下 *Kakka* Your Excellency
4 内 *kakunai* within the cabinet
5 外 *kakugai* outside the cabinet
令 *kakurei* cabinet order
10 員 *kakuin* cabinet member
14 僚 *kakuryō* cabinet members
20 議 *kakugi* cabinet meeting

A **関** 6402 / J3458 / M41297 **關** 6419 / J6f70 / M41470 KAN barrier, gateway. *kan(suru)* related to, be connected with, concern, affect, involve, pertain to. *kaka(waru)* concern oneself in, have to do with; affect, influence; stick to (opinions). *(ni) kan(shite)* concerning. *kaka(wari)* relation, connection. *seki* barrier, checking station.
2 八州 *Kanhasshū* the Eight Provinces of Kantō
3 山 *seki (no) yama* one's utmost. *kanzan* the mountains around one's home; the mountains around a border station.
与 *kan'yo* participation
ケ原 *Sekigahara* name of place where decisive battle was fought; a decisive battle, a Waterloo
4 木 *kangi* gate bar
心 *kanshin* concern, interest, regard
心事 *kanshingoto* a matter of serious concern
5 白 *kampaku* (ancient) chief advisor to the emperor; a domineering husband
市 *kanshi* border market town
6 守 *sekimori* barrier keeper

8 金 長 7【門】阜 阝 隶 隹 雨 青 非

8 門 *kammon* barrier, gateway; Shimonoseki-Moji
所 *sekisho* barrier, checking station
知 *kanchi* concern
取 *sekitori* sumo wrestler in top two divisions
9 連 *kanren* connection, relation, association
連事項 *kanren jikō* related matters
連質問 *kanren shitsumon* related question
係 *kankei* relation, connection, concern, participation; influence, effect; illicit relations. *kankei(naku)* regardless of
係代名詞 *kankei daimeishi* relative pronoun
係会社 *kankei kaisha* affiliated company
係当局 *kankei tōkyoku* the authorities concerned
係形容詞 *kankei keiyōshi* relative adjective
係者 *kankeisha* participant; interested party, the person concerned
係官庁 *kankei kanchō* authorities concerned
係副詞 *kankei fukushi* relative adverb
係湿度 *kankei shitsudo* relative humidity
10 釜 *Kampu* Shimonoseki-Pusan
12 税 *kanzei* customs, duty, tariff
税率 *kanzeiritsu* customs tariff
税障壁 *kanzei shōheki* tariff wall, customs barrier
13 塞 *kansai* border fortification
節 *kansetsu* joint
節炎 *kansetsuen* arthritis
16 頭 *kantō* turning point; parting of the ways; place of execution
17 聯 *kanren* connection, relation, association
25 鑰 *kan'yaku* bolt and key; key (to the solution)

7

閭 6403 / J6f63 / M41334 Ryo rural area.

B **閲** 6404 / J315c / M41341 Etsu inspection, revision. *es(suru)* review, revise. *kemi(suru)* read, look, over; examine; pass, elapse.
7 兵 *eppei* parade, review, inspection of troops
兵式 *eppeishiki* troop review
14 歴 *etsureki* career, personal history
読 *etsudoku* reading, perusal
16 覧 *etsuran* perusal, inspection, reading
覧者 *etsuransha* reader, visitor
覧室 *etsuranshitsu* reading room

8

閾 6405 / J6f67 / M41384 Iki threshold.

閹 6406 / J6f66 / M41372 En eunuch.
2 人 *enjin* eunuch

閼 6407 / J6f64 / M41380 A obstruct, conceal; (used phonetically).
7 伽 *aka* Buddhist water offering
伽桶 *aka oke* Buddhist water-offering receptacle

閻 6408 / J6f65 / M41379 En town.
21 魔 *Emma* King of Hades
魔帳 *emmachō* teacher's black list

9

闊 6409 / J6f68 / M41429 See 濶 3364.

闃 6410 / J6f6a / M41411 Geki deserted, quiet, still.

闍 6411 / J6f6b / M41434 To, Ja tower above outer town gates; area inside outer gates.

闋 6412 / J-X / M41430 Ketsu rest.

闌 6413 / J6f6c / M41433 Ran. *ta(keru)* rise high, be well up; be well along, be well advanced. *takenawa* height of; full swing; the thick of.
3 干 *rankan* railing, balustrade

闇 6414 / J3047 / M41421 An. *kura(garu)* get dark, get gloomy. *yami*

darkness; grief, gloom; disorder, black market. *kura(i)* dark, gloomy, somber; dim, faint; ignorant.
5 打 *yamiu(chi)* assassination, foul murder
仕合 *yamijiai* fighting in the dark; fighting an unknown assailant
市 *yamiichi* black market
市場 *yami ichiba* black market
6 合 *angō* coincidence
行為 *yami kōi* illegal act; black-market dealings
7 売 *yamiu(ri)* black-market selling
売買 *yami baibai* black-market dealing
8 夜 *yamiyo, an'ya* dark night
取引 *yami torihiki* black-market dealings, undercover dealings
価格 *yami kakaku* black-market price
物資 *yami busshi* black-market goods
金融 *yami kin'yū* illegal lending
9 屋 *yamiya* black marketeer
相場 *yami sōba* black-market price
10 値 *yamine* black-market price
冥 *ammei* darkness
弱 *anjaku* weak-mindedness
11 黒 *ankoku* darkness
商人 *yami shōnin* black marketeer
12 買 *yamiga(i)* black-market purchasing
雲 *yamikumo ni* thoughtlessly, haphazardly, at random
13 路 *yamiji* dark road
17 闇 *yamiyami* suddenly, without one's knowledge; easily. *an'an* darkness; stillness in the depths

10

闔 6415 / J6f6e / M41452 Kō doors.
8 国 *kōkoku* the whole country

闖 6416 / J6f6f / M41458 CHIN inquire about.
2 入 *chinnyū* intrusion, trespassing, raiding
入者 *chinnyūsha* intruder, trespasser, raider

闕 6417 / J6f6d / M41456 KETSU imperial palace. *ka(keru)* be broken (off), be chipped; lack, be missing; wane, be vacant (a position).
3 下 *kekka* emperor; palace gate
4 文 *ketsubun* missing part (of a manuscript)
5 本 *keppon* missing volume
6 如 *ketsujo* lack, deficiency, privation
字 *ketsuji* omitted word; courtesy spaces left above famous names
8 所 *kessho* confiscation of an estate
官 *kekkan* vacant post
10 席 *kesseki* absence, default
員 *ketsuin* vacancy, vacant position, opening
11 焉 *ketsuen* lack, deficiency, privation

B **闘** 6418 / J462e / M45649' **鬪** 6825 / J722c / M45649 Tō fighting. *tataka(u)* wage war; fight; engage in a contest; struggle against.
3 士 *tōshi* fighter, boxer, combatant; champion (of truth)
士体型 *tōshi taikei* athletic type
士型 *tōshigata* athletic type
4 犬 *tōken* dogfight; a fighting dog
牛 *tōgyū* bullfight; fighting bull
牛士 *tōgyūshi* matador, bullfighter
牛場 *tōgyūjō* bull ring
6 争 *tōsō* fight, combat, conflict; labor strife
争宣言 *tōsō sengen* strike declaration
7 技 *tōgi* competition, contest
志 *tōshi* fighting spirit
志満満 *tōshi-mamman* full of pep
10 病 *tōbyō suru* fight against an illness
将 *tōshō* a fighting general; brave fighter; champion of a principle
11 魚 *tōgyo* fighting fish
14 歌 *tōka* poetry contest
魂 *tōkon* fighting spirit
19 鶏 *tōkei* cockfight; cockfighting; fighting cock

11

關 6419 / J6f70 / M41470 See **関** 6402.

12

闥 6420 / J6f72 / M41508 TATSU, TACHI small gate; inside the walls; government office.

闡 6421 / J6f71 / M41489 SEN clarify.

[8] 明 *semmei* clarification

13

闢 6422 / J6f73 / M41500 HEKI, BYAKU open.

RAD. 阜 170

Kozato small village (i.e., in contradistinction to Rads. 163 & 166). Except for the radical character itself, it is always used as the left in the modifed form 阝 (2 strokes) *kozato hen*. Nickname: Left Village.

阜 6423 / J496c / M41534 FU hill; mound.

[16] 頭 *futō* wharf

3

阡 6424 / J6f74 / M41548 SEN one thousand.

4

阨 6425 / J6f75 / M41559 YAKU, AI narrow; steep; obstruct; suffer.

阮 6426 / J6f76 / M41569 GEN used in Chinese place and proper names.

阯 6427 / J6f77 / M41570 SHI foundation; foothills; islet.

阪 6428 / J3a65 / M41562 HAN slope. *saka* incline.

[9] 神 *Hanshin* Osaka-Kobe
[13] 路 *hanro* hill road

A 防 6429 / J4b49 / M41576 BŌ *fuse(gu)* defend, protect; resist; keep away, shut out, ward off; prevent.

[2] 人 *sakimori* ancient military guards
[4] 手 *fuse(gi)te* defender
止 *bōshi* prevention
水 *bōsui* waterproof, watertight; holding back flood waters
水布 *bōsuifu* waterproof cloth, oilskin, tarpaulin
水剤 *bōsuizai* waterproofing material
水帽 *bōsuibō* rain hat, waterproof cap
水着 *bōsuigi* raincoat
水隔室 *bōsui kakushitsu* watertight compartment
火 *bōka* fire prevention, fire fighting, fire proof
火戸 *bōkado* fire door
火金庫 *bōka kinko* fireproof safe
火栓 *bōkasen* fire hydrant
火剤 *bōkazai* fireproof stuff
火樹 *bōkaju* firebreak planting
火壁 *bōkaheki* fire wall
[5] 犯 *bōhan* crime prevention
氷 *bōhyō* de-icing
[6] 守 *bōshu* defense; defensive
虫剤 *bōchūzai* insecticide
共 *bōkyō* anti-Communist
共協定 *Bōkyō Kyōtei* Anti-Comintern Pact
[7] 材 *bōzai* protecting boom; bar (to a harbor entrance)
[8] 波堤 *bōhatei* breakwater
毒 *bōdoku* gasproof
毒面 *bōdokumen* gas mask
空 *bōkū* air defense
空対策 *bōkū taisaku* air-raid precautions
空壕 *bōkūgō* air-raid shelter
空警報 *bōkū keihō* air-raid alarm
[9] 音 *bōon* soundproof; soundproofing
音装置 *bōon sōchi* soundproofing
風 *bōfū* wind protection
風林 *bōfūrin* windbreak
砂林 *bōsarin* trees holding drifting sand
砂堤 *bōsatei* sand dike
臭 *bōshū* deodorization
臭剤 *bōshūzai* deodorant, deodorizer
疫 *bōeki* prevention of epidemics, disinfection, quarantine
疫医 *bōekii* health officer
疫線 *bōekisen* sanitary cordon

11 雪 *bōsetsu* snowbreak
雪林 *bōsetsurin* snowbreak forest
雪柵 *bōsetsusaku* snowbreak
雪壁 *bōsetsuheki* snow wall, snowshed
12 遏 *bōatsu suru* prevent, stop, check, repress
備 *bōbi* defense, defense works, guarding
湿 *bōshitsu* dampproofing
塁 *bōrui* fort, stronghold
弾 *bōdan* bulletproof; bombproof
弾室 *bōdanshitsu* bombproof room
寒 *bōkan* protection against the cold
寒具 *bōkangu* cold-protection outfit
寒着 *bōkangi* winter clothing
御 *bōgyo* defense, protection
御物 *bōgyobutsu* shield, barricade, protector
御陣地 *bōgyo jinchi* defensive position
御線 *bōgyosen* defense line
13 楯 *bōjun* gun shield
戦 *bōsen* defensive war
塞 *bōsai* roadblock, barricade
14 塵 *bōjin* dustproof
腐 *bōfu* preservation; embalmment; antisepsis
腐的 *bōfuteki* antiseptic, aseptic
腐剤 *bōfuzai* antiseptic, preservative
15 蝕剤 *bōshokuzai* anticorrosive
潮門 *bōchōmon* tide gate
潮林 *bōchōrin* forest controlling tidewater
16 諜 *bōchō* anti-espionage, counterintelligence
壁 *bōheki* barrier, bulwark, wall of defense
衛 *bōei* defense, protection
衛水域 *bōei suiiki* the defensive waters
衛庁 *Bōeichō* Defense Agency
衛体制 *bōei taisei* a defense system; a defense build-up
衛協定 *bōei kyōtei* a defense agreement
衛隊 *bōeitai* defense corps, defense force
17 禦 *bōgyo* defense, protection
禦物 *bōgyobutsu* shield, barricade, protector
禦陣地 *bōgyo jinchi* defensive position
禦戦 *bōgyosen* defensive war
禦線 *bōgyosen* defense line
20 護 *bōgo* protection, custody
護団 *bōgodan* air-raid defense corps

5

陂 6430 / J6f78 / M41603 HI, HA slope; sea wall; coast; edge; pond; uneven.

阼 6431 / J-X / M41594 So eastern steps; throne.

陀 6432 / J424b / M41600 TA, DA steep.

B **附** 6433 / J496d / M41606 FU. *fu(suru)* give to, submit to, refer to; affix, attach, append. *tsu(keru) vt* attach, join, stick, glue, fasten; sew on; furnish (a house with); wear, put on; make an entry; appraise, set (a price); apply (ointment); bring alongside; place (under guard or a doctor); follow, shadow; add, append, affix; load; give (courage to); keep (an eye on); establish (relations or understanding). *tsu(ku) vi* be connected with; be dyed; be stained; be scarred; be recorded; be attached to; accompany; study with; increase, be added to. (For compounds, see 付 124).

B **阻** 6434 / J414b / M41593 So separate from; prevent, stop. *haba(mu)* obstruct, prevent, impede, deter, hinder, thwart, resist, frustrate.
4 止 *soshi* obstruction, check, hindrance, prevention
10 害 *sogai* hindrance, check, deterrent, obstruction, interference
害気球 *sogai kikyū* barrage balloon
12 隔 *sokaku* alienation, estrangement, separation
喪 *sosō* loss of power, loss of energy, dejection
13 塞気球 *sosai kikyū* barrage balloon
19 礙 *sogai* hindrance, check, deterrent, obstruction, interference

阿 6435 / J3024 / M41599 A. O. *omone(ru), hetsura(u)* flatter, fawn upon. *kuma* corner, nook, recess; indentation, bend, turn; shade, shading; makeup.
4 比 *abi* loon
父様 *otōsan, otōsama* father

片 *ahen* opium
片中毒 *ahen chūdoku* opium addiction; opium poisoning
片吸飲 *ahen kyūin* opium smoking
片吸飲者 *ahen kyūinsha* opium smoker
片売買 *ahen baibai* opium traffic
片酒 *ahenshu* opium wine
片剤 *ahenzai* opiate
片常用 *ahen jōyō* opium habit
片窟 *ahenkutsu* opium den
片戦争 *Ahen Sensō* Opium War
片膏 *ahenkō* opium plaster
5 世 *asei* timeserving
古屋貝 *akoyagai* mother-of-pearl, pearl oyster
6 多福 *otafuku* homely woman
多福風 *otafuku kaze* mumps
7 呆 *ahō* fool, simpleton. *ahora(shii)* foolish
呆臭 *ahōkusa(i)* foolish
呆鳥 *ahōdori* albatross
8 房 *ahō* fool, simpleton
房臭 *ahōkusa(i)* foolish
房鳥 *ahōdori* albatross
弥陀 *Amida* Amida (Buddha); lottery; wearing a hat on the back of the head
弥陀仏 *Amida Butsu* Amida Buddha
弥陀被 *Amidakabu(ri)* wearing a hat on the back of the head
弥陀堂 *Amidadō* Amida temple
弥陀経 *Amidakyō* one of the Pure Land sutras
11 亀 *okame* homely woman, fat-woman's mask
婆擦 *abazure* wickedness; wicked woman
13 媽 *ama* amah, nurse
14 漕 *akogi* frequency; insatiability; cruelty
鼻叫喚 *abikyōkan* agonize in the eighth burning hell of Buddhism
16 諛 *ayu* flattery, adulation
19 羅漢 *arakan* arhat
蘭陀 *Oranda* Holland

6

陌 6436 / J6f79 / M41617 HAKU path between rice fields; road; boundary; 100.

陏 6437 / J6f7a / M41623 DA, ZUI melon; package.

陋 6438 / J6f7b / M41616 RŌ narrowness; meanness; humbleness.
6 宅 *rōtaku* squalid home; my home
劣 *rōretsu* baseness, meanness
7 見 *rōken* narrow view; my humble opinion
8 居 *rōkyo* hovel
拙 *rōsetsu na* vulgar, low-class
9 風 *rōfū* evil custom, abuse
屋 *rōoku* squalid hut, hovel; my humble cottage
巷 *rōkō* narrow alley; slums
11 習 *rōshū* evil custom, abuse
12 策 *rōsaku* poor plan

A **限** 6439 / J3842 / M41627 GEN. *kagi(ru)* limit, restrict, confine. *kagi(ri)* limit(s); as far as possible, as much as possible, to the best of (one's ability). *(ni) kagi(tte)* of all (days, persons, etc.); alone. *-kagi(ri)* insofar as; this time only. *-kiri* (June) delivery.
5 外 *gengai* outside the limits
外発行 *gengai hakkō* excess (currency) issue
7 局 *genkyoku* limiting
8 限 *girigiri* extreme limit
定 *gentei* limitation, qualification, definition, determination
定版 *genteiban* limited edition
9 界 *genkai* boundary, limit, limits, bounds
度 *gendo* limit, limits, limitation
度内 *gendonai* within the limits
11 産 *gensan* production limit
12 無 *kagi(ri)na(i)* eternal, unlimited, endless. *kagi(ri)na(ku)* without end, exceedingly

7

陦 6440 / J7023 / M-X See 島 1476.

陜 6441 / J6f7d / M41656 KYŌ, KŌ narrow.

陝 6442 / J7021 / M41657 SEN used in Chinese place names.

陟 6443 J7022 M41659 CHOKU climb; advance; high.

A 陛 6444 J4a45 M41654 HEI. *kizahashi* steps (of the throne).
3 下 *Heika* His or Her Majesty

陞 6445 J6f7e M41658 SHŌ go up, climb, rise.
9 叙 *shōjo* promotion, advancement
10 進 *shōshin* promotion, advancement

B 陥 6446 J3459 M41676' 陷 6451 J6f7c M41707 KAN. *ochii(ru)* fall into, get into, slide into, lapse into; cave in, sink; fall (a fort). *otoshii(reru)* ensnare, tempt.
2 入 *kannyū suru* subside, collapse, cave in
7 没 *kambotsu* a cave-in; subsidence
9 穽 *kansei* trap, pitfall
12 落 *kanraku* fall, sinking, a cave-in; surrender; giving in

A 院 6447 J3121 M41665 IN mansion; temple; palace; hospital; school; institution; congress; ex-emperor.
4 内 *innai* inside congress; within the institution
内幹事 *innai kanji* whip, floor leader
内総務 *innai sōmu* floor leader, chief whip
5 庁 *inchō, in(no)chō* retired emperor's office
主 *inshu* head priest of a temple; owner of a hospital
本 *impon* drama; play book
外 *ingai* outside congress; nonparliamentary; outside of the institution
外団 *ingaidan* lobbying group
外者 *ingaisha* lobbyist; persons outside congress
8 長 *inchō* head of a hospital, court, or school
9 政 *insei* government by cloistered emperors
宣 *inzen* decree of a cloistered emperor
11 務 *immu* the business of the institution
20 議 *ingi* decision of congress

B 陣 6448 J3f58 M41667 JIN battle array, ranks; camp; position. *jin(suru)* set up (an army) camp.
4 中 *jinchū ni* in the field, in camp
太鼓 *jindaiko* war drum
5 立 *jinda(te)* battle array
払 *jimbara(i)* breaking up camp and withdrawing
6 伍 *jingo* the ranks of the army
列 *jinretsu* arrangement of the camp; encampment
羽織 *jimbaori* coat worn over the armor; coat of arms
地 *jinchi* encampment; position
地戦 *jinchisen* position or stabilized warfare
7 没 *jimbotsu* death in action
形 *jinkei* battle array
8 門 *jimmon* camp gate
所 *jinsho* encampment
歿 *jimbotsu* death in action
法 *jimpō* battle array
取 *jindo(ru)* encamp, take up a position. *jindo(ri)* battle array; playing war
9 風 *jimpū* squall, gust
屋 *jin'ya* encampment
後 *jingo* the rear of the army
10 容 *jin'yō* battle array
11 笠 *jingasa* (ancient) soldier's helmet; rank and file (of a party)
12 痛 *jintsū* labor pains
備 *jinzona(e)* setting up camp
営 *jin'ei* camp; barracks
替 *jinga(e)* moving camp
13 幕 *jimmaku* camp enclosure
16 頭 *jintō* the head of an army; the field of battle
頭指揮 *jintō shiki* a commander personally leading his army into battle

A 除 6449 J3d7c M41669 JI. JO division (in math). *jo(suru)* divide (in math); exclude. *nozo(ku)* remove, abolish, cancel; exclude, except. *no(keru)* get rid of, remove; finish; omit, exclude. *nozo(ite), nozo(ite wa)* except, exclusive of. *-yoke* protection, shelter, charm.
4 毛剤 *jomōzai* depilatory
5 斥 *joseki suru* exclude, expel, reject
去 *nozo(ki)-sa(ru)* remove, take away. *jokyo* removal, exclusion
号 *jogō* sign of division
外 *jogai* exclusive, exception
外例 *jogairei* exceptional case

6 行 *johō* going slowly
名 *jomei* disfellowshipping, expulsion, dropping a name, excommunication
虫菊 *jochūgiku* the vermifuge chrysanthemum
7 役 *joeki* exemption from military service
8 法 *johō* division (in math)
物 *no(ke)mono* outcast
者 *no(ke)mono* outcast
服 *jofuku* going out of mourning
夜 *joya* New Year's Eve
夜祭 *Joyasai* Shinto New Year's Eve ceremony
夜鐘 *joya (no) kane* New Year's midnight bells
9 除 *jojo ni, sorosoro* gradually, steadily, slowly
草 *josō* weeding
草器 *josōki* weeder
11 隊 *jotai* military discharge
隊兵 *jotaihei* discharged soldier
雪 *josetsu* snow removal
雪機関車 *josetsu kikansha* railway snowplow
13 幕式 *jomakushiki* unveiling (ceremony)
14 酵 *jokō ni* unleavened
酵祭 *jokōsai* feast of unleavened bread
17 霜 *josō* defrosting, deicing
20 籍 *joseki suru* remove a name, expel, denationalize; decommission (warships)

A **降** 6450 / J395f / M41620 Kō going down; surrender. *fu(ru)* fall, drop, come down (rain, etc.). *kuda(su)* let down; get down, descend; be given; be less than; have diarrhea; retire; leave the capital. *o(riru)* come down, go down, step down, descend; get off; land. *o(rosu)* take down, lower, pull down, lift down, let down, drop; launch; let off (passengers); wear (for the first time); cause (abortion); grate; invoke; exercise; borrow (in subtraction); lock. *ku(daru)* surrender. *ku(dasu), fu(rasu)* make it rain. *kuda(tte)* on down; as for me (humble).

2 人 *kōjin* prisoner of war
3 口 *o(ri)kuchi, o(ri)guchi* way out (of a station)
下 *kōka* fall, descent; losing altitude; outpouring; (plane) landing; (atmospheric) depression
下部隊 *kōka butai* parachute troops
4 止 *fu(ri)-ya(mu)* stop raining or snowing
込 *fu(ri)-ko(mu)* rain in on; shut people in by raining
水 *kōsui* precipitation
水量 *kōsuiryō* precipitation
5 出 *fu(ri)-da(su)* begin to rain or snow
6 而 *kudatte* as for me (humble)
灰 *kōkai* falling ash
伏 *kōfuku* surrender, submission
伏文書 *kōfuku bunsho* instrument of surrender
伏宣言 *kōfuku sengen* instrument of surrender
伏旗 *kōfukuki* white surrender flag
7 車 *kōsha* alighting
車口 *kōshaguchi* way out, station exit
8 明 *fu(ri)-a(kasu)* rain all night
注 *fu(ri)-soso(gu)* rain on (something)
服 *kōfuku* surrender, submission
参 *kōsan* surrender; giving in; being nonplussed
雨 *kōu* rain, rainfall
雨日 *kōujitsu* rainy day
雨図 *kōuzu* rain chart, rain map
雨期 *kōuki* rainy season
雨量 *kōuryō* amount of precipitation
9 通 *fu(ri)-tō(su)* rain continuously
神術 *kōshinjutsu* spiritism, spiritualism, necromancy
10 将 *kōshō* surrendered commander
11 掛 *fu(ri)-ka(karu)* fall on; befall, happen to; hang over, overhang; impend
雪 *kōsetsu* snow; a snowfall
12 勝 *fu(ri)ga(chi) na* rainy, wet
等 *kōtō* demotion
落 *fu(ri)-o(chiru)* to rain, to fall
着装置 *kōchaku sōchi* landing gear
13 嫁 *kōka* marriage of a princess to a commoner
続 *fu(ri)-tsuzu(ku)* rain or snow continuously
雹 *kōhyō* hailstorm
14 旗 *kōki* lowering the flag; white surrender flag
15 誕 *kōtan* birth, nativity
誕祭 *kōtansai* birthday celebration; Christmas
16 壇 *kōdan suru* leave the rostrum
頻 *fu(ri)-shiki(ru)* rain or snow incessantly
17 濡 *fu(ri)-sobo(tsu)* get soaked in a rain

臨 *kōrin* advent, descent
霜 *kōsō* a frost
18 職 *kōshoku* demotion
20 懸 *fu(ri)-ka(karu)* fall down (on something) from above
22 籠 *fu(ri)-ko(merareru)* be kept in by rain

8

陷 6451 / J6f7c / M41707 See 陥 6446.

陲 6452 / J7024 / M41694 SUI boundary.

陬 6453 / J7025 / M41685 SŪ corner.
12 遠 *sūen* deep rural area

B **陵** 6454 / J4e4d / M41704 RYŌ *misasagi* imperial tomb.
10 辱 *ryōjoku* insult; outrage, rape
11 域 *ryōiki* imperial tomb precincts
13 墓 *ryōbo* imperial tomb
15 駕 *ryōga suru* excel, surpass, outdo

B **隆** 6455 / J4e34 / M41720' **隆** 6463 / J-X / M41746 RYŪ high; noble; prosperity
6 肉 *ryūniku* bunch; hump (as on camels)
8 昌 *ryūshō* energy, vitality; prosperity
10 起 *ryūki* protuberance, bulging, upheaval, elevation
隆 *ryūryū(taru)* prosperous, thriving; brawny
11 運 *ryūun* prosperity, good fortune
盛 *ryūsei* prosperity
12 替 *ryūtai, ryūtei* prosperity and decline
14 鼻術 *ryūbijutsu* nasal plastic surgery
16 興 *ryūkō* continued prosperity

A **険** 6456 / J3831 / M41721' **險** 6483 / J702a / M41874 **嶮** 1513 / J5655 / M8520
KEN inaccessible place, impregnable pass, strategic position; steep place; sharp (eyes); sinister (look). *kewa(shii)* steep; severe, angry.
7 坂 *kenhan* steep hill
阻 *kenso* steepness; precipice
呑 *kennon na* dangerous, unsafe, unsteady
8 固 *kengo* strong defenses
岨 *kenso* steepness; precipice
所 *kensho* steep place
9 恃 *ken (o) tano(mu)* rely on strong fortifications
相 *kensō* uncanny look
要 *ken'yō no* strategic
10 峻 *kenshun* steepness, precipice
11 悪 *ken'aku na* dangerous; inclement; serious, gloomy
12 隘 *ken'ai* steep and narrow place
13 路 *kenro* steep path
塞 *kensai* fort built on a precipice
18 難 *kennan* steep, dangerous place; danger

B **陳** 6457 / J4444 / M41698 CHIN. *no(beru), chin(zuru), chin(jiru)* state, relate, explain. *hineku(reru)* get warped, become distorted. *hine* old grain; old goods; precocity.
5 皮 *chimpi* dried orange peel
弁 *chimben* explanation, defense, justification
6 列 *chinretsu* exhibition, display, show
列会 *chinretsukai* exhibition
列窓 *chinretsu mado* show window, store window
列棚 *chinretsudana* showcase
列館 *chinretsukan* museum
7 述 *chinjutsu* statement, declaration
述書 *chinjutsusho* statement, declaration
10 套 *chintō na* trite, commonplace, worn out, old-fashioned, out-of-date, stereotyped
11 情 *chinjō* petition, appeal
情書 *chinjōsho* petition, memorial
14 腐 *chimpu na* trite, commonplace, worn out, old-fashioned, out-of-date, stereotyped
17 謝 *chinsha* apology

B **陪** 6458 / J4766 / M41680 BAI follow, accompany, attend on.
6 臣 *baishin* samurai's retainer
8 侍 *baiji* attendance on the nobility
9 音 *baion* overtone; harmonics
食 *baishoku* dining with a superior
乗 *baijō* riding with a superior
10 従 *baijū suru* wait upon, accompany
席 *baiseki* sitting with a superior
席判事 *baiseki hanji* associate judge
15 賓 *baihin* accompanying guest

審 *baishin* jury
審公判 *baishin kōhan* trial by jury
審制度 *baishin seido* jury system
審室 *baishinshitsu* jury room
審員 *baishin'in* jury, juror
18 観 *baikan suru* view with one's superior
観者 *baikansha* visitor's guests

B **陶** 6459 / J462b / M41705 Tō. *sue* porcelain, pottery.
3 土 *tōdo* potter's clay, porcelain clay
工 *tōkō* potter, ceramist
5 瓦 *tōga* porcelain tile
7 芸 *tōgei* ceramic art
冶 *tōya* training, education; culture
冶性 *tōyasei* docility
8 画 *tōga* pictures on porcelain
11 酔 *tōsui* intoxication; fascination; rapture
12 棺 *tōkan* earthenware coffin
然 *tōzen* gloriously drunk
13 業 *tōgyō* porcelain industry
14 像 *tōzō* figurine
管 *tōkan* earthenware pipe
碧玉 *tōhekigyoku* porcelain jasper
磁器 *tōjiki* porcelain, pottery
磁器製造法 *tōjiki seizōhō* ceramics
製 *tōsei* ceramic, earthen
製品 *tōseihin* ceramics, earthenware
15 窯 *tōyō* ceramic kiln
器 *tōki* porcelain, pottery
器工 *tōkikō* potter
器師 *tōkishi* potter
器商 *tōkishō* dish store
器製造所 *tōki seizōjo* pottery works
器製造術 *tōki seizōjutsu* ceramics

B **随** 6460 / J3f6f / M41764' **隨** 6481 / J6e2e / M41871 ZUI. *manimani* at the mercy of (the waves). *mama* as it is; as one likes; because. *-naga(ra)* though, notwithstanding; while, during; both, all. *shitaga(u)* obey, submit to, comply with, observe (a law); follow; accompany.
1 一 *zuiichi* the first, the best, number one, the greatest
4 分 *zuibun* very, extremely; tolerably; cruel, terrible; many
5 処 *zuisho ni* everywhere, anywhere, here and there
6 行 *zuikō* attendant, follower. *zuikō suru* attend on, accompany, follow
行者 *zuikōsha* attendants, suite
行員 *zuikōin* attendants, suite
7 身 *zuijin* attendant; attending (on someone)
伴 *zuihan suru* attend on, accompany
伴者 *zuihansha* attendant, follower, suite, retinue
8 所 *zuisho* everywhere
9 神 *kannagara, Kamunagara* like the gods, god-like, godly
神道 *Kannagara (no) Michi, Kamunagara (no) Michi* Shinto, the Way of the Gods
10 時 *zuiji* any time, at all times; whenever required
員 *zuiin* attendants, suite
従 *zuijū suru* follow the lead of, play second fiddle to
従者 *zuijūsha* henchman, satellite, follower
12 順 *zuijun* faithfully following (one's master)
喜 *zuiki* adoration, idolization
筆 *zuihitsu* essays, miscellaneous writings
13 想 *zuisō* occasional thoughts
想録 *zuisōroku* stray notes; essays
感 *zuikan* random thoughts
感録 *zuikanroku* stray notes
意 *zuii* voluntary, optional. *manimani* at the mercy of
意科 *zuiika* elective course
意科目 *zuii kamoku* elective course
意筋 *zuiikin* voluntary muscles
意選択 *zuii sentaku* free choice

A **陸** 6461 / J4e26 / M41708 ROKU. RIKU *oka, kuga* land.
3 上 *rikujō* on shore, land (events)
上生活 *rikujō seikatsu* life ashore
上自衛隊 *Rikujō Jieitai* Ground Self-Defense Force
上班 *rikujōhan* ground crew
上部隊 *rikujō butai* a land force
上動物 *rikujō dōbutsu* land animal
上勤務 *rikujō kimmu* shore duty
上機 *rikujōki* land-based plane
5 生 *rikusei* terrestrial life
田 *okada* vegetable field
6 行 *rikkō* going by land
地 *rikuchi* land
7 兵 *rikuhei* land forces
8 物 *okamono* land products

岸 *rikugan* shore; land
9 颪 *rikufū* land breeze
相 *Rikushō* War Minister
屋根 *rokuyane* flat roof
海 *rikukai* land and sea
海空 *rikukaikū, rikkaikū* land, sea, and air; the three services
海軍 *rikukaigun, rikkaigun* army and navy
海軍人 *rikkaigunjin* military and naval men
軍 *rikugun* army
軍大臣 *Rikugun Daijin* War Minister
軍大学校 *Rikugun Daigakkō* War College
軍士官学校 *Rikugun Shikan Gakkō* Military Academy
軍用地 *rikugun yōchi* army reservation
軍省 *Rikugunshō* War Department
11 運 *rikuun* land transportation
釣 *okazuri* fishing from the shore
産 *rikusan* land products
軟風 *rikunampū* land breeze
12 揚 *rikua(ge)* landing, unloading
棚 *rikubō, rikuhō, rikudana* continental shelf
棲 *rikusei* land (animal), terrestrial
蒸汽 *okajōki* steam train
13 続 *rikuzoku to* continuously, successively
路 *rikuro, kugaji* land route
戦 *rikusen* land battle, land warfare
戦法規 *rikusen hōki* articles of war
戦隊 *rikusentai* landing forces
14 境 *rikuzakai* land frontier ⌈rice
稲 *rikutō, okabo* upland rice, dry-land
16 橋 *rikkyō* overpass; viaduct; land bridge
19 離 *rikuri* dazzling
霧 *rikumu* land fog
蟹 *rikugani* land crab

B **陰** 6462 / J3122 / M41691 ON. AN. IN the yin principle; negative; melancholy; north side of a mountain; sex organs; secret; shadow; south side of a river; negative electrode; earth; bottom; back; inactivity; nighttime; moon. *kage(ru)* darken; cloud up; be obscured. *kage* shade; back; (your) assistance. *(o)kage* indebtedness, favor, help, patronage, support. *hisoka ni, in ni* secretly.

3 口 *kageguchi* malicious gossip
干 *kagebo(shi)* drying in the shade
4 文 *imbun, immon* the lettering of an engraving
日向 *kage-hinata* light and shade
5 弁慶 *kagebenkei* a lion at home but a weakling elsewhere
6 気 *inki* gloom, melancholy
気臭 *inkikusa(i)* gloomy
7 言 *kagegoto* malicious gossip
声 *kage (no) koe* mystery voice; backstage voices
8 門 *immon* vagina
雨 *in'u* dark and rainy
府 *impu, yomi* Hades, realm of the dead
板 *imban* a negative
画 *inga* a negative
茎 *inkei* penis
事 *inji* secret
性 *insei* dormant; negative
性反応 *insei hannō* negative reaction (in a patient)
9 風 *impū* cold wind, north wind
10 唄 *kageuta* song behind the scenes
険 *inken na* tricky, wily, treacherous
陰 *in'in* gloomy and lonely
部 *imbu* pubic region
11 惨 *insan* sadness and gloom
悪 *in'aku* lurking evil, hidden evil
乾 *kagebo(shi)* drying in the shade
陽 *in'yō, on'yō* cosmic dual forces, positive and negative principles, active and passive, male and female, shade and light, sun and moon *in(ni)-yō(ni)* publicly and privately
陽道 *on'yōdō* divination
陽師 *on'yōji* diviner, fortuneteller
12 晴 *insei* unsettled weather, fine weather and cloudy weather
湿 *inshitsu* the dampness of shady places
雲 *in'un* dark or threatening clouds
然 *inzen* hidden power
極 *inkyoku* negative pole
極線 *inkyokusen* cathode rays
13 路 *kagemichi* shady road
電子 *indenshi* negatron
電気 *indenki* negative electricity
14 暦 *inreki* lunar calendar
徳 *intoku* secret charity

歌 *kageuta* song behind the scenes
15 影 *in'ei* shadow; shading; gloom
蔽 *impei* covering up
16 膳 *kagezen* a tray for the absent one
謀 *imbō* plot, intrigue, conspiracy
謀者 *imbōsha* conspirator, intriguer
謀家 *imbōka* schemer
17 翳 *in'ei* shadow; shading; gloom
22 嚢 *innō* scrotum, testicles
26 欝 *in'utsu* gloom, melancholy

9

隆 6463 | J-X | M41746 See **隆** 6455.

隋 6464 | J6721 | M41751 DA, ZUI remains of sacrifice; bury; fall, sag.

隍 6465 | J7026 | M41754 KŌ. *karabori* dry moat.

隈 6466 | J3728 | M41748 WAI. *kuma* corner, nook, recess; indentation, bend, turn; shade, shading; make-up. *kuma(naku)* everywhere; universally.
8 取 *kumado(ru)* tint, shade; make up (the face). *kumadori* shading, makeup
11 隈 *kumaguma* nooks, corners
12 無 *kumana(ku)* completely

B **隅** 6467 | J3679 | M41743 GŪ corner. *sumi, sumi(kko)* corner, nook.
4 木 *sumigi* hip rafter
切 *sumiki(ri)* beveled, octagonal
5 石 *sumi ishi* cornerstone
11 隅 *sumizumi* every nook and corner
12 棟 *sumimune* hip of a roof

A **隊** 6468 | J4262 | M41750 TAI party, company, corps, squad, crew, band, posse, force, unit.
5 付 *taizu(ki), taitsu(ki)* field, regimental
6 伍 *taigo* the ranks, a line, procession
次 *taiji* order, battle formation
列 *tairetsu* ranks, file, procession
名 *taimei* unit designation
7 形 *taikei* battle formation, disposition of troops
8 長 *taichō* captain, leader, commander
10 員 *taiin* members of the group
11 商 *taishō* caravan
商宿 *taishōjuku* caravansary
13 勢 *taisei* (flight) formation
14 旗 *taiki* flag of a unit

A **階** 6469 | J332c | M41755 KAI stair, staircase; round; step; grade; story, floor; counter for stories (in a building). *kizahashi, kidahashi* stairway; ladder; order.
3 下 *kaika* lower floor, downstairs; under the stairway
上 *kaijō* upper floor; the head of the stairs
7 位 *kaii* court rank, rank of officials
9 前 *kaizen* before the stairs; at the garden
段 *kaidan, kizahashi* steps, stairway
段席 *kaidan seki* rows of ascending seats
段教室 *kaidan kyōshitsu* lecture theater
級 *kaikyū* class, estate, caste, rank, grade
級差 *kaikyūsa* class distinction
級意識 *kaikyū ishiki* class consciousness
級闘争 *kaikyūi tōsō* class struggles
11 梯 *kaitei* step, stairs, ladder; threshold, steppingstone; guide, manual, primer
14 層 *kaisō* classes of people

A **陽** 6470 | J4d5b | M41725 YŌ yang principle, positive; male; heaven; daytime; sun; top; movement; facing the sun; sunshine; south face of a mountain; north side of a river; pride; positive electrode. *arawa ni* openly, publicly; frankly, clearly. *yō ni* openly, publicly.
3 子 *yōshi* proton
5 皮 *yō(no)kawa, yōhi* foreskin
6 気 *yōki* season, weather; vivacity, cheerfulness, gaiety
光 *yōkō* sunshine, sunlight; the sun
当 *hiata(ri)* sunny place; exposure to the sun
8 画 *yōga* positive photographic print
炎 *yōen, kagerō, kageroi* simmering of the air
性 *yōsei no* positive, plus
性反応 *yōsei hannō* positive reaction
物 *yōbutsu* phallus; penis
物崇拝 *yōbutsu sūhai* phallicism
9 春 *yōshun* spring, springtime
10 核 *yōkaku* positive nucleus

差 *hizashi* sunlight, sun's height
11 転 *yōten* positive (TB) test
動作戦 *yōdō sakusen* feint operation
12 極 *yōkyoku* anode, positive pole
報 *yōhō* open reward; rewarding openly
13 溜 *hidama(ri)* sunny place; exposure to the sun
電気 *yōdenki* positive electricity
電荷 *yōdenka* positive charge
14 暦 *yōreki* solar calendar; Julian calendar

10

隙 6471 / J3764 / M41792 See **隙** 6477.

隗 6472 / J7029 / M41788 KAI steep; high.

隘 6473 / J7027 / M41791 AI narrow; obstruct.
13 路 *airo* defile, narrow path

隕 6474 / J7028 / M41785 IN fall.
5 石 *inseki* meteorite
9 星 *insei* meteor, falling star
13 鉄 *intetsu* meteoric iron

B **隔** 6475 / J3356 / M-X **隔** 6476 / J-X / M41783 KAKU every other, alternate; distance. *heda(teru)* separate, interpose; screen, shield; estrange. *hedata(ru)* be distant from, be separated from, become estranged. *heda(tari)* distance; interval; gap; gulf, difference, disparity; distance; coolness. *heda(te)* partition; interval; barrier; distinction; discrimination; reserve, coolness.
4 心 *kakushin* reserve, estrangement, alienation
日 *kakujitsu* alternate days
月 *kakugetsu* alternate months
5 世 *kakusei* a distant age; a different world
世遺伝 *kakusei iden* atavism
6 地 *kakuchi* distant place
年 *kakunen* alternate years
8 板 *kakuhan* partition; bulkhead
10 週 *kakushū* biweekly
12 晩 *kakuban* alternate evenings
絶 *kakuzetsu* isolation, separation, blockade
番 *kakuban* alternation. *kakuban ni* in turn, alternately
13 歳 *kakusai* every other year
意 *kakui* reserve, estrangement, alienation
靴搔痒 *kakka-sōyō* irritation, impatience
16 壁 *kakuheki* partition; bulkhead; septum
19 離 *kakuri* isolation, separation

11

隙 6477 / J-X / M41813 **𨻶** 6471 / J3764 / M41792 GEKI crevice, fissure, chink; discord; opportunity. *su(kasu)* leave a space, thin (trees); make transparent; look through. *hima* time; leisure; poor business; leave of absence; dismissal; divorce; opening. *suki* time; leisure; gap, crack; room, space; chance; unpreparedness, unguarded moment.
2 人 *himajin* man of leisure
7 見 *sukimi* peeping, peeking
8 取 *himado(ru)* take time, be delayed
12 間 *sukima* crevice, gap, opening, space
間風 *sukimakaze* draft
13 飽 *hima (ni) a(kasete)* no matter how long it takes

A **際** 6478 / J3a5d / M41820 SAI time, occasion; when. *kiwa* side, edge, verge. *sai(suru)* meet, encounter. *kiwa(doi)* dangerous; adventurous; delicate; indecent. *(ni) sai(shite)* at that time.
5 立 *kiwada(tsu)* be prominent, be conspicuous
払 *kiwabara(i)* paying when due
6 会 *saikai suru* meet, face, confront
8 物 *kiwamono* seasonal goods
限 *saigen* limits, end, bounds
11 涯 *saigai* extremity

A **障** 6479 / J3e63 / M41821 SHŌ. *sawa(ru)* hinder, interfere with; affect; hurt, harm. *sawa(ri)* hindrance, interference; harm, bad aftereffects; menses.
3 子 *shōji* translucent sliding paper door
子紙 *shōjigami* translucent door paper
10 害 *shōgai* obstacle, hindrance, difficulty, handicap; hurdles
害物 *shōgaibutsu* obstacle, obstruction

害物競走 *shōgaibutsu kyōsō* obstacle race; steeplechase; hurdle race; slalom
害競走 *shōgai kyōsō* obstacle race; steeplechase; hurdle race; slalom
13 碍 *shōgai, shōge* obstacle, hindrance, difficulty, handicap; hurdles
16 壁 *shōheki* enclosing wall, barrier
19 礙 *shōgai, shōge* obstacle, hindrance, difficulty, handicap; hurdles

B 隠 6480 J3123 M41836' 隱 6485 J702c M41891 IN. ON. *kaku(su)* hide, conceal, cover, veil, cloak, disguise. *kaku(reru)* hide, disappear; pass away; be anonymous; lurk. *komo(ru)* seclude oneself, be confined in; be implied; be stuffy, be filled with (smoke).
kaku(renaki) well-known, open (secret).

3 士 *inshi* hermit, recluse
女 *kaku(shi) onna* concubine
子 *kaku(shi)go* illegitimate child
亡 *ombō* cremator
4 戸 *kaku(shi)do* hidden door, trap door
文 *kaku(shi)bumi* anonymous letter
元 *ingen* kidney bean
元豆 *ingen mame* kidney bean
5 田 *onden, kaku(shi)da* unregistered rice field
立 *kaku(shi)da(te)* secrecy
句 *inku* enigma
処 *kaku(re)ga* hiding place
世 *insei* retirement, seclusion
目付 *kaku(shi) metsuke* (ancient) spy
6 宅 *intaku* a retreat (of one retired)
7 見 *inken* appearance and disappearance
坊 *kaku(rem)bō, kaku(rem)bo* hide-and-seek. *ombō* cemetery guard; crematory worker
抜 *kaku(shi)-nu(ku)* hide out successfully
男 *kaku(shi) otoko* paramour
芸 *kaku(shi)gei* stunt, trick; an accomplishment unknown to others
忍 *innin* patience, endurance
君子 *inkunshi* hermit
言葉 *kaku(shi) kotoba* secret language, secret jargon
8 居 *inkyo* retirement; retired person; old person
所 *kaku(shi)dokoro* hiding place; nakedness; private parts
岩 *kaku(re) iwa* sunken rock, reef
果 *kaku(shi)-ō(seru)* succeed in hiding
者 *inja* hermit, recluse
事 *kaku(shi)goto, inji* secret
退 *intai* retirement, seclusion
退生活 *intai seikatsu* secluded life
退所 *intaisho* place of seclusion
退蔵物資 *intaizō busshi* hoarded goods
9 食 *kaku(shi)gu(i)* eating on the sly
室 *inshitsu* living in retirement
10 匿 *intoku* concealment
逸 *in'itsu* retirement, seclusion
栖 *insei* secluded life
釘 *kaku(shi) kugi* concealed nail
剣 *onken* concealed sword
家 *kaku(re)ga* retreat, refuge
11 道 *kaku(re) michi* secret passage
遊 *kaku(re) aso(bi)* clandestine visit to a red-light district
設 *kaku(shi)-mō(keru)* spread a net for
密 *ommitsu, immitsu* privacy, secrecy; detective; spy, secret agent
12 遁 *inton* retirement, seclusion
喩 *in'yu* metaphor
棲 *insei* secluded life
然 *inzen toshite* in reality, actually; in secret
場 *kaku(re)ba* refuge, hiding place
場所 *kaku(shi) basho* cache, place to hide (something). *kaku(re) basho* refuge, hiding place
13 微 *imbi* obscurity, abstruseness, mystery
滅 *immetsu* destruction, suppression
蓑 *kaku(re) mino* a magic coat that can make the wearer invisible
14 徳 *intoku* secret charity
語 *ingo* secret language; password
15 縫 *kaku(shi)nu(i)* concealed sewing
蔽 *impei* concealment, suppression, hiding
16 謀 *imbō* plot, intrigue, conspiracy
躾 *kaku(shi) shitsuke* concealed basting
18 顕 *inken* appearance and disappearance
顕砲 *inkenhō* disappearing gun
顕墨 *inkemboku* invisible ink

12

隨 6481 J6e2e M41871 See 随 6460.

隧 6482 J702b M41870 SUI fall; go around.
11 道 *suidō, tonneru* tunnel; fielding error

13

險 6483 / J702a / M41874 See 険 6456.

B 隣 6484 / J4e59 / M41847 鄰 6156 / J6e43 / M39656 RIN neighboring. *tona(ru)* adjoin. *tonari* next-door neighbor; adjoining.

2 人 *rinjin, tonaryūdo,* neighbor
人愛 *rinjin'ai* love of one's neighbors
4 比 *rimpi* nearness; neighborhood; neighboring
5 付合 *tonarizu(ki)a(i)* neighborliness
6 地 *rinchi* adjoining land
好 *rinkō* neighborhood friendship; friendly relations with neighboring countries
邦 *rimpō* neighboring country
交 *rinkō* neighborhood friendship; friendly relations with neighboring countries
合 *tona(ri)-a(u)* adjoin, be next to. *tona(ri)a(i), tona(ri)a(wase)* adjoining
近所 *tonari kinjo* neighborhood
同士 *tonaridōshi* next door to each other
7 村 *tonari mura, rinson* neighboring village
8 国 *ringoku, tonariguni* neighboring country
9 室 *rinshitsu* the next room
県 *rinken* neighboring prefectures
保 *rimpo* neighborhood
保事業 *rimpo jigyō* welfare work, social service
保館 *rimpokan* settlement house
10 席 *rinseki* the next seat
郷 *ringō* neighboring village
家 *rinka* neighboring house
座敷 *tonari zashiki* the next room
11 接 *rinsetsu(shita)* adjacent, adjoining, neighboring; related
組 *tonarigumi* neighborhood association
13 続 *tonaritsuzu(ki)* being neighbors

14

隱 6485 / J702c / M41891 See 隠 6480.

隲 6486 / J702d / M41880 SHITSU stallion; ride a horse; climb.

隰 6487 / J702e / M41889 SHITSU. *sawa* swamp, bog.

16

隴 6488 / J702f / M41904 RŌ. RYŪ. *oka* hill, slope. *une* ridge between rice fields.

RAD. 隶 171

Reizukuri (i.e., the right-hand element of the character for *rei* "servant, slave").
Nickname: Slave.

隶 6489 / J7030 / M41923 TAI extend; give; cast.

8

B 隷 6490 / J4e6c / M41928 隸 6491 / J7031 / M41932 REI servant; criminal; prisoner; follower.

10 従 *reijū* slavery
書 *reisho* ancient squared character
12 属 *reizoku* subordination, dependency
属民 *reizokumin* an oppressed people
属国 *reizokukoku* dependency, subordination

9

隸 6491 / J7031 / M41932 See 隷 6490.

隹 RAD. 172

Furutori old "bird" (i.e., the less complicated "bird," as distinguished from the "long-tailed" bird of Rad. 196). Nickname: Old Bird.

隹 6492/J7032/M41937 SUI. *tori* bird.

2

隼 6493/J483b/M41943 JUN. *hayabusa* a peregrine (falcon).

2 人 *hayato* an ancient tribe in southern Kyushu

B 隻 6494/J4049/M41941 SEKI counter for ships, fish, birds, arrows, etc., and one of a pair.

4 手 *sekishu* one arm, one hand
7 言 *sekigen* just a word
11 眼 *sekigan* one eye; an eye (for pictures, etc.)
脚 *sekkyaku* one leg
12 腕 *sekiwan* one arm
14 語 *sekigo* just a word
15 影 *sekiei* a single shadow, a trace, a sign
18 騎 *sekiki* a lone rider; a lone cavalryman

3

隺 6495/J5565/M-X KAKU. *tsuru* crane (bird).

雀 6496/J3f7d/M41954 JAKU. *suzume* sparrow.

12 斑 *sobakasu* freckles
13 蜂 *suzumebachi* wasp, hornet
21 躍 *jakuyaku suru* leap for joy, exult

4

B 雇 6497/J385b/M41976 KO. *yato(u)* employ, hire. *yatoi* employee.

2 人 *yatoinin* employee
入 *yato(i)-i(reru)* employ, hire; charter (a boat)
3 口 *yato(i)guchi* employment, job
5 主 *yatoinushi* employer
用 *koyō* employment
用主 *koyōnushi* employer
用者 *koyōsha* employer
7 役 *koeki* employing
兵 *yato(i)hei* mercenary soldier
10 員 *koin* employee
11 庸 *koyō* employment, employing
13 傭 *koyō* employment
聘 *kohei suru* employ
賃 *yato(i)chin* wages

雁 6498/J3467/M41960 鴈 6940/J726e/M46734 GAN *kari, karigane* wild goose.

4 文 *kari (no) fumi* a letter
爪 *ganzume* a Japanese rake
木 *gangi* stepped pier; toothing gear; escapement; hooked stick; zigzag
木車 *gangiguruma* escape wheel; pulley
木鑢 *gangi yasuri* rasp
5 皮紙 *gampishi* rice paper, tissue paper
玉章 *kari (no) tamazusa* a letter
6 行 *gankō* the flight formation of geese; lining up shoulder to shoulder like flying geese; leading out
字搦 *ganjigarami ni, ganjigarame ni* (bind) firmly, truss up
8 金 *karigane* wild goose
使 *kari (no) tsuka(i)* a letter
9 音 *karigane* wild goose
首 *gankubi* pipe bowl; head, neck. *gankubi (o soroete)* lined up (in a straight line). *karikubi* goose neck
便 *kari (no) tayori* a letter
10 骨 *kariganebone* scapula, shoulder blade
書 *gansho* letter

B 雄 6499/J4d3a/M41972 YŪ male; hero; great leader; superiority, excellence. *osu, on-, o-* male.

3 大 *yūdai na* grand, majestic, sublime
才 *yūsai* talents
4 心 *yūshin, ogokoro* manly spirit, ambition, aspiration, gallant spirit
牛 *oushi* bull, steer
5 弁 *yūben* oratory, eloquence
6 羊 *ohitsuji* ram

叫 *otake(bi), osake(bi)* war cry; courageous shout; roar of an animal
壮 *yūsō* bravery, heroism
名 *yūmei* fame, great renown
7 図 *yūto* ambitious undertaking
材 *yūzai* outstanding talent
志 *yūshi* high aspiration, ambition
花 *obana* male flower
8 性 *yūsei* male characteristics; manliness
松 *omatsu* black pine, seaside pine, male pine
武 *yūbu* bravery
9 風 *yūfū* strong breeze
飛 *yūhi* flying jump; great achievement
途 *yūto* a courageous departure
勁 *yūkei na* pithy, vigorous (style)
姿 *yūshi* gallant figure
10 馬 *ouma* stallion
峰 *yūhō* high majestic mountain
将 *yūshō* a great general
11 鳥 *ondori* cock, rooster
健 *yūken na* vigorous, virile, sturdy
強 *yūkyō* very strong character
猛 *yūmō* daring, bravery, valor
略 *yūryaku* big plans
断 *yūdan* a manly decision
12 偉 *yūi no* imposing, grand, magnificent
渾 *yūkon na* magnificent, sublime; vigorous, virile, sturdy, bold
雄 *oo(shii)* manly, brave, heroic
筆 *yuhitsu* powerful writing
13 滝 *odaki* the greater of two waterfalls
傑 *yūketsu* something outstanding
蜂 *obachi* drone (bee)
獅子 *ojishi* male lion
14 魂 *yūkon* brave soul; fine manliness
15 編 *yūhen* a masterpiece
篇 *yūhen* a masterpiece
蕊 *oshibe, yūzui* stamen
16 鴨 *ogamo* drake
17 螺旋 *oneji* male screw
18 藩 *yūhan* large fief
26 驢馬 *oroba* male donkey

A **集** 6500 / J3d38 / M41974 SHŪ collection, gathering. *atsu(maru), tsudo(u)* meet, assemble, congregate; swarm, flock or gather together; be collected, be gathered together; converge. *atsu(meru)* gather, collect; focus (something on). *atsu(mari), tsudo(i)* assembly, meeting; collection; gathering.

3 大成 *shūtaisei* compilation
4 中 *shūchū* concentration, convergence, centralization, integration
中打 *shūchūda* a succession of hits (in baseball)
中攻撃 *shūchū kōgeki* concentrated attack
中治療室 *shūchū chiryōshitsu* intensive care unit
中排除 *shūchū haijo* deconcentration
中豪雨 *shūchū gōu* a localized torrential downpour
5 出 *atsu(me)-da(su)* gather out
札係 *shūsatsugakuri* ticket collector
6 成 *shūsei* collection, compilation
合 *shūgō* gathering, meeting, group; collection
合名詞 *shūgō meishi* collective noun
合的 *shūgōteki* collective
会 *shūkai* meeting, assembly
会所 *shūkaijo* meeting place, assembly hall
会室 *shūkaishitsu* assembly hall, meeting room
会場 *shūkaijō* meeting place, assembly hall
団 *shūdan* group, body, mass, crowd, host
団心理 *shūdan shinri* mass psychology
団安全保障 *shūdan anzen hosho* collective security
団的 *shūdanteki* collective
団的自衛権 *shūdanteki jieiken* right of collective self-defense
団軍 *shūdangun* group army
団保険 *shūdan hoken* group insurance
団家屋 *shūdan kaoku* group of houses
団部隊 *shūdan butai* troops in mass formation
団討論 *shūdan tōron* group discussion
団移民 *shūdan imin* mass immigration
団強盗 *shūdan gōtō* gang of robbers
団結婚 *shūdan kekkon* group marriage
団疎開 *shūdan sokai* mass evacuation
団農業 *shūdan nōgyō* collective farming
団意識 *shūdan ishiki* group consciousness
7 来 *tsudo(i)-ku(ru)* come together, assemble
8 注 *shūchū* variorum edition; directing attention to

金 *shūkin* collecting money
金人 *shūkinnin* money collector
9 約 *shūyaku suru* intensify
約的 *shūyakuteki* intensive
計 *shūkei* total
計表 *shūkeihyō* tabulation
10 書 *shūsho* series (of publications); library (of literature)
荷 *shūka* collection of freight
配 *shūhai* collection and delivery
配人 *shūhainin* mail carrier
11 貨 *shūka* collection of freight
魚灯 *shūgyotō* fish-luring light
12 註 *shūchū* variorum edition
落 *shūraku* centers of population, towns and villages
結 *shūketsu* concentration, collection, assembling
結所 *shūketsujo* concentration center
散 *shūsan* collection and distribution
散地 *shūsanchi* collection and distributing center
13 塊 *shūkai* mass, cluster
14 蔵 *shūzō* garnering; collecting
15 権 *shūken* centralization of power
16 録 *shūroku* compilation, editing
積 *shūseki* accumulation, pile
積地 *shūsekichi* storage place
積度 *shūsekido* components per chip
積回路 *shūseki kairo* integrated circuit
20 議 *shūgi* deliberative meeting

5

雋 6501 / J7034 / M41996 SEN fat; grow fat; delicious; be superior.

雎 6502 / J7033 / M42001 SHO. *misago* osprey, fish hawk.

雍 6503 / J7036 / M42000 YŌ. *yawa(ragu) vi* soften, be reconciled; lessen; calm down. *yawa(rageru) vt* soften, moderate, ease, alleviate, mitigate, relax; appease; dilute (wine); tone down (colors); comfort; pacify, quiet.

雉 6504 / J7035 / M41987 CHI. *kiji* pheasant.
3 子 *kiji, kigisu* pheasant

B **雅** 6505 / J326d / M41973 GA elegance, refined taste. *miya(bita), miya(biyakana)* graceful, refined.
2 人 *gajin* writer, man of taste, dilettante
4 文 *gabun* elegant style, classic style
5 兄 *gakei* polite word used in addressing a friend in a letter
号 *gagō* pen name, pseudonym
6 名 *gamei* ornate name
7 言 *gagen* polite expression, refined diction
8 味 *gami* artistry, good taste, elegance, grace, artistic effect; gusto
9 俗 *gazoku* the refined and the vulgar; the classical and the colloquial
客 *gakaku* writer, man of taste, dilettante
10 称 *gashō* correct name; elegant name; name of a poem
致 *gachi* artistry, good taste, elegance, grace, artistic effect; gusto
12 量 *garyō* magnanimity, generosity, tolerance, liberality, broad-mindedness, capacity
13 楽 *gagaku* ceremonial court music
14 語 *gago* polite expression, refined diction
歌 *Gaka* Song of Solomon
15 趣 *gashu* artistry, elegance, taste
談 *gadan* elite conversation
16 懐 *gakai* esthetic sentiment

6

B **雌** 6506 / J3b73 / M41998 SHI female. *mesu, men-, me-* female.
3 山羊 *meyagi* she-goat, nanny goat
4 牛 *meushi* cow, heifer
犬 *mesu inu* female dog, bitch
6 伏 *shifuku suru* remain in obscurity
7 花 *mebana* female flower
8 虎 *metora* tigress
10 馬 *meuma* mare
11 鳥 *mendori* hen; female bird
鹿 *mejika* doe, hind
豚 *mebuta* sow
12 雄 *shiyū, mesu-osu* male and female
象 *mezō* cow elephant
13 蜂 *mebachi* queen bee
獅子 *mejishi* lioness
14 熊 *meguma* she-bear
15 蕊 *meshibe, shizui* pistil
19 蘂 *shizui* pistil

A **雑** 6507 J3b28 M42022 **雜** 6512 J7038 M42122 Zō, Zatsu miscellany; miscellaneous. *ma(zeru)* mix, blend, mingle; include, let in on. *ma(zaru), ma(jiru)* be mixed, be blended; mingle with. *maji(eru)* mix; converse with; cross (swords). *zatsu na* rough, coarse, rude; miscellaneous.

2 人 *zōnin* low-class people
3 巾 *zōkin* mop, scrubbing cloth
巾掛 *zōkinga(ke)* scrubbing
4 文 *zatsubun* literary miscellany
支出 *zatsu shishutsu* miscellaneous expenditures
手当 *zatsu teate* miscellaneous allowances
木 *zōki, zōboku, zatsuboku* miscellaneous trees
木林 *zōkibayashi, zōbokurin* grove of miscellaneous trees
5 用 *zatsuyō* miscellaneous business *zōyō* miscellaneous business, miscellaneous expenses
収入 *zatsu shūnyū, zasshūnyū* miscellaneous income
6 色 *zasshoku* various colors. *zasshiki, zōshiki* various kinds
気 *majirike* mixture, impurity
返 *ma(ze)-kae(su)* stir up; interrupt, interfere with
曲 *zakkyoku* popular song, musical medley
件 *zakken* miscellaneous affairs
多 *zatta na* miscellaneous, various
交 *zakkō* crossing (in biology)
交受精 *zakkō jusei* cross-fertilization
7 言 *zōgon* abuse, insult, slander, evil speaking
作 *zōsaku* interior finishing (of a house)
兵 *zappyō, zōhyō* ordinary soldiers, rank and file
芸 *zatsugei* miscellaneous accomplishments
役 *zatsueki* odd jobs, sundry services
役夫 *zatsuekifu* handy man
役服 *zatsuekifuku* fatigues
役婦 *zatsuekifu* charwoman
8 炊 *zōsui* medley soup; hodgepodge
物 *zatsubutsu* sundries; impurities, mixture. *zōmotsu* inferior goods; entrails. *maza(ri)mono* mixture, impurities
卒 *zassotsu* rank and file, soldiers
念 *zatsunen, zōnen* worldly thoughts
沓 *zattō* congestion, traffic jam, throng
具 *zatsugu* various tools
学 *zatsugaku* wide knowledge
事 *zatsuji* miscellaneous affairs
居 *zakkyo suru* live together (in the same room, area, or country)
居地 *zakkyochi* mixed-residence quarter
9 音 *zatsuon* noise, static, jamming; (heart) murmur
食 *zasshoku no* omnivorous
則 *zassoku* miscellaneous rules
軍 *zatsugun* disorganized army
品 *zappin* sundries, odds and ends
草 *zassō* weeds
10 株 *zatsu kabu, zakkabu* miscellaneous stocks; minor stocks
書 *zassho* miscellaneous books; book on miscellaneous subjects
記 *zakki* miscellaneous notes
記帳 *zakkichō* notebook; exercise book
11 婚 *zakkon* interracial marriage
務 *zatsumu* miscellaneous business
勘定 *zatsu kanjō* miscellaneous accounts
魚 *zako, jako* small fish; various kinds of small fish
魚寝 *zakone suru* sleep together in a group
貨 *zakka* sundries, notions; general cargo; miscellaneous goods
貨店 *zakkaten* emporium, variety store
貨商 *zakkashō* general store
12 税 *zatsuzei* miscellaneous taxes
詠 *zatsuei* miscellaneous poems
筆 *zappitsu* miscellaneous writings
然 *zatsuzen to* promiscuously, in confusion
煮 *zōni* glutenous rice cakes boiled with vegetables
費 *zappi* miscellaneous expenses
報 *zappō* miscellaneous news
13 話 *zatsuwa* chitchat, gossip
感 *zakkan* miscellaneous impressions
楽 *zatsugaku* miscellaneous popular music
業 *zatsugyō* miscellaneous work, miscellaneous enterprises
損益 *zasson'eki* petty gains and losses
14 種 *zasshu* mixed breed, hybrid, mongrel; various kinds
説 *zassetsu* various theories

駁 *zappaku na* confused, incoherent, desultory, hazy
歌 *zōka* miscellaneous poems
誌 *zasshi* magazine, periodical
誌記者 *zasshi kisha* magazine writer
穀 *zakkoku* minor grains
穀商 *zakkokushō* grain merchant
15 鬧 *zattō* congestion, traffic jam, throng
踏 *zattō* congestion, traffic jam, throng
篇 *zappen* miscellaneous writing
輩 *zappai* rank and file; nonentity
談 *zatsudan* chitchat, gossip
談会 *zatsudankai* talkfest
16 録 *zatsuroku* miscellaneous notes
18 観 *zakkan* miscellaneous impressions
題 *zatsudai* miscellaneous subjects
20 纂 *zassan* miscellaneous collection
22 嚢 *zatsunō* duffel bag

8

雞 6508 / J-X / M-X Nonstandard for **鶏** 6980.

雕 6509 / J703a / M42080 Chō carving.

9

雖 6510 / J6a2d / M42104 Sui. *iedo(mo)* though, although, however.

10

雙 6511 / J5256 / M42116 See **双** 673.

雜 6512 / J7038 / M42122 See **雑** 6507.

雞 6513 / J-X / M42124 See **鶏** 6980.

雛 6514 / J3f77 / M42121 Sū. *hina* chick, squab, duckling; doll. *hiyoko* chick; stripling.
2 人形 *hina ningyō* festival dolls
7 形 *hinagata* pattern, model, sample, specimen, form, copy, miniature
9 型 *hinagata* pattern, model, sample, specimen, form, copy, miniature
11 鳥 *hinadori* chick, young bird
遊 *hinaaso(bi)* playing with dolls; playing before the doll tiers
菊 *hinagiku* daisy
祭 *Hinamatsu(ri)* Girls' Festival
13 僧 *hinasō* boy priest
節句 *Hina (no) Sekku* Girls' Festival
16 壇 *hinadan* doll stand; musicians' platform; state ministers' gallery (on the doll stands)

A**難** 6515 / J4671 / M42128' **難** 6516 / J-X / M42145 Nan trouble, difficulty; accident, disaster; defect; criticism. *kata(i)* difficult; impossible. *muzuka(shii), mutsuka(shii)* hard, difficult; delicate; troublesome; doubtful; hopeless; stern; sullen; hard to please; serious; technical. *nan(zuru)* criticize. *haba(mu)* obstruct, prevent, impede, deter, hinder, thwart, resist, frustrate. *nan(naku)* easily, successfully. *-niku(i)* difficult, awkward. *-gata(i)* difficult (to do). *-ka(neru)* cannot; hesitate to; be impatient.
4 中難事 *nanchū (no) nanji* the hardest thing to do
5 句 *nanku* difficult phrase or passage
民 *nammin* needy people, sufferers; displaced persons, refugees
6 色 *nanshoku* hesitation; disapproval
件 *nanken* difficult problem, delicate matter
地 *nanchi* predicament, trouble
字 *nanji* a difficult character
行 *nangyō* penance, austerities
行苦行 *nangyō-kugyō* penance, austerities
行道 *nangyōdō* the way of hardships, salvation by works
7 局 *nankyoku* difficult situation, crisis
攻不落 *nankō-furaku* impregnability
8 所 *nansho, nanjo* steep, difficult, or dangerous places
治 *nanji, nanchi* incurable; rebellious; difficult
物 *nambutsu* hard customer
易 *nan'i* relative difficulty; difficulty and ease
事 *nanji* difficult matter; hardship
9 風 *nampū* adverse wind
点 *nanten* difficult point
10 病 *nambyō* serious illness

症 *nanshō* serious illness
航 *nankō* stormy voyage; rough flight; rough sledding
訓 *nankun* difficult reading of characters
破 *nampa* shipwreck
破船 *nampasen* shipwreck
11 渋 *nanjū* suffering, distress, hardship
球 *nankyū* a batted ball hard to catch
船 *nansen* shipwreck
産 *nanzan* difficult delivery (in childbirth)
問 *nammon* difficult question
問題 *nammondai* difficult problem
12 場 *namba* predicament, difficulty; dangerous path, rough place
無 *nanna(ku)* easily
13 解 *nankai na* hard to understand; unintelligible; illegible
詰 *nankitsu* blame, censure
路 *nanro* difficult road
戦 *nansen* hard fight, hard fighting
義 *nangi* hardship; trouble
14 関 *nankan* strong barrier, obstacle, difficulty
境 *nankyō* difficult situation
語 *nango* difficult word
読 *nandoku* difficult reading
15 儀 *nangi* hardship, trouble
17 聴 *nanchō* hard of hearing
18 癖 *nankuse* fault, bad habit
題 *nandai* difficult topic; hard question; unreasonable charge; unreasonable demand

11

難 6516 / J-X / M42145 See 難 6515.

B 離 6517 / J4e25 / M42140 Ri separation. *hana(reru), saka(ru) vi and vt* separate, part from; come off; become disjoined; digress; get free; become estranged; be (three miles) away; be separated (by three years); leave, quit, depart from. *hana(su) vt* separate, disconnect, sever; detach; keep apart; alienate; isolate; let go, release, set free. *hana(re)* detached (building).

3 山 *rizan* a mountain off by itself; leaving a temple
4 日 *ri-Nichi* departure from Japan
水 *risui* taking off from water
反 *rihan* estrangement, alienation, desertion, revolt
5 去 *hana(re)-sa(ru)* leave, depart from; drift away
6 任 *rinin* leaving one's position
合 *rigō* meeting and parting
7 床 *rishō suru* get up, leave the sickbed
村 *rison* rural exodus
別 *ribetsu* divorce; dissolution of adoption
8 迷 *hana(re)-mayo(u)* wander away; err from
退 *hana(re)-shirizo(ku)* turn back from
京 *rikyō* leaving the capital
岸 *rigan* setting sail
苦 *riku* agony of separation
乳 *rinyū* weaning
乳食 *rinyūshoku* a baby's weaning meal
9 洲 *risu* floating, refloating
叛 *rihan* estrangement, alienation, desertion, revolt
10 郷 *rikyō* leaving one's hometown
島 *hana(re)jima, ritō* outlying island
宮 *rikyū* detached palace
家 *hana(re)ya* detached building, solitary house
宴 *rien* farewell drinking party
党 *ritō* withdrawal from a party
座敷 *hana(re)zashiki* detached room
陸 *ririku* takeoff; pulling out from the shore
陸場 *ririkujō* airstrip
11 脱 *ridatsu* secession; separation; abolition; giving up (one's membership)
船 *risen* leaving a ship
婚 *rikon* divorce
婚届 *rikon todoke* notice of divorce
婚訴訟 *rikon soshō* divorce suit
12 隔 *rikaku* isolation, separation
散 *risan* dispersion, scattering, breakup
塁 *rirui* leading off from the base
着 *richaku* taking off and landing
間 *rikan* estrangement, separation, rupture
間策 *rikansaku* alienation maneuver
13 殿 *hana(re)dono* separate house
路 *riro* deviation (in navigation)
愁 *rishū* the pain of parting
業 *hana(re)waza* stunt, feat
14 魂病 *rikombyō* somnambulism

15 縁 *rien* divorce; separation of an adopted son
縁状 *rienjō* divorce papers
17 礁 *rishō suru* refloat, get off the reef
18 難 *hana(re)gata(i)* inseparable
職 *rishoku* quitting one's job, loss of employment
職手当 *rishoku teate* quitting allowance
職者 *rishokusha* the unemployed
職票 *rishokuhyō* separation notice
19 離 *hana(re)bana(re)* scattered, dispersed, separated, disconnected
20 艦 *rikan* taking off from a carrier
籍 *riseki* removal of a name from a registry

RAD. 雨 173

Ame rain. At top: ⻗ or ⻗ *ame kammuri*. Nickname: Rain.

A **雨** 6518 / J312b / M42210 U. *ame* rain, rainfall. *ama-* rain.
3 上 *ameaga(ri), amaaga(ri)* after the rain
乞 *amagoi* praying for rain
下駄 *amageta* rain clogs, geta for rainy times
4 戸 *amado* shutter, storm door
止 *amaya(mi)* stopping of rain, lull in the rain
水 *amamizu, usui* rainwater
中 *uchū* in the rain
支度 *amajitaku* preparation for rain
天 *uten* rainy weather
天順延 *uten'jun'en* in case of rain postponed to the next good day
5 氷 *uhyō* silver frost, glaze
外套 *amagaitō* raincoat
6 気 *amake* threatening to rain, signs of rain
合 *amaa(i)* between showers
合羽 *amagappa* raincoat, oilcoat
7 足 *ame ashi, amaashi* a passing shower
囲 *amagako(i)* rain shelter
余 *uyo* after the rain
声 *usei* the sound of rain
承 *amau(ke)* water table, gutter
8 押 *amaosa(e)* flashing (in building)
夜 *amayo* rainy evening, rainy night
具 *amagu* rain gear
季 *uki* rainy season
空 *amazora* threatening sky
垂 *amadare* raindrops, eavesdrops
垂石 *amadare ishi* dripstone, weather molding
9 音 *amaoto* sound of falling rain
風 *ame-kaze* rain and wind. *amakaze* rainy wind
飛 *uhi* coming down like rain (bullets)
後 *ugo* after a rain
除 *amayo(ke)* shelter from the rain, shed, cover
降 *amefu(ri)* rainfall; rain; rainy weather
染 *amaji(mi)* rain stain
11 粒 *amatsubu* raindrop
脚 *amaashi, ame ashi* a passing shower
宿 *amayado(ri)* taking shelter from the rain
笠 *amagasa* rain hat
雫 *amashizuku* raindrop
12 間 *amaai* between showers
湿 *amajime(ri)* wet from the rain
疏 *amaha(ke)* rainwater drainage
勝 *amega(chi)* rainy period
蛙 *amagaeru* tree frog, hyla
期 *uki* rainy season
傘 *amagasa* umbrella
着 *amagi* raincoat
落 *amao(chi)* gutter for eavesdrops
雲 *amagumo* rain cloud
量 *uryō* rain, rainfall
量計 *uryōkei* rain gauge
13 催 *amamoyo(i), amemoyo(i), amamoya(i)* sign of rain
続 *amatsuzu(ki), ametsuzu(ki)* long rain, rainy spell
隠 *amagaku(re)* taking shelter from the rain. *amagomo(ri)* rainbound
靴 *amagutsu* overshoes
意 *ui* threat of rain
障子 *amashōji* translucent oiled-paper doors
14 樋 *amadoi* eaves trough
漏 *amamo(ri)* roof leak
滴 *uteki* raindrop
模様 *amamoyō, ame moyō* signs of rain
15 避 *amayo(ke)* taking shelter from the rain

16 曇 *amagumo(ri)* overcast weather
19 曝 *amazara(shi)* exposure to the rain; weather-beaten
覆 *amaōi* tarpaulin, rain cover
21 露 *uro* rain and dew
22 籠 *amagomo(ri)* rainbound

3

雫 6519 / J3c36 / M42219 DA. DAN. *shizuku* drop, trickle, dripping.

A **雪** 6520 / J4063 / M42216' SETSU. *yuki* snow, snowfall. *susu(gu), soso(gu)* rinse, wash, pour on.
2 人形 *yuki ningyō* snowman
3 山 *yuki yama, setsuzan* snowy mountain; mountain of snow
下 *yukioro(shi)* snowy wind; shoveling snow off the roof
女 *yuki onna* snow demon, snow fairy
女郎 *yuki jorō* snow fairy
上 *setsujō* on the snow
上車 *setsujōsha* snow tractor
4 止 *yukido(me)* snowshed, snow guard, roof guard
水 *yuki mizu* slush, thawing snow; snow water
片 *seppen* snowflake
中 *setchū* in the snow; in a snowstorm
仏 *yukibotoke* snow Buddha
月花 *setsugekka* snow, moon, and flowers
日和 *yukibiyori* signs of snow
5 玉 *yukidama* snowball
田 *setsuden* eternal snow fields
白 *seppaku* snow-white. *yukijiro* refined sugar
目 *yukime* snow blindness
氷 *seppyō* snow ice
6 気 *yukige* threat of snow
肌 *yuki (no) hada* smooth skin, fair skin
交 *yukima(jiri)* fall and winter weather; mixture of rain and snow
合戦 *yuki gassen* snowball fight
7 囲 *yukigako(i)* snowshed
庇 *seppi* overhanging snow
折 *yukio(re)* a snowbreak; bent by snow
投 *yukina(ge)* throwing snowballs
見 *yukimi* snow viewing
見灯籠 *yukimidōrō* large-topped three-legged stone lantern
見酒 *yukimizake* drinking saké at a snow scene
花 *sekka* snowflakes
花石膏 *sekka-sekkō* alabaster
花菜 *kirazu* tofu refuse
8 国 *yukiguni* snowy country
明 *yukiaka(ri)* snow light
泥 *setsudei* slush
夜 *yukiyo* snowy night
盲 *setsumō, yuki mekura* snow blindness
沓 *yukigutsu* snowshoes, snow boots
空 *yukizora* snowy sky, leaden sky
9 後 *setsugo* after the snowfall
洞 *bombori* hand lamp; lampstand
除 *yukiyo(ke)* snow guard, snowshed, roof guards (to prevent snow sliding off)
降 *yukifu(ri)* snowfall
10 原 *setsugen* snow field, frozen waste
峰 *seppō* snowy peak
消 *yukige* thaw, melting snow
寃 *setsuen* vindication, exoneration
害 *setsugai* snow damage
留 *yukidama(ri)* snowdrift, snowbank
辱 *setsujoku* vindication of honor, making up for a loss, revenge
辱戦 *setsujokusen* return match; a fight for vindication
11 道 *yukimichi* snowy road
遊 *yukiaso(bi)* playing with snow
袴 *yukibakama* snow trousers
転 *yukikoro(gashi), yukimaro(bashi)* rolling a snowball
崩 *nadu(reru)* incline toward, give way and fall. *nadare, yuki nadare* snowslide, snow avalanche
達磨 *yuki daruma* snowman
眼鏡 *yuki megane* snow glasses
12 間 *yukima* interval between snowfalls; in the snow
堤 *settei* a snow embankment (to prevent further slides)
晴 *yukiba(re)* clearing after a snowfall
焼 *yukiya(ke)* snow tan
颪 *yuki oro(shi)* snowy wind
嵐 *yuki arashi* snowstorm, blizzard
雲 *yukigumo* snow cloud
景 *sekkei* snowscape
景色 *yukigeshiki* snow scene
13 催 *yukimoyo(i)* threatening to snow
傾 *yukinada(re)* snowslide, avalanche

搔 *yukikaki* snow shoveling, snow removal; snow shovel, snow scraper; snowplow
渓 *sekkei* perpetually snowy valley
解 *yukige, yukido(ke)* thaw, melting snow
路 *yukiji, yuki michi* snowy road
靴 *yukigutsu* snowshoes, snow boots
隠 *setchin, setsuin* lavatory, toilet
隠大工 *setchin daiku* a clumsy carpenter
隠詰 *setchinzu(me) ni suru* argue (someone) into a corner
14 駄 *setta* leather-soled sandals
雑 *yukimaji(ri)* (rain) mixed with snow
模様 *yuki moyō* snowflake pattern; threatening to snow
15 線 *sessen* snow line
踏 *setta* leather-soled sandals
輪 *yukiwa* ski disk
16 曇 *yukigumo(ri)* threatening to snow
17 嶺 *setsurei* snow-capped peak
20 礫 *yukitsubute* snowball

4

B **雰** 6521 / J4a37 / M42231 FUN fog.
7 囲気 *fun'iki* atmosphere, environment, surroundings

A **雲** 6522 / J3140 / M42235 UN. *kumo* cloud.
3 山 *unzan* cloud-covered mountains
上 *unjō* above the clouds. *kumo (no) ue* above the clouds; the heavens; the palace
上人 *unjōbito, kumo(no)uebito* nobles
4 水 *unsui* itinerant priest; clouds and water
切 *kumogi(re)* rift in the clouds
丹 *uni* sea urchin
井 *kumoi* sky; palace, court circles
5 外 *ungai* above the clouds; the depths of the sky
母 *ummo, umbo, kirara* isinglass, mica
母引 *kirabi(ki)* mica sheet
母片岩 *ummo hengan* mica schist
6 行 *kumoyu(ki)* cloud movements; situation, turn of events; progress; signs
向 *unkō* direction of cloud movement
合 *kumoa(i)* the look of the sky
7 足 *kumoashi* cloud movements; overhanging clouds
状 *unjō* nebulous, cloudlike
助 *kumosuke* palanquin bearer, coolie, wandering robber
助根性 *kumosuke-konjō* one who enriches himself at the expense of others
形 *kumogata, unkei* cloud formations
形定規 *kumogata jōgi* draftsman's curve
8 突 *kumotsu(ku)* towering
表 *umpyō* above the clouds
泥差 *undei (no) sa* a wide difference
居 *kumoi* a cloudy place; distant place; sky; palace; court circles
居遙 *kumoi-haruka ni* very far away
9 海 *unkai* sea of clouds; sea of clouds meeting the great ocean
級 *unkyū* cloud types
客 *unkaku* a noble
10 高 *unkō* height of clouds
根 *unkon* place where clouds form; the mountains
脂 *fuke* dandruff
峯 *kumo (no) mine* cloud bank, cumulus-cloud columns
11 鳥 *kumo-tori* clouds and birds; birds flying in the sky
梯 *untei* scaling ladder
脚 *unkyaku* cloud movements; overhanging clouds
雀 *hibari* skylark
12 間 *kumoma* rift between clouds
桟 *unsan* a high bridge
量 *unryō* degree of cloudiness
散 *unsan* scattering like clouds
散霧消 *unsan-mushō* vanishing like clouds and mist
集 *unshū suru* swarm, throng, gather in crowds
集霧散 *unshū-musan* people gathering and quickly dispersing
13 煙 *un'en* clouds and smoke; a landscape; a beautiful picture
路 *kumoji* the paths birds or clouds follow
隠 *kumogaku(re)* demise, passing; disappearance
際 *unsai* edge of the clouds; distant sky
15 影 *un'ei* cloud shape

16 霓 *ungei* clouds and a rainbow; sign of showers

17 霞 *unka* clouds and haze. *kumo-kasumi* clouds and fog; disappearance, fleeing

翳 *un'ei* cloud shade

聳 *kumo (ni) sobie(ru)* (buildings or mountains) soar high

19 簾 *kumo sudare* cloud screen (over the moon)

霧 *ummu* clouds and fog

20 壌 *unjō* clouds and earth; heaven and earth; great contrast

5

雹 6523 / J703b / M42248 HAKU. HOKU. *hyō* hail.

10 害 *hyōgai* hail damage

零 6524 / J4e6d / M42242 B REI zero, nothing, cipher; fall. *kobo(reru) vi* spill, overflow, be scattered. *kobo(su) vt* spill; grumble over.

3 下 *reika* below zero, subzero

7 余 *reiyo* residue, remnant

位 *reii* zero

位線 *reiisen* zero line

8 幸 *kobo(re)zaiwa(i)* a godsend, a windfall

9 度 *reido* zero, freezing point

砕 *reisai* a tiny bit

点 *reiten* zero; freezing point; zero grade

10 時 *reiji* twelve o'clock; noon; midnight

11 敗 *reihai* a shutout (in a game); losing out (in love)

細 *reisai na* petty, small, infinitesimal

細企業 *reisai kigyō* a small business

細農 *reisainō* poor peasant

12 落 *ochibure(ru)* be ruined, be reduced to poverty, fall low. *reiraku* ruin, downfall, reduced circumstances, withering

13 戦 *reisen* zero fighter

雷 6525 / J4d6b / M42245 B RAI *ikazuchi* thunder. *kaminari* thunder; thunderbolt.

4 文 *raimon* zigzag

火 *raika* lightning; fire caused by lightning

公 *raikō* the god of thunder

6 同 *raidō* blindly following the crowd

光 *raikō* lightning

名 *raimei* renown, fame; your famous name

7 声 *raisei* noise of thunder

8 雨 *raiu* thunderstorm

9 神 *raijin* the god of thunder

除 *raiyo(ke)* lightning rod

10 師 *raishi* the god of thunder

11 動 *raidō* rumble of thunder; roaring

雪 *raisetsu* snow thunderstorm

12 雲 *raiun* thunderhead

13 電 *raiden* thunder and lightning, thunderbolt

14 鳴 *raimei* thunder

酸 *raisan* fulminic acid

管 *raikan* percussion cap, detonator

15 避 *kaminari-yo(ke)* lightning rod

霆 *raitei* thunder

撃 *raigeki* torpedo attack

撃機 *raigekiki* torpedo-carrying plane

16 親爺 *kaminari oyaji* snarling old man

電 6526 / J4545 / M42253 A DEN electricity. *inazuma* lightning.

2 力 *denryoku* electric power

力学 *denryokugaku* electrodynamics

3 工 *denkō* electrician

工長 *denkōchō* head electrician

子 *denshi* electron

子工学 *denshi kōgaku* electronics

子化辞書 *denshika jisho* computerized dictionary

子内視鏡 *denshi naishikyō* electronic endoscope

子学 *denshigaku* electronics

子図書館 *denshi toshokan* electronic library

子会議 *denshi kaigi* teleconference

子掲示板 *denshi keijiban* electronic bulletin board system

子顕微鏡 *denshi kembikyō* electron microscope

4 文 *dembun* telegram, telegraphic message

化 *denka* electrification

火 *denka* electric spark

火距離 *denka kyori* sparking distance

火間隙 *denka kangeki* spark gap

5 圧 *den'atsu* voltage

6 池 *denchi* electric battery

休日 *denkyūbi* no-electricity day

光 *denkō* electric light; lightning

光石火 *denkō-sekka* an instant, a flash

光形 *denkōkei* zigzag
灯 *dentō* electric light
灯会社 *dentōgaisha* electric-light company
灯料 *dentōryō* electric-light charges
灯料金 *dentō ryōkin* electric-light charges
灯線 *dentōsen* lamp cord
気 *denki* electricity; electric light
気力学 *denki rikigaku* electrodynamics
気工 *denkikō* electrician
気工学 *denki kōgaku* electrical engineering
気分析 *denki bunseki* electroanalysis
気分解 *denki bunkai* electrolysis; electroanalysis
気写字機 *denki shajiki* teletype
気広告 *denki kōkoku* electric sign
気灯 *denkitō* electric light
気死刑 *denki shikei* electrocution (as execution method)
気会社 *denkigaisha* electric company
気自動車 *denki jidōsha* electric car
気技師 *denki gishi* electrical engineer
気店 *denkiten* electric shop
気板 *denkiban* electrotype
気炉 *denkiro* electric furnace; electric oven
気学 *denkigaku* science of electricity
気抵抗 *denki teikō* electrical resistance
気始動機 *denki shidōki* electric starter
気炬燵 *denkigotatsu* electric foot warmer
気係 *denkigakari* electrician
気剃刀 *denki kamisori* electric razor
気通信 *denki tsūshin* telecommunication
気浴 *denkiyoku* electric bath
気料 *denkiryō* charge for electricity
気料金 *denki ryōkin* charge for electricity
気時計 *denkidokei* electric clock
気量 *denkiryō* amount of electricity
気椅子 *denki isu* electric chair
気蒲団 *denkibuton* electric blanket
気照明 *denki shōmei* electric lighting
気暖房 *denki dambō* electric heating
気暖房法 *denki dambōhō* electric heating
気銅 *denkidō* electrolytic copper
気磁石 *denkijishaku* electromagnet
気熔接 *denki yōsetsu* electric welding
気器具 *denki kigu* electrical appliances
気鋼 *denkikō* electric steel
気鍍金 *denki mekki* electroplating, galvanizing
気療法 *denki ryōhō* electrotherapy
気竈 *denki kamado* electric oven
気鰻 *denki unagi* electric eel
7 位 *den'i* electric potential
車 *densha* electric car, streetcar, tramcar, electric train, trolley
車通 *denshadō(ri)* streetcar line
車賃 *denshachin* carfare
8 弧 *denko* electric arc
卓 *dentaku* electronic calculator
命 *demmei* telegraphic instructions
送 *densō* electrical facsimile transmission
送写真 *densō shashin* phototelegraphy
波 *dempa* electric wave, radio wave
波天文学 *dempa temmongaku* radio astronomy
波妨害 *dempa bōgai* jamming
波波長 *dempa hachō* wavelength
波計 *dempakei* wave meter
波料 *dempaŕyō* air-time charge
波探知機 *dempa tanchiki* radar
波望遠鏡 *dempa bōenkyō* radio telescope
9 柱 *denchū* telephone pole
界 *denkai* electric field
信 *denshin* telegraph, telegram, wire, cable, cablegram
信印字機 *denshin injiki* teletype
信柱 *denshimbashira* telegraph pole
信為替 *denshingawase* telegraphic transfer; electronic transfer
信料 *denshinryō* telegram charge
信術 *denshinjutsu* telegraphy
信線 *denshinsen* telegraph line
信機 *denshinki* telegraph
10 閃 *densen* lightning flash
荷 *denka* electric charge
訓令 *denkunrei* telegraphic instructions
流 *denryū* electric current
流計 *denryūkei* galvanometer, ammeter
流密度 *denryū mitsudo* electric current density
流転換器 *denryū tenkanki* commutator
11 探 *dentan* radar
液 *den'eki* electrolyte
球 *denkyū* electric-light bulb

瓶 *dembin* battery jar
動力 *dendōryoku* electromotive power
動機 *dendōki* electric motor
12 場 *demba* electric field
極 *denkyoku* electrode, pole, terminal
量 *denryō* amount of electricity
報 *dempō* telegram
報用紙 *dempō yōshi* telegram blank
報為替 *dempōgawase* telegraphic transfer
報料 *dempōryō* telegram charge
報略号 *dempō ryakugō* telegraphic address
報暗号帳 *dempō angōchō* telegraphic code book
報頼信紙 *dempō raishinshi* telegram blank
13 源 *dengen* source of electricity
路 *denro* electric circuit
鉄 *dentetsu* electric railway
鈴 *denrei* electric bell
飾 *denshoku* illumination; electric decorations
蓄 *denchiku* electric phonograph
解 *denkai* electrolysis
解液 *denkaieki* electrolyte
解質 *denkaishitsu* electrolyte
話 *denwa* telephone
話口 *denwaguchi* mouthpiece; telephone
話加入者 *denwa kanyūsha* telephone subscriber
話交換手 *denwa kōkanshu* telephone operator
話交換局 *denwa kōkankyoku* telephone central, telephone exchanges
話料 *denwaryō* telephone charges
話帳 *denwachō* telephone directory
話術 *denwajutsu* telephony
話管 *denwakan* speaking tube, mouthpiece
話機 *denwaki* telephone
14 髪 *dempatsu* permanent wave
磁石 *denjishaku* electromagnet
磁気 *denjiki* electromagnetism
磁波 *denjiha* electromagnetic waves
磁相互作用 *denji sōgo sayō* electromagnetic interaction
磁鉄 *denjitetsu* electromagnet
15 鋳 *denchū* electrotyping
撃 *dengeki* electric shock
撃作戦 *dengeki sakusen* blitzkrieg
熱 *dennetsu* electric heat
熱器 *dennetsuki* electric heater
線 *densen* electric wire, electric line, telegraph wire, telephone wire, electric cord, cable
線布設 *densen fusetsu* cable laying
16 機 *denki* electrical machinery and appliances
機子 *denkishi* armature
17 鍵 *denken* telegraph key
19 離 *denri* electrolysis, ionization
離層 *denrisō* ionosphere
27 纜 *denran* electric cable

6

霊 6527 J-X M-X Nonstandard for 霊 6532.

需 6528 J3c7b B M42275 Ju request; need.
5 用 *juyō* consumption (of goods)
9 品 *juhin* supplies
要 *juyō* demand (for commodities); requirements
要者 *juyōsha* user
要供給 *juyō-kyōkyū* supply and demand
要家 *juyōka* user
12 給 *jukyū* supply and demand

7

霆 6529 J703d M42299 Tei lightning; thunder.

霄 6530 J703c M42290 Shō sky.
20 壌 *shōjō* heaven and earth

震 6531 J3f4c B M42300 Shin. *furu(eru), furu(u)* shake, tremble, quiver, shiver, shudder; vibrate. *furu(i), furu(e)* shivering, shaking, trembling, shuddering.
3 上 *furu(e)-a(garu)* tremble, shiver; be frightened, be intimidated
4 天 *shinten* heaven-shaking; very energetic; tremendous (voice)
天動地 *shinten-dōchi* stunning heaven and earth
5 付 *furu(i)-tsu(ku)* grapple with
央 *shin'ō* earthquake center

6 死 *shinshi* death by lightning
7 声 *furu(e)goe, furu(i)goe* trembling voice
災 *shinsai* earthquake disaster
災地 *shinsaichi* earthquake disaster area
9 度 *shindo* earthquake magnitude
10 害 *shingai* earthquake damage
恐 *furu(e)-oso(reru)* shudder, quake with fear
11 動 *furu(e)-ugo(ku)* quake, tremble, shake, reel, rock. *shindō* tremor, shock, concussion, vibration
12 幅 *shimpuku* earthquake amplitude
13 慄 *shinritsu* shuddering in fear
戦 *furu(e)-onono(ku), furu(e)-wanana(ku)* fear and tremble, shudder
源 *shingen* earthquake center; center of a disturbance
源地 *shingenchi* earthquake center; center of a disturbance
15 蕩 *shintō* concussion, shock, impact
16 撼 *shinkan* terror, alarm, fright
駭 *shingai* terror, alarm, fright
17 盪 *shintō* concussion, shock, impact
22 顫 *shinsen* tremor
顫麻痺 *shinsen mahi* paralysis agitans

B **霊** 6532 / J4e6e / M42309' **靈** 6553 / J704d / M42532 REI soul, spirit; Holy Spirit. RYŌ spirits who possess humans. *tamashii, tama* soul, spirit.
3 山 *reizan* sacred mountain
4 木 *reiboku* sacred tree; famous tree
水 *reisui* miracle-working water
化 *reika* spiritualization
5 生 *reisei* spiritual life
石 *reiseki* a sacred rock
代 *reidai, tamashiro* visible symbol of the soul
6 肉 *reiniku* soul and body
気 *reiki* an atmosphere (feeling) of mystery
地 *reichi* hallowed ground, sacred place
安室 *reianshitsu* morgue
交 *reikō* communion, spiritual fellowship
交術 *reikōjutsu* spiritualism, spirit communication
7 位 *reii* Buddhist mortuary tablet
妙 *reimyō na* wonderful, marvelous, miraculous
8 雨 *reiu* a good rain
性 *reisei* divine nature, divinity, spirituality
物 *reimotsu* worker of miracles
的 *reiteki* spiritual
宝 *reihō* precious treasure
長 *reichō* a leader with miraculous powers; an outstanding leader; mankind
長類 *reichōrui* primates, man
9 屋 *tamaya* mausoleum, ancestral shrine, tomb
迹 *reiseki* the aftermath of a miracle; the site of a miracle
前 *reizen* before a god; before the spirit of the deceased
界 *reikai* spiritual world; psychic world
泉 *reisen* fountain or hot springs with magical powers
草 *reisō* sacred herb
柩 *reikyū* coffin, casket
柩車 *reikyūsha* hearse
10 峰 *reihō* sacred mountain; beautiful mountain
祠 *reishi* shrine
11 鳥 *reichō* sacred bird
域 *reiiki* hallowed ground, sacred place
液 *reieki* an elixir
動 *reidō* psychic activity
堂 *reidō* shrine or temple
異 *reii* miracle, wonder
12 場 *reijō* hallowed ground, sacred place
筆 *reihitsu* refined style
雲 *reiun* a strange high cloud
媒 *reibai* spirit medium
媒術 *reibaijutsu* spiritualism
智 *reichi* intellect, wisdom
智学 *reichigaku* theopathy
13 園 *reien* cemetery park
殿 *reiden* mausoleum, shrine
瑞 *reizui* miraculous sign
跡 *reiseki* the aftermath of a miracle; the site of a miracle
夢 *reimu* divine revelation, inspired dream, prophetic vision
感 *reikan* inspiration; sacred intuition
14 境 *reikyō* hallowed ground, sacred place
歌 *reika* spiritual (song)
魂 *reikon* soul, spirit
魂不滅 *reikon-fumetsu* immortality of the soul
15 廟 *reibyō* mausoleum, shrine
16 薬 *reiyaku* panacea, wonder medicine

[18]蹟 *reiseki* the aftermath of a miracle; the site of a miracle
験 *reigen, reiken* miracle, miraculous virtue
顕 *reiken* miracle, miraculous virtue

8

霍 6533 / J7039 / M42321 KAKU cry of birds taking off; first; legume leaf.

霎 6534 / J7040 / M42322 SHO light rain, sprinkle; sound of rain; a short time.

霓 6535 / J703f / M42332 GEI rainbow.

霑 6536 / J7041 / M42329 **沾** 3072 / J5d7e / M17259 TEN moisten, water, soak. *uruo(u)* be moistened, be wet; profit by, be benefited. *uruo(su)* wet, moisten, irrigate, dip; profit, enrich, make prosperous.

霈 6537 / J703e / M42301 HAI. *hisame* big rain; long rainy spell.

霙 6538 / J7044 / M42350 EI. *mizore* sleet, rain-and-snow mixture.

霏 6539 / J7042 / M42323 HI falling rain or snow.
[16]霏 *hihi toshite* (falling) thick and fast

霖 6540 / J7043 / M42335 RIN long rainy spell.
[8]雨 *rin'u* long rainy spell

9

霞 6541 / J3262 / M42365 KA. *kasu(mu)* be hazy; grow dim (eyes), be blurred. *kasumi* haze, mist; dimness of sight.
[9]草 *kasumisō* gypsophila, baby's-breath
[13]隠 *kasumigaku(re)* behind or in the mist
[14]関 *Kasumigaseki* Foreign Ministry (Japan)

B**霜** 6542 / J417a / M42363 SŌ. *shimo* frost.
[4]月 *shimotsuki* 11th lunar month
[7]囲 *shimogako(i)* chilblains; frostbite
[8]夜 *shimoyo* frosty night
[9]風 *shimokaze* a cold frosty wind
柱 *shimobashira* frost columns, ice needles
除 *shimoyo(ke)* frost protection
降 *shimofu(ri)* frosting; gray, salt-and-pepper color
枯 *shimoga(reru)* be killed by the frost. *shimoga(re) no* wintry, bleak, frost-nipped
枯時 *shimoga(re)doki* winter, dead season, slack season
[10]害 *sōgai* frost damage
[11]雪 *sōsetsu* frost and snow; white hair or beard; purity of heart
[12]焼 *shimoya(ke)* chilblains; frostbite
割 *shimowa(re)* splitting of trees from freezing
[13]解 *shimodo(ke)* thaw, thawing

10

霤 6543 / J7045 / M42396 RYŪ rain drops; running water; eaves; room.

11

霪 6544 / J7046 / M42430 IN a long period (over ten days) of rain.

B**霧** 6545 / J4c38 / M42418 MU. *kiri* mist, fog, spray. *ki(ru)* get foggy, get cloudy.
[4]中信号 *muchū shingō* fog signal
[5]氷 *muhyō* fog freezing on vegetation; frost flowers
[7]吹 *kirifu(ki)* atomizer, sprayer, vaporizer
吹器 *kirifu(ki)ki* atomizer, sprayer, vaporizer
[8]雨 *kiriame, kirisame* drizzle
[9]海 *mukai* foggy sea
虹 *kiri niji* fogbow, white rainbow
除 *kiriyo(ke)* eaves, entrance eaves
信号所 *kiri shingōjo* fog-signal station
[10]島 *kirishima* wild honeysuckle
[11]笛 *muteki* fog horn
[12]渡 *kiriwata(ru)* fog covers all
散 *musan suru* dissipate, be dispelled
集 *mushū* great crowds gathering like fog
量計 *muryōkei* fog gauge

8 金長門阜阝隶隹【雨】青非 12

[13]暖簾 *kirinoren* sign curtain
[20]鐘 *mushō* fog bell

12

霰 6546 / J7047 / M42458 SEN. SAN. *arare* hail, hailstones; small cubes.
[12]弾 *sandan* buckshot, slugs

13

霸 6547 / J5b31 / M42490 See 覇 5519.

霹 6548 / J7048 / M42491 HEKI thunder.
[24]靂 *hekireki* thunder, thunderclap

B 露 6549 / J4f2a / M42463 RO dew; Russia. *tsuyu* dew; dewdrops; tears; mortality, flimsiness; (with neg.) not a bit. *ara(wa) ni* openly, publicly; frankly, clearly. *tsuyu, tsuyu (hodo mo)* (not) in the least, (not) a particle. *tsuyu(keshi)* dampness. *-Ro-* Russia.
[2]人 *Rojin* a Russian
[4]支 *Ro-Shi* Russia and China
天 *roten* open air
天風呂 *rotemburo* open-air bath
天掘 *rotembo(ri)* strip mining
[5]玉 *tsuyutama* dewdrops
払 *tsuyuhara(i)* herald, pioneer
台 *rodai* outside balcony
出 *roshutsu* exposure; disclosure; outcrop; (photographic) exposure
出計 *roshutsukei* light meter
出症 *roshutsushō* exhibitionism
[6]地 *roji* farming fields
西亜 *Roshia* Russia
光 *rokō* exposure (in photography)
光計 *rokōkei* exposure meter
[7]見 *roken* discovery, detection
里 *Rori* Russian verst (.6629 mile)
助 *Rosuke* a Russian (derogative)
呈 *rotei* exposure, disclosure
[8]国 *Rokoku* Russia
命 *romei* transient life
店 *roten* roadside stand
店商人 *roten shōnin* stall vendor
店街 *rotengai* district of open-air shops
[9]帝 *Rotei* Czar
軍 *Rogun* the Russian army
点 *roten* dew point
[10]骨 *rokotsu na* plain, frank, undisguised; conspicuous, acute; lewd
座 *roza* sitting out in the open
都 *Roto* Russian capital (city)
[11]探 *Rotan* Czarist spy
清 *Ro-Shin* Russia and Qing dynasty China
聊 *tsuyu-isasa(ka) mo* (not) in the least
悪 *roaku* boasting of one's wickedness
宿 *roshuku* sleeping out in the open
貨 *Roka* Russian money
[12]満 *Ro-Man* Russia and Manchuria
営 *roei* bivouac, camping out
[14]暦 *Roreki* Julian calendar
層 *rosō* outcrop
滴 *roteki* dewdrop
語 *Rogo* the Russian language
領 *Roryō* Russian territory
疑 *tsuyu-utaga(wazu)* not a shadow of a doubt
[16]頭 *rotō* outcrop; uncovered head
[17]礁 *roshō* a rock protruding above the surface of the sea
霜 *tsuyujimo* frozen dew
[18]顕 *roken* discovery, detection
[20]艦 *Rokan* Russian warship

14

霾 6550 / J704a / M42507 BAI wind-borne dust falling (like rain).

霽 6551 / J7049 / M42499 SEI. *ha(reru)* clear up; (doubts) vanish; be refreshed. *ha(rasu)* dispel, clear away (gloom); refresh (oneself).

15

靆 6552 / J704c / M42530 TAI.

16

靈 6553 / J704d / M42532 See 霊 6532.

靂 6554 / J704e / M42523 REKI violent thunder or lightning.

靄 6555 / J704b / M42526 AI. *moya* mist, haze, fog.

17

靉 $\frac{6556}{\text{J704f}}$ / M42540 AI.

23 靆 *tanabi(ku)* (clouds) trail, hang over. *aitai(taru)* trailing (clouds)

RAD. 青 174

Aoi blue. Variant: 靑. Nickname: Blue.

A **青** $\frac{6557}{\text{J4044}}$ / M42564' **靑** $\frac{6558}{\text{J-X}}$ / M42564 SEI. SHŌ. *ao* blue, green; green light. *ao(mu)* turn green. *ao(bamu)* turn greenish, be tinged with green. *ao(i)* blue, green; pale; unripe, green, inexperienced. *ao-* unripe; new; immature; novice; blue, green.

2 二才 *aonisai* green youth, stripling
3 女 *seijo* the goddess of frost and snow; frost
山 *aoyama, seizan* blue mountain, green hills. *seizan* cemetery
大将 *aodaishō* a kind of common harmless snake
4 木 *aoki* green tree; gold-leaf plant
丹 *aoni* blue earth, blue-black earth
少年 *seishōnen* youth, younger generation
水無月 *aominazuki* sixth lunar month
天 *seiten* blue sky
天井 *aotenjō* blue sky
天白日 *seiten-hakujitsu* clear weather; clearing of one's reputation
天白日旗 *seiten-hakujitsuki* Nationalist China flag
天霹靂 *seiten-hekireki* a bolt from the blue, a bombshell
5 玉 *seigyoku* sapphire; jacinth
白 *aojiro(i)* pale, pallid; bluish white
目 *aome* blue eyes
史 *seishi* history, annals
写真 *aojashin, aoshashin* blueprint
田 *aota, aoda* green rice fields
田刈 *aotaga(ri)* a green crop
田売 *aotau(ri)* selling unharvested rice
田売買 *aota baibai* dealing in unharvested rice
田買 *aotaga(i)* buying unharvested rice; making offers to recruits still in school
6 米 *aomai* green rice
色 *ao iro, seishoku* blue
虫 *aomushi* green caterpillar, grub
地 *aoji* blue material, blue cloth
光 *aobikari* phosphorescent light, green light
竹 *aodake* green bamboo
竹色 *aodake iro* bluish green
年 *seinen* youth, young people
年子女 *seinen shijo* young men and women
年団 *seinendan* young people's association
年会 *seinenkai* young people's society
年男女 *seinen danjo* young men and women
年期 *seinenki* adolescence
7 豆 *aomame* green beans
貝 *aogai* mother-of-pearl
8 青 *aoao(shita), aoao(toshita)* verdant, fresh and green
松 *seishō* a green pine
波 *aonami* blue waves
空 *aozora, seikū* blue sky
苔 *aogoke* green moss
金石 *seikinseki* lapis lazuli
宝玉 *seihōgyoku* sapphire
物 *aomono* greens, vegetables
物市 *aomono ichi* vegetable market
物市場 *aomono ichiba* vegetable market
物屋 *aomonoya* vegetable store, vegetable dealer
9 柳 *aoyagi, aoyanagi* green willow tree
臭 *aokusa(i)* smelling grassy or unripe; inexperienced, unskilled
茶 *aocha* bluish brown
草 *aokusa* green grass
信号 *aoshingō* a green light
枯病 *aoga(re)byō* wilting disease
春 *seishun* springtime of life, youth. *seishun no* youthful, adolescent

春期 *seishunki* puberty, adolescence
海 *aoumi* blue sea
海苔 *aonori* green edible seaweed
海原 *aounabara* blue expanse of water
海亀 *aoumigame* large green turtle
10 馬 *aouma* gray horse
梅 *aoume* unripe plum
砥 *aoto* blue whetstone
書 *seisho* a "blue book" (government report)
書生 *aoshosei* young inexperienced student
息 *aoiki* an anxious sigh
息吐息 *aoiki-toiki* pitiful dejection
11 黒 *aoguro(i)* pale and dark
眼 *seigan* aiming at the eye (with a sword)
菜 *aona* greens
票 *aohyō* blue vote, opposing vote
瓷 *seiji* celadon porcelain
12 蛙 *aogaeru* tree frog, green frog
嵐 *aoarashi, seiran* wind blowing through new verdure
畳 *aodatami* new mat, green mat
筋 *aosuji* blue vein
葉 *aoba* foliage, greenery, green leaves
雲 *seiun* blue sky; high rank. *aokumo* white clouds in a blue sky
雲志 *seiun (no) kokorozashi* determination to succeed
13 楼 *seirō* brothel
電車 *aodensha* green-lamp car, next to the last streetcar
14 旗 *aohata* blue flag; safety flag
磁 *seiji* celadon porcelain
緑 *aomidori* dark green
褪 *aoza(meru)* turn pale, turn white
鼻汁 *ao(p)pana, aobana* green nasal mucus
酸 *seisan* hydrocyanic acid, prussic acid
酸塩 *seisan'en* cyanide
銅 *seidō, karakane* bronze
銅工 *seidōkō* worker in bronze
銅貨 *seidōka* bronze coin
銅製 *seidōsei* made of bronze
銅器 *seidōki* bronze ware
銅器時代 *Seidōki Jidai* Bronze Age
15 銹 *aosabi* green rust; patina
豌豆 *aoendō* green peas
16 膨 *aobuku(re)* dropsical swelling
瓢箪 *aobyōtan* green gourd; pale-faced weakling
17 藍 *seiran* indigo blue
19 蠅 *aobae, aobai* blowfly
簾 *aosudare* green bamboo screen
23 黴 *aokabi* green mold; penicillium
24 鷺 *aosagi* blue heron

5

靖 6559 / J4c77 / M42570' SEI. *yasu(i)* peaceful.

6

A **静** 6560 / J4045 / M42574' **靜** 6561 / J7050 / M42578 JŌ, SEI quiet, peace, inactivity. *shizu(maru) vi* get quiet, calm down, grow still; subside, die down, be suppressed. *shizu(meru) vt* calm, pacify; soothe, alleviate; appease; suppress, quell. *shizu(kana)* quiet, still, silent; calm, placid; serene, peaceful; soft (rain); gentle (voice); graceful; slow (walk); deserted. *shizu(kesa), shizu(kasa)* stillness, silence, hush; calm, serenity.

2 力学 *seirikigaku* statics
4 心 *shizugokoro* relaxed spirit
止 *seishi* stillness, repose, standing still
止衛星 *seishi eisei* geostationary satellite
水 *seisui* still water, stagnant water
水力学 *seisui rikigaku* hydrostatics
6 返 *shizu(mari)-kae(ru)* become perfectly quiet, be still as death
7 坐 *seiza* sitting quietly; meditation
8 的 *seiteki* static
夜 *seiya* quiet night
物 *seibutsu* object at rest; still life
物画 *seibutsuga* still-life picture
9 思 *seishi* meditation, contemplation
10 座 *seiza* sitting quietly; meditation
修 *seishū* spiritual retreat
脈 *jōmyaku* vein
脈血 *jōmyakuketsu* venous blood
脈炎 *jōmyakuen* phlebitis
脈注射 *jōmyaku chūsha* intravenous injection
11 粛 *seishuku* silence, quiet
寂 *seijaku* silence, quiet, hush
寂主義 *seijaku shugi* quietism
13 電学 *seidengaku* electrostatics
電気 *seidenki* static electricity
電気学 *seidenkigaku* electrostatics

電誘導 *seiden yūdō* electrostatic induction
14 静 *shizushizu to* calmly, quietly
態 *seitai no* static, stationary
15 養 *seiyō* rest, recuperation, convalescence
養中 *seiyōchū* resting, recuperating
16 穏 *seion* calm, tranquility
17 聴 *seichō* quietly listening; attention
謐 *seihitsu* peace, tranquility
18 観 *seikan* serene contemplation; watchful waiting

8

靜 6561 / J7050 / M42578 See **静** 6560.

靛 6562 / J-X / M42577 TEN a blue plant dye.

RAD. 非 175

Arazu not. Nickname: Negative.

A **非** 6563 / J4873 / M42585 HI mistake; misdeed; injustice; wrong; non-, un-, anti-. *ara(zu)* not, not so, not to be. *ara(zaru)* other than. *ara(zareba)* unless, except. *hi (to) suru* condemn, denounce, disapprove.

2 力 *hiriki* disability, incompetence
人 *hinin* beggar; outcast; criminal
人情 *hininjō* heartlessness
人道 *hijindō* inhumanity
人間的 *hiningenteki* inhuman
3 凡 *hibon na* extraordinary, unusual
才 *hisai* lack of ability, incompetence
4 日 *hi-Nichi* un-Japanese
文明 *hibummei na* uncivilized
公式 *hikōshiki* informal, unofficial, exhibition (game)
公開 *hikōkai* closed (meeting)
友誼的 *hiyūgiteki* unfriendly
友誼的行為 *hiyūgiteki kōi* unfriendly act
5 礼 *hirei* impoliteness
民主的 *himinshuteki* undemocratic
生産的 *hiseisanteki* nonproductive, unproductive
立憲 *hirikken* unconstitutional
立憲的 *hirikkenteki* unconstitutional
打所無 *hi(no)u(chi)dokorona(ku)* nothing to criticize
打算的 *hidasanteki* unselfish, disinterested
正統派 *hiseitōha* heterodoxy
正統説 *hiseitōsetsu* heterodoxy
6 米 *hi-Bei* un-American
行 *hikō* misdemeanor, evil deed, immoral act
合法 *higōhō* illegal; out of order
合法的 *higōhōteki* illegal
合理的 *higōriteki* unreasonable, irrational
7 役 *hiyaku, hieki* retirement
妥協的 *hidakyōteki* uncompromising
芸術的 *higeijutsuteki* inartistic
社交的 *hishakōteki* unsociable, retiring
社会的 *hishakaiteki* antisocial
売同盟 *hibai dōmei* sellers' strike
売品 *hibaihin* articles not for sale
8 命 *himei* untimely death
金属 *hikinzoku* nonmetal
学術的 *higakujutsuteki* unscientific
定期船 *hiteikisen* tramp steamer
法 *hihō* unlawfulness, lawlessness
法人 *hihōjin* unincorporated person
実用品 *hijitsuyōhin* unnecessary things
実際的 *hijissaiteki* impractical, unpractical
武装 *hibusō* demilitarization
武装地帯 *hibusō chitai* demilitarized zone
国民 *hikokumin* unpatriotic person, traitor
国家的 *hikokkateki* unpatriotic
国教徒 *hikokkyōto* nonconformists, dissenters
9 急品 *hikyūhin* a nonessential
政治的 *hiseijiteki* nonpolitical
政府機構 *hiseifu kikō* non-governmental organizations
科学的 *hikagakuteki* unscientific
軍人 *higunjin* civilian

軍事化 *higunjika* demilitarization
軍事的 *higunjiteki* nonmilitary, civilian
10 核地帯 *hikakuchitai* nuclear weapon free zone
能率的 *hinōritsuteki* inefficient
党派的 *hitōhateki* nonpartisan
党員 *hitōin* a nonmember (of a party)
11 運 *hiun* bad luck; misfortune
情 *hijō* inanimate nature
理 *hiri* unreasonableness, absurdity
望 *hibō* ulterior motive, evil design
紳士的 *hishinshiteki* ungentlemanly
組合員 *hikumiaiin* non-unionist, nonmember
道 *hido(i)* cruel, harsh, merciless, atrocious; unjust, unfair; severe, intense, bitter, serious, terrible, outrageous, unreasonable. *hidō* tyranny, cruelty, injustice, lawlessness, unfairness
道徳的 *hidōtokuteki* immoral
現実的 *higenjitsuteki* unreal, impracticable
現業 *higengyō* office work
現業員 *higengyōin* office worker
常 *hijō* emergency, unforeseen occurrence, calamity. *hijō na* remarkable, unusual. *hijō ni* exceedingly, extremely, remarkably, unusually
常口 *hijōguchi* emergency exit
常手段 *hijō shudan* emergency measures
常用 *hijōyō* (for) emergency use
常米 *hijōmai* emergency rice
常灯 *hijōtō* emergency light
常号音 *hijō gōon* alarm call
常事態 *hijō jitai* state of emergency
常時 *hijōji* crisis, emergency
常勤 *hijōkin* part-time work
常報知 *hijō hōchi* alarm; emergency report
常電話 *hijō denwa* emergency phone call
常線 *hijōsen* cordon
常識 *hijōshiki* lack of common sense, absurdity, thoughtlessness
12 番 *hiban* off duty, off guard
違 *hii* lawlessness, unlawfulness
統制 *hitōsei* uncontrolled (goods)
買同盟 *hibai dōmei* boycott
営利的 *hieiriteki* nonprofit
13 毀 *hiki* slander, calumny, libel
愛国的 *hiaikokuteki* disloyal, unpatriotic
鉄金属 *hitetsu kinzoku* nonferrous metals
聖書的 *hiseishoteki* un-Biblical
業死 *higōshi* untimely death
業最後 *higō (no) saigo* untimely death
戦 *hisen* war renunciation
戦災 *hisensai* undamaged by the war
戦論 *hisenron* pacifism
戦闘員 *hisentōin* noncombatant
14 認 *hinin* denial, disapproval, repudiation, veto, nonrecognition
関税障壁 *hikanzei shōheki* non-tariff barrier
15 霊的 *hireiteki* unspiritual
課税 *hikazei* tax exemption
衛生的 *hieiseiteki* unsanitary, unhealthful, unwholesome
論理的 *hironriteki* irrational, illogical
16 機密 *hikimitsu* nonsecret
18 職 *hishoku* retired
難 *hinan* criticism, denunciation
難攻撃 *hinan-kōgeki suru* castigate
難者 *hinansha* critic, accuser
20 議 *higi* abusive argument. *higi suru* criticize, blame

7

靠 6564 / J7051 / M42604 Kō. *mota(reru)* lean on, recline on; lie heavy (on the stomach).
11 掛 *mota(re)-ka(karu)* lean on, recline on; rely on

11

靡 6565 / J7353 / M42612 Hɪ. Bɪ. *nabi(ku)* flutter, wave: bow to, yield to, obey, be swayed by. *nabi(kasu)* seduce; win over; conquer.

9-STROKE RADICALS

RAD. 面 176

Men face. Nickname: Face.

A 面 6566 J4c4c M42618 MEN face features; mask; face guard; surface; plane; side, facet; aspect, phase, corner (of a board); page. *men(suru)* face, border, front on. *omo, omote* face, honor, reputation. *tsura* face, surface.

3 子 *mentsu* face, honor

5 立 *omoda(chi), omoda(te)* looks, countenance, features

付 *tsuratsu(ki)* expression, look

皮 *mempi* countenance

皮厚 *tsura (no) kawa (no) atsu(i)* brazen-faced, impudent, shameless

目 *memmoku, memboku* face, honor, dignity; credit; appearance, aspect

目一新 *memboku isshin suru* take on a completely new appearance

目玉 *membokudama* face, honor, dignity

目無 *membokuna(i)* ashamed

白 *omoshiro(i)* interesting; entertaining, delightful, amusing, comical, queer, promising; favorable. *omoshiro(garu)* amuse oneself, be amused. *omoshiro(garaseru)* amuse, entertain

白半分 *omoshirohambun ni* half in fun, jokingly

白可笑 *omoshiro-okashi(i)* amusing, funny

白尽 *omoshirozu(ku) de* for the fun of it

白味 *omoshiromi* interest, fun, enjoyment

6 色 *menshoku* complexion, countenance, expression

伏 *omobu(se)* ashamed, confused, crestfallen

汚 *tsurayogo(shi)* disgrace, dishonor, shame

当 *tsuraa(te)* mean words, innuendo

争 *mensō* pointing out a person's failures before others

会 *menkai* interview, meeting

会人 *menkainin* visitor, caller

会日 *menkaibi* visitors' day

7 疔 *menchō* face carbuncle

体 *mentei* face, looks, features

妖 *men'yō na* strange, mysterious

忘 *omowasu(re)* failing to recognize

8 長 *omonaga na* long-faced, oval-faced

9 面 *memmen* each one, all; every direction

食 *menku(rau)* be confused, be bewildered, be embarrassed. *menku(i)* emphasizing looks in choosing a mate

持 *omomo(chi)* countenance, look, features

映 *omoha(yui)* bashful, ashamed, coy; disgraceful, shameful

相 *mensō* countenance, looks, features

変 *omogawa(ri)* change in one's looks

前 *menzen* presence; before one's eyes

10 部 *membu* face, facial region

容 *men'yō* countenance, looks, features

差 *omoza(shi)* features

倒 *mendō* trouble, difficulty, complications; care, attention. *mendō na, mendō(i)* troublesome, complicated

倒臭 *mendōkusa(i)* troublesome, tiresome

従 *menjū* obeying only when watched

従腹背 *menjū-fukuhai* passive resistance

皰 *nikibi* pimple, acne

11 晤 *mengo* interview, meeting

舵 *omokaji* starboard; turning to starboard

責 *menseki* personal reproof

接 *mensetsu* interview

接試問 *mensetsu shimon* oral examination

12 喰 *menku(rau)* be confused, be bewildered, be embarrassed

訴 *menso* direct appeal

無 *omona(shi)* be ashamed

13 腫 *omoba(ru)* the face swells

5【面】

革韋韭音頁風飛食首香

詰 *menkitsu* personal reproof
隠 *omogaku(shi)* covering the face.
omogaku(re) hiding the face
照 *omode(ru)* (the face) shines; blush
14 憎 *tsuraniku(i)* disgusting, detestable
構 *tsuragama(e)* expression, look
語 *mengo* personal conversation, interview, talk
貌 *membō* looks, features, countenance
魂 *tsuradamashii* countenance, facial expression
15 瘡 *omokusa* facial acne
談 *mendan* personal conversation, interview, talk
謁 *men'etsu* audience (with the emperor)
輪 *omowa* looks, features, face
影 *omokage* visage, face; trace, shadow; memory
罵 *memba suru* abuse (someone) to his face
16 積 *menseki* area
窶 *omoyatsu(re)* careworn look
壁 *mempeki* meditation facing a wall
19 識 *menshiki* acquaintance

5

皰 6567 / J7052 / M42639 Hō scabs or pustules on the face. *nikibi* pimples.

7

靦 6568 / J7053 / M42660 Ten staring; brash; proud.

14

靨 6569 / J7054 / M42698 Yō *ekubo* dimple.

RAD. 革 177

Tsukuri kawa tanned hide or *kaku no kawa* (*kawa* "leather" written with the character read *kaku* as distinguished from Rad. 107). At left: *kawa hen.* Nickname: Shoe Leather (as in 靴 *kutsu* shoe).

A **革** 6570 / J3357 / M42710 Kaku tanned leather. *arata(maru)* become serious (illness). *kawa* skin; hide; leather; fur, pelt; bark; peeling, husk, shell; film, cream.
2 刀 *kawagatana* leather knife
3 工場 *kawa kōba* tannery
4 文庫 *kawa bunko* leather case
5 正 *kakusei* reform
6 色 *kawa iro* greenish blue
8 沓 *kawagutsu* leather shoes
具 *kawagu* leather goods
表紙 *kawabyōshi* leather binding
命 *kakumei* revolution
命児 *kakumeiji* revolutionist
命的 *kakumeiteki* revolutionary, radical
命軍 *kakumeigun* revolutionary army
命家 *kakumeika* revolutionist
命旗 *kakumeiki* revolutionists' flag
命歌 *kakumeika* revolutionary song
9 草履 *kawazōri* leather sandals
10 砥 *kawato* razor strop
紐 *kawahimo* strap; thong; lash; leash
帯 *kawa obi* leather belt
11 張 *kawaba(ri) no* leather-covered
細工 *kawazaiku* leathercraft
13 靴 *kawagutsu* leather shoes or boots
新 *kakushin* reform, innovation
新的 *kakushinteki* reformatory
新派 *kakushinha* reformists; reformer
14 綴 *kawatoji* leather binding
緒 *kawao* sword strap; clog thong
鞄 *kawa kaban* leather bag, suitcase, briefcase
製 *kawasei* made of leather
15 質 *kakushitsu* coriaceous, leathery
16 鞘 *kawazaya* leather sheath, holster
18 鞣 *kawaname(shi)* tanning; tanner
職人 *kawashokunin* leatherworker
22 嚢 *kawabukuro* leather bag

3

靫 6571 / J7056 / M42713 Sai. Sa. Satsu. *utsubo, utsuo* quiver.

靭 6572 J-X M42715 **靱** 6573 J3f59 M-X **靭** 6574 J7057 M-X
JIN soft, pliable. NIN. *utsubo, utsuo* quiver.
8 性 *jinsei* tenacity
10 帯 *jintai* ligament

4

靹 6575 J7058 M42747 See **鞆** 6580.

B **靴** 6576 J3724 M42729 KA shoes. *kutsu* shoes; boots.
3 工 *kutsukō* shoemaker
下 *kutsushita* socks, stockings
下止 *kutsushitado(me)* garters
下留 *kutsushitado(me)* garters
下編機 *kutsushita a(mi)ki* hosiery knitting machine
5 皮 *kutsugawa* shoe leather
8 底 *kutsuzoko* shoe sole
直 *kutsunao(shi)* shoe repair; cobbler
刷毛 *kutsubake* shoebrush
9 音 *kutsu oto* sound of someone walking
屋 *kutsuya* shoemaker, shoe store
拭 *kutsufu(ki), kutsunugu(i)* doormat
型 *kutsugata* shoe last; shoe stretcher
10 師 *kutsushi* shoemaker
紐 *kutsuhimo* shoelaces
釘 *kutsu kugi* shoe peg, shoe nail
11 脱 *kutsunu(gi)* bootjack
13 傷 *kashō* shoe sore
14 箆 *kutsubera* shoehorn
墨 *kutsuzumi* shoe polish; bootblack
15 縫 *kutsunu(i)* sewing shoes
16 磨 *kutsumigaki* shoe polish; bootblack
17 擦 *kutsuzure* shoe sore

5

靺 6577 J705c M42761 MATSU barbarians; Tunguis.

靼 6578 J705a M42764 TAN tanned leather.

鞁 6579 J705b M42776 HI towline; trace; saddle strap.

鞆 6580 J705d M42794 (国字) *tomo* archer's arm protector.

鞅 6581 J7059 M42784 Ō connection.
12 掌 *ōshō suru* be busy with

鞄 6582 J3373 M42781 HAKU. HŌ. BYŌ. *kaban* suitcase, briefcase, bag.
9 持 *kabammo(chi)* private secretary

6

鞐 6583 J7060 M42829 (国字) *kohaze* clasp, fastener.

鞋 6584 J705e M42813 AI *waraji* straw sandals.

鞏 6585 J705f M42819 KYŌ hard.
8 固 *kyōko* firmness, stability, security, strength

鞍 6586 J3048 M42815 AN *kura* saddle.
3 下 *kurashita* saddlecloth; sirloin; saddle (of mutton)
5 尻 *kurajiri* back of the saddle
9 屋 *kuraya* saddler
10 部 *ambu* col, saddle (between mountains)
12 替 *kuraga(e)* changing quarters (by geisha or prostitutes); changing jobs
壺 *kura tsubo* seat of a saddle
13 数 *kura kazu* number of times one has ridden (horses)
15 敷 *kurashi(ki)* saddlecloth
17 擦 *kurazure* saddle sores
22 嚢 *annō* saddlebag

7

鞘 6587 J3e64 M42850 SHŌ. *saya* (sword) sheath, case, cap; margin, difference, brokerage; spread; (bean) shells.
6 当 *sayaa(te)* courtship rivalry
8 取 *sayato(ri)* brokerage

8

鞜 6588 J7061 M42883 TŌ. *kutsu* shoes, boots.

鞠 6589 J3547 M42892 KIKU. KYŪ. *mari* ball.
8育 *kikuiku* bringing up, nurture
10訊 *kikujin* investigation; questioning, interrogation
躬 *kikkyū* bowing respectfully
躬如 *kikkyūjo toshite* reverently, humbly, respectfully

9

鞨 6590 J7062 M42924 KATSU leather shoes.

鞳 6591 J7065 M42966 TŌ weapon; sound of a drum.

鞦 6592 J7063 M42922 SHŪ a crupper.
23韆 *shūsen, buranko* swing

鞫 6593 J6b71 M42931 KIKU investigate a crime.
10訊 *kikujin* investigation; questioning, interrogation
11問 *kikumon* interrogation (of suspects)

鞣 6594 J7064 M42909 JŪ tanned leather. NYU. *name(su)* tan (hides). *nameshigawa* tanned leather.
5皮 *jūhi, name(shi)gawa* tanned leather
皮業 *jūhigyō* tannery
9屋 *name(shi)ya* tanner; tannery

鞭 6595 J4a5c M42937 BEN *muchi* whip, rod. *muchiu(tsu)* whip, flog; urge on, encourage.
5打 *muchiu(tsu)* whip, flog; urge on, encourage
打苦行者 *Muchiu(chi) Kugyōsha* Flagellants
打症 *muchiuchishō* whiplash injury
7声 *bensei* crack of a whip
15撻 *bentatsu* urging, spurring on; whipping

10

鞴 6596 J7066 M42972 HI. BI. *fuigo, fuigō* bellows.

11

鞺 6597 J-X M42997 TŌ sound of drums.
20鞳 *tōtō* drumming; rumbling, roaring

12

韃 6598 J7067 M43053 DATSU whip; proper name.

14

韈 6599 J7069 M43079 BETSU *tabi*, socks, stockings.

韆 6600 J7068 M43075 SEN swing.

RAD. 韋 178

Nameshigawa tanned leather. This rare radical is traditionally a 9-stroke element. Its more common variant 韋 has 10 strokes. (as in 違 *chigau* differ).

韋 6601 J706a M43108 I tanned leather.

8

韓 6602 J345a M43159 KAN *Kara* Korea.

[2]人 *Kanjin, Karabito* ancient word for a Korean
[6]衣 *Kara koromo* ancient Korean clothes
[8]国 *Kankoku, Karakuni* Korea
[9]竿 *karasao* flail
[14]語 *Kara kotoba* ancient Korean words; a foreign language
[15]鋤 *karasuki* plow
[18]櫃 *karabitsu* Korean chest

10

韜 6603 J706b M43189 Tō bag; wrapping.
[11]晦 *tōkai suru* hide (talents, etc.)
略 *tōryaku* strategy, tactics

RAD. 韭 179

Nira leek. Nickname: Leek.

韭 6604 J706c M43236 See 韮 6605.

3

韮 6605 J4723 M43237 韭 6604 J706c M43236 Kyū. *nira* leek.

10

韲 6606 J706e M43249 See 齏 7087.

RAD. 音 180

Oto sound. Variant: 音. At left: *oto hen* Nickname: Noisy.

A 音 6607 J323b M43265 On sound; noise; pronunciation. In sound, tone. *oto* sound, noise, roar; fame. *ne* sound, tone, note, voice, chirping
[2]力 *onryoku* strength of the voice
[3]上 *ne (o) a(geru)* be tired out
叉 *onsa* tuning fork
[4]引 *onbi(ki)* dictionary arranged by the syllabary
太 *nebuto* voice huskiness
[6]色 *neiro, onshoku* tone color, tone quality
曲 *ongyoku, onkyoku* songs accompanied by the samisen; musical performance
字 *onji* phonetic symbol; syllabary
名 *ommei* names of musical notes
吐 *onto* speaking voice
吐朗朗 *onto-rōrō to* sonorously
[7]沙汰 *otosata* news, letter
声 *onsei, onjō* voice
声言語 *onsei gengo* the spoken language
声学 *onseigaku* phonetics
声認識 *onsei ninshiki* speech recognition
[8]波 *ompu* sound wave
物 *immotsu, imbutsu* friendship gift
画 *onga* sound movies
[9]速 *onsoku* speed of sound
便 *ombin* euphony, euphonic change
信 *onshin, inshin, otozure* correspondence, message, news, tidings
律 *onritsu* meter, rhythm
[10]栓 *onsen* organ stop
訓 *onkun* Chinese and Japanese pronunciations of characters
容 *on'yō* voice and countenance; visage
部記号 *ombu kigō* clef (in music)
[11]域 *on'iki* voice range
訳 *on'yaku* transliteration
階 *onkai* musical scale
符 *ompu* note, score, notation

12 揭 *ne(o)a(geru)* be tired out
程 *ontei* musical interval, step
量 *onryō* voice volume
13 痴 *onchi* tone deafness, no ear for music
節 *onsetsu* syllable
勢 *onsei* vocal stress
感 *onkan* sense of sound
楽 *ongaku* music
楽会 *ongakkai, ongakukai* concert, musicale
楽学校 *ongaku gakkō* music school
楽家 *ongakka, ongakuka* musician
楽隊 *ongakutai* orchestra, band
楽堂 *ongakudō* concert hall
楽療法 *ongaku ryōhō* music therapy
14 読 *ondoku* reading aloud. *on'yo(mi)* the *on* or Chinese reading of a character or a compound
管 *onkan* organ pipe
15 締 *neji(me)* tune
調 *onchō* tune, tone, rhythm, melody, harmony, euphony
盤 *omban* phonograph record
質 *onshitsu* tone quality
標文字 *ompyō monji, ompyō moji* phonetic symbols
16 頭 *ondo* songs where someone takes the lead and others sing or dance in response; a song leader
頭取 *ondoto(ri)* chorus leader; leading spirit, leader
19 譜 *ompu* music, notes, notation
韻 *on'in* vocal sound
韻学 *on'ingaku* phonetics
韻論 *on'inron* phonetics
響 *onkyō* sound, noise, echo
響学 *onkyōgaku* acoustics
響爆弾 *onkyō bakudan* scream bomb

4

韵 6608 J7071 M43271 See **韻** 6611.

5

韶 6609 J7070 M43276 Shō tie together, connect; beautiful.

10

B **響** 6610 J3641 M43318' **響** 6612 J-X M-X **響** 6613 J-X M43325

Kyō. *hibi(ku)* sound, resound, reverberate, echo, ring, vibrate; grate on; affect, find an echo in; become known. *hibi(ki)* sound, noise, peal, boom, crash, explosion; echo, reverberation; influence, effect; vibration, shock.
7 応 *kyōō* hurrying to ally oneself with (someone)
11 動 *doyo(mu), doyo(meku), toyo(mu)* be very noisy; resound; stir up (enthusiasm)
12 渡 *hibi(ki)-wata(ru)* resound throughout

B **韻** 6611 J3124 M43307 In rhyme; elegance; tone.
4 文 *imbun* poetry, verse
6 字 *inji* rhyming words
8 学 *ingaku* prosody, versification
事 *inji* artistic pursuits
9 律 *inritsu* rhythm
11 脚 *inkyaku* metrical foot
12 無 *in (no) na(i)* blank (verse)
14 語 *ingo* rhyming words

12

響 6612 J-X M-X **響** 6613 J-X M43325 See **響** 6610.

RAD. 頁 181

Ōgai big "shell" (to distinguish it from Rad. 154), *ichi no kai* (i.e., the character *ichi* "one" plus *kai* "shell"), or *pēji* "page." Nickname: Big Shell.

頁 6614 / J4a47 / M43333 KETSU. *pēji* page, leaf.

8 岩 *ketsugan* shale

— 2 —

頃 6615 / J3a22 / M43338 KEI. *koro* time, period. *koro(shimo)* just at that time. *-goro, -koro* about (regarding time).

6 合 *koroa(i)* suitable time; propriety; moderation

8 刻 *keikoku* a short period

A **頂** 6616 / J443a / M43335 CHŌ. *itadaki* head; top of the head; top, summit, peak; spire. *itada(ku)* be crowned with, wear; live under (a ruler); install (a president); receive, accept; buy; take, eat, drink. *unaji* nape of the neck.

3 上 *chōjō* top, summit, crest, peak, apex; climax, acme

7 角 *chōkaku* vertical angle

8 門一針 *chōmon (no) isshin* admonition concerning one's shortcomings

9 度 *chōdo* exactly, just right

点 *chōten* apex, vertex, peak, climax, acme, top, height

10 華 *chōka* finial

17 戴 *chōdai suru* accept, receive; take, eat, enjoy. *chōdai* please, be good enough to

戴物 *chōdaimono* a gift received

— 3 —

B **項** 6617 / J3960 / M43343 KŌ clause, paragraph; item; term (in math); argument (in math or linguistics). *unaji* nape of the neck.

5 目 *kōmoku* head, item, provision, clause

8 垂 *unada(reru)* bow the head

須 6618 / J3f5c / M43352 SU. SHU. *subeka(raku)* by all means, necessarily.

8 臾 *shuyu* moment, instant

17 彌壇 *shumidan* Buddhist image dais

A **順** 6619 / J3d67 / M43349 JUN order; turn; right; docility, obedience; occasion.

4 化 *junka suru* acclimate

大 *junten* following the way of heaven

5 正 *junsei na* correct and reasonable

礼 *junrei* pilgrimage; pilgrim

礼歌 *junrei uta* pilgrim's song

行 *junkō* progressing in order

次 *junji* gradually. *junji ni* in order, successively

当 *juntō na* proper, right, regular, normal

7 位 *jun'i* order, rank, precedence

良 *junryō na* gentle, peaceful, obedient

応 *junnō* adaptation; sympathy

応性 *junnōsei* adaptability

序 *junjo* order; system; procedure

序不同 *junjo-fudō* random order

序正 *junjotadashi(ku)* in exact order

序書 *junjoga(ki)* program

序数詞 *junjo sūshi* ordinal number

8 延 *jun'en* postponement

逆 *jungyaku* obedience and disobedience, right and wrong

送 *jun'oku(ri)* passing on from person to person

拝 *jumpai* circuit pilgrimage

9 風 *jumpū* favorable wind, tail wind

盃 *jumpai* passing a cup from person to person at a gathering

11 道 *jundō* the right road; following the path of truth

転 *junten* normal winds

12 順 *junjun ni* in order, in turn

番 *jumban* order, turn

13 路 *junro* regular route; itinerary

14 境 *junkyō* favorable circumstances, prosperity

15 調 *junchō* smoothness, favorable condition

養子 *jun'yōshi* younger brother adopted as a son

19 繰 *jungu(ri) ni* in turn, in order

頏 6620 / J7072 / M43371 KŌ go down, fly down; land. *nodo* throat. *kubi* neck.

B 頒 6621 / J4852 / M43378 HAN. *waka(tsu)* divide, separate; share with; distinguish between.
3 与 *waka(chi)-ata(eru)* make available to
5 白 *hampaku* grayish hair
布 *hampu* distribution, circulation, dissemination
6 行 *hankō* distribution, wide dissemination

頌 6622 / J7073 / M43365 JU. SHŌ eulogy. *shō(suru)* extol, praise.
9 栄 *shōei* doxology; the Gloria
12 詞 *shōshi* eulogy, compliment
13 詩 *shōshi* poem of praise
14 徳 *shōtoku* eulogy
徳碑 *shōtokuhi* monument to someone's honor
歌 *shōka* anthem, carol, hymn of praise
歌隊 *shōkatai* choir

頓 6623 / J465c / M43381 TON. *tomi ni, niwaka ni* suddenly, in a hurry, immediately. *ton to* entirely; (neg.) not in the least.
3 才 *tonsai* ready wit, tact
6 死 *tonshi* sudden death
7 狂 *tonkyō na* flurried, hysteric, wild; discordant
8 知 *tonchi* ready wit, tact
服 *tompuku* dose
服薬 *tompukuyaku* dose (of medicine)
9 首 *tonshu* kowtow, very deep bow, your humble servant
珍漢 *tonchinkan* absurdity, contradiction
10 馬 *tomma* dunce, simpleton. *tomma na* silly
挫 *tonza* setback, rebuff, standstill, impasse, deadlock
12 着 *tonjaku, tonchaku* care, heed, concern, anxiety
智 *tonchi* ready wit, tact
13 痴気 *tonchiki* dunce, simpleton

B 頑 6624 / J3468 / M43374 GAN stubborn; foolish. *gan(toshite)* firmly, stubbornly, resolutely. *kataku(na)* obstinate, stubborn.
3 丈 *ganjō na* solid, firm, stout
8 固 *ganko* obstinacy, stubbornness, persistence, bigotry
物 *gambutsu* hardheaded person
迷 *gammei* obstinacy, perversity, bigotry
陋 *ganrō* stubbornness and meanness
9 是無 *ganzena(i)* helpless, innocent, naïve
10 冥 *gammei* bigotry, obstinacy
11 健 *ganken* robust health
張 *gamba(ru)* persist in, insist on, be inflexible
強 *gankyō* obstinacy, persistence
強派 *gankyōha* diehards
13 愚 *gangu* stupid and obstinate
22 癬 *gansen, tamushi* ringworm

A 預 6625 / J4d42 / M43373 YO. *azu(keru) vt* place in custody, deposit, leave with, entrust with, commit to, give. *azu(karu) vi* take charge of; receive on deposit; undertake to do; call off (as a tie); refrain from; receive, enjoy. *azu(kari)* depositing; custody. *azu(ke)* entrusting to, committing to. *(o)azu(ke)* not carrying out a promise; making a dog wait for a command to eat.
2 人 *azu(kari)nin* one placed in charge of a thing. *azu(ke)nin* depositor
入 *azu(ke)-i(reru)* make a deposit
3 子 *azu(kari)go* foster child
5 主 *azu(kari)nushi* possessor. *azu(ke)nushi* depositor
7 言 *yogen* prophecy
言者 *yogensha* prophet
8 物 *azu(ke)mono* checked article, article left in charge of someone. *azu(kari)mono* a thing on deposit; consignment
金 *azu(ke)kin* key money. *yokin* deposit, bank account, credit
金主 *yokinnushi* depositor
金者 *yokinsha* depositor
金通帳 *yokin tsūchō* bankbook
金票 *yokinhyō* deposit slip
金準備率 *yokin jumbiritsu* deposit reserve rate
10 託 *yotaku suru* deposit
託金 *yotakukin* deposit
11 票 *azu(kari)hyō* claim check

12 貯金 *yochokin* deposit, bank account
証 *azu(kari)shō* baggage check; warehouse receipt; deposit certificate
証券 *azu(kari) shōken* warehouse receipt, deposit certificate
証書 *azu(kari) shōsho* baggage check; warehouse receipt, deposit certificate

5

頚 6626 J375b M43434 See 頸 6638.

頗 6627 J3f7c M43415 HA be prejudiced. *sukobu(ru)* exceedingly, extremely.

A 領 6628 J4e4e M43423 RYŌ dominion, territory possession, fief; suit (of armor). *ryō(suru)* govern, reign, be in possession of.
3 土 *ryōdo* territory, dominion, possession
土保全 *ryōdo hozen* territorial integrity
土拡張 *ryōdo kakuchō* territorial expansion
4 水 *ryōsui* territorial waters
内 *ryōnai* domains, territory
分 *ryōbun* territory, dominion, possession; domain, sphere, field
5 外 *ryōgai* outside the territory
民 *ryōmin* population of a fief
主 *ryōshu* lord of a fief, daimyo
主権 *ryōshuken* feudal lord's authority
収 *ryōshū* receipt, voucher
収者 *ryōshūsha* receiver, recipient
収書 *ryōshūsho* receipt, voucher
収証 *ryōshūshō* receipt, voucher
6 地 *ryōchi* territory, dominion, possession; fief
会 *ryōkai* understanding, comprehension
有 *ryōyū* possession
7 邑 *ryōyū* one's land
承 *ryōshō* acknowledgment
8 国 *ryōkoku* the national domain
空 *ryōkū* territorial air
事 *ryōji* consul
事団 *ryōjidan* consular corps
事裁判 *ryōji saiban* consular jurisdiction
事裁判所 *ryōji saibansho* consular court
事裁判権 *ryōji saibanken* consular jurisdiction
事館 *ryōjikan* consulate
9 首 *erikubi* nape of the neck
海 *ryōkai* territorial waters
10 袖 *ryōshū* leader, chief, boss
11 域 *ryōiki* territory, dominion, possession, domain, sphere ⌈comprehension
13 解 *ryōkai suru* understanding,
置 *ryōchi suru* take over documents and material evidence

6

頬 6629 J4b4b M-X Nonstandard for 頰 6637.

頡 6630 J7076 M43452 KETSU fly up.
13 頏 *kekkō* flying up and down; be of equal standing; be unyielding

7

頻 6631 J-X M43519 See 頻 6641.

頷 6632 J7077 M43512 GAN. *unazu(ku)* nod, nod approval.

頤 6633 J7075 M43455 頥 6634 J-X M43523 I. *otogai* chin. *ago* jaw.
8 使 *ishi suru* have a person under one's absolute control

B 頼 6635 J4d6a M43529' 賴 5818 J-X M36861 RAI. *tano(mu)* ask, request, entreat, appeal; entrust to, commission; employ, call in; depend on, have recourse to, trust in. *tayo(ru)* rely on, have recourse to. *tano(moshii)* reliable, trustworthy; hopeful. *tayo(rinai)* forlorn, helpless; vague; unreliable. *tano(mō)* hello there.
2 入 *tano(mi)-i(ru)* earnestly request
4 込 *tano(mi)-ko(mu)* earnestly request
少 *tano(mi)-suku(nai)* not too reliable; hopeless, helpless, forlorn
8 所 *tayo(ri)dokoro* one's resort, dependence
9 信紙 *raishinshi* telegram blank

14 綱 *tano(mi) (no) tsuna* last resort, only hope

頽 6636 / J7078 / M43517 TAI. *kuzu(reru)* decline; crack up (a baseball pitcher); decay, fester. *kuzu(oreru)* be discouraged. *nada(reru)* slope, descend, slide down. *nada(re)* avalanche, snowslide; slope, sloping; surging (crowd).

4 込 *nada(re)-ko(mu)* rush into, crowd
10 唐 *taitō* decadence, decline
11 運 *taiun* declining fortune
12 落 *nada(re)-o(chiru)* slide down
廃 *taihai* deterioration, degeneration, laxness, corruption, decadence, ruin
廃的 *taihaiteki* corrupt
13 勢 *taisei* downward tendency, decline, decay
17 齢 *tairei* declining years

頰 6637 / J-X / M43496 **頬** 6629 / J4b4b / M-X KYŌ. *hō, hoo, hoho* cheek.

4 辺 *ho(p)peta* cheek
6 当 *hōa(te)* (helmet) visor; (fencing) mask
7 杖突 *hōzue (o) tsu(ku)* rest the chin on one's hands
9 紅 *hōbeni* rouge
冠 *hōkabu(ri)* tying a cloth around the cheeks; affecting ignorance
10 骨 *hōbone, kyōkotsu* cheekbone
被 *hōkabu(ri)* tying a cloth around the cheeks; affecting ignorance
11 張 *hōba(ru)* take (food); take a big mouthful
14 摺 *hōzuri* pressing cheeks together
15 髯 *hōhige* sideburns

頸 6638 / J7074 / M43515 KEI. *kubi* neck, head.

3 丈 *kubidake* height to the neck. *kubi(t)take* complete devotion
4 木 *kubiki* yoke
5 玉 *kubitama* ancient necklace; neck bell (for animals); the neck; collar
9 巻 *kubima(ki)* muffler, comforter
10 骨 *keikotsu* neckbone
部 *keibu* neck (region)
11 桶 *kubi oke* box for a severed head
動脈 *keidōmyaku* carotid artery
12 椎 *keitsui* cervical vertebrae
筋 *kubisuji* nape of the neck
13 際 *kubigiwa* the neck
飾 *kubikaza(ri)* necklace
14 綱 *kubizuna* neck tether
静脈 *keijōmyaku* jugular vein
15 輪 *kubiwa* necklace; collar
縄 *kubinawa* neck tether

A **頭** 6639 / J462c / M43490 TŌ head, counter for large mammals. ZU head. *atama* head; brain, mind, intellect; leader; top; head (of boil); idea; hair; idea, point of view, consideration. *kashira* head; hair; leader, chief. *kōbe, kaburi, kabu, tsumuri* head. *atama kara* from the beginning; (not) at all. *atama(dekkachi)* top-heaviness. *atama(gonashi) ni* unsparingly, categorically. *-gashira* the very moment; the beginning.

3 大 *tōdai no* big-headed, top-heavy
巾 *zukin* hood, turban
上 *zujō* overhead
4 分 *kashirabun* leader, chief
文字 *kashira moji* capital letter; initials; first word
5 目 *tōmoku* chief, head, leader
石 *kashira ishi* cornerstone
付 *kashiratsu(ki)* fish cooked with head attached
打 *zu-u(chi), atama-u(chi)* hit the top (stocks)
6 刎 *atamaha(ne)* kickback, squeeze
字 *kashiraji* capital letter; initials; first word
7 角 *tōkaku* top of the head
囲 *tōi* head measurement
位 *tōi* cephalic presentation (obstetrics)
陀袋 *zudabukuro* wallet, (pilgrim's) scrip, beggar's bag
8 金 *atamakin* down payment, key money
注 *tōchū* notes at the top of the page
取 *tōdori* (private bank) president; manager
9 首 *tōshu* boss, head, chief
垢 *fuke* dandruff
重 *zuomo(i)* dull, top-heavy market. *zuomo* a thick head; impoliteness
10 骨 *tōkotsu* skill
振 *kashira (o) fu(ru)* shake the head (negatively)
株 *atamakabu* leader, executives
部 *tōbu, zubu* the head

書 *tōsho* superscription; the above-mentioned. *kashiraga(ki)* top notes; heading
11 脳 *zunō* head, brain
脳流出 *zunō ryūshutsu* brain drain
脳労働者 *zunō rōdōsha* brainworker
脳明晰 *zunō-meiseki na* clearheaded
12 註 *tōchū* notes at the top of the page
割 *atamawa(ri)* sharing, per capita
寒足熱 *zukan-sokunetsu* keeping the head cool and the feet warm
痛 *zutsū, tōtsū* headache; worry
痛持 *zutsūmo(chi)* chronic headache sufferer
13 数 *atamakazu, tōsū* number of persons, numerical strength
蓋 *tōgai, zugai* skull, cranium
蓋骨 *zugaikotsu* skull, cranium
14 領 *tōryō* chief, manager, dictator
髪 *tōhatsu* hair, head of hair
19 韻 *tōin* alliteration

8

顆 6640 / J7079 / M43551 KA a grain (of rice, etc.); small round object; clod of earth.
11 粒 *karyū* granule

B **頻** 6641 / J4931 / M-X **頻** 6631 / J-X / M43519 HIN. *shiki(ru) vi* repeat, occur repeatedly. *shiki(ri) ni* repeatedly, incessantly, insistently, intently.
5 出 *hinshutsu* frequent appearance
6 回 *hinkai* frequent
9 発 *himpatsu* frequent occurrence, frequent
度 *hindo* frequency
度数 *hindosū* frequency
13 数 *hinsū* frequency
16 繁 *himpan* frequency
17 頻 *himpin to, shikushiku to* frequently

9

顋 6642 / J707b / M43576 See **腮** 4844.

顎 6643 / J335c / M43590 GAKU jaw. *ago* jaw, chin. *agito* gill.
10 骨 *agobone, gakkotsu* jawbone
紐 *agohimo* chin strap
22 鬚 *agohige* beard

A **額** 6644 / J335b / M43586 GAKU tablet, plaque, framed picture; sum, quantity, amount, volume; denomination. *hitai* forehead, brow. *nuka(zuku)* bow, kowtow, prostrate oneself.
6 行灯 *gaku andon* horizontal paper lantern
8 突 *nukazu(ku)* bow, kowtow, prostrate oneself
9 面 *gakumen* face value; par; denomination; mere outlook
10 帯鏡 *gakutaikyō* doctor's head mirror
13 殿 *gakuden* votive-picture hall
際 *hitaigiwa* hairline
裏 *gaku ura* back of a framed picture or motto
15 縁 *gakubuchi* picture frame

A **題** 6645 / J426a / M43584 DAI subject, theme, topic; title, caption, heading; question, problem. *dai(suru)* give a title to.
5 目 *daimoku* title (of a book); heading
句 *daiku* prefatory motto
号 *daigō* book title
6 字 *daiji* preface of a book or title
名 *daimei* title
7 言 *daigen* preface; title (of a monument)
材 *daizai* subject matter, theme
8 画 *daiga* title of a picture
12 詠 *daiei* writing a poem on a given theme
詞 *daishi* preface; title (of a monument)
13 辞 *daiji* prefatory motto
意 *daii* meaning of the subject
19 簽 *daisen* book title

B **顕** 6646 / J3832 / M43609' **顯** 6657 / J707d / M43726 KEN. *ara(wareru)* appear, emerge, come in sight, show up; be revealed, be discovered; be mentioned; become famous. *ara(wasu)* show, indicate, display, prove, disclose, express; represent; distinguish oneself.
5 示 *kenji suru* show, unfold, unveil, uncover
6 在 *kenzai suru* reveal
7 位 *ken'i* high office, high rank

花植物 *kenka shokubutsu* flowering plant
8 官 *kenkan* dignitary, high official
9 界 *genkai* this world
要 *ken'yō* prominence, importance
栄 *ken'ei* attaining fame
11 現 *kengen* manifestation
著 *kencho na* remarkable, striking, obvious
12 揚 *ken'yō suru* extol, exalt
然 *kenzen(taru)* obvious, clear, conspicuous
貴 *kenki* position of honor
13 微鏡 *kembikyō* microscope
微鏡写真 *kembikyō shashin* microphotograph
14 彰 *kenshō suru* manifest, display, exalt, honor
15 賞 *kenshō* public rewarding
17 爵 *kenshaku* high rank of nobility
18 職 *kenshoku* important post

A**類** 6647/J4e60/M43608' **類** 6650/J-X/M43636 RUI kind, variety, class, genus; description; parallel case, an equal. *rui(suru)* be similar to, be akin to. *tagu(eru)* compare with. *tagui* kind, sort, class; match, equal. *-rui* resembling.

2 人猿 *ruijin'en* anthropoid ape, orangutan
4 比 *ruihi* analogy; parallel; equal
火 *ruika* spreading fire
化 *ruika suru* assimilate, incorporate
5 句 *ruiku* synonymous expression; similar haiku poems
6 同 *ruidō* similarity; same kind
名 *ruimei* generic name
似 *ruiji* resemblance, analogy, kinship
似点 *ruijiten* points of similarity
似品 *ruijihin* an imitation
似療法 *ruiji ryōhō* homeopathy
7 伴 *ruiban* same kind; companion; accomplice
別 *ruibetsu* classification
8 例 *ruirei* similar example; analogy
9 型 *ruikei* similar type
10 症 *ruishō* similar diseases, similar cases
書 *ruisho* similar books
11 推 *ruisui* analogy
12 焼 *ruishō* spreading fire
14 語 *ruigo* synonym
15 縁 *ruien* affinity, family relationship
18 題 *ruidai* similar question
20 纂 *ruisan* classified collection in book form

A**顔** 6648/J3469/M43591' **顏** 6649/J707a/M43591 GAN. *kambase* face, countenance. *kao* face, countenance, expression; honor, prestige.

5 立 *kaoda(chi)* facial features. *kao (ga) ta(tsu)* save face
付 *kaotsu(ki)* countenance, looks, features
出 *kaoda(shi) suru* visit, put in an appearance
6 色 *kao iro, ganshoku* complexion, countenance, expression, color
向 *kaomu(ke)* facing the public
合 *kaoa(wase)* meeting, presentation, being matched against or paired with
先 *kaosaki* face, countenance; facial protrusions (nose or cheeks); right in front
汚 *kaoyogoshi* a disgrace
気色 *kaokeshiki* looks, countenance
7 作 *kaozuku(ri)* makeup
役 *kaoyaku* leader, boss
利 *kao (ga) ki(ku)* be influential
売 *kao (o) u(ru), kao (ga) u(reru)* become famous
見 *kaomi(se)* meeting for the first time
見世 *kaomise* debut, first stage appearance
見知 *kaomishi(ri)* one whose face one recognizes
9 持 *kaomo(chi)* looks, countenance
変 *kaogawa(ri)* changing one's looks
負 *kaoma(ke) suru* be outshone, be made to blush
造作 *kao (no) zōsaku* countenance
面 *gammen* the face
面角 *gammenkaku* facial angle
10 振 *kaobu(re)* personnel, line-up
料 *ganryō* cosmetics
容 *kaokatachi, kambase* looks, features, countenance
11 寄 *kaoyo(se)* meeting, presentation; being matched against or paired with
12 揃 *kaozoro(i)* galaxy of notables; all present
違 *kaochiga(i)* changed looks
貸 *kao (o) ka(su)* come and assist
13 触 *kaobure* personnel, line-up
14 貌 *kaokatachi, gambō* features, looks, personal appearance

15 潰 *kao (ga) tsubu(reru)* lose face
18 癖 *kaoguse* facial habits
19 繫 *kaotsuna(gi)* getting acquainted

10

類 6650 / J-X / M43636 See 類 6647.

顛 6651 / J-X / M43628 **顚** 6652 / J453f / M-X TEN overturn; summit; origin.
5 末 *temmatsu* circumstances, facts, details
8 沛 *tempai* stumbling and falling; moment of time
10 倒 *tentō suru* fall down violently, upset, overturn, tumble; invert, reverse
12 落 *tenraku suru* stumble and fall; become suddenly poor
18 覆 *tempuku suru* overthrow, overturn; subvert; upset, capsize

A**願** 6653 / J346a / M43623 GAN prayer, petition, vow. *nega(u)* desire, wish, hope; beg, implore. *nega(i)* desire, wish, request, prayer; petition, application. *nega(wakuwa)* I pray. *nega(washii)* desirable.
2 力 *ganriki* the power of prayer (in Buddhism)
3 下 *nega(i)-sa(geru)* withdraw a request
4 文 *gammon* Shinto or Buddhist prayer
5 立 *ganda(te)* Shinto or Buddhist prayer
叶 *nega(ttari)-kana(ttari)* everything working out as desired
主 *ganshu* a temple petitioner
出 *nega(i)-de(ru)* apply for. *nega(i)de* application, petition
7 状 *ganjō* written request
求 *nega(i)-moto(meru)* entreat
8 事 *nega(i)goto* prayer, one's desire
9 面 *gammen* the front page of an application
10 酒 *ganshu* praying at a temple or shrine for help to stop drinking
書 *gansho* written application or petition
11 掛 *ganka(ke)* Shinto or Buddhist prayer
望 *gambō, gammō* desire, wish, aspiration
13 解 *ganhodo(ki)* release from a vow
意 *gan'i* object of an application

12

顥 6654 / J-X / M43682 Kō clarity.

B**顧** 6655 / J385c / M43689' Ko. *kaeri(miru)* look back; turn around, look back upon, review; examine oneself; take notice of.
5 用 *kaeri(mi) mochi(iru)* to favor
9 眄 *koben, komen* looking around
客 *kokyaku, kokaku* customer, patron, client
11 視 *koshi suru* glance back, turn around
望 *kobō suru* look around; hesitate
問 *komon* adviser, consultant
問弁護士 *komon bengoshi* legal adviser
問団 *komondan* advisory group, brain trust
問医 *komon'i* consulting physician
問官 *komonkan* councilor
15 慮 *koryo* concern, solicitude

13

顫 6656 / J707c / M43706 SEN. *furu(eru), furu(u)* tremble, shudder.

14

顯 6657 / J707d / M43726 See 顕 6646.

顬 6658 / J-X / M43716 JU temple (of the head).

15

顰 6659 / J707e / M43737 HIN scowl. *hiso(meru), shika(meru)* raise (the eyebrows), knit (the brows), scowl. *hiso(mi)* scowling
9 面 *shikamezure, shikame(t)tsura* grimace, sullen face
10 笑 *hinshō* forced laugh, laughing while scowling
18 蹙 *hinshuku suru* frown on; be shocked at

16

顱 6660 / J7121 / M43742 RO head, skull.

顴 6661 / J7122 / M43751 KEN cheekbone.

[10]骨 *kenkotsu* cheekbone

顳 6662 / J7123 / M43750 SHŌ temple (of the head).

[23]顬 *komekami* temple (of the head)

RAD. 風 182

Kaze wind. Variant: 風 *fūnyō* "wind" enclosure. Nickname: Wind (cf. Rad. 16).

A **風** 6663 / J4977 / M43756 FU, FŪ wind; air, look, appearance, bearing, mien, deportment; manners, custom; trend, tone, tendency; way, fashion, manner; style, type; disposition, turn of mind; kind; vein; state, condition. *kaze* wind, storm, breeze, draft, current of air; a cold. *furi* form; condition; deportment; pretense; discipline; custom. *kaza-* wind.

[2]入 *kazai(re)* airing, ventilation
力 *fūryoku* wind force
[3]口 *kazaguchi* air intake
子 *kaze (no) ko* open-air creatures; children
下 *kazashimo, kazashita* leeward
上 *kazakami* windward
上置 *kazakami (ni) o(kenu)* despicable, contemptible
土 *fūdo* climate, topography, natural feature
土病 *fūdobyō* endemic disease
土記 *fudoki* topography, description of natural features
土馴化 *fūdo junka* acclimatization
[4]月 *fūgetsu* wind and moon; beauties of nature
引 *kazehi(ki)* catching cold
切 *kazeki(ri)* leading edge of a wing; car radiator ornament. *kaze (o) ki(ru)* strut along
丰 *fūbō* appearance, attire; visage; beautiful form
心地 *kazegokochi* signs of wind; a slight cold
水 *fūsui* wind and flowing water
水害 *fūsuigai* storm and flood damage
化 *fūka* weathering; efflorescence; influence of a ruler on the governed
化作用 *fūka sayō* weathering
[5]穴 *kazaana* air hole, ventilator
立 *kazeda(tsu)* get windy, begin to blow hard
圧 *fūatsu* wind pressure, air pressure; leeway, driftage
[6]色 *fūshoku* scenery, landscape, view. *kaze iro* the wind blowing through the flowers and branches
気 *kazake* slight cold; signs of wind. *kazake, kaze(k)ke* slight cold. *fūki* climate; customs and climate; the spirit of the people; a slight cold; palsy
向 *fūkō, kazamu(ki), kazemu(ki)* wind direction; situation; tendency
光 *fūkō* scenery, natural beauty
当 *kazaa(tari), kazea(tari)* force of the wind; fierce criticism; oppression
防 *fūbō* windshield, windbreak
[7]足 *kazaashi* wind velocity
車 *fūsha* windmill. *kazaguruma* windmill; pinwheel
伯 *fūhaku* wind god
位 *fūi* wind direction
体 *fūtei, fūtai* appearance, looks, dress, posture, attitude
抜 *kazanu(ki), kazenu(ki)* air hole, ventilation
折 *kazao(re)* broken by the wind
邪 *fūja, kaze* a cold
声 *fūsei* the sound of the wind; rumor; false alarm. *kazegoe* huskiness from a cold
災 *fūsai* storm damage
吹回 *kaze (no) fu(ki)mawa(shi)* wind direction; developments
見 *kazami* weather vane
見舞 *kaze mimai* inquiry after a storm
来 *fūrai* the coming of the wind; showing up from nowhere; ill at ease; useless; no place of abode
来人 *fūraijin* a person showing up from nowhere; wanderer; an unsettled person; a worthless person

来坊 *fūraibō* wanderer, vagabond, waif, tramp
来者 *fūraimono* wanderer, vagabond, waif, tramp
呂 *furo* bath; bathtub
呂代 *furodai* bath charge
呂屋 *furoya* bathhouse, public bath
呂釜 *furogama* bath heater, bath boiler
呂桶 *furooke* bathtub
呂場 *furoba* bathroom
呂番 *furoban* one who lights the bath
呂銭 *furosen* bath charge
呂敷 *furoshiki* wrapping cloth, kerchief
8 雨 *fūu* wind and rain
味 *fūmi* taste, flavor
押 *kazaosa(e)* stones to keep things from blowing away
波 *fūha* wind and waves; rough seas; discord, quarrel
炉 *fūro* wind furnace
和 *kazanagi* a calm
刺 *fūshi* sarcasm, innuendo, irony
炎 *fūen* foehn, warm wind from the mountains
采 *fūsai* appearance, mien, bearing
物 *fūbutsu* natural objects, nature, scenery, landscape; scenes and manners
物詩 *fūbutsushi* nature poem
9 面 *kazaomote* wind direction
音 *kazeoto* sound of the wind
食 *fūshoku* weathering, wind erosion
通 *kazetō(shi), kazatō(shi), kazetō(ri)* ventilation
便 *kaze (no) tayo(ri)* rumor
待 *kazamu(chi), kazema(chi)* waiting for a favorable wind
洞 *fūdō* wind tunnel
神 *kaze (no) kami, fūjin* wind god; demon of colds. *fūshin* character
紀 *fūki* discipline, public morals
級 *fūkyū* wind classification
除 *kazayo(ke)* windbreak, windshield
変 *fūgawa(ri)* eccentricity, peculiarity
発 *fūhatsu* sudden gust; voluble speech
姿 *fūshi* appearance, looks, mien
速 *fūsoku* wind velocity
速計 *fūsokukei* anemometer
前 *fūzen* the place the wind strikes
前灯 *fūzen (no) tomoshibi* flickering light; dangerous situation; verge of death
俗 *fūzoku* manners, customs, morals
俗画 *fūzokuga* paintings depicting customs
俗営業 *fūzoku eigyō* business affecting public morals
俗壊乱 *fūzoku kairan* offense against public morals
信 *fūshin* news; wind direction
信子 *fūshinshi* hyacinth
信子鉱 *fūshinshikō* zircon
信旗 *fushinki* weather vane
信器 *fūshinki* weather vane
10 疹 *fushin* German measles
格 *fūkaku* character, personality, appearance, style
浪 *fūrō* wind and waves, heavy seas
流 *fūryū* taste, elegance, refinement
陰 *kazakage* wind shelter
害 *fūgai* storm damage
馬 *fūba* indifference, apathy
馬牛 *fūbagyū* indifference, apathy; something of no concern; widely separated
致 *fūchi* taste, elegance; scenic beauty
致地区 *fūchi chiku* scenic zone
致林 *fūchirin* ornamental forest
11 鳥 *fūchō* bird of paradise
情 *fuzei* appearance, air; taste; elegance; entertainment, hospitality
眼 *fūgan* gonorrheal ophthalmia
脚 *kazaashi* wind velocity
船 *fūsen* balloon
彩 *fūsai* taste, elegance, refinement
教 *fūkyō* public morals
窓 *kazamado* ventilator, small vent
笛 *fūteki, kazabue* bagpipe
習 *fūshū* manners, customs, usage
雪 *fūsetsu* snowstorm, blizzard
袋 *fūtai* weight of packing, tare; exterior; outward appearance
12 間 *kazama, kazema* lull in the wind; windy spell
評 *fūhyō* rumor
落 *kazao(chi)* fruit blown down by the wind
琴 *fūkin* organ; hand organ; accordion
媒 *fūbai* wind fertilization
媒花 *fūbaika* wind-pollinated flower
景 *fūkei* landscape, scenery, view
景画 *fūkeiga* landscape painting
雲 *kazagumo* wind clouds. *fūun* wind and clouds; state of affairs

雲児 *fūunji* a lucky adventurer
13 雅 *fūga* taste, elegance, refinement; literature, poetry
路 *kazamichi* wind lane; draft
隠 *kazagaku(re)* protected from the wind; taking shelter from the wind
鈴 *fūrin* wind bell
鈴草 *fūrinsō* a Canterbury bell, a bell flower
14 聞 *fūbun, kaze (no) ki(koe)* report, rumor
塵 *fūjin* dust; worldly affairs
説 *fūsetsu* rumor, report, hearsay
貌 *fūbō* looks, features, appearance
態 *fūtai* attitude
模様 *kazemoyō, kazamoyō* wind direction; signs of a wind; looks of a windy sky
15 趣 *fūshu* import, meaning, contents, tenor, gist; tone, touch, sentiment, charm; aspect, appearance
儀 *fūgi* manners, customs, habits, morality, demeanor
標 *kazejirushi* weather vane
潮 *fūchō* lee tide; current (of the times), fashion, trend
蝕 *fūshoku* weathering, wind erosion
16 薫 *kazekao(ru)* fragrant breezes blow
薬 *kazagusuri, kazegusuri* medicine for cold
諭 *fūyu* hint, insinuation; allegory
諭法 *fūyuhō* allegory
17 濤 *fūtō* wind and waves, storm
霜 *fūsō* wind and frost; hardships
18 鎮 *fūchin* decorative hanging-scroll weight
19 靡 *fūbi suru* overwhelm, conquer, dominate, sway
韻 *fūin* grace, taste
22 籟 *fūrai* rustle of leaves

3

凪 6664 / J7124 / M43769 (国字) *oroshi* wind blowing down from the mountains.

5

颯 6665 / J7125 / M43808 SATSU. *sat(to)* suddenly, smoothly.
11 爽 *sassō(taru)* gallant, dashing, stately
14 颯 *sassatsu(taru)* rustling; whistling; murmuring

颱 6666 / J7126 / M43815 TAI typhoon.
9 風 *taifū* typhoon
風眼 *taifūgan, taifū (no) me* eye of a typhoon

7

颶 6667 / J-X / M43840 See **颶** 6668.

8

颶 6668 / J7127 / M43876 **颶** 6667 / J-X / M43840 GU storm.
9 風 *gufū* tornado, hurricane, typhoon

11

飄 6669 / J7128 / M43946 **飃** 6670 / J7129 / M43945 HYŌ wavy. *hirugae(ru) vi* turn over, wave, flutter. *hirugae(su) vt* change (one's mind); turn, reverse; wave, flutter; dodge. *tsumuji* whirlwind.
5 乎 *hyō to* aimlessly; unexpectedly
10 逸 *hyōitsu na* buoyant, detached, aloof
12 然 *hyōzen to* aimlessly; unexpectedly
20 飄 *hyōhyō toshite* buoyantly; roaming

12

飆 6671 / J712a / M43963 HYŌ whirlwind; cyclone; tornado.

RAD. 飛 183

Tobu to fly. Nickname: Flying.

A 飛 6672 J4874 M44000 HI. *to(bu)* fly; skip (pages). *to(basu)* fly (a kite); let fly; blow away; scatter; splash; drive fast; skip over, omit; issue, send out. *ton(da)* surprising, extraordinary, shocking, terrible, tremendous, strange, serious. *to(ndemonai)* absurd; unexpected; fantastic; strange, extraordinary.

2 入 *to(bi)-i(ru)* jump into; dive in; fly into; thrust oneself into. *tobii(ri)* outside competitor, volunteer speaker; patches of color (in shrubbery)

入勝手 *tobii(ri) katte* free-for-all, open to all

3 上 *to(bi)-a(garu)* fly up, jump up. *to(bi)a(gari)* an upstart; a rash person

下 *to(bi)-o(riru)* jump down. *to(bi)-sa(garu)* jump down. *to(bi)o(ri)* jumping off a moving vehicle

下自殺 *to(bi)o(ri) jisatsu* committing suicide by jumping off a building

4 火 *to(bi)hi* flying sparks; leaping flames; repercussions

切 *tobiki(ri)* top quality, beyond comparison; a flying shot (at a bird)

込 *to(bi) ko(mu)* jump into; dive in; fly into; thrust oneself into

込台 *tobikomidai* diving board

込自殺 *tobiko(mi) jisatsu* committing suicide by jumping in front of a train

込様 *to(bi)ko(mi)zama ni* just as one jumps in

5 白 *kasuri* splashed pattern; cloth with a splashed pattern

立 *to(bi)-ta(tsu)* jump to one's feet; fly away

付 *to(bi)-tsu(ku)* fly at, leap at, snatch at, spring on

札 *hisatsu* urgent letter

去 *to(bi)-sa(ru)* flee away, scatter

出 *to(bi)-da(su)* fly away; rush out; project, protrude; appear. *to(bi)-de(ru)* protrude, project, stand out of

石 *to(bi)ishi* steppingstones

石伝 *to(bi)ishizuta(i)* following the steppingstones

石作戦 *to(bi)ishi sakusen* island-hopping operations

石攻撃 *to(bi)ishi kōgeki* island-hopping invasion

6 回 *to(bi)-mawa(ru)* fly around; gambol, romp; hustle around

地 *to(bi)chi* isolated land

交 *to(bi)-ka(u)* fly about, flit about

行 *hikō* flight, flying, aviation

行士 *hikōshi* aviator

行甲板 *hikō kampan* flight deck

行免状 *hikō menjō* pilot's license

行服 *hikōfuku* flying suit

行学 *hikōgaku* aeronautics

行学校 *hikō gakkō* flying school

行速度 *hikō sokudo* air speed

行家 *hikōka* aviator, pilot

行郵便 *hikō yūbin* airmail

行時間 *hikō jikan* flying time

行術 *hikōjutsu* aeronautics, aviation

行船 *hikōsen* airship, dirigible

行隊 *hikōtai* flying corps, air force

行基地 *hikō kichi* air base

行場 *hikōjō* airfield, airport

行帽 *hikōbō* flying helmet

行艇 *hikōtei* flying boat, hydroplane

行機 *hikōki* airplane, aircraft

行機雲 *hikōkigumo* a vapor trail, a condensation trail, a contrail

行翼 *hikōyoku* a flying wing

7 言 *higen* groundless rumor

走 *to(bi) hashi(ru)* leap for joy

来 *hirai suru* come flying; come by air. *to(bi)-kita(ru)* come flying, come running, come in a hurry

8 退 *to(bi)-no(ku)* jump back, jump aside

板 *to(bi)ita* springboard

歩 *to(bi)-aru(ku)* gad about; run around

沫 *himatsu* splash, spray

沫伝染 *himatsu densen* droplet-spread infection

9 飛 *to(bi)to(bi) no* desultory, sporadic

降 *to(bi)o(ri)* jumping off a moving vehicle

降自殺 *to(bi)o(ri) jisatsu* committing suicide by jumping off a building

乗 *to(bi)-no(ru)* jump on (a horse); jump on a moving vehicle

泉 *hisen* rapids, cataract, waterfall
10 起 *to(bi)-o(kiru)* jump out of bed; start up, spring to one's feet
竜 *hiryū* flying dragon; enlightened emperor
11 魚 *to(bi)uo* flying fish
鳥 *hichō* flying bird. *Asuka* Asuka Era (593-710)
掛 *to(bi)-ka(karu)* pounce on, turn upon
球 *hikyū* fly ball
移 *to(bi)-utsu(ru)* jump from one thing to another
脚 *hikyaku* runner, courier; (ancient) postman
雪 *hisetsu* blowing snow
道具 *to(bi)dōgu* missile, firearms
12 越 *to(bi)-ko(su)* jump over, fly cross. *to(bi)ko(shi)* leapfrog
違 *to(bi)-chiga(u)* fly around
弾 *hidan* flying bullet
揚 *hiyō* flying; flight
渡 *to(bi)-wata(ru)* come tearing along; be spread all over, fly across
翔 *hishō* flight, flying, soaring
散 *hisan suru, to(bi)-chi(ru)* scatter, disperse
雲 *hiun* fleeting cloud
報 *hihō* urgent message
13 跳 *to(bi)-ha(neru)* jump up; fly away
節 *hisetsu* gambrel, hock (of a horse)
電 *hiden* urgent telegram
14 語 *higo* rumor, gossip
読 *to(bi)yo(mi)* skimming through (a book), reading desultorily
15 蝗 *batta* grasshopper
縄 *to(bi)nawa* jumping rope
16 燕 *hien* flying swallow
燕草 *hiensō* larkspur, delphinium
17 檄 *higeki* urgent manifesto
18 瀑 *hibaku* waterfall
19 離 *to(bi)-hana(reru)* fly apart; tower above; out of the ordinary
簷 *hien* high roof; upturned eaves
20 礫 *tsubute* stone throwing; a thrown stone
21 躍 *hiyaku* leap; activity; rapid progress; flight (of imagination); maneuvers
躍的 *hiyakuteki* rapid

— 12 —

飜 6673 / J664c / M44009 See 翻 4694.

食 RAD. 184

Shoku food. Variant: 食. At left: 飠 or 飠 (8 strokes) *shoku hen*. Nickname: Food.

A 食 6674 / J3f29 / M44014 SHI, JIKI food. SHOKU food, provisions; eating, meal; appetite. *ta(beru), shoku(suru)* eat. *ku(u)* eat; subsist on; support oneself; consume; get (a scolding); encroach; bite at, gnaw at; (shoes) pinch; be cheated. *ku(rau)* eat, drink; receive (a blow). *ku(rawasu)* feed; strike (someone). *ha(mu)* eat, feed on, graze on, live on, prey on, receive (an allowance). *ku(i-chigiru)* eat off, bite off. *ku(enai)* inedible; hard to get along; cunning, crafty. *ku(eru)* edible; can get along. *shoku(pan)* bread.
2 入 *ku(i)-i(ru)* eat into; encroach upon
人種 *shokujinshu* cannibals
3 下 *ku(i)-sa(garu)* hang on to; hold on to (convictions)
上 *ku(i)-a(geru)* eat all
4 手 *ku(i)te* eater; glutton
方 *ta(be)kata, ku(i)kata* manner of eating; how to eat, table manners
止 *ku(i)-to(meru)* restrain, resist, prevent. *ku(i)sa(shi)* food remnants. *ku(i)sa(shi) no* half-eaten
込 *ku(i)-ko(mu)* eat into, eat up; bore into; cut into; be deep-seated; erode, corrode; drain (funds). *kura(i)-ko(mu)* go to jail; shoulder a debt or other load; be deceived; abandon oneself to vice; fall heir to (trouble). *ku(i)ko(mi)* thrust; intrusion; deficit
切 *ku(i)-ki(ru)* gnaw off; bite off; eat up
分 *ku(i)-wa(keru)* eat and taste carefully. *ku(i)bun* food expenses. *shokubun* phase of an eclipse
中 *shokuata(ri)* food poisoning, food disagreement

中毒 *shoku chūdoku* food poisoning
5 代 *ku(i)shiro* food expenses
付 *ta(be)-tsu(keru)* get used to eating. *ku(i)-tsu(ku)* bite at, fasten one's teeth on, snap at, nibble at; hold on to. *kura(i)-tsu(ku)* bite
外 *ku(i)-hazu(su)* miss a meal; lose a job
台 *shokudai* dining table
出 *ha(mi)-da(su), ha(mi)-de(ru)* protrude, project, jut out, bulge out, be forced out, be pressed out, be crowded out. *ku(i)de* size of a serving. *kuide (ga aru)* have plenty of food
生活 *shoku seikatsu* eating habits, dietary life
用 *shokuyō no* edible, used for food
用牛 *shokuyō ushi* beef cattle
用供 *shokuyō (ni) kyō(suru)* use for food
用油 *shokuyō abura* cooking oil, edible oil
用品 *shokuyōhin* foodstuffs, groceries
用蛙 *shokuyōgaeru* edible frog
用植物 *shokuyō shokubutsu* edible plants
6 虫 *shokuchū* insect eating
回 *ku(i)-mawa(ru)* go around eating
尽 *ku(i)-tsu(kusu)* eat up, consume. *shokujin* maximum obscuration (in an eclipse)
気 *ku(i)ki, ku(i)ke* appetite
休 *shokuyasu(mi)* rest after meals
汚 *ta(be)-yogo(su)* making a mess at the table
合 *ku(i) a(waseru)* eating two things together; dovetail. *ku(i)-a(u)* bite each other; engage (gears); fit together exactly. *ku(i)a(i)* fighting; biting each other
肉 *shokuniku* meat eating
肉類 *shokunikurui* carnivorous animals
7 言 *shokugen* eating one's words; breaking one's word; falsifying
足 *ku(i)-ta(rinai)* have not eaten enough; be unsatisfied; be dissatisfied with (someone)
坊 *ku(ishim)bō* gourmand; gluttony
初 *ta(be)zo(me), ku(i)zo(me)* weaning ceremony
余 *ta(be)-ama(su), ku(i)-ama(su)* leave meals unfinished. *ta(be)ama(ri)* leftover food. *ku(i)ama(ri), ku(i)ama(shi)* food remnants
扶持 *ku(i)buchi* food expenses
8 味 *shokumi* flavor (of a food)
延 *ku(i)-no(basu)* save on provisions; conserve (materials)
逃 *ku(i)ni(ge)* run off without paying for food
取 *ku(i)-to(ru)* pick and eat
券 *shokken* meal ticket
放題 *ta(be)hōdai, ku(i)hōdai* overeating
卓 *shokutaku* dining table
卓用 *shokutakuyō* for table use
卓塩 *shokutakuen* table salt
事 *shokuji* meal, diet, board
事中 *shokujichū* while eating, during a meal
事時 *shokujidoki* mealtime
物 *ta(be)mono, ku(i)mono* food, provisions; victim, prey. *ku(u)mono* food, feed. *shokumotsu* food, provisions; diet; feed. *ku(wase)mono* imitation, counterfeit, fraud; impostor, hypocrite, crook (a person)
物中毒 *shokumotsu chūdoku* food poisoning
物連鎖 *shokumotsu rensa* food chain
物繊維 *shokumotsu sen'i* dietary fiber
9 食 *ku(uya)-ku(wazu) de* penniless
通 *shokutsū* connoisseur of food
後 *shokugo* after eating; after a meal
持 *ku(i)-mo(tsu)* hold between the teeth
紅 *shoku beni* food coloring
封 *shokuhō* feudal estate
客 *shokkaku* a dependent
荒 *ku(i)-a(rasu)* devour; eat a little of everything; work at this and that
甚 *shokujin* maximum obscuration (in an eclipse)
指 *shokushi* forefinger, index finger
指動 *shokushi (ga) ugo(ku)* have a desire to secure (something)
思 *shokushi* appetite
思不振 *shokushi fushin* loss of appetite
前 *shokuzen* before meals; at the dinner table
前服用 *shokuzen fukuyō* to be taken before meals
前酒 *shokuzenshu* appetizer wine, apéritif
品 *shokuhin* foodstuffs, groceries
品工業 *shokuhin kōgyō* food industry
品中毒 *shokuhin chūdoku* food poisoning

品化学 *shokuhin kagaku* food chemistry
品加工 *shokuhin kakō* food processing
品店 *shokuhinten* grocery store
品衛生 *shokuhin eisei* food sanitation
10 逸 *ku(i)-hagu(reru)* miss a meal; lose a job
倒 *ku(i)-tao(su)* sponge on. *ku(i)dao(re)* wasting one's money on food
時 *ta(be)doki* season for (certain foods)
残 *ta(be)-noko(su), ku(i)-noko(su)* leave half-eaten. *ta(be)noko(shi)* leftover food
破 *ku(i)-yabu(ru)* bite and tear up
紛 *ku(i)-magira(wasu)* eat and forget one's troubles
殺 *ku(i)-koro(su)* kill and eat; bite to death
兼 *ta(be)-ka(neru), ku(i)-ka(neru)* have more than one can eat; cannot make a living
料 *shokuryō* food; main article of diet. *kuiryō* food, board
料品 *shokuryōhin* foodstuffs, groceries
料品店 *shokuryōhinten* grocery
料品商 *shokuryōhinshō* grocery business
11 過 *ku(i)-su(giru)* overeat
頃 *ta(be)goro, ku(i)goro* time to eat; season for; done to a turn; period of big appetite
得 *ku(i)doku* a windfall for one's stomach
掛 *ku(i)-ka(keru), ku(i)-ka(karu)* begin to eat. *ku(tte)-ka(karu)* defy, challenge, flare up at, go after. *tabekake, kuika(ke)* food remnants. *kuika(ke) no* half-eaten
盛 *ta(be)zaka(ri)* growing period. *ku(i)zaka(ri)* time to eat; season for; done to a turn; period of big appetite
堂 *shokudō* dining hall, mess hall
堂車 *shokudōsha* dining car
習 *ta(be)-nara(u)* get used to eating
習慣 *shokushūkan* dietary habits
道 *shokudō* alimentary canal, esophagus
道楽 *ku(i)dōraku* epicureanism; gourmet
道癌 *shokudōgan* cancer of the esophagus
欲 *shokuyoku* appetite
欲欠乏 *shokuyoku-ketsubō* lack of appetite
欲不振 *shokuyoku-fushin* poor appetite
12 間 *shokkan* between meals
違 *ku(i)-chiga(u)* cross, interlock; run counter to, clash with; go amiss
飲 *ku(i)no(mi)* eating and drinking
散 *ku(i)-chi(rasu)* eat a bit of everything
裂 *ku(i)-sa(ku)* bite and tear up
費 *shokuhi* food expense, board charge
13 傷 *shokushō* food poisoning; food disagreement; surfeiting
嫌 *ku(wazu)gira(i), ta(bezu)gira(i)* disliking without tasting; prejudice, antipathy
溜 *ku(i)da(me)* storing food in the stomach
滅 *ku(i)-horo(bosu)* devour
滞 *shokutai* indigestion
滓 *ta(be)kasu* leavings of food
続 *ku(i)-tsuzu(keru)* continue to eat; continue to make a living
飽 *ku(i)-a(kiru)* be surfeited; have plenty. *ta(be)-a(kiru)* eat to the full
馴 *ku(i)-na(reru)* be used to eating
置 *ku(i)o(ki)* storing food in the stomach
意地 *ku(i)iji* gluttony
塩 *shokuen* table salt, sodium chloride
塩水 *shokuensui* normal salt solution
詰 *ku(i)-tsu(meru)* fail, go broke, lose one's job, be in penury
詰者 *ku(i)tsu(me)mono* a tramp, a failure, a person out of work
14 厭 *ku(i)-a(kiru)* be fed up, have plenty
様 *ta(be)yō* manner of eating, way of eating, table manners
緊 *ku(i)-shiba(ru)* clench (teeth); compress (lips)
15 締 *ku(i)-shiba(ru)* grit one's teeth; staying by (a job)
慾 *shokuyoku* appetite
器 *shokki* tableware, dinner set
養生 *shokuyōjō* taking nourishment; diet therapy. *ku(i)yōjō* dietary care
潰 *ku(i)-tsubu(su)* sponge on. *ku(i)tsubu(shi)* parasite, hanger-on
潰者 *ku(i)tsubu(shi)mono* parasite, hanger-on
餌 *shokuji* food; feed
餌性 *shokujisei* dietary, dietetic
餌療法 *shokuji ryōhō* diet therapy
16 膳 *shokuzen* dining table
18 囓 *ku(i)-kaji(ru)* gnaw, nibble; have a smattering of knowledge
糧 *shokuryō* food, provisions, rations

糧事情 *shokuryō jijō* food situation
糧品 *shokuryōhin* foodstuffs, groceries
19 蟻獣 *arikui* anteater
20 競 *ta(bek)kura* eating contest
22 籠 *jikirō* lunch box; nest of boxes

2

B 飢 6675 / J3532 / M44023 KI. *u(eru)* be hungry, starve.
5 民 *kimin* starving people
6 色 *kishoku* starved look
死 *ueji(ni)* starving to death
10 疲 *u(e)-tsuka(reru)* be famished
11 渇 *kikatsu* hunger and thirst, starvation
12 寒 *kikan* hunger and cold
15 餓 *kiga* hunger, starvation, famine
餓同盟 *kiga dōmei* hunger strike
餓輸出 *kiga yushutsu* exporting at the expense of home consumers
20 饉 *kikin* famine

4

飫 6676 / J712c / M44050 YO become tired of; everyday food.

飩 6677 / J712b / M44047 DON, TON Japanese noodles.

飭 6678 / J522c / M44057 CHOKU arrange.

A 飯 6679 / J4853 / M44064' HAN cooked rice; food; meal. *meshi* cooked rice; meal; food, livelihood. *mamma, mama* cooked rice (a child's word). *ii* cooked grains.
5 台 *handai* dining table
6 米 *hammai* food; farmer's rice for his own consumption; rice for food (not for saké)
8 炊 *meshita(ki)* cooking rice
事 *mamagoto* (children) playing house
9 屋 *meshiya* eating house
前 *meshimae* before a meal; having not yet eaten
茶碗 *meshi chawan* rice bowl
10 時 *meshidoki* mealtime
11 粒 *meshitsubu* grain of boiled rice
盒 *hangō* mess tin, canteen
盛 *meshimo(ri)* maidservant at an inn
12 場 *hamba* worker's temporary quarters
18 櫃 *meshibitsu* cooked-rice tub; boiled-rice box

A 飲 6680 / J307b / M44063' 飮 6681 / J5d3b / M44063 IN drinking; feast. *no(mu)* drink, taste, take; swallow, devour; smoke; conceal (a weapon); accept (an idea); despise. *no(meru)* can drink; be good to drink; drinkable. *non(dakureru)* be dead drunk. *no(mikko)* drinking contest.
3 口 *no(mi)guchi* tap, faucet, spigot, bunghole. *no(mi)kuchi* taste, flavor
干 *no(mi)-ho(su)* drink up, drain (the cup)
下 *no(mi)-kuda(su)* swallow, gulp down
4 込 *no(mi)-ko(mu)* swallow, gulp down; understand
手 *no(mi)te* heavy drinker
止 *no(mi)-sa(su)* stop drinking; stop smoking
水 *no(mi)mizu* drinking water
友達 *no(mi) tomodachi* drinking companion
5 代 *no(mi)shiro* drink money
用 *in'yō* drinking
用水 *in'yōsui* drinking water
用噴水 *in'yō funsui* drinking fountain
6 回 *no(mi)-mawa(ru)* drink at a round of places. *no(mi)-mawa(su)* pass the cup around
尽 *no(mi)-tsu(kusu)* drink up; devour
仲間 *no(mi) nakama* drinking companion
7 抜 *no(mi)nu(ke)* drunkard
助 *no(mi)suke* tippler, drunkard
良 *no(mi)-yo(i)* good to drink
8 逃 *no(mi)ni(ge)* leaving drinks unpaid for
明 *no(mi)-a(kasu)* drink all night
物 *nomimono* beverage, drinks
直 *no(mi)-nao(su)* drink again
9 屋 *no(mi)ya* tavern, grogshop
食 *no(mi)ku(i), inshoku* food and drink, eating and drinking
食店 *inshokuten* restaurant
食物 *inshokubutsu* food and drink
10 倒 *no(mi)-tao(su)* leave drinks unpaid for
残 *no(mi)noko(ri)* dregs, leftover drinks

酒 *inshu* drinking saké
酒家 *inshuka* habitual drinker
料 *no(mi)ryō* drink money; drink reserved for oneself. *inryō* a drink, beverage
料水 *inryōsui* drinking water
11 過 *no(mi)-su(giru)* drink too much
掛 *no(mi)ka(ke)* (a cup) half-drunk; half-smoked (cigarette)
13 続 *no(mi)-tsuzu(keru)* keep on drinking
14 歌 *no(meya)uta(e)* merrymaking
15 潰 *no(mi)-tsubu(reru)* be dead drunk. *no(mi)-tsubu(su)* make (someone) drunk; drink up (a fortune)
16 薬 *no(mi)gusuri* an internal medicine
18 癖 *no(mi)guse* drinking habit
騒 *no(mi)sawa(gi)* revelry
20 競 *no(mi)kura(be)* drinking contest

5

飴 6682 / J303b / M44080 I. *ame* rice jelly, candy.
5 玉 *amedama* taffies, toffies
6 色 *ame iro* light brown, amber
7 売 *ameu(ri)* candy vendor, candy store
9 屋 *ameya* candy vendor, candy store
12 棒 *amembō* stick of candy

B **飾** 6683 / J3e7e / M44111' SHOKU. *kaza(ru)* ornament, decorate, adorn, embellish; exhibit; be ostentatious; whitewash. *kaza(ri)* adornment, decoration, ornament.
2 人形 *kaza(ri) ningyō* decorative doll; figurehead
5 立 *kaza(ri)-ta(teru)* adorn, dress up; play up. *kaza(ri)ta(te)* ornamentation, decoration
付 *kaza(ri)-tsu(keru)* decorate, arrange
6 気 *kaza(ri)ke* showing off, affectation
7 言 *shokugen* ornate writing
8 板 *kaza(ri)ita* plaque
物 *kaza(ri)mono* ornament, decoration; figurehead
9 屋 *kaza(ri)ya* jewelry worker
11 窓 *kaza(ri) mado* show window
12 棚 *kaza(ri)dana* display shelves
15 縁 *kaza(ri)buchi* molding
18 職 *kaza(ri)shoku* precious-metal worker

B **飽** 6684 / J4b30 / M44109' HŌ. *a(kiru), a(ku)* get tired of, lose interest in, have enough. *a(kasu) vt* satiate, surfeit; bore, tire, weary. *a(kumademo)* to the utmost, to the bitter end, persistently, strictly. *a(kunaki)* insatiable, rapacious. *a(kanu)* untiring, reluctant, unwilling, inseparable. *aki(ppoi)* fickle; soon tired of (something).
6 迄 *a(ku)made* to the bitter end, tenaciously, persistently, strictly, exceedingly
気味 *a(ki)gimi* weariness, being tired of
7 足 *a(ki)-ta(ranai)* be unsatisfying, be not content with. *a(ki)-ta(raseru)* eat to the full. *a(ki)-ta(riru)* be satisfied
8 性 *a(ki)shō* fickleness, flightiness
果 *a(ki)-ha(teru)* be tired of
和 *hōwa* saturation
和空気 *hōwa kūki* saturated air
和点 *hōwaten* saturation point
易 *a(ki)yasu(i)* fickle, soon tired of
9 食 *hōshoku* satiety; gluttony
食暖衣 *hōshoku-dan'i* well fed and well clad
12 満 *hōman* satiety
13 飽 *a(ki)a(ki) suru* be tired of, be bored with

A **飼** 6685 / J3b74 / M44107' SHI raising (animals). *ka(u)* raise, keep, feed.
4 手 *ka(i)te* (dog) owner
犬 *ka(i)inu* pet dog
5 付 *ka(i)tsu(ke)* feeding
主 *ka(i)nushi* (dog) owner; shepherd
7 兎 *ka(i)usagi* tame rabbit
8 育 *shiiku suru* breed, raise, rear, keep
育者 *shiikusha* breeder, fancier, raiser
9 草 *ka(i)gusa* hay
10 料 *shiryō* fodder, feed
殺 *ka(i)goro(shi)* caring for till death
畜 *shichiku* cattle raising
11 鳥 *ka(i)dori* poultry
桶 *ka(i)oke* manger
猫 *ka(i)neko* pet cat
12 葉 *ka(i)ba* fodder
葉桶 *ka(i)ba oke* feed tub, manger
13 馴 *ka(i)-na(rasu)* tame, domesticate
15 養 *shiyō* breeding, raising, keeping
17 藁 *ka(i)wara* fodder straw

6

餞 6686 / J-X / M44156 See **餞** 6700.

餉 6687 / J712e / M44140 SHŌ provisions; a meal; boiled rice. *karei, kareii* dried boiled rice.

餃 6688 / J712d / M44131 KŌ, GYŌ. *ame* candy.
3 子 *gyōza* gyoza, meat dumplings

餅 6689 / J4c5f / M44133 **餠** 6698 / J7136 / M44220 HEI. *mochi, mochii* rice cake.
6 肌 *mochihada* soft white skin
9 屋 *mochiya* rice-cake dealer
草 *mochigusa* a mugwort
13 搗 *mochitsu(ki)* making rice cake
14 網 *mochiami* rice-cake net
15 膚 *mochihada* soft white skin

餌 6690 / J3142 / M44146 JI food. *e, eba, esa* feed, food; bait, prey; tempting profit.
5 付 *ezu(ku)* (birds) begin to eat
9 食 *eba(mu)* feed. *ejiki* food, bait, prey, victim
10 料 *jiryō* feed, fodder, storage
差 *esa(shi)* birdcatching; birdcatcher
11 袋 *ebukuro* crop, craw, gizzard
12 壺 *etsubo* bird-feeding receptacle
13 飼 *ega(i)* feeding and raising animals. *eka(u)* hunt and eat; feed and raise animals

A **養** 6691 / J4d5c / M44144 YŌ. *yashina(u)* bring up, rear; adopt, foster; support; promote (health); cultivate, develop. *yashina(i)* nutrition, nurture; rearing; sustenance; manure.
3 女 *yōjo* adopted daughter; stepdaughter; daughter-in-law
子 *yashina(i)go* foster child. *yōshi* adopted son
子先 *yōshisaki* one's adopted home
子縁組 *yōshi engumi* adopting an heir
4 手 *yashina(i)te* supporter
分 *yōbun* nourishment, sustenance
毛剤 *yōmōzai* hair tonic
父 *yōfu* foster father
父母 *yōfubo* adopted parents
5 母 *yōbo* foster mother
兄 *yōkei* elder adopted brother
生 *yōjō* health care, hygiene; recuperation
生法 *yōjōhō* hygiene, sanitation, rules of health
生訓 *yōjōkun* hygiene, sanitation, rules of health
6 成 *yōsei* training, education
成所 *yōseijo* training school
成学校 *yosei gakko* training school
老 *yōrō* provision for the aged
老年金 *yōrō nenkin* endowment annuity, old-age pension
老金 *yōrōkin* old-age pension
老院 *yōrōin* old-folks home
老保険 *yōrō hoken* endowment insurance
老施設 *yōrō shisetsu* old folks' home
老資金 *yōrō shikin* old-age endowment
7 兵 *yōhei* feeding soldiers
兎 *yōto* rabbit raising
兎場 *yōtojō* rabbit warren
8 狐 *yōko* fox farming
育 *yōiku suru, yashina(i)-soda(teru)* bring up, rear; cultivate
育者 *yōikusha* guide, nurse, guardian
育院 *yōikuin* orphanage
育掛 *yōikugakari* guide, nurse, guardian
9 祖父 *yōsofu* foster grandfather
祖母 *yōsobo* foster grandmother
10 家 *yōka* adopted family
蚕 *yosan* silkworm culture
蚕地 *yosanchi* silk-raising district
蚕所 *yōsanjo* cocoonery
蚕室 *yōsanshitsu* silkworm nursery
蚕家 *yōsanka* silk raiser
蚕業 *yōsangyō* sericulture
蚕農家 *yōsan nōka* silk-raising farmer
11 豚 *yōton* hog raising, hogs
豚者 *yōtonsha* hog raiser, swineherd
豚場 *yōtonjō* hog farm
豚業 *yōtongyō* hog-raising industry
魚 *yōgyo* fish farming, fish breeding
魚池 *yōgyochi* fishpond, breeding pond
魚家 *yōgyoka* fish farmer, fish breeder
魚場 *yōgyojō* fish farm; fish hatchery
魚槽 *yōgyosō* fish tank
12 殖 *yōshoku* culture, raising, breeding
殖真珠 *yōshoku shinju* cultured pearl
13 嗣子 *yōshishi* adopted heir

蜂 *yōhō* beekeeping
蜂所 *yōhōjo* apiary
蜂舎 *yōhōsha* beehive stand
蜂家 *yōhōka* beekeeper
蜂植物 *yōhō shokubutsu* plants for bees
蜂園 *yōhōen* bee farm
蜂箱 *yōhōbako* beehive
16 親 *yōshin, yashina(i)oya* foster parents
樹園 *yōjuen* arboretum, tree nursery
19 鶏 *yōkei* poultry
鶏家 *yōkeika* poultryman
鶏場 *yōkeijō* poultry farm
鶏業 *yōkeigyō* poultry farming
20 護 *yōgo* protection, care
護学級 *yōgo gakkyū* class for handicapped children
護学校 *yōgo gakkō* school for handicapped children
護施設 *yōgo shisetsu* children's home
護教諭 *yōgo kyōyu* nurse-teacher

7

餝 6692 J7133 M44212 See **飾** 6683. Also, nonstandard for **飭** 6678.

餘 6693 J7131 M44185 See **余** 168.

餔 6694 J7130 M44173 Ho rice; a meal; eat; feed.

餒 6695 J712f M44163 Dai hunger; spoil.

餐 6696 J3b71 M44160 San eat; drink; swallow.

B **餓** 6697 J326e M44168' Ga. *u(eru), katsu(eru)* be hungry, starve, thirst. *himo(jii)* hungry.
6 死 *gashi, ueji(ni), katsu(e)ji(ni)* death from starvation
死者 *gashisha* people who starved to death
10 殺 *katsu(e)-koro(su)* starve (someone) to death
莩 *gahyō* person who has starved to death

鬼 *gaki* hungry ghost; urchin, brat, mischievous child
鬼道 *gakidō* (Buddhist) hell of hungry spirits

8

餅 6698 J7136 M44220 See **餠** 6689.

餤 6699 J7135 M44229 Tan advance; increase; eat; feed; dumpling.

餞 6700 J7134 M44214 Sen. *hanamuke* farewell gift.
7 別 *sembetsu* farewell gift

A **館** 6701 J345b M44237' **舘** 4923 J345c M30326 Kan mansion, large building, hall. *tachi* mansion; small castle; government housing. *tate* mansion, palace, fort. *yakata* mansion; temporary residence.
4 内 *kannai* in the building
8 長 *kanchō* superintendent of a building
10 員 *kan'in* personnel (of a public building)

餡 6702 J7132 M44224 An bean jam.
3 子 *anko* bean jam
11 掛 *anka(ke)* food topped with bean jam
15 餅 *ammochi* rice cake stuffed with bean jam

9

餮 6703 J7138 M44268 Tetsu devour, gobble.

餬 6704 J7137 M44255 Ko rice broth.
3 口 *kokō* bare existence, livelihood, living on others

10

饗 6705 J3642 M-X Nonstandard for **饗** 6715.

餽 6706 J7139 M44320 Ki, Gi give a gift; a gift.

餾 6707 J713a M44321 RYŪ steaming (rice).

饂 6708 J713b M44339 (国字) *udon* Japanese noodles.
13 飩 *udon* Japanese noodles
飩粉 *udonko* wheat flour
飩粉病 *udonkobyō* mildew

11

饉 6709 J713c M44366 KIN hunger.

饅 6710 J713d M44346 MAN bean-jam dumpling.
16 頭 *manjū* steamed rice-flour dumpling with bean-jam center
頭笠 *manjūgasa* round wicker hat

12

饋 6711 J713f M44382 KI, GI give a gift; a gift; offer; a meal, food.

饌 6712 J7142 M44386 SEN food; offering.

饐 6713 J713e M44396 I, EI. *su(eru)* go bad, turn sour

饒 6714 J7141 M44400 JŌ. NYŌ. *yutaka* abundant, rich, fruitful.
6 舌 *jōzetsu, nyōzetsu* talkativeness
舌家 *jōzetsuka* chatterbox

饗 6715 J-X M44431 饗 6705 J3642 M-X KYŌ banquet. *kyō(suru)* banquet, treat.
7 応 *kyōō* treat, feast, banquet
10 宴 *kyōen* banquet, dinner
13 筵 *kyōen* seats at a banquet

饑 6716 J7140 M44397 KI. *u(eru)* be hungry, starve, thirst. *himo(jii), hidaru(i)* hungry.
6 色 *kishoku* starved look
死 *uejini* death from starvation
11 渇 *kikatsu* hunger and thirst, starvation
12 寒 *kikan* hunger and cold
15 餓 *kiga* hunger, starvation
20 饉 *kikin* famine

13

饕 6717 J7143 M44426 TŌ covet, crave; scoundrel, villain.

14

饜 6718 J-X M44453 EN. *a(kiru)* be surfeited; be fed up with.

RAD. 首 185

Kubi neck. Nickname: Neck.

A 首 6719 J3c73 M44489 SHU head; neck; beginning, the first; poem and song counter. *kubi* neck, head. *kōbe* the head. *kubi ni suru* dismiss (someone). *kubi ni naru* be dismissed.
3 丈 *kubidake, kubi(t)take* up to the neck, ⌈complete devotion
4 引 *kubi(p)pi(ki)* tug of war using necks; constantly using reference books
切 *kubiki(ri)* decapitation, execution; dismissal
5 玉 *kubitama, kubi(t)tama* ancient necklace; neck bell (for animals); the neck; collar
功 *shukō* outstanding achievement
6 曲 *kubimaga(ri)* crooked neck; person with a crooked neck
吊 *kubitsu(ri)* hanging oneself
合点 *kubigatten* nodding assent, nodding agreement
7 足 *shusoku* head and feet; the whole body
位 *shui* first place, head position
陀羅 *sudara* sutra
尾 *shubi* issue, course (of events), arrangements, result; beginning and

end; head and tail; attitude; rendezvous
尾良 *shubiyo(ku)* successfully, smoothly
8 長 *shuchō* leader, chief, head. *kubi (o) naga(ku) suru* wait expectantly
固 *kubikata(me)* half nelson
府 *shufu* capital
肯 *shukō* assent, consent
実検 *kubi jikken* inspection of a severed head; identification of a suspect
9 飛 *kubi (ga) to(bu)* be beheaded
途 *kadode, shuto* departure
相 *shushō* prime minister
枷 *kubikase, kubikashi* pillory; encumbrance, ties
狩 *kubiga(ri)* headhunting
級 *shukyū* decapitated head
巻 *kubimaki* (neck) muffler
10 座 *shuza, shuso* seat of honor. *kubi(no)za* seat for decapitation
席 *shuseki* head seat, head, chief, president, governor, chair
振 *kubifu(ri)* gooseneck. *kubi (o) fu(ru)* shake the head in disagreement
根 *kubine(kko), kubi(no)ne* neck
将 *shushō* commander-in-chief
班 *shuhan* head position; prime minister
都 *shuto* capital
11 捻 *kubi (o) hine(ru)* disagree
桶 *kubioke* box for a severed head
斬 *kubikiri* decapitation, execution; dismissal
釣 *kubitsuri* hanging oneself
唱 *shushō* advocacy, promotion
唱者 *shushōsha* advocate, proponent
脳 *shunō* head, brains, leading spirit
脳者 *shunōsha* leader, head
脳部 *shunōbu* brain trust, leaders
12 筋 *kubisuji* nape of the neck
無 *kubina(shi)* headless
13 鼠 *shuso* sitting on the fence, vacillating
飾 *kubikaza(ri)* necklace
14 魁 *shukai* leader, ringleader
領 *shuryō* head, chief, boss, leader
導 *shudō* main leadership
15 輪 *kubiwa* necklace, collar
16 縊 *kubikuku(ri)* hanging oneself
謀 *shubō* planning; plotting; main planner, ringleader
謀者 *shubōsha* ringleader
18 題 *shudai* the first paragraph

2

馗 6720 / J7144 / M44492 KI cheekbone; road; hide, conceal.

8

馘 6721 / J7145 / M44507 KAKU, KYOKU behead; dismiss.
9 首 *kakushu suru* behead; dismiss

RAD. 香 186

Nioi odor or *kaori* fragrance. Nickname: Perfume.

B **香** 6722 / J3961 / M44518 KŌ incense, fragrance. *ka* smell, scent, odor; aroma, perfume, fragrance, flavor. *kao(ru)* smell, be fragrant. *kōba(shii), kamba(shii)* fragrant; balmy; favorable. *kao(ri)* fragrance, perfume, aroma, odor, scent, smell. *nioi* smell, odor, scent; stench; fragrance, aroma, perfume.
4 木 *kōboku* aromatic tree, scented wood
水 *kōsui* perfume
6 気 *kōki* fragrance, aroma, perfume
合 *kōgō* incense container. *kōa(wase)* incense-smelling game
7 花 *kōge* (Buddhist) flowers and incense
辛料 *kōshinryō* spices, seasoning
8 油 *kōyu* pomade, balm, perfumed oil
炉 *kōro* censer, incense burner
物 *kō(no)mono* pickled vegetables
味 *kōmi* flavor
味料 *kōmiryō* spices, seasoning
具 *kōgu* perfumes, perfumery, (nonreligious) incense set
具師 *kōgushi* perfumer. *yashi* showman, quack, charlatan
典 *kōden* condolence gift

典返 *kōdengae(shi)* return present for a condolence gift
9 香 *kōkō, kōko* pickles, pickled vegetables
柏 *kōhaku* cedars of Lebanon, Himalaya cedar
草 *kōsō* aromatic grasses
10 料 *kōryō* spices; perfumes; condolence gift
脂 *kōshi* hair oil
案 *kōan* incense table
華 *kōge* (Buddhist) flowers and incense
華院 *kōgein* family temple
11 魚 *kōgyo* fresh-water trout, sweet smelt
道 *kōdō* incense-smelling game
液 *kōeki* balsam, balm
盒 *kōgō* incense container
12 壺 *kōgo* perfume receptacle
奠 *kōden* condolence gift
奠返 *kōdengae(shi)* return present for a condolence gift
13 煙 *kōen* incense smoke
腺 *kōsen* scent gland
14 聞 *kōgi(ki)* perfume smelling
膏 *kōkō* balm, balsam
15 箱 *kōbako* incense box
16 壇 *kōdan* altar of incense
22 囊 *kōbukuro* incense bag

9

馥 6723 / J7146 / M44545 FUKU perfume, fragrance.
8 郁 *fukuiku(taru)* fragrant; balmy

11

馨 6724 / J333e / M44559 KEI. *kao(ru)* be fragrant. *kamba(shii), kōba(shii)* fragrant; balmy; favorable.

10-STROKE RADICALS

RAD. 馬 187

Uma horse. At left: *uma hen.* Nickname: Horse.

A 馬 6725 / J4/4t / M44572 ME, BA, MA horse. *uma* horse; horseflesh; stepladder.
2 丁 *batei* groom, footman, stableman
力 *bariki* horsepower; energy; cart, wagon
刀貝 *mategai* jackknife clam, razor clam
3 子 *mago* pack-horse driver
上 *bajō* horseback, mounted
小屋 *umagoya* horse barn
4 手 *mete* right hand, right side
方 *umakata* pack-horse driver, wagon driver
匹 *bahitsu* horses
引 *umahi(ki)* pack-horse driver, wagon driver
5 皮 *bahi, umagawa* horsehide
市 *uma ichi* horse market
6 肉 *baniku* horse meat
返 *umagae(shi)* the place on the mountain where the horses return
印 *umajirushi* (ancient) commander's standard
耳東風 *baji-tōfū* utter indifference
7 足 *uma (no) ashi* human horse; poor actor
身 *bashin* horse length
車 *basha* carriage, coach; cart, wagon
車鉄道 *basha tetsudo* horse tramway
尾毛 *basu* horsehair
尾藻 *hondawara* a kind of seaweed
8 追 *umao(i)* horse driver
肥 *umagoyashi* horse manure
学 *bagaku* hippology
券 *baken* pari-mutuel ticket
券税 *bakenzei* pari-mutuel tax
具 *bagu* harness, saddlery
具屋 *baguya* saddler; saddlery
具師 *bagushi* saddler; saddlery
9 面 *umazura* horse's face; long face
革 *bakaku* horsehide
食 *bashoku* eating like a horse
首 *bashu* a horse's head
屋 *umaya* stable, barn
持 *umamo(chi)* horse owner; horse renter; horse user

10 【馬】 骨高髟門鬯鬲鬼

2 蛀 *umaabu* horsefly
政 *basei* legislation and administration of equestrian affairs
乗 *umano(ri)* horse riding; horseman; astraddle
草 *magusa* hay, fodder, feed
10 骨 *uma (no) hone* person of doubtful origin, a nondescript
耕 *bakō* cultivation with a horse
陸 *yasude* millipede
栗 *umaguri* horse chestnut
11 術 *bajutsu* horsemanship
脚 *bakyaku* horse's legs; true character. *uma (no) ashi* human horse; poor actor
脚露 *bakyaku (o) arawa(su)* reveal a secret
鹿 *baka* dunce, fool; folly, farce, nonsense; benumbed; dull. *baka(geta)* foolish. *baka ni* extremely. *baka(rashii)* foolish, ridiculous
鹿力 *bakajikara* brute force, great strength
鹿丁寧 *baka-teinei* excessively polite
鹿 正直 *baka-shōjiki* simple honesty, foolishly honest, credulity
鹿加減 *baka(sa)-kagen* the extent of one's stupidity
鹿安 *bakayasu(i)* ridiculously cheap
鹿見 *baka (o) mi(ru)* meet an unfortunate experience
鹿声 *bakagoe* wild yell
鹿呼 *bakayo(bawari)* calling (someone) a fool
鹿者 *bakamono* fool
鹿面 *bakazura* foolish face, vacant look, stupid look
鹿臭 *bakakusa(i)* foolish, absurd
鹿高 *bakadaka(i)* ridiculously high
鹿値 *bakane* ridiculous price
鹿笑 *bakawara(i)* horselaugh
鹿馬鹿 *bakabaka(shii)* silly, absurd
鹿遊 *bakaaso(bi)* spree, riotous pleasure
鹿野郎 *bakayarō* fool, simpleton, idiot
鹿強情 *baka-gōjō* pigheadedness, irrational obstinacy
鹿揃 *bakazoroi* a lot of foolishness
鹿景気 *bakageiki* market boom
鹿話 *bakabanashi* idle talk, silly talk
鹿慇懃 *baka-ingin* excessive politeness
鹿騒 *baka-sawa(gi)* spree, uproarious gaiety
鹿囃子 *bakabayashi* festival music; Japanese jazz band
12 喰 *bakurō* horse trader
場 *baba* riding ground, racecourse
13 賊 *bazoku* mounted bandits
跳 *umato(bi)* leapfrog
飼 *umaka(i)* raising horses
鈴薯 *bareisho* Irish potato, white potato
14 銜 *hami* horse's bit
15 槽 *umabune* manger
16 橇 *basori* horse sleigh
頭 *batō* a horse's head; on a horse
蹄 *batei* horse's hoof
蹄石 *bateiseki* obsidian
蹄形 *bateikei* horseshoe shape
蹄磁石 *batei jishaku* horseshoe magnet
17 鍬 *manga, maguwa* harrow, rake
齢 *barei* one's age (humble), insignificant years
糞 *bafun, maguso* horse manure
糞紙 *bafunshi* strawboard, millboard
18 糧 *baryō* fodder
顔 *umagao* extremely long face
19 櫛 *umagushi* currycomb
蠅 *umabae* horsefly
20 籍 *baseki* horse registration

2

馮 6726 / J7148 / M44579 Hyō, Byō (a horse) run fast; despise, disdain; rely on.

馭 6727 / J7147 / M44576 Gyo driving (a horse).

8 法 *gyohō* horsemanship
者 *gyosha* driver, coachman, bus driver

3

駄 6728 / J-X / M44589 See **駄** 6734.

馴 6729 / J466b / M44595 Jun. *na(reru)* get used to, become experienced; be tamed; get too familiar, mature. *na(rasu)* tame, charm (snakes); train, exercise, drill; habituate, accustom to. *nara(u)* experience; become a habit. *na(re)* practice, habit, skill, experience. *na(rekko)* being used to.

4 化 *junka suru* acclimate

6 合 *na(re)-a(u)* conspire with, be intimate. *narea(i)* collusion, conspiracy; illicit intercourse
7 初 *nareso(me)* beginning of a romance. *na(re)-so(meru)* become intimate.
良 *junryō* docile and good
8 育 *jun'iku* taming, domesticating
9 染 *naji(mu)* become familiar with. *najimi* intimacy; friend
10 致 *junchi suru* tame, domesticate; pave the way for
11 鹿 *junroku, tonakai* reindeer
13 馴 *na(re)na(reshii)* familiar, too free, unceremonious
15 養 *jun'yō suru* tame, domesticate

馳 6730 / J435a / M44593 CHI. *ha(seru)* run, gallop; sail; drive (a wagon); win (fame); dispatch.
3 下 *ha(se)-kuda(ru)* run downhill; run out of the metropolis
6 回 *ha(se)-mawa(ru)* run around, jump about, gallop around
向 *ha(se)-muka(u)* ride off in a hurry
7 走 *chisō* treat, banquet, entertainment, feast, dinner; hospitality; good things
8 参 *ha(se)-san(zuru)* hurry to └to eat
11 掛 *ha(se)-ka(keru), ha(se)-ka(karu)* gallop
12 越 *ha(se)-ko(eru)* jump over (on a horse); ride past
散 *ha(se)-chi(rasu)* ride into and disperse (the enemy)
着 *ha(se)-tsu(keru)* come riding at top speed
集 *ha(se)-atsu(maru)* ride or run together to, flock to, rally around
14 駆 *chiku suru* ride fast, run around, play an active part
15 還 *ha(se)-kae(ru)* return running

4

馿 6731 / J-X / M44616 See **驢** 6778.

馼 6732 / J7149 / M44610 BUN, MON a zebra with a red mane and golden eyes.

駁 6733 / J477d / M44619 HAKU, BAKU refutation, contradiction. *buchi* spots, specks, patches.
14 説 *bakusetsu* refutation
15 論 *bakuron* refutation, rebuttal
撃 *bakugeki* refutation, contradiction, attack

B **駄** 6734 / J424c / M44633 **馱** 6728 / J-X / M44589 TA, DA horse load; pack horse; sending by horses.
4 文 *dabun* poor piece of writing
5 目 *dame* useless; impossible; ruined; unsuccessful, hopeless; must not
句 *daku(ru)* write doggerel. *daku* doggerel, poor poem
弁 *dabe(ru)* jabber, chatter, chat with. *daben* foolish talk
7 作 *dasaku* poor piece of writing
8 物 *damono* low-grade goods, trash
法螺 *dabora* bragging, fish story
9 洒落 *dajare* poor joke
10 馬 *daba* draft horse, pack horse; poor horse
荷 *dani* horse load
11 菓子 *dagashi* cheap sweets
13 賃 *dachin* carriage or horse charge; reward, tip
14 駄 *dada* fretfulness, disobedience
駄子 *dada(k)ko* stubborn child, spoiled child
駄児 *dada(k)ko* stubborn child, spoiled child
駄捏 *dada (o) ko(neru)* fret, talk peevishly, ask for the impossible

A **駅** 6735 / J3158 / M44633' **驛** 6775 / J7167 / M15030 EKI post town; stage; station.
4 手 *ekishu* station hand, baggage handler
止 *ekido(me)* station delivery
夫 *ekifu* railway porter, railway employee
5 弁 *ekiben* station lunch
6 伝 *ekiden* stagecoach, post horse; cross-country relay race
伝競走 *ekiden kyōsō* cross-country race
8 長 *ekichō* stationmaster
舎 *ekisha* station building
9 逓 *ekitei* postal service
前 *ekimae* in front of the station
10 員 *ekiin* station employee, station staff
馬 *ekima, ekiba* post horse
馬車 *ekibasha* stagecoach

[12] 渡 *ekiwata(shi)* station delivery
程 *ekitei* distance between stations
[13] 路 *ekiro, umayaji* post road
勢 *ekisei* traffic volume
[16] 頭 *ekitō* station; front of the station

B 駆 6736 J366e M44634 驅 6768 J715c M44968 KU. *ka(keru)* run, gallop; advance. *ka(ru)* drive (a car); spur on, prompt, actuate, inspire, sway, impel. *ka(rareru)* be carried away by, be actuated by. *ka(kezuru)* run around, bustle around. *ka(kekko), ka(kekkura), ka(kekura)* foot race.

[2] 入 *ka(ke)-i(ru)* gallop in on a horse
[3] 下 *ka(ke)-o(riru) ka(ke)-kuda(ru)* run downhill
上 *ka(ke)-a(garu)* run up, dash up
[4] 比 *ka(ke)kura(be)* foot race
込 *ka(ke)-ko(mi)* dash into, seek refuge in, run into
引 *ka(ke)hi(ki)* bargaining, maneuvering; advancing and retreating; dickering
[5] 立 *ka(ke)-ta(tsu)* run, gallop; chase (the enemy). *ka(ri)-ta(teru)* drive, round up; spur on, stir up, chase away
巡 *ka(ke)-megu(ru)* run around, bustle around
付 *ka(ke)-tsu(keru)* hurry to (the place)
出 *ka(ke)-da(su)* run out, start running. *ka(ri)-da(su)* chase away. *kakeda(shi)* beginner; amateur
[6] 回 *ka(ke)-mawa(ru), ka(kezuri)-mawa(ru)* bustle about, run around
合 *ka(ke)-a(wasu)* fight on horseback
虫 *kuchū* deworming
虫剤 *kuchūzai* insecticide, vermicide
虫薬 *kuchūyaku* insecticide, vermicide
[7] 足 *ka(ke)ashi* running fast, double time
抜 *ka(ke)-nu(keru)* run through (a gate)
[8] 使 *kushi suru* order around; use freely
並 *ka(ke)-nara(bu)* gallop abreast
[9] 通 *ka(ke)-tō(ru)* run through. *ka(ke)dō(shi)* riding through, riding on without resting
降 *ka(ke)-o(riru)* come running down
逐 *kuchiku* expulsion, extermination
逐艦 *kuchikukan* destroyer
除 *kujo* extermination, destruction
除剤 *kujozai* insecticide, expellent
[10] 悩 *ka(ke)-naya(masu)* ride into the midst of the enemy and disconcert him
破 *ka(ke)-yabu(ru)* break up with cavalry charge
[11] 寄 *ka(ke)-yo(ru)* ride up (on horseback). *ka(ke)-yo(seru)* come running up
動 *kudō* driving (force)
動装置 *kudō sōchi* running gear
[12] 越 *ka(ke)-ko(su)* run all the way; outdistance
場 *ka(ke)ba* riding grounds
散 *ka(ke)-chi(rasu)* scatter a crowd (on horseback)
落 *kakeo(chi)* defeat and flight; disappearance without a trace; elopement
集 *ka(ri)-atsu(meru)* mobilize, round up
[13] 馳 *kuchi suru* drive swiftly; bustle around
塞 *ka(ke)-fusa(garu)* ride up and block the way
[15] 潜艇 *kusentei* subchaser
[23] 黴 *kubai* antisyphilis
黴法 *kubaihō* venereal disease prevention law
黴薬 *kubaiyaku* antisyphilitic medicine

5

駟 6737 J714a M44683 SHI four horses; four-horse carriage.

駛 6738 J714b M44679 SHI. *ha(seru)* run fast.

駘 6739 J714d M44675 TAI stupid.
[15] 蕩 *taitō(taru)* calm, serene, mild, genial

駝 6740 J714c M44681 DA hunchback; (an animal) load.
[11] 鳥 *dachō* ostrich

駑 6741 J714e M44661 DO slow horse; a foolish fellow.
[10] 馬 *doba* worn-out horse
[12] 鈍 *dodon* dumb and lazy

駒 6742 J3670 M44663 KU. *koma* horse; colt, pony; chessman; frame (of a film); bridge (of a violin).
[3] 下駄 *komageta* low geta
[11] 鳥 *komadori* robin

駕 6743 / J326f / M44667 KA, GA vehicle. *kago* palanquin, litter. *ga(suru)* hitch up an animal.

22 籠 *kago* palanquin, litter
籠屋 *kagoya* palanquin carriers
籠舁 *kagoka(ki)* palanquin bearer
籠脇 *kagowaki* palanquin bearer; the side of the palanquin

駈 6744 / J366f / M44636 KU. *ka(keru)* run, gallop, advance. *ka(ru)* drive, urge on; prompt; inspire.

4 手 *ka(ke)te* runner
引 *ka(ke)hi(ki)* bargaining; maneuvering
5 出 *ka(ke)da(shi)* start; novice
6 回 *ka(ke)-mawa(ru)* run around, ride around; hurry about, campaign
7 足 *ka(ke)ashi* running fast, double quick
抜 *ka(ke)-nu(ku)* run all the way, outdistance
12 登 *ka(ke)-nobo(ru)* run up
落 *kakeo(chi)* elopement; running away

B **駐** 6745 / J4373 / M44660 CHŪ. *todo(maru)* stop; reside in. *chū-* resident in.

4 支 *chū-Shi* resident in China
日 *chū-Nichi* resident in Japan
仏 *chū-Futsu* resident in France
屯 *chūton* stationing (troops), occupation
6 米 *chū-Bei* resident in America
在 *chūzai* residence, stay
在所 *chūzaisho* police substation
7 兵 *chūhei* stationing troops; garrison
車 *chūsha* parking
車場 *chūshajō* parking area
8 英 *chū-Ei* resident in England
9 独 *chū-Doku* resident in Germany
軍 *chūgun* stationing an army
10 留 *chūryū* retention, stationing (of troops)
留軍 *chūryūgun* army of occupation
11 剳 *chūsatsu* ambassador's residence abroad
12 営 *chūei* encampment
14 箚 *chūsatsu* resident at
15 輦 *chūren* stopping of the imperial carriage
輪場 *chūrinjō* public parking area for bicycles
19 蘇 *chū-So* resident in Soviet Russia

6

馴 6746 / J7152 / M-X JUN.

駮 6747 / J7150 / M44726 HAKU. *buchi* spots, specks, patches.

駢 6748 / J7158 / M44696 **騈** 6755 / J-X / M44795 HEN two-horse carriage.

21 儷体 *benreitai* euphemism; ornate style

駱 6749 / J7151 / M44734 RAKU white horse.

15 駝 *rakuda* camel

駭 6750 / J714f / M44725 GAI. *odoro(ku)* be surprised; be frightened.

12 然 *gaizen to* in surprise, in alarm

7

騁 6751 / J7155 / M44778 TEI. *ha(seru)* run (a horse); do as one pleases; develop, expand, extend.

駸 6752 / J7154 / M44759 SHIN speed; horses running.

17 駸 *shinshin to* rapidly, with rapid strides

駻 6753 / J7153 / M44767 KAN rage, run wild.

10 馬 *kumba* unruly horse, bronco

駿 6754 / J3d59 / M44775 SHUN a good horse; speed; a fast person.

3 才 *shunsai* talented person, genius, prodigy
7 足 *shunsoku* swift horse; talented person
10 馬 *shumme, shumba* swift horse
逸 *shun'itsu* swift horse

8

騈 6755 / J-X / M44795 See **駢** 6748.

騅 6756 / J7157 / M44788 SUI. *ashige* grey (horse); dappled-grey horse.

騏 6757 / J7156 / M44818 Ki fast horse.
23 麟 *kirin* fabulous mythical horse; talent

A **験** 6758 / J3833 / M44835 **騐** 6759 / J-X / M44821 **驗** 6776 / J7164 / M45024
Ken effect; testing. Gen beneficial effect (of austerities). *tame(su), ken(suru)* test, attempt. *shirushi* sign, indication, omen.
14 算 *kenzan* verification of accounts, checking figures

B **騒** 6760 / J417b / M44834' **騷** 6764 / J715b / M44935 Sō. *sawa(gu)* make a noise, be boisterous, shout, clamor; raise an uproar; be excited, be agitated; bustle around; make a fuss about; make merry, go on a spree. *sawa(gaseru)* disturb, trouble, agitate, excite, create a sensation. *sawa(gareru)* be made much of. *zawame(ku), zawatsu(ku)* be noisy, be boisterous. *zome(ku), some(ku)* be noisy. *sawa(gashii)* noisy, boisterous; tumultuous, troubled, agitated. *sawa(gi)* noise, uproar; turmoil, trouble, agitation; fuss, ado; affair; dispute; excitement; sensation; merrymaking, spree.
2 人 *sōjin* literary person, poet
5 立 *sawa(gi)-ta(tsu)* be agitated, be stirred up. *sawa(gi)-ta(teru)* make an uproar, make a fuss, make an outcry, raise an alarm
出 *sawa(gi)-da(su)* begin to riot, start tearing around
7 乱 *sōran* commotion, riot
声 *sawa(gi)goe* tumult, outcry
9 音 *sōon* noise, cacophony
11 動 *sōdō* disturbance, strife, riot, rebellion
12 然 *sōzen(taru)* noisy, confused, uproarious
18 騒 *sōzō(shii), zawazawa(toshita)* noisy, boisterous, turbulent
擾 *sōjō* disturbance, commotion, riot
擾罪 *sōjōzai* crime of sedition

B **騎** 6761 / J3533 / M44817 Ki riding on horses; counter for horsemen.
3 士 *kishi* horseman, equestrian, knight
士道 *kishidō* knighthood, chivalry
4 手 *kishu* rider, horseman, jockey
6 行 *kikō* horseback riding
7 兵 *kihei* cavalry, cavalryman, horseman
兵隊 *kiheitai* cavalry
8 虎 *kiko* riding on a tiger
虎勢 *kiko (no) ikio(i) de* by force of circumstances
9 乗 *kijō no* mounted, on horseback
10 従 *kijū* following on a horse; the following rider
射 *kisha* equestrian archery
砲兵 *kihōhei* horse artillery
馬 *kiba* riding on a horse; the rider
馬巡査 *kiba junsa* mounted police
馬武者 *kiba musha* mounted samurai
馬戦 *kibasen* cavalry battle
14 銃 *kijū* carbine

9

驒 6762 / J424d / M-X Dan. Da. dappled horse; white horse with black mane.

騙 6763 / J7159 / M44849 Hen. *dama(su)* deceive, cheat, defraud; bewitch; delude; soothe; calm. *dama(kasu), tabura(kasu)* deceive, cheat, defraud; bewitch; delude. *kata(ru)* swindle, defraud; assume (another's name). *kata(ri)* fraud, swindle; imposter, swindler.
4 込 *dama(shi)-ko(mu)* deceive, cheat, defraud, take in
6 合 *damashia(i)* cheating each other
8 取 *henshu* swindling, defrauding
取者 *henshusha* swindler
10 討 *dama(shi)u(chi)* surprise attack, foul play

10

騷 6764 / J715b / M44935 See **騒** 6760.

騫 6765 / J715a / M44894 Ken break off; error; extract; flippant.

驀 6766 / J715e / M44949 Baku going straight forward; crossing over.
6 地 *masshigura* straight
10 進 *bakushin* dash, rush
12 然 *bakuzen to* dashingly

B騰 6767 / J462d / M44915' Tō rising; price rise. a(gari) advancing, going up.
[8] 奔 tōhon running and jumping; jumping of prices
[9] 降 tōkō rising and falling (prices)
[12] 落 tōraku fluctuations
貴 tōki rise (in prices)
[13] 勢 tōsei rising trend in prices

11

驅 6768 / J715c / M44968 See 駆 6736.

驂 6769 / J715d / M44965 San add an extra horse to the team; an extra horse; an extra driver.

驃 6770 / J715f / M44966 Hyō, Byō a light brown horse with some white hair; run fast; brave

騾 6771 / J7160 / M44957 Ra mule.
[10] 馬 raba mule

12

驍 6772 / J7162 / M44986 Gyō strong; good horse.
[6] 名 gyomei military fame, fame for bravery
[8] 武 gyōbu strong and brave
[9] 勇 gyōyū bravery, valor
[10] 将 gyōshō valiant general, veteran general; a leader

驕 6773 / J7161 / M45008 Kyō. ogo(ru) be proud or haughty. ogo(ri) pride, haughtiness.
[6] 気 kyōki pride
[7] 兵 kyōhei triumphant soldier; boastful soldier
児 kyōji spoiled child
[10] 恣 kyōshi being proud and self-willed
振舞 ogo(ri)-furuma(u) carry on proudly
[12] 奢 kyōsha luxury, extravagance
肆 kyōshi being proud and self-willed
[14] 慢 kyōman pride, arrogance
[15] 横 kyōō pride and stubbornness

B驚 6774 / J3643 / M45013' Kyō. Kei. odoro(ku) be surprised; be frightened, be taken aback; be appalled; be amazed. odoro(kasu) surprise; frighten; create a stir. odoro(kubeki) amazing, surprising, wonderful.
[2] 入 odoro(ki)-i(ru) be filled with amazement
[4] 天動地 kyōten-dōchi world-shaking, astounding, tremendous
[7] 呆 odoro(ki)-aki(reru) be appalled
[8] 怪 odoro(ki)-aya(shimu) marvel
怖 kyōfu fear and surprise
[10] 倒 kyōtō astonishment
破 suwa(ya), suwa exclamation of sudden surprise
[11] 異 kyōi wonder, miracle
異的 kyōiteki wonderful, phenomenal
[12] 慌 odoro(ki)-awa(teru) be surprised and excited
愕 keigaku, kyōgaku surprise, fright, shock
程 odoro(ku) hodo surprisingly, wonderfully
喜 kyōki pleasant surprise
[13] 嘆 kyōtan wonder, admiration
[16] 駭 odoro(ki)-sawa(gu) be surprised and excited. kyōgai surprise, fright
[18] 騒 odoro(ki)-sawa(gu) be surprised and excited

13

驛 6775 / J7163 / M45030 See 駅 6735.

驗 6776 / J7164 / M45024 See 験 6758.

14

驟 6777 / J7165 / M45048 Shū run; suddenly.
[8] 雨 shūu (sudden) shower
[12] 然 shūzen toshite suddenly

16

驢 6778 / J7166 / M45069 駍 6731 / J-X / M44616 Ro donkey.
[10] 馬 roba donkey

驥 6779/J7167/M45076 KI fast horse; talent.

7足 *kisoku* full ability

17

驤 6780/J7168/M45075 JŌ, SHŌ raise, raise head; jump, leap; run.

驩 6781/J7169/M45086 KAN greetings, courtesies.

19

驪 6782/J716b/M45090 RI, REI a jet-black horse; black; set side by side.

20

驫 6783/J716a/M45094 HYŪ, HYŌ, SHŌ many horses.

RAD. 骨 188

Hone bone. At left: *hone hen.* Nickname: Bone.

A 骨 6784/J397c/M45098 KOTSU bone; remains; knack. *hone* bone; skeleton; frame; rib (of an umbrella); grit, backbone; effort, pains.

3子 *kosshi* bones; marrow; essentials, gist
4片 *koppen* pieces of bone
化 *kokka* ossification
太 *honebuto na* large-boned
6肉 *kotsuniku* one's own flesh and blood; flesh and blood
肉腫 *kotsunikushu* osteosarcoma
灰 *kotsubai, kokkai* bone ashes
休 *honeyasu(mi), honeyasu(me)* relaxation, recreation
7材 *kotsuzai* aggregate
身 *honemi* flesh and bones, marrow
折 *honeo(ru)* take pains, exert oneself. *kossetsu* broken bone, bone fracture. *honeo(ri)* pains, exertion. *hone (ga) ore(ru)* be difficult
折損 *honeo(ri)zon* wasted effort
抜 *honenu(ki) no* boned; mutilated; watered down
抜外交 *honenu(ki) gaikō* spineless diplomacy
8法 *koppō* frame, a person's build; good manners; nice technique
肥 *koppi* bone fertilizer
9拾 *kotsuhiro(i)* gathering the ashes (of the deceased)
柄 *kotsugara* build, physique, personal appearance
炭 *kottan* bone charcoal
相 *kossō* physique, features
相学 *kossōgaku* phrenology
10格 *kokkaku* physique, build, frame
粉 *koppun* bone meal, bone dust
11張 *honeba(ru)* get thin. *honeba(tta)* thin, bony. *kotchō* height (of foolishness); Number One
惜 *honeo(shimi)* sparing oneself, laziness
接 *honetsu(gi)* bone setting; bone setter
粗鬆症 *kotsusoshōshō* osteoporosis
細胞 *kotsusaibō* bone cells
瓶 *honegame* cinerary urn
頂 *kotchō* height (of foolishness); Number One
軟化症 *kotsu nankashō* softening of the bones
組 *honegu(mi)* skeleton; framework
組織 *kotsusoshiki* bony tissue
12揚 *kotsua(ge)* gathering the ashes (of the deceased)
牌 *karuta* playing cards. *koppai* bone chessmen
結核 *kotsu kekkaku* tuberculosis of the bones
壺 *kotsutsubo* mortuary urn
無 *honena(shi)* rickets; spineless person; an invertebrate
董 *kottō* curios, antiques
董品 *kottōhin* curios, antiques
13節 *kossetsu, honebushi* joint. *hone(p)pushi* joint; strong character, spirit
幹 *kokkan* physique, build, frame
14関節 *kokkansetsu* bone joint
膜 *kotsumaku* the periosteum
膜炎 *kotsumakuen* periostitis
15箱 *kotsubako* cinerary box; box for cinerary urn

盤 *kotsuban* pelvis; pelvic bone
質 *kosshitsu* bony tissue
16 骼 *kokkaku* physique, build, frame
17 癌 *kotsugan* bone cancer
18 甕 *honegame* cinerary urn
髄 *kotsuzui* marrow; true spirit
髄炎 *kotsuzuien* osteomyelitis
髄移植 *kotsuzui ishoku* bone marrow transplant

3

骭 6785 / J716c / M45111 KAN shinbone, tibia; leg.

4

骰 6786 / J716d / M45127 TŌ. *sai* dice, bones.
3 子 *saikoro, sai* dice
子入 *saikoroi(re)* dice box

5

骶 6787 / J-X / M45155 TEI backbone; hips.

6

骼 6788 / J716e / M45175 KAKU bleached bones.

骸 6789 / J333c / M45164 GAI bone, body. *mukuro* body; corpse.
9 炭 *gaitan* coke
10 骨 *gaikotsu* skeleton
骨乞 *gaikotsu (o) ko(u)* request to resign

8

髀 6790 / J716f / M45205 HI thigh.
6 肉嘆 *hiniku (no) tan* determination to act in the face of frustration

B 髄 6791 / J3f71 / M45240' 髓 6793 / J7172 / M45289 ZUI marrow, pith.
6 虫 *zuimushi* rice borer, pearl moth

11

髏 6792 / J7170 / M45267 RO skull.

12

髓 6793 / J7172 / M45289 See 髄 6791.

13

體 6794 / J7173 / M45291 See 体 165.

髑 6795 / J7171 / M45281 DOKU skull.
21 髏 *dokuro, sharekōbe, sharikōbe, sarekōbe* skull, cranium

10 馬 骨 【高】 髟 門 鬯 鬲 鬼

RAD. 高 189

Takai high. Variant: 髙 (11 strokes). Nickname: High.

A 高 6796 / J3962 / M45313 髙 6797 / J-X / M45314 KŌ high. *taka(i)* high, tall, lofty, raised, elevated, eminent; exalted, noble; loud, stentorian; expensive; widely known. *taka* quantity, volume, amount, sum; rise (in prices); high; fief. *taka(maru)* rise; swell; be elevated, be promoted; increase. *taka(meru)* raise, lift, promote, elevate; improve, enhance; ennoble; heighten; boost. *taka(buru)* be proud, be arrogant; be high. *taka(mi)* height, eminence. *taka(raka ni)* loudly. *(o)taka(ku)* proudly (in a bad sense). *taka(ga)* only, merely, at best, after all. *kō(jiru), kō(zuru)* increase; be proud.
2 人 *kōnin, kōjin* person of high rank; person of noble character
3 士 *kōshi* high-minded person
大 *kōdai na* grand, sublime, excellent; large and tall
上 *takaa(gari)* expensive; occupying a place of honor (at a banquet)

下 *kōge* rise and fall, fluctuations; rank, grade, quality
下駄 *takageta* high geta
山 *kōzan* high mountain, lofty peak
山病 *kōzambyō* mountain sickness
山動物 *kōzan dōbutsu* alpine fauna
山植物 *kōzan shokubutsu* alpine flora
4 木 *takagi, kōboku* tall tree, large tree
止 *taka(ku) to(maru)* be proud
天原 *Takamagahara, Takama(no)hara* the heavens, the abode of the gods
水準 *kōsuijun* high level
手 *takate* upper arm
手小手 *takate-kote* tying (someone's) hands behind the back
5 処 *takami* high place
札 *kōsatsu* placard; bulletin board; highest bid
丘 *kōkyū* high hill
台 *kōdai* tall tower, tall building. *takadai* eminence, high ground, hill
目 *takame no* high (baseball)
目内角球 *takame naikakkyū* high inside
目外角球 *takame gaikakkyū* high outside
圧 *kōatsu* high tension, high voltage; high handedness
圧電流 *kōatsu denryū* high current of electricity
圧線 *kōatsu densen* high-tension line
圧釜 *kōatsugama* high-pressure kiln; pressure cooker
6 次 *kōji* the higher powers (of a number); high standards
地 *kōchi* high ground, plateau, heights
名 *kōmyō* reknown, fame; your name. *kōmei* fame, good reputation
血圧 *kōketsuatsu* high blood pressure
気圧 *kōkiatsu* high atmospheric pressure
気圧病 *kōkiatsubyō* the bends
年 *kōnen* old people; old age
年者 *kōnensha* elderly person
7 見 *kōken* your opinion; excellent idea
言 *kōgen* boastful speech; excellent speech
庇 *kōhi* the shadow of a high tree or building; your favor
吠 *takabo(e)* loud barking
吟 *kōgin* reciting a poem; your poem
坏 *takatsuki* (ancient) serving table
批 *kōhi* your esteemed criticism
材 *kōsai* outstanding talent; talented person; a large, splendid physique
弟 *kōtei* best student; senior disciple
志 *kōshi* kind intention, kindness, favor, good wishes
声 *kōsei, kōjō* loud voice, high voice, loud talking
寿 *kōju* advanced age
角 *kōkaku* high angle, verticle angle, altitude
角砲 *kōkakuhō* high-angle gun, antiaircraft gun
低 *kōtei, takahiku* unevenness, undulations; fluctuations; modulation; height; pitch
低差 *kōteisa* difference in altitude
位 *kōi* honors, high rank
位高官 *kōi kōkan* dignitaries
足 *kōsoku* the outstanding disciple, best student. *takaashi* stilts
足駄 *takaashida* high geta
足蟹 *takaashigani* giant spider crab
利 *kōri* high interest
利金 *kōrikin* high-interest money
利貸 *kōriga(shi)* usury; usurer
8 所 *kōsho* elevation, height; altitude; long view (of things). *taka(ki) tokoro* high places (in ancient Palestinian paganism)
明 *kōmei na* noble and well-versed
枕 *takamakura* high pillow. *takamakura de* peacefully (sleeping)
炉 *kōro* blast furnace
知 *taka (ga) shi(reru)* be insignificant
臥 *kōga suru* live in proud seclusion (from the world)
岳 *kōgaku* high mountain
官 *kōkan* high office; high official, dignitary
尚 *kōshō na* high noble, refined, advanced
空 *kōkū* high altitude. *takazora* clear sky
学年 *kōgakunen* upper grades in school
周波 *kōshūha* high frequency
物価 *kōbukka* high prices
性能 *kōseinō* high (explosives); high efficiency; high fidelity
価 *kōka* high price
価品 *kōkahin* valuables, costly articles

[9] 風 *kōfū* nobel mien; noble character
屋 *kōoku, taka(ki)ya* tall house; your house
度 *kōdo* altitude, height; high degree; high power; intense; advanced (stage)
度計 *kōdokei* altimeter
括 *taka (o) kuku(ru)* belittle, disparage
相 *kōsō* noble looks
飛 *takato(bi)* high jump; dancing and jumping; abscondence; flying high; skipping the country.
飛車 *takabisha na* highhanded
音 *takane, kōon* high tone; high key; loud sound
音部記号 *kōombu kigō* treble clef
砂 *Takasago* Formosa; Taiwan
砂族 *Takasagozoku* Taiwanese natives
点 *kōten* high score
点者 *kōtensha* persons with the highest scores or votes
架 *kōka* elevated (line)
架鉄道 *kōka tetsudō* elevated railway
祖 *kōso* founder of a dynasty or sect
祖父 *kōsofu* great-grandfather
祖母 *kōsobo* great-grandmother
速 *kōsoku* high speed, high gear
速力学 *kōsoku rikigaku* high-speed mechanics
速炉 *kōsokuro* fast reactor
速度 *kōsokudo* high speed
速度撮影 *kōsokudo satsuei* taking slow motion movies
速度鋼 *kōsokudokō* high-speed steel
速道路 *kōsoku dōro* expressway
速増殖炉 *kōsoku zōshokuro* fast breeder reactor
級 *kōkyū* high rank, seniority; high grade, high class
級車 *kyōkyūsha* high-class automobile
級社員 *kōkyū shain* senior clerk
級店 *kōkyūten* fashionable store
級品 *kōkyūhin* high-grade goods
級船員 *kōkyū sen'in* ship's officers
[10] 原 *kōgen* tableland, plateau
座 *kōza* platform; dias; stage; upper seat
這 *takabai* crawling on hands and knees
値 *takane* high price
峰 *kōhō* lofty peak
峻 *kōshun na* high, steep
根 *takane* lofty peak
浪 *takanami* high waves
配 *kōhai* your good offices, your trouble
家 *kōke* noble samurai family; shogunate liaison official
笑 *takawara(i)* loud laughter
書 *kōsho* your letter
恩 *kōon* a great blessing
陵土 *kōryōdo* kaolin, porcelain clay
島田 *takashimada* a coiffure for unmarried girls
射砲 *kōshahō* antiaircraft gun
浮調 *takau(ki)bo(ri)* high relief
校 *kōkō* senior high school
校生 *kōkōsei* senior high school student
高 *takadaka* very high; at most, at best. *takadaka to* aloft, very high; loudly
高指 *takatakayubi* middle finger
[11] 匐 *takabai* crawling on hands and knees
唱 *kōshō suru* sing loudly; advocate, urge, stress
情 *kōjō* nobility of soul
距 *kōkyo* altitude
率 *kōritsu* high rate
商 *kōshō* higher commercial school
堂 *kōdō* beautiful tall building; your beautiful home
著 *kōcho* your literary work
望 *takanozo(mi)* viewing from the heights; high hopes
脚蟹 *takaashigani* giant spider crab
張提灯 *takaha(ri) chōchin* paper lantern on a pole
野豆腐 *kōyadōfu* frozen tofu
野松 *kōyamatsu* umbrella pine
教 *kōkyō* excellent teaching; your excellent teaching
教会 *Kōkyōkai* the High Church
[12] 遠 *kōen na* high and distant; high, lofty, noble; hard to understand
塀 *takabei* high wall
揚 *kōyō suru* enhance, exhalt, promote
温 *kōon* high temperature
禄 *kōroku* high salary
給 *kōkyū* high salary
評 *kōhyō* your esteemed opinion; criticism by famous people
貴 *kōki* nobility
裁 *kōsai* higher court
順位 *kōjun'i ni* in order beginning with the highest
御位 *takamikurai* emperor's throne
御座 *takamikura* the throne
等 *kōtō* high class, high grade

等小学校 *kōtō shōgakkō* (prewar) higher elementary school
等女学校 *kōtō jogakkō* (prewar) girl's high school
等弁務官 *kōtō bemmukan* high commissioner
等批評 *kōtō hihyō* higher criticism
等官 *kōtōkan* higher official
等法院 *kōtō hōin* higher court
等学校 *kōtō gakkō* senior high school
等科 *kōtōka* advanced course
等飛行 *kōtō hikō* stunt flying
等飛行術 *kōtō hikōjutsu* stunt flying
等遊民 *kōtō yūmin* idle rich
等教育 *kōtō kyōiku* higher education
等動物 *kōtō dōbutsu* higher animals
等裁判所 *kōtō saibansho* higher court
等普通教育 *kōtō futsū kyōiku* liberal education
等数学 *kōtō sūgaku* higher mathmatics
等試験 *kōtō shiken* higher civil service examination
等警察 *kōtō keisatsu* secret police
13 厦 *kōka* tall building
殿 *takadono* stately mansion ⌈priest
僧 *kōsō* high priest, prelate; virtuous
楼 *kōrō* tall building,, skyscraper
雅 *kōga na* refined, elegant; chaste
腰 *takagoshi* pride
話 *takabanashi* loud talk
節 *kōsetsu* noble character, lofty virtues
義 *kōgi* high morality; kindness, favor; noble act
楊枝 *takayōji* leisurely using a toothpick when surfeited
蒔絵 *takamakie* raised lacquerwork
障害 *kōshōgai* high hurdles
障碍 *kōshōgai* high hurdles
粱 *kōryō, kaoryan, kōryan* kaoliang, Indian millet, sorghum
14 閣 *kōkaku* high tower
聞 *kōbun* your attention to my speech
鳴 *takana(ru)* ring loud, clang; throb, be filled (with hope)
徳 *kōtoku* eminent virtue
慢 *kōman* pride, insolence, arrogance. *kōman(chiki) na* haughty, arrogant
説 *kōsetsu* valuable opinion; your views
歌 *kōka* loud singing
察 *kōsatsu* your idea
層 *kōsō* high altitude, upper (atmospheric) strata; tall (building)
層気流 *kōsō kiryū* upper air current
層気象学 *kōsō kishōgaku* aerology
層飛行 *kōsō hikō* high-altitude flying
層建築 *kōsō kenchiku* skyscraper
層建築物 *kōsō kenchikubutsu* skyscraper
層雲 *kōsōun* alto-stratus clouds
15 趣 *kōshu* noble otherworldly interests
邁 *kōmai na* high, lofty, noble
嘱 *kōshoku* your request
潔 *kōketsu* purity, nobility
論 *kōron* exhalted view; your opinion
談 *kōdan* lofty discourse; your discourse
誼 *kōgi* your kindness
熱 *kōnetsu* high fever
潮 *kōchō, takashio* spring tide, flood tide. *kōchō* high tide; climax, acme
潮時 *kōchōji* time of high tide
調 *kōchō suru* emphasize, urge
調子 *takachōshi* high pitch; high stockmarket tone
踏 *kōtō* living a holy life aloof from the world
踏主義 *kōtō shugi* transcendentalism
踏的 *kōtōteki* transcendent; high-toned; highbrowed
16 館 *kōkan* lofty structure; your home
覧 *kōran* your perusal
緯度 *kōido* high or cold latitudes
積雲 *kōsekiun* alto-cumulus clouds
17 燥 *kōsō na* elevated, high and dry
聴 *kōchō* your kind attention
鼾 *takaibiki* loud snore
齢 *kōrei* advanced age
齢化社会 *kōreika shakai* aging society
齢者 *kōreisha* senior citizen, old person
嶺 *takane* lofty peak
嶺花 *takane (no) hana* flowers on inaccessible heights; unattainable object
翼 *kōyoku* high wing
翼機 *kōyokuki* high-wing plane
18 額 *kōgaku* high price, expensiveness
19 識 *kōshiki* exhalted views
瀬 *takase* shallows
瀬舟 *takasebune* flatboat, river boat
麗 *Kōrai, Koma* Koguryo (ancient Korean kingdom)

麗鶯 *kōrai uguisu* oriole
[20] 欄 *kōran* railing, balcony
騰 *kōtō* sudden price jump

RAD. 髟 190

Kami hair. At top: *kamigashira* or *kami kammuri*. Nickname: Long Hair (cf. Rad. 59).

髟 6799 / J7175 / M45355 HYŌ (hair) hanging down long; mane.

[14] 綱 *kamizuna* hair rope
[15] 膚 *happu* hair and skin; body
[16] 頭 *kamigashira* head of hair
[18] 癖 *kamikuse* hair twist, kink

3

髢 6800 / J7176 / M45363 TEI. SEKI. *kamoji* false hair, wig.

4

髥 6801 / J-X / M45375 See 髯 6809.

髦 6802 / J7178 / M45377 BŌ. MŌ bangs; mane; surpass, excel, be superior.

髣 6803 / J7177 / M45371 HŌ dimly.
[15] 髴 *hōfutsu suru* closely resemble

D **髪** 6804 / J4831 / M45387 **髮** 6805 / J717b / M45400 HATSU. *kami* the hair.
[3] 上 *kamia(ge), kan'a(ge)* doing up the hair
[4] 毛 *kami(no)ke* the hair
化粧 *kamikeshō* dolling up the hair
切 *kamiki(ri)* haircutting
切虫 *kamiki(ri) mushi* long-horned beetle
[5] 付 *kamitsu(ki)* hairstyle
[7] 床 *kamidoko* barbershop
形 *kamikatachi* hairstyle
[8] 油 *kamiabura* hair oil, pomade
[9] 型 *kamigata* hairstyle
洗 *kamiara(i)* washing the hair
洗粉 *kamiara(i)ko* shampoo powder
[10] 容 *kamikatachi* hairstyle
[12] 筋 *kamisuji* comb lines; a hair
結 *kamiyu(i)* combing the hair; hairdressing; hairdresser
結床 *kamiyu(i)doko* (Edo) barbershop
[13] 際 *kamigiwa* the hairline
飾 *kamikaza(ri)* hair ornament

13

驂 6798 / J7174 / M45344 SŌ hurry; high, tall, lofty.

5

髮 6805 / J717b / M45400 See 髪 6804.

髴 6806 / J717c / M45414 See 彿 1729.

髫 6807 / J717a / M45392 CHŌ. JŌ. *unai* children's hair hanging down the neck; small child.

髱 6808 / J717d / M45410 HŌ. *tabo* topknot; bun, coiled hair knot

髯 6809 / J7179 / M45401 **髥** 6801 / J-X / M45375 ZEN. *hige* beard; mustache; hairspring.
[9] 茫茫 *higebōbō* bushy-bearded

6

髷 6810 / J717e / M45226 KYOKU. *mage* topknot.

髻 6811 / J7221 / M45442 KEI. KITSU. *tabusa* a samurai hairdo. *motodori* topknot.

髭 6812 / J4926 / M45399 SHI. *hige* beard; moustache; hairspring. *hige(zemmai)* hairspring.
[3] 口 *higeguchi* bearded mouth; a man's mouth
[7] 男 *higeotoko* heavily bearded man
[9] 面 *higezura* unshaven face, hairy face
剃 *higesori* shaving

10 馬骨高【髟】[6] 門鬯鬲鬼

8

鬆 6813 / J7222 / M45484 SHŌ, SŌ (hair) disheveled; loose, coarse. *su* pore (in daikon or burdock).

11

鬘 6814 / J7223 / M45568 BAN. MAN. *katsura* wig, false hair.

12

鬛 6815 / J-X / M45584 See 鬣 6820.

鬚 6816 / J7224 / M45580 SHU. *hige* beard; moustache; hairspring.
8 武者 *higemusha* heavily bearded man
15 髯 *shuzen* mustache and beard

13

鬟 6817 / J7225 / M45596 KAN. topknot, ancient male hairstyle with looped ponytails. *mage, wage* topknot, chignon.

14

鬣 6818 / J-X / M-X See 鬣 6820.

鬢 6819 / J7226 / M45607 BIN side locks, sideburns.
5 付 *bintsu(ke)* hair cosmetic
付油 *bintsu(ke) abura* hair cosmetic
8 長 *binnaga* albacore (a fish)

15

鬣 6820 / J7227 / M45613 鬛 6815 / J-X / M45584 RYŌ. *tategami* mane.

RAD. 鬥 191

Tō or *tatakai* fighting. As enclosure: *tōgamae* or *tatakaigamae*.
Nickname: Broken Gate (cf. Rad. 169).

鬥 6821 / J7228 / M45632 TŌ, TSU take arms, fight, battle.

5

鬧 6822 / J7229 / M45639 See 閙 6395.

6

鬨 6823 / J722a / M45641 KŌ. GŌ. GU. fight. *toki* war cry.
7 声 *toki (no) koe* war cry

8

鬩 6824 / J722b / M45644 KEKI. KAKU. GEKI. *seme(gu)* quarrel.
17 牆 *gekishō* internal strife

10

鬪 6825 / J722c / M45649 See 闘 6418.

14

鬭 6826 / J-X / M45657 See 闘 6418.

17

鬮 6827 / J-X / M-X See 鬮 6828.

18

鬮 6828 / J722d / M45659 鬮 6827 / J-X / M-X KYŪ. *kuji* lottery, lot, raffle.

鬯 RAD. 192

Kaorigusa fragrant herbs. Nickname: Herb.

鬯 6829 / J722e / M45661 CHŌ fragrant herbs, saffron; spiced liqueur; grow, spread; bow case.

19

鬱 6830 / J5d35 / M45671 See 欝 2926.

鬲 RAD. 193

Ashi kamae tripod. Nickname: Tripod.

鬲 6831 / J722f / M45672 REKI tripod (kettle); iron pot; caldron. KAKU separate; shield; be choked; armor breast plate.

12

鬻 6832 / J6478 / M45721 JUKU. *hisa(gu)* sell, deal in.

鬼 RAD. 194

Oni devil. Variant: ⻌ *kinyō* "devil" enclosure. Nickname: Devil.

B 鬼 6833 / J3534 / M45758 KI devil, demon; spirits of the dead. *oni* devil, demon, ghost; spirits of the dead; fiend; creditor; the one who is "it" (in games). *oni-* sharp, relentless, crack (detective), tough, extremely competent. *oni(gokko)* tag games.

3 女 *kijo* demoness; witch
才 *kisai* genius, wizard, prodigy
子 *onigo* child born with teeth; a child not resembling his parents; a fierce child; tag games
子母神 *kishimojin, kishibojin* goddess of children
4 心 *onigokoro* wicked heart
火 *onibi* will-o'-the-wisp, *ignis fatuus*
5 瓦 *onigawara* ridge-end tile; gargoyle
6 虫 *onimushi* stag beetle
気 *kiki* weirdness, ghastliness
百合 *oniyuri* tiger lily
8 門 *kimon* unlucky quarter (northeast); anathema; defect, weakness; undesirable person
板 *oniita* wooden ridge-end ornament
物 *kibutsu* ghost, goblin
事 *onigoto* tag games
武者 *onimusha* intrepid warrior, daredevil
9 面 *kimen* devil mask; bluff
神 *kishin, kijin, onigami* terrible god, fierce god; departed spirit; demon, ghost, monster, goblin
界 *kikai* realm of the demons; realm of the dead
10 殺 *onikoro(shi)* strong-minded person; strong person; strength; cheap drink of high alcoholic content
畜 *kichiku* a devil
哭 *kikoku* wail of a ghost
11 遊 *oniaso(bi)* tag games
婆 *onibaba* witch, hag
鹿毛 *onikage* unbroken horse
12 歯 *oniba* protruding tooth
16 録 *kiroku* hell's record book
19 簿 *kibo* death register
20 籍 *kiseki* record of the dead

4

魁 6834 / J3321 / M45785 KAI. *sakigake* charging ahead of others.

10 ¹²傀 *kaii na* brawny, muscular, impressive

B**魂** 6835 / J3a32 / M45787 KON. *tamashii, tama* soul, spirit.
⁶気 *konki* soul
迎 *tamamuka(e)* welcoming the spirits of the dead
⁸送 *tamaoku(ri)* sending off the spirits of the dead
⁹胆 *kontan* soul; plot, intrigue
¹⁰消 *tamage(ru)* be startled, be astonished
¹¹祭 *tama matsu(ri)* memorial service for the dead
¹⁵魄 *kompaku* soul, spirit

5

魃 6836 / J7231 / M45806 HATSU drought; god of drought.

魄 6837 / J7230 / M45810 TAKU, HAKU soul, spirit.
²力 *hakuryoku* force, intensity, appeal

B**魅** 6838 / J4c25 / M45811 MI. *mi(suru)* charm, fascinate, bewitch, enchant. *baka(su)* bewitch, confuse, enchant, delude.
²力 *miryoku* charm, glamor, appeal
了 *miryō suru* charm, fascinate
¹²惑 *miwaku* fascination, enchantment, charm
惑的 *miwakuteki* charming, fascinating, seductive

8

魍 6839 / J7233 / M45869 BŌ, MŌ spirit of nature that deceives humans by imitating voices.

魎 6840 / J7234 / M45870 RYŌ spirit of mountains and rivers.

魏 6841 / J7232 / M45872 GI high, tall, grand; possible; ancient Chinese place name.

10

魑 6842 / J7235 / M45901 CHI ogre, beast, fiend; mountain monster.

11

B**魔** 6843 / J4b62 / M45906' MA demon, devil, evil spirit.
²力 *maryoku* magical power, charm
³女 *majo* witch, sorceress
⁴手 *mashu* evil influence
王 *maō* the devil
⁸性 *mashō* devilishness
物 *mamono* goblin, apparition
法 *mahō* magic, sorcery, witchcraft
法使 *mahōtsukai* magician, sorcerer
法的 *mahōteki* magic (adjective)
法罎 *mahōbin* thermos bottle
⁹風 *makaze, mafū* a storm caused by the devil; an evil wind
神 *mashin, majin* devil, evil spirit
除 *mayo(ke)* charm against evil spirits, talisman, amulet
界 *makai* world of spirits, infernal regions, hell
¹¹道 *madō* heresy; evil ways
球 *makyū* curve (in baseball)
術 *majutsu* magic, sorcery, witchcraft, augury
術師 *majutsushi* magician, conjurer
¹²街 *magai* den (of thieves); brothel, redlight district
訶不思議 *maka-fushigi* profound mystery
¹³睡 *masui* anesthesia
窟 *makutsu* den (of thieves); brothel, redlight district
¹⁴境 *makyō* frightening world, place of evil
¹⁵魅 *mami* a deceiving spirit

14

魘 6844 / J7236 / M45941 EN. YŌ. *una(sareru)* have a nightmare.

11-STROKE RADICALS

RAD. 魚 195

Sakana or *uo* fish. At left: *uo hen.* Nickname: Fish.

A 魚 6845/J357b/M45956 奐 1157/J-X/M45958 GYO *uo, sakana* fish.
4 切 *uo(gire)* sold out of fish
介 *gyokai* marine products, sea food
5 目 *iome, io(no)me, uo(no)me* corn (on the foot)
市 *uoichi* fish market
市場 *uoichiba* fish market
6 肉 *gyoniku* fish meat
灯 *gyotō* fishing lights
7 見 *uomi* fish lookout (the person, place, or act)
貝 *gyokai* marine products, sea food
形 *gyokei* fishlike, fish-shaped
売 *sakanau(ri)* fish peddler
卵 *gyoran* fish eggs, spawn, roe
串 *uogushi* fish skewer
8 板 *gyoban* fish-shaped temple gong
油 *gyoyu* fish oil
狗 *kawasemi* kingfisher
肥 *gyohi* fish fertilizer
毒 *gyodoku* poison in fish
河岸 *uogashi* riverside fish market
9 食 *gyoshoku* fish eating
屋 *sakanaya* fish shop, fish peddler
臭 *gyoshū* fish smell; smell of rotten fish
10 粉 *gyofun* fish meal
脂 *gyoshi* fish fat
座目 *uonome* foot corn
11 鳥 *gyochō* birds and fishes
道 *gyodō* fish paths in the sea; fish ladder, fishway
族 *gyozoku* the fishes
粕 *uokasu* fish cake
釣 *uotsuri* fishing
問屋 *uodon'ya* fish wholesaler
眼写真 *gyogan shashin* fish eye (180-degree) photo
梯 *gyotei* fish ladder, fishway
梯子 *uobashigo* fish ladder
12 棚 *uodana* fish shop; fish shelves
13 塩 *gyoen* fish and salt; fish-and-salt business
鉤 *uokagi* fish gaff, fishhook
群 *gyogun* school of fish
腹 *gyofuku* the entrails of fish
腹葬 *gyofuku (ni) hōmu(rareru)* drown
雷 *gyorai* torpedo
雷艇 *gyoraitei* torpedo boat
14 精 *gyosei* millet
網 *gyomō* fishing net
15 膠 *uo nikawa* fish glue
餌 *gyoji* fish bait
18 類 *gyorui* the fishes
類学 *gyoruigaku* ichthyology
19 繋 *uotsuna(gi)* lined up like fish on a skewer
20 籃 *gyoran* fish basket
22 鰾 *gyohyō* fish bladder
23 鱗 *gyorin* fish scales

4

魴 6846/J7237/M46022 HŌ, BŌ Japanese bitterling. *kagamitai, kagamidai* a kind of sea bream.

魳 6847/J-X/M46020 SHI. *kamasu* barracuda.

魯 6848/J4f25/M46013 RO foolish; Russia.
8 国 *Rokoku* Russia
12 鈍 *rodon* foolishness, stupidity
20 艦 *Rokan* Russian battleship

5

鮖 6849/J723b/M46089 (国字) *kajika* bullhead.

鮗 6850/J723c/M46091 (国字) *konoshiro* a gizzard shad.

11 【魚】 鳥 鹵 鹿 麥 麦 麻

鮑 6851 / J723a / M46074 Hō. *awabi* abalone, ear shell.

鮃 6852 / J7239 / M46044 Hei. *hirame* flatfish, flounder.

鮓 6853 / J7238 / M46076 Sa. *sushi* sushi, vinegared rice with fish or vegetables.

鮒 6854 / J4a2b / M46075 Ho, Fu. *funa* carp.

鮎 6855 / J303e / M46070 Den. Nen. *ayu* fresh-water trout, sweet smelt.
8 並 *ainame* rock trout

6

鮴 6856 / J7240 / M-X (国字) *mebaru* a rock cod, a rock fish.

鮞 6857 / J-X / M46105 Ji. *hararago* fish eggs.

鮪 6858 / J4b6e / M46126 Ki. Yū. *maguro, shibi* tuna, tunny.

鮭 6859 / J3a7a / M46132 Kai. Kei. *sake, shake* salmon.

鮠 6860 / J723e / M46112 Kai. Ge. *hae, haya* dace (of the carp family).

鮟 6861 / J723d / M46108 An. *namazu* catfish; bullhead.
22 鱇 *ankō* an anglerfish, a frogfish

鮨 6862 / J723f / M46123 Shi. Ki. *sushi* sushi, vinegared rice with fish or vegetables.
9 屋 *sushiya* sushi shop
13 詰 *sushizume* packed audience

鮫 6863 / J3b2d / M46127 Kō. *same* shark.
5 皮 *samegawa* sharkskin
6 肌 *samehada* goose flesh (due to cold, etc.)
15 膚 *samehada* goose flesh (due to cold, etc.)
25 鑢 *sameyasuri* sharkskin rasp

B 鮮 6864 / J412f / M46133 Sen Korea. *azaya(ka) na* vivid, clear, brilliant, fresh, graceful, splendid, beautiful.
4 少 *senshō* few, a little
6 肉 *senniku* fresh meat
血 *senketsu* lifeblood; flowing blood
7 花 *senka* beautiful bright flowers
赤色 *sensekishoku* bright red
8 味 *semmi* freshness
明 *semmei* clearness, distinctness
9 度 *sendo* (degree of) freshness
紅 *senkō* scarlet
美 *sembi* bright and beautiful
11 魚 *sengyo* fresh fish
12 満 *Semman* Korea and Manchuria
15 鋭度 *sen'eido* clarity, clearness
19 麗 *senrei na* gorgeous, vivid

7

鯀 6865 / J7241 / M46168 Kon a kind of large fish.

鯆 6866 / J7244 / M46177 Ho, Fu. *iruka* dolphin, porpoise. *saba* mackerel.

鯊 6867 / J7242 / M46186 Sa. Sha. *haze* goby. *same* shark.

鯏 6868 / J7245 / M46201 (国字) *asari* short-necked clam. *ugui* dace, chub.

鯑 6869 / J7246 / M46203 (国字) *kazunoko* herring roe.

鯒 6870 / J7247 / M46204 (国字) *kochi* flathead (a fish).

鮹 6871 / J7243 / M46154 Sho. *tako* octopus, devilfish.

𩸽 6872 / J-X / M-X (国字) *hokke* Atka mackerel, lockington.

鯁 6873 / J-X / M46171 Kō fishbones.
10 骨 *kōkotsu* hard bone; firmness, inflexibility, stubbornness

鯉 6874 / J3871 / M46182 Ri. *koi* carp.

[3] 口 *koiguchi* mouth of a sword sweath

[15] 幟 *koinobori* carp streamer

8

鯵 6875 / J3033 / M-X Nonstandard for  6912.

鯢 6876 / J7249 / M46245 GEI salamander; cow whale; fingerling.

鯤 6877 / J724a / M46247 KON hard roe, fish eggs; an imaginary giant fish.

鯲 6878 / J724e / M46287 (国字) *dojō* a *dojō*, a loach.

鯰 6879 / J7250 / M46285 (国字) *namazu* fresh-water catfish.

鯡 6880 / J724c / M46243 HI. *nishin* herring.

鯣 6881 / J7248 / M46246 EKI. *surume* dried cuttlefish.

鯔 6882 / J724b / M46208 SHI. *bora* mullet.

鯖 6883 / J3b2a / M46210 SEI. *saba* mackerel.

[14] 読 *saba (o) yo(mu)* cheat in counting

鯛 6884 / J4264 / M46226 CHŌ. *tai* sea bream, red snapper.

[12] 飯 *taimeshi* rice and minced sea bream

鯱 6885 / J724f / M46286 (国字) *shachihoko* fabulous dolphin-like fish. *shachi* killer whale.

[5] 立 *shachihokoda(chi)* standing on one's head; exerting extreme effort

[11] 張 *shachikoba(ru), shachihokoba(ru)* be stiff and formal

B鯨 6886 / J375f / M46257 GEI. *kujira* whale.

[4] 尺 *kujirajaku* long foot (14.91 inches) (a cloth measure)

[6] 肉 *geiniku* whale meat

[8] 油 *geiyu* whale oil

波 *geiha* raging waves; tidal wave; shout of victory. *toki* war cry

[10] 浪 *geirō* huge waves

脂 *geishi* blubber

差 *kujirazashi* long foot (14.91 inches) (a cloth measure)

[11] 脳油 *geinōyu* sperm oil

[12] 飲 *geiin suru* drink hard, drink like a fish

飲馬食 *geiin-bashoku* heavy drinking and eating

[13] 幕 *kujiramaku* black and white bunting curtain

[17] 糞 *geifun* ambergris

[19] 臘 *geirō* whale tallow

9

鰛 6887 / J725c / M-X Nonstandard for 鰮 6905.

鰄 6888 / J725a / M46314 I a kind of fish. *Kairagi* sharkskin-like skin of a ray; sharkskin.

鰆 6889 / J7256 / M46317 SHUN a kind of sea fish. *sawara* Spanish mackerel.

鰉 6890 / J7253 / M46323 KŌ, Ō a kind of big fish. *higai* a goby-like fish living in Lake Biwa (a favorite of the Emperor Meiji).

鰔 6891 / J7252 / M46345 KAN. *tara* cod, codfish. *karei* flatfish, turbot. *ugui* dace, chub.

鰕 6892 / J7251 / M46346 KA *ebi* shrimp, prawn, lobster.

鰊 6893 / J7259 / M46325 REN. *nishin* herring.

鯷 6894 / J-X / M46290 TEI. *hishiko* anchovy.

鰍 6895 / J3362 / M46331 SHŪ. SHU. *kajika* bullhead.

鯽 6896 / J-X / M46304 SEKI. SHIKI. SHAKU. SHOKU. *tanago* surf perch.

鰒 6897 / J7258 / M46340 FUKU. *awabi* abalone.

鰈 6898 / J7257 / M46322 CHŌ. *karei* sole, flatfish, flounder.

17 鮫 *chōzame* sturgeon

鰌 6899 / J7255 / M46330 SHŪ. SHU. *dojō* loach.

16 髭 *dojō hige* thin mustache

鰓 6900 / J7254 / M46344 SAI. *era* gills, gill slits.

4 孔 *era ana, saikō* gill slits

鰐 6901 / J4f4c / M46337 鱷 6929 / J-X / M46597 GAKU. *wani* crocodile, alligator.

3 口 *waniguchi* wide mouth; alligator; a temple gong

5 皮 *wanigawa, wanikawa* alligator skin

7 足 *waniashi* bowlegs

11 魚 *gakugyo* crocodile, alligator

17 鮫 *wanizame* shark

10

鰡 6902 / J725f / M46374 RYŪ, RU a kind of fish. *bora* mullet.

鰰 6903 / J7260 / M46414 (国字) *hatahata* sandfish.

鰯 6904 / J3073 / M46413 (国字) *iwashi* sardine.

鰛 6905 / J725b / M46403 ON. *iwashi* sardine.

鰤 6906 / J725e / M46381 SHI. *buri* yellowtail.

鰭 6907 / J4949 / M46400 KI. GI. *hire* fin.

7 足 *hireashi* flipper

鰥 6908 / J725d / M46382 鱞 6924 / J-X / M46520 KAN. *yamome, yamoo* widower, unmarried man.

4 夫 *yamoo* widower

14 寡孤独 *kanka-kodoku* loneliness

11

鰲 6909 / J7262 / M46416 GŌ a kind of fish. Also used as a variant of 鼇 7072.

鱇 6910 / J7261 / M46468 KŌ an anglerfish, a frogfish.

鰾 6911 / J7264 / M46447 HYŌ. *fue, ukibukuro* fish bladder, air bladder.

鰺 6912 / J724d / M46442 SŌ. *aji* horse mackerel.

鱆 6913 / J7263 / M46464 SHŌ. *tako* octopus, devilfish.

鰻 6914 / J3137 / M46443 MAN. *unagi* eel.

3 上 *unaginobo(ri)* rapid promotion

5 丼 *unagi domburi, unadon* rice-and-eel dish

9 屋 *unagiya* eel shop

鰹 6915 / J336f / M46437 KEN. *katsuo* bonito, skipjack.

4 木 *katsuogi* cigar-shaped cross logs on shrine ridgepole

13 節 *katsuobushi, katsubushi* dried bonito

節削 *katsuobushikezu(ri)* dried bonito shavings

鱈 6916 / J432d / M46470 (国字) SETSU. *tara* codfish.

3 子 *tarako* cod roe

12 場蟹 *tarabagani* king crab

13 腹 *tarafuku* to heart's content

12

鱉 6917 / J-X / M46472 See 鼈 7073.

鱚 6918 / J7265 / M46516 (国字) *kisu* a sillaginoid (a kind of small fish).

鱏 6919 / J-X / M46488 JIN. *ei* ray, skate.

鱓 6920 / J-X / M46496 SEN. ZEN. *utsubo* moray eel.

鱒 6921 / J4b70 / M46492 SON. ZON. SEN. ZAN. *masu* trout.

鱘 6922 / J-X / M46504 JIN. sturgeon.
11 魚 *chōzame* sturgeon

鱗 6923 / J1e5a / M46502 RIN. *uroko, koke, kokera* (fish) scales.
4 介 *rinkai* fish and shellfish
7 状 *rinjō* scaly
形 *urokogata* imbricate pattern. *urokogata no* imbricate, scale-like
11 族 *rinzoku* fish, the finny tribe
14 模様 *uroko moyō* imbricate pattern

13

鱞 6924 / J-X / M46520 See 鰥 6908.

鱮 6925 / J-X / M46571 SHO. *tanago* minnow, shiner.

鱧 6926 / J7267 / M46542 REI. *hamo* conger eel, sea eel.

鱠 6927 / J7266 / M46530 KAI. KE. *namasu* minced meat or seafood; a dish of raw fish and vegetables seasoned in vinegar.
5 叩 *namasu (ni) tataku* to mince meat or fish to make *namasu*; to hack (someone), to mangle (someone)
7 作 *namasu (o) tsuku(ru)* to mince meat or fish to make *namasu*; to mince, hack, mangle

15

鱶 6928 / J7268 / M46592 SHŌ. *fuka* shark.

16

鱷 6929 / J-X / M46597 See 鰐 6901.

鱸 6930 / J7269 / M46600 RO. *suzuki* sea bass.

RAD. 鳥 196

Tori bird. Nickname: Bird.

A 鳥 6931 / J443b / M46634 CHŌ bird. *tori* bird; chicken; fowl.
2 人 *chōjin* aviator, pilot
3 小屋 *torigoya* aviary; henhouse
4 毛 *torige* feathers, down
5 目 *torime* night blindness. *chōmoku* an ancient coin; money
打 *toriuchi* fowling, shooting; cap
打帽 *toriu(chi)bō* cap
打帽子 *toriuchi bōshi* cap
6 肉 *chōniku, toriniku* poultry meat
肌 *torihada* goose flesh (due to cold, etc.)
羽絵 *tobae* comic picture, cartoon
7 貝 *torigai* cockle (shell)
声 *chōsei, torigoe* bird's cry, bird-call
8 居 *torii* Shinto shrine gateway
追 *torio(i)* scaring birds; wandering minstrel
9 屋 *toriya* poultry farmer, bird fancier. *toya* hen coop, roost; actors' rest room
威 *toriodo(shi)* scarecrow
竿 *torizao* limed fowling rod
10 差 *torisa(shi)* birdcatcher
11 寄 *toriyo(se)* birdcall
笛 *toribue* birdcall
12 媒 *chōbai* decoy
渡 *chotto* a short time; just a minute
飯 *torimeshi* chicken and rice
葬 *chōsō* Parsee burial (in a tower leaving the body to be defleshed by carnivorous birds)
13 跡 *chōseki* bird tracks; writing
14 網 *tori ami* fowler's net

語 *chōgo* bird chatter, bird songs
銃 *chōjū* fowling piece
15 膚 *torihada* goose flesh
餌 *torie* birdseed, bird food
影 *torikage* shadow of a bird
16 獣 *chōjū, tori-kedamono* birds and animals
17 鍋 *torinabe* chicken cooked in a pan; shallow cooking pan
瞰図 *chōkanzu* bird's-eye view
糞 *chōfun* droppings, guano
糞石 *chōfunseki* guano deposit
18 類 *chōrui* the birds, fowls
類図鑑 *chōrui zukan* bird book
類学 *chōruigaku* ornithology
22 籠 *torikago* bird cage
23 黐 *torimochi* birdlime

2

鳫 6932 / J726f / M46655 See **雁** 6498.

鳬 6933 / J726a / M46643 **鳧** 6934 / J726b / M46644 FU. *keri* wild duck; end, settlement; suffix.

鳰 6935 / J726c / M46658 (国字) *nio* a (little) grebe.
9 海 *Nio (no) Umi* Lake Biwa
12 湖 *Nio (no) Umi* Lake Biwa

鳩 6936 / J4837 / M46648 KYŪ. *hato* dove, pigeon.
3 小屋 *hatogoya* pigeon house
5 目 *hatome* eyelet
6 羽色 *hatoba iro* bluish grey
7 麦 *hatomugi* pearl barley
尾 *kyūbi, mizoochi, mizuochi* solar plexus, pit of the stomach
8 舎 *kyūsha* pigeon house
9 首 *kyūshu suru* go into a huddle
信 *kyūshin* carrier-pigeon communication
便 *hatobin* carrier-pigeon mail
10 胸 *hatomune* pigeon breast, deformed protruding chest

3

鳳 6937 / J4b31 / M46671 HŌ male phoenix bird.
5 仙花 *hōsenka* balsam
7 声 *hōsei* verbal message
11 凰 *hōō* mythical phoenix bird
15 輦 *hōren* imperial carriage
駕 *hōga* imperial carriage

鳶 6938 / J4650 / M46674 EN. *tobi* black kite; fire fighter; hook. *tombi* black kite; cloak; pilferer.
2 人足 *tobi ninsoku* fire fighter
3 口 *tobiguchi* fire ax, fire hook
6 色 *tobi iro* brown, auburn
8 者 *tobi(no)mono* fire fighter
12 衆 *tobi(no)shū* fire fighter
16 頭 *tobigashira* chief fire fighter
18 職 *tobishoku* casual laborer, construction laborer

A **鳴** 6939 / J4c44 / M46672 MEI. *na(ku)* (animals and birds) cry, bark, chirp, etc. *na(ru)* sound, ring, roar; (thunder) rumbles; (clocks) strike; boom; resound, echo; be famous; (fingers) itch for; sonorous, ringing, squeaky. *na(rasu) vt* ring, sound, blow (a whistle), beat (drums), clank, clink, clap, crack (a whip), smack (lips), cluck (one's tongue), honk; air (grievances); attain (celebrity). *na(ri)* sound, ringing.
3 子 *naruko* clapper
4 戸 *naruto* whirlpool, maelstrom
5 出 *na(ki)-da(su)* begin to sing or chirp
6 合 *na(ki)a(wase)* birds' singing contest
7 声 *na(ki)goe* sound of a bird or animal
8 門 *naruto* whirlpool, maelstrom
物 *na(ri)mono* music; musical instruments
物入 *na(ri)monoi(ri)* loud proclamation, bombastic announcement
9 飛 *na(kazu)-to(bazu)* inactive, obscure
神 *na(ru)kami* thunder
11 動 *meidō* rumbling
笛 *meiteki* playing the flute
12 渡 *na(ri)-wata(ru)* resound, re-echo
散 *na(ri)-chi(rasu)* (birds) cry and scatter blossoms with the breeze caused by their wings
13 禽 *meikin* songbird
19 響 *na(ri)-hibi(ku)* reverberate, echo, resound, be sonorous
20 鐘 *meishō* hour bell
21 轟 *na(ri)-todoro(ku)* rage, roar

4

鳫 6940 / J726e / M46734 See 雁 6498.

鴎 6941 / J322a / M-X Nonstandard for 鷗 6998.

鴃 6942 / J7270 / M46723 GEKI. KEKI. *mozu* shrike, butcher-bird.

鴇 6943 / J463e / M46730 HŌ. *nogan* Siberian bustard; bustard; grey horse; procuress. *toki* Japanese crested ibis.
5 母 *hōbo, yarite* a procuress; a matron (of a brothel)

鴆 6944 / J7271 / M46727 CHIN, JIN bird with feathers used to make poison; poisoned saké; poison.
8 毒 *chindoku* the venom of a poisonous bird
10 殺 *chinsatsu* poison, murder with poison
酒 *chinshu* saké, poison with *chin* feathers

5

鴬 6945 / J3229 / M-X Nonstandard for 鶯 6994.

鴣 6946 / J7275 / M46814 KO partridge.

鴥 6947 / J7272 / M46820 ITSU, ICHI (birds) flying fast, swooping.

鴫 6948 / J3c32 / M46831 (国字) *shigi* snipe.

鴒 6949 / J7279 / M46770 REI the wagtail.

鴦 6950 / J7273 / M46822 Ō female mandarin duck.

鴉 6951 / J726d / M46738 A. *karasu* crow, raven.
4 片 *ahen* opium

鴕 6952 / J7278 / M46774 DA ostrich.
11 鳥 *dachō* ostrich

鴛 6953 / J3175 / M46795 EN male mandarin duck.
16 鴦 *oshidori, en'ō* mandarin duck

鴟 6954 / J7276 / M46805 鵄 6958 / J7277 / M46833 [鳥至] 6957 / J-X / M46832
SHI. *tobi* kite.
7 尾 *shibi* ornamental ridge-end tile

鴨 6955 / J337b / M46823 Ō. *kamo* wild duck, easy mark.
5 打 *kamou(chi)* duck hunting
8 居 *kamoi* lintel
11 猟 *kamoryō* duck hunting

6

鵈 6956 / J727e / M-X See 鳶 6938.

[鳥至] 6957 / J-X / M46832 鵄 6958 / J7277 / M46833 See 鴟 6954.

鵁 6959 / J727a / M46888 KŌ, KYŌ a kind of cormorant; a night heron.

鵆 6960 / J727d / M46903 (国字) *chidori* a plover.

鴿 6961 / J727b / M46884 KŌ. *hato, dobato* dove, a temple pigeon.

鴾 6962 / J727c / M46883 BŌ. *toki* crested ibis.
6 色 *toki iro* yellowish pink

鴻 6963 / J3963 / M46874 KŌ large, great; large bird. *ōtori* large wild goose.
3 大 *kōdai na* vast, immense, tremendous
4 毛 *kōmō* goose feathers; something very light
7 図 *kōto* ambitious scheme
8 学 *kōgaku* learning; learned scholar
10 益 *kōeki* great benefit
恩 *kōon* great blessings, great benevolence
11 基 *kōki* foundation of a great enterprise
13 業 *kōgyō* great achievement
16 儒 *kōju* great scholar
18 鵠 *kōkoku* great scholar

7

鵐 6964 J7325 M46922 Bu. Mu. *shitoto* a kind of quail.

鵙 6965 J7326 M46947 Geki. Keki. *mozu* shrike; butcher-bird.

鵤 6966 J7323 M46980 (国字) *ikaruga, ikaru* Japanese grosbeak, hawkfinch.

鵑 6967 J7324 M46924 Ken cuckoo.

鵠 6968 J3974 M46961 Koku swan.

鵞 6969 J7322 M46956 **鵝** 6970 J7321 M46954 Ga goose.
11 鳥 *gachō* goose

鵜 6971 J312d M46952 Tei. *u* cormorant.
5 目鷹目 *u(no)me-taka(no)me de* with sharp eyes
6 舟 *ubune* cormorant-fishing boat
匠 *ushō* cormorant fisher
8 使 *uzuka(i)* cormorant fishing
12 飲 *uno(mi)* swallowing whole
13 飼 *uka(i)* cormorant fishing

8

鵯 6972 J732b M47010 Hi, Hitsu a jungle crow, a rook, a carrion crow. *hiyodori* a brown-eared bulbul.

鶇 6973 J7329 M47054 Tō. *tsugumi* a dusky thrush.

鵡 6974 J4c39 M46963 Bu, Mu cockatoo.

鵲 6975 J7327 M47014 Shaku. *kasasagi* magpie.

鵼 6976 J-X M47034 **鵺** 6977 J732c M47030 Kō. *nue* fabulous night bird; grotesque monster.

鶉 6978 J7328 M47057 Jun. *uzura* quail.
6 衣 *uzuragoromo* patched clothes
7 豆 *uzura mame* mottled kidney beans

鵬 6979 J4b32 M47005 Hō phoenix, huge mythical bird. *ōtori* fabulous bird.
12 程 *hōtei* a great distance
17 翼 *hōyoku* phoenix wings; airplane wings; airplanes

B **鶏** 6980 J375c M47074' **鷄** 6985 J7331 M47209 **雞** 6513 J-X M42124
Kei. *niwatori* chicken.
6 肉 *keiniku* chicken (meat)
助 *keiroku* fowl's breastbone; weakness; worthlessness
7 声 *keisei* cockcrowing
卵 *keiran* hen egg
卵大 *keirandai* the size of a hen's egg
8 林 *Keirin* Korea
舎 *keisha* poultry house
9 冠 *keikan, tosaka* cockscomb
姦 *keikan* sodomy
11 唱 *keishō* cockcrowing
眼 *keigan* foot corn
豚 *keiton* chickens and hogs; domestic animals
13 群 *keigun* flock of chickens
14 鳴 *keimei* cockcrowing
16 頭 *keitō* cockscomb
17 糞 *keifun* chicken manure

9

鶚 6981 J732d M47105 Gaku. *misago* an osprey, a fish hawk.

鶤 6982 J732e M47130 Un. Kon. *tōmaru* a kind of large fowl.

鶫 6983 J732a M47161 (国字) *tsugumi* a dusky thrush.

鶩 6984 J732f M47142 Boku. Bu. *ahiru* domestic duck.

10

鷄 6985 J7331 M47209 See 鶏 6980.

鶲 6986 / J7330 / M47179 Ō. *hitaki* peewee, crested flycatcher.

鶻 6987 / J7333 / M47198 KOTSU. *hayabusa* peregrine falcon, duck hawk.

鷁 6988 / J7332 / M47206 GEKI, GYAKU a kind of waterfowl that soars in the wind; a waterfowl charm against disaster at sea.

鷂 6989 / J7338 / M47207 YŌ. *haitaka, hashitaka* Asiatic sparrow hawk.

鷆 6990 / J7336 / M47213 鷏 6991 / J7337 / M-X TEN. DEN. *kasui, yotaka* Japanese goatsucker, nightjar; whippoorwill.

鶸 6992 / J7334 / M47193 JAKU. *hiwa* light yellowish-green.

鶺 6993 / J7335 / M47197 SEKI wagtail.

16 鴒 *sekirei* wagtail

鶯 6994 / J7274 / M47169 Ō. *uguisu* nightingale, bush warbler.

6 色 *uguisu iro* greenish brown

9 垣 *uguisugaki* brushwood fence

茶 *uguisu cha* greenish brown

11 張 *uguisuba(ri)* singing floor boards

鶴 6995 / J4461 / M47185 KAKU. *tsuru* crane, stork.

9 首 *kakushu* suru stretch out the neck

11 亀 *tsurukame* crane and tortoise; congratulations

亀鶴亀 *tsurukame-tsurukame* That must not be.

14 髪 *kakuhatsu* gray hair

16 嘴 *tsuruhashi, tsurubashi* pick, pickax, mattock

頸 *tsurukubi* long-necked gourd; long-necked person; long-necked bottle

11

鷙 6996 / J7339 / M47275 SHI bird of prey; catch, capture; shoot, fire; rough, wild, ferocious; doubt.

鷚 6997 / J-X / M47278 RYŪ. RU. BŌ. HYŪ. MU. KYŪ. GU. RYŌ. *hibari* skylark. (Listed as an example of the many *on* that have accompanied some characters from China. As a rule, however, this dictionary includes only *on* in current use.)

鷗 6998 / J-X / M47268 Ō. *kamome* sea gull.

鷓 6999 / J733a / M47251 SHA partridge.

16 鴣 *shako* partridge

12

鷦 7000 / J733c / M47312 SHŌ a winter wren, a jenny wren.

鷭 7001 / J733d / M47335 HAN, BAN an Indian water hen; a moor hen; a common gallinule.

鷯 7002 / J733e / M47342 RYŌ a winter wren; a reed warbler; a common quail. quail.

鷸 7003 / J733b / M47359 ITSU. ICHI. *shigi* snipe, longbill. *kawasemi* a common kingfisher.

鷲 7004 / J4f49 / M47345 SHŪ. JU. *washi* eagle.

14 鼻 *washibana* aquiline nose, Roman nose

摑 *washizuka(mi)* clutch, grab

13

鷽 7005 / J733f / M47379 KAKU, GAKU a blue magpie; a long-tailed cock. *uso* a bullfinch.

鷺 7006 / J3a6d / M47362 RO. *sagi* heron.

鷹 7007 / J426b / M47377 YŌ. Ō. *taka* hawk.

6 匠 *takajō* falconer, hawker

9 狩 *takaga(ri)* hawking, falconry

[12] 揚 *ōyō* generosity, largeheartedness; easy-going

— 17 —

鸛 7008 / J7341 / M47500 KAN. *kōnotori* Japanese stork.

鸚 7009 / J7340 / M47489 Ō parrot.

[10] 哥 *inko* parakeet

[19] 鵡 *ōmu* parrot
鵡返 *ōmugae(shi)* parrot-like repetition
鵡貝 *ōmugai* chambered nautilus

— 19 —

鸞 7010 / J7342 / M47508 RAN a Chinese phoenix; bells attached to an emperor's carriage; carriage with bells attached.

RAD. 鹵 197

Shio salt. Nickname: Salt.

鹵 7011 / J7343 / M47528 RO natural salt; salty soil; shield; plunder; poor, barren.

[16] 獲 *rokaku suru* capture, plunder
獲物 *rokakubutsu* booty, trophy, spoils
獲品 *rokakuhin* booty, trophy, spoils
[19] 簿 *robo* imperial procession

— 8 —

塷 7012 / J-X / M47550 See 塩 1075.

鹸 7013 / J3834 / M-X Nonstandard for 鹼 7016.

— 9 —

鹹 7014 / J7344 / M47553 KAN. *kara(i)* salty.

[4] 水 *kansui* brackish water, sea water, salt water
水沼沢 *kansui shōtaku* salt marsh
水魚 *kansuigyo* salt-water fish
水湖 *kansuiko* salt lake
[6] 気 *shioke* saltiness
[7] 沢 *kantaku* salt marsh
[8] 味 *kammi* saltiness
[11] 魚 *kangyo* salted fish
菜 *kansai* vegetables pickled in salt
[12] 湖 *kanko* salt lake, lagoon

— 13 —

鹽 7015 / J7345 / M47579 See 塩 1075.

鹼 7016 / J-X / M47576 KEN saltiness; lye; salt.

[4] 化 *kenka* saponification

RAD. 鹿 198

Shika deer. At left: *shika hen.* As enclosure: 鹿. Nickname: Deer.

鹿 7017 / J3c2f / M47586 ROKU. *shika* deer.

[3] 子 *ka(no)ko* fawn; dapples, white spots
子斑 *ka(no)ko madara no* spotted like a deer
[4] 毛 *kage* fawn-colored horse
爪 *shikatsume(rashii)* formal; solemn, serious
[5] 皮 *shikagawa* deerskin
逐 *shika (o) o(u)* run for office
[10] 島立 *kashimada(chi)* departure on a journey
[11] 砦 *rokusai* abatis; entanglement

— 2 —

麁 7018 / J7346 / M47591 See 麤 7029.

4

麈 7019 J7347 M47616 SHU reindeer, moose; a priest's horsehair flapper.

6

麋 7020 J7348 M47625 BI. MI reindeer; water's edge; eyebrow.

7

麌 7021 J7349 M47634 GU. GO stag, hart; roe deer stag.

8

麕 7022 J734b M47660 KIN *noro* roe deer.

麓 7023 J4f3c M47658 ROKU. *fumoto* foot of a mountain.

麑 7024 J734c M47656 GEI. *kojika* fawn, young deer; Kagoshima.

麒 7025 J734a M47657 KI giraffe.

23 麟 *kirin* giraffe
麟児 *kirinji* infant prodigy

B **麗** 7026 J4e6f M47663 REI. RAI. *urara(ka) na* beautiful, bright and clear, fine, serene. *uruwa(shii)* beautiful, lovely, graceful.

2 人 *reijin* beauty, belle
4 日 *reijitsu* beautiful day
5 句 *reiku* beautiful phrase
6 色 *reishoku* beautiful views; beautiful countenance
8 服 *reifuku* beautiful clothes
9 姿 *reishi* beautiful figure
10 容 *reiyō* beautiful figure
12 筆 *reihitsu* beautifully written poetry; the writing brush (ornate)
13 雅 *reiga* beauty and nobility
辞 *reiji* beautiful words
15 質 *reishitsu* beauty, charms
18 顔 *reigan* beautiful face
19 麗 *reirei to, reirei(shiku)* ostentatiously, pretentiously

10

麝 7027 J734d M47682 JA musk deer.

9 香 *jakō* musk
香水 *jakōsui* musk water, musk scent
香鹿 *jakōjika* musk deer
香猫 *jakō neko* musk cat
香鼠 *jakō nezumi* muskrat
香豌豆 *jakō endō* sweet peas

12

麟 7028 J4e5b M47690 RIN giraffe.

22

麤 7029 J-X M47714 SO rough.

RAD. 麥 199

Mugi wheat. Variant: 麦 (7 strokes). Variants: 麦 and 麦 *bakunyō* "wheat" enclosure. Nickname: Wheat.

A **麦** 7030 J477e M47718 **麥** 7031 J734e M47717 BAKU. *mugi* wheat, barley, oats, rye.

4 刈 *mugika(ri)* wheat harvest
5 田 *mugita* a rice field used for growing wheat
打 *mugiu(chi)* wheat threshing
6 扱 *mugikoki* wheat threshing
7 作 *mugisaku* wheat raising
束 *mugitaba* sheaf of wheat, stacked wheat
8 芽 *bakuga* malt
芽糖 *bakugatō* maltose, malt sugar
9 畑 *mugibatake, mugibata* wheat field; barley field
秋 *mugiaki, mugi (no) aki, bakushū* wheat harvest
茶 *mugicha* parched-barley tea
10 酒 *bakushu, bīru* beer

粉 *mugiko* (wheat) flour
11 笛 *mugibue* wheat-straw whistle
粒腫 *bakuryūshu* sty (on the eyelid)
12 湯 *mugiyu* parched-barley tea
飯 *mugimeshi, bakuhan* boiled barley and rice
焦 *mugikoga(shi)* parched-barley flour
稈 *bakkan, mugiwara* wheat straw
稈細工 *mugiwarazaiku* straw work
稈帽子 *mugiwara bōshi* straw hat
13 搗 *mugitsu(ki)* polishing wheat
蒔 *mugimaki* wheat planting
15 踏 *mugifu(mi)* treading wheat plants
17 藁 *mugiwara* wheat straw
藁帽子 *mugiwara bōshi* straw hat

— 4 —

麪 7032 / J7351 / M47742 See 麵 7038.

麩 7033 / J734f / M47739 麸 7034 / J7350 / M-X Fu light wheat-gluten bread. *fusuma* wheat bran, mash.

15 質 *fushitsu* gluten

— 5 —

麭 7035 / J7352 / M47757 Hō sticky rice ball.

— 8 —

麹 7036 / J396d / M-X 麴 7037 / J-X / M47818 Kiku. *kōji* malt, leaven, yeast.
11 菌 *kōjikin* yeast plant, yeast cell
23 黴 *kōji kabi* yeast plant, yeast cell

— 9 —

麺 7038 / J4c4d / M-X 麵 7039 / J-X / M47827 麪 7032 / J7351 / M47742
Men noodles; wheat flour.
12 棒 *membō* rolling pin
16 麭 *pan* bread
18 類 *menrui* noodles

麻 RAD. 200

Asa hemp. Variants: 𣏟 and 广 *asa kammuri,* used as an enclosure. Nickname: Hemp.

B 麻 7040 / J4b63 / M47888 麻 7041 / J-X / M47887 Ma. *asa* flax, hemp, ramie, jute, linen.
5 布 *mafu, asa nuno* hemp cloth, linen
6 糸 *asa ito* linen thread, hemp yarn
衣 *asagoromo, asaginu, mai* linen robe
10 屑 *asakuzu* oakum, tow
疹 *hashika, mashin* measles
11 雀 *mājan* mahjong
雀屋 *mājan'ya* mahjong parlor
酔 *masui* anesthesia
酔剤 *masuizai* anesthetic; narcotic
酔薬 *masuiyaku* anesthetic; narcotic
13 痺 *mahi* paralysis, palsy, numbness, stupor, anesthesia
睡 *masui* deep sleep
幹 *ogara* hemp reed, hemp stalk
裏 *asaura* hemp-soled sandals
裏草履 *asaura zōri* hemp-soled sandals
14 綱 *asazuna* hemp rope
15 縄 *asa nawa* hemp rope
16 薬 *mayaku* anesthetic; narcotic
薬常用 *mayaku jōyō* narcotic addiction
18 織 *asao(ri)* hemp cloth

— 3 —

麼 7042 / J5677 / M47892 Ma, Mo, Ba fine, small, delicate. *nani* what. *ika ni* how. *ka, ya* interrogative particle.

— 4 —

麾 7043 / J5d60 / M47899 Ki. *sashimane(ku)* beckon to; command, take command.
3 下 *kika* under one's command
7 兵 *kihei* soldiers under one's command

— 7 —

麿 7044 / J4b7b / M47909' (国字) *maro* I; you.

12-STROKE RADICALS

RAD. 黄 201

Kiiroi yellow. Variant: 黄 (11 strokes). Nickname: Yellow.

A 黄 7045 / J322b / M47926' 黃 7046 / J-X / M47926 Kō. ō. *ki* yellow.

ki(bamu) turn yellow. *ki(bami)* yellow tint.

3 土 *ōdo* yellow ocher. *kōdo* the earth; yellow soil, loess; hades

口 *kōkō* a baby chick; a young and inexperienced person

口児 *kōkōji* immature youth

4 水 *kimizu* bile, gall

水仙 *kisuisen* jonquil

水晶 *kizuishō* citrine, yellow quartz

5 瓜 *kyūri* cucumber

玉 *ōgyoku, kōgyoku* topaz

玉石 *ōgyokuseki, kōgyokuseki* topaz

白 *kōhaku* yellow and white; gold and silver; bribery, corruption

白色 *kōhakushoku* pale yellow

6 色 *kiiro, kiiro(i), kōshoku, ōshoku* yellow

色人種 *ōshoku jinshu* yellow race

色声 *kiiro(i) koe* shrill voice

7 身 *kimi* yolk of an egg

吻 *kōfun* young and inexperienced person

花 *kōka* chrysanthemum, yellow flowers

8 味 *kimi(gakatta)* yellowish, cream-colored

昏 *kōkon, tasogare* dusk, twilight

表紙 *kibyōshi* dime novel

金 *kogane* gold. *ōgon* gold; gold pieces; money

金万能 *ōgon bannō* mammonism, anything for a buck

金世界 *ōgon sekai* Utopia

金色 *ōgonshoku, koganeiro* gold color

金国 *ōgonkoku* El Dorado

金律 *ōgonritsu* golden rule

金時代 *ōgon jidai* the golden age

金術 *ōgonjutsu* alchemy

金率 *ōgonritsu* golden mean

金崇拝 *ōgon sūhai* mammon worship

9 海 *Kōkai* Yellow Sea

変米 *ōhemmai* spoiled rice

枯茶 *kigaracha* bluish yellow

泉 *kōsen* underground spring. *kōsen, yomi* hades, realm of the dead

10 疸 *ōdan* jaundice

斑 *ōhan* yellow spot

粉 *kinako* soybean flour

11 鳥 *ōchō* nightingale

麻 *kōma* jute

梢 *kōshō* a sprig of yellow buds

菊 *kigiku* yellow chrysanthemum

雀 *kōjaku* sparrow

菖蒲 *kishōbu* yellow iris

道 *ōdo, kōdō* ecliptic

道十二宮 *kōdō jūnikyū* 12 signs of the zodiac

道色 *kōdōshoku* brassy yellow

道光 *kōdōkō* zodiacal light

道吉日 *kōdō kichinichi* lucky day

道面 *kōdōmen* plane of the ecliptic

道帯 *kōdōtai* zodiac

12 葉 *kōyō* fall colors

13 楊 *tsuge* boxwood, box tree

禍 *Kōka* Yellow Peril

褐色 *ōkasshoku* yellowish brown

鉛 *ōen* chrome yellow

鉄鉱 *ōtekkō* iron pyrites, fool's gold

14 塵 *kōjin* dust (in the air); this dusty world

碧玉 *kōhekigyoku* yellow jasper, beryl

緑色 *ōryokushoku* yellow green, pea green

銅 *ōdō* brass

銅鉱 *ōdōkō* copper pyrites, fool's gold

15 熟 *kōjuku* ripening and turning yellow

熱 *ōnetsu* yellow fever

熱病 *ōnetsubyō, kōnetsubyō* yellow fever
16 燐 *ōrin* yellow phosphorus, white phosphorus
21 蠟 *ōrō* beeswax

13

黌 7047 / J7354 / M47985 Kō, Ō school (building); institute.

RAD. 黍 202

Kibi millet. Nickname: Millet.

黍 7048 / J3550 / M47991 SHO. *kibi* millet.
6 団子 *kibi dango* millet dumplings

3

黎 7049 / J7355 / M47994 REI dark, black; many.
5 民 *reimin* the common people
8 明 *reimei* daybreak, dawn
11 黒 *reikoku* dark complexion

5

黏 7050 / J7356 / M48007 See **粘** 4393.

11

黐 7051 / J7357 / M48027 CHI. *mochi* birdlime.
9 竿 *mochizao* lime stick (to catch insects)

RAD. 黑 203

Kuroi black. Variant: 黒 (11 strokes). Nickname: Black (cf. Rad. 95).

A **黒** 7052 / J3975 / M48040 **黑** 7053 / J-X / M48038 KOKU. *kuro* black; dark. *kuro(zumu), kuro(zuku)* blacken, darken. *kuro(bamu), kuro(maru) vi* blacken, become black. *kuro(meru) vt* blacken; talk wrong into right. *kuro(raka)* blackness, deep black. *kuro(ku) suru vt* blacken. *kuro(i)* black; dark, swarthy, browned; dirty. *kuro(ppoi)* dark, blackish.
2 人 *Kokujin* Black person
人霊歌 *Kokujin reika* a Negro spiritual
3 土 *kokudo, kurotsuchi* black soil
子 *kokushi* face mole; mite. *kurogo* prompter, stagehand. *hokuro* dark mole; beauty spot
山 *kuroyama* a large crowd
丸 *kuromaru* black spot, black dot; bull's eye; failure
4 木 *kuroki* unbarked lumber
円 *kuromaru* black spot, black dot; bull's eye; failure
内障 *kokunaishō* black cataract
水引 *kuromizuhiki* black-and-white string for tying envelopes
水熱 *kokusuinetsu* blackwater fever
5 白 *kokuhaku, kokubyaku, kuro-shiro* black and white; right and wrong
目 *kurome* black iris, black eyes
奴 *kokudo* Black slave, Black person (derogatory), dark-skinned person
6 米 *kurogome* unpolished rice
肉 *kuroniku* black sealing ink; black stamp pad
血 *kurochi* venous blood
地 *kuroji* black ground, black cloth
字 *kuroji* black figures, profit
光 *kurobika(ri)* black luster
死病 *kokushibyō* bubonic plague, black death
色 *kokushoku* black
色人種 *kokushoku jinshu* Black race
衣 *kokui, kokue* black clothes. *kurogo* prompter, stagehand
衣宰相 *kokui (no) saishō* Buddhist priest who is a government minister
7 豆 *kuromame* black soy bean
麦 *kuromugi* rye

坊 *kurombō, kurombo* Black person (derogation); dark-skinned person; prompter, stagehand
8 枠 *kurowaku* black (mourning) borders
松 *kuromatsu* black pine
服 *kurofuku* black suit, mourning clothes
苺 *kuroichigo* blackberry
表 *kokuhyō* black list
金 *kurogane* iron
金剛石 *kuro kongōseki* black diamond, carbon, carbonado
板 *kokuban* blackboard
板拭 *kokubanfu(ki)* blackboard eraser
9 海 *Kokkai* Black Sea
点 *kokuten* black spot, dark spot; sunspot
炭 *kokutan* bituminous coal
茶 *kurocha* deep brown
砂糖 *kurozatō* unrefined sugar
風 *kokufū* sky-darkening dust storm
風白雨 *kokufū-hakuu* sudden shower in a dust storm
10 酒 *kuroki* black saké
莓 *kuroichigo* blackberry
紋付 *kuromontsu(ki)* black crested haori
11 黒 *kuroguro* deep black
船 *kurofune* the black ships (of the Westerners)
蛇 *kurohebi* blacksnake
眼鏡 *kuromegane* dark glasses
12 痣 *kuroaza* black mole
焼 *kuroya(ki), kuroya(ke)* charring; something charred
斑 *kurobuchi, kurofu* black spots
焦 *kuroko(ge)* something burnt black
装束 *kuroshozoku* black clothes
猩猩 *kuroshōjō* chimpanzee
雲 *kokuun, kurokumo* dark clouds, black clouds
雲母 *kuroummo* biotite, black or green mica
13 煙 *kokuen, kurokemuri* black smoke
鉛 *kokuen* black lead, graphite
鉄 *kurogane* iron
幕 *kuromaku* black curtain; wirepuller
褐色 *kokkasshoku* blackish brown
塗 *kuronu(ri)* blackening; blackened thing; *kuronu(ri)* black-lacquered, black-colored
14 漆 *kokushitsu* black lacquer
緑 *kuromidori* blackish green
髪 *kurokami, kokuhatsu* black hair
熊 *kuroguma, kurokuma* black bear
15 潮 *Kuroshio* Japan Current
穂 *kurobo, kuroho* smut
線 *kokusen* black line
縁 *kurobuchi* black rim, black edge
影 *kokuei* silhouette, dark shadow
銹病 *kurosabibyō* black rust
16 頭巾 *kurozukin* black hood
17 檀 *kokutan* ebony, blackwood
鍵 *kokken* the black keys
18 曜石 *kokuyōseki* obsidian
曜岩 *kokuyōgan* obsidian
19 蟻 *kuroari* black ant, carpenter ant
20 繻子 *kurojusu* black satin
23 黴 *kurokabi* bread mold

4

黔 7054 / J7358 / M48056 KEN, KIN, GEN black; become black; blacken.

B **黙** 7055 / J4C5B / M48063' **默** 7056 / J6034 / M48063 MOKU keeping silence. *moku(suru)* be silent. *moda(su)* be silent; leave as it is. *dama(ru), moda(su)* become silent, stop speaking, say nothing. *damma(ri)* silence, reticence.

4 止 *mokushi suru* keep silent. *moda(su)* be silent; leave as it is
5 礼 *mokurei suru* bow silently
示 *mokuji, mokushi* revelation; implication
示文学 *mokuji bungaku* apocalyptic literature
示録 *Mokujiroku, Mokushiroku* Revelation
6 考 *mokkō* contemplation, meditation
7 坐 *mokuza suru* sit in silence
否権 *mokuhiken* the right to keep silent
8 念 *mokunen* remaining silent
9 屋 *dama(ri)ya* silent person
約 *mokuyaku* tacit understanding
思 *mokushi* contemplation
契 *mokkei* secret understanding without speaking
省 *mokusei* quiet reflection
10 殺 *mokusatsu suru* ignore
秘 *mokuhi* secrecy, silence
秘権 *mokuhiken* the right to keep silent
11 過 *mokka* overlooking, connivance
視 *mokushi suru* wink at, overlook, tolerate

12 黄 黄 黍 【黑 黒】 黹

許 *mokkyo* tacit permission, connivance
[12]然 *mokuzen(taru)* silent, tacit, mute
[13]想 *mokusō* meditation, reverie
[14]読 *mokudoku* silent reading
認 *mokunin* tacit approval, admission, connivance
[15]劇 *mokugeki* pantomime
諾 *mokudaku* tacit consent
黙 *mokumoku(taru)* silent, tacit, mute
[18]難 *moda(shi)gata(i)* hard to refuse
[19]禱 *mokutō* silent prayer; silent tribute

5

點 7057 / J735a / M48083 See 点 3412.

黝 7058 / J735b / M48082 Yū. Yu. *aoguro* blue-black; black; black soil.

黜 7059 / J7359 / M48076 Chutsu draw back.

黛 7060 / J4263 / M48075 Tai blackened eyebrows; blue-black. *mayuzumi* blackened eyebrows.
[8]青 *taisei* blackish blue

6

黠 7061 / J735c / M48097 Katsu crafty.

8

黨 7062 / J735e / M48132 See 党 363.

黥 7063 / J735d / M48123 Kei, Gei tattooing. *irezumi* tattooing.

9

黯 7064 / J735f / M48159 An black; dark.
[12]然 *anzen(taru)* tearful, doleful

11

黴 7065 / J7360 / M48196 Bai. *kabi* mold, mildew, must, fungus. *kabi(ru)* get moldy, get musty, mildew.
[4]止 *kabido(me)* fungicide
[8]雨 *tsuyu, baiu* rainy season
毒 *baidoku* syphilis
毒性 *baidokusei* syphilitic
[9]臭 *kabikusa(i)* musty, moldy; hackneyed
[11]菌 *baikin* bacillus, bacteria, germ
菌学 *baikingaku* bacteriology, microbiology
菌説 *baikinsetsu* germ theory

14

黶 7066 / J7361 / M48229 An a tache, a black mark. En. *hokuro* a mole.

15

黷 7067 / J7362 / M48234 Toku, Doku become dirty; be humiliated; dirty; disgrace.

RAD. 黹 204

Nuu to embroider, sew. Nickname: Sewing.

黹 7068 / J7363 / M48248 Chi. *nu(u)* sew, stitch, embroider.

5

黻 7069 / J7364 / M48250 Futsu a lap robe made with tanned skin; a type of embroidery pattern used in ancient ceremonial dress.

7

黼 7070 / J7365 / M48252 Fu, Ho an ax-shaped embroidery pattern used in ancient ceremonial dress; embroidered clothes.

13-STROKE RADICALS

RAD. 黽 205

Aogaeru tree frog. Nickname: Frog.

黽 7071 / J7366 / M48257 Bō, Bin, Ben green frog; industry.

[10]勉 *bimben* industry, diligence

— 11 —

鼇 7072 / J7367 / M48301 Gō a giant turtle or terrapin.

— 12 —

鼈 7073 / J7368 / M48305 **鱉** 6917 / J-X / M46472 Betsu. *suppon* snapping turtle, mud turtle, fresh-water soft-shell turtle.

[5]甲 *bekkō* tortoise shell

甲色 *bekkō iro* amber color

RAD. 鼎 206

Kamae kettle. This is actually a 12-stroke radical but is placed here in its traditional place among the 13-stroke radicals. Nickname: Kettle.

鼎 7074 / J4524 / M48315 **鼑** 7075 / J-X / M48316 Tei. *kanae* three-legged kettle.

[5]立 *teiritsu* triangular position; three-cornered (contest)

立戦 *teiritsusen* three-cornered contest

[7]座 *teiza suru* sit in a triangle

[15]談 *teidan* three-way talk, tripartite talk

談会 *teidankai* three-way talk, tripartite talk

14-STROKE RADICALS

RAD. 鼓 207

Tsuzumi hand-drum. Variant: 皷 (14 strokes). Nickname: Drum.

B**鼓** 7076 / J385d / M48330 **皷** 3881 / J7369 / M22887 Ko *tsuzumi* drum.

ko(su) beat; rouse, muster (courage).

tsuzumi hand drum.

[4]手 *koshu* drummer

手長 *koshuchō* drum major

[7]吹 *kosui* inspiration; advocacy; encouragement

吹者 *kosuisha* advocate, propagator

[9]室 *koshitsu* eardrum

[11]動 *kodō* beat, palpitation, pulsation, throbbing

笛隊 *kotekitai* drum-and-fife band

[13]腸 *kochō* flatulence, bloating

腹 *kofuku suru* be happy and contented

[14]膜 *komaku* eardrum

[15]楼 *korō* drum tower (at a temple)

舞 *kobu* inspiration, stimulation, encouragement

舞激励 *kobu-gekirei* encouragement

— 5 —

鼕 7077 / J736a / M48341 Tō, Zu the sound of a hand drum.

鼠 RAD. 208

Nezumi rat. As enclosure: 鼠. Nickname: Rat.

鼠 7078 / J414d / M48390 **鼡** 1394 / J736b / M-X So. *nezumi, nezu* rat, mouse; dark gray.

2 入 *nezumii(razu)* a ratproof cupboard
6 色 *nezumi iro* dark gray, slate
8 取 *nezumitor(i)* rat poison; mousetrap
9 疫 *soeki* plague, pest
咬症 *sokōshō* ratbite disease
海豚 *nezumi iruka* porpoise
11 盗 *sotō* pilfering
12 落 *nezumioto(shi)* rattrap
13 賊 *sozoku* petty thief, pilferer; sneak thief
嫁入 *nezumi (no) yomei(ri)* a light shower
14 算 *nezumizan* multiplying like rats
15 背 *sohai* small fry, unimportant people
17 蹊 *sokei* the groin
蹊部 *sokeibu* the groin

5

鼬 7079 / J736c / M48427 Yū. *itachi* weasel; skunk; mink; ermine.

9

鼹 7080 / J-X / M48464 See **鼴** 7081.

10

鼴 7081 / J-X / M48480 **鼹** 7080 / J-X / M48464 En mole.

13 鼠 *mogura* mole (the rodent)

鼻 RAD. 209

Hana nose. Variant: 鼻. Nickname: Nose.

A **鼻** 7082 / J4921 / M48498' Bi nasal. *hana* nose; snout, muzzle. *hana(ppashi)* bridge of the nose.

3 口 *bikō* nose and mouth; nostrils; muzzle (of a dog)
下 *bika* under the nose
下長 *bikachō* amorous man; henpecked husband
4 木 *hanagi* nose hitch (for cattle)
毛 *hanage* nostril hairs
水 *hanamizu* nasal discharge
内 *binai* in the nose
孔 *bikō* nostrils
元 *hanamoto* root of the nose
5 白 *hanajiro(mu)* feel let down; feel ashamed
汁 *hanajiru* nasal discharge
出血 *bishukketsu* nosebleed
6 血 *hanaji* nosebleed
向 *hanamu(ke)* smelling (something)
汗 *hanaase* nose sweat
先 *hanasaki* tip of the nose. *hanasaki ni* under one's nose; imminent
7 折 *hana (o) o(ru)* to humble (a person)
声 *hanagoe, bisei* nasal voice
8 明 *hana (o) aka(su)* take advantage of another's misfortune
炎 *bien* nasal inflammation
呼吸 *bikokyū* nasal respiration
9 面 *hanazura* muzzle, snout
革 *hanagawa* toe cover for geta
音 *bion* a nasal sound
屎 *hana kuso* nasal discharge
拭 *hanafu(ki)* handkerchief
持 *hanamo(chinaranu)* intolerable, disgusting
柱 *hana(p)pashira, hanabashira* septum, bridge of the nose
祖 *biso* founder, originator, introducer
茸 *biji, hanatake* nasal polyps, adenoids
凬 *hanakaze* head cold
風邪 *hanakaze* head cold
10 骨 *bikotsu* nasal bone
疾 *bishitsu* diseases of the nose
唄 *hanauta* humming, crooning
根 *bikon* root of the nose
紙 *hanagami* handkerchief paper
高 *hanataka* high nose; person with a

high nose; pride. *hana (ga) taka(i)* proud. *hana (o) taka(ku) suru* be proud
高高 *hanatakadaka* proudly, triumphantly
息 *bisoku, hanaiki* nasal breathing; a person's pleasure
息荒 *hanaiki (ga) ara(i)* imperious, proud
11 張 *hana(p)pa(ri)* overconfidence
許 *hanamoto* root of the nose
梁 *biryō* bridge of the nose
眼鏡 *hana megane* pince-nez glasses
12 腔 *bikō, bikū* nasal cavity
筋 *hanasuji* bridge of the nose
13 詰 *hanatsuma(ri), hanazuma(ri)* nose being clogged up
14 摘 *hanatsuma(mi)* uncouth person, bore
端 *bitan* nose tip
緒 *hanao* geta thong
綱 *hanazuna* halter
歌 *hanauta* humming, crooning
歌交 *hanautamaji(ri)* humming unconcernedly
15 衝 *hanatsu(ki)* meeting head-on
潰 *hanatsubu(re)* flat nose; flat-nosed person
輪 *hanawa* nose ring
16 薬 *hanagusuri* bribe, hush money
髭 *hanahige* mustache
17 縻 *hanazura* halter
糞 *hana kuso* nasal discharge
19 鏡 *hana kagami, bikyō* nasal speculum

3

鼾 7083 / J736d / M48505 KAN. *ibiki* snoring.
7 声 *kansei* snoring
11 酔 *kansui* snoring

齊 RAD. 210

Sai or *hitoshii* alike. Variant: 斉 (8 strokes). Nickname: Mr. Saito (i.e., the first character of this common surname).

齊 7084 / J736e / M48560 See **斉** 2366.

3

齋 7085 / J6337 / M48565 See **斎** 2368.

7

齎 7086 / J6c5a / M48575 **斎** 2372 / J-X / M-X SEI. *mota(rasu)* bring, take; bring about.

9

齏 7087 / J706d / M48578 **韲** 6606 / J706e / M43249 SEI. *a(eru)* dress vegetables (as in salad).
8 物 *aemono* vegetable side dish

15-STROKE RADICALS

RAD. 齒 211

Ha tooth. Variant: 歯 (12 strokes). Nickname: Tooth.

齒 7088 / J736f / M48583 See 歯 2961.

2

齔 7089 / J7370 / M48587 SHIN, CHIN lose milk teeth and gain permanent teeth; a child, a youngster.

5

齠 7090 / J7373 / M48631 CHŌ, JŌ lose milk teeth and gain permanent teeth; a child, a youngster.

齣 7091 / J7371 / M48638 SHAKU a paragraph, a section; frame, scene.

齝 7092 / J-X / M48622 CHI *nire(gamu), nige(kamu)* chew the cud.

B 齢 7093 / J4e70 / M48632' 齡 7094 / J7374 / M48632 REI. *yowai* age.

齟 7095 / J7372 / M48627 SO. uneven; bite; disagree.

22 齬 *sogo* inconsistency, discord, conflict, discrepancy, contradiction; failure, frustration.

6

齦 7096 / J7375 / M48649 GIN. KON. *haguki* gums.

齧 7097 / J7376 / M48651 GETSU. *kaji(ru)* gnaw, nibble, bite at, munch, crunch; have a smattering of.

5 付 *kaji(ri)-tsu(ku)* bite into, stick to

12 散 *kaji(ri)-chi(rasu)* gnaw at and scatter around; start a lot of things and not finish any

7

齬 7098 / J7377 / M48680 GO irregular teeth; discord.

齪 7099 / J7378 / M48669 SAKU, SOKU grating the teeth; fretful.

9

齶 7100 / J737b / M48725 腭 4840 / J-X / M29700 GAKU. *ago* jaw.

齷 7101 / J7379 / M48727 AKU grating the teeth; fretful.

22 齪 *akuseku suru* worry about; be busy about. *akuseku* fussily, busily, sedulously

齲 7102 / J737a / M48716 KU, U *mushiba* decayed tooth; cavity.

12 歯 *ushi, mushiba* decayed tooth; cavity

15 蝕 *ushoku* tooth decay

16-STROKE RADICALS

RAD. 龍 212

Tatsu dragon. Variants: 竜 (10 strokes). Nickname: Big Dragon (cf. Rad. 161).

龍 7103 / J4e36 / M48818 See 竜 4232.

6 ——

龕 7104 / J737c / M48839 GAN niche or alcove for an image.

[6]灯 *gandō* Buddhist altar light

—— 23 ——

龘 7105 / J-X / M48845 DŌ. TŌ. dragons moving.

RAD. 龜 213

Kame turtle. Variant: 亀 (11 strokes). Nickname: Turtle.

龜 7106 / J737d / M48847 See 亀 62.

17-STROKE RADICALS

RAD. 龠 214

Fue flute. Nickname: Flute.

龠 7107 / J737e / M48882 YAKU flute.

APPENDIX 1. HOW TO FIND A CHARACTER

Some three centuries ago the Chinese evolved a system of classifying their characters according to 214 basic elements or radicals. The system was based partially on the character's shape and composition and partially on the meaning of the character. Thus, although most characters involving the enclosure 門 (Rad. 169-gate) are to be found under that radical, 聞 4732 is classified under 耳 (Rad. 128-ear), presumably because hearing is done with the ear. This system is still used today in Chinese, Korean, and Japanese character dictionaries and is followed in the present dictionary also. There have been a large number of attempts to reclassify the characters, either under a new radical system or under a redistribution of the characters within the traditional system. One drawback of these attempts is that it is difficult for one who has learned one of the revised systems to use a traditional Japanese, Korean, or Chinese character dictionary; another in that it separates different versions of the same character that differ only in the arrangement of their component elements. Finding the radical, then, is not a deterministic process and may require some trial and error.

1. Determine the radical of the character (see Appendices 3, 4, 5, and 6), count the strokes of the radical, and find the radical number on the chart inside the front covers.

2. Spin the pages of the dictionary till you come to that radical number in the upper, outer corners of the pages.

> *Another method, replacing the foregoing two steps* (this short cut is recommended only for those familiar enough with the radicals to realize immediately that, for example, the common 3-stroke grass radical is actually a variant of the 6-stroke grass radical—No. 140—and is to be looked for under the larger stroke-count): Having determined the radical and without worrying about its number, spin immediately to the place where all the radicals of the same stroke-count appear in the marginal radical strings, the stroke-count being shown by the large numeral at the head of each string. (*In case of a variant radical, use the stroke-count of its parent radical.*) Now find your radical in the radical string and spin the pages slowly one way or the other till the brackets moving up and down the string reach your radical.

3. Count the number of strokes in the non-radical part of the character and then, as a guide to the eye, place your thumb near the proper radical in the radical string and slowly spin the pages one way or the other till the tiny numeral opposite your radical reaches your stroke-count.

4. Glance through the main-character entries nearby to find the one you want; it will be somewhere in those pages with the proper non-radical stroke-count as indicated either by the tiny marginal numeral or the large numerals in the column-wide dividers. Within any given stroke-count section, the main character entries are arranged with cross-reference and rarer characters first, followed by the more familiar characters in the ascending order of the number of compounds listed under each.

APPENDIX 2. HOW TO FIND A COMPOUND

1. Find the first character of the compound by the procedure described in the preceding appendix.

2. Count the total number of strokes in the second character and then glance down the series of superscript numerals immediately to the left of the list of compounds till you find the proper second-character stroke-count.

3. Look for the second character of your compound among those with this stroke-count. In listing each compound, its first character has been omitted since it is the same as the character shown in the main entry above it. Note also that the character-repetition sign (々) has not been used; since the first character is omitted in listing compounds, in such cases it was felt better to repeat the full character.

4. If there are many compounds listed under the same second-character stroke-count, time can be saved by keeping in mind that within such a grouping the compounds have been arranged in the following order: (a) 2-character compounds, (b) 3-character compounds, (c) 4-character compounds, and (d) "families" of compounds, i.e., a group of compounds whose second characters, as well as the first, are identical.

5. If you cannot find your compound, possible reasons and remedies are:

(a) You may have miscounted the strokes of the second character. So look for it up and down the adjacent stroke-count groups.

(b) The second character of your compound may be in a variant form that differs in shape, and probably in stroke-count as well, from the standard form used in the compounds of this dictionary. For example, it may be a Jōyō Kanji given in its older form, while in our lists of compounds all Jōyō Kanji appear only in their newer forms. Or again, it may be a non-Jōyō Kanji in which, according to the unauthorized usage of some printers, one element has been simplified by analogy with the same element in a Jōyō Kanji, while in our lists non-Jōyō Kanji usually appear only in their original forms. To have included such variations in our lists would have led to endless duplication of entries. But we do give the important variants in our main-character entries. Hence, the surest remedy, which is unfortunately also the most time-consuming, is to look up the second character of your compound in the main-character entries, there ascertain its standard form, and then look for such standard form in your list of compounds. But we recommend first checking quickly through the same stroke-count group and the immediately adjacent groups for a character that looks almost the same as the one you are looking for. This method will usually work when the variation is slight.

(c) The word may be one of the less frequently used ones which do not appear in this dictionary. So either look for it in one of the large Japanese character dictionaries (the M numbers provide ready reference to Morohashi's dictionary) or determine its probable reading by looking up the individual characters of which it is composed and then consult a Japanese-English romanized dictionary like Kenkyūsha's.

(d) In the case of a compound of three or more characters, it may be a "compound compound." So try, for example in the case of four characters, looking for separate compound forms of the first two and the last two.

APPENDIX 3. HOW TO DETERMINE THE RADICAL OF A CHARACTER

Those who are familiar with character dictionaries know how difficult it often is to decide which is the radical of a character. This is due to the fact that nearly every character, excepting only a few, contains from two to seven or eight radicals. The character 截, for example, contains the following seven elements, each of which happens to be a radical (the radical numbers are shown in parentheses): 一 (1), 丨 (2), 丶 (3), ノ (4), 十 (24), 戈 (62), 隹 (172). So it is anybody's guess as to which of these is the traditional radical under which this character would be listed. (In fact, it is listed under 戈 62.) The process of deciding under which radical to search is far too often a time-wasting and discouraging trial-and-error process. We believe that we have solved this problem with the introduction of the **Universal Radical Index**, Appendix 15. The URI allows character look-ups based on virtually any reasonable radical element found in the character. Aimed primarily at the novice user, but useful to anyone frustrated by obscure radicals and difficult-to-remember "radical priorities," the URI lists characters (including characters which consist of one and only one radical) under multiple alternative radicals and plausible miscounts of residual strokes. The following 12 steps run from most likely to least likely radical placment. The rules are not absolute, but are guidelines that will generally lead the user to the correct location. If the character is not found in the first or second try, the user may wish to resort to the Universal Radical Index.

THE 12 STEPS. If you follow these steps, you will be able to choose the radical correctly in most cases and, after a little practice, almost instantaneously. (The numerals given below in parentheses show the numbers of the radicals.)

N.B. If there are two radicals in the same designated position, always take the one with the GREATER *stroke-count.*

STEP 1. ALL? *Is* ALL *the character a radical?* For a complete listing, see Appendix 13. Here are a few examples:

土(32), 方(70), 生(100), 米(119), 辛(160), 高(189), 鼻(209).

STEP 2. LONE? *Does it have only one lone radical?*

メ (丶 3), 乃 (ノ 4), 久 (ノ 4), 了 (亅 6)

STEP 3. ENCLOSURE? *Does it have a completely exterior* ENCLOSURE *radical?* The enclosure may cover two, three, or four sides.

Examples of characters containing all the radicals that *enclose two sides* (the radicals and their numbers shown in parentheses):

勿 (勹 20), 原 (厂 27), 局 (尸 44), 度 (广 53), 廻 (廴 54), 式 (弋 56),
成 (戈 62), 房 (戸 63), 死 (歹 78), 毬 (毛 82), 気 (气 84), 爬 (爪 87),
瓸 (瓦 98), 病 (疒 104), 虎 (虍 141), 起 (走 156), 辱 (辰 161), 速 (辶 162),
颱 (風 182), 魁 (鬼 194), 麝 (鹿 198), 麪 (麦 199), 磨 (麻 200), 鼬 (鼠 208)

Examples of all the radicals that *enclose three sides*:

円 (冂 13), 凶 (凵 17), 医 (匸 22), 閉 (門 169), 齎 (齊 210)

Example of the one radical that *encloses four sides*: 国 (囗 31)

STEP 4. LEFT? *Is there a clearly defined* LEFT *radical?* By "clearly defined" we mean a radical that completely dominates the left side, i.e., one that is unobstructed both above and below, such as 十 in 協. It follows that in the character 截, for example, neither 十 nor 隹 can be chosen as a left radical. Some other examples:
偉—both left and right are radicals; take the left, 亻 (9).
准—both left and right are radicals; take the left, 冫 (15).
杉—both left and right are radicals; take the left, 木 (75).

3. How to Determine the Radical of a Character

釣—right not a radical, take the left, 金 (167).

STEP 5. RIGHT? *Is there a clearly defined* RIGHT *radical?*
和—both left and right are radicals; take the right, 口 (30).
彫—left not a radical; take the right, 彡 (59).
欧—left not a radical; take the right, 欠 (76). Note that we ignore any slight interference with the left by a left-tapering stroke.
頂—left not a radical; take the right, 頁 (181).

STEP 6. TOP? *Is there a clear* TOP *radical?* Examples:
空—take the top, 穴 (116). Note that we take this in place of 宀 (40) because in general it is advantageous to take the more complex of two similarly placed radicals.
云—take 二 (7).
公—both top and bottom are radicals; take the top, 八 (12). Note that Rad. 12 appears in three forms 八, 𠆢, and ソ.
兼—take 八 (12).
套—take 大 (37).
安—both top and bottom are radicals; take the top, 宀 (40).
男—both top and bottom are radicals; take the top, 田 (102).

Note that many top radicals are closed canopies like 人, 冖, 大, 宀, or 穴.

STEP 7. BOTTOM? *Is there a clear* BOTTOM *radical?* Note that this may or not be resting under a canopy. Examples:
急—top not a radical; take the bottom, 心 (61).
思—both top and bottom are radicals; take the bottom, 心 (61).
学—top not a radical; take the bottom, 子 (39).
嚮—top not a radical; take 口 (30) at the bottom under the canopy.
甥—top not a radical; take the bottom, 刀 (18).
朶—top not a radical; take the bottom, 木 (75).

STEP 8. NW? *Is there a radical in the* NORTHWEST *corner?* Examples:
報—Going down our table of steps, we find this is neither ALL, LONE, ENCLOSURE, LEFT, RIGHT, TOP, nor BOTTOM. So we start around the corners clockwise beginning in the NORTHWEST, and there sits 土 (32). This is our radical. There is also 十 (24) in that same corner; but remember, we generally take the more complex of two possible radicals.
梵—The character is not a radical in its own right, has no enclosures, and does not divide into left and right portions. It does divide into top and bottom, but the top as a whole is not a radical, nor is the bottom. Take 木 (75) at the upper left (NW) corner.

STEP 9. NE? *Is there a radical in the* NORTHEAST *corner?* Example: 呉—bottom is also a radical, but take the upper right (NE) corner, 口 (30).

STEP 10. SE? *Is there a radical in the* SOUTHEAST *corner?* Example: 君—Here again we find that 口 (30) is the radical in the SE corner. Note that this is not the case of a lone radical because we also have radicals 丿 (4), 一 (1), 尸 (44), and ヨ (58).

STEP 11. SW? *Is there a radical in the* SOUTHWEST *corner?* Examples:
糶 The upper right, lower right, and lower left (southwest) corners are all radicals; take the lower left, 米, (119)

羅—All four corners are radicals; here, too, take the southwest corner radical, 米, (119).

虱 At first glance, the upper right element may look like an enclosure, however, it is not a radical and we are lead to the lower left corner, 虫 (142).

STEP 12. INSIDE? *Is there a radical in the INTERIOR of the character?* Examples:

周 One would expect the enclosure 冂 (13) to be the relevant radical, but the character is to be found under the bottom inside, 口 (30). In the URI, this character is listed under 冂, 口, and 土.

巡 The obvious radical is 辶 (162), but the character is traditionally classified under 巛 (47).

APPENDIX 4. MORE ABOUT RADICALS

MISCELLANEOUS EXAMPLES OF RADICALS. The following table, arranged by the twelve steps given above, illustrates the process of finding the radical for a given character. In general, following the eleven steps will lead to finding the character quickly and easily. Usually a top radical will be preferred to a bottom one, a left radical to a right one, and an enclosure to the inside, but not every time. When in doubt, consult the Universal Radical Index, where each character is listed under all of its likely radicals.

STEP 1. ALL

木 2531 → 木 75
欠 2928 → 欠 76
高 6796 → 高 189
黑 7052 → 黑 203

STEP 2. LONE

乃 42 → 丿 4
久 47 → 丿 4
了 67 → 亅 6

STEP 3. ENCLOSURE

凧 434 → 几 16
函 446 → 凵 17
匍 575 → 勹 20
匪 592 → 匚 22
厭 662 → 厂 27
園 962 → 囗 31
履 1434 → 尸 44
座 1619 → 广 53
建 1660 → 廴 54
弐 1673 → 弋 56
或 2030 → 戈 62
疱 3791 → 疒 104
趁 5850 → 走 156
[illegible] 6057 → 辶 162
問 6391 → 門 169
鬨 6823 → 鬥 191

STEP 4. LEFT

俐 208 → 人 9
冲 413 → 冫 15
加 523 → 力 19
協 617 → 十 24
味 766 → 口 30
址 982 → 土 32
奴 1174 → 女 38
孩 1294 → 子 39
枉 2584 → 木 75
灯 3395 → 火 86
牾 3543 → 牛 93
疏 3775 → 疋 103
眈 3911 → 目 109
硯 4005 → 石 112
訴 5588 → 言 149
販 5779 → 貝 154
軋 5940 → 車 159
麒 7025 → 鹿 198
鼾 7083 → 鼻 209
齔 7099 → 齒 211

STEP 5. RIGHT

刧 462 → 刀 18
勍 542 → 力 19
卸 641 → 卩 26
彬 1717 → 彡 59
欧 2931 → 欠 76
殺 2994 → 殳 79
状 3556 → 犬 94
視 5525 → 見 147
韓 6602 → 韋 178
頂 6616 → 頁 181
鳰 6935 → 鳥 196

STEP 6. TOP

丁 2 → 一 1
主 38 → 丶 3
乖 53 → 丿 4
交 90 → 亠 8
今 112 → 人 9
兮 370 → 八 12
宣 1328 → 宀 40
彙 1709 → 彐 58
登 3862 → 癶 105
笑 4256 → 竹 118
要 5515 → 襾 146
魯 6848 → 魚 195

STEP 7. BOTTOM

兄 344 → 儿 10
兵 374 → 八 12
分 454 → 刀 18
午 604 → 十 24
呑 737 → 口 30
弄 1668 → 廾 55

4. More about Radicals

当 1706 → ヨ 58
志 1785 → 心 61
擘 2290 → 手 64
泉 3095 → 水 85
砦 4002 → 石 112
紊 4447 → 糸 120
靡 6565 → 非 175
鶩 6984 → 鳥 196
黶 7066 → 黒 203
龕 7104 → 龍 212

STEP 8. NORTHWEST

報 1059 → 土 32
巽 1546 → 己 49
幾 1601 → 幺 52
競 4244 → 立 117
霎 6556 → 雨 173

STEP 9. NORTHEAST

整 2360 → 攵 66
耀 4695 → 羽 124

STEP 10. SOUTHEAST

友 672 → 又 29
君 746 → 口 30
将 1379 → 寸 41
左 1535 → 工 48
幹 1596 → 干 51
炭 3413 → 火 86
産 3716 → 生 100

STEP 11. SOUTHWEST

旬 2415 → 日 72
歸 2966 → 止 77
糶 4430 → 米 119
糴 4429 → 米 119
虱 5276 → 虫 142
鬱 6830 → 鬯 192

STEP 12. INSIDE

夙 1126 → 夕 36
夾 1144 → 大 37
嬲 1275 → 女 38
県 3918 → 目 109
聞 4732 → 耳 128
輿 5983 → 車 159

IMPORTANT RADICALS. Here are the 67 radicals that you will most often encounter. They are classified by stroke-count and arranged by their numbers. It will definitely be worth your while to memorize their numbers and recommended "nicknames"which accompany them. Note that only the parent form of each radical is shown here; consult Appendix 5 and the chart inside the cover for important variant forms.

ONE STROKE
一 1—one
丨 2—rod
丶 3—dot
丿 4—*kana no*

TWO STROKES
亠 8—lid
人 9—man
八 12—eight
刀 18—sword
力 19—strong
十 24—cross
厂 27—cliff

THREE STROKES
口 30—mouth
囗 31—box
土 32—earth
女 38—woman
宀 40—*kana u*
小 42—little
尸 44—flag
山 46—mountain
巾 50—cloth
广 53—dotted cliff
弓 57—bow
彳 60—going man

FOUR STROKES
心 61—heart
手 64—hand
攴 66—folding chair
日 72—sun
木 75—tree
水 85—water
火 86—fire
牛 93—cow
犬 94—dog

FIVE STROKES
玉 96—jewel
田 102—rice field
疒 104—sick
皿 108—dish
目 109—eye
石 112—stone
示 113—showing
禾 115—2-branch tree
立 117—standing

SIX STROKES
竹 118—bamboo
米 119—rice
糸 120—thread
耳 128—ear
肉 130—meat
舟 137—ship
艸 140—grass
虫 142—bug
衣 145—clothing

SEVEN STROKES
見 147—seeing
言 149—speaking
貝 154—small shell
足 157—foot
車 159—car
辵 162—road
邑 163—right village

EIGHT STROKES
金 167—metal
門 169—gate
阜 170—left village
隹 172—old bird
雨 173—rain

NINE STROKES
頁 181—big shell
食 184—food

TEN STROKES
馬 187— horse

ELEVEN STROKES
魚 195—fish
鳥 196—bird

WARNINGS ON UNUSUAL RADICALS. It is well, occasionally, to look over the Step-1 table of Appendix 13 in the book to refresh your memory as to which current characters are their own radicals.

Remember that ⺕ is a variety of ヨ (Rad. 58).

Note the distinct difference between Rads. 71 and 92 as shown on the chart inside the front cover. 牙 is a 5-stroke variant of the 4-stroke 牙 (92) and it is encountered more often than the parent. 旡 is a 5-stroke variant of the 4-stroke 无 (71) and it is also encountered more often than the parent.

Note that 禸 (114) is a 5-stroke, not a 4-stroke, radical and is always counted as 5 whenever it appears in any character.

Remember that 豸 is a 6-stroke variant of the 7-stroke 豕 (152).

Glance over the chart inside the front cover beginning with Rad. 187 and note the many radicals in the 10- to 17-stroke categories. You will encounter them more or less frequently.

Let us repeat that it is very important to be able to recognize a radical when you see one, even though you may not be able to recall its name or its number.

When you are not sure whether an element of a character is a radical or not, consult the chart inside the front cover or the tables in Appendix 13.

LOST RADICALS. In the simplification of characters by the Japanese Government, some have actually lost their traditional radicals, making them most difficult to find in ordinary dictionaries. These have been reclassified according to the standard practice of Japanese character dictionaries and have been entered into the Universal Radical Index.

The following table gives a representative list of characters that have lost their radicals. Each entry shows, first, the original form of the character followed by its traditional radical (now lost) and radical number; and then, following an arrow, are given the present simplified form of the character, the number under which it is entered in this dictionary, and the radical and radical number under which we classify it.

兩	入 (12)	→	両 (23)	一 (1)
豫	豕 (152)	→	予 (68)	亅 (6)
會	日 (72)	→	会 (143)	人 (9)
處	虍 (141)	→	処 (435)	几 (16)
醫	酉 (164)	→	医 (590)	匚 (22)
單	口 (30)	→	単 (620)	十 (24)
嚴	口 (30)	→	厳 (663)	厂 (27)
營	火 (86)	→	営 (857)	口 (30)
聲	耳 (128)	→	声 (989)	士 (32)
壽	士 (32)	→	寿 (1374)	寸 (41)
盡	皿 (108)	→	尽 (1408)	尸 (44)
貳	貝 (154)	→	弐 (1675)	弋 (56)

當	田 (102)	→	当 (1706)	ヨ (58)	
舊	臼 (134)	→	旧 (2412)	日 (72)	
來	人 (9)	→	来 (2565)	木 (75)	
爲	爪 (87)	→	為 (3411)	火 (86)	
縣	糸 (120)	→	県 (3918)	目 (109)	

APPENDIX 5. THE RADICALS CLASSIFIED BY POSITION

The charts which follow are arranged in the same order as the steps suggested above for finding the radical of a character. Only the first seven steps are illustrated because the radicals appearing in the corners and inside are not limited to a definable set.

STEP 1. ALL
The Characters Which Are Also Radicals

1	一 1	乙 5	**2**	二 7	人 9	入 11	八 12	刀 18	力 19	匕 21	十 24
卜 25	厶 28	又 29	**3**	口 30	土 32	士 33	夕 36	大 37	女 38	子 39	寸 41
小 42	尸 44	山 46	川 47	工 48	己 49	已 49	巳 49	巾 50	干 51	廾 55	弋 56
弓 57	彳 60	**4**	心 61	戸 63	戶 63	手 64	文 67	斗 68	斤 69	方 70	日 72
曰 73	月 74	木 75	欠 76	止 77	毋 80	比 81	毛 82	氏 83	水 85	火 86	爪 87
父 88	片 91	牙 92	牛 93	犬 94	王 [96]	**5**	母 [80]	牙 [92]	玄 95	玉 96	瓜 97
瓦 98	甘 99	生 100	用 101	田 102	疋 103	白 106	皮 107	皿 108	目 109	矛 110	矢 111
石 112	示 113	穴 116	立 117	**6**	竹 118	米 119	糸 120	缶 121	羊 123	羽 124	羽 124
老 125	而 126	耒 127	耳 128	肉 130	臣 131	自 132	至 133	臼 134	舌 135	舟 137	色 139
虫 142	血 143	行 144	衣 145	西 146	**7**	臣 [131]	見 147	角 148	言 149	谷 150	豆 151

豕 152	貝 154	赤 155	走 156	足 157	身 158	車 159	辛 160	辛 160	辰 161	邑 163	酉 164
釆 165	里 166	麦 [199]	**8**	金 167	長 168	門 169	阜 170	雨 173	雨 173	青 174	靑 174
非 175	**9**	面 176	革 177	韭 179	音 180	音 180	頁 181	風 182	飛 183	食 184	食 184
首 185	香 186	**10**	馬 187	骨 188	高 189	鬼 194	**11/17**	魚 195	鳥 196	鹵 197	鹿 198
麥 199	麻 200	麻 200	黄 [201]	黒 [203]	黃 201	黍 202	黑 203	鼎 206	鼓 207	鼠 208	皷 [207]
鼻 209	鼻 209	齊 210	齒 211	龍 212	龜 213	龠 214					

STEP 2. LONE

The Common Characters Having But One Radical

(each followed by Its rad. & rad. no.)

メ → 丶 3	乃 → ノ 4	久 → ノ 4	了 → 亅 6

STEP 3. ENCLOSURE

The Radicals Found as Enclosures

1	乚 5	**2**	冂 13	冂 13	冂 13	冂 13	几 16	几 16	凵 17	勹 20	匚 22
匸 22	厂 27	辶 [162]		**3**	口 31	夂 34	尸 44	广 53	廴 54	弋 56	辶 [162]
4	戈 62	戸 63	戶 63	支 65	歹 78	毛 82	气 84	爪 87	**5**	瓦 98	疒 104
6	耳 128	虍 141	**7**	走 156	辰 161	辵 162	麦 [199]	**8**	門 169	**9**	風 182
10	鬥 191	鬼 194		**11**	鹿 198	麥 199	麻 200		**13/14**	鼠 208	齊 210

STEP 4. LEFT
The Radicals Found at the Left

1	丨 2	㇑ 2	丿 4	2	亻 9	冫 15	力 19	十 24	又 29	ヌ 29	阝 [170]
3	口 30	土 32	夕 36	女 38	子 39	山 46	川 47	工 48	己 49	巾 50	干 51
幺 52	弓 57	彡 59	彳 60	忄 [61]	扌 [64]	氵 [85]	丬 [90]	犭 [94]			
4	戸 63	戸 63	手 64	文 67	斤 69	方 70	日 72	木 75	止 77	歹 78	火 86
爻 89	爿 90	片 91	牙 92	牛 93	王 [96]	礻 [113]	月 [130]	月 [130]			
5	牙 [92]	玄 95	瓦 98	甘 99	生 100	田 102	疋 103	白 106	皮 107	目 109	矛 110
矢 111	石 112	示 113	禾 115	立 117	艮 [138]	衤 [145]	6	米 119	糸 120	缶 121	羊 123
羽 124	羽 124	而 126	耒 127	耒 127	耳 128	臣 131	至 133	舌 135	舟 137	虫 142	血 143
7	臣 [131]	角 148	言 149	谷 150	豆 151	豕 152	豸 153	貝 154	赤 155	足 157	身 158
車 159	辛 160	酉 164	釆 165	里 166	長 [168]	8	金 167	隹 172	青 174	靑 174	食 [184]
斉 [210]	9	面 176	革 177	韋 178	音 180	音 180	食 [184]	首 185	香 186		
10	韋 [178]	馬 187	骨 188	鬲 193	魚 [195]	11	魚 195	鳥 196	鹵 197	鹿 198	麦 199
黄 [201]	黒 [203]	12/17	黃 201	黍 202	黑 203	歯 [211]	鼠 208	鼻 209	齊 210	齒 211	龍 212

STEP 5. RIGHT

The Radicals Found at the Right

1	丨 2	丨 2	乚 5	**2**	人 9	几 16	刀 18	刂 18	力 19	匕 21	十 24
卜 25	卩 26	又 29	阝 [163]	**3**	口 30	子 39	寸 41	彡 59	**4**	戈 62	支 65
攴 66	攵 66	斗 68	斤 69	欠 76	殳 79	比 81	毛 82	犬 94	月 [130]	月 [130]	
5	旡 [71]	爪 97	瓦 98	甘 99	皮 107	目 109	立 117	**6**	羊 123	羽 124	羽 124
耳 128	聿 129	艮 138	色 139	虫 142	**7**	見 147	角 148	谷 150	豕 152	辛 160	辛 160
酉 164	里 166	**8**	隶 171	隹 172	青 174	靑 174	**9**	韋 178	頁 181	風 182	飛 183
10	韋 [178]	鬼 194	**11**	鳥 196							

STEP 6. TOP

The Radicals Found at the Top

1	一 1	一 1	丶 3	丿 4	ノ 4	**2**	二 7	亠 8	亠 8	人 9	入 11
八 12	八 12	ソ 12	冖 14	刀 18	力 19	匕 21	十 24	卜 25	厶 28	又 29	
3	口 30	土 32	士 32	夂 34	夕 36	大 37	女 38	子 39	宀 40	小 42	⺌ 42
山 46	巛 47	工 48	己 49	彐 58	⺕ 58	彐 58	彑 58	卄 [140]	**4**	戈 62	攵 66
文 67	日 72	曰 72	木 75	止 77	毋 80	比 81	氏 83	水 85	火 86	罒 87	爫 87

5. The Radicals Classfied by Position

爻 88	牛 93	王 [96]	艹 [140]	**5**	玄 95	甘 99	田 102	癶 105	白 106	目 109	矛 110
石 112	禾 115	穴 116	穴 116	穴 116	立 117	罒 [122]	**6**	竹 118	米 119	羊 123	羽 124
羽 124	老 125	而 126	耳 128	聿 129	自 132	臼 134	虫 142	血 143	衣 145	西 146	襾 146
7	貝 154	車 159	辰 161	釆 165		**8**	隹 172	雨 173	非 175		
9	音 180	音 180	**10**	馬 187	鬲 189	髟 190	**11**	魚 195	鳥 196	鹿 198	麻 200
麻 200	黒 [203]			**12**	黑 203			**13/16**	鼓 207	齊 210	龍 212

STEP 7. BOTTOM

The Radicals Found at the Bottom

1	一 1	丶 3		**2**	二 7	儿 10	八 12	冫 15	几 16	刀 18	力 19
十 24	巳 26	厶 28	又 29	又 29		**3**	口 30	土 32	夂 34	夊 34	夕 36
大 37	女 38	子 39	寸 41	小 42	山 46	工 48	己 49	巾 50	干 51	廾 55	弓 57
彐 58	彡 59		**4**	心 61	㣺 61	手 64	斤 69	方 70	日 72	曰 72	木 75
止 77	毋 80	比 81	毛 82	水 85	火 86	灬 86	牛 93	犬 94	王 [96]	任 [96]	月 [130]
5	母 [80]	氺 [85]	玉 96	瓦 98	甘 99	用 101	田 102	疋 103	白 106	皿 108	目 109
矢 111	石 112	示 113	禾 115		**6**	米 119	糸 120	缶 121	羊 123	羽 124	羽 124
而 126	耳 128	聿 129	肉 130	至 133	臼 134	舌 135	舛 136	艮 138	虫 142	衣 145	豕 [152]

7	舛 [136]	見 147	角 148	言 149	豆 151	豕 152	貝 154	足 157	車 159	辛 160	辛 160
辰 161	酉 164	里 166		8	金 167	隹 172	非 175		9	面 176	革 177
韭 179	音 180	音 180	風 182	食 184	食 184	香 186		10	馬 187	鬲 193	鬼 194
11	魚 195	鳥 196	鹿 198		12	黄 201	黑 203		16	龍 212	

APPENDIX 6. HOW TO COUNT STROKES

Nothing will so much speed up your dictionary work as skill and accuracy in counting strokes, whether of whole characters, radicals, or non-radical elements. Therefore, every effort has been made in this dictionary to make this process free of guesswork. In this connection, some knowledge of how to write characters is needed; such a study is outside the scope of this dictionary, but an excellent treatment can be found in *A Guide to Reading and Writing Japanese* edited by Florence Sakade (Tuttle, 1959).

ACCURACY. The general rule is: No matter how a line may twist and turn nor how complex its printed form, if it is written without lifting your pencil, count it as a single stroke. Examples:

2 strokes: 乃, 辶, 阝
3 strokes: 及, 与, 辶, 弓

STROKE DETAILS TO BE IGNORED. Because of variations in type fonts and other practical considerations the following details are ignored in counting strokes:

1. *Ignore* the little flip at the bottom of the element 𠄌 as found in such characters as the following, thus giving them the stroke-counts shown in parentheses; in handwritten characters, such a little flip is a mere continuation of the vertical member above it and even in printed form it seldom touches or cuts through the next element to the right: 良 (7), 卯 (5), 留 (10), 以 (4), 似 (6), 民 (5), and especially in characters traditionally belonging to the 6-stroke radical 衣, such as 衾 (10), 袈 (11), 袋 (11), and 裂 (12). It also follows logically not to count the similarly situated flip in such characters as 表 (8), 喪 (12), or 畏 (9). *However*, we do count a similar stroke in the following three pairs of characters as the said stroke either cuts through or takes a firm grip on the next element to the right: 叫 or 呌 (6); 収 (5) or 收 (7); and 糾 (9).

2. *Ignore* the little protrusion in the elements 勹 and 彑 in such characters as the following, counting these as 1 and 2 strokes respectively, especially so since in some type fonts the protrusion is scarcely visible: 考 (6), 顎 (18), 互 (4), and 禄 (12).

3. *Ignore* the downward protrusion of 口 as found in characters like the following in some fonts: 啼, 鳴, 啞. We still consider the left member the radical, i.e., 口 (30). The element 艹 is counted as three strokes, in 韋 (Rad. 178), but it is usually counted as four strokes.

4. *Ignore* any interference with another member of a character (usually a left radical) by a left-tapering stroke as such vary in length. These usually involve the radical 口 and examples follow: 吸, 呎, 吹, 呱, 喫, 喀, 毎.

5. *Ignore* the slight left interference with a left radical of an ichi (一) stroke at the bottom of such characters as 岨, 阻, 組, and 粗.

6. *Ignore* any interference of any slightly hooked stroke like the horizontal element in the character 予, where we take 亅 (6) as the radical.

COUNTING STROKES OF PARENT RADICALS AND THEIR VARIANTS.

1. The stroke-count of a *parent radical* is always that shown in the chart inside the front cover. Thus the following radicals whose stroke-count, at least in the printed form, appears to differ from that historically assigned to them are always given the stroke-count indicated in the following examples: 廴 (3), 厶 (2). Thus when the element 厶 appears in the character 宏, it is counted as 2 and not 3 strokes, making this character one of 7 strokes, not 8.

2. *Radical variants*, however, always carry their natural stroke-count wherever they appear. Thus the parent radical 水 is always a 4-stroke element but it has the following variants which carry the indicated stroke-counts: 氵 (3), 氺 (5). Similarly:

Rad. 92, a parent radical of 4 strokes (牙), has a 5-stroke variant in 牙.
Rad. 64, a parent radical of 4 strokes (手), has a 3-stroke variant in 扌.
Rad. 61, a parent radical of 4 strokes (心), has a 3-stroke variant in 忄.
Rad. 125, a parent radical of 6 strokes (老), has a 4-stroke variant in 耂.
Rad. 152, a parent radical of 7 strokes (豕), has a 6-stroke variant in 豸.
Rad. 140, a parent radical of 6 strokes (艸) has a 3-stroke variant in 艹 and a 4-stroke variant in 艹. The latter, however, is always counted as 3 strokes as it is often impossible to detect the space between the two crosses.

APPENDIX 7. HINTS FOR SPEED

Much has been done in the arrangement of this dictionary to speed up the process of finding a character. But much will also depend upon the user, and here a little effort will pay great dividends. When one is reading a Japanese book or magazine, speed in looking up a new word is of the essence if the chain of thought is not to be interrupted. Several suggestions to this end:

Spinning the pages of this book, which has been made strong and flexible for this very purpose, will often get you to your character almost immediately. Many of you will soon have memorized many radical numbers and you will spin quickly to the correct radical area. Some of you will prefer to spin to the proper radical string and locate your radical there. Having located your radical in its proper string, you will now spin again, and perhaps more slowly, until the heavy brackets scurrying up and down the strings crawl around your radical. Spinning further and a bit more slowly, you will see the tiny numeral beside the radical change to the stroke-count of the non-radical part of your character and your compound will not be far away. For you have now arrived at the proper stroke-count group, wherein the characters are arranged in the ascending order of the number of their compounds.

Quick stroke-counting is important in the speeding-up process. You will soon learn the stroke-counts of the more common radicals as you will be using them frequently, and you should also make an effort to memorize the stroke-counts of other elements which, though not radicals, reoccur frequently. Then make a habit of counting the strokes by mentally adding up the number of strokes of their larger components. For example, in 截 you should not laboriously count the strokes one by one but as follows: 2(十) + 4(戈) + 8(隹) = 14.

A good magnifying glass is most helpful in counting strokes, especially when reading type that is small or not clear.

All *cross references are in the Arabic notation* and refer to the serial numbers of the 7107 numbered character entries. These character numbers also appear conveniently at the lower outer corners of the pages, a contribution to speed.

Whenever you are not sure whether an element of a character is a radical or not, consult *the chart inside the front cover* or Appendix 13.

By all means familiarize yourself with the 214 historic radicals as given inside the front cover so that you can always recognize a radical when you see one. And if you wish to quadruple your speed in dictionary work, memorize their numbers. Missionaries in China used to do this as a matter of course during their first year of language study. A few brave souls in Japan have also done so. You should at least memorize the 67 more important radicals as given in Appendix 4.

APPENDIX 8. THE *KANA* SYSTEMS

There are two syllabaries in Japan, called *kana*. One of these is *katakana*, or the squared form, and the other is *hiragana*, or the cursive. They are arranged in two ways, one the A-I-U-E-O, or systematic, arrangement, and the other, the I-RO-HA arrangement, which forms a poem on the Buddhist theme of the transitoriness of life. This latter arrangement is still occasionally used in indices, outlines, and the like, much as the alphabet is used in the West; however, it is rapidly giving way to the easily remembered A-I-U-E-O arrangement.

Katakana are used much like italics are used in English. However, *katakana* are also used to write foreign names and most foreign words that have entered the Japanese language. Additionally, many plant and animal names, as well as onomatopoeia, are usually written in *katakana*. *Hiragana*, however, are more widely used, particularly as *okurigana* to indicate the inflections of verbs and other words whose stems are written in characters. With the limitation of the use of characters since WWII, many words previously written in *kanji* are now written in *hiragana*. Formerly, and to some extent today, *hiragana* have been used along the side of the text to indicate the pronunciation of the characters. When used in this way, they are called *furigana* or *rubi*.

THE HIRAGANA A-I-U-E-O ARRANGEMENT

あ *a*	か *ka*	さ *sa*	た *ta*	な *na*	は *ha*	ま *ma*	や *ya*	ら *ra*	わ *wa*	
い *i*	き *ki*	し *shi*	ち *chi*	に *ni*	ひ *hi*	み *mi*	[1]い *(y)i*	り *ri*	[2]ゐ *(w)i*	
う *u*	く *ku*	す *su*	つ *tsu*	ぬ *nu*	ふ *fu*	む *mu*	ゆ *yu*	る *ru*	[1]う *(w)u*	
え *e*	け *ke*	せ *se*	て *te*	ね *ne*	へ *he*	め *me*	[1]え *e*	れ *re*	[2]ゑ *(w)e*	
お *o*	こ *ko*	そ *so*	と *to*	の *no*	ほ *ho*	も *mo*	よ *yo*	ろ *ro*	[3]を *(w)o*	ん *n*

[1] Pronounced as a simple vowel. A repetition of the corresponding kana in the first column.

[2] Pronounced as a simple vowel. Not used in approved postwar orthography, having been replaced by the corresponding *kana* in the first column.

[3] Pronounced as a simple vowel. In approved orthography, now used only for the particle *o*.

8. The Kana Systems

THE KATAKANA A-I-U-E-O ARRANGEMFNT

ア *a*	カ *ka*	サ *sa*	タ *ta*	ナ *na*	ハ *ha*	マ *ma*	ヤ *ya*	ラ *ra*	ワ *wa*	
イ *i*	キ *ki*	シ *shi*	チ *chi*	ニ *ni*	ヒ *hi*	ミ *mi*	[1]イ *(y)i*	リ *ri*	[2]ヰ *(w)i*	
ウ *u*	ク *ku*	ス *su*	ツ *tsu*	ヌ *nu*	フ *fu*	ム *mu*	ユ *yu*	ル *ru*	[1]ウ *(w)u*	
エ *e*	ケ *ke*	セ *se*	テ *te*	ネ *ne*	ヘ *he*	メ *me*	[1]エ *e*	レ *re*	[2]ヱ *(w)e*	
オ *o*	コ *ko*	ソ *so*	ト *to*	ノ *no*	ホ *ho*	モ *mo*	ヨ *yo*	ロ *ro*	[3]ヲ *(w)o*	ン *n*

[1, 2, 3] See footnotes for *hiragana*.

THE I-RO-HA ARRANGEMENT

The Poem	*Romanization*	*Kana Represented*
色は匂へど	Iro wa nioedo	I-ro ha ni-ho-he-to
散りぬるを	Chirinuru o	Chi-ri-nu-ru (w)o
我世誰ぞ	Waga yo tare zo	Wa-ka yo ta-re so
常ならむ	Tsune naran	Tsu-ne na-ra-mu
有為の奥山	Ui no okuyama	U-(w)i no o-ku-ya-ma
今日越えて	Kyō koete	Ke-fu ko-e-te
浅き夢見じ	Asaki yume miji	A-sa-ki yu-me mi-shi
酔もせず	Ei mo sezu.	(W)e-hi mo se-su

A roughly literal paraphrase might run as follows: "Colors are fragrant, but they fade away. In this world of ours none lasts forever. Today cross the high mountain of life's illusions [i.e., rise above this physical world], and there will be no more shallow dreaming, no more drunkeness [i.e., there will be no more uneasiness, no more temptations]."

SOUND CHANGES. The sounds of the basic *kana* given above, as well as of the *kana* combinations treated hereafter, may be changed in any one of three ways, or in a combination of these ways. (Note that, although all the examples below are given in *hiragana*, the same remarks apply to *katakana* unless otherwise indicated.) The three ways are listed below.

1) By lengthening the vowels. This is done in *hiragana* by adding the appropriate vowel *kana* to sounds ending in *a*, *i*, *e*, or *u*. In the case of sounds ending in *o*, usually the *kana u* is added, but for certain words, it is the *kana o* that is added. For example, か *ka* becomes かあ *kā*; き *ki*, きい *kī*; く *ku*, くう *kū*; ね *ne*, ねえ *nē*; and と *to*, とう *tō* or とお *tō*. In *katakana*, the lengthening of a vowel is indicated by a dash-like symbol in place of the additional *kana*. For example, カ *ka* becomes カー *kā*, etc.

2) By inserting a small っ *tsu* before a *kana* beginning with *k*, *s*, *t*, or *p*, thereby doubling that consonant. For example, また *mata* becomes まった *matta*.

3) By adding two kinds of diacritical marks to certain of the *kana*, to represent other sounds. The first of these two, ゛, is called *dakuten* (literally, "voice marks"),

and the second, ゜, is called *handakuten* (literally, "half voice marks"). Their use is illustrated below.

が *ga*	ざ *za*	だ *da*	ば *ba*	ぱ *pa*
ぎ *gi*	じ *ji*	ぢ *ji*	び *bi*	ぴ *pi*
ぐ *gu*	ず *zu*	づ *zu*	ぶ *bu*	ぷ *pu*
げ *ge*	ぜ *ze*	で *de*	べ *be*	ぺ *pe*
ご *go*	ぞ *zo*	ど *do*	ぼ *bo*	ぽ *po*

***KANA* COMBINATIONS.** Certain *kana* clusters represent given combinations of sounds. The modern combinations are shown below. Note that the preceding sound change rules also apply here.

きゃ *kya*	しゃ *sha*	ちゃ *cha*	ひゃ *hya*	みゃ *mya*	りゃ *rya*
きゅ *kyu*	しゅ *shu*	ちゅ *chu*	ひゅ *hyu*	みゅ *myu*	りゅ *ryu*
きょ *kyo*	しょ *sho*	ちょ *cho*	ひょ *hyo*	みょ *myo*	りょ *ryo*

In addition to the modern *kana* combinations given above, there are certain historical combinations which were used in pre-WWII writing. Though no longer approved, they are still occasionally encountered. Following is a list of many such historical *kana* combinations, in the A-I-U-E-O arrangement, and likewise subject to the sound change rules; also included are a few single *kana* which had special pronunciations in certain words, instead of the standard modern pronunciations shown in parentheses.

あう	*ō*
あふ	*ō*
いふ	*yū (iu)*
おふ	*ō*
かう	*kō*
かふ	*kō*
きう	*kyū*
きふ	*kyū*
くふ	*kū*

けう	*kyō*
けふ	*kyō*
こふ	*kō*
さふ	*sō*
しう	*shū*
しふ	*shū*
すふ	*sū*
せう	*shō*
せふ	*shō*

そふ	*sō*
たう	*tō*
たふ	*tō*
ちう	*chū*
ちふ	*chū*
づふ	*zū*
てう	*chō*
てふ	*chō*
なう	*nō*

なふ	*nō*
にふ	*nyū*
ぬふ	*nū*
ねう	*nyō*
のふ	*nō*
はう	*hō*
はふ	*hō*
ひ	*i (hi)*
ひう	*hyū*

8. The Kana Systems

ふ	*u,o (fu)*
へ	*e (he)*
へう	*hyō*
ほ	*o (ho)*
ほふ	*hō*
まう	*mō*
まふ	*mō*

む	*n (mu)*
めう	*myō*
もふ	*mō*
やう	*yō*
ゆふ	*yū*
よふ	*yō*
らう	*rō*

らふ	*rō*
りう	*ryū*
りふ	*ryū*
るふ	*rū*
れう	*ryō*
れふ	*ryō*
ろふ	*rō*

わう	*ō*
ゐ	*i*
ゑ	*e*
ゑふ	*yō*
をう	*ō*
をふ	*ō*

KANA DERIVATIONS. Both *hiragana* and *katakana* were derived from *kanji*. *Hiragana* were developed from cursive writing of characters; *katakana* were mostly made from parts of characters. Both sets of *kana* and their parent characters are listed below.

HIRAGANA

あ 安	か 加	さ 左	た 太	な 奈	は 波	ま 末	や 也	ら 良	わ 和	
い 以	き 幾	し 之	ち 知	に 仁	ひ 比	み 美		り 利	ゐ 爲	
う 宇	く 久	す 寸	つ 川	ぬ 奴	ふ 不	む 武	ゆ 由	る 留		
え 衣	け 計	せ 世	て 天	ね 祢	へ 部	め 女		れ 礼	ゑ 惠	
お 於	こ 己	そ 曾	と 止	の 乃	ほ 保	も 毛	よ 與	ろ 呂	を 遠	ん 无

KATAKANA

ア 阿	カ 加	サ 散	タ 多	ナ 奈	ハ 八	マ 末	ヤ 也	ラ 良	ワ 和	
イ 伊	キ 幾	シ 之	チ 千	ニ 仁	ヒ 比	ミ 三		リ 利	ヰ 井	
ウ 宇	ク 久	ス 須	ツ 川	ヌ 奴	フ 不	ム 牟	ユ 由	ル 流		
エ 江	ケ 介	セ 世	テ 天	ネ 祢	ヘ 部	メ 女		レ 礼	ヱ 慧	
オ 於	コ 己	ソ 曾	ト 止	ノ 乃	ホ 保	モ 毛	ヨ 與	ロ 呂	ヲ 乎	ン 尓

APPENDIX 9. HISTORICAL TABLES

CHINESE DYNASTIES AND PERIODS. Listed here are the more important of the Chinese dynasties and historic periods. The principal sources used for compiling this table were Edwin O. Reischauer's *Chronological Chart of Far Eastern History* (Harvard Press, 1947), René Grousset's *Chinese Art and Culture* (Orion Press, New York, 1959), and R. H. Matthews' *Chinese-English Dictionary* (Harvard Press, 1950). There is often some question as to exactly when a given dynasty began or ended; in such case the *circa* abbreviation has been prefixed to the date, while the question mark indicates rough conjecture. Japanese readings are given in italics following the Chinese characters.

Xia	夏	*Ka*	?1989 to ?1523 B.C.E.
Shang or Yin	商, 殷	*Shō or In*	?1523 to ?1028
Western Zhou	西周	*Seishū*	?1122 to 770
Eastern Zhou	東周	*Tōshū*	770 to *c.* 256
Spring and Autumn Annals	春秋	*Shunjū*	770 to 403
Warring States	戦国	*Sengoku*	c. 403 to 221
Qin	秦	*Shin*	c. 221 to 206
Former, or Western Han	前漢	*Zenkan*	206 B.C.E. to *c.* C.E. 8
Later or Eastern Han	後漢	*Gokan*	C.E. 25 to 220
Three Kingdoms	三国	*Sangoku*	*c.* 220 to *c.* 280
Six Dynasties	六朝	*Rikuchō*	*c.* 222 to 589
Northern & Southern Dynasties	南北朝	*Nambokuchō*	*c.* 317 to *c.* 589
Sui	隋	*Zui*	*c.* 581 to 618
Tang	唐	*Tō*	618 to *c.* 907
Northern Song	北宋	*Hokusō*	960 to 1126
Southern Song	南宋	*Nansō*	*c.* 1127 to 1279
Yuan (Mongol)	元	*Gen*	*c.* 1280 to 1368
Ming	明	*Min*	1368 to *c.* 1644
Qing (Manchu)	清	*Shin*	*c.* 1644 to 1912
Republic	民国	*Minkoku*	Since 1912
People's Republic	人民共和国	*Jimmin Kyōwakoku*	Since 1949

PERIODS OF JAPANESE HISTORY AND ART. There is often little agreement as to the exact nomenclature for and the years covered by the various periods of Japanese history and art. As a rough guide, the chart presented here has been prepared from the following sources:

(1) G. B. Sansom: *Japan: A Short Cultural History*. Appleton-Century-Crofts, New York, 1943, p. xviii. This list gives the classification of art periods adopted by the Art Research Institute of Tokyo.

(2) Edwin O. Reischauer: *Chronological Chart of Far Eastern History*. Harvard Press, Cambridge, 1947. This is a chart of political rather than art periods.

(3) Chronological chart of art periods published by the Japanese Art Dealers' Association, Tokyo, 1958.

(4) Andrew N. Nelson: *The Origin, History, and Present Status of the Temples of Japan.* Unpublished doctorate thesis, University of Washington, Seattle, 1938.

(5) Suwa Tokutarō: *Nihonshi no Yōryō* (Outline of Japanese History). Ōbunsha, Tokyo, 1957.

(6) Toyota Takeshi: *Yōsetsu Nihonshi* (Japanese History Outline). Chūkyō Shuppan, Tokyo, 1964.

The numerals in parentheses in the chart refer to the foregoing sources.

9. Historical Tables

Jōmon 縄文
(3) To 200 B.C.E.
(5) To A.D. 8

Yayoi 弥生
(3) 200 B.C.E. to C.E. 250
(5) 8–300

Kofun (Tumulus) 古墳
(3) 250–552

Clan or Pre-Asuka
飛鳥前
(2) To 252
(4) Same

Yamato 大和
(5) 300–710

Asuka or Suiko
飛鳥, 推古
(1) 552–646
(3) 552–645
(4) Same

Borrowing from China
(2) 552–866

Early Nara or Hakuhō
奈良前期, 白鳳
(1) 646–710
(3) 645–710
(4) Same

Nara, Late Nara, or Tempyō
奈良後期, 天平
(1) 710–794
(2) 710–784
(3) 710–794
(4) Same
(5) Same

Early Heian or Kōnin
平安前期, 弘仁
(1) 794–897
(2) 794–866
(3) 794–898
(4) Same
(5) Same

Late Heian or Fujiwara
平安後期, 藤原
(2) 866–1160
(3) 897–1185
(4) 898–1185
(5) Same

Main Fujiwara
藤原前期
(1) 897–1086

Late Fujiwara
藤原後期
(1) 1086–1185

Taira 平
(2) 1160–1185

Kamakura or Minamoto
鎌倉, 源
(2) 1185–1333
(3) 1185–1392
(4) 1185–1333
(5) Same

Early Kamakura
鎌倉前期
(1) 1185–1249

Late Kamakura
鎌倉後期
(1) 1249–1382

Yoshino or Nambokuchō (Northern and Southern Courts)
吉野, 南北朝
(2) 1336–1392
(3) Same
(4) Same
(5) Same

Ashikaga or Muromachi
足利, 室町
(1) 1392–1568
(2) 1336–1568
(3) 1473–1568
(4) 1392–1573
(5) 1333–1573

Sengoku (Warring Countries) 戦国
(5) 1482–1558

Momoyama or Azuchi-Momoyama
桃山, 安土桃山
(1) 1568–1615
(2) 1568–1600
(3) Same
(4) 1573–1615
(5) 1573–1603

Tokugawa or Edo
徳川, 江戸
(1) 1615–1867
(2) 1600–1867
(3) 1600–1868
(4) 1615–1867
(5) 1603–1868

Modern 近代
(6) 1868–1945

Contemporary 現代
(6) 1946 to date

JAPANESE SHOGUNATES. Here again there is often reason for choosing different dates. In this case we follow Tōkyōdō's *Sekai Jimmei Jiten: Tōyō Hen* (1952, p. 922), which consistently begins each period with the formal nomination of its first shogun and ends it with the abdication or death of its last shogun. Note that the first three entries are usually known collectively as the Kamakura Shogunate; during much of this period the shoguns themselves had no real power, being ruled in turn by the Hōjō regents from 1205 to 1333.

Minamoto (Kamakura)	源 (鎌倉)	1192–1219
Fujiwara (Kamakura)	藤原(鎌倉)	1226–1252
Imperial Princes (Kamakura)	(鎌倉)	1252–1333
Ashikaga (Muromachi)	足利(室町)	1338–1573
Tokugawa (Edo)	徳川(江戸)	1603–1867

JAPANESE EMPERORS AND ERA NAMES. The following list of the Japanese sovereigns, together with era names (*nengō*), begins with the legendary first emperor, Jimmu. Much of the early chronology before the introduction of writing is legendary rather than historical. Japanese textbooks now usually begin such a list with Emperor Kimmei (reigned 539–571). But legends often play an equal role with history in a nation's literature, and it has been thought well to give the full traditional list.

The list is based on three sources. Nippon Hōsō Kyōkai's *Songō to Nengō no Yobikata* (1953), being based on studies with the Imperial Household, has been taken as the final authority for the reading of all names and for the era dates. Reign dates have been taken from Tōkyōdō's *Sekai Jimmei Jiten: Tōyō Hen* (1952, pp. 919–22) and Shinchōsha's *Shukuyaku Nippon Bungaku Daijiten* (1955, appendix pp. 1–92).

Asterisks indicate empresses. The system of era names was not adopted until the time of the 36th emperor, and there is some confusion regarding the first few eras. Reign dates show: (1) the year of actual accession to the throne if known and, in parentheses, of formal coronation, but the latter date is not repeated when it is the same as the former; and (2) the year in which the reign ended, whether by death or abdication. An era date shows the first year of the era. Era names are indented beneath the names of the respective emperors.

1. 神武 Jimmu, (660)–585 B.C.E.
2. 綏靖 Suizei, 581–549
3. 安寧 Annei, 549–511
4. 懿徳 Itoku, 510–477
5. 孝昭 Koshō, 475–393
6. 孝安 Kōan, 392–291
7. 孝霊 Kōrei, 290–215
8. 孝元 Kōgen, 214–158
9. 開化 Kaika, 158–98
10. 崇神 Sujin, (97)–30
11. 垂仁 Suinin, (29 B.C.E.)–C.E. 70
12. 景行 Keikō, (71)–130
13. 成務 Seimu, (131)–190
14. 仲哀 Chūai, (192)–200
    神功皇后 Jingū Kōgō (Regent), 201-269
15. 応神 Ōjin, (270)–310
16. 仁徳 Nintoku, (313)–399
17. 履中 Richū, (400)–405
18. 反正 Hanzei, (406)–410
19. 允恭 Ingyō, (412)–453
20. 安康 Ankō, 453–456
21. 雄略 Yūryaku, 456–479
22. 清寧 Seinei, (480)–484
23. 顕宗 Kenzō, (485)–487
24. 仁賢 Ninken, (488)–498
25. 武烈 Buretsu, 498–506
26. 継体 Keitai, (507)–531
27. 安閑 Ankan, 531–535
28. 宣化 Senka, 535–539
29. 欽明 Kimmei, 539–571
30. 敏達 Bidatsu, (572)–585
31. 用明 Yōmei, 585–587
32. 崇峻 Sushun, 587–592
33. 推古 *Suiko, 592–628
34. 舒明 Jomei, (629)–641
35. 皇極 *Kōgyoku, (642)–645
36. 孝徳 Kōtoku, 645–654
    大化 Taika 645
    白雉 Hakuchi 650
37. 斉明 *Saimei, (655)–661
38. 天智 Tenji, (662)–671
39. 弘文 Kōbun, 671–672
    白鳳 Hakuhō 672
40. 天武 Temmu, (673)–686
    朱鳥 Shuchō 686
41. 持統 *Jitō, (690)–697
42. 文武 Mommu, 697–707
    大宝 Taihō 701
    慶雲 Keiun 704
43. 元明 *Gemmei, 707–715
    和銅 Wadō 708
44. 元正 *Genshō, 715–724
    霊亀 Reiki 715

養老 Yōrō	717
45. 聖武 Shōmu, 724–749	
神亀 Jinki	724
天平 Tempyō	729
46. 孝謙 *Kōken, 749–758	
天平感宝 Tempyō-kampō	749
天平勝宝 Tempyō-shōhō	749
天平宝字 Tempyō-hōji	757
47. 淳仁 Junnin, 758–764	
48. 称徳 *Shōtoku, 764–770	
天平神護 Tempyō-jingo	765
神護景雲 Jingo-keiun	767
49. 光仁 Kōnin, 770–781	
宝亀 Hōki	770
50. 桓武 Kammu, 781–806	
天応 Ten'ō	781
延暦 Enryaku	782
51. 平城 Heizei, 806–809	
大同 Daidō	806
52. 嵯峨 Saga, 809–823	
弘仁 Kōnin	810
53. 淳和 Junna, 823–833	
天長 Tenchō	824
54. 仁明 Nimmyō, 833–850	
承和 Shōwa	834
嘉祥 Kajō	848
55. 文徳 Montoku, 850–858	
仁寿 Ninju	851
斉衡 Saikō	854
天安 Tennan	857
56. 清和 Seiwa, 858–876	
貞観 Jōgan	859
57. 陽成 Yōzei, 876(877)–884	
元慶 Genkei	877
58. 光孝 Kōkō, 884–887	
仁和 Ninna	885
59. 宇多 Uda, 887–897	
寛平 Kampyō	889
60. 醍醐 Daigo, 897–930	
昌泰 Shōtai	898
延喜 Engi	901
延長 Enchō	923
61. 朱雀 Suzaku, 930–946	
承平 Shōhei	931
天慶 Tengyō	938
62. 村上 Murakami, 946–967	
天暦 Tenryaku	947
天徳 Tentoku	957
応和 Ōwa	961
康保 Kōhō	964
63. 冷泉 Reizei, 967–969	
安和 Anna	968
64. 円融 En'yū, 969–984	
天禄 Tenroku	970
天延 Ten'en	973
貞元 Jōgen	976
天元 Tengen	978
永観 Eikan	983
65. 花山 Kazan, 984–986	
寛和 Kanna	985
66. 一条 Ichijō, 986–1011	
永延 Eien	987
永祚 Eiso	989
正暦 Shōryaku	990
長徳 Chōtoku	995
長保 Chōhō	999
寛弘 Kankō	1004
67. 三条 Sanjō, 1011–1016	
長和 Chōwa	1012
68. 後一条 Goichijō, 1016–1036	
寛仁 Kannin	1017
治安 Jian	1021
万寿 Manju	1024
長元 Chōgen	1028
69. 後朱雀 Gosuzaku, 1036–1045	
長暦 Chōryaku	1037
長久 Chōkyū	1040
寛徳 Kantoku	1044
70. 後冷泉 Goreizei,1045–1068	
永承 Eishō	1046
天喜 Tengi	1053
康平 Kōhei	1058
治暦 Jiryaku	1065
71. 後三条 Gosanjō, 1068–1072	
延久 Enkyū	1069
72. 白河 Shirakawa, 1072–1086	
承保 Jōhō	1074
承暦 Shōryaku	1077
永保 Eihō	1081
応徳 Ōtoku	1084
73. 堀河 Horikawa, 1086–1107	
寛治 Kanji	1087
嘉保 Kahō	1094
永長 Eichō	1096
承徳 Jōtoku	1097
康和 Kōwa	1099
長治 Chōji	1104
嘉承 Kajō	1106
74. 鳥羽 Toba, 1107–1123	
天仁 Tennin	1108
天永 Ten'ei	1110
永久 Eikyū	1113
元永 Gen'ei	1118
保安 Hōan	1120

75. 崇徳 Sutoku, 1123–1141

天治 Tenji	1124
大治 Daiji	1126
天承 Tenshō	1131
長承 Chōshō	1132
保延 Hōen	1135

76. 近衛 Konoe, 1141–1155

永治 Eiji	1141
康治 Kōji	1142
天養 Ten'yō	1144
久安 Kyūan	1145
仁平 Nimpei	1151
久寿 Kyūju	1154

77. 後白河 Goshirakawa, 1155–1158

保元 Hōgen	1156

78. 二条 Nijō, 1158–1165

平治 Heiji	1159
永暦 Eiryaku	1160
応保 Ōhō	1161
長寛 Chōkan	1163

79. 六条 Rokujō, 1165–1168

永万 Eiman	1165
仁安 Ninnan	1166

80. 高倉 Takakura, 1168–1180

嘉応 Kaō	1169
承安 Shōan	1171
安元 Angen	1175
治承 Jishō	1177

81. 安徳 Antoku, 1180–1183

養和 Yōwa	1181
寿永 Juei	1182

82. 後鳥羽 Gotoba, 1183(1184)–1198

元暦 Genryaku	1184
文治 Bunji	1185
建久 Kenkyū	1190

83. 土御門 Tsuchimikado, 1198–1210

正治 Shōji	1199
建仁 Kennin	1201
元久 Genkyū	1204
建永 Ken'ei	1206
承元 Jōgen	1207

84. 順徳 Juntoku, 1210–1221

建暦 Kenryaku	1211
建保 Kempō	1213
承久 Jōkyū	1219

85. 仲恭 Chūkyō, 1221

86. 後堀河 Gohorikawa, 1221–1232

貞応 Jōō	1222
元仁 Gennin	1224
嘉禄 Karoku	1225
安貞 Antei	1227
寛喜 Kanki	1229

87. 四条 Shijō, 1232–1242

貞永 Jōei	1232
天福 Tempuku	1233
文暦 Bunryaku	1234
嘉禎 Katei	1235
暦仁 Ryakunin	1238
延応 En'ō	1239
仁治 Ninji	1240

88. 後嵯峨 Gosaga, 1242–1246

寛元 Kangen	1243

89. 後深草 Gofukakusa, 1246–1259

宝治 Hōji	1247
建長 Kenchō	1249
康元 Kōgen	1256
正嘉 Shōka	1257

90. 亀山 Kameyama, 1259–1274

正元 Shōgen	1259
文応 Bun'ō	1260
弘長 Kōchō	1261
文永 Bun'ei	1264

91. 後宇多 Gouda, 1274–1287

建治 Kenji	1275
弘安 Kōan	1278

92. 伏見 Fushimi, (1288)–1298

正応 Shōō	1288
永仁 Einin	1293

93. 後伏見 Gofushimi, 1298–1301

正安 Shōan	1299

94. 後二条 Gonijō, 1301–1308

乾元 Kengen	1302
嘉元 Kagen	1303
徳治 Tokuji	1306

95. 花園 Hanazono, 1308–1318

延慶 Enkyō	1308
応長 Ōcho	1311
正和 Shōwa	1312
文保 Bumpō	1317

96. 後醍醐 Godaigo, 1318–1339

元応 Gen'ō	1319
元亨 Genkō	1321
正中 Shōchū	1324
嘉暦 Karyaku	1326
元徳 Gentoku	1329
元弘 Genkō	1331
建武 Kemmu	1334
延元 Engen	1336

97. 後村上 Gomurakami, 1339 (coronation?)–1368

興国 Kōkoku	1340
正平 Shōhei	1346

98. 長慶 Chōkei, 1368 (coronation?)–1383

建徳 Kentoku 1370
文中 Bunchū 1372
天授 Tenju 1375
弘和 Kōwa 1381

99. 後亀山 Gokameyama, 1383–1392
元中 Genchū 1384
明徳 Meitoku 1390

100. 後小松 Gokomatsu, 1392–1412
応永 Ōei 1394

101. 称光 Shōkō, 1412(1414)–1428
正長 Shōchō 1428

102. 後花園 Gohanazono, (1429)–1464
永享 Eikyō 1429
嘉吉 Kakitsu 1441
文安 Bunnan 1444
宝徳 Hōtoku 1449
享徳 Kyōtoku 1452
康正 Kōshō 1455
長禄 Chōroku 1457
寛正 Kanshō 1460

103. 後土御門 Gotsuchimikado, (1465)–1500
文正 Bunshō 1466
応仁 Ōnin 1467
文明 Bummei 1469
長享 Chōkyō 1487
延徳 Entoku 1489
明応 Meiō 1492

104. 後柏原 Gokashiwabara, 1500(1521)–1526
文亀 Bunki 1501
永正 Eishō 1504
大永 Daiei 1521

105. 後奈良 Gonara, 1526(1536)–1557
享禄 Kyōroku 1528
天文 Temmon 1532
弘治 Kōji 1555

106. 正親町 Ōgimachi, 1557(1560)–1586
永禄 Eiroku 1558
元亀 Genki 1570
天正 Tenshō 1573

107. 後陽成 Goyōzei, 1586–1611
文禄 Bunroku 1592
慶長 Keichō 1596

108. 後水尾 Gomizunoo, 1611–1629
元和 Genna 1615
寛永 Kan'ei 1624

109. 明正 *Meishō, (1630)–1643

110. 後光明 Gokōmyō, 1643–1654
正保 Shōhō 1644
慶安 Keian 1648
承応 Jōō 1652
明暦 Meireki 1655

111. 後西 Gosai, (1656)–1663
万治 Manji 1658
寛文 Kambun 1661

112. 霊元 Reigen, 1663–1687
延宝 Empō 1673
天和 Tenna 1681
貞享 Jōkyō 1684

113. 東山 Higashiyama, 1687–1709
元禄 Genroku 1688
宝永 Hōei 1704

114. 中御門 Nakamikado, (1710)–1735
正徳 Shōtoku 1711
享保 Kyōhō 1716

115. 桜町 Sakuramachi, 1735–1747
元文 Gembun 1736
寛保 Kampō 1741
延享 Enkyō 1744

116. 桃園 Momozono, 1747–1762
寛延 Kan'en 1748
宝暦 Hōreki 1751

117. 後桜町 Gosakuramachi, (1763)–1770
明和 Meiwa 1764

118. 後桃園 Gomomozono, (1771)–1779
安永 An'ei 1772

119. 光格 Kōkaku, (1780)–1817
天明 Temmei 1781
寛政 Kansei 1789
享和 Kyōwa 1801
文化 Bunka 1804

120. 仁孝 Ninkō, 1817–1846
文政 Bunsei 1818
天保 Tempō 1830
弘化 Kōka 1844

121. 孝明 Kōmei, (1847)–1866
嘉永 Kaei 1848
安政 Ansei 1854
万延 Man'en 1860
文久 Bunkyū 1861
元治 Genji 1864
慶応 Keiō 1865

122. 明治 Meiji, 1866(1868)–1912
明治 Meiji 1868

123. 大正 Taishō, 1912(1915)–1926
大正 Taishō 1912

124. 昭和 Shōwa, 1926(1928)–1989
昭和 Shōwa 1926

125. 今上陛下 The Present Emperor, 1989–
平成 Heisei 1989

THE BRIEF NORTHERN DYNASTY

1. 光厳 Kōgon, 1332–1333
   - 正慶 Shōkei 1332
2. 光明 Kōmyō, (1337)–1348
   - 暦応 Ryakuō 1338
   - 康永 Kōei 1342
   - 貞和 Jōwa 1345
3. 崇光 Sukō, (1349)–1351
   - 観応 Kan'ō 1350
4. 後光厳 Gokōgon, (1353)–1371
   - 文和 Bunna 1352
   - 延文 Embun 1356
   - 康安 Kōan 1361
   - 貞治 Jōji 1362
   - 応安 Ōan 1368
5. 後円融 Goen'yū, (1374)–1382
   - 永和 Eiwa 1375
   - 康暦 Kōryaku 1379
   - 永徳 Eitoku 1381
6. 後小松 Gokomatsu, 1382–1392 (becoming 100th in main line)
   - 至徳 Shitoku 1384
   - 嘉慶 Kakei 1387
   - 康応 Kōō 1389
   - 明徳 Meitoku 1390

APPENDIX 10. JAPANESE GEOGRAPHICAL NAMES

ANCIENT KUNI AND MODERN PREFECTURES

THE ANCIENT KUNI (国)	THE MODERN PREFECTURES (KEN 県)
(東北) THE TŌHOKU AREA	
陸奥 Mutsu	青森 Aomori
羽後 Ugo	秋田 Akita
陸中 Rikuchū	岩手 Iwate
陸前 Rikuzen	宮城 Miyagi
羽前 Uzen	山形 Yamagata
岩代 Iwashiro	福島 Fukushima
磐城 Iwaki	
(関東) THE KANTO AREA	
常陸 Hitachi	茨城 Ibaraki
下野 Shimotsuke	栃木 Tochigi
上野 Kōzuke	群馬 Gumma
武蔵 Musashi	埼玉 Saitama
	東京都 Tōkyō To
相模 Sagami	神奈川 Kanagawa
下総 Shimōsa	千葉 Chiba
上総 Kazusa	
安房 Awa	
(中部) THE CHŪBU AREA	
越後 Echigo	新潟 Niigata
佐渡 Sado	
越中 Etchū	富山 Toyama
加賀 Kaga	石川 Ishikawa
能登 Noto	
越前 Echizen	福井 Fukui
若狭 Wakasa	
駿河 Suruga	静岡 Shizuoka
伊豆 Izu	
甲斐 Kai	山梨 Yamanashi
信濃 Shinano	長野 Nagano
三河 Mikawa	愛知 Aichi
尾張 Owari	
美濃 Mino	岐阜 Gifu
飛驒 Hida	
(近畿) THE KINKI AREA (ŌSAKA-KYŌTO)	
近江 Ōmi	滋賀 Shiga
山城 Yamashiro	京都府 Kyōto Fu
丹波 Tamba	
丹後 Tango	
和泉 Izumi	大阪府 Ōsaka Fu
河内 Kawachi	
大和 Yamato	奈良 Nara
紀伊 Kii	和歌山 Wakayama
伊勢 Ise	三重 Mie
伊賀 Iga	
但馬 Tajima	兵庫 Hyōgo
摂津 Settsu	
播磨 Harima	
淡路 Awaji	
(中国) THE CHŪGOKU AREA	
備前 Bizen	岡山 Okayama
備中 Bitchū	
美作 Mimasaka	
備後 Bingo	広島 Hiroshima
安芸 Aki	
長門 Nagato	山口 Yamaguchi
周防 Suō	
因幡 Inaba	鳥取 Tottori
伯耆 Hōki	
出雲 Izumo	島根 Shimane
石見 Iwami	
隠岐 Oki	
(四国) SHIKOKU	
讃岐 Sanuki	香川 Kagawa
伊予 Iyo	愛媛 Ehime

10. Japanese Geographical Names

阿波 Awa	徳島 Tokushima	肥前 Hizen	長崎 Nagasaki
土佐 Tosa	高知 Kōchi	壱岐 Iki	(the island)
(九州) KYŪSHŪ		対馬 Tsushima	(the island)
筑前 Chikuzen	福岡 Fukuoka	肥後 Higo	熊本 Kumamoto
豊前 Buzen		薩摩 Satsuma	鹿児島 Kagoshima
豊後 Bungo	大分 Ōita	大隅 Ōsumi	
日向 Hyūga	宮崎 Miyazaki	(琉球) RYŪKYŪ	
筑後 Chikugo	佐賀 Saga	琉球 Ryūkyū	沖縄 Okinawa

CITIES OF OVER 100,000 (as of 1992). Listed from north to south.

PREFECTURES	CITIES
北海道 Hokkaidō	北見 Kitami
	旭川 Asahikawa
	小樽 Otaru
	江別 Ebetsu
	札幌 Sapporo
	釧路 Kushiro
	帯広 Obihiro
	苫小牧 Tomakomai
	室蘭 Muroran
	函館 Hakodate
青森 Aomori	青森 Aomori
	弘前 Hirosaki
	八戸 Hachinohe
岩手 Iwate	盛岡 Morioka
宮城 Miyagi	石巻 Ishinomaki
	仙台 Sendai
秋田 Akita	秋田 Akita
山形 Yamagata	酒田 Sakata
	鶴岡 Tsuruoka
	山形 Yamagata
福島 Fukushima	福島 Fukushima
	会津若松 Aizu-Wakamatsu
	郡山 Kōriyama
	いわき Iwaki
茨城 Ibaraki	日立 Hitachi
	勝田 Katsuta
	水戸 Mito
	土浦 Tsuchiura
	つくば Tsukuba
栃木 Tochigi	宇都宮 Utsunomiya
	小山 Oyama
	足利 Ashikaga
群馬 Gumma	桐生 Kiryū
	前橋 Maebashi
	伊勢崎 Isesaki
	高崎 Takasaki
	太田 Ōta
埼玉 Saitama	熊谷 Kumagaya
	春日部 Kasukabe
	上尾 Ageo
	岩槻 Iwatsuki
	大宮 Ōmiya
	川越 Kawagoe
	越谷 Koshigaya
	浦和 Urawa
	狭山 Sayama
	入間 Iruma
	三郷 Misato
	草加 Sōka
	川口 Kawaguchi
	所沢 Tokorozawa
	朝霞 Asaka
	新座 Niiza
千葉 Chiba	野田 Noda
	柏 Kashiwa
	我孫子 Abiko
	流山 Nagareyama
	松戸 Matsudo
	八千代 Yachiyo
	市川 Ichikawa
	佐倉 Sakura
	船橋 Funabashi
	習志野 Narashino
	浦安 Urayasu
	千葉 Chiba
	市原 Ichihara
	木更津 Kisarazu
東京都 Tōkyō To	青梅 Ōme
	東久留米 Higashi-kurume
	東村山 Higashi-murayama
	小平 Kodaira
	武蔵野 Musashino
	国分寺 Kokubunji
	昭島 Akishima
	小金井 Koganei
	立川 Tachikawa
	三鷹 Mitaka
	日野 Hino

	八王子 Hachiōji
	府中 Fuchū
	調布 Chōfu
	多摩 Tama
	町田 Machida
神奈川 Kanagawa	相模原 Sagamihara
	川崎 Kawasaki
	大和 Yamato
	座間 Zama
	横浜 Yokohama
	海老名 Ebina
	厚木 Atsugi
	秦野 Hadano
	藤沢 Fujisawa
	平塚 Hiratsuka
	茅ケ崎 Chigasaki
	鎌倉 Kamakura
	横須賀 Yokosuka
	小田原 Odawara
新潟 Niigata	新潟 Niigata
	長岡 Nagaoka
	上越 Jōetsu
富山 Toyama	高岡 Tukuoka
	富山 Toyama
石川 Ishikawa	金沢 Kanazawa
	小松 Komatsu
福井 Fukui	福井 Fukui
山梨 Yamanashi	甲府 Kōfu
長野 Nagano	長野 Nagano
	上田 Ueda
	松本 Matsumoto
	飯田 Iida
岐阜 Gifu	岐阜 Gifu
	各務原 Kakamigahara
	大垣 Ōgaki
静岡 Shizuoka	富士宮 Fujinomiya
	富士 Fuji
	三島 Mishima
	沼津 Numazu
	清水 Shimizu
	静岡 Shizuoka
	藤枝 Fujieda
	焼津 Yaizu
	浜松 Hamamatsu
愛知 Aichi	一宮 Ichinomiya
	小牧 Komaki
	春日井 Kasugai
	瀬戸 Seto
	名古屋 Nagoya
	豊田 Toyota
	刈谷 Kariya
	安城 Anjō
	岡崎 Okazaki
	半田 Handa
	豊川 Toyokawa
	豊橋 Toyohashi
三重 Mie	四日市 Yokkaichi
	鈴鹿 Suzuka
	津 Tsu
	松阪 Matsuzaka
	伊勢 Ise
滋賀 Shiga	大津 Ōtsu
	彦根 Hikone
京都 Kyōto Fu	京都 Kyōto
	宇治 Uji
大阪 Ōsaka Fu	高槻 Takatsuki
	枚方 Hirakata
	茨木 Ibaraki
	箕面 Minoo
	池田 Ikeda
	豊中 Toyonaka
	吹田 Suita
	寝屋川 Neyagawa
	守口 Moriguchi
	大東 Daitō
	門真 Kadoma
	東大阪 Higashi-ōsaka
	大阪 Ōsaka
	八尾 Yao
	松原 Matsubara
	羽曳野 Habikino
	堺 Sakai
	富田林 Tondabayashi
	和泉 Izumi
	岸和田 Kishiwada
	河内長野 Kawachinagano
兵庫 Hyōgo	川西 Kawanishi
	姫路 Himeji
	宝塚 Takarazuka
	伊丹 Itami
	加古川 Kakogawa
	西宮 Nishinomiya
	尼崎 Amagasaki
	神戸 Kōbe
	明石 Akashi
奈良 Nara	奈良 Nara
	生駒 Ikoma
	橿原 Kashihara
和歌山 Wakayama	和歌山 Wakayama
鳥取 Tottori	鳥取 Tottori

10. Japanese Geographical Names

	米子 Yonago	高知 Kōchi	高知 Kōchi
島根 Shimane	松江 Matsue	福岡 Fukuoka	北九州 Kitakyūshū
岡山 Okayama	岡山 Okayama		福岡 Fukuoka
	倉敷 Kurashiki		久留米 Kurume
広島 Hiroshima	福山 Fukuyama		大牟田 Ōmuta
	広島 Hiroshima	佐賀 Saga	佐賀 Saga
	呉 Kure	長崎 Nagasaki	佐世保 Sasebo
山口 Yamaguchi	岩国 Iwakuni		長崎 Nagasaki
	山口 Yamaguchi	熊本 Kumamoto	熊本 Kumamoto
	徳山 Tokuyama		八代 Yatsushiro
	防府 Hōfu	大分 Ōita	別府 Beppu
	下関 Shimonoseki		大分 Ōita
	宇部 Ube	宮崎 Miyazaki	延岡 Nobeoka
徳島 Tokushima	徳島 Tokushima		宮崎 Miyazaki
香川 Kagawa	高松 Takamatsu		都城 Miyakonojō
愛媛 Ehime	今治 Imabari	鹿児島 Kagoshima	鹿児島 Kagoshima
	新居浜 Niihama	沖縄 Okinawa	那覇 Naha
	松山 Matsuyama		沖縄 Okinawa

MISCELLANEOUS JAPANESE PLACE NAMES

Bays

Ise Wan	伊勢湾	Ise Bay including Nagoya Harbor
Ōsaka Wan	大阪湾	Osaka Bay including the Osaka and Kobe harbors
Tōkyō Wan	東京湾	Tokyo Bay including the Yokohama and Tokyo harbors

Islands

Amami Ōshima	奄美大島	South of Kagoshima
Awaji Shima	淡路島	West side of Osaka Bay
Chishima Rettō	千島列島	The Kurile Islands
Hachijōjima	八丈島	South of Tokyo Bay
Hokkaidō	北海道	
Honshū	本州	
Iki (no) Shima	壱岐島	Between Kyushu and Korea
Karafuto	樺太	Sakhalin
Kunashiritō	国後島	Off the east coast of Hokkaido
Kyūshū	九州	
Ogasawara Shotō	小笠原諸島	The Bonin Islands
Ryūkyū Rettō	琉球列島	The Ryukyu Islands
Oki Guntō	隠岐群島	In the Japan Sea
Ōshima	大島	Off Tokyo Bay
Sado(ga)shima	佐渡島	In the Japan Sea
Shikoku	四国	
Shōdo Shima	小豆島	In the Inland Sea
Tanegashima	種子島	South of Kagoshima
Tsushima	対馬	Between Kyushu and Korea

Rivers

Arakawa	荒川	Flows into Tokyo Bay at Tokyo
Edogawa	江戸川	Flows into Tokyo Bay at Ichikawa
Fujigawa	富士川	At the foot of Mt. Fuji
Ishikarigawa	石狩川	Hokkaido
Kisogawa	木曾川	Flows into Ise Bay at Nagoya

Kitakamigawa	北上川	Tohoku
Kumagawa	球磨川	Kyushu
Mogamigawa	最上川	Tohoku
Nagaragawa	長良川	Famed for the cormorant fishing at Gifu
Ōigawa	大井川	Between Mt. Fuji and Nagoya
Sagamigawa	相模川	Near Odawara
Sumidagawa	隅田川	Flows through Tokyo into Tokyo Bay
Tamagawa	多摩川	Flows into Tokyo Bay
Tenryūgawa	天竜川	Between Mt. Fuji and Nagoya
Tonegawa	利根川	Flows into the Pacific at Choshi in Chiba Ken
Yodogawa	淀川	Flows through Osaka

Seas

Higashi Shinakai	東支那海	East China Sea
Nihonkai	日本海	Japan Sea
Minami Shinakai	南支那海	South China Sea
Kōkai	黄海	Yellow Sea

Straits

Kammon Kaikyō	関門海峡	Between Shimonoseki and Moji
Mamiya Kaikyō	間宮海峡	Between Hokkaido and Sakhalin
Naruto Kaikyō	鳴門海峡	The entrance to Osaka Bay
Sōya Kaikyō	宗谷海峡	Between Hokkaido and Sakhalin
Tsugaru Kaikyō	津軽海峡	Between Honshu and Hokkaido
Tsushima Kaikyō	対馬海峡	Between Iki and Tsushima island

Mountains

Asama Yama	浅間山	Mt. Asama near Karuizawa
Asosan	阿蘇山	Kyushu
Bandaisan	磐梯山	Tohoku near Aizu-Wakamatsu
Daisen	大山	Tottori Ken
Daisetsuzan	大雪山	Hokkaido
Fujisan	富士山	Mt. Fuji
Hakusan	白山	Northwest of Nagoya
Hakone Yama	箱根山	South of Tokyo
Hieizan	比叡山	Near Kyoto
Kōyasan	高野山	Near Kyoto
Tateyama	立山	In the Japan Alps
Unzendake	雲仙岳	Near Nagasaki
Yari(ga)take	槍ケ岳	In the Japan Alps

APPENDIX 11. FOREIGN GEOGRAPHICAL NAMES

For Chinese and Korean place names the Japanese have customarily used the original Chinese characters with Japanese *on* readings as given in the two immediately following lists, but there is a growing tendency to indicate the current Chinese or Korean pronunciations in *katakana*. The Pinyin pronunciations of the Chinese place names are also given. In the case of Western names, for which the characters in the third list were formerly used, the present tendency is to transcribe them phonetically in *katakana*, but the older literature is, of course, always with us.

Although when used today the characters of the names in all three lists would be subject to the Jōyō Kanji rules, they are given here in their older forms since, particularly in the case of the third list, they are more likely to be encountered in the old literature. Those names in the third list that are the most commonly used today are indicated with asterisks.

CHINESE PLACE NAMES

NAME IN PINYIN SYSTEM[1]	NAME IN THOMAS WADE SYSTEM[2]	JAPANESE PRONUNCIATION	CHARACTERS[3]
Anhui (Anwhei)	Anhui	Anki	安徽
Andong	Antung	Antō	安東
Aomen (Macao)	Aomen	Makao	澳門
Beijing (Peking)	Peiching	Pekin, Hokkei, Hokkin	北京
Beiping	Peip'ing	Peipin, Hokuhei	北平
Chahar	Chaha'erh	Chaharu	察哈爾
Changjiang (Yangtze River)	Ch'angchiang	Chōkō	長江
Changchun	Ch'angch'un	Chōshun	長春
Changsha	Ch'angsha	Chōsha	長沙
Chengdu	Ch'engtu	Seito	成都
Chongqing	Ch'ungch'ing	Jūkei	重慶
Dagu	Taku	Tākū	大沽
Dalian	Talien	Dairen	大連
Dandong	Tantung	Tantō	丹東
Dongbei (Manchuria)	Tungpei	Tōhoku	東北
Dunhuang	Tunhuang	Tonkō	敦煌
Fengtian (Mukden)	Fengt'ien	Hōten	奉天
Fujian	Fuchien	Fukken	福建
Fuzhou	Fuchou	Fukushū	福州
Gansu	Kansu	Kanshuku	甘肅
Gaoxiong	Kaohsiung	Takao	高雄
Guangdong	Kuangtung	Kanton, Kantō	廣東
Guangxi	Kuanghsi	Kanshī, Kōsei	廣西
Guangzhou	Kuangchou	Kōshū	廣州
Guilin	Kuilin	Keirin	桂林
Guiyang	Kuiyang	Kiyō	貴陽
Guizhou (Kweichow)	Kuichou	Kishū	貴州
Haikou	Haik'ou	Kaikō	海口
Hainandao	Hainantao	Kainantō	海南島
Hangzhou (Hangchow)	Hangchou	Kōshū	杭州
Hankou (Hankow)	Hank'ou	Kankō	漢口
Hanshui	Hanshui	Kansui	漢水
Harbin	Harpin	Harubin	哈爾濱
Hebei	Hepei	Kahoku	河北
Hefei	Hefei	Gōhi	合肥

Heilongjiang (Amur River)	Heilungchiang	Kokuryūkō	黒龍江
Henan	Henan	Kanan	河南
Huabei (Northern China)	Huapei	Kahoku	華北
Huaihe	Huaihe	Waiga	淮河
Huanan (Southern China)	Huanan	Kanan	華南
Huanghe (Yellow River)	Huanghe	Kōga	黄河
Huazhong (Central China)	Huachung	Kachū	華中
Hubei	Hupei	Kohoku	湖北
Hohhot	Hohhot	Fufuhoto	呼和浩特
Hunan	Hunan	Konan	湖南
Jiangsu	Chiangsu	Kōso	江蘇
Jiangxi	Chianghsi	Kōsei	江西
Jilin (Kirin)	Chilin	Kitsurin	吉林
Jilong (Keelung)	Chilung	Kīrun	基隆
Jinan (Tsinan)	Chinan	Sainan	濟南
Jiulong (Kowloon)	Chiulung	Kyūryū, Kuryū, Kūron	九龍
Kaifeng	K'aifeng	Kaihō	開封
Kunming	K'unming	Kommei	昆明
Lahsa	Lhasa	Rasa	拉薩
Lanzhou	Lanchou	Ranshū	蘭州
Lianyungang	Lienyunkang	Ren'unkō	連雲港
Liaodong Bandao (Liaodong Peninsula)	Liaotung Pantao	Ryōtō Hantō	遼東半島
Liaoning	Liaoning	Ryōnei	遼寧
Lugouqiao (Marco Polo Bridge)	Lukouch'iao	Rokokyō	蘆溝橋
Luoyang	Loyang	Rakuyō	洛陽
Lushun (Port Arthur)	Lushun	Ryojun	旅順
Manzhou (Manchuria)	Manchou	Manshū	満洲
Manzhouli	Manchouli	Manchuri	満洲里
Nanchang	Nanch'ang	Nanshō	南昌
Nanjing (Nanking)	Nanching	Nankin	南京
Nanning	Nanning	Nannei	南寧
Nei Mongol (Inner Mongolia)	Nei Mengku	Nai Mōko, Uchi Mongoru	内蒙古
Ningbo	Ningpo	Neiha, Ninpo	寧波
Ningxia	Ninghsia	Neika	寧夏
Penghu Zhudao (Pescadores)	P'enghu Chutao	Hōko Shotō	澎湖諸島
Pukou (Pukow)	P'uk'ou	Hokō	浦口

11. Foreign Geographical Names

NAME IN PINYIN SYSTEM[1]	NAME IN THOMAS WADE SYSTEM[2]	JAPANESE PRONUNCIATION	CHARACTERS[3]
Qingdao	Ch'ingtao	Chintao, Seitō	青島
Qinghai	Ch'inghai	Seikai	青海
Qinhuangdao	Ch'inghuangtao	Shinnōtō	秦皇島
Rehe (Jehol)	Jehe	Nekka	熱河
Shaanxi	Shaanhsi	Sensei	陝西
Shandong	Shantung	Santō	山東
Shanghai	Shanghai	Shanhai	上海
Shantou (Swatou)	Shant'ou	Suwatō	汕頭
Shanxi	Shanhsi	Sansei	山西
Shenyang (Mukden)	Shenyang	Shin'yō	瀋陽
Shijiazhuang	Shihchiachuang	Sekkasō	石家荘
Sichuan (Szechwan)	Ssuch'uan	Shisen	四川
Songhuajiang (Sungari River)	Sunghuachiang	Shōkakō	松花江
Suiyuan	Suiyuan	Suien	綏遠
Suzhou (Soochow)	Suchou	Soshū	蘇州
Taibei	T'aipei	Taihoku	臺北
Tainan	T'ainan	Tainan	臺南
Taiwan (Formosa)	T'aiwan	Taiwan	臺灣
Taiyuan	T'aiyuan	Taigen	太原
Taizhong	T'aichung	Taichū	臺中
Tianjin	T'ienchin	Tenshin	天津
Urumqi	Wulumuch'i	Urumuchi	烏魯木齊
Wanli Changcheng (The Great Wall)	Wanli Ch'angch'eng	Banri no Chōjō	萬里長城
Weihai	Weihai	Ikai	威海
Wuhan	Wuhan	Bukan	武漢
Wusong	Wusung	Ūsun, Goshō	呉淞
Xiamen (Amoy)	Hsiamen	Amoi	厦門
Xi'an	Hsi'an	Seian	西安
Xianggang (Hong Kong)	Hsiangkang	Honkon	香港
Xikang	Hsik'ang	Seikō	西康
Xining	Hsining	Seinei	西寧
Xinjiang (Sinkiang)	Hsinchiang	Shinkyō	新疆
Xizang (Tibet)	Hsitsang	Chibetto	西藏
Yan'an	Yen'an	En'an	延安
Yangzijiang (Yangtze River)	Yangtzuchiang	Yōsukō	揚子江
Yantai	Yent'ai	Entai	煙臺

Yichang	Ich'ang	Gishō	宜昌
Yinchuan	Yinch'uan	Ginsen	銀川
Yunnan	Yunnan	Unnan	雲南
Zhangjiakou (Kalgan)	Changchiak'ou	Chōkakō	張家口
Zhejiang	Chechiang	Sekkō	浙江
Zhengzhou	Chengchou	Teishū	鄭州
Zhifu	Chihfu	Chīfu	芝罘
Zhongguo (China)	Chungkuo	Chūgoku	中國
Zhonghua Minguo (Republic of China — Taiwan)	Chunghua Minkuo	Chūka Minkoku	中華民國
Zhonghua Renmin Gongheguo (People's Republic of China)	Chunghua Jenmin Kunghekuo	Chūka Jimmin Kyōwakoku	中華人民共和國
Zhujiang (Pearl River)	Chuchiang	Shukō	珠江

[1] The Pinyin system is the official romanization system of the People's Republic of China and of the United Nations.
[2] The Thomas Wade system is the official romanization system of the Republic of China (Taiwan).
[3] The simplified forms of the following characters are shown in parentheses: 廣(広), 濟(済), 臺(台), 萬(万), 國(国), 濱(浜).

KOREAN PLACE NAMES

NAME	JAPANESE PRONUNCIATION	CHARACTERS
Andong	Antō	安東
Cheju Island	Saishūtō	濟州島
Chinnampo	Chinnampo	鎮南補
Han River	Kankō	漢江
Inchon	Jinsen	仁川
Kaesong	Kaijō	開城
Kimpo	Kimpo	金補
Korea	Chōsen	朝鮮
Korea-North	Hokusen	北鮮
	Chōsen Minshushugi Jimmin Kyōwakoku	朝鮮民主主義人民共和國
Korea-South	Nansen	南鮮
	Daikan Minkoku (Kankoku)	大韓民國(韓國)
Kum River	Kinkō	錦江
Panmunjom	Hammonten	板門店
Pusan	Fuzan	釜山
Pyongyang	Heijō	平壤
Seoul	Keijō	京城
Taegu	Taikyū	大邱
Wonsan	Genzan	元山
Yalu River	Ōryokkō	鴨緑江

MISCELLANEOUS FOREIGN PLACE NAMES

NAME	JAPANESE PRONUNCIATION	CHARACTERS
Africa	Afurika	阿弗利加
America	Amerika	亜米利加

11. Foreign Geographical Names

NAME	JAPANESE PRONUNCIATION	CHARACTERS
The Americas	Beishū	米洲
Annam	Annan	安南
Antarctic Ocean	Nampyōyō	南氷洋*
Arabia	Arabiya	亞刺比亞
Arctic Ocean	Hoppyōyō	北氷洋*
Argentina	Aruzenchin	亞爾然丁
Asia	Ajia	亞細亞
Asia Minor	Shōajia	小亞細亞
Atlantic Ocean	Taiseiyō	大西洋*
Australia	Ōsutoraria Gōshū	濠太刺利 濠洲, 豪州*
Austria	Ōsutoria	墺太利
Belgium	Berugii	白耳義
Berlin	Berurin	伯林
Black Sea	Kokkai	黒海*
Brazil	Burajiru	伯刺西爾
California	Kariforunia, Kashū	加州
Cambodia	Kanbojia	柬埔寨
Canada	Kanada	加奈陀
Cape of Good Hope	Kibōhō	喜望峰*
Central America	Chūō Amerika Chūbei	中央亞米利加 中米*
Chicago	Shikago	市俄古
Coral Sea	Sangokai	珊瑚海*
Dead Sea	Shikai	死海*
Denmark	Demm āku	丁抹
East Indies	Higashi Indo Shotō	東印度諸島
Egypt	Ejiputo	埃及
England	Ingurando, Eikoku	英蘭, 英国*
English Channel	Ei-Futsu Kaikyō	英仏海峡*
Europe	Yōroppa Ōshū	歐羅巴 欧州*
Far East	Kyokutō	極東*
France	Furansu, Futsukoku	佛蘭西, 仏国*
French Indo-China	Futsuin	佛印
Germany	Doitsu, Dokkoku	獨逸, 独国*
Golden Gate	Kimmon Kaikyō	金門海峡*
Great Britain	Igirisu, Eikoku	英吉利, 英国*
Greece	Girisha	希臘
Greenland	Gurinrando, Ryokutō	緑島
Hanoi	Hanoi	河内
Hawaii	Hawaii	布哇
Ho Chi Min	Hochimin	胡志明
Holland, The Netherlands	Oranda	和蘭陀
Hungary	Hangarī	洪牙利, 匈牙利*
Iceland	Aisurando	氷洲
India	Indo	印度
Indian Ocean	Indoyō	印度洋
Indo-China	Indo-Shina	印度支那
Ireland	Airurando, Airan	愛蘭
Italy	Itarī Itaria	伊太利 伊太利亞
Java	Jawa	瓜哇
Kurile Current	Oyashio	親潮*

Laos	Raosu	老撾
London	Rondon	倫敦
Los Angeles	Rafu, Rosuanzerusu	羅府
Malayshia	Marēshia	馬來西亞
Mediterranean Sea	Chichūkai	地中海*
Mexico	Mekishiko	墨西哥
Middle East	Chūtō	中東*
Mongolia	Mōko	蒙古*
Myanmar	Myanmā	緬甸
Near East	Kintō	近東*
Newfoundland	Nyūfandorando	新發見島
New York	Nyūyōku	紐育
New Zealand	Nyūjīrando	新西蘭
North America	Hokubei	北米*
Norway	Noruwei	諾威
Pacific Ocean	Taiheiyō	太平洋*
Paris	Pari	巴里
Philadelphia	Firaderufia	費拉府, 費府
Philippines	Firipin	比律賓
	Hitō	比島
Poland	Porando	波蘭
Portugal	Porutogaru	葡萄牙
Prussia	Purosha	普魯西
Persia	Perusha	波斯
Red Sea	Kōkai	紅海*
Rome	Rōma	羅馬
Russia	Roshia	露西亞
	Rokoku	露國, 魯國
Saigon	Saigon	西貢
San Francisco	San Furanshisuko	
	Sōkō	桑港
Siberia	Shiberia	西伯利亞
Singapore	Shingapōru	星港, 新嘉坡
South America	Minami Amerika	南亞米利加
	Nambei	南米*
Spain	Supein	西班牙
Sweden	Suēden	瑞典
Switzerland	Suisu	瑞西
Thailand, Siam	Tai, Taikoku	泰, 泰國
Tibet	Chibetto	西藏
Turkey	Toruko	土耳古
Union of Soviet Socialist Republics	Sorempō, Soren	蘇連邦, 蘇連
United Kingdom	Eikoku	英国*
United States	Beikoku	米国*
Vienna, Wien	Uīn	維也納
Vietnam	Betonamu	
	Etsunan	越南
Washington	Washinton	華聖頓
	Kafu	華府
West Indies	Nishi Indo Shotō	西印度諸島
White Russia	Haku Roshia	白露西亞

Note: Because of the present tendency to use katakana for foreign place names, this list does not include the names of some newer countries.

APPENDIX 12. WEIGHTS AND MEASURES

The metric system is now official in Japan but of course the older units will remain in the literature.

LINEAR MEASURE

1 *rin* (厘)		=.012 inch	= .303 millimeter
10 *rin*	=1 *bu*	= .12 inch	= 3.03 millimeters
10 *bu* (分)	=1 *sun*	= 1.2 inches	= 3.03 centimeters
10 *sun* (寸)	=1 *shaku*	=.994 foot	= 30.3 centimeters
6 *shaku* (尺)	=1 *ken*	=1.99 yards	= 1.82 meters
6 *shaku*	=1 *hiro* (尋)	=.994 fathom	= 1.82 meters
10 *shaku*	=1 *jo* (丈)	=3.31 yards	= 3.03 meters
60 *ken* (間)	=1 *chō*	=119 yards	= 109 meters
36 *chō* (町 or 丁)	=1 *ri* (里)	=2.44 miles	= 3.93 kilometers
1 *kairi* (海里)		= 1 knot	=1852 meters

SQUARE MEASURE

1 square *ken*	=1 *tsubo* (坪)	=3.95 sq. yds.	=3.31 sq. meters
1 square *ken*	=1 *bu*	=3.95 sq. yds.	=3.31 sq. meters
30 *bu* (歩)	=1 *se*	=119 sq. yds.	=99.3 sq. meters
10 *se* (畝)	=1 *tan*	=.245 acres	=993 sq. meters
10 *tan* (段 or 反)	=1 *chō* (町)	=2.45 acres	=.992 hectares
10 *tan*	=1 *chōbu* (町歩)	=2.45 acres	=.992 hectares

CAPACITY

1 *shaku* (勺)		=.0384 pint (u.s.)	=.018 liter
10 *shaku*	=1 *gō*	=.384 pint (u.s.)	= .18 liter
10 *gō* (合)	=1 *shō*	=1.92 quarts (u.s.)	= 1.8 liters
10 *shō* (升)	=1 *to*	=4.8 gallons (u.s.)	= 18. liters
10 *to* (斗)	=1 *koku* (石)	=44.8 gallons (u.s.)	=180. liters

WEIGHTS

1 *momme* (匁)		=.1325 oz.	=3.75 grams
100 *momme*	=*hyakume* (百目)	=13.25 oz.	=375 grams
160 *momme*	=1 *kin* (斤)	=1.32 lb.	= .6 kilogram
1000 *momme*	=1 *kan* (貫 or 〆)		
	or 1 *kamme* (貫目)	=8.72 lb.	=3.75 kilograms
100 *kin* (斤)	=1 *biroku* (擔 or 担)	=132 lb. (1 picul)	= 60 kilograms

METRIC SYSTEM

粍 millimeter	瓱 milligram	竓 milliliter
糎 centimeter	甅 centigram	竰 centiliter
粉 decimeter	瓰 decigram	竕 deciliter
米 meter	瓦 gram	立 liter
籵 decameter	瓧 decagram	竍 decaliter
粨 hectometer	瓸 hectogram	竡 hectoliter
粁 kilometer	瓩 kilogram	竏 kiloliter

APPENDIX 13. JŌYŌ KANJI LISTS

For convenience, particularly when studying characters, we have gathered into this appendix a complete listing of all the Jōyō Kanji as established by the Japanese Government, arranging them under three headings: essential characters, general use characters, and additions for proper names. Also shown, for purpose of speedy reference, is the number under which each character has been listed in the body of this dictionary.

1006 ESSENTIAL CHARACTERS. These have been marked with a small capital A in the body of this dictionary and are here arranged according to the elementary school grades in which they are taught; within each grade the characters are arranged in the order in which they appear in this dictionary.

GRADE ONE — 80 CHARACTERS

一	七	三	下	上	中	九	二	五	人	休
1	3	8	9	10	28	57	72	77	99	142
先	入	八	六	円	出	力	十	千	口	右
350	366	369	371	385	445	521	598	599	685	700
名	四	土	夕	大	天	女	子	字	学	小
716	938	966	1123	1133	1138	1173	1281	1285	1294	1389
山	川	左	年	手	文	日	早	月	木	本
1439	1526	1535	1593	2060	2364	2410	2419	2530	2531	2536
村	林	校	森	正	気	水	火	犬	王	玉
2564	2590	2669	2749	2955	3025	3030	3394	3553	3619	3620
生	田	町	男	白	百	目	石	空	立	竹
3715	3727	3729	3731	3863	3864	3906	3985	4192	4223	4246
糸	耳	花	草	虫	見	貝	赤	足	車	金
4431	4715	4980	5032	5275	5522	5766	5840	5856	5939	6211
雨	青	音								
6518	6557	6607								

GRADE TWO — 160 CHARACTERS

万	丸	交	京	今	会	体	作	何	元	兄
7	34	90	93	112	143	165	167	169	343	344
光	公	内	冬	刀	切	分	前	北	午	半
349	372	386	410	448	453	454	490	581	604	608
南	原	友	台	古	合	同	回	図	国	園
619	652	672	699	702	715	717	941	947	950	962
地	声	売	場	夏	外	多	夜	太	妹	姉
976	989	990	1058	1120	1125	1127	1129	1137	1199	1201
室	家	寺	少	岩	工	市	帰	広	店	弓
1327	1337	1373	1390	1461	1532	1549	1564	1604	1613	1678
引	弟	弱	強	当	形	後	心	思	戸	才
1681	1685	1692	1695	1706	1713	1742	1780	1824	2048	2059

教 2345　数 2353　新 2387　方 2389　明 2435　昼 2450　星 2452　春 2453　時 2462　書 2463　晴 2488

曜 2522　来 2565　東 2596　楽 2790　歌 2945　止 2954　歩 2958　母 3005　毎 3006　毛 3013　池 3042

汽 3068　活 3132　海 3133　点 3412　父 3516　牛 3532　理 3644　用 3721　画 3733　番 3762　直 3908

矢 3976　知 3978　社 4065　科 4130　秋 4131　答 4285　算 4316　米 4380　紙 4455　組 4470　細 4472

絵 4488　線 4548　羽 4675　考 4697　聞 4732　肉 4753　朝 4838　自 4900　船 4939　色 4956　茶 5033

行 5419　西 5514　親 5534　角 5543　言 5552　計 5555　記 5563　話 5608　語 5628　読 5629　谷 5730

買 5793　走 5845　近 6021　通 6063　週 6070　道 6091　遠 6101　里 6206　野 6208　長 6379　門 6381

間 6391　雪 6520　雲 6522　電 6526　頭 6639　顔 6648　風 6663　食 6674　首 6719　馬 6725　高 6796

魚 6845　鳥 6931　鳴 6939　麦 7030　黄 7045　黒 7052

GRADE THREE — 200 CHARACTERS

丁 2　世 20　両 23　主 38　乗 54　予 68　事 71　他 122　仕 123　代 125　全 145

住 164　使 196　係 217　倍 252　具 376　写 400　列 460　助 530　勉 543　動 549　勝 553

化 580　区 585　医 590　去 665　反 674　受 678　取 679　号 692　向 712　君 746　味 766

命 767　和 770　品 792　員 808　問 830　商 832　坂 985　夫 1136　始 1203　委 1204　守 1310

安 1311　定 1323　実 1324　客 1329　宮 1336　宿 1344　寒 1350　対 1375　局 1412　屋 1421　岸 1459

島 1476　州 1529　帳 1568　平 1590　幸 1595　度 1616　庫 1617　庭 1618　式 1676　役 1726　待 1741

急 1823　息 1850　悪 1873　悲 1897　想 1922　意 1926　感 1928　所 2054　打 2063　投 2095　拾 2149

持 2151　指 2152　放 2333　整 2360　旅 2396　族 2399　曲 2418　昔 2433　昭 2446　暑 2484　暗 2503

板 2595　柱 2631　根 2670　植 2751　業 2789　様 2821　横 2854　橋 2879　次 2929　歯 2961　死 2968

氷 3032　決 3070　泳 3090　波 3101　注 3103　油 3106　洋 3130　消 3158　流 3160　深 3206　湖 3240

港 3242　湯 3245　温 3246　漢 3281　炭 3413　物 3538　球 3643　由 3724　申 3726　界 3739　畑 3741

病 3798　発 3860　登 3862　皮 3878　皿 3885　県 3918　相 3920　真 3926　着 3938　短 3982　研 3991

礼 4061	神 4087	祭 4092	福 4105	秒 4129	究 4189	章 4235	童 4239	笛 4268	第 4272	等 4287
筆 4288	箱 4331	級 4437	終 4471	緑 4528	練 4530	羊 4658	美 4660	習 4681	者 4698	有 4756
育 4773	服 4775	期 4836	苦 5009	荷 5059	葉 5129	落 5130	薬 5224	血 5411	表 5422	詩 5610
談 5643	調 5647	豆 5735	負 5769	起 5849	路 5876	身 5928	転 5948	軽 5953	農 6008	返 6020
送 6039	追 6042	速 6060	進 6073	運 6092	遊 6093	部 6146	都 6148	酒 6160	配 6163	重 6207
鉄 6253	銀 6268	開 6393	院 6447	階 6469	陽 6470	集 6500	面 6566	題 6645	飲 6680	館 6701
駅 6735	鼻 7082									

GRADE FOUR — 200 CHARACTERS

不 13	争 69	以 109	令 121	付 124	仲 140	伝 141	位 162	低 166	例 193	便 219
信 221	候 250	倉 255	借 259	停 273	側 275	健 278	働 297	億 321	兆 346	児 355
共 373	兵 374	典 375	冷 419	利 466	別 467	初 469	刷 479	副 503	功 522	加 523
努 527	労 531	勇 541	包 572	卒 615	協 617	単 620	博 621	印 630	参 666	史 697
司 698	各 714	告 744	周 768	唱 829	喜 858	器 898	囲 945	固 949	型 1010	堂 1037
塩 1075	士 1117	変 1119	央 1140	失 1141	好 1180	季 1292	孫 1296	完 1315	官 1322	害 1333
察 1360	差 1537	希 1553	席 1561	帯 1563	府 1611	底 1612	康 1621	建 1660	径 1730	徒 1746
得 1755	街 1759	必 1781	念 1800	愛 1927	成 2025	戦 2037	折 2094	挙 2150	改 2332	敗 2343
救 2344	散 2352	料 2374	旗 2402	昨 2449	景 2487	最 2492	札 2533	末 2534	未 2535	束 2559
材 2561	松 2592	果 2594	栄 2635	梅 2666	案 2667	械 2685	巣 2705	極 2753	標 2852	機 2880
欠 2928	歴 2964	残 2976	殺 2994	毒 3007	氏 3020	民 3021	求 3036	治 3100	泣 3104	法 3107
浅 3129	浴 3153	清 3205	満 3248	漁 3309	灯 3395	然 3435	焼 3438	無 3439	照 3457	熱 3473
牧 3537	特 3541	産 3716	的 3867	省 3916	祝 4085	票 4089	種 4159	積 4176	競 4244	笑 4256
節 4299	管 4317	粉 4390	紀 4439	約 4440	給 4489	結 4492	続 4500	置 4645	老 4696	胃 4793

脈 4805	望 4819	腸 4849	臣 4894	航 4933	良 4954	芸 4978	芽 5002	英 5008	菜 5097	衣 5420
要 5515	覚 5529	観 5538	訓 5562	試 5611	説 5627	課 5644	議 5716	象 5744	貨 5781	費 5786
貯 5791	賞 5815	軍 5943	輪 5973	辞 6000	辺 6011	連 6062	達 6088	選 6114	郡 6143	量 6209
録 6298	鏡 6341	関 6402	陸 6461	隊 6468	静 6560	順 6619	類 6647	願 6653	飛 6672	飯 6679
養 6691	験 6758									

GRADE FIVE — 185 CHARACTERS

久 47	仏 111	件 130	任 136	似 138	仮 144	余 168	価 188	舎 189	保 222	俵 243
個 258	修 260	備 284	像 308	再 391	刊 456	判 465	券 473	制 481	則 487	効 535
務 546	勢 558	厚 651	句 693	可 701	営 857	因 939	団 940	圧 970	在 975	均 988
基 1040	報 1059	墓 1073	境 1085	増 1088	夢 1131	妻 1200	婦 1243	容 1335	寄 1345	富 1349
導 1388	居 1416	属 1430	布 1548	師 1562	常 1569	幹 1596	序 1607	弁 1663	張 1694	往 1733
術 1754	復 1760	徳 1767	衛 1776	志 1785	応 1789	快 1802	性 1822	恩 1851	情 1898	態 1947
慣 1970	承 2088	技 2092	招 2124	授 2208	採 2209	接 2213	提 2237	損 2255	支 2324	故 2334
政 2335	敵 2359	断 2385	旧 2412	易 2432	暴 2511	条 2563	枝 2591	査 2630	桜 2664	格 2668
検 2752	構 2823	武 2959	比 3010	永 3031	河 3102	液 3199	混 3204	測 3244	減 3249	準 3278
演 3310	潔 3332	災 3400	燃 3490	版 3526	犯 3554	状 3556	独 3574	率 3618	現 3645	留 3750
略 3755	益 3891	眼 3935	破 3999	確 4039	示 4060	祖 4083	禁 4098	移 4141	程 4144	税 4146
築 4343	精 4411	素 4456	経 4473	統 4487	絶 4490	綿 4531	総 4532	編 4552	績 4579	織 4596
罪 4644	群 4666	義 4668	耕 4710	職 4742	肥 4774	能 4809	興 4913	舌 4917	製 5476	複 5484
規 5524	解 5548	許 5569	設 5570	評 5587	証 5589	謝 5687	講 5689	識 5704	護 5715	豊 5737
財 5773	責 5780	貧 5782	貿 5788	賀 5790	貸 5792	資 5803	賛 5814	質 5817	輸 5978	述 6030
迷 6037	退 6040	逆 6041	造 6061	過 6090	適 6107	酸 6177	鉱 6252	銭 6264	銅 6266	防 6429

限	険	際	雑	非	預	領	額	飼		
6439	6456	6478	6507	6563	6625	6628	6644	6685		

GRADE SIX — 181 CHARACTERS

並	乱	乳	亡	仁	供	俳	値	傷	優	党
24	60	61	86	110	195	254	257	301	334	363
冊	処	刻	創	割	劇	勤	危	卵	厳	収
389	435	478	506	507	517	552	629	632	663	675
后	吸	否	呼	善	困	垂	城	域	奏	奮
704	713	742	769	859	946	999	1011	1030	1156	1172
姿	存	孝	宅	宇	宙	宝	宗	宣	密	寸
1216	1284	1289	1308	1309	1318	1320	1321	1328	1343	1372
専	将	射	尊	就	尺	届	展	層	己	巻
1377	1379	1380	1386	1401	1404	1413	1425	1432	1540	1545
幕	干	幼	庁	座	延	律	従	忘	忠	憲
1578	1589	1599	1603	1619	1657	1740	1745	1784	1801	1988
我	批	拡	担	拝	捨	探	推	揮	操	敬
2028	2086	2118	2121	2126	2205	2211	2212	2229	2296	2351
映	晩	暖	暮	机	枚	染	株	棒	模	権
2448	2491	2502	2508	2543	2582	2636	2665	2750	2825	2853
樹	欲	段	泉	沿	派	洗	済	源	潮	激
2878	2936	2991	3095	3096	3126	3131	3197	3274	3336	3350
灰	熟	片	班	異	疑	痛	皇	盛	盟	看
3396	3472	3525	3636	3757	3777	3814	3870	3895	3899	3919
砂	磁	私	秘	穀	穴	窓	策	筋	簡	糖
3992	4029	4124	4140	4157	4186	4201	4284	4286	4350	4420
系	紅	納	純	絹	縦	縮	署	翌	聖	肺
4433	4441	4453	4454	4499	4571	4585	4643	4679	4727	4791
背	朗	胸	脳	腹	臓	臨	至	若	著	蒸
4794	4802	4811	4821	4851	4886	4899	4903	5007	5098	5163
蔵	蚕	衆	裁	装	裏	補	視	覧	討	訪
5182	5290	5417	5454	5455	5462	5464	5525	5533	5561	5571
訳	詞	誠	誌	認	誤	誕	論	諸	警	貴
5572	5582	5606	5620	5623	5626	5640	5646	5648	5705	5794
賃	遺	郷	郵	針	鋼	閉	閣	陛	除	降
5802	6115	6145	6147	6218	6302	6385	6401	6444	6449	6450
障	難	革	頂	骨						
6479	6515	6570	6616	6784						

939 GENERAL-USE CHARACTERS. These are the rest of the 1945 Jōyō Kanji, which have been marked with a small capital B in the body of this dictionary. They are arranged here in the order of their appearance in this dictionary.

丈	与	丙	且	丘	衷	丹	乏	乙	乾	了
5	6	16	17	19	31	36	46	56	63	67

互 75 井 76 亜 81 享 92 亭 96 介 108 仙 120 伐 132 企 135 仰 137 伏 139
但 154 佐 155 伺 156 伴 157 伯 158 伸 163 侮 187 併 190 依 191 侍 192 佳 194
侯 211 促 212 俊 216 侵 218 俗 220 倣 235 倫 246 倹 248 俸 249 倒 256 偵 270
偶 274 偽 276 偏 277 傘 283 偉 285 傍 286 傑 293 債 296 催 298 傾 299 僧 300
僕 313 僚 314 舗 322 儀 324 儒 330 償 333 充 348 克 354 免 361 兼 381 冗 399
冠 401 准 426 凍 427 凝 431 凡 433 凶 442 凸 443 凹 444 刃 449 刈 452 刑 461
到 477 刺 480 削 488 剖 492 剤 493 剛 497 剣 498 剰 501 劣 524 励 528 劾 534
勅 540 勘 548 募 551 勧 559 勲 560 勺 565 匁 566 匹 584 匠 588 匿 591 升 603
卓 616 卑 618 占 624 却 631 即 633 卸 641 厄 646 厘 650 又 668 及 670 双 673
叔 677 叙 681 召 695 吏 706 叫 708 吐 709 吉 711 呈 734 吟 740 呉 741 含 743
吹 747 咲 790 哀 791 唆 803 唇 807 哲 811 唐 812 喝 824 啓 828 唯 831 喚 852
喪 853 喫 855 嗣 868 嘆 872 嘱 894 噴 900 嚇 915 囚 937 圏 960 壮 974 壱 983
坊 986 坑 987 坪 998 垣 1009 埋 1020 培 1032 堕 1033 堀 1036 堅 1038 執 1039 塚 1048
塀 1051 塔 1052 堤 1054 塁 1056 堪 1057 塑 1068 塊 1070 塗 1074 墜 1082 塾 1083 墨 1086
墳 1095 墾 1097 壌 1098 壇 1101 壊 1102 壁 1103 奔 1148 奉 1149 奇 1150 契 1155 奥 1165
奨 1167 奪 1171 奴 1174 妃 1176 妄 1177 如 1178 妨 1187 妥 1188 妊 1189 妙 1191 姓 1196
姻 1215 姫 1217 威 1219 娠 1224 娘 1230 娯 1231 婆 1240 婚 1242 婿 1246 媒 1247 嫁 1256
嫌 1257 嫡 1263 嬢 1270 孔 1282 孤 1293 宜 1317 宰 1330 宴 1332 宵 1334 寂 1342 寛 1352
寝 1353 寧 1361 寡 1363 賓 1365 寮 1366 審 1367 寿 1374 封 1376 尉 1383 尋 1385 尚 1395
尼 1405 尽 1408 尿 1410 尾 1411 屈 1415 履 1434 屯 1438 岐 1447 岳 1457 岬 1458 峠 1464
峡 1465 峰 1473 崎 1485 崇 1490 崩 1491 巡 1528 巧 1533 巨 1534 帆 1551 帥 1559 帝 1560
帽 1573 幅 1574 幣 1585 幻 1598 幽 1600 幾 1601 床 1608 廊 1622 庸 1624 庶 1625 廃 1630

廉 1634	廷 1654	弊 1670	弐 1675	弔 1680	弧 1687	弦 1688	弾 1699	彩 1718	彫 1719	彰 1721
影 1722	征 1731	彼 1732	徐 1744	循 1758	御 1761	微 1765	徴 1768	徹 1771	衝 1772	衡 1775
忙 1783	忌 1786	忍 1787	怖 1817	怠 1818	怒 1820	怪 1821	恨 1842	恭 1845	恥 1846	恵 1847
悔 1848	恒 1849	恋 1852	恐 1853	悩 1867	悦 1868	悟 1870	患 1871	悠 1872	悼 1891	惑 1892
惜 1894	惨 1896	慌 1917	愉 1920	惰 1921	愁 1923	慈 1924	愚 1925	慨 1944	慎 1945	慕 1948
慮 1962	慶 1967	慢 1968	憎 1969	憂 1971	慰 1972	憩 1980	憤 1990	憾 1999	憶 2001	懇 2002
懐 2003	懲 2006	懸 2011	戒 2027	戯 2041	戻 2051	房 2053	扇 2056	扉 2058	払 2062	扱 2070
択 2082	把 2083	拒 2084	抄 2087	扶 2089	抑 2090	抗 2091	抜 2093	拐 2107	抹 2112	拠 2113
拍 2114	拓 2115	披 2116	抽 2119	抵 2120	拙 2122	拘 2123	抱 2125	押 2128	拷 2142	括 2143
挑 2145	挟 2146	挿 2167	捜 2168	捕 2170	振 2171	措 2190	掲 2194	据 2195	描 2196	掌 2200
控 2202	掘 2204	掃 2207	排 2210	掛 2214	搭 2228	援 2230	握 2232	換 2233	揺 2235	揚 2236
搬 2249	搾 2251	摂 2252	携 2253	摩 2264	撃 2265	摘 2266	撲 2274	撤 2280	撮 2282	擁 2294
擦 2306	擬 2307	攻 2331	敏 2337	敢 2350	敷 2357	斉 2366	斎 2368	斗 2373	斜 2376	斤 2379
斥 2380	施 2391	旋 2400	既 2407	旨 2414	旬 2415	更 2422	昆 2430	昇 2434	是 2451	曹 2477
晶 2482	暁 2485	替 2486	普 2489	暇 2501	暦 2507	暫 2510	曇 2518	朴 2544	朽 2545	朱 2546
杉 2562	析 2574	枠 2585	杯 2586	枢 2588	柄 2627	某 2628	柳 2629	架 2632	柔 2633	枯 2634
栓 2649	栽 2654	桟 2658	核 2660	桑 2661	桃 2663	棋 2744	棺 2746	棟 2747	棚 2748	楼 2785
棄 2787	概 2824	槽 2844	欄 2914	欧 2931	款 2938	欺 2939	歓 2948	歳 2962	殉 2974	殊 2975
殖 2981	殴 2990	殻 2996	殿 3001	汁 3035	江 3045	汗 3046	汚 3047	沢 3062	沖 3065	没 3066
沈 3069	況 3086	沼 3091	泌 3092	泡 3093	沸 3094	泰 3098	泊 3099	泥 3105	津 3122	洪 3123
洞 3125	浄 3128	浜 3152	涙 3154	浪 3155	浦 3156	浸 3157	浮 3159	涯 3181	渉 3190	淑 3191
渇 3195	渓 3196	涼 3198	渋 3200	添 3201	淡 3202	滋 3238	湾 3239	渦 3241	湿 3243	渡 3247

漠 3268	滝 3273	溝 3275	溶 3277	滅 3279	滞 3280	滑 3282	滴 3299	漬 3301	漂 3303	漆 3304
漸 3305	漏 3307	漫 3308	潟 3328	澄 3333	潤 3334	潜 3337	濁 3348	濃 3349	濯 3360	濫 3366
瀬 3384	炉 3403	炎 3404	炊 3405	為 3411	烈 3420	焦 3436	煮 3437	煩 3454	煙 3456	燥 3493
爆 3505	爵 3514	牲 3539	犠 3550	狂 3562	狭 3572	狩 3573	猫 3586	猟 3587	猛 3588	猶 3593
献 3596	猿 3600	獄 3602	獣 3606	獲 3609	玄 3616	珍 3631	珠 3637	琴 3654	環 3680	璽 3683
瓶 3699	甘 3710	甚 3711	甲 3725	畔 3746	畝 3748	畜 3749	畳 3763	疎 3776	疫 3783	症 3795
疲 3796	疾 3797	痢 3810	痘 3813	痴 3823	療 3842	癒 3847	癖 3848	皆 3869	盆 3889	盗 3894
監 3901	盤 3902	盲 3907	盾 3912	冒 3915	眠 3925	眺 3933	督 3946	睡 3948	瞬 3969	矛 3974
矯 3984	砕 3990	砲 3998	硫 4006	硝 4007	硬 4008	碁 4020	碑 4028	磨 4045	礁 4048	礎 4054
祉 4069	祈 4071	祥 4090	禍 4102	禅 4104	秀 4123	秩 4135	租 4138	称 4139	稚 4154	稲 4158
稿 4166	穂 4168	稼 4169	穏 4175	穫 4180	突 4191	窃 4195	窒 4200	窯 4210	窮 4212	竜 4232
端 4243	符 4270	筒 4283	箇 4315	範 4330	篤 4342	簿 4364	籍 4368	粋 4389	粒 4392	粘 4393
粗 4394	粧 4400	糧 4426	糾 4438	索 4449	紡 4450	紋 4451	紛 4452	紹 4465	紺 4466	紳 4467
累 4469	絡 4484	絞 4485	紫 4486	継 4501	維 4516	緒 4521	緊 4524	綱 4525	網 4527	縄 4547
締 4549	縫 4550	緩 4551	縁 4553	緯 4566	縛 4567	繁 4570	繊 4586	繕 4594	繭 4595	繰 4602
缶 4624	罰 4647	罷 4650	羅 4655	翁 4677	翼 4692	翻 4694	耐 4705	耗 4709	聴 4740	粛 4747
肌 4755	肖 4760	肝 4762	肪 4766	肢 4768	肯 4771	肩 4776	胞 4788	胎 4789	胆 4790	朕 4797
脅 4803	脂 4808	胴 4810	脚 4820	脱 4822	脹 4832	腐 4835	腕 4837	腰 4850	膜 4854	膚 4867
膨 4874	臭 4901	致 4904	舞 4926	舟 4927	般 4931	舶 4936	艇 4941	艦 4950	芝 4961	芋 4964
芳 4979	茎 4991	茂 4998	苗 5004	荘 5031	荒 5034	華 5058	菌 5091	菓 5095	菊 5096	葬 5128
蓄 5161	薦 5219	薪 5222	薫 5223	薄 5225	藩 5242	藻 5254	虐 5267	虚 5269	虞 5272	虜 5273
蚊 5288	蛍 5302	蛇 5303	蛮 5314	融 5371	衰 5432	袋 5443	被 5445	裂 5453	裕 5461	褐 5473

裸 5475	褒 5483	襟 5504	襲 5510	覆 5517	覇 5519	触 5547	訂 5553	託 5560	訟 5565	詔 5581
詠 5584	詐 5585	診 5586	訴 5588	該 5601	誉 5602	誇 5605	詳 5607	詰 5609	誓 5622	誘 5625
謁 5637	諾 5638	請 5645	諮 5660	謡 5666	諭 5667	謀 5671	謄 5685	謙 5686	謹 5688	譜 5703
譲 5714	豚 5743	豪 5749	貞 5768	貢 5772	貫 5778	販 5779	賄 5800	賊 5801	賠 5810	賦 5811
賜 5812	賢 5816	購 5823	贈 5827	赦 5841	赴 5847	越 5851	超 5852	趣 5854	距 5866	践 5873
跡 5875	跳 5877	踊 5882	踏 5889	躍 5921	軌 5941	軒 5944	軟 5947	軸 5952	較 5959	載 5960
輩 5971	輝 5972	轄 5981	辛 5996	辱 6007	込 6010	迅 6014	迎 6019	迭 6029	迫 6031	逃 6038
逝 6051	逓 6055	逐 6056	途 6057	透 6059	逮 6069	逸 6071	遇 6083	遂 6084	遍 6086	遅 6089
違 6099	遺 6100	遭 6105	遮 6106	遵 6112	遷 6113	避 6120	還 6121	邦 6130	邸 6134	邪 6135
郊 6137	郎 6138	郭 6144	酌 6162	酔 6166	酢 6169	酬 6171	酪 6172	酵 6175	酷 6176	醜 6189
醸 6197	釈 6203	釣 6224	鈍 6235	鈴 6247	鉢 6249	鉛 6251	銑 6263	銘 6265	銃 6267	鋭 6279
鋳 6280	錘 6291	錠 6293	錯 6299	錬 6300	鍛 6318	鎖 6325	鎮 6328	鐘 6352	鑑 6361	閑 6390
閥 6398	閲 6404	闘 6418	附 6433	阻 6434	陥 6446	陣 6448	陵 6454	隆 6455	陳 6457	陪 6458
陶 6459	随 6460	陰 6462	隅 6467	隔 6475	隠 6480	隣 6484	隷 6490	隻 6494	雇 6497	雄 6499
雅 6505	雌 6506	離 6517	雰 6521	零 6524	雷 6525	需 6528	震 6531	霊 6532	霜 6542	霧 6545
露 6549	靴 6576	響 6610	韻 6611	項 6617	須 6621	頑 6624	頼 6635	頻 6641	顕 6646	顧 6655
飢 6675	飾 6683	飽 6684	餓 6697	香 6722	駄 6734	駆 6736	駐 6745	騒 6760	騎 6761	騰 6767
驚 6774	髄 6791	髪 6804	鬼 6833	魂 6835	魅 6838	魔 6843	鮮 6864	鯨 6886	鶏 6980	麗 7026
麻 7040	黙 7055	鼓 7076	齢 7093							

284 ADDITIONS FOR PROPER NAMES. The following characters, in addition to the 1945 Jōyō Kanji, have been approved by the Government for use in proper names.

丑 12	丞 22	乃 42	之 48	也 58	亀 62	亘 79	亦 88	亥 89	亨 91	亮 95

伍 131	伎 133	伊 134	伶 149	佑 150	伽 159	侑 177	侃 182	倖 228	倭 242	偲 266
允 342	冴 417	冶 418	凌 424	凜 429	凪 437	凱 440	勁 538	匡 587	尭 614	卯 628
叡 683	叶 689	只 694	呂 728	吾 733	哉 779	啄 793	唄 802	喬 841	嘉 887	圭 973
奈 1147	奎 1152	媛 1244	嬉 1267	孟 1291	宏 1314	宥 1326	寅 1341	峻 1475	崚 1480	嵐 1496
嵯 1500	嵩 1502	嶺 1517	巌 1521	巳 1538	巴 1541	巽 1546	庄 1605	弘 1682	弥 1689	彗 1708
彦 1714	彪 1716	彬 1717	怜 1812	恕 1834	悌 1861	惇 1887	惣 1889	惟 1890	慧 1964	憧 1982
拳 2148	捺 2189	捷 2198	敦 2349	斐 2370	於 2390	旦 2411	旭 2416	昂 2424	旺 2427	昌 2428
昴 2441	晋 2455	晃 2458	晏 2460	晟 2472	晨 2476	智 2490	暉 2499	暢 2506	曙 2519	李 2549
杏 2554	杜 2560	柊 2614	柾 2619	柚 2622	栞 2645	桐 2655	桂 2659	栗 2662	梓 2688	梢 2695
梨 2697	梧 2700	椋 2725	椰 2739	椎 2742	楓 2777	楠 2779	椿 2782	楊 2784	榛 2811	樺 2817
槙 2819	槻 2845	橘 2868	檀 2895	欣 2930	欽 2940	毅 3003	毬 3016	汀 3034	汐 3041	汰 3055
沙 3063	洸 3113	洵 3116	洲 3120	浩 3147	渚 3164	淳 3189	湧 3207	渥 3224	滉 3257	漱 3293
澪 3342	熙 3465	熊 3468	燎 3483	燦 3498	燿 3500	爽 3520	爾 3521	猪 3585	玖 3621	玲 3626
琢 3640	琳 3646	瑛 3647	瑶 3656	瑚 3662	瑞 3665	瑳 3667	璃 3669	瑠 3673	甫 3722	皐 3873
皓 3875	眉 3917	眸 3932	睦 3945	瞭 3960	瞳 3961	矩 3980	碩 4026	碧 4027	磯 4049	祐 4079
禄 4096	禎 4099	秦 4133	稀 4145	稔 4149	稜 4152	穣 4179	竣 4238	笙 4264	笹 4271	紘 4445
紗 4446	紬 4462	絃 4468	絢 4481	緋 4517	綸 4519	綜 4520	綺 4522	綾 4523	翔 4683	翠 4685
耀 4695	耶 4716	聡 4730	肇 4751	朋 4769	胤 4786	胡 4792	朔 4801	脩 4815	舜 4925	艶 4957
芙 4966	芹 4970	茉 4994	茄 4995	苑 4996	茅 5005	茜 5019	莉 5044	莞 5052	菖 5085	菫 5086
萌 5094	蓮 5105	葵 5120	萩 5122	蓉 5135	蒔 5153	蒼 5162	蔦 5178	蕉 5191	蕗 5203	藍 5233
藤 5241	蘭 5255	虎 5265	虹 5279	蝶 5363	衿 5431	袈 5442	裟 5457	詢 5593	誼 5634	諄 5635
諒 5641	赳 5848	輔 5964	辰 6006	迪 6026	遥 6075	遼 6111	邑 6127	那 6129	郁 6136	酉 6157

醇	采	錦	鎌	阿	隼	雛	霞	靖	鞠	須
6181	6201	6301	6326	6435	6493	6514	6541	6559	6589	6618
頌	颯	馨	駒	駿	魁	鮎	鯉	鯛	鳩	鳳
6622	6665	6724	6742	6754	6834	6855	6874	6884	6936	6937
鴻	鵬	鶴	鷹	鹿	麟	麿	黎	黛		
6963	6979	6995	7007	7017	7028	7044	7049	7060		

APPENDIX 14. THE ON-KUN INDEX

This *on-kun* index is a romanized listing of all the *on* (Sino-Japanese) and *kun* (native Japanese and foreign) readings of all the individual characters in alphabetical order. Also included are unpredictable compound readings (e.g., *asu* for 明日). The compounds listed here are only those with readings that are unpredicatable given the readings listed in this dictionary. In many cases, there are other compounds that are used to write the words spelled out by these unpredicatable compounds using predictable readings of their component characters. These common, predictable compounds may be found in any large Japanese-English dictionary. The order of each entry is as follows: the ON (in small capitals) or *kun* (in italics) followed by the various characters having that reading and the Nelson number of each character. Compounds are indexed by Nelson number followed by the stroke-count of the second member of the compound (e.g., 明日 2435.4). In this index, okurigana have not been marked by parentheses, as was done in the entries in the body of the dictionary. As in the body of the dictionary, prefixes, suffixes, verbs, and phrases are printed in italics along with the *kun* readings for simplicity's sake, even though they may contain *on* readings within them.

— A —

— B —

— D —

— G —

— I —

— J —

— K —

— N —

— S —

— T —

— U —

— W —

— Y —

APPENDIX 15: THE UNIVERSAL RADICAL INDEX

One of the innovative features of the revised Nelson's character dictionary is the **Universal Radical Index**, which allows character look-ups based on virtually any reasonable radical element found in the character. Aimed primarily at the novice user, but useful to anyone frustrated by obscure radicals and difficult-to-remember 'radical priorities,' the URI lists characters (including characters which consist of one and only one radical) under multiple alternative radicals and plausible miscounts of residual strokes. To further facilitate look-ups, three nonce radicals "frequently recurring graphical elements that do not have official status" have been added to the traditional 214 radicals. These three have been added at the end of the traditional list and consist of Rad. 301 ク *kana ku*, Rad. 302 マ *kana ma*, and Rad. 303 *santen-gammuri*, (as in the three dots on top of characters such as 覚 and 巣); the numbering serves to clearly distinguish these three as artificial classifiers.

Using the URI requires the reader to identify a salient radical or radical-like element in a character and to count the residual strokes as if doing a traditional character look-up. Each character is then referenced to the place it occurs in the body of the dictionary, which follows traditional radical and stroke-count order. For example, the character 稲 can be found by five means: Rad. 115 plus 9 residual strokes (its traditional listing), Rad. 2 plus 13 residual strokes, Rad. 87 plus 10 residual strokes, and either Rad. 72 or 73 plus 10 residual strokes. The one-radical character 黒 can be accessed not only via the traditional Rad. 203 plus 0 residual strokes, but also by Rad. 86 plus 7 residual strokes, Rad. 102 plus 6 or 7 residual strokes, Rad. 32 plus 8 or 9 residual strokes, and Rad. 166 plus 4 residual strokes. The URI also facilitates searches in cases where unsuspected traditional radicals might frustrate even the experienced user: 聞 is listed under both Rad. 128 plus 8 residual strokes and also under Rad. 169 plus 6 residual strokes.

Attention to detail and a forgiving attitude toward inexperienced users has resulted in an index in excess of 30,000 individual listings, or roughly four to five for any given character. Certain constraints had to be observed, however, to keep the size (and reasonableness) of the index manageable. Not every horizontal line means a character gets listed under Rad. 1, nor is every vertical considered an occurrence of Rad. 2. Attention has also been paid to the relative prominence of radicals and the likelihood of their being recognized as such. Thus, while Rad. 120 characters are never cross-listed under Rad. 52, Rad. 95 characters consistently are.

For each entry the JIS code and the Morohashi index number have been given, together with the Nelson number. Each entry includes the JIS code prefixed with J, and the Morohashi index number with M. For example, the entry 立 is followed by $\frac{\text{J4267}}{\text{M38703}}$ 2610.

In general, the compilation of the index has followed these conventions:

· Use of single-stroke radicals has been limited to cases where the radical either does not touch any other element in the character or extends all the way through the character. Despite these constraints, many hundreds of characters can be located by keying to these simple radicals.

· Characters containing radicals which overlap completely or nearly completely in form with another radical (cf. Rad. 22 & Rad. 23; Rad. 72 & 73; Rad 74 & 130) are usually listed under both possible radicals in the index.

· Characters listed in the index under their traditional "correct" radical have **bold** Nelson numbers.

· Within each radical group in the index, subheadings for residual stroke counts (see

Appendix 6) have been provided, with characters listed in Nelson number order under these subheadings. In some cases, a range of residual stroke counts has been combined into a single subgrouping. Here, too, Nelson number order is used within the subgrouping.

Rad. 1 一

0 residual strokes

一 J306c/M1 **1**

1 residual stroke

丁 J437a/M2 **2**
七 J3c37/M6 **3**
二 J4673/M247 72
亠 J5035/M286 85
十 J3d3d/M2695 598
厂 J524c/M2890 645

2 residual strokes

丂 J-X/M-X **4**
丈 J3e66/M11 **5**
与 J4d3f/M20 **6**
万 J4b7c/M10 **7**
三 J3b30/M12 **8**
下 J323c/M14 **9**
上 J3e65/M13 **10**
于 J5032/M252 73
兀 J513a/M1337 341
千 J4069/M2697 599
土 J455a/M4867 966
士 J3b4e/M5638 1117
大 J4267/M5831 1133
女 J3d77/M6036 1173
子 J3b52/M6930 1281
寸 J4023/M7411 1372
尢 J5577/M7538 1398
工 J3929/M8714 1532
干 J3433/M9165 1589
廾 J5730/M9583 1661
廿 J467b/M9586 1662
弋 J5735/M9656 1671
彑 J5740/M9909 1705
才 J3a4d/M11769 2059

3 residual strokes

与 J4d3f/M20 **6**
丏 J5022/M22 **11**
丑 J312f/M23 **12**
不 J4954/M19 **13**
丗 J5242/M32 **15**
世 J4024/M31 **20**
丞 J3e67/M40 **22**
丰 J-X/M75 27
丹 J4330/M99 36
云 J313e/M254 74
互 J385f/M255 75
井 J3066/M258 76
五 J385e/M257 77
元 J3835/M1340 343
兮 J5142/M1455 370
六 J4f3b/M1453 371
卆 J5240/M2701 600
卐 J-X/M48950 601
卅 J5241/M2700 602
升 J3e23/M2702 603
午 J3861/M2703 604
卍 J5244/M2724 611
友 J4d27/M3119 672
圡 J-X/M4871 967
壬 J3f51/M5639 968
夭 J5470/M5838 1135
夫 J4957/M5835 1136
太 J4240/M5834 1137
天 J4537/M5833 1138
尤 J4c60/M7543 1399
尹 J557a/M7631 1403
廿 J467b/M9586 1662
弌 J5021/M9658 1672
弖 J355d/M9692 1678
弖 J5737/M9703 1679
彑 J5740/M9909 1705
戈 J5879/M11530 2018
戸 J384d/M11696 2048
手 J3c6a/M11768 2060
曰 J5b29/M14278 2529
木 J4c5a/M14415 2531
止 J3b5f/M16253 2954
歹 J5d46/M16359 2967
氏 J3b61/M17026 3020
气 J5d63/M17043 3023
牛 J356d/M19922 3532
王 J3226/M20823 3619
瓦 J3424/M21438 3690
甘 J3445/M21643 3710
辷 J6d68/M38703 6009

4 residual strokes

丏 J5022/M22 **11**
丑 J312f/M23 **12**
业 J-X/M-X **14**
丙 J4a3a/M35 **16**
且 J336e/M29 **17**
丕 J5023/M30 **18**
丘 J3556/M33 **19**
世 J4024/M31 **20**
丞 J3e67/M40 **22**
丼 J5027/M101 37
乎 J3843/M131 49
互 J385f/M255 75
五 J385e/M257 77
亙 J-X/M-X 78
令 J4e61/M387 121
兮 J5142/M1455 370
冉 J5147/M1514 388
冊 J3a7d/M1515 389
册 J5146/M1516 390
写 J3c4c/M1570 400
卐 J-X/M48950 601
卋 J-X/M2713 605
卉 J5243/M2706 606
卌 J-X/M2712 607
半 J483e/M2707 608
𠦄 J-X/M2714 609
叮 J525a/M3244 690
号 J3966/M3256 692
右 J3126/M3250 700
可 J3244/M3245 701
央 J317b/M5840 1140
失 J3c3a/M5844 1141
孕 J5554/M6938 1283
巧 J392a/M8721 1533
左 J3a38/M8720 1535
平 J4a3f/M9167 1590
庁 J4423/M9223 1603
弁 J4a5b/M9588 1663
弁 J4a5b/M9588 1664
弁 J4a5b/M9588 1665
弁 J4a5b/M9588 1666
式 J5031/M9661 1673
弖 J355d/M9692 1678
打 J4247/M11781 2063
旦 J4336/M13734 2411
末 J4b76/M14420 2534
未 J4c24/M14419 2535
本 J4b5c/M14421 2536
正 J4035/M16255 2955
毌 J5d59/M16721 3004
母 J4a6c/M16723 3005
氏 J3b61/M17026 3020
民 J4c31/M17028 3021
気 J-X/M-X 3024
汀 J4475/M17103 3034
牙 J3267/M19909 3531
玉 J364c/M20821 3620
瓦 J3424/M21438 3690
甘 J3445/M21643 3710
生 J4038/M21670 3715
皿 J3b2e/M22941 3885
矢 J4c70/M23929 3976

Char	JIS	Morohashi	No.
石	J4050	M24024	3985
示	J3c28	M24623	4060
立	J4e29	M25721	4223
覀	J6b28	M34762	5513
辷	J6d68	M38703	6009
迂	J312a	M38722	6016

5 residual strokes

Char	JIS	Morohashi	No.
丏	J5022	M22	**11**
且	J336e	M29	**17**
世	J4024	M31	**20**
丗	J-X	M-X	**21**
丞	J3e67	M40	**22**
両	J4e3e	M46	**23**
争	J4168	M236	69
亙	J-X	M-X	78
亘	J4f4b	M262	79
亙	J4f4a	M265	80
光	J3877	M1350	349
先	J4068	M1349	350
共	J3626	M1458	373
再	J3a46	M1524	391
写	J3c4c	M1570	400
[illegible]	J-X	M48950	601
卋	J-X	M2714	609
卉	J-X	M2720	610
卍	J5244	M2724	611
号	J3966	M3256	692
吏	J4d79	M3299	706
合	J3967	M3287	715
同	J4631	M3294	717
因	J3078	M4693	939
在	J3a5f	M4881	975
夸	J5472	M5854	1142
安	J4c51	M6063	1177
奸	J5521	M6045	1179
存	J4238	M6943	1284
字	J3b7a	M6942	1285
孛	J5556	M6949	1288
㝉	J-X	M7076	1307
宇	J3127	M7067	1309
巧	J392a	M8721	1533
师	J-X	M8800	1550
幵	J5674	M9169	1591
并	J5675	M9170	1592
弍	J-X	M9662	1674
弎	J4675	M-X	1675
式	J3c30	M9663	1676
彺	J-X	M-X	1724
戋	J-X	M11542	2021
戍	J587c	M11535	2022
戎	J3d3f	M11539	2024
攷	J5a3f	M13111	2328
朽	J3560	M14439	2545
朱	J3c6b	M14424	2546
死	J3b60	M16365	2968
母	J4a6c	M16723	3005
毎	J4b68	M16724′	3006
民	J4c31	M17028	3021
気	J3524	M17046	3025
求	J3561	M17105	3036
汎	J-X	M-X	3044
汚	J3178	M17133	3047
灯	J4574	M18855	3395
灰	J-X	M18858	3397
百	J4934	M22679	3864
石	J-X	M24026	3986
羊	J4d53	M28425	4658
而	J3c29	M28871	4704
耒	J6650	M28898	4706
耳	J3c2a	M28999	4715
聿	J6666	M29215	4746
有	J4d2d	M14332	4756
至	J3b6a	M30142	4903
舌	J4065	M30277	4917
舟	J3d2e	M30350	4927
血	J376c	M33964	5411
行	J3954	M34029	5419
西	J403e	M34763	5514
迂	J312a	M38722	6016
迃	J-X	M38723	6017
阮	J6f76	M41569	6426

6 residual strokes

Char	JIS	Morohashi	No.
両	J4e3e	M46	**23**
亙	J-X	M-X	78
亘	J4f4b	M262	79
亙	J4f4a	M265	80
亜	J3021	M272	81
但	J4322	M495	154
伺	J3b47	M483	156
克	J396e	M1355	354
兵	J4a3c	M1462	374
冷	J4e64	M1622	419
刪	J5168	M1917	464
励	J4e65	M2326	528
[illegible]	J-X	M2864	637
司	J3b4a	M3257	698
吾	J3863	M3379	733
呑	J465d	M3329	737
吟	J3663	M3330	740
呉	J3862	M3365′	741
否	J485d	M3340	742
含	J345e	M3350	743
囲	J304f	M4722	945
坐	J3a41	M4931	978
坏	J542f	M4930	984
夸	J5472	M5854	1142
夷	J3050	M5852	1143
夾	J5473	M5867	1144
妛	J562c	M6094	1182
孛	J5556	M6949	1288
㝉	J-X	M7076	1307
宏	J3928	M7086	1314
完	J3430	M7079	1315
寿	J3c77	M7419′	1374
尨	J5578	M7554	1400
岑	J562a	M7937	1445
巠	J-X	M8681	1530
巫	J5660	M8728	1536
希	J3475	M8813	1553
弃	J5731	M9594	1667
弄	J4f2e	M9596	1668
形	J3741	M9969	1713
忸	J5759	M10397	1797
抔	J5938	M11886	2076
扶	J495e	M11840	2089
抜	J4834	M11901′	2093
攷	J5a3f	M13111	2328
旱	J5a5d	M13752	2421
更	J3939	M14283	2422
朽	J3560	M14439	2545
朸	J5b3d	M14488′	2547
杋	J-X	M14457	2550
杖	J3e73	M14469	2555
束	J422b	M14480	2559
材	J3a60	M14463	2561
步	J-X	M16264	2957
汚	J3178	M17133	3047
汽	J3525	M17177	3068
泄	J5d75	M17267	3083
犹	J603b	M20259	3558
甫	J4a63	M21706	3722
町	J442e	M21735	3729
甼	J6136	M-X	3730
疔	J614b	M22019	3778
芫	J676b	M30727	4967
芦	J3032	M30716	4975
芸	J375d	M30741′	4978
表	J493d	M34105	5422
言	J3840	M35205	5552
豆	J4626	M36245	5735
豕	J6c35	M36334	5742
車	J3c56	M38172	5939
辛	J-X	M38630′	5997
辰	J4324	M38682	6006
迃	J-X	M38723	6017
邸	J4521	M39347	6134
邪	J3c59	M39357′	6135
酉	J4653	M39763	6157
采	J4850	M40115	6202
長	J4439	M41100	6379
镸	J-X	M41101	6380
阻	J414b	M41593	6434
麦	J477e	M47718	7030

7 residual strokes

Char	JIS	Morohashi	No.
並	J4a42	M54	**24**
乖	J502a	M149	53
事	J3b76	M241	71
亜	J3021	M272	81
亞	J5033	M274	82

Char	J	M	No.
亟	J5034	M279	83
來	J5054	M581	173
佰	J5051	M553	174
侖	J5055	M599	176
佪	J3241	M628′	188
使	J3b48	M573	196
兩	J5140	M1436	368
典	J4535	M1474	375
具	J3671	M1473	376
具	J-X	M-X	377
其	J4236	M1472	378
函	J4821	M1826	446
卑	J-X	M2738	612
兗	J3646	M-X	614
卺	J-X	M2864	637
咀	J5272	M3476	758
呵	J526a	M3459	763
味	J4c23	M3456	766
命	J4c3f	M3473	767
囹	J507a	M4744	948
坩	J5430	M4975	995
坦	J4333	M4971	997
垂	J3162	M5012	999
奈	J4660	M5893	1147
奔	J4b5b	M-X	1148
奉	J4a74	M5894	1149
奇	J3471	M5892	1150
妲	J5527	M6129	1192
姐	J3039	M6172	1195
妹	J4b65	M6138	1199
妻	J3a4a	M6140	1200
宜	J3539	M7111	1317
定	J446a	M7109	1323
実	J3c42	M7124	1324
岻	J562e	M8017	1455

Char	J	M	No.
岨	J413b	M7984	1456
岳	J3359	M8001	1457
岩	J3464	M7985	1461
帙	J5665	M8852	1557
幷	J-X	M-X	1594
底	J446c	M9262	1612
彽	J-X	M10069	1727
徂	J5749	M10078	1728
征	J402c	M10077	1731
忝	J575b	M10348	1796
念	J4730	M10390	1800
怛	J5765	M10458	1807
怜	J4e67	M10461	1812
怖	J495d	M10450	1817
或	J303f	M11563	2030
戻	J4c61	M11707	2051
房	J4b3c	M11714	2053
拔	J5936	M11959	2099
抹	J4b75	M11926	2112
抵	J4471	M11921	2120
担	J4334	M11941	2121
拝	J4752	M11969′	2126
拯	J594e	M11991	2132
拵	J594f	M12001	2140
昊	J5a5f	M13799	2426
昔	J404e	M13816	2433
昇	J3e3a	M13794	2434
昶	J5a64	M13867	2442
枦	J5b45	M-X	2568
枡	J5b46	M14577	2587
東	J456c	M14499	2596
武	J4970	M16273	2959
毒	J4647	M16730	3007
[illegible]	J-X	M17052	3026
氛	J5d64	M17048	3027

Char	J	M	No.
泯	J5e23	M17324	3079
泄	J5d75	M17267	3083
沫	J4b77	M17235	3085
沮	J5d7c	M17238	3089
炉	J4f27	M18902	3403
狙	J4140	M20347	3567
画	J3268	M21739′	3733
画	J-X	M21739	3734
盂	J6233	M22949	3886
肴	J3a68	M29322	4767
肱	J394f	M29315	4770
肩	J382a	M29299	4776
苓	J4e6a	M30777	4981
苒	J6772	M30776	4989
苺	J6775	M30824	4990
苴	J6773	M30813	4992
茉	J677d	M30841	4994
苧	J4377	M30798	5000
苛	J3257	M30785	5006
若	J3e63	M30796′	5007
表	J493d	M34105	5422
辰	J4324	M38682	6006
迠	J-X	M38723	6017
郁	J306a	M39371	6136
長	J4439	M41100	6379
陌	J6f79	M41617	6436
陏	J6f7a	M41623	6437
陋	J6f7b	M41616	6438
隹	J7032	M41937	6492
雨	J312b	M42210	6518

8 residual strokes

Char	J	M	No.
[illegible]	J3e68	M153	54
亞	J5033	M274	82
亟	J5034	M279	83
兪	J5141	M1437	198
俎	J5059	M679	209
便	J4a58	M659	219
剄	J516d	M1990	483
勁	J5226	M2349	538
匍	J5235	M2527	575
兗	J3646	M-X	614
卑	J485c	M2751	618
咸	J5279	M3563	774
哈	J527d	M3594	778
咢	J5278	M3529	782
垰	J543b	M-X	1001
垣	J3340	M5060	1009
夷	J3050	M5852	1143
奏	J4155	M5915	1156
姶	J3028	M6242	1208
宥	J4d28	M7137	1326
宣	J406b	M7132	1328
専	J406a	M-X	1377
屍	J3b53	M7688	1420
峇	J5634	M8020	1462
峠	J463d	M8068	1464
峡	J362e	M8068′	1465
巷	J-X	M8756	1544
巻	J342c	M8759′	1545
彖	J5741	M9920	1707
恫	J5778	M10594	1837
恰	J3366	M10603	1838
恍	J5772	M10546	1840
悔	J3279	M10617′	1848
恒	J3931	M10527	1849
抵	J4471	M11921	2120
拝	J5941	M11969	2127
[illegible]	J-X	M11999	2129

Char	J	M	No.
拯	J594e	M11991	2132
拱	J594a	M11994	2139
拵	J594f	M12001	2140
挟	J3634	M-X	2146
拳	J377d	M11996	2148
拾	J3d26	M12014	2149
政	J402f	M13135	2335
昜	J5a66	M13832	2437
昞	J-X	M13835	2438
昺	J-X	M13836	2439
昶	J5a64	M13867	2442
昧	J4b66	M13846	2444
昼	J436b	M13886	2450
春	J3d55	M13844	2453
柤	J5b4f	M14642	2606
柢	J5b52	M14640	2612
柾	J4b6f	M14675	2619
柵	J3a74	M14665	2620
柄	J4a41	M14603	2627
査	J3a3a	M14643	2630
歪	J4f44	M16286	2960
毒	J4647	M16730	3007
毒	J-X	M-X	3008
洸	J5e2b	M17419	3113
洽	J5e2a	M17426	3114
洪	J393f	M17402	3123
洞	J4636	M17386	3125
浅	J4075	M17452	3129
海	J3324	M17450	3133
炳	J5f5b	M18960	3407
爼	J602c	M19743	3519
牴	J6032	M19988	3540
狭	J3639	M20406′	3572
玲	J4e68	M20888	3626
珊	J3b39	M20917	3630

Char	JIS	Morohashi	No.
甚	J3f53	M21648	3711
畊	J6139	M21773	3736
畏	J-X	M21785	3743
疣	J614f	M22050	3782
癸	J6223	M22660	3859
発	J482f	M22662′	3860
盃	J4756	M22955	3887
矜	J6262	M23852	3975
研	J3826	M24080	3991
祐	J4d34	M24652′	4079
祖	J4144	M24664′	4083
穽	J6357	M25433	4194
紆	J647e	M27244	4436
罘	J6629	M28224	4636
胝	J6673	M29395	4782
胚	J6675	M29390	4787
胆	J4340	M29354	4790
苺	J6775	M30824	4990
苔	J6829	M30937	5015
衿	J365e	M34149	5431
訂	J447b	M35211	5553
訃	J6b3e	M35214	5554
計	J3757	M35220	5555
逋	J6d79	M38871	6047
逕	J6d74	M38883	6052
逗	J3f60	M38887	6053
逐	J4360	M38877′	6056
酊	J6e44	M39764	6158
重	J3d45	M40132	6207
閂	J6f59	M41211	6382
陋	J6f7b	M41616	6438
陏	J7023	M-X	6440
院	J3121	M41665	6447
面	J4c4c	M42618	6566
革	J3357	M42710	6570
韭	J706e	M43236	6604
頁	J4a47	M43333	6614

9 residual strokes

Char	JIS	Morohashi	No.
乘	J502b	M154	55
亞	J5033	M274	82
亟	J5034	M279	83
俎	J5059	M679	209
倫	J4e51	M793	246
倹	J3770	M823	248
兼	J3773	M1483	381
冓	J514a	M1540	396
冥	J4c3d	M1588	405
咢	J5278	M3529	782
啞	J3022	M3743	795
唳	J533a	M-X	797
哽	J532b	M3680	799
唏	J5329	M3707	800
哥	J5327	M3641	801
唇	J3f30	M3697	807
圄	J537d	M4775	953
圃	J4a60	M4774	954
夏	J3246	M5720	1120
套	J4565	M5926	1161
宸	J5562	M7171	1331
峽	J5637	M8122	1466
峺	J5638	M8115	1468
崋	J563c	M8161	1469
峨	J3265	M8071	1471
峩	J5636	M8072	1472
峰	J4a76	M8094	1473
峯	J4a77	M8093	1474
島	J4567	M8108	1476
師	J3b55	M8916	1562
帯	J4253	M8929	1563
彖	J5741	M9920	1707
徑	J574d	M10118	1743
恵	J3743	M10618′	1847
悔	J-X	M10659	1855
悟	J3867	M10680	1870
扇	J4070	M11743′	2056
拿	J593d	M12015	2138
拳	J3573	M12081′	2150
挿	J415e	M12119	2167
振	J3f36	M12093	2171
教	J-X	M13212	2346
旆	J5a53	M13640	2394
晋	J3f38	M13899	2455
晉	J5a69	M13898	2456
晃	J3938	M13891	2458
晄	J5a68	M13892	2459
柢	J5b52	M14640	2612
桧	J4930	M-X	2637
栢	J337c	M14714	2638
栜	J-X	M14796	2648
栴	J4073	M14737	2651
桓	J343c	M14774	2652
栽	J3a4f	M14750	2654
桐	J364d	M14770	2655
毒	J-X	M-X	3008
氣	J5d66	M17059	3028
氤	J5d65	M17060	3029
泰	J4259	M17325	3098
海	J3324	M17450	3133
海	J-X	M17503	3137
涛	J4573	M-X	3138
浜	J494d	M17462	3152
浦	J313a	M17475	3156
烝	J5f5f	M19019	3417
烘	J-X	M19012	3418
烏	J3128	M18998	3421
牴	J6032	M19988	3540
瓸	J6129	M21499	3698
瓶	J4953	M21486	3699
畏	J305a	M21778	3742
畔	J484a	M21801	3746
畢	J492d	M21829	3754
疸	J6155	M22094	3786
疽	J6154	M22106	3787
病	J4942	M22127	3798
痏	J-X	M-X	3799
益	J3157	M22972	3891
看	J-X	M-X	3921
眛	J6246	M23230	3923
真	J3f3f	M23236	3926
砥	J4556	M24093	3997
祗	J632d	M24665	4077
祐	J-X	M24652	4080
祠	J632c	M24676	4081
祖	J-X	M24664	4084
秦	J3f41	M24995	4133
秣	J6342	M24992	4136
租	J4145	M24988	4138
笄	J6422	M25862	4255
笹	J3a7b	M25968	4271
紐	J4933	M27268	4448
紲	J6528	M27347	4461
耘	J6651	M28910	4708
耕	J394c	M28907′	4710
耺	J-X	M29018	4718
耼	J-X	M29025	4719
胝	J6673	M29395	4782
朓	J6679	M29432	4796
朕	J443f	M14361	4797
胼	J6f20	M29453	4798
胯	J6678	M29430	4799
脊	J4054	M29472	4804
胴	J4639	M29436	4810
荳	J683a	M30989	5036
莖	J6833	M31052	5037
莱	J4d69	M-X	5039
莪	J6830	M31077	5047
莓	J6776	M31047	5049
莟	J6831	M31064	5050
莞	J3450	M31063	5052
華	J325a	M31119	5058
蚌	J6953	M32851	5281
蚕	J3b3d	M32869	5290
衄	J6a48	M33973	5414
衰	J3f6a	M34127	5432
衵	J6a58	M34184	5437
袴	J3853	M34236	5448
訌	J6b41	M35228	5558
訊	J3f56	M35224	5559
託	J4277	M35243	5560
討	J4624	M35231	5561
訓	J3731	M35238	5562
記	J352d	M35244	5563
豈	J6c31	M36249	5736
豺	J6c39	M36500	5754
財	J3a62	M36664	5773
辱	J3f2b	M38686	6007
逑	J6d73	M38878	6045
逋	J6d79	M38871	6047
逕	J6d74	M38883	6052
逗	J3f60	M38887	6053
逐	J4360	M38877′	6056
郵	J4d39	M39485	6147
酒	J3c72	M39776	6160

12 residual strokes

暄	J5a77	M14033	2497
暘	J5a78	M14066	2498
暖	J4348	M14064	2502
暢	J442a	M14095	2506
椏	J5b73	M15025	2727
極	J364b	M15181	2753
椹	J5c3b	M15082	2758
楡	J5c40	M15153	2768
楕	J424a	M15133	2780
椿	J4458	M15090	2782
楊	J4d4c	M15112	2784
業	J3648	M15170	2789
瀛	J-X	M18019	3252
溽	J5e69	M17990	3256
滉	J5e66	M18017	3257
滔	J-X	M17922	3262
溥	J5e70	M17957	3266
滄	J5e6b	M18007	3267
溢	J306e	M17951	3270
溝	J3942	M17944	3275
滞	J425a	M18067′	3280
漢	J3441	M18068′	3281
滯	J5e7c	M18075	3285
滙	J3443	M18216	3287
漾	J5f21	M18184	3290
焼	J-X	M-X	3440
煬	J5f6c	M19235	3446
刦	J-X	M19213	3450
煖	J5f6b	M19196	3451
煩	J4851	M19229	3454
牒	J442d	M19871	3529
獅	J3b62	M20609	3599
瑁	J6070	M21096	3661
瑜	J6071	M21129	3663
瑞	J3f70	M21131	3665
痹	J-X	M22279	3821
睅	J-X	M23458	3943
睫	J624c	M23469	3944
睡	J3f67	M23448	3948
碍	J3337	M24283	4016
碁	J386b	M24261	4020
祺	J6332	M24733	4095
福	J4a21	M24768′	4105
稘	J6345	M25118	4147
稔	J4c2d	M25107	4149
筜	J-X	M-X	4289·
粵	J6465	M26935	4399
粳	J646b	M26967	4408
絀	J6528	M27047	4461
組	J4148	M27374	4470
經	J6534	M27508	4493
聘	J665b	M29079	4726
肅	J6669	M29225	4748
腭	J-X	M29700	4840
腫	J3c70	M29697	4848
腸	J4432	M29721	4849
與	J6750	M30212	4911
蕚	J6855	M31361	5119
蓁	J686d	M31639	5134
蓑	J4c2c	M31661	5143
蓐	J686c	M31660	5149
蔭	J307e	M31840	5151
蒙	J4c58	M31555	5154
蒲	J3377	M31611	5156
葦	J3031	M31437	5160
蒼	J4173	M31627	5162
虞	J3673	M32723′	5272
蜃	J6967	M33089	5327
褊	J6a6c	M34356	5469
詆	J6b49	M35356	5574
詇	J-X	M35495	5590
誨	J-X	M-X	5592
詢	J6b4e	M35411	5593
詣	J3758	M35412	5594
詬	J6b4d	M35433	5595
誂	J6b50	M35469	5596
詼	J6b4b	M35462	5597
詫	J4f4d	M35431	5598
誅	J6b4f	M35472	5599
誄	J6b51	M35471	5600
該	J333a	M35445	5601
誉	J4d40	M35498	5602
詭	J6b4c	M35434	5603
詮	J4127	M35405	5604
誇	J3858	M35474	5605
誠	J403f	M35497′	5606
詳	J3e5c	M35446	5607
話	J4f43	M35441	5608
詰	J354d	M35440	5609
詩	J3b6d	M35427	5610
試	J3b6e	M35415	5611
誕	J-X	M35516	5613
豊	J4b2d	M36263	5737
豢	J6c36	M36380	5746
賄	J4f45	M36745	5800
跨	J3859	M37504	5872
践	J4129	M37547′	5873
輀	J-X	M38287	5954
輌	J6d52	M-X	5955
農	J4740	M38688	6008
遘	J6e29	M39031	6096
遣	J382f	M39052′	6100
鄙	J6e41	M39597	6153
殺	J-X	M40271	6240
鉦	J3e60	M40322	6246
鈴	J4e6b	M40267	6247
鉢	J482d	M40317	6249
雅	J326d	M41973	6505
零	J4e6d	M42242	6524
靻	J705a	M42764	6578
頑	J3468	M43374	6624
飩	J712b	M44047	6677
飭	J522c	M44057	6678
飲	J5d3b	M44063	6681
飼	J3b74	M44107′	6685

13 residual strokes

劄	J-X	M-X	511
劃	J3344	M2193	513
喪	J4153	M3985	853
嘈	J-X	M4175	879
噓	J3133	M-X	886
圖	J5426	M4832	963
場	J5447	M5385	1076
壽	J5468	M5672	1077
嫣	J5541	M6659	1261
孳	J555a	M-X	1299
實	J5569	M7294	1356
寨	J5c4d	M7298	1357
寧	J472b	M7296′	1361
寧	J-X	M7296	1362
寡	J3249	M7286	1363
惡	J5828	M10824	1875
愓	J5853	M11133	1952
戠	J-X	M11637	2038
搴	J596b	M12519	2246
旗	J347a	M13687	2402
普	J-X	M-X	2494
榿	J5c48	M15298	2801
榎	J315d	M15219	2810
榛	J3f3a	M15240	2811
樺	J3372	M15497	2817
槙	J4b6a	M-X	2819
槍	J4164	M15319	2822
構	J393d	M15317	2823
歉	J5d3e	M16159	2944
滿	J5e60	M18099	3283
漢	J-X	M18153	3284
滯	J5e7c	M18075	3285
滙	J3443	M18216	3287
漾	J5f21	M18184	3290
滸	J5e77	M18089	3291
澧	J4166	M18131	3306
演	J3169	M18130	3310
煨	J-X	M19228	3447
熏	J5f6d	M19300	3461
爾	J3c24	M19750	3521
甦	J-X	M-X	3720
罍	J-X	M21867	3758
瘀	J6168	M22318	3824
瘧	J616a	M22419	3826
監	J3446	M23032	3901
睿	J624f	M23536	3949
碪	J6274	M24339	4022
福	J-X	M24768	4106
稱	J634a	M25180	4155
窬	J-X	M25582	4207
端	J433c	M25806	4243
箚	J6434	M26149	4305
箕	J4c27	M26143	4307
絖	J652d	M27409	4477
絣	J6533	M27429	4478
絵	J3328	M27464′	4488
給	J356b	M27432	4489

綸	J6545	M27583	4519
罰	J4833	M28315	4647
聘	J665b	M29079	4726
肇	J4825	M29228	4751
膀	J-X	M29700	4840
膌	J-X	M29794	4853
膈	J672d	M29772	4856
蓑	J4c2c	M31661	5143
蓐	J686c	M31660	5149
蔻	J-X	M31741	5171
蔲	J-X	M-X	5172
蔔	J6879	M31785	5173
蜃	J6967	M33089	5327
蜷	J6970	M33199	5339
蝶	J4433	M33333	5363
誨	J-X	M-X	5592
該	J333a	M35445	5601
誇	J3858	M35474	5605
誠	J-X	M35537	5612
誕	J-X	M35516	5613
誨	J6b52	M35553	5616
誡	J6b53	M35538	5617
誣	J6b58	M35542	5618
誑	J6b54	M35510	5619
誌	J3b6f	M35501	5620
誦	J6b56	M35551	5621
誓	J4040	M35514	5622
認	J4727	M35502′	5623
認	J-X	M35502	5624
誘	J4d36	M35525	5625
誤	J386d	M35546′	5626
説	J4062	M35556′	5627
語	J386c	M35533	5628
誕	J4342	M35692′	5640
豨	J-X	M36404	5747
豬	J-X	M36398	5748
賓	J-X	M36788	5804
跨	J3859	M37504	5872
輕	J6d4b	M38346	5961
農	J4740	M38688	6008
銅	J463c	M40361	6266
閣	J395e	M41301	6397
閧	J6f62	M41311	6399
関	J3458	M41297	6402
霊	J-X	M-X	6527
需	J3c7b	M42275	6528
靼	J705a	M42764	6578
鞅	J705d	M42794	6580
頗	J3f7c	M43415	6627
領	J4e4e	M43423	6628
飼	J3b74	M44107′	6685
餅	J4c5f	M44133	6689
髯	J-X	M45375	6801
髪	J4831	M45387′	6804
魂	J3a32	M45787	6835
鳳	J4b31	M46671	6937

14 residual strokes

儉	J512d	M1190	315
僵	J512c	M1158	317
儈	J-X	M1189	319
舗	J4a5e	M30323′	322
劍	J5178	M2228	514
匳	J523d	M2655	596
啞	J-X	M3835	827
嘘	J-X	M4206	885
墟	J5452	M5457	1090
孳	J555a	M-X	1299
實	J5569	M7294	1356
賓	J4950	M-X	1365
嶝	J5653	M8482	1511
嶢	J5652	M8491	1512
廣	J5722	M9493	1640
徵	J-X	M10239	1769
德	J-X	M10243	1770
惡	J5828	M10824	1875
憂	J4d2b	M11170	1971
撲	J4b50	M12755	2274
撓	J597a	M12698	2275
撰	J4071	M12753	2277
撒	J3b35	M12697	2279
撫	J496f	M12743	2281
敷	J-X	M13359	2358
棄	J-X	M-X	2788
橢	J5c73	M15565	2829
樓	J5c6c	M15430	2830
槽	J4165	M15393	2844
槻	J4450	M15390	2845
樺	J3822	M15484	2853
横	J3223	M15484′	2854
殤	J5d4f	M16557	2983
澂	J5f2d	M18313	3312
澑	J5f31	M18335	3313
澆	J5f24	M18317	3327
澄	J4021	M18315	3333
潰	J4459	M18281	3335
瘡	J616c	M22404	3829
瘠	J616b	M22401	3833
監	J3446	M23032	3901
磑	J6276	M24402	4035
磚	J6322	M24418	4043
穀	J-X	M25221	4160
篇	J4a53	M26257	4324
箴	J643e	M26214	4327
經	J6534	M27508	4493
綣	J653c	M27550	4507
緘	J654f	M27730	4540
緬	J4c4b	M27674	4542
緘	J6548	M27638	4545
緩	J344b	M27669	4551
罸	J662f	M28343	4648
羮	J663e	M28536	4669
翫	J3465	M28766	4689
膓	J6736	M29811	4862
舉	J5a2a	M30238	4914
舞	J4971	M30342′	4926
蕁	J6856	M31970	5183
蕘	J687d	M31965	5186
蕪	J4973	M32004	5196
蕩	J4622	M32002	5198
蝨	J697c	M33303	5347
蝪	J6a23	M33305	5350
蝓	J6a21	M33261	5351
蝠	J6975	M33288	5353
蝕	J-X	M33264	5358
蝶	J4433	M33333	5363
[illegible]	J-X	M-X	5485
褥	J6a73	M34495	5487
誨	J6b52	M35553	5616
誘	J4d36	M35525	5625
諌	J3452	M35642	5630
諚	J6b5c	M35682	5631
諏	J3f5b	M35648	5632
諍	J6b5a	M35643	5633
誼	J3543	M35605	5634
諄	J6b59	M35622	5635
諾	J427a	M35687	5638
誹	J4870	M35601	5639
誕	J4342	M35692′	5640
諒	J4e4a	M35653	5641
誰	J432f	M35586	5642
談	J434c	M35633	5643
課	J325d	M35589	5644
請	J4041	M35640′	5645
論	J4f40	M35658	5646
調	J4434	M35609′	5647
諸	J3d74	M35691′	5648
諛	J6b67	M35696	5653
謎	J4666	M35800	5661
諜	J4435	M35697	5665
豌	J6c32	M36273	5738
豎	J6c33	M36280	5739
賦	J496a	M36800	5811
賛	J3b3f	M36841	5814
輛	J6d51	M38361	5969
輪	J4e58	M38400	5973
遶	J6e2d	M39122	6109
還	J3454	M39174′	6121
鋲	J4946	M40503	6277
險	J702a	M41874	6483
震	J3f4c	M42300	6531
霊	J4e6e	M42309′	6532
頬	J4b4b	M-X	6629
餉	J712e	M44140	6687
餃	J712d	M44131	6688
餅	J4c5f	M44133	6689
駈	J366f	M44636	6744
骶	J-X	M45155	6787
髯	J7179	M45404	6809
魃	J7231	M45806	6836
魅	J4c25	M45811	6838
鮃	J-X	M46020	6847
麩	J734f	M47739	7033

15 residual strokes

Char	JIS	Morohashi	No.
儔	J5132	M1224	326
儒	J3c74	M1220	330
劒	J5179	M2245	518
劔	J517a	M2243	519
叡	J3143	M3214	683
嚊	J5367	M4467	913
圜	J5428	M4851	965
壇	J4345	M5528	1101
寰	J556e	M7344	1368
嶮	J5655	M8520	1513
嶼	J5659	M8561	1515
彊	J3630	M9872	1702
惡	J5828	M10824	1875
憂	J4d2b	M11170	1971
憮	J5863	M11259	1981
憾	J3438	M11312	1999
戲	J-X	M11668	2043
擔	J593f	M12828	2286
撼	J597e	M12775	2291
撿	J-X	M12779	2292
擅	J5a23	M12790	2293
整	J-X	M13393	2361
曉	J5a7c	M14176	2513
曇	J465e	M14172	2518
椏	J5b73	M15025	2727
横	J-X	M15594	2857
橊	J-X	M15525	2859
橅	J-X	M15513	2867
橈	J5c76	M15521	2872
樸	J5c77	M15495	2873
橙	J5c74	M15552	2877
歙	J5d40	M16204	2949
殪	J5d50	M16578	2984
滋	J3c22	M17919′	3238
澪	J5f3a	M18398	3342
濛	J5f42	M18491	3345
澹	J5f38	M18421	3346
澱	J4543	M18410	3347
濃	J473b	M18442	3349
燈	J4575	M19402	3476
獣	J3d43	M20714′	3606
獪	J6056	M20729	3608
疊	J614a	M-X	3769
瘻	J6171	M22467	3834
稽	J-X	M-X	4174
窿	J6363	M25660	4213
窶	J6360	M25620	4214
窺	J312e	M25633	4215
簑	J6442	M26387	4334
篳	J644a	M26393	4338
篩	J6441	M26359	4339
篝	J6440	M26320	4340
糂	J6473	M27014	4412
綸	J6545	M27583	4519
縟	J6555	M27779	4561
縉	J6556	M27737	4562
縉	J-X	M-X	4563
縛	J477b	M27771	4567
縊	J6550	M27738	4568
膩	J6737	M29862	4872
興	J363d	M30226	4913
舞	J4971	M30342	4926
艙	J675a	M30516	4943
蕁	J6856	M31970	5183
薇	J692f	M32092	5209
薈	J6927	M32093	5210
薑	J6928	M32110	5212
融	J4d3b	M33384	5371
褥	J6a73	M34495	5487
覦	J6b30	M34904	5532
覧	J4d77	M34928	5533
諄	J6b59	M35622	5635
謁	J-X	M35757	5649
諸	J-X	M35743	5650
諡	J6b6b	M35708	5652
諛	J6b67	M35696	5653
諠	J6b63	M35706	5654
諤	J6b60	M35713	5655
諺	J-X	M35747	5658
諺	J3841	M-X	5659
諮	J3b70	M35728	5660
謎	J4666	M36000	5661
諜	J4435	M35697	5665
諭	J4d21	M35727′	5667
諭	J-X	M35727	5668
謔	J6b62	M35810	5675
諱	J6b61	M35733	5677
踰	J6c7c	M37675	5891
輳	J6d54	M38429	5975
輻	J6d55	M38442	5977
輸	J4d22	M38438′	5978
遶	J6e2d	M39122	6109
還	J3454	M39174′	6121
醗	J4830	M-X	6182
醍	J4269	M39924	6184
錻	J6f27	M40597	6288
錏	J6e7b	M40534	6289
錘	J3f6e	M40547	6291
鋼	J395d	M40509	6302
雞	J-X	M-X	6508
頜	J7077	M43512	6632
頸	J7074	M43515	6638
頭	J462c	M43490	6639
餝	J7133	M44212	6692
餔	J7130	M44173	6694
駢	J7158	M44696	6748
鴒	J7279	M46770	6949
鴉	J726d	M46738	6951
鴟	J7276	M46805	6954
麺	J4c4d	M-X	7038
黔	J7358	M48056	7054

16 residual strokes

Char	JIS	Morohashi	No.
儲	J4c59	M-X	331
優	J4d25	M1261	334
壔	J-X	M5558	1106
彊	J3630	M9872	1702
彌	J373d	M9877	1703
徽	J-X	M10267	1778
懦	J586f	M11390	2005
戲	J5926	M11681	2044
戴	J4257	M11685	2045
擧	J5a29	M12863	2288
擣	J5a2e	M12853	2301
擡	J5a2c	M12851	2302
斂	J5a4c	M13407	2362
曁	J5a7a	M14165	2516
曚	J5b24	M14223	2520
樸	J5c77	M15495	2873
檢	J5c7d	M15684	2883
檬	J5d28	M15710	2887
櫃	J3360	M15629	2889
檜	J5b58	M15676	2894
檀	J4349	M15632	2895
歛	J5d42	M16210	2951
濃	J473b	M18442	3349
濱	J5f40	M18537	3355
瀰	J5f3e	M18482	3357
濮	J5f41	M18526	3358
濘	J5f3f	M18487	3359
濤	J5e39	M18508	3361
濬	J5f3d	M18524	3362
濠	J396a	M18502	3363
濡	J4728	M18504	3365
濫	J4d74	M18521	3366
燒	J5f76	M19420	3475
犧	J353e	M20190′	3550
環	J-X	M21287	3681
盪	J623b	M23062	3905
磴	J6324	M24478	4046
磯	J6323	M24494	4047
禧	J6336	M24828	4112
穗	J634f	M25298	4177
簑	J6443	M-X	4344
篡	J5255	M26490	4345
糟	J416c	M27104	4423
糞	J4a35	M27102	4425
縅	J654f	M27730	4540
緬	J4c4b	M27674	4542
緘	J6548	M27638	4545
緩	J344b	M27669	4551
縮	J3d4c	M27815	4585
翼	J4d63	M28801′	4692
臉	J6740	M29954	4876
膾	J673a	M29937	4879
朦	J5b2f	M14409	4882
膿	J473f	M29938	4884
興	J363d	M30226	4913
舉	J-X	M30241	4915
艱	J6765	M30600	4955
藍	J4d75	M32258	5233
覯	J6b32	M34937	5535

17 residual strokes

18 residual strokes

19 residual strokes

藹 J693d/M32397 5249
蘯 J623c/M32532 5256
蘞 J-X/M32490 5261
蠕 J6a40/M33749 5400
譜 J-X/M-X 5707
譽 J6c25/M36066 5708
蹼 J6d2e/M37889 5909
軆 J6d3d/M38157 5937
轗 J6d5e/M38550 5989
醴 J6e54/M40053 6195
醵 J6e53/M40055 6196
釀 J3e7a/M40064′ 6197
鐚 J6e7b/M40534 6289
鐙 J462a/M40904 6348
鏡 J6f3f/M40867 6350
鐻 J6f3c/M40907 6351
闡 J6f71/M41489 6421
隸 J704c/M42530 6552
饉 J713c/M44366 6709
饅 J713d/M44346 6710
騫 J715a/M44894 6765
驀 J715e/M44949 6766
騰 J462d/M44915′ 6767
鬪 J722c/M45649 6825
鰈 J7257/M46322 6898
鰐 J4f4c/M46337 6901
鶚 J732d/M47105 6981
鹹 J7344/M47553 7014
麒 J734a/M47657 7025
麗 J4e6f/M47663 7026
齢 J4e70/M48632′ 7093
齡 J7374/M48632 7094

20 residual strokes

儷 J5136/M1311 336
儺 J5135/M1317 337
囂 J536f/M4616 930
攘 J5a37/M12989 2316
曩 J5b28/M14258 2527
欖 J-X/M15905 2912
櫸 J-X/M-X 2918
欅 J5d30/M15883 2919
籐 J645b/M26693 4373
繪 J6569/M27939 4597
繿 J6571/M28009 4605
艦 J344f/M30571 4950
蠢 J6a41/M33797 5402
襯 J6b25/M34712 5509
覽 J6b35/M34977 5540
譽 J6c25/M36066 5708
躊 J6d34/M37941 5919
轜 J6d5f/M38571 5990
鐻 J6f3c/M40907 6351
鐶 J6f42/M40946 6358
隸 J704c/M42530 6552
饋 J713f/M44382 6711
饌 J7142/M44386 6712
饐 J713e/M44396 6713
饒 J7141/M44400 6714
饗 J-X/M44431 6715
鰐 J4f4c/M46337 6901
鰤 J725e/M46381 6906
鷂 J7332/M47206 6988
鷄 J7337/M-X 6991
鶺 J7335/M47197 6993

21 residual strokes

儷 J5136/M1311 336
囊 J-X/M4633 933
巔 J565c/M8644 1524
懿 J5874/M11501 2015
灑 J5f53/M18774 3392
疊 J6148/M21983 3772
疉 J6149/M21982 3773
禳 J633a/M24868 4117
繻 J656c/M27996 4609
繿 J6571/M28009 4605
纜 J-X/M28053 4616
罏 J6624/M28189 4631
聽 J6665/M29211 4744
嚢 J4739/M-X 5499
襷 J6b27/M34737 5512
讃 J3b3e/M36110 5720
鑄 J6f49/M40972 6360
鑑 J3455/M40988 6361
鑒 J6f48/M40989 6362
顫 J707c/M43706 6656
饗 J-X/M44431 6715
饕 J7143/M44426 6717
驍 J7162/M44986 6772
髓 J7172/M45289 6793
鬻 J6478/M45721 6832
龕 J737c/M48839 7104

22 residual strokes

戀 J5878/M11504 2017
攣 J5a3b/M13032 2320
曬 J-X/M14266 2528
欒 J5d33/M15947 2922
灑 J5f53/M18774 3392
籥 J6460/M26771 4377
繿 J6571/M28009 4605
纜 J-X/M28053 4616
鬱 J6748/M30049 4893
羈 J-X/M34794 5520
變 J5a4e/M36117 5721
鑑 J3455/M40988 6361
鑒 J6f48/M40989 6362
鑛 J6f4a/M41010 6363
隸 J704c/M42530 6552
靨 J7054/M42698 6569
饗 J-X/M44431 6715
驗 J7164/M45024 6776
髓 J7172/M45289 6793
體 J7173/M45291 6794
鬢 J7225/M46596 6817
鱮 J-X/M46571 6925
鷲 J4f49/M47345 7004

23 residual strokes

攬 J5a30/M13046 2323
曬 J-X/M14266 2528
癲 J6221/M22643 3857
蠱 J6260/M23836 3971
纜 J-X/M28053 4616
艷 J6766/M30637 4958
鱞 J-X/M46520 6924
鱮 J-X/M46571 6925
鱧 J7267/M46542 6926
鱠 J7266/M46530 6927
鹼 J-X/M47576 7016

24 residual strokes

廳 J572c/M9562 1651
攬 J5a30/M13046 2322
欖 J5d34/M15964 2923
灣 J5f54/M18823 3393
纜 J-X/M28053 4616
羈 J6b2b/M34795 5521
鑰 J6f50/M41051 6371
鑲 J-X/M41053 6372
靉 J704f/M42540 6556
鱮 J-X/M46571 6925

25 residual strokes

欖 J5d34/M15964 2923
驥 J7167/M45076 6779
鱝 J7268/M46592 6928

26 residual strokes

戀 J5878/M11504 2017
攣 J5a3b/M13032 2320
欒 J5d33/M15947 2922
纘 J657c/M28100 4623
鬱 J6748/M30049 4893
變 J5a4e/M36117 5721
鱝 J7268/M46592 6928
鱺 J-X/M46597 6929

27–29 residual strokes

灣 J5f54/M18823 3393
纘 J657c/M28100 4623
鑿 J6f58/M41088 6378
驪 J716b/M45090 6782
鸞 J7342/M47508 7010

Rad. 2 丨

0 residual strokes

丿 J502d/M224 66

1 residual stroke

亠 J5035/M286 85
冂 J5144/M1506 384
十 J3d3d/M2695 598
卜 J4b4e/M2774 622
卩 J5247/M2836 626

2 residual strokes

下 J323c/M14 9
上 J3e65/M13 10
个 J5024/M70 **25**
丂 J-X/M71 **26**
ケ J2531/M-X 43
也 J4c69/M171 58
凵 J5161/M1800 441
匚 J5239/M2595 583
千 J4069/M2697 599
口 J387d/M3227 685
囗 J5378/M4675 936
土 J455a/M4867 966
宀 J555f/M7054 1304
山 J3b33/M7869 1439
川 J406e/M8673 1526
工 J3929/M8714 1532
巾 J3652/M8771 1547
干 J3433/M9165 1589
彳 J5746/M10037 1723

3 residual strokes

不 J4954/M19 13
世 J4024/M31 20
丰 J-X/M75 **27**
中 J4366/M73 **28**
丼 J5027/M101 37
井 J3066/M258 76
介 J3270/M359 108
内 J4662/M1512 386
卆 J5240/M2701 600
灰 J-X/M48950 601
卅 J5241/M2700 602
升 J3e23/M2702 603
午 J3861/M2703 604
卍 J5244/M2724 611
口 J387d/M3227 685
弔 J4424/M9698 1680
引 J307a/M9699 1681
斗 J454d/M13489 2373
斤 J3654/M13534 2379
日 J467c/M13733 2410
曰 J5b29/M14278 2529
木 J4c5a/M14415 2531
止 J3b5f/M16253 2954
爪 J445e/M19653 3509
爿 J602d/M19758 3522
牛 J356d/M19922 3532
王 J3226/M20823 3619
甘 J3445/M21643 3710

4 residual strokes

业 J-X/M-X 14
丗 J5242/M32 15
且 J336e/M29 17
丕 J5023/M30 18
丘 J3556/M33 19
世 J4024/M31 20
丱 J5025/M77 **29**
主 J3c67/M100 38
乍 J4663/M130 50
五 J385e/M257 77
以 J304a/M388 109
内 J4662/M1512 386
冉 J5147/M1514 388
冊 J3a7d/M1515 389
凸 J464c/M1809 443
凹 J317a/M1810 444
出 J3d50/M1811 445
北 J4b4c/M2574 581
灰 J-X/M48950 601
卉 J5243/M2706 606
卌 J-X/M2712 607
半 J483e/M2707 608
卯 J312c/M2847 628
收 J3c7d/M3128 675
収 J-X/M3137 676
史 J3b4b/M3249 697
四 J3b4d/M4682 938
央 J317b/M5840 1140
巨 J3570/M8722 1534
市 J3b54/M8775 1549
平 J4a3f/M9167 1590
弗 J4a26/M9708 1683
旧 J356c/M13737 2412
末 J4b76/M14420 2534
未 J4c24/M14419 2535
本 J4b5c/M14421 2536
正 J4035/M16255 2955
玉 J364c/M20821 3620
甘 J3445/M21643 3710
生 J4038/M21670 3715
用 J4d51/M21703 3721
由 J4d33/M21724 3724
甲 J3943/M21725 3725
申 J3f3d/M21726 3726
田 J4544/M21723 3727
皿 J3b2e/M22941 3885
目 J4c5c/M23105 3906
阡 J6f74/M41548 6424

5 residual strokes

且 J336e/M29 17
世 J4024/M31 20
両 J4e3e/M46 23
丱 J5025/M77 **29**
价 J5043/M412 126
仲 J4367/M403 140
冲 J5155/M1616 413
凸 J464c/M1809 443
凹 J317a/M1810 444
灰 J-X/M48950 601
古 J-X/M2714 609
卉 J-X/M2720 610
卍 J5244/M2724 611
卯 J312c/M2847 628
印 J3075/M2848 630
叫 J362b/M3240 708
向 J387e/M3301 712
壮 J4154/M5642 974
在 J3a5f/M4881 975
地 J434f/M4890 976
存 J4238/M6943 1284
州 J3d23/M8678 1529
巨 J3570/M8722 1534
师 J-X/M8800 1550
幵 J5674/M9169 1591
并 J5675/M9170 1592
年 J472f/M9168 1593
弗 J4a26/M9708 1683
彳工 J-X/M-X 1724
佛 J5767/M10486 1813
臾 J-X/M14281 2413
曳 J3148/M14282 2417
曲 J364a/M14280 2418
民 J4c31/M17028 3021
池 J4353/M17141 3042
祁 J3737/M24634 4063
竹 J435d/M25841 4246
羊 J4d53/M28425 4658
耳 J3c2a/M28999 4715
聿 J6666/M29215 4746
臼 J3131/M30173 4907
艸 J6767/M30638 4959
虫 J436e/M32804 5275
那 J4661/M39305 6129
邦 J4b2e/M39310 6130

6 residual strokes

両 J4e3e/M46 23
串 J367a/M80 **30**
乕 J6949/M148 52
亜 J3021/M272 81
伸 J3f2d/M481 163
児 J3b79/M1364 355
凸 J464c/M1809 443
凹 J317a/M1810 444

判 J483d/M1923 465
否 J485d/M3340 742
告 J-X/M3381 745
囬 J-X/M4713 942
囲 J304f/M4722 945
壯 J5463/M5643 977
坚 J-X/M4963 979
妍 J552b/M6075 1186
巫 J5660/M8728 1536
弗 J4a26/M9708 1683
形 J3741/M9969 1713
收 J5a40/M13110 2329
攸 J5a41/M13113 2330
束 J422b/M14480 2559
步 J-X/M16264 2957
沖 J322d/M17209 3065
泄 J5d75/M17267 3083
沛 J5d6f/M17216 3088
状 J3e75/M20257 3556
狆 J603e/M20293 3561
甫 J4a63/M21706 3722
臣 J3f43/M30068 4894
臼 J3131/M30173 4907
芥 J3329/M30715 4977
車 J3c56/M38172 5939
迚 J6d69/M38773 6018
邨 J6e37/M39313 6128
采 J4850/M40115 6202
長 J4439/M41100 6379
镸 J-X/M41101 6380
阼 J-X/M41594 6431

7 residual strokes

並 J4a42/M54 24
乖 J502a/M149 53
亜 J3021/M272 81
來 J5054/M581 173
典 J4535/M1474 375
其 J4236/M1472 378
凸 J464c/M1809 443
卑 J-X/M2738 612
卵 J4d71/M2857 632
卹 J-X/M2862 636
咋 J3a70/M3488 751
呷 J526e/M3461 756
咀 J5272/M3476 758
咄 J5274/M3480 761
呻 J5271/M3470 762
味 J4c23/M3456 766
坤 J3a25/M4969 996
坪 J445a/M4976 998
垂 J3f62/M5012 999
奉 J4a74/M5894 1149
姐 J3009/M6172 1195
妹 J4b65/M6138 1199
宙 J4368/M7108 1318
官 J3431/M7107 1322
巢 J736b/M-X 1394
屈 J367e/M7669 1415
岬 J4c28/M7992 1458
帚 J5664/M8854 1555
幷 J-X/M-X 1594
彿 J574a/M10071 1729
恼 J-X/M10392 1791
忠 J4369/M10353 1801
拂 J5944/M11936 2097
拒 J-X/M11957 2098
拌 J5942/M11951 2102
抽 J436a/M11930 2119
拙 J405b/M11965 2122
拝 J4752/M11969' 2126
押 J3221/M11929 2128
拵 J594f/M12001 2140
斉 J4046/M13454 2366
昇 J3e3a/M13794 2434
枘 J5b46/M14577 2587
果 J324c/M14556 2594
東 J456c/M14499 2596
柹 J-X/M14596 2625
泯 J5e23/M17324 3079
泄 J5d75/M17267 3083
沫 J4b77/M17235 3085
沸 J4a28/M17261 3094
油 J4c7d/M17253 3106
爬 J6028/M19662 3511
牀 J602e/M19763 3523
狀 J-X/M20280 3557
狎 J6040/M20329 3563
狒 J6041/M20338 3564
画 J3268/M21739' 3733
直 J443e/M23136 3908
竏 J6368/M25731 4225
糾 J-X/M27227 4434
耶 J4c6d/M29008 4716
服 J497e/M14345' 4775
良 J4e49/M30597 4954
虱 J694d/M32812 5276
軋 J6d42/M38173 5940
迚 J6d69/M38773 6018
迸 J6d7e/M38867 6036
追 J4449/M38836' 6042
長 J4439/M41100 6379
門 J4c67/M41208 6381
雨 J312b/M42210 6518
非 J4873/M42585 6563

8 residual strokes

乗 J3e68/M153 54
倏 J6047/M762 231
単 J4331/M2752 620
叟 J5257/M3176 682
屆 J-X/M-X 1418
峠 J463d/M8068 1464
巷 J-X/M8756 1544
帥 J3f63/M8886 1559
幽 J4d29/M9205 1600
庲 J-X/M-X 1614
律 J4e27/M10097 1710
怎 J5763/M10431 1803
拜 J5941/M11969 2127
拵 J594f/M12001 2140
施 J3b5c/M13629 2391
昨 J3a72/M13847 2449
柬 J5b4b/M14655 2608
柮 J5b53/M14657 2609
柹 J-X/M14596 2625
歪 J4f44/M16286 2960
段 J434a/M16619 2991
洲 J3d27/M17413 3120
津 J4445/M17396 3122
派 J4749/M17428 3126
炸 J5f5a/M18979 3410
狙 J602c/M19743 3519
牴 J6032/M19988 3540
甚 J3f53/M21648 3711
畊 J6139/M21773 3736
界 J3326/M21775 3739
畍 J6138/M21776 3740
疥 J614e/M22057 3781
矧 J476a/M23938 3979
研 J3826/M24080 3991
神 J3f40/M24673' 4087
穽 J6357/M25433 4194
糾 J356a/M-X 4438
罘 J6629/M28224 4636
胖 J6676/M29381 4780
胛 J6670/M29392 4783
胙 J6672/M29387 4784
胄 J6674/M29349 4785
胚 J6675/M29390 4787
臾 J674c/M30178 4908
虽 J-X/M32836 5278
赳 J6c62/M37030 5848
軌 J-X/M-X 5942
迸 J6d7e/M38867 6036
追 J4449/M38836' 6042
逋 J6d79/M38871 6047
重 J3d45/M40132 6207
陥 J3459/M41676' 6446
降 J395f/M41620 6450
面 J4c4c/M42618 6566
韭 J706c/M43236 6604
飛 J4874/M44000 6672

9 residual strokes

衷 J436f/M-X **31**
乘 J502b/M154 55
候 J3875/M775 250
兼 J3773/M1483 381
啞 J3022/M3743 795
唐 J4562/M3709' 812
娣 J-X/M6329 1226

10 residual strokes

11 residual strokes

12 residual strokes

Rad.2: 21 residual strokes

21–30 residual strokes

Rad. 3 、

0 residual strokes

1 residual stroke

2 residual strokes

3 residual strokes

4 residual strokes

5 residual strokes

6 residual strokes

7 residual strokes

8 residual strokes

Rad.4: 3 residual strokes

7 residual strokes

8 residual strokes

Char	JIS	Morohashi	No.
城	J3e6b	M5086′	1011
奏	J4155	M5915	1156
娜	J5531	M6311	1211
姥	J3138	M6216	1212
孩	J5558	M6977	1295
宥	J4d28	M7137	1326
屏	J5622	M7692	1417
巷	J-X	M8756	1544
庲	J-X	M-X	1614
怎	J5763	M10431	1803
怫	J5767	M10486	1813
怱	J5764	M10494	1815
恠	J575f	M10574	1826
拜	J5941	M11969	2127
挘	J-X	M12081	2137
拵	J594f	M12001	2140
拷	J3969	M12006	2142
捗	J-X	M12160	2161
柞	J5b50	M14636	2605
柬	J5b4b	M14655	2608
栃	J464a	M14687	2613
柨	J-X	M14596	2625
柳	J4c78	M14662	2629
染	J4077	M14621	2636
歪	J4f44	M16286	2960
洩	J314c	M17401	3118
派	J4749	M17428	3126
洗	J4076	M17379	3131
炸	J5f5a	M18979	3410
為	J3059	M18981	3411
狙	J602c	M19743	3519
瓲	J6126	M21467	3694
畊	J6139	M21773	3736
界	J3326	M21775	3739
畍	J6138	M21776	3740
疥	J614e	M22057	3781
疣	J614f	M22050	3782
盃	J4756	M22955	3887
盈	J314e	M22961	3888
盾	J3d62	M23171	3912
眇	J623f	M23188	3914
省	J3e4a	M23179	3916
看	J3447	M23196	3919
研	J3826	M24080	3991
砂	J3a3d	M24046	3992
祢	J472a	M-X	4074
祐	J4d34	M24652′	4079
禹	J633b	M24885	4118
秒	J4943	M24952	4129
穽	J6357	M25433	4194
笂	J6373	M-X	4248
笈	J3568	M25869	4249
級	J3569	M27258′	4437
罘	J6629	M28224	4636
胙	J6672	M29387	4784
胤	J307d	M29405	4786
胚	J6675	M29390	4787
茱	J6825	M30910	5020
軌	J3530	M38176	5941
迸	J6d7e	M38867	6036
逓	J447e	M38881′	6055
透	J4629	M38876′	6059
郡	J3734	M39436	6143
重	J3d45	M40132	6207
陏	J7023	M-X	6440
面	J4c4c	M42618	6566
飛	J4874	M44000	6672

9 residual strokes

Char	JIS	Morohashi	No.
乘	J502b	M154	**55**
兼	J3773	M1483	381
卿	J362a	M2878	642
咳	J3331	M3555	789
哦	J5328	M3642	798
哽	J532b	M3680	799
唏	J5329	M3707	800
埒	J5440	M5124	1019
夏	J3246	M5720	1120
奋	J-X	M5931	1158
娣	J-X	M6329	1226
娑	J5530	M6294	1229
娩	J4a5a	M6337	1233
孫	J4239	M6987	1296
峺	J5638	M8115	1468
峨	J3265	M8071	1471
差	J3a39	M8732	1537
息	J4255	M10469	1818
悌	J4470	M10642	1861
悩	J473a	M10716′	1867
悗	J5824	M10664	1879
挛	J-X	M-X	2130
拷	J3969	M12006	2142
捗	J-X	M12160	2161
挿	J415e	M12119	2167
教	J3635	M13213	2345
教	J-X	M13212	2346
旅	J4e39	M-X	2396
旅	J-X	M13644	2397
既	J347b	M13721	2407
柳	J4c78	M14662	2629
栲	J5b5e	M14734	2642
梅	J4073	M14737	2651
核	J334b	M14743	2660
株	J3374	M14723	2665
欬	J-X	M16061	2932
殺	J-X	M16625	2992
殷	J5d56	M16627	2993
殺	J3b26	M16629	2994
氤	J5d65	M17060	3029
涛	J4573	M-X	3138
涕	J5e38	M17543	3143
浩	J3940	M17479′	3147
班	J4849	M20976	3636
珠	J3c6e	M20956	3637
瓶	J4953	M21486	3699
痏	J-X	M-X	3799
盈	J314e	M22961	3888
看	J-X	M-X	3921
祢	J-X	M24679	4073
祕	J6330	M24663	4075
祚	J632f	M24668	4076
祐	J-X	M24652	4080
祓	J6331	M24658	4082
秡	J6341	M24990	4132
秩	J4361	M24998	4135
称	J3e4e	M25016′	4139
秘	J486b	M24977	4140
窄	J3a75	M25455	4197
笈	J3568	M25869	4249
笋	J6424	M25873	4251
笊	J6375	M25872	4253
笏	J6374	M25882	4254
笄	J6422	M25862	4255
粋	J3f68	M26875	4389
級	J3569	M27258′	4437
紘	J3949	M27289	4445
紗	J3c53	M27287	4446
翆	J6643	M28647	4676
耄	J664e	M28848	4699
耆	J664d	M28849	4701
耕	J394c	M28907′	4710
耾	J-X	M29025	4719
耽	J433f	M29024	4721
胤	J307d	M29405	4786
胼	J6726	M29453	4798
莎	J6835	M31040	5045
莠	J683c	M31065	5046
蚜	J-X	M32882	5280
袁	J6a4f	M34152	5429
託	J4277	M35243	5560
豺	J6c39	M36500	5754
貶	J6c4a	M36707	5771
財	J3a62	M36664	5773
逓	J447e	M38881′	6055
透	J4629	M38876′	6059
逅	J-X	M-X	6065
迸	J-X	M38929	6066
郵	J4d39	M39485	6147
都	J4554	M39497′	6148
釜	J3378	M40164	6215
陲	J7024	M41694	6452
随	J3f6f	M41764′	6460

10 residual strokes

Char	JIS	Morohashi	No.
倬	J506c	M740	234
冕	J514b	M1545	397
剱	J517b	M-X	499
剩	J3e6a	M2107	501
卿	J362a	M2878	642
咳	J3331	M3555	789
唾	J4243	M3785	826
埵	J-X	M5190	1027
執	J3c39	M5193	1039

11 residual strokes

12 residual strokes

Rad.4: 13 residual strokes

Char	JIS	Morohashi	No.
滯	J5e7c	M18075	3285
潅	J3443	M18216	3287
煮	J-X	M19188	3441
煑	J-X	M19187	3442
煖	J5f6b	M19196	3451
牌	J4757	M-X	3528
牒	J442d	M19871	3529
瑟	J606e	M21133	3660
暑	J-X	M21537	3700
痺	J6163	M22280	3820
睥	J-X	M23458	3943
睡	J3f67	M23448	3948
碑	J-X	M24289	4010
稗	J-X	M25113	4151
粳	J646b	M26967	4408
綉	J6535	M27493	4495
署	J3d70	M28311′	4643
罪	J3a61	M28293	4644
群	J3732	M28498	4666
羣	J663a	M28497	4667
肅	J6669	M29225	4748
蒹	J6865	M31621	5133
蔕	J6878	M31789	5169
詬	J6b4d	M35433	5595
詼	J6b4b	M35462	5597
誅	J6b4f	M35472	5599
該	J333a	M35445	5601
豫	J502e	M36425	5751
賎	J4128	M-X	5796
賄	J4f45	M36745	5800
跣	J6c71	M37497	5871
跡	J4057	M37493	5875
酬	J3d37	M39850	6171
鈸	J-X	M40271	6240
鉄	J4534	M40285	6253
隙	J-X	M41813	6477
雅	J326d	M41973	6505
頓	J465c	M43381	6623
飫	J712c	M44050	6676
飩	J712b	M44047	6677
飭	J522c	M44057	6678
馴	J466b	M44595	6729
鳩	J4837	M46648	6936

13 residual strokes

Char	JIS	Morohashi	No.
僑	J3623	M1088	307
劂	J-X	M2190	512
嘆	J-X	M4171	874
塲	J5447	M5385	1076
塀	J-X	M-X	1079
塾	J3d4e	M5402	1083
奬	J547d	M5997	1169
孵	J555b	M7021	1301
愿	J5857	M11100	1938
慯	J5853	M11133	1952
慟	J5856	M11103	1959
搴	J596b	M12519	2246
携	J3748	M12529	2253
摯	J5975	M12632	2260
歎	J5d3e	M16159	2944
滯	J5e7c	M18075	3285
潅	J3443	M18216	3287
瑳	J3a3c	M21170	3667
瘍	J6167	M22327	3825
睹	J6251	M23519	3950
碑	J486a	M24364′	4028
稗	J-X	M25113	4151
稗	J4923	M-X	4156
種	J3c6f	M25174	4159
箅	J-X	M-X	4300
箸	J4824	M-X	4301
絏	J6532	M27397	4476
絣	J6533	M27429	4478
綉	J6535	M27493	4495
絣	J-X	M27607	4502
緒	J3d6f	M27632	4521
塚	J-X	M28319	4646
翡	J6647	M28733	4684
聚	J665c	M29093	4731
翮	J-X	M30310	4921
蜴	J696e	M33190	5335
蜱	J-X	M33182	5336
蜚	J6974	M33138	5340
蜜	J4c2a	M33143	5343
裴	J6a6a	M34362	5465
該	J333a	M35445	5601
豨	J-X	M36404	5747
豬	J-X	M36398	5748
船	J-X	M38089	5933
酷	J3973	M39870′	6176
銑	J412d	M40376	6263
隨	J6e2e	M41871	6481
霊	J-X	M-X	6527
餅	J4c5f	M44133	6689
駁	J477d	M44619	6733
髪	J4831	M45387′	6804
齊	J736e	M48560	7084

14 residual strokes

Char	JIS	Morohashi	No.
嘸	J535f	M4269	893
嘱	J3e7c	M4249	894
墸	J5457	M-X	1093
嬌	J5548	M6739	1268
孵	J555b	M7021	1301
賓	J4950	M-X	1365
衝	J3e57	M34069	1772
戯	J353a	M11665	2041
樇	J5c73	M15565	2829
榕	J5c69	M15428	2846
権	J3822	M15484	2853
歓	J343f	M16197	2948
畿	J3526	M21925	3768
磋	J6278	M24395	4034
稽	J374e	M25218	4163
箸	J-X	M26224	4328
緜	J6544	M27644	4533
緒	J-X	M27633	4535
緲	J654d	M27687	4539
緩	J344b	M27669	4551
餤	J-X	M28744	4687
蜱	J-X	M33182	5336
蝨	J697c	M33303	5347
裵	J6a6a	M34362	5465
諾	J427a	M35687	5638
諸	J3d74	M35691′	5648
賭	J4552	M-X	5807
輩	J475a	M38398	5971
銹	J6e78	M40426	6271
鋳	J4372	M40503′	6280
隨	J6e2e	M41871	6481
靠	J7051	M42604	6564
餅	J4c5f	M44133	6689
駛	J714b	M44679	6738
髴	J717c	M45414	6806
魃	J7231	M45806	6836
鴆	J7271	M46727	6944
鼏	J-X	M48316	7075
齊	J736e	M48560	7084

15 residual strokes

Char	JIS	Morohashi	No.
劍	J517a	M2243	519
嘯	J5362	M4246	904
噯	J-X	M4394	907
噸	J4655	M4429	910
嘷	J5367	M4467	913
壅	J5459	M5524	1096
墺	J5454	M5504	1100
憲	J-X	M11269	1989
戲	J-X	M11668	2043
潴	J5f4c	M18287	3311
熱	J472e	M19360	3473
熱	J-X	M-X	3474
餤	J-X	M19395	3485
稽	J-X	M-X	4174
絣	J-X	M27607	4502
緒	J3d6f	M27632	4521
縣	J6551	M27784	4555
縒	J6553	M27751	4559
膸	J673b	M29924	4869
薯	J3d72	M-X	5202
蕭	J692b	M32012	5218
覩	J6b2f	M34913	5531
諸	J-X	M35743	5650
賭	J-X	M36847	5819
赭	J6c60	M37017	5844
輳	J6d54	M38429	5975
銹	J6e78	M40426	6271
錘	J3f6e	M40547	6291
錫	J3c62	M40573	6292
隲	J702d	M41880	6486
霏	J7042	M42323	6539
駢	J7158	M44696	6748
駭	J714f	M44725	6750

6 residual strokes

乱 J4d70/M187 **60**
乳 J467d/M190 **61**
吼 J5263/M3377 730
吾 J3863/M3379 733
壳 J4764/M5647′ 990
尨 J5578/M7554 1400
弛 J4350/M9724 1684
沌 J4659/M17193 3054
紇 J647d/M27222 4432

7 residual strokes

乳 J467d/M190 **61**
奄 J3162/M5881 1146
庖 J4a79/M9266 1610
弛 J4350/M9724 1684
颮 J6126/M21467 3694
軋 J6d42/M38173 5940

8 residual strokes

乳 J467d/M190 **61**
咤 J5323/M3533 781
施 J3b5c/M13629 2391
染 J4077/M14621 2636
颮 J6126/M21467 3694
竓 J636a/M25738 4228
紇 J647d/M27222 4432
胤 J307d/M29405 4786

9 residual strokes

亳 J5038/M-X 97
悒 J5825/M10655 1859
竜 J4e35/M25751 4232
粍 J4c30/M26881 4387
胤 J307d/M29405 4786
菴 J683f/M31227 5063
訖 J6b3f/M35242 5557
託 J4277/M35243 5560

10 residual strokes

亀 J3535/M210 **62**
乾 J3425/M204 **63**
帶 J5668/M8950 1565
庵 J3043/M9369 1623
掩 J3166/M12285 2192
淹 J5e3b/M17696 3178
紮 J6527/M27341 4463
胤 J307d/M29405 4786
酔 J3f6c/M39807 6166
鈍 J6e61/M40192 6221
飩 J7144/M44492 6720

12 residual strokes

亂 J502c/M214 **64**
塾 J3d4e/M5402 1083
滝 J426c/M18067 3273
滯 J5e7c/M18075 3285
紮 J6527/M27341 4463
罨 J662c/M28288 4641
誂 J6b50/M35469 5596
詫 J4f4d/M35431 5598
跳 J4437/M37533 5877
電 J4545/M42253 6526
馳 J435a/M44593 6730
髦 J7176/M45363 6800
鴇 J4837/M46648 6936
黽 J7366/M48257 7071

13 residual strokes

亂 J502c/M214 **64**
亂 J-X/M-X **65**
塾 J3d4e/M5402 1083
滯 J5e7c/M18075 3285
輒 J6d4c/M38336 5962

14 residual strokes

縄 J466c/M27729 4547
蝿 J4768/M-X 5344

15 residual strokes

穐 J302c/M25281 4170
篭 J4f36/M26371 4332
闔 J6f66/M41372 6406

16 residual strokes

壠 J-X/M5592 1113
竈 J3376/M-X 4216
縄 J466c/M27729 4547
龜 J737d/M48847 7106

18–23 residual strokes

壠 J-X/M5592 1113
穐 J6354/M25381 4184
繩 J656a/M27937 4598
蠅 J6a24/M33690 5394
鷙 J7339/M47275 6996
鼈 J7368/M48305 7073

Rad. 6 亅

0 residual strokes

亅 J502d/M224 **66**

1 residual stroke

丁 J437a/M2 2
了 J4e3b/M226 **67**

2 residual strokes

于 J5032/M252 73
冂 J5144/M1506 384
孑 J5553/M6931 1280
子 J3b52/M6930 1281
寸 J4023/M7411 1372
小 J3e2e/M7473 1389
才 J3a4d/M11769 2059
水 J3f65/M17083 3030

3 residual strokes

丬 J-X/M-X 35
予 J4d3d/M231 **68**
少 J3e2f/M7475 1390
手 J3c6a/M11768 2060
水 J3f65/M17083 3030

4 residual strokes

丞 J3e67/M40 22
争 J4168/M236 **69**
冰 J5156/M1612 412
叮 J525a/M3244 690
可 J3244/M3245 701
尓 J5575/M7478 1392
庁 J4423/M9223 1603
打 J4247/M11781 2063
氷 J4939/M17087 3032
汀 J4475/M17103 3034
牙 J3267/M19909 3531
矛 J4c37/M23846 3974
迂 J312a/M38722 6016

5 residual strokes

丞 J3e67/M40 22
氶 J-X/M139 51
事 J502f/M-X **70**
冰 J5156/M1612 412
冴 J-X/M1615 415
吁 J525e/M3275 705
宇 J3127/M7067 1309
永 J314a/M17088 3031
求 J3561/M17105 3036
汗 J-X/M17132 3048
灯 J4574/M18855 3395
犲 J603c/M20248 3555
竹 J435d/M25841 4246
芋 J3072/M30670′ 4964
行 J3954/M34029 5419
迂 J312a/M38722 6016

Rad. 7 二

汅 J3178/M17133 3047
汙 J-X/M17132 3048
礼 J-X/M24626 4062
缶 J344c/M28108 4624
芋 J3072/M30670′ 4964
行 J3954/M34029 5419
迂 J312a/M38722 6016
迃 J-X/M38723 6017
阮 J6f76/M41569 6426

5 residual strokes

互 J-X/M-X **78**
亘 J4f4b/M262 **79**
亙 J4f4a/M265 **80**
亜 J3021/M272 **81**
伝 J4541/M462′ 141
会 J3271/M460 143
佞 J5524/M521 161
冱 J5154/M1613 414
吁 J525e/M3275 705
吾 J3863/M3379 733
囲 J304f/M4722 945
坐 J3a41/M4931 978
壼 J5467/M5667 1065
夸 J5472/M5854 1142
妍 J552b/M6075 1186
完 J3430/M7079 1315
巫 J5660/M8728 1536
形 J3741/M9969 1713
政 J402f/M13135 2335
汚 J3178/M17133 3047
沍 J5d6c/M17194 3058
芫 J676b/M30727 4967
芸 J375d/M30741′ 4977
迃 J-X/M38723 6017

6 residual strokes

並 J4a42/M54 24
亜 J3021/M272 **81**
亞 J5033/M274 **82**
亟 J5034/M279 **83**
些 J3a33/M268 **84**
其 J4236/M1472 378
卷 J524b/M2860 635
味 J4c23/M3456 766
坪 J445a/M4976 998
奈 J4660/M5893 1147
奉 J4a74/M5894 1149
妹 J4b65/M6138 1199
帙 J5665/M8852 1557
枅 J5b47/M14525 2571
歩 J4a62/M16284 2958
沍 J5d6c/M17194 3058
玩 J3461/M20872 3622
盂 J6233/M22949 3886
竺 J3c33/M25842 4247
迃 J-X/M38723 6017

7 residual strokes

亞 J5033/M274 **82**
亟 J5034/M279 **83**
剏 J516c/M2024 485
咲 J3a69/M3554 790
垣 J3340/M5060 1009
奏 J4155/M5915 1156
娜 J5531/M6311 1211
屏 J5622/M7692 1417
巻 J342c/M8759′ 1545
怜 J4e67/M10461 1812
恆 J5771/M10528 1825
恒 J3931/M10527 1849
爰 J6029/M19672 3512
畊 J6139/M21773 3736
看 J3447/M23196 3919
穽 J6357/M25433 4194
胼 J6676/M29381 4780
院 J3121/M41665 6447

8 residual strokes

亞 J5033/M274 **82**
亟 J5034/M279 **83**
冓 J514a/M1540 396
咢 J5278/M3529 782
唖 J3022/M3743 795
峯 J4a77/M8093 1474
徐 J3d79/M10110 1744
恆 J5771/M10528 1825
恭 J3633/M10596 1845
悍 J577b/M10643 1862
悟 J3867/M10680 1870
晋 J3f38/M13899 2455
晉 J5a69/M13898 2456
桧 J4930/M-X 2637
桓 J343c/M14774 2652
殊 J3c6c/M16451 2975
泰 J4259/M17325 3098
浣 J5e31/M17470 3146
紜 J6522/M27296 4444
耘 J6651/M28910 4708
耺 J-X/M29018 4718
莞 J3450/M31063 5052
蚕 J3b3d/M32869 5290
袴 J3853/M34236 5448

9 residual strokes

咢 J5278/M3529 782
堊 J5441/M5215 1025
基 J3470/M5197 1040
壼 J5467/M5667 1065
寇 J5564/M7209 1339
宼 J-X/M7208 1340
崇 J3f72/M8152 1490
悪 J302d/M10717 1873
惓 J582b/M10795 1882
敍 J5a46/M13205 2340
斜 J3c50/M13509 2376
淙 J5e4a/M17643 3188
瓠 J6121/M21392 3687
票 J493c/M24694 4089
袴 J3853/M34236 5448
裄 J6a62/M34283 5451
貮 J6c49/M-X 5774
転 J453e/M38234′ 5948
鄂 J6e3f/M39520 6150

10 residual strokes

啻 J5341/M3886 835
堊 J5441/M5215 1025
壼 J5467/M5667 1065
廃 J4751/M9425 1630
惡 J5828/M10824 1875
惷 J5836/M10864 1901
愃 J583a/M10891 1903
愕 J5833/M10939 1914
撓 J-X/M-X 2217
晉 J5a69/M13898 2456
普 J4961/M13982 2489
榜 J5b7b/M-X 2711
椏 J5b73/M15025 2727
款 J343e/M16107 2938
湲 J5e53/M17877 3220
湊 J4c2b/M17822 3226
無 J4c35/M19113 3439
瓠 J6121/M21392 3687
蒄 J6857/M31342 5107
鄂 J6e3f/M39520 6150
開 J332b/M41233 6393
雲 J3140/M42235 6522

11 residual strokes

冀 J-X/M1494 382
堊 J5441/M5215 1025
嫣 J553d/M6597 1253
惡 J5828/M10824 1875
慫 J5834/M10900 1911
愕 J5833/M10939 1914
普 J-X/M-X 2494
暄 J5a77/M14033 2497
暖 J4348/M14064 2502
椏 J5b73/M15025 2727
潛 J-X/M17922 3262
煖 J5f6b/M19196 3451
篔 J-X/M-X 4289
貳 J6c48/M36703 5783
頑 J3468/M43374 6624

12 residual strokes

Char	JIS	Morohashi	No.
眈	J623e	M23189	3911
杭	J-X	M24954	4127
育	J3069	M29318	4773
肺	J4759	M29422′	4791
茫	J682b	M30900	5029
荒	J3953	M30953	5034
虻	J303a	M32835	5277
䖟	J-X	M32836	5278
迹	J6d71	M38827	6035
音	J323b	M43265	6607

8 residual strokes

Char	JIS	Morohashi	No.
衷	J436f	M-X	31
亳	J5038	M-X	**97**
倅	J5066	M750	223
倣	J-X	M725	225
凉	J515a	M1665	421
剖	J4b36	M2034	492
剤	J3a5e	M2076′	493
勍	J5227	M2370	542
咳	J3331	M3555	789
哀	J3025	M3580	791
垓	J5436	M5040	1002
変	J4a51	M5703	1119
宰	J3a4b	M7160	1330
弯	J573f	M-X	1690
恋	J4e78	M10537	1852
悋	J5827	M10640	1865
惇	J4657	M10759	1887
挛	J-X	M-X	2130
斋	J-X	M13460	2367
旃	J5a56	M13642	2392
旆	J5a54	M13646	2393
旁	J5a55	M13637	2395
核	J334b	M14743	2660
校	J393b	M14713	2669
效	J-X	M16061	2932
殺	J-X	M16625	2992
氓	J5d62	M17030	3022
流	J4e2e	M17572′	3160
淳	J3d5f	M17690	3189
烹	J4b23	M19049	3425
兹	J-X	M20816	3617
畝	J4026	M21815	3748
痃	J6152	M22124	3790
竝	J636d	M25752	4230
竜	J4e35	M25751	4232
紊	J6524	M27261	4447
航	J3952	M30385	4933
蚊	J3263	M32849	5288
蚉	J-X	M32848	5289
衮	J-X	M34121	5423
衷	J-X	M-X	5424
衰	J3f6a	M34127	5432
郭	J3354	M39474	6144
高	J3962	M45313	6796

9 residual strokes

Char	JIS	Morohashi	No.
偐	J5074	M850	262
停	J4464	M864	273
傚	J507b	M969	280
割	J3364	M2112′	507
商	J3e26	M3803	832
埣	J5443	M5166	1023
培	J475d	M5195	1032
孰	J5559	M6995	1297
弦	J3839	M9754	1688
弯	J573f	M-X	1690
衒	J6a4a	M34045	1753
悴	J582c	M10726	1884
惇	J4657	M10759	1887
掖	J5955	M12262	2185
掠	J4e2b	M12273	2191
敦	J4658	M13276	2349
斎	J3a58	M13467	2368
核	J334b	M14743	2660
梓	J3034	M14845	2688
梳	J5b60	M14886	2704
椁	J5b76	M15003	2722
毫	J5d5d	M16831	3015
淬	J5e43	M17679	3176
淳	J3d5f	M17690	3189
涼	J4e43	M17606	3198
液	J3155	M17586	3199
渟	J5e5b	M17763	3221
烹	J4b23	M19049	3425
牽	J3823	M20025	3544
猝	J604c	M20500	3581
率	J4e28	M20817′	3618
琉	J4e30	M20978	3642
産	J3b3a	M21684′	3716
畩	J613e	M-X	3751
皎	J6229	M22724	3872
竟	J706f	M25757	4234
翌	J4d62	M28657′	4679
望	J4b3e	M14368′	4819
萃	J6844	M31251	5078
衮	J-X	M34121	5423
衷	J-X	M-X	5424
袤	J6a5d	M34213	5436
袞	J6a51	M34203	5441
郭	J3354	M39474	6144
髙	J-X	M45314	6797

10 residual strokes

Char	JIS	Morohashi	No.
傚	J507b	M969	280
傍	J4b35	M948	286
啻	J5341	M3886	835
喨	J534a	M3978	836
啼	J5346	M3887	837
孰	J5559	M6995	1297
孶	J-X	M7011	1300
就	J3d22	M7599	1401
嵜	J563f	M-X	1492
慌	J3932	M11057	1917
敦	J4658	M13276	2349
斐	J4865	M13469	2370
斑	J4843	M13470	2371
景	J374a	M13983	2487
椁	J5b76	M15003	2722
椋	J4c3a	M15020	2725
棄	J-X	M-X	2788
殕	J5d4d	M16498	2979
湾	J4f51	M17920	3239
焠	J-X	M19111	3430
焙	J5f64	M19099	3433
兹	J-X	M20816	3617
疏	J4141	M22000	3775
痃	J6152	M22124	3790
硫	J4e32	M24229	4006
禽	J3659	M24893	4120
童	J4638	M25775	4239
紊	J6524	M27261	4447
絞	J394a	M27421	4485
統	J457d	M27447	4487
腋	J667e	M29615	4833
蒂	J685c	M31495	5101
蛟	J6960	M33009	5311
蛮	J485a	M33044	5314

11 residual strokes

Char	JIS	Morohashi	No.
亶	J5039	M328	**98**
喪	J4153	M3985	853
塙	J4839	M5341	1063
塘	J4564	M5340	1066
塾	J3d4e	M5402	1083
孶	J-X	M7011	1300
嵩	J3f73	M8348	1502
幌	J566d	M9024	1576
廓	J3347	M9461	1633
意	J3055	M10921	1926
新	J3f37	M13572	2387
旒	J5a58	M13676	2401
暗	J3045	M14065	2503
棄	J347e	M14913	2787
椸	J5c3c	M15179	2762
滋	J-X	M18021	3250
溟	J5e72	M17947	3258
滓	J5e68	M18034	3260
滂	J5e71	M18003	3264
漓	J5f22	M18127	3292
琿	J606d	M21093	3658
瘁	J6161	M22294	3816
碎	J626c	M24284	4009
稟	J6349	M24742	4094
禽	J3659	M24893	4120
稾	J6348	M25127	4153
蓑	J4c2c	M31661	5143
蒡	J6870	M31572	5145
蒿	J6866	M31634	5147
蓄	J435f	M31642	5161
裔	J6a63	M34303	5459

Rad. 9 人

8 residual strokes

9 residual strokes

10 residual strokes

11 residual strokes

筱	J642c	M26076	4293
筴	J6429	M26079	4294
筮	J642e	M26070	4298
糀	J6471	M27013	4406
絛	J6536	M27465	4494
蓙	J6868	M31709	5142
蓚	J686b	M-X	5146
蔭	J307e	M31840	5151
蒼	J4173	M31627	5162
蜍	J696b	M33110	5320
諛	J-X	M35495	5590
該	J333a	M35445	5601
詮	J4127	M35435	5606
貅	J6c3c	M36542	5760
賃	J4442	M36743	5802
鈷	J385a	M40270	6236
鉅	J6e6a	M40286	6237
鉐	J6e71	M40298	6238
鉚	J6e76	M40309	6239
鈸	J-X	M40271	6240
鉉	J6e6b	M40290	6241
鉈	J6e6d	M40289	6242
鈿	J6e6f	M40279	6243
鉞	J6e68	M40313	6244
鉗	J6e69	M40306	6245
鉦	J3e60	M40322	6246
鈴	J4e6b	M40267	6247
鉋	J6e70	M40292	6248
鉢	J482d	M40317	6249
鉤	J6e6c	M40319	6250
鉛	J3174	M40310	6251
鉱	J395b	M40340′	6252
鉄	J4534	M40285	6253
零	J4e6d	M42242	6524
靴	J3724	M42729	6576
飫	J712a	M44050	6676
飩	J712b	M44047	6677
飭	J522c	M44057	6678
飯	J4853	M44064′	6679
飲	J307b	M44063′	6680
飮	J5d3b	M44063	6681
飴	J303b	M44080	6682
飾	J3e7e	M44111′	6683
飽	J4b30	M44109′	6684
飼	J3b74	M44107′	6685

12 residual strokes

債	J3a44	M1022	**296**
僞	J5126	M1105	**303**
僧	J-X	M1117	**304**
僣	J5129	M1111	**305**
僖	J5125	M1095	**306**
僑	J3623	M1088	**307**
像	J417c	M1084	**308**
像	J-X	M48923	**309**
僮	J512a	M1132	**310**
僥	J5127	M1113	**311**
儁	J512e	M1175	**312**
僕	J4b4d	M1094	**313**
僚	J4e3d	M1100	**314**
剳	J-X	M-X	511
寥	J556c	M7292	1359
廖	J5721	M9464	1637
慘	J584e	M11094	1949
摎	J5977	M12564	2258
斡	J3036	M13522	2378
楹	J5c45	M15277	2800
榕	J5c57	M15228	2815
槍	J4164	M15319	2822
滌	[illegible]	M18069	3296
漆	J3c3f	M18108	3304
熔	J4d50	M19319	3458
熅	J-X	M19288	3467
睿	J624f	M23536	3949
碣	J6272	M24326	4025
窬	J-X	M25582	4207
竭	J6371	M25803	4242
箚	J6434	M26149	4305
箆	J4a4f	M26114	4310
粹	J646f	M26987	4409
絵	J3328	M27464′	4488
給	J356b	M27432	4489
綸	J6545	M27583	4519
翠	J3f69	M28732	4685
聚	J665c	M29093	4731
腐	J4965	M29625	4835
腈	J-X	M29794	4853
膃	J672c	M29757	4857
蓼	J687a	M31744	5166
蓿	J6872	M31747	5167
蔘	J6875	M31795	5174
蜽	J-X	M33201	5315
蝕	J3f2a	M-X	5333
褐	J-X	M34435	5478
褓	J6a70	M34438	5479
覡	J6b2e	M34875	5530
該	J333a	M35445	5601
誣	J6b58	M35542	5618
銕	J6e6e	M40382	6254
鉼	J4b48	M40353	6255
銖	J6e73	M40383	6256
鋌	J6e7a	M40490	6258
鑑	J-X	M40489	6259
銚	J4438	M40387	6260
銛	[illegible]	M40389	6261
銓	J6e74	M40378	6262
銑	J412d	M40376	6263
銭	J412c	M40413	6264
銘	J4c43	M40385	6265
銅	J463c	M40361	6266
銃	J3d46	M40359	6267
銀	J3664	M40355	6268
閤	J395e	M41301	6397
閥	J4836	M41308	6398
鞆	J705d	M42794	6580
領	J4e4e	M43423	6628
飴	J303b	M44080	6682
飾	J3e7e	M44111′	6683
飽	J4b30	M44109′	6684
飼	J3b74	M44107′	6685
餞	J-X	M44156	6686
餅	J4c5f	M44133	6689
餌	J3142	M44146	6690

13 residual strokes

儉	J512d	M1190	**315**
價	J512b	M1163	**316**
僵	J512c	M1158	**317**
儂	J512f	M1176	**318**
儈	J-X	M1189	**319**
僂	J5133	M1236	**320**
億	J322f	M1178	**321**
舗	J4a5e	M30323′	**322**
僻	J4a48	M1166	**323**
儀	J3537	M1172	**324**
劍	J5178	M2228	514
劉	J4e2d	M2224	515
匳	J323d	M2655	596
慾	J4d5d	M11163	1951
慫	J5851	M11127	1958
戮	J5924	M11655	2040
擒	J5a22	M12816	2289
樅	J-X	M-X	2792
樅	J5c62	M15404	2838
樛	J5c5c	M15445	2842
滲	J5e7a	M18081	3302
瘟	J6169	M22396	3828
瘡	J616c	M22404	3829
瘠	J616b	M22401	3833
穃	J634e	M-X	4164
箆	J4a4f	M26114	4310
篌	J643c	M26272	4322
篋	J643a	M26271	4323
羯	J663b	M28537	4670
膵	J6739	M29920	4865
膠	J6731	M29841	4866
膝	J4928	M29837	4868
舗	J6754	M30323	4922
蝕	J3f2a	M-X	5333
蝎	J6979	M33254	5354
蝕	J-X	M33264	5358
褒	J4b2b	M34437	5483
褞	J6a72	M34475	5486
論	J4f40	M35658	5646
賚	J6c4f	M36805	5809
輪	J4e58	M38400	5973
醉	J6e4d	M39906	6178
鉉	J6e6b	M40290	6241
鑑	J-X	M40489	6259
鋪	J4a5f	M40491	6269
錠	J-X	M40469	6270
銹	J6e78	M40426	6271

14 residual strokes

15 residual strokes

16 residual strokes

17 residual strokes

18 residual strokes

19 residual strokes

20 residual strokes

21 residual strokes

Rad. 10 儿

唆 J3a36/M3696 803
娩 J4a5a/M6337 1233
尅 J5571/M7435 1378
峻 J3d54/M8116 1475
悛 J5822/M10674 1858
悦 J3159/M10629′ 1868
挽 J-X/M12111 2169
挽 J4854/M-X 2172
晁 J5a6a/M13889 2457
晃 J3938/M13891 2458
晄 J5a68/M13892 2459
桃 J456d/M14757 2663
涜 J4642/M-X 3134
浣 J5e31/M17470 3146
浚 J5e34/M17460 3151
祝 J-X/M24672 4086
耽 J433f/M29024 4721
胱 J6679/M29432 4796
莵 J6839/M-X 5035
莞 J3450/M31063 5052
逡 J6d75/M38899 6050
逵 J6d7c/M38948 6068
逸 J306f/M38951′ 6071
逸 J-X/M38951 6072
陵 J4e4d/M41704 6454
陸 J4e26/M41708 6461
鬲 J722f/M45672 6831
鬼 J3534/M45758 6833

9 residual strokes

兜 J3375/M1386 **364**
冕 J514b/M1545 397
冤 J514d/M1587 404
勘 J342a/M2393 548
啌 J5333/M3810 816
商 J3e26/M3803 832
寃 J5563/M7202 1338
寇 J5564/M7209 1339
寇 J-X/M7208 1340
崚 J5645/M8184 1480
彪 J4937/M9993 1716
悗 J5824/M10664 1879
挽 J4854/M-X 2172
控 J3935/M12283 2202
探 J4335/M12276 2211
晩 J-X/M13940 2466
冕 J-X/M-X 2468
梭 J5b68/M14878 2693
梳 J5b60/M14886 2704
涳 J5e4c/M17638 3173
烱 J5f58/M19040 3422
猊 J6049/M20468 3582
琉 J4e30/M20978 3642
現 J383d/M21004 3645
眺 J442f/M23314 3933
窕 J635a/M25496 4199
竟 J706f/M25757 4234
脱 J4326/M29539′ 4822
菟 J-X/M31189 5077
菱 J4929/M31219 5092
覓 J6b2c/M34815 5523
規 J352c/M34810 5524
視 J3b6b/M34827′ 5525
逵 J6d7c/M38948 6068
逸 J306f/M38951′ 6071
逸 J-X/M38951 6072
酖 J6e45/M39792 6165
麻 J-X/M47887 7041

10 residual strokes

傀 J507a/M928 282
兜 J3375/M1386 **364**
冕 J514b/M1545 397
唍 J534a/M3978 836
喚 J342d/M3953 852
堯 J7421/M5272 1041
堪 J342e/M5266 1057
寃 J5563/M7202 1338
尊 J423a/M7445 1386
就 J3d22/M7599 1401
廃 J4751/M9425 1630
慌 J-X/M-X 1918
慌 J-X/M-X 1919
撓 J-X/M-X 2217
換 J3439/M12358 2233
暁 J3647/M14031 2485
晩 J4855/M14030′ 2491
椌 J5b7d/M15021 2726
棱 J-X/M14979 2730
澆 J482e/M-X 3209
渙 J5e52/M17757 3231
湛 J4339/M17846 3234
焼 J3e46/M19166′ 3438
焼 J-X/M-X 3440
琥 J6068/M21061 3651
疏 J4141/M22000 3775
皖 J622a/M22736 3874
皴 J622f/M22866 3880
睍 J-X/M-X 3936
䂓 J-X/M23979 3981
硯 J3827/M24233 4005
硫 J4e32/M24229 4006
税 J4047/M25070′ 4146
窠 I-X/M25556 4205
竣 J3d57/M25773 4238
筅 J6426/M25986 4275
絖 J652d/M27409 4477
統 J457d/M27447 4487
腔 J3950/M29630 4826
菟 J4551/M-X 5102
蒄 J6857/M31342 5107
視 J-X/M34836 5526
覘 J6b2d/M34840 5527
覗 J4741/M34839 5528
覚 J3350/M34846 5529
隗 J7029/M41788 6472
隔 J3356/M-X 6475

11 residual strokes

兜 J3375/M1386 **364**
堪 J342e/M5266 1057
塊 J3274/M5319 1070
寛 J3432/M7276 1352
尠 J5576/M7523 1396
嵬 J564c/M8355 1499
幌 J4b5a/M9022 1577
微 J4879/M10203 1765
愧 J5843/M10982 1941
戡 J5922/M11616 2036
搾 J3a71/M12553 2251
斟 J5a50/M13517 2377
旒 J5a58/M13676 2401
暁 J-X/M-X 2495
樓 J5c24/M15078 2755
椹 J5c3b/M15082 2758
滉 J5e66/M18017 3257
焼 J-X/M-X 3440
煥 J5f65/M19224 3448
痲 J6164/M22254 3818
痹 J-X/M22279 3821
睦 J4b53/M23460 3945
睨 J624b/M23464 3947
稜 J4e47/M25123 4152
筧 J642a/M26059 4296
続 J4233/M27533 4500
蒐 J3d2f/M31539 5159
號 J694b/M32726 5271
蛻 J6968/M33078 5322
蜆 J6964/M33093 5328
裔 J6a63/M34303 5459
跣 J6c71/M37497 5871
遞 J6e2a/M39045 6095
頑 J3468/M43374 6624

12 residual strokes

僥 J5127/M1113 311
兢 J513e/M1395 **365**
嘛 J5357/M4230 876
境 J362d/M5409 1085
寛 J-X/M-X 1355
槐 J5c47/M15323 2803
瑰 J6073/M21164 3672
碁 J6274/M24339 4022
箜 J6433/M26151 4309
絖 J652d/M27409 4477
統 J457d/M27447 4487
綾 J303d/M27591 4523
膈 J672d/M29772 4856
蔆 J6851/M31760 5168
蔲 J-X/M31741 5171
蔻 J-X/M-X 5172

讒 J6c29/M36137 5728
魘 J7236/M45941 6844

23 residual strokes

攙 J5a30/M13046 2323
欃 J5d34/M15964 2923
纔 J-X/M28053 4616
纔 J6578/M28070 4621
讒 J6c29/M36137 5728

24–28 residual strokes

欃 J5d34/M15964 2923
欟 J5d36/M15986 2927
纔 J6578/M28070 4621
纘 J657c/M28100 4623
讚 J6c2d/M36163 5729
鑽 J6f53/M41082 6374
黷 J7362/M48234 7067

Rad. 11 入

0 residual strokes

入 J467e/M1415 **366**

1 residual stroke

久 J3557/M118 47

2 residual strokes

內 J-X/M1418 **367**
内 J4662/M1512 386

込 J397e/M38712 6010

3 residual strokes

仝 J2138/M378 114
叺 J525d/M3267 688
圦 J5429/M-X 969
氽 J-X/M7477 1391
込 J397e/M38712 6010

4 residual strokes

全 J4134/M1424 145
杁 J5b35/M-X 2538

5 residual strokes

吶 J5265/M3370 732
岔 J562b/M7944 1446

6 residual strokes

兩 J5140/M1436 **368**
圀 J537a/M4744 948
枘 J-X/M14552 2579
肭 J666d/M29305 4765

7 residual strokes

兪 J5141/M1437 198
衲 J6a55/M34130 5430
陜 J7021/M41657 6442

8 residual strokes

倆 J506f/M751 229
蚋 J6952/M32850 5286

9 residual strokes

偸 J5079/M901 272
塀 J3a66/M5289 1045
痊 J6159/M22141 3800
訥 J6b44/M35274 5566

10 residual strokes

喩 J5348/M3979 839
塔 J4563/M5332 1052
愉 J-X/M-X 1919
揄 J5969/M12320 2224
渝 J5e61/M17761 3212
筌 J6425/M25995 4278
逾 J6e27/M38977 6076
鞆 J7058/M42747 6575

11 residual strokes

塔 J4563/M5332 1052
塗 J4549/M5338 1074
愈 J4c7c/M10904 1909
楡 J5c40/M15153 2768
瑜 J6071/M21129 3663
褕 J6a6c/M34356 5469
鞆 J7058/M42747 6575
鳰 J726c/M46658 6935

12 residual strokes

滿 J5e60/M18099 3283
瘉 J6168/M22318 3824
[illegible] J-X/M40489 6259
銓 J6e74/M40378 6262

13 residual strokes

蝓 J6a21/M33261 5351
輸 J6d51/M38361 5969
[illegible] J-X/M40489 6259

14–20 residual strokes

懣 J5870/M11384 2004
瞞 J6256/M23649 3956
羅 J647b/M27191 4429
覦 J6b30/M34904 5532
諭 J-X/M35727 5668
踰 J6c7c/M37675 5891
蹣 J6d2a/M37822 5907
鍮 J6f2b/M40645 6308
魎 J7234/M45870 6840

Rad. 12 八

0 residual strokes

八 J482c/M1450 **369**

2 residual strokes

兮 J5142/M1455 **370**
六 J4f3b/M1453 **371**
公 J3878/M1452 **372**
分 J4a2c/M1853 454
少 J3e2f/M7475 1390
父 J4963/M19721 3516

3 residual strokes

兮 J5142/M1455 **370**
半 J483e/M2707 608
叭 J525c/M3242 687
只 J427e/M3239 694
平 J4a3f/M9167 1590
必 J492c/M10299 1781
穴 J376a/M25406 4186
穴 JX/MX 4187
立 J4e29/M25721 4223

4 residual strokes

兊 JX/M1351 345
共 J3626/M1458 **373**
劣 J4e74/M2302 524
尽 J3f54/M7642 1408
并 J5675/M9170 1592
米 J4a46/M26832 4380
羊 J4d53/M28425 4658
辛 J3f49/M38630 5996

5 residual strokes

伴 J483c/M475 157
余 J4d3e/M515 168
兌 J513c/M1356 353
兵 J4a3c/M1462 **374**
判 J483d/M1923 465
吳 JX/M3365 719
呎 J5268/M3423 722
吩 J5266/M3347 725

吳	J3862	M3365′	741
宍	J3c35	M7084	1312
岔	J562b	M7944	1446
弟	J446f	M9737	1685
扮	J4a31	M11830	2080
来	J4d68	M14489	2565
汾	J5d70	M17178	3051
芬	J676e	M30728	4973
谷	J432b	M36102	5730
豆	J4626	M36245	5735
貝	J332d	M36656	5766
述	J3d52	M38803′	6030
逆	J3555	M38849′	6041

6 residual strokes

並	J4a42	M54	24
併	J4a3b	M561	190
供	J3621	M605	195
典	J4535	M1474	**375**
具	J3671	M1473	**376**
具	JX	MX	**377**
其	J4236	M1472	**378**
券	J3774	M1966	473
劵	J5225	M2330	532
巷	JX	MX	634
卷	J524b	M2860	635
呼	J3846	M3471	769
岡	J322c	M7962	1460
幸	J392c	M9176	1595
弟	J446f	M9737	1685
忩	JX	M10366	1792
忿	J575d	M10408	1798
拌	J5942	M11951	2102
拉	J5947	M11946	2109
斧	J4960	M13539	2382
枌	J5b43	M14534	2573
松	J3e3e	M14516	2592
枩	J5b40	MX	2593
毟	J5d5b	M16790	3014
氛	J5d64	M17048	3027
沿	J3168	M17260	3096
瓮	J6125	M21461	3693
瓰	J6127	M21465	3695
羌	J6635	M28429	4659
苹	J6779	M30823	4984
述	J3d52	M38803′	6030
迸	J6d7e	M38867	6036
送	J4177	M38842	6039
逆	J3555	M38849′	6041
金	J3662	M40152	6211

7 residual strokes

俤	J503f	M719	200
俊	J3d53	M674	216
俗	J422f	M695	220
荆	JX	MX	**379**
兹	JX	MX	**380**
剏	J516c	M2024	485
剃	J4466	M1989	489
前	J4130	M2011	490
南	J466e	M2750	619
卻	J524a	M2867	638
叛	J4840	M3166	680
吳	J3862	M3365′	741
咫	J5321	M3542	783
哄	J527c	M3588	786
咬	J527b	M3543	787
咲	J3a69	M3554	790
姘	J543a	M5086	1004
屏	J5622	M7692	1417
屎	J557d	M7689	1419
巷	J392b	MX	1543
巷	JX	M8756	1544
巻	J342c	M8759′	1545
庠	J5679	M9298	1615
弟	J446f	M9737	1685
徉	JX	M10094	1737
忩	JX	M10366	1792
拱	J594a	M11994	2139
挟	J3634	MX	2146
拳	J377d	M11996	2148
枳	J5b4c	M14383	2600
洪	J393f	M17402	3123
洋	J4d4e	M17363	3130
狭	J3639	M20406′	3572
瓮	J6125	M21461	3693
瓰	J6127	M21465	3695
盆	J4e5f	M22959	3889
盼	J623d	M23166	3910
省	J3e4a	M23179	3916
蚡	J6369	M25740	4227
美	J487e	M28435	4660
胖	J6676	M29381	4780
茶	J4363	M30915′	5033
負	JX	M36659	5767
負	J4969	MX	5769
貧	JX	M36660	5770
迸	J6d7e	M38867	6036
送	J4177	M38842′	6039
逗	J3f60	M38887	6053
郤	J6e3c	M39440	6142
酋	J3d36	M39765	6159
頁	J4a47	M43333	6614
首	J3c73	M44489	6719

8 residual strokes

俤	J505f	M719	200
俊	J3d53	M674	216
倶	J3666	M724	245
倦	J3771	M788	251
兼	J3773	M1483	**381**
冥	J4c3d	M1588	405
剃	J4466	M1989	489
剛	J3964	M2042	497
唄	J3134	M3694	802
員	J3077	M3600	808
娣	JX	M6329	1226
娯	J3864	M6307′	1231
宰	J3a4b	M7160	1330
容	J4d46	M7172	1335
屓	J557e	M7713	1423
峪	J563b	M8073	1467
差	J3a39	M8732	1537
従	J3d3e	M10133	1745
恙	J5779	M10565	1835
恭	J3633	M10596	1845
悌	J4470	M10642	1861
悦	J3159	M10629′	1868
拳	J3573	M12081′	2150
旁	J5a55	M13637	2395
晋	J3f38	M13899	2455
涕	J5e38	M17543	3143
浜	J494d	M17462	3152
浴	J4d61	M17496	3153
烘	JX	M19012	3418
狽	J4762	M20433	3576
瓶	J4953	M21486	3699
畔	J484a	M21801	3746
益	J3157	M22972′	3891
盼	J623d	M23166	3910
看	JX	MX	3921
真	J3f3f	M23236	3926
眞	J6243	M23235	3927
祥	J3e4d	M24689′	4090
秤	J4769	M24993	4134
竝	J636d	M25752	4230
粉	J4a34	M26872	4390
紛	J4a36	M27295	4452
羔	J6636	M28447	4661
翁	J3227	M28635′	4677
朕	J443f	M14361	4797
胼	J6726	M29453	4798
朔	J3a73	M14359	4801
舩	J6755	M30384	4930
荳	J683a	M30989	5036
蚣	J694f	M32892	5282
衮	JX	M34121	5423
袢	J6a5b	M34210	5438
貶	J6c4a	M36707	5771
貢	J3957	M36665	5772
財	J3a62	M36664	5773
逧	J6d7a	MX	6044
逗	J3f60	M38887	6053
釖	J6e5b	M40157	6212
釛	J6e5e	M40163	6213
釟	J6e5c	M40167	6214
釜	J3378	M40164	6215
釡	J6e5d	M40170	6216
釘	J4523	M40159	6217
針	J3f4b	M40165	6218

9 residual strokes

俤	J505f	M719	200
剪	J5172	M2088	502
商	J3e26	M3803	832
圈	J5421	M4789	955
圉	J537e	M4793	957
執	J3c39	M5193	1039
基	J3470	M5197	1040
寅	J4652	M7204	1341
崟	J5640	M8199	1481
崗	J563e	M8221	1483
惧	J577c	M10848	1878
惓	J582b	M10795	1882
惘	J5831	M10809	1883
戝	J6c43	M11603	2031
敗	J4754	M13227	2343
曽	J413e	MX	2464
梹	J5b6e	M14909	2677
梯	J4474	M14881	2706
欲	J4d5f	M16080	2936
渕	J5e3c	MX	3165
港	JX	MX	3168
淇	J5e3f	M17620	3170
淞	J5e44	M17651	3174
淦	J5e40	M17667	3193
瓶	J4953	M21486	3699
異	J305b	M21854	3757
痒	J615a	M22163	3802
盖	J6235	M22996	3892
眷	J6247	M23311	3934
祥	JX	M24689	4091
絆	J652b	M27376	4464
羚	J6639	M28463	4662
羞	J6637	M28471	4664
翌	J4d62	M28657′	4679
脰	JX	M29544	4816
脱	J4326	M29539′	4822
船	J4125	M30407	4939
菘	J6845	M31177	5066
萍	J684c	M31266	5076
萁	JX	M31248	5080
衮	JX	M34121	5423
袞	J6a51	M34203	5441
訟	J3e59	M35266	5565
谺	JX	M36193	5731
貶	J6c4a	M36707	5771
貮	J6c49	MX	5774
貭	J6c44	M36694	5775
賢	JX	M36695	5776
販	J484e	M36679	5779
責	J4055	M36682	5780
貨	J325f	M36678	5781
貧	J494f	M36677	5782
貰	J4c63	M36699	5789
逧	J6d7a	MX	6044
逹	J6d7d	MX	6064
選	JX	MX	6074
逎	J6e26	M38993	6082
遂	J3f6b	M38985′	6084
達	J4323	M39011′	6088
道	J463b	M39010′	6091
鈒	J6e5f	MX	6219
釵	J6e60	M40191	6220
鈍	J6e61	M40192	6221
釧	J367c	M40176	6222
釦	J4b55	M40175	6223
釣	J4460	M40172	6224
隊	J4262	M41750	6468
雀	J3f7d	M41954	6496
頃	J3a22	M43338	6615
頂	J443a	M43335	6616
馗	J7144	M44492	6720
麥	J734e	M47717	7031
黄	J322b	M47926′	7045

10 residual strokes

傾	J3739	M1038	299
僖	J5125	M1095	306
勝	J3e21	M2409	553
厥	J5250	M2992	656
厨	J3f5f	M3005	657
啻	J5341	M3886	835
啼	J5346	M3887	837
喃	J5347	M3903	846
喜	J346e	M3957	858
善	J4131	M3904	859
圏	J3777	M4815′	960
壹	J5465	M5661	1044
奠	J547b	M5960	1163
嫌	J3779	M6618	1257
孳	J555a	MX	1299
寒	J3428	M7239	1350
尊	J423a	M7445	1386
屢	J3c48	M7770	1428
巽	J4327	M8765	1546
幀	J566c	M8982	1570
彭	J5745	M10003	1720
惘	J5831	M10809	1883
惷	J5836	M10864	1901
惻	J583c	M10869	1916
捲	J377e	M12208	2193
揃	J4237	M12319	2226
斯	J3b5b	M13563	2386
曾	J413d	M14299	2483
普	J4961	M13982	2489
榜	J5b7b	MX	2711
椣	J5c30	MX	2715
棠	J5c2b	M14953	2718
棡	J5b7c	M14955	2719
椪	J5c2e	MX	2734
棋	J347d	M14922	2744
棊	J5b77	M14921	2745
欺	J353d	M16097	2939
欽	J3656	M16104	2940
渝	J5e61	M17761	3212
滋	J3c22	M17919′	3238
港	J3941	M17783′	3242
測	J422c	M17780	3244
爺	J4c6c	M19734	3517
猶	J4d31	M20557	3593
献	J3825	M20539	3596
痘	J4577	M22185	3813
登	J4550	M22668	3862
睇	J6249	M23360	3937
着	J4365	M23339	3938
短	J433b	M23978	3982
硲	J4823	M24243	4004
税	J4047	M25070′	4146
紛	J4a36	M27295	4452
絣	J6533	M27429	4478
翔	J6646	M28689	4683
腆	J6722	M29602	4825
腔	J3950	M29630	4826
朞	J5b2e	M14377	4828
期	J347c	M14378	4835
蒂	J685c	M31495	5101
蓉	J4d56	M31648	5135
蛬	J695f	M33047	5305
蛟	J6960	M33009	5311
裕	J4d35	M34305	5461
評	J493e	M35383	5587
谺	J6c2e	MX	5732
貫	J3453	M36681	5778
賁	J6c4c	M36727	5784
貽	J6c46	M36719	5785
費	J4871	M36717	5786
貼	J453d	M36718	5787
貿	J4b47	M36721	5788
貰	J4c63	M36699	5789
賀	J326c	M36725	5790
貯	J4379	M36698	5791
貸	J425f	M36709	5792
買	J4763	M36708	5793
貴	J352e	M36704	5794
辜	J6d63	M38636	5998
逹	J6d7d	MX	6064
選	JX	MX	6074
遒	J6e24	M39008	6077
遖	J6e28	M39030	6078
逎	J6e26	M38993	6082
遂	J3f6b	M38985′	6084
達	J4323	M39011′	6088
道	J463b	M39010′	6091
遡	J414c	M39048	6094
釟	J6e65	MX	6225
鈎	J3343	M40220	6226
釿	J6e63	M40203	6227
鈩	J6f4f	MX	6228
鈞	J6e62	M40238	6229
鈕	J6e66	M40228	6230
鈑	J6e67	M40224	6231
鈲	JX	M40200	6232
鈇	JX	M40213	6234

Char	JIS / Morohashi	No.
鈍	J465f / M40219	6235
隘	J7027 / M41791	6473
隕	J7028 / M41785	6474
雰	J4a37 / M42231	6521
項	J3960 / M43343	6617
須	J3f5c / M43352	6618
順	J3d67 / M43349	6619
黄	JX / M47926	7046
黑	JX / M48038	7053
黹	J7363 / M48248	7068

11 residual strokes

Char	JIS / Morohashi	No.
僧	J414e / M1076	300
[illegible]	JX / M1494	302
勦	J522a / M2423	555
嗛	JX / M4088	862
嗔	J5351 / M4074	866
嗟	J534d / M4102	869
圓	J5424 / M4819	961
塞	J3a49 / M5349	1069
塡	JX / M5355	1071
嫌	J3779 / M6610	1257
嵯	J3a37 / M8363	1500
嵳	J564d / M8364	1501
廉	J4e77 / M9436	1634
愈	J4c7c / M10904	1909
愈	JX / MX	1910
慈	J3b7c / M10980′	1924
慊	J5844 / M11051	1939
慎	J3f35 / M11024′	1945
愼	J5846 / M11024	1946
搓	J596d / M12476	2243
損	J423b / M12459	2255
新	J3f37 / M13572	2387
普	JX / MX	2494
棆	J5c3c / M15179	2762
楢	J466a / M15154	2769
楠	J466f / M15152	2779
業	J3648 / M15170	2789
殿	J4542 / M16651	3001
溟	J5e72 / M17947	3258
滓	J5e68 / M18034	3260
溢	J306e / M17951	3270
溯	J5e6a / M17975	3272
溶	J4d4f / M17983	3277
漾	J5f21 / M18184	3290
煎	J4079 / M19184	3453
煩	J4851 / M19229	3454
猷	J4d32 / M20558	3590
碁	J306b / M24261	4020
祺	J6332 / M24733	4095
禎	J4477 / M24767′	4099
稘	J6345 / M25118	4147
絆	J652b / M27376	4464
羨	J4122 / M28503	4665
群	J3732 / M28498	4666
羣	J663a / M28497	4667
義	J3541 / M28504	4668
與	J6750 / M30212	4911
蓊	J6863 / M31650	5136
蒴	JX / M31614	5140
虞	J3673 / M32723′	5272
蛻	J6968 / M33078	5322
解	J6b3b / M35074	5549
誉	J4d40 / M35498	5602
詳	J3e5c / M35446	5607
豊	J4b2d / M36263	5737
豢	J6c36 / M36380	5746
賁	J6c4c / M36727	5784
賎	J4128 / MX	5796
貲	J6c47 / M36702	5797
賈	J6c4b / M36755	5798
賂	J4f28 / M36738	5799
賄	J4f45 / M36745	5800
賊	J4231 / M36759	5801
賃	J4442 / M36743	5802
資	J3b71 / M36730	5803
遡	J414c / M39048	6094
鈔	J6e64 / M40227	6233
鈷	J385a / M40270	6236
鉅	J6e6a / M40286	6237
鉐	J6e71 / M40298	6238
鉚	J6e76 / M40309	6239
鈸	JX / M40271	6240
鉉	J6e6b / M40290	6241
鉈	J6e6d / M40289	6242
鈿	J6e6f / M40279	6243
鉞	J6e68 / M40313	6244
鉗	J6e69 / M40306	6245
鉦	J3e60 / M40322	6246
鈴	J4e6b / M40267	6247
鉋	J6e70 / M40292	6248
鉢	J482d / M40317	6249
鉤	J6e6c / M40319	6250
鉛	J3174 / M40310	6251
鉱	J395b / M40340′	6252
鉄	J4534 / M40285	6253
頎	J7072 / M43371	6620
頒	J4852 / M43378	6621
頌	J7073 / M43365	6622
頓	J465c / M43381	6623
頑	J3468 / M43374	6624
預	J4d42 / M43373	6625
鼓	J385d / M48330	7076

12 residual strokes

Char	JIS / Morohashi	No.
僭	JX / M1117	304
僕	J4b4d / M1094	313
劂	JX / M2190	512
匱	J523c / M2651	595
厮	J5251 / M3026	661
噌	J4139 / MX	873
嘖	J5354 / M4204	882
噓	J3133 / MX	886
嘉	J3245 / M4176	887
増	J417d / M5448′	1088
嫡	J4364 / M6656	1263
孳	J555a / MX	1299
實	J5569 / M7294	1356
寨	J5e4d / M7298	1357
寡	J3249 / M7286	1363
導	J4633 / M7463′	1388
層	J4158 / MX	1432
愬	J5847 / M10988	1932
愼	J5846 / M11024	1946
搴	J596b / M12519	2246
摯	J5975 / M12632	2260
摘	J4526 / M12582	2266
旗	J347a / M13687	2402
普	JX / MX	2494
暝	J5a79 / M14083	2505
樅	JX / MX	2792
槎	J5c4c / M15320	2802
榜	J5c56 / M15241	2804
棚	JX / M15325	2812
槊	J5c4e / M15316	2813
槓	J5c4a / M15343	2814
榕	J5c57 / M15228	2815
槇	J7422 / M15310	2818
槙	J4b6a / MX	2819
様	J4d4d / M15352′	2821
殞	J5d4e / M16535	2982
漾	J5f21 / M18184	3290
滾	J5e78 / M18098	3297
漬	J4452 / M18167	3301
演	J3169 / M18130	3310
熔	J4d50 / M19319	3458
熕	J5f70 / M19321	3462
燧	J5f7c / M19469	3484
獗	J6055 / M20671	3605
瑳	J3a3c / M21170	3667
瑱	JX / M21167	3668
瑣	J6074 / M21147	3674
皴	J7369 / M22887	3881
睿	J624f / M23536	3949
睾	J6250 / M23535	3951
碩	J6273 / MX	4023
磁	J3c27 / M24364	4029
禎	JX / M24767	4100
箕	J4c27 / M26143	4307
絣	J6533 / M27429	4478
綱	J394b / M27576	4525
網	J4c56 / M27577	4527
総	J416d / M27620	4532
聡	J416f / M29109	4730
蜷	J6970 / M33199	5339
誤	J386d / M35546′	5626
説	J4062 / M35556′	5627
賓	JX / M36788	5804
賖	JX / MX	5805
賑	J4678 / M36785	5806
辣	J6d65 / M38646	6001
遵	J3d65 / M39118′	6112
選	J412a / M39127′	6114

13 residual strokes

14 residual strokes

簣 J644f/M26524 4354
簀 J6450/M26541 4356
縢 J6558/M27783 4558
縒 J6553/M27751 4559
縉 JX/MX 4563
縊 J6550/M27738 4568
縦 J3d44/M27804′ 4571
繚 J6567/M27904 4592
繕 J4136/M27893 4594
藤 J4623/M32340′ 5241
蟖 JX/M33578 5385
豐 J6c34/M36304 5740
贓 JX/M36904 5824
贇 J6c53/M36907 5825
贅 J6c54/M36908 5826
贈 J4223/M36920′ 5827
蹟 J4058/M37814 5905
輿 J4d41/M38468 5983
邇 J6d6e/M39193 6122
邃 J6364/M39191 6123
鎚 J444a/MX 6281
鎹 J6f31/M40766 6309
鎚 JX/M40715 6310
鍔 J4457/M40617 6313
鎰 J6f2d/M40747 6319
鎗 J4179/M40709 6320
鎬 J6f2e/M40741 6321
鎍 JX/M40694 6322
鏈 J6f3a/M40779 6323
鎧 J333b/M40735 6324
鎖 J3a3f/M40708′ 6325
鎌 J3379/M40693 6326
鎔 J6f30/M40704 6327
鎮 J4443/M40745 6328
鎭 J6f2f/M40744 6329
闕 J6f6d/M41456 6417
闘 J462e/M45649′ 6418
顋 J707b/M43576 6642
顎 J335c/M43590 6643
額 J335b/M43586 6644
顕 J3832/M43609′ 6646
類 J4e60/M43608′ 6647
顔 J3469/M43591′ 6648
顏 J707a/M43591 6649
騏 J7156/M44818 6757
鬆 J7222/M45484 6813
魍 J7233/M45869 6839
鵙 J7326/M46947 6965
鵜 J312d/M46952 6971
鼕 J736a/M48341 7077

17 residual strokes

嚬 JX/M4562 922
嬾 J554f/M6872 1276
寳 J5570/M7366 1369
寵 J437e/M7368 1370
懶 J5871/M11455 2010
曝 J4778/M14239 2524
曠 J5b25/M14245 2525
櫃 J5d24/M15757 2898
櫝 JX/M15821 2907
瀧 J426d/M18671 3376
瀬 J4025/M18672′ 3384
瀨 JX/M18672 3385
爆 J477a/M19540 3505
犢 J6039/M20196 3551
獺 J605c/M20782 3615
禰 JX/M24851 4115
籔 J4876/M26609 4363
簾 J4e7c/M26616 4365
績 J4053/M27845 4579
繪 J6569/M27939 4597
繹 J6568/M27975 4599
羹 J663d/M28584 4672
臀 JX/M29940 4881
艤 J675f/M30565 4949
艶 J3170/M30632 4957
藾 J6941/M32405 5245
蘋 J6940/M32435 5248
蟻 J3542/M33672 5397
證 J6b7a/M35946 5697
譜 J4968/M35990 5703
譜 JX/MX 5707
譽 J6c25/M36066 5708
谿 J6c30/M36219 5734
贓 JX/M36904 5824
贍 JX/M36929 5828
贊 J6c55/M36935 5829
贋 J6c56/M36909 5831
蹲 J6d2d/M37874 5912
辭 J6d66/M38671 6004
鏈 J6f3a/M40779 6323
鏥 J6f35/M40821 6330
鏁 JX/M40770 6331
鏐 J6f39/M40789 6332
鏑 J452d/M40790 6334
鏨 J6f34/M40824 6335
鏃 J6f37/M40772 6336
鏘 J6f36/M40802 6337
鏤 J6f3b/M40820 6339
鏝 J6f38/M40807 6340
鏡 J3640/M40812 6341
韻 J3124/M43307 6611
顎 J335c/M43590 6643
類 JX/M43636 6650
顚 JX/M43628 6651
顛 J453f/MX 6652
鶉 JX/M47034 6976
麒 J734a/M47657 7025
黼 J7365/M48252 7070

18 residual strokes

瀕 J494e/M18636 3381
瀲 J5f52/M18693 3387
瀰 J5f50/M18690 3389
牘 J6031/M19906 3530
犧 J603a/M20209 3552
礦 J6268/M24564 4057
竇 J6365/M25695 4220
籏 J6459/MX 4366
繚 J6567/M27904 4592
繕 J4136/M27893 4594
辮 J6570/M27991 4604
繽 J656f/M27999 4606
蘭 JX/M32519 5257
蘚 J6945/M32483 5262
襭 J6b23/M34702 5508
譱 J6641/M36028 5706
譽 J6c25/M36066 5708
譯 J6c23/M36023 5709
譬 J6c22/M36019 5712
譲 J3e79/M36037′ 5714
議 J3544/M36027 5716
贍 J6c58/M36945 5832
蹼 J6d2e/M37889 5909
躄 J6d32/M37913 5915
躃 JX/M37912 5916
軆 J6d3d/M38157 5937
醴 J6e54/M40053 6195
醸 J3e7a/M40064′ 6197
釋 J6e59/M40129 6205
鋋 J6e7b/M40534 6289
鎍 JX/M40694 6322
鏗 J6f33/M40801 6333
鐵 J6f45/MX 6342
鐺 J4c7a/MX 6343
鐇 J6f40/M40874 6344
鐐 J6f41/M40886 6345
鐙 J462a/M40904 6348
鐫 J6f43/M40924 6349
鐃 J6f3f/M40867 6350
鐚 J6f3c/M40907 6351
鐘 J3e62/M40902 6352
騫 J715a/M44894 6765
騰 J462d/M44915′ 6767
鬪 J722c/M45649 6825
鰌 J7255/M46330 6899
麒 J734a/M47657 7025

19 residual strokes

囂 J536f/M4616 930
欄 JX/M15904 2915
櫻 J5d2f/M15888 2917
欅 JX/MX 2918
欅 J5d30/M15883 2919
瓔 J607d/M21347 3685
癪 J617b/M22626 3853
癩 J617a/M22622 3854
籐 J645b/M26693 4373
繪 J6569/M27939 4597
繹 J6568/M27975 4599
續 J6574/M28037 4610

20 residual strokes

21 residual strokes

22 residual strokes

23 residual strokes

24 residual strokes

25 residual strokes

26–29 residual strokes

Rad. 13 冂

0 residual strokes

1 residual stroke

2 residual strokes

3 residual strokes

4 residual strokes

5 residual strokes

甫 J4a63/M21706 3722
甬 J6135/M21707 3723
角 J3351/M35003 5543

6 residual strokes

侖 J5055/M599 176
兩 J5140/M1436 368
冐 J666e/M1534 **393**
周 J3c7e/M3441′ 768
尚 J3e30/M7493 1395
岡 J322c/M7962 1460
廻 JX/M9573 1655
柯 JX/MX 2566
枘 JX/M14552 2579
罔 J6628/M28211 4635
肭 J666d/M29305 4765
苒 J6772/M30776 4989
迥 J6d6a/M38786 6025
陋 J6f7b/M41616 6438
雨 J312b/M42210 6518
青 JX/M42564 6558

7 residual strokes

俑 J505c/M683 206
冒 JX/M1538 **394**
冑 J5149/M1537 **395**
南 J466e/M2750 619
咼 J5325/M3573 775
恫 J5778/M10594 1837
扁 J5928/M11724 2055
昞 JX/M13835 2438
昺 JX/M13836 2439
柵 J3a74/M14665 2620
柄 J4a41/M14603 2627
洞 J4636/M17386 3125
炳 J5f5b/M18960 3407
烔 J5f57/M18956 3408
珊 J3b39/M20917 3630
禹 J633b/M24885 4118
禺 J633c/M24886 4119
冐 JX/MX 4777
舡 JX/M30362 4928
衲 J6a55/M34130 5430
逈 J6d6a/M38786 6025
陋 J6f7b/M41616 6438

8 residual strokes

倫 J4e51/M793 246
冓 J514a/M1540 **396**
凋 J437c/M1668 423
剛 J3964/M2042 497
圃 J4a60/M4774 954
敝 J5a49/M13245 2347
旃 J5a53/M13640 2394
栴 J4073/M14737 2651
桐 J364d/M14770 2655
病 J4942/M22127 3798
痌 JX/MX 3799
納 J473c/M27264 4453
胴 J4639/M29436 4810
般 J484c/M30388 4931
舫 J6756/M30386 4932
航 J3952/M30385 4933
蚋 J6952/M32850 5286
週 J3d35/M38937′ 6070
高 J3962/M45313 6796
鬲 J722f/M45672 6831

9 residual strokes

冕 J514b/M1545 **397**
商 J3e26/M3803 832
圊 JX/M4797 958
嵛 J5646/M8183 1478
崘 J5647/M8182 1479
崗 J563e/M8221 1483
彫 J4426/M9995 1719
徜 JX/M10149 1751
惆 J582f/M10757 1881
惘 J5831/M10809 1883
掣 J595a/M12277 2183
敝 J5a49/M13245 2347
敞 J5a48/M13246 2348
淌 J5e45/M17629 3171
淪 J5e4d/M17675 3186
烱 J5f58/M19040 3422
猜 J604a/M20499 3584
箭 JX/M25938 4266
絅 J6525/M27375 4460
舸 J6757/M30404 4934
舳 J6758/M30397 4935
舶 J4775/M30402 4936
舵 J4249/M30400 4937
舷 J383f/M30403 4938
船 J4125/M30407 4939
菁 J6847/M31136 5072
訥 J6b44/M35274 5566
週 J3d35/M38937′ 6070
遇 J3678/M38991′ 6083
遍 J4a57/M39001′ 6086
過 J3261/M39002′ 6090
隅 J3679/M41743 6467
高 JX/M45314 6797

10 residual strokes

喩 J5348/M3979 839
喬 J362c/M3990 841
喃 J5347/M3903 846
喚 J342d/M3953 852
堝 J5446/M5247 1047
寓 J3677/M7243 1348
属 J4230/M7754 1430
嵎 J564a/M8281 1494
徧 JX/M10174 1757
惘 J5831/M10809 1883
惼 JX/M10872 1908
揣 J5965/M12371 2227
換 J3439/M12358 2233
換 JX/MX 2234
敞 J5a48/M13246 2348
棆 J5c32/M14916 2716
棡 J5b7c/M14955 2719
渦 J3132/M17771 3241
滿 J4b7e/M17921′ 3248
猯 J604e/M20540 3591
献 J3825/M20539 3596
筒 J457b/M26004 4283
策 J3a76/M26009 4284
粡 J6469/M26928 4397
納 J473c/M27264 4453
艇 J447a/M30440 4941
萬 J685f/M31339 5103
萵 J6862/M31351 5108
蹁 J6c69/M37477 5863
適 J6e28/M39030 6078
遇 J3678/M38991′ 6083
遍 J4a57/M39001′ 6086
過 J3261/M39002′ 6090
隔 J3356/MX 6475
隔 JX/M41783 6476
鞆 J7058/M42747 6575
黹 J7363/M48248 7068

11 residual strokes

嗣 J3b4c/M4109 868
塙 J4839/M5341 1063
媾 J553d/M6597 1253
嵎 J564a/M8281 1494
嵩 J3f73/M8348 1502
愚 J3672/M10946 1925
搆 J596c/M12447 2242
楠 J466f/M15152 2779
溝 J3942/M17944 3275
漓 J5f22/M18127 3292
瑁 J6070/M21096 3661
瑞 J3f70/M21131 3665
禍 J3252/M24766′ 4102
稠 J6347/M25130 4150
舷 J383f/M30403 4938
艇 J447a/M30440 4941
蒿 J6866/M31634 5147
裔 J6a63/M34303 5459
褊 J6a6c/M34356 5469
輛 JX/M38287 5954
輌 J6d52/MX 5955
遘 J6e29/M39031 6096
適 J452c/M39076′ 6107
鞆 J7058/M42747 6575

12 residual strokes

亂 J502c/M214 64

亂 JX/MX 65
僑 J3623/M1088 307
像 JX/M48923 309
廠 J5252/M3034 658
厲 JX/MX 659
嫡 J4364/M6656 1263
幣 J5672/MX 1586
摘 J4526/M12582 2266
敲 J5a4a/M13337 2354
敵 JX/M13338 2355
槁 J5c49/M15300 2806
構 J393d/M15317 2823
滿 J5e60/M18099 3283
潿 J5f22/M18127 3292
滴 J4529/M18084 3299
爾 J3c24/M19750 3521
犒 J6037/M20114 3549
璃 J4d7e/M21196 3669
禍 JX/M24766 4103
稱 J634a/M25180 4155
窩 J635d/M25579 4208
端 J433c/M25806 4243
綢 J6542/M27546 4506
綸 J6545/M27583 4519
綱 J394b/M27576 4525
網 J4c56/M27577 4527
膈 J672d/M29772 4856
蔽 J4a43/M31888 5193
崗 JX/M33201 5315
蜩 J6973/M33166 5334
蜻 J6971/M33203 5341
裔 J6a63/M34303 5459
製 J403d/M34380 5476
褊 J6a6f/M34420 5481
適 J452c/M39076′ 6107
銅 J463c/M40361 6266
需 J3c7b/M42275 6528
鞆 J705d/M42794 6580
髯 JX/M45375 6801

13 residual strokes

嘱 J3e7c/M4249 894
嬌 J5548/M6739 1268
幣 J4a3e/M9088 1585
廠 J3e33/M9490 1643
擒 J5a22/M12816 2289
敵 J4528/M13354 2359
璃 J4d7e/M21196 3669
稿 J3946/M25220 4166
稾 J634c/M25219 4167
篇 J4a53/M26257 4324
綸 J6545/M27583 4519
綱 J3946/M27576 4525
編 J4a54/M27665 4552
翩 J6649/M28762 4688
艘 J675b/M30511 4942
蔽 J4a43/M31888 5193
蕎 J363e/M31946 5197
蝙 J697e/M33271 5360
蝸 J6977/M33338 5362
製 J403d/M34380 5476
論 J4f40/M35658 5646
輛 J6d51/M38361 5969
輪 J4e58/M38400 5973
邁 J6e32/M39169 6110
餉 J712e/M44140 6687
髯 J7179/M45404 6809

14 residual strokes

儒 J3c74/M1220 330
勵 J522f/M2472 562
嚆 J5365/M4458 908
墺 J5454/M5504 1100
擒 J5a22/M12816 2289
橡 JX/MX 2864
橘 J354c/M15551 2868
橋 J3636/M15526 2879
檎 J3869/M15657 2888
瞞 J6256/M23649 3956
瞥 J4a4d/M23672 3959
篝 J6440/M26320 4340
綸 J6545/M27583 4519
綱 J394b/M27576 4525
網 J4c56/M27577 4527
縞 J3c4a/M27777 4569
艘 J675b/M30511 4942
艙 J673a/M30516 4943
融 J4d3b/M33384 5371
邁 J6e32/M39169 6110
鋼 J395d/M40509 6302
雕 J703a/M42080 6509
静 J7050/M42578 6561
靛 JX/M42577 6562

15 residual strokes

彌 J573d/M9877 1703
懦 J586f/M11390 2005
擿 JX/M12922 2299
檎 J3869/M15657 2888
濔 J5f3e/M18482 3357
濡 J4728/M18504 3365
瞥 J4a4d/M23672 3959
矯 J363a/M24015 3984
篩 J6449/M26494 4349
編 J4a54/M27665 4552
藁 J4f4e/M32222 5234
覯 J6b32/M34937 5535
講 J3956/M35824 5689
購 J3958/M36885 5823
邇 J6d6e/M39193 6122
鍋 J4669/M40603 6315
鮞 JX/M46105 6857
黻 J7364/M48250 7069
龠 J737e/M48882 7107

16 residual strokes

嚮 JX/M4565 919
嚮 J536c/MX 920
彌 J573d/M9877 1703
懣 J5070/M11384 2004
擿 JX/M12922 2299
攜 JX/M12924 2308
礇 J6325/M24505 4051
礪 J626a/M24571 4056
禰 J4729/MX 4116
縞 J3c4a/M27777 4569
繭 J4b7a/M27944 4595
臑 J6742/M29986 4885
藕 J6939/M32298 5239
謫 J6b73/M35868 5694
蹣 J6d2a/M37822 5907
邇 J6d6e/M39193 6122
鎬 J6f2e/M40741 6321
離 J4e25/M42140 6517
魍 J7233/M45869 6839
魎 J7234/M45870 6840

17 residual strokes

彌 J573d/M9877 1703
瀰 JX/M18659 3380
璽 J3c25/M21309 3683
礪 J626a/M24571 4056
禰 JX/M24851 4115
臋 JX/M29940 4881
艨 J6761/M30574 4948
艤 J675f/M30565 4949
襦 J6b21/M34678 5506
謪 J6b79/M35956 5701
轎 J6d5d/M38532 5987
辭 J6d66/M38671 6004
鏑 J452d/M40790 6334
離 J4e25/M42140 6517
騙 J7159/M44849 6763
鯛 J4264/M46226′ 6884
黼 J7365/M48252 7070

18 residual strokes

嚮 JX/M4565 919
濔 J5f50/M18690 3389
糯 J6479/M27173 4428
繭 J4b7a/M27944 4595
繻 J656c/M27996 4609
艦 J344f/M30571 4950
蠣 J695a/M33799 5399
蠕 J6a40/M33749 5400
讁 JX/M36091 5717
魑 J7235/M45901 6842

Rad. 15 冫

椴 J464e / M15075 2772
楓 J4976 / M15126 2779
毀 J544c / M16654 3000
殿 J4542 / M16651 3001
蝋 J4f39 / M-X 5332
凳 J6c6f / M37519 5870
頽 J7072 / M43371 6620
鳬 J726a / M46643 6933

12 residual strokes

廏 J567e / M9453 1635
慇 J5840 / M11045 1942
攄 J-X / M12674 2257
槃 J5c51 / M15303 2805
瘋 J6166 / M22322 3827
穀 J3972 / M25188' 4157
蕁 J-X / M-X 5164
颯 J7125 / M43808 6665
颱 J7126 / M43815 6666
骰 J716d / M45127 6786
鳳 J4b31 / M46671 6937

13 residual strokes

廢 J5726 / M9492 1639
擊 J3762 / M12674' 2265
撥 J597b / M12727 2283
毆 J5d58 / M16674 3002
毅 J3523 / M16673 3003
潑 J-X / M18225 3325
癈 J616d / M22405 3830
盤 J4857 / M23036 3902
磐 J4858 / M24401 4037
穀 J-X / M25221 4160
緞 J654b / M27646 4546
褫 J6a75 / M34504 5488
輦 J705f / M42819 6585

14 residual strokes

澱 J4543 / M18410 3347
磬 J627e / M24454 4042
築 J435b / M26298 4343
縠 J-X / M27067 4417
薇 J692f / M32092 5209
諷 J6b65 / M35741 5669
轂 J6d58 / M38479 5979
頹 J7078 / M43517 6636
颫 J-X / M43840 6667

15 residual strokes

具 J-X / M12800 2287
燬 J5f7b / M19478 3494
瘢 J6173 / M22520 3841
緞 J654b / M27646 4546
緊 J3752 / M-X 4573
翳 J664a / M28796 4691
聲 J6661 / M29166 4736
臀 J673d / M29939 4880
鍛 J4343 / M40625 6318
颶 J7127 / M43876 6668

16 residual strokes

燬 J5f7b / M19478 3494
癜 J6175 / M22570 3845
謦 J6b72 / M35856 5692
醫 J6e50 / M40006 6190

17 residual strokes

瀛 J5f4a / M18656 3378
繋 J3752 / M-X 4573
繫 J-X / M27940 4601
臋 J-X / M29940 4881
醱 J-X / M40041 6194
鯱 J724f / M46286 6885
麗 J4e6f / M47663 7026

18 residual strokes

贏 J6c57 / M36950 5833
飄 J7128 / M43946 6669
飃 J7129 / M43945 6670
馨 J333e / M44559 6724
麗 J4e6f / M47663 7026

19–26 residual strokes

儷 J5136 / M1311 336
巷 J-X / M14266 2528
灑 J5f53 / M18774 3392
繫 J-X / M27940 4601
羸 J6640 / M28583 4674
鑿 J6f58 / M41088 6378
飆 J712a / M43963 6671

Rad. 17 凵

0 residual strokes

凵 J5161 / M1800 **441**

1 residual stroke

山 J3b33 / M7869 1439

2 residual strokes

卅 J5242 / M32 15
凶 J3627 / M1803 **442**
屯 J4656 / M7828 1438

3 residual strokes

凸 J464c / M1809 **443**
凹 J317a / M1810 **444**
出 J3d50 / M1811 **445**
古 J-X / M2714 609

4 residual strokes

兇 J3624 / M1348 347
凸 J464c / M1809 **443**
凹 J317a / M1810 **444**
臼 J3131 / M30173 4907

5 residual strokes

凸 J464c / M1809 **443**
凹 J317a / M1810 **444**
怞 J-X / M10392 1791

6 residual strokes

函 J4821 / M1826 **446**
凾 J5162 / M1830 **447**
咄 J5274 / M3480 761
屆 J557c / M7666 1414
画 J3268 / M21739' 3733

7 residual strokes

凾 J5162 / M1830 **447**
幽 J4d29 / M9205 1600
恟 J576f / M10573 1833
洶 J5e28 / M17417 3112

8 residual strokes

悩 J473a / M10716' 1867
涵 J-X / M17595 3183
胸 J363b / M29442 4811
匘 J722e / M45661 6829

9–10 residual strokes

歯 J3b75 / M16323 2961
涵 J-X / M17595 3183
涵 J5e3e / M-X 3184
脳 J473e / M29567' 4821

11 residual strokes

幽 J4d29 / M9205 1600
樓 J5c24 / M15078 2755
漓 J5f22 / M18127 3292

13–15 residual strokes

擒 J5a22 / M12816 2289
檎 J3869 / M15657 2888

齒 J736f/M48583 7088
齔 J7370/M48587 7089

16–17 residual strokes

嚙 J337a/M-X 888
豐 J6c34/M36304 5740
離 J4e25/M42140 6517
壚 J-X/M47550 7012

18 residual strokes

齠 J7373/M48631 7090
齣 J7371/M48638 7091
齝 J-X/M48622 7092
齢 J4e70/M48632′ 7093
齡 J7374/M48632 7094
齟 J7372/M48627 7095

19–27 residual strokes

囓 J5377/M4659 934
鏤 J6f47/M-X 6359
鬱 J5d35/M45671 6830
齦 J7375/M48649 7096
齧 J7376/M48651 7097
齬 J7377/M48680 7098
齪 J7378/M48669 7099
齶 J737b/M48725 7100
齷 J7379/M48727 7101
齲 J737a/M48716 7102

Rad. 18 刀

0 residual strokes

刀 J4561/M1845 **448**

1 residual stroke

刃 J3f4f/M1850 **449**
刅 J-X/M1848 **450**
刄 J5163/M1849 **451**

2 residual strokes

刈 J3422/M1859 **452**
切 J405a/M1858 **453**
分 J4a2c/M1853 **454**
匁 J4c68/M2502 566
辺 J4a55/M38710′ 6011

3 residual strokes

仞 J5040/M379 115
仭 J-X/M-X 116
仭 J5041/M397 117
刋 J5164/M1866 **455**
刊 J3429/M1865 **456**
叨 J525b/M3237 686
召 J3e24/M3241 695
岃 J5627/M-X 1441
辺 J4a55/M38710′ 6011

4 residual strokes

刕 J-X/M1899 **457**
刔 J5165/M1897 **458**
刎 J5166/M1879 **459**
列 J4e73/M1901 **460**
刑 J373a/M1886 **461**
扨 J592e/M11824 2064
杒 J5b37/M14432 2539

5 residual strokes

兎 J-X/M1358 352
刧 J5167/M1927 **462**
刦 J-X/M1926 **463**
删 J5168/M1917 **464**
判 J483d/M1923 **465**
利 J4d78/M1932 **466**
別 J4a4c/M1924 **467**
䉶 J-X/M1925 **468**
初 J3d69/M1911 **469**
封 J-X/M1955 **470**
劭 J5223/M2318 526
吩 J5266/M3347 725
岔 J562b/M7944 1446
忍 J4726/M10312′ 1787
痴 J-X/M10312 1788
扮 J4a31/M11830 2080
汾 J5d70/M17178 3051
苅 J3423/M30771 4969
芬 J676e/M30728 4973
邵 J6e3a/M39343 6133

6 residual strokes

例 J4e63/M587 193
兔 J-X/M1368′ 360
洌 J5158/M1637 420
封 J-X/M1955 **470**
刮 J-X/M1975 **471**
刮 J5169/M1943 **472**
券 J3774/M1966 **473**
刹 J516b/M1967 **474**
刳 J516a/M1956 **475**
看 J-X/M-X **476**
到 J457e/M1950 **477**
刻 J396f/M1970 **478**
刷 J3a7e/M1964 **479**
刺 J3b49/M1969 **480**
制 J4029/M1961 **481**
忿 J575d/M10408 1798
拐 J327d/M11955 2107
拐 J-X/M-X 2108
招 J3e37/M11968 2124
枌 J5b43/M14534 2573
氛 J5d64/M17048 3027
沼 J3e42/M17257 3091
砐 J6127/M21465 3695
岆 J-X/M-X 5412
迢 J6d6b/M38781 6024

7 residual strokes

俐 J505e/M682 208
荊 J-X/M-X 379
看 J-X/M-X **476**
剅 J-X/M-X **482**
剄 J516d/M1990 **483**
剌 J516f/M2010 **484**
捌 J516c/M2024 **485**
剋 J516e/M2009 **486**
則 J4227/M1994 **487**
削 J3a6f/M2000 **488**
剃 J4466/M1989 **489**
前 J4130/M2011 **490**
勉 J-X/M-X 537
型 J373f/M5030 1010
奕 J5475/M5922 1154
契 J3740/M5917 1155
挈 J594d/M12035 2133
昭 J3e3c/M13855 2446
枴 J5b4a/M14584 2601
洌 J5e30/M17364 3115
砐 J6127/M21465 3695
盆 J4b5f/M22959 3889
砌 J6266/M24062 3988
窃 J4060/M25453 4195
蚡 J6369/M25740 4227
粉 J4c62/M26857 4384
籾 J-X/M26853 4385
荔 J682d/M30866 5024
荊 J3755/M-X 5027
荆 J-X/M30940 5028
峋 J6a49/M33971 5413
貟 J-X/M36660 5770
迢 J6d6b/M38781 6024

8 residual strokes

倒 J455d/M767 256
剅 J-X/M-X **482**
剃 J4466/M1989 **489**
剞 J5170/M2054 **491**
剖 J4b36/M2034 **492**
剤 J3a5e/M2076′ **493**
剔 J5171/M2031 **494**
剝 J-X/M2049 **495**
剥 J476d/M48939 **496**
剛 J3964/M2042 **497**

秕 J633e/M24958 4126
窃 J4060/M25453 4195
背 J4758/M29363 4794
虐 J3554/M32678′ 5266
陛 J4a45/M41654 6444

8 residual strokes

垂 J5431/M5104 1012
埖 J5442/M-X 1014
柴 J3c46/M14664 2657
毘 J487b/M16753 3011
毗 J-X/M16752 3012
皆 J3327/M22699 3869
眤 J6242/M23247 3922
眞 J6243/M23235 3927
砒 J6267/M24068 3989
秕 J633e/M24958 4126
粃 J6463/M26861 4388
紕 J6523/M27279 4443
耄 J664e/M28848 4699
耆 J664d/M28849 4701
脂 J3b69/M29463 4808
能 J473d/M29454 4809
虔 J694a/M32686 5267
陛 J4a45/M41654 6444
鬯 J722e/M45661 6829

9 residual strokes

偕 J5073/M855 269
匙 J3a7c/M2590 **582**
喝 J3365/M-X 824
崑 J5642/M8173 1484
揭 J3747/M12311′ 2194
既 J-X/M13724 2408
既 J-X/M13725 2409
梍 J5b74/M14839 2680
梐 J3371/M15065 2683
欸 J-X/M16085 2933
欸 J5d37/M16090 2934
渴 J3369/M17748 3195
混 J3a2e/M17694 3204
疵 J6153/M22089 3805
皆 J6244/M23250 3929
眦 J6245/M23251 3930
砦 J3a56/M24098 4002
粃 J6463/M26861 4388
紕 J6523/M27279 4443
舵 J4249/M30400 4937
葛 J336b/M-X 5060
菎 J6842/M31160 5088
蓖 J-X/M-X 5089
處 J515d/M32697 5268
蛇 J3c50/M32964 5303
訛 J6b42/M35256 5568
豼 J6c41/M36504 5756
貨 J325f/M36678 5781
階 J332c/M41755 6469
頃 J3a22/M43338 6615
鹿 J3c2f/M47586 7017
麁 J7346/M47591 7018

10 residual strokes

傾 J3739/M1038 299
卿 J-X/M2880 643
卿 J-X/M2879 644
唧 J-X/M3961 844
唧 J5344/M-X 845
崑 J5642/M8173 1484
揩 J5962/M12383 2223
既 J-X/M13724 2408
既 J-X/M13725 2409
棍 J5b7e/M14924 2735
殷 J-X/M16645 2999
混 J3a2e/M17694 3204
焜 J5f63/M19103 3432
琥 J6068/M21061 3651
琵 J487c/M21080 3653
硫 J626d/M-X 4003
紫 J3b67/M27337 4486
菎 J6842/M31160 5088
蓖 J-X/M-X 5089
葬 J4172/M31448′ 5128
蓖 J686f/M31626 5152
虚 J-X/M32709 5270
蛯 J6962/M33061 5306
詑 J4242/M35374 5579
豼 J6c41/M36504 5756
鄉 J-X/M-X 6151
階 J332c/M41755 6469
鹿 J3c2f/M47586 7017
麁 J7346/M47591 7018

11 residual strokes

傾 J3739/M1038 299
厩 J3139/M-X 654
嗔 J5351/M4074 866
嗜 J534f/M4089 870
塡 J-X/M5355 1071
填 J4536/M-X 1072
慎 J5846/M11024 1946
揩 J5962/M12383 2223
棍 J5b7e/M14924 2735
楷 J5c34/M15185 2781
焜 J5f63/M19103 3432
琵 J487c/M21080 3653
糀 J6471/M27013 4406
肆 J6667/M29224 4750
蓍 J6869/M31655 5137
蓖 J686f/M31626 5152
虜 J3673/M32723′ 5272
虜 J4e3a/M32720′ 5273
褐 J336c/M-X 5473
觜 J6b39/M35050 5546
詣 J3758/M35412 5594
貲 J6c47/M36702 5797
遞 J6e2a/M39045 6095
鉈 J6e6d/M40289 6242
靴 J3724/M42729 6576

12 residual strokes

厩 J-X/M3006 660
嘗 J3e28/M4205 878
墟 J-X/M-X 1080
塵 J3f50/M5388 1087
廄 J567e/M9453 1635
廐 J567d/M9454 1636
愼 J5846/M11024 1946
態 J4256/M11052 1947
慨 J-X/M11122 1974
擄 J-X/M12674 2257
楷 J5c34/M15185 2781
槇 J7422/M15310 2818
滬 J3977/M18112 3300
熊 J3727/M19294 3468
瑱 J-X/M21167 3668
疑 J353f/M22007 3777
瘧 J616a/M22419 3826
篦 J6431/M26157 4303
篦 J4a4f/M26114 4310
節 J-X/M26243 4320
紫 J3b67/M27337 4486
遞 J6e2a/M39045 6095
雌 J3b73/M41998 6506

13 residual strokes

噓 J-X/M4206 885
塵 J3f50/M5388 1087
墟 J5452/M5437 1090
廐 J567d/M9454 1636
態 J4256/M11052 1947
慮 J4e38/M11132 1962
慨 J-X/M11122 1974
戲 J353a/M11665 2041
槪 J-X/M15364 2860
穎 J5e73/M18188 3295
滬 J3977/M18112 3300
瞋 J6253/M23568 3953
稽 J374e/M25218 4163
篦 J6431/M26157 4303
篦 J4a4f/M26114 4310
罷 J486d/M28336 4650
膚 J4966/M29829 4867
褫 J6a75/M34504 5488
謁 J315a/M35690′ 5637
錵 J6f26/M40591 6273
駝 J714c/M44681 6740
鴇 J463e/M46730 6943

Rad. 22 匚

Rad. 23 匸

Rad. 24 十

11 residual strokes

12 residual strokes

13 residual strokes

14 residual strokes

15 residual strokes

懐 J327b/M11351 2003
戴 J4257/M11685 2045
擿 J-X/M12922 2299
禪 J6338/M24835 4110
聴 J4430/M29173 4740
蟒 J6a3c/M33724 5373
蟀 J6a2b/M33531 5379
蠎 J-X/M-X 5383
襌 J6a7b/M34593 5500
譁 J6b76/M35928 5674
鞜 J7061/M42883 6588
鞠 J3547/M42892 6589
韓 J345a/M43159 6602

16 residual strokes

嚔 J5369/M4501 917
擿 J-X/M12922 2299
瀟 J5f4f/M18660 3383
瞽 J625c/M23745 3968
禪 J6338/M24835 4110
簟 J6452/M26510 4353
簫 J6454/M26560 4355
簞 J-X/M26509 4357
蟬 J-X/M33616 5388
謫 J6b73/M35868 5694
蹕 J6d2b/M37783 5904
鏉 J-X/M40694 6322
鎮 J4443/M40745 6328
鞫 J6b71/M42931 6593
鞣 J7064/M42909 6594
鞭 J4a5c/M42937 6595
餬 J7137/M44255 6704
髀 J716f/M45205 6790
鼕 J736a/M48341 7077

17 residual strokes

瀚 J5f4b/M18652 3379
簞 J-X/M26509 4357
蟀 J6a2b/M33531 5379
蟬 J-X/M33616 5388
覇 J4746/M34790 5519
譚 J6b7d/M35978 5696
鏑 J452d/M40790 6334
鞴 J7066/M42972 6596
顛 J453f/M-X 6652
驒 J424d/M-X 6762
鶻 J732b/M47010 6972
麴 J-X/M47818 7037

18 residual strokes

廳 J572d/M9552 1649
讁 J-X/M36091 5717
鏉 J-X/M40694 6322
鐵 J6f45/M-X 6342
鐔 J6f3d/M40893 6347
闡 J6f71/M41489 6421
韃 J-X/M42997 6597
麵 J-X/M47827 7039

19 residual strokes

囀 J5373/M4614 927
讁 J-X/M36091 5717
鏽 J-X/M40857 6353
鐵 J6f44/M40945 6354
霸 J5b31/M42490 6547
鶇 J7337/M-X 6991

20 residual strokes

囊 J-X/M4633 933
聽 J6665/M29211 4744
鱆 J7263/M46464 6913

21–23 residual strokes

欄 J-X/M15945 2921
欗 J-X/M15971 2925
矗 J6260/M23836 3971
蠹 J6a45/M33896 5407
覊 J-X/M34794 5520
韈 J707e/M43737 6659
鱣 J-X/M46488 6919
鱓 J-X/M46496 6920

Rad. 25 卜

0 residual strokes

卜 J4b4e/M2774 **622**

1 residual stroke

下 J323c/M14 9
上 J3e65/M13 10

2 residual strokes

丐 J5022/M22 11
仆 J503d/M354 103
卞 J5246/M2778 **623**
支 J5a3d/M13108 2326
止 J3b5f/M16253 2954

3 residual strokes

占 J406a/M2780 **624**
外 J3330/M5750 1125
斥 J-X/M-X 2381
正 J4035/M16255 2955
疋 J4925/M21994 3774

4 residual strokes

丐 J5022/M22 11
圷 J542a/M4900 972
延 J-X/M9569 1653
朴 J4b51/M14428 2544
正 J4035/M16255 2955
此 J3a21/M16259 2956
虍 J6948/M32674 5264
阯 J6f77/M41570 6427

5 residual strokes

帖 J4421/M8849 1558
延 J-X/M9569 1653
扑 J5937/M11860 2077
步 J-X/M16264 2957
沚 J5d6d/M17213 3053
走 J4176/M37034 5845
足 J422d/M37365 5856
迠 J-X/M38777 6028

6 residual strokes

些 J3a33/M268 84
卓 J426e/M2741 616
卦 J3735/M2798 **625**
叔 J3d47/M3154 677
咎 J-X/M-X 760
卣 J-X/M5909 1145
定 J446a/M7109 1323
岾 J5633/M-X 1450
庇 J485f/M9239 1606
店 J4539/M9267 1613
延 J3164/M-X 1657
拈 J5940/M11945 2106
歩 J4a62/M16284 2958
沾 J5d7e/M17259 3072
祉 J3b63/M24641 4069
肯 J394e/M29311 4771
卧 J-X/M-X 4897
苫 J4651/M30802 5003
虎 J3857/M32675 5265
迯 J6d6d/M38802 6023
迠 J-X/M38777 6028

7 residual strokes

垰 J543b/M-X 1001
峠 J463d/M8068 1464
是 J4027/M13859 2451
柾 J4b6f/M14675 2619
歪 J4f44/M16286 2960
眦 J-X/M16752 3012
点 J4540/M18980 3412
祉 J-X/M24641 4070
卧 J-X/M-X 4897
莚 J682f/M31059 5040
虐 J3554/M32678 5267
訃 J6b3e/M35214 5554
貞 J4467/M36658 5768
赴 J496b/M37040 5847

迯 J6d6d/M38802 6023
陟 J7022/M41659 6443

8 residual strokes

倬 J506b/M794 233
俶 J5068/M732 236
冦 J514e/M1590 402
捉 J422a/M12136 2159
捗 J-X/M12160 2161
桛 J-X/M14796 2648
眦 J-X/M16752 3012
涉 J-X/M17530 3136
症 J3e49/M22140 3795
晒 J6240/M23182 3913
砧 J354e/M24099 3996
站 J636b/M25742 4231
莚 J682f/M31059 5040
虔 J694a/M32686 5267
起 J352f/M37048 5849
越 J315b/M37110 5851

9 residual strokes

偵 J4465/M898 270
啅 J5336/M3802 815
寇 J5564/M7209 1339
寂 J3c64/M7200 1342
彪 J4937/M9993 1716
從 J574f/M10152 1747
徙 J5750/M10142 1749
悼 J4569/M10738 1891
戚 J404c/M11594 2032
捗 J443d/M-X 2173
掟 J595d/M12272 2180
掉 J595c/M12243 2186
捷 J3e39/M12216 2198
掛 J335d/M12267 2214
梺 J5b72/M14910 2682
淀 J4d64/M17610 3182
渉 J3e44/M17749′ 3190
淑 J3d4a/M17634 3191
渋 J3d42/M17750 3200
晒 J6240/M23182 3913
笘 J6378/M25911 4259
粘 J4734/M26901 4393
菽 J6843/M31241 5068
處 J515d/M32697 5268
虚 J3575/M32700 5269
蛅 J-X/M32961 5296
蛋 J4341/M32977 5301
裃 J6a61/M34282 5447
趾 J6c66/M37406 5858
遉 J6e26/M38993 6082
閇 J6f6a/M41220 6386
雫 J3c36/M42219 6519
鹵 J7343/M47528 7011

10 residual strokes

堽 J544e/M5298 1042
寔 J5566/M7244 1346
幀 J566c/M8982 1570
提 J4473/M12344 2237
椒 J5c25/M15029 2731
棹 J5c2a/M14992 2738
殸 J-X/M16645 2999
湑 J-X/M17829 3227
琥 J6068/M21061 3651
疏 J4141/M22000 3775
疎 J4142/M22002 3776
筵 J6427/M26080 4297
虛 J-X/M32709 5270
蜓 J6963/M33120 5317
覘 J6b2d/M34840 5527
証 J3e5a/M35341 5589
貼 J453d/M36718 5787
越 J315b/M37110 5851
超 J4436/M37096 5852
跚 J6c69/M37477 5863
跑 J-X/M37461 5864
跛 J6c6c/M37479 5865
跋 J6c6d/M37446 5867
跐 J-X/M37447 5868
遉 J6e26/M38993 6082
颪 J7124/M43769 6664

11 residual strokes

堽 J544e/M5298 1042
楚 J413f/M15141 2771
歳 J3a50/M16326′ 2962
睫 J624c/M23469 3944
碇 J4476/M24275 4019
禎 J4477/M24767′ 4099
筵 J6427/M26080 4297
粲 J646c/M26966 4407
罩 J662d/M28289 4640
罫 J3753/M28295 4642
虜 J3673/M32723′ 5272
虜 J4e3a/M32720′ 5273
蜓 J6963/M33120 5317
褂 J6a68/M34401 5467
越 J315b/M37110 5851
跟 J6c70/M37491 5869
跿 J6c6f/M37519 5870
跣 J6c71/M37497 5871
跨 J3859/M37504 5872
践 J4129/M37547′ 5873
跪 J6c6e/M37516 5874
跡 J4057/M37493 5875
路 J4f29/M37524 5876
跳 J4437/M37533 5877
遞 J6e2a/M39045 6095
鉦 J3e60/M40322 6246

12 residual strokes

劇 J3760/M2210 517
墟 J-X/M-X 1080
攄 J-X/M12674 2257
敲 J5a4a/M13337 2354
樅 J-X/M-X 2792
歴 J4e72/M16334′ 2964
滷 J5f23/M18088 3289
疑 J353f/M22007 3777
瘧 J616a/M22419 3826
睿 J624f/M23536 3949
碵 J6273/M-X 4023
禎 J-X/M24767 4100
綻 J433e/M27587 4514
綽 J653f/M27590 4518
聢 J665e/M29113 4729
蔲 J-X/M-X 5172
跨 J3859/M37504 5872
踉 J6c74/M37585 5880
踴 J6c72/M37548 5881
踊 J4d59/M37587 5882
遞 J6e2a/M39045 6095
鞐 J7060/M42829 6583

13 residual strokes

劇 J3760/M2218 517
噓 J-X/M4206 885
嘘 J3133/M-X 886
慼 J-X/M11158 1955
慫 J5851/M11127 1958
慮 J4e38/M11132 1962
樅 J-X/M-X 2792
槭 J5c65/M15369 2835
樅 J5c62/M15404 2838
澁 J5f27/M18312 3314
膚 J4966/M29829 4867
褫 J6a75/M34504 5488
諚 J6b5c/M35682 5631
趣 J3c71/M37207 5854
踐 J6c78/M37608 5883
踞 J6c77/M37642 5885
踠 J-X/M37646 5886
踪 J6d20/M37668 5887
踝 J6c76/M37641 5888
踏 J4627/M37602 5889
錠 J-X/M40469 6270
靛 J-X/M42577 6562
鞐 J7060/M42829 6583
齒 J736f/M48583 7088

14 residual strokes

叡 J3143/M3214 683
戲 J-X/M11668 2043
據 J5a21/M12839 2284
整 J4030/M13394 2360
整 J-X/M13393 2361
歔 J5d41/M16198 2950

Rad. 26 卩

10 residual strokes

偃 J5122/M-X 302
卿 J-X/M2880 **643**
卿 J-X/M2879 **644**
唧 J5332/M3876 825
喞 J-X/M3961 844
喞 J5344/M-X 845
報 J4a73/M5275 1059
御 J3866/M10157 1761
椀 J4f50/M15001 2732
渡 J454f/M17765 3247
腕 J4f53/M29631 4837

11 residual strokes

僊 J-X/M1055 289
卿 J-X/M2879 **644**
碗 J4f52/M24306 4014
節 J4081/M26102 4299
詭 J6b4c/M35434 5603
跪 J6c6e/M37516 5874
鉚 J6e76/M40309 6239

12 residual strokes

孵 J555b/M7021 1301
節 J4061/M26102 4299
蜿 J696f/M33210 5337
蜷 J6970/M33199 5339
遷 J-X/M-X 6103

13 residual strokes

節 J-X/M-X 4319
節 J-X/M26243 4320
範 J484f/M26253 4330
綣 J653c/M27550 4507
豌 J6c32/M36273 5738
踠 J-X/M37646 5886
遷 J-X/M-X 6103

14–21 residual strokes

櫛 J367b/M-X 2884
櫛 J-X/M15817 2909
禦 J357a/M24820 4111
鋺 J6e7c/M40507 6287
韆 J7068/M43075 6600
鮠 J723e/M46112 6860
鴛 J3175/M46795 6953

Rad. 27 厂

0 residual strokes

厂 J524c/M2890 **645**

1 residual stroke

广 J5678/M9221 1602

2 residual strokes

仄 J503c/M352 107
厄 J4c71/M2893 **646**
反 J483f/M3127 674
斤 J3654/M13534 2379

3 residual strokes

卮 J5248/M2846 627
圧 J3035/M4879′ 970
斥 J-X/M-X 2381

4 residual strokes

仮 J323e/M398 144
危 J346d/M2849 **629**
压 J-X/M-X 647
后 J3921/M3298 704
戊 J587c/M11535 2022
戌 J587b/M11537 2023
成 J402e/M11542′ 2025
成 J-X/M11544 2026
灰 J3325/M18859 3396
虍 J6948/M32674 5264
返 J4a56/M38758′ 6020
阨 J6f75/M41559 6425
阪 J3a65/M41562 6428

5 residual strokes

乕 J6949/M148 52
励 J4e65/M2326 528
坂 J3a64/M4910 985
巵 J5662/M8751 1542
成 J-X/M11544 2026
扼 J592f/M11848 2079
汳 J5d72/M17164 3050
辰 J4324/M38682 6006
返 J4a56/M38758′ 6020

6 residual strokes

厓 J-X/M2930 **648**
厚 J387c/M2949 **651**
岸 J345f/M8009 1459
底 J446c/M9262 1612
彼 J4860/M10066 1732
昃 J5a60/M13785 2425
板 J4844/M14518 2595
版 J4847/M19817 3526
茂 J4c50/M30833′ 4998
虎 J3857/M32675 5265
辰 J4324/M38682 6006

7 residual strokes

厖 J524d/M2942 **649**
厘 J4e52/M2946 **650**
厚 J387c/M2949 **651**
叛 J4040/M3166 680
咸 J5279/M3563 774
垢 J3924/M5058 1008
城 J3e6b/M5086′ 1011
城 J-X/M5120 1013
威 J3052/M6259 1219
彦 J4927/M9981 1714
彥 J-X/M9980 1715
恢 J327a/M10577 1843
栃 J464a/M14687 2613
派 J-X/M17427 3127
炭 J433a/M18953 3413
皈 J6227/M22705 3868
盾 J3d62/M23171 3912
虐 J3554/M32678′ 5267

8 residual strokes

原 J3836/M2973 **652**
唇 J3f30/M3697 807
喝 J-X/M3960 834
城 J-X/M5120 1013
娠 J3f31/M6322 1224
宸 J5562/M7171 1331
振 J3f36/M12093 2171
晟 J5a70/M13950 2472
派 J-X/M17427 3127
砺 J4557/M-X 3993
組 J-X/M27294 4442
脆 J4048/M29468 4800
脈 J4c2e/M29470 4805
脈 J-X/M29469 4806
虔 J694a/M32686 5267
辱 J3f2b/M38686 6007

9 residual strokes

修 J5074/M850 262
厠 J524e/M2981 **653**
厩 J3139/M-X **654**
唇 J3f30/M3697 807
啀 J5331/M3789 820
宸 J5562/M7171 1331
崖 J3333/M8180 1488
崕 J563d/M8179 1489
彪 J4937/M9993 1716
戚 J404c/M11594 2032
振 J3f36/M12093 2171
晨 J5a6f/M13962 2476
梔 J5b69/M14846 2692
涯 J3336/M17582 3181

10 residual strokes

11 residual strokes

12 residual strokes

13 residual strokes

14 residual strokes

15 residual strokes

16 residual strokes

17 residual strokes

9 residual strokes

10 residual strokes

11 residual strokes

12 residual strokes

13 residual strokes

14 residual strokes

髷 J717e/M45426 6810
髻 J7221/M45442 6811
髭 J4926/M45399 6812

15 residual strokes

擡 J5a2c/M12851 2302
檜 J3869/M15657 2888
簒 J5255/M26490 4345
糝 J-X/M27101 4421
緻 J-X/M27700 4543
臺 J6937/M32204 5229
醜 J3d39/M39969 6189
駿 J3d59/M44775 6754
鴲 J-X/M46832 6957
鵄 J7277/M46833 6958
鴾 J727c/M46883 6962

16 residual strokes

嚔 J5369/M4501 917
擺 J5a34/M12910 2313
緻 J654c/M-X 4557
縉 J6556/M27737 4562
繧 J6562/M27936 4591
藝 J693a/M32330 5235
闔 J6f6e/M41452 6415
鬆 J7222/M45484 6813
魍 J7233/M45869 6839
魎 J7234/M45870 6840
魏 J7232/M45872 6841

17 residual strokes

壜 J5460/M5588 1114
瓣 J6122/M21425 3689
轍 J4532/M38524 5988
辭 J6d66/M38671 6004
醯 J6e51/M40036 6193
餽 J7139/M44320 6706
鯵 J3033/M-X 6875

18 residual strokes

辮 J6570/M27991 4604
羆 J6631/M28398 4654
魑 J7235/M45901 6842
齝 J-X/M48622 7092

19 residual strokes

囈 J5374/M4629 931
巍 J565b/M8626 1522
欅 J5d2b/M15823 2906
驂 J715d/M44965 6769
鬘 J7223/M45568 6814
鬢 J7224/M45580 6816
鷚 J7330/M47179 6986

20–26 residual strokes

竊 J6366/M25713 4222
籬 J6461/M26803 4379
罎 J6624/M28189 4631
豔 J-X/M36332 5741
靉 J704f/M42540 6556
鬣 J-X/M-X 6818
鬟 J7226/M45607 6819
鬣 J7227/M45613 6820
魘 J7236/M45941 6844
鰺 J724d/M46442 6912
齷 J7379/M48727 7101

Rad. 29 又

0 residual strokes

又 J4b74/M3115 **668**

1 residual strokes

叉 J3a35/M3116 **669**
夂 J5469/M5691 1118

2 residual strokes

及 J355a/M3118′ **670**
及 J-X/M3118 **671**
友 J4d27/M3119 **672**
双 J4150/M3125 **673**
反 J483f/M3127 **674**
支 J3b59/M13061 2324
攴 J5a3d/M13108 2326
殳 J5d55/M16613 2989

3 residual strokes

冬 J455f/M1610 410
処 J3d68/M1745 435
及 J-X/M3118 **671**
収 J3c7d/M3128 **675**
收 J-X/M3137 **676**
奴 J455b/M6039 1174
皮 J4869/M22823 3878

4 residual strokes

伎 J346c/M436 133
仮 J323e/M398 144
各 J3346/M3281 714
扠 J592d/M11804 2068
杈 J-X/M-X 2537
返 J4a56/M38758 6020
阪 J3a65/M41562 6428

5 residual strokes

努 J4558/M2314 527
吸 J355b/M3370′ 713
吸 J-X/M3372 720
坚 J-X/M4963 979
坂 J3a64/M4910 985
妓 J3538/M6083 1185
孥 J5557/M6967 1290
岌 J5620/M7929 1444
岐 J3474/M7936 1447
役 J4c72/M10057 1726
扱 J-X/M11835 2071
技 J353b/M11855 2092
抜 J4834/M11901′ 2093
投 J456a/M11887 2095
条 J3e72/M14486 2563
汳 J5d72/M17164 3050
没 J4b57/M17233 3066
沒 J5d73/M17204 3067
芟 J676c/M30701 4972
返 J4a56/M38758′ 6020
陂 J6f78/M41603 6430
麦 J477e/M47718 7030

6 residual strokes

亟 J5034/M279 83
函 J5162/M1830 447
叔 J3d47/M3154 **677**
受 J3c75/M3159 **678**
取 J3c68/M3158 **679**
呶 J5273/M3460 755
坡 J5433/M4966 994
孥 J5557/M6967 1290
帑 J5666/M8838 1554
弩 J5738/M9760 1686
径 J3742/M10080′ 1730
彼 J4860/M10066 1732
怪 J3278/M10483 1821
披 J4864/M11909 2116
枝 J3b5e/M14557 2591
板 J4844/M14518 2595
歿 J5d47/M16385 2969
殴 J3225/M16618′ 2990
波 J4748/M17308 3101
版 J4847/M19817 3526
肢 J3b68/M29285 4768
股 J3854/M29284 4772
服 J497e/M14345′ 4775
臤 J-X/M30070 4895
茎 J3754/M30861′ 4990

7 residual strokes

亟 J5034/M279 83
侵 J3f2f/M646 218
函 J5162/M1830 447
叛 J4840/M3166 **680**
叙 J3d76/M3163 **681**

Char	JIS	Morohashi	No.
叟	J5257	M3176	**682**
度	J4559	M9313	1616
弩	J5738	M9760	1686
怒	J455c	M10439	1820
拏	J593c	M11954	2103
段	J434a	M16619	2991
爰	J6029	M19672	3512
玻	J6060	M20899	3628
疫	J3156	M22069	3783
皈	J6227	M22705	3868
盈	J314e	M22961	3888
臤	J-X	M30070	4895

8 residual strokes

Char	JIS	Morohashi	No.
亟	J5034	M279	83
俶	J5068	M732	236
冦	J514e	M1590	402
叟	J5257	M3176	**682**
夏	J3246	M5720	1120
寂	J3c64	M7200	1342
屐	J5621	M7708	1422
弩	J5738	M9760	1686
捜	J415c	M12179′	2168
桑	J372c	M14772	2661
豰	J-X	M16625	2992
殷	J5d56	M16627	2993
殺	J3b26	M16629	2994
溲	J-X	M-X	3135
浸	J3f3b	M17505′	3157
痓	J-X	M-X	3784
疲	J4868	M22084	3796
皰	J622e	M22844	3879
盈	J314e	M22961	3888
破	J474b	M24124	3999
紁	J-X	M27294	4442
翅	J6642	M28642	4678
般	J484c	M30388	4931
菽	J6843	M31241	5068
蚤	J4742	M32893	5287
被	J486f	M34222	5445
陬	J7025	M41685	6453
隻	J4049	M41941	6494

9 residual strokes

Char	JIS	Morohashi	No.
假	J5071	M835	261
啜	J5335	M3832	822
堅	J3778	M5210	1038
娶	J5538	M6365	1236
娵	J5537	M6364	1237
婆	J474c	M6390	1240
寇	J5564	M7209	1339
寂	J3c64	M7200	1342
掻	J415f	M-X	2175
掫	J5958	M12287	2179
授	J3c78	M12242	2208
曼	J5258	M14298	2475
椒	J5c25	M15029	2731
殺	J-X	M16638	2995
淑	J3d4a	M17634	3191
経	J3750	M27392	4473
菔	J-X	M31170	5064
菽	J6843	M31241	5068
菆	J-X	M31146	5074
菠	J684a	M31190	5081
設	J405f	M35293	5570
貧	J-X	M36695	5776
販	J484e	M36679	5779
跂	J6c65	M37416	5857
遐	J6e22	M39005	6080
酘	J6e46	M39797	6164
釵	J6e60	M40191	6220

10 residual strokes

Char	JIS	Morohashi	No.
堅	J3778	M5210	1038
報	J4a73	M5275	1059
媛	J4932	M6516	1244
嫂	J553f	M6603	1252
愎	J583f	M10920	1904
援	J3167	M12407	2230
搜	J5953	M12486	2238
敨	J-X	M13086	2325
最	J3a47	M14301	2492
椒	J5c25	M15029	2731
極	J364b	M15181	2753
殻	J334c	M-X	2996
殽	J-X	M16647	2998
㱿	J-X	M16645	2999
湲	J5e53	M17877	3220
溲	J5e6c	M17979	3265
痩	J4169	M-X	3806
發	J6224	M22669	3861
皴	J622f	M22866	3880
督	J4644	M23457	3946
紁	J-X	M27294	4442
胥	J3f55	M29621	4834
葭	J685b	M31450	5114
葮	J6853	M31449	5124
赧	J6c5f	M37001	5842
跛	J6c6c	M37479	5865
跛	J-X	M37447	5868
軽	J375a	M38281	5953
遐	J6e22	M39005	6080
鈑	J6e67	M40224	6231
靫	J7056	M42713	6571
飯	J4853	M44064′	6679
馭	J7147	M44576	6727

11 residual strokes

Char	JIS	Morohashi	No.
寝	J3f32	M7278′	1353
慤	J5842	M10983	1931
搜	J5953	M12486	2238
搬	J4842	M12507	2249
搔	J-X	M12477	2256
暇	J324b	M14036	2501
暖	J4348	M14064	2502
極	J364b	M15181	2753
椴	J464e	M15075	2772
楹	J5c33	M15188	2775
毀	J544c	M16654	3000
殿	J4542	M16651	3001
煖	J5f6b	M19196	3451
瑕	J606c	M21120	3664
畷	J466d	M21892	3766
督	J4644	M23457	3946
碆	J626e	M24273	4011
竪	J4328	M25790	4240
粲	J646c	M26966	4407
経	J3750	M27392	4473
胥	J3f55	M29621	4834
螋	J6a3f	M33752	5391
鈒	J-X	M40271	6240
飯	J4853	M44064′	6679
鼓	J385d	M48330	7076

12 residual strokes

Char	JIS	Morohashi	No.
寢	J556a	M7289	1354
幔	J566f	M9050	1580
廏	J567e	M9453	1635
慇	J5840	M11045	1942
慳	J584c	M11140	1960
敲	J5a4a	M13337	2354
槃	J5c51	M15303	2805
漫	J4c21	M18166	3308
皷	J7369	M22887	3881
皸	J6230	M22888	3882
皹	J6231	M-X	3883
碬	J-X	M24341	4024
穀	J3972	M25188′	4157
竪	J4328	M25790	4240
箙	J6439	M26148	4306
綬	J3c7a	M27565	4510
緊	J365b	M27603	4524
綴	J4456	M27579	4526
聚	J665c	M29093	4731
膄	J-X	M29758	4855
蔲	J-X	M-X	5172
蔓	J4c22	M31784	5180
頚	J375b	M43434	6626
頗	J3f7c	M43415	6627
骰	J716d	M45127	6786
髪	J4831	M45387′	6804

13 residual strokes

Char	JIS	Morohashi	No.
儂	J512f	M1176	318
廢	J5726	M9492	1639
微	J5755	M10261	1774
慳	J584c	M11140	1960
慢	J4b7d	M11110	1968
憂	J4d2b	M11170	1971

Rad. 30 口

---

4 residual strokes

---

5 residual strokes

哨	J3e25	M3646	**809**
哺	J532e	M3676	**810**
哲	J452f	M3667	**811**
唐	J4562	M3709′	**812**
圄	J537d	M4775	953
姬	J-X	M6230	1220
娟	J552f	M6321	1225
婀	J5534	M6382	1227
娿	J-X	M6381	1228
娛	J3864	M6307′	1231
娩	J4a5a	M6337	1233
害	J3332	M7165	1333
容	J4d46	M7172	1335
宮	J355c	M7156	1336
尅	J5571	M7435	1378
峪	J563b	M8073	1467
帥	J3f63	M8886	1559
師	J3b55	M8916	1562
廻	J3276	M9575	1659
息	J4255	M10469	1818
恕	J3d7a	M10560	1834
恩	J3238	M10591	1851
悁	J577a	M10623	1857
悒	J5825	M10655	1859
悋	J5827	M10640	1865
悦	J3159	M10629′	1868
悟	J3867	M10680	1870
惇	J4657	M10759	1887
拿	J593d	M12015	2138
捐	J5950	M12150	2156
捉	J422a	M12136	2159
捌	J3b2b	M12141	2162
挽	J4854	M-X	2172
敕	J5a45	M13225	2338
桔	J354b	M14777	2653
桐	J364d	M14770	2655
格	J334a	M14749	2668
氤	J5d65	M17060	3029
涓	J5e32	M17541	3145
浩	J3940	M17479′	3147
浴	J4d61	M17496	3153
淳	J3d5f	M17690	3189
烙	J5f60	M19014	3419
烏	J3128	M18998	3421
烹	J4b23	M19049	3425
狷	J6046	M20426	3577
珞	J6064	M20953	3635
甛	J-X	M21655	3713
痌	J-X	M22088	3785
痂	J6150	M22122	3793
痀	J-X	M22120	3794
砺	J4557	M-X	3993
砠	J6269	M24084	3995
砧	J354e	M24099	3996
祜	J-X	M24652	4080
祠	J632c	M24676	4081
祝	J-X	M24672	4086
站	J636b	M25742	4231
笘	J6378	M25911	4259
罟	J662a	M28248	4637
胴	J4639	M29436	4810
舐	J6753	M30283	4919
莧	J6839	M-X	5035
莒	J683a	M30989	5036
荅	J6831	M31064	5050
莫	J6834	M31090	5051
荷	J3259	M31000	5059
蚜	J-X	M32882	5280
蚪	J6951	M32903	5284
蚓	J694e	M32866	5285
蚋	J6952	M32850	5286
蚤	J4742	M32893	5287
蚊	J3263	M32849	5288
蚕	J-X	M32848	5289
衷	J-X	M-X	5424
袁	J6a4f	M34152	5429
衰	J3f6a	M34127	5432
訖	J6b3f	M35242	5557
訌	J6b41	M35228	5558
訊	J3f56	M35224	5559
託	J4277	M35243	5560
討	J4624	M35231	5561
訓	J3731	M35238	5562
記	J352d	M35244	5563
豈	J6c31	M36249	5736
逧	J6d7a	M-X	6044
逞	J6d77	M38896	6048
逗	J3f60	M38887	6053
這	J4767	M38889	6058
速	J422e	M38897′	6060
造	J4224	M38898′	6061
週	J3d35	M38937′	6070
郭	J3354	M39474	6144
部	J4974	M39460	6146
険	J3831	M41721′	6456
陪	J4766	M41680	6458
韋	J706a	M43108	6601
高	J3962	M45313	6796
鬲	J722f	M45672	6831

8 residual strokes

停	J4464	M864	273
劔	J517b	M-X	499
剳	J5175	M2113	500
副	J497b	M2097	503
勒	J7055	M2386	545
匐	J5236	M2545	577
匿	J463f	M2690	591
區	J523f	M2691	593
咢	J5278	M3529	**782**
啄	J426f	M-X	**793**
唇	J3f30	M3697	**807**
售	J5334	M3760	**813**
唹	J5330	M3774	**814**
啅	J5336	M3802	**815**
啌	J5333	M3810	**816**
啝	J533b	M3833	**817**
啗	J5338	M3825	**818**
啖	J5337	M3824	**819**
啀	J5331	M3789	**820**
啄	J-X	M3801	**821**
啜	J5335	M3832	**822**
唸	J5339	M3773	**823**
喝	J3365	M-X	**824**
啣	J5332	M3876	**825**
唾	J4243	M3785	**826**
啞	J-X	M3835	**827**
啓	J373c	M3820	**828**
唱	J3e27	M3765	**829**
問	J4c64	M3814	**830**
唯	J4d23	M3761	**831**
商	J3e26	M3803	**832**
喊	J533f	M3916	**843**
國	J5422	M4798	956
圉	J-X	M4797	958
埼	J3a6b	M5201	1028
域	J3068	M5158	1030
培	J475d	M5195	1032
壷	J445b	M5657	1034
堂	J4632	M5207	1037
器	J-X	M-X	1162
婁	J4f2c	M6383	1235
孰	J5559	M6995	1297
寇	J5563	M7202	1338
寄	J3473	M7203	1345
崎	J3a6a	M8169	1485
常	J3e6f	M8955	1569
座	J-X	M-X	1620
廻	J3276	M9575	1659
強	J362f	M9815	1695
彫	J4426	M9995	1719
徛	J-X	M10148	1750
徜	J-X	M10149	1751
悤	J-X	M10693	1854
悚	J577e	M10672	1860
患	J3435	M10691	1871
悪	J302d	M10717	1873
惆	J582f	M10757	1881
惇	J4657	M10759	1887
扈	J6e3d	M11746	2057
挽	J4854	M-X	2172
掻	J415f	M-X	2175
掄	J595e	M-X	2176
掎	J5956	M12250	2182
掠	J4e2b	M12273	2191
据	J3f78	M12204	2195
捨	J3c4e	M12191′	2205
捨	J-X	M12191	2206
敞	J5a48	M13246	2348
敦	J4658	M13276	2349
晩	J-X	M13940	2466
晚	J-X	M-X	2467
冕	J-X	M-X	2468
晧	J5a6e	M13961	2473

晤	J5a6d	M13956	2474
梠	J5b71	M14862	2671
桾	J5b75	M14821	2679
梏	J5b67	M14841	2684
梮	J-X	M14879	2689
梧	J3868	M14872	2700
椁	J5b76	M15003	2722
欲	J4d5f	M16080	2936
毫	J5d5d	M16831	3015
淌	J5e45	M17629	3171
淸	J5e51	M17782	3179
淳	J3d5f	M17690	3189
涸	J5e41	M17601	3192
涼	J4e43	M17606	3198
渟	J5e5b	M17763	3221
烱	J5f58	M19040	3422
烹	J4b23	M19049	3425
牾	J6033	M20028	3543
猗	J6048	M20493	3580
琣	J6069	M20993	3641
甜	J453c	M21656	3712
甛	J-X	M21655	3713
略	J4e2c	M21839	3755
畧	J6140	M21840	3756
盒	J6236	M22988	3893
笳	J6377	M25950	4260
笴	J-X	M24951	4263
笥	J3f5a	M25934	4265
笿	J637a	M25921	4267
粘	J4734	M26901	4393
紿	J6529	M27369	4459
絅	J6525	M27375	4460
紹	J3e52	M27361	4465
耜	J6653	M28915	4711
脰	J-X	M29544	4816
脫	J4326	M29539′	4822
舐	J6753	M30283	4919
舸	J6757	M30404	4934
船	J4125	M30407	4939
菟	J4551	M31189	5077
菫	J6841	M31207	5086
菩	J4a6e	M31205	5093
蛎	J3342	M-X	5291
蛉	J6959	M32969	5294
蛄	J6956	M32960	5295
蛄	J-X	M32961	5296
蚰	J6958	M32918	5297
蚳	J-X	M-X	5298
蛆	J6957	M32963	5299
蚯	J6955	M32916	5300
蛋	J4341	M32977	5301
蛍	J3756	M32983	5302
蛇	J3c58	M32964	5303
衷	J-X	M-X	5424
裒	J6a51	M34203	5441
袈	J3736	M34166	5442
袷	J3041	M34240	5449
訽	J-X	M35260	5564
訟	J3e59	M35266	5565
訥	J6b44	M35274	5566
訣	J376d	M35272	5567
訛	J6b42	M35256	5568
許	J3576	M35298	5569
設	J405f	M35293	5570
訪	J4b2c	M35284	5571
訳	J4c75	M35324′	5572
谺	J-X	M36193	5731
跂	J6c65	M37416	5857
趾	J6c66	M37406	5858
跌	J6c67	M37392	5859
距	J3577	M37481	5866
逧	J6d7a	M-X	6044
週	J3d35	M38937′	6070
逼	J492f	M38973	6085
過	J3261	M39002′	6090
鄂	J6e3f	M39520	6150
釦	J4b55	M40175	6223
鞆	J7057	M-X	6574
髙	J-X	M45314	6797

9 residual strokes

偉	J304e	M837	285
僖	J5125	M1095	306
剴	J5173	M2122	505
創	J414f	M2127	506
割	J3364	M2112′	507
勤	J3650	M2415′	552
區	J523f	M2691	593
厨	J3f5f	M3005	657
喞	J5332	M3876	**825**
單	J5345	M3993	**833**
喝	J-X	M3960	**834**
啻	J5341	M3886	**835**
喨	J534a	M3978	**836**
啼	J5346	M3887	**837**
喙	J533c	M3951	**838**
喩	J5348	M3979	**839**
啾	J5342	M3892	**840**
喬	J362c	M3990	**841**
喟	J5340	M3963	**842**
喊	J533f	M3916	**843**
喞	J-X	M3961	**844**
喞	J5344	M-X	**845**
喃	J5347	M3903	**846**
喀	J533d	M3896	**847**
喘	J5343	M3946	**848**
喰	J3674	M4015	**849**
喋	J437d	M3917	**850**
喇	J5349	M3909	**851**
喚	J342d	M3953	**852**
喪	J4153	M3985	**853**
喉	J3922	M3913	**854**
喫	J354a	M3987	**855**
喧	J3776	M3976	**856**
営	J3144	M4025	**857**
喜	J346e	M3957	**858**
善	J4131	M3904	**859**
喆	J-X	M4143	**881**
圍	J5423	M4806	959
壹	J5465	M5661	1044
堝	J5446	M5247	1047
堡	J5448	M5254	1050
塔	J4563	M5332	1052
孰	J5559	M6995	1297
寃	J5563	M7202	1338
富	J4959	M7230	1349
尌	J-X	M7448	1384
尋	J3f52	M7447	1385
就	J3d22	M7599	1401
属	J4230	M7754	1430
嵜	J563f	M-X	1492
嵒	J5649	M8294	1495
幅	J497d	M8995	1574
強	J362f	M9815	1695
强	J-X	M9822	1696
弼	J-X	M9825	1698
彭	J5745	M10003	1720
惹	J3c66	M10866	1886
惑	J4f47	M10789	1892
惱	J583d	M10856	1899
愕	J5833	M10939	1914
慥	J5854	M11114	1937
掌	J3e38	M12248	2200
揀	J5963	M12315	2221
揖	J4d2c	M12351	2222
搭	J456b	M12508	2228
敁	J-X	M13086	2325
敞	J5a48	M13246	2348
敦	J4658	M13276	2349
敬	J3749	M13285′	2351
景	J374a	M13983	2487
智	J4352	M14010	2490
椥	J5c29	M-X	2712
棠	J5c2b	M14953	2718
椁	J5b76	M15003	2722
椋	J4c3a	M15020	2725
椅	J3058	M15009	2737
検	J3821	M15065′	2752
極	J364b	M15181	2753
歃	J5d3a	M16093	2937
殕	J5d4d	M16498	2979
殗	J-X	M16517	2980
渕	J5e63	M-X	3211
湖	J3850	M17836	3240
渦	J3132	M17771	3241
減	J383a	M17759	3249
焙	J5f64	M19099	3433
甞	J6133	M21659	3714
疎	J4142	M22002	3776
痾	J615e	M22289	3807
痞	J615d	M22206	3808
痘	J4577	M22185	3813
登	J4550	M22668	3862
皓	J622b	M22732	3875

短	J433b	M23978	3982
硴	J626d	M-X	4003
硲	J4823	M24243	4004
程	J4478	M25081′	4144
税	J4047	M25070′	4146
窗	J6359	M25517	4202
窘	J635b	M25519	4203
窖	J635c	M25516	4204
竦	J6370	M25776	4237
筈	J4826	M25990	4277
筒	J457b	M26004	4283
答	J457a	M26006	4285
粭	J6466	M-X	4395
粡	J6469	M26928	4397
粤	J6465	M26935	4399
絮	J6531	M27443	4479
絡	J4d6d	M27426	4484
給	J356b	M27432	4489
結	J376b	M27398	4492
翕	J6645	M28691	4682
耜	J6653	M28915	4711
聒	J665a	M29062	4725
舒	J5030	M30300	4920
莫	J6834	M31090	5051
菟	J4551	M-X	5077
菀	J-X	M-X	5102
萵	J6862	M31351	5108
葆	J685e	M31381	5110
葫	J6859	M31443	5113
萼	J6855	M31361	5119
葺	J4978	M31465	5125
落	J4d6e	M31362	5130
蓉	J4d56	M31648	5135
蛛	J6961	M33002	5307
蛭	J4948	M33048	5308
蛞	J695d	M33008	5309
蛔	J695c	M32990	5310
蛟	J6960	M33009	5311
蛤	J483a	M33023	5312
蛙	J333f	M32997	5313
蜓	J-X	M33121	5318
蜉	J696a	M33104	5324
衉	J-X	M33985	5416
袈	J3736	M34166	5442
裙	J6a65	M34314	5460
裕	J4d35	M34305	5461
訝	J-X	M35260	5564
覘	J6b2d	M34840	5527
視	J4741	M34839	5528
訝	J6b43	M-X	5573
詒	J6b48	M35376	5575
詈	J6b4a	M35360	5576
訶	J6b45	M35328	5577
詁	J6b46	M35347	5578
詑	J4242	M35374	5579
詛	J6b47	M35390	5580
詔	J3e5b	M35379	5581
詞	J3b6c	M35394	5582
註	J4370	M35340	5583
詐	J3a3e	M35373	5585
診	J3f47	M35337	5586
評	J493e	M35383	5587
訴	J414a	M35325	5588
証	J3e5a	M35341	5589
詠	J-X	M-X	5591
谺	J6c2e	M-X	5732
象	J3e5d	M36372	5744
貂	J6c3a	M36528	5757
貽	J6c46	M36719	5785
貼	J453d	M36718	5787
賀	J326c	M36725	5790
貴	J352e	M36704	5794
超	J4436	M37096	5852
跏	J6c68	M37457	5860
跖	J6c6a	M37469	5861
跌	J6c6b	M37450	5862
跚	J6c69	M37477	5863
跑	J-X	M37461	5864
跛	J6c6c	M37479	5865
距	J3577	M37481	5866
跋	J6c6d	M37446	5867
跛	J-X	M37447	5868
軻	J6d46	M38274	5949
辜	J6d63	M38636	5998
逼	J492f	M38973	6085
過	J3261	M39002′	6090
違	J3063	M39067′	6099
遺	J382f	M39052′	6100
遠	J3173	M39047′	6101
鄂	J6e3f	M39520	6150
隕	J7028	M41785	6474
隔	J3356	M-X	6475
隔	J-X	M41783	6476
靫	J7056	M42713	6571
靭	J-X	M42715	6572
靭	J3f59	M-X	6573
靱	J7057	M-X	6574
靹	J7058	M42747	6575
黑	J-X	M48038	7053

10 residual strokes

亶	J5039	M328	98
傴	J507d	M1020	290
僉	J5121	M1054	291
僅	J-X	M1048	292
勤	J-X	M2424	554
喪	J4153	M3985	**853**
嗇	J5427	M4053	**860**
嘩	J325e	M-X	**861**
喩	J-X	M4088	**862**
嗉	J-X	M4057	**863**
嗤	J5350	M4110	**864**
嗚	J534b	M4084	**865**
嗔	J5351	M4074	**866**
嗄	J534e	M4047	**867**
嗣	J3b4c	M4109	**868**
嗟	J534d	M4102	**869**
嗜	J534f	M4089	**870**
嗅	J534c	M4048	**871**
嘆	J4332	M4138′	**872**
嗹	J5358	M4148	**875**
嗸	J-X	M4143	**881**
圍	J5423	M4806	959
圓	J5424	M4819	961
園	J3160	M4818	962
塔	J4563	M5332	1052
塙	J4839	M5341	1063
塘	J4564	M5340	1066
塩	J3176	M5382	1075
塾	J3d4e	M5402	1083
媼	J553c	M6588	1250
嫦	J5543	M6663	1260
嵩	J3f73	M8348	1502
廚	J-X	M-X	1631
廓	J3347	M9461	1633
強	J362f	M9815	1695
彁	J573b	M-X	1701
衙	J6a4b	M34061	1764
愕	J5833	M10939	1914
感	J3436	M10953	1928
慍	J5832	M11059	1930
慥	J5854	M11114	1937
愴	J5848	M11008	1943
搶	J596f	M12525	2245
損	J423b	M12459	2255
搔	J-X	M12477	2256
極	J364b	M15181	2753
楝	J5c42	M15148	2760
楜	J5c35	M15147	2773
楫	J5c37	M15168	2783
溫	J-X	M17968	3251
溏	J5e6f	M17925	3254
滄	J5e6b	M18007	3267
溶	J4d4f	M17983	3277
漢	J3441	M18068′	3281
煦	J5f68	M19225	3445
煉	J-X	M19178	3455
照	J3e48	M19226	3457
營	J535b	M19457	3491
猿	J316e	M20584	3600
獄	J3976	M20603	3602
瑚	J386a	M21126	3662
甞	J6133	M21659	3714
當	J6144	M21890	3765
畸	J6143	M21893	3767
痼	J6160	M22285	3817
痴	J4354	M22257	3823
碆	J626e	M24273	4011
碚	J6270	M24309	4013
碕	J3a6c	M24296	4015
禀	J6349	M24742	4094
禍	J3252	M24766′	4102
福	J4a21	M24768′	4105
稠	J6347	M25130	4150

稟	J6348	M25127	4153
筥	J6428	M26051	4291
粵	J6465	M26935	4399
紹	J3e52	M27361	4465
絽	J6538	M27474	4498
絹	J3828	M27470	4499
群	J3732	M28498	4666
羣	J663a	M28497	4667
聖	J403b	M29074	4727
腦	J672a	M29681	4839
腭	J-X	M29700	4840
萼	J6855	M31361	5119
蔀	J3c43	M31748	5138
蓑	J4c2c	M31661	5143
蒿	J6866	M31634	5147
蒟	J6867	M31566	5150
葦	J3031	M31437	5160
蒼	J4173	M31627	5162
號	J694b	M32726	5271
虞	J3673	M32723'	5272
蜒	J6963	M33120	5317
蜓	J-X	M33121	5318
蜊	J696d	M33106	5319
蜍	J696b	M33110	5320
蜋	J-X	M33108	5321
蛻	J6968	M33078	5322
蜈	J6965	M33099	5323
蜉	J696a	M33104	5324
蛾	J326b	M33082	5325
蛹	J696c	M33076	5326
蜆	J6964	M33093	5328
蜀	J6966	M33086	5329
蛸	J427d	M33072	5330
蜂	J4b2a	M33088	5331
蝴	J697a	M33328	5356
裔	J6a63	M34303	5459
裾	J3f7e	M34382	5474
触	J3f28	M35070	5547
詇	J-X	M35495	5590
誨	J-X	M-X	5592
詢	J6b4e	M35411	5593
詣	J3758	M35412	5594
詬	J6b4d	M35433	5595
誂	J6b50	M35469	5596
詼	J6b4b	M35462	5597
詫	J4f4d	M35431	5598
誅	J6b4f	M35472	5599
誄	J6b51	M35471	5600
該	J333a	M35445	5601
誉	J4d40	M35498	5602
詭	J6b4c	M35434	5603
詮	J4127	M35435	5604
誇	J3858	M35474	5605
誠	J403f	M35497'	5606
詳	J3e5c	M35446	5607
話	J4f43	M35441	5608
詰	J354d	M35440	5609
詩	J3b6d	M35427	5610
試	J3b6e	M35415	5611
誕	J-X	M35516	5613
豊	J4b2d	M36263	5737
貉	J6c3b	M36549	5759
賂	J4f28	M36738	5799
跟	J6c70	M37491	5869
跫	J6c6f	M37519	5870
跣	J6c71	M37497	5871
跨	J3859	M37504	5872
践	J4129	M37547'	5873
跪	J6c6e	M37516	5874
跡	J4057	M37493	5875
路	J4f29	M37524	5876
跿	J6c75	M37552	5879
輅	J6d4a	M38302	5957
辟	J6d64	M38642	5999
辞	J3c2d	M38638	6000
違	J3063	M39067'	6099
遣	J382f	M39052'	6100
遠	J3173	M39047'	6101
適	J452c	M39076'	6107
鄗	J6e41	M39597	6153
酩	J6e49	M39846	6170
酪	J4d6f	M39847	6172
鈷	J385a	M40270	6236
鉅	J6e6a	M40286	6237
鉐	J6e71	M40298	6238
鉤	J6e6c	M40319	6250
鉛	J3174	M40310	6251
鞅	J7058	M42747	6575
靴	J3724	M42729	6576
靺	J705c	M42761	6577
靼	J705a	M42764	6578
鞁	J705b	M42776	6579
飴	J303b	M44080	6682
飼	J3b74	M44107'	6685
鼓	J385d	M48330	7076

11 residual strokes

僑	J3623	M1088	307
兢	J513e	M1395	365
剳	J-X	M-X	511
匱	J523c	M2651	595
厰	J5252	M3034	658
喪	J4153	M3985	**853**
嗉	J-X	M4057	**863**
噌	J4139	M-X	**873**
嘆	J-X	M4171	**874**
嗹	J5358	M4148	**875**
嘛	J5357	M4230	**876**
嗾	J5355	M4155	**877**
嘗	J3e28	M4205	**878**
嘈	J-X	M4175	**879**
嗷	J5353	M4142	**880**
嗸	J-X	M4143	**881**
嘖	J5354	M4204	**882**
嗽	J5356	M4154	**883**
嘔	J5352	M4200	**884**
噓	J-X	M4206	**885**
嘘	J3133	M-X	**886**
嘉	J3245	M4176	**887**
嘯	J5362	M4246	**904**
圖	J5426	M4832	963
團	J5425	M4834	964
壽	J5468	M5672	1077
塾	J3d4e	M5402	1083
奩	J547e	M5991	1170
嫗	J5542	M6640	1259
嫩	J5544	M6666	1262
嫡	J4364	M6656	1263
寤	J5568	M7291	1358
屢	J-X	M7787	1431
嶇	J564f	M8426	1507
幗	J566e	M9057	1579
幣	J5672	M-X	1586
彄	J573b	M-X	1701
慥	J5854	M11114	1937
慝	J5857	M11100	1938
摑	J-X	M12572	2263
摘	J4526	M12582	2266
敲	J5a4a	M13337	2354
敲	J-X	M13338	2355
榱	J5c63	M15276	2799
榲	J5c45	M15277	2800
榿	J5c48	M15298	2801
槁	J5c49	M15300	2806
榕	J5c57	M15228	2815
槍	J4164	M15319	2822
槨	J5c5a	M15362	2826
歌	J324e	M16167	2945
歎	J4337	M16182	2947
殞	J5d4e	M16535	2982
漢	J-X	M18153	3284
滬	J5e76	M18072	3288
滸	J5e77	M18089	3291
漱	J5e7b	M18171	3293
滾	J5e78	M18098	3297
滴	J4529	M18084	3299
熔	J4d50	M19319	3458
熙	J7426	M-X	3464
熅	J-X	M19288	3467
熟	J3d4f	M19332	3472
犒	J6037	M20114	3549
皷	J7369	M22887	3881
磆	J6275	M24350	4021
禍	J-X	M24766	4103
福	J-X	M24768	4106
窩	J635d	M25579	4208
箚	J6434	M26149	4305
箇	J3255	M26116	4315
絮	J6531	M27443	4479
絡	J4d6d	M27426	4484
給	J356b	M27432	4489
結	J376b	M27398	4492
綢	J6542	M27546	4506
綺	J653a	M27586	4522

罰 J4833/M28315 4647
罨 J665d/M29106 4728
腭 J-X/M29700 4840
膈 J672d/M29772 4855
膃 J672c/M29757 4856
膏 J3951/M29800 4859
臺 J674a/M30161 4905
蓑 J4c2c/M31661 5143
蔔 J6879/M31785 5173
號 J694b/M32726 5271
蜒 J6963/M33120 5317
蜋 J-X/M33108 5321
蝋 J4f39/M-X 5332
蜩 J6973/M33166 5334
蜴 J696e/M33190 5335
蜱 J-X/M33182 5336
蜿 J696f/M33210 5337
蜥 J6972/M33157 5338
蜷 J6970/M33199 5339
蜚 J6974/M33138 5340
蜻 J6971/M33203 5341
蜘 J4358/M33134 5342
蜜 J4c2a/M33143 5343
蝣 J6a22/M33292 5352
蝶 J4433/M33333 5363
裔 J6a63/M34303 5459
裳 J3e58/M34357 5472
裸 J6a70/M34438 5479
誨 J-X/M-X 5592
該 J333a/M35445 5601
誇 J3858/M35474 5605
誠 J-X/M35537 5612
誕 J-X/M35516 5613
誥 J6b55/M35549 5615
誨 J6b52/M35553 5616
誡 J6b53/M35538 5617
誣 J6b58/M35542 5618
誑 J6b54/M35510 5619
誌 J3b6f/M35501 5620
誦 J6b56/M35551 5621
誓 J4040/M35514 5622
認 J4727/M35502′ 5623
認 J-X/M35502 5624
誘 J4d36/M35525 5625
誤 J386d/M35546′ 5626
説 J4062/M35556′ 5627
語 J386c/M35533 5628
読 J4649/M35580′ 5629
誕 J4342/M35692′ 5640
豪 J396b/M36406 5749
跨 J3859/M37504 5872
踈 J6c73/M37579 5878
跬 J6c75/M37552 5879
跟 J6c74/M37585 5880
跼 J6c72/M37548 5881
踊 J4d59/M37587 5882
躳 J-X/M38089 5933
辣 J6d65/M38646 6001
適 J452c/M39076′ 6107
遣 J3064/M39134′ 6115
鄲 J6e42/M39659 6154
酲 J6e4b/M39865 6173
酷 J3973/M39870′ 6176
醇 J3d66/M39901 6181
銛 J6e75/M40389 6261
銘 J4c43/M40385 6265
銅 J463c/M40361 6266
閤 J395e/M41301 6397
閣 J3355/M41300 6401
靺 J705c/M42761 6577
靼 J705a/M42764 6578
鞁 J705b/M42776 6579
鞆 J705d/M42794 6580
鞅 J7059/M42784 6581
鞄 J3373/M42781 6582
鞐 J7060/M42829 6583
韶 J7070/M43276 6609
颱 J7126/M43815 6666
飴 J303b/M44080 6682
飼 J3b74/M44107′ 6685
鳴 J4c44/M46672 6939

---

12 residual strokes

儉 J512d/M1190 315
舗 J4a5e/M30323′ 322
僻 J4a48/M1166 323
凜 J7425/M1717 429
凛 J515b/M1718 430
劍 J5178/M2228 514
劈 J517c/M2223 516
匱 J523c/M2651 595
匳 J523d/M2655 596
啞 J-X/M3835 **827**
嗉 J-X/M4057 **863**
嘖 J5354/M4204 **882**
噓 J-X/M4206 **885**
嚙 J337a/M-X **888**
噌 J-X/M4303 **889**
噚 J-X/M4349 **890**
噀 J-X/M4284 **891**
嘶 J535d/M4260 **892**
嘸 J535f/M4269 **893**
嘱 J3e7c/M4249 **894**
噎 J5359/M4307 **895**
噂 J313d/M4286 **896**
嘲 J535e/M4254 **897**
器 J346f/M4349′ **898**
噐 J535a/M4311 **899**
噴 J4a2e/M4345 **900**
墨 J-X/M5469 1091
嬋 J5549/M6738 1266
嬉 J3472/M6736 1267
嬌 J5548/M6739 1268
層 J-X/M7798 1433
嶇 J564f/M8426 1507
嶝 J5653/M8482 1511
幗 J-X/M-X 1581
廚 J5724/M9479 1638
廠 J3e33/M9490 1643
彈 J573c/M9865 1700
彁 J573b/M-X 1701
影 J3146/M10019 1722
衛 J3152/M34073 1776
憇 J585c/M11187 1950
慾 J4d5d/M11163 1951
慫 J5851/M11127 1958
憎 J-X/M11202 1973
憬 J585d/M11256 1978
憚 J585f/M11222 1985
數 J5a4b/M13363 2356
敷 J495f/M13359′ 2357
敵 J4528/M13354 2359
暾 J5a7d/M14160 2515
槺 J5c63/M15276 2799
樞 J5c64/M15450 2828
樓 J5c6c/M15430 2830
槿 J5c5d/M15395 2848
歐 J5d3f/M16185 2946
毆 J5d58/M16674 3002
滾 J5e78/M18098 3297
澔 J-X/M18338 3315
潯 J5f29/M18280 3318
澎 J5f30/M18332 3331
澄 J4021/M18315 3333
潰 J4459/M18281 3335
熟 J3d4f/M19332 3472
燉 J5f77/M19403 3479
瑾 J6077/M21187 3676
甌 J612e/M21586 3707
瘟 J6169/M22396 3828
瘡 J616c/M22404 3829
皚 J622d/M22765 3877
瞎 J6252/M23586 3952
磅 J627c/M24386 4032
磆 J6277/M24389 4033
磑 J6276/M24402 4035
磊 J627d/M24394 4036
穃 J634e/M-X 4164
稿 J3946/M25220 4166
稾 J634c/M25219 4167
箴 J643e/M26214 4327
糊 J3852/M27037 4415
紹 J6538/M27474 4498
絹 J3828/M27470 4499
練 J-X/M27689 4534
緝 J6549/M27645 4537
緘 J6548/M27638 4545
緯 J305e/M27682 4566
罸 J662f/M28343 4648
翩 J6649/M28762 4688
膕 J6732/M29816 4864
舖 J6754/M30323 4922
蕚 J6856/M31970 5183
蕁 J6921/M31899 5195

蕎	J363e	M31946	5197
蜱	J-X	M33182	5336
蝿	J4768	M-X	5344
蠎	J6a3d	M-X	5345
蝨	J697c	M33303	5347
螂	J6a27	M33362	5348
蝉	J4066	M-X	5349
蝙	J6a21	M33261	5351
蝣	J6a22	M33292	5352
蝠	J6975	M33288	5353
蝎	J6979	M33254	5354
蝮	J697d	M33309	5355
蝌	J6978	M33248	5357
蝕	J-X	M33264	5358
蝟	J6976	M33287	5359
蝗	J697b	M33267	5361
蝸	J6977	M33338	5362
蝶	J4433	M33333	5363
蝦	J325c	M33299	5364
褒	J4b2b	M34437	5483
褞	J6a72	M34475	5486
誨	J6b52	M35553	5616
誘	J4d36	M35535	5625
諌	J3452	M35642	5630
諚	J6b5c	M35682	5631
諏	J3f5b	M35648	5632
諍	J6b5a	M35643	5633
誼	J3543	M35605	5634
諄	J6b59	M35622	5635
謁	J315a	M35690′	5637
諾	J427a	M35687	5638
誹	J4870	M35601	5639
誕	J4342	M35692′	5640
諒	J4e4a	M35653	5641
誰	J432f	M35586	5642
談	J434c	M35633	5643
課	J325d	M35589	5644
請	J4041	M35640′	5645
論	J4f40	M35658	5646
調	J4434	M35609′	5647
諸	J3d74	M35691′	5648
諛	J6b67	M35696	5653
謎	J4666	M35800	5661
豌	J6c32	M36273	5738
豎	J6c33	M36280	5739
賠	J4765	M36818	5810
賞	J3e5e	M36813	5815
踐	J6c78	M37608	5883
踟	J6c79	M37645	5884
踞	J6c77	M37642	5885
踠	J-X	M37646	5886
踪	J6d29	M37668	5887
踝	J6c76	M37641	5888
踏	J4627	M37602	5889
遺	J3064	M39134′	6115
避	J4872	M39163′	6120
還	J3454	M39174′	6121
醇	J3d66	M39901	6181
錠	J-X	M40469	6270
鋭	J3154	M40418′	6279
閭	J6f63	M41334	6403
閲	J315c	M41341′	6404
險	J702a	M41874	6483
靠	J7051	M42604	6564
鞐	J7060	M42829	6583
鞋	J705e	M42813	6584
鞏	J705f	M42819	6585
鞍	J3048	M42815	6586
頡	J7076	M43452	6630
餉	J712e	M44140	6687
駛	J714b	M44679	6738
駘	J714d	M44675	6739
駒	J3670	M44663	6742
駕	J326f	M44667	6743
髫	J717a	M45392	6807
13 residual strokes			
儔	J5132	M1224	326
劒	J5179	M2245	518
劔	J517a	M2243	519
器	J-X	M4376	**901**
噬	J5363	M4382	**902**
噺	J4838	M4433	**903**
嘯	J5362	M4246	**904**
嘴	J535c	M4256	**905**
噪	J5364	M4380	**906**
噯	J-X	M4394	**907**
噫	J5365	M4458	**908**
噤	J5361	M4364	**909**
噸	J4655	M4429	**910**
噫	J5360	M4381	**911**
噶	J5367	M4467	**913**
圜	J5428	M4851	965
墻	J5456	M5505	1099
壇	J4345	M5528	1101
壁	J4a49	M5516	1103
嬖	J554a	M6770	1269
寰	J556e	M7344	1368
嶮	J5655	M8520	1513
廩	J5729	M9515	1647
彈	J573c	M9865	1700
衞	J6a4c	M34074	1777
憙	J585a	M11219	1976
憩	J3746	M11246	1980
懆	J586a	M11325	1992
懀	J586b	M11305	1997
憾	J3438	M11312	1999
戰	J5925	M11667	2042
擔	J593f	M12828	2286
撼	J597e	M12775	2291
撿	J-X	M12779	2292
擅	J5a23	M12790	2293
操	J4160	M12806	2296
整	J4030	M13394	2360
整	J-X	M13393	2361
暾	J5a7d	M14160	2515
樞	J5c64	M15450	2828
橡	J464b	M15564	2863
檀	J5c6f	M15623	2866
橘	J354c	M15551	2868
橤	J5c7b	M15681	2870
橙	J5c74	M15552	2877
樹	J3c79	M15496	2878
橋	J3636	M15526	2879
歙	J5d40	M16204	2949
殪	J5d50	M16578	2984
殫	J5d51	M16581	2985
澡	J5f36	M18379	3340
澹	J5f38	M18421	3346
濁	J4279	M18440	3348
燈	J4575	M19402	3476
熹	J5f74	M19380	3478
燉	J5f77	M19403	3479
燕	J316d	M19429	3489
獣	J3d43	M20714′	3606
獪	J6056	M20729	3608
甌	J612e	M21586	3707
瘻	J6171	M22467	3834
瞠	J6255	M23651	3957
磬	J627e	M24454	4042
窶	J6360	M25628	4214
篦	J6444	M26356	4333
篝	J6442	M26387	4334
糖	J457c	M27070	4420
縊	J653a	M27586	4522
縕	J-X	M27757	4564
緯	J305e	M27682	4566
縞	J3c4a	M27777	4569
膳	J4137	M29891	4873
膨	J4b44	M29861	4874
艙	J675a	M30516	4943
蕁	J6856	M31970	5183
薗	J3172	M32119	5200
蕗	J4979	M31964	5203
薀	J6925	M32071	5205
薛	J6930	M32125	5208
薔	J692c	M32113	5220
螂	J6a27	M33362	5348
螢	J6a25	M33434	5365
螕	J-X	M33410	5366
蟒	J-X	M33572	5367
螟	J6a26	M33429	5368
蟆	J6a32	M33542	5369
蟇	J6a31	M33543	5370
融	J4d3b	M33384	5371
褸	J6a7a	M34530	5492
襁	J6a76	M34545	5494
諄	J6b59	M35622	5635
謁	J-X	M35757	5649
諸	J-X	M35743	5650
謚	J6b6b	M35708	5652
諛	J6b67	M35696	5653
諠	J6b63	M35706	5654
諤	J6b60	M35713	5655

14 residual strokes

15 residual strokes

16 residual strokes

17 residual strokes

18 residual strokes

19 residual strokes

20 residual strokes

21 residual strokes

22 residual strokes

23 residual strokes

24 residual strokes

25–27 residual strokes

Rad. 31 口

0 residual strokes

2 residual strokes

3 residual strokes

4 residual strokes

5 residual strokes

6 residual strokes

7 residual strokes

8 residual strokes

9 residual strokes

10 residual strokes

11 residual strokes

Rad.31: 12 residual strokes

摑 JX / M12572 2263
熅 JX / M19288 3467
箘 J6430 / M26147 4302
箇 J3255 / M26116 4315
膃 J672c / M29757 4857

12 residual strokes

瘟 J6169 / M22396 3828
緬 J4c4b / M27674 4542
膕 J6732 / M29816 4864
褞 J6a72 / M34475 5486
駰 J714a / M44683 6737

13 residual strokes

圜 J5428 / M4851 **965**
墻 J5456 / M5505 1099
壇 J4345 / M5528 1101
擅 J5a23 / M12790 2293
篦 J6444 / M26356 4333
縕 JX / M27757 4564
薗 J3172 / M32119 5200
薔 J692c / M32113 5220
錮 J6e7e / M40578 6285

14 residual strokes

懍 J586e / M11335 1994
檣 J5c7e / M15687 2893
檀 J4349 / M15632 2895
氈 J5d61 / M16982 3019
牆 J602f / M19806 3524
篦 J6444 / M26356 4333
緬 J4c4b / M27674 4542

總 J6541 / M27844 4575
貔 J6c40 / M36606 5764
醞 JX / M39974 6188

15 residual strokes

穡 J6351 / M25325 4181
縕 JX / M27757 4564
貔 J6c40 / M36606 5764

16 residual strokes

牘 J6031 / M19906 3530
總 J6541 / M27844 4575
臘 J6744 / M30009 4888
蘊 J693e / M32434 5250
饂 J713b / M44339 6708
鹼 J3834 / MX 7013
鹽 J734b / M47660 7022

17 residual strokes

鹹 J7344 / M47553 7014
鹽 J734b / M47660 7022

18–23 residual strokes

纜 J6574 / M28037 4610
臘 J6744 / M30009 4888
蘊 J693e / M32434 5250
蠟 JX / M33786 5403
豔 JX / M36332 5741
鑞 J6f4d / M41014 6367
顫 J707c / M43706 6656

鬣 JX / MX 6818
鬣 J7227 / M45613 6820
鰮 J725b / M46403 6905
鹼 JX / M47576 7016
齏 J706d / M48578 7087

Rad. 32 土

0 residual strokes

土 J455a / M4867 **966**
士 J3b4e / M5638 1117

1 residual stroke

圡 JX / M4871 **967**
壬 J3f51 / M5639 **968**

2 residual strokes

主 J3c67 / M100 38
仕 J3b45 / M368 123
去 J356e / M3070 665
圦 J5429 / MX **969**
圧 J3035 / M4879′ **970**
生 J4038 / M21670 3715

3 residual strokes

任 J4724 / M416 136
先 J4068 / M1349 350
吐 J4547 / M3300 709
吉 J3548 / M3289 711
圸 J542b / MX **971**
圷 J542a / M4900 **972**
圭 J373d / M4887 **973**

壮 J4154 / M5642 **974**
在 J3a5f / M4881 **975**
地 J434f / M4890 **976**
寺 J3b7b / M7414 1373
庄 J3e31 / M9234 1605
汢 J5d69 / MX 3037
老 J4f37 / M28842 4696
考 J394d / M28843 4697
至 J3b6a / M30142 4903
赱 J6c61 / M37034′ 5846

4 residual strokes

刧 J5167 / M1927 462
刦 JX / M1926 463
劫 J3965 / M2316 529
却 J3551 / M2856 631
告 J3970 / M3381′ 744
壯 J5463 / M5643 **977**
坐 J3a41 / M4931 **978**
坙 JX / M4963 **979**
圻 J542d / M4903 **980**
坎 J542c / M4928 **981**
址 J542e / M4908 **982**
壱 J306d / M5647 **983**
坏 J542f / M4930 **984**
坂 J3a64 / M4910 **985**
坊 J4b37 / M4924 **986**
坑 J3923 / M4932 **987**
均 J3651 / M4916 **988**
声 J403c / M5645 **989**
売 J4764 / M5647′ **990**
孛 J5556 / M6949 1288
孝 J3927 / M6952 1289
志 J3b56 / M10331 1785

杜 J454e / M14477 2560
牡 J3234 / M19933 3536
社 J3c52 / M24631′ 4065
考 J394d / M28843 4697
肚 J666c / M29270 4759
赤 J4056 / M36993 5840
走 J4176 / M37034 5845
赱 J6c61 / M37034′ 5846
里 J4e24 / M40131 6206

5 residual strokes

佶 J504b / M562 184
舎 J3c4b / M30278′ 189
侍 J3b78 / M589 192
佳 J3242 / M557 194
刲 JX / M1955 470
刮 JX / M1975 471
到 J457e / M1950 477
劼 J5224 / M2338 533
尭 J3646 / M-X 614
卦 J3735 / M2798 625
厓 J-X / M2930 648
周 J3c7e / M3441′ 768
垈 J5432 / M-X **991**
垉 J5435 / M-X **992**
垳 J5434 / M5009 **993**
坡 J5433 / M4966 **994**
坩 J5430 / M4975 **995**
坤 J3a25 / M4969 **996**
坦 J4333 / M4971 **997**
坪 J445a / M4976 **998**
垂 J3f62 / M5012 **999**
孛 J5556 / M6949 1288
屆 J557c / M7666 1414

6 residual strokes

7 residual strokes

8 residual strokes

廻 J3d35/M38937′ 6070
達 J4323/M39011′ 6088
都 J-X/M39509 6149
黒 J3975/M48040 7052

9 residual strokes

傲 J507e/M1015 294
喜 J346e/M3957 858
堊 J5441/M5215 **1025**
堕 J4244/M-X **1033**
堅 J3778/M5210 **1038**
堯 J7421/M5272 **1041**
堽 J544e/M5298 **1042**
壺 J5464/M5662 **1043**
壹 J5465/M5661 **1044**
堺 J3a66/M5289 **1045**
堦 J5466/M5664 **1046**
堝 J5446/M5247 **1047**
塚 J444d/M-X **1048**
堙 J5445/M5239 **1049**
堡 J5448/M5254 **1050**
塀 J4a3d/M5316 **1051**
塔 J4563/M5332 **1052**
堵 J-X/M5279 **1053**
堤 J4469/M5259 **1054**
堰 J3161/M5274 **1055**
塁 J4e5d/M5316′ **1056**
堪 J342e/M5266 **1057**
場 J3e6c/M5278 **1058**
報 J4a73/M5275 **1059**
奢 J547a/M5964 1164
屠 J-X/M7761 1429
幄 J566a/M8994 1571
幇 J5673/M8999 1572
彭 J5745/M10003 1720
街 J3339/M34051 1759
握 J302e/M12366 2232
暑 J3d6b/M14031′ 2484
椡 J5c31/M-X 2714
棱 J-X/M14979 2730
款 J343e/M16107 2938
殼 J334c/M-X 2996
殻 J5d57/M16646 2997
渥 J302f/M17770 3224
渚 J-X/M17758 3228
湮 J5e50/M17873 3233
煮 J3c51/M19165′ 3437
猪 J-X/M20534 3589
珪 J373e/M20972 3638
理 J4d7d/M21014 3644
琺 J606b/M21088 3652
痣 J615c/M22218 3809
痤 J-X/M22221 3811
皓 J622b/M22732 3875
童 J4638/M25775 4239
筅 J6426/M25986 4275
等 J4579/M25992 4287
粧 J3e51/M26945 4400
絓 J-X/M27403 4480
結 J376b/M27398 4492
耋 J664f/M28861 4703
著 J-X/M31410 5104
董 J4621/M31433 5118
蛯 J6962/M33061 5306
蛭 J4948/M33048 5308
蛙 J333f/M32997 5313
裁 J3a5b/M34258 5454
装 J4175/M34283 5455
赧 J6c5f/M37001 5842
趁 J6c63/M37083 5830
越 J315b/M37110 5851
超 J4436/M37096 5852
軽 J375a/M38281 5953
逹 J6d7d/M-X 6064
達 J4323/M39011′ 6088
遠 J3173/M39047′ 6101
野 J4c6e/M40133 6208
量 J4e4c/M40138 6209
黒 J3975/M48040 7052
黑 J-X/M48038 7053

10 residual strokes

傲 J507e/M1015 294
勢 J402a/M2422 558
嗇 J5427/M4053 860
嗸 J-X/M4143 881
園 J3160/M4818 962
堽 J544e/M5298 **1042**
壺 J5464/M5662 **1043**
塔 J4563/M5332 **1052**
堪 J342e/M5266 **1057**
塚 J-X/M5345 **1060**
塢 J5449/M5357 **1061**
塰 J544b/M-X **1062**
塙 J4839/M5341 **1063**
塒 J544d/M5329 **1064**
壼 J5467/M5667 **1065**
塘 J4564/M5340 **1066**
塋 J544a/M5320 **1067**
塑 J413a/M5328 **1068**
塞 J3a49/M5349 **1069**
塊 J3274/M5319 **1070**
塡 J-X/M5355 **1071**
填 J4536/M-X **1072**
墓 J4a68/M5431 **1073**
塗 J4549/M5338 **1074**
塩 J3176/M5382 **1075**
塾 J3d4e/M5402 **1083**
慤 J5842/M10983 1931
暑 J-X/M14051 2496
椌 J5c43/M15217 2765
楮 J5c3a/M15172 2770
殻 J5d57/M16646 2997
毀 J544c/M16654 3000
溘 J5e65/M17936 3255
煮 J-X/M19188 3441
煑 J-X/M19187 3442
煙 J316c/M19203 3456
猿 J316e/M20584 3600
甄 J612b/M21557 3701
睚 J624a/M23437 3939
睦 J4b53/M23460 3945
稜 J4e47/M25123 4152
童 J4638/M25775 4239
経 J3750/M27392 4473
罫 J3753/M28295 4642
腟 J6735/M29667 4842
莝 J6868/M31709 5142
蒔 J3c2c/M31546 5153
蓋 J3338/M31652 5155
装 J4175/M34283 5455
裝 J6a66/M34321 5456
裡 J4e23/M34295 5463
裲 J6a68/M34401 5467
詰 J354d/M35440 5609
詩 J3b6d/M35427 5610
賍 J6c5c/M36774 5795
越 J315b/M37110 5851
跣 J6c71/M37497 3871
輊 J6d49/M38311 5958
載 J3a5c/M38309 5960
遠 J3173/M39047′ 6101
酵 J395a/M39868 6175
量 J4e4c/M40138 6209
鼓 J385d/M48330 7076

11 residual strokes

僖 J5125/M1095 306
僥 J5127/M1113 311
嗷 J5353/M4142 880
嗸 J-X/M4143 881
嘉 J3245/M4176 887
壺 J5464/M5662 **1043**
塢 J5449/M5357 **1061**
壼 J5467/M5667 **1065**
塲 J5447/M5385 **1076**
壽 J5468/M5672 **1077**
墮 J5458/M5481 **1078**
墟 J-X/M-X **1079**
墟 J-X/M-X **1080**
墅 J5450/M5412 **1081**
墜 J4446/M5451 **1082**
塾 J3d4e/M5402 **1083**
塹 J544f/M5394 **1084**
境 J362d/M5409 **1085**
墨 J4b4f/M-X **1086**
塵 J3f50/M5388 **1087**
増 J417d/M5448′ **1088**
對 J5574/M7457 1387
慳 J584c/M11140 1960
截 J5923/M11639 2039
摯 J5975/M12632 2260

12 residual strokes

13 residual strokes

14 residual strokes

15 residual strokes

16 residual strokes

17 residual strokes

18 residual strokes

19 residual strokes

20 residual strokes

21–25 residual strokes

1–5 residual strokes

冬 J455f/M1610 410
処 J3d68/M1745 435
各 J3346/M3281 714
咎 J526b/M3493 759
咎 J-X/M-X 760
夂 J546a/M5708 1122
抛 J3572/M11985 2113
条 J3e72/M14486 2563
苳 J6774/M30811 4982
麦 J477e/M47718 7030

6 residual strokes

俊 J3d53/M674 216
咯 J533e/M3550 784
変 J4a51/M5703 **1119**
客 J3552/M7128 1329
後 J3865/M10098 1742
恪 J576d/M10592 1836
挌 J5948/M12047 2135
柊 J4922/M14610 2614
洛 J4d6c/M17383 3119
狢 J6042/M20366 3569
粂 J3729/M26860 4382
茖 J6823/M30863 5012
逡 J6d75/M38899 6050
逢 J3029/M38901 6054
降 J395f/M41620 6450

7 residual strokes

倏 J6047/M762 231
凌 J4e3f/M1669 424
唆 J3a36/M3696 803
夏 J3246/M5720 **1120**
峰 J4a76/M8094 1473
峯 J4a77/M8093 1474
峻 J3d54/M8116 1475
悛 J5822/M10674 1858
敖 J5a44/M13226 2342
格 J334a/M14749 2668
浚 J5e34/M17460 3151
烙 J5f60/M19014 3419
珞 J6064/M20953 3635
疼 J6156/M22105 3792
逡 J6d75/M38899 6050
逢 J3029/M38901 6054
陵 J4e4d/M41704 6454
隆 J4e34/M41720′ 6455

8 residual strokes

夏 J3246/M5720 **1120**
崚 J5645/M8184 1480
梭 J5b68/M14878 2693
烽 J5f62/M19059 3426
略 J4e2c/M21839 3755
畧 J6140/M21840 3756
終 J3d2a/M27372 4471
菱 J4929/M31219 5092
處 J515d/M32697 5268
麥 J734e/M47717 7031
麸 J7350/M-X 7034

9 residual strokes

厦 J524f/M2993 655
喀 J533d/M3896 847
復 J497c/M10183 1760
愎 J583f/M10920 1904
敞 J5a48/M13246 2348
棱 J-X/M14979 2730
竣 J3d57/M25773 4238
絡 J4d6d/M27426 4484
蓬 J4b29/M-X 5099
落 J4d6e/M31362 5130
蛒 J-X/M33985 5416
麸 J7350/M-X 7034

10 residual strokes

嗄 J534e/M4047 867
廈 J567c/M9435 1632
愛 J3026/M10947 1927
樱 J5c24/M15078 2755
稜 J4e47/M25123 4152
終 J3d2a/M27372 4471
絳 J652c/M27449 4475
腹 J4a22/M29722 4851
蓬 J4b29/M-X 5099
蓬 J-X/M31720 5157
蜂 J4b2a/M33088 5331
貉 J6c3b/M36549 5759
賂 J4f28/M36738 5799
路 J4f29/M37524 5876
輅 J6d4a/M38302 5957
酪 J4d6f/M39847 6172

11 residual strokes

嶐 J5657/M8447 1508
榎 J315d/M15219 2810
絡 J4d6d/M27426 4484
綾 J303d/M27591 4523
蓬 J4b29/M-X 5099
蓬 J-X/M31720 5157
蔆 J6851/M31760 5168
複 J4a23/M34417 5484
酸 J3b40/M39871 6177
閣 J3355/M41300 6401

12 residual strokes

夐 J546b/M5731 **1121**
履 J4d7a/M7799 1434
慶 J3744/M11145 1967
憂 J4d2b/M11170 1971
襁 J6335/M24792 4108
稷 J634d/M25207 4165
窿 J6363/M25660 4213
緻 J-X/M27700 4543
縫 J4b25/M27805′ 4550
蝮 J697d/M33309 5355
鋒 J4b2f/M40455 6275
麩 J734f/M47739 7033
麴 J396d/M-X 7036

13 residual strokes

噯 J-X/M4394 907
窿 J6363/M25660 4213
篠 J-X/M26328 4335
篷 J644b/M26404 4337
綾 J303d/M27591 4523
縫 J4b25/M27805′ 4550
縫 J-X/M27809 4556
蕗 J4979/M31964 5203
薐 J6933/M32108 5206
輹 J6d56/M38440 5974
駱 J7151/M44734 6749
骼 J716e/M45175 6788
鮗 J723c/M46091 6850
麪 J7351/M47742 7032
麭 J7352/M47757 7035
麺 J4c4d/M-X 7038

14 residual strokes

優 J4d25/M1261 334
擱 J5a28/M12892 2305
曖 J5b23/M14206 2521
緻 J-X/M27700 4543
縫 J4b25/M27805′ 4550
縫 J-X/M27809 4556
螽 J6a2a/M33519 5378
駿 J3d59/M44775 6754

15 residual strokes

擾 J3e71/M12920 2314
瓊 J607b/M21328 3682
瞹 J6259/M23727 3963
縫 J4b25/M27805′ 4550
縫 J-X/M27809 4556
謖 J6b6c/M35816 5684
額 J335b/M43586 6644
馥 J7146/M44545 6723
鬉 J736a/M48341 7077

16–22 residual strokes

縫 J4b25/M27805′ 4550

鄭 J4522/M39647 6155
銕 J6e6e/M40382 6254
関 J3458/M41297 6402
鞅 J7059/M42784 6581
駄 J424c/M44633 6734

12 residual strokes

冪 J5151/M1601 408
器 J346f/M4349′ 898
嬌 J5548/M6739 1268
寮 J4e40/M7325 1366
撦 J-X/M12728 2268
擦 J597c/M12741 2272
撲 J4b50/M12755 2274
槻 J4450/M15390 2845
樊 J5c68/M15414 2850
渓 J5e64/M17967 3253
滕 J5e6e/M18036 3261
潦 J5f33/M18259 3317
潜 J4078/M18241 3337
奬 J6052/M20637 3601
獠 J-X/M20692 3604
襖 J-X/M-X 4107
篋 J643a/M26271 4323
羹 J663e/M28536 4669
蕎 J363e/M31946 5197
蟒 J6a3d/M-X 5345
賛 J3b3f/M36841 5814
輦 J6d53/M38393 5970
遷 J-X/M-X 6103
遼 J4e4b/M39137 6111
遷 J412b/M39123′ 6113
鋏 J6e77/M40450 6272
頬 J4b4b/M-X 6629

髮 J717b/M45400 6805
駃 J7270/M46723 6942
麩 J734f/M47739 7033
黙 J4c5b/M48063′ 7055

13 residual strokes

墺 J5454/M5504 1100
奮 J4a33/M6012 **1172**
衡 J3955/M34078 1775
懋 J585b/M11215 1979
懊 J5865/M11332 1998
暸 J5b22/M14148 2517
樸 J5c77/M15495 2873
橋 J3636/M15526 2879
澳 J5f34/M18412 3344
燎 J5f79/M19414 3483
燃 J4733/M19394 3490
璞 J6079/M21245 3678
窺 J312e/M25633 4215
篋 J643a/M26271 4323
篡 J-X/M26330 4341
糢 J6477/M27116 4416
綺 J653a/M27586 4522
縢 J6558/M27783 4558
臻 J674b/M30165 4906
蟒 J-X/M33572 5367
蟆 J6a32/M33542 5369
蟇 J6a31/M33543 5370
躾 J6d3f/M38123 5934
轃 J6d54/M38429 5975
閹 J6f66/M41372 6406
闃 J6f6a/M41411 6410
雜 J-X/M-X 6508
霙 J7044/M42350 6538

頰 J-X/M43496 6637
鴦 J7273/M46822 6950
默 J6054/M48063 7056

14 residual strokes

壓 J545a/M5557 1104
嶽 J5656/M8566 1516
擲 J5a33/M12893 2304
濮 J5f41/M18526 3358
燠 J5f7a/M19458 3497
療 J4e45/M22500 3842
瞭 J4e46/M23697 3960
矯 J363a/M24015 3984
簒 J5255/M26490 4345
簇 J6448/M26437 4351
艱 J6765/M30600 4955
蟒 J6a3c/M33724 5373
襖 J3228/M-X 5498
謨 J6b75/M35864 5680
謄 J4625/M35780′ 5685
谿 J6c30/M36219 5734
貘 J6c42/M36621 5765
蹊 J6c7e/M37747 5896
鎹 J6f31/M40766 6309
闋 J-X/M41430 6412

15 residual strokes

攢 J5a39/M12933 2311
礇 J6325/M24505 4051
縢 J6558/M27783 4558
繚 J6567/M27904 4592
羃 J6632/M28393 4652
艱 J6765/M30600 4955

藤 J4623/M32340′ 5241
襖 J-X/M34629 5503
鎹 J6f31/M40766 6309
雞 J-X/M42124 6513
難 J4671/M42128′ 6515
類 J4e60/M43608′ 6647
騎 J3533/M44817 6761
夔 J7349/M47634 7021

16 residual strokes

攀 J5a35/M12926 2315
爨 J6026/M19648 3508
羹 J663d/M28584 4672
譜 J6b7c/M-X 5699
谿 J6c30/M36219 5734
蹊 J6c7e/M37747 5896
蹼 J6d2e/M37889 5909
轎 J6d5d/M38532 5987
難 J-X/M42145 6516
鯵 J3033/M-X 6875
鶏 J375c/M47074′ 6980
夔 J7349/M47634 7021

17 residual strokes

礬 J6329/M24573 4058
繚 J6567/M27904 4592
纂 J3b3c/M28012 4608
鐐 J6f41/M40886 6345
雞 J-X/M42124 6513
驀 J715e/M44949 6766
騰 J462d/M44915′ 6767
鰆 J7256/M46317 6889

18 residual strokes

儺 J5135/M1317 337
灘 J4667/M18784 3391
籐 J645b/M26693 4373
纘 J6573/M28030 4614
蠢 J6a41/M33797 5402
躑 J6d36/M37963 5920
飆 J712a/M43963 6671
鷄 J7331/M47209 6985

19 residual strokes

籘 J645c/M26733 4374
纂 J3b3c/M28012 4608
羇 J6634/M28412 4656
讃 J3b3e/M36110 5720
韉 J7068/M43075 6600
驕 J7161/M45008 6773
鷄 J7331/M47209 6985

20–23 residual strokes

蠶 J-X/M33891 5406
覊 J-X/M34794 5520
鑽 J6f54/M41009 6368
靨 J7054/M42698 6569
韉 J7068/M43075 6600
饜 J-X/M44453 6718
魘 J7236/M45941 6844
鷯 J733e/M47342 7002
黶 J7361/M48229 7066

Rad. 38 女

0 residual strokes

女 J3d77/M6036 **1173**

2 residual strokes

奴 J455b/M6039 **1174**
好 J3925/M6053 **1180**

3 residual strokes

妁 J5522/M6058 **1175**
妃 J485e/M6061 **1176**
妄 J4c51/M6063 **1177**
如 J4721/M6060 **1178**
奸 J5521/M6045 **1179**
好 J3925/M6053 **1180**
安 J3042/M7072 1311
汝 J4672/M17138 3040

4 residual strokes

努 J4558/M2314 527
妒 J-X/M6082 **1181**
妛 J562c/M6094 **1182**
妝 J5523/M6096 **1183**
妣 J5526/M6103 **1184**
妓 J3538/M6083 **1185**
妍 J552b/M6075 **1186**
妨 J4b38/M6111 **1187**
妥 J4245/M6107 **1188**
妊 J4725/M6072 **1189**
妖 J4d45/M6086 **1190**
妙 J4c2f/M6090 **1191**
姉 J-X/M6164 **1202**
孥 J5557/M6967 1290

5 residual strokes

佞 J5525/M-X 172
呶 J5273/M3460 755
妲 J5527/M6129 **1192**
姆 J5528/M6159 **1193**
姑 J3848/M6174 **1194**
姐 J3039/M6172 **1195**
姓 J402b/M6178 **1196**
妬 J454a/M6121 **1197**
妾 J3e2a/M6147 **1198**
妹 J4b65/M6138 **1199**
妻 J3a4a/M6140 **1200**
姉 J3b50/M6165 **1201**
姊 J-X/M6164 **1202**
始 J3b4f/M6166 **1203**
委 J3051/M6181 **1204**
姍 J552c/M6200 **1205**
孥 J5557/M6967 1290
帑 J5666/M8838 1554
弩 J5738/M9760 1686

6 residual strokes

姸 J-X/M6247 **1206**
姚 J552d/M6202 **1207**
姶 J3028/M6242 **1208**
姪 J4c45/M6226 **1209**
姜 J552a/M6205 **1210**
娜 J5531/M6311 **1211**
姥 J3138/M6216 **1212**
娃 J3023/M6262 **1213**
姨 J5529/M6222 **1214**
姻 J3079/M6250 **1215**
姿 J3b51/M6257 **1216**
姫 J4931/M6229 **1217**
姦 J342f/M6217 **1218**
威 J3052/M6259 **1219**
嫋 J553e/M6614 **1254**
弩 J5738/M9760 1686
怒 J455c/M10439 1820
拏 J593c/M11954 2103
按 J3044/M12038 2147
洳 J5e2e/M17414 3111
茹 J6827/M30921 5030
要 J4d57/M34768 5515

7 residual strokes

倭 J4f41/M796 242
凄 J4028/M1657 425
姨 J5529/M6222 **1214**
姫 J4931/M6229 **1217**
姬 J-X/M6230 **1220**
娉 J5532/M6282 **1221**
娚 J5533/M6306 **1222**
娥 J552e/M6331 **1223**
娠 J3f31/M6322 **1224**
娟 J552f/M6321 **1225**
娣 J-X/M6329 **1226**
婀 J5534/M6382 **1227**
娿 J-X/M6381 **1228**
娑 J5530/M6294 **1229**
娘 J4c3c/M6304 **1230**
娯 J3864/M6307 **1231**
娩 J4a5a/M6337 **1233**
宴 J3163/M7166 1332
弩 J5738/M9760 1686
恕 J3d7a/M10560 1834
晏 J5a67/M13914 2460
桜 J3a79/M14796 2664
案 J3046/M14762 2667
珱 J607e/M-X 3632

8 residual strokes

偃 J5070/M830 271
姨 J5529/M6222 **1214**
娉 J5532/M6282 **1221**
娠 J3f31/M6322 **1224**
娘 J4c3c/M6304 **1230**
娯 J3864/M6307 **1231**
婬 J5535/M6440 **1232**
娩 J4a5a/M6337 **1233**
婪 J553a/M6436 **1234**
婁 J4f2c/M6383 **1235**
娶 J5538/M6365 **1236**
婀 J5537/M6364 **1237**
婢 J5539/M6428 **1238**
婉 J5536/M6396 **1239**
婆 J474c/M6390 **1240**
娼 J3e2b/M6376 **1241**
婚 J3a27/M6418 **1242**
婦 J4958/M6432 **1243**
嫋 J553e/M6614 **1254**
悽 J582e/M10744 1880
接 J405c/M12280 2213
淒 J5e47/M17635 3172
蔞 J6846/M31264 5070
萎 J3060/M31269 5087
逶 J6d7b/M38949 6067

9 residual strokes

偃 J5070/M830 271
堰 J3161/M5274 1055
媛 J4932/M6516 **1244**
媚 J553b/M6513 **1245**
婿 J4c3b/M6470 **1246**
媒 J475e/M6498 **1247**
嫂 J553f/M6603 **1252**
嫌 J3779/M6618 **1257**
屢 J3c48/M7770 1428
椄 J5c26/M15008 2723
棲 J4033/M14980 2743
絮 J6531/M27443 4479
蓖 J686f/M31626 5152
逶 J6d7b/M38949 6067

10 residual strokes

僂 J5124/M1045 288
媛 J4932/M6516 **1244**
嫐 J554c/M6626 **1248**
媽 J5540/M6590 **1249**
嫗 J553c/M6588 **1250**
媳 J-X/M6573 **1251**
嫂 J553f/M6603 **1252**
媾 J553d/M6597 **1253**
嫋 J553e/M6614 **1254**
嫉 J3c3b/M6611 **1255**
嫁 J3247/M6602 **1256**
嫌 J3779/M6618 **1257**
嫦 J5543/M6663 **1260**
数 J3f74/M13319 2353
楼 J4f30/M15212 2785
瘻 J615f/M22290 3815

矮 J6264/M23995 3983
綏 J6537/M27501 4496
腰 J3978/M29705 4850
蓖 J686f/M31626 5152
褄 J6a6d/M34410 5470

11 residual strokes

嫖 J5545/M6637 **1258**
嫗 J5542/M6640 **1259**
嫦 J5543/M6663 **1260**
嫣 J5541/M6659 **1261**
嫩 J5544/M6666 **1262**
嫡 J4364/M6656 **1263**
屢 J-X/M7787 1431
絮 J6531/M27443 4479

12 residual strokes

嫺 J5546/M6710 **1264**
嫻 J5547/M6711 **1265**
嬋 J5549/M6738 **1266**
嬉 J3472/M6736 **1267**
嬌 J5548/M6739 **1268**
數 J5a4b/M13363 2356
樓 J5c6c/M15430 2830
縅 J654f/M27730 4540
鞍 J3048/M42815 6586
駕 J714e/M44661 6741

13 residual strokes

嬖 J554a/M6770 **1269**
嬢 J3e6e/M6807′ **1270**
瘻 J6171/M22467 3834
窶 J6360/M25628 4214
薮 J4c79/M-X 5201
褸 J6a7a/M34530 5492
霎 J7040/M42322 6534
餒 J712f/M44163 6695

14 residual strokes

嬬 J445c/M6821 **1271**
嬪 J554d/M6819 **1272**
嬰 J3145/M6828 **1273**
嬶 J554e/M6849 **1274**
嬲 J554b/M6831 **1275**
簍 J644d/M26456 4347
縅 J654f/M27730 4540
縷 J655f/M27832 4584
螻 J6a33/M33515 5375
鮟 J723d/M46108 6861

15 residual strokes

藪 J692e/M32348 5240
魏 J7232/M45872 6841

16 residual strokes

嬾 J554f/M6872 **1276**
瀛 J5f4a/M18656 3378
縷 J655f/M27832 4584
鏤 J6f3b/M40820 6339

17 residual strokes

嚶 J536d/M4592 925
孃 J5550/M6891 **1277**
孅 J5551/M6893 **1278**
孀 J5552/M6885 **1279**
鰔 J725a/M46314 6888

18–25 residual strokes

巍 J565b/M8626 1522
櫻 J5d2f/M15888 2917
瓔 J607d/M21347 3685
籔 J6458/M26708 4372
纓 J6577/M28067 4620
鸚 J7340/M47489 7009
鼴 J-X/M48464 7080
鼷 J-X/M48480 7081

Rad. 39 子

0 residual strokes

孑 J5553/M6931 **1280**
子 J3b52/M6930 **1281**

1 residual stroke

孔 J3926/M6933 **1282**

2 residual strokes

仔 J3b46/M367 119
孕 J5554/M6938 **1283**

3 residual strokes

好 J3925/M6053 1180
孕 J5554/M6938 **1283**
存 J4238/M6943 **1284**
字 J3b7a/M6942 **1285**

4 residual strokes

吼 J5263/M3377 730
孚 J5555/M6948 **1286**
孜 J3b5a/M6951 **1287**
孛 J5556/M6949 **1288**
孝 J3927/M6952 **1289**
孷 J555d/M13453 2365
李 J4d7b/M14459 2549

5 residual strokes

享 J357d/M298 92
孥 J5557/M6967 **1290**
孟 J4c52/M6960 **1291**
季 J3528/M6965 **1292**
孤 J3849/M6966 **1293**
学 J3358/M6974 **1294**

6 residual strokes

俘 J505a/M697 210
勃 J4b56/M2351 539
厚 J387c/M2949 651
孤 J3849/M6966 **1293**
孩 J5558/M6977 **1295**
拵 J594f/M12001 2140
荐 J6828/M30951 5016
郛 J6e3e/M39428 6140

7 residual strokes

哮 J532c/M3659 804
孩 J5558/M6977 **1295**
孫 J4239/M6987 **1296**
孰 J5559/M6995 **1297**
悖 J5823/M10663 1869
桲 J5b61/M14724 2641
浮 J4962/M17487 3159
荸 J-X/M31076 5048
郭 J3354/M39474 6144

8 residual strokes

孫 J4239/M6987 **1296**
孰 J5559/M6995 **1297**
悸 J5829/M10733 1885
惇 J4657/M10759 1887
教 J3635/M13213 2345
敎 J-X/M13212 2346
桴 J5b6f/M14807 2690
殍 J5d4b/M16464 2977
淳 J3d5f/M17690 3189
猛 J4c54/M20498 3588
菰 J3856/M31217 5079
遊 J4d37/M38994′ 6093

9 residual strokes

孫 J4239/M6987 **1296**
孱 J5623/M7000 **1298**
孳 J555a/M-X **1299**
敦 J4658/M13276 2349
椁 J5b76/M15003 2722
渤 J5e5f/M17769 3213
游 J5e62/M17792 3232
遊 J4d37/M38994′ 6093

遜 J423d/M39038 6098

---

10 residual strokes

孳 J555a/M-X **1299**
孶 J-X/M7011 **1300**
廓 J3347/M9461 1633
脬 J6759/M30431 4940
蜉 J696a/M33104 5324
遜 J423d/M39038 6098

---

11 residual strokes

塾 J3d4e/M5402 1083
孳 J555a/M-X **1299**
孵 J555b/M7021 **1301**
槨 J5c5a/M15362 2826
酵 J395a/M39868 6175

---

12 residual strokes

孳 J555a/M-X **1299**
孵 J555b/M7021 **1301**
潺 J5f25/M18298 3326
熟 J3d4f/M19332 3472
蝣 J6a22/M33292 5352
諄 J6b59/M35622 5635
醇 J3d66/M39901 6181

13–17 residual strokes

孳 J555a/M-X **1299**
孶 J-X/M7011 **1300**
學 J555c/M7033 **1302**
孺 J555e/M7042 **1303**
暾 J5a7d/M14160 2515
燉 J5f77/M19403 3479
鐓 J6f3e/M40891 6346
鶉 J7328/M47057 6978

Rad. 40 宀

0 residual strokes

宀 J555f/M7054 **1304**

---

2 residual strokes

宂 J-X/M7056 **1305**
它 J5560/M7057 **1306**
穴 J376a/M25406 4186
穴 J-X/M-X 4187
宂 J-X/M-X 4188

---

3 residual strokes

字 J3b7a/M6942 1285
宇 J-X/M7076 **1307**
宅 J4270/M7064 **1308**
宇 J3127/M7067 **1309**
守 J3c69/M7071 **1310**
安 J3042/M7072 **1311**

---

4 residual strokes

佇 J504a/M496 152
佗 J5049/M513 160
宇 J-X/M7076 **1307**
宍 J3c35/M7084 **1312**
宋 J4157/M7078 **1313**
宏 J3928/M7086 **1314**
完 J3430/M7079 **1315**
牢 J4f34/M19934 3535
究 J3566/M25409 4189
陀 J424b/M41600 6432

---

5 residual strokes

侘 J504e/M602 181
咜 J-X/M-X 749
宕 J4566/M7103 **1316**
宜 J3539/M7111 **1317**
宙 J4368/M7108 **1318**
宛 J3038/M7110 **1319**
宝 J4a75/M7122 **1320**
宗 J3d21/M7106 **1321**
官 J3431/M7107 **1322**
定 J446a/M7109 **1323**
実 J3c42/M7124 **1324**
沱 J5d7d/M17243 3082
穹 J6356/M25414 4190
突 J464d/M25424 4191
空 J3675/M25415 4192
苧 J4377/M30798 5000

---

6 residual strokes

咤 J5323/M3533 781
宦 J5561/M7138 **1325**
宥 J4d28/M7137 **1326**
室 J3c3c/M7136 **1327**
宣 J406b/M7132 **1328**
客 J3552/M7128 **1329**
按 J3044/M12038 2147
柁 J4248/M14599 2597
狩 J3c6d/M20390 3573
突 J-X/M25439 4193
穽 J6357/M25433 4194
窃 J4060/M25453 4195
穿 J407c/M25436 4198
院 J3121/M41665 6447

---

7 residual strokes

倥 J5065/M787 238
宦 J5561/M7138 **1325**
宰 J3a4b/M7160 **1330**
宸 J5562/M7171 **1331**
宴 J3163/M7166 **1332**
害 J3332/M7165 **1333**
宵 J3e2c/M7168 **1334**
容 J4d46/M7172 **1335**
宮 J355c/M7156 **1336**
家 J3248/M7169 **1337**
寂 J3[illegible]/M7200 **1342**
晏 J5a67/M13914 2460
案 J3046/M14762 2667
浤 J5e33/M17471 3140
浣 J5e31/M17470 3146
窈 J6358/M25463 4196
窄 J3a75/M25455 4197
穿 J407c/M25436 4198
竚 J636c/M25744 4229
莞 J3450/M31063 5052

---

8 residual strokes

啌 J5333/M3810 816
埦 J-X/M5171 1026
婉 J5536/M6396 1239
宸 J5562/M7171 **1331**
寃 J5563/M7202 **1338**
寇 J5564/M7209 **1339**
寇 J-X/M7208 **1340**
寅 J4652/M7204 **1341**
寂 J3c64/M7200 **1342**
密 J4c29/M7205 **1343**
宿 J3d49/M7195 **1344**
寄 J3473/M7203 **1345**
崇 J3f72/M8152 1490
常 J3e6f/M8955 1569
掟 J595d/M12272 2180
捥 J-X/M12181 2188
控 J3935/M12283 2202
淀 J4d64/M17610 3182
窕 J635a/M25496 4199
窒 J4362/M25493 4200
窓 J416b/M25494 4201
紵 J652a/M27353 4458
舵 J4249/M30400 4937
萓 J6840/M31279 5071
菅 J3f7b/M31142 5090
蛇 J3c58/M32964 5303
寉 J5565/M-X 6495

---

9 residual strokes

割 J3364/M2112′ 507
喀 J533d/M3896 847
喧 J3776/M3976 856
寃 J5563/M7202 **1338**
寔 J5566/M7244 **1346**
寐 J5567/M7236 **1347**
寓 J3677/M7243 **1348**
富 J4959/M7230 **1349**

寒 J3428/M7239 **1350**
愃 J583a/M10891 1903
棠 J5c2b/M14953 2718
椌 J5b7d/M15021 2726
椀 J4f50/M15001 2732
棕 J5c23/M14933 2740
棺 J343d/M14993 2746
睆 J622a/M22736 3874
窈 J6358/M25463 4196
窗 J6359/M25517 4202
窘 J635b/M25519 4203
窖 J635c/M25516 4204
腔 J3950/M29630 4826
腕 J4f53/M29631 4837
萓 J337e/M31345 5121
詑 J4242/M35374 5579
貯 J4379/M36698 5791

10 residual strokes

塞 J3a49/M5349 1069
嫁 J3247/M6602 1256
寞 J556b/M7282 **1351**
寬 J3432/M7276 **1352**
寢 J3f32/M7278′ **1353**
搾 J3a71/M12553 2251
暄 J5a77/M14033 2497
榁 J5c43/M15217 2765
滓 J5e68/M18034 3260
溶 J4d4f/M17983 3277
碗 J4f52/M24306 4014
碇 J4476/M24275 4019
窟 J3722/M25552 4206
膣 J6735/M29667 4842
蓉 J4d56/M31648 5135
詑 J4f4d/M35431 5598
鉈 J6e6d/M40289 6242

11 residual strokes

寢 J556a/M7289 **1354**
寬 J-X/M-X **1355**
實 J5569/M7294 **1356**
寨 J5c4d/M7298 **1357**
寣 J5568/M7291 **1358**
寥 J556c/M7292 **1359**
察 J3b21/M7283 **1360**
寧 J472b/M7296′ **1361**
寧 J-X/M7296 **1362**
寡 J3249/M7286 **1363**
審 J3f33/M7316 **1367**
搴 J596b/M12519 2246
榕 J5c57/M15228 2815
演 J3169/M18130 3310
熔 J4d50/M19319 3458
窬 J-X/M25582 4207
窩 J635d/M25579 4208
窪 J3726/M25580 4209
箜 J6433/M26151 4309
管 J3449/M26162 4317
粽 J6470/M26993 4410
綰 J6547/M27575 4512
綻 J433e/M27587 4514
綜 J416e/M27535 4520
聢 J665e/M29113 4729
蓿 J6872/M31747 5167
蔻 J-X/M31741 5171
蔲 J-X/M-X 5172
蜿 J696f/M33210 5337
蜜 J4c2a/M33143 5343
賨 J-Y/M36788 5804

12 residual strokes

實 J5569/M7294 **1356**
寫 J556d/M7320 **1364**
賓 J4950/M-X 1365
寮 J4e40/M7325 **1366**
審 J3f33/M7316 **1367**
榁 J5c69/M15428 2846
瞎 J6252/M23586 3952
榕 J634e/M-X 4164
稼 J3254/M25217 4169
窯 J4d52/M25594 4210
窮 J3567/M25593 4212
窿 J6363/M25660 4213
諚 J6b5c/M35682 5631
誼 J3543/M35605 5634
豌 J6c32/M36273 5738
踠 J-X/M37646 5886
踪 J6d29/M37668 5887
鞍 J3048/M42815 6586
駝 J714c/M44681 6740

13 residual strokes

寫 J556d/M7320 **1364**
寰 J556e/M7344 **1368**
憲 J377b/M11269′ 1988
憲 J-X/M11269 1989
確 J334e/M24366 4039
確 J-X/M-X 4040
窿 J6363/M25660 4213
窶 J6360/M25628 4214
窺 J312e/M25633 4215
糘 J6471/M-X 4418
綰 J6547/M27575 4512
綻 J433e/M27587 4514
綜 J416e/M27535 4520
縡 J6552/M27781 4560
諠 J6b63/M35706 5654
鋺 J6e7c/M40507 6287
錠 J3e7b/M40559 6293
靛 J-X/M42577 6562
館 J345b/M44237′ 6701
鴪 J7272/M46820 6947
鴕 J7278/M46774 6952

14 residual strokes

嚀 J5366/M4445 914
嬪 J554d/M6819 1272
寰 J556e/M7344 **1368**
擯 J5a2f/M12880 2300
擦 J3b24/M12862 2306
濱 J5f40/M18537 3355
濘 J5f3f/M18487 3359
獰 J6058/M20755 3611
竃 J3376/M-X 4216
縮 J3d4c/M27815 4585
舘 J345c/M30326 4923
謇 J6b69/M35791 5678
豁 J6c2f/M36221 5733
賽 J6c50/M36886 5822
蹇 J6d21/M37741 5898
轄 J336d/M38482′ 5981
邃 J6364/M39191 6123
館 J345b/M44237′ 6701
鮟 J723d/M46108 6861

15 residual strokes

櫁 J5c6a/M15754 2896
檸 J5d26/M15742 2899
檳 J5d27/M15734 2901
殯 J5d52/M16596 2986
瀋 J5f44/M18600 3369
瀉 J5f43/M18596 3374
竄 J6362/M25679 4218
邃 J6364/M39191 6123
邊 J6e34/M39216 6124
鎔 J6f30/M40704 6327
額 J335b/M43586 6644

16 residual strokes

寳 J5570/M7366 **1369**
寵 J437e/M7368 **1370**
竆 J-X/M25686 4219
竈 J635e/M25703 4221
縮 J3d4c/M27815 4585
邊 J6e34/M39216 6124
鑌 J6f35/M40821 6330
鶎 J-X/M47034 6976

17 residual strokes

寶 J556f/M7376 **1371**
竄 J6362/M25679 4218
竈 J635e/M25703 4221
聹 J6664/M29199 4743
騫 J715a/M44894 6765

Rad. 42 小

掌 J3e38 M12248 2200
敞 J5a49 M13245 2347
敝 J5a48 M13246 2348
景 J374a M13983 2487
棠 J5c2b M14953 2718
椋 J4c3a M15020 2725
椒 J5c25 M15029 2731
渺 J5e5d M17794 3235
甞 J6133 M21659 3714
睄 J6142 M21861 3761
硝 J3e4b M24201 4007
稍 J6344 M25083 4143
紗 J3c53 M27287 4446
絖 J652d M27409 4477
鈔 J6e64 M40227 6233
隙 J3764 M41792 6471

10 residual strokes

塗 J4549 M5338 1074
嫦 J5543 M6663 1260
尠 J5576 M7523 **1396**
尕 J-X M7522 **1397**
幌 J4b5a M9022 1577
滉 J5e66 M18017 3257
源 J383b M17926 3274
甞 J6133 M21659 3714
當 J6144 M21890 3765
督 J4644 M23457 3946
蜍 J696b M33110 5320
蛸 J427d M33072 5330
裟 J3a40 M34325 5457
隙 J-X M41813 6477

11 residual strokes

僚 J4e3d M1100 314
厰 J5252 M3034 658
嘗 J3e28 M4205 878
幣 J4a3e M9088 1585
幤 J5672 M-X 1586
愿 J5845 M11030 1934
慽 J-X M11159 1956
瑣 J6074 M21147 3674
絖 J652d M27409 4477
裟 J3a40 M34325 5457
裳 J3e58 M34357 5472
誚 J6b57 M35529 5614
趙 J6c64 M37171 5833
遼 J4e4b M39137 6111

12 residual strokes

賓 J4050 M-X 1365
寮 J4e40 M7325 1366
幣 J4a3e M9088 1585
廠 J3e33 M9490 1643
影 J3146 M10019 1722
憾 J-X M11158 1955
憬 J585d M11256 1978
撩 J597c M12741 2272
瞥 J5a7e M14155 2514
槭 J5c65 M15369 2835
潦 J5f33 M18259 3317
獠 J-X M20692 3604
緲 J654d M27687 4539
蔽 J4a43 M31888 5193
諒 J4e4a M35653 5641
賞 J3e5e M36813 5815

踪 J6d29 M37668 5887
輝 J3531 M38372 5972
遼 J4e4b M39137 6111
銷 J6e79 M40424 6276
霄 J703c M42290 6530

13 residual strokes

暸 J5b22 M14148 2517
燎 J5f79 M19414 3483
瞠 J6255 M23651 3957
穆 J4b54 M25251 4171
鍄 J6e7d M-X 6283
隲 J702d M41880 6486
鞘 J3e64 M42850 6387
餘 J7131 M44185 6693

14 residual strokes

儐 J3d7e M1245 333
寞 J-X M-X 916
擦 J3b24 M12862 2306
斃 J5a4d M13417 2363
療 J4e45 M22500 3842
瞥 J4a4d M23672 3959
瞭 J4e46 M23697 3960
螳 J6a30 M33503 5372
蟷 J6a2c M-X 5374
頻 J4951 M-X 6641
鯊 J7242 M46186 6867
齋 J6337 M48565 7085

15 residual strokes

斃 J5a4d M13417 2363

礑 J6327 M24526 4052
繚 J6567 M27904 4592
襠 J6a7d M34649 5502
蹩 J6d26 M37790 5902
蹴 J-X M37791 5903
鎖 J3a3f M40708 6325
鯀 J7241 M46168 6865
鮹 J7243 M46154 6871

16 residual strokes

竇 J5570 M7366 1369
蟷 J6a3b M33665 5393
蹴 J3d33 M37876 5913
願 J346a M43623 6653
鯨 J375f M46257 6886

17 residual strokes

瀕 J494e M18636 3381
繚 J6567 M27904 4592
耀 J4d54 M28828 4695
鐐 J6f41 M40886 6345
黨 J735e M48132 7062
黥 J735d M48123 7063

18–22 residual strokes

儻 J5138 M1323 338
纛 J657b M28093 4622
鐺 J6f46 M40954 6355
顥 J-X M43682 6654
鱉 J-X M46472 6917
鶻 J733e M47342 7002

鷲 J4f49 M47345 7004
鼈 J7368 M48305 7073

Rad. 43 尢

0 residual strokes

尢 J5577 M7538 **1398**

1–6 residual strokes

尨 J524d M2942 649
尤 J4c60 M7543 **1399**
尨 J5578 M7554 **1400**
拋 J5946 M11901 2072
拋 J-X M11948 2117
犹 J603b M20259 3558
疣 J614f M22050 3782

8–16 residual strokes

就 J3d22 M7599 **1401**
慨 J-X M-X 1975
既 J-X M13725 2409
晩 J-X M-X 2467
概 J-X M15364 2860
菟 J-X M31189 5077
蹴 J3d33 M37876 5913

Rad. 44 尸

0 residual strokes

尸 J5579 M7630 **1402**

1 residual stroke

Rad. 45 屮

Rad. 46 山

7 residual strokes

8 residual strokes

9 residual strokes

10 residual strokes

11 residual strokes

12 residual strokes

13 residual strokes

14 residual strokes

15 residual strokes

16 residual strokes

杠 J5b3a/M14481 2551
汞 J5d67/M17139 3039
肛 J666a/M29271 4758

5 residual strokes

拒 J-X/M11957 2098
矼 J6265/M24044 3987
空 J3675/M25415 4192

6 residual strokes

到 J516d/M1990 483
勁 J5226/M2349 538
拭 J3f21/M11989 2144
昻 J-X/M13885 2447
紅 J3948/M27243 4441
缸 J657d/M28112 4625
舡 J-X/M30362 4928
虹 J467a/M32830 5279
逕 J6d74/M38883 6052

7 residual strokes

倥 J5065/M787 238
差 J3a39/M8732 **1537**
徑 J574d/M10118 1743
恐 J3632/M10552 1853
揑 J-X/M-X 2166
涅 J-X/M17574 3149
莖 J6833/M31052 5037
訌 J6b41/M35228 5558
貢 J3957/M36665 5772
逕 J6d74/M38883 6052

8 residual strokes

啌 J5333/M3810 816
惘 J5831/M10809 1883
控 J3935/M12283 2202
筇 J-X/M25918 4258
紅 J3948/M27243 4441
脛 J667a/M29504 4818
隋 J6721/M41751 6464

9 residual strokes

尋 J3f52/M7447 1385
弑 J5736/M9680 1677
惘 J5831/M10809 1883
惰 J4246/M10855 1921
揑 J-X/M12345 2215
椌 J5b7d/M15021 2726
瘂 J615b/M22186 3812
筑 J435e/M26002 4280
腔 J3950/M29630 4826
蛩 J695e/M33037 5304
項 J3960/M43343 6617

10 residual strokes

嗟 J534d/M4102 869
嵯 J3a37/M8363 1500
嵳 J564d/M8364 1501
搓 J596d/M12476 2243
椿 J424a/M15133 2780
箜 J642e/M26070 4298
經 J6534/M27508 4493
蹉 J6c6f/M37519 5870
軾 J6d48/M38285 5956

鉅 J6e6a/M40286 6237

11 residual strokes

壽 J5468/M5672 1077
槎 J5c4c/M15320 2802
槓 J5c4a/M15343 2814
熕 J5f70/M19321 3462
瑳 J3a3c/M21170 3667
箜 J6433/M26151 4309
蕁 J-X/M-X 5164
覡 J6b2e/M34875 5530
誣 J6b58/M35542 5618
輕 J6d4b/M38346 5961
隨 J6e2e/M41871 6481

12 residual strokes

噚 J-X/M4349 890
噐 J535a/M4311 899
櫛 J5c73/M15565 2829
潯 J5f29/M18280 3318
磋 J6278/M24395 4034
經 J6534/M27508 4493
蕁 J6921/M31899 5195
隨 J6e2e/M41871 6481
鞏 J705f/M42819 6585

13 residual strokes

儔 J5132/M1224 326
噬 J5363/M4382 902
墮 J5458/M5481 1078
橵 J5c6d/M15512 2876
築 J435b/M26298 4343

縒 J6553/M27751 4559
膸 J673b/M29924 4869
隱 J702c/M41891 6485
頸 J7074/M43515 6638

14 residual strokes

墮 J5458/M5481 1078
壔 J-X/M5558 1106
擣 J5a2e/M12853 2301
濤 J5e39/M18508 3361
蹉 J6d22/M37745 5899
鴻 J3963/M46874 6963

15 residual strokes

縒 J6553/M27751 4559
魍 J7233/M45869 6839
鵐 J7325/M46922 6964

16 residual strokes

檮 J5b6d/M15713 2897
疇 J6146/M21967 3771
禱 J-X/M24852 4114
穩 J6353/M25344 4183
籌 J6456/M26675 4370
岁 J-X/M47034 6976

17 residual strokes

嚴 J536e/M4589 924
巖 J3460/M8624′ 1521
籌 J6456/M26675 4370
躊 J6d34/M37941 5919

18–21 residual strokes

儼 J5137/M1324 339
巖 J565e/M8649 1525
鑄 J6f49/M40972 6360
靈 J704d/M42532 6553
髓 J7172/M45289 6793
鰐 J-X/M46504 6922

Rad. 49 己

0 residual strokes

巳 J4c26/M8744 **1538**
已 J5661/M8743 **1539**
己 J384a/M8742 **1540**

1 residual stroke

巴 J4743/M8745 **1541**

2 residual strokes

囘 J5145/M1521 387
包 J4a71/M2506′ 572
包 J-X/M2506 573

3 residual strokes

妃 J485e/M6061 1176
巵 J5662/M8751 **1542**
色 J3f27/M30602 4956

4 residual strokes

廻 J-X/M9573 1655
忌 J3477/M10310 1786
把 J4744/M11874 2083
改 J327e/M13114 2332
杞 J5b39/M14479 2552
芭 J474e/M30730 4974
邑 J4d38/M39269 6127

5 residual strokes

庖 J4a79/M9266 1610
廻 J-X/M9573 1655
抱 J4a7a/M11917′ 2125
杷 J4747/M14505 2575
泡 J4b22/M17307 3093
爬 J6028/M19662 3511
祀 J632b/M24633 4064
肥 J486e/M29290 4774
苞 J677a/M30789 4996

6 residual strokes

巷 J-X/M-X 634
巷 J392b/M-X **1543**
巷 J-X/M8756 **1544**
巻 J342c/M8759′ **1545**
枹 J5b54/M14589 2602
炮 J5f5c/M18954 3406
紀 J352a/M27234 4439
胞 J4b26/M29396′ 4788

7 residual strokes

倦 J3771/M788 251
悒 J5825/M10655 1859
疱 J6157/M22082 3791
皰 J622e/M22844 3879
砲 J4b24/M24120 3998
笆 J6376/M25865 4252
耙 J6652/M28911 4707
記 J352d/M35244 5563
起 J352f/M37048 5849
配 J475b/M39771 6163

8 residual strokes

匏 J5237/M2544 576
扈 J6e3d/M11746 2057
梔 J5b69/M14846 2692
紀 J352a/M27234 4439
萢 J684d/M-X 5065
蚫 J695b/M32983 5293

9 residual strokes

匏 J5237/M2544 576
圏 J3777/M4815′ 960
巽 J4327/M8765 **1546**
惓 J582b/M10795 1882
捲 J377e/M12208 2193
港 J3941/M17783′ 3242
琶 J474a/M21081 3649
絶 J4064/M-X 4490
絕 J-X/M27407 4491
葩 J685d/M31441 5112
跑 J-X/M37461 5864

10 residual strokes

巽 J4327/M8765 **1546**
鉋 J6e70/M40292 6248
雹 J703b/M42248 6523
飽 J4b30/M44109′ 6684

11 residual strokes

滬 J5e76/M18072 3288
煕 J7426/M-X 3464
熙 J5f66/M19192 3465
熈 J5f67/M19292 3466
絶 J4064/M-X 4490
絕 J-X/M27407 4491
遷 J412b/M39123′ 6113
選 J412a/M39127′ 6114
靤 J7052/M42639 6567
鞄 J3373/M42781 6582
飽 J4b30/M44109′ 6684

12 residual strokes

噀 J-X/M4284 891
撰 J4071/M12753 2277
遷 J412b/M39123′ 6113
選 J412a/M39127′ 6114
髱 J717d/M45410 6808

13–21 residual strokes

廱 J572b/M9554 1650
癰 J617e/M22638 3856
艶 J3170/M30632 4957
艷 J6766/M30637 4958
饌 J7142/M44386 6712
鮑 J723a/M46074 6851
麭 J7352/M47757 7035

Rad. 50 巾

0 residual strokes

巾 J3652/M8771 **1547**

2 residual strokes

凧 J427c/M1749 434
匝 J4159/M2599 586
布 J495b/M8778 **1548**
市 J3b54/M8775 **1549**

3 residual strokes

匝 J4159/M2599 586
吊 J445f/M3291 710
师 J-X/M8800 **1550**
帆 J4841/M8787 **1551**
朿 J5b33/M14441 2541

4 residual strokes

帋 J5663/M8809 **1552**
希 J3475/M8813 **1553**

5 residual strokes

佩 J5050/M543 186
刷 J3a7e/M1964 479
刺 J3b49/M1969 480
制 J4029/M1961 481
姉 J3b50/M6165 1201
帑 J5666/M8838 **1554**
帚 J5664/M8854 **1555**
帛 J5667/M8855 **1556**
帙 J5665/M8852 **1557**
帖 J4421/M8849 **1558**
怦 J5768/M10476 1808
怖 J495d/M10450 1817
沛 J5d6f/M17216 3088

6 residual strokes

帥 J3f63/M8886 **1559**
帝 J446b/M8865 **1560**
柿 J3341/M14681 2624
肺 J4759/M29422′ 4791
逓 J447e/M38881′ 6055

7 residual strokes

唏 J5329/M3707 800
席 J404a/M8926 **1561**
師 J3b55/M8916 **1562**
帯 J4253/M8929 **1563**
帰 J3522/M8930 **1564**
旆 J5a54/M13646 2393
珮 J6063/M20977 3633
逓 J447e/M38881′ 6055

8 residual strokes

婦 J4958/M6432′ 1243
師 J3b55/M8916 **1562**
帶 J5668/M8950 **1565**
帽 J-X/M8967 **1566**
帷 J5669/M8954 **1567**

帳 J4422/M8939 **1568**
常 J3e6f/M8955 **1569**
掃 J415d/M12237′ 2207
晞 J5a6b/M13949 2471
欷 J5d38/M16087 2935
幕 J6848/M31234 5062

9 residual strokes

啻 J5341/M3886 835
啼 J5346/M3887 837
幀 J566c/M8982 **1570**
幄 J566a/M8994 **1571**
幇 J5673/M8999 **1572**
帽 J4b39/M8971 **1573**
幅 J497d/M8995 **1574**
幃 J566b/M8993 **1575**
棘 J5b79/M14938 2729
棗 J5c27/M14937 2736
棉 J4c49/M14919 2741
滞 J425a/M18067′ 3280
稀 J3529/M25058 4145
蒂 J685c/M31495 5101
適 J6e28/M39030 6078

10 residual strokes

嫦 J5543/M6663 1260
幃 J566b/M8993 **1575**
幎 J566d/M9024 **1576**
幌 J4b5a/M9022 **1577**
幕 J4b6b/M9051 **1578**
楴 J5c3c/M15179 2762
滞 J425a/M18067′ 3280
滯 J5e7c/M18075 3285

獅 [illegible]/M20609 3599
蓆 J686e/M31645 5148
蔕 J6878/M31789 5169
閙 J6f5f/M41264 6395
飾 J3e7e/M44111′ 6683

11 residual strokes

幗 J566e/M9057 **1579**
幔 J566f/M9050 **1580**
幣 J4a3e/M9088 **1585**
幤 J5672/M-X **1586**
滯 J5e7c/M18075 3285
箒 J6436/M26139 4308
箍 J6432/M26130 4311
綿 J4c4a/M27592 4531
豨 J-X/M36404 5747
豬 J-X/M36398 5748
飾 J3e7e/M44111′ 6683

12 residual strokes

冪 J5151/M1601 408
幗 J-X/M-X **1581**
幢 J5671/M9087 **1582**
幟 J5670/M9080 **1583**
幡 J4828/M9086 **1584**
幣 J4a3e/M9088 **1585**
幤 J5672/M-X **1586**
暼 J5a7e/M14155 2514
緜 J6544/M27644 4533
締 J4479/M27651 4549
蔕 J687b/M31898 5184
鬧 J7229/M45639 6822
鯑 J-X/M46020 6847

13 residual strokes

衞 J6a4c/M34074 1777
篩 J6441/M26359 4339
緜 J4c4a/M27592 4531
諦 J447c/M35716 5666
蹄 J447d/M37724 5893
錦 J3653/M40569 6301
霈 J703e/M42301 6537

14–18 residual strokes

幗 J-X/M-X **1587**
幮 J-X/M9134 **1588**
歸 J5d45/M16349 2966
緜 J6544/M27644 4533
締 J4479/M27651 4549
羃 J6632/M28393 4652
蟖 J6a2c/M-X 5374
鯑 J7246/M46203 6869
鰤 J725e/M46381 6906

Rad. 51 干

0 residual strokes

干 J3433/M9165 **1589**

1 residual stroke

午 J3861/M2703 604

2 residual strokes

刊 J3429/M1865 456

平 J4a3f/M9167 **1590**

3 residual strokes

吁 J525e/M3275 705
奸 J5521/M6045 1179
幵 J5674/M9169 **1591**
并 J5675/M9170 **1592**
年 J472f/M9168 **1593**
扞 J592a/M11802 2066
汗 J3440/M17130 3046

4 residual strokes

忓 J5758/M10358 1793
旱 J5a5d/M13752 2421
杆 J5b38/M14449 2557
罕 J6627/M28217 4634
肝 J344e/M29273 4762

5 residual strokes

坪 J445a/M4976 998
岼 J5630/M-X 1448
岸 J345f/M8009 1459
幷 J-X/M-X **1594**
幸 J392c/M9176 **1595**
枰 J354f/M14503 2581
泙 J5e24/M17296 3077
舍 J6752/M30278 4918
苹 J6779/M30823 4984

6 residual strokes

南 J466e/M2750 619

姸 J-X/M6247 1206
竿 J3448/M25854 4250

7 residual strokes

悍 J577b/M10643 1862
捍 J5952/M12143 2155
栞 J5b59/M14708 2645
秤 J4769/M24993 4134
訐 J6b40/M35234 5556
軒 J382e/M38187 5944
迸 J-X/M38929 6066

8 residual strokes

執 J3c39/M5193 1039
屛 J-X/M7734 1427
桿 J5b65/M14823 2674
梓 J3034/M14845 2688
硏 J-X/M24177 4000
萍 J684c/M31266 5076
迸 J-X/M38929 6066

9 residual strokes

喃 J5347/M3903 846
報 J4a73/M5275 1059
搖 J4d49/M12445′ 2235
献 J3825/M20539 3596
稈 J6343/M25074 4142
筓 J-X/M26005 4274
胼 J-X/M29586 4823
舒 J5030/M30300 4920
評 J493e/M35383 5587

10 residual strokes

幹 J3434/M9183 **1596**
楠 J466f/M15152 2779
滓 J5e68/M18034 3260
瑶 J6076/M-X 3656
幵 J716c/M45111 6785

11–15 residual strokes

僻 J4a48/M1166 323
塀 J-X/M-X 1079
滸 J5e77/M18089 3291
澤 J5f37/M18383 3338
澼 J5f35/M18382 3341
絣 J-X/M27607 4502
謡 J4d58/M35779′ 5666
辧 J5221/M38656 6003
餅 J7136/M44220 6698
髀 J7153/M44767 6753
駢 J-X/M44795 6755
鮃 J7239/M46044 6852
鼾 J736d/M48505 7083

Rad. 52 幺

0 residual strokes

幺 J5676/M9189 **1597**

1 residual stroke

幻 J3838/M9190 **1598**

2 residual strokes

幼 J4d44/M9193 **1599**
玄 J383c/M20814 3616

3 residual strokes

玆 J-X/M-X 380
糸 J3b65/M27221 4431

5 residual strokes

呟 J526c/M3427 753
弦 J3839/M9754 1688
拗 J5939/M11962 2111

6 residual strokes

幽 J4d29/M9205 **1600**
後 J3865/M10098 1742
胤 J307d/M29405 4786
茲 J6824/M30911 5011

7 residual strokes

奚 J5478/M5930 1160
畜 J435c/M21814 3749
痃 J6152/M22124 3790
眩 J6241/M23254 3924
窈 J6358/M25463 4196

8 residual strokes

孿 J555a/M-X 1299
孳 J-X/M7011 1300
衒 J6a4a/M34045 1753
牽 J3823/M20025 3544
率 J4e28/M20817′ 3618
絃 J383e/M27373 4468
舷 J383f/M30403 4938

9 residual strokes

孿 J555a/M-X 1299
孳 J-X/M7011 1300
幾 J3476/M9208 **1601**
滋 J3c22/M17919′ 3238

10 residual strokes

孳 J-X/M7011 1300
幾 J3476/M9208 **1601**
慈 J3b7c/M10980′ 1924
滋 J-X/M18021 3250
蓄 J435f/M31642 5161
鉉 J6a6b/M40290 6241
雍 J7036/M42000 6503

11 residual strokes

孿 J555a/M-X 1299
幾 J3476/M9208 **1601**
慈 J-X/M11048 1929
磁 J3c27/M24364 4029
酳 J6e4a/M39866 6174
麼 J5677/M47892 7042

12 residual strokes

樂 J5c5b/M15399 2832
畿 J3526/M21925 3768
磁 J-X/M24382 4031
聯 J665f/M29134 4733

13 residual strokes

繼 J5459/M5524 1096
機 J3521/M15561 2880
聠 J-X/M29066 4724
聯 J4e7e/M29153 4737
隰 J702e/M41889 6487

14 residual strokes

斷 J5a52/M13611 2388
濕 J5f3c/M18483 3353
磯 J306b/M24465 4049
聠 J-X/M29066 4724
聯 J4e7e/M29153 4737
谿 J6c30/M36219 5734
蹊 J6e7a/M37747 5896
黝 J735b/M48082 7058

15 residual strokes

嚮 J-X/M4565 919
嚮 J536c/M-X 920
擽 J5a36/M12919 2312
斷 J5a52/M13611 2388
甕 J6131/M21617 3709
藥 J693b/M32341 5236
關 J6f70/M41470 6419
雞 J-X/M42124 6513
響 J3641/M43318′ 6610

16 residual strokes

爍 J6023/M19549 3504
譏 J6b78/M35958 5702
關 J6f70/M41470 6419
響 J3641/M43318′ 6610

17–20 residual strokes

礫 J632a/M24572 4059
繼 J656b/M27997 4603
轢 J6d60/M38588 5993
鑠 J6f4b/M41019 6366
響 J-X/M43325 6613
顯 J707d/M43726 6657
饗 J3642/M-X 6705
饗 J-X/M44431 6715
饑 J7140/M44397 6716
鷄 J7331/M47209 6985

Rad. 53 广

0 residual strokes

广 J5678/M9221 **1602**

2 residual strokes

庁 J4423/M9223 **1603**
広 J392d/M9224′ **1604**

3 residual strokes

庄 J3e31/M9234 **1605**

4 residual strokes

庇 J485f / M9239 **1606**
序 J3d78 / M9253 **1607**
床 J3e32 / M9242 **1608**
応 J317e / M10347′ 1789

5 residual strokes

庇 J485f / M9239 **1606**
庚 J392e / M9278 **1609**
庖 J4a79 / M9266 **1610**
府 J495c / M9283 **1611**
底 J446c / M9262 **1612**
店 J4539 / M9267 **1613**
拡 J3348 / M11985′ 2118

6 residual strokes

庲 J-X / M-X **1614**
庠 J5679 / M9298 **1615**
度 J4559 / M9313 **1616**
昿 J5b26 / M-X 2436

7 residual strokes

俯 J506d / M722 253
唐 J4562 / M3709′ 812
席 J404a / M8926 1561
庫 J384b / M9330 **1617**
庭 J446d / M9337 **1618**
座 J3a42 / M9319 **1619**
砿 J395c / M-X 3994

8 residual strokes

座 J-X / M-X **1620**
康 J392f / M9376 **1621**
廊 J4f2d / M-X **1622**
庵 J3043 / M9369 **1623**
庸 J4d47 / M9378 **1624**
庶 J3d6e / M9373 **1625**
庶 J-X / M-X **1626**
紘 J6526 / M-X 4457
鹿 J3c2f / M47586 7017
麻 J4b63 / M47888 7040

9 residual strokes

廁 J567a / M9410 **1627**
廊 J-X / M9437 **1628**
廂 J567b / M9416 **1629**
廃 J4751 / M9425 **1630**
椨 J5c2d / M-X 2713
渡 J454f / M17765 3247
粧 J3e51 / M26945 4400
腑 J6725 / M29626 4831
鹿 J3c2f / M47586 7017

10 residual strokes

傭 J4d43 / M1007 295
塘 J4564 / M5340 1066
嫉 J3c3b / M6611 1255
厨 J-X / M-X **1631**
厦 J567c / M9435 **1632**
廓 J3347 / M9461 **1633**
廉 J4e77 / M9436 **1634**
溏 J5e6f / M17925 3254
蓙 J6868 / M31709 5142
蓆 J686e / M31645 5148
賍 J6c5c / M36774 5795
遮 J3c57 / M39086 6106
鉱 J395b / M40340′ 6252

11 residual strokes

嘛 J5357 / M4230 876
塵 J3f50 / M5388 1087
廏 J567e / M9453 **1635**
廐 J567d / M9454 **1636**
廖 J5721 / M9464 **1637**
廡 J5727 / M9491 **1642**
慵 J5859 / M11144 1954
慷 J584d / M11146 1963
漉 J3977 / M18112 3300
腐 J4965 / M29625 4835
蔗 J6874 / M31794 5176
遮 J3c57 / M39086 6106
麼 J5677 / M47892 7042

12 residual strokes

塵 J3f50 / M5388 1087
廐 J567d / M9454 **1636**
廖 J5721 / M9464 **1637**
廚 J5724 / M9479 **1638**
廢 J5726 / M9492 **1639**
廣 J5722 / M9493 **1640**
廝 J5723 / M9487 **1641**
廡 J5727 / M9491 **1642**
廠 J3e33 / M9490 **1643**
廛 J5725 / M9483 **1644**
廟 J4940 / M9489 **1645**
慵 J5859 / M11144 1954
慶 J3744 / M11145 1967
摩 J4b60 / M12613′ 2264
漉 J3977 / M18112 3300
麼 J5677 / M47892 7042
麾 J5d60 / M47899 7043

13 residual strokes

廐 J567d / M9454 **1636**
廨 J5728 / M9510 **1646**
廩 J5729 / M9515 **1647**
濂 J5f32 / M18441 3343
磨 J4b61 / M24449′ 4045
糖 J457c / M27070 4420
薦 J4126 / M32143′ 5219
麈 J7347 / M47616 7019

14 residual strokes

應 J5866 / M11330 1991
糜 J6476 / M27097 4422
糠 J3947 / M27105 4424
縻 J655b / M27839 4580
膺 J673f / M29928 4878
鍍 J4555 / M40607 6312
麈 J7347 / M47616 7019
麋 J7348 / M47625 7020

15 residual strokes

壙 J545d / M5576 1110
幮 J-X / M9134 1588
擴 J5a32 / M12895 2309
蹠 J6d28 / M37815 5906
麋 J7348 / M47625 7020
麕 J7349 / M47634 7021
麿 J4b7b / M47909 7044

16 residual strokes

廬 J572a / M9535 **1648**
曠 J5b25 / M14245 2525
簾 J4e7c / M26616 4365
縻 J655b / M27839 4580
鏖 J6f32 / M40799 6338
靡 J7353 / M42612 6565
麕 J7349 / M47634 7021
麛 J734b / M47660 7022
麓 J4f3c / M47658 7023
麑 J734c / M47656 7024
麒 J734a / M47657 7025
麗 J4e6f / M47663 7026

17 residual strokes

廳 J572d / M9552 **1649**
礦 J6268 / M24564 4057
鏖 J6f32 / M40799 6338
麛 J734b / M47660 7022
麓 J4f3c / M47658 7023
麑 J734c / M47656 7024
麒 J734a / M47657 7025
麗 J4e6f / M47663 7026

18 residual strokes

儷 J5136 / M1311 336
廱 J572b / M9554 **1650**
纏 J453b / M28043 4612

閧 [illegible]/M41311 6399
鼻 J4921/M48498′ 7082

12 residual strokes

噗 J-X/M4284 891
噴 J4a2e/M4345 900
廣 J5722/M9493 1640
弊 J4a40/M9644 **1670**
憤 J4a30/M11239 1990
撰 J4071/M12753 2277
撒 J3b35/M12697 2279
碾 J627a/M24370 4038
聯 J665f/M29134 4733
蟒 J6a3d/M-X 5345
醋 J6e4c/M39911 6179

13 residual strokes

彝 J5734/M9948 1710
碾 J627a/M24370 4038
蟒 J-X/M33572 5367
錯 J3a78/M40579 6299
閧 J722a/M45641 6823

14 residual strokes

彝 J5734/M9948 1710
擤 J-X/M12857 2298
糞 J4a35/M27102 4425
翼 J4d63/M28801 4692
藉 J6934/M32242 5231
蟒 J6a3c/M33724 5373
鍍 J4555/M40607 6312

15 residual strokes

彝 J5733/M9950 1711
瀑 J5f46/M18609 3371
簣 J6450/M26541 4356
蹠 J6d28/M37815 5906

16–20 residual strokes

嘸 J536b/M4545 923
彝 J5733/M9950 1711
曝 J4778/M14239 2524
爆 J477a/M19540 3505
[illegible] J-X/M34021 5418
鑛 J6f4a/M41010 6363
霰 J7047/M42458 6546
饌 J7142/M44386 6712
鵲 J7327/M47014 6975
鷓 J733a/M47251 6999

Rad. 56 弋

0 residual strokes

弋 J5735/M9656 **1671**

1–4 residual strokes

代 J4265/M386 125
弌 J5021/M9658 **1672**
弍 J5031/M9661 **1673**
弎 J-X/M9662 **1674**
弐 J4675/M-X **1675**
式 J3c30/M9663 **1676**
杙 J5b3b/M14473 2553

5–8 residual strokes

垈 J5432/M-X 991
岱 J4252/M7997 1452
岷 J5631/M8007 1454
拭 J3f21/M11989 2144
武 J4970/M16273 2959
玳 J605e/M20889 3627
袋 J425e/M34171 5443
貳 J6c49/M-X 5774

9 residual strokes

弑 J5736/M9680 **1677**
斌 J494c/M13468 2369
袋 J425e/M34171 5443
貳 J6c48/M36703 5783
貸 J425f/M36709 5792

10–16 residual strokes

試 J3b6e/M35415 5611
賦 J496a/M36800 5811
贇 J6c56/M36909 5831
軾 J6d48/M38285 5956
鉽 J6f27/M40597 6288
鳶 J4650/M46674 6938
鵡 J4c39/M46963 6974
黛 J4263/M48075 7060

Rad. 57 弓

0 residual strokes

弓 J355d/M9692 **1678**

1 residual stroke

弖 J5737/M9703 **1679**
弔 J4424/M9698 **1680**
引 J307a/M9699 **1681**

2–4 residual strokes

佛 J5047/M517 146
夷 J3050/M5852 1143
弘 J3930/M9709 **1682**
弗 J4a26/M9708 **1683**
弛 J4350/M9724 **1684**
弟 J446f/M9737 **1685**

5 residual strokes

弩 J5738/M9760 **1686**
弧 J384c/M9757 **1687**
弦 J3839/M9754 **1688**
弥 J4c6f/M9753 **1689**
彿 J574a/M10071 1729
怫 J5767/M10486 1813
拂 J5944/M11936 2097
泓 J5d77/M17288 3075
沸 J4a28/M17251 3094
狒 J6041/M20338 3564
穹 J6356/M25414 4190

6 residual strokes

剃 J4466/M1989 489
姨 J5529/M6222 1214
弯 J573f/M-X **1690**
弭 J5739/M9768 **1691**
洟 [illegible]/M17387 3121
矧 J476a/M23938 3979
粥 J3421/M26938 4402

7 residual strokes

娣 J-X/M6329 1226
弦 J3839/M9754 **1688**
弱 J3c65/M9791′ **1692**
張 J4425/M9812 **1694**
悌 J4470/M10642 1861
涕 J5e38/M17543 3143
蚓 J694e/M32866 5285
躬 J6d3b/M38038 5929

8 residual strokes

弸 J573a/M9817 **1693**
張 J4425/M9812 **1694**
強 J362f/M9815 **1695**
柫 J-X/M14911 2687
梯 J4474/M14881 2706
痍 J6158/M22148 3801
第 J4268/M25943 4272

9 residual strokes

强 J-X/M9822 **1696**
弼 J492b/M9826 **1697**
弻 J-X/M9825 **1698**
弾 J4346/M9836′ **1699**
湾 J4f51/M17920 3239
發 J6224/M22669 3861
睇 J6249/M23360 3937
費 J4871/M36717 5786

10 residual strokes

嫋 J553e/M6614 1254
嵶 J564e/M-X 1498
彁 J573b/M-X **1701**
搦 J596e/M12500 2248
溺 J452e/M17990 3271
漲 J5e7d/M18173 3294
蒻 J686a/M31623 5141

11 residual strokes

漲 J5e7d/M18173 3294
鋹 J6e6e/M40382 6254

12 residual strokes

廢 J5726/M9492 1639
彈 J573c/M9865 **1700**
彁 J573b/M-X **1701**
撥 J597b/M12727 2283
潑 J-X/M18225 3325
窮 J3567/M25593 4212
鬻 J717c/M45414 6806

13–14 residual strokes

彊 J3630/M9872 **1702**
彌 J573d/M9877 **1703**
癈 J6173/M22520 3841
襁 J6a76/M34545 5494
襁 J-X/M-X 5497

5–26 residual strokes

彎 J573e/M9904 **1704**
瀰 J5f50/M18690 3389
灣 J5f54/M18823 3393
疆 J6145/M21961 3770
醱 J-X/M40041 6194
鬻 J6478/M45721 6832
鰯 J3073/M46413 6904
鶸 J312d/M46952 6971
鷄 J7334/M47193 6992

Rad. 58 彐

0 residual strokes

彐 J5740/M9909 **1705**

1 residual stroke

尹 J557a/M7631 1403

2 residual strokes

聿 J6666/M29215 4746

3 residual strokes

伊 J304b/M432 134
冱 J5154/M1613 414
彐 J546c/M5759 1128
当 J4576/M9913 **1706**

4 residual strokes

争 J502f/M-X 70
君 J372f/M3323 746
怛 J5759/M10397 1797
沍 J5d6c/M17194 3058
狃 J603d/M20289 3559

5 residual strokes

事 J3b76/M241 71
妻 J3a4a/M6140 1200
帚 J5664/M8854 1555
庚 J392e/M9278 1609
爭 J6027/M19663 3510
秉 J633d/M24932 4125
隶 J7030/M41923 6489

6 residual strokes

侵 J3f2f/M646 218
律 J4e27/M10097 1740
急 J355e/M10475 1823
津 J4445/M17396 3122
浄 J3e74/M17451 3128
衄 J6a48/M33973 5414
郡 J3734/M39436 6143

7 residual strokes

倢 J-X/M784 227
兼 J3773/M1483 381
凄 J4028/M1657 425
剝 J-X/M2049 495
剥 J476d/M48939 496
唐 J4562/M3709′ 812
帰 J3522/M8930 1564

彖 J5741/M9920 **1707**
書 J3d71/M14294 2463
档 J5b63/M-X 2639
浸 J3f3b/M17505′ 3157
笋 J6424/M25873 4251
逮 J4261/M38931′ 6069

8 residual strokes

婦 J4958/M6432′ 1243
崢 J5644/M8203 1482
康 J392f/M9376 1621
庸 J4d47/M9378 1624
彗 J5742/M9927 **1708**
悽 J582e/M10744 1880
捷 J3e39/M12216 2198
掃 J415d/M12237′ 2207
晝 J5a6c/M13948 2465
椙 J5b75/M14821 2679
淨 J5e46/M17669 3163
淒 J5e47/M17635 3172
菷 J6848/M31234 5062
葬 J6846/M31264 5070
逮 J4261/M38931′ 6069
雪 J4063/M42216′ 6520

9 residual strokes

喙 J533c/M3951 838
嫌 J3779/M6618 1257
尋 J3f52/M7447 1385
棣 J5c28/M14957 2720
棲 J4033/M14980 2743
畫 J6141/M21859 3759
祿 J4f3d/M24741′ 4096

窘 J635b/M25519 4203
筝 J6438/M-X 4273
筆 J492e/M25987 4288
粛 J3d4d/M29223 4747
腱 J6727/M29708 4843
葎 J4e2a/M31397 5111
裙 J6a65/M34314 5460
鈕 J6e66/M40228 6230

10 residual strokes

嗛 J-X/M4088 862
嫌 J3779/M6618 1257
寖 J3f32/M7278′ 1353
廉 J4e77/M9436 1634
彙 J5743/M9936 **1709**
慊 J5844/M11051 1939
搀 J5961/M12313 2220
椽 J5c3d/M15087 2778
溏 J5e6f/M17925 3254
睫 J624c/M23469 3944
碌 J6271/M24282 4017
祿 J6333/M24741 4097
群 J3732/M28498 4666
羣 J663a/M28497 4667
肆 J6668/M29226 4749
腱 J6727/M29708 4843
蒹 J6865/M31621 5133
褄 J6a6d/M34410 5470
隠 J3123/M41836′ 6480

11 residual strokes

寢 J556a/M7289 1354
慵 J5859/M11144 1954

慷 J584d/M11146 1963
歉 J5d3e/M16159 2944
盡 J6238/M23029 3900
箒 J6436/M26139 4308
箏 J6437/M26133 4313
緑 J4e50/M27541′ 4528
綠 J-X/M27541 4529
肇 J4825/M29228 4751
肈 J-X/M29230 4752
蕁 J-X/M-X 5164
静 J4045/M42574′ 6560

12 residual strokes

噚 J-X/M4349 890
慵 J5859/M11144 1954
慧 J3745/M11116 1964
潯 J5f29/M18280 3318
篆 J643f/M26256 4329
縁 J316f/M27656′ 4553
緣 J-X/M27656 4554
膟 J6733/M-X 4863
蕁 J6921/M31899 5195
諍 J6b5a/M35643 5633

13 residual strokes

嘯 J5362/M4246 904
彝 J5734/M9948 **1710**
濂 J5f32/M18441 3343
穏 J323a/M25280′ 4175
糖 J457c/M27070 4420
緑 J4e50/M27541′ 4528
綠 J-X/M27541 4529
蕭 J692b/M32012 5218
錚 J6f23/M40553 6290
録 J4f3f/M40519′ 6298
錄 J-X/M40611 6303
鍵 J3830/M40654 6317
隠 J702c/M41891 6485
靜 J7050/M42578 6561

14 residual strokes

儘 J5056/M1234 327
壗 J545c/M-X 1105
瀞 J4654/M-X 3356
濯 J4275/M18532 3360
糠 J3947/M27105 4424
縁 J316f/M27656′ 4553
緣 J-X/M27656 4554
繍 J3d2b/M-X 4572
艝 J675c/M30536 4945
謙 J382c/M35821′ 5686
賺 J6c51/M36880 5821
鍵 J3830/M40654 6317
隷 J7031/M41932 6491
騷 J7154/M44759 6752
龜 J737d/M48847 7106

15 residual strokes

彝 J5733/M9950 **1711**
歸 J5d45/M16349 2966
瀟 J5f4f/M18660 3383
燼 J5f7e/M19515 3502
簫 J6454/M26560 4355
轌 J6d5a/M-X 5985
鎌 J3379/M40693 6326

16 residual strokes

櫞 J5d29/M15822 2904
瀞 J-X/M18659 3380
穩 J6353/M25344 4183
簾 J4e7c/M26616 4365
繍 J3d2b/M-X 4572
繡 J-X/M27913 4600

17 residual strokes

彝 J5733/M9950 **1711**
靆 J704c/M42530 6552

18 residual strokes

櫞 J5d29/M15822 2904
穐 J6354/M25381 4184
繍 J3d2b/M-X 4572
繡 J-X/M27913 4600
蠡 J6a42/M33796 5401
贐 J6c59/M36956 5834
鏽 J-X/M40857 6353
靆 J704c/M42530 6552
鱇 J7261/M46468 6910

19–25 residual strokes

穐 J6354/M25381 4184
靆 J704c/M42530 6552
鬮 J-X/M-X 6827
鬮 J722d/M45659 6828
鱈 J432d/M46470 6916
鱘 J-X/M46504 6922

Rad. 59 彡

0 residual strokes

彡 J5744/M9962 **1712**

4–5 residual strokes

参 J3b32/M3090 666
尨 J5578/M7554 1400
形 J3741/M9969 **1713**
杉 J3f79/M14452 2562
衫 J6a4e/M34111 5421

6 residual strokes

修 J3d24/M721 260
厖 J524d/M2942 649
彦 J4927/M9981 **1714**
彥 J-X/M9980 **1715**
殄 J5d49/M16413 2971
珍 J4441/M20920 3631

7 residual strokes

修 J3d24/M721 260
畛 J613b/M21810 3744
疹 J3f3e/M22097 3788
袗 J6a57/M34194 5440
髟 J7175/M45355 6799

8 residual strokes

倐 J5074/M850 262
彪 J4937/M9993 **1716**
彬 J494b/M9996 **1717**
彩 J3a4c/M9992 **1718**
彫 J4426/M9995 **1719**
惨 J3b34/M10850 1896
渗 J-X/M-X 3167

9 residual strokes

參 J5254/M3098 667
彭 J5745/M10003 **1720**
診 J3f47/M35337 5586
趁 J6c63/M37083 5850
軫 J6d47/M38243 5950
須 J3f5c/M43352 6618

10 residual strokes

勠 J522d/M2418 556
蓚 J686b/M-X 5146
髢 J7176/M45363 6800

11 residual strokes

寥 J556c/M7292 1359
廖 J5721/M9464 1637
彰 J3e34/M10015 **1721**
慘 J584e/M11094 1948
摎 J5977/M12564 2258
滲 J5e7a/M18081 3302
蓼 J687a/M31744 5166
蔘 J6875/M31795 5174
髥 J-X/M45375 6801
髦 J7178/M45377 6802
髣 J7177/M45371 6803
髪 J4831/M45387′ 6804

- 徽 J-X / M10267 **1778**
- 禦 J357a / M24820 4111
- 縱 J6554 / M27819 4576
- 聳 J6660 / M29167 4739

15–21 residual strokes

- 徽 J-X / M10267 **1778**
- 衢 J6a4d / M34090 **1779**
- 懲 J4428 / M11399′ 2006
- 懲 J-X / M11424 2007
- 縦 J3d44 / M27804′ 4571
- 縱 J6554 / M27819 4576
- 覆 J4a24 / M34789′ 5517
- 蹤 J6d27 / M37823 5901
- 黴 J7360 / M48196 7065

Rad. 61 心

0 residual strokes

- 心 J3f34 / M10295 **1780**

1 residual stroke

- 必 J492c / M10299 **1781**

3 residual strokes

- 忖 J5756 / M10326 **1782**
- 忙 J4b3b / M10334 **1783**
- 忘 J4b3a / M10333 **1784**
- 志 J3b56 / M10331 **1785**
- 忌 J3477 / M10310 **1786**
- 忍 J4726 / M10312′ **1787**
- 忍 J-X / M10312 **1788**
- 応 J317e / M10347′ **1789**
- 怫 J5767 / M10486 **1813**
- 沁 J5d6e / M17182 3056
- 芯 J3f44 / M30732 4976

4 residual strokes

- 忰 J582d / M10381 **1790**
- 忷 J-X / M10392 **1791**
- 忩 J-X / M10366 **1792**
- 忤 J5758 / M10358 **1793**
- 忱 J575a / M10382 **1794**
- 忻 J5757 / M10401 **1795**
- 忝 J575b / M10348 **1796**
- 忸 J5759 / M10397 **1797**
- 忿 J575d / M10408 **1798**
- 忽 J397a / M10405 **1799**
- 念 J4730 / M10390 **1800**
- 忠 J4369 / M10353 **1801**
- 快 J3277 / M10369 **1802**
- 怫 J5767 / M10486 **1813**
- 泌 J4867 / M17279 3092

5 residual strokes

- 忷 J-X / M10392 **1791**
- 忩 J-X / M10366 **1792**
- 忱 J575a / M10382 **1794**
- 怎 J5763 / M10431 **1803**
- 怐 J5761 / M10435 **1804**
- 怕 J5766 / M10448 **1805**
- 怙 J5760 / M10454 **1806**
- 怛 J5765 / M10458 **1807**
- 怦 J5768 / M10476 **1808**
- 怩 J5762 / M10481 **1809**
- 怺 J576a / M10513 **1810**
- 怏 J5769 / M10434 **1811**
- 怜 J4e67 / M10461 **1812**
- 怫 J5767 / M10486 **1813**
- 怡 J575e / M10470 **1814**
- 怱 J5764 / M10494 **1815**
- 怯 J3631 / M10491 **1816**
- 怖 J495d / M10450 **1817**
- 怠 J4255 / M10469 **1818**
- 怨 J3165 / M10479 **1819**
- 怒 J455c / M10439 **1820**
- 怪 J3278 / M10483 **1821**
- 性 J402d / M10478 **1822**
- 急 J355e / M10475 **1823**
- 思 J3b57 / M10462 **1824**
- 悌 J4470 / M10642 **1861**

6 residual strokes

- 怫 J5767 / M10486 **1813**
- 怠 J4255 / M10469 **1818**
- 恆 J5771 / M10528 **1825**
- 恠 J575f / M10574 **1826**
- 恷 J576e / M-X **1827**
- 恁 J576c / M10518 **1828**
- 恂 J5776 / M10520 **1829**
- 恊 J5770 / M10535 **1830**
- 恚 J576b / M10566 **1831**
- 恃 J5774 / M10521 **1832**
- 恟 J576f / M10573 **1833**
- 恕 J3d7a / M10560 **1834**
- 恙 J5779 / M10565 **1835**
- 恪 J576d / M10592 **1836**
- 恫 J5778 / M10594 **1837**
- 恰 J3366 / M10603 **1838**
- 恤 J5775 / M10583 **1839**
- 恍 J5772 / M10546 **1840**
- 恣 J5773 / M10580 **1841**
- 恨 J3a28 / M10588 **1842**
- 恢 J327a / M10577 **1843**
- 恬 J5777 / M10595 **1844**
- 恭 J3633 / M10596 **1845**
- 恥 J4351 / M10585 **1846**
- 恵 J3743 / M10618′ **1847**
- 悔 J3279 / M10617′ **1848**
- 恒 J3931 / M10527 **1849**
- 息 J4229 / M10601 **1850**
- 恩 J3238 / M10591 **1851**
- 恋 J4e78 / M10537 **1852**
- 恐 J3632 / M10552 **1853**
- 悖 J5823 / M10663 **1869**
- 祕 J6330 / M24663 4075
- 秘 J486b / M24977 4140
- 葱 J683b / M30994 5041

7 residual strokes

- 偬 J5078 / M889 263
- 偲 J3c45 / M895 266
- 唸 J5339 / M3773 823
- 密 J4c29 / M7205 1343
- 恆 J5771 / M10528 **1825**
- 悤 J-X / M10693 **1854**
- 悔 J-X / M10659 **1855**
- 悧 J5826 / M10689 **1856**
- 悁 J577a / M10623 **1857**
- 悛 J5822 / M10674 **1858**
- 悒 J5825 / M10655 **1859**
- 悚 J577e / M10672 **1860**
- 悌 J4470 / M10642 **1861**
- 悍 J577b / M10643 **1862**
- 悃 J577d / M10625 **1863**
- 悉 J3c3d / M10635 **1864**
- 悋 J5827 / M10640 **1865**
- 悄 J5821 / M10627 **1866**
- 悩 J473a / M10716′ **1867**
- 悦 J3159 / M10629′ **1868**
- 悖 J5823 / M10663 **1869**
- 悟 J3867 / M10680 **1870**
- 患 J3435 / M10691 **1871**
- 悠 J4d2a / M10681 **1872**
- 悪 J302d / M10717 **1873**
- 悗 J5824 / M10664 **1879**
- 悸 J5829 / M10733 **1885**
- 惇 J4657 / M10759 **1887**
- 捻 J4731 / M12222 2201
- 添 J453a / M17698 3201
- 窓 J416b / M25494 4201

8 residual strokes

- 悳 J575c / M10724 **1874**
- 惡 J5828 / M10824 **1875**
- 惠 J582a / M10822 **1876**
- 惧 J-X / M-X **1877**
- 惧 J577c / M10848 **1878**
- 悗 J5824 / M10664 **1879**
- 悽 J582e / M10744 **1880**
- 惆 J582f / M10757 **1881**
- 惓 J582b / M10795 **1882**
- 惘 J5831 / M10809 **1883**
- 悴 J582c / M10726 **1884**
- 悸 J5829 / M10733 **1885**
- 惹 J3c66 / M10866 **1886**

優 J4d25/M1261 334
嚀 J5366/M4445 914
慈 J3b7c/M10980′ **1924**
慨 J-X/M11122 **1974**
憐 J4e79/M11206 **1987**
應 J5866/M11330 **1991**
懆 J586a/M11325 **1992**
懋 J586c/M11333 **1993**
懍 J586e/M11335 **1994**
懃 J5869/M11321 **1995**
懌 J5864/M11334 **1996**
憺 J586b/M11305 **1997**
懊 J5865/M11332 **1998**
憾 J3438/M11312 **1999**
懈 J5868/M11328 **2000**
憶 J3231/M11295 **2001**
懇 J3a29/M11326 **2002**
懐 J327b/M11351 **2003**
曖 J5b23/M14206 2521
檍 J5c7a/M15656 2885
濘 J5f3f/M18487 3359
獰 J6058/M20755 3611
穗 J634f/M25298 4177
總 J6541/M27844 4575
罹 J586d/M28347 4651
聰 J6662/M29154 4735
聴 J4430/M29173 4740
臆 J3232/M29951 4883
蟋 J6a29/M33550 5380
謐 J6b6d/M35803 5681

---

14 residual strokes

慈 J-X/M11048 **1929**
懇 J3a29/M11326 **2002**
懐 J327b/M11351 **2003**
懣 J5870/M11384 **2004**
懦 J586f/M11390 **2005**
懲 J4428/M11399′ **2006**
擾 J3e71/M12920 2314
檬 J5c6a/M15754 2896
檸 J5d26/M15742 2899
濾 J5f49/M18565 3372
癒 J4c7e/M22545 3847
瞹 J6259/M23727 3963
顋 J707b/M43576 6642
騐 J-X/M44821 6759

---

15 residual strokes

懲 J-X/M11424 **2007**
懱 J5873/M-X **2008**
穩 J6353/M25344 4183
總 J6541/M27844 4575
藥 J6922/M32410 5243
鯰 J7250/M46285 6879

---

16 residual strokes

廳 J572d/M9552 1649
懷 J5867/M11456 **2009**
懶 J5871/M11455 **2010**
懸 J377c/M11462 **2011**
聹 J6664/M29199 4743
轗 J6d5e/M38550 5989
鑁 J6f3c/M40907 6351
鰓 J7254/M46344 6900

---

17 residual strokes

懷 J5867/M11456 **2009**
懺 J5872/M11478 **2012**
懽 J5875/M11497 **2013**
鑁 J6f3c/M40907 6351

---

18 residual strokes

懸 J377c/M11462 **2011**
懾 J5877/M11498 **2014**
懿 J5874/M11501 **2015**
懼 J5876/M11488 **2016**
聽 J6665/M29211 4744

19–23 residual strokes

廳 J572c/M9562 1651
戀 J5878/M11504 **2017**
軈 J6d41/M38167 5938
鑢 J6f4c/M41021 6365
靉 J704f/M42540 6556

Rad. 62 戈

0 residual strokes

戈 J5879/M11530 **2018**

---

1 residual stroke

戉 J587a/M11531 **2019**
戊 J4a6a/M11532 **2020**

---

2 residual strokes

伐 J4832/M439 132
戉 J587a/M11531 **2019**
戋 J-X/M11542 **2021**
戌 J587c/M11535 **2022**
戍 J587b/M11537 **2023**
戎 J3d3f/M11539 **2024**
成 J-X/M11544 **2026**

---

3 residual strokes

成 J402e/M11542′ **2025**
成 J-X/M11544 **2026**
戒 J327c/M11548 **2027**
我 J3266/M11545 **2028**
找 J5932/M11851 2073

---

4 residual strokes

戔 J587d/M11559 **2029**
或 J303f/M11563 **2030**
栈 J-X/M-X 2567
茂 J4c50/M30833′ 4998

---

5 residual strokes

俄 J3264/M665 215
咸 J5279/M3563 774
哉 J3a48/M3596 779
城 J3e6b/M5086′ 1011
城 J-X/M5120 1013
威 J3052/M6259 1219

---

6 residual strokes

哦 J5328/M3642 798
城 J-X/M5120 1013
娥 J552e/M6331 1223
峨 J3265/M8071 1471
峩 J5636/M8072 1472
晟 J5a70/M13950 2472
栽 J3a4f/M14750 2654
桟 J3b37/M14796′ 2658
残 J3b44/M16459 2976
莪 J6830/M31077 5047

---

7 residual strokes

國 J5422/M4798 956
域 J3068/M5158 1030
戝 J6c43/M11603 **2031**
戚 J404c/M11594 **2032**
戛 J587e/M11598 **2033**
械 J3323/M14882 2685
淺 J5e49/M17697 3162
盛 J4039/M23001′ 3895

---

8 residual strokes

喊 J533f/M3916 843
幾 J3476/M9208 1601
惑 J4f47/M10789 1892
戞 J5921/M11605 **2034**
戟 J3761/M11606 **2035**
棧 J5c22/M14963 2708
殘 J5d4c/M16506 2978
減 J383a/M17759 3249
牋 J6030/M19849 3527
盛 J-X/M23005 3897
筬 J642d/M26067 4279
筏 J4835/M26000 4282
絨 J6530/M27435 4483

Rad. 63 戸

0 residual strokes

7 residual strokes

8 residual strokes

9 residual strokes

10 residual strokes

11 residual strokes

Rad.64: 12 residual strokes

Rad. 65 支

Rad. 66 攴

Rad. 67 文

0 residual strokes

Rad.67: 2 residual strokes

文 J4a38/M13450 **2364**

2–5 residual strokes

吝 J5267/M3327 736
対 J4250/M7419 1375
彦 J-X/M9980 1715
李 J555d/M13453 **2365**
斉 J4046/M13454 **2366**
旻 J5a61/M13775 2429

6 residual strokes

剤 J3a5e/M2076′ 493
悋 J5827/M10640 1865
噯 J-X/M13460 **2367**
紊 J6524/M27261 4447
紋 J4c66/M27262 4451
虔 J694a/M32686 5266
蚊 J3263/M32849 5288
蚉 J-X/M32848 5289

7 residual strokes

倏 J5074/M850 262
斎 J3a58/M13467 **2368**
済 J3a51/M17749 3197
產 J-X/M21684 3717

8 residual strokes

斌 J494c/M13468 **2369**
斐 J4865/M13469 **2370**
斑 J4843/M13470 **2371**
紊 J6524/M27261 4447
紋 J4c66/M27262 4451
臍 J-X/M-X 4824
閔 J6f5c/M41251 6387

10–15 residual strokes

嫩 J5544/M6666 1262
憫 J5862/M11252 1986
斖 J-X/M-X **2372**
緕 J656e/M-X 4504
諺 J-X/M35747 5658
贇 J6c56/M36909 5831
顏 J707a/M43591 6649

Rad. 68 斗

0 residual strokes

斗 J454d/M13489 **2373**

3–6 residual strokes

抖 J5935/M11888 2075
科 J324a/M24950 4130
料 J4e41/M13501 **2374**
蚪 J6951/M32903 5284

7–9 residual strokes

斛 J5a4f/M13508 **2375**
斜 J3c50/M13509 **2376**
斟 J5a50/M13517 **2377**
萪 J6854/M31334 5106

10–11 residual strokes

斡 J3036/M13522 **2378**
槲 J5c60/M15375 2836
蝌 J6978/M33248 5357
魁 J3321/M45785 6834

Rad. 69 斤

0 residual strokes

斤 J3654/M13534 **2379**

1–2 residual strokes

丘 J3556/M33 19
匠 J3e22/M2605 588
斥 J404d/M13535 **2380**
斥 J-X/M-X **2381**
近 J3661/M38752′ 6021

3 residual strokes

兵 J4a3c/M1462 374
匠 J3e22/M2605 588
听 J5261/M3352 723
圻 J542d/M4903 980
忻 J5757/M10401 1795
折 J405e/M11890 2094
沂 J5d6b/M17183 3052
芹 J365c/M30742 4970
近 J3661/M38752′ 6021
邱 J6e39/M39335 6132

4 residual strokes

岳 J3359/M8001 1457
所 J3d6a/M11715 2054
拆 J593e/M11943 2101
斧 J4960/M13539 **2382**
析 J404f/M14538 2574
欣 J3655/M16008 2930
泝 J5d7b/M17300 3078
祈 J3527/M24640′ 4071

5 residual strokes

斫 J5a51/M13548 **2383**
柝 J5b51/M14633 2610
祈 J-X/M24640 4072
逝 J4042/M38895 6051

6 residual strokes

哲 J452f/M3667 811
浙 J5e36/M17458 3139
浜 J494d/M17462 3152
逝 J4042/M38895 6051

7 residual strokes

啓 J373c/M3820 828
掀 J5957/M12230 2178
斬 J3b42/M13555 **2384**
断 J4347/M13557 **2385**
晢 J5a71/M13953 2469
晣 J-X/M13954 2470
梹 J5b6e/M14909 2677
淅 J5e48/M17617 3169
蚚 J6955/M32916 5300

8 residual strokes

断 J4347/M13557 **2385**
斯 J3b5b/M13563 **2386**
晰 J5a72/M13990 2481
訴 J414a/M35325 5588
釿 J6e63/M40203 6227

9 residual strokes

新 J3f37/M13572 **2387**
晳 J622c/M22748 3876

10 residual strokes

厮 J5251/M3026 661
塹 J544f/M5394 1084
嶄 J5650/M8413 1509
嶃 J-X/M8412 1510
慚 J5850/M11096 1965
漸 J4132/M18179 3305
誓 J4040/M35514 5622

11 residual strokes

嘶 J535d/M4260 892
慙 J584f/M11095 1966
撕 J5979/M12705 2269
暫 J3b43/M14120 2510
槧 J5c61/M15359 2833
質 J3c41/M36833 5817
鋲 J4946/M40503 6277
駈 J366f/M44636 6744

Kanji	JIS	Morohashi	No.
借	J3c5a	M781	259
冥	J4c3d	M1588	405
凍	J4560	M1670	427
剔	J5171	M2031	494
原	J3836	M2973	652
哽	J532b	M3680	799
宴	J3163	M7166	1332
峺	J5638	M8115	1468
島	J4567	M8108	1476
庫	J384b	M9330	1617
悍	J577b	M10643	1862
捍	J5952	M12143	2155
捏	J5954	M12149	2165
揑	J-X	M-X	2166
挿	J415e	M12119	2167
捜	J415c	M12179′	2168
晦	J3322	M-X	**2454**
晋	J3f38	M13899	**2455**
晉	J5a69	M13898	**2456**
晁	[illegible]	M13889	**2457**
晃	J3938	M13891	**2458**
晄	J5a68	M13892	**2459**
晏	J5a67	M13914	**2460**
晒	J3b2f	M13924	**2461**
時	J3b7e	M13890	**2462**
書	J3d71	M14294	**2463**
晟	J5a70	M13950	**2472**
桓	J343c	M14774	2652
殉	J3d5e	M16448	2974
殷	J5d56	M16627	2993
溲	J-X	M-X	3135
涅	J5e3a	M17521	3148
涅	J-X	M17574	3149
狸	J432c	M20427	3578
畠	J482b	M21827	3747
疸	J6155	M22094	3786
皋	J6228	M22714	3871
神	J-X	M24673	4088
竜	J4e35	M25751	4232
耆	J664d	M28849	4701
脂	J3b69	M29463	4808
莫	J477c	M31078	5057
袙	J6a5a	M34196	5435
袓	J6a58	M34184	5437
軒	J382e	M38187	5944
連	J4f22	M38902′	6062
都	J4554	M39497′	6148
陳	J4444	M41698	6457

7 residual strokes

Kanji	JIS	Morohashi	No.
亀	J3535	M210	62
乾	J3425	M204	63
偖	J5077	M856	265
偈	J5075	M836	267
偃	J5070	M830	271
冕	J514b	M1545	397
勗	J5228	M2392	544
動	J4630	M2390	549
啅	J5336	M3802	815
喝	J3365	M-X	824
唱	J3e27	M3765	829
奢	J547a	M5964	1164
娼	J3e2b	M6376	1241
婚	J3a27	M6418	1242
宿	J3d49	M7195	1344
屠	J454b	M-X	1426
崑	J5642	M8173	1484
帽	J-X	M8967	1566
庵	J3043	M9369	1623
得	J4640	M10137	1755
悼	J4569	M10738	1891
惜	J404b	M10814	1894
捶	J5959	M12215	2177
掉	J595c	M12243	2186
措	J413c	M12286	2190
掩	J3166	M12285	2192
掲	J3747	M12311′	2194
斬	J3b42	M13555	2384
曽	J413e	M-X	**2464**
晝	J5a6c	M13948	**2465**
晩	J-X	M13940	**2466**
晚	J-X	M-X	**2467**
晜	J-X	M-X	**2468**
晢	J5a71	M13953	**2469**
晣	J-X	M13954	**2470**
晞	J5a6b	M13949	**2471**
晧	J5a6e	M13961	**2473**
晤	J5a6d	M13956	**2474**
曼	J5250	M14298	**2475**
晨	J5a6f	M13962	**2476**
曹	J4162	M14297	**2477**
晦	J-X	M13960	**2478**
桿	J5b65	M14823	2674
梗	J393c	M14849	2698
渚	J3d6d	M-X	3164
淹	J5e3b	M17696	3178
渇	J3369	M17748	3195
混	J3a2e	M17694	3204
焰	J316b	M-X	3423
猖	J604b	M20490	3583
猪	J4376	M20511′	3585
皎	J6229	M22724	3872
眴	J-X	M23307	3931
竡	J636e	M25767	4233
竟	J706f	M25757	4234
章	J3e4f	M25761	4235
粕	J4774	M26891	4391
紳	J3f42	M27348	4467
習	J3d2c	M28672′	4681
舶	J4775	M30402	4936
葛	J336b	M-X	5060
菴	J683f	M31227	5063
菖	J3e54	M31174	5085
菎	J6842	M31160	5088
萌	J4b28	M31265	5094
菓	J325b	M31168′	5095
著	J4378	M31302	5098
覃	J6b29	M34770	5516
軎	J6d44	M-X	5945
軛	J6d43	M38207	5946
軟	J4670	M38213	5947
転	J453e	M38234′	5948
遏	J6e21	M39004	6079
遇	J3670	M38991′	6083
運	J313f	M38998′	6092
都	J-X	M39509	6149
隍	J7026	M41754	6465
隅	J3679	M41743	6467
陽	J4d5b	M41725	6470

8 residual strokes

Kanji	JIS	Morohashi	No.
偈	J5075	M836	267
偃	J5070	M830	271
冕	J514b	M1545	397
募	J4a67	M2416	551
卿	J-X	M2880	643
啷	J-X	M3961	844
喧	J3776	M3976	856
堵	J4548	M-X	1021
堵	J-X	M5279	1053
堤	J4469	M5259	1054
堰	J3161	M5274	1055
場	J3e6c	M5278	1058
奢	J547a	M5964	1164
寔	J5566	M7244	1346
寓	J3677	M7243	1348
屠	J-X	M7761	1429
崑	J5642	M8173	1484
帽	J4b39	M8971	1573
徨	J5753	M10178	1756
復	J497c	M10183	1760
恵	J582a	M10822	1876
惷	J5836	M10864	1901
惺	J5839	M10868	1902
愃	J583a	M10891	1903
愎	J583f	M10920	1904
惕	J-X	M10933	1906
愠	J-X	M10954	1907
惶	J5835	M10863	1912
戟	J3761	M11606	2035
揭	J-X	M12389	2216
揩	J5962	M12383	2223
揮	J3478	M12394	2229
揚	J4d48	M12355	2236
提	J4473	M12344	2237
既	J-X	M13725	2409
晉	J5a69	M13898	**2456**
晨	J5a6f	M13962	**2476**
暎	J5a75	M14048	**2479**
暃	J5a73	M-X	**2480**
晰	J5a72	M13990	**2481**
晶	J3e3d	M14000	**2482**
曾	J413d	M14299	**2483**

Rad.72: 9 residual strokes

Kanji	JIS	Morohashi	No.
暑	J3d6b	M14031′	**2484**
晄	J3647	M14031	**2485**
替	J4258	M14300	**2486**
景	J374a	M13983	**2487**
晴	J4032	M13994′	**2488**
普	J4961	M13982	**2489**
智	J4352	M14010	**2490**
晩	J4855	M14030′	**2491**
最	J3a47	M14301	**2492**
棔	J5c21	M14931	2717
椙	J3f7a	M15063	2728
棍	J5b7e	M14924	2735
棹	J5c2a	M14992	2738
棉	J4c49	M14919	2741
棟	J456f	M14949	2747
楳	J4760	M15178	2754
殷	J-X	M16645	2999
混	J3a2e	M17694	3204
渴	J-X	M17788	3208
渣	J5e56	M17767	3223
渚	J-X	M17758	3228
渾	J5e55	M17800	3236
湿	J3c3e	M17920′	3243
湯	J4572	M17874	3245
温	J3239	M17774	3246
煉	J4e7b	M-X	3428
焜	J5f63	M19103	3432
煮	J3c51	M19165′	3437
猪	J-X	M20534	3589
猩	J604f	M20528	3595
甦	J6134	M21691	3718
瘦	J4169	M-X	3806
皖	J622a	M22736	3874
皓	J622b	M22732	3875
睍	J-X	M-X	3936
硬	J3945	M24230	4008
稈	J6343	M25074	4142
筍	J6423	M25997	4281
粨	J646a	M26949	4401
絏	J6532	M27397	4476
絢	J303c	M27427	4481
腊	J-X	M29614	4827
朝	J442b	M14374′	4838
菎	J6842	M31160	5088
萬	J685f	M31339	5103
著	J-X	M31410	5104
蓮	J4f21	M-X	5105
葷	J6858	M31461	5116
董	J4621	M31433	5118
萱	J337e	M31345	5121
葛	J-X	M31420	5126
覃	J6b29	M34778	5516
軻	J6d46	M38274	5949
軫	J6d47	M38243	5950
軼	J6d45	M38275	5951
軸	J3c34	M38269	5952
軽	J375a	M38281	5953
遏	J6e21	M39004	6079
遇	J3678	M38991′	6083
運	J313f	M38998′	6092
鄉	J-X	M-X	6151
間	J3456	M41249	6391
隕	J3764	M41792	6471

9 residual strokes

Kanji	JIS	Morohashi	No.
亶	J5039	M328	98
僧	J414e	M1076	300
傷	J3d7d	M1029	301
匙	J3a7c	M2590	582
嗜	J534f	M4089	870
嗹	J5358	M4148	875
塒	J544d	M5329	1064
墓	J4a68	M5431	1073
寘	J556b	M7282	1351
尟	J-X	M7522	1397
幎	J566d	M9024	1576
幌	J4b5a	M9022	1577
幕	J4b6b	M9051	1578
幹	J3434	M9183	1596
愒	J-X	M10933	1906
愚	J3672	M10946	1925
意	J3055	M10921	1926
戦	J406f	M11631′	2037
揩	J5962	M12383	2223
搨	J5972	M12503	2244
搶	J596f	M12525	2245
搢	J-X	M12494	2247
摸	J4c4e	M12644	2250
旣	J-X	M13725	2409
會	J5072	M14306	**2493**
普	J-X	M-X	**2494**
曉	J-X	M-X	**2495**
暑	J-X	M14051	**2496**
暄	J5a77	M14033	**2497**
暘	J5a78	M14066	**2498**
暉	J5a76	M14038	**2499**
暈	J5a74	M14037	**2500**
暇	J324b	M14036	**2501**
暖	J4348	M14064	**2502**
暗	J3045	M14065	**2503**
暢	J442a	M14095	**2506**
棍	J5b7e	M14924	2735
榊	J3a67	M-X	2756
楮	J5c3a	M15172	2770
楷	J5c34	M15185	2781
椿	J4458	M15090	2782
楊	J4d4c	M15112	2784
款	J343e	M16107	2938
歇	J5d3c	M16141	2943
渴	J-X	M17788	3208
漣	J4e7a	M-X	3210
滉	J5e66	M18017	3257
溟	J5e72	M17947	3258
漣	J-X	M18155	3259
潛	J-X	M17922	3262
漠	J4779	M18149	3268
滝	J426c	M18067	3273
源	J383b	M17926	3274
焜	J5f63	M19103	3432
煮	J-X	M19188	3441
煑	J-X	M19187	3442
煬	J5f6c	M19235	3446
煌	J5f6a	M19181	3449
照	J3e48	M19226	3457
獏	J6053	M20638	3597
琿	J606d	M21093	3658
晳	J622c	M22748	3876
盟	J4c41	M23024	3899
碍	J3337	M24283	4016
禅	J4135	M24787′	4104
窠	J-X	M25556	4205
粳	J646b	M26967	4408
紳	J3f42	M27348	4467
罩	J662d	M28289	4640
罨	J662c	M28288	4641
署	J3d70	M28311′	4643
腥	J6729	M29678	4845
腫	J3c70	M29697	4848
腸	J4432	M29721	4849
腹	J4a22	M29722	4851
蓮	J4f21	M-X	5105
葩	J685d	M31441	5112
蓍	J6869	M31655	5137
蒔	J3c2c	M31546	5153
蓮	J-X	M31722	5158
裼	J6a69	M34379	5466
褐	J336c	M-X	5473
諛	J-X	M35495	5590
詢	J6b4e	M35411	5593
詣	J3758	M35412	5594
豊	J4b2d	M36263	5737
貊	J6c3d	M36550	5758
輌	J-X	M38287	5954
輛	J6d52	M-X	5955
軾	J6d48	M38285	5956
輅	J6d4a	M38302	5957
輊	J6d49	M38311	5958
較	J3353	M38297	5959
農	J4740	M38688	6008
遭	J4178	M39082′	6105
閘	J6f5e	M41263	6396
隙	J-X	M41813	6477
障	J3e63	M41821	6479
電	J4545	M42253	6526
靼	J705a	M42764	6578
韵	J7071	M43271	6608

10 residual strokes

Kanji	JIS	Morohashi	No.
僭	J-X	M1117	304
僣	J5129	M1111	305
僚	J4e3d	M1100	314
厭	J315e	M3025	662
噌	J4139	M-X	873

嗹 J5358/M4148 875
嘗 J3e28/M4205 878
嘈 J-X/M4175 879
塲 J5447/M5385 1076
墅 J5450/M5412 1081
境 J362d/M5409 1085
增 J417d/M5448' 1088
層 J4158/M-X 1432
幛 J5651/M8410 1506
嶄 J5650/M8413 1509
嶃 J-X/M8412 1510
幔 J566f/M9050 1580
彰 J3e34/M10015 1721
愿 J5845/M11030 1934
慕 J4a69/M11088 1948
慯 J5853/M11133 1952
慱 J5855/M11137 1953
慟 J5856/M11103 1959
慴 J5852/M11143 1961
憎 J417e/M11188' 1969
慨 J-X/M11122 1974
戧 J-X/M11637 2038
摹 J-X/M12645 2241
摶 J5976/M12642 2259
摺 J4022/M12647 2262
斡 J3036/M13522 2378
普 J-X/M-X **2494**
暳 J5b21/M14169 **2504**
暝 J5a79/M14083 **2505**
暢 J442a/M14095 **2506**
暦 J4e71/M14111' **2507**
暮 J4a6b/M14128 **2508**
楷 J5c34/M15185 2781
槞 J5c59/M-X 2795
槇 J5c55/M15244 2797
榻 J5c50/M15292 2807
榊 J-X/M15352 2808
模 J4c4f/M15453 2825
漣 J4e7a/M-X 3210
漣 J-X/M18155 3259
潟 J-X/M-X 3286
漸 J4132/M18179 3305
漕 J4166/M18131 3306
漫 J4c21/M18166 3308
煦 J5f68/M19225 3445
瘍 J6167/M22327 3825
皸 J6230/M22888 3882
皹 J6231/M-X 3883
睹 J6251/M23519 3950
碣 J6272/M24326 4025
稲 J3070/M25187' 4158
種 J3c6f/M25174 4159
窬 J-X/M25582 4207
竭 J6371/M25803 4242
箸 J4824/M-X 4301
箆 J6431/M26157 4303
箔 J4773/M26142 4312
節 J-X/M26243 4320
綟 J6532/M27397 4476
絢 J303c/M27427 4481
緍 J-X/M27607 4503
綽 J653f/M27590 4518
緒 J3d6f/M27632 4521
練 J4e7d/M27631' 4530
綿 J4c4a/M27592 4531
署 J-X/M28319 4646
翰 J344d/M28780 4690
膜 J4b6c/M29808' 4854
舓 J-X/M30310 4921
蓮 J-X/M31722 5158
蓴 J6873/M31734 5165
蓿 J6872/M31747 5167
蔓 J4c22/M31784 5180
蜴 J696e/M33190 5335
襌 J6a7c/M-X 5477
褐 J-X/M34435 5478
褌 J6a6e/M34428 5480
複 J4a23/M34417 5484
貌 J4b46/M36556 5762
輕 J6d4b/M38346 5961
輒 J6d4c/M38336 5962
輓 J6d4e/M38337 5963
輔 J4a65/M38342 5964
農 J4740/M38688 6008
遭 J4178/M39082' 6105
遼 J4e4b/M39137 6111
鄲 J6e42/M39659 6154
鞀 J705a/M42764 6578
韶 J7070/M43276 6609

11 residual strokes

僧 J-X/M1189 319
億 J322f/M1178 321
冪 J5151/M1601 408
勲 J372e/M2463 560
噌 J-X/M4303 889
嘲 J535e/M4254 897
增 J-X/M5454 1089
墹 J5451/M-X 1092
嬋 J5549/M6738 1266
寮 J4e40/M7325 1366
屨 J-X/M7798 1433
履 J4d7a/M7799 1434
幟 J5670/M9080 1583
廣 J5722/M9493 1640
廟 J4940/M9489 1645
影 J3146/M10019 1722
衝 J3e57/M34069 1772
慚 J5850/M11096 1965
慙 J584f/M11095 1966
慢 J4b7d/M11110 1968
憎 J-X/M11202 1973
慨 J-X/M11122 1974
慓 J585d/M11256 1978
慳 J585f/M11222 1985
撃 J3762/M12674' 2265
擠 J-X/M12728 2268
撩 J597c/M12741 2272
撮 J3b23/M12748 2282
敷 J495f/M13359' 2357
暹 J5a7b/M14150 **2509**
暫 J3b43/M14120 **2510**
暴 J4b3d/M14137 **2511**
暼 J5a7e/M14155 **2514**
暾 J5a7d/M14160 **2515**
樂 J5c5b/M15399 2832
樗 J5c67/M15366 2834
槹 J5c5f/M15385 2837
槽 J4165/M15393 2844
樟 J3e40/M15451 2851
槪 J-X/M15364 2860
殤 J5d4f/M16557 2983
澔 J-X/M18338 3315
潦 J5f33/M18259 3317
潭 J5f2c/M18271 3324
潤 J3442/M-X 3329
潮 J442c/M18277' 3336
潜 J4078/M18241 3337
潛 J5f2a/M18240 3352
獠 J-X/M20692 3604
璋 J6078/M21211 3675
皚 J622d/M22765 3877
瞑 J6254/M23600 3954
稽 J374e/M25218 4163
穂 J4a66/M25236' 4168
篦 J6431/M26157 4303
箪 J433d/M-X 4321
篁 J643b/M26249 4326
箸 J-X/M26224 4328
範 J484f/M26253 4330
緒 J-X/M27633 4535
緼 J-X/M27701 4536
緝 J654e/M27652 4541
縄 J466c/M27729 4547
線 J407e/M27641 4548
緾 J6561/M27838 4565
翫 J663b/M28537 4670
翦 J-X/M28744 4687
翫 J7165/M28766 4689
膓 J6736/M29811 4862
蕈 J687e/M31928 5190
蕩 J4622/M32002 5198
蝿 J4768/M-X 5344
蝪 J6a23/M33305 5350
蝎 J6979/M33254 5354
蝮 J697d/M33309 5355
蝗 J697b/M33267 5361
諌 J3452/M35642 5630
謁 J315a/M35690' 5637
諸 J3d74/M35691' 5648
賭 J4552/M-X 5807
賜 J3b72/M36809 5812
踏 J4627/M37602 5889
輓 J6d4e/M38337 5963

12 residual strokes

13 residual strokes

14 residual strokes

日 J5b29/M14278 **2529**

1 residual stroke

旦 J4336/M13734 2411
旧 J356c/M13737 2412
由 J4d33/M21724 3724
甲 J3943/M21725 3725
申 J3f3d/M21726 3726
白 J4772/M22678 3863

2 residual strokes

曳 J-X/M14281 2413
旨 J3b5d/M13738 2414
旬 J3d5c/M13746 2415
旭 J3030/M13747 2416
曳 J3148/M14282 2417
曲 J364a/M14280 2418
早 J4161/M13742 2419

3 residual strokes

拑 J593a/M11956 2105
曵 J5b2a/M14284 2420
旱 J5a5d/M13752 2421
更 J3939/M14283 2422
汨 J5d71/M17152 3049
皃 J6226/M22686 3865
皀 J6225/M22683 3866
艮 J3a31/M30596 4953
車 J3c56/M38172 5939
迫 J4777/M38797′ 6031
里 J4e24/M40131 6206

4 residual strokes

卑 J-X/M2738 612
卓 J426e/M2741 616
厚 J387c/M2949 651
呷 J526e/M3461 756
坤 J3a25/M4969 996
坦 J4333/M4971 997
奄 J3162/M5881 1146
妲 J5527/M6129 1192
帕 J562f/M8005 1453
岬 J4c28/M7992 1458
帛 J5667/M8855 1556
怛 J5765/M10458 1807
恵 J3743/M10618′ 1847
抻 J593b/M11928 2100
拍 J476f/M11952 2114
抽 J436a/M11930 2119
担 J4334/M11941 2121
押 J3221/M11929 2128
冐 J-X/M-X 2423
昂 J3937/M13783 2424
昃 J5a60/M13785 2425
昊 J5a5f/M13799 2426
旺 J3222/M13774 2427
昌 J3e3b/M13803 2428
旻 J5a61/M13775 2429
昆 J3a2b/M13792 2430
昏 J3a2a/M13806 2431
易 J3057/M13814 2432
昔 J404e/M13816 2433
昇 J3e3a/M13794 2434
明 J4c40/M13805 2435
昶 J5a64/M13867 2442
杲 J5a5e/M14500 2570
杳 J5a62/M14501 2577
果 J324c/M14556 2594
東 J456c/M14499 2596
沓 J3723/M17206 3060
泊 J4771/M17275 3099
狛 J397d/M20349 3566
的 J452a/M22692 3867
者 J3c54/M28852 4698
艮 J3a31/M30596 4953
良 J4e49/M30597 4954
迫 J4777/M38797′ 6031
陌 J6f79/M41617 6436

5 residual strokes

京 J5037/M307 94
便 J4a58/M659 219
単 J4331/M2752 620
卽 J-X/M2872 639
即 J-X/M2873 640
厚 J387c/M2949 651
垣 J3340/M5060 1009
宣 J406b/M7132 1328
徇 J574e/M10091 1735
恂 J5776/M10520 1829
恒 J3931/M10527 1849
拍 J-X/M11999 2129
指 J3b58/M12034 2152
昂 J3937/M13783 2424
昆 J3a2b/M13792 2430
昏 J3a2a/M13806 2431
昿 J5b26/M-X 2436
昜 J5a66/M13832 2437
昞 J-X/M13835 2438
昺 J-X/M13836 2439
旺 J-X/M-X 2440
昴 J5a65/M13865 2441
昶 J5a64/M13867 2442
曷 J5b2b/M14290 2443
昧 J4b66/M13846 2444
昵 J5a63/M13866 2445
昭 J3e3c/M13855 2446
昪 J-X/M13885 2447
映 J3147/M13838 2448
昨 J3a72/M13847 2449
昼 J436b/M13886 2450
是 J4027/M13859 2451
星 J4031/M13837 2452
春 J3d55/M13844 2453
柏 J4770/M14617 2623
沓 J3723/M17206 3060
泉 J4074/M17274 3095
洵 J5e2d/M17416 3116
洩 J314c/M17401 3118
珀 J6061/M20904 3624
皈 J6227/M22705 3868
皇 J3944/M22701 3870
冒 J4b41/M-X 3915
神 J3f40/M24673′ 4087
者 J-X/M28853 4702
胆 J4340/M29354 4790
良 J4e49/M30597 4954
荀 J6826/M30929 5014
草 J4170/M30945′ 5032
衵 J6a52/M34135 5425
軌 J3530/M38176 5941
連 J4f22/M38902′ 6062
陥 J3459/M41676′ 6446
陣 J3f58/M41667 6448
音 J323b/M43265 6607
香 J3961/M44518 6722

6 residual strokes

倬 J506b/M794 233
借 J3c5a/M781 259
原 J3836/M2973 652
哽 J532b/M3680 799
宴 J3163/M7166 1332
峺 J5638/M8115 1468
庫 J384b/M9330 1617
悍 J577b/M10643 1862
捍 J5952/M12143 2155
捏 J5954/M12149 2165
揑 J-X/M-X 2166
挿 J415e/M12119 2167
捜 J415c/M12179′ 2168
晦 J3322/M-X 2454
晉 J5a69/M13898 2456
晁 J5a6a/M13889 2457
晃 J3938/M13891 2458
晄 J5a68/M13892 2459
晏 J5a67/M13914 2460
晒 J3b2f/M13924 2461
時 J3b7e/M13890 2462
書 J3d71/M14294 2463
晟 J5a70/M13950 2472
晦 J-X/M13960 2478
桓 J343c/M14774 2652
殉 J3d5e/M16448 2974
殷 J5d56/M16627 2993
涄 J-X/M-X 3135
涅 J5e3a/M17521 3148
湼 J-X/M17574 3149
狸 J432c/M20427 3578

7 residual strokes

8 residual strokes

萱 J337e/M31345 5121
葛 J-X/M31420 5126
覃 J6b29/M34778 5516
遏 J6e21/M39004 6079
遇 J3678/M38991′ 6083
量 J4e4c/M40138 6209
間 J3456/M41249 6391
隙 J3764/M41792 6471

9 residual strokes

亶 J5039/M328 98
僧 J414e/M1076 300
傷 J3d7d/M1029 301
匙 J3a7c/M2590 582
嗜 J534f/M4089 870
嗹 J5358/M4148 875
堦 J544d/M5329 1064
墓 J4a68/M5431 1073
寘 J556b/M7282 1351
尟 J-X/M7522 1397
幎 J566d/M9024 1576
幌 J4b5a/M9022 1577
幕 J4b6b/M9051 1578
幹 J3434/M9183 1596
惕 J-X/M10933 1906
愚 J3672/M10946 1925
意 J3055/M10921 1926
戦 J406f/M11631′ 2037
揩 J5962/M12383 2223
搨 J5972/M12503 2244
搶 J596f/M12525 2245
搢 J-X/M12494 2247
摸 J4c4e/M12644 2250
卽 J-X/M13725 2409
曾 J5072/M14306 2493
曉 J-X/M-X 2495
暑 J-X/M14051 2496
暄 J5a77/M14033 2497
暘 J5a78/M14066 2498
暉 J5a76/M14038 2499
暈 J5a74/M14037 2500
暇 J324b/M14036 2501
暖 J4348/M14064 2502
暗 J3045/M14065 2503
暢 J442a/M14095 2506
棍 J5b7e/M14924 2735
榊 J3a67/M-X 2756
楮 J5c3a/M15172 2770
楷 J5c34/M15185 2781
椿 J4458/M15090 2782
楊 J4d4c/M15112 2784
渴 J-X/M17788 3208
漣 J4e7a/M-X 3210
滉 J5e66/M18017 3257
溟 J5e72/M17947 3258
漣 J-X/M18155 3259
潛 J-X/M17922 3262
漠 J4779/M18149 3268
滝 J426c/M18067 3273
源 J383b/M17926 3274
煮 J-X/M19188 3441
煑 J-X/M19187 3442
熘 J-X/M19221 3443
煬 J5f6c/M19235 3446
煌 J5f6a/M19181 3449
照 J3e48/M19226 3457
獏 J6053/M20638 3597
琿 J606d/M21093 3658
晳 J622c/M22748 3876
盟 J4c41/M23024 3899
碍 J3337/M24283 4016
禅 J4135/M24787′ 4104
窠 J-X/M25556 4205
粳 J646b/M26967 4408
紳 J3f42/M27348 4467
罩 J662d/M28289 4640
罨 J662c/M28288 4641
署 J3d70/M28311′ 4643
腥 J6729/M29678 4845
腫 J3c70/M29697 4848
腸 J4432/M29721 4849
腹 J4a22/M29722 4851
葩 J685d/M31441 5112
著 J6869/M31655 5137
蒔 J3c2c/M31546 5153
蓮 J-X/M31722 5158
裼 J6a69/M34379 5466
褐 J336c/M-X 5473
諌 J-X/M35495 5590
詢 J6b4e/M35411 5593
詣 J3758/M35412 5594
豊 J4b2d/M36263 5737
貊 J6c3d/M36550 5758
輌 J6d52/M-X 5955
軾 J6d48/M38285 5956
輅 J6d4a/M38302 5957
農 J4740/M38688 6008
閘 J6f5e/M41263 6396
隙 J-X/M41813 6477
障 J3e63/M41821 6479
電 J4545/M42253 6526
靼 J705a/M42764 6578
韵 J7071/M43271 6608

10 residual strokes

僭 J-X/M1117 304
僣 J5129/M1111 305
僚 J4e3d/M1100 314
噌 J4139/M-X 873
嗹 J5358/M4148 875
嘗 J3e28/M4205 878
嘈 J-X/M4175 879
塲 J5447/M5385 1076
墅 J5450/M5412 1081
境 J362d/M5409 1085
増 J417d/M5448′ 1088
層 J4158/M-X 1432
嶂 J5651/M8410 1506
嶄 J5650/M8413 1509
嶃 J-X/M8412 1510
幔 J566f/M9050 1580
彰 J3e34/M10015 1721
愿 J5845/M11030 1934
慕 J4a69/M11088 1948
慯 J5853/M11133 1952
慱 J5855/M11137 1953
慟 J5856/M11103 1959
慴 J5852/M11143 1961
憎 J417e/M11188′ 1969
慨 J-X/M11122 1974
戩 J-X/M11637 2038
摹 J-X/M12645 2241
摶 J5976/M12642 2259
摺 J4022/M12647 2262
斡 J3036/M13522 2378
暤 J5b21/M14169 2504
暝 J5a79/M14083 2505
暦 J4e71/M14111′ 2507
暮 J4a6b/M14128 2508
楷 J5c34/M15185 2781
槞 J5c59/M-X 2795
榠 J5c55/M15244 2797
榻 J5c50/M15292 2807
榊 J-X/M15352 2808
模 J4c4f/M15453 2825
漣 J4e7a/M-X 3210
漣 J-X/M18155 3259
潟 J-X/M-X 3286
漸 J4132/M18179 3305
漕 J4166/M18131 3306
漫 J4c21/M18166 3308
煦 J5f68/M19225 3445
瘍 J6167/M22327 3825
皹 J6230/M22888 3882
碣 J6272/M24326 4025
稲 J3070/M25187′ 4158
種 J3c6f/M25174 4159
竄 J-X/M25582 4207
竭 J6371/M25803 4242
箸 J4824/M-X 4301
箔 J4773/M26142 4312
節 J-X/M26243 4320
絏 J6532/M27397 4476
絢 J303c/M27427 4481
緍 J-X/M27607 4503
綽 J653f/M27590 4518
緒 J3d6f/M27632 4521
練 J4e7d/M27631′ 4530
綿 J4c4a/M27592 4531
署 J-X/M28319 4646
翰 J344d/M28780 4690
膜 J4b6c/M29808′ 4854
瑒 J-X/M30310 4921

14 residual strokes

15 residual strokes

16 residual strokes

17 residual strokes

鰭 J4949/M46400 6907
黯 J735f/M48159 7064

18 residual strokes

噲 J5375/M-X 932
擽 J5a36/M12919 2312
競 J513f/M25840 4245
鑢 J6624/M28189 4631
藥 J693b/M32341 5236
顯 J-X/M43682 6654
顫 J707c/M43706 6656
鱆 J7263/M46464 6913
鼴 J-X/M48464 7080

19 residual strokes

曬 J-X/M14266 2528
蠣 J6d61/M38593 5994
響 J-X/M-X 6612
響 J-X/M43325 6613
顯 J707d/M43726 6657
驪 I-X/M44453 6718
鱣 J-X/M46488 6919
鷞 J733e/M47342 7002
鼴 J-X/M48464 7080

20 residual strokes

曬 J-X/M14266 2528
蠶 J-X/M33891 5406
蠶 J6a44/M33890 5410
靄 J704b/M42526 6555
顰 J707e/M43737 6659
魘 J7236/M45941 6844

鱠 J7266/M46530 6927
鼴 J-X/M48464 7080

21–23 residual strokes

蠶 J6a44/M33890 5410
鑁 J6f57/M41092 6377
靄 J704b/M42526 6555
顯 J707d/M43726 6657
黶 J7361/M48229 7066

Rad. 74 月

0 residual strokes

月 J376e/M14330 **2530**

2 residual strokes

肋 J4f3e/M29239 4754
肌 J4829/M29242 4755
有 J4d2d/M14332 4756

3 residual strokes

肓 J666b/M29259 4757
肚 J666c/M29270 4759
肘 J492a/M29268 4761
肝 J344e/M29273 4762

4 residual strokes

侑 J5052/M594 177
冐 J666e/M1534 393
冒 J-X/M-X 2423
明 J4c40/M13805 2435
炙 J5f55/M18922 3401
肛 J666a/M29271 4758
肬 J666f/M29304 4763
肫 J-X/M29303 4764
肭 J666d/M29305 4765
肪 J4b43/M29302 4766
肴 J3a68/M29322 4767
肢 J3b68/M29285 4768
朋 J4a7e/M14340′ 4769
肱 J394f/M29315 4770
股 J3854/M29284 4772
育 J3069/M29318 4773
肥 J486e/M29291 4774
服 J497e/M14345′ 4775
肩 J382a/M29299 4776
胃 J305f/M29348 4793
陏 J6f7a/M41623 6437
青 J4044/M42564′ 6557

5 residual strokes

兪 J5141/M1437 198
俏 J-X/M680 204
冐 J-X/M1538 394
冑 J5149/M1537 395
削 J3a6f/M2000 488
前 J4130/M2011 490
囿 J537c/M4756 952
宥 J4d28/M7137 1326
明 J-X/M23178 3909
育 J3069/M29318 4773
冒 J-X/M-X 4777
脉 J6677/M29421′ 4778
胐 J5b2c/M14351 4779
胖 J6676/M29381 4780
胥 J6671/M29406 4781
胝 J6673/M29395 4782
胛 J6670/M29392 4783
胙 J6672/M29387 4784
胄 J6674/M29349 4785
胤 J307d/M29405 4786
胚 J6675/M29390 4787
胞 J4b26/M29396′ 4788
胎 J425b/M29369 4789
胆 J4340/M29354 4790
肺 J4759/M29422′ 4791
胡 J3855/M29400 4792
背 J4758/M29363 4794
逍 J6d76/M38873 6049

6 residual strokes

娟 J552f/M6321 1225
宵 J3e2e/M7168 1334
屑 J367d/M7709 1424
峭 J5639/M8085 1470
悁 J577a/M10623 1857
悄 J5821/M10627 1866
捐 J5950/M12150 2156
涓 J5e32/M17541 3145
消 J3e43/M17529′ 3158
狷 J6046/M20426 3577
胝 J6673/M29395 4782
胤 J307d/M29405 4786
脃 J-X/M29494 4795
胱 J6679/M29432 4796
朕 J443f/M14361 4797
胼 J6726/M29453 4798
胯 J6678/M29430 4799
脆 J4048/M29468 4800
朔 J3a73/M14359 4801
朗 J4f2f/M14362′ 4802
脊 J4054/M29472 4804
脈 J4c2e/M29470 4805
脈 J-X/M29469 4806
脇 J4f46/M29467 4807
脂 J3b69/M29463 4808
能 J473d/M29454 4809
胴 J4639/M29436 4810
胸 J363b/M29442 4811
逍 J6d76/M38873 6049
随 J3f6f/M41764′ 6460
骨 J397c/M45098 6781

7 residual strokes

偸 J5079/M901 272
剪 J5172/M2088 502
堋 J5444/M5217 1024
堕 J4244/M-X 1033
崩 J4a78/M8212 1491
帽 J-X/M8967 1566
弸 J573a/M9817 1693
情 J3e70/M10756′ 1898
梢 J3e3f/M14866 2695
淆 J5e42/M17619 3180
清 J4036/M17695′ 3205
胤 J307d/M29405 4786
胯 J6678/M29430 4799
朗 J4f2f/M14362′ 4802
脈 J-X/M29469 4806
朖 J5b2d/M14363 4812
朗 J-X/M14364 4813
脯 J667d/M29543 4814

臈 J6745/M29953 4870
膰 J6738/M29882 4871
膩 J6737/M29862 4872
膳 J4137/M29891 4873
膨 J4b44/M29861 4874
覦 J6b30/M34904 5532
謂 J3062/M35759 5656
諭 J4d21/M35727′ 5667
諭 J-X/M35727 5668
踰 J6c7c/M37675 5891
輸 J4d22/M38438′ 5978
醑 J6e4a/M39866 6174
醐 J386f/M39930 6183
錆 J3b2c/M40523 6296
鞘 J3e64/M42850 6587
骼 J716e/M45175 6788
骸 J333c/M45164 6789
龍 J4e36/M48818 7103

13 residual strokes

壓 J545a/M5557 1104
壠 J-X/M5592 1113
滕 J4654/M-X 3356
澗 J6172/M22518 3843
繃 J655e/M27852 4582
膽 J673c/M29933 4875
臉 J6740/M29954 4876
臂 J673e/M29944 4877
膾 J673a/M29937 4879
臀 J673d/M29939 4880
朦 J5b2f/M14409 4882
臆 J3232/M29951 4883
膿 J473f/M29938 4884
謄 J4625/M35780′ 5685
蹐 J6d24/M37766 5897
鍮 J6f2b/M40645 6308
骸 J333c/M45164 6789
鮪 J4b6e/M46126 6858

14 residual strokes

揄 J5a31/M12898 2310
擺 J5a34/M12910 2313
癒 J4c7e/M22545 3847
箭 J-X/M26520 4359
縢 J6558/M27783 4558
繖 J6564/M27896 4588
繝 J6563/M27908 4589
羂 J6630/M28386 4653
膿 J473f/M29938 4884
臑 J6742/M29986 4885
臓 J4221/M29995′ 4886
臍 J6741/M29967 4887
藤 J4623/M32240′ 5241
隴 J702f/M41904 6488
餬 J7137/M44255 6704
髀 J716f/M45205 6790
髄 J3f71/M45240′ 6791
鮹 J7243/M46154 6871
鵑 J7324/M46924 6967

15 residual strokes

壟 J5462/M5591 1112
壠 J-X/M5592 1113
寵 J437e/M7368 1370
瀧 J426d/M18671 3376
瀛 J5f4a/M18656 3378
繃 J655e/M27852 4582
臓 J4221/M29995′ 4886
臘 J6744/M30009 4888
蘢 J6944/M32438 5246
覇 J4746/M34790 5519
轍 J4532/M38524 5988
髄 J3f71/M45240′ 6791
鯖 J3b2a/M46210 6883
鵬 J4b32/M47005 6979

16 residual strokes

壠 J-X/M5592 1113
瓏 J607c/M21340 3684
羂 J6630/M28386 4653
羆 J6631/M28398 4654
臚 J6746/M30027 4889
臙 J6743/M30018 4890
朧 J5b30/M14411 4891
贏 J6c57/M36950 5833
霰 J7047/M42458 6546
騰 J462d/M44915′ 6767

17 residual strokes

籐 J645b/M26693 4373
羸 J6640/M28583 4674
臘 J6744/M30009 4888
臟 J6747/M30046 4892
霸 J5b31/M42490 6547
髏 J7170/M45267 6792
鶻 J7333/M47198 6987
鶺 J7335/M47197 6993

18 residual strokes

籘 J645c/M26733 4374
籠 J6446/M26752 4376
聾 J4f38/M29212 4745
臟 J6747/M30046 4892
襲 J3d31/M34717 5510
髓 J7172/M45289 6793
龕 J737c/M48839 7104

19 residual strokes

櫳 J-X/M15945 2921
臠 J6748/M30049 4893
襲 J3d31/M34717 5510
靨 J7054/M42698 6569
饜 J-X/M44453 6718
髓 J7172/M45289 6793
體 J7173/M45291 6794
髑 J7171/M45281 6795

20–44 residual strokes

櫳 J-X/M15971 2925
臠 J6748/M30049 4893
魘 J7236/M45941 6844
黶 J7361/M48229 7066
龘 J-X/M48845 7105

Rad. 75 木

0 residual strokes

木 J4c5a/M14415 **2531**

1 residual stroke

朮 J5b32/M14423 **2532**
札 J3b25/M14422 **2533**
末 J4b76/M14420 **2534**
未 J4c24/M14419 **2535**
本 J4b5c/M14421 **2536**
禾 J3253/M24906 4121

2 residual strokes

休 J3559/M440 142
凩 J515e/M1757 436
权 J-X/M-X **2537**
朳 J5b35/M-X **2538**
朷 J5b37/M14432 **2539**
朸 J5b36/M14433 **2540**
朿 J5b33/M14441 **2541**
朶 J5b34/M14430 **2542**
机 J3479/M14435 **2543**
朴 J4b51/M14428 **2544**
朽 J3560/M14439 **2545**
朱 J3c6b/M14424 **2546**
李 J4d7b/M14459 **2549**
米 J4a46/M26832 4380
耒 J6650/M28898 4706

3 residual strokes

体 J424e/M509 165
呆 J4a72/M3395 738
困 J3a24/M4717 946
宋 J4157/M7078 1313
床 J3e32/M9242 1608
朶 J5b34/M14430 **2542**
朽 J3560/M14439 **2545**
杤 J5b3d/M14488′ **2547**

Char	JIS	Morohashi	No.
桀	J5b5c	M14753	**2678**
梛	J5b6b	M14856	**2681**
桴	J5b6f	M14807	**2690**
梃	J5b6c	M14827	**2691**
梵	J5b70	M14888	**2701**
殊	J3c6c	M16451	2975
殺	J3b26	M16629	2994
烋	J5f5e	M18991	3416
珠	J3c6e	M20956	3637
眛	J6246	M23230	3923
秣	J6342	M24992	4136
耙	J6652	M28911	4707
耘	J6651	M28910	4708
耗	J4c57	M28909′	4709
耕	J394c	M28907′	4710
速	J422e	M38897′	6060
陳	J4444	M41698	6457

---

7 residual strokes

Char	JIS	Morohashi	No.
傑	J3766	M955	293
唻	J533b	M3833	817
埜	J4738	M5154	1022
梦	J546d	M5784	1130
婪	J553a	M6436	1234
彬	J494b	M9996	1717
彩	J3a4c	M9992	1718
徠	J5752	M10155	1748
術	J3d51	M34046′	1754
悸	J5829	M10733	1885
採	J3a4e	M12274	2209
探	J4335	M12276	2211
桍	J5b5d	M14767	**2643**
框	J5b5a	M14760	**2646**
核	J334b	M14743	**2660**

Char	JIS	Morohashi	No.
梅	J475f	M14795′	**2666**
根	J3a2c	M14745	**2670**
梠	J5b71	M14862	**2671**
梼	J456e	M14911	**2672**
桝	J4b71	M-X	**2673**
桿	J5b65	M14823	**2674**
條	J5b6a	M14859	**2675**
梅	J-X	M14830	**2676**
梹	J5b6e	M14909	**2677**
桀	J5b5c	M14753	**2678**
桾	J5b75	M14821	**2679**
梍	J5b74	M14839	**2680**
梛	J5b6b	M14856	**2681**
梺	J5b72	M14910	**2682**
椛	J3371	M15065	**2683**
梏	J5b67	M14841	**2684**
械	J3323	M14882	**2685**
桷	J5b64	M14813	**2686**
梻	J-X	M14911	**2687**
梓	J3034	M14845	**2688**
梮	J-X	M14879	**2689**
桴	J5b6f	M14807	**2690**
梃	J5b6c	M14827	**2691**
梔	J5b69	M14846	**2692**
梭	J5b68	M14878	**2693**
桶	J3233	M14811	**2694**
梢	J3e3f	M14866	**2695**
梱	J3a2d	M14883	**2696**
梨	J4d7c	M14873	**2697**
梗	J393c	M14849	**2698**
梶	J3361	M14889	**2699**
梧	J3868	M14872	**2700**
梵	J5b70	M14888	**2701**
梁	J4e42	M14825	**2702**
梟	J5b66	M14861	**2703**

Char	JIS	Morohashi	No.
梳	J5b60	M14886	**2704**
巣	J4163	M8696′	**2705**
梯	J4474	M14881	**2706**
椁	J5b76	M15003	**2722**
椒	J5c25	M15029	**2731**
棄	J347e	M14913	**2787**
殺	J-X	M16638	2995
淅	J5e48	M17617	3169
淞	J5e44	M17651	3174
淋	J4e54	M17626	3194
深	J3f3c	M17687	3206
渫	J5e58	M17778	3225
渠	J3574	M17764	3230
笨	J637c	M25939	4262
紮	J6527	M27341	4463
耜	J6653	M28915	4711
菘	J6845	M31177	5066
菻	J6852	M31238	5067
萊	J-X	M31262	5073
菓	J325b	M31168′	5095
菜	J3a5a	M31184′	5097
葉	J4d55	M31387	5129
貅	I-X	M36509	5755
集	J3d38	M41974	6500
麥	J734e	M47717	7031
麻	J4b63	M47888	7040

---

8 residual strokes

Char	JIS	Morohashi	No.
傑	J3766	M955	293
啾	J5342	M3892	840
喋	J437d	M3917	850
喇	J5349	M3909	851
堡	J5448	M5254	1050
媒	J475e	M6498	1247

Char	JIS	Morohashi	No.
寐	J5567	M7236	1347
屡	J3c48	M7770	1428
巢	J-X	M8696	1531
廂	J567b	M9416	1629
弑	J5736	M9680	1677
愀	J5837	M10884	1913
揀	J5963	M12315	2221
揉	J5966	M12332	2231
晣	J5a72	M13990	2481
梅	J-X	M14830	2676
巣	J4163	M8696′	**2705**
梱	J-X	M14947	**2707**
棧	J5c22	M14963	**2708**
槌	J4448	M X	**2709**
椢	J5b7a	M-X	**2710**
椦	J5b7b	M-X	**2711**
椥	J5c29	M-X	**2712**
椨	J5c2d	M-X	**2713**
椡	J5c31	M-X	**2714**
椣	J5c30	M X	**2715**
棆	J5c32	M14916	**2716**
棔	J5c21	M14931	**2717**
棠	J5c2b	M14953	**2718**
棡	J5b7c	M14955	**2719**
棣	J5c28	M14957	**2720**
棯	J5c2c	M14977	**2721**
椁	J5b76	M15003	**2722**
棱	J5c26	M15008	**2723**
椈	J5b78	M15014	**2724**
椋	J4c3a	M15020	**2725**
椌	J5b7d	M15021	**2726**
椏	J5b73	M15025	**2727**
椙	J3f7a	M15063	**2728**
棘	J5b79	M14938	**2729**
棱	J-X	M14979	**2730**

Char	JIS	Morohashi	No.
椒	J5c25	M15029	**2731**
椀	J4f50	M15001	**2732**
椚	J5c2f	M15064	**2733**
椪	J5c2e	M-X	**2734**
棍	J5b7e	M14924	**2735**
棗	J5c27	M14937	**2736**
椅	J3058	M15009	**2737**
棹	J5c2a	M14992	**2738**
椰	J5c3f	M15069	**2739**
棕	J5c23	M14933	**2740**
棉	J4c49	M14919	**2741**
椎	J4447	M15024	**2742**
棲	J4033	M14980	**2743**
棋	J347d	M14922	**2744**
棊	J5b77	M14921	**2745**
棺	J343d	M14993	**2746**
棟	J456f	M14949	**2747**
棚	J432a	M14941	**2748**
森	J3f39	M14974	**2749**
棒	J4b40	M14929	**2750**
植	J3f22	M15023	**2751**
検	J3821	M15065′	**2752**
極	J364b	M15181	**2753**
楳	J4760	M15178	**2754**
榔	J4f31	M15226	**2766**
楪	J5c44	M15167	**2774**
棄	J347e	M14913	**2787**
棄	J-X	M-X	**2788**
涮	J5e63	M-X	3211
湘	J3e45	M17842	3216
渣	J5e56	M17767	3223
渠	J3574	M17764	3230
煉	J4e7b	M-X	3428
焚	J4a32	M19100	3434
煠	J-X	M19213	3450

Kanji	JIS	Morohashi	No.
橢	J5c73	M15565	**2829**
樓	J5c6c	M15430	**2830**
樣	J5c6b	M15457	**2831**
樂	J5c5b	M15399	**2832**
槧	J5c61	M15359	**2833**
槫	J5c67	M15366	**2834**
槭	J5c65	M15369	**2835**
槲	J5e60	M15375	**2836**
槹	J5c5f	M15385	**2837**
樅	J5c62	M15404	**2838**
樌	J5c6e	M15416	**2839**
樔	J5c66	M15433	**2840**
樗	J4374	M15438	**2841**
樛	J5c5c	M15445	**2842**
樢	J5c70	M15455	**2843**
槽	J4165	M15393	**2844**
槻	J4450	M15390	**2845**
樒	J5c69	M15428	**2846**
樏	J-X	M15425	**2847**
槿	J5c5d	M15395	**2848**
樫	J335f	M15485	**2849**
樊	J5c68	M15414	**2850**
樟	J3e40	M15451	**2851**
標	J4938	M15442	**2852**
権	J3822	M15484	**2853**
横	J3223	M15484′	**2854**
槪	J-X	M15364	**2860**
概	J-X	M15364′	**2861**
磔	J6279	M24406	4044
箱	J4822	M26209	4331
糅	J6472	M27023	4414
練	J-X	M27689	4534
耦	J-X	M28952	4713
蕀	J687b	M31898	5184
蝶	J4433	M33333	5363
裹	J6a67	M34372	5468
褒	J4b2b	M34437	5483
諌	J3452	M35642	5630
課	J325d	M35589	5644
諜	J4435	M35697	5665
醂	J6e4e	M39891	6180
魅	J4c25	M45811	6838
壓	J5677	M47892	7042

12 residual strokes

Kanji	JIS	Morohashi	No.
嘶	J4838	M4433	903
噪	J5364	M4380	906
噤	J5361	M4364	909
廩	J5720	M9515	1647
憖	J585b	M11215	1979
懆	J586a	M11325	1992
懍	J586e	M11335	1994
操	J4160	M12806	2296
整	J-X	M13393	2361
椪	J5b73	M15025	**2727**
樞	J5c64	M15450	**2828**
樌	J5c6e	M15416	**2839**
樔	J5c66	M15433	**2840**
樗	J4374	M15438	**2841**
樫	J335f	M15485	**2849**
榮	J-X	M15569	**2855**
樣	J-X	M-X	**2856**
橫	J-X	M15594	**2857**
橋	J-X	M15501	**2858**
橊	J-X	M15525	**2859**
槪	J-X	M15364	**2860**
概	J-X	M15364′	**2861**
橊	J5c71	M-X	**2862**
橡	J464b	M15564	**2863**
橡	J-X	M-X	**2864**
樶	J5c70	M15491	**2865**
橲	J5c6f	M15623	**2866**
橅	J-X	M15513	**2867**
橘	J354c	M15551	**2868**
橦	J5c75	M15578	**2869**
檠	J5c7b	M15681	**2870**
樵	J3e41	M15489	**2871**
橈	J5c76	M15521	**2872**
樸	J5c77	M15495	**2873**
橇	J5c72	M15517	**2874**
樽	J432e	M15500	**2875**
橄	J5c6d	M15512	**2876**
橙	J5c74	M15552	**2877**
樹	J3e79	M15496	**2878**
橋	J3636	M15526	**2879**
機	J3521	M15561	**2880**
檎	J3869	M15657	**2888**
潛	J5f26	M18293	3319
澡	J5f36	M18379	3340
磔	J6279	M24406	4044
磨	J4b61	M24449′	4045
篠	J-X	M26328	4335
篥	J6445	M26352	4336
築	J435b	M26298	4343
練	J4e7d	M27631′	4530
耦	J-X	M28952	4713
薪	J3f45	M32149′	5222
薬	J4c74	M32188′	5224
親	J3f46	M34918	5534
課	J325d	M35589	5644
諫	J6b5d	M35724	5664
諜	J4435	M35697	5665
謀	J4b45	M35756	5671
賴	J-X	M36861	5818
踝	J6c76	M37641	5888
蹂	J6c7a	M37718	5892
錬	J4f23	M40576	6300
霖	J7043	M42335	6540
頼	J4d6a	M43529′	6635

13 residual strokes

Kanji	JIS	Morohashi	No.
懋	J586c	M11333	1993
樗	J4374	M15438	**2841**
樏	J-X	M15425	**2847**
樸	J5c77	M15495	**2873**
櫟	J5d2c	M-X	**2881**
縉	J-X	M15690	**2882**
檓	J5c7d	M15684	**2883**
櫛	J367b	M-X	**2884**
檍	J5c7a	M15656	**2885**
檗	J5d21	M15669	**2886**
檬	J5d28	M15710	**2887**
檎	J3869	M15657	**2888**
橿	J3360	M15629	**2889**
檞	J-X	M15679	**2890**
檄	J5c7c	M15639	**2891**
檐	J5c79	M15659	**2892**
檣	J5c7e	M15687	**2893**
檜	J5b58	M15676	**2894**
檀	J4349	M15632	**2895**
燥	J4167	M19467	3493
燦	J3b38	M19468	3498
簗	J644c	M-X	4348
篠	J3c44	M-X	4352
練	J-X	M27689	4534
藉	J6934	M32242	5231
藁	J4f4e	M32222	5234
褻	J6a71	M34552	5489
襍	J7037	M34596	5496
鍊	J-X	M40602	6304
闌	J6f6c	M41433	6413
隸	J7031	M41932	6491
霜	J417a	M42363	6542
顆	J7079	M43551	6640
鮴	J7240	M-X	6856

14 residual strokes

Kanji	JIS	Morohashi	No.
擽	J5a36	M12919	2312
櫛	J367b	M-X	**2884**
櫁	J5c6a	M15754	**2896**
檮	J5b6d	M15713	**2897**
櫃	J5d24	M15757	**2898**
檸	J5d26	M15742	**2899**
櫂	J5d25	M15756	**2900**
檳	J5d27	M15734	**2901**
檻	J5d23	M15745	**2902**
磔	J-X	M-X	4050
礎	J4143	M24522	4054
藥	J693b	M32341	5236
藕	J6939	M32298	5239
襟	J365f	M34647	5504
鏊	J6e5a	M40146	6210
雜	J7038	M42122	6512
鞣	J7064	M42909	6594
顆	J7079	M43551	6640
鬆	J7222	M45484	6813
麿	J4b7b	M47909′	7044

15 residual strokes

Kanji	JIS	Morohashi	No.
嬾	J554f	M6872	1276
懶	J5871	M11455	2010

攀 J5a35/M12926 2315
樂 J5c5b/M15399 **2832**
檮 J5b6d/M15713 **2897**
櫃 J5d24/M15757 **2898**
檻 J5d23/M15745 **2902**
櫑 J5d2a/M15796 **2903**
櫞 J5d29/M15822 **2904**
櫚 J5d2d/M15815 **2905**
櫟 J5d2b/M15823 **2906**
櫝 J-X/M15821 **2907**
櫓 J4f26/M15798 **2908**
櫛 J-X/M15817 **2909**
瀬 J4025/M18672′ 3384
瀨 J-X/M18672 3385
爍 J6023/M19549 3504
獺 J605c/M20782 3615
繰 J372b/M27953 4602
蘂 J6922/M32410 5243
藾 J6941/M32405 5245
藻 J4174/M32401 5254
蘭 J4d76/M32477′ 5255
鏁 J-X/M40770 6331
鰈 J7257/M46322 6898
鶇 J7329/M47054 6973
麓 J4f3c/M47658 7023

16 residual strokes

嬬 J5552/M6885 1279
機 J3521/M15561 **2880**
櫨 J4827/M15844 **2910**
櫪 J5d2e/M15846 **2911**
欖 J-X/M15905 **2912**
櫧 J-X/M15843 **2913**
欄 J4d73/M15880′ **2914**
瀾 J5f51/M18722 3388
礬 J6329/M24573 4058
礫 J632a/M24572 4059
籍 J4052/M26676 4368
蘭 J-X/M32519 5257
蘗 J5d22/M32479 5258
蘖 J5d31/M32478 5260
蠑 J6a3e/M33738 5398
譟 J6c21/M35998 5710
躁 J6d2f/M37906 5917
鐇 J6f40/M40874 6344
鰈 J7257/M46322 6898
鶫 J732a/M47161 6983
麓 J4f3c/M47658 7023

17 residual strokes

巍 J565b/M8626 1522
櫞 J5d29/M15822 **2904**
櫟 J5d2b/M15823 **2906**
欖 J-X/M15905 **2912**
欄 J-X/M15904 **2915**
權 J5c5e/M15926 **2916**
櫻 J5d2f/M15888 **2917**
櫸 J-X/M-X **2918**
櫸 J5d30/M15883 **2919**
櫺 J5d32/M15887 **2920**
爛 J6025/M19604 3507
癩 J617a/M22622 3854
繰 J372b/M27953 4602
襯 J6b25/M34712 5509
韃 J-X/M42997 6597
魔 J4b62/M45906′ 6843

18 residual strokes

囃 J5372/M4619 929
擽 J5a36/M12919 2312
籟 J645d/M26751 4375
藥 J693b/M32341 5236
襴 J6b26/M34728 5511
轢 J6d60/M38588 5993

19 residual strokes

欗 J-X/M15945 **2921**
欒 J5d33/M15947 **2922**
鑠 J6f4b/M41019 6366
髞 J7174/M45344 6798

20–25 residual strokes

欒 J5d33/M15947 **2922**
欖 J5d34/M15964 **2923**
爵 J3135/M-X **2924**
欘 J-X/M15971 **2925**
爵 J-X/M15978 **2926**
欟 J5d36/M15986 **2927**
爨 J6026/M19648 3508
礫 J632a/M24572 4059
轢 J6d60/M38588 5993
鑠 J6f4b/M41019 6366
鬱 J5d35/M45671 6830

Rad. 76 欠

0 residual strokes

欠 J3767/M15991 **2928**

2–4 residual strokes

吹 J3f61/M3373 747
坎 J542c/M4928 981
次 J3c21/M15992′ **2929**
欣 J3655/M16008 **2930**
欧 J3224/M16024′ **2931**
炊 J3f66/M18904 3405

5–6 residual strokes

咨 J527e/M3538 780
姿 J3b51/M6257 1216
恣 J5773/M10580 1841
欬 J-X/M16061 **2932**
瓷 J612a/M21491 3697
茨 J3071/M30896 5017

7 residual strokes

嵌 J5648/M8279 1497
掀 J5957/M12230 2178
欵 J-X/M16085 **2933**
欸 J5d37/M16090 **2934**
欷 J5d38/M16087 **2935**
欲 J4d5f/M16080 **2936**
瓷 J612a/M21491 3697
軟 J4670/M38213 5947

8 residual strokes

厥 J5250/M2992 656
嵌 J5648/M8279 1497
欹 J5d3a/M16093 **2937**
款 J343e/M16107 **2938**
欺 J353d/M16097 **2939**
欽 J3656/M16104 **2940**
盜 J5d39/M23006 3896
粢 J6467/M26932 4398
飲 J307b/M44063′ 6680

9 residual strokes

款 J-X/M16125 **2941**
歃 J5d3d/M16131 **2942**
歇 J5d3c/M16141 **2943**
歉 J5d3e/M16159 **2944**
羨 J4122/M28503 4665
資 J3b71/M36750 5803
飲 J307b/M44063′ 6680
飮 J5d3b/M44063 6681

10 residual strokes

劂 J-X/M2190 512
嗽 J5356/M4154 883
歉 J5d3e/M16159 **2944**
歌 J324e/M16167 **2945**
歎 J4337/M16182 **2947**
漱 J5e7b/M18171 3293
盗 J4570/M23000 3894

11 residual strokes

慾 J4d5d/M11163 1951
歐 J5d3f/M16185 **2946**
歎 J4337/M16182 **2947**
歡 J343f/M16197 **2948**
獗 J6055/M20671 3605

Rad. 82 毛

Rad. 83 氏

Rad. 84 气

0 residual strokes

1–4 residual strokes

6–9 residual strokes

Rad. 85 水

0 residual strokes

1 residual stroke

2 residual strokes

3 residual strokes

4 residual strokes

5 residual strokes

6 residual strokes

烝 J5f5f/M19019 3417
球 J3565/M21011 3643
粛 J3d4d/M29223′ 4747
茫 J682b/M30900 5029

7 residual strokes

娑 J5530/M6294 1229
康 J392f/M9376 1621
救 J355f/M13221 2344
棣 J5c28/M14957 2720
泓 J5d77/M17288 **3075**
派 J-X/M17427 **3127**
海 J3324/M17450 **3133**
浣 J4642/M-X **3134**
洩 J-X/M-X **3135**
涉 J-X/M17530 **3136**
海 J-X/M17503 **3137**
涛 J4573/M-X **3138**
浙 J5e36/M17458 **3139**
浤 J5e33/M17471 **3140**
浹 J5e35/M17506 **3141**
浬 J333d/M17485 **3142**
涕 J5e38/M17543 **3143**
涎 J5e37/M17536 **3144**
涓 J5e32/M17541 **3145**
涜 J5e31/M17470 **3146**
浩 J3940/M17479′ **3147**
涅 J5e3a/M17521 **3148**
涅 J-X/M17574 **3149**
涌 J4d30/M17534 **3150**
浚 J5e34/M17460 **3151**
浜 J494d/M17462 **3152**
浴 J4d61/M17496 **3153**
涙 J4e5e/M17573′ **3154**
浪 J4f32/M17482 **3155**
浦 J313a/M17475 **3156**
浸 J3f3b/M17505′ **3157**
消 J3e43/M17529′ **3158**
浮 J4962/M17487 **3159**
流 J4e2e/M17572′ **3160**
涵 J-X/M17595 **3183**
淳 J3d5f/M17690 **3189**
禄 J4f3d/M24741′ 4096
莎 J6835/M31040 5045
酒 J3c72/M39776 6160
黍 J3550/M47991 7048

8 residual strokes

婆 J474c/M6390 1240
梁 J4e42/M14825 2702
棣 J5c28/M14957 2720
海 J-X/M17503 **3137**
涎 J5e37/M17536 **3144**
浪 J4f32/M17482 **3155**
淚 J-X/M17644 **3161**
淺 J5e49/M17697 **3162**
淨 J5e46/M17669 **3163**
渚 J3d6d/M-X **3164**
渕 J5e3c/M-X **3165**
淵 J5e3d/M17750 **3166**
渗 J-X/M-X **3167**
港 J-X/M-X **3168**
淅 J5e48/M17617 **3169**
淇 J5e3f/M17620 **3170**
淌 J5e45/M17629 **3171**
淒 J5e47/M17635 **3172**
淕 J5e4c/M17638 **3173**
淞 J5e44/M17651 **3174**
淤 J5e4b/M17665 **3175**
淬 J5e43/M17679 **3176**
淮 J5e4e/M17682 **3177**
淹 J5e3b/M17696 **3178**
渮 J5e51/M17782 **3179**
淆 J5e42/M17619 **3180**
涯 J3336/M17582 **3181**
淀 J4d64/M17610 **3182**
涵 J-X/M17595 **3183**
涵 J5e3e/M-X **3184**
淼 J-X/M17699 **3185**
淪 J5e4d/M17675 **3186**
淘 J4571/M17642 **3187**
淙 J5e4a/M17643 **3188**
淳 J3d5f/M17690 **3189**
渉 J3e44/M17749′ **3190**
淑 J3d4a/M17634 **3191**
淍 J5e41/M17601 **3192**
淦 J5e40/M17667 **3193**
淋 J4e54/M17626 **3194**
渇 J3369/M17748 **3195**
渓 J374c/M-X **3196**
済 J3a51/M17749 **3197**
涼 J4e43/M17606 **3198**
液 J3155/M17586 **3199**
渋 J3d42/M17750′ **3200**
添 J453a/M17698 **3201**
淡 J4338/M17660 **3202**
淫 J307c/M17678 **3203**
混 J3a2e/M17694 **3204**
清 J4036/M17695′ **3205**
深 J3f3c/M17687 **3206**
渤 J5e5f/M17769 **3213**
渌 J5e59/M17892 **3219**
渟 J5e5b/M17763 **3221**
渫 J5e58/M17778 **3225**
渠 J3574/M17764 **3230**
游 J5e62/M17792 **3232**
淵 J4a25/M17692 **3237**
碌 J6271/M24282 4017
祿 J6333/M24741 4097
笵 J637b/M25952 4261
萢 J684d/M-X 5065
萍 J684c/M31266 5076
菠 J684a/M31190 5081
裘 J6a64/M34312 5458
詠 J3153/M35409 5584
閑 J6f5d/M41260′ 6388

9 residual strokes

慊 J584d/M11146 1963
椋 J5c39/M15214 2764
様 J4d4d/M15352′ 2821
混 J3a2e/M17694 **3204**
湧 J4d2f/M17862 **3207**
渴 J-X/M17788 **3208**
浇 J482e/M-X **3209**
漣 J4e7a/M-X **3210**
溂 J5e63/M-X **3211**
渝 J5e61/M17761 **3212**
渤 J5e5f/M17769 **3213**
渭 J5e4f/M17781 **3214**
湎 J5e5e/M17826 **3215**
湘 J3e45/M17842 **3216**
湟 J5e54/M17850 **3217**
湫 J5e57/M17867 **3218**
渌 J5e59/M17892 **3219**
湲 J5e53/M17877 **3220**
渟 J5e5b/M17763 **3221**
湃 J5e5c/M17808 **3222**
渣 J5e56/M17767 **3223**
渥 J302f/M17770 **3224**
渫 J5e58/M17778 **3225**
湊 J4c2b/M17822 **3226**
湑 J-X/M17829 **3227**
渚 J-X/M17758 **3228**
湍 J5e5a/M17825 **3229**
渠 J3574/M17764 **3230**
渙 J5e52/M17757 **3231**
游 J5e62/M17792 **3232**
湮 J5e50/M17873 **3233**
湛 J4339/M17846 **3234**
渺 J5e5d/M17794 **3235**
渾 J5e55/M17800 **3236**
淵 J4a25/M17692 **3237**
滋 J3c22/M17919′ **3238**
湾 J4f51/M17920 **3239**
湖 J3850/M17836 **3240**
渦 J3132/M17771 **3241**
港 J3941/M17783′ **3242**
湿 J3c3e/M17920′ **3243**
測 J422c/M17780 **3244**
湯 J4572/M17874 **3245**
温 J3239/M17774 **3246**
渡 J454f/M17765 **3247**
満 J4b7e/M17921′ **3248**
減 J383a/M17759 **3249**
溲 J5e6c/M17979 **3265**
滞 J425a/M18067′ **3280**
潺 J5f25/M18298 **3326**
琺 J606b/M21088 3652
盜 J5d39/M23006 3896
緑 J4e50/M27541′ 4528
綠 J-X/M27541 4529

腺 J4123/M29746 4847
膝 J4928/M29837 4868
落 J4d6e/M31362 5130
蒸 J3e78/M31618′ 5163
裘 J6a64/M34312 5458
詠 J-X/M-X 5591

10 residual strokes

準 J5245/M1695 428
匯 J523b/M2644 594
漊 J544b/M-X 1062
塗 J4549/M5338 1074
㥏 J5834/M10900 1911
様 J4d4d/M15352′ 2821
樣 J-X/M-X 2827
溻 J-X/M17788 **3208**
漣 J4e7a/M-X **3210**
滋 J-X/M18021 **3250**
溫 J-X/M17968 **3251**
滊 J-X/M18019 **3252**
溪 J5e64/M17967 **3253**
溏 J5e6f/M17925 **3254**
溘 J5e65/M17936 **3255**
溽 J5e69/M17996 **3256**
滉 J5e66/M18017 **3257**
溟 J5e72/M17947 **3258**
漣 J-X/M18155 **3259**
滓 J5e68/M18034 **3260**
滕 J5e6e/M18036 **3261**
溍 J-X/M17922 **3262**
溷 J5e67/M17986 **3263**
滂 J5e71/M18003 **3264**
溲 J5e6c/M17979 **3265**
溥 J5e70/M17957 **3266**
滄 J5e6b/M18007 **3267**
漠 J4779/M18149 **3268**
滔 J5e6d/M18035 **3269**
溢 J306e/M17951 **3270**
溺 J452e/M17990 **3271**
溯 J5e6a/M17975 **3272**
滝 J426c/M18067 **3273**
源 J383b/M17926 **3274**
溝 J3942/M17944 **3275**
溜 J4e2f/M17943 **3276**
溶 J4d4f/M17983 **3277**
準 J3d60/M17934 **3278**
滅 J4c47/M18008 **3279**
滞 J425a/M18087′ **3280**
漢 J3441/M18068′ **3281**
滑 J336a/M18032 **3282**
滯 J5e7c/M18075 **3285**
漾 J5f21/M18184 **3290**
漓 J5f22/M18127 **3292**
漲 J5e7d/M18173 **3294**
碆 J626e/M24273 4011
箈 J-X/M-X 4289
粱 J646d/M26962 4405
羨 J4122/M28503 4665
膝 J4928/M29837 4868
蒲 J3377/M31611 5156
裟 J3a40/M34325 5457
黎 J7355/M47994 7049

11 residual strokes

慂 J584a/M11039 1935
暴 J4b3d/M14137 2511
樣 J5c6b/M15457 2831
漣 J4e7a/M-X **3210**
漣 J-X/M18155 **3259**
滿 J5e60/M18099 **3283**
漢 J-X/M18153 **3284**
滯 J5e7c/M18075 **3285**
潟 J-X/M-X **3286**
漼 J3443/M18216 **3287**
滬 J5e76/M18072 **3288**
滷 J5f23/M18088 **3289**
漾 J5f21/M18184 **3290**
滸 J5e77/M18089 **3291**
漓 J5f22/M18127 **3292**
漱 J5e7b/M18171 **3293**
漲 J5e7d/M18173 **3294**
潁 J5e73/M18188 **3295**
滌 J5e7e/M18069 **3296**
滾 J5e78/M18098 **3297**
漿 J5e79/M18185 **3298**
滴 J4529/M18084 **3299**
漉 J3977/M18112 **3300**
漬 J4452/M18167 **3301**
滲 J5e7a/M18081 **3302**
漂 J493a/M18102 **3303**
漆 J3c3f/M18108 **3304**
漸 J4132/M18179 **3305**
漕 J4166/M18131 **3306**
漏 J4f33/M18120 **3307**
漫 J4c21/M18166 **3308**
漁 J3579/M18101 **3309**
演 J3169/M18130 **3310**
漑 J5e74/M18123 **3322**
窪 J3726/M25580 4209
箔 J4773/M26142 4312
緑 J4e50/M27541′ 4528
綠 J-X/M27541 4529
線 J407e/M27641 4548
蔆 J6851/M31760 5168
裟 J3a40/M34325 5457
踏 J4627/M37602 5889
録 J4f3f/M40519′ 6298
錄 J-X/M40611 6303
隷 J4e6c/M41928 6490

12 residual strokes

溪 J5e64/M17967 **3253**
滾 J5e78/M18098 **3297**
漉 J3977/M18112 **3300**
潴 J5f4c/M18287 **3311**
澂 J5f2d/M18318 **3312**
澑 J5f31/M18335 **3313**
澁 J5f27/M18312 **3314**
澔 J-X/M18338 **3315**
潘 J5f2f/M18236 **3316**
潦 J5f33/M18259 **3317**
潯 J5f29/M18280 **3318**
潸 J5f26/M18293 **3319**
潼 J5f2e/M18302 **3320**
澈 J-X/M18319 **3321**
漑 J5e74/M18123 **3322**
潰 J5f39/M-X **3323**
潭 J5f2c/M18271 **3324**
潑 J-X/M18225 **3325**
潺 J5f25/M18298 **3326**
澆 J5f24/M18317 **3327**
潟 J3363/M18247 **3328**
潤 J3442/M-X **3329**
潤 J-X/M18253 **3330**
澎 J5f30/M18332 **3331**
潔 J3769/M18231 **3332**
澄 J4021/M18315 **3333**
潤 J3d61/M18255 **3334**
潰 J4459/M18281 **3335**
潮 J442c/M18277′ **3336**
潜 J4078/M18241 **3337**
潛 J5f2a/M18240 **3352**
盥 J6239/M23041 3904
糠 J3947/M27105 4424
蕩 J4622/M32002 5198
錄 J-X/M40611 6303
隷 J4e6c/M41928 6490
隸 J7031/M41932 6491
黏 J7356/M48007 7050

13 residual strokes

滋 J3c22/M17919′ **3238**
澤 J5f37/M18383 **3338**
澬 J-X/M18446 **3339**
澡 J5f36/M18379 **3340**
澣 J5f35/M18382 **3341**
澪 J5f3a/M18398 **3342**
濂 J5f32/M18441 **3343**
澳 J5f34/M18412 **3344**
濛 J5f42/M18491 **3345**
澹 J5f38/M18421 **3346**
澱 J4543/M18410 **3347**
濁 J4279/M18440 **3348**
濃 J473b/M18442 **3349**
激 J3763/M18438 **3350**
糠 J3947/M27105 4424
線 J407e/M27641 4548
薀 J6925/M32071 5205
薄 J4776/M32083′ 5225
藜 J693c/M32326 5238
藤 J4623/M32340′ 5241

霑 J7041/M42329 6536
霈 J703e/M42301 6537
鞜 J7061/M42883 6588

14 residual strokes

曝 J4778/M14239 2524
滋 J-X/M18021 **3250**
潔 J3769/M18231 **3332**
濃 J473b/M18442 **3349**
澀 J5f28/M18311 **3351**
潛 J5f2a/M18240 **3352**
濕 J5f3c/M18483 **3353**
濟 J5f3b/M18498 **3354**
濱 J5f40/M18537 **3355**
瀞 J4654/M-X **3356**
濔 J5f3e/M18482 **3357**
濮 J5f41/M18526 **3358**
濘 J5f3f/M18487 **3359**
濯 J4275/M18532 **3360**
濤 J5e39/M18508 **3361**
濬 J5f3d/M18524 **3362**
濠 J396a/M18502 **3363**
潤 J6f69/M18547 **3364**
濡 J4728/M18504 **3365**
濫 J4d74/M18521 **3366**
爆 J477a/M19540 3505
盪 J623b/M23062 3905
粱 J644c/M-X 4348
闊 J6f68/M41429 6409
鯊 J7242/M46186 6867
鴻 J3963/M46874 6963

15 residual strokes

懣 J5870/M11384 2004
濫 J4d74/M18521 **3366**
濺 J5f45/M18557 **3367**
瀁 J5f47/M18573 **3368**
瀋 J5f44/M18600 **3369**
瀏 J5f48/M18607 **3370**
瀑 J5f46/M18609 **3371**
濾 J5f49/M18565 **3372**
瀆 J-X/M18591 **3373**
瀉 J5f43/M18596 **3374**
瀦 J4375/M-X **3377**
瀟 J5f4f/M18660 **3383**
藩 J484d/M32346′ 5242

16 residual strokes

濳 J5f2b/M18683 **3375**
瀧 J426d/M18671 **3376**
瀦 J4375/M-X **3377**
瀛 J5f4a/M18656 **3378**
瀚 J5f4b/M18652 **3379**
瀞 J-X/M18659 **3380**
瀕 J494e/M18636 **3381**
瀝 J5f4d/M18658 **3382**
瀟 J5f4f/M18660 **3383**
瀬 J4025/M18672′ **3384**
瀨 J-X/M18672 **3385**
瀘 J5f4e/M18646 **3386**
簿 J4a6d/M26623′ 4364
籐 J645b/M26693 4373
藻 J4174/M32401 5254
霪 J7046/M42430 6544

17 residual strokes

瀕 J494e/M18636 **3381**
瀲 J5f52/M18693 **3387**
瀾 J5f51/M18722 **3388**
瀰 J5f50/M18690 **3389**
灌 J5e75/M18759 **3390**
蘯 J623c/M32532 5256

18–26 residual strokes

濕 J5f3c/M18483 **3353**
灘 J4667/M18784 **3391**
灑 J5f53/M18774 **3392**
灣 J5f54/M18823 **3393**
黐 J7357/M48027 7051

Rad. 86 火

0 residual strokes

火 J3250/M18850 **3394**

2 residual strokes

灯 J4574/M18855 **3395**
灰 J3325/M18859 **3396**
灰 J-X/M18858 **3397**

3 residual strokes

灼 J3c5e/M18878 **3398**
灸 J3564/M18872 **3399**
災 J3a52/M18879 **3400**
狄 J603f/M20290 3560

4 residual strokes

杰 J5b3f/M14498 2569
氣 J-X/M17052 3026
炙 J5f55/M18922 **3401**
炒 J5f56/M18915 **3402**
炉 J4f27/M18902 **3403**
炎 J316a/M18910 **3404**
炊 J3f66/M18904 **3405**
炬 J5f59/M18949 **3409**

5 residual strokes

恢 J327a/M10577 1843
炮 J5f5c/M18954 **3406**
炳 J5f5b/M18960 **3407**
炯 J5f57/M18956 **3408**
炬 J5f59/M18949 **3409**
炸 J5f5a/M18979 **3410**
為 J3059/M18981 **3411**
点 J4540/M18980 **3412**
炭 J433a/M18953 **3413**
畑 J482a/M21797 3741
秋 J3d29/M24940 4131

6 residual strokes

烟 J5f5d/M19022 **3414**
烛 J-X/M19017 **3415**
烋 J5f5e/M18991 **3416**
烝 J5f5f/M19019 **3417**
烘 J-X/M19012 **3418**
烙 J5f60/M19014 **3419**
烈 J4e75/M18987 **3420**
烏 J3128/M18998 **3421**
烹 J4b23/M19049 **3425**
羔 J6636/M28447 4661
耿 J6656/M29026 4720
荻 J322e/M31005 5054
逖 J6d78/M38886 6046
馬 J474f/M44572 6725

7 residual strokes

偽 J3536/M927′ 276
啖 J5337/M3824 819
庶 J3d6e/M9373 1625
庶 J-X/M-X 1626
淡 J4338/M17660 3202
烱 J5f58/M19040 **3422**
焔 J316b/M-X **3423**
焉 J5f61/M19076 **3424**
烹 J4b23/M19049 **3425**
烽 J5f62/M19059 **3426**
焰 J-X/M19141 **3427**
魚 J357b/M45956 6845
鳥 J443b/M46634 6931
黒 J3975/M48040 7052

8 residual strokes

勞 J5229/M2410 550
啾 J5342/M3892 840
愀 J5837/M10884 1913
毯 J5d5f/M16858 3017
湫 J5e57/M17867 3218
焰 J-X/M19141 **3427**
煉 J4e7b/M-X **3428**
[illegible] J-X/M19130 **3429**
焠 J-X/M19111 **3430**

9 residual strokes

10 residual strokes

11 residual strokes

12 residual strokes

13 residual strokes

14 residual strokes

15 residual strokes

16 residual strokes

17 residual strokes

18 residual strokes

19 residual strokes

20–25 residual strokes

Rad. 87 爪

0 residual strokes

2–3 residual strokes

4 residual strokes

5 residual strokes

6 residual strokes

7 residual strokes

8 residual strokes

鈲 J-X/M40200 6232

9 residual strokes

奨 J3e29/M5990′ 1167
媛 J4932/M6516 1244
孵 J555b/M7021 1301
愛 J3026/M10947 1927
暖 J4348/M14064 2502
渓 J5e64/M17967 3253
滔 J5e6d/M18035 3269
熖 J-X/M19221 3443
煖 J5f6b/M19196 3451
焰 J-X/M-X 3460
瑶 J6076/M-X 3656
綏 J6537/M27501 4496
舜 J3d58/M30339 4925
艀 J6759/M30431 4940
蒋 J3e55/M-X 5132
蜉 J696a/M33104 5324
觚 J6b38/M35043 5544
隠 J3123/M41836′ 6480

10 residual strokes

亂 J502c/M214 64
亂 J-X/M-X 65
僞 J5126/M1105 303
孵 J555b/M7021 1301
焰 J-X/M-X 3460
稱 J634a/M25180 4155
稲 J3070/M25187′ 4158
箏 J6437/M26133 4313
綵 J653d/M27580 4509
綬 J3c7a/M27565 4510

11 residual strokes

孵 J555b/M7021 1301
溪 J5e64/M17967 3253
稻 J634b/M25216 4161
緩 J344b/M27669 4551
蕣 J687c/M31991 5204
諍 J6b5a/M35643 5633

12 residual strokes

噯 J-X/M4394 907
墾 J3a26/M5509 1097
穏 J323a/M25280′ 4175
綬 J3c7a/M27565 4510
蕣 J687c/M31991 5204
謡 J4d58/M35779′ 5666
錚 J6f23/M40553 6290
隱 J702c/M41891 6485
雞 J-X/M-X 6508
靜 J7050/M42578 6561
餒 J712f/M44163 6695

13 residual strokes

曖 J5b23/M14206 2521
爵 J3c5f/M19710′ **3514**
瞬 J3d56/M23694 3969
緩 J344b/M27669 4551
謟 J-X/M35831 5682
谿 J6c30/M36219 5734
蹈 J6d25/M37744 5895
蹊 J6c7e/M37747 5896
醤 J3e5f/M-X 6186

14 residual strokes

爵 J3c5f/M19710′ **3514**
爵 J-X/M19711 **3515**
瞹 J6259/M23727 3963
瞬 J3d56/M23694 3969
雞 J-X/M42124 6513

15 residual strokes

濔 J-X/M18659 3380
穩 J6353/M25344 4183
譌 J6b77/M35951 5698
谿 J6c30/M36219 5734
蹊 J6c7e/M37747 5896
辭 J6d66/M38671 6004
霪 J7046/M42430 6544
韜 J706b/M43189 6603
鶏 J375c/M47074′ 6980

16–21 residual strokes

嚼 J5370/M4602 926
雞 J-X/M42124 6513
靉 J704f/M42540 6556
韜 J706b/M43189 6603
鷄 J7331/M47209 6985

Rad. 88 父

0 residual strokes

父 J4963/M19721 **3516**

2–4 residual strokes

交 J3872/M291 90
佼 J3873/M570 175
効 J387a/M2334 535
斧 J4960/M13539 2382
郊 J3959/M39392 6137

5–6 residual strokes

傚 J-X/M725 225
咬 J527b/M3543 787
效 J5a43/M13186 2336
校 J393b/M14713 2669
狡 J6044/M20365 3571
釜 J3378/M40164 6215

7–9 residual strokes

傚 J507b/M969 280
爺 J4c6c/M19734 **3517**
皎 J6229/M22724 3872
絞 J394a/M27421 4485
蛟 J6960/M33009 5311
較 J3353/M38297 5959

10–17 residual strokes

絞 J394a/M27421 4485
纐 J6576/M28050 4615
餃 J712d/M44131 6688
駁 J7149/M44610 6732
駮 J7150/M44726 6747
鮫 J3b2d/M46127 6863
鵁 J727a/M46888 6959

Rad. 89 爻

0 residual strokes

爻 J602b/M19737 **3518**

5–10 residual strokes

俎 J5059/M679 209
爼 J602c/M19743 **3519**
爽 J4156/M19746 **3520**
爾 J3c24/M19750 **3521**
駁 J477d/M44619 6733

12–22 residual strokes

學 J555c/M7033 1302
攀 J5a35/M12926 2315
攪 J5978/M13041 2322
[illegible] J-X/M15978 2926
璽 J3c25/M21309 3683
礬 J6329/M24573 4058
禰 J-X/M24851 4115
禰 J4729/M-X 4116

Rad. 90 爿

0 residual strokes

爿 J602d/M19758 **3522**

2–3 residual strokes

Rad.90: 4 residual strokes

- 祇 J6a54/M34237 5446
- 責 J4055/M36682 5780
- 遑 J6e23/M39006 6081
- 隍 J7026/M41754 6465

8 residual strokes

- 惶 J5835/M10863 1912
- 斑 J4843/M13470 2371
- 晴 J4032/M13994′ 2488
- 湟 J5e54/M17850 3217
- 琅 J6066/M21013 **3639**
- 琳 J4e56/M21077 **3646**
- 琙 J314d/M21127 **3647**
- 琲 J606a/M21075 **3648**
- 琶 J474a/M21081 **3649**
- 琢 J-X/M21058 **3650**
- 琥 J6068/M21061 **3651**
- 琺 J606b/M21088 **3652**
- 琵 J487c/M21080 **3653**
- 琴 J3657/M21079 **3654**
- 睚 J-X/M23310 3928
- 程 J4478/M25081′ 4144
- 筐 J637e/M26001 4276
- 筌 J6425/M25995 4278
- 筺 J6421/M-X 4290
- 素 J4147/M27300 4456
- 艇 J447a/M30440 4941
- 董 J6841/M31207 5086
- 蜓 J-X/M33121 5318
- 註 J4370/M35340 5583
- 遑 J6e23/M39006 6081
- 閏 J313c/M41244 6389
- 閠 J6f60/M-X 6394

9 residual strokes

- 僅 J-X/M1048 292
- 嗟 J534d/M4102 869
- 嗷 J5353/M4142 880
- 嘖 J5354/M4204 882
- 嵯 J3a37/M8363 1500
- 嵳 J564d/M8364 1501
- 煌 J5f6a/M19181 3449
- 琵 J487c/M21080 **3653**
- 瑇 J-X/M21102 **3655**
- 瑤 J6076/M-X **3656**
- 瑯 J6067/M21163 **3657**
- 琿 J606d/M21093 **3658**
- 瑙 J606f/M21125 **3659**
- 瑟 J606e/M21133 **3660**
- 瑁 J6070/M21096 **3661**
- 瑚 J386a/M21126 **3662**
- 瑜 J6071/M21129 **3663**
- 瑕 J606c/M21120 **3664**
- 瑞 J3f70/M21131 **3665**
- 睛 J624d/M23438 3940
- 筐 J637e/M26001 4276
- 筺 J6421/M-X 4290
- 聖 J403b/M29074′ 4727
- 艇 J447a/M30440 4941
- 蜓 J-X/M33121 5318
- 解 J6b3b/M35074 5549
- 詮 J4127/M35435 5604
- 賃 J4442/M36743 5802
- 鈷 J385a/M40270 6236
- 靖 J4c77/M42570′ 6559

10 residual strokes

- 僅 J-X/M1048 292
- 嗉 J-X/M4057 863
- 對 J5574/M7457 1387
- 徵 J4427/M10238′ 1768
- 槎 J5c4c/M15320 2802
- 様 J4d4d/M15352′ 2821
- 漬 J4452/M18167 3301
- 瑇 J-X/M21102 **3655**
- 瑯 J6067/M21163 **3657**
- 瑤 J7424/M21149 **3666**
- 瑳 J3a3c/M21170 **3667**
- 蘭 J-X/M21167 **3668**
- 璃 J4d7e/M21196 **3669**
- 瑩 J6072/M21133 **3670**
- 瑪 J6075/M21156 **3671**
- 瑰 J6073/M21164 **3672**
- 瑠 J4e5c/M21143 **3673**
- 瑣 J6074/M21147 **3674**
- 碧 J4a4b/M24334 4027
- 精 J400a/M26997′ 4411
- 蜻 J6971/M33203 5341
- 誑 J6b54/M35510 5619
- 酲 J6e4b/M39865 6173
- 銓 J6e74/M40378 6262
- 霆 J703d/M42299 6529

11 residual strokes

- 徵 J-X/M10239 1769
- 撲 J4b50/M12755 2274
- 様 J4d4d/M15352′ 2821
- 樣 J-X/M-X 2827
- 樣 J5c6b/M15457 2831
- 槿 J5c5d/M15395 2848
- 澂 J5f2d/M18313 3312
- 潔 J3769/M18231 3332
- 潤 J3d61/M18255 3334
- 璃 J4d7e/M21196 **3669**
- 璋 J6078/M21211 **3675**
- 瑾 J6077/M21187 **3676**
- 篁 J643b/M26249 4326
- 蝗 J697b/M33267 5361
- 請 J4041/M35640′ 5645
- 霆 J703d/M42299 6529
- 駐 J4373/M44660 6745
- 髮 J717b/M45400 6805
- 鬧 J7229/M45639 6822
- 麹 J396d/M-X 7036

12 residual strokes

- 嗉 J-X/M4057 863
- 嶬 J5654/M8510 1514
- 憲 J377b/M11269′ 1988
- 槿 J5c5d/M15395 2848
- 樸 J-X/M-X 2856
- 璢 J6065/M21249 **3677**
- 璞 J6079/M21245 **3678**
- 積 J4051/M25266 4176
- 錆 J3b2c/M40523 6296
- 靜 J7050/M42578 6561
- 靛 J-X/M42577 6562
- 鬨 J722a/M45641 6823
- 麺 J4c4d/M-X 7038

13 residual strokes

- 樸 J5c77/M15495 2873
- 檥 J-X/M15690 2882
- 潔 J3769/M18231 3332
- 瀞 J4654/M-X 3356
- 犠 J353e/M20190′ 3550
- 璧 J607a/M21269 **3679**
- 環 J3444/M-X **3680**
- 環 J-X/M21287 **3681**
- 磧 J6321/M24448 4041
- 簣 J6447/M26419 4350
- 績 J4053/M27845 4579
- 謹 J3660/M35850′ 5688
- 轄 J336d/M38482′ 5981
- 鍠 J6f29/M40630 6307
- 鎚 J-X/M40715 6310

14 residual strokes

- 叢 J4151/M3220 684
- 懲 J4428/M11399′ 2006
- 瀆 J5f47/M18573 3368
- 環 J-X/M21287 **3681**
- 瓊 J607b/M21328 **3682**
- 璽 J3c25/M21309 **3683**
- 礒 J6326/M24527 4053
- 謹 J3660/M35850′ 5688
- 謹 J-X/M35900 5690
- 蹟 J4058/M37814 5905
- 鎚 J-X/M40715 6310
- 鬩 J722b/M45644 6824

15 residual strokes

- 寶 J5570/M7366 1369
- 黴 J-X/M11424 2007
- 詠 J-X/M18659 3380
- 績 J4053/M27845 4579
- 蟶 J6a3a/M33664 5390

13 residual strokes

14 residual strokes

15 residual strokes

16 residual strokes

17 residual strokes

鰾 J7264/M46447 6911
鰺 J724d/M46442 6912
鱆 J7263/M46464 6913
鰻 J3137/M46443 6914
鰹 J336f/M46437 6915
鱈 J432d/M46470 6916
鱉 J-X/M46472 6917

18 residual strokes

纒 J6575/M28058 4617
躚 J6d37/M37970 5922
轤 J6d62/M38596 5995
鑛 J6f4a/M41010 6363
鑢 J6f4c/M41021 6365
霾 J704a/M42507 6550
騾 J7160/M44957 6771
鰹 J336f/M46437 6915
鱉 J-X/M46472 6917
鱚 J7283/M46516 6918
鱏 J-X/M46488 6919
鱓 J-X/M46496 6920
鱒 J4b70/M46497 6921
鱘 J-X/M46504 6922
鱗 J4e5a/M46502 6923
鱮 J-X/M46571 6925
鵠 J733d/M47335 7001

19 residual strokes

纏 J453b/M28043 4612
鑪 J6f4e/M41038 6369
魘 J7236/M45941 6844
鱗 J4e5a/M46502 6923
鱞 J-X/M46520 6924
鱮 J-X/M46571 6925
鱧 J7267/M46542 6926
鱠 J7266/M46530 6927
釁 J7354/M47985 7047

20–22 residual strokes

纒 J6575/M28058 4617
顱 J7121/M43742 6660
驢 J7166/M45069 6778
驥 J7167/M45076 6779
鱮 J-X/M46571 6925
鱶 J7268/M46592 6928
鱺 J-X/M46587 6929
鱸 J7269/M46600 6930

Rad. 103 疋

0 residual strokes

疋 J4925/M21994 **3774**

3–5 residual strokes

倢 J-X/M784 227
定 J446a/M7109 1323
從 J3d3e/M10133 1745
徒 J454c/M10121 1746
是 J4027/M13859 2451
胥 J6671/M29406 4781

6 residual strokes

匙 J3a7c/M2590 582
徙 J5750/M10142 1749
捉 J595d/M12272 2180
旋 J407b/M13656 2400
淀 J4d64/M17610 3182
蛋 J4341/M32977 5301

7 residual strokes

堉 J5466/M5664 1046
堤 J4469/M5259 1054
婿 J4c3b/M6470 1246
寔 J5566/M7244 1346
御 J3866/M10157 1761
提 J4473/M12344 2237
湑 J-X/M17829 3227
疏 J4141/M22000 **3775**
疎 J4142/M22002 **3776**

8 residual strokes

尟 J-X/M7522 1397
楚 J413f/M15141 2771
碇 J4476/M24275 4019

9–10 residual strokes

愿 J5845/M11030 1934
椗 J-X/M-X 2792
疑 J353f/M22007 **3777**
綻 J433e/M27587 4514
聢 J665e/M29113 4729
諚 J6b5c/M35682 5631

11 residual strokes

凝 J3645/M1720 431
綻 J433e/M27587 4514
縱 J3d44/M27804' 4571
聳 J-X/M-X 4734
醍 J4269/M39924 6184
錠 J3e7b/M40559 6293
靛 J-X/M42577 6562

12 residual strokes

噓 J536a/M4493 912
嶷 J5658/M8545 1518
擬 J353c/M12870 2307

13–15 residual strokes

嚏 J5369/M4501 917
癡 J6177/M22591 3849
礎 J4143/M24522 4054
礙 J[illegible]/M24542 4055
縱 J3d44/M27804' 4571
題 J426a/M43584 6645
鯷 J-X/M46290 6894

Rad. 104 疒

2–3 residual strokes

疔 J614b/M22019 **3778**
疚 J614c/M22033 **3779**
疝 J614d/M22040 **3780**

4 residual strokes

疥 J614e/M22057 **3781**
疣 J614f/M22050 **3782**
疫 J3156/M22069 **3783**
疳 J6151/M22085 **3789**

5 residual strokes

痓 J-X/M-X **3784**
疴 J-X/M22088 **3785**
疸 J6155/M22094 **3786**
疽 J6154/M22106 **3787**
疹 J3f3e/M22097 **3788**
疳 J6151/M22085 **3789**
痃 J6152/M22124 **3790**
疱 J6157/M22082 **3791**
疼 J6156/M22105 **3792**
痂 J6150/M22122 **3793**
痀 J-X/M22120 **3794**
症 J3e49/M22140 **3795**
疲 J4868/M22084 **3796**
疾 J3e40/M22112 **3797**
病 J4942/M22127 **3798**
痗 J-X/M-X **3799**

6 residual strokes

痊 J6159/M22141 **3800**
痍 J6158/M22148 **3801**
痒 J615a/M22163 **3802**
痕 J3a2f/M22171 **3803**
痔 J3c26/M22167 **3804**
疵 J6153/M22089 **3805**

7 residual strokes

痃 J6152/M22124 **3790**

饗 J-X / M44431 6715

Rad. 107 皮

0 residual strokes

皮 J4869 / M22823 **3878**

2–4 residual strokes

彼 J4860 / M10066 1732
披 J4864 / M11909 2116
波 J4748 / M17308 3101
玻 J6060 / M20899 3628
陂 J6f78 / M41603 6430

5 residual strokes

疲 J4868 / M22084 3796
皰 J622e / M22844 **3879**
破 J474b / M24124 3999
被 J486f / M34222 5445

6–8 residual strokes

婆 J474c / M6390 1240
皴 J622f / M22866 **3880**
碆 J626e / M24273 4011
菠 J684a / M31190 5081
跛 J6c6c / M37479 5865
鞁 J705b / M42776 6579

9–14 residual strokes

皷 J7369 / M22887 **3881**
皸 J6230 / M22888 **3882**
皹 J6231 / M-X **3883**
皺 J6232 / M22899 **3884**
簸 J4876 / M26609 4363
鞁 J705b / M42776 6579
頗 J3f7c / M43415 6627

Rad. 108 皿

0 residual strokes

皿 J3b2e / M22941 **3885**

1–3 residual strokes

孟 J4c52 / M6960 1291
盂 J6233 / M22949 **3886**
血 J376c / M33964 5411

4 residual strokes

恤 J5775 / M10583 1839
洫 J5e29 / M17403 3110
盃 J4756 / M22955 **3887**
盈 J314e / M22961 **3888**
盆 J4b5f / M22959 **3889**

5 residual strokes

猛 J4c54 / M20498 3588
盈 J314e / M22961 **3888**
盍 J6234 / M22980 **3890**
益 J3157 / M22972' **3891**

6 residual strokes

猛 J4c54 / M20498 3588
盖 J6235 / M22996 **3892**
盒 J6236 / M22988 **3893**
盗 J4570 / M23000 **3894**
盛 J4039 / M23001' **3895**

7 residual strokes

愠 J-X / M10954 1907
温 J3239 / M17774 3246
盜 J5d39 / M23006 **3896**
盛 J-X / M23005 **3897**
隘 J7027 / M41791 6473

8 residual strokes

塩 J3176 / M5382 1075
媪 J553c / M6588 1250
慍 J5832 / M11059 1930
榲 J5c33 / M15188 2775
溫 J-X / M17968 3251
溘 J5e65 / M17936 3255
溢 J306e / M17951 3270
盞 J6237 / M23020 **3898**
盟 J4c41 / M23024 **3899**
葢 J6864 / M31432 5100
蓋 J3338 / M31652 5155

9 residual strokes

寧 J-X / M7296 1362
榲 J5c33 / M15188 2775
榅 J5c45 / M15277 2800
熅 J-X / M19288 3467
盡 J6238 / M23029 **3900**
監 J3446 / M23032 **3901**
膃 J672c / M29757 4857

10 residual strokes

瘟 J6169 / M22396 3828
監 J3446 / M23032 **3901**
盤 J4857 / M23036 **3902**
緼 J-X / M27701 4536
褞 J6a72 / M34475 5486

11 residual strokes

盧 J623a / M23050 **3903**
盥 J6239 / M23041 **3904**
縕 J-X / M27757 4564
縊 J6550 / M27738 4568
蕰 J6925 / M32071 5205
諡 J6b6b / M35708 5652

12 residual strokes

儖 J5130 / M1229 325
儘 J5056 / M1234 327
嚀 J5366 / M4445 914
壗 J545c / M-X 1105
濘 J5f3f / M18487 3359
濫 J4d74 / M18521 3366
獰 J6058 / M20755 3611
盪 J623b / M23062 **3905**
緼 J-X / M27701 4536
藍 J4d75 / M32258 5233
諡 J6b6b / M35708 5652
謚 J6b6a / M35823 5679
謐 J6b6d / M35803 5681
醞 J6e4f / M39981 6187
醖 J-X / M39974 6188

13 residual strokes

檸 J5d26 / M15742 2899
檻 J5d23 / M15745 2902
濫 J4d74 / M18521 3366
燼 J5f7e / M19515 3502
縕 J-X / M27757 4564
縊 J6550 / M27738 4568
藍 J4d75 / M32258 5233
鎰 J6f2d / M40747 6319
闔 J6f6e / M41452 6415

14 residual strokes

廬 J572a / M9535 1648
檻 J5d23 / M15745 2902
濾 J5f4e / M18646 3386
蘆 J6943 / M32425 5244
蘊 J693e / M32434 5250
襤 J6b22 / M34674 5507
醯 J6e51 / M40036 6193
饂 J713b / M44339 6708
鹽 J-X / M47550 7012

15 residual strokes

櫨 J4827 / M15844 2910
爐 J6024 / M19566 3506
籃 J6457 / M26648 4369
纜 J6571 / M28009 4605
聹 J6664 / M29199 4743
臚 J6746 / M30027 4889
艦 J344f / M30571 4950

Rad. 109 目

7 residual strokes

8 residual strokes

9 residual strokes

10 residual strokes

賠 J4765/M36818 5810
賦 J496a/M36800 5811
賜 J3b72/M36809 5812
賤 J6c4d/M36826 5813
賛 J3b3f/M36841 5814
賢 J382d/M36822 5816
質 J3c41/M36833 5817
遺 J3064/M39134′ 6115
頬 J4b4b/M-X 6629
鼏 J-X/M48316 7075

11 residual strokes

叡 J3143/M3214 683
噸 J4655/M4429 910
憩 J3748/M11246 1980
樌 J5c6e/M15416 2839
濆 J-X/M18446 3339
疊 J614a/M-X 3769
瞟 J-X/M23650 **3955**
瞞 J6256/M23649 **3956**
瞠 J6255/M23651 **3957**
瞥 J4a4d/M23672 **3959**
穎 J3150/M24824 4109
穎 J314f/M25267 4173
積 J4051/M25266 4176
窺 J312e/M25633 4215
簒 J-X/M26330 4341
縣 J6551/M27784 4555
膩 J6737/M29862 4872
蕢 J6931/M32054 5214
襀 J-X/M34544 5493
覩 J6b2f/M34913 5531
覦 J6b30/M34904 5532
覧 J4d77/M34928 5533
親 J3f46/M34918 5534
賢 J382d/M36822 5816
賭 J-X/M36847 5819
邉 J6e35/M-X 6116
醍 J7053/M42660 6568
頻 J-X/M43519 6631
頷 J7077/M43512 6632
頤 J7075/M43455 6633
頼 J4d6a/M43529′ 6635
頹 J7078/M43517 6636
頽 J-X/M43496 6637
頸 J7074/M43515 6638
頭 J462c/M43490 6639
颶 J-X/M43840 6667

12 residual strokes

償 J3d7e/M1245 333
優 J4d25/M1261 334
嬪 J554d/M6819 1272
嬰 J3145/M6828 1273
嬶 J554e/M6849 1274
嶺 J4e66/M8553 1517
擤 J-X/M12857 2298
擯 J5a2f/M12880 2300
氈 J5d61/M16982 3019
濱 J5f40/M18537 3355
濬 J5f3d/M18524 3362
瞶 J6258/M23713 **3958**
瞥 J4a4d/M23672 **3959**
瞭 J4e46/M23697 **3960**
瞳 J4637/M23707 **3961**
瞰 J6257/M23704 **3962**
瞬 J3d56/M23694 3969
簒 J5255/M26490 4345
簣 J6447/M26419 4350
績 J4053/M27845 4579
罌 J6622/M28185 4629
覯 J6b32/M34937 5535
覬 J6b31/M34934 5536
覲 J6b33/M34952 5537
賻 J6c52/M36881 5820
賺 J6c51/M36880 5821
賽 J6c50/M36886 5822
購 J3958/M36885 5823
贅 J6c54/M36908 5826
霜 J417a/M42363 6542
顆 J7079/M43551 6640
頻 J4951/M-X 6641
颶 J7127/M43876 6668
鹹 J7143/M44507 6721
鼾 J736d/M48505 7083

13 residual strokes

攅 J5a39/M12933 2311
櫃 J5d24/M15757 2898
檳 J5d27/M15734 2901
殯 J5d52/M16596 2986
濺 J5f45/M18557 3367
瀆 J-X/M18591 3373
瓊 J607b/M21328 3682
瞹 J6259/M23727 **3963**
瞻 J625d/M23742 **3964**
瞿 J625a/M23747 **3965**
瞼 J625b/M23744 **3966**
矇 J625e/M23774 **3967**
瞽 J625c/M23745 **3968**
瞬 J3d56/M23694 **3969**
簀 J644f/M26524 4354
覲 J6b33/M34952 5537
観 J3451/M34955 5538
贓 J-X/M36904 5824
贇 J6c53/M36907 5825
贅 J6c54/M36908 5826
贈 J4223/M36920′ 5827
蹟 J4058/M37814 5905
鎖 J3a3f/M40708′ 6325
鎮 J4443/M40745 6328
鎭 J6f2f/M40744 6329
顋 J707b/M43576 6642
顎 J335c/M43590 6643
額 J335b/M43586 6644
題 J426a/M43584 6645
顕 J3832/M43609′ 6646
類 J4e60/M43608′ 6647
顔 J3469/M43591′ 6648
顏 J707a/M43591 6649
鵙 J7326/M46947 6965

14 residual strokes

嚬 J-X/M4562 922
嬾 J554f/M6872 1276
寳 J5570/M7366 1369
懶 J5871/M11455 2010
擾 J3e71/M12920 2314
櫃 J5d24/M15757 2898
櫝 J-X/M15821 2907
瀬 J4025/M18672′ 3384
瀨 J-X/M18672 3385
牘 J6031/M19906 3530
犢 J6039/M20196 3551
獺 J605c/M20782 3615
績 J4053/M27845 4579
藾 J6941/M32405 5245
蘋 J6940/M32435 5248
贓 J-X/M36904 5824
贈 J-X/M36929 5828
贊 J6c55/M36935 5829
贇 J6c56/M36909 5831
韻 J3124/M43307 6611
顎 J335c/M43590 6643
類 J-X/M43636 6650
顚 J-X/M43628 6651
顛 J453f/M-X 6652
願 J346a/M43623 6653

15 residual strokes

嚶 J536d/M4592 925
孀 J5552/M6885 1279
寶 J556f/M7376 1371
懸 J377c/M11462 2011
櫎 J-X/M15905 2912
瀕 J494e/M18636 3381
矍 J625f/M23792 **3970**
竇 J6365/M25695 4220
繽 J656f/M27999 4606
纂 J3b3c/M28012 4608
嶹 J-X/M34021 5418
襭 J6b23/M34702 5508
覺 J6b34/M34973 5539
贍 J6c58/M36945 5832
齟 J7372/M48627 7095

16 residual strokes

囂 J536f/M4616 930
懼 J5876/M11488 2016

Rad. 110 矛

Rad. 111 矢

祁 J3737/M24634 **4063**

3 residual strokes

奈 J4660/M5893 1147
宗 J3d21/M7106 1321
祀 J632b/M24633 **4064**
社 J3c52/M24631′ **4065**
社 J-X/M24631 **4066**

4 residual strokes

柰 J-X/M14659 2598
祇 J-X/M24639 **4067**
祇 J3540/M-X **4068**
祉 J3b63/M24641′ **4069**
祉 J-X/M24641 **4070**
祈 J3527/M24640′ **4071**
祈 J-X/M24640 **4072**
途 J4553/M38882′ 6057
除 J3d7c/M41669 6449

5 residual strokes

敘 J5a47/M13206 2341
淙 J5e4a/M17643 3188
祇 J-X/M24639 **4067**
祇 J3540/M-X **4068**
祢 J-X/M24679 **4073**
祢 J472a/M-X **4074**
祕 J6330/M24663 **4075**
祚 J632f/M24668 **4076**
祗 J632d/M24665 **4077**
祟 J632e/M24674 **4078**
祐 J4d34/M24652′ **4079**
祐 J-X/M24652 **4080**
祠 J632c/M24676 **4081**
祓 J6331/M24658 **4082**
祖 J4144/M24664′ **4083**
祖 J-X/M24664 **4084**
祝 J3d4b/M24672′ **4085**
祝 J-X/M24672 **4086**
神 J3f40/M24673′ **4087**
神 J-X/M24673 **4088**
途 J4553/M38882′ 6057

6 residual strokes

剽 J5177/M2160 510
尉 J3053/M7440 1383
崇 J3f72/M8152 1490
捺 J4668/M12221 2189
敘 J5a47/M13206 2341
斎 J3a58/M13467 2368
祗 J632d/M24665 **4077**
票 J493c/M24694 **4089**
祥 J3e4d/M24689′ **4090**
祥 J-X/M24689 **4091**
祭 J3a57/M24700 **4092**

7 residual strokes

棕 J5c23/M14933 2740
款 J343e/M16107 2938
祷 J4578/M-X **4093**
視 J3b6b/M34827′ 5525
視 J-X/M34836 5526

8 residual strokes

款 J-X/M16125 2941
禀 J6349/M24742 **4094**
祺 J6332/M24733 **4095**
禄 J4f3d/M24741′ **4096**
祿 J6333/M24741 **4097**
禁 J3658/M24743 **4098**
蒜 J4947/M31562 5144
蜍 J696b/M33110 5320
際 J3a5d/M41820 6478

9 residual strokes

嫖 J5545/M6637 1258
察 J3b21/M7283 1360
慓 J5858/M11084 1957
榊 J3a67/M-X 2756
榊 J-X/M15352 2808
漂 J493a/M18102 3303
禎 J4477/M24767′ **4099**
禎 J-X/M24767 **4100**
禊 J6334/M24760 **4101**
禍 J3252/M24766′ **4102**
禍 J-X/M24766 **4103**
禅 J4135/M24787′ **4104**
福 J4a21/M24768′ **4105**
福 J-X/M24768 **4106**
粽 J6470/M26993 4410
綜 J416e/M27535 4520
蔚 J3136/M31805 5181

10 residual strokes

凜 J515b/M1718 430
慰 J3056/M11135 1972
標 J4938/M15442 2852
熨 J5f71/M19346 3471
禊 J-X/M-X **4107**
禝 J6335/M24792 **4108**
蔡 J6871/M31818 5170
踪 J6d29/M37668 5887

11 residual strokes

嘌 J5361/M4364 909
瓢 J493b/M21419 3688
瘭 J-X/M22440 3835
瞟 J-X/M23650 3955
頴 J3150/M24824 **4109**
綜 J416e/M27535 4520
隷 J4e6c/M41928 6490
餘 J7131/M44185 6693

12 residual strokes

擦 J3b24/M12862 2306
禪 J6338/M24835 **4110**
禦 J357a/M24820 **4111**
禧 J6336/M24828 **4112**
縹 J655d/M27837 4583
隸 J7031/M41932 6491
齋 J6337/M48565 7085

13 residual strokes

禮 J6339/M24844 **4113**
襟 J365f/M34647 5504
齋 J6337/M48565 7085

14 residual strokes

禱 J-X/M24852 **4114**
禰 J-X/M24851 **4115**
禰 J4729/M-X **4116**
縹 J655d/M27837 4583

15–17 residual strokes

禳 J633a/M24868 **4117**
飄 J7128/M43946 6669
飃 J7129/M43945 6670
驃 J715f/M44966 6770
鰰 J7260/M46414 6903
鰾 J7264/M46447 6911

Rad. 114 内

4–6 residual strokes

禹 J633b/M24885 **4118**
禺 J633c/M24886 **4119**
遇 J3678/M38991′ 6083
隅 J3679/M41743 6467

7 residual strokes

偶 J3676/M899 274
寓 J3677/M7243 1348
萬 J685f/M31339 5103
遇 J3678/M38991′ 6083

8–9 residual strokes

亂 J-X/M-X 65
愚 J3672/M10946 1925
漓 J5f22/M18127 3292

禽 J3659/M24893 **4120**

10 residual strokes

漓 J5f22/M18127 3292
璃 J4d7e/M21196 3669
耦 J-X/M28952 4713
邁 J6e32/M39169 6110

11–12 residual strokes

擒 J5a22/M12816 2289
檎 J3869/M15657 2888
癘 J6176/M22556 3839
耦 J-X/M28952 4713
邁 J6e32/M39169 6110

13–15 residual strokes

礪 J626a/M24571 4056
糲 J647a/M27181 4427
藕 J6939/M32298 5239
蠣 J695a/M33799 5399
離 J4e25/M42140 6517

16–20 residual strokes

竊 J6366/M25713 4222
籬 J6461/M26803 4379
糲 J647a/M27181 4427
蠣 J695a/M33799 5399
魑 J7235/M45901 6842
黐 J7357/M48027 7051
齲 J737a/M48716 7102

Rad. 115 禾

0 residual strokes

禾 J3253/M24906 **4121**

2 residual strokes

利 J4d78/M1932 466
季 J3528/M6965 1292
禿 J4645/M24910 **4122**
秀 J3d28/M24911 **4123**
私 J3b64/M24913 **4124**
釆 J4850/M40115 6202

3 residual strokes

和 J4f42/M3490 770
咊 J-X/M3489 771
委 J3051/M6181 1204
季 J3528/M6965 1292
秀 J3d28/M24911 **4123**
秉 J633d/M24932 **4125**

4 residual strokes

俐 J505e/M682 208
秕 J633e/M24958 **4126**
秔 J-X/M24954 **4127**
秬 J6340/M25002 **4128**
秒 J4943/M24952 **4129**
科 J324a/M24950 **4130**
秋 J3d29/M24940 **4131**
透 J4629/M38876 6059
香 J3961/M44518 6722

5 residual strokes

倭 J4f41/M796 242
悧 J5826/M10689 1856
悸 J5829/M10733 1885
秕 J633e/M24958 **4126**
秬 J6340/M25002 **4128**
秡 J6341/M24990 **4132**
秦 J3f41/M24995 **4133**
秤 J4769/M24993 **4134**
秩 J4361/M24998 **4135**
秣 J6342/M24992 **4136**
秧 J633f/M24996 **4137**
租 J4145/M24988 **4138**
称 J3e4e/M25016 **4139**
秘 J486b/M24977 **4140**
莉 J683d/M31034 5044
莠 J683c/M31065 5046
透 J4629/M38876 6059

6 residual strokes

唎 J533b/M3833 817
悸 J5829/M10733 1885
梨 J4d7c/M14873 2697
犁 J6035/M20037 3542
移 J305c/M25045 **4141**
莠 J683c/M31065 5046
萎 J3060/M31269 5087
菌 J365d/M31156 5091
逶 J6d7b/M38949 6067
釈 J3c61/M40120 6203

7 residual strokes

啾 J5342/M3892 840
愀 J5837/M10884 1913
梱 J-X/M14947 2707
湫 J5e57/M17867 3218
犂 J6034/M20048 3547
番 J4856/M21858 3762
痢 J4e21/M22213 3810
稈 J6343/M25074 **4142**
稍 J6344/M25083 **4143**
程 J4478/M25081 **4144**
稀 J3529/M25058 **4145**
税 J4047/M25070 **4146**
萪 J6854/M31334 5106
萩 J476b/M31333 5122
逶 J6d7b/M38949 6067
酥 J6e48/M39835 6167
釉 J6e58/M40121 6204
黍 J3550/M47991 7048

8 residual strokes

愁 J3d25/M10885 1923
楸 J5c36/M15186 2763
甃 J612c/M21554 3703
痿 J615f/M22290 3815
矮 J6264/M23995 3983
稘 J6345/M25118 **4147**
稙 J6346/M25119 **4148**
稔 J4c2d/M25107 **4149**
稠 J6347/M25130 **4150**
稗 J-X/M25113 **4151**
稜 J4e47/M25123 **4152**
稟 J6348/M25127 **4153**
稚 J4355/M25120 **4154**
綉 J6535/M27493 4495
蓁 J686d/M31639 5134
蜊 J696d/M33106 5319

9 residual strokes

榛 J3f3a/M15240 2811
澳 J5f34/M18412 3344
甃 J612c/M21554 3703
稱 J634a/M25180 **4155**
稗 J4923/M-X **4156**
穀 J3972/M25188 **4157**
稲 J3070/M25187 **4158**
種 J3c6f/M25174 **4159**
箘 J6430/M26147 4302
綉 J6535/M27493 4495
誘 J4d36/M35525 5625

10 residual strokes

凜 J7425/M1717 429
穀 J-X/M25221 **4160**
稻 J634b/M25216 **4161**
稺 J-X/M25213 **4162**
稽 J374e/M25218 **4163**
穃 J634e/M-X **4164**
稷 J634d/M25207 **4165**
稿 J3946/M25220 **4166**
稾 J634c/M25219 **4167**
穂 J4a66/M25236 **4168**
稼 J3254/M25217 **4169**
蝌 J6978/M33248 5357
誘 J4d36/M35525 5625
銹 J6e78/M40426 6271

黎 J7355/M47994 7049

---

11 residual strokes

廩 J5729/M9515 1647
懍 J586e/M11335 1994
曆 J-X/M14171 2512
歷 J-X/M16340 2965
穀 J-X/M25221 **4160**
穐 J302c/M25281 **4170**
穆 J4b54/M25251 **4171**
穆 J-X/M25256 **4172**
穎 J314f/M25267 **4173**
稽 J-X/M-X **4174**
穏 J323a/M25280′ **4175**
積 J4051/M25266 **4176**
穉 J6350/M25282 **4178**
羲 J663c/M28552 4671
臻 J674b/M30165 4906
薐 J6933/M32108 5206
銹 J6e78/M40426 6271
頽 J7078/M43517 6636

---

12 residual strokes

穗 J634f/M25298 **4177**
穉 J6350/M25282 **4178**
鍬 J372d/M40643 6314
鞦 J7063/M42922 6592
黏 J7356/M48007 7050

---

13 residual strokes

瀋 J5f44/M18600 3369
礇 J6325/M24505 4051
穂 J3e77/M25335′ **4179**
穫 J334f/M25334′ **4180**
穡 J6351/M25325 **4181**
穢 J6352/M25331 **4182**
藜 J693c/M32326 5238
邌 J-X/M39219 6125
鞦 J7063/M42922 6592
馥 J7146/M44545 6723
魏 J7232/M45872 6841
鯏 J7245/M46201 6868

---

14 residual strokes

瀝 J5f4d/M18658 3382
穩 J6353/M25344 **4183**
蘇 J4149/M32427 5252
蘓 J693f/M-X 5253
邌 J-X/M39219 6125
麕 J734b/M47660 7022

---

15 residual strokes

櫪 J5d2e/M15846 2911
犧 J603a/M20209 3552
鐇 J6f40/M40874 6344
馨 J333e/M44559 6724
鰍 J3362/M46331 6895
麕 J734b/M47660 7022

---

16 residual strokes

巍 J565b/M8626 1522
癧 J617c/M22617 3851
癪 J617b/M22626 3853
龝 J6354/M25381 **4184**
飜 J664c/M44009 6673

17–19 residual strokes

龝 J6354/M25381 **4184**
穰 J6355/M25383 **4185**
轣 J6d61/M38593 5994
靂 J704e/M42523 6554
鷭 J733d/M47335 7001
黐 J7357/M48027 7051

Rad. 116 穴

0 residual strokes

穴 J-X/M-X **4186**
穴 J376a/M25406 **4187**
宂 J-X/M-X **4188**

2–3 residual strokes

究 J3566/M25409 **4189**
穹 J6356/M25414 **4190**
突 J464d/M25424 **4191**
空 J3675/M25415 **4192**

---

4 residual strokes

穾 J-X/M25439 **4193**
穽 J6357/M25433 **4194**
窃 J4060/M25453 **4195**
穿 J407c/M25436 **4198**

---

5 residual strokes

倥 J5065/M787 238
窈 J6358/M25463 **4196**
窄 J3a75/M25455 **4197**
穿 J407c/M25436 **4198**

---

6 residual strokes

控 J3935/M12283 2202
窕 J635a/M25496 **4199**
窒 J4362/M25493 **4200**
窓 J416b/M25494 **4201**

---

7 residual strokes

窈 J6358/M25463 **4196**
窗 J6359/M25517 **4202**
窘 J635b/M25519 **4203**
窖 J635c/M25516 **4204**
腔 J3950/M29630 4826

8–9 residual strokes

搾 J3a71/M12553 2251
窠 J-X/M25556 **4205**
窟 J3722/M25552 **4206**
窬 J-X/M25582 **4207**
窩 J635d/M25579 **4208**
窪 J3726/M25580 **4209**

---

10 residual strokes

窯 J4d52/M25594 **4210**
窰 J635f/M25595 **4211**
窮 J3567/M25593 **4212**
窿 J6363/M25660 **4213**
膣 J6734/M29849 4861

---

11 residual strokes

窿 J6363/M25660 **4213**
窶 J6360/M25628 **4214**
窺 J312e/M25633 **4215**
鴪 J7272/M46820 6947
麋 J7348/M47625 7020

12–13 residual strokes

竃 J3376/M-X **4216**
竅 J6361/M25680 **4217**
竄 J6362/M25679 **4218**
麋 J7348/M47625 7020

14–18 residual strokes

竄 J6362/M25679 **4218**
竆 J-X/M25686 **4219**
竇 J6365/M25695 **4220**
竈 J635e/M25703 **4221**
竊 J6366/M25713 **4222**

Rad. 117 立

0 residual strokes

立 J4e29/M25721 **4223**

---

2 residual strokes

位 J304c/M503 162

簇 J6448/M26437 **4351**
篠 J3c44/M-X **4352**

12 residual strokes

擶 J5a31/M12898 2310
櫛 J367b/M-X 2884
簞 J6452/M26510 **4353**
簣 J644f/M26524 **4354**
簫 J6454/M26560 **4355**
簧 J6450/M26541 **4356**
簟 J-X/M26509 **4357**
簡 J344a/M26520′ **4358**
簡 J-X/M26520 **4359**
擶 J645a/M26646 **4360**
簪 J6451/M26558 **4367**

13 residual strokes

櫛 J-X/M15817 2909
簷 J6453/M26607 **4361**
簽 J6455/M26614 **4362**
簸 J4076/M26609 **4363**
簿 J4a6d/M26623′ **4364**
簾 J4e7c/M26616 **4365**
籌 J6456/M26675 **4370**

14 residual strokes

籏 J6459/M-X **4366**
簪 J6451/M26558 **4367**
籍 J4052/M26676 **4368**
籃 J6457/M26648 **4369**
籌 J6456/M26675 **4370**
籤 J645f/M-X **4371**
纂 J3b3c/M28012 4608

15–19 residual strokes

籃 J6457/M26648 **4369**
籔 J6458/M26708 **4372**
籐 J645b/M26693 **4373**
籘 J645c/M26733 **4374**
籟 J645d/M26751 **4375**
籠 J6446/M26752 **4376**
籥 J6460/M26771 **4377**
籤 J645e/M26769 **4378**
籬 J6461/M26803 **4379**
纂 J3b3c/M28012 4608

Rad. 119 米

0 residual strokes

米 J4a46/M26832 **4380**

1–2 residual strokes

釆 J4850/M40115 6202
籵 J6462/M26837 **4381**
迷 J4c42/M38825′ 6037

3 residual strokes

屎 J557d/M7689 1419
粂 J3729/M26860 **4382**
粁 J364e/M26858 **4383**
籾 J4c62/M26857 **4384**
籾 J-X/M26853 **4385**
迷 J4c42/M38825′ 6037

4 residual strokes

料 J4e41/M13501 2374
氣 J5d66/M17059 3028
粐 J6464/M-X **4386**
粍 J4c30/M26881 **4387**
粃 J6463/M26861 **4388**
粋 J3f68/M26875 **4389**
粉 J4a34/M26872 **4390**
莱 J4d69/M-X 5039

5 residual strokes

悉 J3c3d/M10635 1864
掬 J3545/M12290 2197
断 J4347/M13557 2385
渕 J5e3d/M17750 3166
粃 J6463/M26861 **4388**
粕 J4774/M26891 **4391**
粒 J4e33/M26884 **4392**
粘 J4734/M26901 **4393**
粗 J4146/M26898 **4394**
粛 J3d4d/M29223 4747
菊 J3546/M31153 5096
釈 J3c61/M40120′ 6203

6 residual strokes

奥 J317c/M5981 1165
屡 J3c48/M7770 1428
断 J4347/M13557 2385
椈 J5b78/M15014 2724
歯 J3b75/M16323 2961
番 J4856/M21858 3762
粭 J6466/M-X **4395**
粫 J6468/M-X **4396**
粡 J6469/M26928 **4397**
粢 J6467/M26932 **4398**
粤 J6465/M26935 **4399**
粧 J3e51/M26945 **4400**
粨 J646a/M26949 **4401**
粥 J3421/M26938 **4402**
粟 J3040/M26922 **4403**
粮 J646e/M26952 **4404**
釉 J6e58/M40121 6204

7 residual strokes

奧 J547c/M5985 1166
愾 J5841/M11029 1936
数 J3f74/M13319 2353
楼 J4f30/M15212 2785
滊 J-X/M18019 3252
粤 J6465/M26935 **4399**
粮 J646e/M26952 **4404**
粱 J646d/M26962 **4405**
糀 J6471/M27013 **4406**
粲 J646c/M26966 **4407**
粳 J646b/M26967 **4408**
継 J3751/M27531 4501

8 residual strokes

粥 J3421/M26938 **4402**
粮 J646e/M26952 **4404**
粹 J646f/M26987 **4409**
粽 J6470/M26993 **4410**
精 J403a/M26997′ **4411**
鄰 J6e43/M39656 6156
隣 J4e59/M41847 6484

9 residual strokes

幡 J4828/M9086 1584
憐 J4e79/M11206 1987
糂 J6473/M27014 **4412**
糎 J4138/M27057 **4413**
糅 J6472/M27023 **4414**
糊 J3852/M27037 **4415**
継 J3751/M27531 4501
謎 J4666/M35800 5661
鄰 J6e43/M39656 6156
隣 J4e59/M41847 6484
麹 J396d/M-X 7036

10 residual strokes

墺 J5454/M5504 1100
彝 J5734/M9948 1710
憐 J4e79/M11206 1987
燐 J4e55/M19417 3499
粥 J3421/M26938 **4402**
糂 J6473/M27014 **4412**
糢 J6477/M27116 **4416**
糓 J-X/M27067 **4417**
糘 J6474/M-X **4418**
糒 J6475/M27065 **4419**
糖 J457c/M27070 **4420**
薮 J4c79/M-X 5201
謎 J4666/M35800 5661

11 residual strokes

燦 J3b38/M19468 3498
燐 J4e55/M19417 3499
糝 J-X/M27101 **4421**

糜 J6476/M27097 **4422**
糟 J416c/M27104 **4423**
糠 J3947/M27105 **4424**
糞 J4a35/M27102 **4425**
繍 J3d2b/M-X 4572
襖 J3228/M-X 5498
鞠 J3547/M42892 6589

12 residual strokes

彝 J5733/M9950 1711
糓 J-X/M27067 **4417**
糧 J4e48/M27132 **4426**
繍 J3d2b/M-X 4572
類 J4e60/M43608′ 6647

13 residual strokes

繍 J3d2b/M-X 4572
類 J-X/M43636 6650
麴 J-X/M47818 7037

14 residual strokes

彝 J5733/M9950 1711
糲 J647a/M27181 **4427**
糯 J6479/M27173 **4428**
繍 J3d2b/M-X 4572
鐇 J6f40/M40874 6344
齢 J4e70/M48632′ 7093

16–19 residual strokes

糴 J647b/M27191 **4429**
糶 J647c/M27207 **4430**
鬻 J6478/M45721 6832
鱗 J4e5a/M46502 6923
麟 J4e5b/M47690 7028

Rad. 120 糸

0 residual strokes

糸 J3b65/M27221 **4431**

1–2 residual strokes

糺 J647d/M27222 **4432**
系 J374f/M27223 **4433**
糾 J-X/M27227 **4434**

3 residual strokes

係 J3738/M663 217
紂 J6521/M27239 **4435**
紆 J647e/M27244 **4436**
級 J3569/M27258′ **4437**
糾 J356a/M-X **4438**
紀 J352a/M27234 **4439**
約 J4c73/M27242 **4440**
紅 J3948/M27243 **4441**

4 residual strokes

孫 J4239/M6987 1296
級 J3569/M27258′ **4437**
紉 J-X/M27294 **4442**
紕 J6523/M27279 **4443**
紜 J6522/M27296 **4444**
紘 J3949/M27289 **4445**
紗 J3c53/M27287 **4446**
紊 J6524/M27261 **4447**
紐 J4933/M27268 **4448**
索 J3a77/M27306 **4449**
紡 J4b42/M27305 **4450**
紋 J4c66/M27262 **4451**
紛 J4a36/M27295 **4452**
納 J473c/M27264 **4453**
純 J3d63/M27277 **4454**
紙 J3b66/M27293 **4455**
素 J4147/M27300 **4456**
紲 J6528/M27347 **4461**
紺 J3a30/M27362 **4466**

5 residual strokes

紕 J6523/M27279 **4443**
紙 J3b66/M27293 **4455**
紭 J6526/M-X **4457**
紵 J652a/M27353 **4458**
紿 J6529/M27369 **4459**
絅 J6525/M27375 **4460**
紲 J6528/M27347 **4461**
紬 J445d/M27338 **4462**
紮 J6527/M27341 **4463**
絆 J652b/M27376 **4464**
紹 J3e52/M27361 **4465**
紺 J3a30/M27362 **4466**
紳 J3f42/M27348 **4467**
絃 J383e/M27373 **4468**
累 J4e5f/M27343 **4469**
組 J4148/M27374 **4470**
終 J3d2a/M27372 **4471**
細 J3a59/M27344 **4472**
経 J3750/M27392 **4473**

6 residual strokes

絲 J652f/M27448 **4474**
絳 J652c/M27449 **4475**
絏 J6532/M27397 **4476**
絖 J652d/M27409 **4477**
絣 J6533/M27429 **4478**
絮 J6531/M27443 **4479**
絓 J-X/M27403 **4480**
絇 J303c/M27427 **4481**
絎 J652e/M27396 **4482**
絨 J6530/M27435 **4483**
絡 J4d6d/M27426 **4484**
絞 J394a/M27421 **4485**
紫 J3b67/M27337 **4486**
統 J457d/M27447 **4487**
絵 J3328/M27464′ **4488**
給 J356b/M27432 **4489**
絶 J4064/M-X **4490**
絕 J-X/M27407 **4491**
結 J376b/M27398 **4492**
葯 J6860/M31451 5115
逓 J423d/M39038 6098

7 residual strokes

嗉 J-X/M4057 863
絳 J652c/M27449 **4475**
經 J6534/M27508 **4493**
條 J6536/M27465 **4494**
綉 J6535/M27493 **4495**
綏 J6537/M27501 **4496**
綛 J6539/M27534 **4497**
絽 J6538/M27474 **4498**
絹 J3828/M27470 **4499**
続 J4233/M27533 **4500**
継 J3751/M27531 **4501**
綟 J6546/M27540 **4505**
逓 J423d/M39038 6098

8 residual strokes

綉 J6535/M27493 **4495**
綘 J-X/M27571 **4502**
緍 J-X/M27607 **4503**
綪 J656e/M-X **4504**
綟 J6546/M27540 **4505**
綢 J6542/M27546 **4506**
綣 J653c/M27550 **4507**
綫 J6540/M27564 **4508**
綵 J653d/M27580 **4509**
綬 J3c7a/M27565 **4510**
綮 J653b/M27569 **4511**
綰 J6547/M27575 **4512**
綯 J6543/M27573 **4513**
綻 J433e/M27587 **4514**
緇 J653e/M27600 **4515**
維 J305d/M27568 **4516**
緋 J486c/M27604 **4517**
綽 J653f/M27590 **4518**
綸 J6545/M27583 **4519**
綜 J416e/M27535 **4520**
緒 J3d6f/M27632 **4521**
綺 J653a/M27586 **4522**
綾 J303d/M27591 **4523**
緊 J365b/M27603 **4524**
綱 J394b/M27576 **4525**
綴 J4456/M27579 **4526**
網 J4c56/M27577 **4527**
緑 J4e50/M27541′ **4528**

臠 J6748/M30049 4893
蠻 J6a47/M33914 5409

21–24 residual strokes

纜 J657c/M28100 **4623**
鑾 J6f56/M41083 6375
鑼 J6f55/M41081 6376
鸞 J7342/M47508 7010

Rad. 121 缶

0–4 residual strokes

缶 J344c/M28108 **4624**
缸 J657d/M28112 **4625**
缺 J657e/M28122 **4626**
陶 J462b/M41705 6459

5 residual strokes

掏 J595b/M12251 2187
淘 J4571/M17642 3187
萄 J463a/M31252 5075

7 residual strokes

傜 J5754/M10201 1763
搖 J596a/M12479 2239
遙 J7423/M39035 6097

8 residual strokes

瑤 J7424/M21149 3666
綯 J6543/M27573 4513
遙 J7423/M39035 6097

9–11 residual strokes

窰 J635f/M25595 4211
綯 J6543/M27573 4513
⿰缶隹 J-X/M-X **4627**
罅 J6621/M28169 **4628**
謠 J6b6f/M35832 5673

14–23 residual strokes

寶 J556f/M7376 1371
罌 J6622/M28185 **4629**
罍 J6623/M28187 **4630**
罎 J6624/M28189 **4631**
罐 J6625/M28194 **4632**
鬱 J5d35/M45671 6830
鷂 J7338/M47207 6989

Rad. 122 网

0 residual strokes

网 J6626/M28199 **4633**

3–6 residual strokes

曼 J5258/M14298 2475
罕 J6627/M28217 **4634**
罔 J6628/M28211 **4635**
罘 J6629/M28224 **4636**
罟 J662a/M28248 **4637**
罠 J662b/M28249 **4638**

7 residual strokes

埋 J544e/M5298 1042
詈 J6b4a/M35360 5576
買 J4763/M36708 5793

8 residual strokes

埋 J544e/M5298 1042
夢 J4c34/M5801′ 1131
楞 J5c41/M15149 2761
罧 J662e/M28285 **4639**
罩 J662d/M28289 **4640**
罨 J662c/M28288 **4641**
罫 J3753/M28295 **4642**
署 J3d70/M28311′ **4643**
罪 J3a61/M28293 **4644**
置 J4356/M28298 **4645**
蜀 J6966/M33086 5329

9 residual strokes

寧 J472b/M7296′ 1361
幔 J566f/M9050 1580
徳 J4641/M10237′ 1767
漫 J4c21/M18166 3308
甍 J6130/M21587 3704
署 J-X/M28319 **4646**
罰 J4833/M28315 **4647**
蔑 J4a4e/M31781 5179
蔓 J4c22/M31784 5180

10 residual strokes

儚 J5133/M1236 320
德 J-X/M10243 1770
慢 J4b7d/M11110 1968
甍 J6130/M21587 3704
罸 J662f/M28343 **4648**
罵 J474d/M28333 **4649**
罷 J486d/M28336 **4650**
賣 J6c4e/M36825 5808
還 J3454/M39174′ 6121

11 residual strokes

圜 J5428/M4851 965
壊 J3275/M5541′ 1102
寰 J556e/M7344 1368
憲 J377b/M11269′ 1988
憲 J-X/M11269 1989
懌 J5864/M11334 1996
懐 J327b/M11351 2003
擇 J5a24/M12796 2285
澤 J5f37/M18383 3338
濁 J4279/M18440 3348
獨 J6057/M20725 3607
罹 J586d/M28347 **4651**
薨 J692a/M32147 5216
還 J3454/M39174′ 6121

12 residual strokes

懐 J327b/M11351 2003
曙 J3d6c/M-X 2519
燭 J3f24/M19480 3496
爵 J3c5f/M19710′ 3514
環 J3444/M-X 3680
環 J-X/M21287 3681
繯 J655c/M27829 4577
聴 J4430/M29173 4740

13 residual strokes

擺 J5a34/M12910 2313
曙 J-X/M14220 2523
爵 J3c5f/M19710′ 3514
爵 J-X/M19711 3515
環 J-X/M21287 3681
羃 J6632/M28393 **4652**
羂 J6630/M28386 **4653**
謾 J6b74/M35909 5691

14 residual strokes

壞 J5455/M5590 1111
懷 J5867/M11456 2009
繹 J6568/M27975 4599
羆 J6631/M28398 **4654**
羅 J4d65/M28397 **4655**
襪 J6b24/M34696 5505
鏝 J6f38/M40807 6340

15 residual strokes

壞 J5455/M5590 1111
廳 J572d/M9552 1649
懷 J5867/M11456 2009
羂 J6630/M28386 **4653**
蘰 J6946/M32541 5259
觸 J6b3d/M35181 5551
譯 J6c23/M36023 5709
躅 J6d31/M37917 5914
釋 J6e59/M40129 6205
饅 J713d/M44346 6710

15–21 residual strokes

Rad. 124 羽

0 residual strokes

3–4 residual strokes

5 residual strokes

6–7 residual strokes

8 residual strokes

9 residual strokes

10 residual strokes

11 residual strokes

12 residual strokes

13–14 residual strokes

15–16 residual strokes

17–19 residual strokes

Rad. 125 老

0 residual strokes

2–3 residual strokes

4 residual strokes

5 residual strokes

6 residual strokes

7 residual strokes

8 residual strokes

Rad. 131 臣

Rad. 132 自

Rad.137: 3 residual strokes

Rad. 138 艮

馨 J-X/M-X 6612
饗 J3642/M-X 6705
饗 J-X/M44431 6715
齦 J7375/M48649 7096

16–20 residual strokes

鬱 J3135/M-X 2924
馨 J-X/M-X 6612
饗 J-X/M44431 6715
饕 J7143/M44426 6717
饜 J-X/M44453 6718
鱶 J7268/M46592 6928

Rad. 139 色

0 residual strokes

色 J3f27/M30602 **4956**

6–18 residual strokes

絶 J4064/M-X 4490
艶 J3170/M30632 **4957**
艷 J6766/M30637 **4958**

Rad. 140 艸

0 residual strokes

艸 J6767/M30638 **4959**

2–3 residual strokes

艾 J6768/M30648 **4960**
芝 J3c47/M30699′ **4961**
芒 J676a/M30682 **4962**
芍 J6769/M30674 **4963**
芋 J3072/M30670′ **4964**

4 residual strokes

芝 J3c47/M30699′ **4961**
芽 J-X/M30747 **4965**
芙 J4967/M30694 **4966**
芫 J676b/M30727 **4967**
苡 J676f/M30792 **4968**
苅 J3423/M30771 **4969**
芹 J365c/M30742 **4970**
芻 J676d/M30744 **4971**
芟 J676c/M30701 **4972**
芬 J676e/M30728 **4973**
芭 J474e/M30730 **4974**
芦 J3032/M30716 **4975**
芯 J3f44/M30732 **4976**
芥 J3329/M30715 **4977**
芸 J375d/M30741′ **4978**
芳 J4b27/M30736′ **4979**
花 J3256/M30734′ **4980**
苣 J6770/M30794 **4988**

5 residual strokes

供 J3621/M605 195
巷 J-X/M-X 634
芽 J-X/M30747 **4965**
苡 J676f/M30792 **4968**
苓 J4e6a/M30777 **4981**
苙 J677e/M30783 **4982**
苳 J6774/M30811 **4983**
苹 J6779/M30823 **4984**
苻 J6778/M30825 **4985**
范 J6777/M30834 **4986**
茆 J677b/M30838 **4987**
苣 J6770/M30794 **4988**
苒 J6772/M30776 **4989**
苺 J6775/M30824 **4990**
茎 J3754/M30861′ **4991**
苴 J6773/M30813 **4992**
苜 J677c/M30787 **4993**
茉 J677d/M30841 **4994**
茄 J3258/M30835 **4995**
苑 J3171/M30774 **4996**
苞 J677a/M30789 **4997**
茂 J4c50/M30833′ **4998**
苟 J6771/M30790 **4999**
苧 J4377/M30798 **5000**
苔 J425d/M30778 **5001**
芽 J326a/M30860′ **5002**
苫 J4651/M30802 **5003**
苗 J4944/M30781′ **5004**
茅 J337d/M30836 **5005**
苛 J3257/M30785 **5006**
若 J3c63/M30796′ **5007**
英 J3151/M30808′ **5008**
苦 J366c/M30797′ **5009**
荐 J6828/M30951 **5016**

6 residual strokes

荊 J-X/M-X 379
苺 J6775/M30824 **4990**
莽 J684f/M31130 **5010**
茲 J6824/M30911 **5011**
茖 J6823/M30863 **5012**
茯 J682a/M30906 **5013**
荀 J6826/M30929 **5014**
荅 J6829/M30937 **5015**
荐 J6828/M30951 **5016**
茨 J3071/M30896 **5017**
茵 J6821/M30914 **5018**
茜 J302b/M30871 **5019**
茱 J6825/M30910 **5020**
茴 J6822/M30913 **5021**
荏 J3141/M30950 **5022**
茗 J682c/M30864 **5023**
茘 J682d/M30866 **5024**
荔 J-X/M30865 **5025**
茸 J427b/M30918 **5026**
荊 J3755/M-X **5027**
荆 J-X/M30940 **5028**
茫 J682b/M30900 **5029**
茹 J6827/M30921 **5030**
荘 J4171/M30890 **5031**
草 J4170/M30945′ **5032**
茶 J4063/M30915′ **5033**
荒 J3953/M30953′ **5034**
莚 J682f/M31059 **5040**
莩 J-X/M31076 **5048**
革 J3357/M42710 6570

7 residual strokes

匿 J463f/M2690 591
埖 J5442/M-X 1014
勢 J6839/M-X **5035**
荳 J683a/M30989 **5036**
莖 J6833/M31052 **5037**
莊 J6837/M31035 **5038**
莱 J4d69/M-X **5039**
莚 J682f/M31059 **5040**
莵 J683b/M30994 **5041**
莅 J682e/M31024 **5042**
莇 J6836/M31026 **5043**
莉 J683d/M31034 **5044**
莎 J6835/M31040 **5045**
莠 J683c/M31065 **5046**
莪 J6830/M31077 **5047**
莩 J-X/M31076 **5048**
莓 J6776/M31047 **5049**
莟 J6831/M31064 **5050**
莫 J6834/M31090 **5051**
莞 J3450/M31063 **5052**
荼 J6838/M31008 **5053**
荻 J322e/M31005 **5054**
莢 J6832/M31069 **5055**
莨 J683e/M31075 **5056**
莫 J477c/M31078 **5057**
華 J325a/M31119 **5058**
荷 J3259/M31000′ **5059**
菽 J6843/M31241 **5068**
萇 J6849/M31256 **5069**
菰 J3856/M31217 **5079**

8 residual strokes

剳 J5175/M2113 500
勒 J7055/M2386 545
匿 J463f/M2690 591
椛 J3371/M15065 2683
満 J5e51/M17782 3179
莠 J683c/M31065 **5046**
莓 J6776/M31047 **5049**
莨 J683e/M31075 **5056**
葛 J336b/M-X **5060**
萠 J684e/M-X **5061**

蒂	J6848	M31234	**5062**
菴	J683f	M31227	**5063**
菔	J-X	M31170	**5064**
萢	J684d	M-X	**5065**
菘	J6845	M31177	**5066**
菻	J6852	M31238	**5067**
菽	J6843	M31241	**5068**
萇	J6849	M31256	**5069**
萋	J6846	M31264	**5070**
萓	J6840	M31279	**5071**
菁	J6847	M31136	**5072**
萊	J-X	M31262	**5073**
菆	J-X	M31146	**5074**
萄	J463a	M31252	**5075**
萍	J684c	M31266	**5076**
菟	J-X	M31189	**5077**
萃	J6844	M31251	**5078**
菰	J3856	M31217	**5079**
萁	J-X	M31248	**5080**
菠	J684a	M31190	**5081**
菲	J684b	M31220	**5082**
莽	J-X	M31132	**5083**
莾	J-X	M31133	**5084**
菖	J3e54	M31174	**5085**
菫	J6841	M31207	**5086**
萎	J3060	M31269	**5087**
菎	J6842	M31160	**5088**
菎	J-X	M-X	**5089**
菅	J3f7b	M31142	**5090**
菌	J365d	M31156′	**5091**
菱	J4929	M31219	**5092**
菩	J4a6e	M31205	**5093**
萌	J4b28	M31265	**5094**
菓	J325b	M31168′	**5095**
菊	J3546	M31153′	**5096**
菜	J3a5a	M31184′	**5097**
著	J4378	M31302	**5098**
萸	J6850	M31356	**5109**
葉	J4d55	M31387′	**5129**

9 residual strokes

僅	J364f	M-X	279
備	J4877	M967	284
募	J4a67	M2416	551
勤	J3650	M2415′	552
塔	J4563	M5332	1052
惹	J3c66	M10866	1886
慌	J3932	M11057	1917
慌	J-X	M-X	1918
慌	J-X	M-X	1919
搭	J456b	M12508	2228
敬	J3749	M13285′	2351
暎	J5a75	M14048	2479
瑛	J314d	M21127	3647
硴	J626d	M-X	4003
莫	J6834	M31090	**5051**
菎	J6842	M31160	**5088**
菎	J-X	M-X	**5089**
蓬	J4b29	M-X	**5099**
葢	J6864	M31432	**5100**
蒂	J685c	M31495	**5101**
菟	J4551	M-X	**5102**
萬	J685f	M31339	**5103**
著	J-X	M31410	**5104**
蓮	J4f21	M-X	**5105**
萪	J6854	M31334	**5106**
蒄	J6857	M31342	**5107**
萵	J6862	M31351	**5108**
萸	J6850	M31356	**5109**
葆	J685e	M31381	**5110**
葎	J4e2a	M31397	**5111**
葩	J685d	M31441	**5112**
葫	J6859	M31443	**5113**
葭	J685b	M31450	**5114**
葯	J6860	M31451	**5115**
葷	J6858	M31461	**5116**
葹	J6861	M31464	**5117**
董	J4621	M31433	**5118**
萼	J6855	M31361	**5119**
葵	J302a	M31458	**5120**
萱	J337e	M31345	**5121**
萩	J476b	M31333	**5122**
葱	J472c	M31454	**5123**
葮	J6853	M31449	**5124**
葺	J4978	M31465	**5125**
葛	J-X	M31420	**5126**
葡	J4972	M31430	**5127**
葬	J4172	M31448′	**5128**
葉	J4d55	M31387′	**5129**
落	J4d6e	M31362′	**5130**
蓖	J686f	M31626	**5152**
蒸	J3e78	M31618′	**5163**
賁	J6c4c	M36727	5784
靫	J7056	M42713	6571
靭	J-X	M42715	6572
靱	J3f59	M-X	6573
韮	J4723	M43237	6605

10 residual strokes

僅	J364f	M-X	279
僅	J-X	M1048	292
勤	J-X	M2424	554
嘩	J325e	M-X	861
墓	J4a68	M5431	1073
夢	J4c34	M5801′	1131
寞	J556b	M7282	1351
寛	J3432	M7276	1352
幕	J4b6b	M9051	1578
摸	J4c4e	M12644	2250
漠	J4779	M18149	3268
漢	J3441	M18068′	3281
獏	J6053	M20638	3597
糀	J6471	M27013	4406
茲	J6824	M30911	**5011**
蓬	J4b29	M-X	**5099**
蓮	J4f21	M-X	**5105**
萼	J6855	M31361	**5119**
蒻	J685a	M31598	**5131**
蒋	J3e55	M-X	**5132**
蒹	J6865	M31621	**5133**
蓁	J686d	M31639	**5134**
蓉	J4d56	M31648	**5135**
蓊	J6863	M31650	**5136**
蓍	J6869	M31655	**5137**
蔀	J3c43	M31748	**5138**
蓏	J-X	M31658	**5139**
蒴	J-X	M31614	**5140**
蒻	J686a	M31623	**5141**
蓙	J6868	M31709	**5142**
蓑	J4c2c	M31661	**5143**
蒜	J4947	M31562	**5144**
蒡	J6870	M31572	**5145**
蓚	J686b	M-X	**5146**
蒿	J6866	M31634	**5147**
蓆	J686e	M31645	**5148**
蓐	J686c	M31660	**5149**
蒟	J6867	M31566	**5150**
蔭	J307e	M31840	**5151**
蓖	J686f	M31626	**5152**
蒔	J3c2c	M31546	**5153**
蒙	J4c58	M31555	**5154**
蓋	J3338	M31652	**5155**
蒲	J3377	M31611	**5156**
蓬	J-X	M31720	**5157**
蓮	J-X	M31722	**5158**
蒐	J3d2f	M31539	**5159**
葦	J3031	M31437	**5160**
蓄	J435f	M31642′	**5161**
蒼	J4173	M31627	**5162**
蒸	J3e78	M31618′	**5163**
蓴	J6878	M31789	**5169**
靴	J3724	M42729	6576

11 residual strokes

厲	J-X	M-X	659
愿	J5857	M11100	1938
慕	J4a69	M11088	1948
摹	J-X	M12645	2241
曄	J5b21	M14169	2504
暮	J4a6b	M14128	2508
樺	J3372	M15497	2817
模	J4c4f	M15453	2825
滿	J5e60	M18099	3283
甍	J6130	M21587	3704
膜	J4b6c	M29808′	4854
蓬	J4b29	M-X	**5099**
蓑	J4c2c	M31661	**5143**
蓐	J686c	M31660	**5149**
蓬	J-X	M31720	**5157**
蓮	J-X	M31722	**5158**
蕁	J-X	M-X	**5164**
蕁	J6873	M31734	**5165**

蓼 J687a/M31744 **5166**
蓿 J6872/M31747 **5167**
蔆 J6851/M31760 **5168**
蔕 J6878/M31789 **5169**
蔡 J6871/M31818 **5170**
蔻 J-X/M31741 **5171**
蔲 J-X/M-X **5172**
蔔 J6879/M31785 **5173**
蔘 J6875/M31795 **5174**
蔟 J6877/M31815 **5175**
蔗 J6874/M31794 **5176**
蔣 J-X/M31820 **5177**
蔦 J4455/M31828′ **5178**
蔑 J4a4e/M31781 **5179**
蔓 J4c22/M31704 **5180**
蔚 J3136/M31805 **5181**
蔵 J4222/M31885′ **5182**
蔬 J6876/M31839 **5192**
蔽 J4a43/M31888 **5193**
蟎 J-X/M33201 5315
錊 J6e7a/M40490 6258
鍅 J-X/M40489 6259
鞆 J705d/M42794 6580
鞅 J7059/M42784 6581
鞄 J3373/M42781 6582

12 residual strokes

儚 J5133/M1236 320
冪 J5151/M1601 408
墸 J5457/M-X 1093
慶 J3744/M11145 1967
暴 J4b3d/M14137 2511
槿 J5c5d/M15395 2848
濆 J5f39/M-X 3323
瑾 J6077/M21187 3676
豊 J6130/M21587 3704
膵 J6739/M29920 4865
蓄 J435f/M31642′ **5161**
蔕 J6878/M31789 **5169**
蔡 J6871/M31818 **5170**
蔵 J4222/M31885′ **5182**
蕁 J6856/M31970 **5183**
蕀 J687b/M31898 **5184**
蕕 J6924/M31961 **5185**
蕘 J687d/M31965 **5186**
蕄 J-X/M31954 **5187**
蕊 J3c49/M31939 **5188**
蕋 J6923/M31940 **5189**
蕈 J687e/M31928 **5190**
蕉 J3e56/M31937 **5191**
蔬 J6876/M31839 **5192**
蔽 J4a43/M31888 **5193**
蕨 J4f4f/M32001 **5194**
蕁 J6921/M31899 **5195**
蕪 J4973/M32004 **5196**
蕎 J363e/M31946 **5197**
蕩 J4622/M32002 **5198**
蕃 J4859/M31906 **5199**
蕣 J687c/M31991 **5204**
蟒 J6a3d/M-X 5345
諾 J427a/M35687 5638
邁 J6e32/M39169 6110
鍅 J-X/M40489 6259
錵 J6f26/M40591 6273
鎊 J6f25/M40596 6274
鞋 J705e/M42813 6584
鞏 J705f/M42819 6585
鞍 J3048/M42815 6586

13 residual strokes

勵 J522f/M2472 562
嚆 J5365/M4458 908
憊 J5860/M11195 1977
橫 J-X/M15594 2857
檠 J5c7b/M15681 2870
濛 J5f42/M18491 3345
燕 J316d/M19429 3489
獲 J334d/M20758 3609
瞞 J6256/M23649 3956
糢 J6477/M27116 4416
糯 J6475/M27065 4419
臈 J6745/M29953 4870
蕁 J6856/M31970 **5183**
薗 J3172/M32119 **5200**
薮 J4c79/M-X **5201**
薯 J3d72/M-X **5202**
蕗 J4979/M31964 **5203**
蕣 J687c/M31991 **5204**
蕰 J6925/M32071 **5205**
薐 J6933/M32108 **5206**
薛 J692d/M32120 **5207**
薜 J6930/M32125 **5208**
薇 J692f/M32092 **5209**
薈 J6927/M32093 **5210**
薤 J6926/M32141 **5211**
薑 J6928/M32110 **5212**
薊 J6929/M32095 **5213**
蕷 J6931/M32054 **5214**
蕾 J6932/M32067 **5215**
薨 J692a/M32147 **5216**
薩 J3b27/M32189′ **5217**
蕭 J692b/M32012 **5218**
薦 J4126/M32143′ **5219**
薔 J692c/M32113 **5220**
薙 J4665/M32121 **5221**
薪 J3f45/M32149′ **5222**
薫 J3730/M32173 **5223**
薬 J4c74/M32188′ **5224**
薄 J4776/M32083′ **5225**
蟒 J-X/M33572 5367
蟆 J6a32/M33542 5369
蟇 J6a31/M33543 5370
邁 J6e32/M39169 6110
錨 J4945/M40598 6295
霙 J7044/M42350 6538
鞘 J3e64/M42850 6587
餝 J7133/M44212 6692

14 residual strokes

懃 J5869/M11321 1995
曚 J5b24/M14223 2520
檬 J5d28/M15710 2887
癘 J6176/M22556 3839
朦 J5b2f/M14409 4882
舊 J6751/M30249 4916
艚 J675d/M30523 4944
艱 J6765/M30600 4955
薩 J3b27/M32189′ **5217**
薰 J-X/M32192 **5226**
藏 J6936/M32264 **5227**
薺 J6935/M32208 **5228**
薹 J6937/M32204 **5229**
薯 J-X/M32191 **5230**
藉 J6934/M32242 **5231**
藐 J6938/M32267 **5232**
藍 J4d75/M32258 **5233**
藁 J4f4e/M32222 **5234**
蟒 J6a3c/M33724 5373
蟒 J-X/M-X 5383
譁 J6b76/M35928 5674
謨 J6b75/M35864 5680
謹 J3660/M35850′ 5688
貘 J6c42/M36621 5765
鞜 J7061/M42883 6588
鞠 J3547/M42892 6589
鞳 J7065/M42966 6591

15 residual strokes

懣 J5870/M11384 2004
擴 J5a32/M12895 2309
瀟 J5f4f/M18660 3383
矇 J625e/M23774 3967
礪 J626a/M24571 4056
穫 J334f/M25334′ 4180
繭 J4b7a/M27944 4595
羃 J6632/M28393 4652
臟 J4221/M29995′ 4886
艱 J6765/M30600 4955
藏 J6936/M32264 **5227**
藍 J4d75/M32258 **5233**
藝 J693a/M32330 **5235**
藥 J693b/M32341 **5236**
藷 J3d73/M-X **5237**
藜 J693c/M32326 **5238**
藕 J6939/M32298 **5239**
藪 J692e/M32348 **5240**
藤 J4623/M32340′ **5241**
藩 J484d/M32346′ **5242**
蟒 J-X/M-X 5383
謹 J-X/M35900 5690
蹣 J6d2a/M37822 5907

Rad. 141 虍

16–21 residual strokes

艫 J6763/M30582 4952
轤 J6d62/M38596 5995
鑢 J6f4c/M41021 6365
鑪 J6f4e/M41038 6369
饕 J7143/M44426 6717
驢 J7166/M45069 6778
鱸 J7269/M46600 6930

Rad. 142 虫

0 residual strokes

虫 J436e/M32804 **5275**

1–2 residual strokes

虱 J694d/M32812 **5276**

3 residual strokes

凬 J-X/M-X 1418
浊 J-X/M-X 3108
独 J4648/M20406 3574
虻 J303a/M32835 **5277**
虿 J-X/M32836 **5278**
虹 J467a/M32830 **5279**
蚩 J6950/M32902 **5283**
風 J4977/M43756 6663

4 residual strokes

烛 J-X/M19017 3415
蚜 J-X/M32882 **5280**
蚌 J6953/M32851 **5281**
蚣 J694f/M32892 **5282**
蚩 J6950/M32902 **5283**
蚪 J6951/M32903 **5284**
蚓 J694e/M32866 **5285**
蚋 J6952/M32850 **5286**
蚤 J4742/M32893 **5287**
蚊 J3263/M32849 **5288**
蚕 J-X/M32848 **5289**
蚕 J3b3d/M32869 **5290**

5 residual strokes

強 J362f/M9815 1695
搔 J415f/M-X 2175
蛎 J3342/M-X **5291**
蚶 J6954/M32925 **5292**
蚫 J695b/M32984 **5293**
蛉 J6959/M32969 **5294**
蛄 J6956/M32960 **5295**
蛅 J-X/M32961 **5296**
蚰 J6958/M32918 **5297**
蚜 J-X/M-X **5298**
蛆 J6957/M32963 **5299**
蚯 J6955/M32916 **5300**
蛋 J4341/M32977 **5301**
蛍 J3756/M32983 **5302**
蛇 J3c58/M32964 **5303**

6 residual strokes

属 J4230/M7754 1430
嵐 J4d72/M8289 1496
強 J362f/M9815 1695
强 J-X/M9822 1696
蛩 J695e/M33037 **5304**
蛬 J695f/M33047 **5305**
蛯 J6962/M33061 **5306**
蛛 J6961/M33002 **5307**
蛭 J4948/M33048 **5308**
蛞 J695d/M33008 **5309**
蛔 J695c/M32990 **5310**
蛟 J6960/M33009 **5311**
蛤 J483a/M33023 **5312**
蛙 J333f/M32997 **5313**
蛮 J485a/M33044 **5314**
蜒 J6963/M33120 **5317**
蜓 J-X/M33121 **5318**
蜉 J696a/M33104 **5324**
颪 J7124/M43769 6664

7 residual strokes

嗤 J5350/M4110 864
強 J362f/M9815 1695
搔 J-X/M12477 2256
楓 J4976/M15126 2777
蜽 J-X/M33201 **5315**
蜑 J6969/M33119 **5316**
蜒 J6963/M33120 **5317**
蜓 J-X/M33121 **5318**
蜊 J696d/M33106 **5319**
蜍 J696b/M33110 **5320**
蜋 J-X/M33108 **5321**
蛻 J6968/M33078 **5322**
蜈 J6965/M33099 **5323**
蜉 J696a/M33104 **5324**
蛾 J326b/M33082 **5325**
蛹 J696c/M33076 **5326**
蜃 J6967/M33089 **5327**
蜆 J6964/M33093 **5328**
蜀 J6966/M33086 **5329**
蛸 J427d/M33072 **5330**
蜂 J4b2a/M33088 **5331**
触 J3f28/M35070 5547

8 residual strokes

瘋 J6168/M22322 3827
蜽 J-X/M33201 **5315**
蜋 J-X/M33108 **5321**
蜃 J6967/M33089 **5327**
蝋 J4f39/M-X **5332**
蝕 J3f2a/M-X **5333**
蜩 J6973/M33166 **5334**
蜴 J696e/M33190 **5335**
蜱 J-X/M33182 **5336**
蜿 J696f/M33210 **5337**
蜥 J6972/M33157 **5338**
蜷 J6970/M33199 **5339**
蜚 J6974/M33138 **5340**
蜻 J6971/M33203 **5341**
蜘 J4358/M33134 **5342**
蜜 J4c2a/M33143 **5343**
蝣 J6a22/M33292 **5352**
蝶 J4433/M33333 **5363**
颯 J7125/M43808 6665
颱 J7126/M43815 6666

9 residual strokes

嘱 J3e7c/M4249 894
蝕 J3f2a/M-X **5333**
蜱 J-X/M33182 **5336**
蝿 J4768/M-X **5344**
蟒 J6a3d/M-X **5345**
蝨 J-X/M33318 **5346**
蝨 J697c/M33303 **5347**
蝍 J6a27/M33362 **5348**
蝉 J4066/M-X **5349**
蝪 J6a23/M33305 **5350**
蝓 J6a21/M33261 **5351**
蝣 J6a22/M33292 **5352**
蝠 J6975/M33288 **5353**
蝎 J6979/M33254 **5354**
蝮 J697d/M33309 **5355**
蝴 J697a/M33328 **5356**
蝌 J6978/M33248 **5357**
蝕 J-X/M33264 **5358**
蝟 J6976/M33287 **5359**
蝙 J697e/M33271 **5360**
蝗 J697b/M33267 **5361**
蝸 J6977/M33338 **5362**
蝶 J4433/M33333 **5363**
蝦 J325c/M33299 **5364**

10 residual strokes

濁 J4279/M18440 3348
蝍 J6a27/M33362 **5348**
螢 J6a25/M33434 **5365**
螅 J-X/M33410 **5366**
蟒 J-X/M33572 **5367**
螟 J6a26/M33429 **5368**
蟆 J6a32/M33542 **5369**
蟇 J6a31/M33543 **5370**
融 J4d3b/M33384 **5371**
蟒 J-X/M-X **5383**
襁 J6a76/M34545 5494
颸 J-X/M43840 6667

11 residual strokes

燭 J3f24/M19480 3496
蝹 J-X/M33410 **5366**
螳 J6a30/M33503 **5372**
蟒 J6a3c/M33724 **5373**
蟐 J6a2c/M-X **5374**
螻 J6a33/M33515 **5375**
螯 J6a28/M33496 **5376**
螫 J6a2e/M33491 **5377**
螽 J6a2a/M33519 **5378**
蟀 J6a2b/M33531 **5379**
蟋 J6a29/M33550 **5380**
蟄 J6a2f/M33537 **5381**
螺 J4d66/M33512 **5382**
蟒 J-X/M-X **5383**
襁 J-X/M-X 5497
雖 J6a2d/M42104 6510
颶 J7127/M43876 6668

12 residual strokes

檣 J5c6a/M15754 2896
矇 J6258/M23713 3958
繦 J655a/M-X 4587
繭 J4b7a/M27944 4595
蟲 J6a35/M33633 **5384**
蟖 J-X/M33578 **5385**
蟯 J6a34/M33626 **5386**
蟠 J6a36/M33591 **5387**
蟬 J-X/M33616 **5388**
騷 J417b/M44834′ 6760

13 residual strokes

蟀 J6a2b/M33531 **5379**
螺 J4d66/M33512 **5382**
蠍 J6a38/M33707 **5389**
蟶 J6a3a/M33664 **5390**
蠖 J6a3f/M33752 **5391**
蟾 J6a39/M33676 **5392**
蟷 J6a3b/M33665 **5393**
蠅 J6a24/M33690 **5394**
蟹 J332a/M33668 **5395**
蠏 J6a37/M33669 **5396**
蟻 J3542/M33672 **5397**

14 residual strokes

繭 J4b7a/M27944 4595
蠑 J6a3e/M33738 **5398**
蠣 J695a/M33799 **5399**
蠕 J6a40/M33749 **5400**
觸 J6b3d/M35181 5551
譴 J6c24/M36043 5711
躅 J6d31/M37917 5914
騷 J715b/M44935 6764

15 residual strokes

囀 J5373/M4614 927
屬 J5624/M7821 1435
蠡 J6a42/M33796 **5401**
蠢 J6a41/M33797 **5402**
蠟 J-X/M33786 **5403**
譴 J6c24/M36043 5711

16–17 residual strokes

蠟 J-X/M33786 **5403**
蠹 J6a46/M33824 **5404**
蠱 J6a43/M33867 **5405**
蠶 J-X/M33891 **5406**
髑 J7171/M45281 6795

18 residual strokes

蠶 J-X/M33891 **5406**
蠧 J6a45/M33896 **5407**
蠾 J-X/M33887 **5408**
蠺 J6a44/M33890 **5410**

19–28 residual strokes

囑 J5376/M4654 935
矚 J6261/M23841 3973
蠻 J6a47/M33914 **5409**
蠺 J6a44/M33890 **5410**
𨇾 J-X/M38028 5927

Rad. 143 血

0 residual strokes

血 J376c/M33964 **5411**

2–3 residual strokes

卹 J-X/M2862 636
恤 J5775/M10583 1839
洫 J5e29/M17403 3110
衂 J-X/M-X **5412**
衄 J6a49/M33971 **5413**

4–14 residual strokes

睾 J6250/M23535 3951
衄 J6a48/M33973 **5414**
衃 J-X/M33975 **5415**
衉 J-X/M33985 **5416**
衆 J3d30/M33981 **5417**
衊 J-X/M34021 **5418**

Rad. 144 行

0 residual strokes

行 J3954/M34029 **5419**

3–4 residual strokes

哘 J5326/M-X 772
垳 J5438/M-X 1000
衍 J5e27/M34033 1739
桁 J3765/M14754 2656

5–6 residual strokes

衒 J6a4a/M34045 1753
術 J3d51/M34046′ 1754
街 J3339/M34051 1759
絎 J652e/M27396 4482

7 residual strokes

𧗱 J-X/M-X 1762
衙 J6a4b/M34061 1764
愆 J5834/M10900 1911

8 residual strokes

絎 J652e/M27396 4482
裄 J6a62/M34283 5451
銜 J6e72/M40390 6257

9–18 residual strokes

衝 J3e57/M34069 1772
衡 J3955/M34078 1775
衛 J3152/M34073 1776
衞 J6a4c/M34074 1777
衢 J6a4d/M34090 1779
鵆 J727d/M46903 6960

Rad. 145 衣

0 residual strokes

衣 J3061/M34091 **5420**

2 residual strokes

依 J304d/M607 191
初 J3d69/M1911 469

3 residual strokes

哀 J3025/M3580 791
衫 J6a4e/M34111 **5421**
表 J493d/M34105 **5422**
辰 J4324/M38682 6006

4 residual strokes

衷 J436f/M-X 31

娠 J3f31 / M6322 1224

衮 J-X / M34121 **5423**

衷 J X / M-X **5424**

衵 J6a52 / M34135 **5425**

袂 J6a56 / M34154 **5426**

衽 J6a53 / M34146 **5427**

衾 J6a50 / M34147 **5428**

袁 J6a4f / M34152 **5429**

衲 J6a55 / M34130 **5430**

衿 J365e / M34149 **5431**

衰 J3f6a / M34127 **5432**

5 residual strokes

俵 J4936 / M730 243

唇 J3f30 / M3697 807

娠 J3f31 / M6322 1224

晨 J5a6f / M13962 2476

眤 J613e / M-X 3751

衮 J Y / M34121 **5423**

袮 J6a59 / M-X **5433**

袰 J6a5e / M-X **5434**

袙 J6a5a / M34196 **5435**

袤 J6a5d / M34213 **5436**

袓 J6a58 / M34184 **5437**

袢 J6a5b / M34210 **5438**

袍 J6a5c / M34174 **5439**

袗 J6a57 / M34194 **5440**

袞 J6a51 / M34203 **5441**

袈 J3736 / M34166 **5442**

袋 J425e / M34171 **5443**

袖 J4235 / M34192 **5444**

被 J486f / M34222 **5445**

6 residual strokes

喪 J4153 / M3985 853

展 J4538 / M7715 1425

晨 J5a6f / M13962 2476

袁 J6a4f / M34152 **5429**

袰 J6a5e / M-X **5434**

袵 J6a54 / M34237 **5446**

袿 J6a61 / M34282 **5447**

袴 J3853 / M34236 **5448**

袷 J3041 / M34240 **5449**

袱 J6a60 / M34232 **5450**

裄 J6a62 / M34283 **5451**

裃 J6a5f / M34255 **5452**

裂 J4e76 / M34260 **5453**

裁 J3a5b / M34258 **5454**

装 J4175 / M34283′ **5455**

辱 J3f2b / M38686 6007

7 residual strokes

喪 J4153 / M3985 853

脣 J667c / M29526 4817

蓑 J4c2c / M31661 5143

袴 J3853 / M34236 **5448**

裝 J6a66 / M34321 **5456**

裟 J3a40 / M34325 **5457**

裘 J6a64 / M34312 **5458**

裔 J6a63 / M34303 **5459**

裙 J6a65 / M34314 **5460**

裕 J4d35 / M34305 **5461**

裏 J4e22 / M34294 **5462**

裡 J4e23 / M34295 **5463**

補 J4a64 / M34320 **5464**

8 residual strokes

裴 J6a6a / M34362 **5465**

裼 J6a69 / M34379 **5466**

褂 J6a68 / M34401 **5467**

裹 J6a67 / M34372 **5468**

裲 J6a6c / M34356 **5469**

褄 J6a6d / M34410 **5470**

裨 J6a6b / M34338 **5471**

裳 J3e58 / M34357 **5472**

褐 J336c / M-X **5473**

裾 J3f7a / M34382 **5474**

裸 J4d67 / M34371 **5475**

製 J403d / M34380 **5476**

9 residual strokes

裹 J6a67 / M34372 **5468**

褝 J6a7c / M-X **5477**

褐 J-X / M34435 **5478**

褓 J6a70 / M34438 **5479**

褌 J6a6e / M34428 **5480**

褊 J6a6f / M34420 **5481**

褪 J6a74 / M34503 **5482**

褒 J4b2b / M34437 **5483**

複 J4a23 / M34417 **5484**

農 J4740 / M38688 6008

10 residual strokes

壌 J3e6d / M-X 1098

壊 J3275 / M5541′ 1102

嬢 J3e6e / M6807′ 1270

懐 J327b / M11351 2003

簑 J6442 / M26387 4334

褪 J6a74 / M34503 **5482**

𧝒 J-X / M-X **5485**

褞 J6a72 / M34475 **5486**

褥 J6a73 / M34495 **5487**

褫 J6a75 / M34504 **5488**

11 residual strokes

褥 J6a73 / M34495 **5487**

褽 J6a71 / M34552 **5489**

襄 J6a77 / M34556 **5490**

褻 J6a78 / M34536 **5491**

褸 J6a7a / M34530 **5492**

襀 J-X / M34544 **5493**

褷 J6a76 / M34545 **5494**

褶 J6a79 / M34525 **5495**

12 residual strokes

襄 J6a77 / M34556 **5490**

襆 J7037 / M34596 **5496**

襏 J-X / M-X **5497**

襖 J3228 / M-X **5498**

嚢 J4739 / M-X **5499**

襌 J6a7b / M34593 **5500**

13 residual strokes

懷 J5867 / M11456 2009

擐 J5a37 / M12989 2316

穣 J3e77 / M25335′ 4179

嚢 J4739 / M-X **5499**

襞 J6a7e / M34645 **5501**

襠 J6a7d / M34649 **5502**

襖 J-X / M34629 **5503**

襟 J365f / M34647 **5504**

轘 J6d59 / M38467 5982

14 residual strokes

孃 J5550 / M6891 1277

襪 J6b24 / M34696 **5505**

襦 J6b21 / M34678 **5506**

襤 J6b22 / M34674 **5507**

15 residual strokes

曩 J5b28 / M14258 2527

襤 J6b22 / M34674 **5507**

襭 J6b23 / M34702 **5508**

譲 J3e79 / M36037′ 5714

醸 J3e7a / M40064′ 6197

16 residual strokes

囊 J-X / M4633 933

襯 J6b25 / M34712 **5509**

襲 J3d31 / M34717 **5510**

17–22 residual strokes

襴 J6b26 / M34728 **5511**

襷 J6b27 / M34737 **5512**

讓 J6c2a / M36139 5725

釀 J6e56 / M40099 6199

鑲 J-X / M41053 6372

驤 J7168 / M45075 6780

欖 J5d34/M15964 2923

纜 J-X/M28053 4616

觀 J6b37/M34993 **5542**

19–23 residual strokes

欖 J5d34/M15964 2923

欟 J5d36/M15986 2927

纜 J657c/M28100 4623

Rad. 148 角

0 residual strokes

角 J3351/M35003 **5543**

4–5 residual strokes

斛 J5a4f/M13508 2375

觚 J6b38/M35043 **5544**

觝 J6b3a/M35051 **5545**

6 residual strokes

觚 J6b38/M35043 **5544**

觜 J6b39/M35050 **5546**

触 J3f28/M35070 **5547**

解 J3272/M35067 **5548**

觧 J6b3b/M35074 **5549**

8–9 residual strokes

嘴 J535c/M4256 905

懈 J5868/M11328 2000

槲 J5c60/M15375 2836

邂 J6e30/M39173 6118

10–11 residual strokes

檞 J-X/M15679 2890

邂 J6e30/M39173 6118

觴 J6b3c/M35157 **5550**

鵤 J7323/M46980 6966

12–13 residual strokes

蟹 J332a/M33668 5395

蠏 J6e07/M33669 5396

觸 J6b3d/M35181 **5551**

Rad. 149 言

0 residual strokes

言 J3840/M35205 **5552**

2 residual strokes

信 J3f2e/M707 221

訂 J447b/M35211 **5553**

訃 J6b3e/M35214 **5554**

計 J3757/M35220 **5555**

這 J4767/M38889 6058

3 residual strokes

訐 J6b40/M35234 **5556**

訖 J6b3f/M35242 **5557**

訌 J6b41/M35228 **5558**

訊 J3f56/M35224 **5559**

託 J4277/M35243 **5560**

討 J4624/M35231 **5561**

訓 J3731/M35238 **5562**

記 J352d/M35244 **5563**

這 J4767/M38889 6058

4 residual strokes

訝 J-X/M35260 **5564**

訟 J3e59/M35266 **5565**

訥 J6b44/M35274 **5566**

訣 J376d/M35272 **5567**

訛 J6b42/M35256 **5568**

許 J3576/M35298 **5569**

設 J405f/M35293 **5570**

訪 J4b2c/M35284 **5571**

訳 J4c75/M35324′ **5572**

5 residual strokes

訝 J6b43/M-X **5573**

詆 J6b49/M35356 **5574**

詒 J6b40/M35376 **5575**

詈 J6b4a/M35360 **5576**

訶 J6b45/M35328 **5577**

詁 J6b46/M35347 **5578**

詑 J4242/M35374 **5579**

詛 J6b47/M35390 **5580**

詔 J3e5b/M35379 **5581**

詞 J3b6c/M35394 **5582**

註 J4370/M35340 **5583**

詠 J3153/M35409 **5584**

詐 J3a3e/M35373 **5585**

診 J3f47/M35337 **5586**

評 J493e/M35383 **5587**

訴 J414a/M35325 **5588**

証 J3e5a/M35341 **5589**

詠 J-X/M-X **5591**

6 residual strokes

詆 J6b49/M35356 **5574**

詇 J-X/M35495 **5590**

詠 J-X/M-X **5591**

誨 J-X/M-X **5592**

詢 J6b4e/M35411 **5593**

詣 J3758/M35412 **5594**

詬 J6b4d/M35433 **5595**

誂 J6b50/M35469 **5596**

詼 J6b4b/M35462 **5597**

詫 J4f4d/M35431 **5598**

誅 J6b4f/M35472 **5599**

誄 J6b51/M35471 **5600**

該 J333a/M35445 **5601**

誉 J4d40/M35498 **5602**

詭 J6b4c/M35434 **5603**

詮 J4127/M35435 **5604**

誇 J3858/M35474 **5605**

誠 J403f/M35497′ **5606**

詳 J3e5c/M35446 **5607**

話 J4f43/M35441 **5608**

詰 J354d/M35440 **5609**

詩 J3b6d/M35427 **5610**

試 J3b6e/M35415 **5611**

誠 J-X/M35537 **5612**

誕 J-X/M35516 **5613**

7 residual strokes

滸 J5e77/M18089 3291

獄 J3976/M20603 3602

罰 J4833/M28315 4647

誨 J-X/M-X **5592**

該 J333a/M35445 **5601**

誇 J3858/M35474 **5605**

誠 J-X/M35537 **5612**

誕 J-X/M35516 **5613**

誚 J6b57/M35529 **5614**

誥 J6b55/M35549 **5615**

誨 J6b52/M35553 **5616**

誡 J6b53/M35538 **5617**

誣 J6b58/M35542 **5618**

誑 J6b54/M35510 **5619**

誌 J3b6f/M35501 **5620**

誦 J6b56/M35551 **5621**

誓 J4040/M35514 **5622**

認 J4727/M35502′ **5623**

認 J-X/M35502 **5624**

誘 J4d36/M35525 **5625**

誤 J386d/M35546′ **5626**

説 J4062/M35556′ **5627**

語 J386c/M35533 **5628**

読 J4649/M35580′ **5629**

諄 J6b59/M35622 **5635**

誕 J4342/M35692′ **5640**

8 residual strokes

罸 J662f/M28343 4648

誨 J6b52/M35553 **5616**

誘 J4d36/M35525 **5625**

諫 J3452/M35642 **5630**

諚 J6b5c/M35682 **5631**

諏 J3f5b/M35648 **5632**

19–20 residual strokes

巒 J565d/M8640 1523
戀 J5878/M11504 2017
攣 J5a3b/M13032 2320
欒 J5d33/M15947 2922
孌 J5a4e/M36117 **5721**
讚 J6c2d/M36163 **5729**
鑾 J6f56/M41083 6375

21–23 residual strokes

灣 J5f54/M18823 3393
䜌 J-X/M23931 3972
臠 J6748/M30049 4893
蠻 J6a47/M33914 5409
鸞 J7342/M47508 7010

Rad. 150 谷

0 residual strokes

谷 J432b/M36182 **5730**

2 residual strokes

㕡 J422f/M695 220
卻 J524a/M2867 638
郤 J6e3c/M39440 6142

3 residual strokes

容 J4d46/M7172 1335
峪 J563b/M8073 1467
浴 J4d61/M17496 3153
逧 J6d7a/M-X 6044

4–5 residual strokes

欲 J4d5f/M16080 2936
裕 J4d35/M34305 5461
谺 J-X/M36193 **5731**
谻 J6c2e/M-X **5732**
逧 J6d7a/M-X 6044

6–8 residual strokes

慾 J4d5d/M11163 1951
榕 J5c57/M15228 2815
溶 J4d4f/M17983 3277
熔 J4d50/M19319 3458
褣 J634e/M-X 4164

10–12 residual strokes

壑 J545b/M5554 1107
豁 J6c2f/M36221 **5733**
谿 J6c30/M36219 **5734**
鎔 J6f30/M40704 6327

Rad. 151 豆

0 residual strokes

豆 J4626/M36245 **5735**

2–3 residual strokes

脰 J-X/M29544 4816
荳 J683a/M30989 5036
豈 J6c31/M36249 **5736**
逗 J3f60/M38887 6053

5 residual strokes

凱 J332e/M1790 440
剴 J5173/M2122 505
厨 J3f5f/M3005 657
壴 J5465/M5661 1044
尌 J-X/M7448 1384
痘 J4577/M22185 3813
登 J4550/M22668 3862
短 J433b/M23978 3982

6–7 residual strokes

嘉 J3245/M4176 887
廚 J-X/M-X 1631
榿 J5c48/M15298 2801
豊 J4b2d/M36263 **5737**
鼓 J385d/M48330 7076

8 residual strokes

噎 J5359/M4307 895
嶝 J5653/M8482 1511
幩 J-X/M-X 1581
澄 J4021/M18315 3333
皚 J622d/M22765 3877
磑 J6276/M24402 4035
豌 J6c32/M36273 **5738**
豎 J6c33/M36280 **5739**

9 residual strokes

憙 J585a/M11219 1976
橙 J5c74/M15552 2877
樹 J3c79/M15496 2878
殪 J5d50/M16578 2984
燈 J4575/M19402 3476
熹 J5f74/M19380 3478
頭 J462c/M43490 6639

10 residual strokes

幮 J-X/M-X 1587
磴 J6324/M24478 4046
禧 J6336/M24828 4112
豏 [illegible]/M34934 5536

11 residual strokes

幱 J-X/M9134 1588
禮 J6339/M24044 4113
豐 J6c34/M36304 **5740**
鎧 J333b/M40733 6324
闓 J462e/M45649 6418

12–13 residual strokes

巇 J-X/M8614 1519
艶 J3170/M30632 4957
證 J6b7a/M35946 5697
軆 J6d3d/M38157 5937
醴 J6e54/M40053 6195
鐙 J462a/M40904 6348
鬪 J722c/M45649 6825

14–21 residual strokes

懿 J5874/M11501 2015
豔 J-X/M36332 **5741**
鐵 J6f45/M-X 6342
饐 J713e/M44396 6713
體 J7173/M45291 6794
鱧 J7267/M46542 6926

Rad. 152 豕

0 residual strokes

豕 J6c35/M36334 **5742**

2–3 residual strokes

冢 J514f/M1585 403
家 J3248/M7169 1337
彖 J5741/M9920 1707
逐 J4360/M38877 6056

4 residual strokes

啄 J426f/M-X 793
啄 J-X/M3801 821
彖 J5741/M9920 1707
琢 J4276/M-X 3640
豚 J465a/M36352 **5743**
遂 J3f6b/M38985 6084
隊 J4262/M41750 6468

5 residual strokes

喙 J533c/M3951 838

塚 J444d / M-X 1048
掾 J5961 / M12313 2220
琢 J-X / M21058 3650
遂 J3f6b / M38985′ 6084

6 residual strokes

塚 J-X / M5345 1060
嫁 J3247 / M6602 1256
掾 J5961 / M12313 2220
椽 J5c3d / M15087 2778
溷 J5e67 / M17986 3263
蒙 J4c58 / M31555 5154
象 J3e5d / M36372 **5744**
豙 J-X / M36373 **5745**
豢 J6c36 / M36380 **5746**

7 residual strokes

墜 J4446 / M5451 1082
椽 J5c3d / M15087 2778
豨 J-X / M36404 **5747**
豨 J-X / M-X **5748**
豪 J396b / M36406 **5749**
遯 J6e2c / M39089 6102
隧 J702b / M41870 6482

8 residual strokes

像 J417c / M1084 308
像 J-X / M48923 309
劇 J3760 / M2218 517
墜 J4446 / M5451 1082
毅 J3523 / M16673 3003
燧 J5f7c / M19469 3484
稼 J3254 / M25217 4169
篆 J643f / M26256 4329
緑 J316f / M27656′ 4553
緣 J-X / M27656 4554
遯 J6e2c / M39089 6102
隧 J702b / M41870 6482

9 residual strokes

擄 J5a21 / M12839 2284
濛 J5f42 / M18491 3345
燧 J5f7c / M19469 3484
糘 J6474 / M-X 4418
豬 J6c37 / M36432 **5750**
遽 J6e31 / M39161 6117

10 residual strokes

壕 J3968 / M5559 1108
曚 J5b24 / M14223 2520
橡 J464b / M15564 2863
橡 J-X / M-X 2864
檬 J5d28 / M15710 2887
濠 J396a / M18502 3363
燧 J5f7c / M19469 3484
緑 J316f / M27656′ 4553
緣 J-X / M27656 4554
朦 J5b2f / M14409 4882
豫 J502e / M36425 **5751**
遽 J6e31 / M39161 6117
邃 J6364 / M39191 6123

11 residual strokes

瀦 J4375 / M-X 3377
燹 J6021 / M19508 3501
矇 J625e / M23774 3967
邃 J6364 / M39191 6123

12–15 residual strokes

櫞 J5d29 / M15822 2904
艨 J6761 / M30574 4948
蠡 J6a42 / M33796 5401
醵 J6e53 / M40055 6196

Rad. 153 豸

0 residual strokes

豸 J6c38 / M36496 **5752**

3–5 residual strokes

豹 J493f / M36499 **5753**
豺 J6c39 / M36500 **5754**
貁 J-X / M36509 **5755**
豼 J6c41 / M36504 **5756**
貂 J6c3a / M36528 **5757**

6 residual strokes

貊 J6c3d / M36550 **5758**
貉 J6c3b / M36549 **5759**
貅 J6c3c / M36542 **5760**

7–8 residual strokes

貍 J6c3e / M36561 **5761**
貌 J4b46 / M36556 **5762**
貎 J6c3f / M36572 **5763**

10–15 residual strokes

懇 J3a29 / M11326 2002
藐 J6938 / M32267 5232
貔 J6c40 / M36606 **5764**
貘 J6c42 / M36621 **5765**
霾 J704a / M42507 6550

Rad. 154 貝

0 residual strokes

貝 J332d / M36656 **5766**

2 residual strokes

則 J4227 / M1994 487
貟 J-X / M36659 **5767**
貞 J4467 / M36658 **5768**
負 J4969 / M-X **5769**
負 J-X / M36660 **5770**
頁 J4a47 / M43333 6614

3 residual strokes

唄 J3134 / M3694 802
員 J3077 / M3633 808
厠 J557e / M7713 1423
狽 J4762 / M20433 3576
貶 J6c4a / M36707 **5771**
貢 J3957 / M36665 **5772**
財 J3a62 / M36664 **5773**

4 residual strokes

偵 J4465 / M898 270
側 J4226 / M897 275
厠 J524e / M2981 653
戝 J6c43 / M11603 2031
敗 J4754 / M13227 2343
貶 J6c4a / M36707 **5771**
貮 J6c49 / M-X **5774**
貭 J6c44 / M36694 **5775**
貿 J-X / M36695 **5776**
貪 J6c45 / M36680 **5777**
貫 J3453 / M36681 **5778**
販 J484e / M36679 **5779**
責 J4055 / M36682 **5780**
貨 J325f / M36678 **5781**
貧 J494f / M36677 **5782**
貰 J4c63 / M36699 **5789**
遉 J6e26 / M38993 6082
頃 J3a22 / M43338 6615
頂 J443a / M43335 6616

5 residual strokes

幀 J566c / M8982 1570
廁 J567a / M9410 1627
惻 J583c / M10869 1916
測 J422c / M17780 3244
貫 J3453 / M36681 **5778**
貳 J6c48 / M36703 **5783**
賁 J6c4c / M36727 **5784**
貽 J6c46 / M36719 **5785**
費 J4871 / M36717 **5786**
貼 J453d / M36718 **5787**
貿 J4b47 / M36721 **5788**

6 residual strokes

7 residual strokes

8 residual strokes

9 residual strokes

10 residual strokes

11 residual strokes

12 residual strokes

贊 J6c55/M36935 **5829**
贋 J3466/M36943 **5830**
贇 J6c56/M36909 **5831**
韻 J3124/M43307 6611
顎 J335c/M43590 6643
類 J-X/M43636 6650
顛 J-X/M43628 6651
顛 J453f/M-X 6652
願 J346a/M43623 6653

13 residual strokes

嚶 J536d/M4592 925
寶 J556f/M7376 1371
瀕 J494e/M18636 3381
竇 J6365/M25695 4220
繽 J656f/M27999 4606
罌 J6622/M28185 4629
襭 J6b23/M34702 5508
贍 J6c58/M36945 **5832**
贏 J6c57/M36950 **5833**

14 residual strokes

囂 J536f/M4616 930
櫻 J5d2f/M15888 2917
瓔 J607d/M21347 3685
癪 J617b/M22626 3853
癩 J617a/M22622 3854
纉 J6574/M28037 4610
纈 J6572/M28028 4613
纐 J6573/M28030 4614
纇 J6576/M28050 4615
贐 J6c59/M36956 **5834**
贓 J6c5b/M36962 **5835**

贔 J6c5d/M36963 **5836**
顧 J385c/M43689′ 6655
饋 J713f/M44382 6711
齎 J6c5a/M48575 7086

15 residual strokes

囎 J5375/M-X 932
巓 J565c/M8644 1524
籟 J645d/M26751 4375
覿 J6b36/M34984 5541
讀 J6c26/M36088 5719
讃 J3b3e/M36110 5720
贓 J6c5b/M36962 **5835**
贔 J6c5d/M36963 **5836**
贗 J-X/M36972 **5837**
贖 J6c5e/M36970 **5838**
躓 J6d35/M37967 5923
顥 J-X/M43682 6654
顫 J707c/M43706 6656
鬢 J7224/M45580 6816

16 residual strokes

纉 J6574/M28037 4610
纓 J6577/M28067 4620
鑚 J6f54/M41009 6368
顯 J707d/M43726 6657
顬 J-X/M43716 6658

17 residual strokes

屭 J-X/M7823 1436
癲 J6221/M22643 3857
贜 J-X/M36990 **5839**

鬟 J7226/M45607 6819

18–19 residual strokes

讚 J6c2d/M36163 5729
贜 J-X/M36990 **5839**
顱 J7121/M43742 6660
顴 J7122/M43751 6661

20–21 residual strokes

鑽 J6f53/M41082 6374
顯 J707d/M43726 6657
顳 J7123/M43750 6662
鸚 J7340/M47489 7009
黷 J7362/M48234 7067

Rad. 155 赤

0 residual strokes

赤 J4056/M36993 **5840**

4–10 residual strokes

螫 J6a2e/M33491 5377
赦 J3c4f/M36999 **5841**
赧 J6c5f/M37001 **5842**
赫 J3352/M37010 **5843**
赭 J6c60/M37017 **5844**

Rad. 156 走

0 residual strokes

走 J4176/M37034 **5845**
赱 J6c61/M37034′ **5846**

2–6 residual strokes

赴 J496b/M37040 **5847**
赳 J6c62/M37038 **5848**
起 J352f/M37048 **5849**
趁 J6c63/M37083 **5850**
越 J315b/M37110 **5851**
超 J4436/M37096 **5852**

7–10 residual strokes

趙 J6c64/M37171 **5853**
趣 J3c71/M37207 **5854**
趨 J3f76/M37258 **5855**
跿 J6c75/M37552 5879

Rad. 157 足

0 residual strokes

足 J422d/M37365 **5856**

2–3 residual strokes

促 J4225/M664 212
捉 J422a/M12136 2159

4 residual strokes

跂 J6c65/M37416 **5857**
趾 J6c66/M37406 **5858**
趺 J6c67/M37392 **5859**

距 J3577/M37481 **5866**

5 residual strokes

跏 J6c68/M37457 **5860**
跖 J6c6a/M37469 **5861**
跌 J6c6b/M37450 **5862**
跚 J6c69/M37477 **5863**
跑 J-X/M37461 **5864**
跛 J6c6c/M37479 **5865**
距 J3577/M37481 **5866**
跋 J6c6d/M37446 **5867**
𨀤 J-X/M37447 **5868**

6 residual strokes

跟 J6c70/M37491 **5869**
跫 J6c6f/M37519 **5870**
跣 J6c71/M37497 **5871**
跨 J3859/M37504 **5872**
践 J4129/M37547′ **5873**
跪 J6c6e/M37516 **5874**
跡 J4057/M37493 **5875**
路 J4f29/M37524 **5876**
跳 J4437/M37533 **5877**
跿 J6c75/M37552 **5879**

7 residual strokes

跨 J3859/M37504 **5872**
踈 J6c73/M37579 **5878**
跿 J6c75/M37552 **5879**
踉 J6c74/M37585 **5880**
跼 J6c72/M37548 **5881**
踊 J4d59/M37587 **5882**

8 residual strokes

- 踐 J6c78/M37608 **5883**
- 踘 J6c79/M37645 **5884**
- 踞 J6c77/M37642 **5885**
- 踠 J-X/M37646 **5886**
- 踪 J6d29/M37668 **5887**
- 踝 J6c76/M37641 **5888**
- 踏 J4627/M37602 **5889**
- 錠 J-X/M40469 6270

9 residual strokes

- 蕗 J4979/M31964 5203
- 踴 J6c7d/M37684 **5890**
- 踰 J6c7c/M37675 **5891**
- 蹂 J6c7a/M37718 **5892**
- 踵 J6c7b/M37686 **5893**
- 蹄 J447d/M37724 **5894**

10 residual strokes

- 蹈 J6d25/M37744 **5895**
- 蹊 J6c7e/M37747 **5896**
- 蹐 J6d24/M37766 **5897**
- 蹇 J6d21/M37741 **5898**
- 蹉 J6d22/M37745 **5899**
- 蹌 J6d23/M37755 **5900**
- 蹕 J6d2b/M37783 **5904**

11 residual strokes

- 歸 J5d45/M16349 2966
- 蹤 J6d27/M37823 **5901**
- 蹙 J6d26/M37790 **5902**
- 蹙 J-X/M37791 **5903**
- 蹕 J6d2b/M37783 **5904**
- 蹟 J4058/M37814 **5905**
- 蹠 J6d28/M37815 **5906**
- 蹣 J6d2a/M37822 **5907**

12 residual strokes

- 蹊 J6c7e/M37747 **5896**
- 蹙 J-X/M37791 **5903**
- 蹯 J6d30/M37925 **5908**
- 蹼 J6d2e/M37889 **5909**
- 蹶 J6d2c/M37880 **5910**
- 蹷 J-X/M37881 **5911**
- 蹲 J6d2d/M37874 **5912**
- 蹴 J3d33/M37876 **5913**

13 residual strokes

- 躅 J6d31/M37917 **5914**
- 躄 J6d32/M37913 **5915**
- 躃 J-X/M37912 **5916**
- 躁 J6d2f/M37906 **5917**

14 residual strokes

- 躋 J6d33/M37949 **5918**
- 躊 J6d34/M37941 **5919**
- 躑 J6d36/M37963 **5920**
- 躍 J4c76/M37995′ **5921**
- 露 J4f2a/M42463 6549

15–16 residual strokes

- 躔 J6d37/M37970 **5922**
- 躓 J6d35/M37967 **5923**
- 躙 J6d38/M37983 **5924**
- 齪 J7378/M48669 7099

17–21 residual strokes

- 躡 J6d3a/M38009 **5925**
- 躪 J6d39/M38026 **5926**
- 躅 J-X/M38028 **5927**
- 鷺 J3a6d/M47362 7006

Rad. 158 身

0 residual strokes

- 身 J3f48/M38034 **5928**

3–7 residual strokes

- 射 J3c4d/M7434 1380
- 躬 J6d3b/M38038 **5929**
- 躯 J366d/M-X **5930**
- 躰 J6d3c/M38065 **5931**
- 躱 J6d3e/M38078 **5932**
- 躳 J-X/M38089 **5933**

8–11 residual strokes

- 竆 J3567/M25593 4212
- 謝 J3c55/M35827 5687
- 躾 J6d3f/M38123 **5934**
- 軀 J-X/M38137 **5935**

12–17 residual strokes

- 竆 J-X/M25686 4219
- 軈 J6d40/M-X **5936**
- 軆 J6d3d/M38157 **5937**
- 軅 J6d41/M38167 **5938**
- 麝 J734d/M47682 7027

Rad. 159 車

0–1 residual strokes

- 車 J3c56/M38172 **5939**
- 軋 J6d42/M38173 **5940**

2 residual strokes

- 俥 J5060/M720 201
- 軌 J3530/M38176 **5941**
- 軏 J-X/M-X **5942**
- 軍 J3733/M38179 **5943**
- 連 J4f22/M38902′ 6062
- 陣 J3f58/M41667 6418

3 residual strokes

- 庫 J384b/M9330 1617
- 軒 J382e/M38187 **5944**
- 連 J4f22/M38902′ 6062

4 residual strokes

- 動 J4630/M2390 549
- 斬 J3b42/M13555 2384
- 軎 J6d44/M-X **5945**
- 軛 J6d43/M38207 **5946**
- 軟 J4670/M38213 **5947**
- 転 J453e/M38234′ **5948**
- 運 J313f/M38998′ 6092

5 residual strokes

- 揮 J3478/M12394 2229
- 漣 J4e7a/M-X 3210
- 渾 J5e55/M17800 3236
- 蓮 J4f21/M-X 5105
- 葷 J6858/M31461 5116
- 軻 J6d46/M38274 **5949**
- 軫 J6d47/M38243 **5950**
- 軼 J6d45/M38275 **5951**
- 軸 J3c34/M38269 **5952**
- 軽 J375a/M38281 **5953**
- 運 J313f/M38998′ 6092

6 residual strokes

- 嗹 J5350/M4148 875
- 暉 J5a76/M14030 2499
- 暈 J5a74/M14037 2500
- 漣 J4e7a/M-X 3210
- 漣 J-X/M18155 3259
- 琿 J606d/M21093 3658
- 蓮 J4f21/M-X 5105
- 蓮 J-X/M31722 5158
- 輀 J-X/M38287 **5954**
- 輌 J6d52/M-X **5955**
- 軾 J6d48/M38285 **5956**
- 輅 J6d4a/M38302 **5957**
- 輊 J6d49/M38311 **5958**
- 較 J3353/M38297 **5959**

- 載 J3a5c / M38307 **5960**

7 residual strokes

- 嗹 J5358 / M4148 875
- 塹 J544f / M5394 1084
- 嶄 J5650 / M8413 1509
- 嶃 J-X / M8412 1510
- 慚 J5850 / M11096 1965
- 漣 J-X / M18155 3259
- 漸 J4132 / M18179 3305
- 皸 J6230 / M22888 3882
- 皹 J6231 / M-X 3883
- 蓮 J-X / M31722 5158
- 褌 J6a6e / M34428 5480
- 輕 J6d4b / M38346 **5961**
- 輒 J6d4c / M38336 **5962**
- 輓 J6d4e / M38337 **5963**
- 輔 J4a65 / M38342 **5964**

8 residual strokes

- 勲 J372e / M2463 560
- 塹 J544f / M5394 1084
- 慙 J584f / M11095 1966
- 撃 J3762 / M12674′ 2265
- 暫 J3b43 / M14120 2510
- 槧 J5c61 / M15359 2833
- 範 J484f / M26253 4330
- 輓 J6d4e / M38337 **5963**
- 輙 J6d4d / M38359 **5965**
- 輡 J-X / M38381 **5966**
- 輜 J6d4f / M38368 **5967**
- 輟 J6d50 / M38374 **5968**
- 輛 J6d51 / M38361 **5969**
- 輦 J6d53 / M38393 **5970**
- 輩 J475a / M38398 **5971**
- 輝 J3531 / M38372 **5972**
- 輪 J4e58 / M38400 **5973**

9 residual strokes

- 縺 J6561 / M27838 4565
- 諢 J6b64 / M35709 5657
- 輹 J6d56 / M38440 **5974**
- 輳 J6d54 / M38429 **5975**
- 輯 J3d34 / M38420 **5976**
- 輻 J6d55 / M38442 **5977**
- 輸 J4d22 / M38438′ **5978**
- 輿 J4d41 / M38468 **5983**

10 residual strokes

- 擊 J-X / M12800 2287
- 縺 J6561 / M27838 4565
- 繋 J3752 / M-X 4573
- 轂 J6d58 / M38479 **5979**
- 轅 J6d57 / M38483 **5980**
- 轄 J336d / M38482′ **5981**
- 輾 J6d59 / M38467 **5982**
- 輿 J4d41 / M38468 **5983**
- 鏈 J6f3a / M40779 6323

11 residual strokes

- 縺 J6561 / M27838 4565
- 轉 J6d5b / M38507 **5984**
- 轌 J6d5a / M-X **5985**
- 轆 J6d5c / M38502 **5986**
- 鏈 J6f3a / M40779 6323

12 residual strokes

- 縺 J6561 / M27838 4565
- 繋 J3752 / M-X 4573
- 繫 J-X / M27940 4601
- 轂 J6d58 / M38479 **5979**
- 轆 J6d5c / M38502 **5986**
- 轎 J6d5d / M38532 **5987**
- 轍 J4532 / M38524 **5988**
- 鏈 J6f3a / M40779 6323
- 鏨 J6f34 / M40824 6335

13–14 residual strokes

- 囀 J5373 / M4614 927
- 繫 J-X / M27940 4601
- 轗 J6d5e / M38550 **5989**
- 轜 J6d5f / M38571 **5990**
- 轟 J396c / M38577 **5991**
- 鶇 J732e / M47130 6982

15–19 residual strokes

- 轡 J3725 / M38587 **5992**
- 轢 J6d60 / M38588 **5993**
- 轣 J6d61 / M38593 **5994**
- 轤 J6d62 / M38596 **5995**

Rad. 160 辛

0 residual strokes

- 辛 J3f49 / M38630 **5996**
- 辛 J-X / M38630′ **5997**

3–5 residual strokes

- 宰 J3a4b / M7160 1330
- 辜 J6d63 / M38636 **5998**
- 逹 J6d7d / M-X 6064

6 residual strokes

- 新 J3f37 / M13572 2387
- 滓 J5e68 / M18034 3260
- 睾 J6250 / M23535 3951
- 辟 J6d64 / M38642 **5999**
- 辞 J3c2d / M38638 **6000**

7–8 residual strokes

- 劈 J517c / M2223 516
- 熱 J-X / M-X 3474
- 稗 J-X / M25213 4162
- 辣 J6d65 / M38646 **6001**
- 避 J4872 / M39163′ 6120

9 residual strokes

- 壁 J4a49 / M5516 1103
- 嬖 J554a / M6770 1269
- 縡 J6552 / M27781 4560
- 薛 J692d / M32123 5207
- 薜 J6930 / M32125 5208
- 薪 J3f45 / M32149′ 5222
- 蟄 J6a2f / M33537 5381
- 辨 J517e / M38657 **6002**
- 辦 J5221 / M38656 **6003**
- 避 J4872 / M39163′ 6120

10 residual strokes

- 擘 J5a26 / M12835 2290
- 檗 J5d21 / M15669 2886
- 甓 J6132 / M21609 3708
- 臂 J673e / M29944 4877
- 贇 J6c53 / M36907 5825

11 residual strokes

- 璧 J607a / M21269 3679
- 甓 J6132 / M21609 3708
- 癖 J4a4a / M22550 3848

12 residual strokes

- 瓣 J6122 / M21425 3689
- 襞 J6a7e / M34645 5501
- 譬 J6c23 / M36023 5709
- 辭 J6d66 / M38671 **6004**

13 residual strokes

- 辮 J6570 / M27991 4604
- 蘗 J5d22 / M32479 5258
- 蘖 J5d31 / M32478 5260
- 襞 J6a7e / M34645 5501
- 譬 J6c22 / M36019 5712
- 躄 J6d32 / M37913 5915
- 躃 J-X / M37912 5916

14–15 residual strokes

- 辮 J6570 / M27991 4604

Rad. 163 邑

- 銷 J6e79/M40424 6276
- 鋲 J4946/M40503 6277
- 鋤 J3d7b/M40480 6278
- 鋭 J3154/M40418′ 6279
- 鋳 J4372/M40503′ 6280

8 residual strokes

- 銹 J6e78/M40426 6271
- 鎚 J444a/M-X 6281
- 錢 J6f22/M40563 6282
- 鍄 J6e7d/M-X 6283
- 錙 J6f21/M40548 6284
- 錮 J6e7e/M40570 6285
- 錣 J6f24/M40566 6286
- 鋺 J6e7c/M40507 6287
- 錻 J6f27/M40597 6288
- 錏 J6e7b/M40534 6289
- 錚 J6f23/M40553 6290
- 錘 J3f6a/M40547 6291
- 錫 J3c62/M40573 6292
- 錠 J3e7b/M40559 6293
- 錐 J3f6d/M40536 6294
- 錨 J4945/M40598 6295
- 錆 J3b2c/M40523 6296
- 鋸 J3578/M40505 6297
- 録 J4f3f/M40519′ 6298
- 錯 J3a78/M40579 6299
- 錬 J4f23/M40576 6300
- 錦 J3653/M40569 6301
- 鋼 J395d/M40509 6302
- 錄 J-X/M40611 6303
- 鍵 J3830/M40654 6317

9 residual strokes

- 鎚 J444a/M-X 6281
- 錄 J-X/M40611 6303
- 鍊 J-X/M40602 6304
- 鍖 J6f2c/M40620 6305
- 鍜 J6f28/M40626 6306
- 鍠 J6f29/M40630 6307
- 鍮 J6f2b/M40645 6308
- 鎹 J6f31/M40766 6309
- 鎚 J-X/M40715 6310
- 鍾 J3e61/M40672 6311
- 鍍 J4555/M40607 6312
- 鍔 J4457/M40617 6313
- 鍬 J372d/M40643 6314
- 鍋 J4669/M40603 6315
- 鍼 J6f2a/M40667 6316
- 鍵 J3830/M40654 6317
- 鍛 J4343/M40625 6318
- 鏈 J6f3a/M40779 6323

10 residual strokes

- 嚠 J5368/M4544 918
- 瀏 J5f48/M18607 3370
- 鎚 J444a/M-X 6281
- 鎹 J6f31/M40766 6309
- 鎚 J-X/M40715 6310
- 鍔 J4457/M40617 6313
- 鎰 J6f2d/M40747 6319
- 鎗 J4179/M40709 6320
- 鎬 J6f2e/M40741 6321
- 鎍 J-X/M40694 6322
- 鏈 J6f3a/M40779 6323
- 鎧 J333b/M40735 6324
- 鎖 J3a3f/M40708′ 6325
- 鎌 J3379/M40693 6326
- 鎔 J6f30/M40704 6327
- 鎮 J4443/M40745 6328
- 鎭 J6f2f/M40744 6329

11 residual strokes

- 鏈 J6f3a/M40779 6323
- 鏥 J6f35/M40821 6330
- 鏁 J-X/M40770 6331
- 鏐 J6f39/M40789 6332
- 鏗 J6f33/M40801 6333
- 鏑 J452d/M40790 6334
- 鏨 J6f34/M40824 6335
- 鏃 J6f37/M40772 6336
- 鏘 J6f36/M40802 6337
- 鏖 J6f32/M40799 6338
- 鏤 J6f3b/M40820 6339
- 鏝 J6f38/M40807 6340
- 鏡 J3640/M40812 6341
- 鐓 J6f3e/M40891 6346

12 residual strokes

- 錏 J6e7b/M40534 6289
- 鎍 J-X/M40694 6322
- 鏗 J6f33/M40801 6333
- 鏖 J6f32/M40799 6338
- 鐡 J6f45/M-X 6342
- 鑓 J4c7a/M-X 6343
- 鐇 J6f40/M40874 6344
- 鐐 J6f41/M40886 6345
- 鐓 J6f3e/M40891 6346
- 鐔 J6f3d/M40893 6347
- 鐙 J462a/M40904 6348
- 鐫 J6f43/M40924 6349
- 鐃 J6f3f/M40867 6350
- 鐚 J6f3c/M40907 6351
- 鐘 J3e62/M40902 6352

13 residual strokes

- 鑓 J4c7a/M-X 6343
- 鐫 J6f43/M40924 6349
- 鐚 J6f3c/M40907 6351
- 鏽 J-X/M40857 6353
- 鐵 J6f44/M40945 6354
- 鐺 J6f46/M40954 6355
- 鐸 J4278/M40951 6356
- 鑓 J-X/M40998 6357
- 鐶 J6f42/M40946 6358
- 鑁 J6f47/M-X 6359

14 residual strokes

- 鑓 J4c7a/M-X 6343
- 鐫 J6f43/M40924 6349
- 鑓 J-X/M40998 6357
- 鑄 J6f49/M40972 6360
- 鑑 J3455/M40988 6361
- 鑒 J6f48/M40989 6362

15 residual strokes

- 鐫 J6f43/M40924 6349
- 鑑 J3455/M40988 6361
- 鑒 J6f48/M40989 6362
- 鑛 J6f4a/M41010 6363
- 鑣 J-X/M41022 6364
- 鑢 J6f4c/M41021 6365
- 鑠 J6f4b/M41019 6366
- 鑞 J6f4d/M41014 6367
- 鑚 J6f54/M41009 6368

16–17 residual strokes

- 鑣 J-X/M41022 6364
- 鑪 J6f4e/M41038 6369
- 鑵 J6f51/M41064 6370
- 鑰 J6f50/M41051 6371
- 鑲 J-X/M41053 6372

18–20 residual strokes

- 鑷 J6f52/M41069 6373
- 鑽 J6f53/M41082 6374
- 鑾 J6f56/M41083 6375
- 鑼 J6f55/M41081 6376
- 钁 J6f57/M41092 6377
- 鑿 J6f58/M41088 6378

Rad. 168 長

0 residual strokes

- 長 J4439/M41100 6379
- 镸 J-X/M41101 6380

3 residual strokes

- 套 J4565/M5926 1161
- 帳 J4422/M8939 1568
- 張 J4425/M9812 1694

Rad.168: 4 residual strokes

悵 J5830/M10727 1888
萇 J6849/M31256 5069
髟 J7175/M45355 6799

4–6 residual strokes

張 J4425/M9812 1694
漲 J5e7d/M18173 3294
肆 J6668/M29226 4749
脹 J4431/M29570 4832
髢 J7176/M45363 6800

7 residual strokes

髤 J-X/M45375 6801
髦 J7178/M45377 6802
髣 J7177/M45371 6803
髪 J4831/M45387′ 6804

8 residual strokes

髮 J717b/M45400 6805
髴 J717c/M45414 6806
髫 J717a/M45392 6807
髱 J717d/M45410 6808
髯 J7179/M45404 6809

9–11 residual strokes

髷 J717e/M45426 6810
髻 J7221/M45442 6811
髭 J4926/M45399 6812
鬆 J7222/M45484 6813

14–18 residual strokes

鬘 J7223/M45568 6814
鬛 J-X/M45584 6815
鬚 J7224/M45580 6816
鬟 J7225/M45596 6817
鬛 J-X/M-X 6818
鬢 J7226/M45607 6819
鬣 J7227/M45613 6820

Rad. 169 門

0 residual strokes

門 J4c67/M41208 **6381**

1–2 residual strokes

們 J506e/M766 232
閂 J6f59/M41211 **6382**
閃 J412e/M41214 **6383**

3 residual strokes

問 J4c64/M3814 830
捫 J595f/M12197 2181
閊 J6f5b/M41229 **6384**
閉 J4a44/M41222 **6385**
閇 J6f5a/M41220 **6386**

4 residual strokes

悶 J4c65/M10729 1895
椚 J5c2f/M15064 2733
閔 J6f5c/M41251 **6387**
閖 J6f5d/M41260′ **6388**
閏 J313c/M41244 **6389**
閑 J3457/M41247 **6390**
間 J3456/M41249 **6391**
閒 J-X/M41248 **6392**
開 J332b/M41233 **6393**

5 residual strokes

閠 J6f60/M-X **6394**
閙 J6f5f/M41264 **6395**
閘 J6f5e/M41263 **6396**
閨 J6f61/M41312 **6400**

6 residual strokes

聞 J4a39/M29104 4732
閣 J395e/M41301 **6397**
閥 J4836/M41308 **6398**
閧 J6f62/M41311 **6399**
閨 J6f61/M41312 **6400**
閤 J3355/M41300 **6401**
関 J3458/M41297 **6402**

7 residual strokes

墹 J5451/M-X 1092
嫺 J5546/M6710 1264
嫻 J5547/M6711 1265
憪 J5862/M11252 1986
澗 J3442/M-X 3329
澗 J-X/M18253 3330
潤 J3d61/M18255 3334
蕑 J-X/M31954 5187
閭 J6f63/M41334 **6403**
閲 J315c/M41341′ **6404**

8 residual strokes

燗 J-X/M-X 3487
燗 J5f73/M19431 3488
閾 J6f67/M41384 **6405**
閹 J6f66/M41372 **6406**
閼 J6f64/M41380 **6407**
閻 J6f65/M41379 **6408**
闃 J6f6a/M41411 **6410**

9 residual strokes

擱 J5a28/M12892 2305
濶 J6f69/M18547 3364
癇 J6172/M22518 3843
癎 J-X/M-X 3844
闊 J6f68/M41429 **6409**
闃 J6f6a/M41411 **6410**
闍 J6f6b/M41434 **6411**
闋 J-X/M41430 **6412**
闌 J6f6c/M41433 **6413**
闇 J3047/M41421 **6414**

10 residual strokes

簡 J344a/M26520′ 4358
簡 J-X/M26520 4359
繝 J6563/M27908 4589
闔 J6f6e/M41452 **6415**
闖 J6f6f/M41458 **6416**
闕 J6f6d/M41456 **6417**
闘 J462e/M45649′ **6418**
關 J6f70/M41470 **6419**

11 residual strokes

櫚 J5d2d/M15815 2905
藺 J6942/M32399 5251
蘭 J4d76/M32477′ 5255
關 J6f70/M41470 **6419**
闚 J6f72/M41508 **6420**

12 residual strokes

欄 J4d73/M15880′ 2914
瀾 J5f51/M18722 3388
蘭 J-X/M32519 5257
闡 J6f71/M41489 **6421**

13 residual strokes

欄 J-X/M15904 2915
爛 J6025/M19604 3507
闢 J6f73/M41500 **6422**

14–18 residual strokes

襴 J6b26/M34728 5511
躙 J6d38/M37983 5924
躪 J6d39/M38026 5926
關 J6f70/M41470 **6419**

Rad. 170 阜

0 residual strokes

阜 J496c/M41534 **6423**

3–4 residual strokes

埠 J4956/M5161 1029
阡 J6f74/M41548 **6424**
阨 J6f75/M41559 **6425**
阮 J6f76/M41569 **6426**
阯 J6f77/M41570 **6427**
阪 J3a65/M41562 **6428**
防 J4b49/M41576 **6429**

5 residual strokes

陂 J6f78/M41603 **6430**
阼 J-X/M41594 **6431**
陀 J424b/M41600 **6432**
附 J496d/M41606 **6433**
阻 J414b/M41593 **6434**
阿 J3024/M41599 **6435**

6 residual strokes

陌 J6f79/M41617 **6436**
陏 J6f7a/M41623 **6437**
陋 J6f7b/M41616 **6438**
限 J3842/M41627 **6439**

7 residual strokes

陋 J6f7b/M41616 **6438**
限 J3842/M41627 **6439**
陦 J7023/M-X **6440**
陜 J6f7d/M41656 **6441**
陝 J7021/M41657 **6442**
陟 J7022/M41659 **6443**
陛 J4a45/M41654 **6444**
陞 J6f7e/M41658 **6445**
陥 J3459/M41676′ **6446**
院 J3121/M41665 **6447**
陣 J3f58/M41667 **6448**
除 J3d7c/M41669 **6449**
降 J395f/M41620 **6450**

8 residual strokes

娿 J-X/M6381 1228
陝 J7021/M41657 **6442**
陛 J4a45/M41654 **6444**
陷 J6f7c/M41707 **6451**
陲 J7024/M41694 **6452**
陬 J7025/M41685 **6453**
陵 J4e4d/M41704 **6454**
隆 J4e34/M41720′ **6455**
険 J3831/M41721′ **6456**
陳 J4444/M41698 **6457**
陪 J4766/M41680 **6458**
陶 J462b/M41705 **6459**
随 J3f6f/M41764′ **6460**
陸 J4e26/M41700 **6461**
陰 J3122/M41691 **6462**

9 residual strokes

堕 J4244/M-X 1033
随 J3f6f/M41764′ **6460**
隆 J-X/M41746 **6463**
隋 J6721/M41751 **6464**
隍 J7026/M41754 **6465**
隈 J3728/M41748 **6466**
隅 J3679/M41743 **6467**
隊 J4262/M41750 **6468**
階 J332c/M41755 **6469**
陽 J4d5b/M41725 **6470**

10 residual strokes

痾 J615e/M22289 3807
階 J332c/M41755 **6469**
隙 J3764/M41792 **6471**
隗 J7029/M41788 **6472**
隘 J7027/M41791 **6473**
隕 J7028/M41785 **6474**
隔 J3356/M-X **6475**
隔 J-X/M41783 **6476**

11 residual strokes

墮 J5458/M5481 1078
蔭 J307e/M31840 5151
隟 J-X/M41813 **6477**
際 J3a5d/M41820 **6478**
障 J3e63/M41821 **6479**
隠 J3123/M41836′ **6480**

12 residual strokes

墮 J5458/M5481 1078
墜 J4446/M5451 1082
嶐 J5657/M8447 1508
隨 J6e2e/M41871 **6481**
隧 J702b/M41870 **6482**
隣 J4e59/M41847 **6484**

13 residual strokes

墮 J5458/M5481 1078
橢 J5c73/M15565 2829
窿 J6363/M25660 4213
隨 J6e2e/M41871 **6481**
隧 J702b/M41870 **6482**
險 J702a/M41874 **6483**
隣 J4e59/M41847 **6484**

14–16 residual strokes

嚮 J536c/M-X 920
窿 J6363/M25660 4213
隱 J702c/M41891 **6485**
隮 J702d/M41880 **6486**
隰 J702e/M41889 **6487**
隴 J702f/M41904 **6488**

Rad. 171 隶

0 residual strokes

隶 J7030/M41923 **6489**

2–4 residual strokes

康 J392f/M9376 1621
棣 J5c28/M14957 2720
禄 J4f3d/M24741′ 4096
逮 J4261/M38931′ 6069

6–8 residual strokes

慷 J584d/M11146 1963
緑 J4e50/M27541′ 4528
隷 J4e6c/M41928 **6490**

9–16 residual strokes

糠 J3947/M27105 4424
隸 J7031/M41932 **6491**
靆 J704c/M42530 6552
鱇 J7261/M46468 6910

Rad. 172 隹

0 residual strokes

隹 J7032/M41937 **6492**

2 residual strokes

准 J3d5a/M1661 426
匯 J523b/M2644 594
進 J3f4a/M38943′ 6073
隼 J483b/M41943 **6493**
隻 J4049/M41941 **6494**

3 residual strokes

售 J5334/M3760 813
唯 J4d23/M3761 831
堆 J424f/M5211 1035
崔 J5643/M8178 1477
帷 J5669/M8954 1567
惟 J3054/M10820 1890
推 J3f64/M12284 2212
淮 J5e4e/M17682 3177
進 J3f4a/M38943′ 6073
隺 J5565/M-X **6495**
雀 J3f7d/M41954 **6496**

4 residual strokes

準 J5245/M1695 428
椎 J4447/M15024 2742
焦 J3e47/M19119 3436
雀 J3f7d/M41954 **6496**
雇 J385b/M41976 **6497**
雁 J3467/M41960 **6498**
雄 J4d3a/M41972 **6499**
集 J3d38/M41974 **6500**

5 residual strokes

催 J3a45/M1005 298
勧 J342b/M2433 559
携 J3748/M12529 2253
準 J3d60/M17934 3278
睢 J-X/M23450 3941
碓 J3130/M24294 4012
稚 J4355/M25120 4154
雋 J7034/M41996 **6501**
雎 J7033/M42001 **6502**
雍 J7036/M42000 **6503**
雉 J7035/M41987 **6504**
雅 J326d/M41973 **6505**

6 residual strokes

奪 J4325/M5994 1171
截 J5923/M11639 2039
携 J3748/M12529 2253
摧 J5974/M12609 2261
漼 J3443/M18216 3287
維 J305d/M27568 4516
雋 J7034/M41996 **6501**
雌 J3b73/M41998 **6506**
雑 J3b28/M42022 **6507**

7 residual strokes

儁 J512e/M1175 312
憔 J585e/M11213 1983
遲 J5a7b/M14150 2509
権 J3822/M15484 2853
確 J334e/M24366 4039
蕉 J3e56/M31937 5191
誰 J432f/M35586 5642

8 residual strokes

壅 J5459/M5524 1096
奮 J4a33/M6012 1172
擁 J4d4a/M12781 2294
樵 J3e41/M15489 2871
歓 J343f/M16197 2948
燋 J-X/M19410 3482
獲 J334d/M20758 3609
確 J334e/M24366 4039
確 J-X/M-X 4040
維 J305d/M27568 4516
翟 J586d/M28347 4651
薙 J4665/M32121 5221
錐 J3f6d/M40536 6294
雅 J-X/M-X **6508**
雕 J703a/M42080 **6509**
霍 J7039/M42321 6533

9 residual strokes

應 J5866/M11330 1991
擁 J4d4a/M12781 2294
擢 J4527/M12852 2303
濯 J4275/M18532 3360
礁 J3e4c/M24502 4048
篧 J-X/M-X 4627
膺 J673f/M29928 4878
舊 J6751/M30249 4916
虧 J694c/M32770 5274
襍 J7037/M34596 5496
雖 J6a2d/M42104 **6510**

10 residual strokes

戳 J5927/M11684 2046
擕 J-X/M12924 2308
曜 J4d4b/M14227′ 2522
櫂 J5d25/M15756 2900
燿 J6022/M19520 3500
甕 J6131/M21617 3709
癕 J-X/M22549 3846
瞿 J625a/M23747 3965
穫 J334f/M25334′ 4180
篧 J-X/M-X 4627
虧 J694c/M32770 5274
観 J3451/M34955 5538
雙 J5256/M42116 **6511**
雜 J7038/M42122 **6512**
雞 J-X/M42124 **6513**
雛 J3f77/M42121 **6514**
難 J4671/M42128′ **6515**
離 J4e25/M42140 **6517**
騅 J7157/M44788 6756

11 residual strokes

勸 J5230/M2486 563
羅 J4d65/M28397 4655
藺 J6942/M32399 5251
蠖 J6a3f/M33752 5391
贋 J3466/M36943 5830
軅 J6d40/M-X 5936
難 J-X/M42145 **6516**
離 J4e25/M42140 **6517**

12 residual strokes

懽 J5875/M11497 2013
灌 J5e75/M18759 3390
癕 J-X/M22549 3846
矍 J625f/M23792 3970
耀 J4d54/M28828 4695
護 J386e/M36038′ 5715
鐫 J6f43/M40924 6349
雞 J-X/M42124 **6513**

13 residual strokes

儺 J5135/M1317 337
囃 J5372/M4619 929
廱 J572b/M9554 1650
懼 J5876/M11488 2016
攜 J5a38/M13008 2318
權 J5c5e/M15926 2916
歡 J5d44/M16242 2953
灘 J4667/M18784 3391
癨 J6179/M22618 3852
羅 J4d65/M28397 4655
躍 J4c76/M37955′ 5921
鐫 J6f43/M40924 6349
顧 J385c/M43689′ 6655
鶴 J4461/M47185 6995

14 residual strokes

戳 J-X/M11695 2047
糴 J647b/M27191 4429
蘿 J6947/M32590 5263
邏 J6e36/M39259 6126
鐫 J6f43/M40924 6349
飄 J7128/M43946 6669
鶴 J4461/M47185 6995

15 residual strokes

攤 J5a3a/M13033 2319
攫 J5a3c/M13043 2321
癰 J617e/M22638 3856
罐 J6625/M28194 4632
讐 J3d32/M36125 5722
讎 J6c28/M36124 5723
躙 J6d38/M37983 5924
邏 J6e36/M39259 6126
鐫 J6f43/M40924 6349
鵰 J733c/M47312 7000

16 residual strokes

衢 J6a4d/M34090 1779
籬 J6461/M26803 4379
蘿 J6947/M32590 5263
蠵 J-X/M33887 5408
觀 J6b37/M34993 5542
讙 J6c2c/M36157 5727
軅 J6d41/M38167 5938
鷹 J426b/M47377 7007

17–18 residual strokes

籬 J6461/M26803 4379
糶 J647c/M27207 4430
躪 J6d39/M38026 5926
鑵 J6f51/M41064 6370
钁 J6f57/M41092 6377
顴 J7122/M43751 6661

19–21 residual strokes

欟 J5d36/M15986 2927
鑼 J6f55/M41081 6376
驩 J7169/M45086 6781
鸛 J7341/M47500 7008

Rad. 173 雨

0 residual strokes

雨 J312b/M42210 **6518**

3–4 residual strokes

雫 J3c36/M42219 **6519**
雪 J4063/M42216′ **6520**
雰 J4a37/M42231 **6521**
雲 J3140/M42235 **6522**

5 residual strokes

雹 J703b/M42248 **6523**
零 J4e6d/M42242 **6524**
雷 J4d6b/M42245 **6525**
電 J4545/M42253 **6526**

6 residual strokes

漏 J4f33/M18120 3307
霊 J-X/M-X **6527**
需 J3c7b/M42275 **6528**
霆 J703d/M42299 **6529**

7 residual strokes

樗 J4374/M15438 2841
膤 J6733/M-X 4863
霆 J703d/M42299 **6529**
霄 J703c/M42290 **6530**
震 J3f4c/M42300 **6531**
霊 J4e6e/M42309′ **6532**

8 residual strokes

儒 J3c74/M1220 330
擂 J5a27/M12783 2295
曇 J465e/M14172 2518
樗 J4374/M15438 2841
澪 J5f3a/M18398 3342
蕾 J6932/M32067 5215
霍 J7039/M42321 **6533**
霎 J7040/M42322 **6534**
霓 J703f/M42332 **6535**
霑 J7041/M42329 **6536**
霈 J703e/M42301 **6537**
霙 J7044/M42350 **6538**
霏 J7042/M42323 **6539**
霖 J7043/M42335 **6540**

9 residual strokes

嬬 J445c/M6821 1271
孺 J555e/M7042 1303
懦 J586f/M11390 2005
樗 J4374/M15438 2841
濡 J4728/M18504 3365
艝 J675c/M30536 4945
霞 J3262/M42365 **6541**
霜 J417a/M42363 **6542**

10 residual strokes

縹 J6562/M27936 4591
臑 J6742/M29986 4885
轌 J6d5a/M-X 5985
霤 J7045/M42396 **6543**

11 residual strokes

壜 J5460/M5588 1114
襦 J6b21/M34678 5506
霪 J7046/M42430 **6544**
霧 J4c38/M42418 **6545**

12 residual strokes

孀 J5552/M6885 1279
糯 J6479/M27173 4428
繻 J656c/M27996 4609
蠕 J6a40/M33749 5400
霰 J7047/M42458 **6546**

13 residual strokes

櫺 J5d32/M15887 2920
癨 J6179/M22618 3852
轜 J6d5f/M38571 5990
霸 J5b31/M42490 **6547**
霹 J7048/M42491 **6548**
露 J4f2a/M42463 **6549**

14 residual strokes

繻 J656c/M27996 4609
罎 J6624/M28189 4631
霾 J704a/M42507 **6550**
霽 J7049/M42499 **6551**
靆 J704c/M42530 **6552**
鱈 J432d/M46470 6916

15–16 residual strokes

靆 J704c/M42530 **6552**
靈 J704d/M42532 **6553**
靂 J704e/M42523 **6554**
靄 J704b/M42526 **6555**
顬 J-X/M43716 6658

17 residual strokes

欞 J-X/M15971 2925
靄 J704b/M42526 **6555**
靉 J704f/M42540 **6556**

Rad. 174 青

0 residual strokes

青 J4044/M42564′ **6557**
靑 J-X/M42564 **6558**

2–3 residual strokes

倩 J506a/M791 230
情 J3e70/M10756′ 1898
清 J4036/M17695′ 3205
猜 J604a/M20499 3584
菁 J6847/M31136 5072

4–5 residual strokes

晴 J4032/M13994′ 2488
睛 J624d/M23430 3940
靖 J4c77/M42570′ **6559**

6 residual strokes

精 J403a/M26997′ 4411
蜻 J6071/M33203 5341
静 J4045/M42574′ **6560**

7–8 residual strokes

請 J4041/M35640′ 5645
錆 J3b2c/M40523 6296
靜 J7050/M42578 **6561**
靛 J-X/M42577 **6562**

9–11 residual strokes

瀞 J4654/M-X 3356
瀞 J-X/M18659 3380
鯖 J3b2a/M46210 6883

Rad. 175 非

0 residual strokes

非 J4873/M42585 **6563**

2–3 residual strokes

俳 J4750/M726 254
匪 J485b/M2629 592
彗 J5742/M9927 1708
徘 J5751/M10141 1752
排 J4753/M12256 2210
菲 J684b/M31220 5082

4 residual strokes

悲 J4861/M10720 1897
扉 J4862/M11750 2058
斐 J4865/M13469 2370
琲 J606a/M21075 3648
腓 J6724/M29629 4829

5–6 residual strokes

榧 J5c52/M15258 2798
緋 J486c/M27604 4517
罪 J3a61/M28293 4644
翡 J6647/M28733 4684
蜚 J6974/M33138 5340
裴 J6a6a/M34362 5465

7 residual strokes

罪 J5a73/M-X 2480
裵 J6a6a/M34362 5465

誹 J4870/M35601 5639
輩 J475a/M38398 5971
靠 J7051/M42604 **6564**

8–14 residual strokes

殲 J5d53/M16608 2988
緋 J486c/M27604 4517
霏 J7042/M42323 6539
靡 J7353/M42612 **6565**
鯡 J724c/M46243 6880
齏 J706d/M48578 7087

Rad. 176 面

0 residual strokes

面 J4c4c/M42618 **6566**

3–6 residual strokes

湎 J5e5e/M17826 3215
靤 J7052/M42639 **6567**
緬 J4c4b/M27674 4542

7–14 residual strokes

緬 J4c4b/M27674 4542
靦 J7053/M42660 **6568**
靨 J7054/M42698 **6569**
麺 J4c4d/M-X 7038
麪 J-X/M47827 7039

Rad. 177 革

0 residual strokes

革 J3357/M42710 **6570**

2–3 residual strokes

勒 J7055/M2386 545
靫 J7056/M42713 **6571**
靭 J-X/M42715 **6572**
靭 J3f59/M-X **6573**
靱 J7057/M-X **6574**

4–5 residual strokes

靹 J7058/M42747 **6575**
靴 J3724/M42729 **6576**
靺 J705c/M42761 **6577**
靼 J705a/M42764 **6578**
鞁 J705b/M42776 **6579**
鞆 J705d/M42794 **6580**
鞅 J7059/M42784 **6581**
鞄 J3373/M42781 **6582**

6–8 residual strokes

瑾 J6077/M21187 3676
鞐 J7060/M42829 **6583**
鞋 J705e/M42813 **6584**
鞏 J705f/M42819 **6585**
鞍 J3048/M42815 **6586**
鞘 J3e64/M42850 **6587**
鞜 J7061/M42883 **6588**
鞠 J3547/M42892 **6589**

9 residual strokes

鞨 J7062/M42924 **6590**
鞳 J7065/M42966 **6591**
鞦 J7063/M42922 **6592**
鞫 J6b71/M42931 **6593**
鞣 J7064/M42909 **6594**
鞭 J4a5c/M42937 **6595**

10 residual strokes

覇 J4746/M34790 5519
覈 J6b33/M34952 5537
鞴 J7066/M42972 **6596**

11–13 residual strokes

羈 J6634/M28412 4656
霸 J5b31/M42490 6547
韃 J-X/M42997 **6597**
韃 J7067/M43053 **6598**

14 residual strokes

欛 J-X/M15945 2921
覉 J-X/M34794 5520
韈 J7069/M43079 **6599**
韆 J7068/M43075 **6600**

15–16 residual strokes

欛 J-X/M15971 2925
羇 J6633/M28417 4657
覊 J6b2b/M34795 5521

Rad. 178 韋

0 residual strokes

韋 J706a/M43108 **6601**

2–3 residual strokes

偉 J304e/M837 285
幃 J566b/M8993 1575
葦 J3031/M31437 5160

6–10 residual strokes

圍 J5423/M4806 959
衛 J3152/M34073 1776
韓 J345a/M43159 **6602**
韜 J706b/M43189 **6603**

Rad. 179 韭

0 residual strokes

韭 J706c/M43236 **6604**

3–10 residual strokes

懺 J5873/M-X 2008
殲 J5d54/M-X 2987
薤 J6926/M32141 5211
韮 J4723/M43237 **6605**
韲 J706e/M43249 **6606**

11–12 residual strokes

颪 J7124/M43769 **6664**
颯 J7125/M43808 **6665**
颭 J7126/M43815 **6666**

6–12 residual strokes

佩 J5050/M543 186
諷 J6b65/M35741 5669
颸 J-X/M43840 **6667**
颶 J7127/M43876 **6668**
飄 J7128/M43946 **6669**
飃 J7129/M43945 **6670**
飆 J712a/M43963 **6671**

Rad. 183 飛

飛 J4874/M44000 **6672**
飜 J664c/M44009 **6673**

Rad. 184 食

0 residual strokes

食 J3f29/M44014 **6674**

2–3 residual strokes

喰 J3674/M4015 849
飢 J3532/M44023′ **6675**

4 residual strokes

飫 J712c/M44050 **6676**
飩 J712b/M44047 **6677**
飭 J522c/M44057 **6678**
飯 J4853/M44064′ **6679**
飲 J307b/M44063′ **6680**
飮 J5d3b/M44063 **6681**

5 residual strokes

飴 J303b/M44080′ **6682**
飾 J3e7e/M44111′ **6683**
飽 J4b30/M44109′ **6684**
飼 J3b74/M44107′ **6685**

6 residual strokes

蝕 J3f2a/M-X 5333
蝕 J-X/M33264 5358
餞 J-X/M44156 **6686**
餉 J712e/M44140 **6687**
餃 J712d/M44131 **6688**
餅 J4c5f/M44133 **6689**
餌 J3142/M44146 **6690**
養 J4d5c/M44144 **6691**

7 residual strokes

餝 J7133/M44212 **6692**
餘 J7131/M44185 **6693**
餔 J7130/M44173 **6694**
餕 J712f/M44163 **6695**
餐 J3b41/M44160 **6696**
餓 J326e/M44168′ **6697**

8 residual strokes

餠 J7136/M44220 **6698**
餤 J7135/M44229 **6699**
餞 J7134/M44214 **6700**
館 J345b/M44237′ **6701**
餡 J7132/M44224 **6702**

9–10 residual strokes

餋 J7138/M44268 **6703**
餬 J7137/M44255 **6704**
饗 J3642/M-X **6705**
餽 J7139/M44320 **6706**
餾 J713a/M44321 **6707**
饂 J713b/M44339 **6708**

11 residual strokes

癢 J6178/M22602 3850
饉 J713c/M44366 **6709**
饅 J713d/M44346 **6710**

12 residual strokes

饗 J3642/M-X **6705**
饋 J713f/M44382 **6711**
饌 J7142/M44386 **6712**
饐 J713e/M44396 **6713**
饒 J7141/M44400 **6714**
饗 J-X/M44431 **6715**
饑 J7140/M44397 **6716**

13–17 residual strokes

饗 J-X/M44431 **6715**
饑 J7140/M44397 **6716**
饕 J7143/M44426 **6717**
饜 J-X/M44453 **6718**
鱶 J7268/M46592 6928

Rad. 185 首

0 residual strokes

首 J3c73/M44489 **6719**

2–8 residual strokes

導 J4633/M7463′ 1388
道 J463b/M39010′ 6091
馗 J7144/M44492 **6720**
馘 J7145/M44507 **6721**

Rad. 186 香

香 J3961/M44518 **6722**
馥 J7146/M44545 **6723**
馨 J333e/M44559 **6724**

Rad. 187 馬

0 residual strokes

馬 J474f/M44572 **6725**

2 residual strokes

馮 J7148/M44579 **6726**
馭 J7147/M44576 **6727**

3 residual strokes

媽 J5540/M6590 1249
馱 J-X/M44589 **6728**
馴 J466b/M44595 **6729**
馳 J435a/M44593 **6730**

4 residual strokes

瑪 J6075/M21156 3671
馿 J-X/M44616 **6731**
駁 J7149/M44610 **6732**
駮 J477d/M44619 **6733**
駄 J424c/M44633 **6734**
駅 J3158/M44633′ **6735**
駆 J366e/M44634 **6736**

5 residual strokes

碼 J627b/M24368 4030
罵 J474d/M28333 4649
駆 J366e/M44634 **6736**
駟 J714a/M44683 **6737**
駛 J714b/M44679 **6738**
駘 J714d/M44675 **6739**
駝 J714c/M44681 **6740**
駑 J714e/M44661 **6741**
駒 J3670/M44663 **6742**
駕 J326f/M44667 **6743**
駈 J366f/M44636 **6744**
駐 J4373/M44660 **6745**

6 residual strokes

憑 J5861/M11210 1984
篤 J4646/M26344 4342
隲 J702d/M41880 6486
駲 J7152/M-X **6746**
駮 J7150/M44726 **6747**
駢 J7158/M44696 **6748**

7 residual strokes

8 residual strokes

9–10 residual strokes

11 residual strokes

12 residual strokes

13–14 residual strokes

16–20 residual strokes

Rad. 188 骨

0 residual strokes

3 residual strokes

4–5 residual strokes

6–9 residual strokes

11–13 residual strokes

Rad. 189 高

0 residual strokes

3–4 residual strokes

5–13 residual strokes

Rad. 190 髟

0 residual strokes

3–4 residual strokes

5 residual strokes

6 residual strokes

8–12 residual strokes

13–15 residual strokes

Rad. 191 鬥

0 residual strokes

5–8 residual strokes

鬩 J722b / M45644 **6824**

10–18 residual strokes

鬪 J722c / M45649 **6825**
鬭 J-X / M45657 **6826**
鬮 J-X / M-X **6827**
鬮 J722d / M45659 **6828**

Rad. 192 鬯

鬯 J722e / M45661 **6829**
鬱 J5d35 / M45671 **6830**

Rad. 193 鬲

0 residual strokes

鬲 J722f / M45672 **6831**

2 residual strokes

隔 J3356 / M-X 6475
隔 J-X / M41783 6476

4–12 residual strokes

獻 J605b / M20783 3614
膈 J672d / M29772 4856
融 J4d3b / M33384 5371
鬻 J6478 / M45721 **6832**

Rad. 194 鬼

0 residual strokes

鬼 J3534 / M45758 **6833**

2 residual strokes

傀 J507a / M928 282
隗 J7029 / M41788 6472

3 residual strokes

塊 J3274 / M5319 1070
嵬 J564c / M8355 1499
愧 J5843 / M10982 1941
蒐 J3d2f / M31539 5159

4 residual strokes

槐 J5c47 / M15323 2803
瑰 J6073 / M21164 3672
魁 J3321 / M45785 **6834**
魂 J3a32 / M45787 **6835**

5–7 residual strokes

醜 J3d39 / M39969 6189
魃 J7231 / M45806 **6836**
魄 J7230 / M45810 **6837**
魅 J4c25 / M45811 **6838**

8–10 residual strokes

餽 J7139 / M44320 6706
魍 J7233 / M45869 **6839**
魎 J7234 / M45870 **6840**
魏 J7232 / M45872 **6841**
魑 J7235 / M45901 **6842**

11–14 residual strokes

巍 J565b / M8626 1522
魔 J4b62 / M45906′ **6843**
魘 J7236 / M45941 **6844**

Rad. 195 魚

0 residual strokes

魚 J357b / M45956 **6845**

3–4 residual strokes

漁 J3579 / M18101 3309
魴 J7237 / M46022 **6846**
魳 J-X / M46020 **6847**
魯 J4f25 / M46013 **6848**

5 residual strokes

薊 J6929 / M32095 5213
鮖 J723b / M46089 **6849**
鮗 J723c / M46091 **6850**
鮑 J723a / M46074 **6851**
鮃 J7239 / M46044 **6852**
鮓 J7238 / M46076 **6853**
鮒 J4a2b / M46075 **6854**
鮎 J303e / M46070 **6855**

6 residual strokes

鮴 J7240 / M-X **6856**
鮰 J-X / M46105 **6857**
鮪 J4b6e / M46126 **6858**
鮭 J3a7a / M46132 **6859**
鮠 J723e / M46112 **6860**
鮟 J723d / M46108 **6861**
鮨 J723f / M46123 **6862**
鮫 J3b2d / M46127 **6863**
鮮 J412f / M46133 **6864**

7 residual strokes

鯀 J7241 / M46168 **6865**
鯆 J7244 / M46177 **6866**
鯊 J7242 / M46186 **6867**
鯏 J7245 / M46201 **6868**
鯑 J7246 / M46203 **6869**
鯒 J7247 / M46204 **6870**
鮹 J7243 / M46154 **6871**
鯱 J-X / M-X **6872**
鯁 J-X / M46171 **6873**
鯉 J3871 / M46182 **6874**

8 residual strokes

櫓 J4f26 / M15798 2908
蘇 J4149 / M32427 5252
蘓 J693f / M-X 5253
鯵 J3033 / M-X **6875**
鯢 J7249 / M46245 **6876**
鯤 J724a / M46247 **6877**
鯲 J724e / M46287 **6878**
鯰 J7250 / M46285 **6879**
鯡 J724c / M46243 **6880**
鯣 J7248 / M46246 **6881**
鯔 J724b / M46208 **6882**
鯖 J3b2a / M46210 **6883**
鯛 J4264 / M46226′ **6884**
鯱 J724f / M46286 **6885**
鯨 J375f / M46257 **6886**
鰈 J7257 / M46322 **6898**

9 residual strokes

蘚 J6945 / M32483 5262
鯤 J724a / M46247 **6877**
鰛 J725c / M-X **6887**
鰄 J725a / M46314 **6888**
鰆 J7256 / M46317 **6889**
鰉 J7253 / M46323 **6890**
鰔 J7252 / M46345 **6891**
鰕 J7251 / M46346 **6892**
鰊 J7259 / M46325 **6893**
鯷 J-X / M46290 **6894**
鰍 J3362 / M46331 **6895**
鯽 J-X / M46304 **6896**
鰒 J7258 / M46340 **6897**
鰈 J7257 / M46322 **6898**
鰌 J7255 / M46330 **6899**
鰓 J7254 / M46344 **6900**
鰐 J4f4c / M46337 **6901**

10 residual strokes

艪 J6762 / M30580 4951
鰐 J4f4c / M46337 **6901**
鰡 J725f / M46374 **6902**
鰰 J7260 / M46414 **6903**
鰯 J3073 / M46413 **6904**
鰮 J725b / M46403 **6905**
鰤 J725e / M46381 **6906**
鰭 J4949 / M46400 **6907**
鰥 J725d / M46382 **6908**

Rad. 196 鳥

13–19 residual strokes

鸎 J733f/M47379 **7005**
鷺 J3a6d/M47362 **7006**
鷹 J426b/M47377 **7007**
鸛 J7341/M47500 **7008**
鸚 J7340/M47489 **7009**
鸞 J7342/M47508 **7010**

Rad. 197 鹵

0 residual strokes

鹵 J7343/M47528 **7011**

3–14 residual strokes

滷 J5f23/M18088 3289
塷 J-X/M47550 **7012**
鹸 J3834/M-X **7013**
鹹 J7344/M47553 **7014**
鹽 J7345/M47579 **7015**
鹼 J-X/M47576 **7016**

Rad. 198 鹿

0 residual strokes

鹿 J3c2f/M47586 **7017**

2–6 residual strokes

塵 J3f50/M5388 1087
漉 J3977/M18112 3300
麁 J7346/M47591 **7018**
麈 J7347/M47616 **7019**
麋 J7348/M47625 **7020**

7 residual strokes

慶 J3744/M11145 1967
轆 J6d5c/M38502 5986
麌 J7349/M47634 **7021**

8 residual strokes

鏖 J6f32/M40799 6338
麕 J734b/M47660 **7022**
麓 J4f3c/M47658 **7023**
麑 J734c/M47656 **7024**
麒 J734a/M47657 **7025**
麗 J4e6f/M47663 **7026**

10–11 residual strokes

儷 J5136/M1311 336
灑 J5f53/M18774 3392
麝 J734d/M47682 **7027**

12–22 residual strokes

曬 J-X/M14266 2528
鏕 J-X/M41022 6364
驪 J716b/M45090 6782
麟 J4e5b/M47690 **7028**
麤 J-X/M47714 **7029**

Rad. 199 麥

0 residual strokes

麦 J477e/M47718 **7030**
麥 J734e/M47717 **7031**

4–5 residual strokes

麪 J7351/M47742 **7032**
麩 J734f/M47739 **7033**
麸 J7350/M-X **7034**
麭 J7352/M47757 **7035**

6–9 residual strokes

麹 J396d/M-X **7036**
麴 J-X/M47818 **7037**
麺 J4c4d/M-X **7038**
麵 J-X/M47827 **7039**

Rad. 200 麻

0 residual strokes

麻 J4b63/M47888 **7040**
麻 J-X/M47887 **7041**

2–3 residual strokes

嘛 J5357/M4230 876
痲 J6164/M22254 3818
麼 J5677/M47892 **7042**

4–5 residual strokes

摩 J4b60/M12613′ 2264
磨 J4b61/M24449′ 4045
麼 J5677/M47892 **7042**
麾 J5d60/M47899 **7043**

6–10 residual strokes

縻 J6476/M27097 4422
糜 J655b/M27839 4580
靡 J7353/M42612 6565
魔 J4b62/M45906′ 6843
麿 J4b7b/M47909′ **7044**

Rad. 201 黃

0 residual strokes

黄 J322b/M47926′ **7045**
黃 J-X/M47926 **7046**

4–6 residual strokes

壙 J545d/M5576 1110
擴 J5a32/M12895 2309
横 J3223/M15484′ 2854
橫 J-X/M15594 2857
簧 J6450/M26541 4356

7–13 residual strokes

曠 J5b25/M14245 2525
礦 J6268/M24564 4057
黌 J7354/M47985 **7047**

Rad. 202 黍

黍 J3550/M47991 **7048**
黎 J7355/M47994 **7049**
黏 J7356/M48007 **7050**
黐 J7357/M48027 **7051**

Rad. 203 黑

0 residual strokes

黒 J3975/M48040 **7052**
黑 J-X/M48038 **7053**

3 residual strokes

墨 J4b4f/M-X 1086
墨 J-X/M5469 1091

4 residual strokes

勲 J372e/M2463 560
黔 J7358/M48056 **7054**
黙 J4c5b/M48063′ **7055**
默 J6054/M48063 **7056**

5 residual strokes

勲 J372e/M2463 560
點 J-X/M-X 3492
點 J735a/M48083 **7057**
黝 J735b/M48082 **7058**
黜 J7359/M48076 **7059**
黛 J4263/M48075 **7060**

邇 J6e30/M39173 6118
鮇 J7240/M-X 6856
鮄 J-X/M46105 6857
鮪 J4b6e/M46126 6858
鮭 J3a7a/M46132 6859
鮠 J723e/M46112 6860
鮟 J723d/M46108 6861
鮨 J723f/M46123 6862
鮫 J3b2d/M46127 6863
鮮 J412f/M46133 6864
龜 J737d/M48847 7106

16 residual strokes

瓊 J607b/M21328 3682
瞻 J626d/M23742 3964
觴 J6b3c/M35157 5550
鯀 J7241/M46168 6865
鯆 J7244/M46177 6866
鯊 J7242/M46186 6867
鯏 J7245/M46201 6868
鯑 J7246/M46203 6869
鯒 J7247/M46204 6870
鮹 J7243/M46154 6871
鯁 J-X/M46171 6873
鯉 J3871/M46182 6874
鵤 J7323/M46980 6966

17 residual strokes

櫓 J4f26/M15798 2908
簷 J6453/M26607 4361
艶 J3170/M30632 4957
蘇 J4149/M32427 5252
蘓 J693f/M-X 5253
蟾 J6a39/M33676 5392
蟹 J332a/M33668 5395
蠏 J6a37/M33669 5396
鯢 J7249/M46245 6876
鯲 J724e/M46287 6878
鯰 J7250/M46285 6879
鯡 J724c/M46243 6880
鯣 J7248/M46246 6881
鯔 J724b/M46208 6882
鯖 J3b2a/M46210 6883
鯛 J4264/M46226' 6884
鯱 J724f/M46286 6885
鯨 J375f/M46257 6886
鰈 J7257/M46322 6898

18 residual strokes

巉 J565a/M8618 1520
蘚 J6945/M32483 5262
觸 J6b3d/M35181 5551
譫 J6b7e/M36017 5713
贍 J6c58/M36945 5832
鯤 J724a/M46247 6877
鰛 J725c/M-X 6887
鰄 J725a/M46314 6888
鰆 J7256/M46317 6889
鰉 J7253/M46323 6890
鰔 J7252/M46345 6891
鰕 J7251/M46346 6892
鰊 J7259/M46325 6893
鯷 J-X/M46290 6894
鰍 J3362/M46331 6895
鰂 J-X/M46304 6896
鰒 J7258/M46340 6897
鰈 J7257/M46322 6898
鰌 J7255/M46330 6899
鰓 J7254/M46344 6900
鰐 J4f4c/M46337 6901

19 residual strokes

巉 J565a/M8618 1520
穮 J6354/M25381 4184
艪 J6762/M30580 4951
鯤 J724a/M46247 6877
鰐 J4f4c/M46337 6901
鰡 J725f/M46374 6902
鰤 J7260/M46414 6903
鰯 J3073/M46413 6904
鰮 J725b/M46403 6905
鰣 J725e/M46381 6906
鰭 J4949/M46400 6907
鰥 J725d/M46382 6908
鰱 J7261/M46468 6910

20 residual strokes

癬 J617d/M22629 3855
穮 J6354/M25381 4184
鰲 J7262/M46416 6909
鰾 J7264/M46447 6911
鰺 J724d/M46442 6912
鱆 J7263/M46464 6913
鰻 J3137/M46443 6914
鰹 J336f/M46437 6915
鱈 J432d/M46470 6916
鱉 J-X/M46472 6917

21 residual strokes

鰹 J336f/M46437 6915
鱉 J-X/M46472 6917
鱚 J7265/M46516 6918
鱏 J-X/M46488 6919
鱓 J-X/M46496 6920
鱒 J4b70/M46492 6921
鱘 J-X/M46504 6922
鱗 J4e5a/M46502 6923
鱮 J-X/M46571 6925

22 residual strokes

纔 J6578/M28070 4621
艷 J6766/M30637 4958
讒 J6c29/M36137 5728
鱗 J4e5a/M46502 6923
鱞 J-X/M46520 6924
鱮 J-X/M46571 6925
鱧 J7267/M46542 6926
鱠 J7266/M46530 6927

23–24 residual strokes

纔 J6578/M28070 4621
讒 J6c29/M36137 5728
鱮 J-X/M46571 6925
鱶 J7268/M46592 6928

25–26 residual strokes

纔 J6578/M28070 4621
鸝 J722d/M45659 6828
鱶 J7268/M46592 6928
鱺 J-X/M46597 6929
鱸 J7269/M46600 6930

Rad. 302 マ

2–3 residual strokes

予 J4d3d/M231 68
矛 J4c37/M23846 3974

5–6 residual strokes

勇 J4d26/M2360' 541
序 J3d78/M9253 1607
抒 J5933/M11884 2085
杼 J5b41/M14510 2576
甬 J6135/M21707 3723

7 residual strokes

俑 J505c/M683 206
勇 J4d26/M2360' 541
柔 J3d40/M14622 2633
矜 J6262/M23852 3975
茅 J337d/M30836 5005
通 J444c/M38892' 6063

8–9 residual strokes

桶 J3233/M14811 2694
涌 J4d30/M17534 3150
通 J444c/M38892' 6063
野 J4c6e/M40133 6208

10 residual strokes

ANDREW NATHANIEL NELSON *was born in Great Falls, Montana, in 1893. He received his B.A. from Walla Walla College and his Ph.D. from the University of Washington. As a Seventh-day Adventist missionary in Asia between 1918 and 1961, Dr. Nelson played a prominent role in the fields of education and language training. Throughout his life, Dr. Nelson remained devoted to the study of the Japanese language and the fundamentals of Chinese.*

JOHN H. HAIG *is an associate professor of Japanese in the Department of East Asian Languages and Literatures at the University of Hawai'i at Mānoa, one of the largest departments of its kind in the United States.*

NOTE CONCERNING CHART INSIDE BACK COVER. These charts have been placed here as a handy reference for locating the more common radicals. The radicals are shown classified by the locations in which they most commonly appear (top, bottom, left, right, enclosure, lone). Not shown are the comparatively rare corner radicals or cases where the whole character is a radical.

See Appendices 3 and 4 for help in determining the radical of a character. The characters that are radicals by themselves are included in the charts of Appendix 5.

TOP
The Radicals Found at the Top

1	一 1	一 1	丶 3	乛 4	′ 4	**2**	二 7	亠 8	亠 8	人 9	入 11
八 12	八 12	丷 12	冖 14	刀 18	力 19	匕 21	十 24	卜 25	厶 28	又 29	
3	口 30	土 32	士 32	夂 34	夕 36	大 37	女 38	子 39	宀 40	小 42	⺌ 42
山 46	巛 47	工 48	己 49	彐 58	彐 58	彐 58	彑 58	卄 [140]	**4**	戈 62	攵 66
文 67	日 72	日 72	木 75	止 77	毋 80	比 81	氏 83	水 85	火 86	爫 87	爪 87
父 88	牛 93	王 [96]	艹 [140]	**5**	玄 95	甘 99	田 102	癶 105	白 106	目 109	矛 110
石 112	禾 115	穴 116	穴 116	穴 116	立 117	罒 [122]	**6**	竹 118	米 119	羊 123	羽 124
羽 124	老 125	而 126	耳 128	聿 129	自 132	臼 134	虫 142	血 143	衣 145	西 146	襾 146
7	貝 154	車 159	辰 161	釆 165		**8**	隹 172	雨 173	非 175		
9	音 180	音 180	**10**	馬 187	鬲 189	髟 190	**11**	魚 195	鳥 196	鹿 198	麻 200
麻 200	黒 [203]			**12**	黑 203			**13/16**	鼓 207	齊 210	龍 212

LONE
The Common Characters Having But One Radical

乂 – 丶 3	乃 – 丿 4
久 – ノ 4	了 – 亅 6

BOTTOM
The Radicals Found at the Bottom

1	一 1	丶 3		**2**	二 7	儿 10	八 12	冫 15	几 16	刀 18	力 19
十 24	㔾 26	厶 28	又 29	又 29		**3**	口 30	土 32	夂 34	夊 34	夕 36
大 37	女 38	子 39	寸 41	小 42	山 46	工 48	己 49	巾 50	干 51	廾 55	弓 57
彐 58	彡 59		**4**	心 61	⺗ 61	手 64	斤 69	方 70	日 72	曰 72	木 75
止 77	毋 80	比 81	毛 82	水 85	火 86	灬 86	牛 93	犬 94	王 [96]	任 [96]	月 [130]
5	母 [80]	氺 [85]	玉 96	瓦 98	甘 99	用 101	田 102	疋 103	白 106	皿 108	目 109
矢 111	石 112	示 113	禾 115		**6**	米 119	糸 120	缶 121	羊 123	羽 124	羽 124
而 126	耳 128	聿 129	肉 130	至 133	臼 134	舌 135	舛 136	艮 138	虫 142	衣 145	豸 [152]
7	舛 [136]	見 147	角 148	言 149	豆 151	豕 152	貝 154	足 157	車 159	辛 160	辛 160
辰 161	酉 164	里 166		**8**	金 167	隹 172	非 175		**9**	面 176	革 177
韭 179	音 180	音 180	風 182	食 184	食 184	香 186		**10**	馬 187	鬲 193	鬼 194
11	魚 195	鳥 196	鹿 198		**12**	黃 201	黑 203		**16**	龍 212	

ENCLOSURE
The Radicals Found as Enclosures

1	乚 5	**2**	冂 13	冂 13	冂 13	冂 13	几 16
几 16	凵 17	勹 20	匚 22	匸 22	厂 27	辶 [162]	
3	囗 31	夂 34	尸 44	广 53	廴 54	弋 56	辶 [162]
4	戈 62	戸 63	戶 63	支 65	歹 78	毛 82	气 84
爪 87	**5**	瓦 98	疒 104	**6**	耳 128	虍 141	**7**
走 156	辰 161	辵 162	麦 [199]	**8**	門 169	**9**	風 182
10	鬥 191	鬼 194		**11**	鹿 198	麥 199	麻 200
	13/14	鼠 208	齊 210				